The Oxford Compact Dictionary & Thesaurus

Edited by
Julia Elliott

with
Anne Knight and
Chris Cowley

OXFORD UNIVERSITY PRESS

1997

Oxford University Press, Great Clarendon Street, Oxford OX2 6DP

Oxford New York
Athens Auckland Bangkok Bogota Bombay Buenos Aires
Calcutta Cape Town Dar es Salaam Delhi Florence Hong Kong
Istanbul Karachi Kuala Lumpur Madras Madrid Melbourne
Mexico City Nairobi Paris Singapore Taipei Tokyo Toronto
and associated companies in
Berlin Ibadan

Oxford is a trade mark of Oxford University Press

© Oxford University Press 1997
First published 1997

British Library Cataloguing in Publication Data
Data available

Library of Congress Cataloging in Publication Data
Data available

ISBN 0-19-860116-6

10 9 8 7 6 5 4 3 2 1

Typeset in Monotype Nimrod and Arial
by Selwood Systems
Printed in Great Britain by
Clays Ltd
Bungay, Suffolk

Contents

Editorial Team

Preface

The *Oxford Compact Dictionary & Thesaurus* combines within one volume a concise dictionary and a useful thesaurus. These two elements have been carefully integrated so that a single entry contains information on meaning, spelling, and pronunciation, and also offers, where relevant, lists of words which are related in meaning and from which an alternative word or phrase may be selected.

Language panels and usage notes add invaluable information on grammar and punctuation, and helpful guidance on correct usage.

Also included is a special Reverse Dictionary Supplement, providing a guide to related words, a vocabulary-builder, and a puzzle-solver all in one.

J. A. E.

How to use the Oxford Compact Dictionary & Thesaurus

The entry map below explains the different parts of an entry.

Pronunciation in oblique strokes / /

Part of speech in *italic* type

Headword in **bold** type introduces a new entry

Sense number in **bold** type

Compound and phrase section signalled by □

brief /briːf/ *adjective* 1 of short duration. 2 concise. 3 scanty. ● ~~noun 1 (in *plural*) short~~ pants. 2 summary of case for guidance of barrister. 3 instructions for a task. ● *verb* 1 instruct (barrister) by brief. 2 inform or instruct in advance. □ **in brief** to sum up. □ ~~**briefly** *adverb*.~~ **briefness** *noun*.

New part of speech signalled by ●

Derivative section signalled by □

▪ *adjective* 1 cursory, ephemeral, *literary* evanescent, fast, fleeting, hasty, limited, little, momentary, passing, quick, sharp, short, short-lived, temporary, transient, transitory. 2 abbreviated, abridged, compact, compendious, compressed, concise, condensed, crisp, curt, curtailed, incisive, laconic, pithy, shortened, succinct, terse, thumbnail, to the point. ● *noun* 1 (*briefs*) knickers, *colloquial* panties, pants, *US* shorts, trunks, underpants. 2 argument, case, defence, dossier, summary. 3 directions, information, instructions, orders. ● *verb* advise, coach, direct, enlighten, *colloquial* fill in, give the facts, guide, inform, instruct, prepare, prime, put in the picture.

gut *noun* 1 intestine. 2 (in *plural*) bowels, entrails. 3 ~~(in *plural*) *colloquial* courage and~~ determination. 4 *slang* stomach. 5 (in *plural*) contents; essence. 6 material for violin etc. strings or for fishing line. *adjective* instinctive, fundamental. ● *verb* (**-tt-**) 1 remove or destroy internal fittings of (buildings). 2 remove guts of. ▪ **gutless** *adjective*.

Synonym sense number refers back to defined meaning

Synonym section signalled by ▪

Cross-reference in SMALL CAPITALS

▪ *noun* 1 alimentary canal, bowel, intestine. 2 (*guts*) bowels, entrails, *colloquial* innards, *colloquial* insides, intestines, viscera. 3 (*guts*) see COURAGE. 4 abdomen, belly, paunch, stomach, *colloquial* tummy. ● *verb* 1 clear, despoil, empty, loot, pillage, plunder, ransack, ravage, remove the contents of, sack, strip. 2 clean, disembowel, eviscerate.

Headwords

Words given their own entries are in bold type:

    abandon

or in bold italic type if they are borrowed from another language and are usually printed in italics:

    autobahn

Variant spellings are shown:

    almanac ... (also **almanack**)

Variant American spellings are labelled *US*:

    anaemia ... (*US* **anemia**)

Words that are different but are spelt the same way (homographs) are printed with raised numbers:

    abode[1]

    abode[2]

Inflections

Irregular and difficult forms are given for:

a. *nouns:*

        ability ... (*plural* **-ies**)

        sheep ... (*plural* same)

        tomato ... (*plural* **-es**)

    (Irregular plurals are not given for compounds such as *footman* and *schoolchild*).

b. *verbs:*

        abate ... (**-ting**)

        abut ... (**-tt-**) [indicating **abutted, abutting**]

        ring[2] ... (*past* **rang**; *past participle* **rung**)

c. *adjectives:*

        good ... (**better, best**)

        narrow ... (**-er, -est**)

        able ... (**-r, -st**)

d. *adverbs:*

        well ... (**better, best**)

Definitions

Round brackets are used for:

a. optional words, e.g. at

    back ... *verb* (cause to) go backwards

    (because *back* can mean either 'go backwards' or 'cause to go backwards')

b. typical objects of verbs:

> **bank**[2] ... *verb* deposit (money) at bank

c. typical subjects of verbs:

> **break** ... *verb* (of waves) curl over and foam

d. typical nouns qualified by an adjective:

> **catchy** ... (of tune) easily remembered

Phrases, compounds, and derivatives

a. Phrases are entered under their main word:

> **company** ... **in company with**

A comma in a phrase indicates alternatives:

> **in, to excess**

means that *in excess* and *to excess* are both phrases.

b. Compounds are entered under their main word or element (usually the first):

> **air** ... **air speed** ... **airstrip**

unless they need entries of their own:

> **broad**
>
> **broadcast**
>
> **broadside**

A comma in a compound indicates alternatives:

> **block capitals, letters**

means that *block capitals* and *block letters* are both compounds.

c. Derivatives are put at the end of the entry for the word they are derived from:

> **rob** ... **robber** *noun*

unless they need defining:

> **drive** ...
>
> **driver** *noun* **1** person who drives. **2** golf club for driving from tee.

Labels

If the use of a word is restricted in any way, this is indicated by a label printed in italics.

Some labels indicate that a particular word or sense is used chiefly in the regional English specified, for example:

> **bill** ... *US* banknote.

> **brae** ... *Scottish* hillside.

Subject labels are sometimes included to help define the context in which a word is used:

> **sharp** ... *Music* above true pitch.

Register labels indicate a particular level of usage, such as *slang*, *archaic*, or *literary*:

ace ... *slang* excellent.

raiment ... *archaic* clothing.

bosky ... *literary* wooded.

The same regional and register labels, and some subject labels, are attached to the words when they are listed as synonyms. The label precedes the synonym to which it applies:

note ... **5,6** banknote, *US* bill, draft.

hill ... *Scottish* brae, elevation ...

expert ... able, *slang* ace, brilliant ...

costume ... period dress, *archaic* raiment, robes ...

wooded ... afforested, *literary* bosky, forested ...

Cross-references

Cross-references are printed in small capitals:

anatto = ANNATTO

arose *past* of ARISE

glamour ... see BEAUTY[1]

If the cross-reference is in the defining section, it indicates that a definition will be found at the entry referred to.

If the cross-reference is in the synonym section, it indicates that a synonym list will be found at the entry (and sense) referred to.

Synonym sections

Synonym lists are matched to individual senses of a word and numbered accordingly. Sometimes one list will be applicable to more than one sense of the word and then the senses will be identified by a combination of sense numbers. If a single synonym list covers all the senses of a word then the list will not be given a sense number.

Not all senses and not all words have synonyms.

Synonyms are listed alphabetically. Sometimes a semicolon is used to divide a list according to different contexts, and these are exemplified by phrases in italic type.

Occasionally the synonyms are offered for a form other than the exact form of the headword. In these cases the altered form is given in brackets at the beginning of the synonym list. The use of bold or italic type, which mirrors that in the defining section of the entry, is governed by the type of information being offered. For example, the synonyms at sense 2 of the noun *lodging* are substitutable for the plural *lodgings*;

the synonyms at sense 1 of the verb *consist* are substitutable for the verb + *of* :

> **lodging** *noun* **1** temporary accommodation. **2**
> (in *plural*) room(s) rented for lodging in.
> ■ **1** accommodation, billet, shelter, temporary
> home. **2** (*lodgings*) accommodation,
> apartment(s), billet, boarding house, *colloquial*
> digs, lodging house, *slang* pad, quarters, rooms.

> **consist** /kən'sɪst/ *verb* **1** (+ *of*) be composed of.
> **2** (+ *in, of*) have its essential features in.
> ■ **1** (*consist of*) be composed of, be made of,
> comprise, contain, embody, include, incorporate.

The adjective **absorbing**, which is defined at sense 4 of the entry for the verb **absorb**, is given in bold type in the defining section and at the relevant synonym list:

> **absorb** /əb'sɔːb/ *verb* **1** incorporate, assimilate.
> **2** take in (heat, knowledge, etc.). **3** deal with
> easily; reduce intensity of. **4** (often as **absorbing**
> *adjective*) engross attention of. **5** consume
> (resources).
> ■ **1, 2** assimilate, consume, digest, drink in, hold,
> imbibe, incorporate, ingest, *colloquial* mop up,
> soak up, suck up, take in. **3** cushion, deaden,
> lessen, soften. **4** captivate, engage, engross,
> enthral, fascinate, interest, occupy, preoccupy;
> (**absorbing**) engrossing, fascinating, gripping,
> interesting, spellbinding.

Hyphens

Hyphens introduced because a word is divided at the end of a line are printed sloping (-), while 'permanent' hyphens, as in *accident-prone*, are always printed horizontally (even at the end of a line).

Pronunciation symbols

Pronunciations are given in the International Phonetic Alphabet.

Consonants

b	*b*ut	l	*l*eg	t	*t*op	θ	*th*in
d	*d*og	m	*m*an	v	*v*oice	ð	*th*is
f	*f*ew	n	*n*o	w	*w*e	ŋ	ri*ng*
g	*g*et	p	*p*en	z	*z*oo	x	lo*ch*
h	*h*e	r	*r*ed	ʃ	*sh*e	tʃ	*ch*ip
j	*y*es	s	*s*it	ʒ	vi*s*ion	dʒ	*j*ar
k	*c*at						

Vowels

æ	c*a*t	ɒ	h*o*t	aɪ	m*y*	ɔɪ	b*oy*
ɑː	*ar*m	ɔː	s*aw*	aʊ	h*ow*	ʊə	p*oor*
e	b*e*d	ʌ	r*u*n	eɪ	d*ay*	aɪə	f*ire*
ɜː	h*er*	ʊ	p*u*t	əʊ	n*o*	aʊə	s*our*
ɪ	s*i*t	uː	t*oo*	eə	h*air*		
iː	s*ee*	ə	*a*go	ɪə	n*ear*		

(ə) signifies the indeterminate sound as in gard*e*n, carn*a*l, and
rhyth*m*.

The mark ˜ indicates a nasalized sound, as in the following vowels that
are not natural in English:

  æ̃ (*ing*énue)
  ɑ̃ (él*an*)
  ɔ̃ (b*on* voyage)

The main or primary stress of a word is shown by ' before the relevant
syllable.

Note on proprietary terms

This dictionary includes some words which are, or are asserted to be, proprietary names or trade marks. Their inclusion does not imply that they have acquired for legal purposes a non-proprietary or general significance, nor is any other judgement implied concerning their legal status. In cases where the editor has some evidence that a word is used as a proprietary name or trade mark this is indicated by the label *proprietary term*, but no judgement concerning the legal status of such words is made or implied thereby.

A *abbreviation* ampere(s). □ **A-bomb** atomic bomb. **A level** advanced level in GCE exam.

a /ə, eɪ/ *adjective* (called the indefinite article) (also **an** /æn, ən/ before vowel sound) **1** one, some, any. **2** per.

AA *abbreviation* **1** Automobile Association. **2** Alcoholics Anonymous. **3** anti-aircraft.

aardvark /'ɑ:dvɑ:k/ *noun* mammal with tubular snout and long tongue.

aback /ə'bæk/ *adverb* □ **take aback** disconcert, surprise.

abacus /'æbəkəs/ *noun* (*plural* **-es**) frame with wires along which beads are slid for calculating.

abaft /ə'bɑ:ft/ *Nautical adverb* in or towards stern of ship. ● *preposition* nearer stern than.

abandon /ə'bænd(ə)n/ *verb* **1** desert (person, thing, place). **2** give up (hope, attempt, claim, etc.). ● *noun* freedom from inhibitions. □ **abandonment** *noun*.

  ■ *verb* **1** (*abandon a person*) break with, desert, *slang* ditch, *colloquial* dump, forsake, jilt, leave behind, leave in the lurch, maroon, renounce, throw over; (*abandon a place*) evacuate, leave, quit, vacate, withdraw from. **2** abdicate, cancel, *formal* cede, *colloquial* chuck in, discontinue, disown, *slang* ditch, drop, forfeit, forgo, give up, relinquish, resign, surrender, waive, yield.

abandoned *adjective* **1** deserted. **2** unrestrained.

abase /ə'beɪs/ *verb* (**-sing**) humiliate, degrade. □ **abasement** *noun*.

abash /ə'bæʃ/ *verb* (usually as **abashed** *adjective*) embarrass, disconcert.

abate /ə'beɪt/ *verb* (**-ting**) make or become less strong etc. □ **abatement** *noun*.

abattoir /'æbətwɑ:/ *noun* slaughterhouse.

abbess /'æbɪs/ *noun* female head of abbey of nuns.

abbey /'æbɪ/ *noun* (*plural* **-s**) (building occupied by) community of monks or nuns.

abbot /'æbət/ *noun* head of community of monks.

abbreviate /ə'bri:vɪeɪt/ *verb* shorten. □ **abbreviation** *noun*.

  ■ abridge, compress, condense, cut, edit, précis, reduce, shorten, summarize, truncate.

ABC /eɪbi:'si:/ *noun* **1** alphabet. **2** rudiments of subject. **3** alphabetical guide.

abdicate /'æbdɪkeɪt/ *verb* renounce or resign from (throne etc.). □ **abdication** /-'keɪʃ(ə)n/ *noun*.

  ■ renounce the throne, resign (from), step down.

abdomen /'æbdəmən/ *noun* **1** belly. **2** rear part of insect etc. □ **abdominal** /æb'dɒmɪn(ə)l/ *adjective*.

abduct /əb'dʌkt/ *verb* carry off illegally, kidnap. □ **abduction** *noun*. **abductor** *noun*.

  ■ carry off, kidnap, seize, *slang* snatch.

aberrant /æ'berənt/ *adjective* showing aberration.

aberration /æbə'reɪʃ(ə)n/ *noun* **1** deviation from normal type or accepted standard. **2** distortion.

abet /ə'bet/ *verb* (**-tt-**) **1** encourage (offender). **2** assist (offence). □ **abetter**, *Law* **abettor** *noun*.

abeyance /ə'beɪəns/ *noun* (usually after *in*, *into*) temporary disuse, suspension.

abhor /əb'hɔ:/ *verb* (**-rr-**) detest; regard with disgust.

  ■ detest, execrate, hate, loathe, shudder at.

abhorrence /əb'hɒrəns/ *noun* disgust, detestation.

abhorrent *adjective* (often + *to*) inspiring disgust; detestable.

  ■ abominable, detestable, execrable, hateful, loathsome, nauseating, obnoxious, repellent, revolting.

abide /ə'baɪd/ *verb* (**-ding**, *past & past participle* **abode** /ə'bəʊd/ or **abided**) **1** tolerate. **2** (+ *by*) act in accordance with (rule). **3** (+ *by*) keep (promise). **4** *archaic* remain, dwell.

  ■ **1** accept, bear, endure, put up with, stand, stomach, suffer, tolerate. **2** (*abide by*) see OBEY 1. **4** see STAY¹ *verb* 2.

abiding /ə'baɪdɪŋ/ *adjective* enduring, permanent.

ability /ə'bɪlɪtɪ/ *noun* (*plural* **-ies**) **1** (often + *to do*) capacity, power. **2** cleverness, talent.

  ■ **1** capacity, means, power, resources, scope, strength. **2** aptitude, bent, brains, capability, cleverness, competence, expertise, flair, genius, gift, intelligence, knack, know-how, knowledge, proficiency, prowess, skill, talent, wit.

abject /'æbdʒekt/ *adjective* **1** miserable. **2** degraded. **3** despicable. □ **abjection** /-'dʒek-/ *noun*.

abjure /əb'dʒʊə/ *verb* renounce on oath. □ **abjuration** /-dʒʊ'reɪ-/ *noun*.

ablaze /ə'bleɪz/ *adjective & adverb* **1** on fire. **2** glittering. **3** excited.

  ■ **1** afire, aflame, aglow, alight, blazing, burning, flaming, lit up, on fire, raging. **2** see BRIGHT 1.

able /'eɪb(ə)l/ *adjective* (**-r**, **-st**) **1** (often + *to do*)

having the means or power. **2** talented.
□ **able-bodied** healthy, fit. □ **ably** *adverb*.
■ **1** allowed, at liberty, authorized, available, eligible, fit, free, permitted, willing. **2** accomplished, adept, capable, clever, competent, effective, efficient, experienced, expert, handy, intelligent, masterly, practised, proficient, skilful, skilled, talented.

ablution /əˈbluːʃ(ə)n/ *noun* (usually in *plural*) **1** ceremonial washing of hands etc. **2** *colloquial* washing oneself.

abnegate /ˈæbnɪɡeɪt/ *verb* (**-ting**) **1** give up. **2** renounce. □ **abnegation** *noun*.

abnormal /æbˈnɔːm(ə)l/ *adjective* exceptional; deviating from the norm. □ **abnormality** /-ˈmæl-/ *noun*. **abnormally** *adverb*.
■ aberrant, anomalous, atypical, bizarre, curious, deformed, deviant, distorted, eccentric, exceptional, extraordinary, freak, funny, idiosyncratic, irregular, *colloquial* kinky, malformed, odd, peculiar, perverted, queer, singular, strange, uncharacteristic, unnatural, unorthodox, unrepresentative, untypical, unusual, wayward, *colloquial* weird.

aboard /əˈbɔːd/ *adverb & preposition* on or into (ship, aircraft, etc.).

abode[1] /əˈbəʊd/ *noun* dwelling place.

abode[2] *past & past participle* of ABIDE.

abolish /əˈbɒlɪʃ/ *verb* end existence of. □ **abolition** /æbəˈlɪʃ(ə)n/ *noun*. **abolitionist** /æbəˈlɪʃənɪst/ *noun*.
■ abrogate, annul, delete, destroy, dispense with, *colloquial* do away with, eliminate, end, eradicate, finish, get rid of, liquidate, nullify, overturn, put an end to, quash, remove, suppress, terminate, withdraw.

abominable /əˈbɒmɪnəb(ə)l/ *adjective* **1** detestable, loathsome. **2** *colloquial* very unpleasant. □ **Abominable Snowman** yeti. □ **abominably** *adverb*.
■ **1** abhorrent, appalling, atrocious, *colloquial* awful, base, beastly, brutal, cruel, despicable, detestable, disgusting, dreadful, execrable, foul, hateful, heinous, horrible, inhuman, inhumane, loathsome, nasty, obnoxious, odious, repellent, repugnant, repulsive, revolting, *colloquial* terrible, vile. **2** see UNPLEASANT.

abominate /əˈbɒmɪneɪt/ *verb* (**-ting**) detest, loathe. □ **abomination** *noun*.

aboriginal /æbəˈrɪdʒɪn(ə)l/ *adjective* **1** indigenous. **2** (usually **Aboriginal**) of the Australian Aborigines. ● *noun* aboriginal inhabitant, esp. (usually **Aboriginal**) of Australia.

aborigines /æbəˈrɪdʒɪniːz/ *plural noun* aboriginal inhabitants, esp. (usually **Aborigines**) of Australia.
USAGE It is best to refer to one *Aboriginal* but several *Aborigines*, although *Aboriginals* is also acceptable.

abort /əˈbɔːt/ *verb* **1** (of woman) miscarry; undergo abortion. **2** (of foetus) suffer abortion. **3** effect abortion of. **4** (cause to) end before completion.
■ **2** be born prematurely, die. **4** call off, end, halt, nullify, stop, terminate.

abortion /əˈbɔːʃ(ə)n/ *noun* **1** natural or (esp.) induced expulsion of foetus before it can survive. **2** stunted or misshapen creature. □ **abortionist** *noun*.
■ **1** miscarriage, termination. **2** see MONSTER *noun* 3.

abortive /əˈbɔːtɪv/ *adjective* fruitless, unsuccessful.
■ fruitless, futile, ineffective, stillborn, unfruitful, unsuccessful, vain.

abound /əˈbaʊnd/ *verb* **1** be plentiful. **2** (+ *in*, *with*) be rich in; teem with.
■ **1** be plentiful, flourish, prevail, thrive. **2** (*abound in*, *abound with*) be filled with, be rich in, swarm with, teem with.

about /əˈbaʊt/ *preposition* **1** on subject of. **2** relating to; in relation to. **3** at a time near to. **4** around (in). **5** surrounding. **6** here and there in. ● *adverb* **1** approximately. **2** nearby. **3** in every direction. **4** on the move; in action. **5** all around. □ **about-face, -turn 1** turn made so as to face opposite direction. **2** change of policy etc. **be about to** be on the point of (doing something).

above /əˈbʌv/ *preposition* **1** over, on top of, higher than. **2** more than. **3** higher in rank, importance, etc. than. **4** too great or good for. **5** beyond reach of. ● *adverb* **1** at or to higher point; overhead. **2** earlier on page or in book. □ **above all** more than anything else. **above board** *adjective & adverb* without concealment; fair or fairly.

abracadabra /æbrəkəˈdæbrə/ *interjection* supposedly magic word.

abrade /əˈbreɪd/ *verb* (**-ding**) scrape or wear away by rubbing.

abrasion /əˈbreɪʒ(ə)n/ *noun* **1** rubbing or scraping away. **2** resulting damaged area.

abrasive /əˈbreɪsɪv/ *adjective* **1** capable of rubbing or grinding down. **2** harsh or hurtful in manner. ● *noun* abrasive substance. □ **abrasiveness** *noun*.
■ *adjective* **2** biting, caustic, galling, grating, harsh, hurtful, irritating, rough, sharp.

abreast /əˈbrest/ *adverb* **1** side by side and facing same way. **2** (+ *of*) up to date with.

abridge /əˈbrɪdʒ/ *verb* (**-ging**) shorten (a book etc.). □ **abridgement** *noun*.
■ abbreviate, compress, condense, cut, edit, pot, précis, reduce, shorten, summarize, truncate.

abroad /əˈbrɔːd/ *adverb* **1** in or to foreign country. **2** widely. **3** in circulation.

abrogate /ˈæbrəɡeɪt/ *verb* (**-ting**) repeal, abolish (law etc.). □ **abrogation** *noun*.

abrupt /əˈbrʌpt/ *adjective* **1** sudden, hasty. **2** curt. **3** steep. □ **abruptly** *adverb*. **abruptness** *noun*.

■ **1** hasty, headlong, hurried, precipitate, quick, rapid, sudden, unexpected, unforeseen. **2** blunt, brisk, brusque, curt, discourteous, rude, *colloquial* snappy, terse, uncivil, ungracious. **3** precipitous, sharp, sheer, steep.

abscess /'æbsɪs/ *noun* (*plural* **-es**) swelling containing pus.

abscond /əb'skɒnd/ *verb* flee, esp. to avoid arrest; escape. □ **absconder** *noun*.

abseil /'æbseɪl/ *verb* descend (building etc.) by using doubled rope fixed at higher point. ● *noun* such a descent.

absence /'æbsəns/ *noun* **1** being away. **2** duration of this. **3** (+ *of*) lack of. □ **absence of mind** inattentiveness.

absent *adjective* /'æbsənt/ **1** not present or existing. **2** lacking. **3** inattentive. ● *verb* /əb'sent/ (**absent oneself**) go or stay away. □ **absently** *adverb*.

■ *adjective* **1** away, gone, missing, off, out, playing truant, *slang* skiving. **2** deficient, lacking, missing, non-existent, wanting. **3** see ABSENT-MINDED.

absentee /æbsən'tiː/ *noun* person not present.

absenteeism /æbsən'tiːɪz(ə)m/ *noun* absenting oneself from work, school, etc.

absent-minded *adjective* forgetful, inattentive. □ **absent-mindedly** *adverb*. **absent-mindedness** *noun*.

■ absent, absorbed, abstracted, careless, distracted, dreamy, forgetful, inattentive, oblivious, preoccupied, scatterbrained, unaware, unthinking, vague, withdrawn, wool-gathering.

absinthe /'æbsɪnθ/ *noun* wormwood-based, aniseed-flavoured liqueur.

absolute /'æbsəluːt/ *adjective* **1** complete, utter, perfect. **2** unconditional. **3** despotic. **4** not relative; without exceptions. **5** (of adjective or transitive verb) without expressed noun or object. **6** (of decree etc.) final. □ **absolute majority** one over all rivals combined. **absolute temperature** one measured from **absolute zero**, lowest possible temperature (-273.15°C or 0°K).

■ **1** complete, dead, diametrical (*opposites*), downright, exact, genuine, implicit, inalienable, out and out, perfect, pure, sheer, thorough, total, unadulterated, unmitigated, utter. **2** categorical, unconditional, unqualified, unreserved, unrestricted. **3** autocratic, despotic, dictatorial, omnipotent, totalitarian, tyrannical. **4** certain, conclusive, decided, definite, indubitable, positive, sure, unambiguous, unequivocal.

absolutely *adverb* **1** completely. **2** in an absolute sense. **3** *colloquial* quite so, yes.

absolution /æbsə'luːʃ(ə)n/ *noun* formal forgiveness of sins.

absolutism /'æbsəluːtɪz(ə)m/ *noun* absolute government. □ **absolutist** *noun*.

absolve /əb'zɒlv/ *verb* (**-ving**) (often + *from, of*) free from blame or obligation.

absorb /əb'sɔːb/ *verb* **1** incorporate, assimilate. **2** take in (heat, knowledge, etc.). **3** deal with

easily; reduce intensity of. **4** (often as **absorbing** *adjective*) engross attention of. **5** consume (resources).

■ **1, 2** assimilate, consume, digest, drink in, hold, imbibe, incorporate, ingest, *colloquial* mop up, soak up, suck up, take in. **3** cushion, deaden, lessen, soften. **4** captivate, engage, engross, enthral, fascinate, interest, occupy, preoccupy; (**absorbing**) engrossing, fascinating, gripping, interesting, spellbinding.

absorbent /əb'sɔːbənt/ *adjective* tending to absorb. ● *noun* absorbent substance.

■ *adjective* absorptive, spongy.

absorption /əb'sɔːpʃ(ə)n/ *noun* absorbing, being absorbed. □ **absorptive** *adjective*.

abstain /əb'steɪn/ *verb* **1** (usually + *from*) refrain (from acting or indulging). **2** decline to vote. □ **abstainer** *noun*.

■ **1** (*abstain from*) avoid, *formal* cease, deny oneself, desist from, *formal* eschew, forgo, give up, go without, refrain from, refuse, resist, shun, withhold from.

abstemious /əb'stiːmɪəs/ *adjective* moderate or ascetic, esp. in eating and drinking. □ **abstemiously** *adverb*. **abstemiousness** *noun*.

■ ascetic, frugal, moderate, restrained, self-denying, sparing, temperate.

abstention /əb'stenʃ(ə)n/ *noun* abstaining, esp. from voting.

abstinence /'æbstɪnəns/ *noun* abstaining, esp. from food or alcohol. □ **abstinent** *adjective*.

abstract *adjective* /'æbstrækt/ **1** of or existing in theory rather than practice; not concrete. **2** (of art etc.) not representational. ● *verb* /əb'strækt/ **1** (often + *from*) remove. **2** summarize. ● *noun* /'æbstrækt/ **1** summary. **2** abstract idea, work of art, etc.

■ *adjective* **1** academic, hypothetical, indefinite, intangible, intellectual, metaphysical, notional, philosophical, theoretical, unreal. **2** non-pictorial, non-representational, symbolic. ● *noun* **1** outline, précis, résumé, summary, synopsis.

abstracted *adjective* inattentive. □ **abstractedly** *adverb*.

abstraction /əb'strækʃ(ə)n/ *noun* **1** abstracting. **2** abstract idea. **3** abstract qualities in art. **4** absent-mindedness.

abstruse /əb'struːs/ *adjective* hard to understand; profound.

■ complex, cryptic, deep, devious, difficult, enigmatic, esoteric, hard, incomprehensible, mysterious, obscure, perplexing, problematical, profound, unfathomable.

absurd /əb'sɜːd/ *adjective* **1** wildly inappropriate. **2** ridiculous. □ **absurdity** *noun* (*plural* **-ies**). **absurdly** *adverb*.

■ crazy, daft, eccentric, farcical, foolish, grotesque, illogical, incongruous, irrational, laughable, ludicrous, mad, nonsensical, outlandish, paradoxical, preposterous, ridiculous, senseless, silly, stupid, surreal, unreasonable, zany.

ABTA /'æbtə/ *abbreviation* Association of British Travel Agents.

abundance /ə'bʌnd(ə)ns/ *noun* **1** plenty; more than enough. **2** wealth.

abundant *adjective* **1** plentiful. **2** (+ *in*) rich in. □ **abundantly** *adverb*.

■ **1** ample, bountiful, copious, excessive, flourishing, generous, lavish, liberal, luxuriant, plentiful, profuse, rampant, rank. **2** (*abundant in*) overflowing with, rich in, teeming with, well-supplied with.

abuse *verb* /ə'bjuːz/ (**-sing**) **1** use improperly; misuse. **2** maltreat. **3** insult verbally. ● *noun* /ə'bjuːs/ **1** misuse. **2** maltreatment. **3** insulting language. **4** corrupt practice. □ **abuser** /ə'bjuːzə/ *noun*.

■ *verb* **1** exploit, misuse. **2** assault, damage, harm, hurt, ill-treat, injure, maltreat, mistreat, molest, rape, spoil, treat roughly. **3** affront, berate, be rude to, call names, castigate, curse, defame, denigrate, insult, inveigh against, libel, malign, revile, slander, smear, sneer at, swear at, vilify, vituperate, wrong. ● *noun* **1** misappropriation, misuse, perversion. **2** assault, ill-treatment, maltreatment. **3** execration, invective, obscenity, slander, vilification, vituperation.

abusive /ə'bjuːsɪv/ *adjective* insulting, offensive. □ **abusively** *adverb*.

■ acrimonious, angry, censorious, critical, cruel, defamatory, denigrating, derogatory, disparaging, hurtful, impolite, injurious, insulting, libellous, offensive, opprobrious, pejorative, rude, scathing, scornful, scurrilous, slanderous, vituperative.

abut /ə'bʌt/ *verb* (**-tt-**) **1** (+ *on*) border on. **2** (usually + *on*, *against*) touch; lean on.

abysmal /ə'bɪzm(ə)l/ *adjective* **1** very bad, dire. **2** profound. □ **abysmally** *adverb*.

■ **1** see BAD 6. **2** bottomless, boundless, deep, immeasurable, incalculable, infinite, profound, vast.

abyss /ə'bɪs/ *noun* deep chasm.

■ bottomless pit, chasm, crater, fissure, gulf, hole, pit, rift, void.

AC *abbreviation* alternating current.

a/c *abbreviation* account.

acacia /ə'keɪʃə/ *noun* tree with yellow or white flowers.

academia /ækə'diːmɪə/ *noun* the world of scholars.

academic /ækə'demɪk/ *adjective* **1** scholarly. **2** of learning. **3** of no practical relevance. ● *noun* teacher or scholar in university etc. □ **academically** *adverb*.

■ *adjective* **1** bookish, brainy, clever, erudite, *colloquial* highbrow, intelligent, learned, scholarly, studious. **2** educational, pedagogical, scholastic. **3** abstract, conjectural, hypothetical, impractical, intellectual, speculative, theoretical. ● *noun* don, *colloquial* egghead, *colloquial* highbrow, intellectual, lecturer, professor, reader, scholar, thinker.

academician /əkædə'mɪʃ(ə)n/ *noun* member of Academy.

academy /ə'kædəmɪ/ *noun* (*plural* **-ies**) **1** place of specialized training. **2** (**Academy**) society of distinguished scholars, artists, scientists, etc. **3** *Scottish* secondary school.

acanthus /ə'kænθəs/ *noun* (*plural* **-es**) spring herbaceous plant with spiny leaves.

ACAS /'eɪkæs/ *abbreviation* Advisory, Conciliation, and Arbitration Service.

accede /æk'siːd/ *verb* (**-ding**) (+ *to*) **1** take office, esp. as monarch. **2** assent to.

accelerate /ək'seləreɪt/ *verb* (**-ting**) **1** increase speed (of). **2** (cause to) happen earlier. □ **acceleration** *noun*.

■ **1** *colloquial* get a move on, go faster, hasten, pick up speed, quicken, speed up. **2** bring on, expedite, spur on, step up, stimulate.

accelerator *noun* **1** device for increasing speed, esp. pedal in vehicle. **2** *Physics* apparatus for imparting high speeds to charged particles.

accent *noun* /'æksənt/ **1** style of pronunciation of region or social group (see panel). **2** emphasis. **3** prominence given to syllable by stress or pitch. **4** mark on letter indicating pronunciation (see panel). ● *verb* /æk'sent/ **1** emphasize. **2** write or print accents on.

■ *noun* **1** brogue, dialect, intonation, pronunciation, speech pattern. **2** emphasis, stress, weight. **3** accentuation, beat, emphasis, pulse, rhythm, stress.

accentuate /ək'sentʃʊeɪt/ *verb* (**-ting**) emphasize, make prominent. □ **accentuation** *noun*.

accept /ək'sept/ *verb* **1** willingly receive. **2** answer (invitation etc.) affirmatively. **3** regard favourably. **4** receive as valid or suitable. **5** tolerate. □ **acceptance** *noun*. **accepted** *adjective*.

■ **1** get, receive, take, welcome. **2** agree to, consent to, jump at. **3** receive, welcome. **4** abide by, accede to, acknowledge, acquiesce in, admit, agree to, believe in, be reconciled to, consent to, defer to, grant, recognize, swallow, take in. **5** bear, put up with, reconcile oneself to, resign oneself to, stomach, submit to, suffer, tolerate, undergo. □ **acceptance** acquiescence, agreement, approval, consent. **accepted** acknowledged, agreed, axiomatic, common, indisputable, recognized, standard, undisputed, unquestioned.

acceptable *adjective* **1** worth accepting. **2** tolerable. □ **acceptability** *noun*. **acceptably** *adverb*.

■ **1** agreeable, gratifying, pleasant, pleasing, worthwhile. **2** adequate, admissible, moderate, passable, satisfactory, suitable, tolerable.

access /'ækses/ *noun* **1** way of approach or entry. **2** right or opportunity to reach, use, or visit. ● *verb* gain access to (data) in computer.

accessible /ək'sesɪb(ə)l/ *adjective* **1** reachable or obtainable. **2** easy to understand. □ **accessibility** *noun*.

■ **1** approachable, at hand, attainable, available, close, convenient, handy, within reach.

accession /əkˈseʃ(ə)n/ *noun* **1** taking office, esp. as monarch. **2** thing added.

accessory /əkˈsesərɪ/ *noun* (*plural* **-ies**) **1** additional or extra thing. **2** (usually in *plural*) small attachment or item of dress. **3** (often + *to*) person who abets in or is privy to illegal act.
■ **1, 2** addition, appendage, attachment, component, extra. **3** see ACCOMPLICE.

accident /ˈæksɪd(ə)nt/ *noun* **1** unintentional unfortunate esp. harmful event. **2** event without apparent cause; unexpected event. **3** chance. □ **accident-prone** clumsy. **by accident** unintentionally.
■ **1** blunder, catastrophe, disaster, *Law* misadventure, mischance, mishap, mistake; (*car accident*) collision, crash, *colloquial* pile-up. **2** coincidence, fluke. **3** chance, coincidence, fate, fluke, fortune, luck, potluck, serendipity.

accidental /æksɪˈdent(ə)l/ *adjective* happening or done by chance or accident. ● *noun Music* sharp, flat, or natural indicating momentary departure of note from key signature. □ **accidentally** *adverb*.
■ *adjective* arbitrary, casual, chance, coincidental, fluky, fortuitous, fortunate, haphazard, inadvertent, lucky, random, unexpected, unforeseen, unintended, unintentional, unlucky, unplanned, unpremeditated.

acclaim /əˈkleɪm/ *verb* welcome or applaud enthusiastically. ● *noun* **1** applause. **2** welcome. **3** public praise. □ **acclamation** /æklə-/ *noun*.
■ *verb* applaud, celebrate, cheer, clap, commend, extol, hail, honour, praise, salute, welcome.

acclimatize /əˈklaɪmətaɪz/ *verb* (also **-ise**) (**-zing** or **-sing**) adapt to new climate or conditions. □ **acclimatization** *noun*.

acclivity /əˈklɪvɪtɪ/ *noun* (*plural* **-ies**) upward slope.

accolade /ˈækəleɪd/ *noun* **1** praise given. **2** touch made with sword at conferring of knighthood.

accommodate /əˈkɒmədeɪt/ *verb* (**-ting**) **1** provide lodging or room for. **2** adapt, harmonize, reconcile. **3** do favour to. **4** (+ *with*) supply with.
■ **1** billet, board, house, lodge, provide for, put up, quarter, shelter, take in. **2** accustom, adapt, harmonize, reconcile. **3** assist, help, oblige, serve. **4** (*accommodate with*) equip with, fit out with, fit with, furnish with, provide with, supply with.

accommodating *adjective* obliging.
■ see CONSIDERATE.

accommodation *noun* **1** lodgings. **2** adjustment, adaptation. **3** convenient arrangement. □ **accommodation address** postal address used instead of permanent one.
■ **1** abode, billet, board, *colloquial* digs, home, housing, lodgings, *pied-à-terre*, premises, quarters, residence, shelter.

accompaniment /əˈkʌmpənɪmənt/ *noun* **1** instrumental or orchestral support for solo instrument, voice, or group. **2** accompanying thing.

accompany /əˈkʌmpənɪ/ *verb* (**-ies**, **-ied**) **1** go with, attend. **2** (usually in *passive*; + *with*, *by*) be done or found with. **3** *Music* play accompaniment for. □ **accompanist** *noun Music*. **accompanying** *adjective*.
■ **1** attend, chaperon, conduct, escort, go with, guard, guide, look after, partner, tag along with. **2** be associated with, be linked with, belong with, complement, occur with, supplement.
□ **accompanying** associated, attached, attendant, complementary, related.

accomplice /əˈkʌmplɪs/ *noun* partner in crime.
■ abetter, *Law* abettor, accessory, associate, collaborator, colleague, confederate, conspirator, helper, partner.

Accent

1 A person's accent is the way he or she pronounces words. People from different regions and different groups in society have different accents. For instance, most people in northern England say *path* with a 'short' *a*, while most people in southern England say it with a 'long' *a*. In America and Canada the *r* in *far* and *port* is generally pronounced, while in south-eastern England, for example, it is not. Everyone speaks with an accent, although some accents may be regarded as having more prestige, such as 'Received Pronunciation' (RP) in the UK.

2 An accent on a letter is a mark added to it to alter the sound it stands for. In French, for example, there are

   ´ (acute), as in *état*   ¨ (diaresis), as in *Noël*
   ` (grave), as in *mère*   , (cedilla), as in *français*
   ˆ (circumflex), as in *guêpe*

and German has

   ¨ (umlaut), as in *München*.

There are no accents on native English words, but many words borrowed from other languages still have them, such as *blasé* and *façade*.

accomplish /ə'kʌmplɪʃ/ *verb* succeed in doing; achieve, complete.
■ achieve, attain, bring off, carry out, carry through, complete, consummate, discharge, do, effect, finish, fulfil, realize, succeed in.

accomplished *adjective* clever, skilled.
■ adept, clever, expert, gifted, masterly, polished, proficient, skilful, skilled, talented.

accomplishment *noun* 1 completion (of task etc.). 2 acquired esp. social skill. 3 thing achieved.
■ 2 ability, attainment, expertise, gift, skill, talent. 3 achievement, attainment, feat.

accord /ə'kɔːd/ *verb* 1 (often + *with*) be consistent or in harmony. 2 grant, give. ● *noun* agreement, consent. □ **of one's own accord** on one's own initiative.
■ *noun* agreement, concord, consent, harmony, rapport, understanding.

accordance *noun* □ **in accordance with** in conformity to.

according *adverb* 1 (+ *to*) as stated by. 2 (+ *to*, *as*) in proportion to or as.

accordingly *adverb* 1 as circumstances suggest or require. 2 consequently.

accordion /ə'kɔːdɪən/ *noun* musical reed instrument with concertina-like bellows, keys, and buttons.

accost /ə'kɒst/ *verb* approach and speak boldly to.

account /ə'kaʊnt/ *noun* 1 narration, description. 2 arrangement at bank etc. for depositing and withdrawing money etc. 3 statement of financial transactions with balance. 4 importance. 5 behalf. ● *verb* consider as. □ **account for** 1 explain. 2 answer for. 3 kill, destroy. **on account** 1 to be paid for later. 2 in part payment. **on account of** because of. **on no account** under no circumstances. **take account of**, **take into account** consider.
■ *noun* 1 commentary, description, diary, explanation, history, log, memoir, narrative, record, report, statement, story, tale, write-up. 3 bill, calculation, *US* check, computation, invoice, receipt, reckoning, score, statement. 4 advantage, benefit, concern, consequence, importance, interest, significance, use, value, worth.
□ **account for 1** see EXPLAIN 4.

accountable *adjective* 1 responsible; required to account for one's conduct. 2 explicable. □ **accountability** *noun*.

accountant *noun* professional keeper or verifier of financial accounts. □ **accountancy** *noun*. **accounting** *noun*.

accoutrements /ə'kuːtrəmənts/ *plural noun* equipment, trappings.

accredit /ə'kredɪt/ *verb* (-t-) 1 (+ *to*) attribute to. 2 (+ *with*) credit with. 3 (usually + *to*, *at*) send (ambassador etc.) with credentials.

accredited *adjective* 1 officially recognized. 2 generally accepted.

accretion /ə'kriːʃ(ə)n/ *noun* 1 growth by accumulation or organic enlargement. 2 the resulting whole. 3 matter so added.

accrue /ə'kruː/ *verb* (**-ues**, **-ued**, **-uing**) (often + *to*) come as natural increase or advantage, esp. financial.

accumulate /ə'kjuːmjʊleɪt/ *verb* (**-ting**) 1 acquire increasing number or quantity of; amass, collect. 2 grow numerous; increase. □ **accumulation** *noun*. **accumulative** /-lətɪv/ *adjective*.
■ 1 aggregate, amass, assemble, bring together, collect, gather, heap up, hoard, pile up, stockpile, store up. 2 accrue, build up, come together, grow, increase, multiply, pile up. □ **accumulation** build-up, collection, conglomeration, gathering, heap, hoard, mass, stockpile, store.

accumulator *noun* 1 rechargeable electric cell. 2 bet placed on sequence of events, with winnings and stake from each placed on next.

accurate /'ækjʊrət/ *adjective* 1 precise. 2 conforming exactly with truth etc. □ **accuracy** *noun*. **accurately** *adverb*.
■ authentic, careful, correct, exact, factual, faultless, meticulous, minute, nice, perfect, precise, reliable, scrupulous, sound, *colloquial* spot on, true, truthful, unerring, *formal* veracious.

accursed /ə'kɜːsɪd/ *adjective* 1 under a curse. 2 *colloquial* detestable, annoying.

accusative /ə'kjuːzətɪv/ *Grammar noun* case expressing object of action. ● *adjective* of or in accusative.

accuse /ə'kjuːz/ *verb* (**-sing**) (often + *of*) charge with fault or crime; blame. □ **accusation** /æk-/ *noun*. **accusatory** *adjective*.
■ blame, bring charges against, censure, charge, condemn, denounce, impeach, indict, prosecute, *esp. Law* summons, tax. □ **accusation** allegation, charge, citation, complaint, impeachment, indictment, summons.

accustom /ə'kʌstəm/ *verb* (+ *to*) make used to.

accustomed *adjective* 1 (usually + *to*) used (to a thing). 2 customary. □ **get accustomed to** become used to; adapt to.
■ 1 (*accustomed to*) acclimatized to, familiar with, habituated to, used to. 2 common, customary, established, expected, familiar, habitual, normal, ordinary, prevailing, routine, traditional, usual. □ **get accustomed to** see ADAPT 3.

ace *noun* 1 playing card with single spot. 2 person who excels in some activity. 3 *Tennis* unreturnable service. ● *adjective* *slang* excellent. □ **within an ace of** on the verge of.

acerbic /ə'sɜːbɪk/ *adjective* harsh and sharp, esp. in speech or manner. □ **acerbity** *noun* (*plural* **-ies**).

acetate /'æsɪteɪt/ *noun* 1 compound of acetic acid, esp. the cellulose ester. 2 fabric made from this.

acetic /ə'siːtɪk/ *adjective* of or like vinegar. □ **acetic acid** clear liquid acid in vinegar.

acetone /'æsɪtəʊn/ *noun* colourless volatile solvent of organic compounds.

acetylene /ə'setɪliːn/ *noun* inflammable hydrocarbon gas, used esp. in welding.

ache /eɪk/ *noun* **1** continuous dull pain. **2** mental distress. ● *verb* (**aching**) **1** suffer from or be the source of an ache. **2** yearn.
  ■ *noun* **1** discomfort, hurt, pain, pang, smart, soreness, throbbing, twinge. **2** anguish, distress, pain, pang, sorrow. ● *verb* **1** be painful, be sore, hurt, smart, sting, throb. **2** (*ache for*) see DESIRE *verb* 1.

achieve /ə'tʃiːv/ *verb* (**-ving**) **1** reach or attain by effort. **2** accomplish (task etc.). **3** be successful. □ **achievable** *adjective*. **achiever** *noun*. **achievement** *noun*.
  ■ **1** acquire, attain, earn, gain, get, obtain, reach, win. **2** accomplish, bring off, carry out, complete, conclude, do successfully, effect, engineer, execute, finish, fulfil, manage, succeed in.

Achilles /ə'kɪliːz/ *noun* □ **Achilles heel** vulnerable point. **Achilles tendon** tendon attaching calf muscles to heel.

achromatic /ækrəʊ'mætɪk/ *adjective* **1** transmitting light without separating it into colours. **2** free from colour. □ **achromatically** *adverb*.

achy /'eɪkɪ/ *adjective* (**-ier, -iest**) suffering from aches.

acid /'æsɪd/ *noun* **1** *Chemistry* substance that neutralizes alkalis, turns litmus red, and usually contains hydrogen and is sour. **2** *slang* drug LSD. ● *adjective* **1** having properties of acid. **2** sour. **3** biting, sharp. □ **acid drop** sharp-tasting boiled sweet. **acid house** synthesized music with simple beat, associated with hallucinogenic drugs. **acid rain** rain containing acid formed from industrial waste in atmosphere. **acid test** severe or conclusive test. □ **acidic** /ə'sɪd-/ *adjective*. **acidify** /ə'sɪd-/ *verb* (**-ies, -ied**). **acidity** /ə'sɪd-/ *noun*.
  ■ *adjective* **2** sharp, sour, tangy, tart, vinegary. **3** biting, cutting, mordant, sharp, stinging, tart.

acidulous /ə'sɪdjʊləs/ *adjective* somewhat acid.

acknowledge /ək'nɒlɪdʒ/ *verb* (**-ging**) **1** recognize; accept truth of. **2** confirm receipt of (letter etc.). **3** show that one has noticed. **4** express gratitude for.
  ■ **1** accede to, accept, acquiesce in, admit, allow, concede, confess, confirm, endorse, grant, own up to, profess. **2** answer, react to, reply to, respond to, return. **3** greet, hail, recognize, say hello to.

acknowledgement *noun* (also **acknowledgment**) **1** acknowledging. **2** thing given or done in gratitude. **3** letter etc. confirming receipt. **4** (usually in *plural*) author's thanks, prefacing book.

acme /'ækmɪ/ *noun* highest point.
  ■ apex, crown, height, peak, pinnacle, summit, top, zenith.

acne /'æknɪ/ *noun* skin condition with red pimples.

acolyte /'ækəlaɪt/ *noun* assistant, esp. of priest.

aconite /'ækənaɪt/ *noun* **1** any of various poisonous plants, esp. monkshood. **2** drug made from these.

acorn /'eɪkɔːn/ *noun* fruit of oak.

acoustic /ə'kuːstɪk/ *adjective* **1** of sound or sense of hearing. **2** (of musical instrument etc.) without electrical amplification. □ **acoustically** *adverb*.

acoustics *plural noun* **1** properties (of a room etc.) in transmitting sound. **2** (treated as *singular*) science of sound.

acquaint /ə'kweɪnt/ *verb* (+ *with*) make aware of or familiar with. □ **be acquainted with** know.
  ■ (*acquaint with*) apprise of, brief about, enlighten about, inform of, make aware of, make familiar with, notify of, tell about.

acquaintance *noun* **1** being acquainted. **2** person one knows slightly. □ **acquaintanceship** *noun*.
  ■ **1** awareness, familiarity, knowledge, understanding. **2** see FRIEND 1.

acquiesce /ækwɪ'es/ *verb* (**-cing**) (often + *in*) agree, esp. tacitly. □ **acquiescence** *noun*. **acquiescent** *adjective*.

acquire /ə'kwaɪə/ *verb* (**-ring**) gain possession of. □ **acquired immune deficiency syndrome** = AIDS. **acquired taste** liking developed by experience.
  ■ buy, come by, earn, get, procure, purchase.

acquirement *noun* thing acquired or attained.

acquisition /ækwɪ'zɪʃ(ə)n/ *noun* **1** (esp. useful) thing acquired. **2** acquiring, being acquired.
  ■ **1** accession, addition, *colloquial* buy, gain, possession, purchase.

acquisitive /ə'kwɪzɪtɪv/ *adjective* keen to acquire things. □ **acquisitiveness** *noun*.

acquit /ə'kwɪt/ *verb* (**-tt-**) **1** (often + *of*) declare not guilty. **2** (**acquit oneself**) behave, perform. **3** (**acquit oneself**; + *of*) discharge (duty etc.). □ **acquittal** *noun*.
  ■ **1** absolve, clear, declare innocent, discharge, excuse, exonerate, find innocent, free, let off, release, reprieve, set free, vindicate. **2** (**acquit oneself**) see BEHAVE 1.

acre /'eɪkə/ *noun* measure of land, 4840 sq. yards, 0.405 ha.

acreage /'eɪkərɪdʒ/ *noun* number of acres.

acrid /'ækrɪd/ *adjective* bitterly pungent. □ **acridity** /-'krɪd-/ *noun*.
  ■ bitter, caustic, pungent, sharp, unpleasant.

acrimonious /ækrɪ'məʊnɪəs/ *adjective* bitter in manner or temper. □ **acrimony** /'ækrɪmənɪ/ *noun*.
  ■ abusive, acerbic, angry, bad-tempered, bitter, caustic, hostile, hot-tempered, ill-natured, ill-tempered, irascible, quarrelsome, rancorous, sarcastic, sharp, spiteful, tart, testy, venomous, virulent, waspish.

acrobat /'ækrəbæt/ *noun* performer of acrobatics. □ **acrobatic** /-'bæt-/ *adjective*.

acrobatics /ækrə'bætɪks/ *plural noun* gymnastic feats.

acronym /'ækrənɪm/ *noun* word formed from initial letters of other words (e.g. *laser*, *NATO*).

acropolis /ə'krɒpəlɪs/ *noun* citadel of ancient Greek city.

across /ə'krɒs/ *preposition* **1** to or on other side of. **2** from one side to another side of. ● *adverb* **1** to or on other side. **2** from one side to another. □ **across the board** applying to all.

acrostic /ə'krɒstɪk/ *noun* poem etc. in which first (or first and last) letters of lines form word(s).

acrylic /ə'krɪlɪk/ *adjective* made from acrylic acid. ● *noun* acrylic fibre, fabric, or paint.

acrylic acid *noun* a pungent liquid organic acid.

act *noun* **1** thing done, deed. **2** process of doing. **3** item of entertainment. **4** pretence. **5** main division of play. **6** decree of legislative body. ● *verb* **1** behave. **2** perform actions or functions. **3** (often + *on*) have effect. **4** perform in play etc. **5** pretend. **6** play part of. □ **act for** be (legal) representative of. **act on** perform or carry out. **act out** translate into action. **act up** *colloquial* misbehave, give trouble. **put on an act** *colloquial* carry out pretence.

■ *noun* **1** action, deed, exploit, feat, operation, undertaking. **3** performance, routine, sketch, turn. **6** decree, edict, law, regulation, statute. ● *verb* **1** behave, conduct oneself, deport oneself. **2** do something, function, operate, react, serve, take steps. **3** function, operate, take effect, work. **4** see PERFORM **4**. **5** see PRETEND *verb* **1**. **6** appear as, characterize, enact, impersonate, mimic, perform as, personify, play, portray, pose as, represent.

acting *adjective* serving temporarily as.
■ interim, temporary.

actinism /'æktɪnɪz(ə)m/ *noun* property of short-wave radiation that produces chemical changes, as in photography.

action /'ækʃ(ə)n/ *noun* **1** process of doing or acting. **2** forcefulness, energy. **3** exertion of energy or influence. **4** deed, act. **5** (often after *the*) series of events in story, play, etc. **6** *slang* exciting activity. **7** battle. **8** mechanism of instrument. **9** style of movement. **10** lawsuit. □ **action-packed** full of action or excitement. **action replay** playback of part of television broadcast. **out of action** not functioning.

■ **1** activity, movement, operation, performance. **2** energy, enterprise, liveliness, vigour, vitality. **3** effect, force, influence. **4** act, deed, exertion, exploit, feat, measure, proceeding, step, undertaking, work. **5** events, incidents, plot, story. **6** activity, adventure, drama, excitement. **7** see BATTLE *noun* **1**. **8** mechanism, movement, operation, workings, works.

actionable *adjective* providing grounds for legal action.

activate /'æktɪveɪt/ *verb* (**-ting**) **1** make active. **2** make radioactive. □ **activation** *noun*.
■ **1** actuate, energize, excite, fire, galvanize, initiate, mobilize, rouse, set in motion, set off, start, stimulate, trigger.

active /'æktɪv/ *adjective* **1** marked by action; energetic, diligent. **2** working, operative. **3** *Grammar* (of verb) of which subject performs action (e.g. *saw* in *he saw a film*). ● *noun Grammar* active form or voice. □ **active service** military service in wartime. □ **actively** *adverb*.

■ *adjective* **1** animated, brisk, bustling, busy, committed, dedicated, devoted, diligent, dynamic, energetic, enthusiastic, hard-working, hyperactive, industrious, involved, live, lively, militant, nimble, occupied, *colloquial* on the go, restless, sedulous, sprightly, staunch, strenuous, vigorous, vivacious, zealous. **2** functioning, operative, working.

activism *noun* policy of vigorous action, esp. for a political cause. □ **activist** *noun*.

activity /æk'tɪvɪtɪ/ *noun* (*plural* **-ies**) **1** being active. **2** busy or energetic action. **3** (often in *plural*) occupation, pursuit.

■ **1, 2** action, animation, bustle, commotion, energy, hurly-burly, hustle, industry, life, movement, stir. **3** employment, hobby, interest, job, occupation, pastime, pursuit, task, venture, work.

actor /'æktə/ *noun* person who acts in play, film, etc.

■ actress, artist, artiste, entertainer, performer, player, star, Thespian, trouper; (*actors*) cast, company, troupe.

actress /'æktrɪs/ *noun* female actor.
■ see ACTOR.

actual /'æktʃʊəl/ *adjective* **1** existing, real. **2** current. □ **actuality** /-'æl-/ *noun* (*plural* **-ies**).

■ **1** authentic, bona fide, confirmed, corporeal, definite, existing, factual, genuine, indisputable, legitimate, living, material, real, tangible, true, verifiable. **2** current, existing, present, prevailing.

actually *adverb* in fact, really.

actuary /'æktʃʊərɪ/ *noun* (*plural* **-ies**) statistician, esp. one calculating insurance risks and premiums. □ **actuarial** /-'eər-/ *adjective*.

actuate /'æktʃʊeɪt/ *verb* (**-ting**) cause to move, function, act.

acuity /ə'kjuːɪtɪ/ *noun* acuteness.

acumen /'ækjʊmen/ *noun* keen insight or discernment.

acupuncture /'ækjuːpʌŋktʃə/ *noun* medical treatment using needles in parts of the body. □ **acupuncturist** *noun*.

acute /ə'kjuːt/ *adjective* (**-r, -st**) **1** keen, penetrating; perceptive. **2** (of pain) severe, sharp. **3** (of disease) coming quickly to crisis. **4** (of problem etc.) severe, critical. **5** (of angle) less than 90°. ● *noun* = ACUTE ACCENT. □ **acute accent** mark (´) over letter indicating pronunciation. □ **acutely** *adverb*. **acuteness** *noun*.

■ *adjective* **1** alert, analytical, astute, canny, clever, *colloquial* cute, discerning, incisive, intelligent, keen, penetrating, perceptive, sensitive, sharp, shrewd, subtle. **2** excruciating, exquisite, extreme, intense, keen, piercing, racking, severe, sharp, shooting, violent. **3** critical, sudden. **4** critical, immediate, overwhelming, pressing, serious, urgent. **5** narrow, pointed, sharp.

AD *abbreviation* of the Christian era (*Anno Domini*).

ad *noun colloquial* advertisement.

adage /ˈædɪdʒ/ *noun* proverb, maxim.

adagio /əˈdɑːʒɪəʊ/ *Music adverb & adjective* in slow time. ● *noun* (*plural* **-s**) adagio passage.

adamant /ˈædəmənt/ *adjective* stubbornly resolute. □ **adamantly** *adverb*.

adamantine /ædəˈmæntaɪn/ *adjective* unbreakable; unshakeable.

Adam's apple /ˈædəmz/ *noun* cartilaginous projection at front of neck.

adapt /əˈdæpt/ *verb* **1** (usually + *to*) fit, adjust; alter. **2** (+ *to, for*) make suitable, modify. **3** (usually + *to*) adjust to new conditions. □ **adaptable** *adjective*. **adaptation** /æd-/ *noun*.

■ **1, 2** adjust, alter, amend, change, convert, edit, fit, modify, process, rearrange, rebuild, reconstruct, refashion, remake, reorganize, suit, tailor, transform. **3** (*adapt to*) acclimatize to, accustom to, adjust to, attune to, become conditioned to, become hardened to, become reconciled to, get accustomed to, get used to, habituate to.

adaptor *noun* **1** device for making equipment compatible. **2** *Electricity* device for connecting several electrical plugs to one socket.

add *verb* **1** join as increase or supplement. **2** unite (numbers) to get their total. **3** say further. □ **add in** add, include. **add to** increase. **add up 1** find total of. **2** (+ *to*) amount to.

■ **1** annex, append, attach, combine, integrate, join, tack on, unite. **add to** see INCREASE *verb*. **add up 1** see TOTAL *verb* 2. **2** (*add up to*) see TOTAL *verb* 1.

addendum /əˈdendəm/ *noun* (*plural* **-da**) **1** thing to be added. **2** material added at end of book.

adder /ˈædə/ *noun* small venomous snake.

addict /ˈædɪkt/ *noun* **1** person addicted, esp. to drug. **2** *colloquial* devotee.

■ **1** *slang* junkie, *colloquial* user. **2** see ENTHUSIAST (ENTHUSIASM).

addicted /əˈdɪktɪd/ *adjective* (usually + *to*) **1** dependent on a drug as a habit. **2** devoted to an interest. □ **addiction** *noun*.

■ □ **addiction** compulsion, craving, dependence, fixation, habit, obsession.

addictive /əˈdɪktɪv/ *adjective* causing addiction.

addition /əˈdɪʃ(ə)n/ *noun* **1** adding. **2** person or thing added. □ **in addition** (often + *to*) also, as well.

■ **1** adding up, calculation, computation, reckoning, totalling, totting up. **2** accession, accessory, accretion, addendum, additive, adjunct, admixture, annexe, appendage, appendix, appurtenance, attachment, codicil (*to a will*), continuation, development, expansion, extension, extra, increase, increment, postscript, supplement.

additional *adjective* added, extra. □ **additionally** *adverb*.

■ added, extra, further, increased, more, new, other, spare, supplementary.

additive /ˈædɪtɪv/ *noun* substance added, esp. to colour, flavour, or preserve food.

addle /ˈæd(ə)l/ *verb* (**-ling**) **1** muddle, confuse. **2** (usually as **addled** *adjective*) (of egg) become rotten.

address /əˈdres/ *noun* **1** place where person lives or organization is situated. **2** particulars of this, esp. for postal purposes. **3** speech delivered to an audience. ● *verb* **1** write postal directions on. **2** direct (remarks etc.). **3** speak or write to. **4** direct one's attention to. □ **address oneself to 1** speak or write to. **2** attend to.

■ *noun* **1** directions, location, whereabouts. **3** discourse, harangue, homily, lecture, sermon, speech, talk. ● *verb* **3** accost, approach, *colloquial* buttonhole, give a speech to, greet, hail, harangue, lecture, salute, speak to, talk to. **4** see TACKLE *verb* 1.

addressee /ædreˈsiː/ *noun* person to whom letter etc. is addressed.

adduce /əˈdjuːs/ *verb* (**-cing**) cite as proof or instance. □ **adducible** *adjective*.

adenoids /ˈædɪnɔɪdz/ *plural noun* enlarged lymphatic tissue between nose and throat, often hindering breathing. □ **adenoidal** /-ˈnɔɪ-/ *adjective*.

adept *adjective* /əˈdept, ˈædept/ (+ *at, in*) skilful. ● *noun* /ˈædept/ adept person. □ **adeptness** *noun*.

■ *adjective* clever, competent, expert, gifted, practised, proficient, skilful, talented.

adequate /ˈædɪkwət/ *adjective* sufficient, satisfactory. □ **adequacy** *noun*. **adequately** *adverb*.

■ acceptable, all right, average, competent, fair, middling, *colloquial* OK, passable, presentable, satisfactory, *colloquial* so so, sufficient, tolerable.

adhere /ədˈhɪə/ *verb* (**-ring**) **1** (usually + *to*) stick fast. **2** (+ *to*) behave according to (rule etc.). **3** (+ *to*) give allegiance to.

■ **1** bind, bond, cement, cling, glue, gum, paste, stick. **2** (*adhere to*) see FOLLOW 6.

adherent *noun* supporter. ● *adjective* adhering. □ **adherence** *noun*.

■ *noun* aficionado, devotee, fan, follower, supporter.

adhesion /ədˈhiːʒ(ə)n/ *noun* adhering.

adhesive /əd'hi:sɪv/ *adjective* sticky, causing adhesion. ● *noun* adhesive substance.
■ *adjective* glued, gluey, gummed, sticky.

ad hoc /æd 'hɒk/ *adverb & adjective* for one particular occasion or use.

adieu /ə'dju:/ *interjection* goodbye.

ad infinitum /æd ɪnfɪ'naɪtəm/ *adverb* without limit; for ever.

adipose /'ædɪpəʊz/ *adjective* of fat, fatty. □ **adiposity** /-'pɒs-/ *noun*.

adjacent /ə'dʒeɪs(ə)nt/ *adjective* lying near, adjoining. □ **adjacency** *noun*.

adjective /'ædʒɪktɪv/ *noun* word describing noun or pronoun (see panel). □ **adjectival** /-'taɪv-/ *adjective*.

adjoin /ə'dʒɔɪn/ *verb* (often as **adjoining** *adjective*) be next to and joined with.
■ abut on, border on, touch; (**adjoining**) adjacent, contiguous, juxtaposed, neighbouring, next.

adjourn /ə'dʒɜ:n/ *verb* 1 postpone, break off. 2 (+ *to*) transfer to (another place). □ **adjournment** *noun*.
■ 1 break off, defer, discontinue, interrupt, postpone, put off, suspend. □ **adjournment** break, interruption, pause, postponement, recess, stay, suspension.

adjudge /ə'dʒʌdʒ/ *verb* (**-ging**) 1 pronounce judgement on. 2 pronounce or award judicially. □ **adjudg(e)ment** *noun*.

adjudicate /ə'dʒu:dɪkeɪt/ *verb* (**-ting**) 1 act as judge. 2 adjudge. □ **adjudication** *noun*. **adjudicator** *noun*.

adjunct /'ædʒʌŋkt/ *noun* (+ *to, of*) subordinate or incidental thing.

adjure /ə'dʒʊə/ *verb* (**-ring**) (usually + *to do*) beg or command. □ **adjuration** *noun*.

adjust /ə'dʒʌst/ *verb* 1 order, position; arrange. 2 regulate. 3 (usually + *to*) adapt. 4 harmonize. □ **adjustable** *adjective*. **adjustment** *noun*.
■ 1, 2 adapt, alter, amend, arrange, balance, change, convert, correct, modify, put right, rectify, regulate, remake, remodel, reorganize, reshape, set, tailor, temper, tune. 3 (*adjust to*) acclimatize to, accommodate oneself to, accustom oneself to, adapt to, habituate oneself to, reconcile oneself to.

adjutant /'ædʒʊt(ə)nt/ *noun* army officer assisting superior in administrative duties.

ad lib /æd 'lɪb/ *verb* (**-bb-**) improvise. ● *adjective* improvised. ● *adverb* to any desired extent.

Adm. *abbreviation* Admiral.

administer /əd'mɪnɪstə/ *verb* 1 manage (affairs). 2 formally deliver, dispense.
■ 1 administrate, conduct, control, direct, govern, lead, manage, organize, oversee, preside over, regulate, rule, run, supervise. 2 carry out, deliver, dispense, distribute, execute, give, hand out, implement, measure out, *literary* mete out, provide, supply.

administrate /əd'mɪnɪstreɪt/ *verb* administer; act as administrator.

administration /ədmɪnɪ'streɪʃ(ə)n/ *noun* 1 administering, esp. public affairs. 2 government in power.

administrative /əd'mɪnɪstrətɪv/ *adjective* of the management of affairs.

administrator /əd'mɪnɪstreɪtə/ *noun* manager of business, public affairs, or person's estate.
■ bureaucrat, chief, civil servant, controller, director, executive, manager, mandarin, organizer.

admirable /'ædmərəb(ə)l/ *adjective* 1 deserving admiration. 2 excellent. □ **admirably** *adverb*.

Adjective

An adjective is a word that describes a noun or pronoun, e.g.
   red, clever, German, depressed, battered, sticky, shining

Most can be used either before a noun, e.g.
   the red *house*   *a lazy man*
   a clever *woman*

or after a verb like *be, seem,* or *call,* e.g.
   The house is red.   *I wouldn't call him* lazy.
   She seems very clever.

Some can be used only before a noun, e.g.
   the chief *reason* (one cannot say **the reason is chief*)

Some can be used only after a verb, e.g.
   The ship is still afloat. (one cannot say **an afloat ship*)

A few can be used only immediately after a noun, e.g.
   the president elect (one cannot say either **an elect president* or **The president is elect*)

(See also panels at COMPARATIVE and SUPERLATIVE.)

■ **1** awe-inspiring, commendable, creditable, deserving, estimable, exemplary, honourable, laudable, meritorious, pleasing, praiseworthy, wonderful, worthy. **2** see EXCELLENT.

admiral /'ædmər(ə)l/ *noun* **1** commander-in-chief of navy. **2** high-ranking naval officer; commander.

Admiralty *noun* (*plural* **-ies**) (in full **Admiralty Board**) *historical* committee superintending Royal Navy.

admire /əd'maɪə/ *verb* **1** regard with approval, respect, or satisfaction. **2** express admiration of. □ **admiration** /ædmə'reɪ-/ *noun*. **admirer** *noun*. **admiring** *adjective*. **admiringly** *adverb*.

■ applaud, appreciate, approve of, be delighted by, commend, esteem, have a high opinion of, honour, idolize, laud, look up to, marvel at, praise, respect, revere, think highly of, value, venerate, wonder at. □ **admiration** appreciation, awe, commendation, esteem, hero-worship, high regard, honour, praise, respect. **admiring** see COMPLIMENTARY 1, RESPECTFUL.

admissible /əd'mɪsɪb(ə)l/ *adjective* **1** worth accepting or considering. **2** allowable. □ **admissibility** *noun*.

admission /əd'mɪʃ(ə)n/ *noun* **1** acknowledgement (of error etc.). **2** (right of) entering. **3** entrance charge.

■ **1** acceptance, acknowledgement, affirmation, concession, confession, declaration, disclosure, revelation. **2** access, admittance, entrance, entry.

admit /əd'mɪt/ *verb* (**-tt-**) **1** (often + *to be*, *that*) acknowledge, recognize as true. **2** (+ *to*) confess to. **3** let in. **4** take (patient) into hospital. **5** accommodate. **6** (+ *of*) allow as possible.

■ **1** accept, acknowledge, allow, concede, declare, disclose, recognize, reveal, say reluctantly. **2** (*admit to*) confess to, own up to. **3**, **4** accept, allow in, let in, receive, take in.

admittance *noun* admitting or being admitted, usually to a place.

admittedly *adverb* as must be admitted.

admixture /æd'mɪkstʃə/ *noun* **1** thing added, esp. minor ingredient. **2** adding of this.

admonish /əd'mɒnɪʃ/ *verb* **1** reprove. **2** urge. **3** (+ *of*) warn of. □ **admonishment** *noun*. **admonition** /ædmə'nɪ-/ *noun*. **admonitory** *adjective*.

ad nauseam /æd 'nɔːzɪæm/ *adverb* to a sickening extent.

ado /ə'duː/ *noun* fuss, trouble.

adobe /ə'dəʊbɪ/ *noun* sun-dried brick.

adolescent /ædə'lesənt/ *adjective* between childhood and adulthood. ● *noun* adolescent person. □ **adolescence** *noun*.

■ *adjective* boyish, girlish, immature, juvenile, pubescent, teenage, youthful. ● *noun* boy, girl, juvenile, minor, teenager, youngster, youth. □ **adolescence** boyhood, girlhood, growing up, puberty, teens, youth.

adopt /ə'dɒpt/ *verb* **1** legally take (child) as one's own. **2** take over (another's idea etc.). **3** choose. **4** accept responsibility for. **5** approve (report etc.). □ **adoption** *noun*.

■ **1** foster, take in. **2** appropriate, embrace, espouse, follow, support, take over, take up. **3** choose, go for, take on. **5** accept, approve, back, embrace, endorse, support.

adoptive *adjective* because of adoption.

adorable /ə'dɔːrəb(ə)l/ *adjective* **1** deserving adoration. **2** *colloquial* delightful, charming.

adore /ə'dɔː/ *verb* (**-ring**) **1** love intensely. **2** worship. **3** *colloquial* like very much. □ **adoration** /ædə'reɪ-/ *noun*. **adorer** *noun*.

■ **1** admire, cherish, dote on, idolize, love. **2** exalt, glorify, hallow, honour, revere, venerate, worship.

adorn /ə'dɔːn/ *verb* add beauty to, decorate. □ **adornment** *noun*.

■ beautify, decorate, embellish, garnish, ornament, trim.

adrenal /ə'driːn(ə)l/ *adjective* of adrenal glands. ● *noun* (in full **adrenal gland**) either of two ductless glands above the kidneys.

adrenalin /ə'drenəlɪn/ *noun* stimulative hormone secreted by adrenal glands.

adrift /ə'drɪft/ *adverb* & *adjective* **1** drifting. **2** *colloquial* unfastened. **3** out of order.

■ *adjective* **1** afloat, aimless, anchorless, astray, directionless, drifting, floating, lost, purposeless.

adroit /ə'drɔɪt/ *adjective* dexterous, skilful. □ **adroitness** *noun*.

adsorb /əd'sɔːb/ *verb* attract and hold thin layer of (gas or liquid) on its surface. □ **adsorbent** *adjective* & *noun*. **adsorption** *noun*.

adulate /'ædjʊleɪt/ *verb* hold in high regard; flatter obsequiously. □ **adulatory** *adjective*.

adulation /ædjʊ'leɪʃ(ə)n/ *noun* obsequious flattery.

adult /'ædʌlt/ *adjective* **1** grown-up, mature. **2** of or for adults. ● *noun* adult person. □ **adulthood** *noun*.

■ *adjective* **1** full-grown, full-size, grown-up, mature.

adulterate /ə'dʌltəreɪt/ *verb* (**-ting**) debase (esp. food) by adding other substances. □ **adulteration** *noun*.

■ alloy, contaminate, corrupt, debase, dilute, *colloquial* doctor, pollute, taint, weaken.

adultery /ə'dʌltərɪ/ *noun* voluntary sexual intercourse of married person other than with spouse. □ **adulterer**, **adulteress** *noun*. **adulterous** *adjective*.

adumbrate /'ædʌmbreɪt/ *verb* (**-ting**) **1** indicate faintly or in outline. **2** foreshadow. □ **adumbration** *noun*.

advance /əd'vɑːns/ *verb* (**-cing**) **1** move or put forward. **2** progress. **3** pay or lend beforehand. **4** promote. **5** present (idea etc.). ● *noun* **1** going forward. **2** progress. **3** loan. **4** payment beforehand. **5** (in *plural*) amorous approaches. **6** rise in price. ● *adjective* done etc. beforehand; going before others. □ **advance on** approach threateningly. **in advance** ahead, beforehand.

■ *verb* **1** approach, come near, forge ahead, go forward, move forward, press on, proceed, push on. **2** develop, evolve, forge ahead, gain ground, improve, make headway, make progress, progress, prosper, thrive. **3** lend, offer, pay, provide, supply. **4** accelerate, assist, benefit, boost, further, help the progress of, promote. **5** adduce, give, present, propose, put forward, submit, suggest. ● *noun* **1, 2** development, evolution, forward movement, growth, headway, improvement, progress.

advanced *adjective* **1** well ahead. **2** well developed. **3** not elementary. **4** ahead of the times; progressive. □ **advanced level** high level GCE exam.

■ **2** grown-up, mature, precocious, sophisticated, well developed. **3** complex, difficult, hard, higher. **4** forward-looking, innovative, new, novel, pioneering, progressive.

advancement *noun* promotion of person, cause, etc.

advantage /əd'vɑːntɪdʒ/ *noun* **1** beneficial feature. **2** benefit, profit. **3** (often + *over*) superiority. **4** *Tennis* next point after deuce. ● *verb* (**-ging**) benefit, favour. □ **take advantage of 1** make good use of. **2** exploit. □ **advantageous** /ædvən'teɪdʒəs/ *adjective*.

■ *noun* **1** asset, benefit, bonus, boon, plus, strength. **2** aid, assistance, benefit, gain, help, profit, usefulness. **3** dominance, edge, head start, superiority. □ **take advantage of 2** see EXPLOIT

verb **2**. □ **advantageous** beneficial, favourable, helpful, positive, profitable, salutary, useful, valuable, worthwhile.

Advent /'ædvent/ *noun* **1** season before Christmas. **2** coming of Christ. **3** (**advent**) arrival.

Adventist *noun* member of sect believing in imminent second coming of Christ.

adventitious /ædv(ə)n'tɪʃəs/ *adjective* accidental, casual.

adventure /əd'ventʃə/ *noun* **1** unusual and exciting experience. **2** hazardous activity. **3** danger, excitement. **4** enterprise. ● *verb* (**-ring**) dare, venture. □ **adventure playground** one with climbing frames etc.

■ *noun* **1** experience, incident. **2** enterprise, escapade, exploit, feat, undertaking, venture. **3** adventurousness, danger, excitement, hazard, risk. **4** enterprise, risk, speculation, venture.

adventurer *noun* (*feminine* **adventuress**) **1** person who seeks adventure esp. for personal gain or pleasure. **2** financial speculator.

adventurous *adjective* **1** venturesome, enterprising. **2** marked by adventure. □ **adventurousness** *noun*.

■ **1** audacious, bold, brave, courageous, daredevil, daring, foolhardy, intrepid, reckless, venturesome. **2** challenging, dangerous, difficult, exciting, hazardous, risky.

adverb /'ædvɜːb/ *noun* word indicating manner, degree, circumstance, etc. used to modify verb, adjective, or other adverb (see panel). □ **adverbial** /əd'vɜː-/ *adjective*.

··

Adverb

An adverb is used:

1 with a verb, to say:
   a how something happens, e.g. *He walks* quickly.
   b where something happens, e.g. *I live* here.
   c when something happens, e.g. *They visited us* yesterday.
   d how often something happens, e.g. *We* usually *have coffee.*

2 to strengthen or weaken the meaning of:
   a a verb, e.g. *He* really *meant it. I* almost *fell asleep.*
   b an adjective, e.g. *She is* very *clever. This is a* slightly *better result.*
   c another adverb, e.g. *It comes off* terribly *easily. The boys* nearly *always get home late.*

3 to add to the meaning of a whole sentence, e.g.
   He is probably *our best player.* Luckily, *no one was hurt.*

In writing or in formal speech, it is **incorrect** to use an adjective instead of an adverb. For example, use

   Do it properly.   and not   **Do it* proper.

but note that many words are both an adjective and an adverb, e.g.

adjective	adverb
a fast *horse*	*He ran* fast.
a long *time*	*Have you been here* long?

··

adversary /'ædvəsərɪ/ *noun* (*plural* **-ies**) enemy; opponent. □ **adversarial** /-'seə-/ *adjective*.

■ antagonist, attacker, enemy, foe, opponent, rival.

adverse /'ædvɜːs/ *adjective* **1** unfavourable. **2** harmful. □ **adversely** *adverb*.

■ **1** attacking, censorious, critical, derogatory, disadvantageous, hostile, inimical, negative, opposing, prejudicial, uncomplimentary, uncongenial, unfavourable, unkind, unpropitious, unsympathetic. **2** deleterious, detrimental, harmful, hurtful, injurious.

adversity /əd'vɜːsɪtɪ/ *noun* misfortune.

advert /'ædvɜːt/ *noun colloquial* advertisement.

advertise /'ædvətaɪz/ *verb* (**-sing**) **1** promote publicly to increase sales. **2** make generally known. **3** seek to sell, fill (vacancy), or (+ *for*) buy or employ by notice in newspaper etc.

■ **1** market, merchandise, *colloquial* plug, promote, publicize, push, tout. **2** announce, broadcast, display, flaunt, make known, proclaim, publicize, show off.

advertisement /əd'vɜːtɪsmənt/ *noun* **1** public announcement advertising something. **2** advertising.

■ **1** *colloquial* ad, *colloquial* advert, bill, blurb, circular, commercial, handout, leaflet, notice, placard, *colloquial* plug, poster, sign. **2** marketing, promotion, publicity.

advice /əd'vaɪs/ *noun* **1** recommendation on how to act. **2** information. **3** notice of transaction.

■ **1** admonition, counsel, guidance, help, opinion, recommendation, tip, view, warning. **2** see NEWS 1.

advisable /əd'vaɪzəb(ə)l/ *adjective* to be recommended; expedient. □ **advisability** *noun*.

■ expedient, judicious, politic, prudent, recommended, sensible, wise.

advise /əd'vaɪz/ *verb* (**-sing**) **1** give advice (to); recommend. **2** (usually + *of, that*) inform.

■ **1** admonish, caution, counsel, enjoin, exhort, guide, instruct, recommend, suggest, urge, warn. **2** see INFORM 1.

advisedly /əd'vaɪzɪdlɪ/ *adverb* deliberately.

adviser *noun* person who advises, esp. officially.

■ confidant(e), consultant, counsellor, guide, mentor.

advisory /əd'vaɪzərɪ/ *adjective* giving advice.

advocaat /ædvə'kɑːt/ *noun* liqueur of eggs, sugar, and brandy.

advocacy /'ædvəkəsɪ/ *noun* support or argument for cause etc.

advocate *noun* /'ædvəkət/ **1** (+ *of*) person who speaks in favour of. **2** person who pleads for another, esp. in law court. ● *verb* /'ædvəkeɪt/ (**-ting**) recommend by argument.

■ *noun* **1** apologist, backer, champion, proponent, supporter. **2** see LAWYER. ● *verb* argue for, back, champion, favour, recommend, speak for, uphold.

adze /ædz/ *noun* (*US* **adz**) axe with arched blade at right angles to handle.

aegis /'iːdʒɪs/ *noun* protection, support.

aeolian harp /iː'əʊlɪən/ *noun* (*US* **eolian harp**) stringed instrument sounding when wind passes through it.

aeon /'iːɒn/ *noun* (also **eon**) **1** long or indefinite period. **2** an age.

aerate /'eəreɪt/ *verb* (**-ting**) **1** charge with carbon dioxide. **2** expose to air. □ **aeration** *noun*.

aerated /ɛ'reɪtɪd/ *adjective* **1** (of liquid) charged with gas; effervescent. **2** *slang* agitated; angry.

aerial /'eərɪəl/ *noun* device for transmitting or receiving radio signals. ● *adjective* **1** from the air. **2** existing in the air. **3** like air.

aero- *combining form* **1** air. **2** aircraft.

aerobatics /eərə'bætɪks/ *plural noun* **1** feats of spectacular flying of aircraft. **2** (treated as *singular*) performance of these.

aerobics /eə'rəʊbɪks/ *plural noun* vigorous exercises designed to increase oxygen intake. □ **aerobic** *adjective*.

aerodrome /'eərədrəʊm/ *noun* small airport or airfield.

aerodynamics /eərəʊdaɪ'næmɪks/ *plural noun* (usually treated as *singular*) dynamics of solid bodies moving through air. □ **aerodynamic** *adjective*.

aerofoil /'eərəfɔɪl/ *noun* structure with curved surfaces (e.g. aircraft wing), designed to give lift in flight.

aeronautics /eərəʊ'nɔːtɪks/ *plural noun* (usually treated as *singular*) science or practice of motion in the air. □ **aeronautical** *adjective*.

aeroplane /'eərəpleɪn/ *noun* powered heavier-than-air aircraft with wings.

aerosol /'eərəsɒl/ *noun* pressurized container releasing substance as fine spray.

aerospace /'eərəʊspeɪs/ *noun* **1** earth's atmosphere and outer space. **2** aviation in this.

aesthete /'iːsθiːt/ *noun* person who appreciates beauty.

aesthetic /iːs'θetɪk/ *adjective* **1** of or sensitive to beauty. **2** tasteful. □ **aesthetically** *adverb*. **aestheticism** /-sɪz(ə)m/ *noun*.

■ **1** artistic, cultivated, refined, sensitive. **2** artistic, beautiful, tasteful.

aetiology /iːtɪ'ɒlədʒɪ/ *noun* (*US* **etiology**) study of causation or of causes of disease. □ **aetiological** /-ə'lɒdʒ-/ *adjective*.

afar /ə'fɑː/ *adverb* at or to a distance.

affable /'æfəb(ə)l/ *adjective* **1** friendly. **2** courteous. □ **affability** *noun*. **affably** *adverb*.

affair /ə'feə/ *noun* **1** matter, concern. **2** *colloquial* thing, event. **3** love affair. **4** (in *plural*) business.

■ **1** business, concern, interest, matter. **2** circumstance, episode, event, happening, incident, occurrence, thing. **3** amour, attachment, intrigue, involvement, liaison, *colloquial* relationship, romance. **4** (*affairs*) activities, business, dealings, transactions.

affect /əˈfekt/ *verb* **1** produce effect on. **2** (often as **affected** *adjective*) (of disease etc.) attack. **3** move emotionally. **4** use for effect. **5** pretend to feel. **6** (+ *to do*) pretend to.

USAGE *Affect* is often confused with *effect*, which means 'to bring about'.

■ **1** alter, change, have an effect on, have an impact on, impinge on, influence, relate to. **2** afflict, attack, damage, strike; (**affected**) afflicted, damaged, infected, injured, poisoned, *archaic* stricken, troubled. **3** agitate, concern, disturb, impress, influence, move, perturb, stir, touch, trouble, upset. **4** adopt, assume, use. **5** fake, feign, pretend, put on, sham.

affectation /æfekˈteɪʃ(ə)n/ *noun* **1** artificial manner. **2** pretentious display.

■ **1** artificiality, insincerity, mannerism, posturing. **2** see PRETENCE 4.

affected *adjective* **1** pretended. **2** full of affectation.

■ **1** artificial, contrived, insincere, pretended, put on, studied, unnatural. **2** see PRETENTIOUS, UNNATURAL 4.

affection /əˈfekʃ(ə)n/ *noun* **1** goodwill, fond feeling. **2** disease.

■ **1** attachment, fondness, friendliness, friendship, goodwill, liking, love, partiality, tenderness, warmth.

affectionate /əˈfekʃənət/ *adjective* loving. □ **affectionately** *adverb*.

■ caring, doting, fond, kind, loving, tender, warm.

affidavit /æfɪˈdeɪvɪt/ *noun* written statement on oath.

affiliate /əˈfɪlɪeɪt/ *verb* (**-ting**) (+ *to, with*) attach to, connect to, or adopt as member or branch.

affiliation *noun* affiliating, being affiliated. □ **affiliation order** legal order compelling supposed father to support illegitimate child.

affinity /əˈfɪnɪtɪ/ *noun* (*plural* **-ies**) **1** attraction. **2** relationship. **3** resemblance. **4** *Chemistry* tendency of substances to combine with others.

■ **2** closeness, compatibility, kinship, like-mindedness, rapport, relationship, sympathy. **3** likeness, resemblance, similarity.

affirm /əˈfɜːm/ *verb* **1** state as fact. **2** make solemn declaration in place of oath. □ **affirmation** /æfəˈmeɪʃ(ə)n/ *noun*.

■ assert, *formal* aver, *formal* avow, declare, maintain, state, swear, testify. □ **affirmation** assertion, *formal* avowal, declaration, promise, statement, testimony.

affirmative /əˈfɜːmətɪv/ *adjective* affirming, expressing approval. ● *noun* affirmative statement.

■ *adjective* agreeing, assenting, concurring, confirming, positive.

affix *verb* /əˈfɪks/ **1** attach, fasten. **2** add in writing. ● *noun* /ˈæfɪks/ **1** addition. **2** prefix, suffix.

afflict /əˈflɪkt/ *verb* distress physically or mentally.

■ affect, annoy, beset, bother, burden, distress, harass, harm, hurt, oppress, pain, *colloquial* plague, torment, torture, trouble, try, worry, wound.

affliction *noun* **1** distress, suffering. **2** cause of this.

affluent /ˈæfluənt/ *adjective* rich. □ **affluence** *noun*.

■ *colloquial* flush, *slang* loaded, moneyed, opulent, prosperous, rich, wealthy, *colloquial* well-heeled, well off, well-to-do.

afford /əˈfɔːd/ *verb* **1** (after *can, be able to*) have enough money, time, etc., for; be able to spare (time etc.). **2** (+ *to do*) be in a position to. **3** provide.

■ **1** be rich enough, have the means, manage to give. **3** see PROVIDE 1.

afforest /əˈfɒrɪst/ *verb* **1** convert into forest. **2** plant with trees. □ **afforestation** *noun*.

affray /əˈfreɪ/ *noun* breach of peace by fighting or rioting in public.

affront /əˈfrʌnt/ *noun* open insult. ● *verb* **1** insult openly. **2** embarrass.

Afghan /ˈæfɡæn/ *noun* native, national, or language of Afghanistan. ● *adjective* of Afghanistan. □ **Afghan hound** tall dog with long silky hair.

aficionado /æfɪsjəˈnɑːdəʊ/ *noun* (*plural* **-os**) devotee of particular sport or pastime.

afield /əˈfiːld/ *adverb* to or at a distance.

aflame /əˈfleɪm/ *adverb* & *adjective* **1** in flames. **2** very excited.

afloat /əˈfləʊt/ *adverb* & *adjective* **1** floating. **2** at sea. **3** out of debt.

■ **1** adrift, floating. **2** aboard, on board ship, under sail.

afoot /əˈfʊt/ *adverb* & *adjective* in operation; progressing.

afore /əˈfɔː/ *preposition* & *adverb* archaic before.

afore- *combining form* previously.

aforethought *adjective* (after noun) premeditated.

a fortiori /eɪ fɔːtrˈɔːraɪ/ *adverb* & *adjective* with stronger reason. [Latin]

afraid /əˈfreɪd/ *adjective* alarmed, frightened. □ **be afraid** *colloquial* politely regret.

■ aghast, agitated, alarmed, anxious, apprehensive, cowardly, cowed, daunted, diffident, faint-hearted, fearful, frightened, hesitant, horrified, intimidated, *colloquial* jittery, nervous, panicky, panic-stricken, reluctant, scared, terrified, timid, timorous, trembling, unheroic, *colloquial* windy. □ **be afraid** be apologetic, be regretful, be sorry, regret.

afresh /əˈfreʃ/ *adverb* anew; with fresh start.

African /ˈæfrɪkən/ *noun* **1** native of Africa. **2** person of African descent. ● *adjective* of Africa.

Afrikaans /æfrɪˈkɑːns/ *noun* language derived from Dutch, used in S. Africa.

Afrikaner /æfrɪˈkɑːnə/ *noun* Afrikaans-speaking white person in S. Africa.

Afro /ˈæfrəʊ/ *adjective* (of hair) tightly-curled and bushy. ● *noun* (*plural* **-s**) Afro hairstyle.

Afro- *combining form* African.

aft /ɑːft/ *adverb* at or towards stern or tail.

after /ˈɑːftə/ *preposition* **1** following in time. **2** in view of. **3** despite. **4** behind. **5** in pursuit or quest of. **6** about, concerning. **7** in allusion to or imitation of. ● *conjunction* later than. ● *adverb* **1** later. **2** behind. ● *adjective* later. □ **after all** in spite of everything. **afterbirth** placenta etc. discharged after childbirth. **aftercare** attention after leaving hospital etc. **after-effect** delayed effect of accident etc. **afterlife** life after death. **afters** *colloquial* sweet dessert. **aftershave** lotion applied after shaving. **afterthought** thing thought of or added later.

■ □ **afterthought** addendum, addition, extra, postscript.

aftermath /ˈɑːftəmæθ/ *noun* consequences.

afternoon /ɑːftəˈnuːn/ *noun* time between midday and evening.

afterwards /ˈɑːftəwədz/ *adverb* later, subsequently.

again /əˈgen/ *adverb* **1** another time. **2** as previously. **3** in addition. **4** on the other hand. □ **again and again** repeatedly.

against /əˈgenst/ *preposition* **1** in opposition to. **2** into collision or in contact with. **3** to the disadvantage of. **4** in contrast to. **5** in anticipation of. **6** as compensating factor to. **7** in return for.

agape /əˈgeɪp/ *adjective* gaping.

agate /ˈægət/ *noun* usually hard streaked chalcedony.

agave /əˈgeɪvɪ/ *noun* spiny-leaved plant.

age *noun* **1** length of past life or existence. **2** (often in *plural*) *colloquial* a long time. **3** historical period. **4** old age. ● *verb* (**ageing**) **1** (cause to) show signs of age. **2** grow old. **3** mature. □ **come of age** reach legal adult status. **under age** not old enough.

■ *noun* **1** life span, lifetime. **3** days, epoch, era, time. **4** advancing years, decrepitude, dotage, old age, senility. ● *verb* **1, 2** degenerate, grow older, look older. **3** mature, mellow, ripen.

aged *adjective* **1** /eɪdʒd/ of the age of. **2** /ˈeɪdʒɪd/ old.

■ **2** see OLD 1.

ageism /ˈeɪdʒɪz(ə)m/ *noun* prejudice or discrimination on grounds of age.

ageless /ˈeɪdʒlɪs/ *adjective* never growing or appearing old.

agency /ˈeɪdʒənsɪ/ *noun* (*plural* **-ies**) **1** business or premises of agent. **2** action. **3** intervention.

agenda /əˈdʒendə/ *noun* (*plural* **-s**) **1** list of items to be considered at meeting. **2** things to be done.

■ list, plan, programme, schedule, timetable.

agent /ˈeɪdʒ(ə)nt/ *noun* **1** person acting for another in business etc. **2** person or thing producing effect.

■ **1** broker, delegate, envoy, executor, functionary, go-between, intermediary, mediator, middleman, negotiator, proxy, representative, surrogate, trustee.

agent provocateur /ɑːʒɑ̃ prəvɒkəˈtɜː/ *noun* (*plural* **agents provocateurs** same pronunciation) person tempting suspected offenders to self-incriminating action. [French]

agglomerate /əˈglɒməreɪt/ *verb* (**-ting**) collect into mass. □ **agglomeration** *noun*.

agglutinate /əˈgluːtɪneɪt/ *verb* (**-ting**) stick as with glue. □ **agglutination** *noun*. **agglutinative** /-nətɪv/ *adjective*.

aggrandize /əˈgrændaɪz/ *verb* (also **-ise**) (**-zing** or **-sing**) **1** increase power, rank, or wealth of. **2** make seem greater. □ **aggrandizement** /-dɪz-/ *noun*.

aggravate /ˈægrəveɪt/ *verb* (**-ting**) **1** increase seriousness of. **2** *disputed* annoy. □ **aggravation** *noun*.

USAGE The use of *aggravate* to mean 'annoy' is considered incorrect by some people, but it is common in informal use.

■ **1** add to, augment, compound, exacerbate, exaggerate, increase, inflame, intensify, worsen. **2** see ANNOY 1.

aggregate *noun* /ˈægrɪgət/ **1** sum total. **2** crushed stone etc. used in making concrete. ● *adjective* /ˈægrɪgət/ collective, total. ● *verb* /ˈægrɪgeɪt/ **1** collect together, unite. **2** *colloquial* amount to. □ **aggregation** *noun*.

aggression /əˈgreʃ(ə)n/ *noun* **1** unprovoked attack. **2** hostile act or feeling. □ **aggressor** *noun*.

■ □ **aggressor** assailant, attacker, instigator, invader.

aggressive /əˈgresɪv/ *adjective* **1** given to aggression. **2** forceful, self-assertive. □ **aggressively** *adverb*. **aggressiveness** *noun*.

■ **1** antagonistic, bellicose, belligerent, bullying, destructive, hostile, militant, offensive, pugnacious, quarrelsome, violent, warlike. **2** assertive, bold, forceful, *colloquial* pushy, self-assertive.

aggrieved /ə'griːvd/ *adjective* having grievance.

aggro /'ægrəʊ/ *noun slang* **1** aggression. **2** difficulty.

aghast /ə'gɑːst/ *adjective* amazed and horrified.

agile /'ædʒaɪl/ *adjective* quick-moving, nimble. □ **agility** /ə'dʒɪlɪtɪ/ *noun.*
 ■ acrobatic, adroit, deft, *poetical* or *literary* fleet, graceful, lissom, lithe, mobile, nimble, quick-moving, sprightly, spry, supple.

agitate /'ædʒɪteɪt/ *verb* (**-ting**) **1** (often as **agitated** *adjective*) disturb, excite. **2** (often + *for, against*) campaign, esp. politically. **3** shake briskly. □ **agitation** *noun.* **agitator** *noun.*
 ■ **1** alarm, arouse, confuse, discomfit, disconcert, disturb, excite, fluster, incite, perturb, stir up, trouble, unsettle, upset, worry; (**agitated**) see NERVOUS 1,2,4, EXCITED (EXCITE). **3** beat, churn, ruffle, shake, stimulate, stir, toss, work up. □ **agitator** firebrand, rabble-rouser, revolutionary, troublemaker.

aglow /ə'gləʊ/ *adjective & adverb* glowing; in glow of warmth or excitement.

AGM *abbreviation* annual general meeting.

agnail /'ægneɪl/ *noun* **1** torn skin at root of fingernail. **2** resulting soreness.

agnostic /æg'nɒstɪk/ *noun* person who believes that existence of God is not provable. ● *adjective* of agnosticism. □ **agnosticism** /-sɪz(ə)m/ *noun.*

ago /ə'gəʊ/ *adverb* in the past.

agog /ə'gɒg/ *adjective* eager, expectant.

agonize /'ægənaɪz/ *verb* (also **-ise**) (**-zing** or **-sing**) **1** undergo mental anguish; suffer agony. **2** cause to suffer agony. **3** (as **agonized** *adjective*) expressing agony.
 ■ **1** labour, suffer, worry, wrestle.

agony /'ægənɪ/ *noun* (*plural* **-ies**) **1** extreme physical or mental suffering. **2** severe struggle. □ **agony aunt** *colloquial* writer answering letters in **agony column** *colloquial,* section of magazine etc. offering personal advice.
 ■ **1** anguish, distress, pain, suffering, torment, torture.

agoraphobia /ægərə'fəʊbɪə/ *noun* extreme fear of open spaces. □ **agoraphobic** *adjective.*

agrarian /ə'greərɪən/ *adjective* of land or its cultivation. ● *noun* advocate of redistribution of land.

agree /ə'griː/ *verb* (**-ees**, **-eed**) **1** (often + *with*) hold similar opinion. **2** (often + *with*) be or become in harmony; suit, be compatible. **3** (often + *to, to do*) consent. **4** admit as true. **5** reach agreement about. **6** (+ *on*) decide on.
 ■ **1** be unanimous, be united, concur, see eye to eye; (*agree with*) see ENDORSE 1. **2** accord, correspond, fit, get on, harmonize, match, suit. **3** (*agree to*) accede to, acquiesce in, assent to, be willing to, consent to, make a contract to, pledge oneself to, promise to, undertake to. **4** admit, allow, concede, grant. **6** (*agree on*) see CHOOSE 1.

agreeable *adjective* **1** pleasing. **2** willing to agree. □ **agreeably** *adverb.*
 ■ **1** acceptable, delightful, enjoyable, nice, pleasant.

agreement *noun* **1** act or state of agreeing. **2** arrangement, contract.
 ■ **1** accord, compatibility, concord, conformity, consensus, consent, consistency, correspondence, harmony, similarity, sympathy, unanimity, unity. **2** alliance, armistice, arrangement, bargain, compact, contract, convention, covenant, deal, entente, pact, settlement, treaty, truce, understanding.

agriculture /'ægrɪkʌltʃə/ *noun* cultivation of the soil and rearing of animals. □ **agricultural** /-'kʌl-/ *adjective.* **agriculturalist** /-'kʌl-/ *noun.*
 ■ agronomy, crofting, cultivation, farming, husbandry, tilling. □ **agricultural** agrarian, bucolic, farming, pastoral, rural.

agronomy /ə'grɒnəmɪ/ *noun* science of soil management and crop production. □ **agronomist** *noun.*

aground /ə'graʊnd/ *adjective & adverb* on(to) bottom of shallow water.
 ■ *adjective* beached, grounded, helpless, marooned, shipwrecked, stranded.

ague /'eɪgjuː/ *noun* **1** shivering fit. **2** *historical* malarial fever.

ah /ɑː/ *interjection: expressing surprise, pleasure, or realization.*

aha /ɑː'hɑː/ *interjection: expressing surprise, triumph, mockery, etc.*

ahead /ə'hed/ *adverb* **1** in advance, in front. **2** (often + *on*) in the lead (on points etc.).

ahoy /ə'hɔɪ/ *interjection Nautical* call used in hailing.

AI *abbreviation* **1** artificial insemination. **2** artificial intelligence.

aid *noun* **1** help. **2** person or thing that helps. ● *verb* **1** help. **2** promote (recovery etc.). □ **in aid of 1** in support of. **2** *colloquial* for purpose of.
 ■ *noun* **1** assistance, avail, backing, benefit, cooperation, donation, funding, grant, guidance, help, loan, patronage, relief, sponsorship, subsidy, *archaic* or *formal* succour, support. **2** see HELPER (HELP), TOOL *noun* 1. ● *verb* **1** abet, assist, back, benefit, collaborate with, contribute to, cooperate with, give a hand to, help, lend a hand to, prop up, rally round, relieve, subsidize, *archaic* or *formal* succour, support. **2** assist, encourage, facilitate, help, promote.

aide /eɪd/ *noun* **1** aide-de-camp. **2** assistant.

aide-de-camp /eɪd də 'kɑ̃/ *noun* (*plural* **aides-** same pronunciation) officer assisting senior officer.

aide-mémoire /ˌeɪdmem'wɑː/ *noun* (*plural* **aides-mémoires** or **aides-mémoire** same pronunciation) an aid to the memory.

Aids *noun* (also **AIDS**) acquired immune deficiency syndrome.

ail *verb* be ill or in poor condition. □ **ailing** *adjective.*

■ □ **ailing** feeble, ill, infirm, poorly, sick, unwell, weak.

aileron /'eɪlərɒn/ *noun* hinged flap on aircraft wing.

ailment *noun* illness, esp. minor one.

■ affliction, complaint, disease, disorder, illness, infirmity, malady, sickness.

aim *verb* **1** intend, try. **2** (usually + *at*) direct, point. **3** take aim. ● *noun* **1** purpose, object. **2** directing of weapon etc. at object. □ **take aim** direct weapon etc. at object.

■ *verb* **1** aspire, design, endeavour, *formal* essay, intend, plan, propose, resolve, strive, try, want, wish. **2** address, beam, direct, point, sight, train, turn; (*aim at*) focus on, home in on, zero in on. **3** line up, take aim. ● *noun* **1** ambition, cause, design, destination, direction, dream, focus, goal, hope, intent, intention, mark, object, objective, plan, purpose, wish.

aimless *adjective* purposeless. □ **aimlessly** *adverb.*

■ directionless, purposeless, rambling, random, undisciplined, unfocused.

ain't /emt/ *colloquial* **1** am not, is not, are not. **2** has not, have not.

USAGE The use of *ain't* is incorrect in standard English.

air *noun* **1** mixture chiefly of oxygen and nitrogen surrounding earth. **2** open space. **3** earth's atmosphere, often as place where aircraft operate. **4** appearance, manner. **5** (in *plural*) affected manner. **6** light wind. **7** tune. ● *verb* **1** expose (room, clothes, etc.) to air; ventilate. **2** express and discuss publicly. □ **airbase** base for military aircraft. **air-bed** inflatable mattress. **airborne 1** transported by air. **2** (of aircraft) in the air. **airbrick** brick perforated for ventilation. **Air Commodore** RAF officer next above Group Captain. **air-conditioned** *adjective* equipped with air-conditioning. **air-conditioning 1** regulation of humidity and temperature in building. **2** apparatus for this. **airfield** area with runway(s) for aircraft. **air force** branch of armed forces fighting in the air. **airgun** gun using compressed air to fire pellets. **air hostess** stewardess in aircraft. **air letter** sheet of paper forming airmail letter. **airlift** ● *noun* emergency transport of supplies etc. by air. ● *verb* transport thus. **airline** public air transport company. **airliner** large passenger aircraft. **airlock 1** stoppage of flow by air bubble in pipe etc. **2** compartment giving access to pressurized chamber. **airmail 1** system of transporting mail by air. **2** mail carried thus. **airman** pilot or member of aircraft crew. **Air (Chief, Vice-) Marshal** high ranks in RAF. **airplane** *US* aeroplane. **airport** airfield with facilities for passengers and cargo. **air raid** attack by aircraft. **air rifle** rifle using compressed air to fire pellets. **airs and graces** affected manner. **airship** powered aircraft lighter than air. **airsick** nauseous from air travel. **airspace** air above a country. **air speed** aircraft's speed relative to air. **airstrip** strip of ground for take-off and landing of aircraft. **air terminal** building with transport to and from airport. **air traffic controller** official who controls air traffic by radio. **airway 1** recognized route of aircraft. **2** passage for air into lungs. **airwoman** woman pilot or member of aircraft crew. **by air** by or in aircraft. **on the air** being broadcast. **up in the air** (of projects etc.) uncertain; undecided.

■ *noun* **2, 3** airspace, atmosphere, ether, heavens, sky. **4** ambience, appearance, aspect, aura, bearing, character, demeanour, feeling, impression, look, manner, *literary* mien, mood, style. **6** breath, breeze, draught, wind, *literary* zephyr. ● *verb* **1** aerate, freshen, ventilate. **2** articulate, display, exhibit, express, give vent to, make known, make public, vent, voice. □ **airman** aviator, flyer, pilot. **airport** aerodrome, airfield, airstrip, heliport, landing strip, runway.

aircraft *noun* (*plural* same) aeroplane, helicopter. □ **aircraft carrier** warship that carries and acts as base for aircraft. **aircraftman, aircraftwoman** lowest rank in RAF.

Airedale /'eədeɪl/ *noun* terrier of large rough-coated breed.

airless *adjective* **1** stuffy. **2** still, calm.

airtight *adjective* impermeable to air.

airworthy *adjective* (of aircraft) fit to fly. □ **airworthiness** *noun.*

airy *adjective* (-**ier**, -**iest**) **1** well ventilated. **2** flippant. **3** light as air. □ **airy-fairy** *colloquial* unrealistic, impractical.

■ **1** breezy, draughty, fresh, open, ventilated.

aisle /aɪl/ *noun* **1** side part of church divided by pillars from nave. **2** passage between rows of pews, seats, etc.

■ **2** corridor, passage, passageway.

aitchbone /'eɪtʃbəʊn/ *noun* **1** rump bone of animal. **2** cut of beef over this.

ajar /ə'dʒɑː/ *adverb & adjective* (of door etc.) slightly open.

Akela /ɑː'keɪlə/ *noun* adult leader of Cub Scouts.

akimbo /ə'kɪmbəʊ/ *adverb* (of arms) with hands on hips and elbows out.

akin /ə'kɪn/ *adjective* **1** related by blood. **2** similar.

■ **2** allied, related, similar.

alabaster /'æləbɑːstə/ *noun* translucent usually white form of gypsum. ● *adjective* **1** of alabaster. **2** white, smooth.

à la carte /æ lɑː 'kɑːt/ *adverb & adjective* with individually priced dishes.

alacrity /ə'lækrɪtɪ/ *noun* briskness, readiness.

à la mode /æ lɑː 'məʊd/ *adverb & adjective* in fashion; fashionable.

alarm /ə'lɑːm/ *noun* **1** warning of danger etc. **2** warning sound or device. **3** alarm clock. **4** apprehension. ● *verb* **1** frighten, disturb. **2** warn.

☐ **alarm clock** clock that rings at set time.
☐ **alarming** *adjective*.

■ *noun* **1** alert, signal, warning. **2, 3** alarm clock, bell, horn, siren, tocsin, whistle. **4** anxiety, consternation, dismay, fear, fright, nervousness, panic, uneasiness. ● *verb* **1** agitate, dismay, distress, disturb, frighten, panic, *colloquial* put the wind up, shock, startle, unnerve, worry.

alarmist /əˈlɑːmɪst/ *noun* person spreading unnecessary alarm.

alas /əˈlæs/ *interjection: expressing grief or regret.*

alb *noun* long white vestment worn by Christian priests.

albatross /ˈælbətrɒs/ *noun* **1** long-winged seabird related to petrel. **2** *Golf* score of 3 strokes under par for hole.

albeit /ɔːlˈbiːɪt/ *conjunction* although.

albino /ælˈbiːnəʊ/ *noun* (*plural* **-s**) person or animal lacking pigment in skin, hair, and eyes. ☐ **albinism** /ˈælbɪnɪz(ə)m/ *noun*.

album /ˈælbəm/ *noun* **1** book for displaying photographs etc. **2** long-playing gramophone record. **3** set of recordings issued together.

albumen /ˈælbjʊmm/ *noun* egg white.

albumin /ˈælbjʊmm/ *noun* water-soluble protein found in egg white, milk, blood, etc.

alchemy /ˈælkəmɪ/ *noun* medieval chemistry, esp. seeking to turn base metals into gold. ☐ **alchemist** *noun*.

alcohol /ˈælkəhɒl/ *noun* **1** colourless volatile liquid, esp. as intoxicant present in wine, beer, spirits, etc. and as a solvent, fuel, etc. **2** liquor containing this. **3** other compound of this type.

■ **2** *colloquial* booze, drink, liquor, spirits, wine.

alcoholic /ælkəˈhɒlɪk/ *adjective* of, like, containing, or caused by alcohol. ● *noun* person suffering from alcoholism.

■ *adjective* brewed, distilled, fermented, intoxicating, strong. ● *noun* dipsomaniac, drunkard, inebriate.

alcoholism /ˈælkəhɒlɪz(ə)m/ *noun* condition resulting from addiction to alcohol.

alcove /ˈælkəʊv/ *noun* recess in wall of room, garden, etc.

alder /ˈɔːldə/ *noun* tree related to birch.

alderman /ˈɔːldəmən/ *noun esp. historical* civic dignitary next in rank to mayor.

ale *noun* beer.

alehouse /ˈeɪlhaʊs/ *noun archaic* tavern.

alert /əˈlɜːt/ *adjective* watchful; mentally agile. ● *noun* **1** alarm. **2** state or period of special vigilance. ● *verb* (often + *to*) warn. ☐ **alertness** *noun*.

■ *adjective* active, attentive, awake, careful, eagle-eyed, heedful, lively, observant, on one's guard, on one's toes, on the lookout, on the watch, perceptive, quick, ready, sharp-eyed, vigilant, watchful, wide awake; (*alert to*) alive to, sensitive to, *colloquial* wise to. ● *verb* advise, alarm, forewarn, make aware, notify, signal, tip off, warn.

alfalfa /ælˈfælfə/ *noun* clover-like plant used for fodder.

alfresco /ælˈfreskəʊ/ *adjective & adverb* in the open air.

alga /ˈælgə/ *noun* (*plural* **-gae** /-dʒiː/) (usually in *plural*) non-flowering stemless water plant.

algebra /ˈældʒɪbrə/ *noun* branch of mathematics using letters to represent numbers. ☐ **algebraic** /-ˈbreɪk/ *adjective*.

Algol /ˈælgɒl/ *noun* high-level computer-programming language.

algorithm /ˈælgərɪð(ə)m/ *noun* process or rules for (esp. computer) calculation etc.

alias /ˈeɪlɪəs/ *adverb* also known as. ● *noun* assumed name.

alibi /ˈælɪbaɪ/ *noun* (*plural* **-s**) **1** proof that one was elsewhere. **2** *disputed* excuse.

USAGE The use of *alibi* to mean 'an excuse' is considered incorrect by some people.

■ **2** excuse, explanation.

alien /ˈeɪlɪən/ *adjective* **1** (often + *to*) unfamiliar, repugnant. **2** foreign. **3** of beings from another world. ● *noun* **1** non-naturalized foreigner. **2** a being from another world.

■ *adjective* **1, 2** exotic, foreign, outlandish, strange, unfamiliar. **3** extraterrestrial. ● *noun* **1** foreigner, newcomer, outsider, stranger.

alienate /ˈeɪlɪəneɪt/ *verb* (**-ting**) **1** cause to become unfriendly or hostile. **2** (often as **alienated** *adjective*) cause to feel isolated or estranged. **3** transfer ownership of. ☐ **alienation** *noun*.

alight[1] /əˈlaɪt/ *adjective* **1** on fire. **2** lit up.

■ **1** ablaze, aflame, blazing, burning, fiery, ignited, live, on fire. **2** ablaze, illuminated, lit up.

alight[2] /əˈlaɪt/ *verb* **1** (often + *from*) get down or off. **2** come to earth, settle.

■ **1** descend, disembark, dismount, get down, get off. **2** come down, come to rest, land, perch, settle, touch down.

align /əˈlaɪn/ *verb* **1** place in or bring into line. **2** (usually + *with*) ally (oneself etc.). ☐ **alignment** *noun*.

■ **1** arrange in line, line up, straighten up. **2** affiliate, ally, associate, join, side, sympathize.

alike /əˈlaɪk/ *adjective* similar, like. ● *adverb* in similar way.

■ *adjective* analogous, cognate, comparable, equivalent, identical, indistinguishable, like, matching, parallel, resembling, similar, twin, uniform.

alimentary /ælɪˈmentərɪ/ *adjective* **1** concerning nutrition. **2** nourishing. ☐ **alimentary canal** channel through which food passes during digestion.

alimony /ˈælɪmənɪ/ *noun* money payable to a divorced or separated spouse.

alive /əˈlaɪv/ *adjective* **1** living. **2** lively, active. **3** (usually + *to*) alert to. **4** (usually + *with*) swarming with.

■ **1** animate, breathing, existing, extant, flourishing, in existence, live, living, *archaic* quick. **3** (*alive to*) see ALERT *adjective*.

alkali /'ælkəlaɪ/ *noun* (*plural* **-s**) substance that neutralizes acids, turns litmus blue, and forms caustic solutions in water. □ **alkaline** *adjective*. **alkalinity** /-'lm-/ *noun*.

alkaloid /'ælkəlɔɪd/ *noun* plant-based compound often used as drug, e.g. morphine, quinine.

all /ɔːl/ *adjective* whole amount, number, or extent of. ● *noun* **1** all people or things concerned. **2** (+ *of*) the whole of. ● *adverb* entirely, quite. □ **all along** from the beginning. **all at once 1** suddenly. **2** simultaneously. **all but** very nearly. **all for** *colloquial* strongly in favour of. **all-clear** signal that danger or difficulty is over. **all fours** hands and knees. **all in** exhausted. **all-in** inclusive of all. **all in all** everything considered. **all out** (**all-out** before noun) involving all one's strength etc. **all over 1** completely finished. **2** in or on all parts of one's body. **all-purpose** having many uses. **all right 1** satisfactory; safe and sound; in good condition. **2** satisfactorily. **3** I consent. **all-right** (before noun) *colloquial* acceptable. **all round 1** in all respects. **2** for each person. **all-round** (of person) versatile. **all-rounder** versatile person. **All Saints' Day** 1 Nov. **all set** *colloquial* ready to start. **all the same** nevertheless. **all there** *colloquial* mentally alert or normal. **all together** all at same time; all in one place. **at all** (with negative or in questions) in any way; to any extent. **in all** in total; altogether.

USAGE See note at ALTOGETHER.

Allah /'ælə/ *noun: Muslim name of* God.

allay /ə'leɪ/ *verb* lessen, alleviate.
■ alleviate, calm, check, diminish, ease, lessen, mollify, pacify, quell, quench, quieten, reduce, relieve, slake (*thirst*), subdue.

allege /ə'ledʒ/ *verb* declare, esp. without proof. □ **allegation** /ælɪg'eɪʃ(ə)n/ *noun*. **allegedly** /ə'ledʒɪdlɪ/ *adverb*.
■ assert, asseverate, attest, *formal* aver, *formal* avow, claim, declare, depose, maintain, make a charge, plead, state. □ **allegation** accusation, assertion, charge, claim, declaration, statement, testimony.

allegiance /ə'liːdʒ(ə)ns/ *noun* **1** loyalty. **2** duty of subject.
■ devotion, duty, faithfulness, fidelity, loyalty.

allegory /'ælɪgərɪ/ *noun* (*plural* **-ies**) story with moral represented symbolically. □ **allegorical** /-'gɒr-/ *adjective*. **allegorize** *verb* (also **-ise**) (**-zing** or **-sing**).

allegretto /ælɪ'gretəʊ/ *Music adverb & adjective* in fairly brisk tempo. ● *noun* (*plural* **-s**) allegretto movement or passage.

allegro /ə'legrəʊ/ *Music adverb & adjective* in lively tempo. ● *noun* (*plural* **-s**) allegro movement or passage.

alleluia /ælɪ'luːjə/ (also **hallelujah** /hæl-/) *inter-*

jection God be praised. ● *noun* (*plural* **-s**) song of praise to God.

all-embracing *adjective* including much or all; comprehensive.

allergic /ə'lɜːdʒɪk/ *adjective* **1** (+ *to*) having allergy to. **2** (+ *to*) *colloquial* having strong dislike for. **3** caused by allergy.
■ **2** (*allergic to*) antipathetic to, averse to, hostile to, incompatible with, opposed to.

allergy /'ælədʒɪ/ *noun* (*plural* **-ies**) reaction to certain substances.

alleviate /ə'liːvɪeɪt/ *verb* (**-ting**) make (pain etc.) less severe. □ **alleviation** *noun*.
■ abate, allay, ameliorate, assuage, check, diminish, ease, lessen, lighten, mitigate, moderate, quell, quench, reduce, relieve, slake (*thirst*), soften, subdue, temper.

alley /'ælɪ/ *noun* (*plural* **-s**) **1** narrow street or passage. **2** enclosure for skittles, bowling, etc.

alliance /ə'laɪəns/ *noun* formal union or association of states, political parties, etc. or of families by marriage.
■ affiliation, bloc, cartel, coalition, confederation, connection, consortium, federation, guild, marriage, pact, partnership, relationship, union.

allied /'ælaɪd/ *adjective* **1** connected or related. **2** (also **Allied**) associated in an alliance.

alligator /'ælɪgeɪtə/ *noun* large reptile of crocodile family.

alliteration /əlɪtə'reɪʃ(ə)n/ *noun* recurrence of same initial letter or sound in adjacent or nearby words, as in *The fair breeze blew, the white foam flew, the furrow followed free.* □ **alliterate** /-'lɪt-/ *verb*. **alliterative** /ə'lɪtərətɪv/ *adjective*.

allocate /'æləkeɪt/ *verb* (**-ting**) (usually + *to*) assign. □ **allocation** *noun*.
■ allocate, allow, apportion, assign, deal out, *colloquial* dish out, dispense, distribute, dole out, give out, grant, provide, ration, share out.

allot /ə'lɒt/ *verb* (**-tt-**) apportion or distribute to (person).

allotment /ə'lɒtmənt/ *noun* **1** small plot of land rented for cultivation. **2** share. **3** allotting.

allow /ə'laʊ/ *verb* **1** (often + *to do*) permit. **2** assign fixed sum to. **3** (usually + *for*) provide or set aside for a purpose. **4** admit to be true. □ **allow for** take into consideration.
■ **1** approve, authorize, consent to, enable, grant permission for, license, permit, sanction, stand, tolerate; (*allow to*) let. **2** see ALLOT. **4** acknowledge, admit, concede, grant, own.

allowance *noun* **1** amount or sum allowed, esp. regularly. **2** deduction, discount. □ **make allowances** (often + *for*) judge leniently.
■ **1** alimony, allocation, annuity, grant, measure, payment, pension, pocket money, portion, quota, ration, share. **2** deduction, discount, rebate, reduction. □ **make allowances** (*make allowances for*) see TOLERATE 2,3.

alloy /'ælɔɪ/ *noun* **1** mixture of metals. **2** inferior metal mixed esp. with gold or silver. ● *verb* **1** mix (metals). **2** /ə'lɔɪ/ debase by admixture. **3** /ə'lɔɪ/ spoil (pleasure).

■ *noun* **1** aggregate, amalgam, blend, compound, fusion, mixture. **2** admixture.

all-powerful *adjective* having complete power.

allspice /'ɔːlspaɪs/ *noun* **1** spice made from berry of pimento plant. **2** this berry.

allude /ə'luːd/ *verb* (**-ding**) (+ *to*) make allusion to.

■ (*allude to*) hint at, mention, refer to, speak of, touch on.

allure /ə'ljʊə/ *verb* (**-ring**) attract, charm, entice. ● *noun* attractiveness, charm. □ **allurement** *noun*.

■ *verb* attract, beguile, cajole, charm, decoy, draw, entice, fascinate, lead on, lure, magnetize, seduce, tempt.

allusion /ə'luːʒ(ə)n/ *noun* (often + *to*) passing or indirect reference. □ **allusive** /-sɪv/ *adjective*.

■ mention, reference, suggestion.

alluvium /ə'luːvɪəm/ *noun* (*plural* **-via**) deposit left by flood, esp. in river valley. □ **alluvial** *adjective*.

ally *noun* /'ælaɪ/ (*plural* **-ies**) state or person formally cooperating or united with another, esp. in war. ● *verb* (also /ə'laɪ/) (**-ies, -ied**) (often **ally oneself**; often + *with*) combine in alliance.

■ *noun* abetter, *Law* abettor, accessory, accomplice, associate, backer, collaborator, colleague, companion, comrade, confederate, friend, helper, helpmate, mate, partner, supporter. ● *verb* affiliate, amalgamate, associate, band together, collaborate, combine, confederate, cooperate, form an alliance, fraternize, join, join forces, league, link up, marry, merge, side, team up, unite.

Alma Mater /ælmə 'mɑːtə/ *noun* one's university, school, or college.

almanac /'ɔːlmənæk/ *noun* (also **almanack**) calendar, usually with astronomical data.

almighty /ɔːl'maɪtɪ/ *adjective* **1** infinitely powerful. **2** *slang* very great. ● *noun* (**the Almighty**) God.

■ *adjective* **1** all-powerful, omnipotent, supreme. **2** see BIG *adjective* 1.

almond /'ɑːmənd/ *noun* **1** kernel of nutlike fruit related to plum. **2** tree bearing this.

almoner /'ɑːmənə/ *noun* social worker attached to hospital.

almost /'ɔːlməʊst/ *adverb* all but; very nearly.

■ about, all but, approximately, around, as good as, just about, nearly, not quite, practically, virtually.

alms /ɑːmz/ *plural noun historical* donation of money or food to the poor. □ **almshouse** charitable institution for the poor. **almsgiving** giving of alms.

aloe /'æləʊ/ *noun* **1** plant with toothed fleshy leaves. **2** (in *plural*) strong laxative from aloe juice. □ **aloe vera** /'vɪərə/ variety yielding substance used in cosmetics; this substance.

aloft /ə'lɒft/ *adjective & adverb* high up, overhead.

alone /ə'ləʊn/ *adjective* **1** without company or help. **2** lonely. ● *adverb* only, exclusively.

■ *adjective* **1** apart, by oneself, isolated, on one's own, separate, single, solitary, solo, unaccompanied, unassisted. **2** deserted, desolate, forlorn, friendless, isolated, lonely, *esp. US* lonesome.

along /ə'lɒŋ/ *preposition* beside or through (part of) the length of. ● *adverb* **1** onward; into more advanced state. **2** with oneself or others. **3** beside or through (part of) thing's length. □ **alongside** at or close to side (of). **along with** in addition to.

aloof /ə'luːf/ *adjective* unconcerned, unsympathetic. ● *adverb* away, apart. □ **aloofness** *noun*.

■ *adjective* chilly, cold, cool, detached, *disputed* disinterested, dispassionate, distant, formal, frigid, haughty, inaccessible, indifferent, remote, reserved, reticent, self-contained, self-possessed, stand-offish, supercilious, unapproachable, unconcerned, undemonstrative, unemotional, unforthcoming, unfriendly, uninterested, uninvolved, unresponsive, unsociable, unsympathetic.

aloud /ə'laʊd/ *adverb* audibly.

■ audibly, clearly, distinctly.

alp *noun* high mountain, esp. (**the Alps**) those in Switzerland and adjacent countries.

alpaca /æl'pækə/ *noun* **1** S. American llama-like animal. **2** its long wool. **3** fabric made from this.

alpha /'ælfə/ *noun* first letter of Greek alphabet (*A, a*). □ **alpha and omega** beginning and end. **alpha particle** helium nucleus emitted by radioactive substance.

alphabet /'ælfəbet/ *noun* set of letters or signs used in a language. □ **alphabetical** /-'bet-/ *adjective*.

alphanumeric /ælfənju:'merɪk/ *adjective* containing both letters and numbers.

alpine /'ælpaɪn/ *adjective* of high mountains or (**Alpine**) the Alps. ● *noun* **1** plant suited to mountain regions. **2** = ROCK PLANT.

already /ɔːl'redɪ/ *adverb* **1** before the time in question. **2** as early as this.

alright *adverb* = ALL RIGHT 2.

USAGE Although *alright* is widely used, it is not correct in standard English.

Alsatian /æl'seɪʃ(ə)n/ *noun* large dog of a breed of wolfhound.

also /'ɔːlsəʊ/ *adverb* in addition, besides. □ **also-ran 1** loser in race. **2** undistinguished person.

■ additionally, besides, furthermore, in addition, moreover, too.

altar /'ɔːltə/ *noun* **1** flat table or block for offerings to deity. **2** Communion table.

alter /'ɔ:ltə/ *verb* change in character, shape, etc. □ **alterable** *adjective*. **alteration** /-'reɪʃ(ə)n/ *noun*.

■ adapt, adjust, amend, change, convert, edit, emend, enlarge, modify, reconstruct, reduce, reform, remake, remodel, reorganize, reshape, revise, transform, vary. □ **alteration** adaptation, adjustment, amendment, change, conversion, difference, modification, reorganization, revision, transformation.

altercation /ɔ:ltə'keɪʃ(ə)n/ *noun* dispute, wrangle.

alternate *adjective* /ɔ:l'tɜ:nət/ **1** (with noun in *plural*) every other. **2** (of things of two kinds) alternating. ● *verb* /'ɔ:ltəneɪt/ (**-ting**) **1** (often + *with*) arrange or occur by turns. **2** (+ *between*) go repeatedly from one to another. □ **alternating current** electric current regularly reversing direction. □ **alternately** *adverb*. **alternation** *noun*.

USAGE See note at ALTERNATIVE.

■ *verb* **1** follow each other, interchange, replace each other, rotate, substitute for each other, take turns. **2** fluctuate, oscillate, see-saw, vacillate, waver.

alternative /ɔ:l'tɜ:nətɪv/ *adjective* **1** available as another choice. **2** unconventional. ● *noun* **1** any of two or more possibilities. **2** freedom or opportunity to choose. □ **alternatively** *adverb*.

USAGE The adjective *alternative* is often confused with *alternate*, which is correctly used in 'there will be a dance on alternate Saturdays'.

■ *noun* **1** choice, option, possibility.

alternator /'ɔ:ltəneɪtə/ *noun* dynamo generating alternating current.

although /ɔ:l'ðəʊ/ *conjunction* though.

altimeter /'æltɪmi:tə/ *noun* instrument measuring altitude.

altitude /'æltɪtju:d/ *noun* height, esp. of object above sea level or horizon.

■ elevation, height.

alto /'æltəʊ/ *noun* (*plural* **-s**) **1** = CONTRALTO. **2** highest adult male singing voice. **3** singer with this. ● *adjective* having range of alto.

altogether /ɔ:ltə'geðə/ *adverb* **1** totally. **2** on the whole. **3** in total.

USAGE Note that *altogether* means 'in total', as in *six rooms altogether*, whereas *all together* means 'all at same time' or 'all in one place' as in *six rooms all together*.

■ **1** absolutely, completely, entirely, fully, perfectly, quite, thoroughly, totally, utterly, wholly.

altruism /'æltru:ɪz(ə)m/ *noun* unselfishness as principle of action. □ **altruist** *noun*. **altruistic** /-'ɪs-/ *adjective*.

alumina /ə'lu:mɪnə/ *noun* aluminium oxide, emery.

aluminium /æljʊ'mɪnɪəm/ *noun* (*US* **aluminum** /ə'lu:mɪnəm/) a light silvery metallic element.

alumnus /ə'lʌmnəs/ *noun* (*plural* **-ni** /-naɪ/) former pupil or student.

always /'ɔ:lweɪz/ *adverb* **1** at all times. **2** for all time. **3** whatever the circumstances. **4** repeatedly.

■ **1, 2** consistently, constantly, continuously, endlessly, eternally, everlastingly, evermore, forever, invariably, perpetually, persistently, unceasingly, unfailingly, unremittingly. **3** as a last resort, at any rate, in any case. **4** continually, often, regularly, repeatedly.

Alzheimer's disease /'æltshaɪməz/ *noun* brain disorder causing senility.

AM *abbreviation* amplitude modulation.

am *1st singular present* of BE.

a.m. *abbreviation* before noon (*ante meridiem*).

amalgam /ə'mælgəm/ *noun* **1** mixture, blend. **2** alloy of any metal with mercury.

amalgamate /ə'mælgəmeɪt/ *verb* (**-ting**) mix, unite. □ **amalgamation** *noun*.

■ affiliate, ally, associate, band together, blend, coalesce, combine, come together, compound, confederate, form an alliance, fuse, integrate, join, join forces, league, link up, marry, merge, mix, put together, synthesize, team up, unite.

amanuensis /əmænju:'ensɪs/ *noun* (*plural* **-enses** /-si:z/) assistant, esp. writing from dictation.

amaranth /'æmərænθ/ *noun* **1** plant with green, red, or purple flowers. **2** imaginary unfading flower. □ **amaranthine** /-'rænθaɪn/ *adjective*.

amaryllis /æmə'rɪlɪs/ *noun* plant with lily-like flowers.

amass /ə'mæs/ *verb* heap together, accumulate.

amateur /'æmətə/ *noun* **1** person engaging in pursuit as pastime not profession. **2** person with limited skill. ● *adjective* **1** for amateurs; done by amateurs. **2** unskilful. □ **amateurish** *adjective*. **amateurism** *noun*.

■ *noun* **1** dabbler, dilettante, enthusiast, layman, layperson, laywoman, non-professional. ● *adjective* **1** inexperienced, lay, non-professional, unpaid, unqualified. **2** see AMATEURISH. □ **amateurish** *adjective* clumsy, crude, do-it-yourself, incompetent, inept, inexpert, rough-and-ready, second-rate, shoddy, unpolished, unprofessional, unskilful, unskilled, untrained.

amatory /'æmətərɪ/ *adjective* of sexual love.

amaze /ə'meɪz/ *verb* (**-zing**) fill with surprise or wonder. □ **amazement** *noun*. **amazing** *adjective*.

■ astonish, astound, awe, bewilder, confound, daze, disconcert, dumbfound, *colloquial* flabbergast, perplex, rock, shock, stagger, startle, stun, stupefy, surprise. □ **amazing** astonishing, astounding, awe-inspiring, breathtaking, exceptional, exciting, extraordinary, *colloquial* fantastic, *colloquial* incredible, miraculous, notable, phenomenal, prodigious, remarkable, *colloquial* sensational, shocking, special, staggering, startling, *colloquial* stunning, stupendous, unusual, wonderful.

Amazon /'æməzən/ *noun* **1** one of a mythical race of female warriors. **2** (**amazon**) strong or athletic woman. □ **Amazonian** /-'zəʊ-/ *adjective*.

ambassador /æm'bæsədə/ *noun* **1** diplomat living abroad as representative of his or her country. **2** promoter; messenger. □ **ambassadorial** /-'dɔː-/ *adjective*.
■ **1** agent, attaché, chargé d'affaires, consul, diplomat, emissary, envoy, legate, nuncio, plenipotentiary, representative. **2** agent, messenger, promoter, representative, spokesperson.

amber /'æmbə/ *noun* **1** yellow translucent fossil resin. **2** colour of this. ●*adjective* of or like amber.

ambergris /'æmbəgrɪs/ *noun* waxlike substance from sperm whale, used in perfumes.

ambidextrous /æmbɪ'dekstrəs/ *adjective* able to use either hand equally well.

ambience /'æmbɪəns/ *noun* surroundings, atmosphere.

ambient /'æmbɪənt/ *adjective* surrounding.

ambiguous /æm'bɪgjʊəs/ *adjective* **1** having a double meaning. **2** difficult to classify. □ **ambiguity** /-'gjuː-/ *noun* (*plural* **-ies**).
■ confusing, enigmatic, equivocal, imprecise, inconclusive, indefinite, indeterminate, puzzling, uncertain, unclear, vague, woolly.

ambit /'æmbɪt/ *noun* scope, bounds.

ambition /æm'bɪʃ(ə)n/ *noun* **1** determination to succeed. **2** object of this.
■ **1** commitment, drive, energy, enterprise, enthusiasm, go, initiative, push, self-assertion, thrust, zeal. **2** aim, aspiration, desire, dream, goal, hope, ideal, intention, object, objective, target, wish.

ambitious *adjective* **1** full of ambition. **2** (of scheme etc.) showing or requiring ambition.
■ **1** assertive, committed, eager, energetic, enterprising, enthusiastic, go-ahead, hard-working, industrious, keen, *colloquial* pushy, zealous. **2** *colloquial* big, far-reaching, grand, grandiose, large-scale, unrealistic.

ambivalent /æm'bɪvələnt/ *adjective* having mixed feelings towards person or thing. □ **ambivalence** *noun*.
■ doubtful, equivocal, inconsistent, self-contradictory, uncertain, unclear, uncommitted, unresolved, unsettled, vacillating.

amble /'æmb(ə)l/ *verb* (**-ling**) walk at leisurely pace. ●*noun* leisurely pace.

ambrosia /æm'brəʊzɪə/ *noun* **1** food of the gods in classical mythology. **2** delicious food etc.

ambulance /'æmbjʊləns/ *noun* **1** vehicle for taking patients to hospital. **2** mobile army hospital.

ambulatory /'æmbjʊlətərɪ/ *adjective* of or for walking.

ambuscade /æmbəs'keɪd/ *noun & verb* (**-ding**) ambush.

ambush /'æmbʊʃ/ *noun* **1** surprise attack by people hiding. **2** hiding place for this. ●*verb* **1** attack from ambush. **2** waylay.
■ *noun* **1** ambuscade, attack, snare, surprise attack, trap. **2** cover, hiding place. ●*verb* **1** attack, ensnare, entrap, intercept, pounce on, surprise, swoop on, trap. **2** lie in wait for, waylay.

ameliorate /ə'miːlɪəreɪt/ *verb* (**-ting**) make or become better. □ **amelioration** *noun*. **ameliorative** /-rətɪv/ *adjective*.

amen /ɑː'men/ *interjection* (esp. at end of prayer) so be it.

amenable /ə'miːnəb(ə)l/ *adjective* **1** responsive, docile. **2** (often + *to*) answerable (to law etc.).
■ **1** accommodating, acquiescent, adaptable, agreeable, biddable, *formal* complaisant, compliant, cooperative, deferential, docile, open-minded, persuadable, responsive, submissive, tractable, willing.

amend /ə'mend/ *verb* **1** correct error in. **2** make minor alterations in. **3** improve.
■ **1** correct, emend, put right, rectify. **2** adapt, adjust, alter, change, convert, edit, modify, reform, reorganize, reshape, revise, transform, vary. **3** ameliorate, improve, make better, mend, remedy.

amendment *noun* minor alteration or addition in document etc.

amends *noun* □ **make amends** (often + *for*) give compensation.
■ □ **make amends** see COMPENSATE 2.

amenity /ə'miːnɪtɪ/ *noun* (*plural* **-ies**) **1** pleasant or useful feature or facility. **2** pleasantness (of a place etc.).

American /ə'merɪkən/ *adjective* of America, esp. the US. ●*noun* **1** native, citizen, or inhabitant of America, esp. the US. **2** English as spoken in the US. □ **Americanize** *verb* (also **-ise**) (**-zing** or **-sing**).

Americanism *noun* word etc. of US origin or usage.

amethyst /'æməθɪst/ *noun* purple or violet semiprecious stone.

amiable /'eɪmɪəb(ə)l/ *adjective* friendly and pleasant; likeable. □ **amiability** *noun*. **amiably** *adverb*.
■ affable, agreeable, amicable, friendly, genial, good-natured, kind-hearted, kindly, likeable, pleasant, well disposed.

amicable /'æmɪkəb(ə)l/ *adjective* friendly. □ **amicably** *adverb*.

amid /ə'mɪd/ *preposition* in the middle of.

amidships /ə'mɪdʃɪps/ *adverb* in(to) the middle of a ship.

amidst /ə'mɪdst/ = AMID.

amino acid /ə'miːnəʊ/ *noun* organic acid found in proteins.

amir = EMIR.

amiss /ə'mɪs/ *adjective* out of order, wrong.

● *adverb* wrong(ly), inappropriately. □ **take amiss** be offended by.

amity /'æmɪtɪ/ *noun* friendship.

ammeter /'æmɪtə/ *noun* instrument for measuring electric current.

ammo /'æməʊ/ *noun slang* ammunition.

ammonia /ə'məʊnɪə/ *noun* **1** pungent strongly alkaline gas. **2** solution of this in water.

ammonite /'æmənaɪt/ *noun* coil-shaped fossil shell.

ammunition /æmjʊ'nɪʃ(ə)n/ *noun* **1** bullets, shells, grenades, etc. **2** information usable in argument.

  ■ **1** bullets, cartridges, grenades, missiles, projectiles, shells, shot(s).

amnesia /æm'niːzɪə/ *noun* loss of memory. □ **amnesiac** *adjective & noun*.

amnesty /'æmnɪstɪ/ *noun* (*plural* **-ies**) general pardon, esp. for political offences.

amniocentesis /æmnɪəʊsen'tiːsɪs/ *noun* (*plural* **-teses** /-siːz/) sampling of amniotic fluid to detect foetal abnormality.

amniotic fluid /æmnɪ'ɒtɪk/ *noun* fluid surrounding embryo.

amoeba /ə'miːbə/ *noun* (*plural* **-s**) microscopic single-celled organism living in water.

amok /ə'mɒk/ *adverb* □ **run amok, amuck** /ə'mʌk/ run wild.

among /ə'mʌŋ/ *preposition* (also **amongst**) **1** surrounded by. **2** included in or in the category of. **3** from the joint resources of. **4** between.

amoral /eɪ'mɒr(ə)l/ *adjective* **1** beyond morality; neither moral nor immoral. **2** without moral principles. □ **amorality** /-'rælɪtɪ/ *noun*.

  ■ lax, loose, unethical, unprincipled, without standards.

amorous /'æmərəs/ *adjective* showing or feeling sexual love.

  ■ affectionate, ardent, carnal, doting, enamoured, erotic, fond, impassioned, loving, lustful, passionate, randy, sexual, sexy.

amorphous /ə'mɔːfəs/ *adjective* **1** of no definite shape. **2** vague. **3** non-crystalline.

amount /ə'maʊnt/ *noun* total number, size, value, extent, etc. ● *verb* (+ *to*) be equivalent in number, size, etc. to.

  ■ *noun* aggregate, bulk, entirety, extent, *colloquial* lot, mass, measure, quantity, quantum, reckoning, size, sum, supply, total, value, volume, whole. ● *verb* (**amount to**) add up to, *colloquial* aggregate, be equivalent to, come to, equal, make, mean, total.

amour /ə'mʊə/ *noun* (esp. secret) love affair.

amp *noun* **1** ampere. **2** *colloquial* amplifier.

ampere /'æmpeə/ *noun* SI unit of electric current.

ampersand /'æmpəsænd/ *noun* the sign '&' (= *and*).

amphetamine /æm'fetəmiːn/ *noun* synthetic stimulant drug.

amphibian /æm'fɪbɪən/ *noun* amphibious animal or vehicle.

amphibious /æm'fɪbɪəs/ *adjective* **1** living or operating on land and in water. **2** involving military forces landed from the sea.

amphitheatre /'æmfɪθɪətə/ *noun* round open building with tiers of seats surrounding central space.

amphora /'æmfərə/ *noun* (*plural* **-rae** /-riː/) Greek or Roman two-handled jar.

ample /'æmp(ə)l/ *adjective* (**-r**, **-st**) **1** plentiful, extensive. **2** more than enough. □ **amply** *adverb*.

  ■ abundant, bountiful, broad, capacious, commodious, considerable, copious, extensive, fruitful, generous, great, large, lavish, liberal, munificent, plentiful, profuse, roomy, spacious, substantial, unstinting, voluminous.

amplifier /'æmplɪfaɪə/ *noun* device for amplifying sounds or electrical signals.

amplify /'æmplɪfaɪ/ *verb* (**-ies**, **-ied**) **1** increase strength of (sound or electrical signal). **2** add details to (story etc.). □ **amplification** *noun*.

  ■ **1** boost, heighten, increase, intensify, magnify, make louder, raise the volume of. **2** add to, augment, broaden, develop, dilate upon, elaborate, enlarge, expand, expatiate on, extend, fill out, lengthen, supplement.

amplitude /'æmplɪtjuːd/ *noun* **1** spaciousness. **2** maximum departure from average of oscillation, alternating current, etc. □ **amplitude modulation** modulation of a wave by variation of its amplitude.

ampoule /'æmpuːl/ *noun* small sealed capsule holding solution for injection.

amputate /'æmpjʊteɪt/ *verb* (**-ting**) cut off surgically (limb etc.). □ **amputation** *noun*. **amputee** /-'tiː/ *noun*.

  ■ chop off, cut off, dock, lop off, poll, pollard, remove, sever, truncate.

amuck = AMOK.

amulet /'æmjʊlɪt/ *noun* charm worn against evil.

amuse /ə'mjuːz/ *verb* (**-sing**) **1** cause to laugh or smile; delight. **2** interest, occupy. □ **amusing** *adjective*.

  ■ **1** cheer (up), delight, enliven, gladden, please, tickle. **2** absorb, beguile, divert, engross, entertain, interest, involve, occupy. □ **amusing** see ENJOYABLE, FUNNY 1.

amusement *noun* **1** being amused. **2** thing that amuses, esp. device for entertainment at fairground etc. □ **amusement arcade** indoor area with slot machines etc.

  ■ **1** delight, diversion, enjoyment, entertainment, fun, hilarity, interest, laughter, merriment, mirth, play, pleasure, recreation, sport. **2** distraction, diversion, entertainment, game, hobby, interest, joke, leisure activity, pastime, sport.

an see A.

anabolic steroid /ænə'bɒlɪk/ *noun* synthetic steroid hormone used to build muscle.

anachronism /ə'nækrənɪz(ə)m/ *noun* **1** attribution of custom, event, etc. to wrong period. **2** thing thus attributed. **3** out-of-date person or thing. □ **anachronistic** /-'nɪs-/ *adjective*.

anaconda /ænə'kɒndə/ *noun* large S. American constrictor.

anaemia /ə'niːmɪə/ *noun* (*US* **anemia**) deficiency of red blood cells or their haemoglobin, causing pallor and listlessness. □ **anaemic** *adjective*.
■ □ **anaemic** bloodless, colourless, feeble, frail, pale, pallid, pasty, sallow, sickly, unhealthy, wan, weak.

anaesthesia /ænɪs'θiːzɪə/ *noun* (*US* **anes-**) artificially induced insensibility to pain.

anaesthetic /ænɪs'θetɪk/ (*US* **anes-**) *noun* drug, gas, etc. producing anaesthesia. ● *adjective* producing anaesthesia.

anaesthetist /ə'niːsθətɪst/ *noun* (*US* **anes-**) person who administers anaesthetics.

anaesthetize /ə'niːsθətaɪz/ *verb* (also **-ise**; *US* also **anes-**) (**-zing** or **-sing**) administer anaesthetic to.

anagram /'ænəgræm/ *noun* word or phrase formed by transposing letters of another.

anal /'eɪn(ə)l/ *adjective* of the anus.

analgesia /ænəl'dʒiːzɪə/ *noun* absence or relief of pain.

analgesic /ænəl'dʒiːsɪk/ *noun* pain-killing drug. ● *adjective* pain-killing.

analogous /ə'næləgəs/ *adjective* (usually + *to*) partially similar or parallel.

analogue /'ænəlɒg/ (*US* **analog**) *noun* analogous thing. ● *adjective* (of computer (usually **analog**), watch, etc.) using physical variables (e.g. voltage, position of hands) to represent numbers.

analogy /ə'nælədʒɪ/ *noun* (*plural* **-ies**) **1** correspondence, similarity. **2** reasoning from parallel cases.
■ **1** comparison, likeness, metaphor, parallel, resemblance, similarity, simile.

analyse /'ænəlaɪz/ *verb* (**-sing**) (*US* **analyze**; **-zing**) perform analysis on.
■ assay, break down, criticize, dissect, evaluate, examine, interpret, investigate, scrutinize, separate out, take apart, test.

analysis /ə'nælɪsɪs/ *noun* (*plural* **-lyses** /-siːz/) **1** detailed examination. **2** *Chemistry* determination of constituent parts. **3** psychoanalysis.
■ **1** breakdown, critique, dissection, enquiry, evaluation, examination, interpretation, investigation, *colloquial* post-mortem, scrutiny, study, test. **2** breakdown, division.

analyst /'ænəlɪst/ *noun* person who analyses.

analytical /ænə'lɪtɪkəl/ *adjective* (also **analytic**) of or using analysis.

■ critical, in-depth, inquiring, investigative, logical, methodical, penetrating, questioning, rational, searching, systematic.

analyze *US* = ANALYSE.

anarchism /'ænəkɪz(ə)m/ *noun* belief that government and law should be abolished. □ **anarchist** *noun*. **anarchistic** /-'kɪstɪk/ *adjective*.

anarchy /'ænəkɪ/ *noun* disorder, esp. political. □ **anarchic** /ə'nɑːkɪk/ *adjective*.
■ bedlam, chaos, confusion, disorder, disorganization, lawlessness, pandemonium.

anathema /ə'næθəmə/ *noun* (*plural* **-s**) **1** detested thing. **2** Church's curse.

anatomy /ə'nætəmɪ/ *noun* (*plural* **-ies**) (science of) animal or plant structure. □ **anatomical** /ænə'tɒmɪk(ə)l/ *adjective*. **anatomist** *noun*.

anatto = ANNATTO.

ANC *abbreviation* African National Congress.

ancestor /'ænsestə/ *noun* **1** person, animal, or plant from which another has descended or evolved. **2** prototype.
■ **1** forebear, forefather, predecessor, progenitor. **2** antecedent, forerunner, precursor, predecessor, prototype.

ancestral /æn'sestr(ə)l/ *adjective* inherited from ancestors.

ancestry /'ænsestrɪ/ *noun* (*plural* **-ies**) **1** lineage. **2** ancestors collectively.
■ blood, derivation, descent, extraction, family, genealogy, heredity, line, lineage, origin, parentage, pedigree, roots, stock, strain.

anchor /'æŋkə/ *noun* metal device used to moor ship to sea-bottom. ● *verb* **1** secure with anchor. **2** fix firmly. **3** cast anchor. □ **anchorman**, **anchorperson**, **anchorwoman** coordinator, esp. compère in broadcast.
■ *verb* **1, 2** see FASTEN 1.

anchorage /'æŋkərɪdʒ/ *noun* **1** place for anchoring. **2** lying at anchor.

anchorite /'æŋkəraɪt/ *noun* (*feminine* **anchoress** /-res/) hermit, recluse.

anchovy /'æntʃəvɪ/ *noun* (*plural* **-ies**) small strong-flavoured fish of herring family.

ancien régime /ɑ̃sjæ̃ re'ʒiːm/ *noun* superseded regime, esp. that of pre-Revolutionary France. [French]

ancient /'eɪnʃ(ə)nt/ *adjective* **1** of times long past. **2** very old.
■ **1** bygone, earlier, early, former, immemorial, *archaic* olden, past, prehistoric, primeval, primitive, primordial, remote, *literary* of yore. **2** aged, *colloquial* antediluvian, antiquated, antique, archaic, elderly, *colloquial* fossilized, obsolete, old, old-fashioned, outmoded, out of date, passé, superannuated, time-worn, venerable.

ancillary /æn'sɪlərɪ/ *adjective* **1** subsidiary, auxiliary. **2** (esp. of health workers) providing essential support. ● *noun* (*plural* **-ies**) **1** auxiliary. **2** ancillary worker.

and *conjunction: connecting words, clauses, or sentences.*

andante /æn'dæntɪ/ *Music adverb & adjective* in moderately slow time. ● *noun* andante movement or passage.

androgynous /æn'drɒdʒɪnəs/ *adjective* hermaphrodite.

android /'ændrɔɪd/ *noun* robot with human appearance.

anecdote /'ænɪkdəʊt/ *noun* short, esp. true, story. □ **anecdotal** /-'dəʊt(ə)l/ *adjective.*

anemia *US* = ANAEMIA.

anemic *US* = ANAEMIC.

anemometer /ænɪ'mɒmɪtə/ *noun* instrument for measuring wind force.

anemone /ə'nemənɪ/ *noun* plant related to buttercup.

aneroid barometer /'ænərɔɪd/ *noun* barometer that measures air pressure by registering its action on lid of box containing vacuum.

anesthesia etc. *US* = ANAESTHESIA etc.

aneurysm /'ænjʊrɪz(ə)m/ *noun* (also **aneurism**) excessive enlargement of artery.

anew /ə'njuː/ *adverb* **1** again. **2** in different way.

angel /'eɪndʒ(ə)l/ *noun* **1** attendant or messenger of God usually represented as human with wings. **2** kind or virtuous person. □ **angel cake** light sponge cake. **angelfish** small fish with wing-like fins.

■ **1** archangel, cherub, divine messenger, seraph.

angelic /æn'dʒelɪk/ *adjective* **1** of or like angels. **2** kind or virtuous. □ **angelically** *adverb.*

■ **1** *colloquial* beatific, blessed, celestial, cherubic, divine, ethereal, heavenly, holy, seraphic, spiritual. **2** exemplary, good, holy, innocent, kind, pious, pure, saintly, unworldly, virtuous.

angelica /æn'dʒelɪkə/ *noun* **1** aromatic plant. **2** its candied stalks.

angelus /'ændʒɪləs/ *noun* **1** RC prayers said at morning, noon, and sunset. **2** bell rung for this.

anger /'æŋgə/ *noun* extreme displeasure. ● *verb* make angry.

■ *noun* annoyance, antagonism, bitterness, *archaic* choler, displeasure, exasperation, fury, hostility, indignation, *literary* ire, irritability, outrage, passion, pique, rage, rancour, resentment, spleen, temper, vexation, *literary* wrath. ● *verb disputed* aggravate, annoy, antagonize, *slang* bug, displease, *colloquial* drive mad, enrage, exasperate, incense, incite, inflame, infuriate, irritate, madden, *colloquial* needle, outrage, pique, provoke, *colloquial* rile, vex.

angina /æn'dʒaɪnə/ *noun* (in full **angina pectoris**) chest pain brought on by exertion, owing to poor blood supply to heart.

angle[1] /'æŋg(ə)l/ *noun* **1** space between two meeting lines or surfaces, esp. as measured in degrees. **2** corner. **3** point of view. ● *verb* (**-ling**) **1** move or place obliquely. **2** present (information) in biased way.

■ *noun* **2** bend, corner, crook, nook. **3** approach, outlook, perspective, point of view, position, slant, standpoint, viewpoint. ● *verb* **1** bend, bevel, chamfer, slant, turn, twist.

angle[2] /'æŋg(ə)l/ *verb* (**-ling**) **1** fish with line and hook. **2** (+ *for*) seek objective indirectly. □ **angler** *noun.*

Anglican /'æŋglɪkən/ *adjective* of Church of England. ● *noun* member of Anglican Church. □ **Anglicanism** *noun.*

Anglicism /'æŋglɪsɪz(ə)m/ *noun* English expression or custom.

Anglicize /'æŋglɪsaɪz/ *verb* (also **-ise**) (**-zing** or **-sing**) make English in character etc.

Anglo- *combining form* English or British (and).

Anglo-Catholic /æŋgləʊ'kæθəlɪk/ *adjective* of High Church Anglican group emphasizing its Catholic tradition. ● *noun* member of this group.

Anglo-Indian /æŋgləʊ'ɪndɪən/ *adjective* **1** of England and India. **2** of British descent but Indian residence. ● *noun* Anglo-Indian person.

Anglophile /'æŋgləʊfaɪl/ *noun* admirer of England or the English.

Anglo-Saxon /æŋgləʊ'sæks(ə)n/ *adjective* **1** of English Saxons before Norman Conquest. **2** of English descent. ● *noun* **1** Anglo-Saxon person or language. **2** *colloquial* plain (esp. crude) English.

angora /æŋ'gɔːrə/ *noun* fabric made from hair of angora goat or rabbit. □ **angora cat, goat, rabbit** long-haired varieties.

angostura /æŋgə'stjʊərə/ *noun* aromatic bitter bark of S. American tree.

angry /'æŋgrɪ/ *adjective* (**-ier, -iest**) **1** feeling or showing anger. **2** (of wound etc.) inflamed, painful. □ **angrily** *adverb.*

■ **1** *slang* aerated, annoyed, apoplectic, bad-tempered, bitter, bristling, choked, choleric, cross, disgruntled, enraged, exasperated, excited, fiery, fuming, furious, heated, hostile, hot under the collar, ill-tempered, incensed, indignant, infuriated, in high dudgeon, irascible, irate, *colloquial* livid, *colloquial* mad, outraged, provoked, raging, *colloquial* ratty, raving, resentful, *colloquial* riled, seething, smouldering, sore, splenetic, *colloquial* steamed up, stormy, tempestuous, ugly, up in arms, vexed, *colloquial* wild, *literary* wrathful; (*be angry, become angry*) *colloquial* be in a paddy, *colloquial* blow up, boil, bridle, bristle, flare up, *colloquial* fly off the handle, fulminate, fume, *colloquial* get steamed up, lose one's temper, rage, rant, rave, *colloquial* see red, seethe, snap, storm.

angst /æŋst/ *noun* **1** anxiety, neurotic fear. **2** guilt.

angstrom /'æŋstrəm/ *noun* unit of wavelength measurement.

anguish /'æŋgwɪʃ/ *noun* severe mental or physical pain. □ **anguished** *adjective.*

■ agony, anxiety, distress, grief, heartache, misery, pain, sorrow, suffering, torment, torture, tribulation, woe.

angular /'æŋɡjʊlə/ *adjective* **1** having sharp corners. **2** (of person) having sharp features; bony. **3** (of distance) measured by angle. □ **angularity** /-'lær-/ *noun*.

■ **1** bent, crooked, indented, jagged, zigzag. **2** see BONY 1.

aniline /'ænɪliːn/ *noun* colourless oily liquid used in dyes, drugs, and plastics.

animadvert /ænɪmæd'vɜːt/ *verb* (+ *on*) *literary* criticize, censure. □ **animadversion** *noun*.

animal /'ænɪm(ə)l/ *noun* **1** living organism, esp. other than man, having sensation and usually ability to move. **2** brutish person. ● *adjective* **1** of or like animal. **2** carnal.

■ *noun* **1** beast, being, brute, creature, organism; (*animals*) fauna, wildlife. **2** beast, brute, monster. ● *adjective* **2** carnal, fleshly, physical, sensual.

animality /ænɪ'mælɪtɪ/ *noun* **1** the animal world. **2** animal behaviour.

animate *adjective* /'ænɪmət/ **1** having life. **2** lively. ● *verb* /'ænɪmeɪt/ (**-ting**) **1** enliven. **2** give life to.

■ *adjective* **1** alive, animated, breathing, feeling, live, living, sentient. **2** see ANIMATED 1. ● *verb* activate, arouse, brighten up, *colloquial* buck up, cheer up, encourage, energize, enliven, excite, exhilarate, fire, galvanize, incite, inspire, invigorate, kindle, liven up, make lively, move, *colloquial* pep up, perk up, quicken, rejuvenate, revitalize, revive, rouse, spark, spur, stimulate, stir, urge, vitalize.

animated /'ænɪmeɪtɪd/ *adjective* **1** lively. **2** living. **3** (of film) using animation.

■ **1** active, alive, animate, bright, brisk, bubbly, busy, cheerful, eager, ebullient, energetic, enthusiastic, excited, exuberant, gay, impassioned, lively, passionate, quick, spirited, sprightly, vibrant, vigorous, vivacious, zestful. **2** see ANIMATE 1.

animation /ænɪ'meɪʃ(ə)n/ *noun* **1** liveliness. **2** being alive. **3** technique of film-making by photographing sequence of drawings or positions of puppets etc. to create illusion of movement.

■ **1** activity, briskness, eagerness, ebullience, energy, enthusiasm, excitement, exhilaration, gaiety, high spirits, life, liveliness, *colloquial* pep, sparkle, spirit, sprightliness, verve, vigour, vitality, vivacity, zest.

animator /'ænɪmeɪtə/ *noun* artist who prepares animated films.

animism /'ænɪmɪz(ə)m/ *noun* belief that inanimate objects and natural phenomena have souls. □ **animist** *noun*. **animistic** /-'mɪs-/ *adjective*.

animosity /ænɪ'mɒsɪtɪ/ *noun* (*plural* **-ies**) hostility.

■ acerbity, acrimony, animus, antagonism, antipathy, asperity, aversion, bad blood, bitterness, dislike, enmity, grudge, hate, hatred, hostility, ill will, loathing, malevolence, malice, malignancy, malignity, odium, rancour, resentment, sarcasm, sharpness, sourness, spite, unfriendliness, venom, vindictiveness, virulence.

animus /'ænɪməs/ *noun* hostility, ill feeling.

anion /'ænaɪən/ *noun* negatively charged ion.

anise /'ænɪs/ *noun* plant with aromatic seeds.

aniseed /'ænɪsiːd/ *noun* seed of anise.

ankle /'æŋk(ə)l/ *noun* joint connecting foot with leg.

anklet /'æŋklɪt/ *noun* ornament worn round ankle.

ankylosis /æŋkɪ'ləʊsɪs/ *noun* stiffening of joint by fusing of bones.

annals /'æn(ə)lz/ *plural noun* **1** narrative of events year by year. **2** historical records. □ **annalist** *noun*.

annatto /ə'nætəʊ/ *noun* (also **anatto**) orange-red food colouring made from tropical fruit.

anneal /ə'niːl/ *verb* heat (metal, glass) and cool slowly, esp. to toughen.

annelid /'ænəlɪd/ *noun* segmented worm, e.g. earthworm.

annex /æ'neks/ *verb* **1** (often + *to*) add as subordinate part. **2** take possession of. □ **annexation** *noun*.

■ **2** acquire, appropriate, conquer, occupy, *formal* or *jocular* purloin, seize, take over, usurp.

annexe /'æneks/ *noun* supplementary building.

annihilate /ə'naɪəleɪt/ *verb* (**-ting**) destroy utterly. □ **annihilation** *noun*.

■ destroy, eliminate, eradicate, erase, exterminate, extinguish, extirpate, *colloquial* finish off, kill off, liquidate, nullify, obliterate, raze, slaughter, wipe out.

anniversary /ænɪ'vɜːsərɪ/ *noun* (*plural* **-ies**) **1** yearly return of date of event. **2** celebration of this.

Anno Domini /ænəʊ 'dɒmɪnaɪ/ see AD.

annotate /'ænəteɪt/ *verb* (**-ting**) add explanatory notes to. □ **annotation** *noun*.

■ □ **annotation** comment, commentary, elucidation, explanation, footnote, gloss, interpretation, note.

announce /ə'naʊns/ *verb* (**-cing**) **1** make publicly known. **2** make known the approach of; introduce. □ **announcement** *noun*.

■ **1** advertise, broadcast, declare, disclose, divulge, give notice of, intimate, make public, notify, proclaim, promulgate, propound, publicize, publish, put out, report, reveal, state. **2** introduce, lead into, preface, present. □ **announcement** advertisement, bulletin, communiqué, declaration, disclosure, notification, proclamation, promulgation, publication, report, revelation, statement.

announcer *noun* person who announces, esp. in broadcasting.

■ anchorman, anchorwoman, broadcaster, commentator, compère, disc jockey, DJ, harbinger, herald, Master of Ceremonies, MC, messenger, newscaster, newsreader, reporter.

annoy /ə'nɔɪ/ *verb* **1** (often in *passive* + *at*, *with*) anger or distress slightly. **2** harass. □ **annoyed** *adjective*. **annoying** *adjective*.

■ **1** *disputed* aggravate, anger, antagonize, bother, *slang* bug, chagrin, displease, distress, *colloquial* drive mad, exasperate, fret, gall, grate, infuriate, irk, irritate, jar, madden, make cross, *colloquial* needle, nettle, offend, *colloquial* peeve, pique, put out, rankle, *colloquial* rile, rub up the wrong way, ruffle, spite, trouble, try (person's) patience, upset, vex, worry; (*be annoyed*) *colloquial* go off in a huff, take offence, take umbrage. **2** badger, bother, *slang* bug, harass, harry, molest, pester, *colloquial* plague, provoke, tease, worry. □ **annoyed** angry, chagrined, cross, displeased, exasperated, huffy, irritated, jaundiced, *colloquial* miffed, *colloquial* needled, nettled, offended, *colloquial* peeved, piqued, put out, *colloquial* riled, *colloquial* shirty, sore, upset, vexed. **annoying** *disputed* aggravating, bothersome, displeasing, *colloquial* dreadful, exasperating, galling, grating, inconvenient, infuriating, irksome, irritating, jarring, maddening, offensive, provocative, provoking, *colloquial* tiresome, troublesome, trying, upsetting, vexatious, vexing, wearisome, worrying.

annoyance *noun* **1** annoying, being annoyed. **2** thing which annoys.

■ **1** anger, chagrin, crossness, displeasure, exasperation, irritation, pique, vexation. **2** *disputed* aggravation, bother, harassment, irritant, nuisance, offence, *colloquial* pain in the neck, pest, provocation, worry.

annual /'ænjʊəl/ *adjective* **1** reckoned by the year. **2** recurring yearly. ● *noun* **1** book etc. published yearly. **2** plant living only one year. □ **annually** *adverb*.

annuity /ə'njuːɪtɪ/ *noun* (*plural* **-ies**) **1** yearly grant or allowance. **2** investment yielding fixed annual sum for stated period.

annul /ə'nʌl/ *verb* (**-ll-**) **1** declare invalid. **2** cancel, abolish. □ **annulment** *noun*.

annular /'ænjʊlə/ *adjective* ring-shaped.

annulate /'ænjʊlət/ *adjective* marked with or formed of rings.

annunciation /ənʌnsɪ'eɪʃ(ə)n/ *noun* announcement, esp. (**Annunciation**) that made by the angel Gabriel to Mary.

anode /'ænəʊd/ *noun* positive electrode.

anodize /'ænədaɪz/ *verb* (also **-ise**) (**-zing** or **-sing**) coat (metal) with protective layer by electrolysis.

anodyne /'ænədaɪn/ *adjective* **1** pain-relieving. **2** soothing. ● *noun* anodyne drug etc.

anoint /ə'nɔɪnt/ *verb* apply oil or ointment to, esp. ritually.

anomalous /ə'nɒmələs/ *adjective* irregular, abnormal.

anomaly /ə'nɒməlɪ/ *noun* (*plural* **-ies**) anomalous thing.

anon /ə'nɒn/ *adverb* *archaic* soon.

anon. *abbreviation* anonymous.

anonymous /ə'nɒnɪməs/ *adjective* **1** of unknown name or authorship. **2** featureless. □ **anonymity** /ænə'nɪm-/ *noun*.

■ **1** incognito, nameless, unacknowledged, unattributed, unidentified, unknown, unnamed, unsigned, unspecified, unsung. **2** characterless, featureless, impersonal, nondescript, unidentifiable, unrecognizable, unremarkable.

anorak /'ænəræk/ *noun* waterproof usually hooded jacket.

anorexia /ænə'reksɪə/ *noun* lack of appetite, esp. (in full **anorexia nervosa** /nɜː'vəʊsə/) obsessive desire to lose weight by refusing to eat. □ **anorexic** *adjective* & *noun*.

another /ə'nʌðə/ *adjective* an additional or different. ● *pronoun* an additional or different person or thing.

answer /'ɑːnsə/ *noun* **1** something said or done in reaction to a question, statement, charge, or circumstance. **2** solution to problem. ● *verb* **1** make an answer or response (to). **2** suit. **3** (+ *to*, *for*) be responsible to or for. **4** (+ *to*) correspond to (esp. description). □ **answer back** answer insolently. **answering machine**, **answerphone** tape recorder which answers telephone calls and takes messages.

■ *noun* **1** acknowledgement, *slang* comeback, reaction, rejoinder, reply, response, retort, riposte. **2** explanation, outcome, solution. ● *verb* **1** acknowledge, react, rejoin, reply, respond, retort, return; (*answer a charge*) counter, defend oneself against, rebut, refute. **2** meet, satisfy, serve, suffice for, suit. **4** (*answer to*) correspond to, fit, match up to. □ **answer back** see ARGUE 1.

answerable *adjective* **1** (usually + *to*, *for*) responsible. **2** that can be answered.

ant *noun* small usually wingless insect living in complex social group. □ **anteater** mammal feeding on ants. **anthill** moundlike ants' nest.

antacid /æn'tæsɪd/ *noun* & *adjective* preventive or corrective of acidity.

antagonism /æn'tægənɪz(ə)m/ *noun* active hostility.

■ antipathy, dissension, enmity, friction, hostility, opposition, rancour, rivalry, strife.

antagonist /æn'tægənɪst/ *noun* opponent. □ **antagonistic** /-'nɪs-/ *adjective*.

antagonize /æn'tægənaɪz/ *verb* (also **-ise**) (**-zing** or **-sing**) provoke.

■ alienate, anger, annoy, embitter, estrange, irritate, make an enemy of, offend, provoke, put off, upset.

Antarctic /æn'tɑːktɪk/ *adjective* of south polar region. ● *noun* this region.

ante /'æntɪ/ *noun* **1** stake put up by poker player before receiving cards. **2** amount payable in advance.

ante- /'ænti/ *prefix* before.

antecedent /ænti'si:d(ə)nt/ *noun* **1** preceding thing or circumstance. **2** *Grammar* word, phrase, etc., to which another word refers. **3** (in *plural*) person's ancestors. ● *adjective* previous.

antechamber /'ænti,tʃeimbə/ *noun* ante-room.

antedate /ænti'deit/ *verb* (**-ting**) **1** precede in time. **2** give earlier than true date to.

antediluvian /,æntidi'lu:viən/ *adjective* **1** before the Flood. **2** *colloquial* very old.

antelope /'æntiləup/ *noun* (*plural* same or **-s**) swift deerlike animal.

antenatal /ænti'neitəl/ *adjective* **1** before birth. **2** of pregnancy.

antenna /æn'tenə/ *noun* (*plural* **-tennae** /-ni:/) **1** each of pair of feelers on head of insect or crustacean. **2** (*plural* **-s**) aerial.

anterior /æn'tiəriə/ *adjective* **1** nearer the front. **2** (often + *to*) prior.

ante-room /'æntiru:m/ *noun* small room leading to main one.

anthem /'ænθəm/ *noun* **1** choral composition for church use. **2** song of praise, esp. for nation.
■ **1** canticle, chant, chorale, hymn, psalm.

anther /'ænθə/ *noun* part of stamen containing pollen.

anthology /æn'θɒlədʒi/ *noun* (*plural* **-ies**) collection of poems, essays, stories, etc.
■ collection, compendium, compilation, digest, miscellany, selection, treasury.

anthracite /'ænθrəsait/ *noun* hard kind of coal.

anthrax /'ænθræks/ *noun* disease of sheep and cattle transmissible to humans.

anthropocentric /ænθrəpəu'sentrik/ *adjective* regarding humankind as centre of existence.

anthropoid /'ænθrəpɔid/ *adjective* human in form. ● *noun* anthropoid ape.

anthropology /ænθrə'pɒlədʒi/ *noun* study of humankind, esp. societies and customs. □ **anthropological** /-pə'lɒdʒ-/ *adjective*. **anthropologist** *noun*.

anthropomorphism /ænθrəpə'mɔ:fiz(ə)m/ *noun* attributing of human characteristics to god, animal, or thing. □ **anthropomorphic** *adjective*. **anthropomorphize** *verb* (also **-ise**) (**-zing** or **-sing**).

anthropomorphous /ænθrəpə'mɔ:fəs/ *adjective* human in form.

anti /'ænti/ *preposition* opposed to. ● *noun* (*plural* **antis**) person opposed to particular policy, cause, etc.

anti- *prefix* **1** opposed to. **2** preventing. **3** opposite of. **4** unlike conventional form of.

anti-abortion /-ə'bɔ:ʃ(ə)n/ *adjective* opposing abortion. □ **anti-abortionist** *noun*.

anti-aircraft /-'eəkrɑ:ft/ *adjective* for defence against enemy aircraft.

antibiotic /-bai'ɒtik/ *noun* substance that can inhibit or destroy bacteria etc. ● *adjective* functioning as antibiotic.

antibody /'ænti,bɒdi/ *noun* (*plural* **-ies**) blood protein produced in reaction to antigens.

antic /'æntik/ *noun* (usually in *plural*) foolish behaviour.
■ (*antics*) buffoonery, capers, clowning, escapades, foolery, fooling, *colloquial* larking about, pranks, skylarking, tomfoolery, tricks.

anticipate /æn'tisipeit/ *verb* (**-ting**) **1** deal with or use before proper time. **2** *disputed* expect. **3** forestall. □ **anticipation** *noun*. **anticipatory** *adjective*.
USAGE The use of *anticipate* to mean 'expect' is well established in informal use, but is regarded as incorrect by some people.
■ **2** see FORESEE. **3** forestall, obviate, preclude, pre-empt, prevent.

anticlimax /-'klaimæks/ *noun* disappointing conclusion to something significant.
■ bathos, comedown, disappointment, let-down.

anticlockwise /-'klɒkwaiz/ *adverb* in opposite direction to hands of clock. ● *adjective* moving anticlockwise.

anticyclone /-'saikləun/ *noun* system of winds rotating outwards from area of high pressure, producing fine weather.

antidepressant /-di'pres(ə)nt/ *noun* drug etc. alleviating depression. ● *adjective* alleviating depression.

antidote /'æntidəut/ *noun* medicine used to counteract poison.
■ antitoxin, corrective, countermeasure, cure, drug, remedy.

antifreeze /'æntifri:z/ *noun* substance added to water (esp. in vehicle's radiator) to lower its freezing point.

antigen /'æntidʒ(ə)n/ *noun* foreign substance causing body to produce antibodies.

anti-hero /'ænti,hiərəu/ *noun* (*plural* **-es**) central character in story, lacking conventional heroic qualities.

antihistamine /-'histəmi:n/ *noun* drug that counteracts effect of histamine, used esp. to treat allergies.

antiknock /'æntinɒk/ *noun* substance added to motor fuel to prevent premature combustion.

anti-lock /'æntilɒk/ *adjective* (of brakes) not locking when applied suddenly.

antimony /'æntiməni/ *noun* brittle silvery metallic element.

anti-nuclear /-'nju:kliə/ *adjective* opposed to development of nuclear weapons or power.

antipathy /æn'tipəθi/ *noun* (*plural* **-ies**) (often + *to*, *for*, *between*) strong aversion or dislike. □ **antipathetic** /-'θet-/ *adjective*.

antiperspirant /-'pɜ:spərənt/ *noun* substance inhibiting perspiration.

antiphon /'æntif(ə)n/ *noun* hymn sung alternately by two groups. □ **antiphonal** /-'tɪf-/ *adjective*.

antipodes /æn'tɪpədi:z/ *plural noun* places diametrically opposite each other on the earth, esp. (also **Antipodes**) Australasia in relation to Europe. □ **antipodean** /-'di:ən/ *adjective & noun*.

antiquarian /ˌæntɪ'kweərɪən/ *adjective* of or dealing in rare books. ● *noun* antiquary.

antiquary /'æntɪkwərɪ/ *noun* (*plural* **-ies**) student or collector of antiques etc.

antiquated /'æntɪkweɪtɪd/ *adjective* oldfashioned.

■ anachronistic, ancient, *colloquial* antediluvian, antique, archaic, dated, medieval, obsolete, old, old-fashioned, *colloquial* out, outdated, outmoded, out of date, passé, *colloquial* past it, prehistoric, primeval, primitive, quaint, superannuated, unfashionable.

antique /æn'ti:k/ *noun* old valuable object, esp. piece of furniture etc. ● *adjective* **1** of or existing since old times. **2** old-fashioned.

■ *noun* collectable, collector's item, curio, curiosity, *objet d'art*, rarity. ● *adjective* **1** ancient, antiquarian, collectable, historic, old, traditional, veteran, vintage. **2** see ANTIQUATED.

antiquity /æn'tɪkwətɪ/ *noun* (*plural* **-ies**) **1** ancient times, esp. before Middle Ages. **2** (in *plural*) great age. **3** (in *plural*) remains from ancient times.

■ **1** classical times, days gone by, former times, *archaic* olden days, the past.

antirrhinum /ˌæntɪ'raɪnəm/ *noun* snapdragon.

anti-Semitic /-sɪ'mɪtɪk/ *adjective* prejudiced against Jews. □ **anti-Semite** /-'si:maɪt/ *noun*. **anti-Semitism** /-'sem-/ *noun*.

antiseptic /-'septɪk/ *adjective* **1** counteracting sepsis by destroying germs. **2** sterile; free from germs. ● *noun* antiseptic substance.

■ *adjective* **1** disinfectant, germicidal, sterilizing. **2** aseptic, clean, disinfected, germ-free, hygienic, medicated, sanitized, sterile, sterilized, unpolluted.

antisocial /-'səʊʃ(ə)l/ *adjective* **1** not sociable. **2** opposed or harmful to society.

USAGE It is a mistake to use *antisocial* instead of *unsocial* in the phrase *unsocial hours*.

■ **1** alienated, misanthropic, reclusive, retiring, unfriendly, unsociable, withdrawn. **2** anarchic, disagreeable, disorderly, disruptive, nasty, obnoxious, offensive, rebellious, rude, surly, troublesome, uncooperative, undisciplined, unruly.

antistatic /-'stætɪk/ *adjective* counteracting effect of static electricity.

antithesis /æn'tɪθəsɪs/ *noun* (*plural* **-theses** /-si:z/) **1** (often + *of, to*) direct opposite. **2** contrast. **3** rhetorical use of strongly contrasted words. □ **antithetical** /-'θet-/ *adjective*.

antitoxin /-'tɒksɪn/ *noun* antibody counteracting toxin. □ **antitoxic** *adjective*.

antitrades /-'treɪdz/ *plural noun* winds blowing above and in opposite direction to trade winds.

antiviral /-'vaɪər(ə)l/ *adjective* effective against viruses.

antler /'æntlə/ *noun* branched horn of deer.

antonym /'æntənɪm/ *noun* word opposite in meaning to another, e.g. *wet* is an antonym of *dry*.

anus /'eɪnəs/ *noun* (*plural* **-es**) excretory opening at end of alimentary canal.

anvil /'ænvɪl/ *noun* iron block on which metals are worked.

anxiety /æŋ'zaɪətɪ/ *noun* (*plural* **-ies**) **1** troubled state of mind. **2** worry. **3** eagerness.

■ **1, 2** angst, apprehension, concern, disquiet, distress, doubt, dread, fear, foreboding, fretfulness, misgiving, nervousness, qualm, scruple, strain, stress, tension, uncertainty, unease, worry. **3** desire, eagerness, enthusiasm, impatience, keenness, longing, solicitude, willingness.

anxious /'æŋkʃəs/ *adjective* **1** mentally troubled. **2** marked by anxiety. **3** (+ *to do*) uneasily wanting to. □ **anxiously** *adverb*.

■ **1** afraid, agitated, alarmed, apprehensive, concerned, distracted, distraught, distressed, disturbed, edgy, fearful, fraught, fretful, *colloquial* jittery, nervous, *colloquial* nervy, on edge, overwrought, perturbed, restless, tense, troubled, uneasy, upset, watchful, worried. **3** avid, careful, desirous, desperate, dying, eager, impatient, intent, itching, keen, longing, solicitous, willing, yearning.

any /'enɪ/ *adjective* **1** one or some. **2** no matter which. ● *pronoun* **1** any one. **2** any number or amount. ● *adverb* at all. □ **anybody** ● *pronoun* any person. ● *noun* an important person. **anyhow 1** anyway. **2** at random. **anyone** anybody. **anything 1** any thing. **2** a thing of any kind. **anyway 1** in any way. **2** in any case. **anywhere** (in or to) any place.

AOB *abbreviation* any other business.

aorta /eɪ'ɔ:tə/ *noun* (*plural* **-s**) main artery carrying blood from heart.

apace /ə'peɪs/ *adverb literary* swiftly.

apart /ə'pɑ:t/ *adverb* **1** separately. **2** into pieces. **3** at or to a distance.

apartheid /ə'pɑ:teɪt/ *noun* racial segregation, esp. in S. Africa.

apartment /ə'pɑ:tmənt/ *noun* **1** (*US* or esp. for holidays) flat. **2** (usually in *plural*) room.

apathy /'æpəθɪ/ *noun* lack of interest, indifference. □ **apathetic** /-'θet-/ *adjective*.

■ coolness, inactivity, indifference, lassitude, lethargy, listlessness, passivity, torpor. □ apathetic casual, cool, dispassionate, dull, emotionless, half-hearted, impassive, inactive, indifferent, indolent, languid, lethargic, listless, passive, phlegmatic, slow, sluggish, tepid, torpid, unambitious, uncommitted, unconcerned, unenterprising, unenthusiastic, unfeeling, uninterested, uninvolved, unmotivated, unresponsive.

apatosaurus /əpætə'sɔːrəs/ *noun* (*plural* **-ruses**) large long-necked plant-eating dinosaur.

ape *noun* **1** tailless monkey. **2** imitator. ● *verb* (**-ping**) imitate.

aperient /ə'pɪərɪənt/ *adjective & noun* laxative.

aperitif /əperɪ'tiːf/ *noun* alcoholic drink before meal.

aperture /'æpətʃə/ *noun* opening or gap, esp. variable one letting light into camera.

apex /'eɪpeks/ *noun* (*plural* **-es**) **1** highest point. **2** climax. **3** tip.
 ■ **1** crest, crown, head, peak, pinnacle, summit, top. **2** acme, apogee, climax, consummation, crowning moment, culmination, height, high point, peak, pinnacle, zenith. **3** point, tip, vertex.

aphasia /ə'feɪzɪə/ *noun* loss of verbal understanding or expression.

aphelion /ə'fiːlɪən/ *noun* (*plural* **-lia**) point of orbit farthest from sun.

aphid /'eɪfɪd/ *noun* insect infesting plants.

aphis /'eɪfɪs/ *noun* (*plural* **aphides** /-diːz/) aphid.

aphorism /'æfərɪz(ə)m/ *noun* short wise saying. □ **aphoristic** /-'rɪs-/ *adjective*.

aphrodisiac /æfrə'dɪzɪæk/ *adjective* arousing sexual desire. ● *noun* aphrodisiac substance.
 ■ *adjective* arousing, erotic, sexy, stimulating.

apiary /'eɪpɪərɪ/ *noun* (*plural* **-ies**) place where bees are kept. □ **apiarist** *noun*.

apiculture /'eɪpɪkʌltʃə/ *noun* bee-keeping.

apiece /ə'piːs/ *adverb* for each one.

aplomb /ə'plɒm/ *noun* self-assurance.

apocalypse /ə'pɒkəlɪps/ *noun* **1** destructive event. **2** revelation, esp. about the end of the world. □ **apocalyptic** /-'lɪp-/ *adjective*.

Apocrypha /ə'pɒkrɪfə/ *plural noun* **1** Old Testament books not in Hebrew Bible. **2** (**apocrypha**) writings etc. not considered genuine. □ **apocryphal** *adjective*.

apogee /'æpədʒiː/ *noun* **1** highest point. **2** point farthest from earth in orbit of moon etc.

apolitical /eɪpə'lɪtɪk(ə)l/ *adjective* not interested or involved in politics.

apologetic /əpɒlə'dʒetɪk/ *adjective* expressing regret. □ **apologetically** *adverb*.
 ■ conscience-stricken, contrite, penitent, regretful, remorseful, repentant, rueful, sorry.

apologia /æpə'ləʊdʒə/ *noun* formal defence of conduct or opinions.

apologist /ə'pɒlədʒɪst/ *noun* person who defends by argument.

apologize /ə'pɒlədʒaɪz/ *verb* (also **-ise**) (**-zing** or **-sing**) make apology.
 ■ ask pardon, express regret, repent, say sorry.

apology /ə'pɒlədʒɪ/ *noun* (*plural* **-ies**) **1** regret-ful acknowledgement of offence or failure. **2** explanation.
 ■ **1** acknowledgement, confession. **2** defence, excuse, explanation, justification, plea.

apophthegm /'æpəθem/ *noun* short wise saying.

apoplexy /'æpəpleksɪ/ *noun* sudden paralysis caused by blockage or rupture of brain artery. □ **apoplectic** /-'plek-/ *adjective*.

apostasy /ə'pɒstəsɪ/ *noun* (*plural* **-ies**) abandonment of belief, faith, etc.

apostate /ə'pɒsteɪt/ *noun* person who renounces belief. □ **apostatize** /-tət-/ *verb* (also **-ise**) (**-zing** or **-sing**).

a posteriori /eɪ pɒsterɪ'ɔːraɪ/ *adjective & adverb* from effects to causes.

apostle /ə'pɒs(ə)l/ *noun* **1** (**Apostle**) any of twelve men sent by Christ to preach gospel. **2** leader of reform.
 ■ **2** champion, crusader, evangelist, pioneer, preacher, propagandist, proponent, proselytizer, teacher.

apostolic /æpəs'tɒlɪk/ *adjective* **1** of Apostles. **2** of the Pope.

apostrophe /ə'pɒstrəfɪ/ *noun* punctuation mark (') indicating possession or marking omission of letter(s) or number(s) (see panel).

apostrophize *verb* (also **-ise**) (**-zing** or **-sing**) address (esp. absent person or thing).

apothecary /ə'pɒθəkərɪ/ *noun* (*plural* **-ies**) *archaic* pharmacist.

apotheosis /əpɒθɪ'əʊsɪs/ *noun* (*plural* **-oses** /-siːz/) **1** deification. **2** glorification or sublime example (of thing).

appal /ə'pɔːl/ *verb* (**-ll-**) **1** dismay, horrify. **2** (as **appalling** *adjective*) *colloquial* very bad, shocking.
 ■ **1** alarm, disgust, dismay, distress, frighten, harrow, horrify, nauseate, outrage, revolt, shock, sicken, terrify, unnerve. **2** (**appalling**) see ATROCIOUS 2, BAD 2.

apparatus /æpə'reɪtəs/ *noun* equipment for scientific or other work.
 ■ appliance, contraption, device, equipment, gadget, gear, implement, instrument, machine, machinery, mechanism, system, tackle, tool, utensil.

apparel /ə'pær(ə)l/ *noun* *formal* clothing. □ **apparelled** *adjective*.

apparent /ə'pærənt/ *adjective* **1** obvious. **2** seeming. □ **apparently** *adverb*.
 ■ **1** blatant, clear, conspicuous, detectable, discernible, evident, manifest, noticeable, observable, obvious, overt, patent, perceptible, recognizable, self-explanatory, unconcealed, unmistakable, visible. **2** ostensible, outward, seeming.

apparition /æpə'rɪʃ(ə)n/ *noun* **1** thing that appears, esp. of startling kind. **2** ghost.

■ **1** hallucination, illusion, manifestation, presence, vision. **2** ghost, phantasm, phantom, *literary* shade, spectre, spirit, *colloquial* spook, wraith.

appeal /ə'pi:l/ *verb* **1** make earnest or formal request. **2** (usually + *to*) be attractive. **3** (+ *to*) resort to for support. **4** (often + *to*) apply to higher court for revision of judicial decision. **5** *Cricket* ask umpire to declare batsman out. ● *noun* **1** appealing. **2** request for aid. **3** attractiveness.

■ *verb* **1** ask earnestly, beg, call, cry out, plead, pray; (*appeal to the Queen*) beseech, entreat, implore, invoke, petition, request, solicit, *literary* supplicate. **2** (*appeal to*) see ATTRACT 3. ● *noun* **1** application, call, cry, entreaty, petition, plea, prayer, request, solicitation, *literary* supplication. **3** allure, attractiveness, charisma, charm, pull, seductiveness.

appealing *adjective* attractive, likeable. □ **appealingly** *adverb*.

appear /ə'pɪə/ *verb* **1** become or be visible. **2** seem. **3** present oneself, esp. on stage or in court. **4** be published.

■ **1** arise, arrive, be revealed, be seen, bob up, come, come into view, come out, crop up, enter, develop, emerge, heave in sight, loom, *colloquial* materialize, occur, originate, present oneself,

colloquial show, *colloquial* show up, spring up, surface, turn up. **2** look, seem. **3** see PERFORM 4. **4** be published, come out.

appearance *noun* **1** appearing. **2** outward form. **3** (in *plural*) outward show of prosperity, virtue, etc.

■ **1** arrival, advent, emergence, presence, rise. **2** air, aspect, bearing, demeanour, exterior, impression, likeness, look, *literary* mien, pretence, semblance, show.

appease /ə'pi:z/ *verb* (**-sing**) **1** make calm or quiet, esp. conciliate (aggressor) with concessions. **2** satisfy (appetite etc.). □ **appeasement** *noun*. **appeaser** noun.

■ **1** assuage, calm, conciliate, humour, mollify, pacify, placate, propitiate, quiet, reconcile, satisfy, soothe, sweeten, tranquillize, win over. **2** assuage, relieve, satisfy, slake.

appellant /ə'pelənt/ *noun* person who appeals to higher court.

appellation /æpə'leɪʃ(ə)n/ *noun formal* name, title.

append /ə'pend/ *verb* (usually + *to*) attach, affix, add.

appendage /ə'pendɪdʒ/ *noun* thing attached, addition.

··

Apostrophe ’

This is used:

1 to indicate possession:
  with a singular noun:
    a boy's book; *a week's work*; *the boss's salary*
  with a plural already ending with *s*:
    a girls' school; two weeks' newspapers; the bosses' salaries
  with a plural not already ending with *s*:
    the children's books; women's liberation
  with a singular name:
    Bill's book; *John's coat*; *Barnabas'* (or *Barnabas's*) *book*; *Nicholas'* (or *Nicholas's*) *coat*
  with a name ending in *-es* that is pronounced /-ɪz/:
    Bridges' poems; Moses' mother
  and before the word *sake*;
    for God's sake; *for goodness' sake*; *for Nicholas' sake*
  but it is often omitted in a business name:
    Barclays Bank

2 to mark an omission of one or more letters or numbers:
  he's (*he is* or *he has*)   *haven't* (*have not*)
  can't (*cannot*)   *we'll* (*we shall*)
  won't (*will not*)   *o'clock* (*of the clock*)
  the summer of '68 (*1968*)

3 it is sometimes used to form a plural of individual letters or numbers, although this use is dimishing. It is helpful in:
    cross your t's
  but it is unnecessary in, e.g.:
    MPs; *the 1940s*

··

appendectomy /æpen'dektəmɪ/ *noun* (also **appendicectomy** /əpendɪ'sektəmɪ/) (*plural* **-ies**) surgical removal of appendix.

appendicitis /əpendɪ'saɪtɪs/ *noun* inflammation of appendix.

appendix /ə'pendɪks/ *noun* (*plural* **-dices** /-siːz/) **1** tubular sac attached to large intestine. **2** addition to book etc.

■ **2** addendum, addition, codicil, epilogue, postscript, rider, supplement.

appertain /æpə'teɪn/ *verb* (+ *to*) **1** belong to. **2** relate to.

appetite /'æpɪtaɪt/ *noun* (usually + *for*) **1** desire (esp. for food). **2** inclination, desire.

■ **1** hunger. **2** craving, demand, desire, eagerness, fondness, hankering, hunger, keenness, longing, lust, passion, predilection, proclivity, relish, stomach, taste, thirst, urge, willingness, wish, yearning, *colloquial* yen, zeal, zest.

appetizer /'æpɪtaɪzə/ *noun* (also **-iser**) thing eaten or drunk to stimulate appetite.

appetizing /'æpɪtaɪzɪŋ/ *adjective* (also **-ising**) (esp. of food) stimulating appetite.

■ delicious, mouth-watering, tasty, tempting.

applaud /ə'plɔːd/ *verb* **1** express approval (of) by clapping. **2** express approval of; commend.

■ **1** clap, *colloquial* give (person) a hand. **2** acclaim, approve, cheer, commend, compliment, congratulate, eulogize, extol, hail, laud, praise, salute.

applause /ə'plɔːz/ *noun* warm approval, esp. clapping.

■ acclaim, acclamation, approval, cheering, clapping, éclat, ovation, plaudits, praise.

apple /'æp(ə)l/ *noun* roundish firm fruit. □ **apple of one's eye** cherished person or thing. **apple-pie bed** bed with sheets folded so that one cannot stretch out one's legs. **apple-pie order** extreme neatness.

appliance /ə'plaɪəns/ *noun* device etc. for specific task.

■ apparatus, contraption, device, gadget, implement, instrument, machine, mechanism, tool, utensil.

applicable /'æplɪkəb(ə)l/ *adjective* (often + *to*) that may be applied. □ **applicability** *noun*.

applicant /'æplɪkənt/ *noun* person who applies for job etc.

■ aspirant, candidate, competitor, entrant, interviewee, participant, postulant.

application /æplɪ'keɪʃ(ə)n/ *noun* **1** formal request. **2** applying. **3** thing applied. **4** diligence. **5** relevance. **6** use.

applicator /'æplɪkeɪtə/ *noun* device for applying ointment etc.

appliqué /æ'pliːkeɪ/ *noun* work in which cut-out fabric is fixed on to other fabric. ● *verb* (**-qués**, **-quéd**, **-quéing**) decorate with appliqué.

apply /ə'plaɪ/ *verb* (**-ies**, **-ied**) **1** (often + *for, to, to do*) make formal request. **2** (often + *to*) be relevant. **3** make use of. **4** (often + *to*) put or spread (on). **5** (**apply oneself**; often + *to*) devote oneself.

■ **1** (*apply for*) see REQUEST *verb* 1; (*apply to*) see REQUEST *verb* 2. **2** be relevant, have a bearing, pertain; (*apply to*) appertain to, refer to, relate to. **3** bring into use, employ, exercise, implement, practise, use, utilize, wield. **4** administer, affix, lay on, put on, rub on, spread. **5** (**apply oneself**) see CONCENTRATE 1.

appoint /ə'pɔɪnt/ *verb* **1** assign job or office to. **2** (often + *for*) fix (time etc.). **3** (as **appointed** *adjective*) equipped, furnished.

■ **1** assign, choose, co-opt, delegate, depute, designate, detail, elect, name, nominate, plump for, select, settle on, vote for. **2** arrange, authorize, decide on, determine, establish, fix, ordain, prescribe, settle.

appointment *noun* **1** appointing, being appointed. **2** arrangement for meeting. **3** job available. **4** (in *plural*) equipment, fittings.

■ **1** choice, choosing, commissioning, election, naming, nomination, selection. **2** arrangement, assignation, consultation, *colloquial* date, engagement, fixture, interview, meeting, rendezvous, session, *archaic* tryst. **3** job, office, place, position, post, *formal* situation.

apportion /ə'pɔːʃ(ə)n/ *verb* (often + *to*) share out. □ **apportionment** *noun*.

apposite /'æpəzɪt/ *adjective* (often + *to*) **1** well expressed. **2** appropriate.

apposition /æpə'zɪʃ(ə)n/ *noun* juxtaposition, esp. of syntactically parallel words etc. (e.g. *my friend Sue*).

appraise /ə'preɪz/ *verb* (**-sing**) estimate value or quality of. □ **appraisal** *noun*.

appreciable /ə'priːʃəb(ə)l/ *adjective* significant; considerable.

appreciate /ə'priːʃɪeɪt/ *verb* (**-ting**) **1** (highly) value; be grateful for. **2** understand, recognize. **3** rise in value. □ **appreciation** *noun*. **appreciative** /-ʃətɪv/ *adjective*.

■ **1** admire, approve of, be grateful for, cherish, enjoy, esteem, find worthwhile, like, praise, prize, rate highly, regard highly, respect, treasure, value, welcome. **2** acknowledge, apprehend, be sensitive to, comprehend, know, realize, recognize, see, sympathize with, understand. **3** escalate, gain, go up, grow, improve, increase, inflate, mount, rise, soar, strengthen.

apprehend /æprɪ'hend/ *verb* **1** arrest. **2** understand.

apprehension /æprɪ'henʃ(ə)n/ *noun* **1** fearful anticipation. **2** arrest. **3** understanding.

apprehensive /æprɪ'hensɪv/ *adjective* uneasy, fearful. □ **apprehensively** *adverb*. **apprehensiveness** *noun*.

■ afraid, anxious, concerned, disturbed, edgy, fearful, *colloquial* jittery, nervous, *colloquial* nervy, on edge, troubled, uneasy, worried.

apprentice /əˈprentɪs/ *noun* person learning trade by working for agreed period. ● *verb* (usually + *to*) engage as apprentice. □ **apprenticeship** *noun*.

■ *noun* beginner, learner, novice, probationer, pupil, starter, tiro, trainee.

apprise /əˈpraɪz/ *verb* (**-sing**) (usually + *of*) inform.

approach /əˈprəʊtʃ/ *verb* **1** come nearer (to) in space or time. **2** be similar to. **3** approximate to. **4** set about. **5** make tentative proposal to. ● *noun* **1** act of approaching. **2** means of approaching. **3** approximation. **4** technique. **5** request, proposal. **6** part of aircraft's flight before landing.

■ *verb* **1** advance, bear down on, catch up, come near, draw near, gain on, loom, move towards, near, progress. **4** see BEGIN 1. **5** see CONTACT *verb*. ● *noun* **1** advance, advent, arrival, coming, movement, nearing. **2** access, doorway, entrance, entry, passage, road, way in. **4** attitude, course, manner, means, method, mode, *modus operandi*, procedure, style, system, technique, way. **5** appeal, application, invitation, offer, overture, proposal, proposition.

approachable /əˈprəʊtʃəb(ə)l/ *adjective* friendly; able to be approached.

■ accessible, affable, friendly, informal, kind, open, relaxed, sympathetic, unstuffy, well disposed.

approbation /æprəˈbeɪʃ(ə)n/ *noun* approval, consent.

appropriate *adjective* /əˈprəʊprɪət/ suitable, proper. ● *verb* (**-ting**) /əˈprəʊprɪeɪt/ **1** take possession of. **2** devote (money etc.) to special purpose. □ **appropriately** *adverb*. **appropriateness** *noun*. **appropriation** *noun*.

■ *adjective* applicable, apposite, apropos, apt, becoming, befitting, compatible, correct, decorous, deserved, due, felicitous, fit, fitting, germane, happy, just, *archaic* meet, opportune, pertinent, proper, relevant, right, seasonable, seemly, suitable, tactful, tasteful, timely, well judged, well suited, well timed. ● *verb* **1** annex, arrogate, commandeer, confiscate, expropriate, gain control of, hijack, requisition, seize, steal, take, take over, usurp.

approval /əˈpruːv(ə)l/ *noun* **1** approving. **2** consent. □ **on approval** returnable if not satisfactory.

■ **1** acclaim, acclamation, admiration, applause, appreciation, approbation, commendation, esteem, favour, liking, plaudits, praise, regard, respect, support. **2** acceptance, acquiescence, agreement, assent, authorization, blessing, confirmation, consent, endorsement, go-ahead, green light, licence, mandate, *colloquial* OK, permission, ratification, sanction, seal, support, thumbs up, validation.

approve /əˈpruːv/ *verb* (**-ving**) **1** sanction. **2** (often + *of*) regard with favour.

■ **1** accede to, accept, affirm, agree to, allow, assent to, authorize, back, confirm, consent to, countenance, endorse, give one's blessing to, go along with, pass, permit, ratify, rubber-stamp, sanction, sign, subscribe to, support, tolerate, uphold, validate. **2** (*approve of*) see ADMIRE 1.

approx. *abbreviation* approximate(ly).

approximate *adjective* /əˈprɒksɪmət/ fairly correct; near to the actual. ● *verb* /əˈprɒksɪmeɪt/ (**-ting**) (often + *to*) be or make near. □ **approximately** *adverb*. **approximation** *noun*.

■ *adjective* close, estimated, imprecise, inexact, loose, near, rough. ● *verb* (*approximate to*) approach, be close to, be similar to, border on, come near to, equal roughly, look like, resemble, simulate, verge on. □ **approximately** about, approaching, around, *circa*, close to, just about, loosely, more or less, nearly, *colloquial* pushing, roughly.

appurtenance /əˈpɜːtɪnəns/ *noun* (usually in *plural*) a belonging; an appendage or accessory.

APR *abbreviation* annual(ized) percentage rate.

Apr. *abbreviation* April.

après-ski /æpreɪˈskiː/ *noun* activities after a day's skiing. ● *adjective* suitable for these. [French]

apricot /ˈeɪprɪkɒt/ *noun* **1** small orange-yellow peachlike fruit. **2** its colour. ● *adjective* orange-yellow.

April /ˈeɪpr(ə)l/ *noun* fourth month of year. □ **April Fool** victim of hoax on 1 Apr.

a priori /eɪ praɪˈɔːraɪ/ *adjective* **1** from cause to effect. **2** not derived from experience. **3** assumed without investigation. ● *adverb* **1** deductively. **2** as far as one knows.

apron /ˈeɪprən/ *noun* **1** garment protecting front of clothes. **2** area on airfield for manoeuvring or loading. **3** part of stage in front of curtain.

apropos /æprəˈpəʊ/ *adjective* **1** appropriate. **2** (often + *of*) *colloquial* in respect of. ● *adverb* **1** appropriately. **2** incidentally.

apse /æps/ *noun* arched or domed recess esp. at end of church.

apsis /ˈæpsɪs/ *noun* (*plural* **apsides** /-diːz/) aphelion or perihelion of planet; apogee or perigee of moon.

apt *adjective* **1** suitable, appropriate. **2** (+ *to do*) having a tendency to. **3** quick to learn. □ **aptness** *noun*.

aptitude /ˈæptɪtjuːd/ *noun* talent; ability, esp. specified.

■ ability, bent, capability, facility, fitness, flair, gift, skill, suitability, talent.

aqualung /ˈækwəlʌŋ/ *noun* portable underwater breathing-apparatus.

aquamarine /ækwəməˈriːn/ *noun* **1** bluish-green beryl. **2** its colour. ● *adjective* bluish-green.

aquaplane /ˈækwəpleɪn/ *noun* board for riding on water, pulled by speedboat. ● *verb* (**-ning**) **1**

ride on this. **2** (of vehicle) glide uncontrollably on wet surface.

aquarelle /ˌækwəˈrel/ *noun* painting in transparent watercolours.

aquarium /əˈkweərɪəm/ *noun* (*plural* **-s**) tank for keeping fish etc.

Aquarius /əˈkweərɪəs/ *noun* eleventh sign of zodiac.

aquatic /əˈkwætɪk/ *adjective* **1** growing or living in water. **2** done in or on water.

aquatint /ˈækwətɪnt/ *noun* etched print like watercolour.

aqueduct /ˈækwɪdʌkt/ *noun* water channel, esp. raised structure across valley.

aqueous /ˈeɪkwɪəs/ *adjective* of or like water.

aquiline /ˈækwɪlaɪn/ *adjective* **1** of or like an eagle. **2** (of nose) curved.

Arab /ˈærəb/ *noun* **1** member of Semitic people inhabiting originally Saudi Arabia, now Middle East generally. **2** horse of breed originally native to Arabia. ● *adjective* of Arabia or Arabs.

arabesque /ˌærəˈbesk/ *noun* **1** decoration with intertwined leaves, scrollwork, etc. **2** ballet posture with one leg extended horizontally backwards.

Arabian /əˈreɪbɪən/ *adjective* of Arabia. ● *noun* Arab.

Arabic /ˈærəbɪk/ *noun* language of Arabs. ● *adjective* of Arabs or their language. □ **arabic numerals 1**, 2, 3, etc.

arable /ˈærəb(ə)l/ *adjective* fit for growing crops.

arachnid /əˈræknɪd/ *noun* creature of class comprising spiders, scorpions, etc.

arachnophobia /əˌræknəˈfəʊbɪə/ *noun* extreme fear of spiders.

Aramaic /ˌærəˈmeɪɪk/ *noun* language of Syria at time of Christ. ● *adjective* of or in Aramaic.

arbiter /ˈɑːbɪtə/ *noun* **1** arbitrator. **2** person influential in specific field.

arbitrary /ˈɑːbɪtrərɪ/ *adjective* **1** random; capricious. **2** despotic. □ **arbitrarily** *adverb*.

■ **1** capricious, casual, chance, erratic, fanciful, illogical, indiscriminate, irrational, random, subjective, unplanned, unpredictable, unreasonable, whimsical, wilful. **2** absolute, autocratic, despotic, dictatorial, high-handed, imperious, summary, tyrannical, tyrannous, uncompromising.

arbitrate /ˈɑːbɪtreɪt/ *verb* (**-ting**) settle dispute between others. □ **arbitration** *noun*. **arbitrator** *noun*.

■ adjudicate, decide, intercede, judge, make peace, mediate, negotiate, pass judgement, referee, settle, umpire. □ **arbitration** adjudication, intercession, judgement, mediation, negotiation, settlement. **arbitrator** adjudicator, arbiter, go-between, intermediary, judge, mediator, middleman, negotiator, ombudsman, peacemaker, referee, troubleshooter, umpire.

arboreal /ɑːˈbɔːrɪəl/ *adjective* of or living in trees.

arboretum /ˌɑːbəˈriːtəm/ *noun* (*plural* **-ta**) tree-garden.

arboriculture /ˈɑːbərɪkʌltʃə/ *noun* cultivation of trees and shrubs.

arbour /ˈɑːbə/ *noun* (*US* **arbor**) shady garden alcove enclosed by trees etc.

arc *noun* **1** part of circumference of circle or other curve. **2** luminous discharge between two electrodes. □ **arc lamp**, **arc light** one using electric arc. **arc welding** using electric arc to melt metals to be welded.

arcade /ɑːˈkeɪd/ *noun* **1** covered walk, esp. lined with shops. **2** series of arches supporting or along wall.

Arcadian /ɑːˈkeɪdɪən/ *adjective* ideally rustic.

arcane /ɑːˈkeɪn/ *adjective* mysterious, secret.

arch[1] *noun* curved structure supporting bridge, floor, etc. as opening or ornament. ● *verb* **1** form arch. **2** provide with or form into arch.

■ *noun* arc, archway, bridge, vault. ● *verb* arc, bend, bow, curve.

arch[2] *adjective* self-consciously or affectedly playful.

archaeology /ˌɑːkɪˈɒlədʒɪ/ *noun* (*US* **archeology**) study of ancient cultures, esp. by excavation of physical remains. □ **archaeological** /-əˈlɒdʒ-/ *adjective*. **archaeologist** *noun*.

archaic /ɑːˈkeɪɪk/ *adjective* **1** antiquated. **2** (of word) no longer in ordinary use. **3** of early period in culture.

archaism /ˈɑːkeɪɪz(ə)m/ *noun* **1** archaic word etc. **2** use of the archaic. □ **archaistic** /-ˈɪst-/ *adjective*.

archangel /ˈɑːkeɪndʒ(ə)l/ *noun* angel of highest rank.

archbishop /ɑːtʃˈbɪʃəp/ *noun* chief bishop.

archbishopric *noun* office or diocese of archbishop.

archdeacon /ɑːtʃˈdiːkən/ *noun* church dignitary next below bishop. □ **archdeaconry** *noun* (*plural* **-ies**).

archdiocese /ɑːtʃˈdaɪəsɪs/ *noun* archbishop's diocese. □ **archdiocesan** /-daɪˈɒsɪs(ə)n/ *adjective*.

arch-enemy /ɑːtʃˈenəmɪ/ *noun* (*plural* **-ies**) chief enemy.

archeology *US* = ARCHAEOLOGY.

archer /ˈɑːtʃə/ *noun* person who shoots with bow and arrows.

archery /ˈɑːtʃərɪ/ *noun* shooting with bow and arrows.

archetype /ˈɑːkɪtaɪp/ *noun* original model; typical specimen. □ **archetypal** /-ˈtaɪp-/ *adjective*.

■ classic, example, ideal, model, original, paradigm, pattern, precursor, prototype, standard.

archipelago /ˌɑːkɪˈpeləgəʊ/ *noun* (*plural* **-s**) **1** group of islands. **2** sea with many islands.

architect /ˈɑːkɪtekt/ *noun* **1** designer of buildings etc. **2** (+ *of*) person who brings about specified thing.

architectonic /ɑːkɪtek'tɒnɪk/ *adjective* of architecture.

architecture /'ɑːkɪtektʃə/ *noun* **1** design and construction of buildings. **2** style of building. □ **architectural** /-'tek-/ *adjective*.

architrave /'ɑːkɪtreɪv/ *noun* **1** moulded frame round doorway or window. **2** main beam laid across tops of classical columns.

archive /'ɑːkaɪv/ *noun* (usually in *plural*) **1** collection of documents or records. **2** place where these are kept.

  ■ (*archives*) **1** annals, chronicles, documents, history, papers, records, registers. **2** library, museum.

archivist /'ɑːkɪvɪst/ *noun* keeper of archives.

archway /'ɑːtʃweɪ/ *noun* arched entrance or passage.

Arctic /'ɑːktɪk/ *adjective* **1** of north polar region. **2** (**arctic**) very cold. ● *noun* Arctic region.

ardent /'ɑːd(ə)nt/ *adjective* eager, fervent, passionate; burning. □ **ardently** *adverb*.

  ■ burning, eager, enthusiastic, fervent, hot, impassioned, intense, keen, passionate, warm, zealous.

ardour /'ɑːdə/ *noun* zeal, enthusiasm.

arduous /'ɑːdjʊəs/ *adjective* **1** hard to accomplish. **2** strenuous.

  ■ back-breaking, demanding, difficult, exhausting, gruelling, hard, heavy, Herculean, laborious, onerous, punishing, rigorous, severe, strenuous, taxing, tiring, tough, uphill.

are see BE.

area /'eərɪə/ *noun* **1** extent or measure of surface. **2** region. **3** space set aside for a purpose. **4** scope, range; field of study. **5** space in front of house basement.

  ■ **1** acreage, breadth, expanse, extent, patch, sheet, size, space, stretch, surface, tract, width. **2** district, environs, locality, neighbourhood, part, precinct, province, quarter, region, sector, terrain, territory, vicinity, zone. **4** field, sphere, subject.

arena /ə'riːnə/ *noun* **1** centre of amphitheatre. **2** scene of conflict. **3** sphere of action.

aren't /ɑːnt/ **1** are not. **2** (in questions) am not.

arête /æ'reɪt/ *noun* sharp mountain ridge.

argon /'ɑːgɒn/ *noun* inert gaseous element.

argot /'ɑːgəʊ/ *noun* jargon of group or class.

argue /'ɑːgjuː/ *verb* (**-ues**, **-ued**, **-uing**) **1** exchange views, esp. heatedly. **2** (often + *that*) maintain by reasoning. **3** (+ *for*, *against*) reason. □ **arguable** *adjective*. **arguably** *adverb*.

  ■ **1** answer back, bandy words, bargain, bicker, debate, deliberate, demur, differ, disagree, discuss, dispute, dissent, expostulate, fall out, fight, haggle, have words, object, protest, quarrel, remonstrate, *colloquial* row, spar, squabble, take exception, wrangle. **2** assert, claim, contend, demonstrate, hold, maintain, plead, prove, reason, show, suggest. **3** make a case, plead, reason.

argument /'ɑːgjʊmənt/ *noun* **1** (esp. heated) exchange of views. **2** reason given; reasoning. **3** summary of book etc. □ **argumentation** /-men-/ *noun*.

  ■ **1** altercation, bickering, clash, conflict, contention, controversy, debate, difference (of opinion), disagreement, dispute, expostulation, fight, polemic, protest, quarrel, remonstration, *colloquial* row, *colloquial* set-to, squabble, tiff, wrangle. **2** case, contention, defence, deliberation, dialectic, discussion, exposition, hypothesis, reasoning, thesis. **3** abstract, gist, idea, outline, plot, summary, synopsis, theme.

argumentative /ɑːgjʊ'mentətɪv/ *adjective* fond of arguing.

argy-bargy /ɑːdʒɪ'bɑːdʒɪ/ *noun jocular* dispute, wrangle.

aria /'ɑːrɪə/ *noun* song for one voice in opera, oratorio, etc.

arid /'ærɪd/ *noun* **1** dry, parched. **2** uninteresting. □ **aridity** /ə'rɪd-/ *noun*.

  ■ **1** barren, desert, dry, fruitless, infertile, lifeless, parched, sterile, torrid, unproductive, waste, waterless. **2** boring, dreary, dull, pointless, tedious, uninspired, uninteresting, vapid.

Aries /'eəriːz/ *noun* first sign of zodiac.

aright /ə'raɪt/ *adverb* rightly.

arise /ə'raɪz/ *verb* (**-sing**; *past* **arose** /ə'rəʊz/; *past participle* **arisen** /ə'rɪz(ə)n/) **1** originate. **2** (usually + *from*, *out of*) result. **3** emerge. **4** rise.

  ■ **3** appear, come up, crop up, emerge. **4** get up, rise, stand up.

aristocracy /ærɪs'tɒkrəsɪ/ *noun* (*plural* **-ies**) ruling class, nobility.

aristocrat /'ærɪstəkræt/ *noun* member of aristocracy.

  ■ grandee, lady, lord, noble, nobleman, noblewoman, patrician, peer.

aristocratic /ærɪstə'krætɪk/ *adjective* **1** of the aristocracy. **2** grand, distinguished.

  ■ **1** blue-blooded, courtly, elite, gentle, high-born, lordly, noble, patrician, princely, royal, thoroughbred, titled, upper class.

arithmetic *noun* /ə'rɪθmətɪk/ **1** science of numbers. **2** computation; use of numbers. ● *adjective* /ærɪθ'metɪk/ (also **arithmetical**) of arithmetic.

ark *noun* ship in which Noah escaped the Flood. □ **Ark of the Covenant** wooden chest containing tables of Jewish law.

arm[1] *noun* **1** upper limb of human body. **2** sleeve. **3** raised side part of chair. **4** branch. **5** armlike thing. □ **armchair 1** chair with arms. **2** theoretical rather than active. **arm in arm** with arms linked. **armpit** hollow under arm at shoulder. **at arm's length** at a distance. **with open arms** cordially. □ **armful** *noun*.

  ■ **4** bough, branch, limb, offshoot. **5** appendage, branch, extension, offshoot, projection.

arm[2] *noun* **1** (usually in *plural*) weapon. **2**

branch of military forces. **3** (in *plural*) heraldic devices. ● *verb* **1** equip with arms; equip oneself with arms. **2** make (bomb) ready. □ **armed services** military forces. **up in arms** (usually + *against, about*) actively resisting.

■ *noun* **1** see WEAPON 1. □ **armed services** air force, army, forces, military, militia, navy, troops.

armada /ɑːˈmɑːdə/ *noun* fleet of warships.

armadillo /ɑːməˈdɪləʊ/ *noun* (*plural* **-s**) S. American burrowing mammal with plated body.

Armageddon /ɑːməˈɡed(ə)n/ *noun* huge battle at end of world.

armament /ˈɑːməmənt/ *noun* **1** military weapon etc. **2** equipping for war.

armature /ˈɑːmətʃə/ *noun* **1** rotating coil or coils of dynamo or electric motor. **2** iron bar placed across poles of magnet. **3** framework on which sculpture is moulded.

armistice /ˈɑːmɪstɪs/ *noun* truce.

■ agreement, ceasefire, peace, treaty, truce.

armlet /ˈɑːmlɪt/ *noun* band worn round arm.

armorial /ɑːˈmɔːrəl/ *adjective* of heraldic arms.

armour /ˈɑːmə/ *noun* **1** protective covering formerly worn in fighting. **2** metal plates etc. protecting ship, car, tank, etc. **3** armoured vehicles. □ **armoured** *adjective*.

armourer *noun* **1** maker of arms or armour. **2** official in charge of arms.

armoury /ˈɑːmərɪ/ *noun* (*plural* **-ies**) arsenal.

■ ammunition dump, arsenal, depot, magazine, ordnance depot.

army /ˈɑːmɪ/ *noun* (*plural* **-ies**) **1** organized armed land force. **2** vast number. **3** organized body.

arnica /ˈɑːnɪkə/ *noun* **1** plant with yellow flowers. **2** medicine made from it.

aroma /əˈrəʊmə/ *noun* **1** pleasing smell. **2** subtle quality. □ **aromatic** /ærəˈmætɪk/ *adjective*.

■ **1** bouquet, fragrance, odour, perfume, redolence, savour, scent, smell, whiff.

aromatherapy *noun* use of plant extracts and oils in massage. □ **aromatherapist** *noun*.

arose *past* of ARISE.

around /əˈraʊnd/ *adverb* **1** on every side. **2** all round. **3** *colloquial* in existence. **4** *colloquial* near at hand. ● *preposition* **1** on or along the circuit of. **2** on every side of. **3** here and there in or near. **4** about.

arouse /əˈraʊz/ *verb* (**-sing**) **1** induce (esp. emotion). **2** awake from sleep. **3** stir into activity. **4** stimulate sexually. □ **arousal** *noun*.

■ **1** awaken, call forth, encourage, foment, foster, induce, kindle, provoke, quicken, stimulate, stir up, whip up. **2** see AWAKE *verb* 1. **3** see ANIMATE *verb* 1.

arpeggio /ɑːˈpedʒɪəʊ/ *noun* (*plural* **-s**) notes of chord played in rapid succession.

arrack /ˈærək/ *noun* alcoholic spirit made esp. from rice.

arraign /əˈreɪn/ *verb* **1** indict, accuse. **2** find fault with. □ **arraignment** *noun*.

arrange /əˈreɪndʒ/ *verb* (**-ging**) **1** put in order. **2** plan or provide for. **3** (+ *to do, for*) take measures. **4** (+ *with* person) agree about procedure for. **5** *Music* adapt (piece).

■ **1** adjust, align, array, categorize, classify, collate, display, dispose, distribute, grade, group, lay out, line up, marshal, order, organize, pigeon-hole, position, put in order, range, rank, set out, sort (out), space, systematize, tabulate, tidy up. **2** bring about, contrive, coordinate, devise, manage, organize, plan, prepare, see to, settle, set up. **5** adapt, orchestrate, score.

arrangement *noun* **1** arranging, being arranged. **2** manner in which thing is ordered or placed. **3** deal, agreement. **4** *Music* adaptation (of piece).

■ **1** adjustment, alignment, design, disposition, distribution, grouping, layout, marshalling, organization, planning, positioning, setting out, spacing, tabulation. **2** see ORDER *noun* 1, 2. **3** agreement, bargain, compact, contract, deal, pact, scheme, settlement, terms, understanding. **4** adaptation, orchestration, version.

arrant /ˈærənt/ *adjective literary* downright, utter.

arras /ˈærəs/ *noun* tapestry wall-hanging.

array /əˈreɪ/ *noun* **1** imposing series or display. **2** ordered arrangement, esp. of troops. ● *verb* **1** deck, adorn. **2** set in order. **3** marshal (forces).

■ *noun* **1** assemblage, collection, demonstration, display, exhibition, line-up, panoply, parade, presentation, show, spectacle. **2** arrangement, formation, line-up, muster, parade. ● *verb* **1** adorn, attire, clothe, deck, decorate, dress, equip, fit out, garb, rig out, robe, wrap. **2** see ARRANGE 1.

arrears /əˈrɪəz/ *plural noun* **1** outstanding debt. **2** what remains undone. □ **in arrears** behindhand, esp. in payment.

arrest /əˈrest/ *verb* **1** lawfully seize. **2** stop. **3** catch attention of. ● *noun* **1** arresting, being arrested. **2** stoppage.

■ *verb* **1** apprehend, capture, catch, *colloquial* collar, detain, have up, hold, *slang* nab, *slang* nick, *slang* pinch, *colloquial* run in, seize, take into custody, take prisoner. **2** bar, block, check, delay, end, halt, hinder, impede, inhibit, interrupt, obstruct, prevent, restrain, retard, slow, stem, stop. ● *noun* **1** apprehension, capture, detention, seizure.

arrival /əˈraɪv(ə)l/ *noun* **1** arriving. **2** person or thing arriving.

■ **1** advent, appearance, approach, coming, entrance, landing, return, touchdown. **2** caller, newcomer, visitor.

arrive /əˈraɪv/ *verb* (**-ving**) **1** come to destination. **2** (+ *at*) reach (conclusion). **3** *colloquial* become successful. **4** be born.

■ **1** appear, come, disembark, drive up, enter, get in, land, make an entrance, roll in, *colloquial* roll up, *colloquial* show up, touch down, turn up. **2** (*arrive at*) see REACH *verb* 3,4. **3** see SUCCEED 1.

arrogant /'ærəgənt/ *adjective* aggressively assertive or presumptuous. □ **arrogance** *noun*. **arrogantly** *adverb*.

■ boastful, brash, brazen, bumptious, cavalier, *colloquial* cocky, conceited, condescending, disdainful, egotistic(al), haughty, *colloquial* high and mighty, high-handed, imperious, impudent, insolent, lofty, lordly, overbearing, patronizing, pompous, presumptuous, proud, scornful, self-admiring, self-important, smug, snobbish, *colloquial* snooty, *colloquial* stuck-up, supercilious, superior, vain.

arrogate /'ærəgeɪt/ *verb* (**-ting**) claim without right. □ **arrogation** *noun*.

arrow /'ærəʊ/ *noun* **1** pointed missile shot from bow. **2** representation of this, esp. to show direction. □ **arrowhead** pointed tip of arrow.

arrowroot /'ærəʊruːt/ *noun* nutritious starch.

arse /ɑːs/ *noun* (*US* **ass**) *coarse slang* the buttocks.

arsenal /'ɑːsən(ə)l/ *noun* place where weapons and ammunition are made or stored.

arsenic /'ɑːsənɪk/ *noun* **1** brittle semi-metallic element. **2** its highly poisonous trioxide.

arson /'ɑːsən/ *noun* crime of deliberately setting property on fire. □ **arsonist** *noun*.

■ □ arsonist *colloquial* firebug, fire-raiser, incendiary, pyromaniac.

art *noun* **1** human creative skill; its application. **2** branch of creative activity concerned with imitative and imaginative designs, sounds, or ideas, e.g. painting, music, writing. **3** creative activity resulting in visual representation. **4** thing in which skill can be exercised. **5** (in *plural*) certain branches of learning (esp. languages, literature, history, etc.) as distinct from sciences. **6** knack, skill. **7** cunning. □ **art nouveau** /ɑː nuː'vəʊ/ art style of late 19th c., with flowing lines.

■ **1** artistry, craft, craftsmanship, creativity, workmanship. **5** (*the arts*) humanities. **6** aptitude, cleverness, craft, dexterity, expertise, facility, knack, proficiency, skilfulness, skill, talent, technique, touch, trick.

artefact /'ɑːtɪfækt/ *noun* (also **artifact**) man-made object.

arterial /ɑː'tɪərɪəl/ *adjective* of or like artery. □ **arterial road** important main road.

arteriosclerosis /ɑːtɪərɪəʊsklɪə'rəʊsɪs/ *noun* hardening and thickening of artery walls.

artery /'ɑːtərɪ/ *noun* (*plural* **-ies**) **1** blood vessel carrying blood from heart. **2** main road or railway line.

artesian well /ɑː'tiːzɪən/ well in which water rises by natural pressure through vertically drilled hole.

artful /'ɑːtfʊl/ *adjective* sly, crafty. □ **artfully** *adverb*. **artfulness** *noun*.

■ astute, canny, clever, crafty, cunning, deceitful, designing, devious, *slang* fly, foxy, ingenious, scheming, shrewd, skilful, sly, smart, sophisticated, subtle, tricky, wily.

arthritis /ɑː'θraɪtɪs/ *noun* inflammation of joint. □ **arthritic** /-'θrɪt-/ *adjective & noun*.

arthropod /'ɑːθrəpɒd/ *noun* animal with segmented body and jointed limbs, e.g. insect, spider, crustacean.

artichoke /'ɑːtɪtʃəʊk/ *noun* **1** plant allied to thistle. **2** its partly edible flower. **3** Jerusalem artichoke.

article /'ɑːtɪk(ə)l/ *noun* **1** item or thing. **2** short piece of non-fiction in newspaper etc. **3** clause of agreement etc. **4** = DEFINITE ARTICLE, INDEFINITE ARTICLE. ● *verb* employ under contract as trainee.

■ *noun* **1** item, object, thing. **2** composition, essay, feature, newspaper column, piece, treatise.

articular /ɑː'tɪkjʊlə/ *adjective* of joints.

articulate *adjective* /ɑː'tɪkjʊlət/ **1** fluent and clear in speech. **2** (of speech) in which separate sounds and words are clear. **3** having joints. ● *verb* /ɑː'tɪkjʊleɪt/ (**-ting**) **1** speak distinctly. **2** express clearly. **3** (often as **articulated** *adjective*) connect with joints. □ **articulated lorry** one with sections connected by flexible joint. □ **articulately** *adverb*. **articulation** *noun*.

■ *adjective* **1** clear, coherent, comprehensible, distinct, eloquent, expressive, fluent, intelligible, lucid, understandable, vocal. ● *verb* **1, 2** see SPEAK 1,2. **3** (articulated) bending, flexible, hinged, jointed.

artifact = ARTEFACT.

artifice /'ɑːtɪfɪs/ *noun* **1** trick. **2** cunning. **3** skill.

artificer /ɑː'tɪfɪsə/ *noun* craftsman.

artificial /ɑːtɪ'fɪʃ(ə)l/ *adjective* **1** not natural. **2** imitating nature. **3** insincere. □ **artificial insemination** non-sexual injection of semen into uterus. **artificial intelligence** (use of) computers replacing human intelligence. **artificial respiration** manual or mechanical stimulation of breathing. □ **artificiality** /-ʃɪ'æl-/ *noun*. **artificially** *adverb*.

■ **1, 2** fabricated, man-made, manufactured, synthetic, unnatural. **3** affected, assumed, bogus, contrived, counterfeit, fake, false, feigned, forced, imitation, insincere, laboured, mock, *colloquial* phoney, pretended, pseudo, put on, sham, simulated, spurious, unreal.

artillery /ɑː'tɪlərɪ/ *noun* **1** large guns used in fighting on land. **2** branch of army using these. □ **artilleryman** *noun*.

artisan /ɑːtɪ'zæn/ *noun* skilled worker or craftsman.

artist /'ɑːtɪst/ *noun* **1** person who practises any art, esp. painting. **2** artiste. □ **artistic** *adjective*. **artistically** *adverb*. **artistry** *noun*.

■ **2** see MUSICIAN, PERFORMER (PERFORM).
□ **artistic** aesthetic, attractive, beautiful, creative, cultured, decorative, imaginative, ornamental, tasteful.

artiste /ɑːˈtiːst/ *noun* professional singer, dancer, etc.

artless *adjective* **1** guileless, ingenuous. **2** natural. **3** clumsy. □ **artlessly** *adverb*.

arty *adjective* (**-ier, -iest**) *colloquial* pretentiously or affectedly artistic.

arum /ˈeərəm/ *noun* plant with arrow-shaped leaves.

Aryan /ˈeərɪən/ *noun* speaker of any Indo-European language. ● *adjective* of Aryans.

as /æz, əz/ *adverb* to the same extent. ● *conjunction* **1** in the same way that. **2** while, when. **3** since, seeing that. **4** although. ● *preposition* in the capacity or form of. □ **as … as …** to the same extent that … is, does, etc.

asafoetida /æsəˈfetɪdə/ *noun* (*US* **asafetida**) resinous pungent gum.

asbestos /æsˈbestɒs/ *noun* **1** fibrous silicate mineral. **2** heat-resistant or insulating substance made from this.

ascend /əˈsend/ *verb* **1** slope upwards. **2** go or come up; climb.

■ **1** climb, go up, rise, slope upwards. **2** climb, come up, fly, go up, make an ascent, mount, move up, rise, scale, soar, take off.

ascendancy *noun* (often + *over*) dominant control.

ascendant *adjective* rising. □ **in the ascendant** gaining or having power or authority.

ascension /əˈsenʃ(ə)n/ *noun* ascent, esp. (**Ascension**) of Christ into heaven.

ascent /əˈsent/ *noun* **1** ascending, rising. **2** upward path or slope.

■ **1** ascension, climb, rise. **2** climb, gradient, hill, incline, ramp, rise, slope.

ascertain /æsəˈteɪn/ *verb* find out for certain. □ **ascertainment** *noun*.

■ confirm, determine, discover, establish, find out, identify, learn, make certain, make sure, settle, verify.

ascetic /əˈsetɪk/ *adjective* severely abstinent; self-denying. ● *noun* ascetic person. □ **asceticism** /-tɪs-/ *noun*.

■ *adjective* abstemious, austere, celibate, chaste, frugal, harsh, hermit-like, plain, puritanical, restrained, rigorous, self-controlled, self-denying, self-disciplined, severe, Spartan, strict, temperate.

ascorbic acid /əˈskɔːbɪk/ *noun* vitamin C.

ascribe /əˈskraɪb/ *verb* (**-bing**) (usually + *to*) **1** attribute. **2** regard as belonging. □ **ascription** /-ˈskrɪp-/ *noun*.

asepsis /eɪˈsepsɪs/ *noun* **1** absence of sepsis or harmful bacteria. **2** aseptic method in surgery. □ **aseptic** *adjective*.

asexual /eɪˈseksjʊəl/ *adjective* **1** without sex or sexuality. **2** (of reproduction) not involving fusion of gametes. □ **asexually** *adverb*.

ash¹ *noun* **1** (often in *plural*) powdery residue left after burning. **2** (in *plural*) human remains after cremation. **3** (**the Ashes**) trophy in cricket between England and Australia. □ **ashcan** *US* dustbin. **ashtray** receptacle for tobacco ash. **Ash Wednesday** first day of Lent.

■ **1** (*ashes*) burnt remains, cinders.

ash² *noun* **1** tree with silver-grey bark. **2** its wood.

ashamed /əˈʃeɪmd/ *adjective* **1** embarrassed by shame. **2** (+ *to do*) reluctant owing to shame.

■ **1** abashed, apologetic, blushing, chagrined, chastened, conscience-stricken, contrite, discomfited, distressed, embarrassed, guilty, humbled, humiliated, mortified, penitent, red-faced, remorseful, repentant, rueful, shamefaced, sheepish, sorry, upset.

ashen /ˈæʃ(ə)n/ *adjective* grey, pale.

ashore /əˈʃɔː/ *adverb* to or on shore.

ashram /ˈæʃræm/ *noun* religious retreat for Hindus.

Asian /ˈeɪʃ(ə)n/ *adjective* of Asia. ● *noun* **1** native of Asia. **2** person of Asian descent.

aside /əˈsaɪd/ *adverb* **1** to or on one side. **2** away, apart. ● *noun* words spoken aside, esp. by actor to audience.

asinine /ˈæsɪnaɪn/ *adjective* **1** asslike. **2** stupid.

ask /ɑːsk/ *verb* **1** call for answer to or about. **2** seek to obtain from another person. **3** invite. **4** (+ *for*) seek to obtain or meet. **5** (+ *for*) invite (trouble etc.). □ **ask after** inquire about (esp. person).

■ **1** enquire of, inquire of, interrogate, pose a question to, query, question, quiz. **2, 4** beg, beseech, entreat, implore, importune, petition, pray; (*ask for*) appeal for, apply for, badger for, crave, demand, plead for, press for, request, seek, solicit, sue for, *literary* supplicate (for). **3** invite, summon. **5** (*ask for*) see ATTRACT 2.

askance /əˈskæns/ *adverb* sideways. □ **look askance at** regard suspiciously.

askew /əˈskjuː/ *adverb* crookedly. ● *adjective* oblique; awry.

aslant /əˈslɑːnt/ *adverb* at a slant. ● *preposition* obliquely across.

asleep /əˈsliːp/ *adjective* **1** sleeping. **2** *colloquial* inattentive. **3** (of limb) numb. ● *adverb* into state of sleep.

■ *adjective* **1** comatose, *colloquial* dead to the world, dormant, dozing, hibernating, inactive, *slang* kipping, napping, resting, sedated, sleeping, *poetical* slumbering, *colloquial* snoozing, unconscious, under sedation. **2** see INATTENTIVE. **3** see NUMB *adjective*.

asp *noun* small venomous snake.

asparagus /əsˈpærəgəs/ *noun* **1** plant of lily family. **2** its edible shoots.

aspect /'æspekt/ *noun* 1 viewpoint, feature, etc. to be considered. 2 appearance, look. 3 side facing specified direction.

  ■ 1 angle, attribute, characteristic, circumstance, detail, element, facet, feature, quality, side, standpoint, viewpoint. 2 air, appearance, attitude, bearing, countenance, demeanour, expression, face, look, manner, *literary* mien, *literary* visage. 3 direction, orientation, outlook, position, prospect, situation, view.

aspen /'æspən/ *noun* poplar with fluttering leaves.

asperity /æs'perɪtɪ/ *noun* 1 sharpness of temper or tone. 2 roughness.

  ■ 1 abrasiveness, acerbity, acidity, acrimony, astringency, bitterness, churlishness, crossness, harshness, hostility, irascibility, irritability, peevishness, rancour, roughness, severity, sharpness, sourness, venom, virulence.

aspersion /əs'pɜːʃ(ə)n/ *noun* □ **cast aspersions on** defame.

asphalt /'æsfælt/ *noun* 1 bituminous pitch. 2 mixture of this with gravel etc. for surfacing roads etc. ● *verb* surface with asphalt.

asphodel /'æsfədel/ *noun* kind of lily.

asphyxia /æs'fɪksɪə/ *noun* 1 lack of oxygen in blood. 2 suffocation.

asphyxiate /əs'fɪksɪeɪt/ *verb* (**-ting**) suffocate. □ **asphyxiation** *noun*.

aspic /'æspɪk/ *noun* clear savoury jelly.

aspidistra /æspɪ'dɪstrə/ *noun* house plant with broad tapering leaves.

aspirant /'æspɪrənt/ *adjective* aspiring. ● *noun* person who aspires.

aspirate *noun* /'æspərət/ 1 sound of *h*. 2 consonant blended with this. ● *verb* /'æspəreɪt/ (**-ting**) 1 pronounce with *h*. 2 draw (fluid) by suction from cavity.

aspiration /æspə'reɪʃ(ə)n/ *noun* 1 ambition, desire. 2 aspirating.

  ■ 1 aim, ambition, craving, desire, dream, goal, hope, longing, objective, purpose, wish, yearning.

aspire /ə'spaɪə/ *verb* (**-ring**) (usually + *to, after, to do*) have ambition or strong desire. □ **aspiring** *adjective*.

  ■ (*aspire to*) aim for, crave, desire, dream of, hope for, long for, pursue, seek, set one's sights on, want, wish for, yearn for. □ **aspiring** see POTENTIAL *adjective*.

aspirin /'æsprɪn/ *noun* (*plural* same or **-s**) 1 white powder used to reduce pain and fever. 2 tablet of this.

ass *noun* 1 4-legged animal with long ears, related to horse. 2 donkey. 3 stupid person.

assail /ə'seɪl/ *verb* attack physically or verbally. □ **assailant** *noun*.

  ■ assault, attack, bombard, pelt, set on.

assassin /ə'sæsɪn/ *noun* killer, esp. of political or religious leader.

assassinate /ə'sæsɪneɪt/ *verb* (**-ting**) kill for political or religious motives. □ **assassination** *noun*.

assault /ə'sɔːlt/ *noun* 1 violent physical or verbal attack. 2 *Law* threat or display of violence against person. ● *verb* make assault on. □ **assault and battery** *Law* threatening act resulting in physical harm to person.

  ■ *noun* 1 attack, *Law* battery, GBH, mugging, offensive, onslaught, rape, strike. ● *verb* abuse, assail, attack, beat up, *slang* do over, fight, fly at, jump on, lash out at, *colloquial* lay into, mob, molest, mug, *colloquial* pitch into, pounce on, rape, rush at, *colloquial* set about, set on, strike at, violate, *colloquial* wade into.

assay /ə'seɪ/ *noun* test of metal or ore for ingredients and quality. ● *verb* make assay of.

assegai /'æsɪɡaɪ/ *noun* light iron-tipped S. African spear.

assemblage /ə'semblɪdʒ/ *noun* assembled group.

assemble /ə'semb(ə)l/ *verb* (**-ling**) 1 fit together parts of; fit (parts) together. 2 bring or come together.

  ■ 1 build, construct, erect, fabricate, fit together, make, manufacture, piece together, produce, put together. 2 accumulate, amass, bring together, collect, come together, congregate, convene, converge, crowd, flock, gather, get together, group, herd, join up, marshal, meet, mobilize, muster, pile up, rally (round), round up, swarm, throng (round).

assembly /ə'semblɪ/ *noun* (*plural* **-ies**) 1 assembling. 2 assembled group, esp. as parliament etc. 3 fitting together of parts. □ **assembly line** machinery arranged so that product can be progressively assembled.

  ■ 2 assemblage, conclave, conference, congregation, congress, convention, convocation, council, crowd, gathering, meeting, parliament, rally, synod.

assent /ə'sent/ *noun* consent, approval. ● *verb* (usually + *to*) agree, consent.

  ■ *noun* acceptance, accord, acquiescence, agreement, approbation, approval, compliance, consent, go-ahead, permission, sanction, willingness. ● *verb* accede, accept, acquiesce, agree, approve, be willing, comply, concede, concur, consent, express agreement, say yes, submit, yield.

assert /ə'sɜːt/ *verb* 1 declare. 2 enforce claim to. 3 (**assert oneself**) insist on one's rights.

  ■ 1 affirm, allege, argue, asseverate, attest, claim, contend, declare, emphasize, insist, maintain, proclaim, profess, protest, state, stress, swear, testify. 2 claim, demand, insist on. 3 (**assert oneself**) see INSIST.

assertion /ə'sɜːʃ(ə)n/ *noun* declaration; forthright statement.

assertive *adjective* asserting oneself; forthright, positive. □ **assertively** *adverb*. **assertiveness** *noun*.

■ aggressive, assured, authoritative, bold, *colloquial* bossy, certain, confident, decided, decisive, definite, dogmatic, domineering, emphatic, firm, forceful, forthright, insistent, opinionated, peremptory, positive, *colloquial* pushy, self-assured, strong, strong-willed, stubborn, uncompromising.

assess /ə'ses/ *verb* 1 estimate size or quality of. 2 estimate value of (property etc.) for taxation. □ **assessment** *noun.*
■ 1 appraise, assay (*metal*), calculate, compute, consider, determine, estimate, evaluate, fix, gauge, judge, price, reckon, review, *colloquial* size up, value, *colloquial* weigh up, work out. 2 appraise, evaluate, price, value.

assessor *noun* 1 person who assesses taxes etc. 2 judge's technical adviser in court.

asset /'æset/ *noun* 1 useful or valuable person or thing. 2 (usually in *plural*) property and possessions.
■ 1 advantage, aid, benefit, blessing, boon, godsend, good, help, profit, resource, strength, support. 2 (*assets*) capital, effects, estate, funds, goods, holdings, means, money, possessions, property, resources, savings, securities, valuables, wealth.

asseverate /ə'sevəreɪt/ *verb* declare solemnly. □ **asseveration** /-'reɪʃ(ə)n/ *noun.*

assiduous /ə'sɪdjʊəs/ *adjective* persevering, hard-working. □ **assiduity** /æsɪ'djuːɪtɪ/ *noun.* **assiduously** *adverb.*

assign /ə'saɪn/ *verb* 1 allot. 2 appoint. 3 fix (time, place, etc.). 4 (+ *to*) ascribe to. 5 (+ *to*) *Law* transfer formally to.
■ 1 allocate, allot, apportion, consign, dispense, distribute, give, hand over, share out. 2 appoint, delegate, designate, nominate, ordain, select. 3 appoint, authorize, designate, fix, nominate, ordain, prescribe, put down, select, specify, stipulate. 4 (*assign to*) accredit to, ascribe to, attribute to, credit to.

assignation /æsɪg'neɪʃ(ə)n/ *noun* 1 appointment, esp. made by lovers. 2 assigning, being assigned.

assignee /æsaɪ'niː/ *noun Law* person to whom property or right is assigned.

assignment /ə'saɪnmənt/ *noun* 1 task or mission. 2 assigning, being assigned.
■ 1 chore, commission, duty, errand, job, mission, obligation, post, project, responsibility, task, work.

assimilate /ə'sɪmɪleɪt/ *verb* (**-ting**) 1 absorb or be absorbed into system. 2 (usually + *to*) make like. □ **assimilable** *adjective.* **assimilation** *noun.* **assimilative** /-lətɪv/ *adjective.*

assist /ə'sɪst/ *verb* (often + *in*) help. □ **assistance** *noun.*
■ abet, advance, aid, back, benefit, boost, collaborate with, cooperate with, facilitate, further, give a hand, help, lend a hand, promote, rally round, reinforce, relieve, second, serve, *archaic* or *formal* succour, support, sustain, work

with. □ **assistance** aid, backing, benefit, collaboration, contribution, cooperation, encouragement, help, patronage, reinforcement, relief, sponsorship, subsidy, *archaic* or *formal* succour, support.

assistant *noun* 1 helper. 2 subordinate worker. 3 = SHOP ASSISTANT.
■ 1 abetter, *Law* abettor, accessory, accomplice, acolyte, aide, ally, associate, backer, collaborator, colleague, companion, comrade, confederate, helper, helpmate, *usually derogatory* henchman, mainstay, mate, partner, right-hand man, right-hand woman, standby, supporter. 2 auxiliary, deputy, mate, *derogatory* minion, second, second in command, subordinate.

assizes /ə'saɪzɪz/ *plural noun historical* court periodically administering civil and criminal law.

Assoc. *abbreviation* Association.

associate *verb* /ə'səʊʃɪeɪt/ (**-ting**) 1 connect mentally. 2 join, combine. 3 (usually + *with*) have frequent dealings. ● *noun* /ə'səʊʃɪət/ 1 partner, colleague. 2 friend, companion. ● *adjective* /ə'səʊʃɪət/ joined, allied.
■ *verb* 1 bracket together, connect, put together, relate. 2 combine, join up, link up. 3 (*associate with*) ally oneself with, be friends with, consort with, fraternize with, gang up with, go around with, *slang* hang out with, hobnob with, keep company with, make friends with, mingle with, mix with, side with, socialize with. ● *noun* 1 see ASSISTANT 1. 2 see FRIEND 1.

association /əsəʊsɪ'eɪʃ(ə)n/ *noun* 1 group organized for joint purpose. 2 associating, being associated. 3 fellowship. 4 connection of ideas. □ **association football** kind played with round ball which may be handled only by goalkeeper.
■ 1 alliance, body, brotherhood, cartel, clique, club, coalition, company, confederation, consortium, cooperative, corporation, federation, fellowship, group, league, organization, partnership, party, society, syndicate, trust, union. 2 affiliation, alliance, amalgamation, coalition, combination, confederation, federation, marriage, merger, union. 3 companionship, fellowship, friendship, partnership.

assonance /'æsənəns/ *noun* partial resemblance of sound between syllables, as in *run-up*, or *wary* and *barely*. □ **assonant** *adjective.*

assort /ə'sɔːt/ *verb* arrange in sorts, classify.

assorted /ə'sɔːtɪd/ *adjective* of various sorts; mixed.
■ different, differing, *archaic* divers, diverse, heterogeneous, manifold, miscellaneous, mixed, motley, multifarious, sundry, varied, various.

assortment /ə'sɔːtmənt/ *noun* diverse group or mixture.
■ agglomeration, array, choice, collection, diversity, farrago, jumble, medley, *mélange*, miscellany, mishmash, mixed bag, mixed bunch, mixture, pot-pourri, range, selection, variety.

assuage /əˈsweɪdʒ/ *verb* (**-ging**) **1** soothe. **2** appease. □ **assuagement** *noun*.

assume /əˈsjuːm/ *verb* (**-ming**) **1** take to be true. **2** undertake. **3** simulate. **4** put on (disguise etc.). **5** take on (aspect, attribute, etc.).

■ **1** believe, deduce, expect, guess, imagine, infer, presume, presuppose, suppose, surmise, suspect, think, understand. **2** accept, embrace, take on, undertake. **3** affect, fake, feign, pretend, simulate. **4** adopt, don, dress up in, put on, try on, wear. **5** acquire, take on.

assumption /əˈsʌmpʃ(ə)n/ *noun* **1** assuming. **2** thing assumed. **3** (**Assumption**) reception of Virgin Mary bodily into heaven.

■ **2** belief, conjecture, expectation, guess, hypothesis, premiss, presumption, presupposition, supposition, surmise, theory.

assurance *noun* **1** declaration; promise. **2** insurance, esp. of life. **3** certainty. **4** self-confidence.

■ **1** commitment, guarantee, oath, pledge, promise, undertaking, vow, word (of honour).

assure /əˈʃʊə/ *verb* (**-ring**) **1** (often + *of*) convince. **2** tell (person) confidently. **3** ensure, guarantee (result etc.). **4** insure (esp. life). **5** (as **assured** *adjective*) confident.

■ **1** convince, persuade, reassure. **2** give a promise, guarantee, pledge, promise, swear, vow. **3** ensure, guarantee, make sure, secure. **5** (**assured**) see CONFIDENT 1.

assuredly /əˈʃʊərɪdlɪ/ *adverb* certainly.

aster /ˈæstə/ *noun* plant with bright daisy-like flowers.

asterisk /ˈæstərɪsk/ *noun* symbol (*) used as reference to footnote, to mark omission, etc.

astern /əˈstɜːn/ *adverb* **1** in or to rear of ship or aircraft. **2** backwards.

asteroid /ˈæstərɔɪd/ *noun* any of numerous small planets between orbits of Mars and Jupiter.

asthma /ˈæsmə/ *noun* condition marked by difficulty in breathing. □ **asthmatic** /-ˈmæt-/ *adjective & noun*.

astigmatism /əˈstɪɡmətɪz(ə)m/ *noun* eye or lens defect resulting in distorted images. □ **astigmatic** /ˌæstɪɡˈmætɪk/ *adjective*.

astir /əˈstɜː/ *adverb & adjective* **1** in motion. **2** out of bed.

astonish /əˈstɒnɪʃ/ *verb* amaze, surprise. □ **astonishing** *adjective*. **astonishment** *noun*.

■ amaze, astound, baffle, bewilder, confound, daze, dazzle, dumbfound, electrify, *colloquial* flabbergast, leave speechless, nonplus, shock, stagger, startle, stun, stupefy, surprise, take aback, take by surprise, take person's breath away, *slang* wow. □ **astonishing** see AMAZING (AMAZE).

astound /əˈstaʊnd/ *verb* astonish greatly. □ **astounding** *adjective*.

■ see ASTONISH.

astrakhan /ˌæstrəˈkæn/ *noun* **1** dark curly fleece of Astrakhan lamb. **2** cloth imitating this.

astral /ˈæstr(ə)l/ *adjective* **1** of stars. **2** starry.

astray /əˈstreɪ/ *adverb & adjective* away from right way. □ **go astray** be lost. **lead astray** lead into error.

■ adrift, amiss, awry, lost, off course, wrong. □ **lead astray** see MISLEAD.

astride /əˈstraɪd/ *adverb* (often + *of*) with one leg on each side. ● *preposition* astride of.

astringent /əˈstrɪndʒənt/ *adjective* **1** contracting body tissue, esp. to check bleeding. **2** austere, severe. ● *noun* astringent substance. □ **astringency** *noun*.

astrolabe /ˈæstrəleɪb/ *noun* instrument for measuring altitude of stars etc.

astrology /əˈstrɒlədʒɪ/ *noun* study of supposed planetary influence on human affairs. □ **astrologer** *noun*. **astrological** /ˌæstrəˈlɒdʒ-/ *adjective*.

astronaut /ˈæstrənɔːt/ *noun* space traveller.

astronautics /ˌæstrəˈnɔːtɪks/ *plural noun* (treated as *singular*) science of space travel. □ **astronautical** *adjective*.

astronomical /ˌæstrəˈnɒmɪk(ə)l/ *adjective* (also **astronomic**) **1** of astronomy. **2** vast. □ **astronomically** *adverb*.

astronomy /əˈstrɒnəmɪ/ *noun* science of celestial bodies. □ **astronomer** *noun*.

astrophysics /ˌæstrəʊˈfɪzɪks/ *plural noun* (treated as *singular*) study of physics and chemistry of celestial bodies. □ **astrophysical** *adjective*. **astrophysicist** *noun*.

astute /əˈstjuːt/ *adjective* shrewd. □ **astutely** *adverb*. **astuteness** *noun*.

■ acute, adroit, artful, canny, clever, crafty, cunning, discerning, *slang* fly, foxy, guileful, ingenious, intelligent, knowing, observant, perceptive, perspicacious, sagacious, sharp, shrewd, sly, subtle, wily.

asunder /əˈsʌndə/ *adverb literary* apart.

asylum /əˈsaɪləm/ *noun* **1** sanctuary. **2** = POLITICAL ASYLUM. **3** *historical* mental institution.

■ **1, 2** cover, haven, refuge, protection, retreat, safety, sanctuary, shelter.

asymmetry /eɪˈsɪmətrɪ/ *noun* lack of symmetry. □ **asymmetric(al)** /-ˈmet-/ *adjective*.

■ □ **asymmetric(al)** awry, crooked, distorted, irregular, lopsided, unbalanced, uneven, *slang* wonky.

at /æt, ət/ *preposition: expressing position, point in time or on scale, engagement in activity, value or rate, or motion or aim towards*.

atavism /ˈætəvɪz(ə)m/ *noun* **1** resemblance to remote ancestors. **2** reversion to earlier type. □ **atavistic** /-ˈvɪs-/ *adjective*.

ate *past of* EAT.

atelier /əˈtelɪeɪ/ *noun* workshop; artist's studio.

atheism /ˈeɪθɪɪz(ə)m/ *noun* belief that no God exists. □ **atheist** *noun*. **atheistic** /-ˈɪst-/ *adjective*.

■ □ **atheist** see NON-BELIEVER.

atherosclerosis /ˌæθərəʊsklɪəˈrəʊsɪs/ *noun* formation of fatty deposits in the arteries.

athlete /ˈæθliːt/ *noun* person who engages in athletics, exercises, etc. □ **athlete's foot** fungal foot disease.

athletic /æθˈletɪk/ *adjective* **1** of athletes or athletics. **2** physically strong or agile. □ **athletically** *adverb*. **athleticism** /-ˈletɪsɪz(ə)m/ *noun*.

■ **2** acrobatic, active, energetic, fit, muscular, powerful, robust, sinewy, *colloquial* sporty, strapping, strong, sturdy, vigorous, well built, wiry.

athletics *plural noun* (usually treated as *singular*) physical exercises, esp. track and field events.

atlas /ˈætləs/ *noun* book of maps.

atmosphere /ˈætməsfɪə/ *noun* **1** gases enveloping earth, other planet, etc. **2** tone, mood, etc., of place, book, etc. **3** unit of pressure. □ **atmospheric** /-ˈfer-/ *adjective*.

■ **1** aerospace, air, ether, heavens, ionosphere, sky, stratosphere, troposphere. **2** ambience, aura, character, climate, environment, feeling, mood, spirit, tone, *colloquial* vibes, vibrations.

atmospherics /ˌætməsˈferɪks/ *plural noun* **1** electrical disturbance in atmosphere. **2** interference with telecommunications caused by this.

atoll /ˈætɒl/ *noun* ring-shaped coral reef enclosing lagoon.

atom /ˈætəm/ *noun* **1** smallest particle of chemical element that can take part in chemical reaction. **2** this as source of nuclear energy. **3** minute portion or thing. □ **atom bomb** bomb in which energy is released by nuclear fission.

■ **3** bit, crumb, grain, iota, jot, molecule, morsel, particle, scrap, speck, *colloquial* spot, trace.

atomic /əˈtɒmɪk/ *adjective* **1** of atoms. **2** of or using atomic energy or atom bombs. □ **atomic bomb** atom bomb. **atomic energy** nuclear energy. **atomic number** number of protons in nucleus of atom. **atomic weight** ratio of mass of one atom of element to 1/12 mass of atom of carbon-12.

atomize /ˈætəmaɪz/ *verb* (also **-ise**) (**-zing** or **-sing**) reduce to atoms or fine spray.

atomizer *noun* (also **-iser**) aerosol.

atonal /eɪˈtəʊn(ə)l/ *adjective Music* not written in any key. □ **atonality** /-ˈnæl-/ *noun*.

atone /əˈtəʊn/ *verb* (**-ning**) (usually + *for*) make amends. □ **atonement** *noun*.

■ do penance, make amends, make reparation, pay the penalty, pay the price, redeem oneself; (*atone for*) answer for, compensate for, expiate, make up for, recompense for, redeem, redress.

atrium /ˈeɪtrɪəm/ *noun* (*plural* **-s** or **atria**) either of upper cavities of heart.

atrocious /əˈtrəʊʃəs/ *adjective* **1** wicked, brutal. **2** *colloquial* very bad or unpleasant. □ **atrociously** *adverb*.

■ **1** barbaric, bloodthirsty, brutal, brutish, callous, cruel, diabolical, evil, execrable, fiendish, grim, gruesome, hateful, heartless, heinous, hideous, horrendous, horrible, horrific, horrifying, inhuman, merciless, monstrous, sadistic, savage, terrible, vicious, vile, villainous, wicked. **2** *colloquial* abominable, abysmal, *colloquial* appalling, *colloquial* awful, bad, diabolical, dreadful, *colloquial* frightful, horrendous, *colloquial* horrible, nauseating, revolting, *colloquial* shocking, sickening, *colloquial* terrible, woeful.

atrocity /əˈtrɒsɪtɪ/ *noun* (*plural* **-ies**) wicked or cruel act.

■ crime, cruelty, enormity, evil, offence, outrage.

atrophy /ˈætrəfɪ/ *noun* wasting away, esp. through disuse. ● *verb* (**-ies**, **-ied**) **1** suffer atrophy. **2** cause atrophy in.

atropine /ˈætrəpiːn/ *noun* poisonous alkaloid in deadly nightshade.

attach /əˈtætʃ/ *verb* **1** fasten, affix, join. **2** (in *passive*; + *to*) be very fond of. **3** (+ *to*) attribute or be attributable to.

■ **1** add, affix, anchor, append, bind, combine, connect, couple, fasten, fix, join, link, secure, stick, tie, unite, weld. **2** (*be attached to*) adore, be close to, be fond of, be in love with, dote on, love; (*attached*) see LOVING *adjective*. **3** (*attach to*) ascribe to, assign to, associate with, attribute to, impute to, place on, relate to.

attaché /əˈtæʃeɪ/ *noun* specialist member of ambassador's staff. □ **attaché case** small rectangular document case.

attachment *noun* **1** thing attached, esp. for particular purpose. **2** affection, devotion. **3** attaching, being attached.

attack /əˈtæk/ *verb* **1** try to hurt or deflect using force. **2** criticize adversely. **3** act harmfully on. **4** *Sport* try to score against. **5** vigorously apply oneself to. ● *noun* **1** act of attacking. **2** criticism. **3** sudden onset of illness. □ **attacker** *noun*.

■ *verb* **1** ambush, assail, assault, beat up, bombard, charge, counter-attack, descend on, *slang* do over, engage, fight, fly at, invade, jump on, lash out at, *colloquial* lay into, mob, mug, *colloquial* pitch into, pounce on, raid, round on, rush, *colloquial* set about, set on, storm, strike at, *colloquial* wade into. **2** abuse, censure, criticize, denounce, impugn, inveigh against, *colloquial* lay into, libel, malign, round on, slander, snipe at, traduce, vilify. **5** see BEGIN 1. ● *noun* **1** aggression, ambush, assault, *Law* battery, *colloquial* blitz, bombardment, broadside, cannonade, charge, counter-attack, foray, incursion, invasion, offensive, onset, onslaught, pre-emptive strike, raid, rush, sortie, storm, strike. **2** abuse, censure, criticism, diatribe, invective, outburst, tirade. **3** bout, convulsion, fit, outbreak, paroxysm, seizure, spasm, stroke, *colloquial* turn. □ **attacker** aggressor, assailant, belligerent, critic, detractor, enemy, intruder, invader, mugger, opponent, persecutor, raider, slanderer.

attain /əˈteɪn/ *verb* **1** gain, accomplish. **2** (often

+ *to*) reach, arrive at (goal etc.). □ **attainable** *adjective*.

■ **1** accomplish, achieve, acquire, complete, earn, fulfil, gain, get, grasp, make, obtain, procure, pull off, realize, secure, win. **2** arrive at, come to, get to, *colloquial* make, reach, touch.

attainment *noun* **1** attaining. **2** (often in *plural*) skill, achievement.

attar /'ætɑː/ *noun* perfume made from rose-petals.

attempt /ə'tempt/ *verb* **1** try. **2** try to accomplish or conquer. ● *noun* (often + *at, on*) attempting; endeavour.

■ *verb* **1** aim, aspire, do one's best, endeavour, exert oneself, make a bid, make an effort, seek, spare no effort, strive, try, undertake, venture. **2** *formal* essay, *colloquial* have a crack at, have a go at, make an assault on, tackle, undertake. ● *noun* bid, effort, endeavour, go, start, try.

attend /ə'tend/ *verb* **1** be present at. **2** go regularly to. **3** accompany. **4** wait on. **5** (often + *to*) apply mind or oneself. **6** (+ *to*) deal with; take care of. □ **attender** *noun*.

■ **1, 2** appear at, be present at, frequent, go to, present oneself at, put in an appearance at, visit. **3** accompany, chaperon, conduct, escort, guard, usher. **4** mind, wait on. **5** concentrate, follow, hear, heed, listen, mark, mind, notice, observe, pay attention, think, watch. **6** (*attend to*) assist, care for, help, look after, mind, minister to, nurse, see to, take care of, tend.

attendance *noun* **1** attending. **2** number of people present.

attendant *noun* person attending, esp. to provide service. ● *adjective* **1** accompanying. **2** (often + *on*) waiting.

■ *noun* assistant, escort, helper, servant, usher.

attention /ə'tenʃ(ə)n/ *noun* **1** act or faculty of applying one's mind. **2** notice. **3** consideration, care. **4** *Military* erect attitude of readiness. **5** (in *plural*) acts of politeness; courtesies.

■ **1** alertness, attentiveness, awareness, concentration, diligence, vigilance. **2** awareness, heed, notice, recognition. **3** care, concern, consideration, heed, regard, thought. **5** (*attentions*) civilities, courtesies, gallantry, good manners, kindnesses, politeness, thoughtfulness.

attentive /ə'tentɪv/ *adjective* **1** (often + *to*) paying attention. **2** polite. □ **attentively** *adverb*. **attentiveness** *noun*.

■ **1** alert, awake, concentrating, heedful, intent, observant, watchful. **2** see POLITE 1.

attenuate /ə'tenjʊeɪt/ *verb* (**-ting**) **1** make thin. **2** reduce in force or value. □ **attenuated** *adjective*. **attenuation** *noun*.

attest /ə'test/ *verb* **1** certify validity of. **2** (+ *to*) bear witness to. □ **attestation** /æt-/ *noun*.

attic /'ætɪk/ *noun* room or space immediately under roof of house.

attire /ə'taɪə/ *noun* clothes, esp. formal. ● *verb* clothe.

■ *noun* accoutrements, *formal* apparel, array, clothes, clothing, costume, dress, finery, garb, garments, *colloquial* gear, outfit, *archaic* raiment, wear, *archaic* weeds. ● *verb* see DRESS *verb* 1.

attired *adjective* dressed, esp. formally.

attitude /'ætɪtjuːd/ *noun* **1** opinion; way of thinking. **2** (often + *to*) behaviour reflecting this. **3** bodily posture.

■ **1, 2** approach, belief, demeanour, disposition, feeling, frame of mind, manner, *literary* mien, mood, opinion, orientation, outlook, position, posture, stance, standpoint, thought, view, viewpoint. **3** air, aspect, bearing, carriage, pose, posture, stance.

attitudinize /ætɪ'tjuːdɪnaɪz/ *verb* (also **-ise**) (**-zing** or **-sing**) adopt attitudes.

attorney /ə'tɜːnɪ/ *noun* (*plural* **-s**) **1** person, esp. lawyer, appointed to act for another in business or legal matters. **2** *US* qualified lawyer. □ **Attorney-General** chief legal officer of government.

attract /ə'trækt/ *verb* **1** (of magnet etc.) exert pull on. **2** draw to itself or oneself; invite. **3** arouse interest or admiration in.

■ **1** drag, draw, pull, tug at. **2** ask for, cause, court, encourage, generate, incite, induce, invite, provoke, seek out, stir up. **3** allure, appeal to, beguile, bewitch, bring in, captivate, charm, decoy, enchant, entice, fascinate, interest, inveigle, lure, magnetize, seduce, tempt, *colloquial* turn on.

attraction /ə'trækʃ(ə)n/ *noun* **1** attracting, being attracted. **2** attractive quality. **3** person or thing that attracts.

attractive /ə'træktɪv/ *adjective* **1** attracting esp. interest or admiration. **2** pleasing. □ **attractively** *adverb*. **attractiveness** *adjective*.

■ *colloquial* adorable, alluring, appealing, appetizing, beautiful, becoming, bewitching, captivating, catchy (*tune*), charming, *esp. US colloquial* cute, delightful, desirable, disarming, enchanting, endearing, engaging, enticing, enviable, fascinating, fetching, flattering, glamorous, good-looking, *colloquial* gorgeous, handsome, hypnotic, interesting, inviting, irresistible, lovable, *colloquial* lovely, magnetic, personable, pleasing, prepossessing, pretty, quaint, seductive, sought after, *colloquial* stunning, taking, tasteful, tempting, winning, winsome.

attribute *verb* /ə'trɪbjuːt/ (**-ting**) (usually + *to*) regard as belonging to or as written, said, or caused by, etc. ● *noun* /'ætrɪbjuːt/ **1** quality ascribed to person or thing; characteristic quality. **2** object frequently associated with person, office, or status. □ **attributable** /ə'trɪbjʊtəb(ə)l/ *adjective*. **attribution** /ætrɪ'bjuːʃ(ə)n/ *noun*.

■ *verb* accredit, ascribe, assign, charge, credit, impute, put down, refer, trace back. ● *noun* **1** characteristic, feature, property, quality, trait.

attributive /əˈtrɪbjʊtɪv/ *adjective* **1** expressing an attribute. **2** (of adjective or noun) preceding word it describes.

attrition /əˈtrɪʃ(ə)n/ *noun* **1** gradual wearing down. **2** friction, abrasion.

attune /əˈtjuːn/ *verb* (**-ning**) **1** (usually + *to*) adjust. **2** *Music* tune.

atypical /eɪˈtɪpɪk(ə)l/ *adjective* not typical. □ **atypically** *adverb*.

aubergine /ˈəʊbəʒiːn/ *noun* (plant with) oval usually purple fruit used as vegetable.

aubrietia /ɔːˈbriːʃə/ *noun* (also **aubretia**) dwarf perennial rock plant.

auburn /ˈɔːbən/ *adjective* (usually of hair) reddish-brown.

auction /ˈɔːkʃ(ə)n/ *noun* sale in which each article is sold to highest bidder. ● *verb* sell by auction.

auctioneer /ɔːkʃəˈnɪə/ *noun* person who conducts auctions.

audacious /ɔːˈdeɪʃəs/ *adjective* **1** daring, bold. **2** impudent. □ **audacity** /-ˈdæs-/ *noun*.
■ **1** adventurous, bold, cool, courageous, daring, fearless, foolhardy, intrepid, rash, reckless, venturesome. **2** see IMPUDENT. □ **audacity** boldness, cheek, courage, effrontery, forwardness, *colloquial* guts, impertinence, impudence, *colloquial* nerve, presumptuousness, rashness, *colloquial* sauce, temerity.

audible /ˈɔːdɪb(ə)l/ *adjective* that can be heard. □ **audibility** *noun*. **audibly** *adverb*.
■ clear, detectable, distinct, high, loud, noisy, recognizable.

audience /ˈɔːdɪəns/ *noun* **1** group of listeners or spectators. **2** group of people reached by any spoken or written message. **3** formal interview.
■ **1** assembly, congregation, crowd, gathering, house, listeners, onlookers, spectators, turnout, viewers. **3** interview, meeting.

audio /ˈɔːdɪəʊ/ *noun* (reproduction of) sound. □ **audiotape** magnetic tape for recording sound. **audio typist** person who types from tape recording. **audio-visual** using both sight and sound.

audit /ˈɔːdɪt/ *noun* official scrutiny of accounts. ● *verb* (**-t-**) conduct audit of. □ **auditor** *noun*.

audition /ɔːˈdɪʃ(ə)n/ *noun* test of performer's ability. ● *verb* assess or be assessed at audition.

auditorium /ɔːdɪˈtɔːrɪəm/ *noun* (*plural* **-s**) part of theatre etc. for audience.
■ assembly room, concert hall, hall, theatre.

auditory /ˈɔːdɪtərɪ/ *adjective* of hearing.

au fait /əʊ ˈfeɪ/ *adjective* (usually + *with*) conversant.

Aug. *abbreviation* August.

auger /ˈɔːgə/ *noun* tool with screw point for boring holes in wood.

aught /ɔːt/ *noun archaic* anything.

augment /ɔːgˈment/ *verb* make greater, increase. □ **augmentation** *noun*.

■ add to, amplify, boost, eke out, enlarge, expand, extend, fill out, grow, increase, intensify, magnify, multiply, raise, reinforce, strengthen, supplement, swell.

augur /ˈɔːgə/ *verb* portend; serve as omen.
■ bode, forebode, foreshadow, forewarn, herald, portend, predict, promise, prophesy, signal.

augury /ˈɔːgjʊrɪ/ *noun* (*plural* **-ies**) **1** omen. **2** interpretation of omens.
■ **1** forewarning, omen, portent, sign, warning. **2** see PROPHECY 2.

August /ˈɔːgəst/ *noun* eighth month of year.

august /ɔːˈgʌst/ *adjective* venerable, imposing.

auk /ɔːk/ *noun* black and white seabird with small wings.

aunt /ɑːnt/ *noun* **1** parent's sister. **2** uncle's wife. □ **Aunt Sally 1** game in which sticks or balls are thrown at dummy. **2** target of general abuse.

aunty /ˈɑːntɪ/ *noun* (also **auntie**) (*plural* **-ies**) *colloquial* aunt.

au pair /əʊ ˈpeə/ *noun* young foreign woman who helps with housework in return for room and board.

aura /ˈɔːrə/ *noun* **1** distinctive atmosphere. **2** subtle emanation.

aural /ˈɔːr(ə)l/ *adjective* of ear or hearing. □ **aurally** *adverb*.

aureate /ˈɔːrɪət/ *adjective* **1** golden. **2** brilliant. **3** (of language) elaborate.

aureole /ˈɔːrɪəʊl/ *noun* (also **aureola** /ɔːˈriːələ/) halo.

au revoir /əʊ rəˈvwɑː/ *interjection & noun* goodbye (until we meet again). [French]

auricle /ˈɔːrɪk(ə)l/ *noun* **1** external ear of animal. **2** atrium of heart.

auriferous /ɔːˈrɪfərəs/ *adjective* yielding gold.

aurora /ɔːˈrɔːrə/ *noun* (*plural* **-s** or **-rae** /-riː/) streamers of light above northern (**aurora borealis** /bɒrɪˈeɪlɪs/) or southern (**aurora australis** /ɔːˈstreɪlɪs/) polar region.

auscultation /ɔːskəlˈteɪʃ(ə)n/ *noun* listening to sound of heart etc. to help diagnosis.

auspice /ˈɔːspɪs/ *noun* **1** omen. **2** (in *plural*) patronage.

auspicious /ɔːˈspɪʃəs/ *adjective* promising, favourable.
■ favourable, hopeful, lucky, positive, promising, propitious.

Aussie /ˈɒzɪ/ *noun & adjective slang* Australian.

austere /ɒˈstɪə, ɔːˈstɪə/ *adjective* (**-r**, **-st**) **1** severely simple. **2** lacking comfort. **3** stern. **4** morally strict. □ **austerity** /-ˈter-/ *noun*.
■ **1** modest, plain, simple, unadorned, unfussy. **2** economical, frugal, hard, harsh, parsimonious, rigorous, Spartan, thrifty, unpampered. **3** cold, exacting, forbidding, formal, grave, harsh, serious, severe, stern, strict. **4** abstemious, ascetic, chaste, puritanical, restrained, self-denying, self-disciplined, sober, strait-laced, strict.

austral /ˈɔːstr(ə)l/ *adjective* southern.

Australasian /ɒstrəˈleɪʒ(ə)n/ *adjective* of Australia and SW Pacific islands.

Australian /ɒˈstreɪlɪən/ *adjective* of Australia. ● *noun* native or national of Australia.

autarchy /ˈɔːtɑːkɪ/ *noun* absolute rule.

autarky /ˈɔːtɑːkɪ/ *noun* self-sufficiency.

authentic /ɔːˈθentɪk/ *adjective* **1** of undisputed origin; genuine. **2** reliable. □ **authentically** *adverb*. **authenticity** /-ˈtɪs-/ *noun*.
■ accurate, actual, authoritative, bona fide, certain, dependable, factual, genuine, honest, legitimate, original, real, reliable, true, trustworthy, undisputed, valid.

authenticate /ɔːˈθentɪkeɪt/ *verb* (**-ting**) establish as true, genuine, or valid. □ **authentication** *noun*.
■ certify, confirm, corroborate, endorse, substantiate, validate, verify.

author /ˈɔːθə/ *noun* (*feminine* **authoress** /ˈɔːθrɪs/) **1** writer of book etc. **2** originator. □ **authorship** *noun*.
■ **1** composer, dramatist, novelist, playwright, poet, scriptwriter, writer. **2** architect, *literary* begetter, creator, designer, father, founder, initiator, inventor, maker, organizer, originator, parent, planner, prime mover, producer.

authoritarian /ɔːθɒrɪˈteərɪən/ *adjective* favouring strict obedience to authority. ● *noun* authoritarian person. □ **authoritarianism** *noun*.
■ *adjective* autocratic, *colloquial* bossy, despotic, dictatorial, dogmatic, domineering, strict, tyrannical.

authoritative /ɔːˈθɒrɪtətɪv/ *adjective* reliable, esp. having authority.
■ approved, authentic, certified, definitive, dependable, official, recognized, sanctioned, scholarly.

authority /ɔːˈθɒrɪtɪ/ *noun* (*plural* **-ies**) **1** power or right to enforce obedience. **2** delegated power; permission. **3** (esp. in *plural*) body having this. **4** influence based on recognized knowledge or expertise. **5** expert.
■ **1** charge, command, control, domination, force, influence, jurisdiction, might, power, prerogative, right, sovereignty, supremacy, sway, weight. **2** approval, authorization, consent, licence, mandate, permission, permit, sanction, warrant. **3** (*authorities*) administration, government, management, officialdom. **4** influence, power, sway, weight. **5** *colloquial* boffin, *colloquial* buff, connoisseur, expert, scholar, specialist.

authorize /ˈɔːθəraɪz/ *verb* (also **-ise**) (**-zing** or **-sing**) **1** (+ *to do*) give authority to (person). **2** sanction officially. □ **Authorized Version** English translation (1611) of Bible. □ **authorization** *noun*. **authorized** *adjective*.
■ **1** allow, commission, empower, entitle, license, mandate, permit. **2** accede to, agree to, allow, approve, back, commission, consent to, endorse, legalize, license, make official, *colloquial* OK,

pass, permit, ratify, rubber-stamp, sanction, validate. **authorized** see OFFICIAL *adjective* 3.

autism /ˈɔːtɪz(ə)m/ *noun* condition characterized by self-absorption and withdrawal. □ **autistic** /-ˈtɪs-/ *adjective*.

auto- *combining form* **1** self. **2** one's own. **3** of or by oneself or itself.

autobahn /ˈɔːtəʊbɑːn/ *noun* German, Austrian, or Swiss motorway. [German]

autobiography /ɔːtəʊbaɪˈɒɡrəfɪ/ *noun* (*plural* **-ies**) story of one's own life. □ **autobiographer** *noun*. **autobiographical** /-əˈɡræf-/ *adjective*.

autocracy /ɔːˈtɒkrəsɪ/ *noun* (*plural* **-ies**) absolute rule by one person.

autocrat /ˈɔːtəkræt/ *noun* absolute ruler. □ **autocratic** /-ˈkræt-/ *adjective*. **autocratically** /-ˈkræt-/ *adverb*.

autocross /ˈɔːtəʊkrɒs/ *noun* motor racing across country or on unmade roads.

autograph /ˈɔːtəɡrɑːf/ *noun* signature, esp. of celebrity. ● *verb* write on or sign in one's own handwriting.

automate /ˈɔːtəmeɪt/ *verb* (**-ting**) convert to or operate by automation.

automatic /ɔːtəˈmætɪk/ *adjective* **1** working by itself, without direct human involvement. **2** done spontaneously. **3** following inevitably. **4** (of firearm) that can be loaded and fired continuously. **5** (of vehicle or its transmission) using gears that change automatically. ● *noun* automatic firearm, vehicle, etc. □ **automatically** *adverb*.
■ *adjective* **1** automated, computerized, electronic, mechanical, programmable, programmed, robotic, self-regulating, unmanned. **2** conditioned, habitual, impulsive, instinctive, involuntary, natural, reflex, spontaneous, unconscious, unintentional, unthinking.

automation *noun* use of automatic equipment in place of manual labour.

automaton /ɔːˈtɒmət(ə)n/ *noun* (*plural* **-mata** or **-s**) machine controlled automatically.

automobile /ˈɔːtəməbiːl/ *noun US* motor car.

automotive /ɔːtəˈməʊtɪv/ *adjective* of motor vehicles.

autonomous /ɔːˈtɒnəməs/ *adjective* **1** self-governing. **2** free to act independently. □ **autonomy** *noun*.
■ free, independent, self-determining, self-governing, sovereign.

autopsy /ˈɔːtɒpsɪ/ *noun* (*plural* **-ies**) postmortem.

auto-suggestion /ɔːtəʊsəˈdʒestʃ(ə)n/ *noun* hypnotic or subconscious suggestion made to oneself.

autumn /ˈɔːtəm/ *noun* season between summer and winter. □ **autumnal** /ɔːˈtʌmn(ə)l/ *adjective*.

auxiliary /ɔːɡˈzɪljərɪ/ *adjective* **1** giving help. **2** additional, subsidiary. ● *noun* (*plural* **-ies**) **1** auxiliary person or thing. **2** (in *plural*) foreign or allied troops in service of nation at war. **3** auxiliary verb. □ **auxiliary verb** one used with another verb to form tenses etc. (see panel).

■ *adjective* **1** ancillary, assisting, helping, supporting, supportive. **2** additional, ancillary, backup, emergency, extra, reserve, secondary, spare, subordinate, subsidiary, substitute, supplementary.

avail /ə'veɪl/ *verb* **1** (often + *to*) be of use; help. **2** (**avail oneself of**) use, profit by. ● *noun* use, profit.

available *adjective* **1** at one's disposal. **2** (of person) free, able to be contacted. **3** sexually unattached. □ **availability** *noun*.

■ **1** accessible, at hand, convenient, disposable, free, handy, obtainable, procurable, ready, to hand, uncommitted, unused, usable. **2** accessible, contactable, free, on hand, uncommitted, unengaged.

avalanche /'ævəlɑːntʃ/ *noun* **1** mass of snow and ice rapidly sliding down mountain. **2** sudden abundance.

avant-garde /ævɑ̃'gɑːd/ *noun* innovators, esp. in the arts. ● *adjective* new, pioneering.

avarice /'ævərɪs/ *noun* greed for wealth. □ **avaricious** /-'rɪʃ-/ *adjective*.

■ □ **avaricious** acquisitive, covetous, grasping, greedy, mercenary, miserly.

avatar /'ævətɑː/ *noun Hindu Mythology* descent of god to earth in bodily form.

avenge /ə'vendʒ/ *verb* (**-ging**) **1** inflict retribution on behalf of. **2** exact retribution for.

■ exact punishment for, *colloquial* get one's own back for, repay, requite, take revenge for.

avenue /'ævənjuː/ *noun* **1** road or path, usually tree-lined. **2** way of approach.

aver /ə'vɜː/ *verb* (**-rr-**) *formal* assert, affirm.

average /'ævərɪdʒ/ *noun* **1** usual amount, extent, or rate. **2** number obtained by dividing sum of given numbers by how many there are. ● *adjective* **1** usual, ordinary. **2** mediocre. **3** constituting average. ● *verb* (**-ging**) **1** amount on

average to. **2** do on average. **3** estimate average of. □ **average out (at)** result in average (of). **on average** as an average rate etc.

■ *noun* **1** norm, standard. **2** mean. ● *adjective* **1** common, everyday, normal, ordinary, regular, typical, usual. **2** commonplace, mediocre, medium, middling, moderate, run-of-the-mill, unexceptional. **3** mean.

averse /ə'vɜːs/ *adjective* (usually + *to*) opposed, disinclined.

■ antipathetic, disinclined, hostile, opposed, reluctant, resistant, unwilling.

aversion /ə'vɜːʃ(ə)n/ *noun* **1** (usually + *to, for*) dislike, unwillingness. **2** object of this.

■ **1** antagonism, antipathy, dislike, distaste, hatred, hostility, reluctance, repugnance, unwillingness. **2** dislike, hate.

avert /ə'vɜːt/ *verb* **1** prevent. **2** (often + *from*) turn away.

■ **1** fend off, parry, prevent, stave off, ward off. **2** change the course of, deflect, turn aside, turn away.

aviary /'eɪvɪərɪ/ *noun* (*plural* **-ies**) large cage or building for keeping birds.

aviation /eɪvɪ'eɪʃ(ə)n/ *noun* the flying of aircraft.

aviator /'eɪvɪeɪtə/ *noun* person who flies aircraft.

avid /'ævɪd/ *adjective* eager, greedy. □ **avidity** /-'vɪd-/ *noun*. **avidly** *adverb*.

avocado /ævə'kɑːdəʊ/ *noun* (*plural* **-s**) (in full **avocado pear**) dark green pear-shaped fruit with creamy flesh.

avocation /ævə'keɪʃ(ə)n/ *noun* **1** secondary activity done in addition to a person's main work. **2** *colloquial* person's occupation or calling.

avocet /'ævəset/ *noun* wading bird with long upturned bill.

avoid /ə'vɔɪd/ *verb* **1** keep away or refrain from. **2** escape; evade. □ **avoidable** *adjective*. **avoidance** *noun*.

Auxiliary verb

An auxiliary verb is used in front of another verb to alter its meaning. Mainly, it expresses:

1 when something happens, by forming a tense of the main verb, e.g. *I shall go. He was going.*

2 permission, necessity, or possibility to do something, e.g. *They may go. You must go. I can't go. I might go. She would go if she could.*

3 the likelihood of something happening, e.g. *I might go. She would go if she could.*

The principal auxiliary verbs are:

be	*have*	*must*	*will*
can	*let*	*ought*	*would*
could	*may*	*shall*	
do	*might*	*should*	

■ abstain from, be absent from, bypass, circumvent, dodge, elude, escape, *formal* eschew, evade, find a way round, get out of the way of, get round, give a wide berth to, help (*can't help it*), ignore, keep away from, keep clear of, refrain from, run away from, shirk, shun, sidestep, skirt round, *slang* skive off, steer clear of.

avoirdupois /ˌævədə'pɔɪz/ *noun* system of weights based on pound of 16 ounces.

avow /ə'vaʊ/ *verb formal* declare, confess. □ **avowal** *noun.* **avowedly** /ə'vaʊɪdlɪ/ *adverb.*

avuncular /ə'vʌŋkjʊlə/ *adjective* of or like an uncle.

await /ə'weɪt/ *verb* **1** wait for. **2** be in store for.
■ **1** be ready for, expect, hope for, lie in wait for, look out for, wait for.

awake /ə'weɪk/ *verb* (**-king**; *past* **awoke**; *past participle* **awoken**) **1** rouse from sleep. **2** cease to sleep. **3** (often + *to*) make or become alert, aware, or active. ● *adjective* **1** not asleep. **2** alert.
■ *verb* **1** arouse, call, revive, rouse, wake, waken. **2** awaken, wake, waken. **3** alert, animate, arouse, excite, kindle, revive, rouse, stimulate, stir up.
● *adjective* **1** aware, conscious, insomniac, restless, sleepless, wakeful, wide awake. **2** see ALERT *adjective*.

awaken /ə'weɪkən/ *verb* **1** = AWAKE *verb*. **2** (often + *to*) make aware.

award /ə'wɔːd/ *verb* give or order to be given as payment, penalty, or prize. ● *noun* **1** thing awarded. **2** judicial decision.
■ *verb* accord, allot, assign, bestow on, confer on, decorate with, endow with, give, grant, present.
● *noun* **1** badge, cap, cup, decoration, endowment, grant, medal, prize, reward, scholarship, trophy.

aware /ə'weə/ *adjective* (often + *of, that*) conscious, having knowledge. □ **awareness** *noun.*
■ informed, knowledgeable, observant, responsive, sensitive; (*aware of*) acquainted with, alive to, appreciative of, awake to, *formal* cognizant of, conscious of, conversant with, familiar with, heedful of, mindful of, sensible of, versed in.

awash /ə'wɒʃ/ *adjective* **1** at surface of and just covered by water. **2** (+ *with*) abounding in.

away *adverb* **1** to or at distance. **2** into non-existence. **3** constantly, persistently. ● *adjective* (of match etc.) played on opponent's ground.

awe /ɔː/ *noun* reverential fear or wonder. ● *verb* (**awing**) inspire with awe. □ **awe-inspiring** awesome, magnificent.
■ *noun* admiration, amazement, apprehension, dread, fear, respect, reverence, terror, veneration, wonder. □ **awe-inspiring** awesome, *poetical* awful, breathtaking, dramatic, fearsome, grand, imposing, impressive, magnificent, marvellous, overwhelming, solemn, *colloquial* stunning, stupendous, sublime, wonderful, *poetical* wondrous.

aweigh /ə'weɪ/ *adjective* (of anchor) just lifted from sea bottom.

awesome *adjective* inspiring awe. □ **awesomeness** *noun.*

awful /'ɔːfʊl/ *adjective* **1** *colloquial* very bad. **2** *colloquial* very great. **3** *poetical* inspiring awe. □ **awfulness** *noun.*
■ **1** see BAD 1–2. **3** see AWE-INSPIRING (AWE).

awfully *adverb colloquial* **1** badly. **2** very.

awhile /ə'waɪl/ *adverb* for a short time.

awkward /'ɔːkwəd/ *adjective* **1** difficult to use or handle. **2** clumsy. **3** embarrassing. **4** embarrassed. **5** hard to deal with.
■ **1** bulky, cumbersome, inconvenient, unmanageable, unwieldy. **2** blundering, bungling, clumsy, gauche, gawky, *colloquial* ham-fisted, inelegant, inept, inexpert, maladroit, uncoordinated, ungainly, ungraceful, unskilful, wooden. **3, 4** embarrassing, touchy, tricky, uncomfortable, uneasy. **5** (*awkward problem*) difficult, perplexing, thorny, ticklish, tricky, troublesome, trying, vexatious, vexing; (*awkward customer*) *colloquial* bloody-minded, *slang* bolshie, defiant, disobedient, disobliging, exasperating, intractable, obstinate, perverse, prickly, rebellious, recalcitrant, refractory, stubborn, touchy, uncooperative, unruly, wayward.

awl /ɔːl/ *noun* small tool for pricking holes, esp. in leather.

awning /'ɔːnɪŋ/ *noun* fabric roof, shelter.
■ canopy, flysheet, screen, shade, shelter, tarpaulin.

awoke *past* of AWAKE.

awoken *past participle* of AWAKE.

AWOL /'eɪwɒl/ *abbreviation colloquial* absent without leave.

awry /ə'raɪ/ *adverb* **1** crookedly. **2** amiss. ● *adjective* **1** crooked. **2** unsound.

axe /æks/ *noun* (US **ax**) **1** chopping-tool with heavy blade. **2** (**the axe**) dismissal (of employees). **3** (**the axe**) abandonment of project etc. ● *verb* (**axing**) **1** cut (staff, services, etc.). **2** abandon (project).
■ *noun* **1** battleaxe, chopper, cleaver, hatchet, tomahawk. ● *verb* **1** cancel, cut, discharge, discontinue, dismiss, eliminate, get rid of, *slang* give the chop to, make redundant, rationalize, remove, *colloquial* sack, terminate, withdraw. **2** abandon, cancel, discontinue, terminate.

axial /'æksɪəl/ *adjective* of, forming, or placed round axis.

axiom /'æksɪəm/ *noun* **1** established principle. **2** self-evident truth. □ **axiomatic** /-'mæt-/ *adjective*.

axis /'æksɪs/ *noun* (*plural* **axes** /-siːz/) **1** imaginary line about which object rotates. **2** line dividing regular figure symmetrically. **3** reference line for measurement of coordinates etc.

axle /'æks(ə)l/ *noun* spindle on which wheel turns or is fixed.

| ■ rod, shaft, spindle.

ayatollah /aɪəˈtɒlə/ *noun* religious leader in Iran.

aye /aɪ/ *adverb archaic* or *dialect* yes. ● *noun* affirmative answer or vote.

azalea /əˈzeɪlɪə/ *noun* kind of rhododendron.

azimuth /ˈæzɪməθ/ *noun* angular distance between point below star etc. and north or south. □ **azimuthal** *adjective*.

azure /ˈæʒə/ *adjective & noun* sky blue.

Bb

B *abbreviation* black (pencil lead).

b. *abbreviation* born.

BA *abbreviation* Bachelor of Arts.

baa /bɑː/ *noun & verb* (**baas, baaed** or **baa'd**) bleat.

babble /'bæb(ə)l/ *verb* (**-ling**) **1** talk, chatter, or say incoherently or excessively. **2** (of stream) murmur. **3** repeat foolishly. ● *noun* **1** babbling. **2** murmur of water, voices, etc.

babe *noun* baby.

babel /'beɪb(ə)l/ *noun* confused noise, esp. of voices.

baboon /bə'buːn/ *noun* large kind of monkey.

baby /'beɪbɪ/ *noun* (*plural* **-ies**) **1** very young child. **2** childish person. **3** youngest member of family etc. **4** very young animal. **5** small specimen. □ **baby boom** *colloquial* temporary increase in birth rate. **baby grand** small grand piano. □ **babyhood** *noun*.

■ **1** babe, child, infant, newborn, toddler.

babyish /'beɪbɪʃ/ *adjective* **1** childish, simple. **2** immature. □ **babyishly** *adverb*. **babyishness** *noun*.

■ **1** childish, infantile, simple. **2** immature, infantile, *often derogatory* juvenile, puerile.

babysit *verb* (**-tt-**; *past & past participle* **-sat**) look after child while parents are out. □ **babysitter** *noun*.

baccarat /'bækərɑː/ *noun* gambling card game.

Bacchanalia /bækə'neɪlɪə/ *plural noun* **1** Roman festival of Bacchus, god of wine. **2** (**bacchanalia**) drunken revelry. □ **Bacchanalian** *adjective & noun*.

bachelor /'bætʃələ/ *noun* **1** unmarried man. **2** person with a university first degree. □ **bachelorhood** *noun*.

bacillus /bə'sɪləs/ *noun* (*plural* **bacilli** /-laɪ/) rod-shaped bacterium. □ **bacillary** *adjective*.

back *noun* **1** rear surface of human body from shoulders to hips; spine. **2** upper surface of animal's body. **3** reverse or more distant part. **4** part of garment covering back. **5** defensive player in football etc. ● *adverb* **1** to rear; away from front. **2** in(to) the past or an earlier or normal position or condition. **3** in return. **4** at a distance. ● *verb* **1** help with money or moral support. **2** (often + *up*) (cause to) go backwards. **3** bet on. **4** provide with or serve as back, support, or backing to. **5** *Music* accompany. ● *adjective* **1** situated to rear. **2** past, not current. **3** reversed. □ **backache** ache in back. **backbencher** MP without senior office. **backbiting** malicious talk. **back boiler** one behind domestic fire etc. **backbone 1** spine. **2** main support. **3** firmness of char-

acter. **backchat** *colloquial* verbal insolence. **backcloth** painted cloth at back of stage. **backdate 1** make retrospectively valid. **2** put earlier date to. **back door** secret or ingenious means. **back down** withdraw from confrontation. **backdrop** backcloth. **backfire 1** (of engine or vehicle) undergo premature explosion in cylinder or exhaust pipe. **2** (of plan etc.) have opposite of intended effect. **backhand** *Tennis etc.* (stroke) made with hand across body. **backhanded** indirect, ambiguous. **backhander** *slang* bribe. **backlash** violent, usually hostile, reaction. **backlog** arrears (of work etc.). **back number** old issue of magazine etc. **back out** (often + *of*) withdraw. **backpack** rucksack. **back-pedal** reverse previous action or opinion. **back room** place where (esp. secret) work goes on. **back seat** less prominent or important position. **backside** *colloquial* buttocks. **backslide** return to bad ways. **backstage** behind the scenes. **backstreet** ● *noun* side-street, alley. ● *adjective* illicit, illegal. **backstroke** stroke made by swimmer lying on back. **back to front** with back and front reversed. **backtrack 1** retrace one's steps. **2** reverse one's policy or opinion. **back up 1** give (esp. moral) support to. **2** *Computing* make backup of. **backup 1** support. **2** *Computing* (making of) spare copy of data. **backwash 1** receding waves. **2** repercussions. **backwater 1** peaceful, secluded, or dull place. **2** stagnant water fed from stream. **backwoods** remote uncleared forest land. **turn one's back on 1** abandon. **2** ignore. □ **backer** *noun*.

■ *noun* **1** rear, spine. **3** end, rear, reverse, stern, tail, tail-end, verso. ● *verb* **1** see SUPPORT *verb* 4. **2** back away, back off, beat a retreat, go backwards, move back, recede, recoil, retire, retreat, reverse. ● *adjective* **1** dorsal, end, hind, hinder, hindmost, last, posterior, rear, rearmost. □ **back down** see RETREAT *verb* 1. **back out** see WITHDRAW 5. **backside** see BUTTOCK. □ **backer** advocate, benefactor, patron, promoter, sponsor, supporter.

back-breaking *adjective* (esp. of manual work) extremely hard.

backgammon /'bækgæmən/ *noun* board game with pieces moved according to throw of dice.

background /'bækgraʊnd/ *noun* **1** back part of scene etc. **2** inconspicuous position. **3** person's education, social circumstances, etc. **4** explanatory information; circumstances surrounding thing.

■ **1** setting, surroundings. **3** breeding, circumstances, education, experience, grounding, history, tradition, training, upbringing. **4** circumstances, context, setting.

backing *noun* **1** help or support. **2** material used for thing's back or support. **3** musical accompaniment.

■ **1** aid, approval, assistance, encouragement, endorsement, funding, grant, help, investment, loan, patronage, sponsorship, subsidy, support. **3** accompaniment, orchestration, scoring.

backward *adjective* **1** directed backwards. **2** reverting to inferior state. **3** slow in learning. **4** shy.

■ **1** rearward, retreating, reverse. **2** regressive, retrograde, retrogressive. **3** disadvantaged, handicapped, immature, retarded, slow, subnormal, underdeveloped, undeveloped. **4** afraid, bashful, coy, diffident, hesitant, inhibited, modest, reluctant, reserved, reticent, self-effacing, shy, timid, unassertive, unforthcoming.

backwards *adverb* **1** away from one's front. **2** back foremost. **3** in reverse of usual way. **4** into worse state. **5** into past. **6** back towards starting point. □ **bend over backwards** *colloquial* make every effort.

bacon /'beɪkən/ *noun* cured meat from back and sides of pig.

bacteriology /bæktɪərɪ'ɒlədʒɪ/ *noun* study of bacteria.

bacterium /bæk'tɪərɪəm/ *noun* (*plural* **-ria**) single-celled micro-organism. □ **bacterial** *adjective*.

USAGE It is a mistake to use the plural form *bacteria* when only one bacterium is meant.

bad *adjective* (**worse**, **worst**) **1** wicked, naughty; morally offensive. **2** unpleasant; unfortunate. **3** serious, severe. **4** harmful. **5** decayed; foul. **6** inadequate, defective. **7** incorrect; not valid. **8** ill; injured. **9** regretful; guilty. □ **bad debt** debt that is not recoverable. **bad-tempered** irritable. □ **badness** *noun*.

■ **1** abhorrent, abominable, atrocious, *colloquial* awful, base, beastly, blameworthy, corrupt, criminal, cruel, dangerous, delinquent, deplorable, depraved, detestable, evil, guilty, immoral, infamous, malevolent, malicious, malignant, mean, mischievous, nasty, naughty, offensive, regrettable, reprehensible, rotten, shameful, sinful, unworthy, vicious, vile, villainous, wicked, wrong. **2** *colloquial* appalling, atrocious, *colloquial* awful, deplorable, disagreeable, discouraging, *colloquial* dreadful, *colloquial* frightful, *colloquial* ghastly, harsh, *colloquial* horrible, inappropriate, inauspicious, irksome, *colloquial* lousy, regrettable, *slang* rotten, uncongenial, unfavourable, unfortunate, unhelpful, unpleasant, unpropitious. **3** critical, crucial, dire, grave, grievous, serious, severe. **4** adverse, dangerous, deleterious, destructive, detrimental, harmful, hostile, hurtful, injurious, prejudicial, unhealthy, unwholesome. **5** decayed, decomposing, foul, loathsome, mildewed, mouldy, nauseating, noxious, objectionable, obnoxious, odious, offensive, polluted, putrid, rancid, repellent, repulsive, revolting, rotten, sickening, smelly, sour, spoiled, tainted, vile. **6** abysmal, *colloquial* chronic, defective, deficient, diabolical, disgraceful, dreadful, egregious, execrable, faulty, feeble, *slang* grotty, hopeless, imperfect, inadequate, incompetent, ineffective, inefficient,

inferior, *colloquial* lousy, pitiful, poor, *colloquial* ropy, shoddy, sorry, substandard, unsatisfactory, unsound, *colloquial* useless, weak, worthless. **7** incorrect, invalid, unusable, void, worthless. **8** see ILL *adjective* **1**. **9** see REGRETFUL (REGRET).

□ **bad-tempered** acrimonious, angry, bilious, cantankerous, churlish, crabbed, cross, crotchety, disgruntled, disobliging, dyspeptic, fretful, gruff, grumbling, grumpy, hostile, hot-tempered, ill-humoured, ill-tempered, irascible, irritable, malevolent, malign, moody, morose, peevish, petulant, quarrelsome, querulous, rude, scowling, short-tempered, shrewish, *colloquial* snappy, *colloquial* stroppy, sulky, sullen, testy, truculent, unfriendly, unsympathetic.

baddy /'bædɪ/ *noun* (also **baddie**) (*plural* **-ies**) *colloquial* villain or criminal, esp. in story, film, etc.

bade *archaic past* of BID.

badge *noun* small flat emblem worn as sign of office, membership, etc. or bearing slogan etc.

■ crest, device, emblem, insignia, logo, mark, medal, sign, symbol, token.

badger /'bædʒə/ *noun* nocturnal burrowing mammal with black and white striped head. ● *verb* pester.

badinage /'bædɪnɑːʒ/ *noun* banter. [French]

badly *adverb* (**worse**, **worst**) **1** in bad manner. **2** severely. **3** very much. □ **badly off** poor.

badminton /'bædmɪnt(ə)n/ *noun* game played with rackets and shuttlecock.

baffle /'bæf(ə)l/ *verb* **1** perplex. **2** frustrate. ● *noun* device that hinders flow of fluid or sound. □ **bafflement** *noun*. **baffling** *adjective*.

■ *verb* **1** *colloquial* bamboozle, bemuse, bewilder, confound, confuse, floor, *colloquial* flummox, mystify, perplex, puzzle, stump. **2** defeat, foil, frustrate, thwart. □ **baffling** see INEXPLICABLE.

bag *noun* **1** soft open-topped receptacle. **2** woman's handbag. **3** piece of luggage. **4** (in *plural*; usually + *of*) *colloquial* large amount. **5** animal's sac. **6** amount of game shot by one person. ● *verb* **1** *colloquial* secure, take possession of. **2** bulge, hang loosely. **3** put in bag. **4** shoot (game).

■ *noun* **1** carrier, carrier bag, sack, shopping bag. **2** handbag, *US* purse, shoulder bag. **3** (*bags*) see LUGGAGE. ● *verb* **4** capture, catch, ensnare, snare.

bagatelle /bægə'tel/ *noun* **1** game in which small balls are struck into holes on inclined board. **2** mere trifle.

bagel /'beɪg(ə)l/ *noun* ring-shaped bread roll.

baggage /'bægɪdʒ/ *noun* **1** luggage. **2** portable equipment of army.

■ **1** accoutrements, bags, belongings, gear, impedimenta, luggage, paraphernalia, things.

baggy *adjective* (**-ier**, **-iest**) hanging loosely.

bagpipes /'bægpaɪps/ *plural noun* musical instrument with windbag for pumping air through reeded pipes.

baguette /bæ'get/ *noun* long thin French loaf.

bail[1] *noun* **1** security given for released prisoner's return for trial. **2** person(s) pledging this. ● *verb* (usually + *out*) give bail for and secure release of (prisoner).

bail[2] *noun Cricket* either of two crosspieces resting on stumps.

bail[3] *verb* (also **bale**) (usually + *out*) scoop (water) out of (boat etc.). □ **bail out** = BALE OUT.

bailey /'beɪlɪ/ *noun* (*plural* **-s**) **1** outer wall of castle. **2** court enclosed by this.

bailiff /'beɪlɪf/ *noun* **1** sheriff's officer who executes writs, performs distraints, etc. **2** landlord's agent or steward.

bailiwick /'beɪlɪwɪk/ *noun* district of bailiff.

bairn /beən/ *noun Scottish & Northern English* child.

bait *noun* **1** food to entice prey. **2** allurement. ● *verb* **1** torment (chained animal). **2** harass (person). **3** put bait on or in (fish-hook, trap, etc.).
  ■ *noun* allurement, attraction, bribe, carrot, decoy, enticement, inducement, lure, temptation. ● *verb* **1, 2** annoy, goad, harass, hound, jeer at, *colloquial* needle, persecute, pester, provoke, tantalize, tease, torment.

baize /beɪz/ *noun* usually green felted woollen fabric used for coverings etc.

bake *verb* (**-king**) **1** cook or become cooked by dry heat esp. in oven. **2** *colloquial* be very hot. **3** harden by heat. □ **baking powder** mixture used as raising agent.

Bakelite /'beɪkəlaɪt/ *noun proprietary term* kind of plastic.

baker /'beɪkə/ *noun* professional bread-maker. □ **baker's dozen** thirteen.

bakery /'beɪkərɪ/ *noun* (*plural* **-ies**) place where bread is made or sold.

baksheesh /'bækʃiːʃ/ *noun* gratuity, tip.

Balaclava /bælə'klɑːvə/ *noun* (in full **Balaclava helmet**) woollen covering for head and neck.

balalaika /bælə'laɪkə/ *noun* Russian triangular-bodied guitar-like musical instrument.

balance /'bæləns/ *noun* **1** even distribution of weight or amount. **2** stability of body or mind. **3** weighing apparatus. **4** counteracting weight or force. **5** regulating device in clock etc. **6** decisive weight or amount. **7** difference between credits and debits; remainder. ● *verb* (**-cing**) **1** bring or come into or keep in equilibrium. **2** offset, compare. **3** equal, neutralize. **4** (usually as **balanced** *adjective*) make well proportioned and harmonious. **5** equalize debits and credits of account; have debits and credits equal. □ **balance of payments** difference between payments into and out of a country. **balance of power 1** position in which no country etc. predominates. **2** power held by small group when larger groups are of (almost) equal strength. **balance of trade** difference between exports and imports. **balance sheet** statement giving balance of account. **on balance** all things considered.
  ■ *noun* **1** correspondence, equality, equivalence, evenness, parity, symmetry. **2** equanimity, equilibrium, equipoise, poise, stability, steadiness. **3** scales, weighing machine. **7** difference, excess, remainder, residue, rest, surplus. ● *verb* **1** poise, stabilize, steady, support; (*balanced*) see STABLE *adjective* 1. **2** compare, offset, *colloquial* weigh up. **3** cancel out, compensate for, counteract, counterbalance, counterpoise, equalize, even up, level, match, neutralize, offset, parallel, stabilize, steady; (*balanced*) see EVEN *adjective* 3, IMPARTIAL.

balcony /'bælkənɪ/ *noun* (*plural* **-ies**) **1** outside balustraded or railed platform with access from upper floor. **2** upper tier of seats in theatre etc.

bald /bɔːld/ *adjective* **1** lacking some or all hair on scalp. **2** without fur, feathers, etc. **3** with surface worn away. **4** direct. □ **baldly** *adverb*. **baldness** *noun*.
  ■ **1, 2** bald-headed, bare, hairless, smooth, thin on top. **4** direct, forthright, plain, simple, stark, straightforward, unadorned, uncompromising.

balderdash /'bɔːldədæʃ/ *noun* nonsense.

balding /'bɔːldɪŋ/ *adjective* becoming bald.

bale[1] *noun* bundle of merchandise or hay. ● *verb* (**-ling**) make up into bales. □ **bale out** (also **bail out**) make emergency parachute jump from aircraft.
  ■ *noun* bunch, bundle, pack, package, truss. □ **bale out** eject, jump out, parachute down.

bale[2] = BALE[3].

baleful /'beɪlfʊl/ *adjective* **1** menacing. **2** destructive, malignant.

balk = BAULK.

ball[1] /bɔːl/ *noun* **1** spherical object or mass. **2** usually spherical object used in game. **3** rounded part of foot or hand at base of big toe or thumb. **4** cannon ball. **5** delivery or pass of ball in game. □ **ball-bearing 1** bearing using ring of small balls between its two parts. **2** one such ball. **ballcock** valve operated by floating ball that controls level of water in cistern. **ball game** *US* **1** baseball game. **2** *colloquial* affair or matter. **ballpoint (pen)** pen with tiny ball as writing point.
  ■ **1** drop, globe, globule, orb, sphere, spheroid.

ball[2] /bɔːl/ *noun* **1** formal social gathering for dancing. **2** *slang* enjoyable time.
  ■ **1** dance, *colloquial* disco, party, social.

ballad /'bæləd/ *noun* **1** poem or song narrating popular story. **2** slow sentimental song. □ **balladry** *noun*.

balladeer /bælə'dɪə/ *noun* singer or composer of ballads.

ballast /'bæləst/ *noun* **1** heavy material stabilizing ship, controlling height of balloon, etc. **2** coarse stone etc. as bed of road or railway. ● *verb* provide with ballast.

ballerina /ˌbæləˈriːnə/ *noun* female ballet dancer.

ballet /ˈbæleɪ/ *noun* **1** dramatic or representational style of dancing to music. **2** piece or performance of ballet. □ **ballet dancer** dancer of ballet. □ **balletic** /bəˈletɪk/ *adjective*.

ballistic /bəˈlɪstɪk/ *adjective* of projectiles. □ **ballistic missile** one that is powered and guided but falls by gravity.

ballistics *plural noun* (usually treated as *singular*) science of projectiles and firearms.

balloon /bəˈluːn/ *noun* **1** small inflatable rubber toy or decoration. **2** large inflatable flying bag, esp. one with basket below for passengers. **3** outline containing words or thoughts in strip cartoon. ● *verb* (cause to) swell out like balloon. □ **balloonist** *noun*.

■ *noun* **2** airship, dirigible, hot-air balloon. ● *verb* see BILLOW *verb*.

ballot /ˈbælət/ *noun* **1** voting in writing and usually secret. **2** votes recorded in ballot. ● *verb* (**-t-**) **1** hold ballot. **2** vote by ballot. **3** take ballot of (voters). □ **ballot box** container for **ballot papers**, slips for marking votes.

■ *noun* **1** election, plebiscite, poll, referendum, vote.

ballroom /ˈbɔːlrʊm/ *noun* large room for dancing. □ **ballroom dancing** formal social dancing for couples.

bally /ˈbælɪ/ *adjective & adverb archaic slang:* mild form of BLOODY.

ballyhoo /bælɪˈhuː/ *noun* **1** loud noise, fuss. **2** noisy publicity.

balm /bɑːm/ *noun* **1** aromatic ointment. **2** fragrant oil or resin exuded from some trees. **3** thing that heals or soothes. **4** aromatic herb.

balmy /ˈbɑːmɪ/ *adjective* (**-ier, -iest**) **1** fragrant, mild, soothing. **2** *slang* = BARMY.

balsa /ˈbɔːlsə/ *noun* lightweight tropical American wood used for making models.

balsam /ˈbɔːlsəm/ *noun* **1** balm from trees. **2** ointment. **3** tree yielding balsam. **4** any of several flowering plants.

baluster /ˈbæləstə/ *noun* short pillar supporting rail.

balustrade /bæləˈstreɪd/ *noun* railing supported by balusters, esp. on balcony.

bamboo /bæmˈbuː/ *noun* **1** tropical giant woody grass. **2** its hollow stem.

bamboozle /bæmˈbuːz(ə)l/ *verb* (**-ling**) *colloquial* **1** cheat. **2** mystify.

ban *verb* (**-nn-**) prohibit, esp. formally. ● *noun* formal prohibition.

■ *verb* banish, bar, debar, disallow, exclude, forbid, interdict, make illegal, ostracize, outlaw, prevent, prohibit, proscribe, restrict, stop, suppress, veto. ● *noun* boycott, embargo, interdiction, moratorium, prohibition, proscription, taboo, veto.

banal /bəˈnɑːl/ *adjective* commonplace, trite. □ **banality** /-ˈnæl-/ *noun* (*plural* **-ies**).

■ boring, clichéd, cliché-ridden, commonplace, *colloquial* corny, dull, hackneyed, humdrum, obvious, *colloquial* old hat, ordinary, overused, pedestrian, platitudinous, predictable, stereotyped, trite, unimaginative, uninteresting, unoriginal, vapid.

banana /bəˈnɑːnə/ *noun* **1** long curved yellow tropical fruit. **2** treelike plant bearing it.

band *noun* **1** flat strip or loop of thin material. **2** stripe. **3** group of musicians. **4** organized group of criminals etc. **5** range of values, esp. frequencies or wavelengths. ● *verb* **1** (usually + *together*) unite. **2** put band on. **3** mark with stripes. □ **bandbox** hatbox. **bandmaster** conductor of band. **bandsman** player in band. **bandstand** outdoor platform for musicians.

■ *noun* **1** belt, fillet, hoop, loop, ribbon, ring, strip, swath. **2** border, line, ring, strip, stripe. **3** ensemble, group, orchestra. **4** association, body, clique, club, company, crew, flock, gang, group, *derogatory* herd, *usually derogatory* horde, party, society, troop.

bandage /ˈbændɪdʒ/ *noun* strip of material for binding wound etc. ● *verb* (**-ging**) bind with bandage.

■ *noun* dressing.

bandanna /bænˈdænə/ *noun* large patterned handkerchief.

bandeau /ˈbændəʊ/ *noun* (*plural* **-x** /-z/) narrow headband.

bandit /ˈbændɪt/ *noun* robber, esp. of travellers. □ **banditry** *noun*.

■ brigand, buccaneer, desperado, gangster, gunman, *historical* highwayman, hijacker, marauder, outlaw, pirate, robber, thief.

bandolier /bændəˈlɪə/ *noun* (also **bandoleer**) shoulder belt with loops or pockets for cartridges.

bandwagon *noun* □ **climb, jump on the bandwagon** join popular or successful cause.

bandy[1] /ˈbændɪ/ *adjective* (**-ier, -iest**) (of legs) curved wide apart at knees. □ **bandy-legged** *adjective*.

■ bandy-legged, bowed, bow-legged.

bandy[2] /ˈbændɪ/ *verb* (**-ies, -ied**) **1** (often + *about*) pass (story etc.) to and fro; discuss disparagingly. **2** (often + *about*) throw (ball etc.) to and fro. **3** (often + *with*) exchange (blows, insults, etc.).

■ **2** pass, throw, toss. **3** exchange, interchange, swap; (*bandy words*) see ARGUE 1.

bane *noun* cause of ruin or trouble. □ **baneful** *adjective*.

bang *noun* **1** loud short sound. **2** sharp blow. ● *verb* **1** strike or shut noisily. **2** (cause to) make bang. ● *adverb* **1** with bang. **2** *colloquial* exactly. □ **bang on** *colloquial* exactly right.

■ *noun* **1** blast, boom, clang, clank, clap, crash, explosion, pop, report, thud, thump. **2** blow, box, bump, cuff, hit, knock, punch, slam, smack, stroke, thump, *colloquial* wallop, *colloquial* whack. ● *verb* **1** see HIT *verb* 1.

banger *noun* **1** firework making bang. **2** *slang* sausage. **3** *slang* noisy old car.

bangle /'bæŋg(ə)l/ *noun* rigid bracelet or anklet.

banian = BANYAN.

banish /'bænɪʃ/ *verb* **1** condemn to exile. **2** dismiss from one's mind. □ **banishment** *noun*.

■ **1** deport, drive out, eject, evict, exclude, excommunicate, exile, expatriate, expel, ostracize, oust, outlaw, proscribe, rusticate, send away, ship away, transport. **2** cast out, dismiss, drive out, eliminate, expel, get rid of, remove.

banister /'bænɪstə/ *noun* (also **bannister**) (usually in *plural*) uprights and handrail beside staircase.

banjo /'bændʒəʊ/ *noun* (*plural* **-s** or **-es**) round-bodied guitar-like musical instrument. □ **banjoist** *noun*.

bank¹ *noun* **1** sloping ground on each side of river. **2** raised shelf of ground, esp. in sea; slope. **3** mass of cloud etc. ● *verb* **1** (often + *up*) heap or rise into banks. **2** pack (fire) tightly for slow burning. **3** (cause to) travel round curve with one side higher than the other.

■ *noun* **1** brink, edge, margin, shore, side. **2** camber, declivity, dyke, earthwork, embankment, gradient, incline, mound, ramp, rampart, ridge, rise, slope, tilt. ● *verb* **3** cant, heel, incline, lean, list, pitch, slant, slope, tilt, tip.

bank² *noun* **1** establishment, usually a public company, where money is deposited, withdrawn, and borrowed. **2** pool of money in gambling game. **3** storage place. ● *verb* **1** deposit (money) at bank. **2** (often + *at*, *with*) keep money (at bank). □ **bank card** cheque card. **bank holiday** public holiday when banks are closed. **banknote** piece of paper money. **bank on** *colloquial* rely on.

■ *verb* deposit, save.

bank³ *noun* row (of lights, switches, organ keys, etc.).

■ array, collection, display, file, group, line, panel, rank, row, series.

banker *noun* **1** owner or manager of bank. **2** keeper of bank in gambling game. □ **banker's card** cheque card.

bankrupt /'bæŋkrʌpt/ *adjective* **1** insolvent. **2** (often + *of*) drained (of emotion etc.). ● *noun* insolvent person. ● *verb* make bankrupt. □ **bankruptcy** *noun* (*plural* **-ies**).

■ *adjective* **1** *colloquial* broke, failed, *colloquial* gone bust, gone into liquidation, insolvent, ruined, wound up.

banner /'bænə/ *noun* **1** large portable cloth sign bearing slogan or design. **2** flag.

■ colours, ensign, flag, pennant, pennon, standard, streamer.

bannister = BANISTER.

bannock /'bænək/ *noun* *Scottish & Northern English* round flat loaf, usually unleavened.

banns *plural noun* announcement of intended marriage read in church.

banquet /'bæŋkwɪt/ *noun* sumptuous esp. formal dinner. ● *verb* (**-t-**) **1** give banquet for. **2** attend banquet.

■ *noun* *slang* binge, *slang* blow-out, dinner, feast, meal, *formal* repast, *colloquial* spread.

banquette /bæŋ'ket/ *noun* upholstered bench along wall.

banshee /bæn'ʃi:/ *noun* female spirit whose wail warns of death in a house.

bantam /'bæntəm/ *noun* kind of small domestic fowl. □ **bantamweight** boxing weight (51–54 kg).

banter /'bæntə/ *noun* good-humoured teasing. ● *verb* **1** tease. **2** exchange banter.

■ *noun* badinage, chaffing, joking, persiflage, pleasantry, raillery, repartee, ribbing, ridicule, teasing.

banyan /'bænjən/ *noun* (also **banian**) Indian fig tree with self-rooting branches.

baobab /'beɪəʊbæb/ *noun* African tree with massive trunk and edible fruit.

bap *noun* soft flattish bread roll.

baptism /'bæptɪz(ə)m/ *noun* symbolic admission to Christian Church, with immersing in or sprinkling with water and usually name-giving. □ **baptismal** /-'tɪz-/ *adjective*.

Baptist /'bæptɪst/ *noun* member of Church practising adult baptism by immersion.

baptize /bæp'taɪz/ *verb* (also **-ise**) (**-zing** or **-sing**) **1** administer baptism to. **2** give name to.

bar¹ *noun* **1** long piece of rigid material, esp. used to confine or obstruct. **2** (often + *of*) oblong piece (of chocolate, soap, etc.). **3** band of colour or light. **4** counter for serving alcoholic drinks etc. **5** room or building containing it. **6** counter for particular service. **7** barrier. **8** prisoner's enclosure in law court. **9** section of music between vertical lines. **10** heating element of electric fire. **11** strip below clasp of medal as extra distinction. **12** (**the Bar**) barristers. **13** (**the Bar**) their profession. ● *verb* (**-rr-**) **1** fasten with bar. **2** (usually + *in*, *out*) keep in or out. **3** obstruct, prevent. **4** (usually + *from*) exclude. ● *preposition* except. □ **bar code** machine-readable striped code on packaging etc. **barmaid**, **barman**, **bartender** woman, man, person serving in pub etc.

■ *noun* **1** beam, girder, pole, rail, railing, rod, shaft, stake, stick, strut. **2** block, cake, chunk, hunk, ingot, lump, nugget, piece, slab, wedge. **3** band, belt, line, streak, strip, stripe. **5** café, inn, lounge, *colloquial* pub, public house, *US* saloon, taproom, *archaic* or *literary* tavern, wine bar. **7** barricade, barrier, check, deterrent, hindrance, impediment, obstacle, obstruction. ● *verb* **2** (*bar in*) see CONFINE *verb* 1; (*bar out*) keep out, lock out, shut out. **3** arrest, block, check, deter, halt, hinder, impede, obstruct, prevent, stop, thwart. **4** ban, banish, debar, exclude, forbid, keep out, ostracize, outlaw, prohibit, proscribe. □ **barmaid**, **barman**, **bartender** attendant, server, steward, stewardess, waiter, waitress.

bar² *noun* unit of atmospheric pressure.

barathea /bærə'θi:ə/ *noun* fine wool cloth.

barb *noun* **1** backward-facing point on arrow, fish-hook, etc. **2** hurtful remark. ● *verb* fit with barb. □ **barbed wire** wire with spikes, used for fences.

barbarian /bɑːˈbeərɪən/ *noun* uncultured or primitive person. ● *adjective* uncultured, primitive.

■ *noun* boor, churl, heathen, hun, ignoramus, lout, pagan, philistine, savage, vandal, *slang* yob.
● *adjective* see BARBARIC 1,3.

barbaric /bɑːˈbærɪk/ *adjective* **1** uncultured. **2** cruel. **3** primitive.

■ **1, 3** barbarian, barbarous, crude, primitive, rough, savage, uncivil, uncivilized, uncultivated, uncultured, wild. **2** see CRUEL.

barbarism /ˈbɑːbərɪz(ə)m/ *noun* **1** barbaric state or act. **2** non-standard word or expression.

barbarity /bɑːˈbærɪtɪ/ *noun* (*plural* **-ies**) **1** savage cruelty. **2** barbaric act.

barbarous /ˈbɑːbərəs/ *adjective* **1** uncultured. **2** cruel.

barbecue /ˈbɑːbɪkjuː/ *noun* **1** meal cooked over charcoal etc. out of doors. **2** party for this. **3** grill etc. used for this. ● *verb* (**-cues**, **-cued**, **-cuing**) cook on barbecue.

barber /ˈbɑːbə/ *noun* person who cuts men's hair.

barbican /ˈbɑːbɪkən/ *noun* outer defence, esp. double tower over gate or bridge.

barbiturate /bɑːˈbɪtjʊrət/ *noun* sedative derived from **barbituric acid** /bɑːbɪˈtjʊərɪk/, an organic acid.

bard *noun* **1** poet. **2** *historical* Celtic minstrel. **3** prizewinner at Eisteddfod. □ **bardic** *adjective*.

bare /beə/ *adjective* **1** unclothed, uncovered. **2** leafless. **3** empty. **4** unadorned, plain. **5** scanty, just sufficient. ● *verb* (**-ring**) uncover, reveal. □ **bareback** without saddle. **bare bones** essential part. **barefaced** shameless, impudent. **barefoot** with bare feet. **bareheaded** without hat.

■ *adjective* **1** denuded, exposed, naked, nude, shorn, stark naked, stripped, unclad, unclothed, uncovered, undressed. **2** defoliated, denuded, leafless, stripped. **3** barren, blank, bleak, desolate, empty, featureless, open, treeless, unfurnished, unoccupied, unwooded, vacant, windswept. **4** austere, bald, clean, direct, explicit, hard, honest, literal, open, plain, simple, straightforward, unadorned, unconcealed, undecorated, undisguised, unembellished. **5** basic, essential, just adequate, just sufficient, minimal, minimum, scanty. ● *verb* betray, bring to light, disclose, expose, lay bare, make known, publish, reveal, show, uncover, undress, unmask, unveil.

barely *adverb* **1** scarcely. **2** scantily.

bargain /ˈbɑːgɪn/ *noun* **1** agreement on terms of sale etc. **2** cheap thing. ● *verb* discuss terms of sale etc. □ **bargain for** be prepared for. **into the bargain** moreover.

■ *noun* **1** agreement, arrangement, compact, contract, covenant, deal, negotiation, pact, pledge, promise, settlement, transaction, treaty, understanding. **2** *colloquial* give-away, *colloquial* good buy, good deal, loss-leader, reduced item, *slang* snip, special offer. ● *verb* argue, barter, do a deal, haggle, negotiate. □ **bargain for** see EXPECT 1.

barge /bɑːdʒ/ *noun* **1** large flat-bottomed cargo boat on canal or river. **2** long ornamental pleasure boat. ● *verb* (**-ging**) **1** (+ *in*) intrude or interrupt. **2** (+ *into*) collide with.

bargee /bɑːˈdʒiː/ *noun* person in charge of barge.

baritone /ˈbærɪtəʊn/ *noun* **1** adult male singing voice between tenor and bass. **2** singer with this.

barium /ˈbeərɪəm/ *noun* white metallic element. □ **barium meal** mixture swallowed to reveal digestive tract on X-ray.

bark[1] *noun* sharp explosive cry of dog etc. ● *verb* **1** give a bark. **2** speak or utter sharply or brusquely.

■ *verb* **1** growl, yap.

bark[2] *noun* tough outer layer of tree. ● *verb* **1** graze (shin etc.). **2** strip bark from.

■ *verb* **1** abrade, chafe, graze, rub, scrape, scratch.

barker *noun* tout at auction or sideshow.

barley /ˈbɑːlɪ/ *noun* **1** cereal used as food and in spirits. **2** (also **barleycorn**) its grain. □ **barley sugar** hard sweet made from sugar. **barley water** drink made from boiled barley.

barm *noun* froth on fermenting malt liquor.

bar mitzvah /bɑː ˈmɪtsvə/ *noun* religious initiation of Jewish boy at 13.

barmy /ˈbɑːmɪ/ *adjective* (**-ier**, **-iest**) *slang* crazy.

barn *noun* building for storing grain etc. □ **barn dance** social gathering for country dancing. **barn owl** kind of owl frequenting barns.

barnacle /ˈbɑːnək(ə)l/ *noun* small shellfish clinging to rocks, ships' bottoms, etc. □ **barnacle goose** kind of Arctic goose.

barney /ˈbɑːnɪ/ *noun* (*plural* **-s**) *colloquial* noisy quarrel.

barometer /bəˈrɒmɪtə/ *noun* instrument measuring atmospheric pressure. □ **barometric** /bærəˈmetrɪk/ *adjective*.

baron /ˈbærən/ *noun* **1** member of lowest order of British or foreign nobility. **2** powerful businessman etc. □ **baronial** /bəˈrəʊnɪəl/ *adjective*.

baroness /ˈbærənɪs/ *noun* **1** woman holding rank of baron. **2** baron's wife or widow.

baronet /ˈbærənɪt/ *noun* member of lowest British hereditary titled order. □ **baronetcy** *noun* (*plural* **-ies**).

barony /ˈbærənɪ/ *noun* (*plural* **-ies**) baron's rank or domain.

baroque /bəˈrɒk/ *adjective* (esp. of 17th- & 18th-c. European architecture and music) ornate and extravagant in style. ● *noun* baroque style.

barque /bɑːk/ *noun* kind of sailing ship.

barrack[1] /'bærək/ *noun* (usually in *plural*, often treated as *singular*) **1** housing for soldiers. **2** large bleak building.

■ **1** (*barracks*) billet, camp, garrison, quarters.

barrack[2] /'bærək/ *verb* shout or jeer (at).

barracuda /bærə'ku:də/ *noun* (*plural* same or **-s**) large voracious tropical sea fish.

barrage /'bærɑ:ʒ/ *noun* **1** concentrated artillery bombardment. **2** rapid succession of questions etc. **3** artificial barrier in river etc.

■ **1** assault, attack, bombardment, cannonade, fusillade, gunfire, onslaught, salvo, storm, volley. **3** see BARRIER 1.

barrel /'bær(ə)l/ *noun* **1** cylindrical usually convex container. **2** contents or capacity of this. **3** tube forming part of thing, esp. gun or pen. ● *verb* (**-ll-**; *US* **-l-**) put in barrels. □ **barrel organ** musical instrument with rotating pin-studded cylinder.

■ *noun* **1** butt, cask, drum, hogshead, keg, tank, tub, tun, water-butt.

barren /'bærən/ *adjective* (**-er, -est**) **1** unable to bear young. **2** unable to produce fruit or vegetation. **3** unprofitable. **4** dull. □ **barrenness** *noun*.

■ **1** childless, fruitless, infertile, sterile, sterilized, unfruitful. **2** arid, bare, desert, desolate, dried-up, dry, empty, infertile, lifeless, non-productive, treeless, uncultivated, unproductive, untilled, waste. **3** non-productive, unproductive, unprofitable, useless.

barricade /bærɪ'keɪd/ *noun* barrier, esp. improvised. ● *verb* (**-ding**) block or defend with this.

■ *noun* see BARRIER 1. ● *verb* bar, block off, defend, obstruct.

barrier /'bærɪə/ *noun* **1** fence etc. barring advance or access. **2** obstacle to communication etc. □ **barrier cream** protective skin cream. **barrier reef** coral reef separated from land by channel.

■ **1** bar, barrage, barricade, blockade, boom, bulwark, dam, earthwork, embankment, fence, fortification, frontier, hurdle, obstacle, obstruction, palisade, railing, rampart, stockade, wall. **2** check, drawback, handicap, hindrance, impediment, limitation, restriction, stumbling block.

barrister /'bærɪstə/ *noun* advocate practising in higher courts.

barrow[1] /'bærəʊ/ *noun* **1** two-wheeled handcart. **2** wheelbarrow.

barrow[2] /'bærəʊ/ *noun* ancient grave mound.

Bart. *abbreviation* Baronet.

barter /'bɑ:tə/ *verb* exchange goods, rights, etc., without using money. ● *noun* trade by bartering.

■ *verb* bargain, deal, exchange, negotiate, swap, *US* trade, traffic.

basal /'beɪs(ə)l/ *adjective* of, at, or forming base.

basalt /'bæsɔ:lt/ *noun* dark volcanic rock. □ **basaltic** /bə'sɔ:ltɪk/ *adjective*.

base[1] *noun* **1** what a thing rests or depends on; foundation. **2** principle; starting point. **3** headquarters. **4** main ingredient. **5** number in terms of which other numbers are expressed. **6** substance combining with acid to form salt. ● *verb* (**-sing**) **1** (usually + *on, upon*) found, establish. **2** station. □ **base rate** interest rate set by Bank of England and used as basis for other banks' rates.

■ *noun* **1** basis, bed, bedrock, bottom, essentials, foot, footing, foundation, fundamentals, groundwork, infrastructure, pedestal, plinth, rest, stand, substructure, support, underpinning. **2** basis, ground, premiss, principle, starting point. **3** camp, centre, depot, headquarters, post, station. ● *verb* **1** build, construct, establish, found, ground, secure, set up. **2** locate, position, post, station.

base[2] *adjective* **1** cowardly, despicable. **2** menial. **3** (of coin) alloyed. **4** (of metal) low in value. □ **baseness** *noun*.

■ **1** contemptible, cowardly, depraved, despicable, detestable, dishonourable, evil, ignoble, immoral, low, mean, scandalous, selfish, shabby, shameful, sordid, undignified, unworthy, vulgar, vile, wicked. **2** degrading, ignoble, inferior, low, lowly, mean, unworthy.

baseball *noun* game played esp. in US with bat and ball and circuit of 4 bases.

baseless *adjective* unfounded, groundless.

basement /'beɪsmənt/ *noun* floor below ground level.

■ cellar, crypt, vault.

bases *plural* of BASE[1], BASIS.

bash *verb* **1** strike bluntly or heavily. **2** (often + *up*) *colloquial* attack violently. ● *noun* **1** heavy blow. **2** *slang* attempt. **3** *slang* party.

bashful /'bæʃfʊl/ *adjective* shy, diffident. □ **bashfulness** *noun*.

■ abashed, backward, blushing, coy, demure, diffident, embarrassed, faint-hearted, inhibited, meek, modest, nervous, reserved, reticent, retiring, self-conscious, self-effacing, shamefaced, sheepish, shy, timid, timorous, uneasy, unforthcoming.

BASIC /'beɪsɪk/ *noun* computer programming language using familiar English words.

basic /'beɪsɪk/ *adjective* **1** serving as base. **2** fundamental. **3** simplest; lowest in level. ● *noun* (usually in *plural*) fundamental fact or principle. □ **basically** *adverb*.

■ *adjective* **2** central, chief, crucial, essential, foremost, fundamental, important, intrinsic, key, main, necessary, primary, principal, radical, underlying, vital. **3** elementary, primary, simple.

basil /'bæz(ə)l/ *noun* aromatic herb.

basilica /bə'zɪlɪkə/ *noun* **1** ancient Roman hall with apse and colonnades. **2** similar church.

basilisk /'bæzɪlɪsk/ *noun* **1** mythical reptile with lethal breath and look. **2** American crested lizard.

basin /'beɪs(ə)n/ *noun* **1** round vessel for liquids

or preparing food in. **2** washbasin. **3** hollow depression. **4** sheltered mooring area. **5** round valley. **6** area drained by river.
■ **1** bath, bowl, container, dish, stoup. **2** sink, washbasin.

basis /'beɪsɪs/ *noun* (*plural* **bases** /-siːz/) **1** foundation. **2** main ingredient or principle. **3** starting point for discussion etc.
■ **1, 2** base, core, footing, foundation, ground, infrastructure, principle, support, underpinning. **3** base, premiss, principle, starting point.

bask /bɑːsk/ *verb* **1** relax in warmth and light. **2** (+ *in*) revel in.
■ **1** lie, lounge, relax, sunbathe. **2** (*bask in*) delight in, enjoy, glory in, luxuriate in, revel in, wallow in.

basket /'bɑːskɪt/ *noun* **1** container made of woven canes, wire, etc. **2** amount held by this. □ **basketball** team game in which goals are scored by putting ball through high nets. **basketry**, **basketwork 1** art of weaving cane etc. **2** work so produced.
■ hamper, pannier, punnet, trug.

bas-relief /'bæsrɪliːf/ *noun* carving or sculpture projecting slightly from background.

bass[1] /beɪs/ *noun* **1** lowest adult male voice. **2** singer with this. **3** *colloquial* double bass. **4** *colloquial* bass guitar. **5** low-frequency sound of radio, record player, etc. ● *adjective* **1** lowest in pitch. **2** deep-sounding. □ **bass guitar** electric guitar playing low notes. □ **bassist** *noun*.

bass[2] /bæs/ *noun* (*plural* same or **-es**) **1** common perch. **2** other fish of perch family.

basset /'bæsɪt/ *noun* (in full **basset-hound**) short-legged hunting dog.

bassoon /bə'suːn/ *noun* bass musical instrument of oboe family. □ **bassoonist** *noun*.

bast /bæst/ *noun* fibre from inner bark of tree, esp. lime.

bastard /'bɑːstəd/ *noun* **1** *archaic* or *offensive* person born of parents not married to each other. **2** *slang* person regarded with dislike or pity. **3** *slang* difficult or awkward thing. ● *adjective* **1** *archaic* or *offensive* illegitimate by birth. **2** hybrid. □ **bastardy** *noun*.
■ *noun* **1** illegitimate child, love child, natural child.

bastardize /'bɑːstədaɪz/ *verb* (also **-ise**) (**-zing** or **-sing**) **1** corrupt, debase. **2** declare illegitimate.

baste[1] /beɪst/ *verb* (**-ting**) **1** moisten (roasting meat etc.) with fat etc. **2** beat, thrash.

baste[2] /beɪst/ *verb* (**-ting**) sew with long loose stitches; tack.

bastinado /bæstɪ'neɪdəʊ/ *noun* caning on soles of feet. ● *verb* (**-es**, **-ed**) punish with this.

bastion /'bæstɪən/ *noun* **1** projecting part of fortification. **2** thing regarded as protection.

bat[1] *noun* **1** implement with handle for hitting ball in games. **2** turn at using this. **3** batsman. ● *verb* (**-tt-**) **1** use bat; hit (as) with bat. **2** take one's turn at batting. □ **batsman** person who bats, esp. at cricket.

■ *noun* **1** club, racket.

bat[2] *noun* mouselike nocturnal flying mammal. □ **bats** *slang* crazy.

bat[3] *verb* (**-tt-**) □ **not bat an eyelid** *colloquial* show no reaction.

batch *noun* **1** group, collection, set. **2** loaves baked at one time. ● *verb* arrange in batches.

bated /'beɪtɪd/ *adjective* □ **with bated breath** anxiously.

Bath /bɑːθ/ *noun* □ **Bath bun** round spiced bun with currants. **Bath chair** invalid's wheelchair.

bath /bɑːθ/ *noun* (*plural* **-s** /bɑːðz/) **1** container for sitting in and washing the body. **2** its contents. **3** act of washing in it. **4** (usually in *plural*) building for swimming or bathing. ● *verb* wash in bath. □ **bath cube** cube of **bath salts**, substance for scenting and softening bath water. **bathroom 1** room with bath. **2** *US* room with lavatory.
■ *noun* **1** *proprietary term* Jacuzzi, sauna, shower-bath, *colloquial* tub. **3** shower-bath, soak, wash. **4** (*baths*) lido, pool, swimming pool.

bathe /beɪð/ *verb* (**-thing**) **1** immerse oneself in water etc., esp. to swim or wash. **2** immerse in or treat with liquid. **3** (of sunlight etc.) envelop. ● *noun* swim. □ **bathing costume** garment worn for swimming.
■ *verb* **1** go swimming, paddle, plunge, splash about, swim, take a dip. **2** clean, cleanse, immerse, moisten, rinse, soak, steep, swill, wash.

bathos /'beɪθɒs/ *noun* lapse from sublime to trivial; anticlimax. □ **bathetic** /bə'θetɪk/ *adjective*.
■ anticlimax, comedown, disappointment, let-down.

bathrobe /'bɑːθrəʊb/ *noun* loose robe worn esp. after taking bath; dressing gown.

bathyscaphe /'bæθɪskæf/, **bathysphere** /-sfɪə/ *nouns* vessel for deep-sea diving.

batik /bə'tiːk/ *noun* method of dyeing textiles by waxing parts to be left uncoloured.

batiste /bæ'tiːst/ *noun* fine cotton or linen fabric.

batman /'bætmən/ *noun* army officer's servant.

baton /'bæt(ə)n/ *noun* **1** thin stick for conducting orchestra etc. **2** short stick carried in relay race. **3** stick carried by drum major. **4** staff of office.
■ cane, mace, rod, staff, stick, truncheon, wand.

batrachian /bə'treɪkɪən/ *noun* amphibian that discards gills and tail, esp. frog or toad. ● *adjective* of batrachians.

battalion /bə'tæljən/ *noun* army unit usually of 300–1000 men.

batten[1] /'bæt(ə)n/ *noun* **1** long narrow piece of squared timber. **2** strip for securing tarpaulin over ship's hatchway. ● *verb* strengthen or (often + *down*) fasten with battens.

batten[2] /'bæt(ə)n/ *verb* (often + *on*) thrive at the expense of.

batter /'bætə/ *verb* **1** strike hard and repeatedly. **2** (esp. as **battered** *adjective*) subject to long-term violence. ● *noun* mixture of flour and eggs beaten up with liquid for cooking. ▢ **battering ram** *historical* swinging beam for breaching walls.

■ *verb* **1** beat, bludgeon, *slang* clobber, club, cudgel, hit, keep hitting, pound, *colloquial* wallop.

battery /'bætəri/ *noun* (*plural* **-ies**) **1** portable container of cell or cells for supplying electricity. **2** series of cages etc. for poultry or cattle. **3** set of connected or similar instruments etc. **4** emplacement for heavy guns. **5** *Law* physical violence inflicted on person.

■ **1** accumulator, cell. **5** assault, attack, beating, blows, mugging, onslaught, thrashing, violence.

battle /'bæt(ə)l/ *noun* **1** prolonged fight, esp. between armed forces. **2** contest, struggle. ● *verb* (**-ling**) (often + *with, for*) struggle. ▢ **battleaxe 1** medieval weapon. **2** *colloquial* domineering middle-aged woman. **battlecruiser** *historical* heavy-gunned ship of higher speed and lighter armour than battleship. **battle-cry** cry or slogan of participants in battle or contest. **battledress** soldier's everyday uniform. **battlefield**, **battleground** scene of battle. **battleship** most heavily armed and armoured warship.

■ *noun* **1** action, air raid, Armageddon, attack, *colloquial* blitz, brush, campaign, clash, combat, conflict, confrontation, *historical* crusade, dogfight, encounter, engagement, fight, fray, hostilities, offensive, pitched battle, pre-emptive strike, siege, skirmish, strife, war, warfare. **2** campaign, conflict, confrontation, contest, crusade, encounter, quarrel, struggle, war. ● *verb* see FIGHT *verb* 1. ▢ **battlefield** arena, battleground, theatre of war.

battlement /'bæt(ə)lmənt/ *noun* (usually in *plural*) parapet with gaps at intervals at top of wall.

batty /'bætɪ/ *adjective* (**-ier, -iest**) *slang* crazy.

batwing *adjective* (esp. of sleeve) shaped like a bat's wing.

bauble /'bɔːb(ə)l/ *noun* showy trinket.

baulk /bɔːlk/ (also **balk**) *verb* **1** (often + *at*) jib, hesitate. **2** thwart, hinder. **3** disappoint. ● *noun* **1** hindrance. **2** stumbling block.

bauxite /'bɔːksaɪt/ *noun* claylike mineral, chief source of aluminium.

bawdy /'bɔːdɪ/ *adjective* (**-ier, -iest**) humorously indecent. ● *noun* bawdy talk or writing. ▢ **bawdy house** brothel.

■ *adjective* blue, broad, coarse, dirty, earthy, erotic, immoral, improper, indecent, indecorous, indelicate, lascivious, lecherous, lewd, licentious, lusty, *colloquial jocular* naughty, obscene, pornographic, prurient, racy, *colloquial* raunchy, ribald, risqué, *colloquial* rude, salacious, sexy, smutty, spicy, suggestive, titillating, vulgar.

bawl *verb* shout or weep noisily. ▢ **bawl out** *colloquial* reprimand severely.

■ cry, roar, shout, thunder, wail, weep, yell, yelp.

bay[1] *noun* broad curving inlet of sea.

■ bight, cove.

bay[2] *noun* **1** laurel with deep green leaves. **2** (in *plural*) victor's or poet's bay wreath. **3** (in *plural*) fame. ▢ **bay leaf** leaf of bay tree, used for flavouring.

bay[3] *noun* **1** recess; alcove in wall. **2** compartment. **3** allotted area. ▢ **bay window** window projecting from line of wall.

■ **1** alcove, niche, nook, opening, recess. **2, 3** see COMPARTMENT.

bay[4] *adjective* reddish-brown (esp. of horse). ● *noun* bay horse.

bay[5] *verb* bark loudly. ● *noun* bark of large dog, esp. chorus of pursuing hounds. ▢ **at bay** unable to escape. **keep at bay** ward off.

bayonet /'beɪənet/ *noun* stabbing-blade attachable to rifle. ● *verb* (**-t-**) stab with bayonet. ▢ **bayonet fitting** connecting-part engaged by pushing and twisting.

bazaar /bə'zɑː/ *noun* **1** oriental market. **2** sale of goods, esp. for charity.

■ **1** market, market place. **2** auction, bring-and-buy sale, fair, fête, jumble sale, sale.

bazooka /bə'zuːkə/ *noun* anti-tank rocket launcher.

BBC *abbreviation* British Broadcasting Corporation.

BC *abbreviation* **1** before Christ. **2** British Columbia.

BCG *abbreviation* Bacillus Calmette-Guérin, an anti-tuberculosis vaccine.

be /biː/ *verb* (*present singular 1st* **am**, *2nd* **are** /ɑː/, *3rd* **is** /ɪz/, *plural* **are** /ɑː/; *past singular 1st* **was** /wɒz/, *2nd* **were** /wɜː/, *3rd* **was** /wɒz/, *plural* **were** /wɜː/; *present participle* **being**; *past participle* **been**) **1** exist, live. **2** occur. **3** remain, continue. **4** have specified identity, state, or quality. ● *auxiliary verb* with past participle to form passive, with present participle to form continuous tenses, with infinitive to express duty, intention, possibility, etc. ▢ **be-all and end-all** *colloquial* whole being, essence. **be off** *colloquial* go away; leave.

■ *verb* **1** be alive, breathe, endure, exist, live. **2** arise, *poetical* befall, come about, happen, occur, take place. **3** continue, dwell, inhabit, keep going, last, persist, remain, stay, survive.

beach *noun* sandy or pebbly shore of sea, lake, etc. ● *verb* run or haul (boat etc.) on shore. ▢ **beachcomber** person who searches beaches for articles of value. **beachhead** fortified position set up on beach by landing forces.

■ *noun* bank, coast, foreshore, littoral, sand, sands, seashore, seaside, shore, *esp. poetical* strand.

beacon /'biːkən/ *noun* **1** signal-fire on hill or pole. **2** signal. **3** signal-station. **4** Belisha beacon.

■ **1, 2** bonfire, fire, flare, light, signal. **3** lighthouse.

bead *noun* **1** small ball of glass, stone, etc. pierced for threading with others. **2** drop of liquid. **3** small knob in front sight of gun. ● *verb* adorn with bead(s) or beading.

■ *noun* **1** (*beads*) chaplet, necklace, pearls, rosary. **2** blob, bubble, drip, drop, droplet, globule, pearl.

beading *noun* moulding like series of beads.

beadle /'biːd(ə)l/ *noun* ceremonial officer of church, college, etc.

beady *adjective* (**-ier**, **-iest**) (of eyes) small and bright. □ **beady-eyed 1** with beady eyes. **2** observant.

beagle /'biːg(ə)l/ *noun* small hound used for hunting hares.

beak *noun* **1** bird's horny projecting jaws. **2** *slang* hooked nose. **3** *historical* prow of warship. **4** spout.

beaker /'biːkə/ *noun* **1** tall cup for drinking. **2** lipped glass vessel for scientific experiments.

■ **1** cup, glass, tumbler.

beam *noun* **1** long piece of squared timber or metal used in house-building etc. **2** ray of light or radiation. **3** bright smile. **4** series of radio or radar signals as guide to ship or aircraft. **5** crossbar of balance. **6** (in *plural*) horizontal cross-timbers of ship. ● *verb* **1** emit (light, radio waves, etc.). **2** shine. **3** smile radiantly. □ **off beam** *colloquial* mistaken.

■ *noun* **1** bar, board, boom, brace, girder, joist, plank, post, rafter, spar, stanchion, stud, support, timber. **2** gleam, pencil, ray, shaft, stream. ● *verb* **1** aim, broadcast, direct, emit, radiate, send out, shine, transmit. **2** gleam, glow, radiate, shine. **3** grin, look radiant, smile.

bean *noun* **1** climbing plant with kidney-shaped seeds in long pods. **2** seed of this or of coffee or other plant. □ **beanbag 1** small bag filled with dried beans and used as ball. **2** large bag filled with polystyrene pieces and used as seat. **bean sprout** sprout of bean seed as food. **full of beans** *colloquial* lively, exuberant. **not a bean** *slang* no money.

beano /'biːnəʊ/ *noun* (*plural* **-s**) *slang* party, celebration.

bear[1] /beə/ *verb* (*past* **bore**; *past participle* **borne** or **born**) **1** carry. **2** show. **3** produce, yield (fruit); give birth to. **4** sustain, support. **5** endure, tolerate. □ **bear down** exert downward pressure. **bear down on** approach rapidly or purposefully. **bear out** confirm, support. **bear up** raise one's spirits; not despair. **bear witness** testify.

■ **1** bring, carry, convey, deliver, move, take, transfer, transport. **2** display, exhibit, have, possess, show. **3** breed, bring forth, develop, engender, generate, give birth to, produce, spawn, yield. **4** carry, hold, prop up, shoulder, support, sustain, take. **5** abide, accept, brook, cope with, endure, live with, permit, put up with, reconcile oneself to, stand, stomach, suffer, sustain, tolerate, undergo. □ **bear out** see CONFIRM 1. **bear up** see SURVIVE 1. **bear witness** see TESTIFY.

bear[2] /beə/ *noun* **1** heavy thick-furred mammal. **2** rough surly person. **3** person who sells shares for future delivery in hope of buying them more cheaply before then. □ **beargarden** noisy or rowdy scene. **bear-hug** powerful embrace. **bearskin** guardsman's tall furry cap.

bearable *adjective* endurable.

■ acceptable, endurable, supportable, survivable, sustainable, tolerable.

beard /bɪəd/ *noun* **1** facial hair on chin etc. **2** part on animal (esp. goat) resembling beard. ● *verb* oppose, defy. □ **bearded** *adjective*. **beardless** *adjective*.

bearer *noun* **1** carrier of message, cheque, etc. **2** carrier of coffin, equipment, etc.

bearing *noun* **1** outward behaviour, posture. **2** (usually + *on, upon*) relation, relevance. **3** part of machine supporting rotating part. **4** direction relative to fixed point. **5** (in *plural*) relative position. **6** heraldic device or design.

■ **1** air, appearance, aspect, attitude, behaviour, carriage, demeanour, deportment, look, manner, *literary* mien, poise, posture, presence, stance, style. **2** applicability, application, connection, import, pertinence, reference, relation, relationship, relevance, significance. **5** (*bearings*) orientation, position, sense of direction.

beast *noun* **1** animal, esp. wild mammal. **2** brutal person. **3** *colloquial* disliked person or thing.

■ **1** animal, brute, creature. **2** barbarian, brute, monster, ogre, savage, *colloquial* swine.

beastly *adjective* (**-ier**, **-iest**) **1** like a beast. **2** *colloquial* unpleasant.

■ **1** barbaric, bestial, brutal, cruel, savage. **2** see UNPLEASANT.

beat *verb* (*past* **beat**; *past participle* **beaten**) **1** strike repeatedly or persistently; inflict blows on. **2** overcome, surpass. **3** exhaust, perplex. **4** (often + *up*) whisk (eggs etc.) vigorously. **5** (often + *out*) shape (metal etc.) by blows. **6** pulsate. **7** mark (time of music) with baton, foot, etc. **8** move or cause (wings) to move up and down. ● *noun* **1** main accent in music or verse. **2** strongly marked rhythm of popular music etc. **3** movement of conductor's baton. **4** throbbing. **5** stroke on drum. **6** police officer's appointed course. **7** one's habitual round. ● *adjective colloquial* exhausted, tired out. □ **beat about the bush** not come to the point. **beat a retreat** withdraw. **beat down 1** cause (seller) to lower price by bargaining. **2** (of sun, rain, etc.) shine or fall relentlessly. **beat it** *slang* go away. **beat off** drive back (an attack etc.). **beat up** beat with punches and kicks. **beat-up** *colloquial* dilapidated. □ **beatable** *adjective*.

■ *verb* **1** bash, batter, bludgeon, buffet, cane, *slang* clobber, clout, cudgel, flail, flog, hammer, hit, knock about, lash, *colloquial* lay into, *colloquial* manhandle, pound, punch, scourge, strike, *slang* tan, thrash, thump, trounce, *colloquial* wallop, *colloquial* whack, whip. **2** *colloquial* best, conquer, crush, defeat, get the better of, *colloquial* lick, master, outclass, outdistance, outdo, outpace, outrun, outwit, overcome, overpower, overthrow, overwhelm, rout, subdue, surpass, thrash, trounce, *literary* vanquish, win against, worst. **4** agitate, blend, mix, stir, whip, whisk. **6** palpitate, pound, pulsate, race, throb, thump. **8** flap, flutter. ● *noun* **1, 2** accent, pulse, rhythm, stress, tempo, throb. **4** pulsation, pulse, throb, throbbing. **6, 7** course, itinerary, journey, path, rounds, route, way. □ **beat up** see ATTACK *verb* 1.

beater *noun* **1** whisk. **2** implement for beating carpet. **3** person who rouses game at a shoot.

beatific /biːəˈtɪfɪk/ *adjective* **1** making blessed. **2** *colloquial* blissful.

beatify /biːˈætɪfaɪ/ *verb* (**-ies, -ied**) **1** *RC Church* declare to be blessed as first step to canonization. **2** make happy. □ **beatification** *noun*.

beatitude /biːˈætɪtjuːd/ *noun* **1** blessedness. **2** (in *plural*) blessings in Matthew 5: 3–11.

beau /bəʊ/ *noun* (*plural* **-x** /-z/) **1** boyfriend. **2** dandy.

Beaufort scale /ˈbəʊfət/ *noun* scale of wind speeds.

Beaujolais /ˈbəʊʒəleɪ/ *noun* red or white wine from Beaujolais district of France.

beauteous /ˈbjuːtɪəs/ *adjective poetical* beautiful.

beautician /bjuːˈtɪʃ(ə)n/ *noun* specialist in beauty treatment.

beautiful /ˈbjuːtɪfʊl/ *adjective* **1** having beauty. **2** *colloquial* excellent. □ **beautifully** *adverb*.
■ **1** aesthetic, alluring, appealing, artistic, attractive, becoming, bewitching, brilliant, captivating, charming, *literary* comely, dainty, decorative, delightful, elegant, exquisite, *archaic* fair, fascinating, fetching, fine, good-looking, glamorous, *colloquial* glorious, *colloquial* gorgeous, graceful, handsome, irresistible, lovely, magnificent, neat, picturesque, pleasing, pretty, *literary* pulchritudinous, quaint, radiant, ravishing, scenic, seductive, sensuous, sexy, spectacular, splendid, *colloquial* stunning, superb, tasteful, tempting. **2** see EXCELLENT.

beautify /ˈbjuːtɪfaɪ/ *verb* (**-ies, -ied**) make beautiful, adorn. □ **beautification** *noun*.
■ adorn, bedeck, deck, decorate, embellish, garnish, ornament, prettify, *colloquial* tart up, *colloquial* titivate.

beauty /ˈbjuːtɪ/ *noun* (*plural* **-ies**) **1** combination of qualities that delights the sight or other senses or the mind. **2** person or thing having this. □ **beauty queen** woman judged most beautiful in contest. **beauty parlour, salon** establishment for cosmetic treatment. **beauty spot** beautiful locality.
■ **1** allure, appeal, attractiveness, charm, elegance, fascination, glamour, glory, grace, handsomeness, loveliness, magnificence, picturesqueness, prettiness, *literary* pulchritude, radiance, splendour.

beaver *noun* **1** large amphibious broad-tailed rodent. **2** its fur. **3** hat of this. **4** (**Beaver**) member of most junior branch of Scout Association.

● *verb colloquial* (usually + *away*) work hard.

becalm /bɪˈkɑːm/ *verb* (usually in *passive*) deprive (ship etc.) of wind.
■ (*becalmed*) helpless, idle, motionless, still, unmoving.

became *past* of BECOME.

because /bɪˈkɒz/ *conjunction* for the reason that. □ **because of** by reason of.

beck¹ *noun* brook, mountain stream.

beck² *noun* □ **at (person's) beck and call** subject to his or her constant orders.

beckon /ˈbekən/ *verb* **1** (often + *to*) summon by gesture. **2** entice.
■ **1** gesture, motion, signal, summon, wave.

become /bɪˈkʌm/ *verb* (**-ming**; *past* **became**; *past participle* **become**) **1** come to be; begin to be. **2** (often as **becoming** *adjective*) suit; look well on. □ **become of** happen to.
■ **1** be transformed into, change into, develop into, grow into, mature into, metamorphose into, turn into. **2** be appropriate to, befit, enhance, fit, flatter, harmonize with, set off, suit; (**becoming**) see SUITABLE, ATTRACTIVE.

becquerel /ˈbekərel/ *noun* SI unit of radioactivity.

bed *noun* **1** place to sleep or rest, esp. piece of furniture for sleeping on. **2** garden plot for plants. **3** bottom of sea, river, etc. **4** flat base on which thing rests. **5** stratum. ● *verb* (**-dd-**) **1** (usually + *down*) put or go to bed. **2** (usually + *out*) plant in garden bed. **3** fix firmly. **4** *colloquial* have sexual intercourse with. □ **bedclothes** sheets, blankets, etc. **bedfellow 1** person who shares bed. **2** associate, partner. **bedlinen** sheets, pillowcases, duvet covers, etc. **bedpan** pan for use as toilet by invalid in bed. **bedridden** confined to bed by infirmity. **bedrock 1** solid rock under alluvial deposits etc. **2** basic principles. **bedroom** room for sleeping in. **bed-sitting room, bedsitter** combined bedroom and sitting room. **bedsore** sore developed by lying in bed. **bedspread** cloth for covering bed. **bedstead** framework of bed. **bedtime** hour for going to bed.
■ *noun* **2** border, garden, patch, plot. **3** bottom, channel, watercourse. **4** base, foundation, groundwork, layer, substratum. □ **bedclothes** bedding, bedlinen, covers.

bedaub /bɪˈdɔːb/ *verb* smear with paint etc.

bedding *noun* **1** mattress and bedclothes. **2** litter for cattle etc. □ **bedding plant** annual flowering plant put in garden bed.

bedeck /bɪˈdek/ *verb* adorn, decorate.

bedevil /bɪˈdev(ə)l/ *verb* (**-ll-**; *US* **-l-**) **1** trouble, torment. **2** confuse. □ **bedevilment** *noun*.

bedlam /ˈbedləm/ *noun* scene of confusion or uproar.

Bedouin /ˈbeduːɪn/ *noun* (*plural* same) nomadic Arab of the desert.

bedraggled /bɪˈdræg(ə)ld/ *adjective* dishevelled, untidy.

■ dirty, dishevelled, drenched, messy, muddy, *colloquial* scruffy, sodden, soiled, stained, unkempt, untidy, wet, wringing.

bee *noun* **1** 4-winged stinging insect, collecting nectar and pollen and producing wax and honey. **2** busy worker. **3** meeting for combined work or amusement. □ **beehive** hive. **a bee in one's bonnet** an obsession. **beeswax** wax secreted by bees for honeycomb.

Beeb *noun* (**the Beeb**) *colloquial* the BBC.

beech *noun* **1** smooth-barked glossy-leaved tree. **2** its wood. □ **beechmast** fruit of beech.

beef *noun* **1** meat of ox, bull, or cow. **2** (*plural* **beeves** or *US* **-s**) beef animal. **3** (*plural* **-s**) *slang* protest. ● *verb slang* complain. □ **beefburger** hamburger. **beefeater** warder in Tower of London. **beefsteak** thick slice of beef for grilling or frying. **beef tea** stewed beef extract for invalids. **beef tomato** large tomato.

beefy *adjective* (**-ier**, **-iest**) **1** like beef. **2** solid, muscular.

beeline /'biːlaɪn/ *noun* straight line between two places. □ **make a beeline for** hurry directly to.

been *past participle* of BE.

beep *noun* short high-pitched sound. ● *verb* emit beep.

beer /bɪə/ *noun* alcoholic liquor made from fermented malt etc. flavoured esp. with hops. □ **beer garden** garden where beer is sold and drunk. **beer mat** small mat for beer glass.

■ ale, bitter, lager, porter, stout.

beery *adjective* (**-ier**, **-iest**) **1** showing influence of beer. **2** like beer.

beeswing /'biːzwɪŋ/ *noun* filmy crust on old port wine etc.

beet *noun* plant with succulent root used for salads etc. and sugar-making (see BEETROOT, SUGAR BEET).

beetle[1] /'biːt(ə)l/ *noun* insect with hard protective outer wings. ● *verb* (**-ling**) (+ *about*, *off*, etc.) *colloquial* hurry, scurry.

beetle[2] /'biːt(ə)l/ *adjective* projecting, shaggy, scowling. ● *verb* (usually as **beetling** *adjective*) overhang.

beetle[3] /'biːt(ə)l/ *noun* heavy-headed tool for ramming, crushing, etc.

beetroot *noun* dark red root of beet, used as vegetable.

befall /bɪ'fɔːl/ *verb* (*past* **befell**; *past participle* **befallen**) *poetical* **1** happen. **2** happen to.

■ **1** be the outcome, chance, come about, crop up, happen, occur, take place, *disputed* transpire. **2** become of, *esp. poetical* betide, happen to.

befit /bɪ'fɪt/ *verb* (**-tt-**) be appropriate for.

befog /bɪ'fɒg/ *verb* (**-gg-**) **1** obscure. **2** envelop in fog.

before /bɪ'fɔː/ *conjunction* **1** sooner than. **2** rather than. ● *preposition* **1** earlier than. **2** in front of; ahead of. **3** in presence of. ● *adverb* **1** ahead, in front. **2** previously, already. **3** in the past.

■ *adverb* **2** already, earlier, in advance, previously, sooner.

beforehand *adverb* in anticipation; in readiness; before time.

befoul /bɪ'faʊl/ *verb poetical* **1** make foul. **2** degrade; defile.

befriend /bɪ'frend/ *verb* act as friend to; help.

■ *colloquial* chat up, gang up with, get to know, make friends with, make the acquaintance of, *colloquial* pal up with.

befuddle /bɪ'fʌd(ə)l/ *verb* (**-ling**) **1** make drunk. **2** confuse. □ **befuddlement** *noun*.

beg *verb* (**-gg-**) **1** ask for as gift. **2** live by begging. **3** ask earnestly, entreat. **4** ask formally. □ **beg the question** assume truth of thing to be proved. **go begging** be unwanted.

USAGE The expression *beg the question* is often used incorrectly to mean 'to invite the obvious question (that …)'.

■ **1** *colloquial* cadge, scrounge, solicit, sponge. **3** ask, beseech, crave, entreat, implore, importune, petition, plead, pray, *literary* supplicate. **4** petition, plead, pray, request, *literary* supplicate.

began *past* of BEGIN.

begat *archaic past* of BEGET.

beget /bɪ'get/ *verb* (**-tt-**; *past* **begot**, *archaic* **begat**; *past participle* **begotten**) *literary* **1** be the father of. **2** give rise to. □ **begetter** *noun*.

■ **1** father, procreate, sire. **2** breed, bring about, cause, create, engender, generate, give rise to, produce, propagate, result in, spawn.

beggar /'begə/ *noun* **1** person who begs or lives by begging. **2** *colloquial* person. ● *verb* **1** make poor. **2** be too extraordinary for (belief, description, etc.).

■ *noun* **1** cadger, down-and-out, mendicant, pauper, scrounger, sponger, tramp, vagrant.

beggarly *adjective* **1** mean. **2** poor, needy.

beggary /'begərɪ/ *noun* extreme poverty.

begin /bɪ'gɪn/ *verb* (**-nn-**; *past* **began**; *past participle* **begun**) **1** perform first part of. **2** come into being. **3** (often + *to do*) start; take first step. **4** (usually in negative) *colloquial* show any likelihood.

■ **1** activate, approach, attack, broach, *formal* commence, conceive, create, embark on, enter into, found, inaugurate, initiate, inspire, instigate, introduce, kindle, launch, move into, open, originate, pioneer, precipitate, provoke, set about, set in motion, set up, spark off, start, take up, touch off, trigger off, undertake. **2** appear, arise, break out, come into existence, crop up, emerge, get going, happen, materialize, originate, spring up. **3** be first, *colloquial* get cracking, get going, *colloquial* kick off, lead off, move off, open, set off, set out, start, take steps, take the initiative.

beginner *noun* learner.

■ apprentice, *colloquial* fresher, greenhorn, inexperienced person, initiate, learner, novice, recruit, starter, tiro, trainee.

beginning *noun* **1** time at which thing begins. **2** source, origin. **3** first part.

　■ **1, 2** birth, *formal* commencement, conception, creation, dawn, embryo, emergence, establishment, foundation, genesis, germ, inauguration, inception, initiation, instigation, introduction, launch, onset, opening, origin, outset, point of departure, rise, source, start, starting point, threshold. **3** introduction, opening, preface, prelude, prologue.

begone /bɪˈɡɒn/ *interjection poetical* go away at once!

begonia /bɪˈɡəʊnɪə/ *noun* plant with ornamental foliage and bright flowers.

begot *past* of BEGET.

begotten *past participle* of BEGET.

begrime /bɪˈɡraɪm/ *verb* make grimy.

begrudge /bɪˈɡrʌdʒ/ *verb* (**-ging**) **1** grudge. **2** feel or show resentment at or envy of. **3** be dissatisfied at.

　■ be bitter about, envy, grudge, mind, object to, resent.

beguile /bɪˈɡaɪl/ *verb* (**-ling**) **1** charm. **2** divert. **3** delude, cheat. □ **beguilement** *noun*.

beguine /bɪˈɡiːn/ *noun* W. Indian dance.

begum /ˈbeɪɡəm/ *noun* (in India, Pakistan, and Bangladesh) **1** Muslim woman of high rank. **2** (**Begum**) *title of married Muslim woman*.

begun *past participle* of BEGIN.

behalf /bɪˈhɑːf/ *noun* □ **on behalf of, on (person's) behalf 1** in the interests of. **2** as representative of.

behave /bɪˈheɪv/ *verb* (**-ving**) **1** react or act in specified way. **2** work well (or in specified way). **3** (often **behave oneself**) conduct oneself properly.

　■ **1, 2** acquit oneself, act, *literary* comport oneself, conduct oneself, function, operate, perform, react, respond, run, work. **3** act properly, be good, be on one's best behaviour.

behaviour /bɪˈheɪvjə/ *noun* (*US* **behavior**) manners; conduct, way of behaving. □ **behavioural** *adjective*.

　■ actions, attitude, bearing, *literary* comportment, conduct, demeanour, deportment, manners, performance, reaction, response, ways.

behaviourism *noun* (*US* **behaviorism**) study of human actions by analysis of stimulus and response. □ **behaviourist** *noun*.

behead /bɪˈhed/ *verb* **1** cut head from (person). **2** execute thus.

　■ decapitate, guillotine.

beheld *past & past participle* of BEHOLD.

behest /bɪˈhest/ *noun literary* command, request.

behind /bɪˈhaɪnd/ *preposition* **1** in or to rear of.

2 hidden by; on farther side of. **3** in past in relation to. **4** inferior to. **5** in support of. ● *adverb* **1** in or to rear. **2** on far side. **3** remaining after others' departure. **4** (usually + *with*) in arrears. ● *noun colloquial* buttocks. □ **behindhand 1** in arrears. **2** behind time; too late. **behind time** unpunctual. **behind the times** old-fashioned, antiquated.

behold /bɪˈhəʊld/ *verb* (*past & past participle* **beheld**) *literary* look at; take notice, observe.

　■ descry, discern, espy, look at, note, notice, see, set eyes on, view.

beholden /bɪˈhəʊld(ə)n/ *adjective* (usually + *to*) under obligation.

behove /bɪˈhəʊv/ *verb* (**-ving**) *formal* **1** be incumbent on. **2** befit.

beige /beɪʒ/ *noun* pale sandy fawn colour. ● *adjective* of this colour.

being /ˈbiːɪŋ/ *noun* **1** existence. **2** constitution, nature. **3** existing person etc.

　■ **1** actuality, essence, existence, life, living, reality, solidity, substance. **3** animal, creature, individual, person, spirit, soul.

belabour /bɪˈleɪbə/ *verb* (*US* **belabor**) attack physically or verbally.

belated /bɪˈleɪtɪd/ *adjective* coming (too) late. □ **belatedly** *adverb*.

　■ behindhand, delayed, last-minute, late, overdue, posthumous, tardy, unpunctual.

bel canto /bel ˈkæntəʊ/ *noun* singing marked by full rich tone.

belch *verb* **1** emit wind from stomach through mouth. **2** (of volcano, gun, etc.) emit (fire, smoke, etc.). ● *noun* act of belching.

　■ *verb* **1** *colloquial* burp. **2** discharge, emit, gush, send out, spew out, vomit.

beleaguer /bɪˈliːɡə/ *verb* **1** besiege. **2** vex; harass.

belfry /ˈbelfrɪ/ *noun* (*plural* **-ies**) **1** bell tower. **2** space for bells in church tower.

belie /bɪˈlaɪ/ *verb* (**belying**) **1** give false impression of. **2** fail to confirm, fulfil, or justify.

belief /bɪˈliːf/ *noun* **1** act of believing. **2** what one believes. **3** trust, confidence. **4** acceptance as true.

　■ **2** attitude, conviction, creed, doctrine, dogma, ethos, faith, feeling, ideology, morality, notion, opinion, persuasion, principles, religion, standards, tenet, theory, view. **3** assurance, certainty, confidence, reliance, security, sureness, trust. **4** acceptance, assent, credence.

believe /bɪˈliːv/ *verb* (**-ving**) **1** accept as true. **2** think. **3** (+ *in*) have faith or confidence in. **4** trust word of. **5** have religious faith. □ **believable** *adjective*. **believer** *noun*.

　■ **1** accept, be certain of, credit, swallow, trust. **2** assume, consider, dare say, feel, gather, guess, hold, imagine, judge, know, maintain, postulate, presume, speculate, suppose, take it for granted, think. **3** (*believe in*) count on, depend on, have faith in, reckon on, rely on, subscribe to, *colloquial* swear by, trust in. □ **believer** adherent, devotee, disciple, fanatic, follower, proselyte, supporter, upholder, zealot.

Belisha beacon /bə'liːʃə/ *noun* flashing orange ball on striped post, marking pedestrian crossing.

belittle /bɪ'lɪt(ə)l/ *verb* (**-ling**) disparage. □ **belittlement** *noun*.

■ criticize, decry, denigrate, deprecate, depreciate, detract from, disparage, minimize, play down, slight, speak slightingly of, underrate, undervalue.

bell *noun* **1** hollow esp. cup-shaped metal body emitting musical sound when struck. **2** sound of bell. **3** bell-shaped thing. □ **bell-bottomed** (of trousers) widening below knee. **bell pull** cord pulled to sound bell. **bell push** button pressed to ring electric bell. **give (person) a bell** *colloquial* telephone him or her.

■ *noun* **2** alarm, carillon, chime, knell, peal, ring, signal.

belladonna /belə'dɒnə/ *noun* **1** deadly nightshade. **2** drug obtained from this.

belle /bel/ *noun* **1** handsome woman. **2** reigning beauty.

belles-lettres /bel 'letr/ *plural noun* (also treated as *singular*) writings or studies of purely literary kind.

bellicose /'belɪkəʊs/ *adjective* eager to fight.

belligerent /bɪ'lɪdʒərənt/ *adjective* **1** engaged in war. **2** given to constant fighting; pugnacious. ● *noun* belligerent person or nation. □ **belligerence** *noun*.

■ *adjective* **1** fighting, hostile, militant, warring. **2** aggressive, antagonistic, argumentative, bellicose, bullying, combative, contentious, defiant, disputatious, fierce, hawkish, hostile, jingoistic, martial, militaristic, provocative, pugnacious, quarrelsome, unfriendly, violent, warlike, warmongering.

bellow /'beləʊ/ *verb* emit deep loud roar. ● *noun* bellowing sound.

bellows /'beləʊz/ *plural noun* (also treated as *singular*) **1** device for driving air into fire, organ, etc. **2** expandable part of camera etc.

belly /'belɪ/ *noun* (*plural* **-ies**) **1** cavity of body containing stomach, bowels, etc. **2** stomach. **3** front of body from waist to groin. **4** underside of animal. **5** cavity or bulging part of anything. ● *verb* (**-ies**, **-ied**) (often + *out*) swell, bulge. □ **bellyache** ● *noun colloquial* stomach pain. ● *verb slang* complain noisily or persistently. **belly button** *colloquial* navel. **belly dance** dance by woman (**belly dancer**) with voluptuous movements of belly. **belly laugh** loud unrestrained laugh.

bellyful *noun* **1** enough to eat. **2** *colloquial* more than one can tolerate.

belong /bɪ'lɒŋ/ *verb* **1** (+ *to*) be property of. **2** (+ *to*) be assigned to. **3** (+ *to*) be member of. **4** fit

socially. **5** be rightly placed or classified.

■ **1, 2** (*belong to*) be owned by, go with, pertain to, relate to. **3** (*belong to*) be affiliated with, be a member of, be connected with. **4** be at home, feel welcome, have a place.

belongings *plural noun* possessions, luggage. ■ chattels, effects, gear, goods, impedimenta, possessions, property, things.

beloved /bɪ'lʌvɪd/ *adjective* loved. ● *noun* beloved person.

below /bɪ'ləʊ/ *preposition* **1** under. **2** lower than. **3** less than. **4** of lower rank or importance etc. than. **5** unworthy of. ● *adverb* **1** at or to lower point or level. **2** further on in book etc.

belt *noun* **1** strip of leather etc. worn round waist or across chest. **2** continuous band in machinery. **3** distinct strip of colour etc. **4** zone, district. **5** *slang* heavy blow. ● *verb* **1** put belt round. **2** *slang* thrash. **3** *slang* move rapidly. □ **below the belt** unfair(ly). **belt out** *slang* sing or play (music) loudly. **belt up** **1** *slang* be quiet. **2** *colloquial* put on seat belt. **tighten one's belt** economize. **under one's belt** securely acquired.

■ *noun* **1** *literary* cincture, cummerbund, girdle, girth, sash, strap, waistband, *archaic* zone. **3** band, circle, line, loop, stretch, strip, swath. **4** area, district, tract, zone.

bemoan /bɪ'məʊn/ *verb* lament, complain about.

bemuse /bɪ'mjuːz/ *verb* (**-sing**) make (person) confused. □ **bemusement** *noun*.

■ befuddle, bewilder, confuse, mix up, muddle, perplex, puzzle, stupefy.

bench *noun* **1** long seat of wood or stone. **2** carpenter's or laboratory table. **3** (seat of) judge or magistrate. **4** judges and magistrates collectively. **5** law court. □ **benchmark** **1** surveyor's mark at point in line of levels. **2** standard, point of reference.

■ **1** form, pew, seat, settle. **2** counter, table, workbench, work table, worktop. **3** judge, magistrate. **5** court, courtroom, tribunal.

bend *verb* (*past & past participle* **bent** except in *bended knee*) **1** force into curve or angle. **2** be altered in this way. **3** incline from vertical; bow, stoop. **4** interpret or modify (rule) to suit oneself. **5** (force to) submit. ● *noun* **1** bending, curve. **2** bent part of thing. **3** (**the bends**) *colloquial* symptoms due to too rapid decompression under water. □ **round the bend** *colloquial* crazy, insane. □ **bendable** *adjective*.

■ *verb* **1, 2** arch, be flexible, bow, buckle, coil, contort, crook, curl, curve, deflect, distort, divert, flex, fold, give, loop, mould, refract, shape, turn, twist, warp, wind, yield. **3** bow, crouch, curtsy, duck, genuflect, kneel, lean, stoop. ● *noun* **1, 2** angle, arc, bow, corner, crank, crook, curvature, curve, loop, turn, turning, twist, zigzag. □ **round the bend** see MAD 1.

bender *noun slang* wild drinking spree.

bendy /'bendɪ/ *adjective colloquial* capable of bending; flexible.

beneath /bɪˈniːθ/ *preposition* **1** below, under. **2** unworthy of. ● *adverb* below, underneath.

Benedictine /benɪˈdɪktɪn/ *noun* **1** monk or nun of Order of St Benedict. **2** /-tiːn/ *proprietary term* kind of liqueur. ● *adjective* of St Benedict or his order.

benediction /benɪˈdɪkʃ(ə)n/ *noun* utterance of blessing. □ **benedictory** *adjective*.

benefaction /benɪˈfækʃ(ə)n/ *noun* **1** charitable gift. **2** doing good.

benefactor /ˈbenɪfæktə/ *noun* (*feminine* **benefactress**) person who has given financial or other help.

■ backer, donor, fairy godmother, patron, philanthropist, promoter, sponsor, supporter.

benefice /ˈbenɪfɪs/ *noun* living from a church office.

beneficent /bɪˈnefɪsənt/ *adjective* doing good; actively kind. □ **beneficence** *noun*.

beneficial /benɪˈfɪʃ(ə)l/ *adjective* advantageous. □ **beneficially** *adverb*.

■ advantageous, benign, constructive, favourable, fruitful, good, health-giving, healthy, helpful, improving, nourishing, nutritious, positive, productive, profitable, rewarding, salubrious, salutary, supportive, useful, valuable, wholesome.

beneficiary /benɪˈfɪʃərɪ/ *noun* (*plural* **-ies**) **1** receiver of benefits. **2** holder of church living.

■ **1** heir, heiress, inheritor, legatee, recipient, successor (*to title*).

benefit /ˈbenɪfɪt/ *noun* **1** advantage, profit. **2** payment made under insurance or social security. **3** performance or game etc. of which proceeds go to particular player or charity. ● *verb* (**-t-**; *US* **-tt-**) **1** do good to. **2** receive benefit. □ **benefit of the doubt** assumption of innocence rather than guilt.

■ *noun* **1** advantage, asset, blessing, boon, convenience, gain, good thing, help, privilege, prize, profit, service, use. **2** aid, allowance, assistance, *colloquial* dole, handout, grant, payment, social security, welfare. ● *verb* **1** advance, advantage, aid, assist, better, boost, do good to, enhance, further, help, improve, promote, serve. **2** gain, profit.

benevolent /bɪˈnevələnt/ *adjective* **1** wishing to do good; kind and helpful. **2** (of fund, society, etc.) charitable. □ **benevolence** *noun*.

■ **1** altruistic, beneficent, benign, caring, compassionate, considerate, friendly, generous, helpful, humane, humanitarian, kind, kind-hearted, kindly, liberal, magnanimous, merciful, philanthropic, supportive, sympathetic, unselfish, warm-hearted. **2** charitable, philanthropic.

Bengali /beŋˈɡɔːlɪ/ *noun* (*plural* **-s**) native or language of Bengal. ● *adjective* of Bengal.

benighted /bɪˈnaɪtɪd/ *adjective* intellectually or morally ignorant.

benign /bɪˈnaɪn/ *adjective* **1** kindly, gentle. **2** favourable, salutary. **3** *Medicine* mild, not malignant. □ **benignity** /bɪˈnɪɡnɪtɪ/ *noun*.

■ **1** benevolent, compassionate, gentle, harmless, kind, kind-hearted, kindly, merciful, mild, sympathetic, warm-hearted. **2** see FAVOURABLE 1, BENEFICIAL.

benignant /bɪˈnɪɡnənt/ *adjective* **1** kindly. **2** beneficial. □ **benignancy** *noun*.

bent *past & past participle* of BEND. ● *adjective* **1** curved or having angle. **2** *slang* dishonest. **3** (+ *on*) set on doing or having. ● *noun* **1** inclination, bias. **2** (+ *for*) talent for.

■ *adjective* **1** angled, arched, bowed, buckled, coiled, contorted, crooked, curved, distorted, folded, hunched, looped, twisted, warped. **2** corrupt, criminal, dishonest, immoral, untrustworthy, wicked. ● *noun* **1** see BIAS *noun* 1. **2** see APTITUDE.

benumb /bɪˈnʌm/ *verb* **1** make numb; deaden. **2** paralyse.

benzene /ˈbenziːn/ *noun* chemical got from coal tar and used as solvent.

benzine /ˈbenziːn/ *noun* spirit obtained from petroleum and used as cleaning agent.

benzoin /ˈbenzəʊɪn/ *noun* fragrant resin of E. Asian tree. □ **benzoic** /-ˈzəʊɪk/ *adjective*.

bequeath /bɪˈkwiːð/ *verb* **1** leave by will. **2** transmit to posterity.

■ *Law* devise, endow, hand down, leave, make over, pass on, settle, transmit, will.

bequest /bɪˈkwest/ *noun* bequeathing; thing bequeathed.

■ endowment, gift, inheritance, legacy, settlement.

berate /bɪˈreɪt/ *verb* (**-ting**) scold.

bereave /bɪˈriːv/ *verb* (**-ving**) (esp. as **bereaved** *adjective*) (often + *of*) deprive of relative, friend, etc., esp. by death. □ **bereavement** *noun*.

■ □ **bereavement** death, loss.

bereft /bɪˈreft/ *adjective* (+ *of*) deprived of.

■ (*bereft of*) deprived of, destitute of, devoid of, lacking (in), robbed of, wanting (in).

beret /ˈbereɪ/ *noun* round flat brimless cap of felt etc.

berg *noun* iceberg.

bergamot /ˈbɜːɡəmɒt/ *noun* **1** perfume from fruit of a dwarf orange tree. **2** an aromatic herb.

beriberi /berɪˈberɪ/ *noun* nervous disease caused by deficiency of vitamin B_1.

Bermuda shorts /bəˈmjuːdə/ *plural noun* close-fitting knee-length shorts.

berry /ˈberɪ/ *noun* (*plural* **-ies**) any small round juicy stoneless fruit.

berserk /bəˈzɜːk/ *adjective* (esp. after *go*) wild, frenzied.

■ beside oneself, crazed, crazy, demented, deranged, frantic, frenetic, frenzied, furious, infuriated, insane, mad, maniacal, rabid, violent, wild; (*go berserk*) see RAGE *verb* 1, RAMPAGE *verb*.

berth *noun* **1** sleeping place. **2** ship's place at wharf. **3** sea room. **4** *colloquial* situation, appointment. ● *verb* **1** moor (ship) in berth. **2** provide sleeping berth for. □ **give a wide berth to** stay away from.
■ *noun* **1** bed, bunk, hammock. **2** moorings.
● *verb* **1** dock, moor, tie up. □ **give a wide berth to** see AVOID 1.

beryl /'berɪl/ *noun* **1** transparent (esp. green) precious stone. **2** mineral species including this and emerald.

beryllium /bə'rɪlɪəm/ *noun* hard white metallic element.

beseech /bɪ'siːtʃ/ *verb* (*past & past participle* **besought** /-'sɔːt/ or **beseeched**) entreat; ask earnestly for.
■ ask, beg, entreat, implore, importune, plead, *literary* supplicate.

beset /bɪ'set/ *verb* (**-tt-**; *past & past participle* **beset**) **1** attack or harass persistently. **2** surround, hem in.

beside /bɪ'saɪd/ *preposition* **1** at side of; close to. **2** compared with. **3** irrelevant to. □ **beside oneself** frantic with anger or worry etc.

besides *preposition* in addition to; apart from.
● *adverb* also, as well.

besiege /bɪ'siːdʒ/ *verb* (**-ging**) **1** lay siege to. **2** crowd round eagerly. **3** assail with requests.
■ **1, 2** beleaguer, beset, blockade, cut off, encircle, encompass, hem in, isolate, lay siege to, surround. **3** assail, beleaguer, beset, harass, overwhelm, pester, *colloquial* plague.

besmirch /bɪ'smɜːtʃ/ *verb* soil, dishonour.

besom /'biːz(ə)m/ *noun* broom made of twigs.

besotted /bɪ'sɒtɪd/ *adjective* **1** infatuated. **2** stupefied.

besought *past & past participle* of BESEECH.

bespatter /bɪ'spætə/ *verb* **1** spatter all over. **2** defame.

bespeak /bɪ'spiːk/ *verb* (*past* **bespoke**; *past participle* **bespoken**) **1** engage beforehand. **2** order (goods). **3** be evidence of.

bespectacled /bɪ'spektək(ə)ld/ *adjective* wearing spectacles.

bespoke /bɪ'spəʊk/ *adjective* made to order.

best *adjective* (*superlative* of GOOD) most excellent. ● *adverb* (*superlative* of WELL¹) **1** in the best way. **2** to greatest degree. ● *noun* that which is best. ● *verb colloquial* defeat, outwit. □ **best man** bridegroom's chief attendant at wedding. **best-seller 1** book with large sale. **2** author of such book. **do one's best** do all one can.
■ *adjective* choicest, excellent, finest, first-class, foremost, incomparable, leading, matchless, optimum, outstanding, pre-eminent, superlative, supreme, top, unequalled, unrivalled, unsurpassed.

bestial /'bestɪəl/ *adjective* **1** brutish. **2** of or like beasts. □ **bestiality** /-'æl-/ *noun*.

■ **1** barbaric, beastly, brutal, brutish, callous, cruel, inhuman, savage, subhuman. **2** animal, beast-like, beastly.

bestiary /'bestɪərɪ/ *noun* (*plural* **-ies**) medieval treatise on beasts.

bestir /bɪ'stɜː/ *verb* (**-rr-**) (**bestir oneself**) exert or rouse oneself.

bestow /bɪ'stəʊ/ *verb* (+ *on, upon*) confer as gift. □ **bestowal** *noun*.
■ award, confer, donate, give, grant, present.

bestrew /bɪ'struː/ *verb* (*past participle* **bestrewed** or **bestrewn**) **1** strew. **2** lie scattered over.

bestride /bɪ'straɪd/ *verb* (**-ding**; *past* **bestrode**; *past participle* **bestridden**) **1** sit astride on. **2** stand astride over.

bet *verb* (**-tt-**; *past & past participle* **bet** or **betted**) risk one's money etc. against another's on result of event. ● *noun* **1** such arrangement. **2** sum of money bet.
■ *verb colloquial* chance, gamble, *slang* have a flutter, hazard, lay bets, *colloquial* punt, risk, speculate, stake, venture, wager. ● *noun* **1** *slang* flutter, gamble, punt, speculation, wager. **2** ante, stake, wager.

beta /'biːtə/ *noun* second letter of Greek alphabet (*B, β*). □ **beta-blocker** drug used to prevent unwanted stimulation of the heart in angina etc. **beta particle** fast-moving electron emitted by radioactive substance.

betake /bɪ'teɪk/ *verb* (**-king**; *past* **betook**; *past participle* **betaken**) (**betake oneself**) go.

betatron /'biːtətrɒn/ *noun* apparatus for accelerating electrons.

betel /'biːt(ə)l/ *noun* leaf chewed with betel-nut. □ **betel-nut** seed of tropical palm.

bête noire /beɪt 'nwɑː/ *noun* (*plural* **bêtes noires** same pronunciation) particularly disliked person or thing. [French]

bethink /bɪ'θɪŋk/ *verb* (*past & past participle* **bethought** /-'θɔːt/) (**bethink oneself**) *formal* **1** reflect, stop to think. **2** be reminded.

betide /bɪ'taɪd/ *verb* esp. *poetical* happen to. □ **woe betide (person)** misfortune will befall him or her.

betimes /bɪ'taɪmz/ *adverb literary* in good time; early.

betoken /bɪ'təʊkən/ *verb* be sign of.

betook *past* of BETAKE.

betray /bɪ'treɪ/ *verb* **1** be disloyal to (person, one's country, etc.). **2** give up or reveal treacherously. **3** reveal involuntarily; be evidence of. □ **betrayal** *noun*.
■ **1, 2** be a Judas to, be a traitor to, be false to, cheat, conspire against, deceive, denounce, desert, double-cross, give away, *slang* grass on, incriminate, inform against, inform on, jilt, let down, rat on, report, sell out, *slang* shop, tell tales about. **3** disclose, divulge, expose, give away, indicate, let out, let slip, manifest, reveal, show, tell.

betroth /bɪ'trəʊð/ *verb* (usually as **betrothed** *adjective*) bind with promise to marry. □ **betrothal** *noun*.

better /'betə/ *adjective* (*comparative* of GOOD) **1** more excellent. **2** partly or fully recovered from illness. ● *adverb* (*comparative* of WELL[1]) **1** in better manner. **2** to greater degree. ● *noun* better thing or person. ● *verb* **1** improve upon; surpass. **2** improve. □ **better half** *colloquial* one's wife or husband. **better off** in better (esp. financial) situation. **get the better of** defeat, outwit.

■ *adjective* **1** preferable, recommended, superior. **2** convalescent, cured, fitter, healed, healthier, improved, on the mend, progressing, recovered, recovering, restored. ● *verb* **1** see SURPASS 1. **2** see IMPROVE 1.

betterment *noun* improvement.

between /bɪ'twi:n/ *preposition* **1** in or into space or interval. **2** separating. **3** shared by. **4** to and from. **5** taking one or other of. ● *adverb* (also **in between**) between two or more points; between two extremes.

bevel /'bev(ə)l/ *noun* **1** slope from horizontal or vertical in carpentry etc. **2** sloping edge or surface. **3** tool for marking angles. ● *verb* (**-ll-**; *US* **-l-**) impart bevel to; slant.

beverage /'bevərɪdʒ/ *noun formal* drink.

bevvy /'bevɪ/ *slang noun* (*plural* **-ies**) drink. ● *verb* (**-ies**, **-ied**) drink.

bevy /'bevɪ/ *noun* (*plural* **-ies**) company, flock.

bewail /bɪ'weɪl/ *verb* wail over; mourn for.

beware /bɪ'weə/ *verb* (only in *imperative* or *infinitive*) **1** take heed. **2** (+ *of*) be cautious of.

■ **1** be alert, be careful, be cautious, be on one's guard, look out, take care, take heed, take precautions, watch out, watch one's step. **2** (*beware of*) avoid, guard against, heed, keep clear of, mind, shun, steer away from.

bewilder /bɪ'wɪldə/ *verb* perplex, confuse. □ **bewildering** *adjective*. **bewilderment** *noun*.

■ baffle, *colloquial* bamboozle, bemuse, confound, confuse, daze, disconcert, disorientate, distract, floor, *colloquial* flummox, mislead, muddle, mystify, perplex, puzzle, stump.

bewitch /bɪ'wɪtʃ/ *verb* **1** enchant, greatly delight. **2** cast spell on. □ **bewitching** *adjective*. **bewitchment** *noun*.

■ **1** captivate, charm, delight, enchant, enrapture, enthral, fascinate. **2** cast a spell on, charm, enchant, spellbind.

beyond /bɪ'jɒnd/ *preposition* **1** at or to further side of. **2** outside the range or understanding of. **3** more than. ● *adverb* **1** at or to further side. **2** further on. ● *noun* (**the beyond**) life after death. □ **back of beyond** very remote place.

bezel /'bez(ə)l/ *noun* **1** sloped edge of chisel etc. **2** oblique face of cut gem. **3** groove holding watch-glass or gem.

bezique /bɪ'zi:k/ *noun* card game for two.

biannual /baɪ'ænjʊəl/ *adjective* occurring etc. twice a year.

bias /'baɪəs/ *noun* **1** predisposition, prejudice. **2** distortion of statistical results. **3** edge cut obliquely across weave of fabric. **4** *Sport* bowl's curved course due to its lopsided form. ● *verb* (**-s-** or **-ss-**) **1** give bias to. **2** (esp. as **biased** *adjective*) prejudice; influence (usually unfairly). □ **bias binding** strip of fabric cut obliquely and used to bind edges.

■ *noun* **1** aptitude, bent, bigotry, favouritism, imbalance, inclination, injustice, leaning, liking, one-sidedness, partiality, partisanship, penchant, predilection, predisposition, preference, prejudice, proclivity, proneness, propensity, tendency, unfairness. ● *verb* **2** see INFLUENCE *verb*; (**biased**) bigoted, blinkered, distorted, emotive, influenced, interested, jaundiced, loaded, one-sided, partial, partisan, prejudiced, slanted, *derogatory* tendentious, unfair, unjust, warped.

biathlon /baɪ'æθlən/ *noun* athletic contest in skiing and shooting. □ **biathlete** *noun*.

bib *noun* **1** cloth put under child's chin while eating. **2** upper part of apron etc.

Bible /'baɪb(ə)l/ *noun* **1** Christian scriptures. **2** (**bible**) copy of these. **3** (**bible**) *colloquial* any authoritative book. □ **biblical** /'bɪb-/ *adjective*.

bibliography /bɪblɪ'ɒgrəfɪ/ *noun* (*plural* **-ies**) **1** list of books of any author, subject, etc. **2** history of books, their editions, etc. □ **bibliographer** *noun*. **bibliographical** /-ə'græf-/ *adjective*.

bibliophile /'bɪblɪəfaɪl/ *noun* collector of books; book-lover.

bibulous /'bɪbjʊləs/ *adjective* fond of or addicted to alcoholic drink.

bicameral /baɪ'kæmər(ə)l/ *adjective* having two legislative chambers.

bicarb /'baɪkɑːb/ *noun colloquial* bicarbonate of soda.

bicarbonate /baɪ'kɑːbənɪt/ *noun* **1** any acid salt of carbonic acid. **2** (in full **bicarbonate of soda**) compound used in cooking and as antacid.

bicentenary /baɪsen'ti:nərɪ/ *noun* (*plural* **-ies**) 200th anniversary.

bicentennial /baɪsen'tenɪəl/ *noun* bicentenary. ● *adjective* recurring every 200 years.

biceps /'baɪseps/ *noun* (*plural* same) muscle with double head or attachment, esp. that at front of upper arm.

bicker /'bɪkə/ *verb* quarrel, wrangle pettily.

bicuspid /baɪ'kʌspɪd/ *adjective* having two cusps. ● *noun* bicuspid tooth.

bicycle /'baɪsɪk(ə)l/ *noun* two-wheeled pedal-driven vehicle. ● *verb* (**-ling**) ride bicycle.

■ *noun colloquial* bike, cycle, *colloquial* push-bike.

bid *verb* (**-dd-**; *past* **bid**, *archaic* **bade** /bæd, beɪd/; *past participle* **bid**, *archaic* **bidden**) **1** make offer; make bid. **2** command, invite. **3** *literary* utter (greeting, farewell) to. **4** *Cards* state before play number of tricks intended. ● *noun* **1** act of bidding. **2** amount bid. **3** *colloquial* attempt, effort.

■ *verb* **1** offer, proffer, propose, tender. **2** see COMMAND *verb* 1. ● *noun* **1, 2** offer, price, proposal, proposition, tender. **3** attempt, *colloquial* crack, effort, endeavour, go, try, venture.

biddable *adjective* obedient, docile.

bidding *noun* command, invitation.

bide *verb* (**-ding**) *archaic* or *dialect* stay, remain. □ **bide one's time** wait for good opportunity.

bidet /'biːdeɪ/ *noun* low basin that one can sit astride to wash crotch area.

biennial /baɪ'enɪəl/ *adjective* **1** lasting 2 years. **2** recurring every 2 years. ● *noun* plant that flowers, fruits, and dies in second year.

bier /bɪə/ *noun* movable stand on which coffin or corpse rests.

biff *slang noun* smart blow. ● *verb* strike.

bifid /'baɪfɪd/ *adjective* divided by cleft into two parts.

bifocal /baɪ'fəʊk(ə)l/ *adjective* (of spectacle lenses) with two parts of different focal lengths. ● *noun* (in *plural*) bifocal spectacles.

bifurcate /'baɪfəkeɪt/ *verb* (**-ting**) divide into two branches; fork. □ **bifurcation** *noun*.

big *adjective* (**-gg-**) **1** large (in size, amount, intensity, etc.). **2** important; significant. **3** grown-up. **4** boastful. **5** *colloquial* ambitious. **6** *colloquial* generous. **7** (usually + *with*) advanced in pregnancy. ● *adverb colloquial* **1** in big manner. **2** with great effect; impressively. □ **Big Apple** *US slang* New York City. **Big Brother** seemingly benevolent dictator. **big business** large-scale commerce. **big end** end of connecting rod in engine, encircling crank-pin. **big-head** *colloquial* conceited person. **big-headed** *adjective*. **big-headedness** *noun*. **big-hearted** generous. **big name** famous person. **big shot** *colloquial* important person. **big time** *slang* highest rank among entertainers. **big top** main tent at circus. **bigwig** *colloquial* important person. **in a big way** *colloquial* with great enthusiasm. □ **biggish** *adjective*. **bigness** *noun*.

■ *adjective* **1** (*big thing, person, etc.*) above average, *slang* almighty, ample, broad, bulky, burly, capacious, colossal, commodious, considerable, elephantine, enormous, extensive, fat, formidable, gargantuan, generous, giant, gigantic, grand, great, gross, hearty (*appetite*), heavy, hefty, high, huge, *colloquial* jumbo, king-size, large, largish, lofty, long, mammoth, massive, mighty, monstrous, monumental, mountainous, overgrown, oversized, prodigious, roomy, sizeable, spacious, stupendous, substantial, swingeing (*increase*), tall, *colloquial* terrific, thick, *colloquial* thumping, *colloquial* tidy (*sum*), titanic, towering, *colloquial* tremendous, vast, voluminous, weighty, *colloquial* whacking, *colloquial* whopping, wide; (*big number*) see INFINITE. **2** great, important, influential, main, major, momentous, powerful, prime, principal, serious, significant.

bigamy /'bɪɡəmɪ/ *noun* (*plural* **-ies**) crime of making second marriage while first is still valid.

□ **bigamist** *noun*. **bigamous** *adjective*.

bight /baɪt/ *noun* **1** recess of coast; bay. **2** loop of rope.

bigot /'bɪɡət/ *noun* obstinate and intolerant adherent of creed or view. □ **bigoted** *adjective*. **bigotry** *noun*.

■ dogmatist, fanatic, zealot. □ **bigoted** biased, intolerant, one-sided, partial, prejudiced.

bijou /'biːʒuː/ *noun* (*plural* **-x** same pronunciation) jewel, trinket. ● *adjective* (**bijou**) small and elegant. [French]

bike *colloquial noun* bicycle; motorcycle. ● *verb* (**-king**) ride a bike. □ **biker** *noun*.

bikini /bɪ'kiːnɪ/ *noun* (*plural* **-s**) woman's brief two-piece bathing suit.

bilateral /baɪ'læt(ə)l/ *adjective* **1** of, on, or with two sides. **2** between two parties. □ **bilaterally** *adverb*.

bilberry /'bɪlbərɪ/ *noun* (*plural* **-ies**) **1** N. European heathland shrub. **2** its small dark blue edible berry.

bile *noun* **1** bitter fluid secreted by liver to aid digestion. **2** bad temper, peevishness.

bilge /bɪldʒ/ *noun* **1** nearly flat part of ship's bottom. **2** (in full **bilge-water**) foul water in bilge. **3** *slang* nonsense, rubbish.

bilharzia /bɪl'hɑːtsɪə/ *noun* disease caused by tropical parasitic flatworm.

biliary /'bɪlɪərɪ/ *adjective* of bile.

bilingual /baɪ'lɪŋɡw(ə)l/ *adjective* of, in, or speaking two languages.

bilious /'bɪlɪəs/ *adjective* **1** affected by disorder of the bile. **2** bad-tempered. □ **biliousness** *noun*.

bilk *verb slang* evade payment of; cheat.

bill[1] *noun* **1** statement of charges for goods, work done, etc. **2** draft of proposed law. **3** poster; leaflet. **4** programme of entertainment. **5** *US* banknote. ● *verb* **1** send statement of charges to. **2** announce; put in programme. **3** (+ *as*) advertise as. □ **bill of exchange** written order to pay sum on given date. **bill of fare** menu. **billposter**, **billsticker** person who pastes up advertisements on hoardings etc.

■ *noun* **1** account, invoice, statement, tally. **3** advertisement, broadsheet, bulletin, circular, handout, leaflet, notice, placard, poster, sheet.

bill[2] *noun* **1** beak (of bird). **2** narrow promontory. ● *verb* (of doves etc.) stroke bill with bill. □ **bill and coo** exchange caresses.

bill[3] *noun historical* weapon with hook-shaped blade.

billabong /'bɪləbɒŋ/ *noun Australian* branch of river forming backwater.

billboard *noun* large outdoor board for advertisements.

billet[1] /'bɪlɪt/ *noun* **1** place where soldier etc. is lodged. **2** *colloquial* appointment, job. ● *verb* (**-t-**) quarter (soldiers etc.).

billet[2] /'bɪlɪt/ *noun* **1** thick piece of firewood. **2** small metal bar.

billet-doux /ˌbɪlɪˈduː/ *noun* (*plural* **billets-doux** /-ˈduːz/) love letter.

billhook *noun* concave-edged pruning-instrument.

billiards /ˈbɪljədz/ *noun* game played with cues and 3 balls on cloth-covered table. □ **billiard ball, room, table, etc.** ones used for billiards.

billion /ˈbɪljən/ *noun* (*plural* same) **1** thousand million. **2** million million. **3** (**billions**) *colloquial* very large number. □ **billionth** *adjective & noun*.

billow /ˈbɪləʊ/ *noun* **1** wave. **2** any large mass. ● *verb* rise or move in billows. □ **billowy** *adjective*.
■ *verb* balloon, belly, bulge, fill out, heave, puff out, rise, roll, surge, swell, undulate.

billy[1] /ˈbɪlɪ/ *noun* (*plural* **-ies**) (in full **billycan**) *Australian* tin or enamel outdoor cooking pot.

billy[2] /ˈbɪlɪ/ *noun* (*plural* **-ies**) (in full **billy goat**) male goat.

bin *noun* large receptacle for rubbish or storage. □ **bin-liner** bag for lining rubbish bin. **binman** *colloquial* dustman.

binary /ˈbaɪnərɪ/ *adjective* **1** of two parts; dual. **2** of system using digits 0 and 1 to code information.

bind /baɪnd/ *verb* (*past & past participle* **bound** /baʊnd/) **1** tie or fasten tightly. **2** restrain. **3** (cause to) cohere. **4** compel; impose duty on. **5** edge with braid etc. **6** (often + *up*) put bandage etc. round. **7** fasten (pages of book) into cover. ● *noun colloquial* nuisance; restriction.
■ *verb* **1** attach, clamp, connect, fasten, hitch, hold together, join, lash, link, rope, secure, strap, tie, truss. **3** cohere, combine, consolidate, fuse, unify, unite, weld. **4** compel, constrain, force, necessitate, oblige, require. **6** bandage, cover, dress, encase, swathe, wrap.

binder *noun* **1** cover for loose papers. **2** substance that binds things together. **3** *historical* sheaf-binding machine. **4** bookbinder.

bindery *noun* (*plural* **-ies**) bookbinder's workshop.

binding *noun* **1** book cover. **2** braid etc. for edging. ● *adjective* obligatory.
■ *adjective* see COMPULSORY, FORMAL 5.

bindweed *noun* convolvulus.

binge /bɪndʒ/ *slang noun* bout of excessive eating, drinking, etc.; spree. ● *verb* (**-ging**) indulge in binge.

bingo /ˈbɪŋgəʊ/ *noun* gambling game in which each player marks off numbers on card as they are called.

binnacle /ˈbɪnək(ə)l/ *noun* case for ship's compass.

binocular /baɪˈnɒkjʊlə/ *adjective* for both eyes.

binoculars /bɪˈnɒkjʊləz/ *plural noun* instrument with lens for each eye, for viewing distant objects.

binomial /baɪˈnəʊmɪəl/ *noun* algebraic expression of sum or difference of two terms. ● *adjective* consisting of two terms.

bio- *combining form* **1** biological. **2** life.

biochemistry /baɪəʊˈkemɪstrɪ/ *noun* chemistry of living organisms. □ **biochemical** *adjective*. **biochemist** *noun*.

biodegradable /baɪəʊdɪˈgreɪdəb(ə)l/ *adjective* able to be decomposed by bacteria or other living organisms.

biography /baɪˈɒgrəfɪ/ *noun* (*plural* **-ies**) written life of person. □ **biographer** *noun*. **biographical** /-əˈgræf-/ *adjective*.
■ autobiography, life, life story, memoirs, recollections.

biological /baɪəˈlɒdʒɪk(ə)l/ *adjective* of biology; of living organisms. □ **biological warfare** use of bacteria etc. to spread disease among enemy. □ **biologically** *adverb*.

biology /baɪˈɒlədʒɪ/ *noun* study of living organisms. □ **biologist** *noun*.

bionic /baɪˈɒnɪk/ *adjective* having electronically operated body parts.

biorhythm /ˈbaɪəʊrɪð(ə)m/ *noun* biological cycle thought to affect person's physical or mental state.

biosphere /ˈbaɪəʊsfɪə/ *noun* earth's crust and atmosphere containing life.

bipartite /baɪˈpɑːtaɪt/ *adjective* **1** of two parts. **2** involving two parties.

biped /ˈbaɪped/ *noun* two-footed animal. ● *adjective* two-footed.

biplane /ˈbaɪpleɪn/ *noun* aeroplane with two pairs of wings, one above the other.

birch *noun* **1** tree with thin peeling bark. **2** bundle of birch twigs used for flogging. ● *verb* flog with birch.

bird *noun* **1** feathered vertebrate with two wings and two feet. **2** *slang* young woman. □ **a bird in the hand** something secured or certain. **birdlime** sticky stuff spread to catch birds. **bird of passage 1** migratory bird. **2** person who travels habitually. **bird of prey** one hunting animals for food. **birdseed** seeds as food for caged birds. **bird's-eye view** general view from above. **birds of a feather** similar people. **bird table** platform on which food for wild birds is placed.

birdie /ˈbɜːdɪ/ *noun* **1** *colloquial* little bird. **2** *Golf* hole played in one under par.

biretta /bɪˈretə/ *noun* square cap of RC priest.

Biro /ˈbaɪərəʊ/ *noun* (*plural* **-s**) *proprietary term* kind of ballpoint pen.

birth *noun* **1** emergence of young from mother's body. **2** origin, beginning. **3** ancestry; inherited position. □ **birth control** prevention of undesired pregnancy. **birthday** anniversary of birth. **birthmark** unusual mark on body from birth. **birth rate** number of live births per thousand of population per year. **birthright** rights belonging to one by birth. **give birth** bear child, young, etc. **give birth to 1** produce (young). **2** originate, found.

■ **1** childbirth, confinement, delivery, labour, nativity, *formal* parturition. **2** see BEGINNING 1,2. **3** ancestry, background, blood, breeding, derivation, descent, extraction, family, genealogy, line, lineage, parentage, pedigree, race, stock, strain. □ **give birth to 1** bear, breed, bring forth, drop, produce. **2** begin, develop, engender, found, generate, originate, produce, start, yield.

birthplace *noun* place where person was born.

biscuit /'bɪskɪt/ *noun* **1** flat thin unleavened cake, usually crisp and sweet. **2** fired unglazed pottery. **3** light brown colour.

bisect /baɪ'sekt/ *verb* divide into two (usually equal) parts. □ **bisection** *noun.* **bisector** *noun.*
■ cross, cut in half, divide, halve, intersect.

bisexual /baɪ'seksjʊəl/ *adjective* **1** feeling or involving sexual attraction to members of both sexes. **2** hermaphrodite. ● *noun* bisexual person. □ **bisexuality** /-'æl-/ *noun.*

bishop /'bɪʃəp/ *noun* **1** senior clergyman usually in charge of diocese. **2** mitre-shaped chess piece.

bishopric /'bɪʃəprɪk/ *noun* office or diocese of bishop.

bismuth /'bɪzməθ/ *noun* **1** reddish-white metallic element. **2** compound of it used medicinally.

bison /'baɪs(ə)n/ *noun* (*plural* same) wild ox.

bisque¹ /biːsk/ *noun* rich soup.

bisque² /bɪsk/ *noun* advantage of one free point or stroke in certain games.

bisque³ /bɪsk/ *noun* fired unglazed pottery.

bistre /'bɪstə/ *noun* brown pigment made from soot.

bistro /'biːstrəʊ/ *noun* (*plural* -s) small informal restaurant.

bit¹ *noun* **1** small piece or amount. **2** short time or distance. **3** mouthpiece of bridle. **4** cutting part of tool etc. □ **bit by bit** gradually.
■ **1** atom, bite, chip, crumb, dollop, fraction, fragment, gobbet, grain, helping, iota, modicum, morsel, mouthful, part, particle, piece, portion, sample, scrap, section, segment, share, slice, snippet, soupçon, speck, *colloquial* spot, taste, titbit, trace. **2** flash, instant, *colloquial* jiffy, minute, moment, *colloquial* second, *colloquial* tick, time, while.

bit² *past of* BITE.

bit³ *noun Computing* unit of information expressed as choice between two possibilities.

bitch /bɪtʃ/ *noun* **1** female dog, fox, or wolf. **2** *offensive slang* spiteful woman. ● *verb colloquial* **1** speak spitefully. **2** grumble.

bitchy *adjective slang* spiteful. □ **bitchily** *adverb.* **bitchiness** *noun.*

bite *verb* (-ting; *past* bit; *past participle* bitten) **1** nip or cut into or off with teeth. **2** sting. **3** penetrate, grip. **4** accept bait. **5** be harsh in effect, esp. intentionally. ● *noun* **1** act of biting. **2** wound so made. **3** small amount to eat. **4** pungency. **5** incisiveness. □ **bite the dust** *slang* **1** die. **2** fail.

■ *verb* **1** champ, chew, crunch, gnaw, masticate, munch, nibble, nip, snap, tear at. **2** pierce, sting. **3** grip, hold. ● *noun* **1, 2** nip, pinch, sting. **3** bit, morsel, mouthful, nibble, snack, taste.

bitter /'bɪtə/ *adjective* **1** having sharp pungent taste; not sweet. **2** causing pain or sorrow. **3** showing or feeling resentment; harsh, virulent. **4** piercingly cold. ● *noun* **1** bitter beer, strongly flavoured with hops. **2** (in *plural*) liquor with bitter flavour, esp. of wormwood. □ **bitterly** *adverb.* **bitterness** *noun.*
■ *adjective* **1** acid, acrid, harsh, sharp, sour, unpleasant. **2** distasteful, distressing, galling, hateful, heartbreaking, painful, poignant, sorrowful, unhappy, unwelcome, upsetting. **3** acerbic, acrimonious, angry, cruel, cynical, embittered, envious, harsh, hostile, jaundiced, jealous, malicious, rancorous, resentful, savage, sharp, spiteful, stinging, vicious, violent, virulent, waspish. **4** biting, cold, fierce, freezing, *colloquial* perishing, piercing, raw.

bittern /'bɪt(ə)n/ *noun* wading bird of heron family.

bitty *adjective* (-ier, -iest) made up of bits.

bitumen /'bɪtjʊmɪn/ *noun* tarlike mixture of hydrocarbons derived from petroleum. □ **bituminous** /bɪ'tjuːmɪnəs/ *adjective.*

bivalve /'baɪvælv/ *noun* aquatic mollusc with hinged double shell. ● *adjective* with such a shell.

bivouac /'bɪvʊæk/ *noun* temporary encampment without tents. ● *verb* (-ck-) make, or camp in, bivouac.

bizarre /bɪ'zɑː/ *adjective* **1** strange in appearance or effect. **2** grotesque. □ **bizarreness** *noun.*
■ curious, eccentric, fantastic, freakish, grotesque, odd, outlandish, outré, peculiar, strange, surreal, *colloquial* weird.

blab *verb* (-bb-) talk or tell foolishly or indiscreetly.

black *adjective* **1** very dark; having no colour from absence or complete absorption of light. **2** (**Black**) of human group with dark skin, esp. African. **3** heavily overcast. **4** angry, gloomy. **5** sinister, wicked. **6** declared untouchable by workers in dispute. ● *noun* **1** black colour, paint, clothes, etc. **2** (player using) darker pieces in chess etc. **3** (of tea or coffee) without milk. **4** (**Black**) member of dark-skinned race, esp. African. ● *verb* **1** make black. **2** declare (goods etc.) 'black'. □ **black and blue** badly bruised. **black and white 1** not in colour. **2** comprising only opposite extremes. **3** (after *in*) in print. **black art** (after *the*) black magic. **blackball** exclude from club, society, etc. **black beetle** common cockroach. **black belt** (holder of) highest grade of proficiency in judo, karate, etc. **black box** flight recorder. **black comedy** comedy presenting tragedy in comic terms. **black eye** bruised skin round eye. **blackfly** kind of aphid. **Black Forest gateau** chocolate sponge with cherries and whipped cream. **blackhead** black-topped pimple. **black hole** region of space from which matter and radiation cannot escape.

black ice thin hard transparent ice. **blacklead** graphite. **blackleg** *derogatory* person refusing to join strike etc. **black magic** magic supposed to invoke evil spirits. **Black Maria** *slang* police van. **black mark** mark of discredit. **black market** illicit traffic in rationed, prohibited, or scarce commodities. **black marketeer** person who trades in the black market. **Black Mass** travesty of Mass in worship of Satan. **black out 1** effect blackout on. **2** undergo blackout. **blackout 1** temporary loss of consciousness or memory. **2** loss of electric power, radio reception, etc. **3** compulsory darkness as precaution against air raids. **black pudding** sausage of blood, suet, etc. **Black Rod** chief usher of House of Lords. **black sheep** disreputable member. **blackshirt** *historical* Fascist. **black spot** place of danger or trouble. **blackthorn** thorny shrub bearing white flowers and sloes. **black tie** man's formal evening dress. **black velvet** mixture of stout and champagne. **black widow** venomous spider of which female devours male. **in the black** in credit or surplus. □ **blackness** *noun*.

■ *adjective* **1** blackish, coal-black, dark, ebony, inky, jet, jet-black, moonless, pitch-black, pitch-dark, raven, *esp. poetical* sable, sooty, starless, unlit. **3** dark, dusky, funereal, gloomy, murky, overcast. ● *verb* **2** see BLACKLIST *verb*. □ **blackleg** *colloquial derogatory* scab, strikebreaker, traitor.

blackberry *noun* (*plural* **-ies**) dark edible fruit of bramble.

blackbird *noun* European songbird.

blackboard *noun* board for chalking on in classroom etc.

blackcurrant *noun* **1** small black fruit. **2** shrub on which it grows.

blacken *verb* **1** make or become black. **2** slander.

blackguard /ˈblæɡɑːd/ *noun* villain, scoundrel. □ **blackguardly** *adjective*.

blacking *noun* black polish for boots and shoes.

blacklist *noun* list of people etc. in disfavour. ● *verb* put on blacklist.

■ *verb* ban, bar, black, blackball, boycott, debar, disallow, exclude, ostracize, preclude, proscribe, put an embargo on, repudiate, snub, veto.

blackmail *noun* **1** extortion of payment in return for silence. **2** use of threats or pressure. ● *verb* extort money from (person) thus. □ **blackmailer** *noun*.

blacksmith *noun* smith working in iron.

bladder /ˈblædə/ *noun* sac in humans and other animals, esp. that holding urine.

blade *noun* **1** cutting part of knife etc. **2** razor blade. **3** flat part of oar, spade, propeller, etc. **4** flat narrow leaf of grass and cereals. **5** flat bone in shoulder. **6** *poetical* sword.
■ **6** see SWORD.

blame *verb* (**-ming**) **1** assign fault or responsibility to. **2** (+ *on*) assign responsibility for (error etc.) to. ● *noun* **1** responsibility for bad result. **2**

blaming; attributing of responsibility. □ **blameable** *adjective* (*US* also **blamable**). **blameless** *adjective*.

■ *verb* **1** accuse, admonish, censure, charge, *archaic* chide, condemn, criticize, denounce, hold responsible, incriminate, rebuke, *formal* reprehend, reprimand, reproach, *formal* reprove, round on, scold, tax, upbraid. ● *noun* **1** accountability, culpability, fault, guilt, liability, onus, responsibility. **2** accusation, castigation, censure, charge, complaint, condemnation, criticism, imputation, incrimination, *slang* rap, recrimination, reprimand, reproach, *formal* reproof, *colloquial* stick, stricture. □ **blameless** faultless, guiltless, innocent, irreproachable, moral, unimpeachable, upright.

blameworthy *adjective* deserving blame. □ **blameworthiness** *noun*.

blanch /blɑːntʃ/ *verb* **1** make or grow pale. **2** peel (almonds etc.) by scalding. **3** immerse briefly in boiling water. **4** whiten (plant) by depriving it of light.

blancmange /bləˈmɒndʒ/ *noun* sweet opaque jelly of flavoured cornflour and milk.

bland *adjective* **1** mild; insipid, tasteless. **2** gentle, suave. □ **blandly** *adverb*.

■ **1** banal, boring, characterless, dull, flat, insipid, mild, nondescript, soft, soothing, tasteless, trite, unappetizing, unexciting, uninspiring, uninteresting, vapid, watery, weak, *colloquial* wishy-washy. **2** affable, amiable, calm, gentle, mild, smooth, suave.

blandishment /ˈblændɪʃmənt/ *noun* (usually in *plural*) flattering attention; cajolery.

blank *adjective* **1** not written or printed on. **2** (of form etc.) not filled in. **3** (of space) empty. **4** plain, unadorned. **5** without interest, result, or expression. ● *noun* **1** space to be filled up in form etc. **2** blank cartridge. **3** empty space or surface. **4** dash written in place of word. □ **blank cartridge** one without bullet. **blank cheque** one with amount left for payee to fill in. **blank verse** unrhymed verse, esp. iambic pentameters. □ **blankly** *adverb*.

■ *adjective* **1, 2** clean, unfilled, unmarked, unused. **3, 4** bare, clear, empty, plain, spotless, unadorned, void. **5** apathetic, baffled, baffling, dead, deadpan, emotionless, expressionless, featureless, glazed, immobile, impassive, inane, inscrutable, lifeless, poker-faced, uncomprehending, unresponsive, vacant, vacuous. ● *noun* **1** box, break, gap, line, space. **2** emptiness, nothingness, vacuity, vacuum, void.

blanket /ˈblæŋkɪt/ *noun* **1** large esp. woollen sheet as bed-covering etc. **2** thick covering layer. ● *adjective* general; covering all cases or classes. ● *verb* (**-t-**) cover (as) with blanket. □ **blanket stitch** stitch used to finish edges of blanket etc.

blare *verb* (**-ring**) **1** sound or utter loudly. **2** make sound of trumpet. ● *noun* blaring sound.

blarney /ˈblɑːnɪ/ *noun* cajoling talk; flattery. ● *verb* (**-eys, -eyed**) flatter, use blarney.

blasé /'blɑːzeɪ/ *adjective* bored or indifferent, esp. through familiarity.

blaspheme /blæs'fiːm/ *verb* (**-ming**) **1** treat religious name or subject irreverently. **2** talk irreverently about.

■ curse, execrate, profane, swear.

blasphemy /'blæsfəmɪ/ *noun* (*plural* **-ies**) (instance of) blaspheming. □ **blasphemous** *adjective*.

■ □ **blasphemous** disrespectful, godless, impious, irreligious, irreverent, profane, sacrilegious, sinful, ungodly, wicked.

blast /blɑːst/ *noun* **1** strong gust. **2** explosion. **3** destructive wave of air from this. **4** loud note from wind instrument, car horn, whistle, etc. **5** *colloquial* severe reprimand. ● *verb* **1** blow up with explosive. **2** (of wind) blow fiercely. **3** blight, destroy; curse. **4** (cause to) make explosive sound. **5** *colloquial* reprimand severely. **6** *colloquial* shoot; shoot at. ● *interjection* damn. □ **blast furnace** one for smelting with compressed hot air driven in. **blast off** (of rocket) take off from launching site. □ **blast-off** *noun*.

■ *noun* **1** gale, gust, wind. **2, 3** see EXPLOSION 1–2. **4** blare, din, noise, racket, roar, sound. ● *verb* **1** see EXPLODE 1,2. □ **blast off** see LAUNCH¹ *verb* 2.

blasted *colloquial adjective* annoying. ● *adverb* extremely.

blatant /'bleɪt(ə)nt/ *adjective* flagrant, unashamed. □ **blatantly** *adverb*.

■ apparent, barefaced, bold, brazen, conspicuous, evident, flagrant, glaring, obtrusive, obvious, open, overt, shameless, stark, unconcealed, undisguised, unmistakable, visible.

blather /'blæðə/ *noun* (also **blether** /'bleðə/) foolish talk. ● *verb* talk foolishly.

blaze¹ *noun* **1** bright flame or fire. **2** violent outburst of passion. **3** bright display or light. ● *verb* (**-zing**) **1** burn or shine brightly or fiercely. **2** burn with excitement etc. □ **blaze away** shoot continuously.

■ *noun* **1** conflagration, fire, flame, holocaust, inferno. **2** flare-up, outburst, rush, surge. ● *verb* **1** burn, flame, flare, shine. **2** burn, erupt, flame, flare.

blaze² *noun* white mark on face of horse or chipped in bark of tree. ● *verb* (**-zing**) mark (tree, path) with blaze(s).

blazer *noun* jacket without matching trousers, esp. lightweight and part of uniform.

blazon /'bleɪz(ə)n/ *verb* **1** proclaim. **2** describe or paint (coat of arms). □ **blazonry** *noun*.

bleach *verb* whiten in sunlight or by chemical process. ● *noun* bleaching substance or process.

■ *verb* blanch, discolour, etiolate, fade, lighten, pale, peroxide (*hair*), whiten.

bleak *adjective* **1** exposed, windswept. **2** dreary, grim. □ **bleakness** *noun*.

■ **1** bare, barren, blasted, chilly, cold, desolate, exposed, windswept, wintry. **2** cheerless, comfortless, depressing, dismal, dreary, grim, hopeless, joyless, sombre, uncomfortable, unpromising.

bleary /'blɪərɪ/ *adjective* (**-ier**, **-iest**) **1** dim-sighted. **2** blurred. □ **bleary-eyed** having dim sight.

■ **2** blurred, blurry, cloudy, dim, filmy, fogged, foggy, fuzzy, hazy, indistinct, misty, murky, obscured, smeary, unclear, watery.

bleat *verb* **1** utter cry of sheep, goat, etc. **2** speak plaintively. ● *noun* bleating cry.

bleed *verb* (*past & past participle* **bled**) **1** emit blood. **2** draw blood from. **3** *colloquial* extort money from.

bleep *noun* intermittent high-pitched sound. ● *verb* **1** make bleep. **2** summon by bleep.

bleeper *noun* small electronic device alerting person to message by bleeping.

blemish /'blemɪʃ/ *noun* flaw, defect, stain. ● *verb* spoil, mark, stain.

■ *noun* blot, blotch, defect, deformity, disfigurement, eyesore, fault, flaw, imperfection, mark, mess, scar, smudge, speck, spot, stain. ● *verb* deface, disfigure, flaw, mar, mark, scar, spoil, stain, tarnish.

blench *verb* flinch, quail.

blend *verb* **1** mix (various sorts) into required sort. **2** become one. **3** mingle intimately. ● *noun* mixture.

■ *verb* **1** beat, combine, mix, stir together, whip, whisk. **2** amalgamate, coalesce, combine, compound, fuse, harmonize, integrate, merge, synthesize, unite. **3** *literary* commingle, intermingle, intermix, mingle. ● *noun* alloy, amalgam, amalgamation, combination, composite, compound, concoction, fusion, *mélange*, mix, mixture, synthesis, union.

blender *noun* machine for liquidizing or chopping food.

blenny /'blenɪ/ *noun* (*plural* **-ies**) spiny-finned sea fish.

bless *verb* (*past & past participle* **blessed**, *poetical* **blest**) **1** ask God to look favourably on. **2** consecrate. **3** glorify (God). **4** thank. **5** make happy.

■ **2** anoint, consecrate, dedicate, grace, hallow, make sacred, ordain, sanctify. **3** adore, exalt, extol, glorify, *archaic* magnify, praise.

blessed /'blesɪd/ *adjective* **1** holy. **2** *euphemistic* cursed. **3** *RC Church* beatified. **4** happy, fortunate. □ **blessedness** *noun*.

■ **1** adored, divine, hallowed, holy, revered, sacred, sanctified. **4** see HAPPY 1–2.

blessing *noun* **1** invocation of divine favour. **2** grace said at meals. **3** approval. **4** benefit, advantage.

■ **1** benediction, consecration, prayer. **2** grace, prayer. **3** approbation, approval, backing, concurrence, consent, leave, permission, sanction, support. **4** advantage, asset, benefit, boon, comfort, convenience, godsend, help.

blether = BLATHER.

blew *past* of BLOW¹.

blight /blaɪt/ *noun* **1** disease of plants caused by insects or fungi. **2** insect or fungus causing such disease. **3** harmful or destructive force. ● *verb* **1** affect with blight. **2** spoil, destroy.

■ *noun* **1** canker, mildew, rot, rust. **3** affliction, ailment, bane, cancer, canker, curse, decay, disease, evil, illness, infestation, misfortune, pestilence, plague, pollution, scourge, sickness, trouble. ● *verb* **2** see SPOIL *verb* 1,2.

blighter *noun colloquial* annoying person.

blimey /'blaɪmɪ/ *interjection slang: expressing surprise.*

blimp *noun* **1** small non-rigid airship. **2** (also **(Colonel) Blimp**) reactionary person.

blind /blaɪnd/ *adjective* **1** without sight. **2** without adequate foresight, discernment, or information. **3** (often + *to*) unwilling or unable to appreciate (a factor). **4** not governed by purpose. **5** reckless. **6** concealed. **7** closed at one end. ● *verb* **1** deprive of sight or judgement. **2** deceive. ● *noun* **1** screen for window. **2** thing used to hide truth. **3** obstruction to sight or light. ● *adverb* blindly. □ **blind date** *colloquial* date between two people who have not met before. **blind man's buff** game in which blindfold player tries to catch others. **blind spot 1** spot on retina insensitive to light. **2** area where vision or judgement fails. **blindworm** slow-worm. **turn a blind eye to** pretend not to notice; disregard. □ **blindly** *adverb*. **blindness** *noun*.

■ *adjective* **1** blinded, eyeless, sightless, unseeing, visually handicapped. **2** blinkered, heedless, ignorant, inattentive, indifferent, indiscriminate, insensible, insensitive, irrational, mindless, oblivious, prejudiced, unaware, unobservant, unreasoning. ● *verb* **1** dazzle, make blind. **2** see DECEIVE 1. ● *noun* **1** awning, cover, curtain, screen, shade, shutters.

blindfold *verb* cover eyes of (person) with tied cloth etc. ● *noun* cloth etc. so used. ● *adjective & adverb* **1** with eyes covered. **2** without due care.

blink *verb* **1** shut and open eyes quickly. **2** (often + *back*) prevent (tears) by blinking. **3** shine unsteadily, flicker. ● *noun* **1** act of blinking. **2** momentary gleam. □ **blink at** ignore, shirk. **on the blink** *slang* (of machine etc.) out of order.

■ *verb* **3** coruscate, flash, flicker, flutter, gleam, glimmer, shimmer, sparkle, twinkle.

blinker *noun* (usually in *plural*) either of screens on bridle preventing horse from seeing sideways. ● *verb* **1** obscure with blinkers. **2** (as **blinkered** *adjective*) prejudiced, narrow-minded.

blinking *adjective & adverb slang: expressing mild annoyance.*

blip *noun* **1** minor deviation or error. **2** quick

popping sound. **3** small image on radar screen.

bliss *noun* **1** perfect joy. **2** being in heaven. □ **blissful** *adjective*. **blissfully** *adverb*.

■ blessedness, delight, ecstasy, euphoria, felicity, gladness, glee, happiness, heaven, joy, nirvana, paradise, pleasure, rapture.

blister /'blɪstə/ *noun* **1** small bubble on skin filled with watery fluid. **2** any swelling resembling this. ● *verb* **1** become covered with blisters. **2** raise blister on.

blithe /blaɪð/ *adjective* **1** *poetical* cheerful, happy. **2** carefree, casual. □ **blithely** *adverb*.

blithering /'blɪðərɪŋ/ *adjective colloquial* **1** utter, hopeless. **2** contemptible.

blitz /blɪts/ *colloquial noun* intensive (esp. aerial) attack. ● *verb* inflict blitz on.

blizzard /'blɪzəd/ *noun* severe snowstorm.

bloat *verb* **1** inflate, swell. **2** (as **bloated** *adjective*) puffed up, swollen.

■ **2** (**bloated**) dilated, distended, enlarged, inflated, puffy, swollen.

bloater *noun* herring cured by salting and smoking.

blob *noun* small drop or spot.

bloc *noun* group of governments etc. sharing some common purpose.

block *noun* **1** solid piece of hard material. **2** large building, esp. when subdivided. **3** group of buildings surrounded by streets. **4** obstruction. **5** large quantity as a unit. **6** piece of wood or metal engraved for printing. ● *verb* **1** obstruct (passage etc.); impede. **2** restrict use of. **3** stop (cricket ball) with bat. □ **block and tackle** system of pulleys and ropes used for lifting. **blockboard** board with core of wooden strips. **blockbuster** *slang* very successful film, book, etc. **blockhead** stupid person. **block capitals, letters** separate capital letters. **block out** shut out (light, noise, view, etc.). **block up 1** shut in. **2** fill (window etc.) in. **block vote** vote proportional in size to number of people voter represents. **mental block** mental inability due to subconscious factors.

■ *noun* **1** bar, brick, cake, chock, chunk, hunk, ingot, lump, mass, piece, slab. **4** see BLOCKAGE. ● *verb* **1** (*block a passage*) bar, barricade, bung up, choke, clog, close off, congest, constrict, dam, fill, jam, obstruct, plug, shut off, stop up; (*block a plan*) deter, halt, hamper, hinder, hold back, impede, prevent, prohibit, resist, scotch, stonewall, stop, thwart.

blockade /blɒ'keɪd/ *noun* surrounding or blocking of place by enemy. ● *verb* (**-ding**) subject to blockade.

blockage *noun* obstruction.

■ barrier, block, bottleneck, congestion, constriction, hindrance, impediment, jam, obstacle, obstruction, resistance, stoppage.

bloke *noun slang* man, fellow.

blond (of woman, usually **blonde**) *adjective* light-coloured; fair-haired. ● *noun* blond person.

■ *adjective* bleached, fair, flaxen, golden, light, platinum, silvery, yellow.

blood /blʌd/ *noun* **1** fluid, usually red, circulating in arteries and veins of animals. **2** killing, bloodshed. **3** passion, temperament. **4** race, descent. **5** relationship. ● *verb* **1** give first taste of blood to (hound). **2** initiate (person). □ **bad blood** ill feeling. **blood bank** store of blood for transfusion. **bloodbath** massacre. **blood count** number of corpuscles in blood. **blood-curdling** horrifying. **blood donor** giver of blood for transfusion. **blood group** any of types of human blood. **bloodhound** large keen-scented dog used for tracking. **bloodletting** surgical removal of blood. **blood orange** red-fleshed orange. **blood poisoning** diseased condition due to micro-organisms in blood. **blood pressure** pressure of blood in arteries. **blood relation** one related by birth. **bloodshed** killing. **bloodshot** (of eyeball) inflamed. **blood sport** one involving killing of animals. **bloodstain** discoloration caused by blood. **bloodstained 1** stained with blood. **2** guilty of bloodshed. **bloodstream** circulating blood. **bloodsucker 1** leech. **2** extortioner. **bloodthirsty** eager for bloodshed. **bloodthirstiness** eagerness for bloodshed. **blood vessel** vein, artery, or capillary carrying blood.

■ □ **bloodshed** bloodletting, butchery, carnage, killing, murder, slaughter, slaying, violence. **bloodthirsty** barbaric, brutal, cruel, feral, ferocious, fierce, homicidal, inhuman, murderous, pitiless, ruthless, *colloquial* sadistic, sanguinary, savage, vicious, violent, warlike.

bloodless *adjective* **1** without blood or bloodshed. **2** unemotional. **3** pale.

bloody *adjective* (**-ier, -iest**) **1** of or like blood. **2** running or stained with blood. **3** involving bloodshed, cruel. **4** *coarse slang* annoying. **5** *coarse slang* very great. ● *adverb coarse slang* extremely. ● *verb* (**-ies, -ied**) stain with blood. □ **bloody-minded** *colloquial* deliberately uncooperative.

■ *adjective* **2** bleeding, bloodstained, raw. **3** bloodthirsty, brutal, cruel, gory, sanguinary.

bloom /bluːm/ *noun* **1** flower; flowering state. **2** prime; freshness. **3** fine powder on fruit etc. ● *verb* **1** bear flowers; be in flower. **2** flourish.

■ *noun* **1** blossom, bud, floret, flower. **2** beauty, blush, flush, glow, prime. ● *verb* **1** blossom, bud, burgeon, come out, flower, grow, open, sprout. **2** be healthy, blossom, burgeon, develop, flourish, prosper, thrive.

bloomer[1] *noun slang* blunder.

bloomer[2] *noun* long loaf with diagonal marks.

bloomers *plural noun colloquial* woman's long loose knickers.

blooming *adjective* **1** flourishing, healthy. **2** *slang* annoying. **3** *slang* very great. ● *adverb slang* extremely.

blossom /'blɒsəm/ *noun* **1** flower. **2** mass of flowers on tree. ● *verb* **1** open into flower. **2** flourish.

blot *noun* **1** spot of ink etc. **2** disgraceful act. **3** blemish, ugliness. ● *verb* (**-tt-**) **1** make blot on; stain. **2** dry with blotting paper. □ **blot one's copybook** damage one's reputation. **blot out 1** obliterate. **2** obscure. **blotting paper** absorbent paper for drying wet ink.

■ *noun* **1** blob, blotch, mark, smear, smirch, smudge, *colloquial* splodge, spot, stain. **3** blemish, defect, eyesore, fault, flaw. ● *verb* **1** bespatter, blemish, blotch, blur, disfigure, mar, mark, smudge, spoil, spot, stain. □ **blot out 1** see OBLITERATE. **blot one's copybook** see MISBEHAVE.

blotch *noun* **1** inflamed patch on skin. **2** irregular patch of colour. □ **blotchy** *adjective* (**-ier, -iest**).

■ □ **blotchy** blemished, brindled, discoloured, inflamed, marked, patchy, smudged, spotty, streaked, uneven.

blotter *noun* device holding blotting paper.

blouse /blaʊz/ *noun* **1** woman's shirtlike garment. **2** type of military jacket.

blow[1] /bləʊ/ *verb* (*past* **blew** /bluː/; *past participle* **blown**) **1** send directed air current esp. from mouth. **2** drive or be driven by blowing. **3** move as wind does. **4** sound (wind instrument). **5** (*past participle* **blowed**) *slang* curse, confound. **6** clear (nose) by forceful breath. **7** pant. **8** make or shape by blowing. **9** break or burst suddenly. **10** (cause to) break electric circuit. **11** *slang* squander. ● *noun* **1** blowing. **2** short spell in fresh air. □ **blow-dry** arrange (hair) while using hand-held dryer. **blowfly** bluebottle. **blow in 1** send inwards by explosion. **2** *colloquial* arrive unexpectedly. **blowlamp** device with flame for plumbing, burning off paint, etc. **blow one's own trumpet** praise oneself. **blow one's top** (*US* also **stack**) *colloquial* explode in rage. **blow out 1** extinguish by blowing. **2** send outwards by explosion. **blow-out** *noun* **1** *colloquial* burst tyre. **2** *slang* large meal. **blow over** fade away. **blowpipe** tube for blowing through, esp. one from which dart or arrow is projected. **blowtorch** *US* blowlamp. **blow up 1** explode. **2** *colloquial* rebuke strongly. **3** *colloquial* lose one's temper. **4** inflate. **5** exaggerate. **6** *colloquial* enlarge (photograph). **blow-up** *noun colloquial* enlargement of photograph.

■ *verb* **1** breathe, exhale, puff. **2** drive, fan, waft, whirl. **3** blast, gust, puff, roar, waft, whine, whistle. □ **blow up 1** (*blow up a dam*) blast, bomb, dynamite, shatter; (*the device blew up*) burst, erupt, explode, go off; (*blow up a bomb*) detonate, set off. **3** erupt, get angry, lose one's temper, rage. **4** dilate, enlarge, expand, fill, inflate, pump up. **5** exaggerate, magnify, make worse, overstate.

blow[2] /bləʊ/ *noun* **1** hard stroke with hand or weapon. **2** disaster, shock.

■ **1** bang, bash, *slang* belt, *slang* biff, box (*on ears*), buffet, bump, *colloquial* clip, clout, clump, hit, jolt, knock, punch, rap, slap, *slang* slosh, smack, *colloquial* sock, stroke, swat, *colloquial* swipe, thump, thwack, *colloquial* wallop, welt, *colloquial* whack. **2** affliction, bombshell, calamity, disappointment, disaster, misfortune, shock, surprise, upset.

blower /'bləʊə/ *noun* **1** device for blowing. **2** *colloquial* telephone.

blowy /'bləʊɪ/ *adjective* (**-ier, -iest**) windy.

blowzy /'blaʊzɪ/ *adjective* (**-ier, -iest**) **1** coarse-looking, red-faced. **2** dishevelled.

blub *verb* (**-bb-**) *slang* sob.

blubber /'blʌbə/ *noun* whale fat. ● *verb* sob noisily. □ **blubbery** *adjective*.

bludgeon /'blʌdʒ(ə)n/ *noun* heavy club. ● *verb* **1** beat with bludgeon. **2** coerce.

blue /bluː/ *adjective* (**-r, -st**) **1** coloured like clear sky. **2** sad, depressed. **3** pornographic. ● *noun* **1** blue colour, paint, clothes, etc. **2** person who represents Oxford or Cambridge University at sport. **3** (in *plural*) type of melancholy music of American black origin. **4** (**the blues**) depression. ● *verb* (**blues, blued, bluing** or **blueing**) *slang* squander. □ **blue baby** one with congenital heart defect. **bluebell** woodland plant with bell-shaped blue flowers. **blueberry** small edible blue or blackish fruit of various plants. **blue blood** noble birth. **bluebottle** large buzzing fly. **blue cheese** cheese with veins of blue mould. **blue-collar** manual, industrial. **blue-eyed boy** *colloquial* favourite. **bluegrass** type of country and western music. **Blue Peter** blue flag with central white square hoisted before sailing. **blueprint 1** photographic print of building plans etc. in white on blue paper. **2** detailed plan. **bluestocking** *usually derogatory* intellectual woman. **blue tit** small blue and yellow bird. **blue whale** rorqual (largest known living mammal).

■ *adjective* **1** aquamarine, azure, cerulean, cobalt, indigo, navy, sapphire, sky blue, turquoise, ultramarine. **2** see SAD 1. **3** see BAWDY. ● *verb* see SQUANDER. □ **blueprint** design, draft, model, outline, pattern, pilot, plan, proposal, prototype.

blue blood *noun* noble birth. □ **blue-blooded** *adjective*.

bluff[1] *verb* pretend to have strength, knowledge, etc. ● *noun* bluffing.

■ *verb literary* cozen, deceive, delude, dupe, fool, hoodwink, mislead.

bluff[2] *adjective* **1** blunt, frank, hearty. **2** with steep or vertical broad front. ● *noun* bluff headland.

blunder /'blʌndə/ *noun* serious or foolish mistake. ● *verb* **1** make blunder. **2** move about clumsily.

■ *noun colloquial* boob, botch, *slang* clanger, error, fault, *faux pas*, gaffe, *colloquial* howler, indiscretion, miscalculation, misjudgement, mistake, slip, *colloquial* slip-up, solecism. ● *verb* **1** botch, bumble, bungle, *slang* drop a clanger, err, foul up, *slang* goof, go wrong, make a mistake, mess up, miscalculate, misjudge, *colloquial* put one's foot in it, *colloquial* slip up. **2** flounder, stumble.

blunderbuss /'blʌndəbʌs/ *noun historical* short large-bored gun.

blunt *adjective* **1** without sharp edge or point. **2** plain-spoken. ● *verb* make blunt or less sharp. □ **bluntly** *adverb*. **bluntness** *noun*.

■ *adjective* **1** dull, rounded, thick, unpointed, unsharpened, worn. **2** abrupt, bluff, brusque, candid, curt, direct, downright, forthright, frank, honest, insensitive, outspoken, plain-spoken, rude, straightforward, tactless, unceremonious, undiplomatic. ● *verb* abate, allay, deaden, dull, lessen, numb, soften, take the edge off, weaken.

blur *verb* (**-rr-**) **1** make or become less distinct. **2** smear. ● *noun* indistinct object, sound, memory, etc. □ **blurred** *adjective*. **blurry** *adjective*.

■ *verb* **1** befog, cloud, conceal, confuse, darken, dim, fog, mask, muddle, obscure, unfocus. **2** smear, smudge. □ **blurred** bleary, blurry, clouded, cloudy, confused, dim, faint, foggy, fuzzy, hazy, ill-defined, indefinite, indistinct, misty, nebulous, out of focus, smoky, unclear, unfocused, vague.

blurb *noun* promotional description, esp. of book.

blurt *verb* (usually + *out*) utter abruptly or tactlessly.

■ (*blurt out*) blab, burst out with, come out with, cry out, disclose, divulge, exclaim, give away, let out, let slip, reveal, tell, utter.

blush *verb* **1** be or become red (as) with shame or embarrassment. **2** be ashamed. ● *noun* **1** blushing. **2** pink tinge.

■ *verb* **1** colour, flush, glow, go red, redden.

blusher *noun* coloured cosmetic for cheeks.

bluster /'blʌstə/ *verb* **1** behave pompously. **2** storm boisterously. ● *noun* **1** noisy pompous talk. **2** empty threats. □ **blustering** *adjective*. **blustery** *adjective*.

■ □ **blustering** angry, boasting, boisterous, bragging, bullying, crowing, defiant, domineering, hectoring, noisy, ranting, self-assertive, *colloquial* showing off, storming, swaggering, threatening, *literary* vaunting, violent. **blustery** gusty, squally, unsettled, windy.

BMA *abbreviation* British Medical Association.

BMX *noun* **1** organized bicycle racing on dirt track. **2** bicycle used for this.

BO *abbreviation colloquial* body odour.

boa /'bəʊə/ *noun* **1** large snake that kills its prey by crushing it. **2** long stole of fur or feathers. □ **boa constrictor** species of boa.

boar *noun* **1** male wild pig. **2** uncastrated male pig.

board *noun* **1** thin piece of sawn timber. **2** material resembling this. **3** slab of wood etc., e.g. ironing board, notice board. **4** thick stiff card. **5** provision of meals. **6** directors of company; committee. **7** (**the boards**) stage. ● *verb* **1** go on board (ship etc.). **2** receive, or provide with, meals and usually lodging. **3** (usually + *up*) cover with boards. □ **board game** game played on a board. **boarding house** unlicensed house providing board and lodging. **boarding school** one in which pupils live in term-time. **boardroom** room where board of directors meets. **on board** on or into ship, train, aircraft, etc.

■ *noun* **1, 2** blockboard, chipboard, panel, plank, plywood, sheet, slab, slat, timber, weatherboard. **6** cabinet, committee, council, directorate, jury, panel. ● *verb* **1** catch, embark (on), enter, get on, go aboard. **2** accommodate, billet, feed, house, lodge, put up, quarter, stay.

boarder *noun* person who boards, esp. at boarding school.

boast *verb* **1** declare one's achievements etc. with excessive pride. **2** have (desirable thing). ● *noun* **1** boasting. **2** thing one is proud of. □ **boaster** *noun*. **boastful** *adjective*. **boastfulness** *noun*.

■ *verb* **1** blow one's own trumpet, bluster, brag, crow, exaggerate, gloat, praise oneself, *colloquial* show off, sing one's own praises, swagger, *colloquial* swank, *colloquial* talk big, *literary* vaunt. □ **boaster** *colloquial* big-head, braggart, poser, *colloquial* show-off, swaggerer. **boastful** *colloquial* big-headed, bragging, *colloquial* cocky, conceited, egotistic(al), ostentatious, proud, puffed up, swaggering, *colloquial* swanky, *colloquial* swollen-headed, vain, vainglorious.

boat *noun* **1** small vessel propelled by oars, sails, or engine. **2** ship. **3** long low jug for sauce etc. ● *verb* go in boat, esp. for pleasure. □ **boat-hook** long pole with hook for moving boats. **boathouse** shed at water's edge for boats. **boatman** person who hires out or provides transport by boats. **boat people** refugees travelling by sea. **boat-train** train scheduled to connect with ship.

■ *noun* **1** craft, *colloquial* ship, vessel. □ **boatman** bargee, coxswain, ferryman, gondolier, oarsman, rower, sailor, waterman, yachtsman.

boater *noun* flat straw hat with straight brim.

boatswain /ˈbəʊs(ə)n/ *noun* (also **bosun**) ship's officer in charge of equipment and crew.

bob[1] *verb* (**-bb-**) **1** move up and down. **2** rebound. **3** (usually + *up*) appear suddenly. **4** cut (hair) in bob. **5** curtsy. ● *noun* **1** bobbing movement. **2** curtsy. **3** hairstyle with hair hanging evenly above shoulders. **4** weight on pendulum etc. □ **bobtail 1** docked tail. **2** horse or dog with this.

■ *verb* **1** bounce, dance, hop, jerk, jig about, jolt, jump, leap, nod, twitch. **3** (*bob up*) see APPEAR 1.

bob[2] *noun* (*plural* same) *historical slang* shilling (= 5p).

bobbin /ˈbɒbɪn/ *noun* spool or reel for thread etc.

bobble /ˈbɒb(ə)l/ *noun* small woolly ball on hat etc.

bobby /ˈbɒbɪ/ *noun* (*plural* **-ies**) *colloquial* police officer.

bobsled *noun* US bobsleigh.

bobsleigh *noun* racing sledge steered and braked mechanically.

bod *noun colloquial* person.

bode *verb* (**-ding**) □ **bode well, ill** be good or bad sign.

bodge /bɒdʒ/ = BOTCH.

bodice /ˈbɒdɪs/ *noun* part of woman's dress above waist.

bodily /ˈbɒdɪlɪ/ *adjective* of the body. ● *adverb* **1** as a whole (body). **2** in person.

bodkin /ˈbɒdkɪn/ *noun* blunt thick needle for drawing tape etc. through hem.

body /ˈbɒdɪ/ *noun* (*plural* **-ies**) **1** physical structure of person or animal, alive or dead. **2** person's or animal's trunk. **3** main part. **4** group of people regarded as unit. **5** quantity, mass. **6** piece of matter. **7** *colloquial* person. **8** full or substantial quality of flavour etc. **9** body stocking. □ **body-building** exercises to enlarge and strengthen muscles. **bodyguard** escort or personal guard. **body politic** state, nation. **body shop** workshop where bodywork is repaired. **body stocking** woman's undergarment covering trunk. **bodywork** outer shell of vehicle.

■ **1** build, figure, form, physique, shape; (*dead body*) cadaver, carcass, corpse, mortal remains, remains, *slang* stiff. **2** torso, trunk. **4** association, band, committee, company, corporation, group, society. **5** accumulation, agglomeration, collection, corpus, mass. □ **bodyguard** defender, guard, *slang* minder, protector.

Boer /bɔː/ *noun* S. African of Dutch descent.

boffin /ˈbɒfɪn/ *noun colloquial* research scientist.

bog *noun* **1** (area of) wet spongy ground. **2** *slang* lavatory. ● *verb* (usually in *passive*) **1** cause to be stuck. **2** (+ *down*) hinder. □ **boggy** *adjective* (**-ier**, **-iest**).

■ *noun* **1** fen, marsh, marshland, mire, *literary* morass, mudflat(s), peat bog, quagmire, salt marsh, slough, swamp, wetland(s). ● *verb* **1** (*get bogged*) get stuck, sink. **2** (*get bogged down*) be hampered, be hindered, get into difficulties, get stuck.

bogey[1] /ˈbəʊɡɪ/ *noun* (*plural* **-s**) *Golf* **1** score of one more than par for hole. **2** (formerly) par.

bogey[2] /ˈbəʊɡɪ/ *noun* (also **bogy**) (*plural* **-eys** or **-ies**) **1** evil or mischievous spirit. **2** awkward thing.

bogeyman *noun* (also **bogyman**) person (real or imaginary) causing fear or difficulty.

boggle /ˈbɒɡ(ə)l/ *verb* (**-ling**) *colloquial* be startled or baffled.

bogie /ˈbəʊɡɪ/ *noun* wheeled undercarriage below locomotive etc.

bogus /ˈbəʊɡəs/ *adjective* sham, spurious.

■ counterfeit, fake, false, fictitious, fraudulent, imitation, *colloquial* phoney, sham, spurious.

bogy = BOGEY[2].

Bohemian /bəʊˈhiːmɪən/ *noun* **1** native of Bohemia. **2** (also **bohemian**) socially unconventional person, esp. artist or writer. ● *adjective* **1** of Bohemia. **2** (also **bohemian**) socially unconventional. □ **bohemianism** *noun*.

■ *adjective* **2** *colloquial* arty, bizarre, eccentric, *colloquial* hippie, informal, nonconformist, offbeat, unconventional, unorthodox, *colloquial* way-out, *colloquial* weird.

boil[1] *verb* **1** (of liquid or its vessel) bubble up with heat; reach temperature at which liquid turns to vapour. **2** bring to boiling point. **3** subject to heat of boiling water; cook thus. **4** be agitated, esp. by anger. ● *noun* **1** boiling. **2** boiling point. □ **boiling (hot)** *colloquial* very hot. **boiling point** temperature at which a liquid boils. **boil over** spill over in boiling.

■ *verb* **1** bubble, effervesce, foam, seethe, steam. **3** cook, heat, simmer, stew. **4** see RAGE *verb* 1.

boil[2] *noun* inflamed pus-filled swelling under skin.

■ abscess, blister, carbuncle, chilblain, eruption, gathering, gumboil, inflammation, pimple, pock, pustule, sore, spot, ulcer, *esp. US slang* zit.

boiler *noun* **1** apparatus for heating hot-water supply. **2** tank for heating water or turning it into steam. **3** vessel for boiling things in. □ **boiler suit** protective garment combining trousers and shirt.

boisterous /ˈbɔɪstərəs/ *adjective* **1** noisily cheerful. **2** (of weather, sea, etc.) violent, rough. □ **boisterousness** *noun*.

■ **1** animated, disorderly, exuberant, irrepressible, lively, loud, noisy, obstreperous, riotous, rollicking, rough, rowdy, tumultuous, undisciplined, unrestrained, unruly, uproarious, wild. **2** rough, stormy, tempestuous, violent, wild.

bold /bəʊld/ *adjective* **1** confident; adventurous, courageous. **2** impudent. **3** distinct, vivid. □ **boldly** *adverb*. **boldness** *noun*.

■ **1** adventurous, audacious, brave, confident, courageous, daredevil, daring, dauntless, enterprising, fearless, foolhardy, forceful, gallant, hardy, heroic, intrepid, plucky, rash, reckless, resolute, self-confident, unafraid, valiant, valorous, venturesome. **2** brash, brazen, cheeky, forward, *colloquial* fresh, impertinent, impudent, insolent, pert, presumptuous, rude, saucy, shameless, unashamed. **3** big, bright, clear, conspicuous, *colloquial* eye-catching, large, obvious, prominent, pronounced, showy, striking, strong, vivid.

bole *noun* trunk of tree.

bolero *noun* (*plural* **-s**) **1** /bəˈleərəʊ/ Spanish dance. **2** /ˈbɒlərəʊ/ woman's short jacket without fastenings.

boll /bəʊl/ *noun* round seed vessel of cotton, flax, etc.

bollard /ˈbɒlɑːd/ *noun* **1** short thick post in street etc. **2** post on ship or quay for securing ropes to.

boloney /bəˈləʊnɪ/ *noun slang* nonsense.

bolshie /ˈbɒlʃɪ/ *adjective* (**-r**, **-st**) (also **Bolshie**) *slang* rebellious, uncooperative.

bolster /ˈbəʊlstə/ *noun* long cylindrical pillow. ● *verb* (usually + *up*) **1** encourage. **2** support, prop up.

■ *noun* cushion, pillow. ● *verb* **1** see SUPPORT *verb* 4. **2** see SUPPORT *verb* 1,2.

bolt[1] /bəʊlt/ *noun* **1** door-fastening of metal bar and socket. **2** headed metal pin secured with rivet or nut. **3** discharge of lightning. **4** arrow shot from crossbow. **5** bolting. ● *verb* **1** fasten with bolt. **2** (+ *in*, *out*) keep in or out by bolting door. **3** dart off, run away. **4** (of horse) escape from control. **5** gulp down unchewed. **6** run to seed. □ **bolt from the blue** complete surprise. **bolt-hole** means of escape. **bolt upright** erect.

■ *noun* **1** bar, catch, fastening, latch, lock. **2** peg, pin, rivet, rod, screw. **4** arrow, dart, missile, projectile. ● *verb* **1** bar, close, fasten, latch, lock, secure. **3**, **4** abscond, dart away, dash away, escape, flee, fly, run off, rush off. □ **bolt from the blue** see SURPRISE *noun* 1.

bolt[2] /bəʊlt/ *verb* (also **boult**) sift.

bomb /bɒm/ *noun* **1** container filled with explosive, incendiary material, etc., designed to explode and cause damage. **2** (**the bomb**) the atomic bomb. **3** *slang* large amount of money. ● *verb* **1** attack with bombs; drop bombs on. **2** *colloquial* travel fast. □ **bombshell** great surprise or disappointment.

■ *verb* **1** see BOMBARD 1.

bombard /bɒmˈbɑːd/ *verb* **1** attack with heavy guns etc. **2** question or abuse persistently. **3** subject to stream of high-speed particles. □ **bombardment** *noun*.

■ **1** assail, assault, attack, batter, blast, *colloquial* blitz, bomb, fire at, pelt, pound, shell, shoot at, strafe. **2** badger, beset, harass, importune, pester, *colloquial* plague. □ **bombardment** attack, barrage, *colloquial* blast, *colloquial* blitz, broadside, burst, cannonade, discharge, fusillade, hail, salvo, volley.

bombardier /bɒmbəˈdɪə/ *noun* **1** artillery NCO below sergeant. **2** *US* airman who releases bombs from aircraft.

bombast /ˈbɒmbæst/ *noun* pompous or extravagant language. □ **bombastic** /-ˈbæs-/ *adjective*.

■ □ **bombastic** extravagant, grandiloquent, grandiose, high-flown, inflated, pompous, turgid.

Bombay duck /ˈbɒmbeɪ/ *noun* dried fish eaten as relish, esp. with curry.

bomber *noun* **1** aircraft equipped for bombing. **2** person who throws or plants bomb. □ **bomber jacket** one gathered at waist and cuffs.

bona fide /bəʊnə ˈfaɪdɪ/ *adjective* & *adverb* in good faith; genuine(ly).

bonanza /bəˈnænzə/ *noun* **1** source of great wealth. **2** large output, esp. from mine.

bon-bon *noun* sweet.

bond *noun* **1** thing or force that unites. **2** (usually in *plural*) thing or force that restrains. **3** binding agreement. **4** certificate issued by government or company promising to repay money at fixed rate of interest. **5** adhesiveness. **6** document binding person to pay or repay money. **7** linkage of atoms in molecule. ● *verb* **1** bind or connect together. **2** put in bond. □ **bond paper** high-quality writing paper. **in bond** stored by Customs until duty is paid.

■ *noun* **1** affiliation, affinity, attachment, connection, link, relationship, tie, unity. **2** fastening, restraint; (*bonds*) chains, cords, fetters, handcuffs, manacles, ropes, shackles. **3** agreement, compact, contract, covenant, guarantee, pledge, promise, word. ● *verb* **1** see STICK² 4.

bondage /'bɒndɪdʒ/ *noun* **1** slavery. **2** subjection to constraint.

■ **1** enslavement, *historical* serfdom, servitude, slavery, *literary* thraldom, *historical* vassalage. **2** oppression, subjection, subjugation, suppression.

bondsman /'bɒndzmən/ *noun* serf, slave.

bone *noun* **1** any of separate parts of vertebrate skeleton. **2** (in *plural*) skeleton, esp. as remains. **3** substance of which bones consist. ● *verb* (**-ning**) remove bones from. □ **bone china** fine semi-translucent earthenware. **bone dry** completely dry. **bone idle** completely idle. **bone marrow** fatty substance in cavity of bones. **bonemeal** crushed bone as fertilizer. **boneshaker** jolting vehicle.

bonehead *noun slang* stupid person. □ **boneheaded** *adjective*.

bonfire *noun* open-air fire.

bongo /'bɒŋgəʊ/ *noun* (*plural* **-s** or **-es**) either of pair of small drums played with fingers.

bonhomie /bɒnɒ'mi:/ *noun* geniality.

bonkers /'bɒŋkəz/ *adjective slang* crazy.

bonnet /'bɒnɪt/ *noun* **1** woman's or child's hat tied under chin. **2** Scotsman's floppy beret. **3** hinged cover over engine of vehicle.

bonny /'bɒnɪ/ *adjective* (**-ier, -iest**) *esp. Scottish & Northern English* healthy-looking, attractive.

bonsai /'bɒnsaɪ/ *noun* (*plural* same) **1** dwarfed tree or shrub. **2** art of growing these.

bonus /'bəʊnəs/ *noun* **1** extra benefit. **2** extra payment.

■ **1** addition, advantage, benefit, extra, plus. **2** bounty, commission, dividend, gift, gratuity, handout, honorarium, largesse, payment, *colloquial* perk, reward, supplement, tip.

bon voyage /bɔ̃ vwɑː'jɑːʒ/ *interjection* have a good trip. [French]

bony /'bəʊnɪ/ *adjective* (**-ier, -iest**) **1** thin with prominent bones. **2** having many bones. **3** of or like bone.

■ **1** angular, emaciated, gangling, gawky, lanky, lean, scraggy, scrawny, skinny, thin, ungainly.

boo *interjection* **1** *expressing disapproval or contempt.* **2** *sound intended to surprise.* ● *noun* utterance of 'boo'. ● *verb* (**boos, booed**) utter boos (at).

boob *noun* **1** *colloquial* silly mistake. **2** *slang* woman's breast. ● *verb colloquial* make mistake.

booby /'bu:bɪ/ *noun* (*plural* **-ies**) silly or awkward person. □ **booby prize** prize for coming last. **booby trap 1** practical joke in form of trap. **2** disguised bomb etc. triggered by unknowing victim.

book /bʊk/ *noun* **1** written or printed work with pages bound along one side. **2** work intended for publication. **3** bound set of blank sheets for writing or drawing in. **4** bound set of tickets, stamps, matches, cheques, etc. **5** (in *plural*) set of records or accounts. **6** main division of literary work or Bible. **7** telephone directory. **8** *colloquial* magazine. **9** libretto. **10** record of bets made. ● *verb* **1** reserve (seat etc.) in advance. **2** engage (entertainer etc.). **3** take personal details of (offender). **4** enter in book or list. □ **bookcase** cabinet of shelves for books. **bookend** prop to keep books upright. **bookkeeper** person who keeps accounts. **bookmaker** professional taker of bets. **bookmark** thing for marking place in book. **bookplate** decorative personalized label in book. **book token** voucher exchangeable for books. **bookworm 1** *colloquial* devoted reader. **2** larva that eats through books. **the good book** the Bible.

■ *noun* **1, 2** booklet, copy, edition, hardback, manuscript, paperback, publication, scroll, tome, volume, work, writing. **3** album, diary, exercise book, jotter, journal, ledger, notebook, scrapbook, sketchbook. **8** see MAGAZINE 1. ● *verb* **1** buy, order, organize, reserve. **2** arrange, engage, organize, sign up. **3** arrest, take details of, take name of.

bookie /'bʊkɪ/ *noun colloquial* bookmaker.

bookish *adjective* **1** fond of reading. **2** getting knowledge mainly from books.

booklet /'bʊklɪt/ *noun* small usually paper-covered book.

■ brochure, leaflet, pamphlet.

boom¹ /bu:m/ *noun* deep resonant sound. ● *verb* make or speak with boom.

■ *noun* bang, blast, explosion, reverberation, roar, rumble. ● *verb* bang, bellow, blast, resonate, reverberate, roar, rumble, thunder.

boom² /bu:m/ *noun* period of economic prosperity or activity. ● *verb* be suddenly prosperous.

■ *noun* bonanza, boost, expansion, growth, improvement, increase, prosperity, spurt, upsurge, upturn. ● *verb* see PROSPER.

boom³ /bu:m/ *noun* **1** pivoted spar to which sail is attached. **2** long pole carrying camera, microphone, etc. **3** barrier across harbour etc.

■ **3** see BARRIER 1.

boomerang /'bu:məræŋ/ *noun* flat V-shaped Australian hardwood missile returning to thrower. ● *verb* (of plan) backfire.

boon¹ /bu:n/ *noun* advantage, blessing.

boon² /bu:n/ *adjective* intimate, favourite.

boor /bʊə/ *noun* ill-mannered person. □ **boorish** *adjective*. **boorishness** *noun*.

■ □ boorish barbarian, *colloquial* ignorant, ill-bred, ill-mannered, loutish, oafish, philistine, uncultured, vulgar.

boost /buːst/ *verb* **1** promote, encourage; increase, assist. **2** push from below. ● *noun* **1** increase or advance in value, reputation etc. **2** push.

■ *verb* **1** advance, aid, assist, augment, bolster, build up, buoy up, encourage, enhance, enlarge, expand, foster, further, give an impetus to, heighten, help, improve, increase, inspire, lift, promote, push, raise, support, sustain. **2** heave, hoist, lift, push up, raise. ● *noun* aid, encouragement, fillip, impetus, help, lift, push, stimulus.

booster *noun* **1** device for increasing power or voltage. **2** auxiliary engine or rocket for initial speed. **3** dose renewing effect of earlier one.

boot /buːt/ *noun* **1** outer foot-covering reaching above ankle. **2** luggage compartment of car. **3** *colloquial* firm kick. **4** *colloquial* dismissal. ● *verb* **1** kick. **2** (often + *out*) eject forcefully. **3** (usually + *up*) make (computer) ready. □ **bootlace** cord for lacing boot.

bootee /buːˈtiː/ *noun* baby's soft shoe.

booth /buːð/ *noun* **1** temporary structure used esp. as market stall. **2** enclosure for telephoning, voting, etc.

■ **1** stall, stand. **2** box, compartment, cubicle, hut, kiosk.

bootleg /ˈbuːtleg/ *adjective* smuggled, illicit. ● *verb* (**-gg-**) illicitly make or deal in. □ **bootlegger** *noun*.

bootless /ˈbuːtlɪs/ *adjective archaic* unavailing, useless.

bootstrap /ˈbuːtstræp/ *noun* □ **pull oneself up by one's bootstraps** better oneself by one's unaided effort.

booty /ˈbuːtɪ/ *noun* **1** loot, spoils. **2** *colloquial* prize.

■ **1** contraband, gains, haul, loot, pickings, plunder, spoils, *slang* swag, takings. **2** gains, loot, prize, trophies, winnings.

booze *colloquial noun* alcoholic drink. ● *verb* (**-zing**) drink alcohol, esp. excessively. □ **boozy** *adjective* (**-ier, -iest**).

boozer *noun colloquial* **1** habitual drinker. **2** public house.

bop[1] *colloquial noun* spell of dancing, esp. to pop music. ● *verb* (**-pp-**) dance, esp. to pop music.

bop[2] *colloquial noun* hit, blow. ● *verb* (**-pp-**) hit.

boracic /bəˈræsɪk/ *adjective* of borax. □ **boracic acid** boric acid.

borage /ˈbɒrɪdʒ/ *noun* plant with leaves used as flavouring.

borax /ˈbɔːræks/ *noun* salt of boric acid used as antiseptic.

border /ˈbɔːdə/ *noun* **1** edge, boundary, or part near it. **2** line or region separating countries. **3** distinct edging, esp. ornamental strip. **4** long narrow flower bed. ● *verb* **1** put or be border to. **2** adjoin. □ **borderline** ● *noun* line marking boundary or dividing two conditions. ● *adjective* on borderline.

■ *noun* **1** boundary, brim, brink, edge, frame, fringe, limit, margin, perimeter, periphery, rim, verge. **2** borderline, boundary, frontier, limit. **3** edge, edging, frame, frieze, frill, fringe, hem, margin, surround, trimming. **4** bed, herbaceous border. ● *verb* **1** see EDGE *verb* **2**. **2** abut on, adjoin, be adjacent to, be alongside, join, touch.

bore[1] *verb* (**-ring**) **1** make (hole), esp. with revolving tool. **2** make hole in. ● *noun* **1** hollow of firearm barrel or cylinder. **2** diameter of this. **3** deep hole made to find water etc.

■ *verb* drill, gouge (out), mine, penetrate, perforate, pierce, sink, tunnel.

bore[2] *noun* tiresome or dull person or thing. ● *verb* (**-ring**) weary by tedious talk or dullness. □ **bored** *adjective*. **boring** *adjective*.

■ *verb* exhaust, jade, tire, *colloquial* turn off, weary. □ **boring** arid, commonplace, dead, dreary, dry, dull, flat, humdrum, long-winded, monotonous, prolix, repetitious, repetitive, soporific, stale, tedious, tiresome, trite, uneventful, unexciting, uninspiring, uninteresting, vapid, wearisome, wordy.

bore[3] *noun* very high tidal wave rushing up estuary.

bore[4] *past* of BEAR[1].

boredom *noun* being bored (BORE[2]).

boric acid /ˈbɔːrɪk/ *noun* acid used as antiseptic.

born *adjective* **1** existing as a result of birth. **2** being (specified thing) by nature. **3** (usually + *to do*) destined.

■ **2** congenital, genuine, instinctive, natural, untaught.

borne *past participle* of BEAR[1].

boron /ˈbɔːrɒn/ *noun* non-metallic element.

borough /ˈbʌrə/ *noun* **1** administrative area, esp. of Greater London. **2** *historical* town with municipal corporation.

borrow /ˈbɒrəʊ/ *verb* **1** get temporary use of (something to be returned). **2** use another's (invention, idea, etc.). □ **borrower** *noun*.

■ **1** be lent, have the loan of. **2** adopt, appropriate, copy, *colloquial* crib, make use of, obtain, pirate, plagiarize, take, use, usurp.

Borstal /ˈbɔːst(ə)l/ *noun historical* residential institution for youth custody.

bosky /ˈbɒskɪ/ *adjective literary* wooded.

bosom /ˈbʊz(ə)m/ *noun* **1** person's breasts. **2** *colloquial* each of woman's breasts. **3** enclosure formed by breast and arms. **4** emotional centre. □ **bosom friend** intimate friend.

boss[1] *colloquial noun* employer, manager, or supervisor. ● *verb* (usually + *about, around*) give orders to.

■ *noun* see CHIEF *noun*.

boss[2] *noun* round knob or stud.

boss-eyed *adjective colloquial* **1** cross-eyed. **2** crooked.

bossy *adjective* (**-ier**, **-iest**) *colloquial* domineering. □ **bossiness** *noun*.

■ aggressive, assertive, authoritarian, autocratic, bullying, despotic, dictatorial, domineering, exacting, hectoring, high-handed, imperious, lordly, magisterial, masterful, officious, oppressive, overbearing, peremptory, *colloquial* pushy, self-assertive, tyrannical.

bosun = BOATSWAIN.

botany /'bɒtənɪ/ *noun* study of plants. □ **botanic(al)** /bə'tæn-/ *adjective*. **botanist** *noun*.

botch *verb* **1** bungle. **2** patch clumsily. ● *noun* bungled or spoilt work.

both /bəʊθ/ *adjective & pronoun* the two (not only one). ● *adverb* with equal truth in two cases.

bother /'bɒðə/ *verb* **1** trouble, worry. **2** take trouble. ● *noun* **1** person or thing that bothers; nuisance. **2** trouble, worry. ● *interjection: expressing irritation.* □ **bothersome** /-səm/ *adjective*.

■ *verb* **1** annoy, bewilder, concern, confuse, disconcert, dismay, disturb, exasperate, harass, *colloquial* hassle, inconvenience, irk, irritate, molest, nag, perturb, pester, *colloquial* plague, trouble, upset, vex, worry. **2** be concerned, be worried, care, mind, take trouble, trouble oneself. ● *noun* **1** annoyance, inconvenience, irritation, nuisance, pest, problem, trouble, worry. **2** ado, difficulty, disorder, disturbance, fuss, *colloquial* hassle, to-do, trouble, worry.

bottle /'bɒt(ə)l/ *noun* **1** container, esp. glass or plastic, for storing liquid. **2** liquid in bottle. **3** *slang* courage. ● *verb* (**-ling**) **1** put into bottles. **2** preserve (fruit etc.) in jars. **3** (+ *up*) restrain (feelings etc.). □ **bottle bank** place for depositing bottles for recycling. **bottle green** dark green. **bottleneck 1** narrow congested area esp. on road etc. **2** thing that impedes. **bottle party** one to which guests bring bottles of drink.

■ *noun* **1** carafe, carboy, decanter, flagon, flask, jeroboam, magnum, phial. ● *verb* **3** (*bottle up*) see SUPPRESS 2.

bottom /'bɒtəm/ *noun* **1** lowest point or part. **2** buttocks. **3** less honourable end of table, class, etc. **4** ground under water. **5** basis. **6** essential character. ● *adjective* lowest, last. ● *verb* **1** (usually + *out*) reach its lowest level. **2** find extent of. **3** touch bottom (of). □ **bottom line** *colloquial* underlying truth; ultimate criterion.

■ *noun* **1** base, depth, foot, foundation, lowest point, nadir, pedestal, substructure, underneath, underside. **2** *coarse slang* arse, *colloquial* backside, *colloquial* behind, *slang* bum, buttocks, posterior, *colloquial* rear, rump, seat. **4** bed, floor, ground. **5** basis, grounds, origin, root, source. **6** core, essence, heart. ● *adjective* deepest, last, least, lowest, minimum.

bottomless *adjective* **1** without bottom. **2** inexhaustible.

■ **1** deep, immeasurable, unfathomable, unplumbed. **2** see ENDLESS 1.

botulism /'bɒtjʊlɪz(ə)m/ *noun* poisoning caused by bacillus in badly preserved food.

boudoir /'buːdwɑː/ *noun* woman's private room.

bougainvillaea /buːgən'vɪlɪə/ *noun* tropical plant with large coloured bracts.

bough /baʊ/ *noun* branch of tree.

bought *past & past participle* of BUY.

bouillon /'buːjɒn/ *noun* clear broth.

boulder /'bəʊldə/ *noun* large smooth rock.

boulevard /'buːləvɑːd/ *noun* broad tree-lined street.

boult = BOLT².

bounce /baʊns/ *verb* (**-cing**) **1** (cause to) rebound. **2** *colloquial* (of cheque) be returned to payee by bank when there are no funds to meet it. **3** jump, spring; rush boisterously. ● *noun* **1** rebound. **2** *colloquial* swagger, self-confidence. **3** *colloquial* liveliness. □ **bouncy** *adjective* (**-ier**, **-iest**).

■ *verb* **1** rebound, recoil, ricochet, spring back. **3** bob, bound, jump, leap, spring.

bouncer *noun slang* doorman employed to eject troublemakers from nightclub etc.

bouncing *adjective* big and healthy.

bound¹ /baʊnd/ *verb* **1** spring, leap. **2** (of ball etc.) bounce. ● *noun* **1** springy leap. **2** bounce.

■ *verb* **1** bounce, caper, frisk, frolic, gambol, hop, hurdle, jump, leap, pounce, romp, skip, spring, vault. **2** bounce, rebound, recoil, ricochet.

bound² /baʊnd/ *noun* (usually in *plural*) **1** limitation, restriction. **2** border, boundary. ● *verb* **1** limit. **2** be boundary of. □ **out of bounds** outside permitted area.

bound³ /baʊnd/ *adjective* (usually + *for*) starting or having started.

■ (*bound for*) aimed at, directed towards, going to, heading for, making for, off to, travelling towards.

bound⁴ /baʊnd/ *past & past participle* of BIND. □ **bound to 1** certain to. **2** compelled to. **bound up with** closely associated with.

■ □ **bound to 1** certain to, destined to, doomed to, fated to, sure to. **2** committed to, compelled to, constrained to, forced to, obligated to, obliged to, pledged to, required to.

boundary /'baʊndərɪ/ *noun* (*plural* **-ies**) **1** line marking limits. **2** *Cricket* hit crossing limit of field. **3** *Cricket* runs scored for this.

■ **1** border, borderline, bounds, brink, circumference, confines, demarcation, edge, end, extremity, fringe, frontier, interface, limit, margin, perimeter, threshold, verge.

bounder /'baʊndə/ *noun colloquial* or *jocular* dishonourable person.

boundless *adjective* unlimited. □ **boundlessness** *noun*.

■ endless, everlasting, immeasurable, incalculable, inexhaustible, infinite, limitless, unbounded, unconfined, unflagging, unlimited, unrestricted, untold, vast.

bounteous /ˈbaʊntɪəs/ *adjective poetical* bountiful.

bountiful /ˈbaʊntɪfʊl/ *adjective* **1** generous. **2** ample.

bounty /ˈbaʊntɪ/ *noun* (*plural* **-ies**) **1** generosity. **2** official reward; gift.

■ **1** altruism, beneficence, benevolence, charity, generosity, giving, goodness, kindness, largesse, liberality, munificence, philanthropy, unselfishness.

bouquet /buːˈkeɪ/ *noun* **1** bunch of flowers. **2** scent of wine. **3** compliment. □ **bouquet garni** (/ˈɡɑːnɪ/) bunch or bag of herbs for flavouring.

■ **1** arrangement, bunch, buttonhole, corsage, garland, nosegay, posy, spray. **2** see SMELL *noun* 2.

bourbon /ˈbɜːbən/ *noun US* whisky from maize and rye.

bourgeois /ˈbʊəʒwɑː/ *often derogatory adjective* **1** conventionally middle-class. **2** materialist. **3** capitalist. ● *noun* (*plural* same) bourgeois person.

bourgeoisie /ˌbʊəʒwɑːˈziː/ *noun* bourgeois class.

bourn /bɔːn/ *noun* stream.

bourse /bʊəs/ *noun* money market, esp. (**Bourse**) Stock Exchange in Paris.

bout *noun* **1** spell of work etc. **2** fit of illness. **3** wrestling or boxing match.

■ **1, 2** attack, fit, period, run, spell, stint, stretch, time, turn. **3** battle, competition, contest, encounter, engagement, fight, match, round, *colloquial* set-to, struggle.

boutique /buːˈtiːk/ *noun* small shop selling fashionable clothes etc.

bouzouki /buːˈzuːkɪ/ *noun* (*plural* **-s**) form of Greek mandolin.

bovine /ˈbəʊvaɪn/ *adjective* **1** of cattle. **2** dull, stupid.

bow[1] /bəʊ/ *noun* **1** weapon for shooting arrows. **2** rod with horsehair stretched from end to end for playing violin etc. **3** knot with two loops. **4** ribbon etc. so tied. **5** shallow curve or bend. ● *verb* use bow on (violin etc.). □ **bow-legged** having bandy legs. **bow tie** necktie in form of bow. **bow window** curved bay window.

bow[2] /baʊ/ *verb* **1** incline head or body, esp. in greeting or acknowledgement. **2** submit. **3** incline (head etc.). ● *noun* bowing.

■ *verb* **1** bend, curtsy, genuflect, *historical* kowtow, nod, prostrate oneself, salaam, stoop. **2** see SUBMIT 1. **3** bend, bob, drop, incline, nod.

bow[3] /baʊ/ *noun* **1** (often in *plural*) front end of boat or ship. **2** rower nearest bow.

bowdlerize /ˈbaʊdləraɪz/ *verb* (also **-ise**) (**-zing** or **-sing**) expurgate. □ **bowdlerization** *noun*.

bowel /ˈbaʊəl/ *noun* **1** (often in *plural*) intestine. **2** (in *plural*) innermost parts.

■ **1** gut, intestine; (*bowels*) entrails, guts, *colloquial* innards, *colloquial* insides, viscera, vitals. **2** (*bowels*) centre, core, depths, heart, *colloquial* innards, inside.

bower /ˈbaʊə/ *noun* arbour; summer house. □ **bowerbird** Australasian bird, the male of which constructs elaborate bowers or runs.

■ alcove, arbour, gazebo, grotto, hideaway, pavilion, pergola, recess, retreat, sanctuary, shelter, summer house.

bowie knife /ˈbəʊɪ/ *noun* long hunting knife.

bowl[1] /bəʊl/ *noun* **1** dish, esp. for food or liquid. **2** any deep-sided container. **3** hollow part of tobacco pipe, spoon, etc. **4** natural basin or depression.

■ **1** basin, bath, casserole, container, dish, pan, tureen.

bowl[2] /bəʊl/ *noun* **1** hard heavy ball made with bias to run in curve. **2** (in *plural*; usually treated as *singular*) game with these on grass. ● *verb* **1** roll (ball etc.). **2** play bowls. **3** *Cricket* deliver ball. **4** *Cricket* (often + *out*) put (batsman) out by knocking off bails with bowled ball. **5** (often + *along*) go along rapidly. □ **bowling alley** long enclosure for skittles or tenpin bowling. **bowling green** lawn for playing bowls.

■ *verb* **3** fling, hurl, lob, pitch, throw, toss.

bowler[1] /ˈbəʊlə/ *noun Cricket etc.* player who bowls.

bowler[2] /ˈbəʊlə/ *noun* hard round felt hat.

bowsprit /ˈbəʊsprɪt/ *noun* spar running forward from ship's bow.

box[1] *noun* **1** container, usually flat-sided and firm. **2** amount contained in this. **3** compartment in theatre, law court, etc. **4** telephone box. **5** facility at newspaper office for replies to advertisement. **6** (**the box**) *colloquial* television. **7** enclosed area or space. ● *verb* put in or provide with box. □ **box girder** hollow girder with square cross-section. **box junction** yellow-striped road area which vehicle may enter only if exit is clear. **box office** ticket office at theatre etc. **box pleat** two parallel pleats forming raised band.

■ *noun* **1** caddy, carton, case, casket, chest, coffer, container, crate, pack, package, receptacle, trunk.

box[2] *verb* **1** fight with fists as sport. **2** slap (person's ears). ● *noun* slap on ear.

■ *verb* **1** engage in fisticuffs, fight, punch, *colloquial* scrap, spar. **2** see HIT *verb* 1.

box[3] *noun* **1** evergreen shrub with small dark green leaves. **2** its wood.

boxer *noun* **1** person who boxes. **2** short-haired dog with puglike face. □ **boxer shorts** man's loose underpants.

■ **1** prizefighter, pugilist, sparring partner.

boxing *noun* fighting with fists, esp. as sport. □ **boxing glove** padded glove worn in this.

Boxing Day *noun* first weekday after Christmas Day.

boy *noun* **1** male child, young man. **2** son. **3** male servant. ● *interjection: expressing pleasure, surprise, etc.* □ **boyfriend** person's regular male

companion. **boy scout** Scout. □ **boyhood** *noun*.
boyish *adjective*.

■ *noun* **1** *usually derogatory* brat, *colloquial* kid,
lad, schoolboy, stripling, urchin, youngster, youth.

boycott /ˈbɔɪkɒt/ *verb* **1** refuse social or commercial relations with. **2** refuse to handle
(goods). ● *noun* such refusal.

■ *verb* **1** avoid, blackball, blacklist, exclude, give
the cold shoulder to, ignore, make unwelcome,
ostracize, outlaw, prohibit, spurn, stay away from.
2 avoid, black, reject. ● *noun* ban, blacklist,
embargo, prohibition.

bra /brɑː/ *noun* woman's undergarment supporting breasts.

brace *noun* **1** device that clamps or fastens
tightly. **2** timber etc. strengthening framework.
3 (in *plural*) straps supporting trousers from
shoulders. **4** wire device for straightening teeth.
5 (*plural* same) pair. ● *verb* (**-cing**) **1** make
steady by supporting. **2** fasten tightly. **3** (esp. as
bracing *adjective*) invigorate. **4** (often **brace
oneself**) prepare for difficulty, shock, etc.

■ *verb* **3** (**bracing**) crisp, exhilarating,
health-giving, invigorating, refreshing,
restorative, stimulating, tonic.

bracelet /ˈbreɪslɪt/ *noun* **1** ornamental band or
chain worn on wrist or arm. **2** *slang* handcuff.

brachiosaurus /brækɪəˈsɔːrəs/ *noun* (*plural*
-ruses) huge long-necked plant-eating dinosaur.

bracken /ˈbrækən/ *noun* **1** large coarse fern. **2**
mass of these.

bracket /ˈbrækɪt/ *noun* **1** support projecting
from vertical surface. **2** shelf fixed to wall with
this. **3** punctuation mark used in pairs—( ), [ ],
or { }—enclosing words or figures (see panel).
4 group classified as similar or falling between
limits. ● *verb* (**-t-**) **1** enclose in brackets. **2** group
in same category.

brackish /ˈbrækɪʃ/ *adjective* (of water) slightly
salty.

bract *noun* leaflike part of plant growing before
flower.

brad *noun* thin flat nail.

bradawl /ˈbrædɔːl/ *noun* small boring-tool.

brae /breɪ/ *noun* *Scottish* hillside.

brag *verb* (**-gg-**) talk boastfully. ● *noun* **1** card
game like poker. **2** boastful statement or talk.

■ *verb* blow one's own trumpet, boast, crow, gloat,
colloquial show off, *colloquial* talk big.

braggart /ˈbrægət/ *noun* boastful person.

Brahma /ˈbrɑːmə/ *noun* **1** Hindu Creator. **2**
supreme Hindu reality.

Brahman /ˈbrɑːmən/ *noun* (*plural* **-s**) (also
Brahmin) member of Hindu priestly caste.

braid *noun* **1** woven band as edging or trimming.
2 plait of hair. ● *verb* **1** plait. **2** trim with braid.

Braille /breɪl/ *noun* system of writing and printing for the blind, with patterns of raised dots.

brain *noun* **1** organ of soft nervous tissue in skull
of vertebrates; centre of sensation or thought. **2**
(often in *plural*) intelligence. **3** *colloquial* intelligent person. ● *verb* dash out brains of. □ **brainchild** *colloquial* person's clever idea or
invention. **brain drain** *colloquial* emigration of
skilled people. **brainstorm** ● *noun* mental disturbance. ● *verb* hold brainstorming session
(about). **brainstorming** pooling of spontaneous
ideas about problem etc. **brain-teaser** *colloquial*
puzzle or problem. **brains trust** group of experts
answering questions, usually impromptu. **brainwash** implant ideas or esp. ideology into (person)
by repetition etc. **brainwave** *colloquial* bright
idea.

■ *noun* **1** cerebrum, grey matter. **2** *colloquial* grey
matter, intellect, intelligence, mind, *colloquial*
nous, reason, sense, understanding, wisdom, wit.
□ **brainwash** condition, indoctrinate, re-educate.

brainless *adjective* stupid, foolish.

brainpower *noun* mental ability, intelligence.

brainy *adjective* (**-ier**, **-iest**) intellectually clever.

braise /breɪz/ *verb* (**-sing**) stew slowly in closed
container with little liquid.

Brackets ( ) [ ]

Round brackets, also called parentheses, are used mainly to enclose:

1 explanations and extra information or comment, e.g.

> *Zimbabwe (formerly Rhodesia)*
> *He is (as he always was) a rebel.*
> *This is done using integrated circuits (see page 38).*

2 in this dictionary, the type of word which can be used with the word being defined, e.g.

> **crow** ... (of baby) utter happy sounds
> **pave** ... cover (street, floor, etc.) with durable surface

Square brackets are used mainly to enclose:

1 words added by someone other than the original writer or speaker, e.g.

> *Then the man said, 'He [the police officer] can't prove I did it.'*

2 various special types of information, such as stage directions, e.g.

> HEDLEY: Goodbye! [Exit].

brake *noun* **1** device for stopping or slowing wheel or vehicle. **2** thing that impedes. ● *verb* **(-king) 1** apply brake. **2** slow or stop with brake.

bramble /'bræmb(ə)l/ *noun* wild thorny shrub, esp. blackberry.

bran *noun* husks separated from flour.

branch /brɑːntʃ/ *noun* **1** limb or bough of tree. **2** lateral extension or subdivision of river, railway, family, etc. **3** local office of business. ● *verb* (often + *off*) divide, diverge. □ **branch out** extend one's field of interest.

■ *noun* **1** arm, bough, limb, shoot, sprig, twig. **2** department, division, offshoot, part, ramification, section, subdivision, wing. ● *verb* diverge, divide, fork, ramify, split, subdivide. □ **branch out** see DIVERSIFY 1,2.

brand *noun* **1** particular make of goods; trade mark, label, etc. **2** (usually + *of*) characteristic kind. **3** identifying mark made with hot iron. **4** iron stamp for this. **5** piece of burning or charred wood. **6** stigma. **7** *poetical* torch. ● *verb* **1** mark with hot iron. **2** stigmatize. **3** assign trade mark etc. to. **4** impress unforgettably. □ **brand new** completely new.

■ *noun* **1** kind, label, make, sort, trade mark, type, variety. **2** see KIND *noun* 2. ● *verb* **1** burn, scar. **2** characterize, denounce as, discredit as, stigmatize as, vilify as. **3** identify, label, mark, stamp, tag.

brandish /'brændɪʃ/ *verb* wave or flourish.

brandy /'brændɪ/ *noun* (*plural* **-ies**) strong spirit distilled from wine or fermented fruit juice. □ **brandy snap** crisp rolled gingerbread wafer.

brash *adjective* **1** vulgarly assertive; impudent. **2** rash, reckless. □ **brashly** *adverb*. **brashness** *noun*.

■ **1** arrogant, brazen, bumptious, *colloquial* cocky, impertinent, impudent, insolent, presumptuous, *colloquial* pushy, rude, self-assertive. **2** hasty, impetuous, impulsive, rash, reckless.

brass /brɑːs/ *noun* **1** yellow alloy of copper and zinc. **2** brass objects. **3** brass wind instruments. **4** *slang* money. **5** brass memorial tablet. **6** *colloquial* effrontery. ● *adjective* made of brass. □ **brass band** band of brass instruments. **brass rubbing 1** reproducing of design from engraved brass on paper by rubbing with heelball. **2** impression obtained thus. **brass tacks** *slang* essential details.

brasserie /'bræsərɪ/ *noun* restaurant, originally one serving beer with food.

brassica /'bræsɪkə/ *noun* plant of cabbage family.

brassière /'bræzɪə/ *noun* bra.

brassy /'brɑːsɪ/ *adjective* (**-ier, -iest**) **1** of or like brass. **2** impudent. **3** vulgarly showy. **4** loud and blaring.

brat *noun usually derogatory* child.

bravado /brə'vɑːdəʊ/ *noun* show of boldness.

■ arrogance, bluster, machismo, swagger.

brave *adjective* (**-r, -st**) **1** able to face and endure danger or pain. **2** *formal* splendid, spectacular. ● *verb* (**-ving**) face bravely or defiantly. ● *noun* N. American Indian warrior. □ **bravely** *adverb*. **bravery** *noun*.

■ *adjective* **1** adventurous, audacious, bold, chivalrous, cool, courageous, daring, dauntless, determined, fearless, gallant, game, *colloquial* gutsy, heroic, indomitable, intrepid, lion-hearted, macho, noble, plucky, resolute, spirited, stalwart, stoical, stout-hearted, tough, unafraid, uncomplaining, undaunted, unshrinking, valiant, valorous, venturesome. □ **bravery** audacity, boldness, *slang* bottle, courage, daring, dauntlessness, determination, fearlessness, fibre, firmness, fortitude, gallantry, *colloquial* grit, *colloquial* guts, heroism, intrepidity, mettle, nerve, pluck, prowess, resolution, spirit, *colloquial* spunk, stoicism, tenacity, valour, will-power.

bravo /brɑː'vəʊ/ *interjection & noun* (*plural* **-s**) cry of approval.

bravura /brə'vjʊərə/ *noun* **1** brilliance of execution. **2** music requiring brilliant technique.

brawl *noun* noisy quarrel or fight. ● *verb* **1** engage in brawl. **2** (of stream) flow noisily. □ **brawler** *noun*.

■ *noun* affray, altercation, *colloquial* bust-up, clash, *colloquial* dust-up, fracas, fray, free-for-all, mêlée, *colloquial* punch-up, quarrel, *colloquial* row, *colloquial* scrap, scuffle, *colloquial* set-to, tussle. ● *verb* **1** see FIGHT *verb* 1.

brawn *noun* **1** muscular strength. **2** muscle, lean flesh. **3** jellied meat made esp. from pig's head. □ **brawny** *adjective* (**-ier, -iest**).

bray *noun* **1** cry of donkey. **2** harsh sound. ● *verb* **1** make a bray. **2** utter harshly.

braze *verb* (**-zing**) solder with alloy of brass.

brazen /'breɪz(ə)n/ *adjective* **1** shameless. **2** of or like brass. ● *verb* (+ *out*) face or undergo defiantly. □ **brazenly** *adverb*. **brazenness** *noun*.

■ *adjective* barefaced, blatant, brassy, cheeky, defiant, flagrant, impertinent, impudent, insolent, rude, shameless, unabashed, unashamed.

brazier /'breɪzɪə/ *noun* pan or stand for holding burning coals.

Brazil nut /brə'zɪl/ *noun* large 3-sided S. American nut.

breach /briːtʃ/ *noun* **1** breaking or neglect of rule, duty, promise, etc. **2** breaking off of relations; quarrel. **3** gap. ● *verb* **1** break through. **2** make gap in. **3** break (law etc.).

■ *noun* **1** contravention, infringement, transgression, violation. **2** alienation, difference, disagreement, divorce, drifting apart, estrangement, quarrel, rift, rupture, schism, separation, split. **3** aperture, break, chasm, crack, fissure, gap, hole, opening, rent, space, split.

bread /bred/ *noun* **1** baked dough of flour usually leavened with yeast. **2** necessary food. **3** *slang* money. □ **breadcrumb** small fragment of bread, esp. (in *plural*) for use in cooking. **bread-**

line subsistence level. **breadwinner** person whose work supports a family.

> ■ **2** see FOOD 1.

breadth /bredθ/ *noun* **1** broadness; distance from side to side. **2** freedom from mental limitations or prejudices.

break /breɪk/ *verb* (*past* **broke**; *past participle* **broken** /'brəʊk(ə)n/) **1** separate into pieces under blow or strain; shatter. **2** make or become inoperative. **3** break bone in (limb etc.). **4** interrupt; pause. **5** fail to observe or keep. **6** make or become weak, destroy; tame, subdue. **7** weaken effect of (fall, blow, etc.). **8** surpass (record). **9** reveal or be revealed. **10** come, produce, change, etc., with suddenness or violence. **11** (of waves) curl over and foam. **12** (of voice) change in quality at manhood or with emotion. **13** escape; emerge from. ● *noun* **1** breaking. **2** point where thing is broken; gap. **3** pause in work etc. **4** sudden dash. **5** a chance. **6** *Cricket* deflection of ball on bouncing. **7** points scored in one sequence at billiards etc. □ **break away** make or become free or separate. **break down 1** fail. **2** collapse. **3** demolish. **4** analyse. **break even** make neither profit nor loss. **break in 1** intrude forcibly esp. as thief. **2** interrupt. **3** accustom to habit. **4** tame (animal); accustom (horse) to saddle, bridle, etc. **breakneck** (of speed) dangerously fast. **break off 1** detach by breaking. **2** bring to an end. **3** cease talking etc. **break open** open forcibly. **break out 1** escape by force. **2** begin suddenly. **3** (+ *in*) become covered in (rash etc.). **breakout** forcible escape. **break person's heart** see HEART. **break through** penetrate. **breakthrough** major advance in knowledge etc. **break up 1** break into pieces. **2** disband. **3** part. **break-up** disintegration, collapse. **2** dispersal. **breakwater** barrier breaking force of waves. **break wind** release gas from anus.

> ■ *verb* **1** breach, burst, *colloquial* bust, chip, crack, crumple, crush, damage, demolish, destroy, disintegrate, fracture, fragment, knock down, ruin, shatter, shiver, smash, smash to smithereens, snap, splinter, split, squash, wreck. **2** *colloquial* bust, damage, destroy, disable, ruin, wreck. **5** contravene, defy, disobey, disregard, flout, go back on, infringe, transgress, violate. **8** beat, better, do more than, exceed, excel, go beyond, outdo, outstrip, pass, surpass. ● *noun* **1, 2** breach, breakage, burst, chink, cleft, crack, crevice, cut, fissure, fracture, gap, gash, hole, leak, opening, rent, rift, rupture, slit, split, tear. **3** *colloquial* breather, breathing-space, disruption, halt, hiatus, interlude, intermission, interruption, interval, lapse, *colloquial* let-up, lull, pause, respite, rest, suspension, tea break. □ **break down 3** see DEMOLISH 1. **4** see ANALYSE. **break in 1** see INTRUDE 1. **2** see INTERRUPT 1. **break off 2** see FINISH *verb* 1. **break out 1** see ESCAPE *verb* 1. **break through** see PENETRATE 1. **breakthrough** advance, development, discovery, find, improvement, innovation, invention, leap forward, revolution, success. **break up 1** see DISINTEGRATE 1. **breakwater** groyne, jetty, mole, pier.

breakable *adjective* easily broken.

breakage *noun* **1** broken thing. **2** breaking.

breakdown *noun* **1** mechanical failure. **2** loss of (esp. mental) health. **3** collapse; deterioration. **4** analysis.

> ■ **1** collapse, failure, fault, hitch, malfunction, stoppage. **2** collapse. **3** collapse, destruction, deterioration, disintegration, downfall, failure, ruin. **4** analysis, classification, dissection, itemization, listing, rundown.

breaker *noun* heavy breaking wave.

breakfast /'brekfəst/ *noun* first meal of day. ● *verb* have breakfast.

bream *noun* (*plural* same) **1** yellowish freshwater fish. **2** similar sea fish.

breast /brest/ *noun* **1** either of two milk-secreting organs on woman's chest. **2** chest. **3** part of garment covering this. **4** seat of emotions. ● *verb* **1** contend with. **2** reach top of (hill). □ **breastbone** bone connecting ribs in front. **breastfeed** feed (baby) from breast. **breastplate** armour covering chest. **breaststroke** stroke made while swimming on breast by extending arms forward and sweeping them back. **make a clean breast of** confess fully.

breath /breθ/ *noun* **1** air drawn into or expelled from lungs. **2** one respiration. **3** breath as perceived by senses. **4** slight movement of air. **5** slight rumour. □ **breathtaking** astounding, awe-inspiring. **breath test** test with Breathalyser. **take person's breath away** astonish or delight a person.

> ■ **1, 2** exhalation, inhalation, pant, puff, respiration, sigh. **4** breeze, gust, puff, stir, waft, whiff. **5** hint, murmur, whisper.

breathalyse *verb* give breath test to.

Breathalyser /'breθəlaɪzə/ *noun proprietary term* instrument for measuring alcohol in breath.

breathe /briːð/ *verb* (**-thing**) **1** take air into lungs and send it out again. **2** live. **3** utter or sound, esp. quietly. **4** pause. **5** send out or take in (as) with breathed air. □ **breathing-space** time to recover; pause.

> ■ **1** exhale, inhale, pant, puff, respire. **3** hint, let out, murmur, tell, whisper.

breather /'briːðə/ *noun colloquial* short period of rest.

breathless /'breθlɪs/ *adjective* **1** panting, out of breath. **2** still, windless. □ **breathlessly** *adverb*.

> ■ **1** exhausted, gasping, out of breath, panting, puffed, puffing, tired out, wheezy, winded.

bred *past & past participle* of BREED.

breech /briːtʃ/ *noun* **1** back part of gun or gun barrel. **2** (in *plural*) short trousers fastened below knee. □ **breech birth** birth in which buttocks emerge first.

breed *verb* (*past & past participle* **bred**) **1** produce offspring. **2** propagate; raise (animals). **3** yield, result in. **4** arise, spread. **5** train, bring up. **6** create (fissile material) by nuclear reaction. ● *noun* **1** stock of animals within species. **2** race, lineage. **3** sort, kind. □ **breeder reactor** nuclear reactor creating surplus fissile material. □ **breeder** *noun*.

■ *verb* **1** bear young, *literary* beget young, multiply, procreate, produce young, reproduce. **2** cultivate, propagate, raise, rear. **3** arouse, cause, create, cultivate, develop, engender, foster, generate, induce, nourish, nurture, occasion. ● *noun* **1** stock, strain. **2** ancestry, clan, family, line, lineage, pedigree, race, stock. **3** kind, sort, species, type, variety.

breeding *noun* **1** raising of offspring. **2** social behaviour. **3** ancestry.

breeze[1] *noun* gentle wind. ● *verb* **(-zing)** (+ *in*, *out*, *along*, etc.) *colloquial* saunter casually.

■ *noun* air current, breath, draught, waft, wind, *literary* zephyr.

breeze[2] *noun* small cinders. □ **breeze-block** lightweight building block made from breeze.

breezy *adjective* **(-ier, -iest)** slightly windy.

■ airy, blowy, draughty, fresh, gusty, windy.

Bren *noun* lightweight quick-firing machinegun.

brent *noun* small migratory goose.

brethren SEE BROTHER 3–4.

Breton /ˈbrɛt(ə)n/ *noun* native or language of Brittany. ● *adjective* of Brittany.

breve /briːv/ *noun* **1** *Music* note equal to two semibreves. **2** mark (˘) indicating short or unstressed vowel.

breviary /ˈbriːvɪərɪ/ *noun* (*plural* **-ies**) book containing RC daily office.

brevity /ˈbrɛvɪtɪ/ *noun* conciseness, shortness.

■ briefness, compactness, conciseness, concision, curtness, economy, incisiveness, pithiness, shortness, succinctness, terseness.

brew *verb* **1** make (beer etc.) by infusion, boiling, and fermenting. **2** make (tea etc.) by infusion. **3** undergo these processes. **4** be forming. **5** concoct. ● *noun* **1** amount brewed. **2** liquor brewed. □ **brewer** *noun*.

■ *verb* **1–3** boil, cook, ferment, infuse, make, simmer. **5** concoct, contrive, *colloquial* cook up, develop, devise, foment, hatch, plan, plot, prepare, scheme, stir up. ● *noun* **2** blend, compound, concoction, drink, infusion, liquor, mixture, potion, preparation, punch.

brewery /ˈbruːərɪ/ *noun* (*plural* **-ies**) factory for brewing beer etc.

briar[1,2] = BRIER[1,2].

bribe *verb* **(-bing)** persuade to act improperly by gift of money etc. ● *noun* money or services offered in bribing. □ **bribable** *adjective*. **bribery** *noun*.

■ *verb* buy off, corrupt, entice, influence, pervert, reward, suborn, tempt, tip. ● *noun* *slang* backhander, carrot, enticement, *colloquial* graft, incentive, inducement, *esp. US slang* payola, *colloquial* sweetener.

bric-a-brac /ˈbrɪkəbræk/ *noun* cheap ornaments, trinkets, etc.

brick *noun* **1** small rectangular block of baked clay, concrete, etc., used in building. **2** toy building block. **3** brick-shaped thing. **4** *slang* generous or loyal person. ● *verb* (+ *in*, *up*) close or block with brickwork. ● *adjective* made of bricks. □ **brickbat 1** piece of brick, esp. as missile. **2** insult. **bricklayer** person who builds with bricks. **brickwork** building or work in brick.

■ *noun* **1** block, breeze-block, cube, stone. **2** block, cube.

bridal /ˈbraɪd(ə)l/ *adjective* of bride or wedding.

bride *noun* woman on her wedding day and shortly before and after it. □ **bridegroom** man on his wedding day and shortly before and after it. **bridesmaid** woman or girl attending bride at wedding.

bridge[1] *noun* **1** structure providing way over road, railway, river, etc. **2** thing joining or connecting. **3** superstructure from which ship is directed. **4** upper bony part of nose. **5** prop under strings of violin etc. **6** bridgework. ● *verb* (-ging) be or make bridge over. □ **bridgehead** position held on enemy's side of river etc. **bridgework** dental structure covering gap and joined to teeth on either side. **bridging loan** loan to cover interval between buying one house and selling another.

■ *noun* **1** aqueduct, arch, crossing, flyover, footbridge, overpass, span, suspension bridge, viaduct, way over. **2** connection, link, tie. ● *verb* connect, cross, fill, join, link, pass over, span, straddle, tie together, traverse, unite.

bridge[2] *noun* card games derived from whist.

bridle /ˈbraɪd(ə)l/ *noun* **1** headgear for controlling horse etc. **2** restraining thing. ● *verb* **(-ling) 1** put bridle on. **2** control, curb. **3** express resentment, esp. by throwing up head and drawing in chin. □ **bridle path** (also **bridleway**) rough path for riders or walkers.

■ *verb* **2** check, control, curb, restrain.

Brie /briː/ *noun* flat round soft creamy French cheese.

brief /briːf/ *adjective* **1** of short duration. **2** concise. **3** scanty. ● *noun* **1** (in *plural*) short pants. **2** summary of case for guidance of barrister. **3** instructions for a task. ● *verb* **1** instruct (barrister) by brief. **2** inform or instruct in advance. □ **in brief** to sum up. □ **briefly** *adverb*. **briefness** *noun*.

■ *adjective* **1** cursory, ephemeral, *literary* evanescent, fast, fleeting, hasty, limited, little, momentary, passing, quick, sharp, short, short-lived, temporary, transient, transitory. **2** abbreviated, abridged, compact, compendious, compressed, concise, condensed, crisp, curt, curtailed, incisive, laconic, pithy, shortened, succinct, terse, thumbnail, to the point. ● *noun* **1** (*briefs*) knickers, *colloquial* panties, pants, *US* shorts, trunks, underpants. **2** argument, case, defence, dossier, summary. **3** directions, information, instructions, orders. ● *verb* advise, coach, direct, enlighten, *colloquial* fill in, give the facts, guide, inform, instruct, prepare, prime, put in the picture.

briefcase /'bri:fkeɪs/ *noun* flat document case.

briefing /'bri:fɪŋ/ *noun* **1** meeting for giving information or instructions. **2** information or instructions given.

brier[1] /braɪə/ *noun* (also **briar**) wild-rose bush.

brier[2] /braɪə/ *noun* (also **briar**) **1** white heath of S. Europe. **2** tobacco pipe made from its root.

brig[1] *noun* two-masted square-rigged ship.

brig[2] *noun Scottish & Northern English* bridge.

brigade /brɪ'geɪd/ *noun* **1** military unit forming part of division. **2** organized band of workers etc.

brigadier /brɪgə'dɪə/ *noun* army officer next below major-general.

brigand /'brɪgənd/ *noun* member of robber gang.
- bandit, buccaneer, desperado, gangster, *historical* highwayman, marauder, outlaw, pirate, robber, ruffian, thief.

bright /braɪt/ *adjective* **1** emitting or reflecting much light; shining. **2** vivid. **3** sunny. **4** clever. **5** cheerful. **6** (of prospects etc.) promising. □ **look on the bright side** be optimistic. □ **brightly** *adverb*. **brightness** *noun*.
- **1** ablaze, aglow, alight, beaming, blazing, burnished, dazzling, flashing, flashy, glaring, gleaming, glistening, glittering, glossy, glowing, incandescent, lambent, light, luminous, lustrous, pellucid, polished, radiant, *literary* refulgent, resplendent, scintillating, shimmering, shining, shiny, sparkling, twinkling. **2** see VIVID 1. **3** clear, cloudless, fair, sunny. **4** see CLEVER 1. **5** see CHEERFUL 1–2. **6** auspicious, favourable, good, hopeful, optimistic, rosy.

brighten *verb* (often + *up*) **1** make or become lighter. **2** make or become more cheerful.
- **1** become sunny, clear up, lighten. **2** cheer (up), enliven, gladden, illuminate, light up, liven up, perk up, revitalize, smarten up.

brill[1] *noun* (*plural* same) flatfish resembling turbot.

brill[2] *adjective colloquial* excellent.

brilliant /'brɪlɪənt/ *adjective* **1** bright, sparkling. **2** highly talented. **3** showy. **4** *colloquial* excellent. ● *noun* diamond of finest quality. □ **brilliance** *noun*. **brilliantly** *adverb*.
- *adjective* **1** bright, coruscating, dazzling, glaring, glittering, intense, radiant, resplendent, scintillating, shining, sparkling, vivid. **2** see TALENTED (TALENT). **3** dazzling, gaudy, glaring, glittering, *colloquial* glorious, impressive, showy, splendid, striking. **4** see EXCELLENT.

brilliantine /'brɪljənti:n/ *noun* cosmetic for making hair glossy.

brim *noun* **1** edge of vessel or hollow. **2** projecting edge of hat. ● *verb* (**-mm-**) fill or be full to brim.
- *noun* **1** brink, circumference, edge, limit, lip, margin, perimeter, rim, verge.

brimstone /'brɪmstəʊn/ *noun archaic* sulphur.

brindled /'brɪnd(ə)ld/ *adjective* brown with streaks of other colour.

brine *noun* salt water; sea water.

bring *verb* (*past & past participle* **brought** /brɔːt/) **1** come with; carry, convey. **2** cause to be present. **3** cause, result in. **4** be sold for. **5** submit (criminal charge); initiate (legal action). □ **bring about** cause to happen. **bring-and-buy sale** charity sale at which people bring goods for sale and buy what is brought by others. **bring down** cause to fall. **bring forth 1** produce, emit, cause. **2** give birth to. **bring forward 1** move to earlier time. **2** transfer from previous page or account. **3** draw attention to. **bring in 1** introduce. **2** produce as profit. **bring off** succeed in. **bring on** cause to happen, appear, or progress. **bring out 1** emphasize. **2** produce; publish. **bring round 1** restore to consciousness. **2** win over. **bring to bear** (usually + *on*) direct and concentrate (forces). **bring up 1** raise and educate. **2** vomit. **3** draw attention to.
- **1** accompany, bear, carry, conduct, convey, deliver, escort, fetch, guide, lead, take, transport, usher. **2** attract, draw, get, induce, lead. **3** cause, create, earn, engender, generate, give rise to, lead to, occasion, produce, prompt, provoke, result in. □ **bring about** see CREATE 1. **bring in 1** see INTRODUCE 3. **2** see EARN 2. **bring off** see ACHIEVE 2. **bring on** see ACCELERATE 2, CAUSE *verb* 1. **bring out 1** see EMPHASIZE. **2** see PRODUCE *verb* 1, PUBLISH 1. **bring up 1** see RAISE *verb* 8, EDUCATE. **3** see RAISE *verb* 7.

brink *noun* **1** edge of precipice etc. **2** furthest point before danger, discovery, etc. □ **brinkmanship** policy of pursuing dangerous course to brink of catastrophe.
- **1** bank, border, boundary, brim, circumference, edge, fringe, limit, lip, margin, perimeter, periphery, rim, skirt, threshold, verge.

briny /'braɪnɪ/ *adjective* (**-ier, -iest**) of brine or sea; salt. ● *noun* (**the briny**) *slang* the sea.

briquette /brɪ'ket/ *noun* block of compressed coal dust as fuel.

brisk *adjective* **1** active, lively, quick. **2** (of wind) fresh, invigorating. □ **briskly** *adverb*. **briskness** *noun*.
- **1** active, alert, animated, bright, businesslike, bustling, busy, crisp, decisive, energetic, fast, keen, lively, nimble, quick, rapid, *colloquial* snappy, spanking (*pace*), speedy, spirited, sprightly, spry, vigorous. **2** bracing, enlivening, fresh, invigorating, refreshing, stimulating.

brisket /'brɪskɪt/ *noun* animal's breast, esp. as joint of meat.

brisling /'brɪzlɪŋ/ *noun* (*plural* same or **-s**) small herring or sprat.

bristle /'brɪs(ə)l/ *noun* short stiff hair, esp. one used in brushes etc. ● *verb* (**-ling**) **1** (of hair etc.) (cause to) stand up. **2** show irritation. **3** (usually + *with*) be covered (with) or abundant (in). □ **bristly** *adjective*.

■ *noun* hair, whisker; (*bristles*) stubble. ● *verb* **2** become angry, become defensive, become indignant, bridle, flare up.

British /'brɪtɪʃ/ *adjective* of Britain. ● *plural noun* (**the British**) the British people. □ **British Summer Time** = SUMMER TIME.

Briton /'brɪt(ə)n/ *noun* **1** inhabitant of S. Britain before Roman conquest. **2** native of Great Britain.

brittle /'brɪt(ə)l/ *adjective* apt to break, fragile.
■ breakable, crisp, crumbling, delicate, easily broken, fragile, frail, frangible, weak.

broach /brəʊtʃ/ *verb* **1** raise for discussion. **2** pierce (cask) to draw liquor. **3** open and start using.

broad /brɔːd/ *adjective* **1** large across, extensive. **2** of specified breadth. **3** full, clear. **4** explicit. **5** general, undetailed; wide-ranging. **6** tolerant. **7** coarse. **8** (of accent) marked, strong. ● *noun* **1** broad part. **2** *US slang* woman. **3** (**the Broads**) large areas of water in E. Anglia. □ **broad bean 1** bean with large flat seeds. **2** one such seed. **broadloom** (carpet) woven in broad width. **broadsheet** large-sized newspaper. □ **broaden** *verb*. **broadly** *adverb*. **broadness** *noun*.
■ *adjective* **1** ample, capacious, expansive, extensive, great, large, open, roomy, spacious, sweeping, vast, wide. **3** clear, complete, full, open, plain. **4** clear, direct, explicit, obvious, plain, undisguised. **5** all-embracing, catholic, comprehensive, eclectic, encyclopedic, general, imprecise, indefinite, inexact, non-specific, sweeping, undetailed, universal, vague, wide-ranging. **6** see BROAD-MINDED. **7** bawdy, blue, coarse, earthy, improper, impure, indecent, indelicate, racy, ribald, suggestive, vulgar. □ **broaden** branch out, build up, develop, diversify, enlarge, expand, extend, increase, open up, spread, widen.

broadcast *verb* (*past & past participle* **-cast**) **1** transmit by radio or television. **2** take part in such transmission. **3** scatter (seed) etc. **4** disseminate widely. ● *noun* radio or television programme or transmission. □ **broadcaster** *noun*. **broadcasting** *noun*.
■ *verb* **1** air, radio, relay, screen, send out, televise, transmit. **3** scatter, sow. **4** advertise, announce, circulate, disseminate, make known, make public, proclaim, promulgate, publish, report, send out, spread about. ● *noun* programme, relay, show, telecast, transmission. □ **broadcaster** anchorman, anchorperson, anchorwoman, announcer, commentator, compère, disc jockey, DJ, newsreader, presenter.

broad-minded *adjective* tolerant or liberal in one's views. □ **broad-mindedness** *noun*.
■ broad, enlightened, liberal, open-minded, permissive, tolerant, unbiased, unbigoted, unprejudiced, unshockable.

broadside *noun* **1** vigorous verbal attack. **2** firing of all guns on one side of ship. □ **broadside on** sideways on.

brocade /brə'keɪd/ *noun* fabric woven with raised pattern.

broccoli /'brɒkəlɪ/ *noun* brassica with greenish flower heads.

brochure /'brəʊʃə/ *noun* booklet, pamphlet, esp. containing descriptive information.
■ booklet, catalogue, circular, folder, leaflet, pamphlet, prospectus, tract.

broderie anglaise /brəʊdərɪ ɑ̃'gleɪz/ *noun* open embroidery on usually white cotton or linen.

brogue /brəʊg/ *noun* **1** strong shoe with ornamental perforations. **2** rough shoe of untanned leather. **3** marked local, esp. Irish, accent.

broil *verb* **1** grill (meat). **2** make or be very hot.

broiler *noun* young chicken for broiling.

broke *past* of BREAK. ● *adjective colloquial* having no money, bankrupt.

broken /'brəʊkən/ *past participle* of BREAK. ● *adjective* **1** that has been broken. **2** reduced to despair. **3** (of language) spoken imperfectly. **4** interrupted. □ **broken-hearted** crushed by grief. **broken home** family disrupted by divorce or separation.

broker *noun* **1** middleman, agent. **2** stockbroker. □ **broking** *noun*.

brokerage *noun* broker's fee or commission.

brolly /'brɒlɪ/ *noun* (*plural* **-ies**) *colloquial* umbrella.

bromide /'brəʊmaɪd/ *noun* **1** binary compound of bromine, esp. one used as sedative. **2** trite remark.

bromine /'brəʊmiːn/ *noun* poisonous liquid non-metallic element with choking smell.

bronchial /'brɒŋkɪəl/ *adjective* of two main divisions of windpipe or smaller tubes into which they divide.

bronchitis /brɒŋ'kaɪtɪs/ *noun* inflammation of bronchial mucous membrane.

bronco /'brɒŋkəʊ/ *noun* (*plural* **-s**) wild or half-tamed horse of western US.

brontosaurus /brɒntə'sɔːrəs/ *noun* (*plural* **-ruses**) = APATOSAURUS.

bronze /brɒnz/ *noun* **1** brown alloy of copper and tin. **2** its colour. **3** work of art or medal in it. ● *adjective* made of or coloured like bronze. ● *verb* (**-zing**) **1** make or grow brown. **2** tan. □ **Bronze Age** period when tools were of bronze. **bronze medal** medal given usually as third prize.

brooch /brəʊtʃ/ *noun* ornamental hinged pin.
■ badge, clasp, clip, fastening.

brood /bruːd/ *noun* **1** bird's or other animal's young produced at one hatch or birth. **2** *colloquial* children of a family. ● *verb* **1** (often + *on*, *over*) worry or ponder, esp. resentfully. **2** (of hen) sit on eggs.
■ *noun* **1** clutch (*of eggs*), issue, litter, offspring, progeny, young. **2** children, family, offspring, progeny. ● *verb* **1** agonize, eat one's heart out, fret, mope, ponder, sulk, worry; (*brood on*) dwell on. **2** hatch, incubate, sit on.

broody *adjective* (**-ier, -iest**) **1** (of hen) wanting to brood. **2** sullenly thoughtful. **3** *colloquial* (of woman) wanting pregnancy.

brook[1] /brʊk/ *noun* small stream.
▪ beck, *Scottish* burn, channel, rill, rivulet, runnel, stream, watercourse.

brook[2] /brʊk/ *verb* tolerate, allow.
▪ see TOLERATE 1.

broom /bru:m/ *noun* **1** long-handled brush for sweeping. **2** chiefly yellow-flowered shrub. □ **broomstick** broom-handle.

Bros. *abbreviation* Brothers.

broth /brɒθ/ *noun* thin meat or fish soup.

brothel /'brɒθ(ə)l/ *noun* premises for prostitution.

brother /'brʌðə/ *noun* **1** man or boy in relation to his siblings. **2** close man friend. **3** (*plural* also **brethren** /'breðrm/) member of male religious order. **4** (*plural* also **brethren**) fellow Christian etc. **5** fellow human being. □ **brother-in-law** (*plural* **brothers-in-law**) **1** wife's or husband's brother. **2** sister's husband. □ **brotherly** *adjective*.

brotherhood *noun* **1** relationship (as) between brothers. **2** (members of) association for mutual help etc.

brought *past & past participle* of BRING.

brow /braʊ/ *noun* **1** forehead. **2** (usually in *plural*) eyebrow. **3** summit of hill. **4** edge of cliff etc.

browbeat *verb* (*past* **-beat**, *past participle* **-beaten**) intimidate, bully.
▪ badger, bully, coerce, cow, frighten, hector, intimidate, tyrannize.

brown /braʊn/ *adjective* **1** of colour of dark wood or rich soil. **2** dark-skinned; tanned. ● *noun* brown colour, paint, clothes, etc. ● *verb* make or become brown. □ **brown bread** bread made of wholemeal or wheatmeal flour. **browned off** *colloquial* bored, fed up. **Brown Owl** adult leader of Brownies. **brown rice** unpolished rice. **brown sugar** partially refined sugar. □ **brownish** *adjective*.
▪ *adjective* **1** beige, bronze, buff, chestnut, chocolate, dun, fawn, khaki, ochre, russet, sepia, tan, tawny, terracotta, umber. ● *verb* bronze, burn, grill, sear, suntan, tan, toast.

Brownie /'braʊnɪ/ *noun* **1** junior Guide. **2** (**brownie**) small square of chocolate cake with nuts. **3** (**brownie**) benevolent elf.

browse /braʊz/ *verb* (**-sing**) **1** read or look around desultorily. **2** feed on leaves and young shoots. ● *noun* **1** browsing. **2** twigs, shoots, etc. as fodder.
▪ *verb* **1** dip in, flick through, leaf through, look through, peruse, read here and there, scan, skim, thumb through. **2** crop grass, eat, feed, graze, pasture.

bruise /bru:z/ *noun* **1** discoloration of skin caused by blow or pressure. **2** similar damage on fruit etc. ● *verb* (**-sing**) **1** inflict bruise on. **2** be susceptible to bruises.
▪ *noun* **1** black eye, bump, contusion, discoloration, *colloquial* shiner, welt. ● *verb* **1** blacken, damage, discolour, injure, knock, mark, wound.

bruiser *noun colloquial* tough brutal person.

bruit /bru:t/ *verb* (often + *abroad*, *about*) spread (report or rumour).

brunch *noun* combination of breakfast and lunch.

brunette /bru:'net/ *noun* woman with dark hair.

brunt *noun* chief impact of attack etc.

brush *noun* **1** cleaning or hairdressing or painting implement of bristles etc. set in holder. **2** application of brush. **3** short esp. unpleasant encounter. **4** fox's tail. **5** carbon or metal piece serving as electrical contact. ● *verb* **1** use brush on. **2** touch lightly, graze in passing. □ **brush aside** dismiss or discard lightly. **brush off** dismiss abruptly. **brush-off** *noun* dismissal, rebuff. **brush up 1** clean up or smarten. **2** revise (subject, skill). **brushwood 1** undergrowth, thicket. **2** cut or broken twigs etc. **brushwork** painter's way of using brush.
▪ *noun* **1** besom, broom. **3** see CONFLICT *noun* 1. ● *verb* **1** groom, scrub, sweep. **2** graze, touch. □ **brush aside** see DISMISS 3,4, DISREGARD *verb*. **brush-off** see REBUFF *noun*. **brush up 2** see REVISE 3.

brusque /brʊsk/ *adjective* abrupt, offhand. □ **brusquely** *adverb*. **brusqueness** *noun*.

Brussels sprout /'brʌs(ə)lz/ *noun* **1** brassica with small cabbage-like buds on stem. **2** such bud.

brutal /'bru:t(ə)l/ *adjective* **1** savagely cruel. **2** mercilessly frank. □ **brutality** /-'tæl-/ *noun* (*plural* **-ies**). **brutalize** *verb* (also **-ise**) (**-zing**, **-sing**).
▪ **1** atrocious, barbaric, barbarous, beastly, bestial, bloodthirsty, bloody, brutish, callous, cold-blooded, cruel, dehumanized, ferocious, hard-hearted, heartless, inhuman, inhumane, merciless, murderous, pitiless, remorseless, ruthless, *colloquial* sadistic, savage, uncivilized, unfeeling, vicious, violent, wild. **2** see UNKIND. □ **brutalize** dehumanize, harden.

brute /bru:t/ *noun* **1** cruel person. **2** *colloquial* unpleasant person. **3** animal other than man. ● *adjective* **1** unthinking. **2** cruel, stupid. □ **brutish** *adjective*.
▪ *noun* **1** barbarian, beast, bully, devil, monster, ogre, *colloquial* sadist, savage. **2** *colloquial* rat, *slang* rotter, *colloquial* so-and-so, *slang* stinker, *colloquial* swine. **3** animal, beast, creature. ● *adjective* **1** crude, irrational, mindless, rough, stupid, unfeeling, unthinking. **2** see BRUTISH. □ **brutish** animal, barbaric, barbarous, beastly, bestial, boorish, brutal, coarse, cold-blooded, crude, cruel, gross, inhuman, insensitive, loutish, mindless, savage, senseless, stupid, subhuman, uncouth, unintelligent, unthinking.

bryony /'braɪənɪ/ *noun* (*plural* **-ies**) climbing hedge plant.

B.Sc. *abbreviation* Bachelor of Science.

BST *abbreviation* British Summer Time.

Bt. *abbreviation* Baronet.

bubble /'bʌb(ə)l/ *noun* **1** thin sphere of liquid enclosing air or gas. **2** air-filled cavity in glass etc. **3** transparent domed cavity. ● *verb* (**-ling**) **1** send up or rise in bubbles. **2** make sound of boiling. □ **bubble and squeak** cooked potatoes and cabbage fried together. **bubble bath 1** additive to make bathwater bubbly. **2** bath with this added. **bubblegum** chewing gum that can be blown into bubbles.

■ *noun* **1** (*bubbles*) effervescence, fizz, foam, froth, head, lather, spume, suds. **2** blister, hollow, vesicle. ● *verb* boil, effervesce, fizz, fizzle, foam, froth, gurgle, seethe, sparkle.

bubbly *adjective* (**-ier, -iest**) **1** full of bubbles. **2** exuberant. ● *noun colloquial* champagne.

■ *adjective* **1** carbonated, effervescent, fizzy, foaming, seething, sparkling. **2** see LIVELY 1.

bubonic /bju:'bɒnɪk/ *adjective* (of plague) marked by swellings esp. in groin and armpits.

buccaneer /bʌkə'nɪə/ *noun* pirate; adventurer. □ **buccaneering** *adjective & noun.*

■ adventurer, bandit, brigand, corsair, marauder, pirate, privateer, robber.

buck[1] *noun* male deer, hare, or rabbit. ● *verb* **1** (of horse) jump vertically with back arched. **2** throw (rider) thus. **3** (usually + *up*) *colloquial* cheer up. **4** (usually + *up*) *colloquial* hurry up. □ **buckshot** coarse shot for gun. **buck-tooth** projecting upper tooth.

buck[2] *noun US & Australian slang* dollar.

buck[3] *noun slang* small object placed before dealer at poker. □ **pass the buck** *colloquial* shift responsibility.

bucket /'bʌkɪt/ *noun* **1** usually round open container with handle, for carrying or holding water etc. **2** amount contained in this. **3** (in *plural*) *colloquial* large quantities. **4** compartment or scoop in waterwheel, dredger, or grain elevator. ● *verb* (**-t-**) **1** (often + *down*) *colloquial* (esp. of rain) pour heavily. **2** (often + *along*) move jerkily or bumpily. □ **bucket seat** one with rounded back, to fit one person. **bucket shop 1** agency dealing in cheap airline tickets. **2** unregistered broking agency.

■ *noun* **1, 2** can, pail, scuttle.

buckle /'bʌk(ə)l/ *noun* clasp with usually hinged pin for securing strap or belt etc. ● *verb* (**-ling**) **1** fasten with buckle. **2** (cause to) crumple under pressure. □ **buckle down** make determined effort.

■ *noun* catch, clasp, clip, fastener, fastening. ● *verb* **1** clasp, clip, do up, fasten, hitch up, hook up, secure. **2** bend, bulge, cave in, collapse, contort, crumple, curve, dent, distort, fold, twist, warp.

buckram /'bʌkrəm/ *noun* coarse linen etc. stiffened with paste etc.

buckshee /bʌk'ʃi:/ *adjective & adverb slang* free of charge.

buckwheat *noun* seed of plant related to rhubarb.

bucolic /bju:'kɒlɪk/ *adjective* of shepherds; rustic, pastoral.

bud *noun* **1** projection from which branch, leaf, or flower develops. **2** flower or leaf not fully open. **3** asexual growth separating from organism as new animal. ● *verb* (**-dd-**) **1** form buds. **2** (often as **budding** *adjective*) begin to grow or develop. **3** graft bud of (plant) on another plant.

■ *noun* **1** shoot, sprout. ● *verb* **1** burgeon, develop, shoot, sprout. **2** burgeon, develop; (**budding**) see POTENTIAL *adjective*, PROMISING.

Buddhism /'bʊdɪz(ə)m/ *noun* Asian religion founded by Gautama Buddha. □ **Buddhist** *adjective & noun.*

buddleia /'bʌdlɪə/ *noun* shrub with flowers attractive to butterflies.

buddy /'bʌdɪ/ *noun* (*plural* **-ies**) *colloquial* friend, mate.

budge *verb* (**-ging**) **1** move in slightest degree. **2** cause to move or change opinion. **3** (+ *up*) move to make room for another person.

■ **1** change position, give way, move, shift, stir, yield. **2** alter, change, dislodge, influence, move, persuade, propel, push, remove, shift, sway.

budgerigar /bʌdʒərɪ'gɑ:/ *noun* small parrot often kept as pet.

budget /'bʌdʒɪt/ *noun* **1** amount of money needed or available. **2** (**the Budget**) annual estimate of country's revenue and expenditure. **3** similar estimate for group or person. ● *verb* (**-t-**) (often + *for*) allow or arrange for in budget. □ **budgetary** *adjective*.

■ *noun* **1** allocation, allowance, funds, means, resources. **3** accounts, estimate, financial planning. ● *verb* allocate money, allot resources, estimate expenditure, plan one's spending, ration one's spending; (*budget for*) allow for, provide for.

budgie /'bʌdʒɪ/ *noun colloquial* budgerigar.

buff *adjective* of yellowish beige colour. ● *noun* **1** this colour. **2** *colloquial* enthusiast. **3** velvety dull yellow leather. ● *verb* **1** polish. **2** make (leather) velvety. □ **in the buff** *colloquial* naked.

■ *noun* **2** see ENTHUSIAST (ENTHUSIASM). ● *verb* **1** burnish, clean, polish, rub, shine, smooth.

buffalo /'bʌfələʊ/ *noun* (*plural* same or **-es**) any of various kinds of ox. **2** American bison.

buffer[1] *noun* apparatus for deadening impact esp. of railway vehicles. ● *verb* act as buffer to. □ **buffer state** minor one between two larger ones, regarded as reducing friction.

■ bumper, cushion, pad, shield, shock absorber.

buffer[2] *noun slang* old or incompetent fellow.

buffet[1] /'bʊfeɪ/ *noun* **1** room or counter where refreshments are sold. **2** self-service meal of several dishes set out at once. **3** (also /'bʌfɪt/) sideboard. □ **buffet car** railway coach in which refreshments are served.

■ **1** bar, café, cafeteria, counter, snack bar.

buffet² /'bʌfɪt/ verb (**-t-**) strike repeatedly. ● noun **1** blow with hand. **2** shock.

■ verb see HIT verb 1.

buffoon /bə'fuːn/ noun **1** silly or ludicrous person. **2** jester. □ **buffoonery** noun.

bug noun **1** small insect. **2** concealed microphone. **3** colloquial error in computer program etc. **4** slang micro-organism, or disease caused by it. **5** slang enthusiasm, obsession. ● verb (**-gg-**) **1** conceal microphone in. **2** listen in by means of concealed microphone. **3** slang annoy.

■ noun **1** see INSECT. **3** defect, error, failing, fault, flaw, colloquial gremlin, imperfection, malfunction, mistake, virus. **4** see MICROBE, DISEASE. ● verb **1, 2** intercept, listen in to, spy on, tap. **3** see ANNOY 1–2.

bugbear noun **1** cause of annoyance. **2** object of baseless fear.

buggy /'bʌgɪ/ noun (plural **-ies**) **1** small sturdy motor vehicle. **2** lightweight pushchair. **3** light horse-drawn vehicle for one or two people.

bugle /'bjuːg(ə)l/ noun brass instrument like small trumpet. ● verb (**-ling**) sound bugle. □ **bugler** noun.

build /bɪld/ verb (past & past participle **built** /bɪlt/) **1** construct or cause to be constructed. **2** develop or establish. ● noun **1** physical proportions. **2** style of construction. □ **build in** incorporate. **build up 1** increase in size or strength. **2** praise. **3** gradually establish or be established. **build-up** noun **1** favourable description in advance. **2** gradual approach to climax. **3** accumulation.

■ verb **1** assemble, construct, erect, fabricate, form, knock together, make, put together, put up, raise, rear. **2** develop, establish, found, set up. □ **build up 1** see INTENSIFY.

builder noun **1** contractor who builds houses etc. **2** bricklayer etc. on building site.

■ **2** bricklayer, construction worker, labourer.

building noun house or other structure with roof and walls. □ **building society** financial organization (not public company) that pays interest on savings accounts, lends money esp. for mortgages, etc.

■ construction, edifice, erection, pile, premises, structure.

built /bɪlt/ past & past participle of BUILD. □ **built-in** integral. **built-up** covered with buildings.

bulb noun **1** rounded base of stem of some plants. **2** light bulb. **3** bulb-shaped thing or part.

■ **1** corm.

bulbous /'bʌlbəs/ adjective bulb-shaped, bulging.

■ bloated, bulging, convex, distended, ovoid, pear-shaped, pot-bellied, rotund, rounded, spherical, swollen, tuberous.

bulge noun **1** irregular swelling. **2** colloquial temporary increase. ● verb (**-ging**) swell outwards. □ **bulgy** adjective.

■ noun **1** bump, distension, hump, knob, lump, projection, protrusion, protuberance, rise, swelling. ● verb belly, billow, dilate, distend, enlarge, expand, project, protrude, stick out, swell.

bulimia /bʊ'lɪmɪə/ noun (in full **bulimia nervosa** /nɜː'vəʊsə/) disorder in which overeating alternates with self-induced vomiting, fasting, etc.

bulk noun **1** size, magnitude, esp. when great. **2** (**the bulk**) the greater part. **3** large quantity. ● verb **1** seem (in size or importance). **2** make thicker. □ **bulk buying** buying in quantity at discount. **bulkhead** upright partition in ship, aircraft, etc.

■ noun **1** amplitude, body, dimensions, extent, immensity, magnitude, mass, size, substance, volume, weight. **2** (**the bulk**) the greater part, the lion's share, the majority, most.

bulky /'bʌlkɪ/ adjective (**-ier**, **-iest**) large, unwieldy.

■ awkward, big, chunky, cumbersome, large, unwieldy, weighty.

bull¹ /bʊl/ noun **1** uncastrated male ox. **2** male whale or elephant etc. **3** bull's-eye of target. **4** person who buys shares in hope of selling at higher price later. □ **bulldog 1** short-haired heavy-jowled sturdy dog. **2** tenacious and courageous person. **Bulldog clip** strong sprung clip for papers etc. **bulldoze 1** clear with bulldozer. **2** colloquial intimidate. **3** colloquial make (one's way) forcibly. **bulldozer** powerful tractor with broad upright blade for clearing ground. **bullfight** public baiting, and usually killing, of bulls. **bullfinch** pink and black finch. **bullfrog** large American frog with booming croak. **bullring** arena for bullfight. **bull's-eye 1** centre of target. **2** hard minty sweet. **bull terrier** cross between bulldog and terrier. □ **bullish** adjective.

■ □ **bull's-eye 1** bull, centre, mark, target.

bull² /bʊl/ noun papal edict.

bull³ /bʊl/ noun **1** slang nonsense. **2** slang unnecessary routine tasks. **3** absurdly illogical statement.

bullet /'bʊlɪt/ noun small pointed missile fired from rifle, revolver, etc. □ **bulletproof** resistant to bullets.

bulletin /'bʊlɪtɪn/ noun **1** short official statement. **2** short broadcast news report.

■ **1** announcement, communication, communiqué, dispatch, message, notice, report, statement. **2** newsflash, report.

bullion /'bʊlɪən/ noun gold or silver in lump or valued by weight.

bullock /'bʊlək/ noun castrated bull.

bully¹ /'bʊlɪ/ noun (plural **-ies**) person coercing

others by fear. ● *verb* (**-ies, -ied**) persecute or oppress by force or threats. ● *interjection* (+ *for*) very good.

■ *verb* bludgeon, browbeat, coerce, cow, domineer, frighten, harass, hector, intimidate, oppress, persecute, pick on, *colloquial* push around, terrorize, threaten, torment, tyrannize.

bully[2] /'bʊlɪ/ (in full **bully off**) *noun* (*plural* **-ies**) putting ball into play in hockey. ● *verb* (**-ies, -ied**) start play thus.

bully[3] /'bʊlɪ/ *noun* (in full **bully beef**) corned beef.

bulrush /'bʊlrʌʃ/ *noun* **1** tall rush. **2** *Biblical* papyrus.

bulwark /'bʊlwək/ *noun* **1** defensive wall, esp. of earth. **2** person or principle that protects. **3** (usually in *plural*) ship's side above deck.

■ **1** barrier, defence, earthwork, fortification, parapet, protection, rampart, *Military* redoubt, wall. **2** see SHIELD *noun* 2.

bum[1] *noun slang* buttocks. □ **bumbag** small pouch worn round waist.

bum[2] *US slang noun* loafer, dissolute person. ● *verb* (**-mm-**) **1** (often + *around*) loaf, wander around. **2** cadge. ● *adjective* of poor quality.

bumble /'bʌmb(ə)l/ *verb* (**-ling**) **1** (+ *on*) speak ramblingly. **2** be inept; blunder. □ **bumble-bee** large bee with loud hum.

bump *noun* **1** dull-sounding blow or collision. **2** swelling caused by it. **3** uneven patch on road etc. **4** prominence on skull, thought to indicate mental faculty. ● *verb* **1** come or strike with bump against. **2** hurt thus. **3** (usually + *along*) move along with jolts. □ **bump into** *colloquial* meet by chance. **bump off** *slang* murder. **bump up** *colloquial* increase.

■ *noun* **1** bang, blow, buffet, collision, crash, knock, smash, thud, thump. **2** bulge, distension, hump, knob, lump, projection, protrusion, protuberance, rise, swelling, tumescence, welt. ● *verb* **1, 2** bang, collide with, crash (into), hit, jar, knock, ram, run into, slam (into), smash (into), strike, thump, *colloquial* wallop. **3** bounce, jerk, jolt, shake. □ **bump into** see MEET[1] *verb* 1. **bump off** see KILL *verb* 1.

bumper *noun* **1** horizontal bar on motor vehicle to reduce damage in collisions. **2** *Cricket* ball rising high after pitching. **3** brim-full glass. ● *adjective* unusually large or abundant.

bumpkin /'bʌmpkɪn/ *noun* rustic or awkward person.

bumptious /'bʌmpʃəs/ *adjective* self-assertive, conceited.

■ arrogant, *colloquial* big-headed, boastful, brash, *colloquial* cocky, conceited, egotistic(al), forward, immodest, officious, overbearing, overconfident, pompous, presumptuous, pretentious, *colloquial* pushy, self-assertive, self-important, smug, *colloquial* snooty, *colloquial* stuck-up, swaggering, vain, vainglorious, *literary* vaunting.

bumpy *adjective* (**-ier, -iest**) **1** causing jolts. **2** having many bumps.

■ **1** bouncy, jarring, jerky, jolting. **2** broken, irregular, jagged, knobbly, lumpy, pitted, rocky, rough, rutted, stony, uneven.

bun *noun* **1** small sweet cake or bread roll often with dried fruit. **2** small coil of hair at back of head.

bunch *noun* **1** cluster of things growing or fastened together. **2** lot or set. **3** *colloquial* gang, group. ● *verb* **1** arrange in bunch(es). **2** gather in folds. **3** come, cling, or crowd together.

■ *noun* **1** bundle, clump, cluster, sheaf, tuft; (*bunch of flowers*) bouquet, posy, spray. **2** batch, collection, heap, lot, number, *usually derogatory* pack, quantity, set. **3** band, *colloquial* crowd, gang, gathering, group, *colloquial* mob, party, team, troop. ● *verb* **3** assemble, cluster, collect, congregate, crowd, flock, gather, group, herd, huddle, mass, pack.

bundle /'bʌnd(ə)l/ *noun* **1** collection of things tied or fastened together. **2** set of nerve fibres etc. **3** *slang* large amount of money. ● *verb* (**-ling**) **1** (usually + *up*) tie in bundle. **2** (usually + *into*) throw or move carelessly. **3** (usually + *out, off, away*, etc.) send away hurriedly.

■ *noun* **1** bale, bunch, collection, pack, package, packet, parcel, sheaf, truss. ● *verb* **1** bale, bind, fasten, pack, package, roll, tie, truss, wrap. **3** (*bundle out*) see EJECT 1.

bung *noun* stopper, esp. for cask. ● *verb* **1** stop with bung. **2** *slang* throw. □ **bung up** block up.

■ *noun* cork, plug, stopper. ● *verb* **2** see THROW *verb* 1,2.

bungalow /'bʌŋgələʊ/ *noun* one-storeyed house.

bungee /'bʌndʒɪ/ *noun* elasticated cord. □ **bungee jumping** sport of jumping from great height while secured by bungee.

bungle /'bʌŋg(ə)l/ *verb* (**-ling**) **1** mismanage, fail to accomplish. **2** work awkwardly. ● *noun* bungled work or attempt.

■ *verb* **1** botch, foul up, *slang* fluff, *colloquial* make a hash of, make a mess of, mess up, mismanage, *colloquial* muff, ruin, *slang* screw up, spoil. **2** blunder, bumble, make a mess.

bunion /'bʌnjən/ *noun* swelling on foot, esp. on side of big toe.

bunk[1] *noun* shelflike bed against wall. □ **bunk bed** each of two or more bunks one above the other.

bunk[2] *slang* □ **do a bunk** run away.

bunk[3] *noun slang* nonsense, humbug.

bunker *noun* **1** container for fuel. **2** reinforced underground shelter. **3** sandy hollow in golf course.

bunkum /'bʌŋkəm/ *noun* nonsense, humbug.

bunny /'bʌnɪ/ *noun* (*plural* **-ies**) *childish name for* rabbit.

Bunsen burner /'bʌns(ə)n/ *noun* small adjustable gas burner used in laboratory.

bunting[1] /'bʌntɪŋ/ *noun* small bird related to finches.

bunting[2] /'bʌntɪŋ/ *noun* **1** flags and other decorations. **2** loosely woven fabric for these.

buoy /bɔɪ/ *noun* **1** anchored float as navigational mark etc. **2** lifebuoy. ● *verb* **1** (usually + *up*) keep afloat. **2** (usually + *up*) encourage. **3** (often + *out*) mark with buoy(s).

■ *noun* **1** beacon, float, marker, mooring buoy.
● *verb* **2** (*buoy up*) see RAISE *verb* 11.

buoyant /'bɔɪənt/ *adjective* **1** apt to float. **2** resilient; light-hearted, exuberant. □ **buoyancy** *noun*.

■ **1** floating, light. **2** see CHEERFUL 1.

bur *noun* (also **burr**) **1** clinging seed vessel or flower head. **2** plant producing burs. **3** clinging person.

burble /'bɜːb(ə)l/ *verb* (**-ling**) **1** talk ramblingly. **2** make bubbling sound.

burden /'bɜːd(ə)n/ *noun* **1** thing carried, load. **2** oppressive duty, expense, emotion, etc. **3** refrain of song. **4** theme. ● *verb* load, encumber, oppress. □ **burden of proof** obligation to prove one's case. □ **burdensome** *adjective*.

■ *noun* **1** cargo, encumbrance, load, weight. **2** affliction, anxiety, care, cross, duty, handicap, millstone, obligation, onus, problem, responsibility, sorrow, strain, trial, trouble, worry. ● *verb* afflict, bother, encumber, hamper, handicap, impose on, load, lumber, oppress, overload, saddle, tax, trouble, weigh down, worry. □ **burdensome** bothersome, difficult, exacting, hard, heavy, onerous, oppressive, taxing, tiring, troublesome, trying, wearisome, wearying, weighty, worrying.

burdock /'bɜːdɒk/ *noun* plant with prickly flowers and docklike leaves.

bureau /'bjʊərəʊ/ *noun* (*plural* **-s** or **-x** /-z/) **1** writing desk with drawers. **2** *US* chest of drawers. **3** office or department for specific business. **4** government department.

■ **1** desk, writing desk. **3, 4** agency, department, office, service.

bureaucracy /bjʊə'rɒkrəsɪ/ *noun* (*plural* **-ies**) **1** government by central administration. **2** government officials esp. regarded as oppressive and inflexible. **3** conduct typical of these.

■ **1** administration, government. **2** officialdom. **3** paperwork, red tape, regulations.

bureaucrat /'bjʊərəkræt/ *noun* official in bureaucracy. □ **bureaucratic** /-'krætɪk/ *adjective*.

burgeon /'bɜːdʒ(ə)n/ *verb* grow rapidly, flourish.

burger /'bɜːgə/ *noun colloquial* hamburger.

burgher /'bɜːgə/ *noun* citizen, esp. of foreign town.

burglar /'bɜːglə/ *noun* person who commits burglary.

■ cat burglar, housebreaker, intruder, robber, thief.

burglary *noun* (*plural* **-ies**) illegal entry into building to commit theft or other crime.

■ break-in, forcible entry, housebreaking, larceny, pilfering, robbery, stealing, theft, thieving.

burgle /'bɜːg(ə)l/ *verb* (**-ling**) commit burglary (on).

burgundy /'bɜːgəndɪ/ *noun* (*plural* **-ies**) **1** red or white wine produced in Burgundy. **2** dark red colour.

burial /'berɪəl/ *noun* burying, esp. of corpse; funeral.

■ entombment, funeral, interment, obsequies.

burlesque /bɜː'lesk/ *noun* **1** comic imitation, parody. **2** *US* variety show, esp. with striptease. ● *adjective* of or using burlesque. ● *verb* (**-ques, -qued, -quing**) parody.

■ *noun* **1** caricature, imitation, mockery, parody, pastiche, satire, *colloquial* send-up, *colloquial* spoof, *colloquial* take-off, travesty.

burly /'bɜːlɪ/ *adjective* (**-ier, -iest**) large and sturdy.

■ athletic, beefy, brawny, heavy, hefty, *colloquial* hulking, husky, muscular, powerful, stocky, stout, strapping, strong, sturdy, thickset, tough, well built.

burn[1] *verb* (*past & past participle* **burnt** or **burned**) **1** (cause to) be consumed by fire. **2** blaze or glow with fire. **3** (cause to) be injured or damaged by fire, sun, or great heat. **4** use or be used as fuel. **5** produce (hole etc.) by fire or heat. **6** char in working. **7** brand. **8** give or feel sensation or pain (as) of heat. ● *noun* sore or mark made by burning. □ **burn out 1** be reduced to nothing by burning. **2** (cause to) fail by burning. **3** (usually **burn oneself out**) suffer exhaustion. **burnt offering** sacrifice offered by burning.

■ *verb* **1** carbonize, cremate, destroy by fire, fire, ignite, incinerate, kindle, light, reduce to ashes, set alight, set fire to, set on fire. **2** be alight, blaze, flame, flare, flicker, glow, smoke, smoulder, spark. **3** blister, brand, char, scald, scorch, sear, singe, toast. ● *noun* blister, scald, scorch.

burn[2] *noun Scottish* brook.

burner *noun* part of lamp or cooker etc. that emits flame.

burning *adjective* **1** on fire. **2** causing injury or damage by fire. **3** causing sensation as if on fire. **4** causing damage by action of acid. **5** (of smell) produced by thing being on fire. **6** ardent. **7** important, fervently discussed.

■ **1** ablaze, afire, aflame, alight, blazing, flaming, glowing, incandescent, lit up, on fire, raging, smouldering. **2, 3** biting, blistering, fiery, hot, inflamed, scalding, scorching, searing, smarting, stinging. **4** acid, caustic, corrosive. **5** acrid, pungent, reeking, scorching, smoky. **6** acute, ardent, consuming, eager, fervent, flaming, frenzied, heated, impassioned, intense, passionate, *colloquial* red-hot, vehement. **7** crucial, important, pertinent, pressing, relevant, urgent, vital.

burnish /'bɜːnɪʃ/ *verb* polish by rubbing. ● *noun* shine produced by rubbing; lustre.

burnt *past & past participle* of BURN[1].

burp *verb & noun colloquial* belch.

burr[1] *noun* **1** whirring sound. **2** rough sounding of *r*. **3** rough edge on metal etc.

burr[2] = BUR.

burrow /ˈbʌrəʊ/ *noun* hole dug by animal as dwelling. ● *verb* **1** make burrow. **2** make by digging. **3** (+ *into*) investigate or search.
■ *noun* earth, excavation, hole, retreat, sett, shelter, tunnel, warren. ● *verb* **1, 2** *poetical* delve, dig, excavate, mine, tunnel.

bursar /ˈbɜːsə/ *noun* **1** treasurer of college etc. **2** holder of bursary.

bursary /ˈbɜːsərɪ/ *noun* (*plural* **-ies**) grant, esp. scholarship.

burst *verb* (*past & past participle* **burst**) **1** force or be forced open; fly violently apart or give way suddenly; explode. **2** appear or come suddenly and forcefully. **3** (often + *out*, *into*) let out violent expression of feeling. ● *noun* **1** bursting, explosion, outbreak. **2** spurt.
■ *verb* **1** break, *colloquial* bust, crack, disintegrate, erupt, explode, force open, give way, open suddenly, part suddenly, puncture, rupture, shatter, split, tear. **2** see RUSH[1] *verb* 1.

burton /ˈbɜːt(ə)n/ *noun* □ **go for a burton** *slang* be lost, destroyed, or killed.

bury /ˈberɪ/ *verb* (**-ies**, **-ied**) **1** place (corpse) in ground, tomb, or sea. **2** put underground, hide in earth; cover up. **3** consign to obscurity. □ **bury oneself** or in *passive*; usually + *in*) involve (oneself) deeply. □ **bury the hatchet** cease to quarrel.
■ **1** entomb, inter, lay to rest. **2** cover, embed, enclose, engulf, hide, immerse, implant, insert, plant, put away, secrete, sink, submerge. **4** (*be buried*) be absorbed, be engrossed, be immersed, be involved.

bus *noun* (*plural* **buses**, *US* **busses**) large public passenger vehicle usually plying on fixed route. ● *verb* (**buses** or **busses**, **bussed**, **bussing**) **1** go by bus. **2** *US* transport by bus (esp. to aid racial integration). □ **busman's holiday** leisure spent in same occupation as working hours. **bus shelter** shelter for people waiting for bus. **bus station** centre where buses depart and arrive. **bus stop** regular stopping place of bus.
■ *noun historical* charabanc, coach, double-decker, minibus, *formal* omnibus.

busby /ˈbʌzbɪ/ *noun* (*plural* **-ies**) tall fur cap worn by hussars etc.

bush[1] /bʊʃ/ *noun* **1** shrub; clump of shrubs. **2** clump of hair or fur. **3** *Australian etc.* uncultivated land; woodland. □ **bush-baby** small African lemur. **Bushman** member or language of a S. African aboriginal people. **bushman** dweller or traveller in Australian bush. **bush telegraph** rapid informal spreading of information etc.

bush[2] /bʊʃ/ *noun* **1** metal lining of axle-hole etc. **2** electrically insulating sleeve.

bushel /ˈbʊʃ(ə)l/ *noun* measure of capacity for corn, fruit, etc. (8 gallons, 36.4 litres).

bushy *adjective* (**-ier**, **-iest**) **1** growing thickly or like bush. **2** having many bushes.
■ **1** dense, fluffy, fuzzy, hairy, luxuriant, shaggy, thick.

business /ˈbɪznɪs/ *noun* **1** one's occupation or profession. **2** one's own concern. **3** task, duty; thing(s) needing dealing with. **4** (difficult or unpleasant) matter or affair. **5** serious work. **6** buying and selling; trade. **7** commercial firm. □ **businesslike** practical, systematic. **businessman**, **businesswoman** person engaged in trade or commerce.
■ **1** calling, career, craft, employment, industry, job, line of work, occupation, profession, pursuit, trade, vocation, work. **2** affair, concern, obligation, responsibility. **3** agenda, concern, duty, function, job, matter, point, question, subject, topic. **4** affair, issue, matter, problem, situation, subject, topic. **6** buying and selling, commerce, dealings, industry, marketing, merchandising, selling, trade, trading, transactions. **7** company, concern, corporation, enterprise, establishment, firm, organization, *colloquial* outfit, partnership, practice, venture. □ **businesslike** careful, efficient, hard-headed, logical, methodical, neat, orderly, practical, professional, prompt, systematic, well organized. **businessman**, **businesswoman** dealer, entrepreneur, executive, financier, industrialist, magnate, manager, merchant, trader, tycoon.

busk *verb* perform esp. music in street etc. for tips. □ **busker** *noun*.

bust[1] *noun* **1** human chest, esp. of woman. **2** sculpture of head, shoulders, and chest.

bust[2] *colloquial verb* (*past & past participle* **bust** or **busted**) **1** burst, break. **2** raid, search. **3** arrest. ● *adjective* **1** burst, broken. **2** bankrupt. □ **bust-up** quarrel; violent split or separation. **go bust** become bankrupt; fail.

bustard /bˈʌstəd/ *noun* large swift-running bird.

bustle[1] /ˈbʌs(ə)l/ *verb* (**-ling**) **1** (often + *about*) move busily and energetically. **2** make (person) hurry. **3** (as **bustling** *adjective*) active, lively. ● *noun* excited activity.
■ *verb* **1** dart, dash, fuss, hasten, hurry, hustle, make haste, rush, scamper, scramble, scurry, scuttle, *colloquial* tear, whirl. **2** hurry, hustle, rush. ● *noun* activity, agitation, commotion, excitement, fuss, haste, hurly-burly, hurry, hustle, movement, restlessness, scurrying, toing and froing.

bustle[2] /ˈbʌs(ə)l/ *noun historical* padding worn under skirt to puff it out behind.

busy /ˈbɪzɪ/ *adjective* (**-ier**, **-iest**) **1** occupied or engaged in work etc. **2** full of activity. **3** fussy. ● *verb* (**-ies**, **-ied**) occupy, keep busy. □ **busybody** meddlesome person. **busy Lizzie** house plant with usually red, pink, or white flowers. □ **busily** *adverb*.

■ *adjective* **1** active, assiduous, bustling about, committed, dedicated, diligent, employed, energetic, engaged, engrossed, immersed, industrious, involved, keen, occupied, *colloquial* on the go, pottering, preoccupied, slaving, tied up, tireless, working. **2** bustling, frantic, full, hectic, lively. **3** see ELABORATE *adjective* 2. □ **busybody** gossip, meddler, scandalmonger, *colloquial* snooper, spy; (*be a busybody*) see INTERFERE 1,3.

but *conjunction* **1** however. **2** on the other hand. **3** otherwise than. ● *preposition* except, apart from. ● *adverb* only. □ **but for** without the help or hindrance etc. of. **but then** however.

butane /ˈbjuːteɪn/ *noun* hydrocarbon used in liquefied form as fuel.

butch /bʊtʃ/ *adjective slang* masculine, tough-looking.

butcher /ˈbʊtʃə/ *noun* **1** person who sells meat. **2** slaughterer of animals for food. **3** brutal murderer. ● *verb* **1** slaughter or cut up (animal). **2** kill wantonly or cruelly. **3** *colloquial* ruin through incompetence. □ **butchery** *noun* (*plural* -ies).

butler /ˈbʌtlə/ *noun* chief manservant of household.

butt[1] *verb* **1** push with head or horns. **2** (cause to) meet end to end. ● *noun* push or blow with head or horns. □ **butt in** interrupt, meddle.

■ *verb* **1** buffet, bump, hit, jab, knock, poke, prod, punch, push, ram, shove, strike, thump. □ **butt in** see INTERRUPT 1.

butt[2] *noun* **1** (often + *of*) object of ridicule etc. **2** mound behind target. **3** (in *plural*) shooting range.

■ **1** end, mark, object, subject, target, victim.

butt[3] *noun* **1** thicker end, esp. of tool or weapon. **2** stub of cigarette etc. **3** *US slang* buttocks.

■ **1** haft, handle, shaft, stock. **2** end, remains, remnant, stub.

butt[4] *noun* cask.

■ barrel, cask, water-butt.

butter /ˈbʌtə/ *noun* **1** yellow fatty substance made from cream, used as spread and in cooking. **2** substance of similar texture. ● *verb* spread, cook, etc., with butter. □ **butter-bean** dried large flat white bean. **buttercup** plant with yellow flowers. **butter-fingers** *colloquial* person likely to drop things. **buttermilk** liquid left after butter-making. **butter muslin** thin loosely woven cloth. **butterscotch** sweet made of butter and sugar. **butter up** *colloquial* flatter.

butterfly /ˈbʌtəflaɪ/ *noun* (*plural* -ies) **1** insect with 4 often showy wings. **2** (in *plural*) nervous sensation in stomach. □ **butterfly nut** kind of wing-nut. **butterfly stroke** method of swimming with both arms lifted at same time.

buttery[1] *adjective* like or containing butter.

buttery[2] *noun* (*plural* -ies) food store or snack bar, esp. in college.

buttock /ˈbʌtək/ *noun* (usually in *plural*) **1** either protuberance on lower rear part of human trunk. **2** corresponding part of animal.

■ (*buttocks*) *coarse slang* arse, *colloquial* backside, *colloquial* behind, bottom, *slang* bum, *US slang* butt, haunches, hindquarters, posterior, *colloquial* rear, rump, seat.

button /ˈbʌt(ə)n/ *noun* **1** disc or knob sewn to garment etc. as fastening or for ornament. **2** knob etc. pressed to operate electronic equipment. ● *verb* (often + *up*) fasten with buttons. □ **button mushroom** small unopened mushroom.

buttonhole *noun* **1** slit in cloth for button. **2** flower(s) worn in lapel buttonhole. ● *verb* (-ling) *colloquial* accost and detain (reluctant listener).

buttress /ˈbʌtrɪs/ *noun* support built against wall etc. ● *verb* support or strengthen.

■ *noun* brace, prop up, stay, support. ● *verb* brace, prop up, reinforce, shore up, strengthen, support.

buxom /ˈbʌksəm/ *adjective* plump and rosy; large and shapely.

■ ample, full-figured, healthy-looking, plump, robust, rounded, shapely, voluptuous.

buy /baɪ/ *verb* (**buys, buying**; *past & past participle* **bought** /bɔːt/) **1** obtain in exchange for money etc. **2** procure by bribery; bribe. **3** get by sacrifice etc. **4** *slang* accept, believe. ● *noun colloquial* purchase. □ **buy out** pay (person) for ownership, an interest, etc. **buyout** purchase of controlling share in company. **buy up** buy as much as possible of.

■ *verb* **1** acquire, come by, gain, get, get on hire purchase, invest in, obtain, pay for, procure, purchase.

buyer *noun* person who buys, esp. stock for large shop. □ **buyer's market** time when goods are plentiful and cheap.

■ client, consumer, customer, patron, purchaser, shopper.

buzz *noun* **1** hum of bee etc. **2** sound of buzzer. **3** low murmur. **4** hurried activity. **5** *slang* telephone call. **6** *slang* thrill. ● *verb* **1** hum. **2** summon with buzzer. **3** (often + *about*) move busily. **4** be filled with activity or excitement. □ **buzzword** *colloquial* **1** fashionable technical word. **2** catchword.

buzzard /ˈbʌzəd/ *noun* large bird of hawk family.

buzzer *noun* electrical buzzing device as signal.

by /baɪ/ *preposition* **1** near, beside, along. **2** through action, agency, or means of. **3** not later than. **4** past; via. **5** during. **6** to extent of. **7** according to. ● *adverb* **1** near. **2** aside, in reserve. **3** past. □ **by and by** before long. **by-election** parliamentary election between general elections. **by-product** substance or result produced incidentally in making of something else. **byroad** minor road. **by the by, by the way** incidentally. **byway** byroad or secluded path. **byword** **1** person or thing as notable example. **2** proverb.

■ □ **by-product** adjunct, complement, consequence, corollary, repercussion, result, side effect, spin-off.

bye[1] /baɪ/ *noun* **1** *Cricket* run made from ball that passes batsman without being hit. **2** (in tournament) position of competitor left without opponent in round.

bye[2] /baɪ/ *interjection* (also **bye-bye**) *colloquial* goodbye.

bygone *adjective* past, departed. □ **let bygones be bygones** forgive and forget past quarrels.

by-law *noun* regulation made by local authority etc.

byline *noun* line in newspaper etc. naming writer of article etc.

bypass *noun* main road round town or its centre. ● *verb* avoid.

■ *verb* avoid, circumvent, dodge, evade, find a way round, get out of, go round, ignore, omit, sidestep, skirt.

byre /baɪə/ *noun* cowshed.

bystander *noun* person present but not taking part.

■ eyewitness, looker-on, observer, onlooker, passer-by, spectator, watcher, witness.

byte /baɪt/ *noun Computing* group of 8 binary digits, often representing one character.

Byzantine /bɪˈzæntaɪn/ *adjective* **1** of Byzantium or E. Roman Empire. **2** of architectural etc. style developed in Eastern Empire. **3** complicated. **4** underhand.

Cc

C[1] *noun* (also **c**) (Roman numeral) 100.

C[2] *abbreviation* Celsius, centigrade.

c.[1] *abbreviation* **1** century. **2** cent(s).

c.[2] *abbreviation: circa.*

ca. *abbreviation: circa.*

CAA *abbreviation* Civil Aviation Authority.

cab *noun* **1** taxi. **2** driver's compartment in lorry, train, crane, etc.

cabal /kə'bæl/ *noun* **1** secret intrigue. **2** political clique.

cabaret /'kæbəreɪ/ *noun* entertainment in restaurant etc.

cabbage /'kæbɪdʒ/ *noun* **1** vegetable with green or purple leaves forming a round head. **2** *colloquial* dull or inactive person. □ **cabbage white** kind of white butterfly.

cabby /'kæbɪ/ *noun* (*plural* **-ies**) *colloquial* taxi driver.

caber /'keɪbə/ *noun* tree trunk tossed as sport in Scotland.

cabin /'kæbɪn/ *noun* **1** small shelter or house, esp. of wood. **2** room or compartment in aircraft, ship, etc. □ **cabin boy** boy steward on ship. **cabin cruiser** large motor boat with accommodation.

■ **1** chalet, cottage, hut, lodge, shack, shanty, shed, shelter. **2** berth, compartment, quarters.

cabinet /'kæbɪnɪt/ *noun* **1** cupboard or case for storing or displaying things. **2** casing of radio, television, etc. **3** (**Cabinet**) group of senior ministers in government. □ **cabinetmaker** skilled joiner.

cable /'keɪb(ə)l/ *noun* **1** encased group of insulated wires for transmitting electricity etc. **2** thick rope of wire or hemp. **3** cablegram. ● *verb* (**-ling**) send (message) or inform (person) by cable. □ **cable car** small cabin on loop of cable for carrying passengers up and down mountain etc. **cablegram** message sent by undersea cable etc. **cable stitch** knitting stitch resembling twisted rope. **cable television** transmission of television programmes by cable to subscribers.

■ *noun* **1** cord, flex, lead, wire. **2** chain, cord, guy, hawser, line, mooring, rope, wire. **3** message, telegram, *colloquial* wire.

caboodle /kə'buːd(ə)l/ *noun* □ **the whole caboodle** *slang* the whole lot.

caboose /kə'buːs/ *noun* **1** kitchen on ship's deck. **2** *US* guard's van on train.

cabriolet /kæbrɪə'leɪ/ *noun* car with folding top.

cacao /kə'kaʊ/ *noun* (*plural* **-s**) **1** seed from which cocoa and chocolate are made. **2** tree bearing it.

cache /kæʃ/ *noun* **1** hiding place for treasure, supplies, etc. **2** things so hidden. ● *verb* (**-ching**) place in cache.

cachet /'kæʃeɪ/ *noun* **1** prestige. **2** distinguishing mark or seal. **3** flat capsule for medicine.

cack-handed /kæk'hændɪd/ *adjective colloquial* **1** clumsy. **2** left-handed.

cackle /'kæk(ə)l/ *noun* **1** clucking of hen. **2** raucous laugh. **3** noisy chatter. ● *verb* (**-ling**) **1** emit cackle. **2** chatter noisily.

cacophony /kə'kɒfənɪ/ *noun* (*plural* **-ies**) harsh discordant sound. □ **cacophonous** *adjective.*

■ atonality, caterwauling, din, discord, disharmony, dissonance, harshness, jangle, noise, racket, *colloquial* row, *colloquial* rumpus, tumult. □ **cacophonous** discordant, dissonant, harsh, noisy, unmusical.

cactus /'kæktəs/ *noun* (*plural* **-ti** /-taɪ/ or **-tuses**) plant with thick fleshy stem and usually spines but no leaves.

CAD *abbreviation* computer-aided design.

cad *noun* man who behaves dishonourably. □ **caddish** *adjective.*

cadaver /kə'dævə/ *noun* corpse. □ **cadaverous** *adjective.*

caddie /'kædɪ/ (also **caddy**) *noun* (*plural* **-ies**) golfer's attendant carrying clubs etc. ● *verb* (**caddying**) act as caddie.

caddis /'kædɪs/ *noun* □ **caddis-fly** small nocturnal insect living near water. **caddis-worm** larva of caddis-fly.

caddy[1] /'kædɪ/ *noun* (*plural* **-ies**) small container for tea.

caddy[2] = CADDIE.

cadence /'keɪd(ə)ns/ *noun* **1** fall in pitch of voice. **2** tonal inflection. **3** rhythm. **4** close of musical phrase.

■ **2** inflection, intonation, lilt, rise and fall, tune. **3** accent, beat, metre, pattern, rhythm, stress.

cadenza /kə'denzə/ *noun Music* virtuoso passage for soloist during concerto.

cadet /kə'det/ *noun* young trainee in armed services or police force.

■ beginner, learner, recruit, tiro, trainee.

cadge *verb* (**-ging**) *colloquial* get or seek by begging.

■ ask for, beg, scrounge, sponge.

cadi /'kɑːdɪ/ *noun* (*plural* **-s**) judge in Muslim country.

cadmium /ˈkædmɪəm/ *noun* soft bluish-white metallic element.

cadre /ˈkɑːdə/ *noun* **1** basic unit, esp. of servicemen. **2** group of esp. Communist activists.

caecum /ˈsiːkəm/ *noun* (*US* **cecum**) (*plural* **-ca**) pouch between small and large intestines.

Caerphilly /keəˈfɪlɪ/ *noun* kind of mild pale cheese.

Caesarean /sɪˈzeərɪən/ (*US* **Cesarean**, **Cesarian**) *adjective* (of birth) effected by Caesarean section. ● *noun* (in full **Caesarean section**) delivery of child by cutting into mother's abdomen.

caesura /sɪˈzjʊərə/ *noun* (*plural* **-s**) pause in line of verse.

café /ˈkæfeɪ/ *noun* coffee house, restaurant.
 ■ bar, bistro, brasserie, buffet, cafeteria, canteen, coffee bar, coffee house, coffee shop, *US* diner, restaurant, snack bar, take-away, tearoom, teashop.

cafeteria /kæfɪˈtɪərɪə/ *noun* self-service restaurant.

cafetière /kæfəˈtjeə/ *noun* coffee pot with plunger for pressing grounds to bottom.

caffeine /ˈkæfiːn/ *noun* alkaloid stimulant in tea leaves and coffee beans.

caftan /ˈkæftæn/ *noun* (also **kaftan**) **1** long tunic worn by men in Near East. **2** long loose dress.

cage *noun* **1** structure of bars or wires, esp. for confining animals. **2** open framework, esp. lift in mine etc. ● *verb* (**-ging**) confine in cage.
 ■ *noun* **1** aviary, coop, enclosure, hutch, pen, pound. ● *verb* see CONFINE *verb* 1.

cagey /ˈkeɪdʒɪ/ *adjective* (**-ier**, **-iest**) *colloquial* cautious and non-committal. □ **cagily** *adverb*.

cagoule /kəˈguːl/ *noun* light hooded windproof jacket.

cahoots /kəˈhuːts/ *plural noun* □ **in cahoots** *slang* in collusion.

caiman = CAYMAN.

cairn /keən/ *noun* mound of stones. □ **cairn terrier** small shaggy short-legged terrier.

cairngorm /ˈkeəngɔːm/ *noun* yellow or wine-coloured semiprecious stone.

caisson /ˈkeɪs(ə)n/ *noun* watertight chamber for underwater construction work.

cajole /kəˈdʒəʊl/ *verb* (**-ling**) persuade by flattery, deceit, etc. □ **cajolery** *noun*.
 ■ *colloquial* butter up, coax, flatter, inveigle, persuade, seduce.

cake *noun* **1** mixture of flour, butter, eggs, sugar, etc. baked in oven. **2** flattish compact mass. ● *verb* (**-king**) **1** form into compact mass. **2** (usually + *with*) cover (with sticky mass).
 ■ *noun* **1** bun, gateau. **2** bar, block, chunk, cube, loaf, lump, mass, piece, slab. ● *verb* **1** coagulate, congeal, consolidate, dry, harden, solidify, thicken. **2** coat, clog, cover, encrust.

calabash /ˈkæləbæʃ/ *noun* **1** gourd-bearing

tropical American tree. **2** bowl or pipe made from gourd.

calabrese /ˈkæləbriːs, kæləˈbreɪsɪ/ *noun* variety of broccoli.

calamine /ˈkæləmaɪn/ *noun* powdered zinc carbonate and ferric oxide used in skin lotion.

calamity /kəˈlæmɪtɪ/ *noun* (*plural* **-ies**) disaster. □ **calamitous** *adjective*.
 ■ accident, affliction, cataclysm, catastrophe, disaster, misadventure, mischance, misfortune, mishap, tragedy, tribulation. □ **calamitous** *colloquial* awful, cataclysmic, catastrophic, deadly, devastating, dire, disastrous, distressful, dreadful, fatal, ghastly, ruinous, serious, *colloquial* terrible, tragic, unfortunate, unlucky, woeful.

calcareous /kælˈkeərɪəs/ *adjective* of or containing calcium carbonate.

calceolaria /kælsɪəˈleərɪə/ *noun* plant with slipper-shaped flowers.

calcify /ˈkælsɪfaɪ/ *verb* (**-ies**, **-ied**) harden by deposit of calcium salts. □ **calcification** *noun*.

calcine /ˈkælsaɪn/ *verb* (**-ning**) decompose or be decomposed by roasting or burning. □ **calcination** /-sɪn-/ *noun*.

calcium /ˈkælsɪəm/ *noun* soft grey metallic element.

calculate /ˈkælkjʊleɪt/ *verb* (**-ting**) **1** ascertain or forecast by exact reckoning. **2** plan deliberately. □ **calculable** *adjective*. **calculation** *noun*.
 ■ **1** add up, ascertain, assess, compute, count, determine, enumerate, estimate, evaluate, figure out, find out, gauge, judge, reckon, total, weigh, work out.

calculated *adjective* **1** done with awareness of likely consequences. **2** (+ *to do*) designed to.
 ■ **1** see DELIBERATE *adjective* 1.

calculating *adjective* scheming, mercenary.
 ■ see CRAFTY.

calculator *noun* device (esp. small electronic one) used for making calculations.

calculus /ˈkælkjʊləs/ *noun* (*plural* **-luses** or **-li** /-laɪ/) **1** *Mathematics* particular method of calculation. **2** stone in body.

Caledonian /kælɪˈdəʊnɪən/ *literary adjective* of Scotland. ● *noun* Scot.

calendar /ˈkælɪndə/ *noun* **1** system fixing year's beginning, length, and subdivision. **2** chart etc. showing such subdivisions. **3** list of special dates or events. □ **calendar year** period from 1 Jan. to 31 Dec. inclusive.

calends /ˈkælendz/ *plural noun* (also **kalends**) first of month in ancient Roman calendar.

calf[1] /kɑːf/ *noun* (*plural* **calves** /kɑːvz/) **1** young cow, bull, elephant, whale, etc. **2** calf leather. □ **calf-love** romantic adolescent love.

calf[2] /kɑːf/ *noun* (*plural* **calves** /kɑːvz/) fleshy hind part of human leg below knee.

calibrate /ˈkælɪbreɪt/ *verb* (**-ting**) **1** mark (gauge) with scale of readings. **2** correlate readings of (instrument) with standard. **3** find calibre of (gun). □ **calibration** *noun*.

calibre /'kælɪbə/ *noun* (*US* **caliber**) **1** internal diameter of gun or tube; diameter of bullet or shell. **2** strength or quality of character; ability; importance.

■ **1** bore, diameter, gauge, measure, size. **2** ability, capability, capacity, character, competence, distinction, excellence, genius, gifts, importance, merit, proficiency, quality, skill, stature, talent, worth.

calico /'kælɪkəʊ/ *noun* (*plural* **-es** or *US* **-s**) **1** cotton cloth, esp. white or unbleached. **2** *US* printed cotton cloth. ● *adjective* **1** of calico. **2** *US* multicoloured.

caliper = CALLIPER.

caliph /'keɪlɪf/ *noun historical* chief Muslim civil and religious ruler.

calk *US* = CAULK.

call /kɔːl/ *verb* **1** (often + *out*) cry, shout, speak loudly. **2** emit characteristic sound. **3** communicate with by radio or telephone. **4** summon. **5** (+ *for*) fetch. **6** (often + *on*, *in*, *at*) make brief visit. **7** order to take place. **8** name, describe, or regard as. **9** rouse from sleep. **10** (+ *for*) demand. ● *noun* **1** shout. **2** bird's cry. **3** brief visit. **4** telephone conversation. **5** summons. **6** need, occasion. **7** demand. □ **call box** telephone box. **call-girl** prostitute accepting appointments by telephone. **call in 1** withdraw from circulation. **2** seek advice or services of. **call off 1** cancel. **2** order (pursuer) to desist. **call person names** abuse or insult person. **call the shots, tune** *colloquial* be in control. **call up 1** telephone. **2** recall. **3** summon (esp. to do military service). **call-up** *noun* summons to do military service. □ **caller** *noun*.

■ *verb* **1** bellow, clamour, cry out, exclaim, hail, roar, shout, yell. **3** contact, dial, *colloquial* phone, ring, telephone. **4** convene, gather, invite, order, summon. **5** see FETCH 1. **6** (*call on*) *colloquial* drop in on, look in on, pop in on, visit. **7** arrange, order, organize, set up. **8** baptize, christen, dub, entitle, name, title. **9** arouse, awake, awaken, get up, rouse, wake, waken. **10** (*call for*) see DEMAND *verb* 1–2, REQUEST *verb* 1. ● *noun* **1** bellow, cry, exclamation, roar, scream, shout, yell. **3** stay, stop, visit. **5** bidding, invitation, signal, summons. **6** cause, excuse, justification, need, occasion. **7** demand, need, request, requirement. □ **call off 1** see CANCEL 1. **call person names** see INSULT 1.

calligraphy /kə'lɪɡrəfɪ/ *noun* **1** beautiful handwriting. **2** art of this. □ **calligrapher** *noun*. **calligraphic** /kælɪ'ɡræfɪk/ *adjective*.

■ copperplate, handwriting, illumination, lettering, penmanship, script.

calling *noun* **1** profession, occupation. **2** vocation.

■ **1** business, career, employment, job, line of work, *métier*, occupation, profession, pursuit, trade, work. **2** mission, vocation.

calliper /'kælɪpə/ *noun* (also **caliper**) **1** metal splint to support leg. **2** (in *plural*) compasses for measuring diameters.

callisthenics /kælɪs'θenɪks/ *plural noun* exercises for fitness and grace. □ **callisthenic** *adjective*.

callosity /kə'lɒsɪtɪ/ *noun* (*plural* **-ies**) callus.

callous /'kæləs/ *adjective* **1** unfeeling, unsympathetic. **2** (also **calloused**) (of skin) hardened. □ **callously** *adverb*. **callousness** *noun*.

■ **1** apathetic, cold, cold-hearted, cool, cruel, dispassionate, *colloquial* hardbitten, hard-boiled, hardened, hard-hearted, *colloquial* hard-nosed, heartless, inhuman, insensitive, merciless, pitiless, ruthless, thick-skinned, uncaring, unconcerned, unemotional, unfeeling, unsympathetic.

callow /'kæləʊ/ *adjective* inexperienced, immature.

■ adolescent, green, immature, inexperienced, innocent, *often derogatory* juvenile, naive, raw, unsophisticated, wet behind the ears, young.

callus /'kæləs/ *noun* (*plural* **calluses**) area of hard thick skin.

calm /kɑːm/ *adjective* **1** tranquil, windless. **2** not agitated. ● *noun* calm condition or period. ● *verb* (often + *down*) make or become calm. □ **calmly** *adverb*. **calmness** *noun*.

■ *adjective* **1** airless, even, flat, glassy, halcyon (*days*), motionless, placid, quiet, slow-moving, smooth, still, unclouded, windless. **2** collected, complacent, composed, controlled, cool, dispassionate, equable, impassive, imperturbable, *colloquial* laid-back, level-headed, moderate, pacific, passionless, patient, peaceful, poised, quiet, relaxed, restful, restrained, sedate, self-possessed, serene, tranquil, undemonstrative, unemotional, unexcitable, *colloquial* unflappable, unhurried, unperturbed, unruffled, untroubled. ● *noun* calmness, peace, quietness, serenity, stillness, tranquillity. ● *verb* appease, compose, control, cool, lull, mollify, pacify, placate, quieten, sedate, settle (down), sober down, soothe, tranquillize. □ **calmness** complacency, composure, equability, equanimity, imperturbability, level-headedness, peace of mind, sang-froid, self-possession, serenity, *colloquial* unflappability.

calomel /'kæləmel/ *noun* compound of mercury used as laxative.

Calor gas /'kælə/ *noun proprietary term* liquefied butane under pressure in containers for domestic use.

calorie /'kælərɪ/ *noun* unit of heat, amount required to raise temperature of one gram (**small calorie**) or one kilogram (**large calorie**) of water by 1°C.

calorific /kælə'rɪfɪk/ *adjective* producing heat.

calumniate /kə'lʌmnɪeɪt/ *verb* slander. □ **calumniation** /-'eɪʃ(ə)n/ *noun*. **calumniator** *noun*.

calumny /'kæləmnɪ/ *noun* (*plural* **-ies**) slander; malicious misrepresentation. □ **calumnious** /kə'lʌm-/ *adjective*.

calvados /'kælvədɒs/ *noun* apple brandy.

calve /kɑ:v/ *verb* (**-ving**) give birth to (calf).

calves *plural* of CALF[1],[2].

Calvinism /'kælvɪnɪz(ə)m/ *noun* Calvin's theology, stressing predestination. □ **Calvinist** *noun & adjective.* **Calvinistic** /-'nɪs-/ *adjective.*

calx *noun* (*plural* **calces** /'kælsi:z/) powdery residue left after heating of ore or mineral.

calypso /kə'lɪpsəʊ/ *noun* (*plural* **-s**) W. Indian song with usually topical words.

calyx /'keɪlɪks/ *noun* (*plural* **calyces** /-lɪsi:z/ or **-es**) leaves forming protective case of flower in bud.

cam *noun* projection on wheel etc., shaped to convert circular into reciprocal or variable motion.

camaraderie /kæmə'rɑ:dərɪ/ *noun* friendly comradeship.

camber /'kæmbə/ *noun* convex surface of road, deck, etc. ● *verb* construct with camber.

cambric /'kæmbrɪk/ *noun* fine linen or cotton cloth.

camcorder /'kæmkɔ:də/ *noun* combined portable video camera and recorder.

came *past* of COME.

camel /'kæm(ə)l/ *noun* **1** long-legged ruminant with one hump (**Arabian camel**) or two humps (**Bactrian camel**). **2** fawn colour.

camellia /kə'mi:lɪə/ *noun* evergreen flowering shrub.

Camembert /'kæməmbeə/ *noun* kind of soft creamy cheese.

cameo /'kæmɪəʊ/ *noun* (*plural* **-s**) **1** small piece of hard stone carved in relief. **2** short literary sketch or acted scene. **3** small part in play or film.

camera /'kæmrə/ *noun* apparatus for taking photographs or for making motion film or television pictures. □ **cameraman** operator of film or television camera. **in camera** in private.

camiknickers /'kæmɪnɪkəz/ *plural noun* woman's knickers and vest combined.

camisole /'kæmɪsəʊl/ *noun* woman's underbodice.

camomile /'kæməmaɪl/ *noun* (also **chamomile**) aromatic herb with flowers used to make tea.

camouflage /'kæməflɑ:ʒ/ *noun* **1** disguising of soldiers, tanks, etc., so that they blend into background. **2** such disguise. **3** animal's natural blending colouring. **4** concealment of true nature. ● *verb* (**-ging**) hide by camouflage.

■ *noun* **1, 2** cover, disguise. **3** protective colouring. **4** blind, cloak, concealment, cover, disguise, façade, front, guise, mask, pretence, screen, veil. ● *verb* cloak, conceal, cover up, disguise, hide, mask, obscure, screen, veil.

camp[1] *noun* **1** place where troops are lodged or trained. **2** temporary accommodation of tents, huts, etc., for detainees, holidaymakers, etc. **3** fortified site. **4** party supporters regarded collectively. ● *verb* set up or live in camp. □ **camp bed** portable folding bed. **camp follower 1** civilian worker in military camp. **2** disciple. **campsite** place for camping.

■ *noun* **1** base, bivouac, encampment. **2** camping ground, campsite, settlement.

camp[2] *colloquial adjective* **1** affected; theatrically exaggerated. **2** effeminate; homosexual. ● *noun* camp manner. ● *verb* behave or do in camp way.

campaign /kæm'peɪn/ *noun* **1** organized course of action, esp. to gain publicity. **2** series of military operations. ● *verb* take part in campaign. □ **campaigner** *noun.*

■ *noun* **1** battle, crusade, drive, effort, fight, movement, offensive, push, struggle, war. **2** action, battle, *historical* crusade, fight, manoeuvre, movement, offensive, operation, war.

campanile /kæmpə'ni:lɪ/ *noun* bell tower, usually free-standing.

campanology /kæmpə'nɒlədʒɪ/ *noun* **1** study of bells. **2** bell-ringing. □ **campanologist** *noun.*

campanula /kæm'pænjʊlə/ *noun* plant with bell-shaped flowers.

camper *noun* **1** person who camps. **2** motor vehicle with beds.

camphor /'kæmfə/ *noun* pungent crystalline substance used in medicine and formerly mothballs.

camphorate *verb* (**-ting**) impregnate with camphor.

campion /'kæmpɪən/ *noun* wild plant with usually pink or white notched flowers.

campus /'kæmpəs/ *noun* (*plural* **-es**) grounds of university or college.

■ grounds, setting, site.

camshaft *noun* shaft carrying cam(s).

can[1] *auxiliary verb* (*3rd singular present* **can**; *past* **could** /kʊd/) **1** be able to. **2** have the potential to. **3** be permitted to.

can[2] *noun* **1** metal vessel for liquid. **2** sealed tin container for preservation of food or drink. **3** (in *plural*) *slang* headphones. **4** (**the can**) *slang* prison. **5** (**the can**) *US slang* lavatory. ● *verb* (**-nn-**) preserve (food etc.) in can. □ **canned music** pre-recorded music. **carry the can** bear responsibility. **in the can** *colloquial* completed.

canal /kə'næl/ *noun* **1** artificial inland waterway. **2** tubular duct in plant or animal.

■ **1** channel, waterway.

canalize /'kænəlaɪz/ *verb* (also **-ise**) (**-zing** or **-sing**) **1** convert (river) into canal. **2** provide (area) with canal(s). **3** channel. □ **canalization** *noun.*

canapé /'kænəpeɪ/ *noun* small piece of bread or pastry with savoury topping.

canard /'kænɑ:d/ *noun* unfounded rumour.

canary /kə'neərɪ/ *noun* (*plural* **-ies**) small songbird with yellow feathers.

canasta /kə'næstə/ *noun* card game resembling rummy.

cancan /'kænkæn/ *noun* high-kicking dance.

cancel /'kæns(ə)l/ *verb* (**-ll-**; *US* **-l-**) **1** revoke; discontinue (arrangement); annul. **2** delete. **3** mark (ticket, stamp, etc.) to invalidate it. **4** (often + *out*) neutralize, counterbalance. **5** *Mathematics* strike out (equal factor) on each side of equation etc. □ **cancellation** *noun*.
■ **1** abandon, abolish, abort, abrogate, annul, call off, countermand, drop, eliminate, give up, invalidate, override, overrule, quash, repeal, rescind, revoke, scrap, *colloquial* scrub, wipe out, write off. **2** cross out, delete, erase, expunge, obliterate, wipe out. **4** (*cancel out*) see NEUTRALIZE 2.

cancer /'kænsə/ *noun* **1** malignant tumour. **2** disease caused by this. **3** corruption. **3** (**Cancer**) fourth sign of zodiac. □ **cancerous** *adjective*.
■ **1** carcinoma, growth, malignancy, tumour.

candela /kæn'di:lə/ *noun* SI unit of luminous intensity.

candelabrum /kændr'lɑ:brəm/ *noun* (also **-bra**) (*plural* **-bra**, *US* **-brums**, **-bras**) large branched candlestick or lampholder.

candid /'kændɪd/ *adjective* **1** frank. **2** (of photograph) taken informally, usually without subject's knowledge. □ **candidly** *adverb*.
■ **1** blunt, direct, forthright, frank, honest, ingenuous, no-nonsense, objective, open, outspoken, plain, sincere, straight, straightforward, transparent, true, truthful, unbiased, undisguised, unequivocal, unflattering, unprejudiced.

candidate /'kændɪdət/ *noun* **1** person nominated for, seeking, or likely to gain, office, position, award, etc. **2** person entered for exam. □ **candidacy** *noun*. **candidature** *noun*.
■ **1** applicant, aspirant, competitor, contender, contestant, entrant, nominee, pretender (*to throne*), runner, suitor. **2** entrant, examinee.

candle /'kænd(ə)l/ *noun* (usually cylindrical) block of wax or tallow enclosing wick which gives light when burning. □ **candlelight** light from candle(s). **candlelit** lit by candle(s). **candlestick** holder for candle(s). **candlewick 1** thick soft yarn. **2** tufted material made from this.

candour /'kændə/ *noun* (*US* **candor**) frankness.

candy /'kændɪ/ *noun* (*plural* **-ies**) **1** (in full **sugar-candy**) sugar crystallized by repeated boiling and evaporation. **2** *US* sweets; a sweet. ● *verb* (**-ies**, **-ied**) (usually as **candied** *adjective*) preserve (fruit etc.) in candy. □ **candyfloss** fluffy mass of spun sugar. **candy stripe** alternate white and esp. pink stripes.

candytuft /'kændɪtʌft/ *noun* plant with white, pink, or purple flowers in tufts.

cane *noun* **1** hollow jointed stem of giant reed or grass, or solid stem of slender palm, used for wickerwork or as walking stick, plant support, instrument of punishment, etc. **2** sugar cane. ● *verb* (**-ning**) **1** beat with cane. **2** weave cane into (chair etc.).

■ *noun* **1** rod, stick. ● *verb* **1** see THRASH 1.

canine /'keɪnaɪn/ *adjective* of a dog or dogs. ● *noun* **1** dog. **2** (in full **canine tooth**) tooth between incisors and molars.

canister /'kænɪstə/ *noun* **1** small usually metal box for tea etc. **2** cylinder of shot, tear gas, etc.

canker /'kæŋkə/ *noun* **1** disease of trees and plants. **2** ulcerous ear disease of animals. **3** corrupting influence. ● *verb* **1** infect with canker. **2** corrupt. □ **cankerous** *adjective*.

cannabis /'kænəbɪs/ *noun* **1** hemp plant. **2** parts of it used as narcotic.

cannelloni /kænə'ləʊnɪ/ *plural noun* tubes of pasta stuffed with savoury mixture.

cannibal /'kænɪb(ə)l/ *noun* person or animal that eats its own species. □ **cannibalism** *noun*. **cannibalistic** /-'lɪs-/ *adjective*.

cannibalize /'kænɪbəlaɪz/ *verb* (also **-ise**) (**-zing** or **-sing**) use (machine etc.) as source of spare parts.

cannon /'kænən/ *noun* **1** automatic aircraft gun firing shells. **2** (*plural* usually same) *historical* large gun. **3** hitting of two balls successively by player's ball in billiards. ● *verb* (usually + *against*, *into*) collide. □ **cannon ball** *historical* large ball fired by cannon.

cannonade /kænə'neɪd/ *noun* period of continuous heavy gunfire. ● *verb* bombard with cannonade.

cannot /'kænɒt/ can not.

canny /'kænɪ/ *adjective* (**-ier**, **-iest**) **1** shrewd. **2** thrifty.

canoe /kə'nu:/ *noun* light narrow boat, usually paddled. ● *verb* (**-noes**, **-noed**, **-noeing**) travel in canoe. □ **canoeist** *noun*.
■ *noun* dugout, kayak.

canon /'kænən/ *noun* **1** general law, rule, principle, or criterion. **2** church decree. **3** member of cathedral chapter. **4** set of (esp. sacred) writings accepted as genuine. **5** part of RC Mass containing words of consecration. **6** *Music* piece with different parts taking up same theme successively. □ **canon law** ecclesiastical law.

canonical /kə'nɒnɪk(ə)l/ *adjective* **1** according to canon law. **2** included in canon of Scripture. **3** authoritative, accepted. **4** of (member of) cathedral chapter. ● *noun* (in *plural*) canonical dress of clergy.

canonize /'kænənaɪz/ *verb* (also **-ise**) (**-zing** or **-sing**) declare officially to be saint. □ **canonization** *noun*.

canopy /'kænəpɪ/ *noun* (*plural* **-ies**) **1** suspended covering over throne, bed, etc. **2** overhanging shelter. **3** sky. **4** rooflike projection. ● *verb* (**-ies**, **-ied**) supply or be canopy to.
■ *noun* **1, 2** awning, cover, covering, shade, shelter.

cant[1] *noun* **1** insincere pious or moral talk. **2** language peculiar to class, profession, etc.; jargon. ● *verb* use cant.

cant[2] *noun* **1** slanting surface, bevel. **2** oblique push or jerk. **3** tilted position. ● *verb* push or pitch out of level.

can't /kɑːnt/ can not.

cantabile /kæn'tɑːbɪleɪ/ *Music adverb & adjective* in smooth flowing style. ● *noun* cantabile passage or movement.

cantaloupe /'kæntəluːp/ *noun* (also **cantaloup**) small round ribbed melon.

cantankerous /kæn'tæŋkərəs/ *adjective* bad-tempered, quarrelsome. □ **cantankerously** *adverb.* **cantankerousness** *noun.*

cantata /kæn'tɑːtə/ *noun* composition for vocal soloists and usually chorus and orchestra.

canteen /kæn'tiːn/ *noun* **1** restaurant for employees in office, factory, etc. **2** shop for provisions in barracks or camp. **3** case of cutlery. **4** soldier's or camper's water-flask.

canter /'kæntə/ *noun* horse's pace between trot and gallop. ● *verb* (cause to) go at a canter.

canticle /'kæntɪk(ə)l/ *noun* song or chant with biblical text.

cantilever /'kæntɪliːvə/ *noun* **1** bracket, beam, etc. projecting from wall to support balcony etc. **2** beam or girder fixed at one end only. □ **cantilever bridge** bridge made of cantilevers projecting from piers and connected by girders. □ **cantilevered** *adjective.*

canto /'kæntəʊ/ *noun* (*plural* **-s**) division of long poem.

canton *noun* /'kæntɒn/ subdivision of country, esp. Switzerland. ● *verb* /kæn'tuːn/ put (troops) into quarters.

cantonment /kæn'tuːnmənt/ *noun* lodgings of troops.

cantor /'kæntɔː/ *noun* **1** church choir leader. **2** precentor in synagogue.

canvas /'kænvəs/ *noun* **1** strong coarse cloth used for sails and tents etc. and for oil painting. **2** a painting on canvas.

canvass /'kænvəs/ *verb* **1** solicit votes (from). **2** ascertain opinions of. **3** seek custom from. **4** propose (idea etc.). ● *noun* canvassing. □ **canvasser** *noun.*

■ *verb* **1** campaign, drum up support, electioneer, solicit (votes). **2** see POLL *verb* 3. ● *noun* campaign, census, enquiry, examination, investigation, market research, opinion poll, poll, probe, scrutiny, survey.

canyon /'kænjən/ *noun* deep gorge.

■ defile, gorge, *US* gulch, pass, ravine, valley.

CAP *abbreviation* Common Agricultural Policy (of EC).

cap *noun* **1** soft brimless hat, often with peak. **2** head-covering of nurse etc. **3** cap as sign of membership of sports team. **4** academic mortarboard. **5** cover resembling cap, or designed to close, seal, or protect something. **6** contraceptive diaphragm. **7** percussion cap. **8** dental crown. ● *verb* (**-pp-**) **1** put cap on. **2** cover top or end of. **3** limit. **4** award sports cap to. **5** form top of. **6** surpass.

■ *noun* **1–4** hat, head-covering. **5** covering, lid, top. ● *verb* **2** see COVER *verb* 1.

capable /'keɪpəb(ə)l/ *adjective* **1** competent, able. **2** (+ *of*) having ability, fitness, etc. for. □ **capability** *noun* (*plural* **-ies**). **capably** *adverb.*

■ **1** able, accomplished, adept, clever, competent, effective, efficient, experienced, expert, gifted, handy, intelligent, masterly, practised, proficient, qualified, skilful, skilled, talented, trained. **2** (*capable of*) apt to, disposed to, equal to, liable to.

capacious /kə'peɪʃəs/ *adjective* roomy. □ **capaciousness** *noun.*

capacitance /kə'pæsɪt(ə)ns/ *noun* ability to store electric charge.

capacitor /kə'pæsɪtə/ *noun* type of device for storing electric charge.

capacity /kə'pæsɪtɪ/ *noun* (*plural* **-ies**) **1** power to contain, receive, experience, or produce. **2** maximum amount that can be contained etc. **3** mental power. **4** position or function. ● *adjective* fully occupying available space etc.

■ *noun* **2** content, dimensions, magnitude, room, size, volume. **3** ability, acumen, capability, cleverness, competence, intelligence, potential, power, skill, talent, wit. **4** duty, function, job, office, place, position, post, province, responsibility, role.

caparison /kə'pærɪs(ə)n/ *literary noun* **1** horse's trappings. **2** finery. ● *verb* adorn.

cape¹ *noun* short cloak.

■ cloak, cope, mantle, shawl, wrap.

cape² *noun* **1** headland, promontory. **2** (**the Cape**) Cape of Good Hope.

■ **1** head, headland, peninsula, point, promontory.

caper¹ /'keɪpə/ *verb* jump playfully. ● *noun* **1** playful leap. **2** prank. **3** *slang* illicit activity.

■ *verb* **1** bound, cavort, dance, frisk, frolic, gambol, hop, jig about, jump, leap, play, prance, romp, skip, spring.

caper² /'keɪpə/ *noun* **1** bramble-like shrub. **2** (in *plural*) its pickled buds.

capercaillie /kæpə'keɪlɪ/ *noun* (also **capercailzie** /-'keɪlzɪ/) large European grouse.

capillarity /kæpɪ'lærɪtɪ/ *noun* rise or depression of liquid in narrow tube.

capillary /kə'pɪlərɪ/ *adjective* **1** of hair. **2** of narrow diameter. ● *noun* (*plural* **-ies**) capillary tube or blood vessel. □ **capillary action** capillarity.

capital /'kæpɪt(ə)l/ *noun* **1** chief town or city of a country or region. **2** money etc. with which company starts in business. **3** accumulated wealth. **4** capital letter. **5** head of column or pillar. ● *adjective* **1** involving punishment by death. **2** most important. **3** (of letters) large; used to begin sentence or name. **4** *colloquial* excellent. □ **capital gain** profit from sale of investments or property. **capital goods** machinery, plant, etc. **capital transfer tax** *historical* tax levied on transfer of capital by gift or bequest etc.

■ *noun* **1** centre of government, chief city. **2, 3** assets, cash, finance, funds, investments, money, principal, property, *slang* the ready, resources, riches, savings, stock, wealth, *colloquial* the wherewithal. ● *adjective* **2** chief, controlling, first, foremost, important, leading, main, paramount, pre-eminent, primary, principal. **3** big, block, initial, large, upper-case. **4** see EXCELLENT.

capitalism *noun* economic and political system dependent on private capital and profit-making.

capitalist *noun* **1** person using or possessing capital. **2** advocate of capitalism. ● *adjective* of or favouring capitalism. □ **capitalistic** /-'lɪs-/ *adjective*.

capitalize *verb* (also **-ise**) (**-zing** or **-sing**) **1** convert into or provide with capital. **2** write (letter of alphabet) as capital. **3** begin (word) with capital letter. **4** (+ *on*) use to one's advantage. □ **capitalization** *noun*.

capitulate /kə'pɪtjʊleɪt/ *verb* (**-ting**) surrender. □ **capitulation** *noun*.

■ acquiesce, concede, fall, give in, relent, submit, succumb, surrender, throw in the towel, yield.

capon /'keɪpən/ *noun* castrated cock.

cappuccino /kæpʊ'tʃiːnəʊ/ *noun* (*plural* **-s**) frothy milky coffee.

caprice /kə'priːs/ *noun* **1** whim. **2** lively or fanciful work of music etc.

capricious /kə'prɪʃəs/ *adjective* subject to whims; unpredictable. □ **capriciously** *adverb*. **capriciousness** *noun*.

■ changeable, erratic, fanciful, fickle, fitful, flighty, impulsive, inconstant, mercurial, moody, quirky, uncertain, unpredictable, unreliable, unstable, variable, wayward, whimsical.

Capricorn /'kæprɪkɔːn/ *noun* tenth sign of zodiac.

capsicum /'kæpsɪkəm/ *noun* **1** plant with edible fruits. **2** red, green, or yellow fruit of this.

capsize /kæp'saɪz/ *verb* (**-zing**) **1** (of boat) be overturned. **2** overturn (boat).

■ flip over, invert, keel over, overturn, tip over, turn over, turn turtle, turn upside down.

capstan /'kæpst(ə)n/ *noun* **1** thick revolving cylinder for winding cable etc. **2** revolving spindle controlling speed of tape on tape recorder. □ **capstan lathe** lathe with revolving tool holder.

capsule /'kæpsjuːl/ *noun* **1** small soluble case enclosing medicine. **2** detachable compartment of spacecraft or nose-cone of rocket. **3** enclosing membrane. **4** dry fruit releasing seeds when ripe.

■ **1** lozenge, pill, tablet.

Capt. *abbreviation* Captain.

captain /'kæptɪn/ *noun* **1** chief, leader; leader of team. **2** commander of ship. **3** pilot of civil aircraft. **4** army officer next above lieutenant.

● *verb* be captain of. □ **captaincy** *noun* (*plural* **-ies**).

■ *noun* **1** *colloquial* boss, chief, head, leader. **2** commander, master, officer in charge, pilot, skipper.

caption /'kæpʃ(ə)n/ *noun* **1** wording appended to illustration or cartoon. **2** wording on cinema or television screen. **3** heading of chapter, article, etc. ● *verb* provide with caption.

■ *noun* description, explanation, heading, headline, subtitle, surtitle, title.

captious /'kæpʃəs/ *adjective* fault-finding.

captivate /'kæptɪveɪt/ *verb* (**-ting**) fascinate, charm. □ **captivation** *noun*.

■ attract, beguile, bewitch, charm, delight, enamour, enchant, enrapture, enslave, ensnare, enthral, entrance, fascinate, hypnotize, infatuate, mesmerize, seduce, win.

captive /'kæptɪv/ *noun* confined or imprisoned person or animal. ● *adjective* **1** taken prisoner; confined. **2** unable to escape. □ **captivity** /-'tɪv-/ *noun*.

■ *noun esp. historical* convict, detainee, hostage, internee, prisoner, slave. ● *adjective* **1** caged, captured, chained, confined, detained, enslaved, ensnared, fettered, imprisoned, incarcerated, jailed, restricted, secure, taken prisoner, under lock and key. □ **captivity** bondage, confinement, custody, detention, imprisonment, incarceration, internment, prison, protective custody, remand, restraint, servitude, slavery.

captor /'kæptə/ *noun* person who captures.

capture /'kæptʃə/ *verb* (**-ring**) **1** take prisoner; seize. **2** portray in permanent form. **3** record on film or for use in computer. ● *noun* **1** act of capturing. **2** thing or person captured.

■ *verb* **1** apprehend, arrest, *colloquial* bag, catch, *colloquial* collar, conquer, corner, ensnare, entrap, get, *slang* nab, net, *slang* nick, overpower, secure, seize, snare, take prisoner, trap. ● *noun* **1** apprehension, arrest, seizure.

Capuchin /'kæpjʊtʃɪn/ *noun* **1** friar of branch of Franciscans. **2** (**capuchin**) monkey with hair like black hood.

car *noun* **1** motor vehicle for driver and small number of passengers. **2** railway carriage of specified type. **3** *US* any railway carriage or van. □ **car bomb** terrorist bomb placed in or under parked car. **car boot sale** sale of goods from (tables stocked from) boots of cars. **car park** area for parking cars. **car phone** radio-telephone for use in car etc. **carport** roofed open-sided shelter for car. **carsick** nauseous through car travel.

■ **1** *US* automobile, *slang* banger, *colloquial* jalopy, motor, motor car, motor vehicle, vehicle, *slang* wheels.

caracul = KARAKUL.

carafe /kə'ræf/ *noun* glass container for water or wine.

caramel /'kærəmel/ *noun* **1** burnt sugar or

syrup. **2** kind of soft toffee. □ **caramelize** *verb* (also **-ise**) (**-zing** or **-sing**).

carapace /'kærəpeɪs/ *noun* upper shell of tortoise or crustacean.

carat /'kærət/ *noun* **1** unit of weight for precious stones. **2** measure of purity of gold.

caravan /'kærəvæn/ *noun* **1** vehicle equipped for living in and usually towed by car. **2** people travelling together, esp. across desert. □ **caravanner** *noun*.

caravanserai /kærə'vænsəraɪ/ *noun* Eastern inn with central courtyard.

caravel /'kærəvel/ *noun historical* small light fast ship.

caraway /'kærəweɪ/ *noun* plant with small aromatic fruit (**caraway seed**) used in cakes etc.

carbide /'kɑːbaɪd/ *noun* binary compound of carbon.

carbine /'kɑːbam/ *noun* kind of short rifle.

carbohydrate /kɑːbə'haɪdreɪt/ *noun* energy-producing compound of carbon, hydrogen, and oxygen.

carbolic /kɑː'bɒlɪk/ *noun* (in full **carbolic acid**) kind of disinfectant and antiseptic. □ **carbolic soap** soap containing this.

carbon /'kɑːbən/ *noun* **1** non-metallic element occurring as diamond, graphite, and charcoal, and in all organic compounds. **2** carbon copy. **3** carbon paper. □ **carbon copy 1** copy made with carbon paper. **2** person or thing identical or similar to another. **carbon dating** determination of age of object from decay of carbon-14. **carbon dioxide** gas found in atmosphere and formed by respiration. **carbon fibre** thin filament of carbon used as strengthening material. **carbon-14** radioactive carbon isotope of mass 14. **carbon monoxide** poisonous gas formed by burning carbon incompletely. **carbon paper** thin carbon-coated paper for making copies. **carbon tax** tax on fuels producing greenhouse gases. **carbon-12** stable isotope of carbon used as a standard.

carbonate /'kɑːbəneɪt/ *noun* salt of carbonic acid. ● *verb* (**-ting**) fill with carbon dioxide.

carbonic /kɑː'bɒnɪk/ *adjective* containing carbon. □ **carbonic acid** weak acid formed from carbon dioxide in water.

carboniferous /kɑːbə'nɪfərəs/ *adjective* producing coal.

carbonize /'kɑːbənaɪz/ *verb* (also **-ise**) (**-zing** or **-sing**) **1** reduce to charcoal or coke. **2** convert to carbon. **3** coat with carbon. □ **carbonization** *noun*.

carborundum /kɑːbə'rʌndəm/ *noun* compound of carbon and silicon used esp. as abrasive.

carboy /'kɑːbɔɪ/ *noun* large globular glass bottle.

carbuncle /'kɑːbʌŋk(ə)l/ *noun* **1** severe skin abscess. **2** bright red jewel.

carburettor /kɑːbə'retə/ *noun* apparatus mixing air with petrol vapour in internal-combustion engine.

carcass /'kɑːkəs/ *noun* (also **carcase**) **1** dead body of animal or bird or (*colloquial*) person. **2** framework. **3** worthless remains.

■ **1** body, cadaver, corpse, meat, remains. **2** framework, hulk, remains, shell, skeleton, structure.

carcinogen /kɑː'sɪnədʒ(ə)n/ *noun* substance producing cancer. □ **carcinogenic** /-'dʒen-/ *adjective*.

carcinoma /kɑːsɪ'nəʊmə/ *noun* (*plural* **carcinomata** /-tə/ or **carcinomas**) cancerous growth.

card[1] *noun* **1** thick stiff paper or thin pasteboard. **2** piece of this for writing or printing on, esp. to send greetings, to identify person, or to record information. **3** small rectangular piece of plastic used to obtain cash, credit, etc. **4** playing card. **5** (in *plural*) card-playing. **6** (in *plural*) *colloquial* employee's tax etc. documents. **7** programme of events at race meeting etc. **8** *colloquial* eccentric person. □ **card-carrying** registered as member (esp. of political party). **card index** index with separate card for each item. **cardphone** public telephone operated by card instead of money. **card-sharp** swindler at card games. **card vote** block vote. **on the cards** possible or likely.

■ **1** cardboard, pasteboard. **3** bank card, cash card, charge card, cheque card, credit card.

card[2] *noun* wire brush etc. for raising nap on cloth etc. ● *verb* brush with card.

cardamom /'kɑːdəməm/ *noun* seeds of SE Asian aromatic plant used as spice.

cardboard *noun* pasteboard or stiff paper.

cardiac /'kɑːdɪæk/ *adjective* of the heart.

cardigan /'kɑːdɪgən/ *noun* knitted jacket.

cardinal /'kɑːdɪn(ə)l/ *adjective* **1** chief, fundamental. **2** deep scarlet. ● *noun* one of leading RC dignitaries who elect Pope. □ **cardinal number** number representing quantity (1, 2, 3, etc.); compare ORDINAL.

cardiogram /'kɑːdɪəʊgræm/ *noun* record of heart movements.

cardiograph /'kɑːdɪəʊgrɑːf/ *noun* instrument recording heart movements. □ **cardiographer** /-'ɒgrəfə/ *noun*. **cardiography** /-'ɒgrəfɪ/ *noun*.

cardiology /kɑːdɪ'ɒlədʒɪ/ *noun* branch of medicine concerned with heart. □ **cardiologist** *noun*.

cardiovascular /kɑːdɪəʊ'væskjʊlə/ *adjective* of heart and blood vessels.

care /keə/ *noun* **1** (cause of) anxiety or concern. **2** serious attention; caution. **3** protection, charge. **4** task. ● *verb* (**-ring**) (usually + *about, for, whether*) feel concern or interest or affection. □ **in care** (of child) under local authority supervision. **take care 1** be careful. **2** (+ *to do*) not fail or neglect to. **take care of 1** look after. **2** deal with. **3** dispose of.

■ *noun* **1** anxiety, burden, concern, difficulty, hardship, problem, responsibility, sorrow, stress, tribulation, trouble, vexation, woe, worry. **2** attention, carefulness, caution, circumspection, concentration, concern, diligence, exactness, forethought, heed, meticulousness, pains, prudence, solicitude, thoroughness, thought, vigilance, watchfulness. **3** charge, control, custody, guardianship, keeping, management, protection, safe keeping, *archaic* ward. ● *verb* be troubled, bother, concern oneself, mind, worry; (*care for*) see LOVE *verb* 1, TEND².

careen /kə'ri:n/ *verb* **1** turn (ship) on side for repair. **2** move or swerve wildly.

career /kə'rɪə/ *noun* **1** professional etc. course through life. **2** profession or occupation. **3** swift course. ● *adjective* **1** pursuing or wishing to pursue a career. **2** working permanently in specified profession. ● *verb* move or swerve wildly.
■ *noun* **2** business, calling, craft, employment, job, livelihood, living, *métier*, occupation, profession, trade, vocation, work. ● *verb* see RUSH¹ *verb* 1.

careerist *noun* person predominantly concerned with personal advancement.

carefree *adjective* **1** light-hearted, joyous. **2** free of troubles.
■ **1** blasé, careless, casual, cheery, contented, debonair, easygoing, happy, happy-go-lucky, indifferent, insouciant, *colloquial* laid-back, light-hearted, nonchalant, relaxed, unconcerned, unworried. **2** easy, leisured, peaceful, quiet, relaxing, restful, trouble-free, untroubled.

careful *adjective* **1** painstaking. **2** cautious. **3** taking care; not neglecting. □ **carefully** *adverb*. **carefulness** *noun*.
■ **1** accurate, conscientious, deliberate, diligent, exhaustive, fastidious, fussy, judicious, methodical, meticulous, neat, orderly, organized, painstaking, particular, precise, punctilious, responsible, rigorous, scrupulous, systematic, thorough, well organized. **2** alert, attentive, cautious, chary, circumspect, heedful, mindful, observant, prudent, solicitous, thoughtful, vigilant, wary, watchful; (*be careful*) see BEWARE 1.

careless *adjective* **1** done without care. **2** not taking care or paying attention. **3** unthinking, insensitive. **4** light-hearted. □ **carelessly** *adverb*. **carelessness** *noun*.
■ **1** casual, confused, cursory, disorganized, hasty, imprecise, inaccurate, messy, perfunctory, shoddy, slapdash, slipshod, sloppy, slovenly, thoughtless, untidy. **2** absent-minded, inattentive, incautious, irresponsible, negligent, rash, reckless, scatterbrained, unwary. **3** heedless, ill-considered, imprudent, inconsiderate, thoughtless, uncaring, unguarded, unthinking. **4** see CAREFREE 1. □ **carelessness** haste, inattention, irresponsibility, negligence, recklessness, sloppiness, slovenliness, thoughtlessness, untidiness.

carer *noun* person who cares for sick or elderly person, esp. at home.

caress /kə'res/ *verb* touch lovingly. ● *noun* loving touch.
■ *verb* cuddle, embrace, fondle, hug, kiss, pat, pet, smooth, stroke, touch.

caret /'kærət/ *noun* mark indicating insertion in text.

caretaker *noun* person in charge of maintenance of building. ● *adjective* taking temporary control.
■ *noun* custodian, janitor, keeper, porter.

careworn *adjective* showing effects of prolonged anxiety.
■ gaunt, grim, haggard, weary.

cargo /'kɑ:gəʊ/ *noun* (*plural* **-es** or **-s**) goods carried by ship or aircraft.
■ consignment, freight, goods, load, merchandise, payload, shipment.

Caribbean /kærə'bi:ən/ *adjective* of the West Indies.

caribou /'kærɪbu:/ *noun* (*plural* same) N. American reindeer.

caricature /'kærɪkətʃʊə/ *noun* grotesque usually comically exaggerated representation. ● *verb* (**-ring**) make or give caricature of. □ **caricaturist** *noun*.
■ *noun* burlesque, cartoon, parody, satire, *colloquial* send-up, *colloquial* spoof, *colloquial* take-off, travesty. ● *verb* burlesque, distort, exaggerate, imitate, lampoon, make fun of, mimic, mock, overact, overdo, parody, ridicule, satirize, *colloquial* send up, *colloquial* take off.

caries /'keəri:z/ *noun* (*plural* same) decay of tooth or bone.

carillon /kə'rɪljən/ *noun* **1** set of bells sounded from keyboard or mechanically. **2** tune played on this.

Carmelite /'kɑ:məlaɪt/ *noun* **1** friar of Order of Our Lady of Mount Carmel. **2** nun of similar order. ● *adjective* of Carmelites.

carminative /'kɑ:mmətɪv/ *adjective* relieving flatulence. ● *noun* carminative drug.

carmine /'kɑ:maɪn/ *adjective* of vivid crimson colour. ● *noun* **1** this colour. **2** pigment from cochineal.

carnage /'kɑ:nɪdʒ/ *noun* great slaughter.
■ bloodbath, bloodshed, butchery, holocaust, killing, massacre, pogrom, shambles, slaughter.

carnal /'kɑ:n(ə)l/ *adjective* **1** of the flesh; worldly. **2** sensual, sexual. □ **carnality** *noun*.
■ animal, bodily, erotic, fleshly, lustful, physical, sensual, sexual.

carnation /kɑ:'neɪʃ(ə)n/ *noun* **1** clove-scented pink. **2** rosy-pink colour. ● *adjective* rosy-pink.

carnelian = CORNELIAN.

carnival /'kɑ:nɪv(ə)l/ *noun* **1** festivities or festival, esp. preceding Lent. **2** merrymaking.
■ celebration, fair, festival, festivity, fête, fiesta, gala, jamboree, merrymaking, pageant, parade, procession, revelry, show, spectacle.

carnivore /'kɑ:nɪvɔ:/ *noun* animal or plant that feeds on flesh. □ **carnivorous** /-'nɪvərəs-/ *adjective*.

carob /'kærəb/ *noun* seed pod of Mediterranean tree used as chocolate substitute.

carol /'kær(ə)l/ *noun* joyous song, esp. Christmas hymn. ● *verb* (**-ll-**; *US* **-l-**) **1** sing carols. **2** sing joyfully.

carotene /'kærəti:n/ *noun* orange-coloured pigment in carrots etc.

carotid /kə'rɒtɪd/ *noun* each of two main arteries carrying blood to head. ● *adjective* of these arteries.

carouse /kə'raʊz/ *verb* (**-sing**) have lively drinking party. ● *noun* such party. □ **carousal** *noun*. **carouser** *noun*.

carousel /kærə'sel/ *noun* **1** *US* merry-go-round. **2** rotating delivery or conveyor system.

carp[1] *noun* (*plural* same) freshwater fish often bred for food.

carp[2] *verb* find fault, complain. □ **carper** *noun*.
■ cavil, complain, find fault, *colloquial* go on, *colloquial* gripe, grumble, object, pick holes, quibble, split hairs, *colloquial* whinge.

carpal /'kɑːp(ə)l/ *adjective* of the wrist-bones. ● *noun* wrist-bone.

carpel /'kɑːp(ə)l/ *noun* female reproductive organ of flower.

carpenter /'kɑːpɪntə/ *noun* person skilled in woodwork. ● *verb* do woodwork; make by woodwork. □ **carpentry** *noun*.
■ □ **carpentry** joinery, woodwork.

carpet /'kɑːpɪt/ *noun* **1** thick fabric for covering floors etc. **2** piece of this. **3** thing resembling this. ● *verb* (**-t-**) **1** cover (as) with carpet. **2** *colloquial* rebuke. □ **carpet-bag** travelling bag originally made of carpet-like material. **carpet-bagger** *colloquial* political candidate etc. without local connections. **carpet slipper** soft slipper. **carpet sweeper** implement for sweeping carpets.

carpeting *noun* **1** material for carpets. **2** carpets collectively.

carpus /'kɑːpəs/ *noun* (*plural* **-pi** /-paɪ/) group of small bones forming wrist.

carrageen /'kærəgi:n/ *noun* edible red seaweed.

carriage /'kærɪdʒ/ *noun* **1** railway passenger vehicle. **2** wheeled horse-drawn passenger vehicle. **3** conveying of goods. **4** cost of this. **5** bearing, deportment. **6** part of machine that carries other parts. **7** gun carriage. □ **carriage clock** portable clock with handle. **carriageway** part of road used by vehicles.
■ **1, 2** coach. **5** bearing, demeanour, deportment, gait, manner, *literary* mien, posture, presence, stance.

carrier /'kærɪə/ *noun* **1** person or thing that carries. **2** transport or freight company. **3** carrier bag. **4** framework on bicycle for carrying luggage or passenger. **5** person or animal that may transmit disease without suffering from it. **6** aircraft carrier. □ **carrier bag** plastic or paper bag with handles. **carrier pigeon** pigeon trained to carry messages. **carrier wave** high-frequency electromagnetic wave used to convey signal.

■ **1** bearer, conveyor, courier, delivery man, delivery woman, dispatch rider, errand-boy, errand-girl, haulier, messenger, porter, postman, runner. **5** contact, host, transmitter.

carrion /'kærɪən/ *noun* **1** dead flesh. **2** filth. □ **carrion crow** crow feeding on carrion.

carrot /'kærət/ *noun* **1** plant with edible tapering orange root. **2** this root. **3** incentive. □ **carroty** *adjective*.

carry /'kærɪ/ *verb* (**-ies, -ied**) **1** support or hold up, esp. while moving. **2** have with one. **3** convey. **4** (often + *to*) take (process etc.) to specified point. **5** involve. **6** transfer (figure) to column of higher value. **7** hold in specified way. **8** (of newspaper etc.) publish. **9** (of radio or television station) broadcast. **10** keep (goods) in stock. **11** (of sound) be audible at a distance. **12** win victory or acceptance for. **13** win acceptance from. **14** capture. □ **carry away 1** remove. **2** inspire. **3** deprive of self-control. **carrycot** portable cot for baby. **carry forward** transfer (figure) to new page or account. **carry it off** do well under difficulties. **carry off 1** remove (esp. by force). **2** win. **3** (esp. of disease) kill. **carry on 1** continue. **2** *colloquial* behave excitedly. **3** (often + *with*) *colloquial* flirt. **carry-on** *noun colloquial* fuss. **carry out** put into practice. **carry-out** *noun & adjective* take-away. **carry over 1** carry forward. **2** postpone. **carry through 1** complete. **2** bring safely out of difficulties. **carry weight** be influential or important.

■ **1** bear, hold up, shoulder, support, take. **2** bring, lug, take. **3** bring, cart, convey, ferry, fetch, haul, lug, manhandle, move, remove, ship, take, transfer, transmit, transport. **5** demand, entail, involve, lead to, occasion, require, result in. □ **carry on 1** see CONTINUE 1. **carry out** see DO[1] *verb* 1.

cart *noun* **1** open usually horse-drawn vehicle for carrying loads. **2** light vehicle for pulling by hand. ● *verb* **1** carry in or as in cart; convey. **2** *slang* carry with difficulty. □ **cart horse** horse of heavy build. **cart off** remove esp. by force. **cartwheel 1** wheel of cart. **2** sideways somersault with arms and legs extended.
■ *noun* **1** dray, truck, wagon. **2** barrow, trolley, wheelbarrow. ● *verb* **1** see CARRY 3.

carte blanche /kɑːt 'blɑ̃ʃ/ *noun* full discretionary power.

cartel /kɑː'tel/ *noun* union of suppliers etc. set up to control prices.

Cartesian coordinates /kɑː'ti:zɪən/ *plural noun* system of locating point by its distance from two perpendicular axes.

carthorse /'kɑːθɔːs/ *noun* thickset horse fit for heavy work.

Carthusian /kɑː'θjuːzɪən/ *noun* monk of contemplative order founded by St Bruno. ● *adjective* of this order.

cartilage /'kɑːtɪlɪdʒ/ *noun* firm flexible connective tissue in vertebrates. □ **cartilaginous** /-'lædʒ-/ *adjective*.

cartography /kɑː'tɒgrəfɪ/ *noun* map-drawing.

□ **cartographer** *noun.* **cartographic** /-tə'græf-/ *adjective.*

carton /'kɑːt(ə)n/ *noun* light esp. cardboard container.
   ■ box, case, container, pack, package, packet.

cartoon /kɑː'tuːn/ *noun* **1** humorous esp. topical drawing in newspaper etc. **2** sequence of drawings telling story. **3** such sequence animated on film. **4** full-size preliminary design for work of art. □ **cartoonist** *noun.*
   ■ **1** caricature. **2** comic strip. **3** animation. **4** drawing, sketch.

cartouche /kɑː'tuːʃ/ *noun* **1** scroll-like ornament. **2** oval enclosing name and title of pharaoh.

cartridge /'kɑːtrɪdʒ/ *noun* **1** case containing explosive charge or bullet. **2** sealed container of film etc. **3** component carrying stylus on record player. **4** ink-container for insertion in pen. □ **cartridge-belt** belt with pockets or loops for cartridges. **cartridge paper** thick paper for drawing etc.
   ■ **1** magazine, round, shell. **2** canister, capsule, case, cassette, container, cylinder, tube.

carve *verb* (**-ving**) **1** make or shape by cutting. **2** cut pattern etc. in. **3** (+ *into*) form pattern etc. from. **4** cut (meat) into slices. □ **carve out** take from larger whole. **carve up 1** subdivide. **2** drive aggressively into path of (another vehicle). □ **carver** *noun.*
   ■ **1, 3** chip (away) at, chisel, fashion, hew, sculpture, shape. **2** engrave, incise, inscribe. **4** cut, slice.

carvery *noun* (*plural* **-ies**) restaurant etc. with joints displayed for carving.

carving *noun* carved object, esp. as work of art. □ **carving knife** knife for carving meat.

caryatid /kærɪ'ætɪd/ *noun* (*plural* **-tides** /-tɪdiːz/ or **-tids**) supporting pillar in form of female figure.

cascade /kæs'keɪd/ *noun* waterfall, esp. one in series. ● *verb* (**-ding**) fall in or like cascade.
   ■ *noun* cataract, falls, waterfall. ● *verb* see POUR 1.

case[1] /keɪs/ *noun* **1** instance of something occurring. **2** hypothetical or actual situation; state of affairs. **3** person's illness, circumstances, etc. as regarded by doctor, social worker, etc. **4** such a person. **5** crime etc. investigated by detective or police. **6** suit at law. **7** sum of arguments on one side. **8** (valid) set of arguments. **9** *Grammar* relation of word to others in sentence. **10** *Grammar* form of word expressing this. □ **case law** law as established by decided cases. **casework** social work concerned with individual's background. **in any case** whatever the truth or possible outcome is. **in case 1** in the event that. **2** lest; in provision against a possibility. **in case of** in the event of. **is (not) the case** is (not) so.
   ■ **1** example, illustration, instance, occurrence, specimen. **2** circumstances, context, situation, state, state of affairs. **3** circumstances, condition,

plight, predicament, situation, state. **5** inquiry, investigation. **6** action, cause, dispute, lawsuit, suit.

case[2] /keɪs/ *noun* container or cover enclosing something. ● *verb* (**-sing**) **1** enclose in case. **2** (+ *with*) surround with. **3** *slang* inspect closely, esp. for criminal purpose. □ **case-harden 1** harden surface of (esp. steel). **2** make callous.
   ■ *noun* box, cabinet, carton, casket, chest, container, crate, pack, packaging, piece of luggage, suitcase, trunk.

casein /'keɪsɪn/ *noun* main protein in milk and cheese.

casement /'keɪsmənt/ *noun* (part of) window hinged to open like door.

cash *noun* **1** money in coins or notes. **2** full payment at time of purchase. ● *verb* give or obtain cash for. □ **cash and carry 1** (esp. wholesaling) system of cash payment for goods removed by buyer. **2** store where this operates. **cash card** plastic card for use in cash dispenser. **cash crop** crop produced for sale. **cash desk** counter etc. where goods are paid for. **cash dispenser** automatic machine for withdrawal of cash. **cash flow** movement of money into and out of a business. **cash in 1** obtain cash for. **2** (usually + *on*) *colloquial* profit (from). **cash register** till recording sales, totalling receipts, etc. **cash up** count day's takings.
   ■ *noun* banknotes, bills, change, coins, currency, *slang* dough, funds, legal tender, money, notes, *slang* the ready, *colloquial* the wherewithal. ● *verb* exchange for cash, realize, sell. □ **cash in 2** (*cash in on*) see PROFIT *verb* 2.

cashew /'kæʃuː/ *noun* **1** evergreen tree bearing kidney-shaped edible nut. **2** this nut.

cashier[1] /kæ'ʃɪə/ *noun* person dealing with cash transactions in bank etc.
   ■ checkout person, clerk, teller.

cashier[2] /kæ'ʃɪə/ *verb* dismiss from service.
   ■ see DISMISS 2.

cashmere /kæʃ'mɪə/ *noun* fine soft (material of) wool, esp. of Kashmir goat.

casing *noun* enclosing material or cover.

casino /kə'siːnəʊ/ *noun* (*plural* **-s**) public room etc. for gambling.

cask /kɑːsk/ *noun* barrel, esp. for alcoholic liquor.
   ■ barrel, butt, hogshead, tub, tun, vat.

casket /'kɑːskɪt/ *noun* **1** small box for holding valuables. **2** *US* coffin.

cassava /kə'sɑːvə/ *noun* **1** plant with starchy roots. **2** starch or flour from these.

casserole /'kæsərəʊl/ *noun* **1** covered dish for cooking food in oven. **2** food cooked in this. ● *verb* (**-ling**) cook in casserole.

cassette /kə'set/ *noun* sealed case containing magnetic tape, film, etc., ready for insertion in tape recorder, camera, etc.

cassia /ˈkæsɪə/ *noun* tree whose leaves and pod yield senna.

cassis /kæˈsiːs/ *noun* blackcurrant flavouring for drinks etc.

cassock /ˈkæsək/ *noun* long usually black or red clerical garment.

cassowary /ˈkæsəweərɪ/ *noun* (*plural* **-ies**) large flightless Australian bird.

cast /kɑːst/ *verb* (*past & past participle* **cast**) **1** throw. **2** direct, cause to fall. **3** express (doubts etc.). **4** let down (anchor etc.). **5** shed or lose. **6** register (vote). **7** shape (molten metal etc.) in mould. **8** make (product) thus. **9** (usually + *as*) assign (actor) to role. **10** allocate roles in (play, film, etc.). **11** (+ *in*, *into*) arrange (facts etc.) in specified form. ● *noun* **1** throwing of missile, dice, fishing line, etc. **2** thing made in mould. **3** moulded mass of solidified material. **4** actors in play etc. **5** form, type, or quality. **6** tinge of colour. **7** slight squint. **8** worm-cast. □ **cast about, around** search. **cast aside** abandon. **cast down** depress, cause to feel dejected. **casting vote** deciding vote when votes on two sides are equal. **cast iron** hard but brittle iron alloy. **cast-iron** *adjective* **1** of cast iron. **2** very strong; unchallengeable. **cast off 1** abandon. **2** finish piece of knitting. **3** untie (ship). **cast-off** *noun* abandoned or discarded (thing, esp. garment). **cast on** make first row of piece of knitting.

■ *verb* **1** bowl, *colloquial* chuck, drop, fling, hurl, launch, lob, pelt, pitch, project, scatter, shy, *colloquial* sling, throw, toss. **7**, **8** fashion, form, found, mould, sculpture, shape. ● *noun* **2** see SCULPTURE *noun* 2. **4** actors, actresses, company, dramatis personae, performers, players, troupe. □ **cast off 1** see SHED[2] 1–2. **3** see UNTIE.

castanet /kæstəˈnet/ *noun* (usually in *plural*) each of pair of hand-held wooden or ivory shells clicked together in time with esp. Spanish dancing.

castaway /ˈkɑːstəweɪ/ *noun* shipwrecked person. ● *adjective* **1** shipwrecked. **2** cast aside.
■ *adjective* **1** marooned, shipwrecked, stranded. **2** abandoned, deserted, exiled, rejected.

caste /kɑːst/ *noun* **1** any of Hindu hereditary classes whose members have no social contact with other classes. **2** exclusive social class.
■ class, grade, level, position, rank, standing, station, status, stratum.

castellated /ˈkæstəleɪtɪd/ *adjective* built with battlements. □ **castellation** *noun*.

caster = CASTOR.

castigate /ˈkæstɪgeɪt/ *verb* (**-ting**) rebuke; punish. □ **castigation** *noun*.
■ censure, chasten, chastise, *archaic* chide, correct, criticize, discipline, lash, punish, rebuke, reprimand, scold, *colloquial* tell off.

castle /ˈkɑːs(ə)l/ *noun* **1** large fortified residential building. **2** *Chess* rook. ● *verb* (**-ling**) *Chess* make combined move of king and rook.
■ *noun* **1** chateau, citadel, fort, fortress, mansion, palace, stately home, stronghold, tower.

castor /ˈkɑːstə/ *noun* (also **caster**) **1** small swivelled wheel enabling heavy furniture to be moved. **2** container perforated for sprinkling sugar etc. □ **castor sugar** finely granulated white sugar.

castor oil *noun* vegetable oil used as laxative and lubricant.

castrate /kæsˈtreɪt/ *verb* (**-ting**) remove testicles of. □ **castration** *noun*.
■ emasculate, geld, neuter, sterilize, unsex.

casual /ˈkæʒʊəl/ *adjective* **1** chance. **2** not regular or permanent. **3** unconcerned, careless. **4** (of clothes etc.) informal. ● *noun* **1** casual worker. **2** (usually in *plural*) casual clothes or shoes. □ **casually** *adverb*.
■ *adjective* **1** accidental, chance, fortuitous, incidental, random, serendipitous, unexpected, unforeseen, unintentional, unplanned, unpremeditated. **2** erratic, irregular, occasional, *colloquial* promiscuous, sporadic, temporary, unstructured, unsystematic. **3** apathetic, blasé, careless, easygoing, free and easy, lackadaisical, *colloquial* laid-back, lax, negligent, nonchalant, offhand, relaxed, *colloquial* slap-happy, throw-away, unconcerned, unenthusiastic, unprofessional. **4** comfortable, informal.

casualty /ˈkæʒʊəltɪ/ *noun* (*plural* **-ies**) **1** person killed or injured in war or accident. **2** thing lost or destroyed. **3** casualty department. **4** accident. □ **casualty department** part of hospital for treatment of casualties.
■ **1** dead person, death, fatality, injured person, injury, loss, victim, wounded person.

casuist /ˈkæzʊɪst/ *noun* **1** person who resolves cases of conscience etc., esp. cleverly but falsely. **2** sophist, quibbler. □ **casuistic** *adjective*. **casuistry** /-ˈɪs-/ *noun*.

cat *noun* **1** small furry domestic 4-legged animal. **2** wild animal of same family. **3** *colloquial* malicious or spiteful woman. **4** cat-o'-nine-tails. □ **cat burglar** burglar who enters by climbing to upper storey. **catcall** (make) shrill whistle of disapproval. **catfish** fish with whisker-like filaments round mouth. **cat flap** small flap allowing cat passage through outer door. **catnap** (have) short sleep. **cat-o'-nine-tails** *historical* whip with nine knotted cords. **cat's cradle** child's game with string. **Catseye** *proprietary term* reflector stud set into road. **cat's-paw** person used as tool by another. **catsuit** close-fitting garment with trouser legs, covering whole body. **catwalk** narrow walkway. **rain cats and dogs** *colloquial* rain hard.
■ **1** kitten, *slang* mog, *slang* moggie, *colloquial* pussy, tabby, tom, tom-cat.

catachresis /kætəˈkriːsɪs/ *noun* (*plural* **-chreses** /-siːz/) incorrect use of words. □ **catachrestic** /-ˈkres-/ *adjective*.

cataclysm /ˈkætəklɪz(ə)m/ *noun* violent upheaval. □ **cataclysmic** /-ˈklɪz-/ *adjective*.

catacomb /ˈkætəkuːm/ *noun* (often in *plural*) underground cemetery.

■ crypt, sepulchre, tomb, vault.

catafalque /'kætəfælk/ *noun* decorated bier, esp. for state funeral etc.

Catalan /'kætəlæn/ *noun* native or language of Catalonia in Spain. ● *adjective* of Catalonia.

catalepsy /'kætəlɛpsɪ/ *noun* trance or seizure with rigidity of body. □ **cataleptic** /-'lep-/ *adjective & noun.*

catalogue /'kætəlɒg/ (*US* **catalog**) *noun* complete or extensive list, usually in alphabetical or other systematic order. ● *verb* (**-logues**, **-logued**, **-loguing**; *US* **-logs**, **-loged**, **-loging**) **1** make catalogue of. **2** enter in catalogue.

■ *noun* brochure, directory, index, inventory, list, record, register, roll, schedule, table. ● *verb* classify, codify, file, index, list, make an inventory of, record, register, tabulate.

catalysis /kə'tælɪsɪs/ *noun* (*plural* **-lyses** /-siːz/) acceleration of chemical reaction by catalyst. □ **catalyse** *verb* (**-sing**) (*US* **-lyze**; **-zing**).

catalyst /'kætəlɪst/ *noun* **1** substance speeding chemical reaction without itself permanently changing. **2** person or thing that precipitates change.

catalytic /kætə'lɪtɪk/ *adjective* involving or causing catalysis. □ **catalytic converter** device in vehicle for converting pollutant gases into less harmful ones.

catamaran /kætəmə'ræn/ *noun* boat or raft with two parallel hulls.

catapult /'kætəpʌlt/ *noun* **1** forked stick with elastic for shooting stones. **2** *historical* military machine for hurling stones etc. **3** device for launching glider etc. ● *verb* **1** launch with catapult. **2** fling forcibly. **3** leap or be hurled forcibly.

■ *verb* **1, 2** fire, fling, hurl, launch, throw.

cataract /'kætərækt/ *noun* **1** waterfall, downpour. **2** progressive opacity of eye lens.

■ **1** cascade, falls, rapids, torrent, waterfall.

catarrh /kə'tɑː/ *noun* **1** inflammation of mucous membrane, air-passages, etc. **2** mucus in nose caused by this. □ **catarrhal** *adjective.*

catastrophe /kə'tæstrəfɪ/ *noun* **1** great usually sudden disaster. **2** denouement of drama. □ **catastrophic** /kætə'strɒf-/ *adjective.* **catastrophically** /kætə'strɒf-/ *adverb.*

■ **1** blow, calamity, cataclysm, crushing blow, débâcle, devastation, disaster, fiasco, holocaust, mischance, misfortune, mishap, ruin, ruination, tragedy, upheaval.

catch /kætʃ/ *verb* (*past & past participle* **caught** /kɔːt/) **1** capture in trap, hands, etc. **2** detect or surprise. **3** intercept and hold (moving thing) in hand etc. **4** *Cricket* dismiss (batsman) by catching ball before it hits ground. **5** contract (disease) by infection etc. **6** reach in time and board (train etc.). **7** apprehend. **8** check or be checked. **9** (cause to) become entangled. **10** (of artist etc.) reproduce faithfully. **11** reach or overtake. ● *noun* **1** act of catching. **2** *Cricket* chance or act of catching ball. **3** amount of thing caught. **4** thing or person caught or worth catching. **5** question etc. intended to deceive etc. **6** unexpected difficulty or disadvantage. **7** device for fastening door etc. **8** musical round. □ **catch fire** begin to burn. **catch on** *colloquial* **1** become popular. **2** understand what is meant. **catch out 1** detect in mistake etc. **2** *Cricket* catch. **catchpenny** intended merely to sell quickly. **catchphrase** phrase in frequent use. **catch-22** *colloquial* dilemma from which there is no escape because of mutually conflicting conditions. **catch up 1** (often + *with*) reach (person etc. ahead). **2** (often + *with*) make up arrears. **3** involve. **4** fasten. **catchword 1** phrase or word in frequent use. **2** word so placed as to draw attention.

■ *verb* **1** apprehend, arrest, capture, clutch, *slang* cop, corner, ensnare, entrap, grab, grasp, grip, hang on to, hold, hook, *slang* nab, net, *slang* nobble, seize, snare, snatch, take, trap. **2** come upon, detect, discover, expose, find, surprise, take by surprise, uncover. **3** grab, intercept, seize, snatch, stop, take. **5** become infected by, contract, get. **6** be in time for, get on. **9** entangle, hook, snag, stick, tangle. ● *noun* **3, 4** bag, booty, capture, haul, prey, prize, take. **6** difficulty, disadvantage, drawback, obstacle, problem, snag, trap. **7** bolt, clasp, clip, fastener, fastening, hasp, hook, latch, lock. □ **catch on 1** see SUCCEED 2. **2** see UNDERSTAND 1. **catchphrase** see SAYING. **catch-22** see QUANDARY.

catching *adjective* infectious.

■ communicable, contagious, infectious, transmissible, transmittable.

catchment area *noun* **1** area served by school, hospital, etc. **2** area from which rainfall flows into river etc.

catchy *adjective* (**-ier**, **-iest**) (of tune) easily remembered; attractive.

■ attractive, haunting, memorable, popular, singable, tuneful.

catechism /'kætɪkɪz(ə)m/ *noun* **1** (book containing) principles of a religion in form of questions and answers. **2** series of questions.

catechize /'kætɪkaɪz/ *verb* (also **-ise**) (**-zing** or **-sing**) instruct by question and answer. □ **catechist** *noun.*

catechumen /kætɪ'kjuːmən/ *noun* person being instructed before baptism.

categorical /kætɪ'gɒrɪk(ə)l/ *adjective* unconditional, absolute; explicit. □ **categorically** *adverb.*

■ absolute, authoritative, certain, complete, decided, decisive, definite, direct, dogmatic, downright, emphatic, explicit, express, firm, forceful, out and out, positive, strong, total, unambiguous, unconditional, unequivocal, unmitigated, unqualified, unreserved, utter, vigorous.

categorize /'kætɪgəraɪz/ *verb* (also **-ise**) (**-zing** or **-sing**) place in category. □ **categorization** *noun.*

category /'kætɪgərɪ/ *noun* (*plural* **-ies**) class or division (of things, ideas, etc.).

■ class, classification, division, grade, group, head, heading, kind, order, rank, ranking, section, sector, set, sort, type, variety.

cater /'keɪtə/ *verb* **1** supply food. **2** (+ *for*) provide what is required for. **3** (+ *to*) pander to. □ **caterer** *noun*.

■ **1** cook, provision. **2** (*cater for*) minister to, provide for, serve, supply. **3** (*cater to*) humour, indulge, pander to.

caterpillar /'kætəpɪlə/ *noun* **1** larva of butterfly or moth. **2** (**Caterpillar**) (in full **Caterpillar track**) *proprietary term* articulated steel band passing round wheels of vehicle for travel on rough ground.

caterwaul /'kætəwɔːl/ *verb* howl like cat.

catgut *noun* thread made from intestines of sheep etc. used for strings of musical instruments etc.

catharsis /kə'θɑːsɪs/ *noun* (*plural* **catharses** /-siːz/) **1** emotional release. **2** emptying of bowels.
cathartic /kə'θɑːtɪk/ *adjective* effecting catharsis. ● *noun* laxative.

cathedral /kə'θiːdr(ə)l/ *noun* principal church of diocese.

Catherine wheel /'kæθrɪn/ *noun* rotating firework.

catheter /'kæθɪtə/ *noun* tube inserted into body cavity to introduce or drain fluid.

cathode /'kæθəʊd/ *noun* **1** negative electrode of cell. **2** positive terminal of battery. □ **cathode ray** beam of electrons from cathode of vacuum tube. **cathode ray tube** vacuum tube in which cathode rays produce luminous image on fluorescent screen.

catholic /'kæθlɪk/ *adjective* **1** universal. **2** all-embracing; broad-minded. **3** (**Catholic**) Roman Catholic. **4** (**Catholic**) including all Christians or all of Western Church. ● *noun* (**Catholic**) Roman Catholic. □ **Catholicism** /kə'θɒlɪs-/ *noun*. **catholicity** /-ə'lɪs-/ *noun*.

■ *adjective* **1, 2** all-embracing, all-inclusive, broad, broad-minded, comprehensive, cosmopolitan, eclectic, general, liberal, universal, varied, wide, wide-ranging.

cation /'kætaɪən/ *noun* positively charged ion. □ **cationic** /-'ɒnɪk/ *adjective*.

catkin /'kætkɪn/ *noun* spike of usually hanging flowers of willow, hazel, etc.

catmint *noun* pungent plant attractive to cats.

catnip *noun* catmint.

cattery *noun* (*plural* **-ies**) place where cats are boarded.

cattle /'kæt(ə)l/ *plural noun* large ruminants, bred esp. for milk or meat. □ **cattle grid** grid over ditch, allowing vehicles to pass over but not livestock.

■ bullocks, bulls, calves, cows, heifers, livestock, oxen, steers, stock.

catty *adjective* (**-ier**, **-iest**) spiteful. □ **cattily** *adverb*. **cattiness** *noun*.

■ *slang* bitchy, ill-natured, malevolent, malicious, mean, nasty, rancorous, sly, spiteful, unkind, venomous, vicious.

Caucasian /kɔː'keɪʒ(ə)n/ *adjective* of the white or light-skinned race. ● *noun* Caucasian person.

caucus /'kɔːkəs/ *noun* (*plural* **-es**) **1** *US* meeting of party members to decide policy. **2** *often derogatory* (meeting of) group within larger organization.

caudal /'kɔːd(ə)l/ *adjective* of, like, or at tail.

caudate /'kɔːdeɪt/ *adjective* tailed.

caught *past & past participle* of CATCH.

caul /kɔːl/ *noun* **1** membrane enclosing foetus. **2** part of this sometimes found on child's head at birth.

cauldron /'kɔːldrən/ *noun* large vessel for boiling things in.

cauliflower /'kɒlɪflaʊə/ *noun* cabbage with large white flower head.

caulk /kɔːk/ *verb* (*US* **calk**) **1** stop up (ship's seams). **2** make watertight.

causal /'kɔːz(ə)l/ *adjective* relating to cause (and effect). □ **causality** /-'zæl-/ *noun*.

causation /kɔː'zeɪʃ(ə)n/ *noun* **1** causing. **2** causality.

cause /kɔːz/ *noun* **1** person or thing producing effect or giving rise to something. **2** reason or motive; justification. **3** principle, belief, or purpose. **4** matter to be settled, or case offered, at law. ● *verb* (**-sing**) **1** be cause of; produce. **2** (+ *to do*) make.

■ *noun* **1** agent, author, basis, *literary* begetter, beginning, creator, genesis, initiator, inspiration, inventor, origin, originator, producer, root, source, spring, stimulus. **2** basis, excuse, explanation, grounds, justification, motivation, motive, occasion, pretext, reason. **3** aim, belief, concern, end, ideal, object, purpose, undertaking. ● *verb* **1** arouse, awaken, begin, bring about, bring on, create, effect, effectuate, engender, foment, generate, give rise to, incite, kindle, lead to, occasion, precipitate, produce, provoke, result in, set off, spark off, stimulate, trigger off, whip up. **2** (*cause to*) compel to, force to, induce to, lead to, make, motivate to, stimulate to.

cause célèbre /kɔːz se'lebr/ *noun* (*plural* **causes célèbres** same pronunciation) lawsuit that excites much interest. [French]

causeway /'kɔːzweɪ/ *noun* **1** raised road across low ground or water. **2** raised path by road.

caustic /'kɔːstɪk/ *adjective* **1** corrosive, burning. **2** sarcastic, biting. ● *noun* caustic substance. □ **caustic soda** sodium hydroxide. □ **causticity** /-'tɪs-/ *noun*.

■ *adjective* **1** burning, corrosive, destructive. **2** acerbic, acid, acrimonious, astringent, biting, bitter, critical, cutting, mordant, pungent, sarcastic, scathing, severe, sharp, stinging, trenchant, virulent, waspish.

cauterize /'kɔːtəraɪz/ *verb* (also **-ise**) (**-zing** or **-sing**) burn (tissue), esp. to stop bleeding.

caution /'kɔːʃ(ə)n/ *noun* **1** attention to safety. **2** warning. **3** *colloquial* amusing or surprising person or thing. ● *verb* **1** warn. **2** admonish and warn formally.

■ *noun* **1** alertness, attentiveness, care, carefulness, circumspection, discretion, forethought, heed, heedfulness, prudence, vigilance, wariness, watchfulness. **2** admonition, caveat, *colloquial* dressing down, injunction, reprimand, *colloquial* talking-to, *colloquial* ticking-off, warning. ● *verb* **1** advise, alert, counsel, forewarn, inform, tip off, warn. **2** admonish, censure, give a warning to, *formal* reprehend, reprimand, *colloquial* tell off, *colloquial* tick off.

cautionary *adjective* warning.

cautious /'kɔːʃəs/ *adjective* having or showing caution. □ **cautiously** *adverb*. **cautiousness** *noun*.

■ alert, attentive, *colloquial* cagey, calculating, careful, chary, circumspect, deliberate, discreet, gingerly, grudging, guarded, heedful, hesitant, judicious, noncommittal, prudent, restrained, scrupulous, suspicious, tactful, tentative, unadventurous, vigilant, wary, watchful.

cavalcade /kævəl'keɪd/ *noun* procession of riders, cars, etc.

■ march past, parade, procession, spectacle.

cavalier /kævə'lɪə/ *noun* **1** courtly gentleman. **2** *archaic* horseman. **3** (**Cavalier**) *historical* supporter of Charles I in English Civil War. ● *adjective* offhand, supercilious, curt.

cavalry /'kævəlrɪ/ *noun* (*plural* **-ies**) (usually treated as *plural*) soldiers on horseback or in armoured vehicles. □ **cavalryman** (*plural* **-men**) soldier of cavalry regiment.

cave *noun* large hollow in side of cliff, hill, etc., or underground. ● *verb* (**-ving**) explore caves. □ **cave in 1** (cause to) subside or collapse. **2** yield, submit. **cave-in 1** collapse of wall, earth over hollow, etc. **2** instance of yielding to pressure.

■ *noun* cavern, cavity, den, grotto, hole, pothole, underground chamber. □ **cave in 1** SEE COLLAPSE *verb* 1. **2** SEE SURRENDER *verb* 2.

caveat /'kævɪæt/ *noun* warning; proviso.

cavern /'kæv(ə)n/ *noun* cave, esp. large or dark one.

cavernous *adjective* **1** full of caverns. **2** huge or deep as cavern.

caviar /'kævɪɑː/ *noun* (also **caviare**) pickled sturgeon-roe.

cavil /'kævɪl/ *verb* (**-ll-**; *US* **-l-**) (usually + *at*, *about*) make petty objections. ● *noun* petty objection.

cavity /'kævɪtɪ/ *noun* (*plural* **-ies**) **1** hollow within solid body. **2** decayed part of tooth. □ **cavity wall** two walls separated by narrow space.

■ **1** cave, crater, dent, hole, hollow, pit.

cavort /kə'vɔːt/ *verb* caper.

caw *noun* cry of rook etc. ● *verb* utter this cry.

cayenne /ker'en/ *noun* (in full **cayenne pepper**) powdered red pepper.

cayman /'keɪmən/ *noun* (also **caiman**) (*plural* **-s**) S. American alligator-like reptile.

CB *abbreviation* **1** citizens' band. **2** Commander of the Order of the Bath.

CBE *abbreviation* Commander of the Order of the British Empire.

CBI *abbreviation* Confederation of British Industry.

cc *abbreviation* cubic centimetre(s).

CD *abbreviation* **1** compact disc. **2** *Corps Diplomatique*.

CD-ROM /siːdiːˈrɒm/ *abbreviation* compact disc read-only memory (for retrieval of text or data on VDU screen).

cease /siːs/ *formal verb* (**-sing**) stop; bring or come to an end. □ **ceasefire** (order for) truce. **without cease** unending.

■ break off, call a halt, conclude, cut off, desist, discontinue, end, finish, halt, *slang* kick (*a habit*), *colloquial* knock off, *colloquial* lay off, leave off, *colloquial* pack in, *colloquial* pack up, refrain, stop, terminate.

ceaseless *adjective* without end. □ **ceaselessly** *adverb*.

■ chronic, constant, continual, continuous, endless, everlasting, incessant, interminable, never-ending, non-stop, permanent, perpetual, persistent, relentless, unending, unremitting, untiring.

cedar /'siːdə/ *noun* **1** evergreen conifer. **2** its durable fragrant wood.

cede /siːd/ *verb* (**-ding**) *formal* give up one's rights to or possession of.

cedilla /sɪ'dɪlə/ *noun* mark (¸) under *c* (in French, to show it is pronounced /s/, not /k/).

ceilidh /'keɪlɪ/ *noun* informal gathering for music, dancing, etc.

ceiling /'siːlɪŋ/ *noun* **1** upper interior surface of room or other compartment. **2** upper limit. **3** maximum altitude of aircraft.

celandine /'seləndaɪn/ *noun* yellow-flowered plant.

celebrant /'selɪbrənt/ *noun* person performing rite, esp. priest at Eucharist.

celebrate /'selɪbreɪt/ *verb* (**-ting**) **1** engage in festivities. **2** mark with festivities. **3** perform (rite or ceremony). **4** (esp. as **celebrated** *adjective*) praise publicly. □ **celebration** *noun*. **celebratory** /-'breɪt-/ *adjective*.

■ **1** have a celebration, *colloquial* live it up, make merry, *colloquial* paint the town red, rejoice, revel, *archaic* wassail. **2** commemorate, hold, honour, keep, observe, remember. **3** officiate at, solemnize. **4** (**celebrated**) SEE FAMOUS 1. □ **celebration** banquet, carnival, commemoration, feast, festival, festivity, fête, gala, jamboree, jollification, jubilee, merrymaking, observance, orgy, party, *colloquial* rave-up, revelry, (*church*) service, *colloquial* shindig, solemnization.

celebrity /sɪˈlebrɪtɪ/ *noun* (*plural* **-ies**) **1** well-known person. **2** fame.

  ■ **1** big name, *colloquial* bigwig, dignitary, idol, notable, personality, public figure, star, superstar, VIP, worthy. **2** see FAME.

celeriac /sɪˈlerɪæk/ *noun* variety of celery.

celerity /sɪˈlerɪtɪ/ *noun archaic* swiftness.

celery /ˈselərɪ/ *noun* plant of which stalks are used as vegetable.

celesta /sɪˈlestə/ *noun* keyboard instrument with steel plates struck with hammers.

celestial /sɪˈlestɪəl/ *adjective* **1** of sky or heavenly bodies. **2** heavenly, divinely good.

  ■ **1** astronomical, cosmic, galactic, interplanetary, interstellar, starry, stellar, universal. **2** angelic, blissful, divine, ethereal, godlike, heavenly, seraphic, spiritual, sublime, supernatural, transcendental, visionary.

celibate /ˈselɪbət/ *adjective* unmarried, or abstaining from sexual relations, often for religious reasons. ● *noun* celibate person. □ **celibacy** *noun*.

  ■ *adjective* abstinent, chaste, continent, immaculate, single, unmarried, unwedded, virgin. □ **celibacy** abstinence, chastity, continence, purity, self-restraint, virginity.

cell /sel/ *noun* **1** small room, esp. in prison or monastery. **2** small compartment, e.g. in honeycomb. **3** small active political group. **4** unit of structure of organic matter. **5** enclosed cavity in organism etc. **6** vessel containing electrodes for current-generation or electrolysis. □ **cellphone** portable radio-telephone.

  ■ **1** chamber, cubicle, den, prison, room. **2** cavity, compartment, enclosure, section, space, unit.

cellar /ˈselə/ *noun* **1** underground storage room. **2** stock of wine in cellar.

  ■ **1** basement, crypt, vault, wine cellar.

cello /ˈtʃeləʊ/ *noun* (*plural* **-s**) bass instrument of violin family, held between legs of seated player. □ **cellist** *noun*.

Cellophane /ˈseləfeɪn/ *noun proprietary term* thin transparent wrapping material.

cellular /ˈseljʊlə/ *adjective* **1** consisting of cells. **2** of open texture; porous. □ **cellularity** /-ˈlær-/ *noun*.

cellulite /ˈseljʊlaɪt/ *noun* lumpy fat, esp. on women's hips and thighs.

celluloid /ˈseljʊlɔɪd/ *noun* **1** plastic made from camphor and cellulose nitrate. **2** cinema film.

cellulose /ˈseljʊləʊs/ *noun* **1** carbohydrate forming plant-cell walls. **2** paint or lacquer consisting of cellulose acetate or nitrate in solution.

Celsius /ˈselsɪəs/ *adjective* of scale of temperature on which water freezes at 0° and boils at 100°.

Celt /kelt/ *noun* (also **Kelt**) member of an ethnic group including inhabitants of Ireland, Wales, Scotland, Cornwall, and Brittany.

Celtic /ˈkeltɪk/ *adjective* of the Celts. ● *noun* group of Celtic languages.

cement /sɪˈment/ *noun* **1** substance made from lime and clay, mixed with water, sand, etc. to form mortar or concrete. **2** adhesive. ● *verb* **1** unite firmly. **2** strengthen. **3** apply cement to.

cemetery /ˈsemɪtrɪ/ *noun* (*plural* **-ies**) burial ground, esp. one not in churchyard.

  ■ burial ground, graveyard, necropolis.

cenotaph /ˈsenətɑːf/ *noun* tomblike monument to person(s) whose remains are elsewhere.

Cenozoic /siːnəˈzəʊɪk/ *adjective* of most recent geological era, marked by evolution of mammals etc. ● *noun* this era.

censer /ˈsensə/ *noun* incense-burning vessel.

censor /ˈsensə/ *noun* official with power to suppress or expurgate books, films, news, etc., on grounds of obscenity, threat to security, etc. ● *verb* **1** act as censor of. **2** make deletions or changes in. □ **censorial** /-ˈsɔːr-/ *adjective*. **censorship** *noun*.

  USAGE As a verb, *censor* is often confused with *censure*, which means 'to criticize harshly'.

  ■ *verb* **2** amend, bowdlerize, clean up, cut, edit, exclude, expurgate, remove.

censorious /senˈsɔːrɪəs/ *adjective* severely critical.

  ■ critical, fault-finding, *colloquial* holier-than-thou, judgemental, moralistic, self-righteous.

censure /ˈsenʃə/ *verb* (**-ring**) criticize harshly; reprove. ● *noun* hostile criticism; disapproval.

  ■ *verb* admonish, berate, blame, *colloquial* carpet, castigate, caution, *archaic* chide, condemn, criticize, denounce, lecture, rebuke, reproach, *formal* reprove, scold, take to task, *colloquial* tear (person) off a strip, *colloquial* tell off, *colloquial* tick off, upbraid. ● *noun* admonition, blame, castigation, condemnation, criticism, denunciation, diatribe, disapproval, *colloquial* dressing down, harangue, rebuke, reprimand, reproach, *formal* reproof, *colloquial* slating, stricture, *colloquial* talking-to, *colloquial* telling-off, tirade, verbal attack, vituperation.

census /ˈsensəs/ *noun* (*plural* **-suses**) official count of population etc.

cent /sent/ *noun* one-hundredth of dollar or other decimal unit of currency.

cent. *abbreviation* century.

centaur /ˈsentɔː/ *noun* creature in Greek mythology with head, arms, and trunk of man joined to body and legs of horse.

centenarian /sentɪˈneərɪən/ *noun* person 100 or more years old. ● *adjective* 100 or more years old.

centenary /senˈtiːnərɪ/ *noun* (*plural* **-ies**) (celebration of) 100th anniversary. ● *adjective* **1** of a centenary. **2** recurring every 100 years.

centennial /senˈtenɪəl/ *adjective* **1** lasting 100

years. **2** recurring every 100 years. ● *noun US* centenary.

centi- *combining form* one-hundredth.

centigrade /'sentɪɡreɪd/ *adjective* Celsius.

USAGE *Celsius* is the better term to use in technical contexts.

centilitre /'sentɪliːtə/ *noun* (*US* **centiliter**) one-hundredth of litre (0.018 pint).

centime /'sɑ̃tiːm/ *noun* one-hundredth of franc.

centimetre /'sentɪmiːtə/ *noun* (*US* **centimeter**) one-hundredth of metre (0.394 in.).

centipede /'sentɪpiːd/ *noun* arthropod with wormlike body and many legs.

central /'sentr(ə)l/ *adjective* **1** of, forming, at, or from centre. **2** essential, principal. □ **central bank** national bank issuing currency etc. **central heating** heating of building from central source. **central processor**, **central processing unit** computer's main operating part. □ **centrality** *noun*. **centrally** *adverb*.

■ **1** focal, inner, innermost, interior, medial, middle. **2** chief, crucial, essential, fundamental, important, key, main, major, overriding, pivotal, primary, principal, vital.

centralize *verb* (also **-ise**) (**-zing** or **-sing**) **1** concentrate (administration etc.) at single centre. **2** subject (state etc.) to this system. □ **centralization** *noun*.

■ amalgamate, bring together, concentrate, rationalize, streamline, unify.

centre /'sentə/ (*US* **center**) *noun* **1** middle point. **2** core; point of concentration or dispersion. **3** pivot. **4** place or buildings forming a central point or main area for an activity. **5** political party holding moderate opinions. **6** filling in chocolate etc. ● *verb* (**-ring**) **1** (+ *in, on, round*) have as main centre. **2** place in centre. □ **centrefold** centre spread that folds out, esp. with nude photographs. **centre forward**, **back** *Football etc.* middle player in forward or half-back line. **centre of gravity** point at which the mass of an object effectively acts. **centrepiece 1** ornament for middle of table. **2** main item. **centre spread** two facing middle pages of magazine etc.

■ *noun* **1** bull's-eye, middle, mid-point. **2** core, focal point, focus, heart, hub, inside, interior, kernel, middle, nucleus. **3** axis, hub, pivot. **6** filling, inside, middle. ● *verb* **1** concentrate, converge, focus.

centrifugal /sentrɪ'fjuːɡ(ə)l/ *adjective* moving or tending to move from centre. □ **centrifugal force** apparent force acting outwards on body revolving round centre. □ **centrifugally** *adverb*.

■ dispersing, diverging, moving outwards, scattering, spreading.

centrifuge /'sentrɪfjuːdʒ/ *noun* rapidly rotating machine for separating e.g. cream from milk.

centripetal /sen'trɪpɪt(ə)l/ *adjective* moving or tending to move towards centre. □ **centripetally** *adverb*.

■ converging.

centrist /'sentrɪst/ *noun often derogatory* person holding moderate views. □ **centrism** *noun*.

cents. *abbreviation* centuries.

centurion /sen'tjʊəriən/ *noun* commander of century in ancient Roman army.

century /'sentʃəri/ *noun* (*plural* **-ies**) **1** 100 years. **2** *Cricket* score of 100 runs by one batsman. **3** company in ancient Roman army.

USAGE Strictly speaking, because the 1st century ran from the year 1 to the year 100, the first year of a century ends in 1. However, a century is commonly regarded as starting with a year ending in 00, the 20th century thus running from 1900 to 1999.

cephalic /sə'fælɪk/ *adjective* of or in head.

cephalopod /'sefələpɒd/ *noun* mollusc with tentacles on head, e.g. octopus.

ceramic /sɪ'ræmɪk/ *adjective* **1** made of esp. baked clay. **2** of ceramics. ● *noun* ceramic article.

ceramics *plural noun* **1** ceramic products collectively. **2** (usually treated as *singular*) ceramic art.

cereal /'sɪəriəl/ *noun* **1** edible grain. **2** breakfast food made from cereal. ● *adjective* of edible grain.

■ *noun* **1** corn, grain.

cerebellum /serɪ'beləm/ *noun* (*plural* **-s** or **-bella**) part of brain at back of skull.

cerebral /'serɪbr(ə)l/ *adjective* **1** of brain. **2** intellectual. □ **cerebral palsy** paralysis resulting from brain damage before or at birth.

cerebration /serɪ'breɪʃ(ə)n/ *noun* working of brain. □ **cerebrate** /'serɪbreɪt/ *verb*.

cerebrospinal /serɪbrəʊ'spaɪn(ə)l/ *adjective* of brain and spine.

cerebrum /'serɪbrəm/ *noun* (*plural* **-bra**) principal part of brain, at front of skull.

ceremonial /serɪ'məʊniəl/ *adjective* of or with ceremony; formal. ● *noun* system of rites or ceremonies.

■ *adjective* celebratory, dignified, formal, liturgical, majestic, official, ritual, ritualistic, solemn, stately.

ceremonious /serɪ'məʊniəs/ *adjective* fond of or characterized by ceremony; formal. □ **ceremoniously** *adverb*.

■ civil, courteous, courtly, dignified, formal, grand, polite, pompous, proper, punctilious, starchy.

ceremony /'serɪməni/ *noun* (*plural* **-ies**) **1** formal procedure. **2** formalities, esp. ritualistic. **3** excessively polite behaviour. □ **stand on ceremony** insist on formality.

■ **1** celebration, commemoration, *colloquial* do, event, function, occasion, parade, rite, ritual, service, solemnity. **2** ceremonial, decorum, etiquette, formality, grandeur, pageantry, pomp, pomp and circumstance, protocol, ritual, spectacle.

cerise /sə'ri:z/ *noun & adjective* light clear red.

cert /sɜ:t/ *noun* (esp. **dead cert**) *slang* a certainty.

certain /'sɜ:t(ə)n/ *adjective* **1** convinced. **2** indisputable. **3** (often + *to do*) sure, destined. **4** reliable. **5** particular but not specified. **6** some. □ **for certain** undoubtedly. **make certain** make sure.
■ **1** adamant, assured, confident, convinced, decided, determined, firm, positive, resolved, satisfied, settled, sure, undoubting, unshakeable, unwavering. **2** absolute, authenticated, categorical, certified, clear, clear-cut, conclusive, convincing, definite, dependable, established, genuine, guaranteed, incontestable, incontrovertible, indisputable, indubitable, infallible, irrefutable, known, official, plain, reliable, settled, sure, true, trustworthy, unarguable, undeniable, undisputed, undoubted, unmistakable, unquestionable, valid, verifiable. **3** destined, fated, guaranteed, imminent, inescapable, inevitable, inexorable, predestined, predictable, unavoidable; (*certain to*) bound to, compelled to, obliged to, required to, sure to. **5** individual, particular, specific, unnamed, unspecified. □ **for certain** see DEFINITELY. **make certain** see ENSURE.

certainly *adverb* **1** undoubtedly. **2** (in answer) yes.

certainty *noun* (*plural* **-ies**) **1** undoubted fact. **2** sure prospect. **3** absolute conviction. **4** reliable thing or person.
■ **1** actuality, fact, reality, truth. **2** foregone conclusion, inevitability, necessity, sure thing. **3** assurance, authority, certitude, confidence, conviction, knowledge, positiveness, sureness.

certificate *noun* /sə'tɪfɪkət/ document formally attesting fact. ● *verb* /sə'tɪfɪkeɪt/ (**-ting**) (esp. as **certificated** *adjective*) provide with certificate; license or attest by certificate. □ **certification** /sɜ:-/ *noun*.
■ *noun* authorization, award, credentials, degree, diploma, document, guarantee, licence, pass, permit, warrant.

certify /'sɜ:tɪfaɪ/ *verb* (**-ies, -ied**) **1** attest (to). **2** declare by certificate (to be qualified or competent). **3** officially declare insane. □ **certifiable** *adjective*.
■ **1** affirm, asseverate, attest, authenticate, *formal* aver, *formal* avow, bear witness, confirm, declare, endorse, guarantee, notify, sign, swear, testify, verify, vouch, *formal* vouchsafe, warrant, witness. **2** authorize, charter, commission, franchise, license, recognize, validate.

certitude /'sɜ:tɪtju:d/ *noun* feeling certain.
cerulean /sə'ru:lɪən/ *adjective* sky blue.
cervical /sə'vaɪk(ə)l/ *adjective* of cervix or neck.

□ **cervical smear** specimen from neck of womb for examination.

cervix /'sɜ:vɪks/ *noun* (*plural* **cervices** /-si:z/) **1** necklike structure, esp. neck of womb. **2** neck.

Cesarean (also **Cesarian**) *US* = CAESAREAN.

cessation /se'seɪʃ(ə)n/ *noun* ceasing.

cession /'seʃ(ə)n/ *noun* **1** ceding. **2** territory ceded.

cesspit /'sespɪt/ *noun* pit for liquid waste or sewage.

cesspool /'sespu:l/ *noun* cesspit.

cetacean /sɪ'teɪʃ(ə)n/ *noun* member of order of marine mammals including whales. ● *adjective* of cetaceans.

cf. *abbreviation* compare (Latin *confer*).

CFC *abbreviation* chlorofluorocarbon (compound used as refrigerant, aerosol propellant, etc.).

cg *abbreviation* centigram(s).

CH *abbreviation* Companion of Honour.

Chablis /'ʃæbli:/ *noun* (*plural* same /-li:z/) dry white wine from Chablis in France.

chaconne /ʃə'kɒn/ *noun* **1** musical variations over ground bass. **2** dance to this.

chafe /tʃeɪf/ *verb* (**-fing**) **1** make or become sore or damaged by rubbing. **2** irritate. **3** show irritation, fret. **4** rub (esp. skin) to warm. ● *noun* sore caused by rubbing.

chaff /tʃɑ:f/ *noun* **1** separated grain-husks. **2** chopped hay or straw. **3** good-humoured teasing. **4** worthless stuff. ● *verb* tease, banter.

chaffinch /'tʃæfɪntʃ/ *noun* a common European finch.

chafing dish /'tʃeɪfɪŋ/ *noun* vessel in which food is cooked or kept warm at table.

chagrin /'ʃægrɪn/ *noun* acute vexation or disappointment. ● *verb* affect with this.

chain *noun* **1** connected series of links. **2** thing resembling this. **3** (in *plural*) fetters. **4** (in *plural*) restraining force. **5** sequence, series, or set. **6** unit of length (66 ft). ● *verb* (often + *up*) secure with chain. □ **chain gang** *historical* convicts chained together at work etc. **chain mail** armour made from interlaced rings. **chain reaction 1** reaction forming products which themselves cause further reactions. **2** series of events each due to previous one. **chainsaw** motor-driven saw with teeth on loop of chain. **chain-smoke** smoke continuously, esp. by lighting next cigarette etc. from previous one. **chain store** one of series of shops owned by one firm.
■ *noun* **3**, **4** (*chains*) bonds, fetters, handcuffs, irons, manacles, shackles. **5** column, combination, concatenation, line, progression, row, sequence, series, set, string, succession, train. ● *verb* bind, clap in irons, fasten, fetter, handcuff, manacle, shackle, tether, tie.

chair *noun* **1** seat usually with back for one person. **2** (office of) chairperson. **3** professorship. **4** *US* electric chair. ● *verb* **1** be chairperson of (meeting). **2** carry aloft in triumph. □ **chairlift**

series of chairs on loop of cable for carrying passengers up and down mountain etc. **chairman**, **chairperson**, **chairwoman** person who presides over meeting, board, or committee.

■ *verb* **1** be in charge of, conduct, direct, lead, preside over, run. □ **chairman, chairperson, chairwoman** chair, convenor, director, head, leader, president.

chaise /ʃeɪz/ *noun* horse-drawn usually open carriage for one or two people.

chaise longue /ʃeɪz 'lɒŋg/ *noun* (*plural* **chaise longues** or **chaises longues** /'lɒŋg(z)/) sofa with one arm rest.

chalcedony /kæl'sedənɪ/ *noun* (*plural* -**ies**) type of quartz.

chalet /'ʃæleɪ/ *noun* **1** Swiss hut or cottage. **2** similar house. **3** small cabin in holiday camp etc.

chalice /'tʃælɪs/ *noun* **1** goblet. **2** Eucharistic cup.

chalk /tʃɔːk/ *noun* **1** white soft limestone. **2** (piece of) similar, sometimes coloured, substance for writing or drawing. ● *verb* **1** rub, mark, draw, or write with chalk. **2** (+ *up*) record with chalk; register (success etc.). □ **chalky** *adjective* (-**ier**, -**iest**).

challenge /'tʃælmdʒ/ *noun* **1** call to take part in contest etc. or to prove or justify something. **2** demanding or difficult task. **3** call to respond. ● *verb* (-**ging**) **1** issue challenge to. **2** dispute. **3** (as **challenging** *adjective*) stimulatingly difficult. □ **challenger** *noun*.

■ *verb* **1** confront, dare, defy, provoke, summon, take on. **2** argue against, call in doubt, contest, dispute, dissent from, impugn, object to, oppose, protest against, query, question, take exception to. **3** (**challenging**) demanding, difficult, inspiring, stimulating, taxing, testing, thought-provoking, worthwhile.

chamber /'tʃeɪmbə/ *noun* **1** hall used by legislative or judicial body. **2** body that meets in it, esp. a house of a parliament. **3** (in *plural*) set of rooms for barrister(s), esp. in Inns of Court. **4** (in *plural*) judge's room for hearing cases not needing to be taken in court. **5** *archaic* room, esp. bedroom. **6** cavity or compartment in body, machinery, etc. (esp. part of gun that contains charge). □ **chambermaid** woman who cleans hotel bedrooms. **chamber music** music for small group of instruments. **Chamber of Commerce** association to promote local commercial interests. **chamber pot** vessel for urine etc., used in bedroom.

■ **6** cavity, cell, compartment, niche, nook, space.

chamberlain /'tʃeɪmbəlɪn/ *noun* **1** officer managing royal or noble household. **2** treasurer of corporation etc.

chameleon /kə'miːlɪən/ *noun* lizard able to change colour for camouflage.

chamfer /'tʃæmfə/ *verb* bevel symmetrically. ● *noun* bevelled surface.

chamois *noun* **1** /'ʃæmwɑː/ (*plural* same /-wɑːz/) small mountain antelope. **2** /'ʃæmɪ,

'ʃæmwɑː/ (*plural* same /-mɪz, -wɑːz/) (piece of) soft leather from sheep, goats, etc.

chamomile = CAMOMILE.

champ[1] *verb* munch or bite noisily. ● *noun* chewing noise. □ **champ at the bit** show impatience.

champ[2] *noun slang* champion.

champagne /ʃæm'peɪn/ *noun* white sparkling wine from Champagne in France.

champion /'tʃæmpɪən/ *noun* **1** person or thing that has defeated all rivals. **2** person who fights for cause or another person. **3** *archaic* knight who fought for king. ● *verb* support cause of; defend. ● *adjective colloquial* splendid.

■ *noun* **1** conqueror, hero, medallist, prizewinner, record-breaker, *colloquial* superman, *colloquial* superwoman, title-holder, victor, winner. **2** campaigner, backer, defender, guardian, patron, protector, supporter, upholder. ● *verb* see SUPPORT *verb* 6. ● *adjective* great, leading, record-breaking, supreme, top, unrivalled, victorious, winning, world-beating.

championship *noun* **1** (often in *plural*) contest to decide champion in sport etc. **2** position of champion.

■ **1** competition, contest, series, tournament.

chance /tʃɑːns/ *noun* **1** possibility. **2** (often in *plural*) probability. **3** opportunity. **4** unplanned occurrence. **5** fate. **6** risk. ● *adjective* unplanned. ● *verb* (-**cing**) **1** *colloquial* risk. **2** happen. □ **chance on** happen to find.

■ *noun* **1, 2** danger, liability, likelihood, possibility, probability, prospect, risk. **3** occasion, opportunity, time, turn. **4** accident, coincidence, fluke. **5** destiny, fate, fortune, luck, misfortune, serendipity. **6** gamble, hazard, risk. ● *adjective* accidental, adventitious, casual, coincidental, fluky, fortuitous, haphazard, inadvertent, incidental, lucky, random, unexpected, unforeseen, unlooked-for, unplanned, unpremeditated. ● *verb* **1** see RISK *verb* 2.

chancel /'tʃɑːns(ə)l/ *noun* part of church near altar.

chancellery /'tʃɑːnsələrɪ/ *noun* (*plural* -**ies**) **1** chancellor's department, staff, or residence. **2** *US* office attached to embassy.

chancellor /'tʃɑːnsələ/ *noun* **1** state or legal official. **2** head of government in some European countries. **3** non-resident honorary head of university. **4** (in full **Lord Chancellor**) highest officer of the Crown, presiding in House of Lords. **5** (in full **Chancellor of the Exchequer**) UK finance minister.

Chancery /'tʃɑːnsərɪ/ *noun* Lord Chancellor's division of High Court of Justice.

chancy /'tʃɑːnsɪ/ *adjective* (-**ier**, -**iest**) uncertain; risky.

■ dangerous, *slang* dicey, *colloquial* dodgy, hazardous, *colloquial* iffy, insecure, precarious, risky, speculative, ticklish, tricky, uncertain, unpredictable, unsafe.

chandelier /ˌʃændə'lɪə/ *noun* branched hanging support for lights.

chandler /'tʃɑːndlə/ *noun* dealer in candles, oil, soap, paint, etc.

change /tʃeɪndʒ/ *noun* **1** making or becoming different. **2** low-value money in small coins. **3** money returned as balance of that given in payment. **4** new experience. **5** substitution of one thing or person for another. **6** one of different orders in which bells can be rung. ● *verb* **(-ging)** **1** undergo, show, or subject to change. **2** take or use another instead of. **3** (often + *with*) interchange; exchange. **4** give or get money in exchange for. **5** put fresh clothes or coverings on. □ **change hands** be passed to different owner. **change one's mind** come to different opinion. **changeover** change from one system or situation to another. □ **changeful** *adjective*. **changeless** *adjective*.

■ *noun* **1** adaptation, adjustment, alteration, conversion, deterioration, development, difference, diversion, improvement, innovation, metamorphosis, modification, modulation, mutation, new look, rearrangement, refinement, reformation, reorganization, revolution, shift, substitution, swing, transfiguration, transformation, transition, translation, *jocular* transmogrification, transmutation, transposition, turn-about, U-turn, variation, *literary* vicissitude. **2** see CASH *noun* 1. ● *verb* **1** acclimatize, accommodate, accustom, adapt, adjust, affect, alter, amend, be transformed, chop and change, convert, develop, diversify, fluctuate, influence, metamorphose, modify, mutate, process, rearrange, reconstruct, refashion, reform, remodel, reorganize, reshape, restyle, shift, tailor, transfigure, transform, translate, *jocular* transmogrify, transmute, vary; (*change into*) see BECOME 1. **2, 3** alternate, displace, exchange, replace, substitute, swap, switch, trade, transpose. **4** barter, convert, trade in. □ **change one's mind** see RECONSIDER.

changeable *adjective* **1** inconstant. **2** able to change or be changed. □ **changeableness** *noun*.

■ **1** capricious, chequered (*career*), erratic, fickle, fitful, fluctuating, fluid, inconsistent, inconstant, irregular, mercurial, *literary* mutable, protean, shifting, temperamental, uncertain, unpredictable, unreliable, unsettled, unstable, unsteady, *colloquial* up and down, vacillating, variable, varying, volatile, wavering.

changeling *noun* child believed to be substitute for another.

channel /'tʃæn(ə)l/ *noun* **1** piece of water connecting two seas. **2** (**the Channel**) the English Channel. **3** medium of communication; agency. **4** band of frequencies used for radio and television transmission. **5** course in which thing moves. **6** bed of river, watercourse, etc. **7** navigable part of waterway. **8** passage for liquid. **9** lengthwise strip on recording tape etc. ● *verb* (**-ll-**; *US* **-l-**) **1** guide, direct. **2** form channel(s) in.

■ *noun* **1** narrows, sound, strait. **3** avenue, means, medium, path, route, way. **4** *colloquial* side, station, waveband, wavelength. **5** course, groove,

slot, track. **6, 7** aqueduct, canal, conduit, course, dyke, ditch, duct, gully, gutter, moat, overflow, pipe, sluice, trench, trough, watercourse, waterway. ● *verb* **1** conduct, convey, direct, guide, lead, pass on, route, send, transmit.

chant /tʃɑːnt/ *noun* **1** spoken singsong phrase. **2** melody for reciting unmetrical texts. **3** song. ● *verb* **1** talk or repeat monotonously. **2** sing or intone (psalm etc.).

■ *noun* **3** canticle, hymn, plainsong, psalm, song. ● *verb* **2** intone, sing.

chanter *noun* melody-pipe of bagpipes.

chantry /'tʃɑːntrɪ/ *noun* (*plural* **-ies**) **1** endowment for singing of masses. **2** priests, chapel, etc., so endowed.

chaos /'keɪɒs/ *noun* **1** utter confusion. **2** formless matter supposed to have existed before universe's creation. □ **chaotic** /keɪ'ɒtɪk/ *adjective*.

■ **1** anarchy, bedlam, confusion, disorder, disorganization, lawlessness, mayhem, muddle, pandemonium, *colloquial* shambles, tumult, turmoil. □ **chaotic** anarchic, confused, deranged, disordered, disorderly, disorganized, haphazard, *colloquial* haywire, higgledy-piggledy, jumbled, lawless, muddled, rebellious, riotous, *colloquial* shambolic, topsy-turvy, tumultuous, uncontrolled, ungovernable, unruly, untidy, upside down.

chap¹ *noun colloquial* man; boy.

chap² *verb* (**-pp-**) **1** (esp. of skin) develop cracks or soreness. **2** (of wind etc.) cause this. ● *noun* (usually in *plural*) crack in skin etc.

chaparral /ʃæpə'ræl/ *noun US* dense tangled brushwood.

chapatti /tʃə'pɑːtɪ/ *noun* (also **chupatty**) (*plural* **chapattis** or **chupatties**) flat thin cake of unleavened bread.

chapel /'tʃæp(ə)l/ *noun* **1** place for private worship in cathedral or church, with its own altar. **2** place of worship attached to private house, institution, etc. **3** place or service of worship for Nonconformists. **4** branch of printers' or journalists' trade union at a workplace.

chaperon /'ʃæpərəʊn/ *noun* person, esp. older woman, in charge of young unmarried woman on certain social occasions. ● *verb* act as chaperon to.

chaplain /'tʃæplɪn/ *noun* member of clergy attached to private chapel, institution, ship, regiment, etc. □ **chaplaincy** *noun* (*plural* **-ies**).

chaplet /'tʃæplɪt/ *noun* **1** wreath or circlet for head. **2** string of beads; short rosary.

chapter /'tʃæptə/ *noun* **1** division of book. **2** period of time. **3** canons of cathedral etc. **4** meeting of these.

char¹ *verb* (**-rr-**) **1** blacken with fire; scorch. **2** burn to charcoal.

■ **1** blacken, brown, burn, scorch, sear, singe. **2** burn, carbonize.

char² *colloquial noun* charwoman. ● *verb* (**-rr-**)

work as charwoman. □ **charlady, charwoman** one employed to do housework.

char[3] *noun slang* tea.

char[4] *noun* (*plural* same) a kind of trout.

charabanc /'ʃærəbæŋ/ *noun historical* early form of motor coach.

character /'kærɪktə/ *noun* **1** distinguishing qualities or characteristics. **2** moral strength. **3** reputation. **4** person in novel, play, etc. **5** *colloquial* (esp. eccentric) person. **6** letter, symbol. **7** testimonial. □ **in, out of character** consistent or inconsistent with person's character. □ **characterful** *adjective*. **characterless** *adjective*.

■ **1** attributes, characteristics, constitution, disposition, distinctiveness, flavour, idiosyncrasy, individuality, make-up, manner, nature, peculiarity, personality, quality, stamp, taste, temper, temperament, uniqueness. **2** see INTEGRITY 1. **3** see REPUTATION. **4** part, persona, role. **5** *colloquial* card, eccentric, figure, *colloquial* individual, *slang* nutcase, oddity, person, personality, *colloquial* type, *colloquial* weirdo. **6** cipher, figure, hieroglyphic, ideogram, letter, mark, rune, sign, symbol.

characteristic /kærɪktə'rɪstɪk/ *adjective* typical, distinctive. ● *noun* characteristic feature or quality. □ **characteristically** *adverb*.

■ *adjective* distinctive, distinguishing, essential, idiosyncratic, individual, particular, peculiar, recognizable, representative, singular, special, specific, symptomatic, typical, unique. ● *noun* attribute, feature, hallmark, idiosyncrasy, mark, peculiarity, property, quality, symptom, trait.

characterize *verb* (also **-ise**) (**-zing** or **-sing**) **1** describe character of. **2** (+ *as*) describe as. **3** be characteristic of. □ **characterization** *noun*.

■ **1, 2** brand, delineate, depict, describe, draw, identify, portray, present, represent. **3** differentiate, distinguish, identify, individualize, mark, typify.

charade /ʃə'rɑːd/ *noun* **1** (usually in *plural*; treated as *singular*) game of guessing word(s) from acted clues. **2** absurd pretence.

■ **2** absurdity, deceit, deception, fabrication, farce, make-believe, masquerade, mockery, play-acting, pose, pretence, put-up job, sham.

charcoal *noun* black residue of partly burnt wood etc.

charge *verb* (**-ging**) **1** ask (amount) as price. **2** ask (person) for amount as price. **3** (+ *to, up to*) debit cost of to. **4** (often + *with*) accuse (of offence). **5** (+ *to do*) instruct or urge to do. **6** (+ *with*) entrust with. **7** make rushing attack (on). **8** (often + *up*) give electric charge to; store energy in. **9** (often + *with*) load, fill. ● *noun* **1** price. **2** financial liability. **3** accusation. **4** task. **5** custody. **6** person or thing entrusted. **7** (signal for) impetuous attack, esp. in battle. **8** appropriate amount of material to be put in mechanism at one time, esp. explosive in gun. **9** cause of electrical phenomena in matter. □ **charge card** credit card, esp. used at particular shop. **in**

charge having command. □ **chargeable** *adjective*.

■ *verb* **1, 2** ask for, debit, exact, levy, require. **4** accuse, blame, impeach, indict, prosecute, tax. **5** ask, command, direct, enjoin, exhort, instruct, urge. **6** burden, entrust, give, trust. **7** assail, assault, attack, rush, set on, storm. ● *noun* **1** cost, fare, fee, price, rate, terms, toll. **2** expenditure, expense, payment. **3** accusation, allegation, imputation, indictment. **5** care, command, control, custody, guardianship, jurisdiction, keeping, protection, responsibility, safe keeping, supervision, trust. **7** assault, attack, drive, incursion, invasion, offensive, onslaught, raid, rush, sally, sortie, strike.

chargé d'affaires /ʃɑː'ʒeɪ dæ'feə/ *noun* (*plural* **chargés d'affaires** same pronunciation) **1** ambassador's deputy. **2** envoy to minor country.

charger *noun* **1** cavalry horse. **2** apparatus for charging battery.

chariot /'tʃærɪət/ *noun historical* two-wheeled horse-drawn vehicle used in ancient warfare and racing.

charioteer /tʃærɪə'tɪə/ *noun* chariot driver.

charisma /kə'rɪzmə/ *noun* **1** power to inspire or attract others. **2** divinely conferred power or talent. □ **charismatic** /kærɪz'mætɪk/ *adjective*.

charitable /'tʃærɪtəb(ə)l/ *adjective* **1** generous to those in need. **2** of or connected with a charity. **3** lenient in judging others. □ **charitably** *adverb*.

■ **1** bountiful, generous, humanitarian, kind, liberal, munificent, open-handed, philanthropic, unsparing.

charity /'tʃærɪtɪ/ *noun* (*plural* **-ies**) **1** giving voluntarily to those in need. **2** organization for helping those in need. **3** love of fellow men. **4** lenience in judging others.

■ **1** aid, *historical* alms, almsgiving, assistance, bounty, financial support, largesse, patronage. **2** foundation, fund, good cause, trust. **3** affection, altruism, benevolence, bounty, caring, compassion, consideration, generosity, goodness, helpfulness, humanity, kindness, love, mercy, philanthropy, self-sacrifice, sympathy, tender-heartedness, unselfishness, warm-heartedness. **4** see TOLERANCE 1.

charlatan /'ʃɑːlət(ə)n/ *noun* person falsely claiming knowledge or skill. □ **charlatanism** *noun*.

charlotte /'ʃɑːlɒt/ *noun* pudding of stewed fruit under bread etc.

charm *noun* **1** power of delighting, attracting, or influencing. **2** trinket on bracelet etc. **3** object, act, or word(s) supposedly having magic power. ● *verb* **1** delight, captivate. **2** influence or protect (as) by magic. **3** (often + *into, out of*) obtain or influence by charm. □ **charmer** *noun*.

■ *noun* **1** allure, appeal, attractiveness, charisma, fascination, lure, magic, magnetism, power, pull, seductiveness. **2** ornament, trinket. **3** [*object*] amulet, lucky charm, mascot, talisman; [*act or words*] curse, incantation, spell. ● *verb* **1** allure, attract, beguile, bewitch, captivate, cast a spell on, delight, enchant, enrapture, enthral, entrance, fascinate, hold spellbound, hypnotize, mesmerize, please, seduce, soothe, win over. **3** beguile, cajole, coax, decoy, disarm, intrigue, lure, seduce, win.

charming *adjective* delightful. □ **charmingly** *adverb*.
■ see ATTRACTIVE.

charnel house /'tʃɑːn(ə)l/ *noun* place containing corpses or bones.

chart *noun* **1** map esp. for sea or air navigation or showing weather conditions etc. **2** sheet of information in form of tables or diagrams. **3** (usually in *plural*) *colloquial* list of currently best-selling pop records. ● *verb* make chart of.
■ *noun* **1** map, sketch map. **2** diagram, graph, plan, table.

charter *noun* **1** written grant of rights, esp. by sovereign or legislature. **2** written description of organization's functions etc. ● *verb* **1** grant charter to. **2** hire (aircraft etc.). □ **charter flight** flight by chartered aircraft.
■ *verb* **1** see CERTIFY **2**. **2** employ, engage, hire, lease, rent.

chartered *adjective* qualified as member of professional body that has royal charter.

Chartism *noun* working-class reform movement of 1837–48. □ **Chartist** *noun*.

chartreuse /ʃɑːˈtrɜːz/ *noun* green or yellow brandy liqueur.

chary /'tʃeərɪ/ *adjective* (**-ier**, **-iest**) **1** cautious. **2** sparing.

chase[1] /tʃeɪs/ *verb* (**-sing**) **1** pursue. **2** (+ *from*, *out of*, *to*, etc.) drive. **3** hurry. **4** (usually + *up*) *colloquial* pursue (thing overdue). **5** *colloquial* try to attain. **6** *colloquial* court persistently. ● *noun* **1** pursuit. **2** unenclosed hunting-land.
■ *verb* **1** follow, go after, hound, hunt, pursue, run after, track, trail. **2** (*chase out of*) drive out of, evict from, expel from, send away from, throw out of.

chase[2] /tʃeɪs/ *verb* (**-sing**) emboss or engrave (metal).

chaser *noun* **1** horse for steeplechasing. **2** *colloquial* drink taken after another of different kind.

chasm /'kæz(ə)m/ *noun* **1** deep cleft in earth, rock, etc. **2** wide difference in opinion etc.
■ **1** abyss, canyon, cleft, crater, crevasse, drop, fissure, gulf, hole, hollow, opening, pit, ravine, rift, split. **2** gap, gulf, rift, split.

chassis /'ʃæsɪ/ *noun* (*plural* same /-sɪz/) **1** base frame of vehicle. **2** frame for (radio etc.) components.

chaste /tʃeɪst/ *adjective* **1** abstaining from extramarital or from all sexual intercourse. **2** (of behaviour, speech, etc.) pure, decent. **3** unadorned. □ **chastely** *adverb*. **chasteness** *noun*.

■ **1** abstinent, celibate, continent, immaculate, inexperienced, innocent, undefiled, virgin, virginal. **2** decent, good, innocent, moral, pure, sinless, uncorrupted, undefiled.

chasten /'tʃeɪs(ə)n/ *verb* **1** (esp. as **chastening**, **chastened** *adjectives*) restrain. **2** punish, discipline.
■ **1** humble, humiliate, restrain, subdue. **2** see CHASTISE **1**, PUNISH **1**.

chastise /tʃæsˈtaɪz/ *verb* (**-sing**) **1** rebuke severely. **2** punish, beat. □ **chastisement** *noun*.
■ **1** castigate, chasten, correct, discipline, rebuke, reprimand, *formal* reprove, scold. **2** see PUNISH **1**, THRASH **1**.

chastity /'tʃæstɪtɪ/ *noun* being chaste.
■ abstinence, celibacy, continence, innocence, maidenhood, morality, purity, sinlessness, virginity, virtue.

chasuble /'tʃæzjʊb(ə)l/ *noun* sleeveless outer vestment worn by celebrant of Eucharist.

chat *verb* (**-tt-**) talk in light familiar way. ● *noun* informal talk. □ **chatline** telephone service setting up conversations between groups of people on separate lines. **chat show** television or radio broadcast with informal celebrity interviews. **chat up** *colloquial* chat to, esp. flirtatiously.
■ *verb* chatter, converse, gossip, *colloquial* natter, prattle, talk. ● *noun* chatter, *slang* chinwag, *colloquial* chit-chat, conversation, *colloquial* gab, gossip, heart-to-heart. □ **chat up** court, *archaic* make love to, woo.

chateau /'ʃætəʊ/ *noun* (*plural* **-x** /-z/) large French country house.

chatelaine /'ʃætəleɪn/ *noun* **1** mistress of large house. **2** *historical* appendage to woman's belt for carrying keys etc.

chattel /'tʃæt(ə)l/ *noun* (usually in *plural*) movable possession.

chatter /'tʃætə/ *verb* talk fast, incessantly, or foolishly. ● *noun* such talk. □ **chatterer** *noun*. **chattery** *adjective*.

chatty *adjective* (**-ier**, **-iest**) fond of or resembling chat.

chauffeur /'ʃəʊfə/ *noun* person employed to drive car. ● *verb* drive (car or person).

chauvinism /'ʃəʊvɪnɪz(ə)m/ *noun* **1** exaggerated or aggressive patriotism. **2** excessive or prejudiced support or loyalty for something.

chauvinist /'ʃəʊvɪnɪst/ *noun* **1** person exhibiting chauvinism. **2** (in full **male chauvinist**) man who believes in male superiority. □ **chauvinistic** /-'nɪs-/ *adjective*.
■ **1** bigot, jingoist, patriot, xenophobe.

cheap *adjective* **1** low in price. **2** charging low prices. **3** of low quality or value. **4** easily got; worthless. **5** contemptible. □ **cheap and nasty** of low cost and bad quality. □ **cheaply** *adverb*. **cheapness** *noun*.

■ **1** bargain, budget, cut-price, *colloquial* dirt cheap, discount, economical, economy, fair, inexpensive, *colloquial* knock-down, low-priced, reasonable, reduced, rock-bottom, sale, underpriced. **3** base, inferior, poor, second-rate, shoddy, *colloquial* tatty, tawdry, tinny, *esp. US* trashy, worthless. **4, 5** contemptible, crude, despicable, facile, glib, ill-bred, ill-mannered, mean, silly, tasteless, unworthy, vulgar.

cheapen *verb* make or become cheap; degrade.
■ belittle, debase, degrade, demean, devalue, discredit, downgrade, lower the tone (of), · popularize, prostitute, vulgarize.

cheapskate *noun esp. US colloquial* stingy person.

cheat *verb* **1** (often + *into, out of*) deceive. **2** (+ *of*) deprive of. **3** gain unfair advantage esp. in examination, game, etc. ● *noun* **1** person who cheats. **2** deception. □ **cheat on** *colloquial* be sexually unfaithful to. □ **cheater** *noun*.
■ *verb* **1** *colloquial* bamboozle, beguile, *slang* bilk, *slang* con, deceive, defraud, *colloquial* diddle, *slang* do, double-cross, dupe, *slang* fiddle, fleece, fool, hoax, hoodwink, outwit, *colloquial* rip off, rob, short-change, swindle, take in, trick. **2** (*cheat of*) see DEPRIVE 1. **3** copy, *colloquial* crib, plagiarize. ● *noun* **1** charlatan, cheater, con man, counterfeiter, deceiver, double-crosser, extortioner, forger, fraud, hoaxer, impersonator, impostor, mountebank, *colloquial* phoney, quack, racketeer, rogue, *colloquial* shark, swindler, trickster, *colloquial* twister. **2** artifice, bluff, *slang* con, confidence trick, deceit, deception, *colloquial* fiddle, fraud, hoax, imposture, lie, misrepresentation, pretence, put-up job, *slang* racket, *colloquial* rip-off, ruse, sham, swindle, *colloquial* swizz, treachery, trick.

check *verb* **1** test, examine; verify. **2** stop or slow motion of. **3** *colloquial* rebuke. **4** threaten opponent's king at chess. **5** *US* agree on comparison. **6** *US* deposit (luggage etc.). ● *noun* **1** test for accuracy, quality, etc. **2** stopping or slowing of motion. **3** rebuff. **4** restraint. **5** pattern of small squares. **6** fabric so patterned. **7** (also as *interjection*) exposure of chess king to attack. **8** *US* restaurant bill. **9** *US* cheque. **10** *US* token of identification for left luggage etc. **11** *US* counter used in card games. ● *adjective* patterned with small squares. □ **check in** register at hotel, airport, etc. **check-in** *noun* act or place of checking in. **check out** leave hotel etc. with due formalities. **2** *colloquial* examine, test. **checkout 1** act of checking out. **2** pay-desk in supermarket etc. **check-up** thorough (esp. medical) examination.
■ *verb* **1** audit, *colloquial* check out, cross-check, examine, inspect, investigate, monitor, research, scrutinize, test, verify. **2** arrest, bar, block, bridle, control, curb, delay, foil, govern, halt, hamper, hinder, hold back, impede, inhibit, keep in check, obstruct, regulate, rein, repress, restrain, retard, slow down, stem, stop, stunt (*growth*), thwart. ● *noun* **1** audit, check-up, examination, *colloquial* going-over, inspection, investigation, *colloquial* once-over, scrutiny, test. **2** break, delay, halt,

hesitation, hiatus, interruption, pause, stop, stoppage, suspension. ● *adjective* see CHECKED.

checked *adjective* having a check pattern.
■ check, chequered, tartan.

checker = CHEQUER.

checkmate *noun* (also as *interjection*) check at chess from which king cannot escape. ● *verb* (**-ting**) **1** put into checkmate. **2** frustrate.

Cheddar /'tʃedə/ *noun* kind of firm smooth cheese.

cheek *noun* **1** side of face below eye. **2** impertinence; impertinent speech. **3** *slang* buttock. ● *verb* be impertinent to.
■ *noun* **2** audacity, boldness, brazenness, effrontery, impertinence, impudence, insolence, presumptuousness, rudeness, shamelessness, temerity.

cheeky *adjective* (**-ier, -iest**) impertinent. □ **cheekily** *adverb*. **cheekiness** *noun*.
■ arrogant, audacious, bold, brazen, cool, discourteous, disrespectful, flippant, forward, impertinent, impolite, impudent, insolent, insulting, irreverent, mocking, pert, presumptuous, rude, saucy, shameless, tongue-in-cheek.

cheep *noun* shrill feeble note of young bird. ● *verb* make such cry.

cheer *noun* **1** shout of encouragement or applause. **2** mood, disposition. **3** cheerfulness. **4** (as **cheers** *interjection*) *colloquial: expressing good wishes or thanks*. ● *verb* **1** applaud. **2** (usually + *on*) urge with shouts. **3** shout for joy. **4** gladden, comfort. □ **cheer up** make or become less sad.
■ *noun* **1** acclamation, applause, cry, encouragement, hurrah, ovation, shout. **3** see HAPPINESS. ● *verb* **1** acclaim, applaud, clap, shout, yell. **4** cheer up, comfort, console, delight, encourage, exhilarate, gladden, please, solace, uplift. □ **cheer up** see BRIGHTEN 2, COMFORT *verb*, ENTERTAIN 1; [*as exhortation*] *colloquial* buck up, smile, *slang* snap out of it, take heart.

cheerful *adjective* **1** in good spirits. **2** bright, pleasant. □ **cheerfully** *adverb*. **cheerfulness** *noun*.
■ **1** animated, bouncy, bright, buoyant, cheery, *colloquial* chirpy, contented, convivial, delighted, elated, festive, gay, genial, glad, gleeful, good-humoured, happy, hearty, hopeful, jaunty, *literary* jocund, jolly, jovial, joyful, joyous, jubilant, laughing, light, light-hearted, lively, merry, optimistic, perky, pleased, positive, rapturous, sparkling, spirited, sprightly, sunny, warm-hearted. **2** bright, cheery, gay, pleasant, sunny, warm.

cheerio /tʃɪərɪ'əʊ/ *interjection colloquial* goodbye.

cheerless *adjective* gloomy, dreary.
■ bleak, comfortless, dark, depressing, desolate, dingy, disconsolate, dismal, drab, dreary, dull, forbidding, forlorn, frowning, funereal, gloomy,

grim, joyless, melancholy, miserable, mournful, sad, sober, sombre, sullen, sunless, uncongenial, unhappy, uninviting, unpleasant, unpromising, woeful, wretched.

cheery *adjective* (**-ier, -iest**) cheerful. □ **cheerily** *adverb*.

cheese /tʃiːz/ *noun* **1** food made from milk curds. **2** cake of this with rind. **3** thick conserve of fruit. □ **cheeseburger** hamburger with cheese in or on it. **cheesecake** **1** tart filled with sweetened curds. **2** *slang* sexually stimulating display of women. **cheesecloth** thin loosely woven cloth. **cheesed** (often + *off*) *slang* bored, fed up. **cheese-paring** stingy. **cheese plant** climbing plant with holey leaves. □ **cheesy** *adjective*.

cheetah /tʃiːtə/ *noun* swift-running spotted feline resembling leopard.

chef /ʃef/ *noun* (esp. chief) cook in restaurant etc.

chef-d'œuvre /ʃerˈdəːvr(ə)/ *noun* (*plural* **chefs-d'œuvre** same pronunciation) masterpiece.

Chelsea /tʃelsɪ/ *noun* □ **Chelsea bun** kind of spiral-shaped currant bun. **Chelsea pensioner** inmate of Chelsea Royal Hospital for old or disabled soldiers.

chemical /ˈkemɪk(ə)l/ *adjective* of, made by, or employing chemistry. ● *noun* substance obtained or used in chemistry. □ **chemical warfare** warfare using poison gas and other chemicals. □ **chemically** *adverb*.
■ *noun* compound, element, substance.

chemise /ʃəˈmiːz/ *noun* woman's loose-fitting undergarment or dress.

chemist /ˈkemɪst/ *noun* **1** person or business dealing in medicinal drugs etc. **2** expert in chemistry.
■ **1** *archaic* apothecary, dispensary, dispenser, *US* drugstore, pharmacist, pharmacy.

chemistry /ˈkemɪstrɪ/ *noun* (*plural* **-ies**) **1** science of elements and their laws of combination and change. **2** *colloquial* sexual attraction.

chenille /ʃəˈniːl/ *noun* **1** tufted velvety yarn. **2** fabric made of this.

cheque /tʃek/ *noun* **1** written order to bank to pay sum of money. **2** printed form for this. □ **chequebook** book of forms for writing cheques. **cheque card** card issued by bank to guarantee honouring of cheques up to stated amount.

chequer /ˈtʃekə/ (also **checker**) *noun* **1** (often in *plural*) pattern of squares often alternately coloured. **2** (in *plural*; usually **checkers**) *US* game of draughts. ● *verb* **1** (often as **chequered** *adjective*) mark with chequers, like chessboard. **2** variegate; break uniformity of. **3** (as **chequered** *adjective*) with varied fortunes.
■ *verb* **3** (**chequered**) see CHANGEABLE 1.

cherish /ˈtʃerɪʃ/ *verb* **1** tend lovingly. **2** hold dear. **3** cling to.

■ **1** care for, cosset, foster, keep safe, look after, love, nourish, nurse, nurture, protect, tend. **2** be fond of, hold dear, prize, treasure, value. **3** cling to, foster, harbour, hold on to, nurse, nurture.

cheroot /ʃəˈruːt/ *noun* cigar with both ends open.

cherry /ˈtʃerɪ/ *noun* (*plural* **-ies**) **1** small stone fruit. **2** tree bearing it. **3** wood of this. **4** light red. ● *adjective* of light red colour.

cherub /ˈtʃerəb/ *noun* **1** representation of winged child. **2** beautiful child. **3** (*plural* **-im**) angelic being. □ **cherubic** /tʃɪˈruːbɪk/ *adjective*.

chervil /ˈtʃɜːvɪl/ *noun* herb with aniseed flavour.

chess *noun* game for two players with 16 **chessmen** each, on chequered **chessboard** of 64 squares.

chest *noun* **1** large strong box. **2** part of body enclosed by ribs. **3** front surface of body from neck to bottom of ribs. **4** small cabinet for medicines etc. □ **chest of drawers** piece of furniture with set of drawers in frame.
■ **1** box, caddy, case, casket, coffer, crate, strongbox, trunk. **2, 3** breast, thorax.

chesterfield /ˈtʃestəfiːld/ *noun* sofa with arms and back of same height.

chestnut /ˈtʃesnʌt/ *noun* **1** glossy hard brown edible nut. **2** tree bearing it. **3** horse chestnut. **4** reddish-brown horse. **5** *colloquial* stale joke etc. **6** reddish-brown. ● *adjective* reddish-brown.

chesty *adjective* (**-ier, -iest**) *colloquial* inclined to or symptomatic of chest disease. □ **chestily** *adverb*. **chestiness** *noun*.

cheval glass /ʃəˈvæl/ *noun* tall mirror pivoting in upright frame.

chevalier /ʃevəˈlɪə/ *noun* member of certain orders of knighthood etc.

chevron /ˈʃevrən/ *noun* V-shaped line or stripe.

chew *verb* work (food etc.) between teeth. ● *noun* **1** act of chewing. **2** chewy sweet. □ **chewing gum** flavoured gum for chewing. **chew on** **1** work continuously between teeth. **2** think about. **chew over** **1** discuss. **2** think about.
■ *verb* bite, champ, crunch, gnaw, grind, masticate, munch, nibble. □ **chew over** **2** see CONSIDER 1.

chewy *adjective* (**-ier, -iest**) requiring or suitable for chewing.

chez /ʃeɪ/ *preposition* at the home of. [French]

Chianti /kɪˈæntɪ/ *noun* (*plural* **-s**) red wine from Chianti in Italy.

chiaroscuro /kɪɑːrəˈskʊərəʊ/ *noun* **1** treatment of light and shade in painting. **2** use of contrast in literature etc.

chic /ʃiːk/ *adjective* (**chic-er, chic-est**) stylish, elegant. ● *noun* stylishness, elegance.

chicane /ʃɪˈkeɪn/ *noun* **1** artificial barrier or obstacle on motor-racing course. **2** chicanery. ● *verb* (**-ning**) **1** *archaic* use chicanery. **2** (usually + *into, out of*, etc.) cheat (person).

chicanery /ʃɪˈkeɪnərɪ/ *noun* (*plural* **-ies**) **1** clever but misleading talk. **2** trickery, deception.

chick *noun* **1** young bird. **2** *slang* young woman.
■ **1** fledgling, nestling.

chicken /ˈtʃɪkɪn/ *noun* **1** domestic fowl. **2** its flesh as food. **3** young domestic fowl. **4** youthful person. ● *adjective colloquial* cowardly. ● *verb* (+ *out*) *colloquial* withdraw through cowardice. □ **chicken feed 1** food for poultry. **2** *colloquial* insignificant amount esp. of money. **chicken-hearted** (also **chicken-livered**) lacking nerve or courage. **chickenpox** infectious disease with rash of small blisters. **chicken wire** light wire netting.
■ *noun* **1** bantam, broiler, cockerel, fowl, hen, pullet, rooster. **3** pullet.

chickpea *noun* pealike seed used as vegetable.

chickweed *noun* a small weed.

chicle /ˈtʃɪk(ə)l/ *noun* juice of tropical tree, used in chewing gum.

chicory /ˈtʃɪkərɪ/ *noun* (*plural* **-ies**) **1** salad plant. **2** its root, roasted and ground and used with or instead of coffee. **3** endive.

chide *verb* (**-ding**; *past* **chided** or **chid**; *past participle* **chided** or **chidden**) *archaic* scold, rebuke.

chief /tʃiːf/ *noun* **1** leader, ruler. **2** head of tribe, clan, etc. **3** head of department etc. ● *adjective* **1** first or highest in position, rank, or influence. **2** prominent; most important.
■ *noun* administrator, authority figure, *colloquial* bigwig, *colloquial* boss, captain, chairperson, chieftain, commander, commanding officer, commissioner, controller, director, employer, executive, foreman, forewoman, *colloquial* gaffer, governor, head, king, leader, manager, managing director, master, mistress, organizer, overseer, owner, president, principal, proprietor, ringleader, ruler, superintendent, supervisor, supremo.
● *adjective* **1** arch, best, first, foremost, greatest, head, highest, leading, major, premier, principal, senior, supreme, top, unequalled, unrivalled, uppermost. **2** basic, cardinal, central, dominant, especial, essential, fundamental, high-priority, indispensable, key, leading, main, major, necessary, outstanding, overriding, paramount, predominant, primary, prime, prominent, salient, significant, substantial, vital, weighty.

chiefly *adverb* above all; mainly but not exclusively.
■ especially, essentially, generally, in particular, mainly, mostly, particularly, predominantly, primarily, principally, usually.

chieftain /ˈtʃiːft(ə)n/ *noun* leader of tribe, clan, etc. □ **chieftaincy** *noun* (*plural* **-ies**).

chiffchaff /ˈtʃɪftʃæf/ *noun* small European warbler.

chiffon /ˈʃɪfɒn/ *noun* diaphanous silky fabric.

chignon /ˈʃiːnjɒ̃/ *noun* coil of hair at back of head.

chihuahua /tʃɪˈwɑːwə/ *noun* tiny smooth-coated dog.

chilblain /ˈtʃɪlbleɪn/ *noun* itching swelling on hand, foot, etc., caused by exposure to cold.

child /tʃaɪld/ *noun* (*plural* **children** /ˈtʃɪldrən/) **1** young human being. **2** one's son or daughter. **3** (+ *of*) descendant, follower, or product of. □ **child benefit** regular state payment to parents of child up to certain age. **childbirth** giving birth to child. **child's play** easy task. □ **childless** *adjective*.
■ **1** adolescent, babe, baby, *Scottish & Northern English* bairn, boy, *usually derogatory* brat, girl, guttersnipe, infant, juvenile, *colloquial* kid, lad, *esp. Scottish & Northern English* or *poetical* lass, minor, newborn, *colloquial* nipper, offspring, stripling, toddler, tot, urchin, youngster, youth. **2** daughter, descendant, heir, issue, offspring, progeny, son. **3** descendant, disciple, follower, product.

childhood *noun* state or period of being a child.
■ adolescence, babyhood, boyhood, girlhood, infancy, minority, teens, youth.

childish *adjective* **1** of or like child. **2** immature, silly. □ **childishly** *adverb*. **childishness** *noun*.
■ **1** boyish, childlike, girlish. **2** babyish, credulous, foolish, immature, infantile, juvenile, naive, puerile, silly.

childlike *adjective* innocent, frank, etc., like child.
■ artless, frank, green, guileless, ingenuous, innocent, naive, natural, simple, trustful, unaffected, unsophisticated.

chili = CHILLI.

chill *noun* **1** cold sensation. **2** feverish cold. **3** unpleasant coldness (of air etc.). **4** depressing influence. ● *verb* **1** make or become cold. **2** preserve (food or drink) by cooling. **3** depress; horrify. ● *adjective literary* chilly.
■ *noun* **3** see COLD *noun* 1. ● *verb* **1, 2** cool, freeze, keep cold, make cold, refrigerate.

chilli /ˈtʃɪlɪ/ *noun* (also **chili**) (*plural* **-es**) hot-tasting dried red capsicum pod. □ **chilli con carne** /kɒn ˈkɑːnɪ/ chilli-flavoured mince and beans.

chilly *adjective* (**-ier**, **-iest**) **1** rather cold. **2** sensitive to cold. **3** unfriendly, unemotional.
■ **1** *literary* chill, cold, cool, crisp, fresh, frosty, icy, *colloquial* nippy, *colloquial* or *dialect* parky, raw, sharp, wintry. **3** aloof, cool, dispassionate, frigid, hostile, ill-disposed, remote, reserved, stand-offish, unforthcoming, unfriendly, unresponsive, unsympathetic, unwelcoming.

chime *noun* **1** set of attuned bells. **2** sounds made by this. ● *verb* (**-ming**) **1** (of bells) ring. **2** show (time) by chiming. **3** (usually + *together*, *with*) be in agreement. □ **chime in 1** interject remark. **2** join in harmoniously.
■ *noun* carillon, peal, striking, tintinnabulation, tolling. ● *verb* **1** see RING² *verb* 1.

chimera /kaɪˈmɪərə/ *noun* **1** monster in Greek mythology with lion's head, goat's body, and serpent's tail. **2** bogey. **3** wild impossible scheme or fancy. □ **chimerical** /-'merɪk(ə)l/ *adjective*.

chimney /'tʃɪmnɪ/ *noun* (*plural* **-s**) **1** channel conducting smoke etc. away from fire etc. **2** part of this above roof. **3** glass tube protecting lamp-flame. □ **chimney breast** projecting wall round chimney. **chimney pot** pipe at top of chimney. **chimney sweep** person who clears chimneys of soot.

> ■ **1** flue, funnel. **2** smokestack, stack.

chimp *noun colloquial* chimpanzee.

chimpanzee /tʃɪmpən'zi:/ *noun* manlike African ape.

chin *noun* front of lower jaw. □ **chinless wonder** ineffectual person. **chinwag** *noun & verb slang* chat.

china /'tʃaɪnə/ *noun* **1** fine white or translucent ceramic ware. **2** things made of this. ● *adjective* made of china. □ **china clay** kaolin.

> ■ *noun* **1** porcelain. **2** see CROCKERY.

chinchilla /tʃɪn'tʃɪlə/ *noun* **1** S. American rodent. **2** its soft grey fur. **3** breed of cat or rabbit.

chine *noun* **1** backbone. **2** joint of meat containing this. **3** ridge. ● *verb* (**-ning**) cut (meat) through backbone.

Chinese /tʃaɪ'ni:z/ *adjective* of China. ● *noun* **1** Chinese language. **2** (*plural* same) native or national of China. **3** (*plural* same) person of Chinese descent. □ **Chinese lantern 1** collapsible paper lantern. **2** plant with inflated orange-red calyx. **Chinese leaf** lettuce-like cabbage.

chink[1] *noun* narrow opening.

> ■ cleft, crack, cranny, crevice, cut, fissure, gap, opening, rift, slit, slot, space, split.

chink[2] *verb* (cause to) make sound of glasses or coins striking together. ● *noun* this sound.

chintz *noun* printed multicoloured usually glazed cotton cloth.

chip *noun* **1** small piece cut or broken off. **2** place where piece has been broken off. **3** strip of potato usually fried. **4** *US* potato crisp. **5** counter used as money in some games. **6** microchip. ● *verb* (**-pp-**) **1** (often + *off*) cut or break (piece) from hard material. **2** (often + *at, away at*) cut pieces off (hard material). **3** be apt to break at edge. **4** (usually as **chipped** *adjective*) make (potato) into chips. □ **chipboard** board made of compressed wood chips. **chip in** *colloquial* **1** contribute (money etc.). **2** interrupt.

> ■ *noun* **1** bit, flake, fleck, fragment, piece, scrap, shard, shaving, shiver, slice, sliver, splinter, wedge. **2** crack, flaw, gash, nick, notch, scratch, snick. ● *verb* **1** break, cut, snap. **2** break, crack, damage, gash, nick, notch, scratch, splinter; (*chip at, chip away at*) see CHISEL *verb* 1. **3** break, crack, damage, scratch, splinter. □ **chip in 1** see CONTRIBUTE 1. **2** see INTERRUPT 1.

chipmunk /'tʃɪpmʌŋk/ *noun* N. American striped ground squirrel.

chipolata /tʃɪpə'lɑːtə/ *noun* small thin sausage.

Chippendale /'tʃɪpəndeɪl/ *adjective* of an 18th-c. elegant style of furniture.

chiropody /kɪ'rɒpədɪ/ *noun* treatment of feet and their ailments. □ **chiropodist** *noun*.

chiropractic /kaɪərəʊ'præktɪk/ *noun* treatment of disease by manipulation of spinal column. □ **chiropractor** /'kaɪə-/ *noun*.

chirp *verb* **1** (of small bird etc.) utter short thin sharp note. **2** speak merrily. ● *noun* chirping sound.

chirpy *adjective* (**-ier, -iest**) *colloquial* cheerful. □ **chirpily** *adverb*.

chirrup /'tʃɪrəp/ *verb* (**-p-**) chirp, esp. repeatedly. ● *noun* chirruping sound.

chisel /'tʃɪz(ə)l/ *noun* tool with bevelled blade for shaping wood, stone, or metal. ● *verb* (**-ll-**; *US* **-l-**) **1** cut or shape with chisel. **2** (as **chiselled** *adjective*) (of features) clear-cut. **3** *slang* defraud.

> ■ *verb* **1** carve, chip (away) at, cut, engrave, fashion, model, sculpture, shape.

chit[1] *noun* **1** *derogatory* or *jocular* young small woman. **2** young child.

chit[2] *noun* written note.

chit-chat *noun colloquial* light conversation, gossip.

chivalry /'ʃɪvəlrɪ/ *noun* **1** medieval knightly system. **2** honour and courtesy, esp. to the weak. □ **chivalrous** *adjective*. **chivalrously** *adverb*.

> ■ □ **chivalrous** courageous, courteous, courtly, gallant, generous, gentlemanly, heroic, honourable, *historical* knightly, noble, polite, respectable, true, trustworthy, worthy.

chive *noun* herb related to onion.

chivvy /'tʃɪvɪ/ *verb* (**-ies, -ied**) urge persistently; nag.

chloral /'klɔːr(ə)l/ *noun* compound used in making DDT, sedatives, etc.

chloride /'klɔːraɪd/ *noun* compound of chlorine and another element or group.

chlorinate /'klɔːrmeɪt/ *verb* (**-ting**) impregnate or treat with chlorine. □ **chlorination** *noun*.

chlorine /'klɔːriːn/ *noun* poisonous gas used for bleaching and disinfecting.

chlorofluorocarbon see CFC.

chloroform /'klɒrəfɔːm/ *noun* colourless volatile liquid formerly used as general anaesthetic. ● *verb* render unconscious with this.

chlorophyll /'klɒrəfɪl/ *noun* green pigment in most plants.

choc *noun colloquial* chocolate. □ **choc ice** bar of ice cream covered with chocolate.

chock *noun* block of wood; wedge. ● *verb* make fast with chock(s). □ **chock-a-block** (often + *with*) crammed together, full. **chock-full** (often + *of*) crammed full.

chocolate /'tʃɒklət/ *noun* **1** food made as paste, powder, or solid block from ground cacao seeds. **2** sweet made of or covered with this. **3** drink containing chocolate. **4** dark brown. ● *adjective* **1** made from chocolate. **2** dark brown.

choice *noun* **1** act of choosing. **2** thing or person chosen. **3** range to choose from. **4** power to choose. ● *adjective* of superior quality.

■ *noun* **1** decision, election, nomination, pick, preference, say, selection, vote. **2** nomination, pick, preference, selection. **3** array, assortment, diversity, miscellany, mixture, range, selection, variety. **4** alternative, option, say, voice, vote.
● *adjective* see EXCELLENT.

choir /kwaɪə/ *noun* **1** regular group of singers. **2** chancel in large church. □ **choirboy, choirgirl** boy or girl singer in church choir.

choke *verb* (**-king**) **1** stop breathing of (person or animal). **2** suffer such stoppage. **3** block up. **4** (usually + *back*) hold back (feelings, tears, etc.) with difficulty. **5** (as **choked** *adjective*) speechless from emotion. **6** (as **choked** *adjective*) disgusted, disappointed. ● *noun* **1** valve in carburettor controlling inflow of air. **2** device for smoothing variations of alternating electric current.

■ *verb* **1** asphyxiate, garrotte, smother, stifle, strangle, suffocate, throttle. **2** gag, gasp, retch, suffocate. **3** block, bung up, clog, close, congest, constrict, dam, fill, jam, obstruct, smother, stop up. **4** (*choke back*) see SUPPRESS 2.

choker *noun* close-fitting necklace.

choler /ˈkɒlə/ *noun* **1** *historical* bile. **2** *archaic* anger, irascibility.

cholera /ˈkɒlərə/ *noun* infectious often fatal bacterial disease of small intestine.

choleric /ˈkɒlərɪk/ *adjective* easily angered.

cholesterol /kəˈlestərɒl/ *noun* sterol present in human tissues including the blood.

chomp /tʃɒmp/ *verb* munch noisily.

choose /tʃuːz/ *verb* (**-sing;** *past* **chose** /tʃəʊz/; *past participle* **chosen**) **1** select out of greater number. **2** (usually + *between, from*) take one or another. **3** (usually + *to do*) decide.

■ **1** adopt, agree on, appoint, decide on, determine on, draw lots for, elect, identify, name, nominate, opt for, pick out, plump for, select, settle on, show a preference for, single out, vote for. **2** decide, make up one's mind, reach a decision. **3** decide, determine, elect, opt, vote.

choosy /ˈtʃuːzɪ/ *adjective* (**-ier, -iest**) *colloquial* fussy; hard to please.

■ dainty, discerning, discriminating, exacting, fastidious, finical, finicky, fussy, hard to please, nice, particular, *colloquial* pernickety, *colloquial* picky, selective.

chop[1] *verb* (**-pp-**) **1** (usually + *off, down*, etc.) cut with axe etc. **2** (often + *up*) cut into small pieces. **3** strike (ball) with heavy edgewise blow. ● *noun* **1** cutting blow. **2** thick slice of meat usually including rib. **3** (**the chop**) *slang* dismissal from job. **4** (**the chop**) *slang* killing, being killed.

■ *verb* **1** *literary* cleave, cut, hack, hew, lop, slash, split. **2** cube, cut, dice, mince.

chop[2] *noun* (usually in *plural*) jaw.

chop[3] *verb* (**-pp-**) □ **chop and change** vacillate.

■ □ **chop and change** see CHANGE *verb* 1.

chopper *noun* **1** large-bladed short axe. **2** cleaver. **3** *colloquial* helicopter.

choppy *adjective* (**-ier, -iest**) (of sea etc.) fairly rough.

■ roughish, ruffled, turbulent, uneven, wavy.

chopstick /ˈtʃɒpstɪk/ *noun* each of pair of sticks held in one hand as eating utensils by Chinese, Japanese, etc.

chop suey /tʃɒpˈsuːɪ/ *noun* (*plural* **-s**) Chinese-style dish of meat fried with vegetables.

choral /ˈkɔːr(ə)l/ *adjective* of, for, or sung by choir or chorus.

chorale /kəˈrɑːl/ *noun* **1** simple stately hymn tune. **2** choir.

chord[1] /kɔːd/ *noun* combination of notes sounded together.

chord[2] /kɔːd/ *noun* **1** straight line joining ends of arc. **2** string of harp etc.

chore *noun* tedious or routine task, esp. domestic.

■ burden, duty, errand, job, task, work.

choreography /kɒrɪˈɒɡrəfɪ/ *noun* design or arrangement of ballet etc. □ **choreograph** /ˈkɒrɪəɡrɑːf/ *verb*. **choreographer** /-ˈɒɡrəfə/ *noun*. **choreographic** /-əˈɡræf-/ *adjective*.

chorister /ˈkɒrɪstə/ *noun* member of choir, esp. choirboy.

chortle /ˈtʃɔːt(ə)l/ *noun* gleeful chuckle. ● *verb* (**-ling**) chuckle gleefully.

chorus /ˈkɔːrəs/ *noun* (*plural* **-es**) **1** group of singers; choir. **2** music for choir. **3** refrain of song. **4** simultaneous utterance. **5** group of singers and dancers performing together. **6** group of performers commenting on action in ancient Greek play. **7** any of its utterances. ● *verb* (**-s-**) utter simultaneously.

■ *noun* **1** choir, choral society, vocal ensemble. **3** refrain, response.

chose *past* of CHOOSE.

chosen *past participle* of CHOOSE.

chough /tʃʌf/ *noun* red-legged crow.

choux pastry /ʃuː/ *noun* very light pastry made with eggs.

chow *noun* **1** *slang* food. **2** Chinese breed of dog.

chow mein /tʃaʊ ˈmeɪn/ *noun* Chinese-style dish of fried noodles usually with shredded meat and vegetables.

christen /ˈkrɪs(ə)n/ *verb* **1** baptize. **2** name. □ **christening** *noun*.

■ **1** anoint, baptize. **2** call, dub, name, nickname, term.

Christendom /ˈkrɪsəndəm/ *noun* Christians worldwide.

Christian /ˈkrɪstʃ(ə)n/ *adjective* **1** of Christ's teaching. **2** believing in or following Christian religion. **3** charitable, kind. ● *noun* adherent of Christianity. □ **Christian era** era counted from

Christ's birth. **Christian name** forename, esp. given at christening. **Christian Science** system of belief including power of healing by prayer alone. **Christian Scientist** adherent of this.

Christianity /krɪstɪˈænɪtɪ/ *noun* Christian religion, quality, or character.

Christmas /ˈkrɪsməs/ *noun* (period around) festival of Christ's birth celebrated on 25 Dec. □ **Christmas box** present or tip given at Christmas. **Christmas Day** 25 Dec. **Christmas Eve** 24 Dec. **Christmas pudding** rich boiled pudding with dried fruit. **Christmas rose** white-flowered winter-flowering hellebore. **Christmas tree** evergreen tree decorated at Christmas. □ **Christmassy** *adjective*.

chromatic /krəˈmætɪk/ *adjective* 1 of colour; in colours. 2 *Music* of or having notes not belonging to prevailing key. □ **chromatic scale** scale that proceeds by semitones. □ **chromatically** *adverb*.

chrome /krəʊm/ *noun* 1 chromium. 2 yellow pigment got from a compound of chromium.

chromium /ˈkrəʊmɪəm/ *noun* metallic element used as shiny decorative or protective coating.

chromosome /ˈkrəʊməsəʊm/ *noun* *Biology* threadlike structure occurring in pairs in cell nucleus, carrying genes.

chronic /ˈkrɒnɪk/ *adjective* 1 (of disease) long-lasting. 2 (of patient) having chronic illness. 3 *colloquial* habitual. 4 *colloquial* bad, intense, severe. □ **chronically** *adverb*.
■ 1 ceaseless, constant, continuing, deep-rooted, incessant, incurable, ineradicable, ingrained, lasting, lifelong, lingering, long-lasting, long-lived, long-standing, never-ending, non-stop, permanent, persistent, unending. 4 see BAD 6.

chronicle /ˈkrɒnɪk(ə)l/ *noun* record of events in order of occurrence. ● *verb* (**-ling**) record (events) thus. □ **chronicler** *noun*.
■ *noun* account, annals, chronology, description, diary, history, journal, narrative, record, register, saga, story.

chronological /krɒnəˈlɒdʒɪk(ə)l/ *adjective* according to order of occurrence. □ **chronologically** *adverb*.
■ consecutive, in order, sequential.

chronology /krəˈnɒlədʒɪ/ *noun* (*plural* **-ies**) 1 science of computing dates. 2 arrangement of events etc. according to date. 3 document displaying such arrangement.
■ 2 dating, order, sequence, timing. 3 almanac, calendar, diary, journal, log, schedule, timetable.

chronometer /krəˈnɒmɪtə/ *noun* time-measuring instrument, esp. one used in navigation.

chrysalis /ˈkrɪsəlɪs/ *noun* (*plural* **-lises**) 1 pupa of butterfly or moth. 2 case enclosing it.

chrysanthemum /krɪˈsænθəməm/ *noun* garden plant flowering in autumn.

chub *noun* (*plural* same) thick-bodied river fish.

chubby *adjective* (**-ier, -iest**) plump, round.
■ buxom, dumpy, fat, plump, podgy, portly, rotund, round, stout, tubby.

chuck¹ *verb* 1 *colloquial* fling or throw carelessly. 2 (often + *in, up*) *colloquial* give up. 3 touch playfully, esp. under chin. ● *noun* 1 act of chucking. 2 (**the chuck**) *slang* dismissal. □ **chuck out** *colloquial* 1 expel. 2 discard.

chuck² *noun* 1 cut of beef from neck to ribs. 2 device for holding workpiece or bit. ● *verb* fix in chuck.

chuckle /ˈtʃʌk(ə)l/ *verb* (**-ling**) laugh quietly or inwardly. ● *noun* quiet or suppressed laugh.

chuff *verb* (of engine etc.) work with regular sharp puffing sound.

chuffed *adjective slang* delighted.

chug *verb* (**-gg-**) 1 make intermittent explosive sound. 2 move with this.

chukka /ˈtʃʌkə/ *noun* (*US* **chukker**) period of play in polo.

chum *noun colloquial* close friend. □ **chum up** (**-mm-**) (often + *with*) become close friend (of). □ **chummy** *adjective* (**-ier, -iest**).

chump *noun* 1 *colloquial* foolish person. 2 thick end of loin of lamb or mutton. 3 lump of wood.

chunk *noun* lump cut or broken off.
■ bar, block, brick, chuck, hunk, lump, mass, piece, portion, slab, wedge.

chunky *adjective* (**-ier, -iest**) 1 consisting of or resembling chunks. 2 small and sturdy.

chunter /ˈtʃʌntə/ *verb colloquial* mutter, grumble.

chupatty = CHAPATTI.

church *noun* 1 building for public Christian worship. 2 public worship. 3 (**Church**) Christians collectively. 4 (**Church**) clerical profession. 5 (**Church**) organized Christian society. □ **churchgoer** person attending church regularly. **churchgoing** *noun & adjective*. **churchman, churchwoman** member of clergy or Church. **churchwarden** elected lay representative of Anglican parish. **churchyard** enclosed ground round church, esp. used for burials.
■ 1 abbey, basilica, cathedral, chapel, *Scottish & Northern English* kirk, minster, parish church, shrine, temple. □ **churchyard** burial ground, cemetery, graveyard.

churl *noun* bad-mannered, surly, or stingy person.

churlish /ˈtʃɜːlɪʃ/ *adjective* surly; mean-spirited. □ **churlishness** *noun*.

churn *noun* 1 large milk can. 2 butter-making machine. ● *verb* 1 agitate (milk etc.) in churn. 2 make (butter) in churn. 3 (usually + *up*) upset, agitate. □ **churn out** produce in large quantities.

chute¹ /ʃuːt/ *noun* 1 slide for taking things to lower level. 2 slide into a swimming pool.
■ channel, incline, ramp, slide, slope.

chute² /ʃuːt/ *noun colloquial* parachute.

chutney /'tʃʌtnɪ/ *noun* (*plural* **-s**) relish made of fruits, vinegar, spices, etc.

chyle /kaɪl/ *noun* milky fluid into which chyme is converted.

chyme /kaɪm/ *noun* pulp formed from partly-digested food.

CIA *abbreviation* (in *US*) Central Intelligence Agency.

ciabatta /tʃə'bɑːtə/ *noun* Italian bread made with olive oil.

ciao /tʃaʊ/ *interjection colloquial* **1** goodbye. **2** hello.

cicada /sɪ'kɑːdə/ *noun* winged chirping insect.

cicatrice /'sɪkətrɪs/ *noun* scar of healed wound.

cicely /'sɪsəlɪ/ *noun* (*plural* **-ies**) flowering plant related to parsley and chervil.

CID *abbreviation* Criminal Investigation Department.

cider /'saɪdə/ *noun* drink of fermented apple juice.

cigar /sɪ'gɑː/ *noun* roll of tobacco leaves for smoking.

cigarette /sɪgə'ret/ *noun* finely cut tobacco rolled in paper for smoking.

cilium /'sɪlɪəm/ *noun* (*plural* **cilia**) **1** hairlike structure on animal cells. **2** eyelash. □ **ciliary** *adjective*.

cinch /sɪntʃ/ *noun colloquial* **1** certainty. **2** easy task.

cinchona /sɪŋ'kəʊnə/ *noun* **1** S. American evergreen tree. **2** (drug from) its bark which contains quinine.

cincture /'sɪŋktʃə/ *noun literary* girdle, belt, or border.

cinder /'sɪndə/ *noun* residue of coal etc. after burning.

Cinderella /sɪndə'relə/ *noun* person or thing of unrecognized merit.

cine- /sɪnɪ/ *combining form* cinematographic.

cinema /'sɪnɪmɑː/ *noun* **1** theatre where films are shown. **2** films collectively. **3** art or industry of producing films. □ **cinematic** /-'mæt-/ *adjective*.

■ **2** films, *colloquial* the flicks, *esp. US* motion pictures, *esp. US colloquial* movies, pictures.

cinematography /sɪnɪmə'tɒgrəfɪ/ *noun* art of making films. □ **cinematographer** *noun*. **cinematographic** /-mætə'græfɪk/ *adjective*.

cineraria /sɪnə'reərɪə/ *noun* plant with bright flowers and downy leaves.

cinnabar /'sɪnəbɑː/ *noun* **1** red mercuric sulphide. **2** vermilion.

cinnamon /'sɪnəmən/ *noun* **1** aromatic spice from bark of SE Asian tree. **2** this tree. **3** yellowish-brown.

cinquefoil /'sɪŋkfɔɪl/ *noun* plant with compound leaf of 5 leaflets.

Cinque Port /sɪŋk/ *noun* any of (originally 5) ports in SE England with ancient privileges.

cipher /'saɪfə/ (also **cypher**) *noun* **1** secret or disguised writing. **2** key to this. **3** arithmetical symbol 0. **4** person or thing of no importance. ● *verb* write in cipher.

circa /'sɜːkə/ *preposition* (usually preceding date) about. [Latin]

circle /'sɜːk(ə)l/ *noun* **1** perfectly round plane figure. **2** roundish enclosure, structure, etc. **3** ring. **4** curved upper tier of seats in theatre etc. **5** circular route. **6** cycle. **7** set or restricted group. **8** people grouped round centre of interest. ● *verb* (**-ling**) (often + *round*, *about*) move in or form circle.

■ *noun* **1** circlet, disc, ring, round. **3** band, belt, circlet, coil, girdle, hoop, loop, ring, round, wheel. **5** circuit, circulation, circumnavigation, cycle, gyration, lap, loop, orbit, revolution, rotation, round, tour, turn. **7** association, band, body, clique, club, company, coterie, fellowship, *US* fraternity, gang, group, party, set, society, sphere. ● *verb* circumnavigate, circumscribe, coil, compass, corkscrew, curl, curve, encircle, enclose, encompass, girdle, go round, gyrate, hem in, loop, orbit, pirouette, pivot, reel, revolve, ring, rotate, skirt, spin, spiral, surround, swirl, swivel, tour, turn, wheel, whirl, wind.

circlet /'sɜːklɪt/ *noun* **1** small circle. **2** circular band, esp. as ornament.

circuit /'sɜːkɪt/ *noun* **1** line, course, or distance enclosing an area. **2** path of electric current. **3** apparatus through which current passes. **4** judge's itinerary through district. **5** such a district. **6** chain of theatres, cinemas, etc. under single management. **7** motor-racing track. **8** sphere of operation. **9** sequence of sporting events.

■ **1** circle, circumference, lap, orbit, revolution, round, tour.

circuitous /sɜː'kjuːɪtəs/ *adjective* indirect, roundabout.

■ curving, devious, indirect, labyrinthine, meandering, oblique, roundabout, serpentine, tortuous, twisting, winding, zigzag.

circuitry /'sɜːkɪtrɪ/ *noun* (*plural* **-ies**) system of electric circuits.

circular /'sɜːkjʊlə/ *adjective* **1** having form of or moving in circle. **2** (of reasoning) using point to be proved as argument for its own truth. **3** (of letter etc.) distributed to several people. ● *noun* circular letter etc. □ **circular saw** power saw with rotating toothed disc. □ **circularity** /-'lærɪtɪ/ *noun*.

■ *adjective* **1** annular, ring-like, round. **2** circumlocutory, cyclic, periphrastic, repeating, repetitive, roundabout, tautologous. ● *noun* advertisement, leaflet, letter, notice, pamphlet.

circularize *verb* (also **-ise**) (**-zing** or **-sing**) send circular to.

circulate /'sɜːkjʊleɪt/ *verb* (**-ting**) **1** be in circulation. **2** put in circulation. **3** send circulars to. **4** mingle among guests etc.

■ **1** circle, go round, move about, move round, orbit. **2** advertise, disseminate, distribute, issue, make known, noise abroad, promulgate, publicize, publish, put about, send round, spread about. **4** go round, mingle, mix, move round.

circulation *noun* **1** movement from and back to starting point, esp. that of blood from and to heart. **2** transmission, distribution. **3** number of copies sold. □ **circulatory** *adjective*.

■ **1** flow, movement, pumping, recycling. **2** broadcasting, diffusion, dissemination, distribution, promulgation, publication, spreading, transmission. **3** distribution, sales figures.

circumcise /'sɜːkəmsaɪz/ *verb* (**-sing**) cut off foreskin or clitoris of. □ **circumcision** /-'sɪʒ(ə)n/ *noun*.

circumference /sə'kʌmfərəns/ *noun* **1** line enclosing circle. **2** distance round.

■ **1** border, boundary, circuit, edge, fringe, limit, margin, outline, perimeter, periphery, rim, verge.

circumflex /'sɜːkəmfleks/ *noun* (in full **circumflex accent**) mark (ˆ) over vowel indicating pronunciation.

circumlocution /sɜːkəmlə'kjuːʃ(ə)n/ *noun* **1** roundabout expression. **2** evasive speech. **3** verbosity. □ **circumlocutory** /-'lɒkjʊt-/ *adjective*.

circumnavigate /sɜːkəm'nævɪgeɪt/ *verb* (**-ting**) sail round. □ **circumnavigation** *noun*.

circumscribe /'sɜːkəmskraɪb/ *verb* (**-bing**) **1** enclose or outline. **2** lay down limits of; confine, restrict. □ **circumscription** /-'skrɪpʃ(ə)n/ *noun*.

circumspect /'sɜːkəmspekt/ *adjective* cautious; taking everything into account. □ **circumspection** /-'spekʃ(ə)n/ *noun*. **circumspectly** *adverb*.

circumstance /'sɜːkəmst(ə)ns/ *noun* **1** fact, occurrence, or condition, esp. (in *plural*) connected with or affecting an event etc. **2** (in *plural*) financial condition. **3** ceremony, fuss.

■ **1** *colloquial* affair, event, happening, incident, occasion, occurrence; (*circumstances*) background, causes, conditions, considerations, context, contingencies, details, factors, facts, influences, particulars, position, situation, state of affairs, surroundings. **2** (*circumstances*) finances, income, resources.

circumstantial /sɜːkəm'stænʃ(ə)l/ *adjective* **1** (of account, story) detailed. **2** (of evidence) tending to establish a conclusion by reasonable inference.

■ **2** conjectural, deduced, inferred, unprovable.

circumvent /sɜːkəm'vent/ *verb* **1** evade. **2** outwit.

circus /'sɜːkəs/ *noun* (*plural* **-es**) **1** travelling show of performing acrobats, clowns, animals, etc. **2** *colloquial* scene of lively action. **3** group of people in common activity. **4** open space in town, where several streets converge. **5** *historical* arena for sports and games.

cirrhosis /sɪ'rəʊsɪs/ *noun* chronic liver disease.

cirrus /'sɪrəs/ *noun* (*plural* **cirri** /-raɪ/) white wispy cloud.

cissy = SISSY.

Cistercian /sɪs'tɜːʃ(ə)n/ *noun* monk or nun of strict Benedictine order. ● *adjective* of the Cistercians.

cistern /'sɪst(ə)n/ *noun* **1** tank for storing water. **2** underground reservoir.

■ bath, container, reservoir, tank.

citadel /'sɪtəd(ə)l/ *noun* fortress protecting or dominating city.

■ acropolis, bastion, castle, fort, fortification, fortress, garrison, stronghold, tower.

citation /saɪ'teɪʃ(ə)n/ *noun* **1** citing or passage cited. **2** description of reasons for award.

cite *verb* (**-ting**) **1** mention as example. **2** quote (book etc.) in support. **3** mention in military dispatches. **4** summon to law court.

■ **1, 2** adduce, advance, bring up, enumerate, mention, name, quote, reel off, refer to, specify. **3** mention, name, refer to.

citizen /'sɪtɪz(ə)n/ *noun* **1** native or national of state. **2** inhabitant of particular city. □ **citizen's band** system of local intercommunication by radio. □ **citizenry** *noun*. **citizenship** *noun*.

■ **1** denizen, inhabitant, national, native, passport-holder, subject, taxpayer, voter. **2** burgher, dweller, freeman, householder, inhabitant, ratepayer, resident.

citrate /'sɪtreɪt/ *noun* salt of citric acid.

citric /'sɪtrɪk/ *adjective* □ **citric acid** sharp-tasting acid in citrus fruits.

citron /'sɪtrən/ *noun* **1** tree bearing large lemon-like fruits. **2** this fruit.

citronella /sɪtrə'nelə/ *noun* **1** a fragrant oil. **2** grass from S. Asia yielding it.

citrus /'sɪtrəs/ *noun* (*plural* **-es**) **1** tree of group including orange, lemon, and grapefruit. **2** (in full **citrus fruit**) fruit of such tree.

city /'sɪtɪ/ *noun* (*plural* **-ies**) **1** large town. **2** town created city by charter and containing cathedral. **3** (**the City**) part of London governed by Lord Mayor and Corporation. **4** (**the City**) business quarter of this. **5** (**the City**) commercial circles.

■ **1, 2** conurbation, metropolis, town, urban district.

civet /'sɪvɪt/ *noun* **1** (in full **civet cat**) catlike animal of Central Africa. **2** strong musky perfume got from this.

civic /'sɪvɪk/ *adjective* of city or citizenship.

civics *plural noun* (usually treated as *singular*) study of civic rights and duties.

civil /'sɪv(ə)l/ *adjective* **1** of or belonging to citizens. **2** non-military. **3** polite, obliging. **4** *Law* concerning private rights and not criminal offences. □ **civil defence** organization for protecting civilians in wartime. **civil engineer** person who designs or maintains roads, bridges, etc. **civil list** annual allowance by Parliament for royal family's household expenses. **civil mar-**

riage one solemnized without religious ceremony. **civil rights** rights of citizens to social and political freedom, equal opportunity, and non-discriminatory treatment. **civil servant** member of civil service. **civil service** all non-military and non-judicial branches of state administration. **civil war** one between citizens of same country.

■ **1** communal, domestic, internal, national, public, social, state. **2** civilian. **3** affable, civilized, considerate, courteous, obliging, polite, respectful, urbane, well bred, well mannered. □ **civil servant** administrator, bureaucrat, mandarin.

civilian /sɪ'vɪlɪən/ noun person not in armed forces. ● adjective of or for civilians.

civility /sɪ'vɪlɪtɪ/ noun (plural **-ies**) **1** politeness. **2** act of politeness.

civilization noun (also **-sation**) **1** advanced stage of social development. **2** peoples regarded as having achieved, or been instrumental in evolving, this. **3** customs, achievements, beliefs, etc. of such peoples.

■ **1** cultivation, culture, enlightenment, refinement, sophistication. **2** community, culture, nation, people, society. **3** see CULTURE noun 3.

civilize /'sɪvɪlaɪz/ verb (also **-ise**) (**-zing** or **-sing**) **1** bring out of barbarism. **2** enlighten, refine. □ **civilized** adjective.

■ **1** domesticate, humanize, socialize, tame. **2** cultivate, educate, enlighten, improve, organize, refine. □ **civilized** advanced, cultivated, cultured, developed, domesticated, educated, enlightened, humane, orderly, polite, refined, sociable, social, sophisticated, urbane, well behaved, well run.

cl abbreviation centilitre(s).

clack verb make sharp sound as of boards struck together. ● noun such sound.

clad adjective **1** clothed. **2** provided with cladding.

cladding noun protective covering or coating.

claim verb **1** demand as one's due. **2** assert. **3** represent oneself as having. **4** (+ to do) profess to. ● noun **1** demand. **2** (+ to, on) right or title. **3** assertion. **4** thing claimed.

■ verb **1** ask for, collect, demand, exact, insist on, take. **2–4** affirm, allege, argue, assert, attest, contend, declare, insist, maintain, pretend, profess, state.

claimant noun person making claim, esp. in lawsuit or for state benefit.

clairvoyance /kleə'vɔɪəns/ noun supposed faculty of perceiving the future or the unseen.

clairvoyant noun person having clairvoyance. ● adjective having clairvoyance.

■ noun fortune-teller, oracle, prophet, seer, sibyl, soothsayer. ● adjective extrasensory, oracular, prophetic, psychic, telepathic.

clam noun edible bivalve mollusc. ● verb (**-mm-**) (+ up) colloquial refuse to talk.

clamber /'klæmbə/ verb climb using hands or with difficulty.

■ climb, crawl, scramble.

clammy /'klæmɪ/ adjective (**-ier, -iest**) damp and sticky.

■ close, damp, dank, humid, moist, muggy, slimy, sticky, sweaty, wet.

clamour /'klæmə/ (US **clamor**) noun **1** shouting, confused noise. **2** protest, demand. ● verb make clamour, shout. □ **clamorous** adjective.

■ noun **1** babel, commotion, din, hubbub, hullabaloo, noise, outcry, racket, colloquial row, screeching, shouting, storm, uproar. ● verb call out, cry out, exclaim, shout, yell.

clamp[1] noun **1** device, esp. brace or band of iron etc., for strengthening or holding things together. **2** device for immobilizing illegally parked vehicles. ● verb **1** strengthen or fasten with clamp. **2** place or hold firmly. **3** immobilize (car) with clamp. □ **clamp down** (usually + on) become stricter (about).

clamp[2] noun heap of earth and straw over harvested potatoes etc.

clan noun **1** group of families with common ancestor, esp. in Scotland. **2** family as social group. **3** group with common interest. □ **clansman, clanswoman** member or fellow member of clan. □ **clannish** adjective.

■ **1** family, house, tribe. □ **clannish** cliquish, close, close-knit, insular, isolated, narrow, united.

clandestine /klæn'destɪn/ adjective surreptitious, secret.

clang noun loud resonant metallic sound. ● verb (cause to) make clang.

clanger /'klæŋə/ noun slang mistake; blunder. □ **drop a clanger** commit conspicuous indiscretion.

clangour /'klæŋgə/ noun (US **clangor**) continued clanging. □ **clangorous** adjective.

clank noun sound as of metal on metal. ● verb (cause to) make clank.

clap verb (**-pp-**) **1** strike palms of hands together, esp. as applause. **2** put or place quickly or with determination. **3** (+ on) give friendly slap on. ● noun **1** act of clapping. **2** explosive noise, esp. of thunder. **3** slap. □ **clap eyes on** colloquial see. **clapped out** slang worn out; exhausted.

■ verb **1** applaud, show approval. **3** see HIT verb 1. ● noun **2** bang, crack, crash, report. **3** slap, smack, spank.

clapper noun tongue or striker of bell. □ **clapperboard** device in film-making for making sharp noise to synchronize picture and sound.

claptrap noun insincere or pretentious talk; nonsense.

claque /klæk/ noun people hired to applaud.

claret /'klærət/ noun red Bordeaux wine.

clarify /'klærɪfaɪ/ verb (**-ies, -ied**) **1** make or become clear. **2** free from impurities. **3** make transparent. □ **clarification** noun.

■ **1** clear up, define, elucidate, explain, explicate, gloss, illuminate, simplify, spell out, throw light on. **2** cleanse, clear, filter, purify, refine.

clarinet /klærɪ'net/ *noun* woodwind instrument with single reed. □ **clarinettist** *noun*.

clarion /'klærɪən/ *noun* **1** rousing sound. **2** *historical* war-trumpet.

clarity /'klærɪtɪ/ *noun* clearness.

clash *noun* **1** loud jarring sound as of metal objects struck together. **2** collision. **3** conflict. **4** discord of colours etc. ● *verb* **1** (cause to) make clash. **2** coincide awkwardly. **3** (often + *with*) be discordant or at variance.
■ *verb* **1** bang, clang, clank, crash, resonate, ring. **2** see COINCIDE 1. **3** see CONFLICT *verb*.

clasp /klɑːsp/ *noun* **1** device with interlocking parts for fastening. **2** embrace. **3** handshake. **4** bar on medal-ribbon. ● *verb* **1** fasten (as) with clasp. **2** grasp. **3** embrace. □ **clasp-knife** large folding knife.
■ *noun* **1** brooch, buckle, catch, clip, fastener, fastening, hasp, hook, pin. **2, 3** cuddle, embrace, grasp, grip, hold, hug. ● *verb* **1** see FASTEN 1. **2, 3** cling to, clutch, embrace, enfold, grasp, grip, hold, hug, squeeze.

class /klɑːs/ *noun* **1** any set of people or things grouped together or differentiated from others. **2** division or order of society. **3** *colloquial* high quality. **4** set of students taught together. **5** their time of meeting. **6** their course of instruction. ● *verb* place in a class. □ **classmate** person in same class at school. **classroom** room where class of students is taught. □ **classless** *adjective*.
■ *noun* **1** category, classification, division, domain, genre, genus, grade, group, kind, league, order, quality, rank, set, sort, species, sphere, type. **2** caste, descent, extraction, grouping, lineage, pedigree, standing, station, status. **4** band, form, *US* grade, group, set, stream, year. ● *verb* see CLASSIFY 1.

classic /'klæsɪk/ *adjective* **1** first-class; of lasting importance. **2** typical. **3** of ancient Greek or Latin culture etc. **4** (of style) simple and harmonious. **5** famous because long-established. ● *noun* **1** classic writer, artist, work, or example. **2** (in *plural*) study of ancient Greek and Latin.
■ *adjective* **1** abiding, ageless, deathless, enduring, established, excellent, exemplary, first-class, first-rate, flawless, ideal, immortal, lasting, *colloquial* legendary, masterly, memorable, notable, outstanding, perfect, time-honoured, undying, unforgettable, vintage. **2** archetypal, characteristic, definitive, model, paradigmatic, regular, standard, typical, usual. ● *noun* **1** masterpiece, model.

classical *adjective* **1** of ancient Greek or Latin literature etc. **2** (of language) having form used by standard authors. **3** (of style) harmonious, elegant, simple. **4** (of music) serious or conventional.
■ **1** ancient, Greek, Hellenic, Latin, Roman. **3** austere, dignified, elegant, harmonious, pure, restrained, simple, symmetrical, well proportioned.

classicism /'klæsɪsɪz(ə)m/ *noun* **1** following of classic style. **2** classical scholarship. □ **classicist** *noun*.

classification /klæsɪfɪ'keɪʃ(ə)n/ *noun* **1** arranging in classes. **2** class in which thing or person is placed.
■ **1** categorization, codification, ordering, organization, systematization, tabulation, taxonomy. **2** see CLASS *noun* 1.

classify /'klæsɪfaɪ/ *verb* (**-ies**, **-ied**) **1** arrange in classes; class. **2** (often as **classified** *adjective*) designate as officially secret.
■ **1** arrange, bracket together, catalogue, categorize, class, grade, group, order, organize, pigeon-hole, put into sets, sort, systematize, tabulate. **2** (**classified**) see SECRET *adjective* 1.

classy /'klɑːsɪ/ *adjective* (**-ier**, **-iest**) *colloquial* superior. □ **classiness** *noun*.

clatter /'klætə/ *noun* sound as of hard objects struck together. ● *verb* (cause to) make clatter.

clause /klɔːz/ *noun* **1** group of words including finite verb (see panel). **2** single statement in treaty, law, contract, etc.
■ **2** article, condition, item, paragraph, part, passage, provision, proviso, section, subsection.

claustrophobia /klɔːstrə'fəʊbɪə/ *noun* abnormal fear of confined places. □ **claustrophobic** *adjective*.

clavichord /'klævɪkɔːd/ *noun* small keyboard instrument with very soft tone.

clavicle /'klævɪk(ə)l/ *noun* collar-bone.

claw *noun* **1** pointed nail on animal's foot. **2** foot

Clause

A clause is a group of words that includes a finite verb. If it makes complete sense by itself, it is known as a main clause, e.g.

The sun came out.

Otherwise, it must be attached to a main clause; it is then known as a subordinate clause, e.g.

when the sun came out
(as in *When the sun came out, we went outside.*)

armed with claws. **3** pincers of shellfish. **4** device for grappling, holding, etc. ● *verb* scratch, maul, or pull with claws or fingernails.

■ *noun* **1** nail, talon. ● *verb* lacerate, maul, rip, scrape, scratch, slash, tear.

clay *noun* stiff sticky earth, used for bricks, pottery, etc. □ **clay pigeon** breakable disc thrown into air as target for shooting. □ **clayey** *adjective*.

claymore /'kleɪmɔ:/ *noun historical* Scottish two-edged broad-bladed sword.

clean *adjective* **1** free from dirt. **2** clear. **3** pristine. **4** not obscene or indecent. **5** attentive to cleanliness. **6** clear-cut. **7** without record of crime etc. **8** fair. ● *adverb* **1** completely. **2** simply. **3** in a clean way. ● *verb* make or become clean. ● *noun* process of cleaning. □ **clean-cut 1** sharply outlined. **2** (of person) clean and tidy. **clean out 1** clean thoroughly. **2** *slang* empty or deprive (esp. of money). **clean-shaven** without beard or moustache. **clean up 1** make tidy or clean. **2** *slang* acquire as or make profit. □ **cleaner** *noun*. **cleanness** *noun*.

■ *adjective* **1** decontaminated, disinfected, hygienic, immaculate, laundered, perfect, polished, sanitary, scrubbed, spick and span, spotless, sterile, sterilized, unadulterated, unsoiled, unstained, unsullied, washed, wholesome. **2** clarified, clear, distilled, fresh, pure, purified, unpolluted. **3** blank, new, plain, pristine, unmarked, untouched, unused. **4** chaste, decent, good, innocent, moral, respectable, upright, virtuous. **6** clear-cut, definite, neat, regular, smooth, straight, tidy. **8** chivalrous, fair, honest, honourable, sporting, sportsmanlike. ● *verb* bath, bathe, brush, buff, cleanse, clear up, decontaminate, deodorize, disinfect, dry-clean, dust, filter, flush, groom, hoover, launder, mop, polish, purge, purify, rinse, sandblast, sanitize, scour, scrape, scrub, shampoo, shower, soap, sponge, spring-clean, spruce up, sterilize, swab, sweep, swill, tidy up, *colloquial* vacuum, wash, wipe. □ **clean-shaven** beardless, shaved, shaven, shorn, smooth.

cleanly[1] *adverb* in a clean way.

cleanly[2] /'klenlɪ/ *adjective* (**-ier**, **-iest**) habitually clean; attentive to cleanness and hygiene. □ **cleanliness** *noun*.

cleanse /klenz/ *verb* (**-sing**) make clean or pure. □ **cleanser** *noun*.

clear *adjective* **1** free from dirt or contamination. **2** not clouded. **3** transparent. **4** (of colours) bright. **5** readily perceived; distinct. **6** unambiguous; easily understood. **7** evident, manifest. **8** able to discern readily. **9** free from guilt. **10** unobstructed. **11** (often + *of*) free, unhampered. **12** net, without deduction; complete. ● *adverb* **1** clearly. **2** completely. **3** apart. ● *verb* **1** make or become clear. **2** (often + *of*) free from obstruction etc. **3** remove (obstruction etc.). **4** make or become empty. **5** (often + *of*) show (person) to be innocent. **6** approve (person etc.) for special duty, access, etc. **7** pass through (customs). **8** pass over or by without touching. **9** make (sum) as net gain.

10 pass (cheque) through clearing house. **11** (of fog etc.) disappear. □ **clear away** remove. **clear-cut** sharply defined. **clear off** *colloquial* go away. **clear out 1** empty. **2** remove. **3** *colloquial* go away. **clear-out** *noun* tidying by emptying and sorting. **clear up 1** tidy. **2** solve. **clearway** road where vehicles may not stop. □ **clearly** *adverb*. **clearness** *noun*.

■ *adjective* **1** clarified, clean, distilled, filtered, fresh, pure, purified, unpolluted. **2** cloudless, fair, fine, sunny, starlit, unclouded. **3** colourless, crystalline, glassy, limpid, pellucid, pure, transparent. **4** bright, lustrous, shining, sparkling, strong, vivid. **5** (*clear image*) bold, clean, definite, distinct, explicit, focused, legible, positive, recognizable, sharp, simple, visible, well-defined; (*clear sound*) audible, distinct, penetrating, sharp. **6** clear-cut, coherent, comprehensible, explicit, intelligible, lucid, perspicuous, precise, specific, straightforward, unambiguous, understandable, unequivocal, well presented. **7** apparent, blatant, clear-cut, conspicuous, evident, glaring, indisputable, manifest, noticeable, obvious, palpable, perceptible, plain, pronounced, straightforward, unconcealed, undisguised, unmistakable. **8** see PERCEPTIVE. **9** blameless, easy, guiltless, innocent, quiet, satisfied, sinless, undisturbed, untroubled, unworried. **10** empty, free, open, passable, uncluttered, uncrowded, unhampered, unhindered, unimpeded, unobstructed. ● *verb* **1** brighten, clarify, clean, filter, purify. **2** clean out, free, open up, unblock, unclog, unstop. **3** eliminate, get rid of, remove, strip. **4** empty, evacuate. **5** absolve, acquit, *formal* exculpate, excuse, exonerate, free, let off, liberate, release, vindicate. **8** bound over, jump, leap over, pass over, spring over, vault. **11** disappear, evaporate, fade, melt away, vanish. □ **clear away** see REMOVE *verb* 1. **clear off** see DEPART 1,2. **clear up 1** see CLEAN *verb*. **2** see EXPLAIN 1,2.

clearance *noun* **1** removal of obstructions etc. **2** space allowed for passing of two objects. **3** special authorization. **4** clearing for special duty, of cheque, etc. **5** clearing out.

clearing *noun* treeless area in forest. □ **clearing bank** member of clearing house. **clearing house 1** bankers' institution where cheques etc. are exchanged. **2** agency for collecting and distributing information etc.

■ gap, glade, opening, space.

cleat *noun* device for fastening ropes to projection on gangway, sole, etc. to provide grip.

cleavage *noun* **1** hollow between woman's breasts. **2** division. **3** line along which rocks etc. split.

cleave[1] *verb* (**-ving**; *past* **clove** /kləʊv/, **cleft**, or **cleaved**; *past participle* **cloven**, **cleft**, or **cleaved**) *literary* **1** break or come apart. **2** make one's way through.

■ **1** cut, divide, halve, slit, split.

cleave[2] *verb* (**-ving**) (+ *to*) *literary* adhere to.

cleaver *noun* butcher's heavy chopping tool.

clef *noun Music* symbol at start of staff showing pitch of notes on it.

cleft[1] *adjective* split, partly divided. □ **cleft palate** congenital split in roof of mouth.

cleft[2] *noun* split, fissure.

clematis /'klemətɪs/ *noun* climbing flowering plant.

clement /'klemənt/ *adjective* 1 mild. 2 merciful. □ **clemency** *noun*.

clementine /'klemənti:n/ *noun* small tangerine-like fruit.

clench *verb* 1 close tightly. 2 grasp firmly. ● *noun* 1 clenching action. 2 clenched state.
■ *verb* 2 clasp, grasp, grip, hold.

clergy /'klɜ:dʒɪ/ *noun* (*plural* **-ies**) (usually treated as *plural*) those ordained for religious duties.

clergyman /'klɜ:dʒɪmən/ *noun* (*feminine* **clergywoman**) member of clergy.
■ archbishop, bishop, canon, cardinal, chaplain, churchman, churchwoman, confessor, cleric, curate, deacon, deaconess, dean, divine, ecclesiastic, minister, padre, parson, pastor, preacher, prebendary, prelate, priest, primate, rector, vicar.

cleric /'klerɪk/ *noun* member of clergy.

clerical *adjective* 1 of clergy, clergymen, or clergywomen. 2 of or done by clerks.
■ 1 canonical, ecclesiastical, episcopal, ministerial, pastoral, priestly, sacerdotal, spiritual. 2 office, secretarial, white-collar.

clerihew /'klerɪhju:/ *noun* witty or comic 4-line biographical verse.

clerk /klɑ:k/ *noun* 1 person employed to keep records, accounts, etc. 2 secretary or agent of local council, court, etc. 3 lay officer of church. ● *verb* work as clerk.
■ *noun* 1 assistant, bookkeeper, computer operator, copyist, filing clerk, office worker, *colloquial derogatory* pen-pusher, receptionist, secretary, shorthand typist, *esp. US* stenographer, typist. 2 recorder, scribe, secretary.

clever /'klevə/ *adjective* (**-er**, **-est**) 1 skilful, talented; quick to understand and learn. 2 adroit. 3 ingenious. □ **cleverly** *adverb*. **cleverness** *noun*.
■ 1 able, academic, accomplished, acute, adept, apt, artistic, astute, brainy, bright, brilliant, capable, discerning, expert, gifted, intellectual, intelligent, judicious, keen, knowing, knowledgeable, observant, penetrating, perceptive, percipient, perspicacious, precocious, quick, quick-witted, sagacious, sage, sensible, sharp, shrewd, skilful, skilled, smart, subtle, talented, wise, witty. 2 adroit, deft, dexterous, handy, skilful, skilled. 3 artful, astute, canny, crafty, creative, cunning, *colloquial* cute, foxy, guileful, imaginative, ingenious, inventive, resourceful, shrewd, slick, sly, subtle, wily. □ **cleverness** ability, acuteness, astuteness, brilliance, cunning, expertise, ingenuity, intellect, intelligence, mastery, quickness, sagacity, sharpness, shrewdness, skill, subtlety, talent, wisdom, wit.

cliché /'kli:ʃeɪ/ *noun* hackneyed phrase or opinion.
■ banality, *colloquial* chestnut, commonplace, platitude, stereotype, truism, well-worn phrase.

clichéd *adjective* hackneyed, full of clichés.
■ see HACKNEYED.

click *noun* slight sharp sound. ● *verb* 1 (cause to) make click. 2 *colloquial* become clear or understood. 3 *colloquial* be successful. 4 (+ *with*) *colloquial* become friendly with.

client /'klaɪənt/ *noun* 1 person using services of lawyer or other professional person. 2 customer.
■ consumer, customer, patient, patron, shopper, user; (*clients*) clientele.

clientele /kli:ɒn'tel/ *noun* 1 clients collectively. 2 customers.

cliff *noun* steep rock face, esp. on coast. □ **cliffhanger** story etc. with strong element of suspense.
■ bluff, crag, escarpment, precipice, rock face, scar.

climacteric /klaɪ'mæktərɪk/ *noun* period of life when fertility and sexual activity are in decline.

climate /'klaɪmɪt/ *noun* 1 prevailing weather conditions of an area. 2 region with particular weather conditions. 3 prevailing trend of opinion etc. □ **climatic** /-'mæt-/ *adjective*. **climatically** /-'mæt-/ *adverb*.
■ 1 see WEATHER *noun*. 3 ambience, atmosphere, aura, disposition, environment, feeling, mood, spirit, temper, trend.

climax /'klaɪmæks/ *noun* 1 event or point of greatest intensity or interest, culmination. 2 point of greatest sexual excitement. ● *verb colloquial* reach or bring to a climax. □ **climactic** *adjective*.
■ *noun* 1 acme, apex, apogee, crisis, culmination, head, highlight, high point, peak, summit, zenith. 2 orgasm.

climb /klaɪm/ *verb* 1 (often + *up*) ascend, mount, go up. 2 (of plant) grow up wall etc. by clinging etc. 3 rise, esp. in social rank. 4 slope upwards. 5 reach top of (mountain etc.). ● *noun* 1 action of climbing. 2 hill etc. (to be) climbed. □ **climb down** 1 descend. 2 withdraw from position taken in argument. □ **climber** *noun*.
■ *verb* 1 ascend, clamber up, go up, mount, move up, scale, shin up, soar, swarm up. 4 incline, rise, slope up. 5 conquer, reach top of. ● *noun* 1 ascent. 2 ascent, grade, gradient, hill, incline, pitch, rise, slope. □ **climb down** 1 see DESCEND 1.

clime *noun literary* 1 region. 2 climate.

clinch *verb* 1 confirm or settle conclusively. 2 (of boxers) become too closely engaged. 3 secure (nail or rivet) by driving point sideways when through. ● *noun* 1 clinching. 2 resulting state. 3 *colloquial* embrace.

■ *verb* **1** agree, close, complete, conclude, confirm, decide, determine, finalize, make certain of, ratify, secure, settle, shake hands on, sign, verify.

cling *verb* (*past & past participle* **clung**) **1** (often + *to*) adhere. **2** (+ *to*) be emotionally dependent on or unwilling to give up. **3** (often + *to*) maintain grasp. □ **cling film** thin transparent plastic covering for food. □ **clingy** *adjective* (**-ier, -iest**).
■ **1** adhere, attach, fasten, fix, hold fast, stick. **2** (*cling to*) see KEEP *verb* 1,2. **3** (*cling to*) see HOLD[1] *verb* 1.

clinic /ˈklɪnɪk/ *noun* **1** private or specialized hospital. **2** place or occasion for giving medical treatment or specialist advice. **3** teaching of medicine at hospital bedside.
■ **1** health centre, infirmary, medical centre. **2** infirmary, sickbay, surgery.

clinical *adjective* **1** of or for the treatment of patients. **2** objective, coldly detached. **3** (of room etc.) bare, functional. □ **clinically** *adverb*.

clink[1] *noun* sharp ringing sound. ● *verb* (cause to) make clink.

clink[2] *noun slang* prison.

clinker /ˈklɪŋkə/ *noun* **1** mass of slag or lava. **2** stony residue from burnt coal.

clinker-built *adjective* (of boat) with external planks overlapping downwards.

clip[1] *noun* **1** device for holding things together. **2** piece of jewellery fastened by clip. **3** set of attached cartridges for firearm. ● *verb* (**-pp-**) fix with clip. □ **clipboard** board with spring clip for holding papers etc.
■ *verb* clasp, fasten, pin, staple.

clip[2] *verb* (**-pp-**) **1** cut with shears or scissors. **2** cut hair or wool of. **3** *colloquial* hit sharply. **4** omit (letter) from word; omit parts of (words uttered). **5** punch hole in (ticket) to show it has been used. **6** cut from newspaper etc. ● *noun* **1** clipping. **2** *colloquial* sharp blow. **3** extract from motion picture. **4** yield of wool.
■ *verb* **1, 2** crop, cut, dock, prune, shear, snip, trim. ● *noun* **3** bit, cutting, excerpt, extract, fragment, part, passage, portion, quotation, section, snippet, trailer.

clipper *noun* **1** (usually in *plural*) instrument for clipping. **2** *historical* fast sailing ship.

clipping *noun* piece clipped, esp. from newspaper.

clique /kliːk/ *noun* exclusive group of people. □ **cliquey** *adjective* (**cliquier, cliquiest**). **cliquish** *adjective*.

clitoris /ˈklɪtərɪs/ *noun* small erectile part of female genitals.

Cllr *abbreviation* Councillor.

cloak *noun* **1** loose usually sleeveless outdoor garment. **2** covering. ● *verb* **1** cover with cloak. **2** conceal, disguise. □ **cloakroom 1** room for outdoor clothes or luggage. **2** *euphemistic* lavatory.

■ *noun* **1** cape, cope, mantle, poncho, robe, wrap. **2** see COVERING. ● *verb* **1** cover, mantle, shroud, wrap. **2** conceal, cover, disguise, hide, mantle, mask, screen, shroud, veil, wrap.

clobber[1] /ˈklɒbə/ *verb slang* **1** hit (repeatedly). **2** defeat. **3** criticize severely.

clobber[2] /ˈklɒbə/ *noun slang* clothing, belongings.

cloche /klɒʃ/ *noun* **1** small translucent cover for outdoor plants. **2** woman's close-fitting bell-shaped hat.

clock[1] *noun* **1** instrument measuring and showing time by hands on dial or by digital display. **2** measuring device resembling this. **3** *colloquial* speedometer, taximeter, or stopwatch. **4** seed-head of dandelion. ● *verb colloquial* **1** (often + *up*) attain or register (distance etc.). **2** time (race etc.) by stopwatch. □ **clock in (or on), or out (or off)** register time of arrival, or departure, by automatic clock. **clockwise** (moving) in same direction as hands of clock. **clockwork** mechanism with coiled springs etc. on clock principle. **like clockwork** with mechanical precision.
■ *noun* **1** chronometer, timepiece. **3** meter.

clock[2] *noun* ornamental pattern on side of stocking or sock.

clod *noun* lump of earth or clay.

clog *noun* wooden-soled shoe. ● *verb* (**-gg-**) **1** (often + *up*) (cause to) become obstructed; choke. **2** impede.
■ *verb* **1** block, bung up, choke, close, congest, dam, fill, jam, obstruct, plug, stop up. **2** see IMPEDE.

cloister /ˈklɔɪstə/ *noun* **1** covered walk esp. in college or ecclesiastical building. **2** monastic life; seclusion. ● *verb* seclude.

clone *noun* **1** group of organisms produced asexually from one ancestor. **2** one such organism. **3** *colloquial* person or thing regarded as identical to another. ● *verb* (**-ning**) propagate as clone.

close[1] /kləʊs/ *adjective* **1** (often + *to*) at short distance or interval. **2** having strong or immediate relation. **3** corresponding almost precisely. **4** (almost) in contact. **5** dense, compact. **6** nearly equal. **7** rigorous; concentrated. **8** stifling. **9** shut. **10** secret; secretive. **11** niggardly. ● *adverb* at short distance or interval. ● *noun* **1** street closed at one end. **2** precinct of cathedral. □ **close-fisted** niggardly. **close harmony** singing of parts within an octave. **close-knit 1** tightly interlocked. **2** closely united. **close season** season when killing of game etc. is illegal. **close shave** *colloquial* narrow escape. **close-up** photograph etc. taken at short range. □ **closely** *adverb*. **closeness** *noun*.
■ *adjective* **1** accessible, adjacent, adjoining, at hand, convenient, handy, near, neighbouring, point-blank (*range*). **2** affectionate, attached, dear, devoted, familiar, fond, friendly, intimate, loving, *colloquial* thick. **3** alike, analogous, comparable, compatible, corresponding, related, resembling, similar. **5** compact, compressed, congested,

cramped, crowded, dense, *colloquial* jam-packed, packed, thick. **7** attentive, careful, concentrated, detailed, minute, painstaking, precise, rigorous, searching, thorough. **8** airless, *colloquial* fuggy, humid, muggy, oppressive, stale, stifling, stuffy, suffocating, sweltering, unventilated, warm. **10** confidential, private, reserved, reticent, secret, secretive, taciturn. **11** illiberal, mean, *colloquial* mingy, miserly, niggardly, parsimonious, penurious, stingy, *colloquial* tight, tight-fisted, ungenerous.

close[2] /kləʊz/ *verb* (**-sing**) **1** shut. **2** block up. **3** bring or come to an end. **4** end day's business. **5** bring or come closer or into contact. **6** (often + *up*) (of gap) make or become smaller. **7** make (electric circuit) continuous. ● *noun* conclusion, end. □ **closed-circuit** (of television) transmitted by wires to restricted number of receivers. **close down** discontinue working. **closed shop** business etc. where employees must belong to specified trade union.

■ *verb* **1** bolt, fasten, lock, make inaccessible, padlock, put out of bounds, seal, secure, shut. **2** bar, barricade, block, make impassable, obstruct, seal off, stop up. **3** complete, conclude, culminate, discontinue, end, finish, settle, stop, terminate, wind up. **5** come together, connect, draw together, join up. **6** (*close up*) narrow, reduce, shorten. ● *noun* cadence, cessation, coda, completion, conclusion, culmination, denouement, end, finale, finish, stop, termination.

closet /ˈklɒzɪt/ *noun* **1** small room. **2** cupboard. **3** water-closet. ● *adjective* secret. ● *verb* (**-t-**) shut away, esp. in private consultation etc.

closure /ˈkləʊʒə/ *noun* **1** closing; closed state. **2** procedure for ending debate.

clot *noun* **1** thick lump formed from liquid, esp. blood. **2** *colloquial* foolish person. ● *verb* (**-tt-**) form into clots.

■ *noun* **1** embolism, lump, mass, thrombosis. ● *verb* coagulate, coalesce, congeal, curdle, set, solidify, stiffen, thicken.

cloth /klɒθ/ *noun* **1** woven or felted material. **2** piece of this. **3** (**the cloth**) the clergy.

■ **1** fabric, material, stuff, textile.

clothe /kləʊð/ *verb* (**-thing**; *past & past participle* **clothed** or **clad**) **1** put clothes on; provide with clothes. **2** cover as with clothes.

■ **1** array, attire, cover, deck, drape, dress, fit out, garb, kit out, robe, swathe, wrap up. **2** see COVER *verb* 1.

clothes /kləʊðz/ *plural noun* **1** things worn to cover body and limbs. **2** bedclothes. □ **clothes horse** frame for airing washed clothes.

■ **1** *formal* apparel, attire, *slang* clobber, clothing, costume, dress, ensemble, finery, garb, garments, *colloquial* gear, *colloquial* get-up, outfit, *archaic* raiment, *colloquial* rig-out, suit, *colloquial* togs, trousseau, underclothes, uniform, vestments, wardrobe, wear, *archaic* weeds.

clothier /ˈkləʊðɪə/ *noun* dealer in men's clothes.

clothing /ˈkləʊðɪŋ/ *noun* clothes.

cloud /klaʊd/ *noun* **1** visible mass of condensed watery vapour floating in air. **2** mass of smoke or dust. **3** (+ *of*) great number of (birds, insects, etc.) moving together. **4** state of gloom, trouble, or suspicion. ● *verb* **1** cover or darken with cloud(s). **2** (often + *over*, *up*) become overcast or gloomy. **3** make unclear. □ **cloudburst** sudden violent rainstorm. □ **cloudless** *adjective*.

■ *noun* **1** fog, haze, mist, vapour. **2** billow. ● *verb* **1** cover, darken, dull, eclipse, enshroud, mantle, mist up, obscure, screen, shroud, veil. **2** darken, dim. **3** blur, conceal, confuse, dull, hide, muddy, obfuscate, obscure, veil. □ **cloudless** bright, clear, starlit, sunny, unclouded.

cloudy *adjective* (**-ier**, **-iest**) **1** covered with clouds. **2** not transparent, unclear. □ **cloudiness** *noun*.

■ **1** dark, dismal, dull, gloomy, grey, leaden, lowering, overcast, sullen, sunless. **2** (*cloudy windows*) blurred, blurry, dim, misty, opaque, steamy, unclear; (*cloudy liquid*) hazy, milky, muddy, murky.

clout /klaʊt/ *noun* **1** heavy blow. **2** *colloquial* influence; power of effective action. **3** piece of cloth or clothing. ● *verb* hit hard.

clove[1] /kləʊv/ *noun* dried bud of tropical tree, used as spice.

clove[2] /kləʊv/ *noun* segment of compound bulb, esp. of garlic.

clove[3] *past* of CLEAVE[1].

clove hitch *noun* knot for fastening rope round pole etc.

cloven /ˈkləʊv(ə)n/ *adjective* split. □ **cloven hoof, foot** divided hoof, as of oxen, sheep, etc., or the Devil.

clover /ˈkləʊvə/ *noun* kind of trefoil used as fodder. □ **in clover** in ease and luxury.

clown /klaʊn/ *noun* **1** comic entertainer, esp. in circus. **2** foolish or playful person. ● *verb* (often + *about*, *around*) behave like clown. □ **clownish** *adjective*.

■ *noun* buffoon, comedian, comic, *historical* fool, funny man, funny woman, *historical* jester, joker, wag.

cloy *verb* satiate or sicken by sweetness, richness, etc.

club *noun* **1** heavy stick used as weapon. **2** stick with head, used in golf. **3** association of people for social, sporting, etc. purposes. **4** premises of this. **5** playing card of suit marked with black trefoils. **6** (in *plural*) this suit. ● *verb* (**-bb-**) **1** strike (as) with club. **2** (+ *together*) combine, esp. to make up sum of money. □ **club foot** congenitally deformed foot. **clubhouse** premises of club. **clubland** area with many nightclubs. **clubroot** disease of cabbages etc. **club sandwich** sandwich with 2 layers of filling and 3 slices of bread or toast.

■ *noun* **1** bat, baton, bludgeon, *colloquial* cosh, cudgel, staff, stick, truncheon. **3** association, brotherhood, circle, company, federation, fellowship, *US* fraternity, group, guild, league, order, organization, party, set, sisterhood, society, *US* sorority, union. ● *verb* **1** see HIT *verb* 1. **2** (*club together*) see COMBINE *verb* 1.

clubbable /ˈklʌbəb(ə)l/ *adjective* sociable.

cluck *noun* chattering cry of hen. ● *verb* emit cluck(s).

clue *noun* **1** guiding or suggestive fact. **2** piece of evidence used in detection of crime. **3** word(s) used to indicate word(s) for insertion in crossword. ● *verb* (**clues**, **clued**, **cluing** or **clueing**) provide clue to. □ **clue in, up** *slang* inform.
■ *noun* **1, 2** hint, idea, indication, indicator, inkling, key, lead, *colloquial* pointer, sign, suggestion, suspicion, tip, tip-off, trace.

clueless /ˈkluːlɪs/ *adjective colloquial* ignorant, stupid. □ **cluelessly** *adverb*. **cluelessness** *noun*.

clump *noun* (+ *of*) cluster, esp. of trees. ● *verb* **1** form clump. **2** heap or plant together. **3** tread heavily.
■ *noun* bunch, bundle, cluster, collection, group, mass, shock (*of hair*), thicket, tuft.

clumsy /ˈklʌmzɪ/ *adjective* (**-ier**, **-iest**) **1** awkward in movement or shape. **2** difficult to handle or use. **3** done without skill. **4** tactless. □ **clumsily** *adverb*. **clumsiness** *noun*.
■ **1** awkward, blundering, bumbling, bungling, fumbling, gangling, gawky, graceless, *colloquial* ham-fisted, heavy-handed, *colloquial* hulking, inelegant, lumbering, maladroit, shambling, uncoordinated, ungainly, ungraceful, unskilful. **2** awkward, badly made, bulky, cumbersome, heavy, inconvenient, inelegant, large, ponderous, rough, shapeless, unmanageable, unwieldy. **3** see AMATEURISH (AMATEUR). **4** boorish, gauche, ill-judged, inappropriate, indelicate, indiscreet, inept, insensitive, tactless, uncouth, undiplomatic, unsubtle, unsuitable.

clung *past & past participle* of CLING.

cluster /ˈklʌstə/ *noun* close group or bunch of similar people or things. ● *verb* **1** be in or form into cluster(s). **2** (+ *round*, *around*) gather round.
■ *noun* assembly, batch, bunch, bundle, clump, collection, crowd, gathering, group, knot, tuft.
● *verb* **2** see GATHER *verb* 1.

clutch¹ *verb* **1** seize eagerly; grasp tightly. **2** (+ *at*) snatch at. ● *noun* **1** tight or (in *plural*) cruel grasp. **2** (in vehicle) device for connecting engine to transmission. **3** pedal operating this. □ **clutch bag** handbag without handles.
■ *verb* **1** catch, clasp, cling to, grab, grasp, grip, hang on to, hold on to, seize, snatch, take hold of. **2** (*clutch at*) grab at, grasp at, seize, snatch at. ● *noun* **1** clasp, grasp, grip, hold; (*clutches*) control, possession, power.

clutch² *noun* **1** set of eggs. **2** brood of chickens.

clutter /ˈklʌtə/ *noun* crowded untidy collection

of things. ● *verb* (often + *up*, *with*) crowd untidily; fill with clutter.
■ *noun* chaos, confusion, disorder, jumble, junk, litter, lumber, mess, muddle, odds and ends, rubbish, tangle, untidiness. ● *verb* be scattered about, fill, lie about, litter, make untidy, mess up, muddle, strew.

cm *abbreviation* centimetre(s).

Cmdr. *abbreviation* Commander.

CND *abbreviation* Campaign for Nuclear Disarmament.

CO *abbreviation* Commanding Officer.

Co. *abbreviation* **1** company. **2** county.

co- /kəʊ/ *prefix* **1** (added to nouns) joint, mutual, common. **2** (added to adjectives and adverbs) jointly, mutually. **3** (added to verbs) together with another or others.

c/o *abbreviation* care of.

coach *noun* **1** single-decker bus usually for longer journeys. **2** railway carriage. **3** closed horse-drawn carriage. **4** sports trainer or private tutor. ● *verb* train or teach. □ **coachload** group of tourists etc. travelling by coach. **coachman** driver of horse-drawn carriage. **coachwork** bodywork of road or rail vehicle.
■ *noun* **1** bus, *historical* charabanc. **4** instructor, teacher, trainer, tutor. ● *verb* direct, drill, exercise, guide, instruct, prepare, teach, train, tutor.

coagulate /kəʊˈægjʊleɪt/ *verb* (**-ting**) **1** change from liquid to semi-solid. **2** clot, curdle. □ **coagulant** *noun*. **coagulation** *noun*.
■ **1** *colloquial* jell, set, solidify, stiffen, thicken. **2** clot, congeal, curdle.

coal *noun* **1** hard black mineral used as fuel etc. **2** piece of this. □ **coalface** exposed surface of coal in mine. **coalfield** area yielding coal. **coal gas** mixed gases formerly extracted from coal and used for heating, cooking, etc. **coal mine** place where coal is dug. **coal miner** worker in coal mine. **coal scuttle** container for coal for domestic fire. **coal tar** tar extracted from coal. **coal tit** small bird with greyish plumage.

coalesce /kəʊəˈles/ *verb* (**-cing**) come together and form a whole. □ **coalescence** *noun*. **coalescent** *adjective*.

coalition /kəʊəˈlɪʃ(ə)n/ *noun* **1** temporary alliance, esp. of political parties. **2** fusion into one whole.

coaming /ˈkəʊmɪŋ/ *noun* raised border round ship's hatches etc.

coarse /kɔːs/ *adjective* **1** rough or loose in texture; of large particles. **2** lacking refinement; crude, obscene. □ **coarse fish** freshwater fish other than salmon and trout. □ **coarsely** *adverb*. **coarsen** *verb*. **coarseness** *noun*.
■ **1** bristly, gritty, hairy, harsh, lumpy, prickly, rough, scratchy, sharp, stony, uneven, unfinished. **2** bawdy, blasphemous, boorish, *derogatory* common, crude, earthy, foul, immodest, impolite, improper, impure, indecent, indelicate, offensive, ribald, *colloquial* rude, smutty, uncouth, unrefined, vulgar.

coast *noun* border of land near sea; seashore.
● *verb* 1 ride or move (usually downhill) without use of power. 2 make progress without exertion. 3 sail along coast. □ **coastguard** (member of) group of people employed to keep watch on coasts, prevent smuggling, etc. **coastline** line of seashore, esp. with regard to its shape. □ **coastal** *adjective*.

> ■ *noun* beach, coastline, littoral, seaboard, seashore, seaside, shore. ● *verb* 1 cruise, drift, freewheel, glide, sail, skim, slide, slip. □ *coastal* maritime, nautical, naval, seaside.

coaster *noun* 1 ship that sails along coast. 2 tray or mat for bottle or glass.

coat *noun* 1 sleeved outer garment; overcoat, jacket. 2 animal's fur or hair. 3 layer of paint etc. ● *verb* 1 (usually + *with*, *in*) cover with coat or layer. 2 form covering on. □ **coat of arms** heraldic bearings or shield. **coat-hanger** shaped piece of wood etc. for hanging clothes on.

> ■ *noun* 1 anorak, blazer, cagoule, *historical* doublet, duffle coat, greatcoat, jacket, jerkin, mackintosh, overcoat, parka, raincoat, tailcoat, topcoat, trench coat, tunic, windcheater. 2 fleece, fur, hair, hide, pelt, skin. 3 coating, cover, covering, film, finish, glaze, layer, membrane, overlay, patina, sheet, veneer, wash. ● *verb* see COVER *verb* 1. □ *coat of arms* see CREST *noun* 4.

coating *noun* 1 layer of paint etc. 2 cloth for coats.

coax *verb* 1 (usually + *into*, *to*) persuade gradually or by flattery. 2 (+ *out of*) obtain (thing) from (person) thus. 3 manipulate gently.

> ■ 1 allure, beguile, cajole, charm, decoy, entice, induce, inveigle, manipulate, persuade, tempt, urge, wheedle. 2 (*coax out of*) extract from, prise out of, wheedle out of, winkle out of, worm out of.

coaxial /kəʊˈæksɪəl/ *adjective* 1 having common axis. 2 (of electric cable etc.) transmitting by means of two concentric conductors separated by insulator.

cob *noun* 1 roundish lump. 2 domed loaf. 3 corn cob. 4 large hazelnut. 5 sturdy short-legged riding-horse. 6 male swan.

cobalt /ˈkəʊbɔːlt/ *noun* 1 silvery-white metallic element. 2 (colour of) deep blue pigment made from it.

cobber /ˈkɒbə/ *noun Australian & NZ colloquial* companion, friend.

cobble[1] /ˈkɒb(ə)l/ *noun* (in full **cobblestone**) rounded stone used for paving. ● *verb* (-**ling**) pave with cobbles.

cobble[2] /ˈkɒb(ə)l/ *verb* (-**ling**) 1 mend or patch (esp. shoes). 2 (often + *together*) assemble roughly.

> ■ 1 mend, patch up. 2 (*cobble together*) knock up, put together.

cobbler *noun* 1 mender of shoes. 2 (in *plural*) *slang* nonsense.

COBOL /ˈkəʊbɒl/ *noun* computer language for use in business operations.

cobra /ˈkəʊbrə/ *noun* venomous hooded snake.

cobweb /ˈkɒbweb/ *noun* spider's network or thread. □ **cobwebby** *adjective*.

coca /ˈkəʊkə/ *noun* 1 S. American shrub. 2 its leaves chewed as stimulant.

cocaine /kəʊˈkeɪn/ *noun* drug from coca, used as local anaesthetic and as stimulant.

coccyx /ˈkɒksɪks/ *noun* (*plural* **coccyges** /-dʒiːz/) bone at base of spinal column.

cochineal /kɒtʃɪˈniːl/ *noun* 1 scarlet dye. 2 insects whose dried bodies yield this.

cock[1] *noun* 1 male bird, esp. domestic fowl. 2 *slang* (as form of address) friend, fellow. 3 *slang* nonsense. 4 firing lever in gun released by trigger. 5 tap or valve controlling flow. ● *verb* 1 raise or make upright. 2 turn or move (eye or ear) attentively or knowingly. 3 set (hat etc.) aslant. 4 raise cock of (gun). □ **cock-a-hoop** exultant. **cock-a-leekie** Scottish soup of boiled fowl with leeks. **cockcrow** dawn. **cock-eyed** *colloquial* 1 crooked, askew. 2 absurd.

cock[2] *noun* conical heap of hay or straw.

cockade /kɒˈkeɪd/ *noun* rosette etc. worn in hat.

cockatoo /kɒkəˈtuː/ *noun* crested parrot.

cockchafer /ˈkɒktʃeɪfə/ *noun* large pale brown beetle.

cocker /ˈkɒkə/ *noun* (in full **cocker spaniel**) small spaniel.

cockerel /ˈkɒkər(ə)l/ *noun* young cock.

cockle /ˈkɒk(ə)l/ *noun* 1 edible bivalve shellfish. 2 its shell. 3 (in full **cockleshell**) small shallow boat. 4 pucker or wrinkle. □ **cockles of the heart** innermost feelings.

cockney /ˈkɒknɪ/ *noun* (*plural* **-s**) 1 native of London, esp. East End. 2 cockney dialect. ● *adjective* of cockneys.

cockpit *noun* 1 place for pilot etc. in aircraft or spacecraft or for driver in racing car. 2 arena of war etc.

cockroach /ˈkɒkrəʊtʃ/ *noun* dark brown insect infesting esp. kitchens.

cockscomb /ˈkɒkskəʊm/ *noun* cock's crest.

cocksure /kɒkˈʃʊə/ *adjective* arrogantly confident.

cocktail /ˈkɒkteɪl/ *noun* 1 drink of spirits, fruit juices, etc. 2 appetizer containing shellfish etc. 3 any hybrid mixture. □ **cocktail stick** small pointed stick.

cocky *adjective* (-**ier**, -**iest**) *colloquial* conceited, arrogant. □ **cockiness** *noun*.

coco /ˈkəʊkəʊ/ *noun* (*plural* **-s**) coconut palm.

cocoa /ˈkəʊkəʊ/ *noun* 1 powder of crushed cacao seeds. 2 drink made from this.

coconut /ˈkəʊkənʌt/ *noun* large brown seed of coco, with edible white lining enclosing milky juice. □ **coconut matting** matting made from fibre of coconut husks. **coconut shy** fairground sideshow where balls are thrown to dislodge coconuts.

cocoon /kəˈkuːn/ *noun* 1 silky case spun by

larva to protect it as pupa. **2** protective covering. ● *verb* wrap (as) in cocoon.

cocotte /kə'kɒt/ *noun* small fireproof dish for cooking and serving food.

COD *abbreviation* cash (*US* collect) on delivery.

cod[1] *noun* (also **codfish**) (*plural* same) large sea fish. □ **cod liver oil** medicinal oil rich in vitamins.

cod[2] *noun & verb* (**-dd-**) *slang* **1** hoax. **2** parody.

coda /'kəʊdə/ *noun* final passage of piece of music.

coddle /'kɒd(ə)l/ *verb* (**-ling**) **1** treat as an invalid, pamper. **2** cook in water just below boiling point. □ **coddler** *noun*.

code *noun* **1** system of signals or of symbols etc. used for secrecy, brevity, or computer processing of information. **2** systematic set of laws etc. **3** standard of moral behaviour. ● *verb* (**-ding**) put into code.

■ *noun* **1** cipher, secret language, signals, sign system. **2** laws, regulations, rules, system. **3** etiquette, form, manners, principles, protocol, rules, standard, system.

codeine /'kəʊdi:n/ *noun* alkaloid derived from morphine, used as pain-killer.

codex /'kəʊdeks/ *noun* (*plural* **codices** /'kəʊdɪsi:z/) manuscript volume esp. of ancient texts.

codger /'kɒdʒə/ *noun* (usually in **old codger**) *colloquial* (strange) person.

codicil /'kəʊdɪsɪl/ *noun* addition to will.

codify /'kəʊdɪfaɪ/ *verb* (**-ies**, **-ied**) arrange (laws etc.) into code. □ **codification** *noun*.

codling[1] /'kɒdlɪŋ/ *noun* (also **codlin**) **1** variety of apple. **2** moth whose larva feeds on apples.

codling[2] *noun* (*plural* same) small cod.

co-education /kəʊedjʊ'keɪʃ(ə)n/ *noun* education of both sexes together. □ **co-educational** *adjective*.

coefficient /kəʊɪ'fɪʃ(ə)nt/ *noun* **1** *Mathematics* quantity or expression placed before and multiplying another. **2** *Physics* multiplier or factor by which a property is measured.

coeliac disease /'si:liæk/ *noun* intestinal disease whose symptoms include adverse reaction to gluten.

coequal /kəʊ'i:kw(ə)l/ *adjective & noun* equal.

coerce /kəʊ'ɜ:s/ *verb* (**-cing**) persuade or restrain by force. □ **coercion** /-'ɜ:ʃ(ə)n/ *noun*. **coercive** *adjective*.

■ bludgeon, browbeat, bully, compel, constrain, dragoon, force, frighten, intimidate, press-gang, pressurize, terrorize. □ **coercion** browbeating, brute force, bullying, compulsion, constraint, duress, force, intimidation, pressure, strong-arm tactics, threats.

coeval /kəʊ'i:v(ə)l/ *formal adjective* of the same age; contemporary. ● *noun* coeval person or thing.

coexist /kəʊɪg'zɪst/ *verb* (often + *with*) exist

together, esp. in mutual tolerance. □ **coexistence** *noun*. **coexistent** *adjective*.

coextensive /kəʊɪk'stensɪv/ *adjective* extending over same space or time.

C. of E. *abbreviation* Church of England.

coffee /'kɒfɪ/ *noun* **1** drink made from roasted and ground seeds of tropical shrub. **2** cup of this. **3** the shrub. **4** the seeds. **5** pale brown. □ **coffee bar** café selling coffee and light refreshments from bar. **coffee bean** seed of coffee. **coffee mill** small machine for grinding coffee beans. **coffee morning** morning gathering, esp. for charity, at which coffee is served. **coffee shop** small restaurant, esp. in hotel or store. **coffee table** small low table. **coffee-table book** large illustrated book.

coffer /'kɒfə/ *noun* **1** large box for valuables. **2** (in *plural*) funds, treasury. **3** sunken panel in ceiling etc.

coffin /'kɒfɪn/ *noun* box in which corpse is buried or cremated.

cog *noun* each of series of projections on wheel etc. transferring motion by engaging with another series. □ **cogged** *adjective*.

cogent /'kəʊdʒ(ə)nt/ *adjective* (of argument etc.) convincing, compelling. □ **cogency** *noun*. **cogently** *adverb*.

■ compelling, conclusive, convincing, effective, forceful, forcible, indisputable, irresistible, logical, persuasive, potent, powerful, rational, sound, strong, unanswerable, weighty, well argued.

cogitate /'kɒdʒɪteɪt/ *verb* (**-ting**) ponder, meditate. □ **cogitation** *noun*.

cognac /'kɒnjæk/ *noun* French brandy.

cognate /'kɒgneɪt/ *adjective* descended from same ancestor or root. ● *noun* cognate person or word.

cognition /kɒg'nɪʃ(ə)n/ *noun* knowing, perceiving, or conceiving, as distinct from emotion and volition. □ **cognitive** /'kɒg-/ *adjective*.

cognizance /'kɒgnɪz(ə)ns/ *noun formal* knowledge or awareness.

cognizant /'kɒgnɪz(ə)nt/ *adjective formal* (+ *of*) having knowledge or being aware of.

cognomen /kɒg'nəʊmen/ *noun* **1** nickname. **2** *Roman History* surname.

cohabit /kəʊ'hæbɪt/ *verb* (**-t-**) live together as husband and wife. □ **cohabitation** *noun*.

cohere /kəʊ'hɪə/ *verb* (**-ring**) **1** stick together. **2** (of reasoning) be logical or consistent.

■ **1** bind, cake, cling together, coalesce, combine, fuse, hold together, join, stick together, unite. **2** hang together, hold.

coherent *adjective* **1** intelligible. **2** consistent, easily understood. □ **coherence** *noun*. **coherently** *adverb*.

■ articulate, connected, consistent, intelligible, logical, lucid, orderly, organized, rational, reasonable, reasoned, sound, structured, systematic, well ordered, well structured.

cohesion /kəʊˈhiːʒ(ə)n/ *noun* **1** sticking together. **2** tendency to cohere. □ **cohesive** /-sɪv/ *adjective.*

cohort /ˈkəʊhɔːt/ *noun* **1** one-tenth of Roman legion. **2** people banded together.

coif /kɔɪf/ *noun historical* close-fitting cap.

coiffeur /kwɑːˈfɜː/ *noun* (*feminine* **coiffeuse** /-ˈfɜːz/) hairdresser.

coiffure /kwɑːˈfjʊə/ *noun* hairstyle.

coil *verb* **1** arrange or be arranged in concentric rings. **2** move sinuously. ● *noun* **1** coiled arrangement (of rope, electrical conductor, etc.). **2** single turn of something coiled. **3** flexible contraceptive device in womb.

   ■ *verb* **1** bend, curl, entwine, loop, roll, spiral, turn, twine, twirl, twist, wind. **2** curl, snake, twist, wind, writhe. ● *noun* **1, 2** circle, convolution, corkscrew, curl, helix, kink, loop, ring, roll, screw, spiral, twirl, twist, vortex, whirl, whorl.

coin *noun* **1** stamped disc of metal as official money. **2** metal money. ● *verb* **1** make (coins) by stamping. **2** invent (word, phrase). □ **coin box** telephone operated by coins.

   ■ *noun* **1** bit, piece. **2** cash, change, coppers, loose change, silver, small change. ● *verb* **1** forge, make, mint, mould, stamp. **2** conceive, concoct, create, devise, dream up, fabricate, hatch, introduce, invent, make up, originate, produce, *colloquial* think up.

coinage *noun* **1** coining. **2** system of coins in use. **3** invention of word. **4** invented word.

coincide /kəʊɪnˈsaɪd/ *verb* (**-ding**) **1** occur at same time. **2** (often + *with*) agree or be identical.

   ■ **1** clash, coexist, come together, concur, fall together, happen together, synchronize. **2** accord, agree, be congruent, be identical, be in unison, be the same, concur, correspond, harmonize, match, square, tally.

coincidence /kəʊˈɪnsɪd(ə)ns/ *noun* **1** coinciding; agreement. **2** remarkable concurrence of events etc., apparently by chance. □ **coincident** *adjective.*

   ■ **1** accord, agreement, coexistence, concurrence, conformity, congruence, congruity, correspondence, harmony, similarity. **2** accident, chance, fluke, luck.

coincidental /kəʊɪnsɪˈdent(ə)l/ *adjective* in the nature of or resulting from coincidence. □ **coincidentally** *adverb.*

coir /ˈkɔɪə/ *noun* coconut fibre used for ropes, matting, etc.

coition /kəʊˈɪʃ(ə)n/ *noun* coitus.

coitus /ˈkəʊɪtəs/ *noun* sexual intercourse. □ **coital** *adjective.*

coke[1] *noun* solid left after gases have been extracted from coal. ● *verb* (**-king**) convert (coal) into coke.

coke[2] *noun slang* cocaine.

Col. *abbreviation* Colonel.

col *noun* depression in summit-line of mountain chain.

cola /ˈkəʊlə/ *noun* **1** W. African tree with seeds containing caffeine. **2** carbonated drink flavoured with these.

colander /ˈkʌləndə/ *noun* perforated vessel used as strainer in cookery.

cold /kəʊld/ *adjective* **1** of or at low temperature. **2** not heated; having lost heat. **3** feeling cold. **4** (of colour) suggesting cold. **5** *colloquial* unconscious. **6** lacking ardour or friendliness; apathetic. **7** dispiriting. **8** (of hunting-scent) grown faint. ● *noun* **1** prevalence of low temperature; cold weather. **2** infection of nose or throat. ● *adverb* unrehearsed. □ **cold-blooded 1** having body temperature varying with that of environment. **2** callous. **cold-bloodedness** *noun.* **cold call** marketing call on person not previously interested in product. **cold cream** cleansing ointment. **cold feet** fear, reluctance. **cold fusion** nuclear fusion at room temperature. **cold-hearted** unfriendly, lacking warmth. **cold shoulder** unfriendly treatment. **cold-shoulder** be unfriendly to. **cold sweat** state of sweating induced by fear or illness. **cold turkey** *slang* abrupt withdrawal from addictive drugs. **cold war** hostility between nations without actual fighting. **in cold blood** without emotion. **throw cold water on** discourage. □ **coldly** *adverb.* **coldness** *noun.*

   ■ *adjective* **1** arctic, biting, bitter, bleak, *literary* chill, chilly, cool, crisp, cutting, draughty, freezing, fresh, frosty, glacial, ice-cold, icy, inclement, keen, *colloquial* nippy, numbing, *colloquial* or *dialect* parky, penetrating, *colloquial* perishing, piercing, polar, raw, shivery, snowy, wintry. **2** chilled, unheated. **3** chilled, freezing, frozen, numbed, shivering, shivery. **6** aloof, apathetic, callous, cold-blooded, cold-hearted, cool, cruel, dispassionate, distant, frigid, hard, hard-hearted, heartless, impassive, impersonal, indifferent, inhospitable, inhuman, insensitive, passionless, phlegmatic, reserved, stand-offish, stony, thick-skinned, uncaring, unconcerned, undemonstrative, unemotional, unenthusiastic, unfeeling, unfriendly, unkind, unresponsive, unsympathetic. ● *noun* **1** chill, coldness, coolness, freshness, iciness, wintriness. **2** catarrh, *colloquial* flu, influenza, the sniffles. □ **cold-blooded** barbaric, brutal, callous, cruel, hard-hearted, inhuman, inhumane, merciless, pitiless, ruthless, savage.

coleslaw /ˈkəʊlslɔː/ *noun* salad of sliced raw cabbage etc.

coley /ˈkəʊlɪ/ *noun* (*plural* **-s**) any of several edible fish, esp. rock-salmon.

colic /ˈkɒlɪk/ *noun* spasmodic abdominal pain. □ **colicky** *adjective.*

colitis /kəˈlaɪtɪs/ *noun* inflammation of colon.

collaborate /kəˈlæbəreɪt/ *verb* (**-ting**) (often + *with*) work jointly. □ **collaboration** *noun.* **collaborative** /-rətɪv/ *adjective.* **collaborator** *noun.*

   ■ band together, cooperate, join forces, pull together, team up, work together; (*collaborate with enemy*) collude, connive, conspire.

□ **collaboration** association, concerted effort, cooperation, partnership, teamwork; (*collaboration with enemy*) collusion, connivance, conspiracy, treachery. **collaborator** accomplice, ally, assistant, associate, colleague, confederate, fellow worker, helper, helpmate, partner, partner in crime, team-mate; (*collaborator with enemy*) Judas, quisling, *colloquial* traitor.

collage /'kɒlɑːʒ/ *noun* picture made by gluing pieces of paper etc. on to backing.

collapse /kə'læps/ *noun* **1** falling down of structure. **2** sudden failure of plan etc. **3** physical or mental breakdown. ● *verb* (**-sing**) **1** (cause to) fall down or in, fold up, or give way. **2** undergo physical or mental breakdown. **3** *colloquial* relax completely after effort. **4** (cause to) fail or lose value. □ **collapsible** *adjective*.

■ *noun* **1** breakdown, breakup, cave-in, destruction, disintegration, fall, ruin, subsidence. **2** downfall, end, failure, ruin, ruination. ● *verb* **1** break down, break up, buckle, cave in, crumble, crumple, deflate, disintegrate, double up, fall apart, fall down, fall in, fold up, give way, *slang* go west, sink, subside, tumble down. **2** become ill, black out, break down, *colloquial* crack up, faint, fall apart, founder, go to pieces, go under, keel over, pass out, *literary* swoon. **4** crash, deteriorate, diminish, drop, fail, slump, worsen. □ **collapsible** adjustable, folding, retractable, telescopic.

collar /'kɒlə/ *noun* **1** neckband, upright or turned over, of coat, shirt, dress, etc. **2** leather band round animal's neck. **3** band, ring, or pipe in machinery. ● *verb* **1** seize by the collar or neck. **2** *colloquial* capture. **3** *colloquial* accost. **4** *slang* appropriate. □ **collar-bone** bone joining breastbone and shoulder blade.

collate /kə'leɪt/ *verb* (**-ting**) collect and put in order. □ **collator** *noun*.

collateral /kə'lætər(ə)l/ *noun* security pledged as guarantee for repayment of loan. ● *adjective* **1** side by side. **2** additional but subordinate. **3** descended from same ancestor but by different line. □ **collaterally** *adverb*.

collation *noun* **1** collating. **2** light meal.

colleague /'kɒliːg/ *noun* fellow worker, esp. in profession or business.

■ associate, business partner, collaborator, co-worker, fellow worker.

collect[1] /kə'lekt/ *verb* **1** bring or come together; assemble, accumulate. **2** seek and acquire (books, stamps, etc.). **3** obtain (contributions, taxes, etc.) from people. **4** call for; fetch. **5** concentrate (one's thoughts etc.). **6** (as **collected** *adjective*) not perturbed or distracted. ● *adjective* & *adverb* US (of telephone call, parcel, etc.) to be paid for by recipient.

■ *verb* **1** accumulate, agglomerate, aggregate, amass, assemble, bring together, cluster, come together, concentrate, congregate, convene, converge, crowd, forgather, garner, gather, group, harvest, heap, hoard, lay up, muster, pile up, put by, rally, reserve, save, scrape together, stack up, stockpile, store. **3** be given, obtain, raise, secure,

take. **4** acquire, bring, fetch, get, load up, obtain, pick up. **6** (**collected**) see CALM *adjective* 2.

collect[2] /'kɒlekt/ *noun* short prayer of Anglican or RC Church.

collectable (also **collectible**) /kə'lektɪb(ə)l/ *adjective* worth collecting.

collection /kə'lekʃ(ə)n/ *noun* **1** collecting, being collected. **2** (group of) things collected. **3** collecting of money; money collected, esp. at church service etc.

■ **2** accumulation, array, assemblage, assortment, cluster, conglomeration, group, heap, hoard, mass, pile, set, stack, store. **3** flag day, offertory, voluntary contributions, *colloquial* whip-round.

collective /kə'lektɪv/ *adjective* **1** of or relating to group or society as a whole. **2** joint; shared. ● *noun* **1** cooperative enterprise. **2** its members. □ **collective bargaining** negotiation of wages etc. by organized group of employees. **collective noun** singular noun denoting group of individuals. □ **collectively** *adverb*. **collectivize** *verb* (also **-ise**) (**-zing** or **-sing**).

■ *adjective* combined, common, composite, cooperative, corporate, democratic, group, joint, shared, unified, united.

collectivism *noun* theory or practice of collective ownership of land and means of production. □ **collectivist** *noun* & *adjective*.

collector *noun* **1** person collecting things of interest. **2** person collecting taxes, rents, etc.

colleen /'kɒliːn/ *noun Irish* girl.

college /'kɒlɪdʒ/ *noun* **1** establishment for further, higher, or professional education. **2** teachers and students in a college. **3** school. **4** organized group of people with shared functions and privileges.

■ **1** academy, esp. US conservatory, institute, polytechnic, US school, university.

collegiate /kə'liːdʒɪət/ *adjective* **1** of or constituted as college; corporate. **2** (of university) consisting of different colleges.

collide /kə'laɪd/ *verb* (**-ding**) (often + *with*) come into collision or conflict.

■ (**collide with**) bump into, cannon into, crash into, hit, knock, run into, slam into, smash into, strike, touch.

collie /'kɒli/ *noun* sheepdog originally of Scottish breed.

collier /'kɒliə/ *noun* **1** coal miner. **2** coal ship. **3** member of its crew.

colliery /'kɒliəri/ *noun* (*plural* **-ies**) coal mine and its buildings.

collision /kə'lɪʒ(ə)n/ *noun* **1** violent impact of moving body against another or fixed object. **2** clashing of interests etc.

■ **1** accident, bump, clash, crash, head-on collision, impact, knock, *colloquial* pile-up, smash.

collocate /'kɒləkeɪt/ *verb* (**-ting**) place (word etc.) next to another. □ **collocation** *noun*.

colloid /'kɒlɔɪd/ *noun* **1** substance consisting of minute particles. **2** mixture, esp. viscous solution, of this and another substance. □ **colloidal** *adjective*.

colloquial /kə'ləʊkwɪəl/ *adjective* of ordinary or familiar conversation; informal. □ **colloquially** *adverb*.

■ chatty, conversational, everyday, informal, slangy, vernacular.

colloquialism /kə'ləʊkwɪəlɪz(ə)m/ *noun* colloquial word or phrase.

colloquy /'kɒləkwɪ/ *noun* (*plural* **-quies**) *literary* talk, dialogue.

collude /kə'lu:d/ *verb* (**-ding**) conspire. □ **collusion** /-ʒ(ə)n/ *noun*. **collusive** /-sɪv/ *adjective*.

collywobbles /'kɒlɪwɒb(ə)lz/ *plural noun colloquial* **1** ache or rumbling in stomach. **2** apprehensive feeling.

cologne /kə'ləʊn/ *noun* eau-de-Cologne or similar toilet water.

colon[1] /'kəʊlən/ *noun* punctuation mark (:) used between main clauses or before list or quotation (see panel).

colon[2] /'kəʊlən/ *noun* lower and greater part of large intestine.

colonel /'kɜ:n(ə)l/ *noun* army officer commanding regiment, next in rank below brigadier. □ **colonelcy** *noun* (*plural* **-ies**).

colonial /kə'ləʊnɪəl/ *adjective* **1** of a colony or colonies. **2** of colonialism. ● *noun* inhabitant of colony.

colonialism *noun* policy of having colonies.

colonist /'kɒlənɪst/ *noun* settler in or inhabitant of colony.

■ colonizer, pioneer, settler.

colonize /'kɒlənaɪz/ *verb* (also **-ise**) (**-zing** or **-sing**) **1** establish colony in. **2** join colony. □ **colonization** *noun*. **colonizer** *noun*.

■ **1** occupy, people, populate, settle in.

colonnade /kɒlə'neɪd/ *noun* row of columns, esp. supporting roof. □ **colonnaded** *adjective*.

colony /'kɒlənɪ/ *noun* (*plural* **-ies**) **1** settlement or settlers in new territory remaining subject to mother country. **2** people of one nationality, occupation, etc. forming community in town etc.

3 group of animals that live close together.

■ **1** dependency, dominion, possession, protectorate, province, settlement, territory.

colophon /'kɒləf(ə)n/ *noun* tailpiece in book.

color etc. *US* = COLOUR etc.

Colorado beetle /kɒlə'rɑ:dəʊ/ *noun* small beetle destructive to potato.

coloration /kʌlə'reɪʃ(ə)n/ *noun* (also **colouration**) colouring; arrangement of colours.

coloratura /kɒlərə'tʊərə/ *noun* **1** elaborate passages in vocal music. **2** singer of these, esp. soprano.

colossal /kə'lɒs(ə)l/ *adjective* **1** huge. **2** *colloquial* splendid. □ **colossally** *adverb*.

■ **1** big, elephantine, enormous, gargantuan, giant, gigantic, Herculean, huge, immense, *colloquial* jumbo, mammoth, massive, mighty, monstrous, monumental, prodigious, titanic, towering, vast.

colossus /kə'lɒsəs/ *noun* (*plural* **-ssi** /-saɪ/ or **-ssuses**) **1** statue much bigger than life size. **2** gigantic or remarkable person etc.

colour /'kʌlə/ (*US* **color**) *noun* **1** one, or any mixture, of the constituents into which light is separated in rainbow etc. **2** use of all colours as in photography. **3** colouring substance, esp. paint. **4** skin pigmentation, esp. when dark. **5** ruddiness of face. **6** appearance or aspect. **7** (in *plural*) flag of regiment or ship etc. **8** coloured ribbon, rosette, etc. worn as symbol of school, club, political party, etc. ● *verb* **1** give colour to; paint, stain, dye. **2** blush. **3** influence. □ **colour-blind** unable to distinguish certain colours. **colour-blindness** *noun*. **colour scheme** arrangement of colours. **colour supplement** magazine with colour printing, sold with newspaper.

■ *noun* **1** hue, shade, tincture, tinge, tint, tone. **3** colourant, dye, paint, pigment, stain, tint. **4** coloration, colouring, pigment, pigmentation. **5** bloom, blush, flush, glow, rosiness, ruddiness. **7** (*colours*) see FLAG[1] *noun*. ● *verb* **1** crayon, dye, paint, pigment, shade, stain, tinge, tint. **2** blush, burn, flush, redden. **3** affect, bias, distort, impinge on, influence, pervert, prejudice, slant, sway.

colourant /'kʌlər(ə)nt/ *noun* colouring substance.

....

Colon :

This is used:

1 between two main clauses of which the second explains, enlarges on, or follows from the first, e.g.

> *It was not easy: to begin with I had to find the right house.*

2 to introduce a list of items (a dash should not be added), and after expressions such as *namely*, *for example*, *to resume*, *to sum up*, and *the following*, e.g.

> *You will need: a tent, a sleeping bag, cooking equipment, and a rucksack.*

3 before a quotation, e.g.

> *The poem begins: 'Earth has not anything to show more fair'.*

....

coloured (*US* **colored**) *adjective* **1** having colour. **2** wholly or partly of non-white descent. **3** *South African* of mixed white and non-white descent. ● *noun* coloured person.

colourful *adjective* (*US* **colorful**) **1** full of colour. **2** full of interest; lively. □ **colourfully** *adverb*. **colourfulness** *noun*.

■ **1** bright, brilliant, chromatic, flashy, gaudy, iridescent, multicoloured, psychedelic, showy, vibrant, vivid. **2** dashing, dynamic, eccentric, energetic, exciting, flamboyant, florid, graphic, interesting, lively, picturesque, rich, stimulating, striking, telling, unusual, vigorous, vivid.

colouring *noun* (*US* **coloring**) **1** appearance as regards colour, esp. facial complexion. **2** application of colour. **3** substance giving colour.

■ **1** see COLOUR *noun* 4. **3** colourant, dye, pigment, pigmentation, stain, tincture.

colourless *adjective* (*US* **colorless**) **1** without colour. **2** lacking interest.

■ **1** albino, ashen, blanched, faded, grey, monochrome, neutral, pale, pallid, sickly, wan, washed out, waxen, white. **2** bland, boring, characterless, dingy, dismal, dowdy, drab, dreary, dull, insipid, lacklustre, lifeless, ordinary, tame, uninspiring, uninteresting, vacuous, vapid.

colt /kəʊlt/ *noun* **1** young male horse. **2** *Sport* inexperienced player. □ **coltish** *adjective*.

colter *US* = COULTER.

coltsfoot *noun* (*plural* **-s**) yellow wild flower with large leaves.

columbine /ˈkɒləmbaɪn/ *noun* garden plant with purple-blue flowers.

column /ˈkɒləm/ *noun* **1** pillar, usually round and with base and capital. **2** column-shaped thing. **3** series of numbers, one under the other. **4** vertical division of printed page. **5** part of newspaper regularly devoted to particular subject or written by one writer. **6** long, narrow arrangement of advancing troops, vehicles, etc.

■ **1** pilaster, pile, pillar, pole, post, prop, shaft, support, upright. **5** article, feature, leader, leading article, piece. **6** cavalcade, file, line, procession, queue, rank, row, string, train.

columnist /ˈkɒləmnɪst/ *noun* journalist contributing regularly to newspaper etc.

coma /ˈkəʊmə/ *noun* (*plural* **-s**) prolonged deep unconsciousness.

comatose /ˈkəʊmətəʊs/ *adjective* **1** in coma. **2** sleepy.

comb /kəʊm/ *noun* **1** toothed strip of rigid material for arranging hair. **2** thing like comb, esp. for dressing wool etc. **3** red fleshy crest of fowl, esp. cock etc. **4** honeycomb. ● *verb* **1** draw comb through (hair). **2** dress (wool etc.) with comb. **3** *colloquial* search (place) thoroughly.

■ *verb* **1** arrange, groom, neaten, smarten up, spruce up, tidy, untangle. **3** hunt through, ransack, rummage through, scour, search.

combat /ˈkɒmbæt/ *noun* fight, struggle. ● *verb* (**-t-**) **1** do battle (with). **2** strive against, oppose.

■ *noun* action, battle, bout, clash, conflict, contest, duel, encounter, engagement, fight, skirmish, struggle, war, warfare. ● *verb* battle against, contest, counter, defy, face up to, fight, grapple with, oppose, resist, stand up to, strive against, struggle against, tackle, withstand.

combatant /ˈkɒmbət(ə)nt/ *noun* fighter. ● *adjective* fighting.

combative /ˈkɒmbətɪv/ *adjective* pugnacious.

combe = COOMB.

combination /kɒmbɪˈneɪʃ(ə)n/ *noun* **1** combining, being combined. **2** combined state. **3** combined set of things or people. **4** motorcycle with sidecar. **5** sequence of numbers etc. used to open **combination lock**.

■ **1, 2** aggregate, alloy, amalgam, amalgamation, blend, compound, concoction, conjunction, fusion, marriage, merger, mix, mixture, synthesis, unification, union. **3** alliance, amalgamation, association, coalition, confederacy, confederation, consortium, federation, grouping, merger, partnership, set, syndicate, union.

combine *verb* /kəmˈbaɪn/ (**-ning**) **1** join together; unite. **2** form into chemical compound. ● *noun* /ˈkɒmbaɪn/ combination of esp. businesses. □ **combine harvester** /ˈkɒmbaɪn/ combined reaping and threshing machine.

■ *verb* **1** add together, ally, amalgamate, associate, band together, bind, blend, bring together, club together, coalesce, compound, connect, cooperate, form an alliance, fuse, *colloquial* gang together, *colloquial* gang up, incorporate, integrate, intertwine, interweave, join, join forces, link, lump together, marry, merge, mingle, mix, pool, put together, synthesize, team up, unify, unite. **2** bind, blend, coalesce, compound, synthesize, unite.

combustible /kəmˈbʌstɪb(ə)l/ *adjective* capable of or used for burning. ● *noun* combustible substance. □ **combustibility** *noun*.

■ *adjective* flammable, inflammable.

combustion /kəmˈbʌstʃ(ə)n/ *noun* **1** burning. **2** development of light and heat from combination of substance with oxygen.

come /kʌm/ *verb* (**-ming**; *past* **came**; *past participle* **come**) **1** move or be brought towards or reach a place, time, situation, or result. **2** be available. **3** occur. **4** become. **5** traverse. **6** *colloquial* behave like. □ **come about** happen. **come across 1** meet or find by chance. **2** give specified impression. **3** *colloquial* be effective or understood. **come again** *colloquial* what did you say? **come along 1** make progress. **2** hurry up. **come apart** disintegrate. **come at** attack. **comeback 1** return to success. **2** *slang* retort or retaliation. **come back (to)** recur to memory (of). **come by** obtain. **come clean** *colloquial* confess. **comedown 1** loss of status; decline. **2** disappointment. **come down 1** lose position. **2** be handed down. **3** be reduced. **4** (+ *with*) begin to suffer from (disease). **come forward** offer oneself for task etc. **come in 1** become fashionable or seasonable. **2** prove to be. **come in for** receive. **come into**

inherit. **come off 1** succeed; occur. **2** fare. **come off it** *colloquial: expression of disbelief.* **come on** make progress. **come out 1** emerge, become known. **2** be published. **3** go on strike. **4** (of photograph or its subject) be (re)produced clearly. **5** (of stain) be removed. **come out with** declare, disclose. **come over 1** come some distance to visit. **2** (of feeling) affect. **3** appear or sound in specified way. **come round 1** pay informal visit. **2** recover consciousness. **3** be converted to another's opinion. **come through** survive. **come to 1** recover consciousness. **2** amount to. **come to pass** happen. **come up 1** arise; be mentioned or discussed. **2** attain position. **come up against** be faced with. **come upon** meet or find by chance. **come up with** produce (idea etc.).

■ **1** advance, appear, approach, arrive, draw near, enter, move (towards), near, reach, *colloquial* show up, visit. **3** happen, *colloquial* materialize, occur. □ **come about** see HAPPEN 1. **come across 1** see FIND *verb* 1. **come apart** see DISINTEGRATE 1. **come clean** see CONFESS 2. **come out with** see SAY *verb* 1,2. **come round 2** see RECOVER 2. **come up 1** see ARISE 3. **come upon** see FIND *verb* 1.

comedian /kə'miːdɪən/ *noun* **1** humorous performer. **2** actor in comedy. **3** *slang* buffoon.

■ **1, 3** buffoon, clown, comic, *historical* fool, humorist, *historical* jester, joker, wag.

comedienne /kəmiːdɪ'en/ *noun* female comedian.

comedy /'kɒmədɪ/ *noun* (*plural* **-ies**) **1** play or film of amusing character; humorous kind of drama etc. **2** humour. **3** amusing aspects. □ **comedic** /kə'miːdɪk/ *adjective*.

■ **2** buffoonery, clowning, facetiousness, farce, hilarity, humour, jesting, joking, satire, slapstick, wit.

comely /'kʌmlɪ/ *adjective* (**-ier**, **-iest**) *literary* handsome, good-looking. □ **comeliness** *noun*.

comestibles /kə'mestɪb(ə)lz/ *plural noun formal* things to eat.

comet /'kɒmɪt/ *noun* hazy object with 'tail' moving in path round sun.

comeuppance /kʌm'ʌpəns/ *noun colloquial* deserved punishment.

comfort /'kʌmfət/ *noun* **1** physical or mental well-being. **2** consolation. **3** person or thing bringing consolation. **4** (usually in *plural*) things that make life comfortable. ● *verb* console. □ **comfortless** *adjective*.

■ *noun* **1** affluence, contentment, cosiness, ease, luxury, opulence, plenty, relaxation, well-being. **2** aid, cheer, consolation, encouragement, help, moral support, reassurance, relief, solace, *archaic* or *formal* succour, sympathy. ● *verb* assuage, calm, cheer up, console, encourage, gladden, hearten, help, reassure, relieve, solace, soothe, *archaic* or *formal* succour, sympathize with.

comfortable /'kʌmf(ə)təb(ə)l/ *adjective* **1** giving ease. **2** at ease. **3** having adequate standard of living. **4** appreciable. □ **comfortableness** *noun*. **comfortably** *adverb*.

■ **1** agreeable, *colloquial* comfy, convenient, cosy, easy, homely, informal, pleasant, reassuring, relaxing, restful, snug, soft, warm, well fitting. **2** at ease, *colloquial* comfy, contented, cosy, easy, happy, relaxed, serene, tranquil, untroubled. **3** affluent, luxurious, prosperous, well off.

comforter /'kʌmfətə/ *noun* **1** person who comforts. **2** baby's dummy. **3** *archaic* woollen scarf.

comfrey /'kʌmfrɪ/ *noun* tall bell-flowered plant.

comfy /'kʌmfɪ/ *adjective* (**-ier**, **-iest**) *colloquial* comfortable.

comic /'kɒmɪk/ *adjective* **1** of or like comedy. **2** funny. ● *noun* **1** comedian. **2** periodical in form of comic strips. □ **comic strip** sequence of drawings telling comic story. □ **comical** *adjective*. **comically** *adverb*.

■ *adjective* **2** absurd, amusing, comical, diverting, droll, facetious, farcical, funny, hilarious, humorous, hysterical, jocular, joking, laughable, ludicrous, *colloquial* priceless, rich, ridiculous, sarcastic, sardonic, satirical, side-splitting, silly, uproarious, waggish, witty. ● *noun* **1** see COMEDIAN 1,3. **2** see MAGAZINE 1.

comma /'kɒmə/ *noun* punctuation mark (,) indicating pause or break between parts of sentence (see panel).

command /kə'mɑːnd/ *verb* **1** give formal order to. **2** have authority or control over. **3** have at one's disposal. **4** deserve and get. **5** look down over; dominate. ● *noun* **1** order, instruction. **2** holding of authority, esp. in armed forces. **3** mastery. **4** troops or district under commander. □ **command module** control compartment in spacecraft. **command performance** one given at royal request.

■ *verb* **1** adjure, bid, charge, compel, decree, demand, direct, enjoin, instruct, ordain, order, prescribe, request, require. **2** administer, be in charge of, control, direct, govern, have authority over, head, lead, manage, reign over, rule, supervise. ● *noun* **1** *literary* behest, bidding, commandment, decree, directive, edict, injunction, instruction, mandate, order, requirement, ultimatum, writ. **2** authority, charge, control, direction, government, jurisdiction, management, oversight, power, rule, sovereignty, supervision, sway. **3** grasp, knowledge, mastery.

commandant /'kɒməndænt/ *noun* commanding officer, esp. of military academy.

commandeer /kɒmən'dɪə/ *verb* **1** seize (esp. goods) for military use. **2** take possession of without permission.

■ appropriate, confiscate, hijack, impound, requisition, seize, sequester, take over.

commander *noun* person who commands, esp. naval officer next below captain. □ **commander-in-chief** (*plural* **commanders-in-chief**) supreme commander, esp. of nation's forces.

■ captain, chief, commandant, commanding officer, general, head, leader, officer in charge.

commanding *adjective* **1** impressive. **2** giving wide view. **3** substantial.

commandment *noun* divine command.

commando /kə'mɑːndəʊ/ *noun* (*plural* **-s**) **1** unit of shock troops. **2** member of this.

commemorate /kə'meməreɪt/ *verb* (**-ting**) **1** preserve in memory by celebration or ceremony. **2** be memorial of. □ **commemoration** *noun*. **commemorative** /-rətɪv/ *adjective*.

■ **1** celebrate, honour, immortalize, keep alive the memory of, memorialize, pay homage to, pay one's respects to, pay tribute to, remember, salute, solemnize. **2** be a memorial to, be a reminder of, honour.

commence /kə'mens/ *verb* (**-cing**) *formal* begin. □ **commencement** *noun*.

■ begin, embark on, enter on, inaugurate, initiate, launch, open, set off, set out, set up, start.

commend /kə'mend/ *verb* **1** praise. **2** recommend. **3** entrust. □ **commendation** /kɒmen'deɪʃ(ə)n/ *noun*. **commendatory** /kɒ'mendət(ə)rɪ/ *adjective*.

■ **1** acclaim, applaud, approve of, compliment, congratulate, eulogize, extol, praise. **2** see RECOMMEND 1.

commendable *adjective* praiseworthy. □ **commendably** *adverb*.

Comma ,

The comma marks a slight break between words, phrases, etc. In particular, it is used:

1 to separate items in a list, e.g.

> *red, white, and blue* (or *red, white and blue*)
> *We bought some shoes, socks, gloves, and handkerchiefs.*

2 to separate adjectives that describe something in the same way, e.g.

> *It is a hot, dry, dusty place.*

but not if they describe it in different ways, e.g.

> *a distinguished foreign author*

or if one adjective adds to or alters the meaning of another, e.g.

> *a bright red tie.*

3 to separate a name or word used to address someone, e.g.

> *David, I'm here.*
> *Well, Mr Jones, we meet again.*
> *Have you seen this, my friend?*

4 to separate a phrase from the rest of the sentence, e.g.

> *Having had lunch, we went back to work.*

especially in order to clarify the meaning, e.g.

> *In the valley below, the village looked very small.*

5 after words that introduce direct speech, or after direct speech where there is no question mark or exclamation mark, e.g.

> *They answered, 'Here we are.'*
> *'Here we are,' they answered.*

6 after *Dear Sir, Dear Sarah*, etc., and *Yours faithfully, Yours sincerely*, etc. in letters.

7 to separate a word, phrase, or clause that is secondary or adds information or a comment, e.g.

> *I am sure, however, that it will not happen.*
> *Fred, who is bald, complained of the cold.*

but not with a relative clause (one usually beginning with *who, which,* or *that*) that restricts the meaning of the noun it follows, e.g.

> *Men who are bald should wear hats.*

(See panel at RELATIVE CLAUSE.)

No comma is needed between a month and a year in dates, e.g.

> *in December 1993*

or between a number and a road in addresses, e.g.

> *17 Devonshire Avenue.*

■ admirable, creditable, deserving, good, laudable, meritorious, praiseworthy, worthwhile.

commensurable /kə'menʃərəb(ə)l/ *adjective* **1** (often + *with*, *to*) measurable by same standard. **2** (+ *to*) proportionate to. □ **commensurability** *noun*.

commensurate /kə'menʃərət/ *adjective* **1** (usually + *with*) extending over same space or time. **2** (often + *to*, *with*) proportionate.

comment /'kɒment/ *noun* **1** brief critical or explanatory note or remark; opinion. **2** commenting. ● *verb* (often + *on*, *that*) make comment(s). □ **no comment** *colloquial* I decline to answer your question.

■ *noun* **1** *literary* animadversion, annotation, clarification, commentary, criticism, elucidation, explanation, footnote, gloss, interjection, interpolation, mention, note, observation, opinion, reaction, reference, remark, statement. ● *verb literary* animadvert, criticize, elucidate, explain, interject, interpolate, interpose, mention, note, observe, opine, remark, say, state.

commentary /'kɒməntəri/ *noun* (*plural* **-ies**) **1** broadcast description of event happening. **2** series of comments on book or performance etc.

■ **1** account, broadcast, description, report. **2** analysis, criticism, critique, discourse, elucidation, explanation, interpretation, notes, review.

commentate /'kɒmənteɪt/ *verb* (**-ting**) act as commentator.

commentator *noun* writer or speaker of commentary.

■ announcer, broadcaster, journalist, reporter.

commerce /'kɒmɜːs/ *noun* buying and selling; trading.

■ business, buying and selling, dealings, financial transactions, marketing, merchandising, trade, trading, traffic, trafficking.

commercial /kə'mɜːʃ(ə)l/ *adjective* **1** of, in, or for commerce. **2** done or run primarily for financial profit. **3** (of broadcasting) financed by advertising. ● *noun* television or radio advertisement. □ **commercial broadcasting** broadcasting financed by advertising. **commercial traveller** firm's representative visiting shops etc. to get orders. □ **commercially** *adverb*.

■ *adjective* **1**, **2** business, economic, financial, mercantile, monetary, moneymaking, pecuniary, profitable, trading. ● *noun colloquial* ad, *colloquial* advert, advertisement, break, *colloquial* plug.

commercialize *verb* (also **-ise**) (**-zing** or **-sing**) **1** exploit or spoil for profit. **2** make commercial. □ **commercialization** *noun*.

Commie /'kɒmi/ *noun slang derogatory* Communist.

commingle /kə'mɪŋg(ə)l/ *verb* (**-ling**) *literary* mix, unite.

commiserate /kə'mɪzəreɪt/ *verb* (**-ting**) (usually + *with*) have or express sympathy. □ **commiseration** *noun*.

■ be sympathetic, show sympathy; (*commiserate with*) be sorry for, comfort, condole with, console, feel for, feel sorry for, grieve with, mourn with, sympathize with.

commissar /'kɒmɪsɑː/ *noun historical* head of government department in USSR.

commissariat /kɒmɪ'seərɪət/ *noun* **1** department responsible for supply of food etc. for army. **2** food supplied.

commissary /'kɒmɪsəri/ *noun* (*plural* **-ies**) deputy, delegate.

commission /kə'mɪʃ(ə)n/ *noun* **1** authority to perform task. **2** person(s) given such authority. **3** order for specially produced thing. **4** warrant conferring officer rank in armed forces. **5** rank so conferred. **6** pay or percentage received by agent. **7** committing. ● *verb* **1** empower, give authority to. **2** give (artist etc.) order for work. **3** order (work) to be written etc. **4** give (officer) command of ship. **5** prepare (ship) for active service. **6** bring (machine etc.) into operation. □ **in or out of commission** ready or not ready for active service.

■ *noun* **2** see COMMITTEE. **3** booking, order, request. **4** appointment, promotion, warrant. **6** allowance, *slang* cut, fee, percentage, *colloquial* rake-off, reward.

commissionaire /kəmɪʃə'neə/ *noun* uniformed door attendant.

commissioner *noun* **1** person commissioned to perform specific task. **2** member of government commission. **3** representative of government in district etc.

commit /kə'mɪt/ *verb* (**-tt-**) **1** do or make (crime, blunder, etc.). **2** (usually + *to*) entrust, consign. **3** send (person) to prison. **4** pledge or bind (esp. oneself) to policy or course of action. **5** (as **committed** *adjective*) (often + *to*) dedicated. **6** (as **committed** *adjective*) (often + *to*) obliged.

■ **1** carry out, do, enact, execute, perform, perpetrate. **2** consign, deliver, deposit, entrust, give, hand over, transfer. **4** (*commit oneself*) see PROMISE *verb* **1**. **5** (**committed**) active, ardent, card-carrying, dedicated, devoted, earnest, enthusiastic, fervent, firm, keen, passionate, resolute, single-minded, staunch, unwavering, wholehearted, zealous.

commitment *noun* **1** engagement, obligation. **2** committing oneself; pledge. **3** dedication. **4** committing, being committed.

■ **1** appointment, arrangement, engagement, obligation. **2** assurance, duty, guarantee, liability, pledge, promise, undertaking, vow, word. **3** adherence, dedication, determination, devotion, involvement, loyalty, zeal.

committal *noun* act of committing esp. to prison, grave, etc.

committee /kə'mɪti/ *noun* group of people appointed for special function by (and usually out of) larger body.

■ board, body, cabinet, *often derogatory* caucus, commission, council, group, panel, quango, *colloquial* think-tank, working party.

commode /kə'məʊd/ *noun* 1 chamber pot in chair or box with cover. 2 chest of drawers.

commodious /kə'məʊdɪəs/ *adjective* roomy.

commodity /kə'mɒdɪtɪ/ *noun* (*plural* -ies) article of trade.

commodore /'kɒmədɔː/ *noun* 1 naval officer next above captain. 2 commander of squadron or other division of fleet. 3 president of yacht club.

common /'kɒmən/ *adjective* (-er, -est) 1 occurring often. 2 ordinary; of the most familiar kind. 3 shared by all; belonging to the whole community. 4 *derogatory* low-class; inferior, vulgar. 5 *Grammar* (of gender) referring to individuals of either sex. ● *noun* piece of open public land. □ **common ground** point or argument accepted by both sides. **common law** unwritten law based on custom and precedent. **common-law husband, wife** partner recognized by common law without formal marriage. **Common Market** European Community. **common or garden** *colloquial* ordinary. **common room** room for social use of students or teachers at college etc. **common sense** good practical sense. **common time** *Music* 4 crotchets in a bar. **in common** shared; in joint use.

■ *adjective* 1 customary, daily, everyday, familiar, frequent, habitual, prevalent, regular, routine, usual, widespread. 2 average, *colloquial* common or garden, commonplace, conventional, everyday, familiar, normal, ordinary, plain, regular, routine, run-of-the-mill, standard, stock, traditional, typical, undistinguished, unexceptional, unsurprising, usual, well known, workaday. 3 collective, communal, general, joint, *colloquial* disputed mutual, open, popular, public, shared, universal. 4 boorish, churlish, coarse, crude, disreputable, ill-bred, inferior, loutish, low, lower class, lowly, plebeian, proletarian, rude, uncouth, unrefined, vulgar, *slang* yobbish. ● *noun* heath.

commonalty /'kɒmənəltɪ/ *noun* (*plural* -ies) 1 general community. 2 common people.

commoner *noun* person below rank of peer.

commonly *adverb* usually, frequently.

commonplace /'kɒmənpleɪs/ *adjective* 1 lacking originality. 2 ordinary, usual. ● *noun* 1 event, topic, etc. that is ordinary or usual. 2 trite remark.

■ *adjective* 1 banal, boring, forgettable, hackneyed, humdrum, mediocre, obvious, ordinary, pedestrian, plain, platitudinous, predictable, prosaic, routine, standard, trite, unexciting, unremarkable. 2 see COMMON *adjective* 2. ● *noun* 2 see PLATITUDE.

commons /'kɒmənz/ *plural noun* 1 the common people. 2 (**the Commons**) House of Commons.

commonwealth /'kɒmənwelθ/ *noun* 1 independent state or community. 2 (**the Commonwealth**) association of UK with states previously part of British Empire. 3 republican government of Britain 1649–60.

commotion /kə'məʊʃ(ə)n/ *noun* noisy disturbance.

■ ado, agitation, bedlam, bother, brawl, *colloquial* bust-up, chaos, clamour, confusion, contretemps, din, disorder, disturbance, excitement, ferment, flurry, fracas, fray, furore, fuss, hubbub, hullabaloo, incident, *colloquial* kerfuffle, noise, *colloquial* palaver, pandemonium, *colloquial* punch-up, quarrel, racket, riot, *colloquial* row, *colloquial* rumpus, sensation, stir, to-do, tumult, turbulence, turmoil, unrest, upheaval, uproar, upset.

communal /'kɒmjʊn(ə)l/ *adjective* 1 shared between members of group or community. 2 (of conflict etc.) between communities. □ **communally** *adverb*.

■ 1 collective, common, general, joint, *colloquial* disputed mutual, open, public, shared.

commune[1] /'kɒmjuːn/ *noun* 1 group of people sharing accommodation and goods. 2 small administrative district in France etc.

commune[2] /kə'mjuːn/ *verb* (-ning) (usually + *with*) 1 speak intimately. 2 feel in close touch.

communicable /kə'mjuːnɪkəb(ə)l/ *adjective* (esp. of disease) able to be passed on.

communicant /kə'mjuːnɪkənt/ *noun* receiver of Holy Communion.

communicate /kə'mjuːnɪkeɪt/ *verb* (-ting) 1 impart, transmit (news, feelings, ideas, etc.). 2 transmit (disease). 3 (often + *with*) have social dealings. 4 (often + *with*) (of room) be connected. □ **communicator** *noun*.

■ 1 advise, announce, broadcast, convey, declare, disclose, disseminate, divulge, express oneself, get across, impart, indicate, inform, intimate, make known, mention, network, notify, pass on, proclaim, promulgate, publish, put across, put over, relay, report, reveal, say, show, speak, spread, state, transfer, transmit, write. 2 give, infect with, pass on, spread, transfer, transmit. 3 commune, confer, converse, correspond, get in touch, make contact, speak, talk, write. 4 (*communicate with*) be connected with, lead to.

communication *noun* 1 communicating, being communicated. 2 letter, message, etc.; information communicated. 3 connection or means of access. 4 social dealings. 5 (in *plural*) science and practice of transmitting information. □ **communication cord** cord or chain pulled to stop train in emergency. **communication(s) satellite** artificial satellite used to relay telephone calls, TV, radio, etc.

■ 1 communion, contact, conversation, correspondence, dialogue, interaction, intercourse, transmission. 2 announcement, bulletin, cable, card, communiqué, directive, dispatch, document, fax, letter, *colloquial* memo, memorandum, message, note, notice, proclamation, report, telegram, *colloquial* wire. 5 (*communications*) broadcasting, mass media, the media, the press, telecommunications.

communicative /kəˈmjuːnɪkətɪv/ *adjective* ready to talk and impart information.
- articulate, chatty, frank, informative, loquacious, open, outgoing, responsive, sociable, talkative.

communion /kəˈmjuːnjən/ *noun* **1** sharing, esp. of thoughts, interests, etc.; fellowship. **2** group of Christians of same denomination. **3** (**Holy Communion**) Eucharist.

communiqué /kəˈmjuːnɪkeɪ/ *noun* official communication, esp. news report.

communism /ˈkɒmjʊnɪz(ə)m/ *noun* **1** social system based on public ownership of most property. **2** political theory advocating this. **3** (usually **Communism**) form of socialist society in Cuba, China, etc. □ **communist, Communist** *noun & adjective*. **communistic** /-ˈnɪstɪk/ *adjective*.

community /kəˈmjuːnɪtɪ/ *noun* (*plural* **-ies**) **1** group of people living in one place or having same religion, ethnic origin, profession, etc. **2** commune. **3** joint ownership. □ **community centre** place providing social facilities for neighbourhood. **community charge** *historical* tax levied locally on every adult. **community home** institution housing young offenders. **community singing** singing by large group. **community spirit** feeling of belonging to community.
- **1** colony, commonwealth, country, group, nation, society, state. **2** commune, kibbutz.

commute /kəˈmjuːt/ *verb* (**-ting**) **1** travel some distance to and from work. **2** (usually + *to*) change (punishment) to one less severe.
- **1** see TRAVEL *verb* 1. **2** adjust, alter, curtail, decrease, lessen, lighten, mitigate, reduce, shorten.

commuter *noun* person who commutes to and from work.

compact¹ *adjective* /kəmˈpækt/ **1** closely packed together. **2** economically designed. **3** concise. **4** (of person) small but well proportioned. ● *verb* /kəmˈpækt/ make compact. ● *noun* /ˈkɒmpækt/ small flat case for face powder etc. □ **compact disc** disc from which digital information or sound is reproduced by reflection of laser light. □ **compactly** *adverb*. **compactness** *noun*.
- *adjective* **1** close-packed, compacted, compressed, dense, firm, heavy, packed, solid, tight-packed. **2** handy, neat, portable, small. **3** abbreviated, abridged, brief, compendious, compressed, concentrated, concise, condensed, short, small, succinct, terse.

compact² /ˈkɒmpækt/ *noun* agreement, contract.
- see AGREEMENT 2.

companion /kəmˈpænjən/ *noun* **1** person who accompanies or associates with another. **2** person paid to live with another. **3** handbook, reference book. **4** thing that matches another. **5** (**Companion**) member of some orders of knight-

hood. □ **companionway** staircase from ship's deck to cabins etc.
- **1** accomplice, assistant, associate, chaperon, colleague, comrade, confederate, confidant(e), consort, *often derogatory* crony, escort, fellow, follower, friend, helper, *usually derogatory* henchman, mate, partner, stalwart.

companionable *adjective* sociable, friendly. □ **companionably** *adverb*.

companionship *noun* friendship; being together.

company /ˈkʌmpənɪ/ *noun* (*plural* **-ies**) **1** number of people assembled; crowd. **2** guest(s). **3** companionship. **4** commercial business. **5** actors etc. working together. **6** subdivision of infantry battalion. □ **in company with** together with. **keep company** (often + *with*) associate habitually. **part company** (often + *with*) separate. **ship's company** entire crew.
- **1** assemblage, band, body, circle, crowd, entourage, gang, gathering, throng, troop, troupe (*of actors*). **2** callers, guests, visitors. **3** companionship, fellowship, friendship, society. **4** business, cartel, concern, conglomerate, consortium, corporation, establishment, firm, house, organization, partnership, syndicate.

comparable /ˈkɒmpərəb(ə)l/ *adjective* (often + *with*, *to*) able to be compared. □ **comparability** *noun*. **comparably** *adverb*.

USAGE *Comparable* is often pronounced /kəmˈpærəb(ə)l/ (with the stress on the *-par-*), but this is considered incorrect by some people.
- analogous, cognate, commensurate, compatible, corresponding, equal, equivalent, matching, parallel, proportionate, related, similar, twin.

comparative /kəmˈpærətɪv/ *adjective* **1** perceptible or estimated by comparison. **2** relative. **3** of or involving comparison. **4** *Grammar* (of adjective or adverb) expressing higher degree of a quality (see panel). ● *noun Grammar* comparative expression or word. □ **comparatively** *adverb*.

compare /kəmˈpeə/ *verb* (**-ring**) **1** (usually + *to*) express similarities in. **2** (often + *to*, *with*) estimate degree of similarity of. **3** (often + *with*) bear comparison. ● *noun* comparison. □ **compare notes** exchange ideas or opinions.
- *verb* **1** draw parallels (between), equate, liken, make connections (between). **2** contrast, juxtapose, set side by side; (*compare to* or *with*) correlate with, measure against, relate to, weigh against. **3** (*compare with*) see EQUAL *verb* 2.

comparison /kəmˈpærɪs(ə)n/ *noun* **1** comparing. **2** example of similarity. **3** (in full **degrees of comparison**) *Grammar* positive, comparative, and superlative forms of adjectives and adverbs. □ **bear comparison** (often + *with*) be able to be compared favourably.
- **1** contrast, correlation, distinction, juxtaposition. **2** analogy, comparability, correlation, likeness, parallel, relationship, resemblance, similarity.

compartment /kəm'pɑːtmənt/ *noun* space partitioned off within larger space.

■ alcove, area, bay, cell, chamber, cubby hole, cubicle, division, hole, locker, niche, nook, pigeon-hole, section, slot, space, subdivision.

compartmentalize /kɒmpɑːt'ment(ə)laɪz/ *verb* (also **-ise**) divide into compartments or categories. □ **compartmentalization** /-'zeɪʃ(ə)n/ *noun*.

compass /'kʌmpəs/ *noun* 1 instrument showing direction of magnetic north and bearings from it. 2 (usually in *plural*) V-shaped hinged instrument for drawing circles and taking measurements. 3 scope, range.

compassion /kəm'pæʃ(ə)n/ *noun* pity.

compassionate /kəm'pæʃənət/ *adjective* showing compassion; sympathetic. □ **compassionate leave** leave granted on grounds of bereavement etc. □ **compassionately** *adverb*.

compatible /kəm'pætɪb(ə)l/ *adjective* 1 (often + *with*) able to coexist. 2 consistent. 3 (of equipment) able to be used in combination. □ **compatibility** *noun*.

■ 1 harmonious, like-minded, similar, well matched. 2 congruent, consistent, consonant, matching, reconcilable.

compatriot /kəm'pætrɪət/ *noun* person from one's own country.

compeer /kəm'pɪə/ *noun* 1 peer, equal. 2 comrade.

compel /kəm'pel/ *verb* (**-ll-**) 1 force, constrain. 2 arouse irresistibly. 3 (as **compelling** *adjective*) arousing strong interest.

■ 1 bind, bully, coerce, constrain, dragoon, drive, exact, force, impel, make, necessitate, oblige, order, press, press-gang, pressurize, require, *colloquial* shanghai, urge.

compendious /kəm'pendɪəs/ *adjective* comprehensive but brief.

compendium /kəm'pendɪəm/ *noun* (*plural* **-s** or **-dia**) 1 abridgement; summary. 2 handbook. 3 collection of table games etc.

■ 1 abridgement, abstract, condensation, digest, summary. 3 anthology, collection.

compensate /'kɒmpenseɪt/ *verb* (**-ting**) 1 (often + *for*) recompense. 2 (often + *for*) make amends. 3 counterbalance.

■ 1 indemnify, make reparation, make restitution, pay back, recompense, reimburse, remunerate, repay, requite. 2 atone, make amends, make reparation, make restitution; (*compensate for*) expiate, make good, make up for, redress. 3 counterbalance, counterpoise, even up, neutralize, offset.

compensation *noun* 1 compensating, being compensated. 2 money etc. given as recompense. □ **compensatory** /-'seɪt-/ *adjective*.

■ amends, damages, indemnity, recompense, reimbursement, reparation, repayment, restitution.

compère /'kɒmpeə/ *noun* person introducing variety show. ● *verb* (**-ring**) act as compère (to).

■ *noun* anchorman, anchorwoman, announcer, disc jockey, host, hostess, Master of Ceremonies, MC, presenter.

compete /kəm'piːt/ *verb* (**-ting**) 1 take part in contest etc. 2 (often + *with* or *against* person, *for* thing) strive.

■ 1 be a contestant, enter, participate, perform, take part, take up the challenge. 2 conflict, contend, fight, strive, struggle, vie; (*compete with* or *against*) emulate, oppose, rival, undercut.

competence /'kɒmpɪt(ə)ns/ *noun* being competent; ability.

competent *adjective* adequately qualified or capable; effective. □ **competently** *adverb*.

■ able, acceptable, accomplished, adept, adequate, capable, clever, effective, efficient, experienced, expert, fit, handy, practical, proficient, qualified, satisfactory, skilful, skilled, trained, workmanlike, worthwhile.

competition /kɒmpə'tɪʃ(ə)n/ *noun* 1 (often + *for*) competing. 2 event in which people compete. 3 other people competing; opposition.

■ 1 competitiveness, conflict, contention, emulation, rivalry, struggle. 2 challenge, championship, contest, event, game, heat, match, quiz, race, rally, series, tournament, trial.

competitive /kəm'petɪtɪv/ *adjective* 1 of or involving competition. 2 (of prices etc.) compar-

....

Comparative

The form of an adjective used to compare two people or things in respect of a certain quality is called the comparative. Comparative adjectives are formed in two ways: generally, short words add -*er* to the base form, e.g.

smaller, faster, greater.

Often, the base form alters, e.g.

bigger, finer, easier.

Long words take *more* in front of them, e.g.

more beautiful, more informative.

....

ing well with those of rivals. **3** having strong urge to win. □ **competitiveness** *noun*.

■ **1** cut-throat, hard-fought, keen, lively, well fought. **2** average, fair, keen, moderate, reasonable.

competitor /kəm'petɪtə/ *noun* person who competes; rival, esp. in business.

■ adversary, antagonist, candidate, challenger, contender, contestant, entrant, finalist, opponent, participant, rival.

compile /kəm'paɪl/ *verb* (**-ling**) collect and arrange (material) into list, book, etc. □ **compilation** /kɒmpɪ'leɪʃ(ə)n/ *noun*.

■ accumulate, amass, arrange, assemble, collate, collect, compose, edit, gather, marshal, organize, put together.

complacent /kəm'pleɪs(ə)nt/ *adjective* smugly self-satisfied or contented. □ **complacency** *noun*.

complain /kəm'pleɪn/ *verb* **1** (often + *about*) express dissatisfaction. **2** (+ *of*) say that one is suffering from (an ailment). **3** (+ *of*) state grievance concerning. □ **complainant** *noun*.

■ **1** *slang* beef, *slang* bellyache, carp, cavil, find fault, *colloquial* gripe, groan, *colloquial* grouch, *colloquial* grouse, grumble, *colloquial* moan, object, protest, wail, whine, *colloquial* whinge; (*complain about*) see CRITICIZE 1.

complaint *noun* **1** complaining. **2** grievance; cause of dissatisfaction. **3** formal protest. **4** ailment.

■ **2, 3** accusation, *slang* beef, charge, criticism, grievance, *colloquial* gripe, *colloquial* grouse, grumble, *colloquial* moan, objection, protest, stricture, whine, *colloquial* whinge. **4** affliction, ailment, disease, disorder, illness, infection, malady, malaise, sickness, upset.

complaisant /kəm'pleɪz(ə)nt/ *adjective formal* deferential; willing to please; acquiescent. □ **complaisance** *noun*.

■ accommodating, acquiescent, amenable, biddable, compliant, cooperative, deferential, docile, obedient, obliging, polite, submissive, tractable, willing.

complement *noun* /'kɒmplɪmənt/ **1** thing that completes. **2** full number. **3** word(s) added to verb to complete predicate of sentence. **4** amount by which angle is less than 90°. ● *verb* /-ment/ **1** complete. **2** form complement to. □ **complementary** /-'men-/ *adjective*.

│ ■ *noun* **1** completion, finishing touch, perfection. **2** aggregate, capacity, quota, sum, total. ● *verb*

add to, complete, make whole, perfect, round off, top up. □ **complementary** interdependent, matching, reciprocal, toning, twin.

complete /kəm'pli:t/ *adjective* **1** having all its parts. **2** finished. **3** total. ● *verb* (**-ting**) **1** finish. **2** make complete. **3** fill in (form etc.). □ **completely** *adverb*. **completeness** *noun*. **completion** *noun*.

■ *adjective* **1** comprehensive, entire, exhaustive, full, intact, total, unabbreviated, unabridged, uncut, unedited, unexpurgated, whole. **2** accomplished, achieved, completed, concluded, done, ended, finished, over, perfect. **3** absolute, *literary* arrant, downright, extreme, out and out, outright, pure, rank, sheer, thorough, thoroughgoing, total, unmitigated, unmixed, unqualified, utter, wholesale. ● *verb* **1** accomplish, achieve, carry out, clinch, close, conclude, do, end, finalize, finish, fulfil, perform, round off, terminate, wind up. **2** crown, perfect, round off, top off. **3** answer, fill in.

complex /'kɒmpleks/ *noun* **1** buildings, rooms, etc. made up of related parts. **2** group of usually repressed feelings or thoughts causing abnormal behaviour or mental state. ● *adjective* **1** complicated. **2** consisting of related parts. □ **complexity** /kəm'pleks-/ *noun* (*plural* **-ies**).

■ *adjective* **1** complicated, convoluted, elaborate, heterogeneous, intricate, involved, knotty (*problem*), labyrinthine, ornate, perplexing, problematical, sophisticated, tortuous, tricky. **2** composite, compound, manifold, multifarious, multiple.

complexion /kəm'plekʃ(ə)n/ *noun* **1** natural colour, texture, and appearance of skin, esp. of face. **2** aspect.

■ **1** appearance, colour, colouring, look, pigmentation, skin, texture.

compliance /kəm'plaɪəns/ *noun* **1** obedience to request, command, etc. **2** capacity to yield.

compliant *adjective* obedient, yielding. □ **compliantly** *adverb*.

complicate /'kɒmplɪkeɪt/ *verb* (**-ting**) **1** make difficult or complex. **2** (as **complicated** *adjective*) complex, intricate.

■ **1** compound, confound, confuse, elaborate, entangle, mix up, muddle, *slang* screw up, snarl up, tangle, twist. **2** (**complicated**) see COMPLEX *adjective* 1.

complication *noun* **1** involved or confused condition. **2** complicating circumstance; difficulty. **3** (often in *plural*) disease or condition arising out of another.

Complement

A complement is a word or phrase that comes after a verb but has the same reference as the subject or object, e.g.

the culprit in *The dog was the culprit*.
president in *They elected him president*.

■ **1, 2** complexity, confusion, convolution, difficulty, *disputed* dilemma, intricacy, mix-up, obstacle, problem, ramification, setback, snag, tangle.

complicity /kəm'plɪsɪtɪ/ *noun* partnership in wrongdoing.

compliment *noun* /'kɒmplɪmənt/ **1** polite expression of praise. **2** (in *plural*) formal greetings accompanying gift etc. ● *verb* /-ment/ (often + *on*) congratulate; praise.

■ *noun* **1** accolade, commendation, eulogy, panegyric, tribute; (*compliments*) congratulations, felicitations, plaudits. ● *verb* applaud, commend, congratulate, eulogize, extol, felicitate, flatter, give credit, laud, pay homage to, praise, salute, speak highly of.

complimentary /kɒmplɪ'mentərɪ/ *adjective* **1** expressing compliment. **2** given free of charge.

■ **1** admiring, appreciative, approving, commendatory, congratulatory, eulogistic, favourable, flattering, generous, laudatory, panegyrical, rapturous, supportive.

comply /kəm'plaɪ/ *verb* (**-ies, -ied**) (often + *with*) act in accordance (with request or command).

■ acquiesce, agree, assent, concur, conform, consent, defer, fit in, submit, yield; (*comply with*) abide by, accede to, adhere to, coincide with, correspond to, fall in with, follow, fulfil, harmonize with, keep (to), match, meet, obey, observe, perform, respect, satisfy, square with, suit.

component /kəm'pəʊnənt/ *adjective* being part of larger whole. ● *noun* component part.

■ *noun* bit, constituent, element, ingredient, item, part, piece, spare, spare part, unit.

comport /kəm'pɔːt/ *verb* (**comport oneself**) *literary* conduct oneself, behave. □ **comportment** *noun*.

compose /kəm'pəʊz/ *verb* (**-sing**) **1** create in music or writing. **2** make up; constitute. **3** arrange artistically. **4** set up (type); arrange in type. **5** settle, calm. **6** (as **composed** *adjective*) calm, self-possessed.

■ **1** create, devise, make (up), produce, write. **2** compile, constitute, construct, fashion, form, frame, make (up), put together; (*be composed of*) see COMPRISE. **5** calm, control, pacify, quieten, settle, soothe, tranquillize. **6** (**composed**) see CALM *adjective* 2.

composer *noun* person who composes esp. music.

composite /'kɒmpəzɪt/ *adjective* **1** made up of parts. **2** (of plant) having head of many flowers forming one bloom. ● *noun* composite thing or plant.

composition /kɒmpə'zɪʃ(ə)n/ *noun* **1** act of putting together; constitution of substance. **2** arrangement of parts of picture etc. **3** thing composed, esp. musical work. **4** school essay. **5** compound artificial substance.

■ **1** assembly, constitution, construction, creation, establishment, formation, formulation, make-up, setting up. **2** arrangement, balance, configuration, layout, organization, structure. **3** opus, piece, work. **4** article, essay, piece of writing, story.

compositor /kəm'pɒzɪtə/ *noun* person who sets up type for printing.

compos mentis /kɒmpɒs 'mentɪs/ *adjective* having control of one's mind; sane.

compost /'kɒmpɒst/ *noun* mixture of decayed organic matter used as fertilizer.

composure /kəm'pəʊʒə/ *noun* calm manner.

compote /'kɒmpəʊt/ *noun* fruit in syrup.

compound[1] /'kɒmpaʊnd/ *noun* **1** mixture of two or more things. **2** word made up of two or more existing words. **3** substance formed from two or more elements chemically united. ● *adjective* **1** made up of two or more ingredients or parts. **2** combined, collective. ● *verb* /kəm'paʊnd/ **1** mix or combine. **2** increase (difficulties etc.). **3** make up (whole). **4** settle (matter) by mutual agreement. □ **compound fracture** one complicated by wound. **compound interest** interest paid on capital and accumulated interest.

■ *noun* **1** alloy, amalgam, blend, combination, composite, composition, fusion, mixture, synthesis. ● *adjective* **1** complex, complicated, composite, intricate, involved, multiple. ● *verb* **1** see COMBINE *verb* 1–2. **2** see COMPLICATE 1.

compound[2] /'kɒmpaʊnd/ *noun* enclosure; fenced-in space.

■ corral, enclosure, pen, run.

comprehend /kɒmprɪ'hend/ *verb* **1** understand. **2** include.

■ **1** appreciate, apprehend, conceive, discern, fathom, follow, grasp, know, perceive, realize, see, take in, *colloquial* twig, understand.

comprehensible *adjective* that can be understood.

■ clear, easy, intelligible, lucid, meaningful, plain, self-explanatory, simple, straightforward, understandable.

comprehension *noun* **1** understanding. **2** text set as test of understanding. **3** inclusion.

comprehensive *adjective* **1** including all or nearly all. **2** (of motor insurance) providing protection against most risks. ● *noun* (in full **comprehensive school**) secondary school for children of all abilities. □ **comprehensively** *adverb*.

■ *adjective* **1** all-embracing, broad, catholic, compendious, complete, detailed, encyclopedic, exhaustive, extensive, far-reaching, full, inclusive, indiscriminate, sweeping, thorough, total, universal, wholesale, wide-ranging.

compress *verb* /kəm'pres/ **1** squeeze together. **2** bring into smaller space or shorter time. ● *noun* /'kɒmpres/ pad pressed on part of body to relieve inflammation, stop bleeding, etc. □ **com-**

pressed *adjective*. **compressible** *adjective*.
■ *verb* **1** compact, constrict, cram, crush, flatten, jam, press, squash, squeeze, stuff, telescope. **2** abbreviate, abridge, compact, concentrate, condense, contract, précis, shorten, summarize, telescope, truncate. □ **compressed** see COMPACT[1] *adjective* 1, CONCISE.

compression /kəm'preʃ(ə)n/ *noun* **1** compressing. **2** reduction in volume of fuel mixture in internal-combustion engine before ignition.

compressor *noun* machine for compressing air or other gas.

comprise /kəm'praɪz/ *verb* (**-sing**) include; consist of.

USAGE It is a mistake to use *comprise* to mean 'to compose' or 'to make up'.

■ be composed of, comprehend, consist of, contain, cover, embody, embrace, include, incorporate, involve.

compromise /'kɒmprəmaɪz/ *noun* **1** agreement reached by mutual concession. **2** (often + *between*) intermediate state between conflicting opinions etc. ● *verb* (**-sing**) **1** settle dispute by compromise; modify one's opinions, demands, etc. **2** (often as **compromising** *adjective*) bring into disrepute or danger by indiscretion.
■ *noun* **1** bargain, concession, give and take, settlement. **2** halfway house, middle course, middle way. ● *verb* **1** concede a point, go to arbitration, make concessions, meet halfway, negotiate a settlement, reach a formula, settle, strike a balance. **2** damage, discredit, disgrace, dishonour, imperil, jeopardize, prejudice, risk, undermine, weaken; (**compromising**) see SHAMEFUL.

comptroller /kən'trəʊlə/ *noun* controller.

compulsion /kəm'pʌlʃ(ə)n/ *noun* **1** compelling, being compelled. **2** irresistible urge.
■ **1** coercion, constraint, duress, force, necessity, obligation, pressure. **2** drive, impulse, urge.

compulsive *adjective* **1** compelling. **2** resulting or acting (as if) from compulsion. **3** irresistible. □ **compulsively** *adverb*.
■ **1, 3** besetting, compelling, driving, instinctive, involuntary, irresistible, overpowering, overwhelming, powerful, uncontrollable, urgent. **2** addicted, habitual, incorrigible, incurable, obsessive, persistent.

compulsory *adjective* required by law or rule. □ **compulsorily** *adverb*.
■ binding, contractual, de rigueur, enforceable, essential, imperative, imposed, incumbent, indispensable, inescapable, mandatory, necessary, obligatory, official, prescribed, required, requisite, set, statutory, stipulated, unavoidable.

compunction /kəm'pʌŋkʃ(ə)n/ *noun* guilty feeling; slight regret.
■ contrition, pang of conscience, qualm, regret, remorse, scruple, self-reproach.

compute /kəm'pjuːt/ *verb* (**-ting**) **1** calculate. **2** use computer. □ **computation** /kɒm-/ *noun*.
■ **1** add up, ascertain, assess, calculate, count, determine, estimate, evaluate, measure, reckon, total, work out.

computer *noun* electronic device for storing and processing data, making calculations, or controlling machinery. □ **computer-literate** able to use computers. **computer science** study of computers. **computer virus** code maliciously introduced into program to destroy data etc.

computerize /kəm'pjuːtəraɪz/ *verb* (also **-ise**) (**-zing** or **-sing**) equip with or store, perform, or produce by computer. □ **computerization** *noun*.

comrade /'kɒmreɪd/ *noun* **1** companion in some activity. **2** fellow socialist or communist. □ **comradeship** *noun*.
■ **1** associate, *colloquial* chum, colleague, companion, friend, mate.

con[1] *slang noun* confidence trick. ● *verb* (**-nn-**) swindle, deceive.

con[2] *noun* (usually in *plural*) reason against.

con[3] *verb* (*US* **conn**) (**-nn-**) direct steering of (ship).

concatenation /kɒnkætɪ'neɪʃ(ə)n/ *noun* series of linked things or events.

concave /kɒn'keɪv/ *adjective* curved like interior of circle or sphere. □ **concavity** /-'kæv-/ *noun*.

conceal /kən'siːl/ *verb* hide; keep secret. □ **concealed** *adjective*. **concealment** *noun*.
■ blot out, bury, camouflage, cloak, cover up, disguise, envelop, gloss over, hide, hush up, keep dark, keep quiet, keep secret, mask, obscure, screen, secrete, suppress, veil. □ **concealed** see HIDDEN *adjective* 1.

concede /kən'siːd/ *verb* (**-ding**) **1** admit to be true. **2** admit defeat (in). **3** grant, surrender (points, rights, etc.).
■ **1** accept, acknowledge, admit, agree, allow, confess, grant, own, profess, recognize. **2** capitulate, cave in, give in, give up, resign, surrender. **3** allow, *formal* cede, give up, grant, relinquish, surrender, yield.

conceit /kən'siːt/ *noun* **1** personal vanity. **2** *literary* far-fetched comparison.
■ **1** arrogance, boastfulness, egotism, pride, self-admiration, self-esteem, self-love, vanity.

conceited *adjective* vain. □ **conceitedly** *adverb*.
■ arrogant, *colloquial* big-headed, boastful, bumptious, cocksure, *colloquial* cocky, egocentric, egotistic(al), haughty, *colloquial* high and mighty, immodest, narcissistic, overweening, proud, self-centred, self-important, self-satisfied, smug, snobbish, *colloquial* snooty, *colloquial* stuck-up, supercilious, *colloquial* swollen-headed, *colloquial* toffee-nosed, vain, vainglorious.

conceive /kən'siːv/ *verb* (**-ving**) **1** become pregnant (with). **2** (often + *of*) imagine. **3** (usually in *passive*) formulate (plan etc.). □ **conceivable** *adjective*. **conceivably** *adverb*.

■ **2** envisage, fancy, imagine, realize, think, visualize. **3** conjure up, create, design, devise, dream up, evolve, form, formulate, frame, germinate, hatch, initiate, invent, make up, originate, plan, plot, produce, suggest, *colloquial* think up, work out.

concentrate /'kɒnsəntreɪt/ *verb* (**-ting**) **1** (often + *on*) focus one's attention. **2** bring together to one point. **3** (often as **concentrated** *adjective*) increase strength of (liquid etc.) by removing water etc. **4** (as **concentrated** *adjective*) (of effort, feeling, etc.) intense, intensified. ● *noun* concentrated solution.

■ *verb* **1** apply oneself, attend, be absorbed, be attentive, engross oneself, think, work hard. **2** accumulate, centralize, centre, cluster, collect, congregate, converge, crowd, focus, gather, mass. **3** condense, reduce, thicken; (**concentrated**) condensed, evaporated, reduced, strong, thick, undiluted. **4** (**concentrated**) see INTENSIVE 1. ● *noun* distillation, essence, extract.

concentration *noun* **1** concentrating, being concentrated. **2** weight of substance in given amount of mixture. **3** mental attention. □ **concentration camp** place for detention of political prisoners etc.

concentric /kən'sentrɪk/ *adjective* having common centre. □ **concentrically** *adverb*.

concept /'kɒnsept/ *noun* general notion; abstract idea.

conception /kən'sepʃ(ə)n/ *noun* **1** conceiving, being conceived. **2** idea. **3** understanding.

■ **1** *literary* begetting, beginning, fathering, fertilization, genesis, impregnation, initiation, origin. **2** see IDEA 1–2.

conceptual /kən'septjʊəl/ *adjective* of mental concepts. □ **conceptually** *adverb*.

conceptualize *verb* (also **-ise**) (**-zing** or **-sing**) form concept or idea of. □ **conceptualization** *noun*.

concern /kən'sɜːn/ *verb* **1** be relevant or important to. **2** relate to; be about. **3** worry, affect. **4** (**concern oneself**; often + *with, about, in*) interest or involve oneself. ● *noun* **1** anxiety, worry. **2** care, consideration. **3** matter of interest or importance to one. **4** firm, business.

■ *verb* **1, 2** affect, be important to, be relevant to, interest, involve, matter to, pertain to, refer to, relate to. ● *noun* **1** anxiety, burden, disquiet, distress, fear, malaise, solicitude, worry. **2** attention, care, consideration, heed, interest, regard. **3** affair, business, charge, matter, problem, responsibility, task. **4** business, company, corporation, enterprise, establishment, firm, organization.

concerned *adjective* **1** involved, interested. **2** anxious, troubled.

■ **1** connected, implicated, interested, involved, referred to, relevant, responsible. **2** anxious,

bothered, caring, distressed, disturbed, fearful, perturbed, solicitous, touched, troubled, uneasy, unhappy, upset, worried.

concerning *preposition* about, regarding.

■ about, *colloquial* apropos of, germane to, involving, re, regarding, relating to, relevant to, with reference to, with regard to.

concert /'kɒnsət/ *noun* **1** musical performance. **2** agreement.

■ **1** entertainment, extravaganza, *colloquial* gig, performance, programme, recital, show.

concerted /kən'sɜːtɪd/ *adjective* jointly planned.

■ collaborative, collective, combined, cooperative, joint, *colloquial disputed* mutual, shared, united.

concertina /kɒnsə'tiːnə/ *noun* portable musical instrument like accordion but smaller. ● *verb* (**-nas**, **-naed** /-nəd/ or **-na'd**, **-naing**) compress or collapse in folds like those of concertina.

concerto /kən'tʃeətəʊ/ *noun* (*plural* **-tos** or **-ti** /-tɪ/) composition for solo instrument(s) and orchestra.

concession /kən'seʃ(ə)n/ *noun* **1** conceding, thing conceded. **2** reduction in price for certain category of people. **3** right to use land, sell goods, etc. □ **concessionary** *adjective*.

■ **2** adjustment, allowance, reduction.

conch /kɒntʃ/ *noun* **1** large spiral shell of various marine gastropod molluscs. **2** such gastropod.

conchology /kɒŋ'kɒlədʒɪ/ *noun* study of shells.

conciliate /kən'sɪlɪeɪt/ *verb* (**-ting**) **1** make calm; pacify. **2** reconcile. □ **conciliation** *noun*. **conciliator** *noun*. **conciliatory** *adjective*.

concise /kən'saɪs/ *adjective* brief but comprehensive. □ **concisely** *adverb*. **conciseness** *noun*. **concision** /kən'sɪʒ(ə)n/ *noun*.

■ brief, compact, compendious, compressed, concentrated, condensed, epigrammatic, laconic, pithy, short, small, succinct, terse.

conclave /'kɒŋkleɪv/ *noun* **1** private meeting. **2** assembly or meeting-place of cardinals for election of pope.

conclude /kən'kluːd/ *verb* (**-ding**) **1** bring or come to end. **2** (often + *from, that*) infer. **3** settle (treaty etc.).

■ **1** *formal* cease, close, complete, culminate, end, finish, round off, stop, terminate. **2** assume, decide, deduce, gather, infer, judge, reckon, suppose, surmise, think.

conclusion /kən'kluːʒ(ə)n/ *noun* **1** ending. **2** judgement reached by reasoning. **3** summing-up. **4** settling of peace etc. □ **in conclusion** lastly.

■ **1** close, completion, culmination, end, ending, epilogue, finale, finish, rounding-off, termination. **2** answer, belief, decision, deduction, inference, interpretation, judgement, opinion, outcome, resolution, result, solution, upshot, verdict. **3** peroration, recapitulation, summing-up.

conclusive /kən'klu:sɪv/ *adjective* decisive, convincing. □ **conclusively** *adverb*.
■ certain, convincing, decisive, definite, persuasive, unambiguous, unanswerable, unequivocal, unquestionable.

concoct /kən'kɒkt/ *verb* 1 make by mixing ingredients. 2 invent (story, lie, etc.). □ **concoction** *noun*.
■ 1 make, prepare, put together. 2 contrive, *colloquial* cook up, counterfeit, devise, fabricate, feign, formulate, hatch, invent, make up, plan, put together, *colloquial* think up.

concomitant /kən'kɒmɪt(ə)nt/ *adjective* (often + *with*) accompanying. ● *noun* accompanying thing. □ **concomitance** *noun*.

concord /'kɒŋkɔ:d/ *noun* agreement, harmony. □ **concordant** /kən'kɔ:d(ə)nt/ *adjective*.
■ agreement, euphony, harmony, peace.

concordance /kən'kɔ:d(ə)ns/ *noun* 1 agreement. 2 index of words used in book or by author.

concordat /kən'kɔ:dæt/ *noun* agreement, esp. between Church and state.

concourse /'kɒŋkɔ:s/ *noun* 1 crowd. 2 large open area in railway station etc.

concrete /'kɒŋkri:t/ *adjective* 1 existing in material form; real. 2 definite. ● *noun* mixture of gravel, sand, cement, and water used for building. ● *verb* (**-ting**) cover with or embed in concrete. □ **concretely** *adverb*. **concreteness** *noun*.
■ *adjective* actual, definite, existing, factual, firm, material, objective, palpable, physical, real, solid, substantial, tactile, tangible, touchable, visible.

concretion /kən'kri:ʃ(ə)n/ *noun* 1 hard solid mass. 2 forming of this by coalescence.

concubine /'kɒŋkjʊbaɪn/ *noun* 1 *literary* mistress. 2 (among polygamous peoples) secondary wife.

concupiscence /kən'kju:pɪs(ə)ns/ *noun formal* lust. □ **concupiscent** *adjective*.

concur /kən'kɜ:/ *verb* (**-rr-**) 1 (often + *with*) agree. 2 coincide.
■ 1 accede, accord, agree, assent. 2 see COINCIDE 1.

concurrent /kən'kʌrənt/ *adjective* (often + *with*) existing or in operation at the same time. □ **concurrence** *noun*. **concurrently** *adverb*.
■ coexisting, coinciding, concomitant, contemporaneous, contemporary, overlapping, parallel, simultaneous, synchronous.

concuss /kən'kʌs/ *verb* subject to concussion.

concussion /kən'kʌʃ(ə)n/ *noun* 1 temporary unconsciousness or incapacity due to head injury. 2 violent shaking.

condemn /kən'dem/ *verb* 1 express strong disapproval of. 2 (usually + *to*) sentence (to punishment). 3 (usually + *to*) doom (to something unpleasant). 4 pronounce unfit for use. □ **condemnation** /kɒndem'neɪʃ(ə)n/ *noun*. **condemnatory** /-'demnət(ə)rɪ/ *adjective*.
■ 1 blame, castigate, censure, criticize, damn, decry, denounce, deplore, deprecate, disapprove of, disparage, execrate, rebuke, *formal* reprehend, *formal* reprove, revile, *slang* slam, *colloquial* slate, upbraid. 2 convict, find guilty, prove guilty.

condensation /kɒnden'seɪʃ(ə)n/ *noun* 1 condensing, being condensed. 2 condensed liquid. 3 abridgement.
■ 2 haze, mist, steam, water drops.

condense /kən'dens/ *verb* (**-sing**) 1 make denser. 2 make more concise. 3 reduce or be reduced from gas to liquid.
■ 1 concentrate, reduce, thicken. 2 abbreviate, abridge, compress, contract, curtail, précis, reduce, shorten, summarize.

condescend /kɒndɪ'send/ *verb* 1 (usually + *to do*) graciously consent to do a thing while showing one's superiority. 2 (+ *to*) pretend to be on equal terms with (inferior). 3 (as **condescending** *adjective*) patronizing. □ **condescendingly** *adverb*. **condescension** *noun*.
■ 1 deign, demean oneself, humble oneself, lower oneself, stoop. 3 (**condescending**) see HAUGHTY.

condiment /'kɒndɪmənt/ *noun* seasoning or relish for food.

condition /kən'dɪʃ(ə)n/ *noun* 1 stipulation; thing on fulfilment of which something else depends. 2 state of being or fitness of person or thing. 3 ailment. 4 (in *plural*) circumstances. ● *verb* 1 bring into desired state. 2 accustom. 3 determine. 4 be essential to.
■ *noun* 1 limitation, obligation, prerequisite, proviso, qualification, requirement, requisite, restriction, stipulation. 2 fettle, fitness, form, health, *colloquial* nick, order, shape, state, trim, working order. 3 see ILLNESS 1. 4 (*conditions*) see CIRCUMSTANCE 1. ● *verb* 1 educate, fit, prepare, teach, train. 2 acclimatize, accustom, brainwash, educate, mould, re-educate, teach, train.

conditional *adjective* 1 (often + *on*) dependent; not absolute. 2 *Grammar* (of clause, mood, etc.) expressing condition. □ **conditionally** *adverb*.
■ 1 dependent, limited, provisional, qualified, restricted.

condole /kən'dəʊl/ *verb* (**-ling**) (+ *with*) express sympathy with (person) over loss etc.

USAGE *Condole* is commonly confused with *console*, which means 'to comfort'.

condolence *noun* (often in *plural*) expression of sympathy.

condom /'kɒndɒm/ *noun* contraceptive sheath.

condominium /kɒndə'mɪnɪəm/ *noun* 1 joint rule or sovereignty. 2 *US* building containing individually owned flats.

condone /kən'dəʊn/ *verb* (**-ning**) forgive, overlook.
■ allow, connive at, disregard, endorse, excuse, forgive, ignore, overlook, pardon, tolerate.

condor /'kɒndɔ:/ *noun* large S. American vulture.

conducive /kən'dju:sɪv/ *adjective* (often + *to*) contributing or helping (towards something).

■ advantageous, beneficial, encouraging, favourable, helpful, supportive; (*be conducive to*) see ENCOURAGE 3.

conduct *noun* /'kɒndʌkt/ **1** behaviour. **2** manner of conducting business, war, etc. ● *verb* /kən'dʌkt/ **1** lead, guide. **2** control, manage. **3** be conductor of (orchestra etc.). **4** transmit by conduction. **5** (**conduct oneself**) behave.

■ *noun* **1** actions, attitude, bearing, behaviour, *literary* comportment, demeanour, deportment, manners, ways. **2** administration, control, direction, discharge, government, guidance, handling, leading, management, operation, organization, regulation, running, supervision. ● *verb* **1** accompany, escort, guide, lead, pilot, steer, take, usher. **2** administer, be in charge of, chair, command, control, direct, govern, handle, head, lead, look after, manage, organize, oversee, preside over, regulate, rule, run, steer, superintend, supervise. **4** carry, channel, convey, transmit. **5** (**conduct oneself**) see BEHAVE 1,2.

conduction /kən'dʌkʃ(ə)n/ *noun* transmission of heat, electricity, etc.

conductive /kən'dʌktɪv/ *adjective* transmitting heat, electricity, etc. □ **conductivity** /kɒndʌk'tɪv-/ *noun*.

conductor *noun* **1** director of orchestra etc. **2** (*feminine* **conductress**) person who collects fares on bus etc. **3** conductive thing.

conduit /'kɒndɪt/ *noun* channel or pipe for conveying liquid or protecting insulated cable.

cone *noun* **1** solid figure with usually circular base and tapering to a point. **2** cone-shaped object. **3** dry fruit of pine or fir. **4** ice cream cornet.

coney = CONY.

confab /'kɒnfæb/ *noun colloquial* confabulation.

confabulate /kən'fæbjʊleɪt/ *verb* (**-ting**) talk together. □ **confabulation** *noun*.

confection /kən'fekʃ(ə)n/ *noun* sweet dish or delicacy.

confectioner *noun* dealer in sweets or pastries etc. □ **confectionery** *noun*.

confederacy /kən'fedərəsɪ/ *noun* (*plural* **-ies**) alliance or league, esp. of confederate states.

confederate /kən'fedərət/ *adjective esp. Politics* allied. ● *noun* ally; accomplice. ● *verb* /-reɪt/ (**-ting**) (often + *with*) bring or come into alliance. □ **Confederate States** those which seceded from US in 1860–1.

confederation /kənfedə'reɪʃ(ə)n/ *noun* union or alliance, esp. of states.

confer /kən'fɜ:/ *verb* (**-rr-**) **1** (often + *on*, *upon*) grant, bestow. **2** (often + *with*) meet for discussion.

■ **1** accord, award, bestow, give, grant, honour with, impart, invest, present. **2** compare notes, consult, converse, debate, deliberate, discourse, discuss, exchange ideas, put heads together, seek advice, talk.

conference /'kɒnfər(ə)ns/ *noun* **1** consultation. **2** meeting for discussion.

■ **1** consultation, deliberation, dialogue, discussion. **2** congress, convention, council, forum, meeting, seminar, symposium.

conferment /kən'fɜ:mənt/ *noun* conferring (of honour etc.).

confess /kən'fes/ *verb* **1** acknowledge, admit. **2** declare one's sins, esp. to priest. **3** (of priest) hear confession of.

■ **1** acknowledge, admit, concede, disclose, divulge, make a clean breast of, own (up to). **2** *colloquial* come clean, own up, unbosom oneself, unburden oneself.

confessedly /kən'fesɪdlɪ/ *adverb* by one's own or general admission.

confession /kən'feʃ(ə)n/ *noun* **1** act of confessing; thing confessed. **2** statement of principles etc.

■ **1** acknowledgement, admission, declaration, disclosure, revelation. **2** affirmation, declaration, profession, statement, testimony.

confessional *noun* enclosed place where priest hears confession. ● *adjective* of confession.

confessor *noun* priest who hears confession.

confetti /kən'fetɪ/ *noun* small bits of coloured paper thrown by wedding guests at bride and groom.

confidant /'kɒnfɪdænt/ *noun* (*feminine* **confidante** same pronunciation) person trusted with knowledge of one's private affairs.

confide /kən'faɪd/ *verb* (**-ding**) (usually + *to*) **1** tell (secret). **2** entrust (task). □ **confide in** talk confidentially to.

■ **1** disclose, divulge, entrust, impart, reveal, *colloquial* spill the beans, tell all, tell secrets, trust.

confidence /'kɒnfɪd(ə)ns/ *noun* **1** firm trust. **2** feeling of certainty. **3** self-reliance; boldness. **4** something told as a secret. □ **confidence trick** (also **con-trick**) swindle in which victim is persuaded to trust swindler. **confidence trickster** person using confidence tricks. **in confidence** as a secret. **in (person's) confidence** trusted with his or her secrets.

■ **1** belief, credence, faith, reliance, trust. **2** certainty, conviction, firmness, hope, optimism, positiveness. **3** aplomb, assurance, boldness, composure, nerve, panache, self-assurance, self-confidence, self-possession, self-reliance, spirit, verve.

confident *adjective* **1** feeling or showing confidence. **2** trusting. □ **confidently** *adverb*.

■ **1** assertive, assured, bold, cocksure, composed, cool, definite, fearless, secure, self-assured, self-confident, self-possessed, self-reliant, unafraid. **2** certain, convinced, hopeful, optimistic, positive, sanguine, sure, trusting.

confidential /kɒnfɪˈdenʃ(ə)l/ *adjective* **1** spoken or written in confidence. **2** (of secretary etc.) entrusted with secrets. **3** confiding. □ **confidentiality** /-ʃɪˈæl-/ *noun.* **confidentially** *adjective.*

■ **1** classified, *colloquial* hush-hush, intimate, off the record, personal, private, restricted, secret, suppressed, top secret. **2** personal, private, trusted.

configuration /kənfɪgjʊˈreɪʃ(ə)n/ *noun* **1** manner of arrangement. **2** shape, outline. □ **configure** /-ˈfɪgə/ *verb.*

confine *verb* /kənˈfaɪn/ (**-ning**) **1** keep or restrict within certain limits. **2** imprison. ● *noun* /ˈkɒnfaɪn/ (usually in *plural*) boundary. □ **be confined** be in childbirth.

■ *verb* **1** bar in, bind, box in, cage, circumscribe, constrain, contain, coop up, cordon off, cramp, curb, detain, enclose, hedge in, hem in, hold down, isolate, keep in, limit, localize, restrain, restrict, rope off, shut in, shut up, surround, wall up. **2** see IMPRISON 2.

confinement /kənˈfaɪnmənt/ *noun* **1** confining, being confined. **2** childbirth.

confirm /kənˈfɜːm/ *verb* **1** provide support for truth or correctness of. **2** establish more firmly. **3** formally make definite. **4** administer rite of confirmation to.

■ **1** authenticate, back up, bear out, corroborate, demonstrate, endorse, establish, give credence to, justify, lend force to, prove, reinforce, show, substantiate, support, underline, vindicate, witness to. **2** clinch, establish, fortify, reinforce, settle, strengthen. **3** authorize, formalize, guarantee, make legal, make official, ratify, sanction, validate, verify.

confirmation /kɒnfəˈmeɪʃ(ə)n/ *noun* **1** confirming circumstance or statement. **2** rite confirming baptized person as member of Christian Church.

confirmed *adjective* firmly settled in habit or condition.

confiscate /ˈkɒnfɪskeɪt/ *verb* (**-ting**) take or seize by authority. □ **confiscation** *noun.*

■ appropriate, commandeer, expropriate, impound, remove, seize, sequester, sequestrate, take away, take possession of.

conflagration /kɒnfləˈgreɪʃ(ə)n/ *noun* large destructive fire.

conflate /kənˈfleɪt/ *verb* (**-ting**) fuse together, blend. □ **conflation** *noun.*

conflict *noun* /ˈkɒnflɪkt/ **1** fight, struggle. **2** opposition. **3** (often + *of*) clashing of opposed interests etc. ● *verb* /kənˈflɪkt/ clash, be incompatible.

■ *noun* **1** altercation, battle, brush, clash, combat, confrontation, contest, dispute, encounter, engagement, feud, fight, quarrel, *colloquial* row, *colloquial* set-to, skirmish, struggle, war, warfare, wrangle. **2** antagonism, antipathy, contention, contradiction, difference, disagreement, discord, dissension, friction, hostility, incompatibility, inconsistency, opposition, strife. ● *verb* be at odds, be at variance, be incompatible, clash, compete, contend, contradict each other, contrast, cross swords, differ, disagree, fight, oppose each other, quarrel.

confluent /ˈkɒnfluənt/ *adjective* merging into one. ● *noun* stream joining another. □ **confluence** *noun.*

conform /kənˈfɔːm/ *verb* **1** comply with rules or general custom. **2** (+ *to, with*) be in accordance with.

■ **1** be good, behave conventionally, blend in, do what one is told, fit in, keep in step, toe the line. **2** see COMPLY.

conformable *adjective* **1** (often + *to*) similar. **2** (often + *with*) consistent.

conformation /kɒnfɔːˈmeɪʃ(ə)n/ *noun* thing's structure or shape.

conformist *noun* person who conforms to established practice. ● *adjective* conventional. □ **conformism** *noun.*

■ *noun* traditionalist, *colloquial* yes-man.

conformity *noun* **1** conforming with established practice. **2** suitability.

■ **1** *formal* complaisance, compliance, conventionality, obedience, orthodoxy, submission, uniformity.

confound /kənˈfaʊnd/ *verb* **1** baffle, confuse. **2** *archaic* defeat. □ **confound (person, thing)!** *interjection: expressing annoyance.*

confounded *adjective colloquial* damned.

confront /kənˈfrʌnt/ *verb* **1** meet or stand facing, esp. in hostility or defiance. **2** face up to (problem etc.). **3** (of problem etc.) present itself to. **4** (+ *with*) bring face to face with. □ **confrontation** /kɒn-/ *noun.* **confrontational** /kɒn-/ *adjective.*

■ **1, 2** accost, argue with, attack, brave, challenge, defy, encounter, face up to, meet, oppose, resist, stand up to, take on, withstand.

confuse /kənˈfjuːz/ *verb* (**-sing**) **1** (often as **confused** *adjective*) bewilder. **2** mix up; fail to distinguish. **3** make obscure. **4** (often as **confused** *adjective*) throw into disorder. □ **confusing** *adjective.*

■ **1** addle, agitate, baffle, befuddle, bemuse, bewilder, confound, disconcert, disorientate, distract, *colloquial* flummox, fluster, fuddle, mislead, mystify, perplex, puzzle, *colloquial* rattle, *colloquial* throw; (**confused**) addle-brained, dazed, *colloquial* in a tizzy, muddle-headed, muzzy, nonplussed. **2** mix up, muddle. **4** disarrange, disorder, distort, entangle, garble, jumble, mess up, mingle, mix up, muddle, tangle, throw into disarray, upset; (**confused**) aimless, chaotic, contradictory, disconnected, disjointed, disorderly, disorganized, higgledy-piggledy, incoherent, inconsistent, irrational, messy, misleading, obscure, rambling, *slang* screwed up, *colloquial* shambolic, topsy-turvy, twisted, unclear, unsound, unstructured, woolly. □ **confusing** see PUZZLE *verb* 3.

confusion /kən'fju:ʒ(ə)n/ *noun* 1 mixing up. 2 misunderstanding. 3 disorder; jumble. 4 bewilderment.

■ 3 ado, anarchy, bedlam, bother, chaos, clutter, commotion, confusion, din, disorder, disorganization, disturbance, fuss, hubbub, hullabaloo, jumble, mayhem, mêlée, mess, muddle, pandemonium, racket, riot, *colloquial* rumpus, *colloquial* shambles, tumult, turbulence, turmoil, upheaval, uproar, welter, whirl. 4 bemusement, bewilderment, disorientation, distraction, mystification, perplexity, puzzlement.

confute /kən'fju:t/ *verb* (**-ting**) prove to be false or wrong. □ **confutation** /kɒn-/ *noun*.

conga /'kɒŋgə/ *noun* 1 Latin American dance, usually performed in single file. 2 tall narrow drum beaten with hands.

congeal /kən'dʒi:l/ *verb* 1 make or become semi-solid by cooling. 2 (of blood) coagulate.

■ clot, coagulate, curdle, freeze, harden, *colloquial* jell, set, solidify, stiffen, thicken.

congenial /kən'dʒi:nɪəl/ *adjective* 1 having sympathetic nature, similar interests, etc. 2 (often + *to*) suited or agreeable. □ **congeniality** /-'æl-/ *noun*. **congenially** *adverb*.

■ 1 amicable, companionable, compatible, friendly, genial, kindly, sympathetic, understanding, well suited. 2 acceptable, agreeable, suitable, suited, well suited.

congenital /kən'dʒenɪt(ə)l/ *adjective* existing or as such from birth. □ **congenitally** *adverb*.

■ hereditary, inborn, inbred, inherent, inherited, innate, natural.

conger /'kɒŋgə/ *noun* large sea eel.

congest /kən'dʒest/ *verb* (esp. as **congested** *adjective*) affect with congestion.

■ (**congested**) blocked, choked, clogged, crammed, crowded, full, jammed, obstructed, overcrowded, stuffed.

congestion *noun* abnormal accumulation or obstruction, esp. of traffic etc. or of mucus in nose etc.

conglomerate /kən'glɒmərət/ *adjective* gathered into rounded mass. ● *noun* 1 heterogeneous mass. 2 business etc. corporation of merged firms. ● *verb* /-reɪt/ (**-ting**) collect into coherent mass. □ **conglomeration** *noun*.

congratulate /kən'grætʃʊleɪt/ *verb* (**-ting**) (often + *on*) express pleasure at happiness, excellence, or good fortune of (person). □ **congratulatory** /-lətərɪ/ *adjective*.

■ applaud, compliment, felicitate, praise.

congratulation *noun* 1 congratulating. 2 (usually in *plural*) expression of this.

congregate /'kɒŋgrɪgeɪt/ *verb* (**-ting**) collect or gather in crowd.

■ assemble, cluster, collect, come together, convene, converge, crowd, flock, forgather, gather, get together, herd, mass, meet, muster, rally, rendezvous, swarm, throng.

congregation *noun* 1 assembly of people, esp. for religious worship. 2 group of people regularly attending particular church etc.

congregational *adjective* 1 of a congregation. 2 (**Congregational**) of or adhering to Congregationalism.

Congregationalism *noun* system in which individual churches are self-governing. □ **Congregationalist** *noun*.

congress /'kɒŋgres/ *noun* 1 formal meeting of delegates for discussion. 2 (**Congress**) national legislative body of US etc. □ **congressman**, **congresswoman** member of US Congress. □ **congressional** /kən'greʃ-/ *adjective*.

congruent /'kɒŋgrʊənt/ *adjective* 1 (often + *with*) suitable, agreeing. 2 *Geometry* (of figures) coinciding exactly when superimposed. □ **congruence** *noun*.

congruous /'kɒŋgrʊəs/ *adjective* (often + *with*) suitable, agreeing. □ **congruity** /-'gru:ɪtɪ/ *noun*.

conic /'kɒnɪk/ *adjective* of a cone.

conical *adjective* cone-shaped.

conifer /'kɒnɪfə/ *noun* cone-bearing tree. □ **coniferous** /kə'nɪfərəs/ *adjective*.

conjectural /kən'dʒektʃər(ə)l/ *adjective* involving conjecture.

conjecture /kən'dʒektʃə/ *noun* formation of opinion on incomplete information; guess. ● *verb* (**-ring**) guess.

conjoin /kən'dʒɔɪn/ *verb* *formal* join, combine.

conjoint /kən'dʒɔɪnt/ *adjective* *formal* associated, conjoined.

conjugal /'kɒndʒʊg(ə)l/ *adjective* of marriage; between husband and wife.

conjugate *verb* /'kɒndʒʊgeɪt/ (**-ting**) 1 give the different forms of (verb). 2 unite; become fused. ● *adjective* /-gət/ joined together.

conjugation *noun* *Grammar* system of verbal inflection.

conjunct /kən'dʒʌŋkt/ *adjective* joined; combined; associated.

conjunction *noun* 1 joining, connection. 2 word used to connect sentences, clauses, or words (see panel). 3 combination of events or circumstances. □ **conjunctive** *adjective*.

conjunctiva /kɒndʒʌŋk'taɪvə/ *noun* (*plural* **-s**) mucous membrane covering front of eye and inside of eyelid.

conjunctivitis /kəndʒʌŋktɪ'vaɪtɪs/ *noun* inflammation of conjunctiva.

conjure /'kʌndʒə/ *verb* (**-ring**) 1 perform seemingly magical tricks, esp. by movement of hands. 2 summon (spirit). 3 cause to appear, happen, etc., as if by magic. ◻ **conjure up** produce as if by magic, evoke. ◻ **conjuring** *noun*.

■ **2** bewitch, charm, enchant, invoke, raise, rouse, summon. ◻ **conjure up** see PRODUCE *verb* 1.
◻ **conjuring** illusions, legerdemain, magic, sleight of hand, tricks, wizardry.

conjuror *noun* (also **conjurer**) performer of conjuring tricks.

conk[1] *verb colloquial* (usually + *out*) **1** break down. **2** become exhausted; faint; fall asleep.

conk[2] *slang noun* (punch on) nose or head.
● *verb* hit on nose or head.

conker /'kɒŋkə/ *noun* **1** horse chestnut fruit. **2** (in *plural*) children's game played with conkers on strings.

con man *noun* confidence trickster.

connect /kə'nekt/ *verb* **1** (often + *to, with*) join; be joined. **2** associate mentally or practically. **3** (+ *with*) (of train etc.) arrive in time for passengers to transfer to another. **4** put into communication by telephone. **5** (usually in *passive*; + *with*) unite or associate with (others) in relationship etc. ◻ **connecting rod** rod between piston and crankpin etc. in engine. ◻ **connector** *noun*.

■ **1** attach, combine, couple, engage, fasten, fix, interlock, join, link, put on, tie, unite. **2** associate, bracket together, make a connection between, put together, relate, tie up.

connection *noun* (also **connexion**) **1** connecting, being connected. **2** point at which things are connected. **3** association of ideas; relationship. **4** link, esp. by telephone. **5** (often in *plural*) (esp. influential) relative or associate. **6** connecting train etc.

■ **2** see JOINT *noun* 1,2, LINK *noun* 3. **3** affinity, association, bond, coherence, contact, correlation, correspondence, interrelationship, link, relationship, relevance, tie, tie-up.

connective *adjective* connecting. ◻ **connective tissue** body tissue forming tendons and ligaments, supporting organs, etc.

conning tower /'kɒnɪŋ/ *noun* **1** raised struc-

ture of submarine containing periscope. **2** wheelhouse of warship.

connive /kə'naɪv/ *verb* (**-ving**) **1** (+ *at*) tacitly consent to (wrongdoing). **2** conspire. ◻ **connivance** *noun*.

connoisseur /kɒnə'sɜː/ *noun* (often + *of, in*) person with good taste and judgement.

connote /kə'nəʊt/ *verb* (**-ting**) **1** imply in addition to literal meaning. **2** mean. ◻ **connotation** /kɒnə-/ *noun*. **connotative** /'kɒnəteɪtɪv/ *adjective*.

connubial /kə'njuːbɪəl/ *adjective* conjugal.

conquer /'kɒŋkə/ *verb* **1** overcome, defeat; subjugate. **2** be victorious. **3** reach top of (mountain). ◻ **conquerable** *adjective*. **conqueror** *noun*.

■ **1** annex, beat, *colloquial* best, capture, checkmate, crush, defeat, get the better of, humble, *colloquial* lick, master, occupy, outdo, overcome, overpower, overrun, overthrow, overwhelm, possess, prevail over, quell, rout, seize, silence, subdue, subject, subjugate, succeed against, surmount, take, thrash, triumph over, *literary* vanquish, worst. **2** see WIN *verb* 2. **3** climb, reach top of.

conquest /'kɒŋkwest/ *noun* **1** conquering. **2** something won. **3** person whose affections have been won.

■ **1** annexation, appropriation, capture, defeat, domination, invasion, occupation, overthrow, subjection, subjugation, takeover, triumph, victory. **2** prize, trophy.

consanguineous /kɒnsæŋ'gwɪnɪəs/ *adjective* descended from same ancestor; akin. ◻ **consanguinity** *noun*.

conscience /'kɒnʃ(ə)ns/ *noun* moral sense of right and wrong, esp. as affecting behaviour. ◻ **conscience money** money paid to relieve conscience, esp. in respect of evaded payment etc. **conscience-stricken** made uneasy by bad conscience. ◻ **conscienceless** *adjective*.

■ compunction, ethics, honour, misgivings, morality, morals, principles, qualms, reservations, scruples, standards.

conscientious /kɒnʃɪ'enʃəs/ *adjective* dili-

....

Conjunction

A conjunction is used to join parts of a sentence which usually, but not always, contain their own verbs, e.g.

> *He found it difficult* so *I helped him.*
> *I waited* until *you came.*

There are two types of conjunction. **Coordinating conjunctions** (*and, or, but*) join two equal clauses, phrases, or words. **Subordinating conjunctions** join a subordinate clause to a main clause.

The most common subordinating conjunctions are:

after	*if*	*so*	*unless*
although	*in order that*	*so that*	*until*
as	*like*	*than*	*when*
because	*now*	*that*	*where*
before	*once*	*though*	*whether*
for	*since*	*till*	*while*

....

gent and scrupulous. □ **conscientious objector** person who refuses to do military service on grounds of conscience. □ **conscientiously** *adverb.* **conscientiousness** *noun.*

■ accurate, attentive, careful, diligent, dutiful, exact, hard-working, high-minded, honest, meticulous, painstaking, particular, punctilious, responsible, rigorous, scrupulous, serious, thorough.

conscious /'kɒnʃəs/ *adjective* **1** awake and aware of one's surroundings etc. **2** (usually + *of, that*) aware, knowing. **3** intentional. □ **consciously** *adverb.* **consciousness** *noun.*

■ **1** alert, awake, aware, compos mentis, sensible, waking. **2** aware, *formal* cognizant, knowing. **3** calculated, deliberate, intended, intentional, planned, premeditated, self-conscious, studied, voluntary, wilful.

conscript *verb* /kən'skrɪpt/ summon for compulsory state (esp. military) service. ● *noun* /'kɒnskrɪpt/ conscripted person. □ **conscription** *noun.*

consecrate /'kɒnsɪkreɪt/ *verb* (**-ting**) **1** make or declare sacred; dedicate formally to religious purpose. **2** (+ *to*) devote to (a purpose). □ **consecration** *noun.*

■ **1** bless, dedicate, devote, hallow, sanctify.

consecutive /kən'sekjʊtɪv/ *adjective* following continuously; in unbroken or logical order. □ **consecutively** *adverb.*

■ continuous, following, one after the other, running (*3 days running*), sequential, succeeding, successive.

consensus /kən'sensəs/ *noun* (often + *of*) general agreement or opinion.

consent /kən'sent/ *verb* (often + *to*) express willingness; give permission; agree. ● *noun* agreement; permission.

■ *verb* accede, acquiesce, agree, comply, concede, concur, conform, submit, yield; (*consent to*) see ALLOW **1.** ● *noun* acquiescence, agreement, approval, assent, concurrence, imprimatur, permission, seal of approval.

consequence /'kɒnsɪkwəns/ *noun* **1** result of what has gone before. **2** importance.

■ **1** aftermath, by-product, corollary, effect, end, follow-up, issue, outcome, repercussion, result, sequel, side effect, upshot. **2** account, concern, importance, moment, note, significance, value, weight.

consequent /'kɒnsɪkwənt/ *adjective* **1** that results. **2** (often + *on, upon*) following as consequence. □ **consequently** *adverb.*

■ consequential, ensuing, following, resultant, resulting, subsequent.

consequential /kɒnsɪ'kwenʃ(ə)l/ *adjective* **1** resulting, esp. indirectly. **2** important.

conservancy /kən'sɜːvənsɪ/ *noun* (*plural* **-ies**)

1 body controlling river, port, etc. **2** body concerned with preservation of natural resources. **3** conservation; official preservation (of forests etc.).

conservation /kɒnsə'veɪʃ(ə)n/ *noun* preservation, esp. of natural environment. □ **conservationist** *noun.*

■ economy, husbandry, maintenance, management, preservation, protection, safeguarding, saving, upkeep.
□ **conservationist** ecologist, environmentalist, green.

conservative /kən'sɜːvətɪv/ *adjective* **1** averse to rapid change. **2** (of estimate) purposely low. **3** (usually **Conservative**) of Conservative Party. ● *noun* **1** conservative person. **2** (usually **Conservative**) member or supporter of Conservative Party. □ **Conservative Party** political party promoting free enterprise. □ **conservatism** *noun.*

■ *adjective* **1** conventional, diehard, hidebound, moderate, narrow-minded, old-fashioned, reactionary, sober, traditional, unadventurous. **2** cautious, moderate, reasonable, understated, unexaggerated. **3** *colloquial* Tory. ● *noun* **1** conformist, diehard, reactionary, traditionalist. **2** *colloquial* Tory.

conservatoire /kən'sɜːvətwɑː/ *noun* (usually European) school of music or other arts.

conservatory /kən'sɜːvətərɪ/ *noun* (*plural* **-ies**) **1** greenhouse for tender plants. **2** *esp. US* conservatoire.

conserve /kən'sɜːv/ *verb* (**-ving**) preserve; keep from harm or damage. ● *noun* /'kɒnsɜːv/ fruit etc. preserved in sugar; fresh fruit jam.

■ *verb* be economical with, hold in reserve, keep, look after, maintain, preserve, protect, safeguard, save, store up, use sparingly.

consider /kən'sɪdə/ *verb* **1** contemplate; deliberate thoughtfully. **2** make allowance for; take into account. **3** (+ *that*) have the opinion that. **4** regard as. **5** show consideration for. **6** (as **considered** *adjective*) (esp. of an opinion) formed after careful thought.

■ **1** chew over, cogitate, contemplate, deliberate, discuss, examine, meditate on, mull over, muse on, ponder, puzzle over, reflect on, ruminate on, study, think about, think over, turn over, *colloquial* weigh up. **3** believe, judge, reckon, think. **4** *formal* deem, judge, look upon as, rate, regard as, take to be, think.

considerable *adjective* **1** a lot of. **2** notable, important. □ **considerably** *adverb.*

■ **1** appreciable, big, biggish, comfortable, large, largish, noticeable, perceptible, reasonable, respectable, significant, sizeable, substantial, *colloquial* tidy (*amount*), tolerable. **2** important, notable, noteworthy, significant, worthwhile.

considerate /kən'sɪdərət/ *adjective* giving thought to feelings or rights of others. □ **considerately** *adverb.*

■ accommodating, altruistic, attentive, caring, charitable, cooperative, friendly, generous, gracious, helpful, kind, kind-hearted, kindly, neighbourly, obliging, polite, sensitive, solicitous, sympathetic, tactful, thoughtful, unselfish.

consideration /kənsɪdə'reɪʃ(ə)n/ *noun* **1** careful thought. **2** being considerate. **3** fact or thing taken into account. **4** compensation, payment. □ **take into consideration** make allowance for.

considering *preposition* in view of.

consign /kən'saɪn/ *verb* (often + *to*) **1** commit; deliver. **2** send (goods etc.). □ **consignee** /kɒnsaɪ'niː/ *noun*. **consignor** *noun*.

■ **1** commit, convey, deliver, devote, entrust, give, hand over, pass on, relegate, transfer. **2** convey, deliver, send, ship, transmit.

consignment *noun* consigning; goods consigned.

■ batch, cargo, delivery, load, lorry-load, shipment, van-load.

consist /kən'sɪst/ *verb* **1** (+ *of*) be composed of. **2** (+ *in, of*) have its essential features in.

■ **1** (*consist of*) be composed of, be made of, comprise, contain, embody, include, incorporate.

consistency *noun* (*plural* **-ies**) **1** degree of density or firmness, esp. of thick liquids. **2** being consistent.

consistent *adjective* **1** constant to same principles. **2** (usually + *with*) compatible. □ **consistently** *adverb*

■ **1** constant, dependable, faithful, predictable, regular, reliable, stable, steadfast, steady, unchanging, undeviating, unfailing, uniform, unvarying. **2** compatible, congruous, consonant, in accordance, in agreement, in harmony, of a piece.

consistory *noun* (*plural* **-ies**) *RC Church* council of cardinals.

consolation /kɒnsə'leɪʃ(ə)n/ *noun* **1** alleviation of grief or disappointment. **2** consoling person or thing. □ **consolation prize** one given to competitor just failing to win main prize. □ **consolatory** /kən'sɒl-/ *adjective*.

console[1] /kən'səʊl/ *verb* (**-ling**) bring consolation to.

USAGE *Console* is often confused with *condole*. To condole with someone is to express sympathy with that person.

■ cheer, comfort, encourage, hearten, relieve, solace, soothe, *archaic* or *formal* succour.

console[2] /'kɒnsəʊl/ *noun* **1** panel for switches, controls, etc. **2** cabinet for television etc. **3** cabinet with keys and stops of organ. **4** bracket supporting shelf etc.

consolidate /kən'sɒlɪdeɪt/ *verb* (**-ting**) **1** make or become strong or secure. **2** combine (territories, companies, debts, etc.) into one whole. □ **consolidation** *noun*.

■ **1** reinforce, stabilize, strengthen.

consommé /kən'sɒmeɪ/ *noun* clear meat soup.

consonance /'kɒnsənəns/ *noun* agreement, harmony.

consonant *noun* **1** speech sound that forms syllable only in combination with vowel. **2** letter(s) representing this. ● *adjective* (+ *with, to*) consistent with; in agreement or harmony with. □ **consonantal** /-'næn-/ *adjective*.

consort[1] *noun* /'kɒnsɔːt/ wife or husband, esp. of royalty. ● *verb* /kən'sɔːt/ (usually + *with*, *together*) **1** keep company. **2** harmonize.

■ *verb* **1** (*consort with*) accompany, associate with, befriend, be friends with, be seen with, fraternize with, gang up with, keep company with, mix with.

consort[2] /'kɒnsɔːt/ *noun Music* group of players or instruments.

consortium /kən'sɔːtɪəm/ *noun* (*plural* **-tia** or **-s**) association, esp. of several business companies.

conspicuous /kən'spɪkjʊəs/ *adjective* **1** clearly visible. **2** attracting attention. □ **conspicuously** *adverb*.

■ apparent, blatant, clear, discernible, distinguished, dominant, eminent, evident, flagrant, glaring, impressive, manifest, marked, notable, noticeable, obtrusive, obvious, ostentatious, outstanding, patent, perceptible, plain, prominent, pronounced, self-evident, shining (*example*), showy, striking, unconcealed, unmistakable, visible.

conspiracy /kən'spɪrəsɪ/ *noun* (*plural* **-ies**) **1** act of conspiring. **2** plot.

■ **1** collusion, connivance, insider dealing, intrigue, machinations, treason. **2** cabal, *slang* frame-up, intrigue, plot, *slang* racket, scheme, stratagem.

conspirator /kən'spɪrətə/ *noun* person who takes part in conspiracy. □ **conspiratorial** /-'tɔː-/ *adjective*.

■ plotter, schemer, traitor.

conspire /kən'spaɪə/ *verb* (**-ring**) **1** combine secretly for unlawful or harmful purpose. **2** (of events) seemingly work together.

■ **1** be in league, collude, combine, connive, cooperate, hatch a plot, have designs, intrigue, plot, scheme.

constable /'kʌnstəb(ə)l/ *noun* **1** (also **police constable**) police officer of lowest rank. **2** governor of royal castle. □ **Chief Constable** head of police force of county etc.

constabulary /kən'stæbjʊlərɪ/ *noun* (*plural* **-ies**) police force.

constancy /'kɒnstənsɪ/ *noun* dependability; faithfulness.

constant *adjective* **1** continuous. **2** frequently occurring. **3** having constancy; unchanging. ● *noun Mathematics & Physics* unvarying quantity. □ **constantly** *adverb*.

■ *adjective* **1** ceaseless, chronic, consistent, continuous, endless, *colloquial* eternal, everlasting, incessant, never-ending, non-stop, permanent, perpetual, persistent, relentless, stable, steady, sustained, unbroken, unending, uninterrupted, unremitting. **2** continual, frequent, regular, repeated. **3** dedicated, dependable, determined, devoted, faithful, firm, fixed, immutable, indefatigable, invariable, loyal, predictable, reliable, resolute, stationary, staunch, steadfast, tireless, true, trustworthy, *archaic* or *jocular* trusty, unchanging, unflagging, uniform, unswerving, unvarying, unwavering.

constellation /kɒnstə'leɪʃ(ə)n/ *noun* group of fixed stars.

consternation /kɒnstə'neɪʃ(ə)n/ *noun* amazement, dismay.

constipate /'kɒnstɪpeɪt/ *verb* (**-ting**) (esp. as **constipated** *adjective*) affect with constipation.

constipation *noun* difficulty in emptying bowels.

constituency /kən'stɪtjʊənsɪ/ *noun* (*plural* **-ies**) **1** body electing representative. **2** area represented.

constituent /kən'stɪtjʊənt/ *adjective* **1** making part of whole. **2** appointing; electing. ● *noun* **1** member of constituency. **2** component part.

constitute /'kɒnstɪtjuːt/ *verb* (**-ting**) **1** be essence or components of. **2** amount to. **3** establish.

■ **1** compose, form, make up. **3** appoint, bring together, create, establish, form, found, inaugurate, make, set up.

constitution /kɒnstɪ'tjuːʃ(ə)n/ *noun* **1** composition. **2** set of principles by which state etc. is governed. **3** person's inherent state of health, strength, etc.

constitutional *adjective* **1** of or in line with the constitution. **2** inherent. ● *noun* walk taken as exercise. □ **constitutionally** *adverb*.

constitutive /'kɒnstɪtjuːtɪv/ *adjective* **1** able to form or appoint. **2** constituent.

constrain /kən'streɪn/ *verb* **1** compel. **2** confine. **3** (as **constrained** *adjective*) forced, embarrassed.

constraint *noun* **1** compulsion. **2** restriction. **3** self-control.

constrict /kən'strɪkt/ *verb* make narrow or tight; compress. □ **constriction** *noun*. **constrictive** *adjective*.

constrictor *noun* **1** snake that kills by compressing. **2** muscle that contracts a part.

construct *verb* /kən'strʌkt/ **1** fit together; build. **2** *Geometry* draw. ● *noun* /'kɒnstrʌkt/ thing constructed, esp. by the mind. □ **constructor** /kən'strʌktə/ *noun*.

■ *verb* **1** assemble, build, create, engineer, erect, fabricate, fashion, fit together, form, knock together, make, manufacture, pitch (*tent*), produce, put together, put up, set up.

construction /kən'strʌkʃ(ə)n/ *noun* **1** con-

structing. **2** thing constructed. **3** syntactical arrangement. **4** interpretation. □ **constructional** *adjective*.

■ **1** assembly, building, creation, erecting, erection, manufacture, production. **2** building, edifice, erection, structure.

constructive /kən'strʌktɪv/ *adjective* positive, helpful. □ **constructively** *adverb*.

■ advantageous, beneficial, cooperative, creative, helpful, positive, practical, productive, useful, valuable, worthwhile.

construe /kən'struː/ *verb* (**-strues**, **-strued**, **-struing**) **1** interpret. **2** (often + *with*) combine (words) grammatically. **3** translate literally.

consubstantiation /kɒnsəbstænʃɪ'eɪʃ(ə)n/ *noun* presence of Christ's body and blood together with bread and wine in Eucharist.

consul /'kɒns(ə)l/ *noun* **1** official appointed by state to protect its interests and citizens in foreign city. **2** *historical* either of two annually elected magistrates in ancient Rome. □ **consular** /-sjʊlə/ *adjective*.

consulate /'kɒnsjʊlət/ *noun* offices or position of consul.

consult /kən'sʌlt/ *verb* **1** seek information or advice from. **2** (often + *with*) refer to. **3** take into consideration.

■ **1, 2** confer with, discuss with, exchange views with, refer to, seek advice from, speak to, talk things over with.

consultant /kən'sʌlt(ə)nt/ *noun* **1** person who gives professional advice. **2** senior medical specialist. □ **consultancy** *noun*.

consultation /kɒnsəl'teɪʃ(ə)n/ *noun* (meeting for) consulting.

consultative /kən'sʌltətɪv/ *adjective* of or for consultation.

consume /kən'sjuːm/ *verb* (**-ming**) **1** eat or drink. **2** use up. **3** destroy. □ **consumable** *adjective*.

■ **1** devour, digest, drink, eat, gobble up, guzzle, put away, swallow. **2** absorb, deplete, drain, eat into, employ, exhaust, expend, swallow up, use up, utilize.

consumer *noun* user of product or service. □ **consumer goods** goods for consumers, not for producing other goods.

consumerism *noun* **1** protection or promotion of consumers' interests. **2** (*often derogatory*) continual increase in consumption. □ **consumerist** *adjective*.

consummate *verb* /'kɒnsəmeɪt/ (**-ting**) complete (esp. marriage by sexual intercourse). ● *adjective* /kən'sʌmɪt/ complete, perfect; fully skilled. □ **consummation** /kɒnsə-/ *noun*.

consumption /kən'sʌmpʃ(ə)n/ *noun* **1** consuming, being consumed. **2** purchase and use of goods etc. **3** *archaic* tuberculosis of lungs.

consumptive /kən'sʌmptɪv/ *archaic adjective* suffering or tending to suffer from tuberculosis. ● *noun* consumptive person.

cont. *abbreviation* continued.

contact /'kɒntækt/ *noun* **1** condition or state of touching, meeting, or communicating. **2** person who is, or may be, contacted for information etc. **3** person likely to carry contagious disease through being near infected person. **4** connection for passage of electric current. ● *verb* get in touch with. □ **contact lens** small lens placed on eyeball to correct vision. □ **contactable** *adjective*.

■ *noun* **1** communication, connection, join, junction, meeting, touch, union. ● *verb* apply to, approach, call on, communicate with, correspond to, notify, *colloquial* phone, ring, sound out, speak to, talk to, telephone, write to.

contagion /kən'teɪdʒ(ə)n/ *noun* **1** spreading of disease by contact. **2** moral corruption. □ **contagious** *adjective*.

■ □ **contagious** catching, communicable, infectious, transmittable.

contain /kən'teɪn/ *verb* **1** hold or be capable of holding within itself. **2** include, comprise. **3** prevent from moving or extending. **4** control, restrain.

■ **1** accommodate, enclose, hold. **2** be composed of, comprise, consist of, embody, embrace, include, incorporate, involve. **3** see CONFINE *verb* 1. **4** check, control, curb, hold back, keep back, limit, repress, restrain, stifle.

container *noun* **1** box etc. for holding things. **2** large metal box for transporting goods.

■ **1** holder, receptacle, repository, vessel.

containment /kən'teɪnmənt/ *noun* action or policy of preventing expansion of hostile country or influence.

contaminate /kən'tæmɪneɪt/ *verb* (**-ting**) pollute; infect. □ **contaminant** *noun*. **contamination** *noun*.

■ adulterate, *poetical* befoul, corrupt, debase, defile, dirty, foul, infect, poison, pollute, soil, spoil, stain, sully, taint.

contemplate /'kɒntəmpleɪt/ *verb* (**-ting**) **1** survey with eyes. **2** survey with mind; consider. **3** regard as possible. **4** intend. □ **contemplation** *noun*.

■ **1** eye, gaze at, look at, observe, regard, stare at, survey, view, watch. **2** cogitate, consider, daydream, deliberate, examine, meditate, mull over, muse, ponder, reflect, ruminate, study, think (about), work out. **3** see ENVISAGE, EXPECT 1. **4** intend, plan, propose.

contemplative /kən'templətɪv/ *adjective* of or given to (esp. religious) contemplation.

contemporaneous /kəntempə'reɪnɪəs/ *adjective* (usually + *with*) existing or occurring at same time.

contemporary /kən'tempərərɪ/ *adjective* **1** belonging to same time. **2** of same age. **3** modern in style or design. ● *noun* (*plural* **-ies**) contemporary person or thing.

■ *adjective* **1** formal coeval, coexistent, coinciding, concurrent, contemporaneous, simultaneous, synchronous. **2** formal coeval. **3** current, fashionable, (the) latest, modern, newest, novel, present-day, topical, *colloquial often derogatory* trendy, up to date, *colloquial* with it. ● *noun* formal coeval, peer.

contempt /kən'tempt/ *noun* **1** feeling that person or thing deserves scorn or reproach. **2** condition of being held in contempt. **3** (in full **contempt of court**) disobedience to or disrespect for court of law. □ **contemptible** *adjective*.

■ **1** abhorrence, contumely, derision, detestation, disdain, disgust, dislike, disrespect, hatred, loathing, ridicule, scorn; (*feel contempt for*) see DESPISE. □ **contemptible** base, beneath contempt, despicable, detestable, discreditable, disgraceful, dishonourable, disreputable, hateful, ignominious, inferior, loathsome, low-down, mean, odious, pitiful, shabby, shameful, worthless, wretched.

contemptuous *adjective* feeling or showing contempt. □ **contemptuously** *adverb*.

■ arrogant, belittling, condescending, derisive, disdainful, dismissive, disrespectful, haughty, *colloquial* holier-than-thou, imperious, insolent, insulting, jeering, lofty, patronizing, sarcastic, scathing, scornful, sneering, snide, snobbish, *colloquial* snooty, *slang* snotty, supercilious, superior, withering; (*be contemptuous of*) see DESPISE.

contend /kən'tend/ *verb* **1** compete. **2** (usually + *with*) argue. **3** (+ *that*) maintain that. □ **contender** *noun*.

■ **1, 2** argue, compete, contest, cope, dispute, fight, grapple, oppose, quarrel, rival, strive, struggle, vie. **3** affirm, allege, argue, assert, claim, declare, maintain, plead.

content[1] /kən'tent/ *adjective* **1** satisfied. **2** (+ *to do*) willing to. ● *verb* make content; satisfy. ● *noun* contented state; satisfaction. □ **contentment** *noun*.

■ *adjective* **1** see CONTENTED. **2** see WILLING 1. ● *verb* see SATISFY 1,4. □ **contentment** comfort, content, contentedness, ease, fulfilment, happiness, relaxation, satisfaction, serenity, smugness, tranquillity, well-being.

content[2] /'kɒntent/ *noun* **1** (usually in *plural*) what is contained, esp. in vessel, house, or book. **2** amount contained. **3** substance of book etc. as opposed to form. **4** capacity, volume.

■ **1** (*contents*) constituents, elements, ingredients, parts.

contented /kən'tentɪd/ *adjective* happy, satisfied. □ **contentedly** *adverb*. **contentedness** *noun*.

■ cheerful, comfortable, complacent, content, fulfilled, gratified, happy, peaceful, pleased, relaxed, satisfied, serene, smiling, smug, uncomplaining, untroubled, well fed.

contention /kən'tenʃ(ə)n/ *noun* **1** dispute; rivalry. **2** point contended for in argument.

contentious /kən'tenʃəs/ *adjective* **1** quarrelsome. **2** likely to cause argument.

contest *noun* /'kɒntest/ **1** contending. **2** competition. ● *verb* /kən'test/ **1** dispute. **2** contend or compete for; compete in.

■ *noun* **1** see FIGHT *noun* 1. **2** see COMPETITION 2. ● *verb* **1** argue against, challenge, debate, dispute, doubt, oppose, query, question, resist. **2** compete for, contend for, fight for, make a bid for, strive for, struggle for, take up the challenge of, vie for.

contestant /kən'test(ə)nt/ *noun* person taking part in contest.

■ candidate, competitor, contender, entrant, opponent, participant, player, rival.

context /'kɒntekst/ *noun* **1** what precedes and follows word or passage. **2** relevant circumstances. □ **contextual** /kən'tekstjʊəl/ *adjective*.

■ background, circumstances, environment, frame of reference, framework, milieu, position, setting, situation, surroundings.

contiguous /kən'tɪgjʊəs/ *adjective* (usually + *with*, *to*) touching; in contact.

continent[1] /'kɒntɪnənt/ *noun* **1** any of the earth's main continuous bodies of land. **2** (**the Continent**) the mainland of Europe.

continent[2] /'kɒntɪnənt/ *adjective* **1** able to control bowels and bladder. **2** exercising esp. sexual self-restraint. □ **continence** *noun*.

continental /kɒntɪ'nent(ə)l/ *adjective* of or characteristic of a continent or (**Continental**) the Continent. □ **continental breakfast** light breakfast of coffee, rolls, etc. **continental quilt** duvet. **continental shelf** shallow seabed bordering continent.

contingency /kən'tɪndʒənsɪ/ *noun* (*plural* -ies) **1** event that may or may not occur. **2** something dependent on another uncertain event.

contingent *adjective* **1** (usually + *on*, *upon*) conditional, dependent. **2** that may or may not occur. **3** fortuitous. ● *noun* **1** group (of troops, ships, etc.) forming part of larger group. **2** people sharing interest, origin, etc.

continual /kən'tɪnjʊəl/ *adjective* frequently recurring; always happening. □ **continually** *adverb*.

USAGE *Continual* means 'happening frequently (but with breaks between each occurrence)' while *continuous* means 'uninterrupted, incessant'.

■ constant, *colloquial* eternal, everlasting, frequent, limitless, ongoing, perennial, *colloquial* perpetual, recurrent, regular, repeated.

continuance /kən'tɪnjʊəns/ *noun* **1** continuing in existence or operation. **2** duration.

continuation /kəntɪnjʊ'eɪʃ(ə)n/ *noun* **1** continuing, being continued. **2** thing that continues something else.

■ **1** continuance, extension, maintenance, prolongation, protraction, resumption. **2** addition, appendix, postscript, sequel, supplement.

continue /kən'tɪnju:/ *verb* (-**ues**, -**ued**, -**uing**) **1** maintain. **2** resume. **3** prolong. **4** remain.

■ **1** carry on (with), go on (with), keep on (with), keep up, maintain, persevere with, persist in, proceed with, pursue, *colloquial* stick at, sustain. **2** recommence, restart, resume. **3** extend, lengthen, prolong. **4** carry on, endure, last, linger, persist, remain, stay, survive.

continuity /kɒntɪ'nju:ɪtɪ/ *noun* (*plural* -ies) **1** being continuous. **2** logical sequence. **3** detailed scenario of film. **4** linkage of broadcast items.

continuo /kən'tɪnjʊəʊ/ *noun* (*plural* -s) *Music* bass accompaniment played usually on keyboard instrument.

continuous /kən'tɪnjʊəs/ *adjective* connected without break; uninterrupted. □ **continuously** *adverb*.

USAGE See note at CONTINUAL.

■ ceaseless, constant, continuing, endless, incessant, interminable, lasting, never-ending, non-stop, permanent, persistent, relentless, round the clock, solid, sustained, unbroken, unceasing, unending, uninterrupted, unremitting.

continuum /kən'tɪnjʊəm/ *noun* (*plural* -**nua**) thing with continuous structure.

contort /kən'tɔ:t/ *verb* twist or force out of normal shape. □ **contortion** *noun*.

contortionist *noun* entertainer who adopts contorted postures.

contour /'kɒntʊə/ *noun* **1** outline. **2** (in full **contour line**) line on map joining points at same altitude.

■ **1** curve, form, outline, relief, shape.

contraband /'kɒntrəbænd/ *noun* smuggled goods. ● *adjective* forbidden to be imported or exported.

contraception /kɒntrə'sepʃ(ə)n/ *noun* use of contraceptives.

contraceptive /kɒntrə'septɪv/ *adjective* preventing pregnancy. ● *noun* contraceptive device or drug.

contract *noun* /'kɒntrækt/ **1** written or spoken agreement, esp. one enforceable by law. **2** document recording it. ● *verb* /kən'trækt/ **1** make or become smaller. **2** (usually + *with*) make contract. **3** (often + *out*) arrange (work) to be done by contract. **4** become affected by (a disease). **5** incur (debt). **6** draw together. **7** shorten. □ **contract bridge** type of bridge in which only tricks bid and won count towards game. **contract in (or out)** elect (not) to enter scheme etc.

■ *noun* **1** agreement, bargain, bond, commitment, compact, concordat, covenant, deal, indenture, lease, pact, settlement, treaty, understanding, undertaking. ● *verb* **1** close up, condense, decrease, diminish, draw together, dwindle, fall away, lessen, narrow, reduce, shrink, shrivel, slim down, thin out, wither. **2** agree, arrange, close a deal, covenant, negotiate a deal, promise, sign an agreement, undertake. **4** acquire, become infected with, catch, develop, get, go down with.

contraction /kən'trækʃ(ə)n/ *noun* **1** contracting. **2** shortening of uterine muscles during childbirth. **3** shrinking; diminution. **4** shortened word.

■ **3** diminution, narrowing, shortening, shrinkage, shrivelling. **4** abbreviation, diminutive.

contractor /kən'træktə/ *noun* person who undertakes contract, esp. in building, engineering, etc.

contractual /kən'træktjʊəl/ *adjective* of or in the nature of a contract.

contradict /kɒntrə'dɪkt/ *verb* **1** deny; oppose verbally. **2** be at variance with. □ **contradiction** *noun*. **contradictory** *adjective*.

■ **1** argue with, challenge, confute, controvert, deny, disagree with, dispute, gainsay, impugn, oppose, speak against. □ **contradictory** antithetical, conflicting, contrary, different, discrepant, incompatible, inconsistent, irreconcilable, opposed, opposite.

contradistinction /kɒntrədɪs'tɪŋkʃ(ə)n/ *noun* distinction made by contrasting.

contraflow /'kɒntrəfləʊ/ *noun* transfer of traffic from usual half of road to lane(s) of other half.

contralto /kən'træltəʊ/ *noun* (*plural* **-s**) **1** lowest female singing voice. **2** singer with this voice.

contraption /kən'træpʃ(ə)n/ *noun* machine or device, esp. strange one.

■ apparatus, contrivance, device, gadget, invention, machine, mechanism.

contrapuntal /kɒntrə'pʌnt(ə)l/ *adjective* *Music* of or in counterpoint.

contrariwise /kən'treərɪwaɪz/ *adverb* **1** on the other hand. **2** in the opposite way.

contrary /'kɒntrərɪ/ *adjective* **1** (usually + *to*) opposed in nature, tendency, or direction. **2** /kən'treərɪ/ perverse, self-willed. ● *noun* (**the contrary**) the opposite. ● *adverb* (+ *to*) in opposition. □ **on the contrary** the opposite is true.

■ *adjective* **1** adverse, conflicting, contradictory, converse, different, hostile, inimical, opposed, opposing, opposite, other, reverse, unfavourable. **2** awkward, cantankerous, defiant, difficult, disobedient, disobliging, disruptive, intractable, obstinate, perverse, rebellious, *colloquial* stroppy, stubborn, subversive, uncooperative, unhelpful, wayward, wilful.

contrast *noun* /'kɒntrɑːst/ **1** comparison showing differences. **2** difference so revealed. **3** (often + *to*) thing or person having different qualities. **4** degree of difference between tones in photograph or television picture. ● *verb* /kən'trɑːst/ (often + *with*) **1** compare to reveal contrast. **2** show contrast. □ **contrasting** *adjective*.

■ *noun* **1**, **2** comparison, difference, differentiation, disparity, dissimilarity, distinction, divergence, opposition. **3** antithesis, foil, opposite. ● *verb* **1** compare, differentiate, discriminate,

distinguish, set against. **2** clash, conflict, differ, diverge; (*contrast with*) be set off by, set off, throw into relief. □ **contrasting** see DISSIMILAR.

contravene /kɒntrə'viːn/ *verb* (**-ning**) **1** infringe. **2** conflict with. □ **contravention** /-'ven-/ *noun*.

contretemps /'kɒntrətɒ˜ / *noun* (*plural* same /-tɑ ˜z/) **1** unlucky accident. **2** unfortunate occurrence.

contribute /kən'trɪbjuːt/ *verb* (**-ting**) **1** (often + *to*) give jointly with others to common purpose. **2** supply (article etc.) for publication with others. **3** (+ *to*) help to bring about. □ **contribution** /kɒntrɪ'bjuːʃ(ə)n/ *noun*. **contributory** *adjective*.

USAGE *Contribute* is often pronounced /'kɒntrɪbjuːt/ (with the stress on the *con-*), but this is considered incorrect by some people.

■ **1** bestow, *colloquial* chip in, donate, *slang* fork out, furnish, give, present, provide, put up, subscribe, supply; (*contribute to*) see SUPPORT *verb* 4. **3** (*contribute to*) see AID *verb* 1. □ **contribution** donation, fee, gift, grant, handout, help, input, offering, payment, sponsorship, subscription, support.

contributor /kən'trɪbjʊtə/ *noun* person who contributes (esp. to literary publication).

■ backer, benefactor, donor, giver, helper, patron, sponsor, subscriber, supporter; (*contributor to journal, etc.*) see WRITER.

contrite /kən'traɪt/ *adjective* penitent, feeling guilt. □ **contritely** *adverb*. **contriteness** *noun*. **contrition** /-'trɪʃ-/ *noun*.

contrivance *noun* **1** something contrived, esp. device or plan. **2** act of contriving.

contrive /kən'traɪv/ *verb* (**-ving**) **1** devise, plan. **2** (often + *to do*) manage. □ **contriver** *noun*.

contrived *adjective* artificial, forced.

control /kən'trəʊl/ *noun* **1** power of directing or restraining; self-restraint. **2** means of restraining or regulating. **3** (usually in *plural*) device to operate machine, vehicle, etc. **4** place where something is controlled or verified. **5** standard of comparison for checking results of experiment. ● *verb* (**-ll-**) **1** have control of. **2** regulate. **3** hold in check. **4** verify. □ **in control** (often + *of*) in charge. **out of control** no longer manageable. □ **controllable** *adjective*. **controllability** *noun*.

■ *noun* **1** administration, authority, charge, command, direction, discipline, government, grip, guidance, influence, jurisdiction, leadership, management, mastery, orderliness, organization, oversight, power, regulation, restraint, rule, strictness, supervision, supremacy, sway. **2** check, curb, restraint. **3** button, dial, handle, key, lever, switch. ● *verb* **1**, **2** administer, be at the helm, be in charge, *colloquial* boss, command, conduct, cope with, deal with, direct, dominate, engineer, govern, guide, handle, lead, look after, manage, manipulate, order about, oversee, regiment, regulate, rule, run, superintend, supervise. **3** check, confine, contain, curb, hold back, keep in check, master, repress, restrain, subdue, suppress.

controller *noun* **1** person or thing that controls. **2** person controlling expenditure.

controversial /kɒntrə'vɜːʃ(ə)l/ *adjective* **1** causing or subject to controversy. **2** given to controversy.

■ **1** arguable, contentious, controvertible, debatable, disputable, doubtful, moot, polemical, problematical, provocative, questionable. **2** argumentative, contentious, disputatious, litigious, provocative.

controversy /'kɒntrəvɜːsɪ/ *noun* (*plural* **-ies**) dispute, argument.

USAGE *Controversy* is often pronounced /kən'trɒvəsɪ/ (with the stress on the *-trov-*), but this is considered incorrect by some people.

■ altercation, argument, confrontation, contention, debate, disagreement, dispute, dissension, issue, polemic, quarrel, war of words, wrangle.

controvert /kɒntrə'vɜːt/ *verb* dispute, deny. □ **controvertible** *adjective*.

contumely /'kɒntjuːmlɪ, -tjuːmlɪ/ *noun* **1** insult, rudeness. **2** disgrace.

contuse /kən'tjuːz/ *verb* (**-sing**) bruise. □ **contusion** *noun*.

conundrum /kə'nʌndrəm/ *noun* **1** riddle. **2** hard question.

conurbation /kɒnɜː'beɪʃ(ə)n/ *noun* group of towns united by expansion.

convalesce /kɒnvə'les/ *verb* (**-cing**) recover health after illness.

■ get better, improve, make progress, mend, recover, recuperate, regain strength.

convalescent /kɒnvə'les(ə)nt/ *adjective* recovering from illness. ● *noun* convalescent person. □ **convalescence** *noun*.

■ *adjective* healing, improving, on the mend, recovering, recuperating.

convection /kən'vekʃ(ə)n/ *noun* heat transfer by upward movement of heated medium.

convector /kən'vektə/ *noun* heating appliance that circulates warm air by convection.

convene /kən'viːn/ *verb* (**-ning**) **1** summon. **2** assemble. □ **convener, convenor** *noun*.

■ **1** call, convoke, summon. **2** see GATHER *verb* 1.

convenience /kən'viːnɪəns/ *noun* **1** state of being convenient; suitability. **2** advantage. **3** useful thing. **4** public lavatory. □ **convenience food** food needing little preparation.

convenient *adjective* **1** serving one's comfort or interests; suitable. **2** available or occurring at suitable time or place. **3** well situated. □ **conveniently** *adverb*.

■ **1** appropriate, commodious, expedient, handy, helpful, labour-saving, neat, serviceable, suitable, usable, useful. **2, 3** accessible, at hand, available, handy, nearby, opportune, timely, well situated.

convent /'kɒnv(ə)nt/ *noun* **1** religious community, esp. of nuns. **2** its house.

convention /kən'venʃ(ə)n/ *noun* **1** general agreement on social behaviour etc. by implicit consent of majority; customary practice. **2** assembly, conference. **3** agreement, treaty.

■ **1** custom, etiquette, formality, matter of form, practice, rule, tradition. **2** see ASSEMBLY 2.

conventional *adjective* **1** depending on or according with convention; customary. **2** (of person) bound by social conventions. **3** not spontaneous, original, or sincere. **4** (of weapons etc.) non-nuclear. □ **conventionality** /-'nælɪtɪ/ *noun*. **conventionally** *adverb*.

■ **1** accepted, accustomed, commonplace, correct, customary, decorous, expected, formal, habitual, mainstream, ordinary, orthodox, prevalent, received, standard, traditional, usual. **2** *often derogatory* bourgeois, conservative, formal, hidebound, reactionary, rigid, *colloquial* straight, stuffy. **3** insincere, pedestrian, run-of-the-mill, stereotyped, stock, unadventurous, unimaginative, unoriginal, unsurprising.

converge /kən'vɜːdʒ/ *verb* (**-ging**) **1** come together or towards same point. **2** (+ *on*, *upon*) approach from different directions. □ **convergence** *noun*. **convergent** *adjective*.

■ **1** coincide, combine, come together, join, link up, meet, merge, unite.

conversant /kən'vɜːs(ə)nt/ *adjective* (+ *with*) well acquainted with.

conversation /kɒnvə'seɪʃ(ə)n/ *noun* **1** informal spoken communication. **2** instance of this.

■ **1** chat, *literary* colloquy, communication, dialogue, discourse, discussion, gossip, intercourse, talk. **2** chat, *slang* chinwag, *literary* colloquy, conference, dialogue, discourse, discussion, exchange of views, gossip, heart-to-heart, *colloquial* natter, powwow, talk, tête-à-tête.

conversational *adjective* **1** of or in conversation. **2** colloquial. □ **conversationally** *adverb*.

conversationalist *noun* person fond of or good at conversation.

converse[1] /kən'vɜːs/ *verb* (**-sing**) (often + *with*) talk.

converse[2] /'kɒnvɜːs/ *adjective* opposite, contrary, reversed. ● *noun* converse statement or proposition. □ **conversely** *adverb*.

conversion /kən'vɜːʃ(ə)n/ *noun* **1** converting, being converted. **2** converted (part of) building.

convert *verb* /kən'vɜːt/ **1** (usually + *into*) change. **2** cause (person) to change belief etc. **3** change (money etc.) into different form or currency etc. **4** alter (building) for new purpose. **5** *Rugby* kick goal after (try). ● *noun* /'kɒnvɜːt/ person converted, esp. to religious faith.

■ *verb* **1, 4** see CHANGE *verb* 1. **2** convince, persuade, re-educate, win over.

convertible /kən'vɜːtɪb(ə)l/ *adjective* able to be

converted. ● *noun* car with folding or detachable roof.

convex /'kɒnveks/ *adjective* curved like outside of sphere or circle.

convey /kən'veɪ/ *verb* **1** transport, carry. **2** communicate (meaning etc.). **3** transfer by legal process. **4** transmit (sound etc.).

■ **1** bear, bring, carry, conduct, deliver, drive, export, ferry, fetch, forward, import, move, send, shift, ship, shuttle, take, taxi, transfer, transport. **2** communicate, disclose, impart, imply, indicate, mean, reveal, signify, tell. **4** pass on, relay, send, transmit.

conveyance *noun* **1** conveying, being conveyed. **2** vehicle. **3** legal transfer of property. **4** document effecting this.

conveyancing *noun* branch of law dealing with transfer of property. □ **conveyancer** *noun*.

conveyor *noun* person or thing that conveys. □ **conveyor belt** endless moving belt conveying articles in factory etc.

convict *verb* /kən'vɪkt/ (often + *of*) prove or declare guilty. ● *noun* /'kɒnvɪkt/ *esp. historical* sentenced criminal.

■ *verb* condemn, declare guilty, prove guilty. ● *noun* condemned person, criminal, culprit, felon, malefactor, prisoner, wrongdoer.

conviction /kən'vɪkʃ(ə)n/ *noun* **1** convicting, being convicted. **2** being convinced. **3** firm belief.

■ **2** assurance, certainty, confidence, firmness. **3** belief, creed, faith, opinion, persuasion, position, principle, tenet, view.

convince /kən'vɪns/ *verb* (**-cing**) firmly persuade. □ **convincing** *adjective*. **convincingly** *adverb*.

■ assure, bring round, convert, persuade, prove to, reassure, satisfy, sway, win over. □ **convincing** see PERSUASIVE.

convivial /kən'vɪvɪəl/ *adjective* fond of company; sociable, lively. □ **conviviality** /-'æl-/ *noun*.

convocation /kɒnvə'keɪʃ(ə)n/ *noun* **1** convoking. **2** large formal gathering.

convoke /kən'vəʊk/ *verb* (**-king**) call together; summon to assemble.

convoluted /kɒnvə'luːtɪd/ *adjective* **1** coiled, twisted. **2** complex.

convolution /kɒnvə'luːʃ(ə)n/ *noun* **1** coiling. **2** coil, twist. **3** complexity.

convolvulus /kən'vɒlvjʊləs/ *noun* (*plural* **-es**) twining plant, esp. bindweed.

convoy /'kɒnvɔɪ/ *noun* group of ships, vehicles, etc. travelling together. □ **in convoy** as a group.

convulse /kən'vʌls/ *verb* (**-sing**) affect with convulsions.

convulsion *noun* **1** (usually in *plural*) violent irregular motion of limbs or body caused by involuntary contraction of muscles. **2** violent disturbance. **3** (in *plural*) uncontrollable laugh-

ter. □ **convulsive** *adjective*. **convulsively** *adverb*.

■ **1** attack, fit, paroxysm, seizure, spasm. **2** disturbance, eruption, outburst, tremor, turbulence, upheaval. □ **convulsive** jerky, shaking, spasmodic, twitchy, uncontrolled, uncoordinated, violent.

cony /'kəʊnɪ/ *noun* (*plural* **-ies**) (also **coney**) **1** rabbit. **2** its fur.

coo *noun* soft murmuring sound as of doves. ● *verb* (**coos, cooed**) emit coo.

cooee /'kuːiː/ *interjection:* used to attract attention.

cook /kʊk/ *verb* **1** prepare (food) by heating. **2** undergo cooking. **3** *colloquial* falsify (accounts etc.). ● *noun* person who cooks. □ **cookbook** *US* cookery book. **cooking apple** one suitable for eating cooked. **cook up** *colloquial* concoct (scheme, story, etc.). □ **cooking** *noun*.

■ *verb* **1** concoct, heat up, make, prepare, warm up. □ **cook up** see PLOT *verb* 3. □ **cooking** baking, catering, cookery, cuisine.

cooker *noun* **1** appliance or vessel for cooking food. **2** fruit (esp. apple) suitable for cooking.

cookery *noun* art of cooking. □ **cookery book** book containing recipes.

cookie /'kʊkɪ/ *noun US* sweet biscuit.

cool /kuːl/ *adjective* **1** of or at fairly low temperature. **2** suggesting or achieving coolness. **3** calm. **4** lacking enthusiasm. **5** unfriendly. **6** overconfident, audacious. **7** *slang* marvellous; fashionable. ● *noun* **1** coolness. **2** cool place. **3** *slang* composure. ● *verb* **1** (often + *down, off*) make or become cool. **2** calm; lessen (feelings etc.). □ **cool-headed** calm; not easily excited. □ **coolly** /'kuːllɪ/ *adverb*. **coolness** *noun*.

■ *adjective* **1** chilled, chilly, cold, coldish, iced, refreshing, unheated. **3** calm, collected, composed, dignified, *colloquial* laid-back, level-headed, phlegmatic, quiet, relaxed, self-possessed, sensible, serene, unemotional, unexcited, unflustered, unruffled, urbane. **4** apathetic, dispassionate, half-hearted, indifferent, lukewarm, negative, offhand, reserved, unconcerned, unemotional, unenthusiastic, uninvolved, unresponsive. **5** aloof, cold-blooded, cold-hearted, distant, frigid, offhand, reserved, stand-offish, unfriendly, unsociable, unwelcoming. **6** see AUDACIOUS 1. **7** see EXCELLENT, TRENDY *adjective*. ● *verb* **1** chill, freeze, ice, refrigerate. **2** abate, allay, assuage, calm, diminish, lessen, moderate, quiet, temper.

coolant *noun* cooling agent, esp. fluid.

cooler *noun* **1** vessel in which thing is cooled. **2** *slang* prison cell.

coomb /kuːm/ *noun* (also **combe**) **1** valley on side of hill. **2** short valley running up from coast.

coon /kuːn/ *noun US* racoon.

coop /kuːp/ *noun* cage for keeping poultry. ● *verb* (often + *up, in*) confine.

co-op /'kəʊɒp/ *noun colloquial* cooperative society or shop.

cooper *noun* maker or repairer of casks and barrels.

cooperate /kəʊ'ɒpəreɪt/ *verb* (also **co-operate**) (**-ting**) (often + *with*) work or act together. □ **cooperation** *noun*.

■ act in concert, collaborate, combine, conspire, help each other, join forces, *colloquial* pitch in, play along, *colloquial* play ball, pull together, support each other, unite, work as a team, work together. □ **cooperation** assistance, collaboration, coordination, help, joint action, mutual support, teamwork.

cooperative /kəʊ'ɒpərətɪv/ (also **co-operative**) *adjective* **1** willing to cooperate. **2** based on cooperation. **3** (of business etc.) jointly owned and run by members, with profits shared.
● *noun* cooperative society or enterprise.

■ *adjective* **1** accommodating, comradely, constructive, hard-working, helpful, keen, obliging, supportive, united, willing. **2** collective, combined, communal, concerted, coordinated, corporate, joint, shared.

co-opt /kəʊ'ɒpt/ *verb* appoint to committee etc. by invitation of existing members. □ **co-option** *noun*. **co-optive** *adjective*.

coordinate (also **co-ordinate**) *verb* /kəʊ'ɔ:dmeɪt/ (**-ting**) **1** cause to work together efficiently. **2** work or act together effectively.
● *adjective* /-nət/ equal in status. ● *noun* /-nət/ **1** *Mathematics* each of set of quantities used to fix position of point, line, or plane. **2** (in *plural*) matching items of clothing. □ **coordination** *noun*. **coordinator** *noun*.

coot /ku:t/ *noun* **1** black waterfowl with white horny plate on head. **2** *colloquial* stupid person.

cop *slang noun* **1** police officer. **2** capture. ● *verb* (**-pp-**) catch. □ **cop-out** cowardly evasion. **not much cop** of little value or use.

copal /'kəʊp(ə)l/ *noun* kind of resin used for varnish.

copartner /kəʊ'pɑ:tnə/ *noun* partner, associate. □ **copartnership** *noun*.

cope[1] *verb* (**-ping**) **1** manage. **2** (often + *with*) deal effectively or contend.

■ **1** *colloquial* get by, make do, manage, survive, win through. **2** (*cope with*) see ENDURE 2, MANAGE 5.

cope[2] *noun* priest's long cloaklike vestment.

copeck /'kəʊpek/ *noun* (also **kopek, kopeck**) hundredth of rouble.

copier /'kɒpɪə/ *noun* machine that copies (esp. documents).

copilot /'kəʊpaɪlət/ *noun* second pilot in aircraft.

coping /'kəʊpɪŋ/ *noun* top (usually sloping) course of masonry in wall. □ **coping stone** stone used in coping.

copious /'kəʊpɪəs/ *adjective* **1** abundant. **2** producing much. □ **copiously** *adverb*. **copiousness** *noun*.

■ abundant, ample, bountiful, extravagant, generous, great, huge, inexhaustible, large, lavish, liberal, luxuriant, overflowing, plentiful, profuse, unsparing, unstinting.

copper[1] /'kɒpə/ *noun* **1** red-brown metal. **2** (usually in *plural*) bronze coin, esp. one of little value. **3** large metal vessel for boiling laundry.
● *adjective* made of or coloured like copper. □ **copperplate 1** copper plate for engraving or etching. **2** print taken from it. **3** ornate sloping handwriting.

copper[2] /'kɒpə/ *noun slang* police officer.

coppice /'kɒpɪs/ *noun* area of undergrowth and small trees.

copse /kɒps/ *noun* small wood.

copulate /'kɒpjʊleɪt/ *verb* (**-ting**) (often + *with*) (esp. of animals) have sexual intercourse. □ **copulation** *noun*.

copy /'kɒpɪ/ *noun* (*plural* **-ies**) **1** thing made to look like another. **2** specimen of book etc. **3** material to be printed, esp. regarded as good etc. reading matter. ● *verb* (**-ies, -ied**) **1** make copy of. **2** imitate. □ **copy-typist** typist working from document or recording. **copywriter** writer of copy, esp. for advertisements.

■ *noun* **1** carbon copy, *colloquial* clone, counterfeit, double, duplicate, facsimile, fake, forgery, imitation, likeness, model, pattern, photocopy, print, replica, representation, reproduction, tracing, transcript, twin, *proprietary term* Xerox. **2** edition, volume. ● *verb* **1** borrow, counterfeit, *colloquial* crib, duplicate, emulate, follow, forge, imitate, photocopy, plagiarize, print, repeat, reproduce, simulate, transcribe. **2** see IMITATE *verb* 2.

copyist /'kɒpɪɪst/ *noun* person who makes copies.

copyright *noun* exclusive right to print, publish, perform, etc., material. ● *adjective* protected by copyright. ● *verb* secure copyright for (material).

coquette /kə'ket/ *noun* woman who flirts. □ **coquetry** /'kɒkɪtrɪ/ *noun* (*plural* **-ies**). **coquettish** *adjective*.

coracle /'kɒrək(ə)l/ *noun* small boat of wickerwork covered with waterproof material.

coral /'kɒr(ə)l/ *noun* hard substance built up by marine polyps. ● *adjective* of (red or pink colour of) coral. □ **coral island, reef** one formed by growth of coral.

cor anglais /kɔ:r 'ɒŋgleɪ/ *noun* (*plural* **cors anglais** /kɔ:z/) woodwind instrument like oboe but lower in pitch.

corbel /'kɔ:b(ə)l/ *noun* stone or timber projection from wall, acting as supporting bracket.

cord *noun* **1** thick string. **2** piece of this. **3** similar structure in body. **4** ribbed cloth, esp. corduroy. **5** (in *plural*) corduroy trousers. **6** electric flex.
● *verb* secure with cords.

■ *noun* **1, 2** cable, catgut, lace, line, rope, strand, string, twine. **6** cable, flex, line, wire.

cordial /'kɔ:dɪəl/ *adjective* **1** heartfelt. **2** friendly. ● *noun* fruit-flavoured drink. ◻ **cordiality** /-'æl-/ *noun*. **cordially** *adverb*.

cordite /'kɔ:daɪt/ *noun* smokeless explosive.

cordless *adjective* (of electrical appliance, telephone, etc.) working without connection to mains supply or central unit.

cordon /'kɔ:d(ə)n/ *noun* **1** line or circle of police etc. **2** ornamental cord or braid. **3** fruit tree trained to grow as single stem. ● *verb* (often + *off*) enclose or separate with cordon of police etc. ■ *noun* **1** line, ring, row. ● *verb* (*cordon off*) see ISOLATE 1,2.

cordon bleu /kɔ:dɒn 'blɜ:/ *adjective* (of cooking) first-class.

corduroy /'kɔ:dərɔɪ/ *noun* **1** fabric with velvety ribs. **2** (in *plural*) corduroy trousers.

core *noun* **1** horny central part of certain fruits, containing seeds. **2** centre or most important part. **3** part of nuclear reactor containing fissile material. **4** inner strand of electric cable. **5** piece of soft iron forming centre of magnet etc. ● *verb* (**-ring**) remove core from. ■ *noun* **1** centre, heart, inside, kernel, middle. **2** centre, crux, essence, gist, heart, kernel, *slang* nitty-gritty, nub, nucleus.

co-respondent /kəʊrɪ'spɒnd(ə)nt/ *noun* person cited in divorce case as having committed adultery with respondent.

corgi /'kɔ:gɪ/ *noun* (*plural* **-s**) short-legged breed of dog.

coriander /kɒrɪ'ændə/ *noun* **1** aromatic plant. **2** its seed, used as flavouring.

cork *noun* **1** thick light bark of S. European oak. **2** bottle-stopper made of cork etc. ● *verb* (often + *up*) **1** stop, confine. **2** restrain (feelings etc.). ■ *noun* **2** bung, plug, stopper.

corkage *noun* charge made by restaurant etc. for serving customer's own wine etc.

corked *adjective* (of wine) spoilt by defective cork.

corkscrew *noun* **1** spiral steel device for extracting corks from bottles. **2** thing with spiral shape. ● *verb* move spirally.

corm *noun* swollen underground stem in certain plants, e.g. crocus.

cormorant /'kɔ:mərənt/ *noun* diving seabird with black plumage.

corn[1] *noun* **1** cereal before or after harvesting, esp. chief crop of a region. **2** grain or seed of cereal plant. **3** *colloquial* something corny. ◻ **corn cob** cylindrical centre of maize ear. **corncrake** ground-nesting bird with harsh cry. **corn dolly** plaited straw figure. **cornflakes** breakfast cereal of toasted maize flakes. **cornflour** fine-ground maize flour. **cornflower** blue-flowered plant originally growing in cornfields. **corn on the cob** maize eaten from the corn cob.

corn[2] *noun* small tender hard area of skin, esp. on toe.

cornea /'kɔ:nɪə/ *noun* transparent circular part of front of eyeball.

corned *adjective* preserved in salt or brine.

cornelian /kɔ:'ni:lɪən/ *noun* (also **carnelian** /kɑ:-/) dull red variety of chalcedony.

corner /'kɔ:nə/ *noun* **1** place where converging sides, edges, streets, etc. meet. **2** recess formed by meeting of two internal sides of room, box, etc. **3** difficult or inescapable position. **4** remote or secluded place. **5** action or result of buying whole available stock of a commodity. **6** *Football & Hockey* free kick or hit from corner of pitch. ● *verb* **1** force into difficult or inescapable position. **2** buy whole available stock of (commodity). **3** dominate (market) in this way. **4** go round corner. ◻ **cornerstone 1** stone in projecting angle of wall. **2** indispensable part or basis. ■ *noun* **1** bend, crossroad(s), intersection, junction, turn, turning. **2** angle, crook, joint, nook, recess. **4** hideaway, hiding place, hole, niche, nook, recess, retreat. ● *verb* **1** capture, catch, trap.

cornet /'kɔ:nɪt/ *noun* **1** brass instrument resembling trumpet. **2** conical wafer for holding ice cream.

cornice /'kɔ:nɪs/ *noun* ornamental moulding, esp. along top of internal wall.

Cornish /'kɔ:nɪʃ/ *adjective* of Cornwall. ● *noun* Celtic language of Cornwall. ◻ **Cornish pasty** pastry envelope containing meat and vegetables.

cornucopia /kɔ:njʊ'kəʊpɪə/ *noun* horn overflowing with flowers, fruit, etc., as symbol of plenty.

corny *adjective* (**-ier**, **-iest**) *colloquial* **1** banal. **2** feebly humorous. **3** sentimental.

corolla /kə'rɒlə/ *noun* whorl of petals forming inner envelope of flower.

corollary /kə'rɒlərɪ/ *noun* (*plural* **-ies**) **1** proposition that follows from one proved. **2** (often + *of*) natural consequence.

corona /kə'rəʊnə/ *noun* (*plural* **-nae** /-ni:/) halo round sun or moon, esp. that seen in total eclipse of sun.

coronary /'kɒrənərɪ/ *noun* (*plural* **-ies**) coronary thrombosis. ◻ **coronary artery** artery supplying blood to heart. **coronary thrombosis** blockage of coronary artery by blood clot.

coronation /kɒrə'neɪʃ(ə)n/ *noun* ceremony of crowning sovereign.

coroner /'kɒrənə/ *noun* official holding inquest on deaths thought to be violent or accidental.

coronet /'kɒrənɪt/ *noun* small crown.

corpora *plural* of CORPUS.

corporal[1] /'kɔ:p(ə)r(ə)l/ *noun* army or air-force NCO next below sergeant.

corporal[2] /'kɔ:p(ə)r(ə)l/ *adjective* of human body. ◻ **corporal punishment** physical punishment.

corporate /'kɔ:pərət/ *adjective* of, being, or belonging to a corporation or group.

corporation /kɔ:pə'reɪʃ(ə)n/ *noun* **1** group of

people authorized to act as individual, esp. in business. **2** civic authorities.
■ **1** company, concern, enterprise, firm, organization. **2** council, local government.

corporative /'kɔːpərətɪv/ *adjective* **1** of corporation. **2** governed by or organized in corporations.

corporeal /kɔː'pɔːrɪəl/ *adjective* bodily, physical, material. □ **corporeality** /-'ælɪtɪ/ *noun*.

corps /kɔː/ *noun* (*plural* same /kɔːz/) **1** military unit with particular function. **2** organized group of people.

corpse /kɔːps/ *noun* dead body.
■ body, cadaver, carcass, mortal remains, remains, *slang* stiff.

corpulent /'kɔːpjʊlənt/ *adjective* fleshy; bulky. □ **corpulence** *noun*.

corpus /'kɔːpəs/ *noun* (*plural* **-pora** /-pərə/) body or collection of writings, texts, etc.

corpuscle /'kɔːpʌs(ə)l/ *noun* minute body or cell in organism, esp. (in *plural*) red or white cells in blood of vertebrates. □ **corpuscular** /-'pʌskjʊlə/ *adjective*.

corral /kə'rɑːl/ *noun* **1** US pen for horses, cattle, etc. **2** enclosure for capturing wild animals.
● *verb* (**-ll-**) put or keep in corral.

correct /kə'rekt/ *adjective* **1** true, accurate. **2** proper, in accordance with taste, standards, etc.
● *verb* **1** set right. **2** mark errors in. **3** admonish. **4** counteract. □ **correctly** *adverb*. **correctness** *noun*.
■ *adjective* **1** accurate, authentic, confirmed, exact, factual, faithful, faultless, flawless, genuine, literal, precise, reliable, right, strict, true, truthful, verified. **2** acceptable, appropriate, fitting, just, normal, proper, regular, standard, suitable, tactful, unexceptionable, well mannered. ● *verb* **1** adjust, alter, cure, debug, put right, rectify, redress, remedy, repair. **2** assess, mark. **3** see REPRIMAND *verb*.

correction *noun* **1** correcting, being corrected. **2** thing substituted for what is wrong.

correctitude /kə'rektɪtjuːd/ *noun* consciously correct behaviour.

corrective *adjective* serving to correct or counteract. ● *noun* corrective measure or thing.

correlate /'kɒrəleɪt/ *verb* (**-ting**) (usually + *with*, *to*) have or bring into mutual relation.
● *noun* either of two related or complementary things. □ **correlation** *noun*.

correlative /kə'relətɪv/ *adjective* **1** (often + *with*, *to*) having a mutual relation. **2** (of words) corresponding and regularly used together.
● *noun* correlative thing or word.

correspond /kɒrɪ'spɒnd/ *verb* **1** (usually + *to*) be similar or equivalent. **2** (usually + *to*, *with*) agree. **3** (usually + *with*) exchange letters. □ **corresponding** *adjective*.

■ **1, 2** accord, agree, be congruous, be consistent, coincide, concur, conform, correlate, fit, harmonize, match, parallel, square, tally. **3** (*correspond with*) communicate with, send letters to, write to. □ **corresponding** see EQUIVALENT *adjective*.

correspondence *noun* **1** agreement or similarity. **2** (exchange of) letters. □ **correspondence course** course of study conducted by post.
■ **2** letters, memoranda, *colloquial* memos, messages, notes, writings.

correspondent *noun* **1** person who writes letter(s). **2** person employed to write or report for newspaper or broadcasting.
■ **2** contributor, journalist, reporter, writer.

corridor /'kɒrɪdɔː/ *noun* **1** passage giving access into rooms. **2** passage in train giving access into compartments. **3** strip of territory of one state running through that of another. **4** route for aircraft over foreign country.
■ **1** *esp. US* hall, hallway, passage, passageway.

corrigendum /kɒrɪ'dʒendəm/ *noun* (*plural* **-da**) error to be corrected.

corrigible /'kɒrɪdʒɪb(ə)l/ *adjective* able to be corrected.

corroborate /kə'rɒbəreɪt/ *verb* (**-ting**) give support to; confirm. □ **corroboration** *noun*. **corroborative** /-rətɪv/ *adjective*. **corroboratory** /-rət(ə)rɪ/ *adjective*.

corrode /kə'rəʊd/ *verb* (**-ding**) **1** wear away, esp. by chemical action; decay. **2** destroy gradually.
■ **1** consume, crumble, deteriorate, disintegrate, eat into, erode, oxidize, rot, rust, tarnish.

corrosion /kə'rəʊʒ(ə)n/ *noun* **1** corroding, being corroded. **2** corroded area. □ **corrosive** /-sɪv/ *adjective & noun*.

corrugate /'kɒrəgeɪt/ *verb* (**-ting**) (esp. as **corrugated** *adjective*) bend into wavy ridges. □ **corrugation** *noun*.
■ (**corrugated**) creased, crinkly, fluted, furrowed, lined, puckered, ribbed, ridged, wrinkled.

corrupt /kə'rʌpt/ *adjective* **1** influenced by or using bribery; dishonest. **2** immoral, wicked. **3** (of computer files etc.) having errors or alterations. ● *verb* make or become corrupt. □ **corruptible** *adjective*. **corruptibility** *noun*. **corruption** *noun*. **corruptly** *adverb*.
■ *adjective* **1** *slang* bent, bribable, criminal, *colloquial* crooked, dishonest, dishonourable, false, fraudulent, illegal, unethical, unprincipled, unscrupulous, untrustworthy, venal. **2** debauched, decadent, degenerate, depraved, dirty, dissolute, evil, immoral, iniquitous, low, perverted, profligate, rotten, sinful, unsound, vicious, wicked. ● *verb* bribe, debauch, deprave, *colloquial* fix, influence, lead astray, pervert, seduce, suborn, subvert.

corsage /kɔː'sɑːʒ/ *noun* small bouquet worn by woman.

corsair /kɔː'seə/ *noun* **1** pirate ship. **2** pirate.

corset /'kɔːsɪt/ *noun* tight-fitting supporting undergarment worn esp. by women. □ **corsetry** *noun*.

cortège /kɔː'teɪʒ/ *noun* procession, esp. for funeral.

cortex /'kɔːteks/ *noun* (*plural* **-tices** /-tɪsiːz/) outer part of organ, esp. brain. □ **cortical** /'kɔːtɪk(ə)l/ *adjective*.

cortisone /'kɔːtɪzəʊn/ *noun* hormone used in treating inflammation and allergy.

coruscate /'kɒrəskeɪt/ *verb* **1** flash, sparkle. **2** be showy or brilliant. □ **coruscation** /-'skeɪʃ(ə)n/ *noun*.

corvette /kɔː'vet/ *noun* small naval escort-vessel.

cos[1] /kɒs/ *noun* crisp long-leaved lettuce.

cos[2] /kɒz/ *abbreviation* cosine.

cosh *colloquial noun* heavy blunt weapon. ● *verb* hit with cosh.

cosine /'kəʊsaɪn/ *noun* ratio of side adjacent to acute angle (in right-angled triangle) to hypotenuse.

cosmetic /kɒz'metɪk/ *adjective* **1** beautifying, enhancing. **2** superficially improving. **3** (of surgery etc.) restoring or enhancing normal appearance. ● *noun* cosmetic preparation. □ **cosmetically** *adverb*.

  ■ *noun* (*cosmetics*) make-up, toiletries.

cosmic /'kɒzmɪk/ *adjective* **1** of the cosmos. **2** of or for space travel. □ **cosmic rays** high-energy radiations from outer space.

cosmogony /kɒz'mɒgənɪ/ *noun* (*plural* **-ies**) (theory about) origin of universe.

cosmology /kɒz'mɒlədʒɪ/ *noun* science or theory of universe. □ **cosmological** /-mə'lɒdʒ-/ *adjective*. **cosmologist** *noun*.

cosmonaut /'kɒzmənɔːt/ *noun* Russian astronaut.

cosmopolitan /kɒzmə'pɒlɪt(ə)n/ *adjective* **1** of or knowing all parts of world. **2** free from national limitations or prejudices. ● *noun* cosmopolitan person. □ **cosmopolitanism** *noun*.

  ■ *adjective* catholic, international, multicultural, sophisticated, universal, urbane.

cosmos /'kɒzmɒs/ *noun* universe as a well-ordered whole.

Cossack /'kɒsæk/ *noun* member of S. Russian people famous as horsemen.

cosset /'kɒsɪt/ *verb* (**-t-**) pamper.

cost *verb* (*past & past participle* **cost**) **1** have as price. **2** involve as loss or sacrifice. **3** (*past & past participle* **costed**) fix or estimate cost of. ● *noun* **1** price. **2** loss, sacrifice. **3** (in *plural*) legal expenses. □ **cost-effective** effective in relation to cost. **cost of living** cost of basic necessities of life. **cost price** price paid for thing by person who later sells it.

  ■ *verb* **1** be valued at, be worth, fetch, go for, realize, sell for, *colloquial* set one back. ● *noun* **2** amount, charge, expenditure, expense, fare, figure, outlay, payment, price, rate, tariff, value.

costal /'kɒst(ə)l/ *adjective* of ribs.

costermonger /'kɒstəmʌŋgə/ *noun* person who sells fruit etc. from barrow.

costive /'kɒstɪv/ *adjective* constipated.

costly *adjective* (**-ier**, **-iest**) costing much, expensive. □ **costliness** *noun*.

costume /'kɒstjuːm/ *noun* **1** style of dress, esp. of particular place or period. **2** set of clothes. **3** clothing for particular activity. **4** actor's clothes for part. ● *verb* provide with costume. □ **costume jewellery** artificial jewellery.

  ■ *formal* apparel, attire, clothes, clothing, dress, fancy dress, garb, garments, *colloquial* get-up, livery, outfit, period dress, *archaic* raiment, robes, uniform, vestments.

costumier /kɒs'tjuːmɪə/ *noun* person who deals in or makes costumes.

cosy /'kəʊzɪ/ (*US* **cozy**) *adjective* (**-ier**, **-iest**) snug, comfortable. ● *noun* (*plural* **-ies**) cover to keep teapot etc. hot. □ **cosily** *adverb*. **cosiness** *noun*.

  ■ *adjective* comfortable, *colloquial* comfy, easy, homely, intimate, reassuring, relaxing, restful, secure, snug, soft, warm.

cot *noun* **1** small high-sided bed for child etc. **2** small light bed. □ **cot death** unexplained death of sleeping baby.

cote *noun* shelter for birds or animals.

coterie /'kəʊtərɪ/ *noun* exclusive group of people sharing interests.

cotoneaster /kətəʊnɪ'æstə/ *noun* shrub bearing red or orange berries.

cottage /'kɒtɪdʒ/ *noun* small house, esp. in the country. □ **cottage cheese** soft white lumpy cheese. **cottage industry** small business carried on at home. **cottage pie** shepherd's pie.

cottager *noun* person who lives in cottage.

cotter /'kɒtə/ *noun* (also **cotter pin**) wedge or pin for securing machine part such as bicycle pedal crank.

cotton /'kɒt(ə)n/ *noun* **1** soft white fibrous substance covering seeds of certain plants. **2** such a plant. **3** thread or cloth from this. □ **cotton on** (often + *to*) *colloquial* begin to understand. **cotton wool** wadding originally made from raw cotton.

cotyledon /kɒtɪ'liːd(ə)n/ *noun* first leaf produced by plant embryo.

couch[1] /kaʊtʃ/ *noun* upholstered piece of furniture for several people; sofa. ● *verb* (+ *in*) express in (language of specified kind). □ **couch potato** *US slang* person who likes lazing at home.

couch[2] /kuːtʃ/ *noun* (in full **couch grass**) kind of grass with long creeping roots.

couchette /kuː'ʃet/ *noun* **1** railway carriage with seats convertible into sleeping berths. **2** berth in this.

cougar /'kuːgə/ *noun* *US* puma.

cough /kɒf/ *verb* expel air from lungs with sudden sharp sound. ● *noun* **1** (sound of) coughing. **2** condition of respiratory organs causing coughing. □ **cough mixture** medicine to relieve cough. **cough up 1** eject with coughs. **2** *slang* give (money, information, etc.) reluctantly.

could *past* of CAN[1].

couldn't /'kʊd(ə)nt/ could not.

coulomb /'ku:lɒm/ *noun* SI unit of electrical charge.

coulter /'kəʊltə/ *noun* (*US* **colter**) vertical blade in front of ploughshare.

council /'kaʊns(ə)l/ *noun* **1** (meeting of) advisory, deliberative, or administrative body. **2** local administrative body of county, city, town, etc. □ **council flat, house** one owned and let by local council. **council tax** local tax based on value of property and number of residents.

■ **1** assembly, committee, conclave, convention, convocation, corporation, gathering, meeting.

councillor *noun* member of (esp. local) council.

counsel /'kaʊns(ə)l/ *noun* **1** advice, esp. formal. **2** consultation. **3** (*plural* same) legal adviser, esp. barrister; group of these. ● *verb* (**-ll-**; *US* **-l-**) advise, esp. on personal problems. □ **counsellor** (*US* **counselor**) *noun*.

■ *noun* **3** see LAWYER. ● *verb* advise, discuss with, give help, guide.

counselling /'kaʊns(ə)lɪŋ/ *noun* (*US* **counseling**) process in which esp. professional help is given for emotional or psychological problems.

count[1] *verb* **1** find number of, esp. by assigning successive numerals. **2** repeat numbers in order. **3** (+ *in*) include or be included in reckoning. **4** consider to be. **5** have significance. ● *noun* **1** counting, reckoning. **2** total. **3** *Law* each charge in an indictment. □ **countdown** counting numbers backwards to zero, esp. before launching rocket etc. **count on** rely on. **count out** exclude, disregard.

■ *verb* **1** add up, calculate, check, compute, enumerate, estimate, figure out, keep account of, notch up, number, reckon, score, total, tot up, work out. **5** be important, have significance, matter, signify. □ **count on** see EXPECT 1.

count[2] *noun* foreign noble corresponding to earl.

countable /'kaʊntəb(ə)l/ *adjective* that can be counted.

countenance /'kaʊntməns/ *noun* **1** face or its expression. **2** composure. **3** moral support. ● *verb* (**-cing**) support, approve.

■ *noun* **1** air, appearance, aspect, demeanour, expression, face, features, look, *literary* visage. ● *verb* see APPROVE 1.

counter[1] *noun* **1** flat-topped fitment in shop etc. across which business is conducted. **2** small disc used for playing or scoring in board games, cards, etc. **3** device for counting things.

■ **1** bar, table. **2** chip, disc, piece, token.

counter[2] *verb* **1** oppose, contradict. **2** meet by

countermove. ● *adverb* in opposite direction. ● *adjective* opposite. ● *noun* parry, countermove.

■ *verb* answer, contradict, defend oneself against, hit back at, parry, react to, rebut, refute, reply to, resist, ward off.

counteract /kaʊntə'rækt/ *verb* neutralize or hinder by contrary action. □ **counteraction** *noun*. **counteractive** *adjective*.

■ act against, annul, be an antidote to, cancel out, counterbalance, fight against, foil, invalidate, militate against, negate, neutralize, offset, oppose, resist, thwart, withstand, work against.

counter-attack *verb & noun* attack in reply to enemy's attack.

counterbalance *noun* weight or influence balancing another. ● *verb* (**-cing**) act as counterbalance to.

■ *verb* balance, compensate for, counteract, counterpoise, counterweight, equalize.

counter-clockwise *adverb & adjective US* anticlockwise.

counter-espionage *noun* action taken against enemy spying.

counterfeit /'kaʊntəfɪt/ *adjective* imitation; forged; not genuine. ● *noun* forgery, imitation. ● *verb* imitate fraudulently; forge. □ **counterfeiter** *noun*.

■ *adjective* artificial, bogus, copied, ersatz, fake, false, feigned, forged, fraudulent, imitation, make-believe, meretricious, pastiche, *colloquial* phoney, *colloquial* pretend, pseudo, sham, simulated, spurious, synthetic. ● *verb* copy, fake, falsify, feign, forge, imitate, pretend, put on, sham, simulate.

counterfoil *noun* part of cheque, receipt, etc. retained as record.

counter-intelligence *noun* counter-espionage.

countermand /kaʊntə'mɑ:nd/ *verb* revoke; recall by contrary order.

countermeasure *noun* action taken to counteract danger, threat, etc.

countermove *noun* move or action in opposition to another.

counterpane *noun* bedspread.

counterpart *noun* **1** person or thing equivalent or complementary to another. **2** duplicate.

counterpoint *noun* **1** harmonious combination of melodies in music. **2** melody combined with another. **3** contrasting argument, plot, literary theme, etc.

counterpoise *noun* **1** counterbalance. **2** state of equilibrium. ● *verb* (**-sing**) counterbalance.

counter-productive *adjective* having opposite of desired effect.

counter-revolution *noun* revolution opposing former one or reversing its results.

countersign *verb* add confirming signature to. ● *noun* password spoken to person on guard.

countersink verb (past & past participle **-sunk**) **1** shape (screw-hole) so that screw-head lies level with surface. **2** provide (screw) with countersunk hole.

counter-tenor noun **1** male alto singing voice. **2** singer with this.

countervail /kaʊntə'veɪl/ verb **1** counterbalance. **2** oppose.

counterweight noun counterbalancing weight.

countess /'kaʊntɪs/ noun **1** earl's or count's wife or widow. **2** woman with rank of earl or count.

countless adjective too many to count.
■ endless, immeasurable, incalculable, infinite, innumerable, limitless, many, measureless, *literary* myriad, numberless, numerous, unnumbered, untold.

countrified /'kʌntrɪfaɪd/ adjective rustic.

country /'kʌntrɪ/ noun (plural **-ies**) **1** nation's territory, state. **2** land of person's birth or citizenship. **3** rural districts, as opposed to towns. **4** region with regard to its aspect, associations, etc. **5** national population, esp. as voters. □ **country and western** type of folk music originated by southern US whites. **country dance** traditional dance. **countryman, countrywoman 1** person of one's own country or district. **2** person living in rural area. **countryside** rural areas.
■ **1** commonwealth, domain, empire, kingdom, land, nation, power, principality, *formal* realm, state, territory. **3** countryside, provinces. **4** land, landscape, region, scenery, terrain, territory. **5** nation, people, populace, population, public.

county /'kaʊntɪ/ noun (plural **-ies**) **1** territorial division of country, forming chief unit of local administration. **2** US political and administrative division of State. **3** people, esp. gentry, of county. □ **county council** elected governing body of county. **county court** law court for civil cases. **county town** administrative capital of county.

coup /ku:/ noun (plural **-s** /ku:z/) **1** successful stroke or move. **2** coup d'état.

coup de grâce /ku: də 'grɑːs/ noun finishing stroke. [French]

coup d'état /ku: deɪ'tɑː/ noun (plural **coups d'état** same pronunciation) sudden overthrow of government, esp. by force. [French]

coupé /'ku:peɪ/ noun (US **coupe** /ku:p/) two-door car with hard roof and sloping back.

couple /'kʌp(ə)l/ noun **1** (about) two. **2** two people who are married or in a sexual relationship. **3** pair of partners in a dance etc. ● verb (**-ling**) **1** link, fasten, or associate together. **2** copulate.
■ noun brace, duo, pair, twosome. ● verb **1** combine, connect, fasten, hitch, join, link, match, pair, unite, yoke. **2** see MATE verb.

couplet /'kʌplɪt/ noun two successive lines of rhyming verse.

coupling /'kʌplɪŋ/ noun link connecting railway carriages or parts of machinery.

coupon /'ku:pɒn/ noun ticket or form entitling holder to something.
■ ticket, token, voucher.

courage /'kʌrɪdʒ/ noun ability to disregard fear; bravery. □ **courageous** /kə'reɪdʒəs/ adjective. **courageously** adverb.
■ audacity, boldness, *slang* bottle, bravery, daring, dauntlessness, determination, fearlessness, fibre, firmness, fortitude, gallantry, *colloquial* grit, *colloquial* guts, heroism, indomitability, intrepidity, mettle, nerve, pluck, prowess, resolution, spirit, *colloquial* spunk, stoicism, tenacity, valour, will-power.
□ **courageous** audacious, bold, brave, cool, daring, dauntless, determined, fearless, gallant, game, *colloquial* gutsy, heroic, indomitable, intrepid, lion-hearted, noble, plucky, resolute, spirited, stalwart, stoical, stout-hearted, tough, unafraid, uncomplaining, undaunted, unshrinking, valiant, valorous.

courgette /kʊə'ʒet/ noun small vegetable marrow.

courier /'kʊrɪə/ noun **1** person employed to guide and assist group of tourists. **2** special messenger.

course /kɔːs/ noun **1** onward movement or progression. **2** direction taken. **3** line of conduct. **4** series of lectures, lessons, etc. **5** each successive part of meal. **6** golf course, race-course, etc. **7** sequence of medical treatment etc. **8** continuous line of masonry or bricks at one level of building. **9** channel in which water flows. ● verb (**-sing**) **1** use hounds to hunt (esp. hares). **2** move or flow freely. □ **in the course of** during. **of course** naturally; as expected; admittedly. **on, off course** following or deviating from desired direction or goal.
■ noun **1** advance, continuation, development, movement, passage, passing, progress, progression, succession. **2** circuit, direction, line, orbit, path, route, track, way. **4** curriculum, programme, schedule, sequence, series, syllabus.

court /kɔːt/ noun **1** number of houses enclosing a yard. **2** courtyard. **3** rectangular area for a game. **4** (in full **court of law**) judicial body hearing legal cases. **5** courtroom. **6** sovereign's establishment and retinue. ● verb **1** pay amorous attention to; seek to win favour of. **2** try to win (fame etc.). **3** unwisely invite. □ **court card** playing card that is king, queen, or jack. **courthouse 1** building in which judicial court is held. **2** US county administrative offices. **court martial** (plural **courts martial**) judicial court of military officers. **court-martial** verb (**-ll-**; US **-l-**) try by court martial. **courtroom** room in which court of law sits. **court shoe** woman's light shoe with low-cut upper. **courtyard** space enclosed by walls or buildings.
■ noun **2** see COURTYARD. **4** *historical* assizes, bar, bench, law court, tribunal. **6** entourage, followers, palace, retinue, train. ● verb **1** *colloquial* date, go out with, make advances to, *archaic* make love to,

woo. **3** ask for, attract, invite, provoke, seek, solicit. □ **courtyard** court, enclosure, forecourt, *colloquial* quad, quadrangle, yard.

courteous /'kɜːtɪəs/ *adjective* polite, considerate. □ **courteously** *adverb*. **courteousness** *noun*.
■ civil, considerate, gentlemanly, ladylike, polite, respectful, urbane, well bred, well mannered.

courtesan /kɔːtɪ'zæn/ *noun literary* prostitute, esp. one with wealthy or upper-class clients.

courtesy /'kɜːtəsɪ/ *noun* (*plural* **-ies**) courteous behaviour or act. □ **by courtesy of** with formal permission of. **courtesy light** light in car switched on when door is opened.

courtier /'kɔːtɪə/ *noun* person who attends sovereign's court.
■ attendant, follower, lady, lord, noble, page, steward.

courtly *adjective* (**-ier, -iest**) dignified; refined in manners. □ **courtliness** *noun*.

courtship *noun* courting, wooing.

couscous /'kuːskuːs/ *noun* N. African dish of cracked wheat steamed over broth.

cousin /'kʌz(ə)n/ *noun* (also **first cousin**) child of one's uncle or aunt.

couture /kuː'tjʊə/ *noun* design and making of fashionable garments.

couturier /kuː'tjʊərɪeɪ/ *noun* fashion designer.

cove /kəʊv/ *noun* **1** small bay or inlet. **2** sheltered recess.

coven /'kʌv(ə)n/ *noun* assembly of witches.

covenant /'kʌvənənt/ *noun* **1** agreement. **2** *Law* sealed contract. ● *verb* agree, esp. by legal covenant.

Coventry /'kɒvəntrɪ/ *noun* □ **send to Coventry** refuse to associate with or speak to.

cover /'kʌvə/ *verb* **1** (often + *with*) protect or conceal with cloth, lid, etc. **2** extend over. **3** clothe. **4** include; deal with. **5** (of sum) be large enough to meet (expense). **6** protect by insurance. **7** report on for newspaper, television, etc. **8** travel (specified distance). **9** aim gun etc. at. **10** protect by aiming gun. ● *noun* **1** thing that covers, esp. lid, binding of book, wrapper, etc. **2** (in *plural*) bedclothes. **3** shelter; protection. **4** funds to meet liability or contingent loss. **5** place-setting at table. □ **cover charge** service charge per person in restaurant. **cover note** temporary certificate of insurance. **cover up 1** cover completely. **2** conceal. **cover-up** *noun* concealing of facts. **take cover** find shelter.
■ *verb* **1** blot out, bury, camouflage, cap, carpet, cloak, clothe, cloud, coat, conceal, curtain, disguise, drape, encase, enclose, enshroud, envelop, hide, hood, mantle, mask, obscure, overlay, plaster, protect, screen, shade, sheathe, shield, shroud, surface, tile, veil, veneer, wrap up. **2** extend over, lie over, overspread, spread over, strew. **3** see CLOTHE 1. **4** comprise, contain, deal with, embrace, encompass, include, incorporate, involve, treat. **5** be enough for, match, meet, pay for, suffice for. ● *noun* **1** see COVERING; (*cover for*

jar) cap, lid, top; (*book cover*) binding, dust-jacket, jacket; (*cover for papers*) case, envelope, file, folder, portfolio, wrapper. **2** see BEDCLOTHES. **3** camouflage, cloak, concealment, cover-up, deception, defence, disguise, façade, front, hiding place, mask, pretence, protection, refuge, sanctuary, screen, shelter, smokescreen, support.

coverage *noun* **1** area or amount covered. **2** reporting of events in newspaper etc.

covering *noun* thing that covers, esp. blanket, quilt, or clothes.
■ blanket, canopy, cap, carpet, casing, cladding, cloak, coat, coating, cocoon, cover, crust, facing, film, incrustation, layer, lid, mantle, outside, pall, rind, roof, screen, sheath, sheet, shell, shield, shroud, skin, surface, tarpaulin, top, veil, veneer, wrapping.

covering letter *noun* explanatory letter with other documents.

coverlet /'kʌvəlɪt/ *noun* bedspread.

covert /'kʌvət/ *adjective* secret, disguised. ● *noun* shelter, esp. thicket hiding game. □ **covertly** *adverb*.

covet /'kʌvɪt/ *verb* (**-t-**) desire greatly (esp. thing belonging to another person). □ **covetable** *adjective*.

covetous /'kʌvɪtəs/ *adjective* **1** coveting; greatly desiring. **2** greedy for possessions. □ **covetousness** *noun*.

covey /'kʌvɪ/ *noun* (*plural* **-s**) **1** brood of partridges. **2** family, set.

coving /'kəʊvɪŋ/ *noun* curved surface at junction of wall and ceiling.

cow[1] /kaʊ/ *noun* **1** fully grown female of esp. domestic bovine animal. **2** female of elephant, rhinoceros, whale, seal, etc. □ **cowboy 1** (*feminine* **cowgirl**) person who tends cattle, esp. in western US. **2** *colloquial* unscrupulous or incompetent business person. **cowherd** person who tends cattle. **cowhide** (leather made from) cow's hide. **cow-pat** round flat piece of cow-dung. **cowpox** disease of cows, source of smallpox vaccine.

cow[2] /kaʊ/ *verb* intimidate.

coward /'kaʊəd/ *noun* person easily frightened. □ **cowardly** *adjective*. **cowardliness** *noun*.
■ *colloquial* chicken, *colloquial* wimp.
□ **cowardly** abject, afraid, base, chicken-hearted, cowering, craven, dastardly, faint-hearted, fearful, frightened, *colloquial* gutless, lily-livered, *formal* pusillanimous, spineless, submissive, timid, timorous, unchivalrous, ungallant, unheroic, *colloquial* wimpish, *colloquial* yellow.

cowardice /'kaʊədɪs/ *noun* lack of bravery.
■ cowardliness, faint-heartedness, fear, *slang* funk, spinelessness, timidity.

cower /'kaʊə/ *verb* crouch or shrink back in fear.
■ cringe, crouch, flinch, grovel, hide, quail, shiver, shrink, skulk, tremble.

cowl /kaʊl/ *noun* **1** (hood of) monk's cloak. **2** (also **cowling**) hood-shaped covering of chimney or shaft. □ **cowl neck** wide loose roll neck on garment.

cowrie /ˈkaʊrɪ/ *noun* **1** tropical mollusc with bright shell. **2** its shell as money in parts of Asia etc.

cowslip /ˈkaʊslɪp/ *noun* yellow-flowered primula growing in pastures etc.

cox *noun* coxswain. ● *verb* act as cox (of).

coxcomb /ˈkɒkskəʊm/ *noun* conceited showy person.

coxswain /ˈkɒks(ə)n/ *noun* person who steers esp. rowing boat.

coy *adjective* **1** affectedly shy. **2** irritatingly reticent. □ **coyly** *adverb*. **coyness** *noun*.
> ■ **1** arch, bashful, coquettish, demure, diffident, embarrassed, modest, reserved, retiring, self-conscious, sheepish, shy, timid. **2** evasive, hesitant, reserved, reticent, unforthcoming.

coyote /kɔɪˈəʊtɪ/ *noun* (*plural* same or **-s**) N. American wild dog.

coypu /ˈkɔɪpuː/ *noun* (*plural* **-s**) amphibious rodent like small beaver, originally from S. America.

cozen /ˈkʌz(ə)n/ *verb literary* **1** cheat, defraud. **2** beguile.

cozy *US* = COSY.

crab *noun* **1** shellfish with 10 legs. **2** this as food. **3** (in full **crab-louse**) (often in *plural*) parasite infesting human body. ● *verb* (**-bb-**) *colloquial* **1** criticize; grumble. **2** spoil. □ **catch a crab** (in rowing) get oar jammed under water; miss water. **crab-apple 1** wild apple tree. **2** its sour fruit.

crabbed /ˈkræbɪd/ *adjective* **1** crabby. **2** (of handwriting) ill-formed, illegible.

crabby *adjective* (**-ier, -iest**) morose, irritable. □ **crabbily** *adverb*.

crabwise /ˈkræbwaɪz/ *adverb & adjective* (of movement) sideways like a crab.

crack *noun* **1** sudden sharp noise. **2** sharp blow. **3** narrow opening; break or split. **4** *colloquial* joke; malicious remark. **5** sudden change in vocal pitch. **6** *colloquial* attempt. **7** *slang* crystalline cocaine. ● *verb* **1** (cause to) make crack. **2** suffer crack or partial break. **3** (of voice) change pitch sharply. **4** tell (joke). **5** open (bottle of wine etc.). **6** break into (safe). **7** find solution to (problem). **8** give way; yield. **9** hit sharply. **10** (as **cracked** *adjective*) crazy. **11** (as **cracked** *adjective*) (of wheat) coarsely broken. ● *adjective* excellent; first-rate. □ **crack-brained** crazy. **crackdown** *colloquial* severe measures (esp. against lawbreakers). **crack down on** *colloquial* take severe measures against. **crack of dawn** daybreak. **crackpot** *colloquial* eccentric or impractical person. **crack up** *colloquial* collapse under strain. **get cracking** *colloquial* begin promptly and vigorously.

> ■ *noun* **3** breach, break, chink, chip, cleavage, cleft, cranny, crevice, fissure, flaw, fracture, gap, opening, rift, rupture, slit, split. **4** see JOKE *noun* 1. ● *verb* **2** break, chip, fracture, snap, splinter, split. **9** see HIT *verb* 1. □ **crack up** see DISINTEGRATE 1.

cracker *noun* **1** small paper cylinder containing paper hat, joke, etc., exploding with crack when ends are pulled. **2** explosive firework. **3** thin crisp savoury biscuit.

crackers *adjective slang* crazy.

cracking /ˈkrækɪŋ/ *adjective slang* **1** excellent. **2** fast and exciting.

crackle /ˈkræk(ə)l/ *verb* (**-ling**) make repeated light cracking sound. ● *noun* such a sound. □ **crackly** *adjective*.

crackling *noun* crisp skin of roast pork.

cracknel /ˈkræk(ə)l/ *noun* light crisp biscuit.

cradle /ˈkreɪd(ə)l/ *noun* **1** baby's bed, esp. on rockers. **2** place regarded as origin of something. **3** supporting framework or structure. ● *verb* (**-ling**) contain or shelter as in cradle.

craft /krɑːft/ *noun* **1** special skill or technique. **2** occupation needing this. **3** (*plural* same) boat, vessel, aircraft, or spacecraft. **4** cunning. ● *verb* make using skill.
> ■ *noun* **1** art, craftsmanship, handicraft, skill, technique. **2** job, occupation, trade, vocation. **4** see CUNNING *noun* 2. ● *verb* see MAKE *verb* 1.

craftsman /ˈkrɑːftsmən/ *noun* (*feminine* **craftswoman**) person who practises a craft. □ **craftsmanship** *noun*.
> ■ □ **craftsmanship** art, artistry, cleverness, craft, dexterity, expertise, handiwork, knack, know-how, skill, workmanship.

crafty *adjective* (**-ier, -iest**) cunning, artful. □ **craftily** *adverb*. **craftiness** *noun*.
> ■ artful, astute, calculating, canny, cheating, clever, conniving, cunning, deceitful, designing, devious, *colloquial* dodgy, foxy, furtive, guileful, ingenious, knowing, machiavellian, manipulative, scheming, *colloquial* shifty, shrewd, sly, sneaky, tricky, wily.

crag *noun* steep rugged rock.

craggy *adjective* (**-ier, -iest**) rugged; rough-textured.
> ■ jagged, rocky, rough, rugged, steep, uneven.

cram *verb* (**-mm-**) **1** fill to bursting. **2** (often + *in, into*) force. **3** study or teach intensively for exam.
> ■ **1, 2** compress, crowd, crush, fill, force, jam, overcrowd, overfill, pack, press, squeeze, stuff. **3** see STUDY *verb* 3.

crammer *noun* institution that crams pupils for exam.

cramp *noun* painful involuntary contraction of muscles. ● *verb* **1** affect with cramp. **2** restrict, confine.

cramped *adjective* **1** (of space) small. **2** (of handwriting) small and with the letters close together.

■ **1** close, crowded, narrow, restricted, tight, uncomfortable.

crampon /'kræmpɒn/ *noun* spiked iron plate fixed to boot for climbing on ice.

cranberry /'krænbərɪ/ *noun* (*plural* **-ies**) (shrub bearing) small red acid berry.

crane *noun* **1** machine with projecting arm for moving heavy weights. **2** large long-legged wading bird. ● *verb* (**-ning**) stretch (one's neck) in order to see something. □ **crane-fly** two-winged long-legged fly. **cranesbill** kind of wild geranium.

■ *noun* **1** davit, derrick, hoist.

cranium /'kreɪnɪəm/ *noun* (*plural* **-s** or **-nia**) bones enclosing brain; skull. □ **cranial** *adjective*.

crank *noun* **1** part of axle or shaft bent at right angles for converting rotary into reciprocal motion or vice versa. **2** eccentric person. ● *verb* turn with crank. □ **crankpin** pin attaching connecting rod to crank. **crankshaft** shaft driven by crank. **crank up** start (engine) by turning crank.

cranky *adjective* (**-ier, -iest**) **1** eccentric. **2** shaky. **3** *esp. US* crotchety.

cranny /'krænɪ/ *noun* (*plural* **-ies**) chink, crevice.

crape *noun* crêpe, usually of black silk, formerly used for mourning.

craps *plural noun* (also **crap game**) *US* gambling game played with dice.

crapulent /'kræpjʊlənt/ *adjective* suffering the effects of drunkenness. □ **crapulence** *noun*. **crapulous** *adjective*.

crash *verb* **1** (cause to) make loud smashing noise. **2** (often + *into*) (cause to) collide or fall violently. **3** fail, esp. financially. **4** (of computer, system, etc.) fail suddenly. **5** *colloquial* gatecrash. **6** (often + *out*) *slang* fall asleep; sleep. ● *noun* **1** sudden violent noise. **2** violent fall or impact, esp. of vehicle. **3** ruin, esp. financial. **4** sudden collapse, esp. of computer, system, etc. ● *adjective* done rapidly or urgently. □ **crash barrier** barrier to prevent car leaving road. **crash-dive** ● *verb* **1** (of submarine) dive hastily and steeply. **2** (of aircraft) dive and crash. ● *noun* such a dive. **crash helmet** helmet worn to protect head. **crash-land** land or cause (aircraft etc.) to land with crash. **crash landing** instance of landing with crash.

■ *verb* **2** bump, collapse, collide, crash-dive, dive, fall, knock, lurch, pitch, plummet, plunge, smash, topple; (*crash into*) see HIT *verb* **2**. **3, 4** see FAIL *verb* **1,2;7**. ● *noun* **1** bang, boom, clash, explosion. **2** accident, bump, collision, derailment, disaster, impact, knock, *colloquial* pile-up, smash, wreck. **3** collapse, failure, fall.

crass *adjective* **1** grossly stupid. **2** insensitive. □ **crassly** *adverb*. **crassness** *noun*.

crate *noun* **1** slatted wooden case. **2** *slang* old aircraft, car, etc. ● *verb* (**-ting**) pack in crate.

■ *noun* **1** box, carton, case, tea chest.

crater /'kreɪtə/ *noun* **1** mouth of volcano. **2**

bowl-shaped cavity, esp. hollow on surface of moon etc.

■ **2** cavity, hole, hollow, opening, pit.

cravat /krə'væt/ *noun* man's scarf worn inside open-necked shirt.

crave *verb* (**-ving**) (often + *for*) long or beg for.

craven /'kreɪv(ə)n/ *adjective* cowardly; abject. □ **cravenly** *adverb*. **cravenness** *noun*.

craving *noun* strong desire, longing.

craw *noun* crop of bird or insect.

crawfish *noun* (*plural* same) large spiny sea-lobster.

crawl *verb* **1** move slowly, esp. on hands and knees or with body close to ground. **2** *colloquial* behave obsequiously. **3** (often + *with*) be filled with moving people or things. **4** (esp. of skin) creep. ● *noun* **1** crawling motion. **2** slow rate of motion. **3** fast swimming stroke. □ **crawler** *noun*.

■ *verb* **1** creep, slither, squirm, worm, wriggle. **2** cringe, fawn, flatter, grovel, *colloquial* suck up, toady.

crayfish /'kreɪfɪʃ/ *noun* (*plural* same) **1** lobster-like freshwater crustacean. **2** crawfish.

crayon /'kreɪən/ *noun* stick or pencil of coloured wax, chalk, etc. ● *verb* draw or colour with crayons.

craze *verb* (**-zing**) **1** (usually as **crazed** *adjective*) make insane. **2** produce fine surface cracks on. **3** develop such cracks. ● *noun* **1** usually temporary enthusiasm. **2** object of this.

■ *noun* **1** diversion, enthusiasm, fad, fashion, mania, novelty, obsession, passion, pastime, rage, *colloquial* thing, trend, vogue.

crazy *adjective* (**-ier, -iest**) **1** insane, mad. **2** foolish. **3** (usually + *about*) *colloquial* extremely enthusiastic. □ **crazy paving** paving made of irregular pieces. □ **crazily** *adverb*.

■ **1** berserk, confused, crazed, delirious, demented, deranged, frantic, frenzied, hysterical, insane, lunatic, mad, *slang* potty, unbalanced, unhinged, wild. **2** absurd, daft, eccentric, farcical, foolish, idiotic, ill-considered, illogical, impractical, irrational, ludicrous, ridiculous, senseless, silly, stupid, unrealistic, unreasonable, unwise, *slang* wacky, zany.

creak *noun* harsh scraping or squeaking sound. ● *verb* **1** emit creak. **2** move stiffly. □ **creaky** *adjective* (**-ier, -iest**).

cream *noun* **1** fatty part of milk. **2** its yellowish-white colour. **3** food or drink like or made with cream. **4** creamlike cosmetic etc. **5** (usually after *the*) best part or pick of something. ● *verb* **1** take cream from. **2** make creamy. **3** form cream or scum. ● *adjective* yellowish-white. □ **cream cheese** soft rich cheese made of cream and unskimmed milk. **cream cracker** crisp unsweetened biscuit. **cream off** remove best part of. **cream of tartar** purified tartar, used in medicine, baking powder, etc. **cream tea** afternoon tea with scones, jam, and cream. ▢ **creamy** *adjective* (**-ier, -iest**).

  ■ ▢ **creamy** milky, oily, rich, smooth, thick, velvety.

creamer *noun* **1** cream substitute for use in coffee. **2** jug for cream.

creamery *noun* (*plural* **-ies**) **1** factory producing dairy products. **2** dairy.

crease /kriːs/ *noun* **1** line made by folding or crushing. **2** *Cricket* line defining position of bowler or batsman. ● *verb* (**-sing**) **1** make creases in. **2** develop creases.

  ■ *noun* **1** corrugation, crinkle, fold, furrow, groove, line, pleat, pucker, ridge, ruck, tuck, wrinkle.
  ● *verb* crimp, crinkle, crumple, crush, fold, furrow, pleat, pucker, ridge, ruck, rumple, wrinkle.

create /kriːˈeɪt/ *verb* (**-ting**) **1** bring into existence; originate. **2** invest with rank. **3** *slang* make fuss.

  ■ **1** *literary* beget, begin, breed, bring about, bring into being, build, cause, compose, conceive, concoct, constitute, construct, design, devise, dream up, engender, engineer, establish, father, forge, form, found, generate, give rise to, hatch, imagine, institute, invent, make (up), manufacture, occasion, originate, produce, set up, shape, sire, *colloquial* think up.

creation /kriːˈeɪʃ(ə)n/ *noun* **1** creating, being created. **2** (usually **the Creation**) God's creating of the universe. **3** (usually **Creation**) all created things. **4** product of imaginative work.

  ■ **1** beginning, birth, building, conception, constitution, construction, establishing, formation, foundation, generation, genesis, inception, institution, making, origin, procreation, production, shaping. **4** achievement, *colloquial* brainchild, concept, *colloquial* effort, handiwork, invention, product, work of art.

creative /kriːˈeɪtɪv/ *adjective* inventive, imaginative. ▢ **creatively** *adverb*. **creativity** /-ˈtɪv-/ *noun*.

  ■ artistic, clever, fecund, fertile, imaginative, ingenious, inspired, inventive, original, positive, productive, resourceful, talented.

creator /kriːˈeɪtə/ *noun* **1** person who creates. **2** (**the Creator**) God.

  ■ **1** architect, author, *literary* begetter, builder, composer, designer, deviser, discoverer, initiator, inventor, maker, manufacturer, originator, parent, producer.

creature /ˈkriːtʃə/ *noun* **1** living being, esp. animal. **2** person, esp. one in subservient position. **3** anything created.

  ■ **1** animal, beast, being, brute, mortal being, organism.

crèche /krɛʃ/ *noun* day nursery.

credence /ˈkriːd(ə)ns/ *noun* belief.

credentials /krɪˈdenʃ(ə)lz/ *plural noun* documents attesting to person's education, character, etc.

  ■ authorization, documents, identity card, licence, passport, permit, proof of identity, warrant.

credible /ˈkredɪb(ə)l/ *adjective* believable; worthy of belief. ▢ **credibility** *noun*.

USAGE *Credible* is sometimes confused with *credulous*, which means 'gullible'.

  ■ believable, conceivable, convincing, imaginable, likely, persuasive, plausible, possible, reasonable, tenable, thinkable, trustworthy.

credit /ˈkredɪt/ *noun* **1** belief, trust. **2** good reputation. **3** person's financial standing. **4** power to obtain goods before payment. **5** acknowledgement of payment by entry in account. **6** sum entered. **7** acknowledgement of merit or (usually in *plural*) of contributor's services to film, book, etc. **8** grade above pass in exam. **9** educational course counting towards degree. ● *verb* (**-t-**) **1** believe. **2** (usually + *to, with*) enter on credit side of account. ▢ **credit card** card authorizing purchase of goods on credit. **credit (person) with** ascribe to him or her. **credit rating** estimate of person's suitability for commercial credit. **creditworthy** suitable to receive credit. **on credit** with arrangement to pay later. **to one's credit** in one's favour.

  ■ *noun* **2** approval, commendation, distinction, esteem, fame, glory, honour, *colloquial* kudos, merit, praise, prestige, recognition, reputation, status, tribute. ● *verb* **1** accept, believe, *slang* buy, count on, depend on, have faith in, reckon on, rely on, subscribe to, swallow, *colloquial* swear by, trust. **2** add, enter. ▢ **credit with** ascribe to, attribute to.

creditable *adjective* praiseworthy. ▢ **creditably** *adverb*.

  ■ admirable, commendable, estimable, good, honourable, laudable, meritorious, praiseworthy, respectable, well thought of, worthy.

creditor *noun* person to whom debt is owing.

credo /ˈkriːdəʊ/ *noun* (*plural* **-s**) creed.

credulous /ˈkredjʊləs/ *adjective* too ready to believe; gullible. ▢ **credulity** /krɪˈdjuː-/ *noun*.

USAGE *Credulous* is sometimes confused with *credible*, which means 'believable'.

  ■ easily taken in, green, gullible, naive, soft, trusting, unsuspecting.

creed *noun* **1** set of beliefs; system of beliefs. **2** (often **the Creed**) formal summary of Christian doctrine.

  ■ **1** belief, conviction, doctrine, dogma, faith, principle, teaching, tenet.

creek *noun* **1** inlet on sea-coast. **2** arm of river; stream.

  ■ **1** bay, cove, estuary, harbour, inlet.

creel *noun* fisherman's wicker basket.

creep *verb* (*past & past participle* **crept**) **1** crawl. **2** move stealthily, timidly, or slowly. **3** *colloquial* act obsequiously. **4** (of plant) grow along ground or up wall etc. **5** advance or develop gradually. **6** (of flesh) shudder with horror etc. ● *noun* **1** act of creeping. **2** (**the creeps**) *colloquial* feeling of revulsion or fear. **3** *slang* unpleasant person. **4** gradual change in shape of metal under stress.

■ *verb* **1** crawl, slither, worm, wriggle, writhe. **2** crawl, edge, inch, *colloquial* pussyfoot, slink, slip, sneak, steal, tiptoe.

creeper *noun* creeping or climbing plant.

creepy *adjective* (**-ier, -iest**) *colloquial* feeling or causing horror or fear. □ **creepy-crawly** (*plural* **-crawlies**) small crawling insect etc. □ **creepily** *adverb*.

■ disturbing, eerie, frightening, ghostly, hair-raising, macabre, ominous, *colloquial* scary, sinister, spine-chilling, *colloquial* spooky, supernatural, threatening, uncanny, unearthly, weird.

cremate /krɪˈmeɪt/ *verb* (**-ting**) burn (corpse) to ashes. □ **cremation** *noun*.

crematorium /kreməˈtɔːrɪəm/ *noun* (*plural* **-ria** or **-s**) place where corpses are cremated.

crenellated /ˈkrenəleɪtɪd/ *adjective* having battlements. □ **crenellation** *noun*.

Creole /ˈkriːəʊl/ *noun* **1** descendant of European settlers in W. Indies or Central or S. America, or of French settlers in southern US. **2** person of mixed European and black descent. **3** language formed from a European and African language. ● *adjective* **1** of Creoles. **2** (usually **creole**) of Creole origin etc.

creosote /ˈkriːəsəʊt/ *noun* oily wood-preservative distilled from coal tar. ● *verb* (**-ting**) treat with creosote.

crêpe /kreɪp/ *noun* **1** fine crinkled fabric. **2** thin pancake with savoury or sweet filling. **3** wrinkled sheet rubber used for shoe-soles etc. □ **crêpe de Chine** /də ˈʃiːn/ fine silk crêpe. **crêpe paper** thin crinkled paper.

crept *past & past participle* of CREEP.

crepuscular /krɪˈpʌskjʊlə/ *adjective* **1** of twilight. **2** (of animal) active etc. at twilight.

crescendo /krɪˈʃendəʊ/ *Music noun* (*plural* **-s**) gradual increase in loudness. ● *adjective & adverb* increasing in loudness.

USAGE *Crescendo* is sometimes wrongly used to mean a climax rather than the progress towards it.

crescent /ˈkres(ə)nt/ *noun* **1** sickle shape, as of waxing or waning moon. **2** thing with this shape, esp. curved street. ● *adjective* crescent-shaped.

cress *noun* plant with pungent edible leaves.

crest *noun* **1** comb or tuft on animal's head. **2** plume of helmet. **3** top of mountain, wave, etc. **4** *Heraldry* device above shield or on writing paper etc. ● *verb* **1** reach crest of. **2** crown; serve as crest to. **3** form crest. □ **crestfallen** dejected. □ **crested** *adjective*.

■ *noun* **1** comb, plume, tuft. **3** apex, brow, crown, head, peak, pinnacle, ridge, summit, top. **4** badge, coat of arms, design, device, emblem, insignia, seal, sign, symbol.

cretaceous /krɪˈteɪʃəs/ *adjective* chalky.

cretin /ˈkretɪn/ *noun* **1** person with deformity and mental retardation caused by thyroid deficiency. **2** *colloquial* stupid person. □ **cretinism** *noun*. **cretinous** *adjective*.

cretonne /kreˈtɒn/ *noun* heavy cotton usually floral upholstery fabric.

crevasse /krəˈvæs/ *noun* deep open crack in glacier.

crevice /ˈkrevɪs/ *noun* narrow opening or fissure, esp. in rock.

■ break, chink, cleft, crack, cranny, fissure, furrow, groove, rift, slit, split.

crew[1] /kruː/ *noun* **1** group of people working together, esp. manning ship, aircraft, spacecraft, etc. **2** these, other than the officers. ● *verb* **1** supply or act as crew (member) for. **2** act as crew. □ **crew-cut** close-cropped hairstyle. **crew neck** round close-fitting neckline.

■ *noun* band, company, gang, group, party, team.

crew[2] *archaic past* of CROW.

crewel /ˈkruːəl/ *noun* thin worsted yarn for embroidery.

crib *noun* **1** baby's small bed or cot. **2** model of Nativity with manger. **3** *colloquial* plagiarism. **4** *colloquial* translation. **5** *colloquial* cribbage. ● *verb* (**-bb-**) **1** *colloquial* copy unfairly. **2** confine in small space.

cribbage /ˈkrɪbɪdʒ/ *noun* a card game.

crick *noun* sudden painful stiffness, esp. in neck. ● *verb* cause crick in.

cricket[1] /ˈkrɪkɪt/ *noun* team game, played on grass pitch, in which ball is bowled at wicket defended with bat by player of other team. □ **not cricket** *colloquial* unfair behaviour. □ **cricketer** *noun*.

cricket[2] /ˈkrɪkɪt/ *noun* jumping chirping insect.

cried *past & past participle* of CRY.

crier /ˈkraɪə/ *noun* (also **cryer**) official making public announcements in law court or street.

crikey /ˈkraɪkɪ/ *interjection slang*: expressing astonishment.

crime *noun* **1** act punishable by law. **2** such acts collectively. **3** evil act. **4** *colloquial* shameful act.

■ **1, 2** delinquency, dishonesty, felony, illegality, lawbreaking, lawlessness, misconduct, misdeed, misdemeanour, offence, *slang* racket, sin, transgression of the law, violation, wrongdoing.

criminal /ˈkrɪmɪn(ə)l/ *noun* person guilty of crime. ● *adjective* **1** of, involving, or concerning crime. **2** *colloquial* deplorable. □ **criminality** /-ˈnæl-/ *noun*. **criminally** *adverb*.

■ *noun colloquial* baddy, *esp. historical* convict, *colloquial* crook, culprit, delinquent, desperado, felon, gangster, jailbird, knave, *slang* (old) lag, lawbreaker, malefactor, miscreant, offender, outlaw, recidivist, ruffian, scoundrel, thug, transgressor, *colloquial* villain, wrongdoer.
● *adjective* **1** *slang* bent, corrupt, *colloquial* crooked, culpable, dishonest, felonious, illegal, illicit, indictable, lawless, nefarious, shady, unlawful, wicked, wrong.

criminology /krɪmɪˈnɒlədʒɪ/ *noun* study of crime. □ **criminologist** *noun*.

crimp *verb* **1** press into small folds or waves. **2** corrugate.

Crimplene /ˈkrɪmpliːn/ *noun proprietary term* synthetic crease-resistant fabric.

crimson /ˈkrɪmz(ə)n/ *adjective & noun* rich deep red.

cringe *verb* (**-ging**) **1** cower. **2** (often + *to*) behave obsequiously.
■ **1** blench, cower, crouch, flinch, quail, quiver, recoil, shrink back, shy away, tremble, wince. **2** see GROVEL 1.

crinkle /ˈkrɪŋk(ə)l/ *noun* wrinkle, crease. ● *verb* (**-ling**) form crinkles (in). □ **crinkly** *adjective*.

crinoline /ˈkrɪnəlɪn/ *noun* hooped petticoat.

cripple /ˈkrɪp(ə)l/ *noun* lame person. ● *verb* (**-ling**) **1** lame; disable. **2** damage seriously. □ **crippled** *adjective*.
■ *verb* **1** disable, hamper, hamstring, incapacitate, lame, maim, mutilate, paralyse, weaken. **2** damage, put out of action, sabotage, spoil.

crisis /ˈkraɪsɪs/ *noun* (*plural* **crises** /-siːz/) **1** time of acute danger or difficulty. **2** decisive moment.
■ **1** calamity, catastrophe, danger, difficulty, disaster, emergency, predicament, problem. **2** climax, critical moment, turning point.

crisp *adjective* **1** hard but brittle. **2** bracing. **3** brisk; decisive. **4** clear-cut. **5** crackling. **6** curly. ● *noun* (in full **potato crisp**) very thin fried slice of potato. ● *verb* make or become crisp. □ **crispbread** thin crisp biscuit. □ **crisply** *adverb*. **crispness** *noun*.
■ *adjective* **1** breakable, brittle, crackly, crispy, crunchy, fragile, friable. **2** see BRACE *verb* 3. **3** see BRISK 1.

crispy *adjective* (**-ier**, **-iest**) crisp.

criss-cross *noun* pattern of crossing lines. ● *adjective* crossing; in crossing lines. ● *adverb* crosswise. ● *verb* **1** intersect repeatedly. **2** mark with criss-cross lines.

criterion /kraɪˈtɪərɪən/ *noun* (*plural* **-ria**) principle or standard of judgement.
USAGE It is a mistake to use the plural form *criteria* when only one criterion is meant.
■ measure, principle, standard, touchstone, yardstick.

critic /ˈkrɪtɪk/ *noun* **1** person who criticizes. **2** reviewer of literary, artistic, etc. works.
■ **1** attacker, detractor. **2** analyst, authority, commentator, judge, pundit, reviewer.

critical *adjective* **1** fault-finding; expressing criticism. **2** discerning; analytical. **3** providing textual criticism. **4** of the nature of a crisis; decisive. **5** marking transition from one state to another. □ **critically** *adverb*.
■ **1** captious, carping, censorious, criticizing, deprecatory, depreciatory, derogatory, disapproving, disparaging, fault-finding, judgemental, *colloquial* nit-picking, scathing, slighting, uncomplimentary, unfavourable. **2** analytical, discerning, discriminating, intelligent, judicious, perceptive, probing, sharp. **4** basic, crucial, dangerous, decisive, important, key, momentous, pivotal, vital.

criticism /ˈkrɪtɪsɪz(ə)m/ *noun* **1** finding fault; censure. **2** critical article, remark, etc. **3** work of critic.
■ **1, 2** censure, condemnation, diatribe, disapproval, disparagement, reprimand, reproach, stricture, tirade, verbal attack. **3** analysis, appraisal, appreciation, assessment, commentary, critique, elucidation, evaluation, judgement, review, valuation.

criticize /ˈkrɪtɪsaɪz/ *verb* (also **-ise**) (**-zing** or **-sing**) **1** find fault with. **2** discuss critically.
■ **1** belittle, berate, blame, carp, cast aspersions on, castigate, censure, *archaic* chide, complain about, condemn, decry, disapprove of, disparage, fault, find fault with, flay, *colloquial* get at, impugn, *slang* knock, lash, *colloquial* pan, pick holes in, *colloquial* pitch into, rap, rate, rebuke, reprimand, satirize, scold, *slang* slam, *colloquial* slate, snipe at. **2** analyse, appraise, assess, evaluate, discuss, judge, review.

critique /krɪˈtiːk/ *noun* critical analysis.

croak *noun* deep hoarse sound, esp. of frog. ● *verb* **1** utter or speak with croak. **2** *slang* die. □ **croaky** *adjective* (**-ier**, **-iest**). **croakily** *adverb*.

Croat /ˈkrəʊæt/ (also **Croatian** /krəʊˈeɪʃ(ə)n/) *noun* **1** native of Croatia. **2** person of Croatian descent. **3** Slavonic dialect of Croats. ● *adjective* of Croats or their dialect.

crochet /ˈkrəʊʃeɪ/ *noun* needlework of hooked yarn producing lacy patterned fabric. ● *verb* (**crocheted** /-ʃeɪd/; **crocheting** /-ʃeɪɪŋ/) make by crochet.

crock[1] *noun colloquial* old or worn-out person or vehicle.

crock[2] *noun* **1** earthenware jar. **2** broken piece of this.

crockery *noun* earthenware or china dishes, plates, etc.
■ ceramics, china, crocks, dishes, earthenware, porcelain, pottery, tableware.

crocodile /ˈkrɒkədaɪl/ *noun* **1** large amphibious reptile. **2** *colloquial* line of schoolchildren etc. walking in pairs. □ **crocodile tears** insincere grief.

crocus /'krəʊkəs/ *noun* (*plural* **-es**) small plant with corm and yellow, purple, or white flowers.

croft *noun* **1** small piece of arable land. **2** small rented farm in Scotland or N. England. ● *verb* farm croft.

crofter *noun* person who farms croft.

Crohn's disease /krəʊnz/ *noun* inflammatory disease of alimentary tract.

croissant /'krwʌsɑ̃ / *noun* rich crescent-shaped roll.

cromlech /'krɒmlek/ *noun* **1** dolmen. **2** prehistoric stone circle.

crone *noun* withered old woman.

crony /'krəʊnɪ/ *noun* (*plural* **-ies**) *often derogatory* friend, companion.

crook /krʊk/ *noun* **1** hooked staff of shepherd or bishop. **2** bend, curve. **3** *colloquial* swindler, criminal. ● *verb* bend, curve.

■ *noun* **2** angle, bend, corner, curve, hook. **3** see CRIMINAL *noun*.

crooked /'krʊkɪd/ *adjective* (**-er**, **-est**) **1** not straight, bent. **2** *colloquial* dishonest. □ **crookedly** *adverb*. **crookedness** *noun*.

■ **1** angled, askew, awry, bent, bowed, contorted, curved, curving, deformed, gnarled, lopsided, misshapen, off-centre, tortuous, twisted, twisty, warped, winding, zigzag. **2** see CRIMINAL *adjective* 1.

croon /kruːn/ *verb* hum or sing in low voice. ● *noun* such singing. □ **crooner** *noun*.

crop *noun* **1** produce of any cultivated plant or of land. **2** group or amount produced at one time. **3** handle of whip. **4** very short haircut. **5** pouch in bird's gullet where food is prepared for digestion. ● *verb* (**-pp-**) **1** bite off; eat down. **2** cut off. **3** cut (hair) short. **4** raise crop on (land). **5** (of land) bear crop. □ **crop circle** circle of crops inexplicably flattened. **crop up** occur unexpectedly.

■ *noun* **1** gathering, harvest, produce, vintage, yield. ● *verb* **1** bite off, browse, graze, nibble. **2, 3** see CUT *verb* 2. □ **crop up** see ARISE 3.

cropper *noun slang* □ **come a cropper 1** fall heavily. **2** fail badly.

croquet /'krəʊkeɪ/ *noun* **1** lawn game with hoops, wooden balls, and mallets. **2** croqueting. ● *verb* (**croqueted** /-keɪd/; **croqueting** /-keɪɪŋ/) drive away (opponent's ball) by striking one's own ball placed in contact with it.

croquette /krə'ket/ *noun* fried breaded ball of meat, potato, etc.

crosier /'krəʊzɪə/ *noun* (also **crozier**) bishop's ceremonial hooked staff.

cross *noun* **1** upright stake with transverse bar, used in antiquity for crucifixion. **2** representation of this as emblem of Christianity. **3** cross-shaped thing or mark, esp. two short intersecting lines (+ or x). **4** cross-shaped military etc. decoration. **5** intermixture of breeds; hybrid. **6** (+ *between*) mixture of two things. **7** trial, affliction. ● *verb* **1** (often + *over*) go across. **2** place crosswise. **3** lie across; intersect. **4** draw line(s) across.

5 meet and pass. **6** make sign of cross on or over. **7** thwart. **8** (cause to) interbreed. **9** cross-fertilize (plants). ● *adjective* **1** (often + *with*) peevish, angry. **2** transverse; reaching from side to side. **3** intersecting. **4** reciprocal. □ **at cross purposes** misunderstanding each other. **crossbar** horizontal bar, esp. between uprights. **cross-bench** bench in House of Lords for non-party members. **crossbones** see SKULL AND CROSSBONES. **crossbow** bow fixed across wooden stock with mechanism working string. **cross-breed** (produce) hybrid animal or plant. **cross-check** check by alternative method. **cross-country** ● *adjective & adverb* across fields etc., not following roads. ● *noun* cross-country race. **cross-examine** question (esp. opposing witness in law court). **cross-examination** such questioning. **cross-eyed** having one or both eyes turned inwards. **cross-fertilize** fertilize (animal or plant) from another of same species. **crossfire** firing of guns in two crossing directions. **cross-grained 1** (of wood) with grain running irregularly. **2** (of person) perverse or intractable. **cross-hatch** shade with crossing parallel lines. **cross-legged** (sitting) with legs folded across each other. **cross off, out** cancel, expunge. **crossover** point or process of crossing. **crosspatch** *colloquial* bad-tempered person. **cross-ply** (of tyre) having crosswise layers of cords. **cross-question** cross-examine. **cross-reference** reference to another passage in same book. **crossroad** (usually in *plural*) intersection of roads. **cross-section 1** drawing etc. of thing as if cut through. **2** representative sample. **cross stitch** cross-shaped stitch. **cross swords** argue, clash. **crosswise** intersecting, diagonally. **crossword (puzzle)** puzzle in which words crossing each other vertically and horizontally have to be filled in from clues. **on the cross** diagonally. □ **crossly** *adverb*. **crossness** *noun*.

■ *noun* **2** crucifix, rood. **3** intersection, X. **5** cross-breed, hybrid, mongrel. **6** amalgam, blend, combination, halfway house, mixture. **7** affliction, burden, difficulty, grief, misfortune, problem, sorrow, trial, tribulation, trouble, worry. ● *verb* **1** bridge, ford, go across, pass over, span, traverse. **3** criss-cross, intersect, meet. **1** annoy, block, frustrate, hinder, impede, interfere with, oppose, stand in the way of, thwart. ● *adjective* **1** angry, annoyed, bad-tempered, cantankerous, crotchety, grumpy, ill-tempered, irascible, irate, irritable, peevish, short-tempered, testy, tetchy, upset, vexed. □ **cross out** see CANCEL 2. **crossroad** interchange, intersection, junction. **cross swords** see CONFLICT *verb*.

crossing *noun* **1** place where things (esp. roads) meet. **2** place for crossing street etc. **3** journey across water.

■ **3** see JOURNEY *noun*.

crotch *noun* fork, esp. between legs (of person, trousers, etc.).

crotchet /'krɒtʃɪt/ *noun Music* black-headed note with stem, equal to quarter of semibreve and usually one beat.

crotchety *adjective* peevish.

crouch *verb* stand, squat, etc. with legs bent close to body. ● *noun* this position.
■ *verb* squat, stoop.

croup[1] /kru:p/ *noun* laryngitis in children, with sharp cough.

croup[2] /kru:p/ *noun* rump, esp. of horse.

croupier /'kru:pɪə/ *noun* person in charge of gaming table.

croûton /'kru:tɒn/ *noun* small piece of fried or toasted bread served esp. with soup.

crow /krəʊ/ *noun* **1** any of various kinds of large black-plumaged bird. **2** cry of cock or baby. ● *verb* (*past* **crowed** or *archaic* **crew** /kru:/) **1** (of cock) utter loud cry. **2** (of baby) utter happy sounds. **3** exult. □ **crow's-foot** wrinkle at outer corner of eye. **crow's-nest** shelter for look-out man at ship's masthead.

crowbar *noun* iron bar used as lever.

crowd /kraʊd/ *noun* **1** large gathering of people. **2** *colloquial* particular set of people. **3** group of spectators. ● *verb* **1** (cause to) collect in crowd. **2** (often in *passive*; often + *with*) cram. **3** force way. **4** (+ *into*) force or compress into. **5** *colloquial* come aggressively close to. □ **crowd out** exclude by crowding.
■ *noun* **1** army, assemblage, assembly, cluster, collection, crush, flock, gathering, *usually derogatory* horde, host, mass, mob, multitude, *usually derogatory* pack, press, rabble, swarm, throng. **2** *colloquial* bunch, circle, company, group, lot, set. **3** audience, gate, spectators. ● *verb* **1** assemble, cluster, collect, congregate, flock, gather, get together, herd, huddle, mass, muster, swarm, throng. **2** (*crowded*) congested, crammed, cramped, full, jammed, *colloquial* jam-packed, overcrowded, overflowing, packed, swarming, teeming, thronging. **4** bundle, compress, cram, crush, jam, jostle, pack, pile, press, push, shove, squeeze.

crown /kraʊn/ *noun* **1** monarch's jewelled head-dress. **2** (**the Crown**) monarch as head of state. **3** (**the Crown**) his or her authority. **4** wreath for head as emblem of victory. **5** top part of head, hat, hill, etc. **6** visible part of tooth. **7** artificial replacement for this. **8** coin worth 5 shillings or 25 pence. ● *verb* **1** put crown on. **2** make king or queen. **3** (often as **crowning** *adjective*) be con-summation, reward, or finishing touch to. **4** *slang* hit on head. □ **Crown colony** British colony controlled by the Crown. **Crown Court** court of criminal jurisdiction in England and Wales. **crown jewels** sovereign's regalia. **crown prince** male heir to throne. **crown princess 1** wife of crown prince. **2** female heir to throne.
■ *noun* **1** circlet, coronet, diadem, tiara. **5** apex, brow, head, peak, ridge, summit, top. ● *verb* **2** enthrone, install. **3** cap, complete, conclude, consummate, culminate, finish off, perfect, round off, top.

crozier = CROSIER.

CRT *abbreviation* cathode ray tube.

cruces *plural* of CRUX.

crucial /'kru:ʃ(ə)l/ *adjective* **1** decisive, critical. **2** very important. **3** *slang* excellent. □ **crucially** *adverb*.
■ **1** central, critical, decisive, essential, important, major, momentous, pivotal, serious.

crucible /'kru:sɪb(ə)l/ *noun* melting pot for metals.

cruciferous /kru:'sɪfərəs/ *adjective* with 4 equal petals arranged crosswise.

crucifix /'kru:sɪfɪks/ *noun* image of Christ on Cross.

crucifixion /kru:sɪ'fɪkʃ(ə)n/ *noun* crucifying, esp. of Christ.

cruciform /'kru:sɪfɔ:m/ *adjective* cross-shaped.

crucify /'kru:sɪfaɪ/ *verb* (**-ies**, **-ied**) **1** put to death by fastening to cross. **2** persecute, torment.

crude *adjective* **1** in natural or raw state. **2** lacking finish, unpolished. **3** rude, blunt. **4** in-decent. ● *noun* natural mineral oil. □ **crudely** *adverb*. **crudeness** *noun*. **crudity** *noun*.
■ *adjective* **1** natural, raw, unprocessed, unrefined. **2** amateurish, awkward, bungling, clumsy, inartistic, incompetent, inelegant, inept, makeshift, primitive, rough, rudimentary, unpolished, unskilful, unworkmanlike. **4** see VULGAR 1.

crudités /kru:dɪ'teɪ/ *plural noun* hors d'oeuvre of mixed raw vegetables. [French]

cruel /'kru:əl/ *adjective* (**-ll-** or **-l-**) causing pain or suffering, esp. deliberately; harsh, severe. □ **cruelly** *adverb*. **cruelty** *noun* (*plural* **-ies**).
■ atrocious, barbaric, barbarous, beastly, bestial, bloodthirsty, bloody, brutal, callous, cold-blooded, cold-hearted, diabolical, ferocious, fiendish, fierce, grim, hard, hard-hearted, harsh, heartless, hellish, implacable, inexorable, inhuman, inhumane, malevolent, merciless, murderous, pitiless, relentless, remorseless, ruthless, *colloquial* sadistic, savage, severe, sharp, spiteful, stern, stony-hearted, tyrannical, unfeeling, unjust, unkind, unmerciful, unrelenting, vengeful, venomous, vicious, violent. □ **cruelty** barbarity, bestiality, bloodthirstiness, brutality, callousness, cold-bloodedness, ferocity, hard-heartedness, heartlessness, inhumanity, malevolence, ruthlessness, *colloquial* sadism, savagery, unkindness, viciousness, violence.

cruet /'kru:ɪt/ *noun* set of small salt, pepper, etc. containers for use at table.

cruise /kru:z/ *verb* (**-sing**) **1** sail about, esp. travel by sea for pleasure, calling at ports. **2** travel at relaxed or economical speed. **3** achieve objective with ease. ● *noun* cruising voyage. □ **cruise missile** one able to fly low and guide itself.
■ *noun* sail, voyage.

cruiser *noun* **1** high-speed warship. **2** cabin cruiser. □ **cruiserweight** light heavyweight.

crumb /krʌm/ *noun* **1** small fragment esp. of bread. **2** soft inner part of loaf. **3** (**crumbs** *interjection*) *slang: expressing dismay*. ● *verb* **1**

coat with breadcrumbs. **2** crumble (bread).
□ **crumby** *adjective*.

■ *noun* **1** bit, bite, fragment, grain, morsel, particle, scrap, shred, sliver, speck.

crumble /'krʌmb(ə)l/ *verb* (**-ling**) break or fall into fragments; disintegrate. ● *noun* dish of cooked fruit with crumbly topping. □ **crumbly** *adjective* (**-ier, -iest**).

■ *verb* break apart, break up, crush, decay, decompose, deteriorate, disintegrate, fall apart, fragment, grind, perish, pound, powder, pulverize. □ **crumbly** friable, granular, powdery.

crumhorn = KRUMMHORN.

crummy /'krʌmɪ/ *adjective* (**-ier, -iest**) *slang* squalid, inferior.

crumpet /'krʌmpɪt/ *noun* flat soft yeasty cake eaten toasted.

crumple /'krʌmp(ə)l/ *verb* (**-ling**) **1** (often + *up*) crush or become crushed into creases. **2** give way, collapse.

■ **1** crease, crinkle, crush, dent, fold, mangle, pucker, rumple, wrinkle.

crunch *verb* **1** crush noisily with teeth. **2** make or emit crunch. ● *noun* **1** crunching sound. **2** *colloquial* decisive event. □ **crunchy** *adjective* (**-ier, -iest**).

■ *verb* **1** champ, chew, crush, grind, munch, scrunch.

crupper /'krʌpə/ *noun* strap looped under horse's tail to hold harness back.

crusade /kruː'seɪd/ *noun* **1** *historical* medieval Christian military expedition to recover Holy Land from Muslims. **2** vigorous campaign for cause. ● *verb* (**-ding**) take part in crusade. □ **crusader** *noun*.

■ *noun* **1** campaign, expedition, holy war, war. **2** campaign, drive, movement, struggle, war.

cruse /kruːz/ *noun archaic* earthenware jar.

crush *verb* **1** compress violently so as to break, bruise, etc. **2** crease, crumple. **3** defeat or subdue completely. ● *noun* **1** act of crushing. **2** crowded mass of people. **3** drink made from juice of crushed fruit. **4** (usually + *on*) *colloquial* infatuation. □ **crushable** *adjective*. **crusher** *noun*. **crushing** *adjective* (esp. in sense 3 of *verb*).

■ *verb* **1** break, bruise, compress, crunch, grind, mangle, mash, pound, press, pulp, *colloquial* pulverize, shiver, smash, splinter, squash, squeeze. **2** crease, crinkle, crumple, wrinkle. **3** conquer, defeat, humiliate, mortify, overwhelm, quash, rout, subdue, thrash, *literary* vanquish. ● *noun* **2** congestion, crowd, jam, press, swarm.

crust *noun* **1** hard outer part of thing, esp. bread. **2** pastry covering pie. **3** rocky outer part of the earth. **4** deposit, esp. on sides of wine bottle. ● *verb* cover with, form into, or become covered with crust.

■ *noun* **1** covering, outer layer, outside, rind, scab, shell, skin, surface. **4** deposit, incrustation.

crustacean /krʌ'steɪʃ(ə)n/ *noun* hard-shelled

usually aquatic animal, e.g. crab or lobster. ● *adjective* of crustaceans.

crusty *adjective* (**-ier, -iest**) **1** having a crisp crust. **2** irritable, curt.

crutch *noun* **1** support for lame person, usually with cross-piece fitting under armpit. **2** support. **3** crotch.

crux *noun* (*plural* **-es** or **cruces** /'kruːsiːz/) decisive point at issue.

■ centre, core, crucial issue, essence, heart, nub.

cry /kraɪ/ *verb* (**cries, cried**) **1** (often + *out*) make loud or shrill sound, esp. to express pain, grief, joy, etc. **2** weep. **3** (often + *out*) utter loudly, exclaim. **4** (+ *for*) appeal for. ● *noun* (*plural* **cries**) **1** loud shout of grief, fear, joy, etc. **2** loud excited utterance. **3** urgent appeal. **4** fit of weeping. **5** call of animal. □ **cry-baby** person who weeps frequently. **cry down** disparage. **cry off** withdraw from undertaking. **cry out for** need badly. **cry wolf** see WOLF. **a far cry** a long way.

■ *verb* **1, 3** (*cry out*) see SHOUT *verb*. **2** bawl, blubber, *colloquial* grizzle, howl, keen, shed tears, snivel, sob, wail, weep, whimper, *colloquial* whinge. ● *noun* **1, 2** battle-cry, bellow, call, caterwaul, ejaculation, exclamation, hoot, howl, outcry, roar, scream, screech, shout, shriek, whoop, yell, yelp, yowl. □ **cry off** see WITHDRAW 5.

cryer = CRIER.

crying *adjective* (of injustice etc.) flagrant, demanding redress.

cryogenics /kraɪəʊ'dʒenɪks/ *noun* branch of physics dealing with very low temperatures. □ **cryogenic** *adjective*.

crypt /krɪpt/ *noun* vault, esp. below church, usually used as burial place.

■ basement, catacomb, cellar, grave, sepulchre, tomb, undercroft, vault.

cryptic *adjective* obscure in meaning; secret, mysterious. □ **cryptically** *adverb*.

■ arcane, coded, concealed, enigmatic, esoteric, hidden, mysterious, mystical, obscure, occult, perplexing, puzzling, recondite, secret, unclear, unintelligible, veiled.

cryptogam /'krɪptəgæm/ *noun* plant with no true flowers or seeds, e.g. fern or fungus. □ **cryptogamic** /-'gæm-/ *adjective*.

cryptogram /'krɪptəgræm/ *noun* text written in cipher.

crystal /'krɪst(ə)l/ *noun* **1** (piece of) transparent colourless mineral. **2** (articles of) highly transparent glass. **3** substance solidified in definite geometrical form. ● *adjective* of or as clear as crystal. □ **crystal ball** glass globe used in crystal-gazing. **crystal-gazing** study of glass globe in attempt to see picture of future events. **crystal-gazer** *noun*.

crystalline /'krɪstəlaɪn/ *adjective* of or as clear as crystal.

crystallize /'krɪstəlaɪz/ *verb* (also **-ise**) (**-zing** or **-sing**) **1** form into crystals. **2** make or become definite. **3** preserve or be preserved in sugar. □ **crystallization** *noun*.

CS gas *noun* tear gas used to control riots.

cu. *abbreviation* cubic.

cub *noun* **1** young of fox, bear, lion, etc. **2 Cub (Scout)** junior Scout. **3** *colloquial* young newspaper reporter. ● *verb* give birth to (cubs).

cubbyhole /ˈkʌbɪhəʊl/ *noun* **1** very small room. **2** snug space.

cube /kjuːb/ *noun* **1** solid contained by 6 equal squares. **2** cube-shaped block. **3** product of a number multiplied by its square. ● *verb* (**-bing**) **1** find cube of. **2** cut into small cubes. □ **cube root** number which produces given number when cubed.

cubic /ˈkjuːbɪk/ *adjective* **1** of 3 dimensions. **2** involving cube of a quantity. □ **cubic metre** etc., volume of cube whose edge is one metre etc. □ **cubical** *adjective*.

cubicle /ˈkjuːbɪk(ə)l/ *noun* small screened space, esp. sleeping compartment.

cubism /ˈkjuːbɪz(ə)m/ *noun* art style in which objects are represented geometrically. □ **cubist** *adjective & noun*.

cubit /ˈkjuːbɪt/ *noun* ancient measure of length, approximately length of forearm.

cuboid /ˈkjuːbɔɪd/ *adjective* like a cube; cube-shaped. ● *noun* solid with 6 rectangular faces.

cuckold /ˈkʌkəʊld/ *noun* husband of adulteress. ● *verb* make cuckold of.

cuckoo /ˈkʊkuː/ *noun* bird with characteristic cry and laying eggs in nests of small birds. ● *adjective slang* crazy. □ **cuckoo clock** clock with figure of cuckoo emerging to make call on the hour. **cuckoo-pint** wild arum. **cuckoo-spit** froth exuded by larvae of certain insects.

cucumber /ˈkjuːkʌmbə/ *noun* long green fleshy fruit used in salads.

cud *noun* half-digested food chewed by ruminant.

cuddle /ˈkʌd(ə)l/ *verb* (**-ling**) **1** hug. **2** lie close and snug; nestle. ● *noun* prolonged hug.
■ *verb* **1** caress, clasp lovingly, dandle, embrace, fondle, hold closely, hug, nurse, pet. **2** huddle against, nestle against, snuggle up to.

cuddly *adjective* (**-ier, -iest**) soft and yielding.

cudgel /ˈkʌdʒ(ə)l/ *noun* thick stick used as weapon. ● *verb* (**-ll-**; *US* **-l-**) beat with cudgel.
■ *noun* baton, bludgeon, club, *colloquial* cosh, stick, truncheon. ● *verb* batter, beat, bludgeon, *slang* clobber, *colloquial* cosh, hit, pound, pummel, thrash, thump, thwack.

cue[1] /kjuː/ *noun* **1** last words of actor's speech as signal for another to begin. **2** signal, hint. ● *verb* (**cues, cued, cueing** or **cuing**) give cue to. □ **cue in** insert cue for. **on cue** at correct moment.
■ *noun* hint, prompt, reminder, sign, signal.

cue[2] /kjuː/ *noun* long rod for striking ball in billiards etc. ● *verb* (**cues, cued, cueing** or **cuing**)

strike with cue. □ **cue ball** ball to be struck with cue.

cuff[1] *noun* **1** end part of sleeve. **2** trouser turn-up. **3** (in *plural*) *colloquial* handcuffs. □ **cuff link** either of pair of fasteners for shirt cuffs. **off the cuff** extempore, without preparation.

cuff[2] *verb* strike with open hand. ● *noun* such a blow.

cuisine /kwɪˈziːn/ *noun* style of cooking.

cul-de-sac /ˈkʌldəsæk/ *noun* (*plural* **culs-de-sac** same pronunciation, or **cul-de-sacs** /-sæks/) road etc. closed at one end.

culinary /ˈkʌlɪnərɪ/ *adjective* of or for cooking.

cull *verb* **1** select, gather. **2** pick (flowers). **3** select and kill (surplus animals). ● *noun* **1** culling. **2** animal(s) culled.

culminate /ˈkʌlmɪneɪt/ *verb* (**-ting**) (usually + *in*) reach highest or final point. □ **culmination** *noun*.
■ climax, conclude, end, finish, reach a finale, rise to a peak.

culottes /kjuːˈlɒts/ *plural noun* woman's trousers cut like skirt.

culpable /ˈkʌlpəb(ə)l/ *adjective* deserving blame. □ **culpability** *noun*.
■ blameworthy, criminal, guilty, liable, punishable, reprehensible, wrong.

culprit /ˈkʌlprɪt/ *noun* guilty person.
■ criminal, delinquent, malefactor, miscreant, offender, wrongdoer.

cult *noun* **1** religious system, sect, etc. **2** devotion or homage to person or thing. **3** popular fashion. **4** followers of fashion, religious sect, etc.
■ **1** see DENOMINATION 1. **3** craze, fashion, trend, vogue. **4** devotees, following, party, school.

cultivar /ˈkʌltɪvɑː/ *noun* plant variety produced by cultivation.

cultivate /ˈkʌltɪveɪt/ *verb* (**-ting**) **1** prepare and use (soil) for crops. **2** raise (plant etc.). **3** (often as **cultivated** *adjective*) improve (manners etc.). **4** nurture (friendship etc.). □ **cultivation** *noun*.
■ **1** farm, plough, prepare, till, work. **2** grow, plant, produce, raise, sow, tend. **3** (**cultivated**) see CULTURED. **4** court, develop, encourage, foster, further, improve, nurture, promote, pursue.
□ **cultivation** agriculture, agronomy, breeding, culture, farming, gardening, growing, horticulture, husbandry.

cultivator *noun* agricultural implement for breaking up ground etc.

culture /ˈkʌltʃə/ *noun* **1** intellectual and artistic achievement or expression. **2** refined appreciation of arts etc. **3** customs and civilization of a particular time or people. **4** improvement by mental or physical training. **5** cultivation of plants, rearing of bees etc. **6** quantity of bacteria grown for study. ● *verb* (**-ring**) grow (bacteria) for study. □ **culture shock** disorientation felt by person subjected to unfamiliar way of life. □ **cultural** *adjective*.

■ *noun* **3** art, background, civilization, customs, education, learning, mores, traditions, way of life. **5** see CULTIVATION (CULTIVATE). □ **cultural** aesthetic, artistic, civilized, civilizing, educational, elevating, enlightening, *colloquial* highbrow, improving, intellectual.

cultured *adjective* having refined tastes etc. □ **cultured pearl** one formed by oyster after insertion of foreign body into its shell.

■ artistic, civilized, cultivated, discriminating, educated, elegant, erudite, *colloquial* highbrow, knowledgeable, polished, refined, scholarly, sophisticated, well bred, well educated, well read.

culvert /'kʌlvət/ *noun* underground channel carrying water under road etc.

cumbersome /'kʌmbəsəm/ *adjective* (also **cumbrous** /'kʌmbrəs/) inconveniently bulky, unwieldy.

cumin /'kʌmɪn/ *noun* (also **cummin**) **1** plant with aromatic seeds. **2** these as flavouring.

cummerbund /'kʌməbʌnd/ *noun* waist sash.

cumulative /'kjuːmjʊlətɪv/ *adjective* increasing in force etc. by successive additions. □ **cumulatively** *adverb*.

cumulus /'kjuːmjʊləs/ *noun* (*plural* **-li** /-laɪ/) cloud formation of heaped-up rounded masses.

cuneiform /'kjuːnɪfɔːm/ *noun* writing made up of wedge shapes. ● *adjective* of or using cuneiform.

cunning /'kʌnɪŋ/ *adjective* (**-er, -est**) **1** deceitful, crafty. **2** ingenious. ● *noun* **1** ingenuity. **2** craft. □ **cunningly** *adverb*.

■ *adjective* **1** artful, crafty, devious, *colloquial* dodgy, guileful, insidious, knowing, machiavellian, sly, subtle, tricky, wily. **2** adroit, astute, clever, ingenious, skilful. ● *noun* **1** cleverness, expertise, ingenuity, skill. **2** artfulness, chicanery, craft, craftiness, deceit, deception, deviousness, duplicity, guile, slyness, trickery.

cup *noun* **1** small bowl-shaped drinking vessel. **2** cupful. **3** cup-shaped thing. **4** flavoured usually chilled wine, cider, etc. **5** cup-shaped trophy as prize. ● *verb* (**-pp-**) **1** make cup-shaped. **2** hold as in cup. □ **Cup Final** final match in (esp. football) competition. **cup-tie** match in such competition. □ **cupful** *noun*.

USAGE A *cupful* is a measure, and so *three cupfuls* is a quantity of something; *three cups full* means the actual cups and their contents, as in *He brought us three cups full of water*.

■ *noun* **1** mug, tankard, teacup. **5** award, prize, trophy.

cupboard /'kʌbəd/ *noun* recess or piece of furniture with door and usually shelves.

■ cabinet, closet, dresser, larder, locker, sideboard, wardrobe.

Cupid /'kjuːpɪd/ *noun* Roman god of love, pictured as winged boy with bow.

cupidity /kjuː'pɪdɪtɪ/ *noun* greed, avarice.

cupola /'kjuːpələ/ *noun* **1** small dome. **2** revolving gun-turret on ship or in fort.

cuppa /'kʌpə/ *noun colloquial* cup of (tea).

cur *noun* **1** mangy bad-tempered dog. **2** *colloquial* contemptible person.

curable /'kjʊərəb(ə)l/ *adjective* able to be cured.

■ operable, remediable, treatable.

curaçao /'kjʊərəsəʊ/ *noun* (*plural* **-s**) orange-flavoured liqueur.

curacy /'kjʊərəsɪ/ *noun* (*plural* **-ies**) curate's office or position.

curare /kjʊə'rɑːrɪ/ *noun* vegetable poison used on arrows by S. American Indians.

curate /'kjʊərət/ *noun* assistant to parish priest. □ **curate's egg** thing good in parts.

curative /'kjʊərətɪv/ *adjective* tending to cure. ● *noun* curative agent.

curator /kjʊə'reɪtə/ *noun* custodian of museum etc.

curb *noun* **1** check, restraint. **2** (bit with) chain etc. passing under horse's lower jaw. **3** kerb. ● *verb* **1** restrain. **2** put curb on.

■ *verb* **1** bridle, check, contain, control, deter, hamper, hinder, hold back, impede, inhibit, limit, moderate, repress, restrain, restrict, subdue, suppress.

curd *noun* (often in *plural*) coagulated acidic milk product, made into cheese or eaten as food.

curdle /'kɜːd(ə)l/ *verb* (**-ling**) **1** coagulate. **2** (of milk) go sour. □ **make (person's) blood curdle** horrify.

■ clot, coagulate, congeal, go sour, thicken.

cure /kjʊə/ *verb* **1** (often + *of*) restore to health; relieve. **2** eliminate (evil etc.). **3** preserve (meat etc.) by salting etc. ● *noun* **1** restoration to health. **2** thing that cures. **3** course of treatment.

■ *verb* **1** alleviate, correct, counteract, ease, fix, heal, help, mend, palliate, put right, rectify, relieve, remedy, repair, restore, solve, treat. ● *noun* **1** healing, recovery, recuperation, restoration, revival. **2, 3** antidote, corrective, medication, medicine, nostrum, palliative, panacea, prescription, remedy, restorative, solution, therapy, treatment.

curé /'kjʊəreɪ/ *noun* parish priest in France etc. [French]

curette /kjʊə'ret/ *noun* surgeon's scraping-instrument. ● *verb* (**-tting**) scrape with this. □ **curettage** *noun*.

curfew /'kɜːfjuː/ *noun* signal or time after which people must remain indoors.

curie /'kjʊərɪ/ *noun* unit of radioactivity.

curio /'kjʊərɪəʊ/ *noun* (*plural* **-s**) rare or unusual object.

curiosity /kjʊərɪ'ɒsɪtɪ/ *noun* (*plural* **-ies**) **1** desire to know; inquisitiveness. **2** rare or strange thing.

■ **1** inquisitiveness, interest, interference, meddling, nosiness, prying, *colloquial* snooping.

curious /ˈkjʊərɪəs/ *adjective* **1** eager to learn; inquisitive. **2** strange, surprising. □ **curiously** *adverb*.

■ **1** inquiring, inquisitive, interested, interfering, intrusive, meddlesome, *colloquial* nosy, probing, prying, puzzled, questioning, searching. **2** see STRANGE 1.

curl *verb* **1** (often + *up*) bend or coil into spiral. **2** move in curve. **3** (of upper lip) be raised in contempt. **4** play curling. ● *noun* **1** curled lock of hair. **2** anything spiral or curved inwards. □ **curly** *adjective* (**-ier**, **-iest**).

■ *verb* **1, 2** bend, coil, corkscrew, curve, loop, spiral, turn, twine, twist, wind, writhe; (*curl hair*) crimp, frizz, perm, wave. ● *noun* **1** coil, kink, ringlet, wave. **2** bend, coil, curve, kink, loop, scroll, spiral, swirl, turn, twist, wave, whorl. □ **curly** crimped, curled, curling, frizzy, permed, wavy.

curler *noun* pin, roller, etc. for curling hair.

curlew /ˈkɜːljuː/ *noun* long-billed wading bird with musical cry.

curling *noun* game like bowls played on ice with round flat stones.

curmudgeon /kəˈmʌdʒ(ə)n/ *noun* bad-tempered or miserly person. □ **curmudgeonly** *adjective*.

currant /ˈkʌrənt/ *noun* **1** small seedless dried grape. **2** (fruit of) any of various shrubs producing red, black, or white berries.

currency /ˈkʌrənsɪ/ *noun* (*plural* **-ies**) **1** money in use in a country. **2** being current. **3** prevalence (of ideas etc.).

current *adjective* **1** belonging to present time; happening now. **2** in general circulation or use; not expired. ● *noun* **1** body of moving water, air, etc., passing through still water etc. **2** movement of electrically charged particles. **3** general tendency or course. □ **current account** bank account that may be drawn on by cheque without notice. □ **currently** *adverb*.

■ *adjective* **1** alive, contemporary, continuing, existing, extant, fashionable, living, modern, ongoing, present, present-day, reigning, remaining, surviving, *colloquial often derogatory* trendy, up to date. **2** accepted, prevailing, prevalent, usable, valid. ● *noun* **1** draught, flow, stream, tide, undercurrent, undertow. **3** course, drift, stream, tendency, tide, trend.

curriculum /kəˈrɪkjʊləm/ *noun* (*plural* **-la**) course of study. □ **curriculum vitae** /ˈviːtaɪ/ brief account of one's education, career, etc.

■ course, programme of study, syllabus.

curry[1] /ˈkʌrɪ/ *noun* (*plural* **-ies**) meat, vegetables, etc. cooked in spicy sauce, usually served with rice. ● *verb* (**-ies**, **-ied**) make into or flavour like curry. □ **curry powder** mixture of spices for making curry.

curry[2] /ˈkʌrɪ/ *verb* (**-ies**, **-ied**) **1** groom (horse etc.) with curry-comb. **2** dress (leather). □ **curry-comb** metal device for grooming horses etc. **curry favour** ingratiate oneself.

curse /kɜːs/ *noun* **1** invocation of destruction or punishment. **2** violent or profane exclamation. **3** thing causing evil. ● *verb* (**-sing**) **1** utter curse against. **2** (usually in *passive*; + *with*) afflict with. **3** swear. □ **cursed** /ˈkɜːsɪd/ *adjective*.

■ *noun* **1** *formal* imprecation, malediction. **2** blasphemy, exclamation, expletive, oath, obscenity, profanity, swear-word. **3** see EVIL *noun* 1. ● *verb* **1** blaspheme at, damn, execrate, fulminate against, swear at. **3** blaspheme, execrate, swear. □ **cursed** see HATEFUL.

cursive /ˈkɜːsɪv/ *adjective* (of writing) having joined characters. ● *noun* cursive writing.

cursor /ˈkɜːsə/ *noun* indicator on VDU screen showing particular position in displayed matter.

cursory /ˈkɜːsərɪ/ *adjective* hasty, hurried. □ **cursorily** *adverb*.

■ brief, careless, casual, desultory, fleeting, hasty, hurried, perfunctory, quick, slapdash, superficial.

curt *adjective* noticeably or rudely brief. □ **curtly** *adverb*. **curtness** *noun*.

■ abrupt, blunt, brief, brusque, concise, crusty, gruff, laconic, monosyllabic, offhand, rude, sharp, short, *colloquial* snappy, succinct, tart, terse, unceremonious, uncommunicative, ungracious.

curtail /kɜːˈteɪl/ *verb* cut short, reduce. □ **curtailment** *noun*.

■ abbreviate, abridge, break off, contract, cut short, decrease, diminish, dock, guillotine, halt, lessen, lop, prune, reduce, restrict, shorten, stop, terminate, trim, truncate.

curtain /ˈkɜːt(ə)n/ *noun* **1** piece of cloth etc. hung up as screen, esp. at window. **2** rise or fall of stage curtain. **3** curtain-call. **4** (in *plural*) *slang* the end. ● *verb* provide or (+ *off*) shut off with curtains. □ **curtain-call** audience's applause summoning actors to take bow. **curtain-raiser 1** short opening play etc. **2** preliminary event.

■ *noun* **1** blind, *US* drape, drapery, hanging, screen.

curtsy /ˈkɜːtsɪ/ *noun* (also **curtsey**) *noun* (*plural* **-ies** or **-eys**) woman's or girl's acknowledgement or greeting made by bending knees. ● *verb* (**-ies**, **-ied** or **-eys**, **-eyed**) make curtsy.

■ *verb* bend the knee, genuflect.

curvaceous /kɜːˈveɪʃəs/ *adjective colloquial* (esp. of woman) shapely.

curvature /ˈkɜːvətʃə/ *noun* **1** curving. **2** curved form. **3** deviation of curve from plane.

curve *noun* **1** line or surface of which no part is straight. **2** curved line on graph. ● *verb* (**-ving**) bend or shape so as to form curve. □ **curved** *adjective*. **curvy** *adjective* (**-ier**, **-iest**).

■ *noun* arc, arch, bend, bow, bulge, camber, circle, convolution, corkscrew, crescent, curl, curvature, loop, meander, spiral, swirl, trajectory, turn, twist, undulation, whorl. ● *verb* arc, arch, bend, bow, bulge, camber, circle, coil, corkscrew, curl, loop, meander, snake, spiral, swerve, swirl, turn, twist, wind. □ **curved** concave, convex, convoluted, crescent, crooked, curvilinear, curving, curvy, rounded, serpentine, shaped, sinuous, sweeping, swelling, tortuous, turned, undulating, whorled.

curvet /kɜ:'vet/ *noun* horse's frisky leap. ● *verb* (**-tt-** or **-t-**) perform curvet.

curvilinear /kɜ:vɪ'lɪnɪə/ *adjective* contained by or consisting of curved lines.

cushion /'kʊʃ(ə)n/ *noun* **1** bag stuffed with soft material for sitting on etc. **2** protection against shock. **3** padded rim of billiard table. **4** air supporting hovercraft. ● *verb* **1** provide or protect with cushions. **2** mitigate effects of.

■ *noun* **1** bolster, hassock, pad, pillow. ● *verb* **1** bolster, protect, support. **2** absorb, deaden, lessen, mitigate, muffle, protect from, reduce the effect of, soften.

cushy /'kʊʃɪ/ *adjective* (**-ier, -iest**) *colloquial* (of job etc.) easy, pleasant.

cusp *noun* point at which two curves meet, e.g. horn of crescent moon.

cuss *colloquial noun* **1** curse. **2** awkward person. ● *verb* curse.

cussed /'kʌsɪd/ *adjective colloquial* awkward, stubborn.

custard /'kʌstəd/ *noun* pudding or sweet sauce of eggs or flavoured cornflour and milk.

custodian /kʌs'təʊdɪən/ *noun* guardian, keeper.

■ caretaker, curator, guardian, keeper, overseer, superintendent, warden, warder, watchdog, watchman.

custody /'kʌstədɪ/ *noun* **1** guardianship. **2** imprisonment. □ **custodial** /-'stəʊ-/ *adjective*.

■ **1** care, charge, guardianship, keeping, possession, protection, safe keeping. **2** captivity, confinement, detention, imprisonment, incarceration, remand.

custom /'kʌstəm/ *noun* **1** usual behaviour. **2** established usage. **3** business dealings; customers. **4** (in *plural*; also treated as *singular*) duty on imports. **5** (in *plural*; also treated as *singular*) government department or (part of) building at port etc. dealing with this. □ **custom-built, -made** made to customer's order. **custom house** customs office at frontier etc.

■ **1, 2** convention, etiquette, fashion, form, formality, habit, institution, manner, policy, practice, procedure, routine, tradition, usage, way, *formal* or *jocular* wont. **3** business, buyers, customers, patronage, support, trade.

customary /'kʌstəmərɪ/ *adjective* in accordance with custom; usual. □ **customarily** *adverb*.

■ accepted, accustomed, common, commonplace, conventional, established, everyday, expected, fashionable, general, habitual, normal, ordinary, popular, prevailing, regular, routine, traditional, typical, usual, wonted.

customer *noun* **1** person who buys goods or services. **2** *colloquial* person of specified kind.

■ **1** buyer, client, consumer, patron, purchaser, shopper.

customize *verb* (also **-ise**) (**-zing** or **-sing**) make or modify to order; personalize.

cut *verb* (**-tt-**; *past & past participle* **cut**) **1** divide, detach, wound, or penetrate with edged instrument. **2** trim, reduce size, etc. by cutting. **3** reduce length of (book, film, etc.). **4** (+ *loose, open*, etc.) loosen by cutting. **5** (esp. as **cutting** *adjective*) cause pain to. **6** reduce (prices, wages, services, etc.). **7** make by cutting or removing material. **8** cross, intersect. **9** divide (pack of cards). **10** edit (film). **11** stop cameras. **12** end acquaintance or ignore presence of. **13** *US* deliberately miss (class etc.). **14** chop (ball). **15** switch off (engine etc.). **16** (+ *across, through*, etc.) pass through as shorter route. ● *noun* **1** act of cutting. **2** division or wound made by cutting. **3** stroke with knife, sword, whip, etc. **4** reduction (in price, wages, services, etc.). **5** cessation (of power supply etc.). **6** removal of part of play, film, etc. **7** *slang* commission; share of profits, etc. **8** style in which hair, clothing, etc. is cut. **9** particular piece of meat. **10** cutting of ball. **11** deliberate ignoring of person. □ **a cut above** noticeably superior to. **cut and dried** completely decided; inflexible. **cut and run** *colloquial* run away. **cut back 1** reduce (expenditure). **2** prune. **cutback** reduction in expenditure. **cut both ways** serve both sides. **cut corners** do task perfunctorily. **cut dead** refuse to recognize; ignore. **cut down** (often + *on*) reduce one's consumption. **cut glass** glass with patterns cut on it. **cut in 1** interrupt. **2** pull in too closely in front of another vehicle. **cut no ice** *slang* have no influence. **cut off** ● *verb* **1** remove by cutting. **2** bring to abrupt end. **3** interrupt. **4** disconnect. ● *adjective* isolated. **cut-off** point at which something is cut off. **cut one's losses** abandon an unprofitable scheme. **cut out 1** shape by cutting. **2** (cause to) cease functioning. **3** stop doing or using. **cut-out** device for automatic disconnection. **cut-price** selling at reduced price. **cut short 1** bring to premature end. **2** shorten. **cut-throat** ● *noun* murderer. ● *adjective* **1** murderous. **2** (of competition) intense and merciless. **cut-throat razor** one with long unguarded blade set in handle. **cut a tooth** have it appear through gum. **cut up 1** cut in pieces. **2** (usually in *passive*) greatly distress. **cut up rough** show resentment.

■ *verb* **1** amputate, axe, carve, chip, chisel, chop, *literary* cleave, clip, detach, dice, dissect, divide, engrave, fell, gash, gouge, graze, guillotine, hack, hew, incise, knife, lacerate, lance, lop, mince, nick, notch, open, pierce, reap, saw, *historical* scalp, score, sever, shred, slash, slice, slit, snick, snip, split, stab, subdivide, wound. **2** clip, crop, dock, halve, lop, mow, pare, poll, pollard, prune, shave, shear, trim, whittle. **3** abbreviate, abridge, bowdlerize, censor, condense, curtail, edit, précis, prune, reduce, shorten, summarize, truncate. ● *noun* **2** gash, graze, groove, incision, laceration, nick, notch, opening, rent, rip, slash, slice, slit, snick, snip, split, stab, tear. **4** cutback, decrease, fall, lowering, reduction, saving. □ **cut and dried** see DEFINITE 1. **cut in 1** see INTERRUPT. **cut off 1** see REMOVE *verb* 1. **2** see STOP *verb* 1–2. **cut short** see CURTAIL.

cutaneous /kju:'teɪnɪəs/ *adjective* of the skin.

cute /kju:t/ *adjective colloquial* **1** *esp. US* attract-

ive, sweet. **2** clever, ingenious. □ **cutely** *adverb*.
cuteness *noun*.

cuticle /'kjuːtɪk(ə)l/ *noun* skin at base of fingernail or toenail.

cutlass /'kʌtləs/ *noun historical* short broad-bladed curved sword.

cutlery /'kʌtləri/ *noun* knives, forks, and spoons for use at table.

cutlet /'kʌtlɪt/ *noun* **1** neck-chop of mutton or lamb. **2** small piece of veal etc. for frying. **3** flat cake of minced meat etc.

cutter *noun* **1** person or thing that cuts. **2** (in *plural*) cutting tool. **3** small fast sailing ship. **4** small boat carried by large ship.

> ■ **2** (*cutters*) clippers, scissors, secateurs, shears.

cutting *noun* **1** piece cut from newspaper etc. **2** piece cut from plant for replanting. **3** excavated channel in hillside etc. for railway or road. ● *adjective* **1** that cuts. **2** hurtful. □ **cuttingly** *adverb*.

> ■ *adjective* **2** acute, biting, caustic, hurtful, incisive, keen, mordant, sarcastic, satirical, sharp, trenchant.

cuttlefish /'kʌt(ə)lfɪʃ/ *noun* (*plural* same or **-es**) 10-armed sea mollusc ejecting black fluid when pursued.

cutwater *noun* **1** forward edge of ship's prow. **2** wedge-shaped projection from pier of bridge.

C.V. *abbreviation* (also **CV**) curriculum vitae.

cwm /kʊm/ *noun* (in Wales) coomb.

cwt *abbreviation* hundredweight.

cyanide /'saɪənaɪd/ *noun* highly poisonous substance used in extraction of gold and silver.

cyanosis /saɪə'nəʊsɪs/ *noun* bluish skin due to oxygen-deficient blood.

cybernetics /saɪbə'netɪks/ *plural noun* (usually treated as *singular*) science of control systems and communications in animals and machines. □ **cybernetic** *adjective*.

cyclamen /'sɪkləmən/ *noun* plant with pink, red, or white flowers with backward-turned petals.

cycle /'saɪk(ə)l/ *noun* **1** recurrent round or period (of events, phenomena, etc.). **2** series of related poems etc. **3** bicycle, tricycle, etc. ● *verb* (**-ling**) **1** ride bicycle etc. **2** move in cycles. □ **cycle lane** part of road reserved for bicycles. **cycle track, cycleway** path for bicycles.

> ■ *noun* **1** circle, repetition, revolution, rotation, round, sequence, series. **3** bicycle, *colloquial* bike, moped, *colloquial* motorbike, motorcycle, penny-farthing, scooter, tandem, tricycle.

cyclic /'saɪklɪk/ *adjective* (also **cyclical** /'sɪklɪk(ə)l/) **1** recurring in cycles. **2** belonging to chronological cycle. □ **cyclically** *adverb*.

> ■ circular, recurring, repeating, repetitive, rotating.

cyclist /'saɪklɪst/ *noun* rider of bicycle.

cyclone /'saɪkləʊn/ *noun* **1** winds rotating around low-pressure region. **2** violent destructive form of this. □ **cyclonic** /-'klɒn-/ *adjective*.

cyclotron /'saɪklətrɒn/ *noun* apparatus for acceleration of charged atomic particles revolving in magnetic field.

cygnet /'sɪgnɪt/ *noun* young swan.

cylinder /'sɪlɪndə/ *noun* **1** solid or hollow roller-shaped body. **2** container for liquefied gas etc. **3** piston-chamber in engine. □ **cylindrical** /-'lɪn-/ *adjective*.

cymbal /'sɪmb(ə)l/ *noun* concave disc struck usually with another to make ringing sound.

cynic /'sɪnɪk/ *noun* person with pessimistic view of human nature. □ **cynical** *adjective*. **cynically** *adverb*. **cynicism** /-sɪz(ə)m/ *noun*.

> ■ □ **cynical** doubting, *colloquial* hardbitten, incredulous, misanthropic, mocking, negative, pessimistic, questioning, sceptical, sneering.

cynosure /'saɪnəzjʊə/ *noun* centre of attention or admiration.

cypher = CIPHER.

cypress /'saɪprəs/ *noun* conifer with dark foliage.

Cypriot /'sɪprɪət/ (also **Cypriote** /-əʊt/) *noun* native or national of Cyprus. ● *adjective* of Cyprus.

Cyrillic /sɪ'rɪlɪk/ *adjective* of alphabet used esp. for Russian and Bulgarian. ● *noun* this alphabet.

cyst /sɪst/ *noun* sac formed in body, containing liquid matter.

cystic *adjective* **1** of the bladder. **2** like a cyst. □ **cystic fibrosis** hereditary disease usually with respiratory infections.

cystitis /sɪ'staɪtɪs/ *noun* inflammation of the bladder.

czar = TSAR.

czarina = TSARINA.

Czech /tʃek/ *noun* **1** native or national of Czech Republic or *historical* Czechoslovakia. **2** language of Czech people. ● *adjective* of Czechs or their language; of Czech Republic.

Czechoslovak /tʃekə'sləʊvæk/ (also **Czechoslovakian** /-slə'vækɪən/) *historical noun* native or national of Czechoslovakia. ● *adjective* of Czechoslovaks or Czechoslovakia.

Dd

D *noun* (also **d**) (Roman numeral) 500. □ **D-Day 1** day of Allied invasion of France (6 June 1944). **2** important or decisive day.

d. *abbreviation* **1** died. **2** (pre-decimal) penny.

dab[1] *verb* (**-bb-**) **1** (often + *at*) press briefly and repeatedly with cloth etc. **2** (+ *on*) apply by dabbing. **3** (often + *at*) aim feeble blow. **4** strike lightly. ● *noun* **1** dabbing. **2** small amount (of paint etc.) dabbed on. **3** light blow.

dab[2] *noun* (*plural* same) kind of marine flatfish.

dabble /'dæb(ə)l/ *verb* (**-ling**) **1** (usually + *in*, *at*) engage (in an activity etc.) superficially. **2** move about in shallow water etc. □ **dabbler** *noun*.
■ **1** potter about, tinker, work casually. **2** paddle, splash. □ **dabbler** amateur, dilettante, potterer.

dabchick *noun* little grebe.

dab hand *noun* (usually + *at*) expert.

da capo /dɑː ˈkɑːpəʊ/ *adverb Music* repeat from beginning.

dace *noun* (*plural* same) small freshwater fish.

dacha /'dætʃə/ *noun* Russian country cottage.

dachshund /'dækshʊnd/ *noun* short-legged long-bodied dog.

dactyl /'dæktɪl/ *noun* metrical foot of one long followed by two short syllables. □ **dactylic** /-'tɪl-/ *adjective*.

dad *noun colloquial* father.

daddy /'dædɪ/ *noun* (*plural* **-ies**) *colloquial* father. □ **daddy-long-legs** crane-fly.

dado /'deɪdəʊ/ *noun* (*plural* **-s**) lower, differently decorated, part of interior wall.

daffodil /'dæfədɪl/ *noun* spring bulb with trumpet-shaped yellow flowers.

daft /dɑːft/ *adjective* (**-er**, **-est**) foolish, silly, crazy.

dagger /'dægə/ *noun* **1** short knifelike weapon. **2** obelus. □ **look daggers** (often + *at*) glare angrily.
■ **1** bayonet, dirk, knife, poniard, stiletto.

daguerreotype /də'gerəʊtaɪp/ *noun* early photograph using silvered plate.

dahlia /'deɪlɪə/ *noun* garden plant with large showy flowers.

Dáil (Éireann) /dɔɪl 'eərən/ *noun* lower house of Parliament in Republic of Ireland.

daily /'deɪlɪ/ *adjective* done, produced, or occurring every (week)day. ● *adverb* **1** every day. **2** constantly. ● *noun* (*plural* **-ies**) *colloquial* **1** daily newspaper. **2** cleaning woman.
■ *adjective* diurnal, everyday, quotidian, regular.

dainty /'deɪntɪ/ *adjective* (**-ier**, **-iest**) **1** delicately pretty or small. **2** choice. **3** fastidious. ● *noun* (*plural* **-ies**) delicacy. □ **daintily** *adverb*. **daintiness** *noun*.
■ *adjective* **1** charming, delicate, exquisite, fine, graceful, meticulous, neat, nice, pretty. **2** appealing, appetizing, choice, delectable, delicious. **3** *colloquial* choosy, discriminating, fastidious, finicky, fussy, genteel, sensitive, squeamish.

daiquiri /'dækərɪ/ *noun* (*plural* **-s**) cocktail of rum, lime juice, etc.

dairy /'deərɪ/ *noun* (*plural* **-ies**) place for processing, distributing, or selling milk and milk products. ● *adjective* of, containing, or used for milk and milk products. □ **dairymaid** woman employed in dairy. **dairyman** man looking after cows.

dais /'deɪs/ *noun* low platform, esp. at upper end of hall.

daisy /'deɪzɪ/ *noun* (*plural* **-ies**) flowering plant with white radiating petals. □ **daisy chain** string of field daisies threaded together. **daisy wheel** spoked disc bearing printing characters, used in word processors and typewriters.

dale *noun* valley.

dally /'dælɪ/ *verb* (**-ies**, **-ied**) **1** delay; waste time. **2** (often + *with*) flirt. □ **dalliance** *noun*.
■ **1** dawdle, delay, *colloquial* dilly-dally, hang about, idle, linger, loaf, loiter, procrastinate, saunter, *archaic* tarry, waste time.

Dalmatian /dæl'meɪʃ(ə)n/ *noun* large white dog with dark spots.

dam[1] *noun* barrier across river etc., usually forming reservoir or preventing flooding. ● *verb* (**-mm-**) **1** provide or confine with dam. **2** (often + *up*) block up; obstruct.
■ *noun* barrage, barrier, weir.

dam[2] *noun* mother (of animal).

damage /'dæmɪdʒ/ *noun* **1** harm; injury. **2** (in *plural*) financial compensation for loss or injury. **3** (**the damage**) *slang* cost. ● *verb* (**-ging**) inflict damage on.
■ *noun* **1** destruction, devastation, harm, havoc, hurt, injury, loss, mutilation, sabotage. **2** (*damages*) see COMPENSATION. ● *verb* blemish, break, buckle, burst, *colloquial* bust, chip, crack, cripple, deface, destroy, disable, disfigure, do mischief to, flaw, fracture, harm, hurt, immobilize, impair, incapacitate, injure, mar, mark, mutilate, *colloquial* play havoc with, ruin, rupture, sabotage, scar, scratch, spoil, strain, vandalize, warp, weaken, wound, wreck. □ **damaged** see FAULTY. **damaging** see HARMFUL.

damask /'dæməsk/ *noun* fabric with woven design made visible by reflection of light.

● *adjective* **1** made of damask. **2** velvety pink. □ **damask rose** old sweet-scented rose.

dame *noun* **1** (**Dame**) (title of) woman who has been knighted. **2** comic female pantomime character played by man. **3** *US slang* woman.

damn /dæm/ *verb* **1** (often as *interjection*) curse. **2** censure. **3** condemn to hell. **4** (often as **damning** *adjective*) show or prove to be guilty. ● *noun* uttered curse. ● *adjective* & *adverb* damned. □ **damn all** *slang* nothing.

■ *verb* **1** curse, execrate, swear at. **2** attack, berate, *colloquial* blast, *colloquial* carpet, castigate, censure, criticize, denounce. **3** condemn, doom, sentence.

damnable /'dæmnəb(ə)l/ *adjective* hateful, annoying.

damnation /dæm'neɪʃ(ə)n/ *noun* eternal punishment in hell. ● *interjection*: *expressing anger*.

■ *noun* doom, everlasting fire, hell, perdition, ruin.

damned /dæmd/ *adjective* damnable. ● *adverb* extremely.

damp *adjective* slightly wet. ● *noun* slight diffused or condensed moisture. ● *verb* **1** make damp. **2** (often + *down*) discourage. **3** (often + *down*) make burn less strongly. **4** *Music* stop vibration of (string etc.). □ **damp course** layer of damp-proof material in wall to keep damp from rising. □ **dampness** *noun*.

■ *adjective* clammy, dank, dewy, drizzly, foggy, humid, misty, moist, muggy, perspiring, rainy, steamy, sticky, sweaty, unaired, unventilated, wet, wettish. ● *verb* **1** dampen, humidify, moisten, sprinkle. **2** see DISCOURAGE 1.

dampen *verb* **1** make or become damp. **2** discourage.

damper *noun* **1** device that reduces shock, vibration, or noise. **2** discouraging person or thing. **3** metal plate in flue to control draught.

damsel /'dæmz(ə)l/ *noun archaic* young unmarried woman.

damson /'dæmz(ə)n/ *noun* small dark purple plum.

dance /dɑ:ns/ *verb* (**-cing**) **1** move rhythmically, usually to music. **2** perform (dance role etc.). **3** jump or bob about. ● *noun* **1** dancing as art. **2** style or form of this. **3** social gathering for dancing. **4** lively motion. □ **dance attendance (on)** serve obsequiously. □ **dancer** *noun*.

■ *verb* **1** *colloquial* bop, jive. **3** bob, caper, cavort, frisk, frolic, gambol, jig, jump, leap, prance, skip, whirl. ● *noun* **3** ball, barn dance, ceilidh, *colloquial* disco, discothèque, *colloquial* hop, *colloquial* knees-up, party, *colloquial* shindig, social.

dandelion /'dændɪlaɪən/ *noun* yellow-flowered wild plant.

dander *noun* □ **get one's dander up** *colloquial* become angry.

dandle /'dænd(ə)l/ *verb* (**-ling**) bounce (child) on one's knees etc.

dandruff /'dændrʌf/ *noun* flakes of dead skin in hair.

dandy /'dændɪ/ *noun* (*plural* **-ies**) man excessively devoted to style and fashion. ● *adjective* (**-ier, -iest**) *colloquial* splendid. □ **dandy-brush** stiff brush for grooming horses.

Dane *noun* **1** native or national of Denmark. **2** *historical* Viking invader of England.

danger /'deɪndʒə/ *noun* **1** liability or exposure to harm. **2** thing causing or likely to cause harm. □ **danger list** list of those dangerously ill. **danger money** extra payment for dangerous work.

■ **1** chance, hazard, insecurity, jeopardy, liability, peril, possibility, risk, threat. **2** hazard, menace, peril, pitfall, snare, threat, trouble.

dangerous *adjective* involving or causing danger. □ **dangerously** *adverb*.

■ alarming, breakneck, chancy, critical, desperate, destructive, explosive, grave, *slang* hairy, harmful, hazardous, menacing, nasty, noxious, perilous, precarious, reckless, risky, threatening, toxic, treacherous, uncertain, unmanageable, unpredictable, unsafe, violent, volatile, wild.

dangle /'dæŋg(ə)l/ *verb* (**-ling**) **1** hang loosely. **2** hold or carry swaying loosely. **3** hold out (temptation etc.).

■ **1** be suspended, droop, flap, hang, sway, swing, trail, wave about. **2** swing, trail, wave about.

Danish /'deɪnɪʃ/ *adjective* of Denmark. ● *noun* **1** Danish language. **2** (**the Danish**) (treated as *plural*) the Danish people. □ **Danish blue** white blue-veined cheese. **Danish pastry** yeast cake with icing, nuts, fruit, etc.

dank *adjective* damp and cold. □ **dankness** *noun*.

■ chilly, clammy, damp, moist, unaired.

daphne /'dæfnɪ/ *noun* a flowering shrub.

dapper *adjective* **1** neat and precise, esp. in dress. **2** sprightly.

dapple /'dæp(ə)l/ *verb* (**-ling**) (often as **dappled** *adjective*) mark with spots of colour or shade; mottle. □ **dapple grey** (of horse) grey with darker spots. **dapple grey** such a horse.

■ (**dappled**) blotchy, brindled, dotted, flecked, freckled, marbled, motley, mottled, particoloured, patchy, pied, speckled, spotted, stippled, streaked, variegated.

Darby and Joan *noun* devoted old married couple. □ **Darby and Joan club** social club for pensioners.

dare /deə/ *verb* (**-ring**; *3rd singular present* often **dare**) **1** (+ *(to) do*) have the courage or impudence (to). **2** (usually + *to do*) defy, challenge. ● *noun* challenge. □ **daredevil** reckless (person). **I dare say 1** very likely. **2** I grant that.

■ *verb* **1** risk, take a chance, venture. **2** challenge, defy, provoke, taunt.

daring *noun* adventurous courage. ● *adjective* bold; prepared to take risks. □ **daringly** *adverb*.

■ *adjective* see BOLD 1.

dariole /'dærɪəʊl/ *noun* dish cooked and served in a small mould.

dark *adjective* **1** with little or no light. **2** of deep or sombre colour. **3** (of a person) with dark colouring. **4** gloomy. **5** sinister. **6** angry. **7** secret, mysterious. ● *noun* **1** absence of light or knowledge. **2** unlit place. □ **after dark** after nightfall. **Dark Ages** 5th–10th-c., unenlightened period. **dark horse** little-known person who is unexpectedly successful. **darkroom** darkened room for photographic work. **in the dark** without information or light. □ **darken** *verb*. **darkly** *adverb*. **darkness** *noun*.

> ■ *adjective* **1** black, blackish, cheerless, clouded, cloudy, coal-black, dim, dingy, dismal, drab, dreary, dull, dusky, funereal, gloomy, glowering, inky, moonless, murky, overcast, pitch-black, pitch-dark, *esp. poetical* sable, shadowy, shady, sombre, starless, *literary* Stygian, sullen, sunless, *literary* tenebrous, unilluminated, unlighted, unlit. **2** deep, dull, sombre, strong. **3** black, brown, dark-skinned, dusky, swarthy, tanned. **7** see HIDDEN *adjective* 2, MYSTERIOUS. □ **darken** become overcast, blacken, cloud over, dim, eclipse, obscure, overshadow, shade.

darling /'dɑ:lɪŋ/ *noun* beloved or endearing person or animal. ● *adjective* **1** beloved, lovable. **2** *colloquial* charming.

> ■ *noun* apple of one's eye, beloved, *colloquial* blue-eyed boy, dear, favourite, honey, love, loved one, pet, sweetheart, true love.

darn[1] *verb* mend by interweaving wool etc. across hole. ● *noun* darned area.

darn[2] *verb, interjection, adjective, & adverb* *colloquial: mild form of* DAMN.

darnel /'dɑ:n(ə)l/ *noun* grass growing in cereal crops.

dart *noun* **1** small pointed missile. **2** (in *plural* treated as *singular*) indoor game of throwing darts at a dartboard. **3** sudden rapid movement. **4** tapering tuck in garment. ● *verb* (often + *out, in, past,* etc.) move, send, or go suddenly or rapidly. □ **dartboard** circular target in game of darts.

> ■ *noun* **1** arrow, *archaic* shaft. ● *verb* bound,

dash, fling, flit, fly, hurtle, leap, shoot, spring, whiz, zip.

Darwinian /dɑ:'wɪnɪən/ *adjective* of Darwin's theory of evolution. ● *noun* adherent of this. □ **Darwinism** /'dɑ:-/ *noun*. **Darwinist** /'dɑ:-/ *noun*.

dash *verb* **1** rush. **2** strike or fling forcefully so as to shatter. **3** frustrate, dispirit. **4** *colloquial* (as *interjection*) damn. ● *noun* **1** rush; onset. **2** punctuation mark (—) used to indicate break in sense (see panel). **3** longer signal of two in Morse code. **4** slight admixture. **5** (capacity for) impetuous vigour. □ **dashboard** instrument panel of vehicle or aircraft. **dash off** write hurriedly.

> ■ *verb* **1** bolt, chase, dart, fly, hasten, hurry, race, run, rush, speed, sprint, *colloquial* tear, zoom. **2** see HIT *verb* 1. ● *noun* **1** chase, race, run, rush, sprint, spurt.

dashing *adjective* spirited; showy.

> ■ animated, dapper, dynamic, elegant, lively, smart, spirited, stylish, vigorous.

dastardly /'dæstədlɪ/ *adjective* cowardly, despicable.

data /'deɪtə/ *plural noun* (also treated as *singular*) **1** known facts used for inference or reckoning. **2** quantities or characters operated on by computer. □ **data bank** store or source of data. **database** structured set of data held in computer. **data processing** series of operations on data by computer.

USAGE In scientific, philosophical, and general use, *data* is usually considered to mean a number of items and is treated as plural, with *datum* as its singular. In computing and allied subjects (and sometimes in general use), it is treated as singular, as in *Much useful data has been collected*. However, *data* is not singular, and it is wrong to say *a data* or *every data* or to make the plural form *datas*.

> ■ details, evidence, facts, figures, information, statistics.

date[1] *noun* **1** day of month. **2** historical day or year. **3** day, month, and year of writing etc. at head of document etc. **4** period to which work of art etc. belongs. **5** time when an event takes

. . . .

Dash —

This is used:

1 to mark the beginning and end of an interruption in the structure of a sentence:

> *My son—where has he gone?—would like to meet you.*

2 to show faltering speech in conversation:

> *Yes—well—I would—only you see—it's not easy.*

3 to show other kinds of break in a sentence, often where a comma, semicolon, or colon would traditionally be used, e.g.

> *Come tomorrow—if you can.*
> *The most important thing is this—don't rush the work.*

A dash is not used in this way in formal writing.

. . . .

place. **6** *colloquial* social appointment, esp. with person of opposite sex. **7** *esp. US colloquial* person to be met at this. ● *verb* (**-ting**) **1** mark with date. **2** assign date to. **3** (+ *to*) assign to a particular time, period, etc. **4** (often + *from, back to*, etc.) have origin at a particular time. **5** expose as or appear old-fashioned. **6** *colloquial* make date with. **7** *colloquial* go out together as sexual partners. □ **date line 1** line partly along meridian 180° from Greenwich, to the east of which date is a day earlier than to the west. **2** date and place of writing at head of newspaper article etc. **out of date** (**out-of-date** before noun) old-fashioned; obsolete. **to date** until now. **up to date** (**up-to-date** before noun) fashionable; current.

■ *noun* **6** appointment, assignation, engagement, fixture, meeting, rendezvous. □ **out of date** see OBSOLETE. **up to date** see MODERN *adjective*.

date² *noun* **1** oval stone fruit. **2** (in full **date-palm**) tree bearing this.

dative /'deɪtɪv/ *Grammar noun* case expressing indirect object or recipient. ● *adjective* of or in the dative.

datum /'deɪtəm/ *singular* of DATA.

daub /dɔːb/ *verb* **1** paint or spread (paint etc.) crudely or unskilfully. **2** smear (surface) with paint etc. ● *noun* **1** paint etc. daubed on a surface. **2** crude painting. **3** clay etc. coating wattles to form wall.

daughter /'dɔːtə/ *noun* **1** female child in relation to her parents. **2** female descendant or member of family etc. □ **daughter-in-law** (*plural* **daughters-in-law**) son's wife.

daunt /dɔːnt/ *verb* discourage, intimidate. □ **daunting** *adjective*.

■ alarm, depress, deter, discourage, dishearten, dismay, frighten, intimidate, overawe, put off, unnerve.

dauntless *adjective* intrepid, persevering. □ **dauntlessness** *noun*.

dauphin /'dɔːfɪn/ *noun historical* eldest son of King of France.

Davenport /'dævənpɔːt/ *noun* **1** kind of writing desk. **2** *US* large sofa.

davit /'dævɪt/ *noun* small crane on ship for holding lifeboat.

daw *noun* jackdaw.

dawdle /'dɔːd(ə)l/ *verb* (**-ling**) **1** walk slowly and idly. **2** waste time; procrastinate.

■ be slow, dally, delay, *colloquial* dilly-dally, hang about, idle, lag, linger, loaf about, loiter, procrastinate, straggle, take it easy, take one's time, trail behind.

dawn *noun* **1** daybreak. **2** beginning. ● *verb* **1** (of day) begin; grow light. **2** (often + *on, upon*) become evident (to). □ **dawn chorus** birdsong at daybreak.

■ *noun* **1** daybreak, first light, peep of day, sunrise. **2** see BEGINNING 1,2.

day *noun* **1** time between sunrise and sunset. **2**

24 hours as a unit of time. **3** daylight. **4** time during which work is normally done. **5** (also *plural*) historical period. **6** (**the day**) present time. **7** period of prosperity. □ **daybreak** first light in morning. **day centre** place for care of elderly or handicapped during day. **daydream** (indulge in) fantasy etc. while awake. **day off** day's holiday. **day release** part-time education for employees. **day return** reduced fare or ticket for a return journey in one day. **day school** school for pupils living at home. **daytime** part of day when there is natural light. **day-to-day** mundane, routine. **day trip** trip completed in one day. **day tripper** *noun*.

■ **1** daytime. **3** daylight, daytime, light. **5** age, epoch, era, period, time. □ **daydream** *noun* dream, fantasy, hope, illusion, pipe dream, reverie, vision. ● *verb* dream, fantasize, imagine, meditate.

daylight *noun* **1** light of day. **2** dawn. **3** visible gap between things. **4** (usually in *plural*) *slang* life. □ **daylight robbery** blatantly excessive charge. **daylight saving** longer summer evening daylight, achieved by putting clocks forward.

daze *verb* (**-zing**) stupefy, bewilder. ● *noun* dazed state.

■ *verb* amaze, benumb, bewilder, *colloquial* flabbergast, paralyse, shock, stun, stupefy.

dazzle /'dæz(ə)l/ *verb* (**-ling**) **1** blind or confuse temporarily with sudden bright light. **2** impress or overpower with knowledge, ability, etc. ● *noun* bright confusing light. □ **dazzling** *adjective*.

■ *verb* **1** blind, confuse, disorientate. □ **dazzling** see BRILLIANT *adjective* 1;3.

dB *abbreviation* decibel(s).

DC *abbreviation* **1** direct current. **2** District of Columbia. **3** da capo.

DDT *abbreviation* colourless chlorinated hydrocarbon used as insecticide.

deacon /'diːkən/ *noun* **1** (in episcopal churches) minister below priest. **2** (*feminine* **deaconess** /-'nes/) (in Nonconformist churches) lay officer.

deactivate /diˈæktɪveɪt/ *verb* (**-ting**) make inactive or less reactive.

dead /ded/ *adjective* **1** no longer alive. **2** numb. **3** *colloquial* extremely tired or unwell. **4** (+ *to*) insensitive to. **5** not effective; extinct. **6** extinguished. **7** inanimate. **8** lacking vigour. **9** not resonant. **10** quiet; not transmitting sounds. **11** out of play. **12** abrupt, complete, exact. ● *adverb* **1** absolutely, completely. **2** *colloquial* very. ● *noun* time of silence or inactivity. □ **dead beat** *colloquial* utterly exhausted. **dead-beat** *colloquial* tramp. **dead duck** useless person or thing. **dead end** closed end of road etc. **dead-end** *adjective* having no prospects. **dead heat** race in which competitors tie. **dead letter** law etc. no longer observed. **deadline** time limit. **deadlock** ● *noun* state of unresolved conflict. ● *verb* bring or come to a standstill. **dead loss** useless person or thing. **dead man's handle** handle on electric train etc. disconnecting power supply if released. **dead**

march funeral march. **dead on** exactly right.
deadpan lacking expression or emotion. **dead reckoning** estimation of ship's position from log, compass, etc., when visibility is bad. **dead shot** unerring marksman. **dead to the world** *colloquial* fast asleep. **dead weight 1** inert mass. **2** heavy burden. **dead wood** *colloquial* useless person(s) or thing(s). □ **deadness** *noun*.

■ *adjective* **1** dead and buried, *formal* deceased, departed, *colloquial* done for, killed, late, lifeless, perished. **2** deadened, insensate, insensitive, numb, paralysed, without feeling. **5** defunct, died out, extinct, flat (*battery*), inoperative, not going, not working, obsolete, out of order, unresponsive, used up, useless, worn out. **6** died out, extinguished, out. **7** inanimate, inert, lifeless. **8** boring, dull, moribund, slow, stagnant, uninteresting. **12** see EXACT *adjective*.
□ **deadlock** *noun* halt, impasse, stalemate, standstill, stop, stoppage, tie. **dead to the world** see ASLEEP *adjective* 1.

deaden *verb* **1** deprive of or lose vitality, force, etc. **2** (+ *to*) make insensitive to.
■ **1** blunt, check, cushion, damp, diminish, hush, lessen, mitigate, muffle, mute, quieten, reduce, smother, soften, stifle, suppress, weaken. **2** anaesthetize, desensitize, dull, numb, paralyse.

deadly *adjective* (**-ier**, **-iest**) **1** causing fatal injury or serious damage. **2** intense. **3** accurate. **4** deathlike. **5** dreary. ● *adverb* **1** as if dead. **2** extremely. □ **deadly nightshade** plant with poisonous black berries.
■ *adjective* **1** dangerous, destructive, fatal, harmful, lethal, mortal, noxious, terminal.

deaf /def/ *adjective* **1** wholly or partly unable to hear. **2** (+ *to*) refusing to listen ro or comply with. □ **deaf-aid** hearing aid. **deaf-and-dumb alphabet, language** sign language. **deaf mute** deaf and dumb person. □ **deafness** *noun*.

deafen *verb* (often as **deafening** *adjective*) overpower or make deaf with noise, esp. temporarily. □ **deafeningly** *adverb*.
■ (*deafening*) see LOUD *adjective* 1.

deal[1] *verb* (*past & past participle* **dealt** /delt/) **1** (+ *with*) take measures to resolve, placate, etc. **2** (+ *with*) treat (subject). **3** (+ *with*) do business or associate with. **4** (often + *by*, *with*) behave in specified way. **5** (+ *in*) sell. **6** (often + *out*, *round*) distribute. **7** administer. ● *noun* **1** (usually **a good or great deal**) large amount. **2** (usually **a good or great deal**) considerably. **3** business arrangement etc. **4** specified treatment. **5** dealing of cards. **6** player's turn to deal.
■ *verb* **1** (*deal with*) see MANAGE 5. **2** (*deal with*) see TREAT *verb* 1. **5** (*deal in*) buy and sell, do business in, trade in, traffic in. **6** allot, apportion, assign, dispense, distribute, divide, dole out, give out, share out. **7** administer, deliver, give, inflict, *literary* mete out. ● *noun* **1** amount, quantity, volume. **3** agreement, arrangement, bargain, contract, pact, settlement, transaction, understanding.

deal[2] *noun* fir or pine timber, esp. as boards.

dealer *noun* **1** trader. **2** player dealing at cards.
■ **1** agent, broker, distributor, *esp. US & Scottish* merchant, retailer, shopkeeper, stockist, supplier, trader, tradesman, vendor, wholesaler.

dealings *plural noun* conduct or transactions.

dean *noun* **1** head of ecclesiastical chapter. **2** (usually **rural dean**) clergyman supervising parochial clergy. **3** college or university official with disciplinary functions. **4** head of university faculty.

deanery *noun* (*plural* **-ies**) **1** dean's house or position. **2** parishes presided over by rural dean.

dear *adjective* **1** beloved. **2** *used before person's name, esp. at beginning of letter.* **3** (often + *to*) precious. **4** expensive. ● *noun* dear person. ● *adverb* at great cost. ● *interjection* (usually **oh dear! or dear me!**) *expressing surprise, dismay, etc.* □ **dearly** *adverb*.
■ *adjective* **1** adored, beloved, close, darling, intimate, lovable, loved, venerated. **3** cherished, esteemed, precious, prized, treasured, valued. **4** costly, exorbitant, expensive, highly priced, high-priced, overpriced, *colloquial* pricey. ● *noun* see DARLING *noun*.

dearth /dɜːθ/ *noun* scarcity, lack.

death /deθ/ *noun* **1** dying; end of life. **2** being dead. **3** person killed. **4** cause of death. **5** destruction. □ **death blow 1** blow etc. causing death. **2** action, event etc. ending something. **death mask** cast of dead person's face. **death penalty** capital punishment. **death rate** yearly deaths per 1000 of population. **death rattle** gurgling in throat at death. **death row** part of prison for those sentenced to death. **death squad** paramilitary group. **death trap** unsafe place, vehicle, etc. **death warrant** order of execution. **death-watch beetle** beetle that bores into wood and makes ticking sound. **put to death** kill; cause to be killed. □ **deathless** *adjective*. **deathlike** *adjective*.
■ **1** *esp. Law formal* decease, demise, dying, end. **3** casualty, fatality, victim. □ **put to death** see KILL *verb* 1.

deathly *adjective* (**-ier**, **-iest**) like death. ● *adverb* in deathly manner.

deb *noun colloquial* débutante.

débâcle /deɪˈbɑːk(ə)l/ *noun* **1** utter collapse. **2** confused rush.

debar /dɪˈbɑː/ *verb* (**-rr-**) (+ *from*) exclude from. □ **debarment** *noun*.

debark /diːˈbɑːk/ *verb* land from ship; go ashore. □ **debarkation** /-ˈkeɪʃ(ə)n/ *noun*.

debase /dɪˈbeɪs/ *verb* (**-sing**) **1** lower in character, quality, or value. **2** depreciate (coin) by alloying etc. □ **debasement** *noun*.
■ **1** belittle, degrade, demean, depreciate, devalue, diminish, lower the tone of, pollute, ruin, soil, spoil, sully, vulgarize.

debatable /dɪˈbeɪtəb(ə)l/ *adjective* questionable.

■ arguable, contentious, controversial, controvertible, disputable, doubtful, dubious, moot (*point*), open to doubt, open to question, problematical, questionable, uncertain, unsettled, unsure.

debate /dɪ'beɪt/ *verb* (**-ting**) **1** discuss or dispute, esp. formally. **2** consider, ponder. ● *noun* discussion, esp. formal.

■ *verb* **1** argue, deliberate, discuss, dispute, question, wrangle. **2** chew over, consider, deliberate, mull over, ponder, reflect on, think over, *colloquial* weigh up. ● *noun* argument, conference, controversy, deliberation, discussion, disputation, dispute, polemic.

debauch /dɪ'bɔːtʃ/ *verb* **1** corrupt, deprave, debase. **2** (as **debauched** *adjective*) dissolute. ● *noun* bout of debauchery.

debauchee /dɪbə'tʃiː/ *noun* debauched person.

debauchery *noun* excessive sensual indulgence.

debenture /dɪ'bentʃə/ *noun* company bond providing for payment of interest.

debilitate /dɪ'bɪlɪteɪt/ *verb* (**-ting**) enfeeble. □ **debilitation** *noun*.

debility *noun* feebleness, esp. of health.

debit /'debɪt/ *noun* entry in account recording sum owed. ● *verb* (**-t-**) (+ *against*, *to*) enter on debit side of account.

■ *verb* bill, charge, invoice.

debonair /debə'neə/ *adjective* **1** self-assured. **2** pleasant.

debouch /dɪ'baʊtʃ/ *verb* **1** come out into open ground. **2** (often + *into*) (of river etc.) merge. □ **debouchment** *noun*.

debrief /diː'briːf/ *verb* question (diplomat etc.) about completed mission. □ **debriefing** *noun*.

debris /'debriː/ *noun* scattered fragments; wreckage.

■ bits, detritus, flotsam, fragments, litter, pieces, remains, rubbish, rubble, ruins, waste, wreckage.

debt /det/ *noun* **1** money etc. owing. **2** obligation; state of owing.

■ **1** arrears. **2** indebtedness, liability, obligation; (*in debt*) beholden, defaulting, indebted, insolvent.

debtor *noun* person owing money etc.

debug /diː'bʌg/ *verb* (**-gg-**) **1** remove hidden microphones from. **2** remove defects from.

debunk /diː'bʌŋk/ *verb colloquial* expose as spurious or false.

début /'deɪbjuː/ *noun* first public appearance.

débutante /'debjuːtɑːnt/ *noun* young woman making her social début.

Dec. *abbreviation* December.

deca- *combining form* ten.

decade /'dekeɪd/ *noun* **1** 10 years. **2** set or series of 10.

decadence /'dekəd(ə)ns/ *noun* **1** moral or cul-

tural decline. **2** immoral behaviour. □ **decadent** *adjective*.

■ □ **decadent** corrupt, debased, debauched, declining, degenerate, dissolute, immoral, self-indulgent.

decaffeinated /diː'kæfɪneɪtɪd/ *adjective* with caffeine removed.

decagon /'dekəgən/ *noun* plane figure with 10 sides and angles. □ **decagonal** /-'kæg-/ *adjective*.

decahedron /dekə'hiːdrən/ *noun* solid figure with 10 faces. □ **decahedral** *adjective*.

decamp /dɪ'kæmp/ *verb* **1** depart suddenly. **2** break up or leave camp.

decant /dɪ'kænt/ *verb* pour off (wine etc.) leaving sediment behind.

decanter *noun* stoppered glass container for decanted wine or spirit.

decapitate /dɪ'kæpɪteɪt/ *verb* (**-ting**) behead. □ **decapitation** *noun*.

decarbonize /diː'kɑːbənaɪz/ *verb* (also **-ise**) (**-zing** or **-sing**) remove carbon etc. from (engine of car etc.). □ **decarbonization** *noun*.

decathlon /dɪ'kæθlən/ *noun* athletic contest of 10 events. □ **decathlete** *noun*.

decay /dɪ'keɪ/ *verb* **1** (cause to) rot or decompose. **2** decline in quality, power, etc. ● *noun* **1** rotten state. **2** decline.

■ *verb* **1** break down, corrode, decompose, disintegrate, fall apart, fester, go bad, go off, mortify, moulder, perish, putrefy, rot, spoil. **2** atrophy, crumble, degenerate, deteriorate, disintegrate, dissolve, fall apart, shrivel, waste away, weaken, wither.

decease /dɪ'siːs/ *noun esp. Law formal* death.

deceased *formal adjective* dead. ● *noun* (**the deceased**) person who has died.

deceit /dɪ'siːt/ *noun* **1** deception. **2** trick. □ **deceitful** *adjective*. **deceitfulness** *noun*.

■ **1** artifice, cheating, chicanery, craftiness, cunning, deceitfulness, deception, dishonesty, dissimulation, double-dealing, duplicity, guile, hypocrisy, insincerity, lying, misrepresentation, pretence, sham, slyness, treachery, trickery, underhandedness, untruthfulness. **2** see DECEPTION 2. □ **deceitful** cheating, crafty, cunning, deceiving, deceptive, designing, dishonest, double-dealing, duplicitous, false, fraudulent, furtive, hypocritical, insincere, lying, secretive, *colloquial* shifty, sneaky, treacherous, tricky, two-faced, underhand, unfaithful, untrustworthy, wily.

deceive /dɪ'siːv/ *verb* (**-ving**) **1** make (person) believe what is false; mislead. **2** (**deceive oneself**) persist in mistaken belief. **3** be unfaithful to. □ **deceiver** *noun*.

■ **1** *colloquial* bamboozle, be an impostor, beguile, betray, blind, bluff, cheat, *slang* con, defraud, delude, *colloquial* diddle, double-cross, dupe, fool, fox, *colloquial* have on, hoax, hoodwink, *colloquial* kid, lead on, lie to, mislead, mystify, outsmart, outwit, swindle, *colloquial* take for a ride, take in, trick.

decelerate /diːˈseləreɪt/ *verb* (**-ting**) (cause to) reduce speed. □ **deceleration** *noun*.
■ brake, decrease speed, go slower, lose speed, slow down.

December /dɪˈsembə/ *noun* twelfth month of year.

decency /ˈdiːsənsɪ/ *noun* (*plural* **-ies**) **1** correct, honourable, or modest behaviour. **2** (in *plural*) proprieties, manners.

decennial /dɪˈsenɪəl/ *adjective* **1** lasting 10 years. **2** recurring every 10 years.

decent /ˈdiːs(ə)nt/ *adjective* **1** conforming with standards of decency; not obscene. **2** respectable. **3** acceptable; adequate. **4** kind. □ **decently** *adverb*.
■ **1, 2** acceptable, appropriate, becoming, befitting, chaste, courteous, decorous, delicate, fitting, honourable, modest, polite, presentable, proper, pure, respectable, seemly, sensitive, suitable, tasteful. **3** acceptable, adequate, fair, good, passable, reasonable, satisfactory. **4** see KIND *adjective*.

decentralize /diːˈsentrəlaɪz/ *verb* (also **-ise**) (**-zing** or **-sing**) transfer (power etc.) from central to local authority. □ **decentralization** *noun*.

deception /dɪˈsepʃ(ə)n/ *noun* **1** deceiving, being deceived. **2** thing that deceives.
■ **1** see DECEIT 1. **2** bluff, cheat, *slang* con, confidence trick, cover-up, deceit, fake, feint, *colloquial* fiddle, fraud, hoax, imposture, lie, pretence, ruse, sham, stratagem, subterfuge, swindle, trick, wile.

deceptive /dɪˈseptɪv/ *adjective* likely to mislead.
■ ambiguous, deceiving, delusive, dishonest, distorted, equivocal, evasive, fallacious, false, fraudulent, illusory, insincere, misleading, specious, spurious, treacherous, unreliable, wrong.

deci- *combining form* one-tenth.

decibel /ˈdesɪbel/ *noun* unit used in comparison of sound etc. levels.

decide /dɪˈsaɪd/ *verb* (**-ding**) **1** (usually + *to do, that, on, about*) resolve after consideration. **2** settle (issue etc.). **3** (usually + *between, for, against, in favour of, that*) give judgement.
■ **1** choose, conclude, determine, elect, make up one's mind, opt, resolve; (*decide on*) choose, opt for, pick, select, settle on. **2** determine, resolve, settle. **3** adjudicate, arbitrate, judge, reach a decision.

decided *adjective* **1** definite, unquestionable. **2** positive, resolute. □ **decidedly** *adverb*.
■ see DEFINITE 1–2.

deciduous /dɪˈsɪdjʊəs/ *adjective* **1** (of tree) shedding leaves annually. **2** (of leaves etc.) shed periodically.

decimal /ˈdesɪm(ə)l/ *adjective* **1** (of system of numbers, weights, measures, etc.) based on 10. **2** of tenths or 10. **3** proceeding by tens. ● *noun*

decimal fraction. □ **decimal fraction** fraction expressed in tenths, hundredths, etc., esp. by units to right of decimal point. **decimal point** dot placed before fraction in decimal fraction.

decimalize *verb* (also **-ise**) (**-zing** or **-sing**) **1** express as decimal. **2** convert to decimal system. □ **decimalization** *noun*.

decimate /ˈdesɪmeɪt/ *verb* (**-ting**) destroy large proportion of. □ **decimation** *noun*.
USAGE *Decimate* should not be used to mean 'defeat utterly'.

decipher /dɪˈsaɪfə/ *verb* **1** convert (coded information) into intelligible language. **2** determine the meaning of. □ **decipherable** *adjective*.
■ decode, figure out, read, translate, unravel, unscramble, work out.

decision /dɪˈsɪʒ(ə)n/ *noun* **1** deciding. **2** resolution after consideration. **3** settlement. **4** resoluteness.
■ **2, 3** conclusion, decree, finding, judgement, outcome, result, ruling, verdict.

decisive /dɪˈsaɪsɪv/ *adjective* **1** conclusive; settling an issue. **2** unhesitating. □ **decisively** *adverb*. **decisiveness** *noun*.
■ **1** conclusive, convincing, crucial, final, influential, positive, significant. **2** certain, confident, decided, definite, determined, firm, forceful, forthright, resolute, strong-minded, sure, unhesitating.

deck *noun* **1** platform in a ship serving as a floor. **2** floor of bus etc. **3** section for playing discs or tapes etc. in sound system. **4** *US* pack of cards. ● *verb* (often + *out*) decorate. □ **deck-chair** outdoor folding chair.

declaim /dɪˈkleɪm/ *verb* speak, recite, etc. as if addressing audience. □ **declamation** *noun*. **declamatory** /-ˈklæm-/ *adjective*.

declaration /dekləˈreɪʃ(ə)n/ *noun* **1** declaring. **2** emphatic, deliberate, or formal statement.
■ **1, 2** affirmation, announcement, assertion, *formal* avowal, confirmation, deposition, disclosure, proclamation, profession, promulgation, pronouncement, protestation, revelation, statement. **2** edict, manifesto, notice, testimony.

declare /dɪˈkleə/ *verb* (**-ring**) **1** announce openly or formally. **2** pronounce. **3** (usually + *that*) assert emphatically. **4** acknowledge possession of (dutiable goods, income, etc.). **5** *Cricket* close (innings) voluntarily before team is out. **6** *Cards* name trump suit. □ **declaratory** /-ˈklær-/ *adjective*.
■ **1, 2** announce, broadcast, decree, disclose, make known, proclaim, pronounce, report, reveal, show, trumpet forth. **3** affirm, assert, attest, *formal* avow, certify, claim, confirm, contend, emphasize, insist, maintain, profess, protest, say, state, swear, testify, witness.

declassify /diːˈklæsɪfaɪ/ *verb* (**-ies, -ied**) declare (information etc.) to be no longer secret. □ **declassification** *noun*.

declension /dɪˈklenʃ(ə)n/ *noun* **1** *Grammar* variation of form of noun etc., to show grammatical case. **2** *Grammar* class of nouns with same inflections. **3** deterioration.

declination /deklɪˈneɪʃ(ə)n/ *noun* **1** downward bend. **2** angular distance north or south of celestial equator. **3** deviation of compass needle from true north.

decline /dɪˈklaɪn/ *verb* (**-ning**) **1** deteriorate; lose strength or vigour; decrease. **2** refuse. **3** slope or bend downwards. **4** *Grammar* state case forms of (noun etc.). ● *noun* deterioration. □ **declining years** old age.

■ *verb* **1** decrease, degenerate, deteriorate, die away, diminish, drop away, dwindle, ebb, fail, fall off, flag, lessen, peter out, reduce, shrink, sink, slacken, subside, tail off, taper off, wane, weaken, wilt, worsen. **2** refuse, reject, turn down. ● *noun* decrease, degeneration, deterioration, *Music* diminuendo, diminution, downturn, drop, fall, falling off, loss, recession, reduction, slump, worsening.

declivity /dɪˈklɪvɪtɪ/ *noun* (*plural* **-ies**) downward slope.

declutch /diːˈklʌtʃ/ *verb* disengage clutch of motor vehicle.

decoction /dɪˈkɒkʃ(ə)n/ *noun* **1** concentration or extraction of essence by boiling. **2** extracted essence.

decode /diːˈkəʊd/ *verb* (**-ding**) decipher. □ **decoder** *noun*.

■ crack, decipher, explain, figure out, interpret, make out, read, solve, understand, unravel, unscramble.

decoke /diːˈkəʊk/ *verb* (**-king**) *colloquial* decarbonize.

décolletage /deɪkɒlˈtɑːʒ/ *noun* low neckline of woman's dress. [French]

décolleté /deɪˈkɒlteɪ/ *adjective* (also **décolletée**) having low neckline. [French]

decompose /diːkəmˈpəʊz/ *verb* (**-sing**) **1** rot. **2** separate into elements. □ **decomposition** /diːkɒmpəˈzɪʃ(ə)n/ *noun*.

■ **1** break down, decay, disintegrate, go off, moulder, putrefy, rot.

decompress /diːkəmˈpres/ *verb* subject to decompression.

decompression /diːkəmˈpreʃ(ə)n/ *noun* **1** release from compression. **2** reduction of pressure on deep-sea diver etc. □ **decompression chamber** enclosed space for decompression.

decongestant /diːkənˈdʒest(ə)nt/ *noun* medicine etc. that relieves nasal congestion.

decontaminate /diːkənˈtæmɪneɪt/ *verb* (**-ting**) remove contamination from. □ **decontamination** *noun*.

décor /ˈdeɪkɔː/ *noun* furnishings and decoration of room, stage, etc.

decorate /ˈdekəreɪt/ *verb* (**-ting**) **1** adorn. **2** paint, wallpaper, etc. (room etc.). **3** give medal or award to.

■ **1** adorn, array, beautify, bedeck, colour, deck, embellish, embroider, festoon, garnish, ornament, prettify, smarten up, spruce up, *colloquial* tart up, trim. **2** *colloquial* do up, paint, paper, redecorate, refurbish, renovate, wallpaper. **3** give a medal to, honour, reward.

decoration *noun* **1** decorating. **2** thing that decorates. **3** medal etc. **4** (in *plural*) flags etc. put up on festive occasion.

■ **2** accessory, adornment, arabesque, elaboration, embellishment, flourish, ornament, ornamentation, trimming; (*decorations*) finery, trappings. **3** award, badge, colours, medal, order, ribbon, star.

decorative /ˈdekərətɪv/ *adjective* pleasing in appearance. □ **decoratively** *adverb*.

■ elaborate, fancy, non-functional, ornamental, ornate.

decorator *noun* person who decorates for a living.

decorous /ˈdekərəs/ *adjective* having or showing decorum. □ **decorously** *adverb*.

■ appropriate, becoming, befitting, correct, decent, dignified, fitting, genteel, polite, presentable, proper, refined, respectable, sedate, seemly, staid, suitable, well behaved.

decorum /dɪˈkɔːrəm/ *noun* polite dignified behaviour.

■ correctness, decency, dignity, etiquette, good form, good manners, gravity, modesty, politeness, propriety, protocol, respectability, seemliness.

decoy *noun* /ˈdiːkɔɪ/ thing or person used as lure; bait, enticement. ● *verb* /dɪˈkɔɪ/ lure by decoy.

■ *noun* bait, distraction, diversion, enticement, inducement, lure, red herring, stool-pigeon, trap. ● *verb* allure, attract, bait, draw, entice, inveigle, lead, lure, seduce, tempt, trick.

decrease *verb* /dɪˈkriːs/ (**-sing**) make or become smaller or fewer. ● *noun* /ˈdiːkriːs/ **1** decreasing. **2** amount of this.

■ *verb* abate, condense, contract, curtail, cut, decline, die away, diminish, dwindle, ease off, fall off, lessen, lower, peter out, reduce, shrink, slacken, slim down, subside, tail off, taper off, turn down, wane. ● *noun* abatement, contraction, curtailment, cut, cutback, decline, *Music* diminuendo, diminution, downturn, drop, dwindling, easing off, ebb, fall, falling off, lessening, lowering, reduction, shrinkage, wane.

decree /dɪˈkriː/ *noun* **1** official legal order. **2** legal decision. ● *verb* (**-ees**, **-eed**) ordain by decree. □ **decree absolute** final order for completion of divorce. **decree nisi** /ˈnaɪsaɪ/ provisional order for divorce.

■ *noun* **1** act, command, declaration, dictate, dictum, directive, edict, enactment, fiat, injunction, law, mandate, order, ordinance, proclamation, promulgation, regulation, ruling, statute. **2** see JUDGEMENT 4. ● *verb* command, decide, declare, determine, dictate, direct, ordain, order, prescribe, proclaim, promulgate, pronounce, rule.

decrepit /dɪ'krepɪt/ *adjective* **1** weakened by age or infirmity. **2** dilapidated. ☐ **decrepitude** *noun*.
■ **1** feeble, frail, infirm, old, weak. **2** battered, broken-down, derelict, dilapidated, ramshackle, tumbledown, worn out.

decry /dɪ'kraɪ/ *verb* (**-ies, -ied**) disparage.

dedicate /'dedɪkeɪt/ *verb* (**-ting**) **1** (often + *to*) devote (oneself) to a purpose etc. **2** (often + *to*) address (book etc.) to friend or patron etc. **3** (often + *to*) devote (building etc.) to saint etc. **4** (as **dedicated** *adjective*) having single-minded loyalty or purpose. ☐ **dedicatory** *adjective*.
■ **1** commit, consecrate, devote, give, pledge, set apart. **2** address, inscribe. **3** consecrate, hallow, sanctify. **4** (**dedicated**) see KEEN[1] 1, LOYAL.

dedication *noun* **1** dedicating. **2** words with which book is dedicated.
■ **1** adherence, allegiance, commitment, devotion, enthusiasm, faithfulness, fidelity, loyalty, single-mindedness, zeal. **2** inscription.

deduce /dɪ'djuːs/ *verb* (**-cing**) (often + *from*) infer logically. ☐ **deducible** *adjective*.
■ conclude, divine, draw the conclusion, extrapolate, gather, glean, infer, reason, surmise, *slang* suss out, understand, work out.

deduct /dɪ'dʌkt/ *verb* (often + *from*) subtract, take away, withhold.
■ knock off, subtract, take away, withhold.

deductible *adjective* that may be deducted esp. from tax or taxable income.

deduction /dɪ'dʌkʃ(ə)n/ *noun* **1** deducting. **2** amount deducted. **3** inference from general to particular.
■ **1** removal, subtraction, withdrawal. **2** allowance, discount, reduction. **3** conclusion, finding, inference, reasoning, result.

deductive *adjective* of or reasoning by deduction.

deed *noun* **1** thing done; action. **2** legal document. ☐ **deed of covenant** agreement to pay regular sum, esp. to charity. **deed poll** deed made by one party only, esp. to change one's name.
■ **1** accomplishment, achievement, act, action, adventure, *colloquial* effort, endeavour, enterprise, exploit, feat, performance, stunt, undertaking.

deem *verb formal* consider, judge.

deep *adjective* **1** extending far down or in. **2** to or at specified depth. **3** low-pitched. **4** intense. **5** profound. **6** (+ *in*) fully absorbed in, overwhelmed by. ● *adverb* **1** deeply. **2** far down or in. ● *noun* **1** deep state. **2** (**the deep**) *poetical* the sea. ☐ **deep-freeze** ● *noun* freezer. ● *verb* freeze or store in freezer. **deep-fry** fry with fat covering food. ☐ **deepen** *verb*. **deeply** *adverb*.

■ *adjective* **1** bottomless, fathomless, profound, unfathomable, unplumbed, yawning. **3** bass, booming, growling, low, low-pitched, resonant, reverberating, sonorous. **4** (*deep feelings*) earnest, extreme, genuine, heartfelt, intense, serious, sincere; (*deep colour*) dark, rich, strong, vivid; (*deep sleep*) heavy, sound. **5** abstruse, arcane, difficult, esoteric, intellectual, learned, obscure, profound, recondite. **6** (*deep in*) absorbed in, engrossed in, immersed in, lost in, overwhelmed by, preoccupied with, rapt in.

deer *noun* (*plural* same) 4-hoofed grazing animal, male usually with antlers. ☐ **deerstalker** cloth peaked cap with ear-flaps.

deface /dɪ'feɪs/ *verb* (**-cing**) disfigure. ☐ **defacement** *noun*.
■ blemish, damage, disfigure, harm, impair, injure, mar, mutilate, ruin, spoil, vandalize.

de facto /deɪ 'fæktəʊ/ *adjective* existing in fact, whether by right or not. ● *adverb* in fact.

defame /dɪ'feɪm/ *verb* (**-ming**) attack good name of. ☐ **defamation** /defə'meɪʃ(ə)n/ *noun*. **defamatory** /-'fæm-/ *adjective*.

default /dɪ'fɔːlt/ *noun* **1** failure to act, appear, or pay. **2** option selected by computer program etc. unless given alternative instruction. ● *verb* fail to fulfil obligations. ☐ **by default** because of lack of an alternative etc. ☐ **defaulter** *noun*.

defeat /dɪ'fiːt/ *verb* **1** overcome in battle, contest, etc. **2** frustrate, baffle. ● *noun* defeating, being defeated. ☐ **defeated** *adjective*.
■ *verb* **1** beat, *colloquial* best, be victorious over, checkmate, *slang* clobber, conquer, crush, destroy, *colloquial* flatten, foil, get the better of, *colloquial* hammer, lay low, *colloquial* lick, master, outdo, outvote, outwit, overcome, overpower, overthrow, overwhelm, prevail over, put down, quell, repulse, rout, ruin, smash, subdue, subjugate, suppress, thrash, triumph over, trounce, *literary* vanquish, *slang* whip. **2** baffle, baulk, check, confound, foil, frustrate, stop, thwart. ● *noun* beating, conquest, downfall, drubbing, failure, humiliation, *colloquial* licking, overthrow, *colloquial* put-down, rebuff, repulse, reverse, rout, setback, subjugation, thrashing, trouncing. ☐ **defeated** see UNSUCCESSFUL.

defeatism *noun* readiness to accept defeat. ☐ **defeatist** *noun & adjective*.

defecate /'diːfɪkeɪt/ *verb* (**-ting**) evacuate the bowels. ☐ **defecation** *noun*.

defect *noun* /'diːfekt/ **1** shortcoming. **2** fault. ● *verb* /dɪ'fekt/ desert one's country, cause, etc., for another. ☐ **defection** *noun*. **defector** *noun*.
■ *noun* **1** deficiency, failing, imperfection, inadequacy, lack, shortcoming, shortfall, want, weakness, weak point. **2** blemish, *colloquial* bug, error, fault, flaw, imperfection, irregularity, mark, mistake, spot, stain. ● *verb* change sides, desert, go over.

defective /dɪ'fektɪv/ *adjective* faulty, imperfect. ☐ **defectiveness** *noun*.

■ broken, deficient, faulty, flawed, gone wrong, imperfect, incomplete, *slang* on the blink, unsatisfactory, wanting, weak.

defence /dɪˈfens/ *noun* (*US* **defense**) **1** (means of) defending. **2** justification. **3** defendant's case or counsel. **4** players in defending position. **5** (in *plural*) fortifications. □ **defenceless** *adjective*.

■ **1** barrier, cover, deterrence, deterrent, guard, protection, safeguard, security, shelter, shield. **2** *disputed* alibi, apologia, apology, excuse, explanation, justification, plea, testimony, vindication. □ **defenceless** exposed, helpless, impotent, insecure, powerless, unguarded, unprotected, vulnerable, weak.

defend /dɪˈfend/ *verb* **1** (often + *against*, *from*) resist attack made on; protect. **2** uphold by argument. **3** *Law* conduct defence (of). **4** compete to retain (title). □ **defendable** *adjective*. **defender** *noun*.

■ **1** cover, fight for, fortify, guard, keep safe, preserve, protect, safeguard, screen, secure, shelter, shield, stick up for, watch over. **2, 3** argue for, champion, justify, plead for, speak up for, stand by, stand up for, support, uphold, vindicate.

defendant *noun* person accused or sued in court of law.

■ accused, appellant, offender, prisoner.

defense *US* = DEFENCE.

defensible /dɪˈfensɪb(ə)l/ *adjective* able to be defended or justified.

defensive /dɪˈfensɪv/ *adjective* **1** done or intended for defence. **2** overreacting to criticism. □ **on the defensive 1** expecting criticism. **2** ready to defend. □ **defensively** *adverb*. **defensiveness** *noun*.

■ **1** protective. **2** apologetic, self-justifying.

defer[1] /dɪˈfɜː/ *verb* (**-rr-**) postpone. □ **deferment** *noun*. **deferral** *noun*.

■ adjourn, delay, hold over, lay aside, postpone, prorogue (*parliament*), put off, shelve, suspend.

defer[2] /dɪˈfɜː/ *verb* (**-rr-**) (+ *to*) yield or make concessions to.

■ see YIELD *verb* 3.

deference /ˈdefərəns/ *noun* **1** respectful conduct. **2** compliance with another's wishes. □ **in deference to** out of respect for.

■ **1** see RESPECT *noun* 1. **2** acquiescence, compliance, obedience, submission.

deferential /defəˈrenʃ(ə)l/ *adjective* respectful. □ **deferentially** *adverb*.

defiance /dɪˈfaɪəns/ *noun* open disobedience; bold resistance. □ **defiant** *adjective*. **defiantly** *adverb*.

■ □ **defiant** aggressive, antagonistic, belligerent, bold, brazen, challenging, daring, disobedient, headstrong, insolent, insubordinate, mutinous, obstinate, rebellious, recalcitrant, refractory, self-willed, stubborn, truculent, uncooperative, unruly, unyielding.

deficiency /dɪˈfɪʃənsi/ *noun* (*plural* **-ies**) **1** being deficient. **2** (usually + *of*) lack or shortage. **3** thing lacking. **4** deficit. □ **deficiency disease** disease caused by lack of essential element in diet.

deficient /dɪˈfɪʃ(ə)nt/ *adjective* (often + *in*) incomplete or insufficient.

■ defective, inadequate, insufficient, lacking, meagre, scanty, scarce, short, *colloquial* sketchy, unsatisfactory, wanting, weak.

deficit /ˈdefɪsɪt/ *noun* **1** amount by which total falls short. **2** excess of liabilities over assets.

defile[1] /dɪˈfaɪl/ *verb* (**-ling**) **1** make dirty; pollute. **2** profane. □ **defilement** *noun*.

■ **1** contaminate, dirty, foul, infect, poison, pollute, soil, stain, sully, taint, tarnish. **2** corrupt, degrade, desecrate, dishonour, profane, violate.

defile[2] /dɪˈfaɪl/ *noun* narrow gorge or pass. ● *verb* (**-ling**) march in file.

define /dɪˈfaɪn/ *verb* (**-ning**) **1** give meaning of. **2** describe scope of. **3** outline; mark out the boundary of. □ **definable** *adjective*.

■ **1** clarify, explain. **2** delineate, describe, determine, formulate, specify, spell out. **3** bound, circumscribe, demarcate, determine, fix, limit, mark off, mark out, outline.

definite /ˈdefɪnɪt/ *adjective* **1** certain, firm, settled. **2** clearly defined; precise. □ **definite article** the word (*the* in English) placed before a noun and implying a specific object, person, or idea. □ **definitely** *adverb*.

■ **1** assured, categorical, certain, confident, confirmed, cut and dried, decided, determined, emphatic, firm, fixed, positive, settled, sure, unequivocal. **2** apparent, clear, clear-cut, decided, discernible, distinct, exact, explicit, express, marked, noticeable, obvious, particular, perceptible, plain, precise, pronounced, specific, unambiguous, unmistakable, well defined. □ **definitely** beyond doubt, certainly, doubtless, for certain, indubitably, positively, surely, unquestionably, without doubt, without fail.

definition /defɪˈnɪʃ(ə)n/ *noun* **1** defining. **2** statement of meaning of word etc. **3** distinctness in outline.

■ **1, 2** clarification, elucidation, explanation, interpretation. **3** clarity, clearness, focus, precision, sharpness.

definitive /dɪˈfɪnɪtɪv/ *adjective* **1** decisive, unconditional, final. **2** (of edition etc.) most authoritative.

■ **1** complete, conclusive, decisive, final, last (*word*), permanent, settled, ultimate, unconditional. **2** authoritative, official, reliable, standard.

deflate /dɪˈfleɪt/ *verb* (**-ting**) **1** let air out of (tyre etc.). **2** (cause to) lose confidence. **3** subject (economy) to deflation.

deflation *noun* **1** deflating. **2** reduction of money in circulation to combat inflation. □ **deflationary** *adjective*.

deflect /dɪˈflekt/ *verb* **1** bend or turn aside from purpose or course. **2** (often + *from*) (cause to) deviate. □ **deflection** *noun*.
■ avert, deviate, divert, fend off, head off, intercept, parry, prevent, sidetrack, swerve, switch, turn aside, veer, ward off.

deflower /diːˈflaʊə/ *verb* **1** deprive of virginity. **2** ravage.

defoliate /diːˈfəʊlɪeɪt/ *verb* (**-ting**) destroy leaves of. □ **defoliant** *noun*. **defoliation** *noun*.

deforest /diːˈfɒrɪst/ *verb* clear of forests. □ **deforestation** *noun*.

deform /dɪˈfɔːm/ *verb* (often as **deformed** *adjective*) make ugly or misshapen; disfigure. □ **deformation** /diː-/ *noun*.
■ (deformed) bent, buckled, contorted, crippled, crooked, defaced, disfigured, distorted, gnarled, grotesque, malformed, mangled, misshapen, mutilated, twisted, ugly, warped.

deformity /dɪˈfɔːmɪtɪ/ *noun* (*plural* **-ies**) **1** being deformed. **2** malformation.

defraud /dɪˈfrɔːd/ *verb* (often + *of*) cheat by fraud. □ **defrauder** *noun*.
■ cheat, *slang* con, *literary* cozen, deceive, *colloquial* diddle, embezzle, fleece, *colloquial* rip off, rob, swindle, trick.

defray /dɪˈfreɪ/ *verb* provide money for (cost). □ **defrayal** *noun*.

defrock /diːˈfrɒk/ *verb* deprive (esp. priest) of office.

defrost /diːˈfrɒst/ *verb* **1** remove frost or ice from. **2** unfreeze. **3** become unfrozen.

deft *adjective* dexterous, skilful. □ **deftly** *adverb*. **deftness** *noun*.
■ adept, adroit, agile, clever, dexterous, expert, handy, neat, *colloquial* nifty, nimble, proficient, quick, skilful.

defunct /dɪˈfʌŋkt/ *adjective* **1** no longer existing or in use. **2** dead.

defuse /diːˈfjuːz/ *verb* (**-sing**) **1** remove fuse from (bomb etc.). **2** reduce tension in (crisis etc.).

defy /dɪˈfaɪ/ *verb* (**-ies**, **-ied**) **1** resist openly. **2** present insuperable obstacles to. **3** (+ *to do*) challenge to do or prove something.
■ **1** challenge, confront, disobey, face up to, flout, kick against, rebel against, resist, stand up to, withstand. **2** baffle, beat, defeat, elude, foil, frustrate, repel, repulse, resist, thwart, withstand. **3** challenge, dare.

degenerate /dɪˈdʒenərət/ *adjective* having lost usual or good qualities; immoral. ● *noun* degenerate person etc. ● *verb* /-reɪt/ (**-ting**) become degenerate; get worse. □ **degeneracy** *noun*. **degeneration** *noun*.
■ *adjective* see CORRUPT *adjective* 2. ● *verb* become worse, decline, deteriorate, regress, retrogress, sink, slip, weaken, worsen.

degrade /dɪˈgreɪd/ *verb* (**-ding**) **1** (often as **degrading** *adjective*) humiliate; dishonour. **2** reduce to lower rank. □ **degradation** /degrəˈdeɪʃ(ə)n/ *noun*.
■ **1** abase, cheapen, debase, dishonour, humiliate, mortify; (**degrading**) see SHAMEFUL. **2** cashier, demote, depose, downgrade.

degree /dɪˈgriː/ *noun* **1** stage in scale, series, or process. **2** stage in intensity. **3** unit of measurement of angle or temperature. **4** extent of burns. **5** academic rank conferred by university etc.
■ **1** calibre, class, grade, order, position, rank, standard, standing, station, status. **2** extent, intensity, level, measure.

dehumanize /diːˈhjuːmənaɪz/ *verb* (also **-ise**) (**-zing** or **-sing**) **1** remove human qualities from. **2** make impersonal. □ **dehumanization** *noun*.

dehydrate /diːhaɪˈdreɪt/ *verb* (**-ting**) **1** remove water from. **2** make dry. **3** (often as **dehydrated** *adjective*) deprive of fluids; make very thirsty. □ **dehydration** *noun*.

de-ice /diːˈaɪs/ *verb* (**-cing**) **1** remove ice from. **2** prevent formation of ice on. □ **de-icer** *noun*.

deify /ˈdiːɪfaɪ/ *verb* (**-ies**, **-ied**) make god or idol of. □ **deification** *noun*.
■ idolize, venerate, worship.

deign /deɪn/ *verb* (+ *to do*) condescend to.
■ condescend, demean oneself, lower oneself, stoop, *formal* vouchsafe.

deism /ˈdiːɪz(ə)m/ *noun* reasoned belief in existence of a god. □ **deist** *noun*. **deistic** /-ˈɪstɪk/ *adjective*.

deity /ˈdeɪtɪ/ *noun* (*plural* **-ies**) **1** god or goddess. **2** divine status or nature.
■ **1** creator, divinity, god, goddess, godhead, idol, immortal, power, spirit, supreme being. **2** divinity.

déjà vu /deɪʒɑː ˈvuː/ *noun* illusion of having already experienced present situation. [French]

dejected /dɪˈdʒektɪd/ *adjective* sad, depressed. □ **dejectedly** *adverb*. **dejection** *noun*.
■ depressed, disconsolate, dispirited, *colloquial* down, downcast, downhearted, heavy-hearted, in low spirits, sad.

delay /dɪˈleɪ/ *verb* **1** postpone. **2** make late. **3** be late. ● *noun* **1** delaying, being delayed. **2** time lost by this.
■ *verb* **1** defer, hold over, postpone, put back, put off, set back, stay, suspend. **2** check, detain, hinder, hold up, impede, keep back, retard, set back, slow down, *archaic* or *literary* stay. **3** be slow, bide one's time, dally, dawdle, *colloquial* dilly-dally, drag one's feet, get bogged down, hang about, hang back, hang fire, hesitate, lag, linger, loiter, mark time, pause, play for time, procrastinate, stall, *archaic* tarry, temporize, vacillate, wait. ● *noun* check, deferment, deferral, filibuster, hiatus, hitch, hold-up, interruption, moratorium, pause, postponement, setback, stay (*of execution*), stoppage, wait.

delectable /dɪˈlektəb(ə)l/ *adjective* delightful.

delectation /diːlekˈteɪʃ(ə)n/ *noun* enjoyment.

delegate *noun* /'delɪgət/ **1** elected representative sent to conference. **2** member of delegation etc. ● *verb* /'delɪgeɪt/ (**-ting**) **1** (often + *to*) commit (power etc.) to deputy etc. **2** (often + *to*) entrust (task) to another. **3** send or authorize as representative.

■ *noun* agent, ambassador, emissary, envoy, go-between, legate, messenger, nuncio, plenipotentiary, representative, spokesperson. ● *verb* **1, 2** assign, commit, depute, entrust, give. **3** appoint, authorize, charge, commission, depute, designate, empower, mandate, nominate.

delegation /delɪ'geɪʃ(ə)n/ *noun* **1** group representing others. **2** delegating, being delegated.

■ **1** commission, deputation, mission.

delete /dɪ'liːt/ *verb* (**-ting**) strike out (word etc.). □ **deletion** *noun*.

■ blot out, cancel, cross out, cut out, edit out, efface, eliminate, eradicate, erase, expunge, obliterate, remove, rub out, strike out, wipe out.

deleterious /delɪ'tɪərɪəs/ *adjective* harmful.

delft *noun* (also **delftware**) type of glazed earthenware.

deli /'delɪ/ *noun* (*plural* **-s**) *colloquial* delicatessen.

deliberate *adjective* /dɪ'lɪbərət/ **1** intentional, considered. **2** unhurried. ● *verb* /dɪ'lɪbəreɪt/ (**-ting**) **1** think carefully. **2** discuss. □ **deliberately** *adverb*.

■ *adjective* **1** arranged, calculated, cold-blooded, conscious, contrived, designed, intended, intentional, knowing, organized, planned, pre-arranged, preconceived, premeditated, prepared, purposeful, studied, thought out, wilful, worked out. **2** careful, cautious, circumspect, considered, diligent, measured, methodical, orderly, painstaking, regular, slow, thoughtful, unhurried, watchful. ● *verb* **1** see THINK *verb* **3**. **2** see DISCUSS.

deliberation /dɪlɪbə'reɪʃ(ə)n/ *noun* careful consideration or slowness.

deliberative /dɪ'lɪbərətɪv/ *adjective* (esp. of assembly etc.) of or for deliberation.

delicacy /'delɪkəsɪ/ *noun* (*plural* **-ies**) **1** being delicate. **2** choice food.

■ **1** accuracy, care, cleverness, daintiness, discrimination, exquisiteness, fineness, finesse, fragility, intricacy, precision, sensitivity, subtlety, tact. **2** rarity, speciality, treat.

delicate /'delɪkət/ *adjective* **1** fine in texture, quality, etc. **2** subtle; hard to discern. **3** susceptible; tender. **4** requiring tact. **5** tactful, sensitive. **6** skilful. □ **delicately** *adverb*.

■ **1** dainty, diaphanous, elegant, exquisite, feathery, fine, flimsy, fragile, gauzy, gentle, intricate, light, slender, soft. **2** faint, mild, muted, pale, slight, subtle. **3** feeble, fragile, frail, puny, sickly, susceptible, tender, unhealthy, weak. **4** awkward, confidential, embarrassing, private, problematical, prudish, *colloquial* sticky, ticklish, touchy. **5** considerate, diplomatic, discreet, judicious, prudent, sensitive, tactful. **6** accurate, careful, clever, deft, precise, skilled.

delicatessen /delɪkə'tes(ə)n/ *noun* shop selling esp. exotic cooked meats, cheeses, etc.

delicious /dɪ'lɪʃəs/ *adjective* highly enjoyable esp. to taste or smell. □ **deliciously** *adverb*.

■ appetizing, choice, delectable, enjoyable, luscious, mouth-watering, nice, palatable, savoury, *colloquial* scrumptious, succulent, tasty, tempting, toothsome, *colloquial* yummy.

delight /dɪ'laɪt/ *verb* **1** (often as **delighted** *adjective*) please greatly. **2** (+ *in*) take great pleasure in. ● *noun* **1** great pleasure. **2** thing that delights. □ **delightful** *adjective*. **delightfully** *adverb*.

■ *verb* **1** amuse, bewitch, captivate, charm, cheer, divert, enchant, enrapture, entertain, enthral, entrance, fascinate, gladden, gratify, please, ravish, thrill, transport; (**delighted**) see HAPPY 1, PLEASED (PLEASE). **2** (*delight in*) see ENJOY 1. ● *noun* **1** bliss, delectation, ecstasy, enchantment, enjoyment, felicity, gratification, happiness, joy, paradise, pleasure, rapture, satisfaction. **2** joy, pleasure, satisfaction. □ **delightful** agreeable, attractive, captivating, charming, congenial, delectable, diverting, enjoyable, nice, pleasant, pleasing, pleasurable, rewarding, satisfying, spellbinding.

delimit /dɪ'lɪmɪt/ *verb* (**-t-**) fix limits or boundary of. □ **delimitation** *noun*.

delineate /dɪ'lɪnɪeɪt/ *verb* (**-ting**) portray by drawing or in words. □ **delineation** *noun*.

delinquent /dɪ'lɪŋkwənt/ *noun* offender. ● *adjective* **1** guilty of misdeed. **2** failing in a duty. □ **delinquency** *noun*.

■ *noun* criminal, culprit, hooligan, lawbreaker, malefactor, miscreant, offender, *colloquial* roughneck, ruffian, *colloquial* tearaway, vandal, wrongdoer, young offender.

deliquesce /delɪ'kwes/ *verb* (**-cing**) **1** become liquid. **2** dissolve in moisture from the air. □ **deliquescence** *noun*. **deliquescent** *adjective*.

delirious /dɪ'lɪrɪəs/ *adjective* **1** affected with delirium. **2** wildly excited. □ **deliriously** *adverb*.

■ **1** beside oneself, crazy, demented, deranged, distracted, drunk, feverish, frantic, frenzied, hysterical, incoherent, irrational, light-headed, mad, rambling, wild. **2** ecstatic, excited.

delirium /dɪ'lɪrɪəm/ *noun* **1** disordered state of mind, with incoherent speech etc. **2** wildly excited mood. □ **delirium tremens** /'triːmenz/ psychosis of chronic alcoholism with tremors and hallucinations.

deliver /dɪ'lɪvə/ *verb* **1** convey (letters, goods) to destination. **2** (often + *to*) hand over. **3** (often + *from*) save, rescue, set free. **4** assist in giving birth or at birth of. **5** utter (speech). **6** launch or aim (blow etc.). **7** (in full **deliver the goods**) *colloquial* provide or carry out what is required. □ **deliverer** *noun*.

■ **1, 2** bear, bring, carry, cart, convey, distribute, give out, hand over, make over, present, supply, surrender, take round, transfer, transport, turn cover. **3** see RESCUE *verb* 1. **5** announce, broadcast, give, make, present, read, recite, speak, utter. **6** administer, aim, deal, direct, fire, inflict, launch, strike, throw.

deliverance *noun* rescuing.

delivery /dɪ'lɪvərɪ/ *noun* (*plural* **-ies**) **1** delivering; distribution of letters etc. **2** thing delivered. **3** childbirth. **4** manner of delivering (of speech, ball, etc.).

■ **1** consignment, conveyance, dispatch, distribution, shipment, transmission, transportation. **3** childbirth, confinement, *formal* parturition. **4** enunciation, execution, implementation, performance, presentation.

dell *noun* small wooded valley.

delouse /diː'laʊs/ *verb* (**-sing**) rid of lice.

delphinium /del'fɪnɪəm/ *noun* (*plural* **-s**) garden plant with spikes of usually blue flowers.

delta /'deltə/ *noun* **1** triangular alluvial tract at mouth of river. **2** fourth letter of Greek alphabet (*Δ, δ*). **3** fourth-class mark for work etc. □ **delta wing** triangular swept-back wing of aircraft.

delude /dɪ'luːd/ *verb* (**-ding**) deceive, mislead.

deluge /'deljuːdʒ/ *noun* **1** flood. **2** downpour of rain. **3** overwhelming rush. ● *verb* (**-ging**) flood, inundate.

■ *noun* **1** flood, inundation, spate. **2** downpour, rainstorm, torrent. **3** flood, rush, spate, stream, torrent. ● *verb* drown, engulf, flood, inundate, overwhelm, submerge, swamp.

delusion /dɪ'luːʒ(ə)n/ *noun* false belief or hope. □ **delusive** *adjective*. **delusory** *adjective*.

■ dream, fantasy, hallucination, illusion, mirage, misconception, mistake, self-deception.

de luxe /də 'lʌks/ *adjective* luxurious; superior; sumptuous.

delve *verb* (**-ving**) **1** (often + *in, into*) research, search deeply. **2** *poetical* dig.

■ **1** explore, investigate, probe, research, search. **2** burrow, dig.

demagogue /'deməgɒg/ *noun* political agitator appealing to emotion. □ **demagogic** /-'gɒgɪk/ *adjective*. **demagogy** /-gɒgɪ/) *noun*.

demand /dɪ'mɑːnd/ *noun* **1** insistent and peremptory request. **2** desire for commodity. **3** urgent claim. ● *verb* **1** (often + *of, from, to do, that*) ask for insistently. **2** require. **3** (as **demanding** *adjective*) requiring effort, attention, etc. □ **demand feeding** feeding baby whenever it cries. **in demand** wanted.

■ *noun* **1** *literary* behest, command, expectation, importunity, insistence, order, request, requisition. **2** call, desire, need, requirement, want. **3** call, claim. ● *verb* **1** ask for, call for, claim, exact, insist on, order, request, require, requisition. **2** call for, cry out for, necessitate, need, require, want. **3** (**demanding**) see DIFFICULT 1, IMPORTUNATE. □ **in demand** see POPULAR 1.

demarcation /diːmɑː'keɪʃ(ə)n/ *noun* **1** marking of boundary or limits. **2** trade union practice of restricting job to one union. □ **demarcate** /'diː-/ *verb* (**-ting**).

demean /dɪ'miːn/ *verb* (usually **demean oneself**) lower dignity of. □ **demeaning** *adjective*.

■ abase, cheapen, debase, degrade, disgrace, humble, humiliate, lower, undervalue. □ **demeaning** see SHAMEFUL.

demeanour /dɪ'miːnə/ *noun* (*US* **demeanor**) **1** bearing. **2** outward behaviour.

demented /dɪ'mentɪd/ *adjective* mad.

dementia /dɪ'menʃə/ *noun* chronic insanity. □ **dementia praecox** /'priːkɒks/ schizophrenia.

demerara /demə'reərə/ *noun* light brown cane sugar.

demerit /diː'merɪt/ *noun* fault, defect.

demesne /dɪ'miːn/ *noun* **1** landed property, estate. **2** possession (of land) as one's own.

demigod /'demɪgɒd/ *noun* **1** partly divine being. **2** *colloquial* godlike person.

demijohn /'demɪdʒɒn/ *noun* large wicker-cased bottle.

demilitarize /diː'mɪlɪtəraɪz/ *verb* (also **-ise**) (**-zing** or **-sing**) remove army etc. from (zone etc.).

demi-monde /'demɪmɒnd/ *noun* **1** class of women of doubtful morality. **2** semi-respectable group. [French]

demise /dɪ'maɪz/ *noun* death; termination.

demisemiquaver /demɪ'semɪkweɪvə/ *noun* *Music* note equal to half semiquaver.

demist /diː'mɪst/ *verb* clear mist from (windscreen etc.). □ **demister** *noun*.

demo /'deməʊ/ *noun* (*plural* **-s**) *colloquial* demonstration, esp. political.

demobilize /diː'məʊbɪlaɪz/ *verb* (also **-ise**) (**-zing** or **-sing**) disband (troops etc.). □ **demobilization** *noun*.

democracy /dɪ'mɒkrəsɪ/ *noun* (*plural* **-ies**) **1** government by the whole population, usually through elected representatives. **2** state so governed.

democrat /'deməkræt/ *noun* **1** advocate of democracy. **2** (**Democrat**) member of US Democratic Party.

democratic /demə'krætɪk/ *adjective* **1** of, like, or practising democracy. **2** favouring social equality. □ **democratically** *adverb*. **democratize** /dɪ'mɒkrətaɪz/ *verb* (also **-ise**) (**-zing** or **-sing**). **democratization** *noun*.

■ **1** chosen, elected, elective, popular, representative. **2** classless, egalitarian.

demography /dɪ'mɒgrəfɪ/ *noun* study of statistics of birth, death, disease, etc. □ **demographic** /demə'græfɪk/ *adjective*.

demolish /dɪ'mɒlɪʃ/ *verb* **1** pull down (building); destroy. **2** refute. **3** *jocular* eat up voraciously. □ **demolition** /demə'lɪʃ(ə)n/ *noun*.

■ **1** break down, bulldoze, destroy, dismantle, flatten, knock down, level, pull down, raze, tear down, topple, undo, wreck.

demon /'di:mən/ *noun* **1** devil; evil spirit. **2** forceful or skilful performer. □ **demonic** /dɪ'mɒnɪk/ *adjective*.

■ **1** devil, evil spirit, fiend, goblin, imp, spirit.

demoniac /dɪ'məʊnɪæk/ *adjective* **1** frenzied. **2** supposedly possessed by evil spirit. **3** of or like demons. ● *noun* demoniac person. □ **demoniacal** /di:mə'naɪək(ə)l/ *adjective*.

demonology /di:mə'nɒlədʒɪ/ *noun* study of demons.

demonstrable /'demənstrəb(ə)l/ *adjective* able to be shown or proved. □ **demonstrably** *adverb*.

■ evident, incontrovertible, indisputable, irrefutable, palpable, positive, provable, undeniable, unquestionable, verifiable.

demonstrate /'demənstreɪt/ *verb* (**-ting**) **1** show (feelings etc.). **2** describe and explain by experiment etc. **3** prove truth or existence of. **4** take part in public demonstration.

■ **1** display, embody, evince, exemplify, exhibit, express, indicate, manifest, represent, show, typify. **2** describe, display, exhibit, explain, expound, illustrate, show, teach. **3** confirm, establish, prove, substantiate, verify. **4** march, parade, picket, protest.

demonstration *noun* **1** demonstrating. **2** (+ *of*) show of feeling etc. **3** political public march, meeting, etc. **4** proof by logic, argument, etc.

■ **1** description, display, exhibition, exposition, illustration, presentation, show, test, trial. **2** display, exhibition, expression, indication, manifestation, representation, show. **3** *colloquial* demo, march, parade, picket, protest, rally, sit-in. **4** confirmation, evidence, proof, substantiation, verification.

demonstrative /dɪ'mɒnstrətɪv/ *adjective* **1** showing feelings readily; affectionate. **2** *Grammar* indicating person or thing referred to. □ **demonstratively** *adverb*. **demonstrativeness** *noun*.

■ **1** affectionate, effusive, emotional, loving, open, uninhibited, unreserved, unrestrained.

demonstrator /'demənstreɪtə/ *noun* person making or taking part in demonstration.

demoralize /di:'mɒrəlaɪz/ *verb* (also **-ise**) (**-zing** or **-sing**) destroy morale of. □ **demoralization** *noun*.

demote /di:'məʊt/ *verb* (**-ting**) reduce to lower rank or class. □ **demotion** /-'məʊʃ(ə)n/ *noun*.

■ downgrade, reduce, relegate.

demotic /dɪ'mɒtɪk/ *noun* colloquial form of a language. ● *adjective* colloquial, vulgar.

demotivate /di:'məʊtɪveɪt/ *verb* (**-ting**) cause to lose motivation. □ **demotivation** *noun*.

demur /dɪ'mɜ:/ *verb* (**-rr-**) (often + *to*, *at*) raise objections. ● *noun* (also **demurral**) /dɪ'mʌr(ə)l/ (usually in negative) objection, objecting.

demure /dɪ'mjʊə/ *adjective* (**-r**, **-st**) **1** quiet, modest. **2** coy. □ **demurely** *adverb*. **demureness** *noun*.

■ **1** diffident, modest, quiet, reserved, reticent, retiring, sedate, shy, sober, staid. **2** bashful, coy, prim, prissy.

demystify /di:'mɪstɪfaɪ/ *verb* (**-ies**, **-ied**) remove mystery from.

den *noun* **1** wild animal's lair. **2** place of crime or vice. **3** small private room.

■ **1** burrow, hole, lair. **3** hideaway, hideout, hiding place, private place, retreat, sanctuary, secret place, study.

denarius /dɪ'neərɪəs/ *noun* (*plural* **-rii** /-rɪaɪ/) ancient Roman silver coin.

denationalize /di:'næʃənəlaɪz/ *verb* (also **-ise**) (**-zing** or **-sing**) transfer (industry etc.) from national to private ownership. □ **denationalization** *noun*.

denature /di:'neɪtʃə/ *verb* (**-ring**) **1** change properties of. **2** make (alcohol) unfit for drinking.

dendrology /den'drɒlədʒɪ/ *noun* study of trees. □ **dendrologist** *noun*.

denial /dɪ'naɪəl/ *noun* denying or refusing.

■ abnegation, contradiction, disavowal, disclaimer, negation, refusal, refutation, rejection, renunciation, repudiation, veto.

denier /'denjə/ *noun* unit of weight measuring fineness of silk, nylon, etc.

denigrate /'denɪgreɪt/ *verb* (**-ting**) blacken reputation of. □ **denigration** *noun*. **denigratory** /-'greɪt-/ *adjective*.

■ belittle, criticize, decry, disparage, impugn, malign, *colloquial* put down, *colloquial* run down, sneer at, traduce, vilify.

denim /'denɪm/ *noun* **1** twilled cotton fabric. **2** (in *plural*) jeans etc. made of this.

denizen /'denɪz(ə)n/ *noun* (usually + *of*) inhabitant or occupant.

denominate /dɪ'nɒmɪneɪt/ *verb* (**-ting**) give name to; describe as, call.

denomination *noun* **1** Church or religious sect. **2** class of measurement or money. **3** name, esp. for classification. □ **denominational** *adjective*.

■ **1** church, communion, creed, cult, order, persuasion, schism, school, sect. **2** class, size, unit, value. **3** category, class, classification, designation, kind, sort, species, type.

denominator *noun* number below line in vulgar fraction; divisor.

denote /dɪ'nəʊt/ *verb* (**-ting**) **1** (often + *that*) be sign of; indicate. **2** be name for; signify. □ **denotation** /di:nə'teɪʃ(ə)n/ *noun*.

■ designate, express, indicate, mean, represent, signal, signify, stand for, symbolize.

denouement /deɪ'nu:mɑ̃/ *noun* final resolution in play, novel, etc.

■ climax, *colloquial* pay-off, resolution, solution, sorting out, unravelling.

denounce /dɪ'naʊns/ *verb* (**-cing**) **1** accuse publicly. **2** inform against.

■ **1** accuse, attack, blame, brand, censure, complain about, condemn, criticize, declaim against, decry, fulminate against, hold forth against, impugn, incriminate, inveigh against, pillory, stigmatize, vilify, vituperate. **2** betray, inform against, report, reveal.

dense /dens/ *adjective* **1** closely compacted. **2** crowded together. **3** stupid. □ **densely** *adverb*. **denseness** *noun*.

■ **1** close, compact, concentrated, heavy, impassable, impenetrable, lush, massed, solid, thick, tight, viscous. **2** concentrated, crowded, *colloquial* jam-packed, packed. **3** see STUPID 1.

density /'densɪtɪ/ *noun* (*plural* **-ies**) **1** denseness. **2** quantity of mass per unit volume. **3** opacity of photographic image.

dent *noun* **1** depression in surface. **2** noticeable adverse effect. ● *verb* make dent in.

■ *noun* **1** concavity, depression, dimple, dint, dip, hollow, indentation, pit. ● *verb* bend, buckle, crumple, knock in.

dental /'dent(ə)l/ *adjective* **1** of teeth or dentistry. **2** (of sound) made with tongue-tip against front teeth. □ **dental floss** thread used to clean between teeth. **dental surgeon** dentist.

dentate /'denteɪt/ *adjective* toothed, notched.

dentifrice /'dentɪfrɪs/ *noun* tooth powder or toothpaste.

dentine /'denti:n/ *noun* hard dense tissue forming most of tooth.

dentist /'dentɪst/ *noun* person qualified to treat, extract, etc., teeth. □ **dentistry** *noun*.

denture /'dentʃə/ *noun* (usually in *plural*) removable artificial teeth.

denude /dɪ'nju:d/ *verb* (**-ding**) **1** make naked or bare. **2** (+ *of*) strip of (covering etc.). □ **denudation** /di:-/ *noun*.

■ **1** bare, defoliate, deforest, expose, strip, unclothe, uncover.

denunciation /dɪmʌnsɪ'eɪʃ(ə)n/ *noun* denouncing.

deny /dɪ'naɪ/ *verb* (**-ies**, **-ied**) **1** declare untrue or non-existent. **2** repudiate. **3** (often + *to*) withhold from. **4** (**deny oneself**) be abstinent.

■ **1** contradict, controvert, dispute, gainsay, negate, oppose, rebut, *disputed* refute. **2** disclaim, disown, reject, repudiate. **3** begrudge, deprive of, disallow, refuse, withhold. **4** (**deny oneself**) see ABSTAIN 1.

deodorant /di:'əʊdərənt/ *noun* substance applied to body or sprayed into air to conceal smells.

deodorize /di:'əʊdəraɪz/ *verb* (also **-ise**) (**-zing** or **-sing**) remove smell of. □ **deodorization** *noun*.

deoxyribonucleic acid /di:ɒksɪraɪbəʊnju:'kleɪk/ see DNA.

dep. *abbreviation* **1** departs. **2** deputy.

depart /dɪ'pɑ:t/ *verb* **1** (often + *from*) go away; leave. **2** (usually + *for*) set out. **3** (usually + *from*) deviate. **4** die; leave by death.

■ **1, 2** abscond, check out, *colloquial* clear off, decamp, disappear, embark, emigrate, escape, exit, go away, *slang* hit the road, leave, make off, *colloquial* make oneself scarce, *colloquial* make tracks, migrate, move away, move off, *colloquial* push off, quit, retire, retreat, run away, run off, *slang* scarper, *colloquial* scram, set forth, set off, set out, start, take one's leave, vanish, withdraw. **3** see DEVIATE.

departed *adjective* bygone. ● *noun* (**the departed**) *euphemistic* dead person or people.

■ *adjective* see DEAD *adjective* 1.

department *noun* **1** separate part of complex whole, esp. branch of administration; division of school etc.; section of large store. **2** area of expertise. **3** French administrative district. □ **department store** shop with many departments. □ **departmental** /di:pɑ:t'ment(ə)l/ *adjective*.

■ **1** branch, division, office, part, section, sector, subdivision, unit. **2** area, concern, domain, field, function, job, line, province, responsibility, specialism, sphere.

departure /dɪ'pɑ:tʃə/ *noun* **1** departing. **2** new course of action etc.

■ **1** disappearance, embarkation, escape, exit, exodus, going, retirement, retreat, withdrawal.

depend /dɪ'pend/ *verb* **1** (often + *on*, *upon*) be controlled or determined by. **2** (+ *on*, *upon*) need; rely on.

■ **1** (**depend on**) be contingent on, hinge on, pivot on, rest on. **2** (**depend on**) *colloquial* bank on, count on, need, put one's faith in, reckon on, rely on, trust.

dependable *adjective* reliable. □ **dependability** *noun*.

■ conscientious, consistent, faithful, honest, regular, reliable, safe, sound, steady, true, trustworthy, unfailing.

dependant *noun* person supported, esp. financially, by another.

dependence *noun* **1** depending, being dependent. **2** reliance.

■ **1** see ADDICTION (ADDICTED). **2** confidence, reliance, trust.

dependency *noun* (*plural* **-ies**) **1** country etc. controlled by another. **2** dependence (on drugs etc.).

dependent *adjective* **1** (usually + *on*) depending. **2** unable to do without (esp. drug). **3** maintained at another's cost. **4** (of clause etc.) subordinate to word etc.

■ **1** (**dependent on**) conditional on, connected with, controlled by, determined by, liable to, relative to, subject to, vulnerable to. **2** addicted, enslaved, *slang* hooked, reliant.

depict /dɪ'pɪkt/ *verb* **1** represent in painting etc.
2 describe. □ **depiction** *noun*.

■ **1** delineate, draw, illustrate, paint, picture,
portray, represent, reproduce, show, sketch. **2**
delineate, describe, outline, portray, represent,
sketch.

depilate /'depɪleɪt/ *verb* (**-ting**) remove hair
from. □ **depilation** *noun*. **depilator** *noun*.

depilatory /dɪ'pɪlətərɪ/ *adjective* that removes
unwanted hair. ● *noun* (*plural* **-ies**) depilatory
substance.

deplete /dɪ'pliːt/ *verb* (**-ting**) **1** (esp. as **depleted**
adjective) reduce in numbers, quantity, etc. **2**
exhaust. □ **depletion** *noun*.

■ **1** cut, decrease, lessen, reduce. **2** consume,
drain, exhaust, use up.

deplorable /dɪ'plɔːrəb(ə)l/ *adjective* exceedingly bad. □ **deplorably** *adverb*.

■ *colloquial* awful, bad, blameworthy,
discreditable, disgraceful, disreputable, dreadful,
execrable, lamentable, regrettable, reprehensible,
sad, scandalous, shameful, *colloquial* shocking,
unfortunate, unworthy.

deplore /dɪ'plɔː/ *verb* (**-ring**) **1** find deplorable. **2**
regret.

■ **1** see CONDEMN 1. **2** grieve over, lament, mourn,
regret.

deploy /dɪ'plɔɪ/ *verb* **1** spread out (troops) into
line for action. **2** use (arguments etc.) effectively.
□ **deployment** *noun*.

■ **1** arrange, bring into action, distribute, manage,
position. **2** marshal, muster.

deponent /dɪ'pəʊnənt/ *noun* person making
deposition under oath.

depopulate /diː'pɒpjʊleɪt/ *verb* (**-ting**) reduce
population of. □ **depopulation** *noun*.

deport /dɪ'pɔːt/ *verb* **1** remove forcibly or
exile to another country. **2** (**deport oneself**)
behave (well, badly, etc.). □ **deportation**
/diː-/ *noun*.

■ **1** banish, exile, expatriate, expel, remove, send
abroad, *historical* transport.

deportee /diːpɔː'tiː/ *noun* deported person.

deportment *noun* bearing, demeanour.

depose /dɪ'pəʊz/ *verb* (**-sing**) **1** remove from
office; dethrone. **2** (usually + *to, that*) testify on
oath.

■ **1** demote, dethrone, dismiss, displace, get rid of,
oust, remove, topple.

deposit /dɪ'pɒzɪt/ *noun* **1** money in bank
account. **2** thing stored for safe keeping. **3**
payment as pledge or first instalment. **4** returnable sum paid on hire of item. **5** layer of accumulated matter. ● *verb* (**-t-**) **1** entrust for keeping. **2**
pay or leave as deposit. **3** put or lay down.
□ **deposit account** bank account that pays interest but is not usually immediately accessible.

■ *noun* **3** advance payment, down payment, initial
payment, part payment. **5** accumulation, alluvium,
dregs, lees, precipitate, sediment, silt, sludge.
● *verb* **2** bank, pay in, save. **3** drop, dump, lay
down, leave, park, place, put down, set down.

depositary /dɪ'pɒzɪtərɪ/ *noun* (*plural* **-ies**)
person to whom thing is entrusted.

deposition /depə'zɪʃ(ə)n/ *noun* **1** deposing. **2**
sworn evidence. **3** giving of this. **4** depositing.

depositor *noun* person who deposits money,
property, etc.

depository /dɪ'pɒzɪtərɪ/ *noun* (*plural* **-ies**) **1**
storehouse. **2** store (of wisdom etc.). **3** depositary.

depot /'depəʊ/ *noun* **1** military storehouse or
headquarters. **2** place where vehicles, e.g. buses,
are kept. **3** goods yard.

■ **1** arsenal, base, cache, depository, dump,
headquarters, hoard, store, storehouse. **2** garage,
station, terminus.

deprave /dɪ'preɪv/ *verb* (**-ving**) corrupt morally.

■ brutalize, corrupt, debase, degrade, influence,
pervert.

depravity /dɪ'prævɪtɪ/ *noun* (*plural* **-ies**) moral
corruption; wickedness.

deprecate /'deprɪkeɪt/ *verb* (**-ting**) express disapproval of. □ **deprecation** *noun*. **deprecatory**
/-'keɪtərɪ/ *adjective*.

USAGE *Deprecate* is often confused with *depreciate*.

depreciate /dɪ'priːʃɪeɪt/ *verb* (**-ting**) **1** diminish
in value. **2** belittle. □ **depreciatory** /-ʃətərɪ/
adjective.

USAGE *Depreciate* is often confused with *deprecate*.

■ **1** decrease, deflate, drop, fall, go down, lessen,
lower, reduce, slump, weaken. **2** see DISPARAGE.

depreciation *noun* **1** depreciating. **2** decline in
value.

depredation /deprɪ'deɪʃ(ə)n/ *noun* (usually in
plural) despoiling, ravaging.

depress /dɪ'pres/ *verb* **1** make dispirited. **2**
lower; push down. **3** reduce activity of (esp.
trade). **4** (as **depressed** *adjective*) suffering from
depression. □ **depressing** *adjective*. **depress-
ingly** *adverb*.

■ **1** burden, cast down, discourage, dishearten,
dismay, dispirit, enervate, grieve, oppress,
sadden, tire, upset, weary. **3** bring down, deflate,
push down, undermine, weaken. **4** (**depressed**)
see SAD 1. □ **depressing** see SAD 2.

depressant *adjective* reducing activity, esp. of
body function. ● *noun* depressant substance.

depression /dɪ'preʃ(ə)n/ *noun* **1** extreme dejection. **2** long slump. **3** lowering of atmospheric
pressure. **4** hollow or sunken area on a surface.

■ **1** the blues, dejection, desolation, despair, despondency, gloom, glumness, heaviness, hopelessness, low spirits, melancholy, misery, pessimism, sadness, weariness. **2** decline, hard times, recession, slump. **4** cavity, concavity, dent, dimple, dip, excavation, hole, hollow, impression, indentation, pit, recess, rut.

depressive /dɪˈpresɪv/ *adjective* **1** tending towards depression. **2** tending to depress. ● *noun* chronically depressed person.

deprivation /deprɪˈveɪʃ(ə)n/ *noun* depriving, being deprived.

deprive /dɪˈpraɪv/ *verb* (**-ving**) **1** (usually + *of*) prevent from having or enjoying. **2** (as **deprived** *adjective*) lacking what is needed; underprivileged.

■ **1** (*deprive of*) cheat of, deny, dispossess of, refuse, rob of, starve of, strip of, take away, withdraw, withhold. **2** (**deprived**) see POOR 1.

Dept. *abbreviation* Department.

depth *noun* **1** deepness. **2** measure of this. **3** wisdom. **4** intensity. **5** (usually in *plural*) deep, lowest, or inmost part. **6** (usually in *plural*) middle (of winter etc.). **7** (usually in *plural*) abyss. **8** (usually in *plural*) depressed state. □ **depth-charge** bomb exploding under water. **in-depth** thorough; done in depth.

deputation /depjʊˈteɪʃ(ə)n/ *noun* delegation.

depute /dɪˈpjuːt/ *verb* (**-ting**) (often + *to*) **1** delegate (task, authority). **2** authorize as representative.

deputize /ˈdepjʊtaɪz/ *verb* (also **-ise**) (**-zing** or **-sing**) (usually + *for*) act as deputy.

■ (*deputize for*) cover for, do the job of, replace, represent, stand in for, substitute for, take over from, understudy.

deputy /ˈdepjʊtɪ/ *noun* (*plural* **-ies**) **1** person appointed to act for another. **2** parliamentary representative in some countries.

■ **1** agent, ambassador, assistant, delegate, emissary, locum, proxy, relief, replacement, representative, reserve, second in command, spokesperson, stand-in, substitute, supply, surrogate, understudy, vice-captain, vice-president.

deracinate /dɪˈræsɪneɪt/ *verb literary* **1** tear up by roots. **2** obliterate.

derail /diːˈreɪl/ *verb* cause (train etc.) to leave rails. □ **derailment** *noun*.

derange /dɪˈreɪndʒ/ *verb* (**-ging**) (usually as **deranged** *adjective*) make insane. □ **derangement** *noun*.

Derby /ˈdɑːbɪ/ *noun* (*plural* **-ies**) **1** annual horse race at Epsom. **2** similar race or sporting event.

derelict /ˈderɪlɪkt/ *adjective* **1** abandoned. **2** dilapidated. ● *noun* **1** vagrant. **2** abandoned property.

■ *adjective* **1** abandoned, deserted, desolate, forgotten, forlorn, forsaken, neglected, uncared-for, untended. **2** decrepit, dilapidated, ruined, run-down, tumbledown.

dereliction /derɪˈlɪkʃ(ə)n/ *noun* (usually + *of*) neglect (of duty etc.).

deride /dɪˈraɪd/ *verb* (**-ding**) mock. □ **derision** /-ˈrɪʒ-/ *noun*.

de rigueur /də rɪˈɡɜː/ *adjective* required by fashion or etiquette.

derisive /dɪˈraɪsɪv/ *adjective* scoffing, ironical. □ **derisively** *adverb*.

derisory /dɪˈraɪsərɪ/ *adjective* **1** (of sum offered etc.) ridiculously small. **2** derisive.

derivation /derɪˈveɪʃ(ə)n/ *noun* **1** deriving, being derived. **2** origin or formation esp. of word. **3** tracing of this.

■ **1** extraction. **2, 3** ancestry, beginning, descent, etymology, extraction, origin, root, source.

derivative /dɪˈrɪvətɪv/ *adjective* derived, not original. ● *noun* derived word or thing.

derive /dɪˈraɪv/ *verb* (**-ving**) **1** (usually + *from*) get or trace from a source. **2** (+ *from*) arise from. **3** (usually + *from*) assert origin and formation of (word etc.).

■ **1** acquire, collect, *colloquial* crib, draw, extract, gain, gather, get, glean, *colloquial* lift, obtain, pick up, procure, receive, secure, take. **2** see ORIGINATE 1.

dermatitis /dɜːməˈtaɪtɪs/ *noun* inflammation of skin.

dermatology /dɜːməˈtɒlədʒɪ/ *noun* study of skin diseases. □ **dermatological** /-təˈlɒdʒ-/ *adjective*. **dermatologist** *noun*.

derogatory /dɪˈrɒɡətərɪ/ *adjective* disparaging; insulting.

derrick /ˈderɪk/ *noun* **1** crane. **2** framework over oil well etc. for drilling machinery.

derris /ˈderɪs/ *noun* insecticide made from powdered root of tropical plant.

derv *noun* diesel fuel for road vehicles.

dervish /ˈdɜːvɪʃ/ *noun* member of Muslim fraternity vowed to poverty and austerity.

DES *abbreviation historical* Department of Education and Science.

descale /diːˈskeɪl/ *verb* (**-ling**) remove scale from.

descant /ˈdeskænt/ *noun* harmonizing treble melody above basic hymn tune etc.

descend /dɪˈsend/ *verb* **1** come or go down; sink. **2** slope down. **3** (usually + *on*) make sudden attack or visit. **4** (+ *to*) stoop (to unworthy act). **5** be passed on by inheritance. **6** alight from vehicle. □ **be descended from** have as an ancestor.

■ **1** climb down, come down, drop, fall, get down, go down, move down, plummet, plunge, sink, swoop down. **2** decline, dip, incline, slant, slope. **3** (*descend on*) see ATTACK *verb* 1. **6** see ALIGHT² 1. □ **be descended from** see ORIGINATE 1.

descendant /dɪˈsend(ə)nt/ *noun* person etc. descended from another.

■ child, heir, scion, successor; (*descendants*) family, issue, line, lineage, offspring, posterity, progeny, seed.

descent /dɪ'sent/ *noun* **1** act of descending. **2** downward slope. **3** way down. **4** lineage. **5** decline; fall. **6** sudden attack.
■ **1** dive, drop, fall, plunge. **2** declivity, dip, drop, fall, incline, slant, slope. **4** ancestry, background, blood, derivation, extraction, family, genealogy, heredity, lineage, origin, parentage, pedigree, stock, strain. **5** see FALL *noun* 1.

describe /dɪ'skraɪb/ *verb* (**-bing**) **1** state appearance, characteristics, etc. of. **2** (+ *as*) assert to be. **3** draw or move in (curve etc.).
■ **1** characterize, define, delineate, depict, detail, explain, express, give an account of, narrate, outline, picture, portray, present, recount, relate, report, represent, sketch, speak of, tell about. **2** (*describe as*) call, characterize as, depict as, label, portray as, present as, represent as. **3** draw, mark out, trace.

description /dɪ'skrɪpʃ(ə)n/ *noun* **1** describing, being described. **2** sort, kind.
■ **1** account, characterization, commentary, definition, delineation, depiction, explanation, narration, outline, portrait, portrayal, report, representation, sketch, story.

descriptive /dɪ'skrɪptɪv/ *adjective* describing, esp. vividly.
■ colourful, detailed, explanatory, expressive, graphic, illustrative, pictorial, vivid.

descry /dɪ'skraɪ/ *verb* (**-ies**, **-ied**) catch sight of; discern.

desecrate /'desɪkreɪt/ *verb* (**-ting**) violate sanctity of. □ **desecration** *noun*. **desecrator** *noun*.
■ contaminate, corrupt, debase, defile, degrade, dishonour, pollute, profane, treat blasphemously, treat disrespectfully, treat irreverently, vandalize, violate, vitiate.

desegregate /diː'segrɪgeɪt/ *verb* (**-ting**) abolish racial segregation in. □ **desegregation** *noun*.

deselect /diː'sɪ'lekt/ *verb* reject (esp. sitting MP) in favour of another. □ **deselection** *noun*.

desensitize /diː'sensɪtaɪz/ *verb* (also **-ise**) (**-zing** or **-sing**) reduce or destroy sensitivity of. □ **desensitization** *noun*.

desert[1] /dɪ'zɜːt/ *verb* **1** leave without intending to return. **2** (esp. as **deserted** *adjective*) forsake, abandon. **3** run away from military service. □ **deserter** *noun* *Military*. **desertion** *noun*.
■ **1, 2** abandon, betray, forsake, give up, jilt, leave, leave in the lurch, maroon, quit, rat on, renounce, strand, vacate, walk out on; (**deserted**) see EMPTY *adjective* 2, LONELY 3. **3** abscond, decamp, defect, go absent, run away. □ **deserter** absconder, absentee, backslider, betrayer, defector, escapee, fugitive, outlaw, renegade, runaway, traitor, truant, turncoat.

desert[2] /'dezət/ *noun* dry barren, esp. sandy, tract. ● *adjective* **1** barren. **2** uninhabited. □ **desert island** (usually tropical) uninhabited island.

■ *noun* dust bowl, wasteland, wilderness.
● *adjective* **1** arid, barren, dry, infertile, sterile, uncultivated, waterless, wild. **2** desolate, isolated, lonely, unfrequented, uninhabited.

desertification /dɪzɜːtɪfɪ'keɪʃ(ə)n/ *noun* making or becoming a desert.

deserts /dɪ'zɜːts/ *plural noun* deserved reward or punishment.

deserve /dɪ'zɜːv/ *verb* (**-ving**) **1** (often + *to do*) be worthy of (reward, punishment). **2** (as **deserving** *adjective*) (often + *of*) worthy (esp. of help, praise, etc.). □ **deservedly** /-vɪdlɪ/ *adverb*.
■ **1** be good enough for, be worthy of, earn, justify, merit, rate, warrant. **2** (**deserving**) see WORTHY *adjective* 1,2.

desiccate /'desɪkeɪt/ *verb* (**-ting**) remove moisture from, dry out. □ **desiccation** *noun*.

desideratum /dɪzɪdə'rɑːtəm/ *noun* (*plural* **-ta**) something lacking but desirable.

design /dɪ'zaɪn/ *noun* **1** (art of producing) sketch or plan for product. **2** lines or shapes as decoration. **3** layout. **4** established form of product. **5** mental plan; purpose. ● *verb* **1** produce design for. **2** be designer. **3** intend. **4** (as **designing** *adjective*) crafty, scheming. □ **have designs on** plan to take, seduce, etc.
■ *noun* **1** blueprint, conception, draft, drawing, model, pattern, plan, proposal, prototype, sketch. **3** arrangement, composition, configuration, form, layout, pattern, shape. **4** mark, style, type, version. **5** aim, end, goal, intention, object, objective, purpose, scheme; (*have designs*) see PLOT *verb* 2.
● *verb* **1** conceive, construct, contrive, create, delineate, devise, draft, draw, draw up, fashion, form, invent, lay out, make, map out, originate, outline, plan, project, propose, shape, sketch, *colloquial* think up. **3** intend, mean, plan, plot, purpose. **4** (**designing**) see CRAFTY.

designate *verb* /'dezɪgneɪt/ (**-ting**) **1** (often + *as*) appoint to office or function. **2** specify. **3** (often + *as*) describe as. ● *adjective* /'dezɪgnət/ (after noun) appointed but not yet installed.

designation /dezɪg'neɪʃ(ə)n/ *noun* **1** name or title. **2** designating.

designedly /dɪ'zaɪnɪdlɪ/ *adverb* intentionally.

designer *noun* person who designs e.g. clothing, machines, theatre sets; draughtsman. ● *adjective* bearing label of famous fashion designer; prestigious. □ **designer drug** synthetic equivalent of illegal drug.
■ *noun* architect, artist, author, contriver, creator, deviser, inventor, originator.

desirable /dɪ'zaɪərəb(ə)l/ *adjective* **1** worth having or doing. **2** sexually attractive. □ **desirability** *noun*.

desire /dɪ'zaɪə/ *noun* **1** unsatisfied longing. **2** expression of this; request. **3** thing desired. **4** sexual appetite. ● *verb* (**-ring**) **1** (often + *to do*, *that*) long for. **2** request.

■ *noun* **1** ache, ambition, appetite, covetousness, craving, cupidity, fancy, hankering, hunger, itch, longing, thirst, urge, want, wish, yearning, *colloquial* yen. **2** request, requirement, want, wish. **4** ardour, *formal* concupiscence, libido, love, lust, passion. ● *verb* **1** ache for, aspire to, covet, crave, dream of, *colloquial* fancy, hanker after, *colloquial* have a yen for, hope for, hunger for, itch for, like, long for, lust after, pine for, prefer, set one's heart on, set one's sights on, thirst for, want, wish for, yearn for. **2** ask for, request, require.

desirous /dɪ'spra/ *adjective* **1** (usually + *of*) desiring, wanting. **2** hoping.

desist /dɪ'zɪst/ *verb* (often + *from*) cease.

desk *noun* **1** piece of furniture with writing surface, and often drawers. **2** counter in hotel, bank, etc. **3** section of newspaper office.

desktop *noun* **1** working surface of desk. **2** computer for use on ordinary desk. □ **desktop publishing** printing with desktop computer and high-quality printer.

desolate *adjective* /'desələt/ **1** left alone. **2** uninhabited; dreary. **3** forlorn. ● *verb* /'desəleɪt/ (**-ting**) **1** depopulate; devastate. **2** (esp. as **desolated** *adjective*) make wretched. □ **desolately** /-lətlɪ/ *adverb*. **desolation** *noun*.

■ *adjective* **1** abandoned, alone, bereft, companionless, deserted, forsaken, isolated, lonely, neglected, solitary. **2** bare, barren, bleak, depressing, deserted, dismal, dreary, empty, forsaken, gloomy, godforsaken, inhospitable, isolated, lonely, remote, unfrequented, uninhabited, wild, windswept. **3** cheerless, dejected, depressed, despairing, disconsolate, distressed, forlorn, inconsolable, melancholy, miserable, sad, suicidal, unhappy, wretched.

despair /dɪ'speə/ *noun* **1** loss or absence of hope. **2** cause of this. ● *verb* (often + *of*) lose all hope.

■ *noun* **1** dejection, depression, desperation, despondency, hopelessness, misery, pessimism, resignation, wretchedness. ● *verb* give up, lose heart, lose hope.

despatch = DISPATCH.

desperado /despə'rɑ:dəʊ/ *noun* (*plural* **-es** or *US* **-s**) desperate or reckless criminal etc.

desperate /'despərət/ *adjective* **1** reckless from despair; violent and lawless. **2** extremely dangerous or serious. **3** (usually + *for*) needing or desiring very much. □ **desperately** *adverb*. **desperation** *noun*.

■ **1** at one's wits' end, beyond hope, dangerous, despairing, foolhardy, impetuous, rash, reckless, violent, wild, wretched. **2** acute, bad, critical, dangerous, drastic, grave, hopeless, irretrievable, pressing, serious, severe, urgent. **3** see ANXIOUS 3.

despicable /'despɪkəb(ə)l, dɪ'spɪk-/ *adjective* contemptible. □ **despicably** *adverb*.

despise /dɪ'spaɪz/ *verb* (**-sing**) regard as inferior or contemptible.

■ be contemptuous of, deride, disdain, feel contempt for, hate, have a low opinion of, look down on, *colloquial* put down, scorn, sneer at, spurn, undervalue.

despite /dɪ'spaɪt/ *preposition* in spite of.

despoil /dɪ'spɔɪl/ *verb* (often + *of*) plunder, rob. □ **despoliation** /-spəʊlɪ-/ *noun*.

despondent /dɪ'spɒnd(ə)nt/ *adjective* in low spirits; dejected. □ **despondence** *noun*. **despondency** *noun*. **despondently** *adverb*.

■ dejected, depressed, discouraged, disheartened, down, downcast, *colloquial* down in the mouth, melancholy, miserable, morose, pessimistic, sad, sorrowful.

despot /'despɒt/ *noun* **1** absolute ruler. **2** tyrant. □ **despotic** /-'spɒt-/ *adjective*.

■ □ **despotic** absolute, arbitrary, authoritarian, autocratic, dictatorial, domineering, oppressive, totalitarian, tyrannical.

despotism /'despətɪz(ə)m/ *noun* rule by despot.

dessert /dɪ'zɜ:t/ *noun* sweet course of a meal. □ **dessertspoon 1** medium-sized spoon for dessert. **2** (also **dessertspoonful**) amount held by this.

destabilize /di:'steɪbɪlaɪz/ *verb* (also **-ise**) (**-zing** or **-sing**) **1** make unstable. **2** subvert (esp. foreign government). □ **destabilization** *noun*.

destination /destɪ'neɪʃ(ə)n/ *noun* place to which person or thing is going.

■ goal, objective, purpose, stopping place, target, terminus.

destine /'destɪn/ *verb* (**-ning**) (often + *to, for, to do*) appoint; preordain; intend. □ **be destined to** be fated to. □ **destined** *adjective*.

■ appoint, doom, fate, intend, ordain, predestine, preordain. □ **be destined to** be bound to, be certain to, be doomed to, be fated to, be meant to. □ **destined** ineluctable, inescapable, inevitable, unavoidable.

destiny /'destɪnɪ/ *noun* (*plural* **-ies**) **1** fate. **2** this as power.

■ chance, doom, fate, fortune, *Buddhism & Hinduism* karma, kismet, lot, luck, portion, providence.

destitute /'destɪtju:t/ *adjective* **1** without food or shelter etc. **2** (usually + *of*) lacking. □ **destitution** /-'tju:-/ *noun*.

■ **1** bankrupt, deprived, down and out, homeless, impecunious, impoverished, *formal* indigent, insolvent, needy, penniless, poor, poverty-stricken, *slang* skint.

destroy /dɪ'strɔɪ/ *verb* **1** pull or break down; make useless. **2** end existence of. **3** kill. **4** ruin financially. **5** defeat.

■ **1** break down, burst, *colloquial* bust, crush, decimate, demolish, devastate, devour, dismantle, flatten, fragment, knock down, lay waste, level, nullify, pull down, *colloquial* pulverize, raze, ruin, sabotage, sack, scuttle, shatter, smash, undo, uproot, wipe out, wreck, write off. **2** abolish, annihilate, cancel, dispose of, *colloquial* do away with, eliminate, end, eradicate, erase, exterminate, extinguish, extirpate, finish off, get rid of, liquidate, put an end to, put out of existence, root out, stamp out, vaporize, wipe out. **3** see KILL *verb* 1. **5** see DEFEAT *verb* 1.

destroyer /dɪ'strɔɪə/ *noun* **1** fast medium-sized warship. **2** person or thing that destroys.

destruct /dɪ'strʌkt/ *verb* destroy or be destroyed deliberately. □ **destructible** *adjective*.

destruction *noun* destroying, being destroyed.

■ annihilation, damage, decimation, demolition, depredation, devastation, elimination, end, eradication, erasure, extermination, extinction, extirpation, havoc, holocaust, killing, liquidation, overthrow, pulling down, ruin, ruination, shattering, smashing, undoing, uprooting, wiping out, wrecking.

destructive *adjective* **1** destroying or tending to destroy. **2** negatively critical.

■ **1** baleful, baneful, calamitous, catastrophic, damaging, dangerous, deadly, deleterious, detrimental, devastating, disastrous, fatal, harmful, injurious, internecine, lethal, malignant, pernicious, pestilential, ruinous, violent. **2** adverse, antagonistic, negative.

desuetude /dɪ'sjuːɪtjuːd/ *noun formal* state of disuse.

desultory /'dezəltərɪ/ *adjective* **1** constantly turning from one subject to another. **2** unmethodical.

detach /dɪ'tætʃ/ *verb* **1** (often + *from*) unfasten and remove. **2** send (troops) on separate mission. **3** (as **detached** *adjective*) impartial, unemotional. **4** (as **detached** *adjective*) (of house) standing separate. □ **detachable** *adjective*.

■ **1** cut loose, cut off, disconnect, disengage, disentangle, free, isolate, part, pull off, release, remove, segregate, separate, sever, take off, tear off, uncouple, undo, unfasten, unfix, unhitch. **3** (**detached**) see IMPARTIAL, ALOOF. **4** (**detached**) see SEPARATE *adjective*.

detachment *noun* **1** indifference. **2** impartiality. **3** detaching, being detached. **4** troops etc. detached for special duty.

detail /'diːteɪl/ *noun* **1** small separate item or particular. **2** these collectively. **3** minor or intricate decoration. **4** small part of picture etc. shown alone. **5** small military detachment. ● *verb* **1** give particulars of; relate in detail. **2** (as **detailed** *adjective*) containing many details. **3** (as **detailed** *adjective*) itemized. **4** assign for special duty. □ **in detail** item by item; minutely.

■ *noun* **1** aspect, circumstance, complexity, complication, component, element, fact, factor, feature, ingredient, intricacy, item, nicety, particular, point, refinement, respect, specific, technicality; (*details*) minutiae. ● *verb* **2** (**detailed**) complete, complex, comprehensive, descriptive, exact, exhaustive, full, fussy, hair-splitting, intricate, itemized, minute, particularized, specific.

detain /dɪ'teɪn/ *verb* **1** keep waiting; delay. **2** keep in custody. □ **detainment** *noun*.

■ **1** *colloquial* buttonhole, delay, hinder, hold up, impede, keep, keep waiting, restrain, retard, slow, waylay. **2** arrest, capture, confine, hold, imprison, intern, jail.

detainee /diːteɪ'niː/ *noun* person kept in custody, esp. for political reasons.

detect /dɪ'tekt/ *verb* **1** discover. **2** perceive. □ **detectable** *adjective*. **detection** *noun*. **detector** *noun*.

■ **1** discover, expose, ferret out, find, locate, reveal, track down, uncover, unearth, unmask. **2** ascertain, become aware of, diagnose, discern, feel, hear, identify, note, notice, observe, perceive, recognize, scent, see, sense, sight, smell, sniff out, *colloquial* spot, spy, taste.

detective /dɪ'tektɪv/ *noun* person, usually police officer, investigating crime etc.

■ investigator, policeman, policewoman, *colloquial* private eye, *colloquial* sleuth, *colloquial* snooper.

détente /deɪ'tɑ̃t/ *noun* relaxing of strained international relations. [French]

detention /dɪ'tenʃ(ə)n/ *noun* detaining, being detained. □ **detention centre** short-term prison for young offenders.

■ captivity, confinement, custody, imprisonment, incarceration, internment.

deter /dɪ'tɜː/ *verb* (**-rr-**) (often + *from*) discourage or prevent, esp. through fear.

■ check, daunt, discourage, dismay, dissuade, frighten off, hinder, impede, intimidate, obstruct, prevent, put off, repel, send away, stop, *colloquial* turn off, warn off.

detergent /dɪ'tɜːdʒ(ə)nt/ *noun* synthetic cleansing agent used with water. ● *adjective* cleansing.

deteriorate /dɪ'tɪərɪəreɪt/ *verb* (**-ting**) become worse. □ **deterioration** *noun*.

■ crumble, decay, decline, degenerate, depreciate, disintegrate, fall off, get worse, lapse, relapse, slip, weaken, worsen.

determinant /dɪ'tɜːmɪnənt/ *noun* decisive factor.

determinate /dɪ'tɜːmɪnət/ *adjective* **1** limited. **2** of definite scope or nature.

determination /dɪtɜːmɪ'neɪʃ(ə)n/ *noun* **1** resolute purpose. **2** deciding, determining.

■ **1** backbone, commitment, courage, dedication, doggedness, drive, firmness, fortitude, *colloquial* grit, *colloquial* guts, perseverance, persistence, pertinacity, resoluteness, resolution, resolve, single-mindedness, spirit, steadfastness, stubbornness, tenacity, will-power.

determine /dɪ'tɜːmɪn/ *verb* (**-ning**) **1** find out precisely. **2** settle, decide. **3** (+ *to do*) resolve to. **4** be decisive factor in.

■ **1** ascertain, discover, establish, find out, identify. **2** arbitrate, choose, clinch, conclude, decide, decide on, judge, resolve, select, settle. **4** affect, condition, dictate, govern, influence, regulate.

determined *adjective* resolute. □ **be determined** (usually + *to do*) be resolved. □ **determinedly** *adverb*.

■ adamant, assertive, bent (*on success*), certain, convinced, decided, decisive, definite, dogged, firm, insistent, intent, obstinate, persistent, pertinacious, purposeful, resolute, resolved, single-minded, steadfast, strong-minded, strong-willed, stubborn, sure, tenacious, tough, unwavering.

determinism /dɪˈtɜːmɪnɪz(ə)m/ *noun* theory that action is determined by forces independent of will. □ **determinist** *noun & adjective*. **deterministic** /-ˈnɪs-/ *adjective*.

deterrent /dɪˈterənt/ *adjective* deterring. ● *noun* thing that deters (esp. nuclear weapon). □ **deterrence** *noun*.

■ *noun* barrier, caution, check, curb, difficulty, discouragement, disincentive, hindrance, impediment, obstacle, restraint, threat, *colloquial* turn-off, warning.

detest /dɪˈtest/ *verb* hate, loathe. □ **detestation** /diːtesˈteɪʃ(ə)n/ *noun*.

■ abhor, abominate, despise, execrate, hate, loathe.

detestable /dɪˈtestəb(ə)l/ *adjective* hated, loathed.

dethrone /diːˈθrəʊn/ *verb* (**-ning**) remove from throne or high regard. □ **dethronement** *noun*.

detonate /ˈdetəneɪt/ *verb* (**-ting**) **1** set off (explosive charge). **2** be set off. □ **detonation** *noun*.

detonator *noun* device for detonating.

detour /ˈdiːtʊə/ *noun* divergence from usual route; roundabout course.

■ deviation, diversion, indirect route, roundabout route; (*make a detour*) see DEVIATE.

detoxify /diːˈtɒksɪfaɪ/ *verb* (**-ies**, **-ied**) remove poison or harmful substances from. □ **detoxification** *noun*.

detract /dɪˈtrækt/ *verb* (+ *from*) diminish. □ **detraction** *noun*.

■ (*detract from*) diminish, lessen, lower, reduce, take away from.

detractor *noun* person who criticizes unfairly.

detriment /ˈdetrɪmənt/ *noun* **1** damage, harm. **2** cause of this. □ **detrimental** /-ˈmen-/ *adjective*.

■ □ detrimental damaging, deleterious, disadvantageous, harmful, hurtful, inimical, injurious, prejudicial, unfavourable.

detritus /dɪˈtraɪtəs/ *noun* **1** gravel, rock, etc. produced by erosion. **2** debris.

de **trop** /də ˈtrəʊ/ *adjective* superfluous; in the way. [French]

deuce[1] /djuːs/ *noun* **1** two on dice or cards. **2** *Tennis* score of 40 all.

deuce[2] /djuːs/ *noun* (**the deuce**) (in exclamations) the Devil.

deuterium /djuːˈtɪərɪəm/ *noun* stable isotope of hydrogen with mass about twice that of the usual isotope.

Deutschmark /ˈdɔɪtʃmɑːk/ *noun* chief monetary unit of Germany.

devalue /diːˈvæljuː/ *verb* (**-ues**, **-ued**, **-uing**) reduce value of, esp. currency relative to others or to gold. □ **devaluation** *noun*.

devastate /ˈdevəsteɪt/ *verb* (**-ting**) **1** lay waste; cause great destruction to. **2** (often as **devastated** *adjective*) overwhelm with shock or grief. □ **devastation** *noun*.

■ **1** demolish, destroy, flatten, lay waste, level, obliterate, overwhelm, ravage, raze, ruin, sack, waste, wreck. **2** see DISMAY *verb*.

devastating *adjective* **1** crushingly effective; overwhelming. **2** *colloquial* stunningly beautiful. □ **devastatingly** *adverb*.

develop /dɪˈveləp/ *verb* (**-p-**) **1** make or become fuller, bigger, or more elaborate, etc. **2** bring or come to active, visible, or mature state. **3** begin to exhibit or suffer from. **4** build on (land). **5** convert (land) to new use. **6** treat (photographic film) to make image visible. □ **developing country** poor or primitive country. □ **developer** *noun*.

■ **1** amplify, augment, blow up, branch out, build up, diversify, elaborate (on), enlarge (on), evolve, expand (on), expatiate (on), extend, grow, increase, swell, unfold, work up. **2** advance, age, arise, blossom, come into existence, cultivate, evolve, flourish, foster, get better, grow, improve, mature, progress, ripen. **3** acquire, contract, get, pick up.

development *noun* **1** developing, being developed. **2** stage of growth or advancement. **3** newly developed thing, event, etc. **4** area of developed land, esp. with buildings. □ **developmental** /-ˈment(ə)l/ *adjective*.

■ **1** advance, betterment, building, change, conversion, enlargement, evolution, expansion, exploitation, extension, furtherance, gain, growth, improvement, increase, progress, promotion, regeneration, reinforcement, spread. **3** happening, incident, occurrence, outcome, result, upshot.

deviant /ˈdiːvɪənt/ *adjective* deviating from normal, esp. sexual, behaviour. ● *noun* deviant person or thing. □ **deviance** *noun*. **deviancy** *noun* (*plural* **-ies**).

deviate /ˈdiːvɪeɪt/ *verb* (**-ting**) (often + *from*) turn aside; diverge. □ **deviation** *noun*.

■ branch off, depart, digress, diverge, drift, err, go astray, make a detour, stray, swerve, turn aside, turn off, vary, veer, wander.

device /dɪˈvaɪs/ *noun* **1** thing made or adapted for particular purpose. **2** scheme, trick. **3** heraldic design. □ **leave (person) to his or her own devices** leave (person) to do as he or she wishes.

■ **1** apparatus, appliance, contraption, contrivance, gadget, implement, instrument, invention, machine, tool, utensil. **2** dodge, expedient, gambit, gimmick, manoeuvre, plan, ploy, ruse, scheme, stratagem, stunt, tactic, trick, wile. **3** badge, design, figure, logo, motif, sign, symbol, token.

devil /ˈdev(ə)l/ *noun* **1** (usually **the Devil**) Satan; supreme spirit of evil. **2** personified evil. **3** mischievously clever person. ● *verb* (**-ll-**; *US* **-l-**) (usually as **devilled** *adjective*) cooked with hot spices. □ **devil-may-care** cheerful and reckless. **devil's advocate** person who tests proposition by arguing against it.

■ *noun* **3** demon, fiend, imp, spirit.

devilish *adjective* **1** of or like a devil. **2** mischievous. ● *adverb colloquial* very. □ **devilishly** *adverb*.

■ *adjective* **1** demoniac(al), demonic, diabolic(al), evil, fiendish, hellish, infernal, inhuman, satanic. **2** see MISCHIEVOUS (MISCHIEF).

devilment *noun* mischief; wild spirits.

devilry /ˈdevəlrɪ/ *noun* (*plural* **-ies**) **1** wickedness; reckless mischief. **2** black magic.

devious /ˈdiːvɪəs/ *adjective* **1** not straightforward, underhand. **2** winding, circuitous. □ **deviously** *adverb*. **deviousness** *noun*.

■ **1** calculating, cunning, deceitful, dishonest, evasive, insincere, misleading, scheming, slippery, sly, sneaky, treacherous, underhand, wily. **2** circuitous, crooked, deviating, indirect, periphrastic, roundabout, sinuous, tortuous, wandering, winding.

devise /dɪˈvaɪz/ *verb* (**-sing**) **1** plan or invent. **2** *Law* leave (real estate) by will. □ **deviser** *noun*.

■ **1** arrange, conceive, concoct, contrive, *colloquial* cook up, create, design, engineer, form, formulate, frame, imagine, invent, make up, plan, plot, prepare, project, scheme, think out, *colloquial* think up, work out.

devoid /dɪˈvɔɪd/ *adjective* (+ *of*) lacking, free from.

devolution /diːvəˈluːʃ(ə)n/ *noun* delegation of power esp. to local or regional administration. □ **devolutionist** *noun & adjective*.

devolve /dɪˈvɒlv/ *verb* (**-ving**) **1** (+ *on, upon*, etc.) (of duties etc.) pass or be passed to another. **2** (+ *on, to, upon*) (of property) descend to.

devote /dɪˈvəʊt/ *verb* (**-ting**) (+ *to*) apply or give over to (particular activity etc.).

devoted *adjective* loving, loyal. □ **devotedly** *adverb*. **devotedness** *noun*.

■ committed, dedicated, enthusiastic, faithful, loving, loyal, staunch, true, unswerving, wholehearted, zealous.

devotee /devəʊˈtiː/ *noun* (usually + *of*) enthusiast, supporter. **2** pious person.

■ **1** *colloquial* addict, aficionado, *colloquial* buff, enthusiast, fan, follower, *colloquial* freak, supporter.

devotion /dɪˈvəʊʃ(ə)n/ *noun* **1** (usually + *to*) great love or loyalty. **2** worship. **3** (in *plural*) prayers. **4** devoutness. □ **devotional** *adjective*.

■ **1** allegiance, attachment, commitment, dedication, devotedness, enthusiasm, fanaticism, fervour, love, loyalty, zeal. **4** see PIETY.

devour /dɪˈvaʊə/ *verb* **1** eat voraciously. **2** (of fire etc.) engulf, destroy. **3** take in greedily (with eyes or ears).

■ **1** bolt, *jocular* demolish, eat up, gobble, gorge, gulp, guzzle, swallow, wolf. **2** consume, demolish, destroy, devastate, engulf, ravage.

devout /dɪˈvaʊt/ *adjective* earnestly religious or sincere. □ **devoutly** *adverb*. **devoutness** *noun*.

■ God-fearing, godly, holy, pious, religious, sincere, spiritual.

dew *noun* **1** condensed water vapour forming on cool surfaces at night. **2** similar glistening moisture. □ **dewberry** fruit like blackberry. **dew-claw** rudimentary inner toe on some dogs. **dewdrop** drop of dew. **dew point** temperature at which dew forms. □ **dewy** *adjective* (**-ier, -iest**).

Dewey Decimal system /ˈdjuːɪ/ *noun* system of library classification.

dewlap *noun* fold of loose skin hanging from throat esp. in cattle.

dexter /ˈdekstə/ *adjective* on or of the right-hand side (observer's left) of a heraldic shield etc.

dexterous /ˈdekstrəs/ *adjective* (also **dextrous**) skilful at handling. □ **dexterity** /-ˈter-/ *noun*. **dexterously** *adverb*.

■ adroit, agile, clever, deft, nimble, quick, sharp, skilful.

dhal /dɑːl/ *noun* (also **dal**) **1** kind of split pulse from India. **2** dish made with this.

dharma /ˈdɑːmə/ *noun* **1** right behaviour. **2** Buddhist truth. **3** Hindu moral law.

dhoti /ˈdəʊtɪ/ *noun* (*plural* **-s**) loincloth worn by male Hindus.

dia. *abbreviation* diameter.

diabetes /daɪəˈbiːtiːz/ *noun* disease in which sugar and starch are not properly absorbed by the body.

diabetic /daɪəˈbetɪk/ *adjective* **1** of or having diabetes. **2** for diabetics. ● *noun* diabetic person.

diabolical /daɪəˈbɒlɪk(ə)l/ *adjective* (also **diabolic**) **1** of the Devil. **2** inhumanly cruel or wicked. **3** extremely bad. □ **diabolically** *adverb*.

■ **1** demoniac(al), demonic, devilish, evil, fiendish, hellish, infernal, inhuman, satanic, wicked. **2** see INHUMAN, WICKED **1**.

diabolism /daɪˈæbəlɪz(ə)m/ *noun* **1** worship of the Devil. **2** sorcery.

diaconate /daɪˈækənət/ *noun* **1** office of deacon. **2** deacons collectively.

diacritic /daɪəˈkrɪtɪk/ *noun* sign (e.g. accent) indicating sound or value of letter.

diacritical *adjective* distinguishing.

diadem /ˈdaɪədem/ *noun* crown.

diaeresis /daɪˈɪərəsɪs/ *noun* (*plural* **-reses** /-siːz/) (*US* **dieresis**) mark (¨) over vowel to show it is sounded separately.

diagnose /ˈdaɪəgˈnəʊz/ *verb* (**-sing**) make diagnosis of.
■ detect, determine, distinguish, find, identify, isolate, name, pinpoint, recognize.

diagnosis /daɪəgˈnəʊsɪs/ *noun* (*plural* **-noses** /-siːz/) identification of disease or fault from symptoms etc.
■ analysis, conclusion, explanation, identification, interpretation, opinion, pronouncement, verdict.

diagnostic /daɪəgˈnɒstɪk/ *adjective* of or assisting diagnosis. ● *noun* symptom.

diagnostics *noun* 1 (treated as *plural*) programs etc. used to identify faults in computing. 2 (treated as *singular*) science of diagnosing disease.

diagonal /daɪˈægən(ə)l/ *adjective* crossing a straight-sided figure from corner to corner, oblique. ● *noun* straight line joining two opposite corners. □ **diagonally** *adverb*.

diagram /ˈdaɪəgræm/ *noun* outline drawing, plan, etc. of thing or process. □ **diagrammatic** /-grəˈmætɪk/ *adjective*.
■ chart, drawing, figure, flow chart, graph, illustration, outline, picture, plan, representation, sketch, table.

dial /ˈdaɪəl/ *noun* 1 plate with scale and pointer for measuring. 2 face of clock or watch. 3 numbered disc on telephone for making connection. 4 disc on television etc. for selecting channel etc. ● *verb* (**-ll-**; *US* **-l-**) select (telephone number) with dial. □ **dialling tone** sound indicating that telephone caller may dial.
■ *noun* 1, 2 digital display, face, instrument, meter.

dialect /ˈdaɪəlekt/ *noun* regional form of language (see panel).
■ accent, argot, brogue, cant, creole, idiom, jargon, language, patois, phraseology, pronunciation, slang, speech, tongue, vernacular.

dialectic /daɪəˈlektɪk/ *noun* 1 process or situation involving contradictions or conflict of opposites and their resolution. 2 = DIALECTICS.

dialectical *adjective* of dialectic. □ **dialectical materialism** Marxist theory that historical events arise from conflicting economic (and therefore social) conditions. □ **dialectically** *adverb*.

dialectics *noun* (treated as *singular* or *plural*) art of investigating truth by discussion and logic.

dialogue /ˈdaɪəlɒg/ *noun* (*US* **dialog**) 1 conversation, esp. in a play, novel, etc. 2 discussion between people of different opinions.
■ 1 chat, *slang* chinwag, *literary* colloquy, communication, conversation, discourse, exchange, interchange, intercourse, oral communication, talk, tête-à-tête. 2 *literary* colloquy, communication, conference, conversation, debate, discussion, duologue, meeting, talk.

dialysis /daɪˈæləsɪs/ *noun* (*plural* **-lyses** /-siːz/) 1 separation of particles in liquid by differences in their ability to pass through membrane. 2 purification of blood by this technique.

diamanté /dɪəˈmɑːteɪ/ *adjective* decorated with synthetic diamonds etc.

diameter /daɪˈæmɪtə/ *noun* 1 straight line passing through centre of circle or sphere to its edges. 2 transverse measurement.

diametrical /daɪəˈmetrɪk(ə)l/ *adjective* (also **diametric**) 1 of or along diameter. 2 (of opposites) absolute. □ **diametrically** *adverb*.

diamond /ˈdaɪəmənd/ *noun* 1 transparent very hard precious stone. 2 rhombus. 3 playing card of suit marked with red rhombuses. □ **diamond jubilee, wedding** 60th (or 75th) anniversary of reign or wedding.

diapason /daɪəˈpeɪz(ə)n/ *noun* 1 compass of musical instrument or voice. 2 either of two main organ stops.

diaper /ˈdaɪəpə/ *noun* US baby's nappy.

diaphanous /daɪˈæfənəs/ *adjective* (of fabric etc.) light and almost transparent.

diaphragm /ˈdaɪəfræm/ *noun* 1 muscular partititon between thorax and abdomen in mammals. 2 = DUTCH CAP. 3 vibrating disc in microphone, telephone, loudspeaker, etc. 4 device for varying aperture of camera lens.

diapositive /daɪəˈpɒzɪtɪv/ *noun* positive photographic transparency.

diarist /ˈdaɪərɪst/ *noun* person famous for keeping diary.

diarrhoea /daɪəˈrɪə/ *noun* (*US* **diarrhea**) condition of excessively loose and frequent bowel movements.

diary /ˈdaɪərɪ/ *noun* (*plural* **-ies**) 1 daily record of events etc. 2 book for this or for noting future engagements.

··

Dialect

Everyone speaks a particular dialect: that is, a particular type of English distinguished by its vocabulary and its grammar. Different parts of the world and different groups of people speak different dialects: for example, Australians may say *arvo* while others say *afternoon*, and a London Cockney may say *I done it* while most other people say *I did it*. A dialect is not the same thing as an accent, which is the way a person pronounces words.

(See also panel at STANDARD ENGLISH.)

··

■ **1** annals, calendar, chronicle, journal, log, record. **2** appointment book, engagement book, journal, logbook.

Diaspora /daɪˈæspərə/ *noun* **1** dispersion of the Jews. **2** the dispersed Jews.

diatonic /daɪəˈtɒnɪk/ *adjective Music* (of scale etc.) involving only notes of prevailing key.

diatribe /ˈdaɪətraɪb/ *noun* forceful verbal criticism.

diazepam /daɪˈæzɪpæm/ *noun* tranquillizing drug.

dibble /ˈdɪb(ə)l/ *noun* (also **dibber** /ˈdɪbə/) tool for making small holes for planting. ● *verb* (**-ling**) plant with dibble.

dice *noun* (*plural* same) **1** small cube marked on each face with 1–6 spots, used in games or gambling. **2** game played with dice. ● *verb* (**-cing**) **1** gamble, take risks. **2** cut into small cubes.

dicey /ˈdaɪsɪ/ *adjective* (**dicier**, **diciest**) *slang* risky, unreliable.

dichotomy /daɪˈkɒtəmɪ/ *noun* (*plural* **-ies**) division into two.

dichromatic /daɪkrəʊˈmætɪk/ *adjective* of two colours.

dick[1] *noun colloquial* (esp. in **clever dick**) person.

dick[2] *noun slang* detective.

dickens /ˈdɪkɪnz/ *noun* (**the dickens**) (usually after *how, what, why,* etc.) *colloquial* the Devil.

dicky /ˈdɪkɪ/ *noun* (*plural* **-ies**) *colloquial* false shirt-front. ● *adjective* (**-ier**, **-iest**) *slang* unsound. □ **dicky bow** *colloquial* bow tie.

dicotyledon /daɪkɒtɪˈliːd(ə)n/ *noun* flowering plant with two cotyledons. □ **dicotyledonous** *adjective*.

Dictaphone /ˈdɪktəfəʊn/ *noun proprietary term* machine for recording and playing back dictation for typing.

dictate *verb* /dɪkˈteɪt/ (**-ting**) **1** say or read aloud (material to be recorded etc.). **2** state authoritatively; order peremptorily. ● *noun* /ˈdɪkt-/ (usually in *plural*) authoritative requirement of conscience etc. □ **dictation** *noun*.

■ *verb* **2** command, decree, direct, enforce, give orders, impose, lay down the law, make the rules, ordain, order, prescribe, state categorically.

dictator *noun* **1** usually unelected absolute ruler. **2** omnipotent or domineering person. □ **dictatorship** *noun*.

■ autocrat, Big Brother, despot, tyrant.

dictatorial /dɪktəˈtɔːrɪəl/ *adjective* **1** of or like a dictator. **2** overbearing. □ **dictatorially** *adverb*.

■ **1** absolute, arbitrary, authoritarian, autocratic, despotic, omnipotent, repressive, totalitarian, tyrannical, undemocratic. **2** authoritarian, autocratic, *colloquial* bossy, despotic, dogmatic, dominant, domineering, illiberal, imperious, intolerant, oppressive, overbearing.

diction /ˈdɪkʃ(ə)n/ *noun* manner of enunciation.

dictionary /ˈdɪkʃənərɪ/ *noun* (*plural* **-ies**) **1** book listing (usually alphabetically) and explaining words of a language, or giving corresponding words in another language. **2** similar book of terms for reference.

■ **1** glossary, lexicon, thesaurus, vocabulary. **2** concordance, encyclopedia.

dictum /ˈdɪktəm/ *noun* (*plural* **dicta** or **-s**) **1** formal expression of opinion. **2** a saying.

did *past of* DO[1].

didactic /dɪˈdæktɪk/ *adjective* **1** meant to instruct. **2** (of person) tediously pedantic. □ **didactically** *adverb*. **didacticism** /-sɪz(ə)m/ *noun*.

■ **1** see INSTRUCTIVE. **2** lecturing, pedagogical, pedantic, schoolmasterly.

diddle /ˈdɪd(ə)l/ *verb* (**-ling**) *colloquial* swindle.

didgeridoo /dɪdʒərɪˈduː/ *noun* long tubular Australian Aboriginal musical instrument.

didn't /ˈdɪd(ə)nt/ did not.

die[1] /daɪ/ *verb* (**dying** /ˈdaɪɪŋ/) **1** cease to live or exist. **2** fade away. **3** (of fire) go out. **4** (+ *on*) cease to live or function while in the presence or charge of (person). **5** (+ *of, from, with*) be exhausted or tormented. □ **be dying for, to** desire greatly. **die down** become less loud or strong. **die hard** (of habits etc.) die reluctantly. **die off** die one after another. **die out** become extinct; cease to exist.

■ **1** *slang* bite the dust, breathe one's last, *formal* cease to exist, come to the end, depart, drown, expire, fall, *colloquial* give up the ghost, *slang* kick the bucket, lay down one's life, lose one's life, pass away, *slang* peg out, perish, *slang* snuff it, starve. **2** decline, decrease, die away, disappear, droop, dwindle, ebb, end, fade, fail, fizzle out, languish, lessen, peter out, stop, subside, vanish, wane, weaken, wilt, wither.

die[2] /daɪ/ *noun* **1** engraved device for stamping coins etc. **2** (*plural* **dice**) a dice. □ **die-casting** process or product of casting from metal moulds.

diehard /ˈdaɪhɑːd/ *noun* conservative or stubborn person.

dielectric /daɪɪˈlektrɪk/ *adjective* not conducting electricity. ● *noun* dielectric substance.

dieresis *US* = DIAERESIS.

diesel /ˈdiːz(ə)l/ *noun* **1** (in full **diesel engine**) internal-combustion engine in which heat produced by compression of air in the cylinder ignites the fuel. **2** vehicle driven by or fuel for diesel engine. □ **diesel-electric** driven by electric current from diesel-engined generator. **diesel oil** petroleum fraction used in diesel engines.

diet[1] /ˈdaɪət/ *noun* **1** habitual food. **2** prescribed food. ● *verb* (**-t-**) keep to special diet, esp. to slim. □ **dietary** *adjective*. **dieter** *noun*.

■ *noun* **1** fare, food, intake, nourishment, nutriment, nutrition, sustenance. ● *verb* lose weight, ration oneself, slim.

diet[2] /'daɪət/ *noun* **1** legislative assembly. **2** *historical* congress.

dietetic /daɪə'tetɪk/ *adjective* of diet and nutrition.

dietetics *plural noun* (usually treated as *singular*) study of diet and nutrition.

dietitian /daɪə'tɪʃ(ə)n/ *noun* (also **dietician**) expert in dietetics.

differ /'dɪfə/ *verb* **1** (often + *from*) be unlike or distinguishable. **2** (often + *with*) disagree.

■ **1** be different, be distinct, contrast, deviate, diverge, show differences, vary. **2** argue, be at odds, be at variance, clash, conflict, contradict, disagree, dispute, dissent, fall out, have a difference, oppose each other, quarrel, take issue with each other.

difference /'dɪfrəns/ *noun* **1** being different or unlike. **2** degree of this. **3** way in which things differ; thing which distinguishes. **4** quantity by which amounts differ. **5** remainder after subtraction. **6** disagreement. □ **make a (or all the, no, etc.) difference** have significant (or very significant, no, etc.) effect. **with a difference** having new or unusual feature.

■ **1, 2** alteration, change, comparison, contrast, development, deviation, differential, differentiation, discrepancy, disparity, dissimilarity, distinction, diversity, incompatibility, incongruity, inconsistency, inequality, modification, nuance, unlikeness, variation, variety. **3** see DISTINCTION 2. **4** deficit, differential, discrepancy, disparity, gap, margin. **6** argument, clash, conflict, controversy, debate, disagreement, disharmony, dispute, dissent, quarrel, strife, tiff, wrangle.

different /'dɪfrənt/ *adjective* **1** (often + *from*, *to*) unlike; of another nature. **2** separate. **3** unusual. □ **differently** *adverb*.

USAGE The preferred phrase is *different from*; but *different to* is common in informal use.

■ **1, 2** altered, assorted, changed, clashing, conflicting, contradictory, contrasting, deviating, discordant, discrepant, disparate, dissimilar, distinct, distinguishable, divergent, diverse, heterogeneous, ill-matched, incompatible, inconsistent, miscellaneous, mixed, multifarious, opposed, opposite, poles apart, several, sundry, unlike, varied, various. **3** abnormal, anomalous, atypical, bizarre, distinctive, eccentric, extraordinary, fresh, individual, irregular, new, original, particular, peculiar, personal, revolutionary, separate, singular, special, specific, strange, uncommon, unconventional, unique, unorthodox, unusual.

differential /dɪfə'renʃ(ə)l/ *adjective* **1** constituting or relating to specific difference. **2** of, exhibiting, or depending on a difference. **3** *Mathematics* relating to infinitesimal differences. ● *noun* difference, esp. between rates of interest or wage-rates. □ **differential calculus** method of calculating rates of change, maximum or minimum values, etc. **differential gear** gear enabling wheels to revolve at different speeds on corners.

differentiate /dɪfə'renʃɪeɪt/ *verb* (**-ting**) **1** constitute difference between or in. **2** distinguish. **3** become different. □ **differentiation** *noun*.

■ **2** contrast, discriminate, distinguish, tell apart.

difficult /'dɪfɪk(ə)lt/ *adjective* **1** hard to do or understand. **2** hard to deal with; troublesome.

■ **1** (*difficult task*) arduous, awkward, back-breaking, burdensome, challenging, daunting, demanding, exacting, exhausting, formidable, gruelling, heavy, Herculean, *colloquial* killing, laborious, onerous, punishing, rigorous, severe, strenuous, taxing, tough, uphill; (*difficult problem*) abstruse, advanced, baffling, complex, complicated, deep, *colloquial* dodgy, enigmatic, hard, intractable, intricate, involved, knotty, nasty, obscure, perplexing, problematical, puzzling, thorny, ticklish, tricky. **2** annoying, disruptive, fussy, headstrong, intractable, obstinate, obstreperous, refractory, stubborn, *colloquial* tiresome, troublesome, trying, uncooperative, unfriendly, unhelpful, unresponsive, unruly.

difficulty /'dɪfɪkəltɪ/ *noun* (*plural* **-ies**) **1** being difficult. **2** difficult thing; hindrance. **3** (often in *plural*) distress, esp. financial.

■ **1** adversity, hardship, perplexity, tribulation, trouble. **2** adversity, challenge, complication, *disputed* dilemma, embarrassment, enigma, hardship, hiccup, hindrance, hurdle, impediment, obstacle, perplexity, pitfall, problem, puzzle, quandary, snag, stumbling block, tribulation, trouble, vexed question. **3** (*difficulties*) fix, *colloquial* jam, mess, *colloquial* pickle, plight, predicament, *colloquial* spot, straits, trouble.

diffident /'dɪfɪd(ə)nt/ *adjective* lacking self-confidence. □ **diffidence** *noun*. **diffidently** *adverb*.

■ backward, bashful, coy, distrustful, doubtful, fearful, hesitant, hesitating, inhibited, insecure, introvert, meek, modest, nervous, private, reluctant, reserved, retiring, self-effacing, sheepish, shrinking, shy, tentative, timid, timorous, unadventurous, unassuming, underconfident, unsure, withdrawn.

diffract /dɪ'frækt/ *verb* break up (beam of light) into series of dark and light bands or coloured spectra. □ **diffraction** *noun*. **diffractive** *adjective*.

diffuse *verb* /dɪ'fjuːz/ (**-sing**) **1** spread widely or thinly. **2** intermingle. ● *adjective* /dɪ'fjuːs/ **1** spread out; not concentrated. **2** not concise. □ **diffuseness** *noun*. **diffusible** *adjective*. **diffusion** *noun*. **diffusive** *adjective*.

■ *verb* **1** see SPREAD *verb* 4. ● *adjective* **1** dispersed, scattered, spread out. **2** digressive, discursive, long-winded, meandering, rambling, unstructured, vague, *colloquial* waffly, wandering, wordy.

dig *verb* (**-gg-**; *past & past participle* **dug**) **1** (often + *up*) break up and turn over (ground etc.). **2** make (hole etc.) by digging. **3** excavate. **4** (+ *up, out*) obtain by digging. **5** (+ *up, out*) find, discover. **6** *slang* like; understand. **7** (+ *in, into*) thrust, prod. ● *noun* **1** piece of digging. **2** thrust, poke. **3**

colloquial pointed remark. **4** archaeological excavation. **5** (in *plural*) *colloquial* lodgings. □ **dig in** *colloquial* begin eating. **dig oneself in** prepare defensive position.

■ *verb* **1** cultivate, fork over, grub (up), till, trench, turn over. **2, 3** burrow, *poetical* delve, excavate, gouge, hollow, mine, quarry, scoop, tunnel. **4** (*dig up*) disinter, exhume, grub up, unearth. **5** (*dig out*) see FIND *verb* **1**. **7** jab, nudge, poke, prod, punch, shove, thrust.

digest *verb* /daɪˈdʒest/ **1** assimilate food. **2** assimilate information etc. ● *noun* /ˈdaɪdʒest/ **1** periodical synopsis of current news etc. **2** summary, esp. of laws. □ **digestible** *adjective*.

■ *verb* **2** absorb, assimilate, consider, ponder, study, take in, understand. ● *noun* see SUMMARY *noun*.

digestion *noun* **1** digesting. **2** capacity to digest food.

digestive *adjective* of or aiding digestion. ● *noun* (in full **digestive biscuit**) wholemeal biscuit.

digger /ˈdɪɡə/ *noun* **1** person or machine that digs. **2** *colloquial* Australian, New Zealander.

digit /ˈdɪdʒɪt/ *noun* **1** any numeral from 0 to 9. **2** finger or toe.

■ **1** figure, integer, number, numeral.

digital /ˈdɪdʒɪt(ə)l/ *adjective* **1** of digits. **2** (of clock, etc.) giving a reading by displayed digits. **3** (of computer) operating on data represented by digits. **4** (of recording) sound-information represented by digits for more reliable transmission. □ **digitally** *adverb*.

digitalis /dɪdʒɪˈteɪlɪs/ *noun* heart stimulant made from foxgloves.

digitize *verb* (also **ise**) (**-zing** or **-sing**) convert (computer data etc.) into digital form.

dignified /ˈdɪɡnɪfaɪd/ *adjective* having or showing dignity.

■ august, calm, courtly, decorous, distinguished, elegant, formal, grand, grave, imposing, impressive, lofty, lordly, majestic, noble, proper, refined, regal, sedate, serious, sober, solemn, stately, tasteful, upright.

dignify /ˈdɪɡnɪfaɪ/ *verb* (**ies**, **-ied**) give dignity to.

dignitary /ˈdɪɡnɪtərɪ/ *noun* (*plural* **-ies**) person of high rank or office.

■ important person, luminary, notable, official, VIP, worthy.

dignity /ˈdɪɡnɪtɪ/ *noun* (*plural* **-ies**) **1** composed and serious manner. **2** being worthy of respect. **3** high rank or position.

■ **1** calmness, courtliness, decorum, elegance, formality, gravity, majesty, nobility, propriety, respectability, seriousness, sobriety, solemnity, stateliness. **3** eminence, glory, grandeur, greatness, honour, importance, nobility, regality.

digraph /ˈdaɪɡrɑːf/ *noun* two letters representing one sound, e.g. *sh* in *show*, or *ey* in *key*.

USAGE *Digraph* is sometimes confused with *lig-*

ature, which means 'two or more letters joined'.

digress /daɪˈɡres/ *verb* depart from main subject. □ **digression** *noun*. **digressive** *adjective*.

■ deviate, diverge, drift, get off the subject, go off at a tangent, ramble, stray, veer, wander.

dike = DYKE.

dilapidated /dɪˈlæpɪdeɪtɪd/ *adjective* in disrepair. □ **dilapidation** *noun*.

■ broken down, crumbling, decayed, decrepit, derelict, falling apart, falling down, in disrepair, in ruins, neglected, ramshackle, rickety, ruined, run-down, shaky, tottering, tumbledown, uncared-for.

dilate /daɪˈleɪt/ *verb* (**-ting**) **1** widen or expand. **2** speak or write at length. □ **dilatation** *noun*. **dilation** *noun*.

dilatory /ˈdɪlətərɪ/ *adjective* given to or causing delay.

dilemma /daɪˈlemə, dɪˈlemə/ *noun* **1** situation in which choice has to be made between equally undesirable alternatives. **2** *disputed* difficult situation.

USAGE The use of *dilemma* to mean 'a difficult situation or predicament' is considered incorrect by some people.

■ **1** *colloquial* catch-22. **2** deadlock, difficulty, embarrassment, fix, impasse, *colloquial* jam, mess, *colloquial* pickle, plight, predicament, problem, quandary, *colloquial* spot, stalemate.

dilettante /dɪlɪˈtæntɪ/ *noun* (*plural* **dilettanti** /-tɪ/ or **-s**) dabbler in a subject. □ **dilettantism** *noun*.

diligent /ˈdɪlɪdʒ(ə)nt/ *adjective* **1** hard-working. **2** showing care and effort. □ **diligence** *noun*. **diligently** *adverb*.

■ assiduous, busy, careful, conscientious, constant, devoted, earnest, energetic, hard-working, indefatigable, industrious, meticulous, painstaking, persevering, persistent, pertinacious, punctilious, scrupulous, sedulous, studious, thorough, tireless.

dill *noun* herb with aromatic leaves and seeds.

dilly-dally /dɪlɪˈdælɪ/ *verb* (**-ies**, **-ied**) *colloquial* dawdle; vacillate.

dilute /daɪˈljuːt/ *verb* (**-ting**) **1** reduce strength (of fluid) by adding water etc. **2** weaken in effect. ● *adjective* diluted. □ **dilution** *noun*.

■ *verb* adulterate, thin, water down, weaken.

diluvial /daɪˈluːvɪəl/ *adjective* of flood, esp. Flood in Genesis.

dim *adjective* (**-mm-**) **1** not bright; faintly luminous or visible. **2** ill-defined; indistinctly perceived or remembered. **3** (of eyes) not seeing clearly. **4** *colloquial* stupid. ● *verb* (**-mm-**) make or become dim. □ **take a dim view of** *colloquial* disapprove of. □ **dimly** *adverb*. **dimness** *noun*.

■ *adjective* **1** clouded, cloudy, dark, dingy, dull, faint, fogged, foggy, fuzzy, gloomy, grey, hazy, misty, murky, obscure, obscured, pale, shadowy, sombre. **2** blurred, faint, foggy, fuzzy, hazy, ill-defined, imperceptible, indistinct, indistinguishable, misty, nebulous, obscure, unclear, vague, weak. **3** bleary, blurred, clouded, dull, weak. **4** see STUPID **1**. ● *verb* blacken, cloud, darken, dull, fade, go out, lower, mask, obscure, shade, shroud. □ **take a dim view of** see DISAPPROVE.

dime *noun US* 10-cent coin.

dimension /daɪˈmenʃ(ə)n/ *noun* **1** any measurable extent. **2** (in *plural*) size. **3** aspect. □ **dimensional** *adjective*.

■ **1** see MEASUREMENT **2**. **2** (*dimensions*) capacity, extent, magnitude, measurements, proportions, scale, scope, size.

diminish /dɪˈmɪnɪʃ/ *verb* **1** make or become smaller or less. **2** (often as **diminished** *adjective*) lessen reputation of (person); humiliate.

■ **1** abate, contract, curtail, cut, decline, decrease, depreciate, die down, dwindle, ease off, ebb, fade, lessen, *colloquial* let up, lower, peter out, recede, reduce, shorten, shrink, shrivel, slow down, subside, wane, wind down. **2** belittle, cheapen, demean, deprecate, devalue, disparage, minimize, undervalue.

diminuendo /dɪmɪnjʊˈendəʊ/ *Music noun* (*plural* **-s**) gradual decrease in loudness. ● *adverb & adjective* decreasing in loudness.

diminution /dɪmɪˈnjuːʃ(ə)n/ *noun* diminishing.

diminutive /dɪˈmɪnjʊtɪv/ *adjective* **1** tiny. **2** (of word or suffix) implying smallness or affection. ● *noun* diminutive word or suffix.

■ *adjective* **1** microscopic, midget, miniature, *colloquial* minuscule, minute, small, tiny, undersized.

dimmer *noun* (in full **dimmer switch**) device for varying brightness of electric light.

dimple /ˈdɪmp(ə)l/ *noun* small hollow, esp. in cheek or chin. ● *verb* (**-ling**) produce dimples (in).

dimwit /ˈdɪmwɪt/ *noun colloquial* stupid person. □ **dim-witted** *adjective*.

din *noun* prolonged loud confused noise. ● *verb* (**-nn-**) **1** (+*into*) force (information) into person by repetition. **2** make din.

■ *noun* blaring, clamour, clangour, clatter, commotion, crash, hubbub, hullabaloo, noise, outcry, pandemonium, racket, roar, *colloquial* row, *colloquial* rumpus, shouting, tumult, uproar.

dinar /ˈdiːnɑː/ *noun* chief monetary unit of (former) Yugoslavia and several Middle Eastern and N. African countries.

dine *verb* (**-ning**) **1** eat dinner. **2** (+ *on, upon*) eat for dinner. **3** (esp. in phrase **wine and dine**) entertain with food. □ **dining car** restaurant on train. **dining room** room in which meals are eaten.

diner *noun* **1** person who dines. **2** small dining-room. **3** dining-car. **4** *US* restaurant.

ding-dong /ˈdɪŋdɒŋ/ *noun* **1** sound of chimes. **2** *colloquial* heated argument.

dinghy /ˈdɪŋɡɪ/ *noun* (*plural* **-ies**) small, often inflatable, boat.

dingle /ˈdɪŋɡ(ə)l/ *noun* deep wooded valley.

dingo /ˈdɪŋɡəʊ/ *noun* (*plural* **-es**) wild Australian dog.

dingy /ˈdɪndʒɪ/ *adjective* (**-ier, -iest**) drab; dirty-looking. □ **dinginess** *noun*.

■ dark, depressing, dim, dirty, discoloured, dismal, drab, dreary, dull, faded, gloomy, grimy, murky, seedy, shabby, smoky, soiled, sooty, worn.

dinkum /ˈdɪŋkəm/ *adjective & adverb* (in full **fair dinkum**) *Australian & NZ colloquial* genuine(ly), honest(ly).

dinky /ˈdɪŋkɪ/ *adjective* (**-ier, -iest**) *colloquial* pretty; small and neat.

dinner /ˈdɪnə/ *noun* main meal, at midday or in the evening. □ **dinner dance** formal dinner followed by dancing. **dinner jacket** man's formal evening jacket. **dinner lady** woman who supervises school dinners. **dinner service** set of matching crockery for dinner.

■ banquet, feast, meal.

dinosaur /ˈdaɪnəsɔː/ *noun* extinct usually large reptile.

dint *noun* dent. ● *verb* mark with dints. □ **by dint of** by force or means of.

diocese /ˈdaɪəsɪs/ *noun* district under bishop's pastoral care. □ **diocesan** /daɪˈɒsɪs(ə)n/ *adjective*.

diode /ˈdaɪəʊd/ *noun* **1** semiconductor allowing current in one direction and having two terminals. **2** thermionic valve with two electrodes.

dioxide /daɪˈɒksaɪd/ *noun* oxide with two atoms of oxygen.

Dip. *abbreviation* Diploma.

dip *verb* (**-pp-**) **1** put or lower briefly into liquid etc.; immerse. **2** go below a surface or level. **3** decline slightly or briefly. **4** slope or extend downwards. **5** go briefly under water. **6** (+ *into*) look cursorily into (book, subject, etc.). **7** (+ *into*) put (hand etc.) into (container) to take something out. **8** (+ *into*) use part of (resources). **9** lower or be lowered, esp. in salute. **10** lower beam of (headlights). ● *noun* **1** dipping, being dipped. **2** liquid for dipping. **3** brief bathe in sea etc. **4** downward slope or hollow. **5** sauce into which food is dipped. □ **dip switch** switch for dipping vehicle's headlights.

■ *verb* **1** douse, drop, dunk, immerse, lower, plunge, submerge. **2, 3** decline, descend, dive, fall, go down, sag, sink, slump, subside. **4** decline, descend, drop, fall, go down, slope down. **5** dive, duck, plunge. ● *noun* **1** immersion, plunge. **3** bathe, dive, plunge, swim. **4** concavity, declivity, dent, depression, fall, hole, hollow, incline, slope.

diphtheria /dɪfˈθɪərɪə/ *noun* infectious disease with inflammation of mucous membrane esp. of throat.

diphthong /'dɪfθɒŋ/ *noun* union of two vowels in one syllable.

diplodocus /dɪ'plɒdəkəs/ *noun* (*plural* **-cuses**) huge long-necked plant-eating dinosaur.

diploma /dɪ'pləʊmə/ *noun* **1** certificate of educational qualification. **2** document conferring honour, privilege, etc.

diplomacy /dɪ'pləʊməsɪ/ *noun* **1** management of international relations. **2** tact.

■ **1** foreign affairs, international relations, negotiation. **2** adroitness, delicacy, discretion, finesse, skill, tact, tactfulness.

diplomat /'dɪpləmæt/ *noun* **1** member of diplomatic service. **2** tactful person.

■ **1** ambassador, consul, government representative, minister, negotiator, official, peacemaker, politician, representative, tactician.

diplomatic /dɪplə'mætɪk/ *adjective* **1** of or involved in diplomacy. **2** tactful. □ **diplomatic bag** container for dispatching embassy mail. **diplomatic immunity** exemption of foreign diplomatic staff from arrest, taxation, etc. **diplomatic service** branch of civil service concerned with representing a country abroad. □ **diplomatically** *adverb*.

■ **2** careful, considerate, delicate, discreet, judicious, polite, politic, prudent, sensitive, subtle, tactful, thoughtful, understanding.

diplomatist /dɪ'pləʊmətɪst/ *noun* diplomat.

dipper /'dɪpə/ *noun* **1** diving bird. **2** ladle.

dippy /'dɪpɪ/ *adjective* (**-ier**, **-iest**) *slang* crazy, silly.

dipsomania /dɪpsə'meɪnɪə/ *noun* alcoholism. □ **dipsomaniac** *noun*.

dipstick *noun* rod for measuring depth, esp. of oil in vehicle's engine.

dipterous /'dɪptərəs/ *adjective* two-winged.

diptych /'dɪptɪk/ *noun* painted altarpiece on two hinged panels.

dire *adjective* **1** dreadful. **2** ominous. **3** *colloquial* very bad. **4** urgent.

direct /daɪ'rekt/ *adjective* **1** extending or moving in straight line or by shortest route; not crooked or circuitous. **2** straightforward, frank. **3** without intermediaries. **4** complete, greatest possible. ● *adverb* **1** in a direct way. **2** by direct route. ● *verb* **1** control, guide. **2** (+ *to do, that*) order. **3** (+ *to*) tell way to (place). **4** (+ *to*) address (letter etc.). **5** (+ *at, to, towards*) point, aim, or turn. **6** supervise acting etc. of (film, play, etc.). □ **direct current** electric current flowing in one direction only. **direct debit** regular debiting of bank account at request of payee. **direct-grant school** school funded by government, not local authority. **direct object** primary object of verbal action (see panel at OBJECT). **direct speech** words actually spoken, not reported (see panel). **direct tax** tax on income, paid directly to government. □ **directness** *noun*.

■ *adjective* **1** shortest, straight, undeviating, unswerving. **2** blunt, candid, categorical, clear, decided, explicit, express, forthright, frank, honest, open, outspoken, plain, point-blank, sincere, straightforward, tactless, to the point, unambiguous, uncomplicated, undiplomatic, unequivocal, uninhibited, unqualified, unreserved. **3** empirical, first-hand, personal. **4** absolute, complete, diametrical, exact, utter. ● *verb* **1** administer, be in charge of, command, conduct, control, govern, guide, handle, lead, manage, mastermind, oversee, regulate, rule, run, stage-manage, superintend, supervise, take charge of. **2** bid, charge, command, enjoin, instruct, order, require, tell. **3** escort, guide, indicate the way, point, route, send, show the way, tell the way, usher. **5** aim, focus, level, target, train, turn.

direction /daɪ'rekʃ(ə)n/ *noun* **1** directing. **2** (usually in *plural*) orders, instructions. **3** point to, from, or along which person or thing moves or looks. □ **directionless** *adjective*.

....

Direct speech

Direct speech is the actual words of a speaker quoted in writing.

1 In a novel etc., speech punctuation is used for direct speech:

  a The words spoken are usually put in quotation marks.

  b Each new piece of speech begins with a capital letter.

  c Each paragraph within one person's piece of speech begins with quotation marks, but only the last paragraph ends with them.

For example:

  Christopher looked into the box. 'There's nothing in here,' he said. 'It's completely empty.'

2 In a script (the written words of a play, a film, or a radio or television programme):

  a The names of speakers are written in the margin in capital letters.

  b Each name is followed by a colon.

  c Quotation marks are not needed.

  d Any instructions about the way the words are spoken or about the scenery or the actions of the speakers (stage directions) are written in the present tense in brackets or italics.

For example:

  CHRISTOPHER: [Looks into box.] There's nothing in here. It's completely empty.

....

■ **2** (*directions*) guidance, guidelines, instructions, orders, plans. **3** (compass) bearing, course, orientation, path, road, route, tack, track, way.

directional *adjective* **1** of or indicating direction. **2** sending or receiving radio or sound waves in one direction only.

directive /daɪˈrektɪv/ *noun* order from an authority.

directly *adverb* **1** at once; without delay. **2** presently, shortly. **3** exactly. **4** in a direct way. ● *conjunction colloquial* as soon as.

director *noun* person who directs, esp. for stage etc. or as member of board of company. □ **director-general** chief executive. □ **directorial** /-ˈtɔː-/ *adjective*. **directorship** *noun*.

■ administrator, *colloquial* boss, chief, executive, governor, manager, managing director, organizer, president, principal.

directorate /daɪˈrektərət/ *noun* **1** board of directors. **2** office of director.

directory /daɪˈrektərɪ/ *noun* (*plural* **-ies**) book with list of telephone subscribers, inhabitants of town etc., members of profession, etc. □ **directory enquiries** telephone service providing subscriber's number on request.

■ catalogue, index, list, register.

dirge *noun* **1** lament for the dead. **2** dreary piece of music.

dirham /ˈdɪrəm/ *noun* monetary unit of Morocco and United Arab Emirates.

dirigible /ˈdɪrɪdʒɪb(ə)l/ *adjective* that can be steered. ● *noun* dirigible balloon or airship.

dirk *noun* short dagger.

dirndl /ˈdɜːnd(ə)l/ *noun* **1** dress with close-fitting bodice and full skirt. **2** full gathered skirt with tight waistband.

dirt *noun* **1** unclean matter that soils. **2** earth. **3** foul or malicious talk. **4** excrement. □ **dirt cheap** *colloquial* extremely cheap. **dirt track** racing track with surface of earth or cinders etc.

■ **1** dust, filth, grime, impurity, mess, mire, *colloquial* muck, ooze, pollution, slime, sludge, smut, soot. **2** clay, earth, loam, mud, soil. **3** see OBSCENITY 1. **4** excrement, muck, ordure.

dirty /ˈdɜːtɪ/ *adjective* (**-ier**, **-iest**) **1** soiled, unclean. **2** sordid, obscene. **3** dishonest, unfair. **4** (of weather) rough. **5** muddy-looking. ● *adverb* **1** *slang* very. **2** in a dirty or obscene way. ● *verb* (**-ies**, **-ied**) make or become dirty. □ **dirty look** *colloquial* look of disapproval or disgust. □ **dirtiness** *noun*.

■ *adjective* **1** *poetical* befouled, begrimed, besmirched, bespattered, black, contaminated, dingy, dusty, filthy, foul, grimy, grubby, impure, marked, messy, mucky, muddy, murky, nasty, poisoned, polluted, slatternly, smeary, smudged, soiled, sooty, sordid, spotted, squalid, stained, sullied, tainted, tarnished, uncared-for, unclean, untreated (*water*), unwashed. **2** coarse, crude, filthy, foul, improper, indecent, obscene, offensive, *colloquial* rude, smutty, sordid, vulgar. **3** corrupt,

dishonest, dishonourable, illegal, low-down, mean, nasty, rough, shabby, treacherous, unfair, ungentlemanly, unscrupulous, unsporting, unsportsmanlike. ● *verb poetical* befoul, defile, foul, mark, mess up, muddy, pollute, smear, smudge, soil, spatter, spot, stain, streak, tarnish.

disability /dɪsəˈbɪlɪtɪ/ *noun* (*plural* **-ies**) **1** permanent physical or mental incapacity. **2** lack of some capacity, preventing action.

■ affliction, complaint, defect, disablement, handicap, impairment, incapacity, infirmity, weakness.

disable /dɪˈseɪb(ə)l/ *verb* (**-ling**) **1** deprive of an ability. **2** (often as **disabled** *adjective*) physically incapacitate. □ **disablement** *noun*.

■ **1, 2** cripple, damage, debilitate, enfeeble, hamstring, handicap, immobilize, impair, incapacitate, injure, lame, maim, mutilate, paralyse, put out of action, ruin, weaken. **2** (**disabled**) see HANDICAPPED.

disabuse /dɪsəˈbjuːz/ *verb* (**-sing**) **1** (usually + *of*) free from mistaken idea. **2** disillusion.

disadvantage /dɪsədˈvɑːntɪdʒ/ *noun* **1** unfavourable condition or circumstance. **2** loss; damage. ● *verb* (**-ging**) cause disadvantage to. □ **at a disadvantage** in an unfavourable position. □ **disadvantageous** /dɪsædvənˈteɪdʒəs/ *adjective*.

■ *noun* **1** drawback, handicap, hardship, hindrance, impediment, inconvenience, liability, *colloquial* minus, nuisance, privation, snag, trouble, weakness.

disadvantaged *adjective* lacking normal opportunities through poverty, disability, etc.

disaffected /dɪsəˈfektɪd/ *adjective* discontented, alienated (esp. politically). □ **disaffection** *noun*.

disagree /dɪsəˈɡriː/ *verb* (**-ees**, **-eed**) (often + *with*) **1** hold different opinion. **2** not correspond. **3** upset. □ **disagreement** *noun*.

■ **1** argue, bicker, clash, conflict, contend, differ, dispute, dissent, diverge, fall out, fight, quarrel, squabble, wrangle; (*disagree with*) see OPPOSE 1. **2** clash, conflict, differ, diverge. □ **disagreement** altercation, argument, clash, conflict, contention, controversy, debate, difference, discrepancy, disharmony, disparity, dispute, dissension, dissent, divergence, incompatibility, inconsistency, misunderstanding, opposition, quarrel, squabble, strife, tiff, variance, wrangle.

disagreeable *adjective* **1** unpleasant. **2** bad-tempered. □ **disagreeably** *adverb*.

■ **1** disgusting, distasteful, nasty, objectionable, obnoxious, offensive, off-putting, repellent, sickening, unpleasant, unsavoury.

disallow /dɪsəˈlaʊ/ *verb* refuse to allow or accept; prohibit.

disappear /dɪsəˈpɪə/ *verb* **1** cease to be visible. **2** go missing. **3** cease to exist or be in circulation etc. □ **disappearance** *noun*.

■ **1** disperse, dissolve, *literary* evanesce, evaporate, fade, melt away, pass out of sight, vanish, vaporize, wane. **2** *colloquial* clear off, depart, escape, flee, fly, go, run away, walk away, withdraw. **3** die, die out, vanish.

disappoint /dɪsə'pɔɪnt/ *verb* **1** fail to fulfil desire or expectation of. **2** frustrate. □ **disappointed** *adjective*. **disappointing** *adjective*. **disappointment** *noun*.
■ **1** chagrin, dash hopes of, disenchant, disillusion, dismay, displease, dissatisfy, let down, upset, vex. **2** see FRUSTRATE 2. □ **disappointed** crestfallen, disenchanted, disillusioned, dissatisfied, frustrated, let down, sad, unsatisfied.

disapprobation /dɪsæprə'beɪʃ(ə)n/ *noun* disapproval.

disapprove /dɪsə'pruːv/ *verb* (**-ving**) (usually + *of*) have or express unfavourable opinion. □ **disapproval** *noun*. **disapproving** *adjective*.
■ (*disapprove of*) be displeased by, belittle, censure, condemn, criticize, denounce, deplore, deprecate, dislike, disparage, frown on, jeer at, look askance at, object to, reject, *colloquial* take a dim view of, take exception to. □ **disapproval** anger, censure, condemnation, criticism, disapprobation, disfavour, dislike, displeasure, dissatisfaction, hostility, reproach. **disapproving** see CRITICAL 1.

disarm /dɪ'sɑːm/ *verb* **1** deprive of weapons. **2** abandon or reduce one's own weapons. **3** (often as **disarming** *adjective*) make less hostile; charm, win over. □ **disarmament** *noun*. **disarmingly** *adverb*.
■ **2** demilitarize, demobilize, disband troops. **3** charm, mollify, pacify, placate.

disarrange /dɪsə'reɪndʒ/ *verb* (**-ging**) put into disorder.

disarray /dɪsə'reɪ/ *noun* disorder.

disassociate /dɪsə'səʊʃɪeɪt/ *verb* (**-ting**) dissociate. □ **disassociation** *noun*.

disaster /dɪ'zɑːstə/ *noun* **1** sudden or great misfortune. **2** *colloquial* complete failure. □ **disastrous** *adjective*. **disastrously** *adverb*.
■ **1** accident, blow, calamity, cataclysm, catastrophe, misadventure, mischance, misfortune, mishap, reverse, tragedy. **2** crash, débâcle, failure, fiasco, *slang* flop, *colloquial* wash-out. □ **disastrous** appalling, *colloquial* awful, calamitous, cataclysmic, catastrophic, crippling, destructive, devastating, dire, dreadful, fatal, ruinous, *colloquial* terrible, tragic.

disavow /dɪsə'vaʊ/ *verb* disclaim knowledge or approval of or responsibility for. □ **disavowal** *noun*.

disband /dɪs'bænd/ *verb* break up, disperse.

disbar /dɪs'bɑː/ *verb* (**-rr-**) deprive of status of barrister. □ **disbarment** *noun*.

disbelieve /dɪsbɪ'liːv/ *verb* (**-ving**) **1** refuse to believe; not believe. **2** be sceptical. □ **disbelief** *noun*. **disbeliever** *noun*. **disbelieving** *adjective*. **disbelievingly** *adverb*.

■ **1** be sceptical of, discount, discredit, distrust, doubt, have no faith in, mistrust, reject, suspect. **2** be sceptical, doubt, have no faith. □ **disbelieving** see INCREDULOUS.

disburden /dɪs'bɜːd(ə)n/ *verb* relieve (person, one's mind, etc.) of burden.

disburse /dɪs'bɜːs/ *verb* (**-sing**) pay out (money). □ **disbursement** *noun*.

disc *noun* **1** flat thinnish circular object. **2** round flat or apparently flat surface or mark. **3** layer of cartilage between vertebrae. **4** gramophone record. **5** = COMPACT DISC. **6** *Computing* = DISK. □ **disc brake** one using friction of pads against a disc. **disc jockey** presenter of recorded popular music.
■ **1, 2** circle, counter, plate, token. **4** album, long-playing record, LP, record, single.

discard /dɪs'kɑːd/ *verb* **1** reject as unwanted. **2** remove or put aside.
■ **1** abandon, cast off, *colloquial* chuck away, dispense with, dispose of, *slang* ditch, dump, eliminate, get rid of, jettison, junk, reject, scrap, shed, throw away, toss out.

discern /dɪ'sɜːn/ *verb* **1** perceive clearly with mind or senses. **2** make out. □ **discernible** *adverb*.
■ be aware of, be sensitive to, detect, discover, discriminate, distinguish, make out, mark, notice, observe, perceive, recognize, see, spy. □ **discernible** detectable, distinguishable, measurable, noticeable, perceptible.

discerning *adjective* having good judgement or insight. □ **discernment** *noun*.
■ see PERCEPTIVE.

discharge *verb* /dɪs'tʃɑːdʒ/ (**-ging**) **1** release, let go. **2** dismiss from office or employment. **3** fire (gun etc.). **4** emit, pour out. **5** pay or perform (debt, duty). **6** relieve (bankrupt) of residual liability. **7** release an electrical charge from. **8** relieve of cargo; unload. ● *noun* /'dɪstʃɑːdʒ/ **1** discharging, being discharged. **2** matter or thing discharged. **3** release of electric charge, esp. with spark.
■ *verb* **1** absolve, acquit, clear, dismiss, excuse, exonerate, free, let off, liberate, pardon, release. **2** dismiss, fire, make redundant, remove, *colloquial* sack, throw out. **3** detonate, explode, fire, let off, shoot. **4** belch, eject, emit, expel, exude, give off, give out, pour out, produce, release, secrete, send out, spew out, spit out, throw out. **5** (*discharge a debt*) clear, liquidate, meet, pay, settle; (*discharge a duty*) accomplish, carry out, execute, fulfil, perform. ● *noun* **1** dismissal, release. **2** emission, excretion, ooze, pus, secretion, suppuration.

disciple /dɪ'saɪp(ə)l/ *noun* **1** follower of leader, teacher, philosophy, etc. **2** follower of Christ, esp. one of the twelve Apostles.
■ acolyte, adherent, admirer, Apostle, apprentice, devotee, follower, learner, proselyte, pupil, scholar, student, supporter.

disciplinarian /dɪsɪplɪ'neərɪən/ *noun* enforcer of or believer in strict discipline.

■ authoritarian, autocrat, despot, dictator, hardliner, hard taskmaster, martinet, slave-driver, stickler, tyrant.

disciplinary /dɪsɪ'plɪmərɪ/ *adjective* of or enforcing discipline.

discipline /'dɪsɪplɪn/ *noun* **1** control or order exercised over people or animals. **2** system of rules for this. **3** training or way of life aimed at self-control or conformity. **4** behaviour resulting from such training. **5** branch of learning. **6** punishment. ● *verb* (**-ning**) **1** punish. **2** control by training in obedience. □ **disciplined** *adjective*.

■ *noun* **1, 2** control, management, order, restraint, routine, strictness. **3** drilling, indoctrination, instruction, training. **4** good behaviour, obedience, orderliness, self-control, self-restraint. ● *verb* **1** castigate, chasten, chastise, correct, penalize, punish, rebuke, reprimand, *formal* reprove, scold. **2** break in, coach, control, drill, educate, govern, indoctrinate, instruct, keep in check, manage, restrain, school, train. □ **disciplined** see OBEDIENT.

disclaim /dɪs'kleɪm/ *verb* **1** disown, deny. **2** renounce legal claim to.

■ deny, disown, forswear, reject, renounce, repudiate.

disclaimer *noun* statement disclaiming something.

disclose /dɪs'kləʊz/ *verb* (**-sing**) expose, make known, reveal. □ **disclosure** *noun*.

■ divulge, expose, let out, make known, reveal, tell.

disco /'dɪskəʊ/ *noun* (*plural* **-s**) *colloquial* discothèque.

discolour /dɪs'kʌlə/ *verb* (*US* **discolor**) **1** cause to change from its usual colour. **2** stain or become stained. □ **discoloration** *noun*.

■ bleach, dirty, fade, mark, stain, tarnish, tinge.

discomfit /dɪs'kʌmfɪt/ *verb* (**-t-**) **1** disconcert, baffle. **2** frustrate. □ **discomfiture** *noun*.

discomfort /dɪs'kʌmfət/ *noun* **1** lack of comfort. **2** uneasiness of body or mind. ● *verb* make uneasy; distress.

■ *noun* ache, care, difficulty, distress, hardship, inconvenience, irritation, pain, soreness, uncomfortableness, uneasiness.

discompose /dɪskəm'pəʊz/ *verb* (**-sing**) disturb composure of. □ **discomposure** *noun*.

disconcert /dɪskən'sɜːt/ *verb* disturb composure of; fluster.

■ agitate, bewilder, confuse, discomfit, distract, disturb, fluster, nonplus, perplex, put off, puzzle, *colloquial* rattle, ruffle, *colloquial* throw, throw off balance, trouble, unsettle, upset, worry.

disconnect /dɪskə'nekt/ *verb* **1** break connection of or between. **2** put (apparatus) out of action by disconnecting parts. □ **disconnection** *noun*.

■ **1** break off, cut off, detach, disengage, divide, part, sever, uncouple, undo, unhitch, unhook, unplug. **2** switch off, turn off.

disconnected *adjective* incoherent and illogical.

■ see INCOHERENT.

disconsolate /dɪs'kɒnsələt/ *adjective* **1** forlorn, unhappy. **2** disappointed. □ **disconsolately** *adverb*.

discontent /dɪskən'tent/ *noun* dissatisfaction; lack of contentment. ● *verb* (esp. as **discontented** *adjective*) make dissatisfied. □ **discontentment** *noun*.

■ *verb* (**discontented**) annoyed, disgruntled, displeased, dissatisfied, fed up, restless, sulky, unhappy, unsettled.

discontinue /dɪskən'tɪnjuː/ *verb* (**-ues**, **-ued**, **-uing**) **1** (cause to) cease. **2** not go on with (activity).

discontinuous /dɪskən'tɪnjʊəs/ *adjective* lacking continuity; intermittent. □ **discontinuity** /-kɒntɪ'njuːɪtɪ/ *noun*.

discord /'dɪskɔːd/ *noun* **1** disagreement, strife. **2** harsh noise, clashing sounds; lack of harmony.

■ **1** argument, conflict, contention, difference of opinion, disagreement, disharmony, friction, incompatibility, strife. **2** cacophony, clash, disharmony, jangle, noise.

discordant /dɪs'kɔːdənt/ *adjective* **1** disagreeing; not fitting in. **2** (of sounds) harsh; not in harmony.

■ **1** conflicting, contrary, differing, disagreeing, dissimilar, divergent, incompatible, incongruous, inconsistent, opposed, opposite. **2** cacophonous, clashing, dissonant, grating, grinding, harsh, jangling, jarring, shrill, strident, tuneless, unmusical.

discothèque /'dɪskətek/ *noun* nightclub etc. where pop records are played for dancing.

discount *noun* /'dɪskaʊnt/ amount deducted from normal price. ● *verb* /dɪs'kaʊnt/ **1** disregard as unreliable or unimportant. **2** deduct amount from (price etc.). **3** give or get present value of (investment certificate which has yet to mature). □ **at a discount** below nominal or usual price.

■ *noun* allowance, concession, cut, deduction, rebate, reduction. ● *verb* **1** disbelieve, dismiss, disregard, gloss over, ignore, overlook, reject.

discountenance /dɪs'kaʊntɪnəns/ *verb* (**-cing**) **1** disconcert. **2** refuse to approve of.

discourage /dɪs'kʌrɪdʒ/ *verb* (**-ging**) **1** reduce confidence or spirits of. **2** (usually + *from*) dissuade, deter; try to prevent. **3** show disapproval of. □ **discouragement** *noun*.

■ **1** cow, damp, dampen, daunt, demoralize, depress, disenchant, dishearten, dismay, dispirit, frighten, inhibit, intimidate, overawe, scare, unman, unnerve. **2** deflect, deter, dissuade, hinder, inhibit, prevent, put an end to, put off, restrain, slow down, stop, suppress. **3** deprecate, disapprove of, frown on, throw cold water on.

□ **discouragement** constraint, damper, deterrent, disincentive, hindrance, impediment, obstacle, restraint, setback.

discourse *noun* /'dɪskɔːs/ **1** conversation. **2** lengthy treatment of theme. **3** lecture, speech. ● *verb* /dɪs'kɔːs/ (**-sing**) **1** converse. **2** speak or write at length.
■ *noun* **1** see CONVERSATION 1–2. **2, 3** dissertation, essay, lecture, monograph, paper, speech, thesis, treatise, writing. ● *verb* see SPEAK 3.

discourteous /dɪs'kɜːtɪəs/ *adjective* rude, uncivil. □ **discourteously** *adverb.* **discourtesy** /-əsɪ/ *noun* (*plural* **-ies**).

discover /dɪ'skʌvə/ *verb* **1** find or find out, by effort or chance. **2** be first to find or find out in particular case. **3** find and promote (little-known performer). □ **discoverer** *noun.*
■ **1, 2** ascertain, bring to light, come across, conceive, detect, dig up, disclose, dredge up, explore, expose, ferret out, find, hit on, identify, invent, learn, light (up)on, locate, notice, observe, perceive, recognize, reveal, search out, *colloquial* spot, *slang* suss out, track down, turn up, uncover, unearth. □ **discoverer** creator, explorer, finder, initiator, inventor, originator, pioneer.

discovery *noun* (*plural* **-ies**) **1** discovering, being discovered. **2** person or thing discovered.
■ **1** conception, detection, disclosure, exploration, innovation, invention, recognition, revelation. **2** breakthrough, conception, find, innovation, invention, revelation.

discredit /dɪs'kredɪt/ *verb* (**-t-**) **1** cause to be disbelieved. **2** harm good reputation of. **3** refuse to believe. ● *noun* **1** harm to reputation. **2** cause of this. **3** lack of credibility.
■ *verb* **1** challenge, *colloquial* debunk, disprove, explode, prove false, raise doubts about. **2** attack, calumniate, defame, disgrace, dishonour, show up, slander, *archaic* or *US* slur, smear, vilify. **3** see DISBELIEVE 1.

discreditable *adjective* bringing discredit, shameful.

discreet /dɪ'skriːt/ *adjective* (**-er, -est**) **1** tactful, prudent. **2** cautious in speech or action. **3** unobtrusive. □ **discreetly** *adverb.* **discreetness** *noun.*
■ **1, 2** careful, cautious, chary, circumspect, considerate, delicate, diplomatic, guarded, judicious, polite, politic, prudent, sensitive, tactful, thoughtful, wary. **3** low-key, mild, muted, restrained, soft, subdued, understated, unobtrusive.

discrepancy /dɪ'skrepənsɪ/ *noun* (*plural* **-ies**) difference; inconsistency. □ **discrepant** *adjective.*
■ conflict, difference, disparity, dissimilarity, divergence, incompatibility, incongruity, inconsistency, variance.

discrete /dɪ'skriːt/ *adjective* separate, distinct.
discretion /dɪ'skreʃ(ə)n/ *noun* **1** being discreet.

2 prudence, judgement. **3** freedom or authority to act as one thinks fit. □ **discretionary** *adjective.*
■ **1, 2** circumspection, diplomacy, good sense, judgement, maturity, prudence, responsibility, sensitivity, tact, wisdom.

discriminate /dɪ'skrɪmɪneɪt/ *verb* (**-ting**) **1** (often + *between*) make or see a distinction. **2** (usually + *against, in favour of*) treat badly or well, esp. on the basis of race, gender, etc. □ **discriminating** *adjective.* **discriminatory** /-nətərɪ/ *adjective.*
■ **1** differentiate, distinguish, draw a distinction, separate, tell apart. **2** be biased, be intolerant, be prejudiced. □ **discriminating** see PERCEPTIVE.

discrimination *noun* **1** good taste. **2** biased or unfavourable treatment.
■ **1** discernment, good taste, insight, judgement, perceptiveness, refinement, selectivity, subtlety, taste. **2** bias, bigotry, favouritism, intolerance, prejudice, unfairness.

discursive /dɪs'kɜːsɪv/ *adjective* rambling; tending to digress.

discus /'dɪskəs/ *noun* (*plural* **-cuses**) heavy disc thrown in athletic events.

discuss /dɪs'kʌs/ *verb* **1** talk about. **2** talk or write about (subject) in detail; examine, debate. □ **discussion** *noun.*
■ argue about, confer about, consider, consult about, debate, deliberate, examine, put heads together about, speak about, talk about, thrash out, weigh the pros and cons of, write about. □ **discussion** argument, *literary* colloquy, confabulation, conference, consideration, consultation, conversation, debate, deliberation, dialogue, discourse, examination, exchange of views, powwow, symposium, talk.

disdain /dɪs'deɪn/ *noun* scorn, contempt. ● *verb* **1** regard with disdain. **2** refrain or refuse out of disdain. □ **disdainful** *adjective.*
■ □ **disdainful** contemptuous, jeering, mocking, scornful, sneering, supercilious, superior.

disease /dɪ'ziːz/ *noun* **1** unhealthy condition of organism or part of organism. **2** (specific) disorder or illness. □ **diseased** *adjective.*
■ affliction, ailment, blight, *slang* bug, complaint, condition, contagion, disorder, illness, infection, infirmity, malady, plague, sickness. □ **diseased** ailing, ill, infirm, sick, unwell.

disembark /dɪsɪm'bɑːk/ *verb* **1** put or go ashore. **2** get off aircraft, bus, etc. □ **disembarkation** /-embɑː-/ *noun.*
■ **1** debark, go ashore, land, put ashore. **2** alight, get off.

disembarrass /dɪsɪm'bærəs/ *verb* **1** (usually + *of*) rid or relieve (of a load etc.). **2** free from embarrassment. □ **disembarrassment** *noun.*

disembodied /dɪsɪm'bɒdɪd/ *adjective* (of soul etc.) separated from body or concrete form; without a body.

disembowel /dɪsɪm'baʊəl/ *verb* (**-ll-**; *US* **-l-**) remove entrails of. □ **disembowelment** *noun*.

disenchant /dɪsɪn'tʃɑːnt/ *verb* disillusion. □ **disenchantment** *noun*.

disencumber /dɪsɪn'kʌmbə/ *verb* free from encumbrance.

disenfranchise /dɪsɪn'fræntʃaɪz/ *verb* (**-sing**) deprive of right to vote, of citizen's rights, or of franchise held. □ **disenfranchisement** *noun*.

disengage /dɪsɪn'geɪdʒ/ *verb* (**-ging**) **1** detach, loosen, release. **2** remove (troops) from battle etc. **3** become detached. **4** (as **disengaged** *adjective*) at leisure, uncommitted. □ **disengagement** *noun*.

disentangle /dɪsɪn'tæŋg(ə)l/ *verb* (**-ling**) free or become free of tangles or complications. □ **disentanglement** *noun*.

disestablish /dɪsɪ'stæblɪʃ/ *verb* **1** deprive (Church) of state support. **2** end the establishment of. □ **disestablishment** *noun*.

disfavour /dɪs'feɪvə/ *noun* (*US* **disfavor**) **1** dislike, disapproval. **2** being disliked.

disfigure /dɪs'fɪgə/ *verb* (**-ring**) spoil appearance of. □ **disfigurement** *noun*.

■ blemish, damage, deface, deform, distort, impair, injure, make ugly, mar, mutilate, ruin, scar, spoil.

disgorge /dɪs'gɔːdʒ/ *verb* (**-ging**) **1** eject from throat. **2** pour forth (food, fluid, etc.).

disgrace /dɪs'greɪs/ *noun* **1** shame, ignominy. **2** shameful or very bad person or thing. ● *verb* (**-cing**) **1** bring shame or discredit on. **2** dismiss from position of honour or favour.

■ *noun* **1** contumely, degradation, discredit, dishonour, disrepute, embarrassment, humiliation, ignominy, obloquy, odium, opprobrium, scandal, shame, stigma.

disgraceful *adjective* causing disgrace; shameful. □ **disgracefully** *adverb*.

■ bad, contemptible, degrading, dishonourable, embarrassing, humiliating, ignominious, shameful, shaming, wicked.

disgruntled /dɪs'grʌnt(ə)ld/ *adjective* discontented; sulky. □ **disgruntlement** *noun*.

■ annoyed, bad-tempered, cross, disaffected, disappointed, discontented, dissatisfied, fed up, grumpy, moody, sulky, sullen.

disguise /dɪs'gaɪz/ *verb* (**-sing**) **1** conceal identity of; make unrecognizable. **2** conceal. ● *noun* **1** costume, make-up, etc. used to disguise. **2** action, manner, etc. used to deceive. **3** disguised condition.

■ *verb* **1** camouflage, dress up, mask, screen, shroud, veil; (*disguise oneself as*) see IMPERSONATE. **2** conceal, cover up, falsify, gloss over, hide, misrepresent. ● *noun* **1** camouflage, costume, cover, fancy dress, *colloquial* get-up, make-up, mask. **2** cover, front, pretence, smokescreen.

disgust /dɪs'gʌst/ *noun* strong aversion; repug-

nance. ● *verb* cause disgust in. □ **disgusting** *adjective*. **disgustingly** *adverb*.

■ *noun* abhorrence, antipathy, aversion, contempt, detestation, dislike, distaste, hatred, loathing, nausea, outrage, repugnance, repulsion, revulsion, sickness. ● *verb* appal, be distasteful to, displease, horrify, nauseate, offend, outrage, put off, repel, revolt, shock, sicken, turn (person's) stomach. □ **disgusting** see HATEFUL.

dish *noun* **1** shallow flat-bottomed container for food. **2** food served in dish. **3** particular kind of food. **4** (in *plural*) crockery etc. to be washed etc. after a meal. **5** dish-shaped object or cavity. **6** *colloquial* sexually attractive person. ● *verb* **1** make dish-shaped. **2** *colloquial* outmanoeuvre; frustrate. □ **dish out** *colloquial* distribute, allocate. **dish up** (prepare to) serve meal.

■ *noun* **1** basin, bowl, casserole, container, plate, platter, tureen. **3** concoction, food, recipe. □ **dish out** see DISTRIBUTE 1. **dish up** see SERVE *verb* 9.

disharmony /dɪs'hɑːmənɪ/ *noun* lack of harmony; discord.

dishearten /dɪs'hɑːt(ə)n/ *verb* cause to lose courage or confidence. □ **disheartened** *adjective*.

■ depress, deter, discourage, dismay, put off, sadden. □ **disheartened** see SAD 1.

dishevelled /dɪ'ʃev(ə)ld/ *adjective* (*US* **disheveled**) ruffled, untidy.

■ bedraggled, disarranged, disordered, knotted, matted, messy, ruffled, rumpled, *colloquial* scruffy, slovenly, tangled, tousled, uncombed, unkempt, untidy.

dishonest /dɪs'ɒnɪst/ *adjective* fraudulent; insincere. □ **dishonestly** *adverb*. **dishonesty** *noun*.

■ *slang* bent, cheating, corrupt, criminal, *colloquial* crooked, deceitful, deceiving, deceptive, devious, dishonourable, disreputable, false, fraudulent, hypocritical, immoral, insincere, lying, mendacious, misleading, perfidious, shady, slippery, specious, swindling, thieving, treacherous, two-faced, underhand, unethical, unprincipled, unscrupulous, untrustworthy, untruthful.

dishonour /dɪs'ɒnə/ (*US* **dishonor**) *noun* **1** loss of honour; disgrace. **2** cause of this. ● *verb* **1** disgrace (person, family, etc.). **2** refuse to pay (cheque etc.). **3** *archaic* rape.

■ *noun* **1** degradation, discredit, disgrace, humiliation, ignominy, indignity, loss of face, obloquy, opprobrium, reproach, scandal, shame, slander. ● *verb* **1** abuse, affront, debase, defile, degrade, disgrace, offend, profane, shame, slight. **3** see RAPE[1] *verb*.

dishonourable *adjective* (*US* **dishonorable**) **1** causing disgrace; ignominious. **2** unprincipled. □ **dishonourably** *adverb*.

■ base, blameworthy, compromising, corrupt, despicable, discreditable, disgraceful, disgusting, dishonest, disloyal, disreputable, ignoble, ignominious, improper, infamous, mean, outrageous, perfidious, reprehensible, scandalous, shabby, shameful, shameless, treacherous, unchivalrous, unethical, unprincipled, unscrupulous, untrustworthy, unworthy, wicked.

dishy *adjective* (**-ier, -iest**) *colloquial* sexually attractive.

disillusion /dɪsɪ'lu:ʒ(ə)n/ *verb* free from illusion or mistaken belief, esp. disappointingly. ● *noun* disillusioned state. □ **disillusionment** *noun*.
■ *verb* disabuse, disappoint, disenchant, enlighten, undeceive.

disincentive /dɪsɪn'sentɪv/ *noun* thing that discourages, esp. from a particular line of action.

disincline /dɪsɪn'klaɪn/ *verb* (**-ning**) (usually as **disinclined** *adjective*) make unwilling. □ **disinclination** /-klɪ'neɪ-/ *noun*.

disinfect /dɪsɪn'fekt/ *verb* cleanse of infection. □ **disinfection** *noun*.
■ clean, cleanse, decontaminate, fumigate, purge, purify, sanitize, sterilize.

disinfectant *noun* substance that destroys germs etc. ● *adjective* disinfecting.
■ *noun* antiseptic, fumigant, germicide.

disinformation /dɪsɪnfə'meɪʃ(ə)n/ *noun* false information, propaganda.

disingenuous /dɪsɪn'dʒenjʊəs/ *adjective* insincere; not candid. □ **disingenuously** *adverb*. **disingenuousness** *noun*.

disinherit /dɪsɪn'herɪt/ *verb* (**-t-**) deprive of right to inherit; reject as one's heir. □ **disinheritance** *noun*.
■ cut out of a will, deprive person of his/her birthright.

disintegrate /dɪ'sɪntɪɡreɪt/ *verb* (**-ting**) **1** separate into component parts; break up. **2** *colloquial* break down, esp. mentally. □ **disintegration** *noun*.
■ **1** break into pieces, break up, come apart, crumble, decay, decompose, degenerate, deteriorate, fall apart, moulder, rot, shatter, smash, splinter. **2** break down, collapse, *colloquial* crack up.

disinter /dɪsɪn'tɜ:/ *verb* (**-rr-**) dig up (esp. corpse). □ **disinterment** *noun*.

disinterested /dɪ'sɪntrɪstɪd/ *adjective* **1** impartial. **2** *disputed* uninterested. □ **disinterest** *noun*. **disinterestedly** *adverb*.

USAGE The use of *disinterested* to mean 'uninterested' is common in informal use but is widely considered incorrect. The use of the noun *disinterest* to mean 'lack of interest' is also objected to, but it is rarely used in any other sense and the alternative *uninterest* is rare.
■ **1** detached, dispassionate, impartial, impersonal, neutral, objective, unbiased, uninvolved, unprejudiced.

disjointed /dɪs'dʒɔɪntɪd/ *adjective* disconnected, incoherent.

■ aimless, broken up, confused, desultory, disconnected, dislocated, disordered, disunited, divided, incoherent, jumbled, loose, mixed up, muddled, rambling, separate, split up, unconnected, uncoordinated, wandering.

disjunction /dɪs'dʒʌŋkʃ(ə)n/ *noun* separation.

disjunctive /dɪs'dʒʌŋktɪv/ *adjective* **1** involving separation. **2** (of a conjunction) expressing alternative.

disk /dɪsk/ *noun* (also **disc**) flat circular computer storage device. □ **disk drive** mechanism for rotating disk and reading or writing data from or to it.

dislike /dɪs'laɪk/ *verb* (**-king**) have aversion to; not like. ● *noun* **1** feeling of repugnance or not liking. **2** object of this. □ **dislikable** *adjective*.
■ *verb* despise, detest, disapprove of, hate, object to, scorn, take against, take exception to. ● *noun* **1** animus, antagonism, antipathy, aversion, contempt, detestation, disapproval, disfavour, disgust, distaste, hatred, hostility, ill will, loathing, repugnance, revulsion.

dislocate /'dɪsləkeɪt/ *verb* (**-ting**) **1** disturb normal connection of (esp. a joint in the body). **2** disrupt. □ **dislocation** *noun*.
■ **1** disengage, displace, put out of joint.

dislodge /dɪs'lɒdʒ/ *verb* (**-ging**) disturb or move. □ **dislodgement** *noun*.

disloyal /dɪs'lɔɪəl/ *adjective* unfaithful; lacking loyalty. □ **disloyalty** *noun*.
■ faithless, false, insincere, perfidious, *literary* recreant, renegade, seditious, subversive, treacherous, treasonable, two-faced, unfaithful, unreliable, untrue, untrustworthy. □ **disloyalty** betrayal, double-dealing, duplicity, faithlessness, falseness, inconstancy, infidelity, perfidy, treachery, treason, unfaithfulness.

dismal /'dɪzm(ə)l/ *adjective* **1** gloomy; miserable; dreary. **2** *colloquial* feeble, inept. □ **dismally** *adverb*.
■ **1** bleak, cheerless, depressing, dreary, dull, funereal, gloomy, grey, grim, joyless, miserable, sad, sombre, wretched.

dismantle /dɪs'mænt(ə)l/ *verb* (**-ling**) **1** pull down; take to pieces. **2** deprive of defences, equipment, etc.
■ **1** demolish, knock down, strike, strip down, take apart, take down.

dismay /dɪs'meɪ/ *noun* feeling of intense disappointment and discouragement. ● *verb* affect with dismay.
■ *noun* agitation, alarm, anxiety, apprehension, consternation, depression, disappointment, discouragement, distress, dread, fear, gloom, *colloquial* horror, pessimism, trepidation. ● *verb* alarm, appal, daunt, depress, devastate, disappoint, discompose, discourage, disgust, dishearten, dispirit, distress, frighten, horrify, scare, shock, take aback, unnerve.

dismember /dɪs'membə/ *verb* **1** remove limbs

from. **2** partition (country etc.). □ **dismemberment** *noun*.

dismiss /dɪs'mɪs/ *verb* **1** send away; disband; allow to go. **2** terminate employment of, esp. dishonourably. **3** put out of one's thoughts. **4** treat summarily. **5** *Law* refuse further hearing to. **6** *Cricket* put (batsman, side) out. □ **dismissal** *noun*.

■ **1** disband, discharge, free, let go, pack off, release, send away, *colloquial* send packing. **2** axe, cashier, disband, discharge, fire, get rid of, give notice to, *colloquial* give (person) the boot, *colloquial* give (person) the push, lay off, make redundant, *colloquial* sack. **3, 4** belittle, brush aside, discard, discount, disregard, drop, give up, pooh-pooh, reject, repudiate, set aside, shelve, shrug off, wave aside.

dismissive *adjective* dismissing rudely or casually; disdainful. □ **dismissively** *adverb*.

dismount /dɪs'maʊnt/ *verb* **1** get off or down from cycle or horseback etc. **2** remove (thing) from mounting.

disobedient /dɪsə'biːdɪənt/ *adjective* disobeying; rebellious. □ **disobedience** *noun*. **disobediently** *adverb*.

■ anarchic, contrary, defiant, delinquent, disorderly, disruptive, fractious, headstrong, insubordinate, intractable, mutinous, naughty, obdurate, obstinate, obstreperous, perverse, rebellious, recalcitrant, refractory, riotous, self-willed, stubborn, uncontrollable, undisciplined, ungovernable, unmanageable, unruly, wayward, wild, wilful.

disobey /dɪsə'beɪ/ *verb* fail or refuse to obey.

■ mutiny, protest, rebel, revolt, rise up; (*disobey rules, etc.*) break, contravene, defy, disregard, flout, ignore, infringe, oppose, rebel against, resist, transgress, violate.

disoblige /dɪsə'blaɪdʒ/ *verb* (**-ging**) refuse to help or cooperate with (person). **disobliging** *adjective*.

disorder /dɪs'ɔːdə/ *noun* **1** confusion. **2** tumult, riot. **3** bodily or mental ailment. □ **disordered** *adjective*.

■ **1** anarchy, chaos, confusion, disarray, disorderliness, disorganization, jumble, mess, muddle, *colloquial* shambles, tangle, untidiness. **2** clamour, commotion, disturbance, fighting, fracas, fuss, lawlessness, riot, *colloquial* rumpus, tumult, uproar. **3** see ILLNESS 1.

disorderly *adjective* **1** untidy; confused. **2** riotous. □ **disorderliness** *noun*.

■ **1** see DISORGANIZED (DISORGANIZE). **2** see DISOBEDIENT.

disorganize /dɪs'ɔːgənaɪz/ *verb* (also **-ise**) (**-zing** or **-sing**) **1** throw into confusion or disorder. **2** (as **disorganized** *adjective*) badly organized; untidy. □ **disorganization** *noun*.

■ **2** (**disorganized**) aimless, careless, chaotic, confused, disorderly, haphazard, illogical, jumbled, messy, muddled, rambling, scatterbrained, slapdash, slipshod, sloppy, slovenly, straggling, unmethodical, unplanned, unstructured, unsystematic, untidy.

disorientate /dɪs'ɔːrɪənteɪt/ *verb* (also **disorient**) (**-ting**) confuse (person) as to his or her bearings. □ **disorientation** *noun*.

disown /dɪs'əʊn/ *verb* deny or give up any connection with; repudiate.

■ cast off, deny, disclaim, renounce, repudiate.

disparage /dɪ'spærɪdʒ/ *verb* (**-ging**) criticize; belittle. □ **disparagement** *noun*. **disparaging** *adjective*.

■ belittle, criticize, demean, depreciate, discredit, insult, *colloquial* put down, slight, undervalue. □ **disparaging** see UNCOMPLIMENTARY.

disparate /'dɪspərət/ *adjective* essentially different; unrelated.

disparity /dɪ'spærɪtɪ/ *noun* (*plural* **-ies**) inequality; difference; incongruity.

dispassionate /dɪ'spæʃənət/ *adjective* **1** free from emotion. **2** impartial. □ **dispassionately** *adverb*.

■ **1** calm, composed, cool, equable, even-tempered, level-headed, sober, unemotional. **2** see IMPARTIAL.

dispatch /dɪs'pætʃ/ (also **despatch**) *verb* **1** send off. **2** perform (task etc.) promptly. **3** kill. **4** *colloquial* eat (food) quickly. ● *noun* **1** dispatching, being dispatched. **2** official written message, esp. military or political. **3** promptness, efficiency. □ **dispatch box** case for esp. parliamentary documents. **dispatch rider** motorcyclist etc. carrying messages.

■ *verb* **1** consign, convey, forward, mail, post, send, ship, transmit. **3** see KILL *verb* 1. ● *noun* **2** bulletin, communiqué, document, letter, message, report.

dispel /dɪ'spel/ *verb* (**-ll-**) drive away (esp. unwanted ideas or feelings); scatter.

dispensable /dɪ'spensəb(ə)l/ *adjective* that can be dispensed with.

dispensary /dɪ'spensərɪ/ *noun* (*plural* **-ies**) place where medicines etc. are dispensed.

dispensation /dɪspen'seɪʃ(ə)n/ *noun* **1** distributing, dispensing. **2** exemption from penalty, rule, etc. **3** ordering or management, esp. of world by Providence.

dispense /dɪ'spens/ *verb* (**-sing**) **1** distribute. **2** administer. **3** make up and give out (medicine). **4** (+ *with*) do without; make unnecessary; do away with.

■ **1** allocate, allot, apportion, assign, deal out, disburse, distribute, dole out, give out, issue, measure out, *literary* mete out, parcel out, provide, ration out, share. **4** (**dispense with**) see OMIT 1, REMOVE *verb* 1.

dispenser *noun* **1** person who dispenses something. **2** device that dispenses selected amount at a time.

disperse /dɪ'spɜːs/ *verb* (**-sing**) **1** go or send widely or in different directions; scatter, disseminate. **2** station at different points. **3** separate (light) into coloured constituents. □ **dispersal** *noun.* **dispersion** *noun.*

■ **1** break up, broadcast, decentralize, devolve, disband, dismiss, dispel, dissipate, dissolve, distribute, divide up, drive away, scatter, send away, separate, spread, spread out, stray.

dispirit /dɪˈspɪrɪt/ *verb* (esp. as **dispiriting, dispirited** *adjectives*) make despondent.

displace /dɪsˈpleɪs/ *verb* (**-cing**) **1** move from its place. **2** remove from office. **3** oust; take the place of. □ **displaced person** refugee in war etc. or from persecution.

■ **1** disarrange, dislocate, dislodge, disturb, misplace, move, shift. **2** depose, dispossess, evict, expel, unseat. **3** oust, replace, succeed, supersede, supplant, take the place of, usurp.

displacement *noun* **1** displacing, being displaced. **2** amount of fluid displaced by object floating or immersed in it.

display /dɪˈspleɪ/ *verb* show, exhibit. ● *noun* **1** displaying. **2** exhibition. **3** ostentation. **4** image shown on a visual display unit etc.

■ *verb* advertise, air, betray, demonstrate, disclose, exhibit, expose, flaunt, flourish, give evidence of, parade, present, produce, put on show, reveal, set out, show, show off, unfold, unfurl, unveil, *literary* vaunt. ● *noun* **1** demonstration, exhibition, manifestation, presentation. **2** array, demonstration, exhibition, pageant, parade, presentation, show, spectacle. **3** ceremony, ostentation, pageantry, pomp, showing off.

displease /dɪsˈpliːz/ *verb* (**-sing**) offend; make angry or upset. □ **displeasure** /-ˈpleʒə/ *noun.*

■ anger, annoy, offend, put out, upset.

disport /dɪˈspɔːt/ *verb* (also **disport oneself**) frolic, enjoy oneself.

disposable *adjective* **1** that can be disposed of. **2** designed to be discarded after one use.

■ **1** at one's disposal, available, spendable, usable. **2** biodegradable, expendable, non-returnable, replaceable, throw-away.

disposal *noun* disposing of. □ **at one's disposal** available.

dispose /dɪˈspəʊz/ *verb* (**-sing**) **1** (usually + *to, to do*) (usually in *passive*) incline, make willing. **2** (usually + *to, to do*) (in *passive*) tend. **3** arrange suitably. **4** (as **disposed** *adjective*) having a specified inclination. **5** determine events. □ **dispose of 1** get rid of. **2** deal with. **3** finish.

■ **1, 2** (*be disposed*) be apt, be inclined, *disputed* be liable, be likely, be minded, be prone, be tempted, be willing, tend. **3** adjust, arrange, array, distribute, group, order, organize, place, position, put, set out, situate. □ **dispose of 1** see DESTROY 2, DISCARD 1.

disposition /dɪspəˈzɪʃ(ə)n/ *noun* **1** natural tendency; temperament. **2** arrangement (of parts etc.).

dispossess /dɪspəˈzes/ *verb* **1** (usually + *of*)

(esp. as **dispossessed** *adjective*) deprive. **2** oust, dislodge. □ **dispossession** *noun.*

disproof /dɪsˈpruːf/ *noun* refutation.

disproportion /dɪsprəˈpɔːʃ(ə)n/ *noun* lack of proportion.

disproportionate *adjective* out of proportion; relatively too large or too small. □ **disproportionately** *adverb.*

■ excessive, incommensurate, incongruous, inequitable, inordinate, out of proportion, unbalanced, uneven, unreasonable.

disprove /dɪsˈpruːv/ *verb* (**-ving**) prove (theory etc.) false.

■ confute, contradict, controvert, demolish, discredit, explode, invalidate, negate, rebut, refute.

disputable *adjective* open to question.

disputant *noun* person in dispute.

disputation /dɪspjuːˈteɪʃ(ə)n/ *noun* **1** debate, esp. formal. **2** argument, controversy.

disputatious /dɪspjuːˈteɪʃəs/ *adjective* argumentative.

dispute /dɪˈspjuːt/ *verb* (**-ting**) **1** hold debate. **2** quarrel. **3** question truth or validity of. **4** contend for. **5** resist. ● *noun* **1** controversy, debate. **2** quarrel. **3** disagreement leading to industrial action.

■ *verb* **1** see DEBATE *verb* 1. **2** see QUARREL *verb* 2. **3** argue against, challenge, contest, contradict, controvert, deny, disagree with, doubt, fault, gainsay, impugn, object to, oppose, pick holes in, quarrel with, query, question, raise doubts about, take exception to. ● *noun* **2** see QUARREL *noun* 1.

disqualify /dɪsˈkwɒlɪfaɪ/ *verb* (**-ies, -ied**) make or pronounce (competitor, applicant, etc.) unfit or ineligible. □ **disqualification** *noun.*

■ bar, debar, exclude, preclude, prohibit, reject, turn down.

disquiet /dɪsˈkwaɪət/ *verb* make anxious. ● *noun* uneasiness, anxiety. □ **disquietude** *noun.*

disquisition /dɪskwɪˈzɪʃ(ə)n/ *noun* discursive treatise or discourse.

disregard /dɪsrɪˈɡɑːd/ *verb* ignore; treat as unimportant. ● *noun* indifference, neglect.

■ *verb* brush aside, despise, discount, dismiss, disobey, exclude, fly in the face of, forget, ignore, leave out, make light of, miss out, neglect, omit, overlook, pass over, pay no attention to, pooh-pooh, reject, shrug off, skip, slight, snub, turn a blind eye to.

disrepair /dɪsrɪˈpeə/ *noun* bad condition due to lack of repairs.

disreputable /dɪsˈrepjʊtəb(ə)l/ *adjective* **1** having a bad reputation; not respectable in character. **2** not respectable in appearance. □ **disreputably** *adverb.*

■ **1** dishonest, dishonourable, *colloquial* dodgy, dubious, infamous, questionable, raffish, shady, suspect, suspicious, unconventional, unreliable, unsound, untrustworthy. **2** see SHABBY 1,2, SLOVENLY *adjective*.

disrepute /dɪsrɪ'pjuːt/ *noun* lack of good reputation; discredit.

disrespect /dɪsrɪ'spekt/ *noun* lack of respect. □ **disrespectful** *adjective*.

■ □ **disrespectful** bad-mannered, blasphemous, derisive, discourteous, disparaging, impolite, impudent, inconsiderate, insolent, insulting, irreverent, mocking, rude, scornful, uncivil, uncomplimentary, unmannerly.

disrobe /dɪs'rəʊb/ *verb* (**-bing**) *literary* undress.

disrupt /dɪs'rʌpt/ *verb* **1** interrupt continuity of; bring disorder to. **2** break (thing) apart. □ **disruption** *noun*. **disruptive** *adjective*.

■ **1** agitate, break up, confuse, disconcert, dislocate, disorder, disturb, interfere with, interrupt, intrude on, spoil, throw into disorder, unsettle, upset.

dissatisfy /dɪ'sætɪsfaɪ/ *verb* (**-ies, -ied**) (usually as **dissatisfied** *adjective*) (often + *with*) fail to satisfy; make discontented. □ **dissatisfaction** /-'fæk-/ *noun*.

■ (**dissatisfied**) disaffected, disappointed, discontented, disgruntled, displeased, fed up, frustrated, unfulfilled, unhappy, unsatisfied.

□ **dissatisfaction** annoyance, chagrin, disappointment, discontentment, dismay, displeasure, disquiet, exasperation, frustration, irritation, malaise, regret, unhappiness.

dissect /dɪ'sekt/ *verb* **1** cut in pieces, esp. for examination or post-mortem. **2** analyse or criticize in detail. □ **dissection** *noun*.

USAGE *Dissect* is often wrongly pronounced /dar'sekt/ (and sometimes written with only one *s*) because of confusion with *bisect*.

dissemble /dɪ'semb(ə)l/ *verb* (**-ling**) **1** be hypocritical or insincere. **2** conceal or disguise (a feeling, intention, etc.).

disseminate /dɪ'semɪneɪt/ *verb* (**-ting**) scatter about; spread (esp. ideas) widely. □ **dissemination** *noun*.

dissension /dɪ'senʃ(ə)n/ *noun* angry disagreement.

dissent /dɪ'sent/ *verb* **1** (often + *from*) disagree, esp. openly. **2** differ, esp. from established or official opinion. ● *noun* **1** such difference. **2** expression of this.

dissenter *noun* **1** person who dissents. **2** (**Dissenter**) Protestant dissenting from Church of England.

dissentient /dɪ'senʃ(ə)nt/ *adjective* disagreeing with the established or official view. ● *noun* person who dissents.

dissertation /dɪsə'teɪʃ(ə)n/ *noun* detailed discourse, esp. as submitted for academic degree.

disservice /dɪs'sɜːvɪs/ *noun* harmful action.

dissident /'dɪsɪd(ə)nt/ *adjective* disagreeing, esp. with established government. ● *noun* dissident person.

■ *noun* agitator, apostate, dissenter, independent thinker, nonconformist, protester, rebel, recusant, refusenik, revolutionary.

dissimilar /dɪ'sɪmɪlə/ *adjective* not similar. □ **dissimilarity** /-'lærɪtɪ/ *noun* (*plural* **-ies**).

■ antithetical, clashing, conflicting, contrasting, different, disparate, distinct, distinguishable, divergent, diverse, heterogeneous, incompatible, irreconcilable, opposite, unlike, unrelated, various.

dissimulate /dɪ'sɪmjʊleɪt/ *verb* (**-ting**) dissemble. □ **dissimulation** *noun*.

dissipate /'dɪsɪpeɪt/ *verb* (**-ting**) **1** dispel, disperse. **2** squander. **3** (as **dissipated** *adjective*) dissolute.

■ **1** break up, diffuse, disappear, disperse, scatter. **2** fritter away, squander, throw away, use up, waste. **3** (**dissipated**) see IMMORAL.

dissipation *noun* **1** dissolute way of life. **2** dissipating, being dissipated.

dissociate /dɪ'səʊʃɪeɪt/ *verb* (**-ting**) **1** disconnect or separate; become disconnected. **2** (**dissociate oneself from**) declare oneself unconnected with. □ **dissociation** *noun*.

■ **1** cut off, detach, disconnect, disengage, distance, divorce, isolate, segregate, separate.

dissolute /'dɪsəluːt/ *adjective* lax in morals; licentious.

dissolution /dɪsə'luːʃ(ə)n/ *noun* **1** dissolving, being dissolved. **2** dismissal or dispersal of assembly, esp. parliament. **3** breaking up; abolition (of institution). **4** death.

dissolve /dɪ'zɒlv/ *verb* (**-ving**) **1** make or become liquid, esp. by immersion or dispersion in liquid. **2** (cause to) disappear gradually. **3** dismiss (assembly). **4** put an end to; annul (partnership etc.). **5** (often + *in, into*) be overcome (by tears, laughter, etc.).

■ **1** deliquesce, disperse, liquefy, melt away. **2** diffuse, disappear, disintegrate, disperse, vanish. **3** adjourn, break up, disband, dismiss, suspend, terminate, wind up. **4** annul, break up, cancel, end, sever, split up, terminate, wind up.

dissonant /'dɪsənənt/ *adjective* **1** discordant, harsh-toned. **2** incongruous. □ **dissonance** *noun*.

dissuade /dɪ'sweɪd/ *verb* (**-ding**) (often + *from*) discourage, persuade against. □ **dissuasion** /-'sweɪʒ(ə)n/ *noun*.

■ (**dissuade from**) advise against, argue out of, deter from, discourage from, persuade not to, put off, warn against.

distaff /'dɪstɑːf/ *noun* cleft stick holding wool etc. for spinning by hand. □ **distaff side** female branch of family.

distance /'dɪst(ə)ns/ *noun* **1** being far off; remoteness. **2** space between two points. **3** distant point. **4** aloofness, reserve. **5** remoter field of vision. ● *verb* (**-cing**) **1** place or cause to seem far off. **2** leave behind in race etc. □ **at a distance** far off. **keep one's distance** remain aloof.

■ *noun* **1** isolation, remoteness, separation. **2** breadth, extent, gap, haul, interval, journey, length, measurement, mileage, range, space, span, stretch, width. **4** aloofness, coolness, haughtiness, remoteness, stand-offishness, unfriendliness. ● *verb* **1** detach, dissociate, separate, set apart; (*distance oneself*) be unfriendly, detach oneself, dissociate oneself, keep away, keep one's distance, remove oneself, separate oneself, set oneself apart, stay away.

distant *adjective* **1** at specified distance. **2** remote in space, time, relationship, etc. **3** aloof. **4** abstracted. **5** faint. □ **distantly** *adverb*.

■ **2** far, far-away, far-flung, godforsaken, inaccessible, outlying, out of the way, remote, removed. **3** aloof, cool, formal, frigid, haughty, reserved, reticent, stiff, unapproachable, unenthusiastic, unfriendly, withdrawn.

distaste /dɪs'teɪst/ *noun* (usually + *for*) dislike, aversion. □ **distasteful** *adjective*.

■ □ **distasteful** disgusting, displeasing, nasty, nauseating, objectionable, offensive, off-putting, repugnant, revolting, unpalatable, unpleasant.

distemper[1] /dɪ'stempə/ *noun* paint for walls, using glue etc. as base. ● *verb* paint with distemper.

distemper[2] /dɪ'stempə/ *noun* catarrhal disease of dogs etc.

distend /dɪ'stend/ *verb* swell out by pressure from within. □ **distension** *noun*.

distich /'dɪstɪk/ *noun* verse couplet.

distil /dɪ'stɪl/ *verb* (*US* **distill**) (**-ll-**) **1** purify or extract essence from (substance) by vaporizing and condensing it and collecting remaining liquid. **2** extract gist of (idea etc.). **3** make (whisky, essence, etc.) by distilling. □ **distillation** *noun*.

distiller *noun* person who distils, esp. alcoholic liquor.

distillery *noun* (*plural* **-ies**) factory etc. for distilling alcoholic liquor.

distinct /dɪ'stɪŋkt/ *adjective* **1** (often + *from*) separate; different in quality or kind. **2** clearly perceptible. **3** definite, decided. □ **distinctly** *adverb*.

■ **1** contrasting, detached, different, discrete, dissimilar, distinguishable, individual, separate, special, *sui generis*, unconnected, unique. **2, 3** apparent, clear, clear-cut, decided, definite, evident, noticeable, obvious, palpable, patent, perceptible, plain, precise, recognizable, sharp, unambiguous, unequivocal, unmistakable, visible, well defined.

distinction /dɪ'stɪŋkʃ(ə)n/ *noun* **1** discriminating, distinguishing. **2** difference between things. **3** thing that differentiates. **4** special consideration or honour. **5** excellence; eminence. **6** mark of honour.

■ **1** differentiation, discrimination, division, separation. **2** contrast, difference, dissimilarity, dividing line, separation. **3** distinctiveness, individuality, particularity, peculiarity, uniqueness. **5** celebrity, credit, eminence, excellence, fame, glory, greatness, honour, importance, merit, prestige, renown, reputation, superiority, worth.

distinctive *adjective* distinguishing, characteristic. □ **distinctively** *adverb*. **distinctiveness** *noun*.

■ characteristic, different, distinguishing, idiosyncratic, individual, inimitable, original, peculiar, personal, singular, special, striking, typical, uncommon, unique.

distingué /dɪ'stæŋɡeɪ/ *adjective* having distinguished air, manners, etc. [French]

distinguish /dɪ'stɪŋɡwɪʃ/ *verb* **1** (often + *from*, *between*) see or draw distinctions. **2** characterize. **3** make out by listening or looking etc. **4** (usually **distinguish oneself**; often + *by*) make prominent. □ **distinguishable** *adjective*.

■ **1** differentiate, discriminate, separate, tell apart. **3** ascertain, determine, discern, know, make out, perceive, pick out, recognize, see, single out, tell.

distinguished *adjective* **1** eminent, famous. **2** dignified.

■ **1** see FAMOUS 1.

distort /dɪ'stɔːt/ *verb* **1** pull or twist out of shape. **2** misrepresent (facts etc.). **3** transmit (sound) inaccurately. □ **distorted** *adjective*. **distortion** /-'stɔːʃ(ə)n/ *noun*.

■ **1** bend, buckle, contort, deform, twist, warp, wrench. **2** alter, exaggerate, falsify, garble, misrepresent, pervert, slant, tamper with, twist. **3** garble, scramble. □ **distorted** see FALSE 1.

distract /dɪ'strækt/ *verb* **1** (often + *from*) draw away attention of. **2** bewilder. **3** (as **distracted** *adjective*) confused, mad, or angry. **4** amuse, esp. to divert from pain etc.

■ **1** deflect, divert, sidetrack. **2** bewilder, confound, confuse, disconcert, mystify, perplex, puzzle, *colloquial* rattle. **3** (**distracted**) see DISTRAUGHT, MAD 1. **4** see DIVERT 2.

distraction /dɪ'strækʃ(ə)n/ *noun* **1** distracting, being distracted. **2** thing which distracts. **3** amusement, relaxation. **4** mental confusion. **5** frenzy, madness.

■ **2** disturbance, diversion, interference, interruption, temptation, upset. **3** see DIVERSION 2. **4** agitation, befuddlement, bewilderment, confusion. **5** delirium, frenzy, insanity, madness.

distrain /dɪ'streɪn/ *verb* (usually + *upon*) impose distraint (on person, goods, etc.).

distraint /dɪ'streɪnt/ *noun* seizure of goods to enforce payment.

distrait /dɪ'streɪ/ *adjective* inattentive; distraught. [French]

distraught /dɪ'strɔːt/ *adjective* distracted with worry, fear, etc.; very agitated.

■ agitated, anxious, beside oneself, distracted, distressed, disturbed, emotional, excited, frantic, hysterical, overcome, overwrought, troubled, upset, worked up.

distress /dɪ'stres/ *noun* **1** suffering caused by pain, grief, anxiety, etc. **2** poverty. **3** *Law* distraint. ● *verb* cause distress to; make unhappy. □ **distressed** *adjective*. **distressful** *adjective*. **distressing** *adjective*.

■ *noun* **1** adversity, affliction, angst, anguish, anxiety, danger, desolation, discomfort, dismay, fright, grief, heartache, misery, pain, sadness, sorrow, stress, suffering, torment, tribulation, trouble, unhappiness, woe, worry, wretchedness. **2** adversity, difficulty, hardship, poverty, privation. ● *verb* afflict, alarm, bother, cut up, dismay, disturb, frighten, grieve, harass, harrow, hurt, oppress, pain, perplex, perturb, *colloquial* plague, sadden, scare, shake, shock, terrify, torment, torture, trouble, upset, vex, worry, wound.

distribute /dɪ'strɪbjuːt/ *verb* **(-ting)** **1** give shares of; deal out. **2** spread about; put at different points. **3** arrange; classify. □ **distribution** /-'bjuː-/ *noun*. **distributive** *adjective*.

USAGE *Distribute* is often pronounced /'dɪstrɪbjuːt/ (with the stress on the *dis-*), but this is considered incorrect by some people.

■ **1** allocate, allot, apportion, assign, circulate, deal out, deliver, *colloquial* dish out, dispense, divide out, dole out, give out, hand round, issue, *literary* mete out, partition, pass round, share out, take round. **2** disperse, disseminate, scatter, spread, strew. **3** arrange, class, classify, sort.

distributor *noun* **1** agent who supplies goods. **2** device in internal-combustion engine for passing current to each spark plug in turn.

district /'dɪstrɪkt/ *noun* **1** region. **2** administrative division. □ **district attorney** (in the US) public prosecutor of district. **district nurse** nurse who makes home visits in an area.

■ area, community, department, division, locality, neighbourhood, parish, part, precincts, province, quarter, region, sector, territory, vicinity, ward, zone.

distrust /dɪs'trʌst/ *noun* lack of trust; suspicion. ● *verb* have no confidence in. □ **distrustful** *adjective*.

■ *verb* disbelieve, doubt, have misgivings about, have qualms about, mistrust, question, suspect. □ **distrustful** cautious, chary, cynical, disbelieving, distrusting, doubtful, dubious, sceptical, suspicious, uncertain, uneasy, unsure, wary.

disturb /dɪ'stɜːb/ *verb* **1** break rest or quiet of. **2** worry. **3** disorganize. **4** (as **disturbed** *adjective*) emotionally or mentally unstable.

■ **1** annoy, bother, discompose, disrupt, distract, excite, *colloquial* hassle, interrupt, intrude on, pester, startle, stir up, unsettle, upset. **2** agitate, alarm, bother, distress, fluster, frighten, perturb, ruffle, scare, shake, stir up, trouble, unsettle, upset, worry. **3** confuse, disorder, disorganize, interfere

with, jumble up, mess about with, move, muddle, rearrange, reorganize. **4** (**disturbed**) see DISTRAUGHT.

disturbance *noun* **1** disturbing, being disturbed. **2** tumult; disorder; agitation.

■ **1** disruption, interference, upheaval, upset. **2** see COMMOTION.

disunion /dɪs'juːnɪən/ *noun* **1** separation. **2** lack of union.

disunite /dɪsjuː'naɪt/ *verb* **(-ting)** separate; divide. □ **disunited** *adjective*. **disunity** /-'juː-/ *noun*.

■ □ **disunited** divided, opposed, polarized, split. **disunity** difference, disagreement, discord, disharmony, disintegration, division, fragmentation, incoherence, opposition, polarization.

disuse /dɪs'juːs/ *noun* state of no longer being used.

disused /dɪs'juːzd/ *adjective* no longer in use.

■ abandoned, archaic, closed, dead, discarded, discontinued, idle, neglected, obsolete, superannuated, unused, withdrawn.

disyllable /daɪ'sɪləb(ə)l/ *noun* word or metrical foot of two syllables. □ **disyllabic** /-'læb-/ *adjective*.

ditch *noun* long narrow excavation esp. for drainage or as boundary. ● *verb* **1** make or repair ditches. **2** *slang* abandon, discard.

■ *noun* channel, dyke, drain, gully, gutter, moat, trench, watercourse. ● *verb* **2** see ABANDON *verb* 1–2.

dither /'dɪðə/ *verb* **1** hesitate; be indecisive. **2** tremble, quiver. ● *noun colloquial* state of agitation or hesitation. □ **ditherer** *noun*. **dithery** *adjective*.

dithyramb /'dɪθɪræm/ *noun* **1** ancient Greek wild choral hymn. **2** passionate or inflated poem etc. □ **dithyrambic** /-'ræmbɪk/ *adjective*.

ditto /'dɪtəʊ/ *noun* (*plural* **-s**) the aforesaid; the same (in accounts, lists, etc., or *colloquial* in speech).

ditty /'dɪtɪ/ *noun* (*plural* **-ies**) short simple song.

diuretic /daɪjʊ'retɪk/ *adjective* causing increased output of urine. ● *noun* diuretic drug.

diurnal /daɪ'ɜːn(ə)l/ *adjective* **1** in or of day. **2** daily. **3** occupying one day.

diva /'diːvə/ *noun* (*plural* **-s**) great woman opera singer.

divalent /daɪ'veɪlənt/ *adjective Chemistry* having a valency of 2. □ **divalency** *noun*.

divan /dɪ'væn/ *noun* low couch or bed without back or ends.

dive *verb* **(-ving)** **1** plunge head foremost into water. **2** (of submarine or diver) submerge. **3** (of aircraft) descend fast and steeply. **4** go deeper. **5** (+ *into*) *colloquial* put one's hand into. ● *noun* **1** act of diving; plunge. **2** *colloquial* disreputable nightclub, bar, etc. □ **dive-bomb** bomb (target)

from diving aircraft. **diving board** elevated
board for diving from.

■ *verb* **1–3** crash-dive, descend, dip, drop, duck,
fall, go under, jump, leap, nosedive, pitch,
plummet, plunge, sink, submerge, swoop.

diver *noun* **1** person who dives, esp. one who
works under water. **2** diving bird.

diverge /daɪˈvɜːdʒ/ *verb* (**-ging**) **1** (often + *from*)
depart from set course. **2** (of opinions etc.) differ.
3 take different courses; spread outward from
central point. □ **divergence** *noun.* **divergent**
adjective.

■ **1** depart, deviate, digress, go off at a tangent,
stray, turn aside. **2** see DIFFER 1. **3** branch, deviate,
divide, fork, part, radiate, ramify, separate, split,
spread, subdivide.

divers /ˈdaɪvɜːz/ *adjective archaic* various,
several.

diverse /daɪˈvɜːs/ *adjective* varied.

■ assorted, different, dissimilar, distinct,
divergent, diversified, heterogeneous,
miscellaneous, mixed, multifarious, varied,
various.

diversify /daɪˈvɜːsɪfaɪ/ *verb* (**-ies**, **-ied**) **1** make
diverse; vary. **2** (often + *into*) expand range of
products. **3** spread (investment) over several
enterprises. □ **diversification** *noun.*

■ **1, 2** branch out, broaden out, develop, enlarge,
expand, extend, spread out, vary.

diversion /daɪˈvɜːʃ(ə)n/ *noun* **1** diverting, being
diverted. **2** recreation, pastime. **3** alternative
route when road is temporarily closed. **4** stratagem for diverting attention. □ **diversionary**
adjective.

■ **2** amusement, distraction, entertainment, fun,
game, hobby, interest, pastime, play, recreation,
relaxation, sport. **3** detour, deviation.

diversity /daɪˈvɜːsɪtɪ/ *noun* variety.

divert /daɪˈvɜːt/ *verb* **1** turn aside; deflect. **2** distract (attention). **3** (often as **diverting** *adjective*)
entertain, amuse.

■ **1** alter, avert, deflect, deviate, rechannel,
redirect, reroute, shunt, sidetrack, switch, turn
aside. **2** amuse, beguile, cheer up, delight, distract,
engage, entertain, occupy, regale. **3** (**diverting**)
see FUNNY 1, INTERESTING.

divest /daɪˈvest/ *verb* **1** (usually + *of*) unclothe,
strip. **2** deprive, rid.

divide /dɪˈvaɪd/ *verb* (**-ding**) **1** (often + *in, into*)
separate into parts; split or break up. **2** (often +
out) distribute; deal; share. **3** separate (one thing)
from another; classify into parts or groups. **4**
cause to disagree. **5** (+ *by*) find how many times
number contains another. **6** (+ *into*) be contained
exact number of times. **7** (of parliament) vote (by
members entering either of two lobbies). ● *noun*
dividing line; watershed.

■ *verb* **1** branch, break up, cut up, detach, diverge,
fork, move apart, part, separate, split up, *literary*
sunder. **2** allocate, allot, apportion, deal out,
dispense, distribute, dole out, give out, measure

out, *literary* mete out, parcel out, pass round, share
out. **3** arrange, categorize, classify, grade, group,
sort out, subdivide. **4** disunite, polarize, split.

dividend /ˈdɪvɪdend/ *noun* **1** share of profits paid
to shareholders, football pools winners, etc. **2**
number to be divided.

divider *noun* **1** screen etc. dividing room. **2** (in
plural) measuring compasses.

divination /dɪvɪˈneɪʃ(ə)n/ *noun* supposed foreseeing of the future, using special technique.

divine /dɪˈvaɪn/ *adjective* (**-r**, **-st**) **1** of, from, or
like God or a god; sacred. **2** *colloquial* excellent.
● *verb* (**-ning**) **1** discover by intuition or guessing. **2** foresee. **3** practise divination. ● *noun* theologian. □ **divining-rod** dowser's forked twig.
□ **divinely** *adverb.*

■ *adjective* **1** angelic, celestial, godlike, hallowed,
heavenly, holy, immortal, mystical, religious,
sacred, saintly, spiritual, superhuman,
supernatural, transcendental. ● *verb* **3** see
PROPHESY 1. ● *noun* see CLERGYMAN.

diviner *noun* **1** practitioner of divination. **2**
dowser.

divinity /dɪˈvɪnɪtɪ/ *noun* (*plural* **-ies**) **1** being
divine. **2** god. **3** theology; religious study.

■ **2** see GOD 1. **3** religion, religious studies,
theology.

divisible /dɪˈvɪzɪb(ə)l/ *adjective* capable of being
divided. □ **divisibility** *noun.*

division /dɪˈvɪʒ(ə)n/ *noun* **1** dividing, being
divided. **2** dividing one number by another. **3**
disagreement. **4** one of parts into which thing
is divided. **5** point at which thing is divided. **6**
administrative unit, esp. group of army units or
of teams in sporting league. □ **divisional** *adjective.*

■ **1** allocation, allotment, apportionment, cutting
up, dividing, partition, segmentation, separation,
splitting. **3** disagreement, discord, disunity, feud,
quarrel, rupture, schism, split. **4** compartment,
part, section, segment, subdivision, unit. **5** border,
borderline, boundary line, demarcation, divider,
dividing wall, fence, frontier, margin, partition,
screen. **6** branch, department, section,
subdivision, unit.

divisive /dɪˈvaɪsɪv/ *adjective* causing disagreement. □ **divisively** *adverb.* **divisiveness** *noun.*

divisor /dɪˈvaɪzə/ *noun* number by which
another is to be divided.

divorce /dɪˈvɔːs/ *noun* **1** legal dissolution of marriage. **2** separation. ● *verb* (**-cing**) **1** (usually as
divorced *adjective*) (often + *from*) legally dissolve
marriage of; separate by divorce; end marriage
with by divorce. **2** separate.

■ *noun* **1** annulment, break-up, decree nisi,
dissolution, separation, split-up. ● *verb* **1** annul
marriage, dissolve marriage, part, separate, split
up.

divorcee /dɪvɔːˈsiː/ *noun* divorced person.

divot /ˈdɪvət/ *noun* piece of turf dislodged by head
of golf club.

divulge /daɪˈvʌldʒ/ *verb* (**-ging**) disclose (secret).

divvy /ˈdɪvɪ/ *colloquial noun* (*plural* **-ies**) dividend. ● *verb* (**-ies, -ied**) (often + *up*) share out.

Dixie /ˈdɪksɪ/ *noun* Southern States of US. □ **Dixieland 1** Dixie. **2** kind of jazz.

dixie /ˈdɪksɪ/ *noun* large iron cooking pot.

DIY *abbreviation* do-it-yourself.

dizzy /ˈdɪzɪ/ *adjective* (**-ier, -iest**) **1** giddy; dazed. **2** causing dizziness. ● *verb* (**-ies, -ied**) **1** make dizzy. **2** bewilder. □ **dizzily** *adverb*. **dizziness** *noun*.

■ *adjective* **1** bewildered, confused, dazed, faint, giddy, light-headed, muddled, reeling, shaky, swimming, unsteady, *colloquial* woozy.
□ **dizziness** faintness, giddiness, light-headedness, vertigo.

DJ *abbreviation* **1** disc jockey. **2** dinner jacket.

dl *abbreviation* decilitre(s).

D.Litt. *abbreviation* Doctor of Letters.

DM *abbreviation* Deutschmark.

dm *abbreviation* decimetre(s).

DNA *abbreviation* deoxyribonucleic acid (substance carrying genetic information in chromosomes).

do[1] /duː/ *verb* (*3rd singular present* **does** /dʌz/; *past* **did**; *past participle* **done** /dʌn/; *present participle* **doing**) **1** perform, carry out. **2** produce, make. **3** impart. **4** act, proceed. **5** work at. **6** be suitable; satisfy. **7** attend to, deal with. **8** fare. **9** solve. **10** *colloquial* (often as **done** *adjective*) finish. **11** *colloquial* (often as **done** *adjective*) cook sufficiently. **12** *colloquial* (often as **done** *adjective*) (often + *in*) exhaust. **13** *colloquial* defeat; kill. **14** *colloquial* cater for. **15** *slang* rob. **16** *slang* swindle. **17** *slang* prosecute, convict. ● *auxiliary verb* **1** *used in questions and negative or emphatic statements and commands.* **2** *used as verbal substitute to avoid repetition.* ● *noun* (*plural* **dos** or **do's**) *colloquial* elaborate party or other undertaking. □ **do away with** *colloquial* **1** abolish. **2** kill. **do down** *colloquial* **1** swindle. **2** overcome. **do for 1** be sufficient for. **2** *colloquial* (esp. as **done** for *adjective*) destroy or ruin or kill. **3** *colloquial* do housework for. **do in 1** *slang* kill. **2** *colloquial* exhaust. **do-it-yourself** (to be) done or made by householder etc. **do over** *slang* attack, beat up. **do up 1** fasten. **2** *colloquial* restore; repair. **3** dress up. **do with** (after *could*) would appreciate; would profit by. **do without** forgo; manage without. □ **doable** *adjective*. **doer** *noun*.

■ *verb* **1** accomplish, achieve, bring about, carry out, cause, commit, complete, effect, execute, finish, fulfil, implement, initiate, instigate, organize, perform, undertake. **4** act, behave, conduct oneself, perform, proceed. **6** be acceptable, be enough, be satisfactory, be sufficient, be suitable, satisfy, serve, suffice. **7** arrange, attend to, cope with, deal with, handle, look after, manage, see to, work at. **9** answer, give one's mind to, puzzle out, solve, think out, work out. □ **do away with 1** see ABOLISH. **2** see KILL *verb* 1. **do up 1** see FASTEN 1. **2** see DECORATE 2.

do[2] = DOH.

do. *abbreviation* ditto.

docile /ˈdəʊsaɪl/ *adjective* submissive, easily managed. □ **docility** /-ˈsɪl-/ *noun*.

■ cooperative, domesticated, obedient, submissive, tame, tractable.

dock[1] *noun* **1** enclosed harbour for loading, unloading, and repair of ships. **2** (usually in *plural*) range of docks with wharves, warehouses, etc. ● *verb* **1** bring or come into dock. **2** join (spacecraft) together in space, be thus joined. □ **dockyard** area with docks and equipment for building and repairing ships.

■ *noun* **1** berth, jetty, landing stage, pier, quay, wharf. **2** (*docks*) dockyard, harbour, haven, marina, port. ● *verb* **1** anchor, berth, drop anchor, land, moor, tie up.

dock[2] *noun* enclosure in criminal court for accused.

dock[3] *noun* weed with broad leaves.

dock[4] *verb* **1** cut short (tail). **2** reduce or deduct (money etc.).

■ **1** see CUT *verb* 2. **2** see REDUCE 1.

docker *noun* person employed to load and unload ships.

docket /ˈdɒkɪt/ *noun* document listing goods delivered, jobs done, contents of package, etc. ● *verb* (**-t-**) label with or enter on docket.

doctor /ˈdɒktə/ *noun* **1** qualified medical practitioner. **2** holder of doctorate. ● *verb* **1** *colloquial* tamper with, adulterate. **2** castrate, spay.

■ *noun* **1** general practitioner, GP, medical officer, medical practitioner, MO, physician, *slang* quack, surgeon.

doctoral *adjective* of the degree of doctor.

doctorate /ˈdɒktərət/ *noun* highest university degree in any faculty.

doctrinaire /ˌdɒktrɪˈneə/ *adjective* applying theory or doctrine dogmatically.

doctrine /ˈdɒktrɪn/ *noun* **1** what is taught. **2** principle or set of principles of religious or political etc. belief. □ **doctrinal** /-ˈtraɪn(ə)l/ *adjective*.

■ **1** teaching. **2** axiom, belief, conviction, credo, creed, dogma, maxim, orthodoxy, postulate, precept, principle, tenet, theory, thesis.

document *noun* /ˈdɒkjʊmənt/ something written etc. that provides record or evidence of events, circumstances, etc. ● *verb* /ˈdɒkjʊment/ prove by or support with documents. □ **documentation** *noun*.

■ *noun* certificate, deed, instrument, paper, record. ● *verb* see RECORD *verb* 1.

documentary /ˌdɒkjʊˈmentərɪ/ *adjective* **1** consisting of documents. **2** factual; based on real events. ● *noun* (*plural* **-ies**) documentary film etc.

■ *adjective* **1** authenticated, chronicled, recorded, substantiated, written. **2** factual, historical, non-fiction, real life.

dodder /'dɒdə/ *verb* tremble, totter; be feeble. □ **dodderer** *noun*. **doddery** *adjective*.

doddle /'dɒd(ə)l/ *noun colloquial* easy task.

dodecagon /dəʊ'dekəgən/ *noun* plane figure with 12 sides.

dodecahedron /dəʊdekə'hi:drən/ *noun* solid figure with 12 faces.

dodge *verb* (**-ging**) **1** move quickly to elude pursuer, blow, etc. **2** elude (pursuer, blow, etc.) by moving out of the way. **3** evade by cunning or trickery. ● *noun* **1** quick evasive movement. **2** trick, clever expedient.
■ *verb* **1** duck, sidestep, swerve, turn away, veer, weave. **2** avoid, elude, escape, evade, sidestep. **3** evade, get out of, wriggle out of; (*dodge work*) shirk, *slang* skive; (*dodge a question*) equivocate, hedge, quibble, *colloquial* waffle. ● *noun* **2** contrivance, device, knack, manoeuvre, ploy, *slang* racket, ruse, scheme, stratagem, subterfuge, trick, *colloquial* wheeze.

dodgem /'dɒdʒəm/ *noun* small electrically powered car at funfair, bumped into others in enclosure.

dodgy *adjective* (**-ier, -iest**) *colloquial* unreliable, risky.

dodo /'dəʊdəʊ/ *noun* (*plural* **-s**) large extinct flightless bird.

DoE *abbreviation* Department of the Environment.

doe *noun* (*plural* same or **-s**) female fallow deer, reindeer, hare, or rabbit.

does *3rd singular present of* DO[1].

doesn't /'dʌz(ə)nt/ does not.

doff *verb esp. literary* take off (hat etc.).

dog *noun* **1** 4-legged flesh-eating animal of many breeds akin to wolf etc. **2** male of this or of fox or wolf. **3** *colloquial* despicable person. **4** (**the dogs**) *colloquial* greyhound racing. **5** mechanical device for gripping. ● *verb* (**-gg-**) follow closely; pursue, track. □ **dog cart** two-wheeled driving-cart with cross seats back to back. **dog collar** *colloquial* clergyman's stiff collar. **dog days** hottest period of year. **dog-eared** (of book-page etc.) with worn corners. **dog-end** *slang* cigarette-end. **dogfight** **1** fight between aircraft. **2** rough fight. **dogfish** small shark. **doghouse 1** *US & Australian* kennel. **2** (**in the doghouse**) *slang* in disgrace. **dog rose** wild hedge-rose. **dogsbody** *colloquial* drudge. **dog-star** Sirius. **dog-tired** tired out.
■ *noun* **1** bitch, cur, hound, mongrel, pup, puppy, whelp. ● *verb* see FOLLOW 1.

doge /dəʊdʒ/ *noun historical* chief magistrate of Venice or Genoa.

dogged /'dɒgɪd/ *adjective* tenacious. □ **doggedly** *adverb*. **doggedness** *noun*.

doggerel /'dɒgər(ə)l/ *noun* poor or trivial verse.

doggo /'dɒgəʊ/ *adverb slang* □ **lie doggo** wait motionless or hidden.

doggy *adjective* **1** of or like dogs. **2** devoted to dogs. □ **doggy bag** bag for restaurant customer to take home leftovers. **doggy-paddle** elementary swimming stroke.

dogma /'dɒgmə/ *noun* **1** principle, tenet. **2** doctrinal system.
■ article of faith, belief, conviction, creed, doctrine, orthodoxy, precept, principle, teaching, tenet, truth.

dogmatic /dɒg'mætɪk/ *adjective* imposing personal opinions; authoritative, arrogant. □ **dogmatically** *adverb*. **dogmatism** /'dɒgmətɪz(ə)m/ *noun*. **dogmatist** /'dɒgmətɪst/ *noun*.
■ arbitrary, assertive, authoritarian, authoritative, categorical, certain, dictatorial, doctrinaire, hardline, hidebound, imperious, inflexible, intolerant, narrow-minded, obdurate, opinionated, pontifical, positive, stubborn.

doh /dəʊ/ *noun* (also **do**) *Music* first note of scale in tonic sol-fa.

doily /'dɔɪlɪ/ *noun* (*plural* **-ies**) small lacy paper mat placed on plate for cakes etc.

doings /'du:ɪŋz/ *plural noun* **1** actions, exploits. **2** *slang* thing(s) needed.

Dolby /'dɒlbɪ/ *noun proprietary term* system used esp. in tape-recording to reduce hiss.

doldrums /'dɒldrəmz/ *plural noun* (usually **the doldrums**) **1** low spirits. **2** period of inactivity. **3** equatorial ocean region of calms.

dole *noun* **1** *colloquial* unemployment benefit. **2** charitable (esp. niggardly) gift or distribution. ● *verb* (**-ling**) (usually + *out*) distribute sparingly. □ **on the dole** *colloquial* receiving unemployment benefit.
■ *noun* **1** benefit, income support, social security, unemployment benefit. ● *verb* (*dole out*) see DISTRIBUTE 1. □ **on the dole** see UNEMPLOYED 1.

doleful /'dəʊlfʊl/ *adjective* **1** mournful. **2** dreary, dismal. □ **dolefully** *adverb*.

doll *noun* **1** model of esp. infant human figure as child's toy. **2** ventriloquist's dummy. **3** *colloquial* attractive young woman. ● *verb* (+ *up*) *colloquial* dress smartly.
■ *noun* **1** dolly, rag doll. **2** dummy, figure, puppet.

dollar /'dɒlə/ *noun* chief monetary unit in US, Australia, etc.

dollop /'dɒləp/ *noun* shapeless lump of food etc.

dolly /'dɒlɪ/ *noun* (*plural* **-ies**) **1** *child's word for* doll. **2** movable platform for cine-camera etc.

dolman sleeve /'dɒlmən/ *noun* loose sleeve cut in one piece with bodice.

dolmen /'dɒlmən/ *noun* megalithic tomb with large flat stone laid on upright ones.

dolomite /'dɒləmaɪt/ *noun* mineral or rock of calcium magnesium carbonate.

dolour /'dɒlə/ *noun* (*US* **dolor**) *literary* sorrow. □ **dolorous** *adjective*.

dolphin /'dɒlfɪn/ *noun* large porpoise-like sea mammal.

dolt /dəʊlt/ *noun* stupid person. □ **doltish** *adjective*.

Dom *noun: title prefixed to names of some RC dignitaries and Carthusian and Benedictine monks.*

domain /də'meɪn/ *noun* **1** area ruled over; realm. **2** estate etc. under one's control. **3** sphere of authority.

dome *noun* **1** rounded vault as roof. **2** dome-shaped thing. ● *verb* (**-ming**) (usually as **domed** *adjective*) cover with or shape as dome.

domestic /də'mestɪk/ *adjective* **1** of home, household, or family affairs. **2** of one's own country. **3** (of animal) tamed. **4** fond of home life. ● *noun* household servant.
■ *adjective* **1** family, home, household, private. **2** indigenous, inland, internal, national.

domesticate /də'mestɪkeɪt/ *verb* (**-ting**) (often as **domesticated** *adjective*) **1** tame (animal) to live with humans. **2** accustom to housework etc. □ **domestication** *noun.*
■ **1** (**domesticated**) house-trained, tame, tamed, trained.

domesticity /dɒme'stɪsɪtɪ/ *noun* **1** being domestic. **2** home life.

domicile /'dɒmɪsaɪl/ *noun* **1** dwelling place. **2** place of permanent residence. ● *verb* (**-ling**) (usually as **domiciled** *adjective*) (usually + *at, in*) settle in a place.

domiciliary /dɒmɪ'sɪlɪərɪ/ *adjective formal* (esp. of doctor's etc. visit) to or at person's home.

dominant /'dɒmɪnənt/ *adjective* dominating, prevailing. ● *noun Music* 5th note of diatonic scale. □ **dominance** *noun.*
■ *adjective* ascendant, biggest, chief, commanding, conspicuous, controlling, dominating, domineering, *colloquial* eye-catching, governing, highest, imposing, influential, largest, leading, main, major, obvious, outstanding, powerful, predominant, pre-eminent, presiding, prevailing, primary, principal, reigning, ruling, supreme, tallest, uppermost, widespread.

dominate /'dɒmɪneɪt/ *verb* (**-ting**) **1** command, control. **2** be most influential or obvious. **3** (of place) overlook. □ **domination** *noun.*
■ **1** be dominant, control, direct, govern, influence, lead, manage, master, rule, subjugate, take control of, tyrannize. **2** be in the majority, influence, monopolize, outnumber, preponderate, prevail, stand out. **3** dwarf, look out over, overshadow, tower over.

domineer /dɒmɪ'nɪə/ *verb* (often as **domineering** *adjective*) behave overbearingly.
■ (**domineering**) authoritarian, autocratic, *colloquial* bossy, despotic, dictatorial, high-handed, masterful, oppressive, overbearing, *colloquial* pushy, strict, tyrannical.

Dominican /də'mɪnɪkən/ *noun* friar or nun of order founded by St Dominic. ● *adjective* of this order.

dominion /də'mɪnjən/ *noun* **1** sovereignty. **2** realm, domain. **3** *historical* self-governing territory of British Commonwealth.

domino /'dɒmɪnəʊ/ *noun* (*plural* **-es**) **1** any of 28 small oblong pieces marked with 0–6 pips in each half. **2** (in *plural*) game played with these. **3** loose cloak worn with half-mask.

don[1] *noun* **1** university teacher, esp. senior member of college at Oxford or Cambridge. **2** (**Don**) *Spanish title prefixed to man's name.*

don[2] *verb* (**-nn-**) put on (garment).

donate /dəʊ'neɪt/ *verb* (**-ting**) give (money etc.), esp. to charity.
■ contribute, give, grant, hand over, present, supply.

donation *noun* **1** donating, being donated. **2** thing (esp. money) donated.
■ **1** contribution, giving. **2** *historical* alms, contribution, gift, offering, present.

done /dʌn/ *past participle* of DO[1]. ● *adjective* **1** completed. **2** cooked. **3** *colloquial* socially acceptable. **4** (often + *in*) *colloquial* tired out. **5** (esp. as *interjection* in response to offer etc.) accepted. □ **be done with** have or be finished with. **done for** *colloquial* in serious trouble.

doner kebab /'dɒnə kɪ'bæb/ *noun* spiced lamb cooked on spit and served in slices, often with pitta bread.

donkey /'dɒŋkɪ/ *noun* (*plural* **-s**) **1** domestic ass. **2** *colloquial* stupid person. □ **donkey jacket** thick weatherproof jacket. **donkey's years** *colloquial* very long time. **donkey-work** drudgery.

Donna /'dɒnə/ *noun: title of Italian, Spanish, or Portuguese lady.*

donnish *adjective* **1** like a college don. **2** pedantic.

donor /'dəʊnə/ *noun* **1** person who donates. **2** person who provides blood for transfusion, organ for transplantation, etc.
■ **1** backer, benefactor, contributor, giver, philanthropist, provider, sponsor, supplier, supporter.

don't /dəʊnt/ *verb* do not. ● *noun* prohibition.

doodle /'duːd(ə)l/ *verb* (**-ling**) scribble or draw absent-mindedly. ● *noun* such scribble or drawing.

doom /duːm/ *noun* **1** terrible fate or destiny. **2** ruin; death. ● *verb* **1** (usually + *to*) condemn or destine. **2** (esp. as **doomed** *adjective*) consign to ruin, destruction, etc. □ **doomsday** day of Last Judgement.
■ *noun* **1** destiny, end, fate, fortune, *Buddhism & Hinduism* karma, kismet, lot. ● *verb* **1** condemn, destine, fate, intend, ordain, predestine. **2** (**doomed**) accursed, condemned, cursed, damned, fated, hopeless, ill-fated, ill-starred, luckless, unlucky.

door /dɔː/ *noun* **1** hinged or sliding barrier closing entrance to building, room, cupboard, etc. **2** doorway. □ **doormat 1** mat for wiping shoes on. **2** *colloquial* subservient person. **doorstep 1** step or area immediately outside esp. outer door. **2** *slang* thick slice of bread. **doorstop** device for keeping door open or to keep it from striking wall. **door-to-door** (of selling etc.) done at each house in turn. **doorway** opening filled by door. **out of doors** in(to) open air.

■ **2** doorway, entrance, exit, gate, gateway, opening, portal, *archaic* postern, way out.

doorman /ˈdɔːmən/ *noun* person on duty at entrance to large building.

dope *noun* **1** *slang* drug, esp. narcotic. **2** thick liquid used as lubricant etc. **3** varnish. **4** *slang* stupid person. **5** *slang* information. ● *verb* (**-ping**) **1** give or add drug to. **2** apply dope to.

dopey *adjective* (also **dopy**) (**dopier, dopiest**) *colloquial* **1** half asleep, stupefied. **2** stupid.

doppelganger /ˈdɒp(ə)lgæŋə/ *noun* (also **doppelgänger** /-geŋə/) apparition or double of living person.

Doppler effect /ˈdɒplə/ *noun* change in frequency of esp. sound waves when source and observer are moving closer or apart.

dormant /ˈdɔːmənt/ *adjective* **1** lying inactive; sleeping. **2** inactive; not being used. □ **dormancy** *noun*.

■ **1** asleep, comatose, hibernating, inactive, inert, passive, quiescent, quiet, resting, sleeping, torpid. **2** hidden, latent, potential, unrevealed, untapped, unused.

dormer /ˈdɔːmə/ *noun* (in full **dormer window**) upright window in sloping roof.

dormitory /ˈdɔːmɪtərɪ/ *noun* (*plural* **-ies**) **1** sleeping-room with several beds. **2** (in full **dormitory town** etc.) commuter town or suburb.

dormouse /ˈdɔːmaʊs/ *noun* (*plural* **-mice**) small mouselike hibernating rodent.

dorsal /ˈdɔːs(ə)l/ *adjective* of or on back.

dory /ˈdɔːrɪ/ *noun* (*plural* same or **-ies**) edible sea fish.

dosage *noun* **1** size of dose. **2** giving of dose.

dose /dəʊs/ *noun* **1** single portion of medicine. **2** amount of radiation received. ● *verb* (**-sing**) **1** give medicine to. **2** (+ *with*) treat with.

■ *noun* amount, dosage, measure, portion, quantity.

doss *verb* (often + *down*) *slang* sleep on makeshift bed or in doss-house. □ **doss-house** cheap lodging house. □ **dosser** *noun*.

dossier /ˈdɒsɪə, ˈdɒsɪeɪ/ *noun* file containing information about person, event, etc.

■ file, folder, records.

dot *noun* **1** small spot, esp. as decimal point, part of *i* or *j* etc. **2** shorter signal of the two in Morse code. ● *verb* (**-tt-**) **1** mark or scatter with dot(s). **2** place dot over (letter). **3** (often + *about*) scatter like dots. **4** partly cover as with dots. **5** *slang* hit. □ **dotted line** line of dots for signature etc. on document. **on the dot** exactly on time.

■ *noun* **1** decimal point, fleck, full stop, mark, point, speck, spot. ● *verb* **1, 4** fleck, punctuate, speckle, spot, stipple.

dotage /ˈdəʊtɪdʒ/ *noun* feeble-minded senility.

dote *verb* (**-ting**) (usually + *on* or as **doting** *adjective*) be excessively fond of.

■ (*dote on*) adore, idolize, love, worship.

dotterel /ˈdɒtər(ə)l/ *noun* small plover.

dotty *adjective* (**-ier, -iest**) *colloquial* **1** eccentric, silly, crazy. **2** (+ *about*) infatuated with.

double /ˈdʌb(ə)l/ *adjective* **1** consisting of two things. **2** multiplied by two. **3** twice as much or many or large etc. **4** having twice the usual size, quantity, strength, etc. **5** having some part double. **6** (of flower) with two or more circles of petals. **7** ambiguous; deceitful. ● *adverb* **1** at or to twice the amount. **2** two together. ● *noun* **1** double quantity (of spirits etc.) or thing; twice the amount or quantity. **2** person or thing looking exactly like another. **3** (in *plural*) game between two pairs of players. **4** pair of victories. **5** bet in which winnings and stake from first bet are transferred to second. ● *verb* (**-ling**) **1** make or become double; increase twofold; amount to twice as much as. **2** fold over upon itself. **3** become folded. **4** play (two parts) in same play etc. **5** (usually + *as*) play twofold role. **6** turn sharply. **7** *Nautical* get round (headland). □ **at the double** running. **double agent** spy working for two rival countries etc. **double back** take reverse direction. **double-barrelled 1** (of gun) having two barrels. **2** (of surname) hyphenated. **double bass** largest instrument of violin family. **double-book** mistakenly reserve (seat, room, etc.) for two people at once. **double-breasted** (of garment) overlapping across body. **double chin** chin with fold of flesh below it. **double cream** thick cream with high fat-content. **double-cross** cheat, deceive. **double-crosser** *noun*. **double-dealing** (practising) deceit, esp. in business. **double-decker 1** bus etc. with two decks. **2** *colloquial* sandwich with two layers of filling. **double Dutch** *colloquial* gibberish. **double eagle** figure of eagle with two heads. **double-edged** presenting both a danger and an advantage. **double figures** numbers from 10 to 99. **double glazing** two layers of glass in window. **double negative** *Grammar* negative statement (incorrectly) containing two negative elements (see note below). **double pneumonia** pneumonia of both lungs. **double standard** rule or principle not impartially applied. **double take** delayed reaction to unexpected element of situation. **double-talk** (usually deliberately) ambiguous or misleading speech. **double up 1** bend or curl up (esp. in pain). **2** fold up.

USAGE Double negatives like *He didn't do nothing* and *I'm never going nowhere like that* are mistakes in standard English because one negative element is redundant. However, two negatives are perfectly acceptable in, for instance, *a not ungenerous sum* (meaning 'quite a generous sum').

■ *adjective* **1** coupled, doubled, dual, duple, duplicate, duplicated, paired, twin, twofold, two-ply. **2** twice. **3, 4** doubled, duplicate, twofold, two-ply. ● *noun* **2** *colloquial* clone, copy, counterpart, doppelganger, duplicate, lookalike, *colloquial* spitting image, twin. ● *verb* **1** duplicate, increase, multiply by two, reduplicate, repeat.

□ **double back** see RETURN *verb* 1. **double-cross** betray, cheat, deceive, let down, trick. **double up 1** see COLLAPSE *verb* 1.

double entendre /duːb(ə)l ɑːnˈtɑːndrə/ *noun* phrase capable of two meanings, one usually indecent. [French]

doublet /ˈdʌblɪt/ *noun* **1** *historical* man's close-fitting jacket. **2** one of pair of similar things.

doubloon /dʌˈbluːn/ *noun historical* Spanish gold coin.

doubt /daʊt/ *noun* **1** uncertainty; undecided state of mind. **2** cynicism; feeling of disbelief. **3** uncertain state. ● *verb* **1** feel uncertain or undecided about. **2** hesitate to believe. **3** call in question. □ **in doubt** open to question. **no doubt** certainly; admittedly. □ **doubter** *noun*.
■ *noun* **1** anxiety, apprehension, confusion, diffidence, disquiet, fear, hesitation, indecision, misgiving, perplexity, qualm, reservation, uncertainty, worry. **2** agnosticism, cynicism, disbelief, distrust, incredulity, mistrust, scepticism, suspicion. **3** ambiguity, confusion, uncertainty. ● *verb* **1, 2** be dubious about, be sceptical about, disbelieve, distrust, feel uncertain about, have doubts about, have misgivings about, have reservations about, mistrust, suspect. **3** see QUESTION *verb* 3.

doubtful *adjective* **1** feeling doubt. **2** causing doubt. **3** unreliable. □ **doubtfully** *adverb*.
■ **1** agnostic, cynical, diffident, disbelieving, distrustful, dubious, hesitant, incredulous, irresolute, sceptical, suspicious, tentative, uncertain, unclear, unconvinced, undecided, unsure, vacillating, wavering. **2** ambiguous, debatable, dubious, equivocal, *colloquial* iffy, inconclusive, problematical, questionable, suspect, vague, worrying. **3** dubious, questionable, suspect, uncommitted, undependable, unreliable, untrustworthy.

doubtless *adverb* **1** certainly. **2** probably.

douche /duːʃ/ *noun* **1** jet of liquid applied to part of body for cleansing or medicinal purposes. **2** device for producing this. ● *verb* (**-ching**) **1** treat with douche. **2** use douche.

dough /dəʊ/ *noun* **1** thick paste of flour mixed with liquid for baking. **2** *slang* money. □ **doughnut** (*US* **donut**) small fried cake of sweetened dough. □ **doughy** *adjective* (**-ier, -iest**).

doughty /ˈdaʊtɪ/ *adjective* (**-ier, -iest**) *archaic* valiant. □ **doughtily** *adverb*. **doughtiness** *noun*.

dour /dʊə/ *adjective* stern, grim; obstinate.

douse /daʊs/ *verb* (also **dowse**) (**-sing**) **1** throw water over. **2** plunge into water. **3** extinguish (light).

dove /dʌv/ *noun* **1** bird with short legs and full breast. **2** advocate of peaceful policies. **3** gentle or innocent person. □ **dovecot(e)** pigeon house.

dovetail *noun* mortise-and-tenon joint shaped like dove's spread tail. ● *verb* **1** fit together; combine neatly. **2** join with dovetails.

dowager /ˈdaʊədʒə/ *noun* woman with title or property from her late husband.

dowdy /ˈdaʊdɪ/ *adjective* (**-ier, -iest**) **1** (of clothes) unattractively dull. **2** dressed dowdily. □ **dowdily** *adverb*. **dowdiness** *noun*.
■ **1** colourless, drab, dull, old-fashioned, shabby, sloppy, slovenly, *colloquial* tatty, unattractive, unstylish. **2** frumpish, frumpy, shabby, unattractive, unstylish.

dowel /ˈdaʊəl/ *noun* cylindrical peg for holding parts of structure together.

dowelling *noun* rods for cutting into dowels.

dower /ˈdaʊə/ *noun* widow's share for life of husband's estate.

down[1] /daʊn/ *adverb* **1** towards or into lower place, esp. to ground. **2** in lower place or position. **3** to or in place regarded as lower, esp. southwards or away from major city or university. **4** in or into low or weaker position or condition. **5** losing by. **6** (of a computer system) out of action. **7** from earlier to later time. **8** in written or recorded form. ● *preposition* **1** downwards along, through, or into. **2** from top to bottom of. **3** along. **4** at lower part of. ● *adjective* **1** directed downwards. **2** *colloquial* depressed. ● *verb colloquial* **1** knock or bring etc. down. **2** swallow. ● *noun* **1** reverse of fortune. **2** *colloquial* period of depression. □ **be down to 1** be the responsibility of. **2** have nothing left but. **down and out** destitute. **down-and-out** destitute person. **downcast 1** dejected. **2** (of eyes) looking down. **downfall 1** fall from prosperity or power. **2** cause of this. **downgrade** reduce in rank etc. **downhearted** despondent **downhill** ● *adverb* in descending direction; on a decline. ● *adjective* sloping down, declining. **down in the mouth** *colloquial* looking unhappy. **downmarket** of or to cheaper sector of market. **down payment** partial payment made at time of purchase, booking, etc. **downpour** heavy fall of rain. **downside** negative aspect, drawback. **downstairs** ● *adverb* **1** down the stairs. **2** to or on lower floor. ● *adjective* situated downstairs. **downstream** in direction of flow of stream etc. **down-to-earth** practical, realistic. **down tools** *colloquial* cease working. **downtown** *US* (of) lower or central part of town or city. **downtrodden** oppressed. **downturn** decline, esp. in economic activity. **down under** *colloquial* in Australia or NZ. **downwind** in direction in which wind is blowing. **down with** *expressing rejection of person or thing.* **have a down on** *colloquial* be hostile to. □ **downward** *adjective & adverb*. **downwards** *adverb*.
■ □ **downfall** collapse, defeat, overthrow, ruin, undoing. **downhearted** dejected, depressed, discouraged, *colloquial* down, downcast, miserable, sad, unhappy. □ **downward** *adjective* declining, descending, downhill, falling.

down[2] /daʊn/ *noun* **1** baby bird's fluffy covering. **2** bird's under-plumage. **3** fine soft feathers or hairs.

down[3] /daʊn/ *noun* **1** open rolling land. **2** (in *plural*) chalk uplands of S. England etc.

downright *adjective* **1** plain, straightforward. **2** utter. ● *adverb* thoroughly.

Down's syndrome *noun* congenital disorder with mental retardation and physical abnormalities.

downy *adjective* (**-ier, -iest**) of, like, or covered with down.
■ feathery, fleecy, fluffy, furry, fuzzy, soft, velvety, woolly.

dowry /ˈdaʊərɪ/ *noun* (*plural* **-ies**) property brought by bride to her husband.

dowse[1] /daʊz/ *verb* (**-sing**) search for underground water or minerals by holding stick or rod which dips abruptly when over right spot. □ **dowser** *noun*.

dowse[2] = DOUSE.

doxology /dɒkˈsɒlədʒɪ/ *noun* (*plural* **-ies**) liturgical hymn etc. of praise to God.

doyen /ˈdɔɪən/ *noun* (*feminine* **doyenne** /dɔɪˈen/) senior member of group.

doz. *abbreviation* dozen.

doze *verb* (**-zing**) sleep lightly; be half asleep. ● *noun* short light sleep. □ **doze off** fall lightly asleep.

dozen /ˈdʌz(ə)n/ *noun* **1** (*plural* same (after numeral) or **-s**) set of twelve. **2** (**dozens**, usually + *of*) *colloquial* very many.

D.Phil. *abbreviation* Doctor of Philosophy.

Dr *abbreviation* Doctor.

drab *adjective* (**-bb-**) **1** dull, uninteresting. **2** of dull brownish colour. □ **drabness** *noun*.
■ **1** cheerless, colourless, dingy, dismal, dowdy, dreary, dull, flat, gloomy, grey, grimy, lacklustre, shabby, sombre, unattractive, uninteresting.

drachm /dræm/ *noun* weight formerly used by apothecaries, = ⅛ ounce.

drachma /ˈdrækmə/ *noun* (*plural* **-s**) chief monetary unit of Greece.

Draconian /drəˈkəʊnɪən/ *adjective* (of laws) harsh, cruel.

draft /drɑːft/ *noun* **1** preliminary written outline of scheme or version of speech, document, etc. **2** written order for payment of money by bank. **3** drawing of money on this. **4** detachment from larger group. **5** selection of this. **6** *US* conscription. **7** *US* draught. ● *verb* **1** prepare draft of. **2** select for special duty or purpose. **3** *US* conscript.
■ *noun* **1** notes, outline, plan, sketch. **2** bill of exchange, cheque, order, postal order. ● *verb* **1** compose, delineate, draw up, outline, plan, prepare, put together, sketch out, work out.

draftsman /ˈdrɑːftsmən/ *noun* **1** person who drafts documents. **2** person who makes drawings.

drafty *US* = DRAUGHTY.

drag *verb* (**-gg-**) **1** pull along with effort. **2** (allow to) trail. **3** (of time etc.) pass tediously or slowly. **4** search bottom of (river etc.) with grapnels, nets, etc. **5** (+ *on*, *at*) *slang* draw on (cigarette etc.).

● *noun* **1** obstruction to progress; retarding force. **2** *colloquial* boring or tiresome task, person, etc. **3** lure before hounds as substitute for fox. **4** apparatus for dredging. **5** *slang* a draw on cigarette etc. **6** *slang* women's clothes worn by men. □ **drag one's feet** be slow or reluctant. **drag out** protract.
■ *verb* **1** draw, haul, lug, pull, tow, tug. **2** dangle, stream, trail.

draggle /ˈdræg(ə)l/ *verb* (**-ling**) **1** make dirty and wet by trailing. **2** hang trailing.

dragon /ˈdrægən/ *noun* **1** mythical monster like reptile, usually with wings and able to breathe fire. **2** fierce woman.

dragonfly *noun* (*plural* **-ies**) large long-bodied gauzy-winged insect.

dragoon /drəˈguːn/ *noun* **1** cavalryman. **2** fierce man. ● *verb* (+ *into*) coerce or bully into.

drain *verb* **1** draw off liquid from. **2** draw off (liquid). **3** flow or trickle away. **4** dry or become dry. **5** exhaust. **6** drink to the dregs. **7** empty (glass etc.) by drinking. ● *noun* **1** channel or pipe carrying off liquid, sewage, etc. **2** constant outflow or expenditure. □ **draining board** sloping grooved surface beside sink for draining dishes. **drainpipe** pipe for carrying off water etc.
■ *verb* **2** draw off, empty, extract, pump out, remove, tap. **3** drip, ebb, leak, ooze, seep, trickle. **5** consume, deplete, exhaust, sap, spend, use up. ● *noun* **1** channel, conduit, culvert, ditch, drainpipe, duct, dyke, gutter, outlet, pipe, sewer, trench, watercourse.

drainage *noun* **1** draining. **2** system of drains. **3** what is drained off.

drake *noun* male duck.

dram *noun* **1** small drink of spirits etc. **2** drachm.

drama /ˈdrɑːmə/ *noun* **1** play for stage or broadcasting. **2** art of writing, acting, or presenting plays. **3** dramatic event or quality.
■ **1** dramatization, performance, play, production, radio play, screenplay, show, stage play, TV play. **2** acting, dramatics, histrionics, stagecraft, theatre, theatricals, Thespian arts. **3** *slang* action, crisis, excitement, suspense, turmoil.

dramatic /drəˈmætɪk/ *adjective* **1** of drama. **2** unexpected and exciting. **3** striking. **4** theatrical. □ **dramatically** *adverb*.
■ **1** histrionic, stage, theatrical, Thespian. **2** see EXCITING (EXCITE). **4** exaggerated, flamboyant, histrionic, large, melodramatic, overdone, showy, theatrical.

dramatics *plural noun* (often treated as *singular*) **1** performance of plays. **2** exaggerated behaviour.

dramatis personae /ˈdræmətɪs pɜːˈsəʊnaɪ/ *plural noun* characters in a play.

dramatist /ˈdræmətɪst/ *noun* writer of plays.
■ playwright, scriptwriter.

dramatize /ˈdræmətaɪz/ *verb* (also **-ise**) (**-zing** or **-sing**) **1** convert into play. **2** make dramatic. **3**

behave dramatically. □ **dramatization** *noun*.

■ **1** adapt. **3** exaggerate, make too much of, overdo, overplay, overstate.

drank *past* of DRINK.

drape *verb* (**-ping**) **1** cover or hang or adorn with cloth etc. **2** arrange in graceful folds. ● *noun* (often in *plural*) US curtain.

■ *verb* **1** cover, decorate, festoon, hang, swathe.

draper *noun* retailer of textile fabrics.

drapery *noun* (*plural* **-ies**) **1** clothing or hangings arranged in folds. **2** draper's trade or fabrics.

drastic /'dræstɪk/ *adjective* far-reaching in effect; severe. □ **drastically** *adverb*.

■ desperate, dire, Draconian, extreme, far-reaching, forceful, harsh, radical, rigorous, severe, strong, vigorous.

drat *colloquial verb* (**-tt-**) (usually as *interjection*) curse. ● *interjection: expressing annoyance.*

draught /drɑːft/ *noun* (US **draft**) **1** current of air indoors. **2** traction. **3** depth of water needed to float ship. **4** drawing of liquor from cask etc. **5** single act of drinking or inhaling. **6** amount so drunk. **7** (in *plural*) game for two with 12 pieces each, on **draughtboard** (like chessboard). □ **draught beer** beer drawn from cask, not bottled.

■ **1** breeze, current, puff, wind. **5, 6** dose, drink, gulp, measure, pull, swallow, *colloquial* swig.

draughtsman /'drɑːftsmən/ *noun* **1** person who makes drawings. **2** piece in game of draughts.

draughty *adjective* (US **drafty**) (**-ier, -iest**) (of a room etc.) letting in sharp currents of air.

draw *verb* (*past* **drew** /druː/; *past participle* **drawn**) **1** pull or cause to move towards or after one. **2** pull (thing) up, over, or across. **3** pull (curtains) open or shut. **4** attract; take in. **5** (+ *at, on*) inhale from. **6** extract; take from or out. **7** make (line, mark, or outline). **8** make (picture) in this way. **9** represent (thing) in this way. **10** finish (game etc.) with equal scores. **11** proceed to specified position. **12** infer. **13** elicit, evoke. **14** induce. **15** haul up (water) from well. **16** bring out (liquid from tap, wound, etc.). **17** draw lots. **18** obtain by lot. **19** (of tea) infuse. **20** (of chimney, pipe, etc.) promote or allow draught. **21** (+ *on*) make demand on imagination, skill, experience, etc. **22** write out (bill, cheque, etc.). **23** search (cover) for game etc. **24** (as **drawn** *adjective*) looking strained and tense. ● *noun* **1** act of drawing. **2** person or thing that draws custom or attention. **3** drawing of lots; raffle. **4** drawn game etc. □ **draw back** withdraw. **drawback** disadvantage. **drawbridge** hinged retractable bridge. **draw in 1** (of days etc.) become shorter. **2** (of train etc.) arrive at station. **draw out 1** prolong. **2** induce to talk. **3** (of days etc.) become longer. **drawstring** string or cord threaded through waistband, bag opening, etc. **draw up 1** draft (document etc.). **2** bring into order. **3** come to a halt. **4** (**draw oneself up**) make oneself erect.

■ *verb* **1** drag, haul, lug, pull, tow, tug. **4** allure, attract, bring in, coax, entice, invite, lure, pull in, win over. **6** extract, remove, take out, unsheathe, withdraw. **7–9** depict, map out, mark out, outline, paint, pen, pencil, portray, represent, sketch, trace. **10** be equal, finish equal, tie. **12** (*draw a conclusion*) arrive at a conclusion, come to a conclusion, deduce, gather, infer, reach a conclusion, work out. **16** drain, let (*blood*), pour, pump, siphon, tap. **18** choose, pick, select. ● *noun* **2** attraction, enticement, lure, pull. **3** competition, lottery, raffle. **4** dead heat, deadlock, stalemate, tie. □ **drawback** defect, difficulty, disadvantage, hindrance, hurdle, impediment, obstacle, obstruction, problem, snag, stumbling block. **draw out 1** see EXTEND 1. **draw up 1** see DRAFT *verb* 1. **3** see HALT[1] *verb*.

drawer /'drɔːə/ *noun* **1** person who draws. **2** (also /drɔː/) receptacle sliding in and out of frame (**chest of drawers**) or of table etc. **3** (in *plural*) knickers, underpants.

drawing *noun* **1** art of representing by line with pencil etc. **2** picture etc. made thus. □ **drawing board** board on which paper is fixed for drawing on. **drawing-pin** flat-headed pin for fastening paper to a surface.

■ **1** design, graphics, illustration, sketching. **2** cartoon, design, illustration, outline, picture, sketch.

drawing-room *noun* room in private house for sitting or entertaining in.

drawl *verb* speak with drawn-out vowel sounds. ● *noun* drawling utterance or way of speaking.

dray *noun* low cart without sides for heavy loads, esp. beer barrels.

dread /dred/ *verb* fear greatly, esp. in advance. ● *noun* great fear or apprehension. ● *adjective* **1** dreaded. **2** *archaic* awe-inspiring.

■ *verb* be afraid of, fear, shrink from, view with horror. ● *noun* anxiety, apprehension, awe, dismay, fear, nervousness, perturbation, qualm, trepidation, uneasiness, worry.

dreadful *adjective* **1** terrible. **2** *colloquial* very annoying, very bad. □ **dreadfully** *adverb*.

■ **1** alarming, appalling, *colloquial* awful, dire, distressing, evil, fearful, frightening, frightful, ghastly, grisly, gruesome, harrowing, hideous, horrible, horrifying, indescribable, monstrous, shocking, *colloquial* terrible, tragic, unspeakable, upsetting, wicked. **2** see ANNOYING (ANNOY), BAD 2.

dream *noun* **1** series of scenes in mind of sleeping person. **2** daydream or fantasy. **3** ideal; aspiration. ● *verb* (*past & past participle* **dreamt** /dremt/ or **dreamed**) **1** experience dream. **2** imagine as in dream. **3** (esp. in negative; + *of, that*) consider possible or acceptable. **4** be inactive or unrealistic. □ **dream up** think up, invent. □ **dreamer** *noun*. **dreamlike** *adjective*.

■ *noun* **1** (*bad dream*) nightmare. **2** daydream, delusion, fantasy, hallucination, illusion, mirage, reverie, trance, vision. **3** ambition, aspiration, ideal, pipe dream, wish. ● *verb* **1, 2** daydream, fancy, fantasize, hallucinate, have a vision, imagine, think. □ **dream up** see INVENT 1.

dreamy *adjective* (**-ier, -iest**) **1** given to daydreaming. **2** dreamlike; vague. **3** *colloquial* delightful. □ **dreamily** *adverb*

dreary /'drɪərɪ/ *adjective* (**-ier, -iest**) dismal, gloomy, dull. □ **drearily** *adverb*. **dreariness** *noun*.

■ bleak, boring, cheerless, depressing, dismal, dull, gloomy, joyless, miserable, sombre, uninteresting.

dredge[1] *noun* apparatus used to collect oysters etc., or to clear mud etc., from bottom of sea etc. ● *verb* (**-ging**) **1** bring up or clear (mud etc.) with dredge. **2** (+ *up*) bring up (something forgotten). **3** clean with or use dredge.

dredge[2] *verb* (**-ging**) sprinkle with flour etc.

dredger[1] *noun* **1** boat with dredge. **2** dredge.

dredger[2] *noun* container with perforated lid for sprinkling flour etc.

dregs *plural noun* **1** sediment, grounds. **2** worst part.

■ **1** deposit, grounds (*of coffee*), lees, precipitate, remains, residue, sediment.

drench *verb* **1** wet thoroughly. **2** force (animal) to take medicine. ● *noun* dose of medicine for animal.

■ *verb* **1** douse, drown, flood, inundate, saturate, soak, souse, steep, wet.

dress *verb* **1** put clothes on. **2** have and wear clothes. **3** put on evening or formal dress. **4** arrange or adorn. **5** put dressing on (wound etc.). **6** prepare (poultry, crab, etc.) for cooking or eating. **7** apply manure to. ● *noun* **1** woman's one-piece garment of bodice and skirt. **2** clothing, esp. whole outfit. □ **dress circle** first gallery in theatre. **dressmaker** person who makes women's clothes, esp. for a living. **dressmaking** *noun*. **dress rehearsal** (esp. final) rehearsal in costume. **dress up 1** put on special clothes. **2** make (person, thing) more attractive or interesting.

■ *verb* **1** array, attire, clothe, robe. **5** bandage, bind up, treat. ● *noun* **1** frock, gown, robe, shift. **2** *formal* apparel, attire, clothes, clothing, costume, garb, garments, *colloquial* gear, *colloquial* get-up, outfit, *archaic* raiment.

dressage /'dresɑːʒ/ *noun* training of horse in obedience and deportment.

dresser[1] /'dresə/ *noun* tall kitchen sideboard with shelves.

dresser[2] *noun* person who helps actors or actresses to dress for stage.

dressing *noun* **1** putting one's clothes on. **2** sauce, esp. of oil, vinegar, etc., for salads. **3** bandage, ointment, etc. for wound. **4** compost etc. spread over land. □ **dressing down** *colloquial* scolding. **dressing gown** loose robe worn while one is not fully dressed. **dressing table** table with mirror etc. for use while dressing, applying make-up, etc.

■ **3** bandage, compress, plaster, poultice. □ **dressing gown** bathrobe, housecoat, kimono, *esp. US* robe, wrapper.

dressy *adjective* (**-ier, -iest**) *colloquial* (of clothes or person) smart, elegant.

drew *past* of DRAW.

drey /dreɪ/ *noun* squirrel's nest.

dribble /'drɪb(ə)l/ *verb* (**-ling**) **1** allow saliva to flow from the mouth. **2** flow or allow to flow in drops. **3** *Football etc.* move (ball) forward with slight touches of feet etc. ● *noun* **1** act of dribbling. **2** dribbling flow.

■ *verb* **1** drool, slaver, slobber. **2** drip, leak, ooze, run, seep, trickle.

driblet /'drɪblɪt/ *noun* small quantity (of liquid etc.).

dribs and drabs *plural noun colloquial* small scattered amounts.

dried *past & past participle* of DRY.

drier[1] *comparative* of DRY.

drier[2] /'draɪə/ *noun* (also **dryer**) machine for drying hair, laundry, etc.

driest *superlative* of DRY.

drift *noun* **1** slow movement or variation. **2** this caused by current. **3** intention, meaning, etc. of what is said etc. **4** mass of snow etc. heaped up by wind. **5** state of inaction. **6** deviation of craft etc. due to current, wind, etc. ● *verb* **1** be carried by or as if by current of air or water. **2** progress casually or aimlessly. **3** (of current) carry. **4** heap or be heaped into drifts. □ **drift-net** net for sea fishing, which is allowed to drift. **driftwood** wood floating on moving water or washed ashore.

■ *noun* **3** see GIST. **4** accumulation, bank, dune, heap, mound, pile. ● *verb* **1** coast, float, waft. **2** coast, float, meander, ramble, roam, rove, stray, wander. **4** accumulate, gather, heap up, pile up.

drifter *noun* **1** aimless person. **2** fishing boat with drift-net.

drill[1] *noun* **1** tool or machine for boring holes. **2** instruction in military exercises. **3** thorough training, esp. by repetition. **4** routine procedure in emergency. **5** *colloquial* recognized procedure. ● *verb* **1** make hole in or through with drill. **2** make (hole) with drill. **3** train or be trained by drill.

■ *noun* **2, 3** discipline, exercises, instruction, practice, training. **4, 5** see PROCEDURE. ● *verb* **1, 2** bore, penetrate, perforate, pierce. **3** coach, discipline, exercise, indoctrinate, instruct, practise, rehearse, school, teach, train.

drill[2] *noun* **1** machine for making furrows, sowing, and covering seed. **2** small furrow for sowing seed in. **3** row of seeds sown by drill. ● *verb* plant in drills.

drill[3] *noun* coarse twilled cotton or linen fabric.

drill[4] *noun* W. African baboon related to mandrill.

drily *adverb* (also **dryly**) in a dry way.

drink *verb* (*past* **drank**; *past participle* **drunk**) **1** swallow (liquid). **2** take alcohol, esp. to excess. **3** (of plant etc.) absorb (moisture). ● *noun* **1** liquid for drinking. **2** draught or specified amount of this. **3** alcoholic liquor. **4** glass, portion, etc., of this. **5** (**the drink**) *colloquial* the sea. □ **drink-driver** *colloquial* person driving with excess alcohol in the blood. **drink in** listen eagerly to. **drink to** toast; wish success to. **drink up** drink all or remainder of. □ **drinkable** *adjective*. **drinker** *noun*.

■ *verb* **1** gulp, guzzle, imbibe, *slang* knock back, lap, partake of, *literary* quaff, sip, suck, swallow, *colloquial* swig, swill. **2** *colloquial* booze, carouse, get drunk, imbibe, *colloquial* indulge, tipple, *archaic* or *literary* tope. ● *noun* **1** *formal* beverage, *slang* bevvy, potation. **2, 4** *colloquial* cuppa, dram, draught, glass, gulp, nightcap, nip, *colloquial* pint, sip, swallow, *colloquial* swig, *colloquial* tipple, tot. **3** alcohol, *colloquial* booze, grog, liquor, *colloquial* plonk.

drip *verb* (**-pp-**) **1** fall or let fall in drops. **2** (often + *with*) be so wet as to shed drops. ● *noun* **1** liquid falling in drops. **2** drop of liquid. **3** sound of dripping. **4** *colloquial* dull or ineffectual person.

■ *verb* **1** dribble, drizzle, drop, leak, plop, splash, sprinkle, trickle, weep. ● *noun* **1–3** bead, dribble, drop, leak, splash, spot, tear, trickle.

drip-dry *verb* dry or leave to dry crease-free when hung up. ● *adjective* able to be drip-dried.

drip-feed *verb* feed intravenously in drops. ● *noun* **1** feeding thus. **2** apparatus for doing this.

dripping *noun* fat melted from roasting meat.

drive *verb* (**-ving**; *past* **drove** /drəʊv/; *past participle* **driven** /'drɪv(ə)n/) **1** urge in some direction, esp. forcibly. **2** compel. **3** force into specified state. **4** operate and direct (vehicle etc.). **5** carry or be carried in vehicle. **6** (often + *into*) force (nail etc.) into place by blows; force to penetrate. **7** strike ball from tee. **8** (of wind etc.) carry along, propel. ● *noun* **1** excursion in vehicle. **2** driveway. **3** street, road. **4** motivation and energy; inner urge. **5** forcible stroke of bat etc. **6** organized group effort. **7** transmission of power to machinery or wheels of motor vehicle etc. **8** organized whist, bingo, etc. competition. □ **drive at** seek, intend, mean. **drive-in** (bank, cinema, etc.) used while one sits in one's car. **drive out** force out; take place of. **driveway** private road through garden to house. **driving licence** licence permitting person to drive vehicle. **driving test** official test of competence to drive. **driving wheel** wheel transmitting power of vehicle to ground.

■ *verb* **1** force, herd, propel, push, send, urge. **2** coerce, compel, constrain, force, oblige, press, pressure, pressurize, push, urge. **4** control, direct, guide, handle, manage, operate, pilot, steer. **5** see CONVEY 1. **6** bang, force, hammer, hit, impel, knock, plunge, prod, push, ram, sink, stab, strike, thrust. ● *noun* **1** excursion, jaunt, journey, outing, ride, run, *colloquial* spin, trip. **4** aggressiveness, ambition, determination, energy, enterprise, enthusiasm, *colloquial* get-up-and-go, impetus, industry, initiative, keenness, motivation,

persistence, push, vigour, *colloquial* vim, zeal. **6** campaign, crusade, effort. □ **drive out** see EXPEL 1.

drivel /'drɪv(ə)l/ *noun* silly nonsense. ● *verb* (**-ll-**; *US* **-l-**) **1** talk drivel. **2** run at mouth or nose.

driver *noun* **1** person who drives. **2** golf club for driving from tee.

drizzle /'drɪz(ə)l/ *noun* very fine rain. ● *verb* (**-ling**) fall in very fine drops. □ **drizzly** *adjective*.

droll /drəʊl/ *adjective* **1** quaintly amusing. **2** strange, odd. □ **drollery** *noun* (*plural* **-ies**). **drollness** *noun*.

dromedary /'drɒmɪdərɪ/ *noun* (*plural* **-ies**) one-humped (esp. Arabian) camel bred for riding.

drone *noun* **1** non-working male of honey-bee. **2** idler. **3** deep humming sound. **4** monotonous speaking tone. **5** bass-pipe of bagpipes or its continuous note. ● *verb* (**-ning**) **1** make deep humming sound. **2** speak or utter monotonously.

drool *verb* **1** slobber, dribble. **2** (often + *over*) admire extravagantly.

droop /druːp/ *verb* **1** bend or hang down, esp. from fatigue or lack of food, drink, etc. **2** flag. ● *noun* **1** drooping position. **2** loss of spirit. □ **droopy** *adjective*.

■ *verb* **1** be limp, bend, dangle, fall, flop, hang, sag, slump, wilt, wither. **2** see LANGUISH.

drop *noun* **1** globule of liquid that falls, hangs, or adheres to surface. **2** very small amount of liquid. **3** abrupt fall or slope. **4** amount of this. **5** act of dropping. **6** fall in prices, temperature, etc. **7** drop-shaped thing; pendant or sweet. **8** (in *plural*) liquid medicine measured in drops. ● *verb* (**-pp-**) **1** fall; allow to fall; let go. **2** fall, let fall, or shed in drops. **3** sink down from exhaustion or injury. **4** cease; lapse; abandon. **5** *colloquial* cease to associate with or discuss. **6** set down (passenger etc.). **7** utter or be uttered casually. **8** fall or let fall in direction, amount, degree, pitch, etc. **9** (of person) jump down lightly; let oneself fall. **10** omit. **11** give birth to (lamb). **12** deliver from the air by parachute etc. **13** *Football* send (ball) or score (goal) by drop kick. □ **drop anchor** anchor ship. **drop back, behind** fall back; get left behind. **drop in, by** *colloquial* visit casually. **drop kick** kick at football made by dropping ball and kicking it as it touches ground. **drop off 1** fall asleep. **2** drop (passenger). **drop out** (often + *of*) *colloquial* cease to participate (in). **drop-out** *noun colloquial* person who has dropped out of esp. course of study or conventional society. **drop scone** scone made by dropping spoonful of mixture into pan etc. **drop shot** tennis shot dropping abruptly after clearing net. □ **droplet** *noun*.

■ *noun* **1** bead, blob, drip, droplet, globule, pearl, spot, tear. **2** dash, nip, tot. **3, 4** declivity, descent, dive, escarpment, fall, incline, plunge, precipice, scarp. **6** cut, decrease, reduction, slump. ● *verb* **1** fall, let go, release, relinquish. **3** collapse, fall, sink, slump. **4, 5** abandon, desert, discard, *colloquial* dump, forsake, give up, jilt, leave, reject, scrap, shed. **8** descend, dip, dive, fall, go down, lower, nosedive, plummet, plunge, sink, slump, subside, swoop, tumble. **10** eliminate, exclude, leave out, omit. □ **drop behind** see LAG[1] *verb*. **drop in** (*drop in on*) see VISIT *verb* 1. **drop off 1** see SLEEP *verb* 1.

dropper *noun* device for releasing liquid in drops.

droppings *plural noun* **1** dung. **2** thing that falls or has fallen in drops.

dropsy /ˈdrɒpsɪ/ *noun* oedema. □ **dropsical** *adjective*.

dross *noun* **1** rubbish. **2** scum of molten metal. **3** impurities.

drought /draʊt/ *noun* prolonged absence of rain.

drove[1] *past* of DRIVE.

drove[2] /drəʊv/ *noun* **1** moving crowd. **2** (in *plural*) *colloquial* great number. **3** herd or flock moving together.

drover *noun* herder of cattle.

drown /draʊn/ *verb* **1** kill or die by submersion. **2** submerge; flood; drench. **3** deaden (grief etc.) by drinking alcohol. **4** (often + *out*) overpower (sound) with louder sound.

■ **1** see DIE[1] 1. **2** deluge, drench, engulf, flood, immerse, submerge, swamp. **4** overpower, overwhelm, silence.

drowse /draʊz/ *verb* (**-sing**) be lightly asleep.

drowsy /ˈdraʊzɪ/ *adjective* (**-ier, -iest**) **1** very sleepy; almost asleep. **2** tending to make sleepy. □ **drowsily** *adverb*. **drowsiness** *noun*.

■ **1** dozing, dozy, heavy-eyed, listless, *colloquial* nodding off, sleepy, sluggish, somnolent, tired, weary. **2** see SOPORIFIC *adjective*.

drub *verb* (**-bb-**) **1** thrash, beat. **2** defeat thoroughly. □ **drubbing** *noun*.

drudge *noun* person who does dull, laborious, or menial work. ● *verb* (**-ging**) work hard or laboriously. □ **drudgery** *noun*.

■ □ **drudgery** chores, donkey-work, *colloquial* grind, labour, slavery, slog, toil, *literary* travail, work.

drug *noun* **1** medicinal substance. **2** (esp. addictive) hallucinogen, stimulant, narcotic, etc. ● *verb* (**-gg-**) **1** add drug to (drink, food, etc.). **2** administer drug to. **3** stupefy. □ **drugstore** *US* combined chemist's shop and café.

■ *noun* **1** medicament, medication, medicine, *esp. archaic* physic, remedy, treatment. **2** analgesic, antidepressant, barbiturate, hallucinogen, narcotic, opiate, painkiller, sedative, stimulant, tonic, tranquillizer; (*drugs*) *slang* dope. ● *verb* **2** dose, medicate, treat. **3** anaesthetize, dope, knock out, poison, sedate, stupefy, tranquillize.

drugget /ˈdrʌgɪt/ *noun* coarse woven fabric used for floor coverings etc.

druggist *noun* pharmacist.

Druid /ˈdruːɪd/ *noun* **1** ancient Celtic priest. **2**

member of a modern Druidic order, esp. the Gorsedd. □ **Druidic** /-ˈɪdɪk/ *adjective*. **Druidism** *noun*.

drum *noun* **1** hollow esp. cylindrical percussion instrument covered at one or both ends with plastic, skin, etc. **2** sound of this. **3** cylindrical structure or object. **4** cylinder used for storage etc. **5** eardrum. ● *verb* (**-mm-**) **1** play drum. **2** beat or tap continuously with fingers etc. **3** (of bird etc.) make loud noise with wings. □ **drumbeat** stroke or sound of stroke on drum. **drum brake** kind in which shoes on vehicle press against drum on wheel. **drum into** drive (facts etc.) into (person) by persistence. **drum machine** electronic device that simulates percussion. **drum major** leader of marching band. **drum majorette** female baton-twirling member of parading group. **drum out** dismiss with ignominy. **drumstick 1** stick for beating drum. **2** lower leg of fowl for eating. **drum up** summon or get by vigorous effort.

■ *noun* **2** (*drums*) timpani. **4** see BARREL *noun* 1.

drummer *noun* player of drum.

drunk /drʌŋk/ *past participle* of DRINK. ● *adjective* **1** lacking control as result of drinking alcohol. **2** (often + *with*) overcome with joy, success, power, etc. ● *noun* person who is drunk, esp. habitually.

■ *adjective* **1** delirious, fuddled, *colloquial* high, inebriate, inebriated, intoxicated, *colloquial* merry, *slang* paralytic, *slang* pickled, *slang* pie-eyed, *slang* plastered, *slang* sloshed, *colloquial* soused, *colloquial* sozzled, *slang* stoned, *colloquial* tiddly, *colloquial* tight, tipsy.

drunkard /ˈdrʌŋkəd/ *noun* person habitually drunk.

■ alcoholic, *colloquial* boozer, dipsomaniac, drunk, sot, tippler, *archaic* or *literary* toper.

drunken /ˈdrʌŋkən/ *adjective* **1** drunk. **2** caused by or involving drunkenness. **3** often drunk. □ **drunkenly** *adverb*. **drunkenness** *noun*.

drupe /druːp/ *noun* fleshy stone fruit.

dry *adjective* (**drier, driest**) **1** free from moisture, esp. with moisture having evaporated, drained away, etc. **2** (of eyes) free from tears. **3** (of climate) not rainy. **4** (of river, well, etc.) dried up. **5** (of wine etc.) not sweet. **6** plain, unelaborated. **7** uninteresting. **8** (of sense of humour) ironic, understated. **9** prohibiting sale of alcohol. **10** (of bread) without butter etc. **11** (of provisions etc.) solid, not liquid. **12** *colloquial* thirsty. ● *verb* (**dries, dried**) **1** make or become dry. **2** (usually as **dried** *adjective*) preserve (food) by removing moisture. □ **dry-clean** clean (clothes etc.) with solvents without water. **dry-fly** (of fishing) with floating artificial fly. **dry ice** solid carbon dioxide. **dry out 1** make or become fully dry. **2** treat or be treated for alcoholism. **dry rot 1** decay in wood not exposed to air. **2** fungi causing this. **dry run** *colloquial* rehearsal. **dry-shod** without wetting one's shoes. **dry up 1** make or become completely dry. **2** dry dishes. □ **dryness** *noun*.

■ *adjective* **1** arid, baked, barren, dehydrated, desiccated, parched, scorched, shrivelled, waterless. **7** boring, dreary, dull, flat, prosaic, stale, tedious, tiresome, uninspired, uninteresting. **8** deadpan, droll, ironic, laconic, understated, wry. ● *verb* **1** dehydrate, desiccate, go hard, parch, shrivel, wilt, wither.

dryad /'draɪæd/ *noun* wood nymph.

dryer = DRIER².

dryly = DRILY.

D.Sc. *abbreviation* Doctor of Science.

DSC, DSM, DSO *abbreviations* Distinguished Service Cross, Medal, Order.

DSS *abbreviation* Department of Social Security (formerly DHSS).

DT *abbreviation* (also **DT's** /di:'ti:z/) delirium tremens.

DTI *abbreviation* Department of Trade and Industry.

dual /'dju:əl/ *adjective* **1** in two parts; twofold. **2** double. ● *noun Grammar* dual number or form. □ **dual carriageway** road with dividing strip between traffic flowing in opposite directions. **dual control** two linked sets of controls, esp. of vehicle used for teaching driving etc., enabling operation by either of two people. □ **duality** /-'æl-/ *noun*.

■ *adjective* binary, coupled, double, duplicate, linked, paired, twin.

dub¹ *verb* (**-bb-**) **1** make (person) into knight. **2** give name or nickname to.

dub² *verb* (**-bb-**) **1** provide (film etc.) with alternative, esp. translated, soundtrack. **2** add (sound effects, music) to film or broadcast.

dubbin /'dʌbɪn/ *noun* (also **dubbing**) grease for softening and waterproofing leather.

dubiety /dju:'baɪətɪ/ *noun literary* doubt.

dubious /'dju:bɪəs/ *adjective* **1** doubtful. **2** questionable. **3** unreliable. □ **dubiously** *adverb*. **dubiousness** *noun*.

■ **1** see DOUBTFUL 1–3. **2** see QUESTIONABLE. **3** *slang* fishy, shady, suspect, suspicious, unreliable, untrustworthy.

ducal /'dju:k(ə)l/ *adjective* of or like duke.

ducat /'dʌkət/ *noun* gold coin formerly current in most European countries.

duchess /'dʌtʃɪs/ *noun* **1** duke's wife or widow. **2** woman holding rank of duke.

duchy /'dʌtʃɪ/ *noun* (*plural* **-ies**) duke's or duchess's territory.

duck *noun* (*plural* same or **-s**) **1** swimming bird, esp. domesticated form of mallard or wild duck. **2** female of this. **3** its flesh as food. **4** *Cricket* batsman's score of 0. **5** (also **ducks**) *colloquial* (esp. as form of address) darling. ● *verb* **1** bob down, esp. to avoid being seen or hit. **2** dip head briefly under water. **3** plunge (person) briefly in water. □ **duckweed** any of various plants that grow on surface of still water.

■ *verb* **1** bend, bob down, crouch, dodge, stoop. **2, 3** dip, immerse, plunge, push under, submerge.

duckling *noun* young duck.

duct *noun* **1** channel, tube. **2** tube in body carrying secretions etc.

ductile /'dʌktaɪl/ *adjective* **1** (of metal) capable of being drawn into wire; pliable. **2** easily moulded. **3** docile. □ **ductility** /-'tɪl-/ *noun*.

ductless *adjective* (of gland) secreting directly into bloodstream.

dud *slang noun* **1** useless or broken thing. **2** counterfeit article. **3** (in *plural*) clothes, rags. ● *adjective* defective, useless.

dude /du:d/ *noun* **1** *slang* fellow. **2** *US* dandy. **3** *US* city man staying on ranch.

dudgeon /'dʌdʒ(ə)n/ *noun* resentment; indignation. □ **in high dudgeon** very angry or angrily.

due *adjective* **1** owing, payable. **2** merited, appropriate. **3** (often + *to do*) expected or under obligation to do something or arrive at certain time. ● *noun* **1** what one owes or is owed. **2** (usually in *plural*) fee or amount payable. ● *adverb* (of compass point) exactly, directly. □ **due to** because of; caused by.

USAGE Many people believe that *due to*, meaning 'because of', should only be used after the verb *to be*, as in *The mistake was due to ignorance*, and not as in *All trains may be delayed due to a signal failure*. Instead, *owing to a signal failure* could be used.

■ *adjective* **1** in arrears, outstanding, owed, owing, payable, unpaid. **2** adequate, appropriate, decent, deserved, expected, fitting, just, mature, merited, proper, requisite, right, rightful, scheduled, sufficient, suitable, well earned. ● *noun* **1** deserts, entitlement, merits, reward, rights. **2** (*dues*) see DUTY 2.

duel /'dju:əl/ *noun* **1** armed contest between two people, usually to the death. **2** two-sided contest. ● *verb* (**-ll-**; *US* **-l-**) fight duel. □ **duellist** *noun*.

duenna /dju:'enə/ *noun* older woman acting as chaperon to girls, esp. in Spain.

duet /dju:'et/ *noun* musical composition for two performers.

duff *noun* boiled pudding. ● *adjective slang* worthless, useless, counterfeit.

duffer /'dʌfə/ *noun colloquial* inefficient or stupid person.

duffle /'dʌf(ə)l/ *noun* (also **duffel**) coarse woollen cloth. □ **duffle bag** cylindrical canvas bag closed by drawstring. **duffle coat** hooded overcoat of duffle with toggle fastenings.

dug¹ *past & past participle* of DIG.

dug² *noun* udder, teat.

dugong /'du:gɒŋ/ *noun* (*plural* same or **-s**) Asian sea mammal.

dugout *noun* **1** roofed shelter, esp. for troops in trenches. **2** underground shelter. **3** canoe made from tree trunk.

duke /dju:k/ *noun* **1** person holding highest hereditary title of the nobility. **2** sovereign prince ruling duchy or small state. □ **dukedom** *noun*.

dulcet /'dʌlsɪt/ *adjective* sweet-sounding.

dulcimer /'dʌlsɪmə/ *noun* metal-stringed musical instrument struck with two hand-held hammers.

dull *adjective* **1** tedious; not interesting. **2** (of weather) overcast. **3** (of colour, light, sound, etc.) not bright, vivid, or clear. **4** slow-witted, stupid. **5** (of knife-edge etc.) blunt. **6** listless, depressed. ● *verb* make or become dull. □ **dullard** *noun*. **dullness** *noun*. **dully** /'dʌllɪ/ *adverb*.

■ *adjective* **1** boring, commonplace, dry, monotonous, prosaic, stodgy, tame, tedious, unexciting, uninteresting. **2** cloudy, dismal, grey, heavy, leaden, murky, overcast, sullen, sunless. **3** (*dull colours*) dim, dingy, dowdy, drab, dreary, faded, flat, gloomy, lacklustre, lifeless, matt, plain, shabby, sombre, subdued; (*dull sounds*) deadened, indistinct, muffled, muted. **4** dense, *colloquial* dim, *colloquial* dim-witted, *colloquial* dumb, obtuse, slow, stupid, *colloquial* thick, unimaginative, unintelligent, unresponsive. **5** blunt, blunted, unsharpened.

duly /'dju:lɪ/ *adverb* **1** in due time or manner. **2** rightly, properly.

dumb /dʌm/ *adjective* **1** unable to speak. **2** silent, taciturn. **3** *colloquial* stupid, ignorant. □ **dumb-bell** short bar with weight at each end, for muscle-building etc. **dumbstruck** speechless with surprise. □ **dumbness** *noun*.

■ **1** inarticulate, *colloquial* mum, mute, silent, speechless, tongue-tied. **2** see SILENT 1;4.

dumbfound /dʌm'faʊnd/ *verb* nonplus; make speechless with surprise.

dumdum /'dʌmdʌm/ *noun* (in full **dumdum bullet**) soft-nosed bullet that expands on impact.

dummy /'dʌmɪ/ *noun* (*plural* **-ies**) **1** model of human figure, esp. as used to display clothes or by ventriloquist or as target. **2** imitation object used to replace real or normal one. **3** baby's rubber teat. **4** *colloquial* stupid person. **5** imaginary player in bridge etc., whose cards are exposed and played by partner. ● *adjective* sham, imitation. ● *verb* (**-ies, -ied**) make pretended pass etc. in football. □ **dummy run** trial attempt.

■ *noun* **1** doll, figure, manikin, puppet. **2** copy, counterfeit, duplicate, imitation, mock-up, model, reproduction, sample, sham, simulation, substitute, toy.

dump *noun* **1** place for depositing rubbish. **2** *colloquial* unpleasant or dreary place. **3** temporary store of ammunition etc. ● *verb* **1** put down firmly or clumsily. **2** deposit or discard as rubbish. **3** *colloquial* abandon. **4** sell (surplus goods) to foreign market at low price. **5** copy (contents of computer memory etc.) as diagnostic aid or for security.

■ *noun* **1** rubbish heap, scrapyard, tip. **3** arsenal, cache, depot, hoard, store. ● *verb* **1** deposit, drop, park, place, plonk down, put down, throw down. **2** discard, dispose of, *slang* ditch, get rid of, jettison,

offload, scrap, throw away, tip, *colloquial* unload. **3** abandon, desert, *slang* ditch, *colloquial* drop, jilt, reject, walk out on.

dumpling /'dʌmplɪŋ/ *noun* ball of dough boiled in stew or containing apple etc.

dumps *plural noun* (usually in **down in the dumps**) *colloquial* low spirits.

dumpy /'dʌmpɪ/ *adjective* (**-ier, -iest**) short and stout.

dun *adjective* greyish-brown. ● *noun* **1** dun colour. **2** dun horse.

dunce *noun* person slow at learning.

dunderhead /'dʌndəhed/ *noun* stupid person.

dune /dju:n/ *noun* drift of sand etc. formed by wind.

■ drift, hillock, hummock, mound, sand dune.

dung *noun* excrement of animals; manure. ● *verb* apply dung to (land). □ **dunghill** heap of dung or refuse.

dungarees /dʌŋgə'ri:z/ *plural noun* trousers with bib attached.

dungeon /'dʌndʒ(ə)n/ *noun* underground prison cell.

dunk *verb* **1** dip (food) into liquid before eating it. **2** immerse.

dunlin /'dʌnlɪn/ *noun* red-backed sandpiper.

dunnock /'dʌnək/ *noun* hedge sparrow.

duo /'dju:əʊ/ *noun* (*plural* **-s**) **1** pair of performers. **2** duet.

duodecimal /dju:əʊ'desɪm(ə)l/ *adjective* **1** of twelfths or 12. **2** proceeding by twelves.

duodenum /dju:əʊ'di:nəm/ *noun* (*plural* **-s**) part of small intestine next to stomach. □ **duodenal** *adjective*.

duologue /'dju:əlɒg/ *noun* dialogue between two people.

dupe /dju:p/ *noun* victim of deception. ● *verb* (**-ping**) deceive, trick.

duple /'dju:p(ə)l/ *adjective* of two parts. □ **duple time** *Music* rhythm with two beats to bar.

duplex /'dju:pleks/ *noun* US **1** flat on two floors. **2** house subdivided for two families. ● *adjective* having two elements; twofold.

duplicate *adjective* /'dju:plɪkət/ **1** identical. **2** doubled. ● *noun* /-kət/ identical thing, esp. copy. ● *verb* /-keɪt/ (**-ting**) **1** double. **2** make or be exact copy of. **3** repeat (an action etc.), esp. unnecessarily. □ **in duplicate** in two exact copies. □ **duplication** *noun*.

■ *adjective* copied, identical, matching, twin. ● *noun* carbon copy, *colloquial* clone, copy, double, facsimile, imitation, likeness, lookalike, match, photocopy, *proprietary term* Photostat, replica, reproduction, twin, *proprietary term* Xerox. ● *verb* **2** copy, photocopy, reproduce, xerox. **3** do again, redo, repeat, replicate.

duplicator *noun* machine for producing multiple copies of texts.

duplicity /djuˈplɪsɪtɪ/ *noun* double-dealing; deceitfulness. □ **duplicitous** *adjective*.

durable /ˈdjʊərəb(ə)l/ *adjective* lasting; hard-wearing. □ **durability** *noun*.

■ enduring, hard-wearing, heavy-duty, indestructible, long-lasting, permanent, resilient, stout, strong, substantial, thick, tough.

duration /djʊəˈreɪʃ(ə)n/ *noun* time taken by event. □ **for the duration 1** until end of event. **2** for very long time.

duress /djʊəˈres/ *noun* compulsion, esp. illegal use of force or threats.

Durex /ˈdjʊəreks/ *noun* proprietary term condom.

during /ˈdjʊərɪŋ/ *preposition* throughout; at some point in.

dusk *noun* darker stage of twilight.

■ evening, *poetical* gloaming, gloom, sundown, sunset, twilight.

dusky *adjective* (**-ier, -iest**) **1** shadowy, dim. **2** dark-coloured.

dust *noun* **1** finely powdered earth or other material etc. **2** dead person's remains. ● *verb* **1** wipe the dust from (furniture etc.). **2** sprinkle with powder, sugar, etc. □ **dustbin** container for household refuse. **dust bowl** desert made by drought or erosion. **dustcover 1** dust sheet. **2** dust jacket. **dust jacket** paper cover on hardback book. **dustman** man employed to collect household refuse. **dustpan** pan into which dust is brushed from floor etc. **dust sheet** protective cloth over furniture. **dust-up** *colloquial* fight, disturbance.

■ *noun* **1** dirt, grime, grit, particles, powder.

duster *noun* cloth etc. for dusting furniture etc.

dusty *adjective* (**-ier, -iest**) **1** covered with or full of dust. **2** like dust; powdery.

■ **1** dirty, filthy, grimy, grubby, mucky, uncleaned, unswept. **2** chalky, crumbly, dry, fine, friable, gritty, powdery, sandy, sooty.

Dutch *adjective* of the Netherlands or its people or language. ● *noun* **1** Dutch language. **2** (**the Dutch**) (treated as *plural*) the people of the Netherlands. □ **Dutch auction** one in which price is progressively reduced. **Dutch barn** roof on poles over hay etc. **Dutch cap** dome-shaped contraceptive device fitting over cervix. **Dutch courage** courage induced by alcohol. **Dutchman, Dutchwoman** native or national of the Netherlands. **Dutch treat** party, outing, etc. at which people pay for themselves. **go Dutch** share expenses on outing.

dutiable /ˈdjuːtɪəb(ə)l/ *adjective* requiring payment of duty.

dutiful /ˈdjuːtɪfʊl/ *adjective* doing one's duty; obedient. □ **dutifully** *adverb*.

■ attentive, careful, compliant, conscientious, devoted, diligent, faithful, hard-working, loyal, obedient, obliging, punctilious, reliable, responsible, scrupulous, trustworthy, willing.

duty /ˈdjuːtɪ/ *noun* (*plural* **-ies**) **1** moral or legal obligation; responsibility. **2** tax on certain goods, imports, etc. **3** job or function arising from a business or office. □ **duty-free** (of goods) on which duty is not payable. **on, off duty** working, not working.

■ **1** allegiance, faithfulness, loyalty, obedience, obligation, onus, responsibility, service. **2** charge, customs, dues, fee, impost, levy, tariff, tax, toll. **3** assignment, business, charge, chore, function, job, office, role, task, work.

duvet /ˈduːveɪ/ *noun* thick soft quilt used instead of sheets and blankets.

dwarf /dwɔːf/ *noun* (*plural* **-s** or **dwarves** /dwɔːvz/) **1** person, animal, or plant much below normal size, esp. with normal-sized head and body but short limbs. **2** small mythological being with magical powers. ● *adjective* small; stunted. ● *verb* **1** stunt in growth. **2** make look small by contrast. □ **dwarfish** *adjective*.

■ *noun* **1** midget, pygmy. ● *adjective* see SMALL *adjective* 1. ● *verb* **2** dominate, overshadow, tower over.

dwell *verb* (*past & past participle* **dwelt** or **dwelled**) reside, live. □ **dwell on** think, write, or speak at length on. □ **dweller** *noun*.

■ *archaic* abide, be accommodated, live, lodge, reside, stay; (*dwell in*) see INHABIT.

dwelling *noun* (also **dwelling place**) house, residence.

■ abode, domicile, habitation, home, house, lodging, quarters, residence.

dwindle /ˈdwɪnd(ə)l/ *verb* (**-ling**) **1** become gradually less or smaller. **2** lose importance.

dye /daɪ/ *noun* **1** substance used to change colour of fabric, wood, hair, etc. **2** colour produced by this. ● *verb* (**dyeing, dyed**) **1** colour with dye. **2** dye a specified colour. □ **dyed in the wool** unchangeable, inveterate. □ **dyer** *noun*.

dying /ˈdaɪɪŋ/ *present participle* of DIE[1]. ● *adjective* of, or at the time of, death.

■ *adjective* declining, expiring, fading, failing, moribund, obsolescent.

dyke /daɪk/ (also **dike**) *noun* **1** embankment built to prevent flooding. **2** low wall. ● *verb* (**-king**) provide or protect with dyke(s).

dynamic /darˈnæmɪk/ *adjective* **1** energetic, active. **2** of motive force. **3** of force in operation. **4** of dynamics. □ **dynamically** *adverb*.

■ **1** active, committed, driving, eager, energetic, enterprising, enthusiastic, forceful, go-ahead, high-powered, lively, motivated, powerful, *colloquial* pushy, spirited, vigorous, zealous.

dynamics *plural noun* (usually treated as *singular*) mathematical study of motion and forces causing it.

dynamism /ˈdaɪnəmɪz(ə)m/ *noun* energy; dynamic power.

dynamite /ˈdaɪnəmaɪt/ *noun* high explosive mixture containing nitroglycerine. ● *verb* (**-ting**) charge or blow up with this.

dynamo /'daməməʊ/ *noun* (*plural* **-s**) **1** machine converting mechanical into electrical energy. **2** *colloquial* energetic person.

dynast /'dmɑst/ *noun* **1** ruler. **2** member of dynasty.

dynasty /'dmɑsti/ *noun* (*plural* **-ies**) line of hereditary rulers. □ **dynastic** /-'nɑs-/ *adjective*.

dyne *noun Physics* force required to give a mass of one gram an acceleration of one centimetre per second per second.

dysentery /'dɪsəntri/ *noun* inflammation of bowels, causing severe diarrhoea.

dysfunction /dɪs'fʌŋkʃ(ə)n/ *noun* abnormality or impairment of functioning.

dyslexia /dɪs'leksɪə/ *noun* abnormal difficulty in reading and spelling. □ **dyslectic** /-'lektɪk/ *adjective & noun*. **dyslexic** *adjective & noun*.

dyspepsia /dɪs'pepsɪə/ *noun* indigestion. □ **dyspeptic** *adjective & noun*.

dystrophy /'dɪstrəfɪ/ *noun* defective nutrition.

Ee

E. *abbreviation* (also **E**) east(ern). □ **E-number** number prefixed by letter E identifying food additive.

each *adjective* every one of two or more, regarded separately. ● *pronoun* each person or thing. □ **each way** (of bet) backing horse etc. to win or come second or third.

eager /'iːgə/ *adjective* keen, enthusiastic. □ **eagerly** *adverb*. **eagerness** *noun*.

■ agog, animated, anxious (*to please*), ardent, avid, bursting, committed, craving, desirous, earnest, enthusiastic, excited, fervent, fervid, hungry, impatient, intent, interested, itching, keen, keyed up, longing, motivated, passionate, *colloquial* raring to go, voracious, yearning, zealous. □ **eagerness** alacrity, anxiety, appetite, ardour, avidity, commitment, desire, earnestness, enthusiasm, excitement, fervour, hunger, hurry, impatience, intentness, interest, keenness, longing, motivation, passion, thirst, zeal.

eagle /'iːg(ə)l/ *noun* **1** large bird of prey. **2** *Golf* score of two under par for hole. □ **eagle eye** keen sight, watchfulness. **eagle-eyed** *adjective*.

eaglet /'iːglɪt/ *noun* young eagle.

ear[1] /ɪə/ *noun* **1** organ of hearing, esp. external part. **2** faculty of discriminating sound. **3** attention. □ **all ears** listening attentively. **earache** pain in inner ear. **eardrum** membrane of middle ear. **earphone** (usually in *plural*) device worn on ear to listen to recording, radio, etc. **earplug** device worn in ear as protection from water, noise, etc. **earring** jewellery worn on ear. **earshot** hearing-range. **ear-splitting** excessively loud. **ear-trumpet** trumpet-shaped tube formerly used as hearing aid.

ear[2] /ɪə/ *noun* seed-bearing head of cereal plant.

earl /ɜːl/ *noun* British nobleman ranking between marquess and viscount. □ **earldom** *noun*.

early /'ɜːlɪ/ *adjective & adverb* (**-ier, -iest**) **1** before due, usual, or expected time. **2** not far on in day or night. **3** not far on in development etc.; of first stage. □ **early bird** *colloquial* person who arrives, gets up, etc. early. **early days** too soon to expect results etc.

■ **1** advance, ahead of time, before time, forward, premature. **3** ancient, antiquated, first, initial, old, original, primeval, primitive.

earmark *verb* set aside for special purpose.

earn /ɜːn/ *verb* **1** obtain as reward for work or merit. **2** bring as income or interest. □ **earner** *noun*.

■ **1** attain, be worthy of, deserve, merit, qualify for, warrant, win. **2** be paid, bring in, clear, gain, get, gross, make, make a profit of, net, obtain, pocket, realize, receive, yield.

earnest /'ɜːnɪst/ *adjective* intensely serious. □ **in earnest** serious(ly). □ **earnestly** *adverb*. **earnestness** *noun*.

■ ardent, assiduous, committed, conscientious, dedicated, determined, devoted, diligent, eager, grave, hard-working, heartfelt, impassioned, industrious, involved, purposeful, resolved, serious, sincere, sober, solemn, thoughtful, well meant, zealous.

earnings /'ɜːnɪŋz/ *plural noun* money earned.

■ income, pay, salary, stipend, wages.

earth /ɜːθ/ *noun* **1** planet we live on (also **Earth**). **2** land and sea as opposed to sky. **3** ground. **4** soil, mould. **5** this world as opposed to heaven or hell. **6** *Electricity* connection to earth as completion of circuit. **7** hole of fox etc. ● *verb* **1** *Electricity* connect to earth. **2** cover (roots) with earth. □ **earthwork** bank of earth in fortification. **earthworm** worm living in earth. **run to earth** find after long search.

■ *noun* **4** clay, dirt, ground, humus, loam, mould, soil, topsoil.

earthen *adjective* made of earth or baked clay. □ **earthenware** pottery made of fired clay.

■ □ **earthenware** ceramics, china, crockery, crocks, porcelain, pots, pottery.

earthly *adjective* **1** of earth, terrestrial. **2** *colloquial* (usually with negative) remotely possible. □ **not an earthly** *colloquial* no chance or idea whatever.

■ **1** corporeal, human, material, materialistic, mortal, mundane, physical, secular, temporal, terrestrial, worldly.

earthquake *noun* violent shaking of earth's surface.

■ *colloquial* quake, shock, tremor.

earthy *adjective* (**-ier, -iest**) **1** of or like earth or soil. **2** coarse, crude.

■ **2** bawdy, coarse, crude, frank, lusty, obscene, ribald, uninhibited.

earwig *noun* insect with pincers at rear end.

ease /iːz/ *noun* **1** facility, effortlessness. **2** freedom from pain, trouble, or constraint. ● *verb* (**-sing**) **1** relieve from pain etc. **2** (often + *off, up*) become less burdensome or severe. **3** (often + *off, up*) relax, slacken. **4** move or be moved by gentle force.

■ *noun* **1** dexterity, easiness, effortlessness, facility, simplicity, skill, speed, straightforwardness. **2** aplomb, calmness, comfort, composure, contentment, enjoyment, happiness, leisure, luxury, nonchalance, peace, quiet, relaxation, repose, rest, serenity, tranquillity. ● *verb* **1** allay, alleviate, assuage, calm, comfort, lighten, mitigate, moderate, pacify, quell, quieten, reduce, relax, relieve, soothe, tranquillize. **2** abate, decrease, diminish, lessen, *colloquial* let up. **4** edge, guide, inch, manoeuvre, move gradually, slide, slip, steer.

easel /'iːz(ə)l/ *noun* stand for painting, blackboard, etc.

easement *noun Law* right of way over another's property.

easily /'iːzɪlɪ/ *adverb* **1** without difficulty. **2** by far. **3** very probably.

east *noun* **1** point of horizon where sun rises at equinoxes. **2** corresponding compass point. **3** (usually **the East**) eastern part of world, country, town, etc. ● *adjective* **1** towards, at, near, or facing east. **2** (of wind) from east. ● *adverb* **1** towards, at, or near east. **2** (+ *of*) further east than. □ **eastbound** travelling or leading east. **East End** part of London east of City. **east-north-east**, **east-south-east** point midway between east and north-east or south-east. □ **eastward** *adjective, adverb, & noun.* **eastwards** *adverb.*

Easter /'iːstə/ *noun* festival of Christ's resurrection. □ **Easter egg** artificial usually chocolate egg given at Easter. **Easter Saturday 1** day before Easter. **2** (properly) Saturday after Easter.

easterly /'iːstəlɪ/ *adjective & adverb* **1** in eastern position or direction. **2** (of wind) from east.

eastern /'iːst(ə)n/ *adjective* of or in east. □ **Eastern Church** Orthodox Church. □ **easternmost** *adjective.*

easterner *noun* native or inhabitant of east.

easy /'iːzɪ/ *adjective* (**-ier, -iest**) **1** not difficult. **2** free from pain, trouble, or anxiety. **3** relaxed and pleasant. **4** compliant. ● *adverb* with ease; in an effortless or relaxed way. □ **easy chair** large comfortable armchair. **easygoing** placid and tolerant. **easy on the eye, ear, etc.** *colloquial* pleasant to look at, listen to, etc. **go easy** (usually + *on, with*) be sparing or cautious. **take it easy 1** proceed gently. **2** relax. □ **easiness** *noun.*

■ *adjective* **1** (*easy instructions*) clear, elementary, facile, foolproof, manageable, plain, simple, straightforward, uncomplicated, understandable, user-friendly; (*easy job*) *colloquial* cushy, effortless, light, painless, *colloquial* soft, undemanding, unexacting. **2** carefree, comfortable, contented, cosy, *colloquial* cushy, leisurely, painless, peaceful, relaxed, relaxing, restful, serene, *colloquial* soft, tranquil, unhurried, untroubled. **3** see EASYGOING.
□ **easygoing** accommodating, affable, amenable, calm, carefree, casual, cheerful, docile, even-tempered, flexible, forbearing, free and easy, friendly, genial, happy-go-lucky, indulgent, informal, *colloquial* laid-back, lax, lenient, liberal,

mellow, natural, nonchalant, patient, permissive, placid, pleasant, relaxed, tolerant, unexcitable, unruffled.

eat *verb* (*past* **ate** /et, eɪt/; *past participle* **eaten**) **1** chew and swallow (food). **2** consume food; have meal. **3** (+ *away, into*) destroy. **4** (+ *away, into*) consume. ● *noun* (in *plural*) *colloquial* food. □ **eating apple** one suitable for eating raw. **eat one's heart out** suffer from excessive longing. **eat out** have meal away from home, esp. in restaurant. **eat up** eat completely.

■ **1** consume, devour, digest, feed on, ingest, live on, partake of, swallow. **2** banquet, breakfast, dine, feast, have a meal, lunch, *archaic* sup. **3** (*eat away, eat into*) see ERODE.

eatable *adjective* fit to be eaten. ● *noun* (usually in *plural*) food.

■ *adjective* digestible, edible, fit to eat, good, palatable, safe to eat, wholesome.

eater *noun* **1** person who eats. **2** eating apple.

eau-de-Cologne /əʊdəkə'ləʊn/ *noun* toilet water originally from Cologne.

eaves /iːvz/ *plural noun* underside of projecting roof.

eavesdrop *verb* (**-pp-**) listen to private conversation. ● **eavesdropper** *noun.*

ebb *noun* outflow of tide. ● *verb* **1** flow back. **2** decline.

■ *verb* **1** fall, flow back, go down, recede, retreat, subside. **2** see DECLINE *verb* 1.

ebony /'ebənɪ/ *noun* hard heavy black tropical wood. ● *adjective* made of or black as ebony.

ebullient /ɪ'bʌlɪənt/ *adjective* exuberant. □ **ebullience** *noun.* **ebulliently** *adverb.*

EC *abbreviation* **1** European Community. **2** East Central.

eccentric /ɪk'sentrɪk/ *adjective* **1** odd or capricious in behaviour or appearance. **2** not placed centrally; not having axis etc. placed centrally. **3** not concentric. **4** not circular. ● *noun* eccentric person. □ **eccentrically** *adverb.* **eccentricity** /eksen'trɪs-/ *noun* (*plural* **-ies**).

■ *adjective* **1** aberrant, abnormal, anomalous, atypical, bizarre, capricious, cranky, curious, freakish, grotesque, idiosyncratic, *colloquial* kinky, odd, outlandish, out of the ordinary, peculiar, preposterous, quaint, queer, quirky, singular, strange, unconventional, unorthodox, unusual, *slang* wacky, *colloquial* way-out, *colloquial* weird, zany. **2, 3** irregular, off-centre. ● *noun* *colloquial* character, *colloquial* crackpot, crank, *colloquial* freak, individualist, nonconformist, *colloquial* oddball, oddity, *colloquial* weirdo.

ecclesiastic /ɪkliːzɪ'æstɪk/ *noun* clergyman.

ecclesiastical *adjective* of the Church or clergy.

ECG *abbreviation* electrocardiogram.

echelon /'eʃəlɒn/ *noun* **1** level in organization,

society, etc. **2** wedge-shaped formation of troops, aircraft, etc.

echidna /ɪˈkɪdnə/ *noun* Australian egg-laying spiny mammal.

echo /ˈekəʊ/ *noun* (*plural* **-es**) **1** repetition of sound by reflection of sound waves. **2** reflected radio or radar beam. **3** close imitation. **4** circumstance or event reminiscent of earlier one. ● *verb* (**-es, -ed**) **1** resound with echo. **2** (of sound) be repeated. **3** repeat, imitate.

■ *verb* **1** resound, reverberate, ring, sound again. **3** ape, copy, duplicate, emulate, imitate, mimic, reiterate, repeat, reproduce, say again.

éclair /eɪˈkleə/ *noun* finger-shaped iced cake of choux pastry filled with cream.

éclat /eɪˈklɑː/ *noun* **1** brilliant display. **2** conspicuous success; prestige.

eclectic /ɪˈklektɪk/ *adjective* selecting ideas, style, etc. from various sources. ● *noun* eclectic person. □ **eclecticism** /-tɪs-/ *noun*.

eclipse /ɪˈklɪps/ *noun* **1** obscuring of light of sun by moon (**solar eclipse**) or of moon by earth (**lunar eclipse**). **2** loss of light or importance. ● *verb* (**-sing**) **1** cause eclipse of. **2** intercept (light). **3** outshine, surpass.

■ *verb* **1** block out, blot out, cloud, conceal, cover, darken, dim, extinguish, obscure, veil. **3** excel, outdo, outshine, overshadow, put in the shade, surpass, top.

eclogue /ˈeklɒg/ *noun* short pastoral poem.

ecology /ɪˈkɒlədʒɪ/ *noun* study of relations of organisms to one another and their surroundings. □ **ecological** /iːkəˈlɒdʒ-/ *adjective*. **ecologically** /iːkəˈlɒdʒ-/ *adverb*. **ecologist** *noun*.

economic /iːkəˈnɒmɪk/ *adjective* **1** of economics; connected with trade and industry. **2** profitable. □ **economically** *adverb*.

■ **1** budgetary, business, commercial, financial, fiscal, industrial, mercantile, monetary, trading. **2** moneymaking, paying, profitable, remunerative.

economical /iːkəˈnɒmɪk(ə)l/ *adjective* sparing; avoiding waste. □ **economically** *adverb*.

■ (*economical housekeeper*) careful, cheese-paring, frugal, parsimonious, provident, prudent, sparing, thrifty; (*economical meal*) cheap, cost-effective, inexpensive, low-priced, reasonable.

economics /iːkəˈnɒmɪks/ *plural noun* (treated as *singular*) **1** science of production and distribution of wealth. **2** application of this to particular subject. □ **economist** /ɪˈkɒnəmɪst/ *noun*.

economize /ɪˈkɒnəmaɪz/ *verb* (also **-ise**) (**-zing** or **-sing**) make economies; reduce expenditure.

■ be economical, cut back, cut costs, retrench, save, scrimp, skimp, spend less, tighten one's belt.

economy /ɪˈkɒnəmɪ/ *noun* (*plural* **-ies**) **1** community's system of wealth creation. **2** frugality. **3** instance of this. **4** sparing use.

■ **1** budget, economic affairs, wealth. **2, 3** frugality, parsimony, providence, prudence, restraint, saving, thrift. **4** see BREVITY.

ecosystem /ˈiːkəʊsɪstəm/ *noun* biological community of interacting organisms and their physical environment.

ecru /ˈeɪkruː/ *noun* light fawn colour.

ecstasy /ˈekstəsɪ/ *noun* (*plural* **-ies**) **1** overwhelming joy or rapture. **2** *slang* type of hallucinogenic drug. □ **ecstatic** /ɪkˈstætɪk/ *adjective*.

■ **1** bliss, delight, delirium, elation, enthusiasm, euphoria, exaltation, fervour, frenzy, gratification, happiness, joy, rapture, thrill, trance, transport. □ **ecstatic** blissful, delighted, delirious, elated, enraptured, enthusiastic, euphoric, exhilarated, exultant, fervent, frenzied, gleeful, happy, joyful, orgasmic, overjoyed, over the moon, rapturous, transported.

ECT *abbreviation* electroconvulsive therapy.

ectoplasm /ˈektəʊplæz(ə)m/ *noun* supposed viscous substance exuding from body of spiritualistic medium during trance.

ecu /ˈeɪkjuː/ *noun* (also **Ecu**) (*plural* **-s**) European Currency Unit.

ecumenical /iːkjuːˈmenɪk(ə)l/ *adjective* **1** of or representing whole Christian world. **2** seeking worldwide Christian unity. □ **ecumenism** /iːˈkjuːmən-/ *noun*.

eczema /ˈeksɪmə/ *noun* kind of inflammation of skin.

ed. *abbreviation* **1** edited by. **2** edition. **3** editor.

Edam /ˈiːdæm/ *noun* round Dutch cheese with red rind.

eddy /ˈedɪ/ *noun* (*plural* **-ies**) circular movement of water, smoke etc. ● *verb* (**-ies, -ied**) move in eddies.

■ *noun* maelstrom, swirl, vortex, whirl, whirlpool, whirlwind. ● *verb* spin, swirl, turn, whirl.

edelweiss /ˈeɪd(ə)lvaɪs/ *noun* Alpine plant with woolly white bracts.

edema *US* = OEDEMA.

Eden /ˈiːd(ə)n/ *noun* (in full **Garden of Eden**) **1** home of Adam and Eve. **2** delightful place or state.

edge *noun* **1** boundary line or margin of area or surface. **2** narrow surface of thin object. **3** meeting-line of surfaces. **4** sharpened side of blade. **5** sharpness. **6** brink of precipice. **7** crest of ridge. **8** effectiveness. ● *verb* (**-ging**) **1** advance gradually or furtively. **2** give or form border to. **3** sharpen. □ **edgeways**, **edgewise** with edge foremost or uppermost. **have the edge on, over** have slight advantage over. **on edge** excited or irritable. **set (person's) teeth on edge** cause unpleasant nervous sensation in.

■ *noun* **1** border, boundary, brim, brink, circumference, edging, frame, fringe, hem, kerb, limit, lip, margin, outline, outskirts, perimeter, periphery, rim, selvage, side, verge. **5** acuteness, keenness, sharpness. ● *verb* **1** crawl, creep, inch, move stealthily, sidle, slink, steal, work one's way, worm. **2** bind, border, fringe, hem, trim.

edging *noun* thing forming edge or border.

edgy *adjective* (**-ier**, **-iest**) irritable; anxious. □ **edginess** *noun*.

edible /'edɪb(ə)l/ *adjective* fit to be eaten. ● *noun* (in *plural*) food.
■ digestible, eatable, fit to eat, palatable, safe to eat, wholesome.

edict /'i:dɪkt/ *noun* order proclaimed by authority.

edifice /'edɪfɪs/ *noun* building, esp. imposing one.

edify /'edɪfaɪ/ *verb* (**-ies**, **-ied**) improve morally. □ **edification** *noun*.

edit /'edɪt/ *verb* (**-t-**) **1** prepare for publication or broadcast. **2** be editor of. **3** cut and collate (films, tapes, etc.) to make unified sequence. **4** reword, modify. **5** (+ *out*) remove (part) from text, recording, etc.
■ **1** adapt, annotate, arrange, assemble, compile, dub (*sounds*), format, get ready, organize, prepare, proof-read, put together, select. **3** collate, cut, put together, splice. **4** abridge, adapt, alter, amend, bowdlerize, censor, clean up, condense, correct, cut, emend, expurgate, modify, polish, rearrange, rephrase, revise, reword, rewrite, shorten. **5** (*edit out*) cut out, delete, erase, expunge, expurgate.

edition /ɪ'dɪʃ(ə)n/ *noun* **1** edited or published form of book etc. **2** copies of book or newspaper etc. issued at one time. **3** instance of regular broadcast.
■ **1, 2** copy, issue, number, printing, print run, publication, version.

editor /'edɪtə/ *noun* **1** person who edits. **2** person who directs writing of newspaper or news programme or section of one. **3** person who selects material for publication. □ **editorship** *noun*.

editorial /edɪ'tɔ:rɪəl/ *adjective* of editing or an editor. ● *noun* article giving newspaper's views on current topic.

educate /'edjʊkeɪt/ *verb* (**-ting**) **1** train or instruct mentally and morally. **2** provide systematic instruction for. □ **educable** *adjective*. **educated** *adjective*. **education** *noun*. **educational** *adjective*. **educator** *noun*.
■ bring up, civilize, coach, counsel, cultivate, discipline, drill, edify, enlighten, guide, improve, inculcate, indoctrinate, inform, instruct, lecture, nurture, rear, school, teach, train, tutor. □ **educated** cultured, enlightened, erudite, knowledgeable, learned, literate, numerate, sophisticated, trained, well bred, well read. **education** coaching, curriculum, enlightenment, guidance, indoctrination, instruction, schooling, syllabus, teaching, training, tuition.

educationist *noun* (also **educationalist**) expert in educational methods.

Edwardian /ed'wɔ:dɪən/ *adjective* of or characteristic of reign (1901–10) of Edward VII. ● *noun* person of this period.

EEC *abbreviation* European Economic Community.

EEG *abbreviation* electroencephalogram.

eel *noun* snakelike fish.

eerie /'ɪərɪ/ *adjective* (**-r**, **-st**) strange; weird. □ **eerily** *adjective*. **eeriness** *noun*.
■ *colloquial* creepy, frightening, ghostly, mysterious, *colloquial* scary, spectral, *colloquial* spooky, strange, uncanny, unearthly, unnatural, weird.

efface /ɪ'feɪs/ *verb* (**-cing**) **1** rub or wipe out. **2** surpass, eclipse. **3** (**efface oneself**) treat oneself as unimportant. □ **effacement** *noun*.

effect /ɪ'fekt/ *noun* **1** result, consequence. **2** efficacy. **3** impression. **4** (in *plural*) possessions. **5** (in *plural*) lighting, sound, etc. giving realism to play etc. **6** physical phenomenon. ● *verb* bring about.

USAGE As a verb, *effect* should not be confused with *affect*. *He effected an entrance* means 'He got in (somehow)', but *This won't affect me* means 'My life won't be changed by this'.
■ *noun* **1** aftermath, conclusion, consequence, impact, influence, issue, outcome, repercussion, result, sequel, upshot. **3** feeling, illusion, impression, sensation, sense. ● *verb* accomplish, achieve, bring about, bring in, carry out, cause, create, effectuate, execute, implement, initiate, make, produce, put into effect, secure.

effective *adjective* **1** operative. **2** impressive. **3** actual. **4** producing intended effect. □ **effectively** *adverb*. **effectiveness** *noun*.
■ **1** functional, operational, operative. **2** cogent, compelling, convincing, impressive, persuasive, potent, powerful, striking, strong, telling. **3** actual, real. **4** able, capable, competent, effectual, efficacious, efficient, productive, proficient, serviceable, successful, useful, worthwhile.

effectual /ɪ'fektʃʊəl/ *adjective* **1** producing required effect. **2** valid.

effectuate /ɪ'fektʃʊeɪt/ *verb* cause to happen.

effeminate /ɪ'femɪnət/ *adjective* (of a man) unmanly, womanish. □ **effeminacy** *noun*.
■ *colloquial* camp, effete, girlish, *colloquial* sissy, unmanly, weak, *derogatory* womanish.

effervesce /efə'ves/ *verb* (**-cing**) give off bubbles of gas. □ **effervescence** *noun*. **effervescent** *adjective*.
■ bubble, ferment, fizz, foam, froth, sparkle. □ **effervescent** bubbling, bubbly, carbonated, fizzy, foaming, frothy, gassy, sparkling.

effete /ɪ'fi:t/ *adjective* feeble; effeminate.

efficacious /efɪ'keɪʃəs/ *adjective* producing desired effect. □ **efficacy** /'efɪkəsɪ/ *noun*.

efficient /ɪ'fɪʃ(ə)nt/ *adjective* **1** productive with minimum waste of effort. **2** competent, capable. □ **efficiency** *noun*. **efficiently** *adverb*.
■ **1** cost-effective, economic, effective, productive, streamlined, thrifty. **2** see COMPETENT.

effigy /'efɪdʒɪ/ *noun* (*plural* **-ies**) sculpture or model of person.

effloresce /ˌef*lɔː*ˈres/ *verb* (**-cing**) burst into flower. □ **efflorescence** *noun*.

effluence /ˈeflʊəns/ *noun* **1** flowing out (of light, electricity, etc.). **2** what flows out.

effluent /ˈeflʊənt/ *adjective* flowing out. ● *noun* **1** sewage or industrial waste discharged into river etc. **2** stream flowing from lake etc.

effluvium /ɪˈfluːvɪəm/ *noun* (*plural* **-via**) unpleasant or harmful outflow.

effort /ˈefət/ *noun* **1** exertion. **2** determined attempt. **3** force exerted. **4** *colloquial* something accomplished. □ **effortless** *adjective*. **effortlessly** *adverb*. **effortlessness** *noun*.

■ **1** application, diligence, *colloquial* elbow grease, endeavour, exertion, industry, labour, pains, strain, stress, striving, struggle, toil, *literary* travail, trouble, work. **2** attempt, endeavour, go, try, venture. **4** accomplishment, achievement, exploit, feat, job, outcome, result.

effrontery /ɪˈfrʌntərɪ/ *noun* impudence.

effuse /ɪˈfjuːz/ *verb* (**-sing**) pour forth.

effusion /ɪˈfjuːʒ(ə)n/ *noun* outpouring.

effusive /ɪˈfjuːsɪv/ *adjective* demonstrative; gushing. □ **effusively** *adverb*. **effusiveness** *noun*.

■ demonstrative, ebullient, enthusiastic, exuberant, fulsome, gushing, lavish, over the top, profuse, voluble.

EFL *abbreviation* English as a foreign language.

Efta /ˈeftə/ *noun* (also **EFTA**) European Free Trade Association.

e.g. *abbreviation* for example.

egalitarian /ɪˌɡælɪˈteərɪən/ *adjective* of or advocating equal rights for all. ● *noun* egalitarian person. □ **egalitarianism** *noun*.

egg[1] *noun* **1** body produced by female of birds, insects, etc., capable of developing into new individual. **2** edible egg of domestic hen. **3** ovum. □ **eggcup** cup for holding boiled egg. **egghead** *colloquial* intellectual. **eggplant** aubergine. **egg white** white or clear part round yolk of egg.

egg[2] *verb* (+ *on*) urge.

eglantine /ˈeɡləntaɪn/ *noun* sweet-brier.

ego /ˈiːɡəʊ/ *noun* (*plural* **-s**) **1** the self. **2** part of mind that has sense of individuality. **3** self-esteem.

egocentric /ˌiːɡəʊˈsentrɪk/ *adjective* self-centred. □ **egocentricity** *noun*.

egoism /ˈiːɡəʊɪz(ə)m/ *noun* **1** self-interest as moral basis of behaviour. **2** systematic selfishness. **3** egotism. □ **egoist** *noun*. **egoistic** /-ˈɪs-/ *adjective*.

■ egocentricity, egotism, narcissism, pride, self-centredness, self-importance, self-interest, selfishness, self-love, self-regard, vanity.

egotism /ˈiːɡətɪz(ə)m/ *noun* **1** self-conceit. **2** selfishness. □ **egotist** *noun*. **egotistic(al)** /-ˈtɪs-/ *adjective*.

■ □ **egotistic** conceited, egocentric, overweening, self-admiring, self-centred, selfish.

egregious /ɪˈɡriːdʒəs/ *adjective* **1** extremely bad. **2** *archaic* remarkable.

egress /ˈiːɡres/ *noun* **1** going out. **2** way out.

egret /ˈiːɡrɪt/ *noun* kind of white heron.

Egyptian /ɪˈdʒɪpʃ(ə)n/ *adjective* of Egypt. ● *noun* **1** native or national of Egypt. **2** language of ancient Egyptians.

Egyptology /ˌiːdʒɪpˈtɒlədʒɪ/ *noun* study of ancient Egypt. □ **Egyptologist** *noun*.

eh /eɪ/ *interjection* *colloquial* expressing inquiry, surprise, etc.

eider /ˈaɪdə/ *noun* northern species of duck. □ **eiderdown** quilt stuffed with soft material, esp. down.

eight /eɪt/ *adjective* & *noun* **1** one more than seven. **2** 8-oared boat. **3** its crew. □ **eightsome reel** lively Scottish dance for 8 people. □ **eighth** /eɪtθ/ *adjective* & *noun*.

eighteen /eɪˈtiːn/ *adjective* & *noun* one more than seventeen. □ **eighteenth** *adjective* & *noun*.

eighty /ˈeɪtɪ/ *adjective* & *noun* (*plural* **-ies**) eight times ten. □ **eightieth** *adjective* & *noun*.

eisteddfod /aɪˈstedfəd/ *noun* congress of Welsh poets and musicians gathering for musical and literary competition.

either /ˈaɪðə, ˈiːðə/ *adjective* & *pronoun* **1** one or other of two. **2** each of two. ● *adverb* (with negative) any more than the other. □ **either ... or ...** as one possibility ... and as the other ... .

ejaculate /ɪˈdʒækjʊleɪt/ *verb* (**-ting**) **1** emit (semen) in orgasm. **2** exclaim. □ **ejaculation** *noun*.

eject /ɪˈdʒekt/ *verb* **1** throw out, expel. **2** (of pilot etc.) cause oneself to be propelled from aircraft in emergency. **3** emit. □ **ejection** *noun*.

■ **1** banish, boot out, bundle out, deport, discharge, dismiss, drive out, evict, exile, expel, get rid of, kick out, oust, push out, put out, remove, *colloquial* sack, send out, shoot out, shove out, throw out, turn out. **3** see EMIT.

ejector seat *noun* device in aircraft for emergency ejection of pilot etc.

eke *verb* (**eking**) □ **eke out 1** supplement (income etc.). **2** make (living) or support (existence) with difficulty.

elaborate *adjective* /ɪˈlæbərət/ **1** minutely worked out. **2** complicated. ● *verb* /ɪˈlæbəreɪt/ (**-ting**) **1** work out or explain in detail. **2** make more intricate. □ **elaborately** *adverb*. **elaboration** *noun*.

■ *adjective* **1** detailed, exhaustive, intricate, meticulous, minute, painstaking, thorough. **2** baroque, busy, Byzantine, complex, complicated, decorative, fancy, fantastic, fussy, intricate, involved, ornamental, ornamented, ornate, rococo, showy. ● *verb* add to, adorn, amplify, complicate, decorate, develop, embellish, enlarge on, enrich, expand (on), expatiate on, fill out, flesh out, give details of, improve on, ornament.

élan /eɪˈlɑ̃/ *noun* vivacity, dash. [French]

eland /'iːlənd/ *noun* (*plural* same or -s) large African antelope.

elapse /ɪ'læps/ *verb* (-sing) (of time) pass by.
| ■ go by, lapse, pass, slip by.

elastic /ɪ'læstɪk/ *adjective* 1 able to resume normal bulk or shape after being stretched or squeezed. 2 springy. 3 flexible, adaptable. ● *noun* elastic cord or fabric, usually woven with strips of rubber. □ **elastic band** rubber band. □ **elasticity** /iːlæ'stɪs-/ *noun*.
| ■ *adjective* 1, 2 bouncy, ductile, expandable, flexible, plastic, pliable, pliant, resilient, rubbery, springy, stretchable, stretchy, yielding.

elasticated /ɪ'læstɪkeɪtɪd/ *adjective* (of fabric) made elastic by weaving with rubber thread.

elate /ɪ'leɪt/ *verb* (-ting) (esp. as **elated** *adjective*) make delighted or proud. □ **elation** *noun*.

elbow /'elbəʊ/ *noun* 1 joint between forearm and upper arm. 2 part of sleeve covering elbow. 3 elbow-shaped thing. ● *verb* 1 thrust or jostle (person). 2 make (one's way) thus. □ **elbow grease** *colloquial* vigorous polishing; hard work. **elbow room** *colloquial* adequate space to move or work in.

elder[1] /'eldə/ *adjective* older; senior. ● *noun* 1 older person. 2 official in early Christian and some modern Churches.

elder[2] /'eldə/ *noun* tree with white flowers and black **elderberries**.

elderly /'eldəlɪ/ *adjective* rather old.
| ■ aged, ageing, getting on, old, oldish.

eldest /'eldɪst/ *adjective* first-born; oldest surviving.

eldorado /eldə'rɑːdəʊ/ *noun* (*plural* -s) imaginary land of great wealth.

elect /ɪ'lekt/ *verb* 1 choose by voting. 2 choose, decide. ● *adjective* 1 chosen. 2 select, choice. 3 (after noun) chosen but not yet in office.
| ■ *verb* adopt, appoint, choose, name, nominate, opt for, pick, select, vote for. ● *adjective* 1 chosen, elected, selected. 3 designate, to be.

election /ɪ'lekʃ(ə)n/ *noun* 1 electing, being elected. 2 occasion for this.
| ■ 1 choice, selection, voting. 2 ballot, plebiscite, poll, referendum, vote.

electioneer /ɪlekʃə'nɪə/ *verb* take part in election campaign.
| ■ campaign, canvass.

elective /ɪ'lektɪv/ *adjective* 1 chosen by or derived from election. 2 entitled to elect. 3 optional.

elector /ɪ'lektə/ *noun* person entitled to vote in election. □ **electoral** *adjective*.

electorate /ɪ'lektərət/ *noun* group of electors.
| ■ constituents, electors, voters.

electric /ɪ'lektrɪk/ *adjective* 1 of, worked by, or charged with electricity. 2 causing or charged with excitement. □ **electric blanket** one heated by internal wires. **electric chair** chair used for electrocution of criminals. **electric eel** eel-like fish able to give electric shock. **electric fire** portable electric heater. **electric shock** effect of sudden discharge of electricity through body of person etc. □ **electrically** *adverb*.
| ■ 1 battery-operated, electrical, mains-operated. 2 see EXCITING (EXCITE).

electrical *adjective* of or worked by electricity. □ **electrically** *adverb*.

electrician /ɪlek'trɪʃ(ə)n/ *noun* person who installs or maintains electrical equipment.

electricity /ɪlek'trɪsɪtɪ/ *noun* 1 form of energy present in protons and electrons. 2 science of electricity. 3 supply of electricity.
| ■ 3 current, energy, power, power supply.

electrify /ɪ'lektrɪfaɪ/ *verb* (-ies, -ied) 1 charge with electricity. 2 convert to electric working. 3 startle, excite. □ **electrification** *noun*.

electro- *combining form* of or caused by electricity.

electrocardiogram /ɪlektrəʊ'kɑːdɪəgræm/ *noun* record of electric currents generated by heartbeat. □ **electrocardiograph** instrument for recording such currents.

electroconvulsive /ɪlektrəʊkən'vʌlsɪv/ *adjective* (of therapy) using convulsive response to electric shocks.

electrocute /ɪ'lektrəkjuːt/ *verb* (-ting) kill by electric shock. □ **electrocution** /-'kjuːʃ(ə)n/ *noun*.

electrode /ɪ'lektrəʊd/ *noun* conductor through which electricity enters or leaves electrolyte, gas, vacuum, etc.

electroencephalogram /ɪlektrəʊ'sefələgræm/ *noun* record of electrical activity of brain. □ **electroencephalograph** instrument for recording such activity.

electrolysis /ɪlek'trɒlɪsɪs/ *noun* 1 chemical decomposition by electric action. 2 breaking up of tumours, hair-roots, etc. thus.

electrolyte /ɪ'lektrəlaɪt/ *noun* 1 solution that can conduct electricity. 2 substance that can dissolve to produce this. □ **electrolytic** /-trəʊ'lɪt-/ *adjective*.

electromagnet /ɪlektrəʊ'mægnɪt/ *noun* soft metal core made into magnet by electric current through coil surrounding it.

electromagnetism /ɪlektrəʊ'mægnɪtɪz(ə)m/ *noun* 1 magnetic forces produced by electricity. 2 study of these.

electron /ɪ'lektrɒn/ *noun* stable elementary particle with charge of negative electricity, found in all atoms and acting as primary carrier of electricity in solids. □ **electron microscope** one with high magnification, using electron beam instead of light.

electronic /ɪlek'trɒnɪk/ *adjective* 1 of electrons or electronics. 2 (of music) produced electronically. □ **electronic mail** messages distributed by a computer system. □ **electronically** *adverb*.

electronics *plural noun* (treated as *singular*) science of movement of electrons in vacuum, gas, semiconductor, etc.

electroplate /ɪˈlektrəʊpleɪt/ *verb* (**-ting**) coat with chromium, silver, etc. by electrolysis. ● *noun* electroplated articles.

elegant /ˈelɪgənt/ *adjective* **1** graceful, tasteful, refined. **2** ingeniously simple. □ **elegance** *noun*. **elegantly** *adverb*.
■ **1** artistic, beautiful, chic, courtly, cultivated, dapper, debonair, dignified, exquisite, fashionable, fine, genteel, graceful, gracious, handsome, luxurious, modish, noble, pleasing, *colloquial* plush, *colloquial* posh, refined, smart, *soigné(e)*, sophisticated, splendid, stately, stylish, suave, tasteful, urbane, well bred.

elegiac /elɪˈdʒaɪək/ *adjective* used for elegies; mournful.

elegy /ˈelɪdʒɪ/ *noun* (*plural* **-ies**) sorrowful song or poem, esp. for the dead.
■ dirge, lament, requiem.

element /ˈelɪmənt/ *noun* **1** component part. **2** substance which cannot be resolved by chemical means into simpler substances. **3** any of **the four elements** (earth, water, air, fire) formerly supposed to make up all matter. **4** person's preferred surroundings. **5** wire that gives out heat in electric heater, cooker, etc. **6** (in *plural*) atmospheric agencies. **7** (in *plural*) rudiments, first principles. **8** (in *plural*) bread and wine of Eucharist. □ **in one's element** in one's preferred situation.
■ **1** component, constituent, detail, essential, factor, feature, fragment, ingredient, part, piece, small amount, unit. **4** domain, environment, habitat, medium, sphere, territory. **6** (*elements*) see WEATHER *noun*. **7** (*elements*) see RUDIMENT 1.

elemental /elɪˈment(ə)l/ *adjective* **1** of or like the elements or the forces of nature. **2** basic, essential.

elementary /elɪˈmentərɪ/ *adjective* **1** dealing with simplest facts of subject. **2** unanalysable. □ **elementary particle** *Physics* subatomic particle, esp. one not known to consist of simpler ones.
■ **1** basic, early, easy, first, fundamental, initial, introductory, primary, principal, rudimentary, simple, straightforward, uncomplicated, understandable.

elephant /ˈelɪf(ə)nt/ *noun* (*plural* same or **-s**) largest living land animal, with trunk and ivory tusks.

elephantiasis /elɪfənˈtaɪəsɪs/ *noun* disease causing gross enlargement of limbs etc.

elephantine /elɪˈfæntaɪn/ *adjective* **1** of elephants. **2** huge. **3** clumsy.

elevate /ˈelɪveɪt/ *verb* (**-ting**) **1** lift up, raise. **2** exalt in rank etc. **3** (usually as **elevated** *adjective*) raise morally or intellectually.
■ **1** hold up, jack up, lift, make higher, raise, rear, uplift. **2** boost, exalt, move up, promote, upgrade. **3** (**elevated**) see HIGH *adjective* 1;4, NOBLE *adjective* 2.

elevation *noun* **1** elevating, being elevated. **2** angle above horizontal. **3** height above given level. **4** drawing showing one side of building.

elevator *noun* **1** *US* lift. **2** movable part of tailplane for changing aircraft's altitude. **3** hoisting machine.

eleven /ɪˈlev(ə)n/ *adjective & noun* **1** one more than ten. **2** team of 11 people in cricket etc. □ **eleventh hour** last possible moment. □ **eleventh** *adjective & noun*.

elevenses /ɪˈlevənzɪz/ *noun colloquial* light mid-morning refreshment.

elf *noun* (*plural* **elves** /elvz/) mythological being, esp. small and mischievous one. □ **elfish** *adjective*.

elfin /ˈelfɪn/ *adjective* of elves; elflike.

elicit /ɪˈlɪsɪt/ *verb* (**-t-**) draw out (facts, response, etc.).
■ bring out, call forth, derive, draw out, evoke, extort, extract, get, obtain, wrest, wring.

elide /ɪˈlaɪd/ *verb* (**-ding**) omit in pronunciation.

eligible /ˈelɪdʒɪb(ə)l/ *adjective* **1** (often + *for*) fit or entitled to be chosen. **2** desirable or suitable, esp. for marriage. □ **eligibility** *noun*.
■ **1** acceptable, allowed, authorized, competent, equipped, fit, fitting, proper, qualified, worthy. **2** appropriate, available, desirable, suitable.

eliminate /ɪˈlɪmɪneɪt/ *verb* (**-ting**) **1** remove, get rid of. **2** exclude. □ **elimination** *noun*. **eliminator** *noun*.
■ **1** abolish, annihilate, delete, destroy, dispense with, *colloquial* do away with, eject, end, eradicate, exterminate, extinguish, finish off, get rid of, kill, murder, put an end to, remove, stamp out. **2** cut out, drop, exclude, knock out, leave out, omit, reject.

elision /ɪˈlɪʒ(ə)n/ *noun* omission of vowel or syllable in pronunciation.

elite /ɪˈliːt/ *noun* (also **élite**) **1** best part of larger body or group. **2** (**the elite**) group within society regarded as superior and favoured.
■ **1** best, cream, pick. **2** aristocracy, gentry, jet set, nobility.

elitism *noun* (also **élitism**) advocacy of or reliance on dominance by select group. □ **elitist** *noun & adjective* (also **élitist**).

elixir /ɪˈlɪksɪə/ *noun* **1** alchemist's preparation supposedly able to change metal into gold or prolong life indefinitely. **2** aromatic medicine.

Elizabethan /ɪlɪzəˈbiːθ(ə)n/ *adjective* of time of Elizabeth I or II. ● *noun* person of this time.

elk *noun* (*plural* same or **-s**) large type of deer.

ellipse /ɪˈlɪps/ *noun* regular oval.

ellipsis /ɪˈlɪpsɪs/ *noun* (*plural* **ellipses** /-siːz/) omission of words needed to complete construction or sense.

elliptical /ɪˈlɪptɪk(ə)l/ *adjective* **1** of or like an ellipse. **2** (of language) confusingly concise.

elm *noun* **1** tree with rough serrated leaves. **2** its wood.

elocution /eləˈkjuːʃ(ə)n/ *noun* art of clear and expressive speaking.

elongate /ˈiːlɒŋgeɪt/ *verb* (**-ting**) lengthen, extend. □ **elongation** *noun*.

elope /ɪˈləʊp/ *verb* (**-ping**) run away to marry secretly. □ **elopement** *noun*.

eloquence /ˈeləkwəns/ *noun* fluent and effective use of language. □ **eloquent** *adjective*. **eloquently** *adverb*.

■ □ **eloquent** articulate, expressive, fluent, forceful, glib, moving, persuasive, plausible, powerful, unfaltering.

else /els/ *adverb* 1 besides. 2 instead. 3 otherwise; if not. □ **elsewhere** in or to some other place.

elucidate /ɪˈluːsɪdeɪt/ *verb* (**-ting**) throw light on, explain. □ **elucidation** *noun*.

elude /ɪˈluːd/ *verb* (**-ding**) 1 escape adroitly from. 2 avoid. 3 baffle.

■ 1 avoid, dodge, escape, foil, get away from, give (person) the slip, shake off, slip away from. 2 avoid, circumvent, dodge, evade.

elusive /ɪˈluːsɪv/ *adjective* 1 difficult to find, catch, or remember. 2 avoiding the point raised. □ **elusiveness** *noun*.

■ 1 (*an elusive person*) always on the move, evasive, fugitive, hard to find, shifting, slippery; (*an elusive quality*) baffling, hard to pin down, indefinable, intangible, puzzling. 2 ambiguous, deceptive, evasive, indirect.

elver /ˈelvə/ *noun* young eel.

elves *plural* of ELF.

Elysium /ɪˈlɪzɪəm/ *noun* 1 *Greek Mythology* home of the blessed after death. 2 place of ideal happiness. □ **Elysian** *adjective*.

em *noun Printing* unit of measurement approximately equal to width of M.

emaciate /ɪˈmeɪsɪeɪt/ *verb* (**-ting**) (esp. as **emaciated** *adjective*) make thin or feeble. □ **emaciation** *noun*.

■ (**emaciated**) anorexic, atrophied, bony, cadaverous, gaunt, haggard, shrivelled, skeletal, skinny, thin, underfed, undernourished, wasted away, wizened.

emanate /ˈemaneɪt/ *verb* (**-ting**) (usually + *from*) issue or originate (from source). □ **emanation** *noun*.

emancipate /ɪˈmænsɪpeɪt/ *verb* (**-ting**) free from social, political, or moral restraint. □ **emancipation** *noun*.

■ deliver, discharge, enfranchise, free, give rights to, let go, liberate, loose, release, set free, unchain.

emasculate *verb* /ɪˈmæskjʊleɪt/ (**-ting**) 1 enfeeble. 2 castrate. ● *adjective* /ɪˈmæskjʊlət/ 1 enfeebled. 2 castrated. 3 effeminate. □ **emasculation** *noun*.

embalm /ɪmˈbɑːm/ *verb* 1 preserve (corpse) from decay. 2 preserve from oblivion. 3 make fragrant.

embankment /ɪmˈbæŋkmənt/ *noun* bank constructed to confine water or carry road or railway.

■ bank, causeway, dam, earthwork, mound, rampart.

embargo /ɪmˈbɑːgəʊ/ *noun* (*plural* **-es**) 1 order forbidding ships to enter or leave port. 2 suspension of commerce or other activity. ● *verb* (**-es**, **-ed**) place under embargo.

embark /ɪmˈbɑːk/ *verb* 1 put or go on board ship. 2 (+ *on, in*) begin (enterprise).

■ 1 board, get on, go aboard. 2 (*embark on*) see BEGIN 1.

embarkation /embɑːˈkeɪʃ(ə)n/ *noun* embarking on ship.

embarrass /ɪmˈbærəs/ *verb* 1 make (person) feel awkward or ashamed. 2 (as **embarrassed** *adjective*) feeling ashamed or self-conscious. 3 encumber. 4 (as **embarrassed** *adjective*) encumbered with debts. □ **embarrassing** *adjective*. **embarrassment** *noun*.

■ 1 abash, chagrin, confuse, discomfit, discompose, disconcert, discountenance, disgrace, distress, fluster, humiliate, make (person) blush, mortify, shame, show up, upset. 2 (**embarrassed**) see ASHAMED 1. □ **embarrassing** see AWKWARD 3,4, SHAMEFUL.

embassy /ˈembəsɪ/ *noun* (*plural* **-ies**) 1 ambassador's residence or offices. 2 deputation to foreign government.

embattled /ɪmˈbæt(ə)ld/ *adjective* 1 prepared or arrayed for battle. 2 fortified with battlements. 3 under heavy attack. 4 in trying circumstances.

embed /ɪmˈbed/ *verb* (also **imbed**) (**-dd-**) (esp. as **embedded** *adjective*) fix in surrounding mass.

embellish /ɪmˈbelɪʃ/ *verb* 1 beautify, adorn. 2 improve story etc. with invented details. □ **embellishment** *noun*.

■ 1 adorn, beautify, deck, decorate, embroider, garnish, ornament, *colloquial* tart up, *colloquial* titivate. 2 see ELABORATE *verb*.

ember /ˈembə/ *noun* (usually in *plural*) small piece of glowing coal etc. in dying fire. □ **ember days** days of fasting and prayer in Christian Church, associated with ordinations.

embezzle /ɪmˈbez(ə)l/ *verb* (**-ling**) divert (money) fraudulently to own use. □ **embezzlement** *noun*. **embezzler** *noun*.

■ appropriate, misapply, misappropriate, peculate, steal, take fraudulently. □ **embezzlement** fraud, misappropriation, misuse of funds, peculation, stealing, theft.

embitter /ɪmˈbɪtə/ *verb* arouse bitter feelings in. □ **embittered** *adjective*. **embitterment** *noun*.

■ □ **embittered** angry, bitter, disillusioned, envious, rancorous, resentful, sour.

emblazon /ɪmˈbleɪz(ə)n/ *verb* portray or adorn conspicuously.

emblem /ˈembləm/ *noun* 1 symbol. 2 (+ *of*) type,

embodiment of. **3** distinctive badge. □ **emblematic** /-'mæt-/ *adjective*.

> ■ **1, 3** badge, crest, device, image, insignia, logo, mark, seal, sign, symbol, token.

embody /ɪm'bɒdɪ/ *verb* (**-ies, -ied**) **1** give concrete form to. **2** be expression of. **3** include, comprise. □ **embodiment** *noun*.

> ■ **1** manifest, personify. **2** exemplify, express, represent, stand for, symbolize. **3** bring together, combine, comprise, embrace, enclose, gather together, include, incorporate, integrate, involve, take in, unite.

embolden /ɪm'bəʊld(ə)n/ *verb* encourage.

embolism /'embəlɪz(ə)m/ *noun* obstruction of artery by blood clot etc.

emboss /ɪm'bɒs/ *verb* carve or decorate with design in relief.

embrace /ɪm'breɪs/ *verb* (**-cing**) **1** hold closely in arms. **2** enclose. **3** accept, adopt. **4** include. ● *noun* act of embracing; clasp.

> ■ *verb* **1** clasp, cling to, cuddle, enfold, grasp, hold, hug, kiss, snuggle up to. **3** accept, adopt, espouse, welcome. **4** see EMBODY 3.

embrasure /ɪm'breɪʒə/ *noun* **1** bevelling of wall at sides of window etc. **2** opening in parapet for gun.

embrocation /embrə'keɪʃ(ə)n/ *noun* liquid for rubbing on body to relieve muscular pain.

embroider /ɪm'brɔɪdə/ *verb* **1** decorate with needlework. **2** embellish. □ **embroidery** *noun*.

embroil /ɪm'brɔɪl/ *verb* (often + *in*) involve (in conflict or difficulties). □ **embroilment** *noun*.

embryo /'embrɪəʊ/ *noun* (*plural* -**s**) **1** unborn or unhatched offspring. **2** thing in rudimentary stage. □ **embryonic** /-'ɒn-/ *adjective*.

> ■ □ **embryonic** early, immature, just beginning, rudimentary, underdeveloped, undeveloped, unformed.

emend /ɪ'mend/ *verb* correct; remove errors from (text etc.). □ **emendation** /i:-/ *noun*.

emerald /'emər(ə)ld/ *noun* **1** bright green gem. **2** colour of this. ● *adjective* bright green.

emerge /ɪ'mɜ:dʒ/ *verb* (**-ging**) come up or out into view or notice. □ **emergence** *noun*. **emergent** *adjective*.

> ■ appear, arise, be revealed, come out, come to light, come to notice, emanate, issue forth, leak out, peep (through), pop up, proceed, surface, transpire, turn out.

emergency /ɪ'mɜ:dʒənsɪ/ *noun* (*plural* -**ies**) sudden state of danger etc., requiring immediate action.

> ■ crisis, danger, difficulty, exigency, predicament, serious situation.

emeritus /ɪ'merɪtəs/ *adjective* retired and holding honorary title.

emery /'emərɪ/ *noun* coarse corundum for polishing metal etc. □ **emery board** emery-coated nail-file.

emetic /ɪ'metɪk/ *adjective* that causes vomiting. ● *noun* emetic medicine.

emigrate /'emɪgreɪt/ *verb* (**-ting**) leave own country to settle in another. □ **emigrant** *noun* & *adjective*. **emigration** *noun*.

émigré /'emɪgreɪ/ *noun* emigrant, esp. political exile.

eminence /'emɪnəns/ *noun* **1** recognized superiority. **2** raised ground. **3** (**His, Your Eminence**) *title used of or to cardinal*.

eminent /'emɪnənt/ *adjective* distinguished, notable. ● **eminently** *adverb*.

> ■ august, celebrated, conspicuous, distinguished, elevated, esteemed, exalted, famous, great, honoured, illustrious, important, notable, noted, noteworthy, outstanding, pre-eminent, prominent, renowned, well known.

emir /e'mɪə/ *noun* (also **amir** /ə'mɪə/) *title of various Muslim rulers*.

emirate /'emrət/ *noun* position, reign, or domain of emir.

emissary /'emɪsərɪ/ *noun* (*plural* -**ies**) person sent on diplomatic mission.

emit /ɪ'mɪt/ *verb* (**-tt-**) give or send out; discharge. □ **emission** /ɪ'mɪʃ(ə)n/ *noun*.

> ■ belch, discharge, disgorge, ejaculate, eject, exhale, expel, exude, give off, give out, issue, radiate, send out, spew out, spout, transmit, vent, vomit.

emollient /ɪ'mɒlɪənt/ *adjective* softening, soothing. ● *noun* emollient substance.

emolument /ɪ'mɒljʊmənt/ *noun* fee from employment; salary.

emotion /ɪ'məʊʃ(ə)n/ *noun* **1** strong instinctive feeling such as love or fear. **2** emotional intensity or sensibility. □ **emotionless** *adjective*.

> ■ **1** feeling, passion, sentiment. **2** agitation, excitement, feeling, fervour, intensity, passion, sentiment, warmth.

emotional *adjective* **1** of or expressing emotion(s). **2** especially liable to emotion. **3** arousing emotion. □ **emotionalism** *noun*. **emotionally** *adverb*.

USAGE See note at EMOTIVE.

> ■ **1** ardent, emotive, excited, fervent, heartfelt, heated, impassioned, moved, passionate, sentimental, stirred, subjective, touched. **2** ardent, demonstrative, enthusiastic, excitable, fiery, hot-headed, intense, irrational, moved, passionate, romantic, stirred, touched, warm-hearted, worked up. **3** affecting, biased, emotive, heart-rending, inflammatory, loaded, moving, pathetic, poignant, prejudiced, provocative, sentimental, stirring, tender, touching.

emotive /ɪ'məʊtɪv/ *adjective* of or arousing emotion.

USAGE Although the senses of *emotive* and *emotional* overlap, *emotive* is more common in the sense 'arousing emotion', as in *an emotive issue*, and only *emotional* can mean 'especially liable to emotion', as in *a highly emotional person*.

empanel /ɪm'pæn(ə)l/ *verb* (also **impanel**) (**-ll-**; *US* **-l-**) enter (jury) on panel.

empathize /'empəθaɪz/ *verb* (also **-ise**) (**-zing** or **-sing**) (usually + *with*) exercise empathy.

empathy /'empəθɪ/ *noun* ability to identify with person or object. □ **empathetic** *adjective*.

emperor /'empərə/ *noun* ruler of empire.

emphasis /'emfəsɪs/ *noun* (*plural* **emphases** /-siːz/) **1** importance attached to something. **2** significant stress on word(s). **3** vigour of expression etc.

■ **1** attention, gravity, importance, priority, prominence, stress, urgency, weight. **2** accent, stress. **3** force, intensity, strength, vigour.

emphasize /'emfəsaɪz/ *verb* (also **-ise**) (**-zing** or **-sing**) lay stress on.

■ accent, accentuate, bring out, dwell on, focus on, give emphasis to, highlight, insist on, make obvious, play up, point up, rub it in, spotlight, stress, underline, underscore.

emphatic /ɪm'fætɪk/ *adjective* **1** forcibly expressive. **2** (of word) bearing emphasis (e.g. *myself* in *I did it myself*). □ **emphatically** *adverb*.

■ **1** affirmative, assertive, categorical, confident, definite, dogmatic, firm, forceful, insistent, positive, pronounced, resolute, strong, uncompromising, unequivocal.

emphysema /emfɪ'siːmə/ *noun* disease of lungs causing breathlessness.

empire /'empaɪə/ *noun* **1** large group of states under single authority. **2** supreme dominion. **3** large commercial organization etc. owned or directed by one person.

empirical /ɪm'pɪrɪk(ə)l/ *adjective* based on observation or experiment, not on theory. □ **empiricism** /-rɪs-/ *noun*. **empiricist** /-rɪs-/ *noun*.

■ experiential, experimental, observed, practical, pragmatic.

emplacement /ɪm'pleɪsmənt/ *noun* **1** platform for gun(s). **2** putting in position.

employ /ɪm'plɔɪ/ *verb* **1** use services of (person) in return for payment. **2** use (thing, time, energy, etc.). **3** keep (person) occupied. □ **in the employ of** employed by. □ **employed** *adjective*. **employer** *noun*.

■ **1** commission, engage, enlist, have on the payroll, hire, pay, sign up, take on, use the services of. **2** apply, use, utilize. □ **employed** active, busy, earning, engaged, hired, involved, in work, occupied, practising, working. **employer** *colloquial* boss, chief, *colloquial* gaffer, *slang* governor, head, manager, owner, proprietor, taskmaster.

employee /emplɔɪ'iː/ *noun* person employed for wages.

■ hand, *usually derogatory* underling, worker; (*employees*) staff, workforce.

employment *noun* **1** employing, being employed. **2** person's trade or profession. □ **employment office** government office finding work for the unemployed.

■ **2** business, calling, craft, job, line, livelihood, living, *métier*, occupation, profession, pursuit, trade, vocation, work.

emporium /em'pɔːrɪəm/ *noun* **1** large shop. **2** centre of commerce.

empower /ɪm'paʊə/ *verb* give power to.

empress /'emprɪs/ *noun* **1** wife or widow of emperor. **2** woman emperor.

empty /'emptɪ/ *adjective* (**-ier**, **-iest**) **1** containing nothing. **2** vacant, unoccupied. **3** hollow, insincere. **4** without purpose. **5** *colloquial* hungry. **6** vacuous, foolish. ● *verb* (**-ies**, **-ied**) **1** remove contents of. **2** remove or transfer (contents). **3** become empty. **4** (of river) discharge itself. ● *noun* (*plural* **-ies**) *colloquial* emptied bottle etc. □ **empty-handed** bringing or taking nothing. **empty-headed** foolish. □ **emptiness** *noun*.

■ *adjective* **1** bare, blank, clean, clear, hollow, unfilled, unladen, unused, void. **2** deserted, desolate, forsaken, unfurnished, uninhabited, unoccupied, vacant. **3, 4** futile, hollow, idle, impotent, ineffective, insincere, meaningless, pointless, purposeless, senseless, unreal, worthless. ● *verb* **1** clear, drain, evacuate, exhaust, unload, vacate, void. **2** discharge, drain, eject, pour out, remove, take out, transfer, unload. **4** discharge, drain.

EMS *abbreviation* European Monetary System.

emu /'iːmjuː/ *noun* (*plural* **-s**) large flightless Australian bird.

emulate /'emjʊleɪt/ *verb* (**-ting**) **1** try to equal or excel. **2** imitate. □ **emulation** *noun*. **emulator** *noun*.

emulsify /ɪ'mʌlsɪfaɪ/ *verb* (**-ies**, **-ied**) make emulsion of. □ **emulsifier** *noun*.

emulsion /ɪ'mʌlʃ(ə)n/ *noun* fine dispersion of one liquid in another, esp. as paint, medicine, etc.

en *noun* *Printing* unit of measurement equal to half em.

enable /ɪ'neɪb(ə)l/ *verb* (**-ling**) **1** (+ *to do*) supply with means or authority to. **2** make possible.

■ **1** aid, allow, approve, assist, authorize, charter, empower, entitle, equip, facilitate, franchise, help, license, permit, qualify, sanction.

enact /ɪ'nækt/ *verb* **1** ordain, decree. **2** make (bill etc.) law. **3** play (part). □ **enactment** *noun*.

enamel /ɪ'næm(ə)l/ *noun* **1** glasslike opaque coating on metal. **2** any hard smooth coating. **3** kind of hard gloss paint. **4** hard coating of teeth. ● *verb* (**-ll-**; *US* **-l-**) coat with enamel.

enamour /ɪ'næmə/ *verb* (*US* **enamor**) (usually in *passive*; + *of*) inspire with love or delight.

en bloc /ɑ̃ 'blɒk/ *adverb* in a block; all at same time. [French]

encamp /ɪn'kæmp/ *verb* settle in (esp. military) camp. □ **encampment** *noun*.

encapsulate /ɪn'kæpsjʊleɪt/ *verb* (**-ting**) 1 enclose (as) in capsule. 2 summarize.

encase /ɪn'keɪs/ *verb* (**-sing**) confine (as) in a case.

encash /ɪn'kæʃ/ *verb* convert into cash. □ **encashment** *noun*.

encephalitis /ensefə'laɪtɪs/ *noun* inflammation of brain.

enchant /ɪn'tʃɑ:nt/ *verb* 1 delight. 2 bewitch. □ **enchanting** *adjective*. **enchantment** *noun*.
■ 1 allure, beguile, captivate, charm, delight, enrapture, enthral, entrance, fascinate. 2 bewitch, cast a spell on, charm, hypnotize, mesmerize, spellbind. □ **enchanting** see ATTRACTIVE. **enchantment** charm, delight, magic, rapture, sorcery, spell, witchcraft, wizardry.

enchanter *noun* (*feminine* **enchantress**) person who enchants, esp. by magic.

encircle /ɪn'sɜ:k(ə)l/ *verb* (**-ling**) surround. □ **encirclement** *noun*.

enclave /'enkleɪv/ *noun* 1 part of territory of one state surrounded by that of another. 2 group of people distinct from those surrounding them, esp. ethnically.

enclose /ɪn'kləʊz/ *verb* (**-sing**) 1 surround with wall, fence, etc.; shut in. 2 put in receptacle (esp. in envelope besides letter). 3 (as **enclosed** *adjective*) (of religious community) secluded from outside world.
■ 1 bound, box, cage, case, cocoon, conceal, confine, contain, cover, encase, encircle, encompass, enfold, envelop, fence in, hedge in, hem in, immure, imprison, insert, limit, package, parcel up, pen, restrict, ring, secure, sheathe, shut in, shut up, surround, wall in, wall up, wrap.

enclosure /ɪn'kləʊʒə/ *noun* 1 enclosing. 2 enclosed space or area. 3 thing enclosed.
■ 2 arena, cage, compound, coop, corral, court, courtyard, farmyard, field, fold, paddock, pen, pound, ring, run, stockade, sty, yard. 3 contents, inclusion, insertion.

encode /ɪn'kəʊd/ *verb* (**-ding**) put into code.

encomium /ɪn'kəʊmɪəm/ *noun* (*plural* **-s**) formal praise.

encompass /ɪn'kʌmpəs/ *verb* 1 contain, include. 2 surround.

encore /'ɒŋkɔ:/ *noun* 1 audience's call for repetition of item, or for further item. 2 such item. ● *verb* (**-ring**) call for repetition of or by. ● *interjection* again.

encounter /ɪn'kaʊntə/ *verb* 1 meet by chance. 2 meet as adversary. ● *noun* 1 meeting by chance. 2 meeting in conflict.
■ *verb* 1 chance upon, come upon, happen upon, meet, run into. 2 clash with, confront, contend with, cross swords with, face, grapple with. ● *noun* 1 confrontation, meeting. 2 battle, brush, clash, conflict, dispute, engagement, fight, skirmish, struggle.

encourage /ɪn'kʌrɪdʒ/ *verb* (**-ging**) 1 give courage to. 2 urge. 3 promote. □ **encouragement** *noun*. **encouraging** *adjective*.
■ 1 animate, embolden, give hope to, hearten, inspire, rally, reassure, rouse, support. 2 advocate, egg on, incite, invite, persuade, prompt, spur on, urge. 3 abet, aid, be an incentive to, be conducive to, boost, engender, foster, further, generate, help, increase, induce, promote, stimulate.
□ **encouragement** approval, boost, exhortation, incentive, incitement, inspiration, reassurance, *colloquial* shot in the arm, stimulation, stimulus, support. **encouraging** comforting, favourable, heartening, hopeful, inspiring, optimistic, positive, promising, reassuring.

encroach /ɪn'krəʊtʃ/ *verb* (usually + *on*, *upon*) intrude on other's territory etc. □ **encroachment** *noun*.
■ (*encroach on, upon*) enter, impinge on, infringe on, intrude on, invade, make inroads on, trespass on, violate.

encrust /ɪn'krʌst/ *verb* 1 cover with or form crust. 2 coat with hard casing or deposit.

encumber /ɪn'kʌmbə/ *verb* 1 be burden to. 2 hamper.

encumbrance /ɪn'kʌmbrəns/ *noun* 1 burden. 2 impediment.

encyclical /ɪn'sɪklɪk(ə)l/ *noun* papal letter to all RC bishops.

encyclopedia /ɪnsaɪklə'pi:dɪə/ *noun* (also **-paedia**) book of information on many subjects or on many aspects of one subject.

encyclopedic *adjective* (also **-paedic**) (of knowledge or information) comprehensive.

end *noun* 1 limit; farthest point. 2 extreme point or part. 3 part furthest from front. 4 conclusion. 5 latter part. 6 destruction; death. 7 result. 8 goal, object. 9 remnant. ● *verb* 1 bring to end. 2 put end to. 3 come to end. □ **endmost** nearest the end. **endpaper** blank leaf of paper at beginning or end of book. **end product** final product of manufacture etc. **end up 1** be or become eventually. 2 arrive. **in the end** finally. **make ends meet** live within one's income. **no end** *colloquial* to a great extent.
■ *noun* 1, 2 boundary, edge, extreme, extremity, limit, terminus, tip. 3 back, rear, tail. 5 cessation, close, coda, completion, conclusion, culmination, curtain (*of play*), denouement (*of plot*), ending, expiration, expiry, finale, finish, *colloquial* pay-off, resolution, termination. 6 death, *esp. Law formal* decease, demise, destiny, destruction, doom, extinction, fate, passing, ruin. 7 consequence, effect, outcome, result, upshot. 8 aim, aspiration, design, destination, goal, intention, object, objective, plan, purpose. ● *verb* 1, 2 abolish, break off, bring to an end, close, complete, conclude, cut off, destroy, discontinue, *colloquial* drop, eliminate, exterminate, finalize, finish, get rid of, halt, phase out, put an end to, round off, ruin, scotch, stop, terminate, wind up. 3 break up, *formal* cease, close, come to an end, culminate, die, disappear, expire, fade away, finish, *colloquial* pack up, peter out, run out, stop, terminate.

endanger /ɪnˈdeɪndʒə/ *verb* place in danger. □ **endangered species** one in danger of extinction.
- expose to risk, imperil, jeopardize, put at risk, threaten.

endear /ɪnˈdɪə/ *verb* (usually + *to*) make dear. □ **endearing** *adjective.*
- □ **endearing** appealing, attractive, captivating, charming, disarming, enchanting, engaging, likeable, lovable, sweet, winning, winsome.

endearment *noun* expression of affection.

endeavour /ɪnˈdevə/ (*US* **endeavor**) *verb* try, strive. ● *noun* attempt, effort.
- *verb* aim, aspire, attempt, do one's best, exert oneself, strive, try.

endemic /enˈdemɪk/ *adjective* (often + *to*) regularly found among particular people or in particular area. □ **endemically** *adverb.*

ending *noun* end of word or story.

endive /ˈendaɪv/ *noun* curly-leaved plant used in salads.

endless *adjective* **1** infinite. **2** continual. □ **endlessly** *adverb.* **endlessness** *noun.*
- **1** bottomless, boundless, immeasurable, inexhaustible, infinite, limitless, measureless, unbounded, unfailing, unlimited. **2** abiding, ceaseless, constant, continual, continuous, enduring, eternal, everlasting, immortal, incessant, interminable, never-ending, non-stop, perpetual, persistent, unbroken, undying, unending, uninterrupted.

endocrine /ˈendəʊkraɪn/ *adjective* (of gland) secreting directly into blood.

endogenous /enˈdɒdʒɪnəs/ *adjective* growing or originating from within.

endorse /ɪnˈdɔːs/ *verb* (**-sing**) **1** approve. **2** write on (document), esp. sign (cheque). **3** enter details of offence on (driving licence). □ **endorsement** *noun.*
- **1** advocate, agree with, approve, authorize, back, condone, confirm, *colloquial* OK, sanction, set one's seal of approval to, subscribe to, support. **2** countersign, sign.

endoskeleton /ˈendəʊskelɪtən/ *noun* internal skeleton.

endow /ɪnˈdaʊ/ *verb* **1** give permanent income to. **2** (esp. as **endowed** *adjective*) provide with talent or ability.

endowment *noun* **1** endowing. **2** money with which person or thing is endowed. □ **endowment mortgage** one in which borrower pays only premiums until policy repays mortgage capital. **endowment policy** life insurance policy paying out on set date or earlier death.

endue /ɪnˈdjuː/ *verb* (**-dues**, **-dued**, **-duing**) (+ *with*) provide (person) with (quality etc.).

endurance *noun* power of enduring.
- determination, fortitude, patience, perseverance, persistence, pertinacity, resolution, stamina, staying power, strength, tenacity.

endure /ɪnˈdjʊə/ *verb* (**-ring**) **1** undergo. **2** bear. **3** last. □ **endurable** *adjective.* **enduring** *adjective.*
- **1** experience, face, go through, submit to, suffer, undergo. **2** bear, cope with, put up with, stand, *colloquial* stick, stomach, suffer, tolerate, weather, withstand. **3** carry on, continue, exist, last, live on, persevere, persist, prevail, remain, stay, survive. □ **enduring** see ENDLESS 2.

endways *adverb* with an end facing forwards.

ENE *abbreviation* east-north-east.

enema /ˈenɪmə/ *noun* **1** injection of liquid etc. into rectum, esp. to expel its contents. **2** liquid used for this.

enemy /ˈenəmɪ/ *noun* (*plural* **-ies**) **1** person actively hostile to another. **2** hostile army or nation. **3** member of this. **4** adversary, opponent. ● *adjective* of or belonging to enemy.
- *noun* adversary, antagonist, foe, opponent, opposition, rival.

energetic /enəˈdʒetɪk/ *adjective* full of energy. □ **energetically** *adverb.*
- active, animated, brisk, dynamic, enthusiastic, fast, forceful, hard-working, high-powered, indefatigable, lively, powerful, quick-moving, spirited, strenuous, tireless, unflagging, vigorous, zestful.

energize /ˈenədʒaɪz/ *verb* (also **-ise**) (**-zing** or **-sing**) give energy to.

energy /ˈenədʒɪ/ *noun* (*plural* **-ies**) **1** force, vigour, activity. **2** ability of matter or radiation to do work.
- **1** animation, ardour, dash, drive, dynamism, *élan*, enthusiasm, exertion, fire, force, forcefulness, *colloquial* get-up-and-go, go, life, liveliness, might, *colloquial* pep, spirit, stamina, strength, verve, vigour, *colloquial* vim, vitality, vivacity, zeal, zest. **2** power.

enervate /ˈenəveɪt/ *verb* (**-ting**) deprive of vigour. □ **enervation** *noun.*

en famille /ɑ̃ fæˈmiː/ *adverb* in or with one's family. [French]

enfant terrible /ɑ̃fɑ̃ teˈriːbl/ *noun* (*plural enfants terribles* same pronunciation) indiscreet or unruly person. [French]

enfeeble /ɪnˈfiːb(ə)l/ *verb* (**-ling**) make feeble. □ **enfeeblement** *noun.*

enfilade /enfɪˈleɪd/ *noun* gunfire directed down length of enemy position. ● *verb* (**-ding**) direct enfilade at.

enfold /ɪnˈfəʊld/ *verb* **1** wrap. **2** embrace.

enforce /ɪnˈfɔːs/ *verb* (**-cing**) **1** compel observance of. **2** impose. □ **enforceable** *adjective.* **enforcement** *noun.*
- administer, apply, carry out, compel, execute, implement, impose, inflict, insist on, put into effect, require, stress.

enfranchise /ɪnˈfræntʃaɪz/ *verb* (**-sing**) give (person) right to vote. □ **enfranchisement** /-tʃɪz-/ *noun.*

engage /ɪnˈgeɪdʒ/ *verb* (**-ging**) **1** employ, hire. **2**

occupy. **3** hold (person's attention). **4** (as **engaged** *adjective*) occupied, busy. **5** (as **engaged** *adjective*) having promised to marry. **6** cause parts of (gear) to interlock. **7** fit, interlock. **8** bring into battle. **9** come into battle with (enemy). **10** (usually + *in*) take part. **11** (+ *that*, *to do*) undertake.

■ **1** employ, enlist, hire, recruit, sign up, take on. **2** see OCCUPY 6. **4 (engaged)** see BUSY *adjective* 1. **5 (engaged)** betrothed, *archaic* plighted, *archaic* promised, spoken for. **6, 7** bite, fit together, interlock. **10** (*engage in*) see PARTICIPATE. **11** see PROMISE *verb* 1.

engagement /ɪn'ɡeɪdʒmənt/ *noun* **1** promise to marry. **2** appointment. **3** battle.

■ **1** betrothal, *archaic* troth. **2** appointment, arrangement, commitment, *colloquial* date, fixture, meeting, obligation, rendezvous. **3** see BATTLE *noun* 1.

engender /ɪn'dʒendə/ *verb* give rise to.

engine /'endʒɪn/ *noun* **1** mechanical contrivance of parts working together, esp. as source of power. **2** railway locomotive.

■ **1** machine, motor. **2** locomotive.

engineer /endʒɪ'nɪə/ *noun* **1** person skilled in a branch of engineering. **2** person who makes or is in charge of engines etc. **3** person who designs and constructs military works. **4** mechanic, technician. ● *verb* **1** contrive, bring about. **2** act as engineer. **3** construct or manage as engineer.

■ *verb* **1** see DEVISE 1. **3** see CONSTRUCT *verb* 1.

engineering *noun* application of science to design, building, and use of machines etc.

English /'ɪŋɡlɪʃ/ *adjective* of England. ● *noun* **1** language of England, now used in UK, US, and most Commonwealth countries. **2** (**the English**) (treated as *plural*) the people of England. □ **Englishman, Englishwoman** native of England.

engraft /ɪn'ɡrɑːft/ *verb* (usually + *into*, *on*) **1** graft. **2** implant. **3** incorporate.

engrave /ɪn'ɡreɪv/ *verb* (**-ving**) **1** inscribe or cut (design) on hard surface. **2** inscribe (surface) thus. **3** (often + *on*) impress deeply (on memory etc.). □ **engraver** *noun*.

■ **1, 2** carve, chisel, cut, etch, inscribe.

engraving *noun* print made from engraved plate.

engross /ɪn'ɡrəʊs/ *verb* (usually as **engrossed** *adjective*) (+ *in*) fully occupy.

engulf /ɪn'ɡʌlf/ *verb* flow over and swamp; overwhelm.

enhance /ɪn'hɑːns/ *verb* (**-cing**) intensify; improve. □ **enhancement** *noun*.

enigma /ɪ'nɪɡmə/ *noun* **1** puzzling person or thing. **2** riddle. □ **enigmatic** /enɪɡ'mætɪk/ *adjective*.

■ **1** mystery, puzzle, riddle. **2** conundrum, *colloquial* poser, problem, puzzle, riddle.

enjoin /ɪn'dʒɔɪn/ *verb* command, order.

enjoy /ɪn'dʒɔɪ/ *verb* **1** find pleasure in. **2** (**enjoy oneself**) find pleasure. **3** have use or benefit of. **4** experience. □ **enjoyable** *adjective*. **enjoyably** *adverb*. **enjoyment** *noun*.

■ **1** admire, appreciate, bask in, be happy in, delight in, go in for, indulge in, lap up, like, luxuriate in, rejoice in, relish, revel in, savour, take pleasure from, take pleasure in. **2 (enjoy oneself)** celebrate, gad about, have a good time, make merry. **3** benefit from, have, take advantage of, use. **4** experience, have. □ **enjoyable** agreeable, amusing, delicious, delightful, diverting, entertaining, gratifying, likeable, nice, pleasant, pleasurable, rewarding, satisfying.

enlarge /ɪn'lɑːdʒ/ *verb* (**-ging**) **1** make or become larger. **2** (often + *on*, *upon*) describe in greater detail. **3** reproduce on larger scale. □ **enlargement** *noun*.

■ **1** amplify, augment, blow up, broaden, build up, develop, dilate, distend, diversify, elongate, expand, extend, fill out, grow, increase, inflate, lengthen, magnify, multiply, spread, stretch, supplement, swell, wax, widen. **2** (*enlarge on*) see ELABORATE *verb*.

enlarger *noun* apparatus for enlarging photographs.

enlighten /ɪn'laɪt(ə)n/ *verb* **1** inform. **2** (as **enlightened** *adjective*) progressive. □ **enlightenment** *noun*.

■ **1** edify, illuminate, inform, make aware, teach.

enlist /ɪn'lɪst/ *verb* **1** enrol in armed services. **2** secure as means of help or support. □ **enlistment** *noun*.

■ **1** call up, conscript, *US* draft, enrol, join up, muster, recruit, sign up, volunteer. **2** see OBTAIN 1.

enliven /ɪn'laɪv(ə)n/ *verb* make lively or cheerful. □ **enlivenment** *noun*.

■ animate, arouse, brighten, cheer up, energize, inspire, *colloquial* pep up, quicken, rouse, stimulate, vitalize, wake up.

en masse /ɑ̃ 'mæs/ *adverb* all together. [French]

enmesh /ɪn'meʃ/ *verb* entangle (as) in net.

enmity /'enmɪtɪ/ *noun* (*plural* **-ies**) **1** hostility. **2** state of being an enemy.

ennoble /ɪ'nəʊb(ə)l/ *verb* (**-ling**) make noble. □ **ennoblement** *noun*.

ennui /ɒ'nwiː/ *noun* boredom.

enormity /ɪ'nɔːmɪtɪ/ *noun* (*plural* **-ies**) **1** great wickedness. **2** monstrous crime. **3** great size.

USAGE Many people believe it is wrong to use *enormity* to mean 'great size'.

enormous /ɪ'nɔːməs/ *adjective* huge. □ **enormously** *adverb*. **enormousness** *noun*.

■ big, colossal, elephantine, gargantuan, giant, gigantic, gross, huge, *colloquial* hulking, immense, *colloquial* jumbo, king-size, large, mammoth, massive, mighty, monstrous, mountainous, prodigious, stupendous, titanic, towering, *colloquial* tremendous, vast.

enough /ɪˈnʌf/ *adjective* as much or as many as required. ● *noun* sufficient amount or quantity. ● *adverb* **1** to required degree. **2** fairly. **3** very, quite.
■ *adjective* adequate, ample, as much as necessary, sufficient.

enquire /ɪnˈkwaɪə/ *verb* (**-ring**) **1** seek information; ask question. **2** (+ *after, for*) ask about a person, person's health, etc. **3** seek information formally; inquire.
■ **1** ask, demand, inquire, query, question, quiz, request. **3** see INQUIRE 1; (*enquire into*) see INVESTIGATE.

enquiry *noun* (*plural* **-ies**) **1** asking. **2** inquiry.

enrage /ɪnˈreɪdʒ/ *verb* (**-ging**) make furious.
■ anger, incense, inflame, infuriate, madden, provoke.

enrapture /ɪnˈræptʃə/ *verb* (**-ring**) delight intensely.

enrich /ɪnˈrɪtʃ/ *verb* make rich(er). □ **enrichment** *noun*.

enrol /ɪnˈrəʊl/ *verb* (*US* **enroll**) (**-ll-**) **1** (cause to) join society, course, etc. **2** write one's name on list. **3** write name of (person) on list. □ **enrolment** *noun*.

en route /ɑ̃ ˈruːt/ *adverb* on the way. [French]

ensconce /ɪnˈskɒns/ *verb* (**-cing**) (usually **ensconce oneself** or in *passive*) settle comfortably.

ensemble /ɒnˈsɒmb(ə)l/ *noun* **1** thing viewed as whole. **2** set of clothes worn together. **3** group of performers working together. **4** *Music* passage for ensemble.

enshrine /ɪnˈʃraɪn/ *verb* (**-ning**) **1** enclose in shrine. **2** protect, make inviolable.

enshroud /ɪnˈʃraʊd/ *verb literary* **1** cover with shroud. **2** cover; hide from view.

ensign /ˈensaɪn/ *noun* **1** banner, flag; esp. military or naval flag of nation. **2** standard-bearer. **3** *historical* lowest commissioned infantry officer. **4** *US* lowest commissioned naval officer.

enslave /ɪnˈsleɪv/ *verb* (**-ving**) make slave of. □ **enslavement** *noun*.
■ disenfranchise, dominate, subject, subjugate, take away the rights of.

ensnare /ɪnˈsneə/ *verb* (**-ring**) entrap.

ensue /ɪnˈsjuː/ *verb* (**-sues, -sued, -suing**) happen later or as a result.

en suite /ɑ̃ ˈswiːt/ *adverb* forming single unit. ● *adjective* **1** (of bathroom) attached to bedroom. **2** (of bedroom) with bathroom attached.

ensure /ɪnˈʃʊə/ *verb* (**-ring**) make certain or safe.
■ confirm, guarantee, make certain, make sure, secure.

ENT *abbreviation* ear, nose, and throat.

entail /ɪnˈteɪl/ *verb* **1** necessitate or involve unavoidably. **2** *Law* bequeath (estate) to specified line of beneficiaries. ● *noun* entailed estate.

■ *verb* **1** call for, demand, give rise to, involve, lead to, necessitate, require.

entangle /ɪnˈtæŋg(ə)l/ *verb* (**-ling**) **1** catch or hold fast in snare etc. **2** involve in difficulties. **3** complicate. □ **entanglement** *noun*.

entente /ɒnˈtɒnt/ *noun* friendly understanding between states. □ **entente cordiale** entente, esp. between Britain and France since 1904.

enter /ˈentə/ *verb* **1** go or come in or into. **2** come on stage. **3** penetrate. **4** put (name, fact, etc.) into list or record etc. **5** (usually + *for*) name, or name oneself, as competitor. **6** become member of. □ **enter into 1** engage in. **2** bind oneself by. **3** form part of. **4** sympathize with. **enter (up)on 1** begin; begin to deal with. **2** assume possession of.
■ **1** arrive, come in, get in, go in, infiltrate, invade, move in, step in. **3** dig into, penetrate, pierce, puncture, push into. **4** add, inscribe, insert, note down, put down, record, register, set down, sign, write. **5** engage in, go in for, participate in, take part in. **6** enlist in, enrol in, join, sign up for, volunteer for. □ **enter into 1** see BEGIN 1.

enteric /enˈterɪk/ *adjective* of intestines.

enteritis /entəˈraɪtɪs/ *noun* inflammation of intestines.

enterprise /ˈentəpraɪz/ *noun* **1** bold undertaking. **2** readiness to engage in this. **3** business firm or venture.
■ **1** adventure, effort, endeavour, operation, programme, project, undertaking, venture. **2** adventurousness, ambition, boldness, courage, daring, determination, drive, energy, *colloquial* get-up-and-go, initiative, push. **3** business, company, concern, firm, organization.

enterprising *adjective* showing enterprise.
■ adventurous, ambitious, bold, courageous, daring, determined, eager, energetic, enthusiastic, go-ahead, hard-working, imaginative, indefatigable, industrious, intrepid, keen, purposeful, *colloquial* pushy, resourceful, spirited, venturesome, vigorous, zealous.

entertain /entəˈteɪn/ *verb* **1** amuse. **2** receive as guest. **3** harbour (feelings); consider (idea). □ **entertainer** *noun*. **entertaining** *adjective*.
■ **1** amuse, cheer up, delight, divert, keep amused, make laugh, occupy, please, regale, tickle. **2** accommodate, be hostess to, be host to, cater for, give hospitality to, put up, receive, treat, welcome. **3** accept, agree to, approve, consent to, consider, contemplate, harbour, ponder, support, take seriously. □ **entertainer** artist, artiste, performer, player. **entertaining** see INTERESTING.

entertainment *noun* **1** entertaining, being entertained. **2** thing that entertains; performance.
■ **1** amusement, distraction, diversion, enjoyment, fun, night-life, pastime, play, pleasure, recreation, sport. **2** exhibition, extravaganza, pageant, performance, presentation, production, show, spectacle.

enthral /ɪnˈθrɔːl/ *verb* (*US* **enthrall**) (**-ll-**) captivate, please greatly. □ **enthralment** *noun*.

enthrone /ɪnˈθrəʊn/ *verb* (**-ning**) place on throne. □ **enthronement** *noun*.

enthuse /ɪnˈθjuːz/ *verb* (**-sing**) *colloquial* be or make enthusiastic.

enthusiasm /ɪnˈθjuːzɪæz(ə)m/ *noun* **1** great eagerness or admiration. **2** object of this. □ **enthusiast** *noun*. **enthusiastic** /-ˈæst-/ *adjective*. **enthusiastically** *adverb*.

■ **1** ambition, ardour, avidity, commitment, drive, eagerness, excitement, exuberance, fanaticism, fervour, gusto, keenness, panache, passion, relish, spirit, verve, zeal, zest. **2** craze, diversion, fad, hobby, interest, passion, pastime.
□ **enthusiast** *colloquial* addict, adherent, admirer, aficionado, *colloquial* buff, champion, devotee, fan, fanatic, *slang* fiend, *colloquial* freak, lover, *colloquial* maniac, supporter, zealot.
enthusiastic ambitious, ardent, avid, committed, delighted, devoted, eager, earnest, ebullient, energetic, excited, exuberant, fervent, fervid, hearty, impassioned, interested, involved, irrepressible, keen, lively, motivated, optimistic, passionate, positive, rapturous, *colloquial* raring to go, spirited, unqualified, unstinting, vigorous, wholehearted, zealous; (*be enthusiastic*) *colloquial* enthuse, get excited, go into raptures, *colloquial* go overboard, rave.

entice /ɪnˈtaɪs/ *verb* (**-cing**) attract by offer of pleasure or reward. □ **enticement** *noun*. **enticing** *adjective*. **enticingly** *adverb*.

■ allure, attract, cajole, coax, decoy, inveigle, lead on, lure, persuade, seduce, tempt, trap, wheedle.

entire /ɪnˈtaɪə/ *adjective* **1** complete. **2** unbroken; in one piece. **3** absolute.

■ **1, 2** complete, full, intact, sound, total, unbroken, undivided, uninterrupted, whole.

entirely *adverb* wholly.

entirety /ɪnˈtaɪərətɪ/ *noun* (*plural* **-ies**) **1** completeness. **2** sum total. □ **in its entirety** in its complete form.

entitle /ɪnˈtaɪt(ə)l/ *verb* (**-ling**) **1** (usually + *to*) give (person) right or claim. **2** give title to. □ **entitlement** *noun*.

■ **1** allow, authorize, empower, enable, justify, license, permit, qualify, warrant. **2** call, christen, designate, dub, name, style, term, title.
□ **entitlement** claim, ownership, prerogative, right, title.

entity /ˈentɪtɪ/ *noun* (*plural* **-ies**) **1** thing with distinct existence. **2** thing's existence.

■ **1** article, being, object, organism, thing, whole.

entomb /ɪnˈtuːm/ *verb* **1** place in tomb. **2** serve as tomb for. □ **entombment** *noun*.

entomology /entəˈmɒlədʒɪ/ *noun* study of insects. □ **entomological** /-məˈlɒdʒ-/ *adjective*. **entomologist** *noun*.

entourage /ˈɒntʊrɑːʒ/ *noun* people attending important person.

entr'acte /ˈɒntrækt/ *noun* (music or dance performed in) interval in play.

entrails /ˈentreɪlz/ *plural noun* **1** intestines. **2** inner parts.

■ **1** bowels, guts, *colloquial* innards, inner organs, *colloquial* insides, intestines, viscera.

entrance[1] /ˈentrəns/ *noun* **1** place for entering. **2** coming or going in. **3** right of admission. □ **entrance hall** area of building into which entrance opens.

■ **1** door, doorway, entry, gate, gateway, ingress, opening, portal, way in. **2** appearance, arrival, coming, entry. **3** access, admission, admittance.
□ **entrance hall** ante-room, foyer, lobby, passage, passageway, vestibule.

entrance[2] /ɪnˈtrɑːns/ *verb* (**-cing**) **1** enchant, delight. **2** put into trance.

entrant /ˈentrənt/ *noun* person who enters exam, profession, etc.

■ applicant, candidate, competitor, contender, contestant, entry, participant, player, rival.

entrap /ɪnˈtræp/ *verb* (**-pp-**) catch (as) in trap.

entreat /ɪnˈtriːt/ *verb* ask earnestly, beg.

■ ask, beg, beseech, implore, importune, petition, request, sue, *literary* supplicate.

entreaty *noun* (*plural* **-ies**) earnest request.

entrecôte /ˈɒntrəkəʊt/ *noun* boned steak cut off sirloin.

entrée /ˈɒntreɪ/ *noun* **1** main dish of meal. **2** dish served between fish and meat courses. **3** right of admission.

entrench /ɪnˈtrentʃ/ *verb* **1** establish firmly. **2** (as **entrenched** *adjective*) (of attitude etc.) not easily modified. **3** surround or fortify with trench. □ **entrenchment** *noun*.

entrepreneur /ˌɒntrəprəˈnɜː/ *noun* person who undertakes commercial venture. □ **entrepreneurial** *adjective*.

entropy /ˈentrəpɪ/ *noun* **1** measure of disorganization of universe. **2** measure of unavailability of system's thermal energy for conversion into mechanical work.

entrust /ɪnˈtrʌst/ *verb* **1** (+ *to*) give (person, thing) into care of. **2** (+ *with*) assign responsibility for (person, thing) to.

entry /ˈentrɪ/ *noun* (*plural* **-ies**) **1** coming or going in; entering. **2** item entered. **3** place of entrance. **4** alley. **5** entrant.

■ **1** see ENTRANCE[1] 2. **2** insertion, item, jotting, listing, note, record. **3** see ENTRANCE[1] 1. **5** see ENTRANT.

entwine /ɪnˈtwaɪn/ *verb* (**-ning**) twine round, interweave.

enumerate /ɪˈnjuːməreɪt/ *verb* (**-ting**) **1** specify (items). **2** count. □ **enumeration** *noun*.

enunciate /ɪˈnʌnsɪeɪt/ *verb* (**-ting**) **1** pronounce (words) clearly. **2** state definitely. □ **enunciation** *noun*.

envelop /ɪn'veləp/ *verb* (**-p-**) **1** wrap up, cover. **2** surround. □ **envelopment** *noun*.

> ■ **1** cloak, cover, enclose, enfold, enshroud, hide, shroud, swathe, veil, wrap. **2** see SURROUND *verb*.

envelope /'envələup/ *noun* **1** folded paper cover for letter etc. **2** wrapper, covering.

> ■ **2** cover, sheath, wrapper, wrapping.

enviable /'envɪəb(ə)l/ *adjective* likely to excite envy. □ **enviably** *adverb*.

> ■ attractive, covetable, desirable, favourable, sought after.

envious /'envɪəs/ *adjective* feeling or showing envy.

> ■ begrudging, bitter, covetous, dissatisfied, grudging, jaundiced, jealous, resentful.

environment /ɪn'vaɪərənmənt/ *noun* surroundings and circumstances affecting person's life. □ **environmental** /-'men-/ *adjective*. **environmentally** /-'men-/ *adverb*.

> ■ circumstances, conditions, context, ecosystem, environs, habitat, location, milieu, setting, situation, surroundings, territory.

environmentalist /ɪnvaɪərən'mentəlɪst/ *noun* person concerned with protection of natural environment.

environs /ɪn'vaɪərənz/ *plural noun* district round town etc.

envisage /ɪn'vɪzɪdʒ/ *verb* (**-ging**) visualize, imagine, contemplate.

> ■ *disputed* anticipate, contemplate, dream of, fancy, forecast, foresee, imagine, picture, predict, visualize.

envoy /'envɔɪ/ *noun* **1** messenger, representative. **2** diplomat ranking below ambassador.

envy /'envɪ/ *noun* (*plural* **-ies**) **1** discontent aroused by another's better fortune etc. **2** object or cause of this. ● *verb* (**-ies, -ied**) feel envy of.

> ■ *noun* **1** bitterness, covetousness, cupidity, desire, discontent, dissatisfaction, ill will, jealousy, longing, resentment. ● *verb* begrudge, grudge, resent.

enzyme /'enzaɪm/ *noun* protein catalyst of specific biochemical reaction.

eolian harp *US* = AEOLIAN HARP.

eon = AEON.

EP *abbreviation* extended-play (record).

epaulette /'epəlet/ *noun* (*US* **epaulet**) ornamental shoulder-piece, esp. on uniform.

ephedrine /'efədrɪn/ *noun* alkaloid drug used to relieve asthma etc.

ephemera /ɪ'femərə/ *plural noun* things of only short-lived relevance.

ephemeral *adjective* short-lived, transitory.

> ■ brief, *literary* evanescent, fleeting, fugitive, impermanent, momentary, passing, short-lived, temporary, transient, transitory.

epic /'epɪk/ *noun* **1** long poem narrating adventures of heroic figure etc. **2** book or film based on this. ● *adjective* **1** like an epic. **2** grand, heroic.

epicene /'epɪsiːn/ *adjective* **1** of or for both sexes. **2** having characteristics of both sexes or of neither sex.

epicentre /'epɪsentə/ *noun* (*US* **epicenter**) point at which earthquake reaches earth's surface.

epicure /'epɪkjʊə/ *noun* person with refined taste in food and drink. □ **epicurism** *noun*.

epicurean /epɪkjʊə'riːən/ *noun* person fond of pleasure and luxury. ● *adjective* characteristics of an epicurean. □ **epicureanism** *noun*.

epidemic /epɪ'demɪk/ *noun* widespread occurrence of particular disease etc. in community at particular time. ● *adjective* in the nature of an epidemic.

> ■ *noun* outbreak, pestilence, plague, rash, upsurge. ● *adjective* general, pandemic, prevalent, spreading, universal, widespread.

epidemiology /epɪdiːmɪ'ɒlədʒɪ/ *noun* study of epidemics and their control.

epidermis /epɪ'dɜːmɪs/ *noun* outer layer of skin.

epidiascope /epɪ'daɪəskəʊp/ *noun* optical projector giving images of both opaque and transparent objects.

epidural /epɪ'djʊər(ə)l/ *adjective* (of anaesthetic) injected close to spinal cord. ● *noun* epidural injection.

epiglottis /epɪ'glɒtɪs/ *noun* flap of cartilage at root of tongue that covers windpipe during swallowing. □ **epiglottal** *adjective*.

epigram /'epɪɡræm/ *noun* **1** short poem with witty ending. **2** pointed saying. □ **epigrammatic** /-ɡrə'mæt-/ *adjective*.

epigraph /'epɪɡrɑːf/ *noun* inscription.

epilepsy /'epɪlepsɪ/ *noun* nervous disorder with convulsions and often loss of consciousness. □ **epileptic** /-'lep-/ *adjective & noun*.

epilogue /'epɪlɒg/ *noun* **1** short piece ending literary work. **2** short speech at end of play etc.

Epiphany /ɪ'pɪfənɪ/ *noun* (festival on 6 Jan. commemorating) visit of Magi to Christ.

episcopacy /ɪ'pɪskəpəsɪ/ *noun* (*plural* **-ies**) bishops collectively.

episcopal /ɪ'pɪskəp(ə)l/ *adjective* **1** of bishop or bishops. **2** (of church) governed by bishops. □ **Episcopal Church** Anglican Church in Scotland and US.

Episcopalian /ɪpɪskə'peɪlɪən/ *adjective* of the Episcopal Church or (**episcopalian**) an episcopal church. ● *noun* member of the Episcopal Church.

episcopate /ɪ'pɪskəpət/ *noun* **1** office or tenure of bishop. **2** bishops collectively.

episode /'epɪsəʊd/ *noun* **1** incident in narrative. **2** event as part of sequence. **3** part of serial story. □ **episodic** /-'sɒd-/ *adjective*.

■ **1** incident, part, passage, scene, section. **2** *colloquial* affair, event, happening, incident, occurrence. **3** chapter, instalment, part.

epistemology /ɪpɪstɪ'mɒlədʒɪ/ *noun* philosophy of knowledge. □ **epistemological** /-ə'lɒdʒ-/ *adjective*.

epistle /ɪ'pɪs(ə)l/ *noun* **1** letter. **2** poem etc. in form of letter.

epistolary /ɪ'pɪstələrɪ/ *adjective* of or in form of letters.

epitaph /'epɪtɑːf/ *noun* words in memory of dead person, esp. on tomb.

epithelium /epɪ'θiːlɪəm/ *noun* (*plural* **-s** or **-lia**) *Biology* tissue forming outer layer of body and lining many hollow structures. □ **epithelial** *adjective*.

epithet /'epɪθet/ *noun* adjective etc. expressing quality or attribute.

epitome /ɪ'pɪtəmɪ/ *noun* **1** person or thing embodying a quality etc. **2** abstract of written work.

■ **1** archetype, embodiment, essence, exemplar, incarnation, personification, quintessence, representation. **2** see SUMMARY *noun*.

epitomize *verb* (also **-ise**) (**-zing** or **-sing**) make or be perfect example of (a quality etc.).

EPNS *abbreviation* electroplated nickel silver.

epoch /'iːpɒk/ *noun* **1** period marked by special events. **2** beginning of era. □ **epoch-making** notable, significant.

eponym /'epənɪm/ *noun* **1** word derived from person's name. **2** person whose name is used in this way. □ **eponymous** /ɪ'pɒnɪməs/ *adjective*.

epoxy resin /ɪ'pɒksɪ/ *noun* synthetic thermosetting resin, used esp. as glue.

Epsom salts /'epsəm/ *noun* magnesium sulphate used as purgative.

equable /'ekwəb(ə)l/ *adjective* **1** not varying. **2** moderate. **3** not easily disturbed. □ **equability** *noun*. **equably** *adverb*.

equal /'iːkw(ə)l/ *adjective* **1** same in number, size, merit, level, etc. **2** evenly balanced or matched. **3** having or giving same rights or status. ● *noun* person etc. equal to another. ● *verb* (**-ll-**; *US* **-l-**) **1** be equal to. **2** achieve something equal to. □ **equal opportunity** (often in *plural*) opportunity to compete equally for jobs regardless of race, sex, etc. □ **equally** *adverb*.

USAGE It is a mistake to say *equally as*, as in *She was equally as guilty*. The correct version is *She was equally guilty* or possibly, for example, *She was as guilty as he was*.

■ *adjective* **1** coextensive, commensurate, congruent, corresponding, equivalent, even, identical, indistinguishable, interchangeable, level, like, matching, the same, uniform. **2** balanced, even, matched, regular, symmetrical. **3** egalitarian, even-handed, unbiased. ● *noun* compeer, counterpart, equivalent, fellow, peer, twin. ● *verb* **1** see AMOUNT *verb*. **2** balance, be in the same class as, compare with, correspond to, draw with, match, parallel, resemble, rival, tie with, vie with.

equality /ɪ'kwɒlɪtɪ/ *noun* being equal.

■ balance, congruence, correspondence, egalitarianism, equivalence, even-handedness, evenness, identity, parity, similarity, uniformity.

equalize *verb* (also **-ise**) (**-zing** or **-sing**) **1** make or become equal. **2** (in games) reach opponent's score. □ **equalization** *noun*.

■ **1** balance, compensate, even up, match, regularize, square, standardize. **2** catch up, draw level, even up.

equalizer *noun* (also **-iser**) equalizing goal etc.

equanimity /ekwə'nɪmɪtɪ/ *noun* composure, calm.

equate /ɪ'kweɪt/ *verb* (**-ting**) **1** (usually + *to*, *with*) regard as equal or equivalent. **2** (+ *with*) be equal or equivalent to.

■ **1** assume to be equal, compare, juxtapose, liken, set side by side. **2** (*equate with*) agree with, match, parallel, square with, tally with.

equation /ɪ'kweɪʒ(ə)n/ *noun* **1** making or being equal. **2** *Mathematics* statement that two expressions are equal. **3** *Chemistry* symbolic representation of reaction.

equator /ɪ'kweɪtə/ *noun* imaginary line round the earth or other body, equidistant from poles.

equatorial /ekwə'tɔːrɪəl/ *adjective* of or near equator.

equerry /'ekwərɪ/ *noun* (*plural* **-ies**) officer attending British royal family.

equestrian /ɪ'kwestrɪən/ *adjective* **1** of horse-riding. **2** on horseback. □ **equestrianism** *noun*.

equiangular /iːkwɪ'æŋɡjʊlə/ *adjective* having equal angles.

equidistant /iːkwɪ'dɪst(ə)nt/ *adjective* at equal distances.

equilateral /iːkwɪ'lætər(ə)l/ *adjective* having all sides equal.

equilibrium /iːkwɪ'lɪbrɪəm/ *noun* **1** state of balance. **2** composure.

■ **1** balance, equipoise, evenness, poise, stability, steadiness, symmetry. **2** composure, equanimity.

equine /'ekwaɪn/ *adjective* of or like horse.

equinox /'iːkwɪnɒks/ *noun* time or date at which sun crosses equator and day and night are of equal length.

equip /ɪ'kwɪp/ *verb* (**-pp-**) supply with what is needed.

■ arm, array, attire, *literary* caparison, clothe, dress, fit out, fit up, furnish, kit out, provide, stock, supply.

equipment *noun* **1** necessary tools, clothing, etc. **2** equipping, being equipped.

■ **1** accoutrements, apparatus, appurtenances, *slang* clobber, clothes, furnishings, gear, hardware, implements, instruments, kit, machinery, materials, outfit, paraphernalia, plant, rig, stuff, supplies, tackle, things, tools, trappings.

equipoise /'ekwɪpɔɪz/ *noun* 1 equilibrium. 2 counterbalancing thing.

equitable /'ekwɪtəb(ə)l/ *adjective* 1 fair, just. 2 *Law* valid in equity. □ **equitably** *adverb*.

equitation /ekwɪ'teɪʃ(ə)n/ *noun* horsemanship; horse-riding.

equity /'ekwɪtɪ/ *noun* (*plural* **-ies**) 1 fairness. 2 principles of justice supplementing law. 3 value of shares issued by company. 4 (in *plural*) stocks and shares not bearing fixed interest.

equivalent /ɪ'kwɪvələnt/ *adjective* 1 (often + *to*) equal in value, meaning, etc. 2 corresponding. ● *noun* equivalent amount etc. □ **equivalence** *noun*.
  ■ *adjective* alike, analogous, commensurate, comparable, corresponding, equal, identical, interchangeable, like, parallel, the same, similar, synonymous; (*equivalent to*) tantamount to.

equivocal /ɪ'kwɪvək(ə)l/ *adjective* 1 of double or doubtful meaning. 2 of uncertain nature. 3 (of person etc.) questionable. □ **equivocally** *adverb*.
  ■ 1, 2 ambiguous, circumlocutory, doubtful, dubious, equivocating, evasive, noncommittal, oblique, periphrastic, roundabout, vague. 3 dubious, questionable, suspect.

equivocate /ɪ'kwɪvəkeɪt/ *verb* (**-ting**) use words ambiguously to conceal truth. □ **equivocation** *noun*.
  ■ beat about the bush, be equivocal, dodge the issue, evade the question, fence, hedge, prevaricate, quibble, *colloquial* waffle.

ER *abbreviation* Queen Elizabeth (*Elizabetha Regina*).

era /'ɪərə/ *noun* 1 system of chronology starting from particular point. 2 historical or other period.
  ■ age, day, epoch, period, time.

eradicate /ɪ'rædɪkeɪt/ *verb* (**-ting**) root out, destroy. □ **eradication** *noun*.
  ■ destroy, eliminate, erase, get rid of, root out, uproot.

erase /ɪ'reɪz/ *verb* (**-sing**) 1 rub out, obliterate. 2 remove recording from (magnetic tape etc.).
  ■ 1 cancel, cross out, delete, efface, eradicate, expunge, obliterate, remove, rub out, wipe away, wipe off.

eraser *noun* piece of rubber etc. for removing esp. pencil marks.

erasure /ɪ'reɪʒə/ *noun* 1 erasing. 2 erased word etc.

ere /eə/ *preposition* & *conjunction* *poetical* or *archaic* before.

erect /ɪ'rekt/ *adjective* 1 upright, vertical. 2 (of part of body) enlarged and rigid, esp. from sexual excitement. ● *verb* 1 raise, set upright. 2 build. 3 establish. □ **erection** *noun*.
  ■ *adjective* 1 perpendicular, standing, straight, upright, vertical. 2 enlarged, hard, rigid, stiff, swollen. ● *verb* 1, 2 build, construct, elevate, lift up, make upright, pitch (*a tent*), put up, raise, set up. 3 see FOUND² 1;3.

erectile /ɪ'rektaɪl/ *adjective* that can become erect.

erg *noun* unit of work or energy.

ergo /'ɜːɡəʊ/ *adverb* therefore. [Latin]

ergonomics /ɜːɡə'nɒmɪks/ *plural noun* (treated as *singular*) study of relationship between people and their working environment. □ **ergonomic** *adjective*.

ergot /'ɜːɡət/ *noun* disease of rye etc. caused by fungus.

ERM *abbreviation* Exchange Rate Mechanism.

ermine /'ɜːmɪn/ *noun* (*plural* same or **-s**) 1 stoat, esp. in its white winter fur. 2 this fur.

Ernie /'ɜːnɪ/ *noun* device for drawing prize-winning numbers of Premium Bonds.

erode /ɪ'rəʊd/ *verb* (**-ding**) wear away; gradually destroy. □ **erosion** *noun*. **erosive** *adjective*.
  ■ abrade, corrode, eat away, eat into, gnaw away, grind down, wash away, wear away.

erogenous /ɪ'rɒdʒɪnəs/ *adjective* (of part of body) sexually sensitive.

erotic /ɪ'rɒtɪk/ *adjective* arousing sexual desire or excitement. □ **erotically** *adverb*. **eroticism** /-sɪz-/ *noun*.
  ■ amatory, amorous, aphrodisiac, arousing, lubricious, lustful, randy, *colloquial* raunchy, seductive, sensual, sexy, venereal, voluptuous.

erotica *plural noun* erotic literature or art.

err /ɜː/ *verb* 1 be mistaken or incorrect. 2 sin.
  ■ 1 be mistaken, *colloquial* boob, get it wrong, go astray, go wrong, miscalculate, *colloquial* slip up. 2 go astray, misbehave, sin, transgress, *archaic* trespass.

errand /'erənd/ *noun* 1 short journey, esp. on another's behalf, to take message etc. 2 object of journey. □ **errand-boy, -girl** one who runs errands.
  ■ 1 journey, mission, trip. 2 assignment, commission, duty, job, mission, task.

errant /'erənt/ *adjective* 1 erring. 2 *literary* travelling in search of adventure.

erratic /ɪ'rætɪk/ *adjective* 1 inconsistent in conduct etc. 2 uncertain in movement. □ **erratically** *adverb*.
  ■ 1 aberrant, capricious, changeable, fickle, fitful, fluctuating, inconsistent, irregular, shifting, spasmodic, sporadic, uneven, unpredictable, unreliable, unstable, unsteady, variable, wayward. 2 aimless, directionless, haphazard, meandering, wandering.

erratum /ɪ'rɑːtəm/ *noun* (*plural* **-ta**) error in printing etc.

erroneous /ɪ'rəʊnɪəs/ *adjective* incorrect. □ **erroneously** *adverb*.

error /'erə/ *noun* **1** mistake. **2** condition of being morally wrong. **3** degree of inaccuracy in calculation or measurement.

> ■ **1** *slang* bloomer, blunder, *colloquial* boob, corrigendum, erratum, fallacy, falsehood, fault, flaw, gaffe, *colloquial* howler, inaccuracy, inconsistency, inexactitude, lapse, misapprehension, miscalculation, misconception, misprint, mistake, misunderstanding, omission, oversight, *colloquial* slip-up, solecism. **2** see SIN *noun* 1.

ersatz /'eəzæts/ *adjective & noun* substitute, imitation.

erstwhile /'ɜːstwaɪl/ *adjective* former.

eructation /iːrʌk'teɪʃ(ə)n/ *noun formal* belching.

erudite /'eruːdaɪt/ *adjective* learned. □ **erudition** /-'dɪʃ-/ *noun*.

erupt /ɪ'rʌpt/ *verb* **1** break or burst out. **2** (of volcano) shoot out lava etc. **3** (of rash) appear on skin. □ **eruption** *noun*.

> ■ **1** break out, burst out, explode. **2** blow up, explode. **3** appear, break out. □ **eruption** burst, discharge, emission, explosion, outbreak, outburst, rash.

erysipelas /err'sɪpɪləs/ *noun* disease causing deep red inflammation of skin.

escalate /'eskəleɪt/ *verb* (**-ting**) increase or develop by stages. □ **escalation** *noun*.

escalator *noun* moving staircase.

escalope /'eskəlɒp/ *noun* thin slice of meat, esp. veal.

escapade /'eskəpeɪd/ *noun* piece of reckless behaviour.

> ■ adventure, exploit, *colloquial* lark, practical joke, prank, stunt.

escape /ɪs'keɪp/ *verb* (**-ping**) **1** get free. **2** leak. **3** avoid punishment etc. **4** get free of. **5** elude, avoid. ● *noun* **1** escaping. **2** means of escaping. **3** leakage. **4** avoidance of or distraction from work, problems, etc. □ **escape clause** clause releasing contracting party from obligation in specified circumstances. □ **escaper** *noun*.

> ■ *verb* **1** abscond, *slang* beat it, bolt, break free, break out, *colloquial* cut and run, decamp, disappear, *slang* do a bunk, elope, flee, fly, get away, run, run away, *slang* scarper, slip away, take to one's heels, turn tail. **2** discharge, drain, leak, ooze, pour out, run out, seep. **5** avoid, dodge, elude, evade, get away from, shirk. ● *noun* **1** bolt, breakout, departure, flight, flit, getaway, retreat, running away. **3** discharge, emission, leak, leakage, seepage. **4** avoidance, distraction, diversion, escapism, evasion, relief.

escapee /ɪskeɪ'piː/ *noun* person who has escaped.

escapism *noun* pursuit of distraction and relief from reality. □ **escapist** *adjective & noun*.

> ■ daydreaming, fantasy, pretence, unreality, wishful thinking.

escapology /eskə'pɒlədʒɪ/ *noun* techniques of escaping from confinement, esp. as entertainment. □ **escapologist** *noun*.

escarpment /ɪs'kɑːpmənt/ *noun* long steep slope at edge of plateau etc.

eschatology /eskə'tɒlədʒɪ/ *noun* doctrine of death and final destiny. □ **eschatological** /-tə'lɒdʒ-/ *adjective*.

escheat /ɪs'tʃiːt/ *noun* **1** lapse of property to the state etc. **2** property so lapsing. ● *verb* **1** hand over as escheat. **2** confiscate. **3** revert by escheat.

eschew /ɪs'tʃuː/ *verb formal* abstain from.

escort *noun* /'eskɔːt/ **1** person(s) etc. accompanying another for protection or as courtesy. **2** person accompanying another of opposite sex socially. ● *verb* /ɪ'skɔːt/ act as escort to.

> ■ *noun* **1** attendant, bodyguard, convoy, entourage, guard, guide, pilot, protection, protector, retinue, train. **2** companion, *esp. US colloquial* date, partner. ● *verb* accompany, attend, chaperon, conduct, guard, keep an eye on, *colloquial* keep tabs on, look after, protect, shepherd, stay with, usher, watch.

escritoire /eskrɪ'twɑː/ *noun* writing desk with drawers etc.

escutcheon /ɪ'skʌtʃ(ə)n/ *noun* shield bearing coat of arms.

ESE *abbreviation* east-south-east.

Eskimo /'eskɪməʊ/ *noun* **1** (*plural* same or **-s**) member of people inhabiting N. Canada, Alaska, Greenland, and E. Siberia. **2** their language. ● *adjective* of Eskimos or their language.

USAGE The Eskimos of N. America prefer the name *Inuit*.

ESN *abbreviation historical* educationally subnormal.

esophagus *US* = OESOPHAGUS.

esoteric /esə'terɪk, iːsə'terɪk/ *adjective* intelligible only to those with special knowledge.

ESP *abbreviation* extrasensory perception.

esp. *abbreviation* especially.

espadrille /espə'drɪl/ *noun* light canvas shoe with plaited fibre sole.

espalier /ɪ'spælɪə/ *noun* **1** framework for training tree etc. **2** tree trained on espalier.

esparto /e'spɑːtəʊ/ *noun* kind of grass used to make paper.

especial /ɪ'speʃ(ə)l/ *adjective* special, notable.

especially *adverb* in particular; more than in other cases; particularly.

Esperanto /espə'ræntəʊ/ *noun* artificial universal language.

espionage /'espɪənɑːʒ/ *noun* spying or using spies.

esplanade /esplə'neɪd/ *noun* level space, esp. used as public promenade.

espousal /ɪ'spaʊz(ə)l/ *noun* **1** espousing. **2** *archaic* marriage, betrothal.

espouse /ɪ'spaʊz/ *verb* (**-sing**) **1** support (cause). **2** *archaic* marry.

espresso /e'spresəʊ/ *noun* (*plural* **-s**) coffee made under steam pressure.

esprit de corps /espri: də 'kɔ:/ *noun* devotion to and pride in one's group. [French]

espy /ɪ'spaɪ/ *verb* (**-ies, -ied**) catch sight of.

Esq. *abbreviation* Esquire.

esquire /ɪ'skwaɪə/ *noun: title placed after man's name in writing.*

essay *noun* /'eseɪ/ **1** short piece of writing, esp. on given subject. **2** *formal* attempt. ● *verb* /e'seɪ/ *formal* attempt.

essayist *noun* writer of essays.

essence /'es(ə)ns/ *noun* **1** fundamental nature; inherent characteristics. **2** extract obtained by distillation etc. **3** perfume. □ **in essence** fundamentally.

> ■ **1** centre, character, core, cornerstone, crux, heart, kernel, life, meaning, nature, pith, quintessence, soul, spirit, substance. **2** concentrate, decoction, elixir, extract, flavouring, tincture. **3** fragrance, perfume, scent.

essential /ɪ'sen∫(ə)l/ *adjective* **1** necessary, indispensable. **2** of or constituting a thing's essence. ● *noun* (esp. in *plural*) indispensable element or thing. □ **essential oil** volatile oil with characteristic odour. □ **essentially** *adverb*.

> ■ *adjective* **1** basic, chief, crucial, elementary, fundamental, important, indispensable, irreplaceable, key, leading, main, necessary, primary, principal, requisite, vital. **2** characteristic, inherent, innate, intrinsic, quintessential.

establish /ɪ'stæblɪ∫/ *verb* **1** set up. **2** settle. **3** (esp. as **established** *adjective*) achieve permanent acceptance for. **4** place beyond dispute. □ **Established Church** Church recognized by state.

> ■ **1** base, begin, constitute, construct, create, decree, form, found, inaugurate, initiate, institute, introduce, organize, originate, set up, start. **2** ensconce, entrench, install, lodge, secure, settle, station. **3** (**established**) deep-rooted, deep-seated, indelible, ineradicable, ingrained, long-lasting, long-standing, permanent, proven, reliable, respected, rooted, secure, traditional, well known, well tried. **4** accept, agree, authenticate, certify, confirm, corroborate, decide, demonstrate, fix, prove, ratify, recognize, show to be true, substantiate, verify.

establishment *noun* **1** establishing, being established. **2** public institution. **3** place of business. **4** staff, household, etc. **5** Church system established by law. **6** (**the Establishment**) social group with authority or influence and resisting change.

> ■ **1** composition, constitution, creation, formation, foundation, inauguration, inception, institution, introduction, setting up. **2, 3** business, company, concern, enterprise, factory, institution, office, organization, shop. **4** see HOUSEHOLD 2, STAFF *noun* 3.

estate /ɪ'steɪt/ *noun* **1** landed property. **2** area of homes or businesses planned as a whole. **3** dead person's collective assets and liabilities. □ **estate agent** person whose business is sale and lease of buildings and land on behalf of others. **estate car** car with continuous area for rear passengers and luggage.

> ■ **1** demesne, domain, holding, land, property. **2** area, development. **3** assets, belongings, capital, chattels, effects, fortune, goods, inheritance, lands, possessions, property, wealth.

esteem /ɪ'sti:m/ *verb* **1** (usually in *passive*) think highly of. **2** *formal* consider. ● *noun* high regard.

> ■ *verb* **1** see RESPECT *verb* 1. ● *noun* admiration, credit, estimation, favour, honour, regard, respect, reverence, veneration.

ester /'estə/ *noun* compound formed by replacing the hydrogen of an acid by an organic radical.

estimable /'estɪməb(ə)l/ *adjective* worthy of esteem.

estimate *noun* /'estɪmət/ **1** approximate judgement of cost, value, etc. **2** approximate price stated in advance for work. ● *verb* /'estɪmeɪt/ (**-ting**) **1** form estimate of. **2** (+ *that*) make rough calculation. **3** (+ *at*) put (sum etc.) at by estimating.

> ■ *noun* **1** appraisal, approximation, assessment, calculation, estimation, evaluation, guess, guesstimate, judgement, opinion, reckoning, valuation. **2** price, quotation. ● *verb* **1** appraise, assess, consider, evaluate, gauge, guess, judge, think out, *colloquial* weigh up. **2, 3** assess, calculate, compute, gauge, guess, judge, project, reckon, work out.

estimation /estɪ'meɪ∫(ə)n/ *noun* **1** estimating. **2** judgement of worth.

> ■ **1** appraisal, assessment, calculation, computation, evaluation. **2** appraisal, appreciation, assessment, consideration, estimate, evaluation, judgement, opinion, view.

estrange /ɪ'streɪndʒ/ *verb* (**-ging**) **1** (usually in *passive*; often + *from*) alienate; make hostile or indifferent. **2** (as **estranged** *adjective*) no longer living with spouse. □ **estrangement** *noun*.

estrogen *US* = OESTROGEN.

estuary /'estjʊərɪ/ *noun* (*plural* **-ies**) tidal mouth of river.

> ■ creek, firth, fjord, inlet, *Scottish* loch, river mouth.

ETA *abbreviation* estimated time of arrival.

et al *abbreviation* and others (*et alii*).

etc. *abbreviation* et cetera.

et cetera /et 'setrə/ *adverb* (also **etcetera**) **1** and the rest. **2** and so on. □ **etceteras** *plural noun* the usual extras.

etch *verb* **1** reproduce (picture etc.) by engraving metal plate with acid, esp. to print copies. **2** engrave (plate) thus. **3** practise this craft. **4** (usually + *on, upon*) impress deeply.

etching *noun* print made from etched plate.

eternal /ɪˈtɜːn(ə)l/ *adjective* **1** existing always; without end or beginning. **2** unchanging. **3** *colloquial* constant, too frequent. □ **eternalize** *verb* (also **-ise**). **eternally** *adverb*.

■ **1** ceaseless, deathless, endless, everlasting, immortal, infinite, lasting, limitless, never-ending, permanent, perpetual, timeless, undying, unending, unlimited. **2** immutable, invariable, unchanging. **3** see CONTINUAL.

eternity /ɪˈtɜːnɪtɪ/ *noun* **1** infinite time. **2** endless life after death. **3** (**an eternity**) *colloquial* a very long time.

■ **1** infinity, perpetuity. **2** afterlife, eternal life, immortality.

ethane /ˈiːθeɪn/ *noun* hydrocarbon gas present in petroleum and natural gas.

ethanol /ˈeθənɒl/ *noun* alcohol.

ether /ˈiːθə/ *noun* **1** volatile liquid used as anaesthetic or solvent. **2** clear sky; upper air.

ethereal /ɪˈθɪərɪəl/ *adjective* **1** light, airy. **2** delicate, esp. in appearance. **3** heavenly.

ethic /ˈeθɪk/ *noun* set of moral principles.

ethical *adjective* **1** relating to morals or ethics. **2** morally correct. **3** (of drug etc.) available only on prescription. □ **ethically** *adverb*.

■ **2** decent, fair, good, honest, just, moral, noble, principled, righteous, upright, virtuous.

ethics *plural noun* (also treated as *singular*) **1** moral philosophy. **2** (set of) moral principles.

Ethiopian /iːθɪˈəʊpɪən/ *noun* native or national of Ethiopia. ● *adjective* of Ethiopia.

ethnic /ˈeθnɪk/ *adjective* **1** (of social group) having common national or cultural tradition. **2** (of clothes etc.) resembling those of an exotic people. **3** (of person) having specified origin by birth or descent rather than nationality. □ **ethnic cleansing** *euphemistic* expulsion or murder of people of ethnic or religious group in certain area. □ **ethnically** *adverb*.

■ **1, 2** cultural, folk, national, racial, traditional, tribal.

ethnology /eθˈnɒlədʒɪ/ *noun* comparative study of peoples. □ **ethnological** /-nəˈlɒdʒ-/ *adjective*.

ethos /ˈiːθɒs/ *noun* characteristic spirit of community, people, or system.

ethylene /ˈeθɪliːn/ *noun* flammable hydrocarbon gas.

etiolate /ˈiːtɪəleɪt/ *verb* (**-ting**) **1** make pale by excluding light. **2** give sickly colour to. □ **etiolation** *noun*.

etiology *US* = AETIOLOGY.

etiquette /ˈetɪket/ *noun* conventional rules of social behaviour or professional conduct.

■ ceremony, civility, code of behaviour, conventions, courtesy, decency, decorum, form, formalities, manners, politeness, propriety, protocol, rules, standards of behaviour.

étude /eɪˈtjuːd/ *noun* musical composition designed to develop player's skill.

etymology /etɪˈmɒlədʒɪ/ *noun* (*plural* **-ies**) **1** word's origin and sense-development. **2** account of these. □ **etymological** /-məˈlɒdʒ-/ *adjective*.

eucalyptus /juːkəˈlɪptəs/ *noun* (*plural* **-tuses** or **-ti** /-taɪ/) **1** tall evergreen tree. **2** its oil, used as antiseptic etc.

Eucharist /ˈjuːkərɪst/ *noun* **1** Christian sacrament in which bread and wine are consecrated and consumed. **2** consecrated elements, esp. bread. □ **Eucharistic** /-ˈrɪs-/ *adjective*.

eugenics /juːˈdʒenɪks/ *plural noun* (also treated as *singular*) improvement of qualities of race by control of inherited characteristics. □ **eugenic** *adjective*. **eugenically** *adverb*.

eulogize /ˈjuːlədʒaɪz/ *verb* (also **-ise**) (**-zing** or **-sing**) extol, praise.

eulogy /ˈjuːlədʒɪ/ *noun* (*plural* **-ies**) speech or writing in praise or commendation. □ **eulogistic** /-ˈdʒɪs-/ *adjective*.

eunuch /ˈjuːnək/ *noun* castrated man.

euphemism /ˈjuːfɪmɪz(ə)m/ *noun* mild expression substituted for blunt one. □ **euphemistic** /-ˈmɪs-/ *adjective*. **euphemistically** /-ˈmɪs-/ *adverb*.

euphonium /juːˈfəʊnɪəm/ *noun* brass instrument of tuba family.

euphony /ˈjuːfənɪ/ *noun* pleasantness of sound, esp. in words. □ **euphonious** /-ˈfəʊ-/ *adjective*.

euphoria /juːˈfɔːrɪə/ *noun* intense sense of well-being and excitement. □ **euphoric** /-ˈfɒr-/ *adjective*.

Eurasian /jʊəˈreɪʒ(ə)n/ *adjective* **1** of mixed European and Asian parentage. **2** of Europe and Asia. ● *noun* Eurasian person.

eureka /jʊəˈriːkə/ *interjection* I have found it!

Eurodollar /ˈjʊərəʊdɒlə/ *noun* dollar held in bank in Europe etc.

European /jʊərəˈpɪən/ *adjective* of, in, or extending over Europe. ● *noun* **1** native or inhabitant of Europe. **2** descendant of one.

Eustachian tube /juːˈsteɪʃ(ə)n/ *noun* passage between middle ear and back of throat.

euthanasia /juːθəˈneɪzɪə/ *noun* killing person painlessly, esp. one who has incurable painful disease.

evacuate /ɪˈvækjʊeɪt/ *verb* (**-ting**) **1** remove (people) from place of danger. **2** make empty, clear. **3** withdraw from (place). **4** empty (bowels). □ **evacuation** *noun*.

■ **1** move out, remove, send away. **2** clear, deplete, drain, void. **3** abandon, decamp from, desert, empty, forsake, leave, pull out of, quit, relinquish, vacate, withdraw from.

evacuee /ɪvækjuːˈiː/ *noun* person evacuated.

evade /ɪˈveɪd/ *verb* (**-ding**) **1** escape from, avoid. **2** avoid doing or answering directly. **3** avoid paying (tax) illegally.

■ **1, 2** avoid, *colloquial* chicken out of, circumvent, dodge, elude, escape from, flinch from, get away from, hedge, parry, shirk, shrink from, shun, sidestep, steer clear of; *(evade a question)* see EQUIVOCATE. **3** avoid, dodge, get out of.

evaluate /ɪˈvæljʊeɪt/ *verb* (**-ting**) **1** assess, appraise. **2** find or state number or amount of. □ **evaluation** *noun*.

■ **1** appraise, assess, estimate, judge, value, *colloquial* weigh up. **2** calculate value of, compute, work out.

evanesce /evəˈnes/ *verb* (**-cing**) *literary* fade from sight. □ **evanescence** *noun*. **evanescent** *adjective*.

evangelical /iːvænˈdʒelɪk(ə)l/ *adjective* **1** of or according to gospel teaching. **2** of Protestant groups maintaining doctrine of salvation by faith. ● *noun* member of evangelical group. □ **evangelicalism** *noun*.

evangelist /ɪˈvændʒəlɪst/ *noun* **1** writer of one of the 4 Gospels. **2** preacher of gospel. □ **evangelism** *noun*. **evangelistic** /-ˈlɪs-/ *adjective*.

evangelize *verb* (also **-ise**) (**-zing** or **-sing**) preach gospel to. □ **evangelization** *noun*.

evaporate /ɪˈvæpəreɪt/ *verb* (**-ting**) **1** turn into vapour. **2** (cause to) lose moisture as vapour. **3** (cause to) disappear. □ **evaporation** *noun*.

■ **1** vaporize. **2** dehydrate, desiccate, dry up. **3** disappear, disperse, dissipate, dissolve, *literary* evanesce, melt away, vanish.

evasion /ɪˈveɪʒ(ə)n/ *noun* **1** evading. **2** evasive answer.

evasive /ɪˈveɪsɪv/ *adjective* seeking to evade. □ **evasiveness** *noun*.

■ ambiguous, *colloquial* cagey, circumlocutory, deceptive, devious, disingenuous, equivocal, equivocating, inconclusive, indecisive, indirect, misleading, noncommittal, oblique, prevaricating, roundabout, *colloquial* shifty, sophistical, uninformative.

eve *noun* **1** evening or day before festival etc. **2** time just before event. **3** *archaic* evening.

even /ˈiːv(ə)n/ *adjective* (**-er, -est**) **1** level, smooth. **2** uniform. **3** equal. **4** equable, calm. **5** divisible by two. ● *adverb* **1** still, yet. **2** (with negative) so much as. ● *verb* (often + *up*) make or become even. □ **even-handed** impartial, fair. **even-handedness** *noun*. **even if** in spite of the fact that; no matter whether. **even out 1** become level or regular. **2** spread (thing) over period or among group. **even-tempered** not easily angered. **get even 1** (often + *with*) achieve revenge. **2** equalize score. □ **evenly** *adverb*. **evenness** *noun*.

■ *adjective* **1** flat, flush, horizontal, level, plane, smooth, straight, true. **2** consistent, constant, equalized, measured, metrical, monotonous, proportional, regular, rhythmical, symmetrical, unbroken, uniform, unvarying. **3** balanced, equal, identical, level, matching, the same. **4** balanced, calm, composed, cool, equable, even-tempered, impassive, imperturbable, pacific, peaceable, peaceful, placid, poised, reliable, self-possessed,

serene, stable, steady, tranquil, unemotional, unexcitable, unruffled. ● *verb* (*even up*) see EQUALIZE 1–2. □ **even out 1** see FLATTEN 1. **get even** see RETALIATE.

evening /ˈiːvnɪŋ/ *noun* end part of day, esp. from about 6 p.m. to bedtime. □ **evening class** adult education class held in evening. **evening dress** formal clothes for evening wear. **evening star** planet, esp. Venus, conspicuous in west after sunset.

■ dusk, *archaic* or *poetical* eventide, *poetical* gloaming, nightfall, sundown, sunset, twilight.

evensong *noun* evening service in Church of England.

event /ɪˈvent/ *noun* **1** thing that happens. **2** fact of thing occurring. **3** organized occasion. **4** (item in) sports programme. □ **in any event, at all events** whatever happens. **in the event** as it turns or turned out. **in the event of** if (thing) happens.

■ **1** affair, business, circumstance, episode, experience, happening, incident, occurrence. **2** conclusion, consequence, effect, issue, outcome, result, upshot. **3** activity, ceremony, entertainment, function, occasion. **4** bout, championship, competition, contest, engagement, fixture, game, match, meeting, tournament.

eventful *adjective* marked by noteworthy events.

eventide /ˈiːv(ə)ntaɪd/ *noun archaic* or *poetical* evening.

eventual /ɪˈventʃʊəl/ *adjective* occurring in due course or in the end. □ **eventually** *adverb*.

■ concluding, consequent, destined, due, ensuing, final, last, resultant, resulting, ultimate.

eventuality /ɪventʃʊˈælɪtɪ/ *noun* (*plural* **-ies**) possible event.

ever /ˈevə/ *adverb* **1** at all times; always. **2** at any time. □ **ever since** throughout period since (then). **ever so** *colloquial* very. **ever such a(n)** *colloquial* a very.

evergreen *adjective* retaining green leaves throughout year. ● *noun* evergreen plant.

everlasting *adjective* **1** lasting for ever or a long time. **2** (of flower) retaining shape and colour when dried. □ **everlastingly** *adverb*.

■ **1** ceaseless, deathless, endless, eternal, immortal, incorruptible, infinite, lasting, limitless, measureless, never-ending, permanent, perpetual, persistent, timeless, unchanging, undying, unending.

evermore *adverb* for ever; always.

■ always, eternally, for ever, unceasingly.

every /ˈevrɪ/ *adjective* **1** each. **2** all. □ **everybody** every person. **everyday 1** occurring every day. **2** ordinary. **Everyman** ordinary or typical human being. **every now and again or then** occasionally. **everyone** everybody. **every other** each alternate. **everything 1** all things. **2** the most important thing. **everywhere** in every place.

evict /ɪ'vɪkt/ *verb* expel (tenant) by legal process. □ **eviction** *noun*.
■ boot out, dispossess, eject, expel, kick out, oust, put out, remove, throw out, *colloquial* turf out, turn out.

evidence /'evɪd(ə)ns/ *noun* **1** (often + *for, of*) indication, sign. **2** information given to establish fact etc. **3** statement etc. admissible in court of law. ● *verb* (**-cing**) be evidence of.
■ *noun* **1** indication, manifestation, proof, sign, symptom, token. **2** confirmation, corroboration, data, documentation, facts, grounds, information, statistics, substantiation. **3** attestation, deposition, statement, testimony; (*give evidence*) see TESTIFY.

evident *adjective* obvious, manifest.
■ apparent, certain, clear, discernible, manifest, noticeable, obvious, palpable, patent, perceptible, plain, self-explanatory, unambiguous, undeniable, unmistakable, visible.

evidential /evɪ'denʃ(ə)l/ *adjective* of or providing evidence.

evidently *adverb* **1** seemingly. **2** as shown by evidence.

evil /'iːv(ə)l/ *adjective* **1** wicked. **2** harmful. **3** disagreeable, unpleasant. ● *noun* **1** evil thing. **2** wickedness. □ **evildoer** person who does evil. **evildoing** *noun*. **evil eye** gaze believed to cause harm. □ **evilly** *adverb*.
■ *adjective* **1** amoral, atrocious, bad, base, black-hearted, blasphemous, corrupt, criminal, cruel, depraved, devilish, diabolical, dishonest, fiendish, foul, hateful, heinous, hellish, immoral, impious, infamous, iniquitous, irreligious, machiavellian, malevolent, malicious, nefarious, perverted, reprobate, satanic, sinful, sinister, ungodly, unprincipled, unrighteous, vicious, vile, villainous, wicked, wrong. **2** bad, baleful, destructive, harmful, malignant, noxious, pernicious, pestilential, poisonous, treacherous. **3** disagreeable, foul, nasty, troublesome, unpleasant, unspeakable, vile. ● *noun* **1** affliction, bane, calamity, catastrophe, curse, disaster, enormity, harm, ill, misfortune, wrong. **2** amorality, blasphemy, corruption, crime, criminality, cruelty, depravity, dishonesty, fiendishness, heinousness, immorality, impiety, iniquity, knavery, malevolence, malice, mischief, sin, sinfulness, treachery, *formal* turpitude, ungodliness, unrighteousness, vice, viciousness, villainy, wickedness, wrongdoing.

evince /ɪ'vɪns/ *verb* (**-cing**) show, indicate.

eviscerate /ɪ'vɪsəreɪt/ *verb* (**-ting**) disembowel. □ **evisceration** *noun*.

evocative /ɪ'vɒkətɪv/ *adjective* evoking (feelings etc.).
■ atmospheric, convincing, descriptive, emotive, graphic, imaginative, provoking, realistic, stimulating, suggestive, vivid.

evoke /ɪ'vəʊk/ *verb* (**-king**) call up (feeling etc.). □ **evocation** /evə-/ *noun*.

■ arouse, awaken, call up, conjure up, elicit, excite, inspire, invoke, kindle, produce, provoke, raise, rouse, stimulate, stir up, suggest, summon up.

evolution /iːvə'luːʃ(ə)n/ *noun* **1** evolving. **2** development of species from earlier forms. **3** unfolding of events etc. **4** change in disposition of troops or ships. □ **evolutionary** *adjective*.
■ **1, 2** advance, development, emergence, formation, growth, improvement, maturing, progress. **3** development, unfolding.

evolutionist *noun* person who regards evolution as explaining origin of species.

evolve /ɪ'vɒlv/ *verb* (**-ving**) **1** develop gradually and naturally. **2** devise. **3** unfold, open out.
■ **1** derive, descend, develop, emerge, grow, improve, mature, modify gradually, progress, unfold.

ewe /juː/ *noun* female sheep.

ewer /'juːə/ *noun* water-jug with wide mouth.

ex[1] *preposition* (of goods) sold from (warehouse etc.). □ **ex-directory** not listed in telephone directory at subscriber's wish.

ex[2] *noun colloquial* former husband or wife.

ex- *prefix* formerly.

exacerbate /ek'sæsəbeɪt/ *verb* (**-ting**) **1** make worse. **2** irritate. □ **exacerbation** *noun*.

exact /ɪg'zækt/ *adjective* accurate; correct in all details. ● *verb* **1** demand and enforce payment of (fees etc.). **2** demand, insist on. □ **exactness** *noun*.
■ *adjective* accurate, correct, dead (*centre*), detailed, faithful, faultless, flawless, literal, meticulous, painstaking, perfect, precise, punctilious, right, rigorous, scrupulous, specific, *colloquial* spot on, strict, true, truthful, *formal* veracious. ● *verb* claim, compel, demand, enforce, extort, extract, get, impose, insist on, obtain, require.

exacting *adjective* demanding; requiring much effort.
■ see DIFFICULT 1.

exaction *noun* **1** exacting, being exacted. **2** illegal or exorbitant demand.

exactitude *noun* exactness.

exactly *adverb* **1** precisely. **2** I agree.

exaggerate /ɪg'zædʒəreɪt/ *verb* (**-ting**) **1** make seem larger or greater than it really is. **2** increase beyond normal or due proportions. □ **exaggerated** *adjective*. **exaggeration** *noun*.
■ **1** amplify, embellish, embroider, enlarge, inflate, *colloquial* lay it on thick, magnify, make too much of, maximize, overdo, overemphasize, overestimate, overstate, *colloquial* pile it on. **2** see CARICATURE *verb*. □ **exaggerated** see EXCESSIVE.

exalt /ɪg'zɔːlt/ *verb* **1** raise in rank, power, etc. **2** praise, extol. **3** (usually as **exalted** *adjective*) make lofty or noble. □ **exaltation** /eg-/ *noun*.

■ **1** boost, elevate, lift, promote, raise, uplift. **2** see PRAISE 2. **3 (exalted)** see HIGH *adjective* 4.

exam /ɪɡ'zæm/ *noun* examination, test.

examination /ɪɡzæmɪ'neɪʃ(ə)n/ *noun* **1** examining, being examined. **2** detailed inspection. **3** testing of knowledge or ability by questions. **4** formal questioning of witness etc. in court.

■ **1, 2** analysis, appraisal, assessment, audit, check-up, inspection, investigation, *colloquial* post-mortem, probe, review, scan, scrutiny, study, survey. **3** exam, *colloquial* oral, paper, test, *colloquial* viva, viva voce. **4** cross-examination, interrogation, questioning.

examine /ɪɡ'zæmɪn/ *verb* **(-ning) 1** inquire into. **2** look closely at. **3** test knowledge or ability of. **4** check health of. **5** question formally. □ **examinee** /-'niː/ *noun*. **examiner** *noun*.

■ **1, 2** analyse, appraise, audit (*accounts*), check, *colloquial* check out, explore, inquire into, inspect, investigate, look at, peruse, probe, research, scan, scrutinize, sift, sort out, study, *slang* suss out, vet, *colloquial* weigh up. **3** assess, evaluate, quiz, test. **5** cross-examine, cross-question, grill, interrogate, pump, question, sound out, try.

example /ɪɡ'zɑːmp(ə)l/ *noun* **1** thing illustrating general rule; specimen. **2** model, pattern; precedent. **3** warning to others. □ **for example** by way of illustration.

■ **1** case, illustration, instance, occurrence, sample, specimen. **2** ideal, model, paragon, pattern, precedent, prototype. **3** lesson, warning.

exasperate /ɪɡ'zɑːspəreɪt/ *verb* **(-ting)** irritate intensely. □ **exasperation** *noun*.

■ *disputed* aggravate, annoy, *colloquial* drive mad, gall, infuriate, irk, irritate, *colloquial* needle, pique, provoke, *colloquial* rile, vex.

ex cathedra /eks kə'θiːdrə/ *adjective & adverb* with full authority (esp. of papal pronouncement). [Latin]

excavate /'ekskəveɪt/ *verb* **(-ting) 1** make (hole etc.) by digging. **2** dig out material from (ground). **3** reveal or extract by digging. **4** dig systematically to explore (archaeological site). □ **excavation** *noun*. **excavator** *noun*.

■ **1** burrow, dig, gouge out, hollow out, mine, scoop out. **3** dig up, expose, extract, reveal, uncover, unearth.

exceed /ɪk'siːd/ *verb* **1** be more or greater than. **2** go beyond; do more than is warranted by. **3** surpass.

■ **1** beat, go over, outnumber, overtake, pass. **2** do more than, go beyond, overstep, transcend. **3** excel, outshine, outstrip, surpass, transcend.

exceedingly *adverb* very.

■ amazingly, especially, exceptionally, excessively, extraordinarily, extremely, outstandingly, specially, unusually, very.

excel /ɪk'sel/ *verb* **(-ll-) 1** surpass. **2** be pre-eminent.

■ **1** beat, better, eclipse, exceed, outclass, outdo, outshine, surpass, top. **2** be excellent, be pre-eminent, do best, shine, stand out.

excellence /'eksələns/ *noun* great merit.

Excellency *noun* (*plural* **-ies**) **(His, Her, Your Excellency)** *title used of or to ambassador, governor, etc.*

excellent *adjective* extremely good.

■ *slang* ace, admirable, *colloquial* beautiful, *colloquial* brilliant, *colloquial* capital, *colloquial* champion, choice, consummate, *slang* cool, *slang* cracking, distinguished, esteemed, estimable, exceptional, exemplary, extraordinary, *colloquial* fabulous, *colloquial* fantastic, fine, first-class, first-rate, flawless, *colloquial* gorgeous, *colloquial* great, high-class, ideal, impressive, *colloquial* magnificent, marvellous, model, notable, outstanding, perfect, phenomenal, remarkable, *colloquial* smashing, splendid, sterling, *colloquial* stunning, *colloquial* super, *colloquial* superb, superlative, supreme, surpassing, *colloquial* terrific, *colloquial* tiptop, *colloquial* top-notch, top-ranking, *colloquial* tremendous, unequalled, wonderful.

except /ɪk'sept/ *verb* exclude from general statement etc. ● *preposition* (often + *for*) not including; other than.

■ *verb* exclude, leave out, omit.

excepting *preposition* except.

exception /ɪk'sepʃ(ə)n/ *noun* **1** excepting. **2** thing or case excepted. **3** thing that does not follow rule. □ **take exception** (often + *to*) object.

■ **1** exclusion, omission, rejection. **3** abnormality, anomaly, departure, deviation, eccentricity, freak, irregularity, oddity, peculiarity, quirk, rarity. □ **take exception** see OBJECT *verb*.

exceptionable *adjective* open to objection.

USAGE *Exceptionable* is sometimes confused with *exceptional*.

exceptional *adjective* **1** forming exception. **2** unusual. **3** unusually good. □ **exceptionally** *adverb*.

USAGE *Exceptional* is sometimes confused with *exceptionable*.

■ **1, 2** aberrant, abnormal, anomalous, atypical, curious, deviant, eccentric, extraordinary, extreme, isolated, memorable, notable, odd, out of the ordinary, peculiar, phenomenal, quirky, rare, remarkable, singular, solitary, special, strange, surprising, uncommon, unconventional, unexpected, unheard-of, unique, unparalleled, unprecedented, unpredictable, untypical, unusual. **3** see EXCELLENT.

excerpt *noun* /'eksɜːpt/ short extract from book, film, etc. ● *verb* /ɪk'sɜːpt/ take excerpts from. □ **excerption** /ɪk'sɜːpʃ(ə)n/ *noun*.

■ *noun* citation, clip, extract, fragment, highlight, part, passage, quotation, section, selection, trailer.

excess *noun* /ɪk'ses/ **1** exceeding. **2** amount by

which thing exceeds. **3** intemperance in eating or drinking. ● *adjective* /'eksɪs/ that exceeds limit or given amount. □ **in, to excess** exceeding proper amount or degree. **in excess of** more than.

■ *noun* **1** abundance, glut, over-abundance, overflow, overkill, profit, redundancy, superabundance, superfluity, surfeit, surplus. **3** debauchery, dissipation, extravagance, intemperance, over-indulgence, profligacy, wastefulness.

excessive /ɪk'sesɪv/ *adjective* too much or too great. □ **excessively** *adverb*.

■ disproportionate, exaggerated, exorbitant, extortionate, extravagant, extreme, fanatical, immoderate, inflated, inordinate, intemperate, needless, overdone, prodigal, profligate, profuse, superfluous, undue, unjustifiable, unnecessary, unneeded, unrealistic, unreasonable, wasteful.

exchange /ɪks'tʃeɪmdʒ/ *noun* **1** giving one thing and receiving another in its place. **2** exchanging of money for equivalent, esp. in other currency. **3** centre where telephone connections are made. **4** place where merchants, stockbrokers, etc. transact business. **5** employment office. **6** short conversation. ● *verb* (**-ging**) **1** give or receive in exchange. **2** interchange. □ **exchange rate** price of one currency expressed in another. □ **exchangeable** *adjective*.

■ *noun* **1** deal, interchange, reciprocity, replacement, substitution, swap, switch. ● *verb* bargain, barter, change, convert (*currency*), interchange, reciprocate, replace, substitute, swap, switch, trade, trade in, traffic.

exchequer /ɪks'tʃekə/ *noun* **1** former government department in charge of national revenue. **2** royal or national treasury.

excise[1] /'eksaɪz/ *noun* **1** tax levied on goods produced or sold within the country. **2** tax on certain licences.

excise[2] /ɪk'saɪz/ *verb* (**-sing**) cut out or away. □ **excision** /-'sɪʒ-/ *noun*.

excitable *adjective* easily excited. □ **excitability** *noun*.

■ bubbly, chattery, edgy, emotional, explosive, fidgety, fiery, highly-strung, hot-tempered, irrepressible, jumpy, lively, mercurial, nervous, passionate, quick-tempered, restive, temperamental, unstable, volatile.

excite /ɪk'saɪt/ *verb* (**-ting**) **1** move to strong emotion. **2** arouse (feelings etc.). **3** provoke (action etc.). **4** stimulate to activity. □ **excited** *adjective*. **excitement** *noun*. **exciting** *adjective*.

■ **1** agitate, animate, arouse, awaken, discompose, disturb, elate, electrify, enthral, exhilarate, fluster, get going, incite, inflame, interest, intoxicate, move, perturb, provoke, rouse, stimulate, stir up, thrill, titillate, *colloquial* turn on, upset, urge, *colloquial* wind up, work up. **2** arouse, awaken, cause, elicit, encourage, engender, evoke, fire, generate, kindle, motivate, produce, whet. **3** call forth, cause, elicit, generate, incite, provoke, set off, stimulate. **4** see ACTIVATE 1.
□ **excited** agitated, boisterous, delirious, eager, enthusiastic, excitable, exuberant, feverish, frantic, frenzied, heated, *colloquial* het up, hysterical, impassioned, intoxicated, lively, moved, nervous, overwrought, restless, spirited, vivacious, wild. **excitement** *slang* action, activity, adventure, agitation, animation, commotion, delirium, drama, eagerness, enthusiasm, furore, fuss, heat, intensity, *colloquial* kicks, passion, stimulation, suspense, tension, thrill, unrest. **exciting** dramatic, electric, electrifying, eventful, fast-moving, galvanizing, gripping, hair-raising, heady, inspiring, intoxicating, provocative, riveting, rousing, sensational, spectacular, spine-tingling, stimulating, stirring, suspenseful, tense, thrilling.

exclaim /ɪk'skleɪm/ *verb* **1** cry out suddenly. **2** utter or say thus.

■ bawl, bellow, blurt out, call, cry out, ejaculate, shout, vociferate, yell.

exclamation /eksklə'meɪʃ(ə)n/ *noun* **1** exclaiming. **2** word(s) etc. exclaimed. **3** expletive. □ **exclamation mark** punctuation mark (!) indicating exclamation (see panel). □ **exclamatory** /ɪk'sklæmətərɪ/ *adjective*.

■ **1, 2** bellow, call, cry, ejaculation, interjection, shout, vociferation, yell. **3** expletive, oath, swear word.

exclude /ɪk'sklu:d/ *verb* (**-ding**) **1** shut out, leave out. **2** make impossible, preclude. □ **exclusion** *noun*.

■ **1** ban, banish, bar, blacklist, debar, disown, eject, excommunicate, expel, keep out, leave out, lock out, omit, ostracize, oust, outlaw, proscribe, put an embargo on, refuse, reject, remove, repudiate, shut out. **2** bar, disallow, except, forbid, interdict, outlaw, preclude, prevent, prohibit, proscribe, rule out, stop, veto.

exclusive /ɪk'sklu:sɪv/ *adjective* **1** excluding other things. **2** (+ *of*) not including. **3** (of society etc.) tending to exclude outsiders. **4** high-class. **5** not obtainable or published elsewhere. ● *noun* exclusive item of news, film, etc. □ **exclusively**

Exclamation mark !

This is used instead of a full stop at the end of a sentence to show that the speaker or writer is very angry, enthusiastic, insistent, disappointed, hurt, surprised, etc., e.g.

I am not pleased at all!	*I wish I could have gone!*
I just love sweets!	*Ow!*
Go away!	*He didn't even say goodbye!*

adverb. **exclusiveness** *noun.* **exclusivity**
/eksklu:'sɪvɪtɪ/ *noun.*

■ *adjective* 3 clannish, closed, private, restrictive,
select, selective, snobbish. 4 *colloquial* classy,
fashionable, high-class, *colloquial* posh,
upmarket. 5 limited, restricted, sole, unique,
unshared.

excommunicate /ekskə'mju:nɪkeɪt/ *verb*
(-ting) deprive (person) of membership and sacraments of Church. □ **excommunication** *noun.*

excoriate /eks'kɔːrɪeɪt/ *verb* (-ting) 1 remove
part of skin of by abrasion. 2 remove (skin). 3
censure severely. □ **excoriation** *noun.*

excrement /'ekskrɪmənt/ *noun* faeces.

excrescence /ɪk'skres(ə)ns/ *noun* abnormal
or morbid outgrowth. □ **excrescent** *adjective.*

excreta /ɪk'skri:tə/ *plural noun* faeces and
urine.

■ droppings, dung, excrement, faeces, filth,
manure, sewage, urine, waste matter.

excrete /ɪk'skri:t/ *verb* (-ting) (of animal or
plant) expel (waste). □ **excretion** *noun.* **excretory** *adjective.*

■ defecate, evacuate the bowels, go to the
lavatory, relieve oneself.

excruciating /ɪk'skru:ʃɪeɪtɪŋ/ *adjective*
acutely painful. □ **excruciatingly** *adverb.*

exculpate /'ekskʌlpeɪt/ *verb* (-ting) *formal* free
from blame. □ **exculpation** *noun.*

excursion /ɪk'skɜ:ʃ(ə)n/ *noun* journey to place
and back, made for pleasure.

■ cruise, expedition, jaunt, journey, outing,
ramble, tour, trek, trip, voyage.

excursive /ɪk'skɜ:sɪv/ *adjective literary* digressive.

excuse *verb* /ɪk'skju:z/ (-sing) 1 try to lessen
blame attaching to (person, act); forgive. 2 serve
as reason to judge (person, act) less severely. 3
(often + *from*) grant exemption to. ● *noun*
/ɪk'skju:s/ 1 reason put forward to mitigate or
justify offence. 2 apology. □ **be excused** be
allowed to leave or be absent. **excuse me** *polite
request to be allowed to pass; polite apology for
interrupting or disagreeing.* □ **excusable**
/-'skju:z-/ *adjective.*

■ *verb* 1 absolve, acquit, apologize for, clear,
condone, defend, disregard, *formal* exculpate,
exonerate, forgive, ignore, overlook, pardon, pass
over, sanction, tolerate. 2 explain away, justify,
mitigate, vindicate, warrant. 3 absolve, discharge,
exempt, free, let off, *colloquial* let off the hook,
liberate, release. ● *noun disputed* alibi, apology,
defence, explanation, extenuation, justification,
mitigation, palliation, plea, pretext, rationalization,
reason, vindication.

ex-directory *adjective* not listed in telephone
directory at subscriber's wish.

execrable /'eksɪkrəb(ə)l/ *adjective* abominable.

execrate /'eksɪkreɪt/ *verb* (-ting) 1 express or
feel abhorrence for. 2 curse. □ **execration** *noun.*

execute /'eksɪkju:t/ *verb* (-ting) 1 carry out,
perform. 2 put to death.

■ 1 accomplish, achieve, bring off, carry out,
complete, discharge, do, effect, enact, finish,
implement, perform, pull off. 2 see KILL *verb* 1.

execution /eksɪ'kju:ʃ(ə)n/ *noun* 1 carrying out.
2 performance. 3 capital punishment.

executioner *noun* person carrying out death
sentence.

executive /ɪg'zekjʊtɪv/ *noun* 1 person or body
with managerial or administrative responsibility. 2 branch of government etc. concerned with
executing laws, agreements, etc. ● *adjective* concerned with executing laws, agreements, etc. or
with administration etc.

■ *noun* 1 administrator, *colloquial* boss, chief,
director, manager.

executor /ɪg'zekjʊtə/ *noun* (*feminine* **executrix**
/-trɪks/) person appointed by testator to carry out
terms of will. □ **executorial** /-'tɔːrɪəl/ *adjective.*

exegesis /eksɪ'dʒi:sɪs/ *noun* explanation, esp.
of Scripture. □ **exegetic** /-'dʒetɪk/ *adjective.*

exemplar /ɪg'zemplə/ *noun* 1 model. 2 typical
instance.

exemplary *adjective* 1 outstandingly good. 2
serving as example or warning.

■ 1 admirable, commendable, faultless, flawless,
ideal, model, perfect, praiseworthy,
unexceptionable.

exemplify /ɪg'zemplɪfaɪ/ *verb* (-ies, -ied) give or
be example of. □ **exemplification** *noun.*

■ demonstrate, depict, embody, illustrate,
personify, represent, show, symbolize, typify.

exempt /ɪg'zempt/ *adjective* (often + *from*) free
from obligation or liability imposed on others.
● *verb* (usually + *from*) make exempt. □ **exemption** *noun.*

■ *verb* except, exclude, excuse, free, let off,
colloquial let off the hook, liberate, release, spare.

exercise /'eksəsaɪz/ *noun* 1 use of muscles etc.,
esp. for health. 2 task set for physical or other
training. 3 use or application of faculties etc.;
practice. 4 (often in *plural*) military drill or manoeuvres. ● *verb* (-sing) 1 use. 2 perform
(function). 3 take exercise. 4 give exercise to. 5
tax powers of. 6 perplex, worry.

■ *noun* 1 action, activity, effort, exertion. 2
(*exercises*) aerobics, callisthenics, games,
gymnastics, PE, sport, warm-up, workout. 3
application, discipline, drill, operation, practice,
training, use. 4 (*exercises*) drill, manoeuvres,
training. ● *verb* 1 apply, bring to bear, display,
effect, employ, execute, exert, expend, implement,
put to use, show, use, utilize, wield. 3 drill, exert
oneself, jog, keep fit, practise, train, work out. 6 see
WORRY *verb* 2.

exert /ɪg'zɜ:t/ *verb* 1 use; bring to bear. 2 (**exert
oneself**) make effort. □ **exertion** *noun.*

■ □ **exertion** action, effort, endeavour, strain,
striving, struggle, work.

exfoliate /eks'fəʊlɪeɪt/ *verb* (**-ting**) come off in scales or layers. □ **exfoliation** *noun*.

ex gratia /eks 'greɪʃə/ *adverb* as favour and not under (esp. legal) compulsion. ● *adjective* granted on this basis. [Latin]

exhale /eks'heɪl/ *verb* (**-ling**) **1** breathe out. **2** give off or be given off in vapour. □ **exhalation** /-hə-/ *noun*.

exhaust /ɪg'zɔːst/ *verb* **1** consume, use up. **2** (often as **exhausted** *adjective* or **exhausting** *adjective*) tire out. **3** study or expound completely. **4** empty of contents. ● *noun* **1** waste gases etc. expelled from engine after combustion. **2** pipe or system through which they are expelled. □ **exhaustible** *adjective*. **exhaustion** *noun*.

■ *verb* **1** consume, deplete, dissipate, expend, finish off, run through, sap, spend, use up. **2** debilitate, enervate, *colloquial* fag, fatigue, prostrate, tax, tire, wear out, weary; (**exhausted**) see BREATHLESS 1, WEARY *adjective* 1; (**exhausting**) arduous, back-breaking, crippling, debilitating, demanding, difficult, enervating, fatiguing, gruelling, hard, laborious, punishing, severe, strenuous, taxing, tiring, wearying. **4** drain, empty, void. ● *noun* **1** discharge, emission, fumes, gases, smoke. □ **exhaustion** debility, fatigue, lassitude, tiredness, weakness, weariness.

exhaustive *adjective* complete, comprehensive. □ **exhaustively** *adverb*.

■ all out, complete, comprehensive, extensive, full-scale, intensive, meticulous, thorough.

exhibit /ɪg'zɪbɪt/ *verb* (**-t-**) **1** show, esp. publicly. **2** display. ● *noun* thing exhibited. □ **exhibitor** *noun*.

■ *verb* **1** arrange, display, offer, present, put up, set up, show. **2** air, betray, brandish, demonstrate, disclose, display, evidence, express, flaunt, indicate, manifest, parade, reveal, show off.

exhibition /eksɪ'bɪʃ(ə)n/ *noun* **1** display, public show. **2** exhibiting, being exhibited. **3** scholarship, esp. from funds of college etc.

■ **1** demonstration, display, exposition, presentation, show.

exhibitioner *noun* student receiving exhibition.

exhibitionism *noun* **1** tendency towards attention-seeking behaviour. **2** compulsion to expose genitals in public. □ **exhibitionist** *noun*.

exhilarate /ɪg'zɪləreɪt/ *verb* (**-ting**) (often as **exhilarating** *adjective* or **exhilarated** *adjective*) enliven, gladden. □ **exhilaration** *noun*.

■ (**exhilarating**) bracing, cheering, enlivening, exciting, invigorating, refreshing, rejuvenating, stimulating, tonic, uplifting; (**exhilarated**) see HAPPY 1.

exhort /ɪg'zɔːt/ *verb* (often + *to do*) urge strongly or earnestly. □ **exhortation** /eg-/ *noun*. **exhortative** *adjective*. **exhortatory** *adjective*.

■ advise, encourage, give a pep talk to, harangue, lecture, sermonize, urge.

exhume /eks'hjuːm/ *verb* (**-ming**) dig up. □ **exhumation** *noun*.

exigency /'eksɪdʒənsɪ/ *noun* (*plural* **-ies**) (also **exigence**) **1** urgent need. **2** emergency. □ **exigent** *adjective*.

exiguous /eg'zɪgjʊəs/ *adjective* scanty, small. □ **exiguity** /-'gjuːɪtɪ/ *noun*.

exile /'eksaɪl/ *noun* **1** expulsion or long absence from one's country etc. **2** person in exile. ● *verb* (**-ling**) send into or condemn to exile.

■ *noun* **1** banishment, deportation, expatriation, expulsion, *historical* transportation. **2** deportee, displaced person, émigré, expatriate, outcast, refugee. ● *verb* ban, banish, bar, deport, drive out, eject, evict, expatriate, expel, oust, send away, *historical* transport.

exist /ɪg'zɪst/ *verb* **1** be, have being. **2** occur, be found. **3** live with no pleasure. **4** live. □ **existing** *adjective*.

■ **1** be, be in existence, be real. **2** be found, happen, occur. **4** *archaic* abide, continue, endure, hold out, keep going, last, live, remain alive, subsist, survive. □ **existing** see ACTUAL 1–2, CURRENT *adjective* 1, LIVING *adjective* 1.

existence *noun* **1** fact or manner of existing. **2** all that exists. □ **existent** *adjective*.

■ **1** actuality, being, continuance, life, living, persistence, reality, survival. **2** creation, life, universe.

existential /egzɪ'stenʃ(ə)l/ *adjective* of or relating to existence.

existentialism *noun* philosophical theory emphasizing existence of individual as free and self-determining agent. □ **existentialist** *adjective* & *noun*.

exit /'eksɪt/ *noun* **1** way out. **2** going out, departure. **3** place where vehicles leave motorway etc. ● *verb* (**-t-**) make one's exit.

■ *noun* **1** barrier, door, doorway, egress, gate, gateway, opening, portal, way out. **2** departure, escape, evacuation, exodus, flight, leave-taking, retreat, withdrawal. ● *verb* see DEPART 1,2.

exodus /'eksədəs/ *noun* **1** mass departure. **2** (**Exodus**) that of Israelites from Egypt.

ex officio /eks ə'fɪʃɪəʊ/ *adverb* & *adjective* by virtue of one's office.

exonerate /ɪg'zɒnəreɪt/ *verb* (**-ting**) free or declare free from blame. □ **exoneration** *noun*.

exorbitant /ɪg'zɔːbɪt(ə)nt/ *adjective* grossly excessive.

■ disproportionate, excessive, expensive, extortionate, extravagant, high, inordinate, outrageous, prohibitive, *colloquial* steep, unjustifiable, unrealistic, unreasonable, unwarranted.

exorcize /'eksɔːsaɪz/ *verb* (also **-ise**) (**-zing** or **-sing**) **1** drive out (evil spirit) by prayers etc. **2** free (person, place) thus. □ **exorcism** *noun*. **exorcist** *noun*.

exoskeleton /'eksəʊskelɪtən/ *noun* external skeleton.

exotic /ɪɡ'zɒtɪk/ *adjective* **1** introduced from abroad. **2** strange, unusual. ● *noun* exotic plant etc. □ **exotically** *adverb*.

■ *adjective* **1** alien, far-away, foreign, remote. **2** bizarre, different, extraordinary, foreign-looking, novel, odd, outlandish, peculiar, rare, singular, strange, striking, unfamiliar, unusual, *colloquial* weird.

expand /ɪk'spænd/ *verb* **1** increase in size or importance. **2** (often + *on*) give fuller account. **3** become more genial. **4** write out in full. **5** spread out flat. □ **expandable** *adjective*. **expansion** *noun*.

■ **1** amplify, augment, broaden, build up, develop, dilate, distend, diversify, elaborate, enlarge, extend, fill out, grow, heighten, increase, lengthen, prolong, stretch, swell, thicken, widen. **2** see ELABORATE *verb*. **5** open out, spread out, unfold.

expanse /ɪk'spæns/ *noun* wide area or extent of land, space, etc.

■ area, breadth, extent, range, sheet, space, spread, stretch, surface, sweep, tract.

expansionism *noun* advocacy of expansion, esp. of state's territory. □ **expansionist** *noun & adjective*.

expansive *adjective* **1** able or tending to expand. **2** extensive. **3** genial.

■ **2** see BROAD *adjective* 1. **3** affable, amiable, communicative, effusive, extrovert, friendly, genial, open, outgoing, sociable, talkative, well disposed.

expatiate /ɪk'speɪʃɪeɪt/ *verb* (**-ting**) (usually + *on*, *upon*) speak or write at length. □ **expatiation** *noun*.

expatriate *adjective* /eks'pætrɪət/ **1** living abroad. **2** exiled. ● *noun* /eks'pætrɪət/ expatriate person. ● *verb* /eks'pætrɪeɪt/ (**-ting**) expel from native country. □ **expatriation** /-'eɪʃ(ə)n/ *noun*.

expect /ɪk'spekt/ *verb* **1** regard as likely. **2** look for as one's due. **3** *colloquial* suppose. □ **be expecting** *colloquial* be pregnant.

■ **1** *disputed* anticipate, await, *colloquial* bank on, bargain for, be prepared for, contemplate, count on, envisage, forecast, foresee, have faith in, hope for, imagine, look forward to, plan for, predict, prophesy, reckon on, wait for; (*expected*) see PREDICTABLE (PREDICT). **2** demand, insist on, look for, rely on, require, want. **3** assume, believe, conjecture, guess, imagine, judge, presume, presuppose, suppose, surmise, think.

expectant *adjective* **1** expecting. **2** expecting to become. **3** pregnant. □ **expectancy** *noun*. **expectantly** *adverb*.

■ **1** eager, hopeful, keyed up, on tenterhooks, optimistic, ready. **2** hopeful, optimistic. **3** *colloquial* expecting, pregnant.

expectation /ekspek'teɪʃ(ə)n/ *noun* **1** expecting, anticipation. **2** what one expects. **3** probability. **4** (in *plural*) prospects of inheritance.

expectorant /ek'spektərənt/ *adjective* causing

expectoration. ● *noun* expectorant medicine.

expectorate /ek'spektəreɪt/ *verb* (**-ting**) cough or spit out from chest or lungs; spit. □ **expectoration** *noun*.

expedient /ɪk'spiːdɪənt/ *adjective* advantageous; advisable on practical rather than moral grounds. ● *noun* means of achieving an end; resource. □ **expediency** *noun*.

■ *adjective* advantageous, advisable, appropriate, apropos, beneficial, convenient, desirable, helpful, judicious, opportune, politic, practical, pragmatic, profitable, propitious, prudent, right, sensible, suitable, to one's advantage, useful, worthwhile. ● *noun* contrivance, device, dodge, manoeuvre, means, measure, method, ploy, recourse, resort, ruse, scheme, stratagem, tactic.

expedite /'ekspɪdaɪt/ *verb* (**-ting**) **1** assist progress of. **2** accomplish quickly.

expedition /ekspɪ'dɪʃ(ə)n/ *noun* **1** journey or voyage for particular purpose. **2** people etc. undertaking this. **3** speed.

■ **1** *historical* crusade, excursion, exploration, journey, mission, pilgrimage, quest, raid, safari, tour, trek, trip, undertaking, voyage.

expeditionary *adjective* of or used on expedition.

expeditious /ekspɪ'dɪʃəs/ *adjective* acting or done with speed and efficiency. □ **expeditiously** *adverb*. **expeditiousness** *noun*.

expel /ɪk'spel/ *verb* (**-ll-**) **1** deprive of membership. **2** force out; eject.

■ **1** ban, banish, cast out, *colloquial* chuck out, dismiss, drive out, eject, evict, exile, exorcize, fire, kick out, oust, remove, *colloquial* sack, send away, throw out, *colloquial* turf out, turn out. **2** belch, discharge, emit, exhale, give out, push out, send out, spew out.

expend /ɪk'spend/ *verb* spend (money, time, etc.); use up.

■ consume, disburse, *colloquial* dish out, employ, pay out, spend, use, use up.

expendable *adjective* that may be sacrificed or dispensed with.

■ disposable, inessential, insignificant, replaceable, throw-away, unimportant.

expenditure /ɪk'spendɪtʃə/ *noun* **1** expending. **2** amount expended.

expense /ɪk'spens/ *noun* **1** cost, charge. **2** (in *plural*) costs incurred in doing job etc. **3** reimbursement of this.

■ **1** charge, cost, disbursement, fee, outlay, payment, price, rate. **2** (*expenses*) expenditure, outgoings, overheads, spending.

expensive *adjective* costing or charging much. □ **expensively** *adverb*.

■ costly, dear, exorbitant, extravagant, high-priced, overpriced, precious, *colloquial* pricey, *colloquial* steep, upmarket, valuable.

experience /ɪk'spɪərɪəns/ *noun* **1** personal observation or contact. **2** knowledge or skill based on this. **3** event that affects one. ● *verb* (**-cing**) **1** have experience of; undergo. **2** feel. □ **experiential** /-'en-/ *adjective*.

■ *noun* **1** background, familiarity, involvement, observation, participation, practice, taking part. **2** expertise, know-how, knowledge, *savoir faire*, skill, understanding, wisdom. **3** adventure, circumstance, episode, event, happening, incident, occurrence, ordeal, trial. ● *verb* **1** encounter, endure, face, go through, have a taste of, meet, practise, suffer, test out, try, undergo. **2** feel, know, sample, suffer, taste.

experienced *adjective* **1** having had much experience. **2** skilful through experience.
■ **2** see EXPERT *adjective*.

experiment /ɪk'sperɪmənt/ *noun* procedure adopted to test hypothesis or demonstrate known fact. ● *verb* (also /-ment/) make experiment(s). □ **experimentation** /-men-/ *noun.* **experimenter** *noun.*

■ *noun* demonstration, investigation, practical, research, test, trial, try-out. ● *verb* examine, investigate, make tests, probe, research, test, try out.

experimental /ɪksperɪ'ment(ə)l/ *adjective* **1** based on experiment. **2** done by way of experiment. □ **experimentally** *adverb*.

■ **1** empirical, experiential. **2** exploratory, on trial, pilot, provisional, tentative, trial.

expert /'eksp3:t/ (often + *at, in*) *adjective* well informed or skilful in a subject. ● *noun* expert person. □ **expertly** *adverb*. **expertness** *noun.*

■ *adjective* able, *slang* ace, brilliant, capable, clever, competent, experienced, knowing, knowledgeable, masterful, masterly, practised, professional, proficient, qualified, skilful, skilled, sophisticated, specialized, trained, well versed, worldly-wise. ● *noun* ace, authority, connoisseur, dab hand, genius, *colloquial* know-all, master, old hand, professional, pundit, specialist, veteran, virtuoso, wiseacre, wizard.

expertise /eksp3:'ti:z/ *noun* special skill or knowledge.
■ adroitness, dexterity, expertness, judgement, know-how, knowledge, *savoir faire*, skill.

expiate /'ekspɪeɪt/ *verb* (**-ting**) pay penalty or make amends for (wrong). □ **expiation** *noun*.

expire /ɪk'spaɪə/ *verb* (**-ring**) **1** come to an end. **2** cease to be valid. **3** die. **4** breathe out. □ **expiration** /ekspɪ-/ *noun.*

■ **1** *formal* cease, come to an end, discontinue, end, finish, stop, terminate. **2** become invalid, lapse, run out. **3** see DIE¹ 1.

expiry *noun* end of validity or duration.

explain /ɪks'pleɪn/ *verb* **1** make intelligible. **2** make known. **3** say by way of explanation. **4** account for. □ **explainable** *adjective*.

■ **1, 2** clarify, clear up, decipher, decode, define, demonstrate, describe, disentangle, elucidate, expound, get across, gloss, illustrate, interpret, make clear, make plain, shed light on, simplify, sort out, spell out, teach, translate, unravel. **4** account for, excuse, give reasons for, justify, legitimize, make excuses for, rationalize, vindicate.

explanation /eksplə-/ *noun* **1** explaining; statement or fact which clarifies. **2** excuse or reason.

■ **1** account, analysis, clarification, definition, demonstration, description, elucidation, exegesis, explication, exposition, gloss, illustration, interpretation, key, meaning, rubric, significance, solution, translation. **2** cause, excuse, justification, motivation, motive, rationalization, reason, vindication.

explanatory /ɪk'splænətərɪ/ *adjective* serving to explain.

■ descriptive, helpful, illuminating, illustrative, interpretive, revelatory.

expletive /ɪk'spli:tɪv/ *noun* swear-word or exclamation.

explicable /ɪk'splɪkəb(ə)l/ *adjective* explainable.

explicate /'eksplɪkaɪt/ *verb* develop meaning of; explain. □ **explication** /-'keɪʃ(ə)n/ *noun*.

explicit /ɪk'splɪsɪt/ *adjective* **1** expressly stated; stated in detail. **2** definite. **3** outspoken. □ **explicitly** *adverb*. **explicitness** *noun.*

■ **1, 2** categorical, clear, definite, detailed, exact, express, graphic, manifest, patent, plain, positive, precise, put into words, specific, spelt out, spoken, stated, unconcealed, unhidden, well defined. **3** direct, forthright, frank, open, outspoken, plain-spoken, straightforward, unambiguous, unequivocal, unreserved.

explode /ɪk'spləʊd/ *verb* (**-ding**) **1** expand violently with loud noise. **2** cause (bomb etc.) to do this. **3** give vent suddenly to emotion, esp. anger. **4** (of population etc.) increase suddenly. **5** discredit.

■ **1, 2** backfire, blast, blow up, burst, detonate, erupt, go off, set off, shatter. **3** *colloquial* blow one's top, *colloquial* blow up, *slang* flip one's lid, *colloquial* fly off the handle, *colloquial* lose one's cool, lose one's temper, snap. **5** *colloquial* debunk, destroy, discredit, disprove, put an end to, rebut, refute, reject.

exploit *noun* /'eksplɔɪt/ daring feat. ● *verb* /ɪk'splɔɪt/ **1** use or develop. **2** use for one's own ends; take advantage of (esp. person). □ **exploitation** /-'teɪʃ(ə)n/ *noun.* **exploitative** /ɪk'splɔɪt-/ *adjective*. **exploiter** *noun.*

■ *noun* achievement, adventure, attainment, deed, enterprise, feat. ● *verb* **1** capitalize on, *colloquial* cash in on, develop, make capital out of, make use of, profit by, profit from, trade on, use, utilize, work on. **2** enslave, ill-treat, impose on, keep down, manipulate, milk, misuse, oppress, prey on, *colloquial* rip off, take advantage of, treat unfairly, use.

explore /ɪk'splɔ:/ *verb* (**-ring**) **1** travel through (country etc.) to learn about it. **2** inquire into. **3** examine (part of body); probe (wound). □ **exploration** /eksplə-/ *noun.* **exploratory** /-'splɒr-/ *adjective.* **explorer** *noun.*

■ **1** prospect, reconnoitre, scout, search, survey, tour, travel through. **2** analyse, examine, inquire into, inspect, investigate, look into, probe, research, scrutinize, study.

explosion /ɪk'spləʊʒ(ə)n/ *noun* **1** exploding. **2** loud noise caused by this. **3** outbreak. **4** sudden increase.

■ **1** blast, burst, detonation, discharge, eruption, firing. **2** bang, blast, boom, clap, crack, detonation, report. **3** fit, outbreak, outburst, paroxysm, spasm.

explosive /ɪk'spləʊsɪv/ *adjective* **1** tending to explode. **2** likely to cause violent outburst etc. ● *noun* explosive substance.

■ *adjective* dangerous, highly charged, sensitive, unstable, volatile.

exponent /ɪk'spəʊnənt/ *noun* **1** person promoting idea etc. **2** practitioner of activity, profession, etc. **3** person who explains or interprets. **4** type, representative. **5** *Mathematics* raised number or symbol showing how many of a number are to be multiplied together, e.g. ^{3} in $2^3 = 2 \times 2 \times 2$.

■ **1** advocate, champion, defender, exponder, presenter, propagandist, proponent, supporter, upholder. **2** interpreter, performer, player.

exponential /ekspə'nenʃ(ə)l/ *adjective* (of increase) more and more rapid. □ **exponentially** *adverb.*

export *verb* /ɪk'spɔ:t/ sell or send (goods or services) to another country. ● *noun* /'ekspɔ:t/ **1** exporting. **2** exported article or service. **3** (in *plural*) amount exported. □ **exportation** *noun.* **exporter** /ɪk'spɔ:tə/ *noun.*

expose /ɪk'spəʊz/ *verb* (**-sing**) **1** leave unprotected, esp. from weather. **2** (+ *to*) put at risk of. **3** (+ *to*) subject to (influence etc.). **4** *Photography* subject (film etc.) to light. **5** reveal, disclose. **6** exhibit, display. **7** (**expose oneself**) display one's genitals indecently in public.

■ **5** bare, betray, bring to light, dig up, disclose, lay bare, leak, make known, reveal, show, show up, uncover, unearth, unmask. **6** display, exhibit, show.

exposé /ek'spəʊzeɪ/ *noun* **1** orderly statement of facts. **2** disclosure of discreditable thing.

exposition /ekspə'zɪʃ(ə)n/ *noun* **1** expounding, explanation. **2** *Music* part of movement in which principal themes are presented. **3** exhibition.

ex post facto /eks pəʊst 'fæktəʊ/ *adjective* & *adverb* retrospective(ly). [Latin]

expostulate /ɪk'spɒstjʊleɪt/ *verb* (**-ting**) make protest, remonstrate. □ **expostulation** *noun.*

exposure /ɪk'spəʊʒə/ *noun* **1** exposing, being exposed. **2** physical condition resulting from being exposed to elements. **3** *Photography* length of time film etc. is exposed. **4** *Photography* section of film etc. exposed at one time.

expound /ɪk'spaʊnd/ *verb* **1** set out in detail. **2** explain, interpret. □ **expounder** *noun.*

express /ɪk'spres/ *verb* **1** represent in language, conduct, etc.; put into words. **2** squeeze out (juice, milk, etc.). **3** (**express oneself**) communicate what one thinks, feels, or means. **4** represent by symbols etc. ● *adjective* **1** operating at high speed. **2** definitely stated. **3** delivered by specially fast service. ● *adverb* **1** with speed. **2** by express messenger or train. ● *noun* express train etc. □ **expressible** *adjective.*

■ *verb* **1** air, articulate, communicate, convey, disclose, give vent to, make known, phrase, put into words, vent, ventilate, voice, word. **3** see COMMUNICATE 1. **4** denote, represent, signify, symbolize.

expression /ɪk'spreʃ(ə)n/ *noun* **1** expressing, being expressed. **2** wording, word, phrase. **3** conveying or depiction of feeling. **4** appearance (of face); intonation (of voice). **5** *Mathematics* collection of symbols expressing quantity. □ **expressionless** *adjective.*

■ **1** articulation, confession, declaration, disclosure, revelation, statement. **2** cliché, formula, phrase, phraseology, remark, saying, statement, term, turn of phrase, usage, utterance, wording. **3** depth, emotion, expressiveness, feeling, intensity, nuance, pathos, sensibility, sensitivity, sympathy, tone, understanding. **4** (*expression on one's face*) air, appearance, aspect, countenance, face, look, *literary* mien; (*expression in one's voice*) accent, intonation, note, tone. □ **expressionless** (*expressionless face*) blank, deadpan, emotionless, empty, glassy, impassive, inscrutable, poker-faced, straight-faced, uncommunicative, wooden; (*expressionless voice*) boring, dull, flat, monotonous, uninspiring, unmodulated, unvarying.

expressionism *noun* style of painting etc. seeking to express emotion rather than depict external world. □ **expressionist** *noun & adjective.*

expressive *adjective* **1** full of expression. **2** (+ *of*) serving to express. □ **expressiveness** *noun.*

■ **1** articulate, eloquent, lively, meaningful, mobile, modulated, revealing, sensitive, significant, striking, telling, varied. **2** (*expressive of*) indicative of, revealing of, suggestive of.

expressly *adverb* explicitly.

expropriate /ɪks'prəʊprieɪt/ *verb* (**-ting**) **1** take away (property). **2** dispossess. □ **expropriation** *noun.* **expropriator** *noun.*

expulsion /ɪk'spʌlʃ(ə)n/ *noun* expelling, being expelled.

expunge /ɪk'spʌndʒ/ *verb* (**-ging**) erase, remove.

expurgate /'ekspəgeɪt/ *verb* (**-ting**) **1** remove matter considered objectionable from (book etc.). **2** clear away (such matter). □ **expurgation** *noun.* **expurgator** *noun.*

exquisite /'ekskwɪzɪt, ek'skwɪzɪt/ *adjective* **1** extremely beautiful or delicate. **2** acute, keen. □ **exquisitely** *adverb.* **exquisiteness** *noun.*

■ **1** beautiful, delicate, elegant, fine, intricate, refined, skilful, well crafted.

ex-serviceman /eks'sɜ:vɪsmən/ *noun* (*feminine* **ex-servicewoman**) person formerly member of armed forces.

extant /ek'stænt/ *adjective* still existing.

extempore /ɪk'stempəri/ *adverb & adjective* without preparation.

extemporize /ɪk'stempəraɪz/ *verb* (also **-ise**) (**-zing** or **-sing**) improvise. □ **extemporization** *noun.*

extend /ɪk'stend/ *verb* **1** lengthen in space or time. **2** lay out at full length. **3** reach or be or make continuous over certain area. **4** (+ *to*) have certain scope. **5** offer or accord (feeling, invitation, etc.). **6** tax powers of. □ **extendible** *adjective.* **extensible** *adjective.*

■ **1** add to, broaden, build up, develop, draw out, enlarge, expand, increase, keep going, lengthen, open up, pad out, perpetuate, prolong, protract, spin out, spread, stretch, widen. **2** hold out, lay out, put out, reach out, stick out, stretch out. **3** continue, range, reach. **5** accord, give, offer, present, proffer.

extension /ɪk'stenʃ(ə)n/ *noun* **1** extending. **2** enlargement; additional part. **3** subsidiary telephone on same line as main one. **4** additional period of time.

extensive /ɪk'stensɪv/ *adjective* large, far-reaching. □ **extensively** *adverb.*

■ broad, comprehensive, expansive, far-ranging, far-reaching, large, sweeping, vast, wide, widespread.

extent /ɪk'stent/ *noun* **1** space covered; size, amount. **2** width of application; scope.

■ **1** amount, area, breadth, compass, dimensions, distance, expanse, length, magnitude, measure, measurement, proportions, range, reach, size, space, spread, sweep, width. **2** bounds, compass, degree, limit, range, scale, scope.

extenuate /ɪk'stenjʊeɪt/ *verb* (**-ting**) (often as **extenuating** *adjective*) make (guilt etc.) seem less serious by partial excuse. □ **extenuation** *noun.*

exterior /ɪk'stɪərɪə/ *adjective* **1** outer. **2** coming from outside. ● *noun* **1** exterior aspect or surface. **2** outward demeanour.

■ *adjective* **1** external, outer, outside, outward, superficial. ● *noun* **1** coating, covering, façade, front, outside, shell, skin, surface.

exterminate /ɪk'stɜ:mmeɪt/ *verb* (**-ting**) destroy utterly. □ **extermination** *noun.* **exterminator** *noun.*

■ annihilate, destroy, eliminate, eradicate, extirpate, get rid of, kill, obliterate, put an end to, root out, terminate.

external /ɪk'stɜ:n(ə)l/ *adjective* **1** of or on the outside. **2** coming from outside. **3** relating to a country's foreign affairs. **4** (of medicine) for use on outside of body. ● *noun* (in *plural*) external features or circumstances. □ **externality** /ekstɜ:'nælɪti/ *noun.* **externally** *adverb.*

■ *adjective* **1** exterior, outer, outside, outward, superficial.

externalize *verb* (also **-ise**) (**-zing** or **-sing**) give or attribute external existence to.

extinct /ɪk'stɪŋkt/ *adjective* **1** no longer existing. **2** no longer burning. **3** (of volcano) that no longer erupts. **4** obsolete.

■ **1** dead, defunct, died out, exterminated, gone, vanished. **2** burnt out, extinguished, quenched. **3** dormant, inactive. **4** see OLD 6.

extinction *noun* **1** making or becoming extinct. **2** extinguishing, being extinguished.

extinguish /ɪk'stɪŋgwɪʃ/ *verb* **1** put out (flame, light, etc.). **2** terminate, destroy. **3** wipe out (debt).

■ **1** blow out, damp down, douse, put out, quench, smother, snuff out, switch off. **2** see DESTROY 2.

extinguisher *noun* = FIRE EXTINGUISHER.

extirpate /'ekstəpeɪt/ *verb* (**-ting**) destroy; root out. □ **extirpation** *noun.*

extol /ɪk'stəʊl/ *verb* (**-ll-**) praise enthusiastically.

extort /ɪk'stɔ:t/ *verb* get by coercion.

■ exact, extract, force, obtain by force.

extortion *noun* **1** extorting, esp. of money. **2** illegal exaction. □ **extortioner** *noun.* **extortionist** *noun.*

extortionate /ɪk'stɔ:ʃənət/ *adjective* exorbitant.

extra /'ekstrə/ *adjective* additional; more than usual or necessary. ● *adverb* **1** more than usually. **2** additionally. ● *noun* **1** extra thing. **2** thing for which one is charged extra. **3** person playing one of crowd etc. in film. **4** special edition of newspaper. **5** *Cricket* run not scored from hit with bat.

■ *adjective* accessory, added, additional, ancillary, auxiliary, excess, further, left-over, more, other, reserve, spare, superfluous, supernumerary, supplementary, surplus, temporary, unneeded, unused, unwanted.

extra- *combining form* **1** outside. **2** beyond scope of.

extract *verb* /ɪk'strækt/ **1** take out. **2** obtain (money, confession, etc.) against person's will. **3** obtain from earth. **4** obtain (information from book etc.); copy out, quote. **5** obtain (juice etc.) by pressure, distillation, etc. **6** derive (pleasure etc.). **7** *Mathematics* find (root of number). ● *noun* /'ekstrækt/ **1** passage from book etc. **2** preparation containing concentrated constituent of substance.

■ *verb* **1** draw out, extricate, pull out, remove, take out, withdraw. **2** extort, force out, winkle out, worm out, wrench, wrest, wring. **4** choose, cite, copy out, cull, derive, distil, gather, glean, *colloquial* lift, obtain, quote, select. ● *noun* **1** abstract, citation, clip, clipping, cutting, excerpt, passage, quotation, selection. **2** concentrate, decoction, distillation, essence, quintessence.

extraction /ɪkˈstrækʃ(ə)n/ *noun* **1** extracting. **2** removal of tooth. **3** lineage.

extractor /ɪkˈstræktə/ *noun* machine that extracts. □ **extractor fan** one that extracts bad air etc.

extracurricular /ekstrəkəˈrɪkjʊlə/ *adjective* outside normal curriculum.

extraditable *adjective* **1** liable to extradition. **2** (of crime) warranting extradition.

extradite /ˈekstrədaɪt/ *verb* (**-ting**) hand over (person accused of crime) to state where crime was committed. □ **extradition** /-ˈdɪʃ-/ *noun*.

extramarital /ekstrəˈmærɪt(ə)l/ *adjective* (of sexual relationship) outside marriage.

extramural /ekstrəˈmjʊər(ə)l/ *adjective* additional to ordinary teaching or studies.

extraneous /ɪkˈstreɪnɪəs/ *adjective* **1** of external origin. **2** (often + *to*) separate, irrelevant, unrelated.

extraordinary /ɪkˈstrɔːdɪnərɪ/ *adjective* **1** unusual, remarkable. **2** unusually great. **3** (of meeting etc.) additional. □ **extraordinarily** *adverb*. **extraordinariness** *noun*.

■ **1, 2** abnormal, amazing, astonishing, astounding, awe-inspiring, bizarre, breathtaking, curious, exceptional, extreme, *colloquial* fantastic, funny, *colloquial* incredible, marvellous, miraculous, mysterious, mystical, notable, noteworthy, odd, outstanding, peculiar, phenomenal, prodigious, queer, rare, remarkable, *colloquial* sensational, signal, singular, special, staggering, strange, striking, *colloquial* stunning, stupendous, surprising, unbelievable, uncommon, unheard-of, unimaginable, *disputed* unique, unprecedented, unusual, *colloquial* weird, wonderful. **3** additional, extra, special.

extrapolate /ɪkˈstræpəleɪt/ *verb* (**-ting**) estimate (unknown facts or values) from known data. □ **extrapolation** *noun*.

extrasensory /ekstrəˈsensərɪ/ *adjective* derived by means other than known senses.

extraterrestrial /ekstrətɪˈrestrɪəl/ *adjective* outside the earth or its atmosphere. ● *noun* fictional being from outer space.

extravagant /ɪkˈstrævəgənt/ *adjective* **1** spending (esp. money) excessively. **2** costing much. **3** excessive; absurd. □ **extravagance** *noun*. **extravagantly** *adverb*.

■ **1** immoderate, improvident, lavish, prodigal, profligate, reckless, self-indulgent, spendthrift, uneconomical, unthrifty, wasteful. **2** see EXPENSIVE. **3** exaggerated, excessive, flamboyant, grandiose, immoderate, lavish, outrageous, overblown, overdone, pretentious, profuse, showy, unreasonable. □ **extravagance** excess, immoderation, improvidence, lavishness, over-indulgence, overspending, prodigality, profligacy, self-indulgence, wastefulness.

extravaganza /ɪkstrævəˈgænzə/ *noun* **1** spectacular theatrical or television production. **2** fanciful composition.

extreme /ɪkˈstriːm/ *adjective* **1** reaching high or highest degree. **2** severe, not moderate. **3** outermost. **4** utmost. ● *noun* **1** either of two things as remote or different as possible. **2** thing at either end. **3** highest degree. □ **extreme unction** anointing by priest of dying person. □ **extremely** *adverb*.

■ *adjective* **1** exceptional, extraordinary, greatest, intensest, maximum, outstanding, severest, *colloquial* terrific, utmost. **2** (*extreme pain*) acute, drastic, excessive, intense, severe; (*extreme opinions*) absolute, avant-garde, exaggerated, extravagant, extremist, fanatical, hardline, immoderate, intemperate, intransigent, militant, obsessive, outrageous, radical, uncompromising, *colloquial* way-out, zealous. **3** distant, endmost, farthest, furthermost, furthest, last, outermost, remotest. **4** furthest, greatest, last, maximum, ultimate, utmost, uttermost. ● *noun* **1, 2** bottom, edge, end, extremity, limit, maximum, minimum, pole, top, ultimate. **3** see MAXIMUM *noun*.

extremis see IN EXTREMIS.

extremism *noun* advocacy of extreme measures. □ **extremist** *adjective & noun*.

extremity /ɪkˈstremɪtɪ/ *noun* (*plural* **-ies**) **1** extreme point; end. **2** (in *plural*) hands and feet. **3** condition of extreme adversity.

extricate /ˈekstrɪkeɪt/ *verb* (**-ting**) disentangle, release. □ **extrication** *noun*.

extrinsic /ekˈstrɪnsɪk/ *adjective* **1** not inherent or intrinsic. **2** (often + *to*) extraneous. □ **extrinsically** *adverb*.

extrovert /ˈekstrəvɜːt/ *noun* **1** sociable or unreserved person. **2** person mainly concerned with external things. ● *adjective* typical or having nature of extrovert. □ **extroversion** /-ˈvɜː-/ *noun*. **extroverted** *adjective*.

■ □ **extroverted** gregarious, outgoing, sociable, unreserved.

extrude /ɪkˈstruːd/ *verb* (**-ding**) **1** thrust or squeeze out. **2** shape by forcing through nozzle. □ **extrusion** *noun*.

exuberant /ɪgˈzjuːbərənt/ *adjective* **1** lively, high-spirited. **2** luxuriant, prolific. **3** (of feelings etc.) abounding. **4** ornate. □ **exuberance** *noun*.

■ **1** animated, boisterous, bubbly, buoyant, cheerful, eager, ebullient, effervescent, effusive, energetic, enthusiastic, excited, exhilarated, exultant, high-spirited, irrepressible, lively, spirited, sprightly, vivacious. **2** abundant, copious, lush, luxuriant, profuse, prolific, rank, teeming. **4** baroque, exaggerated, flamboyant, highly decorated, lavish, ornate, overdone, rich.

exude /ɪgˈzjuːd/ *verb* (**-ding**) **1** ooze out. **2** give off. **3** display (emotion) freely. □ **exudation** *noun*.

exult /ɪgˈzʌlt/ *verb* rejoice. □ **exultant** *adjective*. **exultation** /eg-/ *noun*.

■ □ **exultant** delighted, ecstatic, elated, joyful, jubilant, *colloquial* on top of the world, overjoyed, rejoicing.

eye /aɪ/ *noun* **1** organ of sight. **2** iris of eye. **3** region round eye. **4** faculty of sight. **5** gaze. **6** perception. **7** eyelike thing. **8** leaf bud of potato.

9 centre of hurricane. **10** spot, hole, loop. ● *verb*
(**eyes**, **eyed**, **eyeing** or **eying**) (often + *up*)
observe; watch closely or suspiciously. □ **all
eyes** watching intently. **eyeball** ball of eye
within lids and socket. **eyebath** vessel for applying lotion to eye. **eyebrow** hair growing on ridge
over eye. **eye-catching** *colloquial* striking. **eyeglass** lens for defective eye. **eyehole** hole to look
through. **eyelash** any of hairs on edge of eyelid.
eyelid fold of skin that can cover eye. **eyeliner**
cosmetic applied as line round eye. **eye-opener**
colloquial enlightening experience; unexpected
revelation. **eyepiece** lens(es) to which eye is
applied at end of optical instrument. **eye-shade**
device to protect eyes from strong light.
eye-shadow cosmetic for eyelids. **eyesight**
faculty or power of sight. **eyesore** ugly thing.
eye-tooth canine tooth in upper jaw. **eyewash
1** lotion for eyes. **2** *slang* nonsense. **eyewitness**
person who saw thing happen and can tell of it.

have one's eye on wish or plan to obtain. **keep
an eye on 1** watch. **2** look after. **keep an eye open**
(often + *for*) watch out carefully. **see eye to eye**
(often + *with*) agree. **set eyes on** see. □ **eyeless**
adjective.

■ *noun* **4** eyesight, sight, vision. **6** appreciation,
discernment, perception, sensitivity. ● *verb*
contemplate, examine, inspect, look at, observe,
regard, scrutinize, study, watch. □ **eyewitness**
bystander, looker-on, observer, onlooker,
passer-by, spectator, watcher, witness.

eyeful *noun* (*plural* **-s**) *colloquial* **1** good look. **2**
visually striking person or thing.

eyelet /ˈaɪlɪt/ *noun* small hole for passing cord
etc. through.

eyrie /ˈɪərɪ/ *noun* nest of bird of prey, esp. eagle,
built high up.

Ff

F *abbreviation* Fahrenheit.

f *abbreviation* (also **f.**) **1** female. **2** feminine. **3** *Music* forte.

FA *abbreviation* Football Association.

fa = FAH.

fable /'feɪb(ə)l/ *noun* fictional tale, esp. legendary, or moral tale, often with animal characters.

fabled *adjective* celebrated; legendary.

fabric /'fæbrɪk/ *noun* **1** woven material. **2** walls, floor, and roof of building. **3** structure.
  ■ **1** cloth, material, stuff, textile. **2** construction, framework, structure. **3** constitution, construction, framework, make-up, structure, substance.

fabricate /'fæbrɪkeɪt/ *verb* (**-ting**) **1** construct, esp. from components. **2** invent (fact). **3** forge (document). □ **fabrication** *noun*.

fabulous /'fæbjʊləs/ *adjective* **1** *colloquial* marvellous. **2** legendary. □ **fabulously** *adverb*.
  ■ **1** see EXCELLENT. **2** fabled, fairy-tale, fanciful, fictitious, imaginary, legendary, mythical.

façade /fə'sɑːd/ *noun* **1** face or front of building. **2** outward, esp. deceptive, appearance.

face *noun* **1** front of head. **2** facial expression. **3** surface. **4** front or façade of building etc. **5** dial of clock etc. **6** side of mountain. **7** functional side of tool, bat, etc. **8** aspect, feature. ● *verb* (**-cing**) **1** look or be positioned towards. **2** be opposite. **3** meet resolutely, confront. **4** put facing on (garment, wall, etc.). □ **facelift 1** cosmetic surgery to remove wrinkles etc. **2** improvement in appearance. **face up to** accept bravely. **face value 1** nominal value. **2** superficial appearance. **lose face** be humiliated. **loss of face** humiliation. **on the face of it** apparently. **pull a face** distort features. **save face** avoid humiliation.
  ■ *noun* **1** features, lineaments, *slang* mug, physiognomy, *literary* visage. **2** appearance, countenance, expression, look. **3** facet, side, surface. **4** aspect, exterior, façade, front, outside, side. **6** aspect, side. ● *verb* **1** front on to, look towards, overlook. **3** appear before, brave, come to terms with, confront, cope with, defy, encounter, experience, face up to, meet, oppose, stand up to, tackle. **4** clad, coat, cover, dress, finish, overlay, sheathe, veneer.

faceless *adjective* without identity; not identifiable.

facet /'fæsɪt/ *noun* **1** aspect. **2** side of cut gem etc.

facetious /fə'siːʃəs/ *adjective* intended to be amusing, esp. inappropriately. □ **facetiously** *adverb*. **facetiousness** *noun*.
  ■ cheeky, flippant, impudent, irreverent.

facia = FASCIA.

facial /'feɪʃ(ə)l/ *adjective* of or for the face. ● *noun* beauty treatment for the face. □ **facially** *adverb*.

facile /'fæsaɪl/ *adjective* **1** easily achieved but of little value. **2** glib.
  ■ **1** cheap, easy, effortless, hasty, quick, simple, superficial, unconsidered. **2** fluent, glib, insincere, plausible, ready, shallow, slick, smooth.

facilitate /fə'sɪlɪteɪt/ *verb* (**-ting**) ease (process etc.). □ **facilitation** *noun*.

facility /fə'sɪlɪtɪ/ *noun* (*plural* **-ies**) **1** ease; absence of difficulty. **2** dexterity. **3** (esp. in *plural*) opportunity or equipment for doing something.
  ■ **1** ease, effortlessness. **2** adroitness, deftness, dexterity, expertise, fluency, glibness, skill, smoothness. **3** amenity, convenience, help, provision, resource, service.

facing *noun* **1** material over part of garment etc. for contrast or strength. **2** outer covering on wall etc.

facsimile /fæk'sɪmɪlɪ/ *noun* exact copy of writing, picture, etc.

fact *noun* **1** thing known to exist, have occurred, or be true. **2** reality. **3** (usually in *plural*) item of information. □ **factsheet** information leaflet. **in fact 1** in reality. **2** in short. **the facts of life** information on sexual functions etc.
  ■ **1** certainty, event, *fait accompli*, occurrence. **2** actuality, certainty, reality, truth. **3** (*facts*) circumstances, data, details, evidence, information, *colloquial* low-down, particulars, statistics.

faction /'fækʃ(ə)n/ *noun* **1** small dissenting group within larger one, esp. in politics. **2** such dissension. □ **factional** *adjective*.

factious /'fækʃəs/ *adjective* of or inclined to faction.

factitious /fæk'tɪʃəs/ *adjective* **1** specially contrived. **2** artificial.

factor /'fæktə/ *noun* **1** thing contributing to result. **2** whole number etc. that when multiplied produces given number (e.g. 2, 3, 4, and 6 are the factors of 12).
  ■ **1** aspect, cause, circumstance, component, consideration, constituent, contingency, detail, determinant, element, fact, influence, ingredient, item, part, particular.

factorial /fæk'tɔːrɪəl/ *noun* the product of a number and all whole numbers below it.

factory /'fæktərɪ/ *noun* (*plural* **-ies**) building(s) for manufacture of goods. □ **factory farming**

using intensive or industrial methods of rearing livestock.

■ forge, foundry, manufacturing plant, mill, plant, refinery, works, workshop.

factotum /fæk'təʊtəm/ *noun* (*plural* **-s**) employee doing all kinds of work.

factual /'fæktjʊəl/ *adjective* based on or concerned with fact. □ **factuality** /-'ælɪtɪ/ *noun*. **factually** *adverb*.

■ accurate, authentic, bona fide, circumstantial, correct, demonstrable, documentary, empirical, faithful, genuine, objective, realistic, real-life, straightforward, true, unadorned, unbiased, undistorted, unvarnished, valid, verifiable.

faculty /'fækəltɪ/ *noun* (*plural* **-ies**) **1** aptitude for particular activity. **2** physical or mental power. **3** group of related university departments. **4** *US* teaching staff of university etc.

■ **1, 2** ability, aptitude, capability, capacity, flair, genius, gift, knack, power, talent.

fad *noun* **1** craze. **2** peculiar notion.

faddy *adjective* (**-ier, -iest**) having petty likes and dislikes.

fade *verb* (**-ding**) **1** (cause to) lose colour, light, or sound. **2** slowly diminish or disappear. **3** lose freshness or strength. ● *noun* action of fading. □ **fade away 1** die away, disappear. **2** *colloquial* languish, grow thin.

■ *verb* **1** blanch, bleach, dim, discolour, dull, etiolate, grow pale, whiten. **2** become less, decline, decrease, diminish, disappear, dwindle, *literary* evanesce, fail, melt away, vanish, wane. **3** droop, flag, perish, shrivel, waste away, weaken, wilt, wither.

faeces /'fiːsiːz/ *plural noun* (*US* **feces**) waste matter from bowels. □ **faecal** /-k(ə)l/ *adjective*.

fag *noun* **1** *colloquial* tedious task. **2** *slang* cigarette. **3** (at public schools) junior boy who runs errands for a senior. ● *verb* (**-gg-**) **1** (often + *out*) *colloquial* exhaust. **2** act as fag. □ **fag-end** *slang* cigarette-end.

faggot /'fægət/ *noun* (*US* **fagot**) **1** baked or fried ball of seasoned chopped liver etc. **2** bundle of sticks etc.

fah /fɑː/ *noun* (also **fa**) *Music* fourth note of scale in tonic sol-fa.

Fahrenheit /'færənhaɪt/ *adjective* of scale of temperature on which water freezes at 32° and boils at 212°.

faience /'faɪɑ̃s/ *noun* decorated and glazed earthenware and porcelain.

fail *verb* **1** not succeed. **2** be or judge to be unsuccessful in (exam etc.). **3** (+ *to do*) be unable to, neglect to. **4** disappoint. **5** be absent or insufficient. **6** become weaker. **7** cease functioning. **8** become bankrupt. ● *noun* failure in exam. □ **fail-safe** reverting to safe condition when faulty. **without fail** for certain; whatever happens.

■ *verb* **1, 2** abort, be a failure, be unsuccessful, come to grief, come to nothing, crash, fall through, *slang* flop, founder, meet with disaster, miscarry, misfire, miss out. **3** forget, neglect, omit. **4** abandon, disappoint, let down. **5** cut out, give out, peter out, run out, vanish. **6** decay, decline, deteriorate, diminish, disappear, dwindle, ebb, fade, fizzle out, get worse, give out, melt away, peter out, vanish, wane, weaken. **7** break down, close down, come to an end, *colloquial* conk out, crash, cut out, stop working. **8** *colloquial* fold (up), go bankrupt, *colloquial* go bust, go out of business.

failed *adjective* **1** unsuccessful. **2** bankrupt.

failing *noun* fault; weakness. ● *preposition* in default of.

■ *noun* blemish, defect, fault, flaw, foible, imperfection, shortcoming, weakness, weak spot.

failure /'feɪljə/ *noun* **1** lack of success. **2** unsuccessful person or thing. **3** non-performance. **4** breaking down or ceasing to function. **5** running short of supply etc.

■ **1** defeat, disappointment, *colloquial* disaster, downfall, loss, miscarriage. **2** *slang* dud, fiasco, *slang* flop, *colloquial* wash-out, wreck. **3** dereliction, neglect, omission. **4** breakdown, collapse, crash, stoppage.

fain *archaic adjective* (+ *to do*) **1** willing to. **2** obliged to. ● *adverb* gladly.

faint *adjective* **1** dim, pale, indistinct. **2** weak, giddy. **3** slight. **4** timid. ● *verb* **1** lose consciousness. **2** become faint. ● *noun* act or state of fainting. □ **faint-hearted** cowardly, timid. **faint-heartedness** *noun*. □ **faintly** *adverb*. **faintness** *noun*.

■ *adjective* **1** (*faint images, faint colour*) blurred, blurry, dim, faded, feeble, hazy, ill-defined, indistinct, misty, muzzy, pale, pastel, shadowy, unclear, vague; (*faint smell*) delicate, slight; (*faint sounds*) distant, hushed, low, muffled, muted, soft, stifled, subdued, thin, weak. **2** dizzy, exhausted, feeble, giddy, light-headed, unsteady, weak, *colloquial* woozy. ● *verb* **1** become unconscious, black out, collapse, flake out, keel over, pass out, *literary* swoon.

fair[1] *adjective* **1** just, equitable. **2** blond, not dark. **3** moderate in quality or amount. **4** (of weather) fine; (of wind) favourable. **5** *archaic* beautiful. ● *adverb* **1** in a fair or just manner. **2** exactly, completely. □ **fair and square 1** exactly. **2** straightforwardly. **fair copy** transcript free from corrections. **fair game** legitimate target or object. **fair-minded** just. **fair-mindedness** *noun*. **fair play** just treatment or behaviour. **fair-weather friend** friend or ally who deserts in crisis. □ **fairness** *noun*.

■ *adjective* **1** disinterested, equitable, even-handed, fair-minded, honest, honourable, impartial, just, lawful, legitimate, non-partisan, open-minded, proper, right, unbiased, unprejudiced, upright. **2** blond, blonde, flaxen, golden, light, yellow. **3** acceptable, adequate, average, indifferent, mediocre, middling, moderate, passable, reasonable, respectable, satisfactory, *colloquial* so so, tolerable. 4 (*fair weather*) bright, clear, clement, cloudless, dry, fine, pleasant, sunny; (*fair wind*) benign, favourable. 5 see BEAUTIFUL 1.

---

fair² *noun* 1 stalls, amusements, etc. for public entertainment. 2 periodic market, often with entertainments. 3 trade exhibition. □ **fairground** outdoor site for fair.

■ 1 amusement park, carnival, festival, fête, funfair, gala. 2 bazaar, market, sale. 3 exhibition, exposition, show.

Fair Isle *noun* multicoloured knitwear design characteristic of Fair Isle in the Shetland Islands.

fairly *adverb* 1 in a fair way. 2 moderately. 3 to a noticeable degree.

■ 2 moderately, *colloquial* pretty, quite, rather, reasonably, tolerably. 3 quite, rather, somewhat, up to a point.

fairway *noun* 1 navigable channel. 2 mown grass between golf tee and green.

fairy /'feərɪ/ *noun* (*plural* -ies) small winged legendary being. □ **fairy cake** small iced sponge cake. **fairy godmother** benefactress. **fairyland** 1 home of fairies. 2 enchanted region. **fairy lights** small coloured lights for decoration. **fairy ring** ring of darker grass caused by fungi. **fairy story, tale** 1 tale about fairies. 2 unbelievable story; lie.

fait accompli /feɪt ə'kɒmpliː/ *noun* (*plural* *faits accomplis* same pronunciation) thing done and past arguing about. [French]

faith /feɪθ/ *noun* 1 trust. 2 religious belief; creed. 3 loyalty, trustworthiness. □ **faith healing** healing dependent on faith rather than treatment. **faith healer** *noun*.

■ 1 assurance, belief, certitude, confidence, reliance, sureness, trust. 2 belief, conviction, creed, doctrine, dogma, persuasion, religion. 3 allegiance, devotion, faithfulness, loyalty.

faithful *adjective* 1 showing faith. 2 (often + *to*) loyal, trustworthy. 3 accurate. □ **faithfulness** *noun*.

■ 2 constant, dependable, devoted, dutiful, loyal, reliable, staunch, steadfast, trusted, trustworthy, *archaic* or *jocular* trusty, unswerving. 3 accurate, close, consistent, exact, factual, literal, precise, true.

faithfully *adverb* in a faithful way. □ **Yours faithfully** *written before signature at end of business letter*.

faithless *adjective* 1 disloyal. 2 without religious faith. □ **faithlessness** *noun*.

fake *noun* thing or person that is not genuine. ● *adjective* counterfeit, not genuine. ● *verb* (-king) 1 make fake or imitation of. 2 feign.

■ *noun* [thing] copy, counterfeit, duplicate, forgery, hoax, imitation, replica, reproduction, sham, simulation; [person] charlatan, cheat, fraud, hoaxer, humbug, impostor, mountebank, *colloquial* phoney, quack. ● *adjective* artificial,

bogus, concocted, counterfeit, ersatz, factitious, false, fictitious, forged, fraudulent, imitation, invented, made up, mock, *colloquial* phoney, pretended, sham, simulated, spurious, synthetic, trumped-up, unfounded, unreal. ● *verb* 1 copy, counterfeit, fabricate, falsify, forge, fudge, imitate, reproduce. 2 affect, dissemble, feign, make believe, pretend, put on, sham, simulate.

---

fakir /'feɪkɪə/ *noun* Muslim or Hindu religious beggar or ascetic.

falcon /'fɔːlkən/ *noun* small hawk trained to hunt.

falconry *noun* breeding and training of hawks.

fall /fɔːl/ *verb* (*past* **fell**; *past participle* **fallen**) 1 go or come down freely; descend. 2 (often + *over*) lose balance and come suddenly to ground. 3 slope down. 4 hang down. 5 sink lower; subside. 6 diminish. 7 decline in power, status, etc. 8 occur. 9 become. 10 (of face) show dismay etc. 11 be defeated. 12 die. ● *noun* 1 falling. 2 amount or thing that falls. 3 overthrow. 4 (esp. in *plural*) waterfall. 5 *US* autumn. □ **fall about** *colloquial* be helpless, esp. with laughter. **fall apart** 1 break into pieces. 2 (of situation etc.) collapse. 3 lose one's capacity to cope. **fall away** 1 (of ground) slope downwards. 2 become scarce. **fall back** retreat. **fall back on** have recourse to. **fall behind** 1 be outstripped, lag. 2 be in arrears. **fall down** 1 collapse. 2 (often + *on*) *colloquial* fail (in). **fall for** be captivated or deceived by. **fall foul of** come into conflict with. **fall guy** *slang* 1 easy victim. 2 scapegoat. **fall in** 1 collapse inwards. 2 *Military* take place in parade. **fall in with** 1 meet by chance. 2 agree or coincide with. **falling star** meteor. **fall off** decrease, deteriorate. **falling-off** *noun*. **fall out** 1 quarrel. 2 (of hair, teeth, etc.) become detached. 3 result, occur. 4 *Military* come out of formation. **fallout** *noun* radioactive nuclear debris. **fall short of** fail to reach or obtain. **fall through** fail. **fall to** start eating, working, etc.

■ *verb* 1 collapse, come down, crash down, descend, dive, drop down, founder, go down, pitch, plummet, plunge, sink, slump, spiral. 2 *slang* come a cropper, keel over, overbalance, stumble, topple, trip over, tumble. 3 descend, dip, drop, fall away, slope down. 4 be suspended, cascade, dangle, hang. 5, 6 become less, become lower, decline, decrease, diminish, dwindle, ebb, lessen, subside. 8 come, come about, happen, occur, settle. 11 see SURRENDER *verb* 2. 12 see DIE¹ 1. ● *noun* 1 collapse, crash, decline, decrease, depreciation, descent, dip, dive, downturn, drop, lowering, nosedive, plunge, reduction, slant, slump, tumble. 3 capitulation, capture, defeat, overthrow, seizure, submission, surrender. □ **fall apart** 1 see DISINTEGRATE 1. 2 see COLLAPSE *verb* 1. 3 see COLLAPSE *verb* 2. **fall back** see RETREAT *verb* 1. **fall behind** 1 see LAG¹ *verb*. **fall down** 1 see COLLAPSE *verb* 1. **fall in** 1 see COLLAPSE *verb* 1. **fall off** see DECLINE *verb* 1. **fall out** 1 see QUARREL *verb* 2. **fall through** see FAIL *verb* 1,2.

---

fallacy /'fæləsɪ/ *noun* (*plural* -ies) 1 mistaken belief. 2 faulty reasoning; misleading argument. □ **fallacious** /fə'leɪʃəs/ *adjective*.

■ **1** delusion, misconception, mistake. **2** error, flaw, miscalculation, mistake, sophism.

fallible /ˈfælɪb(ə)l/ *adjective* capable of making mistakes. □ **fallibility** *noun*.

■ erring, frail, human, imperfect, uncertain, unpredictable, unreliable, weak.

Fallopian tube /fəˈləʊpɪən/ *noun* either of two tubes along which ova travel from ovaries to womb.

fallow /ˈfæləʊ/ *adjective* (of land) ploughed but left unsown; uncultivated. ● *noun* fallow land.

■ dormant, resting, uncultivated, unplanted, unsown, unused.

fallow deer *noun* small deer with white-spotted reddish-brown summer coat.

false /fɔːls/ *adjective* **1** wrong, incorrect. **2** sham, artificial. **3** (+ *to*) deceitful, treacherous, unfaithful to. **4** deceptive. □ **false alarm** alarm given needlessly. **false name** name taken to deceive. **false pretences** misrepresentations meant to deceive. □ **falsely** *adverb*. **falseness** *noun*. **falsity** *noun*.

■ **1** distorted, erroneous, fabricated, fallacious, faulty, fictitious, flawed, imprecise, inaccurate, incorrect, inexact, invalid, mistaken, spurious, unsound, untrue, wrong. **2** see FAKE *adjective*. **3** deceitful, dishonest, disloyal, double-dealing, faithless, lying, treacherous, two-faced, unfaithful, unreliable, untrustworthy. **4** deceptive, misleading, unreliable, untrustworthy. □ **false name** see PSEUDONYM.

falsehood *noun* **1** untrue thing, lie. **2** lying.

■ **1** fabrication, fib, fiction, lie, *colloquial* story, untruth, *slang* whopper. **2** deceit, deception, duplicity, fibbing, lying, mendacity, perjury, prevarication.

falsetto /fɔːlˈsetəʊ/ *noun* male voice above normal range.

falsify /ˈfɔːlsɪfaɪ/ *verb* (**-ies, -ied**) **1** fraudulently alter. **2** misrepresent. □ **falsification** *noun*.

■ **1** alter, *colloquial* cook (*the books*), counterfeit, fake, forge, fudge, tamper with. **2** distort, exaggerate, imitate, misrepresent, oversimplify, pervert, simulate, slant, tell lies about, twist.

falter /ˈfɔːltə/ *verb* **1** stumble; go unsteadily. **2** lose courage; waver. **3** speak hesitatingly. □ **faltering** *adjective*.

■ **1** stagger, stumble, totter. **2** become weaker, flag, flinch, hesitate, hold back, lose confidence, quail, vacillate, waver. **3** hesitate, pause, stammer, stutter. □ **faltering** see HESITANT.

fame *noun* **1** renown, being famous. **2** *archaic* reputation.

■ acclaim, celebrity, distinction, eminence, glory, honour, illustriousness, importance, *colloquial* kudos, name, notoriety, pre-eminence, prestige, prominence, public esteem, renown, reputation, repute, stardom.

famed *adjective* (+ *for*) much spoken of or famous because of.

familial /fəˈmɪlɪəl/ *adjective* of a family or its members.

familiar /fəˈmɪlɪə/ *adjective* **1** (often + *to*) well known, often encountered. **2** (+ *with*) knowing (a thing) well. **3** (often + *with*) well acquainted; intimate. **4** (excessively) informal. ● *noun* **1** intimate friend. **2** supposed attendant of witch etc. □ **familiarity** /-ˈær-/ *noun* (*plural* -**ies**). **familiarly** *adverb*.

■ *adjective* **1** accustomed, common, conventional, current, customary, everyday, frequent, habitual, mundane, normal, ordinary, predictable, regular, routine, stock, traditional, usual, well known. **2** (*familiar with*) acquainted with, at home with, aware of, conscious of, expert in, informed about, knowledgeable about, trained in, versed in. **3** close, friendly, intimate, near. **4** chatty, forward, free and easy, impudent, informal, presumptuous, relaxed, sociable, unceremonious.

familiarize /fəˈmɪlɪəraɪz/ *verb* (also **-ise**) (-**zing** or -**sing**) (usually + *with*) make (person etc.) conversant. □ **familiarization** *noun*.

family /ˈfæmɪlɪ/ *noun* (*plural* -**ies**) **1** set of relations, esp. parents and children. **2** person's children. **3** household. **4** all the descendants of common ancestor; lineage. **5** group of similar things, people, etc. **6** group of related genera of animals or plants. □ **family credit** regular state payment to low-income family. **family planning** birth control. **family tree** genealogical chart.

■ **1** flesh and blood, kin, kindred, kinsfolk, kinsmen, kinswomen, kith and kin, nearest and dearest, relations, relatives, *usually derogatory* tribe. **2** *colloquial* brood, children, issue, litter, offspring, progeny. **4** ancestors, ancestry, blood, clan, descendants, descent, dynasty, extraction, forebears, genealogy, house, line, lineage, pedigree, race, strain, tribe.

famine /ˈfæmɪn/ *noun* **1** extreme scarcity, esp. of food. **2** *archaic* hunger, starvation.

■ **1** dearth, lack, scarcity, shortage, want. **2** hunger, malnutrition, starvation.

famish /ˈfæmɪʃ/ *verb* (usually as **famished** *adjective colloquial*) make or become extremely hungry.

■ (**famished**) hungry, *colloquial* peckish, ravenous, *colloquial* starved, *colloquial* starving.

famous /ˈfeɪməs/ *adjective* **1** (often + *for*) well known; celebrated. **2** *colloquial* excellent. □ **famously** *adverb*.

■ **1** acclaimed, big, celebrated, distinguished, eminent, exalted, famed, glorious, great, historic, honoured, illustrious, important, *colloquial* legendary, lionized, notable, noted, notorious, outstanding, popular, prominent, proverbial, renowned, revered, time-honoured, venerable, well known, world-famous.

fan[1] *noun* **1** apparatus, usually with rotating blades, for ventilation etc. **2** device, semicircular and folding, waved to cool oneself. **3** fan-shaped thing. ● *verb* (-**nn**-) **1** blow air on, (as) with fan. **2**

(usually + *out*) spread out like fan. □ **fan belt** belt driving fan to cool radiator in vehicle. **fanlight** small, originally semicircular, window over door etc. **fantail** pigeon with broad tail.

■ *noun* 1 blower, extractor, propeller, ventilator.

fan[2] *noun* devotee. □ **fan club** (club of) devotees. **fan mail** letters from fans.

■ *colloquial* addict, admirer, aficionado, *colloquial* buff, devotee, enthusiast, fanatic, *slang* fiend, follower, *colloquial* freak, lover, supporter.

fanatic /fə'nætɪk/ *noun* person obsessively devoted to a belief, activity, etc. ● *adjective* excessively enthusiastic. □ **fanatical** *adjective*. **fanatically** *adverb*. **fanaticism** /-tɪsɪz(ə)m/ *noun*.

■ *noun* activist, adherent, bigot, extremist, *slang* fiend, *colloquial* freak, *colloquial* maniac, militant, zealot. □ **fanatical** bigoted, excessive, extreme, fervent, fervid, immoderate, irrational, *colloquial* maniacal, militant, obsessive, overenthusiastic, passionate, rabid, single-minded, zealous.

fancier /'fænsɪə/ *noun* 1 connoisseur, enthusiast. 2 breeder, esp. of pigeons.

fanciful /'fænsɪfʊl/ *adjective* 1 imaginary. 2 indulging in fancies. □ **fancifully** *adverb*.

■ 1 chimerical, extravagant, fancy, fantastic, illusory, imaginary, imagined, make-believe, unrealistic. 2 capricious, dreamy, unrealistic, whimsical.

fancy /'fænsɪ/ *noun* (*plural* -**ies**) 1 inclination; whim. 2 supposition. 3 imagination. ● *adjective* (-**ier**, -**iest**) 1 extravagant. 2 ornamental. ● *verb* (-**ies**, -**ied**) 1 (+ *that*) imagine, suppose. 2 *colloquial* find attractive, desire. 3 have unduly high opinion of. 4 conceive; picture to oneself. □ **fancy dress** costume for masquerading. **fancy man, woman** woman's or man's lover. □ **fancily** *adverb*.

■ *noun* 1 see WHIM. 3 see IMAGINATION 1.
● *adjective* 1 see FANCIFUL 1. 2 decorative, elaborate, embellished, embroidered, intricate, ornamented, ornate. ● *verb* 1 believe, conjecture, guess, imagine, suppose, think. 2 be attracted to, crave, desire, *colloquial* have a yen for, like, long for, prefer, want, wish for. 4 conjure up, dream of, envisage, imagine, picture, think of, visualize.

fandango /fæn'dæŋɡəʊ/ *noun* (*plural* -**es** or -**s**) lively Spanish dance.

fanfare /'fænfeə/ *noun* short showy sounding of trumpets etc.

fang *noun* 1 canine tooth, esp. of dog or wolf. 2 tooth of venomous snake. 3 (prong of) root of tooth.

fantasia /fæn'teɪzɪə/ *noun* free or improvisatory musical etc. composition.

fantasize /'fæntəsaɪz/ *verb* (also -**ise**) (-**zing** or -**sing**) 1 daydream. 2 imagine; create fantasy about.

fantastic /fæn'tæstɪk/ *adjective* 1 extravagantly fanciful. 2 grotesque; quaint. 3 *colloquial* excellent, extraordinary. □ **fantastically** *adverb*.

■ 1 amazing, elaborate, exaggerated, extraordinary, extravagant, fabulous, fanciful, far-fetched, imaginative, implausible, incredible, rococo, unbelievable, unlikely, unrealistic. 2 absurd, bizarre, grotesque, odd, quaint, remarkable, strange, surreal, *colloquial* weird. 3 see EXCELLENT.

fantasy /'fæntəsɪ/ *noun* (*plural* -**ies**) 1 imagination, esp. when unrelated to reality. 2 mental image, daydream. 3 fantastic invention or composition.

■ 1 fancy, imagination, invention, make-believe. 2 chimera, daydream, delusion, dream, fancy, hallucination, illusion, invention, mirage, pipe dream, reverie, vision.

fanzine /'fænziːn/ *noun* magazine for fans of science fiction, a football team, etc.

far (**further**, **furthest** or **farther**, **farthest**) *adverb* 1 at, to, or by a great distance in space or time. 2 by much. ● *adjective* 1 distant; remote. 2 extreme. □ **far and wide** over large area. **far-away** 1 remote. 2 dreamy. 3 distant. **the Far East** countries of E. Asia. **Far Eastern** *adjective*. **far-fetched** unconvincing, exaggerated, fanciful. **far-flung** widely scattered, remote. **far from** almost the opposite of. **far gone** very ill, drunk, etc. **far-off** remote. **far-out** *slang* 1 unconventional. 2 excellent. **far-ranging** broad, extensive. **far-reaching** widely influential or applicable. **far-seeing** showing foresight. **far-sighted** 1 having foresight. 2 *esp. US* long-sighted. **far-sightedness** *noun*.

■ *adjective* 1 distant, far-away, far-off, outlying, remote.

farad /'færəd/ *noun* SI unit of electrical capacitance.

farce /fɑːs/ *noun* 1 comedy with ludicrously improbable plot. 2 absurdly futile proceedings. 3 pretence. □ **farcical** *adjective*.

■ □ **farcical** absurd, foolish, ludicrous, preposterous, ridiculous, silly.

fare *noun* 1 price of journey on public transport. 2 passenger. 3 food. ● *verb* (-**ring**) progress; get on. □ **fare-stage** 1 section of bus route for which fixed fare is charged. 2 stop marking this.

■ *noun* 1 charge, cost, fee, payment, price, ticket. 3 see FOOD 1.

farewell /feə'wel/ *interjection* goodbye. ● *noun* leave-taking.

■ *noun* departure, goodbye, leave-taking, send-off, *formal* valediction; (*farewell gift*) last, leaving, parting, valedictory.

farina /fə'riːnə/ *noun* flour of corn, nuts, or starchy roots. □ **farinaceous** /færɪ'neɪʃəs/ *adjective*.

farm *noun* 1 land and its buildings used for growing crops, rearing animals, etc. 2 farmhouse. ● *verb* 1 use (land) thus. 2 be farmer. 3 breed (fish etc.) commercially. 4 (+ *out*) delegate or subcontract (work). □ **farm hand** worker on farm. **farmhouse** house attached to farm. **farm-**

land land used for farming. **farmstead** farm and its buildings. **farmyard** yard adjacent to farmhouse. □ **farming** noun.
■ noun 1 croft, farmstead, ranch, smallholding. 2 farmhouse, grange. □ **farming** agriculture, agronomy, crofting, cultivation, food production, husbandry.

farmer noun owner or manager of farm.

faro /ˈfeərəʊ/ noun gambling card game.

farrago /fəˈrɑːgəʊ/ noun (plural **-s** or US **-es**) medley, hotchpotch.

farrier /ˈfærɪə/ noun smith who shoes horses.

farrow /ˈfærəʊ/ verb give birth to (piglets).
● noun litter of pigs.

Farsi /ˈfɑːsɪ/ noun modern Persian language.

farther = FURTHER.

farthest = FURTHEST.

farthing /ˈfɑːðɪŋ/ noun historical coin worth quarter of old penny.

farthingale /ˈfɑːðɪŋgeɪl/ noun historical hooped petticoat.

fascia /ˈfeɪʃə/ noun (also **facia**) (plural **-s**) 1 instrument panel of vehicle. 2 similar panel etc. for operating machinery. 3 long flat surface of wood or stone.

fascicle /ˈfæsɪk(ə)l/ noun instalment of book.

fascinate /ˈfæsɪneɪt/ verb (**-ting**) capture interest of; attract. □ **fascinating** adjective. **fascination** noun.
■ allure, attract, beguile, bewitch, captivate, charm, delight, enchant, engross, enthral, entice, entrance, hypnotize, interest, mesmerize, rivet, spellbind. □ **fascinating** see ATTRACTIVE.

Fascism /ˈfæʃɪz(ə)m/ noun 1 extreme right-wing totalitarian nationalist movement in Italy (1922–43). 2 (also **fascism**) any similar movement. □ **Fascist, fascist** noun & adjective. **Fascistic, fascistic** /-ˈʃɪs-/ adjective.

fashion /ˈfæʃ(ə)n/ noun 1 current popular custom or style, esp. in dress. 2 manner of doing something. ● verb (often + into) form, make. □ **in fashion** fashionable. **out of fashion** not fashionable.
■ noun 1 craze, cut, fad, line, look, mode, pattern, rage, style, taste, trend, vogue. 2 manner, method, mode, way.

fashionable adjective 1 of or conforming to current fashion. 2 of or favoured by high society. □ **fashionably** adverb.
■ à la mode, chic, contemporary, current, in, in vogue, (the) latest, modern, modish, popular, smart, slang snazzy, sophisticated, stylish, colloquial often derogatory trendy, up-to-date, colloquial with it.

fast¹ /fɑːst/ adjective 1 rapid. 2 capable of or intended for high speed. 3 (of clock) ahead of correct time. 4 firm, fixed. 5 (of colour) not fading. 6 pleasure-seeking, dissipated. ● adverb 1 quickly. 2 firmly. 3 soundly, completely. □ **fastback** car with sloping rear. **fast breeder**

(reactor) reactor using neutrons with high kinetic energy. **fast food** food that is prepared and served quickly. **pull a fast one** colloquial try to deceive someone.
■ adjective 1 breakneck, brisk, expeditious, express, hasty, headlong, high-speed, hurried, lively, colloquial nippy, precipitate, quick, rapid, smart, spanking, speedy, supersonic, swift, unhesitating. 4 attached, bound, fastened, firm, fixed, immobile, immovable, secure, tight. 5 indelible, lasting, permanent, stable. 6 see IMMORAL. ● adverb 1 at full tilt, briskly, in no time, post-haste, quickly, rapidly, swiftly.

fast² /fɑːst/ verb abstain from food. ● noun act or period of fasting.

fasten /ˈfɑːs(ə)n/ verb 1 make or become fixed or secure. 2 (+ in, up) shut in; lock securely. 3 (+ off) fix with knot or stitches. 4 (+ on) direct (attention) towards.
■ 1 affix, anchor, attach, batten, bind, bolt, buckle, button, chain, clamp, clasp, cling, close, connect, couple, do up, fix, grip, hitch, hook, join, knot, lace, lash, latch, link, lock, make fast, moor, nail, padlock, paste, peg, pin, rivet, rope, screw, screw down, seal, secure, solder, staple, stick, strap, tack, tape, tether, tie, unite, weld. 2 (fasten up) bolt, do up, lock, padlock, secure, shut. 3 (fasten off) fix, knot, make fast, secure, tack, tie.

fastener noun (also **fastening**) device that fastens.
■ bond, connection, connector, coupling, link.

fastidious /fæˈstɪdɪəs/ adjective 1 fussy. 2 easily disgusted, squeamish.
■ 1 colloquial choosy, discriminating, finical, finicky, fussy, hard to please, nice, particular, colloquial pernickety, colloquial picky, selective. 2 dainty, delicate, squeamish.

fastness /ˈfɑːstnɪs/ noun stronghold.

fat noun 1 oily substance, esp. in animal bodies. 2 part of meat etc. containing this. ● adjective (**-tt-**) 1 plump. 2 containing much fat. 3 thick, substantial. ● verb (**-tt-**) (esp. as **fatted** adjective) make or become fat. □ **fat-head** colloquial stupid person. **fat-headed** stupid. **a fat lot** colloquial very little. □ **fatless** adjective. **fatness** noun. **fatten** verb.
■ adjective 1 bloated, bulky, chubby, corpulent, dumpy, flabby, fleshy, gross, heavy, massive, obese, overweight, paunchy, plump, podgy, portly, pot-bellied, colloquial pudgy, rotund, round, solid, squat, stocky, stout, tubby, weighty. 2 fatty, greasy, oily. 3 bulky, heavy, massive, solid, squat, stout, sturdy, substantial, thick, weighty.

fatal /ˈfeɪt(ə)l/ adjective 1 causing or ending in death. 2 causing disaster or ruin. □ **fatally** adverb.
■ 1 deadly, final, incurable, lethal, malignant, mortal, terminal. 2 see DISASTROUS (DISASTER).

fatalism noun 1 belief in predetermination. 2 submissive acceptance. □ **fatalist** noun. **fatalistic** /-ˈlɪs-/ adjective.

fatality /fə'tælɪtɪ/ *noun* (*plural* -ies) death by accident, in war, etc.
■ casualty, death, loss.

fate *noun* **1** supposed power predetermining events. **2** destiny. **3** death, destruction. ● *verb* (-ting) **1** (usually in *passive*) preordain. **2** (as **fated** *adjective*) unavoidable. **3** (as **fated** *adjective*) doomed.
■ *noun* **1** chance, destiny, fortune, luck, predestination, providence, the stars. **2** destiny, doom, fortune, *Buddhism & Hinduism* karma, kismet, lot, nemesis. **3** death, demise, destruction, disaster, doom, downfall, end, ruin. ● *verb* **1** decree, destine, intend, predestine, predetermine, preordain. **2** (**fated**) certain, inescapable, inevitable, sure, unavoidable. **3** (**fated**) cursed, damned, doomed.

fateful *adjective* **1** decisive, important. **2** controlled by fate.

father /'fɑːðə/ *noun* **1** male parent. **2** (usually in *plural*) forefather. **3** originator. **4** early leader. **5** (also **Father**) priest. **6** (**the Father**) God. **7** (in *plural*) elders. ● *verb* **1** be father of. **2** originate. □ **father-in-law** (*plural* **fathers-in-law**) wife's or husband's father. **fatherland** native country. □ **fatherhood** *noun*. **fatherless** *adjective*.
■ *noun* **1** *literary* begetter, *colloquial* dad, *colloquial* daddy, *colloquial* pa, *archaic* papa, parent, *esp. US colloquial* pop, *archaic* sire.

fatherly *adjective* of or like a father.

fathom /'fæð(ə)m/ *noun* measure of 6ft, esp. in soundings. ● *verb* **1** comprehend. **2** measure depth of (water). □ **fathomable** *adjective*.

fathomless *adjective* too deep to fathom.

fatigue /fə'tiːg/ *noun* **1** extreme tiredness. **2** weakness in metals etc. from repeated stress. **3** non-military army duty. **4** (in *plural*) clothing for this. ● *verb* (-gues, -gued, -guing) (esp. as **fatigued** *adjective*) cause fatigue in.
■ *noun* **1** debility, exhaustion, feebleness, languor, lassitude, lethargy, tiredness, weakness, weariness. ● *verb* debilitate, drain, enervate, exhaust, tire, weaken, weary; (**fatigued**) see WEARY *adjective* 1.

fatty *adjective* (-ier, -iest) like or containing fat. ● *noun* (*plural* -ies) *colloquial* fat person. □ **fatty acid** type of organic compound.

fatuous /'fætjʊəs/ *adjective* vacantly silly; purposeless. □ **fatuity** /fə'tjuːɪtɪ/ *noun* (*plural* -ies). **fatuously** *adverb*. **fatuousness** *noun*.

fatwa /'fætwɑː/ *noun* legal ruling by Islamic religious leader.

faucet /'fɔːsɪt/ *noun esp. US* tap.

fault /fɔːlt/ *noun* **1** defect, imperfection. **2** offence; thing wrongly done. **3** responsibility for wrongdoing, error, etc. **4** break in electric circuit. **5** *Tennis etc.* incorrect service. **6** break in rock strata. ● *verb* find fault with. □ **find fault** (often + *with*) criticize or complain (about). **to a fault** excessively. □ **faultless** *adjective*. **faultlessly** *adverb*. **faultlessness** *noun*.

■ *noun* **1** blemish, defect, deficiency, demerit, failing, failure, fallacy, flaw, foible, frailty, imperfection, inaccuracy, malfunction, snag, weakness. **2** blunder, *colloquial* boob, error, failing, *faux pas*, gaffe, *colloquial* howler, indiscretion, lapse, miscalculation, misdeed, mistake, offence, omission, oversight, peccadillo, shortcoming, sin, slip, transgression, *archaic* trespass, vice, wrongdoing. **3** accountability, blame, culpability, guilt, liability, responsibility. ● *verb* see CRITICIZE 1. □ **faultless** accurate, correct, exemplary, flawless, ideal, in mint condition, irreproachable, perfect, sinless, unimpeachable.

faulty *adjective* (-ier, -iest) having faults. □ **faultily** *adverb*.
■ broken, damaged, defective, deficient, flawed, illogical, imperfect, inaccurate, incomplete, incorrect, inoperative, invalid, not working, out of order, shop-soiled, unusable, useless.

faun /fɔːn/ *noun* Latin rural deity with goat's horns, legs, and tail.

fauna /'fɔːnə/ *noun* (*plural* -s) animal life of a region or period.

faux pas /fəʊ 'pɑː/ *noun* (*plural* same /'pɑːz/) tactless mistake. [French]

favour /'feɪvə/ (*US* **favor**) *noun* **1** kind act. **2** approval, goodwill. **3** partiality. **4** badge, ribbon, etc. as emblem of support. ● *verb* **1** regard or treat with favour. **2** support, facilitate. **3** tend to confirm (idea etc.). **4** (+ *with*) oblige with. **5** (as **favoured** *adjective*) having special advantages. □ **in favour 1** approved of. **2** (+ *of*) in support of or to the advantage of. **out of favour** disapproved of.
■ *noun* **1** courtesy, good deed, good turn, indulgence, kindness, service. **2** acceptance, approbation, approval, friendliness, goodwill, grace, liking, support. **3** bias, favouritism, partiality, preference. ● *verb* **1** approve of, be in sympathy with, champion, choose, commend, esteem, fancy, go for, like, opt for, prefer, show favour to, think well of, value. **2** abet, advance, back, be advantageous to, befriend, facilitate, forward, help, promote, support.

favourable *adjective* (*US* **favorable**) **1** well disposed. **2** approving. **3** promising; satisfactory, pleasing. **4** helpful, suitable. □ **favourably** *adverb*.
■ **1** auspicious, benign, friendly, propitious, well disposed. **2** approving, commendatory, complimentary, congratulatory, encouraging, enthusiastic, laudatory, positive, reassuring, supportive, sympathetic. **3** agreeable, good, pleasing, promising, satisfactory. **4** advantageous, appropriate, beneficial, convenient, following (*wind*), generous, helpful, kind, opportune, suitable, supportive.

favourite /'feɪvərɪt/ (*US* **favorite**) *adjective* preferred to all others. ● *noun* **1** favourite person or thing. **2** competitor thought most likely to win.

■ *adjective* beloved, best, choice, chosen, dearest, esteemed, ideal, liked, loved, popular, preferred, selected, well liked. ● *noun* **1** apple of one's eye, choice, darling, idol, pet, pick, preference.

favouritism *noun* (*US* **favoritism**) unfair favouring of one person etc.

fawn[1] *noun* **1** deer in first year. **2** light yellowish brown. ● *adjective* fawn-coloured. ● *verb* give birth to fawn.

fawn[2] *verb* **1** (often + *on, upon*) behave servilely. **2** (of dog) show extreme affection.

fax *noun* **1** electronic transmission of exact copy of document etc. **2** such copy. **3** (in full **fax machine**) apparatus used for this. ● *verb* transmit in this way.

faze *verb* (**-zing**) (often as **fazed** *adjective*) *colloquial* disconcert.

FBI *abbreviation* (in *US*) Federal Bureau of Investigation.

FC *abbreviation* Football Club.

FCO *abbreviation* Foreign and Commonwealth Office.

FE *abbreviation* further education.

fealty /'fiːəltɪ/ *noun* (*plural* **-ies**) **1** fidelity to feudal lord. **2** allegiance.

fear *noun* **1** panic etc. caused by impending danger, pain, etc. **2** cause of this. **3** alarm, dread. ● *verb* **1** be afraid of; dread. **2** (+ *for*) feel anxiety about. **3** shrink from. **4** have uneasy feeling or expectation. **5** revere (God).

■ *noun* **1, 3** alarm, anxiety, apprehension, apprehensiveness, awe, concern, consternation, cowardice, cravenness, diffidence, dismay, doubt, dread, faint-heartedness, fright, *slang* funk, horror, nervousness, panic, terror, timidity, trepidation, uneasiness, worry. **2** anxiety, concern, doubt, dread, foreboding, horror, misgiving, phobia, qualm, suspicion, terror, worry. ● *verb* **1, 3** be afraid of, dread, quail at, shrink from, tremble at, worry about. **4** be afraid, suspect.

fearful *adjective* **1** afraid. **2** terrible, awful. **3** extremely unpleasant. □ **fearfully** *adverb*. **fearfulness** *noun*.

■ **1** afraid, alarmed, apprehensive, frightened, nervous, panic-stricken, scared, terrified, timid. **2** see FEARSOME.

fearless *adjective* not afraid; brave. □ **fearlessly** *adverb*. **fearlessness** *noun*.

■ bold, brave, courageous, dauntless, intrepid, resolute, stoical, unafraid, unconcerned, undaunted, valiant, valorous.

fearsome *adjective* frightening. □ **fearsomely** *adverb*.

■ appalling, awe-inspiring, awesome, daunting, dreadful, fearful, frightening, frightful, intimidating, terrible, terrifying.

feasible /'fiːzɪb(ə)l/ *adjective* practicable, possible. □ **feasibility** *noun*. **feasibly** *adverb*.

USAGE *Feasible* should not be used to mean

'likely'. *Possible* or *probable* should be used instead.

■ achievable, attainable, easy, possible, practicable, practical, realizable, viable, workable.

feast *noun* **1** sumptuous meal. **2** religious festival. **3** sensual or mental pleasure. ● *verb* **1** (often + *on*) have feast; eat and drink sumptuously. **2** regale.

■ *noun* **1** banquet, *slang* blow-out, dinner, *colloquial* spread. ● *verb* **1** dine, gorge, gormandize, wine and dine. **2** banquet, regale, wine and dine.

feat *noun* remarkable act or achievement.

■ accomplishment, achievement, act, action, attainment, deed, exploit, performance.

feather /'feðə/ *noun* **1** one of structures forming bird's plumage, with fringed horny shaft. **2** these as material. ● *verb* **1** cover or line with feathers. **2** turn (oar) through air edgeways. □ **feather bed** bed with feather-stuffed mattress. **feather-bed** *verb* cushion, esp. financially. **feather-brained, -headed** silly. **featherweight** amateur boxing weight (54–57 kg). □ **feathery** *adjective*.

■ *noun* **1** plume, quill; (*feathers*) down, plumage. □ **feathery** downy, fluffy, light, wispy.

feature /'fiːtʃə/ *noun* **1** characteristic or distinctive part. **2** (usually in *plural*) part of face. **3** specialized article in newspaper etc. **4** (in full **feature film**) main film in cinema programme. ● *verb* (**-ring**) **1** make or be special feature of; emphasize. **2** take part. □ **featureless** *adjective*.

■ *noun* aspect, attribute, characteristic, circumstance, detail, facet, hallmark, idiosyncrasy, mark, peculiarity, point, property, quality, trait. **2** (*features*) see FACE *noun* 1. **3** article, column, item, piece, report, story. ● *verb* emphasize, focus on, give prominence to, highlight, present, promote, show up, spotlight, stress. **2** act, appear, figure, participate, perform, play a role, star, take a part.

Feb. *abbreviation* February.

febrile /'fiːbraɪl/ *adjective* of fever.

February /'februərɪ/ *noun* (*plural* **-ies**) second month of year.

fecal *US* = FAECAL.

feces *US* = FAECES.

feckless /'feklɪs/ *adjective* **1** feeble, ineffectual. **2** irresponsible.

fecund /'fekənd/ *adjective* fertile. □ **fecundity** /fɪ'kʌndɪtɪ/ *noun*.

fecundate /'fekəndeɪt/ *verb* (**-ting**) **1** make fruitful. **2** fertilize. □ **fecundation** *noun*.

fed *past & past participle* of FEED. □ **fed up** (often + *with*) discontented, bored.

federal /'fedər(ə)l/ *adjective* **1** of system of government in which self-governing states unite for certain functions. **2** of such a federation. **3** (**Federal**) *US* of Northern States in Civil War. □ **federalism** *noun*. **federalist** *noun*. **federalize**

verb (also **-ise**) (**-zing** or **-sing**). **federalization** *noun*. **federally** *adverb*.

federate *verb* /ˈfedəreɪt/ (**-ting**) unite on federal basis. ● *adjective* /ˈfedərət/ federally organized. □ **federative** /-rətɪv/ *adjective*.

federation /fedəˈreɪʃ(ə)n/ *noun* **1** federal group. **2** act of federating.

fee *noun* **1** payment for professional advice or services. **2** (often in *plural*) payment for admission, membership, licence, education, exam, etc. **3** money paid for transfer of footballer etc. □ **fee-paying 1** paying fee(s). **2** (of school) charging fees.

■ **1** bill, charge, cost, emolument, payment, price, remuneration, sum, tariff, terms, toll, wage. **2** charge, dues, payment, subscription.

feeble /ˈfiːb(ə)l/ *adjective* (**-r**, **-st**) **1** weak. **2** lacking energy, strength, or effectiveness. □ **feeble-minded** unintelligent. □ **feebleness** *noun*. **feebly** *adverb*.

■ **1** ailing, debilitated, decrepit, delicate, enfeebled, exhausted, faint, fragile, frail, helpless, ill, infirm, languid, listless, poorly, puny, sickly, slight, weak, weedy. **2** (*feeble leader*) effete, feckless, hesitant, impotent, inadequate, incompetent, indecisive, ineffective, ineffectual, irresolute, namby-pamby, powerless, spineless, *colloquial* useless, vacillating, *colloquial* wimpish, *colloquial* wishy-washy; (*feeble excuse*) flimsy, insubstantial, lame, paltry, poor, tame, thin, unconvincing.

feed *verb* (*past & past participle* **fed**) **1** supply with food. **2** put food in mouth of. **3** (usually + *on*) graze; eat. **4** keep supplied with. **5** (+ *into*) supply (material) to machine etc. **6** (often + *on*) nourish; be nourished by. ● *noun* **1** food, esp. for animals or infants. **2** feeding. **3** *colloquial* meal. □ **feedback 1** information about result of experiment; response. **2** *Electronics* return of part of output signal to input.

■ *verb* **1, 2** cater for, give food to, provide for, provision, suckle, wine and dine. **3** graze, pasture; (*feed on*) consume, dine on, eat, live on, partake of. **6** nourish, nurture, strengthen, support, sustain.

feeder *noun* **1** person or thing that feeds in specified way. **2** baby's feeding bottle. **3** bib. **4** tributary. **5** branch road or railway line. **6** electricity main supplying distribution point. **7** feeding apparatus in machine.

feel *verb* (*past & past participle* **felt**) **1** examine, search, or perceive by touch. **2** experience. **3** be affected by. **4** (+ *that*) have impression. **5** consider, think. **6** seem. **7** be consciously. **8** (+ *for*, *with*) have sympathy or pity for. ● *noun* **1** feeling. **2** sense of touch. **3** sensation characterizing something. □ **feel like** have wish or inclination for. **feel up to** be ready to face or deal with.

■ *verb* **1** caress, finger, fondle, fumble, grope, handle, hold, manipulate, maul, *colloquial* paw, pet, stroke, touch. **2** be aware of, be conscious of, detect, discern, experience, know, notice, perceive, sense, suffer, undergo. **4, 5** believe, consider, *formal* deem, guess, have a feeling, have

a hunch, intuit, judge, think. **6** appear, give a feeling of, seem.

feeler *noun* organ in certain animals for touching, foraging, etc. □ **put out feelers** make tentative proposal.

feeling *noun* **1** capacity to feel; sense of touch; physical sensation. **2** emotion. **3** (in *plural*) susceptibilities. **4** emotional atmosphere. **5** sensitivity. **6** notion, opinion. **7** vague awareness. ● *adjective* sensitive; sympathetic. □ **feelingly** *adverb*.

■ *noun* **1** sensation, sense of touch, sensitivity. **2** ardour, emotion, fervour, passion, sentiment, warmth. **4** atmosphere, aura, mood, tone, vibrations. **5** fondness, responsiveness, sensibility, sensitivity, sympathy, understanding. **6** attitude, belief, guess, hunch, idea, impression, instinct, intuition, notion, opinion, perception, thought, view. **7** awareness, consciousness, impression.

feet *plural* of FOOT.

feign /feɪn/ *verb* simulate; pretend.

feint /feɪnt/ *noun* **1** sham attack or diversionary blow. **2** pretence. ● *verb* make a feint. ● *adjective* (of paper etc.) having faintly ruled lines.

feldspar /ˈfeldspɑː/ *noun* (also **felspar** /ˈfelspɑː/) common aluminium silicate.

felicitate /fəˈlɪsɪteɪt/ *verb* (usually + *on*) congratulate. □ **felicitation** /-ˈteɪʃ(ə)n/ *noun*.

felicitous /fəˈlɪsɪtəs/ *adjective* apt; well chosen.

felicity /fəˈlɪsɪtɪ/ *noun* (*plural* **-ies**) **1** great happiness. **2** capacity for apt expression.

feline /ˈfiːlaɪn/ *adjective* **1** of cat family. **2** catlike. ● *noun* animal of cat family.

fell[1] *past* of FALL.

fell[2] *verb* **1** cut down (tree). **2** strike down.

■ **1** chop down, cut down. **2** bring down, *colloquial* flatten, floor, knock down, mow down, prostrate.

fell[3] *noun* hill or stretch of hills in N. England.

fell[4] *adjective* □ **at, in one fell swoop** in a single (originally deadly) action.

fell[5] *noun* animal's hide or skin with hair.

fellow /ˈfeləʊ/ *noun* **1** comrade, associate. **2** counterpart, equal. **3** *colloquial* man, boy. **4** incorporated senior member of college. **5** member of learned society. ● *adjective* of same group etc. □ **fellow-feeling** sympathy. **fellow-traveller 1** person who travels with another. **2** sympathizer with Communist Party.

fellowship /ˈfeləʊʃɪp/ *noun* **1** friendly association, companionship. **2** group of associates. **3** position or income of college fellow.

felon /ˈfelən/ *noun* person who has committed felony.

felony /ˈfelənɪ/ *noun* (*plural* **-ies**) serious usually violent crime. □ **felonious** /fɪˈləʊ-/ *adjective*.

felspar = FELDSPAR.

felt[1] *noun* fabric of matted and pressed fibres of wool etc. ● *verb* **1** make into or cover with felt. **2**

become matted. □ **felt-tip pen** (also **felt-tipped pen**, **felt tip**) pen with fibre point.

felt² *past & past participle* of FEEL.

female /'fiːmeɪl/ *adjective* **1** of the sex that can give birth or produce eggs. **2** (of plants) fruit-bearing. **3** of female people, animals, or plants. **4** (of screw, socket, etc.) hollow to receive inserted part. ● *noun* female person, animal, or plant.
■ *adjective* **1** see FEMININE 1. ● *noun* see WOMAN 1.

feminine /'femmn/ *adjective* **1** of women; womanly. **2** (of a man) effeminate. **3** *Grammar* (of noun) belonging to gender including words for most female people and animals. □ **femininity** /-'nm-/ *noun*.
■ **1** female, girlish, ladylike, womanly. **2** effeminate, unmanly, unmasculine, *derogatory* womanish, womanly.

feminism /'femmɪz(ə)m/ *noun* advocacy of women's rights and sexual equality. □ **feminist** *noun & adjective*.

femme fatale /fæm fæ'tɑːl/ *noun* (*plural femmes fatales* same pronunciation) dangerously seductive woman. [French]

femur /'fiːmə/ *noun* (*plural* **-s** or **femora** /'femərə/) thigh-bone. □ **femoral** /'femər(ə)l/ *adjective*.

fen *noun* low marshy land.
■ bog, marsh, *literary* morass, quagmire, slough, swamp.

fence *noun* **1** barrier or railing enclosing field, garden, etc. **2** jump for horses. **3** *slang* receiver of stolen goods. ● *verb* (**-cing**) **1** surround (as) with fence. **2** (+ *in*) enclose (as) with fence. **3** practise sword play. **4** be evasive. **5** deal in (stolen goods). □ **fencer** *noun*.
■ *noun* **1** barricade, barrier, fencing, paling, palisade, railing, stockade. **2** barricade, barrier, hurdle, jump, obstacle. ● *verb* **1** bound, circumscribe, encircle, enclose, surround, wall in. **2** (*fence in*) confine, coop up, hedge in, pen in. **3** see FIGHT *verb* 1.

fencing *noun* **1** fences. **2** material for fences. **3** sword-fighting, esp. as sport.

fend *verb* **1** (+ *off*) ward off. **2** (+ *for*) look after (esp. oneself).
■ **1** (*fend off*) see REPEL 1. **2** (*fend for oneself*) care for oneself, do for oneself, *colloquial* get by, look after oneself, support oneself.

fender *noun* **1** low frame round fireplace. **2** matting etc. to protect side of ship. **3** *US* bumper of vehicle.

fennel /'fen(ə)l/ *noun* fragrant plant with edible leaf-stalks and seeds.

fenugreek /'fenjuːgriːk/ *noun* leguminous plant with aromatic seeds used for flavouring.

feral /'fer(ə)l/ *adjective* **1** wild. **2** (of animal) escaped and living wild.

ferial /'fɪərɪəl/ *adjective* (of day) not a church festival or fast.

ferment *noun* /'fɜːment/ **1** excitement. **2** fermentation. **3** fermenting agent. ● *verb* /fə'ment/ **1** undergo or subject to fermentation. **2** excite.
■ *noun* **1** see COMMOTION. ● *verb* **1** boil, bubble, effervesce, fizz, foam, froth, rise, seethe, work. **2** agitate, excite, foment, incite, instigate, provoke, rouse, stir up.

fermentation /fɜːmen'teɪʃ(ə)n/ *noun* **1** breakdown of substance by yeasts, bacteria, etc. **2** excitement.

fern *noun* flowerless plant usually with feathery fronds.

ferocious /fə'rəʊʃəs/ *adjective* fierce. □ **ferociously** *adverb*. **ferocity** /-'rɒs-/ *noun*.
■ bestial, bloodthirsty, brutal, cruel, feral, fiendish, fierce, harsh, inhuman, merciless, murderous, pitiless, *colloquial* sadistic, savage, vicious, wild.

ferret /'ferɪt/ *noun* small polecat used in catching rabbits, rats, etc. ● *verb* (**-t-**) **1** hunt with ferrets. **2** (often + *out*, *about*, etc.) rummage. **3** (+ *out*) search out.

ferric /'ferɪk/ *adjective* **1** of iron. **2** containing iron in trivalent form.

Ferris wheel /'ferɪs/ *noun* tall revolving vertical wheel with passenger cars in fairgrounds etc.

ferroconcrete /ferəʊ'kɒŋkriːt/ *noun* reinforced concrete.

ferrous /'ferəs/ *adjective* containing iron, esp. in divalent form.

ferrule /'feruːl/ *noun* ring or cap on end of stick etc.

ferry *noun* (*plural* **-ies**) **1** boat etc. for esp. regular transport across water. **2** ferrying place or service. ● *verb* (**-ies**, **-ied**) **1** take or go in ferry. **2** transport from place to place, esp. regularly. □ **ferryman** *noun*.
■ *verb* carry, convey, export, fetch, import, shift, ship, shuttle, take across, taxi, transport.

fertile /'fɜːtaɪl/ *adjective* **1** (of soil) abundantly productive; fruitful. **2** (of seed, egg, etc.) capable of growth. **3** inventive. **4** (of animal or plant) able to reproduce. □ **fertility** /-'tɪl-/ *noun*.
■ **1** fecund, flourishing, fruitful, luxuriant, productive, prolific, rich, teeming. **3** fecund, fruitful, inventive, prolific, rich. **4** fecund, productive, prolific.

fertilize /'fɜːtɪlaɪz/ *verb* (also **-ise**) (**-zing** or **-sing**) **1** make (soil etc.) fertile. **2** cause (egg, female animal, etc.) to develop new individual. □ **fertilization** *noun*.
■ **1** cultivate, dress, enrich, feed, make fertile, manure, mulch, nourish, top dress. **2** impregnate, inseminate, pollinate.

fertilizer *noun* (also **-iser**) substance added to soil to make it more fertile.

■ *noun* compost, dressing, dung, manure, mulch, nutrient.

fervent /'fɜːv(ə)nt/ *adjective* ardent, intense. □ **fervency** *noun*. **fervently** *adverb*.

■ animated, ardent, avid, burning, committed, devout, eager, earnest, emotional, enthusiastic, excited, fanatical, fervid, fiery, frenzied, heated, impassioned, intense, keen, passionate, rapturous, spirited, vehement, vigorous, warm, wholehearted, zealous.

fervid /'fɜːvɪd/ *adjective* fervent. □ **fervidly** *adverb*.

fervour /'fɜːvə/ *noun* (*US* **fervor**) passion, zeal.

■ ardour, eagerness, energy, enthusiasm, excitement, fervency, fire, heat, intensity, keenness, passion, sparkle, spirit, vehemence, vigour, warmth, zeal.

fescue /'feskjuː/ *noun* pasture and fodder grass.

fester /'festə/ *verb* **1** make or become septic. **2** cause continuing bitterness. **3** rot. **4** stagnate.

■ **1** become infected, become inflamed, become poisoned, discharge, (*of boil*) gather, go septic, ooze, putrefy, rot, run, suppurate, ulcerate. **3** decay, decompose, go bad, mortify, putrefy, rot.

festival /'festɪv(ə)l/ *noun* **1** day or period of celebration. **2** series of cultural events in town etc.

■ **1** anniversary, carnival, celebration, commemoration, fair, feast, festivity, fête, fiesta, gala, holiday, jamboree, jubilee.

festive /'festɪv/ *adjective* **1** of or characteristic of festival. **2** joyous.

■ **1** celebratory, gala, holiday, party. **2** cheerful, cheery, convivial, gay, gleeful, happy, jolly, jovial, joyful, joyous, light-hearted, merry, uproarious.

festivity /fe'stɪvɪtɪ/ *noun* (*plural* **-ies**) **1** gaiety. **2** (in *plural*) celebration. **3** festive occasion, party.

■ **1, 2** celebration, conviviality, entertainment, feasting, gaiety, jollification, jollity, jubilation, merriment, merrymaking, mirth, rejoicing, revelry. **3** celebration, festive occasion, party, revels.

festoon /fe'stuːn/ *noun* curved hanging chain of flowers, ribbons, etc. ● *verb* (often + *with*) adorn with or form into festoons.

feta /'fetə/ *noun* salty white Greek cheese made from ewe's or goat's milk.

fetal *US* = FOETAL.

fetch *verb* **1** go for and bring back. **2** be sold for. **3** draw forth. **4** deal (blow). □ **fetch up** *colloquial* arrive, come to rest.

■ **1** bring, call (for), collect, get, obtain, retrieve, summon. **2** bring in, earn, go for, make, produce, raise, realize, sell for.

fetching *adjective* attractive. □ **fetchingly** *adverb*.
■ see ATTRACTIVE.

fête /feɪt/ *noun* outdoor fund-raising event. ● *verb* (**-ting**) honour or entertain lavishly.

fetid /'fetɪd/ *adjective* (also **foetid**) stinking.

fetish /'fetɪʃ/ *noun* **1** abnormal object of sexual desire. **2** object worshipped by primitive peoples. **3** object of obsessive concern. □ **fetishism** *noun*. **fetishist** *noun*. **fetishistic** /-'ʃɪs-/ *adjective*.

fetlock /'fetlɒk/ *noun* back of horse's leg where tuft of hair grows above hoof.

fetter /'fetə/ *noun* **1** shackle for ankles. **2** (in *plural*) captivity. **3** restraint. ● *verb* **1** put into fetters. **2** restrict.

fettle /'fet(ə)l/ *noun* condition, trim.

fetus *US* = FOETUS.

feud /fjuːd/ *noun* prolonged hostility, esp. between families, tribes, etc. ● *verb* conduct feud.

■ *noun* conflict, dispute, quarrel, vendetta.

feudal /'fjuːd(ə)l/ *adjective* **1** of, like, or according to feudal system. **2** reactionary. □ **feudal system** medieval system in which vassal held land in exchange for allegiance and service to landowner. □ **feudalism** *noun*. **feudalistic** /-'lɪs-/ *adjective*.

fever /'fiːvə/ *noun* **1** abnormally high body temperature. **2** disease characterized by this. **3** nervous agitation. ● *verb* (esp. as **fevered** *adjective*) affect with fever or excitement. □ **fever pitch** state of extreme excitement.

■ *noun* **1** delirium, feverishness, high temperature.

feverfew /'fiːvəfjuː/ *noun* aromatic plant, used formerly to reduce fever, now to treat migraine.

feverish *adjective* **1** having symptoms of fever. **2** excited, restless. □ **feverishly** *adverb*. **feverishness** *noun*.

■ **1** burning, febrile, fevered, flushed, hot, inflamed. **2** agitated, excited, frantic, frenetic, frenzied, hectic, hurried, impatient, passionate, restless.

few *adjective* not many. ● *noun* **1** (treated as *plural*) not many. **2** (**a few**) some but not many. □ **a good few** a considerable number (of). **few and far between** scarce. **quite a few** *colloquial* a fairly large number (of). **very few** a very small number (of).

■ *adjective* few and far between, hardly any, inadequate, infrequent, rare, scarce, sparse, sporadic, thin on the ground, uncommon.

fey /feɪ/ *adjective* strange, other-worldly; whimsical.

fez *noun* (*plural* **fezzes**) man's flat-topped conical red cap, worn by some Muslims.

ff *abbreviation Music* fortissimo.

ff. *abbreviation* following pages etc.

fiancé /fɪ'ɒnseɪ/ *noun* (*feminine* **fiancée** same pronunciation) person one is engaged to.

fiasco /fɪ'æskəʊ/ *noun* (*plural* **-s**) ludicrous or humiliating failure.

fiat /'faɪæt/ *noun* **1** authorization. **2** decree.

fib *noun* trivial lie. ● *verb* (**-bb-**) tell fib. □ **fibber** *noun*.

fibre /'faɪbə/ *noun* (*US* **fiber**) **1** thread or filament forming tissue or textile. **2** piece of threadlike glass. **3** substance formed of fibres. **4** moral character. **5** roughage. □ **fibreboard** board made of compressed wood etc. fibres. **fibreglass 1** fabric made from woven glass fibres. **2** plastic reinforced with glass fibres. **fibre optics** optics using glass fibres, usually to carry signals. □ **fibrous** *adjective*.

■ **1** filament, hair, strand, thread. **4** backbone, character, determination, spirit, tenacity, toughness.

fibril /ˈfaɪbrɪl/ *noun* small fibre.

fibroid /ˈfaɪbrɔɪd/ *adjective* of, like, or containing fibrous tissue or fibres. ● *noun* benign fibrous tumour, esp. in womb.

fibrosis /faɪˈbrəʊsɪs/ *noun* thickening and scarring of connective tissue.

fibrositis /faɪbrəˈsaɪtɪs/ *noun* rheumatic inflammation of fibrous tissue.

fibula /ˈfɪbjʊlə/ *noun* (*plural* **-lae** /-liː/ *or* **-s**) bone on outer side of lower leg.

fiche /fiːʃ/ *noun* microfiche.

fickle /ˈfɪk(ə)l/ *adjective* inconstant, changeable. □ **fickleness** *noun*.

■ capricious, changeable, changing, disloyal, erratic, faithless, flighty, inconsistent, inconstant, mercurial, *literary* mutable, treacherous, undependable, unfaithful, unpredictable, unreliable, unstable, unsteady, *colloquial* up and down, vacillating, variable, volatile.

fiction /ˈfɪkʃ(ə)n/ *noun* **1** non-factual literature, esp. novels. **2** invented idea, thing, etc. **3** generally accepted falsehood. □ **fictional** *adjective*.

■ **2, 3** concoction, deception, fabrication, fantasy, figment of the imagination, flight of fancy, invention, lie(s), storytelling, *colloquial* tall story. □ **fictional** fabulous, fanciful, imaginary, invented, legendary, made up, make-believe, mythical.

fictitious /fɪkˈtɪʃəs/ *adjective* **1** imaginary, unreal. **2** not genuine.

■ **1** apocryphal, fabricated, fictional, imaginary, imagined, invented, made up, unreal, untrue. **2** assumed, bogus, counterfeit, deceitful, fabricated, false, fraudulent, invented, made up, *colloquial* phoney, spurious.

fiddle /ˈfɪd(ə)l/ *noun* **1** *colloquial* violin. **2** *colloquial* cheat, fraud. **3** fiddly task. ● *verb* (**-ling**) **1** (often + *with*, *at*) play restlessly. **2** (often + *about*) move aimlessly. **3** (usually + *with*) tamper, tinker. **4** *slang* falsify, swindle. **5** *slang* get by cheating. **6** play fiddle. □ **fiddler** *noun*.

■ *verb* **1, 3** fidget, interfere, meddle, play about, tamper, tinker.

fiddling *adjective* **1** petty, trivial. **2** *colloquial* fiddly.
■ **1** see TRIVIAL 1.

fiddly *adjective* (**-ier**, **-iest**) *colloquial* awkward to do or use.

fidelity /fɪˈdelɪtɪ/ *noun* **1** faithfulness, loyalty. **2** accuracy. **3** precision in sound reproduction.

fidget /ˈfɪdʒɪt/ *verb* (**-t-**) **1** move restlessly. **2** be or make uneasy. ● *noun* **1** person who fidgets. **2** (**the fidgets**) restless state or mood. □ **fidgety** *adjective*.

■ *verb* **1** be restless, fiddle about, fuss, jiggle, move restlessly, shuffle, squirm, twitch, wriggle about. **2** see WORRY *verb* 1. □ **fidgety** agitated, impatient, *colloquial* jittery, jumpy, nervous, on edge, restive, restless, twitchy, uneasy.

fiduciary /fɪˈdjuːʃərɪ/ *adjective* **1** of a trust, trustee, etc. **2** held or given in trust. **3** (of currency) dependent on public confidence. ● *noun* (*plural* **-ies**) trustee.

fief /fiːf/ *noun* land held under feudal system.

field /fiːld/ *noun* **1** area of enclosed land, esp. for cultivation. **2** area rich in some natural product. **3** area of land for playing game. **4** competitors. **5** expanse of sea, snow, etc. **6** battlefield. **7** area of activity or study. **8** *Computing* part of record, representing item of data. ● *verb* **1** *Cricket etc.* act as fielder(s). **2** *Cricket etc.* stop and return (ball). **3** select (player, candidate, etc.). **4** deal with (questions etc.). □ **field day 1** exciting or successful time. **2** military exercise or review. **field events** athletic events other than races. **field glasses** outdoor binoculars. **Field Marshal** army officer of highest rank. **fieldmouse** small long-tailed rodent. **fieldsman** = FIELDER. **field sports** outdoor sports, esp. hunting, shooting, and fishing. **fieldwork** practical surveying, science, sociology, etc. conducted in natural environment. **fieldworker** person doing fieldwork.

■ *noun* **1** enclosure, meadow, paddock, pasture. **3** arena, ground, pitch, playing-field, recreation ground, stadium. **7** area, department, domain, province, sphere, subject, territory.

fielder *noun* *Cricket etc.* member (other than bowler) of fielding side.

fieldfare *noun* grey thrush.

fiend /fiːnd/ *noun* **1** evil spirit. **2** wicked or cruel person. **3** mischievous or annoying person. **4** *slang* devotee. **5** difficult or unpleasant thing. □ **fiendish** *adjective*. **fiendishly** *adverb*. **fiendishness** *noun*.

■ **1** demon, devil, evil spirit, goblin, hobgoblin, imp, Satan, spirit. **4** see FANATIC *noun*.

fierce *adjective* (**-r**, **-st**) **1** violently aggressive or frightening. **2** eager; intense. □ **fiercely** *adverb*. **fierceness** *noun*.

■ **1** aggressive, angry, barbaric, barbarous, bloodthirsty, bloody, brutal, cruel, dangerous, fearsome, ferocious, fiendish, fiery, homicidal, inhuman, merciless, murderous, pitiless, ruthless, *colloquial* sadistic, savage, untamed, vicious, violent, wild. **2** ardent, competitive, eager, fiery, furious, heated, intense, keen, passionate, relentless, strong, unrelenting.

fiery /ˈfaɪərɪ/ *adjective* (**-ier**, **-iest**) **1** consisting of or flaming with fire. **2** bright red. **3** burning hot. **4** spirited. □ **fieriness** *noun*.

■ **1** ablaze, aflame, blazing, burning, flaming. **2** aglow, flaming, glowing, incandescent, red. **3** burning, hot, red-hot. **4** angry, ardent, choleric, excitable, fervent, fierce, furious, heated, hot-headed, intense, irascible, irritable, *colloquial* livid, *colloquial* mad, passionate, touchy, violent.

fiesta /fɪˈestə/ *noun* festival, holiday.

FIFA /ˈfiːfə/ *abbreviation* International Football Federation (*Fédération Internationale de Football Association*).

fife /faɪf/ *noun* small shrill flute.

fifteen /fɪfˈtiːn/ *adjective & noun* **1** one more than fourteen. **2** *Rugby* team of fifteen players. □ **fifteenth** *adjective & noun*.

fifth *adjective & noun* **1** next after fourth. **2** any of 5 equal parts of thing. □ **fifth column** group working for enemy within country at war. **fifth columnist** *noun*.

fifty /ˈfɪftɪ/ *adjective & noun* (*plural* **-ies**) five times ten. □ **fifty-fifty** half and half; equal(ly). □ **fiftieth** *adjective & noun*.

fig *noun* **1** soft fruit with many seeds. **2** tree bearing it. □ **fig leaf** device concealing genitals.

fig. *abbreviation* figure.

fight /faɪt/ *verb* (*past & past participle* **fought** /fɔːt/) **1** (often + *against, with*) contend with in war, combat, etc. **2** engage in (battle etc.). **3** (+ *for*) strive to secure (something) or on behalf of (something or someone). **4** contest (election). **5** strive to overcome. **6** (as **fighting** *adjective*) able and eager or trained to fight. ● *noun* **1** combat; battle. **2** boxing match. **3** conflict; struggle. **4** power or inclination to fight. □ **fight back 1** counter-attack. **2** suppress (tears etc.). **fighting chance** chance of success if effort is made. **fighting fit** extremely fit. **fight off** repel with effort. **fight shy of** avoid. **put up a fight** offer resistance.

■ *verb* **1** battle, box, brawl, brush, clash, compete, conflict, contend, do battle, duel, engage, exchange blows, fence, feud, grapple, have a fight, *historical* joust, quarrel, *colloquial* row, *colloquial* scrap, scuffle, skirmish, spar, squabble, stand up (to), strive, struggle, tilt, tussle, wage war, wrestle. **3** campaign, strive, struggle, take a stand. **5** campaign against, contest, defy, oppose, protest against, resist, take a stand against. ● *noun* **1** affray, battle, brawl, brush, clash, combat, conflict, confrontation, contest, dogfight, duel, *colloquial* dust-up, encounter, engagement, feud, fisticuffs, fracas, fray, free-for-all, hostilities, *historical* joust, mêlée, *colloquial* punch-up, riot, scramble, *colloquial* scrap, scrimmage, scuffle, *colloquial* set-to, skirmish, struggle, tussle, war. **2** bout, boxing match, contest, fisticuffs, match. **3** see QUARREL *noun* 1.

fighter *noun* **1** person who fights. **2** aircraft designed for attacking other aircraft.

■ **1** aggressor, antagonist, attacker, belligerent, campaigner, combatant, contender, contestant, defender.

figment /ˈfɪgmənt/ *noun* imaginary thing.

figurative /ˈfɪgərətɪv/ *adjective* **1** metaphorical. **2** (of art) not abstract; representational. □ **figuratively** *adverb*.

figure /ˈfɪgə/ *noun* **1** external form; bodily shape. **2** person of specified kind. **3** representation of human form; image. **4** numerical symbol or number, esp. 0–9. **5** value, amount. **6** (in *plural*) arithmetical calculations. **7** diagram, illustration. **8** dance etc. movement or sequence. **9** (in full **figure of speech**) metaphor, hyperbole, etc. ● *verb* (**-ring**) **1** appear, be mentioned. **2** (usually as **figured** *adjective*) embellish with pattern. **3** calculate. **4** *esp. US colloquial* understand, consider. **5** *esp. US colloquial* make sense. □ **figurehead 1** nominal leader. **2** carved image etc. over ship's prow. **figure of fun** ridiculous person. **figure on** *esp. US colloquial* count on, expect. **figure out** work out by arithmetic or logic. **figure skating** skating in prescribed patterns.

■ *noun* **1** body, build, form, outline, physique, shape, silhouette. **2** see PERSON 1. **4** cipher, digit, integer, number, numeral, symbol. **5** amount, sum, value; (*figures*) see STATISTICS 2. **7** diagram, drawing, graph, illustration, picture, plate, representation. ● *verb* **1** see FEATURE *verb* 2. □ **figure out** see CALCULATE 1, UNDERSTAND 1.

figurine /fɪgəˈriːn/ *noun* statuette.

filament /ˈfɪləmənt/ *noun* **1** threadlike strand or fibre. **2** conducting wire in electric bulb.

filbert /ˈfɪlbət/ *noun* (nut of) cultivated hazel.

filch *verb* steal, pilfer.

file[1] *noun* **1** folder, box, etc. for holding loose papers. **2** paper kept in this. **3** collection of related computer data. **4** row of people or things one behind another. ● *verb* (**-ling**) **1** place in file or among records. **2** submit (petition for divorce etc.). **3** walk in line. □ **filing cabinet** cabinet with drawers for storing files.

■ *noun* **1** binder, case, document-case, dossier, folder, portfolio, ring-binder. **2** documentation, documents, dossier, papers. **4** column, line, procession, queue, rank, row, stream, string, train. ● *verb* **1** arrange, categorize, classify, enter, organize, pigeon-hole, put away, record, register, store, systematize. **3** march, parade, proceed in a line, stream, troop.

file[2] *noun* tool with rough surface for smoothing wood, fingernails, etc. ● *verb* (**-ling**) smooth or shape with file.

filial /ˈfɪlɪəl/ *adjective* of or due from son or daughter.

filibuster /ˈfɪlɪbʌstə/ *noun* **1** obstruction of progress in legislative assembly. **2** *esp. US* person who engages in this. ● *verb* act as filibuster.

filigree /ˈfɪlɪgriː/ *noun* **1** fine ornamental work in gold etc. wire. **2** similar delicate work.

filings *plural noun* particles rubbed off by file.

Filipino /fɪlɪˈpiːnəʊ/ *noun* (*plural* **-s**) native or national of Philippines. ● *adjective* of Philippines or Filipinos.

fill *verb* **1** (often + *with*) make or become full. **2** occupy completely. **3** spread over or through. **4** block up (hole, tooth, etc.). **5** appoint to or hold (office etc.). **6** satisfy, fulfil. **7** (as **filling** *adjective*) (of food) satisfying. ● *noun* enough to satisfy or fill. □ **fill in 1** complete (form etc.). **2** fill completely. **3** (often + *for*) act as substitute. **4** *colloquial* inform more fully. **fill out 1** enlarge or become enlarged, esp. to proper size. **2** fill in (form etc.). **fill up 1** fill completely. **2** fill petrol tank (of).

■ *verb* **1** be full of, fill in, fill up, inflate, load, pack, refill, replenish, stock up, stuff, top up. **2** cram, crowd, flood, jam, occupy, pack, stuff. **3** see PERVADE 1. **4** block, bung up, caulk, clog up, close up, jam, obstruct, plug, seal, stop up. **5** execute, hold, occupy, take over, take up. **6** answer, fulfil, furnish, meet, provide, satisfy, supply. □ **fill out 1** see SWELL *verb* 3.

filler *noun* material used to fill cavity or increase bulk.

fillet /ˈfɪlɪt/ *noun* **1** boneless piece of fish or meat. **2** (in full **fillet steak**) undercut of sirloin. **3** ribbon etc. binding hair. **4** narrow flat band between mouldings. ● *verb* (**-t-**) **1** remove bones from (fish etc.) or divide into fillets. **2** bind or provide with fillet(s).

filling *noun* material used to fill tooth, sandwich, pie, etc. □ **filling station** garage selling petrol etc.

■ contents, *colloquial* innards, padding, stuffing, wadding.

fillip /ˈfɪlɪp/ *noun* stimulus, incentive.

filly /ˈfɪlɪ/ *noun* (*plural* **-ies**) young female horse.

film *noun* **1** thin coating or layer. **2** strip or sheet of plastic etc. coated with light-sensitive emulsion for exposure in camera. **3** story etc. on film. **4** (in *plural*) cinema industry. **5** slight veil, haze, etc. ● *verb* **1** make photographic film of. **2** (often + *over*) cover or become covered (as) with film. □ **film star** well-known film actor or actress. □ **filmy** *adjective* (**-ier, -iest**).

■ *noun* **1** coat, coating, cover, covering, layer, membrane, overlay, screen, sheet, skin. **3** *colloquial* flick, *esp. US* motion picture, *esp. US colloquial* movie, picture, video, videotape. **5** haze, mist, veil.

filmsetting *noun* typesetting by projecting characters on to photographic film. □ **filmset** *verb*. **filmsetter** *noun*.

Filofax /ˈfaɪləʊfæks/ *noun* proprietary term personal organizer.

filo pastry /ˈfiːləʊ/ *noun* pastry in very thin sheets.

filter /ˈfɪltə/ *noun* **1** porous esp. paper device for removing impurities from liquid or gas or making coffee. **2** screen for absorbing or modifying light. **3** device for suppressing unwanted electrical or sound waves. **4** arrangement for filtering traffic. ● *verb* **1** pass through filter. **2** (usually as **filtered** *adjective*) make (coffee) by dripping hot water through ground beans. **3** (+ *through, into*, etc.) make way gradually through, into, etc. **4** (of traffic) be allowed to turn left or right at junction when other traffic is held up. □ **filter tip** (cigarette with) filter for removing some impurities.

■ *noun* **1** colander, gauze, membrane, mesh, riddle, screen, sieve, strainer. ● *verb* **1** clarify, filtrate, percolate, purify, refine, screen, sieve, sift, strain.

filth *noun* **1** disgusting dirt. **2** excrement. **3** obscenity.

■ **1** decay, dirt, effluent, *US* garbage, grime, *colloquial* gunge, impurity, *colloquial* muck, mud, ordure, pollution, putrescence, refuse, rubbish, scum, sewage, slime, sludge, *esp. US* trash. **2** see EXCRETA.

filthy *adjective* (**-ier, -iest**) **1** disgustingly dirty. **2** obscene. **3** (of weather) very unpleasant. ● *adverb colloquial* extremely. □ **filthy lucre 1** dishonourable gain. **2** money.

■ *adjective* **1** begrimed, caked, defiled, dirty, disgusting, dusty, foul, grimy, grubby, impure, messy, mucky, muddy, nasty, polluted, scummy, slimy, smelly, soiled, sooty, sordid, squalid, stinking, tainted, uncleaned, unkempt, unwashed, vile. **2** see OBSCENE 1.

filtrate /ˈfɪltreɪt/ *verb* (**-ting**) filter. ● *noun* filtered liquid. □ **filtration** *noun*.

fin *noun* **1** organ, esp. of fish, for propelling and steering. **2** similar projection for stabilizing aircraft etc.

finagle /fɪˈneɪɡ(ə)l/ *verb* (**-ling**) *colloquial* act or obtain dishonestly.

final /ˈfaɪn(ə)l/ *adjective* **1** at the end; coming last. **2** conclusive, decisive. ● *noun* **1** last or deciding heat or game. **2** last edition of day's newspaper. **3** (usually in *plural*) exams at end of degree course. □ **finality** /-ˈnæl-/ *noun*. **finally** *adverb*.

■ *adjective* **1** closing, concluding, dying, end, eventual, finishing, last, terminal, terminating, ultimate. **2** clinching, conclusive, decisive, settled.

finale /fɪˈnɑːlɪ/ *noun* last movement or section of drama, piece of music, etc.

finalist *noun* competitor in final.

finalize *verb* (also **-ise**) (**-zing** or **-sing**) **1** put in final form. **2** complete. □ **finalization** *noun*.

■ **2** clinch, complete, conclude, settle, *colloquial* wrap up.

finance /ˈfaɪnæns/ *noun* **1** management of money. **2** monetary support for enterprise. **3** (in *plural*) money resources. ● *verb* (**-cing**) provide capital for. □ **financial** /-ˈnæn-/ *adjective*. **financially** /-ˈnæn-/ *adverb*.

■ *noun* **1** accounting, banking, business, commerce, economics, investment, stocks and shares. **3** (*finances*) assets, budget, capital, cash, funds, holdings, income, money, resources, wealth, *colloquial* the wherewithal. ● *verb* back, fund, guarantee, invest in, pay for, provide money for, subsidize, support, underwrite. □ **financial** economic, fiscal, monetary, pecuniary.

financier /faˈnænsɪə/ *noun* capitalist; entrepreneur.

finch *noun* small seed-eating bird.

find /faɪnd/ *verb* (*past & past participle* **found**) **1** discover; get by chance or after search. **2** become aware of. **3** obtain; provide. **4** summon up. **5** perceive, experience. **6** (often in *passive*) discover to be present. **7** consider to be. **8** *Law* judge and declare. **9** reach. ● *noun* **1** discovery of treasure etc. **2** valued thing or person newly discovered. □ **all found** (of wages) with board and lodging provided free. **find out** (often + *about*) discover, detect. □ **finder** *noun*.

■ *verb* **1** acquire, arrive at, *colloquial* bump into, chance upon, come across, come upon, detect, diagnose, dig out, dig up, discover, encounter, espy, expose, ferret out, get back, happen on, hit on, identify, light on, locate, meet, recover, rediscover, regain, repossess, retrieve, reveal, *colloquial* spot, stumble on, trace, track down, uncover, unearth. **2** become aware of, detect, discover, learn, note, notice, recognize. **3** acquire, give, obtain, procure, provide, supply. **5** experience, note, notice, observe, perceive. **9** arrive at, reach.

finding *noun* (often in *plural*) conclusion reached by inquiry.

■ conclusion, decision, decree, judgement, pronouncement, verdict.

fine[1] *adjective* **1** of high quality; showing high level of skill. **2** excellent; good, satisfactory. **3** pure, refined. **4** imposing. **5** bright and clear. **6** small or thin; sharp. **7** delicate. **8** in small particles. **9** perceptible with difficulty. **10** smart, showy. **11** flattering. ● *adverb* **1** finely. **2** very well. □ **fine arts** poetry, music, painting, sculpture, architecture, etc. **fine-spun 1** delicate. **2** too subtle. **fine-tune** make small adjustments to. □ **finely** *adverb*. **fineness** *noun*.

■ *adjective* **1** choice, classic, first-class, high-quality, select, superior; (*fine workmanship*) consummate, meticulous, skilful, skilled. **2** see EXCELLENT, GOOD *adjective* 1;7. **5** bright, clear, cloudless, dry, fair, nice, pleasant, sunny. **6** acute, keen, narrow, sharp, slender, slim, thin. **7** dainty, delicate, exquisite, flimsy, fragile, silky. **8** powdery. **9** discriminating, hair-splitting, nice, precise, subtle.

fine[2] *noun* money paid as penalty. ● *verb* (**-ning**) punish by fine.

■ *noun* charge, forfeit, penalty.

finery /ˈfaɪnərɪ/ *noun* showy dress or decoration.

finesse /fɪˈnes/ *noun* **1** refinement. **2** subtlety. **3** artfulness. **4** *Cards* attempt to win trick with card that is not the highest held. ● *verb* (**-ssing**) **1** use or manage by finesse. **2** *Cards* make finesse.

finger /ˈfɪŋɡə/ *noun* **1** any of terminal projections of hand (usually excluding thumb). **2** part of glove for finger. **3** finger-like object. ● *verb* touch, turn about, or play with fingers. □ **finger-bowl** bowl for rinsing fingers during meal. **finger-dry** dry and style hair by running fingers through it. **fingernail** nail on each finger. **fingerprint** impression made on surface by fingers, used in detecting crime. **finger-stall** protective cover for injured finger. **fingertip** tip of finger.

fingering *noun* **1** manner of using fingers in music. **2** indication of this in score.

finial /ˈfɪnɪəl/ *noun* ornamental top to gable, canopy, etc.

finicky /ˈfɪnɪkɪ/ *adjective* (also **finical**, **finicking**) **1** over-particular, fastidious. **2** detailed; fiddly.

finis /ˈfɪnɪs/ *noun* end, esp. of book.

finish /ˈfɪnɪʃ/ *verb* **1** (often + *off*) bring or come to end or end of; complete. **2** (often + *off*) *colloquial* kill; overcome. **3** (often + *off*, *up*) complete consuming. **4** treat surface of. ● *noun* **1** last stage, completion. **2** end of race etc. **3** method etc. of surface treatment. □ **finish off** *colloquial* kill.

■ *verb* **1** accomplish, achieve, break off, bring to an end, *formal* cease, clinch, complete, conclude, discontinue, end, finalize, fulfil, halt, *colloquial* pack up, perfect, phase out, reach the end, round off, say goodbye, sign off, stop, take one's leave, terminate, wind up, *colloquial* wrap up. **3** consume, drink up, eat up, empty, exhaust, expend, get through, polish off, say goodbye to, use up. ● *noun* **1** cessation, close, completion, conclusion, culmination, end, ending, finale, resolution, result, termination. **3** appearance, gloss, lustre, patina, perfection, polish, shine, smoothness, surface, texture. □ **finish off** see KILL *verb* 1.

finite /ˈfaɪnaɪt/ *adjective* **1** limited, not infinite. **2** (of verb) having specific number and person.

■ **1** bounded, calculable, controlled, definable, defined, determinate, fixed, known, limited, measurable, numbered, rationed, restricted.

Finn *noun* native or national of Finland.

finnan /ˈfɪnən/ *noun* (in full **finnan haddock**) smoke-cured haddock.

Finnish *adjective* of Finland. ● *noun* language of Finland.

fiord /fjɔːd/ *noun* (also **fjord**) narrow inlet of sea as in Norway.

fir *noun* **1** evergreen conifer with needles growing singly on the stems. **2** its wood. □ **fir-cone** its fruit.

fire *noun* **1** state of combustion of substance with oxygen, giving out light and heat. **2** flame; glow. **3** destructive burning. **4** burning fuel in grate etc. **5** electric or gas heater. **6** firing of guns. **7** fervour, spirit. **8** burning heat. ● *verb* (**-ring**) **1** shoot (gun etc. or missile from it). **2** (often + *at*) shoot gun or missile. **3** produce (salute etc.) by shooting. **4** (of gun) be discharged. **5** detonate. **6** deliver or utter rapidly. **7** dismiss (employee). **8** set fire to. **9** supply with fuel. **10** stimulate, enthuse. **11** undergo ignition. **12** bake or make (pottery, bricks, etc.). □ **fire alarm** bell etc. warning of fire. **firearm** gun, esp. pistol or rifle. **fireball 1** large meteor. **2** ball of flame. **firebomb** incendiary bomb. **firebrand 1** piece of burning wood. **2** troublemaker. **firebreak** obstacle preventing spread of fire in forest etc. **firebrick** fireproof brick in grate. **fire brigade** group of firefighters. **firebug** *colloquial* pyromaniac. **firedog** support for logs in hearth. **fire door**

fire-resistant door. **fire drill** rehearsal of procedure in case of fire. **fire engine** vehicle carrying hoses, firefighters, etc. **fire escape** emergency staircase etc. for use in fire. **fire extinguisher** apparatus discharging water, foam, etc. to extinguish fire. **firefighter** person who extinguishes fires. **firefly** insect emitting phosphorescent light, e.g. glow-worm. **fire-irons** tongs, poker, and shovel for domestic fire. **fireman 1** male firefighter. **2** person who tends steam engine or steamship furnace. **fireplace** place in wall for domestic fire. **firepower** destructive capacity of guns etc. **fire practice** fire-drill. **fireproof** able to resist fire. **fire-raiser** arsonist. **fire screen 1** ornamental screen for fireplace. **2** screen against direct heat of fire. **fireside** area round fireplace. **fire station** headquarters of local fire brigade. **firestorm** intense fire into which strong air currents are drawn. **fire trap** building without fire escapes etc. **firework 1** device producing flashes, bangs, etc. from burning chemicals. **2** (in *plural*) outburst of anger etc. **on fire 1** burning. **2** excited. **under fire** being shot at or criticized.

■ *noun* **1** blaze, burning, combustion, flames. **3** blaze, bonfire, conflagration, holocaust, inferno, pyre. **7** see PASSION 1,4;3. ● *verb* **1,** 4 catapult, discharge, launch, let off, propel, set off, shoot, trigger off. **2** (*fire at*) see BOMBARD 1. **5** detonate, explode, let off, set off. **7** dismiss, make redundant, *colloquial* sack, throw out. **8** ignite, kindle, light, put a light to, set alight, set fire to, spark off. **10** animate, awaken, enliven, *colloquial* enthuse, excite, incite, inflame, inspire, motivate, rouse, stimulate, stir. □ **fireplace** grate, hearth. **fireproof** flameproof, incombustible, non-flammable. **fire-raiser** arsonist, *colloquial* firebug, pyromaniac.

firing *noun* discharge of guns. □ **firing line 1** front line in battle. **2** centre of criticism etc. **firing squad** soldiers ordered to shoot condemned person.

firm[1] *adjective* **1** solid. **2** fixed, steady. **3** resolute; steadfast. **4** (of offer etc.) definite. ● *adverb* steadily, resolutely. ● *verb* (often + *up*) make or become firm or secure. □ **firmly** *adverb*. **firmness** *noun*.

■ *adjective* **1** compact, compressed, congealed, dense, hard, inelastic, inflexible, rigid, set, solid, stiff, unyielding. **2** anchored, embedded, fast, fastened, fixed, immovable, secure, stable, steady, tight. **3** (*firm convictions*) adamant, decided, determined, dogged, obstinate, persistent, resolute, unshakeable, unwavering; (*firm friends*) constant, dependable, devoted, faithful, loyal, reliable, steadfast. **4** agreed, definite, settled, unchangeable.

firm[2] *noun* **1** business concern. **2** its members.

■ business, company, concern, corporation, establishment, organization, partnership.

firmament /ˈfɜːməmənt/ *noun literary* sky regarded as vault.

first *adjective* **1** foremost in time or order. **2** foremost in importance. ● *noun* **1** (**the first**) first person or thing. **2** beginning; first occurrence of something notable. **3** first-class degree. **4** first gear. **5** first place in race. ● *adverb* **1** before all or something else. **2** for the first time. □ **at first hand** directly from original source. **first aid** emergency medical treatment. **first class 1** best category or accommodation. **2** mail given priority. **3** highest division in exam. **first-class** *adjective & adverb* **1** of or by first class. **2** excellent(ly). **first floor** (*US* **second floor**) floor above ground floor. **first-footing** first crossing of threshold in New Year. **first-hand** direct, original. **first mate** (on merchant ship) second in command. **first name** personal or Christian name. **first night** first public performance of play etc. **first-rate** excellent. **first thing** before anything else; very early. □ **firstly** *adverb*.

■ *adjective* **1** (*first version*) archetypal, earliest, embryonic, oldest, original; (*first inhabitants*) aboriginal, earliest, eldest, oldest, original, primeval; (*first steps*) basic, elementary, fundamental, initial, introductory, preliminary, rudimentary. **2** cardinal, chief, dominant, foremost, head, highest, key, leading, main, outstanding, paramount, predominant, primary, prime, principal, top, uppermost. □ **first-class 2** see EXCELLENT. **first-rate** see EXCELLENT.

firth /fɜːθ/ *noun* **1** inlet. **2** estuary.

fiscal /ˈfɪsk(ə)l/ *adjective* of public revenue. ● *noun Scottish* procurator fiscal. □ **fiscal year** financial year.

fish[1] *noun* (*plural* same or **-es**) **1** vertebrate cold-blooded animal living in water. **2** its flesh as food. **3** person of specified kind. ● *verb* **1** try to catch fish (in). **2** (+ *for*) search for. **3** (+ *for*) seek indirectly. **4** (+ *up, out*) retrieve with effort. □ **fish cake** fried cake of fish and mashed potato. **fish-eye lens** wide-angled lens. **fish farm** place where fish are bred for food. **fish finger** small oblong piece of fish in breadcrumbs. **fish-hook** barbed hook for catching fish. **fish kettle** oval pan for boiling fish. **fish-knife** knife for eating or serving fish. **fishmeal** ground dried fish as fertilizer etc. **fishmonger** dealer in fish. **fishnet** open-meshed fabric. **fish slice** slotted cooking utensil. **fishwife 1** coarse or noisy woman. **2** woman selling fish.

■ *verb* **1** angle, go fishing, trawl.

fish[2] *noun* piece of wood or iron for strengthening mast etc. □ **fish-plate** flat plate of iron etc. holding rails together.

fisherman /ˈfɪʃəmən/ *noun* person who catches fish as occupation or sport.

fishery *noun* (*plural* **-ies**) **1** place where fish are caught or reared. **2** industry of fishing or breeding fish.

fishing *noun* occupation or sport of trying to catch fish. □ **fishing-rod** tapering rod for fishing.

fishy *adjective* (**-ier, -iest**) **1** of or like fish. **2** *slang* dubious, suspect.

fissile /ˈfɪsaɪl/ *adjective* **1** capable of undergoing nuclear fission. **2** tending to split.

fission /ˈfɪʃ(ə)n/ *noun* **1** splitting of atomic

nucleus. **2** division of cell as mode of reproduction. ● *verb* (cause to) undergo fission.

fissure /'fɪʃə/ *noun* narrow crack or split. ● *verb* (-ring) split.

fist *noun* clenched hand. □ **fisticuffs** fighting with the fists. □ **fistful** *noun* (*plural* **-s**).

fistula /'fɪstjʊlə/ *noun* (*plural* **-s** or **fistulae** /-liː/) abnormal or artificial passage in body. □ **fistular** *adjective*. **fistulous** *adjective*.

fit[1] *adjective* (**-tt-**) **1** well suited. **2** proper, right; becoming. **3** qualified, competent. **4** in good health or condition. **5** (+ *for*) good enough, right for. **6** ready. ● *verb* (**-tt-**) **1** be of right size and shape. **2** find room for. **3** (often + *in*, *into*) be correctly positioned. **4** adjust to right shape or size. **5** (+ *on*, *together*) fix in place. **6** (+ *with*) supply with. **7** befit. ● *noun* way thing fits. □ **fit in 1** (often + *with*) be compatible, accommodate. **2** make room or time for. **fit out, up** equip. **see (or think) fit** (often + *to*) decide or choose (specified course of action). □ **fitness** *noun*.

■ *adjective* **1** adapted, adequate, applicable, apposite, appropriate, apropos, apt, befitting, equipped, fitting, right, satisfactory, sound, suitable, suited. **2** appropriate, becoming, befitting, correct, decent, fitting, proper, right, seemly, timely. **3** able, capable, competent, equipped, prepared, qualified. **4** able-bodied, hale and hearty, healthy, in fine fettle, in good form, in good shape, perky, strong, sturdy, well. **5** (*fit for*) befitting, good enough for, right for, suitable for. **6** prepared, ready, set. ● *verb* **3** dovetail, interlock, join, match. **4** adapt, adjust, alter, modify, shape. **5** arrange, assemble, build, construct, dovetail, install, interlock, join, match, position, put in place, put together. **7** accord with, become, be fitting for, conform with, correspond to, correspond with, go with, harmonize with, suit. □ **fit out, up** see EQUIP.

fit[2] *noun* **1** sudden esp. epileptic seizure. **2** sudden brief bout or burst. □ **by or in fits and starts** spasmodically.

■ **1** attack, convulsion, paroxysm, seizure, spasm. **2** attack, bout, eruption, explosion, outbreak, outburst, paroxysm, *colloquial* spasm, spell.

fitful *adjective* spasmodic, intermittent. □ **fitfully** *adverb*.

fitment *noun* (usually in *plural*) fixed item of furniture.

fitted *adjective* **1** made to fit closely. **2** with built-in fittings. **3** built-in.

fitter *noun* **1** mechanic who fits together and adjusts machinery etc. **2** supervisor of cutting, fitting, etc. of garments.

fitting *noun* **1** action of fitting on a garment. **2** (usually in *plural*) fixture, fitment. ● *adjective* proper, befitting. □ **fittingly** *adverb*.

five *adjective & noun* one more than four. □ **five o'clock shadow** beard-growth visible in latter part of day. **five-star** of highest class. **fivestones** jacks played with five pieces of metal etc. and usually no ball.

fiver *noun colloquial* five-pound note.

fives *noun* game in which ball is struck with gloved hand or bat against walls of court.

fix *verb* **1** make firm, stable, or permanent; fasten, secure. **2** settle, specify. **3** mend, repair. **4** (+ *on, upon*) direct (eyes etc.) steadily on. **5** attract and hold (attention etc.). **6** identify, locate. **7** *US colloquial* prepare (food, drink). **8** *colloquial* kill; deal with (person). **9** *colloquial* arrange result fraudulently. ● *noun* **1** dilemma, predicament. **2** position determined by bearings etc. **3** *slang* dose of addictive drug. **4** *colloquial* fraudulently arranged result. □ **fix up 1** arrange. **2** (often + *with*) provide (person). □ **fixer** *noun*.

■ *verb* **1** attach, bind, connect, embed, fasten, implant, install, join, link, make firm, plant, position, secure, stabilize, stick. **2** agree, appoint, arrange, arrive at, conclude, confirm, decide, define, establish, finalize, name, ordain, set, settle, sort out, specify. **3** correct, make good, mend, put right, rectify, remedy, repair. ● *noun* **1** *colloquial* catch-22, corner, difficulty, dilemma, *colloquial* hole, *colloquial* jam, mess, *colloquial* pickle, plight, predicament, problem, quandary.

fixate /fɪk'seɪt/ *verb* (**-ting**) *Psychology* (usually in *passive*; often + *on, upon*) cause to become abnormally attached to person or thing.

fixation /fɪk'seɪʃ(ə)n/ *noun* **1** fixating, being fixated. **2** obsession.

fixative /'fɪksətɪv/ *adjective* tending to fix (colours etc.). ● *noun* fixative substance.

fixedly /'fɪksɪdlɪ/ *adverb* intently.

fixity *noun* **1** fixed state. **2** stability, permanence.

fixture /'fɪkstʃə/ *noun* **1** thing fixed in position. **2** (date fixed for) sporting event. **3** (in *plural*) articles belonging to land or house.

■ **2** date, engagement, event, game, match, meeting.

fizz *verb* **1** make hissing or spluttering sound. **2** effervesce. ● *noun* **1** fizzing sound. **2** effervescence. **3** *colloquial* effervescent drink. □ **fizzy** *adjective* (**-ier**, **-iest**).

■ *verb* **1** fizzle, hiss, sizzle, sputter. **2** bubble, effervesce, foam, froth, sparkle. □ **fizzy** bubbly, effervescent, foaming, sparkling.

fizzle /'fɪz(ə)l/ *verb* (**-ling**) hiss or splutter feebly. ● *noun* fizzling sound. □ **fizzle out** end feebly.

fjord = FIORD.

fl. *abbreviation* **1** fluid. **2** floruit.

flab *noun colloquial* fat, flabbiness.

flabbergast /'flæbəgɑːst/ *verb* (esp. as **flabbergasted** *adjective*) *colloquial* astonish; dumbfound.

flabby /'flæbɪ/ *adjective* (**-ier**, **-iest**) **1** (of flesh) limp, not firm. **2** feeble. □ **flabbiness** *noun*.

flaccid /'flæksɪd/ *adjective* flabby. □ **flaccidity** /-'sɪd-/ *noun*.

flag[1] *noun* piece of cloth attached by one edge to pole or rope as country's emblem, standard, or signal. ● *verb* (**-gg-**) **1** grow tired; lag. **2** droop. **3** mark out with flags. **4** signal with flag. □ **flag day** day when charity collects money and gives stickers to contributors. **flag down** signal to stop. **flag-officer** admiral or vice or rear admiral. **flagpole** flagstaff. **flagship 1** ship with admiral on board. **2** leading example of thing. **flagstaff** pole on which flag is hung. **flag-waving** ● *noun* populist agitation. ● *adjective* chauvinistic.

■ *noun* banner, bunting, colours, ensign, jack, pennant, pennon, standard, streamer. ● *verb* **1** see DECLINE *verb* 1. **4** see SIGNAL¹ *verb*.

flag² *noun* (also **flagstone**) flat paving stone. ● *verb* (**-gg-**) pave with flags.

flag³ *noun* plant with bladed leaf, esp. iris.

flagellant /ˈflædʒələnt/ *noun* person who flagellates himself, herself, or others. ● *adjective* of flagellation.

flagellate /ˈflædʒəleɪt/ *verb* (**-ting**) whip or flog, esp. as religious discipline or sexual stimulus. □ **flagellation** *noun*.

flageolet /flædʒəˈlet/ *noun* small flute blown at end.

flagon /ˈflægən/ *noun* quart bottle or other vessel for wine etc.

flagrant /ˈfleɪɡrənt/ *adjective* blatant; scandalous. □ **flagrancy** *noun*. **flagrantly** *adverb*.

flagrante see IN FLAGRANTE DELICTO.

flail *verb* **1** (often + *about*) wave or swing wildly. **2** beat (as) with flail. ● *noun* staff with heavy stick swinging from it, used for threshing.

flair *noun* **1** natural talent. **2** style, finesse.

flak *noun* **1** anti-aircraft fire. **2** criticism; abuse.

flake *noun* **1** thin light piece of snow etc. **2** thin broad piece peeled or split off. ● *verb* (**-king**) **1** (often + *away, off*) take or come away in flakes. **2** fall in or sprinkle with flakes. □ **flake out** fall asleep or drop from exhaustion; faint.

■ *noun* **2** bit, chip, scale, scurf, shaving, slice, sliver, splinter.

flaky *adjective* (**-ier, -iest**) of, like, or in flakes. □ **flaky pastry** lighter version of puff pastry.

flambé /ˈflɒmbeɪ/ *adjective* (of food) covered with alcohol and set alight briefly.

flamboyant /flæmˈbɔɪənt/ *adjective* **1** ostentatious, showy. **2** florid. □ **flamboyance** *noun*. **flamboyantly** *adverb*.

flame *noun* **1** ignited gas. **2** portion of this. **3** bright light. **4** brilliant orange colour. **5** passion, esp. love. **6** *colloquial* sweetheart. ● *verb* (**-ming**) **1** (often + *out, up*) burn, blaze. **2** (of passion) break out. **3** become angry. **4** shine or glow like flame. □ **flameproof** treated so as to be non-flammable.

■ *noun* **1, 2** blaze, light, tongue; (*flames*) see FIRE *noun* 1. ● *verb* **1** see FLARE *verb* 1.

flamenco /fləˈmeŋkəʊ/ *noun* (*plural* **-s**) Spanish Gypsy guitar music with singing and dancing.

flaming *adjective* **1** emitting flames. **2** very hot. **3** passionate. **4** brightly coloured. **5** *colloquial*: expressing annoyance.

flamingo /fləˈmɪŋɡəʊ/ *noun* (*plural* **-s** or **-es**) tall long-necked wading bird with usually pink plumage.

flammable /ˈflæməb(ə)l/ *adjective* inflammable.

USAGE *Flammable* is often used because *inflammable* could be taken to mean 'not flammable'. The negative of *flammable* is *non-flammable*.

flan *noun* **1** pastry case with savoury or sweet filling. **2** sponge base with sweet topping.

flange /flændʒ/ *noun* projecting flat rim, for strengthening etc.

flank *noun* **1** side of body between ribs and hip. **2** side of mountain, army, etc. ● *verb* (often as **flanked** *adjective*) be at or move along side of.

flannel /ˈflæn(ə)l/ *noun* **1** woven woollen usually napless fabric. **2** (in *plural*) flannel trousers. **3** face-cloth. **4** *slang* nonsense. **5** *slang* flattery. ● *verb* (**-ll-**; *US* **-l-**) **1** *slang* flatter. **2** wash with flannel.

flannelette /flænəˈlet/ *noun* napped cotton fabric like flannel.

flap *verb* (**-pp-**) **1** move or be moved loosely up and down; beat, flutter. **2** *colloquial* be agitated or panicky. **3** *colloquial* (of ears) listen intently. ● *noun* **1** piece of cloth, wood, etc. attached by one side, esp. to cover gap. **2** flapping. **3** *colloquial* agitation. **4** aileron. □ **flapjack 1** sweet oatcake. **2** *esp. US* small pancake.

■ *verb* **1** beat, flutter, oscillate, slap, sway, swing, thrash about, wag, *colloquial* waggle, wave about.

flapper *noun* **1** person apt to panic. **2** *slang* (in 1920s) young unconventional woman.

flare *verb* (**-ring**) **1** blaze with bright unsteady flame. **2** (usually as **flared** *adjective*) widen gradually. **3** burst out, esp. angrily. ● *noun* **1** bright unsteady flame. **2** outburst of this. **3** flame or bright light as signal etc. **4** gradual widening. **5** (in *plural*) wide-bottomed trousers. □ **flare-path** line of lights on runway to guide aircraft. **flare up** burst into blaze, anger, activity, etc. **flare-up** *noun* outburst.

■ *verb* **1** blaze, brighten, burn, flame, shine. **2** see WIDEN. **3** *colloquial* blow up, burst out, erupt, explode, flare up, *colloquial* fly off the handle, *colloquial* get steamed up, *colloquial* lose one's cool, rage, *colloquial* see red, seethe.

flash *verb* **1** (cause to) emit brief or sudden light; gleam. **2** send or reflect like sudden flame. **3** burst suddenly into view etc. **4** move swiftly. **5** send (news etc.) by radio etc. **6** signal (to) with vehicle lights. **7** show ostentatiously. **8** *slang* indecently expose oneself. ● *noun* **1** sudden bright light or flame. **2** an instant. **3** sudden brief feeling or display. **4** newsflash. **5** *Photography* flashlight. ● *adjective colloquial* gaudy; showy; vulgar. □ **flashback** scene set in earlier time than main action. **flash bulb** *Photography* bulb for flashlight. **flashgun** device operating camera flashlight. **flash in the pan** promising start followed by failure. **flash-lamp** portable flashing electric lamp. **flashlight 1** *Photography* light giving intense flash. **2** electric torch. **flashpoint 1** temperature at which vapour from oil etc. will ignite in air. **2** point at which anger is expressed.

■ *verb* **1** coruscate, dazzle, flicker, glare, gleam, glint, glitter, light up, reflect, scintillate, shine, spark, sparkle, twinkle.

flasher *noun* **1** *slang* man who indecently exposes himself. **2** automatic device for switching lights rapidly on and off.

flashing *noun* (usually metal) strip to prevent water penetration at roof joint etc.

flashy *adjective* (**-ier, -iest**) showy; cheaply attractive. □ **flashily** *adverb*. **flashiness** *noun*.

flask /flɑːsk/ *noun* **1** narrow-necked bulbous bottle. **2** hip-flask. **3** vacuum flask.

flat[1] *adjective* (**-tt-**) **1** horizontally level. **2** smooth, even. **3** level and shallow. **4** downright. **5** dull. **6** dejected. **7** having lost its effervescence. **8** (of battery) having exhausted its charge. **9** (of tyre etc.) deflated. **10** *Music* below correct or normal pitch. **11** *Music* having flats in key signature. ● *adverb* **1** spread out. **2** completely. **3** exactly. **4** flatly. ● *noun* **1** flat part. **2** level esp. marshy ground. **3** *Music* note lowered by semitone. **4** *Music* sign (♭) indicating this. **5** flat theatre scenery on frame. **6** punctured tyre. **7** (**the flat**) flat racing. **8** (**the flat**) its season. □ **flatfish** fish with flattened body, e.g. sole, plaice. **flat foot** foot with flattened arch. **flat-footed 1** having flat feet. **2** *colloquial* uninspired. **flat out 1** at top speed. **2** using all one's strength etc. **flat race** horse race over level ground without jumps. **flat rate** unvarying rate or charge. **flat spin 1** aircraft's nearly horizontal spin. **2** *colloquial* state of panic. **flatworm** worm with flattened body, e.g. fluke. □ **flatly** *adverb*. **flatness** *noun*. **flattish** *adjective*.

■ *adjective* **1** horizontal, level, outstretched, plane, prone, prostrate, recumbent, spreadeagled, spread out, supine. **2** calm, even, level, smooth, unbroken, unruffled. **5** bland, boring, dead, dry, dull, featureless, insipid, lacklustre, lifeless, monotonous, spiritless, stale, tedious, tired, unexciting, uninteresting, unmodulated, unvarying. **9** blown out, burst, deflated, punctured.

flat[2] *noun* set of rooms, usually on one floor, as residence. □ **flatmate** person sharing flat. □ **flatlet** *noun*.

■ apartment, bedsitter, flatlet, maisonette, penthouse, rooms, suite.

flatten *verb* **1** make or become flat. **2** *colloquial* humiliate; defeat. **3** *colloquial* knock down.

■ **1** compress, even out, iron, level out, press, roll, smooth, straighten. **2** see DEFEAT *verb* 1. **3** crush, demolish, destroy, devastate, fell, floor, knock down, level, prostrate, raze, run over, squash, trample.

flatter /ˈflætə/ *verb* **1** compliment unduly. **2** enhance appearance of. **3** (usually **flatter oneself**; usually + *that*) congratulate or delude (oneself etc.). □ **flatterer** *noun*. **flattering** *adjective*. **flatteringly** *adverb*. **flattery** *noun*.

■ **1** be flattering to, *colloquial* butter up, compliment, court, curry favour with, fawn on, humour, play up to, praise, *colloquial* suck up to, toady to. □ **flatterer** *colloquial* crawler, *slang* creep, groveller, lackey, sycophant, time-server, toady, *colloquial* yes-man. **flattering** see COMPLIMENTARY 1, OBSEQUIOUS. **flattery** adulation, blandishments, blarney, cajolery, fawning, *slang* flannel, insincerity, obsequiousness, servility, *colloquial* soft soap, sycophancy, unctuousness.

flatulent /ˈflætjʊlənt/ *adjective* **1** causing, caused by, or troubled with, intestinal wind. **2** inflated, pretentious. □ **flatulence** *noun*.

flaunt /flɔːnt/ *verb* display proudly; show off, parade.

USAGE *Flaunt* is often confused with *flout*, which means 'to disobey contemptuously'.

flautist /ˈflɔːtɪst/ *noun* flute-player.

flavour /ˈfleɪvə/ (*US* **flavor**) *noun* **1** mixed sensation of smell and taste; distinctive taste. **2** characteristic quality. ● *verb* give flavour to; season. □ **flavour of the month** temporary trend or fashion. □ **flavourless** *adjective*. **flavoursome** *adjective*.

■ *noun* **1** savour, taste. **2** air, ambience, atmosphere, aura, character, characteristic, feel, feeling, property, quality, spirit, stamp, style. ● *verb* season, spice.

flavouring *noun* (*US* **flavoring**) substance used to flavour food or drink.

■ additive, essence, extract, seasoning.

flaw *noun* **1** imperfection; blemish. **2** crack. **3** invalidating defect. ● *verb* damage; spoil. □ **flawed** *adjective*. **flawless** *adjective*. **flawlessness** *noun*.

■ *noun* **1** blemish, defect, deformity, disfigurement, error, fault, imperfection, inaccuracy, mistake, shortcoming, slip, weakness. **2** break, crack, split. **3** fallacy, loophole, mistake, weakness. □ **flawed** see IMPERFECT *adjective* 1. **flawless** accurate, clean, faultless, immaculate, in mint condition, perfect, pristine, sound, spotless, undamaged, unmarked.

flax *noun* blue-flowered plant grown for its oily seeds (linseed) and for making into linen.

flaxen *adjective* **1** of flax. **2** (of hair) pale yellow.

flay *verb* **1** strip skin or hide off. **2** criticize severely. **3** peel off.

flea *noun* small wingless jumping parasitic insect. □ **flea market** street market selling second-hand goods etc.

fleck *noun* **1** small patch of colour or light. **2** speck. ● *verb* mark with flecks.

flection *US* = FLEXION.

fled *past & past participle* of FLEE.

fledgling /ˈfledʒlɪŋ/ (also **fledgeling**) *noun* young bird. ● *adjective* new, inexperienced.

flee *verb* (**flees**; *past & past participle* **fled**) **1** run away (from). **2** leave hurriedly.

■ abscond, beat a retreat, *slang* beat it, bolt, *colloquial* clear off, *colloquial* cut and run, decamp, disappear, escape, fly, get away, hurry off, make off, retreat, run, run away, *slang* scarper, take flight, take to one's heels, vanish, withdraw.

fleece *noun* **1** woolly coat of sheep etc. **2** this shorn from sheep. **3** fleecy lining etc. ● *verb* **(-cing)** (often + *of*) **1** strip of money etc.; swindle. **2** shear. **3** (as **fleeced** *adjective*) cover as with fleece. □ **fleecy** *adjective* **(-ier, -iest)**.

fleet[1] *noun* **1** warships under one commander-in-chief. **2 (the fleet)** navy. **3** vehicles in one company etc.

■ **1, 2** armada, convoy, flotilla, navy, squadron, task force.

fleet[2] *adjective poetical* or *literary* nimble, swift. □ **fleet-footed** nimble; fast on one's feet. □ **fleetness** *noun*.

fleeting *adjective* transitory; brief. □ **fleetingly** *adverb*.

■ brief, ephemeral, *literary* evanescent, fugitive, impermanent, momentary, *literary* mutable, passing, short, short-lived, temporary, transient, transitory.

Fleming /ˈflemɪŋ/ *noun* **1** native of medieval Flanders. **2** member of Flemish-speaking people of N. and W. Belgium.

Flemish /ˈflemɪʃ/ *adjective* of Flanders. ● *noun* language of the Flemings.

flesh *noun* **1** soft substance between skin and bones. **2** plumpness, fat. **3** body, esp. as sinful. **4** pulpy substance of fruit etc. **5** (also **flesh colour**) yellowish pink colour. □ **flesh and blood 1** human body. **2** human nature, esp. as fallible. **3** humankind. **4** near relations. **flesh out** make or become substantial. **fleshpots** luxurious living. **flesh wound** superficial wound. **in the flesh** in person. □ **fleshy** *adjective* **(-ier, -iest)**.

■ **1** carrion, fat, meat, muscle, tissue.

fleshly /ˈfleʃlɪ/ *adjective* **1** worldly. **2** carnal.

fleur-de-lis /flɜːdəˈliː/ *noun* (also **fleur-de-lys**) (*plural* **fleurs-** same pronunciation) **1** iris flower. **2** *Heraldry* lily of 3 petals. **3** former royal arms of France.

flew *past* of FLY[1].

flews *plural noun* hanging lips of bloodhound etc.

flex[1] *verb* **1** bend (joint, limb). **2** move (muscle) to bend joint.

■ **1** see BEND *verb* 1,2.

flex[2] *noun* flexible insulated cable.

■ cable, cord, extension, lead, wire.

flexible /ˈfleksɪb(ə)l/ *adjective* **1** able to bend without breaking; pliable. **2** variable; adaptable. □ **flexibility** *noun*. **flexibly** *adverb*.

■ **1** bendable, *colloquial* bendy, elastic, floppy, limp, lithe, plastic, pliable, pliant, rubbery, soft, springy, stretchy, supple, willowy, yielding. **2** (*flexible arrangement*) adjustable, alterable, fluid, *literary* mutable, open, provisional, variable; (*flexible person*) accommodating, adaptable,

amenable, compliant, conformable, cooperative, docile, easygoing, malleable, open-minded, responsive, tractable, willing.

flexion /ˈflekʃ(ə)n/ *noun* (*US* **flection**) **1** bending. **2** bent part.

flexitime /ˈfleksɪtaɪm/ *noun* system of flexible working hours.

flibbertigibbet /ˈflɪbətɪˈdʒɪbɪt/ *noun* gossiping, frivolous, or restless person.

flick *noun* **1** light sharp blow. **2** sudden release of bent finger etc. to propel thing. **3** jerk. **4** *colloquial* cinema film. **5 (the flicks)** *colloquial* the cinema. ● *verb* (often + *away*, *off*) strike or move with flick. □ **flick-knife** knife with blade that springs out. **flick through** glance at or through by turning over (pages etc.) rapidly.

flicker /ˈflɪkə/ *verb* **1** shine or burn unsteadily. **2** flutter. **3** waver. ● *noun* **1** flickering light or motion. **2** brief feeling (of hope etc.); slightest reaction or degree. □ **flicker out** die away.

■ *verb* **1** blink, glimmer, shimmer, sparkle, twinkle, waver. **2** flap, flutter, quiver, shake, tremble, vibrate. **3** see WAVER.

flier = FLYER.

flight[1] /flaɪt/ *noun* **1** act or manner of flying; movement, passage, or journey through air or space. **2** timetabled airline journey. **3** flock of birds etc. **4** (usually + *of*) series of stairs etc. **5** imaginative excursion. **6** volley. **7** tail of dart. □ **flight bag** small zipped shoulder bag for air travel. **flight deck 1** cockpit of large aircraft. **2** deck of aircraft carrier. **flight lieutenant** RAF officer next below squadron leader. **flight path** planned course of aircraft etc. **flight recorder** device in aircraft recording technical details of flight. **flight sergeant** RAF rank next above sergeant.

■ **1** journey, trajectory.

flight[2] /flaɪt/ *noun* fleeing; hasty retreat.

■ see ESCAPE *noun* 1.

flightless *adjective* (of bird etc.) unable to fly.

flighty *adjective* **(-ier, -iest)** frivolous, fickle.

flimsy /ˈflɪmzɪ/ *adjective* **(-ier, -iest) 1** insubstantial, rickety. **2** unconvincing. **3** (of clothing) thin. □ **flimsily** *adverb*. **flimsiness** *noun*.

■ **1** breakable, brittle, decrepit, delicate, dilapidated, fragile, frail, gimcrack, insubstantial, jerry-built, loose, makeshift, rickety, shaky, slight, tottering, weak, wobbly. **2** feeble, implausible, inadequate, superficial, trivial, unbelievable, unconvincing, unsatisfactory. **3** delicate, fine, insubstantial, light, sheer, thin.

flinch *verb* **1** draw back in fear etc.; wince. **2** (often + *from*) shrink.

■ **1** blench, cower, cringe, draw back, falter, jerk away, jump, quail, recoil, shrink back, shy away, start, wince. **2** (*flinch from*) see EVADE 1,2.

fling *verb* (*past & past participle* **flung**) **1** throw, hurl. **2** rush, esp. angrily. **3** (+ *away*) discard rashly. ● *noun* **1** flinging; throw. **2** bout of wild behaviour. **3** whirling Scottish dance.

■ *verb* **1** bowl, *slang* bung, cast, *colloquial* chuck, *colloquial* heave, hurl, launch, lob, pelt, pitch, propel, send, shy, *colloquial* sling, throw, toss. **3** (*fling away*) *colloquial* chuck away, throw away, toss away.

flint *noun* **1** hard grey stone. **2** piece of this, esp. as tool or weapon. **3** piece of hard alloy used to produce spark. □ **flintlock** old type of gun fired by spark from flint. □ **flinty** *adjective* (**-ier, -iest**).

flip *verb* (**-pp-**) **1** toss (coin etc.) so that it spins in air. **2** turn or flick (small object) over. **3** *slang* become suddenly angry or excited; go mad. ● *noun* act of flipping. ● *adjective* glib; flippant. □ **flip chart** large pad of paper on stand. **flip-flop** sandal with thong between toes. **flip one's lid** *slang* lose self-control. **2** go mad. **flip side** reverse side of gramophone record etc. **flip through** flick through.

flippant /ˈflɪpənt/ *adjective* frivolous; disrespectful. **flippancy** *noun*. **flippantly** *adverb*.

■ cheeky, disrespectful, facetious, facile, flip, frivolous, light-hearted, shallow, superficial, thoughtless, unserious.

flipper *noun* **1** limb of turtle, penguin, etc., used in swimming. **2** rubber attachment to foot for underwater swimming.

flirt *verb* **1** (usually + *with*) behave in sexually enticing manner but without serious intent. **2** (usually + *with*) superficially interest oneself (with idea, etc.); trifle. ● *noun* person who flirts. □ **flirtation** *noun*. **flirtatious** *adjective*. **flirtatiously** *adverb*. **flirtatiousness** *noun*. **flirty** *adjective*.

■ *verb* **1** (*flirt with*) *colloquial* chat up, lead on, *archaic* make love to, philander with, toy with affections of. ● *noun female* coquette, *male* philanderer, tease. □ **flirtatious** amorous, coquettish, flirty, philandering, playful, promiscuous, teasing.

flit *verb* (**-tt-**) **1** pass lightly or rapidly. **2** make short flights. **3** disappear secretly, esp. to escape creditors. ● *noun* act of flitting.

flitch *noun* side of bacon.

flitter *verb* flit about.

float *verb* **1** (cause to) rest or drift on surface of liquid. **2** move or be suspended freely in liquid or gas. **3** launch (company, scheme). **4** offer (stocks, shares, etc.) on stock market. **5** (cause or allow to) have fluctuating exchange rate. **6** circulate or cause (rumour, idea) to circulate. ● *noun* **1** device or structure that floats. **2** electrically powered vehicle or cart. **3** decorated platform or tableau on lorry in procession etc. **4** supply of loose change; petty cash.

■ *verb* **1** bob, drift, glide, sail, swim; (*float a ship*) launch. **2** be poised, be suspended, drift, glide, hang, hover, waft.

floating *adjective* not settled; variable; not committed. □ **floating rib** lower rib not attached to breastbone.

floaty *adjective* (**-ier, -iest**) (of fabric) light and airy.

flocculent /ˈflɒkjʊlənt/ *adjective* like tufts of wool.

flock[1] *noun* **1** animals, esp. birds or sheep, as group or unit. **2** large crowd of people. **3** people in care of priest, teacher, etc. ● *verb* (often + *to, in, out, together*) congregate; mass; troop.

■ *noun* **1** see GROUP *noun* 1. **2** assembly, congregation, crowd, drove, gathering, *derogatory* herd, *usually derogatory* horde, multitude, swarm. ● *verb* see GATHER *verb* 1.

flock[2] *noun* **1** shredded wool, cotton, etc. used as stuffing. **2** powdered wool used to make pattern on wallpaper.

floe *noun* sheet of floating ice.

flog *verb* (**-gg-**) **1** beat with whip, stick, etc. **2** (often + *off*) *slang* sell.

■ **1** beat, birch, cane, chastise, flagellate, flay, hit, lash, scourge, thrash, whip.

flood /flʌd/ *noun* **1** overflowing or influx of water, esp. over land. **2** (**the Flood**) the flood described in Genesis. **3** outpouring of water. **4** outburst or outpouring (of tears, questions, etc.). **5** abundance, excess. **6** inflow of tide. ● *verb* **1** overflow; cover or be covered with flood. **2** irrigate. **3** deluge. **4** come in great quantities. **5** overfill (carburettor) with petrol. □ **floodgate 1** gate for admitting or excluding water. **2** (usually in *plural*) last restraint against tears, anger, etc. **floodlight** (illuminate with) large powerful light. **floodlit** lit thus.

■ *noun* **1** deluge, inundation, overflow, spate. **3** cataract, deluge, downpour, outburst, outpouring, rush, spate, stream, surge, tidal wave, tide, torrent. **5** abundance, excess, glut, plethora, superfluity, surfeit. ● *verb* **1, 3** cover, deluge, drown, engulf, fill up, immerse, inundate, overflow, overwhelm, saturate, sink, submerge, swamp.

floor /flɔː/ *noun* **1** lower surface of room. **2** bottom of sea, cave, etc. **3** storey. **4** part of legislative chamber where members sit and speak. **5** right to speak in debate. **6** minimum of prices, wages, etc. ● *verb* **1** provide with floor. **2** knock down. **3** baffle. **4** overcome. □ **floor manager** stage manager of television production. **floor plan** diagram of rooms etc. on one storey. **floor show** cabaret.

■ *noun* **1** floorboards, flooring. **3** deck, level, storey, tier.

flooring /ˈflɔːrɪŋ/ *noun* material of which floor is made.

flop *verb* (**-pp-**) **1** sway about heavily or loosely. **2** (often + *down, on, into*) move, fall, sit, etc. awkwardly or suddenly. **3** *slang* collapse, fail. **4** make dull soft thud or splash. ● *noun* **1** flopping motion or sound. **2** *slang* failure. ● *adverb* with a flop.

■ *verb* **1** dangle, droop, drop, flap about, hang down, sag, sway. **2** *colloquial* collapse, drop, fall, flag, slump, topple, tumble, wilt. **3** see FAIL *verb* 1, 2.

floppy *adjective* (**-ier, -iest**) tending to flop; flaccid. ● *noun* (*plural* **-ies**) (in full **floppy disk**) flexible disc for storage of computer data.

■ *adjective* dangling, droopy, flabby, flaccid, flexible, hanging, limp, loose, pliable, soft.

flora /'flɔːrə/ *noun* (*plural* **-s** or **-rae** /-riː/) plant life of region or period.

floral *adjective* of or decorated with flowers.

floret /'flɒrɪt/ *noun* **1** each of small flowers of composite flower head. **2** each stem of head of cauliflower, broccoli, etc.

florid /'flɒrɪd/ *adjective* **1** ruddy. **2** ornate; showy.

florin /'flɒrɪn/ *noun historical* gold or silver coin, esp. British two-shilling coin.

florist /'flɒrɪst/ *noun* person who deals in or grows flowers.

floruit /'flɒrʊɪt/ *verb* (of painter, writer, etc.) lived and worked.

floss *noun* **1** rough silk of silkworm's cocoon. **2** dental floss. ● *verb* clean (teeth) with dental floss. □ **flossy** *adjective* (**-ier**, **-iest**).

flotation /fləʊ'teɪʃ(ə)n/ *noun* launching of commercial enterprise etc.

flotilla /flə'tɪlə/ *noun* **1** small fleet. **2** fleet of small ships.

flotsam /'flɒtsəm/ *noun* floating wreckage. □ **flotsam and jetsam 1** odds and ends. **2** vagrants.

flounce[1] /flaʊns/ *verb* (**-cing**) (often + *off*, *out*, etc.) go or move angrily or impatiently. ● *noun* flouncing movement.

flounce[2] /flaʊns/ *noun* frill on dress, skirt, etc. ● *verb* (**-cing**) (usually as **flounced** *adjective*) trim with flounces.

flounder[1] /'flaʊndə/ *verb* **1** struggle helplessly. **2** do task clumsily; become confused.

■ **1** blunder, flail, fumble, grope, move clumsily, plunge about, stagger, struggle, stumble, tumble. **2** blunder, falter, get confused, make mistakes.

flounder[2] /'flaʊndə/ *noun* (*plural* same) small flatfish.

flour /flaʊə/ *noun* meal or powder from ground wheat etc. ● *verb* sprinkle with flour. □ **floury** *adjective* (**-ier**, **-iest**).

flourish /'flʌrɪʃ/ *verb* **1** grow vigorously. **2** thrive, prosper. **3** wave, brandish. ● *noun* **1** showy gesture. **2** ornamental curve in writing. **3** *Music* ornate passage. **4** *Music* fanfare.

■ *verb* **1** bloom, blossom, burgeon, develop, do well, flower, grow, increase, strengthen, thrive. **2** be fruitful, be successful, boom, burgeon, do well, perk up, progress, prosper, succeed, thrive. **3** brandish, flaunt, gesture with, shake, swing, twirl, wag, wave, wield. ● *noun* **1** see GESTURE *noun*.

flout *verb* disobey (law etc.) contemptuously.

USAGE *Flout* is often confused with *flaunt*, which means 'to display proudly or show off'.

flow /fləʊ/ *verb* **1** glide along; move smoothly. **2** gush out; spring. **3** circulate. **4** be plentiful or in flood. **5** (often + *from*) result. ● *noun* **1** flowing movement or liquid; stream. **2** rise of tide. □ **flow chart, diagram, sheet** diagram of movement or action in complex activity.

■ *verb* **1** course, dribble, drift, ebb, glide, move in a stream, purl, ripple, roll, run, stream, trickle. **2** cascade, drip, flood, flush, gush, issue, leak, ooze, overflow, pour, seep, spill, spring, spurt, squirt, stream, swirl, well, well up. ● *noun* **1** cascade, course, current, drift, ebb, effusion, flood, gush, outpouring, spate, spurt, stream, tide, trickle.

flower /'flaʊə/ *noun* **1** part of plant from which seed or fruit develops. **2** plant bearing blossom. **3** (usually in *plural*) cut stem bearing blossom. ● *verb* **1** bloom. **2** reach peak. □ **flower bed** garden bed for flowers. **the flower of** the best of. **flowerpot** pot for growing plant in. **in flower** blooming. □ **flowered** *adjective*.

■ *noun* **1** bloom, blossom, bud, floret, petal. **3** (*flowers*) arrangement, bouquet, bunch of flowers, corsage, garland, posy, spray, wreath. ● *verb* **1** bloom, blossom, bud, burgeon, come out, have flowers, open out, unfold. **2** see FLOURISH *verb* 1.

flowery *adjective* **1** florally decorated. **2** (of speech etc.) high-flown. **3** full of flowers.

flowing *adjective* **1** fluent. **2** smoothly continuous. **3** (of hair etc.) unconfined.

flown *past participle* of FLY[1].

flu *noun colloquial* influenza.

fluctuate /'flʌktʃʊeɪt/ *verb* (**-ting**) vary, rise and fall. □ **fluctuation** *noun*.

■ alternate, be unsteady, change, go up and down, oscillate, see-saw, shift, swing, vacillate, vary, waver.

flue *noun* **1** smoke duct in chimney. **2** channel for conveying heat.

fluent /'fluːənt/ *adjective* **1** expressing oneself easily and naturally, esp. in foreign language. **2** flowing easily. □ **fluency** *noun*. **fluently** *adverb*.

■ **1** articulate, eloquent, expressive, glib, natural, unhesitating, voluble. **2** effortless, facile, flowing, glib, polished, ready, smooth.

fluff *noun* **1** soft fur, feathers, fabric particles, etc. **2** *slang* mistake in performance etc. ● *verb* **1** (often + *up*) shake into or become soft mass. **2** *slang* make mistake in performance etc. □ **fluffy** *adjective* (**-ier**, **-iest**).

■ *noun* **1** down, dust, feathers, fuzz, thistledown. □ **fluffy** downy, feathery, fleecy, furry, fuzzy, hairy, light, silky, soft, velvety, wispy, woolly.

flugelhorn /'fluːg(ə)lhɔːn/ *noun* brass instrument like cornet.

fluid /'fluːɪd/ *noun* **1** substance, esp. gas or liquid, capable of flowing freely. **2** liquid secretion. ● *adjective* **1** able to flow freely. **2** constantly changing. □ **fluid ounce** twentieth or *US* sixteenth of pint (0.028 litre, *US* 0.03 litre). □ **fluidity** /-'ɪdɪtɪ/ *noun*.

■ *noun* **1** gas, liquid, liquor, vapour. ● *adjective* **1** aqueous, flowing, gaseous, liquefied, liquid, melted, molten, running, runny, sloppy, watery. **2** adjustable, alterable, changing, flexible, *literary* mutable, open, undefined, variable.

fluke[1] /fluːk/ *noun* lucky accident. □ **fluky** *adjective* (**-ier, -iest**).

■ accident, chance, serendipity, stroke of good luck, twist of fate.

fluke[2] /fluːk/ *noun* parasitic flatworm.

flummery /ˈflʌmərɪ/ *noun* (*plural* **-ies**) **1** nonsense; flattery. **2** sweet milk dish.

flummox /ˈflʌməks/ *verb colloquial* bewilder.

flung *past & past participle* of FLING.

flunk *verb US colloquial* fail (esp. exam).

flunkey /ˈflʌŋkɪ/ *noun* (also **flunky**) (*plural* **-eys** or **-ies**) *usually derogatory* footman.

fluorescence /fluəˈres(ə)ns/ *noun* **1** light radiation from certain substances. **2** property of absorbing invisible light and emitting visible light. □ **fluoresce** *verb* (**-scing**). **fluorescent** *adjective*.

fluoridate /ˈfluərɪdeɪt/ *verb* (**-ting**) add fluoride to (water). □ **fluoridation** *noun*.

fluoride /ˈfluəraɪd/ *noun* compound of fluorine with metal, esp. used to prevent tooth decay.

fluorinate /ˈfluərɪneɪt/ *verb* (**-ting**) **1** fluoridate. **2** introduce fluorine into (compound). □ **fluorination** *noun*.

fluorine /ˈfluəriːn/ *noun* poisonous pale yellow gaseous element.

flurry /ˈflʌrɪ/ *noun* (*plural* **-ies**) **1** gust, squall. **2** burst of activity, excitement, etc. ● *verb* (**-ies, -ied**) agitate, confuse.

flush[1] *verb* **1** (often as **flushed** *adjective*) (+ *with*) (cause to) glow or blush (with pride etc.). **2** cleanse (drain, lavatory, etc.) by flow of water. **3** (often + *away, down*) dispose of thus. ● *noun* **1** glow, blush. **2** rush of water. **3** cleansing (of lavatory etc.) thus. **4** rush of esp. elation or triumph. **5** freshness, vigour. **6** (also **hot flush**) sudden hot feeling during menopause. **7** feverish redness or temperature etc. ● *adjective* **1** level; in same plane. **2** *colloquial* having plenty of money.

■ *verb* **1** blush, colour, glow, go red, redden. **2, 3** clean out, cleanse, flood, rinse out, wash out.

flush[2] *noun* hand of cards all of one suit.

flush[3] *verb* (cause to) fly up suddenly. □ **flush out 1** reveal. **2** drive out.

■ chase out, drive out, expel, send up.

fluster /ˈflʌstə/ *verb* confuse, make nervous. ● *noun* confused or agitated state.

■ *verb* agitate, bewilder, bother, confuse, distract, flurry, perplex, put off, put out, *colloquial* rattle, *colloquial* throw, upset.

flute /fluːt/ *noun* **1** high-pitched woodwind instrument held sideways. **2** vertical groove in pillar etc. ● *verb* (**-ting**) **1** (often as **fluted** *adjective*) make grooves in. **2** play on flute. □ **fluting** *noun*.

flutter /ˈflʌtə/ *verb* **1** flap (wings) in flying or trying to fly. **2** fall quiveringly. **3** wave or flap quickly. **4** move about restlessly. **5** (of pulse etc.) beat feebly or irregularly. ● *noun* **1** fluttering. **2** tremulous excitement. **3** *slang* small bet on horse

etc. **4** abnormally rapid heartbeat. **5** rapid variation of pitch, esp. of recorded sound.

■ *verb* **3** bat (*eyelid*), flap, flicker, oscillate, shake, vibrate, wave. **4** flit, move agitatedly, oscillate, shake, tremble, twitch, vacillate. **5** fluctuate, palpitate, quiver, tremble.

fluvial /ˈfluːvɪəl/ *adjective* of or found in rivers.

flux *noun* **1** flowing, flowing out. **2** discharge. **3** continuous change. **4** substance mixed with metal etc. to assist fusion.

fly[1] /flaɪ/ *verb* (**flies**; *past* **flew** /fluː/; *past participle* **flown** /fləʊn/) **1** move or travel through air with wings or in aircraft. **2** control flight of (aircraft). **3** cause to fly or remain aloft. **4** wave. **5** move swiftly. **6** be driven forcefully. **7** flee (from). **8** (+ *at, upon*) attack or criticize fiercely. ● *noun* (*plural* **-ies**) **1** (usually in *plural*) flap to cover front fastening on trousers. **2** (usually in *plural*) this fastening. **3** flap at entrance of tent. **4** (in *plural*) space over stage, for scenery and lighting. **5** act of flying. □ **fly-by-night** unreliable. **fly-half** *Rugby* stand-off half. **fly in the face of** openly disregard. **flyleaf** blank leaf at beginning or end of book. **fly off the handle** *colloquial* suddenly lose one's temper. **flyover** bridge carrying road etc. over another. **fly-past** ceremonial flight of aircraft. **fly-post** fix (posters etc.) illegally. **flysheet 1** canvas cover over tent for extra protection. **2** short tract or circular. **fly-tip** illegally dump (waste). **flywheel** heavy wheel regulating machinery or accumulating power.

■ *verb* **1** ascend, flit, glide, hover, rise, sail, soar, swoop, take flight, take wing. **2** see PILOT *verb*. **3** display, flap, flutter, hang up, hoist, raise, show, wave. **7** escape, flee, hurry, move quickly, run. **8** (*fly at*) see ATTACK *verb* 1. □ **fly in the face of** see DISREGARD *verb*.

fly[2] /flaɪ/ *noun* (*plural* **flies**) **1** two-winged insect. **2** disease caused by flies. **3** (esp. artificial) fly used as bait in fishing. □ **fly-blown** tainted by flies. **flycatcher** bird that catches flies during flight. **fly-fish** *verb* fish with fly. **fly in the ointment** minor irritation or setback. **fly on the wall** unnoticed observer. **fly-paper** sticky treated paper for catching flies. **fly-trap** plant that catches flies. **flyweight** amateur boxing weight (48–51 kg).

fly[3] /flaɪ/ *adjective slang* knowing, clever.

flyer *noun* (also **flier**) **1** airman, airwoman. **2** thing or person that flies in specified way. **3** small leaflet.

flying *adjective* **1** that flies. **2** hasty. ● *noun* flight. □ **flying boat** boatlike seaplane. **flying buttress** (usually arched) buttress running from upper part of wall to outer support. **flying doctor** doctor who uses aircraft to visit patients. **flying fish** fish gliding through air with winglike fins. **flying fox** fruit-eating bat. **flying officer** RAF officer next below flight lieutenant. **flying saucer** supposed alien spaceship. **flying squad** rapidly mobile police detachment, midwifery unit, etc. **flying start 1** start (of race) at full speed. **2** vigorous start.

■ *noun* aeronautics, air travel, aviation, flight, *colloquial* jetting.

FM *abbreviation* **1** Field Marshal. **2** frequency modulation.

FO *abbreviation* Flying Officer.

foal *noun* young of horse or related animal. ● *verb* give birth to (foal).

foam *noun* **1** froth formed in liquid. **2** froth of saliva or sweat. **3** spongy rubber or plastic. ● *verb* emit foam; froth. □ **foam at the mouth** be very angry. □ **foamy** *adjective* (**-ier**, **-iest**).

■ *noun* **1** bubbles, effervescence, froth, head (*on beer*), lather, scum, spume, suds. **2** lather. ● *verb* boil, bubble, effervesce, fizz, froth, lather.

fob[1] *noun* **1** (attachment to) watch-chain. **2** small pocket for watch etc.

fob[2] *verb* (**-bb-**) □ **fob off 1** (often + *with*) deceive into accepting something inferior. **2** (often + *on*, *on to*) offload (unwanted thing on person).

focal /'fəʊk(ə)l/ *adjective* of or at a focus. □ **focal distance, length** distance between centre of lens etc. and its focus. **focal point 1** focus. **2** centre of interest or activity.

fo'c's'le = FORECASTLE.

focus /'fəʊkəs/ *noun* (*plural* **focuses** or **foci** /'fəʊsaɪ/) **1** point at which rays etc. meet after reflection or refraction or from which rays etc. appear to proceed. **2** point at which object must be situated to give clearly defined image. **3** adjustment of eye or lens to produce clear image. **4** state of clear definition. **5** centre of interest or activity. ● *verb* (**-s-** or **-ss-**) **1** bring into focus. **2** adjust focus of (lens, eye). **3** (often + *on*) concentrate or be concentrated on. **4** (cause to) converge to focus.

■ *noun* **4** clarity, correct adjustment, sharpness. **5** centre, core, focal point, heart, hub, pivot, target. ● *verb* **3** (*focus on*) aim at, centre on, concentrate on, direct attention to, fix attention on, home in on, spotlight.

fodder /'fɒdə/ *noun* hay, straw, etc. as animal food.

foe *noun* enemy.

foetid = FETID.

foetus /'fiːtəs/ *noun* (*US* **fetus**) (*plural* **-tuses**) unborn mammalian offspring, esp. human embryo of 8 weeks or more. □ **foetal** *adjective*.

fog *noun* **1** thick cloud of water droplets or smoke suspended at or near earth's surface; thick mist. **2** cloudiness on photographic negative. **3** confused state. ● *verb* (**-gg-**) **1** envelop (as) in fog. **2** perplex. □ **fog-bank** mass of fog at sea. **foghorn 1** horn warning ships in fog. **2** *colloquial* penetrating voice.

■ *noun* **1** cloud, haze, *archaic* miasma, mist, smog, vapour.

fogey /'fəʊgɪ/ *noun* (also **fogy**) (*plural* **-eys** or **-ies**) (esp. **old fogey**) dull old-fashioned person.

foggy *adjective* (**-ier**, **-iest**) **1** full of fog. **2** of or like fog. **3** vague. □ **not the foggiest** *colloquial* no idea.

■ **1, 2** blurred, blurry, clouded, cloudy, dim, hazy, indistinct, misty, murky, obscure.

foible /'fɔɪb(ə)l/ *noun* minor weakness or idiosyncrasy.

foil[1] *verb* frustrate, defeat.

■ baffle, block, check, circumvent, defeat, frustrate, halt, hamper, hinder, obstruct, outwit, prevent, stop, thwart.

foil[2] *noun* **1** thin sheet of metal. **2** person or thing setting off another to advantage.

foil[3] *noun* blunt fencing sword.

foist *verb* (+ *on*) force (thing, oneself) on to (unwilling person).

■ fob off, get rid of, impose, offload, palm off.

fold[1] /fəʊld/ *verb* **1** double (flexible thing) over on itself. **2** bend portion of. **3** become or be able to be folded. **4** (+ *away*, *up*) make compact by folding. **5** (often + *up*) *colloquial* collapse; cease to function. **6** enfold. **7** clasp. **8** (+ *in*) mix in gently. ● *noun* **1** folding. **2** line made by folding. **3** hollow among hills.

■ *verb* **1, 2** bend, crease, crimp, crinkle, double over, overlap, pleat, pucker, tuck in, turn over. **4** close, collapse, let down, put down, shut. **5** see FAIL *verb* **8**. **6, 7** clasp, embrace, enclose, enfold, entwine, envelop, hold, hug, wrap. ● *noun* **2** bend, corrugation, crease, crinkle, furrow, gather, hollow, knife-edge, line, pleat, pucker, wrinkle.

fold[2] /fəʊld/ *noun* **1** sheepfold. **2** religious group or congregation.

■ **1** see ENCLOSURE 2.

folder *noun* folding cover or holder for loose papers.

foliaceous /fəʊlɪ'eɪʃəs/ *adjective* **1** of or like leaves. **2** laminated.

foliage /'fəʊlɪdʒ/ *noun* leaves, leafage.

foliar /'fəʊlɪə/ *adjective* of leaves. □ **foliar feed** fertilizer supplied to leaves.

foliate *adjective* /'fəʊlɪət/ **1** leaflike. **2** having leaves. ● *verb* /'fəʊlɪeɪt/ (**-ting**) split into thin layers. □ **foliation** *noun*.

folio /'fəʊlɪəʊ/ *noun* (*plural* **-s**) **1** leaf of paper etc. numbered only on front. **2** sheet of paper folded once. **3** book of such sheets. ● *adjective* (of book) made of folios.

folk /fəʊk/ *noun* (*plural* same or **-s**) **1** (treated as *plural*) people in general or of specified class. **2** (in *plural*, usually **folks**) one's relatives. **3** (treated as *singular*) a people or nation. **4** (in full **folk music**) (treated as *singular*) traditional, esp. working-class, music, or music in style of this. ● *adjective* of popular origin. □ **folklore 1** traditional beliefs etc. **2** study of these. **folk tale** popular or traditional story. **folkweave** rough loosely woven fabric.

■ *noun* **1** people, the population, the public, society. **3** clan, nation, people, race, society, tribe.

folksy /'fəʊksɪ/ *adjective* (**-ier**, **-iest**) **1** of or like folk art. **2** in deliberately popular style.

follicle /ˈfɒlɪk(ə)l/ *noun* small sac or vesicle, esp. for hair-root. □ **follicular** /fɒˈlɪkjʊlə/ *adjective*.

follow /ˈfɒləʊ/ *verb* **1** go or come after. **2** go along. **3** come next in order or time. **4** practise. **5** understand. **6** take as guide; conform to. **7** take interest in. **8** (+ *with*) provide with (sequel etc.). **9** ensue. **10** (+ *from*) result from. **11** be necessary inference. □ **follow on 1** continue. **2** (of cricket team) bat twice in succession. **follow-on** *noun* instance of this. **follow suit 1** play card of suit led. **2** conform to another's actions. **follow through 1** continue to conclusion. **2** continue movement of stroke after hitting the ball. **follow-through** *noun* instance of this. **follow up** act or investigate further. **follow-up** *noun* subsequent action.

■ **1** chase, come after, dog, go after, hound, hunt, pursue, shadow, stalk, *colloquial* tail, track, trail. **2** go along, keep to, proceed along, trace. **3** come after, replace, succeed, supersede, supplant, take the place of. **5** appreciate, comprehend, grasp, keep up with, take in, understand. **6** (*follow person's example*) adopt, be guided by, conform to, copy, imitate, mimic, mirror; (*follow rules*) abide by, adhere to, attend to, comply with, heed, honour, keep to, obey, observe, pay attention to, submit to, take notice of. **7** admire, be a fan of, keep abreast of, know about, support, take an interest in. **9** come about, ensue, happen, result. **10** (*follow from*) flow from, result from. **11** be inevitable, be logical, have the consequence, mean.

follower *noun* **1** supporter, devotee. **2** person who follows.

following *preposition* **1** after in time. **2** as sequel to. ● *noun* group of supporters. ● *adjective* that follows. □ **the following** what follows, now to be mentioned.

■ *adjective* see SUBSEQUENT.

folly /ˈfɒlɪ/ *noun* (*plural* **-ies**) **1** foolishness. **2** foolish act, idea, etc. **3** building for display only.

■ **1** foolishness, insanity, lunacy, madness, stupidity.

foment /fəˈment/ *verb* instigate; stir up (trouble etc.). □ **fomentation** /fəʊmenˈteɪʃ(ə)n/ *noun*. **fomenter** *noun*.

■ arouse, incite, instigate, kindle, provoke, rouse, stir up.

fond *adjective* **1** (+ *of*) liking. **2** affectionate, doting. **3** foolishly optimistic. □ **fondly** *adverb*. **fondness** *noun*.

■ **1** (*be fond of*) see LOVE *verb* 1. **2** adoring, affectionate, caring, loving, tender, warm. **3** see FOOLISH.

fondant /ˈfɒnd(ə)nt/ *noun* soft sugary sweet.

fondle /ˈfɒnd(ə)l/ *verb* (**-ling**) caress.

■ caress, cuddle, handle, pat, pet, squeeze, touch.

fondue /ˈfɒndju:/ *noun* dish of melted cheese.

font[1] *noun* receptacle for baptismal water.

font[2] = FOUNT[2].

fontanelle /fɒntəˈnel/ *noun* (*US* **fontanel**) space

in infant's skull, which later closes up.

food /fu:d/ *noun* **1** substance taken in to maintain life and growth; solid food. **2** mental stimulus. □ **food chain** series of organisms each dependent on next for food. **food poisoning** illness due to bacteria etc. in food. **food processor** machine for chopping and mixing food. **foodstuff** substance used as food.

■ **1** bread, *formal* comestibles, cooking, cuisine, delicacies, diet, eatables, *colloquial* eats, fare, feed, fodder, foodstuff, forage, *colloquial* grub, *slang* nosh, nourishment, nutriments, *jocular* provender, provisions, rations, refreshments, sustenance, swill, *colloquial* tuck, *formal* viands, victuals.

foodie /ˈfu:dɪ/ *noun colloquial* person who makes a cult of food.

fool[1] *noun* **1** unwise or stupid person. **2** *historical* jester, clown. ● *verb* **1** deceive; trick, cheat. **2** joke; tease. **3** (+ *about, around*) play, trifle. □ **act, play the fool** behave in silly way. **foolproof** incapable of misuse or mistake. **fool's paradise** illusory happiness. **make a fool of** make (person) look foolish; trick.

■ *noun* **1** ass, blockhead, booby, buffoon, *colloquial* dimwit, *slang* dope, dunce, dunderhead, dupe, *colloquial* fat-head, halfwit, idiot, ignoramus, mug, *colloquial* muggins, *slang* mutt, ninny, *slang* nit, *colloquial* nitwit, simpleton, sucker, *slang* twerp, *slang* wally. **2** clown, comedian, comic, coxcomb, entertainer, *historical* jester. ● *verb* **1** *colloquial* bamboozle, bluff, cheat, *slang* con, *literary* cozen, deceive, defraud, delude, dupe, fleece, gull, *colloquial* have on, hoax, hoodwink, *colloquial* kid, mislead, *colloquial* string along, swindle, take in, trick. **2** banter, jest, joke, *colloquial* kid, tease. **3** (*fool about, around*) see MISBEHAVE.

fool[2] *noun* dessert of fruit purée with cream or custard.

foolery *noun* foolish behaviour.

foolhardy *adjective* (**-ier**, **-iest**) foolishly bold; reckless. □ **foolhardily** *adverb*. **foolhardiness** *noun*.

foolish *adjective* lacking good sense or judgement; unwise. □ **foolishly** *adverb*. **foolishness** *noun*.

■ absurd, asinine, brainless, childish, crazy, daft, *colloquial* dopey, *colloquial* dotty, fatuous, feather-brained, feeble-minded, fond, frivolous, half-baked, hare-brained, idiotic, illogical, immature, inane, infantile, *colloquial* insane, irrational, jokey, laughable, light-hearted, ludicrous, lunatic, mad, meaningless, mindless, misguided, naive, nonsensical, playful, pointless, preposterous, ridiculous, scatterbrained, *colloquial* scatty, senseless, shallow, silly, simple, simple-minded, simplistic, *colloquial* soppy, stupid, thoughtless, unintelligent, unreasonable, unsound, unwise, witless.

foolscap /ˈfu:lskæp/ *noun* large size of paper, about 330 mm x 200 (or 400) mm.

foot /fʊt/ *noun* (*plural* **feet**) **1** part of leg below ankle. **2** lower part or end. **3** (*plural* same or **feet**) linear measure of 12 in. (30.48 cm). **4** metrical unit of verse forming part of line. **5** *historical* infantry. ● *verb* **1** pay (bill). **2** (usually as **foot it**) go on foot. □ **foot-and-mouth (disease)** contagious viral disease of cattle etc. **footbridge** bridge for use by pedestrians. **footfall** sound of footstep. **foot-fault** (in tennis) serving with foot over baseline. **foothill** low hill lying at base of mountain or range. **foothold 1** secure place for feet in climbing. **2** secure initial position. **footlights** row of floor-level lights along front of stage. **footloose** free to act as one pleases. **footman** liveried servant. **footmark** footprint. **footnote** note at foot of page. **footpath, footway** path for pedestrians. **footplate** platform for crew in locomotive. **footprint** impression left by foot or shoe. **footslog (-gg-)** walk laboriously esp. for long distance. **footslogger** noun. **footsore** with sore feet, esp. from walking. **footstep** (sound of) step taken in walking. **footstool** stool for resting feet on when sitting. **footwear** shoes, boots, socks, etc. **on foot** walking. **put one's foot down** *colloquial* **1** insist. **2** accelerate. **put one's foot in it** *colloquial* commit blunder. □ **footless** *adjective*.

■ *noun* **1** claw, hoof, paw, trotter. **2** see BASE¹ *noun* **1**. □ **footprint** footmark, spoor, track.

footage *noun* **1** a length of TV or cinema film etc. **2** length in feet.

football *noun* **1** large inflated usually leather ball. **2** team game played with this. □ **football pool(s)** organized gambling on results of football matches. □ **footballer** *noun*.

footing *noun* **1** foothold; secure position. **2** operational basis; relative position or status. **3** (often in *plural*) foundations of wall.

footling /ˈfuːtlɪŋ/ *adjective colloquial* trivial, silly.

Footsie /ˈfʊtsɪ/ *noun* FT-SE.

footsie /ˈfʊtsɪ/ *noun colloquial* amorous play with feet.

fop *noun* dandy. □ **foppery** *noun*. **foppish** *adjective*.

for /fə, fɔː/ *preposition* **1** in interest, defence, or favour of. **2** appropriate to. **3** regarding. **4** representing. **5** at the price of. **6** as consequence or on account of. **7** in order to get or reach. **8** so as to start promptly at. **9** notwithstanding. ● *conjunction* because, since. □ **be for it** be liable or about to be punished.

forage /ˈfɒrɪdʒ/ *noun* **1** food for horses and cattle. **2** searching for food. ● *verb* (**-ging**) **1** (often + *for*) search for food. **2** rummage. **3** collect food from. □ **forage cap** infantry undress cap.

foray /ˈfɒreɪ/ *noun* sudden attack, raid. ● *verb* make foray.

forbade (also **forbad**) *past* of FORBID.

forbear¹ /fɔːˈbeə/ *verb* (*past* **forbore**; *past participle* **forborne**) *formal* abstain or refrain from.

forbear² = FOREBEAR.

forbearance *noun* patient self-control; tolerance.

forbearing *adjective* patient or tolerant.

forbid /fəˈbɪd/ *verb* (**forbidding**; *past* **forbade** /-ˈbæd/ or **forbad**; *past participle* **forbidden**) **1** (+ *to do*) order not to. **2** not allow. **3** refuse entry to.

■ **1** (*forbid to*) ban from, bar from, debar from, exclude from, preclude from, prevent from, prohibit from, stop from. **2** ban, deny, disallow, interdict, outlaw, prohibit, proscribe, refuse, rule out, say no to, veto. **3** deny.

forbidden *adjective* **1** not allowed. **2** having access prohibited. □ **forbidden fruit** thing desired esp. because not allowed.

■ **1** against the law, taboo, unlawful, wrong. **2** closed, out of bounds, restricted, secret.

forbidding *adjective* stern, threatening. □ **forbiddingly** *adverb*.

■ gloomy, grim, menacing, ominous, stern, threatening, unfriendly, uninviting, unwelcoming.

forbore *past* of FORBEAR¹.

forborne *past participle* of FORBEAR¹.

force *noun* **1** strength, power; intense effort. **2** group of soldiers, police, etc. **3** coercion, compulsion. **4** effect, significance. **5** influential person or thing. ● *verb* (**-cing**) **1** compel, coerce. **2** make way; break into or open by force. **3** drive, propel. **4** (+ *on, upon*) impose or press on (person). **5** cause or produce by effort. **6** strain. **7** artificially hasten maturity of. **8** accelerate. □ **forced landing** emergency landing of aircraft. **forced march** lengthy and vigorous march, esp. by troops. **force-feed** feed (prisoner etc.) against his or her will. **force (person's) hand** make him or her act prematurely or unwillingly.

■ *noun* **1** drive, effort, energy, intensity, might, momentum, power, strength, vehemence, vigour. **2** army, body, group; (*forces*) troops. **3** aggression, coercion, compulsion, constraint, duress, pressure, violence. **4** cogency, effect, effectiveness, impact, intensity, persuasiveness, power, rightness, significance, strength, thrust, validity, weight. ● *verb* **1** *colloquial* bulldoze, coerce, compel, constrain, drive, impel, impose on, make, oblige, order, press-gang, pressurize. **2** break open, burst open, prise open, smash, use force on, wrench. **4** impose, inflict.

forceful *adjective* **1** powerful. **2** impressive. □ **forcefully** *adverb*. **forcefulness** *noun*.

force majeure /fɔːs mæˈʒɜː/ *noun* **1** irresistible force. **2** unforeseeable circumstances. [French]

forcemeat /ˈfɔːsmiːt/ *noun* minced seasoned meat for stuffing etc.

forceps /ˈfɔːseps/ *noun* (*plural* same) surgical pincers.

forcible /ˈfɔːsɪb(ə)l/ *adjective* done by or involving force; forceful. □ **forcibly** *adverb*.

ford *noun* shallow place where river etc. may be crossed. ● *verb* cross (water) at ford. □ **fordable** *adjective*.

fore *adjective* situated in front. ● *noun* **1** front part. **2** bow of ship. ● *interjection* (*in golf*) warning to person in path of ball. □ **fore-and-aft**

(of sails or rigging) lengthwise; at bow and stern. **to the fore** conspicuous.

forearm[1] /'fɔːrɑːm/ *noun* arm from elbow to wrist or fingertips.

forearm[2] /fɔːˈrɑːm/ *verb* arm beforehand; prepare.

forebear /'fɔːbeə/ *noun* (also **forbear**) (usually in *plural*) ancestor.

forebode /fɔːˈbəʊd/ *verb* (**-ding**) be advance sign of; portend.

foreboding *noun* expectation of trouble.
■ anxiety, apprehension, dread, fear, foreshadowing, forewarning, intimation, intuition, misgiving, omen, portent, premonition, presentiment, suspicion, warning, worry.

forecast *verb* (*past & past participle* **-cast** or **-casted**) predict; estimate beforehand. ● *noun* prediction, esp. of weather. □ **forecaster** *noun*.
■ *verb* see FORESEE. ● *noun* augury, expectation, outlook, prediction, prognosis, prognostication, projection, prophecy.

forecastle /'fəʊks(ə)l/ *noun* (also **fo'c's'le**) forward part of ship, formerly living quarters.

foreclose /fɔːˈkləʊz/ *verb* (**-sing**) **1** stop (mortgage) from being redeemable. **2** repossess mortgaged property of (person) when loan is not duly repaid. **3** exclude, prevent. □ **foreclosure** *noun*.

forecourt *noun* **1** part of filling-station with petrol pumps. **2** enclosed space in front of building.

forefather *noun* (usually in *plural*) ancestor.

forefinger *noun* finger next to thumb.

forefoot *noun* front foot of animal.

forefront *noun* **1** leading position. **2** foremost part.
■ front, lead, vanguard.

forego = FORGO.

foregoing /fɔːˈgəʊɪŋ/ *adjective* preceding; previously mentioned.

foregone conclusion /'fɔːgɒn/ *noun* easily foreseeable result.

foreground *noun* part of view nearest observer.

forehand *Tennis etc. adjective* (of stroke) played with palm of hand facing forward. ● *noun* forehand stroke.

forehead /'fɒrɪd, 'fɔːhed/ *noun* part of face above eyebrows.

foreign /'fɒrən/ *adjective* **1** of, from, in, or characteristic of country or language other than one's own. **2** dealing with other countries. **3** of another district, society, etc. **4** (often + *to*) unfamiliar, alien. **5** coming from outside. □ **foreign body** extraneous object, esp. one ingested, introduced, etc. into the body. **foreign legion** group of foreign volunteers in (esp. French) army. □ **foreignness** *noun*.

■ **1** alien, distant, exotic, far-away, immigrant, imported, outlandish, overseas, remote. **2** external, international, overseas. **4** alien, exotic, odd, outlandish, strange, uncharacteristic, unfamiliar, unknown, unnatural, untypical, unusual. **5** external, extraneous, incoming, outside.

foreigner *noun* person born in or coming from another country.
■ alien, immigrant, newcomer, outsider, overseas visitor, stranger.

foreknowledge /fɔːˈnɒlɪdʒ/ *noun* knowledge in advance of (an event etc.).

foreleg *noun* animal's front leg.

forelock *noun* lock of hair just above forehead. □ **touch one's forelock** defer to person of higher social rank.

foreman /'fɔːmən/ *noun* (*feminine* **forewoman**) **1** worker supervising others. **2** spokesman of jury.

foremast *noun* mast nearest bow of ship.

foremost *adjective* **1** most notable, best. **2** first, front. ● *adverb* most importantly.
■ *adjective* **1** see CHIEF *adjective* 1. **2** first, front, leading.

forename *noun* first or Christian name.

forensic /fəˈrensɪk/ *adjective* **1** of or used in courts of law. **2** of or involving application of science to legal problems.

foreplay *noun* stimulation preceding sexual intercourse.

forerunner *noun* predecessor.
■ advance messenger, ancestor, harbinger, herald, precursor, predecessor.

foresail *noun* principal sail on foremast.

foresee /fɔːˈsiː/ *verb* (*past* **-saw**; *past participle* **-seen**) see or be aware of beforehand. □ **foreseeable** *adjective*.
■ *disputed* anticipate, envisage, expect, forecast, foretell, picture.

foreshadow /fɔːˈʃædəʊ/ *verb* be warning or indication of (future event).

foreshore *noun* shore between high and low water marks.

foreshorten /fɔːˈʃɔːt(ə)n/ *verb* portray (object) with apparent shortening due to perspective.

foresight *noun* **1** care or provision for future. **2** foreseeing.
■ **1** anticipation, caution, far-sightedness, forethought, perspicacity, planning, preparation, prudence, readiness, vision. **2** looking ahead, vision.

foreskin *noun* fold of skin covering end of penis.

forest /'fɒrɪst/ *noun* **1** large area of trees. **2** large number; dense mass. ● *verb* **1** plant with trees. **2** convert into forest.
■ *noun* **1** coppice, copse, jungle, plantation, trees, woodland, woods.

forestall /fɔːˈstɔːl/ *verb* **1** prevent by advance action. **2** deal with beforehand.

forester *noun* **1** manager of forest. **2** expert in forestry. **3** dweller in forest.

forestry *noun* science or management of forests.

foretaste *noun* small preliminary experience of something.

■ advance warning, augury, example, foreknowledge, forewarning, indication, omen, premonition, preview, sample, specimen, tip-off, trailer, try-out.

foretell /fɔːˈtel/ *verb* (*past & past participle* **-told**) **1** predict, prophesy. **2** indicate approach of.

■ **1** augur, bode, forebode, foresee, foreshadow, forewarn, give a foretaste of, portend, predict, presage, prognosticate, prophesy, signify. **2** herald, presage.

forethought *noun* **1** care or provision for future. **2** deliberate intention.

■ **1** anticipation, caution, far-sightedness, foresight, looking ahead, perspicacity, planning, preparation, prudence, readiness, vision.

forever /fəˈrevə/ *adverb* always, constantly.

forewarn /fɔːˈwɔːn/ *verb* warn beforehand. □ **forewarning** *noun*.

■ □ **forewarning** advance warning, augury, foretaste, omen, premonition, tip-off.

foreword *noun* introductory remarks in book, often not by author.

forfeit /ˈfɔːfɪt/ *noun* (thing surrendered as) penalty. ● *adjective* lost or surrendered as penalty. ● *verb* (**-t-**) lose right to; surrender as penalty. □ **forfeiture** *noun*.

■ *noun* charge, damages, fee, fine, penalty. ● *verb* abandon, give up, let go, lose, pay up, relinquish, renounce, surrender. □ **forfeiture** confiscation, sequestration.

forgather /fɔːˈɡæðə/ *verb* assemble; associate.

forgave *past* of FORGIVE.

forge¹ *verb* (**-ging**) **1** make or write in fraudulent imitation. **2** shape by heating and hammering. ● *noun* **1** furnace etc. for melting or refining metal. **2** blacksmith's workshop. □ **forger** *noun*.

■ *verb* **1** coin, copy, counterfeit, fake, falsify, imitate, make illegally, reproduce. **2** beat into shape, cast, construct, hammer out, manufacture, mould, shape, work. ● *noun* **2** smithy, workshop.

forge² *verb* (**-ging**) advance gradually. □ **forge ahead 1** take lead. **2** progress rapidly.

■ □ **forge ahead 2** see ADVANCE *verb* 1–2.

forgery /ˈfɔːdʒərɪ/ *noun* (*plural* **-ies**) (making of) forged document etc.

■ copy, counterfeit, *slang* dud, fake, fraud, imitation, *colloquial* phoney, replica, reproduction.

forget /fəˈɡet/ *verb* (**forgetting**; *past* **forgot**; *past*

participle **forgotten** or *US* **forgot**) **1** lose remembrance of; not remember. **2** neglect, overlook. **3** omit to bring, mention, etc. **4** cease to think of. **5** (**forget oneself**) act without dignity. □ **forget-me-not** plant with small blue flowers. □ **forgettable** *adjective*.

■ **1** be forgetful, fail to remember, suffer from amnesia. **2** neglect, omit, overlook. **3** be without, leave behind, leave out, lose, miss out, neglect, omit, overlook, skip. **4** dismiss from one's mind, disregard, ignore, unlearn.

forgetful *adjective* **1** apt to forget. **2** (often + *of*) neglectful. □ **forgetfully** *adverb*. **forgetfulness** *noun*.

■ **1** absent-minded, amnesiac, careless, distracted, inattentive, preoccupied, unreliable, vague. **2** careless, neglectful, negligent, oblivious, unconscious, unmindful.

forgive /fəˈɡɪv/ *verb* (**-ving**; *past* **forgave**; *past participle* **forgiven**) **1** cease to resent; pardon. **2** remit (debt). □ **forgivable** *adjective*. **forgiveness** *noun*. **forgiving** *adjective*.

■ **1** (*forgive a person*) absolve, acquit, clear, *formal* exculpate, excuse, exonerate, indulge, let off, pardon, spare; (*forgive an offence*) condone, ignore, make allowances for, overlook, pass over. □ **forgivable** allowable, excusable, justifiable, pardonable, petty, understandable, venial. **forgiveness** absolution, amnesty, clemency, compassion, *formal* exculpation, exoneration, grace, *RC Church* indulgence, leniency, mercy, pardon, tolerance. **forgiving** clement, compassionate, forbearing, generous, kind, lenient, magnanimous, merciful, tolerant, understanding.

forgo /fɔːˈɡəʊ/ *verb* (also **forego**) (**-goes**; *past* **-went**; *past participle* **-gone**) go without, relinquish.

■ abandon, abstain from, do without, forswear, give up, go without, omit, *colloquial* pass up, relinquish, renounce, sacrifice, turn down, waive.

forgot *past* of FORGET.

forgotten *past participle* of FORGET.

fork *noun* **1** pronged item of cutlery. **2** similar large tool for digging etc. **3** forked part, esp. of bicycle frame. **4** (place of) divergence of road etc. ● *verb* **1** form fork or branch. **2** take one road at fork. **3** dig with fork. □ **fork-lift truck** vehicle with fork for lifting and carrying. **fork out** *slang* pay, esp. reluctantly. □ **forked** *adjective*.

■ □ **forked** branched, cleft, divergent, divided, fork-like, pronged, split, V-shaped.

forlorn /fəˈlɔːn/ *adjective* **1** sad and abandoned. **2** pitiful. □ **forlorn hope** faint remaining hope or chance. □ **forlornly** *adverb*.

■ **1** abandoned, alone, bereft, deserted, forsaken, friendless, lonely, outcast, sad, solitary, unloved.

form *noun* **1** shape; arrangement of parts; visible aspect. **2** person or animal as visible or tangible. **3** mode in which thing exists or manifests itself. **4** kind, variety. **5** document with blanks to be filled in. **6** class in school. **7** (often as **the form**) customary or correct behaviour or method. **8** set order of words. **9** (of athlete, horse, etc.) condition of health and training. **10** record of performances. **11** disposition. **12** bench. ● *verb* **1** make; be made. **2** constitute. **3** develop or establish as concept, practice, etc. **4** (+ *into*) organize into. **5** (of troops etc.) bring or move into formation. **6** mould, fashion.

■ *noun* **1** anatomy, appearance, arrangement, build, cast, configuration, design, format, frame, framework, mould, outline, pattern, physique, plan, shape, silhouette, structure, system. **2** body, figure. **3** character, guise, manifestation, manner, nature, semblance, style. **4** genre, kind, model, sort, species, type, variety. **5** document, paper. **6** class, grade, group, level, set, stream. **7** behaviour, convention, custom, etiquette, fashion, manners, practice. **9** condition, fettle, fitness, health. **10** performance. **11** condition, disposition, mood, shape, spirits, state. **12** see SEAT *noun* 1.
● *verb* **1** (*formed objects*) bring into existence, cast, construct, create, design, forge, found, give form to, make, model, mould, produce, shape; (*stalactites formed*) appear, arise, come into existence, develop, grow, materialize, take shape. **2** act as, compose, constitute, make up, serve as. **3** acquire, cultivate, develop, establish, get. **4** arrange, assemble, organize.

formal /ˈfɔːm(ə)l/ *adjective* **1** in accordance with rules, convention, or ceremony. **2** (of garden etc.) symmetrical. **3** prim, stiff. **4** perfunctory. **5** drawn up correctly. **6** concerned with outward form. □ **formally** *adverb*.

■ **1** (*formal occasion*) ceremonial, ceremonious, dignified, official, *colloquial* posh, solemn, stately; (*formal procedure*) conventional, correct, customary, official, orthodox, proper, ritualistic, set; (*formal language*) academic, impersonal, official, precise, specialist, stilted, technical, unemotional. **2** geometrical, orderly, organized, regular, rigid, symmetrical. **3** aloof, ceremonious, conventional, cool, correct, dignified, pretentious, prim, proper, punctilious, sophisticated, starchy, stiff, stilted, unbending, unfriendly. **5** binding, contractual, enforceable, legal, official, precise, signed and sealed.

formaldehyde /fɔːˈmældɪhaɪd/ *noun* colourless gas used as preservative and disinfectant.

formalin /ˈfɔːməlɪn/ *noun* solution of formaldehyde in water.

formalism *noun* strict adherence to external form, esp. in art. □ **formalist** *noun*.

formality /fɔːˈmælɪtɪ/ *noun* (*plural* **-ies**) **1** formal, esp. meaningless, regulation or act. **2** rigid observance of rules or convention.

formalize *verb* (also **-ise**) (**-zing** or **-sing**) **1** give definite (esp. legal) form to. **2** make formal. □ **formalization** *noun*.

format /ˈfɔːmæt/ *noun* **1** shape and size (of book etc.). **2** style or manner of procedure etc. **3** arrangement of computer data etc. ● *verb* (**-tt-**) **1** arrange in format. **2** prepare (storage medium) to receive computer data.

■ *noun* **1** appearance, design, layout, plan, shape, size, style. **2** arrangement, manner, method, organization, plan, structure, style.

formation /fɔːˈmeɪʃ(ə)n/ *noun* **1** forming. **2** thing formed. **3** particular arrangement (e.g. of troops). **4** rocks or strata with common characteristic.

formative /ˈfɔːmətɪv/ *adjective* serving to form; of formation.

former /ˈfɔːmə/ *adjective* **1** of the past. **2** earlier, previous. **3** (**the former**) the first or first-named of two.

■ **1, 2** bygone, departed, ex-, last, late, old, one-time, past, previous, prior, recent. **3** (**the former**) earlier, first, first-mentioned.

formerly *adverb* in former times; previously.

Formica /fɔːˈmaɪkə/ *noun proprietary term* hard plastic laminate for surfaces.

formic acid /ˈfɔːmɪk/ *noun* colourless irritant volatile acid contained in fluid emitted by ants.

formidable /ˈfɔːmɪdəb(ə)l/ *adjective* **1** inspiring awe, respect, or dread. **2** difficult to deal with. □ **formidably** *adverb*.

USAGE *Formidable* is also pronounced /fəˈmɪdəb(ə)l/ (with the stress on the *-mid-*), but this is considered incorrect by some people.

■ **1** awe-inspiring, awesome, daunting, dreadful, fearful, frightening, intimidating, *colloquial* mind-boggling, prodigious. **2** challenging, daunting, difficult, large-scale, onerous, overwhelming, taxing.

formless *adjective* without definite or regular form. □ **formlessness** *noun*.

formula /ˈfɔːmjʊlə/ *noun* (*plural* **-s** or **-lae** /-liː/) **1** chemical symbols showing constituents of substance. **2** mathematical rule expressed in symbols. **3** fixed form of words. **4** list of ingredients; recipe. **5** classification of racing car, esp. by engine capacity. □ **formulaic** /-ˈleɪk/ *adjective*.

■ **3** form of words, rubric, spell, wording. **4** blueprint, method, prescription, procedure, recipe, rule, technique, way.

formulate /ˈfɔːmjʊleɪt/ *verb* **1** express in formula. **2** express clearly and precisely. **3** devise. □ **formulation** *noun*.

■ **1** codify, set out in detail, specify, systematize. **2** articulate, codify, define, express clearly, set out in detail, specify, systematize. **3** concoct, create, devise, evolve, form, invent, map out, originate, plan, work out.

fornicate /ˈfɔːnɪkeɪt/ *verb* (**-ting**) *usually jocular* have extramarital sexual intercourse. □ **fornication** *noun*. **fornicator** *noun*.

forsake /fəˈseɪk/ *verb* (**-king**; *past* **forsook** /-ˈsʊk/; *past participle* **forsaken**) **1** *literary* give up, renounce. **2** desert, abandon.

■ **1** forgo, forswear, give up, jettison, renounce, repudiate, surrender. **2** abandon, desert, jilt, leave, quit, throw over, turn one's back on, vacate.

forswear /fɔːˈsweə/ *verb* (*past* **forswore**; *past*

participle **forsworn**) **1** abjure, renounce. **2** (**forswear oneself**) perjure oneself. **3** (as **forsworn** *adjective*) perjured.

forsythia /fɔːˈsaɪθɪə/ *noun* shrub with bright yellow flowers.

fort *noun* fortified building or position. □ **hold the fort** act as temporary substitute.

> ■ camp, castle, citadel, fortification, fortress, garrison, stronghold, tower.

forte[1] /ˈfɔːteɪ/ *noun* thing in which one excels or specializes.

forte[2] /ˈfɔːteɪ/ *Music adjective* loud. ● *adverb* loudly. ● *noun* loud playing, singing, or passage.

forth /fɔːθ/ *adverb* **1** forward(s). **2** out. **3** onwards in time. □ **forthcoming** /fɔːθˈkʌmɪŋ/ **1** coming or available soon. **2** produced when wanted. **3** informative, responsive.

forthright *adjective* **1** straightforward; outspoken. **2** decisive.

> ■ **1** blunt, candid, decisive, direct, frank, outspoken, straightforward, unequivocal, unhesitating, uninhibited.

forthwith /fɔːθˈwɪθ/ *adverb* immediately, without delay.

fortification /fɔːtɪfɪˈkeɪʃ(ə)n/ *noun* **1** fortifying. **2** (usually in *plural*) defensive works.

fortify /ˈfɔːtɪfaɪ/ *verb* (**-ies, -ied**) **1** provide with fortifications. **2** strengthen. **3** (usually as **fortified** *adjective*) strengthen (wine etc.) with alcohol. **4** (usually as **fortified** *adjective*) increase nutritive value of (food, esp. with vitamins).

> ■ **1** buttress, defend, garrison, protect, reinforce, secure against attack, shore up. **2** bolster, boost, brace, buoy up, cheer, embolden, encourage, hearten, invigorate, lift the morale of, reassure, stiffen the resolve of, strengthen, support, sustain.

fortissimo /fɔːˈtɪsɪməʊ/ *Music adjective* very loud. ● *adverb* very loudly. ● *noun* (*plural* **-mos** or **-mi** /-miː/) very loud playing, singing, or passage.

fortitude /ˈfɔːtɪtjuːd/ *noun* courage in pain or adversity.

> ■ backbone, bravery, courage, determination, endurance, firmness, heroism, patience, resolution, stoicism, tenacity, valour, will-power.

fortnight /ˈfɔːtnaɪt/ *noun* two weeks.

fortnightly *adjective* done, produced, or occurring once a fortnight. ● *adverb* every fortnight. ● *noun* (*plural* **-ies**) fortnightly magazine etc.

Fortran /ˈfɔːtræn/ *noun* (also **FORTRAN**) computer language used esp. for scientific calculations.

fortress /ˈfɔːtrɪs/ *noun* fortified building or town.

fortuitous /fɔːˈtjuːɪtəs/ *adjective* happening by chance. □ **fortuitously** *adverb*. **fortuitousness** *noun*. **fortuity** *noun* (*plural* **-ies**).

fortunate /ˈfɔːtʃənət/ *adjective* lucky, auspicious. □ **fortunately** *adverb*.

> ■ auspicious, blessed, favourable, happy, lucky, opportune, propitious, prosperous, providential, timely.

fortune /ˈfɔːtʃ(ə)n/ *noun* **1** chance or luck in human affairs. **2** person's destiny. **3** prosperity, wealth. **4** *colloquial* large sum of money. □ **fortune-teller** person claiming to foretell one's destiny.

> ■ **1** accident, chance, destiny, fate, fortuity, luck, providence. **2** destiny, fate, *Buddhism & Hinduism* karma, kismet, lot. **3** affluence, assets, estate, holdings, inheritance, means, money, opulence, possessions, property, prosperity, riches, treasure, wealth. **4** *colloquial* millions, *colloquial* packet, *colloquial* pile. □ **fortune-teller** clairvoyant, crystal-gazer, oracle, palmist, prophet, seer, soothsayer, *colloquial usually derogatory* or *jocular* stargazer.

forty /ˈfɔːtɪ/ *adjective & noun* (*plural* **-ies**) four times ten. □ **forty winks** *colloquial* short sleep. □ **fortieth** *adjective & noun*.

forum /ˈfɔːrəm/ *noun* **1** place of or meeting for public discussion. **2** court, tribunal.

forward /ˈfɔːwəd/ *adjective* **1** onward; towards front. **2** bold; precocious; presumptuous. **3** relating to the future. **4** well advanced. ● *noun* attacking player in football etc. ● *adverb* **1** to front; into prominence. **2** so as to make progress. **3** towards future. **4** forwards. ● *verb* **1** send (letter etc.) on; dispatch. **2** help to advance; promote. □ **forwardness** *noun*.

> ■ *adjective* **1** advancing, front, frontal, leading, onward, progressive. **2** advanced, assertive, bold, brazen, cheeky, confident, familiar, *colloquial* fresh, impertinent, impudent, insolent, overconfident, precocious, presumptuous, *colloquial* pushy, shameless, uninhibited. **3** advance, early, forward-looking, future. **4** well advanced, well developed. ● *verb* **1** dispatch, expedite, post on, send, send on, ship, transmit, transport. **2** accelerate, advance, encourage, facilitate, foster, further, give a helping hand to, hasten, help along, lend a helping hand to, promote, speed up, support.

forwards *adverb* in direction one is facing.

forwent *past* of FORGO.

fossil /ˈfɒs(ə)l/ *noun* **1** remains or impression of (usually prehistoric) plant or animal hardened in rock. **2** *colloquial* antiquated or unchanging person or thing. ● *adjective* of or like fossil. □ **fossil fuel** natural fuel extracted from ground. □ **fossilize** *verb* (also **-ise**) (**-zing** or **-sing**). **fossilization** *noun*.

foster /ˈfɒstə/ *verb* **1** promote growth of. **2** encourage or harbour (feeling). **3** bring up (another's child). **4** assign as foster child. ● *adjective* related by or concerned with fostering.

> ■ *verb* **1, 2** advance, cultivate, encourage, further, harbour, help, nurture, promote, stimulate. **3** adopt, bring up, care for, look after, maintain, nourish, nurse, raise, rear, take care of.

fought *past & past participle* of FIGHT.

foul /faʊl/ *adjective* **1** offensive to the senses; loathsome, stinking. **2** dirty, soiled. **3** *colloquial* awful. **4** noxious. **5** morally offensive; obscene. **6** unfair, against rules. **7** (of weather) rough. **8** entangled. ● *noun* **1** foul blow or play. **2** entanglement. ● *adverb* unfairly. ● *verb* **1** make or become foul. **2** commit foul on (player). **3** (often + *up*) (cause to) become entangled or blocked. □ **foul-mouthed** using obscene or offensive language. **foul play 1** unfair play. **2** treacherous or violent act, esp. murder. □ **foully** /ˈfaʊlɪ/ *adverb*. **foulness** *noun*.

■ *adjective* **1** bad, disagreeable, disgusting, fetid, hateful, loathsome, malodorous, mephitic, nasty, nauseating, nauseous, *literary* noisome, obnoxious, *colloquial* off, offensive, *colloquial* pongy, putrid, rank, repellent, repugnant, repulsive, revolting, rotten, sickening, smelly, squalid, stinking, vile. **2** see DIRTY *adjective* 1. **4** contaminated, impure, infected, mephitic, *literary* noisome, noxious, polluted. **5** (*foul crimes*) abhorrent, abominable, atrocious, *colloquial* beastly, cruel, evil, monstrous, scandalous, shameful, vicious, vile, villainous, violent, wicked; (*foul language*) abusive, bawdy, blasphemous, coarse, *derogatory* common, crude, impolite, improper, indecent, insulting, licentious, obscene, offensive, rude, uncouth, vulgar. **6** against the rules, dishonest, forbidden, illegal, invalid, prohibited, unfair, unsportsmanlike. **7** foggy, rainy, rough, stormy, violent, windy. ● *noun* **1** infringement, violation. ● *verb* **1** see DIRTY *verb*. **3** (*foul up*) see MUDDLE *verb* 1.

found[1] *past* and *past participle* of FIND.

found[2] /faʊnd/ *verb* **1** establish, originate. **2** lay base of. **3** base. □ **founder** *noun*.

■ **1** begin, bring about, create, endow, erect, establish, fund, get going, inaugurate, initiate, institute, organize, originate, raise, set up, start. **3** base, build, construct, erect, ground, rest, set.

found[3] /faʊnd/ *verb* **1** melt and mould (metal). **2** fuse (materials for glass). **3** make thus. □ **founder** *noun*.

foundation /faʊnˈdeɪʃ(ə)n/ *noun* **1** solid ground or base under building. **2** (usually in *plural*) lowest part of building, usually below ground. **3** basis; underlying principle. **4** establishing (esp. endowed institution). **5** base for cosmetics. **6** (in full **foundation garment**) woman's supporting undergarment. □ **foundation-stone 1** stone laid ceremonially at founding of building. **2** basis.

■ **1, 2** base, basis, bottom, footing, substructure, underpinning. **3** basic principle, basis, element, essential, fundamental, origin, rudiments. **4** beginning, endowment, establishment, founding, inauguration, initiation, institution, organizing, setting up, starting.

founder /ˈfaʊndə/ *verb* **1** (of ship) fill with water and sink. **2** (of plan) fail. **3** (of horse) stumble, fall lame.

■ **1** be wrecked, go down, sink. **2** abort, come to grief, fail, fall through, miscarry.

foundling /ˈfaʊndlɪŋ/ *noun* abandoned infant of unknown parentage.

foundry /ˈfaʊndrɪ/ *noun* (*plural* **-ies**) workshop for casting metal.

fount[1] /faʊnt/ *noun poetical* source; spring; fountain.

fount[2] /fɒnt/ *noun* (also **font**) set of printing type of same size and face.

fountain /ˈfaʊntɪn/ *noun* **1** jet(s) of water as ornament or for drinking. **2** spring. **3** (often + *of*) source. □ **fountainhead** source. **fountain pen** pen with reservoir or cartridge for ink.

■ **1** *poetical* fount, jet, spout, spray. **2** font, *poetical* fount, spring, well, well-spring. **3** *poetical* fount, fountainhead, source, well, well-spring.

four /fɔː/ *adjective & noun* **1** one more than three. **2** 4-oared boat. **3** its crew. □ **four-letter word** short obscene word. **four-poster** bed with 4 posts supporting canopy. **four-square** *adjective* **1** solidly based. **2** steady. ● *adverb* resolutely. **four-stroke** (of internal-combustion engine) having power cycle completed in two up-and-down movements of piston. **four-wheel drive** drive acting on all 4 wheels of vehicle.

fourfold *adjective & adverb* four times as much or many.

foursome *noun* **1** group of 4 people. **2** golf match between two pairs.

fourteen /fɔːˈtiːn/ *adjective & noun* one more than thirteen. □ **fourteenth** *adjective & noun*.

fourth /fɔːθ/ *adjective & noun* **1** next after third. **2** any of four equal parts of thing. □ **fourthly** *adverb*.

fowl /faʊl/ *noun* (*plural* same or **-s**) **1** chicken kept for eggs and meat. **2** poultry as food.

fox *noun* **1** wild canine animal with red or grey fur and bushy tail. **2** its fur. **3** crafty person. ● *verb* deceive; puzzle. □ **foxglove** tall plant with purple or white flowers. **foxhole** hole in ground as shelter etc. in battle. **foxhound** hound bred to hunt foxes. **fox-hunting** hunting foxes with hounds. **fox-terrier** small short-haired terrier. **foxtrot** ballroom dance with slow and quick steps. □ **foxlike** *adjective*.

foxy *adjective* (**-ier**, **-iest**) **1** foxlike. **2** sly, cunning. **3** reddish-brown. □ **foxily** *adverb*.

foyer /ˈfɔɪeɪ/ *noun* entrance hall in hotel, theatre, etc.

■ ante-room, entrance, entrance hall, hall, lobby, reception.

FPA *abbreviation* Family Planning Association.

Fr. *abbreviation* **1** Father. **2** French.

fr. *abbreviation* franc(s).

fracas /ˈfrækɑː/ *noun* (*plural* same /-kɑːz/) noisy quarrel.

fraction /ˈfrækʃ(ə)n/ *noun* **1** part of whole number. **2** small part, amount, etc. **3** portion of mixture obtainable by distillation etc. □ **fractional** *adjective*. **fractionally** *adverb*.

■ **2** division, part, portion, section, subdivision.

fractious /ˈfrækʃəs/ *adjective* irritable, peevish.

fracture /'fræktʃə/ *noun* breakage, esp. of bone.
● *verb* (**-ring**) cause fracture in; suffer fracture.
■ *noun* break, breakage, chip, cleavage, cleft,
crack, fissure, rift, rupture, split. ● *verb* breach,
break, chip, *literary* cleave, crack, rupture,
separate, split.

fragile /'frædʒaɪl/ *adjective* **1** easily broken. **2**
delicate. □ **fragility** /frə'dʒɪl-/ *noun*.
■ see FRAIL 1.

fragment *noun* /'frægmənt/ **1** part broken off. **2**
incomplete part. **3** remains or unfinished portion
of book etc. ● *verb* /fræg'ment/ break into fragments. □ **fragmental** /-'men-/ *adjective*. **fragmentary** *adjective*. **fragmentation** *noun*.
■ *noun* **1**, **2** atom, bit, chip, crumb, morsel, part,
particle, piece, portion, remnant, scrap, shard,
shiver, shred, sliver, snatch, snippet, speck;
(*fragments*) debris, remains, smithereens. ● *verb*
see BREAK *verb* 1. □ **fragmentary** bitty, broken,
disconnected, disintegrated, disjointed,
fragmented, imperfect, in bits, incoherent,
incomplete, in fragments, partial, scattered,
scrappy, *colloquial* sketchy, uncoordinated.

fragrance /'freɪɡrəns/ *noun* **1** sweetness of
smell. **2** sweet scent.
■ aroma, bouquet, nose (*of wine*), odour,
perfume, redolence, scent, smell.

fragrant *adjective* sweet-smelling.
■ aromatic, odoriferous, odorous, perfumed,
redolent, scented, sweet-smelling.

frail *adjective* **1** fragile, delicate. **2** in weak health.
3 morally weak. □ **frailly** /'freɪlli/ *adverb*. **frail-
ness** *noun*.
■ **1** breakable, brittle, dainty, delicate, flimsy,
fragile, insubstantial, light, puny, rickety, slight,
thin, unsound, unsteady, weedy. **2** see ILL
adjective 1. **3** susceptible, vulnerable, weak.

frailty *noun* (*plural* **-ies**) **1** frail quality. **2** weakness, foible.

frame *noun* **1** case or border enclosing picture
etc. **2** supporting structure. **3** (in *plural*) structure of spectacles holding lenses. **4** build of
person or animal. **5** framework; construction. **6**
(in full **frame of mind**) temporary state. **7** single
picture on photographic film. **8** (in snooker etc.)
triangular structure for positioning balls. **9** (in
snooker etc.) round of play. **10** glazed structure
to protect plants. ● *verb* (**-ming**) **1** set in frame. **2**
serve as frame for. **3** construct; devise. **4** (+ *to*,
into) adapt, fit. **5** *slang* concoct false charge etc.
against. **6** articulate (words). □ **frame-up** *slang*
conspiracy to convict innocent person. **framework 1** essential supporting structure. **2** basic
system.
■ *noun* **1** border, case, casing, edge, edging,
mount, mounting. **2** bodywork, chassis,
construction, framework, scaffolding, shell,
skeleton, structure. **5** see FRAMEWORK. **6** (**frame
of mind**) see ATTITUDE 1,2. ● *verb* **1**, **2** box in,
enclose, mount, set off, surround. **3** see COMPOSE
2. □ **framework 1** bare bones, frame, shell,
skeleton, structure, support, trellis. **2** frame,
outline, plan, structure, system.

franc *noun* French, Belgian, Swiss, etc. unit of
currency.

franchise /'fræntʃaɪz/ *noun* **1** right to vote. **2**
citizenship. **3** authorization to sell company's
goods etc. in particular area. **4** right granted to
person or corporation. ● *verb* (**-sing**) grant
franchise to.

Franciscan /fræn'sɪskən/ *adjective* of (order of)
St Francis. ● *noun* Franciscan friar or nun.

frangible /'fræn(d)ʒɪb(ə)l/ *adjective* breakable,
fragile.

franglais /'frãɡleɪ/ *noun* French with many
English words and idioms. [French]

Frank *noun* member of Germanic people that
conquered Gaul in 6th c. □ **Frankish** *adjective*.

frank *adjective* **1** candid, outspoken. **2** undisguised. **3** open. ● *verb* mark (letter etc.) to record
payment of postage. ● *noun* franking signature
or mark. □ **frankly** *adverb*. **frankness** *noun*.
■ *adjective* **1** blunt, candid, direct, downright,
explicit, forthright, heart-to-heart, open,
outspoken, plain, plain-spoken, straightforward,
straight from the heart. **2** open, outright, revealing,
unconcealed, undisguised, unreserved. **3**
genuine, honest, ingenuous, open, sincere,
straightforward, trustworthy, truthful.

frankfurter /'fræŋkfɜːtə/ *noun* seasoned
smoked sausage.

frankincense /'fræŋkɪnsens/ *noun* aromatic
gum resin burnt as incense.

frantic /'fræntɪk/ *adjective* **1** wildly excited;
frenzied. **2** (of activity, action, etc.) hurried,
anxious; desperate; violent. **3** *colloquial* extreme.
□ **frantically** *adverb*.
■ **1** agitated, anxious, berserk, beside oneself,
crazy, delirious, demented, deranged, desperate,
distraught, excitable, feverish, frenetic, frenzied,
hysterical, *colloquial* mad, overwrought, panicky,
rabid, uncontrollable, wild, worked up. **2** anxious,
desperate, fraught, frenetic, frenzied, furious,
hectic, hurried, violent, wild.

fraternal /frə'tɜːn(ə)l/ *adjective* **1** of brothers,
brotherly. **2** comradely. □ **fraternally** *adverb*.

fraternity /frə'tɜːnɪti/ *noun* (*plural* **-ies**) **1** religious brotherhood. **2** group with common inter-
ests or of same professional class. **3** *US* male
students' society. **4** brotherliness.

fraternize /'frætənaɪz/ *verb* (also **-ise**) (**-zing** or
-sing) (often + *with*) associate, make friends, esp.
with enemy etc. □ **fraternization** *noun*.

fratricide /'frætrɪsaɪd/ *noun* **1** killing of one's
brother or sister. **2** person who does this. □ **frat-
ricidal** /-'saɪd(ə)l/ *adjective*.

Frau /frau/ *noun* (*plural* **Frauen** /'frauən/) *title
used of or to married or widowed German-
speaking woman*.

fraud /frɔːd/ *noun* **1** criminal deception. **2** dishonest trick. **3** impostor.

■ **1** cheating, chicanery, deceit, deception, dishonesty, double-dealing, duplicity, forgery, imposture, pretence, sharp practice, trickery. **2** con-trick, counterfeit, deception, fake, forgery, hoax, imposture, put-up job, ruse, sham, swindle, trick. **3** charlatan, cheat, con man, hoaxer, humbug, impostor, mountebank, *colloquial* phoney, quack, rogue, scoundrel, swindler.

fraudulent /'frɔːdjʊlənt/ *adjective* of, involving, or guilty of fraud. □ **fraudulence** *noun*. **fraudulently** *adverb*.

■ *slang* bent, bogus, cheating, corrupt, counterfeit, criminal, *colloquial* crooked, deceitful, devious, dirty, dishonest, double-dealing, duplicitous, fake, false, forged, illegal, lying, *colloquial* phoney, sham, specious, swindling, underhand, unscrupulous.

fraught /frɔːt/ *adjective* **1** (+ *with*) filled or attended with (danger etc.). **2** distressing; tense.

Fräulein /'frɔɪlaɪn/ *noun: title used of or to unmarried German-speaking woman.*

fray[1] *verb* **1** (often as **frayed** *adjective*) wear or become worn; unravel at edge. **2** (esp. as **frayed** *adjective*) (of nerves) become strained.

■ **1** (frayed) ragged, rough-edged, shabby, tattered, *colloquial* tatty, threadbare, torn, unravelled, worn.

fray[2] *noun* **1** fight, conflict. **2** brawl.

■ **1** see FIGHT *noun* 1. **2** brawl, commotion, disturbance, fracas, mêlée, quarrel, *colloquial* rumpus.

frazzle /'fræz(ə)l/ *colloquial noun* worn, exhausted, or shrivelled state. ● *verb* (**-ling**) (usually as **frazzled** *adjective*) wear out; exhaust.

freak *noun* **1** monstrosity; abnormal person or thing. **2** abnormal occurrence. **3** *colloquial* unconventional person. **4** *colloquial* fanatic of specified kind. ● *verb* (often + *out*) *colloquial* **1** make or become very angry. **2** (cause to) undergo esp. drug-induced hallucinations or strong emotional experience. □ **freakish** *adjective*. **freaky** *adjective* (**-ier**, **-iest**).

■ *noun* **1** aberration, abnormality, abortion, anomaly, curiosity, deformity, irregularity, monster, monstrosity, mutant, oddity, quirk, rarity, variant. **2** (*freak storm*) aberrant, abnormal, anomalous, atypical, bizarre, exceptional, extraordinary, freakish, odd, peculiar, queer, rare, unaccountable, unforeseeable, unpredictable, unusual, *colloquial* weird. **4** see FANATIC *noun*.

freckle /'frek(ə)l/ *noun* light brown spot on skin. ● *verb* (**-ling**) (usually as **freckled** *adjective*) spot or be spotted with freckles. □ **freckly** *adjective* (**-ier**, **-iest**).

free *adjective* (**freer** /'friːə/, **freest** /'friːɪst/) **1** not a slave; having personal rights and social and political liberty. **2** autonomous; democratic. **3** unrestricted, not confined. **4** (+ *of*, *from* or in *combination*) exempt from. **5** (+ *of*, *from* or in *combination*) not containing or subject to. **6** (+ *to do*) permitted, at liberty to. **7** costing nothing. **8** available, not occupied. **9** clear of engagements or obligations. **10** clear of obstructions. **11** spontaneous. **12** lavish, unreserved. **13** (of translation) not literal. ● *adverb* **1** freely. **2** without cost. ● *verb* (**frees, freed**) **1** make free, liberate. **2** disentangle. □ **for free** *colloquial* gratis. **free and easy** informal. **freeboard** part of ship's side between waterline and deck. **freebooter** pirate. **freeborn** inheriting citizen's rights. **Free Church** Nonconformist Church. **free enterprise** freedom of private business from state control. **free fall** movement under force of gravity only. **free-for-all 1** spontaneous fight involving number of people. **2** unrestricted discussion. **free hand** liberty to act at one's own discretion. **freehand** ● *adjective* (of drawing) done without ruler, compasses, etc. ● *adverb* in a freehand way. **free house** public house not controlled by brewery. **freeloader** *slang* sponger. **freeman** holder of freedom of city etc. **free port** port without customs duties, or open to all traders. **free-range 1** (of hens etc.) roaming freely. **2** (of eggs) produced by such hens. **free spirit** independent or uninhibited person. **free-standing** not supported by another structure. **freestyle 1** swimming race in which any stroke may be used. **2** wrestling allowing almost any hold. **freethinker** /-'θɪŋkə/ person who rejects dogma, esp. in religious belief. **freethinking** *noun* & *adjective*. **free trade** trade without import restrictions etc. **freeway** *US* motorway. **freewheel 1** ride bicycle with pedals at rest. **2** act without constraint. **free will** power of acting independently of fate or without coercion.

■ *adjective* **1** at liberty, emancipated, freeborn, liberated, released, unchained, unfettered, unshackled. **2** autonomous, democratic, independent, self-governing, sovereign. **3** at large, at liberty, loose, unconfined, unconstrained, unencumbered, unfixed, unrestrained, unrestricted, untrammelled. **6** able, allowed, at liberty, permitted. **7** complimentary, gratis, without charge. **8** available, empty, uninhabited, unoccupied, vacant. **9** at leisure, idle, independent, not working, uncommitted. **10** accessible, clear, open, permitted, unhindered, unimpeded, unrestricted. **11** spontaneous, unasked-for, unsolicited. **12** *poetical* bounteous, charitable, generous, lavish, liberal, munificent, ready, unstinting, willing. ● *verb* **1** absolve, acquit, clear, deliver, discharge, emancipate, enfranchise, *formal* exculpate, exonerate, let go, let off, let out, liberate, loose, make free, pardon, parole, ransom, release, reprieve, rescue, save, set free, spare, turn loose, unchain, unfetter, unleash, unlock, unloose. **2** clear, disengage, disentangle, extricate, loose, unbind, undo, unknot, untie. □ **free and easy** see INFORMAL 1.

freebie /'friːbɪ/ *noun colloquial* thing given free of charge.

freedom *noun* **1** being free. **2** personal or civil liberty. **3** (often + *to*) liberty of action. **4** (+ *from*) exemption from. **5** (+ *of*) honorary membership or citizenship of. **6** (+ *of*) unrestricted use of (house etc.). □ **freedom fighter** person who violently resists established political system.

■ **1, 2** autonomy, deliverance, emancipation, independence, liberation, liberty, release, self-determination, self-government, sovereignty. **3** ability, carte blanche, discretion, free hand, latitude, leeway, leisure, licence, opportunity, permission, power, privilege, right, scope. **4** exemption, immunity.

freehold *noun* **1** complete ownership of property for unlimited period. **2** such property. □ **freeholder** *noun*.

freelance *noun* person working for no fixed employer. ● *verb* work as freelance. ● *adverb* as freelance.

Freemason /ˈfriːmeɪs(ə)n/ *noun* member of fraternity for mutual help with secret rituals. □ **Freemasonry** *noun*.

freesia /ˈfriːzjə/ *noun* fragrant flowering African bulb.

freeze *verb* (**-zing**; *past* **froze**; *past participle* **frozen** /ˈfrəʊz(ə)n/) **1** turn into ice or other solid by cold. **2** make or become rigid from cold. **3** (esp. as **freezing** *adjective*) be or feel very cold. **4** cover or be covered with ice. **5** refrigerate below freezing point. **6** make or become motionless. **7** (as **frozen** *adjective*) devoid of emotion. **8** make (assets etc.) unrealizable. **9** fix (prices etc.) at certain level. **10** stop (movement in film). ● *noun* **1** period or state of frost. **2** price-fixing etc. **3** (in full **freeze-frame**) still film-shot. □ **freeze-dry** preserve (food) by freezing and then drying in vacuum. **freeze up** obstruct or be obstructed by ice. **freeze-up** *noun* period of extreme cold. **freezing point** temperature at which liquid freezes.

■ *verb* **1** become ice, become solid, congeal, harden, solidify, stiffen. **2** chill, cool, make cold, numb. **3** (**freezing**) see COLD *adjective* 1;3. **4** ice over, ice up. **5** chill, deep-freeze, ice, refrigerate. **6** fix, hold, immobilize, keep still, paralyse, peg, petrify, stand still, stick, stop. **10** fix, hold, stop.

freezer *noun* refrigerated cabinet for preserving food in frozen state.

freight /freɪt/ *noun* **1** transport of goods. **2** goods transported. **3** charge for transport of goods.

■ **1** consignment, shipment, shipping, transport. **2** cargo, consignment, goods, haul, load, merchandise, payload, shipment.

freighter *noun* ship or aircraft for carrying freight.

French *adjective* of France or its people or language. ● *noun* **1** French language. **2** (**the French**) (treated as *plural*) the French people. □ **French bean** kidney or haricot bean as unripe pods or as ripe seeds. **French bread** long crisp loaf. **French dressing** salad dressing of oil and vinegar. **French fried potatoes**, **French fries** chips. **French horn** coiled brass wind instrument. **French letter** *colloquial* condom. **Frenchman**, **Frenchwoman** native or national of France. **French polish** *noun* shellac polish for wood. **French-polish** *verb*. **French window** glazed door in outside wall.

frenetic /frəˈnetɪk/ *adjective* frantic, frenzied. □ **frenetically** *adverb*.

frenzy /ˈfrenzɪ/ *noun* (*plural* **-ies**) wild excitement or fury. ● *verb* (**-ies**, **-ied**) (usually as **frenzied** *adjective*) drive to frenzy. □ **frenziedly** *adverb*.

■ *noun* agitation, delirium, derangement, excitement, fever, fit, fury, hysteria, insanity, lunacy, madness, mania, outburst, paroxysm, passion, turmoil.

frequency /ˈfriːkwənsɪ/ *noun* (*plural* **-ies**) **1** commonness of occurrence. **2** frequent occurrence. **3** rate of recurrence (of vibration etc.). □ **frequency modulation** *Electronics* modulation by varying carrier-wave frequency.

frequent *adjective* /ˈfriːkwənt/ **1** occurring often or in close succession. **2** habitual. ● *verb* /frɪˈkwent/ go to habitually. □ **frequenter** /frɪˈkwentə/*noun*. **frequently** /ˈfriːkwəntlɪ/ *adverb*.

■ *adjective* **1** common, continual, countless, incessant, innumerable, many, numerous, persistent, recurrent, recurring, regular, reiterative, repeated. **2** constant, customary, everyday, familiar, habitual, normal, ordinary, regular, usual. ● *verb* see HAUNT *verb* 1,2.

fresco /ˈfreskəʊ/ *noun* (*plural* **-s**) painting in watercolour on fresh plaster.

fresh *adjective* **1** newly made or obtained. **2** other, different; new, additional. **3** (+*from*) lately arrived from. **4** not stale or faded. **5** (of food) not preserved. **6** (of water) not salty. **7** pure, refreshing. **8** (of wind) brisk. **9** *colloquial* cheeky. **10** *colloquial* amorously impudent. **11** alert. **12** inexperienced. ● *adverb* newly, recently. □ **freshwater** (of fish etc.) not of the sea. □ **freshly** *adverb*. **freshness** *noun*.

■ *adjective* **1** just arrived, (the) latest, new, newly gathered, recent, up-to-date. **2** additional, alternative, different, extra, new, supplementary, unfamiliar. **4** (*fresh sheets*) clean, crisp, laundered, untouched, unused, washed; (*fresh colours*) bright, clean, glowing, just painted, renewed, restored, sparkling, unfaded, vivid. **5** healthy, natural, newly gathered, unprocessed, untreated, wholesome. **6** drinkable, potable, sweet. **7** airy, circulating, clear, cool, invigorating, pure, refreshing, uncontaminated, unpolluted, ventilated. **8** bracing, breezy, brisk, invigorating, moderate, sharp, stiff, strongish. **11** alert, energetic, healthy, invigorated, lively, perky, rested, revived, sprightly, spry, tingling, vigorous, vital. **12** callow, green, inexperienced, naive, raw, unsophisticated, untried, wet behind the ears.

freshen *verb* **1** make or become fresh. **2** (+ *up*) wash, tidy oneself, etc. **3** revive.

fresher *noun colloquial* first-year student at university or (*US*) high school.

freshet /ˈfreʃɪt/ *noun* **1** rush of fresh water into sea. **2** river flood.

freshman /ˈfreʃmən/ *noun* fresher.

fret[1] *verb* (**-tt-**) **1** be worried or distressed. **2** make anxious, irritate. ● *noun* worry, vexation. □ **fretful** *adjective*. **fretfully** *adverb*. **fretfulness** *noun*.

■ *verb* **1** agonize, be anxious, brood, lose sleep, worry. **2** see ANNOY 1. □ **fretful** anxious, distressed, disturbed, edgy, irritable, irritated, *colloquial* jittery, peevish, petulant, restless, testy, touchy, worried.

fret² *noun* ornamental pattern of straight lines joined usually at right angles. ● *verb* (**-tt-**) adorn with fret etc. □ **fretsaw** narrow saw on frame for cutting thin wood in patterns. **fretwork** work done with fretsaw.

fret³ *noun* bar or ridge on finger-board of guitar etc.

Freudian /ˈfrɔɪdɪən/ *adjective* of Freud's theories or method of psychoanalysis. ● *noun* follower of Freud. □ **Freudian slip** unintentional verbal error revealing subconscious feelings.

Fri. *abbreviation* Friday.

friable /ˈfraɪəb(ə)l/ *adjective* easily crumbled. □ **friability** *noun*.

friar /ˈfraɪə/ *noun* member of male non-enclosed religious order. □ **friar's balsam** type of inhalant.

friary /ˈfraɪərɪ/ *noun* (*plural* **-ies**) monastery for friars.

fricassee /ˈfrɪkəseɪ/ *noun* pieces of meat in thick sauce. ● *verb* (**fricassees, fricasseed**) make fricassee of.

fricative /ˈfrɪkətɪv/ *adjective* sounded by friction of breath in narrow opening. ● *noun* such consonant (e.g. *f, th*).

friction /ˈfrɪkʃ(ə)n/ *noun* **1** rubbing of one object against another. **2** resistance so encountered. **3** clash of wills, opinions, etc. □ **frictional** *adjective*.

■ **1** abrasion, attrition, chafing, fretting, grating, rubbing, scraping. **3** see CONFLICT *noun* 2.

Friday /ˈfraɪdeɪ/ *noun* day of week following Thursday.

fridge *noun* *colloquial* refrigerator. □ **fridge-freezer** combined refrigerator and freezer.

friend /frend/ *noun* **1** supportive and respected associate, esp. one for whom affection is felt. **2** ally. **3** kind person. **4** person already mentioned. **5** (**Friend**) Quaker. □ **friendless** *adjective*. **friendlessness** *noun*.

■ **1** acquaintance, associate, boyfriend, *colloquial* buddy, *colloquial* chum, companion, comrade, confidant(e), *often derogatory* crony, girlfriend, intimate, mate, *colloquial* pal, partner, penfriend, playfellow, playmate, supporter, well-wisher. **2** see ALLY. □ **friendless** abandoned, alienated, alone, deserted, estranged, forlorn, forsaken, isolated, lonely, ostracized, shunned, shut out, solitary, unattached, unloved.

friendly *adjective* (**-ier, -iest**) **1** outgoing, kindly. **2** (often + *with*) on amicable terms; not hostile. **3** user-friendly. ● *noun* (*plural* **-ies**) friendly match. □ **-friendly** not harming, helping. **friendly match** match played for enjoyment rather than competition. **Friendly Society**

society for insurance against sickness etc. □ **friendliness** *noun*.

■ *adjective* **1, 2** accessible, affable, affectionate, agreeable, amiable, amicable, approachable, attached, benevolent, benign, *colloquial* chummy, civil, close, clubbable, companionable, compatible, comradely, conciliatory, congenial, convivial, cordial, demonstrative, expansive, familiar, favourable, genial, good-natured, gracious, helpful, hospitable, intimate, kind, kind-hearted, kindly, likeable, loving, matey, neighbourly, outgoing, *colloquial* pally, sociable, sympathetic, tender, *colloquial* thick, warm, welcoming, well disposed. **3** accessible, helpful. □ **friendliness** benevolence, camaraderie, conviviality, devotion, esteem, familiarity, goodwill, helpfulness, hospitality, kindness, neighbourliness, regard, sociability, warmth.

friendship *noun* friendly relationship or feeling.

■ affection, alliance, amity, association, attachment, closeness, comradeship, fellowship, fondness, friendliness, harmony, intimacy, love, rapport, *colloquial* relationship.

frier = FRYER.

Friesian /ˈfriːzɪən/ *noun* one of breed of black and white dairy cattle. ● *adjective* of Friesians.

frieze /friːz/ *noun* **1** part of entablature, often filled with sculpture, between architrave and cornice. **2** band of decoration, esp. at top of wall.

frigate /ˈfrɪgɪt/ *noun* naval escort-vessel.

fright /fraɪt/ *noun* **1** sudden or extreme fear. **2** instance of this. **3** grotesque-looking person or thing. □ **take fright** become frightened.

■ **1** alarm, apprehension, consternation, dismay, dread, fear, horror, panic, terror, trepidation. **2** jolt, scare, shock, surprise.

frighten *verb* **1** fill with fright. **2** (+ *away, off, out of, into*) drive by fright. □ **frightened** *adjective*. **frightening** *adjective*. **frighteningly** *adverb*.

■ **1** agitate, alarm, appal, cow, make (person's) blood curdle, daunt, dismay, distress, horrify, intimidate, make afraid, menace, panic, petrify, *colloquial* put the wind up, scare, *colloquial* scare stiff, shake, shock, startle, terrify, terrorize, threaten, traumatize, tyrannize, unnerve, upset. **2** browbeat, bully, intimidate, menace, scare, terrify. □ **frightened** afraid, aghast, alarmed, anxious, appalled, apprehensive, *colloquial* chicken, cowardly, craven, daunted, fearful, harrowed, horrified, horror-struck, panicky, panic-stricken, petrified, scared, shocked, terrified, terror-stricken, trembling, unnerved, upset, *colloquial* windy. **frightening** alarming, appalling, blood-curdling, *colloquial* creepy, daunting, dire, dreadful, eerie, fearful, fearsome, formidable, ghostly, grim, hair-raising, horrifying, intimidating, petrifying, *colloquial* scary, sinister, spine-chilling, *colloquial* spooky, terrifying, traumatic, uncanny, unnerving, upsetting, weird, worrying.

frightful *adjective* **1** dreadful, shocking. **2** ugly. **3** *colloquial* extremely bad. **4** *colloquial* extreme.

□ **frightfully** *adverb*. **frightfulness** *noun*.
■ **1, 2** *colloquial* awful, ghastly, grisly, gruesome, harrowing, hideous, horrible, horrid, horrific, macabre, shocking, terrible. **3, 4** see BAD 2.

frigid /ˈfrɪdʒɪd/ *adjective* **1** unfriendly, cold. **2** (of woman) sexually unresponsive. **3** cold. □ **frigidity** /-ˈdʒɪd-/ *noun*.

frill *noun* **1** ornamental edging of gathered or pleated material. **2** (in *plural*) unnecessary embellishments. ● *verb* (usually as **frilled** *adjective*) decorate with frill. □ **frilly** *adjective* (**-ier, -iest**).

fringe *noun* **1** border of tassels or loose threads. **2** front hair cut to hang over forehead. **3** outer limit. **4** unimportant area or part. ● *verb* (**-ging**) **1** adorn with fringe. **2** serve as fringe to. □ **fringe benefit** employee's benefit additional to salary.
■ *noun* **3** borders, boundary, edge, limits, *historical* marches, margin, outskirts, perimeter, periphery.

frippery /ˈfrɪpərɪ/ *noun* (*plural* **-ies**) **1** showy finery. **2** empty display. **3** (usually in *plural*) knick-knacks.

frisk *verb* **1** leap or skip playfully. **2** *slang* search (person). ● *noun* playful leap or skip.

frisky *adjective* (**-ier, -iest**) lively, playful.
■ active, animated, coltish, frolicsome, high-spirited, jaunty, lively, perky, playful, skittish, spirited, sprightly.

frisson /ˈfriːsɒn/ *noun* emotional thrill. [French]

fritillary /frɪˈtɪlərɪ/ *noun* (*plural* **-ies**) **1** plant with bell-like flowers. **2** butterfly with red and black chequered wings.

fritter¹ /ˈfrɪtə/ *verb* (usually + *away*) waste triflingly.

fritter² /ˈfrɪtə/ *noun* fruit, meat, etc. coated in batter and fried.

frivolous /ˈfrɪvələs/ *adjective* **1** not serious, shallow, silly. **2** trifling. □ **frivolity** /-ˈvɒl-/ *noun* (*plural* **-ies**).
■ **1** casual, childish, facetious, flighty, flip, flippant, foolish, irresponsible, jocular, joking, puerile, ridiculous, shallow, silly, stupid, superficial, unserious, vacuous. **2** inconsequential, insignificant, minor, nugatory, paltry, petty, pointless, trivial, trumpery, unimportant, worthless. □ **frivolity** childishness, facetiousness, flippancy, levity, light-heartedness, nonsense, playing about, silliness, triviality.

frizz *verb* form (hair) into tight curls. ● *noun* frizzed hair or state. □ **frizzy** *adjective* (**-ier, -iest**).

frizzle¹ /ˈfrɪz(ə)l/ *verb* (**-ling**) **1** fry or cook with sizzling noise. **2** (often + *up*) burn, shrivel.

frizzle² /ˈfrɪz(ə)l/ *verb* (**-ling**) & *noun* frizz.

frock *noun* **1** woman's or girl's dress. **2** monk's or priest's gown. □ **frock-coat** man's long-skirted coat.
■ **1** dress, gown, robe. **2** gown, robe.

frog *noun* tailless leaping amphibian. □ **frog in**

one's throat *colloquial* phlegm in throat that hinders speech. **frogman** underwater swimmer equipped with rubber suit and flippers. **frogmarch** hustle forward with arms pinned behind. **frog-spawn** frog's eggs.

frolic /ˈfrɒlɪk/ *verb* (**-ck-**) play about merrily. ● *noun* merrymaking.
■ *verb* caper, cavort, curvet, dance, frisk about, gambol, have fun, hop about, horse around, jump about, *colloquial* lark around, leap about, *colloquial* make whoopee, play about, prance, revel, romp, skip, skylark, sport.

frolicsome *adjective* playful.

from /frəm/ *preposition: expressing separation or origin.*

fromage frais /ˈfrɒmɑːʒ ˈfreɪ/ *noun* type of soft cheese.

frond *noun* leaflike part of fern or palm.

front /frʌnt/ *noun* **1** side or part most prominent or important, or nearer spectator or direction of motion. **2** line of battle; scene of actual fighting. **3** organized political group. **4** demeanour. **5** pretext; bluff. **6** person etc. as cover for subversive or illegal activities. **7** land along edge of sea or lake, esp. in town. **8** forward edge of advancing cold or warm air. **9** auditorium. **10** breast of garment. ● *adjective* of or at front. ● *verb* **1** (+ *on, to, towards,* etc.) have front facing or directed towards. **2** (+ *for*) *slang* act as front for. **3** (usually as **fronted** *adjective*) (+ *with*) provide with or have front. **4** lead (band, organization, etc.). □ **front bench** seats in Parliament for leading members of government and opposition. **front line** foremost part of army or group under attack. **front runner** favourite in race etc.
■ *noun* **1** anterior, bow (of ship), façade, face, forefront, foreground, frontage, head, nose, obverse, van, vanguard. **2** battle area, danger zone, front line. **4** appearance, aspect, bearing, demeanour, expression, look, show. **5** blind, bluff, cover-up, disguise, mask, pretence, pretext, show. ● *adjective* first, foremost, leading, most advanced.

frontage *noun* **1** front of building. **2** land next to street, water, etc. **3** extent of front.

frontal *adjective* **1** of or on front. **2** of forehead.
■ **1** direct, facing, head-on, oncoming.

frontier /ˈfrʌntɪə/ *noun* **1** border between countries. **2** district on each side of this. **3** limits of attainment or knowledge in subject. **4** *esp. US historical* border between settled and unsettled country. □ **frontiersman, frontierswoman** *noun*.
■ **1, 2** border, borderline, boundary, bounds, limit, *historical* marches, pale. **3** bounds, limit(s).

frontispiece /ˈfrʌntɪspiːs/ *noun* illustration facing title-page of book.

frost *noun* **1** frozen dew or vapour. **2** temperature below freezing point. ● *verb* **1** (usually + *over, up*) become covered with frost. **2** cover (as) with frost. **3** (usually as **frosted** *adjective*) roughen surface of (glass) to make opaque.

◻ **frostbite** injury to body tissue due to freezing. **frostbitten** *adjective*.

frosting *noun* icing for cakes.

frosty *adjective* (**-ier, -iest**) **1** cold or covered with frost. **2** unfriendly.

froth *noun* **1** foam. **2** idle talk. ● *verb* emit or gather froth. ◻ **frothy** *adjective* (**-ier, -iest**).
■ *noun* **1** bubbles, effervescence, foam, head (*on beer*), lather, scum, spume, suds.

frown *verb* **1** wrinkle brows, esp. in displeasure or concentration. **2** (+ *at, on*) disapprove of. ● *noun* act of frowning; frowning look.
■ *verb* **1** *colloquial* give a dirty look, glare, glower, grimace, knit one's brow, look sullen, lour, lower, scowl. **2** (*frown on*) see DISAPPROVE.

frowsty /ˈfraʊstɪ/ *adjective* (**-ier, -iest**) fusty, stuffy.

frowzy /ˈfraʊzɪ/ *adjective* (also **frowsy**) (**-ier, -iest**) **1** fusty. **2** slatternly, dingy.

froze *past* of FREEZE.

frozen *past participle* of FREEZE.

FRS *abbreviation* Fellow of the Royal Society.

fructify /ˈfrʌktɪfaɪ/ *verb* (**-ies, -ied**) **1** bear fruit. **2** make fruitful.

fructose /ˈfrʌktəʊz/ *noun* sugar in fruits, honey, etc.

frugal /ˈfruːg(ə)l/ *adjective* **1** sparing. **2** meagre. ◻ **frugality** /-ˈɡæl-/ *noun*. **frugally** *adverb*.

fruit /fruːt/ *noun* **1** seed-bearing part of plant or tree. **2** this as food. **3** (usually in *plural*) products; profits, rewards. ● *verb* bear fruit. ◻ **fruit cake** cake containing dried fruit. **fruit cocktail** diced fruit salad. **fruit machine** coin-operated gambling machine. **fruit salad** dessert of mixed fruit. **fruit sugar** fructose.

fruiterer /ˈfruːtərə/ *noun* dealer in fruit.

fruitful *adjective* **1** productive. **2** successful. ◻ **fruitfully** *adverb*. **fruitfulness** *noun*.
■ **1** abundant, *poetical* bounteous, bountiful, copious, fecund, fertile, flourishing, luxurious, *literary* plenteous, productive, profuse, prolific, rich. **2** advantageous, beneficial, effective, gainful, profitable, rewarding, successful, useful, well spent, worthwhile.

fruition /fruːˈɪʃ(ə)n/ *noun* realization of aims or hopes.

fruitless *adjective* **1** not bearing fruit. **2** useless, unsuccessful. ◻ **fruitlessly** *adverb*.
■ **1** barren, sterile, unfruitful, unproductive. **2** abortive, *archaic* bootless, disappointing, futile, ineffective, ineffectual, pointless, profitless, unavailing, unprofitable, unrewarding, unsuccessful, useless, vain.

fruity *adjective* (**-ier, -iest**) **1** of or resembling fruit. **2** (of voice) deep and rich. **3** *colloquial* slightly indecent.

frump *noun* dowdy woman. ◻ **frumpish** *adjective*. **frumpy** *adjective* (**-ier, -iest**).

frustrate /frʌsˈtreɪt/ *verb* (**-ting**) **1** make (efforts) ineffective. **2** prevent from achieving purpose. **3** (as **frustrated** *adjective*) discontented; unfulfilled. ◻ **frustrating** *adjective*. **frustratingly** *adverb*. **frustration** *noun*.
■ **1** counteract, negate, neutralize, nullify. **2** baffle, baulk, block, check, circumvent, defeat, disappoint, discourage, foil, halt, hamstring, hinder, impede, inhibit, prevent, stop, stymie, thwart. **3** (**frustrated**) disappointed, embittered, loveless, lovesick, resentful, thwarted, unfulfilled, unsatisfied.

fry[1] *verb* (**fries, fried**) cook in hot fat. ● *noun* fried food, esp. (usually **fries**) chips. ◻ **frying-pan** shallow long-handled pan for frying. **fry-up** *colloquial* fried bacon, eggs, etc.

fry[2] *plural noun* young or freshly hatched fishes.

fryer *noun* (also **frier**) **1** person who fries. **2** vessel for frying esp. fish.

ft *abbreviation* foot, feet.

FT-SE *abbreviation* Financial Times Stock Exchange (100 share index).

fuchsia /ˈfjuːʃə/ *noun* shrub with drooping flowers.

fuddle /ˈfʌd(ə)l/ *verb* (**-ling**) confuse, esp. with alcohol. ● *noun* **1** confusion. **2** intoxication.

fuddy-duddy /ˈfʌdɪdʌdɪ/ *colloquial adjective* fussy, old-fashioned. ● *noun* (*plural* **-ies**) such person.

fudge *noun* **1** soft toffee-like sweet. **2** faking. ● *verb* (**-ging**) make or do clumsily or dishonestly; fake.

fuel /ˈfjuːəl/ *noun* **1** material for burning or as source of heat, power, or nuclear energy. **2** thing that sustains or inflames passion etc. ● *verb* (**-ll-**; *US* **-l-**) **1** supply with fuel. **2** inflame (feeling).
■ *verb* **1** stoke up, supply with fuel. **2** encourage, feed, inflame, keep going, nourish, stimulate, sustain.

fug *noun colloquial* stuffy atmosphere. ◻ **fuggy** *adjective* (**-ier, -iest**).

fugitive /ˈfjuːdʒɪtɪv/ *noun* (often + *from*) person who flees. ● *adjective* **1** fleeing. **2** transient, fleeting.
■ *noun Military* deserter, escapee, escaper, refugee, renegade, runaway. ● *adjective* **2** see TRANSIENT.

fugue /fjuːɡ/ *noun* piece of music in which short melody or phrase is introduced by one part and developed by others. ◻ **fugal** *adjective*.

fulcrum /ˈfʌlkrəm/ *noun* (*plural* **-s** or **-cra**) point on which lever is supported.

fulfil /fʊlˈfɪl/ *verb* (*US* **fulfill**) (**-ll-**) **1** carry out. **2** satisfy. **3** (as **fulfilled** *adjective*) completely happy. **4** (**fulfil oneself**) realize one's potential. ◻ **fulfilment** *noun*.
■ **1** accomplish, achieve, bring about, bring off, carry off, carry out, complete, consummate, discharge, do, effect, effectuate, execute, implement, make come true, perform, realize. **2** answer, comply with, conform to, meet, obey, respond to, satisfy.

full /fʊl/ *adjective* **1** holding all it can. **2** replete. **3** abundant; satisfying. **4** (+ *of*) having abundance of. **5** (+ *of*) engrossed in. **6** complete, perfect. **7** utmost. **8** resonant. **9** plump. **10** (of clothes) ample. ● *adverb* **1** quite. **2** exactly. □ **full back** defensive player near goal in football etc. **full-blooded 1** vigorous, sensual. **2** not hybrid. **full-blown** fully developed. **full board** provision of bed and all meals. **full-bodied** rich in quality, tone, etc. **full frontal 1** (of nude) fully exposed at front. **2** explicit. **full-grown** grown to maturity. **full house 1** maximum attendance at theatre etc. **2** hand in poker with 3 of a kind and a pair. **full-length 1** of normal length, not shortened. **2** (of portrait) showing whole figure. **full moon** moon with whole disc illuminated. **full stop 1** punctuation mark (.) at end of sentence etc. (see panel). **2** complete cessation. **full term** completion of normal pregnancy. **full-time** ● *adjective* for or during whole of working week. ● *adverb* on full-time basis. □ **fullness** *noun*.

■ *adjective* **1** brimming, bursting, chock-a-block, chock-full, congested, crammed, crowded, filled, jammed, *colloquial* jam-packed, loaded, overflowing, packed, replete, solid, stuffed, topped-up, well filled, well stocked, well supplied. **2** gorged, replete, *formal* sated, satiated, satisfied, stuffed, well fed. **3** abundant, comprehensive, copious, detailed, exhaustive, extensive, satisfying, thorough. **6** complete, entire, perfect, plenary (*session*), total, unabridged, uncensored, uncut, unedited, unexpurgated, whole. **7** extreme, greatest, highest, maximum, top, utmost. **9** ample, broad, buxom, fat, large, plump, rounded, voluptuous, well built. **10** ample, baggy, generous,

voluminous, wide. □ **full-grown** adult, grown-up, mature, ready, ripe.

fully *adverb* **1** completely. **2** at least.

fulmar /ˈfʊlmə/ *noun* kind of petrel.

fulminate /ˈfʊlmɪneɪt/ *verb* (**-ting**) **1** criticize loudly and forcibly. **2** explode, flash. □ **fulmination** *noun*.

fulsome /ˈfʊlsəm/ *adjective* excessive, cloying; insincere. □ **fulsomely** *adverb*.

USAGE *Fulsome* is sometimes used wrongly to mean 'generous', as in *fulsome praise*, or 'generous with praise', as in *a fulsome tribute*.

fumble /ˈfʌmb(ə)l/ *verb* (**-ling**) **1** grope about. **2** handle clumsily or nervously. ● *noun* act of fumbling.

■ *verb* **1** feel (about), grope, stumble. **2** grope at, handle awkwardly, mishandle, touch clumsily.

fume *noun* (usually in *plural*) exuded smoke, gas, or vapour. ● *verb* (**-ming**) **1** emit fumes. **2** (often as **fuming** *adjective*) be very angry. **3** subject (oak etc.) to fumes to darken.

■ *noun* (*fumes*) exhaust, fog, gases, pollution, smog, smoke, vapour. ● *verb* **1** smoke, smoulder. **2** (**fuming**) see ANGRY 1.

fumigate /ˈfjuːmɪgeɪt/ *verb* (**-ting**) disinfect or purify with fumes. □ **fumigant** *noun*. **fumigation** *noun*. **fumigator** *noun*.

fun *noun* **1** playful amusement. **2** source of this. **3** mockery. □ **funfair** fair consisting of amusements and sideshows. **fun run** *colloquial* spon-

· ·

Full stop.

This is used:

1 at the end of a sentence, e.g.

I am going to the cinema tonight.
The film begins at seven.

The full stop is replaced by a question mark at the end of a question, and by an exclamation mark at the end of an exclamation.

2 after an abbreviation, e.g.

    H. G. Wells   *p. 19* (= *page 19*)   *Sun.* (= *Sunday*)
    Ex. 6 (= *Exercise 6*)

Full stops are **not** used with:

    a numerical abbreviations, e.g. *1st, 2nd, 15th, 23rd*
    b acronyms, e.g. *FIFA, NATO*
    c abbreviations that are used as ordinary words, e.g. *con, demo, recap*
    d chemical symbols, e.g. Fe, K, H_2O

Full stops are not essential for:

    a abbreviations consisting entirely of capitals, e.g. *BBC, AD, BC, PLC*
    b *C* (= *Celsius*), *F* (= *Fahrenheit*)
    c measures of length, weight, time, etc., except for *in.* (= *inch*), *st.* (= *stone*)
    d contractions (i.e. where the last letter is the same as the last letter of the full word), e.g. *Dr, Revd* (but note *Rev.*), *Mr, Mrs, Mme, Mlle, St* (= *Saint*)
    e certain other conventional abbreviations which are not directly related to the full word, e.g. *Hants, Northants*

· ·

sored run for charity. **make fun of**, **poke fun at** ridicule.

■ **1, 2** amusement, clowning, diversion, enjoyment, entertainment, festivity, fooling around, frivolity, frolic, gaiety, games, high jinks, high spirits, horseplay, jocularity, jokes, joking, jollification, jollity, *colloquial* kicks, laughter, merriment, merrymaking, mirth, pastimes, play, playfulness, pleasure, pranks, recreation, romp, skylarking, sport, teasing, tomfoolery. □ **make fun of**, **poke fun at** see RIDICULE *verb*.

function /'fʌŋkʃ(ə)n/ *noun* **1** proper role etc. **2** official duty. **3** public or social occasion. **4** *Mathematics* quantity whose value depends on varying values of others. ● *verb* fulfil function; operate.

■ *noun* **1** aim, job, purpose, *raison d'être*, role, task, use. **3** *colloquial* affair, ceremony, *colloquial* do, event, occasion, party, reception. ● *verb* act, behave, go, operate, perform, run, work.

functional *adjective* **1** of or serving a function. **2** practical rather than attractive. □ **functionally** *adverb*.

■ **1** functioning, going, operational, working. **2** practical, serviceable, useful, utilitarian.

functionalism *noun* belief that function should determine design. □ **functionalist** *noun* & *adjective*.

functionary *noun* (*plural* **-ies**) official.

fund *noun* **1** permanently available stock. **2** money set apart for purpose. **3** (in *plural*) money resources. ● *verb* **1** provide with money. **2** make (debt) permanent at fixed interest. □ **fundraising** raising money for charity etc. **fundraiser** *noun*.

■ *noun* **1** hoard, mine, pool, reserve, reservoir, stock, store, supply. **2** cache, hoard, kitty, nest egg, pool, reserve. **3** (*funds*) capital, endowments, investments, money, reserves, resources, riches, savings, wealth, *colloquial* the wherewithal.

fundamental /fʌndə'ment(ə)l/ *adjective* of or serving as base or foundation; essential, primary. ● *noun* fundamental principle. □ **fundamentally** *adverb*.

■ *adjective* axiomatic, basic, cardinal, central, crucial, elementary, essential, important, key, main, necessary, primary, prime, principal, quintessential, rudimentary, underlying.

fundamentalism *noun* strict adherence to traditional religious beliefs. □ **fundamentalist** *noun* & *adjective*.

funeral /'fju:nər(ə)l/ *noun* ceremonial burial or cremation of dead. ● *adjective* of or used at funerals. □ **funeral director** undertaker. **funeral parlour** establishment where corpses are prepared for funerals.

■ *noun* burial, cremation, entombment, interment, obsequies, wake.

funerary /'fju:nərərɪ/ *adjective* of or used at funerals.

funereal /fju:'nɪərɪəl/ *adjective* **1** of or appropriate to funeral. **2** dismal, dark.

■ dark, depressing, dismal, gloomy, grave, mournful, sad, sepulchral, solemn, sombre.

fungicide /'fʌndʒɪsaɪd/ *noun* substance that kills fungus. □ **fungicidal** /-'saɪd(ə)l/ *adjective*.

fungus /'fʌŋgəs/ *noun* (*plural* **-gi** /-gaɪ/ or **-guses**) **1** mushroom, toadstool, or allied plant. **2** spongy morbid growth. □ **fungal** *adjective*. **fungoid** *adjective*. **fungous** *adjective*.

funicular /fju:'nɪkjʊlə/ *noun* (in full **funicular railway**) cable railway with ascending and descending cars counterbalanced.

funk *slang noun* fear, panic. ● *verb* evade through fear.

funky *adjective* (**-ier**, **-iest**) *slang* (esp. of jazz etc.) with heavy rhythm.

funnel /'fʌn(ə)l/ *noun* **1** tube widening at top, for pouring liquid etc. into small opening. **2** chimney of steam engine or ship. ● *verb* (**-ll-**; *US* **-l-**) (cause to) move (as) through funnel.

■ *noun* **2** chimney, smokestack. ● *verb* channel, direct, filter, pour.

funny /'fʌnɪ/ *adjective* (**-ier**, **-iest**) **1** amusing, comical. **2** strange, perplexing. **3** *colloquial* unwell; eccentric. □ **funny bone** part of elbow over which very sensitive nerve passes. **funny business** *slang* misbehaviour or deception. □ **funnily** *adverb*.

■ **1** absurd, amusing, comic, comical, crazy, daft, diverting, droll, eccentric, entertaining, facetious, farcical, foolish, grotesque, hilarious, humorous, *colloquial* hysterical, ironic, jocose, jocular, *colloquial* killing, laughable, ludicrous, mad, merry, nonsensical, preposterous, *colloquial* priceless, rich, ridiculous, risible, sarcastic, sardonic, satirical, side-splitting, silly, slapstick, uproarious, waggish, witty, zany.

fur *noun* **1** short fine animal hair. **2** hide with fur on it. **3** garment of or lined with this. **4** coating inside kettle etc. ● *verb* (**-rr-**) **1** (esp. as **furred** *adjective*) line or trim with fur. **2** (often + *up*) (of kettle etc.) become coated with fur.

■ *noun* **1** bristles, coat, down, fleece, hair, wool. **2** hide, pelt, skin.

furbelow /'fɜ:bɪləʊ/ *noun* (in *plural*) showy ornaments.

furbish /'fɜ:bɪʃ/ *verb* (often + *up*) refurbish.

furcate /'fɜ:keɪt/ *adjective* forked, branched. ● *verb* (**-ting**) fork, divide. □ **furcation** *noun*.

furious /'fjʊərɪəs/ *adjective* **1** very angry, raging. **2** frantic, intense. □ **furiously** *adverb*.

■ **1** angry, boiling, enraged, fuming, incensed, infuriated, irate, *colloquial* livid, *colloquial* mad, raging, savage, *literary* wrathful. **2** agitated, fierce, frantic, frenzied, intense, tempestuous, tumultuous, turbulent, violent, wild.

furl *verb* **1** roll up (sail, umbrella). **2** become furled.

furlong /'fɜ:lɒŋ/ *noun* eighth of mile.

furlough /'fɜ:ləʊ/ *noun* leave of absence.

furnace /ˈfɜːnɪs/ *noun* **1** chamber for intense heating by fire. **2** very hot place.

furnish /ˈfɜːnɪʃ/ *verb* **1** provide with furniture. **2** (as **furnished** *adjective*) let with furniture. **3** (often + *with*) supply. □ **furnishings** *plural noun.*
■ **1** equip, fit out. **3** afford, give, grant, provide, supply.

furniture /ˈfɜːnɪtʃə/ *noun* **1** movable contents of building or room. **2** ship's equipment. **3** accessories, e.g. handles and locks.
■ **1** chattels, effects, equipment, fitments, fittings, fixtures, furnishings, household goods, movables, possessions.

furore /fjʊəˈrɔːrɪ/ *noun* (*US* **furor** /ˈfjʊərɔː/) **1** uproar. **2** enthusiasm.

furrier /ˈfʌrɪə/ *noun* dealer in or dresser of furs.

furrow /ˈfʌrəʊ/ *noun* **1** narrow trench made by plough. **2** rut; wrinkle. ● *verb* **1** plough. **2** make furrows in. **3** (esp. as **furrowed** *adjective*) wrinkle (brow).
■ *noun* **1** channel, ditch, drill, trench. **2** channel, corrugation, crease, cut, ditch, drill, fissure, fluting, gash, groove, hollow, line, rut, score, scratch, track, trench, wrinkle. ● *verb* **2** crease, crinkle, corrugate, flute, groove, rut, score. **3** (**furrowed**) frowning, lined, worried, wrinkled.

furry /ˈfɜːrɪ/ *adjective* (**-ier, -iest**) like or covered with fur.
■ fleecy, fluffy, fuzzy.

further /ˈfɜːðə/ *adverb* (also **farther** /ˈfɑːðə/) **1** more distant in space or time. **2** more; to greater extent. **3** in addition. ● *adjective* (also **farther** /ˈfɑːðə/) **1** more distant or advanced. **2** more, additional. ● *verb* promote, favour. □ **further education** education for people above school age. **furthermore** in addition, besides. □ **furthermost** *adjective.*
■ *adjective* **2** accessory, additional, another, auxiliary, extra, fresh, more, new, other, spare, supplementary. □ **furthermore** additionally, also, besides, moreover, too.

furtherance *noun* furthering of scheme etc.

furthest /ˈfɜːðɪst/ (also **farthest** /ˈfɑːðɪst/) *adjective* most distant. ● *adverb* to or at the greatest distance.

furtive /ˈfɜːtɪv/ *adjective* sly, stealthy. □ **furtively** *adverb.*
■ clandestine, concealed, conspiratorial, covert, deceitful, disguised, hidden, mysterious, private, secret, secretive, *colloquial* shifty, sly, sneaky, stealthy, surreptitious, underhand, untrustworthy.

fury /ˈfjʊərɪ/ *noun* (*plural* **-ies**) **1** wild and passionate anger. **2** violence (of storm etc.). **3** (**Fury**) (usually in *plural*) avenging goddess. **4** angry woman.
■ **1** see ANGER *noun*, FRENZY. **2** ferocity, fierceness, force, intensity, power, rage, savagery, tempestuousness, turbulence, vehemence, violence.

furze *noun* gorse. □ **furzy** *adjective* (**-ier, -iest**).

fuse[1] /fjuːz/ *verb* (**-sing**) **1** melt with intense heat. **2** blend by melting. **3** supply with fuse. **4** fail due to melting of fuse. **5** cause fuse(s) of to melt. ● *noun* easily melted wire in circuit, designed to melt when circuit is overloaded.
■ *verb* **2** amalgamate, blend, coalesce, combine, *literary* commingle, compound, consolidate, join, melt, merge, mix, solder, unite, weld.

fuse[2] /fjuːz/ *noun* combustible device for igniting bomb etc. ● *verb* (**-sing**) fit fuse to.

fuselage /ˈfjuːzəlɑːʒ/ *noun* body of aircraft.

fusible /ˈfjuːzɪb(ə)l/ *adjective* that can be melted. □ **fusibility** *noun.*

fusilier /fjuːzɪˈlɪə/ *noun* soldier of any of several regiments formerly armed with light muskets.

fusillade /fjuːzɪˈleɪd/ *noun* continuous discharge of firearms or outburst of criticism etc.
■ barrage, burst, firing, outburst, salvo, volley.

fusion /ˈfjuːʒ(ə)n/ *noun* **1** fusing. **2** blending. **3** coalition. **4** nuclear fusion.

fuss *noun* **1** excited commotion; bustle. **2** excessive concern about trivial thing. **3** sustained protest. ● *verb* **1** behave with nervous concern. **2** agitate, worry. □ **fusspot** *colloquial* person given to fussing. **make a fuss** complain vigorously. **make a fuss of, over** treat affectionately.
■ *noun* **1** see COMMOTION. ● *verb* **1** complain, *slang* create, fidget, *colloquial* flap, get worked up, grumble, make a commotion, worry. **2** agitate, bother, worry.

fussy *adjective* (**-ier, -iest**) **1** inclined to fuss. **2** fastidious. **3** over-elaborate.
■ **1, 2** carping, *colloquial* choosy, difficult, discriminating, faddy, fastidious, finicky, hard to please, niggling, *colloquial* nit-picking, particular, *colloquial* pernickety, scrupulous, squeamish. **3** Byzantine, complicated, detailed, elaborate, fancy, ornate, overdone, rococo.

fustian /ˈfʌstɪən/ *noun* **1** thick usually dark twilled cotton cloth. **2** bombast.

fusty /ˈfʌstɪ/ *adjective* (**-ier, -iest**) **1** musty, stuffy. **2** antiquated.

futile /ˈfjuːtaɪl/ *adjective* useless, ineffectual. □ **futility** /-ˈtɪl-/ *noun.*
■ abortive, absurd, barren, *archaic* bootless, empty, foolish, forlorn, fruitless, hollow, impotent, ineffective, ineffectual, pointless, profitless, silly, sterile, unavailing, unproductive, unprofitable, unsuccessful, useless, vain, wasted, worthless.

futon /ˈfuːtɒn/ *noun* **1** Japanese mattress used as bed. **2** this with frame, convertible into couch.

future /ˈfjuːtʃə/ *adjective* **1** of time to come. **2** about to happen, be, or become. **3** *Grammar* (of tense) describing event yet to happen. ● *noun* **1** time to come. **2** future condition or events etc. **3** prospect of success etc. **4** *Grammar* future tense. **5** (in *plural*) (on stock exchange) goods etc. sold for future delivery. □ **future perfect** *Grammar* tense giving sense 'will have done'.

■ *adjective* **1, 2** approaching, awaited, coming, destined, expected, forthcoming, impending, intended, planned, prospective, subsequent, unborn. ● *noun* **1** time to come, tomorrow. **3** expectations, outlook, prospects.

futurism *noun* 20th-c. artistic movement celebrating technology etc. □ **futurist** *adjective & noun*.

futuristic /fjuːtʃəˈrɪstɪk/ *adjective* **1** suitable for the future; ultra-modern. **2** of futurism.

futurity /fjuːˈtjʊərɪtɪ/ *noun* (*plural* -**ies**) *literary* future time, events, etc.

fuzz *noun* **1** fluff. **2** fluffy or frizzy hair. **3** (**the fuzz**) *slang* police (officer).

■ **1** down, floss, fluff, hair.

fuzzy /ˈfʌzɪ/ *adjective* (-**ier**, -**iest**) **1** fluffy. **2** blurred, indistinct.

■ **1** downy, feathery, fleecy, fluffy, frizzy, furry, woolly. **2** bleary, blurred, cloudy, dim, faint, hazy, ill-defined, indistinct, misty, obscure, out of focus, shadowy, unclear, unfocused, vague.

Gg

G □ **G-man** *US colloquial* FBI special agent.
G-string narrow strip of cloth etc. attached to string round waist for covering genitals.

g *abbreviation* (also **g.**) gram(s).

gab *noun colloquial* talk, chatter. □ **gift of the gab** facility of speaking eloquently or profusely.

gabardine /ˈgæbəˈdiːn/ *noun* **1** a strong twilled cloth. **2** raincoat etc. of this.

gabble /ˈgæb(ə)l/ *verb* (**-ling**) talk or utter unintelligibly or too fast. ● *noun* rapid talk.

gaberdine = GABARDINE.

gable /ˈgeɪb(ə)l/ *noun* triangular part of wall at end of ridged roof. □ **gabled** *adjective*.

gad *verb* (**-dd-**) (+ *about*) go about idly or in search of pleasure. □ **gadabout** person who gads about.

gadfly /ˈgædflaɪ/ *noun* (*plural* **-ies**) fly that bites cattle.

gadget /ˈgædʒɪt/ *noun* small mechanical device or tool. □ **gadgetry** *noun*.

 ■ apparatus, appliance, contraption, contrivance, device, implement, instrument, invention, machine, tool, utensil.

Gael /geɪl/ *noun* Scottish or Gaelic-speaking Celt.

Gaelic /ˈgeɪlɪk/ *noun* Celtic language of Scots (also /ˈgælɪk/) or Irish. ● *adjective* of Gaelic or Gaelic-speaking people.

gaff[1] *noun* **1** stick with hook for landing fish. **2** barbed fishing-spear. ● *verb* seize (fish) with gaff.

gaff[2] *noun slang* □ **blow the gaff** let out secret.

gaffe /gæf/ *noun* blunder, tactless mistake.

gaffer /ˈgæfə/ *noun* **1** old man. **2** *colloquial* foreman, boss. **3** chief electrician in film unit.

gag *noun* **1** thing thrust into or tied across mouth to prevent speech etc. **2** joke or comic scene. ● *verb* (**-gg-**) **1** apply gag to. **2** silence. **3** choke, retch. **4** make jokes.

 ■ *noun* **2** see JOKE *noun* 1. ● *verb* **1** muzzle. **2** check, curb, keep quiet, muffle, muzzle, prevent from speaking, quiet, silence, stifle, still, suppress.

gaga /ˈgɑːgɑː/ *adjective slang* **1** senile. **2** crazy.

gage[1] *noun* **1** pledge, security. **2** challenge.

gage[2] *US* = GAUGE.

gaggle /ˈgæg(ə)l/ *noun* **1** flock (of geese). **2** *colloquial* disorganized group.

gaiety /ˈgeɪətɪ/ *noun* (*US* **gayety**) **1** being gay, mirth. **2** merrymaking. **3** bright appearance.

 ■ **1** brightness, cheerfulness, delight, exhilaration, felicity, glee, happiness, high spirits, hilarity, jollity, joyfulness, joyousness, light-heartedness, liveliness, merriment, mirth. **2** see MERRYMAKING (MERRY). **3** brightness, colourfulness.

gaily /ˈgeɪlɪ/ *adverb* in a gay way.

gain *verb* **1** obtain, win. **2** acquire, earn. **3** (often + *in*) increase, improve. **4** benefit. **5** (of clock etc.) become fast (by). **6** reach. **7** (often + *on*, *upon*) get closer to (person or thing one is following). ● *noun* **1** increase (of wealth); profit. **2** (in *plural*) money made in trade etc.

 ■ *verb* **1** achieve, acquire, attain, capture, collect, garner, gather in, get, harvest, obtain, pick up, procure, reap, receive, secure, win. **2** acquire, bring in, earn, get, make, net, realize, receive. **4** see PROFIT *verb* 2. **6** arrive at, get to, reach. **7** (*gain on*) approach, catch up with, close the gap with, close with. ● *noun* **1** achievement, acquisition, advantage, asset, attainment, benefit, dividend, increase, profit, yield. **2** (*gains*) earnings, income, proceeds, profits, return, revenue, winnings.

gainful /ˈgeɪnfʊl/ *adjective* **1** paid. **2** lucrative. □ **gainfully** *adverb*.

 ■ **2** advantageous, beneficial, fruitful, lucrative, productive, profitable, remunerative, rewarding, worthwhile.

gainsay /geɪnˈseɪ/ *verb* deny, contradict.

gait *noun* manner of walking or proceeding.

gaiter /ˈgeɪtə/ *noun* covering of leather etc. for lower leg.

gal. *abbreviation* gallon(s).

gala /ˈgɑːlə/ *noun* festive occasion or gathering.

 ■ carnival, celebration, fair, festival, festivity, fête, jamboree, party.

galactic /gəˈlæktɪk/ *adjective* of galaxy.

galantine /ˈgæləntiːn/ *noun* cold dish of meat boned, spiced, and covered in jelly.

galaxy /ˈgæləksɪ/ *noun* (*plural* **-ies**) **1** independent system of stars etc. in space. **2** (**the Galaxy**) Milky Way. **3** (+ *of*) gathering of beautiful or famous people.

gale *noun* **1** strong wind. **2** outburst, esp. of laughter.

 ■ **1** blast, cyclone, hurricane, storm, tempest, tornado, typhoon, wind.

gall[1] /gɔːl/ *noun* **1** *colloquial* impudence. **2** rancour. **3** bile. □ **gall bladder** bodily organ containing bile. **gallstone** small hard mass that forms in gall bladder.

gall[2] /gɔːl/ *noun* **1** sore made by chafing. **2** (cause of) vexation. **3** place rubbed bare. ● *verb* **1** rub sore. **2** vex, humiliate.

gall[3] /gɔːl/ *noun* growth produced on tree etc. by insect etc.

gallant /ˈgælənt/ *adjective* **1** brave. **2** fine, stately. **3** (/gəˈlænt/) attentive to women. ● *noun*

(/gə'lænt/) ladies' man. □ **gallantly** *adverb*.
■ *adjective* **1** bold, brave, courageous, daring, dashing, dauntless, fearless, heroic, honourable, intrepid, noble, valiant. **3** attentive, chivalrous, courteous, courtly, gentlemanly, gracious, magnanimous, noble, polite, well bred.

gallantry /'gæləntrɪ/ *noun* (*plural* **-ies**) **1** bravery. **2** courteousness to women. **3** polite act or speech.

galleon /'gælɪən/ *noun historical* (usually Spanish) warship.

galleria /gælə'riːə/ *noun* group of small shops, cafés, etc. under one roof.

gallery /'gælərɪ/ *noun* (*plural* **-ies**) **1** room etc. for showing works of art. **2** balcony, esp. in church, hall, etc. **3** highest balcony in theatre. **4** covered walk, colonnade. **5** passage, corridor.

galley /'gælɪ/ *noun* (*plural* **-s**) **1** *historical* long flat one-decked vessel, usually rowed by slaves or criminals. **2** ship's or aircraft's kitchen. **3** (in full **galley proof**) printer's proof before division into pages.

Gallic /'gælɪk/ *adjective* **1** (typically) French. **2** of Gaul or Gauls.

Gallicism /'gælɪsɪz(ə)m/ *noun* French idiom.

gallimimus /gælɪ'maɪməs/ *noun* (*plural* **-muses**) medium-sized dinosaur that ran fast on two legs.

gallinaceous /gælɪ'neɪʃəs/ *adjective* of order of birds including domestic poultry.

gallivant /'gælɪvænt/ *verb colloquial* gad about.

gallon /'gælən/ *noun* measure of capacity (8 pints, 4.546 litres).

gallop /'gæləp/ *noun* **1** horse's fastest pace. **2** ride at this pace. ● *verb* (**-p-**) **1** (cause to) go at gallop. **2** talk etc. fast. **3** progress rapidly.

gallows /'gæləʊz/ *plural noun* (usually treated as *singular*) structure for hanging criminals.
■ *historical* gibbet, *historical* scaffold.

Gallup poll /'gæləp/ *noun* kind of opinion poll.

galore /gə'lɔː/ *adverb* in plenty.

galosh /gə'lɒʃ/ *noun* waterproof overshoe.

galumph /gə'lʌmf/ *verb colloquial* (esp. as **galumphing** *adjective*) move noisily or clumsily.

galvanic /gæl'vænɪk/ *adjective* **1** producing an electric current by chemical action. **2** (of electric current) produced thus. **3** stimulating; full of energy.

galvanize /'gælvənaɪz/ *verb* (also **-ise**) (**-zing** or **-sing**) **1** (often + *into*) rouse by shock. **2** stimulate (as) by electricity. **3** coat (iron, steel) with zinc to protect from rust.

galvanometer /gælvə'nɒmɪtə/ *noun* instrument for measuring electric currents.

gambit /'gæmbɪt/ *noun* **1** *Chess* opening with sacrifice of pawn etc. **2** trick, device.

gamble /'gæmb(ə)l/ *verb* (**-ling**) **1** play games of chance for money. **2** bet (sum of money). **3** (often + *away*) lose by gambling. ● *noun* **1** risky undertaking. **2** spell of gambling. □ **gambler** *noun*.

■ *verb* **1** bet, draw lots, game, *slang* have a flutter, lay bets, speculate, take a chance, take risks. **2** bet, *colloquial* chance, hazard, lay, risk, stake, venture, wager.

gambol /'gæmb(ə)l/ *verb* (**-ll-**; *US* **-l-**) jump about playfully. ● *noun* caper.

game[1] *noun* **1** form or period of play or sport, esp. competitive one organized with rules. **2** portion of play forming scoring unit. **3** (in *plural*) athletic contests. **4** piece of fun. **5** (in *plural*) tricks. **6** *colloquial* scheme, activity. **7** wild animals or birds etc. hunted for sport or food. **8** their flesh as food. ● *adjective* spirited; eager. ● *verb* (**-ming**) gamble for money. □ **gamekeeper** person employed to breed and protect game. **gamesmanship** art of winning games by psychological means. □ **gamely** *adverb*.
■ *noun* **1** amusement, diversion, entertainment, frolic, pastime, play, recreation, romp, sport. **2** competition, contest, match, round, tournament. **3** see SPORT *noun* 1,2. **4** jest, joke, *colloquial* lark. **7** animals, game birds, prey, quarry. ● *adjective* see BRAVE *adjective* 1, WILLING 1.

game[2] *adjective colloquial* (of leg etc.) crippled.

gamete /'gæmiːt/ *noun* mature germ cell uniting with another in sexual reproduction.

gamin /'gæmɪn/ *noun* **1** street urchin. **2** impudent child.

gamine /gæ'miːn/ *noun* **1** girl gamin. **2** attractively mischievous or boyish girl.

gamma /'gæmə/ *noun* third letter of Greek alphabet ($Γ$, $γ$). □ **gamma rays** very short X-rays emitted by radioactive substances.

gammon /'gæmən/ *noun* back end of side of bacon, including leg.

gammy /'gæmɪ/ *adjective* (**-ier**, **-iest**) *slang* (of leg etc.) crippled.

gamut /'gæmət/ *noun* entire range or scope. □ **run the gamut of** experience or perform complete range of.

gamy /'geɪmɪ/ *adjective* (**-ier**, **-iest**) smelling or tasting like high game.

gander /'gændə/ *noun* male goose.

gang *noun* **1** set of associates, esp. for criminal purposes. **2** set of workers, slaves, or prisoners. ● *verb colloquial* **1** (+ *together*, *up*) combine in gang. **2** (+ *up with*) act together with. **3** (+ *up on*) combine against.
■ *noun* **1** band, crew, *colloquial* crowd, group, *colloquial* mob, *usually derogatory* pack, ring, set, team. ● *verb* **1** (*gang together*, *gang up*) see COMBINE *verb* 1.

ganger /'gæŋə/ *noun* foreman of gang of workers.

gangling /'gæŋglɪŋ/ *adjective* (of person) tall and thin; lanky.

ganglion /'gæŋglɪən/ *noun* (*plural* **ganglia** or **-s**) knot on nerve containing assemblage of nerve cells.

gangly *adjective* (**-ier**, **-iest**) gangling.

gangplank /'gæŋplæŋk/ *noun* plank for walking on to or off boat etc.

gangrene /'gæŋgriːn/ *noun* death of body tissue, usually caused by obstruction of circulation. □ **gangrenous** *adjective*.

gangster /'gæŋstə/ *noun* member of gang of violent criminals.

■ bandit, brigand, criminal, *colloquial* crook, desperado, gunman, hoodlum, hooligan, Mafioso, mugger, racketeer, robber, ruffian, thug, tough.

gangue /gæŋ/ *noun* valueless part of ore deposit.

gangway *noun* **1** passage, esp. between rows of seats. **2** opening in ship's bulwarks. **3** bridge.

gannet /'gænɪt/ *noun* **1** large seabird. **2** *slang* greedy person.

gantry /'gæntrɪ/ *noun* (*plural* **-ies**) structure supporting travelling crane, railway or road signals, rocket-launching equipment, etc.

gaol etc. = JAIL etc.

gap *noun* **1** empty space, interval. **2** deficiency. **3** breach in hedge, wall, etc. **4** wide divergence.

■ **1** breathing-space, discontinuity, gulf, hiatus, interlude, intermission, interruption, interval, lacuna, lapse, lull, pause, recess, respite, rest, space, suspension, wait. **3** aperture, breach, break, cavity, chink, cleft, crack, cranny, crevice, hole, opening, rent, rift, rip, space, void. **4** difference, disagreement, discrepancy, disparity, distance, divergence, division, incompatibility, inconsistency.

gape *verb* (**-ping**) **1** open mouth wide. **2** be or become wide open. **3** (+ *at*) stare at. ● *noun* **1** open-mouthed stare. **2** opening.

■ *verb* **2** open, part, split, yawn. **3** *colloquial* gawp, gaze, goggle, stare.

garage /'gærɑːdʒ/ *noun* **1** building for keeping vehicle(s) in. **2** establishment selling petrol etc. or repairing and selling vehicles. ● *verb* (**-ging**) put or keep in garage.

garb *noun* clothing, esp. of distinctive kind. ● *verb* dress.

garbage /'gɑːbɪdʒ/ *noun* **1** *US* refuse. **2** *colloquial* nonsense.

■ **1** debris, detritus, junk, litter, *colloquial* muck, refuse, rubbish, scrap, *esp. US* trash, waste.

garble /'gɑːb(ə)l/ *verb* (**-ling**) (esp. as **garbled** *adjective*) distort or confuse (facts, statements, etc.).

■ confuse, corrupt, distort, falsify, misconstrue, misquote, misrepresent, mutilate, pervert, slant, twist, warp.

garden /'gɑːd(ə)n/ *noun* **1** piece of ground for growing flowers, fruit, or vegetables, or for recreation. **2** (esp. in *plural*) public pleasure-grounds. ● *verb* cultivate or tend garden. □ **garden centre** place selling plants and garden equipment. □ **gardener** *noun*. **gardening** *noun*.

■ *noun* **1** allotment, patch, plot, *US & Australian* yard. **2** (*gardens*) grounds, park. □ **gardening** cultivation, horticulture.

gardenia /gɑːˈdiːnɪə/ *noun* tree or shrub with fragrant flowers.

gargantuan /gɑːˈgæntjʊən/ *adjective* gigantic.

gargle /'gɑːg(ə)l/ *verb* (**-ling**) rinse (throat) with liquid kept in motion by breath. ● *noun* liquid so used.

gargoyle /'gɑːgɔɪl/ *noun* grotesque carved spout projecting from gutter of building.

garish /'geərɪʃ/ *adjective* obtrusively bright, gaudy. □ **garishly** *adverb*. **garishness** *noun*.

■ bright, cheap, crude, flamboyant, flashy, gaudy, harsh, loud, lurid, meretricious, ostentatious, raffish, showy, startling, tasteless, tawdry, vivid, vulgar.

garland /'gɑːlənd/ *noun* wreath of flowers etc. as decoration. ● *verb* adorn or crown with garland(s).

garlic /'gɑːlɪk/ *noun* plant with pungent bulb used in cookery. □ **garlicky** *adjective colloquial*.

garment /'gɑːmənt/ *noun* **1** article of dress. **2** (in *plural*) clothes.

■ **2** (*garments*) *formal* apparel, attire, clothes, clothing, costume, dress, garb, *colloquial* gear, habit, outfit.

garner /'gɑːnə/ *verb* **1** collect. **2** store. ● *noun* storehouse for corn etc.

garnet /'gɑːnɪt/ *noun* glassy mineral, esp. red kind used as gem.

garnish /'gɑːnɪʃ/ *verb* decorate (esp. food). ● *noun* decoration, esp. to food.

garret /'gærɪt/ *noun* room, esp. small, cold, etc. immediately under roof.

garrison /'gærɪs(ə)n/ *noun* **1** troops stationed in town. **2** building or fort occupied by them. ● *verb* (**-n-**) provide with or occupy as garrison.

■ *noun* **1** contingent, detachment, force, unit. **2** barracks, camp, citadel, fort, fortification, fortress, station, stronghold.

garrotte /gəˈrɒt/ (also **garotte**, *US* **garrote**) *verb* (**garrotting**, *US* **garroting**) execute by strangulation, esp. with wire collar. ● *noun* device for this.

garrulous /'gærələs/ *adjective* talkative. □ **garrulity** /gəˈruːlɪtɪ/ *noun*. **garrulousness** *noun*.

garter /'gɑːtə/ *noun* **1** band to keep sock or stocking up. **2** (**the Garter**) (badge of) highest order of English knighthood. □ **garter stitch** plain knitting stitch.

gas /gæs/ *noun* (*plural* **-es**) **1** any airlike substance (i.e. not liquid or solid). **2** such substance (esp. coal gas or natural gas) used as fuel. **3** gas used as anaesthetic. **4** poisonous gas used in war. **5** *US colloquial* petrol. **6** *slang* empty talk, boasting. **7** *slang* amusing thing or person. ● *verb* (**gases**, **gassed**, **gassing**) **1** expose to gas, esp. to kill. **2** *colloquial* talk emptily or boastfully. □ **gasbag** *slang* empty talker. **gas chamber** room filled with poisonous gas to kill people or animals. **gasholder** gasometer. **gas mask** respirator for protection against harmful gases. **gas ring** ring pierced with gas jet(s) for cooking etc. **gasworks** place where gas is manufactured.

   ■ *noun* **1** exhalation, exhaust, fumes, *archaic* miasma, vapour.

gaseous /'gæsɪəs/ *adjective* of or as gas.

gash *noun* long deep cut or wound. ● *verb* make gash in.

   ■ *verb* cut, incise, lacerate, score, slash, slit, wound.

gasify /'gæsɪfaɪ/ *verb* (**-ies, -ied**) convert into gas. □ **gasification** *noun*.

gasket /'gæskɪt/ *noun* sheet or ring of rubber etc. to seal joint between metal surfaces.

gasoline /'gæsəliːn/ *noun* (also **gasolene**) *US* petrol.

gasometer /gæ'sɒmɪtə/ *noun* large tank from which gas is distributed.

gasp /gɑːsp/ *verb* **1** catch breath with open mouth. **2** utter with gasps. ● *noun* convulsive catching of breath. □ **gasping** *adjective*.

   ■ *verb* **1** breathe with difficulty, choke, fight for breath, gulp, huff and puff, pant, puff, wheeze. □ **gasping** see BREATHLESS 1.

gassy /'gæsɪ/ *adjective* (**-ier, -iest**) **1** of, like, or full of gas. **2** *colloquial* verbose.

gastric /'gæstrɪk/ *adjective* of stomach. □ **gastric flu** *colloquial* intestinal disorder of unknown cause. **gastric juice** digestive fluid secreted by stomach glands.

gastritis /gæ'straɪtɪs/ *noun* inflammation of stomach.

gastroenteritis /gæstrəʊentə'raɪtɪs/ *noun* inflammation of stomach and intestines.

gastronome /'gæstrənəʊm/ *noun* gourmet. □ **gastronomic** /-'nɒm-/ *adjective*. **gastronomical** /-'nɒm-/ *adjective*. **gastronomically** /-'nɒm-/ *adverb*. **gastronomy** /-'strɒn-/ *noun*.

gastropod /'gæstrəpɒd/ *noun* mollusc that moves using underside of abdomen, e.g. snail.

gate *noun* **1** barrier, usually hinged, used to close opening in wall, fence, etc. **2** such opening. **3** means of entrance or exit. **4** numbered place of access to aircraft at airport. **5** device regulating passage of water in lock etc. **6** number of people paying to enter stadium etc. **7** money thus taken. □ **gatekeeper** attendant controlling entrance and exit through gate. **gateleg (table)** table with legs in gatelike frame for supporting folding flaps. **gatepost** post at either side of gate. **gateway 1** opening closed by gate. **2** means of access.

   ■ **1** barrier, door. **2, 3** access, doorway, entrance, entry, exit, gateway, opening, passage, portal, way in, way out.

gateau /'gætəʊ/ *noun* (*plural* **-s** or **-x** /-z/) large rich elaborate cake.

gatecrash *verb* attend (party etc.) uninvited. □ **gatecrasher** *noun*.

gather /'gæðə/ *verb* **1** bring or come together. **2** collect (harvest, dust, etc.). **3** infer, deduce. **4** increase (speed). **5** summon up (energy etc.). **6** draw together in folds or wrinkles. **7** (of boil etc.) come to a head. ● *noun* fold or pleat.

   ■ *verb* **1** accumulate, amass, assemble, bring together, build up, cluster, collect, come together, concentrate, congregate, convene, crowd, flock, forgather, get together, group, grow, heap up, herd, hoard, huddle together, marshal, mass, meet, mobilize, muster, pick up, pile up, rally, round up, stockpile, store up, swarm, throng. **2** collect, cull, garner, glean, harvest, pick, pluck, reap. **3** assume, be led to believe, conclude, deduce, guess, infer, learn, surmise, understand.

gathering *noun* **1** assembly. **2** pus-filled swelling.

   ■ **1** assembly, conclave, congress, convention, convocation, function, *colloquial* get-together, group, meeting, party, rally, social.

GATT /gæt/ *abbreviation* General Agreement on Tariffs and Trade.

gauche /gəʊʃ/ *adjective* **1** socially awkward. **2** tactless. □ **gauchely** *adverb*. **gaucheness** *noun*.

gaucho /'gaʊtʃəʊ/ *noun* (*plural* **-s**) cowboy in S. American pampas.

gaudy /'gɔːdɪ/ *adjective* (**-ier, -iest**) tastelessly showy. □ **gaudily** *adverb*. **gaudiness** *noun*.

   ■ bright, cheap, crude, flamboyant, flashy, garish, loud, lurid, meretricious, ostentatious, raffish, showy, tasteless, tawdry, vivid, vulgar.

gauge /geɪdʒ/ (*US* **gage**) *noun* **1** standard measure. **2** instrument for measuring. **3** distance between rails or opposite wheels. **4** capacity, extent. **5** criterion, test; means of estimating. ● *verb* (**-ging**) **1** measure exactly. **2** measure contents of. **3** estimate.

   ■ *noun* **1** measure, measurement. **4** capacity, dimensions, extent, measure, size, span, thickness, width. **5** benchmark, criterion, guideline, measure, norm, standard, test, yardstick. ● *verb* **1, 2** see MEASURE *verb* 1. **3** see ESTIMATE *verb* 1;2,3.

Gaul /gɔːl/ *noun* inhabitant of ancient Gaul. □ **Gaulish** *adjective & noun*.

gaunt /gɔːnt/ *adjective* **1** lean, haggard. **2** grim, desolate. □ **gauntness** *noun*.

   ■ **1** bony, cadaverous, emaciated, haggard, hollow-eyed, lanky, lean, pinched, raw-boned, scraggy, scrawny, skeletal, starving, thin, underweight, wasted away. **2** bare, bleak, desolate, dreary, forbidding, grim, stark, stern, unfriendly.

gauntlet[1] /'gɔːntlɪt/ *noun* **1** glove with long loose wrist. **2** *historical* armoured glove.

gauntlet[2] /'gɔːntlɪt/ *noun* □ **run the gauntlet 1** undergo criticism. **2** pass between two rows of people wielding sticks etc., as punishment.

gauze /gɔːz/ *noun* **1** thin transparent fabric. **2** fine mesh of wire etc. □ **gauzy** *adjective* (**-ier, -iest**).

gave *past of* GIVE.

gavel /'gæv(ə)l/ *noun* auctioneer's, chairman's, or judge's hammer.

gavotte /gə'vɒt/ *noun* 1 18th-c. French dance. 2 music for this.

gawk *verb colloquial* gawp. ● *noun* awkward or bashful person. □ **gawky** *adjective* (**-ier, -iest**).
  ■ □ **gawky** awkward, blundering, clumsy, gangling, gauche, inept, lumbering, maladroit, uncoordinated, ungainly, ungraceful, unskilful.

gawp *verb colloquial* stare stupidly.

gay *adjective* 1 light-hearted, cheerful. 2 showy. 3 homosexual. 4 *colloquial* carefree, dissolute. ● *noun* (esp. male) homosexual.
  ■ *adjective* 1 animated, bright, carefree, cheerful, festive, fun-loving, happy, jolly, jovial, joyful, light-hearted, lively, merry, sparkling, sunny, vivacious. 2 see VIVID 1. 3 see HOMOSEXUAL.

gayety *US* = GAIETY.

gaze *verb* (**-zing**) (+ *at*, *into*, *on*, etc.) look fixedly. ● *noun* intent look.
  ■ *verb* gape, look, stare; (*gaze at*) contemplate, eye, regard, view, wonder at.

gazebo /gə'zi:bəʊ/ *noun* (*plural* **-s**) summer house etc. giving view.

gazelle /gə'zel/ *noun* (*plural* same or **-s**) small graceful antelope.

gazette /gə'zet/ *noun* 1 newspaper. 2 official publication. ● *verb* (**-tting**) publish in official gazette.

gazetteer /gæzɪ'tɪə/ *noun* geographical index.

gazump /gə'zʌmp/ *verb* 1 *colloquial* raise price after accepting offer from (buyer). 2 swindle.

gazunder /gə'zʌndə/ *verb colloquial* lower an offer made to (seller) just before exchange of contracts.

GB *abbreviation* Great Britain.

GBH *abbreviation* grievous bodily harm.

GC *abbreviation* George Cross.

GCE *abbreviation* General Certificate of Education.

GCSE *abbreviation* General Certificate of Secondary Education.

GDR *abbreviation historical* German Democratic Republic.

gear /gɪə/ *noun* 1 (often in *plural*) set of toothed wheels working together, esp. those connecting engine to road wheels. 2 particular setting of these. 3 equipment. 4 *colloquial* clothing. ● *verb* 1 (+ *to*) adjust or adapt to. 2 (often + *up*) equip with gears. 3 (+ *up*) make ready. □ **gearbox** (case enclosing) gears of machine or vehicle. **gear lever** lever moved to engage or change gear. **in gear** with gear engaged.
  ■ *noun* 3 accessories, accoutrements, apparatus, appliances, baggage, belongings, equipment, *colloquial* get-up, harness, implements, instruments, kit, luggage, materials, paraphernalia, rig, stuff, tackle, things, tools, trappings. 4 see CLOTHES 1.

gecko /'gekəʊ/ *noun* (*plural* **-s**) tropical house-lizard.

gee /dʒi:/ *interjection: expressing surprise etc.*

geese *plural of* GOOSE.

geezer /'gi:zə/ *noun slang* man, esp. old one.

Geiger counter /'gaɪgə/ *noun* instrument for measuring radioactivity.

geisha /'geɪʃə/ *noun* (*plural* same or **-s**) Japanese professional hostess and entertainer.

gel /dʒel/ *noun* 1 semi-solid jelly-like colloid. 2 jelly-like substance for hair. ● *verb* (**-ll-**) 1 form gel. 2 jell.

gelatin /'dʒelətɪn/ *noun* (also **gelatine** /-ti:n/) transparent tasteless substance used in cookery, photography, etc. □ **gelatinous** /dʒɪ'læt-/ *adjective*.

geld /geld/ *verb* castrate.

gelding /'geldɪŋ/ *noun* castrated horse etc.

gelignite /'dʒelɪgnaɪt/ *noun* nitroglycerine explosive.

gem /dʒem/ *noun* 1 precious stone. 2 thing or person of great beauty or worth. ● *verb* (**-mm-**) adorn (as) with gems.
  ■ *noun* 1 jewel, precious stone, *colloquial* sparkler.

Gemini /'dʒemɪnaɪ/ *noun* third sign of zodiac.

Gen. *abbreviation* General.

gen /dʒen/ *slang noun* information. ● *verb* (**-nn-**) (+ *up*) gain or give information on.

gendarme /'ʒɒndɑ:m/ *noun* police officer in France etc.

gender /'dʒendə/ *noun* 1 (grammatical) classification roughly corresponding to the two sexes and sexlessness. 2 one of these classes. 3 person's sex.

gene /dʒi:n/ *noun* unit in chromosome, controlling particular inherited characteristic.

genealogy /dʒi:nɪ'ælədʒɪ/ *noun* (*plural* **-ies**) 1 descent traced continuously from ancestor; pedigree. 2 study of pedigrees. □ **genealogical** /-ə'lɒdʒ-/ *adjective*. **genealogically** /-ə'lɒdʒ-/ *adverb*. **genealogist** *noun*.

genera *plural of* GENUS.

general /'dʒenər(ə)l/ *adjective* 1 including, affecting, or applicable to (nearly) all; not partial or particular. 2 prevalent, usual. 3 vague; lacking detail. 4 chief, head. ● *noun* 1 army officer next below Field Marshal. 2 commander of army. □ **general anaesthetic** one affecting whole body. **general election** national election of representatives to parliament. **general practice** work of **general practitioner**, doctor treating cases of all kinds. **general strike** simultaneous strike of workers in all or most trades. **in general** as a rule; usually.
  ■ *adjective* 1 across the board, all-embracing, blanket, broad-based, catholic, collective, communal, comprehensive, diversified, encyclopedic, extensive, far-ranging, far-reaching, global, heterogeneous, hybrid, inclusive, public, shared, sweeping, universal,

wholesale, wide-ranging, widespread, worldwide. **2** accepted, accustomed, common, conventional, customary, everyday, familiar, habitual, normal, ordinary, popular, prevailing, prevalent, regular, run-of-the-mill, typical, usual, widespread. **3** approximate, broad, ill-defined, imprecise, indefinite, inexact, loose, simplified, superficial, unclear, undefined, unspecific, vague.

generalissimo /dʒenərə'lɪsɪməʊ/ *noun* (*plural* **-s**) commander of combined forces.

generality /dʒenə'rælɪtɪ/ *noun* (*plural* **-ies**) **1** general statement. **2** general applicability. **3** indefiniteness. **4** (+ *of*) majority of.

generalize /'dʒenərəlaɪz/ *verb* (also **-ise**) (**-zing** or **-sing**) **1** speak in general or indefinite terms. **2** form general notion(s). **3** reduce to general statement. **4** infer (rule etc.) from particular cases. **5** bring into general use. □ **generalization** *noun*.

generally /'dʒenərəlɪ/ *adverb* **1** usually; in most cases. **2** in most respects. **3** in general sense.
■ **1** as a rule, chiefly, commonly, in the main, mainly, mostly, normally, on the whole, predominantly, usually. **2** in the main, mainly, mostly, on the whole, predominantly, principally. **3** broadly, roughly.

generate /'dʒenəreɪt/ *verb* (**-ting**) bring into existence; produce.
■ *literary* beget, breed, bring about, cause, create, engender, father, give rise to, make, originate, procreate, produce, propagate, sire, spawn, whip up.

generation *noun* **1** all people born about same time. **2** stage in family history or in (esp. technological) development. **3** period of about 30 years. **4** production, esp. of electricity. **5** procreation.

generative /'dʒenərətɪv/ *adjective* **1** of procreation. **2** productive.

generator *noun* **1** dynamo. **2** apparatus for producing gas, steam, etc.

generic /dʒɪ'nerɪk/ *adjective* **1** characteristic of or relating to class or genus; not specific or special. **2** (of esp. drug) with no brand name. □ **generically** *adverb*.

generous /'dʒenərəs/ *adjective* **1** giving or given freely. **2** magnanimous. **3** abundant. □ **generosity** /-'rɒs-/ *noun*. **generously** *adverb*.
■ **1** (*generous giver*) *poetical* bounteous, bountiful, charitable, free, liberal, munificent, open, open-handed, unselfish, unsparing, unstinting; (*generous gifts*) expensive, handsome, princely, valuable. **2** benevolent, big-hearted, charitable, disinterested, forgiving, kind, liberal, magnanimous, munificent, noble, philanthropic, public-spirited, unmercenary, unprejudiced, unselfish. **3** abundant, ample, big, copious, lavish, plentiful, sizeable, substantial. □ **generosity** bounty, largesse, liberality, munificence, philanthropy.

genesis /'dʒenɪsɪs/ *noun* **1** origin; mode of

formation. **2** (**Genesis**) first book of Old Testament.

genetic /dʒɪ'netɪk/ *adjective* **1** of genetics. **2** of or in origin. □ **genetic engineering** manipulation of DNA to modify hereditary features. **genetic fingerprinting** identification of individuals by DNA patterns. □ **genetically** *adverb*.

genetics *plural noun* (treated as *singular*) study of heredity and variation among animals and plants. □ **geneticist** /-sɪst/ *noun*.

genial /'dʒiːnɪəl/ *adjective* **1** sociable, kindly. **2** (of climate) mild, warm. **3** cheering. □ **geniality** /-'æl-/ *noun*. **genially** *adverb*.
■ **1** affable, agreeable, amiable, cheerful, convivial, cordial, easygoing, friendly, good-natured, happy, jolly, jovial, kindly, pleasant, relaxed, sociable, sunny, warm, warm-hearted. **2** fair, mild, sunny, temperate, warm.

genie /'dʒiːnɪ/ *noun* (*plural* **genii** /-nɪaɪ/) sprite or goblin of Arabian tales.

genital /'dʒenɪt(ə)l/ *adjective* of animal reproduction or reproductive organs. ● *noun* (in *plural*; also **genitalia**) external reproductive organs.
■ *noun* (*genitals*) genitalia, *euphemistic* private parts, pudenda, sex organs.

genitive /'dʒenɪtɪv/ *Grammar noun* case expressing possession, origin, etc., corresponding to *of*, *from*, etc. ● *adjective* of or in this case.

genius /'dʒiːnɪəs/ *noun* (*plural* **-es**) **1** exceptional natural ability. **2** person having this. **3** guardian spirit.
■ **1** ability, aptitude, bent, brains, brilliance, capability, flair, gift, intellect, intelligence, knack, talent, wit. **2** academic, *colloquial* egghead, expert, intellectual, *colloquial* know-all, mastermind, thinker, virtuoso.

genocide /'dʒenəsaɪd/ *noun* mass murder, esp. among particular race or nation.

genre /'ʒɑ̃rə/ *noun* **1** kind or style of art etc. **2** portrayal of scenes from ordinary life.

gent /dʒent/ *noun* **1** *colloquial* gentleman. **2** (**Gents**) *colloquial* men's public lavatory.

genteel /dʒen'tiːl/ *adjective* **1** affectedly refined. **2** of or appropriate to upper classes.
■ **1** affected, mannered, overpolite, *colloquial* posh, refined, stylish. **2** chivalrous, courtly, gentlemanly, ladylike, patrician, polite, upper-class, *colloquial* upper-crust.

gentian /'dʒenʃ(ə)n/ *noun* mountain plant with usually blue flowers. □ **gentian violet** violet dye used as antiseptic.

Gentile /'dʒentaɪl/ *adjective* not Jewish; heathen. ● *noun* non-Jewish person.

gentility /dʒen'tɪlɪtɪ/ *noun* **1** social superiority. **2** genteel habits.

gentle /'dʒent(ə)l/ *adjective* (**-r**, **-st**) **1** not rough or severe; moderate. **2** mild, kind. **3** well born. **4** quiet. □ **gentleness** *noun*. **gently** *adverb*.

■ **1** (*gentle wind*) balmy, delicate, faint, light, soft, warm; (*gentle hill*) easy, gradual, imperceptible, moderate, slight, steady; (*gentle hint*) indirect, polite, subtle, tactful. **2** amiable, biddable, compassionate, docile, easygoing, good-tempered, harmless, humane, kind, kindly, lenient, loving, meek, merciful, mild, moderate, obedient, pacific, passive, peace-loving, pleasant, quiet, soft-hearted, sweet-tempered, sympathetic, tame, tender. **4** low, muted, peaceful, quiet, relaxing, soft, soothing.

gentlefolk /'dʒentəlfəʊk/ *noun* people of good family.

gentleman /'dʒentəlmən/ *noun* **1** man. **2** chivalrous well-bred man. **3** man of good social position. □ **gentlemanly** *adjective*.

gentlewoman *noun archaic* woman of good birth or breeding.

gentrification /dʒentrɪfɪ'keɪʃ(ə)n/ *noun* upgrading of working-class urban area by arrival of affluent residents. □ **gentrify** *verb* (**-ies, -ied**).

gentry /'dʒentrɪ/ *plural noun* **1** people next below nobility. **2** *derogatory* people.

genuflect /'dʒenjuːflekt/ *verb* bend knee, esp. in worship. □ **genuflection**, **genuflexion** /-'flekʃ(ə)n/ *noun*.

genuine /'dʒenjuːm/ *adjective* **1** really coming from its reputed source. **2** properly so called; not sham. **3** candid, sincere. □ **genuinely** *adverb*. **genuineness** *noun*.

■ **1, 2** actual, authentic, authenticated, bona fide, legitimate, original, proper, *colloquial* pukka, real, sterling, true, unaffected, unfeigned, veritable. **3** candid, devout, earnest, frank, heartfelt, honest, sincere.

genus /'dʒiːnəs/ *noun* (*plural* **genera** /'dʒenərə/) **1** group of animals or plants with common structural characteristics, usually containing several species. **2** kind, class.

geocentric /dʒiːə'sentrɪk/ *adjective* **1** considered as viewed from earth's centre. **2** having earth as centre.

geode /'dʒiːəʊd/ *noun* **1** cavity lined with crystals. **2** rock containing this.

geodesic /dʒiːəʊ'diːzɪk/ *adjective* (also **geodetic** /-'det-/) of geodesy. □ **geodesic line** shortest possible line on surface between two points.

geodesy /dʒiː'ɒdɪsɪ/ *noun* study of shape and area of the earth.

geography /dʒiː'ɒgrəfɪ/ *noun* **1** science of earth's physical features, resources, etc. **2** features of place. □ **geographer** *noun*. **geographic(al)** /-ə'græf-/ *adjective*. **geographically** /-ə'græf-/ *adverb*.

geology /dʒɪ'ɒlədʒɪ/ *noun* science of earth's crust, strata, etc. □ **geological** /-ə'lɒdʒ-/ *adjective*. **geologist** *noun*.

geometry /dʒɪ'ɒmətrɪ/ *noun* science of properties and relations of lines, surfaces, and solids. □ **geometric(al)** /-ə'met-/ *adjective*. **geometrician** /-'trɪʃ(ə)n/ *noun*.

Geordie /'dʒɔːdɪ/ *noun* native of Tyneside.

georgette /dʒɔː'dʒet/ *noun* kind of fine dress material.

Georgian /'dʒɔːdʒ(ə)n/ *adjective* of time of George I–IV or George V and VI.

geranium /dʒə'reɪmɪəm/ *noun* (*plural* **-s**) **1** cultivated pelargonium. **2** herb or shrub with fruit shaped like crane's bill.

gerbil /'dʒɜːbɪl/ *noun* mouselike desert rodent with long hind legs.

geriatric /dʒerɪ'ætrɪk/ *adjective* **1** of geriatrics or old people. **2** *derogatory* old. ● *noun often derogatory* old person.

geriatrics /dʒerɪ'ætrɪks/ *plural noun* (usually treated as *singular*) branch of medicine dealing with health and care of old people. □ **geriatrician** /-ə'trɪʃ(ə)n/ *noun*.

germ /dʒɜːm/ *noun* **1** microbe. **2** portion of organism capable of developing into new one. **3** thing that may develop; rudiment, elementary principle.

■ **1** bacterium, *slang* bug, microbe, micro-organism, virus. **3** basis, beginning, embryo, genesis, cause, nucleus, origin, root, seed, source, start.

German /'dʒɜːmən/ *noun* (*plural* **-s**) native, national, or language of Germany. ● *adjective* of Germany. □ **German measles** disease like mild measles. **German shepherd (dog)** Alsatian.

german /'dʒɜːmən/ *adjective* (placed after *brother*, *sister*, or *cousin*) having same two parents or grandparents.

germander /dʒɜː'mændə/ *noun* plant of mint family.

germane /dʒɜː'meɪn/ *adjective* (usually + *to*) relevant.

Germanic /dʒɜː'mænɪk/ *adjective* having German characteristics. ● *noun* group of languages including English, German, Dutch, and Scandinavian languages.

germicide /'dʒɜːmɪsaɪd/ *noun* substance that destroys germs. □ **germicidal** /-'saɪd(ə)l/ *adjective*.

germinal /'dʒɜːmɪn(ə)l/ *adjective* **1** of germs. **2** in earliest stage of development.

germinate /'dʒɜːmɪneɪt/ *verb* (**-ting**) (cause to) sprout or bud. □ **germination** *noun*.

■ bud, develop, grow, root, shoot, spring up, sprout, take root.

gerontology /dʒerɒn'tɒlədʒɪ/ *noun* study of old age and ageing.

gerrymander /'dʒerɪmændə/ *verb* manipulate boundaries of (constituency etc.) to gain unfair electoral advantage.

gerund /'dʒerənd/ *noun* verbal noun, in English ending in *-ing*.

Gestapo /ge'stɑːpəʊ/ *noun historical* Nazi secret police.

gestation /dʒe'steɪʃ(ə)n/ *noun* **1** carrying or being carried in womb between conception and birth. **2** this period. **3** development of plan etc. □ **gestate** *verb* (**-ting**).

gesticulate /dʒeˈstɪkjʊleɪt/ *verb* (**-ting**) use gestures instead of or with speech. □ **gesticulation** *noun*.

gesture /ˈdʒestʃə/ *noun* **1** meaningful movement of limb or body. **2** action performed as courtesy or to indicate intention. ● *verb* (**-ring**) gesticulate.

■ *noun* action, flourish, gesticulation, indication, motion, movement, sign, signal. ● *verb* gesticulate, indicate, motion, sign, signal.

get /get/ *verb* (**getting**; *past* **got**; *past participle* **got** or *US* **gotten**) **1** obtain, earn. **2** fetch, procure. **3** capture, catch. **4** go to reach or catch. **5** prepare (meal). **6** (cause to) reach some state or become. **7** obtain from calculation. **8** contract (disease). **9** contact. **10** have (punishment) inflicted on one. **11** succeed in bringing, placing, etc. **12** (cause to) succeed in coming or going. **13** succeed in persuading; prevail on. **14** *colloquial* understand. **15** *colloquial* make out, hear. **16** *colloquial* annoy. **17** *colloquial* harm. **18** *colloquial* attract. **19** *archaic* beget. □ **get about** go from place to place. **get across** communicate. **get ahead** be or become successful. **get along** (often + *with*) live harmoniously. **get around** = GET ABOUT. **get at 1** reach; get hold of. **2** *colloquial* imply. **3** *colloquial* nag. **get away** escape. **getaway** *noun*. **get by** *colloquial* cope. **get down** descend, alight. **get hold of 1** grasp. **2** understand. **3** make contact with (person). **get in 1** enter. **2** obtain place at college etc. **3** win election. **get off 1** alight (from). **2** *colloquial* escape with little or no punishment. **3** start, depart. **4** (+ *with*) *colloquial* start sexual relationship with. **get on 1** make progress; manage. **2** advance. **3** enter (bus etc.). **4** (often + *with*) live harmoniously. **5** (usually as **be getting on**) age. **get one's own back** *colloquial* have one's revenge. **get out 1** leave. **2** solve. **get out of** avoid; escape. **get over 1** recover from. **2** surmount. **get round 1** coax or cajole (person). **2** evade (law etc.). **3** (+ *to*) deal with (task) in due course. **get through 1** pass (exam etc.). **2** use up (resources). **3** make contact by telephone. **4** (+ *to*) succeed in making (person) understand. **get together** gather. **get-together** *noun colloquial* social assembly. **get up 1** rise esp. from bed. **2** (of wind etc.) strengthen. **3** organize. **4** stimulate. **5** arrange appearance of. **get-up** *noun colloquial* style of dress etc. **get-up-and-go** *colloquial* energy, enthusiasm. **have got 1** possess. **2** (+ *to do*) must.

■ **1** acquire, be given, come by, come in possession of, earn, gain, get hold of, inherit, *colloquial* land, lay hands on, obtain, pick up, receive, secure, take, win. **2** bring, buy, fetch, obtain, pick up, procure, purchase, retrieve. **3** apprehend, arrest, capture, catch, *colloquial* collar, *slang* nab, *slang* pinch, seize. **5** cook, make ready, prepare. **6** become, grow, land up, turn. **8** catch, come down with, contract, develop, fall ill with, suffer from. **9** contact, get in touch with, reach, speak to. **12** arrive, come, go, journey, reach, travel. **13** cajole, cause, induce, influence, persuade, prevail on, wheedle. **14** absorb,

appreciate, apprehend, catch, comprehend, distinguish, fathom, follow, glean, grasp, hear, know, make out, take in, understand, work out. □ **get across** see COMMUNICATE. **1**. **get ahead** see PROSPER. **get at 3** see CRITICIZE **1**. **get away** see ESCAPE *verb* **1**. **getaway** escape, flight, retreat. **get down** see DESCEND **1**, ALIGHT² **1**. **get in 1** see ENTER **1**. **get off 1** see ALIGHT² **1**. **get on 1** see PROSPER. **get out 1** see LEAVE¹ **1**. **get together** see GATHER *verb* **1**.

geyser /ˈgiːzə/ *noun* **1** hot spring. **2** apparatus for heating water.

ghastly /ˈgɑːstlɪ/ *adjective* (**-ier**, **-iest**) **1** horrible, frightful. **2** *colloquial* unpleasant. **3** deathlike, pallid. □ **ghastliness** *noun*.

■ **1** appalling, *colloquial* awful, dreadful, frightening, frightful, grim, grisly, gruesome, hideous, horrible, macabre, nasty, shocking, terrible, upsetting. **2** see UNPLEASANT. **3** ashen, deathlike, grim, pallid, pasty, wan.

ghee /giː/ *noun* Indian clarified butter.

gherkin /ˈgɜːkɪn/ *noun* small cucumber for pickling.

ghetto /ˈgetəʊ/ *noun* (*plural* **-s**) **1** part of city occupied by minority group. **2** *historical* Jews' quarter in city. **3** segregated group or area. □ **ghetto-blaster** large portable radio or cassette player.

ghost /gəʊst/ *noun* **1** apparition of dead person etc.; disembodied spirit. **2** (+ *of*) semblance of. **3** secondary image in defective telescope or television picture. ● *verb* (often + *for*) act as ghost-writer of (book etc.). □ **ghost-writer** writer doing work for which another takes credit. □ **ghostly** *adjective* (**-ier**, **-iest**).

■ *noun* **1** apparition, banshee, bogey, doppelganger, ghoul, hallucination, illusion, phantasm, phantom, poltergeist, *literary* shade, shadow, spectre, spirit, *colloquial* spook, vision, visitant, wraith. □ **ghostly** *colloquial* creepy, disembodied, eerie, frightening, illusory, phantasmal, *colloquial* scary, shadowy, sinister, spectral, *colloquial* spooky, supernatural, uncanny, unearthly, weird, wraith-like.

ghoul /guːl/ *noun* **1** person morbidly interested in death etc. **2** evil spirit. **3** (in Arabic mythology) spirit preying on corpses. □ **ghoulish** *adjective*.

GHQ *abbreviation* General Headquarters.

ghyll = GILL³.

GI /dʒiːˈaɪ/ *noun* soldier in US army.

giant /ˈdʒaɪənt/ *noun* **1** mythical being of human form but superhuman size. **2** person, animal, or thing of extraordinary size, ability, etc. ● *adjective* gigantic.

■ *noun* **1** colossus, monster, ogre, superhuman, Titan. **2** colossus, *colloquial* jumbo, leviathan, monster, *slang* whopper. ● *adjective* see GIGANTIC.

gibber /ˈdʒɪbə/ *verb* chatter inarticulately.

gibberish /ˈdʒɪbərɪʃ/ *noun* unintelligible or meaningless speech or sounds.

gibbet /ˈdʒɪbɪt/ *noun historical* **1** gallows. **2** post with arm from which executed criminal was hung after execution.

gibbon /'gɪbən/ *noun* long-armed ape.

gibbous /'gɪbəs/ *adjective* **1** convex. **2** (of moon etc.) with bright part greater than semicircle.

gibe /dʒaɪb/ (also **jibe**) *verb* (**-bing**) (often + *at*) jeer, mock. ● *noun* jeering remark, taunt.

giblets /'dʒɪblɪts/ *plural noun* liver, gizzard, etc. of bird removed and usually cooked separately.

giddy /'gɪdɪ/ *adjective* (**-ier, -iest**) **1** dizzy; tending to fall or stagger. **2** mentally intoxicated. **3** excitable, flighty. **4** making dizzy. □ **giddiness** *noun*.

■ **1** dizzy, faint, light-headed, reeling, spinning, unbalanced, unsteady, vertiginous. □ **giddiness** *noun* dizziness, faintness, unsteadiness, vertigo.

gift /gɪft/ *noun* **1** thing given, present. **2** talent. **3** *colloquial* easy task.

■ **1** benefaction, bonus, bounty, contribution, donation, favour, *colloquial* give-away, grant, gratuity, handout, honorarium, offering, present, tip. **2** ability, aptitude, bent, capability, capacity, facility, flair, genius, knack, power, strength, talent.

gifted *adjective* talented.

■ able, capable, clever, expert, skilful, skilled, talented.

gig[1] /gɪg/ *noun* **1** light two-wheeled one-horse carriage. **2** light boat on ship. **3** rowing boat, esp. for racing.

gig[2] /gɪg/ *colloquial noun* engagement to play music, usually on one occasion. ● *verb* (**-gg-**) perform gig.

giga- /'gɪgə/ *combining form* one thousand million.

gigantic /dʒaɪ'gæntɪk/ *adjective* huge, giant-like.

■ colossal, elephantine, enormous, gargantuan, giant, Herculean, huge, immense, *colloquial* jumbo, king-size, mammoth, massive, mighty, monstrous, prodigious, titanic, towering, vast.

giggle /'gɪg(ə)l/ *verb* (**-ling**) laugh in half-suppressed spasms. ● *noun* **1** such laugh. **2** *colloquial* amusing person or thing. □ **giggly** *adjective* (**-ier, -iest**).

■ *verb* chuckle, laugh, snicker, snigger, titter.

gigolo /'dʒɪgələʊ/ *noun* (*plural* **-s**) young man paid by older woman to be escort or lover.

gild[1] /gɪld/ *verb* (*past participle* **gilded** or as *adjective* **gilt**) **1** cover thinly with gold. **2** tinge with golden colour.

gild[2] = GUILD.

gill[1] /gɪl/ *noun* (usually in *plural*) **1** respiratory organ of fish etc. **2** vertical radial plate on underside of mushroom etc. **3** flesh below person's jaws and ears.

gill[2] /dʒɪl/ *noun* quarter-pint measure.

gill[3] /gɪl/ *noun* (also **ghyll**) **1** deep wooded ravine. **2** narrow mountain torrent.

gillie /'gɪlɪ/ *noun Scottish* man or boy attending hunter or angler.

gillyflower /'dʒɪlɪflaʊə/ *noun* clove-scented flower, e.g. wallflower.

gilt[1] /gɪlt/ *adjective* overlaid (as) with gold. ● *noun* gilding. □ **gilt-edged** (of securities etc.) having high degree of reliability.

gilt[2] /gɪlt/ *noun* young sow.

gimbals /'dʒɪmb(ə)lz/ *plural noun* contrivance of rings etc. for keeping things horizontal in ship, aircraft, etc.

gimcrack /'dʒɪmkræk/ *adjective* flimsy, tawdry. ● *noun* showy ornament etc.

■ *adjective* cheap, cheap and nasty, flimsy, rubbishy, shoddy, tawdry, *esp. US* trashy, trumpery, *colloquial* useless, worthless.

gimlet /'gɪmlɪt/ *noun* small boring-tool.

gimmick /'gɪmɪk/ *noun* trick or device, esp. to attract attention. □ **gimmickry** *noun*. **gimmicky** *adjective*.

■ device, ploy, ruse, stratagem, stunt, subterfuge, trick.

gimp /'gɪmp/ *noun* twist of silk etc. with cord or wire running through.

gin[1] /dʒɪn/ *noun* spirit distilled from grain or malt and flavoured with juniper berries.

gin[2] /dʒɪn/ *noun* **1** snare, trap. **2** machine separating cotton from seeds. **3** kind of crane or windlass. ● *verb* (**-nn-**) **1** treat (cotton) in gin. **2** trap.

ginger /'dʒɪndʒə/ *noun* **1** hot spicy root used in cooking. **2** plant having this root. **3** light reddish-yellow. ● *adjective* of ginger colour. ● *verb* **1** flavour with ginger. **2** (+ *up*) enliven. □ **ginger ale, beer** ginger-flavoured fizzy drinks. **gingerbread** ginger-flavoured treacle cake. **ginger group** group urging party or movement to stronger action. **ginger-nut** kind of ginger-flavoured biscuit. □ **gingery** *adjective*.

gingerly /'dʒɪndʒəlɪ/ *adverb* in a careful or cautious way. ● *adjective* showing extreme care or caution.

gingham /'gɪŋəm/ *noun* plain-woven usually checked cotton cloth.

gingivitis /dʒɪndʒɪ'vaɪtɪs/ *noun* inflammation of the gums.

ginkgo /'gɪŋkəʊ/ *noun* (*plural* **-s**) tree with fan-shaped leaves and yellow flowers.

ginseng /'dʒɪnseŋ/ *noun* **1** plant found in E. Asia and N. America. **2** medicinal root of this.

Gipsy = GYPSY.

giraffe /dʒɪ'rɑːf/ *noun* (*plural* same or **-s**) tall 4-legged African animal with long neck.

gird /gɜːd/ (*past & past participle* **girded** or **girt**) encircle or fasten (on) with waistbelt etc. □ **gird (up) one's loins** prepare for action.

girder /'gɜːdə/ *noun* iron or steel beam or compound structure for bridge-building etc.

■ bar, beam, joist, rafter.

girdle[1] /'gɜːd(ə)l/ *noun* **1** belt or cord worn round waist. **2** corset. **3** thing that surrounds. **4** bony support for limbs. ● *verb* (**-ling**) surround with girdle.

■ *noun* **1** band, belt, waistband. ● *verb* see SURROUND *verb*.

girdle[2] /'gɜːd(ə)l/ *noun Scottish & Northern English* = GRIDDLE.

girl /gɜːl/ *noun* **1** female child. **2** *colloquial* young woman. **3** *colloquial* girlfriend. **4** female servant. □ **girlfriend** person's regular female companion. **Girl Guide** Guide. **Girl Scout** female Scout. □ **girlhood** *noun*. **girlish** *adjective*. **girly** *adjective*.

■ **1** *archaic* damsel, daughter, female, hoyden, *esp. Scottish & Northern English* or *poetical* lass, *archaic* maid, *archaic* maiden, schoolgirl, tomboy. **2** *slang* bird, *archaic* damsel, daughter, débutante, female, hoyden, *esp. Scottish & Northern English* or *poetical* lass, *archaic* maid, *archaic* maiden, *Australian & NZ slang* sheila, *jocular* wench, woman. **3** fiancée, girlfriend, sweetheart, *colloquial* woman.

giro /'dʒaɪrəʊ/ *noun* (*plural* -s) **1** system of credit transfer between banks, Post Offices, etc. **2** cheque or payment by giro. ● *verb* (-es, -ed) pay by giro.

girt *past & past participle* of GIRD.

girth /gɜːθ/ *noun* **1** distance round a thing. **2** band round body of horse securing saddle.

■ **1** circumference, perimeter.

gist /dʒɪst/ *noun* substance or essence of a matter; general drift (of speech etc.).

■ core, direction, drift, essence, general sense, main idea, meaning, nub, pith, point, quintessence, significance.

git /gɪt/ *noun slang* silly or contemptible person.

gîte /ʒiːt/ *noun* furnished holiday house in French countryside. [French]

give /gɪv/ *verb* (-ving; *past* gave; *past participle* given) **1** transfer possession of freely. **2** provide with. **3** administer. **4** deliver (message). **5** (often + *for*) make over in exchange or payment. **6** confer; accord. **7** pledge. **8** perform (action etc.). **9** utter, declare. **10** yield to pressure; collapse. **11** yield as product. **12** consign. **13** devote. **14** present, offer (one's hand, arm, etc.). **15** impart; be source of. **16** concede. **17** grant. **18** put on (party, meal, etc.). ● *noun* **1** capacity to comply. **2** elasticity. □ **give and take 1** exchange of talk or ideas. **2** ability to compromise. **give away 1** transfer as gift. **2** hand over (bride) to bridegroom. **3** betray or expose. **give-away** *noun colloquial* **1** unintentional disclosure. **2** free or inexpensive thing. **give in 1** yield. **2** hand in. **give off** emit. **give out 1** announce; emit; distribute. **2** be exhausted. **3** run short. **give over 1** *colloquial* desist. **2** hand over. **3** devote. **give the game away** reveal secret. **give up 1** resign; surrender. **2** part with. **3** renounce hope (of). **4** cease (activity). **give up the ghost** *colloquial* die. □ **giver** *noun*.

■ *verb* **1** allocate, allot, allow, apportion, assign, contribute, deal out, *colloquial* dish out, distribute, dole out, donate, *slang* fork out, furnish, give away, give out, grant, hand over, lend, let (person) have, offer, pass on, present, provide, ration out, render, share out, supply. **2** endow with, entrust with, equip with, furnish with, let (person) have, provide with, supply with. **3** (*give medicine*) administer, dispense, dose with, prescribe; (*give a punishment*) impose, inflict, *literary* mete out. **4** deliver, display, express, impart, issue, notify, publish, put across, put into words, reveal, set out, show, tell, transmit. **6** accord, award, bestow, confer, grant. **9** emit, let out, utter, voice. **10** be flexible, bend, buckle, collapse, distort, fail, fall apart, give way, warp, yield. **12** consign, deliver, entrust, give away, hand over. **15** cause, create, engender, occasion. **18** arrange, organize, provide, put on, run, set up. □ **give away 3** see BETRAY 1–3. **give in 1** see SURRENDER *verb* 2. **give off** see EMIT. **give out 1** see EMIT. **give up 1** see SURRENDER *verb* 1–2. **3** see ABANDON *verb* 2. **give up the ghost** see DIE[1] 1.

given *past participle* of GIVE. ● *adjective* **1** (+ *to*) disposed or prone to. **2** assumed as basis of reasoning etc. **3** fixed, specified.

gizmo /'gɪzməʊ/ *noun* (*plural* -s) gadget.

gizzard /'gɪzəd/ *noun* bird's second stomach, for grinding food.

glacé /'glæseɪ/ *adjective* **1** (of fruit) preserved in sugar. **2** (of cloth etc.) smooth, polished.

glacial /'gleɪʃ(ə)l/ *adjective* of ice or glaciers.

glaciated /'gleɪsɪeɪtɪd/ *adjective* **1** marked or polished by moving ice. **2** covered with glaciers. □ **glaciation** *noun*.

glacier /'glæsɪə/ *noun* slowly moving mass of ice on land.

glad *adjective* (-dd-) **1** pleased, willing. **2** joyful, cheerful. □ **glad rags** *colloquial* best clothes. □ **gladden** *verb*. **gladly** *adverb*. **gladness** *noun*.

■ **1** disposed, eager, inclined, keen, pleased, ready, willing. **2** cheerful, content, delighted, gratified, happy, joyful, overjoyed, pleased.

glade *noun* clear space in forest.

gladiator /'glædɪeɪtə/ *noun historical* trained fighter in ancient Roman shows. □ **gladiatorial** /-ɪə'tɔːrɪəl/ *adjective*.

gladiolus /glædɪ'əʊləs/ *noun* (*plural* -li /-laɪ/) plant of lily family with bright flower-spikes.

gladsome *adjective poetical* cheerful, joyful.

Gladstone bag /'glædst(ə)n/ *noun* kind of light portmanteau.

glair *noun* **1** white of egg. **2** similar or derivative viscous substance.

glamour /'glæmə/ *noun* (*US* **glamor**) **1** physical, esp. cosmetic, attractiveness. **2** alluring or exciting beauty or charm. □ **glamorize** *verb* (also **-ise**) (-zing or -sing). **glamorous** *adjective*. **glamorously** *adverb*.

■ **1** see BEAUTY 1. **2** allure, appeal, attraction, brilliance, charm, excitement, fascination, glitter, lustre, magic, romance. □ **glamorize** idealize, romanticize. **glamorous** alluring, appealing, beautiful, colourful, dazzling, enviable, exciting, exotic, fascinating, glittering, prestigious, romantic, smart, spectacular, wealthy.

glance /glɑːns/ *verb* (**-cing**) **1** (often + *down*, *up*, *over*, etc.) look or refer briefly. **2** (often + *off*) hit at fine angle and bounce off. ● *noun* **1** brief look. **2** flash, gleam. **3** swift oblique stroke in cricket. □ **at a glance** immediately on looking.
■ *verb* **1** glimpse, have a quick look, look (briefly), peek, peep, scan, skim.

gland *noun* **1** organ etc. secreting substances for use in body. **2** similar organ in plant.

glanders /ˈglændəz/ *plural noun* contagious horse disease.

glandular /ˈglændjʊlə/ *adjective* of gland(s). □ **glandular fever** infectious disease with swelling of lymph glands.

glare /gleə/ *verb* (**-ring**) **1** look fiercely. **2** shine oppressively. **3** be very evident. ● *noun* **1** oppressive light or public attention. **2** fierce look. **3** tawdry brilliance.
■ *verb* **1** frown, give a nasty look, glower, look daggers, lour, lower, scowl, stare angrily. **2** blaze, dazzle, flare, reflect, shine.

glaring *adjective* **1** looking fiercely. **2** shining oppressively. **3** evident, conspicuous. □ **glaringly** *adverb*
■ **2** see BRIGHT 1. **3** see OBVIOUS.

glasnost /ˈglæznɒst/ *noun* (in former USSR) policy of more open government.

glass /glɑːs/ *noun* **1** hard, brittle, usually transparent substance made by fusing sand with soda and lime etc. **2** glass objects collectively. **3** glass drinking vessel. **4** its contents. **5** window. **6** glazed frame for plants. **7** barometer. **8** covering of watch-face. **9** lens. **10** mirror. **11** (in *plural*) spectacles. **12** (in *plural*) binoculars. ● *verb* (usually as **glassed** *adjective*) fit with glass. □ **glass-blowing** blowing of semi-molten glass to make glass objects. **glass fibre** glass filaments made into fabric or reinforcing plastic. **glasshouse 1** greenhouse. **2** *slang* military prison. **glasspaper** paper covered with powdered glass, for smoothing etc. **glass wool** fine glass fibres for packing and insulation. □ **glassful** *noun* (*plural* **-s**).
■ *noun* **2** crystal. **3** beaker, goblet, tumbler, wineglass. **5** pane, window. **9** eyeglass, lens, magnifying glass, monocle. **10** looking-glass, mirror, reflector. **11** (*glasses*) eyeglasses, *colloquial* specs, spectacles. **12** binoculars, field-glasses, opera-glasses. □ **glasshouse 1** conservatory, greenhouse, hothouse.

glassy /ˈglɑːsɪ/ *adjective* (**-ier**, **-iest**) **1** like glass. **2** (of eye etc.) dull, fixed.
■ **1** glazed, gleaming, glossy, icy, polished, shining, shiny, smooth, vitreous. **2** see EXPRESSIONLESS (EXPRESSION).

glaucoma /glɔːˈkəʊmə/ *noun* eye disease with pressure in eyeball and gradual loss of sight.

glaze *verb* (**-zing**) **1** fit with glass or windows. **2** cover (pottery etc.) with vitreous substance or (surface) with smooth shiny coating. **3** (often + *over*) (of eyes) become glassy. ● *noun* substance used for or surface produced by glazing.

■ *verb* **2** burnish, enamel, gloss, lacquer, polish, shellac, shine, varnish.

glazier /ˈgleɪzɪə/ *noun* person who glazes windows etc.

gleam *noun* faint or brief light or show. ● *verb* emit gleam(s). □ **gleaming** *adjective*.
■ *verb* flash, glimmer, glint, glisten, glow, reflect, shimmer, shine. □ **gleaming** see BRIGHT 1.

glean *verb* **1** gather (facts etc.). **2** gather (corn left by reapers). □ **gleanings** *plural noun*.

glebe *noun* **1** piece of land yielding revenue to benefice. **2** *poetical* earth; land, field.

glee *noun* **1** mirth, delight. **2** musical composition for several voices. □ **gleeful** *adjective*. **gleefully** *adverb*.
■ □ **gleeful** cheerful, delighted, ecstatic, exuberant, exultant, gay, happy, jovial, joyful, jubilant, overjoyed, pleased, rapturous, triumphant.

glen *noun* narrow valley.

glengarry /glenˈgærɪ/ *noun* (*plural* **-ies**) kind of Highland cap.

glib *adjective* (**-bb-**) speaking or spoken fluently but insincerely. □ **glibly** *adverb*. **glibness** *noun*.
■ articulate, facile, fast-talking, fluent, insincere, plausible, quick, ready, shallow, slick, smooth, smooth-tongued, suave, superficial, unctuous.

glide *verb* (**-ding**) **1** move smoothly or continuously. **2** (of aircraft) fly without engine-power. **3** go stealthily. ● *noun* gliding motion.
■ *verb* **1** coast, drift, float, fly, freewheel, glissade, hang, hover, sail, skate, ski, skid, skim, slide, slip, soar, stream.

glider /ˈglaɪdə/ *noun* light aircraft without engine.

glimmer /ˈglɪmə/ *verb* shine faintly or intermittently. ● *noun* **1** faint or wavering light. **2** (also **glimmering**) (usually + *of*) small sign.

glimpse /glɪmps/ *noun* (often + *of*, *at*) **1** brief view. **2** faint transient appearance. ● *verb* (**-sing**) have brief view of.
■ *noun* **1** glance, look, peep, sight, *colloquial* squint, view. ● *verb* discern, distinguish, espy, make out, notice, observe, see briefly, sight, *colloquial* spot, spy.

glint *verb* & *noun* flash, glitter.

glissade /glɪˈsɑːd/ *noun* **1** controlled slide down snow slope. **2** gliding. ● *verb* (**-ding**) perform glissade.

glissando /glɪˈsændəʊ/ *noun* (*plural* **-di** /-dɪ/ or **-s**) *Music* continuous slide of adjacent notes.

glisten /ˈglɪs(ə)n/ *verb* shine like wet or polished surface. ● *noun* glitter.
■ *verb* flash, gleam, glimmer, glint, glitter, reflect, shimmer, shine, sparkle.

glitch *noun* *colloquial* irregularity, malfunction.

glitter /ˈglɪtə/ *verb* **1** shine with brilliant

reflected light; sparkle. **2** (often + *with*) be showy. ● *noun* **1** sparkle. **2** showiness. **3** tiny pieces of glittering material. □ **glittering** *adjective*.

■ *verb* **1** coruscate, flash, glint, glisten, scintillate, spark, sparkle, twinkle. □ **glittering** see BRIGHT 1.

glitz *noun slang* showy glamour. □ **glitzy** *adjective* (-ier, -iest).

gloaming /ˈgləʊmɪŋ/ *noun poetical* twilight.

gloat *verb* (often + *over* etc.) look or ponder with greedy or malicious pleasure.

■ boast, brag, crow, exult, glory, rejoice, rub it in, *colloquial* show off, triumph.

global /ˈgləʊb(ə)l/ *adjective* **1** worldwide. **2** all-embracing. □ **global warming** increase in temperature of earth's atmosphere. □ **globally** *adverb*.

■ **1** international, pandemic, universal, worldwide. **2** all-embracing, broad, far-reaching, total, universal, wide-ranging.

globe *noun* **1** spherical object. **2** spherical map of earth. **3** (**the globe**) the earth. □ **globe artichoke** partly edible head of artichoke plant. **globe-trotter** person travelling widely. **globe-trotting** *noun & adjective*.

■ **1** ball, globule, orb, sphere. **3** earth, planet, world.

globular /ˈglɒbjʊlə/ *adjective* **1** globe-shaped. **2** composed of globules.

globule /ˈglɒbjuːl/ *noun* small globe, round particle, or drop.

glockenspiel /ˈglɒkənspiːl/ *noun* musical instrument of bells or metal bars played with hammers.

gloom /gluːm/ *noun* **1** darkness. **2** melancholy, depression.

■ **1** blackness, cloudiness, darkness, dimness, dullness, dusk, murkiness, obscurity, semi-darkness, shade, shadow, twilight. **2** see DEPRESSION 1.

gloomy /ˈgluːmɪ/ *adjective* (-ier, -iest) **1** dark. **2** depressed. **3** depressing.

■ **1** cloudy, dark, dim, dingy, dull, grey, murky, obscure, overcast, shadowy, shady, sombre. **2** depressed, desolate, dismal, doleful, downhearted, forlorn, glum, heavy-hearted, joyless, lugubrious, miserable, morose, mournful, pessimistic, sad, saturnine, sullen. **3** cheerless, depressing, dismal, dreary, grim.

glorify /ˈglɔːrɪfaɪ/ *verb* (-ies, -ied) **1** make glorious. **2** make seem more splendid than is the case. **3** (as **glorified** *adjective*) treated as more important etc. than it is. **4** extol. □ **glorification** *noun*.

glorious /ˈglɔːrɪəs/ *adjective* **1** possessing or conferring glory. **2** *colloquial* splendid, excellent. □ **gloriously** *adverb*.

■ **1** celebrated, distinguished, eminent, famed, famous, heroic, illustrious, noble, noted, renowned, triumphant. **2** beautiful, bright, brilliant, dazzling, delightful, excellent, fine, *colloquial* gorgeous, grand, impressive, lovely, magnificent, majestic, marvellous, outstanding, pleasurable,

resplendent, spectacular, splendid, *colloquial* super, superb, wonderful.

glory /ˈglɔːrɪ/ *noun* (*plural* **-ies**) **1** (thing bringing) renown, honourable fame, etc. **2** adoring praise. **3** resplendent majesty, beauty, etc. **4** halo of saint. ● *verb* (-ies, -ied) (often + *in*) take pride.

■ *noun* **1** credit, distinction, eminence, fame, honour, *colloquial* kudos, praise, prestige, renown, repute, reputation, success, triumph. **2** adoration, exaltation, glorification, gratitude, homage, praise, thanksgiving, veneration, worship. **3** beauty, brightness, brilliance, grandeur, magnificence, majesty, radiance, splendour, wonder.

gloss[1] *noun* **1** surface lustre. **2** deceptively attractive appearance. **3** (in full **gloss paint**) paint giving glossy finish. ● *verb* make glossy. □ **gloss over** seek to conceal.

■ *noun* **1** brightness, brilliance, burnish, finish, glaze, gleam, lustre, polish, sheen, shine, varnish. □ **gloss over** see CONCEAL.

gloss[2] *noun* **1** explanatory comment added to text. **2** interpretation. ● *verb* add gloss to.

■ *noun* annotation, comment, definition, elucidation, exegesis, explanation, footnote, interpretation, marginal note, note, paraphrase. ● *verb* annotate, comment on, define, elucidate, explain, interpret, paraphrase.

glossary /ˈglɒsərɪ/ *noun* (*plural* **-ies**) dictionary of technical or special words, esp. as appendix.

■ dictionary, phrase book, vocabulary.

glossy *adjective* (-ier, -iest) **1** smooth and shiny. **2** printed on such paper. ● *noun* (*plural* **-ies**) *colloquial* glossy magazine or photograph.

■ *adjective* **1** bright, burnished, glassy, glazed, gleaming, glistening, lustrous, polished, reflective, shiny, silky, sleek, smooth, waxed.

glottal /ˈglɒt(ə)l/ *adjective* of the glottis. □ **glottal stop** sound produced by sudden opening or shutting of glottis.

glottis /ˈglɒtɪs/ *noun* opening at upper end of windpipe between vocal cords.

glove /glʌv/ *noun* **1** hand-covering for protection, warmth, etc. **2** boxing glove. ● *verb* (-ving) cover or provide with gloves. □ **glove compartment** recess for small articles in car dashboard. **glove puppet** small puppet fitted on hand.

■ *noun* **1** gauntlet, mitt, mitten.

glow /gləʊ/ *verb* **1** emit flameless light and heat. **2** (often + *with*) feel bodily heat or strong emotion. **3** show warm colour. ● *noun* **1** glowing state. **2** glowing appearance; warm colour. **3** glowing feeling. **4** ardour. □ **glow-worm** beetle that emits green light from abdomen.

■ *verb* **1** gleam, incandesce, light up, phosphoresce, radiate, shine, smoulder. **2, 3** blush, flush, redden, warm. ● *noun* **1** burning, fieriness, heat, incandescence, luminosity, lustre, phosphorescence, radiation, redness. **2** blush, flush, radiance, redness, rosiness. **4** ardour, enthusiasm, fervour, passion, warmth.

glower /ˈglaʊə/ *verb* (often + *at*) scowl.
■ frown, glare, lour, lower, scowl, stare angrily.

glowing *adjective* **1** emitting flameless light and heat. **2** expressing pride or satisfaction.
■ **1** aglow, bright, hot, incandescent, lambent, luminous, phosphorescent, radiant, red, red-hot, warm, white-hot. **2** complimentary, enthusiastic, favourable, laudatory.

glucose /ˈgluːkəʊs/ *noun* kind of sugar found in blood, fruits, etc.

glue *noun* substance used as adhesive. ● *verb* (**glues**, **glued**, **gluing** or **glueing**) **1** attach (as) with glue. **2** hold closely. ▫ **glue ear** blocking of (esp. child's) Eustachian tube. **glue-sniffing** inhalation of fumes from adhesives as intoxicant. ▫ **gluey** *adjective* (**gluier**, **gluiest**).
■ *noun* adhesive, cement, fixative, gum, paste, sealant, size. ● *verb* **1** affix, bond, cement, fasten, fix, gum, paste, seal, stick.

glum *adjective* (**-mm-**) dejected, sullen. ▫ **glumly** *adverb*. **glumness** *noun*.
■ cheerless, dejected, depressed, dispirited, displeased, gloomy, grim, heavy-hearted, joyless, lugubrious, moody, morose, mournful, out of sorts, sad, saturnine, sullen.

glut *verb* (**-tt-**) **1** feed or indulge to the full; satiate. **2** overstock. ● *noun* excessive supply; surfeit.
■ *noun* abundance, excess, over-abundance, overprovision, superfluity, surfeit, surplus.

gluten /ˈgluːt(ə)n/ *noun* sticky part of wheat flour.

glutinous /ˈgluːtɪnəs/ *adjective* sticky, gluelike.

glutton /ˈglʌt(ə)n/ *noun* **1** excessive eater. **2** (often + *for*) *colloquial* insatiably eager person. **3** voracious animal of weasel family. ▫ **gluttonous** *adjective*. **gluttonously** *adverb*. **gluttony** *noun*.
■ **1** good trencherman, gormandizer, gourmand, guzzler, *colloquial* pig. ▫ **gluttonous** gormandizing, greedy, piggish, voracious.

glycerine /ˈglɪsəriːn/ *noun* (also **glycerol**, *US* **glycerin**) colourless sweet viscous liquid used in medicines, explosives, etc.

gm *abbreviation* gram(s).

GMT *abbreviation* Greenwich Mean Time.

gnarled /nɑːld/ *adjective* knobbly, twisted, rugged.
■ bent, bumpy, contorted, crooked, distorted, knobbly, knotted, knotty, lumpy, rough, rugged, twisted, warped.

gnash /næʃ/ *verb* **1** grind (one's teeth). **2** (of teeth) strike together.

gnat /næt/ *noun* small biting fly.

gnaw /nɔː/ *verb* **1** (often + *at*, *into*) bite persist-

ently. **2** (usually + *away* etc.) wear away by biting. **3** corrode. **4** torment.
■ **1** bite, chew, eat, munch, nibble. **3** consume, corrode, erode, wear away.

gneiss /naɪs/ *noun* coarse-grained rock of feldspar, quartz, and mica.

gnome /nəʊm/ *noun* **1** dwarf, goblin. **2** (esp. in *plural*) *colloquial* person with sinister influence, esp. financial.

gnomic /ˈnəʊmɪk/ *adjective* of aphorisms; sententious.

gnomon /ˈnəʊmɒn/ *noun* rod etc. on sundial, showing time by its shadow.

gnostic /ˈnɒstɪk/ *adjective* **1** of knowledge. **2** having special mystic knowledge. ● *noun* (**Gnostic**) early Christian heretic claiming mystical knowledge. ▫ **Gnosticism** /-sɪz(ə)m/ *noun*.

GNP *abbreviation* gross national product.

gnu /nuː/ *noun* (*plural* same or **-s**) oxlike antelope.

go[1] *verb* (*3rd singular present* **goes** /gəʊz/; *past* **went**; *past participle* **gone** /gɒn/) **1** (start to) walk, travel, proceed. **2** participate in (doing something). **3** extend in a certain direction. **4** depart. **5** move, function. **6** make specified movement or sound. **7** *colloquial* say. **8** be. **9** become. **10** elapse; be traversed. **11** (of song etc.) have specified wording etc. **12** (often + *together*) match. **13** be regularly kept. **14** fit. **15** be successful. **16** be sold. **17** (of money) be spent. **18** be relinquished. **19** fail, decline; collapse. **20** be acceptable or accepted. **21** (often + *by*, *with*, *on*, *upon*) be guided by. **22** (often + *to*) attend regularly. **23** (+ *to*, *towards*) contribute to. **24** (+ *for*) apply to. ● *noun* (*plural* **goes**) **1** animation. **2** vigorous activity. **3** success. **4** turn; attempt. ▫ **get going** start steadily talking, working, etc. **go-ahead** ● *adjective* enterprising. ● *noun* permission to proceed. **go along with** agree to; take same view as. **go around with** be regularly in company of. **go away** depart. **go back on** fail to honour (promise or commitment). **go-between** intermediary. **go down 1** descend. **2** become less. **3** decrease (in price). **4** subside. **5** sink. **6** (of sun) set. **7** deteriorate; cease to function. **8** be recorded. **9** be swallowed. **10** (+ *with*) find acceptance with. **11** *colloquial* leave university. **12** *colloquial* be sent to prison. **13** (+ *with*) become ill with. **go for 1** go to fetch. **2** prefer; choose. **3** pass or be accounted as. **4** *colloquial* attack. **5** *colloquial* strive to attain. **go-getter** *colloquial* pushily enterprising person. **go in for** compete or engage in. **go into 1** enter. **2** investigate. **go-kart** miniature racing car with skeleton body. **go off 1** explode. **2** deteriorate. **3** fall asleep. **4** begin to dislike. **go off well, badly** succeed, fail. **go on 1** continue. **2** proceed. **3** *colloquial* talk at great length. **4** (+ *at*) *colloquial* nag. **5** use as evidence. **go out 1** leave room or house. **2** be extinguished. **3** be broadcast. **4** cease to be fashionable. **5** (often + *with*) have romantic or sexual relationship. **6** (usually + *to*) sympathize. **go over** inspect details of; rehearse. **go round 1** spin, revolve. **2** suffice for all. **go slow** work slowly as industrial protest.

go through experience. **go under** sink; succumb; fail. **go up 1** rise. **2** increase (in price). **3** be consumed (in flames etc.); explode. **4** *colloquial* enter university. **go with 1** be pair with. **2** match. **3** accompany. **go without** manage without or forgo (something). **have a go at 1** attack. **2** attempt. **on the go** *colloquial* active.

■ *verb* **1** advance, begin, *colloquial* be off, *formal* commence, embark, get going, get moving, get out, get under way, move, pass along, pass on, proceed, run, set out, start, travel, walk, wend one's way. **3** extend, lead, reach, stretch. **4** decamp, depart, disappear, escape, get away, leave, make off, retire, retreat, *slang* shove off, take off, take one's leave, vanish, withdraw. **5** act, function, move, operate, perform, run, work. **6, 7** say, sound, utter. **9** become, grow, turn. **10** elapse, lapse, pass. **12** see MATCH[1] *verb* 1. **13** belong, have a proper place, live. **19** collapse, decline, die, fade, fail, give way. ● *noun* **4** attempt, chance, *colloquial* crack, opportunity, *colloquial* shot, *colloquial* stab, try, turn. □ **go-ahead** ● *adjective* ambitious, enterprising, forward-looking, progressive, resourceful. ● *noun* approval, green light, permission, sanction, *colloquial* say-so, thumbs up. **go away** see DEPART 1, 2. **go-between** agent, broker, envoy, intermediary, mediator, messenger, middleman, negotiator. **go down 1** see DESCEND 1. **5** see SINK *verb* 1–2; 4. **go for 2** see LIKE[2] *verb* 2. **go into 2** see INVESTIGATE. **go off 1** see EXPLODE 1, 2. **go on 1** see CONTINUE 1. **go through** see SUFFER 2, 3. **go with 3** see ACCOMPANY 1. **go without** see ABSTAIN 1.

go[2] *noun* Japanese board game.

goad *verb* **1** urge with goad. **2** (usually + *on, into*) irritate; stimulate. ● *noun* **1** spiked stick for urging cattle. **2** thing that torments or incites.

■ *verb* **2** badger, chivvy, egg on, *colloquial* hassle, *colloquial* needle, prod, prompt, spur, stimulate, urge.

goal *noun* **1** object of effort. **2** destination. **3** structure into or through which ball is to be driven in certain games. **4** point(s) so won. **5** point where race ends. □ **goalkeeper** player protecting goal. **goalpost** either post supporting crossbar of goal.

■ **1** aim, ambition, aspiration, design, end, ideal, intention, object, objective, purpose, target. **2** destination, end, target.

goalie *noun colloquial* goalkeeper.

goat *noun* **1** small domesticated mammal with horns and (in male) beard. **2** licentious man. **3** *colloquial* fool. □ **get (person's) goat** *colloquial* irritate him or her.

goatee /ɡəʊˈtiː/ *noun* small pointed beard.

gob[1] *noun slang* mouth. □ **gobsmacked** *slang* flabbergasted. **gob-stopper** large hard sweet.

gob[2] *slang noun* clot of slimy matter. ● *verb* (**-bb-**) spit.

gobbet /ˈɡɒbɪt/ *noun* **1** lump of flesh, food, etc. **2** extract from text set for translation or comment.

gobble[1] /ˈɡɒb(ə)l/ *verb* (**-ling**) eat hurriedly and noisily.

■ bolt, devour, gulp, guzzle, *colloquial* scoff, wolf.

gobble[2] /ˈɡɒb(ə)l/ *verb* (**-ling**) **1** (of turkeycock) make guttural sound. **2** speak thus.

gobbledegook /ˈɡɒbəldɪguːk/ *noun* (also **gobbledeygook**) *colloquial* pompous or unintelligible jargon.

goblet /ˈɡɒblɪt/ *noun* drinking vessel with foot and stem.

goblin /ˈɡɒblɪn/ *noun* mischievous demon.

goby /ˈɡəʊbɪ/ *noun* (*plural* **-ies**) small fish with sucker on underside.

god *noun* **1** superhuman being worshipped as possessing power over nature, human fortunes, etc. **2** (**God**) creator and ruler of universe. **3** idol; adored person. **4** (**the gods**) (occupants of) gallery in theatre. □ **godchild** person in relation to godparent. **god-daughter** female godchild. **godfather** male godparent. **God-fearing** religious. **godforsaken** devoid of all merit; dismal. **godmother** female godparent. **godparent** person who responds on behalf of candidate at baptism. **godsend** unexpected welcome event or acquisition. **godson** male godchild. □ **godlike** *adjective*.

■ **1** deity, divinity, godhead, spirit; (*the gods*) the immortals, the pantheon. **2** (**God**) the Almighty, the Creator, the supreme being. □ **godsend** blessing, boon, gift, miracle, stroke of good fortune, windfall.

goddess /ˈɡɒdɪs/ *noun* **1** female deity. **2** adored woman.

■ **1** deity, divinity, godhead, spirit.

godhead *noun* **1** divine nature. **2** deity.

godless *adjective* **1** impious, wicked. **2** not believing in God. □ **godlessness** *noun*.

godly /ˈɡɒdlɪ/ *adjective* (**-ier, -iest**) pious, devout. □ **godliness** *noun*.

goer /ˈɡəʊə/ *noun* **1** person or thing that goes. **2** *colloquial* lively or sexually promiscuous person. □ **-goer** regular attender.

goggle /ˈɡɒɡ(ə)l/ *verb* (**-ling**) **1** (often + *at*) look with wide-open eyes. **2** (of eyes) be rolled; project. **3** roll (eyes). ● *adjective* (of eyes) protuberant, rolling. ● *noun* (in *plural*) spectacles for protecting eyes. □ **goggle-box** *colloquial* television set.

going /ˈɡəʊɪŋ/ *noun* condition of ground as affecting riding etc. ● *adjective* **1** in action. **2** existing, available. **3** current, prevalent. □ **going concern** thriving business. **going-over** (*plural* **goings-over**) **1** *colloquial* inspection or overhaul. **2** *slang* thrashing. **goings-on** strange conduct.

goitre /ˈɡɔɪtə/ *noun* (*US* **goiter**) abnormal enlargement of thyroid gland.

gold /ɡəʊld/ *noun* **1** precious yellow metal. **2** colour of this. **3** coins or articles of gold. ● *adjective* of or coloured like gold. □ **gold-digger** *slang* woman who goes after men for their money. **gold field** area with naturally occurring gold. **goldfinch** brightly coloured songbird. **goldfish** small golden-red Chinese carp. **gold leaf** gold beaten into thin sheet. **gold medal** medal given usually as first prize. **gold plate 1** vessels of gold. **2** material plated with gold. **gold-plate** plate with gold. **gold-rush** rush to newly discovered gold field. **goldsmith** worker in gold. **gold standard** financial system in which value of money is based on gold.

golden /'gəʊld(ə)n/ adjective **1** of gold. **2** coloured or shining like gold. **3** precious. excellent. □ **golden handshake** colloquial gratuity as compensation for redundancy or compulsory retirement. **golden jubilee** 50th anniversary of reign. **golden mean** principle of moderation. **golden retriever** retriever with gold-coloured coat. **golden wedding** 50th anniversary of wedding. ■ **1** aureate, gilded, gilt. **2** blond, blonde, flaxen, yellow.

golf noun game in which small hard ball is struck with clubs over ground into series of small holes. ● verb play golf. □ **golf ball 1** ball used in golf. **2** spherical unit carrying type in some electric typewriters. **golf course** area of land on which golf is played. **golf club 1** club used in golf. **2** (premises of) association for playing golf. □ **golfer** noun.

golliwog /'gɒlɪwɒg/ noun black-faced soft doll with fuzzy hair.

gonad /'gəʊnæd/ noun animal organ producing gametes, e.g. testis or ovary.

gondola /'gɒndələ/ noun **1** light Venetian canal-boat. **2** car suspended from airship.

gondolier /gɒndə'lɪə/ noun oarsman of gondola.

gone /gɒn/ past participle of GO[1]. ● adjective **1** (of time) past. **2** lost, hopeless. **3** dead. **4** colloquial pregnant for specified time.

goner /'gɒnə/ noun slang person or thing that is doomed or irrevocably lost.

gong noun **1** metal disc giving resonant note when struck. **2** saucer-shaped bell. **3** slang medal.

gonorrhoea /gɒnə'riːə/ noun (US **gonorrhea**) a venereal disease.

goo noun colloquial **1** sticky or slimy substance. **2** sickly sentiment. □ **gooey** adjective (**gooier, gooiest**).

good /gʊd/ adjective (**better, best**) **1** having right or desired qualities; adequate. **2** (of person) competent, effective. **3** (of thing) efficient. **4** kind. **5** morally excellent. **6** well behaved. **7** agreeable, enjoyable. **8** (of book) well written, readable. **9** considerable. **10** not less than. **11** beneficial; healthy; eatable. **12** valid. ● noun **1** (only in singular) good quality or circumstance. **2** (in plural) movable property, merchandise. □ **good-for-nothing** worthless (person). **good humour** genial mood. **good-humoured** adjective. **good-looking** handsome. **good nature** kindly disposition. **good-natured** adjective. **good-tempered** cheerful; not easily angered. **goodwill 1** kindly feeling. **2** established value-enhancing reputation of a business. **good word** (often in phrase **put in a good word for**) words in recommendation or defence of person.

■ adjective **1** acceptable, adequate, admirable, appropriate, commendable, esteemed, fair, fine, gratifying, happy, perfect, praiseworthy, proper, right, satisfactory, suitable, colloquial useful, valuable, worthy. **2** able, accomplished, adept, capable, clever, competent, conscientious, efficient, gifted, proficient, skilful, skilled, talented. **3** careful, competent, creditable, efficient, meritorious, professional, thorough. **4** benevolent, benign, caring, charitable, considerate, decent, dependable, dutiful, friendly, helpful, honest, humane, just, kind, loyal, merciful, personable, reliable, thoughtful, true, trustworthy. **5** chaste, ethical, holy, honourable, incorruptible, innocent, law-abiding, moral, noble, philanthropic, pure, religious, righteous, saintly, upright, virtuous, worthy. **6** angelic, obedient, well behaved, well mannered. **7** agreeable, delightful, enjoyable, excellent, colloquial fabulous, colloquial fantastic, fine, colloquial great, colloquial incredible, colloquial lovely, marvellous, nice, phenomenal, pleasant, pleasing, colloquial sensational, splendid, colloquial super, colloquial superb, wonderful. **8** classic, exciting, great, interesting, readable, well written. **11** beneficial, delicious, eatable, healthy, nourishing, nutritious, tasty, well cooked, wholesome. **12** fair, legitimate, proper, right, sound, valid. ● noun **2** (goods) belongings, chattels, commodities, effects, freight, merchandise, possessions, produce, property, stock, wares. □ **good-humoured** see GOOD-TEMPERED. **good-looking** see HANDSOME 1. **good-natured** see KIND adjective. **good-tempered** accommodating, amenable, amiable, benevolent, benign, cheerful, cheery, considerate, cooperative, cordial, friendly, genial, good-humoured, good-natured, helpful, in a good mood, obliging, patient, pleasant, relaxed, smiling.

goodbye /gʊd'baɪ/ (US **goodby**) interjection: expressing good wishes at parting. ● noun (plural **-byes** or US **-bys**) parting, farewell. ■ interjection adieu, au revoir, bon voyage, colloquial bye, colloquial cheerio, colloquial ciao, farewell, colloquial see you, colloquial so long, colloquial ta-ta. ● noun au revoir, farewell, departure, leave-taking, parting, send-off, formal valediction.

goodly /'gʊdlɪ/ adjective (**-ier, -iest**) **1** handsome. **2** of imposing size etc.

goodness /'gʊdnɪs/ noun **1** virtue; excellence. **2** kindness. **3** nutriment.

goody /'gʊdɪ/ noun (plural **-ies**) **1** colloquial good person. **2** (usually in plural) something good or attractive, esp. to eat. ● interjection: expressing childish delight. □ **goody-goody** colloquial (person who is) smugly or obtrusively virtuous.

goof /guːf/ slang noun foolish or stupid person or mistake. ● verb bungle, blunder. □ **goofy** adjective (**-ier, -iest**).

googly /'guːglɪ/ noun (plural **-ies**) Cricket ball bowled so as to bounce in unexpected direction.

goon /guːn/ noun slang **1** stupid person. **2** esp. US hired ruffian.

goose /guːs/ *noun* (*plural* **geese** /giːs/) **1** large web-footed bird. **2** female of this. **3** *colloquial* simpleton. □ **goose-flesh, -pimples** (*US* **-bumps**) pimply state of skin due to cold or fright. **goose-step** stiff-legged marching step.

gooseberry /ˈgʊzbərɪ/ *noun* (*plural* **-ies**) **1** small green usually sour berry. **2** thorny shrub bearing this.

gopher /ˈgəʊfə/ *noun* American burrowing rodent.

gore[1] *noun* clotted blood.

gore[2] *verb* (**-ring**) pierce with horn, tusk, etc.

gore[3] *noun* **1** wedge-shaped piece in garment. **2** triangular or tapering piece in umbrella etc. ● *verb* (**-ring**) shape with gore.

gorge *noun* **1** narrow opening between hills. **2** surfeit. **3** contents of stomach. ● *verb* (**-ging**) **1** feed greedily. **2** satiate.

> ■ *verb* **1** be greedy, guzzle, indulge oneself, *colloquial* make a pig of oneself, overeat, stuff oneself.

gorgeous /ˈgɔːdʒəs/ *adjective* **1** richly coloured, magnificent. **2** *colloquial* splendid. **3** *colloquial* strikingly beautiful. □ **gorgeously** *adverb*.

> ■ **1** colourful, dazzling, *colloquial* glorious, magnificent, resplendent, showy, splendid, sumptuous. **2** see SPLENDID **1**. **3** see BEAUTIFUL **1**.

gorgon /ˈgɔːgən/ *noun* **1** (in Greek mythology) any of 3 snake-haired sisters able to turn people to stone. **2** frightening or repulsive woman.

Gorgonzola /gɔːgənˈzəʊlə/ *noun* rich blue-veined Italian cheese.

gorilla /gəˈrɪlə/ *noun* largest anthropoid ape.

gormandize /ˈgɔːm(ə)ndaɪz/ (also **-ise**) *verb* **1** eat or devour voraciously. **2** indulge in good eating. ● *noun* = GORMANDISE. □ **gormandizer** *noun*.

gormless /ˈgɔːmlɪs/ *adjective colloquial* foolish, lacking sense. □ **gormlessly** *adverb*.

gorse /gɔːs/ *noun* prickly yellow-flowered shrub.

Gorsedd /ˈgɔːseð/ *noun* Druidic order meeting before eisteddfod.

gory /ˈgɔːrɪ/ *adjective* (**-ier, -iest**) **1** involving bloodshed. **2** bloodstained.

> ■ **1** bloody, grisly, gruesome, sanguinary, savage. **2** bloodstained, bloody.

gosh *interjection: expressing surprise.*

goshawk /ˈgɒshɔːk/ *noun* large short-winged hawk.

gosling /ˈgɒzlɪŋ/ *noun* young goose.

gospel /ˈgɒsp(ə)l/ *noun* **1** teaching or revelation of Christ. **2** (**Gospel**) (each of 4 books giving) account of Christ's life in New Testament. **3** (**Gospel**) portion of this read at church service. **4** thing regarded as absolutely true. □ **gospel music** black American religious singing.

> ■ **3** lesson, message, reading.

gossamer /ˈgɒsəmə/ *noun* **1** filmy substance of small spiders' webs. **2** delicate filmy material. ● *adjective* light and flimsy as gossamer.

gossip /ˈgɒsɪp/ *noun* **1** unconstrained talk or writing, esp. about people. **2** idle talk. **3** person indulging in gossip. ● *verb* (**-p-**) talk or write gossip. □ **gossip column** regular newspaper column of gossip. □ **gossipy** *adjective*.

> ■ *noun* **1, 2** casual talk, chatter, hearsay, prattle, rumour, scandal, small talk, tattle, tittle-tattle. **3** busybody, scandalmonger, tell-tale. ● *verb* blab, chat, chatter, *colloquial* natter, prattle, talk, tattle, tell tales, tittle-tattle.

got *past & past participle* of GET.

Goth *noun* member of Germanic tribe that invaded Roman Empire in 3rd–5th c.

Gothic *adjective* **1** of Goths. **2** *Architecture* in the pointed-arch style prevalent in W. Europe in 12th–16th c. **3** (of novel etc.) in a style popular in 18th & 19th c., with supernatural or horrifying events.

gotten *US past participle* of GET.

gouache /guːˈɑːʃ/ *noun* **1** painting with opaque watercolour. **2** pigments used for this.

Gouda /ˈgaʊdə/ *noun* flat round Dutch cheese.

gouge /gaʊdʒ/ *noun* concave-bladed chisel. ● *verb* (**-ging**) cut or (+ *out*) force out (as) with gouge.

> ■ *verb* chisel, cut, dig, hollow, incise, scoop.

goulash /ˈguːlæʃ/ *noun* stew of meat and vegetables seasoned with paprika.

gourd /gʊəd/ *noun* **1** fleshy fruit of trailing or climbing cucumber-like plant. **2** this plant. **3** dried rind of this fruit used as bottle etc.

gourmand /ˈgʊəmənd/ *noun* **1** glutton. **2** *disputed* gourmet.

USAGE The use of *gourmand* to mean 'gourmet' is considered incorrect by some people.

gourmandise /gʊəmɒ̃ˈdiːz/ *noun* habits of a gourmand; gluttony.

gourmet /ˈgʊəmeɪ/ *noun* connoisseur of good food.

> ■ connoisseur, epicure, gastronome, *disputed* gourmand.

gout /gaʊt/ *noun* disease with inflammation of small joints. □ **gouty** *adjective*.

govern /ˈgʌv(ə)n/ *verb* **1** rule with authority; conduct policy and affairs of. **2** influence or determine. **3** curb, control. □ **governable** *adjective*.

> ■ **1** administer, be in charge of, command, conduct affairs of, control, direct, guide, head, lead, look after, manage, oversee, preside over, reign over, rule, run, steer, superintend, supervise. **3** bridle, check, control, curb, discipline, keep in check, keep under control, master, regulate, restrain, tame.

governance *noun* act, manner, or function of governing.

governess /ˈgʌvənɪs/ *noun* woman employed to teach children in private household.

government *noun* **1** manner or system of governing. **2** group of people governing state. □ **governmental** /-'men-/ *adjective*.

■ **1** administration, authority, bureaucracy, conduct of state affairs, constitution, control, direction, domination, management, oversight, regime, regulation, rule, sovereignty, supervision, surveillance, sway. **2** administration, bureaucracy, leadership, ministry.

governor *noun* **1** ruler. **2** official governing a province, town, etc. **3** executive head of each State of US. **4** member of governing body of institution. **5** *slang* one's employer or father. **6** automatic regulator controlling speed of engine etc. □ **Governor-General** representative of Crown in Commonwealth country regarding Queen as head of state. □ **governorship** *noun*.

gown /gaʊn/ *noun* **1** woman's, esp. formal or elegant, long dress. **2** official robe of alderman, judge, cleric, academic, etc. **3** surgeon's overall.

■ **1** dress, frock. **2** robe, vestment.

goy *noun* (*plural* **-im** or **-s**) *Jewish name for* non-Jew.

GP *abbreviation* general practitioner.

GPO *abbreviation* General Post Office.

gr *abbreviation* (also **gr.**) **1** gram(s). **2** grain(s). **3** gross.

grab *verb* (**-bb-**) **1** seize suddenly. **2** take greedily. **3** *slang* impress. **4** (+ *at*) snatch at. ● *noun* **1** sudden clutch or attempt to seize. **2** device for clutching.

■ *verb* **1** capture, catch, clutch, collar, get hold of, grasp, *slang* nab, pluck, seize, snap up, snatch. **2** appropriate, *colloquial* bag, commandeer, expropriate, get hold of.

grace *noun* **1** elegance of proportions, manner, or movement. **2** courteous good will. **3** attractive feature. **4** unmerited favour of God. **5** goodwill. **6** delay granted. **7** thanksgiving at meals. **8** (**His, Her, Your Grace**) *title used of or to duke, duchess, or archbishop*. ● *verb* (**-cing**) **1** (often + *with*) add grace to. **2** bestow honour on. □ **grace note** *Music* note embellishing melody.

■ *noun* **1** attractiveness, beauty, charm, ease, elegance, fluidity, gracefulness, loveliness, poise, refinement, softness, tastefulness. **2** benevolence, courtesy, decency, goodness, good will, graciousness, kindness, politeness. **4** beneficence, benevolence, compassion, favour, forgiveness, goodness, graciousness, kindness, love, mercy. **7** blessing, prayer, thanksgiving.

graceful *adjective* **1** full of grace or elegance. **2** polite, kind. □ **gracefully** *adverb*. **gracefulness** *noun*.

■ **1** agile, balletic, dignified, easy, elegant, flowing, fluid, lithe, natural, nimble, pliant, smooth, supple, willowy. **2** courteous, courtly, delicate, kind, polite, refined, suave, tactful, urbane.

graceless *adjective* **1** lacking grace. **2** lacking charm.

■ **1** awkward, clumsy, gangling, gawky, inelegant, maladroit, uncoordinated, ungainly, ungraceful. **2** boorish, gauche, inept, rude, tactless, uncouth.

gracious /'greɪʃəs/ *adjective* **1** kindly, esp. to inferiors. **2** merciful. **3** (of way of life) elegant, luxurious. □ **gracious living** elegant way of life. □ **graciously** *adverb*. **graciousness** *noun*.

■ **1** affable, agreeable, beneficent, benevolent, considerate, cordial, courteous, friendly, kind, kindly, good-natured, pleasant, polite. **2** clement, compassionate, forbearing, forgiving, generous, indulgent, lenient, magnanimous, merciful, pitying, sympathetic. **3** affluent, civilized, dignified, elegant, expensive, lavish, luxurious, opulent, sumptuous.

gradate /grə'deɪt/ *verb* (**-ting**) **1** (cause to) pass gradually from one shade to another. **2** arrange in steps or grades.

gradation *noun* (usually in *plural*) **1** stage of transition or advance. **2** degree in rank, intensity, etc. **3** arrangement in grades. □ **gradational** *adjective*.

grade *noun* **1** degree in rank, merit, etc. **2** mark indicating quality of student's work. **3** slope. **4** *US* class in school. ● *verb* (**-ding**) **1** arrange in grades. **2** (+ *up, down, off, into*, etc.) pass between grades. **3** give grade to. **4** reduce to easy gradients. □ **make the grade** succeed.

■ *noun* **1** category, class, degree, echelon, level, notch, point, position, quality, rank, rung, standard, standing, status, step. **2** mark, result, score. **3** see GRADIENT 1. **4** class, form, year. ● *verb* **1** arrange, categorize, classify, differentiate, group, organize, range, size, sort. **3** assess, evaluate, mark, rank, rate.

gradient /'greɪdɪənt/ *noun* **1** sloping road etc. **2** amount of such slope.

■ **1** ascent, bank, declivity, grade, hill, incline, rise, slope.

gradual /'grædʒʊəl/ *adjective* **1** happening by degrees. **2** not steep or abrupt. □ **gradually** *adverb*.

■ **1** continuous, leisurely, regular, slow, steady, unhurried, unspectacular. **2** easy, even, gentle, moderate.

graduate *noun* /'grædʒʊət/ holder of academic degree. ● *verb* /-eɪt/ (**-ting**) **1** obtain academic degree. **2** (+ *to*) move up to. **3** mark in degrees or portions. **4** arrange in gradations. **5** apportion (tax etc.) according to scale. □ **graduation** *noun*.

■ *verb* **3** calibrate, gradate, mark off.

graffiti /grə'fiːtɪ/ *plural noun* (*singular* **graffito**) writing or drawing on wall etc.

USAGE *Graffiti* should be used with plural verbs, as in *Graffiti have appeared everywhere*.

graft[1] /grɑːft/ *noun* **1** shoot or scion planted in slit in another stock. **2** piece of transplanted living tissue. **3** *slang* hard work. ● *verb* **1** (often + *in, on, together*, etc.) insert (graft). **2** transplant (living tissue). **3** (+ *in, on*) insert or fix (thing) permanently to another. **4** *slang* work hard.

■ *verb* **1, 3** implant, insert, join, splice.

graft[2] /grɑːft/ *colloquial noun* **1** practices for securing illicit gains in politics or business. **2** such gains. ● *verb* seek or make graft.

Grail *noun* (in full **Holy Grail**) legendary cup or platter used by Christ at Last Supper.

grain *noun* **1** fruit or seed of cereal. **2** wheat or allied food-grass; corn. **3** particle of sand, salt, etc. **4** unit of weight (0.065 g). **5** least possible amount. **6** texture in skin, wood, stone, etc. **7** arrangement of lines of fibre in wood. ● *verb* **1** paint in imitation of grain of wood. **2** form into grains.

■ *noun* **3** crumb, fleck, granule, mote, particle, seed, speck. **5** atom, bit, fragment, iota, jot, mite, morsel, particle, scrap, trace.

gram *noun* (also **gramme**) metric unit of mass equal to one-thousandth of a kilogram.

grammar /'græmə/ *noun* **1** study or rules of relations between words in (a) language. **2** application of such rules. **3** book on grammar. □ **grammar school** *esp. historical* secondary school with academic curriculum.

grammarian /grə'meərɪən/ *noun* expert in grammar.

grammatical /grə'mætɪk(ə)l/ *adjective* of or according to grammar.

gramophone /'græməfəʊn/ *noun* record player.

grampus /'græmpəs/ *noun* (*plural* **-es**) sea mammal of dolphin family.

gran *noun colloquial* grandmother.

granary /'grænərɪ/ *noun* (*plural* **-ies**) **1** storehouse for grain. **2** region producing much corn.

grand *adjective* **1** splendid, imposing. **2** chief; of chief importance. **3** (**Grand**) of highest rank. **4** *colloquial* excellent. **5** (seeming to be) socially superior. ● *noun* **1** grand piano. **2** (*plural* same) (usually in *plural*) *slang* 1,000 dollars or pounds. □ **grand jury** jury to examine validity of accusation before trial. **grand piano** piano with horizontal strings. **grand slam** winning of all of group of matches. **grand total** sum of other totals. □ **grandly** *adverb*. **grandness** *noun*.

■ *adjective* **1** aristocratic, august, big, dignified, eminent, *colloquial* glorious, great, important, imposing, impressive, lordly, magnificent, majestic, noble, opulent, palatial, regal, royal, splendid, stately, sumptuous, superb. **5** grandiose, great, lofty, majestic, noble, *colloquial* posh, rich, superior, upper-class, *colloquial* upper-crust.

grandad *noun* (also **grand-dad**) *colloquial* grandfather.

grandchild *noun* child of one's son or daughter.

granddaughter *noun* one's child's daughter.

grandee /græn'diː/ *noun* **1** Spanish or Portuguese noble of highest rank. **2** great personage.

grandeur /'grændʒə/ *noun* **1** majesty, splendour, dignity. **2** high rank, eminence.

grandfather *noun* one's parent's father.

□ **grandfather clock** clock in tall wooden case.

grandiloquent /græn'dɪləkwənt/ *adjective* pompous or inflated in language. □ **grandiloquence** *noun*.

■ bombastic, elaborate, florid, flowery, fustian, grandiose, high-flown, inflated, melodramatic, ornate, poetic, pompous, rhetorical, turgid.

grandiose /'grændɪəʊs/ *adjective* **1** (trying to be) imposing. **2** planned on large scale. □ **grandiosity** /-'ɒsɪtɪ/ *noun*.

■ **1** affected, extravagant, flamboyant, flashy, grand, grandiloquent, *colloquial* highfalutin, imposing, ostentatious, pretentious, showy. **2** ambitious, exaggerated, extravagant, grand, imposing, impressive, magnificent, overdone, over the top.

grandma *noun colloquial* grandmother.

grandmother *noun* one's parent's mother.

grandparent *noun* one's parent's parent.

Grand Prix /grɑ̃ 'priː/ *noun* any of several international motor-racing events.

grandson *noun* one's child's son.

grandstand *noun* main stand for spectators at racecourse etc.

grange /greɪndʒ/ *noun* country house with farm buildings.

granite /'grænɪt/ *noun* granular crystalline rock of quartz, mica, etc.

granny /'grænɪ/ *noun* (also **grannie**) (*plural* **-ies**) **1** *colloquial* grandmother. **2** (in full **granny knot**) reef-knot crossed wrong way.

grant /grɑːnt/ *verb* **1** consent to fulfil. **2** allow to have. **3** give formally; transfer legally. **4** (often + *that*) admit, concede. ● *noun* **1** granting. **2** thing, esp. money, granted. □ **take for granted 1** assume to be true. **2** cease to appreciate through familiarity. □ **grantor** /grɑːn'tɔː/ *noun*.

■ *verb* **2, 3** allocate, allot, allow, assign, award, bestow on, confer on, donate, give, pay, provide, supply. **4** accede, accept, acknowledge, admit, agree, concede, consent, *formal* vouchsafe.
● *noun* **2** allocation, allowance, annuity, award, benefaction, bursary, concession, contribution, donation, endowment, gift, honorarium, investment, loan, pension, scholarship, sponsorship, subsidy, subvention.

granular /'grænjʊlə/ *adjective* of or like grains or granules.

granulate /'grænjʊleɪt/ *verb* (**-ting**) **1** form into grains. **2** roughen surface of. □ **granulation** *noun*.

granule /'grænjuːl/ *noun* small grain.

grape *noun* usually green or purple berry growing in clusters on vine. □ **grapeshot** *historical* small balls as scattering charge for cannon etc. **grapevine 1** vine. **2** *colloquial* means of transmission of rumour.

grapefruit /'greɪpfruːt/ *noun* (*plural* same) large round usually yellow citrus fruit.

graph /grɑːf/ *noun* symbolic diagram repre-

senting relation between two or more variables. ● *verb* plot on graph.
■ *noun* chart, diagram, pie chart, table.

graphic /ˈɡræfɪk/ *adjective* **1** of writing, drawing, etc. **2** vividly descriptive. □ **graphic arts** visual and technical arts involving design or lettering. □ **graphically** *adverb*.
■ **1** descriptive, pictorial, representational, visual. **2** clear, descriptive, detailed, lifelike, lucid, photographic, plain, realistic, vivid, well drawn.

graphics *plural noun* (usually treated as *singular*) **1** products of graphic arts. **2** use of diagrams in calculation and design.

graphite /ˈɡræfaɪt/ *noun* crystalline form of carbon used as lubricant, in pencils, etc.

graphology /ɡrəˈfɒlədʒɪ/ *noun* study of handwriting. □ **graphologist** *noun*.

grapnel /ˈɡræpn(ə)l/ *noun* **1** iron-clawed instrument for dragging or grasping. **2** small manyfluked anchor.

grapple /ˈɡræp(ə)l/ *verb* (**-ling**) **1** (often + *with*) fight at close quarters. **2** (+ *with*) try to manage (problem etc.). **3** grip with hands; come to close quarters with; seize. ● *noun* **1** hold (as) of wrestler. **2** contest at close quarters. **3** clutching-instrument. □ **grappling hook, iron** grapnel.
■ *verb* **1** (*grapple with*) fight (with), scuffle with, struggle with, tackle, tussle with, wrestle with. **2** (*grapple with*) attend to, come to grips with, contend with, cope with, deal with, engage with, get involved with, handle, have a go at, manage, try to solve. **3** see GRASP *verb* 1.

grasp /ɡrɑːsp/ *verb* **1** clutch at; seize greedily. **2** hold firmly. **3** understand, realize. ● *noun* **1** firm hold, grip. **2** (+ *of*) mastery, mental hold of.
■ *verb* **1** catch, clutch at, get hold of, grab, grapple, *slang* nab, seize, snatch, take hold of. **2** clasp, clutch, grip, hang on to, hold. **3** appreciate, apprehend, comprehend, *colloquial* cotton on to, follow, *colloquial* get the hang of, get the point of, learn, master, realize, take in, understand.

grasping *adjective* avaricious.
■ see GREEDY 2.

grass /ɡrɑːs/ *noun* **1** (any of several) plants with bladelike leaves eaten by ruminants. **2** pasture land; grass-covered ground. **3** grazing. **4** *slang* marijuana. **5** *slang* informer. ● *verb* **1** cover with turf. **2** *US* pasture. **3** *slang* betray; inform police. □ **grassland** large open area of country covered with grass. **grass roots 1** fundamental level or source. **2** rank and file. **grass snake** small non-poisonous snake. **grass widow, widower** person whose husband or wife is temporarily absent. □ **grassy** *adjective* (**-ier, -iest**).
■ *noun* **2** field, grassland, green, lawn, meadow, pasture, playing-field, prairie, savannah, steppe, *literary* sward, turf, *South African* veld. ● *verb* **3** see INFORM 2.

grasshopper /ˈɡrɑːshɒpə/ *noun* jumping and chirping insect.

grate[1] *verb* (**-ting**) **1** reduce to small particles by rubbing on rough surface. **2** (often + *against, on*) rub with, utter with, or make harsh sound. **3** (often + *on*) have irritating effect. **4** grind, creak. □ **grater** *noun*. **grating** *adjective*.
■ **3** see ANNOY 1. □ **grating** see ANNOYING (ANNOY), HARSH 1.

grate[2] *noun* (metal) frame holding fuel in fireplace etc.
■ fireplace, hearth.

grateful /ˈɡreɪtfʊl/ *adjective* thankful; feeling or showing gratitude. □ **gratefully** *adverb*. **gratefulness** *noun*.
■ appreciative, beholden, gratified, indebted, obliged, thankful.

gratify /ˈɡrætɪfaɪ/ *verb* (**-ies, -ied**) **1** please, delight. **2** indulge. □ **gratification** *noun*.
■ **2** fulfil, indulge, pander to, satisfy.

grating /ˈɡreɪtɪŋ/ *noun* framework of parallel or crossed metal bars.

gratis /ˈɡrɑːtɪs/ *adverb* & *adjective* free, without charge.
■ complimentary, free, free of charge, gratuitous, without charge.

gratitude /ˈɡrætɪtjuːd/ *noun* being thankful.
■ appreciation, gratefulness, thankfulness, thanks.

gratuitous /ɡrəˈtjuːɪtəs/ *adjective* **1** given or done gratis. **2** uncalled-for, motiveless. □ **gratuitously** *adverb*. **gratuitousness** *noun*.
■ **1** see GRATIS. **2** baseless, groundless, needless, unasked-for, uncalled-for, undeserved, unjustifiable, unmerited, unnecessary, unprovoked, unsolicited, unwarranted.

gratuity /ɡrəˈtjuːɪtɪ/ *noun* (*plural* **-ies**) money given for good service.
■ bonus, *colloquial* perk, present, recompense, reward, tip.

grave[1] /ɡreɪv/ *noun* **1** hole dug for burial of corpse. **2** mound or monument over this. **3 (the grave)** death. □ **gravestone** (usually inscribed) stone over grave. **graveyard** burial ground.
■ **2** barrow, burial place, crypt, last resting place, mausoleum, sepulchre, tomb, tumulus, vault. □ **gravestone** headstone, memorial, monument, tombstone. **graveyard** burial ground, cemetery, churchyard, necropolis.

grave[2] /ɡreɪv/ *adjective* **1** serious, weighty. **2** dignified, solemn. **3** threatening. □ **gravely** *adverb*.
■ **1** (*a grave matter*) critical, crucial, important, major, momentous, pressing, serious, severe, significant, urgent, vital, weighty, worrying; (*a grave offence*) criminal, indictable, punishable. **2** dignified, earnest, grim, long-faced, pensive, sad, sedate, serious, severe, sober, solemn, sombre, subdued, thoughtful, unsmiling. **3** acute, critical, dangerous, life-threatening, perilous, terminal (*illness*), threatening, vital.

grave[3] /greɪv/ *verb* (**-ving**; *past participle* **graven** or **graved**) **1** (+ *in, on*) fix indelibly on (memory etc.). **2** *archaic* engrave, carve. □ **graven image** idol.

grave[4] /grɑːv/ *noun* (in full **grave accent**) mark (ˋ) over letter indicating pronunciation.

gravel /ˈgræv(ə)l/ *noun* **1** coarse sand and small stones. **2** formation of crystals in bladder. ● *verb* (**-ll-**; *US* **-l-**) lay with gravel.

■ *noun* **1** grit, pebbles, shingle, stones.

gravelly /ˈgrævəlɪ/ *adjective* **1** of or like gravel. **2** (of voice) deep and rough-sounding.

gravid /ˈgrævɪd/ *adjective* pregnant.

gravitate /ˈgrævɪteɪt/ *verb* (**-ting**) **1** (+ *to, towards*) move, be attracted, or tend by force of gravity to(wards). **2** sink (as) by gravity.

gravitation *noun* **1** attraction between each particle of matter and every other. **2** effect of this, esp. falling of bodies to earth. □ **gravitational** *adjective*.

gravity /ˈgrævɪtɪ/ *noun* **1** force that attracts body to centre of earth etc. **2** intensity of this. **3** weight. **4** importance, seriousness. **5** solemnity.

■ **1, 2** attraction, gravitation, pull. **3** heaviness, ponderousness, weight. **4** acuteness, danger, importance, magnitude, momentousness, seriousness, severity, significance, weightiness. **5** ceremony, dignity, earnestness, pomp, sedateness, sobriety, solemnity.

gravy /ˈgreɪvɪ/ *noun* (*plural* **-ies**) (sauce made from) juices exuding from meat in and after cooking. □ **gravy-boat** long shallow jug for gravy. **gravy train** *slang* source of easy financial benefit.

gray *US* = GREY.

grayling *noun* (*plural* same) silver-grey freshwater fish.

graze[1] *verb* (**-zing**) **1** feed on growing grass. **2** pasture cattle.

graze[2] *verb* (**-zing**) **1** rub or scrape (part of body). **2** (+ *against, along*, etc.) touch lightly in passing. **3** (+ *against, along*, etc.) move with such contact. ● *noun* abrasion.

■ *noun* abrasion, laceration, raw spot, scrape, scratch, wound.

grazier /ˈgreɪzɪə/ *noun* person who feeds cattle for market.

grazing *noun* grassland suitable for pasturage.

grease /griːs/ *noun* **1** oily or fatty matter, esp. as lubricant. **2** melted fat of dead animal. ● *verb* (**-sing**) smear or lubricate with grease. □ **greasepaint** actor's make-up. **greaseproof** impervious to grease.

■ *noun* fat, lubrication, oil.

greasy /ˈgriːsɪ/ *adjective* (**-ier, -iest**) **1** of, like, smeared with, or having too much grease. **2** (of person, manner) unctuous. □ **greasiness** *noun*.

■ **1** buttery, fatty, oily, slippery, slithery, smeary, waxy. **2** fawning, flattering, fulsome, grovelling, ingratiating, slick, *colloquial* smarmy, sycophantic, toadying, unctuous.

great /greɪt/ *adjective* **1** above average in bulk, number, extent. **2** above average in intensity. **3** important, pre-eminent. **4** imposing. **5** distinguished. **6** of remarkable ability etc. **7** (+ *at, on*) competent, well informed. **8** fully deserving name of; doing thing habitually or intensively. **9** *colloquial* very satisfactory. ● *noun* great person or thing. □ **greatcoat** heavy overcoat. **Great Dane** dog of large short-haired breed. □ **greatness** *noun*.

■ *adjective* **1** big, colossal, enormous, extensive, giant, gigantic, grand, huge, immense, large, mammoth, massive, monstrous, prodigious, *colloquial* tremendous, vast. **2** acute, considerable, deep, excessive, extreme, intense, marked, profound, pronounced, severe. **3** chief, critical, important, main, momentous, pre-eminent, serious, significant, weighty. **4** grand, imposing, impressive, large-scale, spectacular. **5** celebrated, distinguished, eminent, famous, notable, noted, prominent, renowned, well known. **6** able, brilliant, classic, excellent, *colloquial* fabulous, *colloquial* famous, *colloquial* fantastic, fine, first-rate, gifted, outstanding, skilled, talented, wonderful. **8** active, ardent, assiduous, dedicated, devoted, eager, enthusiastic, frequent, habitual, keen, passionate, true, zealous. **9** see EXCELLENT, GOOD *adjective* 7.

great- /greɪt/ *combining form* (of family relationships) one degree more remote (*great-grandfather, great-niece*, etc.).

greatly *adverb* much.

grebe *noun* a diving bird.

Grecian /ˈgriːʃ(ə)n/ *adjective* Greek.

greed *noun* **1** excessive desire for food. **2** excessive desire, esp. for wealth.

■ **1** gluttony, gormandizing, piggishness, voraciousness, voracity. **2** acquisitiveness, avarice, covetousness, cupidity, desire, rapacity, self-interest.

greedy /ˈgriːdɪ/ *adjective* (**-ier, -iest**) **1** showing greed for food. **2** showing greed for wealth, pleasure, etc. **3** (+ *for, to do*) eager. □ **greedily** *adverb*.

■ **1** gluttonous, gormandizing, piggish, voracious; (*be greedy*) see GORGE *verb* 1. **2** acquisitive, avaricious, covetous, grasping, materialistic, mean, mercenary, miserly, rapacious, selfish. **3** avid, desirous, eager, keen.

Greek *noun* native, national, or language of Greece. ● *adjective* of Greece.

green *adjective* **1** coloured like grass. **2** unripe, unseasoned. **3** not dried, smoked, or tanned. **4** inexperienced. **5** jealous. **6** (also **Green**) concerned with protection of environment. **7** (also **Green**) not harmful to environment. ● *noun* **1** green colour, paint, clothes, etc. **2** piece of grassy public land. **3** grassy area for special purpose. **4** (in *plural*) green vegetables. **5** (also **Green**) supporter of protection of environment. □ **green belt** area of open land for preservation round city. **green card** motorist's international insurance document. **greenfinch** bird with greenish plumage. **green fingers** *colloquial* skill in gar-

dening. **greenfly** green aphid. **greengage** round green plum. **greenhorn** novice. **green light** signal or permission to proceed. **green pound** the agreed value of the pound for payments to agricultural producers in EC. **green room** room in theatre for actors when off stage. **greensward** grassy turf.
■ *adjective* **1** aquamarine, bottle green, emerald, hazel, jade, lime-green, olive, turquoise, verdant. **4** see IMMATURE 2.

greenery *noun* green foliage.
■ foliage, leaves, plants, vegetation.

greengrocer /'griːngrəʊsə/ *noun* retailer of fruit and vegetables. □ **greengrocery** *noun* (*plural* **-ies**).

greenhouse *noun* structure with sides and roof mainly of glass, for rearing plants. □ **greenhouse effect** trapping of sun's warmth in earth's lower atmosphere. **greenhouse gas** gas contributing to greenhouse effect, esp. carbon dioxide.

greet *verb* **1** address on meeting or arrival. **2** receive or acknowledge in specified way. **3** become apparent to (eye, ear, etc.).
■ **1, 2** acknowledge, address, give a greeting to, hail, meet, receive, salute, say hello to, usher in, welcome.

greeting *noun* **1** act or words used to greet. **2** (often in *plural*) goodwill message. □ **greetings card** decorative card carrying goodwill message etc.
■ **1** *formal* salutation, reception, welcome. **2** (*greetings*) compliments, congratulations, felicitations, good wishes, regards.

gregarious /grɪ'geərɪəs/ *adjective* **1** fond of company. **2** living in flocks etc. □ **gregariousness** *noun*.

Gregorian calendar /grɪ'gɔːrɪən/ *noun* calendar introduced in 1582 by Pope Gregory XIII.

Gregorian chant /grɪ'gɔːrɪən/ *noun* form of plainsong named after Pope Gregory I.

gremlin /'gremlɪn/ *noun colloquial* mischievous sprite said to cause mechanical faults etc.

grenade /grɪ'neɪd/ *noun* small bomb thrown by hand or shot from rifle.

grenadier /grenə'dɪə/ *noun* **1** (**Grenadier**) member of first regiment of royal household infantry. **2** *historical* soldier armed with grenades.

grew *past* of GROW.

grey /greɪ/ (*US* **gray**) *adjective* **1** of colour between black and white. **2** clouded, dull. **3** (of hair) turning white. **4** (of person) having grey hair. **5** anonymous, unidentifiable. **6** undistinguished, boring. ● *noun* **1** grey colour, paint, clothes, etc. **2** grey horse. ● *verb* make or become grey. □ **grey area** indefinite situation or topic. **Grey Friar** Franciscan friar. **grey matter 1** darker tissues of brain. **2** *colloquial* intelligence.
■ *adjective* **1** ashen, blackish, leaden, livid, silver, silvery, slate, smoky, whitish. **2** see GLOOMY 1. **3, 4** greying, grizzled, grizzly, hoary, silver, silvery, whitish.

greyhound *noun* slender swift dog used in racing.

greylag *noun* European wild goose.

grid *noun* **1** grating. **2** system of numbered squares for map references. **3** network of lines, electric power connections, etc. **4** pattern of lines marking starting place on motor-racing track.
■ **1** grating, grille. **3** framework, lattice, network.

griddle /'grɪd(ə)l/ *noun* iron plate placed over heat for baking etc.

gridiron /'grɪdaɪən/ *noun* **1** barred metal frame for broiling or grilling. **2** American football field.

grief /griːf/ *noun* (cause of) intense sorrow. □ **come to grief** meet with disaster.
■ affliction, anguish, dejection, depression, desolation, despondency, distress, heartache, heartbreak, melancholy, misery, mourning, pain, regret, remorse, sadness, sorrow, suffering, tragedy, unhappiness, woe, wretchedness. □ **come to grief** see FAIL *verb* 1,2.

grievance *noun* resented wrong; real or imagined cause for complaint.
■ allegation, charge, complaint, *colloquial* gripe, objection.

grieve /griːv/ *verb* (**-ving**) **1** cause grief to. **2** feel grief.
■ **1** afflict, depress, dismay, distress, hurt, pain, sadden, upset, wound. **2** be in mourning, eat one's heart out, fret, lament, mope, mourn, suffer, wail, weep.

grievous /'griːvəs/ *adjective* **1** severe. **2** causing grief. **3** injurious. **4** flagrant, heinous. □ **grievously** *adverb*.

griffin /'grɪfɪn/ *noun* (also **gryphon** /-f(ə)n/) mythical creature with eagle's head and wings and lion's body.

griffon /'grɪf(ə)n/ *noun* **1** small coarse-haired terrier-like dog. **2** large vulture. **3** griffin.

grill *noun* **1** device on cooker for radiating heat downwards. **2** gridiron. **3** grilled food. **4** (in full **grill room**) restaurant specializing in grills. ● *verb* **1** cook under grill or on gridiron. **2** subject to or experience extreme heat. **3** subject to severe questioning.

grille /grɪl/ *noun* (also **grill**) **1** grating, latticed screen. **2** metal grid protecting vehicle radiator.

grilse /grɪls/ *noun* (*plural* same or **-s**) young salmon that has been to the sea only once.

grim *adjective* (**-mm-**) **1** of stern appearance. **2** harsh, merciless. **3** ghastly, joyless. **4** unpleasant. □ **grimly** *adverb*. **grimness** *noun*.
■ **1** dour, fearsome, fierce, forbidding, formidable, frightening, frowning, gloomy, glum, louring, menacing, ominous, sinister, stern, sullen, surly, threatening, unattractive, unsmiling. **2** cruel, fierce, formidable, harsh, inexorable, inflexible, merciless, pitiless, relentless, ruthless, savage,

severe, uncompromising, unfriendly, unrelenting, unyielding. **3** alarming, appalling, *colloquial* awful, cheerless, depressing, dire, dreadful, fearsome, forbidding, frightening, frightful, ghastly, gloomy, glum, grisly, gruesome, hideous, horrible, horrid, joyless, sinister, stark, terrible, unattractive. **4** see UNPLEASANT.

grimace /ˈgrɪməs/ *noun* distortion of face made in disgust etc. or to amuse. ● *verb* (**-cing**) make grimace.

grime *noun* deeply ingrained dirt. ● *verb* (**-ming**) blacken, befoul. ▫ **grimy** *adjective* (**-ier, -iest**).

■ *noun* dirt, dust, filth, grit, *colloquial* muck, scum, soot.

grin *verb* (**-nn-**) smile broadly. ● *noun* broad smile.

grind /graɪnd/ *verb* (*past* and *past participle* **ground** /graʊnd/) **1** crush to small particles. **2** sharpen, smooth. **3** rub gratingly. **4** (often + *down*) oppress. **5** (often + *away*) work or study hard. ● *noun* **1** grinding. **2** *colloquial* hard dull work. ▫ **grindstone** thick revolving abrasive disc for grinding, sharpening, etc. ▫ **grinder** *noun*.

■ *verb* **1** crumble, crush, granulate, grate, mill, pound, powder, pulverize. **2** abrade, erode, file, polish, rasp, sand, sandpaper, scrape, sharpen, smooth, wear away, whet. **3** gnash, grate, grit, rub together. **4** (*grind down*) see OPPRESS 1,2. **5** (*grind away*) see WORK *verb* 1.

grip *verb* (**-pp-**) **1** grasp tightly; take firm hold. **2** compel attention of. ● *noun* **1** firm hold, grasp. **2** way of holding. **3** power of holding attention. **4** intellectual mastery. **5** control of one's behaviour. **6** part of machine that grips. **7** part of weapon etc. that is gripped. **8** hairgrip. **9** travelling bag. ▫ **come or get to grips with** begin to deal with.

■ *verb* **1** clasp, clutch, get a grip on, grab, grasp, hold, seize, take hold of. **2** absorb, compel, engage, engross, enthral, entrance, fascinate, hypnotize, mesmerize, rivet, spellbind. ● *noun* **1, 2** clasp, clutch, grasp, hold, purchase, stranglehold. **3** see CONTROL *noun* 1. ▫ **come to grips with** see TACKLE *verb* 1.

gripe *verb* (**-ping**) **1** *colloquial* complain. **2** affect with colic. ● *noun* **1** (usually in *plural*) colic. **2** *colloquial* complaint. ▫ **Gripe Water** *proprietary term* medicine to relieve colic in babies.

grisly /ˈgrɪzlɪ/ *adjective* (**-ier, -iest**) causing horror, disgust, or fear.

■ appalling, *colloquial* awful, bloody, disgusting, dreadful, fearful, frightful, ghastly, ghoulish, gory, grim, gruesome, hair-raising, hideous, horrible, horrid, horrifying, macabre, nauseating, repellent, repulsive, revolting, sickening, terrible.

grist *noun* corn for grinding. ▫ **grist to the mill** source of profit or advantage.

gristle /ˈgrɪs(ə)l/ *noun* tough flexible tissue; cartilage. ▫ **gristly** *adjective*.

■ ▫ **gristly** leathery, rubbery, tough, uneatable.

grit *noun* **1** small particles of sand etc. **2** coarse sandstone. **3** *colloquial* pluck, endurance. ● *verb* (**-tt-**) **1** spread grit on (icy roads etc.). **2** clench (teeth). **3** make grating sound. ▫ **gritty** *adjective* (**-ier, -iest**).

■ ▫ **gritty** abrasive, dusty, grainy, granular, gravelly, rough, sandy.

grits *plural noun* **1** coarse oatmeal. **2** unground husked oats.

grizzle /ˈgrɪz(ə)l/ *verb* (**-ling**) *colloquial* cry fretfully. ▫ **grizzly** *adjective* (**-ier, -iest**).

grizzled *adjective* grey-haired.

grizzly /ˈgrɪzlɪ/ *adjective* (**-ier, -iest**) grey-haired. ● *noun* (*plural* **-ies**) (in full **grizzly bear**) large fierce N. American bear.

groan *verb* **1** make deep sound expressing pain, grief, or disapproval. **2** complain. **3** (usually + *under, beneath, with*) be loaded or oppressed. ● *noun* sound made in groaning.

■ *verb* **1** cry out, lament, moan, sigh, wail, whimper, whine. **2** see COMPLAIN 1.

groat *noun historical* silver coin worth 4 old pence.

groats *plural noun* hulled or crushed grain, esp. oats.

grocer /ˈgrəʊsə/ *noun* dealer in food and household provisions.

grocery /ˈgrəʊsərɪ/ *noun* (*plural* **-ies**) grocer's trade, shop, or (in *plural*) goods.

grog *noun* drink of spirit (originally rum) and water.

groggy /ˈgrɒgɪ/ *adjective* (**-ier, -iest**) incapable, unsteady. ▫ **groggily** *adverb*.

groin[1] *noun* **1** depression between belly and thigh. **2** edge formed by intersecting vaults. ● *verb* build with groins.

groin[2] *US* = GROYNE.

grommet /ˈgrɒmɪt/ *noun* **1** eyelet placed in hole to protect or insulate rope or cable passed through it. **2** tube passed through eardrum to middle ear.

groom /gruːm/ *noun* **1** person employed to tend horses. **2** bridegroom. ● *verb* **1** tend (horse). **2** give neat or attractive appearance to. **3** prepare (person) for office or occasion etc.

■ *noun* **1** *historical* ostler, stable lad, stableman. **2** bridegroom, husband. ● *verb* **1** brush, clean, curry, tend. **2** brush, clean, make neat, neaten, preen, smarten up, spruce up, tidy, *colloquial* titivate. **3** coach, drill, educate, get ready, prepare, prime, train, tutor.

groove *noun* **1** channel, elongated hollow. **2** spiral cut in gramophone record for needle. ● *verb* (**-ving**) make groove(s) in.

■ *noun* **1** channel, cut, fluting, furrow, gutter, hollow, indentation, rut, score, scratch, slot, striation, track. **2** track.

groovy /ˈgruːvɪ/ *adjective* (**-ier, -iest**) **1** *slang* excellent. **2** of or like a groove.

grope *verb* (**-ping**) **1** (usually + *for*) feel about or search blindly. **2** (+ *for*, *after*) search mentally. **3** fondle clumsily for sexual pleasure. **4** feel (one's way). ● *noun* act of groping.

■ *verb* **1** cast about, feel about, flounder, fumble; (*grope for*) fish for, search blindly for. **2** (*grope for*) cast about for, look for, search for.

grosgrain /ˈɡrəʊɡreɪn/ *noun* corded fabric of silk etc.

gross /ɡrəʊs/ *adjective* **1** overfed, bloated; disgustingly fat. **2** coarse, indecent. **3** flagrant. **4** total, not net. ● *verb* produce as gross profit. ● *noun* (*plural* same) 12 dozen. □ **grossly** *adverb*. **grossness** *noun*.

■ *adjective* **1** bloated, fat, massive, obese, overweight, repellent, repulsive, revolting. **2** coarse, crude, indecent, *colloquial* rude, unrefined, unsophisticated, vulgar. **3** blatant, flagrant, glaring, manifest, monstrous, obvious, outrageous, shameful. **4** before tax, inclusive, overall, total, whole.

grotesque /ɡrəʊˈtesk/ *adjective* **1** comically or repulsively distorted. **2** incongruous, absurd. ● *noun* **1** decoration interweaving human and animal features. **2** comically distorted figure or design. □ **grotesquely** *adverb*.

■ *adjective* **1** deformed, distorted, freakish, gnarled, malformed, misshapen, monstrous, twisted, ugly. **2** absurd, bizarre, curious, fantastic, incongruous, ludicrous, outlandish, preposterous, queer, ridiculous, strange, surreal, unnatural, *colloquial* weird.

grotto /ˈɡrɒtəʊ/ *noun* (*plural* **-es** or **-s**) **1** picturesque cave. **2** structure imitating cave.

grotty /ˈɡrɒtɪ/ *adjective* (**-ier**, **-iest**) *slang* unpleasant, dirty, ugly.

grouch /ɡraʊtʃ/ *colloquial verb* grumble. ● *noun* **1** grumbler. **2** complaint. **3** sulky grumbling mood. □ **grouchy** *adjective* (**-ier**, **-iest**).

ground[1] /ɡraʊnd/ *noun* **1** surface of earth. **2** area on earth's surface. **3** soil, earth. **4** extent of subject. **5** (often in *plural*) foundation, motive. **6** area of special kind. **7** (in *plural*) enclosed land attached to house etc. **8** area or basis for agreement etc. **9** surface worked on in painting. **10** (in *plural*) dregs. **11** bottom of sea. **12** floor of room etc. ● *verb* **1** prevent from taking off or flying. **2** run aground; strand. **3** (+ *in*) instruct thoroughly in. **4** (often as **grounded** *adjective*) (+ *on*) base cause or principle on. □ **gain or make ground** advance steadily; make progress. **get off the ground** *colloquial* make successful start. **go to ground 1** (of animal) enter its earth, burrow, etc. **2** (of person) become inaccessible; hide. **ground control** personnel directing landing etc. of aircraft etc. **ground cover** low-growing plants. **ground floor** storey at ground level. **ground frost** frost on surface of ground. **groundnut** peanut. **ground rent** rent for land leased for building. **groundsman** person who maintains sports ground. **ground speed** aircraft's speed relative to ground. **groundswell 1** heavy sea due to distant or past storm etc. **2** build-up and strengthening (of opinion, feeling, etc.). **groundwork** preliminary or basic work.

■ *noun* **1** land, terra firma. **2** area, country, terrain, territory. **3** clay, dirt, earth, loam, mud, soil. **5** (*grounds*) argument, base, basis, case, cause, excuse, evidence, foundation, justification, motive, proof, rationale, reason. **6** see SPORTS GROUND (SPORT). **7** (*grounds*) campus, estate, garden, park, property, surroundings. ● *verb* **2** beach, run aground, run ashore, shipwreck, strand, wreck. **3** coach, educate, instruct, prepare, teach, train, tutor. **4** base, establish, found.

ground[2] *past* & *past participle* of GRIND.

grounding *noun* basic instruction.

groundless *adjective* without motive or foundation.

■ baseless, chimerical, false, gratuitous, hypothetical, illusory, imaginary, irrational, motiveless, needless, speculative, suppositional, uncalled-for, unfounded, unjustifiable, unjustified, unproven, unreasonable, unsound, unsubstantiated, unsupported, unwarranted.

groundsel /ˈɡraʊnds(ə)l/ *noun* yellow-flowered weed.

group /ɡruːp/ *noun* **1** number of people or things near, classed, or working together. **2** number of companies under common ownership. **3** pop group. **4** division of air force. ● *verb* **1** form into group. **2** place in group(s). □ **group captain** RAF officer next below air commodore.

■ *noun* **1** *people* alliance, assembly, association, band, body, *colloquial* bunch, circle, clique, club, cluster, company, congregation, corps, coterie, crew, crowd, faction, gang, gathering, huddle, knot, league, organization, party, society, team, throng, troop, union; *animals* flock, herd; *things* accumulation, agglomeration, assortment, batch, category, class, clump, cluster, collection, heap, mass, pile, series, set. **2** alliance, bloc, cartel, consortium, syndicate. **3** see BAND *noun* 3. ● *verb* **1** associate, band, cluster, come together, congregate, crowd, flock, gather, get together, herd, swarm, team up, throng. **2** arrange, assemble, assort, bracket together, bring together, categorize, classify, collect, gather, herd, marshal, order, organize, put together, set out, sort.

groupie *noun slang* ardent follower of touring pop group(s).

grouse[1] /ɡraʊs/ *noun* (*plural* same) game bird with feathered feet.

grouse[2] /ɡraʊs/ *verb* (**-sing**) & *noun colloquial* grumble.

grout /ɡraʊt/ *noun* thin fluid mortar. ● *verb* apply grout to.

grove /ɡrəʊv/ *noun* small wood; group of trees.

grovel /ˈɡrɒv(ə)l/ *verb* (**-ll-**; *US* **-l-**) **1** behave obsequiously. **2** lie prone. □ **groveller** *noun*. **grovelling** *adjective*.

■ **1** abase oneself, be humble, *colloquial* crawl, *colloquial* creep, cringe, demean oneself, fawn, flatter, ingratiate oneself, kowtow, prostrate oneself, snivel, *colloquial* suck up, toady. □ **grovelling** see OBSEQUIOUS.

grow /grəʊ/ *verb* (*past* **grew**; *past participle* **grown**) **1** increase in size, height, amount, etc. **2** develop or exist as living plant or natural product. **3** produce by cultivation. **4** become gradually. **5** (+ *on*) become more favoured by. **6** (in *passive*; + *over*) be covered with growth. □ **grown-up** *adjective* & *noun* adult. **grow up** mature. □ **grower** *noun*.

■ **1** augment, become bigger, broaden, build up, develop, enlarge, evolve, expand, extend, fill out, improve, increase, lengthen, make progress, mature, multiply, mushroom, progress, proliferate, ripen, rise, shoot up, spread, swell, thicken. **2** burgeon, come to life, develop, emerge, exist, flourish, flower, germinate, live, prosper, sprout, survive, thrive. **3** cultivate, farm, help along, nurture, produce, propagate, raise. **4** become, get, turn. □ **grown-up** *adjective* adult, fully grown, mature, well developed.

growl /graʊl/ *verb* **1** (often + *at*) make low guttural sound, usually of anger. **2** rumble. ● *noun* **1** growling sound. **2** angry murmur.

grown *past participle* of GROW.

growth /grəʊθ/ *noun* **1** process of growing. **2** increase. **3** what has grown or is growing. **4** tumour. □ **growth industry** one that is developing rapidly.

■ **1** accretion, advance, augmentation, broadening, burgeoning, development, enlargement, evolution, expansion, extension, flowering, improvement, maturing, progress, proliferation, prosperity, spread, success. **2** accretion, advance, augmentation, enlargement, expansion, extension, increase, progress, rise. **4** cancer, cyst, excrescence, lump, swelling, tumour.

groyne /grɔɪn/ *noun* (*US* **groin**) wall built out into sea to stop beach erosion.

grub *noun* **1** larva of insect. **2** *colloquial* food. ● *verb* (**-bb-**) **1** dig superficially. **2** (+ *up*, *out*) extract by digging.

■ *noun* **1** caterpillar, larva, maggot. **2** see FOOD 1. ● *verb* see DIG *verb* 1;4.

grubby /'grʌbɪ/ *adjective* (**-ier**, **-iest**) dirty.

grudge *noun* persistent resentment or ill will. ● *verb* (**-ging**) **1** be unwilling to give or allow. **2** feel resentful about (doing something). □ **grudging** *adjective*. **grudgingly** *adverb*.

■ *noun* see RESENTMENT (RESENT). ● *verb* begrudge, envy, resent. □ **grudging** envious, guarded, half-hearted, hesitant, jealous, reluctant, resentful, unenthusiastic, ungracious, unkind, unwilling.

gruel /'gruːəl/ *noun* liquid food of oatmeal etc. boiled in milk or water.

gruelling (*US* **grueling**) *adjective* exhausting, punishing.

■ arduous, back-breaking, crippling, demanding, difficult, exhausting, fatiguing, laborious, punishing, severe, stiff, strenuous, taxing, tiring, tough, uphill, wearying.

gruesome /'gruːsəm/ *adjective* grisly, disgusting. □ **gruesomeness** *noun*.

■ appalling, *colloquial* awful, bloody, disgusting, dreadful, fearful, fearsome, frightful, ghastly, ghoulish, gory, grim, grisly, hair-raising, hideous, horrible, horrid, horrific, horrifying, macabre, repellent, repugnant, revolting, shocking, sickening, terrible.

gruff *adjective* **1** rough-voiced. **2** surly. □ **gruffly** *adverb*.

■ **1** guttural, harsh, hoarse, husky, rasping, rough, throaty. **2** see BAD-TEMPERED (BAD).

grumble /'grʌmb(ə)l/ *verb* (**-ling**) **1** complain peevishly. **2** rumble. ● *noun* **1** complaint. **2** rumble. □ **grumbler** *noun*.

■ *verb* **1** *slang* beef, complain, fuss, *colloquial* gripe, groan, *colloquial* grouch, *colloquial* grouse, make a fuss, *colloquial* moan, murmur, mutter, object, protest, whine, *colloquial* whinge.

grumpy /'grʌmpɪ/ *adjective* (**-ier**, **-iest**) ill-tempered.

grunt *noun* low guttural sound characteristic of pig. ● *verb* utter (with) grunt.

Gruyère /'gruːjeə/ *noun* kind of Swiss cheese with holes in.

gryphon = GRIFFIN.

guano /'gwɑːnəʊ/ *noun* (*plural* **-s**) excrement of seabirds, used as manure.

guarantee /gærən'tiː/ *noun* **1** formal promise or assurance. **2** guaranty. **3** giver of guaranty or security. ● *verb* (**-tees**, **-teed**) **1** give or serve as guarantee for. **2** promise. **3** secure. □ **guarantor** *noun*.

■ *noun* **1, 2** assurance, bond, guaranty, oath, obligation, pledge, promise, surety, undertaking, warranty, word of honour. ● *verb* **1** certify, vouch for. **2** assure, pledge, promise, swear, undertake, vow. **3** ensure, make sure of, reserve, secure, stake a claim to.

guaranty /'gærəntɪ/ *noun* (*plural* **-ies**) **1** written or other undertaking to answer for performance of obligation. **2** thing serving as security.

guard /gɑːd/ *verb* **1** (often + *from*, *against*) defend, protect. **2** keep watch. **3** prevent from escaping. **4** keep in check. **5** (+ *against*) take precautions against. ● *noun* **1** vigilant state. **2** protector. **3** soldiers etc. protecting place or person. **4** official in charge of train. **5** (in *plural*) (**Guards**) household troops of monarch. **6** device to prevent injury or accident. **7** defensive posture. □ **be on** (or **keep** or **stand**) **guard** keep watch, guard. **guardhouse**, **guardroom** building or room for accommodating military guard or for detaining prisoners. **guardsman** soldier in guards or Guards. **off** (**one's**) **guard** unprepared for surprise or difficulty. **on** (**one's**) **guard** watchful; prepared for difficulty or danger.

■ *verb* **1** care for, defend, keep safe, look after, mind, oversee, patrol, police, preserve, protect, safeguard, secure, shelter, shield, tend, watch over. **2, 3** be on guard over, keep watch (on), stand guard over, supervise, watch, watch over. ● *noun* **2** bodyguard, *slang* bouncer, custodian, escort, guardian, *colloquial* heavy, lookout, *slang* minder, patrol, picket, *slang* screw, security guard, sentinel, sentry, warder, watchman. **3** escort, patrol, picket, sentries, watch. □ **on one's guard** see ALERT *adjective*.

guarded *adjective* (of remark etc.) cautious. □ **guardedly** *adverb*.

guardian /'gɑːdɪən/ *noun* **1** protector, keeper. **2** person having custody of another, esp. minor. □ **guardianship** *noun*.

■ **1** champion, custodian, defender, guard, keeper, preserver, protector, trustee, warden. **2** adoptive parent, foster parent.

guava /'gwɑːvə/ *noun* **1** edible orange acid fruit. **2** tropical tree bearing this.

gubernatorial /gjuːbənə'tɔːrɪəl/ *adjective* US of governor.

gudgeon[1] /'gʌdʒ(ə)n/ *noun* small freshwater fish.

gudgeon[2] /'gʌdʒ(ə)n/ *noun* **1** kind of pivot or pin. **2** tubular part of hinge. **3** socket for rudder.

guelder rose /'geldə/ *noun* shrub with round bunches of white flowers.

Guernsey /'gɜːnzɪ/ *noun* (*plural* -s) **1** one of breed of cattle from Guernsey. **2** (**guernsey**) type of thick knitted woollen jersey.

guerrilla /gə'rɪlə/ *noun* (also **guerilla**) member of one of several independent groups fighting against regular forces.

guess /ges/ *verb* **1** estimate without calculation or measurement. **2** conjecture, think likely. **3** conjecture rightly. ● *noun* estimate, conjecture. □ **guesswork** guessing.

■ *verb* **1** estimate, figure out, hazard a guess, judge, reckon. **2** assume, conclude, conjecture, divine, *colloquial* expect, fancy, feel, have a hunch, intuit, have a theory, hazard a guess, hypothesize, imagine, judge, postulate, predict, reckon, speculate, suppose, surmise, suspect, think likely. ● *noun* assumption, conjecture, estimate, feeling, guesstimate, hunch, hypothesis, intuition, opinion, prediction, shot in the dark, speculation, supposition, surmise, suspicion, theory.

guesstimate /'gestɪmət/ *noun* (also **guestimate**) estimate based on guesswork and calculation.

guest /gest/ *noun* **1** person invited to visit another's house or have meal etc. at another's expense. **2** person lodging at hotel etc. □ **guest house** superior boarding house.

■ **1** caller, visitor; (*guests*) company. **2** customer, lodger, patron, resident.

guffaw /gʌ'fɔː/ *noun* boisterous laugh. ● *verb* utter guffaw.

guidance /'gaɪd(ə)ns/ *noun* **1** advice; leadership. **2** guiding.

■ **1** advice, briefing, counselling, direction, guidelines, help, instruction, leadership, management, spoon-feeding, teaching, tips. **2** direction, guiding.

guide /gaɪd/ *noun* **1** person who shows the way. **2** conductor of tours. **3** adviser. **4** directing principle. **5** guidebook. **6** (**Guide**) member of girls' organization similar to Scouts. ● *verb* (**-ding**) **1** act as guide to; lead, direct. **2** advise; give guidance to. □ **guidebook** book of information about place etc. **guided missile** missile under remote control or directed by equipment within itself. **guide dog** dog trained to lead blind person. **guideline** principle directing action.

■ *noun* **1, 2** conductor, courier, escort, leader, navigator, pilot. **3** adviser, counsellor, director, guru, mentor. **5** atlas, directory, gazetteer, guidebook, handbook. ● *verb* **1** conduct, direct, escort, lead, manoeuvre, navigate, pilot, shepherd, show the way, steer, usher. **2** advise, brief, control, counsel, educate, govern, help along, influence, instruct, regulate, teach, train, tutor.

Guider /'gaɪdə/ *noun* adult leader of Guides.

guild /gɪld/ *noun* (also **gild**) **1** society for mutual aid or with common object. **2** medieval association of craftsmen. □ **guildhall** meeting-place of medieval guild; town hall.

guilder /'gɪldə/ *noun* monetary unit of Netherlands.

guile /gaɪl/ *noun* sly behaviour; treachery, deceit. □ **guileful** *adjective*. **guileless** *adjective*.

guillemot /'gɪlɪmɒt/ *noun* kind of auk.

guillotine /'gɪlətiːn/ *noun* **1** beheading machine. **2** machine for cutting paper. **3** method of shortening debate in parliament by fixing time of vote. ● *verb* (**-ning**) use guillotine on.

guilt /gɪlt/ *noun* **1** fact of having committed offence. **2** culpability. **3** feeling of culpability.

■ **1** criminality, sinfulness, wickedness, wrongdoing. **2** blame, blameworthiness, culpability, fault, guiltiness, liability, responsibility. **3** bad conscience, contriteness, contrition, guiltiness, guilty conscience, guilty feelings, penitence, regret, remorse, self-accusation, self-reproach, shame, sorrow.

guiltless *adjective* (often + *of*) innocent.

■ above suspicion, blameless, clear, faultless, immaculate, innocent, in the right, irreproachable, pure, sinless, untarnished, untroubled, virtuous.

guilty *adjective* (-ier, -iest) **1** having committed offence. **2** feeling or causing feeling of guilt. □ **guiltily** *adverb*. **guiltiness** *noun*.

■ **1** at fault, blameable, blameworthy, culpable, in the wrong, liable, reprehensible, responsible. **2** apologetic, ashamed, conscience-stricken, contrite, penitent, regretful, remorseful, repentant, rueful, shamefaced, sheepish, sorry.

guinea /'gɪnɪ/ *noun* (*historical* coin worth) £1.05. □ **guinea fowl** domestic fowl with white-spotted grey plumage. **guinea pig 1** domesticated S. American rodent. **2** person used in experiment.

guipure /'giːpjʊə/ *noun* heavy lace of patterned pieces joined by stitches.

guise /gaɪz/ *noun* external, esp. assumed, appearance; pretence.

guitar /gɪˈtɑː/ *noun* usually 6-stringed musical instrument played with fingers or plectrum. □ **guitarist** *noun*.

gulch *noun US* ravine, gully.

gulf *noun* **1** large area of sea with narrow-mouthed inlet. **2** deep hollow, chasm. **3** wide difference of opinion etc. □ **Gulf Stream** warm current from Gulf of Mexico to Europe.

gull[1] *noun* long-winged web-footed seabird.

gull[2] *verb* dupe, fool.

gullet /ˈɡʌlɪt/ *noun* food-passage from mouth to stomach.

gullible /ˈɡʌlɪb(ə)l/ *adjective* easily persuaded or deceived. □ **gullibility** *noun*.

■ credulous, easily taken in, green, impressionable, inexperienced, innocent, naive, suggestible, trusting, unsophisticated, unsuspecting, unwary.

gully /ˈɡʌlɪ/ *noun* (*plural* **-ies**) **1** water-worn ravine. **2** gutter, drain. **3** *Cricket* fielding position between point and slips.

gulp *verb* **1** (often + *down*) swallow hastily or with effort. **2** choke. **3** (+ *down, back*) suppress. ● *noun* **1** act of gulping. **2** large mouthful.

■ *verb* **1** bolt down, devour, gobble, guzzle, *slang* knock back, *literary* quaff, swallow, *colloquial* swig, wolf down. **3** (*gulp back*) check, choke back, stifle, suppress. ● *noun* mouthful, swallow, *colloquial* swig.

gum[1] *noun* **1** sticky secretion of some trees and shrubs, used as glue etc. **2** chewing gum. **3** (also **gumdrop**) hard jelly sweet. ● *verb* (**-mm-**) **1** (usually + *down, together*, etc.) fasten with gum. **2** apply gum to. □ **gum arabic** gum exuded by some kinds of acacia. **gumboot** rubber boot. **gum tree** tree exuding gum, esp. eucalyptus. **gum up** *colloquial* interfere with; spoil.

gum[2] *noun* (usually in *plural*) firm flesh around roots of teeth. □ **gumboil** small abscess on gum.

gummy[1] /ˈɡʌmɪ/ *adjective* (**-ier, -iest**) **1** sticky. **2** exuding gum.

gummy[2] /ˈɡʌmɪ/ *adjective* (**-ier, -iest**) toothless.

gumption /ˈɡʌmpʃ(ə)n/ *noun colloquial* **1** resourcefulness, enterprise. **2** common sense.

■ **1** cleverness, enterprise, initiative, resourcefulness. **2** common sense, judgement, *colloquial* nous, sense, shrewdness, wisdom.

gun *noun* **1** metal tube for throwing missiles with explosive propellant. **2** starting pistol. **3** device for discharging grease, electrons, etc., in desired direction. **4** member of shooting party. ● *verb* (**-nn-**) **1** (usually + *down*) shoot with gun. **2** (+ *for*) seek out determinedly to attack or rebuke. □ **gunboat** small warship with heavy guns. **gun carriage** wheeled support for gun. **gun cotton** cotton steeped in acids, used as explosive. **gun dog** dog trained to retrieve game. **gunfire** firing of guns. **gunman** armed lawbreaker. **gunmetal 1** bluish-grey colour. **2** alloy of copper, tin, and usually zinc. **gunpowder** explosive of saltpetre, sulphur, and charcoal. **gun-runner** person selling or bringing guns into country illegally. **gunshot 1** shot from gun. **2** the range of a gun. **gunslinger** *esp. US* gunman. **gunsmith** maker and repairer of small firearms. **stick to one's guns** *colloquial* maintain one's position in face of opposition.

■ *noun* **1** firearm. ● *verb* **1** (*gun down*) see SHOOT *verb* 3. □ **gunfire** crossfire, firing, gunshots. **gunman** assassin, bandit, criminal, desperado, fighter, gangster, *esp. US* gunslinger, killer, murderer, sniper, terrorist.

gunge /ɡʌndʒ/ *colloquial noun* sticky substance. ● *verb* (**-ging**) (usually + *up*) clog with gunge. □ **gungy** *adjective*.

gung-ho /ɡʌŋˈhəʊ/ *adjective* (arrogantly) eager.

gunner /ˈɡʌnə/ *noun* **1** artillery soldier. **2** *Nautical* warrant officer in charge of battery, magazine, etc. **3** airman who operates gun.

gunnery /ˈɡʌnərɪ/ *noun* construction and management, or firing, of large guns.

gunny /ˈɡʌnɪ/ *noun* (*plural* **-ies**) **1** coarse sacking usually of jute fibre. **2** sack made of this.

gunwale /ˈɡʌn(ə)l/ *noun* upper edge of ship's or boat's side.

guppy /ˈɡʌpɪ/ *noun* (*plural* **-ies**) very small brightly coloured tropical freshwater fish.

gurgle /ˈɡɜːɡ(ə)l/ *verb* (**-ling**) **1** make bubbling sound as of water. **2** utter with such sound. ● *noun* bubbling sound.

■ *verb* **1** babble, bubble, burble, ripple, purl, splash.

gurnard /ˈɡɜːnəd/ *noun* (*plural* same or **-s**) sea fish with large spiny head.

guru /ˈɡʊruː/ *noun* (*plural* **-s**) **1** Hindu spiritual teacher. **2** influential or revered teacher.

gush *verb* **1** flow in sudden or copious stream. **2** speak or behave effusively. ● *noun* **1** sudden or copious stream. **2** effusiveness. □ **gushing** *adjective*.

■ *verb* **1** cascade, flood, flow freely, overflow, pour, run, rush, spout, spurt, squirt, stream. **2** be enthusiastic, be sentimental, fuss, *colloquial* go on, prattle on. ● *noun* **1** burst, cascade, eruption, flood, flow, jet, outpouring, overflow, rush, spout, spurt, squirt, stream, tide, torrent. □ **gushing** see EFFUSIVE, SENTIMENTAL.

gusher /ˈɡʌʃə/ *noun* **1** oil well emitting unpumped oil. **2** effusive person.

gusset /ˈɡʌsɪt/ *noun* piece let into garment etc. to strengthen or enlarge it.

gust *noun* **1** sudden violent rush of wind. **2** burst of rain, smoke, anger, etc. ● *verb* blow in gusts. □ **gusty** *adjective* (**-ier, -iest**).

gusto /ˈɡʌstəʊ/ *noun* zest, enjoyment.

■ appetite, delight, enjoyment, enthusiasm, excitement, liveliness, pleasure, relish, satisfaction, spirit, verve, vigour, zest.

gut *noun* **1** intestine. **2** (in *plural*) bowels,

entrails. **3** (in *plural*) *colloquial* courage and determination. **4** *slang* stomach. **5** (in *plural*) contents; essence. **6** material for violin etc. strings or for fishing line. ● *adjective* instinctive; fundamental. ● *verb* (**-tt-**) **1** remove or destroy internal fittings of (buildings). **2** remove guts of. □ **gutless** *adjective*.

■ *noun* **1** alimentary canal, bowel, intestine. **2** (*guts*) bowels, entrails, *colloquial* innards, *colloquial* insides, intestines, viscera. **3** (*guts*) see COURAGE. **4** abdomen, belly, paunch, stomach, *colloquial* tummy. ● *verb* **1** clear, despoil, empty, loot, pillage, plunder, ransack, ravage, remove the contents of, sack, strip. **2** clean, disembowel, eviscerate.

gutless *adjective colloquial* lacking courage; feeble. □ **gutlessly** *adverb*. **gutlessness** *noun*.

gutsy /ˈgʌtsɪ/ *adjective* (**-ier, iest**) *colloquial* **1** courageous. **2** greedy.

gutta-percha /gʌtəˈpɜːtʃə/ *noun* tough plastic substance made from latex.

gutted *adjective slang* deeply disappointed or upset.

gutter /ˈgʌtə/ *noun* **1** shallow trough below eaves, or channel at side of street, for carrying off rainwater. **2** (**the gutter**) poor or degraded environment. **3** channel, groove. ● *verb* (of candle) burn unsteadily and melt away.

■ *noun* **1, 3** channel, conduit, ditch, drain, duct, guttering, sewer, sluice, trench, trough.

guttering *noun* (material for) gutters.

guttersnipe *noun* street urchin.

guttural /ˈgʌtər(ə)l/ *adjective* **1** throaty, harsh-sounding. **2** (of sound) produced in throat. ● *noun* guttural consonant.

guy[1] /gaɪ/ *noun* **1** *colloquial* man. **2** effigy of Guy Fawkes burnt on 5 Nov. ● *verb* ridicule.

guy[2] /gaɪ/ *noun* rope or chain to secure tent or steady crane-load etc. ● *verb* secure with guy(s).

guzzle /ˈgʌz(ə)l/ *verb* (**-ling**) eat or drink greedily. □ **guzzler** *noun*.

gybe /dʒaɪb/ *verb* (*US* **jibe**) (**-bing**) **1** (of fore-and-aft sail or boom) swing across boat, momentarily pointing into wind. **2** cause (sail) to do this. **3** (of boat etc.) change course thus.

gym /dʒɪm/ *noun colloquial* **1** gymnasium. **2** gymnastics. □ **gymslip, gym tunic** schoolgirl's sleeveless dress.

gymkhana /dʒɪmˈkɑːnə/ *noun* horse-riding competition.

gymnasium /dʒɪmˈneɪzɪəm/ *noun* (*plural* **-siums** or **-sia**) room etc. equipped for gymnastics.

gymnast /ˈdʒɪmnæst/ *noun* expert in gymnastics.

gymnastic /dʒɪmˈnæstɪk/ *adjective* of gymnastics. □ **gymnastically** *adverb*.

gymnastics *plural noun* (also treated as *singular*) exercises to develop or demonstrate physical (or mental) agility.

gynaecology /gaɪnɪˈkɒlədʒɪ/ *noun* (*US* **gynecology**) science of physiological functions and diseases of women. □ **gynaecological** /-kəˈlɒdʒ-/ *adjective*. **gynaecologist** *noun*.

gypsum /ˈdʒɪpsəm/ *noun* mineral used esp. to make plaster of Paris.

Gypsy /ˈdʒɪpsɪ/ *noun* (also **Gipsy**) (*plural* **-ies**) **1** member of nomadic dark-skinned people of Europe. **2** (**gipsy**) person living like Gypsy.

■ **1** Romany, traveller. **2** (**gypsy**) nomad, traveller, wanderer.

gyrate /dʒaɪəˈreɪt/ *verb* (**-ting**) move in circle or spiral. □ **gyration** *noun*. **gyratory** *adjective*.

● circle, pirouette, revolve, rotate, spin, spiral, swivel, turn, twirl, wheel, whirl.

gyro /ˈdʒaɪərəʊ/ *noun* (*plural* **-s**) *colloquial* gyroscope.

gyroscope /ˈdʒaɪərəskəʊp/ *noun* rotating wheel whose axis is free to turn but maintains fixed direction unless perturbed, esp. used for stabilization.

H *abbreviation* **1** hard (pencil lead). **2** (water) hydrant. **3** *slang* heroin. □ **H-bomb** hydrogen bomb.

h *abbreviation* (also **h.**) **1** height. **2** hour(s). **3** hot. □ **h. & c.** hot and cold (water).

ha[1] /hɑː/ (also **hah**) *interjection: expressing surprise, triumph, etc.*

ha[2] *abbreviation* hectare(s).

habeas corpus /ˌheɪbɪəs ˈkɔːpəs/ *noun* writ requiring person to be brought before judge etc., esp. to investigate lawfulness of his or her detention.

haberdasher /ˈhæbədæʃə/ *noun* dealer in dress accessories and sewing goods. □ **haberdashery** *noun* (*plural* **-ies**).

habit /ˈhæbɪt/ *noun* **1** settled tendency or practice. **2** practice that is hard to give up. **3** mental constitution or attitude. **4** clothes, esp. of religious order.

■ **1** convention, custom, inclination, manner, mannerism, pattern, penchant, policy, practice, predisposition, proclivity, propensity, quirk, routine, rule, tendency, usage, way, *formal* or *jocular* wont. **2** addiction, compulsion, dependence, fixation, obsession, vice. **3** attitude, bent, constitution, disposition, inclination, make-up, manner, predisposition.

habitable /ˈhæbɪtəb(ə)l/ *adjective* suitable for living in. □ **habitability** *noun*.

■ in good repair, inhabitable, *colloquial* liveable, usable.

habitat /ˈhæbɪtæt/ *noun* natural home of plant or animal.

habitation /ˌhæbɪˈteɪʃ(ə)n/ *noun* **1** inhabiting. **2** house, home.

habitual /həˈbɪtʃʊəl/ *adjective* **1** done as a habit. **2** usual. **3** given to a habit. □ **habitually** *adverb*.

■ **1** established, ineradicable, ingrained, obsessive, persistent, recurrent. **2** accustomed, common, conventional, customary, established, expected, familiar, fixed, frequent, natural, normal, ordinary, predictable, regular, ritual, routine, set, settled, standard, traditional, typical, usual, wonted. **3** addicted, *colloquial* chronic, conditioned, confirmed, dependent, hardened, *slang* hooked, inveterate, persistent.

habituate /həˈbɪtʃʊeɪt/ *verb* (**-ting**) (often + *to*) accustom. □ **habituation** *noun*.

habitué /həˈbɪtʃʊeɪ/ *noun* (often + *of*) frequent visitor or resident. [French]

háček /ˈhætʃek/ *noun* mark (ˇ) used over letter to modify its sound in some languages.

hacienda /ˌhæsɪˈendə/ *noun* (in Spanish-speaking countries) plantation etc. with dwelling house.

hack[1] *verb* **1** cut or chop roughly. **2** kick shin of. **3** (often + *at*) deal cutting blows. **4** cut (one's way) through. **5** *colloquial* gain unauthorized access to (computer data). **6** *slang* manage, tolerate. ● *noun* **1** kick with toe of boot. **2** wound from this. □ **hacksaw** saw for cutting metal.

■ *verb* **1** carve, chop, cut, gash, hew, mangle, mutilate, slash.

hack[2] *noun* **1** horse for ordinary riding. **2** hired horse. **3** person hired to do dull routine work, esp. as writer. ● *adjective* **1** used as hack. **2** commonplace. ● *verb* ride on horseback on road at ordinary pace.

hacker *noun colloquial* **1** computer enthusiast. **2** person who gains unauthorized access to computer network.

hacking *adjective* (of cough) short, dry, and frequent.

hackle /ˈhæk(ə)l/ *noun* (in *plural*) **1** hairs on animal's neck which rise when it is angry or alarmed. **2** long feather(s) on neck of domestic cock etc. **3** steel flax-comb. □ **make (person's) hackles rise** arouse anger or indignation.

hackney /ˈhækni/ *noun* (*plural* **-s**) horse for ordinary riding. □ **hackney carriage** taxi.

hackneyed /ˈhæknɪd/ *adjective* overused, trite.

■ banal, clichéd, cliché-ridden, commonplace, conventional, *colloquial* corny, familiar, obvious, overused, pedestrian, platitudinous, predictable, stale, stereotyped, stock, threadbare, tired, trite, uninspired, unoriginal.

had *past & past participle* of HAVE.

haddock /ˈhædək/ *noun* (*plural* same) common edible sea fish.

Hades /ˈheɪdiːz/ *noun* (in Greek mythology) the underworld.

hadj = HAJJ.

hadji = HAJJI.

hadn't /ˈhæd(ə)nt/ had not.

haematite /ˈhiːmətaɪt/ *noun* (*US* **hem-**) red or brown iron ore.

haematology /ˌhiːməˈtɒlədʒɪ/ *noun* (*US* **hem-**) study of the blood. □ **haematologist** *noun*.

haemoglobin /ˌhiːməˈgləʊbɪn/ *noun* (*US* **hem-**) oxygen-carrying substance in red blood cells.

haemophilia /ˌhiːməˈfɪlɪə/ *noun* (*US* **hem-**) hereditary tendency to severe bleeding from even a slight injury through failure of blood to clot. □ **haemophiliac** *noun*.

haemorrhage /ˈhemərɪdʒ/ (*US* **hem-**) *noun*

profuse bleeding. ● *verb* (**-ging**) suffer haemor-rhage.

haemorrhoids /ˈhemərɔɪdz/ *plural noun* (*US* **hem-**) swollen veins near anus; piles.

haft /hɑːft/ *noun* handle of knife etc.

hag *noun* **1** ugly old woman. **2** witch. □ **hag-ridden** afflicted by nightmares or fears.

haggard /ˈhæɡəd/ *adjective* looking exhausted and distraught.

■ careworn, drawn, emaciated, exhausted, gaunt, hollow-cheeked, hollow-eyed, pinched, run-down, scraggy, scrawny, shrunken, thin, tired out, ugly, unhealthy, wasted, weary, withered, worn out.

haggis /ˈhæɡɪs/ *noun* Scottish dish of offal boiled in bag with oatmeal etc.

haggle /ˈhæɡ(ə)l/ *verb* (**-ling**) (often + *over*, *about*) bargain persistently. ● *noun* haggling.

■ *verb* argue, bargain, barter, discuss terms, negotiate, quarrel, quibble, wrangle.

hagiography /hæɡɪˈɒɡrəfɪ/ *noun* writing about saints' lives. □ **hagiographer** *noun*.

hah = HA¹.

ha-ha /ˈhɑːhɑː/ *noun* ditch with wall in it bounding park or garden.

ha ha /hɑːˈhɑː/ *interjection: representing laugh-ter*.

haiku /ˈhaɪkuː/ *noun* (*plural* same) Japanese 3-line poem of usually 17 syllables.

hail¹ *noun* **1** pellets of frozen rain. **2** (+ *of*) barrage, onslaught of. ● *verb* **1** (after *it*) hail falls. **2** pour down as or like hail. □ **hailstone** pellet of hail. **hailstorm** period of heavy hail.

hail² *verb* **1** signal (taxi etc.) to stop. **2** greet enthu-siastically. **3** acclaim. **4** (+ *from*) originate from. ● *interjection archaic or jocular: expressing greet-ing*. ● *noun* act of hailing.

■ *verb* **1** call to, flag down, signal to. **2** address, greet. **3** see ACCLAIM *verb*.

hair *noun* **1** any or all of fine filaments growing from skin of mammals, esp. of human head. **2** hairstyle. **3** hairlike thing. □ **haircut** (style of) cutting hair. **hairdo** style of or act of styling hair. **hairdresser** person who cuts and styles hair. **hairdressing** *noun*. **hairdrier, hairdryer** device for drying hair with warm air. **hairgrip** flat hairpin with ends close together. **hairline 1** edge of person's hair on forehead. **2** very narrow crack or line. **hairnet** piece of netting for confining hair. **hair of the dog** further alcoholic drink taken to cure effects of previous drinking. **hair-piece** false hair augmenting person's natural hair. **hairpin** U-shaped pin for fastening the hair. **hairpin bend** U-shaped bend in road. **hair-raising** terrifying. **hair's breadth** minute distance. **hair shirt** ascetic's or penitent's shirt made of hair. **hairslide** clip for keeping hair in position. **hair-splitting** quibbling. **hairspray** liquid sprayed on hair to keep it in place. **hairspring** fine spring regulating balance-wheel of watch. **hairstyle** particular way of arranging hair. **hair-stylist** *noun*. **hair-trigger** trigger acting on very

slight pressure. □ **hairless** *adjective*.

■ **1** beard, bristles, curls, fleece, fur, fuzz, locks, mane, mop, moustache, shock, tresses, whiskers; (*false hair*) hairpiece, toupee, wig. □ **hairdo** coiffure, cut, hair, haircut, hairstyle, style. **hairdresser** barber, coiffeur, coiffeuse, stylist. □ **hairless** bald, bare, clean-shaven, naked, shaved, shaven, smooth.

hairy /ˈheːrɪ/ *adjective* (**-ier, -iest**) **1** covered with or having feel of hair. **2** *slang* alarmingly diffi-cult. □ **hairiness** *noun*.

■ **1** bearded, bristly, downy, fleecy, furry, fuzzy, hirsute, long-haired, shaggy, stubbly, woolly.

hajj /hædʒ/ *noun* (also **hadj**) Islamic pilgrimage to Mecca.

hajji /ˈhædʒɪ/ *noun* (also **hadji**) (*plural* **-s**) Muslim who has made pilgrimage to Mecca.

haka /ˈhɑːkə/ *noun NZ* **1** Maori ceremonial war dance. **2** similar dance by sports team before match.

hake *noun* (*plural* same) codlike sea fish.

halal /hɑːˈlɑːl/ *noun* (also **hallal**) meat from animal killed according to Muslim law.

halberd /ˈhælbəd/ *noun historical* combined spear and battleaxe.

halcyon /ˈhælsɪən/ *adjective* **1** calm, peaceful. **2** happy.

hale *adjective* strong and healthy (esp. in **hale and hearty**).

half /hɑːf/ *noun* (*plural* **halves** /hɑːvz/) **1** either of two (esp. equal) parts into which a thing is divided. **2** *colloquial* half pint, esp. of beer. **3** *Sport* either of two equal periods of play. **4** *Sport* half-back. **5** half-price (esp. child's) ticket. ● *adjective* forming a half. ● *adverb* partly. □ **half and half** being half one thing and half another. **half-back** player between forwards and full back(s) in football etc. **half-baked** not thor-oughly thought out. **half board** provision of bed, breakfast, and one main meal. **half-brother, -sister** one having only one parent in common. **half-crown** *historical* coin worth 2 shillings and 6 pence (= 12½p). **half-dozen** (about) six. **half-hearted** lacking courage or zeal. **half-heartedly** *adverb*. **half holiday** half day as holi-day. **half-hour, half an hour 1** 30 minutes. **2** point of time 30 minutes after any hour o'clock. **half-hourly** *adjective & adverb*. **half-life** time after which radioactivity etc. is half its original value. **half mast** position of flag halfway down mast as symbol of mourning. **half measures** unsatisfactory compromise etc. **half-moon** (shape of) moon with disc half illuminated. **half nelson** see NELSON. **half-term** short holiday halfway through school term. **half-timbered** having walls with timber frame and brick or plaster filling. **half-time** (short break at) mid-point of game or contest. **halftone** photo-graph representing tones by large or small dots. **half-truth** statement that conveys only part of truth. **half-volley** playing of ball as soon as it bounces off ground. **halfwit** stupid person.

half-witted *adjective*. **not half 1** *slang* very much, very. **2** not nearly. **3** *colloquial* not at all.

halfpenny /'heɪpnɪ/ *noun* (*plural* **-pennies** or **-pence** /'heɪpəns/) *historical* coin worth half penny (withdrawn in 1984).

halfway *adverb* **1** at a point midway between two others. **2** to some extent. ● *adjective* situated halfway. □ **halfway house 1** compromise. **2** halfway point. **3** rehabilitation centre. **4** inn etc. between two towns.

halibut /'hælɪbət/ *noun* (*plural* same) large flatfish.

halitosis /hælɪ'təʊsɪs/ *noun* bad breath.

hall /hɔːl/ *noun* **1** entrance area of house. **2** *esp.* US corridor. **3** large room or building for meetings, concerts, etc. **4** large country house or estate. **5** (in full **hall of residence**) residence for students. **6** college dining-room. **7** large public room in palace etc. □ **hallmark 1** mark used to show standard of gold, silver, and platinum. **2** distinctive feature. **hallway** entrance hall or corridor.

■ **1** corridor, entrance hall, foyer, hallway, lobby, passage, passageway, vestibule. **3** auditorium, concert hall, lecture room, theatre.

hallal = HALAL.

hallelujah = ALLELUIA.

hallo = HELLO.

hallow /'hæləʊ/ *verb* (usually as **hallowed** *adjective*) make or honour as holy.

■ (**hallowed**) blessed, consecrated, dedicated, holy, honoured, revered, reverenced, sacred, sacrosanct, worshipped.

Hallowe'en /hæləʊ'iːn/ *noun* eve of All Saints' Day, 31 Oct.

hallucinate /hə'luːsɪneɪt/ *verb* (**-ting**) experience hallucinations.

■ daydream, dream, fantasize, *slang* have a trip, see things, see visions.

hallucination *noun* **1** illusion of seeing or hearing something not actually present. **2** thing perceived in this way. □ **hallucinatory** /hə'luːsɪnətərɪ/ *adjective*.

■ apparition, chimera, daydream, delusion, dream, fantasy, figment of the imagination, ghost, illusion, mirage, phantasm, phantom, vision.

hallucinogen /hə'luːsɪnədʒ(ə)n/ *noun* drug causing hallucinations. □ **hallucinogenic** /-'dʒen-/ *adjective*.

halm = HAULM.

halo /'heɪləʊ/ *noun* (*plural* **-es**) **1** disc of light shown round head of sacred person. **2** glory associated with idealized person. **3** circle of light round sun or moon etc. ● *verb* (**-es, -ed**) surround with halo.

halogen /'hæləʊdʒ(ə)n/ *noun* any of the non-metallic elements (fluorine, chlorine, etc.) which form a salt when combined with a metal.

halon /'heɪlɒn/ *noun* gaseous halogen compound used to extinguish fires.

halt[1] /hɔːlt/ *noun* **1** stop (usually temporary). **2** minor stopping place on local railway line. ● *verb* (cause to) make a halt.

■ *noun* **1** break, cessation, close, end, interruption, pause, standstill, stop, stoppage, termination. ● *verb* arrest, block, break off, *formal* cease, check, come to a halt, come to rest, desist, discontinue, draw up, end, impede, obstruct, pull up, quit, stop, terminate, wait.

halt[2] /hɔːlt/ *verb* (esp. as **halting** *adjective*) proceed hesitantly. □ **haltingly** *adverb*.

■ (**halting**) see HESITANT, IRREGULAR *adjective* 2.

halter /'hɔːltə/ *noun* **1** rope with headstall for leading or tying up horses etc. **2** strap passing round back of neck holding dress etc. up. **3** (also **halterneck**) dress etc. held by this.

halva /'hælvə/ *noun* confection of sesame flour, honey, etc.

halve /hɑːv/ *verb* (**-ving**) **1** divide into halves. **2** reduce to half.

■ **1** bisect, cut in half, divide into halves, share equally, split in two. **2** cut by half, reduce by half.

halves *plural* of HALF.

halyard /'hæljəd/ *noun* rope or tackle for raising and lowering sail etc.

ham *noun* **1** upper part of pig's leg cured for food. **2** back of thigh; thigh and buttock. **3** *colloquial* inexpert or unsubtle performer or actor. **4** *colloquial* operator of amateur radio station. ● *verb* (**-mm-**) (usually in **ham it up**) *colloquial* overact. □ **ham-fisted, -handed** *colloquial* clumsy.

hamburger /'hæmbɜːgə/ *noun* cake of minced beef, usually eaten in soft bread roll.

hamlet /'hæmlɪt/ *noun* small village, esp. without church.

hammer /'hæmə/ *noun* **1** tool with heavy metal head at right angles to handle, used for driving nails etc. **2** similar device, as for exploding charge in gun, striking strings of piano, etc. **3** auctioneer's mallet. **4** metal ball attached to a wire for throwing as athletic contest. ● *verb* **1** strike or drive (as) with hammer. **2** *colloquial* defeat utterly. □ **hammer and tongs** *colloquial* with great energy. **hammerhead** shark with flattened hammer-shaped head. **hammerlock** wrestling hold in which twisted arm is bent behind back. **hammer-toe** toe bent permanently downwards. □ **hammering** *noun*.

■ *noun* **1** mallet, sledgehammer. ● *verb* **1** bash, batter, beat, drive, hit, knock, pound, smash, strike. **2** see DEFEAT *verb* 1.

hammock /'hæmək/ *noun* bed of canvas or netting suspended by cords at ends.

hamper[1] /'hæmpə/ *noun* large basket, usually with hinged lid and containing food.

hamper[2] /'hæmpə/ *verb* **1** obstruct movement of. **2** hinder.

■ baulk, block, curb, curtail, delay, encumber, entangle, fetter, foil, frustrate, handicap, hinder, hold back, hold up, impede, inhibit, interfere with, obstruct, prevent, restrain, restrict, retard, shackle, slow down, thwart, trammel.

hamster /ˈhæmstə/ *noun* short-tailed mouse-like rodent often kept as pet.

hamstring *noun* 1 any of 5 tendons at back of human knee. 2 (in quadruped) tendon at back of hock. ● *verb* (*past & past participle* **-strung** or **-stringed**) 1 cripple by cutting hamstrings. 2 impair efficiency of.

hand *noun* 1 end part of human arm beyond wrist. 2 similar member of monkey. 3 (often in *plural*) control, disposal; agency. 4 share in action; active support. 5 handlike thing, esp. pointer of clock etc. 6 right or left side, direction, etc. 7 skill or style, esp. of writing. 8 person who does or makes something. 9 person etc. as source. 10 manual worker in factory etc. 11 pledge of marriage. 12 playing cards dealt to player. 13 round or game of cards. 14 *colloquial* round of applause. 15 measure of horse's height, = 4 in. (10.16 cm). ● *verb* (+ *in, to, over, round*, etc.) deliver or transfer (as) with hand. □ **at hand** close by. **by hand** 1 by person not machine. 2 not by post. **give or lend a hand** help. **handbag** small bag carried esp. by woman. **handball** 1 game with ball thrown by hand. 2 *Football* foul touching of ball. **handbell** small bell for ringing by hand. **handbook** short manual or guidebook. **handbrake** brake operated by hand. **handcuff** secure (prisoner) with **handcuffs**, pair of lockable metal rings joined by short chain. **hand down** pass on use or ownership of. **handgrip** 1 a grasp with the hand. 2 handle. **handgun** small firearm held in one hand. **handhold** something for hand to grip. **hand in glove** in collusion. **handmade** made by hand (rather than machine). **hand-me-down** article passed on from another person. **handout** 1 thing given to needy person. 2 information etc. distributed to press etc. 3 notes given out in class. **handover** act of handing over. **hand over fist** *colloquial* with rapid progress. **hand-picked** carefully chosen. **handrail** rail along edge of stairs etc. **hands down** without effort. **handset** part of telephone held in hand. **handshake** clasping of person's hand, esp. as greeting etc. **hands-on** practical rather than theoretical. **handstand** act of supporting oneself vertically on one's hands. **hand-to-hand** (of fighting) at close quarters. **handwriting** (style of) writing by hand. **on hand** 1 available. 2 in attendance. **take in hand** 1 start doing or dealing with. 2 undertake control or reform of. **to hand** within reach.

■ *noun* 1, 2 fist, *slang* mitt, palm, *colloquial* paw. 5 indicator, pointer. 10 see WORKER 1. ● *verb* (**hand in**) deliver, give in, offer, present, submit, tender; (**hand to**) convey to, deliver to, give to, offer to, pass to, present to; (**hand over**) see SURRENDER *verb* 1; (**hand round**) see DISTRIBUTE 1. □ **at hand** see HANDY 2. **give or lend a hand** see HELP *verb* 1. **hand down** see BEQUEATH. **to hand** see HANDY 2.

-handed /ˈhændɪd/ *adjective* (in *combination*) 1 for or involving specified number of hands. 2 using the hand specified. □ **-handedly** *adverb*. **-handedness** *noun*.

handful *noun* (*plural* **-s**) 1 enough to fill the hand. 2 small number or quantity. 3 *colloquial* troublesome person or task.

handicap /ˈhændɪkæp/ *noun* 1 physical or mental disability. 2 thing that makes progress difficult. 3 disadvantage imposed on superior competitor to equalize chances. 4 race etc. in which this is imposed. ● *verb* (**-pp-**) 1 impose handicap on. 2 place at disadvantage.

■ *noun* 1 defect, disability, impairment. 2 barrier, burden, disadvantage, difficulty, drawback, encumbrance, hindrance, impediment, inconvenience, limitation, *colloquial* minus, nuisance, obstacle, problem, restraint, restriction, shortcoming, stumbling block. ● *verb* burden, check, curb, disable, disadvantage, encumber, hamper, hinder, hold back, impede, limit, restrain, restrict, retard, trammel.

handicapped *adjective* suffering from physical or mental disability.

■ crippled, disabled, disadvantaged.

handicraft /ˈhændɪkrɑːft/ *noun* work requiring manual and artistic skill.

handiwork /ˈhændɪwɜːk/ *noun* work done or thing made by hand, or by particular person.

■ achievement, creation, invention, production, responsibility, work.

handkerchief /ˈhæŋkətʃɪf/ *noun* (*plural* **-s** or **-chieves** /-tʃiːvz/) square of cloth used to wipe nose etc.

handle /ˈhænd(ə)l/ *noun* part by which thing is held. ● *verb* (**-ling**) 1 touch, feel, operate, etc. with hands. 2 manage, deal with. 3 be able to be operated. 4 deal in (goods etc.). □ **handlebar** (usually in *plural*) steering-bar of bicycle etc.

■ *noun* grip, haft, handgrip, hilt, knob, stock (*of rifle*). ● *verb* 1 caress, feel, finger, fondle, grasp, hold, manipulate, maul, operate, pat, *colloquial* paw, stroke, touch, treat. 2 conduct, contend with, control, cope with, deal with, direct, guide, look after, manage, manipulate, organize, tackle, treat. 3 manoeuvre, operate, respond, steer, work. 4 deal in, do trade in, market, sell, stock, touch, traffic in.

handler *noun* person in charge of trained dog etc.

handsome /ˈhænsəm/ *adjective* (**-r, -st**) 1 good-looking. 2 imposing. 3 generous; considerable. □ **handsomely** *adverb*. **handsomeness** *noun*.

■ 1 attractive, beautiful, *literary* comely, elegant, *archaic* fair, fine-looking, good-looking, personable, tasteful. 3 big, bountiful, considerable, generous, goodly, gracious, large, liberal, magnanimous, munificent, sizeable, unselfish, valuable.

handy *adjective* (**-ier, -iest**) 1 convenient to handle. 2 ready to hand. 3 clever with hands. □ **handyman** person able to do odd jobs.

■ 1 convenient, easy to use, helpful, manageable, practical, serviceable, useful, well designed, worth having. 2 accessible, at hand, available, close at hand, easy to reach, nearby, reachable, ready, to hand. 3 adept, capable, clever, competent, practical, proficient, skilful.

hang *verb* (*past & past participle* **hung** except as below) **1** (cause to) be supported from above; attach by suspending from top. **2** set up on hinges etc. **3** place (picture) on wall or in exhibition. **4** attach (wallpaper). **5** (*past & past participle* **hanged**) suspend or be suspended by neck, esp. as capital punishment. **6** let droop. **7** remain or be hung. **8** remain in air. ● *noun* way thing hangs. □ **get the hang of** *colloquial* get knack of; understand. **hang about, around** loiter; not move away. **hang back 1** remain behind. **2** hesitate; be reluctant to act. **hangdog** shamefaced. **hang fire** delay acting. **hang-glider** fabric wing on light frame from which pilot is suspended. **hang-gliding** *noun*. **hangman** executioner by hanging. **hangnail** agnail. **hang on 1** (often + *to*) continue to hold. **2** (+ *to*) retain. **3** wait for short time. **4** not ring off during pause in telephoning. **hang out 1** hang from window, clothes line, etc. **2** protrude or cause to protrude downwards. **3** (+ *of*) lean out of (window etc.). **4** *slang* reside, be often present. **5** (+ *with*) *slang* associate with. **hangover** after-effects of excess of alcohol. **hang together 1** make sense. **2** remain associated. **hang up 1** hang from hook etc. **2** end telephone conversation. **hang-up** *noun slang* emotional inhibition.

▪ *verb* **1** attach, drape, fasten, fix, peg, pin up, stick up, suspend. **1, 7** be suspended, dangle, droop, fall, flap, flop, sway, swing, trail down. **6** droop, flop. **8** drift, float, hover. □ **hang about, around** see DAWDLE. **hang back 2** see HESITATE 2. **hang fire** see DELAY *verb* 3. **hang on 2** (*hang on to*) see KEEP *verb* 1,2. **3** see WAIT *verb* 1.

hangar /'hæŋə/ *noun* building for housing aircraft etc.

hanger *noun* **1** person or thing that hangs. **2** (in full **coat-hanger**) shaped piece of wood etc. for hanging clothes on. □ **hanger-on** (*plural* **hangers-on**) follower, dependant.

hanging *noun* **1** execution by suspending by neck. **2** (usually in *plural*) drapery for walls etc. ● *adjective* suspended.

▪ *adjective* see PENDENT 1.

hank *noun* coil of yarn etc.

▪ coil, length, loop, piece, skein.

hanker /'hæŋkə/ *verb* (+ *for, after, to do*) crave, long for. □ **hankering** *noun*.

▪ (*hanker for, after*) ache for, covet, crave, desire, *colloquial* fancy, *colloquial* have a yen for, hunger for, itch for, long for, pine for, thirst for, want, wish for, yearn for.

hanky /'hæŋkɪ/ *noun* (also **hankie**) (*plural* -**ies**) *colloquial* handkerchief.

hanky-panky /hæŋkɪ'pæŋkɪ/ *noun slang* **1** misbehaviour. **2** trickery.

Hansard /'hænsɑːd/ *noun* verbatim record of parliamentary debates.

hansom /'hænsəm/ *noun* (in full **hansom cab**) *historical* two-wheeled horse-drawn cab.

haphazard /hæp'hæzəd/ *adjective* casual, random. □ **haphazardly** *adverb*.

▪ accidental, adventitious, arbitrary, casual, chance, chaotic, confusing, disorderly, disorganized, fortuitous, higgledy-piggledy, hit-and-miss, illogical, irrational, random, serendipitous, unforeseen, unplanned, unstructured, unsystematic.

hapless /'hæplɪs/ *adjective* unlucky.

happen /'hæpən/ *verb* **1** occur. **2** (+ *to do*) have the (good or bad) fortune to. **3** (+ *to*) be fate or experience of. **4** (+ *on*) come by chance on. □ **happening** *noun*.

▪ **1** arise, *poetical* befall, come about, come to pass, crop up, emerge, ensue, follow, materialize, occur, result, take place, *disputed* transpire, turn out. **2** chance. **3** (*happen to*) become of, *poetical* befall, *esp. poetical* betide. **4** (*happen on*) see FIND *verb* 1. □ **happening** accident, *colloquial* affair, chance, circumstance, episode, event, incident, occasion, occurrence, phenomenon.

happy /'hæpɪ/ *adjective* (-**ier**, -**iest**) **1** feeling or showing pleasure or contentment. **2** fortunate. **3** (of words etc.) apt, pleasing. □ **happy-go-lucky** taking things cheerfully as they happen. **happy hour** time of day when drinks are sold at reduced prices. **happy medium** compromise. □ **happily** *adverb*. **happiness** *noun*.

▪ **1** *colloquial* beatific, blessed, blissful, *poetical* blithe, buoyant, cheerful, cheery, contented, delighted, ecstatic, elated, enraptured, euphoric, exhilarated, exuberant, exultant, felicitous, festive, gay, glad, gleeful, good-humoured, gratified, grinning, halcyon (*days*), heavenly, high-spirited, idyllic, jocose, jocular, *literary* jocund, joking, jolly, jovial, joyful, joyous, jubilant, laughing, light-hearted, lively, merry, *colloquial* on top of the world, overjoyed, over the moon, pleased, proud, radiant, rapturous, rejoicing, relaxed, satisfied, smiling, *colloquial* starry-eyed, sunny, thrilled, triumphant. **2** advantageous, auspicious, beneficial, blessed, convenient, favourable, fortuitous, fortunate, lucky, opportune, propitious, timely, welcome, well timed. **3** appropriate, apt, felicitous, pleasing. □ **happiness** bliss, cheer, cheerfulness, contentment, delight, ecstasy, elation, enjoyment, euphoria, exhilaration, exuberance, felicity, gaiety, gladness, glee, heaven, high spirits, joy, joyfulness, joyousness, jubilation, light-heartedness, merriment, pleasure, pride, rapture, well-being.

hara-kiri /hærə'kɪrɪ/ *noun historical* Japanese suicide by ritual disembowelling.

harangue /hə'ræŋ/ *noun* lengthy and earnest speech. ● *verb* (-**guing**) make harangue to.

▪ *noun* diatribe, exhortation, lecture, pep talk, speech, tirade. ● *verb* chivvy, encourage, exhort, lecture, pontificate, preach, sermonize.

harass /'hærəs/ *verb* **1** trouble, annoy. **2** attack repeatedly. □ **harassed** *adjective*. **harassment** *noun*.

USAGE *Harass* is often pronounced /hə'ræs/ (with the stress on the -*rass*), but this is considered incorrect by some people.

■ **1** annoy, badger, bait, bother, chivvy, disturb, harry, *colloquial* hassle, hound, irritate, molest, nag, persecute, pester, pick on, *colloquial* plague, torment, trouble, vex, worry. **2** assail, attack, beset, besiege, molest. □ **harassed** at the end of one's tether, careworn, distraught, distressed, exhausted, frayed, pressured, strained, stressed, tired, weary, worn out.

harbinger /'hɑːbɪndʒə/ *noun* person or thing announcing another's approach; forerunner.

harbour /'hɑːbə/ (*US* **harbor**) *noun* **1** place of shelter for ships. **2** shelter. ● *verb* **1** give shelter to. **2** entertain (thoughts etc.).

■ *noun* **1** anchorage, dock, haven, jetty, landing stage, marina, mooring, pier, port, quay, wharf. **2** asylum, haven, refuge, shelter. ● *verb* **1** conceal, give asylum to, give refuge to, give sanctuary to, hide, protect, shelter, shield. **2** cherish, cling (on) to, entertain, hold on to, keep in mind, maintain, nurse, nurture, retain.

hard *adjective* **1** firm, solid. **2** difficult to bear, do, or understand. **3** unfeeling. **4** harsh, severe. **5** strenuous; enthusiastic. **6** *Politics* extreme, radical. **7** (of drinks) strongly alcoholic. **8** (of drug) potent and addictive. **9** (of water) difficult to lather. **10** (of currency etc.) not likely to fall in value. **11** (of facts) not disputable. ● *adverb* strenuously, severely, intensely. □ **hard and fast** (of rule etc.) strict. **hardback** (book) bound in stiff covers. **hardbitten** *colloquial* tough; cynical. **hardboard** stiff board of compressed wood pulp. **hard-boiled 1** (of eggs) boiled until yolk and white are solid. **2** (of person) tough, shrewd. **hard cash** coins and banknotes, not cheques etc. **hard copy** printed material produced by computer. **hard core 1** stones, rubble, etc. as foundation. **2** central or most enduring part. **hard disk** *Computing* rigid storage disk, esp. fixed in computer. **hard-done-by** unfairly treated. **hard feelings** feelings of resentment. **hard-headed** practical, not sentimental. **hard-hearted** unfeeling. **hard-heartedness** *noun*. **hard line** firm adherence to policy. **hardline** unyielding. **hardliner** *noun*. **hard luck** worse fortune than one deserves. **hard-nosed** *colloquial* realistic, uncompromising. **hard of hearing** somewhat deaf. **hard-pressed 1** closely pursued. **2** burdened with urgent business. **hard sell** aggressive salesmanship. **hard shoulder** strip at side of motorway for emergency stops. **hard up** short of money. **hardware 1** tools, weapons, machinery, etc. **2** mechanical and electronic components of computer. **hard-wearing** able to withstand much wear. **hardwood** wood of deciduous tree. □ **hardness** *noun*.

■ *adjective* **1** adamantine, compact, compressed, dense, firm, flinty, frozen, hardened, impenetrable, impervious, inflexible, rigid, rocky, solid, solidified, steely, stiff, stony, unbreakable, unyielding. **2** (*hard times*) austere, bad, calamitous, disagreeable, distressing, grim, intolerable, painful, unhappy, unpleasant; (*hard labour*) arduous, back-breaking, exhausting, fatiguing, formidable, gruelling, harsh, heavy, laborious, onerous, rigorous, severe, stiff, strenuous, taxing,

tiring, tough, uphill, wearying; (*a hard problem*) baffling, complex, complicated, confusing, difficult, enigmatic, insoluble, intricate, involved, knotty, perplexing, puzzling, tangled, thorny. **3** callous, cold, cruel, hard-boiled, hard-hearted, harsh, heartless, hostile, inflexible, intolerant, merciless, obdurate, pitiless, ruthless, severe, stern, strict, unbending, unfeeling, unfriendly, unkind. **5** (*a hard blow*) forceful, heavy, powerful, strong, violent; (*a hard worker*) assiduous, conscientious, devoted, enthusiastic, indefatigable, industrious, keen, persistent, unflagging, untiring, zealous. □ **hard-headed** see BUSINESSLIKE (BUSINESS). **hard-hearted** see CRUEL. **hard up** see POOR **1**. **hardware 1** equipment, implements, instruments, ironmongery, machinery, tools. **hard-wearing** see DURABLE.

harden *verb* make or become hard or unyielding.

■ bake, cake, clot, coagulate, congeal, freeze, gel, *colloquial* jell, ossify, petrify, reinforce, set, solidify, stiffen, strengthen, toughen.

hardihood /'hɑːdɪhʊd/ *noun* boldness.

hardly *adverb* **1** scarcely. **2** with difficulty.

■ **1** barely, faintly, only just, rarely, scarcely, seldom. **2** barely, only just, with difficulty.

hardship *noun* severe suffering or privation.

■ adversity, affliction, austerity, bad luck, deprivation, destitution, difficulty, distress, misery, misfortune, need, privation, suffering, trial, tribulation, trouble, unhappiness, want.

hardy /'hɑːdɪ/ *adjective* (**-ier**, **-iest**) **1** robust; capable of endurance. **2** intrepid, bold. **3** (of plant) able to grow in the open all year. □ **hardiness** *noun*.

■ **1** durable, fit, healthy, hearty, resilient, robust, rugged, strong, sturdy, tough, vigorous. **2** see BOLD **1**.

hare /heə/ *noun* mammal like large rabbit, with long ears, short tail, and long hind legs. ● *verb* (**-ring**) run rapidly. □ **hare-brained** rash, wild.

harebell *noun* plant with pale blue bell-shaped flowers.

harem /'hɑːriːm/ *noun* **1** women of Muslim household. **2** their quarters.

haricot /'hærɪkəʊ/ *noun* (in full **haricot bean**) **1** French bean with small white seeds. **2** these as vegetable.

hark *verb* (usually in *imperative*) *archaic* listen. □ **hark back** revert to earlier topic.

Harlequin /'hɑːlɪkwɪn/ *noun* masked pantomime character in diamond-patterned costume. ● *adjective* (**harlequin**) in varied colours.

harlot /'hɑːlət/ *noun archaic* prostitute.

harm *noun & verb* damage, hurt.

■ *noun* abuse, damage, detriment, disadvantage, disservice, havoc, hurt, inconvenience, injury, loss, mischief, misfortune, pain, unhappiness, upset, wrong. ● *verb* abuse, be harmful to, damage, hurt, ill-treat, impair, injure, maltreat, misuse, ruin, spoil, wound.

harmful *adjective* causing or likely to cause harm. ◻ **harmfully** *adverb*.
■ bad, baleful, damaging, dangerous, deadly, deleterious, destructive, detrimental, disadvantageous, evil, fatal, hurtful, injurious, lethal, malign, negative, noxious, pernicious, poisonous, prejudicial, ruinous, unfavourable, unhealthy, unpleasant, unwholesome.

harmless *adjective* not able or likely to harm. ◻ **harmlessly** *adverb*. **harmlessness** *noun*.
■ benign, gentle, innocent, innocuous, inoffensive, mild, non-toxic, safe, tame, unobjectionable.

harmonic /hɑːˈmɒnɪk/ *adjective* of or relating to harmony; harmonious. ● *noun Music* overtone accompanying (and forming a note with) a fundamental at a fixed interval.

harmonica /hɑːˈmɒnɪkə/ *noun* small rectangular musical instrument played by blowing and sucking air through it.

harmonious /hɑːˈməʊnɪəs/ *adjective* **1** sweet-sounding, tuneful. **2** forming a pleasant or consistent whole. **3** free from dissent. ◻ **harmoniously** *adverb*.
■ **1** concordant, *colloquial* easy on the ear, euphonious, harmonizing, melodious, musical, sweet-sounding, tonal, tuneful. **2** agreeable, congruous, consistent, consonant, integrated. **3** amicable, compatible, congenial, cooperative, friendly, like-minded, sympathetic.

harmonium /hɑːˈməʊnɪəm/ *noun* keyboard instrument with bellows and metal reeds.

harmonize /ˈhɑːmənaɪz/ *verb* (also **-ise**) (**-zing** or **-sing**) **1** add notes to (melody) to produce harmony. **2** bring into or be in harmony. ◻ **harmonization** *noun*.
■ **2** agree, balance, blend, cooperate, coordinate, correspond, go together, match, suit each other, tally, tone in.

harmony /ˈhɑːmənɪ/ *noun* (*plural* **-ies**) **1** combination of notes to form chords. **2** melodious sound. **3** agreement, concord.
■ **2** assonance, euphony, tunefulness. **3** accord, agreement, amity, balance, compatibility, concord, conformity, congruence, consonance, cooperation, friendliness, goodwill, like-mindedness, peace, rapport, sympathy, togetherness, understanding.

harness /ˈhɑːnɪs/ *noun* **1** straps etc. by which horse is fastened to cart etc. and controlled. **2** similar arrangement for fastening thing to person. ● *verb* **1** put harness on; control. **2** utilize (natural forces), esp. to produce energy.
■ *noun* **1** equipment, gear, straps, tackle. ● *verb* **2** exploit, make use of, mobilize, use, utilize.

harp *noun* large upright stringed instrument plucked with fingers. ● *verb* (+ *on, on about*) dwell on tediously. ◻ **harpist** *noun*.

harpoon /hɑːˈpuːn/ *noun* spearlike missile for shooting whales etc. ● *verb* spear with harpoon.

harpsichord /ˈhɑːpsɪkɔːd/ *noun* keyboard instrument with strings plucked mechanically. ◻ **harpsichordist** *noun*.

harpy /ˈhɑːpɪ/ *noun* (*plural* **-ies**) **1** mythological monster with woman's face and bird's wings and claws. **2** grasping unscrupulous person.

harridan /ˈhærɪd(ə)n/ *noun* bad-tempered old woman.

harrier /ˈhærɪə/ *noun* **1** hound used in hunting hares. **2** kind of falcon.

harrow /ˈhærəʊ/ *noun* frame with metal teeth or discs for breaking clods of earth. ● *verb* **1** draw harrow over. **2** (usually as **harrowing** *adjective*) distress greatly.

harry /ˈhærɪ/ *verb* (**-ies**, **-ied**) **1** ravage, despoil. **2** harass.

harsh *adjective* **1** rough to hear, taste, etc. **2** severe, cruel. ◻ **harshly** *adverb*. **harshness** *noun*.
■ **1** (*harsh sounds*) cacophonous, croaking, croaky, disagreeable, discordant, dissonant, grating, gravelly, grinding, gruff, guttural, hoarse, husky, irritating, jarring, rasping, raucous, rough, screeching, shrill, squawking, stertorous, strident, unpleasant; (*harsh to the touch*) abrasive, bristly, coarse, hairy, rough, scratchy; (*harsh colours, light*) bright, brilliant, dazzling, gaudy, glaring, lurid; (*harsh smell*) acrid, bitter, sour. **2** (*harsh conditions*) arduous, austere, comfortless, difficult, hard, severe, stressful, tough; (*harsh criticism, treatment*) abusive, acerbic, bitter, blunt, brutal, cruel, Draconian, frank, hard-hearted, hurtful, impolite, merciless, outspoken, pitiless, severe, sharp, stern, strict, uncivil, unforgiving, unkind, unrelenting, unsympathetic.

hart *noun* (*plural* same or **-s**) male of (esp. red) deer.

hartebeest /ˈhɑːtɪbiːst/ *noun* large African antelope with curved horns.

harum-scarum /heərəmˈskeərəm/ *adjective colloquial* reckless, wild.

harvest /ˈhɑːvɪst/ *noun* **1** gathering in of crops etc. **2** season for this. **3** season's yield. **4** product of any action. ● *verb* reap and gather in.
■ *noun* **1** gathering in, reaping. **3** crop, produce, yield. **4** fruit, outcome, product, result, return. ● *verb* bring in, collect, garner, gather, glean, mow, pick, reap, take in.

harvester *noun* **1** reaper. **2** reaping machine.

has *3rd singular present* of HAVE.

hash[1] *noun* **1** dish of reheated pieces of cooked meat. **2** mixture, jumble. **3** recycled material. ● *verb* (often + *up*) recycle (old material). ◻ **make a hash of** *colloquial* make a mess of; bungle.
■ *noun* **1** goulash, stew. **2** botch, confusion, farrago, hotchpotch, jumble, mess, mishmash, mixture. ◻ **make a hash of** see BUNGLE *verb* 1.

hash[2] *noun colloquial* hashish.

hashish /ˈhæʃɪʃ/ *noun* narcotic drug got from hemp.

hasn't /ˈhæz(ə)nt/ has not.

hasp /hɑːsp/ *noun* hinged metal clasp passing over staple and secured by padlock.

hassle /ˈhæs(ə)l/ *colloquial noun* **1** trouble, problem. **2** argument. ● *verb* (**-ling**) **1** harass. **2** quarrel.

■ *noun* **1** bother, confusion, difficulty, disturbance, fuss, harassment, inconvenience, nuisance, persecution, problem, struggle, trouble, upset. **2** altercation, argument, disagreement, fight. ● *verb* **1** see HARASS 1. **2** see QUARREL *verb* 2.

hassock /ˈhæsək/ *noun* kneeling-cushion.

haste /heɪst/ *noun* **1** urgency of movement. **2** hurry. □ **make haste** be quick.

■ **1** dispatch, quickness, rapidity, speed, swiftness, urgency. **2** hurry, impetuosity, precipitateness, rashness, recklessness, rush.

hasten /ˈheɪs(ə)n/ *verb* (cause to) proceed or go quickly.

hasty /ˈheɪstɪ/ *adjective* (**-ier, -iest**) **1** hurried. **2** said, made, or done too quickly. □ **hastily** *adverb*. **hastiness** *noun*.

■ **1** abrupt, brief, brisk, fast, hurried, immediate, instantaneous, quick, rapid, short, speedy, sudden, swift. **2** careless, cursory, foolhardy, headlong, hot-headed, hurried, ill-considered, impetuous, impulsive, incautious, pell-mell, perfunctory, precipitate, rash, reckless, rushed, slapdash, summary (*justice*), superficial, thoughtless, unthinking.

hat *noun* (esp. outdoor) head-covering. □ **hat trick 1** *Cricket* taking 3 wickets with successive balls. **2** *Football* scoring of 3 goals in one match by same player. **3** 3 consecutive successes.

hatch[1] *noun* **1** opening in wall between kitchen and dining-room for serving food. **2** opening or door in aircraft etc. **3** (cover for) hatchway. □ **hatchback** car with rear door hinged at top. **hatchway** opening in ship's deck for lowering cargo.

hatch[2] *verb* **1** (often + *out*) emerge from egg. **2** (of egg) produce young animal. **3** incubate. **4** (also + *up*) devise (plot). ● *noun* **1** hatching. **2** brood hatched.

■ *verb* **3** brood, incubate. **4** conceive, concoct, contrive, *colloquial* cook up, design, devise, dream up, formulate, invent, plan, plot, scheme, *colloquial* think up.

hatch[3] *verb* mark with parallel lines. □ **hatching** *noun*.

hatchet /ˈhætʃɪt/ *noun* light short axe.

hate *verb* (**-ting**) dislike intensely. ● *noun* **1** hatred. **2** *colloquial* person or thing hated.

■ *verb* abhor, abominate, be averse to, be hostile to, be revolted by, can't bear, can't stand, deplore, despise, detest, dislike, execrate, fear, find intolerable, loathe, object to, recoil from, resent, scorn, shudder at. ● *noun* **1** see HATRED. **2** abomination, aversion, *bête noire*, dislike, loathing.

hateful *adjective* arousing hatred.

■ abhorrent, abominable, *colloquial* accursed, *colloquial* awful, contemptible, cursed, damnable, despicable, detestable, disgusting, distasteful, execrable, foul, hated, heinous, *colloquial* horrible, *colloquial* horrid, loathsome, nasty, nauseating, obnoxious, odious, offensive, repellent, repugnant, repulsive, revolting, vile.

hatred /ˈheɪtrɪd/ *noun* intense dislike; ill will.

■ abhorrence, animosity, antagonism, antipathy, aversion, contempt, detestation, dislike, enmity, execration, hate, hostility, ill will, intolerance, loathing, misanthropy, odium, repugnance, revulsion.

hatter *noun* maker or seller of hats.

haughty /ˈhɔːtɪ/ *adjective* (**-ier, -iest**) proud, arrogant. □ **haughtily** *adverb*. **haughtiness** *noun*.

■ arrogant, boastful, bumptious, cavalier, *colloquial* cocky, conceited, condescending, disdainful, egotistic(al), *colloquial* high and mighty, hoity-toity, imperious, lofty, lordly, offhand, patronizing, pompous, presumptuous, pretentious, proud, self-admiring, self-important, smug, snobbish, *colloquial* snooty, *colloquial* stuck-up, supercilious, superior, *colloquial* uppity, vain.

haul /hɔːl/ *verb* **1** pull or drag forcibly. **2** transport by lorry, cart, etc. ● *noun* **1** hauling. **2** amount gained or acquired. **3** distance to be traversed.

■ *verb* **1** drag, draw, heave, lug, pull, tow, trail, tug. **2** carry, cart, convey, move, transport.

haulage *noun* (charge for) commercial transport of goods.

haulier /ˈhɔːlɪə/ *noun* person or firm engaged in transport of goods.

haulm /hɔːm/ *noun* (also **halm**) **1** stalk or stem. **2** stalks of beans, peas, potatoes, etc. collectively.

haunch /hɔːntʃ/ *noun* **1** fleshy part of buttock and thigh. **2** leg and loin of deer etc. as food.

haunt /hɔːnt/ *verb* **1** (of ghost etc.) visit regularly. **2** frequent (place). **3** linger in mind of. ● *noun* place frequented by person.

■ *verb* **1, 2** frequent, hang around, keep returning to, loiter about, patronize, spend time at, visit regularly. **3** beset, linger in, obsess, *colloquial* plague, prey on, torment.

haunting *adjective* (of memory, melody, etc.) lingering; poignant, evocative.

haute couture /əʊt kuːˈtjʊə/ *noun* (world of) high fashion.

hauteur /əʊˈtɜː/ *noun* haughtiness.

have /hæv/ *verb* (**having**; *3rd singular present* **has** /hæz/; *past & past participle* **had**) **1** hold in possession or relationship; be provided with. **2** contain as part or quality. **3** experience. **4** (come to) be subjected to a specified state. **5** engage in. **6** hold (party, meeting, etc.). **7** eat, drink. **8** tolerate; permit to. **9** receive. **10** provide accommodation; entertain. **11** obtain or know (qualification, language, etc.). **12** give birth to. **13** *colloquial* get the better of. **14** (usually in *passive*) cheat. ● *aux-iliary verb: used with past participle to form past tenses.* ● *noun* **1** (usually in *plural*) colloquial wealthy person. **2** *slang* swindle. □ **have on 1** wear (clothes). **2** have (engagement). **3** *colloquial* hoax. **have-not** (usually in *plural*) person lacking wealth. **have to** be obliged to, must. **have up** bring (person) before court, interviewer, etc.

■ *verb* **1** be in possession of, keep, maintain, own, possess, use, utilize. **2** comprise, consist of, contain, embody, hold, include, incorporate, involve. **3** be subject to, endure, enjoy, experience, feel, go through, live through, put up with, suffer, tolerate, undergo. **6** arrange, hold, organize, prepare, set up. **7** consume, eat, drink, partake of, swallow. **9** accept, acquire, be given, gain, get, obtain, procure, receive. **10** be host to, cater for, entertain, put up. □ **have on 3** see HOAX *verb*. **have to** be compelled to, be forced to, have an obligation to, must, need to, ought to, should. **have up** see ARREST *verb* 1.

haven /ˈheɪv(ə)n/ *noun* **1** refuge. **2** harbour.
■ **1** asylum, refuge, retreat, safety, sanctuary, shelter. **2** see HARBOUR *noun* 1.

haven't /ˈhæv(ə)nt/ have not.

haver /ˈheɪvə/ *verb* **1** hesitate. **2** talk foolishly.

haversack /ˈhævəsæk/ *noun* canvas bag carried on back or over shoulder.

havoc /ˈhævək/ *noun* devastation, confusion.
□ **play havoc with** *colloquial* cause confusion to.
■ chaos, confusion, damage, desolation, destruction, devastation, disorder, disruption, mayhem, rack and ruin, ruin, *colloquial* shambles, upset, waste, wreckage.

haw *noun* hawthorn berry.

hawk[1] *noun* **1** bird of prey with rounded wings. **2** *Politics* person who advocates aggressive policy. ● *verb* hunt with hawk. □ **hawkish** *adjective*. **hawkishness** *noun*.

hawk[2] *verb* carry (goods) about for sale.

hawk[3] *verb* **1** clear throat noisily. **2** (+ *up*) bring (phlegm etc.) up thus.

hawker *noun* person who hawks goods.

hawser /ˈhɔːzə/ *noun* thick rope or cable for mooring ship.

hawthorn *noun* thorny shrub with red berries.

hay *noun* grass mown and dried for fodder. □ **haycock** conical heap of hay. **hay fever** allergic irritation of nose, throat, etc. caused by pollen, dust, etc. **haymaking** mowing grass and spreading it to dry. **hayrick**, **haystack** packed pile of hay. **haywire** *colloquial* badly disorganized; out of control.

hazard /ˈhæzəd/ *noun* **1** danger; risk. **2** obstacle on golf course. ● *verb* **1** venture on (guess etc.). **2** risk.
■ *noun* **1** chance, danger, jeopardy, peril, risk, threat. ● *verb* **1** chance, dare, risk, stake, venture. **2** endanger, gamble with, imperil, jeopardize, risk, take a chance with.

hazardous *adjective* risky.

■ chancy, dangerous, *slang* dicey, fraught with danger, *slang* hairy, *archaic* parlous, perilous, precarious, risky, ticklish, tricky, uncertain, unpredictable, unsafe.

haze *noun* **1** slight mist. **2** mental obscurity, confusion.
■ **1** cloud, film, fog, mist, steam, vapour.

hazel /ˈheɪz(ə)l/ *noun* **1** nut-bearing hedgerow shrub. **2** greenish-brown. □ **hazelnut** nut of hazel.

hazy *adjective* (**-ier, -iest**) **1** misty. **2** vague. **3** confused. □ **hazily** *adverb*. **haziness** *noun*.
■ **1** blurred, blurry, clouded, cloudy, dim, faint, foggy, fuzzy, indefinite, milky, misty, obscure, unclear. **2** see VAGUE 1. **3** see UNCERTAIN 1–2.

HB *abbreviation* hard black (pencil lead).

HE *abbreviation* **1** His or Her Excellency. **2** high explosive.

he /hiː/ *pronoun* **1** (as subject of verb) the male person or animal in question. **2** person of unspecified sex. □ **he-man** masterful or virile man.

head /hed/ *noun* **1** uppermost part of human body, or foremost part of body of animal, containing brain, sense organs, etc. **2** seat of intellect. **3** thing like head in form or position. **4** top, front, or upper end. **5** source of river. **6** person in charge, esp. of school. **7** position of command. **8** individual as unit. **9** side of coin bearing image of head. **10** (in *plural*) this as call when tossing coin. **11** signal-converting device on tape recorder etc. **12** foam on top of beer etc. **13** confined body of water or steam. **14** pressure exerted by this. **15** (usually in **come to a head**) climax, crisis. ● *adjective* principal, chief. ● *verb* **1** be at front or in charge of. **2** (often + *for*) move or send in specified direction. **3** provide with heading. **4** *Football* strike (ball) with head. □ **headache 1** continuous pain in head. **2** *colloquial* troublesome problem. **headachy** *adjective*. **headband** band worn round head as decoration or to confine hair. **headboard** upright panel at head of bed. **headcount** (counting of) total number of people. **headdress** (esp. ornamental) covering for head. **headhunting 1** collecting of enemies' heads as trophies. **2** seeking of staff by approaching people employed elsewhere. **headlamp, headlight** (main) light at front of vehicle. **headland** promontory. **headline 1** heading at top of page, newspaper article, etc. **2** (in *plural*) summary of broadcast news. **headlock** wrestling hold round opponent's head. **headlong 1** with head foremost. **2** in a rush. **headman** tribal chief. **headmaster, headmistress** head teacher. **head off 1** get ahead of and deflect. **2** avert. **head-on** (of collision etc.) with front foremost. **headphones** pair of earphones fitting over head. **headquarters** (treated as *singular* or *plural*) organization's administrative centre. **headroom** overhead space. **headset** headphones, often with microphone. **headshrinker** *slang* psychiatrist. **headstall** part of bridle or halter fitting round horse's head. **head start** advantage granted or gained at early stage. **headstone** stone set up at head of grave. **headstrong** self-willed. **head**

teacher teacher in charge of school. **headway** progress. **headwind** one blowing from directly in front. **lose one's head** panic, lose control. **off one's head** *colloquial* crazy. **put heads together** consult together.

■ *noun* **1** brain, cranium, skull. **2** ability, brains, capacity, imagination, intelligence, intellect, mind, understanding. **4** apex, crown, highest point, peak, summit, top, vertex. **5** see SOURCE 1. **6** authority figure, *colloquial* boss, captain, chief, commander, director, employer, leader, manager, ruler, superintendent, supervisor, supremo; (*head of a school*) headmaster, headmistress, head teacher, principal. ● *adjective* see CHIEF *adjective* 1. ● *verb* **1** be in charge of, command, control, direct, govern, guide, lead, manage, rule, run, superintend, supervise. **2** aim, go, point, proceed, set out, start, steer, turn; (*head for*) make for, make a beeline for. □ **head off 1** see DEFLECT.
headquarters base, depot, head office, HQ, main office. nerve centre. **lose one's head** see PANIC *verb*. **off one's head** see MAD 1.

header *noun* **1** *Football* act of heading ball. **2** *colloquial* headlong dive or plunge.

heading *noun* title at head of page etc.
■ caption, headline, rubric, title.

heady *adjective* (**-ier, -iest**) **1** (of liquor etc.) potent. **2** exciting, intoxicating. **3** impetuous. **4** headachy.

heal *verb* **1** (often + *up*) become healthy again. **2** cure. **3** put right (differences). □ **healer** *noun*.
■ **1** become healthy, get better, improve, knit, mend, recover, recuperate. **2** cure, make better, minister to, nurse, rejuvenate, remedy, renew, restore, revitalize, tend, treat. **3** patch up, put right, reconcile, repair, settle.

health /helθ/ *noun* **1** state of being well in body or mind. **2** mental or physical condition. □ **health centre** building containing local medical services. **health food** natural food, thought to promote good health. **health service** public medical service. **health visitor** nurse who visits mothers and babies, the elderly, etc. at home.
■ **1** fitness, robustness, soundness, strength, vigour, well-being. **2** condition, constitution, fettle, form, shape, trim.

healthful /'helθfʊl/ *adjective* conducive to good health; beneficial. □ **healthfully** *adverb*. **healthfulness** *noun*.

healthy *adjective* (**-ier, -iest**) having, conducive to, or indicative of, good health. □ **healthily** *adverb*. **healthiness** *noun*.
■ (*a healthy creature*) active, blooming, fine, fit, flourishing, good, hale and hearty, hearty, in fine fettle, in good shape, lively, perky, robust, sound, strong, sturdy, vigorous, well; (*healthy living conditions*) bracing, health-giving, hygienic, invigorating, salubrious, sanitary, wholesome.

heap *noun* **1** disorderly pile. **2** (esp. in *plural*) *colloquial* large number or amount. **3** *slang* dilapidated vehicle. ● *verb* **1** (+ *up, together*, etc.) pile

or collect in heap. **2** (+ *with*) load copiously with. **3** (+ *on, upon*) offer copiously.
■ *noun* **1** accumulation, assemblage, bank, collection, hill, hoard, mass, mound, mountain, pile, stack. **2** (*heaps*) see PLENTY *noun* 1. ● *verb* **1** (*heap up*) accumulate, amass, bank up, collect, gather, hoard, mass, pile, stack, stockpile, store.

hear *verb* (*past & past participle* **heard** /hɜːd/) **1** perceive with ear. **2** listen to. **3** listen judicially to and try (case). **4** be informed. **5** (+ *from*) receive message etc. from. □ **hearsay** rumour, gossip. □ **hearer** *noun*.
■ **1** catch, overhear, pick up. **2** attend to, heed, listen to, pay attention to. **3** examine, investigate, judge, try. **4** be told, be informed, discover, find out, gather, learn; (*hear of*) get wind of.

hearing *noun* **1** faculty of perceiving sounds. **2** range within which sounds may be heard. **3** opportunity to state one's case. **4** trial of case before court. □ **hearing aid** small sound-amplifier worn by partially deaf person.
■ **4** case, inquest, inquiry, trial.

hearse /hɜːs/ *noun* vehicle for carrying coffin.

heart /hɑːt/ *noun* **1** organ in body keeping up circulation of blood by contraction and dilation. **2** region of heart; breast. **3** seat of thought, feeling, or emotion (esp. love). **4** capacity for feeling emotion. **5** courage. **6** mood. **7** central or innermost part; essence. **8** tender inner part of vegetable etc. **9** (conventionally) heart-shaped thing. **10** playing card of suit marked with red hearts. □ **at heart** in inmost feelings. **break person's heart** overwhelm person with sorrow. **by heart** from memory. **have the heart** (usually in negative, + *to do*) be hard-hearted enough to. **heartache** mental anguish. **heart attack** sudden heart failure. **heartbeat** pulsation of heart. **heartbreak** overwhelming distress. **heartbreaking** *adjective*. **heartbroken** *adjective*. **heartburn** burning sensation in chest from indigestion. **heartfelt** sincere. **heart-rending** very distressing. **heartsick** despondent. **heartstrings** deepest affections or pity. **heart-throb** *colloquial* object of (esp. immature) romantic feelings. **heart-to-heart** frank (talk). **heart-warming** emotionally moving and encouraging. **take to heart** be much affected by.
■ **1** *colloquial* ticker. **4** affection, compassion, concern, feeling, goodness, humanity, kindness, love, pity, sensitivity, sympathy, tenderness, understanding, warmth. **7** centre, core, crux, essence, focus, hub, kernel, *slang* nitty-gritty, nub, nucleus, pith. □ **heartbreaking** bitter, distressing, grievous, heart-rending, pitiful, tragic. **heartbroken** broken-hearted, dejected, desolate, despairing, dispirited, grief-stricken, grieved, heartsick, inconsolable, miserable, shattered.

hearten *verb* make or become more cheerful. □ **heartening** *adjective*.
■ boost, cheer up, encourage, strengthen, uplift.

hearth /hɑːθ/ *noun* floor of fireplace. □ **hearth-rug** rug laid before fireplace.

heartless *adjective* unfeeling, pitiless. □ **heartlessly** *adverb.* **heartlessness** *noun.*
■ callous, cold, cruel, hard-hearted, icy, inhuman, pitiless, ruthless, steely, stony, unconcerned, unemotional, unfeeling, unkind, unsympathetic.

hearty *adjective* (**-ier, -iest**) **1** strong, vigorous. **2** (of meal or appetite) large. **3** warm, friendly; enthusiastic. **4** sincere, genuine. □ **heartily** *adverb.* **heartiness** *noun.*
■ **1** energetic, healthy, robust, strong, vigorous. **2** see BIG *adjective* **1. 3** enthusiastic, exuberant, friendly, lively, positive, spirited, warm. **4** genuine, heartfelt, sincere, wholehearted.

heat *noun* **1** condition or sensation of being hot. **2** energy arising from motion of molecules. **3** hot weather. **4** warmth of feeling. **5** anger. **6** most intense part or period of activity. **7** preliminary round in contest. ● *verb* **1** make or become hot. **2** inflame. □ **heatproof** able to resist great heat. **heatwave** period of very hot weather. **on heat** (of female animals) sexually receptive.
■ *noun* **1** fever, fieriness, glow, hotness, incandescence, warmth. **2** calorific value. **3** closeness, heatwave, high temperature, hot weather, humidity, sultriness, torridity, warmth. **4** ardour, eagerness, enthusiasm, excitement, fervour, feverishness, impetuosity, intensity, passion, vehemence, violence. **5** anger, fury. ● *verb* **1** bake, blister, boil, burn, cook, frizzle, fry, grill, melt, reheat, roast, scald, scorch, simmer, sizzle, smoulder, steam, stew, swelter, toast, warm.

heated *adjective* angry, impassioned. □ **heatedly** *adverb.*
■ see FERVENT, HOT *adjective* 4.

heater *noun* device for heating room, water, etc.

heath /hi:θ/ *noun* **1** flattish tract of uncultivated land with low shrubs. **2** plant growing on heath, esp. heather.
■ **1** common, moor, moorland, open country.

heathen /'hi:ð(ə)n/ *noun* **1** person not belonging to predominant religion. **2** unenlightened person. ● *adjective* **1** not belonging to any of the predominant religions; having no religion. **2** unenlightened.
■ *noun* **1** Gentile, heretic, idolater, infidel, pagan, sceptic, unbeliever. **2** barbarian, philistine, savage. ● *adjective* **1** Gentile, godless, idolatrous, infidel, irreligious, pagan. **2** barbaric, philistine, savage, unenlightened.

heather /'heðə/ *noun* purple-flowered plant of moors and heaths.

heating *noun* equipment used to heat building.

heave *verb* (**-ving**; *past & past participle* **heaved** or *esp. Nautical* **hove** /həʊv/) **1** lift, haul, or utter with effort. **2** *colloquial* throw. **3** rise and fall periodically. **4** *Nautical* haul by rope. **5** retch. ● *noun* heaving. □ **heave in sight** come into view. **heave to** bring vessel to standstill.

■ *verb* **1** drag, draw, haul, hoist, lift, lug, move, pull, raise, tow, tug. **2** see THROW *verb* 1, 2. **5** see VOMIT *verb* 1. □ **heave in sight** see APPEAR 1.

heaven /'hev(ə)n/ *noun* **1** home of God and of blessed after death. **2** place or state of bliss. **3** delightful thing. **4** (**the heavens**) sky as seen from earth. □ **heavenly** *adjective.*
■ **1** afterlife, *Greek Mythology* Elysium, the hereafter, the next world, nirvana, paradise. **3** bliss, contentment, delight, ecstasy, felicity, happiness, joy, paradise, perfection, pleasure, rapture, Utopia. □ **heavenly** angelic, *colloquial* beatific, beautiful, blissful, celestial, delightful, divine, exquisite, glorious, lovely, other-worldly, *colloquial* out of this world, saintly, spiritual, sublime, unearthly, wonderful.

heavy /'hevɪ/ *adjective* (**-ier, -iest**) **1** of great weight; difficult to lift. **2** of great density. **3** abundant. **4** severe, extensive. **5** striking or falling with force. **6** (of machinery etc.) very large of its kind. **7** needing much physical effort. **8** hard to digest. **9** hard to read or understand; dull, tedious. **10** (of ground) difficult to travel over. **11** oppressive. **12** depressed, weighed down. **13** coarse, ungraceful. ● *noun* (*plural* **-ies**) **1** *colloquial* thug (esp. hired). **2** villain. □ **heavy-duty** designed to withstand hard use. **heavy-handed 1** clumsy. **2** oppressive. **heavy-hearted** unhappy, depressed. **heavy hydrogen** deuterium. **heavy industry** that concerned with production of metal and machines etc. **heavy metal** *colloquial* loud rock music with pounding rhythm. **heavy water** water composed of deuterium and oxygen. **heavyweight** amateur boxing weight (over 81 kg). □ **heavily** *adverb.* **heaviness** *noun.*
■ *adjective* **1** bulky, burdensome, fat, hefty, immovable, large, leaden, massive, ponderous, unwieldy, weighty. **2** compact, concentrated, dense, solid. **3** abundant, copious, laden, loaded, profuse, thick. **4** concentrated, excessive, extensive, intensive, severe. **5** (*a heavy blow*) forceful, hard, powerful, strong, violent; (*heavy rain*) pouring, severe, torrential. **7** arduous, demanding, difficult, hard, exhausting, laborious, onerous, strenuous, tough. **9** deep, dull, intellectual, intense, serious, tedious, wearisome. **12** burdened, depressed, gloomy, miserable, sad, sorrowful, troubled, unhappy. □ **heavy-handed 1** see CLUMSY 1. **heavy-hearted** see SAD 1.

Hebraic /hi:'breɪk/ *adjective* of Hebrew or the Hebrews.

Hebrew /'hi:bru:/ *noun* **1** member of a Semitic people in ancient Palestine. **2** their language. **3** modern form of this, used esp. in Israel. ● *adjective* **1** of or in Hebrew. **2** of the Jews.

heckle /'hek(ə)l/ *verb* (**-ling**) interrupt or harass (speaker). ● *noun* act of heckling. □ **heckler** *noun.*

hectare /'hekteə/ *noun* metric unit of square measure (2.471 acres).

hectic /'hektɪk/ *adjective* **1** busy and confused; excited. **2** feverish. □ **hectically** *adverb.*

■ **1** animated, boisterous, brisk, bustling, busy, chaotic, excited, feverish, frantic, frenetic, frenzied, hurried, hyperactive, lively, mad, over-active, restless, riotous, *colloquial* rumbustious, turbulent, wild. **2** febrile, feverish, flushed.

hecto- /ˈhektəʊ/ *combining form* one hundred.

hector /ˈhektə/ *verb* bluster, bully. □ **hectoring** *adjective*.

he'd /hiːd/ **1** he had. **2** he would.

hedge *noun* **1** fence of bushes or low trees. **2** protection against possible loss. ● *verb* (**-ging**) **1** surround with hedge. **2** (+ *in*) enclose. **3** secure oneself against loss on (bet etc.). **4** avoid committing oneself. □ **hedgehog** small spiny insect-eating mammal. **hedge-hop** fly at low altitude. **hedgerow** row of bushes forming hedge. **hedge sparrow** common brown-backed bird.

■ *noun* **1** hedgerow. ● *verb* **2** (*hedge in*) see ENCLOSE 1. **4** beat about the bush, be evasive, equivocate, hum and haw, quibble, stall, temporize, *colloquial* waffle.

hedonism /ˈhiːdənɪz(ə)m/ *noun* (behaviour based on) belief in pleasure as humankind's proper aim. □ **hedonist** *noun.* **hedonistic** /-ˈnɪs-/ *adjective*.

■ □ **hedonistic** epicurean, extravagant, intemperate, luxurious, pleasure-loving, self-indulgent, sensual, sybaritic, voluptuous.

heed *verb* attend to; take notice of. ● *noun* care, attention. □ **heedful** *adjective.* **heedfully** *adverb.* **heedfulness** *noun.* **heedless** *adjective.* **heed-lessly** *adverb*.

■ *verb* attend to, bear in mind, concern oneself about, consider, follow, keep to, listen to, mark, mind, note, notice, obey, observe, pay attention to, regard, take notice of. □ **heedful** attentive, careful, concerned, considerate, mindful, observant, sympathetic, vigilant, watchful. **heedless** blind, careless, deaf, inattentive, inconsiderate, neglectful, oblivious, reckless, regardless, thoughtless, uncaring, unconcerned, unmindful, unobservant, unsympathetic.

hee-haw /ˈhiːhɔː/ *noun & verb* bray.

heel[1] *noun* **1** back of foot below ankle. **2** part of sock etc. covering this, or of shoe etc. supporting it. **3** crust end of loaf. **4** *colloquial* scoundrel. **5** (as *interjection*) *command to dog to walk near owner's heel.* ● *verb* **1** fit or renew heel on (shoe). **2** touch ground with heel. **3** (+ *out*) *Rugby* pass ball with heel. □ **cool, kick one's heels** be kept waiting. **heelball** shoemaker's polishing mixture of wax etc., esp. used in brass rubbing. **take to one's heels** run away.

heel[2] *verb* **1** (often + *over*) (of ship etc.) lean over. **2** (often + *over*) cause (ship) to do this. ● *noun* heeling.

■ *verb* careen, incline, lean, list, tilt, tip.

hefty /ˈheftɪ/ *adjective* (**-ier, -iest**) **1** (of person) big, strong. **2** (of thing) heavy, powerful.

■ **1** beefy, big, brawny, burly, *colloquial* hulking, husky, large, mighty, muscular, powerful, robust, rugged, solid, strapping, strong, tough. **2** big, bulky, heavy, huge, large, massive, powerful, sizeable, substantial.

hegemony /hɪˈgemənɪ/ *noun* leadership.

heifer /ˈhefə/ *noun* young cow, esp. one that has not had more than one calf.

height /haɪt/ *noun* **1** measurement from base to top. **2** elevation above ground or other level. **3** high place. **4** top; highest point or degree. **5** extreme example.

■ **1** tallness, vertical measurement. **2** altitude, elevation, level. **3** crag, fell, hill, mound, mountain, peak, prominence, ridge, summit, top. **4, 5** acme, apex, apogee, climax, crest, culmination, extreme, high point, maximum, peak, pinnacle, zenith.

heighten *verb* make or become higher or more intense.

■ add to, amplify, augment, boost, build up, elevate, enhance, improve, increase, intensify, lift up, magnify, maximize, raise, reinforce, sharpen, strengthen, supplement.

heinous /ˈheməs/ *adjective* atrocious. □ **hein-ousness** *noun*.

heir /eə/ *noun* (*feminine* **heiress**) person entitled to property or rank as legal successor of former holder. □ **heir apparent** one whose claim cannot be superseded by birth of nearer heir. **heirloom** piece of property that has been in family for generations. **heir presumptive** one whose claim may be superseded by birth of nearer heir.

held *past & past participle* of HOLD[1].

helical /ˈhelɪk(ə)l/ *adjective* spiral.

helices *plural* of HELIX.

helicopter /ˈhelɪkɒptə/ *noun* wingless aircraft lifted and propelled by overhead blades revolving horizontally.

heliograph /ˈhiːlɪəɡrɑːf/ *noun* signalling apparatus reflecting flashes of sunlight. ● *verb* send (message) thus.

heliotrope /ˈhiːlɪətrəʊp/ *noun* plant with fragrant purple flowers.

heliport /ˈhelɪpɔːt/ *noun* place where helicopters take off and land.

helium /ˈhiːlɪəm/ *noun* light non-flammable gaseous element.

helix /ˈhiːlɪks/ *noun* (*plural* **helices** /ˈhiːlɪsiːz/) spiral or coiled curve.

hell *noun* **1** home of the damned after death. **2** place or state of misery. □ **hellish** *adjective.* **hell-ishly** *adverb*.

■ **1** Hades, infernal regions, netherworld, underworld. **2** see MISERY 1.

he'll /hiːl/ he will; he shall.

hellebore /ˈhelɪbɔː/ *noun* evergreen plant of kind including Christmas rose.

Hellene /ˈheliːn/ *noun* Greek. □ **Hellenic** /-ˈlen-/ *adjective.* **Hellenism** /-lɪm-/ *noun.* **Hellenist** /-lɪm-/ *noun*.

Hellenistic /helɪˈnɪstɪk/ *adjective* of Greek history, language, and culture of late 4th to late 1st c. BC.

hello /həˈləʊ/ (also **hallo, hullo**) *interjection: expressing informal greeting or surprise, or calling attention.* ● *noun* (*plural* **-s**) cry of 'hello'.

helm *noun* tiller or wheel for managing rudder. □ **at the helm** in control. **helmsman** person who steers ship.

helmet /ˈhelmɪt/ *noun* protective headcover of policeman, motorcyclist, etc.

help *verb* **1** provide with means to what is needed or sought. **2** be useful to. **3** improve, alleviate. **4** (usually in negative) prevent, refrain from. **5** (**help oneself**; often + *to*) serve oneself. **6** (**help oneself**; often + *to*) take without permission. ● *noun* **1** act of helping. **2** person or thing that helps. **3** *colloquial* domestic assistant or assistance. **4** remedy etc. □ **helpline** telephone service providing help with problems. □ **helper** *noun*.

■ *verb* **1** abet, advise, aid, assist, back, befriend, boost, collaborate with, contribute to, cooperate with, encourage, facilitate, forward, further the interests of, give a hand, lend a hand, profit, promote, prop up, rally round, serve, side with, spoon-feed, stand by, subsidize, *archaic* or *formal* succour, support, take pity on. **2** avail, be useful to, serve. **3** alleviate, benefit, cure, ease, improve, lessen, make easier, relieve, remedy. **4** see PREVENT, AVOID. ● *noun* **1** advice, aid, assistance, backing, boost, collaboration, contribution, cooperation, encouragement, friendship, guidance, moral support, patronage, relief, *archaic* or *formal* succour, support. **2** advantage, asset, assistant, avail (*of no avail*), benefit, boon, boost, guide, helper, prop, support. **4** see REMEDY *noun* 2. □ **helper** abetter, *Law* abettor, accessory, accomplice, aid, ally, assistant, associate, collaborator, colleague, confederate, deputy, help, helpmate, *usually derogatory* henchman, partner, right-hand man, second, supporter.

helpful *adjective* giving help, useful. □ **helpfully** *adverb*. **helpfulness** *noun*.

■ (*a helpful person*) accommodating, benevolent, caring, considerate, cooperative, favourable, friendly, helping, kind, neighbourly, obliging, practical, supportive, sympathetic, thoughtful, willing; (*a helpful comment*) advantageous, beneficial, constructive, informative, instructive, profitable, valuable, worthwhile; (*a helpful tool*) convenient, handy, practical, serviceable, useful.

helping *adjective* giving help, helpful. ● *noun* portion of food.

■ *adjective* see HELPFUL. ● *noun* amount, dollop, plateful, portion, ration, serving, share.

helpless *adjective* **1** lacking help, defenceless. **2** unable to act without help. □ **helplessly** *adverb*. **helplessness** *noun*.

■ **1** abandoned, defenceless, deserted, destitute, exposed, in difficulties, marooned, stranded, unprotected, vulnerable. **2** crippled, dependent, disabled, feeble, handicapped, impotent, incapable, infirm, lame, powerless.

helpmate /ˈhelpmeɪt/ *noun* helpful companion or partner (usually spouse).

helter-skelter /heltəˈskeltə/ *adverb* & *adjective* in disorderly haste. ● *noun* spiral slide at funfair.

hem[1] *noun* border of cloth where edge is turned under and sewn down. ● *verb* (**-mm-**) sew edge thus. □ **hem in** confine, restrict. **hemline** lower edge of skirt etc. **hemstitch** (make hem with) ornamental stitch.

hem[2] *interjection: expressing hesitation or calling attention by slight cough.*

hemisphere /ˈhemɪsfɪə/ *noun* **1** half sphere. **2** half earth, esp. as divided by equator or by line passing through poles. **3** each half of brain. □ **hemispherical** /-ˈsfer-/ *adjective*.

hemlock /ˈhemlɒk/ *noun* **1** poisonous plant with small white flowers. **2** poison made from it.

hemp *noun* **1** (in full **Indian hemp**) Asian herbaceous plant. **2** its fibre used for rope etc. **3** narcotic drug made from it.

hempen *adjective* made of hemp.

hen *noun* female bird, esp. of domestic fowl. □ **henbane** poisonous hairy plant. **hen-party** *colloquial* party of women only.

hence *adverb* **1** from now. **2** for this reason. □ **henceforth, henceforward** from this time onwards.

henchman /ˈhentʃmən/ *noun usually derogatory* trusted supporter.

henge *noun* prehistoric circle of wood or stone uprights, as at *Stonehenge*.

henna /ˈhenə/ *noun* **1** tropical shrub. **2** reddish dye made from it and used esp. to colour hair. ● *verb* (**hennaed, hennaing**) dye with henna.

henpeck /ˈhenpek/ *verb* (usually as **henpecked** *adjective*) constantly harass; nag.

henry /ˈhenrɪ/ *noun* (*plural* **-s, -ies**) SI unit of inductance.

hep = HIP[4].

hepatitis /hepəˈtaɪtɪs/ *noun* inflammation of the liver.

hepta- *combining form* seven.

heptagon /ˈheptəgən/ *noun* plane figure with 7 sides and angles. □ **heptagonal** /-ˈtæg-/ *adjective*.

her *pronoun* **1** (as object of verb) the female person or thing in question. **2** *colloquial* she. ● *adjective* of or belonging to her.

herald /ˈher(ə)ld/ *noun* **1** messenger. **2** forerunner. **3** official. ● *verb* **1** proclaim approach of. **2** usher in. □ **heraldic** /-ˈræld-/ *adjective*.

■ *noun* **1** announcer, courier, messenger. **2** forerunner, harbinger, omen, precursor, sign. ● *verb* **1** advertise, announce, foretell, indicate, make known, proclaim, promise, publicize.

heraldry /ˈherəldrɪ/ *noun* (science or art of) armorial bearings.

herb *noun* **1** non-woody seed-bearing plant. **2** plant with leaves, seeds, or flowers used for flavouring, medicine, etc.

herbaceous /hɜ:'beɪʃəs/ *adjective* of or like herbs. □ **herbaceous border** border in garden etc. containing flowering plants.

herbage *noun* vegetation collectively, esp. pasturage.

herbal *adjective* of herbs. ● *noun* book about herbs.

herbalist *noun* **1** dealer in medicinal herbs. **2** writer on herbs.

herbarium /hɜ:'beərɪəm/ *noun* (*plural* **-ria**) collection of dried plants.

herbicide /'hɜ:bɪsaɪd/ *noun* poison used to destroy unwanted vegetation.

herbivore /'hɜ:bɪvɔ:/ *noun* plant-eating animal. □ **herbivorous** /-'bɪvərəs/ *adjective*.

Herculean /hɜ:kjʊ'li:ən/ *adjective* having or requiring great strength or effort.

herd *noun* **1** number of cattle etc. feeding or travelling together. **2** (often as **the herd**) *derogatory* large number of people. ● *verb* **1** (cause to) go in herd. **2** tend. □ **herdsman** keeper of herds.

■ *noun* **2** bunch, crowd, flock, *usually derogatory* horde, mass, mob, pack, rabble, swarm, throng.
● *verb* **1** assemble, collect, congregate, drive, gather, group together, round up. **2** look after, shepherd, tend.

here *adverb* **1** in or to this place. **2** *indicating a person or thing*. **3** at this point. ● *noun* this place. □ **hereabout(s)** somewhere near here. **hereafter 1** (in) future. **2** (in) next world. **hereby** by this means. **herein** *formal* in this place, book, etc. **hereinafter** *formal* from this point on. **2** below (in document). **hereof** *formal* of this. **hereto** *formal* to this. **heretofore** *formal* formerly. **hereupon** after or in consequence of this. **herewith** with this.

hereditary /hɪ'redɪtərɪ/ *adjective* **1** transmitted genetically from one generation to another. **2** descending by inheritance. **3** holding position by inheritance.

■ **1** congenital, constitutional, genetic, inborn, inbred, inherent, inheritable, innate, transmissible, transmittable. **2** ancestral, bequeathed, family, handed down, inherited, passed down, passed on, willed.

heredity /hɪ'redɪtɪ/ *noun* **1** genetic transmission of physical or mental characteristics. **2** these characteristics. **3** genetic constitution.

heresy /'herəsɪ/ *noun* (*plural* **-ies**) **1** *esp. RC Church* religious belief contrary to orthodox doctrine. **2** opinion contrary to what is normally accepted.

■ dissent, nonconformity, rebellion, stepping out of line, unorthodoxy.

heretic /'herətɪk/ *noun* believer in heresy. □ **heretical** /hɪ'ret-/ *adjective*.

■ apostate, dissenter, freethinker, iconoclast, nonconformist, rebel, renegade, unorthodox thinker. □ **heretical** atheistic, dissenting, freethinking, heathen, heterodox, iconoclastic, nonconformist, pagan, rebellious, unorthodox.

heritable /'herɪtəb(ə)l/ *adjective* that can be inherited.

heritage /'herɪtɪdʒ/ *noun* **1** what is or may be inherited. **2** inherited circumstances, benefits, etc. **3** nation's historic buildings, countryside, etc.

■ **1, 2** birthright, inheritance, legacy. **3** culture, history, past, tradition.

hermaphrodite /hɜ:'mæfrədaɪt/ *noun* person, animal, or plant with organs of both sexes. ● *adjective* combining both sexes. □ **hermaphroditic** /-'dɪt-/ *adjective*.

hermetic /hɜ:'metɪk/ *adjective* with an airtight seal. □ **hermetically** *adverb*.

hermit /'hɜ:mɪt/ *noun* person living in solitude. □ **hermit crab** crab which lives in mollusc's cast-off shell.

■ anchoress, anchorite, recluse, solitary.

hermitage *noun* **1** hermit's dwelling. **2** secluded residence.

hernia /'hɜ:nɪə/ *noun* protrusion of part of organ through wall of cavity containing it.

hero /'hɪərəʊ/ *noun* (*plural* **-es**) **1** person admired for courage, outstanding achievements, etc. **2** chief male character in play, story, etc. □ **hero-worship** *noun* idealization of admired person. ● *verb* worship as hero.

■ **1** champion, conqueror, daredevil, exemplar, heroine, ideal, idol, luminary, star, superstar, victor, winner. **2** heroine, lead, protagonist, star.

heroic /hɪ'rəʊɪk/ *adjective* **1** fit for, or like, a hero. **2** very brave. ● *noun* (in *plural*) overdramatic talk or behaviour. □ **heroically** *adverb*.

■ *adjective* adventurous, audacious, bold, brave, chivalrous, courageous, daring, dauntless, *archaic* doughty, epic, fearless, gallant, Herculean, intrepid, lion-hearted, noble, selfless, staunch, steadfast, stout-hearted, superhuman, unafraid, valiant, valorous.

heroin /'herəʊɪn/ *noun* sedative addictive drug prepared from morphine.

heroine /'herəʊɪn/ *noun* **1** female hero. **2** chief female character in play, story, etc.

■ **1** see HERO 1. **2** see HERO 2.

heroism /'herəʊɪz(ə)m/ *noun* heroic conduct.

heron /'herən/ *noun* long-necked long-legged wading bird.

herpes /'hɜ:pi:z/ *noun* virus disease causing blisters.

Herr /heə/ *noun* (*plural* **Herren** /'herən/) *title of German man.*

herring /'herɪŋ/ *noun* (*plural* same or **-s**) N. Atlantic edible fish. □ **herring-bone** stitch or weave of small 'V' shapes making zigzag pattern.

hers /hɜ:z/ *pronoun* the one(s) belonging to her.

herself /hə'self/ *pronoun* **1** *emphatic form of* SHE *or* HER. **2** *reflexive form of* HER.

hertz *noun* (*plural* same) SI unit of frequency (one cycle per second).

he's /hiːz/ **1** he is. **2** he has.

hesitant /ˈhezɪt(ə)nt/ *adjective* hesitating. □ **hesitance** *noun.* **hesitancy** *noun.* **hesitantly** *adverb.*

■ cautious, diffident, dithering, faltering, half-hearted, halting, hesitating, indecisive, irresolute, nervous, shilly-shallying, shy, stammering, stumbling, stuttering, tentative, timid, uncertain, uncommitted, undecided, underconfident, unsure, vacillating, wary, wavering.

hesitate /ˈhezɪteɪt/ *verb* (**-ting**) **1** feel or show indecision; pause. **2** (often + *to do*) be reluctant. **3** falter in speaking. □ **hesitatingly** *adverb.* **hesitation** /-ˈteɪʃ(ə)n/ *noun.*

■ **1** be hesitant, be indecisive, be in two minds, delay, *colloquial* dilly-dally, dither, equivocate, falter, halt, haver, hum and haw, pause, put it off, shilly-shally, temporize, think twice, vacillate, wait, waver. **2** demur, hang back; (*hesitate to*) baulk at, be reluctant to, jib at, shrink from. **3** falter, hum and haw, stammer, stumble, stutter. □ **hesitation** caution, delay, diffidence, dithering, doubt, indecision, irresolution, nervousness, reluctance, shilly-shallying, uncertainty, vacillation, wavering.

hessian /ˈhesɪən/ *noun* strong coarse hemp or jute sacking.

heterodox /ˈhetərəʊdɒks/ *adjective* not orthodox. □ **heterodoxy** *noun.*

heterogeneous /hetərəʊˈdʒiːnɪəs/ *adjective* **1** diverse. **2** varied in content. □ **heterogeneity** /-dʒɪˈniːɪtɪ/ *noun.*

heteromorphic /hetərəʊˈmɔːfɪk/ *adjective* (also **heteromorphous** /-ˈmɔːfəs/) *Biology* of dissimilar forms.

heterosexual /hetərəʊˈsekʃʊəl/ *adjective* feeling or involving sexual attraction to opposite sex. ● *noun* heterosexual person. □ **heterosexuality** /-ˈæl-/ *noun.*

het up *adjective colloquial* overwrought.

heuristic /hjʊəˈrɪstɪk/ *adjective* **1** serving to discover. **2** using trial and error.

hew *verb* (*past participle* **hewn** /hjuːn/ or **hewed**) **1** chop or cut with axe, sword, etc. **2** cut into shape.

hex *verb* **1** practise witchcraft. **2** bewitch. ● *noun* magic spell.

hexa- *combining form* six.

hexagon /ˈheksəgən/ *noun* plane figure with 6 sides and angles. □ **hexagonal** /-ˈsæg-/ *adjective.*

hexagram /ˈheksəgræm/ *noun* 6-pointed star formed by two intersecting equilateral triangles.

hexameter /hekˈsæmɪtə/ *noun* verse line of 6 metrical feet.

hey /heɪ/ *interjection: calling attention or expressing surprise, inquiry, etc.* □ **hey presto!** *conjuror's phrase on completing trick.*

heyday /ˈheɪdeɪ/ *noun* time of greatest success; prime.

HF *abbreviation* high frequency.

HGV *abbreviation* heavy goods vehicle.

HH *abbreviation* **1** Her or His Highness. **2** His Holiness. **3** double-hard (pencil lead).

hi /haɪ/ *interjection: calling attention or as greeting.*

hiatus /haɪˈeɪtəs/ *noun* (*plural* **-tuses**) **1** gap in series etc. **2** break between two vowels coming together but not in same syllable.

hibernate /ˈhaɪbəneɪt/ *verb* (**-ting**) (of animal) spend winter in dormant state. □ **hibernation** *noun.*

Hibernian /haɪˈbɜːnɪən/ *archaic poetical adjective* of Ireland. ● *noun* native of Ireland.

hibiscus /hɪˈbɪskəs/ *noun* (*plural* **-cuses**) cultivated shrub with large brightly coloured flowers.

hiccup /ˈhɪkʌp/ (also **hiccough**) *noun* **1** involuntary audible spasm of respiratory organs. **2** temporary or minor stoppage or difficulty. ● *verb* (**-p-**) make hiccup.

hick *noun esp. US colloquial* yokel.

hickory /ˈhɪkərɪ/ *noun* (*plural* **-ies**) **1** N. American tree related to walnut. **2** its wood.

hid *past of* HIDE[1].

hidden *past participle of* HIDE[1]. ● *adjective* **1** concealed, invisible. **2** obscure in meaning; secret. □ **hidden agenda** secret motivation behind policy etc.; ulterior motive.

■ *adjective* **1** camouflaged, concealed, covered, disguised, enclosed, invisible, obscured, out of sight, private, shrouded, under wraps, undetectable, unnoticeable, unseen, veiled. **2** abstruse, arcane, coded, covert, cryptic, dark, esoteric, implicit, mysterious, mystical, obscure, occult, recondite, secret, unclear.

hide[1] *verb* (**-ding**; *past* **hid**; *past participle* **hidden** /ˈhɪd(ə)n/) **1** put or keep out of sight. **2** conceal oneself. **3** (usually + *from*) conceal (fact). ● *noun* camouflaged shelter for observing wildlife. □ **hide-and-seek** game in which players hide and another searches for them. **hideaway** hiding place, retreat. **hideout** *colloquial* hiding place. **hiding place** place to hide.

■ *verb* **1** blot out, bury, camouflage, cloak, conceal, cover, curtain, disguise, eclipse, enclose, mantle, mask, obscure, put away, put out of sight, screen, secrete, shelter, shroud, veil, wrap up. **2** go to ground, *US colloquial* hole up, lie low, lurk, shut oneself away, take cover. **3** censor, hush up, repress, silence, suppress, withhold. □ **hiding place** den, haven, hide, hideaway, hideout, lair, refuge, retreat, sanctuary.

hide[2] *noun* **1** animal's skin, esp. tanned. **2** *colloquial* human skin. □ **hidebound** rigidly conventional.

■ **1** fur, leather, pelt, skin.

hideous /ˈhɪdɪəs/ *adjective* repulsive, revolting. □ **hideously** *adverb.* **hideousness** *noun.*

■ appalling, *colloquial* beastly, disgusting, dreadful, frightful, ghastly, grim, grisly, grotesque, gruesome, macabre, nauseous, odious, repellent, repulsive, revolting, shocking, sickening, terrible, ugly.

hiding *noun colloquial* thrashing.

hierarchy /'haɪərɑːkɪ/ *noun* (*plural* **-ies**) system of grades of authority ranked one above another. □ **hierarchical** /-'rɑːk-/ *adjective*.

■ grading, ladder, pecking order, ranking, scale, sequence, series, social order, system.

hieroglyph /'haɪərəglɪf/ *noun* picture representing word or syllable, esp. in ancient Egyptian. □ **hieroglyphic** /-'glɪf-/ *adjective*. **hieroglyphics** /-'glɪf-/ *plural noun*.

hi-fi /'haɪfaɪ/ *colloquial adjective* of high fidelity. ● *noun* (*plural* **-s**) equipment for such sound reproduction.

higgledy-piggledy /hɪgəldɪ'pɪgəldɪ/ *adverb & adjective* in disorder.

high /haɪ/ *adjective* 1 of great or specified upward extent. 2 far above ground or sea level. 3 coming above normal level. 4 of exalted rank or position. 5 of superior quality. 6 extreme, intense. 7 (often + *on*) *colloquial* intoxicated by alcohol or drugs. 8 (of price) greater than normal. 9 (of sound) shrill. 10 (of period etc.) at its peak. 11 (of meat etc.) beginning to go bad. ● *noun* 1 high or highest level or number. 2 area of high barometric pressure. 3 *slang* euphoric state, esp. drug-induced. ● *adverb* 1 far up; aloft. 2 in or to high degree. 3 at high price. 4 (of sound) at high pitch. □ **high altar** chief altar in church. **high and dry** 1 stranded without resources. 2 (of ship) out of the water, esp. stranded. **high and mighty** *colloquial* arrogant. **highball** *US* drink of spirits and soda etc. **high-born** of noble birth. **high chair** child's chair with long legs and meal-tray. **High Church** section of Church of England emphasizing ritual, priestly authority, and sacraments. **high-class** of high quality. **high command** army commander-in-chief and associated staff. **High Commission** embassy from one Commonwealth country to another. **High Court** supreme court of justice for civil cases. **highfalutin(g)** *colloquial* pompous, pretentious. **high fidelity** high-quality sound reproduction. **high-flown** extravagant, bombastic. **high-flyer, -flier** person of great potential or ambition. **high frequency** *Radio* 3–30 megahertz. **high-handed** overbearing. **high-handedly** *adverb*. **high-handedness** *noun*. **high heels** shoes with high heels. **high jump** 1 athletic event consisting of jumping over high bar. 2 *colloquial* drastic punishment. **high-level** 1 conducted by people of high rank. 2 (of computer language) close to ordinary language. **high-minded** of firm moral principles. **high-mindedness** *noun*. **high-pitched** 1 (of sound) high. 2 (of roof) steep. **high point** maximum or best state reached. **high-powered** 1 having great power. 2 influential. **high pressure** 1 high degree of activity. 2 atmospheric condition with pressure above average. **high priest** 1 chief priest. 2 head of cult. **high-rise** (of building) having many storeys. **high road** main road. **high school** secondary school. **high sea(s)** seas outside territorial waters. **high-speed** operating or moving at great speed. **high spirits** vivacity; cheerfulness. **high-spirited** *adjective*. **high spot** *colloquial* most enjoyable feature, moment, or experience. **high street** principal shopping street of town. **high tea** early evening meal of tea and cooked food. **high-tech** 1 employing, requiring, or involved in high technology. 2 imitating its style. **high technology** advanced (esp. electronic) technology. **high tension, voltage** electrical potential large enough to injure or damage. **high tide, water** time or level of tide at its peak. **high water mark** level reached at high water.

■ *adjective* 1 elevated, high-rise, lofty, raised, soaring, tall, towering. 4 aristocratic, chief, distinguished, elevated, eminent, exalted, important, leading, powerful, prominent, royal, senior, superior, top, upper. 5 (*a high reputation*) favourable, good, noble, respected, virtuous. 6 exceptional, extreme, great, intense, powerful, strong. 8 dear, excessive, exorbitant, expensive, extravagant, outrageous, *colloquial* steep, unreasonable. 9 acute, high-pitched, penetrating, piercing, sharp, shrill, soprano, squeaky, treble. □ **high and mighty** see ARROGANT. **high-class** see EXCELLENT. **high-handed** see ARROGANT. **high-minded** see MORAL *adjective* 2. **high-powered** see POWERFUL. **high-speed** see FAST¹ *adjective* 1. **high-spirited** see LIVELY 1;3.

highbrow *colloquial noun* person of superior intellect or culture. ● *adjective* 1 intellectual; cultured. 2 cultural.

■ *adjective* 1 academic, bookish, brainy, cultured, intellectual, pretentious, sophisticated. 2 classical, cultural, deep, difficult, educational, improving, serious.

highland /'haɪlənd/ *noun* (usually in *plural*) mountainous country, esp. (**the Highlands**) of N. Scotland. ● *adjective* of highland or Highlands. □ **highlander, Highlander** *noun*.

highlight *noun* 1 moment or detail of vivid interest. 2 bright part of picture. 3 bleached streak in hair. ● *verb* 1 bring into prominence. 2 mark with highlighter.

■ *noun* 1 best moment, climax, high point, high spot, peak.

highlighter *noun* coloured marker pen for emphasizing printed word.

highly *adverb* 1 in high degree. 2 favourably. □ **highly-strung** sensitive, nervous.

highness *noun* 1 state of being high. 2 (**His, Her, Your Highness**) *title of prince, princess, etc.*

highway *noun* 1 public road. 2 main route. □ **Highway Code** official handbook for road-users. **highwayman** *historical* (usually mounted) robber of stagecoaches.

hijack /'haɪdʒæk/ *verb* 1 seize control of (vehicle, aircraft, etc.), esp. to force it to different destination. 2 steal (goods) in transit. ● *noun* hijacking. □ **hijacker** *noun*.

hike *noun* 1 long walk, esp. in country for pleasure. 2 rise in prices etc. ● *verb* (**-king**) go on hike. □ **hiker** *noun*.

hilarious /hɪ'leərɪəs/ *adjective* 1 extremely funny. 2 boisterously merry. □ **hilariously** *adverb*. **hilarity** /-'lær-/ *noun*.

■ **1** cheering, comical, entertaining, funny, humorous, side-splitting, uproarious. **2** boisterous, cheerful, jolly, jovial, lively, merry, mirthful, rollicking.

hill *noun* **1** natural elevation of ground, lower than mountain. **2** heap, mound. **3** slope. □ **hill-billy** *US colloquial often derogatory* person from remote rural area. □ **hilly** *adjective* (**-ier**, **-iest**).

■ **1** *Scottish* brae, elevation, eminence, fell, foothill, height, hillock, hillside, hummock, knoll, mound, *archaic* mount, mountain, peak, prominence, ridge, summit, tor, wold; (*hills*) downs, highlands, uplands. **2** heap, mound, pile, stack. **3** acclivity, ascent, declivity, drop, gradient, incline, ramp, rise, slope.

hillock /'hɪlək/ *noun* small hill, mound.

hillside /'hɪlsaɪd/ *noun* sloping side of hill.

hilt *noun* handle of sword, dagger, etc.

him *pronoun* **1** (as object of verb) the male person or animal in question. **2** (as object of verb) person of unspecified sex. **3** *colloquial* he.

himself /hɪm'self/ *pronoun* **1** *emphatic form of* HE *or* HIM. **2** *reflexive form of* HIM.

hind[1] /haɪnd/ *adjective* at back. □ **hindquarters** rump and hind legs of quadruped. **hindsight** wisdom after event. □ **hindmost** *adjective*.

hind[2] /haɪnd/ *noun* female (esp. red) deer.

hinder[1] /'hɪndə/ *verb* impede; delay.

■ arrest, bar, check, curb, delay, deter, endanger, frustrate, get in the way of, hamper, handicap, hold back, hold up, impede, keep back, limit, obstruct, oppose, prevent, restrain, restrict, retard, sabotage, slow down, slow up, stand in the way of, stop, thwart.

hinder[2] /'haɪndə/ *adjective* rear, hind.

Hindi /'hɪndɪ/ *noun* **1** group of spoken languages in N. India. **2** one of official languages of India; literary form of Hindustani.

hindrance /'hɪndrəns/ *noun* obstruction.

■ bar, barrier, burden, check, curb, deterrent, difficulty, disadvantage, drag, drawback, encumbrance, handicap, hitch, impediment, inconvenience, limitation, obstacle, obstruction, restraint, restriction, snag, stumbling block.

Hindu /'hɪnduː/ *noun* (*plural* **-s**) follower of Hinduism. ● *adjective* of Hindus or Hinduism.

Hinduism /'hɪnduːɪz(ə)m/ *noun* main religious and social system of India, including belief in reincarnation and worship of several gods.

Hindustani /hɪnduˈstɑːnɪ/ *noun* language based on Hindi, used in much of India.

hinge *noun* **1** movable joint on which door, lid, etc. swings. **2** principle on which all depends. ● *verb* (**-ging**) **1** (+ *on*) depend on (event etc.). **2** attach or be attached with hinge.

■ *noun* **1** articulation, joint, pivot. ● *verb* **1** (*hinge on*) depend on, hang on, rest on, turn on.

hinny /'hɪnɪ/ *noun* (*plural* **-ies**) offspring of female donkey and male horse.

hint *noun* **1** indirect suggestion; slight indication. **2** small piece of practical information. **3** faint trace. ● *verb* suggest indirectly. □ **hint at** refer indirectly to.

■ *noun* **1** allusion, clue, idea, implication, indication, inkling, innuendo, insinuation, *colloquial* pointer, sign, suggestion, tip, tip-off. **2** *colloquial* pointer, suggestion, tip, *colloquial* wrinkle. **3** dash, shadow, suggestion, suspicion, taste, tinge, touch, trace, undertone, whiff. ● *verb* imply, indicate, insinuate, intimate, mention, suggest, tip off. □ **hint at** see ALLUDE.

hinterland /'hɪntəlænd/ *noun* district behind that lying along coast etc.

hip[1] *noun* projection of pelvis and upper part of thigh-bone. □ **hip-flask** small flask for spirits.

hip[2] *noun* fruit of rose.

hip[3] *interjection: used to introduce cheer.*

hip[4] *adjective* (also **hep**) (**-pp-**) *slang* trendy, stylish. □ **hip hop**, **hip-hop** subculture combining rap music, graffiti art, and break-dancing.

hippie /'hɪpɪ/ *noun* (also **hippy**) (*plural* **-ies**) *colloquial* person (esp. in 1960s) rejecting convention, typically with long hair, jeans, etc.

hippo /'hɪpəʊ/ *noun* (*plural* **-s**) *colloquial* hippopotamus.

Hippocratic oath /hɪpəˈkrætɪk/ *noun* statement of ethics of medical profession.

hippodrome /'hɪpədrəʊm/ *noun* **1** music-hall, dance hall, etc. **2** *historical* course for chariot races etc.

hippopotamus /hɪpəˈpɒtəməs/ *noun* (*plural* **-muses** or **-mi** /-maɪ/) large African mammal with short legs and thick skin, living by rivers etc.

hippy = HIPPIE.

hipster[1] /'hɪpstə/ *adjective* (of garment) hanging from hips rather than waist. ● *noun* (in *plural*) such trousers.

hipster[2] /'hɪpstə/ *noun slang* hip person.

hire *verb* (**-ring**) obtain use of (thing) or services of (person) for payment. ● *noun* **1** hiring, being hired. **2** payment for this. □ **hire out** grant temporary use of (thing) for payment. **hire purchase** system of purchase by paying in instalments. □ **hirer** *noun*.

■ *verb* book, charter, employ, engage, lease, pay for the use of, rent, sign on, take on. □ **hire out** lease out, let, rent out, take payment for.

hireling /'haɪəlɪŋ/ *noun usually derogatory* person who works for hire.

hirsute /'hɜːsjuːt/ *adjective* hairy.

his /hɪz/ *adjective* of or belonging to him. ● *pronoun* the one(s) belonging to him.

Hispanic /hɪˈspænɪk/ *adjective* **1** of Spain or Spain and Portugal. **2** of Spain and other Spanish-speaking countries. ● *noun* Spanish-speaking person living in US.

hiss /hɪs/ *verb* **1** make sharp sibilant sound, as of letter *s*. **2** express disapproval of thus. **3** whisper urgently or angrily. ● *noun* sharp sibilant sound.

■ *verb* **1** buzz, fizz, rustle, sizzle, swish, whiz.

histamine /'hɪstəmiːn/ *noun* chemical compound in body tissues associated with allergic reactions.

histology /hɪ'stɒlədʒɪ/ *noun* study of tissue structure.

historian /hɪ'stɔːrɪən/ *noun* **1** writer of history. **2** person learned in history.

historic /hɪ'stɒrɪk/ *adjective* **1** famous in history or potentially so. **2** *Grammar* (of tense) used to narrate past events.

■ **1** celebrated, eminent, epoch-making, famed, famous, important, momentous, notable, outstanding, remarkable, renowned, significant, well known.

historical *adjective* **1** of history. **2** belonging to or dealing with the past; not legendary. **3** studying development over period of time. □ **historically** *adverb*.

■ **1, 2** actual, authentic, documented, factual, real, real-life, recorded, true, verifiable.

historicity /hɪstə'rɪsɪtɪ/ *noun* historical genuineness or accuracy.

historiography /hɪstɔːrɪ'ɒɡrəfɪ/ *noun* **1** writing of history. **2** study of this. □ **historiographer** *noun*.

history /'hɪstərɪ/ *noun* (*plural* **-ies**) **1** continuous record of (esp. public) events. **2** study of past events. **3** total accumulation of these. **4** the past. **5** (esp. eventful) past or record.

■ **1** annals, biography, chronicles, diaries, narratives, records. **4** antiquity, bygone days, heritage, historical events, the old days, the past. **5** background, past, record.

histrionic /hɪstrɪ'ɒnɪk/ *adjective* (of behaviour) theatrical, dramatic. ● *noun* (in *plural*) insincere and dramatic behaviour designed to impress.

■ *adjective* dramatic, theatrical.

hit *verb* (**-tt-**; *past & past participle* **hit**) **1** strike with blow or missile. **2** (of moving body) strike with force. **3** affect adversely. **4** (often + *at*) aim blow. **5** propel (ball etc.) with bat etc. **6** achieve, reach. **7** *colloquial* encounter. **8** *colloquial* arrive at. ● *noun* **1** blow. **2** shot that hits target. **3** *colloquial* popular success. □ **hit it off** (often + *with*, *together*) get on well. **hit-and-miss**, **hit-or-miss** random. **hit-and-run 1** (of person) causing damage or injury and leaving immediately. **2** (of accident etc.) caused by such person(s). **hit back** retaliate. **hit man** (*plural* **hit men**) *slang* hired assassin. **hit on (or upon)** find. **hit the road** (*US* **trail**) *slang* depart.

■ *verb* **1** bang, bash, baste, batter, beat, *slang* belt, *slang* biff, birch, box, bludgeon, buffet, bump, butt, cane, clap, clip, *slang* clobber, clout, club, *colloquial* cosh, crack, cudgel, cuff, dash, deliver a blow, drive, elbow, flagellate, flail, flick, flip, flog, hammer, impact, jab, jar, jog, kick, knee, knock,

slang lam, *colloquial* lambaste, lash, nudge, pat, poke, pound, prod, pummel, punch, punt, putt, ram, rap, scourge, slam, slap, slog, *slang* slosh, *US* slug, smack, smash, *esp. archaic* or *literary* smite, *colloquial* sock, spank, stab, strike, stub, swat, *colloquial* swipe, *slang* tan, tap, thrash, thump, thwack, *colloquial* wallop, *colloquial* whack, *colloquial* wham, whip. **2** bang into, bump into, cannon into, collide with, crash into, ram into, run into, slam into, smash into, strike. **3** affect, attack, bring disaster to, check, damage, do harm to, harm, have an effect on, hinder, hurt, make suffer, ruin. ● *noun* **1** blow, collision, impact, stroke. **2** bull's-eye, shot. **3** success, triumph, winner. □ **hit back** see RETALIATE. **hit on** see DISCOVER 1,2.

hitch *verb* **1** fasten with loop etc. **2** move (thing) with jerk. **3** *colloquial* hitchhike. **4** obtain (lift). ● *noun* **1** temporary difficulty, snag. **2** jerk. **3** kind of noose or knot. **4** *colloquial* free ride in vehicle. □ **get hitched** *colloquial* marry. **hitchhike** travel by means of free lifts in passing vehicles. **hitchhiker** *noun*.

hi-tech /'haɪtek/ *adjective* high-tech.

hither /'hɪðə/ *adverb formal* to this place. □ **hitherto** up to now.

HIV *abbreviation* human immunodeficiency virus, either of two viruses causing Aids.

hive *noun* beehive. □ **hive off** (**-ving**) separate from larger group.

hives /haɪvz/ *plural noun* skin eruption, esp. nettle-rash.

HM *abbreviation* Her or His Majesty('s).

HMG *abbreviation* Her or His Majesty's Government.

HMI *abbreviation historical* Her or His Majesty's Inspector (of Schools).

HMS *abbreviation* Her or His Majesty's Ship.

HMSO *abbreviation* Her or His Majesty's Stationery Office.

HNC, HND *abbreviations* Higher National Certificate, Diploma.

ho /həʊ/ *interjection: expressing triumph, derision, etc., or calling attention etc.*

hoard /hɔːd/ *noun* store (esp. of money or food). ● *verb* amass and store. □ **hoarder** *noun*.

■ *noun* accumulation, cache, collection, fund, heap, pile, reserve, stockpile, store, supply, treasure trove. ● *verb* accumulate, amass, assemble, collect, gather, keep, lay in, lay up, mass, pile up, put away, put by, save, stockpile, store, treasure.

hoarding /'hɔːdɪŋ/ *noun* **1** structure erected to carry advertisements. **2** temporary fence round building site etc.

hoar-frost /'hɔːfrɒst/ *noun* frozen water vapour on lawns.

hoarse /hɔːs/ *adjective* **1** (of voice) rough, husky. **2** (of person) having hoarse voice. □ **hoarsely** *adverb*. **hoarseness** *noun*.

■ croaking, grating, gravelly, growling, gruff, harsh, husky, rasping, raucous, rough, throaty.

hoary /'hɔːrɪ/ *adjective* (**-ier, -iest**) **1** white or grey with age. **2** aged. **3** old and trite.

hoax *noun* humorous or malicious deception. ● *verb* deceive with hoax. □ **hoaxer** *noun*.

■ *noun* cheat, *slang* con, confidence trick, deception, fake, fraud, humbug, imposture, joke, *colloquial* leg-pull, practical joke, *colloquial* spoof, swindle, trick. ● *verb* bluff, cheat, *slang* con, *literary* cozen, deceive, defraud, delude, dupe, fool, gull, *colloquial* have on, hoodwink, lead on, mislead, pull (person's) leg, swindle, *colloquial* take for a ride, take in, tease, trick. □ **hoaxer** cheat, con man, deceiver, impostor, joker, practical joker, swindler, trickster.

hob *noun* **1** hotplates etc. on cooker or as separate unit. **2** flat metal shelf at side of fire for heating pans etc. □ **hobnail** heavy-headed nail for boot-sole.

hobble /'hɒb(ə)l/ *verb* (**-ling**) **1** walk lamely, limp. **2** tie together legs of (horse etc.) to keep it from straying. ● *noun* **1** limping gait. **2** rope etc. used to hobble horse.

■ *verb* **1** dodder, falter, limp, shamble, shuffle, stagger, stumble, totter.

hobby /'hɒbɪ/ *noun* (*plural* **-ies**) leisure-time activity pursued for pleasure. □ **hobby horse 1** stick with horse's head, used as toy. **2** favourite subject or idea.

■ amateur interest, avocation, diversion, interest, pastime, pursuit, recreation, relaxation, sideline.

hobgoblin /'hɒbgɒblɪn/ *noun* mischievous imp; bogy.

hobnob /'hɒbnɒb/ *verb* (**-bb-**) (usually + *with*) mix socially or informally.

hobo /'həʊbəʊ/ *noun* (*plural* **-es** or **-s**) *US* wandering worker; tramp.

hock[1] *noun* joint of quadruped's hind leg between knee and fetlock.

hock[2] *noun* German white wine.

hock[3] *verb esp. US colloquial* pawn. □ **in hock 1** in pawn. **2** in debt. **3** in prison.

hockey /'hɒkɪ/ *noun* team game played with ball and hooked sticks.

hocus-pocus /həʊkəs'pəʊkəs/ *noun* trickery.

hod *noun* **1** trough on pole for carrying bricks etc. **2** portable container for coal.

hodgepodge = HOTCHPOTCH.

hoe *noun* long-handled tool for weeding etc. ● *verb* (**hoes, hoed, hoeing**) weed (crops), loosen (soil), or dig up etc. with hoe.

hog *noun* **1** castrated male pig. **2** *colloquial* greedy person. ● *verb* (**-gg-**) *colloquial* take greedily; monopolize. □ **go the whole hog** *colloquial* do thing thoroughly. **hogwash** *colloquial* nonsense. □ **hoggish** *adjective*.

hogmanay /'hɒgmənɪ/ *noun Scottish* New Year's Eve.

hogshead /'hɒgzhed/ *noun* **1** large cask. **2** liquid or dry measure (about 50 gals.).

ho-ho /həʊ'həʊ/ *interjection: representing deep*

jolly laugh or expressing surprise, triumph, or derision.

hoick *verb colloquial* (often + *out*) lift or jerk.

hoi polloi /hɔɪ pə'lɔɪ/ *noun* the masses; ordinary people. [Greek]

hoist *verb* **1** raise or haul up. **2** raise with ropes and pulleys etc. ● *noun* **1** act of hoisting. **2** apparatus for hoisting. □ **hoist with one's own petard** caught by one's own trick etc.

■ *verb* elevate, heave, lift, pull up, raise, winch up. ● *noun* **2** block and tackle, crane, davit, jack, lift, pulley, tackle, winch, windlass.

hoity-toity /hɔɪtɪ'tɔɪtɪ/ *adjective* haughty.

hokum /'həʊkəm/ *noun esp. US slang* **1** sentimental or unreal material in film etc. **2** bunkum, rubbish.

hold[1] /həʊld/ *verb* (*past & past participle* **held**) **1** keep fast; grasp. **2** keep in particular position. **3** maintain (position etc.). **4** contain; have capacity for. **5** possess, have (property, qualifications, job, opinion, etc.). **6** conduct; celebrate. **7** detain. **8** think, believe. **9** not give way. **10** persist; continue; remain valid. **11** reserve. ● *noun* **1** grasp. **2** manner or means of holding. **3** (+ *on, over*) power over. □ **holdall** large soft travelling bag. **hold back 1** impede. **2** keep for oneself. **3** (often + *from*) refrain. **hold down 1** repress. **2** *colloquial* be competent enough to keep (job). **hold forth** speak at length or tediously. **hold on 1** maintain grasp. **2** wait. **3** not ring off. **hold one's ground** not give way. **hold one's tongue** *colloquial* remain silent. **hold out 1** stretch forth (hand etc.). **2** offer (inducement etc.). **3** maintain resistance. **4** (+ *for*) continue to demand. **hold over** postpone. **hold up 1** sustain. **2** display. **3** obstruct. **4** stop and rob by force. **hold-up** *noun* **1** stoppage, delay. **2** robbery by force. **hold with** (usually in negative) *colloquial* approve of.

■ *verb* **1** bear, carry, clasp, clench, cling to, clutch, cradle, embrace, enfold, grasp, grip, hang on to, have, hug, keep, retain, seize, support, take. **3** continue, keep up, maintain, preserve, retain, sustain. **4** contain, enclose, have a capacity of, include. **5** (*hold a job*) have, *colloquial* hold down, keep, occupy, possess; (*hold an opinion*) believe in, have, maintain, subscribe to. **6** celebrate, conduct, convene, have, organize. **7** arrest, confine, coop up, detain, imprison, keep in custody, restrain. **8** see BELIEVE 2. **10** be unaltered, carry on, continue, endure, hold out, keep on, last, persist, remain unchanged, stay. ● *noun* **1** clasp, clutch, grasp, grip. **2** foothold, grip, purchase, toe-hold. **3** (*hold on, hold over*) ascendancy over, authority over, control over, dominance over, influence over, leverage on, mastery over, power over, sway over. □ **hold back 1** see RESTRAIN 1,2. **hold forth** see SPEAK 7, TALK *verb* 1. **hold out 2** see OFFER *verb* 1. **3** PERSIST. **hold over** see DELAY *verb* 1. **hold up 3** see DELAY *verb* 2. **hold-up 2** see ROBBERY (ROB).

hold[2] /həʊld/ *noun* cavity in lower part of ship or aircraft for cargo.

holder *noun* **1** device for holding something. **2**

possessor of title, shares, etc. **3** occupant of office etc.

holding *noun* **1** tenure of land. **2** stocks, property, etc. held. □ **holding company** one formed to hold shares of other companies.

hole *noun* **1** hollow place in solid body. **2** opening in or through something. **3** burrow. **4** *colloquial* small or gloomy place. **5** *colloquial* awkward situation. **6** (in games) cavity or receptacle for ball. **7** *Golf* section of course from tee to hole. □ **hole up (-ling)** *US colloquial* hide oneself. □ **holey** *adjective*.

■ **1** abyss, cave, cavern, cavity, chamber, chasm, crater, dent, depression, excavation, fault, hollow, indentation, niche, pit, pocket, pothole, recess, shaft, tunnel. **2** aperture, breach, break, chink, crack, cut, eyelet, fissure, gap, gash, leak, opening, orifice, perforation, puncture, rip, slit, slot, split, tear, vent. **3** burrow, tunnel, warren.

holiday /ˈhɒlɪdeɪ/ *noun* **1** (often in *plural*) extended period of recreation, esp. spent away from home; break from work or school. **2** day of recreation or festivity. ● *verb* spend holiday. □ **holidaymaker** person on holiday.

■ *noun* **1** break, furlough, half-term, leave, recess, respite, rest, sabbatical, time off, vacation. **2** bank holiday, celebration, day off, feast, festival.

holier-than-thou *adjective colloquial* self-righteous.

holiness /ˈhəʊlɪnɪs/ *noun* **1** being holy or sacred. **2** (**His, Your Holiness**) *title of Pope*.

■ **1** devotion, divinity, faith, godliness, piety, religiosity, sacredness, saintliness, sanctimoniousness, sanctity, venerability.

holism /ˈhəʊlɪz(ə)m/ *noun* (also **wholism**) **1** theory that certain wholes are greater than sum of their parts. **2** *Medicine* treating of whole person rather than symptoms of disease. □ **holistic** /-ˈlɪst-/ *adjective*.

hollandaise sauce /hɒlənˈdeɪz/ *noun* creamy sauce of butter, egg yolks, vinegar, etc.

holler /ˈhɒlə/ *verb & noun US colloquial* shout.

hollow /ˈhɒləʊ/ *adjective* **1** having cavity; not solid. **2** sunken. **3** echoing. **4** empty. **5** hungry. **6** meaningless. **7** insincere. ● *noun* **1** hollow place; hole. **2** valley. ● *verb* (often + *out*) make hollow; excavate. ● *adverb colloquial* completely.

■ *adjective* **2** concave, depressed, dimpled, indented, recessed, sunken. **4** empty, unfilled, vacant, void. **6** empty, futile, insubstantial, meaningless, pointless, valueless, worthless. **7** cynical, false, insincere. ● *noun* **1** bowl, cavity, concavity, crater, dent, depression, dimple, dint, dip, dish, excavation, furrow, hole, indentation, pit, trough. **2** see VALLEY. ● *verb* (*hollow out*) see EXCAVATE 1.

holly /ˈhɒlɪ/ *noun* (*plural* **-ies**) evergreen prickly-leaved shrub with red berries.

hollyhock /ˈhɒlɪhɒk/ *noun* tall plant with showy flowers.

holm /həʊm/ *noun* (in full **holm-oak**) evergreen oak.

holocaust /ˈhɒləkɔːst/ *noun* **1** wholesale destruction or slaughter. **2** (**the Holocaust**) mass murder of Jews by Nazis 1939–45.

■ **1** annihilation, bloodbath, carnage, conflagration, destruction, devastation, extermination, firestorm, genocide, inferno, massacre, pogrom, slaughter.

hologram /ˈhɒləgræm/ *noun* photographic pattern having 3-dimensional effect.

holograph /ˈhɒləgrɑːf/ *adjective* wholly in handwriting of person named as author. ● *noun* such document.

holography /həˈlɒgrəfɪ/ *noun* study or production of holograms.

holster /ˈhəʊlstə/ *noun* leather case for pistol or revolver on belt etc.

holy /ˈhəʊlɪ/ *adjective* (**-ier, -iest**) **1** morally and spiritually excellent. **2** belonging or devoted to God. **3** consecrated, sacred. □ **Holy Ghost** Holy Spirit. **Holy Land** area between River Jordan and Mediterranean. **holy of holies 1** inner chamber of Jewish temple. **2** thing regarded as most sacred. **holy orders** those of bishop, priest, and deacon. **Holy Saturday** day before Easter. **Holy See** papacy; papal court. **Holy Spirit** Third Person of Trinity. **Holy Week** that preceding Easter. **Holy Writ** Bible.

■ **1, 2** devoted, devout, faithful, God-fearing, godly, immaculate, pietistic, pious, prayerful, pure, religious, reverent, reverential, righteous, saintly, sanctimonious, sinless, unsullied. **3** blessed, consecrated, dedicated, divine, hallowed, heavenly, revered, sacred, sacrosanct, sanctified, venerable.

homage /ˈhɒmɪdʒ/ *noun* **1** tribute. **2** expression of reverence.

Homburg /ˈhɒmbɜːg/ *noun* man's felt hat with narrow curled brim and lengthwise dent in crown.

home *noun* **1** place where one lives; residence. **2** (esp. good or bad) family circumstances. **3** native land. **4** institution caring for people or animals. **5** place where thing originates, is kept, is most common, etc. **6** (in games) finishing line in race. **7** (in games) goal. **8** (in games) home match or win etc. ● *adjective* **1** of or connected with home. **2** carried on or done at home. **3** not foreign. **4** played etc. on team's own ground. ● *adverb* **1** to or at home. **2** to point aimed at. ● *verb* (**-ming**) **1** (of pigeon) return home. **2** (often + *on, in on*) (of missile etc.) be guided to destination. □ **at home 1** in one's house or native land. **2** at ease. **3** well informed. **4** available to callers. **at-home** *noun* social reception in person's home. **home-brew** beer etc. brewed at home. **Home Counties** those lying round London. **home economics** study of household management. **homeland 1** native land. **2** any of several areas formerly set aside for Black South Africans. **Home Office** British government department concerned with immigration, law and order, etc. **home rule** self-government. **Home Secretary** minister in charge of Home Office. **homesick** depressed by absence from home. **homesickness** such depres-

sion. **homestead** house with outbuildings; farm.
homework lessons to be done by schoolchild at
home. □ **homeward** *adjective & adverb*. **home-wards** *adverb*.

> ■ *noun* **1** abode, accommodation, base, domicile,
> dwelling, dwelling place, habitation, house,
> household, lodging, quarters, residence. **3**
> birthplace, fatherland, homeland, mother country,
> native land.

homeless *adjective* having no home. ● *noun*
(after *the*) homeless people.

homely *adjective* (**-ier, -iest**) **1** plain. **2** unpretentious. **3** informal, cosy. **4** *US* unattractive.
□ **homeliness** *noun*.

> ■ **2, 3** comfortable, congenial, cosy, easygoing,
> familiar, friendly, informal, intimate, modest,
> natural, relaxed, simple, unaffected, unassuming,
> unpretentious, unsophisticated.

homeopathy etc. *US* = HOMOEOPATHY etc.

Homeric /həʊˈmerɪk/ *adjective* **1** of or in style of
the ancient Greek poet Homer. **2** of Bronze Age
Greece.

homey *adjective* (**-mier, -miest**) suggesting
home; cosy.

homicide /ˈhɒmɪsaɪd/ *noun* **1** killing of person
by another. **2** person who kills another. □ **homicidal** /-ˈsaɪd-/ *adjective*.

homily /ˈhɒmɪlɪ/ *noun* (*plural* **-ies**) **1** short
sermon. **2** moralizing lecture. □ **homiletic** /-ˈlet-/
adjective.

homing *adjective* **1** (of pigeon) trained to fly
home. **2** (of device) for guiding to target etc.

hominid /ˈhɒmɪnɪd/ *adjective* of mammal family
of existing and fossil man. ● *noun* member of
this.

hominoid /ˈhɒmɪnɔɪd/ *adjective* like a human.
● *noun* animal resembling human.

homoeopathy /həʊmɪˈɒpəθɪ/ *noun* (*US*
homeopathy) treatment of disease by drugs that
in healthy person would produce symptoms of
the disease. □ **homoeopath** /ˈhəʊmɪəʊpæθ/
noun. **homoeopathic** /-ˈpæθ-/ *adjective*.

homogeneous /hɒməˈdʒiːnɪəs/ *adjective* **1** of
same kind or nature. **2** having parts of same kind;
uniform. □ **homogeneity** /-dʒɪˈniːɪtɪ/ *noun*.
homogeneously *adverb*.

> **USAGE** *Homogeneous* is often confused with
> *homogenous* (and pronounced /həˈmɒdʒənəs/,
> with the stress on the *-mog-*), but that is a term
> in biology meaning 'similar owing to common
> descent'.

> ■ **1** akin, alike, comparable, compatible, identical,
> indistinguishable, matching, similar. **2** consistent,
> uniform, unvarying.

homogenize /həˈmɒdʒmaɪz/ *verb* (also **-ise**)
(**-zing** or **-sing**) **1** make homogeneous. **2** treat
(milk) so that cream does not separate.

homologous /həˈmɒləgəs/ *adjective* **1** having
same relation, relative position, etc. **2** corresponding.

homology /həˈmɒlədʒɪ/ *noun* homologous relation; correspondence.

homonym /ˈhɒmənɪm/ *noun* word spelt or pronounced like another but of different meaning.

homophobia /hɒməˈfəʊbɪə/ *noun* hatred or
fear of homosexuals. □ **homophobe** /ˈhɒm-/
noun. **homophobic** *adjective*.

homophone /ˈhɒməfəʊn/ *noun* word pronounced like another but having different
meaning, e.g. *beach, beech*.

Homo sapiens /həʊməʊ ˈsæpɪenz/ *noun*
modern humans regarded as a species. [Latin]

homosexual /hɒməˈseksjʊəl/ *adjective* feeling
or involving sexual attraction to people of same
sex. ● *noun* homosexual person. □ **homosexuality** /-ˈæl-/ *noun*.

> ■ *adjective* colloquial camp, gay, (*of women*)
> lesbian, *offensive slang* queer.

Hon. *abbreviation* **1** Honorary. **2** Honourable.

hone *noun* whetstone, esp. for razors. ● *verb*
(**-ning**) sharpen (as) on hone.

honest /ˈɒnɪst/ *adjective* **1** not lying, cheating, or
stealing; fair. **2** sincere. **3** fairly earned. ● *adverb*
colloquial genuinely, really. □ **honestly** *adverb*.
> ■ *adjective* **1** conscientious, equitable, fair, good,
> honourable, impartial, incorruptible, just,
> law-abiding, moral, *colloquial* on the level,
> principled, pure, reliable, respectable, scrupulous,
> straight, trustworthy, *archaic* or *jocular* trusty,
> truthful, unbiased, unprejudiced, upright, *formal*
> veracious, virtuous. **2** blunt, candid, direct,
> forthright, frank, genuine, *colloquial* on the level,
> open, outspoken, plain, sincere, straight,
> straightforward, unequivocal. **3** above board,
> legal, legitimate, square (*deal*).

honesty /ˈɒnɪstɪ/ *noun* **1** being honest, truthfulness. **2** openness, sincerity. **3** plant with
purple or white flowers and flat round pods.
> ■ **1** fairness, goodness, honour, integrity, morality,
> probity, rectitude, reliability, scrupulousness,
> sense of justice, trustworthiness, truthfulness,
> uprightness, veracity, virtue. **2** bluntness,
> candour, directness, frankness, openness,
> outspokenness, plainness, sincerity,
> straightforwardness.

honey /ˈhʌnɪ/ *noun* (*plural* **-s**) **1** sweet sticky
yellowish fluid made by bees from nectar. **2**
colour of this. **3** sweetness. **4** darling.

honeycomb *noun* **1** beeswax structure of hexagonal cells for honey and eggs. **2** pattern
arranged hexagonally. ● *verb* **1** fill with cavities.
2 mark with honeycomb pattern.

honeydew *noun* **1** sweet substance excreted by
aphids. **2** variety of melon.

honeyed *adjective* **1** sweet. **2** sweet-sounding.

honeymoon *noun* **1** holiday of newly married
couple. **2** initial period of enthusiasm or goodwill. ● *verb* spend honeymoon.

honeysuckle *noun* climbing shrub with fragrant flowers.

honk *noun* **1** sound of car horn. **2** cry of wild goose. ● *verb* (cause to) make honk.

honky-tonk /ˈhɒŋkɪtɒŋk/ *noun colloquial* ragtime piano music.

honor *US* = HONOUR.

honorable *US* = HONOURABLE.

honorarium /ɒnəˈreərɪəm/ *noun* (*plural* **-s** or **-ria**) voluntary payment for professional services.

honorary /ˈɒnərərɪ/ *adjective* **1** conferred as honour. **2** unpaid.

■ **2** unpaid, unsalaried.

honorific /ɒnəˈrɪfɪk/ *adjective* **1** conferring honour. **2** implying respect.

honour /ˈɒnə/ (*US* **honor**) *noun* **1** high respect; public regard. **2** adherence to what is right. **3** nobleness of mind. **4** thing conferred as distinction (esp. official award for bravery or achievement). **5** privilege. **6** (**His, Her, Your Honour**) *title of judge etc.* **7** person or thing that brings honour. **8** chastity. **9** reputation for this. **10** (in *plural*) specialized degree course or special distinction in exam. **11** (in *plural*) (in card games) 4 or 5 highest-ranking cards. **12** *Golf* right of driving off first. ● *verb* **1** respect highly. **2** confer honour on. **3** accept or pay (bill, cheque) when due. □ **do the honours** perform duties of host etc.

■ *noun* **1** acclaim, credit, distinction, esteem, fame, good name, *colloquial* kudos, regard, renown, reputation, repute, respect, reverence, veneration. **2, 3** decency, dignity, honesty, integrity, loyalty, morality, nobility, principle, rectitude, righteousness, sincerity, uprightness, virtue. **4** award, commendation, decoration, distinction. **5** distinction, pleasure, privilege. ● *verb* **1** admire, esteem, respect, revere, reverence, value, venerate. **2** acclaim, applaud, celebrate, commemorate, commend, dignify, give credit to, glorify, pay homage to, pay respects to, pay tribute to, praise, remember, salute, sing the praises of, worship.

honourable *adjective* (*US* **honorable**) **1** deserving, bringing, or showing honour. **2** (**Honourable**) *courtesy title of MPs, certain officials, and children of certain ranks of the nobility.* □ **honourably** *adverb*.

■ **1** admirable, chivalrous, creditable, decent, estimable, ethical, fair, good, high-minded, honest, irreproachable, just, law-abiding, loyal, moral, noble, principled, proper, reputable, respectable, respected, righteous, sincere, trustworthy, *archaic* or *jocular* trusty, upright, venerable, virtuous, worthy.

hooch /huːtʃ/ *noun US colloquial* alcoholic spirits, esp. inferior or illicit.

hood[1] /hʊd/ *noun* **1** covering for head and neck, esp. as part of garment. **2** separate hoodlike garment. **3** folding top of car etc. **4** *US* bonnet of car etc. **5** protective cover. ● *verb* cover with hood. □ **hooded** *adjective*.

hood[2] /hʊd/ *noun US slang* gangster, gunman.

-hood /hʊd/ *suffix* forming nouns indicating: **1** condition or state. **2** collection or group.

hoodlum /ˈhuːdləm/ *noun* **1** hooligan. **2** gangster.

hoodoo /ˈhuːduː/ *noun US* **1** bad luck. **2** thing or person that brings this.

hoodwink *verb* deceive, delude.

■ bluff, cheat, *slang* con, *literary* cozen, deceive, defraud, delude, dupe, fool, gull, *colloquial* have on, hoax, lead on, mislead, swindle, *colloquial* take for a ride, take in, trick.

hoof /huːf/ *noun* (*plural* **-s** or **hooves** /huːvz/) horny part of foot of horse etc. □ **hoof it** *slang* go on foot.

hook /hʊk/ *noun* **1** bent piece of metal etc. for catching hold or for hanging things on. **2** curved cutting instrument. **3** hook-shaped thing. **4** hooking stroke. **5** *Boxing* short swinging blow. ● *verb* **1** grasp, secure, or fasten, with hook. **2** catch with hook. **3** (in sports) send (ball) in curving or deviating path. **4** *Rugby* secure (ball) in scrum with foot. □ **hook and eye** small hook and loop as fastener. **hook, line, and sinker** completely. **hook-up** connection, esp. of broadcasting equipment. **hookworm** worm infesting intestines of humans and animals. **off the hook 1** *colloquial* no longer in difficulty or trouble. **2** (of telephone receiver) not on its rest.

■ *noun* **1** barb, fastener, hanger, holder, peg. ● *verb* **1** see FASTEN 1. **2** capture, catch, take.

hookah /ˈhʊkə/ *noun* tobacco pipe with long tube passing through water to cool smoke.

hooked *adjective* **1** hook-shaped. **2** (often + *on*) *slang* addicted or captivated.

hooker *noun* **1** *Rugby* player in front row of scrum who tries to hook ball. **2** *slang* prostitute.

hooligan /ˈhuːlɪɡən/ *noun* young ruffian. □ **hooliganism** *noun*.

■ bully, delinquent, hoodlum, lout, mugger, rough, ruffian, *colloquial* tearaway, thug, tough, troublemaker, vandal, *slang* yob.

hoop /huːp/ *noun* **1** circular band of metal, wood, etc., esp. as part of framework. **2** wooden etc. circle bowled by child or used by circus performer etc. **3** arch through which balls are hit in croquet. ● *verb* bind with hoop(s). □ **hoopla** game with rings thrown to encircle prizes.

■ *noun* **1, 2** band, circle, girdle, loop, ring.

hoopoe /ˈhuːpuː/ *noun* bird with variegated plumage and fanlike crest.

hooray = HURRAH.

hoot /huːt/ *noun* **1** owl's cry. **2** sound of car's horn etc. **3** shout of derision etc. **4** *colloquial* (cause of) laughter. **5** (also **two hoots**) *slang* anything; in the slightest. ● *verb* **1** utter hoot(s). **2** greet or drive away with hoots. **3** sound (horn).

hooter *noun* **1** thing that hoots, esp. car's horn or siren. **2** *slang* nose.

Hoover /ˈhuːvə/ *noun proprietary term* vacuum cleaner. ● *verb* (**hoover**) clean or (+ *up*) suck up with vacuum cleaner.

hooves *plural* of HOOF.

hop[1] *verb* (**-pp-**) **1** (of bird, frog, etc.) spring with all feet at once. **2** (of person) jump on one foot. **3** move or go quickly; leap. ● *noun* **1** hopping movement. **2** *colloquial* dance. **3** short journey, esp. flight. □ **hop in, out** *colloquial* get into or out of car etc. **hopscotch** child's game of hopping over squares marked on ground.

■ *verb* **1** bound, jump, leap, spring, vault.

hop[2] *noun* **1** climbing plant with bitter cones used to flavour beer etc. **2** (in *plural*) these cones.

hope *noun* **1** expectation and desire. **2** person or thing giving cause for hope; ground of hope. **3** what is hoped for. ● *verb* (**-ping**) **1** feel hope. **2** expect and desire.

■ *noun* **1, 3** ambition, aspiration, craving, daydream, desire, dream, expectation, longing, wish, yearning. **2** assumption, conviction, faith, likelihood, optimism, promise, prospect. ● *verb* *disputed* anticipate, trust, wish; (*hope for*) aspire to, count on, desire, expect, look forward to, want.

hopeful *adjective* **1** feeling hope. **2** inspiring hope; promising.

■ **1** assured, confident, expectant, optimistic, positive, sanguine. **2** auspicious, cheering, encouraging, favourable, heartening, promising, propitious, reassuring.

hopefully *adverb* **1** in a hopeful way. **2** *disputed* it is to be hoped.

USAGE The use of *hopefully* to mean 'it is to be hoped' is common, but it is considered incorrect by some people.

■ **1** confidently, expectantly, optimistically, with hope.

hopeless *adjective* **1** feeling no hope. **2** admitting no hope. **3** inadequate, incompetent. □ **hopelessly** *adverb*. **hopelessness** *noun*.

■ **1** defeatist, demoralized, despairing, desperate, disconsolate, fatalistic, negative, pessimistic, resigned, wretched. **2** daunting, depressing, impossible, incurable, irremediable, irreparable, irreversible. **3** feeble, inadequate, incompetent, inefficient, poor, *colloquial* useless, weak, worthless.

hopper *noun* **1** funnel-like device for feeding grain into mill etc. **2** hopping insect.

horde *noun* *usually derogatory* large group, gang.

■ band, crowd, drove, gang, mob, swarm, throng, tribe.

horehound /ˈhɔːhaʊnd/ *noun* herb with aromatic bitter juice.

horizon /həˈraɪz(ə)n/ *noun* **1** line at which earth and sky appear to meet. **2** limit of mental perception, interest, etc.

horizontal /ˌhɒrɪˈzɒnt(ə)l/ *adjective* parallel to plane of horizon; level, flat. ● *noun* horizontal line, plane, etc. □ **horizontally** *adverb*.

■ *adjective* even, flat, level, lying down, prone, prostrate, supine.

hormone /ˈhɔːməʊn/ *noun* **1** substance produced by body and transported in tissue fluids to stimulate cells or tissues to growth etc. **2** similar synthetic substance. □ **hormone replacement therapy** treatment with hormones to relieve menopausal symptoms. □ **hormonal** /-ˈməʊn-/ *adjective*.

horn *noun* **1** hard outgrowth, often curved and pointed, on head of animal. **2** hornlike projection. **3** substance of horns. **4** musical wind instrument originally made of horn, now usually of brass. **5** instrument giving warning. □ **hornbeam** tough-wooded hedgerow tree. **hornbill** bird with hornlike excrescence on bill. **horn of plenty** cornucopia. **horn-rimmed** (of spectacles) having rims of horn or similar substance. □ **horned** *adjective*.

hornblende /ˈhɔːnblend/ *noun* dark brown etc. mineral constituent of granite etc.

hornet /ˈhɔːnɪt/ *noun* large species of wasp.

hornpipe *noun* (music for) lively dance associated esp. with sailors.

horny *adjective* (**-ier, -iest**) **1** of or like horn. **2** hard. **3** *slang* sexually excited. □ **horniness** *noun*.

horology /həˈrɒlədʒɪ/ *noun* clock-making. □ **horological** /ˌhɒrəˈlɒdʒ-/ *adjective*.

horoscope /ˈhɒrəskəʊp/ *noun* prediction of person's future based on position of planets at his or her birth.

horrendous /həˈrendəs/ *adjective* horrifying. □ **horrendously** *adverb*.

horrible /ˈhɒrɪb(ə)l/ *adjective* **1** causing horror. **2** *colloquial* unpleasant. □ **horribly** *adverb*.

■ **1** see HORRIFIC. **2** *colloquial* abominable, *colloquial* awful, *colloquial* beastly, despicable, detestable, disagreeable, dreadful, ghastly, hateful, hellish, *colloquial* horrid, loathsome, *colloquial* lousy, nasty, objectionable, obnoxious, odious, offensive, revolting, *colloquial* terrible, unkind, unpleasant.

horrid /ˈhɒrɪd/ *adjective* **1** horrible. **2** *colloquial* unpleasant.

horrific /həˈrɪfɪk/ *adjective* horrifying. □ **horrifically** *adverb*.

■ appalling, atrocious, blood-curdling, disgusting, dreadful, frightening, frightful, grisly, gruesome, hair-raising, harrowing, hideous, horrendous, horrible, horrifying, nauseating, shocking, sickening, spine-chilling, unacceptable, unnerving, *colloquial* unthinkable.

horrify /ˈhɒrɪfaɪ/ *verb* (**-ies, -ied**) arouse horror in; shock. □ **horrifying** *adjective*.

■ alarm, appal, disgust, frighten, harrow, nauseate, outrage, scare, shock, sicken, stun, terrify, unnerve. □ **horrifying** see HORRIFIC.

horror /ˈhɒrə/ *noun* **1** intense fear. **2** (often + *of*) deep dislike or loathing. **3** *colloquial* intense dismay. **4** horrifying thing. **5** quality of being horrifying. ● *adjective* (of films etc.) designed to arouse feelings of horror. □ **horror-struck** (also **horror-stricken**) horrified.

■ *noun* **1** alarm, apprehension, dread, fear, panic, terror. **2** abhorrence, antipathy, aversion, detestation, disgust, dislike, distaste, dread, hatred, loathing, repugnance, revulsion. **3** see DISMAY. **5** *colloquial* awfulness, frightfulness, ghastliness, gruesomeness, hideousness.

hors d'oeuvre /ɔː'dɜːvr/ *noun* appetizer served at start of meal.

horse *noun* **1** large 4-legged hoofed mammal with mane, used for riding etc. **2** adult male horse. **3** vaulting-block. **4** supporting frame. ● *verb* (**-sing**) (+ *around*) fool about. □ **horsebox** closed vehicle for transporting horse(s). **horse brass** brass ornament originally for horse's harness. **horse chestnut 1** tree with conical clusters of flowers. **2** its dark brown fruit. **horse-drawn** pulled by horse(s). **horsefly** biting insect troublesome to horses. **Horse Guards** cavalry brigade of British household troops. **horsehair** (padding etc. of) hair from mane or tail of horse. **horseman** (skilled) rider on horseback. **horsemanship** skill in riding. **horseplay** boisterous play. **horsepower** (*plural* same) unit of rate of doing work. **horse race** race between horses with riders. **horse racing** sport of racing horses. **horseradish** plant with pungent root used to make sauce. **horse sense** *colloquial* plain common sense. **horseshoe 1** U-shaped iron shoe for horse. **2** thing of this shape. **horsetail** (plant resembling) horse's tail. **horsewhip** ● *noun* whip for horse. ● *verb* beat (person) with this. **horsewoman** (skilled) woman rider on horseback.

■ □ **horseman, horsewoman** cavalryman, equestrian, jockey, rider.

horsy *adjective* (**-ier, -iest**) **1** of or like horse. **2** concerned with horses.

horticulture /'hɔːtɪkʌltʃə/ *noun* art of gardening. □ **horticultural** /-'kʌlt-/ *adjective*. **horticulturist** /-'kʌlt-/ *noun*.

hosanna /həʊ'zænə/ *noun & interjection* cry of adoration.

hose /həʊz/ *noun* **1** (also **hose-pipe**) flexible tube for conveying liquids. **2** (treated as *plural*) stockings and socks collectively. **3** *historical* breeches. ● *verb* (**-sing**) (often + *down*) water, spray, or drench with hose.

hosier /'həʊzɪə/ *noun* dealer in stockings and socks. □ **hosiery** *noun*.

hospice /'hɒspɪs/ *noun* **1** home for (esp. terminally) ill or destitute people. **2** travellers' lodging kept by religious order etc.

hospitable /hɒs'pɪtəb(ə)l/ *adjective* giving hospitality. □ **hospitably** *adverb*.

■ cordial, courteous, friendly, generous, gracious, receptive, sociable, welcoming.

hospital /'hɒspɪt(ə)l/ *noun* **1** institution providing medical and surgical treatment and nursing for ill and injured people. **2** *historical* hospice.

■ **1** clinic, convalescent home, dispensary, health centre, hospice, infirmary, medical centre, nursing home, sanatorium, sickbay.

hospitality /hɒspɪ'tælɪtɪ/ *noun* friendly and generous reception of guests or strangers.

■ (*thank for hospitality*) cordiality, courtesy, friendliness, generosity, sociability, warmth, welcome; (*offer hospitality*) accommodation, catering, entertainment.

hospitalize /'hɒspɪtəlaɪz/ *verb* (also **-ise**) (**-zing** or **-sing**) send or admit to hospital. □ **hospitalization** *noun*.

host[1] /həʊst/ *noun* (usually + *of*) large number of people or things.

■ army, crowd, mob, multitude, swarm, throng, troop.

host[2] /həʊst/ *noun* **1** person who entertains another as guest. **2** compère. **3** animal or plant having parasite. **4** recipient of transplanted organ. **5** landlord of inn. ● *verb* be host to (person) or of (event).

■ *noun* **2** see COMPÈRE.

host[3] /həʊst/ *noun* (usually **the Host**) bread consecrated in Eucharist.

hostage /'hɒstɪdʒ/ *noun* person seized or held as security for fulfilment of a condition.

■ captive, pawn, prisoner, surety.

hostel /'hɒst(ə)l/ *noun* **1** house of residence for students etc. **2** youth hostel.

hostelling *noun* (*US* **hosteling**) practice of staying in youth hostels. □ **hosteller** *noun*.

hostelry *noun* (*plural* **-ies**) *archaic* inn.

hostess /'həʊstɪs/ *noun* woman who entertains guests, or customers at nightclub.

hostile /'hɒstaɪl/ *adjective* **1** of enemy. **2** (often + *to*) unfriendly, opposed.

■ **1** attacking, belligerent, combative, militant, opposing, rival, warring. **2** adverse, aggressive, angry, antagonistic, antipathetic, averse, bellicose, confrontational, contrary, ill-disposed, inhospitable, inimical, malevolent, opposed, opposing, oppressive, pugnacious, resentful, unfavourable, unfriendly, unhelpful, unpropitious, unsympathetic, unwelcoming, warlike.

hostility /hɒ'stɪlɪtɪ/ *noun* (*plural* **-ies**) **1** being hostile; enmity. **2** warfare. **3** (in *plural*) acts of war.

■ **1** aggression, animosity, animus, antagonism, bad feeling, belligerence, confrontation, dissension, enmity, estrangement, friction, hatred, incompatibility, malevolence, malice, opposition, pugnacity, rancour, resentment, strife, unfriendliness. **3** (*hostilities*) see WAR *noun* 1.

hot *adjective* (**-tt-**) **1** having high temperature; very warm. **2** causing sensation of or feeling heat. **3** pungent. **4** excited, ardent. **5** (often + *on, for*) eager. **6** (of news) fresh. **7** skilful, formidable. **8** (+ *on*) knowledgeable about. **9** *slang* (of stolen goods) difficult to dispose of. ● *verb* (**-tt-**) **1** (usually + *up*) *colloquial* make or become hot. **2** become more active, exciting, or dangerous. □ **hot air** *slang* empty or boastful talk. **hot-air balloon** balloon containing air heated by burners, causing it to rise. **hotbed 1** (+ *of*) environment conducive to (vice etc.). **2** bed of earth heated by fermenting manure. **hot cross bun** bun marked with cross, eaten on Good Friday. **hot dog** *colloquial* hot sausage in bread roll. **hotfoot** in eager haste. **hothead** impetuous person. **hot-headed** impetuous. **hot-headedness** *noun*. **hothouse 1** heated (mainly glass) building for growing plants. **2** environment conducive to rapid growth. **hotline** direct telephone line. **hotplate** heated metal plate for cooking food or keeping it hot. **hotpot** dish of stewed meat and vegetables. **hot rod** vehicle modified for extra power and speed. **hot seat** *slang* **1** awkward or responsible position. **2** electric chair. **hot-tempered** becoming angry easily. **hot under the collar** angry, embarrassed, or resentful. **hot water** *colloquial* difficulty, trouble. **hot-water bottle** container filled with hot water to warm bed etc. □ **hotly** *adverb*. **hotness** *noun*.

■ *adjective* **1** *colloquial* baking, blistering, *colloquial* boiling, burning, fiery, flaming, oppressive, piping hot, red-hot, roasting, scalding, *colloquial* scorching, searing, sizzling, steamy, stifling, sultry, summery, sweltering, thermal, torrid, tropical, warm, white-hot. **3** acrid, biting, gingery, peppery, piquant, pungent, spicy, strong. **4** ardent, eager, emotional, excited, fervent, fervid, feverish, fierce, heated, hot-headed, impatient, impetuous, inflamed, intense, passionate, violent. □ **hot-tempered** see BAD-TEMPERED (BAD). **hot under the collar** see ANGRY 1.

hotchpotch /ˈhɒtʃpɒtʃ/ *noun* (also **hodgepodge** /ˈhɒdʒpɒdʒ/) confused mixture, jumble, esp. of ideas.

hotel /həʊˈtel/ *noun* (usually licensed) place providing meals and accommodation for payment.

■ guest house, hostel, *archaic* hostelry, inn, lodge, motel, pension.

hotelier /həʊˈteliə/ *noun* hotel-keeper.

houmous = HUMMUS.

hound /haʊnd/ *noun* **1** dog used in hunting. **2** *colloquial* despicable man. ● *verb* harass or pursue.

■ *noun* **1** see DOG *noun* 1. ● *verb* annoy, badger, chase, harass, harry, hunt, nag, persecute, pester, pursue.

hour /aʊə/ *noun* **1** twenty-fourth part of day and night; 60 minutes. **2** time of day; point in time. **3** (in *plural* with preceding numerals in form 18.00, 20.30, etc.) this number of hours and minutes past midnight on the 24-hour clock. **4** period set aside for some purpose. **5** (in *plural*) working or open period. **6** short time. **7** time for action etc. **8** (**the hour**) each time o'clock of a whole number of hours. □ **hourglass** two connected glass bulbs containing sand that takes an hour to pass from upper to lower bulb. □ **hourly** *adjective & adverb*.

houri /ˈhʊəri/ *noun* (*plural* **-s**) beautiful young woman in Muslim paradise.

house *noun* /haʊs/ (*plural* /ˈhaʊzɪz/) **1** building for human habitation. **2** building for special purpose or for keeping animals or goods. **3** (buildings of) religious community. **4** section of boarding school etc. **5** division of school for games etc. **6** royal family; dynasty. **7** (premises of) firm or institution. **8** (building for) legislative etc. assembly. **9** audience or performance in theatre etc. ● *verb* /haʊz/ (**-sing**) **1** provide house for. **2** store. **3** enclose or encase (part etc.). **4** fix in socket etc. □ **house arrest** detention in one's own house. **houseboat** boat equipped for living in. **housebound** confined to one's house through illness etc. **housebreaker** burglar. **housebreaking** burglary. **housefly** common fly. **househusband** man who does wife's traditional duties. **housekeeper** woman managing affairs of house. **housekeeping 1** management of house. **2** money for this. **3** record-keeping etc. **houseman** resident junior doctor of hospital. **house martin** bird which builds nests on house walls etc. **housemaster, housemistress** teacher in charge of house in boarding school. **house music** pop music with synthesized drums and bass and fast beat. **House of Commons** elected chamber of Parliament. **House of Lords** chamber of Parliament that is mainly hereditary. **house plant** one grown indoors. **house-proud** attentive to care etc. of home. **house-trained** (of domestic animal) trained to be clean in house. **house-warming** party celebrating move to new house. **housewife** woman whose chief occupation is managing household. **housewifely** *adjective*. **housework** regular cleaning and cooking etc. in home. **Lower House** larger and usually elected body in legislature, esp. the House of Commons. **Upper House** higher house in legislature, esp. House of Lords.

■ *noun* **1** abode, domicile, dwelling, dwelling place, habitation, home, homestead, household, place, residence. ● *verb* **1** accommodate, billet, board, domicile, harbour, keep, lodge, place, put up, quarter, shelter, take in.

housecoat /ˈhaʊskəʊt/ *noun* woman's long loose garment for informal wear.

household *noun* **1** occupants of house. **2** house and its affairs. □ **household name** well-known name. **household troops** those nominally guarding sovereign. **household word** well-known saying or name.

■ **1** family, ménage. **2** establishment, home, set-up.

householder *noun* **1** person who owns or rents house. **2** head of household.

housing /ˈhaʊzɪŋ/ *noun* **1** (provision of) houses. **2** protective casing. □ **housing estate** residential area planned as a unit.

hove *past* of HEAVE.

hovel /ˈhɒv(ə)l/ *noun* small miserable dwelling.

■ *colloquial* dump, *colloquial* hole, hut, shack, shanty.

hover /ˈhɒvə/ *verb* **1** (of bird etc.) remain in one place in air. **2** (often + *about*, *round*) linger. **3** be undecided.

■ **1** be suspended, drift, float, flutter, fly, hang, poise. **2** dally, hang about, hang around, linger, loiter, wait about. **3** be indecisive, dither, hesitate, pause, vacillate, waver.

hovercraft *noun* (*plural* same) vehicle moving on air-cushion provided by downward blast.

hoverport *noun* terminal for hovercraft.

how /haʊ/ *interrogative & relative adverb* **1** by what means; in what way. **2** in what condition. **3** to what extent. □ **however 1** nevertheless. **2** in whatever way. **3** to whatever extent.

howdah /'haʊdə/ *noun* (usually canopied) seat for riding elephant or camel.

howitzer /'haʊɪtsə/ *noun* short gun firing shells at high elevation.

howl /haʊl/ *noun* **1** long doleful cry of dog etc. **2** prolonged wailing noise. **3** loud cry of pain, rage, derision, or laughter. ● *verb* **1** make howl. **2** weep loudly. **3** utter with howl.

■ *verb* bay, bellow, cry, roar, shout, ululate, wail, yowl.

howler *noun colloquial* glaring mistake.

hoy *interjection: used to call attention.*

hoyden /'hɔɪd(ə)n/ *noun* boisterous girl.

HP *abbreviation* **1** hire purchase. **2** (also **hp**) horsepower.

HQ *abbreviation* headquarters.

hr. *abbreviation* hour.

HRH *abbreviation* Her or His Royal Highness.

HRT *abbreviation* hormone replacement therapy.

HT *abbreviation* high tension.

hub *noun* **1** central part of wheel, rotating on or with axle. **2** centre of interest, activity, etc.

■ **2** axis, centre, core, focal point, focus, heart, middle, nucleus, pivot.

hubble-bubble /'hʌb(ə)lbʌb(ə)l/ *noun* **1** simple hookah. **2** confused sound or talk.

hubbub /'hʌbʌb/ *noun* **1** confused noise of talking. **2** disturbance.

hubby /'hʌbɪ/ *noun* (*plural* **-ies**) *colloquial* husband.

hubris /'hju:brɪs/ *noun* arrogant pride, presumption.

huckleberry /'hʌkəlbərɪ/ *noun* (*plural* **-ies**) **1** low N. American shrub. **2** its fruit.

huckster /'hʌkstə/ *noun* **1** hawker. **2** aggressive salesman. ● *verb* **1** haggle. **2** hawk (goods).

huddle /'hʌd(ə)l/ *verb* (**-ling**) **1** (often + *up*, *together*) crowd together. **2** (often + *up*, *together*) nestle closely. **3** (often + *up*) curl one's body up. ● *noun* **1** confused mass. **2** *colloquial* secret conference.

■ *verb* **1** cluster, converge, crowd, flock, gather, group, heap, herd, jam, pile, press, squeeze, swarm, throng. **2** curl up, nestle, snuggle. ● *noun* **1** see GROUP *noun* 1.

hue *noun* colour, tint.

■ cast, colour, complexion, dye, nuance, shade, tincture, tinge, tint, tone.

hue and cry *noun* loud outcry.
■ see OUTCRY.

huff *noun* fit of petulance. ● *verb* **1** blow air, steam, etc. **2** (esp. **huff and puff**) bluster. **3** remove (opponent's man) as forfeit in draughts. □ **huffy** *adjective* (**-ier, -iest**).

hug *verb* (**-gg-**) **1** squeeze tightly in one's arms, esp. with affection. **2** keep close to. **3** fit tightly around. ● *noun* close clasp.

■ *verb* **1** clasp, cling to, cuddle, embrace, enfold, fold in one's arms, hold close, nurse, squeeze.

huge /hju:dʒ/ *adjective* very large or great.

■ astronomical, big, colossal, elephantine, enormous, gargantuan, giant, gigantic, *colloquial* hulking, immeasurable, immense, imposing, impressive, *colloquial* jumbo, majestic, mammoth, massive, mighty, monster, monstrous, monumental, mountainous, prodigious, stupendous, titanic, towering, *colloquial* tremendous, unlimited, vast, weighty, *colloquial* whopping.

hugely *adverb* extremely, very much.

hugger-mugger /'hʌgəmʌgə/ *adjective* & *adverb* **1** in secret. **2** in confusion.

Huguenot /'hju:gənəʊ/ *noun historical* French Protestant.

hula /'hu:lə/ *noun* (also **hula-hula**) Polynesian women's dance. □ **hula hoop** large hoop spun round the body.

hulk *noun* **1** body of dismantled ship. **2** *colloquial* large clumsy-looking person or thing.

■ **1** body, carcass, frame, hull, shell, wreck. **2** lout, lump, oaf.

hulking *adjective colloquial* bulky, clumsy.

■ awkward, big, bulky, clumsy, cumbersome, heavy, hefty, large, massive, ungainly, unwieldy.

hull[1] *noun* body of ship etc.
■ body, framework, structure.

hull[2] *noun* outer covering of fruit. ● *verb* remove hulls of.

hullabaloo /hʌləbə'lu:/ *noun* uproar.

hullo = HELLO.

hum *verb* (**-mm-**) **1** make low continuous sound like bee or spinning top. **2** sing with closed lips. **3** make slight inarticulate sound. **4** *colloquial* be active. **5** *colloquial* smell unpleasantly. ● *noun* humming sound. □ **hum and haw** hesitate, esp. in speaking. **hummingbird** small tropical bird whose wings hum.

■ *verb* **1** buzz, drone, murmur, purr, sing, vibrate, whirr. □ **hum and haw** see HESITATE 1;3.

human /'hju:mən/ *adjective* **1** of or belonging to species *Homo sapiens*. **2** consisting of human beings. **3** having characteristics of humankind, as being weak, fallible, mortal, etc.; not divine. **4** having better characteristics of humankind, as being kind, sympathetic, etc. ● *noun* (*plural* **-s**) human being. ◻ **human being** man, woman, or child. **human chain** line of people for passing things along etc. **humankind** human beings collectively. **human rights** those held to belong to all people. **human shield** person(s) placed in line of fire to discourage attack.

■ *adjective* **1** anthropoid, hominid, hominoid. **3** fallible, mortal, vulnerable, weak. **4** compassionate, feeling, humane, kind, rational, reasonable, sensible, sensitive, sympathetic, tender, thoughtful. ◻ **human being** child, human, individual, man, mortal, person, woman; (*human beings*) folk, humanity, humankind, mankind, people.

humane /hjuːˈmeɪn/ *adjective* **1** benevolent, compassionate. **2** inflicting minimum pain. **3** (of studies) tending to civilize. ◻ **humanely** *adverb*. **humaneness** *noun*.

■ **1** altruistic, benevolent, charitable, civilized, compassionate, feeling, forgiving, good, human, humanitarian, kind, kind-hearted, loving, magnanimous, merciful, philanthropic, pitying, sympathetic, tender, understanding, unselfish, warm-hearted.

humanism /ˈhjuːmənɪz(ə)m/ *noun* **1** non-religious philosophy based on liberal human values. **2** (often **Humanism**) literary culture, esp. in Renaissance. ◻ **humanist** *noun*. **humanistic** /-ˈnɪst-/ *adjective*.

humanitarian /hjuːmænɪˈteərɪən/ *noun* person who seeks to promote human welfare. ● *adjective* of humanitarians. ◻ **humanitarianism** *noun*.

humanity /hjuːˈmænɪtɪ/ *noun* (*plural* **-ies**) **1** human race. **2** human nature. **3** humaneness, benevolence. **4** (usually in *plural*) subjects concerned with human culture.

humanize *verb* (also **-ise**) (**-zing** or **-sing**) make human or humane. ◻ **humanization** *noun*.

humanly *adverb* **1** within human capabilities. **2** in a human way.

humble /ˈhʌmb(ə)l/ *adjective* (**-r**, **-st**) **1** having or showing low estimate of one's importance. **2** lowly, modest. ● *verb* (**-ling**) **1** make humble. **2** lower rank of. ◻ **eat humble pie** apologize humbly; accept humiliation. ◻ **humbleness** *noun*. **humbly** *adverb*.

■ *adjective* **1** deferential, docile, meek, modest, obsequious, polite, reserved, respectful, self-effacing, servile, submissive, subservient, sycophantic, unassertive, unassuming, unostentatious, unpresuming, unpretentious. **2** base, commonplace, ignoble, inferior, insignificant, low, lowly, mean, modest, obscure, ordinary, plebeian, poor, simple, undistinguished, unimportant, unprepossessing, unremarkable. ● *verb* **1** see HUMILIATE.

humbug /ˈhʌmbʌɡ/ *noun* **1** deception, hypocrisy. **2** impostor. **3** striped peppermint-flavoured boiled sweet. ● *verb* (**-gg-**) **1** be impostor. **2** hoax.

humdinger /ˈhʌmdɪŋə/ *noun slang* remarkable person or thing.

humdrum /ˈhʌmdrʌm/ *adjective* dull, commonplace.

humerus /ˈhjuːmərəs/ *noun* (*plural* **-ri** /-raɪ/) bone of upper arm.

humid /ˈhjuːmɪd/ *adjective* warm and damp.

■ clammy, damp, moist, muggy, steamy, sticky, sultry, sweaty.

humidifier /hjuːˈmɪdɪfaɪə/ *noun* device for keeping atmosphere moist.

humidify /hjuːˈmɪdɪfaɪ/ *verb* (**-ies**, **-ied**) make (air etc.) humid.

humidity /hjuːˈmɪdɪtɪ/ *noun* (*plural* **-ies**) **1** dampness. **2** degree of moisture, esp. in atmosphere.

humiliate /hjuːˈmɪlɪeɪt/ *verb* (**-ting**) injure dignity or self-respect of. ◻ **humiliating** *adjective*. **humiliation** *noun*.

■ abase, abash, break, break (person's) spirit, bring down, chagrin, chasten, crush, deflate, degrade, demean, discredit, disgrace, embarrass, humble, make ashamed, make eat humble pie, make feel small, mortify, *colloquial* put down, shame, show up. ◻ **humiliating** see SHAMEFUL. **humiliation** abasement, chagrin, degradation, discredit, disgrace, dishonour, embarrassment, ignominy, indignity, loss of face, mortification, obloquy, shame.

humility /hjuːˈmɪlɪtɪ/ *noun* humbleness; meekness.

■ deference, humbleness, lowliness, meekness, modesty, self-abasement, self-effacement, servility, shyness, unpretentiousness.

hummock /ˈhʌmək/ *noun* hillock, hump.

hummus /ˈhʊmʊs/ *noun* (also **houmous**) dip of chickpeas, sesame paste, lemon juice, and garlic.

humor *US* = HUMOUR.

humorist /ˈhjuːmərɪst/ *noun* humorous writer, talker, or actor.

humorous /ˈhjuːmərəs/ *adjective* showing humour, comic. ◻ **humorously** *adverb*.

■ absurd, amusing, comic, comical, diverting, droll, entertaining, facetious, farcical, funny, hilarious, *colloquial* hysterical, ironic, jocose, jocular, *colloquial* killing, laughable, merry, *colloquial* priceless, risible, sarcastic, sardonic, satirical, side-splitting, slapstick, uproarious, waggish, whimsical, witty, zany.

humour /ˈhjuːmə/ (*US* **humor**) *noun* **1** quality of being amusing. **2** expression of humour in literature etc. **3** (in full **sense of humour**) ability to perceive or express humour. **4** state of mind; mood. **5** each of 4 fluids formerly held to determine physical and mental qualities. ● *verb* gratify or indulge (person, taste, etc.). ◻ **humourless** *adjective*.

■ *noun* **1** absurdity, comedy, drollness, facetiousness, incongruity, jocularity, waggishness, wittiness. **2** badinage, banter, comedy, irony, jesting, jokes, joking, merriment, quips, raillery, repartee, satire, wit, witticism. **3** fun, sense of fun. **4** disposition, frame of mind, mood, spirits, state of mind, temper.

hump *noun* **1** rounded lump, esp. on back. **2** rounded raised mass of earth etc. **3** (**the hump**) *slang* fit of depression or annoyance. ● *verb* **1** (often + *about*) *colloquial* lift or carry with difficulty. **2** make hump-shaped. □ **over the hump** past the most difficult stage.

■ *noun* **1** bulge, bump, curve, growth, hunch, knob, lump, node, projection, protrusion, protuberance, swelling, tumescence. **2** barrow, hillock, hummock, mound, rise, tumulus. ● *verb* **1** drag, heave, hoist, lift, lug, raise, shoulder. **2** arch, bend, crook, curl, curve, hunch, raise.

humpback /ˈhʌm(p)bæk/ *noun* back deformed by hump; person having this. □ **humpback bridge** small bridge with steep ascent and descent. □ **humpbacked** *adjective*.

humph /həmf/ *interjection & noun* inarticulate sound of dissatisfaction etc.

humus /ˈhjuːməs/ *noun* organic constituent of soil formed by decomposition of plants.

hunch *verb* bend or arch into a hump. ● *noun* **1** hump. **2** intuitive feeling.

■ *verb* arch, bend, crook, curl, curve, huddle, hump, raise, shrug. ● *noun* **1** see HUMP *noun* 1. **2** feeling, guess, idea, impression, inkling, intuition, premonition, presentiment, suspicion.

hunchback /ˈhʌn(t)ʃbæk/ *noun* = HUMPBACK. □ **hunchbacked** *adjective*.

hundred /ˈhʌndrəd/ *adjective & noun* (*plural* same in first sense) **1** ten times ten. **2** *historical* subdivision of county. **3** (**hundreds**) *colloquial* large number. □ **hundreds and thousands** tiny coloured sweets. **hundredweight** (*plural* same or **-s**) 112 lb (50.80 kg); *US* 100 lb (45.4 kg). □ **hundredth** *adjective & noun*.

hundredfold *adjective & adverb* a hundred times as much or many.

hung *past & past participle* of HANG. □ **hung-over** suffering from hangover. **hung parliament** parliament in which no party has clear majority.

Hungarian /hʌŋˈgeəriən/ *noun* native, national, or language of Hungary. ● *adjective* of Hungary or its people or language.

hunger /ˈhʌŋgə/ *noun* **1** lack of food. **2** discomfort or exhaustion caused by this. **3** (often + *for*, *after*) strong desire. ● *verb* **1** (often + *for*, *after*) crave, desire. **2** feel hunger. □ **hunger strike** refusal of food as protest.

■ *noun* **1, 2** appetite, deprivation, emptiness, *archaic* famine, hungriness, malnutrition, ravenousness, starvation, voracity. **3** see DESIRE *noun* 1. ● *verb* **1** (*hunger for*) see DESIRE *verb* 1.

hungry /ˈhʌŋgrɪ/ *adjective* (**-ier**, **-iest**) **1** feeling, showing, or inducing hunger. **2** craving. □ **hungrily** *adverb*. **hungriness** *noun*.

■ **1** emaciated, *colloquial* empty, *colloquial* famished, greedy, hollow, *colloquial* peckish, ravenous, *colloquial* starved, *colloquial* starving, underfed, undernourished, voracious. **2** aching, avid, covetous, craving, eager, longing, thirsty, yearning.

hunk *noun* **1** large piece cut off. **2** *colloquial* sexually attractive man.

hunt *verb* **1** pursue wild animals for food or sport. **2** (of animal) pursue prey. **3** (+ *after*, *for*) search. **4** (as **hunted** *adjective*) (of look) frightened. ● *noun* **1** hunting. **2** hunting district or society. □ **huntsman**, **huntswoman 1** hunter. **2** person in charge of hounds. □ **hunting** *noun*.

■ *verb* **1, 2** chase, course, dog, ferret, hound, poach, pursue, stalk, track, trail. **3** (*hunt for*, *after*) ferret out, look for, search for, seek. ● *noun* **1** chase, hunting, pursuit, quest, search. □ **hunting** blood sports, coursing, poaching, stalking, trapping.

hunter *noun* (*feminine* **huntress**) **1** person who hunts. **2** horse ridden for hunting.

■ **1** huntsman, huntswoman, predator, stalker, trapper.

hurdle /ˈhɜːd(ə)l/ *noun* **1** frame to be jumped over by athlete in race. **2** (in *plural*) hurdle race. **3** obstacle. **4** portable rectangular frame used as temporary fence. ● *verb* (**-ling**) run in hurdle race. □ **hurdler** *noun*.

■ *noun* **1** barricade, jump. **3** bar, barrier, complication, difficulty, handicap, hindrance, impediment, obstacle, obstruction, problem, restraint, snag, stumbling block. **4** barricade, barrier, fence.

hurdy-gurdy /hɜːdɪˈgɜːdɪ/ *noun* (*plural* **-ies**) **1** droning musical instrument played by turning handle. **2** *colloquial* barrel organ.

hurl *verb* throw violently. ● *noun* violent throw.

■ *verb* cast, catapult, *colloquial* chuck, dash, fire, fling, *colloquial* heave, launch, let fly, pelt, pitch, project, propel, send, shy, *colloquial* sling, throw, toss.

hurley /ˈhɜːlɪ/ *noun* (*plural* **-s**) (also **hurling**) (stick used in) Irish game resembling hockey.

hurly-burly /hɜːlɪˈbɜːlɪ/ *noun* boisterous activity; commotion.

hurrah /huˈrɑː/ (also **hooray**, **hurray** /huˈreɪ/) *interjection*: expressing joy or approval. ● *noun* utterance of 'hurrah'.

hurricane /ˈhʌrɪkən/ *noun* storm with violent wind, esp. W. Indian cyclone. □ **hurricane lamp** lamp with flame protected from wind.

■ cyclone, storm, tempest, tornado, typhoon, whirlwind.

hurry /ˈhʌrɪ/ *noun* **1** great haste. **2** (with negative or in questions) need for haste. **3** eagerness. ● *verb* (**-ies**, **-ied**) **1** move or act hastily. **2** cause to move or act hastily. **3** (as **hurried** *adjective*) hasty; done rapidly. □ **hurriedly** *adverb*.

■ *noun* **1** see HASTE 2. **3** see EAGERNESS. ● *verb* **1** *slang* belt, *colloquial* buck up, chase, dash, dispatch, fly, *colloquial* get a move on, hasten, hurtle, hustle, make haste, move quickly, rush, *slang* shift, speed up, *colloquial* step on it, work faster. **2** accelerate, expedite, hasten, press on with, quicken, rush, speed up. **3** (**hurried**) see HASTY 1–2.

hurt *verb* (*past & past participle* **hurt**) **1** cause pain, injury, or distress to. **2** suffer pain. **3** cause damage to. ● *noun* **1** injury. **2** harm. □ **hurtful** *adjective*. **hurtfully** *adverb*.
■ *verb* **1** (*hurt physically*) abuse, afflict, agonize, bruise, cripple, cut, disable, injure, maim, misuse, mutilate, torture, wound; (*hurt mentally*) affect, be hurtful to, cut to the quick, depress, distress, grieve, humiliate, insult, offend, pain, sadden, torment, upset. **2** ache, be painful, burn, pinch, smart, sting, throb, tingle. **3** damage, harm, impair, mar, ruin, sabotage, spoil. □ **hurtful** biting, cruel, cutting, damaging, derogatory, detrimental, distressing, hard to bear, harmful, injurious, malicious, nasty, painful, sarcastic, scathing, spiteful, uncharitable, unkind, upsetting, vicious, wounding.

hurtle /'hɜ:t(ə)l/ *verb* (**-ling**) **1** move or hurl rapidly or noisily. **2** come with crash.
■ **1** charge, chase, dash, fly, plunge, race, rush, shoot, speed, *colloquial* tear.

husband /'hʌzbənd/ *noun* married man in relation to his wife. ● *verb* use (resources) economically.

husbandry *noun* **1** farming. **2** management of resources.

hush *verb* make, become, or be silent. ● *interjection: calling for silence.* ● *noun* silence. □ **hush-hush** *colloquial* highly secret. **hush money** *slang* sum paid to ensure discretion. **hush up** suppress (fact).
■ *verb* see SILENCE *verb*. ● *interjection* be quiet! be silent! *colloquial* hold one's tongue! *colloquial* pipe down! *colloquial* shut up! ● *noun* see SILENCE *noun* 1. □ **hush up** see SUPPRESS 2.

husk *noun* dry outer covering of fruit or seed. ● *verb* remove husk from.

husky[1] /'hʌskɪ/ *adjective* (**-ier, -iest**) **1** dry in the throat, hoarse. **2** strong, hefty. □ **huskily** *adverb*.

husky[2] /'hʌskɪ/ *noun* (*plural* **-ies**) powerful dog used for pulling sledges.

hussar /hʊ'zɑː/ *noun* light-cavalry soldier.

hussy /'hʌsɪ/ *noun* (*plural* **-ies**) **1** pert girl. **2** promiscuous woman.

hustings /'hʌstɪŋz/ *noun* election proceedings.

hustle /'hʌs(ə)l/ *verb* (**-ling**) **1** bustle; jostle. **2** (+ *into, out of*, etc.) force, hurry. **3** *slang* solicit business. ● *noun* act or instance of hustling. □ **hustler** *noun*.
■ *verb* **1** bustle, hasten, hurry, jostle, push, rush, scamper, scurry, shove. **2** coerce, compel, force, hurry, push, shove, thrust.

hut *noun* small simple or crude house or shelter.
■ cabin, den, hovel, lean-to, shack, shanty, shed, shelter.

hutch *noun* box or cage for rabbits etc.

hyacinth /'haɪəsɪnθ/ *noun* bulbous plant with bell-shaped flowers.

hybrid /'haɪbrɪd/ *noun* **1** offspring of two animals or plants of different species etc. **2** thing of mixed origins. ● *adjective* **1** bred as hybrid. **2** heteroge-neous. □ **hybridism** *noun*. **hybridization** *noun*. **hybridize** *verb* (also **-ise**) (**-zing** or **-sing**).
■ *noun* **1** cross, cross-breed, mongrel. **2** amalgam, combination, composite, compound, mixture.

hydra /'haɪdrə/ *noun* **1** freshwater polyp. **2** something hard to destroy.

hydrangea /haɪ'dreɪndʒə/ *noun* shrub with globular clusters of white, blue, or pink flowers.

hydrant /'haɪdrənt/ *noun* outlet for drawing water from main.

hydrate /'haɪdreɪt/ *noun* chemical compound of water with another compound etc. ● *verb* (**-ting**) (cause to) combine with water. □ **hydration** *noun*.

hydraulic /haɪ'drɔːlɪk/ *adjective* **1** (of water etc.) conveyed through pipes etc. **2** operated by movement of liquid. □ **hydraulically** *adverb*.

hydraulics *plural noun* (usually treated as *singular*) science of conveyance of liquids through pipes etc., esp. as motive power.

hydro /'haɪdrəʊ/ *noun* (*plural* **-s**) *colloquial* **1** hotel etc. originally providing hydropathic treatment. **2** hydroelectric powerplant.

hydro- *combining form* **1** water. **2** combined with hydrogen.

hydrocarbon /haɪdrəʊ'kɑːbən/ *noun* compound of hydrogen and carbon.

hydrocephalus /haɪdrə'sefələs/ *noun* accumulated fluid in brain, esp. in young children. □ **hydrocephalic** /-sɪ'fælɪk/ *adjective*

hydrochloric acid /haɪdrə'klɒrɪk/ *noun* solution of hydrogen chloride in water.

hydrodynamics /haɪdrəʊdaɪ'næmɪks/ *plural noun* (usually treated as *singular*) science of forces acting on or exerted by liquids. □ **hydrodynamic** *adjective*.

hydroelectric /haɪdrəʊ'lektrɪk/ *adjective* **1** generating electricity by water-power. **2** (of electricity) so generated. □ **hydroelectricity** /-'trɪs-/ *noun*.

hydrofoil /'haɪdrəfɔɪl/ *noun* **1** boat equipped with planes for raising hull out of water at speed. **2** such a plane.

hydrogen /'haɪdrədʒ(ə)n/ *noun* light colourless odourless gas combining with oxygen to form water. □ **hydrogen bomb** immensely powerful bomb utilizing explosive fusion of hydrogen nuclei. **hydrogen peroxide** see PEROXIDE 1.

hydrogenate /haɪ'drɒdʒɪneɪt/ *verb* (**-ting**) charge with or cause to combine with hydrogen. □ **hydrogenation** *noun*.

hydrography /haɪ'drɒgrəfɪ/ *noun* science of surveying and charting seas, lakes, rivers, etc. □ **hydrographer** *noun*. **hydrographic** /-drə'græf-/ *adjective*.

hydrology /haɪ'drɒlədʒɪ/ *noun* science of relationship between water and land.

hydrolyse /'haɪdrəlaɪz/ *verb* (**-sing**) (*US* **-lyze**, **-zing**) decompose by hydrolysis.

hydrolysis /haɪˈdrɒlɪsɪs/ *noun* decomposition by chemical reaction with water.

hydrometer /haɪˈdrɒmɪtə/ *noun* instrument for measuring density of liquids.

hydropathy /haɪˈdrɒpəθɪ/ *noun* (medically unorthodox) treatment of disease by water. □ **hydropathic** /-drəˈpæθ-/ *adjective*.

hydrophobia /haɪdrəˈfəʊbɪə/ *noun* **1** aversion to water, esp. as symptom of rabies in humans. **2** rabies. □ **hydrophobic** *adjective*.

hydroplane /ˈhaɪdrəpleɪn/ *noun* **1** light fast motor boat. **2** finlike device enabling submarine to rise or fall.

hydroponics /haɪdrəˈpɒnɪks/ *noun* growing plants without soil, in sand, water, etc. with added nutrients.

hydrostatic /haɪdrəˈstætɪk/ *adjective* of the equilibrium of liquids and the pressure exerted by liquids at rest.

hydrostatics *plural noun* (usually treated as *singular*) study of hydrostatic properties of liquids.

hydrotherapy /haɪdrəˈθerəpɪ/ *noun* use of water, esp. swimming, in treatment of disease.

hydrous /ˈhaɪdrəs/ *adjective* containing water.

hyena /haɪˈiːnə/ *noun* doglike flesh-eating mammal.

hygiene /ˈhaɪdʒiːn/ *noun* **1** conditions or practices conducive to maintaining health; cleanliness. **2** sanitary science. □ **hygienic** /-ˈdʒiːn-/ *adjective*. **hygienically** /-ˈdʒiːn-/ *adverb*. **hygienist** *noun*.

■ **1** cleanliness, health, sanitariness, sanitation, wholesomeness. □ **hygienic** aseptic, clean, disinfected, germ-free, healthy, pure, salubrious, sanitary, sterile, sterilized, unpolluted, wholesome.

hygrometer /haɪˈgrɒmɪtə/ *noun* instrument for measuring humidity of air etc.

hygroscopic /haɪgrəˈskɒpɪk/ *adjective* tending to absorb moisture from air.

hymen /ˈhaɪmen/ *noun* membrane at opening of vagina, usually broken at first sexual intercourse.

hymenopterous /haɪmeˈnɒptərəs/ *adjective* of order of insects with 4 membranous wings, including bees and wasps.

hymn /hɪm/ *noun* song of esp. Christian praise. ● *verb* praise or celebrate in hymns.

hymnal /ˈhɪmn(ə)l/ *noun* book of hymns.

hymnology /hɪmˈnɒlədʒɪ/ *noun* composition or study of hymns. □ **hymnologist** *noun*.

hyoscine /ˈhaɪəsiːn/ *noun* alkaloid used to prevent motion sickness etc.

hype /haɪp/ *slang noun* intensive promotion of product etc. ● *verb* (**-ping**) promote with hype. □ **hyped up** excited.

hyper /ˈhaɪpə/ *adjective slang* hyperactive.

hyper- /ˈhaɪpə/ *prefix* **1** over, above. **2** too.

hyperactive /haɪpərˈæktɪv/ *adjective* abnormally active.

hyperbola /haɪˈpɜːbələ/ *noun* (*plural* **-s** or **-lae** /-liː/) curve produced when cone is cut by plane making larger angle with base than side of cone makes. □ **hyperbolic** /-pəˈbɒl-/ *adjective*.

hyperbole /haɪˈpɜːbəlɪ/ *noun* exaggeration, esp. for effect. □ **hyperbolical** /-ˈbɒl-/ *adjective*.

hyperglycaemia /haɪpəglaɪˈsiːmɪə/ *noun* (*US* **hyperglycemia**) excess of glucose in bloodstream.

hypermarket /ˈhaɪpəmɑːkɪt/ *noun* very large supermarket.

hypermedia /ˈhaɪpəmiːdɪə/ *noun* provision of several media (audio, video, etc.) on one computer system.

hypersensitive /haɪpəˈsensɪtɪv/ *adjective* excessively sensitive. □ **hypersensitivity** /-ˈtɪv-/ *noun*.

hypersonic /haɪpəˈsɒnɪk/ *adjective* of speeds more than 5 times that of sound.

hypertension /haɪpəˈtenʃ(ə)n/ *noun* **1** abnormally high blood pressure. **2** extreme tension.

hypertext /ˈhaɪpətekst/ *noun* provision of several texts on one computer system.

hyperthermia /haɪpəˈθɜːmɪə/ *noun* abnormally high body-temperature.

hyperthyroidism /haɪpəˈθaɪrɔɪdɪz(ə)m/ *noun* overactivity of thyroid gland.

hyperventilation /haɪpəventɪˈleɪʃ(ə)n/ *noun* abnormally rapid breathing. □ **hyperventilate** *verb* (**-ting**).

hyphen /ˈhaɪf(ə)n/ *noun* punctuation mark (-) used to join or divide words (see panel). ● *verb* hyphenate.

hyphenate /ˈhaɪfəneɪt/ *verb* (**-ting**) join or divide with hyphen. □ **hyphenation** *noun*.

hypnosis /hɪpˈnəʊsɪs/ *noun* **1** state like sleep in which subject acts only on external suggestion. **2** artificially induced sleep.

hypnotherapy /hɪpnəʊˈθerəpɪ/ *noun* treatment of mental disorders by hypnosis.

hypnotic /hɪpˈnɒtɪk/ *adjective* **1** of or causing hypnosis. **2** sleep-inducing. ● *noun* hypnotic drug or influence. □ **hypnotically** *adverb*.

■ *adjective* **1** fascinating, irresistible, magnetic, mesmerizing, spellbinding. **2** narcotic, sleep-inducing, soothing, soporific.

hypnotism /ˈhɪpnətɪz(ə)m/ *noun* study or practice of hypnosis. □ **hypnotist** *noun*.

hypnotize /ˈhɪpnətaɪz/ *verb* (also **-ise**) (**-zing** or **-sing**) **1** produce hypnosis in. **2** fascinate.

■ **2** bewitch, captivate, cast a spell over, dominate, enchant, entrance, fascinate, gain power over, magnetize, mesmerize, spellbind, stupefy.

hypo /ˈhaɪpəʊ/ *noun* sodium thiosulphate, used as photographic fixer.

hypo- /'haɪpəʊ/ *prefix* **1** under. **2** below normal. **3** slightly.

hypochondria /haɪpə'kɒndrɪə/ *noun* abnormal anxiety about one's health.

hypochondriac /haɪpə'kɒndrɪæk/ *noun* person given to hypochondria. ● *adjective* of hypochondria.

hypocrisy /hɪ'pɒkrɪsɪ/ *noun* (*plural* **-ies**) simulation of virtue; insincerity.

■ cant, deceit, deception, double-dealing, double standards, double-talk, double-think, duplicity, falsity, humbug, inconsistency, insincerity.

hypocrite /'hɪpəkrɪt/ *noun* person guilty of hypocrisy. □ **hypocritical** /-'krɪt-/ *adjective*. **hypocritically** /-'krɪt-/ *adverb*.

■ □ hypocritical deceptive, double-dealing, double-faced, duplicitous, false, inconsistent, insincere, Pharisaic, *colloquial* phoney, self-deceiving, self-righteous, two-faced.

hypodermic /haɪpə'dɜːmɪk/ *adjective* (of drug, syringe, etc.) introduced under the skin. ● *noun* hypodermic injection or syringe.

hypotension /haɪpəʊ'tenʃ(ə)n/ *noun* abnormally low blood pressure.

hypotenuse /haɪ'pɒtənjuːz/ *noun* side opposite right angle of right-angled triangle.

hypothalamus /haɪpə'θæləməs/ *noun* (*plural*

-mi /-maɪ/) region of brain controlling body temperature, thirst, hunger, etc.

hypothermia /haɪpəʊ'θɜːmɪə/ *noun* abnormally low body-temperature.

hypothesis /haɪ'pɒθɪsɪs/ *noun* (*plural* **-theses** /-siːz/) supposition made as basis for reasoning etc. □ **hypothesize** *verb* (also **-ise**) (**-zing** or **-sing**).

■ conjecture, guess, postulate, premise, proposition, speculation, supposition, theory, thesis.

hypothetical /haɪpə'θetɪk(ə)l/ *adjective* of or resting on hypothesis. □ **hypothetically** *adverb*.

■ academic, alleged, assumed, conjectural, groundless, imaginary, presumed, *formal* putative, speculative, supposed, suppositional, theoretical, unreal.

hypothyroidism /haɪpəʊ'θaɪrɔɪdɪz(ə)m/ *noun* subnormal activity of the thyroid gland.

hypoventilation /haɪpəʊventɪ'leɪʃ(ə)n/ *noun* abnormally slow breathing.

hyssop /'hɪsəp/ *noun* small bushy aromatic herb.

hysterectomy /hɪstə'rektəmɪ/ *noun* (*plural* **-ies**) surgical removal of womb.

hysteria /hɪ'stɪərɪə/ *noun* **1** uncontrollable emotion or excitement. **2** functional disturbance of nervous system.

....

Hyphen -

This is used:

1 to join two or more words so as to form a compound or single expression, e.g.
   mother-in-law, non-stick
This use is growing less common; often you can do without such hyphens:
   treelike, dressing table

2 to join words in an attributive compound (one put before a noun, like an adjective), e.g.
   a well-known man (but *the man is well known*)
   an out-of-date list (but *the list is out of date*)

3 to join a prefix etc. to a proper name, e.g.
   anti-Darwinian; half-Italian; non-British

4 to make a meaning clear by linking words, e.g.
   twenty-odd people/twenty odd people
or by separating a prefix, e.g.
   re-cover/recover; re-present/represent; re-sign/resign

5 to separate two identical letters in adjacent parts of a word, e.g.
   pre-exist, Ross-shire

6 to represent a common second element in the items of a list, e.g.
   two-, three-, or fourfold

7 to divide a word if there is no room to complete it at the end of a line, e.g.
   ... diction-
   ary ...
The hyphen comes at the end of the line, not at the beginning of the next line. In general, words should be divided at the end of a syllable; *dicti-onary* would be quite wrong. In handwriting, typing, and word processing, it is safest (and often neatest) not to divide words at all.

●●●

■ **1** frenzy, hysterics, madness, mania, panic.

hysteric /hɪˈsterɪk/ *noun* **1** (in *plural*) fit of hysteria. **2** (in *plural*) *colloquial* overwhelming laughter. **3** hysterical person. □ **hysterical** *adjective.* **hysterically** *adverb.*

■ □ **hysterical** berserk, beside oneself, crazed, delirious, demented, distraught, frantic, frenzied, irrational, mad, over-emotional, rabid, raving, uncontrollable, wild.

Hz *abbreviation* hertz.

I[1] *noun* (also **i**) (Roman numeral) 1.

I[2] /aɪ/ *pronoun: used by speaker or writer to refer to himself or herself as subject of verb.*

I[3] *abbreviation* **1** (also **I.**) Island(s). **2** Isle(s).

iambic /aɪˈæmbɪk/ *adjective* of or using iambuses. ● *noun* (usually in *plural*) iambic verse.

iambus /aɪˈæmbəs/ *noun* (*plural* **-buses** or **-bi** /-baɪ/) metrical foot of one short followed by one long syllable.

IBA *abbreviation* Independent Broadcasting Authority.

ibex /ˈaɪbeks/ *noun* (*plural* **-es**) wild mountain goat with large backward-curving ridged horns.

ibid. /ˈɪbɪd/ *abbreviation* in same book or passage etc. (*ibidem*).

ibis /ˈaɪbɪs/ *noun* (*plural* **-es**) storklike bird with long curved bill.

ice *noun* **1** frozen water. **2** portion of ice cream etc. ● *verb* (**icing**) **1** mix with or cool in ice. **2** (often + *over*, *up*) cover or become covered (as) with ice; freeze. **3** cover (a cake etc.) with icing. □ **ice age** glacial period. **icebox 1** compartment in refrigerator for making or storing ice. **2** *US* refrigerator. **ice-breaker** boat designed to break through ice. **ice cap** mass of thick ice permanently covering polar region etc. **ice-cold** as cold as ice. **ice cream** sweet creamy frozen food. **ice field** extensive sheet of floating ice. **ice hockey** form of hockey played on ice with flat disc instead of ball. **ice lolly** flavoured ice on stick. **ice rink** area of ice for skating etc. **ice-skate** ● *noun* boot with blade attached for gliding over ice. ● *verb* move on ice-skates. **on ice 1** performed by ice-skaters. **2** *colloquial* in reserve.

iceberg /ˈaɪsbɜːɡ/ *noun* mass of floating ice at sea. □ **tip of the iceberg** small perceptible part of something very large or complex.

Icelander /ˈaɪsləndə/ *noun* native of Iceland.

Icelandic /aɪsˈlændɪk/ *adjective* of Iceland. ● *noun* language of Iceland.

ichneumon /ɪkˈnjuːmən/ *noun* **1** (in full **ichneumon fly**) wasplike insect parasitic on other insects. **2** mongoose of N. Africa etc.

ichthyology /ɪkθɪˈɒlədʒɪ/ *noun* study of fishes. □ **ichthyological** /-əˈlɒdʒɪk(ə)l/ *adjective.* **ichthyologist** *noun.*

ichthyosaur /ˈɪkθɪəsɔː/ *noun* large extinct reptile like dolphin.

icicle /ˈaɪsɪk(ə)l/ *noun* tapering hanging spike of ice, formed from dripping water.

icing *noun* **1** sugar etc. coating for cake etc. **2** formation of ice on ship or aircraft. □ **icing sugar** finely powdered sugar.

icon /ˈaɪkɒn/ *noun* (also **ikon**) **1** sacred painting, mosaic, etc. **2** image, statue. □ **iconic** /-ˈkɒn-/ *adjective.*

iconoclast /aɪˈkɒnəklæst/ *noun* **1** person who attacks cherished beliefs. **2** *historical* breaker of religious images. □ **iconoclasm** *noun.* **iconoclastic** /-ˈklæstɪk/ *adjective.*

iconography /aɪkəˈnɒɡrəfɪ/ *noun* **1** illustration of subject by drawings etc. **2** study of portraits, esp. of one person, or of artistic images or symbols.

icy /ˈaɪsɪ/ *adjective* (**-ier**, **-iest**) **1** very cold. **2** covered with or abounding in ice. **3** (of manner) unfriendly. □ **iciness** *noun.*
■ **1** arctic, chilling, freezing, frigid, frosty, frozen, glacial, polar. **2** frozen, glassy, slippery, *colloquial* slippy.

ID *abbreviation* identification, identity.

I'd /aɪd/ **1** I had. **2** I should; I would.

id *noun Psychology* part of mind comprising instinctive impulses of individual etc.

idea /aɪˈdɪə/ *noun* **1** plan etc. formed by mental effort. **2** mental impression or concept; vague belief or fancy. **3** purpose, intention. **4** pattern; archetype. □ **have no idea** *colloquial* **1** not know at all. **2** be completely incompetent.
■ **1** *colloquial* brainwave, conception, design, inspiration, plan, proposal, scheme, suggestion. **2** abstraction, attitude, belief, clue, concept, conception, conjecture, construct, conviction, doctrine, fancy, guess, hypothesis, impression, inkling, intimation, notion, opinion, perception, philosophy, principle, sentiment, suspicion, teaching, tenet, theory, thought, view, vision. **3** intention, meaning, point, purpose. **4** guidelines, impression, model, pattern.

ideal /aɪˈdiːəl/ *adjective* **1** perfect. **2** existing only in idea; visionary. ● *noun* **1** perfect type, thing, principle, etc., esp. as standard for imitation. **2** (often in *plural*) moral principle.
■ *adjective* **1** best, classic, complete, excellent, faultless, model, optimum, perfect, supreme, unsurpassable. **2** chimerical, dream, hypothetical, illusory, imaginary, unattainable, unreal, Utopian, visionary. ● *noun* **1** acme, criterion, epitome, exemplar, model, paragon, pattern, standard. **2** see PRINCIPLE 2.

idealism *noun* **1** forming or pursuing ideals. **2** representation of things in ideal form. **3** philosophy in which objects are held to be dependent on mind. □ **idealist** *noun.* **idealistic** /-ˈlɪst-/ *adjective.*
■ □ **idealistic** high-minded, impractical, over-optimistic, quixotic, romantic, *colloquial* starry-eyed, unrealistic.

idealize *verb* (also **-ise**) (**-zing** or **-sing**) regard or represent as ideal. □ **idealization** *noun*
■ deify, exalt, glamorize, glorify, put on a pedestal, romanticize.

identical /aɪ'dentɪk(ə)l/ *adjective* **1** (often + *with*) absolutely alike. **2** same. **3** (of twins) developed from single ovum and very similar in appearance. □ **identically** *adverb*.
■ **1** alike, comparable, congruent, corresponding, duplicate, equal, equivalent, indistinguishable, interchangeable, like, matching, the same, similar, twin. **2** same, selfsame.

identify /aɪ'dentɪfaɪ/ *verb* (**-ies, -ied**) **1** establish identity of. **2** select, discover. **3** (+ *with*) closely associate with. **4** (+ *with*) regard oneself as sharing basic characteristics with. **5** (often + *with*) treat as identical. □ **identifiable** *adjective*. **identification** *noun*.
■ **1** distinguish, label, mark, name, put a name to, recognize. **2** detect, diagnose, discover, establish, isolate, pick out, pinpoint, recognize, select, single out, specify, *colloquial* spot. **4** (*identify with*) empathize with, feel for, relate to, sympathize with. □ **identifiable** detectable, discernible, distinctive, distinguishable, familiar, known, named, noticeable, perceptible, recognizable, unmistakable.

identity /aɪ'dentɪtɪ/ *noun* (*plural* **-ies**) **1** being specified person or thing. **2** individuality. **3** identification or the result of it. **4** absolute sameness.
■ **1** ID, name. **2** character, distinctiveness, individuality, nature, particularity, personality, selfhood, singularity, uniqueness.

ideogram /'ɪdɪəgræm/ *noun* (also **ideograph** /-grɑːf/) symbol representing thing or idea without indicating sounds in its name (e.g. Chinese character, or '=' for 'equals').

ideology /aɪdɪ'ɒlədʒɪ/ *noun* (*plural* **-ies**) **1** scheme of ideas at basis of political etc. theory or system. **2** characteristic thinking of class etc. □ **ideological** /-ə'lɒdʒ-/ *adjective*.
■ assumptions, beliefs, creed, convictions, ideas, philosophy, principles, tenets, theories, underlying attitudes.

idiocy /'ɪdɪəsɪ/ *noun* (*plural* **-ies**) **1** utter foolishness; foolish act. **2** mental condition of idiot.

idiom /'ɪdɪəm/ *noun* **1** phrase etc. established by usage and not immediately comprehensible from the words used. **2** form of expression peculiar to a language. **3** language. **4** characteristic mode of expression. □ **idiomatic** /-'mæt-/ *adjective*.
■ **1** expression, locution, phrase. **2, 3** argot, cant, choice of words, dialect, jargon, language, manner of speaking, parlance, phraseology, phrasing, turn of phrase, usage. □ **idiomatic** colloquial, natural, vernacular, well phrased.

idiosyncrasy /ɪdɪəʊ'sɪŋkrəsɪ/ *noun* (*plural* **-ies**) attitude or form of behaviour peculiar to person. □ **idiosyncratic** /-'kræt-/ *adjective*.

■ characteristic, eccentricity, feature, habit, mannerism, oddity, peculiarity, quirk, trait. □ **idiosyncratic** characteristic, distinctive, eccentric, individual, odd, peculiar, personal, quirky, singular, unique.

idiot /'ɪdɪət/ *noun* **1** stupid person. **2** person too deficient in mind to be capable of rational conduct. □ **idiotic** /-'ɒt-/ *adjective*.
■ **1** ass, blockhead, *slang* bonehead, booby, *colloquial* chump, *colloquial* clot, *colloquial* cretin, *colloquial* dimwit, dolt, *slang* dope, *colloquial* duffer, *colloquial* dummy, dunce, dunderhead, *colloquial* fat-head, fool, halfwit, ignoramus, *colloquial* imbecile, *colloquial* moron, nincompoop, ninny, *colloquial* nitwit, simpleton, *slang* twerp, *slang* twit. □ **idiotic** see STUPID 1–2.

idle /'aɪd(ə)l/ *adjective* (**-r, -st**) **1** lazy, indolent. **2** not in use; not working. **3** (of time) unoccupied. **4** useless, purposeless. ● *verb* (**-ling**) **1** be idle. **2** (of engine) run slowly without doing any work. **3** pass (time) in idleness. □ **idleness** *noun*. **idler** *noun*. **idly** *adverb*.
■ *adjective* **1** apathetic, indolent, lackadaisical, lazy, shiftless, slothful, slow, sluggish, torpid, work-shy. **2** dormant, inactive, inoperative, in retirement, not working, redundant, retired, unemployed, unoccupied, unproductive, unused. **3** free, unfilled, unoccupied. **4** frivolous, futile, pointless, unproductive, useless, worthless. ● *verb* **1** be lazy, dawdle, do nothing, hang about, laze, loaf, loll, lounge about, mess about, potter about, *colloquial* slack, stagnate, take it easy, vegetate. □ **idler** good-for-nothing, layabout, *colloquial* lazybones, loafer, malingerer, shirker, *slang* skiver, slacker, sluggard, wastrel.

idol /'aɪd(ə)l/ *noun* **1** image as object of worship. **2** object of devotion.
■ **1** effigy, fetish, graven image, icon, statue. **2** celebrity, darling, deity, favourite, god, hero, pin-up, star, superstar.

idolater /aɪ'dɒlətə/ *noun* **1** worshipper of idols. **2** devout admirer. □ **idolatrous** *adjective*. **idolatry** *noun*.

idolize *verb* (also **-ise**) (**-zing** or **-sing**) **1** venerate or love to excess. **2** treat as idol. □ **idolization** *noun*.
■ adore, adulate, deify, hero-worship, lionize, look up to, revere, reverence, venerate, worship.

idyll /'ɪdɪl/ *noun* **1** account of picturesque scene or incident etc. **2** such scene etc. □ **idyllic** /ɪ'dɪlɪk/ *adjective*.
■ □ **idyllic** Arcadian, bucolic, charming, delightful, happy, idealized, lovely, pastoral, peaceful, perfect, picturesque, rustic, unspoiled.

i.e. *abbreviation* that is to say (*id est*).

if *conjunction* **1** on condition or supposition that. **2** (*with past tense*) *implying that the condition is not fulfilled.* **3** even though. **4** whenever. **5** whether. **6** *expressing wish, request, or (with negative) surprise.* □ **if only 1** even if for no other reason than. **2** I wish that.

iffy /'ɪfɪ/ *adjective* (**-ier**, **-iest**) *colloquial* **1** uncertain. **2** of questionable quality.

igloo /'ɪgluː/ *noun* Eskimo dome-shaped snow house.

igneous /'ɪgnɪəs/ *adjective* **1** of fire. **2** (esp. of rocks) produced by volcanic action.

ignite /ɪg'naɪt/ *verb* (**-ting**) **1** set fire to. **2** catch fire. **3** provoke or excite (feelings etc.).

> ■ **1** burn, fire, kindle, light, set alight, set on fire, spark off, touch off. **2** burn, catch fire, fire, kindle.

ignition /ɪg'nɪʃ(ə)n/ *noun* **1** mechanism for starting combustion in cylinder of motor engine. **2** igniting.

ignoble /ɪg'nəʊb(ə)l/ *adjective* (**-r**, **-st**) **1** dishonourable. **2** of low birth or position.

> ■ **1** base, churlish, cowardly, despicable, disgraceful, dishonourable, infamous, low, mean, selfish, shabby, uncharitable, unchivalrous, unworthy.

ignominious /ɪgnə'mɪnɪəs/ *adjective* humiliating. ☐ **ignominiously** *adverb*.

ignominy /'ɪgnəmɪnɪ/ *noun* dishonour, infamy.

ignoramus /ɪgnə'reɪməs/ *noun* (*plural* **-muses**) ignorant person.

ignorant /'ɪgnərənt/ *adjective* **1** lacking knowledge. **2** (+ *of*) uninformed about. **3** *colloquial* uncouth. ☐ **ignorance** *noun*.

> ■ **1** benighted, *colloquial* clueless, ill-informed, illiterate, innocent, stupid, uneducated, unenlightened, uninformed, unlettered, unscholarly, unsophisticated, unwitting. **2** (*ignorant of*) oblivious of *or* to, unacquainted with, unaware of, unconscious of, unfamiliar with. **3** ill-bred, ill-mannered, impolite, uncivil, uncouth, uncultivated. ☐ **ignorance** inexperience, innocence, naivety, stupidity, unawareness, unconsciousness, unfamiliarity.

ignore /ɪg'nɔː/ *verb* (**-ring**) refuse to take notice of.

> ■ disobey, disregard, leave out, miss out, neglect, omit, overlook, pass over, reject, shut one's eyes to, skip, slight, snub, take no notice of, turn a blind eye to.

iguana /ɪg'wɑːnə/ *noun* large Central and S. American tree lizard.

iguanodon /ɪg'wɑːnədɒn/ *noun* large planteating dinosaur.

ikebana /ɪkɪ'bɑːnə/ *noun* Japanese art of flower arrangement.

ikon = ICON.

ilex /'aɪleks/ *noun* (*plural* **-es**) **1** plant of genus including holly. **2** holm-oak.

iliac /'ɪlɪæk/ *adjective* of flank or hip-bone.

ilk *noun colloquial* sort, kind. ☐ **of that ilk** *Scottish* of ancestral estate of same name as family.

I'll /aɪl/ I shall; I will.

ill *adjective* **1** in bad health; sick. **2** harmful, unfavourable. **3** hostile, unkind. **4** faulty, deficient. ● *adverb* **1** badly, unfavourably. **2** scarcely. ● *noun* **1** harm. **2** evil. ☐ **ill-advised** unwise. **ill**

at ease embarrassed, uneasy. **ill-bred** rude. **ill-fated** unlucky. **ill-favoured** unattractive. **ill feeling** bad feeling; animosity. **ill-gotten** gained unlawfully or wickedly. **ill health** poor physical condition. **ill humour** bad temper. **ill-humoured** *adjective*. **ill-mannered** rude. **ill-natured** churlish. **ill-omened** unlucky. **ill-tempered** morose, irritable. **ill-timed** done or occurring at unsuitable time. **ill-treat, -use** treat badly. **ill-treatment** *noun*. **ill use** bad treatment. **ill-use** *verb*.

> ■ *adjective* **1** ailing, bad, bedridden, bilious, *slang* dicky, diseased, feeble, frail, *colloquial* funny, groggy, indisposed, infected, infirm, invalid, languishing, nauseated, nauseous, off colour, out of sorts, pasty, poorly, queasy, queer, *colloquial* seedy, sick, sickly, suffering, *colloquial* under the weather, unhealthy, unwell, valetudinarian, weak. **2** bad, damaging, detrimental, evil, harmful, injurious, unfavourable, unfortunate, unlucky. ☐ **ill-advised** see MISGUIDED. **ill-bred** see RUDE 1. **ill-fated** see UNLUCKY 3. **ill-humoured** see BAD-TEMPERED (BAD). **ill-mannered** see RUDE 1. **ill-natured** see UNKIND. **ill-omened** see UNLUCKY 3. **ill-tempered** see BAD-TEMPERED (BAD). **ill-treat** see MISTREAT.

illegal /ɪ'liːg(ə)l/ *adjective* contrary to law. ☐ **illegality** /-'gæl-/ *noun* (*plural* **-ies**). **illegally** *adverb*.

> ■ actionable, against the law, banned, black-market, criminal, felonious, forbidden, illegitimate, illicit, invalid, irregular, outlawed, prohibited, proscribed, unauthorized, unconstitutional, unlawful, unlicensed, wrong, wrongful.

illegible /ɪ'ledʒɪb(ə)l/ *adjective* not legible, unreadable. ☐ **illegibility** *noun*. **illegibly** *adverb*.

> ■ indecipherable, indistinct, obscure, unclear, unreadable.

illegitimate /ɪlɪ'dʒɪtɪmət/ *adjective* **1** born of parents not married to each other. **2** unlawful. **3** improper. **4** wrongly inferred. ☐ **illegitimacy** *noun*.

> ■ **1** *archaic* or *offensive* bastard, born out of wedlock, natural. **2** see ILLEGAL. **3** against the rules, improper, irregular, unauthorized, unjustifiable, unreasonable, unwarranted. **4** inadmissible, incorrect, invalid, spurious.

illiberal /ɪ'lɪbər(ə)l/ *adjective* **1** narrow-minded. **2** stingy. ☐ **illiberality** /-'ræl-/ *noun*.

illicit /ɪ'lɪsɪt/ *adjective* unlawful, forbidden. ☐ **illicitly** *adverb*.

illiterate /ɪ'lɪtərət/ *adjective* **1** unable to read. **2** uneducated. ● *noun* illiterate person. ☐ **illiteracy** *noun*.

> ■ *adjective* **1** unlettered. **2** benighted, ignorant, uneducated, unenlightened, unlettered, unschooled.

illness *noun* **1** disease. **2** ill health.

> ■ **1** affliction, ailment, *slang* bug, complaint, condition, disease, disorder, health problem, indisposition, infection, infirmity, malady, malaise, pestilence, plague, sickness. **2** disability, infirmity, indisposition, sickness, weakness.

illogical /ɪˈlɒdʒɪk(ə)l/ *adjective* devoid of or contrary to logic. □ **illogicality** /-ˈkæl-/ *noun* (*plural* **-ies**). **illogically** *adverb*.

■ absurd, fallacious, inconsequential, inconsistent, invalid, irrational, senseless, silly, unreasonable, unsound.

illuminate /ɪˈluːmɪneɪt/ *verb* (**-ting**) **1** light up. **2** decorate with lights. **3** decorate (manuscript etc.) with gold, colour, etc. **4** help to explain (subject etc.). **5** enlighten spiritually or intellectually. □ **illuminating** *adjective*. **illumination** *noun*.

■ **1** brighten, light up, make brighter. **4** clarify, clear up, elucidate, enlighten, explain, explicate, reveal, throw light on. **5** see ENLIGHTEN 1.

illumine /ɪˈljuːmɪn/ *verb* (**-ning**) *literary* **1** light up. **2** enlighten.

illusion /ɪˈluːʒ(ə)n/ *noun* **1** false belief. **2** deceptive appearance. □ **be under the illusion** (+ *that*) believe mistakenly that. □ **illusive** *adjective*. **illusory** *adjective*.

■ **1** error, false impression, misapprehension, misconception, mistake. **2** apparition, conjuring trick, daydream, deception, delusion, dream, fancy, fantasy, figment of the imagination, hallucination, mirage. □ **illusory** chimerical, deceptive, deluding, delusive, fallacious, false, fanciful, illusive, imaginary, imagined, misleading, mistaken, sham, unreal, untrue.

illusionist *noun* conjuror.

illustrate /ˈɪləstreɪt/ *verb* (**-ting**) **1** provide with pictures. **2** make clear, esp. by examples or drawings. **3** serve as example of. □ **illustrator** *noun*.

■ **1** adorn, decorate, depict, draw, embellish, illuminate, ornament, picture, portray. **2** demonstrate, elucidate, explain, show. **3** exemplify, instance, represent.

illustration *noun* **1** drawing etc. in book. **2** explanatory example. **3** illustrating.

■ **1** diagram, drawing, figure, image, photograph, picture, sketch. **2** demonstration, example, exemplar, instance, sample, specimen. **3** decoration, depiction, illumination.

illustrative /ˈɪləstrətɪv/ *adjective* (often + *of*) explanatory.

illustrious /ɪˈlʌstrɪəs/ *adjective* distinguished, renowned. □ **illustriousness** *noun*.

I'm /aɪm/ I am.

image /ˈɪmɪdʒ/ *noun* **1** representation of object, esp. figure of saint or divinity. **2** reputation or persona of person, company, etc. **3** appearance as seen in mirror or through lens. **4** person or thing closely resembling another. **5** idea, conception. **6** simile, metaphor. ● *verb* (**-ging**) **1** make image of. **2** mirror. **3** picture.

■ *noun* **1** carving, effigy, figure, icon, idol, imitation, representation, statue. **3** likeness, picture, projection, reflection, representation. **4** counterpart, double, likeness, *colloquial* spitting image, twin.

imagery /ˈɪmɪdʒərɪ/ *noun* **1** figurative illustration; use of images in literature etc. **2** images,

statuary. **3** mental images collectively.

imaginable /ɪˈmædʒɪnəb(ə)l/ *adjective* that can be imagined.

imaginary /ɪˈmædʒɪnərɪ/ *adjective* existing only in imagination.

■ fabulous, fanciful, fictional, fictitious, hypothetical, illusory, imagined, insubstantial, invented, legendary, made up, mythical, mythological, non-existent, supposed, unreal, visionary.

imagination /ɪmædʒɪˈneɪʃ(ə)n/ *noun* **1** mental faculty of forming images of objects not present to senses. **2** creative faculty of mind.

■ **1** fancy, fantasy. **2** artistry, creativity, ingenuity, insight, inspiration, inventiveness, originality, resourcefulness, sensitivity, thought, vision.

imaginative /ɪˈmædʒɪnətɪv/ *adjective* having or showing high degree of imagination. □ **imaginatively** *adverb*.

■ artistic, clever, creative, fanciful, ingenious, innovative, inspired, inspiring, inventive, original, poetic, resourceful, sensitive, thoughtful, unusual, visionary, vivid.

imagine /ɪˈmædʒɪn/ *verb* (**-ning**) **1** form mental image of; conceive. **2** suppose, think.

■ **1** conceive, conjure up, create, dream up, envisage, fancy, fantasize, invent, make believe, make up, picture, pretend, see, think of, *colloquial* think up, visualize. **2** assume, believe, conjecture, guess, infer, judge, presume, suppose, surmise, suspect, think.

imago /ɪˈmeɪgəʊ/ *noun* (*plural* **-s** or **imagines** /ɪˈmædʒɪniːz/) fully developed stage of insect.

imam /ɪˈmɑːm/ *noun* **1** prayer-leader of mosque. **2** *title of some Muslim leaders*.

imbalance /ɪmˈbæləns/ *noun* **1** lack of balance. **2** disproportion.

imbecile /ˈɪmbɪsiːl/ *noun* **1** *colloquial* stupid person. **2** adult with mental age of about 5. ● *adjective* mentally weak, stupid. □ **imbecilic** /-ˈsɪlɪk/ *adjective*. **imbecility** /-ˈsɪlɪtɪ/ *noun* (*plural* **-ies**).

imbed = EMBED.

imbibe /ɪmˈbaɪb/ *verb* (**-bing**) **1** drink. **2** drink in; absorb. **3** inhale.

imbroglio /ɪmˈbrəʊlɪəʊ/ *noun* (*plural* **-s**) confused or complicated situation.

imbue /ɪmˈbjuː/ *verb* (**-bues**, **-bued**, **-buing**) (often + *with*) **1** inspire. **2** saturate, dye.

imitate /ˈɪmɪteɪt/ *verb* (**-ting**) **1** follow example of. **2** mimic. **3** make copy of. **4** be like. □ **imitable** *adjective*. **imitative** /-tətɪv/ *adjective*. **imitator** *noun*.

■ **1** copy, emulate, follow, match, model oneself on. **2** ape, burlesque, caricature, counterfeit, duplicate, echo, impersonate, mimic, parody, parrot, portray, reproduce, satirize, *colloquial* send up, simulate, *colloquial* take off, travesty. **3** see COPY *verb* 1.

imitation *noun* **1** imitating, being imitated. **2**

copy; counterfeit. ● *adjective* made in imitation of thing.

■ *noun* 1 copying, duplication, emulation, mimicry, repetition. 2 *colloquial* clone, copy, counterfeit, dummy, duplicate, fake, forgery, impersonation, impression, likeness, mock-up, model, parody, replica, reproduction, sham, simulation, *colloquial* take-off, toy, travesty. ● *adjective* artificial, copied, counterfeit, dummy, ersatz, man-made, mock, model, *colloquial* phoney, reproduction, sham, simulated, synthetic.

immaculate /ɪˈmækjʊlət/ *adjective* 1 perfectly clean, spotless. 2 faultless. 3 innocent, sinless. □ **immaculately** *adverb*. **immaculateness** *noun*.

immanent /ˈɪmənənt/ *adjective* 1 inherent. 2 (of God) omnipresent. □ **immanence** *noun*.

immaterial /ɪməˈtɪərɪəl/ *adjective* 1 unimportant; irrelevant. 2 not material. □ **immateriality** /-ˈæl-/ *noun*.

immature /ɪməˈtjʊə/ *adjective* 1 not mature. 2 undeveloped, esp. emotionally. □ **immaturity** *noun*.

■ 1 adolescent, undeveloped, unripe, young, youthful. 2 babyish, backward, callow, childish, green, inexperienced, infantile, *often derogatory* juvenile, puerile.

immeasurable /ɪˈmeʒərəb(ə)l/ *adjective* not measurable; immense. □ **immeasurably** *adverb*.

immediate /ɪˈmiːdɪət/ *adjective* 1 occurring at once. 2 direct; without intermediary. 3 nearest. 4 having priority. □ **immediacy** *noun*. **immediately** *adverb*.

■ 1 instant, instantaneous, prompt, quick, speedy, sudden, swift, unhesitating, unthinking. 3 adjacent, close, closest, direct, near, nearest, neighbouring, next. 4 current, present, pressing, top-priority, urgent. □ **immediately** at once, directly, forthwith, instantly, now, promptly, right away, straight away, unhesitatingly.

immemorial /ɪmɪˈmɔːrɪəl/ *adjective* ancient beyond memory.

immense /ɪˈmens/ *adjective* vast, huge. □ **immensity** *noun*.

■ big, colossal, elephantine, enormous, gargantuan, giant, gigantic, great, huge, *colloquial* hulking, immeasurable, imposing, impressive, incalculable, *colloquial* jumbo, large, mammoth, massive, mighty, monster, monstrous, monumental, mountainous, prodigious, stupendous, titanic, towering, *colloquial* tremendous, vast, *colloquial* whopping.

immensely *adverb colloquial* 1 vastly. 2 very much.

immerse /ɪˈmɜːs/ *verb* (-sing) 1 (often + *in*) dip, plunge. 2 put under water. 3 (often **immerse oneself** or in *passive*; often + *in*) involve deeply. 4 (often + *in*) embed.

■ 1, 2 bathe, dip, drench, drown, duck, dunk, plunge, sink, submerge. 3 (*immersed*) see BUSY *adjective* 1, INTERESTED.

immersion /ɪˈmɜːʃ(ə)n/ *noun* immersing, being immersed. □ **immersion heater** electric heater designed to be immersed in liquid to be heated.

■ dipping, ducking, dunking, plunge, submersion.

immigrant /ˈɪmɪɡrənt/ *noun* person who immigrates. ● *adjective* 1 immigrating. 2 of immigrants.

■ *noun* alien, arrival, newcomer, outsider, settler.

immigrate /ˈɪmɪɡreɪt/ *verb* (-ting) enter a country to settle permanently. □ **immigration** *noun*.

imminent /ˈɪmɪnənt/ *adjective* soon to happen. □ **imminence** *noun*. **imminently** *adverb*.

■ about to happen, approaching, close, coming, foreseeable, forthcoming, impending, looming, menacing, near, threatening.

immobile /ɪˈməʊbaɪl/ *adjective* 1 motionless. 2 immovable. □ **immobility** *noun*.

■ 1 frozen, inflexible, motionless, rigid. 2 see IMMOVABLE 1.

immobilize /ɪˈməʊbɪlaɪz/ *verb* (also **-ise**) (**-zing** or **-sing**) prevent from being moved. □ **immobilization** *noun*.

immoderate /ɪˈmɒdərət/ *adjective* excessive. □ **immoderately** *adverb*. **immoderation** *noun*.

immodest /ɪˈmɒdɪst/ *adjective* 1 conceited. 2 indecent. □ **immodesty** *noun*.

immolate /ˈɪməleɪt/ *verb* (-ting) kill as sacrifice. □ **immolation** *noun*.

immoral /ɪˈmɒr(ə)l/ *adjective* opposed to, or not conforming to, (esp. sexual) morality; dissolute. □ **immorality** /ɪməˈrælɪtɪ/ *noun*.

■ abandoned, base, conscienceless, corrupt, debauched, degenerate, depraved, dishonest, dissipated, dissolute, evil, fast, impure, indecent, irresponsible, licentious, loose, low, profligate, promiscuous, rotten, sinful, unchaste, unethical, unprincipled, unscrupulous, vicious, villainous, wanton, wicked, wrong.

immortal /ɪˈmɔːt(ə)l/ *adjective* 1 living for ever. 2 unfading. 3 divine. 4 famous for all time. ● *noun* immortal being, esp. (in *plural*) gods of antiquity. □ **immortality** /-ˈtæl-/ *noun*. **immortalize** *verb* (also **-ise**) (**-zing** or **-sing**).

■ *adjective* 1 ageless, ceaseless, deathless, endless, eternal, everlasting, indestructible, never-ending, perpetual, timeless, undying, unending. 2 incorruptible, indestructible, lasting, unchanging, unfading. 3 divine, godlike. 4 classic, legendary, mythical, timeless. □ **immortalize** RC *Church* beatify, canonize, commemorate, deify, enshrine, keep alive, make immortal, make permanent, memorialize, perpetuate.

immovable /ɪˈmuːvəb(ə)l/ *adjective* 1 not movable. 2 unyielding. □ **immovability** *noun*.

■ 1 anchored, fast, firm, fixed, immobile, immobilized, motionless, paralysed, riveted, rooted, secure, set, settled, static, stationary, still, stuck, unmoving. 2 see IMMUTABLE, INFLEXIBLE 2.

immune /ɪˈmjuːn/ *adjective* 1 having immunity. 2 relating to immunity. 3 exempt.

■ **1** immunized, inoculated, invulnerable, protected, resistant, safe, vaccinated. **3** (*immune from* or *to*) exempt from, free from, protected from, resistant to, safe from, unaffected by.

immunity *noun* (*plural* **-ies**) **1** living organism's power of resisting and overcoming infection. **2** (often + *from*) freedom, exemption.

immunize /'ɪmjuːnaɪz/ *verb* (also **-ise**) (**-zing** or **-sing**) make immune. □ **immunization** *noun*.
■ inoculate, vaccinate.

immure /ɪ'mjʊə/ *verb* (**-ring**) imprison.

immutable /ɪ'mjuːtəb(ə)l/ *adjective* unchangeable. □ **immutability** *noun*.
■ constant, dependable, enduring, eternal, fixed, immovable, invariable, lasting, obdurate, permanent, perpetual, reliable, resolute, settled, stable, steadfast, unalterable, unchangeable, unswerving, unvarying.

imp *noun* **1** mischievous child. **2** little devil.

impact *noun* /'ɪmpækt/ **1** collision, striking. **2** (immediate) effect or influence. ● *verb* /ɪm'pækt/ **1** drive or wedge together. **2** (as **impacted** *adjective*) (of tooth) wedged between another tooth and jaw. □ **impaction** /ɪm'pækʃ(ə)n/ *noun*.
■ *noun* **1** bang, blow, bump, collision, contact, crash, knock, smash. **2** bearing, consequence, effect, force, impression, influence, repercussions, reverberations. ● *verb* **1** see HIT *verb* 1.

impair /ɪm'peə/ *verb* damage, weaken. □ **impairment** *noun*.
■ cripple, damage, harm, injure, mar, ruin, spoil, weaken.

impala /ɪm'pɑːlə/ *noun* (*plural* same or **-s**) small African antelope.

impale /ɪm'peɪl/ *verb* (**-ling**) transfix on stake. □ **impalement** *noun*.
■ pierce, run through, skewer, spear, spike, spit, stab, stick, transfix.

impalpable /ɪm'pælpəb(ə)l/ *adjective* **1** not easily grasped. **2** imperceptible to touch.

impart /ɪm'pɑːt/ *verb* **1** communicate (news etc.). **2** give share of.

impartial /ɪm'pɑːʃ(ə)l/ *adjective* fair, not partial. □ **impartiality** /-ʃɪ'æl-/ *noun*. **impartially** *adverb*.
■ balanced, detached, disinterested, dispassionate, equitable, even-handed, fair, fair-minded, judicial, just, neutral, non-partisan, objective, open-minded, unbiased, uninvolved, unprejudiced.

impassable /ɪm'pɑːsəb(ə)l/ *adjective* that cannot be traversed. □ **impassability** *noun*.
■ blocked, closed, obstructed, unusable.

impasse /'æmpæs/ *noun* deadlock.

impassioned /ɪm'pæʃ(ə)nd/ *adjective* filled with passion; ardent.

impassive /ɪm'pæsɪv/ *adjective* not feeling or showing emotion. □ **impassively** *adverb*. **impassivity** /-'sɪv-/ *noun*.

impasto /ɪm'pæstəʊ/ *noun* technique of laying on paint thickly.

impatiens /ɪm'peɪʃɪenz/ *noun* any of several plants including busy Lizzie.

impatient /ɪm'peɪʃ(ə)nt/ *adjective* **1** not patient; intolerant. **2** restlessly eager. □ **impatience** *noun*. **impatiently** *adverb*.
■ **1** abrupt, brusque, curt, hasty, intolerant, irascible, irritable, precipitate, quick-tempered, short-tempered, snappish, *colloquial* snappy, testy. **2** agitated, chafing, edgy, fidgety, fretful, impetuous, nervous, restive, restless, uneasy; (*impatient to*) anxious to, eager to, keen to, *colloquial* raring to go.

impeach /ɪm'piːtʃ/ *verb* **1** accuse, esp. of treason etc. **2** call in question; disparage. □ **impeachment** *noun*.

impeccable /ɪm'pekəb(ə)l/ *adjective* faultless, exemplary. □ **impeccability** *noun*. **impeccably** *adverb*.

impecunious /ɪmpɪ'kjuːnɪəs/ *adjective* having little or no money. □ **impecuniousness** *noun*.

impedance /ɪm'piːd(ə)ns/ *noun* total effective resistance of electric circuit etc. to alternating current.

impede /ɪm'piːd/ *verb* (**-ding**) obstruct; hinder.
■ arrest, bar, be an impediment to, check, clog (up), curb, delay, deter, frustrate, get in the way of, hamper, handicap, hinder, hold back, hold up, keep back, limit, obstruct, oppose, prevent, restrain, restrict, retard, sabotage, slow down, slow up, stand in the way of, stop, thwart.

impediment /ɪm'pedɪmənt/ *noun* **1** hindrance. **2** defect in speech, esp. lisp or stammer.
■ **1** bar, barrier, check, curb, difficulty, disadvantage, drag, drawback, encumbrance, hindrance, inconvenience, limitation, obstacle, obstruction, restraint, restriction, snag, stumbling block. **2** defect, disability, handicap, impairment.

impedimenta /ɪmpedɪ'mentə/ *plural noun* **1** encumbrances. **2** baggage, esp. of army.

impel /ɪm'pel/ *verb* (**-ll-**) **1** drive, force. **2** propel.

impend /ɪm'pend/ *verb* **1** be imminent. **2** hang. □ **impending** *adjective*.
■ □ **impending** about to happen, approaching, close, coming, foreseeable, forthcoming, imminent, looming, menacing, near, threatening.

impenetrable /ɪm'penɪtrəb(ə)l/ *adjective* **1** not penetrable. **2** inscrutable. **3** inaccessible to influences etc. □ **impenetrability** *noun*.
■ **1** dense, impassable, impervious, impregnable, resistant, safe, secure, solid, strong, thick. **2** inaccessible, incomprehensible, inscrutable, unfathomable, *colloquial* unget-at-able.

impenitent /ɪm'penɪt(ə)nt/ *adjective* not penitent. □ **impenitence** *noun*.

imperative /ɪm'perətɪv/ *adjective* **1** urgent. **2** obligatory. **3** peremptory. **4** *Grammar* (of mood) expressing command. ● *noun* **1** *Grammar* imperative mood. **2** command. **3** essential or urgent thing.

imperceptible /ɪmpə'septɪb(ə)l/ *adjective* **1** not perceptible. **2** very slight or gradual. □ **imperceptibility** *noun*. **imperceptibly** *adverb*.

■ faint, gradual, inaudible, indistinguishable, infinitesimal, insignificant, invisible, microscopic, minute, negligible, slight, small, subtle, tiny, unclear, undetectable, unnoticeable, vague.

imperfect /ɪm'pɜːfɪkt/ *adjective* **1** not perfect; incomplete; faulty. **2** *Grammar* (of past tense) implying action going on but not completed. ● *noun* imperfect tense. □ **imperfectly** *adverb*.

■ *adjective* **1** blemished, broken, chipped, cracked, damaged, defective, deficient, faulty, flawed, incomplete, incorrect, marred, partial, patchy, shop-soiled, spoilt, unfinished, wanting.

imperfection /ɪmpə'fekʃ(ə)n/ *noun* **1** imperfectness. **2** fault, blemish.

■ **1** deficiency, inadequacy, incompleteness. **2** blemish, defect, deficiency, error, failing, fault, flaw, foible, frailty, infirmity, peccadillo, shortcoming, weakness.

imperial /ɪm'pɪərɪəl/ *adjective* **1** of empire or sovereign state ranking with this. **2** of emperor. **3** majestic. **4** (of non-metric weights and measures) used by statute in UK.

imperialism *noun* **1** imperial system of government etc. **2** (*usually derogatory*) policy of dominating other nations by acquisition of dependencies or through trade etc. □ **imperialist** *noun* & *adjective*.

imperil /ɪm'perɪl/ *verb* (**-ll-**; *US* **-l-**) endanger.

imperious /ɪm'pɪərɪəs/ *adjective* overbearing, domineering. □ **imperiously** *adverb*.

imperishable /ɪm'perɪʃəb(ə)l/ *adjective* that cannot perish.

impermanent /ɪm'pɜːmənənt/ *adjective* not permanent. □ **impermanence** *noun*.

■ changeable, changing, ephemeral, *literary* evanescent, fleeting, inconstant, momentary, passing, shifting, short-lived, temporary, transient, transitory, unstable.

impermeable /ɪm'pɜːmɪəb(ə)l/ *adjective* not permeable. □ **impermeability** *noun*.

impersonal /ɪm'pɜːsən(ə)l/ *adjective* **1** having or showing no personal feelings. **2** having no personal reference; objective. **3** *Grammar* (of verb) used esp. with *it* as subject. □ **impersonality** /-'næl-/ *noun*.

■ **1** aloof, detached, distant, remote, stiff, unapproachable, unemotional, unfriendly, unsympathetic, without emotion, wooden. **2** bland, businesslike, formal, neutral, objective, official.

impersonate /ɪm'pɜːsəneɪt/ *verb* (**-ting**) **1** pretend to be. **2** play part of. □ **impersonation** *noun*. **impersonator** *noun*.

■ disguise oneself as, do impressions of, dress up as, imitate, masquerade as, mimic, portray, pose as, pretend to be, *colloquial* take off.

impertinent /ɪm'pɜːtɪnənt/ *adjective* **1** insolent, saucy. **2** irrelevant. □ **impertinence** *noun*. **impertinently** *adverb*.

■ **1** bold, brazen, cheeky, *colloquial* cocky, cool, discourteous, disrespectful, forward, *colloquial* fresh, impolite, impudent, insolent, insubordinate, insulting, irreverent, pert, rude, saucy.

imperturbable /ɪmpə'tɜːbəb(ə)l/ *adjective* not excitable; calm. □ **imperturbability** *noun*. **imperturbably** *adverb*.

impervious /ɪm'pɜːvɪəs/ *adjective* **1** (usually + *to*) impermeable. **2** not responsive.

■ **1** impermeable, non-porous, waterproof, water-repellent, watertight. **2** (*impervious to*) see RESISTANT (RESISTANCE).

impetigo /ɪmpɪ'taɪgəʊ/ *noun* contagious skin disease.

impetuous /ɪm'petjʊəs/ *adjective* **1** acting or done rashly or suddenly. **2** moving violently or fast. □ **impetuosity** /-'ɒs-/ *noun*. **impetuously** *adverb*.

■ **1** abrupt, careless, eager, hasty, headlong, hot-headed, impulsive, incautious, offhand, precipitate, quick, rash, reckless, speedy, spontaneous, thoughtless, unplanned, unpremeditated, unthinking.

impetus /'ɪmpɪtəs/ *noun* **1** moving force; momentum. **2** impulse.

■ **1** drive, energy, force, momentum, power, thrust. **2** boost, drive, encouragement, fillip, force, impulse, incentive, inspiration, momentum, motivation, push, spur, stimulation, stimulus, thrust.

impiety /ɪm'paɪətɪ/ *noun* (*plural* **-ies**) **1** lack of piety. **2** act showing this.

■ **1** blasphemy, godlessness, irreverence, profanity, sacrilege, sinfulness, ungodliness, unrighteousness, wickedness. **2** see SIN *noun* 1.

impinge /ɪm'pɪndʒ/ *verb* (**-ging**) **1** (usually + *on*) make impact. **2** (usually + *upon*) encroach.

impious /'ɪmpɪəs/ *adjective* **1** not pious. **2** wicked.

■ **1** blasphemous, godless, irreligious, irreverent, profane, sacrilegious, sinful, unholy. **2** see WICKED 1.

impish *adjective* of or like imp; mischievous. □ **impishly** *adverb*. **impishness** *noun*.

implacable /ɪm'plækəb(ə)l/ *adjective* not appeasable. □ **implacability** *noun*. **implacably** *adverb*.

implant *verb* /ɪm'plɑːnt/ **1** insert, fix. **2** instil. **3** plant. **4** (in *passive*) (of fertilized ovum) become attached to wall of womb. ● *noun* /'ɪmplɑːnt/ thing implanted. □ **implantation** *noun*.

implausible /ɪm'plɔːzɪb(ə)l/ *adjective* not plausible. □ **implausibly** *adverb*.

■ doubtful, dubious, far-fetched, feeble, improbable, questionable, suspect, unconvincing, unlikely, unreasonable, weak.

implement *noun* /'ɪmplɪmənt/ tool, utensil.

● *verb* /'ɪmplɪment/ carry into effect. □ **implementation** *noun*.

■ *noun* apparatus, appliance, contrivance, device, gadget, instrument, mechanism, tool, utensil. ● *verb* accomplish, achieve, bring about, carry out, effect, enforce, execute, fulfil, perform, put into effect, put into practice, realize, try out.

implicate /'ɪmplɪkeɪt/ *verb* (**-ting**) **1** (often + *in*) show (person) to be involved (in crime etc.). **2** imply.

■ **1** associate, concern, connect, embroil, enmesh, ensnare, entangle, include, incriminate, inculpate, involve, show involvement in.

implication *noun* **1** thing implied. **2** implying. **3** implicating.

■ **1** hidden meaning, hint, innuendo, insinuation, overtone, purport, significance. **3** association, connection, embroilment, entanglement, inclusion, involvement.

implicit /ɪm'plɪsɪt/ *adjective* **1** implied though not expressed. **2** unquestioning. □ **implicitly** *adverb*.

■ **1** hinted at, implied, indirect, inherent, insinuated, tacit, understood, undeclared, unexpressed, unsaid, unspoken, unstated, unvoiced. **2** see ABSOLUTE 1.

implode /ɪm'pləʊd/ *verb* (**-ding**) (cause to) burst inwards. □ **implosion** /ɪm'pləʊʒ(ə)n/ *noun*.

implore /ɪm'plɔː/ *verb* (**-ring**) beg earnestly.

imply /ɪm'plaɪ/ *verb* (**-ies, -ied**) **1** (often + *that*) insinuate, hint. **2** mean.

■ **1** hint, indicate, insinuate, intimate, point to, suggest. **2** see SIGNIFY 1–3.

impolite /ɪmpə'laɪt/ *adjective* uncivil, rude. □ **impolitely** *adverb*. **impoliteness** *noun*.

■ discourteous, disrespectful, ill-bred, ill-mannered, impudent, insolent, rude, uncivil, vulgar.

impolitic /ɪm'pɒlɪtɪk/ *adjective* inexpedient, not advisable. □ **impoliticly** *adverb*.

imponderable /ɪm'pɒndərəb(ə)l/ *adjective* **1** that cannot be estimated. **2** very light. ● *noun* (usually in *plural*) imponderable thing. □ **imponderability** *noun*. **imponderably** *adverb*.

import *verb* /ɪm'pɔːt/ **1** bring in (esp. foreign goods) from abroad. **2** imply, mean. ● *noun* /'ɪmpɔːt/ **1** article or (in *plural*) amount imported. **2** importing. **3** meaning, implication. **4** importance. □ **importation** *noun*. **importer** /-'pɔːtə/ *noun*.

■ *verb* **1** bring in, buy in, introduce, ship in.

important /ɪm'pɔːt(ə)nt/ *adjective* **1** (often + *to*) of great consequence; momentous. **2** (of person) having position of authority or rank. **3** pompous. □ **importance** *noun*. **importantly** *adverb*.

■ **1** basic, big, cardinal, central, chief, consequential, critical, crucial, epoch-making, essential, foremost, fundamental, grave, historic, key, main, major, momentous, newsworthy, noteworthy, once in a lifetime, outstanding,

pressing, primary, principal, rare, salient, serious, signal, significant, strategic, substantial, urgent, valuable, vital, weighty. **2** celebrated, distinguished, eminent, famous, great, high-ranking, influential, known, leading, notable, noted, powerful, pre-eminent, prominent, renowned, top-level, well known.

importunate /ɪm'pɔːtjʊnət/ *adjective* making persistent or pressing requests. □ **importunity** /-'tjuːn-/ *noun*.

■ demanding, impatient, insistent, persistent, pressing, relentless, urgent, unremitting.

importune /ɪmpə'tjuːn/ *verb* (**-ning**) **1** pester (person) with requests. **2** solicit as prostitute.

■ **1** ask, badger, harass, hound, pester, *colloquial* plague, plead with, press, solicit, urge.

impose /ɪm'pəʊz/ *verb* (**-sing**) **1** enforce compliance with. **2** (often + *on*) inflict; lay (tax etc.). **3** (+ *on, upon*) take advantage of.

■ **1, 2** decree, dictate, enforce, exact, fix, foist, force, inflict, insist on, introduce, lay, levy, prescribe, set; (*impose on*) see BURDEN *verb*. **3** (*impose on*) see EXPLOIT *verb* 2.

imposing *adjective* impressive, esp. in appearance.

■ see IMPRESSIVE.

imposition /ɪmpə'zɪʃ(ə)n/ *noun* **1** imposing, being imposed. **2** unfair demand or burden. **3** tax, duty.

impossible /ɪm'pɒsɪb(ə)l/ *adjective* **1** not possible. **2** not easy or convenient. **3** *colloquial* outrageous, intolerable. □ **impossibility** *noun*. **impossibly** *adverb*.

■ **1** hopeless, impracticable, impractical, inconceivable, insoluble, insuperable, insurmountable, *colloquial* not on, out of the question, unachievable, unattainable, unimaginable, unobtainable, unthinkable, unviable, unworkable.

impost /'ɪmpəʊst/ *noun* tax, duty.

impostor /ɪm'pɒstə/ *noun* (also **imposter**) **1** person who assumes false character. **2** swindler.

imposture /ɪm'pɒstʃə/ *noun* fraudulent deception.

impotent /'ɪmpət(ə)nt/ *adjective* **1** powerless. **2** (of male) unable to achieve erection of penis or have sexual intercourse. □ **impotence** *noun*.

■ **1** debilitated, decrepit, emasculated, enervated, helpless, inadequate, incapable, incompetent, ineffective, ineffectual, inept, infirm, powerless, unable, weak.

impound /ɪm'paʊnd/ *verb* **1** confiscate. **2** shut up in pound.

impoverish /ɪm'pɒvərɪʃ/ *verb* make poor. □ **impoverishment** *noun*.

impracticable /ɪm'præktɪkəb(ə)l/ *adjective* impossible in practice. □ **impracticability** *noun*. **impracticably** *adverb*.

■ impossible, unachievable, unattainable, unworkable, useless.

impractical /ɪmˈpræktɪk(ə)l/ *adjective* **1** not practical. **2** *esp. US* not practicable. □ **impracticality** /-ˈkæl-/ *noun.*
　■ **1** academic, idealistic, quixotic, romantic, theoretical, unrealistic, visionary.

imprecation /ɪmprɪˈkeɪʃ(ə)n/ *noun formal* curse.

imprecise /ɪmprɪˈsaɪs/ *adjective* not precise.
　■ ambiguous, approximate, careless, estimated, fuzzy, guessed, hazy, ill-defined, inaccurate, inexact, inexplicit, loose, sloppy, undefined, unscientific, vague, *colloquial* waffly, woolly.

impregnable /ɪmˈpregnəb(ə)l/ *adjective* safe against attack. □ **impregnability** *noun.*
　■ impenetrable, invincible, inviolable, invulnerable, safe, secure, strong, unassailable, unconquerable.

impregnate /ˈɪmpregneɪt/ *verb* (**-ting**) **1** fill, saturate. **2** make pregnant. □ **impregnation** *noun.*

impresario /ɪmprɪˈsɑːrɪəʊ/ *noun* (*plural* **-s**) organizer of public entertainments.

impress *verb* /ɪmˈpres/ **1** affect or influence deeply. **2** arouse admiration or respect in. **3** (often + *on*) emphasize. **4** imprint, stamp. ● *noun* /ˈɪmpres/ **1** mark impressed. **2** characteristic quality.
　■ *verb* **1** affect, be memorable to, excite, influence, inspire, leave its mark on, move, persuade, stick in the mind of, stir, touch. **4** emboss, engrave, imprint, mark, print, stamp.

impression /ɪmˈpreʃ(ə)n/ *noun* **1** effect produced on mind. **2** belief. **3** imitation of person or sound, esp. done to entertain. **4** impressing; mark impressed. **5** unaltered reprint of book etc. (as opposed to edition). **6** issue of book or newspaper etc. **7** print from type or engraving.
　■ **1** effect, impact, influence, mark. **2** belief, consciousness, fancy, feeling, hunch, idea, memory, notion, opinion, recollection, sense, suspicion, view. **3** imitation, impersonation, mimicry, parody, *colloquial* take-off. **4** dent, hollow, imprint, indentation, mark, print, stamp. **5** printing, reprint.

impressionable *adjective* easily influenced.
　■ gullible, inexperienced, naive, persuadable, receptive, responsive, suggestible, susceptible.

impressionism *noun* **1** school of painting concerned with conveying effect of natural light on objects. **2** style of music or writing seeking to convey esp. fleeting feelings or experience. □ **impressionist** *noun.* **impressionistic** /-ˈnɪs-/ *adjective.*

impressive /ɪmˈpresɪv/ *adjective* arousing respect, approval, or admiration. □ **impressively** *adverb.* **impressiveness** *noun.*
　■ affecting, august, awe-inspiring, awesome, commanding, distinguished, evocative, exciting, formidable, grand, grandiose, great, imposing, magnificent, majestic, memorable, moving, powerful, redoubtable, remarkable, splendid, stately, stirring, striking, touching.

imprimatur /ɪmprɪˈmɑːtə/ *noun* **1** licence to print. **2** official approval.

imprint *verb* /ɪmˈprɪnt/ **1** (often + *on*) impress firmly, esp. on mind. **2** make impression of (figure etc.) on thing. **3** make impression on with stamp etc. ● *noun* /ˈɪmprɪnt/ **1** impression. **2** printer's or publisher's name in book etc.

imprison /ɪmˈprɪz(ə)n/ *verb* (**-n-**) **1** put into prison. **2** confine. □ **imprisonment** *noun.*
　■ **1** commit to prison, detain, immure, incarcerate, intern, jail, keep in custody, keep under house arrest, keep under lock and key, lock away, lock up, put away, remand, send down, shut up. **2** box in, cage, confine, coop up, shut in, shut up.
　□ **imprisonment** confinement, custody, detention, house arrest, incarceration, internment, jail, remand, restraint.

improbable /ɪmˈprɒbəb(ə)l/ *adjective* not likely; difficult to believe. □ **improbability** *noun.* **improbably** *adverb.*
　■ absurd, doubtful, dubious, far-fetched, hard to believe, implausible, incredible, preposterous, questionable, unbelievable, unconvincing, unexpected, unlikely.

improbity /ɪmˈprəʊbɪtɪ/ *noun* (*plural* **-ies**) **1** wickedness. **2** dishonesty. **3** wicked or dishonest act.

impromptu /ɪmˈprɒmptjuː/ *adverb & adjective* unrehearsed. ● *noun* (*plural* **-s**) **1** impromptu performance or speech. **2** short, usually solo, musical piece, often improvisatory in style.
　■ *adjective* ad lib, extempore, extemporized, improvised, impulsive, offhand, off the cuff, on the spur of the moment, spontaneous, unplanned, unpremeditated, unprepared, unrehearsed, unscripted.

improper /ɪmˈprɒpə/ *adjective* **1** unseemly, indecent. **2** inaccurate, wrong. □ **improperly** *adverb.*
　■ **1** ill-judged, ill-timed, impolite, inappropriate, indecent, infelicitous, inopportune, offensive, out of place, risqué, suggestive, uncalled-for, unfit, unseemly, unsuitable, unwarranted. **2** erroneous, false, imprecise, inaccurate, incorrect, inexact, irregular, mistaken, wrong.

impropriety /ɪmprəˈpraɪətɪ/ *noun* (*plural* **-ies**) **1** indecency. **2** instance of this. **3** incorrectness, unfitness.
　■ **1** immorality, indecency, indelicacy, insensitivity, obscenity, rudeness, unseemliness, vileness. **3** inappropriateness, incorrectness, infelicity, irregularity, unfitness, unsuitability.

improve /ɪmˈpruːv/ *verb* (**-ving**) **1** make or become better. **2** (+ *on*) produce something better than. **3** (as **improving** *adjective*) giving moral benefit. □ **improvement** *noun.*
　■ **1** (*business improved*) advance, develop, grow, increase, look up, progress, take a turn for the better; (*improve after illness*) convalesce, get better, pick up, rally, recover, recuperate, revive, strengthen, turn the corner; (*improve one's ways*) ameliorate, amend, better, correct, enhance,

enrich, mend, polish (up), rectify, refine, reform, revise; (*improve a home*) decorate, extend, modernize, recondition, refurbish, renovate, repair, touch up, update, upgrade. □ **improvement** advance, alteration, amelioration, betterment, correction, development, enhancement, extension, facelift, gain, increase, lift, modernization, modification, progress, rally, recovery, reformation, renovation, upswing, upturn.

improvident /ɪmˈprɒvɪd(ə)nt/ *adjective* **1** lacking foresight. **2** wasteful. □ **improvidence** *noun.* **improvidently** *adverb.*

improvise /ˈɪmprəvaɪz/ *verb* (**-sing**) **1** compose extempore. **2** provide or construct from materials etc. not intended for the purpose. □ **improvisation** *noun.* **improvisational** *adjective.* **improvisatory** /-ˈzeɪtərɪ/ *adjective.*
■ **1** ad lib, extemporize, perform impromptu, play (it) by ear, vamp. **2** concoct, contrive, devise, invent, make do, make up, throw together.

imprudent /ɪmˈpruːd(ə)nt/ *adjective* rash, indiscreet. □ **imprudence** *noun.* **imprudently** *adverb.*

impudent /ˈɪmpjʊd(ə)nt/ *adjective* impertinent. □ **impudence** *noun.* **impudently** *adverb.*
■ audacious, bold, cheeky, disrespectful, forward, *colloquial* fresh, impertinent, insolent, pert, presumptuous, rude, saucy.

impugn /ɪmˈpjuːn/ *verb* challenge; call in question.

impulse /ˈɪmpʌls/ *noun* **1** sudden urge; tendency to follow such urges. **2** impelling. **3** impetus.
■ **1** caprice, desire, instinct, urge, whim. **3** drive, force, impetus, motive, pressure, push, stimulus, thrust.

impulsive /ɪmˈpʌlsɪv/ *adjective* **1** apt to act on impulse. **2** done on impulse. **3** tending to impel. □ **impulsively** *adverb.* **impulsiveness** *noun.*
■ **1** capricious, emotional, foolhardy, hot-headed, impetuous, rash, reckless, unthinking. **2** automatic, hare-brained, hasty, headlong, impromptu, instinctive, intuitive, involuntary, madcap, precipitate, rash, reckless, snap, spontaneous, sudden, thoughtless, unconscious, unplanned, unpremeditated, wild.

impunity /ɪmˈpjuːnɪtɪ/ *noun* exemption from punishment or injurious consequences. □ **with impunity** without punishment etc.

impure /ɪmˈpjʊə/ *adjective* **1** adulterated. **2** dirty. **3** unchaste.
■ **1** adulterated, contaminated, defiled, foul, infected, polluted, tainted, unclean, unwholesome. **2** see DIRTY *adjective* 1. **3** see IMMORAL.

impurity *noun* (*plural* **-ies**) **1** being impure. **2** impure thing or part.
■ **1** adulteration, contamination, defilement, infection, pollution, taint. **2** contaminant, dirt, foreign body, pollutant.

impute /ɪmˈpjuːt/ *verb* (**-ting**) (+ *to*) ascribe (fault etc.) to. □ **imputation** *noun.*

in *preposition* **1** *expressing inclusion or position within limits of space, time, circumstance, etc.* **2** after (specified period of time). **3** with respect to. **4** as proportionate part of. **5** with form or arrangement of. **6** as member of. **7** involved with. **8** within ability of. **9** having the condition of. **10** affected by. **11** having as aim. **12** by means of. **13** meaning. **14** into (with verb of motion or change). ● *adverb* **1** *expressing position bounded by certain limits, or movement to point enclosed by them.* **2** into room etc. **3** at home etc. **4** so as to be enclosed. **5** as part of a publication. **6** in fashion, season, or office. **7** (of player etc.) having turn or right to play. **8** (of transport) at platform etc. **9** (of season, harvest, ordered goods, etc.) having arrived or been received. **10** (of fire etc.) burning. **11** (of tide) at highest point. ● *adjective* **1** internal; living etc. inside. **2** fashionable. **3** (of joke etc.) confined to small group. □ **in-between** *colloquial* intermediate. **in-house** within an institution, company, etc. **ins and outs** (often + *of*) details. **in so far as** to the extent that. **in that** because; in so far as. **in-tray** tray for incoming documents etc. **in with** on good terms with.

in. *abbreviation* inch(es).

inability /ɪnəˈbɪlɪtɪ/ *noun* being unable.

inaccessible /ɪnækˈsesɪb(ə)l/ *adjective* **1** not accessible. **2** unapproachable. □ **inaccessibility** *noun.*
■ **1** cut off, deserted, desolate, godforsaken, impassable, impenetrable, inconvenient, isolated, lonely, outlying, out of reach, out of the way, private, remote, solitary, unavailable, unfrequented, *colloquial* unget-at-able, unobtainable, unreachable, unusable. **2** aloof, antisocial, distant, private, remote, solitary, unapproachable, unavailable, unsociable.

inaccurate /ɪnˈækjʊrət/ *adjective* not accurate. □ **inaccuracy** *noun* (*plural* **-ies**). **inaccurately** *adverb.*
■ erroneous, fallacious, false, faulty, flawed, imperfect, imprecise, incorrect, inexact, misleading, mistaken, unfaithful, unreliable, unsound, untrue, vague, wrong.

inaction /ɪnˈækʃ(ə)n/ *noun* absence of action.

inactive /ɪnˈæktɪv/ *adjective* not active; not operating. □ **inactivity** /-ˈtɪv-/ *noun.*
■ asleep, dormant, hibernating, idle, immobile, inanimate, indolent, inert, languid, lazy, lethargic, out of action, passive, quiescent, quiet, sedentary, sleepy, slothful, slow, sluggish, somnolent, torpid, unemployed, unoccupied, vegetating.

inadequate /ɪnˈædɪkwət/ *adjective* **1** insufficient. **2** incompetent. □ **inadequacy** *noun* (*plural* **-ies**). **inadequately** *adverb.*
■ **1** deficient, disappointing, faulty, imperfect, incomplete, insufficient, limited, meagre, mean, niggardly, *colloquial* pathetic, scanty, scarce, skimpy, sparse, unacceptable, unsatisfactory. **2** incapable, incompetent, ineffective, inept, unsuitable.

inadmissible /ɪnədˈmɪsɪb(ə)l/ *adjective* not

allowable. □ **inadmissibility** *noun.* **inadmissibly** *adverb.*

inadvertent /məd'vɜːt(ə)nt/ *adjective* **1** unintentional. **2** inattentive. □ **inadvertence** *noun.* **inadvertently** *adverb.*

inadvisable /məd'vaɪzəb(ə)l/ *adjective* not advisable. □ **inadvisability** *noun.*
■ foolish, ill-advised, imprudent, misguided, silly, unsound, unwise.

inalienable /ɪn'eɪlɪənəb(ə)l/ *adjective* that cannot be transferred to another or taken away.

inane /ɪ'neɪn/ *adjective* **1** silly, senseless. **2** empty. □ **inanity** /-'næn-/ *noun* (*plural* **-ies**).

inanimate /ɪn'ænɪmət/ *adjective* **1** not endowed with animal life. **2** spiritless, dull.
■ **1** dead, insentient, lifeless. **2** *colloquial* cold, dead, dull, lifeless, soulless, spiritless.

inapplicable /mə'plɪkəb(ə)l/ *adjective* not applicable, irrelevant. □ **inapplicability** *noun.*

inapposite /ɪn'æpəzɪt/ *adjective* not apposite.

inappropriate /mə'prəʊprɪət/ *adjective* not appropriate. □ **inappropriately** *adverb.* **inappropriateness** *noun.*
■ ill-judged, ill-suited, ill-timed, improper, inapplicable, inapposite, incompatible, incongruous, incorrect, inept, inopportune, irrelevant, out of place, tactless, tasteless, unbecoming, unbefitting, unfit, unseasonable, unseemly, unsuitable, unsuited, untimely, wrong.

inapt /ɪn'æpt/ *adjective* **1** not suitable. **2** unskilful. □ **inaptitude** *noun.*

inarticulate /mɑː'tɪkjʊlət/ *adjective* **1** unable to express oneself clearly. **2** (of speech) not articulate, indistinct. **3** dumb. **4** not jointed. □ **inarticulately** *adverb.*
■ **1** faltering, halting, hesitant, mumbling, shy, stammering, stuttering. **2** *see* INCOHERENT. **3** dumb, mute, silent, speechless, tongue-tied, voiceless.

inartistic /mɑː'tɪstɪk/ *adjective* lacking skill in art; not appreciating art.

inasmuch /ɪnəz'mʌtʃ/ *adverb* (+ *as*) **1** since, because. **2** to the extent that.

inattentive /mə'tentɪv/ *adjective* **1** not paying attention. **2** neglecting to show courtesy. □ **inattention** *noun.* **inattentively** *adverb.*
■ absent-minded, abstracted, *colloquial* asleep, careless, daydreaming, distracted, dreaming, drifting, heedless, in a world of one's own, lacking concentration, negligent, preoccupied, remiss, slack, thoughtless, unobservant, vague, wandering, wool-gathering.

inaudible /ɪn'ɔːdɪb(ə)l/ *adjective* that cannot be heard. □ **inaudibly** *adverb.*
■ faint, imperceptible, muffled, mumbled, quiet, silenced, silent, stifled, undetectable, undistinguishable, unheard.

inaugural /ɪn'ɔːgjʊr(ə)l/ *adjective* of inauguration. ● *noun* inaugural speech or lecture.

inaugurate /ɪn'ɔːgjʊreɪt/ *verb* (**-ting**) **1** admit (person) to office. **2** initiate use of or begin with ceremony. **3** begin, introduce. □ **inauguration** *noun.*

inauspicious /mɔː'spɪʃəs/ *adjective* **1** not of good omen. **2** unlucky.

inborn /'mbɔːn/ *adjective* existing from birth; innate.

inbred /ɪn'bred/ *adjective* **1** inborn. **2** produced by inbreeding.

inbreeding /ɪn'briːdɪŋ/ *noun* breeding from closely related animals or people.

inbuilt /mbɪlt/ *adjective* incorporated as part of structure.

Inc. *abbreviation US* Incorporated.

incalculable /ɪn'kælkjʊləb(ə)l/ *adjective* **1** too great for calculation. **2** not calculable beforehand. **3** uncertain. □ **incalculability** *noun.* **incalculably** *adverb.*

incandesce /mkæn'des/ *verb* (**-cing**) (cause to) glow with heat.

incandescent *adjective* **1** glowing with heat. **2** shining. **3** (of artificial light) produced by glowing filament etc. □ **incandescence** *noun.*

incantation /mkæn'teɪʃ(ə)n/ *noun* spell, charm. □ **incantational** *adjective.*

incapable /ɪn'keɪpəb(ə)l/ *adjective* **1** not capable. **2** too honest, kind, etc. to do something. **3** not capable of rational conduct. □ **incapability** *noun.*
■ **1** clumsy, helpless, impotent, inadequate, incompetent, ineffective, ineffectual, inept, powerless, stupid, unable, unfit, unqualified, *colloquial* useless, weak.

incapacitate /mkə'pæsɪteɪt/ *verb* (**-ting**) make incapable or unfit.

incapacity /mkə'pæsɪtɪ/ *noun* **1** inability. **2** legal disqualification.

incarcerate /ɪn'kɑːsəreɪt/ *verb* (**-ting**) imprison. □ **incarceration** *noun.*

incarnate /ɪn'kɑːnət/ *adjective* in esp. human form.

incarnation /mkɑː'neɪʃ(ə)n/ *noun* **1** embodiment in flesh. **2** (**the Incarnation**) embodiment of God in Christ. **3** (often + *of*) living type (of a quality etc.).

incautious /ɪn'kɔːʃəs/ *adjective* rash. □ **incautiously** *adverb.*

incendiary /ɪn'sendɪərɪ/ *adjective* **1** (of bomb) filled with material for causing fires. **2** of arson. **3** guilty of arson. **4** inflammatory. ● *noun* (*plural* **-ies**) incendiary person or bomb.

incense[1] /'msens/ *noun* **1** gum or spice giving sweet smell when burned. **2** smoke of this, esp. in religious ceremony.

incense[2] /ɪn'sens/ *verb* (**-sing**) make angry.

incentive /ɪn'sentɪv/ *noun* **1** motive, incitement. **2** payment etc. encouraging effort in work. ● *adjective* serving to motivate or incite.

■ *noun* bait, carrot, encouragement, enticement, impetus, incitement, inducement, lure, motivation, reward, stimulus, *colloquial* sweetener.

inception /ɪnˈsepʃ(ə)n/ *noun* beginning.

incessant /ɪnˈses(ə)nt/ *adjective* unceasing, continual, repeated. □ **incessantly** *adverb*.

■ ceaseless, chronic, constant, continual, continuous, endless, eternal, everlasting, interminable, never-ending, non-stop, perennial, permanent, perpetual, persistent, relentless, unbroken, unceasing, unending, unremitting.

incest /ˈɪnsest/ *noun* crime of sexual intercourse between people prohibited from marrying because of closeness of their blood relationship.

incestuous /ɪnˈsestjʊəs/ *adjective* **1** of or guilty of incest. **2** having relationships restricted to a particular group etc.

inch *noun* **1** twelfth of (linear) foot (2.54 cm). **2** this used as unit of map-scale (e.g. 1 inch to 1 mile) or as unit of rainfall (= 1 inch depth of water). ● *verb* move gradually. □ **every inch** entirely. **within an inch of one's life** almost to death.

inchoate /ɪnˈkəʊeɪt/ *adjective* **1** just begun. **2** undeveloped. □ **inchoation** *noun*.

incidence /ˈɪnsɪd(ə)ns/ *noun* **1** range, scope, extent, manner, or rate of occurrence. **2** falling of line, ray, particles, etc. on surface. **3** coming into contact with thing.

incident /ˈɪnsɪd(ə)nt/ *noun* **1** event, occurrence. **2** violent episode, civil or military. **3** episode in play, film, etc. ● *adjective* **1** (often + *to*) apt to occur, naturally attaching. **2** (often + *on, upon*) (of light etc.) falling.

■ *noun* **1** *colloquial* affair, circumstance, episode, event, fact, happening, occasion, occurrence, proceeding. **2** accident, commotion, confrontation, disturbance, fight, *colloquial* kerfuffle, scene, to-do, upset. **3** episode, scene.

incidental /ɪnsɪˈdent(ə)l/ *adjective* (often + *to*) **1** minor, supplementary. **2** happening by chance. **3** not essential. □ **incidental music** music played during or between scenes of play, film, etc.

■ **1** attendant, minor, secondary, subordinate, subsidiary, supplementary. **2** accidental, adventitious, casual, chance, fortuitous, odd, random, serendipitous, unplanned. **3** dispensable, inessential, insignificant, non-essential.

incidentally *adverb* **1** by the way. **2** in an incidental way.

incinerate /ɪnˈsɪnəreɪt/ *verb* (-ting) burn to ashes. □ **incineration** *noun*.

incinerator *noun* furnace or device for incineration.

incipient /ɪnˈsɪpɪənt/ *adjective* beginning; in early stage.

■ beginning, developing, early, embryonic, growing, new, rudimentary, starting.

incise /ɪnˈsaɪz/ *verb* (-sing) **1** make cut in. **2** engrave.

incision /ɪnˈsɪʒ(ə)n/ *noun* **1** cutting, esp. by surgeon. **2** cut.

incisive /ɪnˈsaɪsɪv/ *adjective* **1** sharp. **2** clear and effective. □ **incisiveness** *noun*.

■ acute, clear, concise, cutting, decisive, direct, penetrating, percipient, precise, sharp, telling, trenchant.

incisor /ɪnˈsaɪzə/ *noun* cutting-tooth, esp. at front of mouth.

incite /ɪnˈsaɪt/ *verb* (-ting) (often + *to*) urge on, stir up. □ **incitement** *noun*. **inciter** *noun*.

■ awaken, encourage, excite, fire, foment, inflame, inspire, prompt, provoke, rouse, spur on, stimulate, stir, urge, whip up, work up.

incivility /ɪnsɪˈvɪlɪtɪ/ *noun* (*plural* -ies) **1** rudeness. **2** impolite act.

inclement /ɪnˈklemənt/ *adjective* (of weather) severe, stormy. □ **inclemency** *noun*.

inclination /ɪnklɪˈneɪʃ(ə)n/ *noun* **1** propensity. **2** liking, affection. **3** slope, slant.

■ **1** bent, bias, disposition, habit, instinct, leaning, penchant, predisposition, proclivity, propensity, readiness, tendency, trend, willingness. **2** affection, desire, fondness, liking, partiality, penchant, predilection, preference.

incline *verb* /ɪnˈklaɪn/ (-ning) **1** (usually in *passive*) dispose, influence; have specified tendency. **2** be disposed; tend. **3** (cause to) lean or bend. ● *noun* /ˈɪnklaɪn/ slope.

■ *verb* **1** dispose, influence, lead, predispose; (*inclined*) see LIABLE 4–5. **3** angle, ascend, bank, bend, bow, descend, drop, gravitate, lean, rise, slant, slope, tend, tilt, tip, veer. ● *noun* acclivity, ascent, declivity, descent, drop, grade, gradient, hill, pitch, ramp, rise, slope.

include /ɪnˈkluːd/ *verb* (-ding) comprise; regard or treat as part of whole. □ **inclusion** /-ʒ(ə)n/ *noun*.

■ add in, allow for, combine, comprehend, comprise, consist of, contain, count, cover, embody, embrace, encompass, incorporate, involve, make room for, subsume, take in, take into account.

inclusive /ɪnˈkluːsɪv/ *adjective* **1** (often + *of*) including. **2** including the limits stated. **3** comprehensive. **4** including all accessory payments. □ **inclusively** *adverb*. **inclusiveness** *noun*.

incognito /ɪnkɒgˈniːtəʊ/ *adjective* & *adverb* with one's name or identity concealed. ● *noun* (*plural* -s) **1** person who is incognito. **2** pretended identity.

incoherent /ɪnkəʊˈhɪərənt/ *adjective* **1** unintelligible. **2** lacking logic or consistency. **3** not clear. □ **incoherence** *noun*. **incoherently** *adverb*.

■ confused, disconnected, disjointed, disordered, disorganized, garbled, illogical, inarticulate, incomprehensible, inconsistent, irrational, jumbled, mixed up, muddled, rambling, scrambled, unclear, unconnected, unintelligible, unstructured, unsystematic.

incombustible /ɪnkəmˈbʌstɪb(ə)l/ *adjective* that cannot be burnt.
- fireproof, fire-resistant, flameproof, non-flammable.

income /ˈɪnkʌm/ *noun* money received, esp. periodically, from work, investments, etc. □ **income tax** tax levied on income.
- earnings, gain, interest, pay, pension, proceeds, profits, receipts, return, revenue, salary, takings, wages.

incoming *adjective* 1 coming in. 2 succeeding another.
- 1 approaching, arriving, entering, coming, landing, returning, rising (*tide*). 2 new, next, succeeding.

incommensurable /ɪnkəˈmenʃərəb(ə)l/ *adjective* 1 (often + *with*) not comparable in size, value, etc. 2 having no common factor. □ **incommensurability** *noun*.

incommensurate /ɪnkəˈmenʃərət/ *adjective* 1 (often + *with*, *to*) out of proportion; inadequate. 2 incommensurable.

incommode /ɪnkəˈməʊd/ *verb* (**-ding**) *formal* 1 inconvenience. 2 trouble, annoy.

incommodious /ɪnkəˈməʊdɪəs/ *adjective* *formal* too small for comfort; inconvenient.

incommunicable /ɪnkəˈmjuːnɪkəb(ə)l/ *adjective* that cannot be shared or communicated.

incommunicado /ɪnkəmjuːnɪˈkɑːdəʊ/ *adjective* 1 without means of communication. 2 in solitary confinement.

incomparable /ɪnˈkɒmpərəb(ə)l/ *adjective* without an equal; matchless. □ **incomparability** *noun*. **incomparably** *adverb*.

incompatible /ɪnkəmˈpætɪb(ə)l/ *adjective* not compatible. □ **incompatibility** *noun*.
- antipathetic, at variance, clashing, conflicting, contradictory, contrasting, different, discordant, discrepant, incongruous, inconsistent, irreconcilable, mismatched, opposed, unsuited.

incompetent /ɪnˈkɒmpɪt(ə)nt/ *adjective* 1 inept; showing lack of skill. 2 (often + *to*) lacking the necessary skill; not legally qualified. □ **incompetence** *noun*.
- 1 bungled, inadequate, inept, inexpert, unacceptable, unsatisfactory, unskilful, *colloquial* useless. 2 bungling, clumsy, feckless, gauche, helpless, hopeless, incapable, ineffective, ineffectual, inefficient, inexperienced, maladroit, unfit, unqualified, unskilled, untrained.

incomplete /ɪnkəmˈpliːt/ *adjective* not complete. □ **incompleteness** *noun*.
- abbreviated, abridged, bitty, deficient, edited, expurgated, fragmentary, imperfect, insufficient, partial, selective, shortened, *colloquial* sketchy, unfinished, unpolished, wanting.

incomprehensible /ɪnkɒmprɪˈhensɪb(ə)l/ *adjective* that cannot be understood.
- abstruse, arcane, baffling, beyond comprehension, cryptic, deep, enigmatic, esoteric, illegible, impenetrable, indecipherable, meaningless, mysterious, mystifying, obscure, opaque, perplexing, puzzling, recondite, strange, too difficult, unclear, unfathomable, unintelligible.

incomprehension /ɪnkɒmprɪˈhenʃ(ə)n/ *noun* failure to understand.

inconceivable /ɪnkənˈsiːvəb(ə)l/ *adjective* that cannot be imagined. □ **inconceivably** *adverb*.
- implausible, incredible, *colloquial* mind-boggling, staggering, unbelievable, undreamed-of, unimaginable, unthinkable.

inconclusive /ɪnkənˈkluːsɪv/ *adjective* (of argument etc.) not convincing or decisive.
- ambiguous, equivocal, indecisive, indefinite, open, open-ended, questionable, uncertain, unconvincing, unresolved, up in the air.

incongruous /ɪnˈkɒŋɡrʊəs/ *adjective* 1 out of place; absurd. 2 (often + *with*) out of keeping. □ **incongruity** /-ˈɡruːɪtɪ/ *noun* (*plural* **-ies**). **incongruously** *adverb*.
- absurd, clashing, conflicting, contrasting, discordant, ill-matched, ill-suited, inappropriate, incompatible, inconsistent, irreconcilable, nonsensical, odd, out of keeping, out of place, preposterous, surprising, uncoordinated, unsuited.

inconsequent /ɪnˈkɒnsɪkwənt/ *adjective* 1 irrelevant. 2 not following logically. 3 disconnected. □ **inconsequence** *noun*.

inconsequential /ɪnkɒnsɪˈkwenʃ(ə)l/ *adjective* 1 unimportant. 2 inconsequent. □ **inconsequentially** *adverb*.

inconsiderable /ɪnkənˈsɪdərəb(ə)l/ *adjective* 1 of small size, value, etc. 2 not worth considering. □ **inconsiderably** *adverb*.

inconsiderate /ɪnkənˈsɪdərət/ *adjective* 1 not considerate of others. 2 thoughtless. □ **inconsiderately** *adverb*. **inconsiderateness** *noun*.
- 1 insensitive, intolerant, negligent, rude, self-centred, selfish, tactless, thoughtless, uncaring, unconcerned, unfriendly, ungracious, unhelpful, unkind, unsympathetic, unthinking. 2 careless, heedless, negligent, thoughtless, unthinking.

inconsistent /ɪnkənˈsɪst(ə)nt/ *adjective* 1 not consistent, variable. 2 (often + *with*) not compatible; not in keeping. □ **inconsistency** *noun* (*plural* **-ies**). **inconsistently** *adverb*.
- 1 capricious, changeable, erratic, fickle, inconstant, patchy, unpredictable, unreliable, unstable, *colloquial* up and down, variable. 2 see INCOMPATIBLE.

inconsolable /ɪnkənˈsəʊləb(ə)l/ *adjective* that cannot be consoled. □ **inconsolably** *adverb*.

inconspicuous /ɪnkənˈspɪkjʊəs/ *adjective* not conspicuous; not easily noticed. □ **inconspicuously** *adverb*. **inconspicuousness** *noun*.

■ camouflaged, concealed, discreet, hidden, insignificant, in the background, invisible, modest, ordinary, out of sight, plain, restrained, retiring, self-effacing, small, unassuming, unobtrusive, unostentatious.

inconstant /ɪnˈkɒnst(ə)nt/ *adjective* **1** fickle. **2** variable. □ **inconstancy** *noun* (*plural* **-ies**).

incontestable /ɪnkənˈtestəb(ə)l/ *adjective* that cannot be disputed. □ **incontestably** *adverb*.

incontinent /ɪnˈkɒntɪnənt/ *adjective* **1** unable to control bowels or bladder. **2** lacking self-restraint. □ **incontinence** *noun*.

incontrovertible /ɪnkɒntrəˈvɜːtɪb(ə)l/ *adjective* indisputable. □ **incontrovertibly** *adverb*.

inconvenience /ɪnkənˈviːnɪəns/ *noun* **1** lack of ease or comfort; trouble. **2** cause or instance of this. ● *verb* (**-cing**) cause inconvenience to.

■ *noun* **1** bother, discomfort, trouble. **2** annoyance, bother, discomfort, disruption, drawback, encumbrance, hindrance, impediment, irritation, nuisance, trouble. ● *verb* annoy, bother, disturb, *formal* incommode, irk, irritate, put out, trouble.

inconvenient *adjective* **1** causing trouble, difficulty, or discomfort. **2** awkward. □ **inconveniently** *adverb*.

■ **1** annoying, bothersome, difficult, embarrassing, ill-timed, inopportune, irksome, irritating, *colloquial* tiresome, troublesome, unsuitable, untimely, untoward. **2** awkward, burdensome, cumbersome, troublesome, unwieldy.

incorporate *verb* /ɪnˈkɔːpəreɪt/ (**-ting**) **1** include as part or ingredient. **2** (often + *in, with*) unite (in one body). **3** admit as member of company etc. **4** (esp. as **incorporated** *adjective*) constitute as legal corporation. ● *adjective* /ɪnˈkɔːpərət/ incorporated. □ **incorporation** *noun*.

■ *verb* **1** admit, combine, comprehend, comprise, consist of, contain, embody, embrace, encompass, include, involve, mix in, subsume, take in, unite. **2** see UNITE 1.

incorporeal /ɪnkɔːˈpɔːrɪəl/ *adjective* without substance or material existence. □ **incorporeally** *adverb*.

incorrect /ɪnkəˈrekt/ *adjective* **1** untrue, inaccurate. **2** improper, unsuitable. □ **incorrectly** *adverb*. **incorrectness** *noun*.

■ **1** erroneous, fallacious, false, faulty, imprecise, inaccurate, inexact, misleading, mistaken, specious, untrue, wrong. **2** see INAPPROPRIATE.

incorrigible /ɪnˈkɒrɪdʒɪb(ə)l/ *adjective* **1** that cannot be corrected or improved. **2** incurably bad. □ **incorrigibility** *noun*. **incorrigibly** *adverb*.

■ **1** confirmed, dyed in the wool, habitual, hardened, hopeless, impenitent, incurable, intractable, inveterate, irredeemable, obdurate, shameless, unalterable, unreformable, unrepentant. **2** see NAUGHTY 1, WICKED 1.

incorruptible /ɪnkəˈrʌptɪb(ə)l/ *adjective* **1** that cannot decay. **2** that cannot be corrupted. □ **incorruptibility** *noun*. **incorruptibly** *adverb*.

■ **1** see EVERLASTING 1. **2** honest, honourable, just, moral, sound, true, trustworthy, unbribable, upright.

increase *verb* /ɪnˈkriːs/ (**-sing**) become or make greater or more numerous. ● *noun* /ˈɪnkriːs/ **1** growth, enlargement. **2** (of people, animals, or plants) multiplication. **3** increased amount. □ **on the increase** increasing.

■ *verb* add to, advance, amplify, augment, boost, broaden, build up, develop, enlarge, escalate, expand, extend, gain, get bigger, grow, improve, intensify, lengthen, magnify, make bigger, maximize, multiply, proliferate, prolong, put up, raise, snowball, spread, step up, strengthen, stretch, swell, wax, widen. ● *noun* **1** addition, amplification, augmentation, boost, build-up, *Music* crescendo, development, enlargement, escalation, expansion, extension, gain, growth, inflation, intensification, rise, spread, upsurge, upturn. **2** growth, multiplication, proliferation, spread. **3** addition, extension, gain, growth, increment, rise.

increasingly /ɪnˈkriːsɪŋlɪ/ *adverb* more and more.

incredible /ɪnˈkredɪb(ə)l/ *adjective* **1** that cannot be believed. **2** *colloquial* surprising; extremely good. □ **incredibility** *noun*. **incredibly** *adverb*.

■ **1** beyond belief, far-fetched, implausible, impossible, improbable, inconceivable, miraculous, surprising, unbelievable, unconvincing, unimaginable, unlikely, untenable, unthinkable. **2** see EXTRAORDINARY 1,2.

incredulous /ɪnˈkredjʊləs/ *adjective* unwilling to believe; showing disbelief. □ **incredulity** /ɪnkrɪˈdjuːlɪtɪ/ *noun*. **incredulously** *adverb*.

■ disbelieving, distrustful, doubtful, dubious, mistrustful, questioning, sceptical, suspicious, unbelieving, unconvinced.

increment /ˈɪŋkrɪmənt/ *noun* **1** amount of increase. **2** added amount. □ **incremental** /-ˈment(ə)l/ *adjective*.

incriminate /ɪnˈkrɪmɪneɪt/ *verb* (**-ting**) **1** indicate as guilty. **2** charge with crime. □ **incrimination** *noun*. **incriminatory** *adjective*.

■ **1** blame, embroil, implicate, inculpate, involve. **2** accuse, charge, inculpate, indict.

incrustation /ɪnkrʌˈsteɪʃ(ə)n/ *noun* (also **encrustation**) **1** encrusting, being encrusted. **2** crust, hard coating. **3** deposit on surface.

incubate /ˈɪŋkjʊbeɪt/ *verb* (**-ting**) **1** hatch (eggs) by sitting on them or by artificial heat. **2** cause (bacteria etc.) to develop. **3** develop slowly.

incubation *noun* **1** incubating, being incubated. **2** period between infection and appearance of first symptoms.

incubator *noun* apparatus providing warmth for hatching eggs, rearing premature babies, or developing bacteria.

incubus /'ɪŋkjʊbəs/ *noun* (*plural* **-buses** or **-bi** /-baɪ/) **1** demon or male spirit formerly believed to have sexual intercourse with sleeping women. **2** nightmare. **3** oppressive person or thing.

inculcate /'ɪnkʌlkeɪt/ *verb* (**-ting**) (often + *upon*, *in*) urge; impress persistently. ▫ **inculcation** *noun*.

inculpate /'ɪnkʌlpeɪt/ *verb* involve in charge; accuse.

incumbency /ɪn'kʌmbənsɪ/ *noun* (*plural* **-ies**) office or tenure of incumbent.

incumbent /ɪn'kʌmbənt/ *adjective* **1** lying, pressing. **2** currently holding office. ● *noun* holder of office, esp. benefice. ▫ **it is incumbent on a person** (+ *to do*) it is a person's duty.

incur /ɪn'kɜː/ *verb* (**-rr-**) bring on oneself.
■ earn, expose oneself to, get, lay oneself open to, provoke, run up, suffer.

incurable /ɪn'kjʊərəb(ə)l/ *adjective* that cannot be cured. ● *noun* incurable person. ▫ **incurability** *noun.* **incurably** *adverb*.
■ *adjective* (*incurable disease*) fatal, hopeless, inoperable, irremediable, irreparable, terminal, untreatable; (*incurable flirt*) incorrigible, irredeemable, unreformable.

incurious /ɪn'kjʊərɪəs/ *adjective* lacking curiosity.

incursion /ɪn'kɜːʃ(ə)n/ *noun* invasion; sudden attack. ▫ **incursive** *adjective*.

indebted /ɪn'detɪd/ *adjective* (usually + *to*) owing money or gratitude. ▫ **indebtedness** *noun*.
■ beholden, bound, grateful, obliged, thankful, under an obligation.

indecent /ɪn'diːs(ə)nt/ *adjective* **1** offending against decency. **2** unbecoming; unsuitable. ▫ **indecent assault** sexual attack not involving rape. ▫ **indecency** *noun*. **indecently** *adverb*.
■ **1** blue, coarse, crude, dirty, immodest, impolite, improper, impure, indelicate, insensitive, *colloquial jocular* naughty, obscene, offensive, risqué, *colloquial* rude, sexy, smutty, suggestive, titillating, unprintable, unrepeatable, vulgar. **2** see INDECOROUS 1.

indecipherable /ɪndɪ'saɪfərəb(ə)l/ *adjective* that cannot be deciphered.

indecision /ɪndɪ'sɪʒ(ə)n/ *noun* inability to decide; hesitation.

indecisive /ɪndɪ'saɪsɪv/ *adjective* **1** irresolute. **2** not conclusive. ▫ **indecisively** *adverb*. **indecisiveness** *noun*.
■ **1** doubtful, equivocal, evasive, hesitant, in two minds, irresolute, undecided. **2** see INDEFINITE 1.

indecorous /ɪn'dekərəs/ *adjective* **1** improper, undignified. **2** in bad taste. ▫ **indecorously** *adverb*.
■ **1** churlish, ill-bred, improper, inappropriate, indecent, unbecoming, uncouth, undignified, unseemly. **2** in bad taste, indelicate, offensive, tasteless, vulgar.

indeed /ɪn'diːd/ *adverb* **1** in truth; really. **2** admittedly. ● *interjection: expressing irony, incredulity, etc.*

indefatigable /ɪndɪ'fætɪgəb(ə)l/ *adjective* unwearying, unremitting. ▫ **indefatigably** *adverb*.

indefeasible /ɪndɪ'fiːzɪb(ə)l/ *adjective literary* (esp. of claim, rights, etc.) that cannot be forfeited or annulled.

indefensible /ɪndɪ'fensɪb(ə)l/ *adjective* that cannot be defended. ▫ **indefensibility** *noun.* **indefensibly** *adverb*.
■ inexcusable, insupportable, unjustifiable, unpardonable, unreasonable, unsound, untenable, vulnerable, weak, wrong.

indefinable /ɪndɪ'faɪnəb(ə)l/ *adjective* that cannot be defined; mysterious. ▫ **indefinably** *adverb*.

indefinite /ɪn'defɪnɪt/ *adjective* **1** vague, undefined. **2** unlimited. **3** (of adjectives, adverbs, and pronouns) not determining the person etc. referred to. ▫ **indefinite article** word (*a*, *an* in English) placed before noun and meaning 'one, some, any'.
■ **1** ambiguous, blurred, confused, dim, general, ill-defined, imprecise, indecisive, indeterminate, inexact, inexplicit, neutral, obscure, uncertain, unclear, undefined, unsettled, unspecific, unspecified, unsure, vague.

indefinitely *adverb* **1** for an unlimited time. **2** in an indefinite manner.

indelible /ɪn'delɪb(ə)l/ *adjective* **1** that cannot be rubbed out or removed. **2** permanent. ▫ **indelibly** *adverb*.
■ **1** fast, fixed, indestructible, ineradicable, ingrained, lasting, unfading, unforgettable. **2** see PERMANENT.

indelicate /ɪn'delɪkət/ *adjective* **1** coarse, unrefined. **2** tactless. ▫ **indelicacy** *noun* (*plural* **-ies**). **indelicately** *adverb*.

indemnify /ɪn'demnɪfaɪ/ *verb* (**-ies**, **-ied**) **1** (often + *against*, *from*) secure against loss or legal responsibility. **2** (often + *for*) exempt from penalty. **3** compensate. ▫ **indemnification** *noun*.

indemnity /ɪn'demnɪtɪ/ *noun* (*plural* **-ies**) **1** compensation for damage. **2** sum exacted by victor in war. **3** security against damage or loss. **4** exemption from penalties.

indent *verb* /ɪn'dent/ **1** make or impress notches, dents, or recesses in. **2** set back (beginning of line) inwards from margin. **3** draw up (legal document) in duplicate. **4** (often + *for*) make requisition. ● *noun* /'ɪndent/ **1** order (esp. from abroad) for goods. **2** official requisition for stores. **3** indented line. **4** indentation. **5** indenture.

indentation /ɪnden'teɪʃ(ə)n/ *noun* **1** indenting, being indented. **2** notch.
■ **2** cut, dent, depression, dimple, dip, furrow, groove, hollow, indent, mark, nick, notch, pit, recess, score, serration, tooth-mark, zigzag.

indenture /ɪnˈdentʃə/ *noun* **1** (usually in *plural*) sealed agreement. **2** formal list, certificate, etc. ● *verb* (**-ring**) *historical* bind by indentures, esp. as apprentice.

independent /ɪndɪˈpend(ə)nt/ *adjective* **1** (often + *of*) not depending on authority. **2** (often + *of*) self-governing. **3** not depending on another person for one's livelihood or opinions. **4** (of income) making it unnecessary to earn one's livelihood. **5** unwilling to be under obligation to others. **6** not depending on something else for validity etc. **7** not belonging to social, political, or religious organization. **8** (of institution) not supported by public funds. ● *noun* politician etc. independent of any political party. □ **independence** *noun*. **independently** *adverb*.
  ■ *adjective* **2** autonomous, liberated, neutral, non-aligned, self-determining, self-governing, sovereign. **3, 5** footloose, free, freethinking, individualistic, open-minded, self-confident, self-reliant, unbeholden, uncommitted, unconventional, untrammelled, without ties. **7** nonconformist, non-partisan, unaffiliated, unbiased, unprejudiced. **8** non-governmental, private. □ **independence** autarchy, autonomy, freedom, home rule, individualism, liberty, nonconformity, self-confidence, self-determination, self-government, self-reliance, self-rule, self-sufficiency, sovereignty.

indescribable /ɪndɪˈskraɪbəb(ə)l/ *adjective* **1** beyond description. **2** that cannot be described; vague. □ **indescribably** *adverb*.
  ■ **1** beyond words, indefinable, inexpressible, *colloquial* stunning, unspeakable, unutterable. **2** see VAGUE 1.

indestructible /ɪndɪˈstrʌktɪb(ə)l/ *adjective* that cannot be destroyed. □ **indestructibility** *noun*. **indestructibly** *adverb*.
  ■ durable, enduring, eternal, everlasting, immortal, imperishable, ineradicable, lasting, permanent, shatter-proof, solid, strong, tough, toughened, unbreakable.

indeterminable /ɪndɪˈtɜːmɪnəb(ə)l/ *adjective* that cannot be ascertained or settled.

indeterminate /ɪndɪˈtɜːmɪnət/ *adjective* **1** not fixed in extent, character, etc. **2** vague. □ **indeterminacy** *noun*.

index /ˈɪndeks/ *noun* (*plural* **-es** or **indices** /ˈɪndɪsiːz/) **1** alphabetical list of subjects etc. with references, usually at end of book. **2** card index. **3** measure of prices or wages compared with a previous month, year, etc. **4** *Mathematics* exponent. ● *verb* **1** furnish (book) with index. **2** enter in index. **3** relate (wages, investment income, etc.) to a price index. □ **index finger** finger next to thumb. **index-linked** related to value of price index.
  ■ *noun* **1** catalogue, directory, guide, key, listing, register, table (*of contents*). **3** see INDICATOR 2.

Indian /ˈɪndɪən/ *noun* **1** native or national of India. **2** person of Indian descent. **3** (in full **American Indian**) original inhabitant of America. ● *adjective* **1** of India. **2** of the subcontinent comprising India, Pakistan, and Bangladesh. **3** of the original inhabitants of America. □ **Indian corn** maize. **Indian file** single file. **Indian ink 1** black pigment. **2** ink made from this. **Indian summer 1** period of calm dry warm weather in late autumn. **2** happy tranquil period late in life.

indiarubber *noun* rubber, esp. for rubbing out pencil marks etc.

indicate /ˈɪndɪkeɪt/ *verb* (**-ting**) **1** point out; make known; show. **2** state briefly. **3** be sign of. **4** require, call for. **5** give as reading or measurement. **6** point by hand. **7** use a vehicle's indicator. □ **indication** *noun*.
  ■ **1, 2** announce, communicate, convey, designate, display, express, give notice of, intimate, make known, manifest, notify, point out, register, reveal, say, show, signal, signify, specify, spell out, suggest, warn. **3** betoken, denote, designate, evidence, express, imply, mean, signify, spell, stand for, symbolize. **5** display, read, record, register, show. **6, 7** point, signal.
  □ **indication** augury, clue, evidence, forewarning, hint, inkling, intimation, omen, portent, sign, signal, suggestion, symptom, token, warning.

indicative /ɪnˈdɪkətɪv/ *adjective* **1** (+ *of*) suggestive; giving indications of. **2** *Grammar* (of mood) stating thing as fact. ● *noun* **1** *Grammar* indicative mood. **2** verb in this mood.

indicator *noun* **1** flashing light on vehicle showing direction in which it is about to turn. **2** person or thing that indicates. **3** device indicating condition of machine etc. **4** recording instrument. **5** board giving current information.
  ■ **2** index, marker, needle, pointer, sign, signal. **3, 4** clock, dial, display, gauge, instrument, meter. **5** board, screen.

indices *plural* of INDEX.

indict /ɪnˈdaɪt/ *verb* accuse formally by legal process.

indictable *adjective* **1** (of an offence) rendering person liable to be indicted. **2** so liable.

indictment *noun* **1** indicting. **2** accusation. **3** document containing this. **4** thing that serves to condemn or censure.

indifference /ɪnˈdɪfrəns/ *noun* **1** lack of interest or attention. **2** unimportance.

indifferent *adjective* **1** (+ *to*) showing indifference to. **2** neither good nor bad. **3** of poor quality or ability. □ **indifferently** *adverb*.
  ■ **1** aloof, apathetic, blasé, bored, casual, cold, cool, detached, *disputed* disinterested, dispassionate, distant, half-hearted, impartial, impassive, incurious, insouciant, neutral, nonchalant, non-partisan, not bothered, objective, uncaring, unconcerned, unemotional, unenthusiastic, unexcited, unimpressed, uninterested, uninvolved, unmoved. **2** commonplace, fair, mediocre, middling, moderate, nondescript, ordinary, undistinguished, unexciting. **3** see POOR 3.

indigenous /ɪnˈdɪdʒɪnəs/ *adjective* (often + *to*) native or belonging naturally to a place.

indigent /ˈɪndɪdʒ(ə)nt/ *adjective formal* needy, poor. □ **indigence** *noun*.

indigestible /ɪndɪˈdʒestɪb(ə)l/ *adjective* difficult or impossible to digest.

indigestion /ɪndɪˈdʒestʃ(ə)n/ *noun* **1** difficulty in digesting food. **2** pain caused by this.
■ dyspepsia, flatulence, heartburn.

indignant /ɪmˈdɪɡnənt/ *adjective* feeling or showing indignation. □ **indignantly** *adverb*.
■ *slang* aerated, angry, annoyed, cross, disgruntled, exasperated, furious, heated, hot under the collar, infuriated, in high dudgeon, irate, irked, irritated, *colloquial* livid, *colloquial* mad, *colloquial* miffed, *colloquial* peeved, piqued, provoked, put out, *colloquial* riled, sore, up in arms, upset, vexed.

indignation /ɪndɪɡˈneɪʃ(ə)n/ *noun* anger at supposed injustice etc.

indignity /ɪmˈdɪɡnɪtɪ/ *noun* (*plural* **-ies**) **1** humiliating treatment. **2** insult.

indigo /ˈɪndɪɡəʊ/ *noun* (*plural* **-s**) **1** deep violet-blue. **2** dye of this colour.

indirect /ɪndaɪˈrekt/ *adjective* **1** not going straight to the point. **2** (of route etc.) not straight. □ **indirect object** word or phrase representing person or thing affected by action of verb but not acted on (see panel at OBJECT). **indirect speech** reported speech. **indirect tax** tax on goods and services, not income. □ **indirectly** *adverb*.
■ **1** ambiguous, backhanded, circumlocutory, disguised, equivocal, euphemistic, evasive, implicit, implied, oblique. **2** circuitous, devious, erratic, long, meandering, oblique, roundabout, roving, tortuous, twisting, winding, zigzag.

indiscernible /ɪndɪˈsɜːnɪb(ə)l/ *adjective* that cannot be discerned.

indiscipline /ɪmˈdɪsɪplɪn/ *noun* lack of discipline.

indiscreet /ɪndɪˈskriːt/ *adjective* not discreet; injudicious, unwary. □ **indiscreetly** *adverb*.
■ careless, foolish, ill-advised, ill-considered, ill-judged, impolite, impolitic, incautious, injudicious, insensitive, tactless, undiplomatic, unguarded, unthinking, unwise.

indiscretion /ɪndɪˈskreʃ(ə)n/ *noun* indiscreet conduct or action.

indiscriminate /ɪndɪˈskrɪmɪnət/ *adjective* **1** making no distinctions. **2** done or acting at random. □ **indiscriminately** *adverb*.
■ **1** uncritical, undiscerning, undiscriminating, uninformed, unperceptive, unselective. **2** aimless, careless, casual, confused, desultory, general, haphazard, hit-and-miss, miscellaneous, mixed, promiscuous, random, undifferentiated, unplanned, unsystematic, wholesale.

indispensable /ɪndɪˈspensəb(ə)l/ *adjective* that cannot be dispensed with; necessary. □ **indispensably** *adverb*.
■ basic, central, compulsory, crucial, essential, imperative, important, key, mandatory, necessary, needed, obligatory, required, requisite, vital.

indisposed /ɪndɪˈspəʊzd/ *adjective* **1** slightly unwell. **2** averse, unwilling. □ **indisposition** /-spəˈzɪʃ(ə)n/ *noun*.

indisputable /ɪndɪˈspjuːtəb(ə)l/ *adjective* that cannot be disputed. □ **indisputably** *adverb*.
■ absolute, accepted, acknowledged, axiomatic, beyond doubt, certain, clear, definite, evident, incontestable, incontrovertible, indubitable, irrefutable, positive, proved, proven, self-evident, sure, unanswerable, unarguable, undeniable, undisputed, undoubted, unimpeachable, unquestionable.

indissoluble /ɪndɪˈsɒljʊb(ə)l/ *adjective* **1** that cannot be dissolved. **2** lasting, stable. □ **indissolubly** *adverb*.

indistinct /ɪndɪˈstɪŋkt/ *adjective* **1** not distinct. **2** confused, obscure. □ **indistinctly** *adverb*.
■ **2** (*indistinct shapes*) bleary, blurred, confused, dim, dull, faint, fuzzy, hazy, ill-defined, indefinite, misty, obscure, shadowy, unclear, vague; (*indistinct sounds*) deadened, muffled, mumbled, muted, slurred, unintelligible, woolly.

indistinguishable /ɪndɪˈstɪŋɡwɪʃəb(ə)l/ *adjective* (often + *from*) not distinguishable.
■ alike, identical, interchangeable, the same, twin, undifferentiated.

indite /ɪnˈdaɪt/ *verb* (**-ting**) *formal* or *jocular* **1** put into words. **2** write (letter etc.).

individual /ɪndɪˈvɪdʒʊəl/ *adjective* **1** of, for, or characteristic of single person or thing. **2** having distinct character. **3** particular. **4** designed for use by one person. **5** single; separate. ● *noun* **1** single member of class, group, etc. **2** single human being. **3** *colloquial* person. **4** distinctive person.
■ *adjective* **1–3** characteristic, different, distinct, distinctive, exclusive, idiosyncratic, individualistic, particular, peculiar, personal, private, singular, special, specific, unique. **4** personal, private, separate, single. ● *noun* **2–4** SEE PERSON 1.

individualism *noun* **1** social theory favouring free action by individuals. **2** being independent or different. □ **individualist** *noun*. **individualistic** /-ˈlɪs-/ *adjective*.

individuality /ɪndɪvɪdʒʊˈælɪtɪ/ *noun* **1** individual character, esp. when strongly marked. **2** separate existence.

individualize *verb* (also **-ise**) (**-zing** or **-sing**) **1** give individual character to. **2** (esp. as **individualized** *adjective*) personalize.

individually *adverb* **1** one by one. **2** personally. **3** distinctively.

indivisible /ɪndɪˈvɪzɪb(ə)l/ *adjective* not divisible.

indoctrinate /ɪnˈdɒktrɪneɪt/ *verb* (**-ting**) teach to accept a particular belief uncritically. □ **indoctrination** *noun*.
■ brainwash, instruct, re-educate, teach, train.

Indo-European /ɪndəʊjʊərəˈpɪən/ *adjective* **1** of family of languages spoken over most of

Europe and Asia as far as N. India. **2** of hypothetical parent language of this family. ● *noun* **1** Indo-European family of languages. **2** hypothetical parent language of these.

indolent /'ɪndələnt/ *adjective* lazy; averse to exertion. □ **indolence** *noun.* **indolently** *adverb.*

indomitable /ɪn'dɒmɪtəb(ə)l/ *adjective* unconquerable; unyielding. □ **indomitability** /-'bɪlɪtɪ/ *noun.* **indomitably** *adverb.*

indoor /'ɪndɔː/ *adjective* done etc. in building or under cover.

indoors /ɪn'dɔːz/ *adverb* in(to) a building.

indubitable /ɪn'djuːbɪtəb(ə)l/ *adjective* that cannot be doubted. □ **indubitably** *adverb.*

induce /ɪn'djuːs/ *verb* (**-cing**) **1** prevail on; persuade. **2** bring about. **3** bring on (labour) artificially. **4** bring on labour in (mother). **5** speed up birth of (baby). **6** produce by induction. **7** infer. □ **inducible** *adjective.*
- **1** coax, encourage, incite, influence, inspire, motivate, persuade, press, prevail on, stimulate, sway, talk into, tempt, urge. **2** bring about, bring on, cause, effect, engender, generate, give rise to, lead to, occasion, produce, provoke.

inducement *noun* **1** attractive offer. **2** incentive; bribe.
- attraction, bait, bribe, encouragement, enticement, incentive, spur, stimulus, *colloquial* sweetener.

induct /ɪn'dʌkt/ *verb* install into office etc.

inductance *noun* property of electric circuit in which variation in current produces electromotive force.

induction /ɪn'dʌkʃ(ə)n/ *noun* **1** inducting, inducing. **2** act of bringing on (esp. labour) artificially. **3** general inference from particular instances. **4** formal introduction to new job etc. **5** production of electric or magnetic state by proximity to electric circuit or magnetic field.

inductive /ɪn'dʌktɪv/ *adjective* **1** (of reasoning etc.) based on induction. **2** of electric or magnetic induction.

indulge /ɪn'dʌldʒ/ *verb* (**-ging**) **1** (often + *in*) take one's pleasure freely. **2** yield freely to (desire etc.). **3** gratify by compliance with wishes. **4** *colloquial* take alcoholic liquor.
- **1** be self-indulgent, drink too much, eat too much, give in to temptation, *colloquial* overdo it, overeat, spoil oneself; (*indulge in*) see ENJOY 1. **2** give in to, gratify, succumb to, yield to. **3** be indulgent to, cosset, favour, give in to, gratify, humour, mollycoddle, pamper, pander to, spoil, spoon-feed, treat.

indulgence *noun* **1** indulging. **2** thing indulged in. **3** *RC Church* remission of punishment still due after absolution. **4** privilege granted.

indulgent *adjective* **1** lenient; willing to overlook faults. **2** indulging. □ **indulgently** *adverb.*
- compliant, easygoing, fond, forbearing, forgiving, genial, kind, lenient, liberal, overgenerous, patient, permissive, tolerant.

industrial /ɪn'dʌstrɪəl/ *adjective* **1** of, engaged in, for use in, or serving the needs of, industry. **2** having highly developed industries. □ **industrial action** strike or disruptive action by workers as protest. **industrial estate** area of land zoned for factories etc. □ **industrially** *adverb.*

industrialism *noun* system in which manufacturing industries predominate.

industrialist *noun* owner or manager in industry.

industrialize *verb* (also **-ise**) (**-zing** or **-sing**) make (nation etc.) industrial. □ **industrialization** *noun.*

industrious /ɪn'dʌstrɪəs/ *adjective* hardworking. □ **industriously** *adverb.* **industriousness** *noun.*
- assiduous, busy, conscientious, diligent, dynamic, earnest, energetic, enterprising, hard-working, keen, laborious, persistent, pertinacious, productive, sedulous, tireless, unflagging, untiring, zealous.

industry /'ɪndəstrɪ/ *noun* (*plural* **-ies**) **1** branch of trade or manufacture; commercial enterprise. **2** trade or manufacture collectively. **3** concerted activity. **4** diligence.
- **1, 2** business, commerce, manufacturing, production, trade. **3** activity, effort, labour, toil, work. **4** application, commitment, determination, diligence, dynamism, effort, energy, enterprise, industriousness, keenness, perseverance, persistence, sedulousness, tirelessness, zeal.

inebriate *verb* /ɪ'niːbrɪeɪt/ (**-ting**) **1** make drunk. **2** excite. ● *adjective* /ɪ'niːbrɪət/ drunken. ● *noun* /ɪ'niːbrɪət/ drunkard. □ **inebriation** *noun.*

inedible /ɪn'edɪb(ə)l/ *adjective* not suitable for eating.
- harmful, indigestible, nauseating, *colloquial* off, poisonous, rotten, tough, uneatable, unpalatable, unwholesome.

ineducable /ɪn'edjʊkəb(ə)l/ *adjective* incapable of being educated.

ineffable /ɪn'efəb(ə)l/ *adjective* **1** too great for description in words. **2** that must not be uttered. □ **ineffability** *noun.* **ineffably** *adverb.*

ineffective /ɪnɪ'fektɪv/ *adjective* **1** not achieving desired effect. **2** (of person) inefficient. □ **ineffectively** *adverb.* **ineffectiveness** *noun.*
- **1** fruitless, futile, hopeless, unconvincing, unproductive, unsuccessful, useless, vain, worthless. **2** disorganized, feckless, feeble, idle, impotent, inadequate, incapable, incompetent, ineffectual, inefficient, inept, powerless, shiftless, unenterprising, weak.

ineffectual /ɪnɪ'fektʃʊəl/ *adjective* ineffective; feeble. □ **ineffectually** *adverb.*

inefficient /ɪnɪ'fɪʃ(ə)nt/ *adjective* **1** not efficient or fully capable. **2** (of machine etc.) wasteful. □ **inefficiency** *noun.* **inefficiently** *adverb.*
- **1** see INEFFECTIVE 2. **2** extravagant, prodigal, uneconomic, wasteful.

inelastic /ˌɪnɪˈlæstɪk/ *adjective* **1** not elastic. **2** unadaptable, inflexible.

inelegant /ɪnˈelɪɡənt/ *adjective* ungraceful, unrefined. □ **inelegance** *noun*. **inelegantly** *adverb*.

- awkward, clumsy, crude, gauche, graceless, inartistic, rough, ugly, uncouth, ungainly, unpolished, unskilful, unsophisticated, unstylish.

ineligible /ɪnˈelɪdʒɪb(ə)l/ *adjective* not eligible or qualified. □ **ineligibility** *noun*.

- disqualified, inappropriate, out of the running, ruled out, unacceptable, unauthorized, unfit, unqualified, unsuitable, unworthy.

ineluctable /ˌɪnɪˈlʌktəb(ə)l/ *adjective* inescapable, unavoidable.

inept /ɪˈnept/ *adjective* **1** unskilful. **2** absurd, silly. **3** out of place. □ **ineptitude** *noun*. **ineptly** *adverb*.

- **1** awkward, bumbling, bungling, clumsy, gauche, incompetent, inexpert, maladroit, unskilful, unskilled. **3** see INAPPROPRIATE.

inequality /ˌɪnɪˈkwɒlɪtɪ/ *noun* (*plural* **-ies**) **1** lack of equality. **2** variability. **3** unevenness.

- **1** contrast, difference, discrepancy, disparity, dissimilarity, imbalance, incongruity, prejudice. **2** inconsistency, unreliability, variability. **3** irregularity, unevenness.

inequitable /ɪnˈekwɪtəb(ə)l/ *adjective* unfair, unjust.

inequity /ɪnˈekwɪtɪ/ *noun* (*plural* **-ies**) unfairness, injustice.

ineradicable /ˌɪnɪˈrædɪkəb(ə)l/ *adjective* that cannot be rooted out.

inert /ɪˈnɜːt/ *adjective* **1** without inherent power of action, motion, etc. **2** chemically inactive. **3** sluggish, slow; lifeless.

- **1** immobile, inactive, inanimate, lifeless, passive, quiescent, static, stationary, still. **3** apathetic, dormant, idle, inactive, lifeless, quiescent, quiet, slow, sluggish, supine, torpid.

inertia /ɪˈnɜːʃə/ *noun* **1** property by which matter continues in existing state of rest or motion unless acted on by external force. **2** inertness. **3** tendency to remain unchanged. □ **inertia reel** reel allowing seat belt to unwind freely but locking on impact. **inertia selling** sending of unsolicited goods in hope of making a sale.

- **2** apathy, deadness, idleness, immobility, inactivity, indolence, lassitude, laziness, lethargy, listlessness, numbness, passivity, sluggishness, torpor.

inescapable /ˌɪnɪˈskeɪpəb(ə)l/ *adjective* that cannot be escaped or avoided. □ **inescapably** *adverb*.

inessential /ˌɪnɪˈsenʃ(ə)l/ *adjective* not necessary; dispensable. ● *noun* inessential thing.

- *adjective* dispensable, expendable, minor, needless, non-essential, optional, ornamental, secondary, spare, superfluous, unimportant, unnecessary.

inestimable /ɪnˈestɪməb(ə)l/ *adjective* too great etc. to be estimated. □ **inestimably** *adverb*.

inevitable /ɪnˈevɪtəb(ə)l/ *adjective* **1** unavoidable; bound to happen or appear. **2** *colloquial* tiresomely familiar. □ **inevitability** *noun*. **inevitably** *adverb*.

- **1** assured, certain, destined, fated, ineluctable, inescapable, inexorable, ordained, predictable, sure, unavoidable.

inexact /ˌɪnɪɡˈzækt/ *adjective* not exact. □ **inexactitude** *noun*.

inexcusable /ˌɪnɪkˈskjuːzəb(ə)l/ *adjective* that cannot be justified. □ **inexcusably** *adverb*.

- see UNFORGIVABLE.

inexhaustible /ˌɪnɪɡˈzɔːstɪb(ə)l/ *adjective* that cannot be used up.

inexorable /ɪnˈeksərəb(ə)l/ *adjective* relentless. □ **inexorably** *adverb*.

inexpedient /ˌɪnɪkˈspiːdɪənt/ *adjective* not expedient.

inexpensive /ˌɪnɪkˈspensɪv/ *adjective* cheap.

- see CHEAP 1.

inexperience /ˌɪnɪkˈspɪərɪəns/ *noun* lack of experience. □ **inexperienced** *adjective*.

- □ **inexperienced** callow, green, immature, inexpert, innocent, naive, new, probationary, raw, unaccustomed, unfledged, uninitiated, unskilled, unsophisticated, untried, wet behind the ears, young.

inexpert /ɪnˈekspɜːt/ *adjective* unskilful.

inexpiable /ɪnˈekspɪəb(ə)l/ *adjective* that cannot be expiated.

inexplicable /ˌɪnɪkˈsplɪkəb(ə)l/ *adjective* that cannot be explained. □ **inexplicably** *adverb*.

- baffling, bewildering, confusing, enigmatic, incomprehensible, inscrutable, insoluble, mysterious, mystifying, perplexing, puzzling, strange, unaccountable, unexplainable, unfathomable, unsolvable.

inexplicit /ˌɪnɪkˈsplɪsɪt, mek-/ *adjective* not definitely or clearly expressed.

inexpressible /ˌɪnɪkˈspresɪb(ə)l/ *adjective* that cannot be expressed. □ **inexpressibly** *adverb*.

in extremis /ɪn ɪkˈstriːmɪs/ *adjective* **1** at point of death. **2** in great difficulties. [Latin]

inextricable /ˌɪnɪkˈstrɪkəb(ə)l/ *adjective* **1** that cannot be separated, loosened, or resolved. **2** inescapable. □ **inextricably** *adverb*.

infallible /ɪnˈfælɪb(ə)l/ *adjective* **1** incapable of error. **2** unfailing, sure. □ **infallibility** *noun*. **infallibly** *adverb*.

- **1** faultless, impeccable, perfect, unerring. **2** certain, dependable, faultless, foolproof, impeccable, perfect, reliable, sound, sure, trustworthy, unbeatable, unerring, unfailing.

infamous /ˈɪnfəməs/ *adjective* **1** notoriously vile; evil. **2** abominable. □ **infamously** *adverb*. **infamy** *noun* (*plural* **-ies**).

■ **1** disgraceful, disreputable, ill-famed, notorious, outrageous. **2** see WICKED 1.

infant /'ɪnf(ə)nt/ *noun* **1** child during earliest period of life. **2** thing in early stage of development. **3** *Law* person under 18. □ **infancy** *noun*.
■ **1** babe, baby, *Scottish & Northern English* bairn, child, *colloquial* kid, newborn, *colloquial* nipper, toddler, tot.

infanta /ɪn'fæntə/ *noun historical* daughter of Spanish or Portuguese king.

infanticide /ɪn'fæntɪsaɪd/ *noun* **1** killing of infant, esp. soon after birth. **2** person guilty of this.

infantile /'ɪnfəntaɪl/ *adjective* of or like infants. □ **infantile paralysis** poliomyelitis.
■ babyish, childish, immature, *often derogatory* juvenile, puerile.

infantry /'ɪnfəntrɪ/ *noun* (*plural* **-ies**) (group of) foot-soldiers. □ **infantryman** soldier of infantry regiment.

infatuate /ɪn'fætjʊeɪt/ *verb* (**-ting**) (usually as **infatuated** *adjective*) inspire with intense fondness. □ **infatuation** *noun*.
■ (**infatuated**) besotted, charmed, enchanted, in love, mad, obsessed, *esp. archaic or literary* smitten. □ **infatuation** *colloquial* crush, love, obsession, passion.

infect /ɪn'fekt/ *verb* **1** affect or contaminate with germ, virus, or disease. **2** imbue, taint. □ **infected** *adjective*.
■ **1** blight, contaminate, defile, poison, pollute, spoil, taint. **2** affect, imbue, influence, inspire, touch. □ **infected** see SEPTIC.

infection /ɪn'fekʃ(ə)n/ *noun* **1** infecting, being infected. **2** disease. **3** communication of disease.
■ **1** contamination, pollution. **2** blight, *slang* bug, contagion, disease, illness, pestilence, virus. **3** contagion.

infectious *adjective* **1** infecting. **2** transmissible by infection. **3** apt to spread. □ **infectiously** *adverb*.
■ **2, 3** catching, communicable, contagious, transmissible, transmittable.

infelicity /ɪnfɪ'lɪsɪtɪ/ *noun* (*plural* **-ies**) **1** inapt expression. **2** unhappiness. □ **infelicitous** *adjective*.

infer /ɪn'fɜː/ *verb* (**-rr-**) deduce, conclude.
USAGE It is a mistake to use *infer* to mean 'imply', as in *Are you inferring that I'm a liar?*
■ assume, conclude, deduce, derive, draw a conclusion, extrapolate, gather, guess, reach the conclusion, surmise, understand, work out.

inference /'ɪnfərəns/ *noun* **1** act of inferring. **2** thing inferred. □ **inferential** /-'ren(ə)l/ *adjective*.

inferior /ɪn'fɪərɪə/ *adjective* **1** lower in rank etc. **2** of poor quality. **3** situated below. ● *noun* inferior person.

■ *adjective* **1** humble, junior, lesser, lower, lowly, mean, menial, secondary, second-class, servile, subordinate, subsidiary, unimportant. **2** cheap, indifferent, mediocre, poor, shoddy, tawdry, tinny. ● *noun* see SUBORDINATE.

inferiority /ɪnfɪərɪ'ɒrɪtɪ/ *noun* being inferior. □ **inferiority complex** feeling of inadequacy, sometimes marked by compensating aggressive behaviour.

infernal /ɪn'fɜːn(ə)l/ *adjective* **1** of hell. **2** hellish. **3** *colloquial* detestable, tiresome. □ **infernally** *adverb*.

inferno /ɪn'fɜːnəʊ/ *noun* (*plural* **-s**) **1** raging fire. **2** scene of horror or distress. **3** hell.

infertile /ɪn'fɜːtaɪl/ *adjective* not fertile. □ **infertility** /-fə'tɪl-/ *noun*.
■ barren, sterile, unfruitful, unproductive.

infest /ɪn'fest/ *verb* overrun in large numbers. □ **infestation** *noun*. **infested** *adjective*.
■ infiltrate, overrun, pervade, plague. □ **infested** verminous; (*infested with*) alive with, crawling with, swarming with, teeming with.

infidel /'ɪnfɪd(ə)l/ *noun* disbeliever in esp. the supposed true religion. ● *adjective* **1** of infidels. **2** unbelieving.

infidelity /ɪnfɪ'delɪtɪ/ *noun* (*plural* **-ies**) being unfaithful.
■ adultery, betrayal, disloyalty, faithlessness, unfaithfulness.

infighting *noun* **1** conflict or competitiveness in organization. **2** boxing within arm's length.

infiltrate /'ɪnfɪltreɪt/ *verb* (**-ting**) **1** enter (territory, political party, etc.) gradually and imperceptibly. **2** cause to do this. **3** permeate by filtration. **4** (often + *into, through*) introduce (fluid) by filtration. □ **infiltration** *noun*. **infiltrator** *noun*.
■ **1** enter secretly, insinuate oneself into, intrude into, penetrate.

infinite /'ɪnfɪnɪt/ *adjective* **1** boundless; endless. **2** very great or many. □ **infinitely** *adverb*.
■ astronomical, big, boundless, colossal, countless, endless, eternal, everlasting, huge, immeasurable, immense, incalculable, indeterminate, inestimable, inexhaustible, innumerable, interminable, limitless, multitudinous, never-ending, numberless, perpetual, uncountable, undefined, unending, unfathomable, unlimited, unnumbered, untold, vast.

infinitesimal /ɪnfɪnɪ'tesɪm(ə)l/ *adjective* infinitely or very small. □ **infinitesimally** *adverb*.

infinitive /ɪn'fɪnɪtɪv/ *noun* verb-form expressing verbal notion without particular subject, tense, etc. ● *adjective* having this form.

infinitude /ɪn'fɪnɪtjuːd/ *noun literary* **1** infinite number etc. **2** being infinite.

infinity /ɪn'fɪnɪtɪ/ *noun* (*plural* **-ies**) **1** infinite number or extent. **2** being infinite; boundlessness. **3** infinite distance. **4** *Mathematics* infinite quantity.

■ **2** boundlessness, endlessness, eternity, *literary* infinitude, perpetuity.

infirm /ɪnˈfɜːm/ *adjective* weak.

■ ailing, bedridden, crippled, decrepit, elderly, feeble, frail, lame, old, poorly, senile, sickly, unwell, weak.

infirmary /ɪnˈfɜːmərɪ/ *noun* (*plural* **-ies**) **1** hospital. **2** sickbay in school etc.

infirmity *noun* (*plural* **-ies**) **1** being infirm. **2** particular physical weakness.

in flagrante delicto /ɪn fləˈɡræntɪ dɪˈlɪktəʊ/ *adverb* in act of committing offence. [Latin]

inflame /ɪnˈfleɪm/ *verb* (**-ming**) **1** provoke to strong feeling. **2** (esp. as **inflamed** *adjective*) cause inflammation in. **3** aggravate. **4** make hot. **5** (cause to) catch fire.

■ **1** anger, arouse, encourage, exasperate, excite, fire, foment, goad, ignite, incense, incite, infuriate, kindle, madden, provoke, rouse, stimulate, stir up, work up; (*inflamed*) see PASSIONATE. **2** (**inflamed**) see SEPTIC.

inflammable /ɪnˈflæməb(ə)l/ *adjective* easily set on fire or excited. □ **inflammability** *noun*.

USAGE Because *inflammable* could be taken to mean 'not easily set on fire', *flammable* is often used instead. The negative of *flammable* is *non-flammable*.

■ burnable, combustible, flammable, volatile.

inflammation /ɪnfləˈmeɪʃ(ə)n/ *noun* **1** inflaming. **2** disordered bodily condition marked by heat, swelling, redness, and usually pain.

■ **2** abscess, boil, infection, irritation, redness, sore, soreness, swelling.

inflammatory /ɪnˈflæmətərɪ/ *adjective* **1** tending to inflame. **2** of inflammation.

inflatable *adjective* that can be inflated. ● *noun* inflatable object.

inflate /ɪnˈfleɪt/ *verb* (**-ting**) **1** distend with air or gas. **2** (usually + *with*; usually in *passive*) puff up (with pride etc.). **3** resort to inflation of (currency) **4** raise (prices) artificially. **5** (as **inflated** *adjective*) (esp. of language, opinions, etc.) bombastic, exaggerated.

■ **1** blow up, dilate, distend, enlarge, puff up, pump up, swell. **2** puff up, swell. **5** (**inflated**) see BOMBASTIC, EXCESSIVE.

inflation *noun* **1** inflating, being inflated. **2** general rise in prices. **3** increase in supply of money regarded as cause of such rise. □ **inflationary** *adjective*.

inflect /ɪnˈflekt/ *verb* **1** change or vary pitch of (voice). **2** modify (word) to express grammatical relation. **3** undergo such modification.

inflection /ɪnˈflekʃ(ə)n/ *noun* (also **inflexion**) **1** inflecting, being inflected. **2** inflected form. **3** inflecting suffix etc. **4** modulation of voice. □ **inflectional** *adjective*.

inflexible /ɪnˈfleksɪb(ə)l/ *adjective* **1** un-

bendable. **2** unbending; unyielding. □ **inflexibility** *noun*. **inflexibly** *adverb*.

■ **1** adamantine, firm, hard, hardened, immovable, rigid, solid, stiff, unbendable. **2** adamant, entrenched, fixed, immovable, immutable, inexorable, intractable, intransigent, obdurate, obstinate, pig-headed, refractory, resolute, rigorous, strict, stubborn, unalterable, unbending, unchangeable, uncompromising, unhelpful, unyielding.

inflexion = INFLECTION.

inflict /ɪnˈflɪkt/ *verb* **1** deal (blow etc.). **2** (usually + *on*, *upon*) impose (penalty, oneself, etc.). □ **infliction** *noun*.

■ **1** administer, deal, *colloquial* land, wreak. **2** administer, apply, deal out, enforce, impose, *literary* mete out; (*inflict oneself on*) force oneself on, thrust oneself on.

inflight *adjective* occurring or provided during a flight.

inflorescence /ɪnfləˈres(ə)ns/ *noun* **1** collective flower head of plant. **2** arrangement of flowers on plant. **3** flowering.

inflow *noun* **1** flowing in. **2** that which flows in.

influence /ˈɪnflʊəns/ *noun* **1** (usually + *on*) effect a person or thing has on another. **2** (usually + *over*, *with*) ascendancy, moral power. **3** thing or person exercising this. ● *verb* (**-cing**) exert influence on; affect. □ **under the influence** *colloquial* drunk.

■ *noun* **1** effect, impact. **2** ascendancy, authority, control, direction, dominance, guidance, hold, leverage, power, pressure, pull, sway, weight. ● *verb* affect, bias, change, control, direct, dominate, guide, impinge on, impress, induce, manipulate, modify, motivate, move, persuade, prejudice, prompt, put pressure on, stir, sway.

influential /ɪnflʊˈenʃ(ə)l/ *adjective* having great influence.

■ authoritative, compelling, controlling, convincing, dominant, effective, far-reaching, forceful, guiding, important, inspiring, leading, moving, persuasive, potent, powerful, prestigious, significant, strong, telling, weighty.

influenza /ɪnflʊˈenzə/ *noun* infectious viral disease with fever, severe aching, and catarrh.

influx /ˈɪnflʌks/ *noun* flowing in.

■ flood, flow, inflow, inundation, invasion, rush, stream.

inform /ɪnˈfɔːm/ *verb* **1** tell. **2** (usually + *against*, *on*) give incriminating information about person to authorities.

■ **1** advise, apprise, brief, communicate to, enlighten, *colloquial* fill in, instruct, notify, put in the picture, teach, tell, tip off. **2** blab, *slang* grass, *colloquial* peach, rat, sneak, *colloquial* split, tell, tell tales; (*inform on*) see BETRAY 1,2.

informal /ɪnˈfɔːm(ə)l/ *adjective* **1** without formality. **2** (of language) not formal. **3** (of garden, design, etc.) not precise or symmetrical.

□ **informality** /-'mæl-/ *noun* (*plural* **-ies**). **informally** *adverb*.

■ **1** approachable, casual, comfortable, cosy, easy, easygoing, everyday, familiar, free and easy, friendly, homely, natural, ordinary, relaxed, simple, unceremonious, unofficial, unpretentious, unsophisticated. **2** chatty, colloquial, personal, slangy, vernacular. **3** asymmetrical, flexible, fluid, intuitive, irregular, spontaneous.

informant *noun* giver of information.

information /ɪnfə'meɪʃ(ə)n/ *noun* **1** what is told; news. **2** knowledge. **3** formal charge or accusation. □ **information retrieval** tracing of information stored in books, computers, etc. **information technology** study or use of processes (esp. computers etc.) for storing, retrieving, and sending information. □ **informational** *adjective*.

■ **1** briefing, communication, enlightenment, instruction, message, news, report, *archaic or jocular* tidings, word. **2** data, evidence, facts, intelligence, knowledge, statistics.

informative /ɪn'fɔ:mətɪv/ *adjective* giving information; instructive.

■ communicative, edifying, educational, enlightening, factual, helpful, illuminating, instructive, meaningful, revealing, useful.

informed *adjective* **1** knowing the facts. **2** having some knowledge.

■ see KNOWLEDGEABLE.

informer *noun* person who informs, esp. against others.

■ *slang* grass, informant, spy, stool-pigeon, tell-tale, traitor.

infraction /ɪn'frækʃ(ə)n/ *noun* infringement.

infra dig /ɪnfrə 'dɪg/ *adjective colloquial* beneath one's dignity.

infrared /ɪnfrə'red/ *adjective* of or using radiation just beyond red end of spectrum.

infrastructure /'ɪnfrəstrʌktʃə/ *noun* **1** structural foundations of a society or enterprise. **2** roads, bridges, sewers, etc., regarded as country's economic foundation. **3** permanent installations as basis for military etc. operations.

infrequent /ɪn'fri:kwənt/ *adjective* not frequent. □ **infrequently** *adverb*.

■ exceptional, intermittent, irregular, occasional, rare, spasmodic, uncommon, unusual.

infringe /ɪn'frɪndʒ/ *verb* (**-ging**) **1** break or violate (law, another's rights, etc.). **2** (usually + *on*) encroach, trespass. □ **infringement** *noun*.

■ **1** breach, break, contravene, defy, disobey, disregard, flout, ignore, overstep, sin against, transgress, violate. **2** see ENCROACH.

infuriate /ɪn'fjʊərɪeɪt/ *verb* (**-ting**) enrage; irritate greatly. □ **infuriating** *adjective*.

infuse /ɪn'fju:z/ *verb* (**-sing**) **1** (usually + *with*) fill (with a quality). **2** steep or be steeped in liquid to extract properties. **3** (usually + *into*) instil (life etc.).

infusible /ɪn'fju:zɪb(ə)l/ *adjective* that cannot be melted. □ **infusibility** *noun*.

infusion /ɪn'fju:ʒ(ə)n/ *noun* **1** infusing. **2** liquid extract so obtained. **3** infused element.

ingenious /ɪn'dʒi:nɪəs/ *adjective* **1** clever at contriving. **2** cleverly contrived. □ **ingeniously** *adverb*.

USAGE *Ingenious* is sometimes confused with *ingenuous*.

■ adroit, artful, astute, brilliant, clever, crafty, creative, cunning, deft, imaginative, inspired, intelligent, inventive, neat, original, resourceful, shrewd, skilful, smart, subtle, talented.

ingénue /æʒeɪ'nju:/ *noun* artless young woman, esp. as stage type. [French]

ingenuity /ɪndʒɪ'nju:ɪtɪ/ *noun* inventiveness, cleverness.

ingenuous /ɪn'dʒenjʊəs/ *adjective* **1** artless. **2** frank. □ **ingenuously** *adverb*.

USAGE *Ingenuous* is sometimes confused with *ingenious*.

■ **1** artless, childlike, guileless, innocent, naive, plain, simple, sincere, trusting, unaffected, uncomplicated, unsophisticated. **2** frank, honest, open, plain, straightforward.

ingest /ɪn'dʒest/ *verb* **1** take in (food etc.). **2** absorb (knowledge etc.). □ **ingestion** *noun*.

inglenook /'ɪŋgəlnʊk/ *noun* space within opening either side of old-fashioned wide fireplace.

inglorious /ɪn'glɔ:rɪəs/ *adjective* **1** shameful. **2** not famous.

ingoing *adjective* going in.

ingot /'ɪŋgət/ *noun* (usually oblong) mass of cast metal, esp. gold, silver, or steel.

ingrained /ɪn'greɪnd/ *adjective* **1** deeply rooted, inveterate. **2** (of dirt etc.) deeply embedded.

ingratiate /ɪn'greɪʃɪeɪt/ *verb* (**-ting**) (**ingratiate oneself**; usually + *with*) bring oneself into favour. □ **ingratiating** *adjective*.

ingratitude /ɪn'grætɪtju:d/ *noun* lack of due gratitude.

ingredient /ɪn'gri:dɪənt/ *noun* component part in mixture.

■ component, constituent, element, factor, part; (*ingredients*) contents, makings.

ingress /'ɪngres/ *noun* **1** going in. **2** right to go in.

ingrowing *adjective* (of nail) growing into the flesh.

inhabit /ɪn'hæbɪt/ *verb* (**-t-**) dwell in, occupy. □ **inhabitable** *adjective*. **inhabitant** *noun*.

■ *archaic* abide in, colonize, dwell in, live in, make one's home in, occupy, people, populate, reside in, settle in, set up home in. □ **inhabitable** habitable, in good repair, *colloquial* liveable, usable. **inhabitant** citizen, denizen, dweller, inmate, native, occupant, occupier, resident, settler, tenant; (*inhabitants*) population, townspeople.

inhalant /ɪnˈheɪlənt/ *noun* medicinal substance to be inhaled.

inhale /ɪnˈheɪl/ *verb* (**-ling**) breathe in. □ **inhalation** /-həˈleɪʃ(ə)n/ *noun*.

inhaler *noun* device for administering inhalant, esp. to relieve asthma.

inhere /ɪnˈhɪə/ *verb* (**-ring**) be inherent.

inherent /ɪnˈherənt/ *adjective* (often + *in*) existing in something as essential or permanent attribute. □ **inherently** *adverb*.
- built-in, congenital, essential, fundamental, hereditary, immanent, inborn, inbred, ingrained, intrinsic, native, natural.

inherit /ɪnˈherɪt/ *verb* (**-t-**) **1** receive as heir. **2** derive (characteristic) from ancestors. **3** derive or take over (situation) from predecessor. □ **inherited** *adjective*. **inheritor** *noun*.
- **1** be the inheritor of, be left, come into, receive as an inheritance, succeed to. **3** succeed, take over. □ **inherited** see HEREDITARY 2.

inheritable /ɪnˈherɪtəb(ə)l/ *adjective* **1** capable of being inherited. **2** capable of inheriting.

inheritance *noun* **1** what is inherited. **2** inheriting.
- **1** bequest, birthright, estate, fortune, heritage, legacy, patrimony.

inhibit /ɪnˈhɪbɪt/ *verb* (**-t-**) **1** hinder, restrain, prevent. **2** (as **inhibited** *adjective*) suffering from inhibition. **3** (usually + *from*) prohibit.
- **1** bridle, check, control, curb, discourage, frustrate, hinder, hold back, prevent, quell, repress, restrain. **2** (**inhibited**) see REPRESSED, SHY[1] *adjective*.

inhibition /ɪnhɪˈbɪʃ(ə)n/ *noun* **1** restraint of direct expression of instinct. **2** *colloquial* emotional resistance to thought or action. **3** inhibiting, being inhibited.
- **1** bar, barrier, check, constraint, curb, impediment, interference, restraint, stricture. **2** diffidence, *slang* hang-up, repression, reserve, self-consciousness, shyness.

inhospitable /ɪnhɒsˈpɪtəb(ə)l/ *adjective* **1** not hospitable. **2** affording no shelter.
- **1** antisocial, reclusive, reserved, solitary, stand-offish, unfriendly, unkind, unsociable, unwelcoming. **2** bleak, cold, comfortless, desolate, grim, hostile, lonely.

inhuman /ɪnˈhjuːmən/ *adjective* brutal; unfeeling; barbarous. □ **inhumanity** /-ˈmæn-/ *noun* (*plural* **-ies**). **inhumanly** *adverb*.
- animal, barbaric, barbarous, bestial, bloodthirsty, brutal, brutish, diabolical, fiendish, inhumane, merciless, pitiless, ruthless, savage, unfeeling, unnatural, vicious.

inhumane /ɪnhjuːˈmeɪn/ *adjective* not humane, callous.
- callous, cold-hearted, cruel, hard, hard-hearted, heartless, inconsiderate, insensitive, merciless, ruthless, uncaring, uncharitable, uncivilized, unfeeling, unkind, unsympathetic.

inimical /ɪˈnɪmɪk(ə)l/ *adjective* **1** hostile. **2** harmful.

inimitable /ɪˈnɪmɪtəb(ə)l/ *adjective* that cannot be imitated. □ **inimitably** *adverb*.

iniquity /ɪˈnɪkwɪtɪ/ *noun* (*plural* **-ies**) **1** wickedness. **2** gross injustice. □ **iniquitous** *adjective*.

initial /ɪˈnɪʃ(ə)l/ *adjective* of or at beginning. ● *noun* first letter, esp. of person's name. ● *verb* (**-ll-**; *US* **-l-**) mark or sign with one's initials. □ **initially** *adverb*.
- *adjective* beginning, commencing, earliest, first, inaugural, incipient, introductory, opening, original, primary, starting.

initiate *verb* /ɪˈnɪʃɪeɪt/ (**-ting**) **1** originate, set going. **2** admit into society, office, etc., esp. with ritual. **3** (+ *into*) instruct in subject. ● *noun* /ɪˈnɪʃɪət/ initiated person. □ **initiation** /-ˈeɪʃ(ə)n/ *noun*. **initiator** *noun*. **initiatory** /ɪˈnɪʃjətərɪ/ *adjective*.
- **1** activate, actuate, begin, *formal* commence, enter upon, get going, get under way, inaugurate, instigate, institute, introduce, launch, originate, set going, set in motion, set up, start, take the initiative, trigger.

initiative /ɪˈnɪʃətɪv/ *noun* **1** ability to initiate; enterprise. **2** first step. **3** (**the initiative**) power or right to begin. □ **take the initiative** take first step.
- **1** ambition, drive, dynamism, enterprise, *colloquial* get-up-and-go, inventiveness, lead, leadership, originality, resourcefulness. □ **take the initiative** see INITIATE 1.

inject /ɪnˈdʒekt/ *verb* **1** (usually + *into*) force (medicine etc.) (as) by syringe. **2** administer medicine etc. to (person) by injection. **3** place (quality etc.) where needed in something. □ **injection** *noun*.
- □ **injection** inoculation, *colloquial* jab, vaccination.

injudicious /ɪndʒuːˈdɪʃəs/ *adjective* unwise, ill-judged.

injunction /ɪnˈdʒʌŋkʃ(ə)n/ *noun* **1** authoritative order. **2** judicial order restraining from specified act or compelling restitution etc.

injure /ˈɪndʒə/ *verb* (**-ring**) **1** hurt, harm, impair. **2** do wrong to.
- **1** break, crush, cut, damage, deface, disfigure, harm, hurt, impair, mar, ruin, spoil, vandalize, wound. **2** see WRONG *verb* 1.

injurious /ɪnˈdʒʊərɪəs/ *adjective* **1** hurtful. **2** defamatory. **3** wrongful.
- **1** damaging, deleterious, destructive, detrimental, harmful, hurtful, insalubrious, painful, ruinous. **2** see ABUSIVE.

injury /'ɪndʒərɪ/ *noun* (*plural* **-ies**) **1** physical damage, harm. **2** offence to feelings etc. **3** *esp. Law* wrongful treatment. □ **injury time** extra time at football match etc. to compensate for that lost in dealing with injuries.

■ **1, 2** damage, harm, hurt, mischief, trauma, wound.

injustice /ɪn'dʒʌstɪs/ *noun* **1** unfairness. **2** unjust act.

■ **1** bias, bigotry, discrimination, dishonesty, favouritism, illegality, inequality, inequity, one-sidedness, oppression, partiality, partisanship, prejudice, unfairness, unlawfulness, wrong, wrongness. **2** abuse, unfairness, wrong.

ink *noun* **1** coloured fluid or paste for writing or printing. **2** black liquid ejected by cuttlefish etc. ● *verb* mark, cover, or smear with ink. □ **ink-jet printer** printing machine firing tiny jets of ink at paper. **inkwell** pot for ink, esp. in hole in desk. □ **inky** *adjective* (**-ier, -iest**).

inkling /'ɪŋklɪŋ/ *noun* (often + *of*) hint; slight knowledge or suspicion.

inland *adjective* /'ɪnlənd/ **1** remote from sea or border within a country. **2** carried on within country. ● *adverb* /ɪn'lænd/ in or towards interior of country. □ **Inland Revenue** government department assessing and collecting taxes.

in-laws /'ɪnlɔːz/ *plural noun* relatives by marriage.

inlay *verb* /ɪn'leɪ/ (*past & past participle* **inlaid** /ɪn'leɪd/) **1** embed (thing in another). **2** decorate (thing) thus. ● *noun* /'ɪnleɪ/ **1** inlaid material or work. **2** filling shaped to fit tooth-cavity.

inlet /'ɪnlət/ *noun* **1** small arm of sea etc. **2** piece inserted. **3** way of admission.

inmate /'ɪnmeɪt/ *noun* occupant of house, hospital, prison, etc.

in memoriam /ɪn mɪ'mɔːrɪæm/ *preposition* in memory of.

inmost /'ɪnməʊst/ *adjective* most inward.

inn *noun* **1** pub, sometimes with accommodation. **2** *historical* house providing lodging etc. for payment, esp. for travellers. □ **innkeeper** keeper of inn. **Inns of Court** 4 legal societies admitting people to English bar.

■ **1** *archaic* hostelry, hotel, *colloquial* local, *colloquial* pub, *archaic* or *literary* tavern.

innards /'ɪnədz/ *plural noun colloquial* entrails.

innate /ɪ'neɪt/ *adjective* inborn; natural. □ **innately** *adverb*.

inner /'ɪnə/ *adjective* **1** interior, internal. **2** (of thoughts etc.) deeper. ● *noun* circle nearest bull's-eye of target. □ **inner city** central area of city, esp. regarded as having social problems. **inner tube** separate inflatable tube in pneumatic tyre. □ **innermost** *adjective*.

■ *adjective* **1** central, inside, interior, internal, middle. **2** concealed, deeper, hidden, innermost, intimate, inward, mental, private, secret.

innings /'ɪnɪŋz/ *noun* (*plural* same) **1** *esp.*

Cricket batsman's or side's turn at batting. **2** term of office etc. when person, party, etc. can achieve something.

innocence *noun* **1** condition of being free from moral wrong. **2** state of being guiltless. **3** naivety. **4** harmlessness.

■ **1** goodness, honesty, incorruptibility, purity, righteousness, sinlessness, virtue. **3** gullibility, inexperience, naivety, simple-mindedness, simplicity, unsophistication.

innocent /'ɪnəs(ə)nt/ *adjective* **1** free from moral wrong. **2** not guilty. **3** guileless. **4** harmless. ● *noun* innocent person, esp. young child. □ **innocently** *adverb*.

■ *adjective* **1** angelic, blameless, chaste, childlike, faultless, honest, immaculate, pure, righteous, sinless, spotless, untainted, virginal, virtuous. **2** above suspicion, blameless, free from blame, guiltless, honest. **3** artless, childlike, credulous, green, guileless, gullible, inexperienced, ingenuous, naive, simple, simple-minded, trusting, unsophisticated. **4** harmless, innocuous, inoffensive.

innocuous /ɪ'nɒkjʊəs/ *adjective* harmless.

innovate /'ɪnəveɪt/ *verb* (**-ting**) **1** bring in new ideas etc. **2** make changes. □ **innovation** /-'veɪʃ(ə)n/ *noun*. **innovative** /-vətɪv/ *adjective*. **innovator** *noun*. **innovatory** /-veɪt(ə)rɪ/ *adjective*.

■ □ **innovation** change, departure, invention, new feature, novelty, reform, revolution. **innovator** discoverer, experimenter, inventor, pioneer, reformer, revolutionary.

innuendo /ɪnjʊ'endəʊ/ *noun* (*plural* **-es** or **-s**) allusive (usually depreciatory or sexually suggestive) remark.

innumerable /ɪ'njuːmərəb(ə)l/ *adjective* countless.

■ countless, infinite, many, numberless, uncountable, unnumbered, untold.

innumerate /ɪ'njuːmərət/ *adjective* not knowing basic mathematics. □ **innumeracy** *noun*.

inoculate /ɪ'nɒkjʊleɪt/ *verb* (**-ting**) treat with vaccine or serum to promote immunity against a disease. □ **inoculation** *noun*.

inoffensive /ɪnə'fensɪv/ *adjective* not objectionable; harmless.

inoperable /ɪ'nɒpərəb(ə)l/ *adjective* that cannot be cured by surgical operation.

inoperative /ɪ'nɒpərətɪv/ *adjective* not working or taking effect.

inopportune /ɪ'nɒpətjuːn/ *adjective* not appropriate, esp. as regards time.

inordinate /ɪ'nɔːdɪnət/ *adjective* excessive. □ **inordinately** *adverb*.

inorganic /ɪnɔː'gænɪk/ *adjective* **1** *Chemistry* not organic. **2** without organized physical structure. **3** extraneous.

input /'ɪnpʊt/ *noun* **1** what is put in. **2** place of entry of energy, information, etc. **3** action of putting in or feeding in. **4** contribution of information etc. ● *verb* (**inputting**; *past & past participle* **input** or **inputted**) **1** put in. **2** supply (data, programs, etc.) to computer.

inquest /'ɪŋkwest/ *noun* inquiry held by coroner into cause of death.
■ hearing, inquiry.

inquietude /ɪn'kwaɪətjuːd/ *noun* uneasiness.

inquire /ɪn'kwaɪə/ *verb* (**-ring**) **1** seek information formally; make inquiry. **2** ask question.
■ **1** ask, enquire, explore, investigate, seek information, probe, search, survey. **2** ask, demand, enquire, query, question, quiz.

inquiry /ɪn'kwaɪərɪ/ *noun* (*plural* -**ies**) **1** investigation, esp. official. **2** asking; question.
■ **1** cross-examination, examination, inquest, inquisition, interrogation, investigation, *colloquial* post-mortem, probe, review, study, survey. **2** enquiry, query, question.

inquisition /ɪnkwɪ'zɪʃ(ə)n/ *noun* **1** investigation. **2** official inquiry. **3** (**the Inquisition**) *RC Church historical* ecclesiastical tribunal for suppression of heresy. □ **inquisitional** *adjective*.

inquisitive /ɪn'kwɪzɪtɪv/ *adjective* **1** curious, prying. **2** seeking knowledge. □ **inquisitively** *adverb*. **inquisitiveness** *noun*.
■ **1** curious, impertinent, indiscreet, interfering, intrusive, meddlesome, meddling, *colloquial* nosy, prying, *colloquial* snooping, spying. **2** curious, inquiring, investigative, probing, questioning, sceptical, searching.

inquisitor /ɪn'kwɪzɪtə/ *noun* **1** investigator. **2** *historical* officer of Inquisition.

inquisitorial /ɪnkwɪzɪ'tɔːrɪəl/ *adjective* **1** inquisitor-like. **2** prying.

inroad *noun* **1** (often in *plural*) encroachment; using up of resources etc. **2** hostile incursion.

inrush *noun* rapid influx.

insalubrious /ɪnsə'luːbrɪəs/ *adjective* (of climate or place) unhealthy.

insane /ɪn'seɪn/ *adjective* **1** mad. **2** *colloquial* extremely foolish. □ **insanely** *adverb*. **insanity** /ɪn'sænɪtɪ/ *noun* (*plural* -**ies**).
■ **1** berserk, crazy, demented, deranged, lunatic, mad, *colloquial* mental, non compos mentis, psychotic, unbalanced, unhinged. **2** see FOOLISH.

insanitary /ɪn'sænɪtərɪ/ *adjective* not sanitary.

insatiable /ɪn'seɪʃəb(ə)l/ *adjective* **1** that cannot be satisfied. **2** extremely greedy. □ **insatiability** *noun*. **insatiably** *adverb*.

insatiate /ɪn'seɪʃɪət/ *adjective* never satisfied.

inscribe /ɪn'skraɪb/ *verb* (**-bing**) **1** (usually + *in*, *on*) write or carve (words etc.) on surface. **2** mark (surface) with characters. **3** (usually + *to*) write informal dedication in or on (book etc.). **4** enter on list. **5** *Geometry* draw (figure) within another so that some points of their boundaries coincide.

inscription /ɪn'skrɪpʃ(ə)n/ *noun* **1** words inscribed. **2** inscribing.
■ **1** dedication, engraving, epigraph, writing.

inscrutable /ɪn'skruːtəb(ə)l/ *adjective* mysterious, impenetrable. □ **inscrutability** *noun*. **inscrutably** *adverb*.

insect /'ɪnsekt/ *noun* small invertebrate animal with segmented body, 6 legs, and usually wings.
■ bug, *colloquial* creepy-crawly.

insecticide /ɪn'sektɪsaɪd/ *noun* preparation used for killing insects.

insectivore /ɪn'sektɪvɔː/ *noun* animal or plant that feeds on insects. □ **insectivorous** /-'tɪvərəs/ *adjective*.

insecure /ɪnsɪ'kjʊə/ *adjective* **1** not safe. **2** not secure; unprotected. **3** not feeling safe; not confident. □ **insecurity** /-'kjʊr-/ *noun*.
■ **1** dangerous, flimsy, loose, precarious, rickety, *colloquial* rocky, shaky, unsafe, unsound, unstable, unsteady, unsupported, weak, wobbly. **2** defenceless, exposed, open, unprotected, vulnerable. **3** anxious, apprehensive, diffident, uncertain, underconfident, worried.

inseminate /ɪn'semɪneɪt/ *verb* (**-ting**) **1** introduce semen into. **2** sow (seed etc.). □ **insemination** *noun*.

insensate /ɪn'senseɪt/ *adjective* **1** without esp. physical sensibility. **2** stupid.

insensible /ɪn'sensɪb(ə)l/ *adjective* **1** unconscious. **2** unaware. **3** callous. **4** imperceptible. □ **insensibility** *noun*. **insensibly** *adverb*.
■ **1** anaesthetized, benumbed, knocked out, numb, *colloquial* out, senseless, unconscious. **2** see OBLIVIOUS.

insensitive /ɪn'sensɪtɪv/ *adjective* **1** unfeeling. **2** not responsive to stimuli. □ **insensitively** *adverb*. **insensitiveness** *noun*. **insensitivity** /-'tɪv-/ *noun*.
■ **1** boorish, callous, crass, cruel, obtuse, tactless, thick-skinned, thoughtless, uncaring, unfeeling, unperceptive, unsympathetic. **2** anaesthetized, dead, numb, unresponsive.

insentient /ɪn'senʃ(ə)nt/ *adjective* inanimate.

inseparable /ɪn'sepərəb(ə)l/ *adjective* that cannot be separated. □ **inseparability** *noun*. **inseparably** *adverb*.
■ always together, attached, indissoluble, indivisible, integral.

insert *verb* /ɪn'sɜːt/ place or put (thing into another). ● *noun* /'ɪnsɜːt/ thing inserted.
■ *verb* drive in, embed, implant, interject, interleave, interpolate, interpose, introduce, place in, pop in, push in, put in, stick in, tuck in.

insertion /ɪn'sɜːʃ(ə)n/ *noun* **1** inserting. **2** thing inserted.

inset *noun* /'ɪnset/ **1** extra piece inserted in book, garment, etc. **2** small map etc. within border of larger. ● *verb* /ɪn'set/ (**insetting**; *past* and *past participle* **inset** or **insetted**) **1** put in as inset. **2** decorate with inset.

inshore /ɪn'ʃɔː/ *adverb & adjective* at sea but close to shore.

inside *noun* /ɪn'saɪd/ **1** inner side or part; interior. **2** side of path away from road. **3** (usually in *plural*) *colloquial* stomach and bowels. ● *adjective* /'ɪnsaɪd/ **1** of, on, or in the inside. **2** nearer to centre of games field. ● *adverb* /ɪn'saɪd/ **1** on, in, or to the inside. **2** *slang* in prison. ● *preposition* /ɪn'saɪd/ **1** within; on the inside of. **2** in less than. □ **inside out** with inner side turned outwards. **know inside out** know thoroughly.

■ *noun* **1** bowels, centre, contents, core, heart, indoors, interior, lining, middle. **3** (*insides*) see ENTRAILS 1. ● *adjective* **1** indoor, inner, innermost, interior, internal. **2** central, centre.

insider /ɪn'saɪdə/ *noun* **1** person within organization etc. **2** person privy to secret.

insidious /ɪn'sɪdɪəs/ *adjective* proceeding inconspicuously but harmfully. □ **insidiously** *adverb*.

■ crafty, creeping, cunning, deceptive, furtive, pervasive, secretive, sneaky, stealthy, subtle, surreptitious, treacherous, underhand.

insight *noun* **1** capacity for understanding hidden truths etc. **2** instance of this.

insignia /ɪn'sɪgnɪə/ *plural noun* badges or marks of office etc.

insignificant /ɪnsɪg'nɪfɪkənt/ *adjective* unimportant; trivial. □ **insignificance** *noun*.

■ forgettable, inconsiderable, irrelevant, insubstantial, lightweight, meaningless, minor, negligible, paltry, small, trifling, trivial, undistinguished, unimportant, unimpressive, valueless, worthless.

insincere /ɪnsɪn'sɪə/ *adjective* not sincere. □ **insincerely** *adverb*. **insincerity** /-'ser-/ *noun*

■ artful, crafty, deceitful, deceptive, devious, dishonest, disingenuous, dissembling, false, feigned, flattering, foxy, hollow, hypocritical, lying, mealy-mouthed, mendacious, perfidious, *colloquial* phoney, pretended, put on, *colloquial* smarmy, sycophantic, treacherous, two-faced, untrue, untruthful, wily.

insinuate /ɪn'sɪnjʊeɪt/ *verb* (**-ting**) **1** hint obliquely. **2** (usually + *into*) introduce subtly or deviously. □ **insinuation** *noun*.

insipid /ɪn'sɪpɪd/ *adjective* **1** dull, lifeless. **2** flavourless. □ **insipidity** /-'pɪd-/ *noun*. **insipidly** *adverb*.

insist /ɪn'sɪst/ *verb* (often + *on*) demand or maintain emphatically. □ **insistence** *noun*. **insistent** *adjective*. **insistently** *adverb*.

■ assert oneself, asseverate, *formal* aver, *formal* avow, command, declare, emphasize, hold, maintain, persist, *colloquial* put one's foot down, stand firm, state, *colloquial* stick to one's guns, stress, *colloquial* swear, *archaic* vow; (*insist on*) see DEMAND *verb* 1. □ **insistent** assertive, demanding, dogged, emphatic, firm, forceful, importunate, inexorable, obstinate, peremptory, persistent, relentless, repeated, resolute, stubborn, unrelenting, unremitting, urgent.

in situ /ɪn 'sɪtjuː/ *adverb* in its original place. [Latin]

insobriety /ɪnsə'braɪətɪ/ *noun* intemperance, esp. in drinking.

insole *noun* removable inner sole for use in shoe.

insolent /'ɪnsələnt/ *adjective* impertinently insulting. □ **insolence** *noun*. **insolently** *adverb*.

■ arrogant, audacious, bold, brazen, cheeky, contemptuous, defiant, disdainful, disrespectful, forward, *colloquial* fresh, impertinent, impolite, impudent, insubordinate, insulting, offensive, pert, presumptuous, rude, saucy, shameless, sneering, uncivil. □ **insolence** arrogance, boldness, cheek, defiance, disrespect, effrontery, impertinence, impudence, incivility, insubordination, *colloquial* lip, presumptuousness, rudeness, *colloquial* sauce.

insoluble /ɪn'sɒljʊb(ə)l/ *adjective* **1** that cannot be solved. **2** that cannot be dissolved. □ **insolubility** *noun*. **insolubly** *adverb*.

■ **1** baffling, enigmatic, incomprehensible, inexplicable, mystifying, puzzling, strange, unaccountable, unanswerable, unfathomable, unsolvable.

insolvent /ɪn'sɒlv(ə)nt/ *adjective* unable to pay debts. ● *noun* insolvent debtor. □ **insolvency** *noun*.

■ *adjective* bankrupt, *colloquial* broke, *colloquial* bust, failed, ruined.

insomnia /ɪn'sɒmnɪə/ *noun* sleeplessness.

insomniac /ɪn'sɒmnɪæk/ *noun* person suffering from insomnia.

insouciant /ɪn'suːsɪənt/ *adjective* carefree, unconcerned. □ **insouciance** *noun*.

inspect /ɪn'spekt/ *verb* **1** look closely at. **2** examine officially. □ **inspection** *noun*.

■ check, examine, *colloquial* give it the once-over, investigate, peruse, pore over, scan, scrutinize, study, survey, vet. □ **inspection** check, check-up, examination, *colloquial* going-over, investigation, review, scrutiny, survey.

inspector *noun* **1** official employed to inspect or supervise. **2** police officer next above sergeant in rank. □ **inspectorate** *noun*.

■ **1** controller, examiner, investigator, official, scrutineer, superintendent, supervisor, tester.

inspiration /ɪnspə'reɪʃ(ə)n/ *noun* **1** creative force or influence. **2** person etc. stimulating creativity etc. **3** divine influence, esp. on writing of Scripture. **4** sudden brilliant idea. □ **inspirational** *adjective*.

■ **1, 2** creativity, enthusiasm, genius, imagination, impulse, incitement, influence, motivation, muse, prompting, spur, stimulation, stimulus. **4** *colloquial* brainwave, idea, insight, revelation, thought.

inspire /ɪn'spaɪə/ *verb* (**-ring**) **1** stimulate (person) to esp. creative activity. **2** (usually + *with*) animate. **3** (usually + *in, into*) instil thought or feeling into. **4** prompt; give rise to. **5** (as **inspired** *adjective*) characterized by inspiration. □ **inspiring** *adjective*.

■ 1–3 animate, arouse, awaken, egg on, encourage, energize, *colloquial* enthuse, fire, galvanize, influence, inspirit, kindle, motivate, provoke, quicken, reassure, spur, stimulate, stir, support. **4** activate, give rise to, instigate, prompt, provoke, set off, spark off, stimulate.

inspirit /ɪnˈspɪrɪt/ *verb* (**-t-**) **1** put life into; animate. **2** encourage.

inst. *abbreviation* instant, of current month.

instability /ɪnstəˈbɪlɪtɪ/ *noun* lack of stability.
■ capriciousness, change, changeableness, fickleness, fluctuation, flux, impermanence, inconstancy, insecurity, mutability, precariousness, shakiness, transience, uncertainty, unpredictability, unreliability, unsteadiness, vacillation, variability, variations, weakness.

install /ɪnˈstɔːl/ *verb* **1** place (equipment etc.) in position ready for use. **2** place (person) in office with ceremony. **3** settle (person, oneself, etc.) in position. □ **installation** /-stəˈleɪ-/ *noun*.
■ **1** fit, fix, put in, set up. **2** inaugurate, induct, instate, institute, invest, swear in. **3** ensconce, establish, place, position, settle, station.

instalment *noun* (*US* **installment**) **1** any of several usually equal payments for something. **2** any of several parts, esp. of broadcast or published story.
■ **2** chapter, episode, part.

instance /ˈɪnstəns/ *noun* **1** example. **2** particular case. ● *verb* (**-cing**) cite as instance.
■ *noun* **1** case, example, exemplar, illustration, precedent, sample. **2** case, occasion, occurrence.

instant /ˈɪnst(ə)nt/ *adjective* **1** occurring immediately. **2** (of food etc.) processed for quick preparation. **3** urgent, pressing. **4** of current month. ● *noun* **1** precise moment. **2** short space of time.
■ *adjective* **1** direct, fast, immediate, instantaneous, on the spot, prompt, quick, rapid, speedy, split-second, swift, unhesitating. **3** pressing, urgent. ● *noun* **1** minute, moment, point of time, second. **2** flash, *colloquial* jiffy, moment, *colloquial* second, split second, *colloquial* tick, trice, twinkling (of an eye).

instantaneous /ɪnstənˈteɪnɪəs/ *adjective* occurring or done in an instant. □ **instantaneously** *adverb*.

instantly *adverb* immediately.

instate /ɪnˈsteɪt/ *verb* (often + *in*) install, establish.

instead /ɪnˈsted/ *adverb* (+ *of*) in place of; as substitute or alternative for.

instep /ˈɪnstep/ *noun* **1** inner arch of foot between toes and ankle. **2** part of shoe etc. fitting this.

instigate /ˈɪnstɪɡeɪt/ *verb* (**-ting**) **1** bring about by persuasion. **2** incite. □ **instigation** *noun*. **instigator** *noun*.

■ activate, begin, bring about, cause, encourage, foment, generate, incite, induce, initiate, inspire, kindle, prompt, provoke, set up, start, stimulate, stir up, urge, whip up. □ **instigator** agitator, fomenter, inciter, initiator, leader, mischief-maker, provoker, ringleader, troublemaker.

instil /ɪnˈstɪl/ *verb* (*US* **instill**) (**-ll-**) **1** (often + *into*) put (ideas etc. into mind etc.) gradually. **2** put in by drops. □ **instillation** *noun*. **instilment** *noun*.
■ **1** din, implant, inculcate, infuse, inject, insinuate, introduce. **2** dribble, drip.

instinct /ˈɪnstɪŋkt/ *noun* **1** inborn pattern of behaviour; innate impulse. **2** (often + *for*) intuition. □ **instinctive** /-ˈstɪŋktɪv/ *adjective*. **instinctively** /-ˈstɪŋktɪvlɪ/ *adverb*. **instinctual** /-ˈstɪŋktjʊəl/ *adjective*.
■ **1** impulse, inclination, instinctive urge, propensity, tendency, urge. **2** bent, faculty, feel, feeling, hunch, intuition, presentiment, sixth sense. □ **instinctive** automatic, congenital, constitutional, gut, impulsive, inborn, inbred, inherent, innate, instinctual, intuitive, involuntary, irrational, mechanical, native, natural, reflex, spontaneous, subconscious, unconscious, unreasoning, unthinking, visceral.

institute /ˈɪnstɪtjuːt/ *noun* organized body for promotion of science, education, etc. ● *verb* (**-ting**) **1** establish. **2** initiate (inquiry etc.). **3** (usually + *to*, *into*) appoint (person) as cleric in church etc.
■ academy, college, establishment, foundation, organization, school. ● *verb* **1** create, establish, found, inaugurate, launch, organize, set up. **2** begin, initiate, instigate, introduce, open, originate, pioneer, set up, start.

institution /ɪnstɪˈtjuːʃ(ə)n/ *noun* **1** (esp. charitable) organization or society. **2** established law or custom. **3** *colloquial* well-known person. **4** instituting, being instituted.
■ **1** academy, college, establishment, foundation, home, hospital, institute, organization, society. **2** convention, custom, habit, practice, ritual, routine, rule, tradition. **4** creation, establishing, formation, founding, inauguration, inception, initiation, introduction, launching, opening, setting up.

institutional *adjective* **1** of or like an institution. **2** typical of institutions.

institutionalize *verb* (also **-ise**) (**-zing** or **-sing**) **1** (as **institutionalized** *adjective*) made dependent by long period in institution. **2** place or keep in institution. **3** make institutional.

instruct /ɪnˈstrʌkt/ *verb* **1** teach. **2** (usually + *to do*) direct, command. **3** employ (lawyer). **4** inform. □ **instructor** *noun*.
■ **1** coach, drill, educate, indoctrinate, inform, lecture, prepare, school, teach, train, tutor. **2** authorize, brief, charge, command, direct, enjoin, give the order, order, require, tell. □ **instructor** adviser, coach, demonstrator, educator, guide, teacher, trainer, tutor.

instruction /ɪnˈstrʌkʃ(ə)n/ *noun* **1** (often in *plural*) order, direction (as to how thing works

etc.). **2** teaching. □ **instructional** *adjective*.
■ **1** authorization, brief, charge, command, direction, directive, order, requisition. **2** briefing, coaching, drill, education, guidance, indoctrination, lessons, schooling, teaching, training, tuition, tutoring.

instructive /ɪn'strʌktɪv/ *adjective* tending to instruct; enlightening.
■ didactic, edifying, educational, enlightening, helpful, illuminating, improving, informational, informative, instructional, revealing.

instrument /'ɪnstrəmənt/ *noun* **1** tool, implement. **2** (in full **musical instrument**) contrivance for producing musical sounds. **3** thing used in performing action. **4** person made use of. **5** measuring device, esp. in aircraft. **6** formal (esp. legal) document.
■ **1** apparatus, appliance, contraption, device, gadget, implement, machine, mechanism, tool, utensil.

instrumental /ɪnstrə'ment(ə)l/ *adjective* **1** serving as instrument or means. **2** (of music) performed on instruments.
■ **1** active, advantageous, beneficial, contributory, helpful, influential, supportive, useful, valuable.

instrumentalist *noun* performer on musical instrument.

instrumentality /ɪnstrəmen'tælɪtɪ/ *noun* agency, means.

instrumentation /ɪnstrəmen'teɪʃ(ə)n/ *noun* **1** provision or use of instruments. **2** arrangement of music for instruments. **3** particular instruments used in piece.

insubordinate /ɪnsə'bɔːdɪnət/ *adjective* disobedient; unruly. □ **insubordination** *noun*.
■ defiant, disobedient, insurgent, mutinous, rebellious, recalcitrant, refractory, riotous, seditious, undisciplined, unruly.

insubstantial /ɪnsəb'stænʃ(ə)l/ *adjective* **1** lacking solidity or substance. **2** not real.

insufferable /ɪn'sʌfərəb(ə)l/ *adjective* **1** unbearable. **2** unbearably conceited etc. □ **insufferably** *adverb*.

insufficient /ɪnsə'fɪʃ(ə)nt/ *adjective* not enough, inadequate. □ **insufficiency** *noun*. **insufficiently** *adverb*.
■ deficient, disappointing, inadequate, incomplete, meagre, mean, niggardly, *colloquial* pathetic, poor, scanty, scarce, short, skimpy, sparse, too little, unsatisfactory.

insular /'ɪnsjʊlə/ *adjective* **1** of or like an island. **2** separated, remote. **3** narrow-minded. □ **insularity** /-'lær-/ *noun*.
■ **2** closed, cut off, isolated, remote, separated. **3** limited, narrow, narrow-minded, parochial, provincial, restricted.

insulate /'ɪnsjʊleɪt/ *verb* (**-ting**) **1** cover, esp. with non-conductor, to prevent passage of electricity, heat, sound, etc. **2** isolate. □ **insulation** *noun*. **insulator** *noun*.

■ **1** cocoon, cover, cushion, enclose, isolate, lag, protect, shield, surround, wrap up. **2** cut off, detach, isolate, keep apart, quarantine, segregate, separate.

insulin /'ɪnsjʊlɪn/ *noun* hormone regulating the amount of glucose in the blood, the lack of which causes diabetes.

insult *verb* /ɪn'sʌlt/ **1** abuse scornfully; treat with indignity. **2** offend self-respect etc. of. ● *noun* /'ɪnsʌlt/ insulting remark or action. □ **insulting** *adjective*. **insultingly** *adverb*.
■ *verb* **1** abuse, be rude to, call names, *slang* cock a snook at, defame, dishonour, disparage, libel, mock, patronize, revile, slander, slang, slight, sneer at, snub, vilify. **2** affront, offend, outrage.
● *noun* affront, aspersion, indignity, libel, *colloquial* put-down, slight, slur, snub; (*insults*) abuse, cheek, contumely, defamation, impudence, insulting behaviour, rudeness, slander.
□ **insulting** see RUDE 1.

insuperable /ɪn'suːpərəb(ə)l/ *adjective* **1** impossible to surmount. **2** impossible to overcome. □ **insuperability** *noun*. **insuperably** *adverb*.
■ insurmountable, overwhelming, unconquerable.

insupportable /ɪnsə'pɔːtəb(ə)l/ *adjective* **1** unbearable. **2** unjustifiable.

insurance /ɪn'ʃʊərəns/ *noun* **1** procedure or contract securing compensation for loss, damage, injury, or death on payment of premium. **2** sum paid to effect insurance.
■ **1** assurance, cover, indemnification, indemnity, policy, protection, security.

insure /ɪn'ʃʊə/ *verb* (**-ring**) (often + *against*) effect insurance with respect to.
■ cover, indemnify, protect.

insurgent /ɪn'sɜːdʒ(ə)nt/ *adjective* in revolt; rebellious. ● *noun* rebel. □ **insurgence** *noun*. **insurgency** *noun* (*plural* **-ies**).

insurmountable /ɪnsə'maʊntəb(ə)l/ *adjective* insuperable.

insurrection /ɪnsə'rekʃ(ə)n/ *noun* rising in resistance to authority; incipient rebellion. □ **insurrectionary** *adjective*. **insurrectionist** *noun*.

intact /ɪn'tækt/ *adjective* **1** unimpaired; entire. **2** untouched.
■ **1** complete, entire, integral, perfect, solid, sound, unbroken, undamaged, unharmed, unscathed, whole.

intaglio /ɪn'tɑːlɪəʊ/ *noun* (*plural* **-s**) **1** gem with incised design. **2** engraved design.

intake *noun* **1** action of taking in. **2** people, things, or quantity taken in. **3** place where water is taken into pipe, or fuel or air into engine.

intangible /ɪn'tændʒɪb(ə)l/ *adjective* that cannot be touched or mentally grasped. □ **intangibility** *noun*. **intangibly** *adverb*.

■ abstract, airy, disembodied, elusive, ethereal, *literary* evanescent, fleeting, impalpable, imperceptible, imponderable, incorporeal, indefinite, insubstantial, invisible, shadowy, unreal, vague.

integer /ˈɪntɪdʒə/ *noun* whole number.

integral /ˈɪntɪgr(ə)l/ *adjective* **1** of or essential to a whole. **2** complete. **3** of or denoted by an integer.

USAGE *Integral* is often pronounced /ɪnˈtegr(ə)l/ (with the stress on the *-teg-*), but this is considered incorrect by some people.

■ **1** basic, constituent, essential, fundamental, indispensable, intrinsic, irreplaceable, necessary, requisite. **2** complete, full, indivisible, intact, whole.

integrate /ˈɪntɪgreɪt/ *verb* (**-ting**) **1** combine (parts) into whole. **2** complete by adding parts. **3** bring or come into equal membership of society. **4** desegregate (school etc.), esp. racially. □ **integrated circuit** small piece of material replacing electrical circuit of many components. □ **integration** *noun*.

■ amalgamate, assemble, blend, bring together, coalesce, combine, desegregate, consolidate, fuse, harmonize, incorporate, join, knit, merge, mix, put together, unify, unite, weld.

integrity /ɪnˈtegrɪtɪ/ *noun* **1** honesty; moral strength. **2** wholeness; soundness.

■ **1** character, decency, fidelity, goodness, honesty, honour, incorruptibility, loyalty, morality, principle, probity, rectitude, reliability, righteousness, sincerity, trustworthiness, uprightness, veracity, virtue. **2** completeness, oneness, soundness, unity, wholeness.

integument /ɪnˈtegjʊmənt/ *noun* skin, husk, or other (natural) covering.

intellect /ˈɪntəlekt/ *noun* faculty of knowing and reasoning; understanding.

■ brains, cleverness, discernment, genius, intelligence, judgement, mind, rationality, reason, sagacity, sense, understanding, wisdom, wit.

intellectual /ɪntəˈlektʃʊəl/ *adjective* **1** of, requiring, or using intellect. **2** having highly developed intellect. ● *noun* intellectual person. □ **intellectualize** *verb* (also **-ise**) (**-zing** or **-sing**). **intellectually** *adverb*.

■ *adjective* **1** academic, bookish, cerebral, cultural, cultured, deep, difficult, educated, educational, *colloquial* highbrow, improving, scholarly, studious, thinking, thoughtful, thought-provoking. **2** see INTELLIGENT. ● *noun* academic, *colloquial* egghead, genius, *colloquial* highbrow, mastermind, savant, thinker; (*intellectuals*) the intelligentsia.

intelligence /ɪnˈtelɪdʒ(ə)ns/ *noun* **1** intellect; quickness of understanding. **2** collecting of information, esp. secretly for military or political purposes. **3** people employed in this. **4** information collected. □ **intelligence quotient** number denoting ratio of person's intelligence to the average.

■ **1** ability, acumen, alertness, astuteness, brainpower, brains, brightness, brilliance, capacity, cleverness, discernment, genius, *colloquial* grey matter, insight, intellect, judgement, keenness, mind, *colloquial* nous, perceptiveness, perspicaciousness, perspicacity, quickness, reason, sagacity, sense, sharpness, shrewdness, understanding, wisdom, wit, wits. **2, 3** espionage, secret service, spying. **4** data, facts, information, knowledge, *colloquial* low-down, news, notification, report, warning.

intelligent *adjective* having or showing intelligence, clever. □ **intelligently** *adverb*.

■ able, acute, alert, astute, brainy, bright, brilliant, canny, clever, discerning, educated, intellectual, knowing, penetrating, perceptive, percipient, perspicacious, profound, quick, rational, reasonable, sagacious, sensible, sharp, shrewd, smart, thinking, thoughtful, trenchant, wise, *colloquial* with it, witty.

intelligentsia /ɪntelɪˈdʒentsɪə/ *noun* class of intellectuals regarded as cultured and politically enterprising.

intelligible /ɪnˈtelɪdʒɪb(ə)l/ *adjective* that can be understood. □ **intelligibility** *noun*. **intelligibly** *adverb*.

■ clear, comprehensible, decipherable, fathomable, legible, logical, lucid, meaningful, plain, straightforward, unambiguous, understandable.

intemperate /ɪnˈtempərət/ *adjective* **1** immoderate. **2** excessive in consumption of alcohol, or in general indulgence of appetite. □ **intemperance** *noun*.

intend /ɪnˈtend/ *verb* **1** have as one's purpose. **2** (usually + *for*, *as*, *to do*) design, destine.

■ aim, aspire, contemplate, design, determine, have in mind, mean, plan, plot, propose, purpose, resolve, scheme.

intended *adjective* done on purpose. ● *noun colloquial* fiancé(e).

intense /ɪnˈtens/ *adjective* (**-r, -st**) **1** existing in high degree; extreme; vehement; violent, forceful. **2** very emotional. □ **intensity** *noun* (*plural* **-ies**). **intensely** *adverb*.

USAGE *Intense* is sometimes confused with *intensive*, and wrongly used to describe a course of study etc.

■ **1** (*intense pain*) acute, agonizing, excruciating, extreme, fierce, great, harsh, keen, severe, sharp; (*intense feelings*) ardent, burning, consuming, deep, eager, earnest, fervent, fervid, passionate, powerful, profound, serious, strong, towering, vehement, violent. **2** ardent, earnest, emotional, fanatical, fervent, fervid, impassioned, passionate, serious, vehement, zealous.

intensify *verb* (**-ies, -ied**) make or become (more) intense. □ **intensification** *noun*

■ add to, aggravate, augment, boost, build up, deepen, emphasize, escalate, exacerbate, fire, focus, fuel, heighten, increase, magnify, quicken, raise, redouble, reinforce, sharpen, step up, strengthen, whet.

intensive /ɪn'tensɪv/ *adjective* **1** thorough, vigorous; concentrated. **2** of or relating to intensity. **3** increasing production relative to cost. □ **-intensive** making much use of. **intensive care** medical treatment with constant supervision of dangerously ill patient. □ **intensively** *adverb*.

■ all out, comprehensive, concentrated, detailed, exhaustive, high-powered, thorough, unremitting.

intent /ɪn'tent/ *noun* intention; purpose. ● *adjective* **1** (usually + *on*) resolved, bent. **2** attentively occupied. **3** eager. □ **to all intents and purposes** practically. □ **intently** *adverb*. **intentness** *noun*.

■ *noun* see INTENTION 1. ● *adjective* **1** bent, committed, determined, firm, focused, keen, resolute, resolved, set. **2** absorbed, attentive, concentrated, concentrating, engrossed, occupied, preoccupied, steadfast, watchful. **3** eager, earnest, enthusiastic, keen, zealous.

intention /ɪn'tenʃ(ə)n/ *noun* **1** purpose, aim. **2** intending.

■ **1** aim, ambition, design, end, goal, intent, object, objective, plan, point, purpose, target.

intentional *adjective* done on purpose. □ **intentionally** *adverb*.

■ calculated, conscious, contrived, deliberate, designed, intended, knowing, planned, pre-arranged, preconceived, premeditated, prepared, studied, wilful.

inter /ɪn'tɜ:/ *verb* (**-rr-**) bury (corpse etc.).

inter- *combining form* **1** among, between. **2** mutually, reciprocally.

interact /ɪntər'ækt/ *verb* act on each other. □ **interaction** *noun*.

interactive *adjective* **1** reciprocally active. **2** (of computer etc.) allowing two-way flow of information between itself and user. □ **interactively** *adverb*.

interbreed /ɪntə'bri:d/ *verb* (*past & past participle* **-bred**) (cause to) produce hybrid individual.

intercalary /ɪn'tɜ:kələrɪ/ *adjective* **1** inserted to harmonize calendar with solar year. **2** having such addition. **3** interpolated.

intercede /ɪntə'si:d/ *verb* (**-ding**) intervene on behalf of another; plead.

intercept /ɪntə'sept/ *verb* **1** seize, catch, stop, etc. in transit. **2** cut off. □ **interception** *noun*. **interceptor** *noun*.

■ ambush, arrest, block, catch, check, cut off, deflect, head off, impede, interrupt, obstruct, stop, thwart, trap.

intercession /ɪntə'seʃ(ə)n/ *noun* interceding. □ **intercessor** *noun*.

interchange *verb* /ɪntə'tʃeɪndʒ/ (**-ging**) **1** (of two people) exchange (things) with each other. **2** make exchange of (two things); alternate. ● *noun* /'ɪntətʃeɪndʒ/ **1** reciprocal exchange. **2** alterna-

tion. **3** road junction where traffic streams do not cross. □ **interchangeable** *adjective*.

inter-city /ɪntə'sɪtɪ/ *adjective* existing or travelling between cities.

intercom /'ɪntəkɒm/ *noun colloquial* system of intercommunication by telephone or radio.

intercommunicate /ɪntəkə'mju:nɪkeɪt/ *verb* (**-ting**) **1** have communication with each other. **2** (of rooms etc.) open into each other. □ **intercommunication** *noun*.

intercommunion /ɪntəkə'mju:nɪən/ *noun* mutual communion, esp. between religious bodies.

interconnect /ɪntəkə'nekt/ *verb* connect with each other. □ **interconnection** *noun*.

intercontinental /ɪntəkɒntɪ'nent(ə)l/ *adjective* connecting or travelling between continents.

intercourse /'ɪntəkɔ:s/ *noun* **1** social, international, etc. communication or dealings. **2** sexual intercourse.

■ **1** communication, conversation, dealings, interaction, traffic. **2** carnal knowledge, coition, coitus, copulation, intimacy, lovemaking, mating, *colloquial* sex, sexual intercourse, union.

interdenominational /ɪntədɪnɒmɪ'neɪʃən(ə)l/ *adjective* of or involving more than one Christian denomination.

interdependent /ɪntədɪ'pend(ə)nt/ *adjective* mutually dependent. □ **interdependence** *noun*.

interdict *noun* /'ɪntədɪkt/ **1** formal prohibition. **2** *RC Church* sentence debarring person, or esp. place, from ecclesiastical functions and privileges. ● *verb* /ɪntə'dɪkt/ **1** prohibit (action). **2** forbid use of. **3** (usually + *from*) restrain (person). □ **interdiction** /-'dɪk-/ *noun*. **interdictory** /-'dɪk-/ *adjective*.

interdisciplinary /ɪntədɪsɪ'plɪnərɪ/ *adjective* of or involving different branches of learning.

interest /'ɪntrəst/ *noun* **1** concern; curiosity. **2** quality causing this; significance. **3** subject, hobby, etc., towards which one feels it. **4** advantage. **5** money paid for use of money borrowed etc. **6** thing in which one has stake or concern. **7** financial stake. **8** legal concern, title, or right. ● *verb* **1** arouse interest of. **2** (usually + *in*) cause to take interest.

■ *noun* **1** attention, attentiveness, concern, curiosity, involvement, notice, regard, scrutiny. **2** consequence, importance, moment, note, noteworthiness, significance, value. **3** activity, diversion, hobby, pastime, preoccupation, pursuit, relaxation. ● *verb* **1** absorb, appeal to, arouse the curiosity of, attract, capture the imagination of, captivate, concern, divert, enchant, engage, engross, entertain, enthral, excite, fascinate, intrigue, involve, occupy, preoccupy, stimulate, *colloquial* turn on.

interested *adjective* **1** having curiosity aroused. **2** having private interest; not impartial.

■ **1** absorbed, attentive, curious, engrossed, enthusiastic, immersed, intent, involved, keen, occupied, preoccupied, rapt, responsive, riveted. **2** biased, concerned, involved, partial, partisan.

interesting *adjective* causing curiosity; holding the attention. □ **interestingly** *adverb*.

■ absorbing, appealing, attractive, compelling, curious, diverting, engaging, engrossing, entertaining, enthralling, fascinating, gripping, intriguing, inviting, original, piquant, riveting, spellbinding, unusual.

interface /ˈɪntəfeɪs/ *noun* **1** surface forming common boundary of two regions. **2** place where interaction occurs between two systems etc. **3** apparatus for connecting two pieces of esp. computing equipment so they can be operated jointly. ● *verb* (**-cing**) **1** connect by means of interface. **2** interact.

interfere /ɪntəˈfɪə/ *verb* (**-ring**) **1** (often + *with*) meddle. **2** (often + *with*) be an obstacle. **3** (often + *in*) intervene. **4** (+ *with*) molest sexually. □ **interfering** *adjective*.

■ **1, 3** be a busybody, butt in, interrupt, intervene, intrude, meddle, obtrude, *colloquial* poke one's nose in, put one's oar in, pry, *colloquial* snoop, tamper. **2** (*interfere with*) see OBSTRUCT 3. □ **interfering** see NOSY.

interference *noun* **1** interfering. **2** fading of received radio signals.

interferon /ɪntəˈfɪərɒn/ *noun* protein inhibiting development of virus in cell.

interfuse /ɪntəˈfjuːz/ *verb* (**-sing**) mix, blend. □ **interfusion** *noun*.

interim /ˈɪntərɪm/ *noun* intervening time. ● *adjective* provisional, temporary.

■ *adjective* half-time, halfway, provisional, stopgap, temporary.

interior /ɪnˈtɪərɪə/ *adjective* **1** inner. **2** inland. **3** internal; domestic. ● *noun* **1** inner part; inside. **2** inland region. **3** home affairs of country. **4** representation of inside of room etc.

■ *adjective* **1** see INTERNAL 1. ● *noun* **1** centre, core, depths, heart, inside, middle, nucleus.

interject /ɪntəˈdʒekt/ *verb* **1** make (remark etc.) abruptly or parenthetically. **2** interrupt.

interjection /ɪntəˈdʒekʃ(ə)n/ *noun* exclamation.

interlace /ɪntəˈleɪs/ *verb* (**-cing**) bind intricately together; interweave.

interlard /ɪntəˈlɑːd/ *verb* mix (speech etc.) with unusual words or phrases.

interleave /ɪntəˈliːv/ *verb* (**-ving**) insert (usually blank) leaves between leaves of (book).

interline /ɪntəˈlaɪn/ *verb* (**-ning**) put extra layer of material between fabric of (garment) and its lining.

interlink /ɪntəˈlɪŋk/ *verb* link together.

interlock /ɪntəˈlɒk/ *verb* **1** engage with each other by overlapping etc. **2** lock together. ● *noun* machine-knitted fabric with fine stitches.

interlocutor /ɪntəˈlɒkjʊtə/ *noun formal* person who takes part in conversation. □ **interlocutory** *adjective*.

interloper /ˈɪntələʊpə/ *noun* **1** intruder. **2** person who thrusts himself or herself into others' affairs.

interlude /ˈɪntəluːd/ *noun* **1** interval between parts of play etc. **2** performance filling this. **3** contrasting time, event, etc. in middle of something.

■ **1, 2** entr'acte, *Music* intermezzo, intermission, interval. **3** see INTERVAL 2.

intermarry /ɪntəˈmærɪ/ *verb* (**-ies, -ied**) (+ *with*) (of races, castes, families, etc.) become connected by marriage. □ **intermarriage** /-rɪdʒ/ *noun*.

intermediary /ɪntəˈmiːdɪərɪ/ *noun* (*plural* **-ies**) mediator. ● *adjective* **1** acting as mediator. **2** intermediate.

■ *noun* agent, ambassador, arbiter, arbitrator, broker, go-between, mediator, middleman, negotiator, referee, spokesperson, umpire.

intermediate /ɪntəˈmiːdɪət/ *adjective* coming between in time, place, order, etc. ● *noun* intermediate thing.

■ *adjective* average, halfway, intermediary, intervening, mean, medial, median, middle, midway, neither one thing nor the other, neutral, transitional.

interment /ɪnˈtɜːmənt/ *noun* burial.

intermezzo /ɪntəˈmetsəʊ/ *noun* (*plural* **-mezzi** /-sɪ/ or **-s**) *Music* short connecting movement or composition.

interminable /ɪnˈtɜːmɪnəb(ə)l/ *adjective* **1** endless. **2** tediously long. □ **interminably** *adverb*.

intermingle /ɪntəˈmɪŋg(ə)l/ *verb* (**-ling**) mix together; mingle.

intermission /ɪntəˈmɪʃ(ə)n/ *noun* **1** pause, cessation. **2** interval in cinema etc.

intermittent /ɪntəˈmɪt(ə)nt/ *adjective* occurring at intervals; not continuous or steady. □ **intermittently** *adverb*.

■ broken, discontinuous, erratic, fitful, irregular, occasional, on and off, periodic, random, recurrent, spasmodic, sporadic.

intermix /ɪntəˈmɪks/ *verb* mix together.

intern *noun* /ˈɪntɜːn/ *US* resident junior doctor in hospital. ● *verb* /ɪnˈtɜːn/ confine within prescribed limits. □ **internee** /-ˈniː/ *noun*. **internment** *noun*.

internal /ɪnˈtɜːn(ə)l/ *adjective* **1** of or in the inside of thing. **2** relating to inside of the body. **3** private; kept from public knowledge. **4** of domestic affairs of country. **5** (of students) attending a university as well as taking its exams. **6** used or applying within an organization. **7** intrinsic. **8** of mind or soul. □ **internal-combustion engine** engine in which motive power comes from explosion of gas or vapour with air in cylinder. □ **internally** *adverb*.

■ **1** inner, inside, interior, inward. **3** confidential, hidden, in-house, intimate, personal, private, secret, undisclosed.

international /ɪntəˈnæʃən(ə)l/ *adjective* **1** existing or carried on between nations. **2** agreed on by many nations. ● *noun* **1** contest (usually in sports) between representatives of different nations. **2** such representative. **3** (**International**) any of 4 successive associations for socialist or communist action. □ **internationality** /-ˈnæl-/ *noun*. **internationally** *adverb*.

■ *adjective* cosmopolitan, global, intercontinental, universal, worldwide.

internationalism *noun* advocacy of community of interests among nations. □ **internationalist** *noun*.

internationalize *verb* (also **-ise**) (**-zing** or **-sing**) **1** make international. **2** bring under joint protection etc. of different nations.

internecine /ɪntəˈniːsaɪn/ *adjective* mutually destructive.

interpenetrate /ɪntəˈpenɪtreɪt/ *verb* (**-ting**) **1** penetrate each other. **2** pervade. □ **interpenetration** *noun*.

interpersonal /ɪntəˈpɜːsən(ə)l/ *adjective* between people.

interplanetary /ɪntəˈplænɪtərɪ/ *adjective* between planets.

interplay /ˈɪntəpleɪ/ *noun* reciprocal action.

Interpol /ˈɪntəpɒl/ *noun* International Criminal Police Organization.

interpolate /ɪnˈtɜːpəleɪt/ *verb* (**-ting**) **1** insert or introduce between other things. **2** make (esp. misleading) insertions in. □ **interpolation** *noun*.

interpose /ɪntəˈpəʊz/ *verb* (**-sing**) **1** insert (thing between others). **2** introduce, use, say, etc. as interruption or interference; interrupt. **3** advance (objection etc.) so as to interfere. **4** intervene. □ **interposition** /-pəˈzɪʃ(ə)n/ *noun*.

interpret /ɪnˈtɜːprɪt/ *verb* (**-t-**) **1** explain the meaning of (esp. words). **2** render, represent. **3** act as interpreter. □ **interpretation** *noun*. **interpretive** *adjective*.

■ **1, 2** clarify, clear up, construe, decipher, decode, define, elucidate, explain, explicate, expound, gloss, make clear, make sense of, paraphrase, render, rephrase, reword, simplify, sort out, translate, understand, unravel, work out. **3** translate. □ **interpretation** clarification, definition, elucidation, explanation, gloss, paraphrase, reading, rendering, translation, understanding, version.

interpreter *noun* person who translates orally.

interracial /ɪntəˈreɪʃ(ə)l/ *adjective* between or affecting different races.

interregnum /ɪntəˈregnəm/ *noun* (*plural* **-s**) **1** interval with suspension of normal government between successive reigns or regimes. **2** interval, pause.

interrelated /ɪntərɪˈleɪtɪd/ *adjective* related to each other. □ **interrelation** *noun*. **interrelationship** *noun*.

interrogate /ɪnˈterəgeɪt/ *verb* (**-ting**) question closely or formally. □ **interrogation** *noun*. **interrogator** *noun*.

■ □ **interrogation** cross-examination, debriefing, examination, grilling, inquisition, questioning, third degree.

interrogative /ɪntəˈrɒgətɪv/ *adjective* **1** of, like, or used in questions. **2** *Grammar* (of adjective or pronoun) asking question (see panel). ● *noun* interrogative word.

■ *adjective* **1** asking, inquiring, inquisitive, interrogatory, investigatory, questioning.

interrogatory /ɪntəˈrɒgətərɪ/ *adjective* questioning. ● *noun* (*plural* **-ies**) set of questions.

interrupt /ɪntəˈrʌpt/ *verb* **1** break continuity of (action, speech, etc.). **2** obstruct (view etc.). □ **interruption** *noun*.

■ **1** barge in, break in, break off, butt in, call a halt to, chime in, *colloquial* chip in, cut in, cut off, cut short, discontinue, disrupt, disturb, halt, heckle, hold up, interfere, intervene, intrude, punctuate, obstruct, spoil, stop, suspend, terminate. □ **interruption** break, check, disruption, division, gap, halt, hiatus, interference, interval, intrusion, stop, suspension.

intersect /ɪntəˈsekt/ *verb* **1** divide by passing or lying across. **2** cross or cut each other.

■ **1** bisect, cross, divide. **2** bisect each other, converge, criss-cross, cross, meet, pass across each other.

intersection /ɪntəˈsekʃ(ə)n/ *noun* **1** intersecting. **2** place where two roads intersect. **3** point or line common to lines or planes that intersect.

intersperse /ɪntəˈspɜːs/ *verb* (**-sing**) **1** (usually + *between, among*) scatter. **2** (+ *with*) vary (thing) by scattering others among it.

interstate /ˈɪntəsteɪt/ *adjective* existing etc. between states, esp. of US.

● ●

Interrogative pronoun

Interrogative pronouns (*who, whom, which, what*) introduce direct and indirect questions:

> *What did he say?*
> *She asked him what he had said.*
> *Who are you?*
> *She asked him who he was.*

A question mark is used after a direct question, but not after an indirect question.

● ●

interstellar /ɪntə'stelə/ *adjective* between stars.

interstice /ɪn'tɜːstɪs/ *noun* **1** gap. **2** chink, crevice.

interstitial /ɪntə'stɪʃ(ə)l/ *adjective* forming or in interstices.

intertwine /ɪntə'twaɪn/ *verb* (**-ning**) (often + *with*) twine closely together.

interval /'ɪntəv(ə)l/ *noun* **1** intervening time or space. **2** pause; break. **3** *Music* difference of pitch between two sounds. □ **at intervals** here and there, now and then.

■ **1** delay, distance, gap, hiatus, interruption, lapse, opening, space, void, wait. **2** adjournment, break, *colloquial* breather, breathing-space, entr'acte, interlude, *Music* intermezzo, intermission, lull, pause, recess, respite, rest.

intervene /ɪntə'viːn/ *verb* (**-ning**) **1** occur in meantime. **2** interfere. **3** prevent or modify events. **4** come between people or things. **5** mediate.

■ **2, 4** butt in, interfere, interrupt, intrude, step in. **5** arbitrate, intercede, interpose, mediate, step in.

intervention /ɪntə'venʃ(ə)n/ *noun* **1** intervening. **2** interference. **3** mediation.

interview /'ɪntəvjuː/ *noun* **1** oral examination of applicant. **2** conversation with reporter, for broadcast or publication. **3** meeting of people, esp. for discussion. ● *verb* hold interview with. □ **interviewee** /-vjuː'iː/ *noun*. **interviewer** *noun*.

■ *noun* **1** appraisal, *colloquial* oral, questioning, selection procedure, vetting. **2** audience, conversation, talk. **3** conference, consultation, duologue, formal discussion, meeting. ● *verb* appraise, ask questions of, evaluate, examine, interrogate, question, sound out, vet.

interweave /ɪntə'wiːv/ *verb* (**-ving**; *past* **-wove**; *past participle* **-woven**) **1** weave together. **2** blend intimately.

■ **1** criss-cross, entwine, interlace, intertwine, knit, tangle, weave together.

intestate /ɪn'testeɪt/ *adjective* not having made a will before death. ● *noun* person who has died intestate. □ **intestacy** /-təsɪ/ *noun*.

intestine /ɪn'testɪn/ *noun* (in *singular* or *plural*) lower part of alimentary canal. □ **intestinal** *adjective*.

■ (*intestines*) bowels, entrails, guts, *colloquial* innards, *colloquial* insides, offal.

intimate[1] *adjective* /'ɪntɪmət/ **1** closely acquainted; familiar. **2** closely personal. **3** (usually + *with*) having sexual relations. **4** (of knowledge) thorough. **5** (of relationship between things) close. ● *noun* intimate friend. □ **intimacy** /-məsɪ/ *noun*. **intimately** *adverb*.

■ *adjective* **1** *colloquial* chummy, close, familiar, friendly, informal, *colloquial* thick. **2** confidential, personal, private, secret. **3** amorous, loving, physical, sexual. **4** detailed, exhaustive, extensive, thorough. ● *noun* see FRIEND 1.

intimate[2] /'ɪntɪmeɪt/ *verb* (**-ting**) **1** state or make known. **2** imply. □ **intimation** *noun*.

■ see INDICATE 1,2.

intimidate /ɪn'tɪmɪdeɪt/ *verb* (**-ting**) frighten, esp. in order to influence conduct. □ **intimidation** *noun*.

■ alarm, browbeat, bully, coerce, cow, daunt, dismay, frighten, hector, make afraid, menace, overawe, persecute, petrify, scare, terrify, terrorize, threaten, tyrannize.

into /'ɪntʊ, 'ɪntə/ *preposition* **1** *expressing motion or direction to point within, direction of attention, or change of state.* **2** after the beginning of. **3** *colloquial* interested in.

intolerable /ɪn'tɒlərəb(ə)l/ *adjective* that cannot be endured. □ **intolerably** *adverb*.

■ excruciating, impossible, insufferable, insupportable, unacceptable, unbearable, unendurable.

intolerant /ɪn'tɒlərənt/ *adjective* not tolerant. □ **intolerance** *noun*.

■ biased, bigoted, chauvinistic, discriminatory, dogmatic, illiberal, narrow-minded, one-sided, opinionated, prejudiced, racist, sexist, uncharitable, unsympathetic, xenophobic.

intonation /ɪntə'neɪʃ(ə)n/ *noun* **1** modulation of voice; accent. **2** intoning.

■ **1** accent, delivery, inflection, modulation, pronunciation, sound, speech pattern, tone.

intone /ɪn'təʊn/ *verb* (**-ning**) recite with prolonged sounds, esp. in monotone.

in toto /ɪn 'təʊtəʊ/ *adverb* entirely. [Latin]

intoxicant /ɪn'tɒksɪkənt/ *adjective* intoxicating. ● *noun* intoxicating substance.

intoxicate /ɪn'tɒksɪkeɪt/ *verb* (**-ting**) **1** make drunk. **2** excite or elate beyond self-control. □ **intoxicated** *adjective*. **intoxicating** *adjective*. **intoxication** *noun*.

■ **1** addle, inebriate, stupefy. □ **intoxicated** see DRUNK *adjective* 1, EXCITED (EXCITE). **intoxicating** see ALCOHOLIC *adjective*, EXCITING (EXCITE).

intractable /ɪn'træktəb(ə)l/ *adjective* **1** not easily dealt with. **2** stubborn. □ **intractability** *noun*.

intramural /ɪntrə'mjʊər(ə)l/ *adjective* situated or done within walls of institution etc.

intransigent /ɪn'trænsɪdʒ(ə)nt/ *adjective* uncompromising. ● *noun* such person. □ **intransigence** *noun*.

Intransitive verb

See panel at TRANSITIVE VERB.

intransitive /ɪnˈtrænsɪtɪv/ *adjective* (of verb) not taking direct object (see panel at TRANSITIVE VERB).

intrauterine /ɪntrəˈjuːtəraɪn/ *adjective* within the womb.

intravenous /ɪntrəˈviːnəs/ *adjective* in(to) vein(s). □ **intravenously** *adverb*.

intrepid /ɪnˈtrepɪd/ *adjective* fearless; brave. □ **intrepidity** /-trɪˈpɪdɪtɪ/ *noun*.

intricate /ˈɪntrɪkət/ *adjective* complicated; perplexingly detailed. □ **intricacy** /-kəsɪ/ *noun* (*plural* **-ies**). **intricately** *adverb*.

■ complex, complicated, convoluted, delicate, detailed, elaborate, entangled, fancy, *colloquial* fiddly, involved, knotty, labyrinthine, ornate, sophisticated, tangled, tortuous.

intrigue *verb* /ɪnˈtriːg/ (**-gues, -gued, -guing**) **1** carry on underhand plot. **2** use secret influence. **3** rouse curiosity of. ● *noun* /ˈɪntriːg/ **1** underhand plotting or plot. **2** secret arrangement, esp. with romantic associations. □ **intriguing** *adjective*. **intriguingly** *adverb*.

■ *verb* **1** see PLOT *verb* 2. **3** appeal to, arouse the curiosity of, attract, beguile, captivate, capture the interest of, engage, engross, excite the curiosity of, fascinate, interest, stimulate, *colloquial* turn on. ● *noun* **1** see PLOT *noun* 3.

intrinsic /ɪnˈtrɪnzɪk/ *adjective* inherent; essential. □ **intrinsically** *adverb*.

■ basic, essential, fundamental, immanent, inborn, inbred, in-built, inherent, native, natural, proper, real.

intro /ˈɪntrəʊ/ *noun* (*plural* **-s**) *colloquial* introduction.

introduce /ɪntrəˈdjuːs/ *verb* (**-cing**) **1** make (person) known by name to another. **2** announce or present to audience. **3** bring (custom etc.) into use. **4** bring (bill etc.) before Parliament. **5** (+ *to*) initiate (person) in subject. **6** insert. **7** bring in; usher in; bring forward. □ **introducible** *adjective*.

■ **1** (*introduce to*) acquaint with, make known to, present to. **2** announce, lead into, preface. **3** begin, bring in, create, establish, inaugurate, initiate, institute, launch, phase in, pioneer, set up, start. **6** inject, insert, interpose, place in. **7** add, advance, begin, bring in, bring out, broach, make available, offer, present, put forward, suggest, usher in.

introduction /ɪntrəˈdʌkʃ(ə)n/ *noun* **1** introducing, being introduced. **2** formal presentation of one person to another. **3** preliminary matter in book. **4** introductory treatise. **5** preliminary section in piece of music. □ **introductory** *adjective*.

■ **1** see BEGINNING 1,2. **3** foreword, *colloquial* intro, preamble, preface, prolegomenon, prologue. **5** *colloquial* intro, lead-in, opening, overture, prelude. □ **introductory** basic, early, first, fundamental, inaugural, initial, opening, prefatory, preliminary, preparatory, starting.

introspection /ɪntrəˈspekʃ(ə)n/ *noun* examination of one's own thoughts. □ **introspective** *adjective*.

introvert *noun* **1** person chiefly concerned with his or her own thoughts. **2** shy thoughtful person. ● *adjective* (also **introverted**) characteristic of an introvert. □ **introversion** /-ˈvɜːʃ(ə)n/ *noun*.

■ *adjective* (**introverted**) contemplative, introspective, inward-looking, meditative, pensive, quiet, reserved, retiring, self-contained, shy, thoughtful, unsociable, withdrawn.

intrude /ɪnˈtruːd/ *verb* (**-ding**) (+ *on, upon, into*) **1** come uninvited or unwanted. **2** force on a person. □ **intrusion** /-ʒ(ə)n/ *noun*. **intrusive** /-sɪv/ *adjective*.

■ **1** break in, butt in, encroach, gatecrash, interfere, interpose, interrupt, intervene, obtrude, *colloquial* snoop.

intruder /ɪnˈtruːdə/ *noun* person who intrudes, esp. into a building with criminal intent.

■ burglar, gatecrasher, housebreaker, infiltrator, interloper, invader, prowler, raider, robber, *colloquial* snooper, thief, trespasser, uninvited guest.

intuition /ɪntjuːˈɪʃ(ə)n/ *noun* **1** immediate apprehension by mind without reasoning. **2** immediate insight. □ **intuit** /ɪnˈtjuːɪt/ *verb*. **intuitional** *adjective*.

■ **1** see INSTINCT 2. **2** insight, perceptiveness, percipience.

intuitive /ɪnˈtjuːɪtɪv/ *adjective* of, having, or perceived by intuition. □ **intuitively** *adverb*. **intuitiveness** *noun*.

Inuit /ˈɪnjuːɪt/ *noun* (*plural* same or **-s**) **1** N. American Eskimo. **2** language of Inuit. ● *adjective* of Inuit or their language.

inundate /ˈɪnʌndeɪt/ *verb* (**-ting**) (often + *with*) **1** flood. **2** overwhelm. □ **inundation** *noun*.

inure /ɪˈnjʊə/ *verb* (**-ring**) habituate, accustom. □ **inurement** *noun*.

invade /ɪnˈveɪd/ *verb* (**-ding**) **1** enter (country etc.) with arms to control or subdue it. **2** swarm into. **3** (of disease etc.) attack. **4** encroach on. □ **invader** *noun*.

■ **1** attack, descend on, enter, infiltrate, march into, occupy, overrun, raid, subdue. **2** crowd into, infest, overrun, pervade, swarm into. **3** afflict, attack, infect. **4** encroach on, impinge on, infringe on, intrude on, trespass on, violate.

invalid[1] /ˈɪnvəlɪd, -liːd/ *noun* person enfeebled or disabled by illness or injury. ● *adjective* **1** of or for invalids. **2** sick; disabled. ● *verb* (**-d-**) **1** (often + *out* etc.) remove from active service. **2** disable (person) by illness. □ **invalidism** *noun*. **invalidity** /-ˈlɪd-/ *noun*.

■ *noun* cripple, incurable, patient, sufferer, valetudinarian. ● *adjective* **2** see ILL *adjective* 1.

invalid[2] /ɪnˈvælɪd/ *adjective* **1** not legally acceptable. **2** not sound or well grounded. □ **invalidity** /-vəˈlɪd-/ *noun*.

■ **1** null and void, out of date, unacceptable, unusable, void, worthless. **2** fallacious, false, illogical, incorrect, irrational, spurious, unconvincing, unfounded, unreasonable, unscientific, unsound, untenable, untrue, wrong.

invalidate /ɪnˈvælɪdeɪt/ *verb* (**-ting**) make invalid. □ **invalidation** *noun*.

invaluable /ɪnˈvæljʊəb(ə)l/ *adjective* beyond price; very valuable.

■ costly, incalculable, inestimable, irreplaceable, precious, priceless, useful, valuable.

invariable /ɪnˈveərɪəb(ə)l/ *adjective* unchangeable; always the same. □ **invariably** *adverb*.

■ changeless, constant, eternal, even, immutable, inflexible, permanent, predictable, regular, reliable, rigid, solid, stable, steady, unalterable, unchangeable, unchanging, unfailing, uniform, unvarying, unwavering.

invasion /ɪnˈveɪʒ(ə)n/ *noun* **1** invading, being invaded. **2** arrival of large number of things or people. □ **invasive** /-sɪv/ *adjective*

■ **1** assault, attack, encroachment, foray, incursion, infiltration, inroad, intrusion, onslaught, raid, violation. **2** flood, *usually derogatory* horde, infestation, influx, spate, stream, swarm, throng. □ **invasive** intrusive, meddlesome, *colloquial* nosy, obtrusive, prying.

invective /ɪnˈvektɪv/ *noun* violent attack in words.

inveigh /ɪnˈveɪ/ *verb* (+ *against*) speak or write with strong hostility against.

inveigle /ɪnˈveɪɡ(ə)l/ *verb* (**-ling**) (+ *into, to do*) entice, persuade by guile. □ **inveiglement** *noun*.

invent /ɪnˈvent/ *verb* **1** create by thought; originate. **2** fabricate (story etc.). □ **inventor** *noun*.

■ **1** coin, conceive, concoct, construct, contrive, create, design, devise, discover, dream up, formulate, hit upon, imagine, improvise, make, originate, plan, put together, *colloquial* think up. **2** concoct, *colloquial* cook up, fabricate, make up, manufacture, trump up. □ **inventor** architect, author, *colloquial* boffin, creator, designer, discoverer, maker, originator.

invention /ɪnˈvenʃ(ə)n/ *noun* **1** inventing, being invented. **2** thing invented. **3** invented story. **4** inventiveness.

■ **1** coinage, creation, design, discovery, innovation. **2** *colloquial* brainchild, coinage, contraption, contrivance, creation, device, gadget. **3** deceit, fabrication, falsehood, fantasy, fib, fiction, figment, lie. **4** see INVENTIVENESS (INVENTIVE).

inventive *adjective* **1** able to invent. **2** imaginative. □ **inventively** *adverb*. **inventiveness** *noun*.

■ clever, creative, enterprising, fertile (*mind*), imaginative, ingenious, innovative, inspired, original, resourceful. □ **inventiveness** creativity, genius, imagination, ingenuity, inspiration, invention, originality, resourcefulness.

inventory /ˈɪnvəntərɪ/ *noun* (*plural* **-ies**) list of

goods etc. ● *verb* (**-ies, -ied**) **1** make inventory of. **2** enter in inventory.

inverse /ɪnˈvɜːs/ *adjective* inverted in position, order, or relation. ● *noun* **1** inverted state. **2** (often + *of*) direct opposite. □ **inverse proportion, ratio** relation between two quantities such that one increases in proportion as the other decreases.

■ *adjective* opposite, reversed, transposed.

inversion /ɪnˈvɜːʃ(ə)n/ *noun* inverting, esp. reversal of normal order of words.

invert /ɪnˈvɜːt/ *verb* **1** turn upside down. **2** reverse position, order, or relation of. □ **inverted commas** quotation marks (see panel at QUOTATION MARKS).

■ **1** capsize, overturn, upset. **2** reverse, transpose.

invertebrate /ɪnˈvɜːtɪbrət/ *adjective* without backbone. ● *noun* invertebrate animal.

invest /ɪnˈvest/ *verb* **1** (often + *in*) put money for profit (into shares, stocks, etc.). **2** (often + *in*) apply or use (money) for profit. **3** devote (time etc.) to an enterprise. **4** (+ *in*) buy (something useful or otherwise rewarding). **5** (+ *with*) endue with qualities etc. **6** (often + *with, in*) clothe with insignia of office. □ **investor** *noun*.

■ **1** buy stocks and shares, play the market, speculate. **2** lay out, put to work, sink, use profitably, venture. **4** (*invest in*) see BUY *verb* 1.

investigate /ɪnˈvestɪɡeɪt/ *verb* (**-ting**) inquire into; examine. □ **investigation** *noun*. **investigative** /-ɡətɪv/ *adjective*. **investigator** *noun*. **investigatory** /-ɡət(ə)rɪ/ *adjective*.

■ analyse, consider, enquire into, examine, explore, follow up, gather evidence about, go into, inquire into, look into, probe, research, scrutinize, sift (*evidence*), study, *slang* suss out, *colloquial* weigh up. □ **investigation** enquiry, examination, inquiry, inquisition, inspection, *colloquial* post-mortem, probe, quest, research, review, scrutiny, search, study, survey.

investiture /ɪnˈvestɪtʃə/ *noun* formal investing of person with honours etc.

investment *noun* **1** investing. **2** money invested. **3** property etc. in which money is invested.

inveterate /ɪnˈvetərət/ *adjective* **1** (of person) confirmed in (usually undesirable) habit etc. **2** (of habit etc.) long-established. □ **inveteracy** *noun*.

invidious /ɪnˈvɪdɪəs/ *adjective* likely to excite ill will against performer, possessor, etc.

■ undesirable, unenviable.

invigilate /ɪnˈvɪdʒɪleɪt/ *verb* (**-ting**) supervise examinees. □ **invigilation** *noun*. **invigilator** *noun*.

invigorate /ɪnˈvɪɡəreɪt/ *verb* (**-ting**) give vigour to. □ **invigorating** *adjective*.

invincible /ɪnˈvɪnsɪb(ə)l/ *adjective* unconquerable. □ **invincibility** *noun*. **invincibly** *adverb*.

■ impregnable, indestructible, indomitable, insuperable, invulnerable, strong, unassailable, unbeatable, unconquerable, unstoppable.

inviolable /ɪnˈvaɪələb(ə)l/ *adjective* not to be violated. □ **inviolability** *noun*.

inviolate /ɪnˈvaɪələt/ *adjective* not violated; safe (from harm). □ **inviolacy** *noun*.

invisible /ɪnˈvɪzɪb(ə)l/ *adjective* that cannot be seen. □ **invisible exports, imports** items for which payment is made by or to another country but which are not goods. □ **invisibility** /-ˈbɪlɪtɪ/ *noun*. **invisibly** *adverb*.

■ camouflaged, concealed, covered, disguised, hidden, imperceptible, inconspicuous, obscured, out of sight, secret, undetectable, unnoticeable, unnoticed, unseen.

invite *verb* /ɪnˈvaɪt/ (**-ting**) **1** request courteously to come, to do, etc. **2** solicit courteously. **3** tend to evoke unintentionally. **4** attract. ● *noun* /ˈɪnvaɪt/ *colloquial* invitation. □ **invitation** /ɪnvɪˈteɪʃ(ə)n/ *noun*.

■ *verb* **1** ask, encourage, request, summon, urge. **2** see SOLICIT 1. **4** attract, entice, tempt.

inviting *adjective* attractive. □ **invitingly** *adverb*.

■ see ATTRACTIVE.

in vitro /ɪn ˈviːtrəʊ/ *adverb* (of biological processes) taking place in test-tube or other laboratory environment. [Latin]

invocation /ɪnvəˈkeɪʃ(ə)n/ *noun* **1** invoking. **2** calling on, esp. in prayer or for inspiration etc. □ **invocatory** /ɪnˈvɒkətərɪ/ *adjective*.

invoice /ˈɪnvɔɪs/ *noun* bill for usually itemized goods etc. ● *verb* (**-cing**) **1** send invoice to. **2** make invoice of.

■ *noun* account, bill, list, statement.

invoke /ɪnˈvəʊk/ *verb* (**-king**) **1** call on in prayer or as witness. **2** appeal to (law, authority, etc.). **3** summon (spirit) by charms. **4** ask earnestly for (vengeance, justice, etc.).

■ **1, 2** appeal to, entreat, implore, petition, pray to, solicit, *literary* supplicate. **3** call up, conjure, summon. **4** appeal for, call for, cry out for, plead for, pray for.

involuntary /ɪnˈvɒləntərɪ/ *adjective* **1** done etc. without exercise of will. **2** not controlled by will. □ **involuntarily** *adverb*.

■ automatic, conditioned, impulsive, instinctive, mechanical, reflex, spontaneous, unconscious, uncontrollable, unintentional, unthinking, unwitting.

involute /ˈɪnvəluːt/ *adjective* **1** intricate. **2** curled spirally.

involution /ɪnvəˈluːʃ(ə)n/ *noun* **1** involving. **2** intricacy. **3** curling inwards. **4** part so curled.

involve /ɪnˈvɒlv/ *verb* (**-ving**) **1** (often + *in*) cause (person, thing) to share experience or effect. **2** (as **involved** *adjective*) concerned, interested. **3** imply, make necessary. **4** (often + *in*) implicate (person) in charge, crime, etc. **5** include or affect

in its operation. **6** (as **involved** *adjective*) complicated. □ **involvement** *noun*.

■ **2** (**involved**) see BUSY *adjective* 1, INTERESTED 1. **3** call for, demand, entail, imply, necessitate, require. **4** embroil, implicate, include, incriminate, inculpate, mix up. **5** affect, comprise, concern, contain, embrace, hold, include, incorporate, interest, take in, touch. **6** (**involved**) see COMPLEX *adjective* 1. □ **involvement** association, complicity, entanglement, interest, participation, partnership.

invulnerable /ɪnˈvʌlnərəb(ə)l/ *adjective* that cannot be wounded. □ **invulnerability** *noun*.

inward /ˈɪnwəd/ *adjective* **1** directed towards inside; going in. **2** situated within. **3** mental, spiritual. ● *adverb* (also **inwards**) **1** towards inside. **2** in mind or soul.

inwardly *adverb* **1** on the inside. **2** in mind or spirit. **3** not aloud.

inwrought /ɪnˈrɔːt/ *adjective* **1** (often + *with*) decorated (with pattern). **2** (often + *in*, *on*) (of pattern) wrought (in or on fabric).

iodine /ˈaɪədiːn/ *noun* **1** black solid halogen element forming violet vapour. **2** solution of this used as antiseptic.

IOM *abbreviation* Isle of Man.

ion /ˈaɪən/ *noun* atom or group of atoms that has lost or gained one or more electrons.

ionic /aɪˈɒnɪk/ *adjective* of or using ions.

ionize *verb* (also **-ise**) (**-zing** or **-sing**) convert or be converted into ion(s). □ **ionization** *noun*.

ionosphere /aɪˈɒnəsfɪə/ *noun* ionized region in upper atmosphere. □ **ionospheric** /-ˈsfer-/ *adjective*.

iota /aɪˈəʊtə/ *noun* **1** ninth letter of Greek alphabet (*I*, ι). **2** (usually with negative) a jot.

IOU /aɪəʊˈjuː/ *noun* (*plural* **-s**) signed document acknowledging debt.

IOW *abbreviation* Isle of Wight.

IPA *abbreviation* International Phonetic Alphabet.

ipecacuanha /ɪpɪkækjʊˈɑːnə/ *noun* root of S. American plant used as emetic etc.

ipso facto /ɪpsəʊ ˈfæktəʊ/ *adverb* by that very fact. [Latin]

IQ *abbreviation* intelligence quotient.

IRA *abbreviation* Irish Republican Army.

Iranian /ɪˈreɪnɪən/ *adjective* **1** of Iran (formerly Persia). **2** of group of languages including Persian. ● *noun* native or national of Iran.

Iraqi /ɪˈrɑːkɪ/ *adjective* of Iraq. ● *noun* (*plural* **-s**) native or national of Iraq.

irascible /ɪˈræsɪb(ə)l/ *adjective* irritable; hot-tempered. □ **irascibility** *noun*.

irate /aɪˈreɪt/ *adjective* angry, enraged.

ire /ˈaɪə/ *noun literary* anger.

iridescent /ɪrɪˈdes(ə)nt/ *adjective* **1** showing rainbow-like glowing colours. **2** changing colour with position. □ **iridescence** *noun*.

iris /ˈaɪərɪs/ *noun* **1** circular coloured membrane

surrounding pupil of eye. **2** bulbous or tuberous plant with sword-shaped leaves and showy flowers.

Irish /ˈaɪərɪʃ/ *adjective* of Ireland. ● *noun* **1** Celtic language of Ireland. **2** (**the Irish**) (treated as *plural*) the Irish people. □ **Irish coffee** coffee with dash of whiskey and a little sugar, topped with cream. **Irishman**, **Irishwoman** native of Ireland. **Irish stew** dish of stewed mutton, onions, and potatoes.

irk *verb* irritate, annoy.

irksome *adjective* annoying, tiresome.

iron /ˈaɪən/ *noun* **1** common strong grey metallic element. **2** this as symbol of strength or firmness. **3** tool etc. of iron. **4** implement heated to smooth clothes etc. **5** golf club with iron or steel head. **6** (in *plural*) fetters. **7** (in *plural*) stirrups. **8** (often in *plural*) leg-support to rectify malformations. ● *adjective* **1** of iron. **2** robust. **3** unyielding. ● *verb* smooth (clothes etc.) with heated iron. □ **Iron Age** era characterized by use of iron weapons etc. **Iron Curtain** *historical* notional barrier to passage of people and information between Soviet bloc and West. **ironing board** narrow folding table etc. for ironing clothes on. **iron lung** rigid case over patient's body for administering prolonged artificial respiration. **ironmonger** dealer in **ironmongery**, household and building hardware. **iron rations** small emergency supply of food. **ironstone 1** hard iron ore. **2** kind of hard white pottery.

ironic /aɪˈrɒnɪk/ *adjective* (also **ironical**) using or displaying irony. □ **ironically** *adverb*.
■ derisive, double-edged, mocking, sarcastic, satirical, wry.

irony /ˈaɪərəni/ *noun* (*plural* **-ies**) **1** expression of meaning, usually humorous or sarcastic, by use of words normally conveying opposite meaning. **2** apparent perversity of fate or circumstances.
■ **1** double meaning, mockery, sarcasm, satire.

irradiate /ɪˈreɪdɪeɪt/ *verb* (**-ting**) **1** subject to radiation. **2** shine on. **3** throw light on. **4** light up. □ **irradiation** *noun*.

irrational /ɪˈræʃən(ə)l/ *adjective* **1** unreasonable, illogical. **2** not endowed with reason. **3** *Mathematics* not expressible as an ordinary fraction. □ **irrationality** /-ˈnæl-/ *noun*. **irrationally** *adverb*.
■ **1, 2** absurd, arbitrary, biased, crazy, emotional, emotive, illogical, insane, mad, nonsensical, prejudiced, senseless, silly, subjective, surreal, unconvincing, unintelligent, unreasonable, unreasoning, unsound, unthinking, wild.

irreconcilable /ɪˈrekənsaɪləb(ə)l/ *adjective* **1** implacably hostile. **2** (of ideas etc.) incompatible. □ **irreconcilably** *adverb*.

irrecoverable /ɪrɪˈkʌvərəb(ə)l/ *adjective* that cannot be recovered or remedied.

irredeemable /ɪrɪˈdiːməb(ə)l/ *adjective* that cannot be redeemed, hopeless. □ **irredeemably** *adverb*.

irreducible /ɪrɪˈdjuːsɪb(ə)l/ *adjective* not able to be reduced or simplified.

irrefutable /ɪˈrefjuːtəb(ə)l/ *adjective* that cannot be refuted. □ **irrefutably** *adverb*.

irregular /ɪˈregjʊlə/ *adjective* **1** not regular; unsymmetrical, uneven; varying in form. **2** not occurring at regular intervals. **3** contrary to rule. **4** (of troops) not in regular army. **5** (of verb, noun, etc.) not inflected according to usual rules. ● *noun* (in *plural*) irregular troops. □ **irregularity** /-ˈlær-/ *noun* (*plural* **-ies**). **irregularly** *adverb*.
■ *adjective* **1** asymmetrical, broken, bumpy, jagged, lopsided, lumpy, patchy, pitted, ragged, rough, uneven, up and down. **2** erratic, fitful, fluctuating, halting, haphazard, intermittent, occasional, random, spasmodic, sporadic, unequal, unpredictable, unpunctual, variable, varying, wavering. **3** abnormal, anomalous, eccentric, exceptional, extraordinary, illegal, improper, odd, peculiar, quirky, unconventional, unofficial, unplanned, unscheduled, unusual.

irrelevant /ɪˈrelɪv(ə)nt/ *adjective* not relevant. □ **irrelevance** *noun*. **irrelevancy** *noun* (*plural* **-ies**).
■ beside the point, extraneous, immaterial, impertinent, inapplicable, inapposite, inappropriate, inessential, pointless, unconnected, unnecessary, unrelated.

irreligious /ɪrɪˈlɪdʒəs/ *adjective* **1** lacking or hostile to religion. **2** irreverent.
■ **1** agnostic, atheistic, godless, heathen, humanist, pagan, unbelieving, uncommitted, unconverted. **2** impious, irreverent, profane, sacrilegious, sinful, ungodly, unrighteous, wicked.

irremediable /ɪrɪˈmiːdɪəb(ə)l/ *adjective* that cannot be remedied. □ **irremediably** *adverb*.

irremovable /ɪrɪˈmuːvəb(ə)l/ *adjective* not removable. □ **irremovably** *adverb*.

irreparable /ɪˈrepərəb(ə)l/ *adjective* that cannot be rectified or made good. □ **irreparably** *adverb*.
■ hopeless, incurable, irrecoverable, irremediable, irretrievable, irreversible, lasting, permanent, unalterable.

irreplaceable /ɪrɪˈpleɪsəb(ə)l/ *adjective* that cannot be replaced.
■ inimitable, invaluable, priceless, rare, unique.

irrepressible /ɪrɪˈpresɪb(ə)l/ *adjective* that cannot be repressed. □ **irrepressibly** *adverb*.
■ boisterous, bouncy, bubbly, buoyant, ebullient, lively, resilient, uncontrollable, ungovernable, uninhibited, unmanageable, unrestrainable, unstoppable, vigorous.

irreproachable /ɪrɪˈprəʊtʃəb(ə)l/ *adjective* faultless, blameless. □ **irreproachably** *adverb*.

irresistible /ɪrɪˈzɪstɪb(ə)l/ *adjective* too strong, convincing, charming, etc. to be resisted. □ **irresistibility** /-ˈbɪlɪti/ *noun*. **irresistibly** *adverb*.

■ compelling, inescapable, inexorable, irrepressible, not to be denied, overpowering, overriding, overwhelming, persuasive, powerful, relentless, seductive, strong, unavoidable, uncontrollable.

irresolute /ɪˈrezəluːt/ *adjective* hesitating; lacking in resolution. □ **irresoluteness** *noun*. **irresolution** /-ˈluːʃ(ə)n/ *noun*.

■ doubtful, fickle, hesitant, indecisive, open to compromise, shilly-shallying, tentative, uncertain, undecided, vacillating, wavering, weak, weak-willed.

irrespective /ɪrɪˈspektɪv/ *adjective* (+ *of*) not taking into account; regardless of.

irresponsible /ɪrɪˈspɒnsɪb(ə)l/ *adjective* **1** acting or done without due sense of responsibility. **2** not responsible. □ **irresponsibility** *noun*. **irresponsibly** *adverb*.

■ **1** antisocial, careless, conscienceless, devil-may-care, feckless, immature, immoral, inconsiderate, negligent, rash, reckless, selfish, shiftless, thoughtless, unethical, unreliable, unthinking, untrustworthy, wild.

irretrievable /ɪrɪˈtriːvəb(ə)l/ *adjective* that cannot be retrieved or restored. □ **irretrievably** *adverb*.

irreverent /ɪˈrevərənt/ *adjective* lacking in reverence. □ **irreverence** *noun*. **irreverently** *adverb*.

■ blasphemous, disrespectful, impious, irreligious, profane, rude, sacrilegious, ungodly, unholy.

irreversible /ɪrɪˈvɜːsɪb(ə)l/ *adjective* that cannot be reversed or altered. □ **irreversibly** *adverb*.

irrevocable /ɪˈrevəkəb(ə)l/ *adjective* **1** unalterable. **2** gone beyond recall. □ **irrevocably** *adverb*.

■ **1** binding, final, fixed, hard and fast, immutable, irreparable, irreversible, permanent, settled, unalterable, unchangeable. **2** irrecoverable, irretrievable, lost.

irrigate /ˈɪrɪɡeɪt/ *verb* (**-ting**) **1** water (land) by system of artificial channels. **2** (of stream etc.) supply (land) with water. **3** *Medicine* moisten (wound etc.) with constant flow of liquid. □ **irrigable** *adjective*. **irrigation** *noun*. **irrigator** *noun*.

■ **1, 2** flood, inundate, supply water to, water.

irritable /ˈɪrɪtəb(ə)l/ *adjective* **1** easily annoyed. **2** very sensitive to contact. □ **irritability** *noun*. **irritably** *adverb*.

■ **1** bad-tempered, cantankerous, choleric, crabby, cross, crotchety, crusty, curmudgeonly, dyspeptic, edgy, fractious, grumpy, ill-humoured, ill-tempered, impatient, irascible, over-sensitive, peevish, pettish, petulant, prickly, querulous, *colloquial* ratty, short-tempered, *colloquial* snappy, testy, tetchy, touchy, waspish.

irritant /ˈɪrɪt(ə)nt/ *adjective* causing irritation. ● *noun* irritant substance or agent.

irritate /ˈɪrɪteɪt/ *verb* (**-ting**) **1** excite to anger; annoy. **2** stimulate discomfort in (part of body).

□ **irritating** *adjective*. **irritation** *noun*.
■ **1** see ANNOY 1.

Is. *abbreviation* Island(s); Isle(s).

is *3rd singular present* of BE.

-ish /ɪʃ/ *suffix* forming adjectives: **1** (*from nouns*) having the qualities or characteristics of; of the nationality of. **2** (*from adjectives*) somewhat. **3** (*from numbers, times of day, etc.*) *colloquial* in the region of; approximately.

isinglass /ˈaɪzɪŋɡlɑːs/ *noun* kind of gelatin obtained from sturgeon etc.

Islam /ˈɪzlɑːm/ *noun* **1** religion of Muslims, proclaimed by Prophet Muhammad. **2** the Muslim world. □ **Islamic** /-ˈlæm-/ *adjective*.

island /ˈaɪlənd/ *noun* **1** piece of land surrounded by water. **2** traffic island. **3** detached or isolated thing.

■ **1** atoll, *literary* isle, islet; (*islands*) archipelago.

islander *noun* native or inhabitant of island.

isle /aɪl/ *noun literary* (usually small) island.

islet /ˈaɪlɪt/ *noun* small island.

isn't /ˈɪz(ə)nt/ is not.

isobar /ˈaɪsəbɑː/ *noun* line on map connecting places with same atmospheric pressure. □ **isobaric** /-ˈbær-/ *adjective*.

isolate /ˈaɪsəleɪt/ *verb* (**-ting**) **1** place apart or alone. **2** separate (esp. infectious patient from others). **3** insulate (electrical apparatus), esp. by gap. **4** disconnect. □ **isolated** *adjective*. **isolation** *noun*.

■ **1, 2** cloister, cordon off, cut off, detach, exclude, insulate, keep apart, place apart, quarantine, seclude, segregate, separate, sequester, set apart, shut off, shut out, single out. **3** see INSULATE 1. □ **isolated** see SOLITARY 1–2.

isolationism *noun* policy of holding aloof from affairs of other countries or groups. □ **isolationist** *noun*.

isomer /ˈaɪsəmə/ *noun* one of two or more compounds with same molecular formula but different arrangement of atoms. □ **isomeric** /-ˈmer-/ *adjective*. **isomerism** /aɪˈsɒmərɪz(ə)m/ *noun*.

isosceles /aɪˈsɒsɪliːz/ *adjective* (of triangle) having two sides equal.

isotherm /ˈaɪsəθɜːm/ *noun* line on map connecting places with same temperature. □ **isothermal** /-ˈθɜːm(ə)l/ *adjective*.

isotope /ˈaɪsətəʊp/ *noun* any of two or more forms of chemical element with different relative atomic mass and different nuclear but not chemical properties. □ **isotopic** /-ˈtɒp-/ *adjective*.

Israeli /ɪzˈreɪlɪ/ *adjective* of modern state of Israel. ● *noun* (*plural* **-s**) native or national of Israel.

issue /ˈɪʃuː/ *noun* **1** giving out or circulation of shares, notes, stamps, etc. **2** copies of journal etc. circulated at one time. **3** each of regular series of magazine etc. **4** outgoing, outflow. **5** point in question; essential subject of dispute. **6** result; outcome. **7** offspring. ● *verb* (**issues, issued,**

issuing) 1 go or come out. **2** give or send out; publish; circulate. **3** (often + *with*) supply. **4** (+ *from*) be derived, result from. **5** (+ *from*) emerge from.

■ *noun* **2, 3** copy, edition, instalment, number, printing, publication, version. **5** affair, argument, controversy, dispute, matter, point, problem, question, subject, topic. **6** conclusion, consequence, effect, end, impact, outcome, *colloquial* pay-off, repercussions, result, upshot. ● *verb* **1** appear, come out, emerge, erupt, flow out, gush, leak, rise, spring. **2** announce, bring out, broadcast, circulate, declare, disseminate, distribute, give out, make public, print, produce, promulgate, publicize, publish, put out, release, send out; (*issue with*) equip with, furnish with, provide with, supply with.

isthmus /ˈɪsməs/ *noun* (*plural* **-es**) neck of land connecting two larger land masses.

IT *abbreviation* information technology.

it *pronoun* **1** the thing in question. **2** indefinite, undefined, or impersonal subject, action, condition, object, etc. **3** *substitute for deferred subject or object.* **4** exactly what is needed. **5** perfection. **6** *slang* sexual intercourse; sex appeal. □ **that's it** *colloquial* **1** that is what is required. **2** that is the difficulty. **3** that is the end, enough.

Italian /ɪˈtæljən/ *noun* native, national, or language of Italy. ● *adjective* of Italy.

italic /ɪˈtælɪk/ *adjective* **1** (of type etc.) of sloping kind. **2** (of handwriting) neat and pointed. **3** (**Italic**) of ancient Italy. ● *noun* (usually in *plural*) italic type.

italicize /ɪˈtælɪsaɪz/ *verb* (also **-ise**) (**-zing** or **-sing**) print in italics.

itch *noun* **1** irritation in skin. **2** restless desire. **3** disease with itch. ● *verb* **1** feel irritation. **2** feel restless desire.

■ *noun* **1** irritation, prickling, tickle, tingling. **2** ache, craving, desire, hankering, hunger, impatience, impulse, longing, need, restlessness, thirst, urge, wish, yearning, *colloquial* yen. ● *verb*

1 be irritated, prickle, tickle, tingle. **2** (*itch for*) see DESIRE *verb* 1.

itchy *adjective* (**-ier, -iest**) having or causing itch. □ **have itchy feet** *colloquial* **1** be restless. **2** have urge to travel.

it'd /ˈɪtəd/ **1** it had. **2** it would.

item /ˈaɪtəm/ *noun* **1** any one of enumerated things. **2** separate or distinct piece of news etc. ■ **1** article, bit, component, contribution, entry, ingredient, lot, matter, object, particular, thing. **2** account, article, feature, notice, piece, report.

itemize *verb* (also **-ise**) (**-zing** or **-sing**) state by items. □ **itemization** *noun*.

iterate /ˈɪtəreɪt/ *verb* (**-ting**) repeat; state repeatedly. □ **iteration** *noun*. **iterative** /-rətɪv/ *adjective*.

itinerant /aɪˈtɪnərənt/ *adjective* travelling from place to place. ● *noun* itinerant person.

itinerary /aɪˈtɪnərərɪ/ *noun* (*plural* **-ies**) **1** route. **2** record of travel. **3** guidebook.

it'll /ˈɪt(ə)l/ it will; it shall.

its *adjective* of or belonging to it.

it's /ɪts/ **1** it is. **2** it has.

USAGE Because it has an apostrophe, *it's* is easily confused with *its*. Both are correctly used in *Where's the dog? — It's in its kennel, and it's eaten its food* (= *It is in its kennel, and it has eaten its food.*)

itself /ɪtˈself/ *pronoun: emphatic and reflexive form of* IT.

ITV *abbreviation* Independent Television.

IUD *abbreviation* intrauterine (contraceptive) device.

I've /aɪv/ I have.

ivory /ˈaɪvərɪ/ *noun* (*plural* **-ies**) **1** white substance of tusks of elephant etc. **2** colour of this. **3** (in *plural*) *slang* things made of or resembling ivory, esp. dice, piano keys, or teeth. □ **ivory tower** seclusion from harsh realities of life.

ivy /ˈaɪvɪ/ *noun* (*plural* **-ies**) climbing evergreen with shiny 5-angled leaves.

Jj

jab *verb* (**-bb-**) **1** poke roughly. **2** stab. **3** (+ *into*) thrust (thing) hard or abruptly into. ● *noun* **1** abrupt blow or thrust. **2** *colloquial* hypodermic injection.
  ■ *verb* **1** dig, elbow, nudge, poke, prod, stab. **3** see THRUST *verb* 3.

jabber *verb* **1** chatter volubly. **2** utter fast and indistinctly. ● *noun* chatter, gabble.

jabot /ˈʒæbəʊ/ *noun* frill on front of shirt or blouse.

jacaranda /dʒækəˈrændə/ *noun* tropical American tree with blue flowers or one with hard scented wood.

jacinth /ˈdʒæsmθ/ *noun* reddish-orange zircon used as gem.

jack *noun* **1** device for lifting heavy objects, esp. vehicles. **2** lowest-ranking court card. **3** ship's flag, esp. showing nationality. **4** device using single-pronged plug to connect electrical equipment. **5** small white target ball in bowls. **6** (in *plural*) game played with jackstones. ● *verb* (usually + *up*) raise (as) with jack. □ **jackboot** boot reaching above knee. **jack in** *slang* abandon (attempt etc.). **jack-in-the-box** toy figure that springs out of box. **jack of all trades** person with many skills. **jack plug** electrical plug with single prong. **jackstone** metal etc. piece used in tossing games.

jackal /ˈdʒæk(ə)l/ *noun* African or Asian wild animal of dog family.

jackass *noun* **1** male ass. **2** stupid person.

jackdaw *noun* grey-headed bird of crow family.

jacket /ˈdʒækɪt/ *noun* **1** short coat with sleeves. **2** covering round boiler etc. **3** outside wrapper of book. **4** skin of potato. □ **jacket potato** one baked in its skin.
  ■ **1** see COAT *noun* 1. **2** casing, cover, covering, sheath, wrapping. **3** cover, folder, wrapper. **4** skin.

jackknife *noun* large clasp-knife. ● *verb* (**-fing**) (of articulated vehicle) fold against itself in accident.

jackpot *noun* large prize, esp. accumulated in game, lottery, etc.

Jacobean /dʒækəˈbiːən/ *adjective* of reign of James I.

Jacobite /ˈdʒækəbaɪt/ *noun* *historical* supporter of James II in exile, or of Stuarts.

Jacuzzi /dʒəˈkuːzɪ/ *noun* (*plural* **-s**) *proprietary term* large bath with massaging underwater jets.

jade[1] *noun* **1** hard usually green stone for ornaments. **2** green colour of jade.

jade[2] *noun* inferior or worn-out horse.

jaded *adjective* **1** tired out. **2** surfeited.
  ■ **1** see WEARY *adjective* 1. **2** bored, fed up, gorged, listless, *formal* sated, satiated, surfeited.

jag *noun* sharp projection of rock etc. ● *verb* (**-gg-**) **1** cut or tear unevenly. **2** make indentations in.

jagged /ˈdʒægɪd/ *adjective* unevenly cut or torn. □ **jaggedly** *adverb*. **jaggedness** *noun*.
  ■ barbed, broken, chipped, indented, irregular, notched, ragged, rough, serrated, sharp, snagged, spiky, toothed, uneven, zigzag.

jaguar /ˈdʒægjʊə/ *noun* large American spotted animal of cat family.

jail /dʒeɪl/ (also **gaol**) *noun* **1** place for detention of prisoners. **2** confinement in jail. ● *verb* put in jail. □ **jailbird** prisoner; habitual criminal. □ **jailer** (also **gaoler**) *noun*.
  ■ *noun* **1** *historical* Borstal, cell, custody, dungeon, guardhouse, *US* penitentiary, prison. ● *verb* confine, detain, imprison, incarcerate, intern, send down, send to prison, shut away, shut up. □ **jailer** guard, prison officer, *slang* screw, warder.

jalap /ˈdʒæləp/ *noun* purgative drug.

jalopy /dʒəˈlɒpɪ/ *noun* (*plural* **-ies**) *colloquial* dilapidated old motor vehicle.

jalousie /ˈʒæluːziː/ *noun* slatted blind or shutter.

jam[1] *verb* (**-mm-**) **1** (usually + *into*, *together*, etc.) squeeze or cram into space. **2** become wedged. **3** cause (machinery) to become wedged and so unworkable. **4** become wedged in this way. **5** block (exit, road, etc.) by crowding. **6** (usually + *on*) apply (brakes) suddenly. **7** make (radio transmission) unintelligible with interference. ● *noun* **1** squeeze. **2** stoppage. **3** crowded mass, esp. of traffic. **4** *colloquial* predicament. □ **jam-packed** *colloquial* full to capacity. **jam session** (in jazz etc.) improvised ensemble playing.
  ■ *verb* **1, 2** cram, crowd, crush, force, pack, ram, *colloquial* squash, squeeze, stick, stuff, wedge. **5** block, bung up, clog, congest, fill, obstruct, overcrowd, stop up. ● *noun* **1** crush, press, squeeze. **2** blockage, stoppage. **3** blockage, bottleneck, congestion, crowd, obstruction, throng. **4** difficulty, *disputed* dilemma, fix, *colloquial* hole, *colloquial* hot water, *colloquial* pickle, plight, predicament, quandary, tight corner, trouble.

jam[2] *noun* **1** conserve of boiled fruit and sugar. **2** *colloquial* easy or pleasant thing.

■ **1** conserve, jelly, marmalade, preserve.

jamb /dʒæm/ *noun* side post or side face of doorway or window frame.

jamboree /dʒæmbə'ri:/ *noun* **1** celebration. **2** large rally of Scouts.

jammy *adjective* (**-ier**, **-iest**) **1** covered with jam. **2** *colloquial* lucky. **3** *colloquial* profitable.

Jan. *abbreviation* January.

jangle /'dʒæŋg(ə)l/ *verb* (**-ling**) (cause to) make harsh metallic sound. ● *noun* such sound.

janitor /'dʒænɪtə/ *noun* **1** doorkeeper. **2** caretaker.

January /'dʒænjʊərɪ/ *noun* (*plural* **-ies**) first month of year.

japan /dʒə'pæn/ *noun* hard usually black varnish. ● *verb* (**-nn-**) make black and glossy (as) with japan.

Japanese /dʒæpə'ni:z/ *noun* (*plural* same) native, national, or language of Japan. ● *adjective* of Japan or its people or language.

jape *noun* practical joke.

japonica /dʒə'pɒnɪkə/ *noun* flowering shrub with red flowers and edible fruits.

jar¹ *noun* container, usually of glass and cylindrical.

■ amphora, bottle, carafe, container, crock, glass, jug, pot, receptacle, urn, vase, vessel.

jar² *verb* (**-rr-**) **1** (often + *on*) (of sound, manner, etc.) strike discordantly; grate. **2** (often + *against*, *on*) (cause to) strike (esp. part of body) with vibration or shock. **3** (often + *with*) be at variance. ● *noun* jarring sound, shock, or vibration. □ **jarring** *adjective*.

■ *verb* **1** grate, grind, jangle. **2** jerk, jog, jolt, rattle, shake, shock. □ **jarring** see HARSH 1.

jardinière /ʒɑ:dɪ'njeə/ *noun* ornamental pot or stand for plants.

jargon /'dʒɑ:gən/ *noun* **1** words used by particular group or profession. **2** debased or pretentious language.

■ argot, cant, creole, dialect, idiom, language, patois, slang, vernacular.

jasmine /'dʒæzmɪn/ *noun* shrub with white or yellow flowers.

jasper /'dʒæspə/ *noun* red, yellow, or brown opaque quartz.

jaundice /'dʒɔ:ndɪs/ *noun* yellowing of skin caused by liver disease, bile disorder, etc. ● *verb* (as **jaundiced** *adjective*) **1** affected with jaundice. **2** envious, resentful.

jaunt /dʒɔ:nt/ *noun* pleasure trip. ● *verb* take a jaunt.

■ *noun* excursion, expedition, journey, outing, tour, trip.

jaunty *adjective* (**-ier**, **-iest**) **1** cheerful and

self-confident. **2** sprightly. □ **jauntily** *adverb*. **jauntiness** *noun*.

■ alert, breezy, bright, brisk, buoyant, carefree, cheeky, cheerful, debonair, frisky, lively, perky, self-confident, spirited, sprightly.

javelin /'dʒævəlɪn/ *noun* light spear thrown in sport or, formerly, as weapon.

jaw *noun* **1** bony structure containing teeth. **2** (in *plural*) mouth. **3** (in *plural*) gripping parts of tool etc. **4** *colloquial* tedious talk. ● *verb* *slang* speak at tedious length. □ **jawbone** lower jaw in most mammals.

jay *noun* noisy European bird of crow family with vivid plumage. □ **jaywalk** walk across road carelessly or dangerously. **jaywalker** person who does this.

jazz *noun* rhythmic syncopated esp. improvised music of American black origin. □ **and all that jazz** *colloquial* and other related things. **jazz up** enliven.

jazzy *adjective* (**-ier**, **-iest**) **1** of or like jazz. **2** vivid.

■ **1** animated, lively, rhythmic, spirited, swinging, syncopated, vivacious. **2** bold, flashy, gaudy, loud, showy, vivid.

jealous /'dʒeləs/ *adjective* (often + *of*) **1** envious (of person etc.). **2** resentful of rivalry in love. **3** protective (of rights etc.). □ **jealously** *adverb*. **jealousy** *noun* (*plural* **-ies**).

■ **1, 2** bitter, covetous, envious, grudging, jaundiced, resentful. **3** careful, possessive, protective, vigilant, watchful.

jeans /dʒi:nz/ *plural noun* casual esp. denim trousers.

Jeep *noun* *proprietary term* small sturdy esp. military vehicle with 4-wheel drive.

jeer *verb* (often + *at*) scoff, deride. ● *noun* taunt.

■ *verb* barrack, boo, chaff, deride, gibe, heckle, hiss, *slang* knock, laugh, make fun (of), mock, ridicule, scoff, sneer, taunt, twit.

Jehovah /dʒə'həʊvə/ *noun* (in Old Testament) God. □ **Jehovah's Witness** member of unorthodox Christian sect.

jejune /dʒɪ'dʒu:n/ *adjective* (of ideas, writing, etc.) shallow, naïve, or dry and uninteresting.

jell *verb colloquial* **1** set as jelly. **2** (of ideas etc.) take definite form. **3** cohere.

jellied /'dʒelɪd/ *adjective* (of food etc.) set as or in jelly.

jelly /'dʒelɪ/ *noun* (*plural* **-ies**) **1** (usually fruit-flavoured) semi-transparent dessert set with gelatin. **2** similar preparation as jam or condiment. **2** *slang* gelignite. □ **jelly baby** jelly-like baby-shaped sweet. **jellyfish** (*plural* same or **-es**) marine animal with jelly-like body and stinging tentacles.

jemmy /'dʒemɪ/ *noun* (*plural* **-ies**) burglar's crowbar.

jeopardize *verb* (also **-ise**) (**-zing** or **-sing**) endanger.

■ endanger, gamble, imperil, menace, put at risk, risk, threaten, venture.

jeopardy /'dʒepədɪ/ *noun* danger, esp. severe.

jerboa /dʒɜː'bəʊə/ *noun* small jumping desert rodent.

Jeremiah /dʒerɪ'maɪə/ *noun* dismal prophet.

jerk[1] *noun* **1** sharp sudden pull, twist, etc. **2** spasmodic muscular twitch. **3** *slang* fool. ● *verb* move, pull, throw, etc. with jerk. □ **jerky** *adjective* (**-ier, -iest**). **jerkily** *adverb*. **jerkiness** *noun*.

■ *verb* jar, jiggle, jog, jolt, lurch, move jerkily, move suddenly, pluck, pull, tug, tweak, twist, twitch, wrench, *colloquial* yank. □ **jerky** bouncy, bumpy, convulsive, erratic, fitful, jolting, jumpy, rough, shaky, spasmodic, stopping and starting, twitchy, uncontrolled, uneven.

jerk[2] *verb* cure (beef) by cutting in long slices and drying in the sun.

jerkin /'dʒɜːkɪn/ *noun* sleeveless jacket.

jeroboam /dʒerə'bəʊəm/ *noun* wine bottle of 4–12 times ordinary size.

jerry-building *noun* building of shoddy houses with bad materials. □ **jerry-builder** *noun*. **jerry-built** *adjective*.

jerrycan *noun* kind of petrol- or water-can.

jersey /'dʒɜːzɪ/ *noun* (*plural* **-s**) **1** knitted usually woollen pullover. **2** knitted fabric. **3** (**Jersey**) dairy cow from Jersey.

Jerusalem artichoke /dʒə'ruːsələm/ *noun* **1** kind of sunflower with edible tubers. **2** this tuber as vegetable.

jest *noun* **1** joke. **2** fun. **3** banter. **4** object of derision. ● *verb* **1** joke. **2** fool about. □ **in jest** in fun.

■ *noun* **1** see JOKE *noun* 1. ● *verb* see JOKE *verb*.

jester *noun* *historical* professional clown at medieval court etc.

■ buffoon, clown, comedian, comic, *historical* fool, joker.

Jesuit /'dʒezjʊɪt/ *noun* member of RC Society of Jesus. □ **Jesuitical** /-'ɪt-/ *adjective*.

jet[1] *noun* **1** stream of water, steam, gas, flame, etc. shot esp. from small opening. **2** spout or nozzle for this purpose. **3** jet engine or plane. ● *verb* (**-tt-**) **1** spurt out in jet(s). **2** *colloquial* send or travel by jet plane. □ **jet engine** one using jet propulsion. **jet lag** exhaustion felt after long flight across time zones. **jet-lagged** *adjective*. **jet plane** one with jet engine. **jet-propelled 1** having jet propulsion. **2** very fast. **jet propulsion** propulsion by backward ejection of high-speed jet of gas etc. **jet set** wealthy people who travel widely, esp. for pleasure. **jet-setter** such a person.

■ *noun* **1** flow, fountain, gush, rush, spout, spray, spurt, squirt, stream. **2** nozzle, spout, sprinkler.

jet[2] *noun* **1** hard black lignite, often carved and highly polished. **2** deep glossy black colour. ● *adjective* (also **jet-black**) of this colour.

■ *adjective* see BLACK *adjective* 1.

jetsam /'dʒetsəm/ *noun* objects washed ashore, esp. jettisoned from ship.

jettison /'dʒetɪs(ə)n/ *verb* **1** throw (cargo, fuel, etc.) from ship or aircraft to lighten it. **2** abandon; get rid of.

jetty /'dʒetɪ/ *noun* (*plural* **-ies**) **1** pier or breakwater protecting or defending harbour etc. **2** landing pier.

■ **1** breakwater, groyne, mole, pier. **2** landing stage, pier, quay, wharf.

Jew /dʒuː/ *noun* person of Hebrew descent or whose religion is Judaism.

jewel /'dʒuːəl/ *noun* **1** precious stone. **2** this used in watchmaking. **3** jewelled personal ornament. **4** precious person or thing. ● *verb* (**-ll-**; *US* **-l-**) (esp. as **jewelled** *adjective*) adorn or set with jewels.

■ *noun* **1** brilliant, gem, precious stone, rock, *colloquial* sparkler. **3** (*jewels*) see JEWELLERY.

jeweller *noun* (*US* **jeweler**) maker of or dealer in jewels or jewellery.

■ goldsmith, silversmith.

jewellery /'dʒuːəlrɪ/ *noun* (also **jewelry**) rings, brooches, necklaces, etc. collectively.

■ gems, jewels, ornaments, treasure, *colloquial* sparklers.

Jewish *adjective* of Jews or Judaism. □ **Jewishness** *noun*.

Jewry /'dʒʊərɪ/ *noun* Jews collectively.

Jezebel /'dʒezəbəl/ *noun* shameless or immoral woman.

jib *noun* **1** projecting arm of crane. **2** triangular staysail. ● *verb* (**-bb-**) **1** (esp. of horse) stop and refuse to go on. **2** (+ *at*) show aversion to.

jibe[1] = GIBE.

jibe[2] *US* = GYBE.

jiffy /'dʒɪfɪ/ *noun* (*plural* **-ies**) (also **jiff**) *colloquial* short time; moment. □ **Jiffy bag** *proprietary term* padded envelope.

jig *noun* **1** lively dance. **2** music for this. **3** device that holds piece of work and guides tools operating on it. ● *verb* (**-gg-**) **1** dance jig. **2** (often + *about*) move quickly up and down. **3** (often + *about*) fidget.

jigger /'dʒɪgə/ *noun* small glass for measure of spirits.

jiggery-pokery /dʒɪgərɪ'pəʊkərɪ/ *noun* *colloquial* trickery; swindling.

jiggle /'dʒɪg(ə)l/ *verb* (**-ling**) (often + *about*) **1** rock or jerk lightly. **2** fidget. ● *noun* light shake.

jigsaw *noun* **1** (in full **jigsaw puzzle**) picture on board etc. cut into irregular interlocking pieces to be reassembled as pastime. **2** mechanical fine-bladed fret saw.

jihad /dʒɪ'hæd/ *noun* Muslim holy war against unbelievers.

jilt *verb* abruptly reject or abandon (esp. lover).

■ abandon, break with, desert, *slang* ditch, *colloquial* drop, *colloquial* dump, forsake, give (person) the brush-off, leave behind, leave in the lurch, reject, throw over.

jingle /ˈdʒɪŋg(ə)l/ *noun* **1** mixed ringing or clinking noise. **2** repetition of sounds in phrase. **3** short catchy verse in advertising etc. ● *verb* (**-ling**) (cause to) make jingling sound.

■ *noun* **1** chinking, clinking, jangling, ringing, tinkling, tintinnabulation. **3** doggerel, rhyme, song, tune, verse. ● *verb* chime, chink, clink, jangle, ring, tinkle.

jingo /ˈdʒɪŋgəʊ/ *noun* (*plural* **-es**) blustering patriot. □ **jingoism** *noun*. **jingoist** *noun*. **jingoistic** /-ˈɪs-/ *adjective*.

jink *verb* **1** move elusively. **2** elude by dodging. ● *noun* jinking. □ **high jinks** boisterous fun.

jinnee /dʒɪˈniː/ *noun* (also **jinn, djinn** /dʒɪn/) (*plural* **jinn** or **djinn**) (in Muslim mythology) spirit of supernatural power in human or animal form.

jinx *colloquial noun* person or thing that seems to bring bad luck. ● *verb* (esp. as **jinxed** *adjective*) subject to bad luck.

jitter /ˈdʒɪtə/ *colloquial noun* (**the jitters**) extreme nervousness. ● *verb* be nervous; act nervously. □ **jittery** *adjective*.

jive *noun* **1** lively dance of 1950s. **2** music for this. ● *verb* (**-ving**) dance to or play jive music. □ **jiver** *noun*.

Jnr. *abbreviation* Junior.

job *noun* **1** piece of work (to be) done. **2** something one has to do. **3** paid employment. **4** *colloquial* difficult task. **5** *slang* a crime, esp. a robbery. ● *verb* (**-bb-**) **1** do jobs; do piece-work. **2** buy and sell (stocks etc.). **3** deal corruptly with (matter). □ **jobcentre** local government office advertising available jobs. **job-hunt** *colloquial* seek employment. **job lot** mixed lot bought at auction etc.

■ *noun* **1, 2** activity, assignment, charge, chore, duty, errand, function, mission, operation, project, pursuit, responsibility, role, stint, task, undertaking, work. **3** appointment, business, calling, career, craft, employment, livelihood, living, *métier*, occupation, position, post, profession, sinecure, trade, vocation, work.

jobber /ˈdʒɒbə/ *noun* **1** person who jobs. **2** *historical* principal or wholesaler on Stock Exchange.

jobbery *noun* corrupt dealing.

jobless *adjective* unemployed. □ **joblessness** *noun*.

■ out of work, redundant, unemployed, unwaged.

job-sharing *noun* sharing of full-time job by two or more people. □ **job-share** *noun & verb*.

jockey /ˈdʒɒkɪ/ *noun* (*plural* **-s**) rider in horse races. ● *verb* (**-eys, -eyed**) cheat, trick. □ **jockey for position** manoeuvre for advantage.

jockstrap /ˈdʒɒkstræp/ *noun* support or protection for male genitals worn esp. in sport.

jocose /dʒəˈkəʊs/ *adjective* **1** playful. **2** jocular.

□ **jocosely** *adverb*. **jocosity** /-ˈkɒs-/ *noun* (*plural* **-ies**).

jocular /ˈdʒɒkjʊlə/ *adjective* **1** fond of joking; merry. **2** humorous. □ **jocularity** /-ˈlær-/ *noun* (*plural* **-ies**). **jocularly** *adverb*.

■ **1** cheerful, gay, glad, gleeful, happy, *literary* jocund, jokey, joking, jolly, jovial, joyous, jubilant, merry, overjoyed, rejoicing. **2** see HUMOROUS.

jocund /ˈdʒɒkənd/ *adjective literary* merry, cheerful. □ **jocundity** /dʒəˈkʌn-/ *noun* (*plural* **-ies**). **jocundly** *adverb*.

jodhpurs /ˈdʒɒdpəz/ *plural noun* riding breeches tight below knee.

jog *verb* (**-gg-**) **1** run slowly, esp. as exercise. **2** push, jerk. **3** nudge, esp. to alert. **4** stimulate (person's memory). ● *noun* **1** spell of jogging. **2** slow walk or trot. **3** push, jerk. **3** nudge. □ **jogtrot** slow regular trot. □ **jogger** *noun*.

■ *verb* **1** exercise, lope, run, trot. **2** jar, jerk, joggle, jolt, knock. **3** see NUDGE *verb*. **4** activate, arouse, prompt, refresh, remind, set off, stimulate, stir.

joggle /ˈdʒɒg(ə)l/ *verb* (**-ling**) move in jerks. ● *noun* slight shake.

joie de vivre /ʒwɑː də ˈviːvrə/ *noun* exuberance; high spirits. [French]

join *verb* **1** (often + *to, together*) put together; fasten, unite. **2** connect (points) by line etc. **3** become member of (club etc.). **4** take one's place with (person, group, etc.). **5** (+ *in, for*, etc.) take part with (others) in activity etc. **6** (often + *with, to*) come together; be united. **7** (of river etc.) become connected or continuous with. ● *noun* point, line, or surface of junction. □ **join in** take part in (activity). **join up** enlist for military service.

■ *verb* **1** add, amalgamate, attach, combine, connect, couple, dock, dovetail, fasten, fit, fix, knit, link, marry, merge, put together, splice, tack on, unite, yoke. **3** affiliate with, become a member of, enlist in, enrol in, participate in, register for, sign up for, subscribe to, volunteer for. **4** accompany, associate with, follow, go with, *colloquial* latch on to, tag along with, team up with. **7** abut, adjoin, border on, come together, converge, meet, touch, verge on. ● *noun* connection, joint, knot, link, mend, seam.

joiner *noun* maker of furniture and light woodwork. □ **joinery** *noun*.

joint *noun* **1** place at which two or more things are joined. **2** device by which things are joined. **3** point at which two bones fit together. **4** division of animal carcass as meat. **5** *slang* restaurant, bar, etc. **6** *slang* marijuana cigarette. ● *adjective* **1** held by, done by, or belonging to two or more people etc. **2** sharing with another. ● *verb* **1** connect by joint(s). **2** divide at joint or into joints. □ **joint stock** capital held jointly. □ **jointly** *adverb*.

■ *noun* **1, 2** articulation, connection, hinge, junction, union. ● *adjective* collaborative, collective, combined, common, communal, concerted, cooperative, corporate, general, *colloquial* disputed mutual, shared, united.

jointure /'dʒɔmtʃə/ *noun* estate settled on wife by husband for use after his death.

joist *noun* supporting beam in floor, ceiling, etc.
■ beam, girder, rafter.

jojoba /həʊ'həʊbə/ *noun* plant with seeds yielding oil used in cosmetics etc.

joke *noun* 1 thing said or done to cause laughter; witticism. 2 ridiculous person or thing. ● *verb* (**-king**) make jokes. □ **jokily** *adverb*. **jokiness** *noun*. **jokingly** *adverb*. **jokey, joky** *adjective*.
■ *noun* 1 *colloquial* crack, funny story, gag, jape, jest, laugh, pleasantry, pun, quip, *colloquial* wisecrack, witticism. ● *verb* banter, be facetious, clown, fool about, have a laugh, jest, make jokes, quip, tease.

joker *noun* 1 person who jokes. 2 playing card used in some games.

jollification /dʒɒlɪfɪ'keɪʃ(ə)n/ *noun* merrymaking.

jolly /'dʒɒlɪ/ *adjective* (**-ier, -iest**) 1 cheerful; festive, jovial. 2 *colloquial* pleasant, delightful. ● *adverb colloquial* very. ● *verb* (**-ies, -ied**) (usually + *along*) *colloquial* coax, humour. □ **jollity** *noun* (*plural* **-ies**).
■ *adjective* 1 cheerful, delighted, festive, gay, glad, gleeful, good-humoured, grinning, happy, high-spirited, jocose, jocular, *literary* jocund, joking, jovial, joyful, joyous, jubilant, laughing, merry, playful, rejoicing, rosy-faced, smiling, sportive.

jolt /dʒəʊlt/ *verb* 1 shake (esp. in vehicle) with jerk. 2 shock, perturb. 3 move along jerkily. ● *noun* 1 jerk. 2 surprise, shock.
■ *verb* 1 bounce, bump, jar, jerk, jog, shake, twitch. 2 astonish, disturb, nonplus, perturb, shake up, shock, startle, stun, surprise.

jonquil /'dʒɒŋkwɪl/ *noun* narcissus with white or yellow fragrant flowers.

josh *slang verb* tease; make fun of. ● *noun* good-natured joke.

joss *noun* Chinese idol. □ **joss-stick** incense stick for burning.

jostle /'dʒɒs(ə)l/ *verb* (**-ling**) 1 (often + *against*) knock; push, elbow. 2 (+ *with*) struggle with. ● *noun* jostling.
■ 1 crowd, elbow, hustle, press, push, shove.

jot *verb* (**-tt-**) (usually + *down*) write briefly or hastily. ● *noun* very small amount.
■ *verb* (*jot down*) note, scribble, take down, write down.

jotter *noun* small pad or notebook.

joule /dʒuːl/ *noun* SI unit of work and energy.

journal /'dʒɜːn(ə)l/ *noun* 1 newspaper, periodical. 2 daily record of events; diary. 3 account book. 4 part of shaft or axle resting on bearings.
■ 1 gazette, magazine, monthly, newsletter, newspaper, paper, periodical, publication, review, weekly. 2 account, annals, chronicle, diary, dossier, history, log, record.

journalese /dʒɜːnə'liːz/ *noun* hackneyed style of writing characteristic of newspapers.

journalism /'dʒɜːnəlɪz(ə)m/ *noun* work of journalist.

journalist /'dʒɜːnəlɪst/ *noun* person writing for or editing newspapers etc. □ **journalistic** /-'lɪs-/ *adjective*.
■ broadcaster, columnist, contributor, correspondent, hack, *colloquial* news hound, newspaperman, newspaperwoman, reporter, writer.

journey /'dʒɜːnɪ/ *noun* (*plural* **-s**) 1 act of going from one place to another. 2 distance travelled, time taken. ● *verb* (**-s, -ed**) make journey; travel. □ **journeyman** qualified mechanic or artisan working for another.
■ *noun* crossing, drive, expedition, flight, mission, odyssey, passage, ride, run, travelling, trek, trip, voyage. ● *verb* see TRAVEL *verb* 1.

joust /dʒaʊst/ *historical noun* combat with lances between two mounted knights. ● *verb* engage in joust. □ **jouster** *noun*.

jovial /'dʒəʊvɪəl/ *adjective* merry; convivial; hearty. □ **joviality** /-'æl-/ *noun*. **jovially** *adverb*.

jowl /dʒaʊl/ *noun* 1 jaw, jawbone. 2 cheek. 3 loose skin on throat.

joy *noun* 1 gladness, pleasure. 2 thing causing joy. 3 *colloquial* satisfaction. □ **joyride** *colloquial* (go for) pleasure ride in esp. stolen car. **joystick** 1 *colloquial* control column of aircraft. 2 lever for moving image on VDU screen. □ **joyful** *adjective*. **joyfully** *adverb*. **joyfulness** *noun*. **joyless** *adjective*. **joyous** *adjective*. **joyously** *adverb*. **joyousness** *noun*.
■ 1 bliss, cheer, cheerfulness, delight, ecstasy, elation, euphoria, exaltation, exhilaration, exultation, felicity, gaiety, gladness, glee, gratification, happiness, high spirits, hilarity, jocularity, joviality, joyfulness, joyousness, jubilation, light-heartedness, merriment, mirth, pleasure, rapture, rejoicing, triumph. □ **joyful** buoyant, cheerful, delighted, ecstatic, elated, euphoric, exhilarated, exultant, gay, glad, gleeful, happy, *literary* jocund, jolly, jovial, joyous, jubilant, light-hearted, merry, overjoyed, pleased, rapturous, rejoicing, triumphant.

JP *abbreviation* Justice of the Peace.

Jr. *abbreviation* Junior.

jubilant /'dʒuːbɪlənt/ *adjective* exultant, rejoicing. □ **jubilantly** *adverb*. **jubilation** *noun*.

jubilee /'dʒuːbɪliː/ *noun* 1 anniversary (esp. 25th or 50th). 2 time of rejoicing.
■ 2 celebration, commemoration, festival.

Judaic /dʒuː'deɪɪk/ *adjective* of or characteristic of Jews.

Judaism /'dʒuːdeɪɪz(ə)m/ *noun* religion of Jews.

Judas /'dʒuːdəs/ *noun* traitor.

judder /'dʒʌdə/ *verb* shake noisily or violently. ● *noun* juddering.

judge /dʒʌdʒ/ *noun* 1 public official appointed to

hear and try legal cases. **2** person appointed to decide dispute or contest. **3** person who decides question. **4** person having judgement of specified type. ● *verb* **(-ging) 1** form or give opinion (about). **2** estimate. **3** act as judge (of). **4** try (legal case). **5** pronounce sentence on. **6** (often + *to do, that*) conclude, consider.

■ *noun* **1** justice, magistrate. **2** adjudicator, arbiter, arbitrator, moderator, referee, umpire. **4** authority, connoisseur, critic, expert, reviewer. ● *verb* **1** appraise, assess, criticize, evaluate, give one's opinion of, rate, *colloquial* size up, weigh up. **2** assess, estimate, gauge, guess, reckon. **3** adjudicate, mediate, moderate, referee, umpire. **4** examine, try. **5** pass judgement on, pronounce judgement on, sentence. **6** believe, conclude, consider, decide, decree, *formal* deem, determine, guess, reckon, rule, suppose.

judgement *noun* (also **judgment**) **1** critical faculty; discernment. **2** good sense. **3** opinion. **4** sentence of court of justice. **5** *often jocular* deserved misfortune. □ **Judgement Day** day on which God will judge humankind. □ **judgemental** /-'men-/ *adjective*.

■ **1, 2** acumen, common sense, discernment, discretion, discrimination, expertise, good sense, intelligence, reason, wisdom. **3** assessment, belief, estimation, evaluation, idea, impression, mind, notion, opinion, point of view, valuation. **4** arbitration, conclusion, decision, decree, finding, outcome, penalty, result, ruling, verdict.

judicature /'dʒuːdɪkətʃə/ *noun* **1** administration of justice. **2** judge's position. **3** judges collectively.

judicial /dʒuːˈdɪʃ(ə)l/ *adjective* **1** of, done by, or proper to court of law. **2** of or proper to a judge. **3** having function of judge. **4** impartial. □ **judicially** *adverb*.

■ **1** forensic, legal, official. **4** see IMPARTIAL.

judiciary /dʒuːˈdɪʃərɪ/ *noun* (*plural* **-ies**) judges collectively.

judicious /dʒuːˈdɪʃəs/ *adjective* sensible, prudent. □ **judiciously** *adverb*. **judiciousness** *noun*.

■ astute, careful, circumspect, considered, diplomatic, discerning, discreet, discriminating, enlightened, expedient, politic, prudent, reasonable, sage, sensible, shrewd, sober, sound, thoughtful, well advised, well judged, wise.

judo /'dʒuːdəʊ/ *noun* sport derived from ju-jitsu.

jug *noun* **1** deep vessel for liquids, with handle and lip. **2** contents of this. **3** *slang* prison. ● *verb* **(-gg-)** (usually as **jugged** *adjective*) stew (hare) in casserole. □ **jugful** *noun* (*plural* **-s**).

■ *noun* **1** carafe, container, decanter, ewer, flagon, jar, pitcher, vessel.

juggernaut /'dʒʌɡənɔːt/ *noun* **1** large heavy lorry. **2** overwhelming force or object.

juggle /'dʒʌɡ(ə)l/ *verb* **(-ling) 1** (often + *with*) keep several objects in the air at once by throwing and catching. **2** manipulate or

rearrange (facts). ● *noun* **1** juggling. **2** fraud. □ **juggler** *noun*.

■ *verb* **2** alter, *colloquial* cook, *colloquial* doctor, falsify, *colloquial* fix, manipulate, misrepresent, move about, rearrange, rig, tamper.

jugular /'dʒʌɡjʊlə/ *adjective* of neck or throat. ● *noun* jugular vein. □ **jugular vein** any of large veins in neck carrying blood from head.

juice /dʒuːs/ *noun* **1** liquid part of vegetable, fruit, or meat. **2** animal fluid, esp. secretion. **3** *colloquial* petrol, electricity.

■ **1** extract, fluid, liquid, sap.

juicy /'dʒuːsɪ/ *adjective* **(-ier, -iest) 1** full of juice. **2** *colloquial* interesting, scandalous. **3** *colloquial* profitable. □ **juicily** *adverb*.

■ **1** lush, moist, soft, squelchy, succulent.

ju-jitsu /dʒuːˈdʒɪtsuː/ *noun* Japanese system of unarmed combat.

ju-ju /'dʒuːdʒuː/ *noun* (*plural* **-s**) **1** charm or fetish of some W. African peoples. **2** supernatural power attributed to this.

jujube /'dʒuːdʒuːb/ *noun* flavoured jelly-like lozenge.

jukebox /'dʒuːkbɒks/ *noun* coin-operated machine playing records or compact discs.

Jul. *abbreviation* July.

julep /'dʒuːlep/ *noun* **1** sweet drink, esp. medicated. **2** *US* spirits and water iced and flavoured.

julienne /dʒuːlɪˈen/ *noun* vegetables cut into thin strips. ● *adjective* cut into thin strips.

Juliet cap /'dʒuːlɪət/ *noun* small close-fitting cap worn by brides etc.

July /dʒuːˈlaɪ/ *noun* (*plural* **Julys**) seventh month of year.

jumble /'dʒʌmb(ə)l/ *verb* **(-ling)** (often + *up*) mix; confuse; muddle. ● *noun* **1** confused heap etc.; muddle. **2** articles in jumble sale. □ **jumble sale** sale of second-hand articles, esp. for charity.

■ *verb* confuse, disarrange, disorganize, mess up, mingle, mix up, muddle, shuffle, tangle. ● *noun* **1** chaos, clutter, confusion, disarray, disorder, farrago, hotchpotch, mess, muddle, tangle.

jumbo /'dʒʌmbəʊ/ *colloquial noun* (*plural* **-s**) big animal (esp. elephant), person, or thing. ● *adjective* very or extra large. □ **jumbo jet** large airliner for several hundred passengers, esp. Boeing 747.

jump *verb* **1** spring from ground etc. **2** (often + *up, from, in, out*, etc.) rise or move suddenly. **3** jerk from shock or excitement. **4** pass over (obstacle) by jumping. **5** (+ *to, at*) reach (conclusion) hastily. **6** (of train etc.) leave (rails). **7** pass (red traffic light). **8** get on or off (train etc.) quickly, esp. illegally. **9** (often + *on*) attack (person) unexpectedly. ● *noun* **1** act of jumping. **2** sudden movement caused by shock etc. **3** abrupt rise in price, status, etc. **4** obstacle to be jumped, esp. by horse. **5** gap in series etc. □ **jump at** accept eagerly. **jumped-up** *colloquial* upstart. **jump the gun** start prematurely. **jump jet** vertical take-off jet plane. **jump lead** cable for carrying current from one battery to another. **jump-off** deciding round in show-jumping. **jump the queue** take unfair precedence. **jump ship** (of seaman) desert. **jumpsuit** one-piece garment for whole body. **jump to it** *colloquial* act promptly and energetically.

■ *verb* **1** bounce, bound, caper, frisk, frolic, gambol, hop, leap, pounce, prance, skip, spring. **3** flinch, jerk, recoil, start, wince. **4** clear, hurdle, vault. **9** (*jump on*) see ATTACK *verb* 1. ● *noun* **1** bounce, bound, hop, leap, pounce, skip, spring, vault. **3** see RISE *noun* 3. **4** ditch, fence, gap, gate, hurdle, obstacle.

jumper /'dʒʌmpə/ *noun* **1** knitted pullover. **2** loose outer jacket worn by sailors. **3** *US* pinafore dress.

jumpy *adjective* (**-ier**, **-iest**) nervous, easily startled. □ **jumpiness** *noun*.

Jun. *abbreviation* **1** June. **2** Junior.

junction /'dʒʌŋkʃ(ə)n/ *noun* **1** joining-point. **2** place where railway lines or roads meet. □ **junction box** box containing junction of electric cables etc.

■ **1** connection, joining, juncture, meeting, union. **2** confluence, corner, crossroad(s), interchange, intersection, points, T-junction.

juncture /'dʒʌŋktʃə/ *noun* **1** point in time, esp. critical one. **2** joining-point.

June *noun* sixth month of year.

jungle /'dʒʌŋg(ə)l/ *noun* **1** land overgrown with tangled vegetation, esp. in tropics. **2** tangled mass. **3** place of bewildering complexity or struggle.

■ **1** forest, rainforest. **2** see TANGLE *noun*.

junior /'dʒuːnɪə/ *adjective* **1** (often + *to*) lower in age, standing, or position. **2** the younger (esp. after name). **3** (of school) for younger pupils. ● *noun* junior person.

■ *adjective* **1** inferior, lesser, lower, minor, secondary, subordinate, subsidiary, younger.

juniper /'dʒuːnɪpə/ *noun* prickly evergreen shrub or tree with purple berry-like cones.

junk¹ *noun* **1** discarded articles; rubbish. **2** anything regarded as of little value. **3** *slang* narcotic drug, esp. heroin. ● *verb* discard as junk. □ **junk food** food which is not nutritious. **junk mail** unsolicited advertising sent by post.

■ *noun* **1, 2** clutter, debris, flotsam and jetsam, *US* garbage, litter, lumber, oddments, odds and ends, refuse, rubbish, scrap, *esp. US* trash, waste. ● *verb* see DISCARD 1.

junk² *noun* flat-bottomed sailing vessel in China seas.

junket /'dʒʌŋkɪt/ *noun* **1** pleasure outing. **2** official's tour at public expense. **3** sweetened and flavoured milk curds. **4** feast. ● *verb* (**-t-**) feast, picnic.

junkie /'dʒʌŋkɪ/ *noun slang* drug addict.

junta /'dʒʌntə/ *noun* (usually military) clique taking power after *coup d'état*.

juridical /dʒʊə'rɪdɪk(ə)l/ *adjective* **1** of judicial proceedings. **2** relating to the law.

jurisdiction /dʒʊərɪs'dɪkʃ(ə)n/ *noun* **1** (often + *over*) administration of justice. **2** legal or other authority. **3** extent of this.

jurisprudence /dʒʊərɪs'pruːd(ə)ns/ *noun* science or philosophy of law.

jurist /'dʒʊərɪst/ *noun* expert in law. □ **juristic** /-'rɪs-/ *adjective*.

juror /'dʒʊərə/ *noun* member of jury.

jury /'dʒʊərɪ/ *noun* (*plural* **-ies**) **1** group of people giving verdict in court of justice. **2** judges of competition. □ **jury-box** enclosure in court for jury.

just *adjective* **1** morally right, fair. **2** deserved. **3** well grounded; justified. ● *adverb* **1** exactly. **2** very recently. **3** barely. **4** quite. **5** *colloquial* simply, merely, positively. □ **just now 1** at this moment. **2** a little time ago. □ **justly** *adverb*.

■ *adjective* **1** equitable, ethical, even-handed, fair, fair-minded, honest, impartial, lawful, legal, legitimate, neutral, proper, reasonable, right-minded, unbiased, unprejudiced, upright. **2** apt, deserved, merited, rightful. **3** justified, legitimate, reasonable, well grounded.

justice /'dʒʌstɪs/ *noun* **1** fairness. **2** authority exercised in maintenance of right. **3** judicial proceedings. **4** magistrate; judge. □ **do justice to 1** treat fairly. **2** appreciate properly. **Justice of the Peace** lay magistrate.

■ **1** equity, even-handedness, fair-mindedness, fair play, impartiality, integrity, legality, neutrality, objectivity, right. **2** the law, legal proceedings, the police, punishment, retribution, vengeance.

justify /'dʒʌstɪfaɪ/ *verb* (**-ies**, **-ied**) **1** show justice or truth of. **2** (esp. in *passive*) be adequate grounds for; vindicate. **3** *Printing* adjust (line of type) to fill space evenly. **4** (as **justified** *adjective*) just, right. □ **justifiable** *adjective*. **justification** /-fɪ'keɪʃ(ə)n/ *noun*.

■ **1, 2** condone, defend, *formal* exculpate, excuse, exonerate, explain, explain away, forgive, legitimate, legitimize, pardon, rationalize, substantiate, support, sustain, uphold, validate, vindicate, warrant. □ **justifiable** acceptable, allowable, defensible, excusable, forgivable, justified, lawful, legitimate, pardonable, permissible, reasonable, understandable, warranted.

jut *verb* (**-tt-**) (often + *out*) protrude. ● *noun* projection.

■ *verb* beetle, extend, overhang, poke out, project, protrude, stick out.

jute /dʒuːt/ *noun* **1** fibre from bark of E. Indian plant, used for sacking, mats, etc. **2** plant yielding this.

juvenile /'dʒuːvənaɪl/ *adjective* **1** youthful. **2** of or for young people. **3** *often derogatory* immature. ● *noun* **1** young person. **2** actor playing juvenile part. □ **juvenile delinquency** offences committed by people below age of legal responsibility. **juvenile delinquent** such offender.

■ *adjective* **1** adolescent, teenage, young, youthful. **2** adolescent, teenage, young people's, young person's. **3** babyish, childish, immature, infantile, puerile, unsophisticated.

juvenilia /dʒuːvəˈnɪlɪə/ *plural noun* youthful works of author or artist.

juxtapose /dʒʌkstəˈpəʊz/ *verb* (**-sing**) **1** put side by side. **2** (+ *with*) put (thing) beside another. □ **juxtaposition** /-pəˈzɪʃ(ə)n/ *noun*.

Kk

K *abbreviation* (also **K.**) **1** kelvin(s). **2** Köchel (list of Mozart's works). **3** (also **k**) 1,000.

k *abbreviation* **1** kilo-. **2** knot(s).

kaftan = CAFTAN.

kaiser /'kaɪzə/ *noun historical* emperor, esp. of Germany or Austria.

kale *noun* variety of cabbage, esp. with wrinkled leaves.

kaleidoscope /kə'laɪdəskəʊp/ *noun* **1** tube containing angled mirrors and pieces of coloured glass producing reflected patterns when shaken. **2** constantly changing scene, group, etc. □ **kaleidoscopic** /-'skɒp-/ *adjective*.

kalends = CALENDS.

kamikaze /kæmɪ'kɑːzɪ/ *noun historical* **1** explosive-laden Japanese aircraft deliberately crashed on to target in 1939–45 war. **2** pilot of this. ● *adjective* reckless, esp. suicidal.

kangaroo /kæŋgə'ruː/ *noun* (*plural* **-s**) Australian marsupial with strong hind legs for jumping. □ **kangaroo court** illegal court held by strikers, mutineers, etc.

kaolin /'keɪəlɪn/ *noun* fine white clay used esp. for porcelain and in medicines.

kapok /'keɪpɒk/ *noun* fine cotton-like material from tropical tree, used to stuff cushions etc.

kaput /kə'pʊt/ *adjective slang* broken, ruined.

karabiner /kærə'biːnə/ *noun* coupling link used by mountaineers.

karakul /'kærəkʊl/ *noun* (also **caracul**) **1** Asian sheep whose lambs have dark curled fleece. **2** fur of this.

karaoke /kærɪ'əʊkɪ/ *noun* entertainment in nightclubs etc. with customers singing to backing music.

karate /kə'rɑːtɪ/ *noun* Japanese system of unarmed combat.

karma /'kɑːmə/ *noun Buddhism & Hinduism* **1** person's actions in one life, believed to decide fate in next. **2** destiny.

kauri /kaʊ'rɪ/ *noun* (*plural* **-s**) coniferous NZ timber tree.

kayak /'kaɪæk/ *noun* Eskimo one-man canoe.

kazoo /kə'zuː/ *noun* toy musical instrument into which player sings wordlessly.

KBE *abbreviation* Knight Commander of the Order of the British Empire.

kea /'kiːə/ *noun* green and red NZ parrot.

kebab /kɪ'bæb/ *noun* pieces of meat and sometimes vegetables grilled on skewer.

kedge *verb* (**-ging**) move (ship) with hawser attached to small anchor. ● *noun* (in full **kedge-anchor**) small anchor for this purpose.

kedgeree /kedʒə'riː/ *noun* dish of fish, rice, hard-boiled eggs, etc.

keel *noun* main lengthwise member of base of ship etc. ● *verb* (often + *over*) **1** (cause to) fall down or over. **2** turn keel upwards. □ **keelhaul** drag (person) under keel as punishment. **on an even keel** steady, balanced.

keen[1] *adjective* **1** enthusiastic, eager; intense. **2** (often + *on*) enthusiastic about; fond of. **3** (of senses) sharp; sensitive. **4** acute, penetrating. **5** (of knife) sharp. **6** (of wind etc.) piercingly cold. **7** (of price) competitive. □ **keenly** *adverb*. **keenness** *noun*.

■ **1** active, ambitious, anxious, ardent, assiduous, avid, committed, dedicated, devoted, diligent, eager, enthusiastic, fervent, fervid, industrious, intense, intent, interested, motivated, passionate, zealous. **4** acute, bright, clever, discerning, incisive, intelligent, penetrating, quick, sharp, shrewd. **5** razor-sharp, sharp, sharpened. **6** bitter, cold, extreme, icy, intense, penetrating, piercing, severe. **7** competitive, low, rock-bottom.

keen[2] *noun* Irish wailing funeral song. ● *verb* (often + *over*, *for*) wail mournfully, esp. at funeral.

keep *verb* (*past & past participle* **kept**) **1** have charge of; retain possession of. **2** (+ *for*) retain or reserve (for future). **3** maintain or remain in specified condition, position, etc. **4** (of food) remain in good condition. **5** restrain, prevent. **6** detain. **7** (often + *to*) observe or respect (law, secret, etc.). **8** celebrate (special day, feast, etc.). **9** own and look after (animal). **10** clothe, feed, etc. (person). **11** carry on (a business). **12** maintain. **13** guard, protect. **14** continue, do repeatedly. ● *noun* **1** maintenance; food. **2** *historical* tower, stronghold. □ **for keeps** *colloquial* permanently. **keep at** (cause to) persist with. **keep away** (often + *from*) **1** avoid. **2** prevent from being near. **keep-fit** regular physical exercises. **keep off 1** (cause to) stay away from. **2** abstain from. **3** avoid. **keep on 1** continue. **2** (+ *at*) nag. **keep out** (cause to) stay outside. **keep under** hold in subjection. **keep up 1** maintain. **2** prevent from going to bed. **3** (often + *with*) not fall behind. **keep up with the Joneses** compete socially with neighbours.

■ *verb* **1** be responsible for, have charge of, look after, maintain, manage, mind, take charge of. **1, 2** accumulate, amass, cling to, conserve, hang on to, hoard, hold, maintain, preserve, put aside, put away, reserve, retain, safeguard, save, store, stow away, withhold. **3** remain, stay. **4** be preserved, be usable, last, survive, stay fresh, stay good. **5** block, check, curb, deter, get in the way of, hamper, hinder, impede, obstruct, prevent, restrain. **6** delay, detain, hold up, retard. **7** see OBSERVE 3; (*keep to*) see FOLLOW 6, OBEY 1. **8** celebrate, commemorate, mark, observe, solemnize. **9** care for, look after, own, raise, rear, tend. **10** be responsible for, care for, feed, finance, foster, look after, maintain, pay for, provide for, subsidize, support. **11** carry on, maintain, manage, run. **13** guard, protect, safeguard, watch over. **14** carry on, continue, do again and again, do for a long time, keep on, persevere in, persist in. □ **keep up 1** see PROLONG 1, SUSTAIN 8.

keeper *noun* **1** person who looks after or is in charge of an animal, person, or thing. **2** custodian of museum, forest, etc. **3** wicket-keeper. **4** goalkeeper. **5** ring holding another on finger.
■ **1, 2** caretaker, curator, custodian, guard, guardian, jailer, minder, warden, warder.

keeping *noun* **1** custody, charge. **2** (esp. **in or out of keeping with**) agreement, harmony.

keepsake *noun* souvenir, esp. of person.

keg *noun* small barrel. □ **keg beer** beer kept in pressurized metal keg.

kelp *noun* large seaweed suitable for manure.

kelpie /'kelpɪ/ *noun* **1** *Scottish* malevolent water-spirit. **2** Australian sheepdog.

Kelt = CELT.

kelter = KILTER.

kelvin /'kelvɪn/ *noun* SI unit of temperature.

ken *noun* range of knowledge or sight. ● *verb* (**-nn-**; *past & past participle* **kenned** or **kent**) *Scottish & Northern English* recognize, know.

kendo /'kendəʊ/ *noun* Japanese fencing with bamboo swords.

kennel /'ken(ə)l/ *noun* **1** small shelter for dog. **2** (in *plural*) breeding or boarding place for dogs. ● *verb* (**-ll-**; *US* **-l-**) put or keep in kennel.

Kenyan /'kenjən/ *adjective* of Kenya. ● *noun* native or national of Kenya.

kept *past & past participle* of KEEP.

keratin /'kerətɪn/ *noun* fibrous protein in hair, hooves, claws, etc.

kerb *noun* stone etc. edging to pavement etc. □ **kerb-crawling** *colloquial* driving slowly to pick up prostitute. **kerb drill** rules taught to children about crossing roads.

kerfuffle /kə'fʌf(ə)l/ *noun colloquial* fuss, commotion.

kermes /'kɜːmɪz/ *noun* **1** female of insect with berry-like appearance that feeds on **kermes oak**, evergreen oak. **2** red dye made from these insects.

kernel /'kɜːn(ə)l/ *noun* **1** (usually soft) edible centre within hard shell of nut, fruit stone, seed, etc. **2** central or essential part.
■ **2** centre, core, essence, heart, middle, nub, pith.

kerosene /'kerəsiːn/ *noun esp. US* fuel oil distilled from petroleum etc.; paraffin oil.

kestrel /'kestr(ə)l/ *noun* small hovering falcon.

ketch *noun* kind of two-masted sailing boat.

ketchup /'ketʃəp/ *noun* (*US* **catsup** /'kætsəp/)

spicy sauce made esp. from tomatoes.

kettle /'ket(ə)l/ *noun* vessel for boiling water in. □ **kettledrum** large bowl-shaped drum.

key /kiː/ *noun* (*plural* **-s**) **1** instrument for moving bolt of lock, operating switch, etc. **2** instrument for winding clock etc. or grasping screw, nut, etc. **3** finger-operated button or lever on typewriter, piano, computer terminal, etc. **4** explanation, word, or system for understanding list of symbols, code, etc. **5** *Music* system of related notes based on particular note. **6** roughness of surface helping adhesion of plaster etc. ● *adjective* essential; of vital importance. ● *verb* **1** fasten with pin, wedge, bolt, etc. **2** (often + *in*) enter (data) by means of (computer) keyboard. **3** roughen (surface) to help adhesion of plaster etc. □ **keyed up** tense, excited. **keyhole** hole by which key is put into lock. **keynote 1** prevailing tone or idea. **2** *Music* note on which key is based. **keypad** miniature keyboard etc. for telephone, portable computer, etc. **keyring** ring for keeping keys on. **keystone 1** central principle of policy, system, etc. **2** central stone of arch.
■ *noun* **4** (key to problem) answer, clarification, clue, explanation, indicator, *colloquial* pointer, secret, solution; (key to map) glossary, guide, index, legend.

keyboard *noun* set of keys on typewriter, computer, piano, etc. ● *verb* enter (data) by means of keyboard. **keyboarder** *noun Computing*.

KG *abbreviation* Knight of the Order of the Garter.

kg *abbreviation* kilogram(s).

KGB *noun historical* secret police of USSR.

khaki /'kɑːkɪ/ *adjective* dull brownish-yellow. ● *noun* (*plural* **-s**) khaki colour, cloth, or uniform.

khan /kɑːn/ *noun: title of ruler or official in Central Asia.* □ **khanate** *noun*.

kHz *abbreviation* kilohertz.

kibbutz /kɪ'bʊts/ *noun* (*plural* **-im** /-iːm/) communal esp. farming settlement in Israel.

kibosh /'kaɪbɒʃ/ *noun slang* nonsense. □ **put the kibosh on** put an end to.

kick *verb* **1** strike, strike out, or propel forcibly with foot or hoof. **2** (often + *at*, *against*) protest, rebel. **3** *slang* give up (habit). **4** (often + *out*) expel, dismiss. **5** (**kick oneself, could kick oneself**) be annoyed with oneself. **6** score (goal) by kicking. ● *noun* **1** kicking action or blow. **2** recoil of gun. **3** *colloquial* temporary enthusiasm. **4** *colloquial* sharp stimulant effect. **5** *colloquial* (often in *plural*) thrill. □ **kick about 1** drift idly. **2** discuss informally. **kickback 1** recoil. **2** payment esp. for illegal help. **kick the bucket** *slang* die. **kick off 1** begin football game. **2** remove (shoes etc.) by kicking. **3** *colloquial* start. **kick-off** *noun* start, esp. of football game. **kick-start(er)** (pedal on) device to start engine of motorcycle etc. **kick up a fuss** *colloquial* create disturbance; object. **kick upstairs** get rid of by promotion.
■ *verb* **1** boot, heel, punt.

kid[1] *noun* **1** young goat. **2** leather from this. **3** *colloquial* child. ● *verb* (**-dd-**) (of goat) give birth to kid.

kid[2] *verb* (**-dd-**) *colloquial* **1** deceive. **2** tease. □ **no kidding** *slang* that is the truth.

kidnap /ˈkɪdnæp/ *verb* (**-pp-**; *US* **-p-**) carry off (person) illegally, esp. to obtain ransom. □ **kidnapper** *noun*.

■ abduct, capture, carry off, run away with, seize, *slang* snatch.

kidney /ˈkɪdnɪ/ *noun* (*plural* **-s**) **1** either of two organs serving to excrete urine. **2** animal's kidney as food. □ **kidney bean** red-skinned kidney-shaped bean. **kidney machine** apparatus able to perform function of damaged kidney. **kidney-shaped** having one side concave and the other convex.

kill *verb* **1** deprive of life or vitality. **2** end. **3** (**kill oneself**) *colloquial* overexert oneself. **4** (**kill oneself**) *colloquial* laugh heartily. **5** *colloquial* overwhelm with amusement. **6** switch off. **7** pass (time) while waiting. **8** *Computing* delete. **9** *Sport* stop (ball) dead. ● *noun* **1** (esp. in hunting) act of killing. **2** animal(s) killed thus. □ **killjoy** depressing person. **kill off 1** destroy completely. **2** bring about death of (fictional character).

■ *verb* **1** annihilate, assassinate, be the killer of, *slang* bump off, butcher, cull, decimate, destroy, dispatch, *colloquial* do away with, *slang* do in, drown, execute, exterminate, *colloquial* finish off, *slang* knock off, liquidate, martyr, massacre, murder, put down, put to death, slaughter, slay, take life.

killer *noun* person or thing that kills; murderer. □ **killer whale** dolphin with prominent dorsal fin.

■ assassin, butcher, cut-throat, destroyer, executioner, exterminator, *slang* hit man, murderer, slayer.

killing *noun* **1** causing of death. **2** *colloquial* great financial success. ● *adjective colloquial* **1** very funny. **2** exhausting.

■ *noun* **1** annihilation, assassination, bloodbath, bloodshed, butchery, carnage, decimation, destruction, elimination, eradication, euthanasia, execution, extermination, extinction, homicide, liquidation, manslaughter, martyrdom, massacre, murder, pogrom, slaughter, unlawful killing.

kiln *noun* oven for burning, baking, or drying esp. pottery.

kilo /ˈkiːləʊ/ *noun* (*plural* **-s**) kilogram.

kilo- *combining form* one thousand.

kilobyte /ˈkɪləbaɪt/ *noun Computing* 1,024 bytes as measure of memory size etc.

kilocalorie /ˈkɪləkælərɪ/ *noun* large calorie (see CALORIE).

kilocycle /ˈkɪləsaɪk(ə)l/ *noun historical* kilohertz.

kilogram /ˈkɪləgræm/ *noun* SI unit of mass (2.205 lb).

kilohertz /ˈkɪləhɜːts/ *noun* 1,000 hertz.

kilolitre /ˈkɪləliːtə/ *noun* (*US* **-liter**) 1,000 litres.

kilometre /ˈkɪləmiːtə/ *noun* (*US* **-meter**) 1,000 metres (0.6214 mile).

USAGE *Kilometre* is often pronounced /kɪˈlɒmɪtə/ (with the stress on the *-lom-*), but this is considered incorrect by some people.

kiloton /ˈkɪlətʌn/ *noun* (also **kilotonne**) unit of explosive power equal to that of 1,000 tons of TNT.

kilovolt /ˈkɪləvəʊlt/ *noun* 1,000 volts.

kilowatt /ˈkɪləwɒt/ *noun* 1,000 watts. □ **kilowatt-hour** electrical energy equal to 1 kilowatt used for 1 hour.

kilt *noun* pleated skirt usually of tartan, traditionally worn by Highland man. ● *verb* **1** tuck up (skirts) round body. **2** (esp. as **kilted** *adjective*) gather in vertical pleats.

kilter /ˈkɪltə/ *noun* (also **kelter** /ˈkeltə/) good working order.

kimono /kɪˈməʊnəʊ/ *noun* (*plural* **-s**) **1** wide-sleeved Japanese robe. **2** similar dressing gown.

kin *noun* one's relatives or family. ● *adjective* related.

■ *noun* clan, family, folks, kindred, kith and kin, relations, relatives.

kind /kaɪnd/ *noun* **1** species; natural group of animals, plants, etc. **2** class, type, variety. ● *adjective* (often + *to*) friendly, benevolent. □ **in kind 1** in same form. **2** (of payment) in goods etc. instead of money. □ **kindness** *noun*.

■ *noun* **1** breed, class, family, genus, group, race, species. **2** brand, breed, category, class, description, family, form, genre, genus, make, manner, nature, persuasion, race, set, sort, species, style, type, variety. ● *adjective* accommodating, affable, affectionate, agreeable, altruistic, amenable, amiable, amicable, approachable, attentive, avuncular, beneficent, benevolent, benign, bountiful, brotherly, caring, charitable, comforting, compassionate, congenial, considerate, cordial, courteous, decent, encouraging, fatherly, favourable, friendly, generous, genial, gentle, good-natured, good-tempered, gracious, helpful, hospitable, humane, humanitarian, indulgent, kind-hearted, kindly, lenient, loving, merciful, mild, motherly, neighbourly, nice, obliging, patient, philanthropic, pleasant, polite, public-spirited, sensitive, sisterly, soft-hearted, sweet, sympathetic, tactful, tender, tender-hearted, thoughtful, tolerant, understanding, unselfish, warm, warm-hearted, well intentioned, well meaning, well meant.

kindergarten /ˈkɪndəgɑːt(ə)n/ *noun* class or school for young children.

kind-hearted *adjective* of kind disposition. □ **kind-heartedly** *adverb*. **kind-heartedness** *noun*.

kindle /ˈkɪnd(ə)l/ *verb* (**-ling**) **1** set on fire; light. **2** inspire. **3** become aroused or animated.

■ **1** fire, ignite, light, set alight, set fire to, spark off. **2** see AROUSE 1.

kindling /'kɪndlɪŋ/ *noun* small sticks etc. for lighting fires.

kindly /'kaɪndlɪ/ *adverb* **1** in a kind way. **2** please. ● *adjective* (**-ier, -iest**) **1** kind. **2** (of climate etc.) pleasant, mild.

kindred /'kɪndrɪd/ *adjective* related, allied, similar. ● *noun* **1** blood relationship. **2** one's relations.

kinetic /kɪ'netɪk/ *adjective* of or due to motion. □ **kinetic energy** energy of motion. □ **kinetically** *adverb*.

kinfolk *US* = KINSFOLK.

king *noun* **1** (as title usually **King**) male sovereign, esp. hereditary. **2** outstanding man or thing in specified field. **3** largest kind of a thing. **4** chess piece which must be checkmated for a win. **5** crowned piece in draughts. **6** court card depicting king. **7** (**the King**) national anthem when sovereign is male. □ **King Charles spaniel** small black and tan kind. **kingcup** marsh marigold. **kingpin 1** main or large bolt. **2** essential person or thing. **king-size** (also **king-sized**) larger than normal; very large. □ **kingly** *adjective*. **kingliness** *noun*. **kingship** *noun*.

■ **1** crowned head, monarch, ruler, sovereign. **2** see CHIEF *noun*.

kingdom *noun* **1** state or territory ruled by king or queen. **2** spiritual reign of God. **3** domain. **4** division of natural world. □ **kingdom come** *colloquial* the next world.

■ **1** country, empire, land, monarchy, *formal* realm.

kingfisher *noun* small river bird with brilliant blue plumage, which dives for fish.

kink *noun* **1** twist or bend in wire etc. **2** tight wave in hair. **3** mental peculiarity. ● *verb* (cause to) form kink.

■ *noun* **1, 2** bend, coil, crinkle, curl, knot, loop, tangle, twist, wave. **3** see QUIRK 1.

kinky *adjective* (**-ier, -iest**) *colloquial* **1** sexually perverted or unconventional. **2** (of clothing) bizarre and sexually provocative. □ **kinkily** *adverb*. **kinkiness** *noun*.

kinsfolk /'kɪnzfəʊk/ *plural noun* (also *US* **kinfolk** /'kɪnfəʊk/) one's relations by blood.

kinship *noun* **1** blood relationship. **2** similarity.

kinsman /'kɪnzmən/ *noun* (*feminine* **kinswoman**) blood relation.

kiosk /'kiːɒsk/ *noun* **1** open-fronted booth selling newspapers, food, etc. **2** telephone box.

■ **1** booth, stall, stand. **2** call box, telephone box.

kip *slang noun* **1** sleep. **2** bed. ● *verb* (**-pp-**) (often + *down*) sleep.

kipper /'kɪpə/ *noun* fish, esp. herring, split, salted, dried, and usually smoked. ● *verb* treat (herring etc.) this way.

kir /kɪə/ *noun* dry white wine with blackcurrant liqueur.

kirk *noun Scottish & Northern English* church. □ **Kirk-session** lowest court in Church of Scotland.

kirsch /kɪəʃ/ *noun* spirit distilled from cherries.

kismet /'kɪzmet/ *noun* destiny.

kiss *verb* **1** touch with lips, esp. as sign of love, reverence, etc. **2** touch lightly. ● *noun* **1** touch of lips. **2** light touch. □ **kiss-curl** small curl of hair on forehead or nape of neck. **kiss of life** mouth-to-mouth resuscitation.

■ *verb* **1** caress, *colloquial* neck. **2** see TOUCH *verb* 2.

kisser *noun slang* mouth; face.

kissogram *noun* novelty greeting delivered with kiss.

kit *noun* **1** equipment, clothing, etc. for particular purpose. **2** specialized, esp. sports, clothing or uniform. **3** set of parts needed to assemble furniture, model, etc. ● *verb* (**-tt-**) **1** supply. **2** (often + *out*) equip with kit. □ **kitbag** usually cylindrical canvas etc. bag for carrying soldier's etc. kit.

■ *noun* **1** accoutrements, apparatus, appurtenances, baggage, effects, equipment, gear, impedimenta, implements, luggage, outfit, paraphernalia, rig, supplies, tackle, tools, tools of the trade, utensils.

kitchen /'kɪtʃɪn/ *noun* **1** place where food is cooked. **2** kitchen fitments. □ **kitchen garden** garden for growing fruit and vegetables.

■ **1** galley, kitchenette, scullery.

kitchenette /kɪtʃɪ'net/ *noun* small kitchen or cooking area.

kite *noun* **1** light framework with thin covering flown on long string in wind. **2** soaring bird of prey.

kith /kɪθ/ *noun* □ **kith and kin** friends and relations.

kitsch /kɪtʃ/ *noun* vulgar, pretentious, or worthless art.

kitten /'kɪt(ə)n/ *noun* young cat, ferret, etc. ● *verb* give birth to (kittens).

kittenish *adjective* **1** playful. **2** flirtatious.

kittiwake /'kɪtɪweɪk/ *noun* kind of small gull.

kitty[1] /'kɪtɪ/ *noun* (*plural* **-ies**) **1** joint fund. **2** pool in some card games.

kitty[2] /'kɪtɪ/ *noun* (*plural* **-ies**) *childish name for* kitten or cat.

kiwi /'kiːwiː/ *noun* **1** flightless NZ bird. **2** (**Kiwi**) *colloquial* New Zealander. □ **kiwi fruit** green-fleshed fruit.

Klaxon /'klæks(ə)n/ *noun proprietary term* horn, warning hooter.

Kleenex /'kliːneks/ *noun* (*plural* same or **-es**) *proprietary term* disposable paper handkerchief.

kleptomania /kleptə'meɪnɪə/ *noun* irresistible urge to steal. □ **kleptomaniac** /-nɪæk/ *adjective* & *noun*.

km *abbreviation* kilometre(s).

knack /næk/ *noun* **1** acquired faculty of doing something skilfully. **2** habit of action, speech, etc.

■ **1** ability, adroitness, aptitude, art, bent, dexterity, expertise, facility, flair, genius, gift, intuition, know-how, skill, talent. **2** habit, trick, way.

knacker /'nækə/ *noun* buyer of useless horses for slaughter. ● *verb slang* (esp. as **knackered** *adjective*) exhaust, wear out.

knapsack /'næpsæk/ *noun* soldier's or hiker's bag carried on back.

■ backpack, haversack, rucksack.

knapweed /'næpwiːd/ *noun* plant with thistle-like flower.

knave /neɪv/ *noun* **1** rogue, scoundrel. **2** jack (in playing cards). □ **knavery** *noun*. **knavish** *adjective*.

knead /niːd/ *verb* **1** work into dough, paste, etc., esp. by hand. **2** make (bread, pottery) thus. **3** massage.

■ **1** manipulate, pound, press, pummel, squeeze, work. **3** manipulate, massage, rub.

knee /niː/ *noun* **1** joint between thigh and lower leg. **2** lap of sitting person. **3** part of garment covering knee. ● *verb* (**knees, kneed, kneeing**) touch or strike with knee. □ **kneecap** convex bone in front of knee. **knees-up** *colloquial* lively party or gathering.

kneel /niːl/ *verb* (*past & past participle* **knelt**) rest or lower oneself on knee(s).

kneeler *noun* cushion for kneeling on.

knell /nel/ *noun* **1** sound of bell, esp. for death or funeral. **2** event etc. seen as bad omen.

knelt *past & past participle* of KNEEL.

knew *past* of KNOW.

knickerbockers /'nɪkəbɒkəz/ *plural noun* loose-fitting breeches gathered in at knee. □ **Knickerbocker Glory** ice cream and fruit in tall glass.

knickers /'nɪkəz/ *plural noun* woman's or girl's undergarment for lower torso.

■ *colloquial* bloomers, briefs, drawers, *colloquial* panties, pants, underpants.

knick-knack /'nɪknæk/ *noun* (also **nick-nack**) trinket, small ornament.

knife /naɪf/ *noun* (*plural* **knives**) **1** cutting blade or weapon with long sharpened edge fixed in handle. **2** cutting-blade in machine. **3** (**the knife**) *colloquial* surgery. ● *verb* (**-fing**) cut or stab with knife. □ **knife-edge 1** edge of knife. **2** position of extreme uncertainty. **knife-pleat** overlapping narrow flat pleat.

■ *verb* cut, pierce, slash, stab, wound.

knight /naɪt/ *noun* **1** man awarded non-hereditary title (*Sir*) by sovereign. **2** *historical* man raised to honourable military rank. **3** *historical* lady's champion in tournament etc. **4** chess piece usually in shape of horse's head. ● *verb* confer knighthood on. □ **knighthood** *noun*. **knightly** *adjective*.

knit /nɪt/ *verb* (**-tt-**; *past & past participle* **knitted** or **knit**) **1** make (garment etc.) by interlocking loops of esp. wool with knitting-needles or knit-

ting machine. **2** make (plain stitch) in knitting. **3** wrinkle (brow). **4** (often + *together*) make or become close. **5** (often + *together*) (of broken bone) become joined. □ **knit one's brow or brows** frown. **knitwear** knitted garments.

■ **4** bind, combine, connect, fasten, interlace, interweave, join, knit, link, marry, tie, unite. **5** heal, join, mend. □ **knit one's brow** see FROWN *verb* 1.

knitting *noun* work being knitted. □ **knitting-needle** thin pointed rod used usually in pairs for knitting.

knob /nɒb/ *noun* **1** rounded protuberance, e.g. door handle, radio control, etc. **2** small lump (of butter, coal, etc.). □ **knobby** *adjective*.

■ **1** boss, bulge, bump, lump, projection, protrusion, protuberance, stud, swelling; (*door knob*) handle. **2** lump, pat.

knobbly /'nɒblɪ/ *adjective* (**-ier, -iest**) hard and lumpy.

knock /nɒk/ *verb* **1** strike with audible sharp blow. **2** (often + *at*) strike (door etc.) for admittance. **3** (usually + *in, off,* etc.) drive by striking. **4** make (hole) by knocking. **5** (of engine) make thumping etc. noise. **6** *slang* criticize. ● *noun* **1** audible sharp blow. **2** rap, esp. at door. □ **knock about, around 1** treat roughly. **2** wander about aimlessly. **3** (usually + *with*) associate socially. **knock back** *slang* eat or drink, esp. quickly. **knock down 1** strike (esp. person) to ground. **2** demolish. **3** (usually + *to*) (at auction) sell to bidder. **4** *colloquial* lower price of. **knock-down** *adjective colloquial* (of price) very low. **knock knees** legs curved inward at the knee. **knock-kneed** with knock knees. **knock off 1** strike off with blow. **2** *colloquial* finish work. **3** *colloquial* do or make rapidly. **4** (often + *from*) deduct (amount) from price. **5** *slang* steal. **6** *slang* kill. **knock on the head** put end to (scheme etc.). **knock on wood** *US* touch wood. **knock out 1** make unconscious. **2** defeat (boxer) by knocking down for count of 10. **3** defeat in knockout competition. **4** *colloquial* tire out. **knockout** *noun* **1** blow that knocks boxer out. **2** competition in which loser of each match is eliminated. **3** *slang* outstanding person or thing. **knock together** construct hurriedly. **knock up 1** make hastily. **2** arouse by knock at door. **3** practise tennis etc. before formal game begins. **4** *US slang* make pregnant. **knock-up** *noun* practice at tennis etc.

■ *verb* **1** bang, bash, buffet, bump, hammer, hit, pound, rap, smack, *esp. archaic* or *literary* smite, strike, tap, thump. **6** see CRITICIZE 1. □ **knock down 2** see DEMOLISH 1. **knock off 2** see CEASE. **5** see STEAL *verb* 1. **6** see KILL *verb* 1. **knock out 1, 2** see STUN 1.

knocker *noun* hinged metal device on door for knocking with.

knoll /nəʊl/ *noun* small hill, mound.

knot /nɒt/ *noun* **1** intertwining of rope, string, etc. so as to fasten. **2** set method of this. **3** tangle in hair, knitting, etc. **4** unit of ship's or aircraft's speed equal to one nautical mile per hour. **5** hard mass formed in tree trunk where branch grows out. **6** round cross-grained piece in board caused by this. **7** (usually + *of*) cluster. ● *verb* (**-tt-**) **1** tie in knot. **2** entangle. □ **knotgrass** wild plant with creeping stems and pink flowers. **knot-hole** hole in timber where knot has fallen out.

■ *noun* **1** bond, bow, ligature, tie. **3** see TANGLE *noun.* **7** see GROUP *noun* 1. ● *verb* **1** bind, do up, fasten, join, knit, lash, link, tether, tie, unite. **2** entangle, entwine, snarl up, tangle.

knotty *adjective* (**-ier**, **-iest**) **1** full of knots. **2** puzzling.

know /nəʊ/ *verb* (*past* **knew** /njuː/; *past participle* **known**) **1** (often + *that, how, what,* etc.) have in the mind; have learnt. **2** (often + *that*) feel certain. **3** be acquainted with. **4** recognize, identify. **5** (often + *from*) be able to distinguish. **6** (as **known** *adjective*) publicly acknowledged. □ **in the know** *colloquial* having inside information. **know-all** *colloquial* person who seems to know everything. **know-how** practical knowledge or skill.

■ **1** be cognizant of, be familiar with, be knowledgeable about, comprehend, discern, have experience of, have in mind, realize, remember, understand. **2** be certain, have confidence, have no doubt. **3** be acquainted with, be a friend of, be friends with. **4, 5** differentiate, distinguish, identify, make out, perceive, recognize, see. □ **know-all** expert, pundit, *colloquial* show-off, wiseacre.

knowing *adjective* showing knowledge; shrewd; cunning.

■ astute, aware, clever, conspiratorial, cunning, discerning, experienced, expressive, informed, *colloquial* in the know, knowledgeable, meaningful, perceptive, shrewd, wise.

knowingly *adverb* **1** in a knowing way. **2** consciously, intentionally.

knowledge /ˈnɒlɪdʒ/ *noun* **1** (usually + *of*) awareness, familiarity. **2** person's range of information, understanding (of subject). **3** information. **4** sum of what is known.

■ **1** acquaintance, awareness, background, cognition, competence, consciousness, education, erudition, experience, expertise, familiarity, grasp, insight, know-how, learning, lore, memory, science, scholarship, skill, training. **3** data, facts, information, intelligence, *colloquial* low-down.

knowledgeable *adjective* (also **knowledgable**) well informed; intelligent. □ **knowledgeably** *adverb*.

■ au fait, aware, *formal* cognizant, conversant, educated, enlightened, erudite, experienced, expert, familiar (with), *slang* genned up, informed, *colloquial* in the know, learned, scholarly, versed (in), well informed.

known *past participle* of KNOW.

knuckle /ˈnʌk(ə)l/ *noun* **1** bone at finger-joint. **2** knee- or ankle-joint of quadruped. **3** this as joint of meat. ● *verb* (**-ling**) strike, rub, etc. with knuckles. □ **knuckle down** (often + *to*) apply oneself earnestly. **knuckleduster** metal guard worn over knuckles in fighting, esp. to inflict greater damage. **knuckle under** give in; submit.

KO *abbreviation* knockout.

koala /kəʊˈɑːlə/ *noun* (also **koala bear**) small Australian bearlike marsupial with thick grey fur.

kohl /kəʊl/ *noun* black powder used as eye make-up, esp. in Eastern countries.

kohlrabi /kəʊlˈrɑːbɪ/ *noun* (*plural* **-bies**) cabbage with edible turnip-like stem.

kookaburra /ˈkʊkəbʌrə/ *noun* Australian kingfisher with strange laughing cry.

Koran /kɔːˈrɑːn/ *noun* Islamic sacred book.

Korean /kəˈriːən/ *noun* **1** native or national of N. or S. Korea. **2** language of Korea. ● *adjective* of Korea or its people or language.

kosher /ˈkəʊʃə/ *adjective* **1** (of food or food-shop) fulfilling requirements of Jewish law. **2** *colloquial* correct, genuine. ● *noun* kosher food or shop.

kowtow /kaʊˈtaʊ/ *noun* *historical* Chinese custom of touching ground with forehead, esp. in submission. ● *verb* **1** (usually + *to*) act obsequiously. **2** *historical* perform kowtow.

k.p.h. *abbreviation* kilometres per hour.

kraal /krɑːl/ *noun South African* **1** village of huts enclosed by fence. **2** enclosure for cattle etc.

kremlin /ˈkremlɪn/ *noun* **1** citadel within Russian town. **2** (**the Kremlin**) that in Moscow; Russian government.

krill *noun* tiny plankton crustaceans eaten by whales etc.

krugerrand /ˈkruːɡərænd/ *noun* S. African gold coin.

krummhorn /ˈkrʌmhɔːn/ *noun* (also **crumhorn**) medieval musical wind instrument.

krypton /ˈkrɪptɒn/ *noun* gaseous element used in lamps etc.

Kt. *abbreviation* Knight.

kts. *abbreviation* knots.

kudos /ˈkjuːdɒs/ *noun* *colloquial* glory, renown.

kumquat /ˈkʌmkwɒt/ *noun* (also **cumquat**) small orange-like fruit.

kung fu /kʌŋ ˈfuː/ *noun* Chinese form of karate.

kV *abbreviation* kilovolt(s).

kW *abbreviation* kilowatt(s).

kWh *abbreviation* kilowatt-hour(s).

Ll

L[1] *noun* (also **l**) (Roman numeral) 50.

L[2] *abbreviation* Lake. □ **L-plate** sign bearing letter L, attached to vehicle to show that driver is learner.

l *abbreviation* **1** left. **2** line. **3** litre(s).

LA *abbreviation* Los Angeles.

la = LAH.

Lab. *abbreviation* Labour.

lab *noun colloquial* laboratory.

label /'leɪb(ə)l/ *noun* **1** piece of paper attached to object to give information about it. **2** classifying phrase etc. **3** logo, title, or trade mark of company. ● *verb* (**-ll-**; *US* **-l-**) **1** attach label to. **2** (usually + *as*) assign to category.
- *noun* **1** docket, identification, marker, sticker, tag, ticket. **3** brand, hallmark, imprint, logo, trade mark. ● *verb* **1** brand, docket, identify, mark, stamp, tag. **2** brand, call, categorize, class, classify, define, describe, identify, name, pigeon-hole.

labial /'leɪbɪəl/ *adjective* **1** of lips. **2** *Phonetics* pronounced with (closed) lips. ● *noun Phonetics* labial sound.

labium /'leɪbɪəm/ *noun* (*plural* **labia**) each fold of skin of pairs enclosing vulva.

labor etc. *US & Australian* = LABOUR etc.

laboratory /lə'bɒrətərɪ/ *noun* (*plural* **-ies**) place used for scientific experiments and research.

laborious /lə'bɔːrɪəs/ *adjective* **1** needing hard work. **2** (esp. of literary style) showing signs of effort. □ **laboriously** *adverb*.
- **1** arduous, back-breaking, difficult, exhausting, fatiguing, gruelling, hard, heavy, Herculean, onerous, stiff, strenuous, taxing, tough, uphill, wearisome, wearying. **2** artificial, contrived, forced, heavy, laboured, overdone, overworked, pedestrian, ponderous, strained, unnatural.

labour /'leɪbə/ (*US & Australian* **labor**) *noun* **1** physical or mental work; exertion. **2** workers, esp. as political force. **3** (**Labour**) the Labour Party. **4** process of giving birth. **5** task. ● *verb* **1** work hard; exert oneself. **2** elaborate needlessly. **3** proceed with difficulty. **4** (as **laboured** *adjective*) done with great effort. **5** (+ *under*) suffer because of. □ **labour camp** prison camp enforcing hard labour. **Labour Exchange** *colloquial* or *historical* jobcentre. **Labour Party** political party formed to represent workers' interests. **labour-saving** designed to reduce or eliminate work.
- *noun* **1** donkey-work, drudgery, effort, exertion, industry, pains, slavery, strain, *colloquial* sweat, toil, work. **2** employees, hands, wage earners, workers, workforce. **4** childbirth, contractions, delivery, labour pains, *formal* parturition, *literary* travail. ● *verb* **1** drudge, exert oneself, slave, strain, strive, struggle, sweat, toil, *literary* travail, work. **4** (**laboured**) see LABORIOUS 2.
- □ **labour-saving** convenient, handy, helpful, time-saving.

labourer *noun* (*US* **laborer**) person doing unskilled paid manual work.
- blue-collar worker, employee, hand, manual worker, navvy, wage earner, worker.

Labrador /'læbrədɔː/ *noun* dog of retriever breed with black or golden coat.

laburnum /lə'bɜːnəm/ *noun* tree with drooping golden flowers and poisonous seeds.

labyrinth /'læbərɪnθ/ *noun* **1** complicated network of passages. **2** intricate or tangled arrangement. □ **labyrinthine** /-'rɪnθaɪn/ *adjective*.
- **1** complex, maze, network. **2** jungle, tangle.

lac *noun* resinous substance from SE Asian insect, used to make varnish and shellac.

lace *noun* **1** open patterned fabric or trimming made by twisting, knotting, or looping threads. **2** cord etc. passed through eyelets or hooks for fastening shoes etc. ● *verb* (**-cing**) **1** (usually + *up*) fasten or tighten with lace(s). **2** add spirits to (drink). **3** (+ *through*) pass (shoelace etc.) through. □ **lace-up** shoe fastened with lace.
- *noun* **1** filigree, mesh, net, netting, openwork, tatting, web. **2** bootlace, cord, shoelace, string. ● *verb* **1** see FASTEN 1.

lacerate /'læsəreɪt/ *verb* (**-ting**) **1** tear (esp. flesh etc.) roughly. **2** wound (feelings etc.). □ **laceration** *noun*.
- **1** claw, cut, gash, mangle, rip, scratch, slash, tear. **2** see HURT *verb* 1.

lachrymal /'lækrɪm(ə)l/ *adjective* (also **lacrimal**) of tears.

lachrymose /'lækrɪməʊs/ *adjective formal* often weeping; tearful.

lack *noun* (usually + *of*) deficiency, want. ● *verb* be without or deficient in. □ **lacklustre** (*US* **lackluster**) dull; lacking in vitality etc.
- *noun* absence, dearth, deficiency, famine, insufficiency, need, paucity, scarcity, shortage, want. ● *verb* be lacking in, be short of, be without, miss, need, require, want.

lackadaisical /lækə'deɪzɪk(ə)l/ *adjective* languid; unenthusiastic.

lackey /'lækɪ/ *noun* (*plural* **-s**) **1** servile follower. **2** footman, manservant.

lacking *adjective* **1** (often + *in*) undesirably absent; deficient. **2** mentally deficient.

■ **1** deficient, inadequate, insufficient, short, unsatisfactory, weak. **2** see STUPID 1.

laconic /lə'kɒnɪk/ *adjective* using few words. □ **laconically** *adverb*.

lacquer /'lækə/ *noun* **1** hard shiny shellac or synthetic varnish. **2** substance sprayed on hair to keep it in place. ● *verb* coat with lacquer.

lacrimal = LACHRYMAL.

lacrosse /lə'krɒs/ *noun* hockey-like game played with ball carried in net at end of stick.

lactate /læk'teɪt/ *verb* (**-ting**) (of mammals) secrete milk. □ **lactation** *noun*.

lactic /'læktɪk/ *adjective* of milk.

lactose /'læktəʊs/ *noun* sugar present in milk.

lacuna /lə'kju:nə/ *noun* (*plural* **-s** or **-nae** /-ni:/) **1** missing part, esp. in manuscript. **2** gap.

lacy /'leɪsɪ/ *adjective* (**-ier**, **-iest**) like lace fabric.

lad *noun* **1** boy, youth. **2** *colloquial* man.

ladder /'lædə/ *noun* **1** set of horizontal bars fixed at intervals between two uprights for climbing up and down. **2** unravelled stitching in stocking etc. **3** means of advancement in career etc. ● *verb* cause or develop ladder in (stocking etc.).

lade *verb* (**-ding**; *past participle* **laden**) **1** load (ship). **2** ship (goods). **3** (as **laden** *adjective*) (usually + *with*) loaded, burdened.

■ **3** (**laden**) burdened, chock-full, full, loaded, oppressed, piled high, weighed down.

la-di-da /lɑ:dɪ'dɑ:/ *adjective colloquial* pretentious or affected, esp. in manner or speech.

ladle /'leɪd(ə)l/ *noun* deep long-handled spoon for serving liquids. ● *verb* (**-ling**) (often + *out*) transfer with ladle.

lady /'leɪdɪ/ *noun* (*plural* **-ies**) **1** woman regarded as having superior status or refined manner. **2** woman. **3** (in *plural*) *polite form of address for women*. **4** *colloquial* wife, girlfriend. **5** (**Lady**) *title used before name of peeresses, peers' female relatives, wives and widows of knights, etc.* **6** (**Ladies**) women's public lavatory. □ **ladybird** small beetle, usually red with black spots. **Lady chapel** chapel dedicated to Virgin Mary. **Lady Day** Feast of the Annunciation, 25 Mar. **ladylike** like or appropriate to lady.

■ **1** aristocrat, noblewoman, peeress. **2** see WOMAN 1. **4** girlfriend, wife, *colloquial* woman. □ **ladylike** aristocratic, courtly, cultured, dainty, decorous, elegant, genteel, modest, noble, polished, polite, *colloquial* posh, prim, prissy, proper, refined, respectable, well born, well bred.

Ladyship *noun* □ **Her** or **Your Ladyship** *title used of or to Lady*.

lag[1] *verb* (**-gg-**) fall behind; not keep pace. ● *noun* delay.

■ *verb* be slow, bring up the rear, come last, dally, dawdle, delay, drop behind, fall behind, go too slow, hang back, linger, loiter, saunter, straggle, trail.

lag[2] *verb* (**-gg-**) enclose (boiler etc.) with heat-insulating material.

■ insulate, wrap up.

lag[3] *noun slang* habitual convict.

lager /'lɑ:gə/ *noun* kind of light beer. □ **lager lout** *colloquial* youth behaving violently through drinking too much.

laggard /'lægəd/ *noun* person lagging behind.

lagging *noun* insulating material for boiler etc.

lagoon /lə'gu:n/ *noun* salt-water lake separated from sea by sandbank, reef, etc.

lah *noun* (also **la**) *Music* sixth note of scale in tonic sol-fa.

laid *past & past participle* of LAY[1]. □ **laid-back** *colloquial* relaxed, easy-going.

lain *past participle* of LIE[1].

lair *noun* **1** wild animal's home. **2** person's hiding place.

■ den, hideout, hiding place, refuge, resting place, retreat, shelter.

laird /'leəd/ *noun Scottish* landed proprietor.

laissez-faire /leɪseɪ'feə/ *noun* (also **laisser-faire**) policy of non-interference. [French]

laity /'leɪtɪ/ *noun* lay people, as distinct from clergy.

lake[1] *noun* large body of water surrounded by land. □ **Lake District** region of lakes in Cumbria.

■ *Scottish* loch, *dialect* or *poetical* mere, pool, pond, reservoir, sea, tarn, water.

lake[2] *noun* reddish pigment originally made from lac.

lam *verb* (**-mm-**) *slang* hit hard, thrash.

lama /'lɑ:mə/ *noun* Tibetan or Mongolian Buddhist monk.

lamasery /'lɑ:məsərɪ/ *noun* (*plural* **-ies**) lama monastery.

lamb /læm/ *noun* **1** young sheep. **2** its flesh as food. **3** gentle, innocent, or weak person. ● *verb* (of sheep) give birth.

lambaste /læm'beɪst/ *verb* (**-ting**) (also **lambast** /-'bæst/) *colloquial* thrash, beat.

lambent /'læmbənt/ *adjective* **1** (of flame etc.) playing on a surface. **2** (of eyes, wit, etc.) gently brilliant. □ **lambency** *noun*.

lambswool *noun* soft fine wool from young sheep.

lame *adjective* **1** disabled in foot or leg. **2** (of excuse etc.) unconvincing. **3** (of verse etc.) halting. ● *verb* (**-ming**) make lame; disable. □ **lame duck** helpless person or firm. □ **lamely** *adverb*. **lameness** *noun*.

■ *adjective* **1** (*lame animal*) crippled, disabled, handicapped, hobbled, hobbling, incapacitated, limping, maimed; (*lame leg*) game, *slang* gammy, injured. **2** feeble, flimsy, inadequate, poor, tame, thin, unconvincing, weak. **3** halting, stiff, uneven. ● *verb* cripple, disable, hobble, incapacitate, maim.

lamé /ˈlɑːmeɪ/ *noun* fabric with gold or silver thread woven in.

lament /ləˈment/ *noun* **1** passionate expression of grief. **2** song etc. of mourning. ● *verb* **1** express or feel grief for or about; utter lament. **2** (as **lamented** *adjective*) recently dead. □ **lamentation** /læmən-/ *noun*.

■ *noun* **2** dirge, elegy, keen, lamentation, monody, requiem, threnody. ● *verb* **1** bemoan, bewail, cry, deplore, express one's sorrow, grieve, keen, mourn, regret, shed tears, sorrow, wail, weep.

lamentable /ˈlæməntəb(ə)l/ *adjective* deplorable, regrettable. □ **lamentably** *adverb*.

■ deplorable, regrettable, sad, unfortunate, unhappy.

lamina /ˈlæmmə/ *noun* (*plural* **-nae** /-niː/) thin plate or layer. □ **laminar** *adjective*.

laminate *verb* /ˈlæmmeɪt/ (**-ting**) **1** beat or roll into thin plates. **2** overlay with plastic layer etc. **3** split into layers. ● *noun* /ˈlæmmət/ laminated structure, esp. of layers fixed together. □ **lamination** *noun*.

lamp *noun* **1** device for giving light from electricity, gas, oil, etc. **2** apparatus producing esp. ultraviolet or infra-red radiation. □ **lamp-post** post supporting street light. **lampshade** usually partial cover for lamp.

| ■ **1** lantern, light.

lampoon /læmˈpuːn/ *noun* satirical attack on person etc. ● *verb* satirize. □ **lampoonist** *noun*.

lamprey /ˈlæmprɪ/ *noun* (*plural* **-s**) eel-like fish with sucker mouth.

Lancastrian /læŋˈkæstrɪən/ *noun* native of Lancashire or Lancaster. ● *adjective* **1** of Lancashire or Lancaster. **2** of House of Lancaster in Wars of Roses.

lance /lɑːns/ *noun* long spear, esp. one used by horseman. ● *verb* (**-cing**) prick or open with lancet. □ **lance-corporal** army NCO below corporal.

lanceolate /ˈlɑːnsɪələt/ *adjective* shaped like spearhead, tapering to each end.

lancer /ˈlɑːnsə/ *noun* **1** *historical* soldier of cavalry regiment originally armed with lances. **2** (in *plural*) quadrille.

lancet /ˈlɑːnsɪt/ *noun* small broad two-edged surgical knife with sharp point.

land *noun* **1** solid part of earth's surface, not covered by sea. **2** ground, soil. **3** expanse of country. **4** nation, state. **5** landed property. **6** (in *plural*) estates. ● *verb* **1** set or go ashore. **2** bring (aircraft) down. **3** alight on ground etc. **4** bring (fish) to land. **5** (also *reflexive*; often + *up*) bring to, arrive at, or find oneself in certain situation

or place. **6** *colloquial* deal (person etc. a blow etc.). **7** (+ *with*) present (person) with (problem etc.). **8** *colloquial* win (prize, appointment, etc.). □ **landfall** approach to land after sea or air journey. **landfill 1** waste material used to landscape or reclaim land. **2** disposing of waste in this way. **landlocked** (almost) enclosed by land. **landlubber** person unfamiliar with sea and ships. **landmine** explosive mine laid in or on ground. **landslide** (also **landslip**) sliding down of mass of land from cliff or mountain. **2** overwhelming majority in election.

■ *noun* **1** coast, ground, shore, terra firma. **2** earth, ground, soil. **3** country, ground, landscape, region, terrain, territory. **4** country, fatherland, homeland, motherland, nation, region, state, territory. **5, 6** estate(s), grounds, property. ● *verb* **1, 3** alight, arrive, berth, come ashore, come to rest, disembark, dismount, dock, end a journey, get down, go ashore, reach landfall, settle, touch down. **5** bring, get, lead; (*land oneself*) arrive, find oneself; (*land up*) become, end up, *colloquial* fetch up, finish up, grow. **8** see GET 1.

landau /ˈlændɔː/ *noun* (*plural* **-s**) 4-wheeled enclosed carriage with divided top.

landed *adjective* owning or consisting of land.

landing /ˈlændɪŋ/ *noun* **1** coming or bringing to land. **2** platform or passage at top of or part way up stairs. **3** place for ships to load and unload. □ **landing craft** craft used for putting troops and equipment ashore. **landing gear** undercarriage of aircraft. **landing stage** platform for disembarking passengers and goods. **landing strip** airstrip.

■ **1** arrival, docking, return, splashdown, touchdown. **3** see LANDING STAGE. □ **landing stage** berth, dock, harbour, jetty, landing, pier, quay, wharf.

landlady *noun* **1** woman owning rented property. **2** woman keeping pub, guest house, etc.

■ **1** see LANDLORD 1. **2** host, hostess, hotelier, innkeeper, licensee, manager, manageress, proprietor, proprietress, publican, restaurateur.

landlord *noun* **1** person owning rented property. **2** person keeping pub, guest house, etc.

■ **1** landowner, lessor, letter, owner. **2** host, hotelier, innkeeper, licensee, manager, proprietor, publican, restaurateur.

landmark *noun* **1** conspicuous object. **2** notable event.

■ **1** feature, visible feature. **2** milestone, turning point, watershed.

landowner /ˈlændəʊnə/ *noun* owner of land.

landscape /ˈlændskeɪp/ *noun* **1** scenery in area of land. **2** picture of it. ● *verb* (**-ping**) improve (piece of land) by **landscape gardening**, laying out of grounds to resemble natural scenery.

■ *noun* **1** aspect, countryside, outlook, panorama, prospect, rural scene, scene, scenery, view, vista.

lane *noun* **1** narrow road. **2** division of road for one line of traffic. **3** strip of track or water for competitor in race. **4** regular course followed by ship or aircraft.

language /ˈlæŋgwɪdʒ/ *noun* **1** use of words in agreed way as means of human communication. **2** system of words of particular community, country, etc. **3** faculty of speech. **4** style of expression. **5** system of symbols and rules for computer programs. □ **language laboratory** room with tape recorders etc. for learning foreign language.

■ **1, 3** see SPEECH **1**. **2** argot, cant, dialect, idiom, jargon, *colloquial* lingo, parlance, patois, slang, speech, tongue, vernacular. **4** see STYLE *noun* 2.

languid /ˈlæŋgwɪd/ *adjective* lacking vigour; idle. □ **languidly** *adverb*.

■ apathetic, droopy, feeble, idle, inactive, inert, lackadaisical, lazy, lethargic, slow, sluggish, torpid, unenthusiastic, weak.

languish /ˈlæŋgwɪʃ/ *verb* lose or lack vitality. □ **languish for** long for. **languish under** live under (depression etc.).

■ decline, droop, flag, lose momentum, mope, pine, slow down, stagnate, suffer, sulk, waste away, weaken, wither.

languor /ˈlæŋgə/ *noun* **1** lack of energy; idleness. **2** soft or tender mood or effect. □ **languorous** *adjective*.

lank *adjective* **1** (of grass, hair, etc.) long and limp. **2** thin and tall.

■ **1** drooping, lifeless, limp, long, straight, thin. **2** see LANKY.

lanky *adjective* (**-ier, -iest**) ungracefully thin and long or tall.

■ angular, awkward, bony, gangling, gaunt, lank, lean, long, scraggy, scrawny, skinny, tall, thin, ungraceful, weedy.

lanolin /ˈlænəlɪn/ *noun* fat from sheep's wool used in cosmetics, ointments, etc.

lantern /ˈlænt(ə)n/ *noun* **1** lamp with transparent case protecting flame etc. **2** glazed structure on top of dome or room. **3** light-chamber of lighthouse. □ **lantern jaws** long thin jaws.

lanyard /ˈlænjəd/ *noun* **1** cord round neck or shoulder for holding knife etc. **2** *Nautical* short rope.

lap¹ *noun* **1** front of sitting person's body from waist to knees. **2** clothing covering this. □ **lapdog** small pet dog. **laptop** (microcomputer) suitable for use while travelling.

■ **1** knees, thighs.

lap² *noun* **1** one circuit of racetrack etc. **2** section of journey etc. **3** amount of overlap. ● *verb* (**-pp-**) **1** overtake (competitor in race who is a lap behind). **2** (often + *about, around*) fold or wrap (garment etc.).

■ *noun* **1** circle, circuit, course, orbit, revolution.

lap³ *verb* (**-pp-**) **1** (esp. of animal) drink by scooping with tongue. **2** (usually + *up, down*) drink greedily. **3** (usually + *up*) receive (gossip, praise, etc.) eagerly. **4** (of waves etc.) ripple. **5** make

lapping sound against (shore). ● *noun* act or sound of lapping.

■ *verb* **1, 2** see DRINK *verb* 1.

lapel /ləˈpel/ *noun* part of coat-front folded back.

lapidary /ˈlæpɪdərɪ/ *adjective* **1** concerned with stones. **2** engraved on stone. **3** concise; well expressed. ● *noun* (*plural* **-ies**) cutter, polisher, or engraver of gems.

lapis lazuli /ˌlæpɪs ˈlæzjʊlɪ/ *noun* **1** bright blue gem. **2** its colour.

lapse /læps/ *noun* **1** slight error; slip of memory etc. **2** weak or careless decline into inferior state. **3** passage or interval of time. ● *verb* (**-sing**) **1** fail to maintain position or standard. **2** (+ *into*) fall back into (inferior or previous state). **3** (of right etc.) become invalid.

■ *noun* **1** blunder, error, failing, fault, flaw, mistake, omission, shortcoming, slip, *colloquial* slip-up, temporary failure, weakness. **2** backsliding, decline, relapse, slump. **3** break, gap, hiatus, hold-up, intermission, interruption, interval, lacuna, lull, pause. ● *verb* **1** decline, deteriorate, diminish, drop, fall, sink, slide, slip, slump, subside. **2** see RELAPSE *verb*. **3** become invalid, expire, finish, run out, stop, terminate.

lapwing /ˈlæpwɪŋ/ *noun* plover with shrill cry.

larceny /ˈlɑːsənɪ/ *noun* (*plural* **-ies**) theft of personal property. □ **larcenous** *adjective*.

larch *noun* **1** deciduous coniferous tree with bright foliage. **2** its wood.

lard *noun* pig fat used in cooking etc. ● *verb* **1** insert strips of bacon in (meat etc.) before cooking. **2** (+ *with*) embellish (talk etc.) with (strange terms etc.).

larder *noun* room or cupboard for storing food.

lardy-cake *noun* cake made with lard, currants, etc.

large *adjective* **1** of relatively great size or extent. **2** of larger kind. **3** comprehensive. □ **at large 1** at liberty. **2** as a body or whole. **large as life** in person, esp. prominently. **large-scale** made or occurring on a large scale or in large amounts. □ **largeness** *noun*. **largish** *adjective*.

■ **1, 2** above average, abundant, ample, big, broad, bulky, burly, capacious, colossal, commodious, considerable, copious, elephantine, enormous, extensive, fat, formidable, gargantuan, generous, giant, gigantic, grand, great, heavy, hefty, high, huge, *colloquial* hulking, immense, immeasurable, impressive, incalculable, infinite, *colloquial* jumbo, king-size, largish, lofty, long, mammoth, massive, mighty, monstrous, monumental, mountainous, outsize, overgrown, oversized, prodigious, roomy, sizeable, spacious, substantial, swingeing (*increase*), tall, thick, *colloquial* thumping, *colloquial* tidy (*sum*), titanic, towering, *colloquial* tremendous, vast, voluminous, weighty, *colloquial* whacking, *colloquial* whopping, wide.

largely *adverb* to a great extent.

largesse /lɑːˈʒes/ *noun* (also **largess**) money or gifts freely given.

largo /'lɑːgəʊ/ *Music adverb & adjective* in slow time and dignified style. ● *noun* (*plural* **-s**) largo movement or passage.

lariat /'lærɪət/ *noun* **1** lasso. **2** tethering-rope.

lark[1] *noun* small bird with tuneful song, esp. skylark.

lark[2] *colloquial noun* **1** frolic; amusing incident. **2** type of activity. ● *verb* (+ *about, around*) play tricks.

larkspur *noun* plant with spur-shaped calyx.

larva /'lɑːvə/ *noun* (*plural* **-vae** /-viː/) insect in stage between egg and pupa. □ **larval** *adjective*.

■ caterpillar, grub, maggot.

laryngeal /lə'rɪndʒɪəl/ *adjective* of the larynx.

laryngitis /lærɪn'dʒaɪtɪs/ *noun* inflammation of larynx.

larynx /'lærɪŋks/ *noun* (*plural* **larynges** /lə'rɪndʒiːz/ or **-xes**) cavity in throat holding vocal cords.

lasagne /lə'sænjə/ *noun* pasta sheets.

lascivious /lə'sɪvɪəs/ *adjective* lustful. □ **lasciviously** *adverb*. **lasciviousness** *noun*.

laser /'leɪzə/ *noun* device producing intense beam of special kind of light. □ **laser printer** printing machine using laser to produce image.

lash *verb* **1** make sudden whiplike movement. **2** beat with whip. **3** (often + *against, down*) (of rain etc.) beat, strike. **4** criticize harshly. **5** rouse, incite. **6** (often + *together, down*) fasten with rope etc. ● *noun* **1** sharp blow with whip etc. **2** flexible part of whip. **3** eyelash. □ **lash out 1** speak or hit out angrily. **2** *colloquial* spend money extravagantly.

■ *verb* **2** beat, birch, cane, flail, flog, scourge, strike, thrash, whip. **4** see CRITICIZE 1. ● *noun* **2** see WHIP *noun* 1.

lashings *plural noun* (often + *of*) *colloquial* plenty.

lass *noun esp. Scottish & Northern English* or *poetical* girl.

lassitude /'læsɪtjuːd/ *noun* **1** languor. **2** disinclination to exert oneself.

lasso /læ'suː/ *noun* (*plural* **-s** or **-es**) rope with running noose used esp. for catching cattle. ● *verb* (**-es, -ed**) catch with lasso.

last[1] /lɑːst/ *adjective* **1** after all others; coming at end. **2** most recent. **3** only remaining. ● *adverb* **1** after all others. **2** on most recent occasion. ● *noun* **1** last, last-mentioned, or most recent person or thing. **2** last mention, sight, etc. **3** end; death. □ **at (long) last** in the end; after much delay. **the last straw** slight addition to task etc. making it unbearable.

■ *adjective* **1** closing, concluding, final, furthest, hindmost, rearmost, terminal, terminating, ultimate. **2** latest, most recent, newest. **3** final, ultimate.

last[2] /lɑːst/ *verb* remain unexhausted, adequate, or alive for specified or long time. □ **last out** be sufficient for whole of given period.

■ carry on, continue, endure, hold, hold out, keep on, linger, live, persist, remain, stay, survive, wear well.

last[3] /lɑːst/ *noun* shoemaker's model for shaping shoe etc. □ **stick to one's last** keep to what one understands.

lasting *adjective* **1** permanent. **2** durable.

■ **1** see PERMANENT.

lastly *adverb* finally.

lat. *abbreviation* latitude.

latch *noun* **1** bar with catch as fastening of gate etc. **2** spring-lock as fastening of outer door. ● *verb* fasten with latch. □ **latchkey** key of outer door. **latch on to** *colloquial* **1** attach oneself to. **2** understand.

late *adjective* **1** after due or usual time. **2** far on in day, night, period, etc. **3** flowering, ripening, etc. towards end of season. **4** no longer alive or having specified status. **5** of recent date. ● *adverb* **1** after due or usual time. **2** far on in time. **3** at or till late hour. **4** at late stage of development. **5** formerly but not now. □ **late in the day** at late stage of proceedings etc. **the latest** the most recent news, fashion, etc. □ **lateness** *noun*.

■ *adjective* **1** behindhand, belated, delayed, dilatory, overdue, slow, tardy, unpunctual. **4** dead, *formal* deceased, departed, ex-, former, past, previous. **5** current, last, new, recent, up-to-date.

lateen sail /lə'tiːn/ *noun* triangular sail on long yard at angle of 45° to mast.

lately *adverb* not long ago; recently.

latent /'leɪt(ə)nt/ *adjective* **1** existing but not developed or manifest. **2** concealed, dormant. □ **latency** *noun*.

■ dormant, hidden, invisible, potential, undeveloped, undiscovered.

lateral /'lætər(ə)l/ *adjective* of, at, towards, or from side(s). ● *noun* lateral shoot or branch. □ **lateral thinking** method of solving problems by indirect or illogical methods. □ **laterally** *adverb*.

latex /'leɪteks/ *noun* **1** milky fluid of esp. rubber tree. **2** synthetic substance like this.

lath /lɑːθ/ *noun* thin flat strip of wood.

lathe /leɪð/ *noun* machine for shaping wood, metal, etc. by rotating article against cutting tools.

lather /'lɑːðə/ *noun* **1** froth made by agitating soap etc. and water. **2** frothy sweat. **3** state of agitation. ● *verb* **1** (of soap) form lather. **2** cover with lather. **3** *colloquial* thrash.

Latin /'lætɪn/ *noun* language of ancient Rome. ● *adjective* **1** of or in Latin. **2** of countries or peoples speaking languages developed from Latin. **3** of RC Church. □ **Latin America** parts of Central and S. America where Spanish or Portuguese is main language.

Latinate /'lætɪneɪt/ *adjective* having character of Latin.

latitude /'lætɪtjuːd/ *noun* **1** angular distance N. or S. of equator. **2** (usually in *plural*), regions,

climes. 3 freedom from restriction in action or opinion.

■ **3** *colloquial* elbow room, freedom, leeway, liberty, room, scope, space.

latrine /ləˈtriːn/ *noun* communal lavatory, esp. in camp.

latter /ˈlætə/ *adjective* **1** second-mentioned of two. **2** nearer the end. ● *noun* (**the latter**) the latter thing or person. □ **latter-day** modern, contemporary.

■ *adjective* **1** last, last-mentioned, second. **2** closing, concluding, later, recent.

latterly *adverb* **1** recently. **2** in latter part of life or period.

lattice /ˈlætɪs/ *noun* **1** (in full **lattice-work**) structure of crossed laths or bars with spaces between, used as fence, screen, etc. **2** arrangement resembling this. □ **lattice window** one with small panes set in lead. □ **latticed** *adjective*.

■ criss-cross, framework, grid, mesh, trellis.

Latvian /ˈlætvɪən/ *noun* native, national, or language of Latvia. ● *adjective* of Latvia.

laud /lɔːd/ *verb* praise, extol.

laudable *adjective* praiseworthy. □ **laudably** *adverb*.

laudanum /ˈlɔːdənəm/ *noun* solution prepared from opium.

laudatory /ˈlɔːdətərɪ/ *adjective* praising.

laugh /lɑːf/ *verb* **1** make sounds etc. usual in expressing amusement, scorn, etc. **2** express by laughing. **3** (+ *at*) make fun of, ridicule. ● *noun* **1** sound or act of laughing. **2** *colloquial* comical person or thing. □ **laugh off** shrug off (embarrassment etc.) by joking.

■ *verb* **1** burst into laughter, chortle, chuckle, *colloquial* fall about, giggle, guffaw, roar with laughter, snicker, snigger, split one's sides, titter. **3** (*laugh at*) see RIDICULE *verb*.

laughable *adjective* **1** amusing. **2** ridiculous. □ **laughably** *adverb*.

■ **1** see FUNNY 1. **2** absurd, derisory, ludicrous, preposterous, ridiculous.

laughing *noun* laughter. □ **laughing gas** nitrous oxide as anaesthetic. **laughing jackass** kookaburra. **laughing stock** object of general derision. □ **laughingly** *adverb*.

■ □ **laughing stock** butt, figure of fun.

laughter /ˈlɑːftə/ *noun* act or sound of laughing.

■ chuckling, giggling, guffawing, hilarity, *colloquial* hysterics, laughing, laughs, merriment, mirth, snickering, sniggering, tittering.

launch[1] /lɔːntʃ/ *verb* **1** set (vessel) afloat. **2** hurl or send forth (rocket etc.). **3** start or set in motion (enterprise, person, etc.). **4** formally introduce (new product) with publicity. **5** (+ *into*) make start on. **6** (+ *out*) make start on new enterprise. ● *noun* launching. □ **launch pad** platform with structure for launching rockets from.

■ *verb* **1** float, set afloat, set in motion. **2** blast off, catapult, dispatch, fire, propel, send off, set off, shoot. **3** begin, embark on, establish, float, found, inaugurate, initiate, open, organize, set in motion, set off, set up, start.

launch[2] /lɔːntʃ/ *noun* large motor boat.

launder /ˈlɔːndə/ *verb* **1** wash and iron etc. (clothes etc.). **2** *colloquial* transfer (money) to conceal its origin.

launderette /lɔːnˈdret/ *noun* (also **laundrette**) establishment with coin-operated washing machines and driers for public use.

laundress /ˈlɔːndrɪs/ *noun* woman who launders.

laundry /ˈlɔːndrɪ/ *noun* (*plural* **-ies**) **1** place where clothes etc. are laundered. **2** clothes etc. that need to be or have been laundered.

laurel /ˈlɒr(ə)l/ *noun* **1** any of various kinds of shrub with dark green glossy leaves. **2** (in *singular* or *plural*) wreath of bay-leaves as emblem of victory or poetic merit. □ **look to one's laurels** beware of losing one's pre-eminence. **rest on one's laurels** stop seeking further success.

lava /ˈlɑːvə/ *noun* matter flowing from volcano and solidifying as it cools.

lavatorial /lævəˈtɔːrɪəl/ *adjective* **1** of or like lavatories. **2** (esp. of humour) relating to excretion.

lavatory /ˈlævətərɪ/ *noun* (*plural* **-ies**) **1** receptacle for urine and faeces, usually with means of disposal. **2** room etc. containing this.

■ **1** bowl, *colloquial* loo, pan, *colloquial* potty, privy, toilet, urinal, water-closet, WC. **2** *US* bathroom, *euphemistic* cloakroom, convenience, Gents, Ladies, latrine, *colloquial* loo, privy, public convenience, toilet, urinal, water-closet, WC.

lave *verb* (**-ving**) *literary* **1** wash, bathe. **2** wash against; flow along.

lavender /ˈlævɪndə/ *noun* **1** evergreen fragrant-flowered shrub. **2** its dried flowers used to scent linen. **3** pale purplish colour. □ **lavender-water** light perfume.

laver /ˈleɪvə/ *noun* kind of edible seaweed.

lavish /ˈlævɪʃ/ *adjective* **1** profuse; abundant. **2** generous. **3** excessive. ● *verb* (often + *on*) bestow or spend (money, praise, etc.) abundantly. □ **lavishly** *adverb*. **lavishness** *noun*.

■ *adjective* **1** abundant, copious, exuberant, liberal, luxuriant, luxurious, opulent, plentiful, profuse, sumptuous. **2** bountiful, free, generous, liberal, munificent, unselfish, unsparing, unstinting. **3** excessive, extravagant, improvident, prodigal, self-indulgent, wasteful.

law *noun* **1** rule or set of rules established in a community, demanding or prohibiting certain actions. **2** such rules as social system or branch of study; science or philosophy of law. **3** binding force. **4** (**the law**) legal profession. **5** (**the law**) *colloquial* police. **6** law courts; legal remedy. **7** statement of regularity of natural occurrences. □ **law-abiding** obedient to the laws. **law court** court of law. **Law Lord** member of House of Lords qualified to perform its legal work. **lawsuit**

bringing of claim etc. before law court. **lay down the law** give dogmatic opinions. **take the law into one's own hands** get one's rights without help of the law.

■ **1** (*a country's laws*) act, by-law, commandment, decree, directive, edict, injunction, mandate, measure, order, ordinance, pronouncement, regulation, rule, statute; (*laws of decency*) code, convention, practice. **6** justice, litigation. **7** axiom, formula, postulate, principle, proposition, theory. □ **law-abiding** compliant, decent, disciplined, good, honest, obedient, orderly, peaceable, peaceful, respectable, well behaved. **lay down the law** see DICTATE *verb* 2.

lawbreaker /ˈlɔːbreɪkə/ *noun* person who breaks the law. □ **lawbreaking** *noun & adjective*.

lawful *adjective* permitted, appointed, or recognized by law; not illegal. □ **lawfully** *adverb*. **lawfulness** *noun*.

■ allowable, allowed, authorized, constitutional, just, justifiable, legal, legitimate, permissible, permitted, prescribed, proper, recognized, regular, right, rightful, valid.

lawless *adjective* **1** having no laws. **2** disregarding laws; uncontrolled. □ **lawlessness** *noun*.

■ **1** anarchic, chaotic, disorderly, ungoverned, unregulated. **2** badly behaved, disobedient, disorderly, insubordinate, mutinous, rebellious, riotous, rowdy, seditious, turbulent, uncontrolled, undisciplined, ungoverned, unregulated, unrestrained, unruly, wicked, wild. □ **lawlessness** anarchy, chaos, disobedience, disorder, mob law, mob rule, rebellion, rioting.

lawmaker /ˈlɔːmeɪkə/ *noun* person who makes laws or takes part in making laws. □ **law-making** *adjective & noun*.

lawn[1] *noun* piece of close-mown grass in garden etc. □ **lawnmower** machine for cutting lawns. **lawn tennis** tennis played with soft ball on grass or hard court.

lawn[2] *noun* kind of fine linen or cotton.

lawyer /ˈlɔɪə/ *noun* person practising law, esp. solicitor.

■ advocate, barrister, counsel, legal representative, member of the Bar, solicitor.

lax *adjective* **1** lacking care or precision. **2** not strict. **3** loose, relaxed. □ **laxity** *noun*. **laxly** *adverb*. **laxness** *noun*.

■ **1** careless, casual, neglectful, negligent, relaxed, remiss, slack, slipshod, unreliable, vague. **2** casual, easygoing, indulgent, lenient, permissive, relaxed, slack. **3** flexible, loose, relaxed, slack.

laxative /ˈlæksətɪv/ *adjective* helping evacuation of bowels. ● *noun* laxative medicine.

■ *noun* aperient, enema, purgative.

lay[1] *verb* (*past & past participle* **laid**) **1** place on surface, esp. horizontally. **2** put or bring into required position or state. **3** make by laying. **4** (of bird) produce (egg). **5** cause to subside or lie flat. **6** (usually + *on*) attribute (blame etc.). **7** make ready (trap, plan). **8** prepare (table) for meal. **9** put fuel ready to light (fire). **10** put down as bet. ● *noun* way, position, or direction in which something lies. □ **lay bare** expose, reveal. **lay by** store; set aside. **lay-by** extra strip beside road where vehicles may park. **lay claim to** claim as one's own. **lay down 1** relinquish. **2** make (rule). **3** store (wine) in cellar. **4** sacrifice (one's life). **lay hands on** seize. **lay hold of** seize. **lay in** provide oneself with stock of. **lay into** *colloquial* attack violently with blows or verbally. **lay it on thick or with a trowel** *colloquial* flatter, exaggerate grossly. **lay low** overthrow; kill. **lay off 1** discharge (workers) temporarily. **2** *colloquial* desist. **lay on 1** provide. **2** spread on. **lay one's hands on** locate, acquire. **lay out 1** spread. **2** expose to view. **3** prepare (body) for burial. **4** *colloquial* knock unconscious. **5** expend (money). **layout** way in which land, building, printed matter, etc., is arranged or set out. **lay to rest** bury. **lay up 1** store, save (money). **2** (as **laid up** *adjective*) confined to bed or the house. **lay waste** ravage, destroy.

USAGE It is incorrect in standard English to use *lay* to mean 'lie', as in *She was laying on the floor*.

■ *verb* **1, 2** arrange, deposit, leave, place, position, put down, rest, set down, set out, spread. **3** build, construct, establish. **6** ascribe, assign, attribute, charge, impose. **7** concoct, create, design, organize, plan, set up. **10** see GAMBLE *verb* 2. □ **lay bare** see REVEAL 1. **lay by, lay in** see STORE *verb* 1. **lay into** see ATTACK *verb* 1–2. **lay low** see DEFEAT *verb* 1. **lay off 1** see DISMISS 2. **2** see CEASE. **lay to rest** see BURY 1. **lay up 2** see STORE *verb* 1. **lay waste** see DESTROY 1.

lay[2] *adjective* **1** not ordained into the clergy. **2** not professionally qualified. **3** of or done by such people. □ **layman, laywoman** layperson. **lay reader** layperson licensed to conduct some religious services.

■ □ **layman, laywoman** see LAYPERSON.

lay[3] *noun* **1** short poem meant to be sung. **2** song.

lay[4] *past* of LIE[1].

layabout /ˈleɪəbaʊt/ *noun* habitual idler.

layer *noun* **1** thickness of matter, esp. one of several, covering surface. **2** hen that lays eggs. ● *verb* **1** arrange in layers. **2** propagate (plant) by fastening shoot down to take root. □ **layered** *adjective*.

■ *noun* **1** coat, coating, covering, film, sheet, skin, seam, stratum, substratum, surface, thickness. □ **layered** laminated, sandwiched, stratified.

layette /leɪˈet/ *noun* clothes etc. prepared for newborn child.

lay figure *noun* **1** artist's jointed wooden model of human figure. **2** unrealistic character in novel etc.

layperson /ˈleɪpɜːs(ə)n/ *noun* (*plural* **-s** or **laypeople**) **1** person not in holy orders. **2** person without professional or special knowledge.

■ **1** layman, laywoman, member of the congregation, parishioner, unordained person. **2** amateur, layman, laywoman, non-specialist, untrained person.

laze *verb* (**-zing**) spend time idly. ● *noun* spell of lazing.

■ *verb* be lazy, do nothing, idle, lie about, loaf, lounge, relax, sit about, *colloquial* unwind.

lazy *adjective* (**-ier**, **-iest**) **1** disinclined to work; doing little work. **2** of or inducing idleness. □ **lazybones** *colloquial* lazy person. □ **lazily** *adverb*. **laziness** *noun*.

■ **1** easygoing, idle, inactive, indolent, languid, lethargic, listless, shiftless, *slang* skiving, slack, slothful, slow, sluggish, torpid, unenterprising, work-shy. **2** peaceful, quiet, relaxing. □ **lazybones** see SLACKER. □ **laziness** idleness, inactivity, indolence, lethargy, loafing, lounging about, shiftlessness, slackness, sloth, slowness, sluggishness, torpor.

lb *abbreviation* pound(s) weight.

USAGE It is a common mistake to write *lbs* as an abbreviation for *pounds*. *28 lb* is correct.

l.b.w. *abbreviation* leg before wicket.

l.c. *abbreviation* **1** loc. cit. **2** lower case.

LCD *abbreviation* liquid crystal display.

L/Cpl *abbreviation* Lance-Corporal.

LEA *abbreviation* Local Education Authority.

lea *noun poetical* meadow, field.

leach *verb* **1** make (liquid) percolate through some material. **2** subject (bark, ore, ash, soil) to this. **3** (usually + *away*, *out*) remove (soluble matter) or be removed in this way.

lead[1] /liːd/ *verb* (*past & past participle* **led**) **1** conduct, esp. by going in front. **2** direct actions or opinions of. **3** (often + *to*) guide by persuasion. **4** provide access to. **5** pass or spend (life etc.). **6** have first place in. **7** go or be first. **8** play (card) as first player in trick. **9** (+ *to*) result in. **10** (+ *with*) (of newspapers or broadcast) have as main story. ● *noun* **1** guidance; example. **2** leader's place. **3** amount by which competitor is ahead of others. **4** clue. **5** strap etc. for leading dog etc. **6** *Electricity* conductor carrying current to place of use. **7** chief part in play etc. **8** *Cards* act or right of playing first. □ **lead by the nose** make (person) do all one wishes them to. **lead-in** introduction, opening. **lead off** begin. **lead on** entice dishonestly. **lead up the garden path** *colloquial* mislead. **lead up to 1** form preparation for. **2** direct conversation towards.

■ *verb* **1** conduct, escort, guide, pilot, show the way, steer, usher. **2** be in charge of, captain, command, direct, govern, head, manage, preside over, rule, skipper, superintend, supervise. **3** draw, guide, influence, persuade, prompt. **6** beat, defeat, excel, outdo, outstrip, precede, surpass, *literary* vanquish. **7** be first, be in front, be in the lead, go first. ● *noun* **1** direction, example, guidance, leadership, model, pattern, precedent. **2** first place, front, spearhead, van, vanguard. **4** clue, hint, line,

tip, tip-off. **5** chain, leash, strap. **6** cable, flex, wire. **7** chief part, hero, heroine, principal, protagonist, starring role, title role. □ **lead off** see BEGIN 3.

lead[2] /led/ *noun* **1** heavy soft grey metal. **2** graphite used in pencils. **3** lump of lead used in sounding. **4** (in *plural*) strips of lead covering roof; pieces of lead-covered roof. **5** blank space between lines of print. ● *verb* cover, frame, or space with lead(s). □ **lead-free** (of petrol) without added lead compounds.

leaded /'ledɪd/ *adjective* **1** (of petrol) with added lead compounds. **2** (of window pane) framed with lead.

leaden /'led(ə)n/ *adjective* **1** of or like lead. **2** heavy, slow. **3** lead-coloured.

leader /'liːdə/ *noun* **1** person or thing that leads. **2** leading performer in orchestra, quartet, etc. **3** leading article. □ **leadership** *noun*.

■ **1** ayatollah, *colloquial* boss, captain, chief, chieftain, commander, conductor, courier, demagogue, director, figurehead, guide, head, patriarch, premier, prime minister, principal, ringleader, ruler, superior, supremo. **3** editorial, leading article.

leading /'liːdɪŋ/ *adjective* chief; most important. □ **leading aircraftman** one ranking just below NCO in RAF. **leading article** newspaper article giving editorial opinion. **leading light** prominent influential person. **leading note** *Music* seventh note of ascending scale. **leading question** one prompting the answer wanted.

USAGE *Leading question* does not mean a 'principal' or 'loaded' or 'searching' question.

■ see CHIEF *adjective* 1–2, INFLUENTIAL.

leaf *noun* (*plural* **leaves**) **1** flat usually green part of plant growing usually on stem. **2** foliage. **3** single thickness of paper, esp. in book. **4** very thin sheet of metal etc. **5** hinged part, extra section, or flap of table etc. ● *verb* **1** (of plants etc.) begin to grow leaves. **2** (+ *through*) turn over pages of (book etc.). □ **leaf-mould** soil composed chiefly of decaying leaves. □ **leafage** *noun*. **leafless** *adjective*. **leafy** *adjective* (**-ier**, **-iest**).

■ *noun* **2** foliage, greenery. **3** folio, page, sheet.

leaflet /'liːflɪt/ *noun* **1** sheet of paper, pamphlet, etc., giving information. **2** young leaf.

■ **1** advertisement, bill, booklet, brochure, circular, flyer, folder, handout, notice, pamphlet.

league[1] /liːg/ *noun* **1** people, countries, etc., joining together for particular purpose. **2** group of sports clubs who contend for championship. **3** class of contestants. ● *verb* (**-gues**, **-gued**, **-guing**) (often + *together*) join in league. □ **in league** allied, conspiring. **league table** list in order of success.

■ *noun* **1, 2** alliance, association, coalition, confederation, federation, fraternity, group, guild, society, union. □ **in league** (*be in league*) see CONSPIRE.

league[2] /liːg/ *noun archaic* measure of travelling distance, usually about 3 miles.

leak *noun* **1** hole through which liquid etc. passes accidentally in or out. **2** liquid etc. thus passing through. **3** similar escape of electric charge. **4** disclosure of secret information. ● *verb* **1** (let) pass out or in through leak. **2** disclose (secret). **3** (often + *out*) become known. □ **leaky** *adjective* (**-ier, -iest**).

■ *noun* **1** aperture, break, chink, crack, crevice, cut, fissure, flaw, hole, opening, perforation, puncture, rent, split, tear. **2** discharge, drip, emission, escape, exudation, leakage, oozing, seepage, trickle. **4** disclosure, revelation. ● *verb* **1** discharge, drip, escape, exude, ooze, percolate, seep, spill, trickle. **2** disclose, divulge, give away, let out, let slip, make known, pass on, reveal, *colloquial* spill the beans about. □ **leaky** cracked, dripping, holey, perforated, punctured.

leakage *noun* action or result of leaking.

lean[1] *verb* (*past & past participle* **leaned** or **leant** /lent/) **1** (often + *across, back, over,* etc.) be or place in sloping position. **2** (usually + *against, on*) rest for support against. **3** (usually + *on, upon*) rely, depend. **4** (usually + *to, towards*) be inclined or partial. ● *noun* inclination, slope. □ **lean on** *colloquial* put pressure on (person) to act in certain way. **lean-to** building with roof resting against larger building or wall.

■ *verb* **1** bank, careen, heel over, incline, keel over, list, slant, slope, tilt, tip. **2** loll, prop oneself up, recline, rest, support oneself.

lean[2] *adjective* **1** (of person etc.) having no superfluous fat. **2** (of meat) containing little fat. **3** meagre. ● *noun* lean part of meat. □ **lean years** time of scarcity. □ **leanness** *noun*.

■ *adjective* **1** angular, bony, emaciated, gangling, gaunt, hungry-looking, lanky, rangy, scraggy, scrawny, skinny, slender, slim, spare, thin, weedy, wiry.

leaning *noun* tendency or inclination; partiality.

■ bent, bias, favouritism, inclination, instinct, liking, partiality, penchant, predilection, preference, propensity, readiness, taste, tendency, trend.

leap *verb* (*past & past participle* **leaped** or **leapt** /lept/) **1** jump, spring forcefully. **2** jump across. **3** (+ *on*) attack. ● *noun* forceful jump. □ **by leaps and bounds** with very rapid progress. **leapfrog** ● *noun* game in which player vaults with parted legs over another bending down. ● *verb* **1** perform such a vault. **2** vault over. **leap year** year with 29 Feb. as extra day.

■ *verb* **1** bound, caper, cavort, dance, frisk, frolic, gambol, hop, jump, prance, romp, skip, spring, vault. **2** bound, clear (*a fence*), hop over, hurdle, jump, leapfrog, vault. **3** (*leap on*) ambush, attack, jump on, pounce on.

learn /lɜːn/ *verb* (*past & past participle* **learned** /lɜːnt, lɜːnd/ or **learnt**) **1** get knowledge of or skill in by study, experience, or being taught. **2** commit to memory. **3** (usually + *of, about*) be told about; find out.

■ **1** acquire, assimilate, become proficient in, be taught, *colloquial* catch on, gain understanding of, grasp, master, *slang* mug up, pick up, study, *colloquial* swot up. **2** commit to memory, memorize, remember. **3** (*learn of*) ascertain, become aware of, discover, find out, gather.

learned /ˈlɜːnɪd/ *adjective* **1** having much knowledge from studying. **2** showing or requiring learning.

■ **1** see EDUCATED (EDUCATE). **2** see ACADEMIC *adjective* 1.

learner *noun* **1** person learning; beginner. **2** (in full **learner driver**) person who is learning to drive but has not yet passed driving test.

■ **1** apprentice, beginner, cadet, initiate, novice, pupil, scholar, starter, student, trainee, tiro.

learning *noun* knowledge got by study.

■ culture, education, erudition, information, knowledge, lore, scholarship, wisdom.

lease /liːs/ *noun* contract by which owner of land or building allows another to use it for specified time, usually for rent. ● *verb* (**-sing**) grant or take on lease. □ **leasehold** holding of property by lease. **leaseholder** *noun*. **new lease of** (*US* **on**) **life** improved prospect of living, or of use after repair.

■ *noun* agreement, contract. ● *verb* charter, hire out, let, rent out, sublet.

leash *noun* strap for holding dog(s). ● *verb* **1** put leash on. **2** restrain. □ **straining at the leash** eager to begin.

least *adjective* smallest, slightest. ● *noun* least amount. ● *adverb* in the least degree. □ **at least** at any rate. **to say the least** putting the case moderately.

■ *adjective* fewest, lowest, minimum, poorest, slightest, smallest, tiniest.

leather /ˈleðə/ *noun* **1** material made from skin of animal by tanning etc. **2** piece of leather for cleaning esp. windows. **3** *slang* cricket ball; football. ● *verb* **1** beat, thrash. **2** cover or polish with leather. □ **leatherjacket** larva of crane-fly.

■ *noun* **1** chamois, hide, skin, suede. **2** chamois.

leatherette /leðəˈret/ *noun* imitation leather.

leathery *adjective* **1** like leather. **2** tough.

leave[1] *verb* (**-ving**; *past & past participle* **left**) **1** go away (from). **2** cause or allow to remain; depart without taking. **3** cease to reside at, belong to, work for, etc. **4** abandon. **5** (usually + *to*) commit to another person. **6** bequeath. **7** deposit or entrust (object, message, etc.) to be dealt with in one's absence. **8** not consume or deal with. □ **leave off 1** come to or make an end. **2** stop. **leave out** omit.

■ **1** *colloquial* be off, check out, decamp, depart, disappear, *slang* do a bunk, escape, get away, get out, go away, go out, pull out, *colloquial* push off, retire, retreat, run away, say goodbye, set off, take off, take one's leave, withdraw. **2** allow to stay, deposit, forget, let alone, let be, lose, mislay, place, position, put down, set down. **3** *colloquial* chuck in, *colloquial* drop out of, give up, quit, relinquish, renounce, resign from, retire from, walk out of, wash one's hands of. **4** abandon, desert, evacuate, forsake, vacate. **5** assign, *formal* cede, commit, consign, entrust, refer, relinquish. **6** bequeath, hand down, will. **7** deposit, entrust, lodge. □ **leave off 2** see STOP *verb* **1**. **leave out** see OMIT **1**.

leave² *noun* **1** permission. **2** (in full **leave of absence**) permission to be absent from duty. **3** period for which this lasts. □ **leave-taking** act of saying goodbye. **on leave** legitimately absent from duty. **take one's leave (of)** say goodbye (to).
- **1** authorization, consent, dispensation, licence, permission, sanction. **2, 3** free time, furlough, holiday, recess, sabbatical, time off, vacation.

leaven /ˈlev(ə)n/ *noun* **1** substance used to make dough ferment and rise. **2** transforming influence. ● *verb* **1** ferment (dough) with leaven. **2** permeate, transform.

leavings *plural noun* what is left.

Lebanese /lebəˈniːz/ *adjective* of Lebanon. ● *noun* (*plural* same) native or inhabitant of Lebanon.

lecher /ˈletʃə/ *noun* lecherous man.

lecherous *adjective* lustful. □ **lecherously** *adverb*. **lechery** *noun*.

lectern /ˈlekt(ə)n/ *noun* **1** stand for holding Bible etc. in church. **2** similar stand for lecturer etc.

lecture /ˈlektʃə/ *noun* **1** talk giving information to class etc. **2** admonition, reprimand. ● *verb* (**-ring**) **1** (often + *on*) deliver lecture(s). **2** admonish, reprimand.
- *noun* **1** address, discourse, disquisition, lesson, paper, sermon, speech, talk. **2** admonition, diatribe, *colloquial* dressing down, harangue, reprimand, *formal* reproof, sermon, *colloquial* talking-to, *colloquial* telling-off. ● *verb* **1** discourse, give a lecture, harangue, hold forth, pontificate, preach, sermonize, speak, talk formally, teach. **2** see REPRIMAND *verb*.

lecturer *noun* person who lectures, esp. as teacher in higher education.
- don, fellow, instructor, professor, speaker, teacher.

lectureship *noun* university post as lecturer.

led *past & past participle* of LEAD¹.

ledge *noun* narrow shelf or projection from vertical surface.
- mantel, overhang, projection, ridge, shelf, sill, step.

ledger /ˈledʒə/ *noun* book in which firm's accounts are kept.

lee *noun* **1** shelter given by neighbouring object. **2** side of thing away from the wind. □ **leeway 1** allowable deviation. **2** drift of ship to leeward.

leech *noun* **1** bloodsucking worm formerly used medicinally for bleeding. **2** person who sponges on others.

leek *noun* vegetable of onion family with long cylindrical white bulb.

leer *verb* look slyly, lasciviously, or maliciously. ● *noun* leering look.

leery *adjective* (**-ier, -iest**) *slang* **1** knowing, sly. **2** (usually + *of*) wary.

lees /liːz/ *plural noun* **1** sediment of wine etc. **2** dregs.

leeward /ˈliːwəd, *Nautical* ˈluːəd/ *adjective & adverb* on or towards sheltered side. ● *noun* this direction.

left¹ *adjective* **1** on or towards west side of person or thing facing north. **2** (also **Left**) *Politics* of the Left. ● *adverb* on or to left side. ● *noun* **1** left part, region, or direction. **2** *Boxing* left hand. **3** *Boxing* blow with this. **4** (often **Left**) *Politics* group favouring socialism; radicals collectively. □ **left-hand** on left side. **left-handed 1** naturally using left hand for writing etc. **2** made by or for left hand. **3** turning to left. **4** (of screw) turned anticlockwise to tighten. **5** awkward, clumsy. **6** (of compliment etc.) ambiguous. **left-handedness** *noun*. **left-hander** left-handed person or blow. **left wing 1** more radical section of political party. **2** left side of army, football team, etc. **left-wing** socialist, radical. **left-winger** member of left wing. □ **leftward** *adjective & adverb*. **leftwards** *adverb*.
- *adjective* **2** communist, Labour, left-wing, liberal, Marxist, progressive, radical, *colloquial* red, revolutionary, socialist. ● *noun* **1** left hand, port = *left side facing bow of ship*. **4** communists, Labour, left wing, left-wingers, liberals, Marxists, progressives, radicals, *colloquial* reds, revolutionaries, socialists.

left² *past & past participle* of LEAVE¹.

leftover /ˈleftəʊvə/ *noun* (usually in *plural*) item (esp. of food) remaining after rest has been used or eaten. ● *adjective* remaining over, surplus.

leg *noun* **1** each of limbs on which person or animal walks and stands. **2** leg of animal as food. **3** part of garment covering leg. **4** support of chair, table, etc. **5** section of journey, race, competition, etc. **6** *Cricket* half of field behind batsman's back. □ **leg before wicket** *Cricket* (of batsman) declared out for illegal obstruction of ball that would have hit wicket. **leg it** (**-gg-**) *colloquial* walk or run hard. **leg-pull** *colloquial* hoax. **leg warmer** either of pair of tubular knitted garments covering leg from ankle to thigh. □ **legged** *adjective*.
- **1** limb, member. **4** brace, column, pillar, prop, support, upright. **5** lap, length, part, section, stage, stretch.

legacy /ˈlegəsɪ/ *noun* (*plural* **-ies**) **1** gift left by will. **2** anything handed down by predecessor.
- **1** bequest, endowment, estate, inheritance.

legal /ˈliːg(ə)l/ *adjective* **1** of, based on, or concerned with law. **2** appointed, required, or permitted by law. □ **legal aid** state help with cost of legal advice. **legal tender** currency that cannot legally be refused in payment of debt. □ **legality** /lɪˈɡælɪtɪ/ *noun*. **legally** *adverb*.

■ **1** forensic, judicial, judiciary. **2** above board, acceptable, admissible, allowable, allowed, authorized, constitutional, just, lawful, legalized, legitimate, licensed, *formal* licit, permitted, permissible, proper, regular, right, rightful, valid.

legalize /ˈliːɡəlaɪz/ *verb* (also **-ise**) (**-zing** or **-sing**) **1** make lawful. **2** bring into harmony with law. □ **legalization** *noun*.

■ allow, authorize, legitimate, legitimize, license, normalize, permit, regularize, validate.

legate /ˈlɛɡət/ *noun* papal ambassador.

legatee /lɛɡəˈtiː/ *noun* recipient of legacy.

legation /lɪˈɡeɪʃ(ə)n/ *noun* **1** diplomatic minister and his or her staff. **2** this minister's official residence.

legato /lɪˈɡɑːtəʊ/ *Music adverb & adjective* in smooth flowing manner. ● *noun* (*plural* **-s**) legato passage.

legend /ˈlɛdʒ(ə)nd/ *noun* **1** traditional story, myth. **2** *colloquial* famous or remarkable person or event. **3** inscription. **4** explanation on map etc. of symbols used.

■ **1** epic, folk-tale, myth, saga, story, tradition.

legendary *adjective* **1** existing in legend. **2** *colloquial* remarkable, famous.

■ **1** apocryphal, epic, fabled, fabulous, fictional, fictitious, imaginary, invented, made up, mythical, non-existent, traditional. **2** see FAMOUS 1.

legerdemain /lɛdʒədəˈmeɪn/ *noun* **1** sleight of hand. **2** trickery, sophistry.

leger line /ˈlɛdʒə/ *noun Music* short line added for notes above or below range of staff.

legging *noun* (usually in *plural*) **1** close-fitting trousers for women or children. **2** outer covering of leather etc. for lower leg.

leggy *adjective* (**-ier**, **-iest**) **1** long-legged. **2** long-stemmed and weak.

legible /ˈlɛdʒɪb(ə)l/ *adjective* easily read. □ **legibility** *noun*. **legibly** *adverb*.

■ clear, decipherable, distinct, intelligible, neat, plain, readable, understandable.

legion /ˈliːdʒ(ə)n/ *noun* **1** division of 3,000–6,000 men in ancient Roman army. **2** other large organized body. ● *adjective* great in number.

legionary *adjective* of legions. ● *noun* (*plural* **-ies**) member of legion.

legionnaire /liːdʒəˈneə/ *noun* member of foreign legion. □ **legionnaires' disease** form of bacterial pneumonia.

legislate /ˈlɛdʒɪsleɪt/ *verb* (**-ting**) make laws. □ **legislator** *noun*.

legislation *noun* **1** making laws. **2** laws made.

legislative /ˈlɛdʒɪslətɪv/ *adjective* of or empowered to make legislation.

legislature /ˈlɛdʒɪsleɪtʃə/ *noun* legislative body of a state.

legitimate /lɪˈdʒɪtɪmət/ *adjective* **1** (of child)

born of parents married to one another. **2** lawful, proper, regular. **3** logically admissible. ● *verb* /lɪˈdʒɪtɪmeɪt/ **1** make lawful. **2** justify. □ **legitimacy** *noun*. **legitimately** *adverb*.

■ *adjective* **2** authentic, ethical, just, genuine, lawful, legal, *formal* licit, moral, proper, real, regular, true. **3** justifiable, logical, reasonable, right, valid. ● *verb* **1** see LEGALIZE.

legitimize /lɪˈdʒɪtɪmaɪz/ *verb* (also **-ise**) (**-zing** or **-sing**) **1** make legitimate. **2** serve as justification for. □ **legitimization** *noun*.

legume /ˈlɛɡjuːm/ *noun* **1** leguminous plant. **2** edible part of this.

leguminous /lɪˈɡjuːmməs/ *adjective* of the family of plants with seeds in pods, e.g. peas and beans.

lei /ˈleɪ/ *noun* Polynesian garland of flowers.

leisure /ˈlɛʒə/ *noun* free time; time at one's own disposal. □ **at leisure** not occupied, in an unhurried way. **at one's leisure** when one has time. **leisure centre** public building with sports facilities etc. **leisurewear** informal clothes, esp. sportswear.

■ breathing-space, ease, holiday, liberty, opportunity, quiet, recreation, relaxation, relief, repose, respite, rest, spare time, time off.

leisured *adjective* having ample leisure.

leisurely *adjective* relaxed, unhurried. ● *adverb* without hurry.

■ *adjective* easy, gentle, lingering, peaceful, relaxed, relaxing, restful, slow, unhurried.

leitmotif /ˈlaɪtməʊtiːf/ *noun* (also **leitmotiv**) recurring theme in musical etc. composition representing particular person, idea, etc.

lemming /ˈlɛmɪŋ/ *noun* Arctic rodent reputed to rush, during migration, in large numbers into sea and drown.

lemon /ˈlɛmən/ *noun* **1** acid yellow citrus fruit. **2** tree bearing it. **3** pale yellow colour. □ **lemon cheese, curd** thick creamy lemon spread. □ **lemony** *adjective*.

lemonade /lɛməˈneɪd/ *noun* **1** drink made from lemons. **2** synthetic substitute for this, often fizzy.

lemon sole /ˈlɛmən/ *noun* (*plural* same or **-s**) fish of plaice family.

lemur /ˈliːmə/ *noun* tree-dwelling primate of Madagascar.

lend *verb* (*past & past participle* **lent**) **1** grant temporary use of (thing). **2** allow use of (money) in return for interest. **3** bestow, contribute. **4** (**lend itself to**) be suitable for. □ **lend an ear** listen. □ **lender** *noun*.

■ **1, 2** advance, loan.

length *noun* **1** measurement from end to end. **2** extent in or of time. **3** length of horse, boat, etc. as measure of lead in race. **4** long stretch or extent. **5** degree of thoroughness in action. □ **at length 1** in detail. **2** after a long time. □ **lengthways** *adverb*. **lengthwise** *adverb & adjective*.

■ **1** distance, extent, footage, measure, measurement, mileage, reach, size, span, stretch. **2** duration, period, span, stretch, term.

lengthen *verb* make or become longer.
■ continue, drag out, draw out, elongate, enlarge, expand, extend, increase, pad out, prolong, protract, pull out, stretch.

lengthy *adjective* (**-ier, -iest**) **1** of unusual length. **2** prolix, tedious.

lenient /ˈliːnɪənt/ *adjective* merciful, not severe, mild. □ **lenience** *noun.* **leniency** *noun.* **leniently** *adverb.*
■ charitable, easygoing, forbearing, forgiving, gentle, humane, indulgent, kind, merciful, mild, permissive, soft, soft-hearted, sparing, tolerant.

lens /lenz/ *noun* **1** piece of transparent substance with one or both sides curved, used in spectacles, telescopes, cameras, etc. **2** combination of lenses used in photography.

Lent *noun* religious period of fasting and penitence from Ash Wednesday to Easter Eve. □ **Lenten** *adjective.*

lent *past & past participle* of LEND.

lentil /ˈlentɪl/ *noun* **1** edible seed of leguminous plant. **2** this plant.

lento /ˈlentəʊ/ *Music adjective* slow. ● *adverb* slowly. ● *noun* lento movement or passage.

Leo /ˈliːəʊ/ *noun* fifth sign of zodiac.

leonine /ˈliːənaɪn/ *adjective* **1** lionlike. **2** of lions.

leopard /ˈlepəd/ *noun* large animal of cat family with dark-spotted fawn or all black coat; panther.

leotard /ˈliːətɑːd/ *noun* close-fitting one-piece garment worn by dancers etc.

leper /ˈlepə/ *noun* person with leprosy.

leprechaun /ˈleprəkɔːn/ *noun* small mischievous sprite in Irish folklore.

leprosy /ˈleprəsɪ/ *noun* contagious disease of skin and nerves. □ **leprous** *adjective.*

lesbian /ˈlezbɪən/ *noun* homosexual woman. ● *adjective* of homosexuality in women. □ **lesbianism** *noun.*

lesion /ˈliːʒ(ə)n/ *noun* **1** damage, injury. **2** change in part of body due to injury or disease.

less *adjective* **1** smaller. **2** of smaller quantity; not so much. ● *adverb* to smaller extent; in lower degree. ● *noun* smaller amount, quantity, or number. ● *preposition* minus, deducting.

USAGE The use of *less* to mean 'fewer', as in *There are less people than yesterday*, is incorrect in standard English.
■ *adjective* reduced, shorter, smaller.

-less /les/ *suffix* forming adjectives and adverbs: **1** (*from nouns*) not having, without. **2** (*from verbs*) not affected by or doing (the action of the verb). □ **-lessly** *suffix* forming adverbs. **-lessness** *suffix* forming nouns.

lessee /leˈsiː/ *noun* (often + *of*) person holding property by lease.

lessen /ˈles(ə)n/ *verb* make or become less; diminish.
■ abate, assuage, cut, deaden, decline, decrease, die away, diminish, dwindle, ease, ease off, *colloquial* let up, lighten, lower, minimize, mitigate, moderate, reduce, relieve, slacken, subside, tail off, tone down, weaken.

lesser *adjective* not so great as the other(s).

lesson /ˈles(ə)n/ *noun* **1** period of teaching. **2** (in *plural*; usually + *in*) systematic instruction. **3** thing learnt or to be learnt by pupil. **4** experience that serves to warn or encourage. **5** passage from Bible read aloud during church service.
■ **1** class, lecture, practical, seminar, session, tutorial, workshop. **2** (*lessons*) classes, instruction, teaching. **3** drill, task. **4** admonition, example, moral, warning.

lessor /leˈsɔː/ *noun* person who lets property by lease.

lest *conjunction* in order that not; for fear that.

let[1] *verb* (**-tt-**; *past & past participle* **let**) **1** allow, enable, or cause to. **2** grant use of (rooms, land, etc.) for rent or hire. ● *auxiliary verb: in exhortations, commands, assumptions, etc.* ● *noun* act of letting. □ **let alone 1** not to mention. **2** let be. **let be** not interfere with. **let down 1** lower. **2** fail to support or satisfy; disappoint. **let-down** *noun* disappointment. **let fly 1** (often + *at*) attack physically or verbally. **2** discharge (missile). **let go 1** release. **2** lose hold of. **3** cease to think or talk about (something). **let in 1** allow to enter. **2** (usually + *for*) involve (person, often oneself) in loss, problem, etc. **3** (usually + *on*) allow (person) to share secret etc. **let loose** release. **let off 1** fire (gun). **2** cause (steam etc.) to escape. **3** not punish or compel. **let on** *colloquial* reveal secret. **let out 1** release. **2** reveal (secret etc.). **3** slacken. **4** put out to rent. **let-out** *noun colloquial* opportunity to escape. **let up** *colloquial* **1** become less severe. **2** diminish. **let-up** *noun colloquial* **1** relaxation of effort. **2** diminution.
■ *verb* **1** agree to, allow to, authorize to, consent to, enable to, give permission to, license to, permit to, sanction to. **2** charter, contract out, hire, lease, rent. □ **let alone 2** see LEAVE[1] 2. **let be** see LEAVE[1] 2. **let-down** anticlimax, disappointment, disillusionment, *colloquial* wash-out. **let go 1** see LIBERATE 1. **let loose** see LIBERATE 1. **let off 1** see FIRE *verb* 1,4;5. **3** see ACQUIT 1. **let out 1** see LIBERATE 1. **let up** see LESSEN.

let[2] *noun* obstruction of ball or player in tennis etc. after which ball must be served again. ● *verb* (**-tt-**; *past & past participle* **letted** or **let**) *archaic* hinder, obstruct. □ **without let or hindrance** unimpeded.

lethal /ˈliːθ(ə)l/ *adjective* causing or sufficient to cause death. □ **lethally** *adverb.*
■ deadly, fatal, mortal.

lethargy /ˈleθədʒɪ/ *noun* **1** lack of energy. **2** unnatural sleepiness. □ **lethargic** /lɪˈθɑːdʒɪk/ *adjective.* **lethargically** /lɪˈθɑːdʒɪkəlɪ/ *adverb.*

■ **1** apathy, idleness, inactivity, indolence, inertia, laziness, listlessness, slothfulness, slowness, sluggishness, torpor, weariness. **2** see SLEEPINESS. □ **lethargic** apathetic, comatose, dull, heavy, inactive, indifferent, indolent, languid, lazy, listless, phlegmatic, sleepy, slow, slothful, sluggish, torpid, weary.

letter /'letə/ *noun* **1** character representing one or more of sounds used in speech. **2** written or printed communication, usually sent in envelope by post. **3** precise terms of statement. **4** (in *plural*) literature. ● *verb* **1** inscribe letters on. **2** classify with letters. □ **letter bomb** terrorist explosive device sent by post. **letter box 1** box for delivery or posting of letters. **2** slit in door for delivery of letters. **letterhead** printed heading on stationery. **letterpress 1** printed words in illustrated book. **2** printing from raised type. **to the letter** keeping to every detail.

■ *noun* **1** character, sign, symbol. **2** communication, dispatch, epistle, message, *jocular* missive, note; (*letters*) correspondence, mail, post.

lettuce /'letɪs/ *noun* plant with crisp leaves used in salad.

leucocyte /'lu:kəsaɪt/ *noun* white blood cell.

leukaemia /lu:'ki:mɪə/ *noun* (*US* **leukemia**) malignant progressive disease in which too many white blood cells are produced.

Levant /lɪ'vænt/ *noun* (**the Levant**) *archaic* East-Mediterranean region.

Levantine /'levəntaɪn/ *adjective* of or trading to the Levant. ● *noun* native or inhabitant of the Levant.

levee /'levɪ/ *noun US* embankment against river floods.

level /'lev(ə)l/ *noun* **1** horizontal line or plane. **2** height or value reached. **3** position on real or imaginary scale. **4** social, moral, or intellectual standard. **5** plane of rank or authority. **6** instrument giving line parallel to plane of horizon. **7** level surface. **8** flat country. **9** floor or storey (in building, ship, etc.). ● *adjective* **1** flat; not bumpy. **2** horizontal. **3** (often + *with*) on same horizontal plane as something else. **4** (often + *with*) having equality with something else. **5** even, uniform, well balanced. ● *verb* (**-ll-**; *US* **-l-**) **1** make level. **2** raze, completely destroy. **3** (usually + *at*) aim (gun etc.). **4** (usually + *at, against*) direct (accusation etc.). □ **do one's level best** *colloquial* do one's utmost. **find one's level** reach right social, intellectual, etc., position. **level crossing** crossing of road and railway etc. at same level. **level-headed** mentally well balanced; cool. **level-headedness** *noun*. **level pegging** equality of scores etc. **on the level** *colloquial* ● *adverb* honestly, without deception. ● *adjective* honest, truthful.

■ *noun* **1** plane. **2** altitude, depth, elevation, height, value. **3** degree, echelon, grade, position, rank, stage, standard, standing, status. **9** floor, storey. ● *adjective* **1** even, flat, flush, plane, regular, smooth, straight, true, uniform. **5** balanced, even, equal, matching, neck and neck, the same. ● *verb*

1 even out, flatten, rake, smooth. **2** bulldoze, demolish, destroy, devastate, knock down, lay low, raze, tear down, wreck. □ **level-headed** see SENSIBLE 1.

lever /'li:və/ *noun* **1** bar pivoted about fulcrum to transfer force. **2** bar used on pivot to prise or lift. **3** projecting handle used to operate mechanism. **4** means of exerting moral pressure. ● *verb* **1** use lever. **2** lift, move, etc. (as) with lever.

■ *verb* **2** force, prise, wrench.

leverage *noun* **1** action or power of lever. **2** means of accomplishing a purpose.

leveret /'levərɪt/ *noun* young hare.

leviathan /lɪ'vaɪəθ(ə)n/ *noun* **1** *Biblical* sea monster. **2** very large or powerful thing.

Levis /'li:vaɪz/ *plural noun proprietary term* type of (originally blue) denim jeans.

levitate /'levɪteɪt/ *verb* (**-ting**) (cause to) rise and float in air. □ **levitation** *noun*.

levity /'levɪtɪ/ *noun* lack of serious thought; frivolity.

levy /'levɪ/ *verb* (**-ies, -ied**) **1** impose or collect (payment etc.) compulsorily. **2** enrol (troops etc.). ● *noun* (*plural* **-ies**) **1** levying. **2** payment etc. or (in *plural*) troops levied.

lewd /lju:d/ *adjective* **1** lascivious. **2** indecent. □ **lewdly** *adverb*. **lewdness** *noun*.

lexical /'leksɪk(ə)l/ *adjective* **1** of the words of a language. **2** (as) of a lexicon.

lexicography /leksɪ'kɒɡrəfɪ/ *noun* compiling of dictionaries. □ **lexicographer** *noun*.

lexicon /'leksɪkən/ *noun* dictionary.

Leyden jar /'laɪd(ə)n/ *noun* early kind of capacitor.

LF *abbreviation* low frequency.

liability /laɪə'bɪlɪtɪ/ *noun* (*plural* **-ies**) **1** being liable. **2** troublesome person or thing; handicap. **3** (in *plural*) debts for which one is liable.

liable /'laɪəb(ə)l/ *adjective* **1** legally bound. **2** (+ *to*) subject to. **3** (+ *to do*) under an obligation to. **4** (+ *to*) exposed or open to (something undesirable). **5** *disputed* (+ *to do*) likely to. **6** (+ *for*) answerable for.

USAGE The use of *liable* to mean 'likely', as in *It is liable to rain* is considered incorrect by some people.

■ **4** disposed, exposed, inclined, open, predisposed, prone, subject, susceptible, vulnerable. **5** apt, inclined, in the habit of, likely, minded, ready, tempted, willing. **6** accountable, answerable, blameworthy, responsible.

liaise /lɪ'eɪz/ *verb* (**-sing**) (usually + *with, between*) *colloquial* establish cooperation; act as link.

liaison /lɪ'eɪzɒn/ *noun* **1** communication, co-operation. **2** illicit sexual relationship.

■ **1** communication, contact, cooperation, linkage, links, mediation, relationship, tie. **2** see AFFAIR 3.

liana /lɪˈɑːnə/ *noun* climbing plant in tropical forests.

liar /ˈlaɪə/ *noun* person who tells lies.
■ deceiver, false witness, fibber, perjurer, *colloquial* storyteller.

Lib. *abbreviation* Liberal.

lib *noun colloquial* liberation.

libation /laɪˈbeɪʃ(ə)n/ *noun* (pouring out of) drink-offering to a god.

libel /ˈlaɪb(ə)l/ *noun* **1** *Law* published false statement damaging to person's reputation. **2** *Law* publishing of this. **3** false defamatory statement. ● *verb* (**-ll-**: *US* **-l-**) **1** *Law* publish libel against. **2** defame. □ **libellous** *adjective*.
■ *noun* calumny, defamation, denigration, insult, lie, misrepresentation, obloquy, scandal, slander, slur, smear, vilification. ● *verb* blacken the name of, calumniate, defame, denigrate, disparage, malign, misrepresent, slander, *archaic* or *US* slur, smear, write lies about, traduce, vilify. □ **libellous** calumnious, damaging, defamatory, disparaging, false, hurtful, insulting, lying, malicious, mendacious, scurrilous, slanderous, untrue, vicious.

liberal /ˈlɪbər(ə)l/ *adjective* **1** abundant. **2** giving freely; generous. **3** open-minded. **4** not rigorous. **5** (of studies) for general broadening of mind. **6** *Politics* favouring moderate reforms. ● *noun* person of liberal views, esp. (**Liberal**) member of a Liberal Party. □ **Liberal Democrat** member of **Liberal Democrats**, UK political party. □ **liberalism** *noun*. **liberality** /-ˈræl-/ *noun*. **liberally** *adverb*.
■ *adjective* **1** abundant, ample, *poetical* bounteous, copious, lavish, plentiful. **2** big-hearted, bountiful, charitable, free, generous, indulgent, lavish, magnanimous, munificent, open-handed, philanthropic, unselfish, unstinting. **3** broad-minded, easygoing, enlightened, fair-minded, humanitarian, impartial, lenient, magnanimous, open-minded, permissive, tolerant, unbiased, unbigoted, unopinionated, unprejudiced. **6** progressive, radical, reformist.

liberalize *verb* (also **-ise**) (**-zing** or **-sing**) make or become more liberal or less strict. □ **liberalization** *noun*.
■ broaden, ease, enlarge, moderate, open up, relax, soften, widen.

liberate /ˈlɪbəreɪt/ *verb* (**-ting**) **1** (often + *from*) set free. **2** free (country etc.) from aggressor. **3** (as **liberated** *adjective*) (of person etc.) freed from oppressive social conventions. □ **liberation** *noun*. **liberator** *noun*.
■ **1** deliver, discharge, emancipate, enfranchise, free, let go, let loose, let out, loose, ransom, redeem, release, rescue, save, set free, untie. **2** deliver, emancipate, free.

libertine /ˈlɪbətiːn/ *noun* licentious person.

liberty /ˈlɪbətɪ/ *noun* (*plural* **-ies**) **1** being free, freedom. **2** right or power to do as one pleases. **3** (in *plural*) privileges granted by authority. □ **at liberty 1** free. **2** (+ *to do*) permitted to. **take liber-**

ties (often + *with*) behave in unacceptably familiar way. **take the liberty** presume, venture.
■ **1** autonomy, emancipation, freedom, independence, liberation, release, self-determination, self-rule. **2** see FREEDOM 1,2. □ **at liberty 1** see FREE *adjective* 3;6.

libidinous /lɪˈbɪdɪnəs/ *adjective* lustful.

libido /lɪˈbiːdəʊ/ *noun* (*plural* **-s**) psychic impulse or drive, esp. that associated with sex instinct. □ **libidinal** /lɪˈbɪdɪn(ə)l/ *adjective*.

Libra /ˈliːbrə/ *noun* seventh sign of zodiac.

librarian /laɪˈbreərɪən/ *noun* person in charge of or assistant in library. □ **librarianship** *noun*.

library /ˈlaɪbrərɪ/ *noun* (*plural* **-ies**) **1** a collection of books, films, records, etc. **2** room or building etc. where these are kept. **3** series of books issued in similar bindings.

libretto /lɪˈbretəʊ/ *noun* (*plural* **-ti** /-tɪ/ or **-s**) text of opera etc. □ **librettist** *noun*.

lice *plural* of LOUSE.

licence /ˈlaɪs(ə)ns/ *noun* (*US* **license**) **1** official permit to own, use, or do, something, or carry on trade. **2** permission. **3** excessive liberty of action. **4** writer's etc. deliberate deviation from fact.
■ **1** certificate, credentials, document, papers, permit, warrant. **3** see FREEDOM 3.

license /ˈlaɪs(ə)ns/ *verb* (**-sing**) **1** grant licence to. **2** authorize use of (premises) for certain purpose. ● *noun US* = LICENCE.
■ *verb* **1** allow, authorize, certify, empower, entitle, permit, sanction.

licensee /laɪsənˈsiː/ *noun* holder of licence, esp. to sell alcoholic liquor.

licentiate /laɪˈsenʃɪət/ *noun* holder of certificate of professional competence.

licentious /laɪˈsenʃəs/ *adjective* sexually promiscuous. □ **licentiously** *adverb*. **licentiousness** *noun*.

lichee = LYCHEE.

lichen /ˈlaɪkən/ *noun* plant composed of fungus and alga in association, growing on rocks, trees, etc.

lich-gate /ˈlɪtʃɡeɪt/ *noun* (also **lych-gate**) roofed gateway of churchyard.

licit /ˈlɪsɪt/ *adjective formal* lawful, permitted.

lick *verb* **1** pass tongue over. **2** bring into specified condition by licking. **3** (of flame etc.) play lightly over. **4** *colloquial* thrash, defeat. ● *noun* **1** act of licking with tongue. **2** *colloquial* pace, speed. **3** smart blow. □ **lick one's lips, chops** look forward with great pleasure.

licorice = LIQUORICE.

lid *noun* **1** hinged or removable cover, esp. at top of container. **2** eyelid. □ **put the lid on** *colloquial* **1** be the culmination of. **2** put stop to. □ **lidded** *adjective*.
■ **1** cap, cover, covering, top.

lido /ˈliːdəʊ/ *noun* (*plural* **-s**) public open-air swimming pool or bathing beach.

lie[1] /laɪ/ *verb* (**lying**; *past* **lay**; *past participle* **lain**) **1** be in or assume horizontal position on supporting surface. **2** (of thing) rest on flat surface. **3** remain undisturbed or undiscussed. **4** be kept, remain, or be in specified place etc. **5** (of abstract things) be in certain relation. **6** be situated or spread out to view etc. ● *noun* way, position, or direction in which something lies. □ **lie in** stay in bed late in morning. **lie-in** *noun*. **lie low** keep quiet or unseen. **lie of the land** state of affairs.

USAGE It is incorrect in standard English to use *lie* to mean 'lay', as in *lie her on the bed*.

■ *verb* **1** be horizontal, be prone, be prostrate, be recumbent, be supine, lean back, lounge, recline, repose, rest, sprawl, stretch out. **6** be, be found, be located, be situated, exist. □ **lie low** see HIDE[1] *verb* 2.

lie[2] /laɪ/ *noun* **1** intentional false statement. **2** something that deceives. ● *verb* (**lies**, **lied**, **lying**) **1** tell lie(s). **2** (of thing) be deceptive. □ **give the lie to** show the falsity of.

■ *noun* **1** fabrication, falsehood, falsification, fib, fiction, invention, misrepresentation, prevarication, untruth, *slang* whopper. **2** see DECEPTION 2. ● *verb* **1** bluff, commit perjury, deceive, falsify the facts, fib, perjure oneself, prevaricate, tell lies.

lied /liːd/ *noun* (*plural* **lieder**) German song of Romantic period for voice and piano.

liege /liːdʒ/ *historical adjective* entitled to receive, or bound to give, feudal service or allegiance. ● *noun* **1** (in full **liege lord**) feudal superior. **2** (usually in *plural*) vassal, subject.

lien /'liːən/ *noun Law* right to hold another's property till debt on it is paid.

lieu /ljuː/ *noun* □ **in lieu 1** instead. **2** (+ *of*) in place of.

Lieut. *abbreviation* Lieutenant.

lieutenant /lef'tenənt/ *noun* **1** army officer next below captain. **2** naval officer next below lieutenant commander. **3** deputy. □ **lieutenant colonel, commander, general** officers ranking next below colonel etc. □ **lieutenancy** *noun* (*plural* **-ies**).

life *noun* (*plural* **lives**) **1** capacity for growth, functional activity, and continual change until death. **2** living things and their activity. **3** period during which life lasts; period from birth to present time or from present time to death. **4** duration of thing's existence or ability to function. **5** person's state of existence. **6** living person. **7** business and pleasures of the world. **8** energy, liveliness. **9** biography. **10** *colloquial* imprisonment for life. □ **come to life 1** emerge from inactivity; begin operating. **2** (of inanimate object) assume imaginary animation. **life assurance** life insurance. **lifebelt** buoyant ring to keep person afloat. **lifeblood 1** blood as necessary to life. **2** vital factor or influence. **lifeboat 1** boat for rescues at sea. **2** ship's boat for emergency use. **lifebuoy** buoyant support to keep person afloat. **life cycle** series of changes in life of organism. **lifeguard** expert swimmer employed to rescue

bathers from drowning. **Life Guards** regiment of royal household cavalry. **life insurance** insurance which makes payment on death of insured person. **life jacket** buoyant jacket for keeping person afloat. **lifeline 1** rope etc. used for life-saving. **2** sole means of communication or transport. **lifelong** lasting a lifetime. **life peer** peer whose title lapses on death. **life sentence** imprisonment for life. **life-size(d)** of same size as person or thing represented. **lifestyle** way of life. **life-support machine** respirator. **lifetime** duration of person's life.

■ **1** being, existence, living. **8** activity, animation, dash, *élan*, energy, enthusiasm, exuberance, go, liveliness, soul, sparkle, spirit, sprightliness, verve, vigour, vitality, vivacity, zest. **9** autobiography, biography, memoir, story.

lifeless *adjective* **1** dead; without life. **2** unconscious. **3** lacking movement or vitality. □ **lifelessly** *adverb*.

■ **1** (*lifeless bodies*) dead, *formal* deceased, inanimate, inert, killed; (*lifeless desert*) arid, bare, barren, desolate, empty, sterile, uninhabited, waste. **2** comatose, insensate, insensible, motionless, unconscious. **3** apathetic, boring, dull, flat, heavy, lacklustre, lethargic, slow, torpid, unexciting, wooden.

lifelike *adjective* closely resembling life or person or thing represented.

■ authentic, convincing, faithful, graphic, natural, photographic, realistic, true to life, vivid.

lifer *noun slang* person serving life sentence.

lift *verb* **1** (often + *up*, *off*, etc.) raise to higher position. **2** go up; be raised; yield to upward force. **3** give upward direction to (eyes etc.). **4** add interest to; improve. **5** (of fog etc.) rise, disperse. **6** remove (barrier etc.). **7** transport supplies, troops, etc. by air. **8** *colloquial* steal. **9** *colloquial* plagiarize. ● *noun* **1** lifting. **2** ride in another person's vehicle. **3** apparatus for raising and lowering people or things to different floors of building, or for carrying people up or down mountain etc. **4** transport by air. **5** upward pressure on aerofoil. **6** supporting or elevating influence. **7** elated feeling. □ **lift-off** vertical take-off of spacecraft or rocket.

■ *verb* **1** carry, elevate, heave up, hoist, jack up, pick up, pull up, raise, rear. **2** ascend, fly, rise, soar. **4** boost, cheer, enhance, improve, promote. **8** see STEAL *verb* 1. ● *noun* **3** *US* elevator, hoist.

ligament /'lɪgəmənt/ *noun* band of tough fibrous tissue linking bones.

ligature /'lɪgətʃə/ *noun* **1** tie, bandage. **2** *Music* slur, tie. **3** *Printing* two or more letters joined, e.g. æ.

USAGE *Ligature*, in the *Printing* sense, is sometimes confused with *digraph*, which means 'two letters representing one sound'.

light[1] /laɪt/ *noun* **1** electromagnetic radiation that stimulates sight and makes things visible. **2** medium in which this is present. **3** appearance of brightness. **4** source of light. **5** (often in *plural*) traffic light. **6** flame, spark, or device for igniting. **7** aspect in which thing is regarded. **8** mental or spiritual illumination. **9** vivacity, esp. in person's eyes. ● *verb* (*past* **lit**; *past participle* **lit** or **lighted**) **1** set burning; begin to burn. **2** (often + *up*) give light to; make prominent by light. **3** show (person) way etc. with light. **4** (usually + *up*) (of face or eyes) brighten with pleasure etc. ● *adjective* **1** well provided with light; not dark. **2** (of colour) pale. □ **bring or come to light** reveal or be revealed. **half-light** dim imperfect light. **in the light of** taking account of. **light bulb** glass bulb containing metal filament giving light when current is passed through it. **lighthouse** tower with beacon light to warn or guide ships at sea. **lightship** anchored ship with beacon light. **light year** distance light travels in one year. **shed light on** see SHED².

■ *noun* **3** beam, blaze, brightness, brilliance, flare, flash, fluorescence, glare, gleam, glint, glitter, glow, halo, illumination, incandescence, luminosity, lustre, phosphorescence, radiance, ray, reflection, scintillation, shine, sparkle, twinkle. **4** beacon, bulb, candle, chandelier, electric light, flare, floodlight, headlamp, headlight, lamp, lantern, moon, neon light, searchlight, spotlight, standard lamp, star, street light, sun, torch. **6** match, pilot light, spill, taper. ● *verb* **1** fire, ignite, kindle, put a match to, set alight, set fire to, switch on. **2** see LIGHTEN² 1. **4** (*light up*) see LIGHTEN² 2 ● *adjective* **1** bright, illuminated, lit up, well lit. **2** see PALE¹ *adjective* 2–4. □ **bring to light** see DISCOVER 1,2. **lighthouse** beacon, light, lightship.

light² /laɪt/ *adjective* **1** not heavy. **2** relatively low in weight, amount, density, or intensity. **3** (of railway) suitable for small loads. **4** carrying only light arms. **5** (of food) easy to digest. **6** (of music etc.) intended only as entertainment; not profound. **7** (of sleep or sleeper) easily disturbed. **8** easily done. **9** nimble. **10** cheerful. ● *adverb* **1** lightly. **2** with light load. ● *verb* (*past & past participle* **lit** or **lighted**) (+ *on*, *upon*) come upon or find by chance. □ **light-fingered** given to stealing. **light flyweight** amateur boxing weight (up to 48 kg). **light-headed** giddy; delirious. **light-headedness** *noun*. **light-hearted** cheerful. **light-heartedness** *noun*. **light heavyweight** amateur boxing weight (75–81 kg). **light industry** manufacture of small or light articles. **light middleweight** amateur boxing weight (67–71 kg). **lightweight** ● *adjective* **1** below average weight. **2** of little importance. ● *noun* **1** lightweight person or thing. **2** amateur boxing weight (57–60kg). **make light of** treat as unimportant. □ **lightly** *adverb*. **lightness** *noun*.

■ *adjective* **1** lightweight, portable, underweight. **2** (*light traffic*) see SPARSE; (*a light wind*) see GENTLE 1; (*a light touch*) see DELICATE 1. **8** see EASY *adjective* 1. **10** see CHEERFUL 1. ● *verb* (*light on*, *upon*) see DISCOVER 1,2. □ **light-headed** see DIZZY *adjective* 1. **light-hearted** see CHEERFUL 1.

lighten¹ *verb* **1** make or become lighter in weight. **2** reduce weight or load of.
■ **1** see LESSEN.

lighten² *verb* **1** shed light on. **2** make or grow bright.
■ **1** cast light on, floodlight, illuminate, irradiate, light (up), shed light on, shine on. **2** become lighter, brighten, cheer up, clear, light up.

lighter¹ *noun* device for lighting cigarettes etc.

lighter² *noun* boat for transporting goods between ship and wharf etc.

lightning /ˈlaɪtnɪŋ/ *noun* flash of light produced by electric discharge between clouds or between clouds and ground. □ **lightning-conductor** metal rod or wire fixed to building or mast to divert lightning to earth or sea.

lights *plural noun* lungs of sheep, pigs, etc. as food, esp. for pets.

ligneous /ˈlɪɡnɪəs/ *adjective* of the nature of wood.

lignite /ˈlɪɡnaɪt/ *noun* brown coal of woody texture.

lignum vitae /ˌlɪɡnəm ˈvaɪtɪ/ *noun* a hard-wooded tree.

like¹ *adjective* (**more like**, **most like**) **1** similar to another, each other, or original. **2** resembling; such as. **3** characteristic of. **4** in suitable state or mood for. ● *preposition* in manner of; to same degree as. ● *adverb* **1** *slang* so to speak. **2** *colloquial* probably. ● *conjunction colloquial disputed* as; as if (see note below). ● *noun* **1** counterpart; equal. **2** similar person or thing.

USAGE It is incorrect in standard English to use *like* as a conjunction, as in *Tell it like it is* or *He's spending money like it was going out of fashion*.

■ *adjective* **1** akin to, analogous to, close to, cognate with, comparable to, congruent with, corresponding to, equal to, equivalent to, identical to, parallel to, similar to.

like² *verb* (**-king**) **1** find agreeable or enjoyable; feel attracted by. **2** choose to have; prefer. ● *noun* (in *plural*) things one likes or prefers.
■ *verb* **1** admire, approve of, appreciate, be attracted to, be fond of, be interested in, be keen on, be partial to, be pleased by, delight in, enjoy, find pleasant, go in for, have a high regard for, have a weakness for, love, relish, revel in, take pleasure in, take to, welcome. **2** choose, go for, prefer. ● *noun* liking, partiality, predilection, preference.

-like /laɪk/ *combining form* forming adjectives from nouns: similar to; characteristic of.

likeable *adjective* (also **likable**) pleasant; easy to like. □ **likeably** *adverb*.
■ attractive, charming, congenial, endearing, friendly, interesting, lovable, nice, personable, pleasant, pleasing.

likelihood /ˈlaɪklɪhʊd/ *noun* probability.
■ chance, hope, possibility, probability, prospect.

likely /ˈlaɪklɪ/ *adjective* (**-ier**, **-iest**) **1** probable; such as may well happen or be true. **2** (+ *to do*) to be expected to. **3** promising; apparently suitable. ● *adverb* probably. □ **not likely!** *colloquial* certainly not.

■ **1** convincing, credible, expected, foreseeable, plausible, possible, predictable, probable, reasonable, unsurprising. **2** apt, disposed, expected, inclined, *disputed* liable, prone, ready. **3** able, acceptable, appropriate, fitting, hopeful, promising, qualified, suitable.

like-minded *adjective* having same tastes, opinions, etc. □ **like-mindedly** *adverb*. **like-mindedness** *noun*.

liken *verb* (+ *to*) point out resemblance between (person, thing) and (another).
■ compare, equate, match.

likeness *noun* **1** (usually + *between, to*) resemblance. **2** (+ *of*) semblance, guise of. **3** portrait, representation.
■ **1** affinity, analogy, correspondence, resemblance, similarity. **3** copy, depiction, drawing, duplicate, facsimile, image, model, picture, portrait, replica, representation, reproduction, study.

likewise *adverb* **1** also, moreover. **2** similarly.

liking *noun* **1** what one likes; one's taste. **2** (+ *for*) fondness, taste, fancy for.
■ **1** fancy, taste. **2** affection, affinity, appetite, fondness, inclination, love, partiality, penchant, predilection, predisposition, preference, propensity, soft spot, taste, weakness.

lilac /ˈlaɪlək/ *noun* **1** shrub with fragrant pinkish-violet or white flowers. **2** pale pinkish-violet colour. ● *adjective* of this colour.

liliaceous /lɪlɪˈeɪʃəs/ *adjective* of the lily family.

lilliputian /lɪlɪˈpjuːʃ(ə)n/ *noun* diminutive person or thing. ● *adjective* diminutive.

lilt *noun* **1** light springing rhythm. **2** tune with this. ● *verb* (esp. as **lilting** *adjective*) speak etc. with lilt.

lily /ˈlɪlɪ/ *noun* (*plural* **-ies**) **1** tall bulbous plant with large trumpet-shaped flowers. **2** heraldic fleur-de-lis. □ **lily-livered** cowardly. **lily of the valley** plant with fragrant white bell-shaped flowers.

limb[1] /lɪm/ *noun* **1** leg, arm, wing. **2** large branch of tree. **3** branch of cross. □ **out on a limb** isolated. □ **limbless** *adjective*.
■ **2** bough, branch.

limb[2] /lɪm/ *noun* specified edge of sun, moon, etc.

limber[1] /ˈlɪmbə/ *adjective* **1** lithe, flexible. **2** agile. ● *verb* (usually + *up*) **1** make oneself supple. **2** warm up for athletic etc. activity.
■ *verb* (*limber up*) exercise, get ready, loosen up, prepare, warm up.

limber[2] /ˈlɪmbə/ *noun* detachable front of gun-carriage. ● *verb* attach limber to.

limbo[1] /ˈlɪmbəʊ/ *noun* (*plural* **-s**) **1** supposed abode of souls of unbaptized infants, and of the just who died before Christ. **2** (esp. after *in*) intermediate state or condition of awaiting decision.
■ **2** (*in limbo*) forgotten, in abeyance, left out, neglected, neither one thing nor the other, unattached.

limbo[2] /ˈlɪmbəʊ/ *noun* (*plural* **-s**) W. Indian dance in which dancer bends backwards to pass under progressively lowered horizontal bar.

lime[1] *noun* white caustic substance got by heating limestone. ● *verb* (**-ming**) treat with lime. □ **limekiln** kiln for heating limestone. □ **limy** *adjective* (**-ier, -iest**).

lime[2] *noun* **1** round green acid fruit. **2** tree producing this fruit. □ **lime-green** yellowish-green colour.

lime[3] *noun* (in full **lime tree**) tree with heart-shaped leaves and fragrant creamy blossom.

limelight *noun* **1** intense white light used formerly in theatres. **2** glare of publicity.

limerick /ˈlɪmərɪk/ *noun* humorous 5-line verse.

limestone *noun* rock composed mainly of calcium carbonate.

limit /ˈlɪmɪt/ *noun* **1** point, line, or level beyond which something does not or may not extend or pass. **2** greatest or smallest amount permitted. ● *verb* (**-t-**) **1** set or serve as limit to. **2** (+ *to*) restrict to. □ **limited** *adjective*. **limitless** *adjective*.
■ *noun* **1** border, boundary, bounds, brink, ceiling, confines, cut-off point, deadline, demarcation line, edge, end, extent, extreme point, frontier, limitation, margin, perimeter, restriction, stop, threshold. **2** maximum, minimum. ● *verb* **1** bridle, check, circumscribe, confine, control, curb, define, fix, hold in check, ration, restrain, restrict. **2** (*limit to*) confine to, ration to, restrict to. □ **limited** see FINITE 1, INADEQUATE 1, MARGINAL 5. **limitless** boundless, countless, endless, everlasting, extensive, immeasurable, incalculable, inexhaustible, infinite, innumerable, never-ending, numberless, perpetual, renewable, unbounded, unconfined, unending, unimaginable, unlimited, unrestricted, vast.

limitation /lɪmɪˈteɪʃ(ə)n/ *noun* **1** limiting, being limited. **2** limit of ability. **3** limiting circumstance.
■ **1** check, curb, inhibition, limit, restraint, restriction, stop. **2, 3** deficiency, inadequacy, shortcoming, weakness.

limn /lɪm/ *verb archaic* paint.

limousine /lɪmʊˈziːn/ *noun* large luxurious car.

limp[1] *verb* walk or proceed lamely or awkwardly. ● *noun* lame walk.
■ *verb* be lame, falter, hobble, hop, stagger, totter.

limp[2] *adjective* **1** not stiff or firm. **2** without will or energy. □ **limply** *adverb*. **limpness** *noun*.
■ **1** *colloquial* bendy, drooping, flabby, flaccid, flexible, floppy, lax, loose, pliable, sagging, slack, soft, weak, wilting, yielding. **2** see WEARY *adjective* 1.

limpet /ˈlɪmpɪt/ *noun* mollusc with conical shell sticking tightly to rocks.

limpid /ˈlɪmpɪd/ *adjective* clear, transparent. □ **limpidity** /-ˈpɪd-/ *noun*.

linage /ˈlaɪnɪdʒ/ *noun* **1** number of lines in

printed or written page etc. **2** payment by the line.

linchpin /ˈlɪntʃpɪn/ *noun* **1** pin passed through axle-end to keep wheel on. **2** person or thing vital to organization etc.

linctus /ˈlɪŋktəs/ *noun* syrupy medicine, esp. soothing cough mixture.

linden /ˈlɪnd(ə)n/ *noun* = LIME³.

line¹ *noun* **1** continuous mark made on surface. **2** furrow, wrinkle. **3** use of lines in art. **4** straight or curved track of moving point. **5** outline. **6** limit, boundary. **7** row of persons or things. **8** *US* queue. **9** mark defining area of play or start or finish of race. **10** row of printed or written words. **11** portion of verse written in line. **12** (in *plural*) piece of poetry. **13** (in *plural*) words of actor's part. **14** length of cord, rope, etc. serving specified purpose. **15** wire or cable for telephone or telegraph. **16** connection by means of this. **17** single track or branch of railway. **18** regular succession of buses, ships, aircraft, etc., plying between certain places. **19** company conducting this. **20** several generations (of family); stock. **21** manner of procedure, conduct, thought, etc. **22** channel. **23** department of activity; branch of business. **24** type of product. **25** connected series of military field works. **26** arrangement of soldiers or ships side by side. **27** each of very narrow horizontal sections forming television picture. ● *verb* (**-ning**) **1** mark with lines. **2** position or stand at intervals along. □ **line printer** machine that prints computer output a line at a time. **linesman** umpire's or referee's assistant who decides whether ball has fallen within playing area or not. **line up 1** arrange or be arranged in lines. **2** have ready. **line-up** *noun* **1** line of people for inspection. **2** arrangement of persons in team, performance, etc.

■ *noun* **1** band, dash, mark, streak, striation, strip, stripe, stroke, trail. **2** corrugation, crease, crow's-foot, fold, furrow, groove, score, wrinkle. **5** contour, contour line, outline. **6** borderline, boundary, edge, limit. **7, 8** chain, column, cordon, *colloquial* crocodile, file, procession, queue, rank, row, series. **15** cable, wire. **17** branch, route, track. ● *verb* **1** rule, score, streak, underline. **2** border, edge, fringe.

line² *verb* (**-ning**) **1** apply layer of usually different material to cover inside of (garment, box, etc.). **2** serve as lining for. **3** *colloquial* fill (purse etc.).

■ **1** interline, pad, reinforce.

lineage /ˈlɪnɪdʒ/ *noun* lineal descent, ancestry.

lineal /ˈlɪnɪəl/ *adjective* **1** in direct line of descent or ancestry. **2** linear. □ **lineally** *adverb*.

lineament /ˈlɪnɪəmənt/ *noun* (usually in *plural*) distinctive feature or characteristic, esp. of face.

linear /ˈlɪnɪə/ *adjective* **1** of or in lines. **2** long and narrow and of uniform breadth.

linen /ˈlɪnɪn/ *noun* **1** cloth woven from flax. **2** articles made or originally made of linen, as sheets, shirts, underwear, etc. ● *adjective* made of linen.

liner¹ *noun* ship or aircraft carrying passengers on regular line.

liner² *noun* removable lining.

ling¹ *noun* (*plural* same) long slender marine fish.

ling² *noun* kind of heather.

linger /ˈlɪŋgə/ *verb* **1** stay about. **2** (+ *over*, *on*, etc.) dally. **3** be protracted. **4** (often + *on*) die slowly.

■ **1, 2** dally, dawdle, delay, dither, hang about, hover, idle, lag, loiter, pause, procrastinate, remain, shilly-shally, stay, stay behind, *colloquial* stick around, temporize, wait about. **3** continue, endure, last, persist. **4** last, survive.

lingerie /ˈlæʒərɪ/ *noun* women's underwear and nightclothes.

lingo /ˈlɪŋgəʊ/ *noun* (*plural* **-s** or **-es**) *colloquial* foreign language.

lingual /ˈlɪŋgw(ə)l/ *adjective* **1** of tongue. **2** of speech or languages.

linguist /ˈlɪŋgwɪst/ *noun* person skilled in languages or linguistics.

linguistic /lɪŋˈgwɪstɪk/ *adjective* of language or the study of languages. □ **linguistically** *adverb*.

linguistics *noun* study of language and its structure.

liniment /ˈlɪnɪmənt/ *noun* embrocation.

lining *noun* material used to line surface.

link *noun* **1** one loop or ring of chain etc. **2** one in series. **3** means of connection. **4** state of connection. ● *verb* **1** (+ *together*, *to*, *with*) connect, join. **2** clasp or intertwine (hands etc.).

■ *noun* **3** bond, connection, connector, coupling, fastener, join, joint, linkage, tie, yoke. **4** affiliation, alliance, association, communication, interdependence, liaison, partnership, relationship, tie-up, twinning, union. ● *verb* **1** amalgamate, associate, attach, connect, couple, fasten, interlink, join, juxtapose, merge, relate, twin, unite, yoke.

linkage *noun* linking or being linked.

links *noun* (treated as *singular* or *plural*) golf course.

Linnaean /lɪˈniːən/ *adjective* of Linnaeus or his system of classifying plants and animals.

linnet /ˈlɪnɪt/ *noun* brown-grey finch.

lino /ˈlaɪnəʊ/ *noun* (*plural* **-s**) linoleum. □ **linocut 1** design carved in relief on block of linoleum. **2** print made from this.

linoleum /lɪˈnəʊlɪəm/ *noun* canvas-backed material coated with linseed oil, cork, etc.

linseed /ˈlɪnsiːd/ *noun* seed of flax.

lint *noun* **1** linen or cotton with one side made fluffy, used for dressing wounds. **2** fluff.

lintel /ˈlɪnt(ə)l/ *noun* horizontal timber, stone, etc. over door or window.

lion /ˈlaɪən/ *noun* (*feminine* **lioness**) **1** large tawny flesh-eating wild cat of Africa and S. Asia. **2** brave or celebrated person. □ **lion-hearted**

brave and generous. **the lion's share** the largest and best part.

lionize *verb* (also **-ise**) (**-zing** or **-sing**) treat as celebrity.

lip *noun* **1** either edge of opening of mouth. **2** edge of cup, vessel, cavity, etc., esp. part shaped for pouring from. **3** *colloquial* impudent talk. □ **lip-read** understand (speech) by observing speaker's lip movements. **lip-service** insincere expression of support. **lipstick** stick of cosmetic for colouring lips.
  ■ **2** brim, brink, edge, rim.

liquefy /ˈlɪkwɪfaɪ/ *verb* (**-ies**, **-ied**) make or become liquid. □ **liquefaction** /-ˈfækʃ(ə)n/ *noun*.
  ■ dissolve, liquidize, melt, run, thaw.

liqueur /lɪˈkjʊə/ *noun* any of several strong sweet alcoholic spirits.

liquid /ˈlɪkwɪd/ *adjective* **1** having consistency like that of water or oil, flowing freely but of constant volume. **2** having appearance of water. **3** (of sounds) clear, pure. **4** (of assets) easily convertible into cash. ● *noun* **1** liquid substance. **2** *Phonetics* sound of *l* or *r*. □ **liquid crystal** liquid in state approaching that of crystalline solid. **liquid crystal display** visual display in some electronic devices.
  ■ *adjective* **1** aqueous, flowing, fluid, liquefied, melted, molten, running, runny, sloppy, sloshy, thin, watery, wet. **2** aqueous, watery. ● *noun* **1** fluid, juice, liquor, solution, stock.

liquidate /ˈlɪkwɪdeɪt/ *verb* (**-ting**) **1** wind up affairs of (firm etc.). **2** pay off (debt). **3** wipe out; kill. □ **liquidator** *noun*.
  ■ **3** annihilate, destroy, *colloquial* do away with, get rid of, kill, remove, silence, wipe out.

liquidation /lɪkwɪˈdeɪʃ(ə)n/ *noun* liquidating, esp. of firm. □ **go into liquidation** be wound up and have assets apportioned.

liquidity /lɪˈkwɪdɪtɪ/ *noun* (*plural* **-ies**) **1** state of being liquid. **2** having liquid assets.

liquidize *verb* (also **-ise**) (**-zing** or **-sing**) reduce to liquid state.

liquidizer *noun* (also **-iser**) machine for liquidizing foods.

liquor /ˈlɪkə/ *noun* **1** alcoholic (esp. distilled) drink. **2** other liquid, esp. that produced in cooking.
  ■ **1** alcohol, *colloquial* booze, intoxicants, *colloquial* shorts, spirits, strong drink. **2** see LIQUID *noun* 1.

liquorice /ˈlɪkərɪs/ *noun* (also **licorice**) **1** black root extract used as sweet and in medicine. **2** plant from which it is obtained.

lira /ˈlɪərə/ *noun* chief monetary unit of Italy (*plural* **lire** /-rɪ/) and Turkey (*plural* **-s**).

lisle /laɪl/ *noun* fine cotton thread for stockings etc.

lisp *noun* speech defect in which *s* is pronounced like *th* in *thick* and *z* like *th* in *this*. ● *verb* speak or utter with lisp.

lissom /ˈlɪsəm/ *adjective* lithe, agile.

list[1] *noun* **1** number of items, names, etc. written or printed together as record. **2** (in *plural*) palisades enclosing tournament area. ● *verb* **1** arrange as or enter in list. **2** (as **listed** *adjective*) approved for Stock Exchange dealings. **3** (as **listed** *adjective*) (of a building) of historical importance and officially protected. □ **enter the lists** issue or accept challenge.
  ■ *noun* **1** catalogue, column, directory, file, index, inventory, listing, register, roll, roster, rota, schedule, shopping list, table. ● *verb* **1** catalogue, enumerate, index, itemize, note, record, register, tabulate, write down.

list[2] *verb* (of ship etc.) lean over to one side. ● *noun* listing position, tilt.
  ■ *verb* bank, careen, heel, incline, keel over, lean, slant, slope, tilt, tip.

listen /ˈlɪs(ə)n/ *verb* **1** make effort to hear something. **2** attentively hear person speaking. **3** (+ *to*) give attention with ear to. **4** (+ *to*) take notice of. □ **listen in 1** tap telephonic communication. **2** use radio receiving set. □ **listener** *noun*.
  ■ attend, concentrate, eavesdrop, *archaic* hark, hear, heed, lend an ear, overhear, pay attention, take notice.

listless /ˈlɪstlɪs/ *adjective* lacking energy or enthusiasm. □ **listlessly** *adverb*. **listlessness** *noun*.
  ■ apathetic, enervated, feeble, heavy, languid, lazy, lethargic, lifeless, phlegmatic, sluggish, tired, torpid, unenthusiastic, uninterested, weak, weary.

lit *past* & *past participle* of LIGHT[1,2].

litany /ˈlɪtənɪ/ *noun* (*plural* **-ies**) **1** series of supplications to God used in church services. **2** (**the Litany**) that in Book of Common Prayer.

litchi = LYCHEE.

liter *US* = LITRE.

literacy /ˈlɪtərəsɪ/ *noun* ability to read and write.

literal /ˈlɪtər(ə)l/ *adjective* **1** taking words in their basic sense without metaphor etc. **2** corresponding exactly to original words. **3** prosaic; matter-of-fact. □ **literalism** *noun*. **literally** *adverb*.
  ■ **2** close, exact, faithful, strict, verbatim, word for word. **3** matter-of-fact, prosaic, unimaginative.

literary /ˈlɪtərərɪ/ *adjective* of or concerned with or interested in literature.
  ■ (*literary person*) cultured, educated, erudite, learned, refined, scholarly, well-read, widely-read; (*literary style*) ornate, poetic, polished, rhetorical, sophisticated, stylish.

literate /ˈlɪtərət/ *adjective* able to read and write. ● *noun* literate person.
  ■ *adjective* educated, well read.

literati /lɪtəˈrɑːtɪ/ *plural noun* the class of learned people.

literature /ˈlɪtərətʃə/ *noun* **1** written works, esp. those valued for form and style. **2** writings of country or period or on particular subject. **3** *colloquial* printed matter, leaflets, etc.
■ **1, 2** books, creative writing, letters, works, writings. **3** brochures, circulars, handouts, information, leaflets, pamphlets, papers, propaganda.

lithe /laɪð/ *adjective* flexible, supple.
■ agile, flexible, limber, lissom, loose-jointed, pliable, pliant, supple.

litho /ˈlaɪθəʊ/ *colloquial noun* lithography.
● *verb* (**-oes, -oed**) lithograph.

lithograph /ˈlɪθəɡrɑːf/ *noun* lithographic print.
● *verb* print by lithography.

lithography /lɪˈθɒɡrəfɪ/ *noun* process of printing from plate so treated that ink sticks only to design to be printed. □ **lithographer** *noun*. **lithographic** /lɪθəˈɡræfɪk/ *adjective*.

Lithuanian /lɪθjuːˈeɪnɪən/ *noun* native, national, or language of Lithuania. ● *adjective* of Lithuania.

litigant /ˈlɪtɪɡənt/ *noun* party to lawsuit.
● *adjective* engaged in lawsuit.

litigate /ˈlɪtɪɡeɪt/ *verb* (**-ting**) **1** go to law. **2** contest (point) at law. □ **litigation** *noun*. **litigator** *noun*.

litigious /lɪˈtɪdʒəs/ *adjective* **1** fond of litigation. **2** contentious.

litmus /ˈlɪtməs/ *noun* dye turned red by acid and blue by alkali.

litre /ˈliːtə/ *noun* (*US* **liter**) metric unit of capacity (1.76 pints).

litter /ˈlɪtə/ *noun* **1** refuse, esp. paper, discarded in public place. **2** odds and ends lying about. **3** young animals brought forth at one birth. **4** vehicle containing couch and carried on men's shoulders or by animals. **5** kind of stretcher for sick and wounded. **6** straw etc. as bedding for animals. **7** material for animal's, esp. cat's, indoor toilet. ● *verb* **1** make (place) untidy. **2** give birth to (puppies etc.). **3** provide (horse etc.) with bedding.
■ *noun* **1, 2** bits and pieces, clutter, debris, fragments, *US* garbage, jumble, junk, mess, odds and ends, refuse, rubbish, *esp. US* trash, waste. ● *verb* **1** clutter, mess up, scatter, strew.

little /ˈlɪt(ə)l/ *adjective* (**-r, -st**; **less** or **lesser**, **least**) **1** small in size, amount, degree, etc. **2** short in stature. **3** of short distance or duration. **4** (**a little**) certain but small amount of. **5** trivial. **6** only small amount. **7** operating on small scale. **8** humble, ordinary. **9** young, younger. ● *noun* **1** not much; only small amount. **2** short time or distance. ● *adverb* (**less, least**) **1** to small extent only. **2** not at all. □ **little by little** by degrees; gradually. **the little people** fairies.
■ *adjective* **1, 2** diminutive, dwarf, lilliputian, midget, *colloquial* pint-sized, pygmy, short, small, *colloquial* teeny, tiny, undersized, *esp. Scottish* wee, *colloquial* weeny. **1** baby, bantam, compact,

concise, *colloquial* dinky, fine, fractional, infinitesimal, lean, microscopic, *colloquial* mini, miniature, *colloquial* minuscule, minute, narrow, petite (*woman*), pocket-sized, poky, portable, slender, slight, thin, toy. **3** fractional, infinitesimal, short. **5** inconsequential, insignificant, minor, negligible, nugatory, slight, trifling, trivial, unimportant. **6** exiguous, inadequate, insufficient, meagre, mean, *colloquial* measly, miserly, modest, niggardly, *colloquial* piddling, scanty, skimpy, stingy, ungenerous, unsatisfactory.

littoral /ˈlɪtər(ə)l/ *adjective* of or on the shore.
● *noun* region lying along shore.

liturgy /ˈlɪtədʒɪ/ *noun* (*plural* **-ies**) **1** fixed form of public worship. **2** (**the Liturgy**) the Book of Common Prayer. □ **liturgical** /-ˈtɜːdʒ-/ *adjective*.

live[1] /lɪv/ *verb* (**-ving**) **1** have life; be or remain alive. **2** have one's home. **3** (often + *on, off*) subsist. **4** (+ *on*) feed on. **5** keep one's position. **6** pass, spend. **7** conduct oneself in specified way. **8** enjoy life to the full. □ **live down** cause (scandal etc.) to be forgotten through blameless behaviour thereafter. **live it up** *colloquial* live exuberantly and extravagantly.
■ **1** breathe, continue, endure, exist, function, last, persist, remain, stay alive, survive. **2** be accommodated, dwell, lodge, reside, *US* room, stay; (*live in*) see INHABIT. **3** exist, fare, get along, keep going, make a living, subsist, sustain oneself. **4** (*live on*) see EAT 1.

live[2] /laɪv/ *adjective* **1** that is alive; living. **2** (of broadcast, performance, etc.) heard or seen while happening or with audience present. **3** of current interest. **4** glowing, burning. **5** (of match, bomb, etc.) not yet kindled or exploded. **6** charged with electricity. ● *adverb* as live performance. □ **livestock** (usually treated as *plural*) animals kept on farm for use or profit. **live wire** spirited person.
■ *adjective* **1** see LIVING 1. **3** contemporary, current, important, pressing, relevant, topical, vital. **4** see ALIGHT[1] 1. □ **livestock** farm animals, stock.

liveable /ˈlɪvəb(ə)l/ *adjective* (also **livable**) **1** (usually **liveable-in**) *colloquial* (of house etc.) fit to live in. **2** (of life) worth living. **3** (usually **liveable-with**) *colloquial* (of person) easy to live with.

livelihood /ˈlaɪvlɪhʊd/ *noun* means of living; job, income.

livelong /ˈlɪvlɒŋ/ *adjective* in its entire length.

lively /ˈlaɪvlɪ/ *adjective* (**-ier, -iest**) **1** full of life; energetic. **2** (of imagination) vivid. **3** cheerful. **4** *jocular* exciting, dangerous. □ **liveliness** *noun*.
■ **1** active, agile, alert, animated, boisterous, bubbly, bustling, busy, dashing, eager, energetic, enthusiastic, exciting, exuberant, frisky, high-spirited, irrepressible, nimble, perky, playful, quick, spirited, sprightly, stimulating, vigorous, vital, vivacious. **2** colourful, expressive, strong, vivid. **3** bubbly, cheerful, exuberant, gay, happy, high-spirited, jaunty, jolly, merry, perky. □ **liveliness** activity, animation, boisterousness, bustle, dynamism, energy, enthusiasm,

exuberance, go, gusto, high spirits, spirit, sprightliness, verve, vigour, vitality, vivacity, zeal.

liven /'laɪv(ə)n/ *verb* (often + *up*) make or become lively; cheer up.

liver[1] /'lɪvə/ *noun* **1** large glandular organ in abdomen of vertebrates. **2** liver of some animals as food.

liver[2] /'lɪvə/ *noun* person who lives in specified way.

liverish /'lɪvərɪʃ/ *adjective* **1** suffering from liver disorder. **2** peevish, glum.

liverwort *noun* mosslike plant sometimes lobed like liver.

livery /'lɪvərɪ/ *noun* (*plural* **-ies**) **1** distinctive uniform of member of City Company or servant. **2** distinctive guise or marking. **3** distinctive colour scheme for company's vehicles etc. □ **at livery** (of horse) kept for owner at fixed charge. **livery stable** stable where horses are kept at livery or let out for hire.

lives *plural* of LIFE.

livid /'lɪvɪd/ *adjective* **1** *colloquial* furious. **2** of bluish leaden colour.

living /'lɪvɪŋ/ *noun* **1** being alive. **2** livelihood. **3** position held by member of clergy, providing income. ● *adjective* **1** contemporary; now alive. **2** (of likeness) exact. **3** (of language) still in vernacular use. □ **living room** room for general day use. **living wage** wage on which one can live without privation. **within living memory** within memory of living people.

■ *noun* **2** income, livelihood, subsistence.
● *adjective* **1** actual, alive, animate, breathing, existing, extant, functioning, live, *archaic* quick, sentient, surviving.

lizard /'lɪzəd/ *noun* reptile with usually long body and tail, 4 legs, and scaly hide.

llama /'lɑːmə/ *noun* S. American ruminant kept for carrying loads and for woolly fleece.

Lloyd's /lɔɪdz/ *noun* incorporated society of underwriters in London. □ **Lloyd's Register** annual classified list of all ships.

lo *interjection archaic* look.

loach *noun* (*plural* same or **-es**) small freshwater fish.

load *noun* **1** what is (to be) carried. **2** amount usually or actually carried. **3** burden of work, responsibility, care, etc. **4** (in *plural*; often + *of*) plenty. **5** (**a load of**) a quantity of. **6** amount of power carried by electrical circuit or supplied by generating station. ● *verb* **1** put load on or aboard. **2** place (load) aboard ship or on vehicle etc. **3** (often + *up*) (of vehicle or person) take load aboard. **4** (often + *with*) burden, strain, overwhelm. **5** put ammunition in (gun), film in (camera), cassette in (tape recorder), program in (computer), etc. □ **load line** Plimsoll line.

■ *noun* **1, 2** burden, cargo, consignment, freight, shipment. **3** anxiety, burden, care, cross, encumbrance, millstone, onus, trouble, weight, worry. ● *verb* **1, 2** fill, heap, pack, pile, ply, stack, stow. **4** burden, encumber, oppress, overwhelm, saddle, strain, weigh down. **5** charge, prime.

loaded *adjective* **1** *slang* rich. **2** *slang* drunk. **3** *US slang* drugged. **4** (of dice etc.) weighted. **5** (of question or statement) carrying hidden implication. **6** bearing load.

■ **1** see WEALTHY. **4** see BIASED (BIAS). **6** see LADEN (LADE).

loadstone = LODESTONE.

loaf[1] *noun* (*plural* **loaves**) **1** unit of baked bread, usually of standard size or shape. **2** other cooked food in loaf shape. **3** *slang* head.

loaf[2] *verb* (often + *about*) spend time idly; hang about. □ **loafer** *noun*.

■ □ **loafer** idler, good-for-nothing, layabout, *colloquial* lazybones, shirker, *slang* skiver, vagrant, wastrel.

loam *noun* rich soil of clay, sand, and humus. □ **loamy** *adjective*.

loan *noun* **1** thing lent, esp. money. **2** lending, being lent. ● *verb* lend (money, works of art, etc.). □ **on loan** being lent.

■ *noun* advance, credit, mortgage. ● *verb* advance, allow, credit, lend.

loath *adjective* (also **loth**) disinclined, reluctant.

loathe /ləʊð/ *verb* (**-thing**) detest, hate. □ **loathing** *noun*.

■ abhor, abominate, be revolted by, despise, detest, execrate, hate, recoil from, resent, scorn, shudder at.

loathsome /'ləʊðsəm/ *adjective* arousing hatred or disgust; repulsive.

loaves *plural* of LOAF[1].

lob *verb* (**-bb-**) hit or throw (ball etc.) slowly or in high arc. ● *noun* such ball.

lobar /'ləʊbə/ *adjective* of a lobe, esp. of lung.

lobate /'ləʊbeɪt/ *adjective* having lobe(s).

lobby /'lɒbɪ/ *noun* (*plural* **-ies**) **1** porch, anteroom, entrance hall, corridor. **2** (in House of Commons) large hall used esp. for interviews between MPs and the public. **3** (also **division lobby**) each of two corridors to which MPs retire to vote. **4** group of lobbyists. ● *verb* (**-ies, -ied**) **1** solicit support of (influential person). **2** inform (legislators etc.) in order to influence them. □ **lobby correspondent** journalist who receives unattributable briefings from government.

■ *noun* **1** ante-room, corridor, entrance hall, entry, foyer, hall, hallway, porch, reception, vestibule. **4** campaigners, pressure group, supporters. ● *verb* appeal to, persuade, petition, pressurize, urge.

lobbyist *noun* person who lobbies MP etc.

lobe *noun* **1** lower soft pendulous part of outer ear. **2** similar part of other organs. □ **lobed** *adjective*.

lobelia /lə'biːlɪə/ *noun* plant with bright, esp. blue, flowers.

lobotomy /lə'bɒtəmɪ/ *noun* (*plural* **-ies**) incision into frontal lobe of brain to relieve mental disorder.

lobster /'lɒbstə/ *noun* **1** marine crustacean with

two pincer-like claws. **2** its flesh as food. □ **lobster pot** basket for trapping lobsters.

lobworm *noun* large earthworm used as fishing bait.

local /'ləʊk(ə)l/ *adjective* **1** belonging to, existing in, or peculiar to particular place. **2** of the neighbourhood. **3** of or affecting a part and not the whole. **4** (of telephone call) to nearby place and at lower charge. ● *noun* **1** inhabitant of particular place. **2** (often **the local**) *colloquial* local public house. □ **local authority** administrative body in local government. **local colour** touches of detail in story etc. designed to provide realistic background. **local government** system of administration of county, district, parish, etc. by elected representatives of those who live there. □ **locally** *adverb*.

■ *adjective* **1, 2** community, nearby, neighbourhood, neighbouring, parochial, provincial, regional. **3** limited, localized, narrow, particular, restricted. ● *noun* **1** inhabitant, resident, townsman, townswoman. **2** see PUB.

locale /ləʊ'kɑːl/ *noun* scene or locality of event or occurrence.

locality /ləʊ'kælɪtɪ/ *noun* (*plural* **-ies**) **1** district. **2** thing's site or scene. **3** thing's position.

■ **1** area, catchment area, community, district, neighbourhood, parish, region, residential area, town, vicinity, zone. **2, 3** see LOCATION 1.

localize /'ləʊkəlaɪz/ *verb* (also **-ise**) (**-zing** or **-sing**) **1** restrict or assign to particular place. **2** invest with characteristics of place. **3** decentralize.

■ **1** concentrate, confine, contain, enclose, keep within bounds, limit, narrow down, pin down, restrict.

locate /ləʊ'keɪt/ *verb* (**-ting**) **1** discover exact place of. **2** establish in a place; situate. **3** state locality of.

USAGE In standard English, it is incorrect to use *locate* to mean merely 'find' as in *I can't locate my key*.

■ **1** come across, detect, discover, find, identify, lay one's hands on, run to earth, search out, track down, unearth. **2** establish, find a place for, found, place, position, put, set up, site, situate, station.

location *noun* **1** particular place. **2** locating. **3** natural, not studio, setting for film etc.

■ **1** locale, locality, place, point, position, setting, site, situation, spot, venue, whereabouts.

loc. cit. *abbreviation* in the passage cited (*loco citato*).

loch /lɒx, lɒk/ *noun Scottish* lake or narrow inlet of the sea.

lock[1] *noun* **1** mechanism for fastening door etc. with bolt requiring key of particular shape. **2** section of canal or river confined within sluice-gates for moving boats from one level to another. **3** turning of vehicle's front wheels. **4** interlocked or jammed state. **5** wrestling hold. ● *verb* **1** fasten with lock. **2** (+ *up*) shut (house etc.) thus. **3** (of door etc.) be lockable. **4** (+ *up, away, in, into*) enclose (person, thing) by locking. **5** (often + *up, away*) store inaccessibly. **6** make or become rigidly fixed. **7** (cause to) jam or catch. □ **lockjaw** form of tetanus in which jaws become rigidly closed. **lock-keeper** keeper of river or canal lock. **lock on to** (of missile etc.) automatically find and then track (target). **lock out 1** keep out by locking door. **2** (of employer) subject (employees) to lockout. **lockout** *noun* employer's exclusion of employees from workplace until certain terms are accepted. **locksmith** maker and mender of locks. **lock-up 1** house or room for temporary detention of prisoners. **2** premises that can be locked up. **under lock and key** securely locked up; confined. □ **lockable** *adjective*.

■ *noun* **1** bar, bolt, catch, clasp, fastening, hasp, latch, padlock. ● *verb* **1, 2** bolt, close, fasten, padlock, seal, secure, shut. **4** (*lock away, lock up*) see IMPRISON 1. □ **lock out** see EXCLUDE 1.

lock[2] *noun* **1** portion of hair that hangs together. **2** (in *plural*) the hair.

locker *noun* (usually lockable) cupboard, esp. for public use.

locket /'lɒkɪt/ *noun* small ornamental case for portrait etc., usually on chain round neck.

locomotion /ləʊkə'məʊʃ(ə)n/ *noun* motion or power of motion from place to place.

locomotive /ləʊkə'məʊtɪv/ *noun* engine for pulling trains. ● *adjective* of, having, or bringing about locomotion.

locum tenens /ləʊkəm 'tiːnenz/ *noun* (*plural* **locum tenentes** /tɪ'nentiːz/) (also **locum**) deputy acting esp. for doctor or member of clergy.

locus /'ləʊkəs/ *noun* (*plural* **loci** /-saɪ/) **1** position, place. **2** line or curve etc. made by all points satisfying certain conditions or by defined motion of point, line, or surface.

locust /'ləʊkəst/ *noun* African or Asian grasshopper migrating in swarms and consuming all vegetation.

locution /lə'kjuːʃ(ə)n/ *noun* **1** word, phrase, or idiom. **2** style of speech.

lode *noun* vein of metal ore. □ **lodestar** star used as guide in navigation, esp. pole star. **lodestone, loadstone 1** magnetic oxide of iron. **2** piece of this as magnet.

lodge *noun* **1** small house, esp. one for gatekeeper at entrance to park or grounds of large house. **2** porter's room etc. **3** members or meeting place of branch of society such as Freemasons. **4** beaver's or otter's lair. ● *verb* (**-ging**) **1** reside, esp. as lodger. **2** provide with sleeping quarters. **3** submit (complaint etc.). **4** become fixed or caught. **5** deposit for security. **6** settle, place.

■ *verb* **1** *archaic* abide, dwell, live, put up, reside, stay, *colloquial* stop. **2** accommodate, billet, board, house, put up. **3** enter, file, make, put on record, record, register, submit.

lodger *noun* person paying for accommodation in another's house.

■ boarder, guest, inmate, paying guest, resident, tenant.

lodging *noun* **1** temporary accommodation. **2** (in *plural*) room(s) rented for lodging in.

■ **1** accommodation, billet, shelter, temporary home. **2** (*lodgings*) accommodation, apartment(s), billet, boarding house, *colloquial* digs, lodging house, *slang* pad, quarters, rooms.

loft *noun* **1** attic. **2** room over stable. **3** gallery in church or hall. **4** pigeon house. ● *verb* send (ball etc.) high up.

lofty *adjective* (**-ier, -iest**) **1** of imposing height. **2** haughty, aloof. **3** exalted, noble. □ **loftily** *adverb*. **loftiness** *noun*.

■ **1** elevated, high, soaring, tall, towering. **2** see ARROGANT. **3** elevated, exalted, imposing, majestic, noble.

log[1] *noun* **1** unhewn piece of felled tree; any large rough piece of wood. **2** *historical* floating device for ascertaining ship's speed. **3** record of ship's or aircraft's voyage. **4** any systematic record of experiences etc. ● *verb* (**-gg-**) **1** enter (ship's speed or other transport details) in logbook. **2** enter (data etc.) in regular record. **3** cut into logs. □ **logbook 1** book containing record or log. **2** vehicle registration document. **log on or off, log in or out** begin or end operations at terminal of esp. multi-access computer.

■ *noun* **3, 4** account, diary, journal, record.

log[2] *noun* logarithm.

logan /ˈləʊgən/ *noun* (in full **logan-stone**) poised heavy stone rocking at a touch.

loganberry /ˈləʊgənbərɪ/ *noun* (*plural* **-ies**) dark red fruit, hybrid of blackberry and raspberry.

logarithm /ˈlɒgərɪð(ə)m/ *noun* an arithmetic exponent used in computation. □ **logarithmic** /-ˈrɪðmɪk/ *adjective*.

loggerhead /ˈlɒgəhed/ *noun* □ **at loggerheads** (often + *with*) disagreeing or disputing.

loggia /ˈləʊdʒə/ *noun* open-sided gallery or arcade.

logging *noun* work of cutting and preparing forest timber.

logic /ˈlɒdʒɪk/ *noun* **1** science of reasoning. **2** chain of reasoning. **3** use of or ability in argument. **4** inexorable force. **5** principles used in designing computer etc. **6** circuits based on these. □ **logician** /ləˈdʒɪʃ(ə)n/ *noun*.

■ **2, 3** clarity, deduction, intelligence, *literary* ratiocination, rationality, reasonableness, reasoning, sense, validity.

logical *adjective* **1** of or according to logic. **2** correctly reasoned, consistent. **3** capable of correct reasoning. □ **logicality** /-ˈkæl-/ *noun*. **logically** *adverb*.

■ **1, 2** clear, cogent, coherent, consistent, deductive, methodical, rational, reasonable, sound, step by step, structured, systematic, valid, well reasoned, well thought out. **3** intelligent, rational, reasonable, sensible, wise.

logistics /ləˈdʒɪstɪks/ *plural noun* organization of (originally military) services and supplies. □ **logistic** *adjective*. **logistical** *adjective*. **logistically** *adverb*.

logo /ˈləʊgəʊ/ *noun* (*plural* **-s**) organization's emblem used in display material.

loin *noun* **1** (in *plural*) side and back of body between ribs and hip-bones. **2** joint of meat from this part of animal. □ **loincloth** cloth worn round hips, esp. as sole garment.

loiter /ˈlɔɪtə/ *verb* stand about idly; linger. □ **loiter with intent** linger to commit felony.

■ be slow, dally, dawdle, hang back, linger, loaf about or around, mess about or around, skulk, stand about or around, straggle.

loll *verb* **1** (often + *about, around*) stand, sit, or recline in lazy attitude. **2** hang loosely.

lollipop /ˈlɒlɪpɒp/ *noun* hard sweet on stick. □ **lollipop man, lady** *colloquial* warden using circular sign on pole to stop traffic for children to cross road.

lollop /ˈlɒləp/ *verb* (**-p-**) *colloquial* **1** flop about. **2** move in ungainly bounds.

lolly /ˈlɒlɪ/ *noun* (*plural* **-ies**) **1** *colloquial* lollipop. **2** *colloquial* ice lolly. **3** *slang* money.

lone *adjective* **1** solitary; without companions. **2** isolated. **3** unmarried. □ **lone hand 1** hand played or player playing against the rest at cards. **2** person or action without allies. **lone wolf** loner.

■ **1** separate, single, solitary, solo, unaccompanied. **2** see LONELY 3.

lonely /ˈləʊnlɪ/ *adjective* (**-ier, -iest**) **1** without companions. **2** sad because of this. **3** isolated; uninhabited. □ **loneliness** *noun*.

■ **1** abandoned, alone, forlorn, forsaken, friendless, *esp. US* lonesome, loveless, neglected, outcast, reclusive, retiring, solitary, unsociable, withdrawn. **2** see SAD 1. **3** cut off, deserted, desolate, distant, far-away, isolated, lone, out of the way, remote, secluded, unfrequented, uninhabited.

loner *noun* person or animal preferring to be alone.

lonesome *adjective* **1** *esp. US* lonely. **2** causing loneliness.

long[1] *adjective* (**longer** /ˈlɒŋgə/, **longest** /ˈlɒŋgɪst/) **1** measuring much from end to end in space or time. **2** (following measurement) in length or duration. **3** consisting of many items. **4** tedious. **5** reaching far back or forward in time. **6** of elongated shape. **7** involving great interval or difference. ● *noun* long interval or period. ● *adverb* (**longer** /ˈlɒŋgə/, **longest** /ˈlɒŋgɪst/) **1** by or for a long time. **2** (following nouns of duration) throughout specified time. **3** (in *comparative*) after implied point of time. □ **as, so long as** provided that. **before long** soon. **in the long run** eventually. **longboat** sailing ship's largest boat. **longbow** one drawn by hand and shooting long arrow. **long-distance** travelling or operating between distant places. **long-drawn** (also

long-drawn-out) prolonged, esp. unduly. **long face** dismal expression. **long-faced** *adjective*. **longhand** ordinary handwriting. **long johns** *colloquial* long underpants. **long jump** athletic contest of jumping along ground in one leap. **long-lasting** durable. **long-life** (of milk etc.) treated to prolong shelf-life. **long-lived** having a long life. **long odds** chances with low probability. **long-playing** (of gramophone record) playing for about 20–30 minutes on each side. **long-range 1** having a long range. **2** relating to period of time far into future. **longshore** existing on or frequenting the shore. **long shot** wild guess or venture. **long sight** ability to see clearly only what is comparatively distant. **long-sighted 1** having long sight. **2** far-sighted. **long-standing** that has existed for a long time. **long-suffering** bearing provocation patiently. **long-term** of or for long period of time. **long-winded** (of speech or writing) tediously lengthy. **long-windedness** *noun*.

■ *adjective* **1, 3, 7** big, endless, extensive, great, interminable, large, lengthy, longish, prolonged, protracted, unending. **4, 5** drawn-out, endless, extended, extensive, interminable, lasting, lengthy, longish, prolonged, protracted, slow, sustained, time-consuming, unending. **6** elongated, extended, lengthy, longish, stretched.
□ **long-lasting, long-lived** see PERMANENT. **long-standing** see OLD 4. **long-suffering** see PATIENT *adjective*. **long-winded** see TEDIOUS.

long[2] *verb* (+ *for*, *to do*) have strong wish or desire for. □ **longing** *noun* & *adjective*. **longingly** *adverb*.

■ crave, hanker, have a longing, hunger, itch, pine, thirst, wish, yearn; (*long for*) see DESIRE *verb* 1.
□ **longing** appetite, craving, desire, hankering, hunger, itch, need, thirst, urge, wish, yearning, *colloquial* yen.

long. *abbreviation* longitude.

longevity /lɒnˈdʒevɪtɪ/ *noun formal* long life.

longitude /ˈlɒŋgɪtjuːd/ *noun* angular distance E. or W. of (esp. Greenwich) meridian.

longitudinal /lɒŋgɪˈtjuːdɪn(ə)l/ *adjective* **1** of or in length. **2** running lengthwise. **3** of longitude. □ **longitudinally** *adverb*.

longways *adverb* (also **longwise**) in direction parallel with thing's length.

loo *noun colloquial* lavatory.

loofah /ˈluːfə/ *noun* rough bath-sponge made from dried pod of type of gourd.

look /lʊk/ *verb* **1** (often + *at*, *down*, *up*, etc.) use or direct one's eyes; examine. **2** (+ *at*) consider. **3** make visual or mental search. **4** (+ *for*) seek. **5** have specified appearance; seem. **6** (+ *into*) investigate. **7** (of thing) face some direction. **8** indicate (emotion) by looks. **9** (+ *to do*) expect. ● *noun* **1** act of looking. **2** gaze, glance. **3** appearance of face; expression. **4** (in *plural*) personal appearance. □ **look after** attend to. **lookalike** person or thing closely resembling another. **look back** (+ *on*, *to*) turn one's thoughts to (something

past). **look down (up)on** regard with contempt. **looker-on** mere spectator. **look forward to** await (expected event) eagerly or with specified feelings. **look in** make short visit. **look-in** *noun colloquial* chance of participation or success. **looking-glass** mirror. **look on** be spectator. **look out** (often + *for*) be vigilant or prepared. **lookout** *noun* **1** watch. **2** observation-post. **3** person etc. stationed to keep watch. **4** prospect. **5** *colloquial* person's own concern. **look up 1** search for (esp. information in book). **2** *colloquial* visit (person). **3** improve in prospect. **look up to** respect.

■ *verb* **1** gape, *colloquial* gawp, gaze, glance, goggle, have a look, ogle, peek, peep, peer, squint, stare. **1, 2** (*look at*) *literary* behold, cast one's eye over, consider, contemplate, examine, eye, glimpse, inspect, observe, pay attention to, read, regard, scan, scrutinize, see, skim through, study, survey, take note of, view, watch. **3** have a look, search. **4** (*look for*) see SEEK 1. **5** appear, seem. **6** (*look into*) see INVESTIGATE. **7** face, point. ● *noun* **1, 2** gaze, glance, glimpse, observation, peek, peep, sight, *colloquial* squint, view. **3** air, appearance, aspect, bearing, complexion, countenance, demeanour, expression, face, manner, *literary* mien; (*looks*) attractiveness, beauty. □ **look after** see TEND[2]. **look down on** see DESPISE. **look out** see BEWARE 1. **lookout 3** guard, sentinel, sentry, watchman. **look up to** see ADMIRE.

loom[1] /luːm/ *noun* apparatus for weaving.

loom[2] /luːm/ *verb* **1** appear dimly, esp. as vague often tall or threatening shape. **2** (of an event) be ominously close.

■ **1** appear, arise, dominate, emerge, hover, *colloquial* materialize, menace, rise, stand out, stick up, take shape, threaten, tower. **2** impend, menace, threaten.

loon /luːn/ *noun* **1** kind of diving bird. **2** *colloquial* crazy person.

loony /ˈluːnɪ/ *slang noun* (*plural* **-ies**) lunatic. ● *adjective* (**-ier**, **-iest**) crazy.

loop /luːp/ *noun* **1** figure produced by curve or doubled thread etc. crossing itself. **2** thing, path, etc. forming this figure. **3** similarly shaped attachment used as fastening. **4** contraceptive coil. **5** endless band of tape or film allowing continuous repetition. **6** repeated sequence of computer operations. ● *verb* **1** form or bend into loop. **2** fasten with loop(s). **3** form loop. □ **loop line** railway or telegraph line that diverges from main line and joins it again.

■ *noun* **1–3** bend, bow, circle, coil, curl, eye, hoop, kink, noose, ring, turn, twist, whorl. ● *verb* bend, coil, curl, entwine, turn, twist, wind.

loophole *noun* **1** means of evading rule etc. without infringing it. **2** narrow vertical slit in wall of fort etc.

■ **1** escape, *colloquial* let-out, outlet, way out.

loopy *adjective* (**-ier**, **-iest**) *slang* crazy.

loose /luːs/ *adjective* **1** not tightly held. **2** not held together. **3** free from bonds or restraint. **4** (of clothes) not tight-fitting. **5** not compact or dense. **6** inexact. **7** morally lax. ● *verb* (**-sing**) **1**

untie, detach. **2** free, release. **3** relax (hold etc.). □ **at a loose end** unoccupied. **loose change** money as coins for casual use. **loose cover** removable cover for armchair etc. **loose-leaf** (of notebook etc.) with pages that can be removed and replaced. **on the loose 1** escaped from captivity. **2** enjoying oneself freely. □ **loosely** *adverb.* **looseness** *noun.*

■ *adjective* **1, 2** detachable, detached, disconnected, insecure, loosened, movable, moving, scattered, shaky, unattached, unconnected, unfastened, unsteady, wobbly; (*loose hair*) dangling, hanging, spread out, straggling, trailing. **3** at large, at liberty, escaped, free, free-range, independent, released, roaming, uncaged, unconfined, unfettered, unrestricted, untied. **4** baggy, floppy, loose-fitting, slack. **6** broad, careless, casual, diffuse, general, ill-defined, illogical, imprecise, inexact, informal, lax, rambling, rough, sloppy, unscientific, unstructured, vague. **7** see IMMORAL. ● *verb* **1** see LOOSEN. **2** see FREE *verb* 1–2.

loosen *verb* make or become loose or looser. □ **loosen up 1** limber up. **2** relax.

■ come adrift, detach, ease off, free, let go, loose, open up, relax, release, separate, slacken, undo, unfasten, unloose, untie.

loot /luːt/ *noun* **1** spoil, booty. **2** *slang* money. ● *verb* **1** rob or steal, esp. after rioting etc. **2** plunder. □ **looter** *noun.*

■ *noun* **1** booty, contraband, haul, ill-gotten gains, plunder, prize, spoils, *slang* swag, takings. ● *verb* despoil, pillage, plunder, raid, ransack, ravage, rifle, rob, sack, steal from.

lop *verb* (**-pp-**) **1** (often + *off*) cut or remove (part or parts) from whole, esp. branches from tree. **2** prune (tree).

lope *verb* (**-ping**) run with long bounding stride. ● *noun* such stride.

lop-eared *adjective* having drooping ears.

lopsided *adjective* unevenly balanced.

■ askew, asymmetrical, awry, *colloquial* cock-eyed, crooked, one-sided, tilting, unbalanced, unequal, uneven.

loquacious /ləˈkweɪʃəs/ *adjective* talkative. □ **loquacity** /-ˈkwæsɪtɪ/ *noun.*

lord *noun* **1** master, ruler. **2** *historical* feudal superior, esp. of manor. **3** peer of realm; person with title *Lord*. **4** (**Lord**) (often **the Lord**) God, Christ. **5** (**Lord**) *title used before name of certain male peers and officials.* **6** (**the Lords**) House of Lords. ● *interjection: expressing surprise, dismay, etc.* □ **lord it over** domineer. **Lord Mayor** *title of mayor in some large cities.* **Lord's Day** Sunday. **Lord's Prayer** the prayer taught by Christ to his disciples. **Lord's Supper** Eucharist.

■ *noun* **1** see RULER 1. **3** aristocrat, baron, earl, marquess, noble, peer, *historical* thane, viscount.

lordly *adjective* (**-ier, -iest**) **1** haughty, imperious. **2** suitable for a lord.

Lordship *noun* □ **His, Your Lordship** *title used of or to man with rank of Lord.*

lore *noun* body of tradition and information on a subject or held by particular group.

lorgnette /lɔːˈnjet/ *noun* pair of eyeglasses or opera-glasses on long handle.

lorn *adjective archaic* desolate, forlorn.

lorry /ˈlɒrɪ/ *noun* (*plural* **-ies**) large vehicle for transporting goods etc.

lose /luːz/ *verb* (**-sing**; *past & past participle* **lost**) **1** be deprived of; cease to have, esp. by negligence. **2** be deprived of (person) by death. **3** become unable to find, follow, or understand. **4** let pass from one's control. **5** be defeated in. **6** evade; get rid of. **7** forfeit (right to something). **8** suffer loss or detriment. **9** cause (person) the loss of. **10** (of clock etc.) become slow. **11** (in *passive*) disappear, perish. **12** (as **lost** *adjective*) gone, mislaid; strayed. **13** (as **lost** *adjective*) absorbed. **14** (as **lost** *adjective*) damned. □ **be lost for words** be too surprised, shocked, etc. to know what to say. **be lost in** be engrossed in. **be lost without** be dependent on. **lose heart** be discouraged. **lose one's cool** *colloquial* lose one's composure. **lose one's head** lose self-control. **lose one's nerve** become timid or irresolute.

■ **1** be deprived of, *formal* cease to have, find oneself without. **3** forget, leave (somewhere), mislay, misplace, miss, stray from. **4** fritter, let slip, squander, waste. **5** admit defeat, be defeated, capitulate, come to grief, fail, get beaten, succumb, suffer defeat; (*losing*) see UNSUCCESSFUL. **6** escape from, evade, get rid of, give (person) the slip, leave behind, outrun, shake off, throw off. **7** see FORFEIT *verb.* **12** (**lost**) abandoned, departed, destroyed, disappeared, extinct, forgotten, gone, irrecoverable, irretrievable, left behind, mislaid, misplaced, missing, strayed, untraceable, vanished. **13** (**lost**) absorbed, daydreaming, dreamy, distracted, engrossed, preoccupied, rapt. **14** (**lost**) corrupt, damned, fallen, irredeemable.

loser *noun* **1** person or thing that loses esp. contest. **2** *colloquial* person who regularly fails.

loss *noun* **1** losing, being lost. **2** what is lost. **3** detriment resulting from losing. □ **at a loss** (sold etc.) for less than was paid for it. **be at a loss** be puzzled or uncertain. **loss-leader** item sold at a loss to attract customers.

■ **1** bereavement, defeat, depletion, deprivation, destruction, diminution, disappearance, erosion, failure, forfeiture, impairment, privation, reduction, sacrifice. **2** (*losses*) casualties, deaths, death toll, fatalities. **3** damage, detriment, disadvantage, harm, impairment.

lost *past & past participle* of LOSE.

lot *noun* **1** (**a lot, or lots**) *colloquial* large number or amount. **2** each of set of objects used to make chance selection. **3** this method of deciding. **4** share or responsibility resulting from it. **5** destiny, fortune, condition. **6** *esp. US* plot; allotment. **7** article or set of articles for sale at auction etc. **8** group of associated people or things. □ **draw, cast lots** decide by lots. **the (whole) lot** total number or quantity.

USAGE *A lot of*, as in *a lot of people*, is fairly

informal, though acceptable in serious writing, but *lots of people* is not acceptable.

■ **1 (a lot, lots)** see PLENTY *noun* 1. **7** see ITEM 1. □ **draw lots** see GAMBLE *verb* 1. **the (whole) lot** all, everything, the whole thing, *colloquial* the works.

loth = LOATH.

lotion /'ləʊʃ(ə)n/ *noun* medical or cosmetic liquid preparation applied externally.

■ balm, cream, embrocation, liniment, ointment, pomade, salve, unguent.

lottery /'lɒtərɪ/ *noun* (*plural* -ies) **1** means of raising money by selling numbered tickets and giving prizes to holders of numbers drawn at random. **2** thing whose outcome is governed by chance.

■ **1** raffle, sweepstake. **2** gamble, speculation, venture.

lotto /'lɒtəʊ/ *noun* game of chance like bingo.

lotus /'ləʊtəs/ *noun* **1** legendary plant inducing luxurious langour when eaten. **2** kind of water lily. □ **lotus position** cross-legged position of meditation.

loud *adjective* **1** strongly audible; noisy. **2** (of colours etc.) gaudy, obtrusive. ● *adverb* loudly. □ **loudspeaker** apparatus that converts electrical signals into sounds. □ **loudly** *adverb*. **loudness** *noun*.

■ *adjective* **1** audible, big, blaring, booming, clamorous, clarion (*call*), deafening, ear-splitting, echoing, *Music* fortissimo, noisy, penetrating, piercing, raucous, resounding, reverberant, reverberating, roaring, rowdy, shrieking, sonorous, stentorian, strident, thundering, thunderous, vociferous. **2** see GAUDY.

lough /lɒk, lɒx/ *noun* Irish lake, sea inlet.

lounge *verb* (-ging) **1** recline comfortably; loll. **2** (often + *about*, *around*) idle; stand or move idly. ● *noun* **1** place for lounging, esp. sitting room in house. **2** public room (in hotel etc.). **3** place in airport etc. with seats for waiting passengers. **4** spell of lounging. □ **lounge suit** man's suit for ordinary day wear.

■ *verb* be idle, be lazy, hang about or around, idle, laze, loaf, lie around, loll (about or around), *colloquial* mooch (about or around), relax, slouch, slump, sprawl, stand about or around, take it easy, vegetate. ● *noun* **1** drawing-room, front room, living room, *archaic* parlour, salon, sitting room.

lour /laʊə/ *verb* (also **lower** /laʊə/) **1** frown, look sullen. **2** (of sky etc.) look dark and threatening.

louse /laʊs/ *noun* **1** (*plural* lice) parasitic insect. **2** (*plural* louses) *slang* contemptible person. ● *verb* (-sing) delouse.

lousy /'laʊzɪ/ *adjective* (-ier, -iest) **1** *colloquial* very bad; disgusting; ill. **2** (often + *with*) *colloquial* well supplied. **3** infested with lice.

lout *noun* rough-mannered person. □ **loutish** *adjective*.

■ boor, churl, oaf, *slang* yob.

louvre /'lu:və/ *noun* (also **louver**) **1** each of set of overlapping slats designed to admit air and exclude rain. **2** domed structure on roof with side openings for ventilation etc.

lovable /'lʌvəb(ə)l/ *adjective* (also **loveable**) inspiring affection.

■ adorable, appealing, attractive, charming, cuddly, *esp. US colloquial* cute, darling, dear, enchanting, endearing, engaging, fetching, likeable, lovely, pleasing, taking, winning, winsome.

lovage /'lʌvɪdʒ/ *noun* herb used for flavouring etc.

love /lʌv/ *noun* **1** deep affection or fondness. **2** sexual passion. **3** sexual relations. **4** beloved one; sweetheart. **5** *colloquial: form of address regardless of affection.* **6** *colloquial* person of whom one is fond. **7** affectionate greetings. **8** (in games) no score, nil. ● *verb* (-ving) **1** feel love for. **2** delight in; admire. **3** *colloquial* like very much. □ **fall in love** (often + *with*) suddenly begin to love. **in love** (often + *with*) enamoured (of). **love affair** romantic or sexual relationship between two people. **love-bird** kind of parakeet. **love child** illegitimate child. **love-in-a-mist** blue-flowered cultivated plant. **lovelorn** pining from unrequited love. **lovesick** languishing with love. **make love 1** (often + *to*, *with*) have sexual intercourse (with). **2** (often + *to*) *archaic* pay amorous attention (to). □ **loved** *adjective*.

■ *noun* **1** admiration, adoration, adulation, affection, attachment, attraction, devotion, fancy, fondness, friendship, liking, regard, tenderness, warmth. **2** ardour, desire, fervour, infatuation, passion. **4** beloved, darling, dear, loved one, lover, sweetheart. ● *verb* **1** admire, adore, be charmed by, be fond of, be infatuated by, be in love with, care for, cherish, desire, dote on, *colloquial* fancy, *colloquial* have a crush on, have a passion for, idolize, lust after, treasure, value, want, worship. **2, 3** see LIKE² *verb* 1. □ **in love** besotted, devoted, enamoured, fond, infatuated. **love affair** affair, amour, courtship, intrigue, liaison, *colloquial* relationship, romance. **lovesick** frustrated, languishing, lovelorn, pining. **make love 1** be intimate, copulate, *usually jocular* fornicate, have intercourse, *colloquial* have sex, have sexual intercourse, mate. **2** caress, court, cuddle, embrace, flirt, kiss, *colloquial* neck, pet, philander, woo. □ **loved** beloved, cherished, darling, dear, dearest, esteemed, favourite, precious, treasured, valued, wanted.

loveable = LOVABLE.

loveless *adjective* unloving or unloved or both.

■ cold, forsaken, frigid, heartless, lovelorn, passionless, rejected, undemonstrative, unfeeling, unloved, unloving, unresponsive.

lovely *adjective* (-ier, -iest) **1** *colloquial* pleasing, delightful. **2** beautiful. □ **loveliness** *noun*.

■ **1** appealing, attractive, charming, delightful, enjoyable, fine, good, nice, pleasant, pretty, sweet. **2** see BEAUTIFUL 1.

lovemaking /'lʌvmeɪkɪŋ/ *noun* **1** amorous

sexual activity, esp. sexual intercourse. **2** *archaic* courtship.

lover *noun* **1** person in love with another. **2** person having sexual relations with another. **3** (in *plural*) unmarried couple in love or having sexual relations. **4** person who enjoys specified thing.

■ **1** admirer, boyfriend, companion, fiancé(e), friend, girlfriend, *colloquial* intended, suitor, sweetheart, valentine. **2** *literary* concubine, gigolo, mistress, *archaic* paramour, *colloquial* toy boy.

loving *adjective* feeling or showing love; affectionate. ● *noun* affection. □ **loving cup** two-handled drinking cup passed round at banquets. □ **lovingly** *adverb*.

■ *adjective* admiring, adoring, affectionate, amorous, ardent, attached, brotherly, caring, close, concerned, dear, demonstrative, devoted, doting, fatherly, fond, friendly, inseparable, kind, maternal, motherly, passionate, paternal, protective, sisterly, tender, warm.

low[1] /ləʊ/ *adjective* **1** not high or tall. **2** not elevated in position. **3** (of sun) near horizon. **4** of humble rank. **5** of small or less than normal amount, extent, or intensity. **6** dejected; lacking vigour. **7** (of sound) not shrill or loud. **8** commonplace. **9** (of opinion) unfavourable. **10** mean, vulgar. ● *noun* **1** low or lowest level or number. **2** area of low pressure. ● *adverb* **1** in or to low position. **2** in low tone. **3** at low pitch. □ **low-born** of humble birth. **lowbrow** *colloquial* not intellectual or cultured. **Low Church** section of Church of England attaching little importance to ritual, priestly authority, and sacraments. **low-class** of low quality or social class. **Low Countries** Netherlands, Belgium, and Luxembourg. **low-down** ● *adjective* mean, dishonourable. ● *noun* (**the low-down**; usually + *on*) *colloquial* relevant information. **lower case** small letters, not capitals. **low frequency** *Radio* 30–300 kilohertz. **low-grade** of low quality or strength. **low-key** lacking intensity or prominence. **low pressure** **1** low degree of activity. **2** atmospheric condition with pressure below average. **low spirits** dejection, depression. **Low Sunday** Sunday after Easter. **low tide, water** time or level of tide at its ebb. **low water mark** level reached at low water.

■ *adjective* **1** little, short, squat, stumpy, stunted. **2** flat, low-lying, sunken. **4** abject, base, degraded, humble, inferior, junior, lesser, lower, lowly, menial, miserable, modest, servile. **7** (*low notes*) bass, deep, reverberant; (*low sounds*) gentle, indistinct, muffled, murmurous, muted, *Music* pianissimo, quiet, soft, subdued, whispered. **10** base, churlish, coarse, *derogatory* common, cowardly, crude, dastardly, disreputable, ignoble, immoral, mean, nasty, vulgar, wicked. □ **in low spirits** see SAD 1. **lowbrow** accessible, easy, ordinary, pop, popular, rubbishy, simple, straightforward, uncultured, undemanding, unpretentious, unsophisticated.

low[2] /ləʊ/ *noun* sound made by cattle; moo. ● *verb* make this sound.

lower[1] *verb* **1** let or haul down. **2** make or become lower. **3** degrade.

■ **1** dip, drop, haul down, let down, take down. **2** (*lower prices*) bring down, cut, decrease, discount, drop, lessen, mark down, reduce, slash; (*lower the volume*) abate, diminish, quieten, tone down, turn down. **3** abase, belittle, debase, degrade, demean, discredit, disgrace, humble, humiliate.

lower[2] = LOUR.

lowland /ˈləʊlənd/ *noun* (usually in *plural*) low-lying country. ● *adjective* of or in lowland. □ **lowlander** *noun*.

lowly *adjective* (**-ier, -iest**) **1** humble. **2** unpretentious. □ **lowliness** *noun*.

■ **1** base, humble, insignificant, little known, low, low-born, meek, modest, obscure, unimportant. **2** see ORDINARY.

loyal /ˈlɔɪəl/ *adjective* **1** (often + *to*) faithful. **2** steadfast in allegiance etc. □ **loyally** *adverb*. **loyalty** *noun* (*plural* **-ies**).

■ committed, constant, dedicated, dependable, devoted, dutiful, faithful, honest, patriotic, reliable, sincere, stable, staunch, steadfast, steady, true, trustworthy, *archaic* or *jocular* trusty, unswerving, unwavering. □ **loyalty** allegiance, constancy, dedication, dependability, devotion, duty, faithfulness, fealty, fidelity, honesty, patriotism, reliability, staunchness, steadfastness, trustworthiness.

loyalist *noun* **1** person remaining loyal to legitimate sovereign etc. **2** (**Loyalist**) supporter of union between Great Britain and Northern Ireland. □ **loyalism** *noun*.

lozenge /ˈlɒzɪndʒ/ *noun* **1** rhombus. **2** small sweet or medicinal tablet to be dissolved in mouth. **3** lozenge-shaped object.

LP *abbreviation* long-playing (record).

LSD *abbreviation* lysergic acid diethylamide, a powerful hallucinogenic drug.

Lt. *abbreviation* **1** Lieutenant. **2** light.

Ltd. *abbreviation* Limited.

lubber /ˈlʌbə/ *noun* clumsy fellow, lout.

lubricant /ˈluːbrɪkənt/ *noun* substance used to reduce friction.

lubricate /ˈluːbrɪkeɪt/ *verb* (**-ting**) **1** apply oil, grease, etc. to. **2** make slippery. □ **lubrication** *noun*.

■ grease, oil.

lubricious /luːˈbrɪʃəs/ *adjective* **1** slippery, evasive. **2** lewd. □ **lubricity** *noun*.

lucerne /luːˈsɜːn/ *noun* alfalfa.

lucid /ˈluːsɪd/ *adjective* **1** expressing or expressed clearly. **2** sane. □ **lucidity** /-ˈsɪd-/ *noun*. **lucidly** *adverb*.

luck *noun* **1** chance as the bringer of good or bad fortune. **2** circumstances brought by this. **3** success due to chance.

■ **1, 2** accident, chance, coincidence, destiny, fate, fluke, fortune, serendipity. **3** break, good fortune, happiness, prosperity, success.

luckless *adjective* unlucky; ending in failure.

lucky *adjective* (**-ier, -iest**) **1** having good luck. **2** resulting from good luck. **3** bringing good luck. □ **lucky dip** tub containing articles from which one chooses at random. □ **luckily** *adverb*.

■ **1** blessed, favoured, fortunate, successful. **2** accidental, appropriate, chance, fluky, fortuitous, happy, opportune, providential, timely, unintentional, unplanned, welcome. **3** advantageous, auspicious.

lucrative /'luːkrətɪv/ *adjective* profitable. □ **lucratively** *adverb*.

lucre /'luːkə/ *noun derogatory* financial gain.

ludicrous /'luːdɪkrəs/ *adjective* absurd, ridiculous, laughable. □ **ludicrously** *adverb*. **ludicrousness** *noun*.

ludo /'luːdəʊ/ *noun* board game played with dice and counters.

lug *verb* (**-gg-**) **1** drag or carry with effort. **2** pull hard. ● *noun* **1** hard or rough pull. **2** *colloquial* ear. **3** projection on object by which it may be carried, fixed in place, etc.

luggage /'lʌgɪdʒ/ *noun* suitcases, bags, etc., for traveller's belongings.

■ baggage, bags, belongings, gear, impedimenta, paraphernalia, things.

lugger /'lʌgə/ *noun* small ship with 4-cornered sails (**lugsails**).

lugubrious /lʊˈguːbrɪəs/ *adjective* doleful. □ **lugubriously** *adverb*. **lugubriousness** *noun*.

lukewarm /luːkˈwɔːm/ *adjective* **1** moderately warm, tepid. **2** unenthusiastic.

■ **1** room temperature, tepid, warm. **2** apathetic, cool, half-hearted, indifferent, unenthusiastic.

lull *verb* **1** soothe; send to sleep. **2** (usually + *into*) deceive (person) into undue confidence. **3** allay (suspicions etc.). **4** (of noise, storm, etc.) lessen, fall quiet. ● *noun* temporary quiet period.

■ *verb* **1, 3** calm, hush, pacify, quell, quieten, soothe, subdue, tranquillize. ● *noun* break, calm, delay, gap, halt, hiatus, interlude, interruption, interval, lapse, *colloquial* let-up, pause, respite, rest, silence.

lullaby /'lʌləbaɪ/ *noun* (*plural* **-ies**) soothing song to send child to sleep.

lumbago /lʌmˈbeɪgəʊ/ *noun* rheumatic pain in muscles of lower back.

lumbar /'lʌmbə/ *adjective* of lower back. □ **lumbar puncture** withdrawal of spinal fluid from lower back for diagnosis.

lumber /'lʌmbə/ *noun* **1** disused and cumbersome articles. **2** partly prepared timber. ● *verb* **1** (usually + *with*) encumber (person). **2** move in slow clumsy way. **3** cut and prepare forest timber for transporting. □ **lumberjack** person who fells and transports lumber. **lumber-room** room where things in disuse are kept.

■ *noun* **1** bits and pieces, clutter, jumble, junk, litter, odds and ends, rubbish, trash, white elephants. **2** beams, boards, planks, timber, wood. ● *verb* **1** see BURDEN *verb*. **2** blunder, move clumsily, shamble, trudge.

lumen /'luːmen/ *noun* SI unit of luminous flux.

luminary /'luːmɪnərɪ/ *noun* (*plural* **-ies**) **1** *literary* natural light-giving body. **2** wise person. **3** celebrated member of group.

luminescence /luːmɪˈnes(ə)ns/ *noun* emission of light without heat. □ **luminescent** *adjective*.

luminous /'luːmɪnəs/ *adjective* **1** shedding light. **2** phosphorescent; visible in darkness. □ **luminosity** /-ˈnɒs-/ *noun*.

■ bright, glowing, luminescent, lustrous, phosphorescent, radiant, *literary* refulgent, shining.

lump[1] *noun* **1** compact shapeless mass. **2** tumour, swelling, bruise. **3** heavy ungainly person etc. ● *verb* (usually + *together* etc.) class, mass. □ **lump sugar** sugar in small lumps or cubes. **lump sum** sum including number of items or paid down all at once.

■ *noun* **1** ball, bar, bit, block, cake, chunk, clod, clot, cube, dollop, *slang* gob, gobbet, hunk, ingot, mass, nugget, piece, slab, wad, wedge. **2** boil, bulge, bump, carbuncle, cyst, excrescence, growth, hump, knob, node, nodule, protrusion, protuberance, spot, swelling, tumescence, tumour. ● *verb* (*lump together*) see COMBINE 1.

lump[2] *verb colloquial* (in contrast with *like*) put up with ungraciously.

lumpish *adjective* **1** heavy, clumsy. **2** stupid.

lumpy *adjective* (**-ier, -iest**) full of or covered with lumps. □ **lumpily** *adverb*. **lumpiness** *noun*.

lunacy /'luːnəsɪ/ *noun* (*plural* **-ies**) **1** insanity. **2** great folly.

■ **1** delirium, dementia, derangement, frenzy, hysteria, illogicality, insanity, madness, mania, psychosis, unreason. **2** see STUPIDITY.

lunar /'luːnə/ *adjective* of, like, concerned with, or determined by the moon. □ **lunar module** craft for travelling between moon and orbiting spacecraft. **lunar month** period of moon's revolution, (in general use) 4 weeks.

lunate /'luːneɪt/ *adjective* crescent-shaped.

lunatic /'luːnətɪk/ *noun* **1** insane person. **2** wildly foolish person. ● *adjective* **1** insane. **2** very reckless or foolish.

■ *noun colloquial* crackpot, crank, *slang* loony, madman, madwoman, maniac, *slang* nutcase, *slang* nutter, psychopath, psychotic. ● *adjective* **1** see MAD 1. **2** see FOOLISH.

lunation /luːˈneɪʃ(ə)n/ *noun* interval between new moons, about 29½ days.

lunch *noun* midday meal. ● *verb* **1** take lunch. **2** provide lunch for.

luncheon /'lʌntʃ(ə)n/ *noun formal* lunch. □ **luncheon voucher** voucher issued to employees and exchangeable for food at restaurant etc.

lung *noun* either of pair of respiratory organs in humans and many other vertebrates.

lunge *noun* 1 sudden movement forward. 2 attacking move in fencing. ● *verb* (**-ging**) (usually + *at*) 1 deliver lunge. 2 make lunge.
■ *verb* 1 jab, stab, strike, thrust. 2 charge, dash, dive, lurch, plunge, pounce, rush, spring, throw oneself.

lupin /ˈluːpɪn/ *noun* cultivated plant with long tapering spikes of flowers.

lupine /ˈluːpaɪn/ *adjective* of or like wolves.

lupus /ˈluːpəs/ *noun* inflammatory skin disease.

lurch[1] *noun* stagger; sudden unsteady movement or tilt. ● *verb* stagger; move unsteadily.
■ *verb* heave, lean, list, lunge, pitch, plunge, reel, roll, stagger, stumble, sway, totter.

lurch[2] *noun* □ **leave in the lurch** desert (friend etc.) in difficulties.
■ □ **leave in the lurch** see ABANDON *verb* 1.

lurcher /ˈlɜːtʃə/ *noun* crossbred dog, usually working dog crossed with greyhound.

lure *verb* (**-ring**) 1 (usually + *away*, *into*) entice. 2 recall with lure. ● *noun* 1 thing used to entice. 2 enticing quality (of chase etc.). 3 falconer's apparatus for recalling hawk.
■ *verb* allure, attract, bait, charm, coax, decoy, draw, entice, induce, inveigle, invite, lead on, persuade, seduce, tempt.

lurid /ˈljʊərɪd/ *adjective* 1 bright and glaring in colour. 2 sensational, shocking. 3 ghastly, wan. □ **luridly** *adverb*.
■ 1 bright, gaudy, glaring, glowing, striking, vivid. 2 see SENSATIONAL 1.

lurk *verb* 1 linger furtively. 2 lie in ambush. 3 (usually + *in*, *about*, etc.) hide, esp. for sinister purpose. 4 (as **lurking** *adjective*) latent.
■ 1–3 crouch, hide, lie in wait, lie low, prowl, skulk.

luscious /ˈlʌʃəs/ *adjective* 1 richly sweet in taste or smell. 2 voluptuously attractive.
■ 1 appetizing, delectable, delicious, juicy, mouth-watering, rich, succulent, sweet, tasty.

lush[1] *adjective* luxuriant and succulent.

lush[2] *noun slang* alcoholic, drunkard.

lust *noun* 1 strong sexual desire. 2 (usually + *for*, *of*) passionate desire for or enjoyment of. 3 sensuous appetite seen as sinful. ● *verb* (usually + *after*, *for*) have strong or excessive (esp. sexual) desire. □ **lustful** *adjective*. **lustfully** *adverb*.
■ *noun* 1, 3 carnality, *formal* concupiscence, desire, lasciviousness, lechery, libido, licentiousness, passion, sensuality, sexuality. 2 appetite, craving, greed, hunger, itch, longing. □ **lustful** carnal, *formal* concupiscent, erotic, lascivious, lecherous, lewd, libidinous, licentious, on heat, passionate, randy, salacious, sensual, sexy, *colloquial* turned on.

lustre /ˈlʌstə/ *noun* (*US* **luster**) 1 gloss, shining surface. 2 brilliance, splendour. 3 iridescent glaze on pottery and porcelain. □ **lustrous** *adjective*.
■ □ **lustrous** burnished, glazed, gleaming, glossy, metallic, polished, reflective, shiny.

lusty *adjective* (**-ier**, **-iest**) 1 healthy and strong. 2 vigorous, lively. □ **lustily** *adverb*.

lute[1] /luːt/ *noun* guitar-like instrument with long neck and pear-shaped body.

lute[2] /luːt/ *noun* clay or cement for making joints airtight. ● *verb* (**-ting**) apply lute to.

lutenist /ˈluːtənɪst/ *noun* lute-player.

Lutheran /ˈluːθərən/ *noun* 1 follower of Martin Luther. 2 member of Lutheran Church. ● *adjective* of Luther, the doctrines associated with him, or the Protestant Reformation. □ **Lutheranism** *noun*.

lux /lʌks/ *noun* (*plural* same) SI unit of illumination.

luxuriant /lʌgˈzjʊərɪənt/ *adjective* 1 growing profusely. 2 exuberant. 3 florid. □ **luxuriance** *noun*. **luxuriantly** *adverb*.

USAGE *Luxuriant* is sometimes confused with *luxurious*.

■ 1 dense, green, lush, rank, thick, verdant. 1, 2 abundant, ample, copious, exuberant, fertile, flourishing, opulent, *literary* plenteous, plentiful, profuse, prolific, rich, teeming, thriving. 3 see ORNATE.

luxuriate /lʌgˈzjʊərɪeɪt/ *verb* (**-ting**) (+ *in*) take self-indulgent delight in; enjoy as luxury.

luxurious /lʌgˈzjʊərɪəs/ *adjective* 1 supplied with luxuries. 2 very comfortable. 3 fond of luxury. □ **luxuriously** *adverb*.

USAGE *Luxurious* is sometimes confused with *luxuriant*.

■ 1, 2 comfortable, costly, expensive, extravagant, grand, lavish, magnificent, opulent, *colloquial* plush, *colloquial* posh, rich, splendid, sumptuous. 3 hedonistic, pampered, self-indulgent, sybaritic, voluptuous.

luxury /ˈlʌkʃərɪ/ *noun* (*plural* **-ies**) 1 choice or costly surroundings, possessions, etc.; luxuriousness. 2 thing giving comfort or enjoyment but inessential. ● *adjective* comfortable, expensive, etc.
■ *noun* 1 affluence, comfort, ease, enjoyment, extravagance, grandeur, hedonism, indulgence, magnificence, opulence, pleasure, self-indulgence, splendour, sumptuousness, voluptuousness. 2 extravagance, indulgence, pleasure.

LV *abbreviation* luncheon voucher.

lychee /ˈlaɪtʃɪ/ *noun* (also **litchi**, **lichee**) 1 sweet white juicy brown-skinned fruit. 2 tree bearing this.

lych-gate = LICH-GATE.

Lycra /ˈlaɪkrə/ *noun proprietary term* elastic polyurethane fabric.

lye /laɪ/ *noun* **1** water made alkaline with wood ashes. **2** any alkaline solution for washing.

lying *present participle* of LIE[1,2]. ● *adjective* deceitful, false. ● *noun* telling lies.

> ■ *adjective colloquial* crooked, deceitful, deceptive, dishonest, double-dealing, duplicitous, false, hypocritical, insincere, mendacious, misleading, perfidious, unreliable, untrustworthy, untruthful. ● *noun* deceit, deception, dishonesty, duplicity, falsehood, fibbing, hypocrisy, mendacity, perfidy, perjury, prevarication.

lymph /lɪmf/ *noun* **1** colourless fluid from tissues of body, containing white blood cells. **2** this fluid as vaccine.

lymphatic /lɪmˈfætɪk/ *adjective* **1** of, secreting, or carrying lymph. **2** (of person) pale, flabby. ◻ **lymphatic system** vessels carrying lymph.

lynch /lɪntʃ/ *verb* put (person) to death by mob action without legal trial. ◻ **lynching** *noun*.

lynx /lɪŋks/ *noun* (*plural* same or **-es**) wild cat with short tail, spotted fur, and proverbially keen sight.

lyre /laɪə/ *noun* ancient U-shaped musical stringed instrument.

lyric /ˈlɪrɪk/ *adjective* **1** (of poetry) expressing writer's emotion, usually briefly. **2** (of poet) writing in this way. **3** meant or fit to be sung; songlike. ● *noun* **1** lyric poem. **2** (in *plural*) words of song.

lyrical *adjective* **1** lyric. **2** resembling, or using language appropriate to, lyric poetry. **3** *colloquial* highly enthusiastic. ◻ **lyrically** *adverb*.

> ■ **1, 2** emotional, expressive, impassioned, inspired, melodious, musical, poetic, rapturous, rhapsodic, sweet, tuneful. **3** emotional, enthusiastic, impassioned, rapturous, rhapsodic.

lyricism /ˈlɪrɪsɪz(ə)m/ *noun* quality of being lyrical.

lyricist /ˈlɪrɪsɪst/ *noun* writer of lyrics.

Mm

M[1] *noun* (also **m**) (Roman numeral) 1,000.

M[2] *abbreviation* (also **M.**) **1** Master. **2** *Monsieur*. **3** motorway. **4** mega-.

m *abbreviation* (also **m.**) **1** male; masculine. **2** married. **3** mile(s). **4** metre(s). **5** million(s). **6** minute(s). **7** milli-.

MA *abbreviation* Master of Arts.

ma /mɑ:/ *noun colloquial* mother.

ma'am /mæm/ *noun* madam (esp. used in addressing royal lady).

mac *noun* (also **mack**) *colloquial* mackintosh.

macabre /mə'kɑ:br/ *adjective* gruesome, grim.
■ eerie, fearsome, frightful, ghoulish, grim, grisly, grotesque, gruesome, morbid, *colloquial* sick, unhealthy, weird.

macadam /mə'kædəm/ *noun* **1** broken stone as material for road-making. **2** tarmacadam. □ **macadamize** *verb* (also **-ise**) (**-zing** or **-sing**).

macaroni /mækə'rəʊnɪ/ *noun* pasta tubes.

macaroon /mækə'ru:n/ *noun* biscuit made of ground almonds etc.

macaw /mə'kɔ:/ *noun* kind of parrot.

mace[1] *noun* staff of office, esp. symbol of Speaker's authority in House of Commons.

mace[2] *noun* dried outer covering of nutmeg as spice.

macédoine /'mæsɪdwɑ:n/ *noun* mixture of fruits or vegetables, esp. cut up small.

macerate /'mæsəreɪt/ *verb* (**-ting**) soften by soaking. □ **maceration** *noun*.

machete /mə'ʃetɪ/ *noun* broad heavy knife used in Central America and W. Indies.

machiavellian /mækɪə'velɪən/ *adjective* unscrupulous, cunning.

machinate /'mækɪneɪt, 'mæʃ-/ *verb* lay plots; intrigue. □ **machination** /-'neɪʃ(ə)n/ *noun*.

machine /mə'ʃi:n/ *noun* **1** apparatus for applying mechanical power, having several interrelated parts. **2** aircraft. **3** bicycle, motorcycle, etc. **4** computer. **5** controlling system of an organization. ● *verb* (**-ning**) make or operate on with machine. □ **machine-gun** automatic gun giving continuous fire. **machine-readable** in form that computer can process. **machine tool** mechanically operated tool.
■ *noun* **1** apparatus, appliance, contraption, contrivance, device, engine, gadget, implement, instrument, mechanism, motor, robot, tool. **5** machinery, organization, system.

machinery *noun* (*plural* **-ies**) **1** machines. **2** mechanism. **3** organized system. **4** means arranged.

■ **1** apparatus, equipment, gear, machines, plant. **3, 4** constitution, means, method, organization, procedure, structure, system.

machinist *noun* person who works machine.

machismo /mə'kɪzməʊ/ *noun* being macho; masculine pride.

macho /'mætʃəʊ/ *adjective* aggressively masculine.

macintosh = MACKINTOSH.

mack = MAC.

mackerel /'mækr(ə)l/ *noun* (*plural* same or **-s**) edible sea fish. □ **mackerel sky** sky dappled with rows of small fleecy white clouds.

mackintosh /'mækɪntɒʃ/ *noun* (also **macintosh**) **1** waterproof coat or cloak. **2** cloth waterproofed with rubber.
■ **1** anorak, *colloquial* mac, raincoat, waterproof.

macramé /mə'krɑ:mɪ/ *noun* **1** art of knotting cord or string in patterns. **2** work so made.

macrobiotic /mækrəʊbaɪ'ɒtɪk/ *adjective* of diet intended to prolong life, esp. consisting of wholefoods.

macrocosm /'mækrəʊkɒz(ə)m/ *noun* **1** universe. **2** whole of a complex structure.

mad *adjective* (**-dd-**) **1** insane; frenzied. **2** wildly foolish. **3** infatuated; enthusiastic. **4** *colloquial* angry, annoyed. □ **madcap** *adjective* wildly impulsive. ● *noun* reckless person. **madhouse 1** *colloquial* confused uproar. **2** *archaic* mental home or hospital. **madman, madwoman** mad person. □ **madly** *adverb*. **madness** *noun*.
■ **1** *slang* batty, berserk, *slang* bonkers, certified, *slang* crackers, crazed, crazy, daft, delirious, demented, deranged, disordered, distracted, *colloquial* dotty, eccentric, fanatical, frantic, frenzied, hysterical, insane, irrational, *slang* loony, lunatic, maniacal, manic, *colloquial* mental, moonstruck, non compos mentis, *slang* nutty, *colloquial* off one's head, out of one's mind, possessed, *slang* potty, psychotic, *colloquial* round the bend, *slang* screwy, *colloquial* touched, unbalanced, unhinged, unstable, wild. **2** see FOOLISH, ABSURD. **3** see INFATUATED, ENTHUSIASTIC. **4** see ANGRY 1. □ **madman, madwoman** *colloquial* crackpot, crank, *slang* loony, lunatic, maniac, *slang* nut, *slang* nutcase, *slang* nutter, psychopath, psychotic. □ **madness** delirium, dementia, derangement, eccentricity, folly, foolishness, frenzy, hysteria, idiocy, illogicality, insanity, lunacy, mania, mental illness, psychosis, stupidity, unreason.

madam /'mædəm/ *noun* **1** *polite formal address to woman*. **2** *colloquial* conceited or precocious girl or young woman. **3** woman brothel-keeper.

Madame /mə'dɑːm/ *noun* (*plural* **Mesdames** /meɪ'dɑːm/) *title used of or to French-speaking woman.*

madden *verb* **1** make mad. **2** irritate. □ **maddening** *adjective.*
  ■ **1** craze, derange, unhinge. **2** anger, drive crazy, enrage, exasperate, excite, incense, inflame, infuriate, irritate, *colloquial* make (person) see red, provoke, *colloquial* send (person) round the bend, vex.

madder /'mædə/ *noun* **1** herbaceous climbing plant. **2** red dye from its root. **3** synthetic substitute for this dye.

made *past & past participle* of MAKE.

Madeira /mə'dɪərə/ *noun* **1** fortified wine from Madeira. **2** (in full **Madeira cake**) kind of sponge cake.

Mademoiselle /mædəmwə'zel/ *noun* (*plural* **Mesdemoiselles** /meɪdm-/) *title used of or to unmarried French-speaking woman.*

made up *adjective* (**made-up** before noun) **1** invented; not true. **2** wearing make-up. **3** (of meal) already prepared. **4** (of road) surfaced.

Madonna /mə'dɒnə/ *noun* **1** (**the Madonna**) the Virgin Mary. **2** (**madonna**) picture or statue of her.

madrigal /'mædrɪg(ə)l/ *noun* part-song for several voices, usually unaccompanied.

maelstrom /'meɪlstrəm/ *noun* great whirlpool.

maestro /'maɪstrəʊ/ *noun* (*plural* **maestri** /-striː/ or **-s**) eminent musician, esp. teacher or conductor.

Mafia /'mæfɪə/ *noun* organized international group of criminals.

Mafioso /mæfɪ'əʊsəʊ/ *noun* (*plural* **Mafiosi** /-siː/) member of the Mafia.

mag *noun colloquial* magazine.

magazine /mægə'ziːn/ *noun* **1** periodical publication containing contributions by various writers. **2** chamber containing cartridges fed automatically to breech of gun. **3** similar device in slide projector etc. **4** store for explosives, arms, or military provisions.
  ■ **1** *colloquial* book, comic, journal, monthly, periodical, publication, quarterly, weekly. **4** ammunition dump, armoury, arsenal, storehouse.

magenta /mə'dʒentə/ *noun* **1** shade of crimson. **2** aniline dye of this colour.

maggot /'mægət/ *noun* larva, esp. of bluebottle. □ **maggoty** *adjective.*

Magi /'meɪdʒaɪ/ *plural noun* (**the Magi**) the 'wise men from the East' in the Gospel.

magic /'mædʒɪk/ *noun* **1** art of influencing events supernaturally. **2** conjuring tricks. **3** inexplicable influence. ● *adjective* **1** of magic. **2** enchanting, wonderful. □ **magic lantern** simple form of slide projector.
  ■ *noun* **1** black magic, charms, enchantment, incantations, necromancy, occultism, sorcery, spells, voodoo, witchcraft, witchery, wizardry. **2** conjuring, hocus-pocus, illusion, legerdemain, sleight of hand, trickery, tricks. ● *adjective* **1** conjuring, magical, miraculous, mystic, necromantic, supernatural. **2** bewitching, charming, enchanting, entrancing, magical, spellbinding.

magical *adjective* **1** of magic. **2** resembling, or produced as if by, magic. **3** wonderful, enchanting. □ **magically** *adverb.*

magician /mə'dʒɪʃ(ə)n/ *noun* **1** person skilled in magic. **2** conjuror.
  ■ **1** enchanter, enchantress, magus, necromancer, sorcerer, *archaic* warlock, witch, witch-doctor, wizard. **2** conjuror, illusionist, *formal* prestidigitator.

magisterial /mædʒɪ'stɪərɪəl/ *adjective* **1** imperious. **2** authoritative. **3** of a magistrate.

magistracy /'mædʒɪstrəsi/ *noun* (*plural* **-ies**) **1** magisterial office. **2** magistrates.

magistrate /'mædʒɪstreɪt/ *noun* civil officer administering law, esp. one trying minor offences etc.

magnanimous /mæg'nænɪməs/ *adjective* nobly generous; not petty in feelings or conduct. □ **magnanimity** /-nə'nɪm-/ *noun.*

magnate /'mægneɪt/ *noun* person of wealth, authority, etc.

magnesia /mæg'niːʃə/ *noun* **1** magnesium oxide. **2** hydrated magnesium carbonate, used as antacid and laxative.

magnesium /mæg'niːzɪəm/ *noun* silvery metallic element.

magnet /'mægnɪt/ *noun* **1** piece of iron, steel, etc., having properties of attracting iron and of pointing approximately north when suspended. **2** lodestone. **3** person or thing that attracts.

magnetic /mæg'netɪk/ *adjective* **1** having properties of magnet. **2** produced or acting by magnetism. **3** capable of being attracted by or acquiring properties of magnet. **4** very attractive. □ **magnetic field** area of influence of magnet. **magnetic north** point indicated by north end of compass needle. **magnetic storm** disturbance of earth's magnetic field. **magnetic tape** coated plastic strip for recording sound or pictures.
  ■ **4** alluring, attractive, bewitching, captivating, charismatic, charming, compelling, engaging, enthralling, entrancing, fascinating, hypnotic, inviting, irresistible, seductive, spellbinding.

magnetism /'mægnɪtɪz(ə)m/ *noun* **1** magnetic phenomena; science of these. **2** personal charm.
  ■ **2** allure, appeal, attractiveness, charisma, charm, fascination, irresistibility, lure, power, pull, seductiveness.

magnetize /'mægnɪtaɪz/ *verb* (also **-ise**) (**-zing** or **-sing**) **1** make into magnet. **2** attract like magnet. □ **magnetization** *noun.*

magneto /mæg'niːtəʊ/ *noun* (*plural* **-s**) electric

generator using permanent magnets (esp. for ignition in internal-combustion engine).

magnificent /mæg'nɪfɪs(ə)nt/ *adjective* **1** splendid; imposing. **2** *colloquial* excellent. □ **magnificence** *noun*. **magnificently** *adverb*.

> ■ **1** awe-inspiring, beautiful, distinguished, fine, *colloquial* glorious, gorgeous, grand, grandiose, great, imposing, impressive, majestic, noble, opulent, *colloquial* posh, regal, resplendent, rich, spectacular, splendid, stately, sumptuous, superb. **2** see EXCELLENT.

magnify /'mægnɪfaɪ/ *verb* (**-ies, -ied**) **1** make (thing) appear larger than it is, as with lens (**magnifying glass**) etc. **2** exaggerate. **3** intensify. **4** *archaic* extol. □ **magnification** *noun*.

> ■ **1** *colloquial* blow up, enlarge. **2** blow up out of proportion, dramatize, exaggerate, heighten, inflate, make too much of, maximize, overdo, overestimate, overstate. **3** amplify, augment, blow up, enlarge, expand, increase, intensify.

magnitude /'mægnɪtjuːd/ *noun* **1** largeness, size. **2** importance.

> ■ **1** bigness, enormousness, extent, greatness, immensity, size. **2** consequence, importance, significance, weight.

magnolia /mæg'nəʊlɪə/ *noun* **1** kind of flowering tree. **2** very pale pinkish colour of its flowers.

magnum /'mægnəm/ *noun* (*plural* **-s**) wine bottle twice normal size.

magpie /'mægpaɪ/ *noun* **1** crow with long tail and black and white plumage. **2** chatterer. **3** indiscriminate collector.

magus /'meɪgəs/ *noun* (*plural* **magi** /meɪdʒaɪ/) **1** priest of ancient Persia. **2** sorcerer.

Magyar /'mægjɑː/ *noun* **1** member of the chief ethnic group in Hungary. **2** their language. ● *adjective* of this people.

maharaja /mɑːhə'rɑːdʒə/ *noun* (also **maharajah**) *historical title of some Indian princes*.

maharanee /mɑːhə'rɑːnɪ/ *noun* (also **maharani**) (*plural* **-s**) *historical* maharaja's wife or widow.

maharishi /mɑːhə'rɪʃɪ/ *noun* (*plural* **-s**) great Hindu sage.

mahatma /mə'hætmə/ *noun* (in India etc.) revered person.

mah-jong /mɑː'dʒɒŋ/ *noun* (also **-jongg**) originally Chinese game played with 136 or 144 pieces.

mahogany /mə'hɒgənɪ/ *noun* (*plural* **-ies**) **1** reddish-brown wood used for furniture etc. **2** colour of this.

mahout /mə'haʊt/ *noun* elephant driver.

maid *noun* **1** female servant. **2** *archaic* girl, young woman. □ **maidservant** female servant.

maiden /'meɪd(ə)n/ *noun* **1** *archaic* girl; young unmarried woman. **2** *Cricket* maiden over. ● *adjective* **1** unmarried. **2** (of voyage, speech by MP, etc.) first. □ **maidenhair** delicate kind of fern. **maiden name** woman's surname before marriage. **maiden over** *Cricket* over in which no runs are scored. □ **maidenhood** *noun*. **maidenly** *adjective*.

mail[1] *noun* **1** letters etc. conveyed by post. **2** the post. ● *verb* send by mail. □ **mail order** purchase of goods by post.

> ■ *noun* correspondence, letters, parcels, post. ● *verb* dispatch, forward, post, send.

mail[2] *noun* armour of metal rings or plates.

maim *verb* cripple, mutilate.

> ■ cripple, disable, hamstring, handicap, incapacitate, lame, mutilate, wound.

main *adjective* chief, principal. ● *noun* **1** principal channel for water, gas, etc., or (usually in *plural*) electricity. **2** (in *plural*) domestic electricity supply as distinct from batteries. **3** *archaic* high seas. □ **in the main** mostly, on the whole. **main clause** *Grammar* clause forming complete sentence (see panel at CLAUSE). **mainframe 1** central processing unit of large computer. **2** large computer system. **mainland** continuous extent of land excluding neighbouring islands etc. **mainmast** principal mast. **mainsail** lowest sail or sail set on after part of mainmast. **mainspring 1** principal spring of watch or clock. **2** chief motive power etc. **mainstay** chief support. **mainstream** prevailing trend of opinion, fashion, etc.

> ■ *adjective* basic, biggest, cardinal, central, chief, critical, crucial, dominant, dominating, essential, first, foremost, fundamental, greatest, largest, leading, major, most important, outstanding, paramount, predominant, pre-eminent, prevailing, primary, prime, principal, special, strongest, supreme, top, vital.

mainly *adverb* mostly; chiefly.

> ■ above all, as a rule, chiefly, especially, essentially, first and foremost, generally, in the main, largely, mostly, normally, on the whole, predominantly, primarily, principally, usually.

maintain /meɪn'teɪn/ *verb* **1** keep up; keep going. **2** keep in repair. **3** support. **4** assert as true.

> ■ **1** carry on, continue, hold to, keep going, keep up, perpetuate, persevere in, persist in, preserve, retain, *colloquial* stick at, sustain. **2** care for, keep in good condition, look after, service, take care of. **3** feed, keep, pay for, provide for, stand by, support. **4** affirm, allege, argue, assert, *formal* aver, claim, contend, declare, insist, proclaim, profess, state, uphold.

maintenance /'meɪntənəns/ *noun* **1** main-

Main clause

See panel at CLAUSE.

taining, being maintained. **2** provision of enough to support life. **3** alimony.

■ **1** care, conservation, looking after, preservation, repairs, servicing, upkeep. **2, 3** alimony, allowance, contribution, keep, subsistence, support.

maiolica /mə'jɒlɪkə/ *noun* (also **majolica**) kind of decorated Italian earthenware.

maisonette /meɪzə'nɛt/ *noun* **1** flat on more than one floor. **2** small house.

maize *noun* **1** N. American cereal plant. **2** cobs or grain of this.

Maj. *abbreviation* Major.

majestic /mə'dʒɛstɪk/ *adjective* stately and dignified; imposing. □ **majestically** *adverb*.

■ august, awe-inspiring, awesome, dignified, elevated, exalted, *colloquial* glorious, grand, grandiose, imperial, imposing, impressive, kingly, lofty, lordly, magisterial, magnificent, monumental, noble, pompous, princely, queenly, regal, royal, splendid, stately, striking, sublime.

majesty /'mædʒɪstɪ/ *noun* (*plural* **-ies**) **1** stateliness of aspect, language, etc. **2** sovereign power. **3** (**His, Her, Your Majesty**) *title used of or to sovereign or sovereign's wife or widow.*

■ **1** awesomeness, dignity, glory, grandeur, kingliness, loftiness, magnificence, nobility, pomp, royalty, splendour, stateliness, sublimity.

majolica = MAIOLICA.

major /'meɪdʒə/ *adjective* **1** greater or relatively great in size etc. **2** unusually serious or significant. **3** *Music* of or based on scale having semitone next above third and seventh notes. **4** of full legal age. ● *noun* **1** army officer next below lieutenant colonel. **2** person of full legal age. **3** *US* student's main subject or course. **4** *US* student of this. ● *verb* (+ *in*) *US* study or qualify in as a major. □ **major-domo** /-'dəʊməʊ/ (*plural* **-s**) housesteward. **major-general** army officer next below lieutenant general.

■ *adjective* **1** bigger, chief, considerable, extensive, greater, important, key, larger, leading, main, outstanding, principal, significant. **2** critical, crucial, grave, important, serious, significant, vital.

majority /mə'dʒɒrɪtɪ/ *noun* (*plural* **-ies**) **1** (usually + *of*) greater number or part. **2** number by which winning vote exceeds next. **3** full legal age.

USAGE *Majority* should strictly be used of a number of people or things, as in *the majority of people*, and not of a quantity of something, as in *the majority of the work*.

■ **1** bulk, lion's share, mass, preponderance; (*be in the majority*) see DOMINATE **2**. **3** adulthood, coming of age, manhood, maturity, womanhood.

make *verb* (**-king**; *past & past participle* **made**) **1** construct, frame, create, esp. from parts or other substance. **2** compel. **3** bring about; give rise to. **4** cause to become or seem. **5** (usually + *into*) change. **6** appoint. **7** write; compose. **8** constitute;

amount to. **9** undertake; perform. **10** gain, acquire, obtain as result. **11** prepare for consumption or use. **12** proceed. **13** *colloquial* arrive at or in time for. **14** *colloquial* manage to attend. **15** *colloquial* achieve place in. **16** establish, enact. **17** consider to be; estimate as. **18** secure success or advancement of. **19** accomplish. **20** become. **21** represent as. **22** form in the mind. ● *noun* **1** origin of manufactured goods; brand. **2** way thing is made. □ **make believe** pretend. **make-believe** ● *noun* pretence. ● *adjective* pretended. **make do** (often + *with*) manage (with substitute etc.). **make for 1** tend to result in. **2** proceed towards. **make friends** (often + *with*) become friendly. **make good 1** compensate for. **2** repair. **3** succeed in an undertaking. **make it 1** *colloquial* succeed in reaching, esp. in time. **2** *colloquial* be successful. **3** (usually + *with*) *slang* have sexual intercourse (with). **make money** acquire wealth. **make off** depart hastily. **make off with** steal; carry away. **make out 1** discern. **2** understand. **3** assert; pretend. **4** write out; fill in. **5** *colloquial* progress. **make over 1** transfer possession of (thing) to person. **2** refashion (garment etc.). **makeshift** (serving as) temporary substitute or device. **make up 1** put together; prepare. **2** invent (story). **3** apply cosmetics (to). **4** act to overcome (deficiency). **5** complete. **6** be reconciled. **7** (+ *for*) compensate for. **make-up** *noun* **1** cosmetics. **2** similar preparation used as disguise by actor. **3** person's temperament etc. **4** composition. **make up one's mind** decide. **make-weight** small quantity added to make full weight. **on the make** *colloquial* intent on gain.

■ *verb* **1** assemble, build, compose, construct, contrive, craft, create, devise, erect, fabricate, fashion, forge, form, frame, invent, make up, manufacture, mass-produce, originate, produce, put together, *colloquial* think up; (*make clothes*) knit, run up, sew, weave; (*make an effigy*) carve, cast, model, mould, sculpt, shape. **2** coerce, compel, constrain, force, induce, oblige, order, pressurize, prevail on, require. **3** *literary* beget, bring about, cause, create, engender, generate, give rise to, initiate, originate, produce, provoke, result in. **4** render. **5** alter, change, convert, modify, transform, turn. **6** appoint, elect, nominate, ordain. **7** compile, compose, create, devise, draw up, write. **8** add up to, amount to, come to, constitute, total. **9** (*make a curtsy*) carry out, do, execute, perform, undertake; (*make a speech*) deliver, present, pronounce, utter. **10** acquire, earn, gain, get, obtain, procure, receive, win. **11** concoct, cook, *US colloquial* fix, prepare. **16** arrange, codify, decide on, devise, enact, establish, fix, formulate, write. **19** accomplish, achieve, arrive at, attain, get to, reach, score, win. **20** become, change into, grow into, turn into. ● *noun* **1** brand, kind, model, sort, type, variety. □ **make believe** see IMAGINE **1**. **make-believe** ● *noun* dream, fantasy, play-acting, pretence, self-deception, unreality. ● *adjective* fanciful, feigned, imaginary, made up, mock, *colloquial* pretend, pretended, sham, simulated, unreal. **make good 1** see COMPENSATE **2**. **3** see PROSPER. **make off** see DEPART **1,2**. **make off with** see STEAL *verb* **1**. **make out 2** see UNDERSTAND **1**. **makeshift** emergency, improvised, provisional, stopgap, temporary.

make up 2 see INVENT 2. **7** (*make up for*) see COMPENSATE 2. **make up one's mind** see DECIDE 1.

maker *noun* person who makes, esp. (**Maker**) God.
■ architect, author, builder, creator, director, manufacturer, originator, producer.

making *noun* (in *plural*) **1** earnings, profit. **2** essential qualities for becoming. □ **be the making of** ensure success of. **in the making** in the course of being made.

malachite /ˈmæləkaɪt/ *noun* green mineral used for ornament.

maladjusted /mæləˈdʒʌstɪd/ *adjective* (of person) unable to cope with demands of social environment. □ **maladjustment** *noun*.
■ disturbed, neurotic, unbalanced.

maladminister /mælədˈmɪnɪstə/ *verb* manage badly or improperly. □ **maladministration** *noun*.

maladroit /mæləˈdrɔɪt/ *adjective* bungling, clumsy.

malady /ˈmælədɪ/ *noun* (*plural* **-ies**) ailment, disease.

malaise /məˈleɪz/ *noun* feeling of illness or uneasiness.

malapropism /ˈmæləprɒpɪz(ə)m/ *noun* comical confusion between words.

malaria /məˈleərɪə/ *noun* fever transmitted by mosquitoes. □ **malarial** *adjective*.

Malay /məˈleɪ/ *noun* **1** member of a people predominating in Malaysia and Indonesia. **2** their language. ● *adjective* of this people or language.

malcontent /ˈmælkəntent/ *noun* discontented person. ● *adjective* discontented.

male *adjective* **1** of the sex that can beget offspring by fertilizing. **2** (of plants or flowers) containing stamens but no pistil. **3** of men; masculine. **4** (of parts of machinery) designed to enter or fill corresponding hollow part. ● *noun* male person or animal.
■ *adjective* **3** manly, masculine, virile. ● *noun* slang bloke, boy, *colloquial* chap, *colloquial* fellow, gentleman, *colloquial* guy, *colloquial* lad, man.

malediction /mælɪˈdɪkʃ(ə)n/ *noun* curse. □ **maledictory** *adjective*.

malefactor /ˈmælɪfæktə/ *noun* criminal; evildoer. □ **malefaction** /-ˈfækʃ(ə)n/ *noun*.
■ criminal, delinquent, evildoer, lawbreaker, offender, villain, wrongdoer.

malevolent /məˈlevələnt/ *adjective* wishing evil to others. □ **malevolence** *noun*.

malformation /mælfɔːˈmeɪʃ(ə)n/ *noun* faulty formation. □ **malformed** /-ˈfɔːmd/ *adjective*.

malfunction /mælˈfʌŋkʃ(ə)n/ *noun* failure to function normally. ● *verb* function faultily.

malice /ˈmælɪs/ *noun* ill will; desire to do harm.

■ animosity, *slang* bitchiness, bitterness, cattiness, enmity, hatred, hostility, ill will, malevolence, maliciousness, malignity, nastiness, rancour, spite, spitefulness, vengefulness, venom, viciousness, vindictiveness.

malicious /məˈlɪʃəs/ *adjective* given to or arising from malice. □ **maliciously** *adverb*. **maliciousness** *noun*.
■ *slang* bitchy, bitter, catty, evil, hateful, ill-natured, malevolent, malignant, mischievous, nasty, rancorous, revengeful, sly, spiteful, vengeful, venomous, vicious, villainous, vindictive, wicked.

malign /məˈlaɪn/ *adjective* **1** injurious. **2** malignant. **3** malevolent. ● *verb* speak ill of; slander. □ **malignity** /məˈlɪɡnɪtɪ/ *noun*.

malignant /məˈlɪɡnənt/ *adjective* **1** (of disease) very virulent. **2** (of tumour) spreading; recurring; cancerous. **3** feeling or showing intense ill will. □ **malignancy** *noun*.
■ **1, 2** dangerous, deadly, destructive, fatal, harmful, injurious, life-threatening, poisonous, terminal, uncontrollable, virulent. **3** see MALICIOUS.

malinger /məˈlɪŋɡə/ *verb* pretend to be ill, esp. to escape duty. □ **malingerer** *noun*.

mall /mæl, mɔːl/ *noun* **1** sheltered walk. **2** shopping precinct.

mallard /ˈmælɑːd/ *noun* (*plural* same) kind of wild duck.

malleable /ˈmælɪəb(ə)l/ *adjective* **1** that can be shaped by hammering. **2** pliable. □ **malleability** *noun*.
■ **1** ductile, plastic, pliable, soft, tractable, workable. **2** see PLIABLE 2.

mallet /ˈmælɪt/ *noun* **1** hammer, usually of wood. **2** implement for striking croquet or polo ball.

mallow /ˈmæləʊ/ *noun* flowering plant with hairy stems and leaves.

malmsey /ˈmɑːmzɪ/ *noun* a strong sweet wine.

malnutrition /mælnjuːˈtrɪʃ(ə)n/ *noun* lack of foods necessary for health.
■ *archaic* famine, hunger, starvation, undernourishment.

malodorous /mælˈəʊdərəs/ *adjective* evil-smelling.

malpractice /mælˈpræktɪs/ *noun* improper, negligent, or criminal professional conduct.

malt /mɔːlt/ *noun* **1** barley or other grain prepared for brewing etc. **2** *colloquial* malt whisky. ● *verb* convert (grain) into malt. □ **malted milk** drink made from dried milk and extract of malt. **malt whisky** whisky made from malted barley.

Maltese /mɔːlˈtiːz/ *noun* native, national, or language of Malta. ● *adjective* of Malta. □ **Maltese cross** one with equal arms broadened at ends.

maltreat /mælˈtriːt/ *verb* ill-treat. □ **maltreatment** *noun*.

mama /məˈmɑː/ *noun* (also **mamma**) *colloquial* mother.

mamba /ˈmæmbə/ *noun* venomous African snake.

mamma = MAMA.

mammal /ˈmæm(ə)l/ *noun* animal of class secreting milk to feed young. □ **mammalian** /-ˈmeɪlɪən/ *adjective*.

mammary /ˈmæmərɪ/ *adjective* of breasts.

Mammon /ˈmæmən/ *noun* wealth regarded as god or evil influence.

mammoth /ˈmæməθ/ *noun* large extinct elephant. ● *adjective* huge.

man *noun* (*plural* **men**) **1** adult human male. **2** human being; person. **3** the human race. **4** employee, workman. **5** (usually in *plural*) soldier, sailor, etc. **6** suitable or appropriate person. **7** husband. **8** *colloquial* boyfriend. **9** human being of specified type. **10** piece in chess, draughts, etc. ● *verb* (**-nn-**) supply with person(s) for work or defence. □ **manhole** opening giving person access to sewer, conduit, etc. **man-hour** work done by one person in one hour. **man in the street** ordinary person. **man-made** artificial, synthetic. **man-of-war** warship. **manpower** number of people available for work or military service. **manservant** (*plural* **menservants**) male servant. **mantrap** trap set to catch esp. trespassers.

　■ *noun* **1** see MALE *noun*. **2** see PERSON **1**. **3** see MANKIND. ● *verb* crew, provide staff for, staff. □ **man-made** artificial, imitation, manufactured, processed, simulated, synthetic, unnatural.

manacle /ˈmænək(ə)l/ *noun* (usually in *plural*) handcuff. ● *verb* (**-ling**) put manacles on.

manage /ˈmænɪdʒ/ *verb* (**-ging**) **1** organize; regulate. **2** succeed in achieving; contrive. **3** succeed with limited resources; cope. **4** succeed in controlling. **5** cope with. **6** be able to spare (money, time, etc.). □ **managing director** director with executive control or authority. □ **manageable** *adjective*.

　■ **1** administer, be in charge of, command, conduct, control, direct, dominate, govern, head, lead, look after, mastermind, operate, organize, oversee, preside over, regulate, rule, run, superintend, supervise, take care of, take control of. **2** accomplish, achieve, bring about, carry out, contrive, do, finish, get through, muddle through, perform, succeed in, undertake. **3** cope, fend for oneself, scrape by, shift for oneself, succeed, survive. **4** control, dominate, govern, handle, manipulate, take control of. **5** contend with, cope with, deal with, handle. **6** afford, spare. □ **manageable** amenable, compliant, controllable, docile, governable, obedient, submissive, tame, tractable.

management *noun* **1** managing, being managed. **2** administration. **3** people managing a business.

manager *noun* **1** person controlling or administering business etc. **2** person controlling activities of person, team, etc. **3** person who manages money etc. in specified way. □ **managerial** /-ˈdʒɪərɪəl/ *adjective*.

　■ **1** administrator, *colloquial* boss, chief, controller, director, executive, foreman, forewoman, *slang* governor, head, manageress, organizer, overseer, proprietor, proprietress, ruler, superintendent, supervisor.

manageress /mænɪdʒəˈres/ *noun* woman manager, esp. of shop, hotel, etc.

mañana /mænˈjɑːnə/ *adverb* & *noun* some time in the future. [Spanish]

manatee /mænəˈtiː/ *noun* large aquatic plant-eating mammal.

Mancunian /mæŋˈkjuːnɪən/ *noun* native of Manchester. ● *adjective* of Manchester.

mandarin /ˈmændərɪn/ *noun* **1** (**Mandarin**) official language of China. **2** *historical* Chinese official. **3** influential person, esp. bureaucrat. **4** (in full **mandarin orange**) tangerine.

mandate /ˈmændeɪt/ *noun* **1** official command. **2** authority given by electors to government etc. **3** authority to act for another. ● *verb* (**-ting**) instruct (delegate) how to act or vote.

mandatory /ˈmændətərɪ/ *adjective* **1** compulsory. **2** of or conveying a command.

　■ **1** compulsory, essential, necessary, needed, obligatory, required, requisite.

mandible /ˈmændɪb(ə)l/ *noun* **1** jaw, esp. lower one. **2** either part of bird's beak. **3** either half of crushing organ in mouth-parts of insect etc.

mandolin /mændəˈlɪn/ *noun* kind of lute with paired metal strings plucked with a plectrum.

mandrake /ˈmændreɪk/ *noun* narcotic plant with forked root.

mandrill /ˈmændrɪl/ *noun* large W. African baboon.

mane *noun* **1** long hair on horse's or lion's neck. **2** *colloquial* person's long hair.

manège /mæˈneɪʒ/ *noun* **1** riding-school. **2** movements of trained horse. **3** horsemanship.

maneuver *US* = MANOEUVRE.

manful *adjective* brave, resolute. □ **manfully** *adverb*.

manganese /ˈmæŋɡəniːz/ *noun* **1** grey brittle metallic element. **2** black oxide of this.

mange /meɪndʒ/ *noun* skin disease of dogs etc.

mangel-wurzel /ˈmæŋɡ(ə)l wɜːz(ə)l/ *noun* large beet used as cattle food.

manger /ˈmeɪndʒə/ *noun* eating-trough in stable.

mangle[1] /ˈmæŋɡ(ə)l/ *verb* (**-ling**) **1** hack, cut about; crush. **2** mutilate, spoil.

　■ **1** butcher, cripple, crush, cut, damage, deform, disfigure, hack, injure, lacerate, maim, maul, mutilate, squash, tear, wound. **2** damage, mutilate, ruin, spoil, wreck.

mangle[2] /ˈmæŋɡ(ə)l/ *noun* machine with rollers for pressing water out of washed clothes. ● *verb* (**-ling**) put through mangle.

mango /ˈmæŋɡəʊ/ *noun* (*plural* **-es** or **-s**) **1** tropical fruit with yellowish flesh. **2** tree bearing it.

mangold /ˈmæŋɡ(ə)ld/ *noun* mangel-wurzel.

mangrove /ˈmæŋɡrəʊv/ *noun* tropical seashore tree with many tangled roots above ground.

mangy /ˈmeɪndʒɪ/ *adjective* (**-ier, -iest**) **1** having mange. **2** squalid, shabby.
■ **1** scabby. **2** dirty, filthy, moth-eaten, nasty, *colloquial* scruffy, shabby, slovenly, squalid, *colloquial* tatty, unkempt, wretched.

manhandle *verb* (**-ling**) **1** *colloquial* handle roughly. **2** move by human effort.
■ **1** abuse, batter, beat up, ill-treat, knock about, maltreat, mistreat, misuse, *slang* rough up. **2** carry, haul, heave, *colloquial* hump, lift, manoeuvre, pull, push.

manhood *noun* **1** state of being a man. **2** manliness. **3** a man's sexual potency. **4** men of a country.

mania /ˈmeɪnɪə/ *noun* **1** mental illness marked by excitement and violence. **2** (often + *for*) excessive enthusiasm, obsession.
■ **1** see MADNESS (MAD). **2** craving, craze, enthusiasm, fad, fetish, infatuation, obsession, passion, preoccupation, rage.

maniac /ˈmeɪnɪæk/ *noun* **1** *colloquial* person behaving wildly. **2** *colloquial* obsessive enthusiast. **3** person suffering from mania. ● *adjective* of or behaving like maniac. □ **maniacal** /məˈnaɪək(ə)l/ *adjective*.
■ *noun* **1, 3** see MADMAN, MADWOMAN (MAD). **2** see ENTHUSIAST (ENTHUSIASM), FANATIC *noun*.

manic /ˈmænɪk/ *adjective* of or affected by mania. □ **manic-depressive** *adjective* relating to mental disorder with alternating periods of elation and depression. ● *noun* person having such disorder.

manicure /ˈmænɪkjʊə/ *noun* cosmetic treatment of the hands. ● *verb* (**-ring**) give manicure to. □ **manicurist** *noun*.

manifest /ˈmænɪfest/ *adjective* clear to sight or mind; indubitable. ● *verb* **1** make manifest. **2** (**manifest itself**) reveal itself. ● *noun* cargo or passenger list. □ **manifestation** *noun*. **manifestly** *adverb*.
■ *adjective* apparent, blatant, clear, conspicuous, discernible, evident, explicit, glaring, indubitable, noticeable, obvious, patent, plain, recognizable, undeniable, undisguised, visible. ● *verb* **1** see SHOW *verb* 2,3;4.

manifesto /mænɪˈfestəʊ/ *noun* (*plural* **-s**) declaration of policies.
■ declaration, platform, policy statement.

manifold /ˈmænɪfəʊld/ *adjective* **1** many and various. **2** having various forms, applications, parts, etc. ● *noun* **1** manifold thing. **2** pipe etc. with several outlets.

manikin /ˈmænɪkɪn/ *noun* little man, dwarf.

Manila /məˈnɪlə/ *noun* **1** strong fibre of Philippine tree. **2** (also **manila**) strong brown paper made of this.

manipulate /məˈnɪpjʊleɪt/ *verb* (**-ting**) **1**

handle, esp. with skill. **2** manage to one's own advantage, esp. unfairly. □ **manipulation** *noun*. **manipulator** *noun*.
■ **1** control, handle, manage, operate, wield, work. **2** control, direct, engineer, exploit, guide, handle, influence, manage, manoeuvre, orchestrate, steer.

manipulative /məˈnɪpjʊlətɪv/ *adjective* tending to exploit a situation, person, etc., for one's own ends.

mankind *noun* human species.
■ *Homo sapiens*, human beings, humanity, humankind, the human race, man, men and women, mortals, people.

manly *adjective* (**-ier, -iest**) having qualities associated with or befitting a man. □ **manliness** *noun*.
■ brave, chivalrous, gallant, heroic, macho, male, mannish, masculine, swashbuckling, virile.

manna /ˈmænə/ *noun* food miraculously supplied to Israelites in wilderness.

mannequin /ˈmænɪkɪn/ *noun* **1** fashion model. **2** dummy for display of clothes.

manner /ˈmænə/ *noun* **1** way thing is done or happens; style. **2** (in *plural*) social behaviour; polite behaviour. **3** outward bearing, way of speaking, etc. **4** kind, sort.
■ **1** approach, fashion, means, method, mode, procedure, process, style, technique, way. **2** (*manners*) behaviour, breeding, civility, conduct, courtesy, decorum, etiquette, gentility, politeness, protocol, refinement, social graces. **3** air, aspect, attitude, bearing, behaviour, character, conduct, demeanour, deportment, disposition, look, *literary* mien. **4** genre, kind, sort, type, variety.

mannered *adjective* **1** behaving in specified way. **2** showing mannerisms.

mannerism *noun* **1** distinctive gesture or feature of style. **2** excessive use of these in art etc.
■ **1** characteristic, habit, idiosyncrasy, peculiarity, quirk, trait.

mannerly *adjective* well behaved, polite.

mannish *adjective* **1** (of woman) masculine in appearance or manner. **2** characteristic of man as opposed to woman.

manoeuvre /məˈnuːvə/ (*US* **maneuver**) *noun* **1** planned movement of vehicle or troops. **2** (in *plural*) large-scale exercise of troops etc. **3** agile or skilful movement. **4** artful plan. ● *verb* (**-ring**) **1** move (thing, esp. vehicle) carefully. **2** perform or cause to perform manoeuvres. **3** manipulate by scheming or adroitness. **4** use artifice. □ **manoeuvrable** *adjective*.
■ *noun* **1, 3** exercise, move, movement, operation. **2** (*manoeuvres*) army exercise, operation, training. **4** device, dodge, gambit, intrigue, move, operation, plan, plot, ploy, ruse, scheme, stratagem, strategy, tactic, trick. ● *verb* **1** guide, manipulate, move, navigate, negotiate, pilot, steer. **3, 4** contrive, engineer, manipulate, plot, scheme.

manor /'mænə/ *noun* **1** (also **manor house**) large country house with lands. **2** *historical* feudal lordship over lands. ◻ **manorial** /mə'nɔːrɪəl/ *adjective*.

mansard /'mænsɑːd/ *noun* roof with 4 sloping sides, each of which becomes steeper halfway down.

manse /mæns/ *noun* (esp. Scottish Presbyterian) minister's house.

mansion /'mænʃ(ə)n/ *noun* **1** large grand house. **2** (in *plural*) block of flats.

▪ **1** castle, chateau, manor, manor house, palace, stately home, villa.

manslaughter *noun* unintentional but not accidental unlawful killing of human being.

mantel /'mænt(ə)l/ *noun* mantelpiece; mantelshelf. ◻ **mantelpiece 1** structure above and around fireplace. **2** mantelshelf. **mantelshelf** shelf above fireplace.

mantilla /mæn'tɪlə/ *noun* Spanish woman's lace scarf worn over head and shoulders.

mantis /'mæntɪs/ *noun* (*plural* same or **mantises**) kind of predatory insect.

mantle /'mænt(ə)l/ *noun* **1** loose sleeveless cloak. **2** covering. **3** fragile tube round gas jet to give incandescent light. ● *verb* (**-ling**) clothe; conceal, envelop.

▪ *noun* **1** cape, cloak, shawl, wrap. **2** cloak, covering, sheet, shroud. ● *verb see* COVER *verb* 1.

manual /'mænjʊəl/ *adjective* of or done with hands. ● *noun* **1** reference book. **2** organ keyboard played with hands, not feet. ◻ **manually** *adverb*.

manufacture /mænjʊ'fæktʃə/ *noun* **1** making of articles, esp. in factory etc. **2** branch of industry. ● *verb* (**-ring**) **1** make, esp. on industrial scale. **2** invent, fabricate. ◻ **manufactured** *adjective*. **manufacturer** *noun*.

▪ *verb* **1** assemble, build, construct, create, fabricate, make, mass-produce, prefabricate, process, put together, turn out. **2** *see* INVENT 2. ◻ **manufactured** see MAN-MADE (MAN). **manufacturer** factory owner, industrialist, maker, producer.

manure /mə'njʊə/ *noun* fertilizer, esp. dung. ● *verb* (**-ring**) treat with manure.

▪ *noun* compost, dung, fertilizer, muck.

manuscript /'mænjʊskrɪpt/ *noun* book or document written by hand or typed, not printed. ● *adjective* written by hand.

▪ *noun* book, document, papers, script.

Manx *adjective* of Isle of Man. ● *noun* Celtic language of Isle of Man. ◻ **Manx cat** tailless variety.

many /'menɪ/ *adjective* (**more**, **most**) numerous; great in number. ● *noun* (treated as *plural*) **1** many people or things. **2** (**the many**) the majority of people.

▪ *adjective* abundant, assorted, copious, countless, diverse, frequent, innumerable, multifarious, *literary* myriad, numberless, numerous, profuse, *colloquial* umpteen, uncountable, untold, varied, various.

Maori /'maʊrɪ/ *noun* (*plural* same or **-s**) **1** member of aboriginal NZ race. **2** their language. ● *adjective* of this people.

map *noun* **1** flat representation of (part of) earth's surface, or of sky. **2** diagram. ● *verb* (**-pp-**) represent on map. ◻ **map out** plan in detail. **map-read** consult and interpret map.

▪ *noun* chart, diagram, plan.

maple /'meɪp(ə)l/ *noun* kind of tree. ◻ **maple leaf** emblem of Canada. **maple sugar** sugar got by evaporating sap of some kinds of maple. **maple syrup** syrup got from maple sap or maple sugar.

maquette /mə'ket/ *noun* preliminary model or sketch.

Mar. *abbreviation* March.

mar *verb* (**-rr-**) spoil; disfigure.

▪ blight, blot, damage, deface, disfigure, harm, hurt, impair, ruin, spoil, stain, taint, tarnish, wreck.

marabou /'mærəbuː/ *noun* (*plural* **-s**) **1** large W. African stork. **2** its down as trimming etc.

maraca /mə'rækə/ *noun* clublike bean-filled gourd etc., shaken as percussion instrument.

maraschino /mærə'skiːnəʊ/ *noun* (*plural* **-s**) liqueur made from cherries. ◻ **maraschino cherry** one preserved in maraschino.

marathon /'mærəθ(ə)n/ *noun* **1** long-distance foot race. **2** long-lasting, esp. difficult, undertaking.

maraud /mə'rɔːd/ *verb* **1** make raid. **2** pillage. ◻ **marauder** *noun*.

▪ ◻ **marauder** bandit, buccaneer, invader, pirate, plunderer, raider.

marble /'mɑːb(ə)l/ *noun* **1** kind of limestone used in sculpture and architecture. **2** anything of or like marble. **3** small ball of glass etc. as toy. **4** (in *plural*; treated as *singular*) game played with these. **5** (in *plural*) *slang* one's mental faculties. **6** (in *plural*) collection of sculptures. ● *verb* (**-ling**) (esp. as **marbled** *adjective*) give veined or mottled appearance to (esp. paper).

marcasite /'mɑːkəsaɪt/ *noun* **1** crystalline iron sulphide. **2** crystals of this used in jewellery.

March *noun* third month of year. ◻ **March hare** hare in breeding season.

march[1] *verb* **1** walk in military manner or with regular paces. **2** proceed steadily. **3** cause to march or walk. ● *noun* **1** act of marching. **2** uniform military step. **3** long difficult walk. **4** procession as demonstration. **5** (usually + *of*) progress, continuity. **6** piece of music suitable for marching to. ◻ **march past** ceremonial march of troops past saluting point. ◻ **marcher** *noun*.

■ *verb* **1** file, pace, parade, step, stride, strut, troop, walk. ● *noun* **1** cortège, march past, parade, procession. **4** *colloquial* demo, demonstration, procession. **5** see PROGRESS *noun* 1.

march² *noun historical* **1** (often in *plural*) boundary. **2** tract of (often disputed) land between countries etc.

marchioness /mɑːʃəˈnes/ *noun* **1** marquess's wife or widow. **2** woman holding rank of marquess.

mare /meə/ *noun* female equine animal, esp. horse. □ **mare's nest** illusory discovery.

margarine /mɑːdʒəˈriːn/ *noun* butter substitute made from edible oils etc.

marge /mɑːdʒ/ *noun colloquial* margarine.

margin /ˈmɑːdʒɪn/ *noun* **1** edge or border of surface. **2** plain space round printed page etc. **3** amount by which thing exceeds, falls short, etc. □ **margin of error** allowance for miscalculation or mischance.

■ **1** border, boundary, brink, edge, perimeter, periphery, rim, side, verge. **3** allowance, latitude, leeway, room, scope, space.

marginal *adjective* **1** written in margin. **2** of or at edge. **3** (of constituency) having elected MP with small majority. **4** close to limit, esp. of profitability. **5** insignificant. **6** barely adequate. □ **marginally** *adverb*.

■ **2** borderline, peripheral. **5** borderline, doubtful, insignificant, limited, minimal, negligible, peripheral, slight, small, unimportant.

marginalize *verb* (also **-ise**) (**-zing** or **-sing**) make or treat as insignificant. □ **marginalization** *noun*.

marguerite /mɑːɡəˈriːt/ *noun* ox-eye daisy.

marigold /ˈmærɪɡəʊld/ *noun* plant with golden or bright yellow flowers.

marijuana /mærɪˈhwɑːnə/ *noun* dried leaves etc. of hemp smoked as drug.

marimba /məˈrɪmbə/ *noun* **1** African and Central American xylophone. **2** orchestral instrument developed from this.

marina /məˈriːnə/ *noun* harbour for pleasure boats.

marinade /mærɪˈneɪd/ *noun* mixture of wine, vinegar, oil, spices, etc., for soaking fish or meat. ● *verb* (**-ding**) soak in marinade.

marinate /ˈmærɪneɪt/ *verb* (**-ting**) marinade.

marine /məˈriːn/ *adjective* **1** of, found in, or produced by, the sea. **2** of shipping. **3** for use at sea. ● *noun* **1** member of corps trained to fight on land or sea. **2** country's shipping, fleet, or navy.

mariner /ˈmærɪnə/ *noun* seaman.

marionette /mærɪəˈnet/ *noun* puppet worked with strings.

marital /ˈmærɪt(ə)l/ *adjective* of or between husband and wife; of marriage.

■ conjugal, matrimonial, nuptial.

maritime /ˈmærɪtaɪm/ *adjective* **1** connected with the sea or seafaring. **2** living or found near the sea.

marjoram /ˈmɑːdʒərəm/ *noun* aromatic herb used in cookery.

mark¹ *noun* **1** visible sign left by person or thing; stain, scar, etc. **2** written or printed symbol. **3** number or letter denoting conduct or proficiency. **4** (often + *of*) sign, indication. **5** lasting effect. **6** target; thing aimed at. **7** line etc. serving to indicate position. **8** (followed by numeral) particular design of piece of equipment. ● *verb* **1** make mark on; distinguish with mark. **2** correct and assess (student's work etc.). **3** attach price to. **4** notice, observe. **5** characterize. **6** acknowledge, celebrate. **7** indicate on map etc. **8** keep close to (opposing player) in games. **9** (in *passive*) have natural marks. □ **mark down** reduce price of. **mark off** separate by boundary. **mark out 1** plan (course). **2** destine. **3** trace out (boundaries etc.). **mark time 1** march on spot without moving forward. **2** await opportunity to advance. **mark up** increase price of. **mark-up** *noun* amount added to price by retailer for profit.

■ *noun* **1** blemish, blot, blotch, dent, dot, fingerprint, impression, line, marking, print, scar, scratch, scribble, smear, smudge, smut, splotch, spot, stain, streak, trace, vestige; (*marks*) graffiti, stigmata. **2** badge, brand, device, emblem, hallmark, label, seal, sign, stamp, standard, symbol, trade mark. **4** characteristic, feature, indication, indicator, marker, sign, token. ● *verb* **1** blemish, blot, brand, bruise, cut, damage, deface, dent, dirty, disfigure, draw on, mar, scar, scratch, scrawl over, scribble on, smudge, spot, stain, stamp, streak, tattoo, write on. **2** appraise, assess, correct, evaluate, grade, tick. **4** attend to, heed, listen to, mind, note, notice, observe, pay attention to, take note of, take to heart, watch.

mark² *noun* Deutschmark.

marked /mɑːkt/ *adjective* **1** having a visible mark. **2** clearly noticeable. □ **markedly** /-kɪdlɪ/ *adverb*.

marker *noun* **1** thing that marks a position. **2** person or thing that marks. **3** pen with broad felt tip. **4** scorer, esp. at billiards.

market /ˈmɑːkɪt/ *noun* **1** gathering for sale of commodities, livestock, etc. **2** space for this. **3** (often + *for*) demand for commodity etc. **4** place or group providing such demand. **5** conditions for buying and selling. **6** stock market. ● *verb* (**-t-**) **1** offer for sale. **2** *archaic* buy or sell goods in market. □ **market garden** place where vegetables are grown for market. **market place 1** open space for market. **2** commercial world. **market research** surveying of consumers' needs and preferences. **market town** town where market is held. **market value** value as saleable thing. **on the market** offered for sale. □ **marketing** *noun*.

■ *noun* **1** auction, bazaar, exchange, fair, mart, sale. **2** bazaar, market place, mart. ● *verb* **1** advertise, deal in, make available, merchandise, peddle, promote, retail, sell, tout, trade, trade in, vend.

marketable *adjective* able or fit to be sold.

marking *noun* (usually in *plural*) **1** identification mark. **2** colouring of fur, feathers, etc.

marksman /ˈmɑːksmən/ (*feminine* **markswoman**) *noun* skilled shot, esp. with rifle. □ **marksmanship** *noun*.
■ crack shot, gunman, sharpshooter, sniper.

marl *noun* soil composed of clay and lime, used as fertilizer.

marlinspike /ˈmɑːlɪnspaɪk/ *noun* pointed tool used to separate strands of rope or wire.

marmalade /ˈmɑːməleɪd/ *noun* preserve of oranges or other citrus fruit.

Marmite /ˈmɑːmaɪt/ *noun proprietary term* thick brown spread made from yeast and vegetable extract.

marmoreal /mɑːˈmɔːrɪəl/ *adjective* of or like marble.

marmoset /ˈmɑːməzet/ *noun* small bushy-tailed monkey.

marmot /ˈmɑːmət/ *noun* burrowing rodent with short bushy tail.

marocain /ˈmærəkeɪn/ *noun* fabric of ribbed crêpe.

maroon[1] /məˈruːn/ *adjective & noun* brownish-crimson.

maroon[2] /məˈruːn/ *verb* **1** put and leave ashore on desolate island or coast. **2** leave stranded.
■ abandon, desert, forsake, isolate, leave, put ashore, strand.

marquee /mɑːˈkiː/ *noun* large tent.

marquess /ˈmɑːkwəs/ *noun* British nobleman ranking between duke and earl.

marquetry /ˈmɑːkɪtrɪ/ *noun* inlaid work in wood etc.

marquis /ˈmɑːkwɪs/ *noun* (*plural* **-quises**) foreign nobleman ranking between duke and count.

marquise /mɑːˈkiːz/ *noun* **1** marquis's wife or widow. **2** woman holding rank of marquis.

marriage /ˈmærɪdʒ/ *noun* **1** legal union of man and woman for the purpose of living together. **2** act or ceremony establishing this. **3** particular matrimonial union. □ **marriage certificate, lines** certificate stating that marriage has taken place. **marriage guidance** counselling of people with marital problems.
■ **1** matrimony, wedlock. **2** nuptials, wedding. **3** partnership, union.

marriageable *adjective* free, ready, or fit for marriage.
■ nubile.

marrow /ˈmærəʊ/ *noun* **1** large fleshy gourd, cooked as vegetable. **2** bone marrow. □ **marrowbone** bone containing edible marrow. **marrowfat** kind of large pea.

marry /ˈmærɪ/ *verb* (**-ies, -ied**) **1** take, join, or give in marriage. **2** enter into marriage. **3** (+ *into*) become member of (family) by marriage. **4** unite intimately.

■ **1** *archaic* espouse, join in matrimony, unite, wed. **2** *colloquial* get hitched, *usually formal* or *literary* wed. **4** see UNITE 1.

Marsala /mɑːˈsɑːlə/ *noun* dark sweet fortified wine.

Marseillaise /mɑːseɪˈjeɪz/ *noun* French national anthem.

marsh *noun* low watery ground. □ **marsh gas** methane. **marshland** land consisting of marshes. **marsh mallow** shrubby herb. **marshmallow** soft sweet made from sugar, albumen, gelatin, etc. □ **marshy** *adjective* (**-ier, -iest**).
■ bog, fen, marshland, *literary* morass, mudflats, quagmire, saltings, salt marsh, slough, swamp, wetland.

marshal /ˈmɑːʃ(ə)l/ *noun* **1** (**Marshal**) high-ranking officer of state or in armed forces. **2** officer arranging ceremonies, controlling procedure at races, etc. ● *verb* (**-ll-**) **1** arrange in due order. **2** conduct (person) ceremoniously. □ **marshalling yard** yard in which goods trains etc. are assembled.
■ *verb* **1** arrange, assemble, collect, deploy, draw up, gather, group, line up, muster, organize, set out.

marsupial /mɑːˈsuːpɪəl/ *noun* mammal giving birth to underdeveloped young subsequently carried in pouch. ● *adjective* of or like a marsupial.

mart *noun* **1** trade centre. **2** auction-room. **3** market.

Martello tower /mɑːˈteləʊ/ *noun* small circular coastal fort.

marten /ˈmɑːtɪn/ *noun* weasel-like flesh-eating mammal with valuable fur; its fur.

martial /ˈmɑːʃ(ə)l/ *adjective* **1** of warfare. **2** warlike. □ **martial arts** fighting sports such as judo or karate. **martial law** military government with ordinary law suspended.
■ **1** fighting, military, soldierly. **2** aggressive, bellicose, belligerent, militant, pugnacious, warlike.

Martian /ˈmɑːʃ(ə)n/ *adjective* of planet Mars. ● *noun* hypothetical inhabitant of Mars.

martin /ˈmɑːtɪn/ *noun* bird of swallow family.

martinet /mɑːtɪˈnet/ *noun* strict disciplinarian.

Martini /mɑːˈtiːnɪ/ *noun* (*plural* **-s**) **1** *proprietary term* type of vermouth. **2** cocktail of gin and vermouth.

martyr /ˈmɑːtə/ *noun* **1** person who undergoes death or suffering for great cause. **2** (+ *to*) *colloquial* constant sufferer from. ● *verb* **1** put to death as martyr. **2** torment. □ **martyrdom** *noun*.

marvel /ˈmɑːv(ə)l/ *noun* **1** wonderful thing. **2** (+ *of*) wonderful example of. ● *verb* (**-ll-**; *US* **-l-**) (+ *at, that*) feel surprise or wonder.
■ *noun* **1** miracle, phenomenon, wonder. **2** miracle, wonder. ● *verb* (**marvel at**) admire, applaud, be amazed by, be astonished by, be surprised by, gape at, praise, wonder at.

marvellous /ˈmɑːvələs/ *adjective* (*US*

marvelous) **1** astonishing. **2** excellent. □ **mar-vellously** *adverb*.

■ **1** amazing, astonishing, astounding, breathtaking, extraordinary, *colloquial* incredible, miraculous, out of the ordinary, phenomenal, prodigious, remarkable, staggering, *colloquial* stunning, stupendous, surprising, unbelievable, wonderful, *poetical* wondrous. **2** admirable, excellent, exceptional, *colloquial* fabulous, *colloquial* fantastic, *colloquial* glorious, impressive, *colloquial* magnificent, *colloquial* out of this world, praiseworthy, *colloquial* sensational, spectacular, splendid, *colloquial* super, superb, *colloquial* terrific.

Marxism /'mɑːksɪz(ə)m/ *noun* doctrines of Marx, predicting common ownership of means of production. □ **Marxist** *noun & adjective*.

marzipan /'mɑːzɪpæn/ *noun* paste of ground almonds, sugar, etc.

mascara /mæs'kɑːrə/ *noun* cosmetic for darkening eyelashes.

mascot /'mæskɒt/ *noun* person, animal, or thing supposed to bring luck.

masculine /'mæskjʊlɪn/ *adjective* **1** of men. **2** manly. **3** *Grammar* belonging to gender including words for most male people and animals. □ **masculinity** /-'lɪn-/ *noun*.

■ **1** male. **2** boyish, *slang* butch, gentlemanly, macho, male, manly, mannish, virile.

maser /'meɪzə/ *noun* device for amplifying or generating microwaves.

mash *noun* **1** soft or confused mixture. **2** mixture of boiled bran etc. fed to horses. **3** *colloquial* mashed potatoes. ● *verb* crush (potatoes etc.) to pulp.

■ *verb* beat, crush, grind, mangle, pound, pulp, pulverize, smash, squash.

mask /mɑːsk/ *noun* **1** covering for all or part of face, worn as disguise or for protection, or by surgeon etc. to prevent infection of patient. **2** respirator. **3** likeness of person's face, esp. one made by taking mould from face. **4** disguise. ● *verb* **1** cover with mask. **2** conceal. **3** protect.

■ *noun* **1** cover, covering, screen, shield, visor. **4** camouflage, cloak, cover, cover-up, disguise, façade, front, guise, screen, veil. ● *verb* **1, 2** blot out, camouflage, cloak, conceal, cover, disguise, hide, obscure, screen, shield, shroud, veil.

masochism /'mæsəkɪz(ə)m/ *noun* pleasure in suffering physical or mental pain, esp. as form of sexual perversion. □ **masochist** *noun*. **masochistic** /-'kɪs-/ *adjective*.

mason /'meɪs(ə)n/ *noun* **1** person who builds with stone. **2** (**Mason**) Freemason.

Masonic /mə'sɒnɪk/ *adjective* of Freemasons.

masonry /'meɪsənrɪ/ *noun* **1** stonework; mason's work. **2** (**Masonry**) Freemasonry.

■ **1** bricks, brickwork, stone, stonework.

masque /mɑːsk/ *noun* musical drama with mime, esp. in 16th & 17th c.

masquerade /mæskə'reɪd/ *noun* **1** false show; pretence. **2** masked ball. ● *verb* (**-ding**) **1** appear in disguise. **2** assume false appearance. □ **masquerader** *noun*.

mass[1] *noun* **1** cohesive body of matter. **2** dense aggregation. **3** (in *singular* or *plural*; usually + *of*) large number or amount. **4** (usually + *of*) unbroken expanse (of colour etc.). **5** (**the mass**) the majority. **6** (**the masses**) ordinary people. **7** *Physics* quantity of matter body contains. ● *verb* **1** gather into mass. **2** assemble into one body. ● *adjective* of or relating to large numbers of people or things. □ **mass media** means of communication to large numbers of people. **mass production** mechanical production of large quantities of standardized article. **mass-produce** *verb*.

■ *noun* **1, 2** accumulation, agglomeration, aggregation, body, bulk, chunk, collection, concretion, conglomeration, dollop, heap, hoard, hunk, lot, lump, mound, mountain, pile, stack. **3** abundance, collection, *colloquial* heap, *usually derogatory* horde, load, *colloquial* lot, mob, mountain, multitude, *colloquial* pile, profusion, quantity, sea, *colloquial* stack, swarm, throng, *colloquial* ton, volume. ● *verb* **1** accumulate, aggregate, amass, collect, pile up. **2** assemble, collect, congregate, convene, flock together, gather, marshal, meet, mobilize, muster, rally. ● *adjective* comprehensive, general, large-scale, popular, universal, wholesale, widespread. □ **mass media** see COMMUNICATION 5.

mass[2] *noun* (often **Mass**) **1** Eucharist, esp. in RC Church. **2** (musical setting of) liturgy used in this.

massacre /'mæsəkə/ *noun* general slaughter. ● *verb* (**-ring**) make massacre of.

■ *verb* annihilate, butcher, execute, kill, murder, slaughter, slay.

massage /'mæsɑːʒ/ *noun* kneading and rubbing of muscles etc., usually with hands. ● *verb* (**-ging**) treat thus.

■ *verb* knead, manipulate, rub.

masseur /mæ'sɜː/ *noun* (*feminine* **masseuse** /mæ'sɜːz/) person who gives massage.

massif /'mæsiːf/ *noun* mountain heights forming compact group.

massive /'mæsɪv/ *adjective* **1** large and heavy or solid. **2** unusually large or severe. **3** substantial. □ **massively** *adverb*.

mast[1] /mɑːst/ *noun* **1** upright to which ship's yards and sails are attached. **2** tall metal structure supporting radio or television aerial. **3** flagpole.

■ **2** aerial, pylon, transmitter. **3** see POLE[1] 1.

mast[2] /mɑːst/ *noun* fruit of beech, oak, etc., esp. as food for pigs.

mastectomy /mæ'stektəmɪ/ *noun* (*plural* -**ies**) surgical removal of a breast.

master /'mɑːstə/ *noun* **1** person having control or ownership. **2** ship's captain. **3** male teacher. **4** prevailing person. **5** skilled workman. **6** skilled practitioner. **7** holder of university degree above bachelor's. **8** revered teacher. **9** great artist. **10** *Chess etc.* player at international level. **11** thing from which series of copies is made. **12 (Master)** *title prefixed to name of boy.* ● *adjective* **1** commanding; controlling others. **2** main, principal. ● *verb* **1** overcome, conquer. **2** acquire complete knowledge of. □ **master key** one opening several different locks. **mastermind** ● *noun* person with outstanding intellect. ● *verb* plan and direct (enterprise). **Master of Ceremonies** person introducing speakers at banquet or entertainers at variety show. **masterpiece 1** outstanding piece of artistry. **2** one's best work. **master switch** switch controlling electricity etc. supply to entire system.

■ *noun* **1** *colloquial* boss, chief, employer, governor, head, keeper, leader, lord, overseer, owner, proprietor, ruler, taskmaster. **2** captain, skipper. **3** see TEACHER. **5, 6** ace, authority, expert, genius, maestro, mastermind, virtuoso. ● *verb* **1** break in, bridle, check, conquer, control, curb, defeat, dominate, get the better of, govern, manage, overcome, overpower, quell, regulate, repress, rule, subdue, subjugate, suppress, tame, triumph over, *literary* vanquish. **2** become expert in, *colloquial* get the hang of, grasp, have off pat, know, learn, learn by heart, understand.
□ **mastermind** ● *noun* architect, brains, contriver, creator, engineer, expert, genius, intellectual, inventor, manager, originator, planner, prime mover. ● *verb* carry through, conceive, contrive, devise, direct, engineer, execute, manage, organize, originate, plan, plot.
masterpiece best work, *chef-d'oeuvre*, classic, *colloquial* hit, pièce de résistance.

masterful *adjective* **1** imperious, domineering. **2** very skilful. □ **masterfully** *adverb*.

USAGE *Masterful* is normally used of a person, whereas *masterly* is used of achievements, abilities, etc.

■ **1** see DOMINEERING (DOMINEER). **2** accomplished, adept, adroit, consummate, dexterous, expert, masterly, practised, proficient, skilful, skilled.

masterly *adjective* very skilful.

USAGE See note at MASTERFUL.

■ see MASTERFUL 2.

mastery *noun* **1** control, dominance. **2** (often + *of*) comprehensive skill or knowledge.

mastic /'mæstɪk/ *noun* **1** gum or resin from certain trees. **2** such tree. **3** waterproof filler and sealant.

masticate /'mæstɪkeɪt/ *verb* (**-ting**) chew. □ **mastication** *noun*.

mastiff /'mæstɪf/ *noun* large strong kind of dog.

mastodon /'mæstədɒn/ *noun* (*plural* same or **-s**) extinct animal resembling elephant.

mastoid /'mæstɔɪd/ *adjective* shaped like woman's breast. ● *noun* **1** (in full **mastoid process**) conical prominence on temporal bone. **2** (usually in *plural*) *colloquial* inflammation of mastoid.

masturbate /'mæstəbeɪt/ *verb* (**-ting**) produce sexual arousal (of) by manual stimulation of genitals. □ **masturbation** *noun*.

mat[1] *noun* **1** piece of coarse fabric on floor, esp. for wiping shoes on. **2** piece of material laid on table etc. to protect surface. ● *verb* (**-tt-**) (esp. as **matted** *adjective*) bring or come into thickly tangled state. □ **on the mat** *slang* being reprimanded.

■ *verb* (**matted**) dishevelled, knotted, tangled, uncombed, unkempt.

mat[2] = MATT.

matador /'mætədɔː/ *noun* bullfighter whose task is to kill bull.

match[1] *noun* **1** contest, game. **2** person or thing equal to, exactly resembling, or corresponding to another. **3** correspondence. **4** marriage. **5** person viewed as marriage prospect. ● *verb* **1** (often as **matching** *adjective*) be equal; correspond. **2** be or find match for. **3** (+ *against, with*) place in conflict or competition with. □ **matchboard** tongued and grooved board fitting into others. **matchmaker** person who arranges marriages or schemes to bring couples together. **match point** state of game when one side needs only one point to win match. **match up** (often + *with*) fit to form whole; tally. **match up to** be equal to.

■ *noun* **1** bout, competition, contest, duel, game, test match, tie, tournament, tourney. **2** complement, counterpart, double, equal, equivalent, twin. **3** correspondence, fit, pair, similarity. **4** alliance, marriage, partnership, relationship, union. ● *verb* **1** agree, accord, be compatible, be equal, be equivalent, be similar, be the same, blend, coincide, coordinate, correspond, fit, go, go together, harmonize, suit, tally, tie in, tone in; (**matching**) see SIMILAR. **2** combine, fit, join, link up, marry, mate, pair off, pair up, put together, team up.

match[2] *noun* short thin piece of wood etc., tipped with substance that ignites when rubbed on rough or specially prepared surface. □ **matchbox** box for holding matches. **matchstick** stem of match. **matchwood 1** wood suitable for matches. **2** minute splinters.

matchless *adjective* incomparable.

mate[1] *noun* **1** companion, fellow worker. **2** *colloquial: form of address, esp. to another man.* **3** each of a breeding pair, esp. of birds. **4** *colloquial* partner in marriage. **5** subordinate officer on merchant ship. **6** assistant to worker. ● *verb* (**-ting**) come or bring together for breeding.

■ *noun* **1** associate, *colloquial* chum, collaborator, colleague, companion, comrade, *often derogatory* crony, friend, *colloquial* pal. **4** *colloquial* better half, companion, consort, helpmate, husband, partner, spouse, wife. **6** see ASSISTANT 1–2. ● *verb* become partners, copulate, couple, have intercourse, *colloquial* have sex, join, marry, pair up, unite, wed.

mate[2] *noun* & *verb* (**-ting**) checkmate.

material /mə'tɪərɪəl/ *noun* **1** that from which thing is made. **2** cloth, fabric. **3** (in *plural*) things needed for activity. **4** person or thing of specified kind or suitable for purpose. **5** (in *singular* or *plural*) information etc. for book etc. **6** (in *singular* or *plural*) elements. ● *adjective* **1** of matter. **2** not spiritual. **3** of bodily comfort etc. **4** important, relevant.

■ *noun* **1** matter, stuff, substance. **2** cloth, fabric, stuff, textile. **3** (*materials*) equipment, gear, resources, stuff, supplies, things. **5** content, data, facts, ideas, information, matter, notes, statistics, subject matter, substance. **6** (*materials*) components, constituents, elements, ingredients, parts. ● *adjective* **1** concrete, corporeal, palpable, physical, solid, substantial, tangible. **2** see WORLDLY 1. **3** bodily, corporeal, physical.

materialism *noun* **1** greater interest in material possessions and comfort than in spiritual values. **2** theory that nothing exists but matter. □ **materialist** *noun*. **materialistic** /-ˈlɪs-/ *adjective*.

materialize *verb* (also **-ise**) (**-zing** or **-sing**) **1** become fact; happen. **2** *colloquial* appear, be present. **3** represent in or assume bodily form. □ **materialization** *noun*.

■ **1** come to pass, happen, occur, take place. **2, 3** appear, become visible, emerge, take shape, turn up.

maternal /məˈtɜːn(ə)l/ *adjective* **1** of or like a mother. **2** motherly. **3** related on mother's side.

maternity /məˈtɜːnɪtɪ/ *noun* **1** motherhood. **2** motherliness. ● *adjective* for women in pregnancy or childbirth.

matey *adjective* (also **maty**) (**-tier**, **-tiest**) familiar and friendly. □ **matily** *adverb*.

math *noun* US *colloquial* mathematics.

mathematics /mæθəˈmætɪks/ *plural noun* (also treated as *singular*) science of space, number, and quantity. □ **mathematical** *adjective*. **mathematician** /-məˈtɪʃ(ə)n/ *noun*.

maths *noun colloquial* mathematics.

matinée /ˈmætɪneɪ/ *noun* (US **matinee**) theatrical etc. performance in afternoon. □ **matinée coat** baby's short coat.

matins /ˈmætɪnz/ *noun* (also **mattins**) morning prayer.

matriarch /ˈmeɪtrɪɑːk/ *noun* female head of family or tribe. □ **matriarchal** /-ˈɑːk(ə)l/ *adjective*.

matriarchy /ˈmeɪtrɪɑːkɪ/ *noun* (*plural* **-ies**) female-dominated system of society.

matrices *plural* of MATRIX.

matricide /ˈmeɪtrɪsaɪd/ *noun* **1** killing of one's mother. **2** person who does this.

matriculate /məˈtrɪkjʊleɪt/ *verb* (**-ting**) **1** admit (student) to university. **2** be thus admitted. □ **matriculation** *noun*.

matrimony /ˈmætrɪmənɪ/ *noun* marriage. □ **matrimonial** /-ˈməʊnɪəl/ *adjective*.

matrix /ˈmeɪtrɪks/ *noun* (*plural* **matrices** /-siːz/ or **-es**) **1** mould in which thing is cast or shaped. **2** place etc. in which thing is developed. **3** rock in which gems etc. are embedded. **4** *Mathematics* rectangular array of quantities treated as single quantity.

matron /ˈmeɪtrən/ *noun* **1** woman in charge of nursing in hospital. **2** married, esp. staid, woman. **3** woman nurse and housekeeper at school etc.

matronly *adjective* like a matron, esp. portly or staid.

matt *adjective* (also **mat**) dull; not shiny or glossy.

matter /ˈmætə/ *noun* **1** physical substance. **2** thing(s); material. **3** (**the matter**; often + *with*) thing that is amiss. **4** content as opposed to form; substance. **5** affair, concern. **6** purulent discharge. ● *verb* (often + *to*) be of importance. □ **a matter of 1** approximately. **2** amounting to. **matter of course** natural or expected thing. **matter-of-fact 1** prosaic, unimaginative. **2** unemotional. **no matter** (+ *when, how*, etc.) regardless of.

■ *noun* **1, 2** material, stuff, substance. **3** difficulty, problem, trouble, upset, worry. **4** content, material, substance. **5** affair, business, concern, episode, event, fact, incident, issue, occurrence, question, situation, subject, thing, topic. **6** discharge, pus, suppuration. ● *verb* be important, be of consequence, be significant, count, make a difference, mean something, signify. □ **matter-of-fact 1** see PROSAIC 2.

matting *noun* fabric for mats.

mattins = MATINS.

mattock /ˈmætək/ *noun* tool like pickaxe with adze and chisel edge as ends of head.

mattress /ˈmætrɪs/ *noun* fabric case filled with soft or firm material or springs, used on or as bed.

mature /məˈtʃʊə/ *adjective* (**-r**, **-st**) **1** fully developed; ripe. **2** adult. **3** careful, considered. **4** (of bill etc.) due for payment. ● *verb* (**-ring**) bring to or reach mature state. □ **maturity** *noun*.

■ *adjective* **1** mellow, ready, ripe, seasoned. **2** adult, advanced, experienced, full-grown, grown-up, nubile, sophisticated, well developed. ● *verb* age, come to fruition, develop, grow up, mellow, ripen. □ **maturity** adulthood, completion, majority, mellowness, perfection, readiness, ripeness.

matutinal /mætjuːˈtaɪn(ə)l/ *adjective* of or in morning.

maty = MATEY.

maudlin /ˈmɔːdlɪn/ *adjective* weakly sentimental.

maul /mɔːl/ *verb* **1** injure by clawing etc. **2** handle roughly. **3** damage. ● *noun* **1** *Rugby* loose scrum. **2** brawl. **3** heavy hammer.

■ *verb* **1** claw, injure, lacerate, mangle, mutilate, paw, savage, wound. **2** knock about, *colloquial* manhandle, mistreat.

maulstick /ˈmɔːlstɪk/ *noun* stick held to support hand in painting.

maunder /ˈmɔːndə/ *verb* talk ramblingly.

Maundy /'mɔːndɪ/ *noun* distribution of **Maundy money**, silver coins minted for English sovereign to give to the poor on **Maundy Thursday**, Thursday before Easter.

mausoleum /mɔːsə'liːəm/ *noun* magnificent tomb.

mauve /məʊv/ *adjective & noun* pale purple.

maverick /'mævərɪk/ *noun* **1** unorthodox or independent-minded person. **2** *US* unbranded calf etc.

maw *noun* stomach of animal.

mawkish /'mɔːkɪʃ/ *adjective* feebly sentimental. □ **mawkishly** *adverb*. **mawkishness** *noun*.

maxillary /mæk'sɪlərɪ/ *adjective* of the jaw.

maxim /'mæksɪm/ *noun* general truth or rule of conduct briefly expressed.

maxima *plural* of MAXIMUM.

maximal /'mæksɪm(ə)l/ *adjective* greatest possible in size, duration, etc.

maximize /'mæksɪmaɪz/ *verb* (also **-ise**) **(-zing** or **-sing**) make as large or great as possible. □ **maximization** *noun*.

USAGE *Maximize* should not be used in standard English to mean 'to make as good as possible' or 'to make the most of'.

■ add to, augment, boost, build up, exaggerate, improve, increase, inflate, magnify, overdo, overstate.

maximum /'mæksɪməm/ *noun* (*plural* **maxima**) highest possible amount, size, etc. ● *adjective* greatest in amount, size, etc.

■ *noun* apex, ceiling, climax, extreme, highest point, peak, pinnacle, top, upper limit, zenith. ● *adjective* biggest, extreme, full, fullest, greatest, highest, largest, maximal, most, peak, supreme, top, topmost, utmost, uttermost.

May *noun* **1** fifth month of year. **2** (**may**) hawthorn, esp. in blossom. □ **May Day** 1 May as Spring festival or as international holiday in honour of workers. **mayfly** insect living briefly in spring as adult. **maypole** decorated pole danced round on May Day. **May queen** girl chosen to preside over May Day festivities.

may *auxiliary verb* (*3rd singular present* **may**; *past* **might** /maɪt/) expressing possibility, permission, request, wish, etc. □ **be that as it may** although that is possible.

USAGE Both *can* and *may* are used for asking permission, as in *Can I move?* and *May I move?*, but *may* is better in formal English because *Can I move?* also means 'Am I physically able to move?'

maybe /'meɪbiː/ *adverb* perhaps.

■ conceivably, *archaic* perchance, perhaps, possibly.

mayday /'meɪdeɪ/ *noun* international radio distress signal.

mayhem /'meɪhem/ *noun* destruction, havoc.

mayonnaise /meɪə'neɪz/ *noun* **1** creamy dressing of oil, egg yolk, vinegar, etc. **2** dish dressed with this.

mayor /meə/ *noun* **1** head of corporation of city or borough. **2** head of district council with status of borough. □ **mayoral** *adjective*.

mayoralty /'meərəltɪ/ *noun* (*plural* **-ies**) **1** office of mayor. **2** period of this.

mayoress /'meərɪs/ *noun* **1** woman mayor. **2** wife or official consort of mayor.

maze *noun* **1** network of paths and hedges designed as puzzle; labyrinth. **2** confused network, mass, etc.

■ **1** labyrinth, network. **2** complex, confusion, tangle, web.

mazurka /mə'zɜːkə/ *noun* **1** lively Polish dance in triple time. **2** music for this.

MB *abbreviation* Bachelor of Medicine.

MBE *abbreviation* Member of the Order of the British Empire.

MC *abbreviation* **1** Master of Ceremonies. **2** Military Cross.

MCC *abbreviation* Marylebone Cricket Club.

MD *abbreviation* **1** Doctor of Medicine. **2** Managing Director.

me[1] /miː/ *pronoun* **1** *used by speaker or writer to refer to himself or herself as object of verb*. **2** *colloquial* I.

USAGE Some people consider it correct to use only *It is I*, but this is very formal or old-fashioned in most situations, and *It is me* is normally quite acceptable. On the other hand, it is not standard English to say *Me and him went* rather than *He and I went*.

me[2] /mi/ *noun* (also **mi**) *Music* third note of scale in tonic sol-fa.

mead *noun* alcoholic drink of fermented honey and water.

meadow /'medəʊ/ *noun* **1** piece of grassland, esp. used for hay. **2** low ground, esp. near river. □ **meadowsweet** a fragrant flowering plant.

■ **1** field, paddock, pasture.

meagre /'miːgə/ *adjective* (*US* **meager**) scanty in amount or quality.

■ deficient, inadequate, insufficient, lean, mean, paltry, poor, puny, scanty, skimpy, slight, small, sparse, thin, unsatisfying.

meal[1] *noun* **1** occasion when food is eaten. **2** the food eaten on one occasion. □ **meal ticket** *colloquial* source of income.

■ banquet, *slang* blow-out, collation, *formal* repast, *colloquial* spread.

meal[2] *noun* grain or pulse ground to powder.

mealy *adjective* (**-ier**, **-iest**) of, like, or containing meal. □ **mealy-mouthed** afraid to speak plainly.

mean[1] *verb* (*past & past participle* **meant** /ment/) **1** have as one's purpose or design. **2** intend to convey or indicate. **3** (of word) have as equivalent in same or another language. **4** involve. **5** portend. **6** (+ *to*) be of specified significance to.

■ **1** aim, desire, have in mind, hope, intend, plan, propose, purpose, want, wish. **2, 3** betoken, communicate, connote, convey, denote, drive at, express, hint at, imply, indicate, intimate, refer to, represent, say, show, signal, signify, specify, spell out, stand for, suggest, symbolize. **4** entail, involve, necessitate. **5** augur, betoken, foretell, herald, portend, presage, signal, spell.

mean[2] *adjective* **1** niggardly; not generous. **2** ignoble. **3** of low degree or poor quality. **4** malicious. **5** *US* vicious, aggressive. □ **meanness** *noun.*

■ **1** beggarly, cheese-paring, close, close-fisted, illiberal, *colloquial* mingy, miserly, niggardly, parsimonious, penny-pinching, selfish, sparing, stingy, *colloquial* tight, tight-fisted, uncharitable, ungenerous. **2** base, churlish, contemptible, despicable, ignoble, shabby, shameful, small-minded, uncharitable. **3** base, *derogatory* common, humble, inferior, insignificant, low, lowly, miserable, poor, shabby, squalid, wretched. **4, 5** callous, churlish, cruel, hard-hearted, ill-tempered, malicious, nasty, sneaky, spiteful, uncharitable, unkind, vicious.

mean[3] *noun* **1** condition, quality, or course of action equally far from two extremes. **2** term midway between first and last terms of progression. **3** quotient of the sum of several quantities and their number. ● *adjective* **1** (of quantity) equally far from two extremes. **2** calculated as mean.

meander /mɪˈændə/ *verb* **1** wander at random. **2** wind about. ● *noun* **1** (in *plural*) sinuous windings. **2** circuitous journey.

■ *verb* **1** ramble, rove, wander. **2** snake, twist and turn, wind, zigzag.

meaning *noun* **1** what is meant. **2** significance. ● *adjective* expressive; significant. □ **meaningful** *adjective.* **meaningfully** *adverb.* **meaningless** *adjective.* **meaninglessness** *noun.*

■ *noun* connotation, content, definition, denotation, drift, explanation, force, gist, idea, implication, import, importance, interpretation, message, point, purport, purpose, relevance, sense, significance, signification, substance, thrust, value. □ **meaningful** deep, eloquent, expressive, meaning, pointed, positive, pregnant, relevant, serious, significant, suggestive, telling, tell-tale, weighty, worthwhile. **meaningless** absurd, empty, hollow, incomprehensible, incoherent, inconsequential, irrelevant, nonsensical, pointless, senseless, shallow, silly, vacuous, worthless.

means *plural noun* **1** (often treated as *singular*) action, agent, device, or method producing result. **2** money resources. □ **means test** inquiry into financial resources of applicant for assistance etc.

■ **1** agency, channel, course, fashion, instrument, machinery, manner, medium, method, mode, process, way. **2** see WEALTH 1.

meantime *adverb* meanwhile. ● *noun* intervening period.

meanwhile *adverb* **1** in the intervening time. **2** at the same time.

measles /ˈmiːz(ə)lz/ *plural noun* (also treated as *singular*) infectious viral disease with red rash.

measly /ˈmiːzlɪ/ *adjective* (**-ier, -iest**) *colloquial* meagre, contemptible.

measure /ˈmeʒə/ *noun* **1** size or quantity found by measuring. **2** system or unit of measuring. **3** vessel, rod, tape, etc., for measuring. **4** degree, extent. **5** prescribed extent or amount. **6** standard serving as basis of evaluation, comparison, etc.; test, criterion. **7** (usually in *plural*) suitable action. **8** legislative enactment. **9** poetic metre. ● *verb* (**-ring**) **1** find size, quantity, proportions, etc. of by comparison with known standard. **2** be of specified size. **3** estimate (quality etc.) by some criterion. **4** (often + *off*) mark (line etc. of given length). **5** (+ *out*) distribute in measured quantities. **6** (+ *with, against*) bring into competition with. □ **measure up 1** take measurements (of). **2** (often + *to*) have necessary qualifications (for). □ **measurable** *adjective.*

■ *noun* **1** amount, amplitude, dimension(s), extent, magnitude, measurement, quantity, range, scope, size. **2** standard, system, unit. **4** amount, degree, extent. **5** allocation, allowance, amount, extent, portion, quantity, quota, ration. **6** criterion, gauge, indication, standard, test, touchstone, yardstick. **7** action, course of action, expedient, means, procedure, step. **8** act, bill, law. ● *verb* **1** assess, calculate, calibrate, compute, count, determine, estimate, gauge, judge, mark out, meter, plumb (*depth*), quantify, rank, rate, reckon, survey, weigh. **3** assess, determine, estimate, evaluate, gauge, judge, rank, rate, reckon, weigh. **5** (*measure out*) see DISPENSE 1. □ **measurable** appreciable, considerable, perceptible, quantifiable, reasonable, significant.

measured *adjective* **1** rhythmical. **2** (of language) carefully considered.

measureless *adjective* not measurable; infinite.

measurement *noun* **1** measuring. **2** amount measured; size.

■ **1** assessment, calculation, evaluation, mensuration. **2** amount, amplitude, area, breadth, bulk, capacity, depth, dimension, distance, extent, height, length, magnitude, mass, measure, mileage, size, speed, time, volume, weight, width.

meat *noun* **1** animal flesh as food. **2** (often + *of*) chief part.

meaty *adjective* (**-ier, -iest**) **1** full of meat; fleshy. **2** of or like meat. **3** substantial, satisfying.

Mecca /ˈmekə/ *noun* place one aspires to visit.

mechanic /mɪˈkænɪk/ *noun* person skilled in using or repairing machinery.

■ engineer, technician.

mechanical *adjective* **1** of, working, or produced by, machines or mechanism. **2** (of person or action) automatic; lacking originality. **3** of mechanics as a science. □ **mechanically** *adverb.*

■ **1** automated, automatic, machine-driven, technological. **2** automatic, cold, habitual, impersonal, inhuman, instinctive, lifeless, matter-of-fact, perfunctory, reflex, routine, soulless, unconscious, unemotional, unfeeling, unimaginative, uninspired, unthinking.

mechanics /mɪˈkænɪks/ *plural noun* (usually treated as *singular*) **1** branch of applied mathematics dealing with motion. **2** science of machinery. **3** routine technical aspects of thing.

mechanism /ˈmekənɪz(ə)m/ *noun* **1** structure or parts of machine. **2** system of parts working together. **3** process, method.

mechanize /ˈmekənaɪz/ *verb* (also **-ise**) (**-zing** or **-sing**) **1** introduce machines in. **2** make mechanical. **3** equip with tanks, armoured cars, etc. □ **mechanization** *noun*.

medal /ˈmed(ə)l/ *noun* commemorative metal disc etc., esp. awarded for military or sporting prowess.

■ award, decoration, honour, medallion, prize, reward, trophy.

medallion /mɪˈdæljən/ *noun* **1** large medal. **2** thing so shaped, e.g. portrait.

medallist /ˈmedəlɪst/ *noun* (*US* **medalist**) winner of (specified) medal.

■ champion, victor, winner.

meddle /ˈmed(ə)l/ *verb* (**-ling**) (often + *with*, *in*) interfere in others' concerns. □ **meddler** *noun*.

■ be a busybody, butt in, interfere, *colloquial* poke one's nose in, pry, *colloquial* snoop, tamper.

meddlesome *adjective* interfering.

media *plural* of MEDIUM.

USAGE It is a mistake to use *media* with a singular verb, as in *The media is biased*.

mediaeval = MEDIEVAL.

medial /ˈmiːdɪəl/ *adjective* **1** situated in middle. **2** of average size.

median /ˈmiːdɪən/ *adjective* situated in the middle. ● *noun* **1** straight line from angle of triangle to middle of opposite side. **2** middle value of series.

mediate /ˈmiːdɪeɪt/ *verb* (**-ting**) act as go-between or peacemaker. □ **mediation** *noun*. **mediator** *noun*.

■ arbitrate, intercede, *colloquial* liaise, negotiate. □ **mediator** arbiter, arbitrator, broker, conciliator, go-between, intercessor, intermediary, judge, liaison officer, middleman, moderator, negotiator, peacemaker, referee, umpire.

medical /ˈmedɪk(ə)l/ *adjective* of medicine in general or as distinct from surgery. ● *noun colloquial* medical examination. □ **medical certificate** certificate of fitness or unfitness to work etc. **medical examination** examination to determine person's physical fitness. □ **medically** *adverb*.

medicament /mɪˈdɪkəmənt/ *noun* substance used in curative treatment.

medicate /ˈmedɪkeɪt/ *verb* (**-ting**) **1** treat medic-

ally. **2** impregnate with medicinal substance.

medication /medɪˈkeɪʃ(ə)n/ *noun* **1** medicinal drug. **2** treatment using drugs.

medicinal /məˈdɪsɪn(ə)l/ *adjective* (of substance) healing.

■ curative, healing, medical, remedial, restorative, therapeutic.

medicine /ˈmeds(ə)n/ *noun* **1** science or practice of diagnosis, treatment, and prevention of disease, esp. as distinct from surgery. **2** substance, esp. one taken by mouth, used in this. □ **medicine man** witch-doctor.

■ **1** *esp. archaic* physic, treatment. **2** antidote, cure, dose, drug, medicament, medication, nostrum, panacea, *esp. archaic* physic, prescription, remedy, treatment.

medieval /medɪˈiːv(ə)l/ *adjective* (also **mediaeval**) of Middle Ages.

mediocre /miːdɪˈəʊkə/ *adjective* **1** indifferent in quality. **2** second-rate.

■ **1** average, *colloquial* common or garden, commonplace, everyday, fair, indifferent, medium, middling, moderate, ordinary, passable, pedestrian, run-of-the-mill, *colloquial* so so, undistinguished, unexceptional, unexciting, uninspired, unremarkable. **2** amateurish, inferior, second-rate.

mediocrity /miːdɪˈɒkrɪtɪ/ *noun* (*plural* **-ies**) **1** being mediocre. **2** mediocre person.

meditate /ˈmedɪteɪt/ *verb* (**-ting**) **1** engage in (esp. religious) contemplation. **2** plan mentally. □ **meditation** *noun*. **meditative** /-tətɪv/ *adjective*.

■ **1** be lost in thought, brood, cerebrate, cogitate, contemplate, deliberate, mull things over, muse, ponder, pray, reflect, ruminate, think. **2** chew over, consider, contemplate, ponder, turn over. □ **meditation** cerebration, contemplation, deliberation, musing, prayer, reflection, rumination, thought. **meditative** brooding, contemplative, pensive, prayerful, rapt, reflective, ruminative, thoughtful.

Mediterranean /medɪtəˈreɪnɪən/ *adjective* of the sea between Europe and N. Africa, or the countries bordering on it.

medium /ˈmiːdɪəm/ *noun* (*plural* **media** or **-s**) **1** middle quality, degree, etc. between extremes. **2** environment. **3** means of communication. **4** physical material or form used by artist, composer, etc. **5** (*plural* **-s**) person claiming to communicate with the dead. ● *adjective* **1** between two qualities etc. **2** average. □ **medium-range** (of aircraft, missile, etc.) able to travel medium distance.

■ *noun* **1** average, centre, compromise, mean, middle, mid-point, norm. **3** agency, approach, channel, form, means, method, mode, vehicle, way; (*the media*) see COMMUNICATION 5. **5** clairvoyant, seer, spiritualist. ● *adjective* average, intermediate, mean, medial, median, middle, middling, middle-sized, midway, moderate, normal, ordinary, standard, usual.

medlar /'medlə/ *noun* **1** tree bearing fruit like apple, eaten when decayed. **2** such fruit.

medley /'medlɪ/ *noun* (*plural* **-s**) varied mixture.

medulla /mɪ'dʌlə/ *noun* **1** inner part of certain bodily organs. **2** soft internal tissue of plants. □ **medulla oblongata** /ɒblɒŋ'gɑːtə/ lowest part of brainstem. □ **medullary** *adjective*.

meek *adjective* humble and submissive or gentle. □ **meekly** *adverb*. **meekness** *noun*.

■ acquiescent, compliant, deferential, docile, forbearing, gentle, humble, long-suffering, lowly, mild, modest, non-militant, obedient, patient, peaceable, quiet, resigned, retiring, self-effacing, shy, soft, spineless, submissive, tame, timid, tractable, unambitious, unassuming, unprotesting, weak, *colloquial* wimpish.

meerschaum /'mɪəʃəm/ *noun* **1** soft white clay-like substance. **2** tobacco pipe with bowl made from this.

meet[1] *verb* (*past & past participle* **met**) **1** encounter. **2** (of two or more people) come together. **3** be present at arrival of (person, train, etc.). **4** come into contact (with). **5** make acquaintance of. **6** deal with (demand etc.). **7** satisfy (need etc.). **8** (often + *with*) experience, receive. ● *noun* **1** assembly for a hunt. **2** assembly for athletics.

■ *verb* **1** *colloquial* bump into, chance upon, come across, confront, encounter, face, happen on, run across, run into, see. **2** assemble, collect, come together, congregate, convene, forgather, gather, muster, rally, rendezvous. **3** come and fetch, greet, pick up, rendezvous with, welcome. **4** abut, adjoin, come together, connect, converge, cross, intersect, join, link up, merge, touch, unite. **5** be introduced to, make the acquaintance of. **6, 7** answer, comply with, deal with, fulfil, measure up to, observe, pay, satisfy, settle, take care of. **8** (*meet with*) encounter, endure, experience, face, go through, suffer, undergo.

meet[2] *adjective archaic* fitting, proper.

meeting *noun* **1** coming together. **2** coming into contact; junction. **3** assembly of esp. a society, committee, etc. **4** persons assembled. **5** race meeting.

■ **1** appointment, assignation, confrontation, *colloquial* date, encounter, engagement, rendezvous, *archaic* tryst. **2** confluence (*of rivers*), contact, convergence, crossing, crossroads, intersection, joining, junction, T-junction, union. **3, 4** assembly, audience, board, cabinet, *often derogatory* caucus, committee, conclave, conference, congregation, congress, convention, council, forum, gathering, *colloquial* get-together, powwow, rally, seminar, synod.

mega- *combining form* **1** large. **2** one million. **3** *slang* extremely. **4** *slang* very big.

megabyte /'megəbaɪt/ *noun* 2^{20} bytes (approx. 1,000,000) as unit of computer storage.

megalith /'megəlɪθ/ *noun* large stone, esp. as prehistoric monument. □ **megalithic** /-'lɪθ-/ *adjective*.

megalomania /megələ'meɪnɪə/ *noun* **1** mental disorder producing delusions of grandeur. **2** passion for grandiose schemes. □ **megalomaniac** *adjective & noun*.

megaphone /'megəfəʊn/ *noun* large funnel-shaped device for amplifying voice.

megaton /'megətʌn/ *noun* unit of explosive power equal to that of 1,000,000 tons of TNT.

meiosis /maɪ'əʊsɪs/ *noun* (*plural* **meioses** /-siːz/) **1** cell division resulting in gametes with half normal chromosome number. **2** ironical understatement.

melamine /'meləmiːn/ *noun* **1** crystalline compound producing resins. **2** plastic made from this.

melancholia /melən'kəʊlɪə/ *noun* depression and anxiety.

melancholy /'melənkəlɪ/ *noun* **1** pensive sadness; depression. **2** tendency to this. ● *adjective* **1** sad. **2** depressing. □ **melancholic** /-'kɒl-/ *adjective*.

■ *noun* see SADNESS. ● *adjective* **1** dejected, depressed, despondent, disconsolate, dismal, dispirited, *colloquial* down, downhearted, forlorn, gloomy, glum, joyless, low, lugubrious, melancholic, miserable, moody, morose, mournful, sad, sombre, sorrowful, unhappy, woebegone, woeful. **2** cheerless, depressing, dismal, dispiriting, gloomy, saddening.

mélange /mei'lɒ̃ʒ/ *noun* mixture; medley. [French]

mêlée /'melei/ *noun* (US **melee**) **1** confused fight or scuffle. **2** muddle.

mellifluous /mɪ'lɪfluəs/ *adjective* (of voice etc.) pleasing, musical.

mellow /'meləʊ/ *adjective* **1** (of sound, colour, light, or flavour) soft and rich; free from harshness. **2** (of character) gentle. **3** genial. **4** mature. ● *verb* make or become mellow. □ **mellowness** *noun*.

■ *adjective* **1** rich, ripe, smooth, soft, sweet. **2, 3** agreeable, amiable, comforting, cordial, genial, gentle, happy, jovial, kindly, peaceful, pleasant, reassuring, soft, subdued, warm. **4** aged, mature, ripe, ripened. ● *verb* age, develop, mature, ripen, soften, sweeten.

melodic /mɪ'lɒdɪk/ *adjective* **1** of melody. **2** melodious.

melodious /mɪ'ləʊdɪəs/ *adjective* **1** of, producing, or having melody. **2** sweet-sounding. □ **melodiously** *adverb*.

■ dulcet, *colloquial* easy on the ear, euphonious, harmonious, lyrical, mellifluous, melodic, sweet, tuneful.

melodrama /'melədrɑːmə/ *noun* **1** sensational play etc. appealing blatantly to emotions. **2** this type of drama. □ **melodramatic** /-drə'mæt-/ *adjective*.

■ □ **melodramatic** emotional, exaggerated, histrionic, overdone, overdrawn, over the top, sensationalized, sentimental, theatrical.

melody /'melədɪ/ *noun* (*plural* **-ies**) **1** arrangement of notes to make distinctive musical pattern. **2** tune. **3** principal part in harmonized music. **4** tunefulness.
■ **1–3** air, song, strain, subject, theme, tune.

melon /'melən/ *noun* sweet fleshy fruit of various climbers of gourd family.

melt *verb* **1** become liquid or change from solid to liquid by action of heat. **2** dissolve. **3** (as **molten** *adjective*) (esp. of metals etc.) liquefied by heat. **4** (of person, feelings, etc.) soften; be softened. **5** (usually + *into*) merge. **6** (often + *away*) leave unobtrusively. □ **melt down 1** melt (esp. metal) for reuse. **2** become liquid and lose structure. **melting point** temperature at which solid melts. **melting pot** place for mixing races, theories, etc.
■ **1, 2** deliquesce, dissolve, liquefy, soften, thaw, unfreeze. **4** mollify, soften, thaw. **6** (*melt away*) see DISAPPEAR 1.

member /'membə/ *noun* **1** person etc. belonging to society, team, group, etc. **2** (**Member**) person elected to certain assemblies. **3** part of larger structure. **4** part or organ of body, esp. limb.
■ **1** associate, colleague, fellow.

membership *noun* **1** being a member. **2** number or group of members.

membrane /'membreɪn/ *noun* **1** pliable tissue connecting or lining organs in plants and animals. **2** pliable sheet or skin. □ **membranous** /-brən-/ *adjective*.

memento /mɪ'mentəʊ/ *noun* (*plural* **-es** or **-s**) souvenir of person or event.

memo /'meməʊ/ *noun* (*plural* **-s**) *colloquial* memorandum.

memoir /'memwɑː/ *noun* **1** historical account etc. written from personal knowledge or special sources. **2** (in *plural*) autobiography.

memorable /'memərəb(ə)l/ *adjective* **1** worth remembering. **2** not easily forgotten. □ **memorably** *adverb*.
■ **1** distinguished, extraordinary, historic, impressive, never-to-be-forgotten, notable, outstanding, remarkable, striking, unforgettable. **2** catchy (*tune*), haunting, indelible, ineradicable, never-to-be-forgotten, striking, unforgettable.

memorandum /memə'rændəm/ *noun* (*plural* **-da** or **-s**) **1** note or record for future use. **2** informal written message, esp. in business etc.

memorial /mɪ'mɔːrɪəl/ *noun* object etc. established in memory of person or event. ● *adjective* commemorative.
■ *noun* cairn, cenotaph, gravestone, headstone, monument, plaque, reminder, statue, tablet, tomb.

memorialize /mɪ'mɔːrɪəlaɪz/ *verb* (also **-ise**) **1** commemorate. **2** address memorial to (person or body).

memoriam see IN MEMORIAM.

memorize /'meməraɪz/ *verb* (also **-ise**) (**-zing** or **-sing**) commit to memory.

■ learn, learn by heart, learn by rote, learn parrot-fashion, remember, retain.

memory /'memərɪ/ *noun* (*plural* **-ies**) **1** faculty by which things are recalled to or kept in mind. **2** store of things remembered. **3** remembrance, esp. of person etc. **4** storage capacity of computer etc. **5** posthumous reputation.
■ **1** recall, retention. **3** impression, recollection, remembrance, reminiscence. **5** *archaic* fame, honour, name, reputation.

memsahib /'memsɑːb/ *noun historical* European married woman in India.

men *plural* of MAN.

menace /'menɪs/ *noun* **1** threat. **2** dangerous thing or person. **3** *jocular* nuisance. ● *verb* (**-cing**) threaten. □ **menacingly** *adverb*.
■ *noun* **1** danger, peril, threat, warning. ● *verb* alarm, bully, cow, frighten, intimidate, terrify, terrorize, threaten.

ménage /meɪ'nɑːʒ/ *noun* household.

menagerie /mɪ'nædʒərɪ/ *noun* small zoo.

mend *verb* **1** restore to good condition; repair. **2** regain health. **3** improve. ● *noun* darn or repair in material etc. □ **on the mend** recovering, esp. in health.
■ *verb* **1** fix, patch up, put right, rectify, remedy, renew, renovate, repair, restore. **2** convalesce, get better, heal, improve, recover, recuperate. **3** ameliorate, amend, correct, cure, improve, reform, revise.

mendacious /men'deɪʃəs/ *adjective* lying, untruthful. □ **mendacity** /-'dæs-/ *noun* (*plural* **-ies**).

mendicant /'mendɪkənt/ *adjective* **1** begging. **2** (of friar) living solely on alms. ● *noun* **1** beggar. **2** mendicant friar.

menfolk *plural noun* men, esp. men of family.

menhir /'menhɪə/ *noun* usually prehistoric monument of tall upright stone.

menial /'miːnɪəl/ *adjective* (of work) degrading, servile. ● *noun* domestic servant.
■ *adjective* base, boring, *derogatory* common, degrading, demeaning, humble, inferior, insignificant, low, lowly, servile, slavish, subservient, unskilled, unworthy. ● *noun colloquial* dogsbody, lackey, *derogatory* minion, servant, slave, *usually derogatory* underling.

meningitis /menɪn'dʒaɪtɪs/ *noun* (esp. viral) infection and inflammation of membranes enclosing brain and spinal cord.

meniscus /mɪ'nɪskəs/ *noun* (*plural* **menisci** /-saɪ/) **1** curved upper surface of liquid in tube. **2** lens convex on one side and concave on the other.

menopause /'menəpɔːz/ *noun* **1** ceasing of menstruation. **2** period in woman's life when this occurs. □ **menopausal** /-'pɔːz(ə)l/ *adjective*.

menses /'mensiːz/ *plural noun* flow of menstrual blood etc.

menstrual /'menstruəl/ *adjective* of menstruation.

menstruate /'menstrʊeɪt/ *verb* (**-ting**) undergo menstruation.

menstruation *noun* discharge of blood etc. from uterus, usually at monthly intervals.

mensuration /mensjʊə'reɪʃ(ə)n/ *noun* **1** measuring. **2** measuring of lengths, areas, and volumes.

mental /'ment(ə)l/ *adjective* **1** done by the mind. **2** of or in the mind. **3** caring for mental patients. **4** *colloquial* insane. □ **mental age** degree of mental development in terms of average age at which such development is attained. **mental deficiency** abnormally low intelligence. **mental patient** sufferer from mental illness. □ **mentally** *adverb*.

■ **1, 2** cerebral, cognitive, conceptual, intellectual, psychological, rational, *esp. Philosophy* subjective. **4** see MAD 1.

mentality /men'tælɪtɪ/ *noun* (*plural* **-ies**) mental character or disposition.

■ attitude, bent, character, disposition, frame of mind, inclination, make-up, outlook, personality, predisposition, propensity, psychology, temperament, way of thinking.

menthol /'menθɒl/ *noun* mint-tasting organic alcohol found in oil of peppermint etc., used as flavouring and to relieve local pain.

mention /'menʃ(ə)n/ *verb* **1** refer to briefly or by name. **2** disclose. ● *noun* reference, esp. by name.

■ *verb* **1** acknowledge, allude to, *literary* animadvert on, bring up, broach, cite, comment on, draw attention to, enumerate, hint at, make mention of, name, note, observe, pay tribute to, point out, quote, refer to, remark, report, say, speak about, touch on, write about. **2** disclose, divulge, let out, make known, reveal.

mentor /'mentɔː/ *noun* experienced and trusted adviser.

menu /'menjuː/ *noun* (*plural* **-s**) **1** list of dishes available in restaurant etc., or to be served at meal. **2** *Computing* list of options displayed on VDU.

MEP *abbreviation* Member of European Parliament.

mephitis /mɪ'faɪtɪs/ *noun* noxious emanation; stench. □ **mephitic** /-'fɪtɪk/ *adjective*.

mercantile /'mɜːkəntaɪl/ *adjective* **1** of trade, trading. **2** commercial. □ **mercantile marine** merchant shipping.

mercenary /'mɜːsɪnərɪ/ *adjective* primarily concerned with or working for money etc. ● *noun* (*plural* **-ies**) hired soldier in foreign service.

■ *adjective* acquisitive, avaricious, covetous, grasping, greedy, venal.

mercer /'mɜːsə/ *noun* dealer in textile fabrics.

mercerize /'mɜːsəraɪz/ *verb* (also **-ise**) (**-zing** or **-sing**) treat (cotton) with caustic alkali to strengthen and make lustrous.

merchandise /'mɜːtʃəndaɪz/ *noun* goods for sale. ● *verb* (**-sing**) **1** trade (in). **2** promote (goods, ideas, etc.).

■ *noun* commodities, goods, produce, products, stock. ● *verb* **2** see ADVERTISE 1.

merchant /'mɜːtʃ(ə)nt/ *noun* **1** wholesale trader, esp. with foreign countries. **2** *esp. US & Scottish* retail trader. □ **merchant bank** bank dealing in commercial loans and finance. **merchantman** merchant ship. **merchant navy** nation's commercial shipping. **merchant ship** ship carrying merchandise.

■ **1** broker, dealer, distributor, supplier, trader, wholesaler. **2** dealer, retailer, seller, shopkeeper, stockist, trader, tradesman, tradeswoman, vendor.

merchantable *adjective* saleable.

merciful /'mɜːsɪfʊl/ *adjective* showing mercy. □ **mercifulness** *noun*.

■ beneficent, benevolent, charitable, clement, compassionate, forbearing, forgiving, generous, gracious, humane, humanitarian, indulgent, kind, kind-hearted, kindly, lenient, liberal, magnanimous, mild, pitying, soft, soft-hearted, sympathetic, tender-hearted, tolerant.

mercifully *adverb* **1** in a merciful way. **2** fortunately.

merciless /'mɜːsɪləs/ *adjective* showing no mercy. □ **mercilessly** *adverb*.

■ barbaric, barbarous, brutal, callous, cold, cruel, cut-throat, hard, hard-hearted, harsh, heartless, indifferent, inexorable, inflexible, inhuman, inhumane, intolerant, malevolent, pitiless, relentless, remorseless, rigorous, ruthless, savage, severe, stern, stony-hearted, strict, tyrannical, unbending, unfeeling, unforgiving, unkind, unmerciful, unrelenting, unremitting, vicious.

mercurial /mɜː'kjʊərɪəl/ *adjective* **1** (of person) volatile. **2** of or containing mercury.

mercury /'mɜːkjʊrɪ/ *noun* **1** silvery heavy liquid metal used in barometers, thermometers, etc. **2** (**Mercury**) planet nearest to the sun. □ **mercuric** /-'kjʊər-/ *adjective*. **mercurous** *adjective*.

mercy /'mɜːsɪ/ *noun* (*plural* **-ies**) **1** compassion towards defeated enemies or offenders or as quality. **2** act of mercy. **3** thing to be thankful for. □ **at the mercy of** in the power of. **mercy killing** killing done out of pity.

■ **1** beneficence, benignity, charity, clemency, compassion, feeling, forbearance, forgiveness, generosity, grace, humaneness, humanity, indulgence, kind-heartedness, kindness, leniency, love, pity, quarter, sympathy, understanding.

mere[1] /mɪə/ *adjective* (**-st**) being only what is specified. □ **merely** *adverb*.

mere[2] /mɪə/ *noun* *dialect* or *poetical* lake.

meretricious /merə'trɪʃəs/ *adjective* showily but falsely attractive.

merganser /mɜː'gænsə/ *noun* (*plural* same or **-s**) a diving duck.

merge *verb* (**-ging**) **1** (often + *with*) combine; join or blend gradually. **2** (+ *in*) (cause to) lose character and identity in (something else).

■ **1** amalgamate, blend, coalesce, combine, come together, confederate, consolidate, converge, fuse, integrate, join, link up, meet, mingle, mix, pool, put together, unite.

merger *noun* combining, esp. of two commercial companies etc. into one.

meridian /məˈrɪdɪən/ *noun* **1** circle of constant longitude passing through given place and N. and S. Poles. **2** corresponding line on map etc.

meridional /məˈrɪdɪən(ə)l/ *adjective* **1** of or in the south (esp. of Europe). **2** of a meridian.

meringue /məˈræŋ/ *noun* **1** sugar, whipped egg whites, etc. baked crisp. **2** cake of this.

merino /məˈriːnəʊ/ *noun* (*plural* **-s**) **1** variety of sheep with long fine wool. **2** soft material, originally of merino wool. **3** fine woollen yarn.

merit /ˈmerɪt/ *noun* **1** quality of deserving well. **2** excellence, worth. **3** (usually in *plural*) thing that entitles to reward or gratitude. ● *verb* (**-t-**) deserve.

■ *noun* **1, 2** credit, distinction, excellence, good, goodness, importance, quality, value, virtue, worth, worthiness. **3** asset, quality, strength, virtue. ● *verb* be entitled to, be worthy of, deserve, earn, have a right to, justify, rate, warrant.

meritocracy /merɪˈtɒkrəsɪ/ *noun* (*plural* **-ies**) **1** government by those selected for merit. **2** group selected in this way.

meritorious /merɪˈtɔːrɪəs/ *adjective* praiseworthy.

■ admirable, commendable, estimable, exemplary, honourable, laudable, praiseworthy, worthy.

merlin /ˈmɜːlɪn/ *noun* kind of small falcon.

mermaid /ˈmɜːmeɪd/ *noun* legendary creature with woman's head and trunk and fish's tail.

merry /ˈmerɪ/ *adjective* (**-ier, -iest**) **1** joyous; full of laughter or gaiety. **2** *colloquial* slightly drunk. □ **merry-go-round** fairground ride with revolving model horses, cars, etc. **merrymaking** festivity. □ **merrily** *adverb*. **merriment** *noun*.

■ **1** bright, bubbly, carefree, cheerful, cheery, *colloquial* chirpy, convivial, festive, fun-loving, gay, glad, happy, hilarious, jocular, jolly, jovial, joyful, joyous, light-hearted, lively, mirthful, rollicking, spirited, vivacious. □ **merrymaking** carousing, celebration, conviviality, festivity, frolic, fun, gaiety, jollification, junketing, merriment, revelry, roistering, *archaic* wassailing. □ **merriment** amusement, cheerfulness, conviviality, exuberance, gaiety, glee, good cheer, high spirits, hilarity, jocularity, joking, jollity, joviality, *colloquial* larking about, laughter, levity, light-heartedness, liveliness, merrymaking, mirth, vivacity.

mésalliance /meɪˈzælɪɑ̃s/ *noun* marriage with social inferior. [French]

mescal /ˈmeskæl/ *noun* peyote cactus.

□ **mescal buttons** disc-shaped dried tops from mescal, esp. as intoxicant.

mescaline /ˈmeskəlɪn/ *noun* (also **mescalin**) hallucinogenic alkaloid present in mescal buttons.

Mesdames, Mesdemoiselles *plural* of MADAME, MADEMOISELLE.

mesh *noun* **1** network structure. **2** each of open spaces in net, sieve, etc. **3** (in *plural*) network. **4** (in *plural*) snare. ● *verb* **1** (often + *with*) (of teeth of wheel) be engaged. **2** be harmonious. **3** catch in net.

■ *noun* **1, 2** grid, lace, lattice, lattice-work, net, netting, network, reticulation, screen, sieve, tangle, tracery, trellis, web, webbing.

mesmerize /ˈmezməraɪz/ *verb* (also **-ise**) (**-zing** or **-sing**) **1** hypnotize. **2** fascinate. □ **mesmerism** *noun*.

meso- *combining form* middle, intermediate.

mesolithic /mezəʊˈlɪθɪk/ *adjective* of Stone Age between palaeolithic and neolithic periods.

meson /ˈmiːzɒn/ *noun* elementary particle with mass between that of electron and proton.

Mesozoic /mesəʊˈzəʊɪk/ *adjective* of geological era marked by development of dinosaurs. ● *noun* this era.

mess *noun* **1** dirty or untidy state. **2** state of confusion or trouble. **3** something spilt etc. **4** disagreeable concoction. **5** soldiers etc. dining together. **6** army dining-hall. **7** meal taken there. **8** domestic animal's excreta. **9** *archaic* portion of liquid or pulpy food. ● *verb* **1** (often + *up*) make mess of, dirty. **2** (often + *up*) muddle. **3** *US* (+ *with*) interfere with. **4** take one's meals. **5** *colloquial* defecate. □ **make a mess of** bungle. **mess about, around** potter.

■ *noun* **1** chaos, clutter, confusion, dirt, disarray, disorder, hotchpotch, jumble, litter, mishmash, muddle, *colloquial* shambles, tangle, untidiness. **2** botch, difficulty, fix, hash, *colloquial* jam, mix-up, muddle, *colloquial* pickle, plight, predicament, trouble. ● *verb* **1** (*mess up*) see DIRTY *verb*. **2** (*mess up*) see MUDDLE *verb* 1. □ **make a mess of** see BUNGLE *verb* 1, MUDDLE *verb* 1. **mess about, around** amuse oneself, loaf, loiter, lounge about, monkey about, *colloquial* muck about, play about, potter about.

message /ˈmesɪdʒ/ *noun* **1** communication sent by one person to another. **2** exalted or spiritual communication.

■ **1** announcement, bulletin, cable, communication, communiqué, dispatch, information, intelligence, letter, *colloquial* memo, memorandum, *jocular* missive, news, note, notice, report, statement, *archaic or jocular* tidings.

messenger /ˈmesɪndʒə/ *noun* person who carries message(s).

■ bearer, carrier, courier, dispatch rider, emissary, envoy, errand-boy, errand-girl, go-between, harbinger, herald, intermediary, legate, nuncio, postman, runner.

Messiah /mɪˈsaɪə/ *noun* **1** promised deliverer

of Jews. **2** Jesus regarded as this. □ **Messianic** /mesɪˈænɪk/ *adjective*.

Messieurs *plural* of MONSIEUR.

Messrs /ˈmesəz/ *plural* of MR.

messy *adjective* (**-ier, -iest**) **1** untidy, dirty. **2** causing or accompanied by a mess. **3** difficult to deal with; awkward. □ **messily** *adverb*.

> ■ **1** blowzy, careless, chaotic, cluttered, dirty, dishevelled, disorderly, grubby, mucky, muddled, *colloquial* shambolic, slapdash, sloppy, slovenly, unkempt, untidy.

met *past & past participle* of MEET¹.

metabolism /mɪˈtæbəlɪz(ə)m/ *noun* all chemical processes in living organism producing energy and growth. □ **metabolic** /metəˈbɒlɪk/ *adjective*.

metacarpus /metəˈkɑːpəs/ *noun* (*plural* **-carpi** /-paɪ/) set of bones forming part of hand between wrist and fingers. □ **metacarpal** *adjective*.

metal /ˈmet(ə)l/ *noun* **1** any of class of mainly workable elements such as gold, silver, iron, or tin. **2** alloy of any of these. **3** (in *plural*) rails of railway. **4** road-metal. ● *adjective* made of metal. ● *verb* (**-ll-**; *US* **-l-**) **1** make or mend (road) with road-metal. **2** cover or fit with metal.

metallic /mɪˈtælɪk/ *adjective* **1** of or like metal(s). **2** sounding like struck metal.

> ■ **1** gleaming, lustrous, shiny. **2** clanking, clinking, ringing.

metallurgy /mɪˈtælədʒɪ/ *noun* **1** science of metals and their application. **2** extraction and purification of metals. □ **metallurgic** /metəˈlɜːdʒɪk/ *adjective*. **metallurgical** /metəˈlɜːdʒɪk(ə)l/ *adjective*. **metallurgist** *noun*.

metamorphic /metəˈmɔːfɪk/ *adjective* **1** of metamorphosis. **2** (of rock) transformed naturally. □ **metamorphism** *noun*.

metamorphose /metəˈmɔːfəʊz/ *verb* (**-sing**) (often + *to*, *into*) change in form or nature.

metamorphosis /metəˈmɔːfəsɪs/ *noun* (*plural* **-phoses** /-siːz/) **1** change of form, esp. from pupa to insect. **2** change of character, conditions, etc.

metaphor /ˈmetəfə/ *noun* application of name* or description to something to which it is not literally applicable (see panel). □ **metaphoric** /-ˈfɒr-/ *adjective*. **metaphorical** /-ˈfɒr-/ *adjective*. **metaphorically** /-ˈfɒr-/ *adverb*.

> ■ □ **metaphorical** allegorical, figurative, non-literal, symbolic.

metaphysics /metəˈfɪzɪks/ *plural noun* (usually treated as *singular*) philosophy dealing with nature of existence, truth, and knowledge. □ **metaphysical** *adjective*.

metatarsus /metəˈtɑːsəs/ *noun* (*plural* **-tarsi** /-saɪ/) set of bones forming part of foot between ankle and toes. □ **metatarsal** *adjective*.

mete *verb* (**-ting**) (usually + *out*) *literary* apportion, allot.

meteor /ˈmiːtɪə/ *noun* small solid body from outer space becoming incandescent when entering earth's atmosphere.

meteoric /miːtɪˈɒrɪk/ *adjective* **1** rapid; dazzling. **2** of meteors.

meteorite /ˈmiːtɪəraɪt/ *noun* fallen meteor; fragment of rock or metal from outer space.

meteorology /miːtɪəˈrɒlədʒɪ/ *noun* study of atmospheric phenomena, esp. for forecasting weather. □ **meteorological** /-rəˈlɒdʒ-/ *adjective*. **meteorologist** *noun*.

meter¹ /ˈmiːtə/ *noun* **1** instrument that measures or records, esp. gas, electricity, etc. used, distance travelled, etc. **2** parking meter. ● *verb* measure or record by meter.

meter² *US* = METRE.

methane /ˈmiːθeɪn/ *noun* colourless odourless inflammable gaseous hydrocarbon, the main constituent of natural gas.

methanol /ˈmeθənɒl/ *noun* colourless inflammable organic liquid, used as solvent.

methinks /mɪˈθɪŋks/ *verb* (*past* **methought** /mɪˈθɔːt/) *archaic* it seems to me.

method /ˈmeθəd/ *noun* **1** way of doing something; procedure. **2** orderliness.

> ■ **1** approach, fashion, knack, manner, means, methodology, mode, *modus operandi*, plan, procedure, process, programme, recipe, routine, scheme, style, system, technique, trick, way. **2** design, discipline, neatness, order, orderliness, organization, pattern, structure.

methodical /mɪˈθɒdɪk(ə)l/ *adjective* characterized by method or order. □ **methodically** *adverb*.

> ■ businesslike, careful, deliberate, disciplined, logical, meticulous, neat, ordered, orderly, organized, painstaking, precise, rational, regular, structured, systematic, tidy.

Metaphor

A metaphor is a figure of speech that goes further than a simile, either by saying that something is something else that it could not normally be called, e.g.

> *The moon was a ghostly galleon tossed upon cloudy seas.*
> *Stockholm, the Venice of the North*

or by suggesting that something appears, sounds, or behaves like something else, e.g.

> *burning ambition*   *blindingly obvious*
> *the long arm of the*
> *law*

Methodist /'meθədɪst/ *noun* member of Protestant denomination originating in 18th-c. Wesleyan evangelistic movement. ● *adjective* of Methodists or Methodism. □ **Methodism** *noun*.

methodology /meθə'dɒlədʒɪ/ *noun* (*plural* **-ies**) **1** science of method. **2** body of methods used in particular branch of activity.

methought *past* of METHINKS.

meths *noun colloquial* methylated spirit.

methyl /'meθɪl/ *noun* hydrocarbon radical CH₃. □ **methyl alcohol** methanol.

methylate /'meθɪleɪt/ *verb* (**-ting**) **1** mix or impregnate with methanol. **2** introduce methyl group into (molecule).

meticulous /mə'tɪkjʊləs/ *adjective* **1** giving great attention to detail. **2** very careful and precise. □ **meticulously** *adverb*. **meticulousness** *noun*.

■ accurate, exact, fastidious, finicky, painstaking, particular, perfectionist, precise, punctilious, scrupulous, thorough.

métier /'metjeɪ/ *noun* **1** one's trade, profession, or field of activity. **2** one's forte. [French]

metonymy /mɪ'tɒnɪmɪ/ *noun* substitution of name of attribute for that of thing meant.

metre /'miːtə/ *noun* (*US* **meter**) **1** SI unit of length (about 39.4 in.). **2** any form of poetic rhythm. **3** basic rhythm of music.

metric /'metrɪk/ *adjective* of or based on the metre. □ **metric system** decimal measuring system with metre, litre, and gram or kilogram as units of length, volume, and mass. **metric ton** 1,000 kg.

metrical *adjective* **1** of or composed in metre. **2** of or involving measurement. □ **metrically** *adverb*.

metronome /'metrənəʊm/ *noun* device ticking at selected rate to mark musical time.

metropolis /mɪ'trɒpəlɪs/ *noun* chief city; capital.

metropolitan /metrə'pɒlɪt(ə)n/ *adjective* **1** of metropolis. **2** of mother country as distinct from colonies. ● *noun* bishop with authority over bishops of province.

mettle /'met(ə)l/ *noun* **1** quality or strength of character. **2** spirit, courage. □ **mettlesome** *adjective*.

mew¹ *noun* cat's cry. ● *verb* utter this sound.

mew² *noun* gull, esp. common gull.

mewl /mjuːl/ *verb* (also **mule**) cry feebly, whimper.

mews /mjuːz/ *noun* (treated as *singular*) stabling round yard etc., now used esp. for housing.

mezzanine /'metsəniːn/ *noun* storey between two others (usually ground and first floors).

mezzo /'metsəʊ/ *Music adverb* half, moderately. ● *noun* (in full **mezzo-soprano**) (*plural* **-s**) **1** female singing voice between soprano and contralto. **2** singer with this voice. □ **mezzo forte** fairly loud(ly). **mezzo piano** fairly soft(ly).

mezzotint /'metsəʊtɪnt/ *noun* **1** method of copper or steel engraving. **2** print so produced.

mf *abbreviation* mezzo forte.

mg *abbreviation* milligram(s).

Mgr. *abbreviation* **1** Manager. **2** *Monseigneur*. **3** Monsignor.

MHz *abbreviation* megahertz.

mi = ME².

miaow /mɪ'aʊ/ *noun* characteristic cry of cat. ● *verb* make this cry.

miasma /mɪ'æzmə/ *noun* (*plural* **-mata** /-mətə/ or **-s**) *archaic* infectious or noxious vapour. □ **miasmic** *adjective*.

mica /'maɪkə/ *noun* silicate mineral found as glittering scales in granite etc. or crystals separable into thin plates.

mice *plural* of MOUSE.

Michaelmas /'mɪkəlməs/ *noun* feast of St Michael, 29 Sept. □ **Michaelmas daisy** autumn-flowering aster.

mickey /'mɪkɪ/ *noun* (also **micky**) □ **take the mickey** (often + *out of*) *slang* tease, mock.

micro /'maɪkrəʊ/ *noun* (*plural* **-s**) *colloquial* **1** microcomputer. **2** microprocessor.

micro- *combining form* **1** small. **2** one-millionth.

microbe /'maɪkrəʊb/ *noun* micro-organism (esp. bacterium) causing disease or fermentation. □ **microbial** /-'krəʊb-/ *adjective*.

■ bacillus, bacterium, bug, germ, micro-organism, virus.

microbiology /maɪkrəʊbaɪ'ɒlədʒɪ/ *noun* study of micro-organisms. □ **microbiologist** *noun*.

microchip /'maɪkrəʊtʃɪp/ *noun* small piece of semiconductor used to carry integrated circuits.

microcomputer /'maɪkrəʊkəmpjuːtə/ *noun* small computer with microprocessor as central processor.

microcosm /'maɪkrəkɒz(ə)m/ *noun* **1** (often + *of*) miniature representation, e.g. humankind seen as small-scale model of universe. **2** epitome. □ **microcosmic** /-'kɒz-/ *adjective*.

microdot /'maɪkrəʊdɒt/ *noun* microphotograph of document etc. reduced to size of dot.

microfiche /'maɪkrəʊfiːʃ/ *noun* small flat piece of film bearing microphotographs of documents etc.

microfilm /'maɪkrəʊfɪlm/ *noun* length of film bearing microphotographs of documents etc. ● *verb* photograph on microfilm.

microlight /'maɪkrəʊlaɪt/ *noun* kind of motorized hang-glider.

micrometer /maɪ'krɒmɪtə/ *noun* gauge for accurate small-scale measurement.

micron /'maɪkrɒn/ *noun* millionth of a metre.

micro-organism /maɪkrəʊ'ɔːɡənɪz(ə)m/ *noun* microscopic organism.

microphone /'maɪkrəfəʊn/ *noun* instrument for converting sound waves into electrical energy for reconversion into sound.

microphotograph /ˈmaɪkrəʊˈfəʊtəɡrɑːf/ *noun* photograph reduced to very small size.

microprocessor /ˈmaɪkrəʊˈprəʊsesə/ *noun* data processor using integrated circuits contained on microchip(s).

microscope /ˈmaɪkrəskəʊp/ *noun* instrument with lenses for magnifying objects or details invisible to naked eye.

microscopic /ˈmaɪkrəˈskɒpɪk/ *adjective* **1** visible only with microscope. **2** extremely small. **3** of the microscope. □ **microscopically** *adverb*.

microscopy /maɪˈkrɒskəpɪ/ *noun* use of microscopes.

microsurgery /ˈmaɪkrəʊsɜːdʒərɪ/ *noun* intricate surgery using microscopes.

microwave /ˈmaɪkrəʊweɪv/ *noun* **1** electromagnetic wave of length between 1 mm and 30 cm. **2** (in full **microwave oven**) oven using microwaves to cook or heat food quickly. ● *verb* (**-ving**) cook in microwave oven.

micturition /ˌmɪktjʊəˈrɪʃ(ə)n/ *noun formal* urination.

mid- *combining form* middle of. □ **mid-life** middle age. **mid-off, -on** *Cricket* position of fielder near bowler on off or on side.

midday /mɪdˈdeɪ/ *noun* middle of the day; noon.

midden /ˈmɪd(ə)n/ *noun* **1** dunghill. **2** refuse heap.

middle /ˈmɪd(ə)l/ *adjective* **1** at equal distance, time, or number from extremities; central. **2** intermediate in rank, quality, etc. **3** average. ● *noun* **1** (often + *of*) middle point, position, or part. **2** waist. □ **in the middle of** in the process of. **middle age** period between youth and old age. **the Middle Ages** period of European history from *c.* 1000 to 1453. **middle class** social class between upper and lower, including professional and business workers. **middle-class** *adjective*. **the Middle East** countries from Egypt to Iran inclusive. **middle-of-the-road 1** moderate. **2** unadventurous. **middleweight** amateur boxing weight (71–75 kg).

■ *adjective* **1** central, centre, halfway, inner, inside, intermediate, intervening, mean, medial, median, midway. **2, 3** average, intermediate, medium, middle-of-the-road, moderate, neutral. ● *noun* **1** bull's eye, centre, core, crown (*of road*), focus, halfway point, heart, hub, inside, mid-point, midst, nucleus.

middleman /ˈmɪd(ə)lmæn/ *noun* **1** trader who handles commodity between producer and consumer. **2** intermediary.

middling *adjective* moderately good. ● *adverb* fairly, moderately.

■ *adjective* average, fair, fair to middling, indifferent, mediocre, moderate, modest, ordinary, passable, run-of-the-mill, *colloquial* so so, unremarkable.

midge *noun* gnatlike insect.

midget /ˈmɪdʒɪt/ *noun* extremely small person or thing.

midland /ˈmɪdlənd/ *noun* **1** (**the Midlands**) inland counties of central England. **2** middle part of country. ● *adjective* of or in midland or Midlands.

midnight *noun* middle of night; 12 o'clock at night. □ **midnight sun** sun visible at midnight during summer in polar regions.

midriff /ˈmɪdrɪf/ *noun* front of body just above waist.

midshipman /ˈmɪdʃɪpmən/ *noun* naval officer ranking next above cadet.

midst *noun* middle. □ **in the midst of** among.

midsummer *noun* period of or near summer solstice, about 21 June. □ **Midsummer Day, Midsummer's Day** 24 June.

midway /ˈmɪdweɪ, mɪdˈweɪ/ *adverb* in or towards middle of distance between two points.

midwife /ˈmɪdwaɪf/ *noun* (*plural* **-wives**) person trained to assist at childbirth. □ **midwifery** /-ˈwɪfrɪ/ *noun*.

midwinter *noun* period of or near winter solstice, about 22 Dec.

mien /miːn/ *noun literary* person's look or bearing.

miff /mɪf/ *colloquial verb* offend. ● *noun* **1** petty quarrel. **2** huff.

might[1] *past* of MAY.

might[2] /maɪt/ *noun* strength, power.

■ capability, capacity, energy, force, muscle, potency, power, strength, superiority, vigour.

mightn't /ˈmaɪt(ə)nt/ might not.

mighty *adjective* (**-ier, -iest**) **1** powerful, strong. **2** massive. ● *adverb colloquial* very. □ **mightily** *adverb*.

■ *adjective* **1** brawny, dominant, *archaic* doughty, energetic, forceful, hefty, muscular, potent, powerful, robust, strapping, strong, sturdy, vigorous, weighty. **2** see BIG *adjective* 1.

mignonette /ˌmɪnjəˈnet/ *noun* plant with fragrant grey-green flowers.

migraine /ˈmiːɡreɪn/ *noun* recurrent throbbing headache often with nausea and visual disturbance.

migrant /ˈmaɪɡrənt/ *adjective* migrating. ● *noun* migrant person or animal, esp. bird.

migrate /maɪˈɡreɪt/ *verb* (**-ting**) **1** move from one place, esp. one country, to settle in another. **2** (of bird etc.) change habitation seasonally. □ **migration** *noun*. **migratory** /ˈmaɪɡrətərɪ/ *adjective*.

■ emigrate, go, immigrate, move, relocate, resettle, settle, travel.

mikado /mɪˈkɑːdəʊ/ *noun* (*plural* **-s**) *historical* emperor of Japan.

mike *noun colloquial* microphone.

milch *adjective* (of cow etc.) giving milk.

mild /maɪld/ *adjective* **1** (esp. of person) gentle. **2** not severe or harsh. **3** (of weather) moderately warm. **4** (of flavour) not sharp or strong. □ **mild**

steel tough low-carbon steel. □ **mildly** *adverb.* **mildness** *noun.*

■ **1** affable, amiable, conciliatory, docile, easygoing, equable, forbearing, forgiving, gentle, good-tempered, harmless, indulgent, inoffensive, kind, kindly, lenient, meek, merciful, modest, non-violent, pacific, peaceable, placid, quiet, serene, soft, soft-hearted, submissive, sympathetic, tractable, unassuming, understanding, yielding. **2** (*mild illness*) insignificant, minor, modest, slight, trivial, unimportant; (*mild punishment*) gentle, lenient, merciful. **3** balmy, calm, clement, fair, peaceful, pleasant, temperate, warm. **4** bland, delicate, faint, mellow, soothing, subtle. □ **mildness** affability, amiability, clemency, docility, forbearance, gentleness, kindness, leniency, moderation, placidity, softness, sympathy, tenderness.

mildew /ˈmɪldjuː/ *noun* destructive growth of minute fungi on plants, damp paper, leather, etc. ● *verb* taint or be tainted with mildew.

mile *noun* **1** unit of linear measure (1,760 yds, approx. 1.6 km). **2** (in *plural*) *colloquial* great distance or amount. **3** race extending over one mile. □ **milestone 1** stone beside road to mark distance in miles. **2** significant point (in life, history, etc.).

mileage *noun* (also **milage**) **1** number of miles travelled. **2** *colloquial* profit, advantage.

miler *noun colloquial* person or horse specializing in races of one mile.

milfoil /ˈmɪlfɔɪl/ *noun* common yarrow.

milieu /ˈmiːljɜː/ *noun* (*plural* **-x** or **-s** /-z/) person's environment or social surroundings.

militant /ˈmɪlɪt(ə)nt/ *adjective* **1** combative. **2** aggressively active in support of cause. **3** engaged in warfare. ● *noun* militant person. □ **militancy** *noun.* **militantly** *adverb.*

■ *adjective* **1, 2** active, aggressive, assertive, combative, pugnacious. **3** attacking, belligerent, combatant, fighting, warring. ● *noun* activist, extremist, hawk, partisan.

militarism /ˈmɪlɪtərɪz(ə)m/ *noun* **1** aggressively military policy etc. **2** military spirit. □ **militarist** *noun.* **militaristic** /-ˈrɪst-/ *adjective.*

■ □ **militaristic** bellicose, belligerent, combative, hawkish, hostile, pugnacious, warlike.

military /ˈmɪlɪtərɪ/ *adjective* of or characteristic of soldiers or armed forces. ● *noun* (treated as *singular* or *plural*; **the military**) the army.

■ *adjective* armed, belligerent, combatant, enlisted, fighting, martial, soldierly, uniformed, warlike.

militate /ˈmɪlɪteɪt/ *verb* (**-ting**) (usually + *against*) have force or effect.

USAGE *Militate* is often confused with *mitigate*, which means 'to make less intense or severe'.

■ (*militate against*) cancel out, counter, counteract, countervail, discourage, hinder, oppose, prevent, resist.

militia /mɪˈlɪʃə/ *noun* military force, esp. one conscripted in emergency. □ **militiaman** *noun.*

milk *noun* **1** opaque white fluid secreted by female mammals for nourishing young. **2** milk of cows, goats, etc. as food. **3** milklike liquid of coconut etc. ● *verb* **1** draw milk from (cow etc.). **2** exploit (person, situation). **3** draw sap from (tree). □ **milk chocolate** chocolate made with milk. **milk float** small usually electric vehicle used in delivering milk. **milkmaid** woman who milks cows or works in dairy. **milkman** person who sells or delivers milk. **milk run** routine expedition etc. **milk shake** drink of whisked milk, flavouring, etc. **milksop** weak or timid man or youth. **milk tooth** temporary tooth in young mammals.

■ *verb* **2** *colloquial* bleed, exploit, tap.

milky *adjective* (**-ier**, **-iest**) **1** of, like, or mixed with milk. **2** (of gem or liquid) cloudy. □ **Milky Way** luminous band of stars; the Earth's galaxy.

■ **2** chalky, cloudy, misty, opaque, whitish.

mill *noun* **1** building fitted with mechanical device for grinding corn. **2** such device. **3** device for grinding any solid to powder. **4** building fitted with machinery for manufacturing processes etc. **5** such machinery. ● *verb* **1** grind or treat in mill. **2** (esp. as **milled** *adjective*) produce ribbed edge on (coin). **3** (often + *about*, *round*) move aimlessly. □ **millpond** pond retained by dam for operating mill-wheel. **mill-race** current of water driving mill-wheel. **millstone 1** each of two circular stones for grinding corn. **2** heavy burden; great responsibility. **mill-wheel** wheel used to drive water-mill.

■ *noun* **1–3** crusher, grinder, quern, water-mill, windmill. **4** factory, foundry, plant, shop, works, workshop. ● *verb* **1** crush, granulate, grind, pound, powder, pulverize. **3** (*mill about*) seethe, swarm, throng, wander.

millennium /mɪˈlenɪəm/ *noun* (*plural* **-s** or **millennia**) **1** thousand-year period. **2** (esp. future) period of happiness on earth. □ **millennial** *adjective.*

miller /ˈmɪlə/ *noun* **1** person who owns or works mill, esp. corn-mill. **2** person operating milling machine.

millesimal /mɪˈlesɪm(ə)l/ *adjective* **1** thousandth. **2** of, belonging to, or dealing with, thousandth or thousandths. ● *noun* thousandth part.

millet /ˈmɪlɪt/ *noun* **1** cereal plant bearing small nutritious seeds. **2** seed of this.

milli- *combining form* one-thousandth.

millibar /ˈmɪlɪbɑː/ *noun* unit of atmospheric pressure equivalent to 100 pascals.

milligram /ˈmɪlɪɡræm/ *noun* (also **-gramme**) one-thousandth of a gram.

millilitre /ˈmɪlɪliːtə/ *noun* (*US* **-liter**) one-thousandth of a litre (0.002 pint).

millimetre /ˈmɪlɪmiːtə/ *noun* (*US* **-meter**) one-thousandth of a metre.

milliner /ˈmɪlɪnə/ *noun* maker or seller of women's hats. □ **millinery** *noun.*

million /'mɪljən/ *noun* **1** (*plural* same) one thousand thousand. **2** (**millions**) *colloquial* very large number. □ **millionth** *adjective & noun.*

millionaire /mɪljə'neə/ *noun* (*feminine* **millionairess**) person possessing over a million pounds, dollars, etc.

millipede /'mɪlɪpiːd/ *noun* (also **millepede**) small crawling invertebrate with many legs.

millisecond /'mɪlɪsekənd/ *noun* one-thousandth of a second.

milometer /maɪ'lɒmɪtə/ *noun* instrument for measuring number of miles travelled by vehicle.

milt *noun* **1** spleen in mammals. **2** reproductive gland or sperm of male fish.

mime *noun* **1** acting without words, using only gestures. **2** performance using mime. ● *verb* (**-ming**) express or represent by mime.

mimeograph /'mɪmɪəɡrɑːf/ *noun* **1** machine which duplicates from stencil. **2** copy so produced. ● *verb* reproduce in this way.

mimetic /mɪ'metɪk/ *adjective* of or practising imitation or mimicry.

mimic /'mɪmɪk/ *verb* (**-ck-**) **1** imitate (person, gesture, etc.), esp. to entertain or ridicule. **2** copy minutely or servilely. **3** resemble closely. ● *noun* person who mimics. □ **mimicry** *noun.*

■ *verb* **1** ape, caricature, do impressions of, imitate, impersonate, lampoon, make fun of, mock, parody, parrot, ridicule, satirize, *colloquial* take off. **2** ape, copy, duplicate, imitate, reproduce, simulate. **3** echo, look like, mirror, resemble, sound like. ● *noun* caricaturist, imitator, impersonator, impressionist.

mimosa /mɪ'məʊzə/ *noun* **1** shrub with globular usually yellow flowers. **2** acacia plant.

Min. *abbreviation* **1** Minister. **2** Ministry.

min. *abbreviation* **1** minute(s). **2** minimum. **3** minim (fluid measure).

minaret /mɪnə'ret/ *noun* tall slender turret next to mosque, used by muezzin.

minatory /'mɪnətərɪ/ *adjective formal* threatening.

mince *verb* (**-cing**) **1** cut or grind (meat etc.) finely. **2** (usually as **mincing** *adjective*) walk or speak in affected way. ● *noun* minced meat. □ **mincemeat** mixture of currants, sugar, spices, suet, etc. **mince pie** (usually small) pie containing mincemeat. □ **mincer** *noun.*

mind /maɪnd/ *noun* **1** seat of consciousness, thought, volition, and feeling. **2** attention, concentration. **3** intellect. **4** memory. **5** opinion. **6** sanity. ● *verb* **1** object to. **2** remember; take care to. **3** (often + *out*) be careful. **4** look after. **5** concern oneself with. **6** heed; notice. □ **be in two minds** be undecided. **in one's mind's eye** in one's imagination. **mind-boggling** *colloquial* overwhelming; startling. **out of one's mind** insane.

■ *noun* **1** brain, head, mentality, psyche. **3** astuteness, brain, brainpower, brains, cleverness, *colloquial* grey matter, head, insight, intellect, intelligence, judgement, mentality, mental power, perception, rationality, reason, reasoning, sagacity, sapience, sense, shrewdness, thinking,

understanding, wisdom, wit, wits. **4** memory, recollection, remembrance. **5** attitude, belief, bias, disposition, humour, inclination, intention, opinion, outlook, persuasion, point of view, position, view, viewpoint, way of thinking, wishes. ● *verb* **1** be annoyed by, be bothered by, be offended by, be resentful of, be upset by, disapprove of, dislike, object to, resent. **3** (*mind out*) be careful, look out, take care, watch out. **4** attend to, babysit, care for, guard, keep an eye on, look after, take care of, take charge of, watch over. **6** be careful about, beware of, heed, listen to, look out for, mark, note, notice, obey, pay attention to, remember, take notice of, watch out for. □ **be in two minds** see HESITATE 1. **out of one's mind** see MAD 1.

minded *adjective* (usually + *to do*) disposed, inclined. □ **-minded** inclined to think in specified way, or with specified interest.

minder *noun* **1** person employed to look after person or thing. **2** *slang* bodyguard.

mindful *adjective* (often + *of*) taking heed or care.

■ alert, attentive, aware, careful, conscious, heedful, on the lookout, vigilant, watchful.

mindless *adjective* **1** lacking intelligence; stupid. **2** not requiring thought or skill. □ **mindlessly** *adverb.* **mindlessness** *noun.*

■ **1** brainless, fatuous, idiotic, obtuse, senseless, stupid, *colloquial* thick, thoughtless, unintelligent, unthinking, witless.

mine[1] *pronoun* the one(s) belonging to me.

mine[2] *noun* **1** hole dug to extract metal, coal, salt, etc. **2** abundant source (of information etc.). **3** military explosive device placed in ground or water. ● *verb* (**-ning**) **1** (often + *for*) dig in (earth etc.) for ore etc. or to tunnel. **2** obtain (minerals) from mine. **3** lay explosive mines under or in. □ **minefield** area planted with explosive mines. **minesweeper** ship for clearing explosive mines from sea. □ **mining** *noun.*

■ *noun* **1** coalfield, colliery, excavation, pit, quarry, shaft, tunnel, working. **2** fund, repository, source, store, storehouse, supply, treasury, wealth. ● *verb* **1, 2** dig, excavate, extract, quarry, remove, scoop out, unearth.

miner *noun* worker in mine.

mineral /'mɪnər(ə)l/ *noun* **1** inorganic substance. **2** substance obtained by mining. **3** (often in *plural*) artificial mineral water or other carbonated drink. □ **mineral water** water naturally or artificially impregnated with dissolved salts. ■ **2** metal, ore, rock.

mineralogy /mɪnə'rælədʒɪ/ *noun* study of minerals. □ **mineralogical** /-rə'lɒdʒ-/ *adjective.* **mineralogist** *noun.*

minestrone /mɪnɪ'strəʊnɪ/ *noun* soup containing vegetables and pasta, beans, or rice.

mingle /'mɪŋɡ(ə)l/ *verb* (**-ling**) **1** mix, blend. **2** move about (among people).

■ **1** amalgamate, blend, combine, *literary* commingle, intermingle, intermix, join, merge, mix, unite. **2** associate, circulate, fraternize, get together, hobnob, mix, socialize.

mingy /'mɪndʒɪ/ *adjective* (**-ier**, **-iest**) *colloquial* stingy.

mini /'mɪnɪ/ *noun* (*plural* **-s**) **1** *colloquial* miniskirt. **2** (**Mini**) *proprietary term* make of small car. ● *adjective colloquial* very small.

mini- *combining form* miniature; small of its kind.

miniature /'mɪnɪtʃə/ *adjective* **1** much smaller than normal. **2** represented on small scale. ● *noun* **1** miniature object. **2** detailed small-scale portrait. □ **in miniature** on small scale.

■ *adjective* baby, diminutive, dwarf, pocket, pygmy, reduced, scaled-down, small, small-scale, tiny, toy.

miniaturist *noun* painter of miniatures.

miniaturize *verb* (also **-ise**) (**-zing** or **-sing**) produce in smaller version; make small. □ **miniaturization** *noun*.

minibus /'mɪnɪbʌs/ *noun* small bus for about 12 passengers.

minicab /'mɪnɪkæb/ *noun* car used as taxi, hireable only by telephone.

minicomputer /'mɪnɪkəmpjʊtə/ *noun* computer of medium power, more than microcomputer but less than mainframe.

minim /'mɪnɪm/ *noun* **1** *Music* note equal to two crotchets or half a semibreve. **2** one-sixtieth of fluid drachm.

minimal /'mɪnɪm(ə)l/ *adjective* **1** very minute or slight. **2** being a minimum. □ **minimally** *adverb*.

■ least, minimum, minutest, negligible, nominal, slightest, token.

minimize /'mɪnɪmaɪz/ *verb* (also **-ise**) (**-zing** or **-sing**) **1** reduce to or estimate at minimum. **2** estimate or represent at less than true value etc.

■ **1** cut down, decrease, diminish, lessen, pare, prune, reduce. **2** belittle, decry, depreciate, devalue, gloss over, make light of, play down, underestimate, undervalue.

minimum /'mɪnɪməm/ *noun* (*plural* **minima**) least possible or attainable amount. ● *adjective* that is a minimum. □ **minimum wage** lowest wage permitted by law or agreement.

■ *noun* base, bottom, least, lowest, nadir, rock-bottom. ● *adjective* bottom, least, littlest, lowest, minimal, minutest, nominal, rock-bottom, slightest, smallest.

minion /'mɪnjən/ *noun derogatory* servile subordinate.

miniskirt /'mɪnɪskɜːt/ *noun* very short skirt.

minister /'mɪnɪstə/ *noun* **1** head of government department. **2** member of clergy, esp. in Presbyterian and Nonconformist Churches. **3** diplomat, usually ranking below ambassador. ● *verb* (usually + *to*) help, serve, look after. □ **ministerial** /-'stɪər-/ *adjective*.

■ *noun* **2** see CLERGYMAN. **3** see DIPLOMAT 1. ● *verb* (*minister to*) aid, assist, attend to, care for, help, look after, nurse, see to, support, wait on.

ministration /mɪnɪ'streɪʃ(ə)n/ *noun* **1** (usually in *plural*) help, service. **2** ministering, esp. in religious matters.

ministry /'mɪnɪstrɪ/ *noun* (*plural* **-ies**) **1** government department headed by minister. **2** building for this. **3** (**the ministry**) profession of religious minister. **4** (**the ministry**) ministers of government or religion.

mink *noun* (*plural* same or **-s**) **1** small semi-aquatic stoatlike animal. **2** its fur. **3** coat of this.

minke /'mɪŋkɪ/ *noun* small whale.

minnow /'mɪnəʊ/ *noun* (*plural* same or **-s**) small freshwater carp.

Minoan /mɪ'nəʊən/ *adjective* of Cretan Bronze Age civilization. ● *noun* person of this civilization.

minor /'maɪnə/ *adjective* **1** lesser or comparatively small in size or importance. **2** *Music* (of scale) having semitone above second, fifth, and seventh notes. **3** *Music* (of key) based on minor scale. ● *noun* **1** person under full legal age. **2** *US* student's subsidiary subject or course. ● *verb* (+ *in*) *US* study (subject) as subsidiary.

■ *adjective* **1** inconsequential, inferior, insignificant, lesser, little, negligible, petty, secondary, small, smaller, subordinate, subsidiary, trivial, unimportant. ● *noun* **1** see ADOLESCENT *noun*, CHILD 1.

minority /maɪ'nɒrɪtɪ/ *noun* (*plural* **-ies**) **1** (often + *of*) smaller number or part, esp. in politics. **2** smaller group of people differing from larger in race, religion, language, etc. **3** being under full legal age. **4** period of this.

minster /'mɪnstə/ *noun* **1** large or important church. **2** church of monastery.

minstrel /'mɪnstr(ə)l/ *noun* **1** medieval singer or musician. **2** musical entertainer with blacked face.

■ balladeer, bard, entertainer, musician, singer, troubadour.

mint[1] *noun* **1** aromatic herb used in cooking. **2** peppermint. **3** peppermint sweet. □ **minty** *adjective* (**-ier**, **-iest**).

mint[2] *noun* **1** (esp. state) establishment where money is coined. **2** *colloquial* vast sum. ● *verb* **1** make (coin). **2** invent (word, phrase, etc.). □ **in mint condition 1** freshly minted. **2** as new.

■ *noun* **2** *colloquial* fortune, heap, *colloquial* packet, *colloquial* pile, *colloquial* stack. ● *verb* **1** cast, coin, forge, make, manufacture, produce, stamp out, strike. □ **in mint condition** brand new, first-class, fresh, immaculate, new, perfect, unblemished, unmarked, unused.

minuet /mɪnjʊ'et/ *noun* **1** slow stately dance in triple time. **2** music for this.

minus /'maɪnəs/ *preposition* **1** with subtraction of. **2** less than zero. **3** *colloquial* lacking. ● *adjec-*

tive Mathematics negative. ● *noun* **1** minus sign. **2** negative quantity. **3** *colloquial* disadvantage. □ **minus sign** symbol (-) indicating subtraction or negative value.

minuscule /ˈmɪnəskjuːl/ *adjective colloquial* extremely small or unimportant.

minute[1] /ˈmɪnɪt/ *noun* **1** sixtieth part of hour. **2** distance covered in minute. **3** moment. **4** sixtieth part of angular degree. **5** (in *plural*) summary of proceedings of meeting. **6** official memorandum. ● *verb* (**-ting**) **1** record in minutes. **2** send minutes to. □ **up to the minute** up to date.
■ *noun* **5** (*minutes*) log, notes, proceedings, record, résumé, summary, transactions.

minute[2] /maɪˈnjuːt/ *adjective* (**-est**) **1** very small. **2** accurate, detailed. □ **minutely** *adverb*.
■ **1** diminutive, dwarf, infinitesimal, insignificant, lilliputian, microscopic, *colloquial* mini, miniature, *colloquial* minuscule, *colloquial* pint-sized, pocket, pygmy, small, tiny.

minutiae /maɪˈnjuːʃiː/ *plural noun* very small, precise, or minor details.

minx /mɪŋks/ *noun* pert, sly, or playful girl.

miracle /ˈmɪrək(ə)l/ *noun* **1** extraordinary, supposedly supernatural, event. **2** remarkable happening. □ **miracle play** medieval play on biblical themes.
■ marvel, mystery, wonder.

miraculous /mɪˈrækjʊləs/ *adjective* **1** being a miracle. **2** supernatural. **3** surprising. □ **miraculously** *adverb*.
■ **1, 2** abnormal, extraordinary, incredible, inexplicable, magic, magical, mysterious, paranormal, phenomenal, preternatural, supernatural, unaccountable, unbelievable, unexplainable. **3** see MARVELLOUS 1.

mirage /ˈmɪrɑːʒ/ *noun* **1** optical illusion caused by atmospheric conditions, esp. appearance of water in desert. **2** illusory thing.
■ hallucination, illusion, vision.

mire *noun* **1** area of swampy ground. **2** mud. ● *verb* (**-ring**) **1** sink in mire. **2** bespatter with mud. □ **miry** *adjective*.
■ *noun* **1** bog, fen, marsh, *literary* morass, quagmire, slough, swamp. **2** see MUD.

mirror /ˈmɪrə/ *noun* **1** polished surface, usually of coated glass, reflecting image. **2** anything reflecting state of affairs etc. ● *verb* reflect in or as in mirror. □ **mirror image** identical image or reflection with left and right reversed.
■ *noun* **1** glass, looking-glass, reflector. ● *verb* echo, reflect, repeat, send back.

mirth *noun* merriment, laughter. □ **mirthful** *adjective*.

misadventure /mɪsədˈventʃə/ *noun* **1** *Law* accident without crime or negligence. **2** (case of) bad luck. **3** misfortune.
■ **3** accident, calamity, disaster, ill fortune, mischance, misfortune, mishap.

misalliance /mɪsəˈlaɪəns/ *noun* unsuitable alliance, esp. marriage.

misanthrope /ˈmɪsənθrəʊp/ *noun* (also **misanthropist** /mɪˈsænθrəpɪst/) person who hates humankind. □ **misanthropic** /-ˈθrɒp-/ *adjective*.
■ □ **misanthropic** antisocial, cynical, mean, nasty, surly, unfriendly, unpleasant, unsociable.

misanthropy /mɪˈsænθrəpɪ/ *noun* condition or habits of misanthrope.

misapply /mɪsəˈplaɪ/ *verb* (**-ies, -ied**) apply (esp. funds) wrongly. □ **misapplication** /-æplɪˈkeɪ-/ *noun*.

misapprehend /mɪsæprɪˈhend/ *verb* misunderstand (words, person). □ **misapprehension** *noun*.

misappropriate /mɪsəˈprəʊprɪeɪt/ *verb* (**-ting**) take (another's money etc.) for one's own use; embezzle. □ **misappropriation** *noun*.
■ embezzle, peculate, steal.

misbegotten /mɪsbɪˈɡɒt(ə)n/ *adjective* **1** illegitimate, bastard. **2** contemptible.

misbehave /mɪsbɪˈheɪv/ *verb* (**-ving**) behave badly. □ **misbehaviour** *noun*.
■ be a nuisance, be bad, be mischievous, blot one's copybook, commit an offence, disobey, do wrong, err, fool about, make mischief, mess about, *colloquial* muck about, offend, play about, play up, sin, transgress. □ **misbehaviour** badness, delinquency, disobedience, disorderliness, horseplay, indiscipline, insubordination, mischief, mischief-making, misconduct, naughtiness, rowdyism, rudeness, sin, vandalism, wrongdoing.

miscalculate /mɪsˈkælkjʊleɪt/ *verb* (**-ting**) calculate wrongly. □ **miscalculation** *noun*.
■ *colloquial* boob, err, get it wrong, go wrong, make a mistake, miscount, misjudge, misread, overestimate, overrate, overvalue, *colloquial* slip up, underestimate, underrate.

miscarriage /ˈmɪskærɪdʒ/ *noun* **1** spontaneous abortion. **2** failure to attain desired end; mistake. □ **miscarriage of justice** failure of judicial system.
■ **2** breakdown, collapse, defeat, error, failure, perversion.

miscarry /mɪsˈkærɪ/ *verb* (**-ies, -ied**) **1** (of woman) have miscarriage. **2** (of plan etc.) fail.
■ **1** abort, lose a baby. **2** break down, come to grief, come to nothing, fail, fall through, founder, go wrong, misfire.

miscast /mɪsˈkɑːst/ *verb* (*past & past participle* **-cast**) allot unsuitable part to (actor) or unsuitable actors to (play etc.).

miscegenation /mɪsɪdʒɪˈneɪʃ(ə)n/ *noun* interbreeding of races.

miscellaneous /mɪsəˈleɪnɪəs/ *adjective* **1** of mixed composition or character. **2** (+ *plural noun*) of various kinds. □ **miscellaneously** *adverb*.

■ **1** diverse, heterogeneous, mixed, motley, multifarious, varied. **2** assorted, different, *archaic* divers, manifold, mixed, multifarious, sundry, varied, various.

miscellany /mɪˈselənɪ/ *noun* (*plural* **-ies**) mixture, medley.
■ assortment, diversity, hotchpotch, jumble, medley, *mélange*, mixed bag, mixed bunch, mixture, pot-pourri, ragbag, variety.

mischance /mɪsˈtʃɑːns/ *noun* **1** bad luck. **2** instance of this.

mischief /ˈmɪstʃɪf/ *noun* **1** troublesome, but not malicious, conduct, esp. of children. **2** playfulness. **3** malice. **4** harm, injury. □ **make mischief** create discord or trouble. **mischiefmaker** person who encourages discord, esp. by gossip etc. **mischief-making** *noun*. □ **mischievous** /ˈmɪstʃɪvəs/ *adjective*. **mischievously** /ˈmɪstʃɪvəslɪ/ *adverb*.
■ **1, 2** devilment, devilry, impishness, misbehaviour, misconduct, *colloquial* monkey business, naughtiness, playfulness, roguishness, trouble. **4** damage, difficulty, evil, harm, hurt, injury, misfortune, trouble. □ **mischievous** annoying, badly behaved, boisterous, devilish, disobedient, elfish, fractious, frolicsome, impish, lively, naughty, playful, puckish, rascally, roguish, sportive, uncontrollable, wicked.

misconceive /mɪskənˈsiːv/ *verb* (**-ving**) **1** (often + *of*) have wrong idea or conception. **2** (as **misconceived** *adjective*) badly organized etc. □ **misconception** /-ˈsep-/ *noun*.

misconduct /mɪsˈkɒndʌkt/ *noun* improper or unprofessional conduct.

misconstrue /mɪskənˈstruː/ *verb* (**-strues, -strued, -struing**) interpret wrongly. □ **misconstruction** /-ˈstrʌk-/ *noun*.

miscount /mɪsˈkaʊnt/ *verb* count inaccurately. ● *noun* inaccurate count.

miscreant /ˈmɪskrɪənt/ *noun* wretch, villain.

misdeed /mɪsˈdiːd/ *noun* evil deed, wrongdoing.

misdemeanour /mɪsdɪˈmiːnə/ *noun* (US **misdemeanor**) **1** misdeed. **2** *historical* indictable offence less serious than felony.

misdirect /mɪsdaɪˈrekt/ *verb* direct wrongly. □ **misdirection** *noun*.

miser /ˈmaɪzə/ *noun* person who hoards wealth and lives miserably. □ **miserly** *adjective*. **miserliness** *noun*.
■ hoarder, niggard, skinflint. □ **miserly** avaricious, cheese-paring, close, close-fisted, covetous, grasping, greedy, mean, mercenary, *colloquial* mingy, niggardly, parsimonious, penny-pinching, penurious, sparing, stingy, *colloquial* tight, tight-fisted.

miserable /ˈmɪzərəb(ə)l/ *adjective* **1** wretchedly unhappy or uncomfortable. **2** (of person) mean; ill-tempered. **3** contemptible; inadequate; of poor quality. **4** (esp. of weather) causing discomfort. □ **miserably** *adverb*.

■ **1** broken-hearted, crestfallen, cut up, dejected, depressed, desolate, despairing, despondent, disappointed, disconsolate, dismayed, dispirited, distressed, doleful, *colloquial* down, downcast, downhearted, *colloquial* down in the dumps, forlorn, friendless, gloomy, glum, grief-stricken, heartbroken, hopeless, in low spirits, in the doldrums, joyless, *formal* lachrymose, languishing, lonely, low, melancholy, moping, mournful, sad, sorrowful, suicidal, tearful, uneasy, unfortunate, unhappy, unlucky, woebegone, woeful, wretched. **2** churlish, cross, disagreeable, discontented, grumpy, ill-natured, mean, miserly, morose, pessimistic, sour, sulky, sullen, surly, taciturn, unfriendly, unhelpful, unsociable. **3** abject, *colloquial* awful, bad, contemptible, deplorable, disgraceful, distressing, heartbreaking, hopeless, inadequate, inhuman, lamentable, pathetic, pitiable, pitiful, poor, shameful, sordid, soul-destroying, squalid, uncivilized, vile, worthless, wretched. **4** cheerless, depressing, dismal, dreary, uncomfortable, unpleasant; *of weather* damp, grey, inclement, sunless, wet.

misericord /mɪˈzerɪkɔːd/ *noun* projection under hinged choir stall seat to support person standing.

misery /ˈmɪzərɪ/ *noun* (*plural* **-ies**) **1** condition or feeling of wretchedness. **2** cause of this. **3** *colloquial* constantly grumbling person.
■ **1** angst, anguish, anxiety, bitterness, dejection, depression, despair, desperation, despondency, discomfort, distress, *literary* dolour, gloom, grief, heartache, heartbreak, hell, hopelessness, melancholy, sadness, sorrow, suffering, unhappiness, woe, wretchedness. **2** adversity, affliction, deprivation, destitution, hardship, indigence, misfortune, need, oppression, penury, poverty, privation, squalor, suffering, trial, tribulation, trouble, want.

misfire /mɪsˈfaɪə/ *verb* (**-ring**) **1** (of gun, motor engine, etc.) fail to go off, start, or function smoothly. **2** (of plan etc.) fail to be effective. ● *noun* such failure.
■ **2** abort, fail, fall through, *slang* flop, founder, go wrong, miscarry.

misfit /ˈmɪsfɪt/ *noun* **1** person unsuited to surroundings, occupation, etc. **2** garment etc. that does not fit.

misfortune /mɪsˈfɔːtʃuːn, -tʃ(ə)n/ *noun* **1** bad luck. **2** instance of this.
■ **1** adversity, bad luck, hard luck, hardship, ill luck, misadventure, mischance. **2** accident, adversity, affliction, blow, calamity, catastrophe, contretemps, curse, disappointment, disaster, evil, hardship, misadventure, mischance, mishap, reverse, setback, tragedy, trouble, *literary* vicissitude.

misgiving *noun* (usually in *plural*) feeling of mistrust or apprehension.

misgovern /mɪsˈgʌv(ə)n/ *verb* govern badly. □ **misgovernment** *noun*.

misguided /mɪsˈgaɪdɪd/ *adjective* mistaken in

thought or action. □ **misguidedly** *adverb*.
■ erroneous, foolish, ill-advised, inappropriate, incorrect, inexact, misinformed, misled, mistaken, unfounded, unjust, unsound, unwise, wrong.

mishandle /mɪsˈhænd(ə)l/ *verb* (**-ling**) 1 deal with incorrectly or inefficiently. 2 handle roughly.

mishap /ˈmɪshæp/ *noun* unlucky accident.

mishear /mɪsˈhɪə/ *verb* (*past & past participle* **-heard** /-ˈhɜːd/) hear incorrectly or imperfectly.

mishmash /ˈmɪʃmæʃ/ *noun* confused mixture.

misinform /mɪsɪnˈfɔːm/ *verb* give wrong information to; mislead. □ **misinformation** /-fəˈm-/ *noun*.

misinterpret /mɪsɪnˈtɜːprɪt/ *verb* (**-t-**) interpret wrongly. □ **misinterpretation** *noun*.

misjudge /mɪsˈdʒʌdʒ/ *verb* (**-ging**) judge wrongly. □ **misjudgement** *noun*.
■ get wrong, guess wrongly, jump to the wrong conclusion, make a mistake, miscalculate, misinterpret, overestimate, overvalue, underestimate, undervalue.

mislay /mɪsˈleɪ/ *verb* (*past & past participle* **-laid**) accidentally put (thing) where it cannot readily be found.
■ lose, misplace.

mislead /mɪsˈliːd/ *verb* (*past & past participle* **-led**) cause to infer what is not true; deceive. □ **misleading** *adjective*.
■ bluff, confuse, deceive, delude, fool, lead astray, *colloquial* lead up the garden path, lie to, misdirect, misinform, outwit, puzzle, *colloquial* take for a ride, take in, trick. □ **misleading** see DECEPTIVE.

mismanage /mɪsˈmænɪdʒ/ *verb* (**-ging**) manage badly or wrongly. □ **mismanagement** *noun*.

mismatch *verb* /mɪsˈmætʃ/ match unsuitably, esp. in marriage. ● *noun* /ˈmɪsmætʃ/ bad match.

misnomer /mɪsˈnəʊmə/ *noun* wrongly used name or term.

misogyny /mɪˈsɒdʒɪnɪ/ *noun* hatred of women. □ **misogynist** *noun*.

misplace /mɪsˈpleɪs/ *verb* (**-cing**) 1 put in wrong place. 2 bestow (affections, confidence, etc.) on inappropriate object. □ **misplacement** *noun*.

misprint *noun* /ˈmɪsprɪnt/ printing error. ● *verb* /mɪsˈprɪnt/ print wrongly.

mispronounce /mɪsprəˈnaʊns/ *verb* (**-cing**) pronounce (word etc.) wrongly. □ **mispronunciation** /-nʌnsɪˈeɪ-/ *noun*.

misquote /mɪsˈkwəʊt/ *verb* (**-ting**) quote inaccurately. □ **misquotation** *noun*.

misread /mɪsˈriːd/ *verb* (*past & past participle* **-read** /-ˈred/) read or interpret wrongly.

misrepresent /mɪsreprɪˈzent/ *verb* represent wrongly; give false account of. □ **misrepresentation** *noun*.

misrule /mɪsˈruːl/ *noun* bad government. ● *verb* (**-ling**) govern badly.

Miss *noun*: title of girl or unmarried woman.

miss *verb* 1 fail to hit, reach, find, catch, or perceive. 2 fail to seize (opportunity etc.), meet (person etc.), attend (meeting etc.), or keep (appointment etc.). 3 regret absence of. 4 avoid. 5 (of engine etc.) misfire. ● *noun* failure. □ **give (thing) a miss** *colloquial* avoid. **miss out** omit.
■ *verb* 1 (*miss a target*) be wide of, fall short of; (*miss a mistake*) overlook, pass over. 2 (*miss an opportunity*) forgo, let go, lose, *colloquial* pass up; (*miss an appointment*) absent oneself from, be absent from, be too late for, forget, play truant from, *colloquial* skip, *slang* skive off. 3 grieve for, long for, need, pine for, want, yearn for. 4 avoid, bypass, dodge, escape, evade, sidestep. □ **miss out** see OMIT 1.

missal /ˈmɪs(ə)l/ *noun RC Church* 1 book of texts for Mass. 2 book of prayers.

misshapen /mɪsˈʃeɪpən/ *adjective* deformed, distorted.
■ awry, bent, contorted, crippled, crooked, crumpled, deformed, disfigured, distorted, gnarled, grotesque, knotted, malformed, monstrous, screwed up, tangled, twisted, twisty, ugly, warped.

missile /ˈmɪsaɪl/ *noun* 1 object, esp. weapon, suitable for throwing at target or discharging from machine. 2 weapon directed by remote control or automatically.
■ brickbat, projectile, weapon.

missing *adjective* 1 not in its place; lost. 2 not present. 3 (of person) not traced but not known to be dead.
■ 1 absent, disappeared, gone, lost, mislaid, misplaced, removed. 2 absent, *slang* skiving, straying, truant. 3 disappeared, unaccounted-for.

mission /ˈmɪʃ(ə)n/ *noun* 1 task or goal assigned to person or group. 2 journey undertaken as part of this. 3 person's vocation. 4 military or scientific expedition. 5 group of people sent to conduct negotiations or to evangelize. 6 missionary post.
■ 1 aim, assignment, commission, duty, function, goal, job, objective, purpose, quest, undertaking. 3 calling, life's work, *métier*, occupation, profession, vocation. 4 campaign, *historical* crusade, expedition, journey, sortie, voyage. 5 delegation, deputation, task force.

missionary /ˈmɪʃənərɪ/ *adjective* of or concerned with religious missions, esp. abroad. ● *noun* (*plural* **-ies**) person doing missionary work.
■ *noun* evangelist, minister, preacher, proselytizer.

missis = MISSUS.

missive /ˈmɪsɪv/ *noun* 1 *jocular* letter. 2 official letter.

misspell /mɪsˈspel/ *verb* (*past & past participle* **-spelt** or **-spelled**) spell wrongly.

misspend /mɪsˈspend/ verb (past & past parti-ciple **-spent**) (esp. as **misspent** adjective) spend wrongly or wastefully.

misstate /mɪsˈsteɪt/ verb (**-ting**) state wrongly or inaccurately. □ **misstatement** noun.

missus /ˈmɪsɪz/ noun (also **missis**) colloquial or jocular **1** form of address to woman. **2** (**the missis**) colloquial my or your wife.

mist noun **1** water vapour in minute drops limit-ing visibility. **2** condensed vapour obscuring glass etc. **3** dimness or blurring of sight caused by tears etc. ● verb cover or be covered (as) with mist.

■ noun **1** cloud, drizzle, fog, haze, smog, vapour. **2** condensation, film, steam.

mistake /mɪˈsteɪk/ noun incorrect idea or opinion; thing incorrectly done, thought, or judged. ● verb (**-king**; past **mistook** /-ˈstʊk/; past participle **mistaken**) **1** misunderstand meaning of. **2** (+ for) wrongly take (person, thing) for another.

■ noun slang bloomer, blunder, colloquial boob, botch, slang clanger, erratum, error, false step, fault, faux pas, gaffe, colloquial howler, inaccuracy, indiscretion, lapse, misapprehension, miscalculation, misconception, misjudgement, misprint, misspelling, misunderstanding, omission, oversight, slip, colloquial slip-up, solecism, wrong move. ● verb **1** get wrong, misconstrue, misinterpret, misjudge, misread, misunderstand, take the wrong way. **2** (mistake for) confuse with, mix up with, take for.

mistaken /mɪˈsteɪkən/ adjective **1** wrong in opinion or judgement. **2** based on or resulting from error. □ **mistakenly** adverb.

■ erroneous, distorted, false, faulty, ill-judged, inaccurate, inappropriate, incorrect, inexact, misguided, misinformed, unfounded, unjust, unsound, wrong.

mister /ˈmɪstə/ noun colloquial or jocular: form of address to man.

mistime /mɪsˈtaɪm/ verb (**-ming**) say or do at wrong time. □ **mistimed** adjective.

■ □ **mistimed** early, inconvenient, inopportune, late, unseasonable, untimely.

mistle thrush /ˈmɪs(ə)l/ noun large thrush that eats mistletoe berries.

mistletoe /ˈmɪs(ə)ltəʊ/ noun parasitic white-berried plant.

mistook past of MISTAKE.

mistral /ˈmɪstr(ə)l, mɪˈstrɑːl/ noun cold N. or NW wind in S. France.

mistreat /mɪsˈtriːt/ verb treat badly. □ **mis-treatment** noun.

■ abuse, batter, damage, harm, hurt, ill-treat, ill-use, injure, knock about, maltreat, colloquial manhandle, misuse, molest.

mistress /ˈmɪstrɪs/ noun **1** female head of household. **2** woman in authority. **3** female

owner of pet. **4** female teacher. **5** woman having illicit sexual relationship with (usually married) man.

■ **3** keeper, owner. **4** see TEACHER. **5** see LOVER 2.

mistrial /mɪsˈtraɪəl/ noun trial made invalid by error.

mistrust /mɪsˈtrʌst/ verb **1** be suspicious of. **2** feel no confidence in. ● noun **1** suspicion. **2** lack of confidence. □ **mistrustful** adjective. **mistrust-fully** adverb.

■ verb be sceptical about, be suspicious of, be wary of, disbelieve, distrust, doubt, fear, have doubts about, have misgivings about, have reservations about, question, suspect. ● noun apprehension, distrust, doubt, misgiving, reservation, scepticism, suspicion, uncertainty, unsureness, wariness.

misty adjective (**-ier**, **-iest**) **1** of or covered with mist. **2** dim in outline. **3** obscure. □ **mistily** adverb.

■ bleary, blurred, blurry, clouded, cloudy, dim, faint, foggy, fuzzy, hazy, indistinct, murky, obscure, opaque, shadowy, smoky, steamy, unclear, vague.

misunderstand /mɪsʌndəˈstænd/ verb (past & past participle **-stood** /-ˈstʊd/) **1** understand incorrectly. **2** misinterpret words or actions of (person).

■ get wrong, misapprehend, miscalculate, misconceive, misconstrue, mishear, misinterpret, misjudge, misread, mistake.

misunderstanding noun **1** failure to under-stand correctly. **2** slight disagreement.

■ **1** error, false impression, misapprehension, miscalculation, misconception, misconstruction, misinterpretation, misjudgement, misreading, mistake, mix-up, wrong idea. **2** argument, contretemps, controversy, difference of opinion, disagreement, discord, dispute, quarrel.

misuse verb /mɪsˈjuːz/ (**-sing**) **1** use wrongly. **2** ill-treat. ● noun /mɪsˈjuːs/ wrong or improper use.

■ verb **1** fritter away, misapply, misappropriate, mishandle, misspend, pervert, squander, waste. **2** abuse, batter, damage, harm, hurt, ill-treat, ill-use, injure, knock about, maltreat, colloquial manhandle, mistreat, molest. ● noun abuse, corruption, ill-treatment, ill-use, maltreatment, misapplication, misappropriation, mishandling, mistreatment, perversion.

mite[1] noun small arachnid, esp. of kind found in cheese etc.

mite[2] noun **1** small monetary unit. **2** small object or child. **3** modest contribution.

miter US = MITRE.

mitigate /ˈmɪtɪgeɪt/ verb (**-ting**) make less intense or severe. □ **mitigation** noun.

USAGE Mitigate is often confused with militate, which means 'to have force or effect'.

■ abate, allay, alleviate, decrease, ease, extenuate, lessen, lighten, moderate, palliate, qualify, reduce, relieve, soften, take the edge off, temper, tone down.

mitre /'maɪtə/ (*US* **miter**) *noun* **1** bishop's or abbot's tall deeply cleft headdress. **2** joint of two pieces of wood at angle of 90°, such that line of junction bisects this angle. ● *verb* (**-ring**) **1** bestow mitre on. **2** join with mitre.

mitt *noun* (also **mitten**) **1** glove with only one compartment for the 4 fingers and another for thumb. **2** glove leaving fingers and thumb-tip bare. **3** *slang* hand. **4** baseball glove.

mix *verb* **1** combine or put together (two or more substances or things) so that constituents of each are diffused among those of the other(s). **2** prepare (compound, cocktail, etc.) by combining ingredients. **3** combine (activities etc.). **4** join, be mixed. **5** be compatible. **6** be sociable. **7** (+ *with*) be harmonious with. **8** combine (two or more sound signals) into one. ● *noun* **1** mixing, mixture. **2** proportion of materials in mixture. **3** ingredients prepared commercially for making cake, concrete, etc. □ **mix up 1** mix thoroughly. **2** confuse. **mix-up** misunderstanding, mistake.

■ *verb* **1, 4** alloy, amalgamate, blend, coalesce, combine, *literary* commingle, compound, confuse, diffuse, emulsify, fuse, go together, homogenize, incorporate, integrate, intermingle, join, jumble up, merge, mingle, mix up, muddle, put together, shuffle, stir together, unite. **3** combine, confuse, mingle, unite. **6** see SOCIALIZE 1. ● *noun* **1** amalgam, assortment, blend, combination, compound, mixture, range, variety.

mixed /mɪkst/ *adjective* **1** of diverse qualities or elements. **2** containing people from various backgrounds, of both sexes, etc. □ **mixed bag or bunch** diverse assortment of things or persons. **mixed marriage** marriage between people of different race or religion. **mixed-up** *colloquial* mentally or emotionally confused; socially ill-adjusted.

■ **1** (*mixed sweets*) assorted, different, diverse, heterogeneous, miscellaneous, varied, various; (*mixed teams*) amalgamated, combined, composite, integrated, joint, united; (*mixed breed*) hybrid, mongrel; (*mixed feelings*) ambiguous, ambivalent, confused, equivocal, muddled, uncertain.

mixer *noun* **1** machine for mixing foods etc. **2** person who manages socially in specified way. **3** (usually soft) drink to be mixed with spirit. **4** device combining separate signals from microphones etc.

mixture /'mɪkstʃə/ *noun* **1** process of mixing. **2** result of mixing; combination of ingredients, qualities, etc.

■ **1** amalgamation, association, combination, conglomeration, fusion, intermingling, merger, mingling, mixing, synthesis. **2** alloy, amalgam, amalgamation, assortment, blend, collection, combination, composite, compound, concoction, conglomeration, cross-breed, emulsion, farrago, fusion, hotchpotch, hybrid, jumble, medley,

mélange, merger, mess, miscellany, mishmash, mix, mongrel, motley collection, pastiche, pot-pourri, selection, suspension, synthesis, variety.

mizen-mast /'mɪz(ə)n/ *noun* mast next aft of mainmast.

ml *abbreviation* **1** millilitre(s). **2** mile(s).

Mlle *abbreviation* (*plural* **-s**) Mademoiselle.

MM *abbreviation* **1** Messieurs. **2** Military Medal.

mm *abbreviation* millimetre(s).

Mme *abbreviation* (*plural* **-s**) Madame.

mnemonic /nɪ'mɒnɪk/ *adjective* of or designed to aid memory. ● *noun* mnemonic word, verse, etc. □ **mnemonically** *adverb*.

MO *abbreviation* **1** Medical Officer. **2** money order.

mo /məʊ/ *noun* (*plural* **-s**) *colloquial* moment.

moan *noun* **1** low murmur expressing physical or mental suffering or pleasure. **2** *colloquial* complaint. ● *verb* **1** make moan or moans. **2** *colloquial* complain, grumble. □ **moaner** *noun*.

■ *noun* **2** complaint, grievance, *colloquial* gripe. ● *verb* **1** cry, groan, keen, sigh, ululate, wail, weep, whimper, whine. **2** complain, grieve, *colloquial* gripe, *colloquial* grouse, grumble, whine, *colloquial* whinge.

moat *noun* defensive ditch round castle etc., usually filled with water.

mob *noun* **1** disorderly crowd; rabble. **2** (**the mob**) *usually derogatory* the populace. **3** *colloquial* gang, group. **4** (**the Mob**) *colloquial* the Mafia or similar criminal organization. ● *verb* (**-bb-**) crowd round to attack or admire. □ **mob law or rule** law or rule imposed and enforced by mob.

■ *noun* **1** *colloquial* bunch, crowd, *derogatory* herd, *usually derogatory* horde, host, multitude, *usually derogatory* pack, press, rabble, swarm, throng. ● *verb* besiege, crowd round, hem in, jostle, surround, swarm round, throng round.

mob-cap *noun* *historical* woman's indoor cap covering all the hair.

mobile /'məʊbaɪl/ *adjective* **1** movable. **2** able to move easily. **3** (of face etc.) readily changing expression. **4** (of shop etc.) accommodated in vehicle to serve various places. **5** (of person) able to change social status. ● *noun* decoration that may be hung so as to turn freely. □ **mobility** /mə'bɪl/ *noun*.

■ *adjective* **1** motorized, movable, portable, transportable, unfixed. **2** active, agile, independent, nimble, *colloquial* on the go, up and about. **3** animated, changeable, changing, expressive, flexible, fluid, shifting. **4** itinerant, travelling.

mobilize /'məʊbɪlaɪz/ *verb* (also **-ise**) (**-zing** or **-sing**) make or become ready for (esp. military) service or action. □ **mobilization** *noun*.

■ activate, assemble, call up, conscript, enlist, enrol, gather, get together, levy, marshal, muster, organize, rally, stir up, summon.

mobster /'mɒbstə/ *noun slang* gangster.

moccasin /'mɒkəsɪn/ *noun* soft flat-soled shoe originally worn by N. American Indians.

mock *verb* 1 (often + *at*) ridicule, scoff (at); treat with scorn or contempt. 2 mimic contemptuously. ● *adjective* 1 sham, imitation. 2 as a trial run. □ **mock turtle soup** soup made from calf's head etc. **mock-up** experimental model of proposed structure etc. □ **mocking** *adjective*. **mockingly** *adverb*.

■ *verb* 1 decry, deride, disparage, flout, gibe at, insult, jeer at, lampoon, laugh at, make fun of, make sport of, parody, poke fun at, ridicule, satirize, scoff at, scorn, *colloquial* send up, sneer at, tantalize, taunt, tease, travesty. 2 see MIMIC *verb* 1. ● *adjective* 1 artificial, counterfeit, ersatz, fake, false, imitation, make-believe, man-made, *colloquial* pretend, sham, simulated, substitute. 2 simulated, trial. □ **mocking** contemptuous, derisive, disparaging, disrespectful, insulting, irreverent, jeering, rude, sarcastic, satirical, scornful, taunting, teasing, uncomplimentary, unkind.

mockery *noun* (*plural* **-ies**) 1 derision. 2 counterfeit or absurdly inadequate representation; travesty.

■ 1 derision, insults, jeering, laughter, ridicule, sarcasm, scorn. 2 burlesque, caricature, lampoon, parody, satire, *colloquial* send-up, *colloquial* spoof, *colloquial* take-off, travesty.

mode *noun* 1 way in which thing is done. 2 prevailing fashion. 3 *Music* any of several types of scale.

■ 1 approach, configuration, manner, medium, method, *modus operandi*, procedure, set-up, system, technique, way. 2 see FASHION *noun* 1.

model /'mɒd(ə)l/ *noun* 1 representation in 3 dimensions of existing person or thing or of proposed structure, esp. on smaller scale. 2 simplified description of system etc. 3 clay, wax, etc. figure for reproduction in another material. 4 particular design or style, esp. of car. 5 exemplary person or thing. 6 person employed to pose for artist or photographer, or to wear clothes etc. for display. 7 (copy of) garment etc. by well-known designer. ● *adjective* exemplary; ideally perfect. ● *verb* (**-ll-**; *US* **-l-**) 1 fashion or shape (figure) in clay, wax, etc. 2 (+ *after*, *on*, etc.) form (thing) in imitation of. 3 act or pose as model. 4 (of person acting as model) display (garment).

■ *noun* 1, 3 archetype, copy, dummy, effigy, facsimile, image, imitation, likeness, miniature, mock-up, prototype, replica, representation, scale model, toy; (*model village*) imitation, miniature, scaled-down, toy. 4 brand, design, kind, mark, style, type, version. 5 byword, epitome, example, exemplar, ideal, nonpareil, paragon, pattern, standard, yardstick. 6 mannequin, poser, sitter, subject. ● *adjective* exemplary, ideal, perfect, unequalled. ● *verb* 1 carve, fashion, form, make, mould, sculpt, shape. 2 (*model oneself on*) see IMITATE 1.

modem /'məʊdem/ *noun* device for sending and receiving computer data by means of telephone line.

moderate /'mɒdərət/ *adjective* 1 avoiding extremes; temperate in conduct or expression. 2 fairly large or good; medium. 3 (of wind) of medium strength. 4 (of prices) fairly low. ● *noun* person of moderate views. ● *verb* /-reɪt/ (**-ting**) 1 make or become less violent, intense, rigorous, etc. 2 act as moderator of or to. □ **moderately** /-rətlɪ/ *adverb*. **moderation** *noun*.

■ *adjective* 1 balanced, calm, cautious, cool, deliberate, judicious, middle-of-the-road, modest, normal, ordinary, rational, reasonable, respectable, sensible, sober, steady, temperate. 2 average, fair, medium, middling, modest, normal, ordinary, reasonable, respectable, tolerable, unexceptional. 3 gentle, light, mild. ● *verb* 1 abate, blunt, calm, check, curb, decline, decrease, die down, dull, ease, ease off, keep down, lessen, mitigate, modify, modulate, mollify, reduce, regulate, restrain, slacken, subdue, subside, temper, tone down. □ **moderately** comparatively, fairly, passably, *colloquial* pretty, quite, rather, reasonably, somewhat, to some extent. **moderation** balance, caution, common sense, fairness, reasonableness, restraint, reticence, sobriety, temperance.

moderator *noun* 1 arbitrator, mediator. 2 presiding officer. 3 Presbyterian minister presiding over ecclesiastical body.

modern /'mɒd(ə)n/ *adjective* 1 of present and recent times. 2 in current fashion; not antiquated. ● *noun* person living in modern times. □ **modernity** /mə'dɜːnɪ-/ *noun*.

■ *adjective* advanced, avant-garde, contemporary, current, fashionable, forward-looking, fresh, futuristic, in vogue, (the) latest, modish, new, newfangled, novel, present, present-day, progressive, recent, stylish, *colloquial often derogatory* trendy, up to date, up to the minute, *colloquial* with it.

modernism /'mɒd(ə)nɪz(ə)m/ *noun* modern ideas or methods. □ **modernist** *noun & adjective*. **modernistic** /-'rɪstɪk/ *adjective*.

modernize *verb* (also **-ise**) (**-zing** or **-sing**) make modern; adapt to modern needs or habits. □ **modernization** *noun*.

■ bring up to date, *colloquial* do up, improve, rebuild, redesign, redo, refurbish, regenerate, rejuvenate, renovate, revamp, update.

modest /'mɒdɪst/ *adjective* 1 having humble or moderate estimate of one's own merits. 2 bashful. 3 decorous. 4 not excessive. 5 unpretentious; not extravagant. □ **modestly** *adverb*. **modesty** *noun*.

■ 1 humble, lowly, meek, quiet, self-effacing, simple, unassuming, unobtrusive, unostentatious, unpretentious. 2 bashful, coy, demure, diffident, reserved, restrained, reticent, retiring, self-conscious, shy. 3 chaste, decent, demure, discreet, proper, seemly. 4 limited, medium, middling, moderate, normal, ordinary, reasonable, unexceptional. 5 humble, inconspicuous, lowly, plain, simple, unassuming, unobtrusive, unostentatious, unpretentious. □ **modesty** bashfulness, coyness, decency, demureness, discretion, humbleness, humility, lowliness, meekness, propriety, reserve, restraint, reticence, seemliness, self-consciousness, self-effacement, shame, shyness, simplicity.

modicum /'mɒdɪkəm/ *noun* (+ *of*) small quantity of.

modify /'mɒdɪfaɪ/ *verb* (**-ies**, **-ied**) **1** make less severe. **2** make partial changes in. □ **modification** *noun*.
■ **1** see MODERATE *verb* 1. **2** adapt, adjust, alter, amend, change, convert, improve, reconstruct, redesign, remake, remodel, reorganize, revise, reword, rework, transform, vary.

modish /'məʊdɪʃ/ *adjective* fashionable. □ **modishly** *adverb*.

modulate /'mɒdjʊleɪt/ *verb* (**-ting**) **1** regulate, adjust. **2** moderate. **3** adjust or vary tone or pitch of (speaking voice). **4** alter amplitude or frequency of (wave) by using wave of lower frequency to convey signal. **5** *Music* pass from one key to another. □ **modulation** *noun*.
■ **1–3** adjust, balance, moderate, regulate, soften, tone down.

module /'mɒdju:l/ *noun* **1** standardized part or independent unit in construction, esp. of furniture, building, spacecraft, or electronic system. **2** unit or period of training or education. □ **modular** *adjective*.

modus operandi /ˌməʊdəs ɒpəˈrændɪ/ *noun* (*plural* **modi operandi** /ˌməʊdɪ/) method of working. [Latin]

modus vivendi /ˌməʊdəs vɪˈvendɪ/ *noun* (*plural* **modi vivendi** /ˌməʊdɪ/) **1** way of living or coping. **2** compromise between people agreeing to differ. [Latin]

mog *noun* (also **moggie**) *slang* cat.

mogul /'məʊg(ə)l/ *noun colloquial* important or influential person.

mohair /'məʊheə/ *noun* **1** hair of angora goat. **2** yarn or fabric from this.

Mohammedan = MUHAMMADAN.

moiety /'mɔɪətɪ/ *noun* (*plural* **-ies**) **1** half. **2** each of two parts of thing.

moiré /'mwɑːreɪ/ *adjective* **1** (of silk) watered. **2** (of metal) having clouded appearance.

moist *adjective* slightly wet; damp. □ **moisten** *verb*.
■ clammy, damp, dank, dewy, humid, misty, muggy, rainy, runny, steamy, watery, wet, wettish. □ **moisten** damp, dampen, humidify, moisturize, soak, spray, wet.

moisture /'mɔɪstʃə/ *noun* water or other liquid diffused as vapour or within solid, or condensed on surface.
■ condensation, damp, dampness, dankness, dew, humidity, liquid, precipitation, spray, steam, vapour, water, wet, wetness.

moisturize *verb* (also **-ise**) (**-zing** or **-sing**) make

less dry (esp. skin by use of cosmetic). □ **moisturizer** *noun*.

molar /'məʊlə/ *adjective* (usually of mammal's back teeth) serving to grind. ● *noun* molar tooth.

molasses /məˈlæsɪz/ *plural noun* (treated as *singular*) **1** uncrystallized syrup extracted from raw sugar. **2** *US* treacle.

mold *US* = MOULD^{1,2,3}.

molder *US* = MOULDER.

molding *US* = MOULDING.

moldy *US* = MOULDY.

mole^1 *noun* **1** small burrowing animal with dark velvety fur and very small eyes. **2** *slang* spy established in position of trust in organization. □ **molehill** small mound thrown up by mole in burrowing.

mole^2 *noun* small permanent dark spot on skin.

mole^3 *noun* **1** massive structure as pier, breakwater, or causeway. **2** artificial harbour.

mole^4 *noun* SI unit of amount of substance.

molecule /'mɒlɪkju:l/ *noun* group of atoms forming smallest fundamental unit of chemical compound. □ **molecular** /məˈlekjʊlə/ *adjective*.

molest /məˈlest/ *verb* **1** annoy or pester (person). **2** attack or interfere with (person), esp. sexually. □ **molestation** *noun*. **molester** *noun*.
■ **1** annoy, badger, bother, disturb, harass, harry, *colloquial* hassle, hector, irk, irritate, *colloquial* needle, persecute, pester, *colloquial* plague, tease, torment, vex, worry. **2** abuse, assault, attack, ill-treat, interfere with, *colloquial* manhandle, mistreat, set on.

moll *noun slang* **1** gangster's female companion. **2** prostitute.

mollify /'mɒlɪfaɪ/ *verb* (**-ies**, **-ied**) **1** soften. **2** appease. □ **mollification** *noun*.

mollusc /'mɒləsk/ *noun* (*US* **mollusk**) invertebrate with soft body and usually hard shell, e.g. snail or oyster.

mollycoddle /'mɒlɪkɒd(ə)l/ *verb* (**-ling**) coddle, pamper.

molt *US* = MOULT.

molten /'məʊlt(ə)n/ *adjective* melted, esp. made liquid by heat.
■ fluid, liquefied, liquid, melted, soft.

molto /'mɒltəʊ/ *adverb Music* very.

molybdenum /məˈlɪbdɪnəm/ *noun* silver-white metallic element added to steel to give strength and resistance to corrosion.

moment /'məʊmənt/ *noun* **1** very brief portion of time. **2** exact point of time. **3** importance. **4** product of force and distance from its line of action to a point.
■ **1** flash, instant, *colloquial* jiffy, minute, *colloquial* second, split second, *colloquial* tick, trice, twinkling of an eye. **2** hour, juncture, occasion, opportunity, point in time, stage, time.

momentary *adjective* **1** lasting only a moment. **2** transitory. □ **momentarily** *adverb*.

■ brief, ephemeral, *literary* evanescent, fleeting, fugitive, hasty, passing, quick, short, short-lived, temporary, transient, transitory.

momentous /məˈmentəs/ *adjective* very important. □ **momentousness** *noun*.

■ consequential, critical, crucial, decisive, epoch-making, fateful, grave, historic, important, portentous, serious, significant, weighty.

momentum /məˈmentəm/ *noun* (*plural* **-ta**) **1** quantity of motion of moving body, the product of its mass and velocity. **2** impetus gained by movement or initial effort.

Mon. *abbreviation* Monday.

monarch /ˈmɒnək/ *noun* sovereign with title of king, queen, emperor, empress, or equivalent. □ **monarchic** /məˈnɑːk-/ *adjective*. **monarchical** /məˈnɑːk-/ *adjective*.

■ crowned head, emperor, empress, king, potentate, queen, ruler, sovereign, *historical* tsar, *historical* tsarina.

monarchist *noun* advocate of monarchy.

monarchy *noun* (*plural* **-ies**) **1** government headed by monarch. **2** state with this.

■ **2** domain, empire, kingdom, *formal* realm.

monastery /ˈmɒnəstrɪ/ *noun* (*plural* **-ies**) residence of community of monks.

monastic /məˈnæstɪk/ *adjective* of or like monasteries or monks, nuns, etc. □ **monastically** *adverb*. **monasticism** /-sɪz(ə)m/ *noun*.

Monday /ˈmʌndeɪ/ *noun* day of week following Sunday.

monetarism /ˈmʌnɪtərɪz(ə)m/ *noun* control of supply of money as chief method of stabilizing economy. □ **monetarist** *adjective & noun*.

monetary /ˈmʌnɪtərɪ/ *adjective* **1** of the currency in use. **2** of or consisting of money.

money /ˈmʌnɪ/ *noun* (*plural* **-s** or **monies**) **1** coins and banknotes as medium of exchange. **2** wealth. **3** profit, payment. **4** (in *plural*) sums of money. □ **moneylender** person lending money at interest. **moneymaker 1** person who earns much money. **2** thing, idea, etc. that produces much money. **moneymaking** *noun & adjective*. **money market** trade in short-term stocks, loans, etc. **money order** order for payment of specified sum, issued by bank or Post Office. **money-spinner** thing that brings in a profit.

■ **1** banknotes, *slang* bread, cash, change, coins, coppers, currency, *slang* dough, legal tender, *slang* lolly, *derogatory* lucre, notes, *slang* the ready, silver. **2** affluence, assets, capital, finance, fortune, funds, means, resources, riches, wealth, *colloquial* the wherewithal. **3** see PAY *noun*, REVENUE 1.

moneyed /ˈmʌnɪd/ *adjective* rich.

Mongol /ˈmɒŋg(ə)l/ *adjective* **1** of Asian people now inhabiting Mongolia. **2** resembling this people. ● *noun* Mongolian.

Mongolian /mɒŋˈgəʊlɪən/ *noun* native, national, or language of Mongolia. ● *adjective* of or relating to Mongolia or its people or language.

Mongoloid /ˈmɒŋgəlɔɪd/ *adjective* characteristic of Mongolians, esp. in having broad flat yellowish face. ● *noun* Mongoloid person.

mongoose /ˈmɒŋguːs/ *noun* (*plural* **-s**) small flesh-eating civet-like mammal.

mongrel /ˈmʌŋgr(ə)l/ *noun* **1** dog of no definable type or breed. **2** any animal or plant resulting from crossing of different breeds or types. ● *adjective* of mixed origin or character.

■ *noun* cross, cross-breed, hybrid, mixed breed.

monies *plural* of MONEY.

monitor /ˈmɒnɪtə/ *noun* **1** person or device for checking. **2** school pupil with disciplinary etc. duties. **3** television set used to select or verify picture being broadcast or to display computer data. **4** person who listens to and reports on foreign broadcasts etc. **5** detector of radioactive contamination. ● *verb* **1** act as monitor of. **2** maintain regular surveillance over.

■ *noun* **1** detector, guardian, supervisor, watchdog. **2** prefect. **3** screen, set, television, TV, VDU, visual display unit. ● *verb* audit, check, examine, keep an eye on, oversee, record, supervise, trace, track, watch.

monk /mʌŋk/ *noun* member of religious community of men living under vows. □ **monkish** *adjective*.

■ brother, friar.

monkey /ˈmʌŋkɪ/ *noun* (*plural* **-eys**) **1** any of various primates, e.g. baboons, marmosets. **2** mischievous person, esp. child. ● *verb* (**-eys**, **-eyed**) **1** (often + *with*) tamper; play mischievous tricks. **2** (+ *about*, *around*) fool about. □ **monkey business** *colloquial* mischief. **monkey-nut** peanut. **monkey-puzzle** tree with hanging prickly branches. **monkey wrench** wrench with adjustable jaw.

■ *noun* **1** ape, primate, simian.

monkshood /ˈmʌŋkshʊd/ *noun* poisonous plant with hood-shaped flowers.

mono /ˈmɒnəʊ/ *colloquial adjective* monophonic. ● *noun* monophonic reproduction.

mono- *combining form* (usually **mon-** before vowel) one, alone, single.

monochromatic /mɒnəkrəˈmætɪk/ *adjective* **1** (of light or other radiation) of single colour or wavelength. **2** containing only one colour.

monochrome /ˈmɒnəkrəʊm/ *noun* photograph or picture in one colour, or in black and white only. ● *adjective* having or using one colour or black and white only.

monocle /ˈmɒnək(ə)l/ *noun* single eyeglass.

monocular /məˈnɒkjʊlə/ *adjective* with or for one eye.

monody /ˈmɒnədɪ/ *noun* (*plural* **-ies**) **1** ode sung by one actor in Greek tragedy. **2** poem lamenting person's death.

monogamy /məˈnɒgəmɪ/ *noun* practice or state

of being married to one person at a time. □ **monogamous** *adjective*.

monogram /ˈmɒnəɡræm/ *noun* two or more letters, esp. initials, interwoven.

monograph /ˈmɒnəɡrɑːf/ *noun* treatise on single subject.

monolith /ˈmɒnəlɪθ/ *noun* **1** single block of stone, esp. shaped into pillar etc. **2** person or thing like monolith in being massive, immovable, or solidly uniform. □ **monolithic** /-ˈlɪθ-/ *adjective*.

monologue /ˈmɒnəlɒɡ/ *noun* **1** scene in drama in which person speaks alone. **2** dramatic composition for one performer. **3** long speech by one person in conversation etc.

monomania /mɒnəˈmeɪnɪə/ *noun* obsession by single idea or interest. □ **monomaniac** *noun & adjective*.

monophonic /mɒnəˈfɒnɪk/ *adjective* (of sound-reproduction) using only one channel of transmission.

monoplane /ˈmɒnəpleɪn/ *noun* aeroplane with one set of wings.

monopolist /məˈnɒpəlɪst/ *noun* person who has or advocates monopoly. □ **monopolistic** /-ˈlɪs-/ *adjective*.

monopolize /məˈnɒpəlaɪz/ *verb* (also **-ise**) (**-zing** or **-sing**) **1** obtain exclusive possession or control of (trade etc.). **2** dominate (conversation, attention, etc.). □ **monopolization** *noun*. **monopolizer** *noun*.
  ■ control, corner the market in, dominate, *colloquial* hog, keep for oneself, own, shut others out of, take over.

monopoly /məˈnɒpəlɪ/ *noun* (*plural* **-ies**) **1** exclusive possession or control of trade in commodity or service. **2** (+ *of*, *US on*) sole possession or control.

monorail /ˈmɒnəʊreɪl/ *noun* railway with single-rail track.

monosodium glutamate /mɒnəʊˈsəʊdɪəm ˈɡluːtəmeɪt/ *noun* sodium salt of glutamic acid used to enhance flavour of food.

monosyllable /ˈmɒnəsɪləb(ə)l/ *noun* word of one syllable. □ **monosyllabic** /-ˈlæb-/ *adjective*.

monotheism /ˈmɒnəθiːɪz(ə)m/ *noun* doctrine that there is only one God. □ **monotheist** *noun*. **monotheistic** /-ˈɪst-/ *adjective*.

monotone /ˈmɒnətəʊn/ *noun* sound continuing or repeated on one note or without change of pitch.

monotonous /məˈnɒtənəs/ *adjective* lacking in variety; tedious through sameness. □ **monotonously** *adverb*. **monotony** *noun*.
  ■ boring, colourless, dreary, dull, featureless, flat, level, repetitious, repetitive, soporific, tedious, tiresome, tiring, toneless, unchanging, uneventful, unexciting, uniform, uninteresting, unvarying, wearisome.

monoxide /məˈnɒksaɪd/ *noun* oxide containing one oxygen atom.

Monseigneur /mɒnsenˈjɜː/ *noun* (*plural* **Messeigneurs** /mesenˈjɜː/) *title given to eminent French person, esp. prince, cardinal, etc.* [French]

Monsieur /məˈsjɜː/ *noun* (*plural* **Messieurs** /mesˈjɜː/) *title used of or to French-speaking man.*

Monsignor /mɒnˈsiːnjə/ *noun* (*plural* **-nori** /-ˈnjɔːrɪ/) *title of various RC priests and officials.*

monsoon /mɒnˈsuːn/ *noun* **1** wind in S. Asia, esp. in Indian Ocean. **2** rainy season accompanying summer monsoon.

monster /ˈmɒnstə/ *noun* **1** imaginary creature, usually large and frightening. **2** inhumanly wicked person. **3** misshapen animal or plant. **4** large, usually ugly, animal or thing. ● *adjective* huge.
  ■ *noun* **1** beast, bogeyman, demon, fiend, giant, ogre, troll. **2** beast, brute, demon, devil, fiend, ogre. **3** abortion, freak, monstrosity, mutant. **4** giant, monstrosity.

monstrance /ˈmɒnstrəns/ *noun* *RC Church* vessel in which host is exposed for veneration.

monstrosity /mɒnˈstrɒsɪtɪ/ *noun* (*plural* **-ies**) huge or outrageous thing.

monstrous /ˈmɒnstrəs/ *adjective* **1** like a monster; abnormally formed. **2** huge. **3** outrageously wrong; atrocious. □ **monstrously** *adverb*.
  ■ **2** colossal, elephantine, enormous, gargantuan, giant, gigantic, great, huge, *colloquial* hulking, immense, *colloquial* jumbo, mammoth, mighty, prodigious, titanic, towering, *colloquial* tremendous, vast. **3** abhorrent, atrocious, *colloquial* awful, beastly, brutal, cruel, devilish, disgusting, dreadful, evil, execrable, gross, gruesome, heinous, hideous, horrendous, horrible, horrific, horrifying, inhuman, obscene, outrageous, repulsive, shocking, terrible, ugly, villainous, wicked.

montage /mɒnˈtɑːʒ/ *noun* **1** selection, cutting, and arrangement as consecutive whole, of separate sections of cinema or television film. **2** composite whole made from juxtaposed photographs etc.

month /mʌnθ/ *noun* **1** (in full **calendar month**) each of 12 divisions of year. **2** period of time between same dates in successive calendar months. **3** period of 28 days.

monthly *adjective* done, produced, or occurring once every month. ● *adverb* every month. ● *noun* (*plural* **-ies**) monthly periodical.

monument /ˈmɒnjʊmənt/ *noun* anything enduring that serves to commemorate, esp. structure, building, or memorial stone.
  ■ cairn, cenotaph, cross, gravestone, headstone, mausoleum, memorial, obelisk, shrine, tomb, tombstone.

monumental /mɒnjʊˈment(ə)l/ *adjective* **1** extremely great; stupendous. **2** massive and permanent. **3** of or serving as monument.

■ **1, 2** awe-inspiring, awesome, classic, enduring, epoch-making, grand, great, historic, impressive, large-scale, lasting, major, memorable, stupendous, unforgettable. **3** commemorative, memorial.

moo *noun* (*plural* **-s**) characteristic sound of cattle. ● *verb* (**moos, mooed**) make this sound.

mooch *verb colloquial* **1** (usually + *about, around*) wander aimlessly. **2** *esp. US* cadge.

mood[1] *noun* **1** state of mind or feeling. **2** fit of bad temper or depression. □ **in the mood** inclined.
■ **1** atmosphere, attitude, disposition, feeling, frame of mind, humour, inclination, nature, spirit, state of mind, temper, tone, vein. □ **in the mood** see READY *adjective* 3.

mood[2] *noun Grammar* form(s) of verb indicating whether it expresses fact, command, wish, etc.

moody *adjective* (**-ier, -iest**) **1** given to changes of mood. **2** gloomy, sullen.
■ **1** capricious, changeable, erratic, fickle, inconstant, mercurial, temperamental, unpredictable, unreliable, unstable, volatile. **2** abrupt, bad-tempered, cantankerous, crabby, cross, crotchety, depressed, depressive, disgruntled, grumpy, huffy, ill-humoured, irritable, melancholy, miserable, morose, peevish, petulant, sad, short, short-tempered, *colloquial* snappy, sulky, sullen, temperamental, testy, touchy.

moon *noun* **1** natural satellite of the earth, orbiting it monthly, illuminated by and reflecting sun. **2** satellite of any planet. ● *verb* (often + *about, around*) wander aimlessly or listlessly. □ **moonbeam** ray of moonlight. **moonlight** ● *noun* light of moon. ● *verb colloquial* have other paid occupation, esp. one by night as well as one by day. **moonlit** lit by the moon. **moonshine 1** foolish or visionary talk. **2** illicit alcohol. **moonshot** launching of spacecraft to moon. **moonstone** feldspar of pearly appearance. **moonstruck** slightly mad. **over the moon** delighted. □ **moonless** *adjective*.

moony *adjective* (**-ier, -iest**) listless; stupidly dreamy.

Moor /mʊə/ *noun* member of a Muslim people of NW Africa. □ **Moorish** *adjective*.

moor[1] /mʊə/ *noun* open uncultivated upland, esp. when covered with heather. □ **moorhen** small waterfowl. **moorland** large area of moor.
■ fell, heath, moorland.

moor[2] /mʊə/ *verb* attach (boat etc.) to fixed object. □ **moorage** *noun*.
■ anchor, berth, dock, fasten, make fast, secure, tie up.

mooring *noun* **1** (often in *plural*) place where boat etc. is moored. **2** (in *plural*) set of permanent anchors and chains.

moose *noun* (*plural* same) N. American deer; elk.

moot *adjective* debatable, undecided. ● *verb*

raise (question) for discussion. ● *noun historical* assembly.

mop *noun* **1** bundle of yarn or cloth or a sponge on end of stick for cleaning floors etc. **2** thick mass of hair. ● *verb* (**-pp-**) wipe or clean (as) with mop. □ **mop up 1** wipe with mop. **2** *colloquial* absorb. **3** dispose of. **4** complete occupation of (area etc.) by capturing or killing enemy troops left there.

mope *verb* (**-ping**) be depressed or listless. ● *noun* person who mopes. □ **mopy** *adjective* (**-ier, -iest**).
■ *verb* brood, despair, grieve, languish, moon, pine, sulk.

moped /ˈməʊped/ *noun* low-powered motorized bicycle.

moquette /mɒˈket/ *noun* thick pile or looped material used for upholstery etc.

moraine /məˈreɪn/ *noun* area of debris carried down and deposited by glacier.

moral /ˈmɒr(ə)l/ *adjective* **1** concerned with goodness or badness of character or behaviour, or with difference between right and wrong. **2** virtuous in conduct. ● *noun* **1** moral lesson of story etc. **2** (in *plural*) moral principles or behaviour. □ **moral support** psychological rather than physical help. □ **morally** *adverb*.
■ *adjective* **1** ethical, moralistic, moralizing. **2** blameless, chaste, decent, ethical, good, high-minded, honest, honourable, incorruptible, innocent, irreproachable, just, law-abiding, noble, principled, proper, pure, respectable, responsible, right, righteous, sinless, trustworthy, truthful, upright, upstanding, virtuous. ● *noun* **1** lesson, maxim, meaning, message, point, precept, principle, teaching. **2** (*morals*) see MORALITY 1–3.

morale /məˈrɑːl/ *noun* confidence, determination, etc. of person or group.
■ attitude, cheerfulness, confidence, *esprit de corps*, heart, mood, self-confidence, self-esteem, spirit, state of mind.

moralist /ˈmɒrəlɪst/ *noun* person who practises or teaches morality. □ **moralistic** /-ˈlɪs-/ *adjective*.

morality /məˈrælɪtɪ/ *noun* (*plural* **-ies**) **1** (system of) moral principles. **2** degree of conformity to moral principles. **3** moral conduct. **4** science of morals.
■ **1–3** behaviour, conduct, decency, ethics, ethos, fairness, goodness, honesty, ideals, integrity, justice, morals, principles, propriety, rectitude, righteousness, rightness, scruples, standards, uprightness, virtue. **4** ethics, morals.

moralize /ˈmɒrəlaɪz/ *verb* (also **-ise**) (**-zing** or **-sing**) (often + *on*) indulge in moral reflection or talk. □ **moralization** *noun*.
■ lecture, philosophize, pontificate, preach, sermonize.

morass /məˈræs/ *noun* **1** entanglement. **2** *literary* bog.

moratorium /mɒrəˈtɔːrɪəm/ *noun* (*plural* **-s** or

-ria) **1** (often + *on*) temporary prohibition or suspension (of activity). **2** legal authorization to debtors to postpone payment.

morbid /'mɔːbɪd/ *adjective* **1** (of mind, ideas, etc.) unwholesome. **2** *colloquial* melancholy. **3** of or indicative of disease. □ **morbidity** /-'bɪd-/ *noun*. **morbidly** *adverb*.

■ **1** black (*humour*), ghoulish, grim, grotesque, gruesome, macabre, monstrous, *colloquial* sick, unhealthy, unpleasant, unwholesome. **2** brooding, dejected, depressed, gloomy, lugubrious, melancholy, morose, pessimistic, sombre, unhappy. **3** diseased, pathological, unhealthy.

mordant /'mɔːd(ə)nt/ *adjective* **1** (of sarcasm etc.) caustic, biting. **2** smarting. **3** corrosive, cleansing. ● *noun* mordant substance.

more /mɔː/ *adjective* **1** greater in quantity or degree. **2** additional. ● *noun* greater quantity, number, or amount. ● *adverb* **1** to greater degree or extent. **2** *forming comparative of adjectives and adverbs*. □ **more or less 1** in greater or lesser degree. **2** approximately.

■ *adjective* added, additional, extra, further, increased, longer, new, other, renewed, supplementary.

morello /mə'reləʊ/ *noun* (*plural* -s) sour kind of dark cherry.

moreover /mɔː'rəʊvə/ *adverb* besides, in addition.

■ also, as well, besides, further, furthermore, in addition, too.

mores /'mɔːreɪz/ *plural noun* customs or conventions of community.

morganatic /mɔːgə'nætɪk/ *adjective* (of marriage) between person of high rank and one of lower rank, the latter and the latter's children having no claim to possessions of former.

morgue /mɔːg/ *noun* **1** mortuary. **2** room or file of miscellaneous information kept by newspaper office.

moribund /'mɒrɪbʌnd/ *adjective* **1** at point of death. **2** lacking vitality.

Mormon /'mɔːmən/ *noun* member of Church of Jesus Christ of Latter-Day Saints. □ **Mormonism** *noun*.

morn *noun poetical* morning.

morning /'mɔːnɪŋ/ *noun* early part of day till noon or lunchtime. □ **morning coat** tailcoat with front cut away. **morning dress** man's morning coat and striped trousers. **morning glory** climbing plant with trumpet-shaped flowers. **morning sickness** nausea felt in morning in pregnancy. **morning star** planet, usually Venus, seen in east before sunrise.

morocco /mə'rɒkəʊ/ *noun* (*plural* -s) fine flexible leather of goatskin tanned with sumac.

moron /'mɔːrɒn/ *noun* **1** *colloquial* very stupid person. **2** adult with mental age of 8–12. □ **moronic** /mə'r-/ *adjective*.

morose /mə'rəʊs/ *adjective* sullen, gloomy. □ **morosely** *adverb*. **moroseness** *noun*.

■ bad-tempered, churlish, depressed, gloomy, glum, grim, humourless, ill-natured, melancholy, moody, mournful, pessimistic, sad, saturnine, sour, sulky, sullen, surly, taciturn, unhappy, unsociable.

morphia /'mɔːfɪə/ *noun* morphine.

morphine /'mɔːfiːn/ *noun* narcotic drug from opium.

morphology /mɔː'fɒlədʒɪ/ *noun* study of forms of things, esp. of animals and plants and of words and their structure. □ **morphological** /-fə'lɒdʒ-/ *adjective*.

morris dance /'mɒrɪs/ *noun* traditional English dance in fancy costume. □ **morris dancer** *noun*. **morris dancing** *noun*.

morrow /'mɒrəʊ/ *noun* (usually **the morrow**) *literary* following day.

Morse /mɔːs/ *noun* (in full **Morse code**) code in which letters, numbers, etc. are represented by combinations of long and short light or sound signals.

morsel /'mɔːs(ə)l/ *noun* mouthful; small piece (esp. of food).

■ bit, bite, crumb, fragment, gobbet, mouthful, nibble, piece, sample, scrap, soupçon, spoonful, taste, titbit.

mortal /'mɔːt(ə)l/ *adjective* **1** subject to death. **2** causing death. **3** (of combat) fought to the death. **4** (of enemy) implacable. ● *noun* human being. □ **mortal sin** sin depriving soul of salvation. □ **mortally** *adverb*.

■ *adjective* **1** ephemeral, human, passing, temporal, transient. **2** deadly, fatal, lethal, terminal. **4** deadly, implacable, irreconcilable, remorseless, sworn, unrelenting. ● *noun* creature, human being, man, person, soul, woman.

mortality /mɔː'tælɪtɪ/ *noun* (*plural* -ies) **1** being subject to death. **2** loss of life on large scale. **3** (in full **mortality rate**) death rate.

■ **1** humanity, impermanence, transience. **2** death, dying, loss of life. **3** death rate, fatalities.

mortar /'mɔːtə/ *noun* **1** mixture of lime or cement, sand, and water, for bonding bricks or stones. **2** short cannon for firing shells at high angles. **3** vessel in which ingredients are pounded with pestle. □ **mortarboard 1** stiff flat square-topped academic cap. **2** flat board for holding mortar.

mortgage /'mɔːgɪdʒ/ *noun* **1** conveyance of property to creditor as security for debt (usually one incurred by purchase of property). **2** sum of money lent by this. ● *verb* (-ging) convey (property) by mortgage.

mortgagee /mɔːgɪ'dʒiː/ *noun* creditor in mortgage.

mortgager /'mɔːgɪdʒə/ *noun* (also **mortgagor** /-'dʒɔː/) debtor in mortgage.

mortice = MORTISE.

mortician /mɔː'tɪʃ(ə)n/ *noun US* undertaker.

mortify /'mɔːtɪfaɪ/ *verb* (-ies, -ied) **1** humiliate; wound (person's feelings). **2** bring (body etc.) into subjection by self-denial. **3** (of flesh) be affected by gangrene. □ **mortification** *noun.* **mortifying** *adjective.*

■ **1** abash, chagrin, chasten, crush, deflate, embarrass, humble, humiliate, *colloquial* put down, shame.

mortise /ˈmɔːtɪs/ (also **mortice**) *noun* hole in framework to receive end of another part, esp. tenon. ● *verb* (**-sing**) **1** join, esp. by mortise and tenon. **2** cut mortise in. □ **mortise lock** lock recessed in frame of door etc.

mortuary /ˈmɔːtjʊərɪ/ *noun* (*plural* **-ies**) room or building in which dead bodies are kept until burial or cremation. ● *adjective* of death or burial.

Mosaic /məʊˈzeɪɪk/ *adjective* of Moses.

mosaic /məʊˈzeɪɪk/ *noun* **1** picture or pattern made with small variously coloured pieces of glass, stone, etc. **2** diversified thing.

moselle /məʊˈzel/ *noun* dry German white wine.

Moslem = MUSLIM.

mosque /mɒsk/ *noun* Muslim place of worship.

mosquito /mɒsˈkiːtəʊ/ *noun* (*plural* **-es**) biting insect, esp. with long proboscis to suck blood. □ **mosquito-net** net to keep off mosquitoes.

moss *noun* **1** small flowerless plant growing in dense clusters in bogs and on trees, stones, etc. **2** *Scottish & Northern English* peatbog. □ **mossy** *adjective* (**-ier**, **-iest**).

most /məʊst/ *adjective* **1** greatest in quantity or degree. **2** the majority of. ● *noun* **1** greatest quantity or number. **2** the majority. ● *adverb* **1** in highest degree. **2** *forming superlative of adjectives and adverbs.*

mostly *adverb* **1** mainly. **2** usually.

■ chiefly, commonly, generally, largely, mainly, normally, predominantly, primarily, principally, typically, usually.

MOT *abbreviation* (in full **MOT test**) compulsory annual test, instituted by Ministry of Transport, of vehicles over specified age.

mot /məʊ/ *noun* (*plural* **mots** same pronunciation) (usually as **bon mot** /bɔ ˜/) witty saying. □ **mot juste** /ˈʒuːst/ most appropriate expression. [French]

mote *noun* speck of dust.

motel /məʊˈtel/ *noun* roadside hotel for motorists.

moth /mɒθ/ *noun* **1** nocturnal insect like butterfly. **2** insect of this type breeding in cloth etc., on which its larva feeds. □ **mothball** ball of naphthalene etc. kept with stored clothes to deter moths. **moth-eaten 1** damaged by moths. **2** time-worn.

■ □ **moth-eaten** antiquated, decrepit, holey, mangy, ragged, shabby, *colloquial* tatty.

mother /ˈmʌðə/ *noun* **1** female parent. **2** condition etc. giving rise to something else. **3** (in full **Mother Superior**) head of female religious community. ● *verb* treat as mother does. □ **mother**

country country in relation to its colonies. **mother-in-law** (*plural* **mothers-in-law**) husband's or wife's mother. **motherland** native country. **mother-of-pearl** iridescent substance forming lining of oyster and other shells. **mother tongue** native language. □ **motherhood** *noun.* **motherly** *adjective.*

■ *noun* **1** dam (of *animal*), *colloquial* ma, *colloquial* mama, *colloquial* mamma, *colloquial* mum, *colloquial* mummy, parent. ● *verb* care for, cherish, coddle, comfort, cuddle, fuss over, indulge, look after, love, nourish, nurse, nurture, pamper, protect, spoil, take care of. □ **motherly** caring, kind, loving, maternal, protective.

motif /məʊˈtiːf/ *noun* **1** theme repeated and developed in artistic work. **2** decorative design. **3** ornament sewn separately on garment.

■ decoration, design, device, figure, idea, leitmotif, ornament, pattern, symbol, theme.

motion /ˈməʊʃ(ə)n/ *noun* **1** moving; changing position. **2** gesture. **3** formal proposal put to committee etc. **4** application to court for order. **5** evacuation of bowels. ● *verb* (often + *to do*) direct (person) by gesture. □ **motion picture** *esp. US* cinema film. □ **motionless** *adjective.*

■ *noun* **1** action, activity, agitation, change, commotion, development, evolution, move, movement, progress, rise and fall, shift, stir, stirring, travel, travelling, trend. **2** see GESTURE *noun.* ● *verb* see GESTURE *verb.* □ **motionless** at rest, calm, frozen, immobile, inanimate, inert, lifeless, paralysed, peaceful, resting, stagnant, static, stationary, still, stock-still, unmoving.

motivate /ˈməʊtɪveɪt/ *verb* (**-ting**) **1** supply motive to; be motive of. **2** cause (person) to act in particular way. **3** stimulate interest of (person in activity). □ **motivation** *noun.*

■ activate, actuate, arouse, cause, drive, egg on, encourage, excite, galvanize, goad, incite, induce, influence, inspire, instigate, move, occasion, persuade, prompt, provoke, push, rouse, spur, stimulate, stir, urge.

motive /ˈməʊtɪv/ *noun* **1** what induces person to act. **2** motif. ● *adjective* tending to initiate movement. □ **motiveless** *adjective.*

■ *noun* **1** aim, ambition, cause, drive, end, enticement, grounds, impulse, incentive, incitement, inducement, inspiration, instigation, intention, lure, motivation, object, provocation, purpose, push, rationale, reason, spur, stimulation, stimulus.

motley /ˈmɒtlɪ/ *adjective* (**-lier**, **-liest**) **1** diversified in colour. **2** of varied character. ● *noun historical* jester's particoloured costume.

motor /ˈməʊtə/ *noun* **1** thing that imparts motion. **2** machine (esp. using electricity or internal combustion) supplying motive power for vehicle or other machine. **3** car. ● *adjective* **1** giving, imparting, or producing motion. **2** driven by motor. **3** of or for motor vehicles. ● *verb* go or convey by motor vehicle. □ **motorbike** *colloquial,* **motorcycle** two-wheeled motor vehicle without pedal propulsion. **motor boat**

motor-driven boat. **motor car** car. **motor vehicle** road vehicle powered by internal-combustion engine. **motorway** fast road with separate carriageways limited to motor vehicles.

■ *noun* **2** engine. **3** see CAR 1. ● *verb* drive, go by car, travel.

motorcade /'məʊtəkeɪd/ *noun* procession of motor vehicles.

motorist *noun* driver of car.

motorize *verb* (also **-ise**) (**-zing** or **-sing**) **1** equip with motor transport. **2** provide with motor.

mottle /'mɒt(ə)l/ *verb* (**-ling**) (esp. as **mottled** *adjective*) mark with spots or smears of colour.

■ **(mottled)** blotchy, brindled, dappled, flecked, freckled, marbled, patchy, spattered, speckled, spotted, spotty, streaked, streaky, variegated.

motto /'mɒtəʊ/ *noun* (*plural* **-es**) **1** maxim adopted as rule of conduct. **2** words accompanying coat of arms. **3** appropriate inscription. **4** joke, maxim, etc. in paper cracker.

■ **1–3** adage, aphorism, catchphrase, maxim, precept, proverb, rule, saw, saying, slogan.

mould[1] /məʊld/ (*US* **mold**) *noun* **1** hollow container into which substance is poured or pressed to harden into required shape. **2** pudding etc. shaped in mould. **3** form, shape. **4** character, type. ● *verb* **1** shape (as) in mould. **2** give shape to. **3** influence development of.

■ *verb* **1, 2** cast, fashion, forge, form, model, sculpt, shape, stamp, work. **3** form, influence, make, shape.

mould[2] /məʊld/ *noun* (*US* **mold**) furry growth of fungi, esp. in moist warm conditions.

■ blight, fungus, growth, mildew.

mould[3] /məʊld/ *noun* (*US* **mold**) **1** loose earth. **2** upper soil of cultivated land, esp. when rich in organic matter.

moulder /'məʊldə/ *verb* (*US* **molder**) **1** decay to dust. **2** (+ *away*) rot, crumble away.

moulding *noun* (*US* **molding**) **1** ornamental strip of plaster etc. applied as architectural feature, esp. in cornice. **2** similar feature in woodwork etc.

mouldy *adjective* (*US* **moldy**) (**-ier, -iest**) **1** covered with mould. **2** stale; out of date. **3** *colloquial* dull, miserable. □ **mouldiness** *noun*.

■ **1** decaying, decomposing, fusty, mildewed, mouldering, musty, putrefying, rotten, stale. **2** see STALE *adjective* 1.

moult /məʊlt/ (*US* **molt**) *verb* shed (feathers, hair, shell, etc.) in renewing plumage, coat, etc. ● *noun* moulting.

mound /maʊnd/ *noun* **1** raised mass of earth, stones, etc. **2** heap, pile. **3** hillock.

■ **1, 2** barrow, cairn, heap, pile, stack, tumulus. **3** bank, dune, elevation, hill, hillock, hummock, hump, knoll.

mount[1] *verb* **1** ascend. **2** climb on to; get up on (horse etc.). **3** set on horseback. **4** (as **mounted** *adjective*) serving on horseback. **5** (often + *up*) accumulate, increase. **6** set in frame etc., esp. for viewing. **7** organize, arrange (exhibition, attack, etc.). ● *noun* **1** backing etc. on which picture etc. is set for display. **2** horse for riding. **3** setting for gem etc.

■ *verb* **1** ascend, clamber up, climb, fly up, go up, rise, rocket upwards, scale, shoot up, soar. **2** climb on to, get astride, get on, jump on to. **5** accumulate, build up, escalate, expand, get bigger, grow, increase, intensify, multiply, pile up, swell. **6** display, exhibit, frame, install, put in place. **7** arrange, organize, launch, prepare, put on, set up, stage.

mount[2] *noun* (*archaic* except before name) mountain, hill.

■ see MOUNTAIN 1.

mountain /'maʊntɪn/ *noun* **1** large abrupt elevation of ground. **2** large heap or pile. **3** huge quantity. **4** large surplus stock. □ **mountain ash** tree with scarlet berries. **mountain bike** sturdy bicycle with straight handlebars and many gears.

■ **1** alp, elevation, eminence, height, hill, mound, *archaic* mount, peak, prominence, summit, tor, volcano.

mountaineer /maʊntɪ'nɪə/ *noun* person practising mountain climbing. ● *verb* climb mountains as sport. □ **mountaineering** *noun*.

mountainous *adjective* **1** having many mountains. **2** huge.

■ **1** alpine, craggy, high, hilly. **2** daunting, enormous, formidable, gigantic, huge, immense, towering.

mountebank /'maʊntɪbæŋk/ *noun* swindler, charlatan.

Mountie /'maʊntɪ/ *noun colloquial* member of Royal Canadian Mounted Police.

mourn /mɔːn/ *verb* **1** (often + *for, over*) feel or show sorrow or regret. **2** grieve for loss of (dead person etc.).

■ bemoan, bewail, fret, grieve, keen, lament, mope, pine, regret, wail, weep.

mourner *noun* person who mourns, esp. at funeral.

mournful *adjective* doleful, sad. □ **mournfully** *adverb*. **mournfulness** *noun*.

■ dismal, distressed, distressing, doleful, funereal, gloomy, grief-stricken, grieving, heartbreaking, heartbroken, lamenting, lugubrious, melancholy, plaintive, *literary* plangent, sad, sorrowful, tearful, tragic, unhappy, woeful.

mourning *noun* **1** expression of sorrow for dead, esp. by wearing black clothes. **2** such clothes.

mouse /maʊs/ *noun* (*plural* **mice**) **1** small rodent. **2** timid or feeble person. **3** *Computing* small device controlling cursor on VDU screen. ● *verb* (also /maʊz/) (**-sing**) (of cat etc.) hunt mice. □ **mouser** *noun*. **mousy** *adjective*.

mousse /muːs/ *noun* dish of whipped cream, eggs, etc., flavoured with fruit, chocolate, etc., or with meat or fish purée.

moustache /məˈstɑːʃ/ *noun* (*US* **mustache**) hair left to grow on upper lip.

mouth *noun* /maʊθ/ (*plural* **mouths** /maʊðz/) **1** external opening in head, for taking in food and emitting sound. **2** cavity behind it containing teeth and vocal organs. **3** opening of container, cave, trumpet, volcano, etc. **4** place where river enters sea. ● *verb* /maʊð/ (**-thing**) **1** say or speak very distinctly. **2** form words by moving lips silently. **3** utter insincerely or without understanding. □ **mouth-organ** harmonica. **mouthpiece 1** part of musical instrument, telephone, etc., placed next to lips. **2** person who speaks for others. **mouthwash** liquid antiseptic etc. for rinsing mouth. **mouth-watering 1** (of food etc.) having delicious smell or appearance. **2** tempting.

■ *noun* **1** chops, *slang* gob, jaws, *slang* kisser, lips, muzzle. **3** aperture, door, doorway, entrance, exit, gate, gateway, inlet, opening, orifice, outlet, vent, way in. ● *verb* **1** articulate, declaim, enunciate, pronounce, say, speak, utter.

mouthful *noun* (*plural* **-s**) **1** quantity of food etc. that fills the mouth. **2** *colloquial* something difficult to say.

■ **1** bite, gobbet, gulp, morsel, sip, spoonful, swallow, taste.

movable /ˈmuːvəb(ə)l/ *adjective* **1** that can be moved. **2** variable in date. ● *noun* **1** article of furniture that is not a fixture. **2** (in *plural*) personal property.

move /muːv/ *verb* (**-ving**) **1** (cause to) change position, posture, home, or place of work. **2** put or keep in motion. **3** rouse, stir. **4** (often + *about, away, off,* etc.) go, proceed. **5** take action. **6** (+ *in*) be socially active in. **7** affect with emotion. **8** (cause to) change attitude. **9** prompt, incline. **10** propose as resolution. ● *noun* **1** act or process of moving. **2** change of house, premises, etc. **3** step taken to secure object. **4** moving of piece in board game. □ **get a move on** *colloquial* **1** hurry. **2** make a start. **move in 1** take possession of new house etc. **2** get into position of influence. **move in with** start to share accommodation with. **move out** leave one's home. **on the move 1** progressing. **2** moving about. □ **movable** *adjective*.

■ *verb* **1** budge, carry, change places, change position, convey, export, import, relocate, shift, ship, stir, switch, transfer, transplant, transport, transpose. **2** be agitated, be astir, budge, fidget, flap, roll, shake, stir, swing, toss, tremble, turn, twist, twitch, wag, *colloquial* waggle, wave, *colloquial* wiggle. **3** see STIR *verb* 4. **4** advance, go, make headway, make progress, pass, proceed, progress, set off, sweep, travel; (*move away*) see DEPART 1,2; (*move back*) see RETREAT *verb* 1; (*move down*) see DESCEND 1; (*move in*) see ENTER 1; (*move round*) see CIRCULATE 1;4, ROTATE 1; (*move towards*) see APPROACH *verb* 1; (*move up*) see ASCEND 2. **5** act, do something, make a move, take action. **7** affect, arouse, enrage, fire, rouse, stir, touch. **9** encourage, impel, incline, influence,

inspire, persuade, prompt, stimulate, stir, urge.
● *noun* **1** action, gesture, manoeuvre, motion, movement. **2** change, changeover, relocation, shift, transfer. **3** act, action, deed, device, dodge, gambit, initiative, manoeuvre, measure, ploy, ruse, step, stratagem, tack, tactic. **4** chance, go, opportunity, turn. □ **movable** adjustable, changeable, detachable, floating, mobile, portable, transferable, transportable, unfixed, variable.

movement *noun* **1** moving, being moved. **2** moving parts of mechanism. **3** group of people with common object. **4** (in *plural*) person's activities and whereabouts. **5** chief division of longer musical work. **6** bowel motion. **7** rise or fall of stock-market prices. **8** *Military* change of position of troops. **9** progression; trend.

■ **1** action, activity, gesticulation, gesture, manoeuvre, migration, motion, move, shift, shifting, stirring. **3** campaign, crusade, drive, faction, group, lobby, organization, party. **8** exercise, manoeuvre, operation. **9** change, development, drift, evolution, progress, shift, swing, tendency, trend.

movie /ˈmuːvɪ/ *noun esp. US colloquial* cinema film.

■ film, *colloquial* flick, *esp. US* motion picture.

moving *adjective* **1** that moves; able to move. **2** emotionally affecting. □ **moving picture** continuous picture of events obtained by projecting sequence of photographs taken at very short intervals.

■ **1** active, alive, astir, dynamic, flowing, going, in motion, mobile, movable, on the move, travelling, under way. **2** affecting, emotional, emotive, exciting, heart-rending, heart-warming, inspirational, inspiring, pathetic, poignant, spine-tingling, stirring, thrilling, touching.

mow /məʊ/ *verb* (*past participle* **mowed** or **mown**) cut (grass, hay, etc.) with scythe or machine. □ **mow down** kill or destroy randomly or in great numbers. □ **mower** *noun*.

■ clip, cut, scythe, shear, trim.

MP *abbreviation* Member of Parliament.

mp *abbreviation* mezzo piano.

m.p.g. *abbreviation* miles per gallon.

m.p.h. *abbreviation* miles per hour.

Mr /ˈmɪstə/ *noun* (*plural* **Messrs**) *title prefixed to name of man or to designation of office etc.*

Mrs /ˈmɪsɪz/ *noun* (*plural* same) *title of married woman.*

MS *abbreviation* (*plural* **MSS** /emˈesɪz/) **1** manuscript. **2** multiple sclerosis.

Ms /mɪz/ *noun: title of married or unmarried woman.*

M.Sc. *abbreviation* Master of Science.

Mt. *abbreviation* Mount.

much *adjective* existing or occurring in great quantity. ● *noun* **1** great quantity. **2** (usually in negative) noteworthy example. ● *adverb* **1** in great degree. **2** for large part of one's time; often. □ **a bit much** *colloquial* excessive. **much of a muchness** very nearly the same.

mucilage /'mju:sɪlɪdʒ/ *noun* **1** viscous substance obtained from plants. **2** adhesive gum.

muck *noun* **1** *colloquial* dirt, filth; anything disgusting. **2** manure. ● *verb* **1** (usually + *up*) *colloquial* bungle. **2** (usually + *up*) make dirty. **3** (+ *out*) remove manure from. □ **muck about, around** *colloquial* potter or fool about. **muck in** (often + *with*) *colloquial* share tasks etc. **muck-raking** seeking out and revealing of scandals etc. □ **mucky** *adjective* (**-ier, -iest**).

■ *noun* **1** dirt, filth, grime, *colloquial* gunge, mess, mire, mud, ooze, rubbish, scum, slime, sludge. **2** droppings, dung, excrement, faeces, manure, mess, ordure, sewage. □ **mucky** dirty, filthy, foul, grimy, grubby, messy, muddy, scummy, slimy, soiled, sordid, squalid.

mucous /'mju:kəs/ *adjective* of or covered with mucus. □ **mucous membrane** mucus-secreting tissue lining body cavities etc.

mucus /'mju:kəs/ *noun* slimy substance secreted by mucous membrane.

mud *noun* soft wet earth. □ **mudguard** curved strip over wheel to protect against mud. **mud-slinging** abuse, slander.

■ clay, dirt, mire, *colloquial* muck, ooze, silt, slime, sludge, slurry, soil.

muddle /'mʌd(ə)l/ *verb* (**-ling**) **1** (often + *up*) bring into disorder. **2** bewilder; confuse. ● *noun* disorder; confusion. □ **muddle along** progress in haphazard way. **muddle-headed** confused. **muddle through** achieve aims through perseverance rather than skill.

■ *verb* **1** disarrange, disorder, disorganize, entangle, foul up, jumble, make a mess of, mess up, mix up, scramble, shuffle, tangle. **2** bemuse, bewilder, confound, confuse, disorient, disorientate, mislead, perplex, puzzle. ● *noun* chaos, clutter, confusion, disorder, hotchpotch, jumble, mess, mishmash, *colloquial* shambles, tangle, untidiness.

muddy *adjective* (**-ier, -iest**) **1** like mud. **2** covered in or full of mud. **3** (of liquid, colour, or sound) not clear. **4** confused. ● *verb* (**-ies, -ied**) make muddy.

■ *adjective* **2** boggy, caked, dirty, filthy, marshy, messy, mucky, sloppy, sodden, soft, soiled, waterlogged, wet. **3** cloudy, impure, misty, opaque.

mudflat /'mʌdflæt/ *noun* (usually in *plural*) stretch of muddy land left uncovered at low tide.

muesli /'mju:zlɪ/ *noun* breakfast food of crushed cereals, dried fruit, nuts, etc.

muezzin /mu:'ezɪn/ *noun* Muslim crier who proclaims hours of prayer.

muff[1] *noun* covering, esp. of fur, for keeping hands or ears warm.

muff[2] *verb colloquial* **1** bungle. **2** miss (catch etc.).

muffin /'mʌfɪn/ *noun* **1** light flat round spongy cake, eaten toasted and buttered. **2** *US* similar cake made from batter or dough.

muffle /'mʌf(ə)l/ *verb* (**-ling**) **1** (often + *up*) wrap for warmth. **2** wrap or cover to deaden sound. □ **muffled** *adjective*.

■ **1** cloak, cover, enclose, enfold, envelop, shroud, swaddle, swathe, wrap up. **2** damp, deaden, disguise, dull, hush, mask, mute, quieten, silence, soften, stifle, still, suppress, tone down. □ **muffled** damped, deadened, dull, fuzzy, indistinct, muted, silenced, stifled, suppressed, unclear, woolly.

muffler *noun* **1** wrap or scarf worn for warmth. **2** thing used to deaden sound.

mufti /'mʌftɪ/ *noun* civilian clothes.

mug[1] *noun* **1** drinking vessel, usually cylindrical with handle and no saucer. **2** its contents. **3** gullible person. **4** *slang* face, mouth. ● *verb* (**-gg-**) attack and rob, esp. in public place. □ **mugger** *noun*. **mugging** *noun*.

■ *noun* **1** beaker, cup, flagon, pot, tankard. ● *verb* assault, attack, beat up, jump on, molest, rob, set on, steal from. □ **mugger** attacker, hooligan, robber, ruffian, thief, thug. **mugging** attack, robbery.

mug[2] *verb* (**-gg-**) (usually + *up*) *slang* learn (subject) by concentrated study.

■ (**mug up**) see LEARN 1.

muggins /'mʌgɪnz/ *noun* (*plural* same or **mugginses**) *colloquial* gullible person (often meaning oneself).

muggy /'mʌgɪ/ *adjective* (**-ier, -iest**) (of weather etc.) oppressively humid.

■ clammy, close, damp, humid, moist, oppressive, steamy, sticky, stuffy, sultry.

Muhammadan /mə'hæməd(ə)n/ *noun* & *adjective* (also **Mohammedan**) Muslim.

USAGE The term *Muhammadan* is not used by Muslims and is often regarded as offensive.

mulatto /mju:'lætəʊ/ *noun* (*plural* **-s** or **-es**) person of mixed white and black parentage.

mulberry /'mʌlbərɪ/ *noun* (*plural* **-ies**) **1** tree bearing edible purple or white berries. **2** its fruit. **3** dark red; purple.

mulch *noun* layer of wet straw, leaves, plastic, etc., put round plant's roots to enrich or insulate soil. ● *verb* treat with mulch.

mule[1] /mju:l/ *noun* **1** offspring of male donkey and female horse or (in general use) vice versa. **2** obstinate person. **3** kind of spinning machine.

mule[2] /mju:l/ *noun* backless slipper.

muleteer /mju:lə'tɪə/ *noun* mule driver.

mulish *adjective* stubborn.

mull[1] *verb* (often + *over*) ponder.

mull[2] *verb* heat and spice (wine, beer).

mullah /'mʌlə/ *noun* Muslim learned in theology and sacred law.

mullet /'mʌlɪt/ *noun* (*plural* same) edible sea fish.

mulligatawny /mʌlɪɡəˈtɔːnɪ/ *noun* highly seasoned soup originally from India.

mullion /ˈmʌljən/ *noun* vertical bar between panes in window. □ **mullioned** *adjective*.

multi- *combining form* many.

multicoloured /ˈmʌltɪkʌləd/ *adjective* of many colours.

multicultural /mʌltɪˈkʌltʃ(ə)r(ə)l/ *adjective* of or relating to or including several cultural or ethnic groups.

multifarious /mʌltɪˈfeərɪəs/ *adjective* **1** many and various. **2** of great variety.

multiform /ˈmʌltɪfɔːm/ *adjective* **1** having many forms. **2** of many kinds.

multilateral /mʌltɪˈlætər(ə)l/ *adjective* **1** (of agreement etc.) in which 3 or more parties participate. **2** having many sides. □ **multilaterally** *adverb*.

multilingual /mʌltɪˈlɪŋɡw(ə)l/ *adjective* in, speaking, or using many languages.

multinational /mʌltɪˈnæʃən(ə)l/ *adjective* **1** operating in several countries. **2** of several nationalities. ● *noun* multinational company.

multiple /ˈmʌltɪp(ə)l/ *adjective* **1** having several parts, elements, or components. **2** many and various. ● *noun* quantity exactly divisible by another. □ **multiple sclerosis** see SCLEROSIS 2.
■ *adjective* **1** complex, composite, compound. **2** manifold, many, numerous, plural, various.

multiplicand /mʌltɪplɪˈkænd/ *noun* quantity to be multiplied.

multiplication /mʌltɪplɪˈkeɪʃ(ə)n/ *noun* multiplying.

multiplicity /mʌltɪˈplɪsɪtɪ/ *noun* (*plural* **-ies**) **1** manifold variety. **2** (+ *of*) great number of.
■ **1** array, diversity, variety. **2** abundance, number, plurality, profusion.

multiplier /ˈmʌltɪplaɪə/ *noun* quantity by which given number is multiplied.

multiply /ˈmʌltɪplaɪ/ *verb* (**-ies**, **-ied**) **1** obtain from (number) another a specified number of times its value. **2** increase in number, esp. by procreation.
■ **2** breed, increase, proliferate, propagate, reproduce, spread.

multi-purpose /mʌltɪˈpɜːpəs/ *adjective* having several purposes.

multiracial /mʌltɪˈreɪʃ(ə)l/ *adjective* of several races.

multitude /ˈmʌltɪtjuːd/ *noun* **1** (often + *of*) great number. **2** large gathering of people. **3** (**the multitude**) the common people. □ **multitudinous** /-ˈtjuːdɪnəs/ *adjective*.
■ **1** crowd, host, legion, *colloquial* lots, mass, *literary* myriad, swarm, throng. **2** see CROWD *noun* 1.

mum[1] *noun colloquial* mother.

mum[2] *adjective colloquial* silent. □ **mum's the word** say nothing.

mumble /ˈmʌmb(ə)l/ *verb* (**-ling**) speak or utter indistinctly. ● *noun* indistinct utterance.
■ *verb* be inarticulate, murmur, mutter.

mumbo-jumbo /mʌmbəʊˈdʒʌmbəʊ/ *noun* (*plural* **-s**) **1** meaningless ritual. **2** meaningless or unnecessarily complicated language. **3** nonsense.

mummer /ˈmʌmə/ *noun* actor in traditional play or mime.

mummery /ˈmʌmərɪ/ *noun* (*plural* **-ies**) **1** ridiculous (esp. religious) ceremonial. **2** performance by mummers.

mummify /ˈmʌmɪfaɪ/ *verb* (**-ies**, **-ied**) preserve (body) as mummy. □ **mummification** *noun*.

mummy[1] /ˈmʌmɪ/ *noun* (*plural* **-ies**) *colloquial* mother.

mummy[2] /ˈmʌmɪ/ *noun* (*plural* **-ies**) dead body preserved by embalming, esp. in ancient Egypt.

mumps *plural noun* (treated as *singular*) infectious disease with swelling of neck and face.

munch *verb* chew steadily.
■ chew, champ, chomp, crunch, eat, gnaw, masticate.

mundane /mʌnˈdeɪn/ *adjective* **1** dull, routine. **2** of this world. □ **mundanely** *adverb*.
■ **1** banal, common, commonplace, down-to-earth, dull, everyday, familiar, ordinary, practical, quotidian, routine. **2** human, material, physical, temporal, worldly.

municipal /mjuːˈnɪsɪp(ə)l/ *adjective* of municipality or its self-government.
■ borough, city, civic, community, district, local, public, town, urban.

municipality /mjuːnɪsɪˈpælɪtɪ/ *noun* (*plural* **-ies**) **1** town or district with local self-government. **2** its governing body.

munificent /mjuːˈnɪfɪs(ə)nt/ *adjective* (of giver or gift) splendidly generous. □ **munificence** *noun*.

muniment /ˈmjuːnɪmənt/ *noun* (usually in *plural*) document kept as evidence of rights or privileges.

munition /mjuːˈnɪʃ(ə)n/ *noun* (usually in *plural*) military weapons, ammunition, etc.

mural /ˈmjʊər(ə)l/ *noun* painting executed directly on wall. ● *adjective* of, on, or like wall.

murder /ˈmɜːdə/ *noun* **1** intentional unlawful killing of human being by another. **2** *colloquial* unpleasant or dangerous state of affairs. ● *verb* **1** kill (human being) intentionally and unlawfully. **2** *colloquial* utterly defeat. **3** *colloquial* spoil by bad performance, mispronunciation, etc. □ **murderer**, **murderess** *noun*. **murderous** *adjective*.
■ *noun* **1** assassination, fratricide, genocide, homicide, infanticide, killing, matricide, parricide, patricide, regicide, unlawful killing. ● *verb* **1** see KILL *verb* 1. □ **murderer**, **murderess** assassin, butcher, cut-throat, gunman, homicide, killer, slayer. **murderous** barbarous, bloodthirsty,

bloody, brutal, cruel, dangerous, deadly, ferocious, fierce, homicidal, inhuman, pitiless, ruthless, savage, vicious, violent.

murky /'mɜːkɪ/ *adjective* (**-ier**, **-iest**) **1** dark, gloomy. **2** (of liquid etc.) dirty, muddy. □ **murkiness** *noun*.

■ **1** clouded, cloudy, dark, dim, dismal, dreary, dull, foggy, funereal, gloomy, grey, misty, obscure, overcast, shadowy, sombre. **2** clouded, cloudy, dirty, muddy, thick, turbid.

murmur /'mɜːmə/ *noun* **1** subdued continuous sound. **2** softly spoken utterance. **3** subdued expression of discontent. ● *verb* **1** make murmur. **2** utter in low voice. **3** grumble in subdued voice. □ **murmurous** *adjective*.

■ *noun* **1** background noise, buzz, drone, grumble, hum, mutter, rumble. **2** undertone, whisper. **3** grumble, mutter. ● *verb* **1, 2** drone, hum, moan, mumble, mutter, rumble, speak in an undertone, whisper. **3** see GRUMBLE *verb* 1.

murrain /'mʌrɪn/ *noun* infectious disease of cattle.

Muscadet /'mʌskədeɪ/ *noun* **1** dry white wine of France from Loire region. **2** variety of grape used for this.

muscat /'mʌskət/ *noun* **1** sweet usually fortified white wine made from musk-flavoured grapes. **2** this grape.

muscatel /mʌskə'tel/ *noun* **1** muscat wine or grape. **2** raisin made from muscat grape.

muscle /'mʌs(ə)l/ *noun* **1** fibrous tissue producing movement in or maintaining position of animal body. **2** part of body composed of muscles. **3** strength, power. ● *verb* (**-ling**) (+ *in*, *in on*) *colloquial* force oneself on others. □ **muscle-bound** with muscles stiff and inelastic through excessive exercise. **muscle-man** man with highly developed muscles.

Muscovite /'mʌskəvaɪt/ *noun* native or citizen of Moscow. ● *adjective* of Moscow.

muscular /'mʌskjʊlə/ *adjective* **1** of or affecting muscles. **2** having well-developed muscles. □ **muscular dystrophy** hereditary progressive wasting of muscles. □ **muscularity** /-'lær-/ *noun*.

■ **2** athletic, beefy, brawny, broad-shouldered, burly, hefty, *colloquial* hulking, husky, powerful, robust, sinewy, strapping, strong, sturdy, tough, well built, well developed, wiry.

muse[1] /mjuːz/ *verb* (**-sing**) (usually + *on*, *upon*) ponder, reflect.

■ cogitate, deliberate, meditate, ponder, reflect, ruminate, think; (*muse on*, *upon*) consider, contemplate, mull over, study.

muse[2] /mjuːz/ *noun* **1** *Greek & Roman Mythology* any of 9 goddesses inspiring poetry, music, etc. **2** (usually **the muse**) poet's inspiration.

museum /mjuː'zɪəm/ *noun* building for storing and exhibiting objects of historical, scientific, or cultural interest. □ **museum piece 1** object fit for museum. **2** *derogatory* old-fashioned person etc.

mush *noun* **1** soft pulp. **2** feeble sentimentality. **3** *US* maize porridge. □ **mushy** *adjective* (**-ier**, **-iest**).

■ □ **mushy** *colloquial* gooey, pulpy, sloppy, soft, spongy, squashy, *colloquial* squidgy, *colloquial* squishy.

mushroom /'mʌʃrʊm/ *noun* **1** edible fungus with stem and domed cap. **2** pinkish-brown colour. ● *verb* appear or develop rapidly. □ **mushroom cloud** mushroom-shaped cloud from nuclear explosion.

music /'mjuːzɪk/ *noun* **1** art of combining vocal or instrumental sounds in harmonious or expressive way. **2** sounds so produced. **3** musical composition. **4** written or printed score of this. **5** pleasant sound. □ **music centre** equipment combining radio, record player, tape recorder, etc. **music hall 1** variety entertainment. **2** theatre for this.

■ **5** euphony, harmony.

musical *adjective* **1** of music. **2** (of sounds) melodious, harmonious. **3** fond of or skilled in music. **4** set to or accompanied by music. ● *noun* musical film or play. □ **musicality** /-'kæl-/ *noun*. **musically** *adverb*.

■ *adjective* **2** euphonious, harmonious, lyrical, melodious, pleasant, sweet-sounding, tuneful.

musician /mjuː'zɪʃ(ə)n/ *noun* person skilled in practice of music, esp. professional instrumentalist. □ **musicianship** *noun*.

■ artist, instrumentalist, maestro, minstrel, music-maker, performer, player, virtuoso.

musicology /mjuːzɪ'kɒlədʒɪ/ *noun* study of history and forms of music. □ **musicological** /-kə'lɒdʒ-/ *adjective*. **musicologist** *noun*.

musk *noun* **1** substance secreted by male musk deer and used in perfumes. **2** plant which originally had smell of musk. □ **musk deer** small hornless Asian deer. **muskrat 1** large N. American aquatic rodent with smell like musk. **2** its fur. **musk-rose** rambling rose smelling of musk. □ **musky** *adjective* (**-ier**, **-iest**).

musket /'mʌskɪt/ *noun historical* infantryman's (esp. smooth-bored) light gun.

musketeer /mʌskə'tɪə/ *noun historical* soldier armed with musket.

musketry /'mʌskɪtrɪ/ *noun* **1** muskets. **2** soldiers armed with muskets. **3** knowledge of handling small arms.

Muslim /'mʊzlɪm/ (also **Moslem** /'mɒzləm/) *noun* follower of Islamic religion. ● *adjective* of Muslims or their religion.

muslin /'mʌzlɪn/ *noun* fine delicately woven cotton fabric.

musquash /'mʌskwɒʃ/ *noun* **1** muskrat. **2** its fur.

mussel /'mʌs(ə)l/ *noun* edible bivalve mollusc.

must[1] *auxiliary verb* (*3rd singular present* **must**; *past* **had to**) **1** be obliged to. **2** be certain to. **3** ought to. ● *noun colloquial* thing that should not be missed.

USAGE The negative *I must not go* means 'I am not allowed to go'. To express a lack of obligation, use *I am not obliged to go, I need not go, I don't have to go*, or *I haven't got to go*.

must² *noun* grape juice before fermentation is complete.

mustache *US* = MOUSTACHE.

mustang /ˈmʌstæŋ/ *noun* small wild horse of Mexico and California.

mustard /ˈmʌstəd/ *noun* **1** plant with yellow flowers. **2** seeds of this crushed into paste and used as spicy condiment. □ **mustard gas** colourless oily liquid whose vapour is powerful irritant.

muster /ˈmʌstə/ *verb* **1** collect (originally soldiers). **2** come together. **3** summon (courage etc.). ● *noun* assembly of people for inspection. □ **pass muster** be accepted as adequate.
  ■ *verb* **1, 2** assemble, call together, collect, come together, convene, convoke, gather, get together, group, marshal, mobilize, rally, round up, summon. **3** gather, marshal, summon.

mustn't /ˈmʌs(ə)nt/ must not.

musty /ˈmʌstɪ/ *adjective* (**-ier, -iest**) **1** mouldy, stale. **2** dull, antiquated. □ **mustiness** *noun*.
  ■ **1** airless, damp, dank, fusty, mildewed, mouldy, smelly, stale, stuffy, unventilated.

mutable /ˈmjuːtəb(ə)l/ *adjective literary* liable to change. □ **mutability** *noun*.

mutant /ˈmjuːt(ə)nt/ *adjective* resulting from mutation. ● *noun* mutant organism or gene.
  ■ *noun* abortion, anomaly, deviant, freak, monster, monstrosity, variant.

mutate /mjuːˈteɪt/ (cause to) undergo mutation.

mutation *noun* **1** change. **2** genetic change which when transmitted to offspring gives rise to heritable variations.
  ■ alteration, change, deviance, evolution, metamorphosis, modification, transfiguration, transformation, transmutation, variation.

mute /mjuːt/ *adjective* **1** silent; refraining from or temporarily bereft of speech. **2** dumb. **3** soundless. ● *noun* **1** dumb person. **2** device for damping sound of musical instrument. ● *verb* (**-ting**) **1** muffle or deaden sound of. **2** (as **muted** *adjective*) (of colours etc.) subdued. □ **mute swan** common white swan. □ **mutely** *adverb*. **muteness** *noun*.
  ■ *adjective* **1, 2** dumb, quiet, silent, speechless, tacit, taciturn, tight-lipped, tongue-tied, voiceless. ● *verb* **1** damp, deaden, dull, hush, mask, muffle, quieten, silence, soften, stifle, still, suppress, tone down. **2** (**muted**) faint, pale, pastel, soft, subdued, toned down, unobtrusive.

mutilate /ˈmjuːtɪleɪt/ *verb* (**-ting**) **1** deprive (person, animal) of limb etc. **2** destroy usefulness of (limb etc.). **3** excise or damage part of (book etc.). □ **mutilation** *noun*.
  ■ **1, 2** cripple, damage, disable, disfigure, dismember, injure, lame, maim, mangle, wound. **3** damage, deface, expurgate, hack, mar, ruin, spoil, vandalize.

mutineer /mjuːtɪˈnɪə/ *noun* person who mutinies.

mutinous /ˈmjuːtɪnəs/ *adjective* rebellious.
  ■ defiant, disobedient, insubordinate, insurgent, insurrectionary, rebellious, refractory, revolutionary, seditious, subversive, ungovernable, unmanageable, unruly.

mutiny /ˈmjuːtɪnɪ/ *noun* (*plural* **-ies**) open revolt, esp. by soldiers or sailors against officers. ● *verb* (**-ies, -ied**) engage in mutiny.
  ■ *noun* defiance, disobedience, insubordination, insurgency, insurrection, rebellion, revolt, revolution, sedition, subversion, unruliness, uprising. ● *verb* agitate, disobey, rebel, revolt, rise up, strike.

mutt *noun slang* stupid person.

mutter /ˈmʌtə/ *verb* **1** speak in barely audible manner. **2** (often + *against, at*) grumble. ● *noun* **1** muttered words etc. **2** muttering.
  ■ *verb* **1** drone, mumble, murmur, speak in an undertone, whisper. **2** see GRUMBLE *verb* 1.

mutton /ˈmʌt(ə)n/ *noun* flesh of sheep as food.

mutual /ˈmjuːtʃʊəl/ *adjective* **1** (of feelings, actions, etc.) experienced or done by each of two or more parties to the other(s). **2** *colloquial disputed* common to two or more people. **3** having same (specified) relationship to each other. □ **mutuality** /-ˈæl-/ *noun*. **mutually** *adverb*.

USAGE The use of *mutual* to mean 'common to two or more people' is considered incorrect by some people, who use *common* instead.
  ■ **1** interactive, reciprocal, reciprocated, requited. **2** common, joint, shared. **3** reciprocal.

muzzle /ˈmʌz(ə)l/ *noun* **1** projecting part of animal's face, including nose and mouth. **2** guard put over animal's nose and mouth. **3** open end of firearm. ● *verb* (**-ling**) **1** put muzzle on. **2** impose silence on.
  ■ *noun* **1** jaws, mouth, nose, snout. ● *verb* **2** censor, gag, restrain, silence, stifle, suppress.

muzzy /ˈmʌzɪ/ *adjective* (**-ier, -iest**) **1** confused, dazed. **2** blurred, indistinct. □ **muzzily** *adverb*.

MW *abbreviation* **1** megawatt(s). **2** medium wave.

my /maɪ/ *adjective* of or belonging to me.

mycology /maɪˈkɒlədʒɪ/ *noun* **1** study of fungi. **2** fungi of particular region.

mynah /ˈmaɪnə/ *noun* (also **myna**) talking bird of starling family.

myopia /maɪˈəʊpɪə/ *noun* **1** short-sightedness. **2** lack of imagination. □ **myopic** /-ˈɒp-/ *adjective*.

myriad /ˈmɪrɪəd/ *literary noun* indefinitely great number. ● *adjective* innumerable.

myrrh /mɜː/ *noun* gum resin used in perfume, medicine, incense, etc.

myrtle /ˈmɜːt(ə)l/ *noun* evergreen shrub with shiny leaves and white scented flowers.

myself /maɪˈself/ *pronoun* **1** *emphatic form of* I² *or* ME¹. **2** *reflexive form of* ME¹.

mysterious /mɪsˈtɪərɪəs/ *adjective* full of or

wrapped in mystery. □ **mysteriously** *adverb*.
mysteriousness *noun*.

■ arcane, baffling, bewildering, bizarre, confusing, cryptic, curious, dark, enigmatic, incomprehensible, inexplicable, inscrutable, insoluble, magical, miraculous, mystical, mystifying, obscure, perplexing, puzzling, recondite, secret, strange, uncanny, unexplained, unfathomable, unknown, weird.

mystery /ˈmɪstərɪ/ *noun* (*plural* -ies) **1** hidden or inexplicable matter. **2** secrecy, obscurity. **3** fictional work dealing with puzzling event, esp. murder. **4** religious truth divinely revealed. **5** (in *plural*) secret ancient religious rites. □ **mystery play** miracle play. **mystery tour** pleasure trip to unspecified destination.

■ **1** conundrum, enigma, problem, puzzle, question, riddle, secret.

mystic /ˈmɪstɪk/ *noun* person who seeks unity with deity through contemplation etc., or believes in spiritual apprehension of truths beyond understanding. □ **mysticism** /-sɪz(ə)m/ *noun*.

mystical *adjective* **1** of mystics or mysticism. **2** of hidden meaning. **3** spiritually symbolic.

■ arcane, esoteric, metaphysical, mysterious, occult, other-worldly, preternatural, religious, spiritual, supernatural, symbolic.

mystify /ˈmɪstɪfaɪ/ *verb* (-ies, -ied) bewilder, confuse. □ **mystification** *noun*.

■ baffle, *colloquial* bamboozle, beat, bewilder, confound, confuse, *colloquial* flummox, fool, hoax, perplex, puzzle, stump.

mystique /mɪsˈtiːk/ *noun* atmosphere of mystery and veneration attending some activity, person, profession, etc.

myth /mɪθ/ *noun* **1** traditional story usually involving supernatural or imaginary people and embodying popular ideas on natural or social phenomena. **2** such stories collectively. **3** widely held but false idea. **4** fictitious person, thing, or idea. □ **mythic** *adjective*. **mythical** *adjective*.

■ **1, 2** allegory, fable, legend, mythology. **4** fabrication, falsehood, fiction, invention, pretence, untruth. □ **mythic, mythical** allegorical, fabled, fabulous, fanciful, fictional, imaginary, invented, legendary, make-believe, mythological, non-existent, poetic, pretended, symbolic, unreal.

mythology /mɪˈθɒlədʒɪ/ *noun* (*plural* -ies) body or study of myths. □ **mythological** /-θəˈlɒdʒ-/ *adjective*. **mythologize** *verb* (also -ise) (-zing or -sing).

myxomatosis /mɪksəməˈtəʊsɪs/ *noun* viral disease of rabbits.

Nn

N. *abbreviation* (also **N**) north(ern).

n *noun* indefinite number.

n. *abbreviation* (also **n**) **1** noun. **2** neuter.

NAAFI /'næfɪ/ *abbreviation* Navy, Army, and Air Force Institutes (canteen or shop for servicemen).

nab *verb* (**-bb-**) *slang* **1** arrest; catch in wrongdoing. **2** grab.

nacre /'neɪkə/ *noun* mother-of-pearl from any shelled mollusc. □ **nacreous** /'neɪkrɪəs/ *adjective*.

nadir /'neɪdɪə/ *noun* **1** point on celestial sphere directly below observer. **2** lowest point. **3** time of despair.
■ **2** bottom, depths, low point.

naff *adjective slang* **1** unfashionable. **2** rubbishy.

nag[1] *verb* (**-gg-**) **1** persistently criticize or scold. **2** (often + *at*) find fault or urge, esp. continually. **3** (of pain) be persistent.
■ **1, 2** annoy, badger, chivvy, find fault with, goad, *colloquial* go on at, harass, hector, henpeck, pester, *colloquial* plague, scold, worry.

nag[2] *noun colloquial* horse.

naiad /'naɪæd/ *noun* water nymph.

nail *noun* **1** small metal spike hammered in to fasten things. **2** horny covering on upper surface of tip of human finger or toe. ● *verb* **1** fasten with nail(s). **2** fix or hold tight. **3** secure, catch (person, thing).
■ *noun* **1** pin, spike, stud, tack. ● *verb* **1** see FASTEN 1.

naive /naɪ'iːv/ *adjective* (also **naïve**) **1** innocent; unaffected. **2** foolishly credulous. □ **naively** *adverb*. **naivety** *noun*.
■ artless, candid, childlike, credulous, green, guileless, gullible, inexperienced, ingenuous, innocent, open, simple, simple-minded, stupid, trustful, trusting, unsophisticated, unsuspecting, unwary.

naked /'neɪkɪd/ *adjective* **1** unclothed, nude. **2** without usual covering. **3** undisguised. **4** (of light, flame, sword, etc.) unprotected. □ **nakedly** *adverb*. **nakedness** *noun*.
■ **1** bare, *literary* disrobed, exposed, in the nude, nude, *slang* starkers, stark naked, stripped, unclad, unclothed, undraped, undressed. **2** bare, denuded, exposed, stripped, unconcealed, uncovered. **3** bare, open, plain, unadorned, unconcealed, undisguised.

namby-pamby /næmbɪ'pæmbɪ/ *adjective* **1** insipidly pretty or sentimental. **2** weak. ● *noun* (*plural* **-ies**) namby-pamby person.

name *noun* **1** word by which individual person, animal, place, or thing is spoken of etc. **2** (usually abusive) term used of person. **3** word denoting object or class of objects. **4** reputation, esp. good. ● *verb* (**-ming**) **1** give name to. **2** state name of. **3** mention; specify; cite. **4** nominate. □ **in name or name only** as mere formality; hardly at all. **name-day** feast-day of saint after whom person is named. **namesake** person or thing having same name as another. □ **nameable** *adjective*. **named** *adjective*.
■ *noun* **1** alias, *formal* appellation, Christian name, first name, forename, given name, identity, nickname, *nom de plume*, pen-name, pseudonym, sobriquet, surname, title. **3** denomination, designation, epithet, term. ● *verb* **1** baptize, call, christen, dub, entitle, label, style. **3** see SPECIFY. **4** appoint, choose, commission, delegate, designate, elect, nominate, select, single out, specify. □ **named** see SPECIFIC *adjective* 1,3.

nameless *adjective* **1** having, or showing, no name. **2** left unnamed. **3** too horrible to be named.
■ **1, 2** anonymous, incognito, unheard-of, unidentified, unnamed, unsung. **3** dreadful, horrible, indescribable, inexpressible, shocking, unmentionable, unspeakable, unutterable.

namely *adverb* that is to say; in other words.

nanny /'nænɪ/ *noun* (*plural* **-ies**) **1** child's nurse. **2** *colloquial* grandmother. **3** (in full **nanny goat**) female goat.

nano- /'nænəʊ/ *combining form* one thousand millionth.

nap[1] *noun* short sleep, esp. by day. ● *verb* (**-pp-**) have nap.
■ *noun* catnap, doze, *colloquial* forty winks, rest, *colloquial* shut-eye, siesta, sleep, *colloquial* snooze.

nap[2] *noun* raised pile on cloth, esp. velvet.

nap[3] *noun* **1** card game. **2** racing tip claimed to be almost a certainty. ● *verb* (**-pp-**) name (horse) as probable winner. □ **go nap 1** try to take all 5 tricks in nap. **2** risk everything.

napalm /'neɪpɑːm/ *noun* thick jellied hydrocarbon mixture used in bombs.

nape *noun* back of neck.

naphtha /'næfθə/ *noun* inflammable hydrocarbon distilled from coal etc.

naphthalene /'næfθəliːn/ *noun* white crystalline substance produced by distilling tar.

napkin /'næpkɪn/ *noun* **1** piece of linen etc. for wiping lips, fingers, etc. at table. **2** baby's nappy.

nappy /'næpɪ/ *noun* (*plural* **-ies**) piece of towelling etc. wrapped round baby to absorb urine and faeces.

narcissism /'nɑːsɪsɪz(ə)m/ *noun* excessive or erotic interest in oneself. ◻ **narcissistic** /-'sɪstɪk/ *adjective*.

narcissus /nɑː'sɪsəs/ *noun* (*plural* -**cissi** /-saɪ/) any of several flowering bulbs, including daffodil.

narcosis /nɑː'kəʊsɪs/ *noun* **1** unconsciousness. **2** induction of this.

narcotic /nɑː'kɒtɪk/ *adjective* **1** (of substance) inducing drowsiness etc. **2** (of drug) affecting the mind. ● *noun* narcotic substance or drug.

nark *slang noun* police informer. ● *verb* annoy.

narrate /nə'reɪt/ *verb* (-**ting**) **1** give continuous story or account of. **2** provide spoken accompaniment for (film etc.). ◻ **narration** *noun*. **narrator** *noun*.

■ **1** chronicle, describe, detail, recount, rehearse, relate, repeat, report, retail, tell, unfold. ◻ **narration** commentary, reading, recital, recitation, relation, storytelling, telling, voice-over. **narrator** chronicler, commentator, raconteur, reporter, storyteller.

narrative /'nærətɪv/ *noun* ordered account of connected events. ● *adjective* of or by narration. ■ *noun* account, chronicle, description, history, report, story, tale, *colloquial* yarn.

narrow /'nærəʊ/ *adjective* (-**er**, -**est**) **1** of small width. **2** constricted. **3** restricted; of limited scope. **4** with little margin. **5** precise; exact. **6** narrow-minded. ● *noun* (usually in *plural*) narrow part of strait, river, pass, etc. ● *verb* (often + *down*) become or make narrower; contract; lessen. ◻ **narrow boat** canal boat. **narrow-minded** rigid or restricted in one's views; intolerant. **narrow-mindedness** *noun*. ◻ **narrowly** *adverb*. **narrowness** *noun*.

■ *adjective* **1** attenuated, fine, slender, slim, thin. **2** close, confined, constricted, constricting, cramped, enclosed, tight. **3** circumscribed, limited, restricted. **4** close, near. ◻ **narrow-minded** biased, bigoted, conservative, conventional, hidebound, illiberal, inflexible, insular, intolerant, narrow, old-fashioned, parochial, petty, prejudiced, prim, prudish, puritanical, reactionary, rigid, small-minded, strait-laced, stuffy.

narwhal /'nɑːw(ə)l/ *noun* Arctic white whale, male of which has long tusk.

nasal /'neɪz(ə)l/ *adjective* **1** of nose. **2** (of letter or sound) pronounced with breath passing through nose, e.g. *m*, *n*, *ng*. **3** (of voice etc.) having many nasal sounds. ● *noun* nasal letter or sound. ◻ **nasally** *adverb*.

nascent /'næs(ə)nt/ *adjective* **1** in act of being born. **2** just beginning to be. ◻ **nascency** /-ənsɪ/ *noun*.

nasturtium /nə'stɜːʃəm/ *noun* trailing garden plant with edible leaves and bright orange, red, or yellow flowers.

nasty /'nɑːstɪ/ *adjective* (-**ier**, -**iest**) **1** unpleasant. **2** difficult to negotiate. **3** (of illness) serious, dan-

gerous. **4** (of person or animal) ill-natured, spiteful. ● *noun* (*plural* -**ies**) *colloquial* violent horror film, esp. on video. ◻ **nastily** *adverb*. **nastiness** *noun*.

■ *adjective* **1** bad, *colloquial* beastly, dirty, disagreeable, disgusting, distasteful, foul, hateful, *colloquial* horrible, loathsome, *colloquial* lousy, nauseating, objectionable, obnoxious, obscene, offensive, off-putting, repulsive, revolting, *colloquial* shocking, sickening, unkind, unpalatable, unpleasant, unsavoury, vile. **2** bad, dangerous, difficult, hard, problematical, tricky. **3** see SERIOUS **3**. **4** see SPITEFUL.

Nat. *abbreviation* National(ist).

natal /'neɪt(ə)l/ *adjective* of or from birth.

nation /'neɪʃ(ə)n/ *noun* community of people having mainly common descent, history, language, etc., forming state or inhabiting territory. ◻ **nationwide** extending over whole nation.

■ country, domain, land, people, population, power, race, *formal* realm, state, superpower.

national /'næʃən(ə)l/ *adjective* **1** of nation. **2** characteristic of particular nation. ● *noun* citizen of specified country. ◻ **national anthem** song adopted by nation, intended to inspire patriotism. **national grid** network of high-voltage electric power lines between major power stations. **National Insurance** system of compulsory payments from employee and employer to provide state assistance in sickness, retirement, etc. **national service** *historical* conscripted peacetime military service. ◻ **nationally** *adverb*.

■ *adjective* **1** country-wide, general, nationwide, state, widespread. **2** ethnic, racial. ● *noun* citizen, inhabitant, native, resident, subject.

nationalism *noun* **1** patriotic feeling, principles, etc. **2** policy of national independence. ◻ **nationalist** *noun*. **nationalistic** /-'lɪs-/ *adjective*.

■ **1** chauvinism, jingoism, loyalty, patriotism.

nationality /næʃə'nælɪtɪ/ *noun* (*plural* -**ies**) **1** membership of nation. **2** being national. **3** ethnic group within one or more political nations.

nationalize /'næʃənəlaɪz/ *verb* (also -**ise**) (-**zing** or -**sing**) **1** take (industry etc.) into state ownership. **2** make national. ◻ **nationalization** *noun*.

native /'neɪtɪv/ *noun* **1** (usually + *of*) person born in specified place. **2** local inhabitant. **3** indigenous animal or plant. ● *adjective* **1** inherent; innate. **2** of one's birth. **3** (usually + *to*) belonging to specified place. **4** born in a place.

■ *noun* **1, 2** aboriginal, local, national. ● *adjective* **1** congenital, hereditary, inborn, inbred, inherent, inherited, innate, natural. **4** aboriginal, indigenous, local, original.

nativity /nə'tɪvɪtɪ/ *noun* (*plural* -**ies**) **1** (esp. **the Nativity**) Christ's birth. **2** birth.

NATO /'neɪtəʊ/ *abbreviation* (also **Nato**) North Atlantic Treaty Organization.

natter /'nætə/ *colloquial verb* chatter idly. ● *noun* aimless chatter.

natty /'nætɪ/ *adjective* (**-ier, -iest**) *colloquial* trim; smart.

natural /'nætʃər(ə)l/ *adjective* **1** existing in or caused by nature; unprocessed; not artificial. **2** not surprising; to be expected. **3** unaffected. **4** innate. **5** (of person) having certain innate quality. **6** physically existing. **7** related genetically; illegitimate. **8** *Music* not flat or sharp. ● *noun* **1** (usually + *for*) *colloquial* person or thing naturally suitable, adept, etc. **2** *Music* sign (♮) showing return to natural pitch; natural note. □ **natural gas** gas found in earth's crust. **natural history** study of animals and plants. **natural number** whole number greater than 0. **natural selection** process favouring survival of organisms best adapted to environment.

■ *adjective* **1** crude (*oil*), raw, unadulterated, unprocessed, unrefined. **2** common, everyday, habitual, normal, ordinary, predictable, regular, routine, standard, typical, usual. **3** artless, candid, genuine, guileless, sincere, spontaneous, unaffected, unpretentious, unselfconscious, unstudied. **4** hereditary, inborn, inherited, innate, instinctive, intuitive, native. **5** born, congenital, untaught.

naturalism *noun* **1** realistic representation in art and literature. **2** philosophy based on nature alone. □ **naturalistic** /-'lɪs-/ *adjective*.

naturalist *noun* student of natural history.

naturalize *verb* (also **-ise**) (**-zing** or **-sing**) **1** admit (foreigner) to citizenship. **2** introduce (plant etc.) into another region. **3** adopt (foreign word, custom, etc.). □ **naturalization** *noun*.

naturally *adverb* **1** in a natural way. **2** as might be expected; of course.

nature /'neɪtʃə/ *noun* **1** thing's or person's essential qualities or character. **2** physical power causing material phenomena. **3** these phenomena. **4** kind, class. □ **nature reserve** tract of land managed so as to preserve its flora and fauna.

■ **1** attributes, character, constitution, disposition, essence, humour, make-up, manner, personality, properties, quality, temperament, traits. **2, 3** countryside, creation, ecology, environment, natural history, scenery, wildlife. **4** category, class, description, kind, sort, species, type, variety.

naturism *noun* nudism. □ **naturist** *noun*.

naught /nɔːt/ *archaic noun* nothing. ● *adjective* worthless.

naughty /'nɔːtɪ/ *adjective* (**-ier, -iest**) **1** (esp. of children) disobedient; badly behaved. **2** *colloquial jocular* indecent. □ **naughtily** *adverb*. **naughtiness** *noun*.

■ **1** bad, bad-mannered, boisterous, contrary, defiant, delinquent, disobedient, disorderly, disruptive, fractious, headstrong, impish, impolite, incorrigible, insubordinate, intractable, misbehaved, mischievous, obstinate, obstreperous, perverse, playful, puckish, rascally, rebellious, refractory, roguish, rude, self-willed, stubborn, troublesome, uncontrollable, undisciplined, ungovernable, unmanageable,

unruly, wayward, wicked, wild, wilful. **2** cheeky, improper, indecent, obscene, ribald, risqué, *colloquial* rude, shocking, smutty, vulgar.

nausea /'nɔːsɪə/ *noun* **1** inclination to vomit. **2** revulsion.

nauseate /'nɔːsɪeɪt/ *verb* (**-ting**) affect with nausea. □ **nauseating** *adjective*.

■ disgust, offend, repel, revolt, sicken.

nauseous /'nɔːsɪəs/ *adjective* **1** causing nausea. **2** inclined to vomit. **3** disgusting.

■ **1, 3** disgusting, foul, loathsome, nauseating, offensive, repulsive, revolting, sickening, stomach-turning.

nautical /'nɔːtɪk(ə)l/ *adjective* of sailors or navigation. □ **nautical mile** unit of approx. 2,025 yards (1,852 metres).

■ marine, maritime, naval, seafaring, seagoing, yachting.

nautilus /'nɔːtɪləs/ *noun* (*plural* **nautiluses** or **nautili** /-laɪ/) kind of mollusc with spiral shell.

naval /'neɪv(ə)l/ *adjective* **1** of navy. **2** of ships.

nave[1] *noun* central part of church excluding chancel and side aisles.

nave[2] *noun* hub of wheel.

navel /'neɪv(ə)l/ *noun* depression in belly marking site of attachment of umbilical cord. □ **navel orange** one with navel-like formation at top.

navigable /'nævɪɡəb(ə)l/ *adjective* **1** (of river etc.) suitable for ships. **2** seaworthy. **3** steerable. □ **navigability** *noun*.

navigate /'nævɪɡeɪt/ *verb* (**-ting**) **1** manage or direct course of (ship, aircraft). **2** sail on (sea, river, etc.). **3** fly through (air). **4** help car-driver etc. by map-reading etc. □ **navigator** *noun*.

■ **1** captain, direct, drive, guide, handle, manoeuvre, pilot, sail, skipper, steer.

navigation *noun* **1** act or process of navigating. **2** art or science of navigating.

navvy /'nævɪ/ *noun* (*plural* **-ies**) labourer employed in building roads, canals, etc.

navy /'neɪvɪ/ *noun* (*plural* **-ies**) **1** state's warships with their crews, maintenance systems, etc. **2** (in full **navy blue**) dark blue colour.

nay *adverb* **1** or rather; and even. **2** *archaic* no. ● *noun* 'no' vote.

Nazi /'nɑːtsɪ/ *noun* (*plural* **-s**) *historical* member of German National Socialist party. ● *adjective* of Nazis or Nazism. □ **Nazism** *noun*.

NB *abbreviation* note well (*nota bene*).

NCB *abbreviation historical* National Coal Board.

NCO *abbreviation* non-commissioned officer.

NE *abbreviation* north-east(ern).

Neanderthal /nɪ'ændətɑːl/ *adjective* of type of human found in palaeolithic Europe.

neap *noun* (in full **neap tide**) tide with smallest rise and fall.

Neapolitan /nɪə'pɒlɪt(ə)n/ *noun* native of Naples. ● *adjective* of Naples.

near /nɪə/ *adverb* 1 (often + *to*) to or at short distance in space or time. 2 closely. ● *preposition* to or at a short distance from in space, time, condition, or resemblance. ● *adjective* 1 close (to); not far in place or time. 2 closely related. 3 (of part of vehicle, animal, or road) on left side. 4 *colloquial* stingy. 5 with little margin. ● *verb* approach; draw near to. □ **the Near East** countries of eastern Mediterranean. **nearest and dearest** one's closest relatives and friends collectively. **near-sighted** short-sighted. □ **nearness** *noun*.

■ *adjective* 1 *near in place* abutting, adjacent, adjoining, bordering, close, connected, contiguous, immediate, nearby, neighbouring, next door; *near in time* approaching, coming, forthcoming, imminent, impending, looming. 2 close, familiar, intimate, related.

nearby *adjective* near in position. ● *adverb* close.

nearly *adverb* 1 almost. 2 closely. □ **not nearly** nothing like; far from.

■ 1 about, all but, almost, approaching, approximately, around, as good as, close to, just about, not quite, practically, roughly, virtually.

neat *adjective* 1 tidy, methodical. 2 elegantly simple. 3 brief and clear. 4 cleverly done. 5 dexterous. 6 (of alcoholic liquor) undiluted. □ **neaten** *verb*. **neatly** *adverb*. **neatness** *noun*.

■ 1 clean, methodical, meticulous, *colloquial* natty, orderly, organized, shipshape, smart, spick and span, spruce, straight, systematic, tidy, trim, uncluttered, well kept. 2 elegant, simple, smart. 3 see SUCCINCT. 4, 5 adroit, clever, deft, dexterous, expert, ingenious, *colloquial* nifty, skilful. 6 pure, straight, unadulterated, undiluted.

neath *preposition poetical* beneath.

nebula /'nebjʊlə/ *noun* (*plural* **nebulae** /-liː/) cloud of gas and dust seen in night sky, appearing luminous or as dark silhouette. □ **nebular** *adjective*.

nebulous /'nebjʊləs/ *adjective* 1 cloudlike. 2 indistinct, vague.

necessary /'nesəsərɪ/ *adjective* 1 requiring to be done; essential. 2 inevitable. ● *noun* (*plural* **-ies**) (usually in *plural*) any of basic requirements of life. □ **necessarily** *adverb*.

■ *adjective* 1 compulsory, essential, imperative, important, indispensable, mandatory, needed, needful, obligatory, required, requisite, vital. 2 destined, fated, ineluctable, inescapable, inevitable, inexorable, predestined, unavoidable.

necessitate /nɪ'sesɪteɪt/ *verb* (**-ting**) make necessary (esp. as result).

necessitous /nɪ'sesɪtəs/ *adjective* poor, needy.

necessity /nɪ'sesɪtɪ/ *noun* (*plural* **-ies**) 1 indispensable thing. 2 pressure of circumstances. 3 imperative need. 4 poverty. 5 constraint or compulsion seen as natural law governing human action.

■ 1 essential, *colloquial* must, need, prerequisite, requirement, requisite, *sine qua non*. 3 demand, need, requirement, want. 4 beggary, destitution, hardship, indigence, need, penury, poverty, privation, shortage, suffering, want. 5 compulsion, inevitability, obligation.

neck *noun* 1 part of body connecting head to shoulders. 2 part of garment round neck. 3 narrow part of anything. ● *verb colloquial* kiss and caress amorously. □ **neck and neck** running level in a race etc. **neckline** outline of garment-opening at neck. **necktie** strip of material worn round shirt-collar, knotted at front.

necklace /'nekləs/ *noun* 1 string of beads, precious stones, etc. worn round neck. 2 *South African* petrol-soaked tyre placed round victim's neck and lighted.

necromancy /'nekrəʊmænsɪ/ *noun* 1 divination by supposed communication with the dead. 2 magic. □ **necromancer** *noun*. **necromantic** /-'mæntɪk/ *adjective*.

necrophilia /nekrə'fɪlɪə/ *noun* morbid esp. sexual attraction to corpses.

necropolis /ne'krɒpəlɪs/ *noun* ancient cemetery.

necrosis /ne'krəʊsɪs/ *noun* death of tissue. □ **necrotic** /-'krɒt-/ *adjective*.

nectar /'nektə/ *noun* 1 sugary substance produced by plants and made into honey by bees. 2 *Mythology* drink of gods.

nectarine /'nektərɪn/ *noun* smooth-skinned variety of peach.

NEDC *abbreviation historical* National Economic Development Council.

née /neɪ/ *adjective* (*US* **nee**) (before married woman's maiden name) born.

need *verb* 1 stand in want of; require. 2 (usually + *to do*) be under necessity or obligation. ● *noun* 1 requirement. 2 circumstances requiring action. 3 destitution, poverty. 4 emergency.

■ *verb* 1 be short of, call for, crave, demand, depend on, lack, miss, rely on, require, want. ● *noun* 1, 2 call, demand, lack, necessity, requirement, want. 3 see NECESSITY 4.

needful *adjective* requisite.

needle /'niːd(ə)l/ *noun* 1 very thin pointed rod with slit ('eye') for thread, used in sewing. 2 knitting-needle. 3 pointer on dial. 4 any small thin pointed instrument, esp. end of hypodermic syringe. 5 obelisk. 6 pointed rock or peak. 7 leaf of fir or pine. ● *verb* (**-ling**) *colloquial* annoy, provoke. □ **needlecord** fine-ribbed corduroy fabric. **needlework** sewing or embroidery.

needless *adjective* unnecessary. □ **needlessly** *adverb*.

■ excessive, gratuitous, pointless, redundant, superfluous, unnecessary.

needy *adjective* (**-ier, -iest**) poor, destitute.

■ badly off, destitute, hard up, impecunious, impoverished, *formal* indigent, necessitous, penurious, poor, poverty-stricken, underpaid.

ne'er /neə/ *adverb poetical* never. □ **ne'er-do-well** good-for-nothing person.

nefarious /nɪ'feərɪəs/ *adjective* wicked.

negate /nɪ'geɪt/ *verb* (**-ting**) **1** nullify. **2** deny existence of.
 ■ **1** annul, cancel out, invalidate, negative, neutralize, nullify. **2** deny, disprove, gainsay, oppose.

negation *noun* **1** absence or opposite of something positive. **2** act of denying. **3** negative statement. **4** negative or unreal thing.

negative /'negətɪv/ *adjective* **1** expressing or implying denial, prohibition, or refusal. **2** lacking positive attributes; opposite to positive. **3** (of quantity) less than zero; to be subtracted. **4** *Electricity* of, containing, or producing, kind of charge carried by electrons. ● *noun* **1** negative statement or word. **2** *Photography* image with black and white reversed or colours replaced by complementary ones. ● *verb* (**-ving**) **1** refuse to accept; veto. **2** disprove. **3** contradict. **4** neutralize. □ **negatively** *adverb*. **negativeness** *noun*.
 ■ *adjective* **1** contradictory, disagreeing, dissenting, nullifying, opposing. **2** adversarial, antagonistic, destructive, grudging, obstructive, pessimistic, uncooperative, unenthusiastic, unresponsive, unwilling. ● *noun* **1** denial, no, refusal, rejection, veto.

neglect /nɪ'glekt/ *verb* **1** fail to care for or do. **2** (+ *to do*) fail to. **3** pay no attention to; disregard. ● *noun* **1** negligence. **2** neglecting, being neglected. □ **neglectful** *adjective*. **neglectfully** *adverb*.
 ■ *verb* **1** abandon, be remiss about, forget, leave alone, lose sight of, miss, omit, overlook, shirk, skip. **2** fail, forget, omit. **3** disregard, forget, ignore, overlook. ● *noun* carelessness, dereliction, disregard, inadvertence, inattention, indifference, negligence, oversight, slackness.

negligée /'neglɪʒeɪ/ *noun* (also **négligé**) woman's flimsy dressing gown.

negligence /'neglɪdʒ(ə)ns/ *noun* **1** lack of proper care or attention. **2** culpable carelessness. □ **negligent** *adjective*. **negligently** *adverb*.
 ■ □ **negligent** careless, forgetful, heedless, inattentive, inconsiderate, indifferent, irresponsible, lax, offhand, reckless, remiss, slack, sloppy, slovenly, thoughtless, uncaring, unthinking.

negligible /'neglɪdʒɪb(ə)l/ *adjective* not worth considering; insignificant.
 ■ imperceptible, inconsequential, inconsiderable, insignificant, minor, nugatory, paltry, petty, slight, small, tiny, trifling, trivial, unimportant.

negotiate /nɪ'gəʊʃɪeɪt/ *verb* (**-ting**) **1** confer in order to reach agreement. **2** obtain (result) by negotiating. **3** deal successfully with (obstacle etc.). **4** convert (cheque etc.) into money. □ **negotiable** /-ʃəb-/ *adjective*. **negotiation** *noun*. **negotiator** *noun*.

 ■ **1** arbitrate, bargain, come to terms, confer, deal, discuss terms, haggle, make arrangements, mediate, parley. □ **negotiation** arbitration, bargaining, conciliation, debate, diplomacy, discussion, mediation, parleying, transaction. **negotiator** agent, ambassador, arbitrator, broker, conciliator, diplomat, go-between, intercessor, intermediary, mediator, middleman.

Negress /'niːgrɪs/ *noun* female Negro.

USAGE The term *Negress* is often considered offensive; *black* is usually preferred.

Negro /'niːgrəʊ/ *noun* (*plural* **-es**) member of dark-skinned (originally) African race; black. ● *adjective* of this race; black.

USAGE The term *Negro* is often considered offensive; *black* is usually preferred.

Negroid /'niːgrɔɪd/ *adjective* (of physical features etc.) characteristic of black people. ● *noun* black person.

neigh /neɪ/ *noun* cry of horse. ● *verb* make a neigh.

neighbour /'neɪbə/ (*US* **neighbor**) *noun* **1** person living next door or nearby. **2** fellow human being. ● *verb* border on; adjoin. □ **neighbouring** *adjective*.
 ■ □ **neighbouring** adjacent, adjoining, attached, bordering, close, closest, connecting, contiguous, near, nearby, nearest, next door, surrounding.

neighbourhood *noun* (*US* **neighborhood**) **1** district, vicinity. **2** people of a district.
 ■ **1** area, community, district, environs, locality, place, purlieus, quarter, region, surroundings, vicinity, zone. **2** community.

neighbourly *adjective* (*US* **neighborly**) like good neighbour; friendly, helpful. □ **neighbourliness** *noun*.
 ■ civil, considerate, friendly, helpful, kind, sociable, thoughtful, well disposed.

neither /'naɪðə/ *adjective, pronoun, & adverb* not either.

nelson /'nels(ə)n/ *noun* wrestling hold in which arm is passed under opponent's arm from behind and hand applied to neck (**half nelson**), or both arms and hands are applied (**full nelson**).

nem. con. *abbreviation* with no one dissenting (*nemine contradicente*). [Latin]

nemesis /'neməsɪs/ *noun* justice bringing deserved punishment.

neo- *combining form* **1** new. **2** new form of.

neolithic /niːə'lɪθɪk/ *adjective* of later Stone Age.

neologism /niːˈɒlədʒɪz(ə)m/ *noun* **1** new word. **2** coining of new words.

neon /'niːɒn/ *noun* inert gas giving orange glow when electricity is passed through it.

neophyte /'niːəfaɪt/ *noun* **1** new convert. **2** novice of religious order. **3** beginner.

nephew /'nefjuː/ *noun* son of one's brother or sister or of one's spouse's brother or sister.

nephritic /nɪ'frɪtɪk/ *adjective* of or in kidneys.

nephritis /nɪˈfraɪtɪs/ *noun* inflammation of kidneys.

nepotism /ˈnepətɪz(ə)m/ *noun* favouritism to relatives in conferring offices.

nereid /ˈnɪərɪd/ *noun* sea nymph.

nerve *noun* **1** fibre or bundle of fibres conveying impulses of sensation or motion between brain and other parts of body. **2** coolness in danger. **3** *colloquial* impudence. **4** (in *plural*) nervousness; mental or physical stress. ● *verb* (**-ving**) (usually **nerve oneself**) brace or prepare (oneself). □ **nerve cell** cell transmitting impulses in nerve tissue. **nerve centre 1** group of closely connected nerve cells. **2** centre of control of organization etc. **nerve-racking** stressful; frightening.

■ *noun* **2** coolness, courage, determination, firmness, fortitude, resolution, resolve, will-power.

nerveless *adjective* lacking vigour.

nervous *adjective* **1** easily upset; timid; highly strung. **2** anxious. **3** affecting the nerves. **4** (+ *of*) afraid of. □ **nervous breakdown** period of mental illness, usually after stress. **nervous system** body's network of nerves. □ **nervously** *adverb*. **nervousness** *noun*.

■ **1, 2, 4** afraid, agitated, anxious, apprehensive, disturbed, edgy, excitable, fearful, fidgety, flustered, fretful, frightened, highly-strung, ill at ease, *colloquial* in a tizzy, insecure, *colloquial* jittery, jumpy, *colloquial* nervy, neurotic, on edge, on tenterhooks, *colloquial* rattled, restive, restless, ruffled, shaky, shy, strained, tense, timid, touchy, twitchy, uneasy, unnerved, unsettled, *colloquial* uptight, worried.

nervy *adjective* (**-ier**, **-iest**) *colloquial* nervous; easily excited.

nest *noun* **1** structure or place where bird lays eggs and shelters young. **2** breeding-place, lair. **3** snug retreat, shelter. **4** brood, swarm. **5** group or set of similar objects. ● *verb* **1** use or build nest. **2** (of objects) fit one inside another. □ **nest egg** money saved up as reserve.

nestle /ˈnes(ə)l/ *verb* (**-ling**) **1** settle oneself comfortably. **2** press oneself against another in affection etc. **3** (+ *in*, *into*, etc.) push (head, shoulders, etc.) affectionately or snugly. **4** lie half hidden or embedded.

■ **1, 2** cuddle, curl up, huddle, nuzzle, snuggle.

nestling /ˈnestlɪŋ/ *noun* bird too young to leave nest.

net[1] *noun* **1** open-meshed fabric of cord, rope, etc. **2** piece of net used esp. to contain, restrain, or delimit, or to catch fish. **3** structure with net used in various games. ● *verb* (**-tt-**) **1** cover, confine, or catch with net. **2** hit (ball) into net, esp. of goal. □ **netball** game similar to basketball.

■ *noun* **1** lace, lattice-work, mesh, netting, network, web. ● *verb* **1** capture, catch, enmesh, ensnare, trammel, trap.

net[2] (also **nett**) *adjective* **1** remaining after necessary deductions. **2** (of price) not reducible. **3** (of weight) excluding packaging etc. ● *verb* (**-tt-**) gain or yield (sum) as net profit.

■ *verb* accumulate, bring in, clear, earn, gain, get, make, realize, receive, yield.

nether /ˈneðə/ *adjective* *archaic* lower. □ **netherworld** (also **nether world**) hell.

nett = NET[2].

netting *noun* meshed fabric of cord or wire.

nettle /ˈnet(ə)l/ *noun* **1** plant covered with stinging hairs. **2** plant resembling this. ● *verb* (**-ling**) irritate, provoke. □ **nettle-rash** skin eruption like nettle stings.

network *noun* **1** arrangement of intersecting horizontal and vertical lines. **2** complex system of railways etc. **3** people connected by exchange of information etc. **4** group of broadcasting stations connected for simultaneous broadcast of a programme. **5** system of interconnected computers. ● *verb* broadcast on network.

■ *noun* **1** criss-cross, grid, labyrinth, lattice, maze, mesh, net, netting, tangle, tracery, web. **2** complex, organization, system.

neural /ˈnjʊər(ə)l/ *adjective* of nerve or central nervous system.

neuralgia /njʊəˈrældʒə/ *noun* intense pain along a nerve, esp. in face or head. □ **neuralgic** *adjective*.

neuritis /njʊəˈraɪtɪs/ *noun* inflammation of nerve(s).

neuro- /ˈnjʊərəʊ/ *combining form* nerve(s).

neurology /njʊəˈrɒlədʒɪ/ *noun* study of nerve systems. □ **neurological** /-rəˈlɒdʒ-/ *adjective*. **neurologist** *noun*.

neuron /ˈnjʊərɒn/ *noun* (also **neurone** /-rəʊn/) nerve cell.

neurosis /njʊəˈrəʊsɪs/ *noun* (*plural* **-roses** /-siːz/) disturbed behaviour pattern associated with nervous distress.

■ anxiety, depression, mental condition, obsession, phobia.

neurotic /njʊəˈrɒtɪk/ *adjective* **1** caused by or relating to neurosis. **2** suffering from neurosis. **3** *colloquial* abnormally sensitive or obsessive. ● *noun* neurotic person.

■ *adjective* **2, 3** anxious, distraught, disturbed, irrational, maladjusted, nervous, obsessive, overwrought, unbalanced, unstable.

neuter /ˈnjuːtə/ *adjective* neither masculine nor feminine. ● *verb* castrate, spay.

■ *adjective* asexual, sexless. ● *verb* castrate, doctor, emasculate, geld, spay, sterilize.

neutral /ˈnjuːtr(ə)l/ *adjective* **1** supporting neither of two opposing sides; impartial. **2** vague, indeterminate. **3** (of a gear) in which engine is disconnected from driven parts. **4** (of colours) not strong or positive. **5** *Chemistry* neither acid nor alkaline. **6** *Electricity* neither positive nor negative. ● *noun* neutral state or person. □ **neutrality** /-ˈtræl-/ *noun*.

■ *adjective* **1** detached, disinterested, dispassionate, impartial, indifferent, non-aligned, non-belligerent, non-partisan, objective, unaffiliated, unaligned, unbiased, uncommitted, uninvolved, unprejudiced. **2, 4** characterless, colourless, drab, dull, indefinite, indeterminate, intermediate, neither one thing nor the other, pale, vague.

neutralize *verb* (also **-ise**) (**-zing** or **-sing**) **1** make neutral. **2** make ineffective by opposite force. □ **neutralization** *noun*.

■ **2** annul, cancel out, compensate for, counteract, counterbalance, invalidate, make up for, negate, nullify, offset, wipe out.

neutrino /njuːˈtriːnəʊ/ *noun* (*plural* **-s**) elementary particle with zero electric charge and probably zero mass.

neutron /ˈnjuːtrɒn/ *noun* elementary particle of about same mass as proton but without electric charge.

never /ˈnevə/ *adverb* **1** at no time; on no occasion; not ever. **2** not at all. **3** *colloquial* surely not. □ **the never-never** *colloquial* hire purchase.

nevermore *adverb* at no future time.

nevertheless /nevəðəˈles/ *adverb* in spite of that; notwithstanding.

new *adjective* **1** of recent origin or arrival. **2** made, discovered, acquired, or experienced for first time. **3** not used or worn. **4** renewed; reinvigorated. **5** different. **6** unfamiliar. **7** additional. □ **New Age** set of alternative beliefs replacing traditional Western culture. **newborn** recently born. **newcomer** person recently arrived. **newfangled** different from what one is used to. **new moon** moon when first seen as crescent. **New Testament** part of Bible concerned with Christ and his followers. **New World** N. and S. America. **New Year's Day, Eve** 1 Jan., 31 Dec. □ **newness** *noun*.

■ **1** advanced, contemporary, current, fashionable, fresh, just arrived, (the) latest, modern, modernistic, newfangled, recent, *colloquial often derogatory* trendy, up to date. **2** brand new, different, fresh, novel, original, revolutionary. **3** brand new, in mint condition, untried, unused, unworn. **4** changed, refreshed, reinvigorated, renewed, renovated. **5** different, other. **6** strange, unfamiliar, unheard-of, unknown, untried. **7** added, additional, extra, further, supplementary. □ **newcomer** alien, arrival, immigrant, new boy, new girl, outsider, settler, stranger.

newel /ˈnjuːəl/ *noun* **1** supporting central post of winding stairs. **2** top or bottom post of stair-rail.

newly *adverb* **1** recently. **2** afresh.

news /njuːz/ *plural noun* (usually treated as *singular*) **1** information about important or interesting recent events, esp. when published or broadcast. **2** (**the news**) broadcast report of news. □ **newsagent** seller of newspapers etc. **newscast** radio or television broadcast of news reports. **newscaster**, **newsreader** person who reads out broadcast news bulletins. **newsflash** single item of important news. **news hound** *colloquial* news reporter. **newsletter** informal printed bulletin of club etc. **newspaper** /ˈnjuːs-/ printed publication of loose folded sheets with news etc. **newspaperman**, **newspaperwoman** journalist. **newsprint** low-quality paper for printing newspapers. **newsreel** short cinema film of recent events. **newsroom** room where news is prepared for publication or broadcasting. **newsworthy** topical; worth reporting as news.

■ **1** account, advice, announcement, bulletin, communication, communiqué, dispatch, headlines, information, intelligence, the latest, message, newsletter, notice, press release, proclamation, report, rumour, statement, *archaic* or *jocular* tidings, word. **2** bulletin, newscast, newsflash, newsreel. □ **newspaper** *colloquial* daily, gazette, journal, paper, periodical, *derogatory* rag, tabloid.

newsy *adjective* (**-ier**, **-iest**) *colloquial* full of news.

newt /njuːt/ *noun* small tailed amphibian.

newton /ˈnjuːt(ə)n/ *noun* SI unit of force.

next *adjective* **1** (often + *to*) being, placed, or living nearest. **2** nearest in time. ● *adverb* **1** (often + *to*) nearest in place or degree. **2** on first or soonest occasion. ● *noun* next person or thing. ● *preposition colloquial* next to. □ **next door** in next house or room. **next of kin** closest living relative(s).

■ *adjective* **1** adjacent, adjoining, closest, nearest, neighbouring, next door. **2** following, soonest, subsequent, succeeding.

nexus /ˈneksəs/ *noun* (*plural* same) connected group or series.

NHS *abbreviation* National Health Service.

NI *abbreviation* **1** Northern Ireland. **2** National Insurance.

niacin /ˈnaɪəsɪn/ *noun* nicotinic acid.

nib *noun* **1** pen-point. **2** (in *plural*) crushed coffee or cocoa beans.

nibble /ˈnɪb(ə)l/ *verb* (**-ling**) **1** (+ *at*) take small bites at. **2** eat in small amounts. **3** bite gently or playfully. ● *noun* **1** act of nibbling. **2** very small amount of food.

nice *adjective* **1** pleasant, satisfactory. **2** kind, good-natured. **3** (of distinctions) subtle, fine. **4** requiring care. **5** fastidious. □ **nicely** *adverb*. **niceness** *noun*.

■ **1** acceptable, agreeable, attractive, beautiful, delicious, enjoyable, good, gratifying, pleasant, satisfactory, welcome. **2** agreeable, amiable, attractive, compassionate, congenial, delightful, friendly, genial, good, good-natured, kind, kind-hearted, kindly, likeable, pleasant, polite, sympathetic, winsome. **3** accurate, careful, delicate, discriminating, exact, fine, hair-splitting, minute, precise, subtle. **5** dainty, fastidious, fussy, meticulous, particular, *colloquial* pernickety, punctilious, scrupulous.

nicety /ˈnaɪsɪtɪ/ *noun* (*plural* **-ies**) **1** subtle distinction or detail. **2** precision. □ **to a nicety** exactly.

niche /niːʃ/ *noun* **1** shallow recess, esp. in wall. **2** comfortable or apt position in life or employment.

| ■ **1** alcove, corner, hollow, nook, recess.

nick *noun* **1** small cut or notch. **2** *slang* prison. **3** *slang* police station. **4** *colloquial* state, condition. ● *verb* **1** make nick(s) in. **2** *slang* steal. **3** *slang* arrest, catch. □ **in the nick of time** only just in time.

nickel /ˈnɪk(ə)l/ *noun* **1** silver-white metallic element used esp. in magnetic alloys. **2** *colloquial* US 5-cent coin.

nickname /ˈnɪkneɪm/ *noun* familiar or humorous name added to or substituted for real name of person or thing. ● *verb* (**-ming**) give nickname to.

| ■ *noun* alias, sobriquet.

nicotine /ˈnɪkətiːn/ *noun* poisonous alkaloid present in tobacco.

nicotinic acid /nɪkəˈtɪnɪk/ *noun* vitamin of B group.

nictitate /ˈnɪktɪteɪt/ *verb* (**-ting**) blink, wink. □ **nictitation** *noun.*

niece /niːs/ *noun* daughter of one's brother or sister or of one's spouse's brother or sister.

nifty /ˈnɪftɪ/ *adjective* (**-ier, -iest**) *colloquial* **1** clever, adroit. **2** smart, stylish.

niggard /ˈnɪɡəd/ *noun* stingy person.

niggardly *adjective* stingy. □ **niggardliness** *noun.*

| ■ mean, miserly, parsimonious, stingy.

niggle /ˈnɪɡ(ə)l/ *verb* (**-ling**) **1** fuss over details. **2** find fault in petty way. **3** *colloquial* nag. □ **niggling** *adjective.*

nigh /naɪ/ *adverb & preposition archaic* near.

night /naɪt/ *noun* **1** period of darkness from one day to next; time from sunset to sunrise. **2** nightfall. **3** darkness of night. **4** evening. □ **nightcap 1** *historical* cap worn in bed. **2** drink before going to bed. **nightclub** club providing entertainment etc. late at night. **nightdress** woman's or child's loose garment worn in bed. **nightfall** end of daylight. **nightjar** nocturnal bird with harsh cry. **night-life** entertainment available at night. **nightmare** terrifying dream or *colloquial* experience. **night safe** safe with access from outer wall of bank for deposit of money when bank is closed. **nightshade** any of various plants with poisonous berries. **nightshirt** long shirt worn in bed. **nightwatchman** person who keeps watch at night.

nightingale /ˈnaɪtɪŋɡeɪl/ *noun* small reddish-brown bird, of which the male sings tunefully, esp. at night.

nightly *adjective* **1** happening, done, or existing in the night. **2** recurring every night. ● *adverb* every night.

nihilism /ˈnaɪɪlɪz(ə)m/ *noun* rejection of all religious and moral principles. □ **nihilist** *noun.* **nihilistic** /-ˈlɪs-/ *adjective.*

nil *noun* nothing.

nimble /ˈnɪmb(ə)l/ *adjective* (**-r, -st**) **1** quick and light in movement or function; agile. **2** (of mind) quick. □ **nimbly** *adverb.*

| ■ **1** acrobatic, active, adroit, agile, brisk, deft, dexterous, limber, lithe, lively, *colloquial* nippy, quick-moving, sprightly, spry, swift.

nimbus /ˈnɪmbəs/ *noun* (*plural* **nimbi** /-baɪ/ or **nimbuses**) **1** halo. **2** rain-cloud.

nincompoop /ˈnɪŋkəmpuːp/ *noun* foolish person.

nine *adjective & noun* one more than eight. □ **ninepins** (usually treated as *singular*) kind of skittles. □ **ninth** /naɪnθ/ *adjective & noun.*

nineteen /naɪnˈtiːn/ *adjective & noun* one more than eighteen. □ **nineteenth** *adjective & noun.*

ninety /ˈnaɪntɪ/ *adjective & noun* (*plural* **-ies**) nine times ten. □ **ninetieth** *adjective & noun.*

ninny /ˈnɪnɪ/ *noun* (*plural* **-ies**) foolish person.

nip[1] *verb* (**-pp-**) **1** pinch, squeeze sharply, bite. **2** (often + *off*) remove by pinching etc. **3** *colloquial* go nimbly. ● *noun* **1** pinch, sharp squeeze, bite. **2** biting cold. □ **nip in the bud** suppress or destroy at very beginning.

| ■ *verb* **1, 2** bite, clip, pinch, snap, squeeze.

nip[2] *noun* small quantity of spirits.

nipper *noun* **1** person or thing that nips. **2** claw of crab etc. **3** *colloquial* young child. **4** (in *plural*) tool with jaws for gripping or cutting.

nipple /ˈnɪp(ə)l/ *noun* **1** small projection in mammals from which in females milk for young is secreted. **2** teat of feeding-bottle. **3** device like nipple in function. **4** nipple-like protuberance.

nippy *adjective* (**-ier, -iest**) *colloquial* **1** quick, nimble. **2** chilly.

nirvana /nɪəˈvɑːnə/ *noun* (in Buddhism) perfect bliss attained by extinction of individuality.

nit *noun* **1** egg or young of louse or other parasitic insect. **2** *slang* stupid person. □ **nit-picking** *colloquial* fault-finding in a petty way.

niter *US* = NITRE.

nitrate /ˈnaɪtreɪt/ *noun* **1** salt of nitric acid. **2** potassium or sodium nitrate as fertilizer.

nitre /ˈnaɪtə/ *noun* (*US* **niter**) saltpetre.

nitric acid /ˈnaɪtrɪk/ *noun* colourless corrosive poisonous liquid.

nitrogen /ˈnaɪtrədʒ(ə)n/ *noun* gaseous element forming four-fifths of atmosphere. □ **nitrogenous** /-ˈtrɒdʒɪnəs/ *adjective.*

nitroglycerine /naɪtrəʊˈɡlɪsərɪn/ *noun* (*US* **nitroglycerin**) explosive yellow liquid.

nitrous oxide /ˈnaɪtrəs/ *noun* colourless gas used as anaesthetic.

nitty-gritty /nɪtɪˈɡrɪtɪ/ *noun slang* realities or practical details of a matter.

nitwit *noun colloquial* stupid person.

NNE *abbreviation* north-north-east.

NNW *abbreviation* north-north-west.

No = NOH.

No. *abbreviation* number.

no /nəʊ/ *adjective* **1** not any. **2** not a. **3** hardly any. **4** *used to forbid thing specified.* ● *adverb* by no amount; not at all. ● *interjection: expressing negative reply to question, request, etc.* ● *noun* (*plural* **noes**) **1** utterance of word *no.* **2** denial or refusal. **3** 'no' vote. □ **no-ball** unlawfully delivered ball in cricket etc. **no longer** not now as formerly. **no-nonsense** sensible; without flippancy. **no one** nobody. **no way** *colloquial* it is impossible.

nob¹ *noun slang* person of wealth or high social position.

nob² *noun slang* head.

nobble /'nɒb(ə)l/ *verb* (**-ling**) *slang* **1** try to influence (e.g. judge). **2** tamper with (racehorse etc.). **3** steal. **4** seize; catch.

nobility /nəʊ'bɪlɪtɪ/ *noun* (*plural* **-ies**) **1** nobleness of character, birth, or rank. **2** (usually after *a, the*) class of nobles.

> ■ **1** dignity, glory, grandeur, greatness, high-mindedness, integrity, magnanimity, nobleness, uprightness, virtue, worthiness. **2** (*the nobility*) the aristocracy, the elite, the gentry, the nobles, the peerage, the ruling classes, *colloquial* the upper crust.

noble /'nəʊb(ə)l/ *adjective* (**-r, -st**) **1** belonging to the aristocracy. **2** of excellent character; magnanimous. **3** of imposing appearance. ● *noun* nobleman; noblewoman. □ **nobleman** peer. **noblewoman** peeress. □ **nobleness** *noun.* **nobly** *adverb.*

> ■ *adjective* **1** aristocratic, blue-blooded, courtly, distinguished, elite, gentle, high-born, high-ranking, patrician, princely, royal, thoroughbred, titled, upper-class. **2** chivalrous, elevated, exalted, gallant, heroic, honourable, lofty, lordly, magnanimous, upright, virtuous, worthy. **3** dignified, elegant, grand, great, imposing, impressive, magnificent, majestic, splendid, stately. ● *noun* aristocrat, grandee, lady, lord, nobleman, noblewoman, patrician, peer, peeress.

noblesse oblige /nəʊbles ɒ'bliːʒ/ *noun* privilege entails responsibility. [French]

nobody /'nəʊbədɪ/ *pronoun* no person. ● *noun* (*plural* **-ies**) person of no importance.

noctambulist /nɒk'tæmbjʊlɪst/ *noun* sleepwalker.

nocturnal /nɒk'tɜːn(ə)l/ *adjective* of or in the night; done or active by night.

nocturne /'nɒktɜːn/ *noun Music* **1** short romantic composition, usually for piano. **2** picture of night scene.

nod *verb* (**-dd-**) **1** incline head slightly and briefly. **2** let head droop in drowsiness; be drowsy. **3** show (assent etc.) by nod. **4** (of flowers etc.) bend and sway. **5** make momentary slip or mistake. ● *noun* nodding of head. □ **nod off** *colloquial* fall asleep.

> ■ *verb* **1** bend, bob, bow. □ **nod off** see SLEEP *verb* 1.

noddle /'nɒd(ə)l/ *noun colloquial* head.

node *noun* **1** part of plant stem from which leaves emerge. **2** knob on root or branch. **3** natural swelling. **4** intersecting point, esp. of planet's orbit with plane of celestial equator. **5** point or line of least disturbance in vibrating system. **6** point at which curve crosses itself. **7** component in computer network. □ **nodal** *adjective.*

nodule /'nɒdjuːl/ *noun* **1** small rounded lump of anything. **2** small tumour, ganglion, swelling on legume root. □ **nodular** *adjective.*

noggin /'nɒgɪn/ *noun* **1** small mug. **2** small measure of spirits.

Noh /nəʊ/ *noun* (also **No**) traditional Japanese drama.

noise /nɔɪz/ *noun* **1** sound, esp. loud or unpleasant one. **2** confusion of loud sounds. ● *verb* (**-sing**) (usually in *passive*) make public, spread abroad. □ **noiseless** *adjective.* **noiselessness** *noun.*

> ■ *noun* **1** see SOUND¹ *noun* 1. **2** babel, bawling, bedlam, blare, cacophony, caterwauling, clamour, clangour, clatter, commotion, din, discord, fracas, hubbub, hullabaloo, outcry, pandemonium, racket, *colloquial* row, *colloquial* rumpus, screaming, screeching, shouting, shrieking, tumult, uproar, yelling. □ **noiseless** inaudible, mute, muted, quiet, silent, soft, soundless, still.

noisome /'nɔɪsəm/ *adjective literary* **1** harmful, noxious. **2** evil-smelling.

noisy *adjective* (**-ier, -iest**) **1** making much noise. **2** full of noise. □ **noisily** *adverb.*

> ■ blaring, boisterous, booming, cacophonous, chattering, clamorous, deafening, discordant, dissonant, ear-splitting, *Music* fortissimo, harsh, loud, raucous, resounding, reverberating, rowdy, screaming, screeching, shrieking, shrill, strident, talkative, thunderous, tumultuous, unmusical, uproarious, vociferous.

nomad /'nəʊmæd/ *noun* **1** member of tribe roaming from place to place for pasture. **2** wanderer. □ **nomadic** /-'mæd-/ *adjective.*

> ■ □ **nomadic** itinerant, peripatetic, roving, travelling, vagrant, wandering, wayfaring.

nom de plume /nɒm də 'pluːm/ *noun* (*plural* ***noms de plume*** same pronunciation) writer's assumed name. [French]

nomenclature /nəʊ'menklətʃə/ *noun* **1** system of names for things. **2** terminology of a science etc.

nominal /'nɒmɪn(ə)l/ *adjective* **1** existing in name only; not real or actual. **2** (of sum of money etc.) very small. **3** of, as, or like noun. □ **nominally** *adverb.*

> ■ **1** formal, in name only, ostensible, self-styled, so-called, supposed, theoretical, titular. **2** insignificant, minimal, minor, small, token.

nominate /'nɒmɪneɪt/ *verb* (**-ting**) **1** propose (candidate) for election. **2** appoint to office. **3** appoint (date or place). □ **nomination** *noun.* **nominator** *noun.*

■ appoint, choose, designate, elect, name, propose, put forward, put up, recommend, select, specify.

nominative /'nɒmɪnətɪv/ *Grammar noun* case expressing subject of verb. ● *adjective* of or in this case.

nominee /nɒmɪ'ni:/ *noun* person who is nominated.

non- *prefix* giving negative sense of words with which it is combined. For words starting with *non-* that are not found below, the root-words should be consulted.

nonagenarian /nəʊnədʒɪ'neərɪən/ *noun* person from 90 to 99 years old.

non-believer /nɒnbɪ'li:və/ *noun* person who does not believe; person who has no faith.

■ agnostic, atheist, disbeliever, freethinker, heathen, infidel, pagan, sceptic, unbeliever.

non-belligerent /nɒnbə'lɪdʒərənt/ *adjective* not engaged in hostilities. ● *noun* non-belligerent state etc.

nonce /nɒns/ *noun* □ **for the nonce** for the time being, for the present. **nonce-word** word coined for one occasion.

nonchalant /'nɒnʃələnt/ *adjective* calm and casual. □ **nonchalance** *noun*. **nonchalantly** *adverb*.

non-combatant /nɒn'kʌmbət(ə)nt/ *noun* person not fighting in a war, esp. civilian, army chaplain, etc.

non-commissioned /nɒnkə'mɪʃ(ə)nd/ *adjective* (of officer) not holding commission.

noncommittal /nɒnkə'mɪt(ə)l/ *adjective* avoiding commitment to definite opinion or course of action.

non compos mentis /ˌnɒn kɒmpɒs 'mentɪs/ *adjective* not in one's right mind.

non-conductor /nɒnkən'dʌktə/ *noun* substance that does not conduct heat or electricity.

nonconformist /nɒnkən'fɔ:mɪst/ *noun* **1** person who does not conform to doctrine of established Church, esp. (**Nonconformist**) member of Protestant sect dissenting from Anglican Church. **2** person not conforming to prevailing principle.

nonconformity /nɒnkən'fɔ:mɪtɪ/ *noun* **1** nonconformists as body. **2** (+ *to*) failure to conform to.

non-contributory /nɒnkən'trɪbjʊtərɪ/ *adjective* not involving contributions.

nondescript /'nɒndɪskrɪpt/ *adjective* lacking distinctive characteristics; not easily classified. ● *noun* such person or thing.

none /nʌn/ *pronoun* **1** (often + *of*) not any. **2** no person(s). □ **none the** (+ *comparative*), **none too** not in the least.

USAGE The verb following *none* can be singular or plural when it means 'not any of several', e.g. *None of us knows* or *None of us know.*

nonentity /nɒ'nentɪtɪ/ *noun* (*plural* **-ies**) **1** person or thing of no importance. **2** non-existence. **3** non-existent thing.

nonet /nəʊ'net/ *noun* **1** musical composition for 9 performers. **2** the performers. **3** any group of 9.

nonetheless /nʌnðə'les/ *adverb* nevertheless.

non-event /nɒnɪ'vent/ *noun* insignificant event, esp. contrary to hopes or expectations.

non-existent /nɒnɪg'zɪst(ə)nt/ *adjective* not existing. □ **non-existence** *noun*.

■ chimerical, fictional, fictitious, hypothetical, imaginary, imagined, legendary, made up, mythical, unreal.

non-fiction /nɒn'fɪkʃ(ə)n/ *noun* literary work other than fiction.

non-interference /nɒnɪntə'fɪərəns/ *noun* non-intervention.

non-intervention /nɒnɪntə'venʃ(ə)n/ *noun* policy of not interfering in others' affairs.

nonpareil /nɒnpə'reɪl/ *adjective* unrivalled, unique. ● *noun* such person or thing.

non-party /nɒn'pɑ:tɪ/ *adjective* independent of political parties.

nonplus /nɒn'plʌs/ *verb* (**-ss-**) completely perplex.

■ amaze, baffle, confound, disconcert, dumbfound, *colloquial* flummox, perplex, puzzle.

nonsense /'nɒns(ə)ns/ *noun* **1** (often as *interjection*) absurd or meaningless words or ideas. **2** foolish conduct. □ **nonsensical** /-'sen-/ *adjective*.

■ **1** absurdity, balderdash, *slang* bilge, *slang* boloney, *slang* bunk, bunkum, claptrap, *colloquial* double Dutch, drivel, *slang* eyewash, foolishness, gibberish, *colloquial* gobbledegook, inanity, mumbo-jumbo, *colloquial* piffle, *slang* poppycock, *slang* rot, rubbish, silliness, stuff and nonsense, stupidity, *esp. US* trash, *colloquial* tripe, twaddle. **2** absurdity, foolishness, inanity, senselessness, silliness, stupidity. □ **nonsensical** absurd, asinine, crazy, daft, fatuous, foolish, idiotic, illogical, impractical, inane, incomprehensible, irrational, laughable, ludicrous, mad, meaningless, preposterous, ridiculous, senseless, silly, stupid, unreasonable, wild.

non sequitur /nɒn 'sekwɪtə/ *noun* conclusion that does not logically follow from the premisses. [Latin]

non-slip /nɒn'slɪp/ *adjective* **1** that does not slip. **2** that prevents slipping.

non-smoker /nɒn'sməʊkə/ *noun* **1** person who does not smoke. **2** train compartment etc. where smoking is forbidden. □ **non-smoking** *adjective*.

non-starter /nɒn'stɑ:tə/ *noun colloquial* person or scheme not worth considering.

non-stick /nɒn'stɪk/ *adjective* that does not allow things to stick to it.

non-stop /nɒn'stɒp/ *adjective* **1** (of train etc.) not stopping at intermediate stations. **2** done without stopping. ● *adverb* without stopping.

■ *adjective* **2** ceaseless, constant, continual, continuous, endless, *colloquial* eternal, incessant, interminable, perpetual, persistent, round the clock, steady, unbroken, unending, uninterrupted, unremitting.

noodle[1] /'nuːd(ə)l/ *noun* strip or ring of pasta.

noodle[2] /'nuːd(ə)l/ *noun* simpleton.

nook /nʊk/ *noun* corner or recess; secluded place.

noon *noun* 12 o'clock in day, midday. □ **noonday** midday.

noose *noun* **1** loop with running knot. **2** snare. ● *verb* (**-sing**) catch with or enclose in noose.

nor *conjunction* and not.

Nordic /'nɔːdɪk/ *adjective* of tall blond Germanic people of Scandinavia.

norm *noun* **1** standard, type. **2** standard amount of work etc. **3** customary behaviour.

  ■ **1, 2** criterion, measure, model, pattern, rule, standard, type, yardstick. **3** custom, practice, rule.

normal /'nɔːm(ə)l/ *adjective* **1** conforming to standard; regular, usual, typical. **2** free from mental disorder. **3** *Geometry* (of line) at right angles. ● *noun* **1** normal value of a temperature etc. **2** usual state, level, etc. □ **normalcy** *noun* *esp. US.* **normality** /-'mæl-/ *noun.* **normalize** *verb* (also **-ise**) (**-zing** or **-sing**). **normally** *adverb.*

  ■ *adjective* **1** accepted, accustomed, average, common, commonplace, conventional, customary, established, everyday, familiar, general, habitual, natural, ordinary, orthodox, predictable, prosaic, quotidian, regular, routine, run-of-the-mill, standard, typical, universal, unsurprising, usual. **2** balanced, healthy, rational, reasonable, sane, stable, well adjusted.
  □ **normalize** regularize, regulate, standardize.

Norman /'nɔːmən/ *noun* (*plural* **-s**) **1** native of medieval Normandy. **2** descendant of people established there in 10th c. ● *adjective* **1** of Normans. **2** of style of medieval architecture found in Britain under Normans.

Norse *noun* **1** Norwegian language. **2** Scandinavian language group. ● *adjective* of ancient Scandinavia, esp. Norway. □ **Norseman** *noun.*

north *noun* **1** point of horizon 90° anticlockwise from east. **2** corresponding compass point. **3** (usually **the North**) northern part of world, country, town, etc. ● *adjective* **1** towards, at, near, or facing north. **2** (of wind) from north. ● *adverb* **1** towards, at, or near north. **2** (+ *of*) further north than. □ **northbound** travelling or leading north. **north-east, -west** point midway between north and east or west. **north-north-east, north-north-west** point midway between north and north-east or north-west. **North Star** pole star. □ **northward** *adjective, adverb, & noun.* **northwards** *adverb.*

northerly /'nɔːðəlɪ/ *adjective & adverb* **1** in northern position or direction. **2** (of wind) from north.

northern /'nɔːð(ə)n/ *adjective* of or in the north.

□ **northern lights** aurora borealis. □ **northernmost** *adjective.*

northerner *noun* native or inhabitant of north.

Norwegian /nɔː'wiːdʒ(ə)n/ *noun* native, national, or language of Norway. ● *adjective* of or relating to Norway.

nose /nəʊz/ *noun* **1** organ above mouth, used for smelling and breathing. **2** sense of smell. **3** odour or perfume of wine etc. **4** projecting part or front end of car, aircraft, etc. ● *verb* (**-sing**) **1** (usually + *about* etc.) search. **2** (often + *out*) perceive smell of; discover by smell. **3** thrust nose against or into. **4** make one's way cautiously forward. □ **nosebag** fodder-bag hung on horse's head. **nosebleed** bleeding from nose. **nosedive** (make) steep downward plunge. **turn up one's nose** (often + *at*) *colloquial* show disdain.

  ■ *noun* **1** nostrils, proboscis, snout. **4** front; [*of boat*] bow, prow. ● *verb* **1** (*nose about*) see PRY. **4** edge, insinuate oneself, penetrate, probe, push.

nosegay *noun* small bunch of flowers.

nosh *slang verb* eat. ● *noun* food or drink. □ **nosh-up** large meal.

nostalgia /nɒs'tældʒə/ *noun* **1** (often + *for*) yearning for past period. **2** homesickness. □ **nostalgic** *adjective.*

  ■ **1** longing, pining, reminiscence, yearning.
  □ **nostalgic** homesick, wistful, yearning.

nostril /'nɒstr(ə)l/ *noun* either of two openings in nose.

nostrum /'nɒstrəm/ *noun* **1** quack remedy; patent medicine. **2** pet scheme.

nosy *adjective* (**-ier, -iest**) *colloquial* inquisitive, prying. □ **nosiness** *noun.*

  ■ curious, eavesdropping, inquisitive, interfering, meddlesome, prying, *colloquial* snooping.

not *adverb: expressing negation, refusal, or denial.* □ **not quite** almost.

notable /'nəʊtəb(ə)l/ *adjective* **1** worthy of note; remarkable. **2** eminent. ● *noun* eminent person. □ **notability** *noun.* **notably** *adverb.*

  ■ *adjective* celebrated, conspicuous, distinctive, distinguished, eminent, evident, extraordinary, famous, illustrious, important, impressive, memorable, noted, noteworthy, noticeable, obvious, outstanding, pre-eminent, prominent, rare, remarkable, renowned, singular, striking, uncommon, unforgettable, unusual, well known.

notary /'nəʊtərɪ/ *noun* (*plural* **-ies**) solicitor etc. who certifies deeds etc. □ **notarial** /-'teər-/ *adjective.*

notation /nəʊ'teɪʃ(ə)n/ *noun* **1** representation of numbers, quantities, musical notes, etc. by symbols. **2** set of such symbols.

notch *noun* V-shaped indentation on edge or surface. ● *verb* **1** make notches in. **2** (usually + *up*) score, win, achieve (esp. amount or quantity).

note *noun* **1** brief written record as memory aid. **2** short letter. **3** formal diplomatic communication. **4** additional explanation in book. **5** banknote. **6** notice of payment. **7** notice, attention. **8** eminence. **9** single musical tone of definite pitch. **10** written sign representing its pitch and duration. **11** quality or tone of speaking. ● *verb* (**-ting**) **1** observe, notice. **2** (often + *down*) record as thing to be remembered. **3** (in *passive*; often + *for*) be well known. **4** (as **noted** *adjective*) famous. □ **notebook** book for making notes in. **notecase** wallet for banknotes. **notelet** small folded card for informal letter. **notepaper** paper for writing letters. **noteworthy** worthy of attention; remarkable. **noteworthiness** *noun*.

> ■ *noun* **1** chit, jotting, *colloquial* memo, memorandum, minute, record, reminder. **2** billet-doux, communication, epistle, letter, line, *colloquial* memo, memorandum, message, postcard. **4** annotation, comment, commentary, explanation, footnote, gloss, jotting, marginal note. **5, 6** banknote, *US* bill, draft. **11** feeling, quality, sound, tone. ● *verb* **1** detect, discern, discover, feel, find, heed, mark, mind, notice, observe, pay attention to, *archaic* remark, register, see, spy, take note of. **2** enter, jot down, record, scribble, write down. **4** (**noted**) see FAMOUS 1.
> □ **noteworthy** exceptional, extraordinary, rare, remarkable, uncommon, *disputed* unique, unusual.

nothing /ˈnʌθɪŋ/ *noun* **1** no thing; not anything. **2** person or thing of no importance. **3** non-existence. **4** no amount; nought. ● *adverb* not at all; in no way.

> ■ *noun* **4** *archaic* naught, nil, nought, zero, *esp. US slang* zilch.

nothingness *noun* **1** non-existence. **2** worthlessness.

notice /ˈnəʊtɪs/ *noun* **1** attention. **2** displayed sheet etc. with announcement. **3** intimation, warning. **4** formal declaration of intention to end agreement or employment at specified time. **5** short published review of new play, book, etc. ● *verb* (**-cing**) (often + *that*, *how*, etc.) perceive, observe. □ **noticeable** *adjective*. **noticeably** *adverb*.

> ■ *noun* **1** attention, awareness, *formal* cognizance, consciousness, heed, note, regard. **2** advertisement, handout, leaflet, message, note, placard, poster, sign. **3, 4** announcement, indication, intimation, notification, sign, warning; (*give notice*) see NOTIFY 1, WARN. ● *verb* be aware, detect, discern, discover, feel, find, heed, make out, mark, mind, note, observe, pay attention to, perceive, register, *archaic* remark, see, spy, take note. □ **noticeable** appreciable, audible, clear, clear-cut, considerable, conspicuous, detectable, discernible, distinct, distinguishable, manifest, marked, measurable, notable, observable, obtrusive, obvious, overt, palpable, perceivable, perceptible, plain, prominent, pronounced, salient, significant, striking, unconcealed, unmistakable, visible.

notifiable /ˈnəʊtɪfaɪəb(ə)l/ *adjective* (esp. of disease) that must be notified to authorities.

notify /ˈnəʊtɪfaɪ/ *verb* (**-ies**, **-ied**) **1** (often + *of*,

that) inform; give notice to (person). **2** make known. □ **notification** *noun*.

> ■ **1** acquaint, advise, alert, apprise, give notice, inform, tell, warn. **2** announce, make known, proclaim, publish, report.

notion /ˈnəʊʃ(ə)n/ *noun* **1** concept, idea; opinion; vague understanding. **2** intention.

> ■ **1** apprehension, belief, concept, conception, fancy, hypothesis, idea, impression, inkling, opinion, sentiment, theory, thought, understanding, view. **2** design, intention, thought.

notional *adjective* hypothetical, imaginary. □ **notionally** *adverb*.

notorious /nəʊˈtɔːrɪəs/ *adjective* well known, esp. unfavourably. □ **notoriety** /-təˈraɪətɪ/ *noun*. **notoriously** *adverb*.

> ■ disgraceful, disreputable, famous, flagrant, ill-famed, infamous, outrageous, scandalous, shocking, undisguised, undisputed, well known.

notwithstanding /nɒtwɪðˈstændɪŋ/ *preposition* in spite of. ● *adverb* nevertheless.

nougat /ˈnuːgɑː/ *noun* sweet made from nuts, egg white, and sugar or honey.

nought /nɔːt/ *noun* **1** digit 0; cipher. **2** *poetical* or *archaic* nothing.

noun /naʊn/ *noun* word used to name person or thing (see panel).

nourish /ˈnʌrɪʃ/ *verb* **1** sustain with food. **2** foster, cherish (feeling etc.). □ **nourishing** *adjective*.

> ■ **1** feed, maintain, nurse, nurture, provide for, strengthen, support, sustain. **2** cherish, foster, harbour, nurse, nurture. □ **nourishing** see NUTRITIOUS.

nourishment *noun* sustenance, food.

> ■ food, goodness, nutriment, nutrition, sustenance, victuals.

nous /naʊs/ *noun colloquial* common sense.

Nov. *abbreviation* November.

nova /ˈnəʊvə/ *noun* (*plural* **novae** /-viː/ or **-s**) star showing sudden burst of brightness and then subsiding.

novel /ˈnɒv(ə)l/ *noun* fictitious prose story of book length. ● *adjective* of new kind or nature.

> ■ *noun* novelette, novella, romance, story. ● *adjective* different, fresh, imaginative, innovative, new, odd, original, rare, singular, startling, strange, surprising, uncommon, unconventional, unfamiliar, untested, unusual.

novelette /nɒvəˈlet/ *noun* short (esp. romantic) novel.

novelist /ˈnɒvəlɪst/ *noun* writer of novels.

novella /nəˈvelə/ *noun* (*plural* **-s**) short novel or narrative story.

novelty /ˈnɒvəltɪ/ *noun* (*plural* **-ies**) **1** newness. **2** new thing or occurrence. **3** small toy etc.

> ■ **1** freshness, newness, oddity, originality, strangeness, unfamiliarity, uniqueness. **3** bauble, curiosity, gimmick, knick-knack, ornament, souvenir, trifle, trinket.

November /nəʊ'vembə/ *noun* eleventh month of year.

novena /nə'vi:nə/ *noun RC Church* special prayers or services on 9 successive days.

novice /'nɒvɪs/ *noun* **1** probationary member of religious order. **2** beginner.

> ■ **1** noviciate. **2** amateur, apprentice, beginner, greenhorn, initiate, learner, probationer, tiro, trainee.

noviciate /nə'vɪʃɪət/ *noun* (also **novitiate**) **1** period of being a novice. **2** religious novice. **3** novices' quarters.

now *adverb* **1** at present or mentioned time. **2** immediately. **3** by this time. **4** in the immediate past. ● *conjunction* (often + *that*) because. ● *noun* this time; the present. □ **now and again or then** occasionally.

> ■ *adverb* **1** at present, here and now, just now, nowadays, today. **2** at once, immediately, instantly, promptly, straight away.

nowadays /'naʊədeɪz/ *adverb* at present time or age. ● *noun* the present time.

nowhere /'nəʊweə/ *adverb* in or to no place. ● *pronoun* no place.

nowt *noun colloquial* or *dialect* nothing.

noxious /'nɒkʃəs/ *adjective* harmful, unwholesome.

> ■ foul, harmful, nasty, *literary* noisome, objectionable, poisonous, polluting, unwholesome.

nozzle /'nɒz(ə)l/ *noun* spout on hose etc.

nr. *abbreviation* near.

NSPCC *abbreviation* National Society for Prevention of Cruelty to Children.

NSW *abbreviation* New South Wales.

NT *abbreviation* **1** New Testament. **2** Northern Territory (of Australia). **3** National Trust.

nuance /'nju:ɑ ̃s/ *noun* subtle shade of meaning, feeling, colour, etc.

nub *noun* point or gist (of matter or story).

> ■ centre, core, crux, essence, gist, heart, kernel, nucleus, pith, point.

nubile /'nju:baɪl/ *adjective* (of woman) marriageable; sexually attractive. □ **nubility** *noun*.

nuclear /'nju:klɪə/ *adjective* **1** of, relating to, or constituting a nucleus. **2** using nuclear energy. □ **nuclear energy** energy obtained by nuclear fission or fusion. **nuclear family** couple and their child(ren). **nuclear fission** nuclear reaction in which heavy nucleus splits with release of energy. **nuclear fuel** source of nuclear energy. **nuclear fusion** nuclear reaction in which nuclei of low atomic number fuse with release of energy. **nuclear physics** physics of atomic nuclei. **nuclear power 1** power derived from nuclear energy. **2** country that has nuclear weapons.

nucleic acid /nju:'kli:ɪk/ *noun* either of two complex organic molecules (DNA and RNA) present in all living cells.

nucleon /'nju:klɪɒn/ *noun* proton or neutron.

nucleus /'nju:klɪəs/ *noun* (*plural* **nuclei** /-lɪaɪ/) **1** central part or thing round which others collect; kernel. **2** initial part. **3** central core of atom. **4** part of cell containing genetic material.

> ■ **1** centre, core, heart, kernel, middle.

....

Noun

A noun denotes a person or thing. There are four kinds:

1 common nouns (the words for objects and creatures), e.g.

shoe	in	*The red shoe was left on the shelf.*
box	in	*The large box stood in the corner.*
plant	in	*The plant grew to two metres.*
horse	in	*A horse and rider galloped by.*

2 proper nouns (the names of people, places, ships, institutions, and animals, which always begin with a capital letter), e.g.

Jane	*USS Enterprise*	*Bambi*
London	*Grand Hotel*	

3 abstract nouns (the words for qualities, things we cannot see or touch, and things which have no physical reality), e.g.

truth	*absence*
explanation	*warmth*

4 collective nouns (the words for groups of things), e.g.

committee	*squad*	*the Cabinet*
herd	*swarm*	*the clergy*
majority	*team*	*the public*

....

nude /njuːd/ *adjective* naked, unclothed. ● *noun* **1** painting etc. of nude human figure. **2** nude person. □ **in the nude** naked. □ **nudity** *noun*.

■ *adjective* bare, *literary* disrobed, exposed, in the nude, naked, stark naked, stripped, unclothed, uncovered, undressed.

nudge *verb* (**-ging**) **1** prod gently with elbow to draw attention. **2** push gradually. ● *noun* gentle push.

■ *verb* bump, dig, elbow, hit, jab, jog, jolt, poke, prod, push, shove, touch.

nudist /ˈnjuːdɪst/ *noun* person who advocates or practises going unclothed. □ **nudism** *noun*.

nugatory /ˈnjuːgətərɪ/ *adjective* **1** futile, trifling. **2** inoperative; not valid.

nugget /ˈnʌgɪt/ *noun* **1** lump of gold etc., as found in earth. **2** lump of anything.

nuisance /ˈnjuːs(ə)ns/ *noun* person, thing, or circumstance causing annoyance.

■ annoyance, bother, burden, inconvenience, irritant, irritation, *colloquial* pain, pest, plague, trouble, vexation, worry.

null *adjective* **1** (esp. **null and void**) invalid. **2** non-existent. **3** expressionless. □ **nullity** *noun*.

nullify /ˈnʌlɪfaɪ/ *verb* (**-ies**, **-ied**) neutralize, invalidate. □ **nullification** *noun*.

■ abolish, annul, cancel, do away with, invalidate, negate, neutralize, quash, repeal, rescind, revoke, stultify.

numb /nʌm/ *adjective* **1** deprived of feeling. **2** paralysed. ● *verb* **1** make numb. **2** stupefy, paralyse. □ **numbness** *noun*.

■ *adjective* anaesthetized, asleep, benumbed, cold, dead, deadened, frozen, immobile, insensible, insensitive, paralysed, senseless. ● *verb* anaesthetize, benumb, deaden, desensitize, drug, dull, freeze, immobilize, paralyse, stun, stupefy.

number /ˈnʌmbə/ *noun* **1** arithmetical value representing a quantity. **2** word, symbol, or figure representing this. **3** total count or aggregate. **4** numerical reckoning. **5** quantity, amount. **6** person or thing having place in a series, esp. single issue of magazine, item in programme, etc. ● *verb* **1** include. **2** assign number(s) to. **3** amount to specified number. **4** count. □ **number one** *colloquial* oneself. **number plate** plate bearing number esp. of motor vehicle.

USAGE The phrase *a number of* is normally used with a plural verb, as in *a number of problems remain*.

■ *noun* **2** digit, figure, integer, numeral, unit. **3** aggregate, amount, count, sum, total. **5** amount, *colloquial* bunch, collection, crowd, group, multitude, quantity, sum, total. **6** (*musical number*) item, piece, song; (*magazine number*) copy, edition, impression, issue, publication. ● *verb* **3** add up to, total, work out at. **4** see COUNT¹ *verb* 1.

numberless *adjective* innumerable.

numeral /ˈnjuːmər(ə)l/ *noun* symbol or group of symbols denoting a number. ● *adjective* of or denoting a number.

numerate /ˈnjuːmərət/ *adjective* familiar with basic principles of mathematics. □ **numeracy** *noun*.

numeration /njuːməˈreɪʃ(ə)n/ *noun* **1** process of numbering. **2** calculation.

numerator /ˈnjuːməreɪtə/ *noun* number above line in vulgar fraction.

numerical /njuːˈmerɪk(ə)l/ *adjective* of or relating to number(s). □ **numerically** *adverb*.

numerology /njuːməˈrɒlədʒɪ/ *noun* study of supposed occult significance of numbers.

numerous /ˈnjuːmərəs/ *adjective* **1** many. **2** consisting of many.

■ **1** abundant, copious, countless, endless, incalculable, infinite, innumerable, many, multitudinous, *literary* myriad, numberless, plentiful, several, uncountable, untold.

numinous /ˈnjuːmɪnəs/ *adjective* **1** indicating presence of a god. **2** awe-inspiring.

numismatic /njuːmɪzˈmætɪk/ *adjective* of or relating to coins or medals.

numismatics *plural noun* (usually treated as *singular*) study of coins and medals. □ **numismatist** /-ˈmɪzmətɪst/ *noun*.

nun *noun* member of community of women living under religious vows.

■ abbess, Mother Superior, novice, prioress, sister.

nuncio /ˈnʌnsɪəʊ/ *noun* (*plural* **-s**) papal ambassador.

nunnery *noun* (*plural* **-ies**) religious house of nuns.

nuptial /ˈnʌpʃ(ə)l/ *adjective* of marriage or weddings. ● *noun* (usually in *plural*) wedding.

nurse /nɜːs/ *noun* **1** person trained to care for sick and help doctors or dentists. **2** nursemaid. ● *verb* (**-sing**) **1** work as nurse. **2** attend to (sick person). **3** feed or be fed at breast. **4** hold or treat carefully. **5** foster; harbour. □ **nursing home** private hospital or home.

■ *noun* **1** matron, sister. **2** nanny, nursemaid. ● *verb* **2** care for, look after, minister to, nurture, tend, treat. **3** breastfeed, feed, suckle, wet-nurse. **4** cherish, coddle, cradle, cuddle, dandle, hold, hug, mother, pamper.

nursemaid *noun* woman in charge of child(ren).

nursery /ˈnɜːsərɪ/ *noun* (*plural* **-ies**) **1** room or place equipped for young children. **2** place where plants are reared for sale. □ **nurseryman** grower of plants for sale. **nursery rhyme** traditional song or rhyme for young children. **nursery school** school for children between ages of 3 and 5.

■ **1** crèche, kindergarten, nursery school. **2** garden centre, market garden.

nurture /ˈnɜːtʃə/ *noun* **1** bringing up; fostering care. **2** nourishment. ● *verb* (**-ring**) bring up, rear.

■ *verb* bring up, cultivate, educate, feed, look after, nourish, nurse, rear, tend, train.

nut *noun* **1** fruit consisting of hard shell or pod around edible kernel or seeds. **2** this kernel. **3** small usually hexagonal flat piece of metal with threaded hole through it for screwing on end of bolt to secure it. **4** *slang* head. **5** *slang* crazy person. **6** small lump (of coal etc.). □ **nutcase** *slang* crazy person. **nutcracker** (usually in *plural*) device for cracking nuts. **nuthatch** small bird which climbs up and down tree trunks. **nuts** *slang* crazy.

■ □ **nutcase** see MADMAN, MADWOMAN (MAD).

nutmeg /'nʌtmeg/ *noun* **1** hard aromatic seed used as spice etc. **2** E. Indian tree bearing this.

nutria /'njuːtrɪə/ *noun* coypu fur.

nutrient /'njuːtrɪənt/ *noun* substance providing essential nourishment. ● *adjective* serving as or providing nourishment.

nutriment /'njuːtrɪmənt/ *noun* nourishing food.

■ food, nourishment, nutrition, sustenance.

nutrition /njuːˈtrɪʃ(ə)n/ *noun* food, nourishment. □ **nutritional** *adjective*. **nutritionist** *noun*.

nutritious /njuːˈtrɪʃəs/ *adjective* efficient as food.

■ alimentary, beneficial, health-giving, healthy, nourishing, sustaining, wholesome.

nutritive /'njuːtrɪtɪv/ *adjective* **1** of nutrition. **2** nutritious.

nutshell *noun* hard covering of nut. □ **in a nutshell** in few words.

nutter *noun slang* crazy person.

nutty *adjective* (**-ier, -iest**) **1** full of nuts. **2** tasting like nuts. **3** *slang* crazy.

nux vomica /nʌks ˈvɒmɪkə/ *noun* **1** E. Indian tree. **2** its seeds, containing strychnine.

nuzzle /'nʌz(ə)l/ *verb* (**-ling**) **1** prod or rub gently with nose. **2** nestle, lie snug.

NW *abbreviation* north-west(ern).

NY *abbreviation US* New York.

nylon /'naɪlɒn/ *noun* **1** strong light synthetic fibre. **2** nylon fabric. **3** (in *plural*) stockings of nylon.

nymph /nɪmf/ *noun* **1** mythological semi-divine female spirit associated with rivers, woods, etc. **2** immature form of some insects.

nymphomania /nɪmfəˈmeɪnɪə/ *noun* excessive sexual desire in a woman. □ **nymphomaniac** *noun & adjective*.

NZ *abbreviation* New Zealand.

O¹ □ **O level** *historical* ordinary level in GCE exam.

O² /əʊ/ *interjection* **1** = OH. **2** *used before name in exclamation.*

oaf *noun* (*plural* -s) awkward lout. □ **oafish** *adjective.* **oafishly** *adverb.* **oafishness** *noun.*

oak *noun* **1** acorn-bearing hardwood tree with lobed leaves. **2** its wood. □ **oak-apple, -gall** abnormal growth produced on oak trees by insects.

oakum /ˈəʊkəm/ *noun* loose fibre got by picking old rope to pieces.

OAP *abbreviation* old-age pensioner.

oar /ɔː/ *noun* **1** pole with blade used to propel boat by leverage against water. **2** rower. □ **put (or stick) one's oar in** interrupt; meddle (in).

oarsman /ˈɔːzmən/ *noun* (*feminine* **oarswoman**) rower. □ **oarsmanship** *noun.*

oasis /əʊˈeɪsɪs/ *noun* (*plural* **oases** /-siːz/) **1** fertile spot in desert. **2** pleasant or calm place or period in midst of trouble.
■ **1** spring, watering hole, well. **2** asylum, haven, refuge, resort, retreat, safe harbour, sanctuary.

oast *noun* hop-drying kiln. □ **oast house** building containing this.

oat *noun* **1** cereal plant grown as food. **2** (in *plural*) grain of this. **3** tall grass resembling this. □ **oatcake** thin oatmeal biscuit. **oatmeal 1** meal ground from oats. **2** greyish-fawn colour. **sow one's wild oats** indulge in youthful follies before becoming steady. □ **oaten** *adjective.*

oath /əʊθ/ *noun* (*plural* -s /əʊðz/) **1** solemn declaration naming God etc. as witness. **2** curse. □ **on, under oath** having sworn solemn oath.
■ **1** assurance, *formal* avowal, guarantee, pledge, promise, undertaking, vow, word of honour. **2** blasphemy, curse, exclamation, expletive, four-letter word, *formal* imprecation, malediction, obscenity, profanity, swear word.

ob. *abbreviation* died (*obiit*).

obbligato /ɒblɪˈgɑːtəʊ/ *noun* (*plural* -s) *Music* accompaniment forming integral part of a composition.

obdurate /ˈɒbdjʊrət/ *adjective* **1** stubborn. **2** hardened. □ **obduracy** *noun.*

OBE *abbreviation* Officer of the Order of the British Empire.

obedient /əʊˈbiːdɪənt/ *adjective* **1** obeying or ready to obey. **2** submissive to another's will. □ **obedience** *noun.* **obediently** *adverb.*

■ acquiescent, amenable, biddable, compliant, conformable, deferential, disciplined, docile, dutiful, law-abiding, manageable, submissive, subservient, tamed, tractable, well behaved, well trained.

obeisance /əʊˈbeɪs(ə)ns/ *noun* **1** gesture expressing submission, respect, etc. **2** homage. □ **obeisant** *adjective.*

obelisk /ˈɒbəlɪsk/ *noun* tapering usually 4-sided stone pillar.

obelus /ˈɒbələs/ *noun* (*plural* **obeli** /-laɪ/) dagger-shaped mark of reference (†).

obese /əʊˈbiːs/ *adjective* very fat. □ **obesity** *noun.*
■ corpulent, fat, gross, overweight, podgy, portly, rotund.

obey /əʊˈbeɪ/ *verb* **1** carry out command of; carry out (command). **2** do what one is told to do.
■ **1** abide by, accept, acquiesce in, act in accordance with, adhere to, agree to, be ruled by, bow to, carry out, comply with, conform to, defer to, execute, follow, fulfil, give in to, heed, honour, implement, keep to, mind, observe, perform, submit to, take orders from. **2** comply, conform, give in, knuckle under, submit, take orders, toe the line.

obfuscate /ˈɒbfʌskeɪt/ *verb* (-ting) **1** obscure, confuse. **2** bewilder. □ **obfuscation** *noun.*

obituary /əˈbɪtjʊərɪ/ *noun* (*plural* -ies) **1** notice of death(s). **2** brief biography of deceased person. ● *adjective* of or serving as obituary.

object *noun* /ˈɒbdʒɪkt/ **1** material thing. **2** person or thing to which action or feeling is directed. **3** thing sought or aimed at. **4** word or phrase representing person or thing affected by action of verb (see panel). ● *verb* /əbˈdʒekt/ (often + *to*, *against*) express opposition, disapproval, or reluctance; protest. □ **no object** not an important factor. □ **objector** *noun.*
■ *noun* **1** article, body, entity, item, thing. **2** butt, destination, focus, target. **3** aim, end, goal, intent, intention, objective, point, purpose, reason, target. ● *verb* argue, be opposed, carp, cavil, complain, demur, disapprove, dispute, dissent, expostulate, *colloquial* grouse, grumble, mind, *colloquial* moan, oppose, protest, quibble, raise questions, remonstrate, take a stand, take exception.

objectify /əbˈdʒektɪfaɪ/ *verb* (-ies, -ied) **1** present as an object. **2** embody.

objection /əbˈdʒekʃ(ə)n/ *noun* **1** expression of disapproval or opposition. **2** objecting. **3** adverse reason or statement.

■ argument, cavil, challenge, complaint, demur, demurral, disapproval, exception, opposition, outcry, protest, query, question, quibble, refusal, remonstration.

objectionable *adjective* **1** unpleasant, offensive. **2** open to objection. ▫ **objectionably** *adverb*.
    ■ **1** abhorrent, detestable, disagreeable, disgusting, dislikable, displeasing, distasteful, foul, hateful, insufferable, intolerable, loathsome, nasty, nauseating, *literary* noisome, obnoxious, odious, offensive, off-putting, repellent, repugnant, repulsive, revolting, sickening, unacceptable, undesirable, unpleasant, unwanted. **2** contentious, controversial, exceptionable, questionable.

objective /əb'dʒektɪv/ *adjective* **1** external to the mind; actually existing. **2** dealing with outward things uncoloured by opinions or feelings. **3** *Grammar* (of case or word) in form appropriate to object. ● *noun* **1** object or purpose. **2** *Grammar* objective case. ▫ **objectively** *adverb*. **objectivity** /ɒbdʒek'tɪvɪti/ *noun*.
    ■ *adjective* **1** actual, empirical, existing, observable, real. **2** detached, disinterested, dispassionate, factual, impartial, impersonal, neutral, open-minded, outward-looking, rational, scientific, unbiased, uncoloured, unemotional, unprejudiced. ● *noun* **1** aim, ambition, aspiration, design, destination, end, goal, hope, intent, intention, object, point, purpose, target.

objet d'art /ɒbʒeɪ 'dɑː/ *noun* (*plural objets d'art* same pronunciation) small decorative object. [French]

oblate /'ɒbleɪt/ *adjective* (of spheroid) flattened at poles.

oblation /əʊ'bleɪʃ(ə)n/ *noun* thing offered to a divine being.

obligate /'ɒblɪgeɪt/ *verb* (-ting) bind (person) legally or morally.

obligation /ɒblɪ'geɪʃ(ə)n/ *noun* **1** compelling power of law, duty, etc. **2** duty. **3** binding agreement. **4** indebtedness for service or benefit.
    ■ **1, 2** compulsion, constraint, duty, liability, need, onus, requirement, responsibility. **3** agreement, commitment, contract, pledge, promise.

obligatory /ə'blɪgətərɪ/ *adjective* binding, compulsory. ▫ **obligatorily** *adverb*.
    ■ binding, compulsory, essential, mandatory, necessary, required, requisite, unavoidable.

oblige /ə'blaɪdʒ/ *verb* (-ging) **1** compel, require. **2** be binding on. **3** do (person) small favour. **4** (as **obliged** *adjective*) grateful.
    ■ **1, 2** bind, coerce, compel, constrain, force, make, require. **3** accommodate, gratify, indulge, please. **4** (**obliged**) see GRATEFUL.

obliging *adjective* helpful, accommodating. ▫ **obligingly** *adverb*.
    ■ see HELPFUL, POLITE 1.

oblique /ə'bliːk/ *adjective* **1** slanting; at an angle. **2** not going straight to the point; indirect. **3** *Grammar* (of case) other than nominative or vocative. ● *noun* oblique stroke. ▫ **obliquely** *adverb*. **obliqueness** *noun*. **obliquity** /ə'blɪkwɪtɪ/ *noun*.
    ■ *adjective* **1** angled, askew, aslant, canted, declining, diagonal, inclined, leaning, listing, raked, rising, skewed, slanted, slanting, slantwise, sloping, tilted. **2** backhanded, circuitous, circumlocutory, devious, evasive, implicit, implied, indirect, roundabout.

obliterate /ə'blɪtəreɪt/ *verb* (-ting) **1** blot out. **2** leave no clear trace of. ▫ **obliteration** *noun*.
    ■ blot out, cancel, cover over, delete, destroy, efface, eliminate, eradicate, erase, expunge, extirpate, rub out, wipe out.

oblivion /ə'blɪvɪən/ *noun* **1** state of being forgotten. **2** state of having forgotten or being unaware.

• •

Object

There are two types of object:

1 A direct object refers to a person or thing directly affected by the verb and can usually be identified by asking the question 'whom or what?' after the verb, e.g.
    The electors chose Mr Smith.
    Charles wrote a letter.

2 An indirect object usually refers to a person or thing receiving something from the subject of the verb, e.g.
    He gave me *the pen.*
    (*me* is the indirect object, and *the pen* is the direct object.)
    I sent my bank *a letter.*
    (*my bank* is the indirect object, and *a letter* is the direct object.)
Sentences containing an indirect object usually contain a direct object as well, but not always, e.g.
    Pay me.
'Object' on its own usually means a direct object.

• •

■ **1** anonymity, darkness, disregard, extinction, limbo, neglect, obscurity. **2** amnesia, coma, forgetfulness, ignorance, insensibility, obliviousness, unawareness, unconsciousness.

oblivious /ə'blɪvɪəs/ *adjective* unaware or unconscious. □ **obliviously** *adverb*. **obliviousness** *noun*.

■ forgetful, heedless, ignorant, insensible, insensitive, unacquainted, unaware, unconscious, unfeeling, uninformed, unmindful, unresponsive.

oblong /'ɒblɒŋ/ *adjective* rectangular with adjacent sides unequal. ● *noun* oblong figure or object.

obloquy /'ɒbləkwɪ/ *noun* abuse; being ill spoken of.

obnoxious /əb'nɒkʃəs/ *adjective* offensive, objectionable. □ **obnoxiously** *adverb*. **obnoxiousness** *noun*.

oboe /'əʊbəʊ/ *noun* double-reeded woodwind instrument. □ **oboist** *noun*.

obscene /əb'siːn/ *adjective* **1** offensively indecent. **2** *colloquial* highly offensive. **3** *Law* (of publication) tending to deprave and corrupt. □ **obscenely** *adverb*.

■ **1** bawdy, blue, coarse, corrupting, crude, debauched, degenerate, depraved, dirty, disgusting, distasteful, filthy, foul, foul-mouthed, gross, immodest, immoral, improper, impure, indecent, indecorous, indelicate, *colloquial* kinky, lecherous, lewd, *US* off colour, offensive, perverted, pornographic, prurient, ribald, risqué, *colloquial* rude, salacious, scatological, scurrilous, sexy, shameful, shameless, shocking, *colloquial* sick, smutty, suggestive, unchaste, vile, vulgar. **2** *colloquial* abominable, distasteful, loathsome, nasty, objectionable, offensive, outrageous, repugnant, repulsive, shocking.

obscenity /əb'senɪtɪ/ *noun* (*plural* **-ies**) **1** being obscene. **2** obscene word, action, etc.

■ **1** blasphemy, coarseness, dirt, dirtiness, evil, filth, foulness, grossness, immorality, impropriety, indecency, lewdness, licentiousness, offensiveness, outrage, perversion, pornography, profanity, scurrility, vileness. **2** see SWEAR WORD (SWEAR).

obscure /əb'skjʊə/ *adjective* **1** not clearly expressed or easily understood. **2** unexplained. **3** dark, indistinct. **4** hidden. **5** undistinguished. ● *verb* (**-ring**) make obscure or invisible. □ **obscurity** *noun*.

■ *adjective* **1, 2** arcane, baffling, complex, cryptic, enigmatic, esoteric, incomprehensible, mystifying, perplexing, puzzling, recondite, strange, unclear. **3** blurred, clouded, dark, dim, faint, foggy, hazy, indefinite, indistinct, misty, murky, nebulous, shadowy, shady, unclear, unlit, unrecognizable, vague. **4** concealed, covered, hidden, inconspicuous, masked, secret, shrouded, veiled. **5** forgotten, minor, undistinguished, unfamiliar, unheard of, unimportant, unknown, unnoticed. *verb* block out, blur, cloak, cloud, conceal, cover, darken,

disguise, eclipse, envelop, hide, mask, obfuscate, overshadow, screen, shade, shroud, veil.

obsequies /'ɒbsɪkwɪz/ *plural noun* funeral.

obsequious /əb'siːkwɪəs/ *adjective* fawning, servile. □ **obsequiously** *adverb*. **obsequiousness** *noun*.

■ abject, *colloquial* crawling, cringing, deferential, fawning, flattering, fulsome, greasy, grovelling, ingratiating, insincere, mealy-mouthed, menial, oily, servile, *colloquial* smarmy, submissive, subservient, sycophantic, unctuous.

observance /əb'zɜːv(ə)ns/ *noun* **1** keeping or performance of law, duty, etc. **2** rite; ceremonial act.

observant *adjective* good at observing. □ **observantly** *adverb*.

■ alert, astute, attentive, aware, careful, eagle-eyed, heedful, mindful, on the lookout, on the qui vive, perceptive, percipient, quick, sharp-eyed, shrewd, vigilant, watchful.

observation /ɒbzə'veɪʃ(ə)n/ *noun* **1** observing, being observed. **2** power of perception. **3** comment, remark. □ **observational** *adjective*.

■ **1** attention, examination, inspection, monitoring, scrutiny, study, surveillance, viewing, watching. **3** comment, note, opinion, reaction, reflection, remark, response, sentiment, statement, thought, utterance.

observatory /əb'zɜːvətərɪ/ *noun* (*plural* **-ies**) building for astronomical or other observation.

observe /əb'zɜːv/ *verb* (**-ving**) **1** perceive; become aware of. **2** watch. **3** keep (rules etc.). **4** celebrate (rite, anniversary, etc.). **5** remark. **6** take note of scientifically. □ **observable** *adjective*.

■ **1** detect, discern, note, notice, perceive, see, *colloquial* spot, spy, witness. **2** consider, contemplate, examine, keep an eye on, look at, monitor, regard, scrutinize, see, spy on, stare at, study, view, watch, witness. **3** abide by, adhere to, comply with, conform to, follow, heed, honour, keep, obey, pay attention to, respect. **4** celebrate, commemorate, keep, mark, recognize, remember. **5** *literary* animadvert (on), comment, declare, explain, mention, reflect, remark, say, state.

observer *noun* **1** person who observes. **2** interested spectator. **3** person attending meeting to note proceedings but without participating.

■ beholder, bystander, commentator, eyewitness, looker-on, onlooker, spectator, viewer, watcher, witness.

obsess /əb'ses/ *verb* fill mind of (person) all the time; preoccupy. □ **obsession** *noun*. **obsessional** *adjective*. **obsessive** *adjective*. **obsessively** *adverb*. **obsessiveness** *noun*.

■ bedevil, consume, control, dominate, grip, haunt, monopolize, *colloquial* plague, possess, preoccupy, rule, take hold of. □ **obsession** addiction, bee in one's bonnet, conviction, fetish, fixation, *slang* hang-up, hobby horse, infatuation, mania, passion, phobia, preoccupation, *colloquial* thing. **obsessive** addictive, compulsive, consuming, controlling, dominating, haunting, passionate.

obsidian /ɒbˈsɪdɪən/ *noun* dark glassy rock formed from lava.

obsolescent /ɒbsəˈles(ə)nt/ *adjective* becoming obsolete. □ **obsolescence** *noun*.
■ ageing, declining, dying out, fading, moribund, waning.

obsolete /ˈɒbsəliːt/ *adjective* no longer used; antiquated.
■ anachronistic, antiquated, antique, archaic, dated, dead, discarded, disused, extinct, old, old-fashioned, *colloquial* old hat, outdated, outmoded, out of date, passé, primitive, superannuated, superseded, unfashionable.

obstacle /ˈɒbstək(ə)l/ *noun* thing obstructing progress.
■ bar, barrier, block, blockage, catch, check, difficulty, hindrance, hurdle, impediment, obstruction, problem, restriction, snag, stumbling block.

obstetrics /əbˈstetrɪks/ *plural noun* (usually treated as *singular*) branch of medicine or surgery dealing with childbirth. □ **obstetric** *adjective*. **obstetrician** /ɒbstəˈtrɪʃ(ə)n/ *noun*.

obstinate /ˈɒbstmət/ *adjective* stubborn, intractable. □ **obstinacy** *noun*. **obstinately** *adverb*.
■ adamant, *colloquial* bloody-minded, defiant, determined, dogged, firm, headstrong, immovable, inflexible, intractable, intransigent, mulish, obdurate, persistent, pertinacious, perverse, pig-headed, refractory, resolute, rigid, self-willed, single-minded, stiff-necked, stubborn, tenacious, uncooperative, unreasonable, unyielding, wilful, wrong-headed.

obstreperous /əbˈstrepərəs/ *adjective* noisy, unruly. □ **obstreperously** *adverb*. **obstreperousness** *noun*.
■ boisterous, disorderly, irrepressible, naughty, noisy, rough, rowdy, *colloquial* stroppy, turbulent, uncontrollable, undisciplined, unmanageable, unruly, vociferous, wild.

obstruct /əbˈstrʌkt/ *verb* **1** block up. **2** make hard or impossible to pass along or through. **3** retard or prevent progress of.
■ **1, 2** block (up), choke, clog (up), jam, plug (up), occlude, stop (up). **3** arrest, bar, block, bring to a standstill, check, curb, delay, deter, frustrate, halt, hamper, hinder, hold up, impede, inhibit, interfere with, interrupt, prevent, restrict, retard, slow down, stand in the way of, stonewall, stop, stymie, thwart.

obstruction /əbˈstrʌkʃ(ə)n/ *noun* **1** obstructing, being obstructed. **2** thing that obstructs. **3** *Sport* unlawfully obstructing another player.

obstructive *adjective* causing or meant to cause obstruction.

obtain /əbˈtem/ *verb* **1** acquire, get; have granted to one. **2** be prevalent or established. □ **obtainable** *adjective*.
■ **1** acquire, attain, be given, buy, capture, come by, come into possession of, earn, elicit, enlist (*help*), extort, extract, find, gain, get, get hold of, lay one's hands on, pick up, procure, purchase, receive, secure, seize, take possession of, win. **2** apply, be in force, be in use, be relevant, be valid, exist, prevail, stand.

obtrude /əbˈtruːd/ *verb* (**-ding**) (often + *on, upon*) thrust (oneself etc.) importunately forward. □ **obtrusion** *noun*.

obtrusive /əbˈtruːsɪv/ *adjective* **1** unpleasantly noticeable. **2** obtruding oneself. □ **obtrusively** *adverb*. **obtrusiveness** *noun*.
■ **1** blatant, conspicuous, inescapable, intrusive, noticeable, obvious, out of place, prominent, unwanted, unwelcome. **2** forward, importunate, interfering, intrusive, meddling, meddlesome.

obtuse /əbˈtjuːs/ *adjective* **1** dull-witted. **2** (of angle) between 90° and 180° **3** blunt; not sharp or pointed. □ **obtuseness** *noun*.
■ **1** dense, dull, slow, slow-witted, stupid, unperceptive.

obverse /ˈɒbvɜːs/ *noun* **1** counterpart; opposite. **2** side of coin or medal that bears head or principal design. **3** front or top side.

obviate /ˈɒbvɪeɪt/ *verb* (**-ting**) get round or do away with (need, inconvenience, etc.).
■ avert, forestall, preclude, prevent, remove, take away.

obvious /ˈɒbvɪəs/ *adjective* easily seen, recognized, or understood. □ **obviously** *adverb*. **obviousness** *noun*.
■ apparent, bald, blatant, clear, clear-cut, conspicuous, distinct, evident, *colloquial* eye-catching, flagrant, glaring, gross, inescapable, intrusive, manifest, notable, noticeable, obtrusive, open, overt, palpable, patent, perceptible, plain, prominent, pronounced, recognizable, self-evident, self-explanatory, straightforward, transparent, unconcealed, undisguised, undisputed, unmistakable, visible.

OC *abbreviation* Officer Commanding.

ocarina /ɒkəˈriːnə/ *noun* egg-shaped musical wind instrument.

occasion /əˈkeɪʒ(ə)n/ *noun* **1** special event or happening. **2** time of this. **3** reason, need. **4** suitable juncture; opportunity. ● *verb* cause, esp. incidentally.
■ *noun* **1** *colloquial* affair, celebration, ceremony, event, function, *colloquial* get-together, happening, incident, occurrence. **3** call, cause, excuse, grounds, justification, need, reason. **4** chance, circumstance, moment, occurrence, opportunity, time.

occasional *adjective* **1** happening irregularly and infrequently. **2** made or meant for special occasion(s). **3** acting on special occasion. □ **occasional table** small table for use as required. □ **occasionally** *adverb*.

■ **1** casual, desultory, fitful, infrequent, intermittent, irregular, odd, periodic, random, rare, scattered, spasmodic, sporadic, uncommon, unpredictable.

Occident /ˈɒksɪd(ə)nt/ *noun* (**the Occident**) West, esp. Europe and America as distinct from the Orient. □ **occidental** /-ˈden-/ *adjective*.

occiput /ˈɒksɪpʌt/ *noun* back of head. □ **occipital** /-ˈsɪpɪt-/ *adjective*.

occlude /əˈkluːd/ *verb* (**-ding**) **1** stop up; obstruct. **2** *Chemistry* absorb (gases). **3** (as **occluded** *adjective*) *Meteorology* (of frontal system) formed when cold front overtakes warm front, raising warm air. □ **occlusion** *noun*.

occult /ɒˈkʌlt, ˈɒkʌlt/ *adjective* **1** involving the supernatural; mystical. **2** esoteric. □ **the occult** occult phenomena generally. □ **occultism** *noun*. **occultist** *noun*.

■ **1** see SUPERNATURAL. □ **the occult** the black art, black magic, diabolism, occultism, sorcery, the supernatural, witchcraft.

occupant /ˈɒkjʊpənt/ *noun* person occupying dwelling, office, or position. □ **occupancy** *noun* (*plural* **-ies**).

■ denizen, householder, incumbent, inhabitant, lessee, lodger, occupier, owner, resident, tenant.

occupation /ɒkjʊˈpeɪʃ(ə)n/ *noun* **1** profession or employment. **2** pastime. **3** occupying or being occupied. **4** taking or holding military possession (of another country etc.). **5** placing oneself in building etc. without authority as protest etc.

■ **1** appointment, business, calling, career, employment, job, line, *métier*, position, post, profession, *formal* situation, trade, vocation, work. **2** activity, diversion, entertainment, hobby, interest, pastime, pursuit, recreation. **3** incumbency, occupancy, possession, tenancy, tenure, use. **4** annexation, appropriation, colonization, conquest, invasion, oppression, seizure, subjection, subjugation, takeover, usurpation. **5** sit-in.

occupational *adjective* of or connected with one's occupation. □ **occupational disease, hazard** one to which a particular occupation renders someone especially liable. **occupational therapy** programme of mental or physical activity to assist recovery from disease or injury.

occupier /ˈɒkjʊpaɪə/ *noun* person living in house etc. as owner or tenant.

occupy /ˈɒkjʊpaɪ/ *verb* (**-ies, -ied**) **1** live in; be tenant of. **2** take up, fill (space, time, or place). **3** take military possession of. **4** place oneself in (building etc.) without authority as protest etc. **5** hold (office). **6** keep busy.

■ **1** dwell in, inhabit, live in, reside in, take up residence in. **2** fill, take up, use, utilize. **3** annex, capture, conquer, garrison, invade, overrun, possess, subjugate, take over, take possession of. **4** sit in. **6** absorb, busy, divert, engage, engross, involve, preoccupy.

occur /əˈkɜː/ *verb* (**-rr-**) **1** take place, happen. **2** be met with or found in some place or conditions. **3** (+ *to*) come into one's mind.

■ **1** arise, *poetical* befall, chance, come about, come to pass, crop up, develop, happen, materialize, take place, *disputed* transpire, turn out, turn up. **2** appear, be found, crop up, exist, manifest itself, *colloquial* show up, turn up.

occurrence /əˈkʌrəns/ *noun* happening, incident.

■ *colloquial* affair, case, circumstance, development, event, happening, incident, instance, manifestation, matter, occasion, phenomenon, proceeding.

ocean /ˈəʊʃ(ə)n/ *noun* **1** large expanse of sea, esp. one of the 5 named divisions of this, e.g. Atlantic Ocean. **2** (often in *plural*) *colloquial* immense expanse or quantity. □ **oceanic** /əʊʃɪˈænɪk/ *adjective*.

oceanography /əʊʃəˈnɒgrəfi/ *noun* study of the oceans. □ **oceanographer** *noun*.

ocelot /ˈɒsɪlɒt/ *noun* S. American leopard-like cat.

ochre /ˈəʊkə/ *noun* (*US* **ocher**) **1** earth used as pigment. **2** pale brownish-yellow colour. □ **ochreous** /ˈəʊkrɪəs/ *adjective*.

o'clock /əˈklɒk/ *adverb* of the clock (used to specify hour).

Oct. *abbreviation* October.

octa- *combining form* (also **oct-** before vowel) eight.

octagon /ˈɒktəgən/ *noun* plane figure with 8 sides and angles. □ **octagonal** /-ˈtæg-/ *adjective*.

octahedron /ɒktəˈhiːdrən/ *noun* (*plural* **-s**) solid figure contained by 8 (esp. triangular) plane faces. □ **octahedral** *adjective*.

octane /ˈɒkteɪn/ *noun* colourless inflammable hydrocarbon occurring in petrol. □ **high-octane** (of fuel used in internal-combustion engines) not detonating rapidly during power stroke. **octane number, rating** figure indicating antiknock properties of fuel.

octave /ˈɒktɪv/ *noun* **1** *Music* interval of 8 diatonic degrees between two notes. **2** *Music* 8 notes occupying this interval. **3** *Music* each of two notes at this interval's extremes. **4** 8-line stanza.

octavo /ɒkˈteɪvəʊ/ *noun* (*plural* **-s**) size of book or page with sheets folded into 8 leaves.

octet /ɒkˈtet/ *noun* **1** musical composition for 8 performers. **2** the performers. **3** any group of 8.

octo- *combining form* (also **oct-** before vowel) eight.

October /ɒkˈtəʊbə/ *noun* tenth month of year.

octogenarian /ɒktəʊdʒɪˈneərɪən/ *noun* person from 80 to 89 years old.

octopus /ˈɒktəpəs/ *noun* (*plural* **-puses**) mollusc with 8 suckered tentacles.

ocular /ˈɒkjʊlə/ *adjective* of, for, or by the eyes; visual.

oculist /ˈɒkjʊlɪst/ *noun* specialist in treatment of eyes.

OD /əʊ'diː/ *slang noun* drug overdose. ● *verb* (**OD's, OD'd, Od'ing**) take overdose.

odd *adjective* **1** extraordinary, strange. **2** (of job etc.) occasional, casual. **3** not normally considered; unconnected. **4** (of numbers) not divisible by 2. **5** left over; detached from set etc. **6** (added to weight, sum, etc.) rather more than. □ **oddball** *colloquial* eccentric person. □ **oddly** *adverb.* **oddness** *noun.*

■ **1** abnormal, anomalous, atypical, bizarre, cranky, curious, deviant, different, eccentric, exceptional, extraordinary, freak, funny, idiosyncratic, incongruous, inexplicable, *colloquial* kinky, outlandish, out of the ordinary, peculiar, puzzling, queer, rare, singular, strange, uncharacteristic, uncommon, unconventional, unexpected, unusual, *colloquial* weird. **2** casual, irregular, miscellaneous, occasional, part-time, random, sporadic, sundry, varied, various. **5** extra, left over, remaining, single, spare, superfluous, surplus, unmatched, unused.

oddity /'ɒdɪtɪ/ *noun* (*plural* **-ies**) **1** strange person, thing, or occurrence. **2** peculiar trait. **3** strangeness.

oddment *noun* odd article; something left over.
■ (**oddments**) bits, bits and pieces, fragments, junk, leftovers, litter, odds and ends, offcuts, remnants, scraps, shreds.

odds *plural noun* **1** ratio between amounts staked by parties to a bet. **2** chances in favour of or against result. **3** balance of advantage. **4** difference giving an advantage. □ **at odds** (often + *with*) in conflict. **odds and ends** remnants; stray articles; **odds-on** state when success is more likely than failure. **over the odds** above general price etc.

ode *noun* lyric poem of exalted style and tone.

odious /'əʊdɪəs/ *adjective* hateful, repulsive. □ **odiously** *adverb.* **odiousness** *noun.*
■ abhorrent, abominable, detestable, execrable, hateful, loathsome, offensive, repugnant, repulsive.

odium /'əʊdɪəm/ *noun* general dislike or disapproval.

odor *US* = ODOUR.

odoriferous /əʊdə'rɪfərəs/ *adjective* diffusing (usually pleasant) odours.

odour /'əʊdə/ *noun* (*US* **odor**) **1** smell or fragrance. **2** favour or repute. □ **odorous** *adjective.* **odourless** *adjective.*
■ **1** aroma, bouquet, fragrance, nose, redolence, scent, smell, stench, stink. □ **odorous** aromatic, fragrant, odoriferous, perfumed, redolent, scented, smelly. **odourless** deodorized, unscented.

odyssey /'ɒdɪsɪ/ *noun* (*plural* **-s**) long adventurous journey.

OED *abbreviation* Oxford English Dictionary.

oedema /ɪ'diːmə/ *noun* (*US* **edema**) excess fluid in body cavities or tissues.

Oedipus complex /'iːdɪpəs/ *noun* attraction of child to parent of opposite sex (esp. son to mother). □ **Oedipal** *adjective.*

oesophagus /iː'sɒfəgəs/ *noun* (*US* **esophagus**) (*plural* **-gi** /-dʒaɪ/ or **-guses**) passage from mouth to stomach; gullet.

oestrogen /'iːstrədʒ(ə)n/ *noun* (*US* **estrogen**) **1** sex hormone developing and maintaining female physical characteristics. **2** this produced artificially for medical use.

oeuvre /'ɜːvr/ *noun* works of creative artist considered collectively. [French]

of /ɒv/ *preposition* **1** belonging to; from. **2** concerning. **3** out of. **4** among. **5** relating to. **6** *US* (of time in relation to following hour) to. □ **be of** possess; give rise to. **of late** recently. **of old** formerly.

off *adverb* **1** away; at or to distance. **2** out of position; loose, separate, gone. **3** so as to be rid of. **4** discontinued, stopped. **5** not available on menu. ● *preposition* **1** from. **2** not on. ● *adjective* **1** further; far. **2** right-hand. **3** *colloquial* annoying; not acceptable. **4** *colloquial* unwell. **5** *colloquial* (of food etc.) no longer fresh; bad. **6** *Cricket* of, in, or into half of field which batsman faces. ● *noun* **1** start of race. **2** *Cricket* the off side. □ **off and on** now and then. **offbeat 1** unconventional. **2** *Music* not coinciding with beat. **off-centre** not quite coinciding with central position. **off chance** remote possibility. **off colour 1** unwell. **2** *US* rather indecent. **off-licence** shop selling alcoholic drink for consumption away from premises. **off-line** *Computing* ● *adjective* not on-line. ● *adverb* with delay between data production and its processing. **off-peak** (of electricity, traffic, etc.) used or for use at times of lesser demand. **offprint** reprint of part of publication. **off-putting 1** disconcerting. **2** repellent. **offshoot 1** side-shoot or branch. **2** derivative. **offside** (of player in field game) in position where he or she may not play the ball. **off the wall** *slang* crazy, absurd. **off white** white with grey or yellowish tinge.
■ □ **offshoot 1** branch. **2** by-product, derivative, development, spin-off.

offal /'ɒf(ə)l/ *noun* **1** edible organs of animal, esp. heart, liver, etc. **2** refuse; scraps.

offcut /'ɒfkʌt/ *noun* remnant of timber, paper, etc. after cutting.

offence /ə'fens/ *noun* (*US* **offense**) **1** illegal act. **2** transgression. **3** upsetting of person's feelings, insult; resentment. **4** aggressive action. □ **give offence** offend. **take offence** be offended.
■ **1, 2** breach, crime, fault, felony, infringement, lapse, malefaction, misdeed, misdemeanour, outrage, peccadillo, sin, transgression, *archaic* trespass, violation, wrong, wrongdoing. **3** anger, annoyance, disgust, displeasure, hard feelings, indignation, irritation, pique, resentment, umbrage, upset.

offend /ə'fend/ *verb* **1** cause offence to; upset. **2**

displease, anger. **3** (often + *against*) do wrong. □ **offender** *noun*. **offending** *adjective*.

■ **1, 2** affront, anger, annoy, chagrin, disgust, displease, embarrass, give offence, hurt (person's) feelings, insult, irritate, *colloquial* miff, outrage, pain, provoke, revolt, *colloquial* rile, sicken, slight, snub, upset, vex. **3** do wrong, transgress, violate. □ **offender** criminal, culprit, delinquent, evildoer, guilty party, lawbreaker, malefactor, miscreant, outlaw, sinner, transgressor, wrongdoer.

offense *US* = OFFENCE.

offensive /əˈfensɪv/ *adjective* **1** causing offence; insulting. **2** disgusting. **3** aggressive. **4** (of weapon) for attacking. ● *noun* aggressive attitude, action, or campaign. □ **offensively** *adverb*. **offensiveness** *noun*.

■ *adjective* **1** abusive, coarse, disrespectful, embarrassing, impolite, improper, indecent, insulting, obscene, *colloquial* rude, vulgar. **2** annoying, antisocial, detestable, disagreeable, disgusting, displeasing, foul, loathsome, nasty, nauseating, nauseous, noxious, objectionable, obnoxious, off-putting, repugnant, repulsive, revolting, sickening, unpleasant, unsavoury, vile. **3** aggressive, antagonistic, attacking, belligerent, hostile, threatening, warlike. ● *noun* see ATTACK *noun* 1.

offer /ˈɒfə/ *verb* **1** present for acceptance, refusal, or consideration. **2** (+ *to do*) express readiness; show intention to. **3** attempt. **4** (often + *up*) present by way of sacrifice. ● *noun* **1** expression of readiness to do or give if desired, or buy or sell. **2** amount offered. **3** proposal, esp. of marriage. **4** bid. □ **on offer** for sale at certain (esp. reduced) price.

■ *verb* **1** bid, extend, hold out, make available, proffer, put forward, put up, suggest, tender. **2** come forward, propose, show oneself willing, volunteer. ● *noun* bid, proposal, proposition, suggestion, tender.

offering *noun* contribution, gift; thing offered.

■ contribution, donation, gift, oblation, offertory, present, sacrifice.

offertory /ˈɒfətərɪ/ *noun* (*plural* **-ies**) **1** offering of bread and wine at Eucharist. **2** collection of money at religious service.

offhand *adjective* **1** without preparation. **2** casual, curt. □ **offhanded** *adjective*.

■ **1** see IMPROMPTU. **2** abrupt, aloof, careless, casual, cavalier, cool, curt, offhanded, perfunctory, unceremonious, uncooperative, uninterested.

office /ˈɒfɪs/ *noun* **1** room or building where administrative or clerical work is done. **2** place for transacting business. **3** department or local branch, esp. for specified purpose. **4** position with duties attached to it. **5** tenure of official position. **6** duty, task, function. **7** (usually in *plural*) piece of kindness; service. **8** authorized form of worship. □ **office worker** employee in business office.

■ **1** bureau, study, workplace, workroom. **4, 6** appointment, assignment, commission, duty, function, job, occupation, place, position, post, responsibility, role, *formal* situation, task, work.

officer /ˈɒfɪsə/ *noun* **1** person holding position of authority or trust, esp. one with commission in armed forces. **2** policeman or policewoman. **3** president, treasurer, etc. of society etc.

■ **1** functionary, office-holder, official. **2** constable, PC, policeman, police officer, policewoman, WPC.

official /əˈfɪʃ(ə)l/ *adjective* **1** of office or its tenure. **2** characteristic of people in office. **3** properly authorized. ● *noun* person holding office or engaged in official duties. □ **official secrets** confidential information involving national security. □ **officialdom** *noun*. **officially** *adverb*.

■ *adjective* **2** see FORMAL 1. **3** accredited, approved, authentic, authoritative, authorized, bona fide, certified, formal, lawful, legal, legitimate, licensed, organized, proper, recognized, true, trustworthy, valid. ● *noun* administrator, agent, bureaucrat, dignitary, executive, functionary, mandarin, officer, organizer, representative.

officialese /əfɪʃəˈliːz/ *noun derogatory* officials' jargon.

officiate /əˈfɪʃɪeɪt/ *verb* (**-ting**) **1** act in official capacity. **2** conduct religious service.

■ **1** adjudicate, be in charge, be responsible, have authority, preside, referee, umpire; (*officiate at*) chair, conduct, manage, run.

officious /əˈfɪʃəs/ *adjective* **1** domineering. **2** intrusive in correcting etc. □ **officiously** *adverb*. **officiousness** *noun*.

■ *colloquial* bossy, bumptious, *colloquial* cocky, dictatorial, forward, impertinent, interfering, meddlesome, meddling, overzealous, *colloquial* pushy, self-appointed, self-important.

offing /ˈɒfɪŋ/ *noun* □ **in the offing** at hand; ready or likely to happen etc.

offload /ˈɒfləʊd, ɒfˈləʊd/ *verb* **1** get rid of. **2** unload (cargo etc.).

offset *noun* **1** side-shoot of plant used for propagation. **2** compensation. **3** sloping ledge. ● *verb* (**-setting**; *past* and *past participle* **-set**) counterbalance, compensate.

■ *verb* balance, cancel out, compensate for, counteract, counterbalance, make amends for, make good, make up for, redress.

offspring *noun* (*plural* same) **1** person's child, children, or descendants. **2** animal's young or descendants.

■ babies, baby, *colloquial* brood, child, children, descendant(s), family, heir(s), issue, *colloquial* kid(s), litter, progeny, seed, successor(s), young.

oft *adverb archaic* often.

often /ˈɒf(ə)n/ *adverb* (**oftener**, **oftenest**) **1** frequently; many times. **2** at short intervals. **3** in many instances.

■ again and again, all the time, commonly, constantly, continually, frequently, generally, habitually, many times, regularly, repeatedly, time after time, time and again, usually.

ogee /ˈəʊdʒiː/ *noun* S-shaped curve or moulding.

ogive /ˈəʊdʒaɪv/ *noun* **1** pointed arch. **2** diagonal rib of vault.

ogle /ˈəʊg(ə)l/ *verb* (**-ling**) look lecherously or flirtatiously (at). ● *noun* flirtatious glance.

ogre /ˈəʊgə/ *noun* (*feminine* **ogress** /-grɪs/) man-eating giant. □ **ogreish, ogrish** /ˈəʊgərɪʃ/ *adjective*.

oh /əʊ/ *interjection* (also **O**) *expressing surprise, pain, etc.*

ohm /əʊm/ *noun* SI unit of electrical resistance.

OHMS *abbreviation* On Her or His Majesty's Service.

oho /əʊˈhəʊ/ *interjection: expressing surprise or exultation.*

OHP *abbreviation* overhead projector.

oil *noun* **1** viscous usually inflammable liquid insoluble in water. **2** petroleum. ● *verb* **1** apply oil to; lubricate. **2** treat with oil. □ **oilcake** compressed linseed etc. as cattle food or manure. **oilfield** district yielding mineral oil. **oil paint** paint made by mixing pigment with oil. **oil painting** use of or picture in oil paints. **oil rig** equipment for drilling an oil well. **oilskin 1** cloth waterproofed with oil. **2** garment or (in *plural*) suit of it. **oil slick** patch of oil, esp. on sea. **oil well** well from which mineral oil is drawn.

■ *verb* **1** grease, lubricate.

oily *adjective* (**-ier, -iest**) **1** of, like, covered or soaked with, oil. **2** (of manner) fawning.

■ **1** buttery, fat, fatty, greasy, oleaginous. **2** see OBSEQUIOUS.

ointment /ˈɔɪntmənt/ *noun* smooth greasy healing or cosmetic preparation for skin.

■ balm, cream, embrocation, emollient, liniment, lotion, salve, unguent.

OK /əʊˈkeɪ/ (also **okay**) *colloquial adjective & adverb* all right. ● *noun* (*plural* **OKs**) approval, sanction. ● *verb* (**OK's, OK'd, OK'ing**) approve, sanction.

okapi /əʊˈkɑːpɪ/ *noun* (*plural* same or **-s**) African partially striped ruminant mammal.

okay = OK.

okra /ˈəʊkrə/ *noun* tall originally African plant with edible seed pods.

old /əʊld/ *adjective* (**-er, -est**) **1** advanced in age; not young or near its beginning. **2** worn, dilapidated, or shabby from age. **3** practised, inveterate. **4** dating from far back; long established. **5** former. **6** no longer used; obsolete. **7** *colloquial: used to indicate affection.* □ **old age** later part of normal lifetime. **old-age pension** state retirement pension. **old-age pensioner** person receiving this. **Old Bill** *slang* the police. **old boy 1** former male pupil of school. **2** *colloquial* elderly man. **old-fashioned** in or according to fashion

no longer current; antiquated. **old girl 1** former female pupil of school. **2** *colloquial* elderly woman. **Old Glory** *US* Stars and Stripes. **old guard** original, past, or conservative members of group. **old hand** experienced or practised person. **old hat** *colloquial* hackneyed. **old maid 1** *derogatory* elderly unmarried woman. **2** prim and fussy person. **old-maidish** *adjective*. **old man** *colloquial* one's father, husband, or employer etc. **old man's beard** wild clematis. **old master 1** great painter of former times. **2** painting by such painter. **Old Testament** part of Bible dealing with pre-Christian times. **old wives' tale** unscientific belief. **old woman** *colloquial* **1** one's wife or mother. **2** fussy or timid man. **Old World** Europe, Asia, and Africa. **old-world** of or associated with old times. □ **oldish** *adjective*. **oldness** *noun*.

■ **1** advanced in years, aged, doddery, elderly, *derogatory* geriatric, getting on, grey-haired, hoary, in one's dotage, long-lived, oldish, *colloquial* past it, senile, senior; (*old person*) centenarian, fogey, nonagenarian, octogenarian, *colloquial* oldie, pensioner, senior, senior citizen, septuagenarian. **2** crumbling, decayed, decaying, decrepit, dilapidated, moth-eaten, ragged, ruined, *colloquial* scruffy, shabby, stale, threadbare, time-worn, worn, worn out. **3** experienced, expert, familiar, inveterate, mature, practised, skilled, veteran. **4** age-old, ancient, *colloquial* antediluvian, antiquated, antique, archaic, classical, early, enduring, established, historic, lasting, long-standing, medieval, old-fashioned, prehistoric, primeval, primitive, primordial, quaint, time-honoured, traditional, venerable, veteran, vintage, well established. **5** bygone, forgotten, former, (*time*) immemorial, *archaic* olden, past, previous, remote. **6** cancelled, disused, expired, extinct, invalid, obsolete, superannuated, superseded, used. □ **old age** declining years, decrepitude, dotage, senility. **old-fashioned** anachronistic, antiquated, archaic, backward-looking, conventional, dated, *colloquial* fuddy-duddy, fusty, hackneyed, narrow-minded, obsolete, old, *colloquial* old hat, outdated, outmoded, out of date, passé, pedantic, prim, proper, prudish, reactionary, *slang* square, time-honoured, traditional, unfashionable.

olden *adjective archaic* old; of old.

oldie *noun colloquial* old person or thing.

oleaginous /əʊlɪˈædʒɪnəs/ *adjective* like or producing oil; oily.

oleander /əʊlɪˈændə/ *noun* evergreen flowering Mediterranean shrub.

olfactory /ɒlˈfæktərɪ/ *adjective* of the sense of smell.

oligarch /ˈɒlɪgɑːk/ *noun* member of oligarchy.

oligarchy /ˈɒlɪgɑːkɪ/ *noun* (*plural* **-ies**) **1** government by small group of people. **2** members of such government. **3** state so governed. □ **oligarchic(al)** /-ˈgɑːk-/ *adjective*.

olive /ˈɒlɪv/ *noun* **1** oval hard-stoned fruit yielding oil. **2** tree bearing this. **3** dull yellowish green. ● *adjective* **1** olive-green. **2** (of complexion) yellowish-brown. □ **olive branch** gesture of peace or reconciliation.

Olympiad /əˈlɪmpiæd/ *noun* **1** period of 4 years between Olympic Games. **2** celebration of modern Olympic Games.

Olympian /əˈlɪmpiən/ *adjective* **1** of Olympus. **2** magnificent, condescending; aloof.

Olympic /əˈlɪmpɪk/ *adjective* of the Olympic Games. ● *plural noun* (**the Olympics**) Olympic Games. □ **Olympic Games** ancient Greek athletic festival held every 4 years, or modern international revival of this.

OM *abbreviation* Order of Merit.

ombudsman /ˈɒmbʊdzmən/ *noun* official appointed to investigate complaints against public authorities.

omega /ˈəʊmɪgə/ *noun* **1** last letter of Greek alphabet (Ω, ω). **2** last of series.

omelette /ˈɒmlɪt/ *noun* beaten eggs fried and often folded over filling.

omen /ˈəʊmən/ *noun* **1** event supposedly warning of good or evil. **2** prophetic significance.

■ **1** augury, auspice, foreboding, forewarning, harbinger, indication, portent, premonition, presage, prognostication, sign, token, warning, writing on the wall.

ominous /ˈɒmɪnəs/ *adjective* **1** threatening. **2** inauspicious. □ **ominously** *adverb*.

■ baleful, dire, fateful, forbidding, foreboding, grim, ill-omened, ill-starred, inauspicious, louring, menacing, portentous, prophetic, sinister, threatening, unfavourable, unlucky, unpromising, unpropitious, warning.

omit /əʊˈmɪt/ *verb* (**-tt-**) **1** leave out; not include. **2** leave undone. **3** (+ *to do*) neglect to. □ **omission** /əʊˈmɪʃ(ə)n/ *noun*.

■ **1** dispense with, drop, except, exclude, ignore, leave out, miss out, overlook, pass over, skip. **2** neglect, skip. **3** fail, forget, neglect. □ **omission** exclusion, failure, gap, neglect, negligence, oversight, shortcoming.

omni- *combining form* all.

omnibus /ˈɒmnɪbəs/ *noun* **1** *formal* bus. **2** volume containing several novels etc. previously published separately. ● *adjective* **1** serving several purposes at once. **2** comprising several items.

omnipotent /ɒmˈnɪpət(ə)nt/ *adjective* all-powerful. □ **omnipotence** *noun*.

■ all-powerful, almighty, invincible, supreme, unconquerable.

omnipresent /ɒmnɪˈprez(ə)nt/ *adjective* present everywhere. □ **omnipresence** *noun*.

omniscient /ɒmˈnɪsɪənt/ *adjective* knowing everything. □ **omniscience** *noun*.

omnivorous /ɒmˈnɪvərəs/ *adjective* **1** feeding on both plant and animal material. **2** *jocular* reading everything that comes one's way. □ **omnivore** /ˈɒmnɪvɔː/ *noun*. **omnivorousness** *noun*.

on *preposition* **1** (so as to be) supported by, covering, attached to, etc. **2** (of time) exactly at; during. **3** close to. **4** in direction of. **5** at, near. **6** concerning, about. **7** added to. ● *adverb* **1** (so as to be) on something. **2** in some direction; forward. **3** in advance. **4** with movement. **5** in operation or activity. **6** *colloquial* willing to participate, approve, bet, etc. **7** *colloquial* practicable, acceptable. **8** being shown or performed. ● *adjective* Cricket of, in, or into half of field behind batsman's back. ● *noun* Cricket the on side. □ **be on about** *colloquial* discuss, esp. tiresomely. **on and off** intermittent(ly). **on-line** directly controlled by or connected to computer. **onscreen** when being filmed. **on to** to a position on.

USAGE See note at ONTO.

ONC *abbreviation* Ordinary National Certificate.

once /wʌns/ *adverb* **1** on one occasion only. **2** at some time in past. **3** ever or at all. ● *conjunction* as soon as. ● *noun* one time or occasion. □ **at once 1** immediately. **2** simultaneously. **once-over** *colloquial* rapid inspection.

oncology /ɒŋˈkɒlədʒɪ/ *noun* study of tumours.

oncoming *adjective* approaching from the front.

■ advancing, approaching, facing, looming, nearing.

OND *abbreviation* Ordinary National Diploma.

one /wʌn/ *adjective* **1** single and integral in number. **2** only such. **3** without others. **4** identical. **5** forming a unity. ● *noun* **1** lowest cardinal numeral. **2** thing numbered with it. **3** unit; unity. **4** single thing, person, or example. **5** *colloquial* drink. ● *pronoun* any person. □ **one-armed bandit** *colloquial* fruit machine with long handle. **one-horse** *colloquial* small, poorly equipped. **one-man** involving or operated by one person only. **one-off** made as the only one; not repeated. **one-sided** unfair, partial. **one-sidedness** *noun*. **one-time** former. **one-way** allowing movement etc. in one direction only.

■ □ **one-sided** (*one-sided game*) ill-matched, unbalanced, unequal, uneven; (*one-sided umpire*) biased, bigoted, partial, partisan, prejudiced.

oneness *noun* **1** singleness. **2** uniqueness. **3** agreement. **4** sameness.

onerous /ˈəʊnərəs/ *adjective* burdensome. □ **onerousness** *noun*.

■ burdensome, demanding, difficult, exacting, heavy, laborious, taxing.

oneself *pronoun: emphatic and reflexive form of* ONE. □ **be oneself** act in one's natural manner.

ongoing *adjective* continuing; in progress.

onion /ˈʌnjən/ *noun* vegetable with edible bulb of pungent smell and flavour.

onlooker *noun* spectator. □ **onlooking** *adjective*.

■ bystander, eyewitness, looker-on, observer, spectator, watcher, witness.

only /'əʊnlɪ/ *adverb* solely, merely, exclusively. ● *adjective* existing alone of its or their kind. ● *conjunction colloquial* **1** except that. **2** but then. □ **if only 1** even if for no other reason than. **2** I wish that.

> ■ *adverb* barely, exclusively, just, merely, simply, solely. ● *adjective* lone, one, single, sole, solitary, unique.

o.n.o. *abbreviation* or near offer.

onomatopoeia /ɒnəmætə'piːə/ *noun* formation of word from sound associated with thing named, e.g. *whizz, cuckoo.* □ **onomatopoeic** *adjective.*

onrush /'ɒnrʌʃ/ *noun* onward rush.

onset *noun* **1** attack. **2** impetuous beginning.

onslaught /'ɒnslɔːt/ *noun* fierce attack.

onto *preposition* = ON TO.

> USAGE *Onto* is much used but is still not as widely accepted as *into.* It is, however, useful in distinguishing between, e.g., *We drove on to the beach* (i.e. towards it) and *we drove onto the beach* (i.e. into contact with it).

ontology /ɒn'tɒlədʒɪ/ *noun* branch of metaphysics concerned with the nature of being. □ **ontological** /-tə'lɒdʒ-/ *adjective.* **ontologically** /-tə'lɒdʒ-/ *adverb.* **ontologist** *noun.*

onus /'əʊnəs/ *noun* (*plural* **onuses**) burden, duty, responsibility.

onward /'ɒnwəd/ *adverb* (also **onwards**) **1** advancing. **2** into the future. ● *adjective* **1** forward. **2** advancing.

onyx /'ɒnɪks/ *noun* semiprecious variety of agate with coloured layers.

oodles /'uːd(ə)lz/ *plural noun colloquial* very great amount.

ooh /u/ *interjection: expressing surprised pleasure, pain, excitement, etc.*

oolite /'əʊəlaɪt/ *noun* granular limestone. □ **oolitic** /-'lɪt-/ *adjective.*

oomph /ʊmf/ *noun slang* **1** energy, enthusiasm. **2** attractiveness, esp. sex appeal.

ooze[1] *verb* (**-zing**) **1** trickle or leak slowly out. **2** (of substance) exude fluid. **3** (often + *with*) give off (a feeling) freely. ● *noun* sluggish flow. □ **oozy** *adjective.*

> ■ *verb* **1, 2** discharge, emit, exude, leak, secrete, seep, weep. **3** (*ooze with*) exude, give off.

ooze[2] *noun* wet mud. □ **oozy** *adjective.*

op *noun colloquial* operation.

op. *abbreviation* opus.

opacity /əʊ'pæsɪtɪ/ *noun* opaqueness.

opal /'əʊp(ə)l/ *noun* semiprecious milk-white or bluish stone with iridescent reflections.

opalescent /əʊpə'les(ə)nt/ *adjective* iridescent. □ **opalescence** *noun.*

opaline /'əʊpəlaɪn/ *adjective* opal-like, opalescent.

opaque /əʊ'peɪk/ *adjective* (**-r, -st**) **1** not transmitting light. **2** impenetrable to sight. **3** unintelligible. **4** stupid. □ **opaquely** *adverb.* **opaqueness** *noun.*

> ■ **1, 2** cloudy, dark, dim, dull, filmy, hazy, impenetrable, muddy, murky, obscure, turbid, unclear.

op. cit. *abbreviation* in the work already quoted (*opere citato*).

OPEC /'əʊpek/ *abbreviation* Organization of Petroleum Exporting Countries.

open /'əʊpən/ *adjective* **1** not closed, locked, or blocked up. **2** not covered or confined. **3** exposed. **4** (of goal etc.) undefended. **5** undisguised, public. **6** unfolded, spread out. **7** (of fabric) with gaps. **8** frank. **9** open-minded. **10** (of question) undecided. **11** accessible to visitors or customers. **12** (of meeting, competition, etc.) not restricted. **13** (+ *to*) willing to receive. **14** (+ *to*) vulnerable to. ● *verb* **1** make or become open or more open. **2** (+ *into* etc.) give access to. **3** establish; set going; start. **4** ceremonially declare open. ● *noun* **1** (**the open**) open air. **2** open competition etc. □ **open air** outdoors. **open-air** *adjective* outdoor. **open day** day when public may visit place normally closed to them. **open-ended** with no limit or restriction. **open-handed** generous. **open-heart surgery** surgery with heart exposed and blood made to bypass it. **open house** hospitality for all visitors. **open letter** one addressed to individual and printed in newspaper etc. **open-minded** accessible to new ideas; unprejudiced. **open-mindedness** *noun.* **open-plan 1** (of house, offices, etc.) having large undivided rooms. **2** (of room, office, etc.) undivided. **open prison** one with few physical restraints on prisoners. **open question** matter on which different views are legitimate. **open sandwich** one without bread on top. **open sea** expanse of sea away from land. □ **openness** *noun.*

> ■ *adjective* **1** agape, ajar, gaping, unbolted, unfastened, unlocked, unsealed, unwrapped, wide, wide open, yawning. **2, 3** accessible, bare, broad, clear, empty, exposed, extensive, free, revealed, spacious, treeless, unconfined, uncovered, uncrowded, undefended, unenclosed, unfenced, unobstructed, unprotected, unrestricted, vacant. **5** apparent, barefaced, blatant, conspicuous, downright, evident, flagrant, obvious, outspoken, overt, plain, public, unconcealed, undisguised, visible. **6** extended, outstretched, spread out, unfolded. **7** artless, candid, communicative, frank, guileless, honest, innocent, sincere, straightforward, transparent, uninhibited. **9** broad-minded, flexible, generous, magnanimous, open-minded, receptive, responsive, unbiased, unprejudiced. **10** arguable, debatable, moot, problematical, unanswered, undecided, unresolved, unsettled. **11, 12** accessible, free, public, unrestricted. ● *verb* **1** unbar, unblock, unbolt, unclose, uncork, undo, unfasten, unfold, unfurl, unlatch, unlock, unroll, unseal, untie, unwrap. **3** activate, begin, *formal* commence, establish, get going, inaugurate, initiate, *colloquial* kick off, launch, set in motion, set up, start.

opener *noun* device for opening tins or bottles etc.

opening *noun* **1** gap, aperture. **2** opportunity. **3** beginning, initial part. ● *adjective* initial, first.

■ *noun* **1** aperture, breach, break, chink, cleft, crack, crevice, cut, door, doorway, fissure, gap, gash, gate, gateway, hatch, hole, leak, mouth, orifice, outlet, rent, rift, slit, slot, space, split, tear, vent. **2** break, chance, opportunity, way in. **3** beginning, birth, *formal* commencement, dawn, inauguration, inception, initiation, launch, outset, start. ● *adjective* first, inaugural, initial, introductory.

openly *adverb* publicly, frankly.

openwork /'əʊp(ə)nwɜːk/ *noun* pattern with intervening spaces in metal, leather, lace, etc.

opera[1] /'ɒpərə/ *noun* musical drama with sung or spoken dialogue. □ **opera-glasses** small binoculars for use in theatres etc. **opera house** theatre for operas.

opera[2] *plural* of OPUS.

operable /'ɒpərəb(ə)l/ *adjective* **1** that can be operated. **2** suitable for treatment by surgical operation.

operate /'ɒpəreɪt/ *verb* (**-ting**) **1** work, control (machine etc.). **2** be in action. **3** perform surgical operation(s). **4** direct military etc. action. □ **operating theatre** room for surgical operations.

■ **1** control, drive, handle, manage, use, work. **2** act, function, go, perform, run, work.

operatic /ɒpə'rætɪk/ *adjective* of or like opera.

operation *noun* **1** action, working. **2** performance of surgery on a patient. **3** military manoeuvre. **4** financial transaction. □ **operational** *adjective.* **operationally** *adverb.*

■ **1** action, activity, control, direction, effort, exercise, function, functioning, management, movement, performance, procedure, proceeding, process, running, working. **3** action, campaign, exercise, manoeuvre, movement. **4** action, business, deal, enterprise, proceeding, project, transaction, undertaking, venture. □ **operational** functioning, going, in operation, in use, in working order, operative, running, usable, working.

operative /'ɒpərətɪv/ *adjective* **1** in operation. **2** having principal relevance. **3** of or by surgery. ● *noun* worker, artisan.

■ *adjective* **1** see OPERATIONAL (OPERATION). **2** crucial, important, key, principal, relevant, significant. ● *noun* see WORKER 1.

operator *noun* **1** person operating machine, esp. connecting lines in telephone exchange. **2** person engaging in business.

operetta /ɒpə'retə/ *noun* light opera.

ophidian /əʊ'fɪdɪən/ *noun* member of suborder of reptiles including snakes. ● *adjective* of this order.

ophthalmia /ɒf'θælmɪə/ *noun* inflammation of eye.

ophthalmic /ɒf'θælmɪk/ *adjective* of or relating to the eye and its diseases. □ **ophthalmic optician** one qualified to prescribe as well as dispense spectacles.

ophthalmology /ɒfθæl'mɒlədʒɪ/ *noun* study of the eye. □ **ophthalmologist** *noun.*

ophthalmoscope /ɒf'θælməskəʊp/ *noun* instrument for examining the eye.

opiate /'əʊpɪət/ *adjective* **1** containing opium. **2** soporific. ● *noun* **1** drug containing opium, usually to ease pain or induce sleep. **2** soothing influence.

opine /əʊ'paɪn/ *verb* (**-ning**) (often + *that*) express or hold as opinion.

opinion /ə'pɪnjən/ *noun* **1** unproven belief. **2** view held as probable. **3** professional advice. **4** estimation. □ **opinion poll** assessment of public opinion by questioning representative sample.

■ assessment, attitude, belief, comment, conclusion, conjecture, conviction, estimate, estimation, feeling, guess, idea, impression, judgement, notion, perception, point of view, sentiment, theory, thought, view, viewpoint, way of thinking.

opinionated /ə'pɪnjəneɪtɪd/ *adjective* unduly confident in one's opinions.

opium /'əʊpɪəm/ *noun* drug made from juice of certain poppy, used as narcotic or sedative.

opossum /ə'pɒsəm/ *noun* **1** tree-living American marsupial. **2** *Australian & NZ* marsupial resembling this.

opponent /ə'pəʊnənt/ *noun* person who opposes.

■ adversary, antagonist, challenger, competitor, contender, contestant, enemy, foe, opposer, rival; (*opponents*) opposition.

opportune /'ɒpətjuːn/ *adjective* **1** well chosen; specially favourable. **2** (of action, event, etc.) well timed.

■ **1** advantageous, appropriate, auspicious, beneficial, favourable, felicitous, fortunate, good, happy, lucky, propitious, right, suitable. **2** convenient, seasonable, timely, well timed.

opportunism /ɒpə'tjuːnɪz(ə)m/ *noun* adaptation of policy to circumstances, esp. regardless of principle. □ **opportunist** *noun.* **opportunistic** /-'nɪs-/ *adjective.* **opportunistically** /-'nɪs-/ *adverb.*

opportunity /ɒpə'tjuːnɪtɪ/ *noun* (*plural* **-ies**) favourable chance or opening offered by circumstances.

■ break, chance, moment, occasion, opening, possibility, time.

oppose /ə'pəʊz/ *verb* (**-sing**) **1** set oneself against; resist; argue against. **2** (+ *to*) place in opposition or contrast to. □ **as opposed to** in contrast with. □ **opposed** *adjective.* **opposer** *noun.*

■ **1** argue with, attack, be at variance with, challenge, combat, compete against, confront, contend with, contest, contradict, controvert, counter, counter-attack, defy, disagree with, disapprove of, dissent from, face, fight, object to, obstruct, quarrel with, resist, rival, stand up to, take a stand against, take issue with, withstand. □ **opposed** see HOSTILE 2, OPPOSITE *adjective* 2.

opposite /'ɒpəzɪt/ *adjective* **1** facing; on other side. **2** (often + *to, from*) contrary; diametrically different. ● *noun* opposite thing, person, or term. ● *adverb* in opposite position. ● *preposition* opposite to. □ **opposite number** person in corresponding position in another group etc. **the opposite sex** either sex in relation to the other.
  ■ *adjective* **2** antithetical, conflicting, contradictory, contrary, contrasting, converse, different, hostile, incompatible, inconsistent, opposed, opposing, reverse, rival. ● *noun* antithesis, contrary, converse, reverse.

opposition /ɒpə'zɪʃ(ə)n/ *noun* **1** antagonism, resistance. **2** being in conflict or disagreement. **3** contrast. **4** group or party of opponents. **5** chief parliamentary party, or group of parties, opposed to party in office. **6** act of placing opposite.
  ■ **1** antagonism, antipathy, competition, defiance, disapproval, enmity, hostility, objection, resistance, scepticism, unfriendliness. **3** see CONTRAST *noun* 1,2. **4** see OPPONENT.

oppress /ə'pres/ *verb* **1** govern tyrannically. **2** treat with gross harshness or injustice. **3** weigh down. □ **oppressed** *adjective*. **oppression** *noun*. **oppressor** *noun*.
  ■ **1, 2** abuse, crush, enslave, exploit, grind down, harass, intimidate, keep under, maltreat, persecute, ride roughshod over, subdue, subjugate, terrorize, trample on, tyrannize. **3** afflict, burden, depress, encumber, overburden, weigh down. □ **oppressed** browbeaten, downtrodden, enslaved, exploited, misused, persecuted, subjugated, tyrannized. **oppression** abuse, despotism, enslavement, exploitation, harassment, injustice, maltreatment, persecution, subjection, subjugation, suppression, tyranny.

oppressive *adjective* **1** that oppresses. **2** (of weather) sultry, close. □ **oppressively** *adverb*. **oppressiveness** *noun*.
  ■ **1** brutal, cruel, despotic, harsh, repressive, tyrannical, undemocratic, unjust. **2** airless, close, heavy, humid, muggy, stifling, stuffy, suffocating, sultry.

opprobrious /ə'prəʊbrɪəs/ *adjective* (of language) severely scornful; abusive.

opprobrium /ə'prəʊbrɪəm/ *noun* **1** disgrace. **2** cause of this.

opt *verb* (usually + *for*) make choice; decide. □ **opt out (of)** choose not to take part etc. (in).

optic /'ɒptɪk/ *adjective* of eye or sight.

optical *adjective* **1** visual. **2** of or according to optics. **3** aiding sight. □ **optical fibre** thin glass fibre used to carry light signals. **optical illusion 1** image which deceives the eye. **2** mental misapprehension caused by this.

optician /ɒp'tɪʃ(ə)n/ *noun* maker, seller, or prescriber of spectacles, contact lenses, etc.

optics *plural noun* (treated as *singular*) science of light and vision.

optimal /'ɒptɪm(ə)l/ *adjective* best, most favourable.

optimism /'ɒptɪmɪz(ə)m/ *noun* inclination to hopefulness and confidence. □ **optimist** *noun*. **optimistic** /-'mɪs-/ *adjective*. **optimistically** /-'mɪs-/ *adverb*.
  ■ buoyancy, cheerfulness, confidence, hope, idealism, positiveness. □ **optimistic** buoyant, cheerful, confident, expectant, hopeful, idealistic, positive, sanguine; (*be optimistic*) look on the bright side.

optimize /'ɒptɪmaɪz/ *verb* (also **-ise**) (**-zing** or **-sing**) make best or most effective use of. □ **optimization** *noun*.

optimum /'ɒptɪməm/ *noun* (*plural* **-ma**) **1** most favourable conditions. **2** best practical solution. ● *adjective* optimal.
  ■ *adjective* best, finest, first-class, first-rate, ideal, most favourable, optimal, perfect, prime, superlative.

option /'ɒpʃ(ə)n/ *noun* **1** choice, choosing. **2** right to choose. **3** right to buy, sell, etc., on specified conditions at specified time. □ **keep, leave one's options open** not commit oneself.
  ■ **1, 2** alternative, choice, election, possibility, selection.

optional *adjective* not obligatory. □ **optionally** *adverb*.
  ■ avoidable, discretionary, dispensable, elective, inessential, possible, unforced, unnecessary, voluntary.

opulent /'ɒpjʊlənt/ *adjective* **1** wealthy. **2** luxurious. **3** abundant. □ **opulence** *noun*.

opus /'əʊpəs/ *noun* (*plural* **opuses** or **opera** /'ɒpərə/) **1** musical composition numbered as one of composer's works. **2** any artistic work.

or *conjunction: introducing alternatives*. □ **or else 1** otherwise. **2** *colloquial: expressing threat*.

oracle /'ɒrək(ə)l/ *noun* **1** place at which ancient Greeks etc. consulted gods for advice or prophecy. **2** response received there. **3** person or thing regarded as source of wisdom etc. □ **oracular** /ɒ'rækjʊlə/ *adjective*.

oral /'ɔːr(ə)l/ *adjective* **1** spoken, verbal; by word of mouth. **2** done or taken by mouth. ● *noun colloquial* spoken exam. □ **orally** *adverb*.
  ■ *adjective* **1** said, spoken, unwritten, uttered, verbal, vocal, voiced.

orange /'ɒrɪndʒ/ *noun* **1** roundish reddish-yellow citrus fruit. **2** its colour. **3** tree bearing it. ● *adjective* orange-coloured.

orangeade /ɒrɪndʒ'eɪd/ *noun* drink made from or flavoured like oranges, usually fizzy.

orang-utan /ɔːˌræŋuː'tæn/ *noun* (also **orang-outang** /-uː'tæŋ/) large anthropoid ape.

oration /ɔː'reɪʃ(ə)n/ *noun* formal or ceremonial speech.

orator /ˈɒrətə/ *noun* **1** maker of a formal speech. **2** eloquent public speaker.

oratorio /ɒrəˈtɔːrɪəʊ/ *noun* (*plural* **-s**) semi-dramatic musical composition usually on sacred theme.

oratory /ˈɒrətərɪ/ *noun* (*plural* **-ies**) **1** art or practice of public speaking. **2** small private chapel. □ **oratorical** /-ˈtɒr-/ *adjective*.

■ **1** declamation, eloquence, enunciation, fluency, gift of the gab, grandiloquence, public speaking, rhetoric, speech-making.

orb *noun* **1** globe surmounted by cross as part of coronation regalia. **2** sphere, globe. **3** *poetical* celestial body. **4** *poetical* eye.

orbicular /ɔːˈbɪkjʊlə/ *adjective formal* spherical; circular.

orbit /ˈɔːbɪt/ *noun* **1** curved course of planet, comet, satellite, etc. **2** one complete passage round another body. **3** range or sphere of action. ● *verb* (**-t-**) **1** go round in orbit. **2** put into orbit. □ **orbiter** *noun*.

■ *noun* **1, 2** circuit, course, path, revolution. ● *verb* **1** circle, encircle, go round, travel round.

orbital *adjective* **1** of orbits. **2** (of road) passing round outside of city.

■ **1** circular, encircling.

Orcadian /ɔːˈkeɪdɪən/ *adjective* of Orkney. ● *noun* native of Orkney.

orchard /ˈɔːtʃəd/ *noun* enclosed piece of land with fruit trees.

orchestra /ˈɔːkɪstrə/ *noun* large group of instrumental performers. □ **orchestra pit** part of theatre where orchestra plays. □ **orchestral** /ɔːˈkestr(ə)l/ *adjective*.

orchestrate /ˈɔːkɪstreɪt/ *verb* (**-ting**) **1** compose or arrange for orchestral performance. **2** arrange (elements) for desired effect. □ **orchestration** /-ˈstreɪʃ(ə)n/ *noun*.

■ **2** see ORGANIZE 3.

orchid /ˈɔːkɪd/ *noun* any of various plants, often with brilliantly coloured or grotesquely shaped flowers.

ordain /ɔːˈdeɪn/ *verb* **1** confer holy orders on. **2** decree, order.

ordeal /ɔːˈdiːl/ *noun* severe trial; painful or horrific experience.

■ affliction, anguish, difficulty, distress, hardship, misery, *colloquial* nightmare, pain, suffering, test, torture, trial, tribulation, trouble.

order /ˈɔːdə/ *noun* **1** condition in which every part, unit, etc. is in its right place; tidiness. **2** specified sequence. **3** state of repair. **4** authoritative direction or instruction. **5** state of obedience to law, authority, etc. **6** direction to supply something. **7** thing(s) (to be) supplied. **8** social class or rank. **9** kind, sort. **10** constitution or nature of the world, society, etc. **11** *Biology* grouping of animals or plants below class and above family. **12** religious fraternity. **13** grade of Christian ministry. **14** any of 5 classical styles of architec-

ture. **15** company of people distinguished by particular honour, etc. **16** insignia worn by its members. **17** stated form of divine service. **18** system of rules etc. (at meetings etc.). ● *verb* **1** command, prescribe. **2** command or direct (person) to specified destination. **3** direct manufacturer, tradesman, etc. to supply. **4** direct waiter to serve. **5** (often as **ordered** *adjective*) put in order. **6** (of God, fate, etc.) ordain. □ **in order** in correct sequence. **of or in the order of** approximately. **order about** dominate; command officiously. **out of order 1** in incorrect sequence. **2** not working.

■ *noun* **1, 2** arrangement, array, classification, codification, disposition, layout, line-up, neatness, organization, pattern, progression, sequence, series, succession, system, tidiness. **3** condition, repair, state. **4** command, decree, direction, directive, edict, fiat, injunction, instruction, law, mandate, ordinance, regulation, requirement, rule. **5** calm, control, discipline, good behaviour, government, harmony, law and order, obedience, orderliness, peace, peacefulness, quiet, rule. **6** commission, demand, request, requisition. **8** caste, class, group, hierarchy, level, rank, status. **9** category, class, group, kind, quality, sort. **12** brotherhood, community, fraternity, group, sisterhood, society. ● *verb* **1** bid, charge, command, compel, decree, demand, direct, enjoin, instruct, ordain, prescribe, tell. **2** command, direct. **3** apply for, ask for, requisition, send away for. **5** arrange, categorize, classify, codify, lay out, organize, put in order, sort out, tidy up.

orderly *adjective* **1** methodically arranged; tidy. **2** not unruly. ● *noun* (*plural* **-ies**) **1** soldier in attendance on officer. **2** hospital attendant. □ **orderly room** room in barracks for company's business. □ **orderliness** *noun*.

■ *adjective* **1** careful, methodical, neat, organized, regular, symmetrical, systematic, tidy, well arranged, well organized, well prepared. **2** civilized, controlled, decorous, disciplined, law-abiding, peaceable, polite, restrained, well behaved, well mannered.

ordinal /ˈɔːdɪn(ə)l/ *noun* (in full **ordinal number**) number defining position in a series; compare CARDINAL NUMBER.

ordinance /ˈɔːdɪnəns/ *noun* **1** decree. **2** religious rite.

ordinand /ˈɔːdɪnænd/ *noun* candidate for ordination.

ordinary /ˈɔːdɪnərɪ/ *adjective* normal; not exceptional; commonplace. □ **ordinary level** *historical* lowest in GCE exam. **ordinary seaman** sailor of lowest rank. **out of the ordinary** unusual. □ **ordinarily** *adverb*. **ordinariness** *noun*.

■ accustomed, average, common, *colloquial* common or garden, commonplace, conventional, customary, established, everyday, fair, familiar, habitual, humble, humdrum, indifferent, lowly, mediocre, medium, middling, moderate, modest, mundane, nondescript, normal, orthodox, passable, pedestrian, plain, prosaic, quotidian, reasonable, regular, routine, run-of-the-mill, satisfactory, simple, *colloquial* so so, standard, stock, traditional, typical, undistinguished, unexceptional, unexciting, unimpressive, uninspired, uninteresting, unpretentious, unremarkable, unsurprising, usual, workaday.

ordination /ˌɔːdɪˈneɪʃ(ə)n/ *noun* conferring of holy orders; ordaining.

ordnance /ˈɔːdnəns/ *noun* **1** artillery and military supplies. **2** government service dealing with these. □ **Ordnance Survey** government survey of UK producing detailed maps.

ordure /ˈɔːdjʊə/ *noun* dung.

ore *noun* naturally occurring mineral yielding metal or other valuable minerals.

oregano /ɒrɪˈɡɑːnəʊ/ *noun* dried wild marjoram as seasoning.

organ /ˈɔːɡən/ *noun* **1** musical instrument consisting of pipes that sound when air is forced through them, operated by keys and pedals. **2** similar instrument producing sound electronically. **3** part of body serving some special function. **4** medium of opinion, esp. newspaper. □ **organ-grinder** player of barrel organ.

organdie /ˈɔːɡəndɪ/ *noun* fine translucent muslin, usually stiffened.

organic /ɔːˈɡænɪk/ *adjective* **1** of or affecting bodily organ(s). **2** (of animals and plants) having organs or organized physical structure. **3** (of food) produced without artificial fertilizers or pesticides. **4** (of chemical compound etc.) containing carbon. **5** organized. **6** inherent, structural. □ **organic chemistry** that of carbon compounds. □ **organically** *adverb*.

■ **2** animate, biological, growing, live, living, natural. **5** coherent, coordinated, integrated, methodical, organized, structured, systematic. **6** inherent, integral, intrinsic, structural.

organism /ˈɔːɡənɪz(ə)m/ *noun* **1** individual animal or plant. **2** living being with interdependent parts. **3** system made up of interdependent parts.

■ **1, 2** animal, being, creature, living thing, plant.

organist *noun* player of organ.

organization /ˌɔːɡənaɪˈzeɪʃ(ə)n/ *noun* (also **-isation**) **1** organized body, system, or society. **2** organizing, being organized.

■ **1** alliance, association, body, business, club, combine, company, concern, confederation, conglomerate, consortium, corporation, federation, firm, group, institute, institution, league, network, *colloquial* outfit, party, society, syndicate, union. **2** arrangement, categorization, classification, codification, composition, coordination, design, logistics, plan, planning, regimentation, running, structure, structuring, system, systematization.

organize /ˈɔːɡənaɪz/ *verb* (also **-ise**) (**-zing** or **-sing**) **1** give orderly structure to. **2** make arrangements for (person, oneself). **3** initiate, arrange for. **4** (as **organized** *adjective*) make organic or into living tissue. □ **organizer** *noun*.

■ **1** arrange, catalogue, categorize, classify, codify, compose, coordinate, group, order, pigeon-hole, put in order, rearrange, regiment, run, sort, sort out, structure, systematize, tabulate, tidy up. **3** arrange for, coordinate, create, deal with, establish, initiate, manage, mobilize, orchestrate, plan, put together, run, see to, set up, take care of.

orgasm /ˈɔːɡæz(ə)m/ *noun* climax of sexual excitement. ● *verb* have sexual orgasm. □ **orgasmic** /-ˈɡæz-/ *adjective*.

orgy /ˈɔːdʒɪ/ *noun* (*plural* **-ies**) **1** wild party with indiscriminate sexual activity. **2** excessive indulgence in an activity. □ **orgiastic** /-ˈæs-/ *adjective*.

■ **1** bacchanalia, debauch, party, *colloquial* rave-up, revel, revelry, saturnalia, *colloquial* spree. **2** *slang* binge, fling, frenzy, *colloquial* splurge, *colloquial* spree.

oriel /ˈɔːrɪəl/ *noun* window projecting from wall at upper level.

orient /ˈɔːrɪənt/ *noun* (**the Orient**) **1** the East. **2** countries east of Mediterranean, esp. E. Asia. ● *verb* **1** place or determine position of with aid of compass; find bearings of. **2** (often + *towards*) direct. **3** place (building etc.) to face east. **4** turn eastward or in specified direction. **5** (**orient oneself**; often + *to*) accustom oneself to new situation; get one's bearings.

■ *verb* **1** orientate, position. **5** (**orient oneself**) acclimatize, accommodate oneself, accustom oneself, adapt, adjust, condition oneself, familiarize oneself, get one's bearings, orientate oneself.

oriental /ˌɔːrɪˈent(ə)l/ (often **Oriental**) *adjective* of the East, esp. E. Asia; of the Orient. ● *noun* native of Orient.

■ *adjective* Asian, eastern, Far Eastern.

orientate /ˈɔːrɪənteɪt/ *verb* (**-ting**) orient.

orientation *noun* **1** orienting, being oriented. **2** relative position. **3** person's adjustment in relation to circumstances. **4** briefing.

orienteering /ˌɔːrɪənˈtɪərɪŋ/ *noun* competitive sport of running across rough country with map and compass.

orifice /ˈɒrɪfɪs/ *noun* aperture; mouth of cavity.

origami /ɒrɪˈɡɑːmɪ/ *noun* Japanese art of folding paper into decorative shapes.

origanum /əˈrɪɡənəm/ *noun* wild marjoram.

origin /ˈɒrɪdʒɪn/ *noun* **1** source; starting point. **2** (often in *plural*) parentage.

■ **1** base, basis, beginning, birth, cause, *formal* commencement, cradle, creation, dawn, derivation, foundation, *poetical* fount, fountainhead, genesis, inauguration, inception, launch, outset, provenance, root, source, start, well-spring. **2** ancestry, background, descent, extraction, family, genealogy, heritage, lineage, parentage, pedigree, stock.

original /əˈrɪdʒɪn(ə)l/ *adjective* **1** existing from the beginning; earliest. **2** innate. **3** not imitative or derived; creative not copied; by artist etc.

himself or herself. ● *noun* original pattern, picture, etc. from which another is copied or translated. □ **original sin** innate sinfulness held to be common to all human beings after the Fall. □ **originality** /-'næl-/ *noun*. **originally** *adverb*.

■ *adjective* **1** aboriginal, archetypal, earliest, first, initial, native, primal, primitive, primordial. **3** actual, archetypal, authentic, creative, first-hand, fresh, genuine, imaginative, ingenious, innovative, inspired, inventive, new, novel, real, resourceful, thoughtful, true, unconventional, unfamiliar, unique, unusual.

originate /ə'rɪdʒmeɪt/ *verb* (**-ting**) **1** (usually + *from, in*) begin. **2** initiate or give origin to; be origin of. □ **origination** *noun*. **originator** *noun*.

■ **1** arise, be born, be derived, be descended, begin, come, *formal* commence, crop up, derive, emanate, emerge, issue, proceed, spring up, start, stem. **2** *literary* beget, be the inventor of, bring about, coin, conceive, create, design, discover, engender, found, give birth to, inaugurate, initiate, inspire, institute, introduce, invent, launch, mastermind, pioneer, produce, *colloquial* think up.

oriole /'ɔːrɪəʊl/ *noun* kind of bird, esp. **golden oriole** with black and yellow plumage in male.

ormolu /'ɔːməluː/ *noun* **1** gilded bronze. **2** gold-coloured alloy. **3** articles made of or decorated with these.

ornament *noun* /'ɔːnəmənt/ **1** thing used to adorn or decorate; decoration. **2** quality or person bringing honour or distinction. ● *verb* /-ment/ adorn, beautify. □ **ornamental** /-'men-/ *adjective*. **ornamentation** *noun*.

■ *noun* **1** accessory, adornment, bauble, beautification, decoration, embellishment, embroidery, enhancement, frill, frippery, garnish, ornamentation, trimming, trinket. ● *verb* adorn, beautify, deck, decorate, dress up, elaborate, embellish, embroider, enhance, festoon, garnish, prettify, trim. □ **ornamental** attractive, decorative, fancy, flashy, pretty, showy.

ornate /ɔː'neɪt/ *adjective* **1** elaborately adorned. **2** (of literary style) flowery. □ **ornately** *adverb*.

■ arabesque, baroque, busy, decorated, elaborate, fancy, flamboyant, florid, flowery, fussy, luxuriant, ornamented, overdone, pretentious, rococo.

ornithology /ɔːnɪ'θɒlədʒɪ/ *noun* study of birds. □ **ornithological** /-θə'lɒdʒ-/ *adjective*. **ornithologist** *noun*.

orotund /'ɒrətʌnd/ *adjective* **1** (of voice) full, round; imposing. **2** (of writing, style, etc.) pompous; pretentious.

orphan /'ɔːf(ə)n/ *noun* child whose parents are dead. ● *verb* bereave of parents.

orphanage *noun* home for orphans.

orrery /'ɒrərɪ/ *noun* (*plural* **-ies**) clockwork model of solar system.

orris root /'ɒrɪs/ *noun* fragrant iris root used in perfumery.

ortho- *combining form* **1** straight. **2** correct.

orthodontics /ɔːθə'dɒntɪks/ *plural noun* (usually treated as *singular*) correction of irregularities in teeth and jaws.

orthodox /'ɔːθədɒks/ *adjective* holding usual or accepted views, esp. on religion, morals, etc.; conventional. □ **Orthodox Church** Eastern Church headed by Patriarch of Constantinople, including Churches of Russia, Romania, Greece, etc. □ **orthodoxy** *noun*.

■ accepted, accustomed, approved, authorized, common, conformist, conservative, conventional, customary, established, mainstream, normal, official, ordinary, prevailing, recognized, regular, standard, traditional, usual, well established.

orthography /ɔː'θɒgrəfɪ/ *noun* (*plural* **-ies**) spelling, esp. with reference to its correctness. □ **orthographic** /-'græf-/ *adjective*.

orthopaedics /ɔːθə'piːdɪks/ *plural noun* (treated as *singular*) (*US* **-pedics**) branch of medicine dealing with correction of diseased or injured bones or muscles. □ **orthopaedic** *adjective*. **orthopaedist** *noun*.

OS *abbreviation* **1** old style. **2** Ordinary Seaman. **3** Ordnance Survey. **4** outsize.

Oscar /'ɒskə/ *noun* statuette awarded annually in US for excellence in film acting, directing, etc.

oscillate /'ɒsɪleɪt/ *verb* (**-ting**) **1** (cause to) swing to and fro. **2** vacillate. **3** *Electricity* (of current) undergo high-frequency alternations. □ **oscillation** *noun*. **oscillator** *noun*.

oscilloscope /ə'sɪləskəʊp/ *noun* device for viewing oscillations usually on screen of cathode ray tube.

osier /'əʊzɪə/ *noun* **1** willow used in basketwork. **2** shoot of this.

osmosis /ɒz'məʊsɪs/ *noun* **1** passage of solvent through semipermeable partition into another solution. **2** process by which something is acquired by absorption. □ **osmotic** /-'mɒt-/ *adjective*.

osprey /'ɒspreɪ/ *noun* (*plural* **-s**) large bird preying on fish.

osseous /'ɒsɪəs/ *adjective* **1** of bone; bony. **2** having bones.

ossify /'ɒsɪfaɪ/ *verb* (**-ies, -ied**) **1** turn into bone; harden. **2** make or become rigid or unprogressive. □ **ossification** *noun*.

ostensible /ɒ'stensɪb(ə)l/ *adjective* professed; used to conceal real purpose or nature. □ **ostensibly** *adverb*.

■ alleged, apparent, outward, pretended, professed, reputed, specious, supposed, visible.

ostentation /ɒsten'teɪʃ(ə)n/ *noun* **1** pretentious display of wealth. **2** showing off. □ **ostentatious** *adjective*.

■ affectation, display, exhibitionism, flamboyance, flashiness, flaunting, parade, pomp, pretension, pretentiousness, self-advertisement, show, *colloquial* showing off, *colloquial* swank. □ **ostentatious** boastful, flamboyant, flashy, pretentious, showy, *colloquial* swanky, vainglorious.

osteoarthritis /ˌɒstɪəʊɑːˈθraɪtɪs/ *noun* degenerative disease of the joints. □ **osteoarthritic** /-ˈθrɪt-/ *adjective*.

osteopath /ˈɒstɪəpæθ/ *noun* person who treats disease by manipulation of bones. □ **osteopathy** /-ˈɒp-/ *noun*.

osteoporosis /ˌɒstɪəʊpəˈrəʊsɪs/ *noun* brittle bones caused by hormonal change or deficiency of calcium or vitamin D.

ostler /ˈɒslə/ *noun historical* stableman at inn.

ostracize /ˈɒstrəsaɪz/ *verb* (also **-ise**) (**-zing** or **-sing**) exclude from society; refuse to associate with. □ **ostracism** /-sɪz(ə)m/ *noun*.

■ avoid, banish, blackball, blacklist, boycott, cast out, cold-shoulder, cut, exclude, excommunicate, expel, isolate, reject, send to Coventry, shun, shut out, snub.

ostrich /ˈɒstrɪtʃ/ *noun* **1** large flightless swift-running African bird. **2** person refusing to acknowledge awkward truth.

OT *abbreviation* Old Testament.

other /ˈʌðə/ *adjective* **1** further, additional. **2** different. **3** (**the other**) the only remaining. ● *noun* other person or thing. □ **the other day, week, etc.** a few days etc. ago. **other half** *colloquial* one's wife or husband. **other than** apart from.

otherwise /ˈʌðəwaɪz/ *adverb* **1** or else; in different circumstances. **2** in other respects. **3** in a different way. **4** as an alternative. ● *adjective* different.

other-worldly *adjective* **1** of imaginary world. **2** relating to life after death. □ **other-worldliness** *noun*.

otiose /ˈəʊtɪəʊs/ *adjective* not required; serving no practical purpose.

OTT *abbreviation colloquial* over-the-top.

otter /ˈɒtə/ *noun* furred aquatic fish-eating mammal.

Ottoman /ˈɒtəmən/ *adjective historical* of Turkish Empire. ● *noun* (*plural* **-s**) **1** Turk of Ottoman period. **2** (**ottoman**) cushioned seat without back or arms; storage-box with padded top.

OU *abbreviation* **1** Open University. **2** Oxford University.

oubliette /uːblɪˈet/ *noun* secret dungeon with trapdoor entrance.

ouch /aʊtʃ/ *interjection: expressing sharp or sudden pain.*

ought /ɔːt/ *auxiliary verb: expressing duty, rightness, probability, etc.*

oughtn't /ˈɔːt(ə)nt/ ought not.

Ouija /ˈwiːdʒə/ *noun* (in full **Ouija board**) *proprietary term* board marked with letters or signs used with movable pointer to try to obtain messages in seances.

ounce /aʊns/ *noun* **1** unit of weight (1/16 lb, 28.35 g). **2** very small quantity.

our /aʊə/ *adjective* of or belonging to us.

ours /aʊəz/ *pronoun* the one(s) belonging to us.

ourselves /aʊəˈselvz/ *pronoun* **1** *emphatic form of* WE *or* US. **2** *reflexive form of* US.

ousel = OUZEL.

oust /aʊst/ *verb* drive out of office or power, esp. by seizing place of.

■ banish, drive out, eject, expel, kick out, remove, replace, *colloquial* sack, supplant, take over from, unseat.

out /aʊt/ *adverb* **1** away from or not in place. **2** not at home, office, etc. **3** into open, sight, notice, etc. **4** to or at an end. **5** not burning. **6** in error. **7** *colloquial* unconscious. **8** (+ *to do*) determined to. **9** (of limb etc.) dislocated. **10** *colloquial* unfashionable. ● *preposition* out of. ● *noun* way of escape. ● *verb* emerge. □ **out and out** thorough(ly); surpassing(ly). **out for** intent on; determined to get. **out of 1** from inside. **2** not inside. **3** from among. **4** lacking; having no more of. **5** because of.

USAGE The use of *out* as a preposition, as in *He walked out the room*, is not standard English. *Out of* should be used instead.

out- *prefix* **1** so as to surpass. **2** external. **3** out of.

outback *noun Australian* remote inland areas.

outbalance /aʊtˈbæləns/ *verb* (**-cing**) outweigh.

outbid /aʊtˈbɪd/ *verb* (**-dd-**; *past & past participle* **-bid**) bid higher than.

outboard motor *noun* portable engine attached to outside of boat.

outbreak /ˈaʊtbreɪk/ *noun* sudden eruption of emotion, war, disease, fire, etc.

■ epidemic, eruption, flare-up, plague, rash, upsurge.

outbuilding *noun* shed, barn, etc. detached from main building.

outburst *noun* bursting out, esp. of emotion in vehement words.

■ attack, effusion, eruption, explosion, fit, flood, gale, outbreak, outpouring, paroxysm, rush, spasm, surge, upsurge.

outcast *noun* person cast out from home and friends. ● *adjective* homeless; rejected.

■ *noun* displaced person, exile, *historical* outlaw, outsider, pariah, refugee, reject, untouchable.

outclass /aʊtˈklɑːs/ *verb* surpass in quality.

outcome *noun* result.

■ conclusion, consequence, effect, end product, result, sequel, upshot.

outcrop *noun* **1** rock etc. emerging at surface. **2** noticeable manifestation.

outcry *noun* (*plural* **-ies**) loud public protest.

■ dissent, hue and cry, objection, opposition, protest, protestation, remonstrance.

outdated /aʊtˈdeɪtɪd/ *adjective* out of date; obsolete.

outdistance /aʊtˈdɪst(ə)ns/ *verb* (**-cing**) leave (competitor) behind completely.

outdo /aʊt'duː/ *verb* (**-doing**; *3rd singular present* **-does**; *past* **-did**; *past participle* **-done**) surpass, excel.

■ beat, defeat, exceed, excel, get the better of, outbid, outdistance, outrun, outshine, outstrip, outweigh, overcome, surpass, top, *colloquial* trump.

outdoor *adjective* **1** done, existing, or used out of doors. **2** fond of the open air.

■ **1** alfresco, open-air, out of doors, outside.

outdoors /aʊt'dɔːz/ *adverb* in(to) the open air. ● *noun* the open air.

outer *adjective* **1** outside, external. **2** farther from centre or inside. □ **outer space** universe beyond earth's atmosphere. □ **outermost** *adjective*.

■ **1** exterior, external, outside, outward, superficial, surface. **2** distant, further, outlying, peripheral, remote.

outface /aʊt'feɪs/ *verb* (**-cing**) disconcert by staring or by confident manner.

outfall *noun* outlet of river, drain, etc.

outfield *noun* outer part of cricket or baseball pitch. □ **outfielder** *noun*.

outfit *noun* **1** set of equipment or clothes. **2** *colloquial* (organized) group or company.

■ **1** accoutrements, attire, costume, ensemble, equipment, garb, *colloquial* gear, *colloquial* get-up, rig, suit, trappings. **2** see ORGANIZATION 1.

outfitter *noun* supplier of clothing.

outflank /aʊt'flæŋk/ *verb* **1** get round the flank of (enemy). **2** outmanoeuvre.

outflow *noun* **1** outward flow. **2** what flows out.

outgoing *adjective* **1** friendly. **2** retiring from office. **3** going out. ● *noun* (in *plural*) expenditure.

■ *adjective* **1** see SOCIABLE. **2** departing, emeritus, ex-, former, last, leaving, past, retiring. **3** [*of tide*] ebbing, falling, retreating. ● *noun* (**outgoings**) see EXPENSE 2.

outgrow /aʊt'ɡrəʊ/ *verb* (*past* **-grew**; *past participle* **-grown**) **1** get too big for (clothes etc.). **2** leave behind (childish habit etc.). **3** grow faster or taller than.

outgrowth *noun* offshoot.

outhouse *noun* shed etc., esp. adjoining main house.

outing *noun* pleasure trip.

■ excursion, expedition, jaunt, picnic, ride, tour, trip.

outlandish /aʊt'lændɪʃ/ *adjective* bizarre, strange. □ **outlandishly** *adverb*. **outlandishness** *noun*.

outlast /aʊt'lɑːst/ *verb* last longer than.

■ outlive, survive.

outlaw *noun* **1** fugitive from law. **2** *historical* person deprived of protection of law. ● *verb* **1** declare (person) an outlaw. **2** make illegal; proscribe.

■ *noun* **1** bandit, brigand, criminal, *Military* deserter, desperado, fugitive, *historical* highwayman, marauder, renegade, robber. **2** outcast, pariah. ● *verb* **1** see BANISH 1. **2** ban, exclude, forbid, prohibit, proscribe.

outlay *noun* expenditure.

outlet *noun* **1** means of exit. **2** means of expressing feelings. **3** market for goods.

■ **1** channel, duct, egress, escape route, exit, mouth, opening, orifice, safety valve, vent, way out. **3** see SHOP *noun* 1.

outline *noun* **1** rough draft. **2** summary. **3** line(s) enclosing visible object. **4** contour. **5** external boundary. **6** (in *plural*) main features. ● *verb* (**-ning**) **1** draw or describe in outline. **2** mark outline of.

■ *noun* **1** bare bones, diagram, draft, framework, plan, rough idea, skeleton, sketch. **2** abstract, digest, précis, résumé, rundown, scenario, summary, synopsis, thumbnail sketch. **3–5** contour, figure, form, profile, shadow, shape, silhouette. ● *verb* **1** delineate, draft, give the gist of, plan out, précis, rough out, sketch out, summarize, trace.

outlive /aʊt'lɪv/ *verb* (**-ving**) live longer than, beyond, or through.

outlook *noun* **1** view, prospect. **2** mental attitude. **3** future prospects.

■ **1** aspect, panorama, prospect, scene, sight, view, vista. **2** angle, attitude, frame of mind, opinion, perspective, point of view, position, slant, standpoint, viewpoint. **3** expectations, forecast, lookout, prediction, prognosis, prospect.

outlying *adjective* **1** far from centre. **2** remote.

■ distant, far-away, far-flung, far-off, outer, outermost, remote.

outmanoeuvre /aʊtmə'nuːvə/ *verb* (**-ring**) (*US* **-maneuver**) outdo by skilful manoeuvring.

outmatch /aʊt'mætʃ/ *verb* be more than a match for.

outmoded /aʊt'məʊdɪd/ *adjective* outdated; out of fashion.

outnumber /aʊt'nʌmbə/ *verb* exceed in number.

outpace /aʊt'peɪs/ *verb* (**-cing**) **1** go faster than. **2** outdo in contest.

outpatient *noun* non-resident hospital patient.

outplacement *noun* help in finding new job after redundancy.

outpost *noun* **1** detachment on guard at some distance from army. **2** outlying settlement etc.

outpouring *noun* (usually in *plural*) copious expression of emotion.

output *noun* **1** amount produced (by machine, worker, etc.). **2** electrical power etc. supplied by apparatus. **3** printout, results, etc. from computer. **4** place where energy, information, etc., leaves a system. ● *verb* (**-tt-**; *past & past participle*

-put or **-putted**) (of computer) supply (results etc.).

■ *noun* **1** achievement, crop, harvest, production, productivity, result, yield.

outrage *noun* **1** forcible violation of others' rights, sentiments, etc. **2** gross offence or indignity. **3** fierce resentment or anger. ● *verb* **(-ging) 1** subject to outrage. **2** insult. **3** shock and anger.

■ *noun* **1** atrocity, crime, enormity, violation. **2** disgrace, indignity, insult, offence, scandal, sensation. **3** anger, bitterness, disgust, fury, horror, indignation, resentment, revulsion, shock, *literary* wrath. ● *verb* **2** see INSULT *verb* 2. **3** see ANGER *verb*.

outrageous /aʊtˈreɪdʒəs/ *adjective* **1** immoderate. **2** grossly offensive, immoral, cruel, etc.; shocking. □ **outrageously** *adverb*.

■ **1** excessive, extortionate, extravagant, immoderate, inordinate, preposterous, unreasonable. **2** abominable, atrocious, barbaric, beastly, bestial, criminal, cruel, disgraceful, disgusting, execrable, infamous, iniquitous, monstrous, nefarious, notorious, offensive, revolting, scandalous, shocking, unspeakable, *colloquial* unthinkable, vile, villainous, wicked.

outrank /aʊtˈræŋk/ *verb* be superior in rank to.

outré /ˈuːtreɪ/ *adjective* eccentric; violating decorum. [French]

outrider *noun* motorcyclist or mounted guard riding ahead of car(s) etc.

outrigger *noun* **1** spar or framework projecting from or over side of ship, canoe, etc. to give stability. **2** boat with this.

outright *adverb* **1** altogether, entirely. **2** not gradually. **3** without reservation. ● *adjective* **1** downright, complete. **2** undisputed.

outrun /aʊtˈrʌn/ *verb* (**-nn-**; *past* **-ran**; *past participle* **-run**) **1** run faster or farther than. **2** go beyond.

outsell /aʊtˈsel/ *verb* (*past & past participle* **-sold**) **1** sell more than. **2** be sold in greater quantities than.

outset *noun* □ **at, from the outset** at or from the beginning.

outshine /aʊtˈʃaɪn/ *verb* (**-ning**; *past & past participle* **-shone**) be more brilliant than.

outside *noun* /aʊtˈsaɪd, ˈaʊtsaɪd/ **1** external surface; outer part(s). **2** external appearance. **3** position on outer side. ● *adjective* /ˈaʊtsaɪd/ **1** of, on, or nearer outside. **2** not belonging to particular circle or institution. **3** (of chance etc.) remote. **4** greatest existent or possible. ● *adverb* /aʊtˈsaɪd/ **1** on or to outside. **2** out of doors. **3** not within or enclosed. ● *preposition* /aʊtˈsaɪd/ **1** not in; to or at the outside of. **2** external to; beyond limits of. □ **at the outside** (of estimate etc.) at the most. **outside interest** hobby etc. unconnected with one's work.

■ *noun* **1** case, casing, exterior, façade, face, front, shell, skin, surface. **2** appearance, exterior, façade, face, front, look. ● *adjective* **1** exterior, external, outer, outward, superficial, surface,

visible. **2** alien, external, extraneous, foreign. **3** see REMOTE 4.

outsider /aʊtˈsaɪdə/ *noun* **1** non-member of circle, party, profession, etc. **2** competitor thought to have little chance.

■ **1** alien, foreigner, gatecrasher, guest, immigrant, interloper, intruder, invader, newcomer, non-member, non-resident, stranger, trespasser, visitor.

outsize *adjective* unusually large.

outskirts *plural noun* outer area of town etc.

■ borders, edge, environs, fringe, margin, periphery, purlieus, suburbs.

outsmart /aʊtˈsmɑːt/ *verb* outwit; be too clever for.

outspoken /aʊtˈspəʊkən/ *adjective* saying openly what one thinks; frank. □ **outspokenly** *adverb*. **outspokenness** *noun*.

■ blunt, candid, direct, explicit, forthright, frank, honest, plain-spoken, tactless, unambiguous, undiplomatic, unequivocal, unreserved.

outspread /aʊtˈspred/ *adjective* spread out.

outstanding /aʊtˈstændɪŋ/ *adjective* **1** conspicuous, esp. from excellence. **2** still to be dealt with. **3** (of debt) not yet settled. □ **outstandingly** *adverb*.

■ **1** above the rest, celebrated, conspicuous, distinguished, dominant, eminent, excellent, exceptional, extraordinary, famous, first-class, first-rate, great, important, impressive, memorable, notable, noteworthy, noticeable, predominant, pre-eminent, prominent, remarkable, singular, special, striking, superior, *colloquial* top-notch, unrivalled. **2, 3** see OVERDUE 2.

outstation *noun* remote branch or outpost.

outstay /aʊtˈsteɪ/ *verb* stay longer than (one's welcome etc.).

outstretched /aʊtˈstretʃt/ *adjective* stretched out.

outstrip /aʊtˈstrɪp/ *verb* (**-pp-**) **1** go faster than. **2** surpass in progress, competition, etc.

out-take *noun* film or tape sequence cut out in editing.

out-tray *noun* tray for outgoing documents.

outvote /aʊtˈvəʊt/ *verb* (**-ting**) defeat by majority of votes.

outward /ˈaʊtwəd/ *adjective* **1** directed towards outside. **2** going out. **3** physical; external, apparent. ● *adverb* (also **outwards**) in outward direction; towards outside. □ **outwardly** *adverb*.

■ *adjective* **3** apparent, evident, exterior, external, manifest, noticeable, observable, obvious, ostensible, outer, outside, superficial, surface, visible.

outweigh /aʊtˈweɪ/ *verb* exceed in weight, value, influence, etc.

outwit /aʊtˈwɪt/ *verb* (**-tt-**) be too clever for; overcome by greater ingenuity.

■ cheat, deceive, dupe, fool, get the better of, gull, hoax, hoodwink, make a fool of, outmanoeuvre, outsmart, take in, trick.

outwith /aʊt'wɪθ/ *preposition Scottish* outside.

outwork *noun* **1** advanced or detached part of fortress etc. **2** work done off premises of shop, factory, etc. supplying it.

outworn /aʊt'wɔːn/ *adjective* **1** worn out. **2** obsolete.

ouzel /'uːz(ə)l/ *noun* (also **ousel**) small bird of thrush family.

ouzo /'uːzəʊ/ *noun* (*plural* **-s**) Greek aniseed-flavoured alcoholic spirit.

ova *plural* of OVUM.

oval /'əʊv(ə)l/ *adjective* shaped like egg; elliptical. ● *noun* **1** elliptical closed curve. **2** thing with oval outline.
■ *adjective* egg-shaped, elliptical, oviform, ovoid.

ovary /'əʊvərɪ/ *noun* (*plural* **-ies**) **1** either of two ovum-producing organs in female. **2** seed vessel in plant. □ **ovarian** /əʊ'veər-/ *adjective*.

ovation /əʊ'veɪʃ(ə)n/ *noun* enthusiastic applause or reception.
■ acclaim, acclamation, applause, cheering, plaudits, praise.

oven /'ʌv(ə)n/ *noun* enclosed chamber for cooking food in. □ **ovenproof** heat-resistant. **oven-ready** (of food) prepared before sale for immediate cooking. **ovenware** dishes for cooking food in oven.

over /'əʊvə/ *adverb* **1** outward and downward from brink or from erect position. **2** so as to cover whole surface. **3** so as to produce fold or reverse position. **4** above in place or position. **5** from one side, end, etc. to other. **6** from beginning to end with repetition. **7** in excess. **8** settled, finished. ● *preposition* **1** above. **2** out and down from. **3** so as to cover. **4** across; on or to other side, end, etc. of. **5** concerning. ● *noun Cricket* **1** sequence of 6 balls bowled from one end before change is made to other. **2** play during this time. □ **over the way** (in street etc.) facing or across from.

over- *prefix* added to verbs, nouns, adjectives, and adverbs, indicating: **1** excessively. **2** upper, outer. **3** over. **4** completely.

overact /əʊvə'rækt/ *verb* act (role) with exaggeration.

over-active /əʊvə'ræktɪv/ *adjective* too active.

overall *adjective* /'əʊvərɔːl/ taking everything into account; inclusive; total. ● *adverb* /əʊvər'ɔːl/ including everything; on the whole. ● *noun* /'əʊvərɔːl/ **1** protective outer garment. **2** (in *plural*) protective trousers or suit.

overarm *adjective & adverb* with arm raised above shoulder.

overawe /əʊvə'rɔː/ *verb* (**-wing**) awe into submission.

overbalance /əʊvə'bæləns/ *verb* (**-cing**) **1** lose balance and fall. **2** cause to do this.

overbearing /əʊvə'beərɪŋ/ *adjective* **1** domineering. **2** oppressive.

overblown /əʊvə'bləʊn/ *adjective* **1** inflated, pretentious. **2** (of flower etc.) past its prime.

overboard *adverb* from ship into water. □ **go overboard** *colloquial* **1** show extreme enthusiasm. **2** behave immoderately.

overbook /əʊvə'bʊk/ *verb* make too many bookings for (aircraft, hotel, etc.).

overcame *past* of OVERCOME.

overcast *adjective* **1** (of sky) covered with cloud. **2** (in sewing) edged with stitching.
■ **1** black, clouded, cloudy, dark, dismal, dull, gloomy, grey, leaden, louring, murky, sombre, starless, stormy, sunless, threatening.

overcharge /əʊvə'tʃɑːdʒ/ *verb* (**-ging**) **1** charge too high a price to. **2** put too much charge into (battery, gun, etc.).

overcoat *noun* warm outdoor coat.
■ greatcoat, mackintosh, topcoat, trench coat.

overcome /əʊvə'kʌm/ *verb* (**-coming**; *past* **-came**; *past participle* **-come**) **1** prevail over, master. **2** be victorious. **3** (usually as **overcome** *adjective*) make faint. **4** (usually as **overcome** *adjective*) (often + *with*) make weak or helpless.
■ **1** see OVERTHROW 2. **2** (**overcome**) at a loss, beaten, exhausted, overwhelmed, prostrate, speechless.

overcrowd /əʊvə'kraʊd/ *verb* (usually as **overcrowded** *adjective*) cause too many people or things to be in (a place). □ **overcrowding** *noun*.
■ (**overcrowded**) congested, crammed, crawling, jammed, *colloquial* jam-packed, overloaded, packed.

overdevelop /əʊvədɪ'veləp/ *verb* (**-p-**) develop too much.

overdo /əʊvə'duː/ *verb* (**-doing**; *3rd singular present* **-does**; *past* **-did**; *past participle* **-done**) **1** carry to excess. **2** (as **overdone** *adjective*) overcooked. □ **overdo it, things** *colloquial* exhaust oneself.

overdose *noun* excessive dose of drug etc. ● *verb* (**-sing**) take overdose.

overdraft *noun* **1** overdrawing of bank account. **2** amount by which account is overdrawn.

overdraw /əʊvə'drɔː/ *verb* (*past* **-drew**; *past participle* **-drawn**) **1** draw more from (bank account) than amount in credit. **2** (as **overdrawn** *adjective*) having overdrawn one's account.

overdress /əʊvə'dres/ *verb* dress ostentatiously or with too much formality.

overdrive *noun* **1** mechanism in vehicle providing gear above top gear for economy at high speeds. **2** state of high activity.

overdue /əʊvə'djuː/ *adjective* **1** past the time when due or ready. **2** late, in arrears.
■ **1** belated, delayed, late, slow, tardy, unpunctual. **2** due, in arrears, outstanding, owing, unpaid, unresolved, unsettled.

overeat /əʊvər'iːt/ *verb* (*past* **-ate**; *past participle* **-eaten**) eat too much.
■ be greedy, feast, gorge, gormandize, guzzle, indulge oneself, *colloquial* make a pig of oneself, over-indulge, stuff oneself.

overestimate *verb* /əʊvər'estɪmeɪt/ (**-ting**) form too high an estimate of. ● *noun* /əʊvər'estɪmət/ too high an estimate. □ **overestimation** *noun*.

overexpose /əʊvərɪk'spəʊz/ *verb* (**-sing**) **1** expose too much to public. **2** expose (film) for too long.

overfish /əʊvə'fɪʃ/ *verb* deplete (stream etc.) by too much fishing.

overflow *verb* /əʊvə'fləʊ/ **1** flow over. **2** be so full that contents overflow. **3** (of crowd etc.) extend beyond limits or capacity of. **4** flood. **5** (of kindness, harvest, etc.) be very abundant. ● *noun* /'əʊvəfləʊ/ **1** what overflows or is superfluous. **2** outlet for excess liquid.
■ *verb* **1** flood, pour over, run over, spill, well up. **2** brim over, spill over. **4** see FLOOD *verb* 1,3.

overgrown /əʊvə'grəʊn/ *adjective* **1** grown too big. **2** covered with weeds etc. □ **overgrowth** *noun*.
■ **1** outsize, oversized. **2** overrun, rank, tangled, uncut, unkempt, untidy, untrimmed, unweeded, weedy, wild.

overhang *verb* /əʊvə'hæŋ/ (*past & past participle* **-hung**) project or hang over. ● *noun* /'əʊvəhæŋ/ fact or amount of overhanging.
■ *verb* beetle, bulge, jut, project, protrude, stick out.

overhaul *verb* /əʊvə'hɔːl/ **1** check over thoroughly and make repairs to if necessary. **2** overtake. ● *noun* /'əʊvəhɔːl/ thorough examination, with repairs if necessary.
■ *verb* **1** check over, examine, fix, inspect, mend, rebuild, recondition, refurbish, renovate, repair, restore, service. **2** see OVERTAKE 1.

overhead *adverb* /əʊvə'hed/ **1** above one's head. **2** in sky. ● *adjective* /'əʊvəhed/ placed overhead. ● *noun* /'əʊvəhed/ (in *plural*) routine administrative and maintenance expenses of a business. □ **overhead projector** projector for producing enlarged image of transparency above and behind user.
■ *adjective* aerial, elevated, high, overhanging, raised, upper.

overhear /əʊvə'hɪə/ *verb* (*past & past participle* **-heard**) hear as hidden or unintentional listener.

over-indulge /əʊvərɪn'dʌldʒ/ *noun* (**-ging**) indulge to excess. □ **over-indulgence** *noun*.

overjoyed /əʊvə'dʒɔɪd/ *adjective* filled with great joy.

overkill *noun* **1** excess of capacity to kill or destroy. **2** excess.

overland *adjective & adverb* by land and not sea.

overlap *verb* /əʊvə'læp/ (**-pp-**) **1** partly cover. **2** cover and extend beyond. **3** partly coincide.

● *noun* /'əʊvəlæp/ **1** overlapping. **2** overlapping part or amount.

overlay *verb* /əʊvə'leɪ/ (*past & past participle* **-laid**) **1** lay over. **2** (+ *with*) cover (thing) with (coating etc.). ● *noun* /'əʊvəleɪ/ thing laid over another.

overleaf /əʊvə'liːf/ *adverb* on other side of page of book.

overlie /əʊvə'laɪ/ *verb* (**-lying**; *past* **-lay**; *past participle* **-lain**) lie on top of.

overload *verb* /əʊvə'ləʊd/ **1** load too heavily (with baggage, work, etc.). **2** put too great a demand on (electrical circuit etc.). ● *noun* /'əʊvələʊd/ excessive quantity or demand.

overlook /əʊvə'lʊk/ *verb* **1** fail to observe. **2** condone, tolerate; ignore. **3** have view of from above.
■ **1** fail to notice, forget, leave out, miss, neglect, omit. **2** condone, disregard, excuse, gloss over, ignore, let pass, make allowances for, pardon, pass over, pay no attention to, shut one's eyes to, turn a blind eye to, write off. **3** face, front, look at, look down on, look on to.

overlord *noun* supreme lord.

overly *adverb* excessively.

overman /əʊvə'mæn/ *verb* (**-nn-**) provide with too large a crew, staff, etc.

overmuch /əʊvə'mʌtʃ/ *adverb & adjective* too much.

overnight /əʊvə'naɪt/ *adverb* **1** for a night. **2** during the night. **3** suddenly. ● *adjective* **1** for use or done etc. overnight. **2** instant.

over-particular /əʊvəpə'tɪkjʊlə/ *adjective* fussy or excessively particular.

overpass *noun* bridge by which road or railway line crosses another.

overplay /əʊvə'pleɪ/ *verb* give undue importance or emphasis to. □ **overplay one's hand** act on unduly optimistic estimate of one's chances.

overpower /əʊvə'paʊə/ *verb* **1** subdue; reduce to submission. **2** (esp. as **overpowering** *adjective*) be too intense or overwhelming for.
■ **1** see OVERTHROW 2. **2** (**overpowering**) compelling, consuming, inescapable, insupportable, irrepressible, irresistible, overriding, overwhelming, powerful, strong, unbearable, uncontrollable, unendurable.

overproduce /əʊvəprə'djuːs/ *verb* (**-cing**) produce in excess of demand or of defined amount. □ **overproduction** *noun*.

overrate /əʊvə'reɪt/ *verb* (**-ting**) **1** assess or value too highly. **2** (as **overrated** *adjective*) not as good as it is said to be.

overreach /əʊvə'riːtʃ/ *verb* (**overreach oneself**) fail by attempting too much.

overreact /əʊvərɪ'ækt/ *verb* respond more violently etc. than is justified. □ **overreaction** *noun*.

override *verb* /əʊvə'raɪd/ (**-ding**; *past* **-rode**; *past participle* **-ridden**) **1** have priority over. **2** intervene and make ineffective. **3** interrupt action of (automatic device). ● *noun* /'əʊvəraɪd/ suspension of automatic function.

overrider *noun* each of pair of projecting pieces on bumper of car.

overrule /əʊvə'ru:l/ *verb* (**-ling**) **1** set aside (decision etc.) by superior authority. **2** reject proposal of (person) in this way.

overrun /əʊvə'rʌn/ *verb* (**-nn-**; *past* **-ran**; *past participle* **-run**) **1** spread over. **2** conquer (territory) by force. **3** exceed time etc. allowed.

overseas *adverb* /əʊvə'si:z/ across or beyond sea. ● *adjective* /'əʊvəsi:z/ of places across sea; foreign.

oversee /əʊvə'si:/ *verb* (**-sees**; *past* **-saw**; *past participle* **-seen**) superintend (workers etc.).
□ **overseer** *noun*.
 ■ administer, be in charge of, control, direct, invigilate, keep an eye on, preside over, superintend, supervise, watch over.

over-sensitive /əʊvə'sensɪtɪv/ *adjective* excessively sensitive; easily hurt; quick to react.
□ **over-sensitiveness** *noun*. **over-sensitivity** /-'tɪv-/ *noun*.

oversew *verb* (*past participle* **-sewn** or **-sewed**) sew (two edges) with stitches lying over them.

oversexed /əʊvə'sekst/ *adjective* having unusually strong sexual desires.

overshadow /əʊvə'ʃædəʊ/ *verb* **1** appear much more prominent or important than. **2** cast into shade.

overshoe *noun* shoe worn over another for protection in wet weather etc.

overshoot /əʊvə'ʃu:t/ *verb* (*past & past participle* **-shot**) **1** pass or send beyond (target or limit). **2** go beyond runway when landing or taking off. □ **overshoot the mark** go beyond what is intended or proper.

oversight *noun* **1** failure to notice; inadvertent omission or mistake. **2** supervision.
 ■ **1** carelessness, dereliction of duty, error, failure, fault, mistake, omission. **2** administration, control, direction, management, supervision, surveillance.

oversimplify /əʊvə'sɪmplɪfaɪ/ *verb* (**-ies**, **-ied**) distort (problem etc.) by putting it in too simple terms. □ **oversimplification** *noun*.

oversleep /əʊvə'sli:p/ *verb* (*past & past participle* **-slept**) sleep beyond intended time of waking.

overspend /əʊvə'spend/ *verb* (*past & past participle* **-spent**) spend beyond one's means.

overspill *noun* **1** what is spilt over or overflows. **2** surplus population leaving one area for another.

overspread /əʊvə'spred/ *verb* (*past & past participle* **-spread**) **1** cover surface of. **2** (as **overspread** *adjective*) (usually + *with*) covered.

overstate /əʊvə'steɪt/ *verb* (**-ting**) **1** state too strongly. **2** exaggerate. □ **overstatement** *noun*.
 ■ blow up out of proportion, embroider, exaggerate, magnify, make too much of, maximize, overemphasize, overstress.

overstep /əʊvə'step/ *verb* (**-pp-**) pass beyond.
□ **overstep the mark** go beyond conventional behaviour.

overstrain /əʊvə'strem/ *verb* **1** damage by exertion. **2** stretch too far.

overstrung *adjective* **1** /əʊvə'strʌŋ/ (of person, nerves, etc.) too highly strung. **2** /'əʊvəstrʌŋ/ (of piano) with strings crossing each other obliquely.

oversubscribe /əʊvəsəb'skraɪb/ *verb* (**-bing**) (usually as **oversubscribed** *adjective*) subscribe for more than available amount or number of (offer, shares, places, etc.).

overt /əʊ'vɜ:t/ *adjective* openly done; unconcealed. □ **overtly** *adverb*.
 ■ apparent, blatant, clear, evident, manifest, obvious, open, patent, plain, unconcealed, undisguised, visible.

overtake /əʊvə'teɪk/ *verb* (**-king**; *past* **-took**; *past participle* **-taken**) **1** catch up and pass. **2** (of bad luck etc.) come suddenly upon.
 ■ **1** leave behind, outdistance, outpace, outstrip, overhaul, pass.

overtax /əʊvə'tæks/ *verb* **1** make excessive demands on. **2** tax too highly.

overthrow *verb* /əʊvə'θrəʊ/ (*past* **-threw**; *past participle* **-thrown**) **1** remove forcibly from power. **2** conquer. ● *noun* /'əʊvəθrəʊ/ defeat; downfall.
 ■ *verb* **1** bring down, depose, dethrone, oust, overturn, *colloquial* send packing, topple, unseat. **2** beat, conquer, crush, defeat, get the better of, *colloquial* lick, master, overcome, overpower, overwhelm, rout, subdue, triumph over, *literary* vanquish, win against. ● *noun* conquest, defeat, destruction, rout, subjugation, suppression, unseating.

overtime *noun* **1** time worked in addition to regular hours. **2** payment for this. ● *adverb* in addition to regular hours.

overtone *noun* **1** *Music* any of tones above lowest in harmonic series. **2** subtle extra quality or implication.
 ■ **2** association, connotation, hint, implication, innuendo, suggestion, undertone.

overture /'əʊvətjʊə/ *noun* **1** orchestral prelude. **2** (usually in *plural*) opening of negotiations. **3** formal proposal or offer.

overturn /əʊvə'tɜ:n/ *verb* **1** (cause to) fall down or over. **2** upset, overthrow.
 ■ **1** capsize, flip, invert, keel over, knock over, spill, tip over, topple, turn over, turn turtle, turn upside down, up-end, upset. **2** see OVERTHROW 1.

overview *noun* general survey.

overweening /əʊvə'wi:nɪŋ/ *adjective* arrogant.

overweight *adjective* /əʊvə'weɪt/ above the weight allowed or desirable. ● *noun* /'əʊvəweɪt/ excess weight.

overwhelm /əʊvə'welm/ *verb* **1** overpower

with emotion. **2** overcome by force of numbers. **3** bury; submerge utterly.

■ **2** see OVERTHROW **2**. **3** engulf, flood, immerse, inundate, submerge, swamp.

overwhelming *adjective* **1** too great to resist or overcome. **2** by a great number. □ **overwhelmingly** *adverb*.

■ **1** see OVERPOWERING.

overwork /əʊvə'wɜːk/ *verb* **1** (cause to) work too hard. **2** weary or exhaust with work. **3** (esp. as **overworked** *adjective*) make excessive use of. ● *noun* excessive work.

overwrought /əʊvə'rɔːt/ *adjective* **1** overexcited, nervous, distraught. **2** too elaborate.

oviduct /'əʊvɪdʌkt/ *noun* tube through which ova pass from ovary.

oviform /'əʊvɪfɔːm/ *adjective* egg-shaped.

ovine /'əʊvaɪn/ *adjective* of or like sheep.

oviparous /əʊ'vɪpərəs/ *adjective* egg-laying.

ovoid /'əʊvɔɪd/ *adjective* (of solid) egg-shaped.

ovulate /'ɒvjʊleɪt/ *verb* (**-ting**) produce ova or ovules, or discharge them from ovary. □ **ovulation** *noun*.

ovule /'ɒvjuːl/ *noun* structure containing germ cell in female plant.

ovum /'əʊvəm/ *noun* (*plural* **ova** /'əʊvə/) female egg cell from which young develop after fertilization with male person.

ow /aʊ/ *interjection: expressing sudden pain.*

owe /əʊ/ *verb* (**owing**) **1** be under obligation to (re)pay or render. **2** (usually + *for*) be in debt. **3** (usually + *to*) be indebted to person, thing, etc. for.

■ **2** be in debt, have debts. **3** (*owe to*) be beholden to, be indebted to, be under an obligation to.

owing /'əʊɪŋ/ *adjective* **1** owed; yet to be paid. **2** (+ *to*) caused by; because of.

■ **1** due, outstanding, overdue, owed, payable, unpaid, unsettled. **2** (*owing to*) because of, caused by, on account of, resulting from, thanks to, through.

owl /aʊl/ *noun* **1** night bird of prey. **2** solemn or wise-looking person. □ **owlish** *adjective*.

owlet /'aʊlɪt/ *noun* small or young owl.

own /əʊn/ *adjective* (after *my, your*, etc.) belonging to myself, yourself, etc.; not another's. ● *verb* **1** have as property; possess. **2** acknowledge as true or belonging to one. □ **come into**

one's own **1** achieve recognition. **2** receive one's due. **hold one's own** maintain one's position; not be defeated. **on one's own 1** alone. **2** independently; unaided. **own goal 1** goal scored by mistake against scorer's own side. **2** action etc. having unintended effect of harming person's own interests. **own up** confess.

■ *verb* **1** have, hold, possess. □ **own up** see CONFESS **1–2**.

owner *noun* possessor. □ **owner-occupier** person who owns and occupies house. □ **ownership** *noun*.

■ freeholder, holder, landlady, landlord, possessor, proprietor, proprietress.

ox *noun* (*plural* **oxen**) **1** large usually horned ruminant. **2** castrated male of domestic species of cattle. □ **ox-eye daisy** daisy with large white petals and yellow centre. **oxtail** tail of ox, often used in making soup.

oxalic acid /ɒk'sælɪk/ *noun* intensely sour poisonous acid found in wood sorrel and rhubarb leaves.

oxidation /ɒksɪ'deɪʃ(ə)n/ *noun* oxidizing, being oxidized.

oxide /'ɒksaɪd/ *noun* compound of oxygen with another element.

oxidize /'ɒksɪdaɪz/ *verb* (also **-ise**) (**-zing** or **-sing**) **1** combine with oxygen. **2** rust. **3** cover with coating of oxide. □ **oxidization** *noun*.

oxyacetylene /ɒksɪə'setɪliːn/ *adjective* of or using mixture of oxygen and acetylene, esp. in cutting or welding metals.

oxygen /'ɒksɪdʒ(ə)n/ *noun* colourless odourless tasteless gaseous element essential to life and to combustion. □ **oxygen tent** enclosure to allow patient to breathe air with increased oxygen content.

oxygenate /'ɒksɪdʒəneɪt/ *verb* (**-ting**) supply, treat, or mix with oxygen; oxidize.

oyez /əʊ'jes/ *interjection* (also **oyes**) *uttered by public crier or court officer to call for attention.*

oyster /'ɔɪstə/ *noun* bivalve mollusc living on seabed, esp. edible kind. ● *adjective* (in full **oyster-white**) greyish white.

oz *abbreviation* ounce(s).

ozone /'əʊzəʊn/ *noun* **1** form of oxygen with pungent odour. **2** *colloquial* invigorating seaside air. □ **ozone-friendly** not containing chemicals destructive to ozone layer. **ozone layer** layer of ozone in stratosphere that absorbs most of sun's ultraviolet radiation.

Pp

p *abbreviation* (also **p.**) **1** penny, pence. **2** page. **3** piano (softly). □ **p. & p.** postage and packing.

PA *abbreviation* **1** personal assistant. **2** public address.

pa /pɑː/ *noun colloquial* father.

p.a. *abbreviation* per annum.

pace[1] *noun* **1** single step in walking or running. **2** distance covered in this. **3** speed; rate of progression. **4** gait. ● *verb* **(-cing) 1** walk (over, about), esp. with slow or regular step. **2** set pace for. **3** (+ *out*) measure (distance) by pacing. □ **pacemaker 1** person who sets pace. **2** natural or electrical device for stimulating heart muscle.
■ *noun* **1, 2** step, stride. **3** *colloquial* lick, quickness, rate, speed, tempo, velocity. **4** gait, walk. ● *verb* **1** see WALK *verb* 1–5.

pace[2] /ˈpɑːtʃeɪ/ *preposition* with all due deference to. [Latin]

pachyderm /ˈpækɪdɜːm/ *noun* large thick-skinned mammal, esp. elephant or rhinoceros. □ **pachydermatous** /-ˈdɜːmətəs/ *adjective*.

pacific /pəˈsɪfɪk/ *adjective* **1** tending to peace, peaceful. **2** (**Pacific**) of or adjoining the Pacific. ● *noun* (**the Pacific**) ocean between America to the east and Asia to the west.

pacifist /ˈpæsɪfɪst/ *noun* person opposed to war. □ **pacifism** *noun*.

pacify /ˈpæsɪfaɪ/ *verb* (**-ies, -ied**) **1** appease (person, anger, etc.). **2** bring (country etc.) to state of peace. □ **pacification** *noun*.
■ appease, assuage, calm, conciliate, humour, mollify, placate, quell, quieten, soothe, subdue, tame, tranquillize.

pack *noun* **1** collection of things wrapped or tied together for carrying. **2** backpack. **3** set of packaged items. **4** set of playing cards. **5** *usually derogatory* lot or set (of similar things or persons). **6** group of wild animals or hounds. **7** organized group of Cub Scouts or Brownies. **8** forwards of Rugby team. **9** area of large crowded pieces of floating ice in sea. ● *verb* **1** put together in suitcase, box, etc. **2** fill with clothes etc., for transport or storing. **3** cram; crowd together; form into pack. **4** (esp. in *passive*; often + *with*) fill. **5** wrap tightly. □ **packed out** full, crowded. **packhorse** horse for carrying loads. **pack in** *colloquial* stop; give up. **pack it in, up** *colloquial* end or stop it. **pack off** send away. **pack up** *colloquial* **1** stop working; break down. **2** retire from contest, activity, etc. **send packing** *colloquial* dismiss summarily.
■ *noun* **1, 3** bale, box, bundle, package, packet, parcel. **2** backpack, haversack, kitbag, knapsack, rucksack. ● *verb* **1, 2** bundle (up), fill, load, package, parcel up, put together, store, stow, wrap

up. **3** compress, cram, crowd, jam, overcrowd, press, ram, squeeze, stuff, tamp down, wedge. □ **pack off** see DISMISS 1. **pack up 2** see FINISH *verb* 1.

package *noun* **1** parcel; box etc. in which goods are packed. **2** (in full **package deal**) set of proposals or items offered or agreed to as a whole. ● *verb* **(-ging)** make up into or enclose in package. □ **package holiday, tour, etc.** one with fixed inclusive price. □ **packaging** *noun*.

packet /ˈpækɪt/ *noun* **1** small package. **2** *colloquial* large sum of money. **3** *historical* mail-boat.

pact *noun* agreement, treaty.
■ agreement, alliance, armistice, arrangement, bargain, compact, concord, concordat, contract, covenant, deal, entente, league, peace, settlement, treaty, truce, understanding.

pad[1] *noun* **1** piece of soft stuff used to diminish jarring, raise surface, absorb fluid, etc. **2** sheets of blank paper fastened together at one edge. **3** fleshy cushion forming sole of foot of some animals. **4** leg-guard in games. **5** flat surface for helicopter take-off or rocket-launching. **6** *slang* lodging. ● *verb* **(-dd-) 1** provide with pad or padding; stuff. **2** (+ *out*) fill out (book etc.) with superfluous matter.
■ *noun* **1** cushion, filler, hassock, kneeler, padding, pillow, stuffing, wad. **2** jotter, notebook, writing pad. ● *verb* **1** cushion, fill, line, pack, protect, stuff, upholster, wad. **2** (*pad out*) see EXTEND 1.

pad[2] *verb* **(-dd-) 1** walk softly. **2** tramp (along) on foot. **3** travel on foot. ● *noun* sound of soft steady steps.

padding *noun* **1** material used to pad. **2** superfluous matter in book etc. used to lengthen it.
■ **1** filling, protection, upholstery, stuffing, wadding. **2** prolixity, *derogatory* verbiage, verbosity, *colloquial* waffle, wordiness.

paddle[1] /ˈpæd(ə)l/ *noun* **1** short oar with broad blade at one or each end. **2** paddle-shaped instrument. **3** fin, flipper. **4** board on paddle-wheel or mill-wheel. **5** action or spell of paddling. ● *verb* **(-ling) 1** move on water or propel (boat etc.) with paddle(s). **2** row gently. □ **paddle-wheel** wheel for propelling ship, with boards round circumference.
■ *noun* **1** oar, scull. ● *verb* propel, row, scull.

paddle[2] /ˈpæd(ə)l/ *verb* **(-ling)** wade about in shallow water. ● *noun* action or spell of paddling.
■ *verb* dabble, splash about, wade.

paddock /ˈpædək/ *noun* **1** small field, esp. for

keeping horses in. **2** enclosure where horses or cars are assembled before race.

■ **1** enclosure, field, meadow, pasture. **2** enclosure, yard.

paddy[1] /'pædɪ/ *noun* (*plural* **-ies**) **1** (in full **paddy field**) field where rice is grown. **2** rice before threshing or in the husk.

paddy[2] /'pædɪ/ *noun* (*plural* **-ies**) *colloquial* rage, temper.

padlock /'pædlɒk/ *noun* detachable lock hanging by pivoted hook. ● *verb* secure with padlock.

padre /'pɑːdrɪ/ *noun* chaplain in army etc.

paean /'piːən/ *noun* (*US* **pean**) song of praise or triumph.

paediatrics /piːdɪ'ætrɪks/ *plural noun* (treated as *singular*) (*US* **pediatrics**) branch of medicine dealing with children's diseases. □ **paediatric** *adjective*. **paediatrician** /-ə'trɪʃ(ə)n/ *noun*.

paedophile /'piːdəfaɪl/ *noun* (*US* **pedophile**) person feeling sexual attraction towards children.

paella /par'elə/ *noun* Spanish dish of rice, saffron, chicken, seafood, etc.

paeony = PEONY.

pagan /'peɪgən/ *noun* **1** heathen. **2** pantheist. ● *adjective* **1** of pagans; heathen. **2** pantheistic. □ **paganism** *noun*.

■ *noun* **1** heathen, infidel, savage, unbeliever. ● *adjective* **1** godless, heathen, idolatrous, infidel, irreligious, polytheistic, unchristian.

page[1] *noun* **1** leaf of book etc. **2** each side of this. ● *verb* (**-ging**) number pages of.

■ *noun* **1** folio, leaf, sheet. **2** recto, side, verso.

page[2] *noun* boy or man employed as liveried servant or personal attendant. ● *verb* (**-ging**) call name of (person sought) in public rooms of hotel etc. □ **page-boy 1** boy attending bride etc. **2** woman's short hairstyle.

■ *noun* errand-boy, messenger, page-boy.

pageant /'pædʒ(ə)nt/ *noun* **1** spectacular performance, usually illustrative of historical events. **2** brilliant show; parade.

■ ceremony, display, extravaganza, parade, procession, show, spectacle, tableau.

pageantry *noun* spectacular show or display.

■ ceremony, display, formality, grandeur, magnificence, pomp, ritual, show, spectacle, splendour.

pager *noun* bleeping device calling bearer to telephone etc.

paginate /'pædʒɪneɪt/ *verb* (**-ting**) number pages of (book etc.). □ **pagination** *noun*.

pagoda /pə'gəʊdə/ *noun* **1** temple or sacred tower in China etc. **2** ornamental imitation of this.

pah *interjection: expressing disgust.*

paid *past & past participle* of PAY.

pail *noun* bucket.

pain *noun* **1** bodily suffering caused by injury, pressure, illness, etc. **2** mental suffering. **3** (also **pain in the neck**) *colloquial* troublesome person or thing. ● *verb* cause pain to. □ **be at or take pains** take great care. **in pain** suffering pain. **painkiller** pain-relieving drug.

■ *noun* **1** ache, aching, affliction, agony, cramp, crick, discomfort, hurt, irritation, pang, smart, smarting, soreness, spasm, stab, sting, suffering, tenderness, throb, throes, torture, twinge. **2** affliction, agony, anguish, distress, hurt, ordeal, suffering, throes, torment, torture. ● *verb* see HURT *verb* 1. □ **painkiller** anaesthetic, analgesic, anodyne, palliative, sedative.

painful *adjective* **1** causing or (esp. of part of body) suffering pain. **2** causing trouble or difficulty. □ **painfully** *adverb*.

■ **1** aching, achy, agonizing, burning, cruel, distressing, excruciating, grievous, harrowing, hurtful, hurting, inflamed, piercing, raw, severe, sharp, smarting, sore, splitting (*head*), stabbing, stinging, tender, throbbing, traumatic, upsetting, vexing. **2** difficult, hard, laborious, troublesome, trying, unpleasant.

painless *adjective* not causing pain. □ **painlessly** *adverb*.

■ comfortable, easy, effortless, pain-free, simple, trouble-free, undemanding.

painstaking /'peɪnzteɪkɪŋ/ *adjective* careful, industrious, thorough. □ **painstakingly** *adverb*.

paint *noun* colouring matter, esp. in liquid form, for applying to surface. ● *verb* **1** cover surface of with paint. **2** portray or make pictures in colours. **3** describe vividly. **4** apply liquid or cosmetic to. □ **paintbox** box holding dry paints for painting pictures. **painted lady** butterfly with spotted orange-red wings. **paint the town red** *colloquial* enjoy oneself flamboyantly. **paintwork** painted, esp. wooden, surface or area in building etc.

■ *noun* colour, colouring, dye, emulsion, pigment, stain, tint. ● *verb* **1** coat, colour, cover, daub, decorate, dye, redecorate, stain, tint, touch up. **2** delineate, depict, picture, portray, represent. **3** delineate, depict, describe, picture, portray, represent.

painter[1] *noun* person who paints, esp. as artist or decorator.

■ artist, decorator, illustrator, miniaturist.

painter[2] *noun* rope at bow of boat for tying it up.

painting *noun* **1** process or art of using paint. **2** painted picture.

■ **2** fresco, landscape, miniature, mural, oil painting, portrait, still life, watercolour.

pair *noun* **1** set of two people or things. **2** thing with two joined or corresponding parts. **3** engaged or married or mated couple. **4** two playing cards of same denomination. **5** (either of) two MPs etc. on opposite sides agreeing not to vote on certain occasions. ● *verb* **1** (often + *off*, *up*) arrange or unite as pair, in pairs, or in marriage. **2** mate.

■ *noun* **1** brace, couple, duet, duo, mates, partners, partnership, set of two, twins, twosome. ● *verb* **1** (*pair off*, *pair up*) couple, double up, get together, join up, match up, *colloquial* pal up, partner, team up.

Paisley /ˈpeɪzlɪ/ *noun* (*plural* **-s**) pattern of curved feather-shaped figures.

pajamas *US* = PYJAMAS.

Pakistani /pɑːkɪsˈtɑːnɪ/ *noun* (*plural* **-s**) **1** native or national of Pakistan. **2** person of Pakistani descent. ● *adjective* of Pakistan.

pal *colloquial noun* friend. ● *verb* (**-ll-**) (+ *up*) make friends.

palace /ˈpælɪs/ *noun* **1** official residence of sovereign, president, archbishop, or bishop. **2** stately or spacious building.

■ **2** castle, chateau, court, hall, manor, mansion, stately home.

palaeo- *combining form* (*US* **paleo-**) ancient; prehistoric.

palaeography /pælɪˈɒgrəfɪ/ *noun* (*US* **paleography**) study of ancient writing and documents.

palaeolithic /pælɪəʊˈlɪθɪk/ *adjective* (*US* **paleolithic**) of earlier Stone Age.

palaeontology /pælɪɒnˈtɒlədʒɪ/ *noun* (*US* **paleontology**) study of life in geological past. □ **palaeontologist** *noun*.

Palaeozoic /pælɪəʊˈzəʊɪk/ (*US* **Paleozoic**) *adjective* of geological era marked by appearance of plants and animals, esp. invertebrates. ● *noun* this era.

palais /ˈpæleɪ/ *noun colloquial* public dance hall.

palanquin /pælənˈkiːn/ *noun* (also **palankeen**) Eastern covered litter for one.

palatable /ˈpælətəb(ə)l/ *adjective* **1** pleasant to taste. **2** (of idea etc.) acceptable, satisfactory.

■ **1** appetizing, eatable, edible, tasty. **2** acceptable, agreeable, attractive, pleasant, satisfactory.

palatal /ˈpælət(ə)l/ *adjective* **1** of the palate. **2** (of sound) made with tongue against palate. ● *noun* palatal sound.

palate /ˈpælət/ *noun* **1** roof of mouth in vertebrates. **2** sense of taste. **3** liking.

palatial /pəˈleɪʃ(ə)l/ *adjective* like palace, splendid.

■ aristocratic, grand, large-scale, luxurious, majestic, opulent, *colloquial* posh, splendid, stately, upmarket.

palaver /pəˈlɑːvə/ *noun colloquial* tedious fuss and bother.

pale[1] *adjective* **1** (of complexion etc.) whitish. **2** faintly coloured. **3** (of colour) faint. **4** (of light) dim. ● *verb* (**-ling**) **1** grow or make pale. **2** (often + *before*, *beside*) seem feeble in comparison (with). □ **palely** *adverb*.

■ *adjective* **1** anaemic, ashen, blanched, bloodless, cadaverous, colourless, corpse-like, deathly, drained, etiolated, ghastly, ghostly, ill-looking, pallid, pasty, peaky, sallow, sickly, unhealthy, wan, washed out, whey-faced, white, whitish. **2–4** bleached, dim, faded, faint, light, pastel, subtle, weak. ● *verb* **1** blanch, dim, etiolate, fade, lighten, whiten.

pale[2] *noun* **1** pointed piece of wood for fencing etc.; stake. **2** boundary. □ **beyond the pale** outside bounds of acceptable behaviour.

paleo- *US* = PALAEO-.

Palestinian /pælɪˈstɪnɪən/ *adjective* of Palestine. ● *noun* native or inhabitant of Palestine.

palette /ˈpælɪt/ *noun* **1** artist's flat tablet for mixing colours on. **2** range of colours used by artist. □ **palette-knife** knife with long round-ended flexible blade, esp. for mixing colours or applying or removing paint.

palimony /ˈpælɪmənɪ/ *noun esp. US colloquial* allowance paid by either of a separated unmarried couple to the other.

palimpsest /ˈpælɪmpsest/ *noun* writing material used for second time after original writing has been erased.

palindrome /ˈpælɪndrəʊm/ *noun* word or phrase that reads same backwards as forwards. □ **palindromic** /-ˈdrɒm-/ *adjective*.

paling *noun* (in *singular* or *plural*) **1** fence of pales. **2** pale.

palisade /pælɪˈseɪd/ *noun* fence of pointed stakes. ● *verb* (**-ding**) enclose or provide with palisade.

pall[1] /pɔːl/ *noun* **1** cloth spread over coffin etc. **2** ecclesiastical vestment. **3** dark covering. □ **pallbearer** person helping to carry or escort coffin at funeral.

■ **3** cloth, covering, mantle, shroud, veil.

pall[2] /pɔːl/ *verb* (often + *on*) become uninteresting.

■ (*pall on*) bore, tire, weary.

pallet[1] /ˈpælɪt/ *noun* **1** straw mattress. **2** makeshift bed.

pallet[2] /ˈpælɪt/ *noun* portable platform for transporting and storing loads.

palliasse /ˈpælɪæs/ *noun* straw mattress.

palliate /ˈpælɪeɪt/ *verb* (**-ting**) **1** alleviate without curing. **2** excuse, extenuate. □ **palliation** /-ˈeɪʃ(ə)n/ *noun*.

palliative /ˈpælɪətɪv/ *adjective* alleviating. ● *noun* thing which alleviates anxiety, pain, etc.

■ *adjective* alleviating, calming, reassuring, sedative, soothing. ● *noun* painkiller, sedative, tranquillizer.

pallid /ˈpælɪd/ *adjective* pale, sickly-looking.

pallor /ˈpælə/ *noun* paleness.

pally *adjective* (**-ier**, **-iest**) *colloquial* friendly.

palm[1] /pɑːm/ *noun* **1** (also **palm tree**) (usually tropical) treelike plant with unbranched stem and crown of large esp. sickle- or fan-shaped leaves. **2** leaf of this as symbol of victory. □ **Palm Sunday** Sunday before Easter.

palm² /pɑːm/ *noun* inner surface of hand between wrist and fingers. ● *verb* conceal in hand. □ **palm off** (often + *on*) impose fraudulently (on person).

palmate /'pælmeɪt/ *adjective* shaped like open hand.

palmetto /pæl'metəʊ/ *noun* (*plural* **-s**) small palm tree.

palmist /'pɑːmɪst/ *noun* teller of character or fortune from lines etc. in palm of hand. □ **palmistry** *noun*.

palmy /'pɑːmɪ/ *adjective* (**-ier, -iest**) **1** of, like, or abounding in palms. **2** flourishing.

palomino /pælə'miːnəʊ/ *noun* (*plural* **-s**) golden or cream-coloured horse with light-coloured mane and tail.

palpable /'pælpəb(ə)l/ *adjective* **1** that can be touched or felt. **2** readily perceived. □ **palpably** *adverb*.

■ **1** corporeal, physical, real, solid, substantial, tangible, touchable. **2** apparent, evident, manifest, obvious, patent, visible.

palpate /'pælpeɪt/ *verb* (**-ting**) examine (esp. medically) by touch. □ **palpation** *noun*.

palpitate /'pælpɪteɪt/ *verb* (**-ting**) **1** pulsate, throb. **2** tremble. □ **palpitation** *noun*.

■ **1** beat, pound, pulsate, throb, vibrate. **2** flutter, quiver, shiver, tremble, vibrate.

palsy /'pɔːlzɪ/ *noun* (*plural* **-ies**) paralysis, esp. with involuntary tremors. ● *verb* (**-ies, -ied**) affect with palsy.

paltry /'pɔːltrɪ/ *adjective* (**-ier, -iest**) worthless, contemptible, trifling.

■ contemptible, inconsequential, insignificant, petty, *colloquial* piddling, pitiable, puny, small, trifling, unimportant, worthless.

pampas /'pæmpəs/ *plural noun* large treeless S. American plains. □ **pampas grass** large ornamental grass.

pamper /'pæmpə/ *verb* over-indulge.

■ coddle, cosset, humour, indulge, mollycoddle, over-indulge, pander to, pet, spoil, spoon-feed.

pamphlet /'pæmflɪt/ *noun* small unbound booklet, esp. controversial treatise.

■ booklet, brochure, bulletin, catalogue, circular, flyer, folder, handout, leaflet, notice, tract.

pamphleteer /pæmflɪ'tɪə/ *noun* writer of (esp. political) pamphlets.

pan¹ *noun* **1** flat-bottomed usually metal vessel used in cooking etc. **2** shallow receptacle or tray. **3** bowl of scales or of lavatory. ● *verb* (**-nn-**) **1** *colloquial* criticize harshly. **2** (+ *off, out*) wash (gold-bearing gravel) in pan. **3** search for gold in this way. □ **pan out** turn out; work out well or in specified way.

■ *noun* **1** *Australian* billy, casserole, container, frying-pan, pot, saucepan, skillet. ● *verb* **1** see CRITICIZE 1.

pan² *verb* (**-nn-**) **1** swing (camera) horizontally to give panoramic effect or follow moving object. **2** (of camera) be moved thus. ● *noun* panning movement.

pan- *combining form* **1** all. **2** the whole of (esp. referring to a continent, racial group, religion, etc.).

panacea /pænə'siːə/ *noun* universal remedy.

panache /pə'næʃ/ *noun* assertively flamboyant or confident style.

■ animation, confidence, dash, *élan*, energy, enthusiasm, flair, flamboyance, flourish, *savoir faire*, self-assurance, spirit, style, swagger, verve, zest.

panama /'pænəmɑː/ *noun* hat of strawlike material with brim and indented crown.

panatella /pænə'telə/ *noun* long thin cigar.

pancake *noun* thin flat cake of fried batter, usually folded or rolled up with filling. □ **Pancake Day** Shrove Tuesday (when pancakes are traditionally eaten). **pancake landing** *colloquial* emergency aircraft landing with undercarriage still retracted.

panchromatic /pænkrəʊ'mætɪk/ *adjective* (of film etc.) sensitive to all visible colours of spectrum.

pancreas /'pæŋkrɪəs/ *noun* gland near stomach supplying digestive fluid and insulin. □ **pancreatic** /-'æt-/ *adjective*.

panda /'pændə/ *noun* **1** (also **giant panda**) large rare bearlike black and white mammal native to China and Tibet. **2** (also **red panda**) racoon-like Himalayan mammal. □ **panda car** police patrol car.

pandemic /pæn'demɪk/ *adjective* (of disease) widespread; universal.

pandemonium /pændɪ'məʊnɪəm/ *noun* **1** uproar; utter confusion. **2** scene of this.

■ babel, bedlam, chaos, commotion, confusion, hubbub, noise, *colloquial* rumpus, turmoil, uproar.

pander /'pændə/ *verb* (+ *to*) indulge (person or weakness). ● *noun* procurer, pimp.

■ *verb* (*pander to*) bow to, cater for, fulfil, gratify, humour, indulge, please, provide, satisfy.

pandit = PUNDIT.

pane *noun* single sheet of glass in window or door.

panegyric /pænɪ'dʒɪrɪk/ *noun* eulogy; speech or essay of praise. □ **panegyrical** *adjective*.

panel /'pæn(ə)l/ *noun* **1** distinct, usually rectangular, section of surface, esp. of wall, door, or vehicle. **2** group or team of people assembled for discussion, consultation, etc. **3** strip of material in garment. **4** list of available jurors; jury. ● *verb* (**-ll-**; *US* **-l-**) fit with panels. □ **panel game** broadcast quiz etc. played by panel. □ **panelling** *noun*.

■ *noun* **2** committee, group, team. □ **panelling** wainscot, wainscoting.

panellist *noun* (*US* **panelist**) member of panel.

pang *noun* sudden sharp pain or distressing emotion.

pangolin /pæŋ'gəʊlɪn/ *noun* scaly anteater.

panic /'pænɪk/ *noun* **1** sudden alarm. **2** infectious fright. ● *verb* (**-ck-**) (often + *into*) affect or be affected with panic. □ **panic-stricken, -struck** affected with panic. □ **panicky** *adjective*.

■ *noun* alarm, consternation, fear, *colloquial* flap, fright, horror, hysteria, stampede, terror. ● *verb* alarm, fall apart, *colloquial* flap, frighten, go to pieces, lose one's head, lose one's nerve, overreact, scare, stampede. □ **panic-stricken, panic-struck** alarmed, beside oneself, frantic, frenzied, frightened, horrified, hysterical, in a cold sweat, *colloquial* in a tizzy, jumpy, overexcited, panicky, terror-stricken, unnerved, worked up.

panicle /'pænɪk(ə)l/ *noun* loose branching cluster of flowers.

panjandrum /pæn'dʒændrəm/ *noun: mock title of great personage.*

pannier /'pænɪə/ *noun* one of pair of baskets or bags etc. carried on bicycle or motorcycle or by mule, donkey, etc.

panoply /'pænəplɪ/ *noun* (*plural* **-ies**) **1** complete or splendid array. **2** full armour.

panorama /pænə'rɑːmə/ *noun* **1** unbroken view of surrounding region. **2** picture or photograph containing wide view. □ **panoramic** /-'ræm-/ *adjective*.

■ landscape, perspective, prospect, scene, view, vista. □ **panoramic** commanding, extensive, scenic, sweeping, wide.

pansy /'pænzɪ/ *noun* (*plural* **-ies**) garden plant of violet family with richly coloured flowers.

pant *verb* **1** breathe with quick breaths. **2** yearn. ● *noun* panting breath.

■ *verb* **1** blow, gasp, huff and puff, puff, wheeze.

pantaloons /pæntə'luːnz/ *plural noun* baggy trousers gathered at ankles.

pantechnicon /pæn'teknɪkən/ *noun* large furniture van.

pantheism /'pænθiɪz(ə)m/ *noun* doctrine that God is everything and everything is God. □ **pantheist** *noun*. **pantheistic** /-'ɪs-/ *adjective*.

pantheon /'pænθiən/ *noun* **1** building with memorials of illustrious dead. **2** deities of a people collectively. **3** temple of all gods.

panther /'pænθə/ *noun* **1** leopard, esp. black. **2** *US* puma.

panties /'pæntɪz/ *plural noun colloquial* short-legged or legless knickers.

pantile /'pæntaɪl/ *noun* curved roof-tile.

pantograph /'pæntəgrɑːf/ *noun* instrument for copying plan etc. on any scale.

pantomime /'pæntəmaɪm/ *noun* **1** dramatic usually Christmas entertainment based on fairy tale. **2** *colloquial* absurd or outrageous behaviour. **3** gestures and facial expressions conveying meaning.

pantry /'pæntrɪ/ *noun* (*plural* **-ies**) room in which provisions, crockery, cutlery, etc. are kept.

pants *plural noun* **1** underpants; knickers. **2** *US* trousers.

■ **1** *colloquial* bloomers, boxer shorts, briefs, camiknickers, drawers, knickers, *colloquial* panties, *US* shorts, *colloquial* smalls, trunks, underpants, *colloquial* undies. **2** see TROUSERS.

pap[1] *noun* **1** soft or semi-liquid food. **2** trivial reading matter.

pap[2] *noun archaic* nipple.

papa /pə'pɑː/ *noun archaic: child's name for father.*

papacy /'peɪpəsɪ/ *noun* (*plural* **-ies**) **1** Pope's office or tenure. **2** papal system.

papal /'peɪp(ə)l/ *adjective* of the Pope or his office.

paparazzo /pæpə'rætsəʊ/ *noun* (*plural* **-zzi** /-tsɪ/) freelance photographer who pursues celebrities to photograph them.

papaya = PAWPAW.

paper /'peɪpə/ *noun* **1** substance made in very thin sheets from pulp of wood etc., used for writing, printing, wrapping, etc. **2** newspaper. **3** (usually in *plural*) document. **4** set of exam questions or answers. **5** wallpaper. **6** essay. ● *adjective* not actual, theoretical. ● *verb* decorate (wall etc.) with paper. □ **paper boy, girl** one who delivers or sells newspapers. **paper clip** clip of bent wire or plastic for holding sheets of paper together. **paper knife** blunt knife for opening envelopes etc. **paper money** banknotes etc. **paper round 1** job of regularly delivering newspapers. **2** route for doing this. **paperweight** small heavy object to hold papers down. **paperwork** office administration and record-keeping.

■ *noun* **2** *colloquial* daily, journal, newspaper, *derogatory* rag, tabloid. **3** certificate, deed, document, form, ID, identification, licence, record; (*papers*) credentials, dossier, file. **6** article, dissertation, essay, monograph, thesis, treatise.

paperback *adjective* bound in stiff paper, not boards. ● *noun* paperback book.

papier mâché /pæpɪeɪ 'mæʃeɪ/ *noun* moulded paper pulp used for making models etc.

papilla /pə'pɪlə/ *noun* (*plural* **papillae** /-liː/) small nipple-like protuberance. □ **papillary** *adjective*.

papoose /pə'puːs/ *noun* young N. American Indian child.

paprika /'pæprɪkə, pə'priːkə/ *noun* **1** red pepper. **2** condiment made from this.

papyrus /pə'paɪərəs/ *noun* (*plural* **papyri** /-raɪ/) **1** aquatic plant of N. Africa. **2** ancient writing material made from stem of this. **3** manuscript written on this.

par *noun* **1** average or normal value, degree, condition, etc. **2** equality; equal footing. **3** *Golf* number of strokes needed by first-class player for hole or course. **4** face value. □ **par for the course** *colloquial* what is normal or to be expected.

para /'pærə/ *noun colloquial* paratrooper.

para- *prefix* beside, beyond.

parable /'pærəb(ə)l/ *noun* story used to illustrate moral or spiritual truth.
- ■ allegory, fable, moral tale.

parabola /pə'ræbələ/ *noun* plane curve formed by intersection of cone with plane parallel to its side. □ **parabolic** /pærə'bɒlɪk/ *adjective*.

paracetamol /pærə'si:təmɒl/ *noun* **1** compound used to relieve pain and reduce fever. **2** tablet of this.

parachute /'pærəʃu:t/ *noun* usually umbrella-shaped apparatus allowing person or heavy object to descend safely from a height, esp. from aircraft. ● *verb* (**-ting**) convey or descend by parachute. □ **parachutist** *noun*.

parade /pə'reɪd/ *noun* **1** public procession. **2** muster of troops etc. for inspection. **3** parade ground. **4** display, ostentation. **5** public square; row of shops. ● *verb* (**-ding**) **1** march ceremonially. **2** assemble for parade. **3** display ostentatiously. □ **parade ground** place for muster of troops.
- ■ *noun* **1** cavalcade, column, cortège, file, march past, motorcade, pageant, procession. **4** display, exhibition, show, spectacle. ● *verb* **1** file past, march past, process, walk. **2** assemble, form up, line up, muster, present oneself. **3** see DISPLAY *verb*.

paradigm /'pærədaɪm/ *noun* example or pattern, esp. of inflection of word. □ **paradigmatic** /-dɪg'mætɪk/ *adjective*.

paradise /'pærədaɪs/ *noun* **1** heaven. **2** place or state of complete bliss. **3** Garden of Eden.
- ■ **1** *Greek Mythology* Elysium, heaven. **2** Eden, Elysium, heaven, Utopia.

paradox /'pærədɒks/ *noun* seemingly absurd or self-contradictory though often true statement etc. □ **paradoxical** /-'dɒks-/ *adjective*. **paradoxically** /-'dɒks-/ *adverb*.
- ■ absurdity, anomaly, contradiction, incongruity, inconsistency, self-contradiction. □ **paradoxical** absurd, anomalous, conflicting, contradictory, illogical, improbable, incongruous, self-contradictory.

paraffin /'pærəfɪn/ *noun* inflammable waxy or oily substance got by distillation from petroleum etc., used in liquid form esp. as fuel. □ **paraffin wax** solid paraffin.

paragon /'pærəgən/ *noun* (often + *of*) model of excellence.

paragraph /'pærəgrɑːf/ *noun* **1** distinct passage in book etc. usually marked by indentation of first line. **2** mark of reference (¶). **3** short separate item in newspaper etc.

parakeet /'pærəki:t/ *noun* small usually long-tailed parrot.

parallax /'pærəlæks/ *noun* **1** apparent difference in position or direction of object caused by change of observer's position. **2** angular amount of this.

parallel /'pærəlel/ *adjective* **1** (of lines) continuously equidistant. **2** precisely similar, analogous, or corresponding. **3** (of processes etc.) occurring or performed simultaneously. ● *noun* **1** person or thing analogous to another. **2** comparison. **3** imaginary line on earth's surface or line on map marking degree of latitude. ● *verb* (**-l-**) **1** be parallel or correspond to. **2** represent as similar; compare. □ **parallelism** *noun*.
- ■ *adjective* **2** analogous, cognate, corresponding, equivalent, like, matching, similar. **3** see SIMULTANEOUS. ● *noun* **1** analogue, counterpart, equal, likeness, match. **2** analogy, comparison, correspondence, equivalence, kinship, resemblance, similarity. ● *verb* **1** compare with, correspond to, duplicate, echo, equate with, keep pace with, match, remind one of, run alongside. **2** compare, equate, liken, match.

parallelepiped /pærəlelə'paɪped/ *noun* solid bounded by parallelograms.

parallelogram /pærə'leləgræm/ *noun* 4-sided rectilinear figure whose opposite sides are parallel.

paralyse /'pærəlaɪz/ *verb* (**-sing**) (*US* **-lyze**; **-zing**) **1** affect with paralysis. **2** render powerless; cripple. □ **paralysed** *adjective*.
- ■ **1** cripple, disable, immobilize, incapacitate, lame. **2** cripple, deactivate, deaden, desensitize, disable, freeze, halt, immobilize, incapacitate, numb, petrify, stop, stun. □ **paralysed** crippled, dead, desensitized, disabled, handicapped, immobile, immovable, incapacitated, numb, palsied, paralytic, paraplegic, rigid, unusable, useless.

paralysis /pə'rælɪsɪs/ *noun* **1** impairment or loss of esp. motor function of nerves, causing immobility. **2** powerlessness.
- ■ **1** deadness, immobility, numbness, palsy, paraplegia.

paralytic /pærə'lɪtɪk/ *adjective* **1** affected with paralysis. **2** *slang* very drunk. ● *noun* person affected with paralysis.

paramedic /pærə'medɪk/ *noun* paramedical worker.

paramedical /pærə'medɪk(ə)l/ *adjective* supplementing and supporting medical work.

parameter /pə'ræmɪtə/ *noun* **1** *Mathematics* quantity constant in case considered, but varying in different cases. **2** (esp. measurable or quantifiable) characteristic or feature. **3** (loosely) boundary, esp. of subject for discussion.

paramilitary /pærə'mɪlɪtərɪ/ *adjective* similarly organized to military forces. ● *noun* (*plural* **-ies**) member of unofficial paramilitary organization.

paramount /'pærəmaʊnt/ *adjective* supreme; most important or powerful.

paramour /'pærəmʊə/ *noun archaic* illicit lover of married person.

paranoia /pærə'nɔɪə/ *noun* **1** mental derangement with delusions of grandeur, persecution, etc. **2** abnormal tendency to suspect and mistrust others. □ **paranoiac** *adjective & noun.* **paranoid** /'pærənɔɪd/ *adjective & noun.*

paranormal /pærə'nɔ:m(ə)l/ *adjective* beyond the scope of normal scientific investigations etc.

parapet /'pærəpɪt/ *noun* **1** low wall at edge of roof, balcony, bridge, etc. **2** mound along front of trench etc.

paraphernalia /pærəfə'neɪlɪə/ *plural noun* (also treated as *singular*) personal belongings, miscellaneous accessories, etc.

  ■ accessories, apparatus, baggage, belongings, chattels, *slang* clobber, effects, equipment, gear, impedimenta, materials, odds and ends, possessions, property, rig, stuff, tackle, things, trappings.

paraphrase /'pærəfreɪz/ *noun* restatement of sense of passage etc. in other words. ● *verb* (**-sing**) express meaning of in other words.

  ■ *verb* explain, interpret, rephrase, restate, reword, rewrite, translate.

paraplegia /pærə'pli:dʒə/ *noun* paralysis below waist. □ **paraplegic** *adjective & noun.*

parapsychology /pærəsaɪ'kɒlədʒɪ/ *noun* study of mental phenomena outside sphere of ordinary psychology.

paraquat /'pærəkwɒt/ *noun* quick-acting highly toxic herbicide.

parasite /'pærəsaɪt/ *noun* **1** animal or plant living in or on another and feeding on it. **2** person exploiting another or others. □ **parasitic** /-'sɪt-/ *adjective.* **parasitism** *noun.*

parasol /'pærəsɒl/ *noun* light umbrella giving shade from the sun.

paratroops /'pærətru:ps/ *plural noun* airborne troops landing by parachute. □ **paratrooper** *noun.*

paratyphoid /pærə'taɪfɔɪd/ *noun* fever resembling typhoid.

parboil /'pa:bɔɪl/ *verb* partly cook by boiling.

parcel /'pa:s(ə)l/ *noun* **1** goods etc. packed up in single wrapping. **2** piece of land. ● *verb* (**-ll-**; US **-l-**) **1** (+ *up*) wrap into parcel. **2** (+ *out*) divide into portions.

  ■ *noun* **1** bale, box, bundle, carton, case, pack, package, packet. ● *verb* **1** (*parcel up*) see PACK *verb* 1,2. **2** (*parcel out*) see DIVIDE *verb* 2.

parch *verb* **1** make or become hot and dry. **2** slightly roast.

  ■ **1** bake, burn, dehydrate, desiccate, dry, scorch, shrivel, wither.

parched *adjective* **1** hot and dry. **2** *colloquial* thirsty.

  ■ **1** see DRY *adjective* 1. **2** see THIRSTY 1.

parchment /'pa:tʃmənt/ *noun* **1** skin, esp. of

sheep or goat, prepared for writing etc. **2** manuscript written on this.

pardon /'pa:d(ə)n/ *noun* **1** forgiveness. **2** remission of punishment. ● *verb* **1** forgive; excuse. **2** release from legal consequences of offence etc. ● *interjection* (also **pardon me** or **I beg your pardon**) **1** *formula of apology or disagreement.* **2** *request to repeat something said.* □ **pardonable** *adjective.*

  ■ *noun* **1** absolution, *formal* exculpation, exoneration, forgiveness, *RC Church* indulgence, mercy. **2** amnesty, discharge, release, remission, reprieve. ● *verb* **1** absolve, *formal* exculpate, excuse, exonerate, forgive, overlook. **2** absolve, free, let off, release, remit, reprieve, set free, spare. □ **pardonable** allowable, excusable, forgivable, justifiable, minor, negligible, petty, understandable, venial (*sin*).

pare /peə/ *verb* (**-ring**) **1** trim or reduce by cutting away edge or surface of. **2** (often + *away*, *down*) whittle away.

parent /'peərənt/ *noun* **1** person who has had or adopted a child; father, mother. **2** source, origin. □ **parent company** company of which others are subsidiaries. **parent-teacher association** social and fund-raising organization of school's teachers and parents. □ **parental** /pə'rent(ə)l/ *adjective.* **parenthood** *noun.*

  ■ *noun* **1** *literary* begetter, father, mother, procreator, progenitor.

parentage *noun* lineage; descent from or through parents.

  ■ ancestry, birth, descent, extraction, family, line, lineage, pedigree, stock.

parenthesis /pə'renθəsɪs/ *noun* (*plural* **-theses** /-si:z/) **1** word, clause, or sentence inserted as explanation etc. into passage independently of grammatical sequence. **2** (in *plural*) round brackets used to mark this. **3** interlude. □ **parenthetic** /pærən'θetɪk/ *adjective.*

par excellence /pa:r eksə'lɑ̃s/ *adverb* superior to all others so called. [French]

parfait /'pa:feɪ/ *noun* **1** rich iced pudding of whipped cream, eggs, etc. **2** layers of ice cream, meringue, etc., served in tall glass.

pariah /pə'raɪə/ *noun* **1** social outcast. **2** *historical* member of low or no caste.

parietal /pə'raɪət(ə)l/ *adjective* of wall of body or any of its cavities. □ **parietal bone** either of pair forming part of skull.

paring *noun* strip pared off.

parish /'pærɪʃ/ *noun* **1** division of diocese having its own church and clergyman. **2** local government district. **3** inhabitants of parish.

parishioner /pə'rɪʃənə/ *noun* inhabitant of parish.

parity /'pærɪtɪ/ *noun* (*plural* **-ies**) **1** equality; equal status etc. **2** equivalence; being at par.

park *noun* **1** large public garden in town for recreation. **2** large enclosed piece of ground attached to country house or laid out or preserved for public use. **3** place where vehicles may be parked. **4** area for specified purpose. ● *verb* place and leave (esp. vehicle) temporarily. □ **parking lot** *US* outdoor car park. **parking meter** coin-operated meter allocating period of time for which a vehicle may be parked in street. **parking ticket** notice of fine etc. imposed for parking vehicle illegally. **parkland** open grassland with trees etc. **park oneself** *colloquial* settle; sit down.

> ■ *noun* **1, 2** common, estate, gardens, green, national park, nature reserve, parkland, recreation ground, reserve. ● *verb* deposit, leave, place, position, put, station, store. □ **park oneself** see SETTLE[1] **5**, SIT **1**.

parka /ˈpɑːkə/ *noun* jacket with hood, as worn by Eskimos, mountaineers, etc.

parkin /ˈpɑːkɪn/ *noun* oatmeal gingerbread.

parky /ˈpɑːkɪ/ *adjective* (**-ier, -iest**) *colloquial* or *dialect* chilly.

parlance /ˈpɑːləns/ *noun* way of speaking.

parley /ˈpɑːlɪ/ *noun* (*plural* **-s**) meeting between representatives of opposed forces to discuss terms. ● *verb* (**-leys, -leyed**) (often + *with*) hold parley.

parliament /ˈpɑːləmənt/ *noun* **1** body consisting of House of Commons and House of Lords and forming (with Sovereign) legislature of UK. **2** similar legislature in other states.

> ■ **2** assembly, congress, council, diet, legislature, Lower House, senate, Upper House.

parliamentarian /pɑːləmenˈteərɪən/ *noun* member of parliament.

parliamentary /pɑːləˈmentərɪ/ *adjective* of, in, concerned with, or enacted by parliament.

parlour /ˈpɑːlə/ *noun* (*US* **parlor**) **1** *archaic* sitting-room in private house. **2** *esp. US* shop providing specified goods or services. □ **parlour game** indoor game, esp. word game.

parlous /ˈpɑːləs/ *adjective archaic* perilous; hard to deal with.

Parmesan /pɑːmɪˈzæn/ *noun* hard Italian cheese usually used grated.

parochial /pəˈrəʊkɪəl/ *adjective* **1** of a parish. **2** of narrow range; merely local. □ **parochialism** *noun*.

parody /ˈpærədɪ/ *noun* (*plural* **-ies**) **1** humorous exaggerated imitation of author, style, etc. **2** travesty. ● *verb* (**-ies, -ied**) **1** write parody of. **2** mimic humorously. □ **parodist** *noun*.

> ■ *noun* **1** burlesque, caricature, imitation, lampoon, mimicry, satire, *colloquial* send-up, *colloquial* spoof, *colloquial* take-off. **2** distortion, mockery, travesty. ● *verb* ape, burlesque, caricature, imitate, lampoon, mimic, ridicule, satirize, *colloquial* send up, *colloquial* take off, travesty.

parole /pəˈrəʊl/ *noun* **1** temporary or permanent release of prisoner before end of sentence, on promise of good behaviour. **2** such promise. ● *verb* (**-ling**) put (prisoner) on parole.

parotid /pəˈrɒtɪd/ *adjective* situated near ear.

● *noun* (in full **parotid gland**) salivary gland in front of ear.

paroxysm /ˈpærəksɪz(ə)m/ *noun* (often + *of*) fit (of pain, rage, coughing, etc.).

parquet /ˈpɑːkeɪ/ *noun* flooring of wooden blocks arranged in a pattern. ● *verb* (**-eted** /-eɪd/, **-eting** /-eɪɪŋ/) floor (room) thus.

parricide /ˈpærɪsaɪd/ *noun* **1** killing of near relative, esp. parent. **2** person who commits parricide. □ **parricidal** /-ˈsaɪd(ə)l/ *adjective*.

parrot /ˈpærət/ *noun* **1** mainly tropical bird with short hooked bill, of which some species can be taught to repeat words. **2** unintelligent imitator or chatterer. ● *verb* (**-t-**) repeat mechanically. □ **parrot-fashion** (learning or repeating) mechanically, by rote.

parry /ˈpærɪ/ *verb* (**-ies, -ied**) ward off; avert. ● *noun* (*plural* **-ies**) act of parrying.

> ■ *verb* avert, block, counter, deflect, fend off, push away, repel, repulse, stave off, ward off.

parse /pɑːz/ *verb* (**-sing**) describe (word) or analyse (sentence) in terms of grammar.

parsec /ˈpɑːsek/ *noun* unit of stellar distance, about 3.25 light years.

parsimony /ˈpɑːsɪmənɪ/ *noun* **1** carefulness in use of money etc. **2** meanness. □ **parsimonious** /-ˈməʊn-/ *adjective*.

parsley /ˈpɑːslɪ/ *noun* herb used for seasoning and garnishing.

parsnip /ˈpɑːsnɪp/ *noun* **1** plant with pale yellow tapering root used as vegetable. **2** this root.

parson /ˈpɑːs(ə)n/ *noun* **1** parish clergyman. **2** *colloquial* any clergyman. □ **parson's nose** fatty flesh at rump of cooked fowl.

parsonage *noun* parson's house.

part *noun* **1** some but not all. **2** component, division, portion. **3** portion of body. **4** section of book, serial, etc., esp. as much as is issued at one time. **5** share, allotted portion. **6** person's share in an action etc. **7** assigned character or role. **8** *Music* one of melodies making up harmony of concerted music. **9** side in agreement or dispute. **10** (usually in *plural*) region; direction, way. **11** (in *plural*) abilities. ● *verb* **1** divide into parts. **2** separate; leave one another's company. **3** (+ *with*) give up; hand over. **4** make parting in (hair). ● *adverb* partly, in part. □ **on the part of** made or done by. **part and parcel** (usually + *of*) essential part. **part-exchange** ● *noun* transaction in which article is given as part of payment for more expensive one. ● *verb* give (article) thus. **part of speech** grammatical class of words (noun, pronoun, adjective, adverb, verb, etc.). **part-song** song for 3 or more voice parts. **part-time** employed for or occupying less than normal working week etc. **part-timer** part-time worker. **take part** be involved.

> ■ *noun* **1** bit, some. **2** bit, branch, component, constituent, department, division, element, fraction, fragment, ingredient, parcel, particle, percentage, piece, portion, ramification, scrap, section, sector, segment, shard, share, subdivision, unit. **3** limb, member, organ,

4 chapter, episode, instalment. **5** allotment, bit, percentage, portion, share. **9** faction, party, side. **10** area, district, neighbourhood, quarter, region, *Military* sector, vicinity. ● *verb* **1** detach, disconnect, divide, pull apart, separate, sever, split, *literary* sunder. **2** break away, depart, go away, leave, part company, quit, say goodbye, separate, split up, withdraw. **3** (*part with*) see RELINQUISH. □ **take part** see PARTICIPATE.

partake /pɑːˈteɪk/ *verb* (**-king**; *past* **partook**; *past participle* **partaken**) **1** (+ *of, in*) take share of. **2** (+ *of*) eat or drink some of.

parterre /pɑːˈteə/ *noun* **1** level garden space filled with flower-beds etc. **2** *US* pit of theatre.

partial /ˈpɑːʃ(ə)l/ *adjective* **1** not total or complete. **2** biased, unfair. **3** (+ *to*) having a liking for. □ **partiality** /-ʃɪˈæl-/ *noun*. **partially** *adverb*.

■ **1** imperfect, incomplete, limited, qualified, unfinished. **2** biased, one-sided, partisan, prejudiced, unfair. **3** (*be partial to*) see LIKE[2] *verb* 1.

participate /pɑːˈtɪsɪpeɪt/ *verb* (**-ting**) (often + *in*) have share or take part. □ **participant** *noun*. **participation** *noun*.

■ assist, be active, be involved, cooperate, help, partake, take part; (*participate in*) contribute to, engage in, enter into, join in, share in. □ **participation** activity, assistance, complicity, contribution, cooperation, engagement, involvement, partnership, sharing.

participle /ˈpɑːtɪsɪp(ə)l/ *noun* word (either **present participle**, e.g. *writing*, or **past participle**, e.g. *written*) formed from verb and used in complex verb-forms or as adjective (see panel). □ **participial** /-ˈsɪp-/ *adjective*.

particle /ˈpɑːtɪk(ə)l/ *noun* **1** minute portion of matter. **2** smallest possible amount. **3** minor esp. indeclinable part of speech.

■ **1** atom, electron, molecule, neutron, proton, quark. **2** atom, bit, crumb, dot, drop, fragment, grain, hint, iota, jot, mite, molecule, morsel, mote, piece, scintilla, scrap, shred, sliver, *colloquial* smidgen, spark, speck, trace.

particoloured /ˈpɑːtɪkʌləd/ *adjective* (*US* **-colored**) of more than one colour.

particular /pəˈtɪkjʊlə/ *adjective* **1** relating to or considered as one as distinct from others. **2** special. **3** scrupulously exact. **4** fastidious. ● *noun* **1** detail, item. **2** (in *plural*) detailed account. □ **in particular** specifically. □ **particularity** /-ˈlær-/ *noun*.

■ *adjective* **1** distinct, idiosyncratic, individual, peculiar, personal, singular, specific, unique, unmistakable. **2** especial, exceptional, important, marked, notable, noteworthy, outstanding, significant, special, unusual. **3** exact, meticulous, painstaking, precise, rigorous, scrupulous, thorough. **4** *colloquial* choosy, critical, discriminating, fastidious, finical, finicky, fussy, nice, *colloquial* pernickety, selective. ● *noun* **2** (*particulars*) circumstances, details, facts, information, *colloquial* low-down.

particularize /pəˈtɪkjʊləraɪz/ *verb* (also **-ise**) (**-zing** or **-sing**) **1** name specially or one by one. **2** specify (items). □ **particularization** *noun*.

particularly *adverb* **1** very. **2** specifically. **3** in a fastidious way.

parting *noun* **1** leave-taking. **2** dividing line of combed hair.

■ **1** departure, farewell, going away, leave-taking, leaving, saying goodbye, separation, splitting up, *formal* valediction.

partisan /pɑːtɪˈzæn/ *noun* **1** strong supporter of party, side, or cause. **2** guerrilla. ● *adjective* **1** of partisans. **2** biased. □ **partisanship** *noun*.

■ *noun* **1** adherent, devotee, fanatic, follower, supporter, zealot. **2** freedom fighter, guerrilla, resistance fighter, underground fighter. ● *adjective* biased, bigoted, blinkered, factional, fanatical, narrow-minded, one-sided, partial, prejudiced, sectarian, unfair.

partition /pɑːˈtɪʃ(ə)n/ *noun* **1** division into parts. **2** structure dividing a space, esp. light interior wall. ● *verb* **1** divide into parts. **2** (+ *off*) separate with partition.

Participle

There are two kinds of participle in English: the *present participle*, which consists of *-ing* added to the base form of a verb, and the *past participle*, which for most verbs consists of *-ed* added to the base form.

There are three main uses of participles:

1 with *be* or *have* to form different tenses:

She is relaxing.
She has relaxed.

2 to form verbal adjectives:

a relaxing *drink*
a leaving *present*

3 to form verbal nouns:

I don't want your leavings.

■ *noun* **1** break-up, division, separation, splitting up, split-up. **2** barrier, panel, room divider, screen, wall. ● *verb* **1** cut up, divide, parcel out, separate, share out, split up, subdivide. **2** (*partition off*) screen off, separate off, wall off.

partitive /'pɑːtɪtɪv/ *adjective* (of word) denoting part of collective whole. ● *noun* partitive word.

partly *adverb* **1** with respect to a part. **2** to some extent.

partner /'pɑːtnə/ *noun* **1** sharer; person associated with others in business. **2** either of pair in marriage etc. or dancing or game. ● *verb* be partner of. □ **partnership** *noun*.

■ *noun* **1** accessory, accomplice, ally, assistant, associate, bedfellow, collaborator, colleague, companion, comrade, confederate, helper, mate, *colloquial* sidekick. **2** consort, husband, *colloquial* mate, spouse, wife. □ **partnership** affiliation, alliance, association, collaboration, combination, complicity, confederation, cooperation, cooperative, marriage, relationship, syndicate, union.

partridge /'pɑːtrɪdʒ/ *noun* (*plural* same or **-s**) kind of game bird.

parturition /ˌpɑːtjʊˈrɪʃ(ə)n/ *noun formal* childbirth.

party /'pɑːtɪ/ *noun* (*plural* **-ies**) **1** social gathering. **2** group of people travelling or working together. **3** political group putting forward candidates in elections and usually organized on national basis. **4** each side in agreement or dispute. □ **party line 1** set policy of political party etc. **2** shared telephone line. **party wall** wall common to adjoining rooms, buildings, etc.

■ **1** ball, celebration, dance, *colloquial* do, festivity, function, gathering, *colloquial* get-together, jollification, *colloquial* knees-up, orgy, *colloquial* rave-up, reception, *colloquial* shindig, social gathering. **2** see GROUP *noun* 1. **3** alliance, association, bloc, cabal, camp, *often derogatory* caucus, clique, coalition, faction, junta, league, sect, side. **4** camp, faction, side.

parvenu /'pɑːvənjuː/ *noun* (*plural* **-s**; *feminine* **parvenue**, *plural* **-s**) **1** newly rich social climber. **2** upstart.

pascal /'pæsk(ə)l/ *noun* **1** SI unit of pressure. **2** (**Pascal** /pæsˈkɑːl/) computer language designed for training.

paschal /'pæsk(ə)l/ *adjective* **1** of Passover. **2** of Easter.

pasha /'pɑːʃə/ *noun historical* Turkish officer of high rank.

pasque-flower /'pæskflaʊə/ *noun* kind of anemone.

pass[1] /pɑːs/ *verb* **1** move onward; proceed. **2** go past; leave on one side or behind. **3** (cause to) be transferred from one place or person to another. **4** surpass. **5** go unremarked or uncensured; be accepted as adequate. **6** move; cause to go. **7** be successful (in exam). **8** allow (bill in Parliament) to proceed. **9** be approved. **10** elapse. **11** happen.

12 spend (time etc.). **13** *Football etc.* kick, hand, or hit (ball etc.) to player of one's own side. **14** (+ *into, from*) change. **15** come to an end. **16** discharge from body as or with excreta. **17** utter (judgement etc.). **18** forgo one's turn. ● *noun* **1** passing, esp. of exam. **2** status of degree without honours. **3** written permission, ticket, or order. **4** *Football etc.* passing of ball. **5** critical position. □ **make a pass at** *colloquial* make sexual advances to. **pass away** die. **passbook** book recording customer's transactions with bank etc. **passer-by** (*plural* **passers-by**) person who goes past, esp. by chance. **pass for** be accepted as. **pass-key 1** private key to gate etc. **2** master key. **pass off 1** fade away. **2** be carried through (in specified way). **3** lightly dismiss. **4** (+ *as*) misrepresent as something false. **pass on 1** proceed. **2** die. **3** transmit to next person in a series. **pass out 1** become unconscious. **2** complete military training. **pass over 1** omit. **2** overlook. **3** make no remark on. **4** die. **pass round 1** distribute. **2** give to one person after another. **pass up** *colloquial* refuse or neglect (opportunity etc.). **password** pre-arranged word or phrase to secure recognition, admission, etc.

■ *verb* **1** move on, proceed, progress, thread one's way. **2** go beyond, go past, move past, outstrip, overhaul, overtake. **3** circulate, deal out, deliver, give, hand over, offer, present, share, submit, supply, transfer. **8** agree, approve, authorize, confirm, decree, enact, establish, ordain, pronounce, ratify, validate. **10** elapse, go by, lapse, slip away, tick by. **15** come to an end, disappear, fade, go away, melt away, vanish. **18** give in, opt out, say nothing, waive one's rights. ● *noun* **3** authority, authorization, clearance, ID, ID card, licence, passport, permission, permit, ticket, warrant. □ **pass away** see DIE[1] 1. **passer-by** bystander, onlooker, witness. **pass on 3** see TRANSFER *verb* 1,2. **pass out 1** see FAINT *verb* 1. **pass over 1, 2** see IGNORE.

pass[2] /pɑːs/ *noun* narrow way through mountains.

■ canyon, col, cut, defile, gap, gorge, gully, opening, passage, ravine, valley.

passable *adjective* **1** adequate, fairly good. **2** (of road etc.) that can be passed. □ **passably** *adverb*.

■ **1** acceptable, adequate, admissible, allowable, all right, fair, indifferent, mediocre, middling, moderate, not bad, ordinary, satisfactory, *colloquial* so so, tolerable. **2** clear, navigable, open, traversable, unblocked, unobstructed, usable.

passage /'pæsɪdʒ/ *noun* **1** process or means of passing; transit. **2** passageway. **3** right to pass through. **4** journey by sea or air. **5** transition from one state to another. **6** short part of book or piece of music etc. **7** duct etc. in body.

■ **1** advance, flow, lapse (*of time*), march, crossing, movement, moving on, passing, progress, transit. **2** corridor, *esp. US* hall, hallway, lobby, passageway, route, tunnel, vestibule, way through. **4** crossing, cruise, journey, voyage. **5** change, passing, progression, transition. **6** citation, episode, excerpt, extract, paragraph, part, piece, portion, quotation, scene, section, selection.

passageway *noun* narrow way for passing along; corridor.

passé /'pæseɪ/ *adjective* **1** outmoded. **2** past its prime.

passenger /'pæsɪndʒə/ *noun* **1** traveller in or on vehicle (other than driver, pilot, crew, etc.). **2** *colloquial* idle member of team etc.

> ■ **1** commuter, rider, traveller, voyager.

passerine /'pæsəri:n/ *noun* bird able to grip branch etc. with claws. ● *adjective* of passerines.

passim /'pæsɪm/ *adverb* throughout. [Latin]

passion /'pæʃ(ə)n/ *noun* **1** strong emotion. **2** outburst of anger. **3** intense sexual love. **4** strong enthusiasm. **5** object arousing this. **6** (**the Passion**) sufferings of Christ during his last days. **7** (**the Passion**) Gospel narrative of this or musical setting of it. □ **passion flower** plant with flower supposed to suggest instruments of Crucifixion. **passion fruit** edible fruit of some species of passion flower. □ **passionless** *adjective*.

> ■ **1, 4** appetite, ardour, avidity, commitment, craving, craze, drive, eagerness, emotion, enthusiasm, fanaticism, feeling, fervency, fervour, fire, flame, frenzy, greed, heat, hunger, infatuation, intensity, keenness, love, mania, obsession, thirst, urge, urgency, vehemence, zeal, zest. **3** ardour, desire, fire, infatuation, love, lust.

passionate /'pæʃənət/ *adjective* dominated by, easily moved to, or showing passion. □ **passionately** *adverb*.

> ■ ardent, aroused, avid, burning, committed, desirous, eager, emotional, enthusiastic, excited, fanatical, fervent, fiery, frenzied, heated, hot, impassioned, infatuated, inflamed, intense, lustful, manic, obsessive, roused, sexy, urgent, vehement, violent, worked up, zealous.

passive /'pæsɪv/ *adjective* **1** acted upon; not acting. **2** submissive. **3** inert. **4** *Grammar* (of verb) of which subject undergoes action (see panel). □ **passive smoking** involuntary inhalation of others' cigarette smoke. □ **passively** *adverb*. **passiveness** *noun*. **passivity** /-'sɪv-/ *noun*.

> ■ **2** apathetic, calm, *formal* complaisant, compliant, deferential, docile, impassive, long-suffering, malleable, non-violent, patient,

phlegmatic, pliable, receptive, resigned, submissive, tame, tractable, unassertive, unmoved, unresisting, yielding. **3** inert, inactive, quiescent, supine.

Passover /'pɑːsəʊvə/ *noun* Jewish spring festival commemorating Exodus from Egypt.

passport /'pɑːspɔːt/ *noun* official document showing holder's identity and nationality etc. and authorizing travel abroad.

past /pɑːst/ *adjective* **1** gone by. **2** just over. **3** of former time. **4** *Grammar* expressing past action or state. ● *noun* **1** past time or events. **2** person's past life or career. **3** past tense. ● *preposition* beyond. ● *adverb* so as to pass by. □ **past it** *colloquial* old and useless. **past master** expert.

> ■ *adjective* **1** bygone, ended, finished, gone, historical, *archaic* olden (*days*), over and done with. **2** last, recent. **3** earlier, former, late, previous, sometime. ● *noun* **1** antiquity, days gone by, former times, history, old days, *archaic* olden days.

pasta /'pæstə/ *noun* dried flour paste in various shapes.

paste /peɪst/ *noun* **1** any moist fairly stiff mixture. **2** dough of flour with fat, water, etc. **3** flour and water or other mixture as adhesive. **4** meat or fish spread. **5** hard glasslike material used for imitation gems. ● *verb* (**-ting**) **1** fasten or coat with paste. **2** *slang* beat, thrash. □ **pasteboard** stiff substance made by pasting together sheets of paper. □ **pasting** *noun*.

> ■ *noun* **3** adhesive, fixative, glue, gum. **4** pâté, spread. ● *verb* **1** fasten, fix, glue, stick.

pastel /'pæst(ə)l/ *noun* **1** pale shade of colour. **2** crayon made of dry pigment-paste. **3** drawing in pastel. ● *adjective* of pale shade of colour.

pastern /'pæst(ə)n/ *noun* part of horse's foot between fetlock and hoof.

pasteurize /'pɑːstʃəraɪz/ *verb* (also **-ise**) (**-zing** or **-sing**) partially sterilize (milk etc.) by heating. □ **pasteurization** *noun*.

pastiche /pæs'tiːʃ/ *noun* **1** picture or musical composition made up from various sources. **2** literary or other work imitating style of author or period etc.

> ■ **1** blend, composite, compound, hotchpotch, medley, mess, miscellany, mixture, patchwork, selection.

pastille /'pæstɪl/ *noun* small sweet or lozenge.

Passive

A verb in the passive takes the object or person affected by the action as its subject. Passive verbs are formed by placing a form of the auxiliary verb *be* in front of the past participle:

> *This proposal* will *probably* be accepted.
> *Several people* were injured.
> *He* was hit *by a train*.

The passive is often used when the writer does not want to say who exactly is responsible for the action in question:

> *I'm afraid your ideas* have been rejected.

pastime /'pɑːstaɪm/ *noun* recreation; hobby.
■ activity, amusement, avocation, distraction, diversion, entertainment, fun, game, hobby, leisure activity, occupation, play, recreation, relaxation, sport.

pastor /'pɑːstə/ *noun* minister, esp. of Nonconformist church.

pastoral /'pɑːstər(ə)l/ *adjective* 1 of shepherds. 2 of (esp. romanticized) rural life. 3 of pastor.
● *noun* 1 pastoral poem, play, picture, etc. 2 letter from bishop or other pastor to clergy or people.
■ *adjective* 2 agrarian, agricultural, Arcadian, bucolic, country, farming, idyllic, outdoor, peaceful, provincial, rural, rustic. 3 clerical, ecclesiastical, ministerial, parochial, priestly.

pastrami /pæ'strɑːmɪ/ *noun* seasoned smoked beef.

pastry /'peɪstrɪ/ *noun* (*plural* -ies) 1 dough of flour, fat, and water. 2 (item of) food made wholly or partly of this.

pasturage *noun* 1 pasture land. 2 pasturing.

pasture /'pɑːstʃə/ *noun* 1 land covered with grass etc. for grazing animals. 2 herbage for animals. ● *verb* (-ring) 1 put (animals) to pasture. 2 graze.
■ *noun* 1 field, grassland, grazing, meadow, paddock, pasturage.

pasty[1] /'pæstɪ/ *noun* (*plural* -ies) pie of meat etc. wrapped in pastry and baked without dish.

pasty[2] /'peɪstɪ/ *adjective* (-ier, -iest) pallid.

pat[1] *verb* (-tt-) strike gently with flat palm or other flat surface, esp. in affection etc. ● *noun* 1 light stroke or tap, esp. with hand in affection etc. 2 patting sound. 3 small mass, esp. of butter, made (as) by patting.
■ *verb* caress, dab, stroke, tap, touch.

pat[2] *adjective* 1 known thoroughly. 2 apposite, opportune, esp. glibly so. ● *adverb* in a pat way. □ **have off pat** have memorized perfectly.

patch *noun* 1 piece put on in mending or as reinforcement. 2 cover protecting injured eye. 3 large or irregular spot on surface. 4 distinct area or period. 5 small plot of ground. ● *verb* 1 mend with patch(es). 2 (often + *up*) piece together. 3 (+ *up*) settle (quarrel etc.), esp. hastily. □ **not a patch on** *colloquial* very much inferior to. **patchwork** stitching together of small pieces of differently coloured or textured cloth to form pattern.
■ *noun* 1 piece, reinforcement. ● *verb* 1 cover, darn, fix, mend, reinforce, repair, sew up, stitch up.

patchy *adjective* (-ier, -iest) 1 uneven in quality. 2 having patches. □ **patchily** *adverb*.
■ 1 bitty, changing, erratic, inconsistent, irregular, uneven, unpredictable, variable, varied, varying. 2 blotchy, dappled, mottled, speckled, spotty.

pate *noun* *colloquial* head.

pâté /'pæteɪ/ *noun* smooth paste of meat etc. □ **pâté de foie gras** /də fwɑː 'grɑː/ pâté made from livers of fatted geese.

patella /pə'telə/ *noun* (*plural* **patellae** /-liː/) kneecap.

paten /'pæt(ə)n/ *noun* plate for bread at Eucharist.

patent /'peɪt(ə)nt, 'pæt-/ *noun* 1 official document conferring right, title, etc., esp. sole right to make, use, or sell some invention. 2 invention or process so protected. ● *adjective* /'peɪt(ə)nt/ 1 plain, obvious. 2 conferred or protected by patent. 3 (of food, medicine, etc.) proprietary. ● *verb* obtain patent for (invention). □ **patent leather** glossy varnished leather. □ **patently** *adverb*.
■ *adjective* 1 apparent, blatant, clear, conspicuous, evident, flagrant, manifest, obvious, open, plain, self-evident, transparent, undisguised, visible.

patentee /peɪtən'tiː/ *noun* holder of patent.

paterfamilias /peɪtəfə'mɪlɪæs/ *noun* male head of family etc.

paternal /pə'tɜːn(ə)l/ *adjective* 1 of father, fatherly. 2 related through father.

paternalism *noun* policy of restricting freedom and responsibility by well-meant regulations. □ **paternalistic** /-'lɪs-/ *adjective*.

paternity /pə'tɜːnɪtɪ/ *noun* 1 fatherhood. 2 one's paternal origin.

paternoster /pætə'nɒstə/ *noun* Lord's Prayer, esp. in Latin.

path /pɑːθ/ *noun* (*plural* **paths** /pɑːðz/ 1 footway, track. 2 line along which person or thing moves. □ **pathway** 1 path. 2 its course.
■ 1 alley, bridle path, bridleway, footpath, footway, pathway, pavement, *US* sidewalk, towpath, track, trail, walk, walkway, way. 2 course, orbit, route, trajectory, way.

pathetic /pə'θetɪk/ *adjective* 1 exciting pity, sadness, or contempt. 2 *colloquial* inadequate. □ **pathetically** *adverb*.
■ 1 affecting, distressing, emotional, emotive, heartbreaking, heart-rending, lamentable, moving, piteous, pitiable, pitiful, plaintive, poignant, sad, stirring, touching, tragic. 2 see INADEQUATE 1.

pathogen /'pæθədʒ(ə)n/ *noun* agent causing disease. □ **pathogenic** /-'dʒen-/ *adjective*.

pathological /pæθə'lɒdʒɪk(ə)l/ *adjective* 1 of pathology. 2 of or caused by mental or physical disorder. □ **pathologically** *adverb*.

pathology /pə'θɒlədʒɪ/ *noun* study of disease. □ **pathologist** *noun*.

pathos /'peɪθɒs/ *noun* quality that excites pity or sadness.
■ poignancy, sadness, tragedy.

patience /'peɪʃ(ə)ns/ *noun* 1 ability to endure delay, hardship, provocation, pain, etc. 2 perseverance. 3 solo card game.

■ **1** calmness, composure, endurance, equanimity, forbearance, fortitude, resignation, restraint, self-control, serenity, stoicism, tolerance, toleration, *colloquial* unflappability. **2** assiduity, determination, diligence, doggedness, endurance, firmness, perseverance, persistence, pertinacity, tenacity.

patient *adjective* having or showing patience. ● *noun* person under medical etc. treatment. □ **patiently** *adverb*.

■ *adjective* accommodating, acquiescent, assiduous, calm, compliant, composed, determined, diligent, docile, dogged, easygoing, even-tempered, forbearing, forgiving, long-suffering, mild, persevering, persistent, philosophical, quiet, resigned, self-possessed, serene, steady, stoical, submissive, tenacious, tolerant, uncomplaining, unhurried, untiring.

● *noun* case, invalid, sufferer.

patina /ˈpætɪnə/ *noun* (*plural* -s) **1** film, usually green, on surface of old bronze etc. **2** gloss produced by age on woodwork etc.

patio /ˈpætɪəʊ/ *noun* (*plural* -s) **1** paved usually roofless area adjoining house. **2** roofless inner courtyard.

patisserie /pəˈtiːsərɪ/ *noun* **1** shop where pastries are made and sold. **2** pastries collectively.

patois /ˈpætwɑː/ *noun* (*plural* same /-wɑːz/) regional dialect differing from literary language.

patriarch /ˈpeɪtrɪɑːk/ *noun* **1** male head of family or tribe. **2** chief bishop in Orthodox and RC Churches. **3** venerable old man. □ **patriarchal** /-ˈɑːk-/ *adjective*.

patriarchate /ˈpeɪtrɪɑːkət/ *noun* **1** office, see, or residence of patriarch. **2** rank of tribal patriarch.

patriarchy /ˈpeɪtrɪɑːkɪ/ *noun* (*plural* **-ies**) male-dominated social system, with descent reckoned through male line.

patrician /pəˈtrɪʃ(ə)n/ *noun* person of noble birth, esp. in ancient Rome. ● *adjective* of nobility; aristocratic.

patricide /ˈpætrɪsaɪd/ *noun* **1** killing of one's father. **2** person who commits patricide. □ **patricidal** /-ˈsaɪd(ə)l/ *adjective*.

patrimony /ˈpætrɪmənɪ/ *noun* (*plural* **-ies**) **1** property inherited from father or ancestors. **2** heritage.

patriot /ˈpeɪtrɪət/ *noun* person devoted to and ready to defend his or her country. □ **patriotic** /-ˈɒt-/ *adjective*. **patriotism** *noun*.

❙ chauvinist, jingo, jingoist, loyalist, nationalist.

patrol /pəˈtrəʊl/ *noun* **1** act of walking or travelling round area etc. to protect or supervise it. **2** person(s) or vehicle(s) sent out on patrol. **3** unit of usually 6 in Scout troop or Guide company. ● *verb* (**-ll-**) **1** carry out patrol of. **2** act as patrol. □ **patrol car** car used by police etc. for patrol.

■ *noun* **1** beat, guard, policing, sentry duty, surveillance, vigilance, watch. **2** guard, lookout, sentinel, sentry, watchman. ● *verb* **1** defend, guard, inspect, police, protect, tour, watch over. **2** keep a lookout, make the rounds, stand guard, walk the beat.

patron /ˈpeɪtrən/ *noun* (*feminine* **patroness**) **1** person who gives financial or other support. **2** customer of shop etc. □ **patron saint** saint regarded as protecting person, place, activity, etc.

■ **1** advocate, backer, benefactor, champion, defender, helper, philanthropist, promoter, sponsor, subscriber, supporter. **2** client, customer, frequenter, *colloquial* regular, shopper.

patronage /ˈpætrənɪdʒ/ *noun* **1** patron's or customer's support. **2** right of bestowing or recommending for appointments. **3** condescending manner.

■ **1** backing, business, custom, help, sponsorship, support, trade.

patronize /ˈpætrənaɪz/ *verb* (also **-ise**) (**-zing** or **-sing**) **1** treat condescendingly. **2** act as patron to. **3** be customer of. □ **patronizing** *adjective*.

■ **1** humiliate, look down on, *colloquial* put down, talk down to. **2** back, encourage, promote, sponsor, support. **3** bring trade to, buy from, deal with, frequent, shop at. □ **patronizing** see SUPERIOR *adjective* 3.

patronymic /pætrəˈnɪmɪk/ *noun* name derived from that of father or ancestor.

patten /ˈpæt(ə)n/ *noun historical* wooden sole mounted on iron ring for raising wearer's shoe above mud etc.

patter[1] /ˈpætə/ *noun* sound of quick light taps or steps. ● *verb* (of rain etc.) make this sound.

patter[2] /ˈpætə/ *noun* rapid often glib or deceptive talk. ● *verb* say or talk glibly.

pattern /ˈpæt(ə)n/ *noun* **1** decorative design on surface. **2** regular or logical form, order, etc. **3** model, design, or instructions from which thing is to be made. **4** excellent example. ● *verb* **1** decorate with pattern. **2** model (thing) on design etc.

■ *noun* **1** decoration, design, device, figure, motif, ornamentation. **2** arrangement, order, plan, regularity, sequence, shape, system. **3** archetype, example, exemplar, guide, model, original, precedent, prototype, sample, specimen. **4** criterion, ideal, model, paragon, standard, yardstick.

patty /ˈpætɪ/ *noun* (*plural* **-ies**) small pie or pasty.

paucity /ˈpɔːsɪtɪ/ *noun* smallness of number or quantity.

paunch /pɔːntʃ/ *noun* belly, stomach. □ **paunchy** *adjective*.

pauper /ˈpɔːpə/ *noun* very poor person. □ **pauperism** *noun*.

pause /pɔːz/ *noun* **1** temporary stop or silence. **2** *Music* mark denoting lengthening of note or rest. ● *verb* (**-sing**) make a pause; wait.

■ *noun* **1** break, *colloquial* breather, breathing space, caesura, check, delay, gap, halt, hesitation, hiatus, hold-up, interlude, intermission, interruption, interval, lacuna, lapse, *colloquial* let-up, lull, moratorium, respite, rest, standstill, stop, stoppage, suspension, wait. ● *verb* break off, delay, falter, halt, hang back, hesitate, mark time, rest, stop, take a break, *colloquial* take a breather, wait.

pavane /pə'vɑːn/ *noun* (also **pavan** /'pæv(ə)n/) **1** *historical* stately dance. **2** music for this.

pave *verb* (**-ving**) cover (street, floor, etc.) with durable surface. □ **pave the way** (usually + *for*) make preparations. □ **paving** *noun*.

■ asphalt, concrete, flag, macadamize, surface, tarmac, tile. □ **pave the way** see PREPARE 1.

pavement *noun* paved footway at side of road. □ **pavement artist** artist who draws in chalk on pavement for tips.

■ footpath, *US* sidewalk.

pavilion /pə'vɪljən/ *noun* **1** building on sports ground for spectators or players. **2** summer house etc. in park. **3** large tent. **4** building or stand at exhibition.

pavlova /pæv'ləʊvə/ *noun* meringue dessert with cream and fruit filling.

paw *noun* **1** foot of animal with claws. **2** *colloquial* person's hand. ● *verb* **1** touch with paw. **2** *colloquial* fondle awkwardly or indecently.

pawn[1] *noun* **1** chessman of smallest size and value. **2** person subservient to others' plans.

pawn[2] *verb* **1** deposit (thing) as security for money borrowed. **2** pledge. □ **in pawn** held as security. **pawnbroker** person who lends money at interest on security of personal property. **pawnshop** pawnbroker's place of business.

pawpaw /'pɔːpɔː/ *noun* (also **papaya** /pə'paɪə/) **1** pear-shaped mango-like fruit with pulpy orange flesh. **2** tropical tree bearing this.

pay *verb* (*past & past participle* **paid**) **1** discharge debt to. **2** give as due. **3** render, bestow (attention etc.). **4** make (visit, call, etc.). **5** yield adequate return. **6** let out (rope) by slackening it. **7** reward or punish. ● *noun* wages. □ **in the pay of** employed by. **pay-as-you-earn** collection of income tax by deduction at source from wages etc. **pay back 1** return (money). **2** take revenge on (person). **pay claim** demand for increase in pay. **pay day** day on which wages are paid. **pay for 1** hand over money for. **2** bear cost of. **3** suffer or be punished for. **paying guest** lodger. **payload** part of (esp. aircraft's) load from which revenue is derived. **paymaster** official who pays troops, workmen, etc. **Paymaster General** Treasury minister responsible for payments. **pay off 1** pay in full and discharge. **2** *colloquial* yield good results. **pay-off** *noun colloquial* **1** payment. **2** climax. **3** end result. **pay out** spend. **payphone** coin box telephone. **payroll** list of employees receiving regular pay. **pay up** pay full amount (of). □ **payee** /peɪ'iː/ *noun*.

■ *verb* **1** compensate, indemnify, pay back, pay off, recompense, reimburse, remunerate, repay, requite. **2** bear the cost of, *slang* cough up, foot, *slang* fork out, honour, meet, pay back, pay off, pay up, refund, reimburse, repay, settle, spend, *colloquial* stump up. **5** avail, benefit, be profitable, *colloquial* pay off, produce results, prove worthwhile, yield a return. ● *noun* earnings, emolument, fee, gain, honorarium, income, money, payment, profit, recompense, reimbursement,

remittance, remuneration, return, salary, settlement, stipend, take-home pay, wages. □ **pay back 1** see REPAY 1–3. **2** see RETALIATE. **pay for 3** atone for, be punished for, make amends for, make up for, suffer for.

payable *adjective* that must or may be paid.

PAYE *abbreviation* pay-as-you-earn.

payment *noun* **1** paying; amount paid. **2** recompense.

■ **1** advance, alimony, allowance, charge, commission, contribution, cost, deposit, disbursement, donation, expenditure, fare, fee, figure, fine, instalment, loan, outgoings, outlay, pocket money, premium, price, ransom, rate, remittance, remuneration, royalty, *colloquial* sub, subscription, supplement, surcharge, tip, toll, wage. **2** compensation, recompense, return, reward.

payola /peɪ'əʊlə/ *noun esp. US slang* bribe offered for unofficial media promotion of product etc.

PC *abbreviation* **1** Police Constable. **2** personal computer. **3** politically correct; political correctness. **4** Privy Councillor.

p.c. *abbreviation* **1** per cent. **2** postcard.

pd. *abbreviation* paid.

PE *abbreviation* physical education.

pea *noun* **1** climbing plant bearing round edible seeds in pods. **2** one of its seeds. **3** similar plant. □ **pea-souper** *colloquial* thick yellowish fog.

peace *noun* **1** quiet, calm. **2** freedom from or cessation of war. **3** treaty ending war. **4** civil order. **5** state of harmony. □ **peacemaker** person who brings about peace. **peacetime** time when country is not at war.

■ **1** calm, calmness, peacefulness, placidity, quiet, repose, serenity, silence, stillness, tranquillity. **2, 5** accord, agreement, amity, conciliation, concord, friendliness, harmony. **3** alliance, armistice, ceasefire, pact, treaty, truce. **4** see ORDER *noun* 5. □ **peacemaker** adjudicator, appeaser, arbitrator, conciliator, diplomat, intercessor, intermediary, mediator, reconciler, referee, umpire.

peaceable *adjective* disposed or tending to peace; peaceful.

■ amicable, civil, conciliatory, cooperative, friendly, gentle, harmonious, inoffensive, mild, non-violent, pacific, peaceful, peace-loving, placid, temperate, understanding.

peaceful *adjective* **1** characterized by peace; serene. **2** not infringing peace. □ **peacefully** *adverb*. **peacefulness** *noun*.

■ **1** balmy, calm, easy, gentle, pleasant, quiet, relaxing, restful, serene, slow-moving, soothing, still, tranquil, undisturbed, unruffled, untroubled. **2** see PEACEABLE.

peach[1] *noun* **1** roundish juicy fruit with downy yellow or rosy skin. **2** tree bearing it. **3** yellowish-pink colour. **4** *colloquial* person or thing of superlative merit. □ **peach Melba** dish of ice cream and peaches. □ **peachy** *adjective* (**-ier, -iest**).

peach[2] *verb colloquial* turn informer; inform.

peacock /'piːkɒk/ *noun* (*plural* same or **-s**) male peafowl; bird with brilliant plumage and erectile fanlike tail. □ **peacock blue** bright lustrous greenish blue of peacock's neck. **peacock butterfly** butterfly with eyelike markings resembling those on peacock's tail.

peafowl /'piːfaʊl/ *noun* **1** kind of pheasant. **2** peacock or peahen.

peahen /'piːhen/ *noun* female peafowl.

peak[1] *noun* **1** pointed top, esp. of mountain. **2** stiff projecting brim at front of cap. **3** highest point of achievement, intensity, etc. ● *verb* reach highest value, quality, etc.

■ *noun* **1** apex, brow, cap, crest, crown, eminence, hill, mountain, pinnacle, point, ridge, summit, tip, top. **3** acme, apex, apogee, climax, consummation, crown, culmination, height, pinnacle, zenith.

peak[2] *verb* **1** waste away. **2** (as **peaked** *adjective*) pinched-looking.

peaky *adjective* (**-ier, -iest**) sickly, puny.

peal *noun* **1** loud ringing of bell(s). **2** set of bells. **3** loud repeated sound, esp. of laughter, thunder, etc. ● *verb* **1** (cause to) sound in peal. **2** utter sonorously.

■ *noun* **1** carillon, chime, chiming, clangour, knell, ringing, tintinnabulation, toll. **3** clangour, clap, crash, reverberation, roar, thunder. ● *verb* **1** chime, clang, resonate, ring, sound, toll.

peanut *noun* **1** plant bearing underground pods containing seeds used as food and yielding oil. **2** its seed. **3** (in *plural*) *colloquial* trivial amount, esp. of money. □ **peanut butter** paste of ground roasted peanuts.

pear /peə/ *noun* **1** fleshy fruit tapering towards stalk. **2** tree bearing it.

pearl /pɜːl/ *noun* **1** rounded lustrous usually white solid formed in shell of certain oysters and prized as gem. **2** imitation of this. **3** precious thing; finest example. ● *verb* **1** *poetical* (of moisture) form drops; form drops on. **2** fish for pearls. □ **pearl barley** barley rubbed into small rounded grains. **pearl button** button of (real or imitation) mother-of-pearl.

pearly *adjective* (**-ier, -iest**) **1** resembling a pearl. **2** adorned with pearls. ● *noun* (*plural* **-ies**) **1** pearly king or queen. **2** (in *plural*) pearly king's or queen's clothes. □ **Pearly Gates** *colloquial* gates of Heaven. **pearly king**, **queen** London costermonger, or his wife, wearing clothes covered with pearl buttons.

peasant /'pez(ə)nt/ *noun* **1** (in some countries) worker on land; farm labourer; small farmer. **2** *derogatory* lout, boor. □ **peasantry** *noun* (*plural* **-ies**).

■ **1** rustic, *historical* serf, *archaic* swain. **2** boor, bumpkin, churl, lout, oaf, yokel.

pease-pudding /piːz/ *noun* dried peas boiled in cloth.

peat *noun* **1** vegetable matter decomposed by water and partly carbonized. **2** piece of this as fuel. □ **peatbog** bog composed of peat. □ **peaty** *adjective*.

pebble /'peb(ə)l/ *noun* small stone made smooth by action of water. □ **pebble-dash** mortar with pebbles in it as wall-coating. □ **pebbly** *adjective*.

■ (*pebbles*) cobbles, gravel, stones.

pecan /'piːkən/ *noun* **1** pinkish-brown smooth nut. **2** kind of hickory producing it.

peccadillo /pekə'dɪləʊ/ *noun* (*plural* **-es** or **-s**) trivial offence.

peck[1] *verb* **1** strike, pick up, pluck out, or make (hole) with beak. **2** kiss hastily or perfunctorily. **3** (+ *at*) *colloquial* eat (meal) listlessly or fastidiously. ● *noun* **1** stroke with beak. **2** hasty or perfunctory kiss. □ **pecking order** social hierarchy.

peck[2] *noun* measure of capacity for dry goods (2 gallons, 9.092 litres).

pecker *noun* □ **keep your pecker up** *colloquial* stay cheerful.

peckish *adjective colloquial* hungry.

pectin /'pektɪn/ *noun* soluble gelatinous substance in ripe fruits, causing jam etc. to set.

pectoral /'pektər(ə)l/ *adjective* of or for breast or chest. ● *noun* pectoral fin or muscle.

peculate /'pekjʊleɪt/ *verb* embezzle (money). □ **peculation** /-'leɪʃ(ə)n/ *noun*. **peculator** *noun*.

peculiar /pɪ'kjuːlɪə/ *adjective* **1** odd. **2** (usually + *to*) belonging exclusively; belonging to the individual. **3** particular; special.

■ **1** aberrant, abnormal, anomalous, atypical, bizarre, curious, deviant, eccentric, exceptional, freakish, funny, odd, offbeat, outlandish, out of the ordinary, quaint, queer, quirky, strange, surprising, uncommon, unconventional, unusual, *colloquial* weird. **2, 3** characteristic, different, distinctive, identifiable, idiosyncratic, individual, natural, particular, personal, private, singular, special, unique, unmistakable.

peculiarity /pɪkjuːlɪ'ærɪtɪ/ *noun* (*plural* **-ies**) **1** oddity. **2** characteristic. **3** being peculiar.

■ **1** aberration, abnormality, eccentricity, foible, idiosyncrasy, oddity, quirk. **2** characteristic, feature, idiosyncrasy, mannerism, property, quality, singularity, speciality, trait. **3** difference, distinctiveness, outlandishness, strangeness, uniqueness.

peculiarly *adverb* **1** more than usually; especially. **2** oddly.

pecuniary /pɪ'kjuːnɪərɪ/ *adjective* of or in money.

pedagogue /'pedəgɒg/ *noun* **1** *archaic* schoolmaster. **2** pedantic teacher. □ **pedagogical** /-'gɒdʒɪk(ə)l, -'gɒgɪk(ə)l/ *adjective*.

pedagogy /'pedəgɒdʒɪ/ *noun* science of teaching. □ **pedagogics** /-'gɒdʒɪks, -'gɒgɪks/ *adjective*.

pedal /'ped(ə)l/ *noun* lever or key operated by foot, esp. in bicycle, motor vehicle, or some musical instruments. ● *verb* (**-ll-**; *US* **-l-**) **1** work pedals (of). **2** ride bicycle. ● *adjective* /'pi:d(ə)l/ of foot or feet.

pedant /'ped(ə)nt/ *noun derogatory* person who insists on strict adherence to literal meaning or formal rules. □ **pedantic** /prˈdæntɪk/ *adjective*. **pedantry** *noun*.

■ □ **pedantic** academic, bookish, doctrinaire, donnish, dry, exact, fastidious, formal, fussy, hair-splitting, inflexible, learned, *colloquial* nit-picking, pompous, precise, punctilious, scholarly, schoolmasterly, stiff, stilted, strict, stuffy, unimaginative.

peddle /'ped(ə)l/ *verb* (**-ling**) **1** sell as pedlar; engage in selling, esp. as pedlar. **2** advocate. **3** sell (drugs) illegally.

■ *slang* flog, hawk, market, *colloquial* push, sell, traffic in, vend.

peddler *noun* **1** person who sells drugs illegally. **2** *US* = PEDLAR.

pedestal /'pedɪst(ə)l/ *noun* **1** base of column. **2** block on which something stands. □ **put (or set) on a pedestal** idolize.

pedestrian /prˈdestrɪən/ *noun* walker, esp. in town. ● *adjective* **1** of or for pedestrians. **2** prosaic, dull. □ **pedestrian crossing** part of road where pedestrians have right of way to cross. □ **pedestrianize** *verb* (also **-ise**) (**-zing** or **-sing**).

■ *noun* footslogger, walker. ● *adjective* **1** pedestrianized, traffic-free. **2** banal, boring, dreary, dull, commonplace, lifeless, mundane, ordinary, prosaic, run-of-the-mill, tedious, unimaginative, uninteresting.

pedicure /'pedɪkjʊə/ *noun* care or treatment of feet, esp. of toenails.

pedigree /'pedɪgri:/ *noun* **1** recorded (esp. distinguished) line of descent of person or animal. **2** genealogical table. **3** *colloquial* thing's history. ● *adjective* (of animal) having recorded line of descent showing pure breeding.

■ *noun* **1** ancestry, blood, descent, extraction, family, family history, genealogy, line, lineage, parentage, roots, stock, strain. ● *adjective* pure-bred, thoroughbred.

pediment /'pedɪmənt/ *noun* triangular part crowning front of building, esp. over portico.

pedlar /'pedlə/ *noun* (*US* **peddler**) travelling seller of small wares.

■ door-to-door salesman, hawker, *colloquial* pusher, seller, trafficker, vendor.

pedometer /prˈdɒmɪtə/ *noun* instrument for estimating distance travelled on foot.

pedophile *US* = PAEDOPHILE.

peduncle /prˈdʌŋk(ə)l/ *noun* stalk of flower, fruit, or cluster, esp. main stalk bearing solitary flower.

pee *colloquial verb* (**pees, peed**) urinate. ● *noun* **1** urination. **2** urine.

peek *noun & verb* peep, glance.

peel *verb* **1** strip rind etc. from. **2** (usually + *off*) take off (skin etc.). **3** become bare of bark, skin,

etc. **4** (often + *off*) flake off. **5** (often + *off*) *colloquial* undress, strip. ● *noun* rind or outer coating of fruit, potato, etc.

■ *verb* **1, 2** denude, flay, hull, pare, skin, strip. **5** see UNDRESS *verb* **1**. ● *noun* coating, rind, skin.

peeling *noun* (usually in *plural*) piece peeled off.

peep[1] *verb* **1** look furtively or through narrow aperture. **2** come cautiously or partly into view; emerge. ● *noun* **1** furtive or peering glance. **2** (usually + *of*) first appearance. □ **peephole** small hole to peep through. **Peeping Tom** furtive voyeur. **peep-show** exhibition of pictures etc. viewed through lens or peephole.

■ *verb* **1** glance, have a look, look, peek, squint. **2** see SHOW *verb* **1**, EMERGE.

peep[2] *verb* cheep, squeak. ● *noun* **1** cheep, squeak. **2** slight sound, utterance, or complaint.

peer[1] *verb* look closely or with difficulty.

■ gaze, have a look, look, spy, squint.

peer[2] *noun* **1** (*feminine* **peeress**) duke, marquis, earl, viscount, or baron. **2** equal (esp. in civil standing or rank). □ **peer group** person's associates of same status.

■ **1** aristocrat, baron, baroness, count, countess, duchess, duke, earl, grandee, lady, lord, marchioness, marquis, noble, nobleman, noblewoman, patrician, viscount, viscountess; (*peers*) aristocracy, nobility, peerage. **2** colleague, compeer, equal, fellow.

peerage *noun* **1** peers as a class. **2** rank of peer or peeress.

peerless *adjective* unequalled.

peeve *colloquial verb* (**-ving**) (usually as **peeved** *adjective*) irritate. ● *noun* cause or state of annoyance.

peevish *adjective* querulous, irritable. □ **peevishly** *adverb*. **peevishness** *noun*.

■ bad-tempered, cantankerous, churlish, crabby, crusty, curmudgeonly, grumpy, ill-humoured, irritable, petulant, querulous, testy, touchy, waspish.

peewit /'pi:wɪt/ *noun* lapwing.

peg *noun* **1** wooden, metal, etc. bolt or pin for holding things together, hanging things on, etc. **2** each of pins used to tighten or loosen strings of violin etc. **3** forked wooden peg etc. for hanging washing on line. **4** drink, esp. of spirits. ● *verb* (**-gg-**) **1** (usually + *down, in,* etc.) fix, mark, or hang out (as) with peg(s). **2** keep (prices etc.) stable. □ **off the peg** (of clothes) ready-made. **peg away** (often + *at*) work persistently. **pegboard** board with holes for pegs. **peg out 1** *slang* die. **2** mark out boundaries of.

■ *noun* **1** bolt, dowel, pin, rod, stick, thole-pin. ● *verb* **1** see FASTEN **1**.

pejorative /prˈdʒɒrətɪv/ *adjective* derogatory. ● *noun* derogatory word.

peke *noun colloquial* Pekingese.

Pekingese /pi:kɪˈni:z/ *noun* (also **Pekinese**)

(*plural* same) dog of small short-legged snub-nosed breed with long silky hair.

pelargonium /pelə'gəʊnɪəm/ *noun* plant with showy flowers; geranium.

pelf *noun* money, wealth.

pelican /'pelɪkən/ *noun* large waterfowl with pouch below bill for storing fish. □ **pelican crossing** road crossing-place with traffic lights operated by pedestrians.

pellagra /pə'lægrə/ *noun* deficiency disease with cracking of skin.

pellet /'pelɪt/ *noun* **1** small compressed ball of a substance. **2** pill. **3** small shot.

pellicle /'pelɪk(ə)l/ *noun* thin skin, membrane, film.

pell-mell /pel'mel/ *adverb* **1** headlong. **2** in disorder.

pellucid /pɪ'luːsɪd/ *adjective* transparent, clear.

pelmet /'pelmɪt/ *noun* hanging border concealing curtain-rods etc.

pelt[1] *verb* **1** assail with missiles, abuse, etc. **2** (of rain) come down hard. **3** run at full speed. ● *noun* pelting.

■ *verb* **1** assail, bombard, shower, strafe, throw.

pelt[2] *noun* skin of animal, esp. with hair or fur still on it.

■ coat, fur, hide, skin.

pelvis /'pelvɪs/ *noun* lower abdominal cavity in most vertebrates, formed by haunch bones etc. □ **pelvic** *adjective*.

pen[1] *noun* implement for writing with ink. ● *verb* (**-nn-**) write. □ **penfriend** friend with whom one communicates by letter only. **pen-knife** small folding knife. **pen-name** literary pseudonym. **pen pal** *colloquial* penfriend. **pen-pusher** *colloquial derogatory* clerical worker.

■ *noun* ballpoint, *proprietary term* Biro, felt-tip pen, fountain pen, quill.

pen[2] *noun* small enclosure for cows, sheep, poultry, etc. ● *verb* (**-nn-**) enclose; put or keep in confined space.

■ *noun* coop, *US* corral, enclosure, fold, hutch, pound.

pen[3] *noun* female swan.

penal /'piːn(ə)l/ *adjective* **1** of or involving punishment. **2** punishable.

penalize /'piːnəlaɪz/ *verb* (also **-ise**) (**-zing** or **-sing**) **1** subject to penalty or disadvantage. **2** make punishable.

■ **1** discipline, fine, impose a penalty on, punish.

penalty /'penltɪ/ *noun* (*plural* **-ies**) **1** fine or other punishment. **2** disadvantage, loss, etc., esp. as result of one's own actions. **3** disadvantage imposed in sports for breach of rules etc. □ **penalty area** *Football* area in front of goal within which breach of rules involves award of penalty kick for opposing team. **penalty kick** free kick at goal from close range.

■ *noun* **1** fine, forfeit, punishment. **2** disadvantage, price.

penance /'penəns/ *noun* act of self-punishment, esp. one imposed by priest, performed as expression of penitence. □ **do penance** perform penance.

■ amends, atonement, contrition, penitence, punishment, reparation. □ **do penance** see ATONE.

pence *plural* of PENNY.

penchant /'pɑ̃ʃɑ̃/ *noun* (+ *for*) inclination or liking for.

pencil /'pens(ə)l/ *noun* **1** instrument for drawing or writing, esp. of graphite enclosed in wooden cylinder or metal case with tapering end. **2** something used or shaped like this. ● *verb* (**-ll-**; *US* **-l-**) write, draw, or mark with pencil.

pendant /'pend(ə)nt/ *noun* ornament hung from necklace etc.

pendent /'pend(ə)nt/ *adjective formal* **1** hanging; overhanging. **2** pending.

■ **1** dangling, hanging, loose, pendulous, suspended, swaying, swinging, trailing.

pending /'pendɪŋ/ *adjective* awaiting decision or settlement. ● *preposition* **1** until. **2** during.

■ *adjective* about to happen, forthcoming, imminent, impending, in the offing, undecided.

pendulous /'pendjʊləs/ *adjective* hanging down; swinging.

pendulum /'pendjʊləm/ *noun* (*plural* **-s**) body suspended so as to be free to swing, esp. regulating movement of clock's works.

penetrate /'penɪtreɪt/ *verb* (**-ting**) **1** make way into or through; pierce. **2** permeate. **3** see into or through. **4** be absorbed by the mind. **5** (as **penetrating** *adjective*) having or suggesting insight. **6** (as **penetrating** *adjective*) (of voice) easily heard above other sounds; piercing. □ **penetrable** /-trəb(ə)l/ *adjective*. **penetration** *noun*.

■ **1** bore through, break through, drill into, enter, get into, get through, infiltrate, lance, perforate, pierce, probe, puncture, stab, stick in. **2** filter through, impregnate, percolate through, permeate, pervade, seep into, suffuse.

penguin /'peŋgwɪn/ *noun* flightless seabird of southern hemisphere.

penicillin /penɪ'sɪlɪn/ *noun* antibiotic obtained from mould.

peninsula /pɪ'nɪnsjʊlə/ *noun* piece of land almost surrounded by water or projecting far into sea etc. □ **peninsular** *adjective*.

penis /'piːnɪs/ *noun* sexual and (in mammals) urinary organ of male animal.

penitent /'penɪt(ə)nt/ *adjective* repentant. ● *noun* **1** penitent person. **2** person doing penance. □ **penitence** *noun*. **penitently** *adverb*.

■ *adjective* apologetic, conscience-stricken, contrite, regretful, remorseful, repentant, rueful, shamefaced, sorry.

penitential /penɪ'tenʃ(ə)l/ *adjective* of penitence or penance.

penitentiary /penɪ'tenʃərɪ/ *noun* (*plural* **-ies**) *US* prison. ● *adjective* of penance or reformatory treatment.

penman *noun* **1** person who writes by hand with specified skill. **2** author. □ **penmanship** *noun*.

pennant /'penənt/ *noun* tapering flag, esp. that at masthead of ship in commission.

penniless /'penɪlɪs/ *adjective* destitute.

pennon /'penən/ *noun* **1** long narrow triangular or swallow-tailed flag. **2** long pointed streamer on ship.

> ■ banner, flag, pennant, standard, streamer.

penny /'penɪ/ *noun* (*plural* **pence** or, for separate coins only, **pennies**) British coin worth 1/100 of pound, or formerly 1/240 of pound. □ **penny-farthing** early kind of bicycle with large front wheel and small rear one. **penny-pinching** *noun* meanness. ● *adjective* mean. **a pretty penny** a large sum of money.

pennyroyal /penɪ'rɔɪəl/ *noun* creeping kind of mint.

penology /piː'nɒlədʒɪ/ *noun* study of punishment and prison management.

pension[1] /'penʃ(ə)n/ *noun* periodic payment made by government, ex-employer, private fund, etc. to person above specified age or to retired, widowed, disabled, etc. person. ● *verb* grant pension to. □ **pension off** dismiss with pension.

> ■ *noun* annuity, benefit, superannuation.

pension[2] /pɑ̃'sjɔ̃/ *noun* European, esp. French, boarding house. [French]

pensionable *adjective* entitled or entitling person to pension.

pensioner *noun* recipient of (esp. retirement) pension.

pensive /'pensɪv/ *adjective* deep in thought. □ **pensively** *adverb*. **pensiveness** *noun*.

> ■ brooding, cogitating, contemplative, daydreaming, far-away, lost in thought, meditative, reflective, ruminative, thoughtful.

pent *adjective* (often + *in*, *up*) closely confined; shut in.

penta- *combining form* five.

pentacle /'pentək(ə)l/ *noun* figure used as symbol, esp. in magic, e.g. pentagram.

pentagon /'pentəgən/ *noun* **1** plane figure with 5 sides and angles. **2** (**the Pentagon**) (pentagonal headquarters of) leaders of US defence forces. □ **pentagonal** /-'tæg-/ *adjective*.

pentagram /'pentəgræm/ *noun* 5-pointed star.

pentameter /pen'tæmɪtə/ *noun* line of verse with 5 metrical feet.

Pentateuch /'pentətjuːk/ *noun* first 5 books of Old Testament.

pentathlon /pen'tæθlən/ *noun* athletic contest of 5 events. □ **pentathlete** *noun*.

Pentecost /'pentɪkɒst/ *noun* **1** Whit Sunday. **2** Jewish harvest festival 50 days after second day of Passover.

pentecostal /pentɪ'kɒst(ə)l/ *adjective* (of religious group) emphasizing divine gifts, esp. healing, and often fundamentalist.

penthouse /'penthaʊs/ *noun* flat on roof or top floor of tall building.

penultimate /pɪ'nʌltɪmət/ *adjective & noun* last but one.

penumbra /pɪ'nʌmbrə/ *noun* (*plural* **-s** or **-brae** /-briː/) **1** partly shaded region round shadow of opaque body. **2** partial shadow. □ **penumbral** *adjective*.

penurious /pɪ'njʊərɪəs/ *adjective* **1** poor. **2** stingy.

penury /'penjʊrɪ/ *noun* (*plural* **-ies**) destitution, poverty.

> ■ beggary, destitution, impoverishment, indigence, need, poverty, want.

peon /'piːən/ *noun* Spanish-American day-labourer.

peony /'piːənɪ/ *noun* (also **paeony**) (*plural* **-ies**) plant with large globular red, pink, or white flowers.

people /'piːp(ə)l/ *plural noun* **1** persons in general. **2** (*singular*) race or nation. **3** (**the people**) ordinary people, esp. as electorate. **4** parents or other relatives. **5** subjects. ● *verb* (**-ling**) **1** (usually + *with*) fill with people; populate. **2** (esp. as **peopled** *adjective*) inhabit.

> ■ *noun* **1** folk, human beings, humanity, humans, individuals, ladies and gentlemen, mankind, men and women, mortals, persons. **2** nation, race, tribe. **3** (**the people**) citizenry, citizens, community, electorate, grass roots, *hoi polloi*, the masses, nation, *colloquial* the plebs, populace, population, the public, society, subjects. **4** clan, family, folk, kinsmen, kith and kin, parents, relations, relatives, *usually derogatory* tribe. ● *verb* colonize, fill, inhabit, occupy, populate, settle.

PEP /pep/ *abbreviation* Personal Equity Plan.

pep *colloquial noun* vigour, spirit. ● *verb* (**-pp-**) (usually + *up*) fill with vigour. □ **pep pill** one containing stimulant drug. **pep talk** exhortation to greater effort or courage.

pepper /'pepə/ *noun* **1** hot aromatic condiment from dried berries of some plants. **2** capsicum plant. **3** its fruit. ● *verb* **1** sprinkle or flavour with pepper. **2** pelt with missiles. □ **pepper-and-salt** of closely mingled dark and light colour. **peppercorn 1** dried pepper berry. **2** (in full **peppercorn rent**) nominal rent. **pepper-mill** mill for grinding peppercorns by hand.

peppermint *noun* **1** species of mint grown for its strong-flavoured oil. **2** sweet flavoured with this oil. **3** the oil.

pepperoni /pepə'rəʊnɪ/ *noun* sausage seasoned with pepper.

peppery *adjective* **1** of, like, or abounding in pepper. **2** hot-tempered.

pepsin /'pepsɪn/ *noun* enzyme contained in gastric juice.

peptic /'peptik/ *adjective* digestive. ◻ **peptic ulcer** one in stomach or duodenum.

per *preposition* **1** for each. **2** by, by means of, through.

peradventure /pərəd'ventʃə/ *adverb archaic* perhaps.

perambulate /pə'ræmbjʊleɪt/ *verb* (**-ting**) walk through, over, or about. ◻ **perambulation** *noun*.

perambulator *noun formal* pram.

per annum /pər 'ænəm/ *adverb* for each year.

per capita /pə 'kæpɪtə/ *adverb & adjective* for each person.

perceive /pə'siːv/ *verb* (**-ving**) **1** become aware of by one of senses. **2** apprehend; understand. ◻ **perceivable** *adjective*.

■ **1** become aware of, catch sight of, descry, detect, discern, discover, distinguish, espy, glimpse, hear, identify, make out, note, notice, observe, recognize, see, *colloquial* spot. **2** appreciate, apprehend, comprehend, deduce, feel, figure out, gather, grasp, infer, know, realize, sense, understand.

per cent /pə 'sent/ (*US* **percent**) *adverb* in every hundred. ● *noun* **1** percentage. **2** one part in every hundred.

percentage *noun* **1** rate or proportion per cent. **2** proportion.

percentile /pə'sentaɪl/ *noun* **1** each of 99 points at which a range of data is divided to make 100 groups of equal size. **2** each of these groups.

perceptible /pə'septɪb(ə)l/ *adjective* that can be perceived. ◻ **perceptibility** *noun*. **perceptibly** *adverb*.

■ appreciable, audible, detectable, discernible, distinct, distinguishable, evident, identifiable, manifest, marked, notable, noticeable, observable, obvious, palpable, perceivable, plain, recognizable, unmistakable, visible.

perception /pə'sepʃ(ə)n/ *noun* act or faculty of perceiving. ◻ **perceptual** /-'septʃʊəl/ *adjective*.

■ appreciation, apprehension, awareness, cognition, comprehension, consciousness, discernment, insight, instinct, intuition, knowledge, observation, realization, recognition, sensation, sense, understanding, view.

perceptive /pə'septɪv/ *adjective* **1** sensitive; discerning. **2** capable of perceiving. ◻ **perceptively** *adverb*. **perceptiveness** *noun*.

■ acute, alert, astute, attentive, aware, clear, clever, discerning, discriminating, intelligent, observant, penetrating, percipient, perspicacious, quick, responsive, sensitive, sharp, sharp-eyed, shrewd, sympathetic, understanding.

perch[1] *noun* **1** bird's resting place above ground. **2** high place for person or thing to rest on. **3** *historical* measure of length (5½ yds). ● *verb* rest or place on perch.

■ *noun* **1** rest, resting place, roost. ● *verb* balance, rest, roost, settle, sit.

perch[2] *noun* (*plural* same or **-es**) edible spiny-finned freshwater fish.

perchance /pə'tʃɑːns/ *adverb archaic* maybe.

percipient /pə'sɪpɪənt/ *adjective* perceiving; conscious. ◻ **percipience** *noun*. **percipiently** *adverb*.

percolate /'pɜːkəleɪt/ *verb* (**-ting**) **1** (often + *through*) filter gradually. **2** (of idea etc.) permeate gradually. **3** prepare (coffee) in percolator. ◻ **percolation** *noun*.

percolator *noun* apparatus for making coffee by circulating boiling water through ground beans.

percussion /pə'kʌʃ(ə)n/ *noun* **1** playing of music by striking instruments with sticks etc. **2** such instruments collectively. **3** gentle tapping of body in medical diagnosis. **4** forcible striking of body against another. ◻ **percussionist** *noun*. **percussive** *adjective*.

perdition /pə'dɪʃ(ə)n/ *noun* damnation.

■ damnation, doom, downfall, hell, ruin, ruination.

peregrine /'perɪgrɪn/ *noun* (in full **peregrine falcon**) kind of falcon.

peremptory /pə'remptərɪ/ *adjective* **1** admitting no denial or refusal. **2** imperious. ◻ **peremptorily** *adverb*.

perennial /pə'renɪəl/ *adjective* **1** lasting through the year. **2** (of plant) living several years. **3** lasting long or for ever. ● *noun* perennial plant. ◻ **perennially** *adverb*.

perestroika /pere'strɔɪkə/ *noun* (in former USSR) reform of economic and political system.

perfect *adjective* /'pɜːfɪkt/ **1** complete; not deficient. **2** faultless. **3** very enjoyable. **4** exact; precise. **5** entire; unqualified. **6** *Grammar* (of tense) expressing completed action. ● *verb* /pə'fekt/ **1** make perfect. **2** complete. ● *noun* /'pɜːfɪkt/ perfect tense. ◻ **perfect pitch** *Music* ability to recognize pitch of note.

■ *adjective* **1** absolute, complete, completed, consummate, finished, whole. **2** blameless, excellent, exemplary, faultless, flawless, ideal, immaculate, incomparable, in mint condition, irreproachable, matchless, pure, sinless, spotless, superlative, unbeatable, undamaged, unexceptionable, unimpeachable. **4** accurate, authentic, correct, exact, faithful, immaculate, impeccable, precise, tailor-made, true. **5** absolute, complete, entire, thorough, unqualified, utter.
● *verb* **1** see REFINE 2. **2** bring to fruition, carry through, complete, consummate, effect, execute, finish, fulfil, realize, see through.

perfection /pə'fekʃ(ə)n/ *noun* **1** being or making perfect. **2** perfect state. **3** perfect person, specimen, etc.

■ **1** accomplishment, achievement, completion, consummation, end, fruition, fulfilment, realization. **2** beauty, completeness, excellence, faultlessness, flawlessness, ideal, precision, purity, wholeness.

perfectionism *noun* uncompromising pursuit of perfection. ◻ **perfectionist** *noun*.

perfectly *adverb* **1** quite, completely. **2** in a perfect way.

perfidy /'pɜːfɪdɪ/ *noun* breach of faith; treachery. □ **perfidious** /-'fɪd-/ *adjective*.

perforate /'pɜːfəreɪt/ *verb* (**-ting**) **1** pierce; make hole(s) through. **2** make row of small holes in (paper etc.). □ **perforation** *noun*,
■ **1** bore through, drill, penetrate, pierce, prick, punch, puncture, riddle.

perforce /pə'fɔːs/ *adverb archaic* unavoidably, necessarily.

perform /pə'fɔːm/ *verb* **1** carry into effect. **2** go through, execute. **3** function. **4** act, sing, etc., esp. in public. **5** (of animals) do tricks etc. □ **performing arts** drama, music, dance, etc. □ **performable** *adjective*. **performer** *noun*.
■ **1, 2** accomplish, achieve, bring about, carry on, carry out, commit, complete, discharge, dispatch, do, effect, execute, finish, fulfil, pull off. **3** behave, function, go, operate, run, work. **4** act, appear, dance, enact, feature, mount, play, present, produce, put on, render, represent, sing, stage, take part. □ **performer** actor, actress, artist, artiste, entertainer, player, singer, star, superstar, Thespian, trouper.

performance *noun* **1** act, process, or manner of doing or functioning. **2** execution (of duty etc.). **3** performing of or in play etc. **4** *colloquial* fuss; emotional scene.
■ **1** accomplishment, achievement, act, behaviour, conduct, exploit, feat, functioning, running. **2** carrying out, completion, discharge, doing, execution, fulfilment. **3** act, acting, concert, impersonation, interpretation, play, play-acting, playing, portrayal, presentation, production, rendition, representation, show, turn. **4** act, *colloquial* carry-on, exhibition, fuss, scene.

perfume /'pɜːfjuːm/ *noun* **1** sweet smell. **2** fragrant liquid, esp. for application to the body, scent. ● *verb* (**-ming**) impart perfume to.
■ *noun* **1** aroma, bouquet, fragrance, odour, scent, smell. **2** aftershave, scent, toilet water.

perfumer /pə'fjuːmə/ *noun* maker or seller of perfumes. □ **perfumery** *noun* (*plural* **-ies**).

perfunctory /pə'fʌŋktərɪ/ *adjective* **1** done merely out of duty. **2** superficial. □ **perfunctorily** *adverb*. **perfunctoriness** *noun*.
■ apathetic, automatic, brief, cursory, dutiful, fleeting, half-hearted, hurried, inattentive, indifferent, mechanical, offhand, routine, superficial, uncaring, unenthusiastic, uninterested, uninvolved, unthinking.

pergola /'pɜːgələ/ *noun* arbour or covered walk arched with climbing plants.

perhaps /pə'hæps/ *adverb* it may be; possibly.
■ conceivably, maybe, *archaic* peradventure, *archaic* perchance, possibly.

perianth /'perɪænθ/ *noun* outer part of flower.

perigee /'perɪdʒiː/ *noun* point nearest to earth in orbit of moon etc.

perihelion /perɪ'hiːlɪən/ *noun* (*plural* **-lia**) point nearest to sun in orbit of planet, comet, etc. round it.

peril /'perɪl/ *noun* serious and immediate danger. □ **perilous** *adjective*. **perilously** *adverb*.
■ danger, hazard, insecurity, jeopardy, risk, susceptibility, threat, vulnerability. □ **perilous** dangerous, hazardous, insecure, risky, uncertain, unsafe, vulnerable.

perimeter /pə'rɪmɪtə/ *noun* **1** circumference or outline of closed figure. **2** length of this. **3** outer boundary.
■ **1** circumference, edge, outline. **3** border, borderline, boundary, bounds, circumference, confines, edge, fringe, frontier, limit, margin, periphery, verge.

period /'pɪərɪəd/ *noun* **1** amount of time during which something runs its course. **2** distinct portion of history, life, etc. **3** occurrence of menstruation. **4** time of this. **5** complete sentence. **6** *esp. US* full stop. ● *adjective* characteristic of past period.
■ *noun* **1** duration, interval, phase, season, session, span, spell, stage, stint, stretch, term, time, while. **2** aeon, age, epoch, era, time.

periodic /pɪərɪ'ɒdɪk/ *adjective* appearing or recurring at intervals. □ **periodic table** arrangement of chemical elements by atomic number and chemical properties. □ **periodicity** /-rɪə'dɪsɪtɪ/ *noun*.
■ cyclical, intermittent, occasional, recurrent, repeated, spasmodic, sporadic.

periodical *noun* magazine etc. published at regular intervals. ● *adjective* periodic. □ **periodically** *adverb*.

peripatetic /perɪpə'tetɪk/ *adjective* **1** (of teacher) working in more than one establishment. **2** going from place to place. **3** itinerant.

peripheral /pə'rɪfər(ə)l/ *adjective* **1** of minor importance. **2** of periphery. ● *noun* input, output, or storage device connected to computer.
■ *adjective* **1** borderline, incidental, inessential, irrelevant, marginal, minor, non-essential, secondary, tangential, unimportant, unnecessary. **2** distant, outer, outermost, outlying.

periphery /pə'rɪfərɪ/ *noun* (*plural* **-ies**) **1** bounding line, esp. of round surface. **2** outer or surrounding area.

periphrasis /pə'rɪfrəsɪs/ *noun* (*plural* **-phrases** /-siːz/) circumlocution; roundabout speech or phrase. □ **periphrastic** /perɪ'fræstɪk/ *adjective*.

periscope /'perɪskəʊp/ *noun* apparatus with tube and mirrors or prisms for viewing objects otherwise out of sight.

perish /'perɪʃ/ *verb* **1** suffer destruction; die. **2** lose natural qualities. **3** (cause to) rot or deteriorate. **4** (in *passive*) suffer from cold.

■ **1** be destroyed, be killed, die, expire, fall, lose one's life, meet one's death, pass away. **2, 3** crumble away, decay, decompose, disintegrate, go bad, rot.

perishable *adjective* subject to speedy decay; liable to perish. ● *noun* perishable thing (esp. food).

■ *adjective* biodegradable, destructible.

perisher *noun slang* annoying person.

perishing *colloquial adjective* **1** confounded. **2** intensely cold. ● *adverb* confoundedly.

peritoneum /ˌperɪtə'niːəm/ *noun* (*plural* **-s** or **-nea**) membrane lining abdominal cavity. □ **peritoneal** *adjective*.

peritonitis /ˌperɪtə'naɪtɪs/ *noun* inflammation of peritoneum.

periwig /'perɪwɪg/ *noun historical* wig.

periwinkle[1] /'perɪwɪŋk(ə)l/ *noun* evergreen trailing plant with blue or white flower.

periwinkle[2] /'perɪwɪŋk(ə)l/ *noun* winkle.

perjure /'pɜːdʒə/ *verb* (**-ring**) **1** (**perjure oneself**) commit perjury. **2** (as **perjured** *adjective*) guilty of perjury. □ **perjurer** *noun*.

perjury /'pɜːdʒərɪ/ *noun* (*plural* **-ies**) wilful lying while on oath.

■ lying, mendacity.

perk[1] *verb* □ **perk up 1** (cause to) recover courage. **2** smarten up. **3** raise (head etc.) briskly.

perk[2] *noun colloquial* perquisite.

perky *adjective* (**-ier, -iest**) lively and cheerful.

perm[1] *noun* permanent wave. ● *verb* give permanent wave to.

perm[2] *colloquial noun* permutation. ● *verb* make permutation of.

permafrost /'pɜːməfrɒst/ *noun* permanently frozen subsoil, as in polar regions.

permanent /'pɜːmənənt/ *adjective* lasting or intended to last indefinitely. □ **permanent wave** long-lasting artificial wave in hair. □ **permanence** *noun*. **permanently** *adverb*.

■ abiding, ceaseless, changeless, chronic, constant, continual, continuous, durable, endless, enduring, eternal, everlasting, fixed, immutable, incessant, incurable, indelible, indestructible, indissoluble, ineradicable, interminable, invariable, irreparable, irreversible, lasting, lifelong, long-lasting, long-lived, never-ending, non-stop, ongoing, perennial, perpetual, persistent, stable, steady, unalterable, unceasing, unchanging, undying, unending.

permeable /'pɜːmɪəb(ə)l/ *adjective* capable of being permeated. □ **permeability** *noun*.

permeate /'pɜːmɪeɪt/ *verb* (**-ting**) **1** penetrate; saturate; pervade. **2** be diffused. □ **permeation** *noun*.

■ diffuse through, filter through, flow through, impregnate, infiltrate, penetrate, percolate through, pervade, saturate, soak through, spread through.

permissible /pə'mɪsɪb(ə)l/ *adjective* allowable. □ **permissibility** *noun*.

■ acceptable, admissible, allowable, allowed, excusable, lawful, legal, legitimate, *formal* licit, permitted, proper, right, sanctioned, tolerable, valid, venial (*sin*).

permission /pə'mɪʃ(ə)n/ *noun* consent; authorization.

■ acquiescence, agreement, approbation, approval, assent, authority, authorization, consent, dispensation, franchise, go-ahead, green light, leave, licence, rubber stamp, sanction, seal of approval, support.

permissive /pə'mɪsɪv/ *adjective* **1** tolerant, liberal. **2** giving permission. □ **permissiveness** *noun*.

■ **1** easygoing, indulgent, lenient, liberal, tolerant. **2** acquiescent, consenting.

permit *verb* /pə'mɪt/ (**-tt-**) **1** give consent to; authorize. **2** allow; give opportunity. **3** (+ *of*) allow as possible. ● *noun* /'pɜːmɪt/ written order giving permission or allowing entry.

■ *verb* **1, 2** agree to, allow, approve of, authorize, consent to, endorse, enfranchise, give an opportunity for, give permission for, give one's blessing to, legalize, license, sanction, support, tolerate. **3** (*permit of*) admit of, allow, support. ● *noun* authority, authorization, certification, charter, licence, order, pass, passport, ticket, visa, warrant.

permutation /ˌpɜːmjʊ'teɪʃ(ə)n/ *noun* **1** one of possible ordered arrangements of set of things. **2** combination or selection of specified number of items from larger group.

pernicious /pə'nɪʃəs/ *adjective* destructive, injurious. □ **pernicious anaemia** defective formation of red blood cells through lack of vitamin B.

pernickety /pə'nɪkɪtɪ/ *adjective colloquial* fastidious, over-precise.

peroration /ˌperə'reɪʃ(ə)n/ *noun* concluding part of speech.

peroxide /pə'rɒksaɪd/ *noun* **1** (in full **hydrogen peroxide**) colourless liquid used in water solution, esp. to bleach hair. **2** oxide containing maximum proportion of oxygen. ● *verb* (**-ding**) bleach (hair) with peroxide.

perpendicular /ˌpɜːpən'dɪkjʊlə/ *adjective* **1** (usually + *to*) at right angles. **2** upright. **3** very steep. **4** (**Perpendicular**) of or in style of English Gothic architecture of 15th & 16th c. ● *noun* perpendicular line etc. □ **perpendicularity** /-'lærɪtɪ/ *noun*. **perpendicularly** *adverb*.

■ *adjective* **2** erect, plumb, straight up and down, upright, vertical.

perpetrate /'pɜːpɪtreɪt/ *verb* (**-ting**) commit. □ **perpetration** *noun*. **perpetrator** *noun*.

perpetual /pə'petʃʊəl/ *adjective* **1** lasting for ever or indefinitely. **2** continuous. **3** *colloquial* frequent. □ **perpetually** *adverb*.

■ **1** abiding, ageless, chronic, endless, enduring, eternal, everlasting, immortal, immutable, incurable, indestructible, ineradicable, interminable, invariable, lasting, long-lasting, never-ending, perennial, permanent, protracted, timeless, unchanging, undying, unending, unfailing. **2** ceaseless, constant, continuous, endless, incessant, never-ending, non-stop, ongoing, persistent, unceasing, unending, uninterrupted, unremitting. **3** continual, frequent, persistent, recurrent, recurring, repeated.

perpetuate /pə'petʃʊeɪt/ *verb* (**-ting**) **1** make perpetual. **2** cause to be always remembered. □ **perpetuation** *noun*.
■ **1** continue, eternalize, extend, keep going, maintain, preserve. **2** immortalize, memorialize.

perpetuity /pɜːpɪ'tjuːɪtɪ/ *noun* (*plural* **-ies**) perpetual continuance or possession. □ **in perpetuity** for ever.

perplex /pə'pleks/ *verb* **1** bewilder, puzzle. **2** complicate. **3** tangle. □ **perplexing** *adjective*. **perplexity** *noun*.
■ **1** baffle, *colloquial* bamboozle, befuddle, bewilder, confound, confuse, disconcert, distract, dumbfound, muddle, mystify, nonplus, puzzle, stump, *colloquial* throw, worry.

per pro. /pɜː 'prəʊ/ *abbreviation* through the agency of (used in signatures) (*per procurantionem*). [Latin]

USAGE The abbreviation *per pro.* (or *p.p.*) is frequently written before the wrong name. The correct sequence of signatures is A *per pro.* B, where B is signing on behalf of A.

perquisite /'pɜːkwɪzɪt/ *noun* **1** extra profit additional to main income etc. **2** customary extra right or privilege.

USAGE *Perquisite* is sometimes confused with *prerequisite*, which means 'a thing required as a precondition'.
■ benefit, bonus, consideration, emolument, extra, fringe benefit, gratuity, *colloquial* perk, tip.

perry /'perɪ/ *noun* (*plural* **-ies**) drink made from fermented pear juice.

per se /pɜː 'seɪ/ *adverb* by or in itself; intrinsically. [Latin]

persecute /'pɜːsɪkjuːt/ *verb* (**-ting**) **1** subject to constant hostility and ill-treatment. **2** harass; worry. □ **persecution** /-'kjuːʃ(ə)n/ *noun*. **persecutor** *noun*.
■ **1** abuse, afflict, bully, discriminate against, ill-treat, maltreat, martyr, molest, oppress, suppress, terrorize, torment, torture, tyrannize, victimize. **2** annoy, badger, bother, bully, harass, hector, hound, intimidate, pester, trouble, worry.

persevere /pɜːsɪ'vɪə/ *verb* (**-ring**) continue steadfastly; persist. □ **perseverance** *noun*.

Persian /'pɜːʃ(ə)n/ *noun* **1** native, national, or language of Persia (now Iran). **2** (in full **Persian cat**) cat with long silky hair. ● *adjective* of Persia

(Iran). □ **Persian lamb** silky curled fur of young karakul.

persiflage /'pɜːsɪflɑːʒ/ *noun* banter; light raillery.

persimmon /pɜː'sɪmən/ *noun* **1** tropical tree. **2** its edible orange tomato-like fruit.

persist /pə'sɪst/ *verb* (often + *in*) continue to exist or do something in spite of obstacles.
■ be diligent, be steadfast, carry on, continue, endure, go on, hang on, hold out, keep going, keep on, last, linger, persevere, *colloquial* plug away, remain, *colloquial* soldier on, stand firm, stay, *colloquial* stick at it.

persistent *adjective* **1** continuous; long-lasting. **2** continuing steadfastly. □ **persistence** *noun*. **persistently** *adverb*.
■ **1** ceaseless, chronic, constant, continual, continuous, endless, eternal, everlasting, incessant, interminable, lasting, long-lasting, never-ending, obstinate, permanent, perpetual, persisting, recurrent, recurring, remaining, repeated, unending, unrelenting, unrelieved, unremitting. **2** assiduous, determined, dogged, hard-working, indefatigable, patient, persevering, pertinacious, relentless, resolute, steadfast, steady, stubborn, tenacious, tireless, unflagging, untiring, unwavering, zealous.

person /'pɜːs(ə)n/ *noun* **1** individual human being. **2** living body of human being. **3** *Grammar* one of 3 classes of pronouns, verb-forms, etc., denoting person etc. speaking, spoken to, or spoken of. □ **in person** physically present.
■ **1** adolescent, adult, baby, being, *colloquial* body, character, child, *colloquial* customer, figure, human, human being, individual, infant, man, mortal, personage, soul, *colloquial* type, woman; (*persons*) see PEOPLE *noun* 1.

persona /pə'səʊnə/ *noun* (*plural* **-nae** /-niː/) aspect of personality as perceived by others. □ **persona grata** /'grɑːtə/ (*plural* **personae gratae** /-niː, -tiː/) person acceptable to certain others. **persona non grata** /nɒn/ (*plural* **personae non gratae**) person not acceptable.
■ character, exterior, façade, guise, identity, image, part, personality, role, self-image.

personable *adjective* pleasing in appearance or demeanour.

personage *noun* person, esp. important one.

personal /'pɜːsən(ə)l/ *adjective* **1** one's own; individual; private. **2** done etc. in person. **3** directed to or concerning individual. **4** referring (esp. in hostile way) to individual's private life. **5** intimate. **6** *Grammar* of or denoting one of the 3 persons. □ **personal column** part of newspaper devoted to private advertisements and messages. **personal computer** computer designed for use by single individual. **personal equity plan** scheme for tax-free personal investments. **personal organizer** means of keeping track of personal affairs, esp. loose-leaf notebook divided into sections. **personal pronoun** pronoun replacing subject, object, etc., of clause etc. **personal property** all property except land.

■ **1** distinct, distinctive, exclusive, idiosyncratic, individual, inimitable, particular, peculiar, private, special, unique. **2** actual, bodily, first-hand, in the flesh, live, physical. **3** confidential, individual, intimate, private, secret. **4** belittling, critical, derogatory, disparaging, insulting, offensive, pejorative, rude, slighting, unfriendly. **5** bosom, close, dear, familiar, intimate, known.

personality /pɜːsəˈnælɪtɪ/ *noun* (*plural* **-ies**) **1** distinctive personal character. **2** well-known person. **3** (in *plural*) personal remarks.

■ **1** attractiveness, character, charisma, charm, disposition, identity, individuality, magnetism, make-up, nature, persona, psyche, temperament. **2** big name, celebrity, idol, luminary, name, public figure, star, superstar.

personalize *verb* (also **-ise**) (**-zing** or **-sing**) identify as belonging to particular person.

personally *adverb* **1** in person. **2** for one's own part. **3** in a personal way.

personification /pəsɒnɪfɪˈkeɪʃ(ə)n/ *noun* type of metaphor in which human qualities are attributed to object, plant, animal, nature, etc., e.g. *Life can play some nasty tricks.*

■ embodiment, epitome, incarnation, manifestation.

personify /pəˈsɒnɪfaɪ/ *verb* (**-ies**, **-ied**) **1** attribute human characteristics to. **2** symbolize by human figure. **3** (usually as **personified** *adjective*) embody; exemplify typically. □ **personification** *noun*.

■ **1** anthropomorphize, personalize. **3** embody, epitomize, exemplify, manifest, represent, stand for, symbolize, typify.

personnel /pɜːsəˈnel/ *noun* **1** staff of an organization. **2** people engaged in particular service, profession, etc. □ **personnel department** department of firm etc. dealing with appointment, training, and welfare of employees.

■ employees, manpower, people, staff, workers, workforce.

perspective /pəˈspektɪv/ *noun* **1** art of drawing so as to give effect of solidity and relative position and size. **2** relation as to position and distance, or proportion between visible objects, parts of subject, etc. **3** mental view of relative importance of things. **4** view, prospect. ● *adjective* of or in perspective. □ **in or out of perspective 1** according or not according to rules of perspective. **2** in or not in proportion.

■ *noun* **3** angle, approach, attitude, outlook, point of view, position, prospect, slant, standpoint, view, viewpoint. **4** outlook, prospect, view.

Perspex /ˈpɜːspeks/ *noun proprietary term* tough light transparent plastic.

perspicacious /pɜːspɪˈkeɪʃəs/ *adjective* having mental penetration or discernment. □ **perspicaciousness** *noun*. **perspicacity** /-ˈkæs-/ *noun*.

perspicuous /pəˈspɪkjʊəs/ *adjective* lucid; clearly expressed. □ **perspicuity** /-ˈkjuː-/ *noun*.

perspire /pəˈspaɪə/ *verb* (**-ring**) sweat. □ **perspiration** /pɜːspɪˈreɪʃ(ə)n/ *noun*.

persuade /pəˈsweɪd/ *verb* (**-ding**) cause (person) by argument etc. to believe or do something; convince. □ **persuadable** *adjective*.

■ bring round, cajole, coax, convert, convince, entice, exhort, importune, induce, influence, inveigle, press, prevail upon, prompt, talk into, tempt, urge, wheedle, win over.

persuasion /pəˈsweɪʒ(ə)n/ *noun* **1** persuading. **2** conviction. **3** religious belief or sect.

■ **1** argument, blandishment, brainwashing, cajolery, coaxing, conditioning, enticement, exhortation, inducement, propaganda, reasoning. **2** belief, conviction, creed, opinion. **3** affiliation, belief, conviction, creed, denomination, faith, religion, sect.

persuasive /pəˈsweɪsɪv/ *adjective* able or tending to persuade. □ **persuasively** *adverb*. **persuasiveness** *noun*.

■ cogent, compelling, conclusive, convincing, credible, effective, efficacious, eloquent, forceful, influential, logical, plausible, potent, reasonable, sound, strong, telling, unarguable, valid, watertight.

pert *adjective* **1** saucy, impudent. **2** jaunty. □ **pertly** *adverb*. **pertness** *noun*.

pertain /pəˈteɪn/ *verb* **1** (+ *to*) belong. **2** (+ *to*) relate.

■ **2** (*pertain to*) affect, appertain to, apply to, be relevant to, concern, have bearing on, have reference to, have relevance to, refer to.

pertinacious /pɜːtɪˈneɪʃəs/ *adjective* persistent; obstinate. □ **pertinacity** /-ˈnæs-/ *noun*.

pertinent /ˈpɜːtɪmənt/ *adjective* relevant. □ **pertinence** *noun*. **pertinency** *noun*.

■ apposite, appropriate, apropos, apt, fitting, germane, relevant, suitable.

perturb /pəˈtɜːb/ *verb* throw into agitation; disquiet. □ **perturbation** *noun*.

■ agitate, alarm, bother, confuse, discomfit, discompose, disconcert, disquiet, distress, disturb, fluster, frighten, ruffle, scare, shake, trouble, unnerve, unsettle, upset, vex, worry.

peruke /pəˈruːk/ *noun historical* wig.

peruse /pəˈruːz/ *verb* (**-sing**) read; scan. □ **perusal** *noun*.

■ examine, inspect, look over, read, run one's eye over, scan, scrutinize, study.

pervade /pəˈveɪd/ *verb* (**-ding**) **1** spread through; permeate. **2** be rife among. □ **pervasion** *noun*. **pervasive** *adjective*.

■ **1** affect, diffuse through, fill, filter through, flow through, impregnate, penetrate, percolate through, permeate, saturate, spread through, suffuse. □ **pervasive** general, inescapable, insidious, omnipresent, penetrating, permeating, prevalent, rife, ubiquitous, universal, widespread.

perverse /pəˈvɜːs/ *adjective* obstinately or wilfully in the wrong; wayward. □ **perversely** *adverb*. **perversity** *noun*.

■ adamant, contradictory, contrary, disobedient, fractious, headstrong, illogical, inappropriate, inflexible, intractable, intransigent, obdurate, obstinate, peevish, pig-headed, rebellious, refractory, self-willed, stubborn, *colloquial* tiresome, uncooperative, unhelpful, unreasonable, wayward, wilful, wrong-headed.

perversion /pə'vɜːʃ(ə)n/ *noun* **1** perverting, being perverted. **2** preference for abnormal form of sexual activity.

■ **1** corruption, deviation, distortion, falsification, misrepresentation, misuse, twisting. **2** aberration, abnormality, depravity, deviance, deviation, immorality, impropriety, *colloquial* kinkiness, perversity, unnaturalness, vice, wickedness.

pervert *verb* /pə'vɜːt/ **1** turn (thing) aside from proper or normal use. **2** lead astray from right behaviour or belief etc. **3** (as **perverted** *adjective*) showing perversion. ● *noun* /'pɜːvɜːt/ person who is perverted, esp. sexually.

■ *verb* **1** bend, deflect, distort, divert, falsify, misrepresent, perjure, subvert, twist, undermine. **2** bribe, corrupt, lead astray. **3** (**perverted**) abnormal, amoral, bad, corrupt, debauched, degenerate, depraved, deviant, evil, immoral, improper, *colloquial* kinky, *colloquial* sick, twisted, unnatural, unprincipled, warped, wicked, wrong. ● *noun* debauchee, degenerate, deviant.

pervious /'pɜːvɪəs/ *adjective* **1** permeable. **2** allowing passage or access.

peseta /pə'seɪtə/ *noun* Spanish monetary unit.

peso /'peɪsəʊ/ *noun* (*plural* -**s**) monetary unit in several Latin American countries.

pessary /'pesərɪ/ *noun* (*plural* -**ies**) **1** device worn in vagina. **2** vaginal suppository.

pessimism /'pesɪmɪz(ə)m/ *noun* tendency to take worst view or expect worst outcome. □ **pessimist** *noun*. **pessimistic** /-'mɪst-/ *adjective*.

■ cynicism, despair, despondency, fatalism, gloom, hopelessness, negativeness, resignation, unhappiness. □ **pessimistic** bleak, cynical, defeatist, despairing, despondent, fatalistic, gloomy, hopeless, melancholy, *colloquial* morbid, negative, resigned, unhappy.

pest *noun* **1** troublesome person or thing. **2** destructive animal, esp. insect.

■ **1** annoyance, bane, bother, curse, irritation, nuisance, *colloquial* pain in the neck, trial, vexation. **2** bug, *colloquial* creepy-crawly, insect, parasite; (*pests*) vermin.

pester /'pestə/ *verb* trouble or annoy, esp. with persistent requests.

■ annoy, badger, bait, besiege, bother, harass, harry, *colloquial* hassle, irritate, molest, nag, nettle, *colloquial* plague, provoke, torment, trouble, worry.

pesticide /'pestɪsaɪd/ *noun* substance for destroying harmful insects etc.

pestilence /'pestɪləns/ *noun* fatal epidemic disease, esp. bubonic plague.

■ epidemic, pandemic, plague.

pestilent /'pestɪlənt/ *adjective* **1** deadly. **2** harmful or morally destructive.

pestilential /pestɪ'lenʃ(ə)l/ *adjective* **1** of pestilence. **2** pestilent.

pestle /'pes(ə)l/ *noun* instrument for pounding substances in a mortar.

pet[1] *noun* **1** domestic animal kept for pleasure or companionship. **2** favourite. ● *adjective* **1** as, of, or for a pet. **2** favourite. **3** *expressing fondness*. ● *verb* (**-tt-**) **1** fondle, esp. erotically. **2** treat as pet.

■ *noun* **2** apple of one's eye, darling, favourite, idol. ● *verb* **1** caress, cuddle, fondle, kiss, nuzzle, pat, stroke, touch.

pet[2] *noun* fit of ill humour.

petal /'pet(ə)l/ *noun* each division of flower corolla.

peter /'piːtə/ *verb* □ **peter out** diminish; come to an end.

petersham /'piːtəʃəm/ *noun* thick ribbed silk ribbon.

petiole /'petɪəʊl/ *noun* leaf-stalk.

petite /pə'tiːt/ *adjective* (of woman) of small dainty build.

petit four /petɪ 'fɔː/ *noun* (*plural* **petits fours** /'fɔːz/) very small fancy cake.

petition /pə'tɪʃ(ə)n/ *noun* **1** request, supplication. **2** formal written request, esp. one signed by many people, to authorities etc. ● *verb* **1** make petition to. **2** ask humbly.

■ *noun* **1** appeal, application, entreaty, plea, request, solicitation, *literary* supplication. ● *verb* appeal to, ask, call upon, entreat, importune, solicit, sue, *literary* supplicate.

petit point /petɪ 'pwæ/ *noun* embroidery on canvas using small stitches.

petrel /'petr(ə)l/ *noun* seabird, usually flying far from land.

petrify /'petrɪfaɪ/ *verb* (**-ies**, **-ied**) **1** paralyse with terror or astonishment etc. **2** turn or be turned into stone. □ **petrifaction** /-'fækʃ(ə)n/ *noun*.

petrochemical /petrəʊ'kemɪk(ə)l/ *noun* substance obtained from petroleum or natural gas.

petrodollar /'petrəʊdɒlə/ *noun* notional unit of currency earned by petroleum-exporting country.

petrol /'petr(ə)l/ *noun* refined petroleum used as fuel in motor vehicles, aircraft, etc.

petroleum /pɪ'trəʊlɪəm/ *noun* hydrocarbon oil found in upper strata of earth, refined for use as fuel etc. □ **petroleum jelly** translucent solid mixture of hydrocarbons got from petroleum and used as lubricant etc.

petticoat /'petɪkəʊt/ *noun* woman's or girl's undergarment hanging from waist or shoulders.

pettifogging /'petɪfɒgɪŋ/ *adjective* **1** quibbling; petty. **2** dishonest.

pettish *adjective* fretful, peevish.

petty /'petɪ/ *adjective* (**-ier, -iest**) **1** unimportant, trivial. **2** small-minded. **3** minor, inferior. ◻ **petty cash** money kept for small items of expenditure. **petty officer** naval NCO. ◻ **pettiness** *noun*.

■ **1** inconsequential, insignificant, minor, niggling, small, trivial, trifling, unimportant. **2** grudging, mean, *colloquial* nit-picking, small-minded, ungenerous. **3** see MINOR *adjective* 1.

petulant /'petjʊlənt/ *adjective* peevishly impatient or irritable. ◻ **petulance** *noun*. **petulantly** *adverb*.

petunia /pɪ'tjuːnɪə/ *noun* cultivated plant with vivid funnel-shaped flowers.

pew *noun* **1** (in church) enclosed compartment or fixed bench with back. **2** *colloquial* seat.

pewter /'pjuːtə/ *noun* **1** grey alloy of tin, antimony, and copper. **2** articles made of this.

peyote /per'əʊtɪ/ *noun* **1** a Mexican cactus. **2** hallucinogenic drug prepared from it.

pfennig /'fenɪɡ/ *noun* one-hundredth of Deutschmark.

PG *abbreviation* (of film) classified as suitable for children subject to parental guidance.

pH /piː'eɪtʃ/ *noun* measure of acidity or alkalinity of a solution.

phagocyte /'fæɡəsaɪt/ *noun* blood corpuscle etc. capable of absorbing foreign matter.

phalanx /'fælæŋks/ *noun* (*plural* **phalanxes** or **phalanges** /fə'lændʒiːz/) **1** group of infantry in close formation. **2** united or organized party or company.

phallus /'fæləs/ *noun* (*plural* **phalli** /-laɪ/ or **phalluses**) **1** (esp. erect) penis. **2** image of this. ◻ **phallic** *adjective*.

phantasm /'fæntæz(ə)m/ *noun* illusion; phantom. ◻ **phantasmal** /-'tæzm(ə)l/ *adjective*.

phantasmagoria /fæntæzmə'ɡɔːrɪə/ *noun* shifting scene of real or imaginary figures. ◻ **phantasmagoric** /-'ɡɒrɪk/ *adjective*.

phantom /'fæntəm/ *noun* **1** spectre; apparition. **2** mental illusion. ● *adjective* illusory.

Pharaoh /'feərəʊ/ *noun* ruler of ancient Egypt.

Pharisee /'færɪsiː/ *noun* **1** member of ancient Jewish sect distinguished by strict observance of traditional and written law. **2** self-righteous person; hypocrite. ◻ **Pharisaic** /-'seɪɪk/ *adjective*.

pharmaceutical /fɑːmə'sjuːtɪk(ə)l/ *adjective* **1** of pharmacy. **2** of use or sale of medicinal drugs. ◻ **pharmaceutics** *noun*.

pharmacist /'fɑːməsɪst/ *noun* person qualified to practise pharmacy.

pharmacology /fɑːmə'kɒlədʒɪ/ *noun* study of action of drugs on the body. ◻ **pharmacological** /-kə'lɒdʒ-/ *adjective*. **pharmacologist** *noun*.

pharmacopoeia /fɑːməkə'piːə/ *noun* **1** book with list of drugs and directions for use. **2** stock of drugs.

pharmacy /'fɑːməsɪ/ *noun* (*plural* **-ies**) **1** preparation and dispensing of drugs. **2** pharmacist's shop; dispensary.

pharynx /'færɪŋks/ *noun* (*plural* **pharynges** /-rɪndʒiːz/ or **-xes**) cavity behind mouth and nose. ◻ **pharyngeal** /færɪn'dʒiːəl/ *adjective*.

phase /feɪz/ *noun* **1** stage of development, process, or recurring sequence. **2** aspect of moon or planet. ● *verb* (**-sing**) carry out by phases. ◻ **phase in, out** bring gradually into or out of use.

■ *noun* **1** period, season, spell, stage, state, step, time. ◻ **phase in** see INTRODUCE 3. **phase out** see FINISH *verb* 1.

Ph.D. *abbreviation* Doctor of Philosophy.

pheasant /'fez(ə)nt/ *noun* long-tailed game bird.

phenomenal /fɪ'nɒmɪn(ə)l/ *adjective* **1** extraordinary, remarkable. **2** of or concerned with phenomena. ◻ **phenomenally** *adverb*.

■ **1** amazing, astonishing, astounding, exceptional, extraordinary, *colloquial* fantastic, *colloquial* incredible, marvellous, *colloquial* mind-boggling, miraculous, notable, outstanding, prodigious, rare, remarkable, *colloquial* sensational, singular, staggering, *colloquial* stunning, unbelievable, unorthodox, unusual, wonderful.

phenomenon /fɪ'nɒmɪnən/ *noun* (*plural* **-mena**) **1** observed or apparent object, fact, or occurrence. **2** remarkable person or thing.

USAGE It is a mistake to use the plural form *phenomena* when only one phenomenon is meant.

■ **1** circumstance, event, experience, fact, happening, incident, occasion, occurrence, sight. **2** curiosity, marvel, miracle, prodigy, rarity, sensation, spectacle, wonder.

phew /fjuː/ *interjection:* expressing disgust, relief, etc.

phial /'faɪəl/ *noun* small glass bottle.

philander /fɪ'lændə/ *verb* flirt or have casual affairs with women. ◻ **philanderer** *noun*.

philanthropy /fɪ'lænθrəpɪ/ *noun* **1** love of all humankind. **2** practical benevolence. ◻ **philanthropic** /-'θrɒp-/ *adjective*. **philanthropist** *noun*.

■ ◻ **philanthropic** altruistic, beneficent, benevolent, bountiful, caring, charitable, generous, humane, humanitarian, kind, magnanimous, munificent, public-spirited, ungrudging. **philanthropist** altruist, benefactor, donor, giver, good Samaritan, humanitarian, patron, provider, sponsor.

philately /fɪ'lætəlɪ/ *noun* stamp-collecting. ◻ **philatelist** *noun*.

philharmonic /fɪlhɑː'mɒnɪk/ *adjective* devoted to music.

philippic /fɪ'lɪpɪk/ *noun* bitter verbal attack.

philistine /'fɪlɪstaɪn/ *noun* person who is hostile or indifferent to culture. ● *adjective* hostile or indifferent to culture. □ **philistinism** /-stm-/ *noun*.

■ *adjective* boorish, ignorant, *colloquial* lowbrow, materialistic, uncivilized, uncultivated, uncultured, unenlightened, unlettered, vulgar.

Phillips /'fɪlɪps/ *noun proprietary term* □ **Phillips screw** screw with cross-shaped slot. **Phillips screwdriver** corresponding screwdriver.

philology /fɪ'lɒlədʒɪ/ *noun* study of language. □ **philological** /-lə'lɒdʒ-/ *adjective*. **philologist** *noun*.

philosopher /fɪ'lɒsəfə/ *noun* **1** expert in or student of philosophy. **2** person who acts philosophically.

■ **1** sage, thinker.

philosophical /fɪlə'sɒfɪk(ə)l/ *adjective* (also **philosophic**) **1** of or according to philosophy. **2** calm under adverse circumstances. □ **philosophically** *adverb*.

■ **1** abstract, academic, analytical, erudite, esoteric, ideological, impractical, intellectual, learned, logical, metaphysical, rational, reasoned, scholarly, theoretical, thoughtful, wise. **2** calm, collected, composed, detached, equable, imperturbable, judicious, patient, reasonable, resigned, serene, sober, stoical, unemotional, unruffled.

philosophize /fɪ'lɒsəfaɪz/ *verb* (also **-ise**) (**-zing** or **-sing**) **1** reason like philosopher. **2** theorize.

■ moralize, rationalize, reason, theorize, think things out.

philosophy /fɪ'lɒsəfɪ/ *noun* (*plural* **-ies**) **1** use of reason and argument in seeking truth and knowledge, esp. of ultimate reality or of general causes and principles. **2** philosophical system; system for conduct of life.

■ **1** epistemology, ideology, logic, metaphysics, rationalism, thinking. **2** attitude, convictions, outlook, set of beliefs, tenets, values, viewpoint, wisdom.

philtre /'fɪltə/ *noun* (*US* **philter**) love potion.

phlebitis /flɪ'baɪtɪs/ *noun* inflammation of vein. □ **phlebitic** /-'bɪt-/ *adjective*.

phlegm /flem/ *noun* **1** bronchial mucus ejected by coughing. **2** calmness. **3** sluggishness.

phlegmatic /fleg'mætɪk/ *adjective* calm; not excitable; sluggish.

■ apathetic, cold, cool, frigid, impassive, imperturbable, indifferent, lethargic, passive, placid, slow, sluggish, stoical, stolid, torpid, undemonstrative, unemotional, unenthusiastic, unfeeling, *colloquial* unflappable, uninvolved, unresponsive.

phlox /flɒks/ *noun* (*plural* same or **-es**) plant with clusters of white or coloured flowers.

phobia /'fəʊbɪə/ *noun* abnormal fear or aversion. □ **phobic** *adjective & noun*.

■ anxiety, aversion, dislike, dread, fear, *slang* hang-up, hatred, horror, loathing, neurosis, obsession, repugnance, revulsion.

phoenix /'fiːnɪks/ *noun* bird, the only one of its kind, fabled to burn itself and rise from its ashes.

phone *noun & verb* (**-ning**) *colloquial* telephone. □ **phone book** telephone directory. **phonecard** card holding prepaid units for use with cardphone. **phone-in** broadcast programme in which listeners or viewers participate by telephone.

■ *verb* call, dial, *slang* give a buzz, ring, telephone.

phonetic /fə'netɪk/ *adjective* **1** of or representing vocal sounds. **2** (of spelling) corresponding to pronunciation. □ **phonetically** *adverb*.

phonetics *plural noun* (usually treated as *singular*) study or representation of vocal sounds. □ **phonetician** /fəʊnɪ'tɪʃ(ə)n/ *noun*.

phoney /'fəʊnɪ/ (also **phony**) *colloquial adjective* (**-ier, -iest**) false, sham, counterfeit. ● *noun* (*plural* **-eys** or **-ies**) phoney person or thing. □ **phoniness** *noun*.

■ *adjective* affected, artificial, assumed, bogus, contrived, counterfeit, deceitful, ersatz, factitious, fake, faked, false, fictitious, fraudulent, hypocritical, imitation, insincere, mock, pretended, pseudo, put-up, sham, spurious, synthetic, trick, unreal.

phonic /'fɒnɪk/ *adjective* of (vocal) sound.

phonograph /'fəʊnəɡrɑːf/ *noun* early form of gramophone.

phonology /fə'nɒlədʒɪ/ *noun* study of sounds in language. □ **phonological** /fəʊnə'lɒdʒɪk(ə)l/ *adjective*.

phony = PHONEY.

phosphate /'fɒsfeɪt/ *noun* salt of phosphoric acid, esp. used as fertilizer.

phosphorescence /fɒsfə'res(ə)ns/ *noun* emission of light without combustion or perceptible heat. □ **phosphoresce** *verb* (**-cing**). **phosphorescent** *adjective*.

phosphorus /'fɒsfərəs/ *noun* non-metallic element occurring esp. as waxlike substance appearing luminous in dark. □ **phosphoric** /-'fɒrɪk/ *adjective*. **phosphorous** *adjective*.

photo /'fəʊtəʊ/ *noun* (*plural* **-s**) photograph. □ **photo finish** close finish of race in which winner is distinguishable only on photograph. **photofit** picture of suspect constructed from composite photographs.

photo- *combining form* **1** light. **2** photography.

photocopier /'fəʊtəʊkɒpɪə/ *noun* machine for photocopying documents.

photocopy /'fəʊtəʊkɒpɪ/ *noun* (*plural* **-ies**) photographic copy of document. ● *verb* (**-ies, -ied**) make photocopy of.

■ *verb* copy, duplicate, photostat, print off, reproduce, run off.

photoelectric /fəʊtəʊɪ'lektrɪk/ *adjective* with or using emission of electrons from substances exposed to light. □ **photoelectric cell** device using this effect to generate current. □ **photoelectricity** /-'trɪsɪtɪ/ *noun*.

photogenic /fəʊtəʊ'dʒenɪk/ *adjective* **1** looking

attractive in photographs. **2** producing or emitting light.

photograph /ˈfəʊtəɡrɑːf/ *noun* picture formed by chemical action of light on sensitive film. ● *verb* take photograph (of). □ **photographer** /fəˈtɒɡrəfə/ *noun.* **photography** /fəˈtɒɡrəfɪ/ *noun.*

■ *noun* enlargement, photo, picture, print, shot, snap, snapshot. ● *verb* film, shoot, snap.

photographic /fəʊtəˈɡræfɪk/ *adjective* **1** of, used in, or produced by photography. **2** having accuracy of photograph.

■ **2** accurate, exact, faithful, graphic, lifelike, natural, naturalistic, pictorial, realistic, representational, true to life, visual.

photogravure /fəʊtəʊɡrəˈvjʊə/ *noun* **1** picture produced from photographic negative transferred to metal plate and etched in. **2** this process.

photojournalism /fəʊtəʊˈdʒɜːnəlɪz(ə)m/ *noun* reporting of news by photographs in magazines etc. □ **photojournalist** *noun.*

photolithography /fəʊtəʊlɪˈθɒɡrəfɪ/ *noun* lithography using plates made photographically.

photometer /fəʊˈtɒmɪtə/ *noun* instrument for measuring light. □ **photometric** /fəʊtəʊˈmetrɪk/ *adjective.* **photometry** /-ˈtɒmɪtrɪ/ *noun.*

photon /ˈfəʊtɒn/ *noun* quantum of electromagnetic radiation energy.

Photostat /ˈfəʊtəʊstæt/ *noun proprietary term* **1** type of photocopier. **2** copy made by it. ● *verb* (**photostat**) (**-tt-**) make Photostat of.

photosynthesis /fəʊtəʊˈsɪnθəsɪs/ *noun* process in which energy of sunlight is used by green plants to form carbohydrates from carbon dioxide and water. □ **photosynthesize** *verb* (also **-ise**) (**-zing** or **-sing**).

phrase /freɪz/ *noun* **1** group of words forming conceptual unit but not sentence (see panel). **2** short pithy expression. **3** *Music* short sequence of notes. ● *verb* (**-sing**) **1** express in words. **2** divide (music) into phrases. □ **phrase book** book listing phrases and their foreign equivalents, for use by tourists etc. □ **phrasal** *adjective.*

■ *noun* **1** clause, expression, locution. **2** see SAYING. ● *verb* **1** see SAY *verb* 1,2.

phraseology /freɪzɪˈɒlədʒɪ/ *noun* (*plural* **-ies**) choice or arrangement of words. □ **phraseological** /-zɪəˈlɒdʒ-/ *adjective.*

■ expression, idiom, language, parlance, phrasing, style, turn of phrase, wording.

phrenology /frɪˈnɒlədʒɪ/ *noun historical* study of external form of cranium as supposed indication of mental faculties etc. □ **phrenologist** *noun.*

phut /fʌt/ *adverb colloquial* □ **go phut** collapse, break down.

phylactery /frɪˈlæktərɪ/ *noun* (*plural* **-ies**) small box containing Hebrew texts, worn by Jewish man at prayer.

phylum /ˈfaɪləm/ *noun* (*plural* **phyla**) major division of plant or animal kingdom.

physic /ˈfɪzɪk/ *noun esp. archaic* **1** medicine. **2** medical art or profession.

physical /ˈfɪzɪk(ə)l/ *adjective* **1** of the body. **2** of matter. **3** of nature or according to its laws. **4** of physics. ● *noun US* medical examination. □ **physical education** instruction in physical exercise and games. **physical training** exercises promoting fitness and strength. □ **physically** *adverb.*

■ *adjective* **1** bodily, carnal, corporal, corporeal, fleshly, incarnate, physiological. **2** actual, concrete, corporeal, earthly, material, palpable, real, solid, substantial, tangible.

physician /frɪˈzɪʃ(ə)n/ *noun* doctor, esp. specialist in medical diagnosis and treatment.

■ consultant, doctor, general practitioner, GP, medical practitioner, specialist.

physics /ˈfɪzɪks/ *plural noun* (usually treated as *singular*) science of properties and interaction of matter and energy. □ **physicist** *noun.*

physiognomy /fɪzɪˈɒnəmɪ/ *noun* (*plural* **-ies**) **1** features or type of face. **2** art of judging character from face etc.

physiology /fɪzɪˈɒlədʒɪ/ *noun* science of functioning of living organisms. □ **physiological** /-əˈlɒdʒ-/ *adjective.* **physiologist** *noun.*

■ □ **physiological** anatomical, bodily, physical.

physiotherapy /fɪzɪəʊˈθerəpɪ/ *noun* treatment

Phrase

A phrase is a group of words that has meaning but does not have a subject, main verb, or object (unlike a clause or sentence). It can be:

1 a noun phrase, functioning as a noun, e.g.

I went to see my friend Tom.
The only ones they have *are too small.*

2 an adjective phrase, functioning as an adjective, e.g.

I was very pleased indeed.
This one is better than mine.

3 an adverb phrase, functioning as an adverb, e.g.

They drove off in their car.
I was there ten days ago.

of injury or disease by exercise, heat, or other physical agencies. □ **physiotherapist** *noun*.

physique /fɪˈziːk/ *noun* bodily structure and development.
■ body, build, figure, form, frame, shape.

pi /paɪ/ *noun* **1** sixteenth letter of Greek alphabet (*Π, π*). **2** (as *π*) symbol of ratio of circumference of circle to diameter (approx. 3.14).

pia mater /paɪə ˈmeɪtə/ *noun* inner membrane enveloping brain and spinal cord.

pianissimo /pɪəˈnɪsɪməʊ/ *Music adjective* very soft. ● *adverb* very softly. ● *noun* (*plural* **-s** or **-mi** /-mɪ/) very soft playing, singing, or passage.

pianist /ˈpɪənɪst/ *noun* player of piano.

piano[1] /pɪˈænəʊ/ *noun* (*plural* **-s**) keyboard instrument with metal strings struck by hammers. □ **piano-accordion** accordion with small keyboard like that of piano.

piano[2] /ˈpjɑːnəʊ/ *Music adjective* soft. ● *adverb* softly. ● *noun* (*plural* **-s** or **-ni** /-nɪ/) soft playing, singing, or passage.

pianoforte /pɪænəʊˈfɔːtɪ/ *noun formal* or *archaic* = PIANO[1].

piazza /pɪˈætsə/ *noun* public square or market-place.

pibroch /ˈpiːbrɒk/ *noun* martial or funeral bagpipe music.

picador /ˈpɪkədɔː/ *noun* mounted man with lance in bullfight.

picaresque /pɪkəˈresk/ *adjective* (of style of fiction) dealing with episodic adventures of rogues.

piccalilli /pɪkəˈlɪlɪ/ *noun* (*plural* **-s**) pickle of chopped vegetables, mustard, and spices.

piccolo /ˈpɪkələʊ/ *noun* (*plural* **-s**) small high-pitched flute.

pick *verb* **1** select carefully. **2** pluck, gather (flower, fruit, etc.). **3** probe with fingers or instrument to remove unwanted matter. **4** clear (bone etc.) of scraps of meat etc. **5** eat (food, meal, etc.) in small bits. ● *noun* **1** picking, selection. **2** (usually + *of*) best. **3** pickaxe. **4** *colloquial* plectrum. **5** instrument for picking. □ **pick a lock** open lock with instrument other than proper key, esp. with criminal intent. **pick holes** (often + *in*) find fault. **pick-me-up 1** tonic. **2** experience or news that cheers. **pick on 1** nag at; find fault with. **2** select. **pick out 1** select from larger number. **2** distinguish. **pickpocket** person who steals from pockets. **pick up 1** take hold of and lift. **2** acquire casually. **3** learn routinely. **4** stop for and take with one. **5** make acquaintance of casually. **6** recover, improve. **7** arrest. **8** detect; manage to receive (broadcast signal etc.). **9** accept responsibility of paying (bill etc.). **10** resume. **pickup 1** person met casually. **2** small open truck. **3** part of record player carrying stylus. **4** device on electric guitar etc. that converts string vibrations into electrical signals. **5** act of picking up. **pick-your-own** (of fruit and vegetables) dug or picked by customer at farm etc.

■ *verb* **1** cast (*actor*), choose, decide on, elect, name, nominate, opt for, select, settle on, single out, vote for. **2** collect, cull, cut, gather, harvest, pluck, pull off, take. ● *noun* **1** choice, election, option, preference, selection. **2** best, cream, elite, favourite, pride. □ **pick on 1** see BULLY[1] *verb*. **pick up 2** see GET 1–2. **6** see IMPROVE 1.

pickaxe /ˈpɪkæks/ *noun* (*US* **pickax**) tool with sharp-pointed iron cross-bar for breaking up ground etc.

picket /ˈpɪkɪt/ *noun* **1** one or more people stationed to dissuade workers from entering workplace during strike etc. **2** pointed stake driven into ground. **3** small group of troops sent to watch for enemy. ● *verb* (**-t-**) **1** place or act as picket outside. **2** post as military picket. **3** secure with stakes. □ **picket line** boundary established by workers on strike, esp. at workplace entrance, which others are asked not to cross.

pickings *plural noun* **1** perquisites. **2** gleanings.

pickle /ˈpɪk(ə)l/ *noun* **1** (often in *plural*) vegetables etc. preserved in vinegar etc. **2** liquid used for this. **3** *colloquial* plight. ● *verb* (**-ling**) **1** preserve in or treat with pickle. **2** (as **pickled** *adjective*) *slang* drunk.

picky *adjective* (**-ier, -iest**) *colloquial* highly fastidious.

picnic /ˈpɪknɪk/ *noun* **1** outing including outdoor meal. **2** such meal. **3** something pleasantly or easily accomplished. ● *verb* (**-ck-**) eat meal outdoors.

pictograph /ˈpɪktəɡrɑːf/ *noun* (also **pictogram** /-ɡræm/) pictorial symbol used as form of writing.

pictorial /pɪkˈtɔːrɪəl/ *adjective* of, expressed in, or illustrated with a picture or pictures. □ **pictorially** *adverb*.
■ diagrammatic, graphic, illustrated, realistic, representational, vivid.

picture /ˈpɪktʃə/ *noun* **1** painting, drawing, photograph, etc., esp. as work of art; portrait. **2** beautiful object. **3** scene; mental image. **4** cinema film. **5** (**the pictures**) cinema (performance). ● *verb* (**-ring**) **1** represent in picture. **2** imagine. **3** describe graphically. □ **in the picture** fully informed or noticed. **picture postcard** postcard with picture on one side. **picture window** large window of one pane of glass.
■ *noun* **1** delineation, depiction, drawing, illustration, image, likeness, outline, painting, photograph, portrait, portrayal, profile, representation, sketch; (*pictures*) graffiti, graphics. **4** film, *colloquial* flick, *esp. US* motion picture, *esp. US colloquial* movie, moving picture, video. ● *verb* **1** delineate, depict, draw, illustrate, outline, paint, portray, represent, show, sketch. **2** conceive, dream up, envisage, fancy, imagine, see in one's mind's eye, *colloquial* think up, visualize. **3** see DESCRIBE 1.

picturesque /pɪktʃəˈresk/ *adjective* **1** striking and pleasant to look at. **2** (of language etc.) strikingly graphic. □ **picturesqueness** *noun*.

■ **1** attractive, beautiful, charming, idyllic, lovely, pleasant, pretty, quaint, scenic. **2** colourful, descriptive, expressive, graphic, imaginative, poetic, vivid.

piddle /'pɪd(ə)l/ *verb* (**-ling**) **1** *colloquial* urinate. **2** (as **piddling** *adjective*) *colloquial* trivial. **3** work or act in trifling way.

pidgin /'pɪdʒɪn/ *noun* simplified language, esp. used between speakers of different languages.

pie *noun* dish of meat, fruit, etc., encased in or covered with pastry etc. and baked. □ **pie chart** diagram representing relative quantities as sectors of circle. **pie-eyed** *slang* drunk.
■ flan, pasty, patty, quiche, tart, tartlet, turnover, vol-au-vent.

piebald /'paɪbɔːld/ *adjective* having irregular patches of two colours, esp. black and white.
● *noun* piebald animal.

piece /piːs/ *noun* **1** distinct portion forming part of or broken off from larger object. **2** coin. **3** picture; literary or musical composition. **4** example, item. **5** chessman; man at draughts, etc.
● *verb* (**-cing**) (usually + *together*) form into a whole; join. □ **go to pieces** collapse emotionally; suffer breakdown. **in one piece** unbroken; unharmed. **of a piece** uniform or consistent. **piecework** work paid for according to amount done.
■ *noun* **1** bar, bit, bite, block, chip, chunk, component, constituent, crumb, division, dollop, element, fraction, fragment, grain, helping, hunk, length, lump, morsel, part, particle, portion, quantity, remnant, sample, scrap, section, segment, shard, share, shred, slab, slice, sliver, snippet, speck, stick, tablet, titbit, unit, wedge. **3** article, composition, creation, number, opus, passage, work. **4** example, instance, item, specimen. ● *verb* (*piece together*) see ASSEMBLE 1.

pièce de résistance /pjes də rer'ziːstãs/ *noun* (*plural* **pièces de résistance** same pronunciation) most important or remarkable item.

piecemeal *adverb* piece by piece; part at a time.
● *adjective* gradual; unsystematic.

pied /paɪd/ *adjective* of mixed colours.
■ dappled, flecked, mottled, particoloured, patchy, piebald, spotted, variegated.

pied-à-terre /pjeɪdɑː'teə/ *noun* (*plural* **pieds-** same pronunciation) (usually small) flat, house, etc. kept for occasional use. [French]

pier /pɪə/ *noun* **1** structure built out into sea etc. used as promenade and landing stage or breakwater. **2** support of arch or of span of bridge; pillar. **3** solid part of wall between windows etc. □ **pier glass** large tall mirror.
■ **1** breakwater, jetty, landing stage, quay, wharf. **2** buttress, column, pile, pillar, post, support, upright.

pierce /pɪəs/ *verb* (**-cing**) **1** go through or into like spear or needle. **2** make hole in. **3** make (hole

etc.). **4** (as **piercing** *adjective*) penetrating, sharp.
■ **1–3** bayonet, bore through, cut, drill, enter, go through, impale, jab, lance, penetrate, perforate, poke through, prick, punch, puncture, riddle, skewer, spear, spike, spit, stab, stick into, thrust into, transfix, tunnel through, wound. **4** (**piercing**) see SHARP 5;7.

pierrot /'pɪərəʊ/ *noun* (*feminine* **pierrette** /pɪə'ret/) **1** French white-faced pantomime character with clown's costume. **2** itinerant entertainer so dressed.

pietà /pɪe'tɑː/ *noun* representation of Virgin Mary holding dead body of Christ. [Italian]

pietism /'paɪətɪz(ə)m/ *noun* extreme or affected piety. □ **pietistic** /-'tɪstɪk/ *adjective*.

piety /'paɪətɪ/ *noun* piousness.
■ dedication, devotedness, devotion, devoutness, faith, godliness, holiness, piousness, religion, religiosity, saintliness, sanctity.

piffle /'pɪf(ə)l/ *colloquial noun* nonsense. ● *verb* (**-ling**) talk or act feebly.

piffling /'pɪflɪŋ/ *adjective colloquial* trivial.

pig *noun* **1** wild or domesticated animal with broad snout and stout bristly body. **2** *colloquial* greedy, dirty, obstinate, or annoying person. **3** oblong mass of smelted iron or other metal. ● *verb* (**-gg-**) *colloquial* eat (food) greedily. □ **pig-headed** obstinate. **pig-iron** crude iron from smelting-furnace. **pig it** *colloquial* live in disorderly fashion. **pig out** *esp. US slang* eat gluttonously. **pigsty** sty for pigs. **pigtail** plait or bunch of hair hanging from back or each side of head.
■ *noun* **1** boar, hog, piggy, piglet, runt, sow, *formal or US* swine.

pigeon /'pɪdʒ(ə)n/ *noun* bird of dove family. □ **pigeon-hole** *noun* each of set of compartments in cabinet etc. for papers etc. ● *verb* **1** classify mentally. **2** put in pigeon-hole. **3** put aside for future consideration. **pigeon-toed** having toes turned inwards.

piggery *noun* (*plural* **-ies**) **1** pig farm. **2** pigsty.

piggish *adjective* **1** greedy. **2** dirty. **3** mean.

piggy *noun* (*plural* **-ies**) *colloquial* little pig. ● *adjective* (**-ier, -iest**) **1** like a pig. **2** (of features etc.) like those of a pig. □ **piggyback** (a ride) on shoulders and back of another person. **piggy bank** pig-shaped money box.

piglet /'pɪglɪt/ *noun* young pig.

pigment /'pɪgmənt/ *noun* coloured substance used as paint etc., or occurring naturally in plant or animal tissue. ● *verb* colour (as) with natural pigment. □ **pigmentation** *noun*.

pigmy = PYGMY.

pike *noun* (*plural* same or **-s**) **1** large voracious freshwater fish. **2** spear formerly used by infantry. □ **pikestaff** wooden shaft of pike. **plain as a pikestaff** quite obvious.

pilaff = PILAU.

pilaster /pɪˈlæstə/ *noun* rectangular column, esp. one fastened into wall.

pilau /pɪˈlaʊ/ *noun* (also **pilaff** /pɪˈlɑːf/) Middle Eastern or Indian dish of rice with meat, spices, etc.

pilchard /ˈpɪltʃəd/ *noun* small sea fish related to herring.

pile[1] *noun* 1 heap of things laid on one another. 2 large imposing building. 3 *colloquial* large amount, esp. of money. 4 series of plates of dissimilar metals laid alternately for producing electric current. 5 nuclear reactor. 6 pyre. ● *verb* (-ling) 1 heap. 2 (+ *with*) load with. 3 (+ *in, into, on, out of*, etc.) crowd. □ **pile it on** *colloquial* exaggerate. **pile up** accumulate; heap up. **pile-up** *noun colloquial* collision of several motor vehicles.

■ *noun* 1 accumulation, agglomeration, collection, concentration, conglomeration, deposit, heap, hoard, load, mass, mound, mountain, *colloquial* stack, stockpile. 3 abundance, heap, hoard, load, *colloquial* lot, mass, mound, mountain, plethora, quantity, stack, stockpile, supply, *colloquial* tons. ● *verb* 1 accumulate, amass, assemble, bring together, collect, concentrate, deposit, gather, heap, hoard, load, mass, stack (up), stockpile, store. 2 (*pile with*) heap with, load with, stack with.

pile[2] *noun* heavy beam driven vertically into ground as support for building etc.

■ column, pier, post, support, upright.

pile[3] *noun* soft projecting surface of velvet, carpet, etc.

piles *plural noun colloquial* haemorrhoids.

pilfer /ˈpɪlfə/ *verb* steal or thieve in petty way. □ **pilferer** *noun*.

■ filch, *slang* pinch, rob, shoplift, steal.

pilgrim /ˈpɪlgrɪm/ *noun* 1 person who journeys to sacred place. 2 traveller. □ **Pilgrim Fathers** English Puritans who founded colony in Massachusetts in 1620.

■ 2 see TRAVELLER 1.

pilgrimage *noun* pilgrim's journey.

pill *noun* 1 ball or flat piece of medicinal substance to be swallowed whole. 2 (usually **the pill**) *colloquial* contraceptive pill. □ **pillbox** 1 small round shallow box for pills. 2 hat shaped like this. 3 *Military* small round concrete shelter, mainly underground.

■ 1 capsule, lozenge, pastille, pellet, tablet.

pillage /ˈpɪlɪdʒ/ *verb* (-ging) & *noun* plunder. □ **pillager** *noun*.

■ *noun* buccaneering, depredation, despoliation, devastation, looting, marauding, piracy, plunder, plundering, ransacking, rape, *rhetorical* rapine, robbery, robbing, sacking, stealing, stripping. ● *verb* despoil, devastate, loot, maraud, plunder, raid, ransack, ravage, raze, rob, sack, steal, strip, vandalize.

pillar /ˈpɪlə/ *noun* 1 slender upright structure used as support or ornament. 2 person regarded as mainstay. 3 upright mass. □ **pillar box** public postbox shaped like pillar.

■ 1 baluster, caryatid, column, pier, pilaster, pile, post, prop, shaft, stanchion, support, upright.

pillion /ˈpɪljən/ *noun* seat for passenger behind motorcyclist etc.

pillory /ˈpɪlərɪ/ *noun* (*plural* -ies) *historical* frame with holes for head and hands, allowing an offender to be exposed to public ridicule. ● *verb* (-ies, -ied) 1 expose to ridicule. 2 *historical* set in pillory.

pillow /ˈpɪləʊ/ *noun* 1 cushion as support for head, esp. in bed. 2 pillow-shaped support. ● *verb* rest (as) on pillow. □ **pillowcase, pillowslip** washable cover for pillow.

pilot /ˈpaɪlət/ *noun* 1 person operating controls of aircraft. 2 person in charge of ships entering or leaving harbour etc. 3 experimental or preliminary study or undertaking. 4 guide, leader. ● *adjective* experimental, preliminary. ● *verb* (-t-) 1 act as pilot to. 2 guide course of. □ **pilot light** 1 small gas burner kept alight to light another. 2 electric indicator light. **pilot officer** lowest commissioned rank in RAF.

■ *noun* 1 airman, aviator, captain, flier. 2 coxswain, helmsman, navigator, steersman. ● *verb* conduct, convey, direct, drive, fly, guide, lead, navigate, shepherd, steer.

pimento /pɪˈmentəʊ/ *noun* (*plural* -s) 1 allspice. 2 sweet pepper.

pimiento /pɪmɪˈentəʊ/ *noun* (*plural* -s) sweet pepper.

pimp *noun* person who lives off earnings of prostitute or brothel. ● *verb* act as pimp, esp. procure clients for prostitute.

pimpernel /ˈpɪmpənel/ *noun* scarlet pimpernel.

pimple /ˈpɪmp(ə)l/ *noun* small hard inflamed spot on skin. □ **pimply** *adjective*.

■ blackhead, boil, eruption, pustule, spot, swelling, *esp. US slang* zit; (*pimples*) acne.

pin *noun* 1 small thin pointed piece of metal with head, used as fastening. 2 wooden or metal peg, rivet, etc. 3 (in *plural*) *colloquial* legs. ● *verb* (-nn-) 1 fasten with pin(s). 2 transfix with pin, lance, etc. 3 (usually + *on*) fix (responsibility, blame, etc.). 4 seize and hold fast. □ **pinball** game in which small metal balls are shot across board and strike obstacles. **pincushion** small pad for holding pins. **pin down** 1 (often + *to*) bind (person etc.) to promise, arrangement, etc. 2 make (person) declare position or intentions. **pin money** small sum of money, esp. earned by woman. **pinpoint** ● *noun* very small or sharp thing. ● *adjective* precise. ● *verb* locate with precision. **pinprick** petty irritation. **pins and needles** tingling sensation in limb recovering from numbness. **pinstripe** very narrow stripe in cloth. **pin-table** table used in pinball. **pintail** duck or grouse with pointed tail. **pin-tuck** narrow ornamental tuck. **pin-up** picture of attractive or famous person, pinned up on wall etc. **pinwheel** small Catherine wheel.

■ *noun* **1** brooch, clip, drawing-pin, nail, safety pin, tiepin. **2** bolt, dowel, nail, peg, rivet, spike, thole.
● *verb* **1, 2** clip, fasten, fix, nail, pierce, staple, tack, transfix.

pina colada /pi:nə kə'lɑ:də/ *noun* cocktail of pineapple juice, rum, and coconut.

pinafore /'pɪnəfɔ:/ *noun* **1** apron, esp. with bib. **2** (in full **pinafore dress**) dress without collar or sleeves, worn over blouse or jumper.

pince-nez /'pænsneɪ/ *noun* (*plural* same) pair of eyeglasses with spring that clips on nose.

pincers /'pɪnsəz/ *plural noun* **1** gripping-tool forming pair of jaws. **2** pincer-shaped claw in crustaceans etc. □ **pincer movement** converging movement by two wings of army against enemy position.

pinch *verb* **1** grip tightly, esp. between finger and thumb. **2** constrict painfully. **3** (of cold etc.) affect painfully. **4** *slang* steal. **5** *slang* arrest. **6** stint. **7** be niggardly. ● *noun* **1** pinching. **2** (as **pinched** *adjective*) (of features) drawn. **3** amount that can be taken up with fingers and thumb. **4** stress of poverty etc. □ **at a pinch** in an emergency.

■ *verb* **1, 2** crush, grip, nip, press, squeeze, tweak. **4** see STEAL *verb* 1.

pinchbeck /'pɪntʃbek/ *noun* goldlike copper and zinc alloy used in cheap jewellery etc.
● *adjective* spurious, sham.

pine[1] *noun* **1** evergreen needle-leaved coniferous tree. **2** its wood. □ **pine cone** fruit of pine. **pine nut, kernel** edible seed of some pines.

pine[2] *verb* (**-ning**) **1** (often + *away*) waste away with grief, disease, etc. **2** (usually + *for*) long.

■ **1** mope, mourn, waste away. **2** (*pine for*) see WANT *verb* 1.

pineal /'pɪnɪəl/ *adjective* shaped like pine cone. □ **pineal gland, body** conical gland in brain, secreting hormone-like substance.

pineapple /'paɪnæp(ə)l/ *noun* large juicy tropical fruit with yellow flesh and tough skin.

ping *noun* abrupt single ringing sound. ● *verb* (cause to) emit ping.

ping-pong *noun colloquial* table tennis.

pinion[1] /'pɪnjən/ *noun* **1** outer part of bird's wing. **2** *poetical* wing; flight feather. ● *verb* **1** cut off pinion of (wing or bird) to prevent flight. **2** restrain by binding arms to sides.

pinion[2] /'pɪnjən/ *noun* small cogwheel engaging with larger.

pink[1] *noun* **1** pale red colour. **2** garden plant with clove-scented flowers. **3** (**the pink**) the most perfect condition. ● *adjective* **1** pink-coloured. **2** *colloquial* mildly socialist. □ **in the pink** *colloquial* in very good health. □ **pinkish** *adjective*. **pinkness** *noun*.

pink[2] *verb* **1** pierce slightly. **2** cut scalloped or zigzag edge on. □ **pinking shears** dressmaker's serrated shears for cutting zigzag edge.

pink[3] *verb* (of vehicle engine) emit high-pitched explosive sounds caused by faulty combustion.

pinnace /'pɪnɪs/ *noun* ship's small boat.

pinnacle /'pɪnək(ə)l/ *noun* **1** culmination, climax. **2** natural peak. **3** small ornamental turret crowning buttress, roof, etc.

■ **1** apex, apex, climax, consummation, crowning point, culmination, height, peak, summit, top, zenith. **2** apex, cap, crest, crown, peak, summit, tip. **3** spire, steeple, turret.

pinnate /'pɪneɪt/ *adjective* (of compound leaf) with leaflets on each side of leaf-stalk.

pinny /'pɪnɪ/ *noun* (*plural* **-ies**) *colloquial* pinafore.

pint /paɪnt/ *noun* **1** measure of capacity (⅛ gal., 0.568 litre). **2** *colloquial* pint of beer. □ **pint-sized** *colloquial* very small.

pinta /'paɪntə/ *noun colloquial* pint of milk.

pintle /'pɪnt(ə)l/ *noun* bolt or pin, esp. one on which some other part turns.

Pinyin /pɪn'jɪn/ *noun* system of romanized spelling for transliterating Chinese.

pioneer /paɪə'nɪə/ *noun* **1** beginner of enterprise etc. **2** explorer or settler. ● *verb* **1** initiate (enterprise etc.) for others to follow. **2** act as pioneer.

■ *noun* **1** innovator, inventor, originator, trailblazer, trend-setter. **2** colonist, discoverer, explorer, frontiersman, frontierswoman, settler, trailblazer. ● *verb* **1** begin, create, develop, discover, establish, experiment with, found, inaugurate, initiate, institute, introduce, invent, launch, open up, originate, set up, start.

pious /'paɪəs/ *adjective* **1** devout, religious. **2** sanctimonious. **3** dutiful. □ **piously** *adverb*. **piousness** *noun*.

■ **1** dedicated, devoted, devout, faithful, God-fearing, godly, good, holy, moral, religious, reverent, reverential, saintly, sincere, spiritual, virtuous. **2** *colloquial* goody-goody, *colloquial* holier-than-thou, hypocritical, insincere, mealy-mouthed, pietistic, sanctimonious, self-righteous, self-satisfied.

pip[1] *noun* seed of apple, pear, orange, etc.
■ seed, stone.

pip[2] *noun* short high-pitched sound.
■ bleep, blip.

pip[3] *verb* (**-pp-**) **1** *colloquial* hit with a shot. **2** (also **pip at or to the post**) defeat narrowly.

pip[4] *noun* **1** each spot on dominoes, dice, or playing cards. **2** star on army officer's shoulder.

pip[5] *noun* **1** disease of poultry etc. **2** (esp. **the pip**) *colloquial* (fit of) depression, boredom, or bad temper.

pipe *noun* **1** tube of earthenware, metal, etc., esp. for carrying gas, water, etc. **2** narrow tube with bowl at one end containing tobacco for smoking. **3** quantity of tobacco held by this. **4** musical wind instrument of single tube. **6** each tube by which sound is produced in organ. **7** (in *plural*) bagpipes. **8** tubular organ etc. in body. **9** high note or song, esp. of bird. **10** boatswain's whistle. **11**

measure of capacity for wine (105 gals., 477 litres). ● *verb* (**-ping**) **1** convey (as) through pipes. **2** play on pipe. **3** (esp. as **piped** *adjective*) transmit (recorded music etc.) by wire or cable. **4** utter shrilly. **5** summon, lead, etc. by sound of pipe or whistle. **6** trim with piping. **7** furnish with pipe(s). □ **pipeclay** fine white clay for tobacco pipes or for whitening leather etc. **pipe-cleaner** piece of flexible tuft-covered wire to clean inside tobacco pipe. **pipe down** *colloquial* be quiet. **pipe dream** unattainable or fanciful hope or scheme. **pipeline 1** pipe conveying oil etc. across country. **2** channel of supply or communication. **pipe up** begin to speak, play, sing, etc.

> ■ *noun* **1** conduit, channel, duct, hose, line, main, pipeline, piping, tube. ● *verb* **1** channel, convey, deliver, supply, transmit. **2** blow, play, sound, tootle, whistle. □ **pipe up** see SPEAK 1,2.

piper *noun* person who plays on pipe, esp. bagpipes.

pipette /pɪˈpet/ *noun* slender tube for transferring or measuring small quantities of liquid.

piping *noun* **1** ornamentation of dress, upholstery, etc. by means of cord enclosed in pipelike fold. **2** ornamental cordlike lines of sugar etc. on cake etc. **3** length or system of pipes. ● *adjective* shrill. □ **piping hot** (of food, water, etc.) very or suitably hot.

> ■ *adjective* see SHRILL *adjective*. □ **piping hot** see HOT *adjective* 1.

pipit /ˈpɪpɪt/ *noun* small bird resembling lark.

pippin /ˈpɪpɪn/ *noun* **1** apple grown from seed. **2** dessert apple.

piquant /ˈpiːkənt/ *adjective* **1** agreeably pungent, sharp, appetizing. **2** stimulating. □ **piquancy** *noun*.

> ■ **1** appetizing, poignant, pungent, sharp, spicy, tangy, tart, tasty. **2** arresting, exciting, interesting, provocative, stimulating.

pique /piːk/ *verb* (**piques, piqued, piquing**) **1** wound pride of. **2** stir (curiosity). ● *noun* resentment; hurt pride.

piquet /pɪˈket/ *noun* card game for two players.

piracy /ˈpaɪrəsɪ/ *noun* (*plural* **-ies**) activity of pirate.

piranha /pɪˈrɑːnə/ *noun* voracious S. American freshwater fish.

pirate /ˈpaɪrət/ *noun* **1** seafaring robber attacking ships. **2** ship used by pirate. **3** person who infringes copyright or regulations or encroaches on rights of others etc. ● *verb* (**-ting**) reproduce (book etc.) or trade (goods) without permission. □ **piratical** /-ˈræt-/ *adjective*.

> ■ *noun* **1** buccaneer, corsair, privateer. ● *verb* see PLAGIARIZE.

pirouette /pɪrʊˈet/ *noun* dancer's spin on one foot or point of toe. ● *verb* (**-tting**) perform pirouette.

piscatorial /pɪskəˈtɔːrɪəl/ *adjective* of fishing.

Pisces /ˈpaɪsiːz/ *noun* twelfth sign of zodiac.

piscina /pɪˈsiːnə/ *noun* (*plural* **-nae** /-niː/ or **-s**) stone basin near altar in church, for draining water after use.

pistachio /pɪsˈtɑːʃɪəʊ/ *noun* (*plural* **-s**) kind of nut with green kernel.

piste /piːst/ *noun* ski run of compacted snow.

pistil /ˈpɪstɪl/ *noun* female organ in flowers. □ **pistillate** *adjective*.

pistol /ˈpɪst(ə)l/ *noun* small firearm.

piston /ˈpɪst(ə)n/ *noun* **1** sliding cylinder fitting closely in tube and moving up and down in it, used in steam or petrol engine to impart motion. **2** sliding valve in trumpet etc. □ **piston rod** rod connecting piston to other parts of machine.

pit[1] *noun* **1** large hole in ground. **2** covered hole as trap. **3** coal mine. **4** depression in skin or any surface. **5** orchestra pit. **6** (**the pits**) *slang* worst imaginable place, situation, person, etc. **7** area to side of track where racing cars are refuelled etc. during race. **8** sunken area in floor of workshop etc. for inspection or repair of underside of vehicle etc. ● *verb* (**-tt-**) **1** (usually + *against*) set (one's wits, strength, etc.) in competition. **2** (usually as **pitted** *adjective*) make pit(s) in. **3** store in pit. □ **pit bull terrier** small American dog noted for ferocity. **pitfall 1** unsuspected danger or drawback. **2** covered pit as trap. **pithead 1** top of shaft of coal mine. **2** area surrounding this. **pit of the stomach** hollow below base of breastbone.

> ■ *noun* **1** abyss, chasm, crater, depression, ditch, excavation, hole, hollow, pothole, rut, trench, well. **3** coal mine, colliery, mine, quarry, working. ● *verb* **2** (**pitted**) dented, eaten away, eroded, holey, marked, pock-marked, rough, scarred, uneven. □ **pitfall 1** catch, danger, difficulty, hazard, peril, snag, trap.

pit[2] *verb* (**-tt-**) (usually as **pitted** *adjective*) remove stones from (fruit).

pita = PITTA.

pit-a-pat /ˈpɪtəpæt/ (also **pitter-patter** /ˈpɪtəpætə/) *adverb* **1** with sound as of light quick steps. **2** falteringly. ● *noun* such sound.

pitch[1] *verb* **1** set up (esp. tent, camp, etc.) in chosen position. **2** throw. **3** express in particular style or at particular level. **4** fall heavily. **5** (of ship etc.) plunge in lengthwise direction. **6** set at particular musical pitch. ● *noun* **1** area of play in esp. outdoor game. **2** height, degree, intensity, etc. **3** gradient, esp. of roof. **4** *Music* degree of highness or lowness of tone. **5** act or process of pitching. **6** *colloquial* salesman's persuasive talk. **7** place, esp. in street or market, where one is stationed. **8** distance between successive points, lines, etc. □ **pitched battle 1** vigorous argument etc. **2** planned battle between sides in prepared positions. **pitched roof** sloping roof. **pitchfork** ● *noun* fork with long handle and two prongs for tossing hay etc. ● *verb* (+ *into*) thrust forcibly or hastily into office, position, etc. **pitch in** *colloquial* **1** set to work vigorously. **2** cooperate. **pitch into** *colloquial* attack vigorously.

■ *verb* **1** erect, put up, raise, set up. **2** bowl, *slang* bung, cast, *colloquial* chuck, fling, *colloquial* heave, hurl, launch, lob, *colloquial* sling, throw, toss. **4** dive, drop, fall headlong, nosedive, plummet, plunge, topple. **5** see TOSS *verb* 2. ● *noun* **1** arena, ground, playing-field, stadium. **3** angle, gradient, incline, slope, steepness, tilt. □ **pitch in 2** see COOPERATE. **pitch into** see ATTACK *verb* 1.

pitch² *noun* dark resinous tarry substance. ● *verb* coat with pitch. □ **pitch-black, -dark** intensely dark. **pitch pine** resinous kinds of pine. □ **pitchy** *adjective* (**-ier, -iest**).
■ *noun* bitumen, tar.

pitchblende /ˈpɪtʃblend/ *noun* uranium oxide yielding radium.

pitcher¹ /ˈpɪtʃə/ *noun* large jug; ewer.

pitcher² *noun* player who delivers ball in base-ball.

piteous /ˈpɪtɪəs/ *adjective* deserving or arousing pity. □ **piteously** *adverb*. **piteousness** *noun*.
■ affecting, distressing, heartbreaking, heart-rending, lamentable, miserable, moving, pathetic, pitiable, pitiful, plaintive, poignant, sad, touching, woeful, wretched.

pith *noun* **1** spongy tissue in stems of plants or lining rind of orange etc. **2** chief part. **3** vigour, energy. □ **pith helmet** sun-helmet made from dried pith of plants.

pithy /ˈpɪθɪ/ *adjective* (**-ier, -iest**) condensed and forcible, terse. □ **pithily** *adverb*. **pithiness** *noun*.

pitiable /ˈpɪtɪəb(ə)l/ *adjective* deserving or arousing pity or contempt. □ **pitiably** *adverb*.

pitiful /ˈpɪtɪfʊl/ *adjective* **1** arousing pity. **2** contemptible. □ **pitifully** *adverb*.
■ **1** see PITEOUS. **2** abject, contemptible, deplorable, hopeless, inadequate, incompetent, insignificant, laughable, mean, miserable, *colloquial* pathetic, pitiable, ridiculous, sorry, trifling, unimportant, *colloquial* useless, worthless.

pitiless /ˈpɪtɪlɪs/ *adjective* showing no pity. □ **pitilessly** *adverb*.
■ bloodthirsty, brutal, callous, cruel, ferocious, hard, heartless, inexorable, inhuman, merciless, relentless, ruthless, *colloquial* sadistic, unfeeling, unrelenting, unrelieved, unremitting, unsympathetic.

piton /ˈpiːtɒn/ *noun* peg driven in to support climber or rope.

pitta /ˈpɪtə/ *noun* (also **pita**) originally Turkish unleavened bread which can be split and filled.

pittance /ˈpɪt(ə)ns/ *noun* **1** scanty allowance. **2** small amount.

pitter-patter = PIT-A-PAT.

pituitary /pɪˈtjuːɪtərɪ/ *noun* (*plural* **-ies**) (in full **pituitary gland**) small ductless gland at base of brain.

pity /ˈpɪtɪ/ *noun* **1** sorrow for another's suffering. **2** cause for regret. ● *verb* (**-ies, -ied**) feel pity for.

□ **take pity on** feel or act compassionately towards. □ **pitying** *adjective*.
■ *noun* **1** charity, clemency, commiseration, compassion, condolence, feeling, forbearance, forgiveness, grace, humanity, kindness, leniency, love, mercy, regret, softness, sympathy, tenderness, understanding, warmth. ● *verb* commiserate with, feel for, feel sorry for, show pity for, sympathize with, weep for.

pivot /ˈpɪvət/ *noun* **1** shaft or pin on which something turns. **2** crucial person or point. ● *verb* (**-t-**) **1** turn (as) on pivot. **2** provide with pivot. **3** (+ *on*) depend on. □ **pivotal** *adjective*.
■ *noun* **1** axis, axle, centre, fulcrum, gudgeon, hinge, spindle, swivel. **2** centre, heart, hub, kingpin. ● *verb* **1** revolve, rotate, spin, swivel, turn, twirl, whirl. **3** see DEPEND 1.

pixie /ˈpɪksɪ/ *noun* (also **pixy**) (*plural* **-ies**) fairy-like being.

pizza /ˈpiːtsə/ *noun* flat piece of dough baked with topping of cheese, tomatoes, etc.

pizzeria /piːtsəˈriːə/ *noun* pizza restaurant.

pizzicato /pɪtsɪˈkɑːtəʊ/ *Music adverb* plucking. ● *adjective* performed thus. ● *noun* (*plural* **-s** or **-ti** /-tɪ/) pizzicato note or passage.

pl. *abbreviation* **1** plural. **2** place. **3** plate.

placable /ˈplækəb(ə)l/ *adjective* easily appeased; mild-tempered. □ **placability** *noun*.

placard /ˈplækɑːd/ *noun* large notice for public display. ● *verb* post placards on.
■ *noun colloquial* advert, advertisement, bill, notice, poster, sign.

placate /pləˈkeɪt/ *verb* (**-ting**) conciliate, pacify. □ **placatory** *adjective*.
■ appease, calm, conciliate, humour, mollify, pacify, soothe.

place *noun* **1** particular part of space. **2** space or room of or for person etc. **3** city, town, village; country. **4** residence. **5** rank, station, position. **6** building or spot devoted to specified purpose. **7** office, employment. **8** duties of this. ● *verb* (**-cing**) **1** put or dispose in place. **2** assign rank, order, or class to. **3** identify, remember. **4** give (order for goods etc.) to firm etc. **5** (in *passive*) be among first 3 (or 4) in race. □ **in place 1** suitable. **2** in the right position. **in place of** instead of. **out of place 1** unsuitable. **2** in the wrong position. **place-kick** *Football* kick made with ball placed on ground. **place mat** small mat on table at person's place. **place setting** set of cutlery etc. for one person to eat with. **take place** happen. **take the place of** be substituted for. □ **placement** *noun*.
■ *noun* **1** address, area, locale, locality, location, locus, part, point, position, scene, setting, site, situation, spot, venue, whereabouts. **2** chair, position, room, seat, space, spot. **3** area, city, country, district, locale, locality, neighbourhood, part, quarter, region, town, vicinity, village. **4** see HOUSE *noun* 1. **5** condition, grade, niche, position, rank, slot, standing, station, status. **7** *colloquial* billet, function, job, office, position, post, role.

● *verb* **1** deposit, dispose, dump, lay, leave, locate, pinpoint, plant, position, put down, rest, set down, set out, settle, situate, stand, station, *colloquial* stick. **2** arrange, categorize, class, classify, grade, order, position, rank, sort. **3** identify, put a name to, put into context, recognize, remember. □ **take place** see HAPPEN 1.

placebo /pləˈsiːbəʊ/ *noun* (*plural* **-s**) **1** medicine with no physiological effect prescribed for psychological reasons. **2** dummy pill etc. used in controlled trial.

placenta /pləˈsentə/ *noun* (*plural* **-tae** /-tiː/ or **-s**) organ in uterus of pregnant mammal that nourishes foetus. □ **placental** *adjective*.

placid /ˈplæsɪd/ *adjective* **1** calm, unruffled. **2** not easily disturbed. □ **placidity** /pləˈsɪdɪtɪ/ *noun*. **placidly** *adverb*.

■ **1** calm, motionless, peaceful, quiet, tranquil, unruffled, untroubled. **2** collected, composed, cool, equable, even-tempered, imperturbable, level-headed, mild, phlegmatic, restful, sensible, stable, steady, unexcitable.

placket /ˈplækɪt/ *noun* opening or slit in garment, for fastenings or access to pocket.

plagiarize /ˈpleɪdʒəraɪz/ *verb* (also **-ise**) (**-zing** or **-sing**) take and use (another's writings etc.) as one's own. □ **plagiarism** *noun*. **plagiarist** *noun*. **plagiarizer** *noun*.

■ appropriate, borrow, copy, *colloquial* crib, imitate, *colloquial* lift, pirate, *formal* or *jocular* purloin, reproduce, steal.

plague /pleɪɡ/ *noun* **1** deadly contagious disease. **2** (+ *of*) *colloquial* infestation of. **3** great trouble or affliction. ● *verb* (**plaguing**) **1** *colloquial* annoy, bother. **2** afflict, hinder.

■ *noun* **1** contagion, epidemic, infection, pandemic, pestilence. **2** infestation, invasion, scourge, swarm. **3** affliction, bane, blight, calamity, curse, nuisance, tribulation, trouble. ● *verb* **1**, **2** afflict, annoy, be a nuisance to, bother, distress, disturb, harass, harry, hound, irritate, molest, nag, persecute, pester, torment, torture, trouble, vex, worry.

plaice /pleɪs/ *noun* (*plural* same) marine flatfish.

plaid /plæd/ *noun* **1** chequered or tartan, esp. woollen, cloth. **2** long piece of this as part of Highland costume.

plain *adjective* **1** clear; evident. **2** readily understood; simple. **3** not beautiful or distinguished-looking. **4** straightforward in speech. **5** not luxurious or elaborate. ● *adverb* **1** clearly. **2** simply. ● *noun* **1** level tract of country. **2** ordinary stitch in knitting. □ **plain chocolate** chocolate made without milk. **plain clothes** ordinary clothes as distinct from esp. police uniform. **plain flour** flour with no raising agent. **plain sailing** simple situation or course of action. **plainsong** traditional church music sung in unison in medieval modes and free rhythm. **plain-spoken** frank. □ **plainly** *adverb*. **plainness** *noun*.

■ *adjective* **1**, **2** apparent, audible, certain, clear, comprehensible, definite, distinct, evident, intelligible, legible, lucid, manifest, obvious, patent, simple, transparent, unambiguous, understandable, unmistakable, visible, well defined. **3** *US* homely, ugly, unattractive, unprepossessing. **4** blunt, candid, direct, downright, explicit, forthright, frank, honest, informative, outspoken, plain-spoken, prosaic, sincere, straightforward, unequivocal, unvarnished. **5** austere, drab, everyday, frugal, homely, modest, ordinary, simple, Spartan, stark, unadorned, undecorated, unexciting, unpretentious, unremarkable, workaday. ● *noun* **1** grassland, pampas, pasture, prairie, savannah, steppe, tundra, *South African* veld.

plaint *noun* **1** *Law* accusation; charge. **2** *literary* lamentation.

plaintiff /ˈpleɪntɪf/ *noun* person who brings case against another in law court.

plaintive /ˈpleɪntɪv/ *adjective* mournful-sounding. □ **plaintively** *adverb*.

■ doleful, melancholy, mournful, *literary* plangent, sad, sorrowful, wistful.

plait /plæt/ *noun* length of hair, straw, etc. in 3 or more interlaced strands. ● *verb* form into plait.

plan *noun* **1** method or procedure for doing something. **2** drawing exhibiting relative position and size of parts of building etc.; diagram. **3** map (of district, town, etc.). ● *verb* (**-nn-**) **1** arrange beforehand; scheme; intend. **2** make plan of; design. **3** (as **planned** *adjective*) in accordance with plan. **4** make plans. □ **plan on** (often + *present participle*) *colloquial* aim at; intend. □ **planning** *noun*.

■ *noun* **1** aim, course of action, design, formula, idea, intention, method, plot, policy, procedure, programme, project, proposal, proposition, scenario, scheme, strategy, system. **2** bird's-eye view, blueprint, chart, design, diagram, drawing, layout, representation. **3** chart, map, sketch map. ● *verb* **1** aim, arrange, conspire, contemplate, contrive, envisage, expect, intend, mean, organize, plot, prepare, propose, scheme, think of. **2** contrive, design, devise, draw up, formulate, invent, map out, mastermind, outline, think out, work out. **3** (**planned**) see DELIBERATE *adjective* 1. □ **planning** arrangement, design, drafting, forethought, organization, preparation, setting up, thinking out.

planchette /plɑːnˈʃet/ *noun* small board on castors, with pencil, said to write messages from spirits when person's fingers rest on it.

plane[1] *noun* **1** flat surface (not necessarily horizontal). **2** *colloquial* aeroplane. **3** level of attainment etc. ● *adjective* level as or lying in a plane.

■ *noun* **1** flat, level, surface. ● *adjective* even, flat, flush, level, smooth, uniform.

plane[2] *noun* tool for smoothing surface of wood by paring shavings from it. ● *verb* (**-ning**) smooth or pare with plane.

plane[3] *noun* tall spreading broad-leaved tree.

planet /'plænɪt/ *noun* heavenly body orbiting star. □ **planetary** *adjective*.

planetarium /plænɪ'teərɪəm/ *noun* (*plural* **-s** or **-ria**) **1** building in which image of night sky as seen at various times and places is projected. **2** device for such projection.

plangent /'plændʒ(ə)nt/ *adjective literary* **1** loudly reverberating. **2** lamenting; plaintive.

plank *noun* **1** long flat piece of timber. **2** item of political or other programme. ● *verb* **1** provide or cover with planks. **2** (usually + *down*) *esp. US colloquial* put down roughly. **3** (usually + *down*) *esp. US colloquial* deposit (esp. money).
■ *noun* **1** beam, board, timber.

plankton /'plæŋkt(ə)n/ *noun* chiefly microscopic organisms drifting in sea or fresh water.

planner *noun* **1** person who plans new town etc. **2** person who makes plans. **3** list, table, chart, etc. with information helpful in planning.

plant /plɑːnt/ *noun* **1** organism capable of living wholly on inorganic substances and lacking power of locomotion. **2** small plant (other than trees and shrubs). **3** equipment for industrial process. **4** factory. **5** *colloquial* thing deliberately placed for discovery, esp. to incriminate another. ● *verb* **1** place (seed etc.) in ground to grow. **2** fix firmly, establish; place in position. **3** cause (idea etc.) to be established, esp. in another person's mind. **4** deliver (blow etc.). **5** *colloquial* place (something incriminating) for later discovery.
■ *noun* **1, 2** (*plants*) flora, greenery, growth, vegetation. **3** apparatus, equipment, machinery, machines. **4** factory, foundry, mill, shop, works, workshop. ● *verb* **1** bed out, sow, transplant. **2** locate, place, position, put, situate, station.

plantain[1] /'plæntɪn/ *noun* herb yielding seed used as food for birds.

plantain[2] /'plæntɪn/ *noun* **1** plant related to banana. **2** banana-like fruit of this.

plantation /plɑːn'teɪʃ(ə)n/ *noun* **1** estate for cultivation of cotton, tobacco, etc. **2** number of growing plants, esp. trees, planted together. **3** *historical* colony.

planter *noun* **1** owner or manager of plantation. **2** container for house-plants.

plaque /plæk/ *noun* **1** ornamental tablet of metal, porcelain, etc. **2** deposit on teeth, where bacteria proliferate.

plasma /'plæzmə/ *noun* (also **plasm** /'plæz(ə)m/) **1** colourless fluid part of blood etc. in which corpuscles etc. float. **2** protoplasm. **3** gas of positive ions and free electrons in about equal numbers. □ **plasmic** *adjective*.

plaster /'plɑːstə/ *noun* **1** mixture esp. of lime, sand, and water spread on walls etc. **2** sticking plaster. **3** plaster of Paris. ● *verb* **1** cover with or like plaster. **2** apply, stick, etc. like plaster to. **3** (as **plastered** *adjective*) *slang* drunk. □ **plasterboard** two boards with core of plaster used for walls etc. **plaster cast** bandage stiffened with plaster of Paris and wrapped round broken limb etc. **plaster of Paris** fine white gypsum powder for plaster casts etc. □ **plasterer** *noun*.
■ *noun* **1** mortar, stucco. **2** dressing, sticking plaster. ● *verb* **1, 2** apply, bedaub, coat, cover, daub, smear, spread.

plastic /'plæstɪk/ *noun* **1** synthetic resinous substance that can be given any shape. **2** (in full **plastic money**) *colloquial* credit card(s). ● *adjective* **1** made of plastic. **2** capable of being moulded. **3** giving form to clay, wax, etc. □ **plastic arts** those involving modelling. **plastic explosive** putty-like explosive. **plastic surgery** repair or restoration of lost or damaged etc. tissue. □ **plasticity** /-'tɪs-/ *noun*. **plasticize** /-saɪz/ *verb* (also **-ise**) (**-zing** or **-sing**). **plasticky** *adjective*.
■ *adjective* **2** ductile, flexible, malleable, pliable, shapable, soft, supple, workable.

Plasticine /'plæstəsiːn/ *noun proprietary term* pliant substance used for modelling.

plate *noun* **1** shallow usually circular vessel from which food is eaten or served. **2** similar vessel used for collection in church etc. **3** table utensils of gold, silver, or other metal. **4** objects of plated metal. **5** piece of metal with inscription, for fixing to door etc. **6** illustration on special paper in book. **7** thin sheet of metal, glass, etc. coated with sensitive film for photography. **8** flat thin sheet of metal etc. **9** part of denture fitting to mouth and holding teeth. **10** each of several sheets of rock thought to form earth's crust. ● *verb* (**-ting**) **1** cover (other metal) with thin coating of silver, gold, etc. **2** cover with plates of metal. □ **plate glass** thick fine-quality glass for mirrors, windows, etc. **platelayer** workman laying and repairing railway lines. □ **plateful** *noun* (*plural* **-s**).
■ *noun* **1** dinner plate, dish, platter, salver, *historical* trencher. **5** plaque, slab, tablet. **6** illustration, photo, photograph, picture, print. **8** lamina, layer, leaf, pane, panel, sheet, slab. ● *verb* **1** anodize, coat, cover, electroplate, galvanize (*with zinc*), gild (*with gold*).

plateau /'plætəʊ/ *noun* (*plural* **-x** or **-s** /-z/) **1** area of level high ground. **2** state of little variation following an increase. ● *verb* (**plateaus**, **plateaued**, **plateauing**) (often + *out*) reach level or static state after period of increase.

platelet /'pleɪtlɪt/ *noun* small disc in blood, involved in clotting.

platen /'plæt(ə)n/ *noun* **1** plate in printing press by which paper is pressed against type. **2** corresponding part in typewriter etc.

platform /'plætfɔːm/ *noun* **1** raised level surface, esp. one from which speaker addresses audience, or one along side of line at railway station. **2** floor area at entrance to bus etc. **3** thick sole of shoe. **4** declared policy of political party.
■ **1** dais, podium, rostrum, stage, stand. **4** see POLICY[1] 1.

platinum /'plætɪnəm/ *noun* white heavy precious metallic element that does not tarnish.

□ **platinum blonde** *adjective* silvery-blond.
● *noun* person with such hair.

platitude /'plætɪtjuːd/ *noun* commonplace remark. □ **platitudinous** /-'tjuːd-/ *adjective*.
▮ banality, cliché, commonplace, truism.

Platonic /plə'tɒnɪk/ *adjective* **1** of Plato or his philosophy. **2** (**platonic**) (of love or friendship) not sexual.

platoon /plə'tuːn/ *noun* subdivision of infantry company.

platter /'plætə/ *noun* flat plate or dish.

platypus /'plætɪpəs/ *noun* (*plural* **-puses**) Australian aquatic egg-laying mammal with duck-like beak.

plaudit /'plɔːdɪt/ *noun* (usually in *plural*) **1** round of applause. **2** commendation.

plausible /'plɔːzɪb(ə)l/ *adjective* **1** reasonable, probable. **2** (of person) persuasive but deceptive. □ **plausibility** *noun*. **plausibly** *adverb*.
▮ **1** acceptable, believable, conceivable, credible, imaginable, likely, logical, possible, probable, rational, reasonable, sensible, tenable, thinkable. **2** deceptive, glib, meretricious, misleading, persuasive, specious, smooth, sophistical.

play *verb* **1** occupy or amuse oneself pleasantly. **2** (+ *with*) act light-heartedly or flippantly with (feelings etc.). **3** perform on (musical instrument). **4** perform (piece of music etc.). **5** cause (record etc.) to produce sounds. **6** perform (drama, role). **7** (+ *on*) perform (trick or joke etc.) on. **8** *colloquial* cooperate; do what is wanted. **9** take part in game. **10** have as opponent in game. **11** move (piece) in game, put (card) on table, strike (ball), etc. **12** move about in lively or unrestrained way. **13** (often + *on*) touch gently. **14** pretend to be. **15** allow (fish) to exhaust itself pulling against line. ● *noun* **1** recreation; amusement. **2** playing of game. **3** dramatic piece for stage etc. **4** freedom of movement. **5** fitful or light movement. **6** gambling. □ **play about 1** behave irresponsibly. **2** flirt. **play-act 1** act in play. **2** behave insincerely or affectedly. **play along** pretend to cooperate. **play back** play (what has been recorded). **playback** *noun*. **play ball** *colloquial* cooperate. **playbill** poster announcing play etc. **playboy** pleasure-seeking usually wealthy man. **play by ear 1** perform (music) without having seen it written down. **2** (also **play it by ear**) *colloquial* proceed gradually according to results. **play one's cards right** *colloquial* make best use of opportunities and advantages. **play down** minimize. **playfellow** playmate. **play for time** seek to gain time by delaying. **play the game** behave honourably. **playground** outdoor area for children to play in. **playgroup** group of preschool children who play together under supervision. **playhouse** theatre. **playing card** small usually oblong card used in games, one of set of usually 52 divided into 4 suits. **play it cool** *colloquial* appear relaxed or indifferent. **playmate** child's companion in play. **play-off** extra match played to decide draw or tie. **play the market** speculate in stocks etc. **plaything** toy. **play up 1** behave mischievously. **2** annoy in this

way. **3** cause trouble. **4** emphasize. **play up to** flatter. **play with fire** take foolish risks. **playwright** dramatist.
▮ *verb* **1** amuse oneself, caper, cavort, disport oneself, enjoy oneself, fool about, frisk, frolic, gambol, have a good time, have fun, mess about, romp, sport. **3** perform on, strum. **5** listen to, operate, put on, switch on. **6** act, depict, impersonate, perform, portray, pretend to be, represent, take the part of. **9** join in, participate, take part. **10** challenge, compete against, oppose, rival, take on, vie with. ● *noun* **1** amusement, diversion, entertainment, frivolity, fun, horseplay, joking, make-believe, merrymaking, pretending, recreation, revelry, skylarking, sport. **3** see DRAMA 1. **4** flexibility, freedom, give, latitude, leeway, looseness, movement, tolerance. □ **play about 1** see MISBEHAVE. **play along, play ball** see COOPERATE. **play by ear 2** see IMPROVISE 1. **play down** see MINIMIZE 2. **play for time** see DELAY *verb* 3. **play up 1** see MISBEHAVE. **play up to** see FLATTER 1.

player *noun* **1** person playing sport. **2** actor. **3** person playing musical instrument.
▮ **1** competitor, contestant, participant, sportsman, sportsperson, sportswoman. **2** actor, actress, artist, artiste, entertainer, Thespian, trouper. **3** instrumentalist, musician, performer, soloist.

playful *adjective* **1** fond of or inclined to play. **2** done in fun. □ **playfully** *adverb*. **playfulness** *noun*.
▮ **1** active, cheerful, coltish, flirtatious, frisky, frolicsome, fun-loving, good-natured, high-spirited, impish, kittenish, light-hearted, lively, mischievous, puckish, roguish, skittish, spirited, sportive, sprightly, vivacious, waggish. **2** facetious, humorous, jesting, jokey, joking, teasing, tongue-in-cheek.

playing field *noun* field used for outdoor team games.

plc *abbreviation* (also **PLC**) Public Limited Company.

plea *noun* **1** appeal, entreaty. **2** *Law* formal statement by or on behalf of defendant. **3** excuse.
▮ **1** appeal, entreaty, invocation, petition, prayer, request, solicitation, *literary* supplication. **3** argument, excuse, explanation, justification, pretext, reason.

pleach *verb* entwine or interlace (esp. branches to form a hedge).

plead *verb* **1** (+ *with*) make earnest appeal to. **2** address court as advocate or party. **3** allege as excuse. **4** (+ *guilty*, *not guilty*) declare oneself to be guilty or not guilty of a charge. **5** make appeal or entreaty.
▮ **1** (**plead with**) appeal to, ask, beg, beseech, entreat, implore, importune, petition, request, solicit, *literary* supplicate. **3** allege, argue, assert, *formal* aver, declare, maintain, reason, *colloquial* swear. **5** (**plead for**) appeal for, ask for, beg for, cry out for, demand, request, seek, solicit, *literary* supplicate (for).

pleading noun (usually in plural) formal statement of cause of action or defence.

pleasant /'plez(ə)nt/ adjective (-er, -est) agreeable; giving pleasure. □ **pleasantly** adverb.
■ acceptable, affable, agreeable, amiable, approachable, attractive, balmy, beautiful, charming, cheerful, congenial, decent, delicious, delightful, enjoyable, entertaining, excellent, fine, friendly, genial, gentle, good, gratifying, heavenly, hospitable, kind, likeable, colloquial lovely, mellow, mild, nice, palatable, peaceful, pleasing, pleasurable, pretty, reassuring, relaxed, satisfying, soothing, sympathetic, warm, welcome, welcoming.

pleasantry noun (plural -ies) joking remark; polite remark.

please /pli:z/ verb (-sing) 1 be agreeable to; give joy or gratification to. 2 think fit; want, desire. 3 (in passive) be willing; like. 4 used in polite requests. □ **pleased** adjective. **pleasing** adjective.
■ 1 amuse, cheer up, content, delight, divert, entertain, give pleasure to, gladden, gratify, humour, satisfy, suit. 2 like, see fit, think fit, want, wish. 3 (be pleased) be delighted, be glad, be happy, be willing, like. □ **pleased** slang chuffed, complacent, contented, delighted, elated, euphoric, glad, grateful, gratified, happy, over the moon, satisfied, thankful, thrilled. **pleasing** see PLEASANT.

pleasurable /'pleʒərəb(ə)l/ adjective causing pleasure. □ **pleasurably** adverb.

pleasure /'pleʒə/ noun 1 satisfaction, delight. 2 sensuous enjoyment. 3 source of gratification. 4 will, choice. ● adjective done or used for pleasure.
■ 1, 2 bliss, comfort, contentment, delight, ecstasy, enjoyment, euphoria, fulfilment, gladness, gratification, happiness, joy, rapture, satisfaction, solace. 3 amusement, comfort, delight, diversion, entertainment, fun, joy, luxury, recreation, self-indulgence, solace.

pleat noun flattened fold in cloth etc. ● verb make pleat(s) in.
■ noun crease, flute, fold, gather, tuck.

pleb noun colloquial plebeian.

plebeian /plɪ'bi:ən/ noun 1 commoner, esp. in ancient Rome. 2 working-class person (esp. uncultured). ● adjective 1 of the common people. 2 uncultured, coarse.

plebiscite /'plebɪsaɪt/ noun referendum.
■ ballot, poll, referendum, vote.

plectrum /'plektrəm/ noun (plural -s or -tra) thin flat piece of plastic etc. for plucking strings of musical instrument.

pledge noun 1 solemn promise. 2 thing given as security for payment of debt etc. 3 thing put in pawn. 4 token. 5 drinking of health. ● verb (-ging) 1 deposit as security. 2 pawn. 3 promise solemnly by pledge. 4 bind by solemn promise. 5 drink to the health of.

■ noun 1 assurance, covenant, guarantee, oath, pact, promise, undertaking, vow, warranty, word. 2 bail, bond, collateral, deposit, pawn, security, surety. ● verb 3 agree, commit oneself, contract, give one's word, guarantee, promise, swear, undertake, vouch, formal vouchsafe, vow.

Pleiades /'plaɪədi:z/ plural noun cluster of stars in constellation Taurus.

plenary /'pli:nərɪ/ adjective 1 (of assembly) to be attended by all members. 2 entire, unqualified.
■ 1 full, general, open.

plenipotentiary /plenɪpə'tenʃərɪ/ noun (plural -ies) person (esp. diplomat) having full authority to act. ● adjective having such power.

plenitude /'plenɪtju:d/ noun literary 1 fullness. 2 completeness. 3 abundance.

plenteous /'plentɪəs/ adjective literary plentiful.

plentiful /'plentɪfʊl/ adjective existing in ample quantity. □ **plentifully** adverb. **plentifulness** noun.
■ abounding, abundant, ample, poetical bounteous, bountiful, bumper (crop), copious, generous, inexhaustible, lavish, liberal, overflowing, literary plenteous, profuse, prolific.

plenty /'plentɪ/ noun 1 abundance. 2 quite enough. ● adjective colloquial plentiful. ● adverb colloquial fully.
■ noun 1 abundance, affluence, cornucopia, excess, fertility, flood, fruitfulness, glut, colloquial heaps, colloquial lashings, loads, colloquial a lot, colloquial lots, masses, much, colloquial oceans, colloquial oodles, colloquial piles, literary plenitude, plentifulness, plethora, prodigality, profusion, prosperity, quantities, colloquial stacks, superabundance, surfeit, surplus, colloquial tons, wealth. 2 adequacy, sufficiency.

plenum /'pli:nəm/ noun full assembly of people or a committee etc.

pleonasm /'pli:ənæz(ə)m/ noun use of more words than are needed. □ **pleonastic** /-'næstɪk/ adjective.

plesiosaur /'pli:sɪəsɔ:/ noun large extinct reptile with flippers and long neck.

plethora /'pleθərə/ noun over-abundance.

pleurisy /'plʊərəsɪ/ noun inflammation of membrane enclosing lungs. □ **pleuritic** /-'rɪt-/ adjective.

plexus /'pleksəs/ noun (plural same or **plexuses**) network of nerves or blood vessels.

pliable /'plaɪəb(ə)l/ adjective 1 easily bent; supple. 2 easily influenced; compliant. □ **pliability** noun.
■ 1 bendable, colloquial bendy, ductile, flexible, plastic, pliant, springy, supple. 2 adaptable, compliant, docile, impressionable, malleable, manageable, persuadable, receptive, responsive, suggestible, susceptible, tractable, yielding.

pliant /'plaɪənt/ adjective pliable. □ **pliancy** noun.

pliers /'plaɪəz/ *plural noun* pincers with parallel flat surfaces for bending wire etc.

plight[1] /plaɪt/ *noun* unfortunate condition or state.

plight[2] /plaɪt/ *verb archaic* pledge. □ **plight one's troth** promise to marry.

plimsoll /'plɪms(ə)l/ *noun* rubber-soled canvas shoe. □ **Plimsoll line, mark** marking on ship's side showing limit of legal submersion under various conditions.

plinth *noun* base supporting column, vase, statue, etc.

plod *verb* (**-dd-**) **1** walk laboriously. **2** work steadily or laboriously. □ **plodder** *noun*.

■ **1** slog, tramp, trudge. **2** drudge, labour, peg away, persevere, *colloquial* plug away, slave away, toil, work.

plonk[1] *verb* **1** set down hurriedly or clumsily. **2** (usually + *down*) set down firmly. ● *noun* heavy thud.

plonk[2] *noun colloquial* cheap or inferior wine.

plop *noun* sound as of smooth object dropping into water. ● *verb* (**-pp-**) (cause to) fall with plop. ● *adverb* with a plop.

plot *noun* **1** small piece of land. **2** plan or interrelationship of main events of tale, play, etc. **3** secret plan; conspiracy. ● *verb* (**-tt-**) **1** make chart, diagram, graph, etc. of. **2** hatch secret plans. **3** devise secretly. **4** mark on chart or diagram. □ **plotter** *noun*.

■ *noun* **1** acreage, allotment, area, estate, garden, *esp. US* lot, parcel, patch, smallholding, tract. **2** narrative, scenario, story, storyline. **3** cabal, conspiracy, intrigue, machination, plan, scheme. ● *verb* **1** chart, draw, map out, mark, outline. **2** collude, conspire, have designs, intrigue, machinate, scheme. **3** arrange, brew, conceive, concoct, *colloquial* cook up, design, devise, dream up, hatch.

plough /plaʊ/ (*US* **plow**) *noun* **1** implement for furrowing and turning up soil. ● *verb* **1** (often + *up, out*, etc.) turn up or extract with plough. **2** furrow; make (furrow). **3** (+ *through*) advance laboriously or cut or force way through. **4** *colloquial* fail in exam. □ **plough back** reinvest (profits) in business. **ploughman** user of plough. **ploughman's lunch** meal of bread, cheese, pickles, etc. **ploughshare** blade of plough.

plover /'plʌvə/ *noun* plump-breasted wading bird.

plow *US* = PLOUGH.

ploy *noun* manoeuvre to gain advantage.

pluck *verb* **1** pick or pull out or away. **2** strip (bird) of feathers. **3** pull at, twitch. **4** (+ *at*) tug or snatch at. **5** sound (string of musical instrument) with finger or plectrum. ● *noun* **1** courage. **2** twitch. **3** animal's heart, liver, and lungs. □ **pluck up** summon up (one's courage etc.).

■ *verb* **1** collect, gather, harvest, pick, pull off, pull out, remove. **2** denude, strip. **3** jerk, pull at, tweak, twitch, *colloquial* yank. **4** (*pluck at*) grab at, pull at, snatch at, tug at. ● *noun* **1** see COURAGE.

plucky *adjective* (**-ier, -iest**) brave, spirited.

plug *noun* **1** something fitting into hole or filling cavity. **2** device of metal pins etc. for making electrical connection. **3** spark plug. **4** *colloquial* piece of free publicity. **5** cake or stick of tobacco. ● *verb* (**-gg-**) **1** (often + *up*) stop with plug. **2** *slang* shoot. **3** *colloquial* seek to popularize by frequent recommendation. □ **plug away** (often + *at*) *colloquial* work steadily. **plughole** hole for plug, esp. in sink or bath. **plug in** connect electrically by inserting plug into socket. **plug-in** *adjective* designed to be plugged into socket. **pull the plug** *colloquial* **1** flush toilet. **2** (+ *on*) put an end to by withdrawing resources etc.

■ *noun* **1** bung, cork, stopper. **4** see ADVERTISEMENT 1. ● *verb* **1** block up, bung up, close, cork, fill, jam, seal, stop up. **3** advertise, commend, promote, publicize, puff, recommend. □ **plug away** see WORK *verb* 1.

plum *noun* **1** roundish fleshy stone fruit. **2** tree bearing this. **3** reddish-purple colour. **4** raisin. **5** *colloquial* prized thing. □ **plum pudding** Christmas pudding.

plumage /'pluːmɪdʒ/ *noun* bird's feathers.

plumb /plʌm/ *noun* lead ball attached to line for testing water's depth or whether wall etc. is vertical. ● *adverb* **1** exactly. **2** vertically. **3** *US slang* quite, utterly. ● *adjective* vertical. ● *verb* **1** provide with plumbing. **2** fit as part of plumbing system. **3** work as plumber. **4** test with plumb. **5** experience (extreme feeling). **6** learn detailed facts about. □ **plumb line** string with plumb attached.

■ *adverb* **1** accurately, dead, exactly, precisely, slap. **2** perpendicularly, vertically. ● *verb* **4** fathom, measure, penetrate, probe, sound.

plumber *noun* person who fits and repairs apparatus of water supply, heating, etc.

plumbing *noun* **1** system or apparatus of water supply etc. **2** plumber's work.

■ **1** heating system, pipes, water supply.

plume /pluːm/ *noun* **1** feather, esp. large and showy one. **2** feathery ornament in hat, hair, etc. **3** feather-like formation, esp. of smoke. ● *verb* (**-ming**) **1** furnish with plume(s). **2** (**plume oneself on, upon**) pride oneself on.

■ *noun* **1** feather, quill; (*plumes*) plumage.

plummet /'plʌmɪt/ *noun* **1** plumb; plumb line. **2** sounding line. ● *verb* (**-t-**) fall rapidly.

plummy *adjective* (**-ier, -iest**) **1** rich in plums. **2** *colloquial* (of voice) affectedly rich in tone. **3** *colloquial* good, desirable.

plump[1] *adjective* having full rounded shape; fleshy. ● *verb* (often + *up, out*) make or become plump. □ **plumpness** *noun*.

■ *adjective* ample, buxom, chubby, dumpy, fat, fleshy, overweight, podgy, portly, *colloquial* pudgy, roly-poly, rotund, round, squat, stout, tubby.

plump[2] *verb* (+ *for*) decide on, choose. ● *noun* abrupt or heavy fall. ● *adverb colloquial* with plump.

■ *verb* (*plump for*) see CHOOSE 1.

plunder /'plʌndə/ *verb* **1** rob or steal, esp. in war. **2** embezzle. ● *noun* **1** plundering. **2** property plundered. □ **plunderer** *noun*.

■ *verb* **1** capture, despoil, devastate, lay waste, loot, maraud, pillage, raid, ransack, ravage, rifle, rob, sack, seize, steal from, strip, vandalize. ● *noun* **2** booty, contraband, loot, pickings, pillage, prize, spoils, *slang* swag, takings.

plunge *verb* (**-ging**) **1** (usually + *in*, *into*) thrust forcefully. **2** (usually + *in*, *into*) dive. **3** immerse completely. **4** (cause to) enter into impetuously; (cause to) enter certain state of mind. **5** move suddenly downward. **6** move with a rush. **7** *colloquial* run up gambling debts. ● *noun* **1** plunging; dive. **2** decisive step.

■ *verb* **1** force, push, stick, thrust. **2, 5** descend, dip, dive, drop, fall, fall headlong, jump, leap, lower, nosedive, pitch, plummet, swoop, tumble. **3** engulf, immerse, sink, submerge. **6** charge, dash, hurtle, rush, tear.

plunger *noun* **1** part of mechanism that works with plunging or thrusting motion. **2** rubber cup on handle for removing blockages by plunging action.

pluperfect /plu:'pɜ:fɪkt/ *Grammar adjective* expressing action completed prior to some past point of time. ● *noun* pluperfect tense.

plural /'plʊər(ə)l/ *adjective* **1** more than one in number. **2** denoting more than one. ● *noun* plural word, form, or number.

pluralism *noun* **1** form of society in which minority groups retain independent traditions. **2** holding of more than one office at a time. □ **pluralist** *noun*. **pluralistic** /-'lɪst-/ *adjective*.

plurality /plʊə'rælɪtɪ/ *noun* (*plural* **-ies**) **1** state of being plural. **2** pluralism. **3** large number. **4** non-absolute majority (of votes etc.).

pluralize *verb* (also **-ise**) (**-zing** or **-sing**) **1** make plural. **2** express as plural.

plus *preposition* **1** with addition of. **2** (of temperature) above zero. **3** *colloquial* having gained. ● *adjective* **1** (after number) at least. **2** (after grade) better than. **3** *Mathematics* positive. **4** additional, extra. ● *noun* **1** plus sign. **2** advantage. □ **plus sign** symbol (+) indicating addition or positive value.

USAGE The use of *plus* as a conjunction, as in *they arrived late, plus they wanted a meal*, is considered incorrect except in very informal use.

plush *noun* cloth of silk, cotton, etc., with long soft pile. ● *adjective* **1** made of plush. **2** *colloquial* plushy.

plushy *adjective* (**-ier**, **-iest**) *colloquial* stylish, luxurious.

plutocracy /plu:'tɒkrəsɪ/ *noun* (*plural* **-ies**) **1** state in which power belongs to rich. **2** wealthy elite. □ **plutocrat** /'plu:təkræt/ *noun*. **plutocratic** /-tə'kræt-/ *adjective*.

plutonium /plu:'təʊnɪəm/ *noun* radioactive metallic element.

pluvial /'plu:vɪəl/ *adjective* of or caused by rain.

ply[1] /plaɪ/ *noun* (*plural* **-ies**) **1** thickness, layer. **2** strand.

ply[2] /plaɪ/ *verb* (**-ies**, **-ied**) **1** wield. **2** work at. **3** (+ *with*) supply continuously or approach repeatedly with. **4** (often + *between*) (of vehicle etc.) go to and fro.

plywood *noun* strong thin board made by gluing layers of wood with the direction of the grain alternating.

PM *abbreviation* prime minister.

p.m. *abbreviation* after noon (*post meridiem*).

PMS *abbreviation* premenstrual syndrome.

PMT *abbreviation* premenstrual tension.

pneumatic /nju:'mætɪk/ *adjective* **1** filled with air or wind. **2** operated by compressed air.

pneumonia /nju:'məʊnɪə/ *noun* inflammation of lung(s).

PO *abbreviation* **1** Post Office. **2** postal order. **3** Petty Officer. **4** Pilot Officer.

po *noun* (*plural* **-s**) *colloquial* chamber pot. □ **po-faced 1** solemn-faced, humourless. **2** smug.

poach[1] *verb* **1** cook (egg) without shell in boiling water. **2** cook (fish etc.) by simmering in small amount of liquid. □ **poacher** *noun*.

poach[2] *verb* **1** catch (game or fish) illicitly. **2** (often + *on*) trespass; encroach. **3** appropriate (another's ideas, staff, etc.). □ **poacher** *noun*.

■ **1** hunt, steal. **3** see STEAL *verb* 1.

pock *noun* (also **pock-mark**) small pus-filled spot, esp. in smallpox. □ **pock-marked** *adjective*.

pocket /'pɒkɪt/ *noun* **1** small bag sewn into or on garment for carrying small articles. **2** pouchlike compartment in suitcase, car door, etc. **3** financial resources. **4** isolated group or area. **5** cavity in earth etc. containing ore. **6** pouch at corner or on side of billiard or snooker table into which balls are driven. ● *adjective* small, esp. small enough for carrying in pocket. ● *verb* (**-t-**) **1** put into pocket. **2** appropriate. **3** submit to (affront etc.). **4** conceal (feelings). □ **in or out of pocket** having gained or lost in transaction. **pocket-book 1** notebook. **2** folding case for papers, paper money, etc. **pocket knife** small folding knife. **pocket money** money for minor expenses, esp. given to child.

■ *noun* **1** bag, container, pouch, receptacle. ● *verb* **2** see TAKE *verb* 10.

pod *noun* long seed vessel, esp. of pea or bean. ● *verb* (**-dd-**) **1** form pods. **2** remove (peas etc.) from pods.

■ *noun* case, hull, shell.

podgy /'pɒdʒɪ/ *adjective* (**-ier**, **-iest**) short and fat.

podium /'pəʊdɪəm/ *noun* (*plural* **-s** or **podia**) rostrum.

poem /'pəʊɪm/ *noun* **1** metrical composition. **2** elevated composition in verse or prose. **3** something with poetic qualities.

■ **1** ballad, eclogue, elegy, epic, haiku, lay, limerick, lyric, ode, pastoral, rhyme, sonnet, verse.

poesy /'pəʊəzɪ/ *noun archaic* poetry.

poet /'pəʊɪt/ *noun* (*feminine* **poetess**) writer of poems. □ **Poet Laureate** poet appointed to write poems for state occasions.
  ■ bard, lyricist, minstrel, poetaster, rhymer, versifier.

poetaster /pəʊɪ'tæstə/ *noun* inferior poet.

poetic /pəʊ'etɪk/ *adjective* (also **poetical**) of or like poetry or poets. □ **poetic justice** well-deserved punishment or reward. **poetic licence** departure from truth etc. for effect. □ **poetically** *adverb*.
  ■ emotive, flowery, imaginative, lyrical, metrical, musical.

poetry /'pəʊɪtrɪ/ *noun* **1** poet's art or work. **2** poems. **3** poetic or tenderly pleasing quality.

pogo /'pəʊgəʊ/ *noun* (*plural* **-s**) (also **pogo stick**) stiltlike toy with spring, used to jump about on.

pogrom /'pɒgrəm/ *noun* organized massacre (originally of Jews in Russia).

poignant /'pɔɪnjənt/ *adjective* **1** painfully sharp; deeply moving. **2** arousing sympathy. **3** pleasantly piquant. □ **poignance** *noun*. **poignancy** *noun*. **poignantly** *adverb*.
  ■ **1, 2** affecting, distressing, heartbreaking, heartfelt, heart-rending, moving, painful, pathetic, piteous, pitiful, sad, stirring, tender, touching, upsetting. **3** see PIQUANT 1.

poinsettia /pɔɪn'setɪə/ *noun* plant with large scarlet bracts surrounding small yellowish flowers.

point *noun* **1** sharp end; tip. **2** geometric entity with position but no magnitude. **3** particular place. **4** precise moment. **5** very small mark on surface. **6** decimal point. **7** stage or degree in progress or increase. **8** single item or particular. **9** unit of scoring in games etc., or in evaluation etc. **10** significant or essential thing; thing actually intended or under discussion. **11** sense, purpose, advantage. **12** characteristic. **13** each of 32 directions marked on compass. **14** (usually in *plural*) pair of tapering movable rails to direct train from one line to another. **15** power point. **16** *Cricket* (position of) fielder near batsman on off side. **17** promontory. ● *verb* **1** (usually + *to*, *at*) direct (finger, weapon, etc.). **2** direct attention. **3** (+ *at*, *towards*) aim or be directed to. **4** (+ *to*) indicate; be evidence of. **5** give force to (words, action). **6** fill joints of (brickwork) with smoothed mortar or cement. **7** (of dog) indicate presence of game by acting as pointer. □ **at or on the point of** on the verge of. **beside the point** irrelevant. **point-blank 1** at close range. **2** directly, flatly. **point duty** traffic control by police officer. **point of view 1** position from which thing is viewed. **2** way of considering a matter. **point out** indicate; draw attention to. **point-to-point** steeplechase for hunting horses. **point up** emphasize. **to the point** relevant(ly). **up to a point** to some extent but not completely.

  ■ *noun* **1** apex, peak, prong, sharp end, spike, spur, tine, tip. **3** location, place, position, site, situation, spot. **4** instant, juncture, moment, second, stage, time. **5** dot, mark, speck, spot. **6** dot, full stop. **8** aspect, detail, idea, issue, item, matter, particular, question, topic. **10** burden, crux, drift, essence, gist, heart, import, meaning, nub, pith, subject, substance, theme, thrust. **11** advantage, aim, end, goal, intention, motive, object, objective, purpose, relevance, sense, significance, use, usefulness, value. **12** attribute, characteristic, facet, feature, peculiarity, property, quality, trait. ● *verb* **1** aim, direct, guide, lead, level, steer; (*point to*) call attention to, direct attention to, draw attention to, indicate, point out, show, signal. **4** (*point to*) indicate, signal, signify, suggest. □ **to the point** see RELEVANT.

pointed *adjective* **1** having point. **2** (of remark etc.) cutting. **3** emphasized. □ **pointedly** *adverb*.
  ■ **1** see SHARP *adjective* 1,2. **2** see SHARP *adjective* 8.

pointer *noun* **1** indicator on gauge etc. **2** rod for pointing at features on screen etc. **3** *colloquial* hint. **4** dog of breed trained to stand rigid looking at game.
  ■ **1** arrow, hand (*of clock*), indicator.

pointless *adjective* **1** purposeless, meaningless. **2** ineffective. □ **pointlessly** *adverb*. **pointlessness** *noun*.
  ■ **1** aimless, fatuous, inane, meaningless, purposeless, senseless, silly, stupid, worthless. **2** fruitless, futile, ineffective, unproductive, useless, vain.

poise /pɔɪz/ *noun* **1** composure. **2** equilibrium. **3** carriage (of head etc.). ● *verb* (**-sing**) **1** balance; hold suspended or supported. **2** be balanced or suspended.
  ■ *noun* **1** aplomb, assurance, calmness, composure, coolness, dignity, equanimity, equilibrium, imperturbability, presence, sang-froid, self-confidence, self-control, self-possession, serenity. **2** balance, equilibrium, equipoise, steadiness. ● *verb* **1** balance, keep in balance, support, suspend. **2** balance, hover.

poised *adjective* **1** self-assured; carrying oneself with dignity. **2** (often + *for*) ready.
  ■ **1** assured, calm, composed, cool, cool-headed, dignified, self-confident, self-possessed, serene, suave, *colloquial* unflappable, unruffled, urbane. **2** keyed up, prepared, ready, set, standing by, waiting.

poison /'pɔɪz(ə)n/ *noun* **1** substance that when absorbed by living organism kills or injures it. **2** *colloquial* harmful influence. ● *verb* **1** administer poison to. **2** kill or injure with poison. **3** treat (weapon) with poison. **4** corrupt, pervert. **5** spoil. □ **poison ivy** N. American climbing plant secreting irritant oil from leaves. **poison pen letter** malicious anonymous letter. □ **poisoner** *noun*. **poisonous** *adjective*.
  ■ *noun* **1** toxin, venom. ● *verb* **1** adulterate,

contaminate, infect, pollute, taint. **4** corrupt, defile, deprave, pervert, prejudice, subvert, warp.

□ **poisonous** deadly, fatal, infectious, lethal, mephitic, miasmic, mortal, noxious, poisoned, toxic, venomous, virulent.

poke *verb* (**-king**) **1** push with (end of) finger, stick, etc. **2** (+ *out, up*, etc.) (be) thrust forward. **3** (+ *at* etc.) make thrusts. **4** (+ *in*) produce (hole etc.) in by poking. **5** (+ *about*) search, pry. **6** stir (fire). ● *noun* **1** poking. **2** thrust, nudge. □ **poke fun at** ridicule. **poke one's nose in(to)** *colloquial* pry or intrude (into).

■ *verb* **1** butt, dig, elbow, goad, jab, jog, nudge, prod, stab, stick, thrust. **2** (*poke out*) see PROTRUDE 2. **5** (*poke about*) see SEARCH *verb* 2.

poker[1] *noun* metal rod for stirring fire.

poker[2] /'pəʊkə/ *noun* card game in which players bet on value of their hands. □ **poker-face** impassive countenance assumed by poker player. **poker-faced** *adjective*.

poky /'pəʊkɪ/ *adjective* (**-ier, -iest**) (of room etc.) small and cramped.

■ confined, cramped, restrictive, small.

polar /'pəʊlə/ *adjective* **1** of or near either pole of earth etc. **2** having magnetic or electric polarity. **3** directly opposite in character. **4** (of weather) very cold. □ **polar bear** large white bear living in Arctic.

■ **4** Antarctic, Arctic, chilly, freezing, glacial, icy.

polarity /pə'lærɪtɪ/ *noun* (*plural* **-ies**) **1** tendency of magnet etc. to point to earth's magnetic poles or of body to lie with axis in particular direction. **2** possession of two poles having contrary qualities. **3** possession of two opposite tendencies, opinions, etc. **4** electrical condition of body (positive or negative).

polarize /'pəʊləraɪz/ *verb* (also **-ise**) (**-zing** or **-sing**) **1** restrict vibrations of (light-waves etc.) to one direction. **2** give polarity to. **3** divide into two opposing groups. □ **polarization** *noun*.

■ **3** diverge, divide, separate, split.

Polaroid /'pəʊlərɔɪd/ *noun* **1** *proprietary term* material in thin sheets polarizing light passing through it. **2** camera that produces print immediately after each exposure. **3** (in *plural*) sunglasses with Polaroid lenses.

Pole *noun* native or national of Poland.

pole[1] *noun* **1** long slender rounded piece of wood, metal, etc., esp. as support etc. **2** *historical* measure of length (5½ yds). □ **pole-vault** jump over high bar with aid of pole held in hands.

■ **1** bar, column, mast, post, rod, shaft, spar, staff, stake, standard, stick, stilt, upright.

pole[2] *noun* **1** each of two points in celestial sphere (in full **north, south pole**) about which stars appear to revolve. **2** each end of axis of earth (in full **North, South Pole**) or of other body. **3** each of two opposite points on surface of magnet at which magnetic forces are strongest. **4** positive or negative terminal of electric cell, battery, etc. **5** each of two opposed principles. □ **be poles**

apart differ greatly, esp. in opinion. **pole star 1** star near N. pole of heavens. **2** thing serving as guide.

■ **5** end, extreme, limit.

poleaxe /'pəʊlæks/ (*US* **-ax**) *noun* **1** *historical* battleaxe. **2** butcher's axe. ● *verb* (**-xing**) **1** hit or kill with poleaxe. **2** (esp. as **poleaxed** *adjective*) *colloquial* dumbfound; overwhelm.

polecat /'pəʊlkæt/ *noun* small dark brown mammal of weasel family.

polemic /pə'lemɪk/ *noun* **1** verbal attack. **2** controversy. **3** (in *plural*) art of controversial discussion. ● *adjective* (also **polemical**) involving dispute; controversial. □ **polemicist** /-sɪst/ *noun*.

police /pə'liːs/ *noun* (treated as *plural*) **1** civil force responsible for maintaining public order. **2** its members. **3** force with similar functions. ● *verb* (**-cing**) **1** control or provide with police. **2** keep in order; control, administer. □ **police dog** dog used in police work. **police force** body of police of country, district, or town. **policeman, police officer, policewoman** member of police force. **police state** totalitarian state controlled by political police. **police station** office of local police force.

■ *noun* **1** *slang* Old Bill, constabulary, *slang* the fuzz, *colloquial* the law, police force, policemen, police officers, policewomen. ● *verb* **1** guard, keep the peace, patrol, protect, provide a police presence. **2** control, keep in order, monitor, oversee, supervise, watch over. □ **policeman, police officer, policewoman** *colloquial* bobby, constable, *slang* cop, *slang* copper, detective, gendarme, inspector, officer, PC, police constable, woman police constable, WPC.

policy[1] /'pɒlɪsɪ/ *noun* (*plural* **-ies**) **1** course of action adopted by government, business, person, etc. **2** prudent conduct.

■ **1** approach, code of conduct, custom, guidelines, intentions, line, manifesto, method, plan, platform, practice, principles, procedure, programme, proposals, protocol, regulations, rules, stance, strategy, tactics.

policy[2] /'pɒlɪsɪ/ *noun* (*plural* **-ies**) (document containing) contract of insurance. □ **policy-holder** person or body holding insurance policy.

polio /'pəʊlɪəʊ/ *noun* poliomyelitis.

poliomyelitis /pəʊlɪəʊmaɪə'laɪtɪs/ *noun* infectious viral disease of grey matter of central nervous system, with temporary or permanent paralysis.

Polish /'pəʊlɪʃ/ *adjective* of Poland. ● *noun* language of Poland.

polish /'pɒlɪʃ/ *verb* (often + *up*) **1** make or become smooth or glossy by rubbing. **2** refine, improve, revise. ● *noun* **1** substance used for polishing. **2** smoothness, glossiness. **3** refinement. □ **polish off** finish quickly.

■ *verb* **1** brighten, brush up, buff, burnish, gloss, rub down, rub, shine, smooth, wax. **2** see IMPROVE 1. ● *noun* **1** beeswax, wax. **2** brightness, brilliance, finish, glaze, gleam, gloss, lustre, sheen, shine, smoothness, sparkle. **3** *colloquial* class, elegance, finesse, grace, refinement, sophistication, style, suavity, urbanity. □ **polish off** see FINISH *verb* 3.

polished *adjective* **1** smooth, glossy. **2** refined, perfected.
■ **1** bright, burnished, glassy, gleaming, glossy, lustrous, shining, shiny. **2** civilized, *colloquial* classy, cultivated, cultured, debonair, elegant, expert, faultless, fine, finished, flawless, genteel, gracious, impeccable, perfect, perfected, polite, *colloquial* posh, refined, *soigné(e)*, sophisticated, suave, urbane.

polite /pə'laɪt/ *adjective* (**-r**, **-st**) **1** having good manners; courteous. **2** cultivated, refined. □ **politely** *adverb*. **politeness** *noun*.
■ **1** agreeable, attentive, chivalrous, civil, considerate, correct, courteous, deferential, diplomatic, discreet, euphemistic, formal, gallant, gentlemanly, gracious, ladylike, obliging, proper, respectful, tactful, thoughtful, well mannered, well-spoken. **2** courtly, cultivated, cultured, genteel, polished, refined, well bred.

politic /'pɒlɪtɪk/ *adjective* **1** judicious, expedient. **2** prudent, sagacious. ● *verb* (**-ck-**) engage in politics.

political /pə'lɪtɪk(ə)l/ *adjective* **1** of state or its government; of public affairs. **2** of, engaged in, or taking a side in politics. **3** relating to pursuit of power, status, etc. □ **political asylum** state protection for foreign refugee. **political correctness** avoidance of language or action which excludes ethnic or cultural minorities. **political economy** study of economic aspects of government. **political geography** geography dealing with boundaries etc. of states. **political prisoner** person imprisoned for political reasons.
■ **1** administrative, civil, diplomatic, governmental, legislative, parliamentary, state. **2** factional, militant, partisan.

politically *adverb* in a political way. □ **politically correct** exhibiting political correctness.

politician /pɒlɪ'tɪʃ(ə)n/ *noun* person engaged in politics.

politicize /pə'lɪtɪsaɪz/ *verb* (also **-ise**) (**-zing** or **-sing**) give political character or awareness to.

politics /'pɒlɪtɪks/ *plural noun* **1** (treated as *singular* or *plural*) art and science of government. **2** (treated as *singular* or *plural*) political life and affairs. **3** political principles, beliefs, etc. **4** activities relating to pursuit of power, status, etc.
■ **1, 2** diplomacy, government, political affairs, political science, public affairs, statesmanship.

polity /'pɒlɪtɪ/ *noun* (*plural* **-ies**) **1** form of civil administration. **2** organized society; state.

polka /'pɒlkə/ *noun* **1** lively dance. **2** music for this. ● *verb* (**-kas**, **-kaed** /-kəd/ or **-ka'd**, **-kaing** /-kəɪŋ/) dance polka. □ **polka dot** round dot as one of many forming regular pattern on textile fabric etc.

poll /pəʊl/ *noun* **1** (often in *plural*) voting. **2** counting of votes. **3** result of voting. **4** number of votes recorded. **5** questioning of sample of popu-lation to estimate trend of public opinion. **6** head. ● *verb* **1** take or receive vote(s) of. **2** vote. **3** record opinion of (person, group). **4** cut off top of (tree etc.) or (esp. as **polled** *adjective*) horns of (cattle). □ **polling booth** cubicle where voter stands to mark ballot paper. **polling station** building used for voting. **poll tax** *historical* tax levied on every adult.
■ *noun* **1** ballot, election, plebiscite, referendum, vote. **5** canvass, census, opinion poll, survey. ● *verb* **1, 2** ballot. **3** ballot, canvass, question, sample, survey.

pollack /'pɒlək/ *noun* (also **pollock**) (*plural* same or **-s**) edible marine fish related to cod.

pollard /'pɒləd/ *noun* **1** hornless animal. **2** tree polled to produce close head of young branches. ● *verb* make pollard of (tree).

pollen /'pɒlən/ *noun* fertilizing powder discharged from flower's anther. □ **pollen count** index of amount of pollen in air.

pollinate /'pɒlɪneɪt/ *verb* (**-ting**) sprinkle (stigma of flower) with pollen. □ **pollination** *noun*.

pollock = POLLACK.

pollster *noun* person who organizes opinion poll.

pollute /pə'luːt/ *verb* (**-ting**) **1** contaminate; make impure. **2** corrupt. □ **pollutant** *noun*. **polluter** *noun*. **pollution** *noun*.
■ **1** adulterate, *poetical* befoul, blight, contaminate, defile, dirty, foul, infect, poison, soil, taint. **2** corrupt, defile, profane, sully, taint.

polo /'pəʊləʊ/ *noun* game like hockey played on horseback. □ **polo-neck** (sweater with) high round turned-over collar.

polonaise /pɒlə'neɪz/ *noun* **1** slow processional dance. **2** music for this.

poltergeist /'pɒltəgaɪst/ *noun* noisy mischievous ghost.

poltroon /pɒl'truːn/ *noun* coward. □ **poltroonery** *noun*.

poly- *combining form* **1** many. **2** polymerized.

polyandry /'pɒlɪændrɪ/ *noun* polygamy in which one woman has more than one husband.

polyanthus /pɒlɪ'ænθəs/ *noun* (*plural* **-thuses**) cultivated primula.

polychromatic /pɒlɪkrəʊ'mætɪk/ *adjective* many-coloured.

polychrome /'pɒlɪkrəʊm/ *adjective* in many colours. ● *noun* polychrome work of art.

polyester /pɒlɪ'estə/ *noun* synthetic fibre or resin.

polyethylene /pɒlɪ'eθɪliːn/ *noun* polythene.

polygamy /pə'lɪgəmɪ/ *noun* practice of having more than one wife or husband at once. □ **polygamist** *noun*. **polygamous** *adjective*.

polyglot /'pɒlɪglɒt/ *adjective* knowing, using, or written in several languages. ● *noun* polyglot person.

polygon /'pɒlɪgən/ *noun* figure with many sides and angles. □ **polygonal** /pə'lɪg-/ *adjective.*

polyhedron /pɒlɪ'hiːdrən/ *noun* (*plural* **-dra**) solid figure with many faces. □ **polyhedral** *adjective.*

polymath /'pɒlɪmæθ/ *noun* person of great or varied learning.

polymer /'pɒlɪmə/ *noun* compound of molecule(s) formed from repeated units of smaller molecules. □ **polymeric** /-'mer-/ *adjective.* **polymerization** *noun.* **polymerize** *verb* (also **-ise**) (**-zing** or **-sing**).

polyp /'pɒlɪp/ *noun* **1** simple organism with tube-shaped body. **2** small growth on mucous membrane.

polyphony /pə'lɪfənɪ/ *noun* (*plural* **-ies**) contrapuntal music. □ **polyphonic** /pɒlɪ'fɒnɪk/ *adjective.*

polypropylene /pɒlɪ'prəʊpɪliːn/ *noun* any of various thermoplastic materials used for films, fibres, or moulding.

polystyrene /pɒlɪ'staɪəriːn/ *noun* kind of hard plastic.

polysyllabic /pɒlɪsɪ'læbɪk/ *adjective* **1** having many syllables. **2** using polysyllables.

polysyllable /'pɒlɪsɪləb(ə)l/ *noun* polysyllabic word.

polytechnic /pɒlɪ'teknɪk/ *noun* college providing courses in esp. vocational subjects up to degree level.

polytheism /'pɒlɪθiːɪz(ə)m/ *noun* belief in or worship of more than one god. □ **polytheistic** /-'ɪst-/ *adjective.*

polythene /'pɒlɪθiːn/ *noun* a tough light plastic.

polyunsaturated /pɒlɪʌn'sætʃəreɪtɪd/ *adjective* (of fat) containing several double or triple bonds in each molecule and therefore capable of combining with hydrogen and not associated with accumulation of cholesterol.

polyurethane /pɒlɪ'jʊərəθeɪn/ *noun* synthetic resin or plastic used esp. in paints or foam.

polyvinyl chloride /pɒlɪ'vaɪnɪl/ *noun* see PVC.

pomade /pə'mɑːd/ *noun* scented ointment for hair.

pomander /pə'mændə/ *noun* **1** ball of mixed aromatic substances. **2** container for this.

pomegranate /'pɒmɪgrænɪt/ *noun* **1** tropical tough-rinded many-seeded fruit. **2** tree bearing this.

pommel /'pʌm(ə)l/ *noun* **1** knob of sword hilt. **2** projecting front of saddle.

pomp *noun* **1** splendid display; splendour. **2** specious glory.

■ **1** brilliance, ceremonial, ceremony, display, formality, glory, grandeur, magnificence, pageantry, ritual, show, solemnity, spectacle, splendour. **2** see OSTENTATION.

pom-pom /'pɒmpɒm/ *noun* automatic quick-firing gun.

pompon /'pɒmpɒn/ *noun* (also **pompom**) decorative tuft or ball on hat, shoe, etc.

pompous /'pɒmpəs/ *adjective* **1** self-important; affectedly grand or solemn. **2** (of language) affectedly grand; pretentious. □ **pomposity** /-'pɒs-/ *noun* (*plural* **-ies**). **pompously** *adverb.* **pompousness** *noun.*

■ **1** affected, arrogant, conceited, grandiose, haughty, *colloquial* highfalutin, imperious, magisterial, overbearing, pontifical, *colloquial* posh, pretentious, proud, self-important, sententious, showy, smug, snobbish, *colloquial* snooty, *colloquial* stuck-up, stuffy, supercilious, vain, vainglorious. **2** bombastic, grandiloquent, *colloquial* highfalutin, high-flown, long-winded, ornate, ostentatious, pedantic, pretentious, sententious, turgid.

ponce *slang noun* man who lives off prostitute's earnings. ● *verb* act as ponce. □ **ponce about** move about effeminately.

poncho /'pɒntʃəʊ/ *noun* (*plural* **-s**) cloak of rectangular piece of material with slit in middle for head.

pond *noun* small body of still water.

ponder /'pɒndə/ *verb* think over; muse.

ponderable /'pɒndərəb(ə)l/ *adjective literary* having appreciable weight.

ponderous /'pɒndərəs/ *adjective* **1** heavy and unwieldy. **2** laborious; dull. □ **ponderously** *adverb.* **ponderousness** *noun.*

■ **1** awkward, bulky, burdensome, cumbersome, elephantine, heavy, hefty, huge, massive, unwieldy, weighty. **2** dreary, dull, humourless, inflated, laboured, lifeless, long-winded, overdone, pedestrian, plodding, prolix, slow, stilted, stodgy, tedious, tiresome, verbose, *colloquial* windy.

pong *noun* & *verb colloquial* stink. □ **pongy** *adjective* (**-ier**, **-iest**).

poniard /'pɒnjəd/ *noun* dagger.

pontiff /'pɒntɪf/ *noun* Pope.

pontifical /pɒn'tɪfɪk(ə)l/ *adjective* **1** papal. **2** pompously dogmatic.

pontificate *verb* /pɒn'tɪfɪkeɪt/ (**-ting**) be pompously dogmatic. ● *noun* /pɒn'tɪfɪkət/ **1** office of bishop or Pope. **2** period of this.

pontoon[1] /pɒn'tuːn/ *noun* card game in which players try to acquire cards with face value totalling 21.

pontoon[2] /pɒn'tuːn/ *noun* **1** flat-bottomed boat. **2** boat etc. as one of supports of temporary bridge.

pony /'pəʊnɪ/ *noun* (*plural* **-ies**) horse of any small breed. □ **pony-tail** hair drawn back, tied, and hanging down behind head. **pony-trekking** travelling across country on ponies for pleasure.

poodle /'puːd(ə)l/ *noun* dog of breed with thick curling hair.

pooh /puː/ *interjection: expressing contempt or disgust.* □ **pooh-pooh** express contempt for; ridicule.

pool[1] *noun* **1** small body of still water. **2** small shallow body of any liquid. **3** swimming pool. **4** deep place in river.

■ **1** lagoon, lake, *dialect* or *poetical* mere, oasis, pond, puddle, tarn.

pool[2] *noun* **1** common supply of people, vehicles, etc., for sharing by group. **2** group of people sharing duties etc. **3** common fund, e.g. of profits or of gamblers' stakes. **4** arrangement between competing parties to fix prices and share business. **5** game like billiards with usually 16 balls. **6** (**the pools**) football pool. ● *verb* **1** put into common fund. **2** share in common.
■ *verb* **1** see COMBINE *verb* **1**.

poop *noun* **1** stern of ship. **2** furthest aft and highest deck.

poor /pʊə/ *adjective* **1** having little money or means. **2** (+ *in*) deficient in. **3** inadequate; inferior. **4** unproductive. **5** deserving pity. **6** despicable. □ **poor man's** inferior substitute for.
■ **1** badly off, bankrupt, beggarly, *colloquial* broke, deprived, destitute, disadvantaged, down and out, hard up, impecunious, impoverished, *formal* indigent, insolvent, necessitous, needy, *colloquial* on one's uppers, penniless, penurious, poverty-stricken, *slang* skint, straitened, underpaid, underprivileged. **2** (*poor in*) deficient in, lacking in, wanting. **3** (*a poor salary*) inadequate, insufficient, low, meagre, mean, scanty, small, sparse, unprofitable, unrewarding; (*poor quality*) amateurish, bad, cheap, defective, deficient, disappointing, faulty, imperfect, indifferent, inferior, low-grade, mediocre, paltry, second-rate, shoddy, substandard, unacceptable, unsatisfactory, *colloquial* useless, worthless. **4** barren, exhausted, infertile, sterile, unfruitful, unproductive. **5** forlorn, hapless, ill-fated, luckless, miserable, pathetic, pitiable, sad, unfortunate, unhappy, unlucky, wretched.

poorly *adverb* in poor manner; badly. ● *adjective* unwell.

pop[1] *noun* **1** abrupt explosive sound. **2** *colloquial* effervescent drink. ● *verb* (**-pp-**) **1** (cause to) make pop. **2** (+ *in, out, up*, etc.) move, come, or put unexpectedly or suddenly. **3** *slang* pawn. ● *adverb* with the sound pop. □ **popcorn 1** maize kernels which burst open when heated. **2** these kernels when burst. **pop-eyed** *colloquial* with eyes bulging or wide open. **popgun** toy gun shooting pellet etc. by compressed air or spring. **popping crease** *Cricket* line in front of and parallel to wicket. **pop-up** involving parts that pop up automatically.

pop[2] *noun colloquial* **1** (in full **pop music**) highly successful commercial music. **2** pop record or song. □ **pop art** art based on modern popular culture and the mass media. **pop culture** commercial culture based on popular taste. **pop group** ensemble playing pop music.

pop[3] *noun esp. US colloquial* father.

popadam = POPPADAM.

pope *noun* (also **Pope**) head of RC Church.

popinjay /ˈpɒpɪndʒeɪ/ *noun* fop; conceited person.

poplar /ˈpɒplə/ *noun* slender tree with straight trunk and often tremulous leaves.

poplin /ˈpɒplɪn/ *noun* closely woven corded fabric.

poppadam /ˈpɒpədəm/ *noun* (also **poppadom**, **popadam**) thin crisp spiced Indian bread.

popper *noun* **1** *colloquial* press-stud. **2** thing that pops.

poppet /ˈpɒpɪt/ *noun colloquial* (esp. as term of endearment) small or dainty person.

poppy /ˈpɒpɪ/ *noun* (*plural* **-ies**) **1** plant with bright flowers and milky narcotic juice. **2** artificial poppy worn on Remembrance Sunday. □ **Poppy Day** Remembrance Sunday.

poppycock /ˈpɒpɪkɒk/ *noun slang* nonsense.

populace /ˈpɒpjʊləs/ *noun* the common people.
■ commonalty, *hoi polloi*, masses, people, public, rabble, riff-raff.

popular /ˈpɒpjʊlə/ *adjective* **1** generally liked or admired. **2** of, for, or prevalent among the general public. □ **popularity** /-ˈlærɪtɪ/ *noun*. **popularize** *verb* (also **-ise**) (**-zing** or **-sing**). **popularly** *adverb*.
■ **1** accepted, acclaimed, all the rage, approved, celebrated, famous, fashionable, favoured, favourite, in, in demand, liked, lionized, loved, renowned, sought after, *colloquial often derogatory* trendy, well known, well liked, well received. **2** average, common, conventional, current, democratic, general, of the people, ordinary, predominant, prevailing, representative, standard, universal. □ **popularize** promote, simplify, spread, tart up.

populate /ˈpɒpjʊleɪt/ *verb* (**-ting**) **1** form population of. **2** supply with inhabitants.
■ **1** dwell in, inhabit, live in, occupy, reside in. **2** colonize, fill, people, settle.

population /pɒpjʊˈleɪʃ(ə)n/ *noun* **1** inhabitants of town, country, etc. **2** total number of these.
■ **1** citizenry, citizens, community, denizens, folk, inhabitants, natives, occupants, people, populace, public, residents.

populous /ˈpɒpjʊləs/ *adjective* thickly inhabited.
■ crowded, full, heavily populated, jammed, overcrowded, overpopulated, packed, swarming, teeming.

porcelain /ˈpɔːsəlɪn/ *noun* **1** fine translucent ceramic. **2** things made of this.

porch *noun* covered entrance to building.

porcine /ˈpɔːsaɪn/ *adjective* of or like pigs.

porcupine /ˈpɔːkjʊpaɪn/ *noun* large rodent with body and tail covered with erectile spines.

pore[1] *noun* minute opening in surface through which fluids may pass.

pore[2] *verb* (**-ring**) (+ *over*) be absorbed in studying (book etc.).
■ (*pore over*) examine, go over, peruse, read, scrutinize, study.

pork *noun* flesh of pig used as food.

porker *noun* pig raised for food.

porn (also **porno**) *colloquial noun* pornography. ● *adjective* pornographic.

pornography /pɔːˈnɒgrəfɪ/ *noun* explicit presentation of sexual activity in literature, films, etc., to stimulate erotic rather than aesthetic feelings. □ **pornographic** /-nəˈgræf-/ *adjective*.

■ □ **pornographic** arousing, blue, erotic, explicit, indecent, obscene, salacious, sexy, titillating.

porous /ˈpɔːrəs/ *adjective* **1** having pores. **2** permeable. □ **porosity** /-ˈrɒs-/ *noun*.

■ **1** cellular, holey, spongy. **2** absorbent, penetrable, permeable, pervious, spongy.

porphyry /ˈpɔːfɪrɪ/ *noun* (*plural* **-ies**) hard rock with feldspar crystals in fine-grained red mass.

porpoise /ˈpɔːpəs/ *noun* sea mammal of whale family.

porridge /ˈpɒrɪdʒ/ *noun* oatmeal or other cereal boiled in water or milk.

porringer /ˈpɒrɪndʒə/ *noun* small soup-bowl.

port[1] *noun* **1** harbour. **2** town possessing harbour.

■ **1** dock, dockyard, harbour, haven, marina. **2** seaport.

port[2] *noun* strong sweet fortified wine.

port[3] *noun* left-hand side of ship or aircraft looking forward. ● *verb* turn (helm) to port.

port[4] *noun* **1** opening in ship's side for entrance, loading, etc. **2** porthole. □ **porthole** (esp. glazed) aperture in ship's side to admit light.

portable /ˈpɔːtəb(ə)l/ *adjective* **1** easily movable; convenient for carrying. **2** adaptable in altered circumstances. □ **portability** *noun*.

■ **1** compact, convenient, handy, light, lightweight, manageable, mobile, movable, pocket, pocket-sized, small, transportable.

portage /ˈpɔːtɪdʒ/ *noun* carrying of boats or goods between two navigable waters.

Portakabin /ˈpɔːtəkæbɪn/ *noun proprietary term* prefabricated small building.

portal /ˈpɔːt(ə)l/ *noun* doorway; gate.

portcullis /pɔːtˈkʌlɪs/ *noun* strong heavy grating lowered in defence of fortress gateway.

portend /pɔːˈtend/ *verb* **1** foreshadow as an omen. **2** give warning of.

portent /ˈpɔːtent/ *noun* **1** omen, significant sign. **2** marvellous thing.

portentous /pɔːˈtentəs/ *adjective* **1** like or being portent. **2** pompously solemn.

porter[1] /ˈpɔːtə/ *noun* **1** person employed to carry luggage etc. **2** dark beer brewed from charred or browned malt. □ **porterhouse steak** choice cut of beef.

■ **1** baggage-handler, bearer, carrier.

porter[2] /ˈpɔːtə/ *noun* gatekeeper or doorkeeper, esp. of large building.

■ caretaker, doorman, gatekeeper, janitor, security guard, watchman.

porterage *noun* (charge for) hire of porters.

portfolio /pɔːtˈfəʊlɪəʊ/ *noun* (*plural* **-s**) **1** folder for loose sheets of paper, drawings, etc. **2** samples of artist's work. **3** list of investments held by investor etc. **4** office of government minister. □ **Minister without Portfolio** government minister not in charge of department.

portico /ˈpɔːtɪkəʊ/ *noun* (*plural* **-es** or **-s**) colonnade; roof supported by columns, usually serving as porch to building.

portion /ˈpɔːʃ(ə)n/ *noun* **1** part, share. **2** helping. **3** destiny or lot. ● *verb* **1** divide into portions. **2** (+ *out*) distribute.

■ *noun* **1** allocation, allowance, bit, chunk, division, fraction, fragment, hunk, measure, part, percentage, piece, quota, ration, scrap, section, segment, share, slice, sliver, subdivision, wedge. **2** helping, ration, serving. ● *verb* **2** (*portion out*) see SHARE *verb* 1,2.

Portland /ˈpɔːtlənd/ *noun* □ **Portland cement** cement manufactured from chalk and clay. **Portland stone** a valuable building limestone.

portly /ˈpɔːtlɪ/ *adjective* (**-ier**, **-iest**) corpulent.

portmanteau /pɔːtˈmæntəʊ/ *noun* (*plural* **-s** or **-x** /-z/) case for clothes etc., opening into two equal parts. □ **portmanteau word** word combining sounds and meanings of two others.

portrait /ˈpɔːtrɪt/ *noun* **1** drawing, painting, photograph, etc. of person or animal. **2** description.

■ **1** depiction, image, likeness, picture, portrayal, profile, representation. **2** see DESCRIPTION 1.

portraiture /ˈpɔːtrɪtʃə/ *noun* **1** portraying. **2** description. **3** portrait.

portray /pɔːˈtreɪ/ *verb* **1** make likeness of. **2** describe. **3** represent dramatically. □ **portrayal** *noun*.

■ **1, 2** delineate, depict, describe, evoke, illustrate, paint, picture, represent, show. **3** see IMPERSONATE.

Portuguese /pɔːtʃʊˈgiːz/ *noun* (*plural* same) native, national, or language of Portugal. ● *adjective* of Portugal.

pose /pəʊz/ *verb* (**-sing**) **1** assume attitude, esp. for artistic purpose. **2** (+ *as*) pretend to be. **3** behave affectedly for effect. **4** propound (question, problem). **5** arrange in required attitude. ● *noun* **1** attitude of body or mind. **2** affectation, pretence.

■ *verb* **1** model, sit. **2** (*pose as*) see IMPERSONATE. **3** attitudinize, posture, put on airs, *colloquial* show off. **4** advance, ask, broach, posit, postulate, present, propound, put forward, submit, suggest. ● *noun* **1** attitude, position, posture, stance. **2** act, affectation, attitudinizing, façade, masquerade, pretence.

poser *noun* **1** poseur. **2** *colloquial* puzzling question or problem.

■ **1** see POSEUR. **2** dilemma, enigma, problem, puzzle, question, riddle.

poseur /pəʊˈzɜː/ *noun* person who behaves affectedly.

■ exhibitionist, fraud, impostor, masquerader, *colloquial* phoney, poser, pretender, *colloquial* show-off.

posh *colloquial adjective* **1** smart. **2** upper-class. ● *adverb* in an upper-class way. □ **poshly** *adverb*. **poshness** *noun*.
■ **1** *colloquial* classy, elegant, fashionable, formal, grand, lavish, luxurious, ostentatious, rich, showy, smart, stylish, sumptuous, *colloquial* swanky, *colloquial* swish. **2** see SNOBBISH.

posit /ˈpɒzɪt/ *verb* (-t-) assume as fact; postulate.
position /pəˈzɪʃ(ə)n/ *noun* **1** place occupied by person or thing. **2** way thing is placed. **3** proper place. **4** advantage. **5** mental attitude. **6** situation. **7** rank, status. **8** paid employment. **9** strategic location. ● *verb* place in position. □ **in a position to** able to. □ **positional** *adjective*.
■ *noun* **1** locality, location, locus, niche, place, placement, point, reference, site, situation, spot, whereabouts. **2** angle, pose, posture, stance. **5** assertion, attitude, contention, hypothesis, opinion, outlook, perspective, principle, proposition, stance, standpoint, thesis, view, viewpoint. **6** circumstances, condition, situation, state. **7** grade, level, place, rank, standing, station, status, title. **8** appointment, job, niche, occupation, post, role, *formal* situation. ● *verb* arrange, deploy, dispose, fix, locate, place, put, settle, site, situate, stand, station.

positive /ˈpɒzɪtɪv/ *adjective* **1** explicit, definite, unquestionable. **2** convinced, confident, cocksure. **3** absolute; not relative. **4** *Grammar* (of adjective or adverb) expressing simple quality without comparison. **5** constructive; favourable. **6** marked by presence and not absence of qualities. **7** dealing only with matters of fact; practical. **8** *Mathematics* (of quantity) greater than zero. **9** *Electricity* of, containing, or producing kind of charge produced by rubbing glass with silk. **10** *Photography* showing lights and shades or colours as seen in original image. ● *noun* positive adjective, photograph, quantity, etc. □ **positive discrimination** making distinctions in favour of groups believed to be underprivileged. **positive vetting** inquiry into background etc. of candidate for post involving national security. □ **positively** *adverb*. **positiveness** *noun*.
■ *adjective* **1** affirmative, categorical, certain, clear, conclusive, decided, definite, emphatic, explicit, firm, incontestable, incontrovertible, irrefutable, real, undeniable, unequivocal. **2** assured, certain, confident, convinced, sure. **5** beneficial, constructive, helpful, optimistic, practical, useful, worthwhile. **6** affirmative.

positivism *noun* philosophical system recognizing only facts and observable phenomena. □ **positivist** *noun & adjective*.
positron /ˈpɒzɪtrɒn/ *noun* elementary particle with same mass as but opposite charge to electron.
posse /ˈpɒsɪ/ *noun* **1** strong force or company. **2** group of law-enforcers.
possess /pəˈzes/ *verb* **1** hold as property; own,

have. **2** occupy; take over (territory). **3** dominate mind of. □ **possessor** *noun*.
■ **1** be gifted with, embody, embrace, enjoy, have, hold, include, own. **2** acquire, control, dominate, govern, invade, occupy, rule, seize, take over. **3** bewitch, captivate, cast a spell over, charm, enthral, haunt, hypnotize, obsess.

possession /pəˈzeʃ(ə)n/ *noun* **1** possessing, being possessed. **2** occupancy. **3** thing possessed. **4** (in *plural*) property. **5** control of ball by player.
■ **4** (*possessions*) assets, belongings, chattels, effects, estate, fortune, goods, property, riches, things, wealth.

possessive /pəˈzesɪv/ *adjective* **1** wanting to retain what one possesses. **2** jealous and domineering. **3** *Grammar* indicating possession. ● *noun* *Grammar* possessive case or word. □ **possessive pronoun** pronoun indicating possession (see panel). □ **possessiveness** *noun*.
■ **1** acquisitive, greedy, proprietorial, selfish, stingy. **2** clinging, dominating, domineering, jealous, overbearing, protective.

possibility /ˌpɒsɪˈbɪlɪtɪ/ *noun* (*plural* -ies) **1** state or fact of being possible. **2** thing that may exist or happen. **3** (usually in *plural*) capability of being used.
■ **1** chance, danger, feasibility, likelihood, odds, opportunity, plausibility, practicality, probability, risk. **3** (*possibilities*) capability, potential, promise.

possible /ˈpɒsɪb(ə)l/ *adjective* **1** capable of existing, happening, being done, etc. **2** potential. ● *noun* **1** possible candidate, member of team, etc. **2** highest possible score.
■ *adjective* **1** achievable, admissible, attainable, conceivable, credible, doable, feasible, imaginable, obtainable, plausible, practicable, practical, realizable, reasonable, tenable, thinkable, viable, workable. **2** likely, potential, probable.

possibly *adverb* **1** perhaps. **2** in accordance with possibility.
■ **1** *disputed* hopefully, if possible, maybe, *archaic* peradventure, *archaic* perchance, perhaps.

possum /ˈpɒsəm/ *noun colloquial* opossum. □ **play possum** *colloquial* pretend to be unconscious or unaware.

post[1] /pəʊst/ *noun* **1** upright of timber or metal as support in building, to mark boundary, carry notices, etc. **2** pole etc. marking start or finish of race. ● *verb* **1** (often + *up*) display (notice etc.) in prominent place. **2** advertise by poster or list.
■ *noun* **1** baluster, bollard, brace, capstan, column, leg, newel, pale, paling, picket, pier, pile, pillar, pole, prop, pylon, shaft, stake, stanchion, standard, strut, support, upright. **2** starting post, winning post. ● *verb* **1** display, pin up, put up, stick up. **2** advertise, announce, proclaim, promulgate, publicize, publish.

post[2] /pəʊst/ *noun* **1** official conveying of parcels, letters, etc. **2** single collection or delivery of these; letters etc. dispatched. **3** place where letters etc. are collected. ● *verb* **1** put (letter etc.) into post. **2** (esp. as **posted** *adjective*) (often + *up*) supply with information. **3** enter in ledger. □ **postbox** public box for posting mail. **postcard** card for posting without envelope. **postcode** group of letters and figures in postal address to assist sorting. **post-haste** with great speed. **postman, postwoman** person who collects or delivers post. **postmark** official mark on letters to cancel stamp. **postmaster, postmistress** official in charge of post office. **post office** room or building for postal business. **Post Office** public department or corporation providing postal services.

■ *noun* **2** collection, delivery, letters, mail. ● *verb* **1** dispatch, mail, send, transmit.

post³ /pəʊst/ *noun* **1** appointed place of soldier etc. on duty. **2** occupying force. **3** fort. **4** paid employment. **5** trading post. ● *verb* **1** place (soldier etc.) at post. **2** appoint to post or command.

■ *noun* **1** location, place, point, position, station. **4** appointment, assignment, employment, job, occupation, office, place, position, *formal* situation, task, work. ● *verb* appoint, assign, locate, place, position, set, situate, station.

post- *prefix* after, behind.

postage *noun* charge for sending letter etc. by post. □ **postage stamp** small adhesive label indicating amount of postage paid.

postal *adjective* of or by post. □ **postal order** money order issued by Post Office.

postdate /pəʊst'deɪt/ *verb* (**-ting**) **1** give later than actual date to. **2** follow in time.

poster *noun* **1** placard in public place. **2** large printed picture. □ **poster paint** gummy opaque paint.

■ **1** advertisement, announcement, bill, broadsheet, circular, display, flyer, notice, placard, sign.

poste restante /pəʊst re'stɑ̃t/ *noun* department in post office where letters are kept till called for.

posterior /pɒ'stɪərɪə/ *adjective* **1** later in time or order. **2** at the back. ● *noun* (in *singular* or *plural*) buttocks.

posterity /pɒ'sterɪtɪ/ *noun* **1** later generations. **2** descendants.

■ **2** descendants, heirs, issue, offspring, progeny, successors.

postern /'pɒst(ə)n/ *noun archaic* back or side entrance.

postgraduate /pəʊst'grædjʊət/ *noun* person on course of study after taking first degree. ● *adjective* relating to postgraduates.

posthumous /'pɒstjʊməs/ *adjective* **1** occurring after death. **2** published after author's death. **3** born after father's death. □ **posthumously** *adverb*.

postilion /pɒ'stɪljən/ *noun* (also **postillion**) rider on near horse of team drawing coach etc. without coachman.

post-impressionism /pəʊstɪm'preʃənɪz(ə)m/ *noun* art intending to express individual artist's conception of objects represented. □ **post-impressionist** *noun & adjective*.

post-industrial /pəʊstɪn'dʌstrɪəl/ *adjective* of society or economy no longer reliant on heavy industry.

post-mortem /pəʊst'mɔ:təm/ *noun* **1** examination of body made after death. **2** *colloquial* discussion analysing course and result of event. ● *adverb & adjective* after death.

postnatal /pəʊst'neɪt(ə)l/ *adjective* existing or occurring after birth.

postpone /pəʊst'pəʊn/ *verb* (**-ning**) cause to take place at later time. □ **postponement** *noun*.

■ adjourn, defer, delay, hold over, keep in abeyance, lay aside, put back, put off, shelve, stay, suspend.

postscript /'pəʊstskrɪpt/ *noun* addition at end of letter etc. after signature.

■ addendum, addition, afterthought, codicil (*to will*), epilogue, PS.

postulant /'pɒstjʊlənt/ *noun* candidate, esp. for admission to religious order.

postulate *verb* /'pɒstjʊleɪt/ (**-ting**) **1** (often + *that*) assume or require to be true; take for granted. **2** claim. ● *noun* /'pɒstjʊlət/ **1** thing postulated. **2** prerequisite.

■ *verb* **1** assume, hypothesize, posit, propose, suppose, theorize.

posture /'pɒstʃə/ *noun* **1** relative position of parts, esp. of body; bearing. **2** mental attitude. **3** condition or state (of affairs etc.). ● *verb* (**-ring**) **1** assume posture, esp. for effect. **2** pose (person).

■ *noun* **1** appearance, bearing, carriage, deportment, pose, position, stance. **2** see ATTITUDE 1,2.

postwar /pəʊst'wɔ:/ *adjective* occurring or existing after a war.

....

Possessive pronoun

A possessive pronoun is a word such as *mine, yours*, or *theirs*, functioning as subject, complement, or direct or indirect object in a clause.

    This one is mine.
    That one is yours.
    Hers *is no good.*

....

posy /'pəʊzɪ/ *noun* (*plural* **-ies**) small bunch of flowers.

■ bouquet, buttonhole, corsage, nosegay, spray.

pot[1] *noun* **1** rounded ceramic, metal, or glass vessel. **2** flowerpot, teapot, etc. **3** contents of pot. **4** chamber pot. **5** total amount bet in game etc. **6** (usually in *plural*) *colloquial* large sum. **7** *slang* cup etc. as prize. ● *verb* (**-tt-**) **1** plant in pot. **2** (usually as **potted** *adjective*) preserve (food) in sealed pot. **3** pocket (ball) in billiards etc. **4** abridge, epitomize. **5** shoot at, hit, or kill (animal). □ **go to pot** *colloquial* be ruined. **pot belly** protuberant belly. **pot-bellied** *adjective*. **potboiler** work of literature etc. done merely to earn money. **pot-herb** herb grown in kitchen garden. **pothole 1** deep hole in rock. **2** hole in road surface. **potluck** whatever is available. **pot plant** plant grown in flowerpot. **pot roast** piece of braised meat. **pot-roast** *verb* braise. **potsherd** broken piece of ceramic material. **pot-shot** random shot. □ **potful** *noun* (*plural* **-s**).

■ *noun* **1** basin, bowl, casserole, cauldron, container, crock, crucible, dish, jar, pan, saucepan, urn, vessel.

pot[2] *noun slang* marijuana.

potable /'pəʊtəb(ə)l/ *adjective* drinkable.

potash /'pɒtæʃ/ *noun* any of various compounds of potassium.

potassium /pə'tæsɪəm/ *noun* soft silver-white metallic element.

potation /pə'teɪʃ(ə)n/ *noun* **1** a drink. **2** drinking.

potato /pə'teɪtəʊ/ *noun* (*plural* **-es**) **1** edible plant tuber. **2** plant bearing this. □ **potato crisp** crisp.

poteen /pɒ'tʃiːn/ *noun Irish* illicit distilled spirit.

potent /'pəʊt(ə)nt/ *adjective* **1** powerful, strong. **2** cogent. **3** (of male) able to achieve erection of penis or have sexual intercourse. □ **potency** *noun*.

■ **1** effective, forceful, formidable, influential, intoxicating (*drink*), mighty, overpowering, overwhelming, powerful, *literary* puissant, strong, vigorous. **2** see PERSUASIVE.

potentate /'pəʊtənteɪt/ *noun* monarch, ruler.

potential /pə'tenʃ(ə)l/ *adjective* capable of coming into being; latent. ● *noun* **1** capability or resources for use or development. **2** quantity determining energy of mass in gravitational field or of charge in electric field. □ **potentiality** /-ʃɪ'æl-/ *noun*. **potentially** *adverb*.

■ *adjective* aspiring, budding, embryonic, hopeful, latent, likely, possible, probable, promising, would-be. ● *noun* **1** aptitude, capability, capacity, possibility, promise, resources.

pother /'pɒðə/ *noun literary* din, fuss.

potion /'pəʊʃ(ə)n/ *noun* liquid dose of medicine, poison, etc.

■ brew, concoction, decoction, draught, drink, drug, elixir, liquid, medicine, mixture, philtre, potation, tonic.

pot-pourri /pəʊ'pʊərɪ/ *noun* (*plural* **-s**) **1** scented mixture of dried petals and spices. **2** musical or literary medley.

pottage /'pɒtɪdʒ/ *noun archaic* soup, stew.

potter[1] /'pɒtə/ *verb* (*US* **putter**) **1** (often + *about, around*) work etc. in aimless or desultory manner. **2** go slowly. □ **potterer** *noun*.

■ **1** dabble, do odd jobs, fiddle about, mess about, tinker. **2** amble, loiter, saunter, stroll.

potter[2] /'pɒtə/ *noun* maker of ceramic vessels.

pottery /'pɒtərɪ/ *noun* (*plural* **-ies**) **1** vessels etc. made of baked clay. **2** potter's work or workshop.

■ **1** ceramics, china, crockery, crocks, earthenware, porcelain, stoneware, terracotta.

potty[1] /'pɒtɪ/ *adjective* (**-ier**, **-iest**) *slang* **1** crazy. **2** insignificant. □ **pottiness** *noun*.

potty[2] *noun* (*plural* **-ies**) *colloquial* chamber pot, esp. for child.

pouch *noun* **1** small bag; detachable pocket. **2** baggy area of skin under eyes etc. **3** baglike receptacle in which marsupials carry un-developed young. **4** other baglike natural structure. ● *verb* **1** put or make into pouch. **2** take possession of.

■ *noun* **1** bag, pocket, purse, sack, wallet.

pouffe /puːf/ *noun* firm cushion as low seat or footstool.

poulterer /'pəʊltərə/ *noun* dealer in poultry and usually game.

poultice /'pəʊltɪs/ *noun* soft usually hot dressing applied to sore or inflamed part of body. ● *verb* (**-cing**) apply poultice to.

poultry /'pəʊltrɪ/ *noun* domestic fowls.

pounce *verb* (**-cing**) **1** spring, swoop. **2** (often + *on, upon*) make sudden attack. **3** (often + *on, upon*) seize eagerly. ● *noun* act of pouncing.

■ *verb* **1** jump, leap, spring, swoop. **2, 3** (*pounce on*) ambush, attack, drop on, jump on, leap on, seize, snatch, spring at, strike, swoop down on, take by surprise.

pound[1] *noun* **1** unit of weight equal to 16 oz (454 g). **2** (in full **pound sterling**) monetary unit of UK etc.

pound[2] *verb* **1** crush or beat with repeated strokes. **2** (+ *at, on*) deliver heavy blows or gunfire to. **3** (+ *along* etc.) walk, run, etc. heavily.

■ **1** batter, beat, crush, grind, hammer, hit, knead, mash, powder, pulp, pulverize, smash.

pound[3] *noun* enclosure where stray animals or officially removed vehicles are kept until claimed.

■ compound, corral, enclosure, pen.

poundage *noun* commission or fee of so much per pound sterling or weight.

-pounder *combining form* **1** thing or person

weighing specified number of pounds. **2** gun firing shell weighing specified number of pounds.

pour /pɔː/ *verb* **1** (usually + *down, out, over*, etc.) (cause to) flow in stream or shower. **2** dispense (drink). **3** rain heavily. **4** (usually + *in, out*, etc.) come or go in profusion or in a rush. **5** discharge copiously.

■ **1** cascade, course, discharge, disgorge, flood, flow, gush, run, spew, spill, spout, spurt, stream. **2** decant, dispense, serve, tip. **4** flood, rush, stream, swarm.

pout *verb* **1** push lips forward, esp. as sign of displeasure. **2** (of lips) be pushed forward. ● *noun* pouting expression.

pouter *noun* kind of pigeon able to inflate crop.

poverty /ˈpɒvətɪ/ *noun* **1** being poor; want. **2** (often + *of, in*) scarcity, lack. **3** inferiority, poorness. □ **poverty-stricken** very poor. **poverty trap** situation in which increase of income incurs greater loss of state benefits.

■ **1** beggary, bankruptcy, destitution, hardship, impecuniousness, indigence, insolvency, necessity, need, penury, privation, want. **2** absence, dearth, insufficiency, lack, paucity, scarcity, shortage.

POW *abbreviation* prisoner of war.

powder /ˈpaʊdə/ *noun* **1** mass of fine dry particles. **2** medicine or cosmetic in this form. **3** talcum powder. **4** gunpowder. ● *verb* **1** apply powder to. **2** (esp. as **powdered** *adjective*) reduce to powder. □ **powder blue** pale blue. **powder puff** soft pad for applying cosmetic powder to skin. **powder room** *euphemistic* women's lavatory. □ **powdery** *adjective*.

■ *noun* **1** dust, particles. ● *verb* **1** coat, dredge, dust, sprinkle. **2** atomize, crush, granulate, grind, pound, pulverize. □ **powdery** chalky, crumbly, crushed, disintegrating, dry, dusty, fine, friable, granular, granulated, ground, loose, powdered, pulverized, sandy.

power /ˈpaʊə/ *noun* **1** ability to do or act. **2** mental or bodily faculty. **3** influence, authority; ascendancy. **4** authorization. **5** influential person etc. **6** state with international influence. **7** vigour, energy. **8** *colloquial* large number or amount. **9** capacity for exerting mechanical force. **10** mechanical or electrical energy. **11** electricity supply. **12** particular source or form of energy. **13** product obtained by multiplying a number by itself a specified number of times. **14** magnifying capacity of lens. ● *verb* **1** supply with mechanical or electrical energy. **2** (+ *up, down*) increase or decrease power supplied to (device); switch on or off. □ **power cut** temporary withdrawal or failure of electric power supply. **powerhouse 1** power station. **2** person or thing of great energy. **power of attorney** authority to act for another in legal and financial matters. **power point** socket for connection of electrical appliance etc. to mains. **power-sharing** coalition government. **power station** building where electric power is generated for distribution.

■ *noun* **1, 2** ability, capability, capacity, competence, faculty, potential, skill, talent. **3** ascendancy, authority, *colloquial* clout, command, control, dominance, domination, dominion, influence, mastery, omnipotence, potency, rule, sovereignty, supremacy, sway. **4** authority, authorization, licence, permission, privilege, right. **7** drive, energy, force, might, muscle, strength, vigour.

powerful *adjective* having great power or influence. □ **powerfully** *adverb*. **powerfulness** *noun*.

■ authoritative, cogent, commanding, compelling, consuming, convincing, dominant, dynamic, effective, effectual, energetic, forceful, high-powered, influential, invincible, irresistible, mighty, muscular, omnipotent, overpowering, overwhelming, persuasive, potent, sovereign, strong, vigorous, weighty.

powerless *adjective* **1** without power. **2** (often + *to*) wholly unable. □ **powerlessness** *noun*.

■ **1** defenceless, disabled, feeble, helpless, impotent, incapacitated, ineffective, ineffectual, paralysed, weak. **2** (*powerless to*) incapable of, unable to, unfit to.

powwow /ˈpaʊwaʊ/ *noun* meeting for discussion (originally among N. American Indians). ● *verb* hold powwow.

pox *noun* **1** virus disease leaving pocks. **2** *colloquial* syphilis.

pp *abbreviation* pianissimo.

pp. *abbreviation* pages.

p.p. *abbreviation* (also **pp**) *per pro*.

PPS *abbreviation* **1** Parliamentary Private Secretary. **2** further postscript (*post-postscriptum*).

PR *abbreviation* **1** public relations. **2** proportional representation.

practicable /ˈpræktɪkəb(ə)l/ *adjective* that can be done or used. □ **practicability** *noun*.

■ achievable, attainable, doable, feasible, performable, possible, practical, realistic, sensible, viable, workable.

practical /ˈpræktɪk(ə)l/ *adjective* **1** of or concerned with practice rather than theory. **2** functional. **3** good at making, organizing, or mending things. **4** realistic; that can be done. **5** that is such in effect; virtual. ● *noun* practical exam. □ **practical joke** trick played on person. **practical joker** *noun*. □ **practicality** /-ˈkæl-/ *noun* (*plural* **-ies**).

■ **1** applied, empirical, experimental. **2** convenient, functional, handy, usable, useful, utilitarian. **3** businesslike, capable, competent, down-to-earth, efficient, expert, hard-headed, matter-of-fact, no-nonsense, pragmatic, proficient, realistic, sensible, skilled. **4** see PRACTICABLE. □ **practical joke** see TRICK *noun* 6.

practically *adverb* **1** virtually, almost. **2** in a practical way.

■ **1** almost, close to, just about, nearly, to all intents and purposes, virtually.

practice /'præktɪs/ *noun* **1** habitual action. **2** repeated exercise to improve skill. **3** rehearsal. **4** action as opposed to theory. **5** doctor's or lawyer's professional business etc. **6** procedure, esp. of specified kind. □ **in practice 1** when applied; in reality. **2** skilled from recent practice. **out of practice** lacking former skill. **put into practice** apply (idea, method, etc.).
■ **1** convention, custom, habit, routine, tradition, way, *formal* or *jocular* wont. **2, 3** drill, dummy run, exercise, preparation, rehearsal, run-through, training, trial, try-out. **4** action, actuality, application, doing, effect, operation, reality, use. **5** business, office, work. **6** method, *modus operandi*, procedure, routine, technique, way.

practise /'præktɪs/ *verb* (**-sing**) (*US* **-tice**; **-cing**) **1** carry out in action. **2** do repeatedly to improve skill; exercise oneself in or on. **3** (as **practised** *adjective*) expert. **4** engage in (profession, religion, etc.).
■ **1** apply, carry out, do, make a practice of, perform, put into practice. **2** drill, exercise, prepare, rehearse, run through, train. **4** engage in, follow, pursue.

practitioner /præk'tɪʃənə/ *noun* professional worker, esp. in medicine.
praesidium = PRESIDIUM.
praetorian guard /priː'tɔːrɪən/ *noun* bodyguard of ancient Roman emperor etc.
pragmatic /præg'mætɪk/ *adjective* dealing with matters from a practical point of view. □ **pragmatically** *adverb*.
pragmatism /'prægmətɪz(ə)m/ *noun* **1** pragmatic attitude or procedure. **2** *Philosophy* doctrine that evaluates assertions according to their practical consequences. □ **pragmatist** *noun*.
prairie /'preərɪ/ *noun* large treeless tract of grassland, esp. in N. America.
praise /preɪz/ *verb* (**-sing**) **1** express warm approval or admiration of. **2** glorify. ● *noun* praising; commendation. □ **praiseworthy** worthy of praise.
■ *verb* **1** acclaim, admire, applaud, cheer, clap, commend, compliment, congratulate, eulogize, extol, marvel at, pay tribute to, rave about, recommend, say nice things about. **2** adore, exalt, glorify, honour, laud, *archaic* magnify, worship. ● *noun* acclaim, acclamation, accolade, admiration, adoration, adulation, applause, approbation, approval, commendation, compliment, congratulation, devotion, encomium, eulogy, glorification, homage, honour, ovation, panegyric, plaudits, testimonial, thanks, tribute, worship. □ **praiseworthy** admirable, commendable, creditable, deserving, laudable, meritorious, worthy.

praline /'prɑːliːn/ *noun* sweet made of nuts browned in boiling sugar.
pram *noun* carriage for baby, pushed by person on foot.
■ baby carriage, *formal* perambulator, pushchair.

prance /prɑːns/ *verb* (**-cing**) **1** (of horse) spring

from hind legs. **2** (of person) caper. **3** walk or behave in an elated or arrogant way. ● *noun* prancing; prancing movement.
■ *verb* **1, 2** bound, caper, cavort, dance, frisk, frolic, gambol, hop, jig about, jump, leap, play, romp, skip, spring. **3** parade, *colloquial* show off, strut, swagger, *colloquial* swan, *colloquial* swank.

prank *noun* practical joke.
prat *noun slang* fool.
prate *verb* (**-ting**) **1** talk too much. **2** chatter foolishly. ● *noun* idle talk.
prattle /'præt(ə)l/ *verb* (**-ling**) talk in childish or inconsequential way. ● *noun* prattling talk.
■ *verb* babble, blather, chatter, gabble, maunder, *colloquial* natter, rattle on, *colloquial* witter on.

prawn *noun* edible shellfish like large shrimp.
pray *verb* (often + *for, to do, that*) **1** say prayers; make devout supplication. **2** entreat.
■ appeal (to), ask, beg, beseech, call upon, entreat, implore, invoke, petition, plead (with), *literary* supplicate.

prayer /preə/ *noun* **1** request or thanksgiving to God or object of worship. **2** formula used in praying. **3** act of praying. **4** entreaty. □ **prayer book** book of set prayers. **prayer mat** small carpet on which Muslims kneel when praying. **prayer shawl** one worn by male Jews when praying.
■ **1** collect, entreaty, intercession, invocation, litany, petition, request, *literary* supplication, thanksgiving. **3** devotion, intercession, meditation, praise, *literary* supplication, thanksgiving, worship. **4** appeal, entreaty, petition, plea, request, *literary* supplication. □ **prayer book** breviary, *RC Church* missal.

prayerful /'preəfʊl/ *adjective* given to praying; devout.
pre- *prefix* before (in time, place, order, degree, or importance).
preach *verb* **1** deliver (sermon); proclaim (the gospel etc.). **2** give moral advice obtrusively. **3** advocate, inculcate. □ **preacher** *noun*.
■ **1** deliver, expound, proclaim; (*preach gospel to*) evangelize, proselytize. **2** harangue, lay down the law, lecture, moralize, pontificate, sermonize. □ **preacher** clergyman, clergywoman, cleric, crusader, divine, ecclesiastic, evangelist, minister, missionary, moralist, pastor.

preamble /priː'æmb(ə)l/ *noun* **1** preliminary statement. **2** introductory part of statute, deed, etc.
pre-arrange /priːə'reɪndʒ/ *verb* (**-ging**) arrange beforehand. □ **pre-arranged** *adjective*. **pre-arrangement** *noun*.
■ □ **pre-arranged** fixed, planned, predetermined, prepared, rehearsed, thought out.

prebend /'prebənd/ *noun* **1** stipend of canon or member of chapter. **2** portion of land etc. from which this is drawn. □ **prebendal** /prɪ'bend(ə)l/ *adjective*.

prebendary /ˈprebəndərɪ/ noun (plural **-ies**) **1** holder of prebend. **2** honorary canon.

Precambrian /priːˈkæmbrɪən/ adjective of earliest geological era. ● noun this era.

precarious /prɪˈkeərɪəs/ adjective **1** uncertain; dependent on chance. **2** perilous. □ **precariously** adverb. **precariousness** noun.

■ dangerous, slang dicey, colloquial dodgy, dubious, hazardous, insecure, perilous, risky, colloquial rocky, shaky, slippery, treacherous, uncertain, unreliable, unsafe, unstable, unsteady, vulnerable, wobbly.

precast /priːˈkɑːst/ adjective (of concrete) cast in required shape before positioning.

precaution /prɪˈkɔːʃ(ə)n/ noun action taken beforehand to avoid risk or ensure good result. □ **precautionary** adjective.

■ preventive measure, safeguard, safety measure.

precede /prɪˈsiːd/ verb (**-ding**) **1** come or go before in time, order, importance, etc. **2** (+ by) cause to be preceded by.

■ **1** be in front of, come before, go ahead of, go before, go in front of, herald, introduce, lead, lead into, pave the way for, preface, prefix, start, usher in.

precedence /ˈpresɪd(ə)ns/ noun **1** priority. **2** right of preceding others. □ **take precedence** (often + over, of) have priority.

precedent noun /ˈpresɪd(ə)nt/ previous case taken as guide or justification etc. ● adjective /prɪˈsiːd(ə)nt/ preceding.

precentor /prɪˈsentə/ noun leader of singing or (in synagogue) prayers of congregation.

precept /ˈpriːsept/ noun rule for action or conduct.

preceptor /prɪˈseptə/ noun teacher, instructor. □ **preceptorial** /priːsepˈtɔːrɪəl/ adjective.

precession /prɪˈseʃ(ə)n/ noun **1** slow movement of axis of spinning body around another axis. **2** such change causing equinoxes to occur earlier in each successive sidereal year.

precinct /ˈpriːsɪŋkt/ noun **1** enclosed area, esp. around building. **2** district in town, esp. where traffic is excluded. **3** (in plural) environs.

preciosity /preʃɪˈɒsɪtɪ/ noun affected refinement in art.

precious /ˈpreʃəs/ adjective **1** of great value. **2** much prized. **3** affectedly refined. ● adverb colloquial extremely, very.

■ adjective **1** costly, expensive, invaluable, irreplaceable, priceless, valuable. **2** adored, beloved, darling, dear, loved, prized, treasured, valued, venerated.

precipice /ˈpresɪpɪs/ noun vertical or steep face of rock, cliff, mountain, etc.

■ bluff, cliff, crag, drop, escarpment.

precipitate verb /prɪˈsɪpɪteɪt/ (**-ting**) **1** hasten occurrence of. **2** (+ into) cause to go into (war etc.) hurriedly or violently. **3** throw down headlong. **4** Chemistry cause (substance) to be deposited in solid form from solution. **5** Physics condense (vapour) into drops. ● adjective /prɪˈsɪpɪtət/ **1** headlong. **2** hasty, rash. ● noun /prɪˈsɪpɪtət/ **1** solid matter precipitated. **2** moisture condensed from vapour. □ **precipitately** /prɪˈsɪpɪtətlɪ/ adverb. **precipitateness** /prɪˈsɪpɪtətnɪs/ noun.

■ verb **1** accelerate, advance, bring on, cause, encourage, expedite, further, hasten, hurry, incite, induce, instigate, occasion, provoke, spark off, trigger off. ● adjective **1** breakneck, fast, headlong, meteoric, premature, quick, rapid. **2** see HASTY 2.

precipitation /prɪsɪpɪˈteɪʃ(ə)n/ noun **1** precipitating, being precipitated. **2** rash haste. **3** rain, snow, etc., falling to ground.

■ **3** dew, drizzle, hail, rain, sleet, snow.

precipitous /prɪˈsɪpɪtəs/ adjective of or like precipice; steep.

■ abrupt, perpendicular, sharp, sheer, steep, vertical.

précis /ˈpreɪsiː/ noun (plural same /-siːz/) summary, abstract. ● verb (**-cises** /-siːz/, **-cised** /-siːd/, **-cising** /-siːɪŋ/) make précis of.

precise /prɪˈsaɪs/ adjective **1** accurately worded; definite, exact. **2** punctilious.

■ **1** accurate, clear-cut, correct, defined, definite, distinct, exact, explicit, fixed, measured, right, specific, unambiguous, unequivocal, well defined. **2** careful, critical, exacting, fastidious, finicky, meticulous, nice, punctilious, rigorous, scrupulous.

precisely adverb **1** in a precise way; exactly. **2** quite so.

precision /prɪˈsɪʒ(ə)n/ noun accuracy. ● adjective designed for or produced by precise work.

preclude /prɪˈkluːd/ verb (**-ding**) (often + from) prevent; make impossible.

■ avert, avoid, bar, debar, exclude, forestall, frustrate, impede, obviate, pre-empt, prevent, prohibit, rule out, thwart.

precocious /prɪˈkəʊʃəs/ adjective prematurely developed in some respect. □ **precociously** adverb. **precociousness** noun. **precocity** /-ˈkɒs-/ noun.

■ advanced, forward, gifted, mature, quick.

precognition /priːkɒɡˈnɪʃ(ə)n/ noun (esp. supernatural) foreknowledge.

preconceive /priːkənˈsiːv/ verb (**-ving**) form (opinion etc.) beforehand.

preconception /priːkənˈsepʃ(ə)n/ noun **1** preconceived idea. **2** prejudice.

■ assumption, bias, expectation, predisposition, prejudgement, prejudice, presupposition.

precondition /priːkənˈdɪʃ(ə)n/ noun condition that must be fulfilled beforehand.

precursor /priːˈkɜːsə/ noun **1** forerunner. **2** person who precedes in office etc. **3** harbinger.

predate /priːˈdeɪt/ verb (**-ting**) precede in time.

predator /'prɛdətə/ *noun* **1** predatory animal. **2** exploiter of others.

predatory /'prɛdətərɪ/ *adjective* **1** (of animal) preying naturally on others. **2** plundering or exploiting others.

■ **1** hunting, preying, rapacious, ravening, ravenous, voracious. **2** acquisitive, avaricious, covetous, extortionate, greedy, marauding, pillaging, plundering, rapacious, ravenous.

predecease /priːdɪˈsiːs/ *verb* (**-sing**) die before (another).

predecessor /'priːdɪsesə/ *noun* **1** previous holder of office or position. **2** ancestor. **3** thing to which another has succeeded.

■ **1** forerunner, precursor. **2** ancestor, antecedent, forebear, forefather, progenitor. **3** antecedent, forerunner, precursor.

predestine /priːˈdɛstɪn/ *verb* (**-ning**) **1** determine beforehand. **2** ordain by divine will or as if by fate. □ **predestination** *noun*.

predetermine /priːdɪˈtɜːmɪn/ *verb* (**-ning**) **1** decree beforehand. **2** predestine.

■ **1** agree, pre-arrange, set up. **2** fate, destine, doom, ordain, predestine.

predicament /prɪˈdɪkəmənt/ *noun* difficult or unpleasant situation.

■ crisis, difficulty, *disputed* dilemma, embarrassment, emergency, fix, impasse, *colloquial* jam, mess, *colloquial* pickle, plight, problem, quandary, situation, state.

predicate *verb* /'prɛdɪkeɪt/ (**-ting**) **1** assert (something) about subject of proposition. **2** (+ *on*) base (statement etc.) on. ● *noun* /'prɛdɪkət/ *Grammar* & *Logic* what is said about subject of sentence or proposition. □ **predicable** *adjective*. **predication** *noun*.

predicative /prɪˈdɪkətɪv/ *adjective* **1** *Grammar* (of adjective or noun) forming part or all of predicate. **2** that predicates.

predict /prɪˈdɪkt/ *verb* forecast, prophesy. □ **predictable** *adjective*. **predictably** *adverb*. **prediction** *noun*. **predictive** *adjective*.

■ augur, forebode, forecast, foresee, foreshadow, foretell, forewarn, hint, intimate, presage, prognosticate, prophesy. □ **predictable** *disputed* anticipated, certain, expected, foreseeable, foreseen, likely, on the cards, probable, sure, unsurprising.

predilection /priːdɪˈlɛkʃ(ə)n/ *noun* (often + *for*) preference, special liking.

predispose /priːdɪsˈpəʊz/ *verb* (**-sing**) **1** influence favourably in advance. **2** (+ *to*, *to do*) render liable or inclined beforehand to. □ **predisposition** /-pəˈzɪʃ(ə)n/ *noun*.

predominate /prɪˈdɒmɪneɪt/ *verb* (**-ting**) **1** (+ *over*) have control over. **2** preponderate, prevail. □ **predominance** *noun*. **predominant** *adjective*. **predominantly** *adverb*.

■ **1** (*predominate over*) control, dominate, have the upper hand on, hold sway over, lead, prevail over, reign over, rule over. **2** be in the majority, dominate, preponderate, prevail; (*predominate over*) outnumber, outweigh. □ **predominant** ascendant, chief, dominating, leading, main, preponderant, prevailing, prevalent, primary, ruling, sovereign.

pre-eminent /priːˈɛmɪnənt/ *adjective* excelling others; outstanding. □ **pre-eminence** *noun*. **pre-eminently** *adverb*.

■ distinguished, eminent, excellent, incomparable, matchless, outstanding, peerless, supreme, unrivalled, unsurpassed.

pre-empt /priːˈɛmpt/ *verb* **1** forestall. **2** obtain by pre-emption.

USAGE *Pre-empt* is sometimes used to mean *prevent*, but this is considered incorrect in standard English.

■ **1** anticipate, forestall. **2** appropriate, arrogate, expropriate, seize, take over.

pre-emption /priːˈɛmpʃ(ə)n/ *noun* purchase or taking of thing before it is offered to others.

pre-emptive /priːˈɛmptɪv/ *adjective* **1** pre-empting. **2** *Military* intended to prevent attack by disabling enemy.

preen *verb* **1** (of bird) tidy (feathers, itself) with beak. **2** (of person) smarten or admire (oneself, one's hair, clothes, etc.). **3** (often + *on*) pride (oneself).

prefab /'priːfæb/ *noun colloquial* prefabricated building.

prefabricate /priːˈfæbrɪkeɪt/ *verb* (**-ting**) manufacture sections of (building etc.) prior to assembly on site.

preface /'prɛfəs/ *noun* **1** introduction to book stating subject, scope, etc. **2** preliminary part of speech. ● *verb* (**-cing**) **1** (often + *with*) introduce or begin (as) with preface. **2** (of event etc.) lead up to (another). □ **prefatory** /-t(ə)rɪ/ *adjective*.

■ *noun* foreword, introduction, lead-in, preamble, prolegomenon, prologue. ● *verb* **1** begin, introduce, lead into, open, precede, prefix, start. **2** lead up to, precede.

prefect /'priːfɛkt/ *noun* **1** chief administrative officer of district in France etc. **2** senior pupil in school, authorized to maintain discipline.

prefecture /'priːfɛktʃə/ *noun* **1** district under government of prefect. **2** prefect's office or tenure.

prefer /prɪˈfɜː/ *verb* (**-rr-**) **1** (often + *to*, *to do*) like better. **2** submit (information, accusation, etc.). **3** promote (person).

■ **1** be partial to, choose, fancy, favour, go for, incline towards, like better, opt for, pick out, plump for, select, single out, vote for.

preferable /'prɛfərəb(ə)l/ *adjective* to be preferred; more desirable. □ **preferably** *adverb*.

■ advantageous, better, better-liked, chosen, favoured, nicer, preferred.

preference /'prefərəns/ *noun* **1** preferring, being preferred. **2** thing preferred. **3** favouring of one person etc. before others. **4** prior right.

■ **1** inclination, liking, partiality, predilection, proclivity. **2** choice, fancy, favourite, option, pick, selection, wish; (*preferences*) likes. **3** bias, favouritism, partiality, prejudice.

preferential /prefə'renʃ(ə)l/ *adjective* of, giving, or receiving preference. □ **preferentially** *adverb*.

■ advantageous, better, biased, favourable, favoured, privileged, special, superior.

preferment /prɪ'fɜ:mənt/ *noun formal* promotion to higher office.

prefigure /priː'fɪgə/ *verb* (**-ring**) represent or imagine beforehand.

prefix /'priː.fɪks/ *noun* **1** part-word added to beginning of word to alter meaning, e.g. *re-* in *retake*, *ex-* in *ex-president*. **2** title before name. ● *verb* **1** (often + *to*) add as introduction. **2** join (word, element) as prefix.

pregnant /'pregnənt/ *adjective* **1** having child or young developing in womb. **2** significant, suggestive. □ **pregnancy** *noun* (*plural* **-ies**).

■ **1** expectant, *colloquial* expecting, gestating, gravid, *literary* with child. **2** see MEANINGFUL (MEANING).

preheat /priː'hiːt/ *verb* heat beforehand.

prehensile /prɪ'hensaɪl/ *adjective* (of tail, limb, etc.) capable of grasping.

prehistoric /priː.hɪs'tɒrɪk/ *adjective* of period before written records. □ **prehistory** /-'hɪstərɪ/ *noun*.

prejudge /priː'dʒʌdʒ/ *verb* (**-ging**) form premature judgement on (person etc.). □ **prejudgement** *noun*.

prejudice /'predʒʊdɪs/ *noun* **1** preconceived opinion. **2** (+ *against*, *in favour of*) bias. **3** harm (possibly) resulting from action or judgement. ● *verb* (**-cing**) **1** impair validity of. **2** (esp. as **prejudiced** *adjective*) cause (person) to have prejudice. □ **prejudicial** /-'dɪʃ-/ *adjective*.

■ *noun* **1, 2** bias, bigotry, discrimination, dogmatism, fanaticism, favouritism, intolerance, leaning, narrow-mindedness, partiality, partisanship, predilection, predisposition, prejudgement, unfairness. ● *verb* **1** damage, harm, injure, ruin, spoil, undermine. **2** bias, colour, incline, influence, predispose, sway; (**prejudiced**) biased, bigoted, discriminatory, illiberal, intolerant, jaundiced, narrow-minded, one-sided, parochial, partial, partisan, *derogatory* tendentious, unfair. □ **prejudicial** damaging, deleterious, detrimental, disadvantageous, harmful, inimical, injurious, unfavourable.

prelacy /'preləsɪ/ *noun* (*plural* **-ies**) **1** church government by prelates. **2** (**the prelacy**) prelates collectively. **3** office or rank of prelate.

prelate /'prelət/ *noun* high ecclesiastical dignitary, e.g. bishop.

preliminary /prɪ'lɪmɪnərɪ/ *adjective* introductory, preparatory. ● *noun* (*plural* **-ies**) (usually in *plural*) **1** preliminary action or arrangement. **2** preliminary trial or contest.

■ *adjective* advance, earliest, early, experimental, exploratory, first, inaugural, initial, introductory, opening, prefatory, preparatory, tentative, trial. ● *noun* **1** see PRELUDE *noun* **1**.

prelude /'preljuːd/ *noun* **1** (often + *to*) action, event, etc. serving as introduction. **2** introductory part of poem etc. **3** *Music* introductory piece of suite. **4** *Music* short piece of similar type. ● *verb* (**-ding**) **1** serve as prelude to. **2** introduce with prelude.

■ *noun* **1** beginning, curtain-raiser, introduction, opener, opening, precursor, preliminary, preparation, prologue, start, starter, warm-up. **2** beginning, foreword, introduction, opening, overture, preamble, preface, prolegomenon, prologue, start.

premarital /priː'mærɪt(ə)l/ *adjective* occurring etc. before marriage.

premature /'premətʃə/ *adjective* **1** occurring or done before usual or right time; too hasty. **2** (of baby) born 3 or more weeks before expected time. □ **prematurely** *adverb*.

■ **1** before time, early, hasty, ill-timed, precipitate, *colloquial* previous, too early, too soon, undeveloped, untimely.

premed /priː'med/ *noun colloquial* premedication.

premedication /priː.medr'keɪʃ(ə)n/ *noun* medication in preparation for operation.

premeditate /priː'medɪteɪt/ *verb* (**-ting**) think out or plan beforehand. □ **premeditated** *adjective*. **premeditation** *noun*.

■ □ **premeditated** calculated, conscious, considered, contrived, deliberate, intended, intentional, planned, pre-arranged, preconceived, predetermined, studied, wilful.

premenstrual /priː'menstrʊəl/ *adjective* of the time immediately before menstruation.

premier /'premɪə/ *noun* prime minister. ● *adjective* first in importance, order, or time. □ **premiership** *noun*.

première /'premɪeə/ *noun* first performance or showing of play or film. ● *verb* (**-ring**) give première of.

premise /'premɪs/ *noun* **1** premiss. **2** (in *plural*) house or other building with its grounds etc. **3** (in *plural*) *Law* previously specified houses, lands, or tenements. □ **on the premises** in the house etc. concerned.

premiss /'premɪs/ *noun* previous statement from which another is inferred.

■ assertion, assumption, basis, grounds, hypothesis, proposition, supposition, thesis.

premium /'priːmɪəm/ *noun* **1** amount to be paid for contract of insurance. **2** sum added to interest, wages, etc. **3** reward, prize. ● *adjective* of best quality and highest price. □ **at a premium** highly valued; above usual or nominal price. **Premium**

(Savings) Bond government security not bearing interest but with periodic prize draw.

premonition /premə'nɪʃ(ə)n/ *noun* forewarning; presentiment. □ **premonitory** /prɪ'mɒnɪtərɪ/ *adjective*.

■ foreboding, forewarning, hunch, indication, intuition, misgiving, omen, portent, presentiment, suspicion, warning.

prenatal /pri:'neɪt(ə)l/ *adjective* existing or occurring before birth.

preoccupy /pri:'ɒkjʊpaɪ/ *verb* (**-ies, -ied**) **1** dominate mind of. **2** (as **preoccupied** *adjective*) otherwise engrossed. □ **preoccupation** *noun*.

■ **2** (**preoccupied**) absent-minded, absorbed, abstracted, daydreaming, distracted, engaged, engrossed, far-away, immersed, inattentive, involved, lost in thought, musing, obsessed, pensive, pondering, rapt, reflecting, taken up, thoughtful, wrapped up.

preordain /pri:ɔ:'deɪn/ *verb* ordain or determine beforehand.

prep *noun colloquial* **1** homework. **2** time when this is done.

prepack /pri:'pæk/ *verb* (also **pre-package** /-'pækɪdʒ/) pack (goods) before retail.

preparation /prepə'reɪʃ(ə)n/ *noun* **1** preparing, being prepared. **2** (often in *plural*) thing done to make ready. **3** substance specially prepared.

■ **1** briefing, gearing up, getting ready, groundwork, making provision, organization, practice, setting up, spadework, training. **2** (*preparations*) arrangements, measures, plans, provisions.

preparatory /prɪ'pærətərɪ/ *adjective* (often + *to*) serving to prepare; introductory. ● *adverb* (often + *to*) as a preparation. □ **preparatory school** private primary or (*US*) secondary school.

prepare /prɪ'peə/ *verb* (**-ring**) **1** make or get ready. **2** train, fit, equip. **3** (often **prepare oneself**) get oneself ready.

■ **1** arrange, cook, devise, do what's necessary, fix up, get ready, make, make arrangements, make ready, organize, pave the way, plan, pre-arrange, process, set up. **2** brief, coach, educate, equip, fit, instruct, practise, prime, rehearse, teach, train, tutor. **3** (**prepare oneself**) brace oneself, discipline oneself, fortify oneself, steel oneself.

prepay /pri:'peɪ/ *verb* (*past & past participle* **prepaid**) **1** pay (charge) beforehand. **2** pay postage on beforehand. □ **prepayment** *noun*.

preponderate /prɪ'pɒndəreɪt/ *verb* (**-ting**) (often + *over*) **1** be superior in influence, quantity, or number. **2** predominate. □ **preponderance** *noun*. **preponderant** *adjective*.

preposition /prepə'zɪʃ(ə)n/ *noun* word used before noun or pronoun to indicate its relationship to another word (see panel). □ **prepositional** *adjective*.

prepossess /pri:pə'zes/ *verb* **1** (usually in *passive*) take possession of. **2** prejudice, usually favourably. **3** (as **prepossessing** *adjective*) attractive. □ **prepossession** *noun*.

preposterous /prɪ'pɒstərəs/ *adjective* **1** utterly absurd. **2** contrary to nature or reason. □ **preposterously** *adverb*.

■ absurd, bizarre, excessive, extreme, grotesque, ludicrous, monstrous, outrageous, ridiculous, surreal, unreasonable, *colloquial* unthinkable.

prepuce /'pri:pju:s/ *noun* foreskin.

Pre-Raphaelite /pri:'ræfəlaɪt/ *noun* member of group of 19th-c. English artists. ● *adjective* **1** of Pre-Raphaelites. **2** (**pre-Raphaelite**) (esp. of woman) of type painted by Pre-Raphaelites.

pre-record /pri:rɪ'kɔ:d/ *verb* record in advance.

prerequisite /pri:'rekwɪzɪt/ *adjective* required as precondition. ● *noun* prerequisite thing.

USAGE *Prerequisite* is sometimes confused with *perquisite*, which means 'an extra profit, right, or privilege'.

Preposition

A preposition is used in front of a noun or pronoun to form a phrase. It often describes the position or movement of something, e.g. *under the chair*, or the time at which something happens, e.g. *in the evening*.

Prepositions in common use are:

about	*behind*	*into*	*through*
above	*beside*	*like*	*till*
across	*between*	*near*	*to*
after	*by*	*of*	*towards*
against	*down*	*off*	*under*
along	*during*	*on*	*underneath*
among	*except*	*outside*	*until*
around	*for*	*over*	*up*
as	*from*	*past*	*upon*
at	*in*	*round*	*with*
before	*inside*	*since*	*without*

■ *adjective* compulsory, essential, indispensable, mandatory, necessary, obligatory, prescribed, required, requisite, specified, stipulated. ● *noun* condition, essential, necessity, precondition, proviso, qualification, requirement, requisite, *sine qua non*, stipulation.

prerogative /prɪˈrɒgətɪv/ *noun* right or privilege exclusive to individual or class.

Pres. *abbreviation* President.

presage /ˈpresɪdʒ/ *noun* **1** omen. **2** presentiment. ● *verb* (**-ging**) **1** portend. **2** indicate (future event etc.). **3** foretell, foresee.

presbyopia /prezbɪˈəʊpɪə/ *noun* long-sightedness. □ **presbyopic** *adjective*.

presbyter /ˈprezbɪtə/ *noun* **1** priest of Episcopal Church. **2** elder of Presbyterian Church.

Presbyterian /prezbɪˈtɪərɪən/ *adjective* (of Church, esp. Church of Scotland) governed by elders all of equal rank. ● *noun* member of Presbyterian Church. □ **Presbyterianism** *noun*.

presbytery /ˈprezbɪtərɪ/ *noun* (*plural* **-ies**) **1** eastern part of chancel. **2** body of presbyters. **3** RC priest's house.

prescient /ˈpresɪənt/ *adjective* having foreknowledge or foresight. □ **prescience** *noun*.

prescribe /prɪˈskraɪb/ *verb* (**-bing**) **1** advise use of (medicine etc.). **2** lay down authoritatively.

USAGE *Prescribe* is sometimes confused with *proscribe*, which means 'forbid'.

■ **1** advise, recommend, suggest. **2** assign, command, demand, dictate, direct, fix, impose, instruct, lay down, ordain, order, require, specify, stipulate.

prescript /ˈpriːskrɪpt/ *noun* ordinance, command.

prescription /prɪˈskrɪpʃ(ə)n/ *noun* **1** prescribing. **2** doctor's (usually written) instruction for composition and use of medicine. **3** medicine thus prescribed.

prescriptive /prɪˈskrɪptɪv/ *adjective* **1** prescribing. **2** laying down rules. **3** arising from custom.

presence /ˈprez(ə)ns/ *noun* **1** being present. **2** place where person is. **3** personal appearance; force of personality. **4** person or spirit that is present. □ **presence of mind** calmness and quick-wittedness in sudden difficulty etc.

■ **1** attendance, closeness, companionship, company, nearness, propinquity, proximity, society. **3** air, appearance, aura, bearing, *literary* comportment, demeanour, impressiveness, *literary* mien, personality, poise, self-assurance, self-possession.

present[1] /ˈprez(ə)nt/ *adjective* **1** being in place in question. **2** now existing, occurring, or being dealt with etc. **3** *Grammar* expressing present action or state. ● *noun* (**the present**) **1** now. **2** present tense. □ **at present** now. **for the present** just now. **present-day** of this time; modern.

■ *adjective* **1** at hand, here, in attendance. **2** contemporary, current, existing, extant, present-day. ● *noun* **1** (**the present**) here and now, now, today.

present[2] /prɪˈzent/ *verb* **1** introduce. **2** exhibit; reveal; offer for consideration. **3** offer or give (thing) to. **4** (+ *with*) provide (person) with. **5** put (play, film, etc.) before public. **6** deliver (cheque etc.) for payment etc. □ **present arms** hold rifle etc. in saluting position. **present oneself** appear.

■ **1** announce, introduce, make known. **2** adduce, bring forward, demonstrate, display, exhibit, furnish, proffer, put forward, reveal, set out, show, submit. **3, 4** award, bestow, confer, dispense, distribute, donate, give, hand over, offer. **5** act, bring out, perform, put on, stage. □ **present oneself** see APPEAR 1, REPORT *verb* 4.

present[3] /ˈprez(ə)nt/ *noun* gift.

■ *historical* alms, bonus, bounty, contribution, donation, endowment, gift, grant, gratuity, handout, offering, tip.

presentable /prɪˈzentəb(ə)l/ *adjective* of good appearance; fit to be shown. □ **presentability** *noun*. **presentably** *adverb*.

■ acceptable, adequate, all right, clean, decent, decorous, good enough, neat, passable, proper, respectable, satisfactory, suitable, tidy, tolerable, up to scratch, worthy.

presentation /prezənˈteɪʃ(ə)n/ *noun* **1** presenting, being presented. **2** thing presented. **3** manner or quality of presenting. **4** demonstration of materials etc.; lecture.

presenter *noun* person introducing broadcast programme.

presentiment /prɪˈzentɪmənt/ *noun* vague expectation; foreboding.

presently *adverb* **1** before long. **2** *US & Scottish* at present.

■ **1** *archaic* anon, before long, by and by, *colloquial* in a jiffy, shortly, soon.

preservative /prɪˈzɜːvətɪv/ *noun* substance for preserving food etc. ● *adjective* tending to preserve.

preserve /prɪˈzɜːv/ *verb* (**-ving**) **1** keep safe or free from decay. **2** maintain, retain. **3** treat (food) to prevent decomposition or fermentation. **4** treat (corpse) to prevent decomposition. **5** keep (game etc.) undisturbed for private use. ● *noun* **1** (in *singular* or *plural*) preserved fruit, jam. **2** place where game etc. is preserved. **3** sphere of activity regarded by person as his or hers alone. □ **preservation** /prezəˈveɪʃ(ə)n/ *noun*. **preserver** *noun*.

■ *verb* **1** care for, defend, guard, look after, protect, safeguard, save, secure, watch over. **2** conserve, keep, lay up, maintain, perpetuate, retain, save, stockpile, store, support, sustain, uphold. **3** bottle, can, chill, conserve, cure, dehydrate, dry, freeze, freeze-dry, irradiate, jam, pickle, refrigerate, salt, tin. **4** embalm, mummify. ● *noun* **1** conserve, jam, jelly, marmalade. **2** reservation, reserve, sanctuary.

preshrunk /priːˈʃrʌŋk/ *adjective* (of fabric etc.) treated so as to shrink during manufacture and not in use.

preside /prɪ'zaɪd/ *verb* (**-ding**) (often + *at*, *over*) **1** be chairperson or president. **2** exercise control or authority.
■ **1** be in charge, chair, officiate, take charge, take the chair. **2** (*preside over*) see GOVERN 1.

presidency /'prezɪdənsɪ/ *noun* (*plural* **-ies**) **1** office of president. **2** period of this.

president /'prezɪd(ə)nt/ *noun* **1** head of republic. **2** head of society or council etc., of certain colleges, or (*US*) of university, company, etc. **3** person in charge of meeting. □ **presidential** /-'den-/ *adjective*.

presidium /prɪ'sɪdɪəm/ *noun* (also **praesidium**) standing committee, esp. in Communist country.

press[1] *verb* **1** apply steady force to. **2** flatten, shape, smooth (esp. clothes). **3** (+ *out of*, *from*, etc.) squeeze (juice etc.). **4** embrace, caress firmly. **5** (+ *on*, *against*, etc.) exert pressure on. **6** be urgent; urge. **7** (+ *for*) demand insistently. **8** (+ *up*, *round*, etc.) crowd. **9** (+ *on*, *forward*, etc.) hasten. **10** (+ *on*, *upon*) force (offer etc.) on. **11** manufacture (gramophone record, car part, etc.) using pressure. ● *noun* **1** pressing. **2** device for compressing, flattening, extracting juice, etc. **3** machine for printing. **4** printing house; publishing company. **5** (**the press**) newspapers. **6** publicity in newspapers. **7** crowding; crowd. **8** pressure of affairs. **9** large usually shelved cupboard. □ **press agent** person employed to manage advertising and press publicity. **press conference** meeting with journalists. **press gallery** gallery for reporters, esp. in legislative assembly. **press release** statement issued to newspapers etc. **press stud** small device fastened by pressing to engage two parts. **press-up** exercise in which prone body is raised by pressing down on hands to straighten arms.
■ *verb* **1** compress, condense, crush, depress, force, push, shove, *colloquial* squash, squeeze. **2** flatten, iron, smooth. **6, 7** ask, beg, bully, coerce, constrain, dragoon, entreat, exhort, implore, importune, induce, *colloquial* lean on, persuade, pressure, pressurize, put pressure on, request, require, urge. **8** cram, crowd, flock, gather, jam, pack, throng. ● *noun* **5** (**the press**) magazines, the media, newspapers.

press[2] *verb* **1** *historical* force to serve in army or navy. **2** bring into use as makeshift. □ **press-gang** *noun historical* group of men employed to press men for navy. ● *verb* force into service.

pressing *adjective* **1** urgent. **2** insistent. ● *noun* **1** thing made by pressing, e.g. gramophone record. **2** series of these made at one time. **3** act of pressing. □ **pressingly** *adverb*.
■ *adjective* see URGENT 1.

pressure /'preʃə/ *noun* **1** exertion of continuous force. **2** force so exerted. **3** amount of this. **4** urgency. **5** affliction, difficulty. **6** constraining or compelling influence. ● *verb* (**-ring**) **1** (often + *into*) apply pressure to. **2** (often + *into*) coerce; persuade. □ **pressure cooker** pan for cooking quickly under high pressure. **pressure group** group formed to influence public policy.
■ *noun* **1, 2** burden, compression, force, heaviness, load, might, power, stress, weight. **4, 5** adversity, affliction, constraints, demands, difficulties, exigencies, *colloquial* hassle, hurry, oppression, problems, strain, stress, urgency. ● *verb* ask, beg, bully, coerce, constrain, dragoon, entreat, exhort, implore, importune, induce, *colloquial* lean on, persuade, press, pressurize, request, require, urge.

pressurize *verb* (also **-ise**) (**-zing** or **-sing**) **1** (esp. as **pressurized** *adjective*) maintain normal atmospheric pressure in (aircraft cabin etc.) at high altitude. **2** raise to high pressure. **3** pressure (person).

prestidigitator /prestɪ'dɪdʒɪteɪtə/ *noun formal* conjuror. □ **prestidigitation** *noun*.

prestige /pres'tiːʒ/ *noun* respect or reputation. ● *adjective* having or conferring prestige. □ **prestigious** /-'stɪdʒəs/ *adjective*.
■ *noun* cachet, celebrity, credit, distinction, eminence, esteem, fame, glory, good name, honour, importance, influence, *colloquial* kudos, regard, renown, reputation, respect, standing, stature, status. □ **prestigious** acclaimed, august, celebrated, creditable, distinguished, eminent, esteemed, estimable, famed, famous, high-ranking, honourable, honoured, important, influential, pre-eminent, prestige, renowned, reputable, respected, significant, well known.

presto /'prestəʊ/ *Music adverb & adjective* in quick tempo. ● *noun* (*plural* **-s**) presto movement or passage.

prestressed /priː'strest/ *adjective* (of concrete) strengthened by stretched wires in it.

presumably /prɪ'zjuːməblɪ/ *adverb* as may reasonably be presumed.

presume /prɪ'zjuːm/ *verb* (**-ming**) **1** (often + *that*) suppose to be true; take for granted. **2** (often + *to do*) venture. **3** be presumptuous. **4** (+ *on*, *upon*) make unscrupulous use of.
■ **1** assume, believe, conjecture, gather, guess, hypothesize, imagine, infer, postulate, suppose, surmise, suspect, take for granted, take it, think. **2** be presumptuous enough, dare, have the effrontery, take the liberty, venture.

presumption /prɪ'zʌmpʃ(ə)n/ *noun* **1** arrogance; presumptuous behaviour. **2** taking for granted. **3** thing presumed to be true. **4** ground for presuming.

presumptive /prɪ'zʌmptɪv/ *adjective* giving grounds for presumption.

presumptuous /prɪ'zʌmptʃʊəs/ *adjective* unduly confident; arrogant. □ **presumptuously** *adverb*. **presumptuousness** *noun*.
■ arrogant, bold, brazen, cheeky, conceited, forward, impertinent, impudent, insolent, overconfident, *colloquial* pushy, shameless, unauthorized, unwarranted.

presuppose /priːsə'pəʊz/ *verb* (**-sing**) **1** assume beforehand. **2** imply. □ **presupposition** /-sʌpə'zɪʃ(ə)n/ *noun*.

pre-tax /priːˈtæks/ *adjective* (of income) before deduction of taxes.

pretence /prɪˈtens/ *noun* (*US* **pretense**) **1** pretending, make-believe. **2** pretext; guise. **3** (+ *to*) (esp. false) claim to. **4** ostentation.

■ **1** acting, artifice, camouflage, charade, counterfeiting, deceit, deception, dissembling, dissimulation, falsification, feigning, fiction, humbug, hypocrisy, insincerity, invention, lying, make-believe, sham, simulation, trickery. **2** act, appearance, blind, cover, deception, disguise, excuse, façade, feint, front, guise, hoax, masquerade, pose, pretext, ruse, subterfuge, wile. **4** affectation, display, ostentation, posing, posturing, pretentiousness, show.

pretend /prɪˈtend/ *verb* **1** claim or assert falsely. **2** imagine in play. **3** (as **pretended** *adjective*) falsely claimed to be. **4** (+ *to*) profess to have. ● *adjective colloquial* pretended.

■ *verb* **1** act, affect, allege, bluff, counterfeit, disguise, dissemble, dissimulate, fake, feign, hoax, lie, make believe, make out, profess, purport, sham, simulate; (*pretend to be*) imitate, impersonate, masquerade as, pose as. **2** act, imagine, make believe, perform, play, play-act, play a part, *colloquial* put on an act. **4** (*pretend to*) claim, lay claim to, profess, purport to have.

pretender *noun* person who claims throne, title, etc.

■ aspirant, claimant, rival, suitor.

pretense *US* = PRETENCE.

pretension /prɪˈtenʃ(ə)n/ *noun* (often + *to*) **1** assertion of claim. **2** pretentiousness.

pretentious /prɪˈtenʃəs/ *adjective* **1** making excessive claim to merit or importance. **2** ostentatious. □ **pretentiously** *adverb*. **pretentiousness** *noun*.

■ affected, *colloquial* arty, conceited, exaggerated, extravagant, grandiose, *colloquial* highfalutin, inflated, ostentatious, overblown, over the top, pompous, showy, snobbish, superficial.

preternatural /priːtəˈnætʃər(ə)l/ *adjective* extraordinary; supernatural.

pretext /ˈpriːtekst/ *noun* ostensible reason; excuse.

■ cloak, cover, disguise, excuse, pretence.

pretty /ˈprɪtɪ/ *adjective* (**-ier**, **-iest**) **1** attractive in delicate way. **2** fine, good. **3** considerable. ● *adverb colloquial* fairly, moderately. ● *verb* (**-ies**, **-ied**) (often + *up*) make pretty. □ **pretty-pretty** *colloquial* too pretty. □ **prettify** *verb* (**-ies**, **-ied**). **prettily** *adverb*. **prettiness** *noun*.

■ *adjective* **1** appealing, attractive, beautiful, *esp. Scottish & Northern English* bonny, charming, *esp. US colloquial* cute, dainty, delicate, *colloquial* easy on the eye, fetching, good-looking, *colloquial* lovely, nice, pleasing, *colloquial* pretty-pretty, winsome. ● *adverb* fairly, moderately, quite, rather, reasonably, somewhat, tolerably.

pretzel /ˈprets(ə)l/ *noun* crisp knot-shaped salted biscuit.

prevail /prɪˈveɪl/ *verb* **1** (often + *against*, *over*) be victorious. **2** be the more usual or predominant. **3** exist or occur in general use. **4** (+ *on*, *upon*) persuade. **5** (as **prevailing** *adjective*) predominant; widespread; in general use.

■ **1** succeed, triumph, win, win the day. **2** hold sway, predominate, preponderate. **3** be current, be prevalent, be widespread, exist, obtain. **5** (**prevailing**) accepted, ascendant, chief, commonest, current, dominant, dominating, general, governing, influential, main, mainstream, predominant, prevalent, principal, ruling.

prevalent /ˈprevələnt/ *adjective* generally existing or occurring. □ **prevalence** *noun*.

■ common, current, customary, established, extensive, familiar, fashionable, general, normal, ordinary, orthodox, pervasive, popular, prevailing, ubiquitous, universal, usual, widespread.

prevaricate /prɪˈværɪkeɪt/ *verb* (**-ting**) speak or act evasively or misleadingly. □ **prevarication** *noun*. **prevaricator** *noun*.

USAGE *Prevaricate* is often confused with *procrastinate*, which means 'to defer action'.

■ beat about the bush, be evasive, cavil, deceive, equivocate, fib, hedge, lie, mislead, quibble, temporize.

prevent /prɪˈvent/ *verb* (often + *from doing*) stop, hinder. □ **preventable** *adjective* (also **preventible**). **prevention** *noun*.

USAGE The use of *prevent* without 'from' as in *She prevented me going* is informal. An acceptable further alternative is *She prevented my going*.

■ avert, avoid, baffle, bar, block, check, control, curb, deter, fend off, foil, forbid, forestall, frustrate, hamper, head off, help (*can't help it*), hinder, impede, inhibit, intercept, nip in the bud, obstruct, obviate, preclude, prohibit, put a stop to, restrain, save, stave off, stop, thwart, ward off.

preventative /prɪˈventətɪv/ *adjective* & *noun* preventive.

preventive /prɪˈventɪv/ *adjective* serving to prevent, esp. disease. ● *noun* preventive agent, measure, drug, etc.

■ *adjective* counteractive, deterrent, obstructive, precautionary, pre-emptive, preventative.

preview /ˈpriːvjuː/ *noun* showing of film, play, etc. before it is seen by general public. ● *verb* view or show in advance.

previous /ˈpriːvɪəs/ *adjective* **1** (often + *to*) coming before in time or order. **2** *colloquial* hasty, premature. ● *adverb* (+ *to*) before. □ **previously** *adverb*.

■ *adjective* **1** above-mentioned, aforementioned, aforesaid, antecedent, earlier, erstwhile, foregoing, former, past, preceding, prior. **2** see PREMATURE 1.

pre-war /priːˈwɔː/ *adjective* existing or occurring before a war.

prey /preɪ/ *noun* **1** animal hunted or killed by

another for food. **2** (often + *to*) victim. ● *verb* (+ *on*, *upon*) **1** seek or take as prey. **2** make victim of. **3** exert harmful influence on.

■ *noun* **1** kill, quarry, victim. **2** quarry, target, victim. ● *verb* (*prey on*) **1** eat, feed on, hunt, kill, live off. **2** see EXPLOIT *verb* 2.

price *noun* **1** amount of money for which thing is bought or sold; value. **2** what must be given, done, etc. to obtain thing. **3** odds. ● *verb* (**-cing**) **1** fix or find price of. **2** estimate value of. □ **at a price** at high cost. **price tag** label on item showing its price.

■ *noun* **1** amount, charge, cost, *slang* damage, estimate, expenditure, expense, fare, fee, figure, outlay, payment, quotation, rate, sum, terms, toll, valuation, value, worth. **2** cost, toll; (*pay the price*) see ATONE.

priceless *adjective* **1** invaluable. **2** *colloquial* very amusing or absurd.

■ **1** costly, dear, expensive, incalculable, inestimable, invaluable, irreplaceable, precious, *colloquial* pricey, rare, valuable. **2** see FUNNY 1.

pricey *adjective* (**pricier**, **priciest**) *colloquial* expensive.

prick *verb* **1** pierce slightly; make small hole in. **2** (+ *off*, *out*) mark with pricks or dots. **3** trouble mentally. **4** tingle. ● *noun* **1** pricking. **2** mark of it. **3** pain caused as by pricking. **4** mental pain. □ **prick out** plant (seedlings etc.) in small holes pricked in earth. **prick up one's ears 1** (of dog) erect the ears when alert. **2** (of person) become suddenly attentive.

■ *verb* **1** jab, lance, perforate, pierce, punch, puncture, riddle, stab, sting. **3** see STIMULATE.

prickle /ˈprɪk(ə)l/ *noun* **1** small thorn. **2** hard-pointed spine. **3** prickling sensation. ● *verb* (**-ling**) cause or feel sensation as of prick(s).

■ *noun* **1, 2** barb, needle, spike, spine, thorn. **3** irritation, itch, pricking, tingle, tingling. ● *verb* irritate, itch, scratch, sting, tingle.

prickly *adjective* (**-ier**, **-iest**) **1** having prickles. **2** irritable. **3** tingling. □ **prickly heat** itchy inflammation of skin near sweat glands. **prickly pear 1** cactus with pear-shaped edible fruit. **2** its fruit. □ **prickliness** *noun*.

■ **1** barbed, bristly, rough, scratchy, sharp, spiky, spiny, stubbly, thorny, unshaven. **2** see IRRITABLE 1.

pride *noun* **1** elation or satisfaction at one's achievements, possessions, etc. **2** object of this. **3** unduly high opinion of oneself. **4** proper sense of one's own worth, position, etc. **5** group (of lions etc.). ● *verb* (**-ding**) (**pride oneself on**, **upon**) be proud of. □ **pride of place** most important position. **take (a) pride in** be proud of.

■ *noun* **1** delight, elation, gratification, happiness, joy, pleasure, satisfaction. **2** delight, jewel, joy, treasure, treasured possession. **3** arrogance, *colloquial* big-headedness, boastfulness, conceit, egotism, haughtiness, hubris, megalomania, narcissism, overconfidence, presumption, self-admiration, self-importance, self-love, self-satisfaction, smugness, snobbery, snobbishness, vainglory, vanity. **4** dignity, honour, self-esteem, self-respect.

prie-dieu /priːˈdjɜː/ *noun* (*plural* **-x** same pronunciation) kneeling-desk for prayer.

priest /priːst/ *noun* **1** ordained minister of some Christian churches (above deacon and below bishop). **2** (*feminine* **priestess**) official minister of non-Christian religion. □ **priesthood** *noun*. **priestly** *adjective*.

■ **1** see CLERGYMAN.

prig *noun* self-righteous or moralistic person. □ **priggish** *adjective*. **priggishness** *noun*.

■ □ **priggish** conservative, fussy, *colloquial* goody-goody, haughty, moralistic, prim, prudish, self-righteous, sententious, stiff-necked, stuffy.

prim *adjective* (**-mm-**) **1** stiffly formal and precise. **2** prudish. □ **primly** *adverb*. **primness** *noun*.

■ **1** fastidious, formal, precise, prissy, proper, starchy. **2** demure, inhibited, narrow-minded, proper, prudish, strait-laced.

prima /ˈpriːmə/ *adjective* □ **prima ballerina** chief female dancer in ballet. **prima donna 1** chief female singer in opera. **2** temperamental person.

primacy /ˈpraɪməsɪ/ *noun* (*plural* **-ies**) **1** pre-eminence. **2** office of primate.

prima facie /praɪmə ˈfeɪʃɪ/ *adverb* at first sight. ● *adjective* (of evidence) based on first impression.

primal /ˈpraɪm(ə)l/ *adjective* **1** primitive, primeval. **2** fundamental.

■ **1** early, earliest, first, original, primeval, primitive, primordial. **2** see PRIMARY *adjective* 1.

primary /ˈpraɪmərɪ/ *adjective* **1** of first importance; fundamental. **2** original. ● *noun* (*plural* **-ies**) **1** primary colour, feather, school, etc. **2** *US* primary election. □ **primary colour** one not obtained by mixing others. **primary education** education for children under 11. **primary election** *US* election to select candidate(s) for principal election. **primary feather** large flight feather of bird's wing. **primary school** school for primary education. □ **primarily** /ˈpraɪmərɪlɪ, praɪˈmeərɪlɪ/ *adverb*.

■ *adjective* **1** basic, cardinal, chief, dominant, first, foremost, fundamental, greatest, important, initial, leading, main, major, outstanding, paramount, predominant, pre-eminent, primal, prime, principal, supreme, top. □ **primarily** basically, chiefly, especially, essentially, firstly, fundamentally, generally, mainly, mostly, particularly, predominantly, pre-eminently, principally.

primate /ˈpraɪmeɪt/ *noun* **1** member of highest order of mammals, including apes, man, etc. **2** archbishop.

prime[1] *adjective* **1** chief, most important. **2** of highest quality. **3** primary, fundamental. **4** (of number etc.) divisible only by itself and unity. ● *noun* best or most vigorous stage. □ **prime minister** chief minister of government. **prime mover**

1 initial source of motive power. **2** author of fruitful idea. **prime time** time when television etc. audience is largest.
■ *adjective* **1, 3** see PRIMARY *adjective* 1. **2** best, excellent, first-class, first-rate, foremost, select, superior, top, top-quality.

prime² *verb* (**-ming**) **1** prepare (thing) for use. **2** prepare (gun) for firing or (explosive) for detonation. **3** pour liquid into (pump) to start it working. **4** cover (wood, metal, etc.) with primer. **5** equip (person) with information etc.
■ **1** get ready, prepare. **5** see PREPARE 2.

primer¹ *noun* substance applied to bare wood, metal, etc. before painting.

primer² *noun* **1** elementary school-book. **2** introductory book.

primeval /praɪˈmiːv(ə)l/ *adjective* **1** of first age of world. **2** ancient, primitive.

primitive /ˈprɪmɪtɪv/ *adjective* **1** at early stage of civilization; ancient. **2** crude, simple. ● *noun* **1** untutored painter with naive style. **2** picture by such painter. □ **primitively** *adverb*. **primitiveness** *noun*.
■ *adjective* **1** aboriginal, ancient, *colloquial* antediluvian, backward, barbarian, behind the times, early, first, obsolete, old, prehistoric, primeval, savage, uncivilized, uncultivated. **2** basic, childlike, crude, elementary, naive, rough, rudimentary, simple, simplistic, undeveloped, unpolished, unrefined, unsophisticated.

primogeniture /praɪməʊˈdʒenɪtʃə/ *noun* **1** being first-born. **2** first-born's right to inheritance.

primordial /praɪˈmɔːdɪəl/ *adjective* existing at or from beginning; primeval.

primrose /ˈprɪmrəʊz/ *noun* **1** plant bearing pale yellow spring flower. **2** this flower. **3** pale yellow. □ **primrose path** pursuit of pleasure.

primula /ˈprɪmjʊlə/ *noun* cultivated plant with flowers of various colours.

Primus /ˈpraɪməs/ *noun proprietary term* portable cooking stove burning vaporized oil.

prince *noun* (as title usually **Prince**) **1** male member of royal family other than king. **2** ruler of small state. **3** nobleman of some countries. **4** (often + *of*) the greatest. □ **Prince Consort** husband of reigning queen who is himself a prince.

princely *adjective* (**-ier, -iest**) **1** of or worthy of a prince. **2** sumptuous, splendid.

princess /prɪnˈses/ *noun* (as title usually **Princess** /ˈprɪnses/) **1** prince's wife. **2** female member of royal family other than queen.

principal /ˈprɪnsɪp(ə)l/ *adjective* **1** first in importance; chief. **2** leading. ● *noun* **1** chief person. **2** head of some institutions. **3** principal actor, singer, etc. **4** capital sum lent or invested. **5** person for whom another is agent etc. □ **principal boy** (usually actress playing) leading male role in pantomime. □ **principally** *adverb*.

■ *adjective* basic, cardinal, chief, dominant, dominating, first, foremost, fundamental, greatest, highest, important, key, leading, main, major, outstanding, paramount, predominant, pre-eminent, prevailing, primary, prime, starring, supreme, top. ● *noun* **1** see CHIEF *noun*. **3** diva, hero, heroine, lead, leading role, prima ballerina, prima donna, protagonist, star.

principality /prɪnsɪˈpælɪtɪ/ *noun* (*plural* **-ies**) **1** state ruled by prince. **2** (**the Principality**) Wales.

principle /ˈprɪnsɪp(ə)l/ *noun* **1** fundamental truth or law as basis of reasoning or action. **2** personal code of conduct. **3** fundamental source or element. □ **in principle** in theory. **on principle** from moral motive.
■ **1** assumption, axiom, belief, creed, criterion, doctrine, dogma, ethic, idea, ideal, law, maxim, notion, precept, proposition, rule, standard, teaching, tenet, theory, truism, truth. **2** conscience, high-mindedness, honesty, honour, ideals, integrity, morality, philosophy, probity, scruples, standards, uprightness, values, virtue. **3** (*principles*) basics, elements, essentials, fundamentals.

principled *adjective* based on or having (esp. praiseworthy) principles of behaviour.

prink *verb* (usually **prink oneself**; often + *up*) smarten, dress up.

print *verb* **1** produce by applying inked type, plates, etc. to paper etc. **2** express or publish in print. **3** (often + *on, with*) impress, stamp. **4** write in letters that are not joined. **5** (often + *off*) produce (image) from negative. **6** (usually + *out*) produce computer output in printed form. **7** mark (fabric) with design. ● *noun* **1** mark left on surface by pressure. **2** printed lettering, words, or publication (esp. newspaper). **3** engraving; printed picture. **4** photograph. **5** printed fabric. □ **in print** (of book etc.) available from publisher, in printed form. **out of print** (of book etc.) no longer available from publisher. **printed circuit** electric circuit with thin conducting strips printed on flat sheet. **printing press** machine for printing from type, plates, etc. **printout** computer output in printed form.
■ *verb* **1** copy, reproduce, run off. **2** issue, publish. **3** engrave, impress, imprint, stamp. ● *noun* **1** impression, imprint, indentation, mark, stamp. **2** characters, fount, lettering, letters, printing, text, type, typeface. **3** copy, duplicate, engraving, etching, facsimile, linocut, lithograph, picture, reproduction, woodcut. **4** see PHOTOGRAPH *noun*.

printer *noun* **1** person who prints books etc. **2** owner of printing business. **3** device that prints esp. computer output.

prior /ˈpraɪə/ *adjective* **1** earlier. **2** (often + *to*) coming before in time, order, or importance. ● *adverb* (+ *to*) before. ● *noun* (*feminine* **prioress**) **1** superior of religious house. **2** (in abbey) deputy of abbot.
■ *adjective* earlier, erstwhile, former, late, old, one-time, previous.

priority /praɪˈɒrɪtɪ/ *noun* (*plural* **-ies**) **1** thing considered more important than others. **2** precedence in time, rank, etc. **3** right to do something before other people. □ **prioritize** *verb* (also **-ise**) (**-zing** or **-sing**).

■ **2** first place, precedence, preference, prerogative, seniority, superiority, urgency. **3** right of way.

priory /ˈpraɪərɪ/ *noun* (*plural* **-ies**) religious house governed by prior or prioress.

prise /praɪz/ *verb* (also **prize**) (**-sing** or **-zing**) force open or out by leverage.

■ force, lever, wrench.

prism /ˈprɪz(ə)m/ *noun* **1** solid figure whose two ends are equal parallel rectilinear figures, and whose sides are parallelograms. **2** transparent body of this form with refracting surfaces.

prismatic /prɪzˈmætɪk/ *adjective* **1** of, like, or using prism. **2** (of colours) distributed (as if) by transparent prism.

prison /ˈprɪz(ə)n/ *noun* **1** place of captivity, esp. building to which people are consigned while awaiting trial or for punishment. **2** confinement.

■ **1** *historical* Borstal, cell, *slang* clink, custody, detention centre, dungeon, guardhouse, jail, lock-up, *US* penitentiary, oubliette, *US historical* reformatory, youth custody centre. **2** see CAPTIVITY (CAPTIVE).

prisoner /ˈprɪznə/ *noun* **1** person kept in prison. **2** person or thing confined by illness, another's grasp, etc. **3** (in full **prisoner of war**) person captured in war. □ **take prisoner** seize and hold as prisoner.

■ **1** captive, *esp. historical* convict, detainee, hostage, inmate, internee, jailbird, *slang* lifer, *slang* (old) lag, trusty.

prissy /ˈprɪsɪ/ *adjective* (**-ier**, **-iest**) prim, prudish. □ **prissily** *adverb*. **prissiness** *noun*.

pristine /ˈprɪstiːn/ *adjective* **1** in original condition; unspoilt. **2** ancient.

privacy /ˈprɪvəsɪ/ *noun* **1** (right to) being private. **2** freedom from intrusion or publicity.

■ concealment, isolation, monasticism, quietness, retirement, retreat, seclusion, secrecy, solitude.

private /ˈpraɪvət/ *adjective* **1** belonging to an individual; personal. **2** confidential, secret. **3** not public. **4** secluded. **5** retiring, reserved. **6** not holding public office or official position. **7** not supported, managed, or provided by state. ● *noun* **1** private soldier. **2** (in *plural*) *colloquial* genitals. □ **in private** privately. **private detective** detective outside police force. **private enterprise** business(es) not under state control. **private eye** *colloquial* private detective. **private means** unearned income from investments etc. **private member** MP not holding government office. **private parts** *euphemistic* genitals. **private soldier** ordinary soldier, not officer. □ **privately** *adverb*.

■ *adjective* **1** exclusive, individual, particular, personal. **2** classified, confidential, *colloquial* hush-hush, off the record, restricted, secret, top secret, undisclosed. **3** clandestine, closed, covert, exclusive, intimate, restricted, surreptitious. **4** concealed, hidden, inaccessible, isolated, little known, quiet, secluded, sequestered, solitary, unknown. **5** quiet, reserved, retiring, solitary, withdrawn.

privateer /praɪvəˈtɪə/ *noun* (commander of) privately owned and government-commissioned warship.

privation /praɪˈveɪʃ(ə)n/ *noun* lack of comforts or necessities.

privatize /ˈpraɪvətaɪz/ *verb* (also **-ise**) (**-zing** or **-sing**) transfer from state to private ownership. □ **privatization** *noun*.

privet /ˈprɪvɪt/ *noun* bushy evergreen shrub used for hedges.

privilege /ˈprɪvɪlɪdʒ/ *noun* **1** right, advantage, or immunity belonging to person, class, or office. **2** special benefit or honour. ● *verb* (**-ging**) invest with privilege. □ **privileged** *adjective*.

■ *noun* **1** advantage, benefit, concession, entitlement, exemption, freedom, immunity, licence, prerogative, right. **2** see HONOUR *noun* 5. □ **privileged** advantaged, affluent, authorized, elite, entitled, favoured, honoured, immune, licensed, powerful, protected, sanctioned, special, superior, wealthy.

privy /ˈprɪvɪ/ *adjective* **1** (+ *to*) sharing secret of. **2** *archaic* hidden, secret. ● *noun* (*plural* **-ies**) lavatory. □ **Privy Council** group of advisers appointed by sovereign. **Privy Councillor, Counsellor** member of this. **privy purse** allowance from public revenue for monarch's private expenses. **privy seal** state seal formerly affixed to minor documents.

prize[1] *noun* **1** reward in competition, lottery, etc. **2** reward given as symbol of victory or superiority. **3** thing (to be) striven for. ● *adjective* **1** to which prize is awarded. **2** excellent of its kind. ● *verb* (**-zing**) value highly.

■ *noun* accolade, award, jackpot, purse, reward, trophy, winnings. ● *verb* appreciate, cherish, esteem, hold dear, like, rate highly, revere, treasure, value.

prize[2] *noun* ship or property captured in naval warfare.

prize[3] = PRISE.

prizefight /ˈpraɪzfaɪt/ boxing match fought for money. □ **prizefighter** *noun*.

prizewinner /ˈpraɪzwɪnə/ *noun* winner of prize. □ **prizewinning** *adjective*.

PRO *abbreviation* **1** Public Record Office. **2** public relations officer.

pro[1] *noun* (*plural* **-s**) *colloquial* professional.

pro[2] *adjective* in favour. ● *noun* (*plural* **-s**) reason in favour. ● *preposition* in favour of. □ **pros and cons** reasons for and against.

proactive /prəʊˈæktɪv/ *adjective* (of person, policy, etc.) taking the initiative.

probability *noun* (*plural* **-ies**) **1** being probable. **2** likelihood. **3** (most) probable event. **4** *Mathematics* extent to which thing is likely to occur, measured by ratio of favourable cases to all cases possible. □ **in all probability** most probably.

probable /'prɒbəb(ə)l/ *adjective* (often + *that*) that may be expected to happen or prove true; likely. ● *noun* probable candidate, member of team, etc. □ **probably** *adverb*.

■ *adjective* believable, convincing, credible, expected, likely, odds-on, plausible, possible, predictable, presumed, undoubted, unquestioned.

probate /'prəʊbeɪt/ *noun* **1** official proving of will. **2** verified copy of will.

probation /prə'beɪʃ(ə)n/ *noun* **1** system of supervising behaviour of offenders as alternative to prison. **2** testing of character and abilities of esp. new employee. □ **probation officer** official supervising offenders on probation. □ **probationary** *adjective*.

probationer *noun* person on probation.

■ apprentice, beginner, learner, novice, tiro.

probe *noun* **1** investigation. **2** device for measuring, testing, etc. **3** blunt-ended surgical instrument for exploring wound etc. **4** unmanned exploratory spacecraft. ● *verb* (**-bing**) **1** examine closely. **2** explore with probe.

■ *noun* **1** enquiry, examination, exploration, inquiry, investigation, scrutiny, study. ● *verb* **1** examine, explore, go into, inquire into, investigate, look into, research into, scrutinize, study. **2** delve, dig, explore, penetrate, plumb, poke, prod.

probity /'prəʊbɪtɪ/ *noun* uprightness, honesty.

problem /'prɒbləm/ *noun* **1** doubtful or difficult question. **2** thing hard to understand or deal with. ● *adjective* causing problems.

■ *noun* **1** *colloquial* brain-teaser, conundrum, enigma, mystery, *colloquial* poser, puzzle, question, riddle. **2** burden, complication, difficulty, *disputed* dilemma, dispute, *colloquial* headache, predicament, quandary, setback, snag, trouble, worry.

problematic /prɒblə'mætɪk/ *adjective* (also **problematical**) **1** attended by difficulty. **2** doubtful, questionable.

■ **1** complicated, difficult, hard to deal with, intractable, sensitive, taxing, tricky, unsettling, worrying. **2** controversial, debatable, disputed, doubtful, enigmatic, *colloquial* iffy, moot (*point*), puzzling, questionable, uncertain.

proboscis /prəʊ'bɒsɪs/ *noun* (*plural* **-sces**) **1** long flexible trunk or snout, e.g. of elephant. **2** elongated mouth-parts of some insects.

procedure /prə'si:dʒə/ *noun* **1** way of conducting business etc. or performing task. **2** set series of actions. □ **procedural** *adjective*.

■ approach, conduct, course of action, *colloquial* drill, formula, method, methodology, *modus operandi*, plan of action, policy, practice, process, routine, scheme, strategy, system, technique, way.

proceed /prə'si:d/ *verb* **1** (often + *to*) go forward or on further; make one's way. **2** (often + *with, to do*) continue or resume. **3** adopt course of action. **4** go on to say. **5** (+ *against*) start lawsuit against. **6** (often + *from*) originate.

■ **1** advance, carry on, continue, forge ahead, get going, go ahead, go on, make headway, make progress, move along, move forward, press on, progress. **6** arise, be derived, begin, develop, emerge, grow, issue, originate, result, spring up, start.

proceeding *noun* **1** action; piece of conduct. **2** (in *plural*) legal action. **3** (in *plural*) published report of discussions or conference.

■ **1** act, action, deed, event, goings-on, happening, operation, procedure, undertaking. **2** (*proceedings*) action, lawsuit, process. **3** (*proceedings*) annals, business, dealings, minutes, records, report, transactions.

proceeds /'prəʊsi:dz/ *plural noun* profits from sale etc.

■ earnings, gain, gate, income, money, profit(s), receipts, return(s), revenue, takings.

process[1] /'prəʊses/ *noun* **1** course of action or proceeding, esp. series of stages in manufacture etc. **2** progress or course. **3** natural or involuntary course of change. **4** action at law; summons, writ. **5** *Biology* natural appendage or outgrowth of organism. ● *verb* **1** subject to particular process. **2** (as **processed** *adjective*) (of food) treated, esp. to prevent decay.

■ *noun* **1** function, method, operation, procedure, system, technique. **2** course, development, experience, progress, progression. ● *verb* **1** alter, change, convert, deal with, make usable, manage, modify, organize, prepare, refine, transform, treat.

process[2] /prə'ses/ *verb* walk in procession.
■ see PARADE *verb* 1.

procession /prə'seʃ(ə)n/ *noun* people etc. advancing in orderly succession, esp. at ceremony, demonstration, or festivity.

■ cavalcade, chain, column, cortège, file, line, march, march past, motorcade, pageant, parade, sequence, string, succession, train.

processional *adjective* **1** of processions. **2** used, carried, or sung in processions. ● *noun* processional hymn (book).

processor /'prəʊsesə/ *noun* **1** machine that processes things. **2** central processor. **3** food processor.

proclaim /prə'kleɪm/ *verb* **1** (often + *that*) announce publicly or officially. **2** declare to be. □ **proclamation** /prɒklə-/ *noun*.

■ **1** announce, advertise, assert, declare, make known, profess, promulgate, pronounce, publish. **2** brand, characterize as, declare, decree, pronounce.

proclivity /prə'klɪvɪtɪ/ *noun* (*plural* **-ies**) natural tendency.

procrastinate /prəʊ'kræstɪneɪt/ *verb* (**-ting**) defer action. □ **procrastination** *noun*.

■ be dilatory, be indecisive, dally, delay, *colloquial* dilly-dally, dither, drag one's feet, equivocate, hesitate, hum and haw, pause, play for time, put things off, shilly-shally, stall, temporize, vacillate, waver.

procreate /'prəʊkrɪeɪt/ *verb* (**-ting**) produce (offspring) naturally. □ **procreation** /-'eɪʃ(ə)n/ *noun.* **procreative** *adjective.* **procreator** *noun.*

proctor /'prɒktə/ *noun* university disciplinary official. □ **proctorial** /-'tɔːrɪəl/ *adjective.*

procuration /prɒkjʊ'reɪʃ(ə)n/ *noun* **1** *formal* procuring. **2** action of attorney.

procurator /'prɒkjʊreɪtə/ *noun* agent or proxy, esp. with power of attorney. □ **procurator fiscal** (in Scotland) local coroner and public prosecutor.

procure /prə'kjʊə/ *verb* (**-ring**) **1** succeed in getting. **2** bring about. **3** act as procurer. □ **procurable** *adjective.* **procurement** *noun.*

■ **1** acquire, buy, come by, find, get, get hold of, lay one's hands on, obtain, pick up, purchase, requisition.

procurer *noun* (*feminine* **procuress**) person who obtains women for prostitution.

prod *verb* (**-dd-**) **1** poke with finger, stick, etc. **2** stimulate to action. ● *noun* **1** poke, thrust. **2** stimulus to action.

■ *verb* **1** dig, elbow, goad, jab, nudge, poke, push. **2** see URGE *verb* 1.

prodigal /'prɒdɪg(ə)l/ *adjective* **1** wasteful. **2** (+ *of*) lavish of. ● *noun* spendthrift. □ **prodigal son** repentant wastrel. □ **prodigality** /-'gæl-/ *noun.*

■ *adjective* **1** excessive, extravagant, immoderate, improvident, irresponsible, lavish, profligate, reckless, self-indulgent, wasteful.

prodigious /prə'dɪdʒəs/ *adjective* **1** marvellous. **2** enormous. **3** abnormal.

prodigy /'prɒdɪdʒɪ/ *noun* (*plural* **-ies**) **1** exceptionally gifted person, esp. precocious child. **2** marvellous thing. **3** (+ *of*) wonderful example of.

■ **1** genius, marvel, talent, virtuoso, *colloquial* whiz-kid, wonder. **2** curiosity, freak, marvel, miracle, phenomenon, rarity, sensation, wonder.

produce *verb* /prə'djuːs/ (**-cing**) **1** manufacture or prepare. **2** bring forward for inspection etc. **3** bear, yield, or bring into existence. **4** cause or bring about. **5** *Geometry* extend or continue (line). **6** bring (play etc.) before public. ● *noun* /'prɒdjuːs/ **1** what is produced, esp. agricultural products. **2** amount produced. **3** (often + *of*) result.

■ *verb* **1** assemble, bring out, compose, conjure up, construct, create, cultivate, develop, fabricate, form, generate, grow, invent, make, manufacture, originate, prepare, supply, *colloquial* think up, turn out. **2** advance, bring out, disclose, display, exhibit,

furnish, introduce, offer, present, provide, put forward, reveal, show, supply, throw up. **3** bear, *literary* beget, breed, give birth to, raise, rear, yield. **4** bring about, cause, create, generate, give rise to, initiate, originate, provoke, result in. **6** direct, mount, present, put on, stage. ● *noun* **1** crop, goods, harvest, merchandise, output, products, yield.

producer *noun* **1** person who produces goods etc. **2** person who supervises production of play, film, broadcast, etc.

product /'prɒdʌkt/ *noun* **1** thing or substance produced, esp. by manufacture. **2** result. **3** *Mathematics* quantity obtained by multiplying.

■ **1** artefact, by-product, commodity, end product; (*products*) goods, merchandise, output, produce. **2** consequence, effect, fruit, issue, outcome, result, upshot, yield.

production /prə'dʌkʃ(ə)n/ *noun* **1** producing, being produced. **2** total yield. **3** thing produced, esp. play etc. □ **production line** systematized sequence of operations to produce commodity.

productive /prə'dʌktɪv/ *adjective* **1** producing, esp. abundantly. **2** profitable; useful. □ **productively** *adverb.* **productiveness** *noun.*

■ **1** abundant, *poetical* bounteous, bountiful, creative, fecund, fertile, fruitful, inventive, prolific, vigorous. **2** beneficial, constructive, effective, efficient, gainful (*employment*), profitable, remunerative, rewarding, useful, valuable, worthwhile.

productivity /prɒdʌk'tɪvɪtɪ/ *noun* **1** capacity to produce. **2** effectiveness of industry, workforce, etc.

Prof. *abbreviation* Professor.

profane /prə'feɪn/ *adjective* **1** irreverent, blasphemous. **2** obscene. **3** not sacred. ● *verb* (**-ning**) **1** treat irreverently. **2** violate, pollute. □ **profanation** /prɒfə-/ *noun.*

profanity /prə'fænɪtɪ/ *noun* (*plural* **-ies**) **1** blasphemy. **2** swear-word.

profess /prə'fes/ *verb* **1** claim openly to have. **2** (often + *to do*) pretend. **3** declare. **4** affirm one's faith in or allegiance to.

■ **2** allege, claim, make out, pretend, purport. **3** affirm, announce, assert, asseverate, *formal* aver, confess, confirm, declare, maintain, state, *archaic* vow.

professed *adjective* **1** self-acknowledged. **2** alleged, ostensible. □ **professedly** /-sɪdlɪ/ *adverb.*

profession /prə'feʃ(ə)n/ *noun* **1** occupation or calling, esp. learned or scientific. **2** people in a profession. **3** declaration, avowal.

■ **1** business, calling, career, craft, employment, job, line of work, *métier*, occupation, trade, vocation, work. **3** acknowledgement, affirmation, announcement, assertion, *formal* avowal, confession, declaration, statement, testimony.

professional *adjective* **1** of, belonging to, or connected with a profession. **2** competent; worthy of professional. **3** engaged in specified activity as paid occupation, or (*derogatory*) fanatically. ● *noun* professional person. ◻ **professionally** *adverb*.

■ *adjective* **1** authorized, experienced, licensed, official, qualified, trained. **2** able, businesslike, competent, conscientious, educated, efficient, expert, knowledgeable, masterly, proficient, proper, skilful, skilled, thorough. **3** paid. ● *noun* expert, master, *colloquial* pro, specialist.

professionalism *noun* qualities of professionals, esp. competence, skill, etc.

professor /prə'fesə/ *noun* **1** highest-ranking academic in university department. **2** *US* university teacher. **3** person who professes a religion etc. ◻ **professorial** /prɒfɪ'sɔːrɪəl/ *adjective*. **professorship** *noun*.

proffer /'prɒfə/ *verb* offer.

proficient /prə'fɪʃ(ə)nt/ *adjective* (often + *in, at*) adept, expert. ◻ **proficiency** *noun*. **proficiently** *adverb*.

■ able, accomplished, adept, capable, competent, efficient, expert, gifted, professional, skilled, talented.

profile /'prəʊfaɪl/ *noun* **1** side view or outline, esp. of human face. **2** short biographical sketch. ● *verb* (**-ling**) represent by profile. ◻ **keep a low profile** remain inconspicuous.

■ *noun* **1** contour, outline, shape, silhouette. **2** account, biography, curriculum vitae, sketch, study.

profit /'prɒfɪt/ *noun* **1** advantage, benefit. **2** financial gain; excess of returns over outlay. ● *verb* (**-t-**) **1** be beneficial to. **2** obtain advantage. ◻ **at a profit** with financial gain. **profit margin** profit after deduction of costs. ◻ **profitless** *adjective*.

■ *noun* **1** advantage, benefit, good, use, value. **2** excess, gain, interest, proceeds, return, revenue, surplus, yield. ● *verb* **1** advance, avail, benefit, help, pay, serve. **2** *colloquial* cash in, earn money, gain, *colloquial* make a killing, make money; (*profit by, from*) see EXPLOIT *verb* 1.

profitable *adjective* **1** yielding profit. **2** beneficial. ◻ **profitability** *noun*. **profitably** *adverb*.

■ **1** commercial, fruitful, gainful, lucrative, moneymaking, paying, productive, remunerative, well paid. **2** advantageous, beneficial, enriching, fruitful, productive, rewarding, useful, valuable, worthwhile.

profiteer /prɒfɪ'tɪə/ *verb* make or seek excessive profits, esp. illegally. ● *noun* person who profiteers.

■ *verb colloquial* cash in, earn money, *colloquial* make a killing, make money; (*profiteer from*) exploit, fleece, overcharge. ● *noun* black marketeer, exploiter, extortionist, racketeer.

profiterole /prə'fɪtərəʊl/ *noun* small hollow cake of choux pastry with filling.

profligate /'prɒflɪgət/ *adjective* **1** recklessly extravagant. **2** licentious, dissolute. ● *noun* profligate person. ◻ **profligacy** *noun*. **profligately** *adverb*.

■ *adjective* **1** extravagant, prodigal, reckless, spendthrift, wasteful. **2** abandoned, debauched, degenerate, depraved, dissolute, immoral, libertine, licentious, loose, perverted, promiscuous, sinful, sybaritic, unprincipled, wanton.

pro forma /prəʊ 'fɔːmə/ *adverb & adjective* for form's sake. ● *noun* (in full **pro forma invoice**) invoice sent in advance of goods supplied.

profound /prə'faʊnd/ *adjective* (**-er, -est**) **1** having or demanding great knowledge, study, or insight. **2** intense, thorough. **3** deep. ◻ **profoundly** *adverb*. **profoundness** *noun*. **profundity** /-'fʌndɪtɪ/ *noun* (*plural* **-ies**).

■ **1** abstruse, arcane, erudite, esoteric, imponderable, informed, intellectual, knowledgeable, learned, penetrating, philosophical, recondite, sagacious, scholarly, serious, thoughtful, wise. **2** absolute, complete, deep, extreme, fundamental, heartfelt, intense, perfect, sincere, thorough, total, unqualified. **3** see DEEP *adjective* 5.

profuse /prə'fjuːs/ *adjective* **1** (often + *in, of*) lavish; extravagant. **2** copious. ◻ **profusely** *adverb*. **profusion** *noun*.

■ abundant, ample, bountiful, copious, extravagant, exuberant, generous, lavish, luxuriant, plentiful, productive, prolific, superabundant, thriving, unsparing, unstinting.

progenitor /prəʊ'dʒenɪtə/ *noun* **1** ancestor. **2** predecessor. **3** original.

progeny /'prɒdʒɪnɪ/ *noun* **1** offspring. **2** descendants. **3** outcome, issue.

progesterone /prəʊ'dʒestərəʊn/ *noun* a sex hormone that helps to initiate and maintains pregnancy.

prognosis /prɒg'nəʊsɪs/ *noun* (*plural* **-noses** /-siːz/) forecast, esp. of course of disease.

prognostic /prɒg'nɒstɪk/ *noun* **1** (often + *of*) advance indication. **2** prediction. ● *adjective* (often + *of*) foretelling, predictive.

prognosticate /prɒg'nɒstɪkeɪt/ *verb* (**-ting**) **1** (often + *that*) foretell. **2** betoken. ◻ **prognostication** *noun*.

programme /'prəʊgræm/ (*US* **program**) *noun* **1** list of events, performers, etc. **2** radio or television broadcast. **3** plan of events. **4** course or series of studies, lectures, etc. **5** (usually **program**) series of instructions for computer. ● *verb* (**-mm-**; *US* **-m-**) **1** make programme of. **2** (usually **program**) express (problem) or instruct (computer) by means of program. ◻ **programmable** *adjective*. **programmer** *noun*.

■ *noun* **1, 3** agenda, bill of fare, calendar, line-up, listing, menu, plan, routine, schedule, scheme, timetable. **2** broadcast, performance, presentation, production, show, transmission. **4** course, curriculum, schedule, syllabus, timetable.

progress *noun* /'prəʊgres/ **1** forward movement. **2** advance, development, improvement. **3** *historical* state journey, esp. by royalty. ● *verb* /prə'gres/ **1** move forward or onward. **2** advance, develop, improve. □ **in progress** developing; going on.

■ *noun* **1** advance, advancement, headway, march (*of time*), progression. **2** advance, advancement, betterment, development, elevation, evolution, furtherance, gain, growth, headway, improvement, promotion, rise. ● *verb* **1** advance, forge ahead, go forward, go on, make headway, press forward, press on, proceed. **2** advance, come on, develop, improve, prosper.

progression /prəˈgreʃ(ə)n/ *noun* **1** progressing. **2** succession, series.

■ **1** see PROGRESS *noun* 1. **2** chain, concatenation, course, flow, order, row, sequence, series, string, succession.

progressive /prəˈgresɪv/ *adjective* **1** moving forward. **2** proceeding step by step; cumulative. **3** (of disease etc.) increasing in severity or extent. **4** favouring rapid reform. **5** modern; efficient. **6** (of taxation) increasing with the sum taxed. ● *noun* (also **Progressive**) advocate of progressive policy. □ **progressively** *adverb*.

■ *adjective* **1** accelerating, advancing, continuing, continuous, ongoing. **2** cumulative, developing, escalating, gradual, growing, increasing, steady. **4** avant-garde, dynamic, enterprising, forward-looking, go-ahead, radical, reformist, *often derogatory* revisionist, revolutionary. **5** advanced, contemporary, modern, modernistic, up to date.

prohibit /prəˈhɪbɪt/ *verb* (**-t-**) **1** (often + *from*) forbid. **2** prevent.

■ **1** ban, bar, censor, debar, disallow, forbid, interdict, outlaw, place an embargo on, proscribe, taboo, veto. **2** block, check, cut out, exclude, foil, hinder, impede, inhibit, preclude, prevent, restrict, rule out, shut out, stop.

prohibition /prəʊhɪˈbɪʃ(ə)n/ *noun* **1** forbidding, being forbidden. **2** edict or order that forbids. **3** (usually **Prohibition**) legal ban on manufacture and sale of alcohol. □ **prohibitionist** *noun*.

prohibitive /prəˈhɪbɪtɪv/ *adjective* **1** prohibiting. **2** (of prices, taxes, etc.) extremely high. □ **prohibitively** *adverb*.

■ **2** excessive, exorbitant, *colloquial* impossible, out of reach, out of the question, unreasonable, *colloquial* unthinkable.

project *noun* /ˈprɒdʒekt/ **1** plan, scheme. **2** undertaking. **3** extensive essay, piece of research, etc. by student(s). ● *verb* /prəˈdʒekt/ **1** protrude; jut out. **2** throw; impel. **3** forecast. **4** plan. **5** cause (light, image, etc.) to fall on surface. **6** cause (voice etc.) to be heard at distance.

■ *noun* **1, 2** contract, design, enterprise, idea, job, plan, programme, proposal, scheme, task, undertaking, venture. **3** assignment, exercise, task. ● *verb* **1** beetle, bulge, extend, jut out, overhang, protrude, stand out, stick out. **2** cast, *colloquial* chuck, fling, hurl, launch, lob, propel, shoot, throw. **3** estimate, forecast, predict. **4** concoct, contrive, design, devise, invent, plan, propose, scheme, *colloquial* think up. **5** cast, flash, shine, throw out.

projectile /prəˈdʒektaɪl/ *noun* object to be fired (esp. by rocket) or hurled. ● *adjective* **1** of or serving as projectile. **2** projecting; impelling.

projection /prəˈdʒekʃ(ə)n/ *noun* **1** projecting, being projected. **2** thing that protrudes. **3** presentation of image(s) etc. on surface. **4** forecast, estimate. **5** mental image viewed as objective reality. **6** transfer of feelings to other people etc. **7** representation of earth etc. on plane surface.

projectionist *noun* person who operates projector.

projector /prəˈdʒektə/ *noun* apparatus for projecting image or film on screen.

prolactin /prəʊˈlæktɪn/ *noun* hormone that stimulates milk production after childbirth.

prolapse *noun* /ˈprəʊlæps/ (also **prolapsus** /-ˈlæpsəs/) **1** slipping forward or downward of part or organ. **2** prolapsed womb, rectum, etc. ● *verb* /prəˈlæps/ (**-sing**) undergo prolapse.

prolate /ˈprəʊleɪt/ *adjective* (of spheroid) lengthened along polar diameter.

prolegomenon /prəʊlɪˈgɒmmən/ *noun* (*plural* **-mena**) (usually in *plural*) preface to book etc., esp. discursive or critical.

proletarian /prəʊlɪˈteərɪən/ *adjective* of proletariat. ● *noun* member of proletariat.

proletariat /prəʊlɪˈteərɪət/ *noun* **1** working class. **2** *esp. derogatory* lowest class.

proliferate /prəˈlɪfəreɪt/ *verb* (**-ting**) **1** reproduce. **2** produce (cells etc.) rapidly. **3** increase rapidly, multiply. □ **proliferation** *noun*.

■ **1, 3** burgeon, flourish, grow, increase, multiply, mushroom, reproduce, thrive.

prolific /prəˈlɪfɪk/ *adjective* **1** producing many offspring or much output. **2** (often + *of*) abundantly productive. **3** copious.

■ **1** creative, fecund, fertile, fruitful, productive. **3** abundant, *poetical* bounteous, bountiful, copious, numerous, *literary* plenteous, profuse, rich.

prolix /ˈprəʊlɪks/ *adjective* lengthy; tedious. □ **prolixity** /-ˈlɪks-/ *noun*.

prologue /ˈprəʊlɒg/ *noun* **1** introduction to poem, play, etc. **2** (usually + *to*) introductory event.

prolong /prəˈlɒŋ/ *verb* **1** extend. **2** (as **prolonged** *adjective*) (tediously) lengthy. □ **prolongation** /prəʊlɒŋˈgeɪʃ(ə)n/ *noun*.

■ **1** drag out, draw out, elongate, extend, increase, keep up, lengthen, pad out, protract, spin out, stretch out.

prom *noun colloquial* **1** promenade. **2** promenade concert.

promenade /prɒməˈnɑːd/ *noun* **1** paved public walk, esp. at seaside. **2** leisure walk. ● *verb* (**-ding**) **1** make promenade (through). **2** lead about, esp. for display. □ **promenade concert** one at which (part of) audience is not seated. **promenade deck** upper deck on liner.

promenader *noun* **1** person who promenades. **2** regular attender at promenade concerts.

prominent /ˈprɒmɪnənt/ *adjective* **1** jutting out.

2 conspicuous. **3** distinguished. □ **prominence** noun.

■ **1** bulging, jutting out, projecting, protruding, protuberant, sticking out. **2** conspicuous, discernible, distinguishable, evident, colloquial eye-catching, large, notable, noticeable, obtrusive, obvious, pronounced, recognizable, salient, significant, striking. **3** celebrated, distinguished, eminent, familiar, famous, foremost, illustrious, important, leading, major, notable, noted, outstanding, public, renowned.

promiscuous /prə'mɪskjʊəs/ adjective **1** having frequent casual sexual relationships. **2** mixed and indiscriminate. **3** colloquial casual. □ **promiscuously** adverb. **promiscuity** /prɒmɪs-'kjuːɪtɪ/ noun.

■ **1** see IMMORAL. **2, 3** casual, haphazard, indiscriminate, irresponsible, non-selective, random, undiscriminating.

promise /'prɒmɪs/ noun **1** explicit undertaking to do or not to do something. **2** favourable indications. ● verb (**-sing**) **1** (usually + to do, that) make promise. **2** (often + to do) seem likely; give hope of. **3** colloquial assure. **4** archaic betroth.

■ noun **1** assurance, commitment, compact, contract, covenant, guarantee, oath, pledge, undertaking, vow, word, word of honour. **2** capability, latent ability, potential, talent. ● verb **1** agree, assure, commit oneself, consent, contract, engage, give one's word, guarantee, pledge, swear, take an oath, undertake, vow. **2** augur, betoken, forebode, foretell, hint at, indicate, presage, prophesy, show signs of, suggest.

promising adjective **1** likely to turn out well. **2** hopeful; full of promise. □ **promisingly** adverb.

■ auspicious, budding, encouraging, favourable, hopeful, likely, optimistic, propitious, talented, colloquial up-and-coming.

promissory /'prɒmɪsərɪ/ adjective expressing or implying promise. □ **promissory note** signed document containing promise to pay stated sum.

promontory /'prɒməntərɪ/ noun (plural **-ies**) point of high land jutting out into sea etc.; headland.

■ cape, headland, peninsula, point, projection, spit.

promote /prə'məʊt/ verb (**-ting**) **1** (often + to) advance (person) to higher office or position. **2** help forward, encourage. **3** publicize and sell.

■ **1** advance, elevate, exalt, move up, prefer, raise, upgrade. **2** back, boost, champion, encourage, endorse, further, help, patronize, sponsor, support. **3** advertise, make known, market, colloquial plug, popularize, publicize, push, recommend, sell, sponsor.

promoter noun person who promotes, esp. sporting event, theatrical production, etc., or formation of joint-stock company.

■ backer, champion, patron, sponsor, supporter.

promotion noun **1** advancement to higher office or position. **2** publicity; backing. □ **promotional** adjective.

■ **1** advancement, elevation, formal preferment, rise, upgrading. **2** advertising, backing, encouragement, furtherance, marketing, publicity, recommendation, sponsorship.

prompt adjective acting, made, or done immediately; ready. ● adverb punctually. ● verb **1** (usually + to, to do) incite. **2** supply (actor, speaker) with next words or with suggestion. **3** inspire. ● noun **1** prompting. **2** thing said to prompt actor etc. **3** sign on computer screen inviting input. □ **promptitude** noun. **promptly** adverb. **promptness** noun.

■ adjective eager, efficient, expeditious, immediate, instantaneous, on time, punctual, quick, ready, timely, unhesitating, willing. ● verb **1** coax, egg on, encourage, exhort, help, incite, influence, inspire, motivate, persuade, prod, provoke, rouse, spur, stimulate, urge. **2** cue, jog (person's) memory, remind. **3** elicit, give rise to, inspire, provoke, stimulate. ● noun **2** cue, reminder.

prompter noun person who prompts actors.

promulgate /'prɒməlgeɪt/ verb (**-ting**) **1** make known to the public. **2** proclaim. □ **promulgation** noun.

prone adjective **1** lying face downwards. **2** lying flat; prostrate. **3** (usually + to, to do) disposed, liable. □ **-prone** likely to suffer. □ **proneness** noun.

■ **1** face down, on one's front, prostrate. **2** flat, horizontal, lying, prostrate, stretched out. **3** apt, disposed, given, inclined, liable, likely, predisposed, subject, susceptible, tending, vulnerable.

prong noun spike of fork.

■ point, spike, spur, tine.

pronominal /prəʊ'nɒmɪn(ə)l/ adjective of, concerning, or being a pronoun.

pronoun /'prəʊnaʊn/ noun word used as substitute for noun or noun phrase usually already mentioned or known (see panel).

pronounce /prə'naʊns/ verb (**-cing**) **1** utter or speak, esp. in approved manner. **2** utter formally. **3** state (as) one's opinion. **4** (usually + on, for, against, etc.) pass judgement. □ **pronounceable** adjective. **pronouncement** noun.

■ **1** articulate, enunciate, say, sound, speak, utter, vocalize, voice. **2, 3** announce, assert, asseverate, declare, decree, judge, make known, proclaim, say, state.

pronounced adjective strongly marked.

■ clear, conspicuous, decided, definite, distinct, evident, inescapable, marked, noticeable, obvious, prominent, recognizable, striking, unambiguous, undisguised, unmistakable, well defined.

pronto /'prɒntəʊ/ adverb colloquial promptly, quickly.

pronunciation /prənʌnsɪ'eɪʃ(ə)n/ noun **1** pronouncing of word, esp. with reference to standard. **2** act of pronouncing. **3** way of pronouncing words.

■ accent, articulation, delivery, diction, elocution, enunciation, inflection, intonation, modulation, speech.

proof /pruːf/ *noun* **1** fact, evidence, reasoning, or demonstration that proves something. **2** test, trial. **3** standard of strength of distilled alcohol. **4** trial impression of printed matter for correction. ● *adjective* (often + *against*) impervious to penetration, damage, etc. by a specified thing. ● *verb* make proof, esp. against water or bullets. □ **proof-read** read and correct (printed proof). **proof-reader** person who does this.

■ *noun* **1** authentication, certification, confirmation, corroboration, demonstration, evidence, facts, grounds, substantiation, testimony, validation, verification. **2** criterion, judgement, measure, test, trial.

prop[1] *noun* **1** rigid support. **2** person or thing that supports, comforts, etc. ● *verb* (-**pp**-) (often + *against, up*, etc.) support (as) with prop.

■ *noun* **1** brace, buttress, crutch, post, stay, strut, support, truss, upright. ● *verb* (*prop up*) bolster, brace, buttress, hold up, reinforce, shore up, support, sustain; (*prop against*) lean against, rest against, stand against.

prop[2] *noun colloquial* stage property.

prop[3] *noun colloquial* propeller.

propaganda /prɒpəˈɡændə/ *noun* **1** organized propagation of a doctrine etc. **2** *usually derogatory* ideas etc. so propagated. □ **propagandist** *noun*.

■ advertising, brainwashing, disinformation, indoctrination, persuasion, publicity.

propagate /ˈprɒpəɡeɪt/ *verb* (-**ting**) **1** breed from parent stock. **2** (often **propagate itself**) (of plant etc.) reproduce itself. **3** disseminate. **4** transmit. □ **propagation** *noun*. **propagator** *noun*.

■ **1, 2** breed, generate, increase, multiply, produce, proliferate, reproduce. **3** circulate,

disseminate, pass on, promote, promulgate, publish, spread, transmit.

propane /ˈprəʊpeɪn/ *noun* gaseous hydrocarbon used as fuel.

propel /prəˈpel/ *verb* (-**ll**-) **1** drive or push forward. **2** urge on. □ **propellant** *noun & adjective*.

■ **1** drive, force, impel, launch, move, pitchfork, push, send, set in motion, shoot, thrust. **2** see URGE *verb* 1.

propeller *noun* revolving shaft with blades, esp. for propelling ship or aircraft.

■ rotor, screw, vane.

propensity /prəˈpensɪtɪ/ *noun* (*plural* -**ies**) inclination, tendency.

proper /ˈprɒpə/ *adjective* **1** accurate, correct. **2** suitable, appropriate, right. **3** decent, respectable. **4** (usually + *to*) belonging, relating; particular. **5** strictly so called; genuine. **6** *colloquial* thorough. □ **proper name, noun** name of person, place, etc. □ **properly** *adverb*.

■ **1** accurate, correct, exact, precise, right. **2** acceptable, accepted, advisable, apposite, appropriate, apropos, apt, deserved, fair, fitting, just, lawful, legal, normal, orthodox, rational, right, sensible, suitable, unexceptionable, usual, valid. **3** conventional, decent, decorous, delicate, dignified, formal, genteel, gentlemanly, grave, in good taste, ladylike, modest, polite, prim, prudish, respectable, sedate, seemly, serious, solemn, tactful, tasteful. **4** allocated, distinctive, individual, own, particular, reserved, separate, special, unique.

property /ˈprɒpətɪ/ *noun* (*plural* -**ies**) **1** thing(s) owned. **2** landed estate. **3** quality, characteristic. **4** movable article used on theatre stage or in film.

■ **1** assets, belongings, capital, chattels, effects, fortune, gear, goods, holdings, patrimony, possessions, resources, riches, wealth. **2** acreage, buildings, estate, land, premises. **3** attribute, characteristic, feature, hallmark, idiosyncrasy, oddity, peculiarity, quality, quirk, trait.

prophecy /ˈprɒfɪsɪ/ *noun* (*plural* -**ies**) **1** proph-

Pronoun

A pronoun is used as a substitute for a noun or a noun phrase, e.g.

He *was upstairs*.   *Did you see* that?
Anything *can happen now*.   It's *lovely weather*.

Using a pronoun often avoids repetition, e.g.

I found Jim—he *was upstairs*.
(instead of *I found Jim—Jim was upstairs*.)

Where are your keys?—*I've got* them.
(instead of *Where are your keys?—I've got my keys*.)

Pronouns are the only words in English which have different forms when used as the subject (*I, we, he, she*, etc.) and as the object (*me, us, him, her*, etc.).

See also language panels at INTERROGATIVE PRONOUN, POSSESSIVE PRONOUN, REFLEXIVE PRONOUN, and RELATIVE CLAUSE.

etic utterance; prediction. **2** prophesying.
■ **1** forecast, oracle, prediction, prognosis. **2** augury, crystal-gazing, divination, foretelling, fortune-telling, prognostication.

prophesy /ˈprɒfɪsaɪ/ *verb* (**-ies, -ied**) **1** (usually + *that, who,* etc.) foretell. **2** speak as prophet.
■ **1** augur, bode, divine, forecast, foresee, foreshadow, foretell, portend, predict, presage, prognosticate, promise.

prophet /ˈprɒfɪt/ *noun* (*feminine* **prophetess**) **1** teacher or interpreter of divine will. **2** person who predicts. **3** (**the Prophet**) Muhammad.
■ **2** clairvoyant, forecaster, fortune-teller, oracle, seer, sibyl, soothsayer.

prophetic /prəˈfetɪk/ *adjective* **1** (often + *of*) containing a prediction; predicting. **2** of prophet.
■ **1** apocalyptic, far-seeing, oracular, predictive, prescient, prognostic.

prophylactic /prɒfɪˈlæktɪk/ *adjective* tending to prevent disease etc. ● *noun* **1** preventive medicine or action. **2** *esp. US* condom.

prophylaxis /prɒfɪˈlæksɪs/ *noun* preventive treatment against disease.

propinquity /prəˈpɪŋkwɪtɪ/ *noun* **1** nearness. **2** close kinship. **3** similarity.

propitiate /prəˈpɪʃɪeɪt/ *verb* (**-ting**) appease. □ **propitiation** *noun.* **propitiatory** /-ʃətərɪ/ *adjective.*

propitious /prəˈpɪʃəs/ *adjective* **1** favourable, auspicious. **2** (often + *for, to*) suitable.
■ **1** advantageous, auspicious, favourable, fortunate, happy, lucky, promising, providential, rosy. **2** appropriate, opportune, suitable, timely, well timed.

proponent /prəˈpəʊnənt/ *noun* person advocating proposal etc.

proportion /prəˈpɔːʃ(ə)n/ *noun* **1** comparative part; share. **2** comparative ratio. **3** correct relation between things or parts of thing. **4** (in *plural*) dimensions. ● *verb* (usually + *to*) make proportionate.
■ *noun* **1** allocation, fraction, part, percentage, piece, quota, ration, section, share. **2** balance, comparison, correlation, correspondence, distribution, equivalence, ratio, relationship. **4** (*proportions*) dimensions, extent, magnitude, measurements, size, volume.

proportional *adjective* in correct proportion; comparable. □ **proportional representation** representation of parties in parliament in proportion to votes they receive. □ **proportionally** *adverb.*
■ analogous, balanced, commensurate, comparable, corresponding, equitable, in proportion, just, proportionate, relative, symmetrical.

proportionate /prəˈpɔːʃənət/ *adjective* proportional. □ **proportionately** *adverb.*

proposal /prəˈpəʊz(ə)l/ *noun* **1** proposing. **2** scheme etc. proposed. **3** offer of marriage.

■ **2** bid, declaration, draft, motion, offer, plan, project, proposition, recommendation, scheme, statement, suggestion, tender.

propose /prəˈpəʊz/ *verb* (**-sing**) **1** put forward for consideration. **2** (usually + *to do*) purpose. **3** (usually + *to*) offer marriage. **4** nominate as member of society etc. □ **propose a toast** ask people to drink to health or in honour of person or thing. □ **proposer** *noun.*
■ **1** advance, come up with, present, propound, put forward, recommend, submit, suggest. **2** aim, have in mind, intend, mean, offer, plan, purpose. **4** nominate, put forward, put up, sponsor.

proposition /prɒpəˈzɪʃ(ə)n/ *noun* **1** statement, assertion. **2** scheme proposed; proposal. **3** statement subject to proof or disproof. **4** *colloquial* problem, opponent, prospect, etc. **5** *Mathematics* formal statement of theorem or problem. **6** likely commercial enterprise, person, etc. **7** sexual proposal. ● *verb colloquial* put (esp. sexual) proposal to.

propound /prəˈpaʊnd/ *verb* offer for consideration.

proprietary /prəˈpraɪətərɪ/ *adjective* **1** of or holding property. **2** of proprietor. **3** held in private ownership. **4** manufactured by one particular firm. □ **proprietary name, term** name of product etc. registered as trade mark.

proprietor /prəˈpraɪətə/ *noun* (*feminine* **proprietress**) owner. □ **proprietorial** /-ˈtɔːr-/ *adjective.*

propriety /prəˈpraɪətɪ/ *noun* (*plural* **-ies**) **1** fitness, rightness. **2** correctness of behaviour or morals. **3** (in *plural*) rules of polite behaviour.
■ **1** appropriateness, aptness, correctness, fitness, suitability. **2** courtesy, decency, decorum, delicacy, dignity, formality, gentility, good form, good manners, gravity, modesty, politeness, prudishness, refinement, respectability, sedateness, seemliness, sensitivity, tact, tastefulness. **3** (*proprieties*) etiquette, formalities, niceties.

propulsion /prəˈpʌlʃ(ə)n/ *noun* **1** driving or pushing forward. **2** force causing this. □ **propulsive** /-ˈpʌlsɪv/ *adjective.*

pro rata /prəʊ ˈrɑːtə/ *adjective* proportional. ● *adverb* proportionally. [Latin]

prorogue /prəˈrəʊg/ *verb* (**-gues, -gued, -guing**) **1** discontinue meetings of (parliament etc.) without dissolving it. **2** be prorogued. □ **prorogation** /prəʊrə-/ *noun.*

prosaic /prəˈzeɪɪk/ *adjective* **1** like prose. **2** unromantic; commonplace. □ **prosaically** *adverb.*
■ **2** characterless, clear, clichéd, commonplace, direct, down-to-earth, dry, dull, factual, flat, hackneyed, lifeless, matter-of-fact, monotonous, mundane, ordinary, pedestrian, plain, prosy, routine, simple, stereotyped, straightforward, to the point, trite, unadorned, understandable, unemotional, unfeeling, unimaginative, uninspired, uninspiring, unpoetic, unromantic, unsentimental, unvarnished.

proscenium /prəˈsiːnɪəm/ *noun* (*plural* **-s** or

-nia) part of theatre stage in front of curtain and enclosing arch.

proscribe /prəˈskraɪb/ *verb* (**-bing**) **1** forbid. **2** denounce. **3** outlaw. □ **proscription** /-ˈskrɪp-/ *noun*. **proscriptive** /-ˈskrɪp-/ *adjective*.

USAGE *Proscribe* is sometimes confused with *prescribe* which means 'to impose'.

prose /prəʊz/ *noun* **1** ordinary language not in verse form. **2** passage of this, esp. for translation. **3** dullness. ● *verb* (**-sing**) talk tediously.

prosecute /ˈprɒsɪkjuːt/ *verb* (**-ting**) **1** institute legal proceedings against. **2** *formal* carry on (trade etc.). □ **prosecutor** *noun*.
  ■ **1** accuse, arraign, bring an action against, bring to trial, charge, indict, prefer charges against, put on trial, sue, take to court. **2** see PURSUE 3,4.

prosecution /prɒsɪˈkjuːʃ(ə)n/ *noun* **1** prosecuting, being prosecuted. **2** prosecuting party.

proselyte /ˈprɒsəlaɪt/ *noun* **1** convert, esp. recent. **2** convert to Jewish faith. □ **proselytism** /-lɪtɪz(ə)m/ *noun*.

proselytize /ˈprɒsələtaɪz/ *verb* (also **-ise**) (**-zing** or **-sing**) (seek to) convert. □ **proselytizer** *noun*.

prosody /ˈprɒsədɪ/ *noun* science of versification. □ **prosodist** *noun*.

prospect *noun* /ˈprɒspekt/ **1** (often in *plural*) expectation. **2** extensive view. **3** mental picture. **4** possible or likely customer etc. ● *verb* /prəˈspekt/ (usually + *for*) explore (for gold etc.). □ **prospector** *noun*.
  ■ *noun* **1** chance, expectation, hope, likelihood, opportunity, outlook, possibility, probability, promise. **2** aspect, landscape, outlook, panorama, perspective, scene, seascape, sight, spectacle, view, vista. ● *verb* explore, quest, search, survey.

prospective /prəsˈpektɪv/ *adjective* some day to be; expected; future.
  ■ *disputed* anticipated, approaching, awaited, coming, expected, forthcoming, future, imminent, impending, intended, likely, looked-for, pending, possible, potential, probable.

prospectus /prəsˈpektəs/ *noun* (*plural* **-tuses**) pamphlet etc. advertising or describing school, business, etc.
  ■ brochure, catalogue, leaflet, manifesto, pamphlet.

prosper /ˈprɒspə/ *verb* succeed; thrive.
  ■ be successful, boom, burgeon, develop, do well, fare well, flourish, get ahead, get on, go from strength to strength, grow, make good, make one's fortune, profit, progress, strengthen, succeed, thrive.

prosperity /prɒˈsperɪtɪ/ *noun* prosperous state.
  ■ affluence, good fortune, growth, opulence, plenty, profitability, riches, success, wealth.

prosperous /ˈprɒspərəs/ *adjective* **1** rich. **2** successful; thriving. **3** auspicious. □ **prosperously** *adverb*.

  ■ **1** affluent, moneyed, rich, wealthy, *colloquial* well-heeled, well off, well-to-do. **2** blooming, booming, buoyant, expanding, flourishing, fruitful, healthy, moneymaking, productive, profitable, prospering, successful, thriving, vigorous.

prostate /ˈprɒsteɪt/ *noun* (in full **prostate gland**) gland secreting component of semen. □ **prostatic** /-ˈstæt-/ *adjective*.

prostitute /ˈprɒstɪtjuːt/ *noun* person who offers sexual intercourse for payment. ● *verb* (**-ting**) **1** make prostitute of. **2** misuse. **3** offer for sale unworthily. □ **prostitution** *noun*.
  ■ *noun* call-girl, camp follower, *literary* courtesan, *archaic* harlot, *slang* hooker, streetwalker, *archaic* strumpet, *slang* tart, trollop, whore. ● *verb* **2, 3** cheapen, debase, degrade, demean, devalue, lower, misuse.

prostrate *adjective* /ˈprɒstreɪt/ **1** lying face downwards, esp. in submission. **2** lying horizontally. **3** overcome, esp. exhausted. ● *verb* /prɒsˈtreɪt/ (**-ting**) **1** lay or throw flat. **2** overcome; make weak. □ **prostration** *noun*.
  ■ *adjective* **1, 2** see PRONE 1–2. **3** see OVERCOME 4. ● *verb* **1** (*prostrate oneself*) abase oneself, bow, grovel, kneel, *historical* kowtow, lie flat.

prosy /ˈprəʊzɪ/ *adjective* (**-ier**, **-iest**) tedious; commonplace; dull.

protagonist /prəˈtægənɪst/ *noun* **1** chief person in drama, story, etc. **2** *disputed* supporter of cause.

USAGE The use of *protagonist* to mean 'a supporter of a cause' is considered incorrect by some people.
  ■ **1** chief actor, hero, heroine, lead, leading figure, principal, title role.

protean /ˈprəʊˈtɪən/ *adjective* **1** variable. **2** versatile.

protect /prəˈtekt/ *verb* (often + *from*, *against*) keep (person etc.) safe; shield.
  ■ care for, cherish, conserve, cover, defend, escort, guard, harbour, keep, keep safe, look after, mind, preserve, safeguard, screen, secure, shield, stand up for, support, take care of, tend, watch over.

protection /prəˈtekʃ(ə)n/ *noun* **1** protecting, being protected; defence. **2** person etc. that protects. **3** protectionism. **4** *colloquial* immunity from violence etc. by paying gangsters etc.; (also **protection money**) money so paid.
  ■ **1** care, conservation, custody, defence, guardianship, patronage, preservation, safe keeping, safety, security, tutelage. **2** barrier, buffer, bulwark, cloak, cover, guard, screen, shelter, shield.

protectionism *noun* theory or practice of protecting home industries. □ **protectionist** *noun* & *adjective*.

protective /prəˈtektɪv/ *adjective* protecting; intended for or giving protection. □ **protective custody** detention of person for his or her own protection. □ **protectively** *adverb.* **protective-ness** *noun.*

■ (*protective material*) fireproof, insulating, preservative, protecting, sheltering, shielding, waterproof; (*protective person*) careful, defensive, jealous, paternalistic, possessive, solicitous, vigilant, watchful.

protector *noun* (*feminine* **protectress**) **1** person or thing that protects. **2** *historical* regent ruling during minority or absence of sovereign. □ **protectorship** *noun.*

■ **1** benefactor, bodyguard, champion, defender, guard, guardian, minder, patron.

protectorate /prə'tektərət/ *noun* **1** state controlled and protected by another. **2** such protectorship. **3** *historical* office of protector of kingdom or state. **4** period of this.

protégé /'prɒtɪʒeɪ/ *noun* (*feminine* **protégée** same pronunciation) person under protection, patronage, etc. of another.

protein /'prəʊtiːn/ *noun* any of a class of nitrogenous compounds essential in all living organisms.

pro tem /prəʊ 'tem/ *adjective & adverb colloquial* for the time being (*pro tempore*).

protest *noun* /'prəʊtest/ **1** expression of dissent or disapproval. **2** demonstration of objection. **3** legal written refusal to pay or accept bill. ● *verb* /prə'test/ **1** (usually + *against, at, about,* etc.) make protest. **2** affirm (innocence etc.). **3** write or get protest relating to (bill). **4** *US* object to. □ **protester, protestor** *noun.*

■ *noun* **1** complaint, demur, demurral, dissent, grievance, *colloquial* gripe, *colloquial* grouse, grumble, objection, opposition, outcry, protestation, remonstrance. **2** *colloquial* demo, demonstration, march, rally. ● *verb* **1** appeal, argue, complain, cry out, demonstrate, expostulate, fulminate, *colloquial* gripe, *colloquial* grouse, grumble, *colloquial* moan, object, remonstrate, take exception. **2** affirm, assert, asseverate, *formal* aver, declare, insist on, profess, *colloquial* swear.

Protestant /'prɒtɪst(ə)nt/ *noun* member or adherent of any of Churches separated from RC Church in Reformation. ● *adjective* of Protestant Churches or Protestants. □ **Protestantism** *noun.*

protestation /prɒtɪs'teɪʃ(ə)n/ *noun* **1** strong affirmation. **2** protest.

proto- *combining form* first.

protocol /'prəʊtəkɒl/ *noun* **1** official formality and etiquette. **2** draft, esp. of terms of treaty. ● *verb* (**-ll-**) draft or record in protocol.

proton /'prəʊtɒn/ *noun* elementary particle with positive electric charge equal to electron's, and occurring in all atomic nuclei.

protoplasm /'prəʊtəplæz(ə)m/ *noun* viscous translucent substance comprising living part of cell in organism. □ **protoplasmic** /-'plæzmɪk/ *adjective.*

prototype /'prəʊtətaɪp/ *noun* **1** original as pattern for copy, improved form, etc. **2** trial model of vehicle, machine, etc. □ **prototypic** /-'tɪp-/ *adjective.* **prototypical** /-'tɪp-/ *adjective.*

protozoan /prəʊtə'zəʊən/ *noun* (*plural* **-s**) (also **protozoon** /-'zəʊɒn/, *plural* **-zoa** /-'zəʊə/) one-celled microscopic organism. ● *adjective* (also **protozoic** /-'zəʊɪk/) of protozoa.

protract /prə'trækt/ *verb* (often as **protracted** *adjective*) prolong, lengthen. □ **protraction** *noun.*

■ (**protracted**) drawn-out, endless, extended, interminable, long, long-drawn(-out), long-winded, never-ending, prolonged, spun-out.

protractor *noun* instrument for measuring angles, usually in form of graduated semicircle.

protrude /prə'truːd/ *verb* (**-ding**) **1** thrust forward. **2** stick out. □ **protruding** *adjective.* **protrusion** *noun.* **protrusive** *adjective.*

■ **2** balloon, bulge, extend, jut out, overhang, poke out, project, stand out, stick out, stick up. □ **protruding** bulbous, bulging, distended, gibbous, humped, jutting, overhanging, projecting, prominent, protuberant, swollen, tumescent.

protuberant /prə'tjuːbərənt/ *adjective* bulging out; prominent. □ **protuberance** *noun.*

proud /praʊd/ *adjective* **1** feeling greatly honoured. **2** haughty, arrogant. **3** (often + *of*) feeling or showing (proper) pride; self-respecting. **4** imposing, splendid. **5** (often + *of*) slightly projecting. □ **do (person) proud** *colloquial* treat with great generosity or honour. □ **proudly** *adverb.*

■ **1** delighted, glad, gratified, happy, honoured, pleased, satisfied. **2** arrogant, *colloquial* big-headed, boastful, bumptious, cocksure, *colloquial* cocky, conceited, disdainful, egocentric, egotistic(al), haughty, *colloquial* high and mighty, immodest, lordly, narcissistic, self-centred, self-important, self-satisfied, smug, snobbish, *colloquial* snooty, *colloquial* stuck-up, supercilious, *colloquial* swollen-headed, *colloquial* toffee-nosed, vain, vainglorious. **3** dignified, independent, self-respecting. **4** august, distinguished, glorious, great, honourable, illustrious, imposing, noble, reputable, respected, splendid, worthy.

prove /pruːv/ *verb* (**-ving**; *past participle* **proved** or *esp. US & Scottish* **proven** /'pruːv(ə)n/) **1** (often + *that*) demonstrate to be true by evidence or argument. **2** (**prove oneself**) show one's abilities etc. **3** (usually + *to be*) be found. **4** test accuracy of. **5** establish validity of (will). **6** (of dough) rise. □ **provable** *adjective.* **proven** *adjective.*

USAGE The use of *proven* as the past participle is uncommon except in certain expressions, such as *of proven ability.* It is, however, standard in Scots and American English.

■ **1** ascertain, attest, authenticate, bear out, certify, check, confirm, corroborate, demonstrate, establish, show to be true, substantiate, verify. □ **provable** demonstrable, verifiable. **proven** accepted, reliable, tried and tested, trustworthy, undoubted, unquestioned, valid, verified.

provenance /'prɒvɪnəns/ *noun* (place of) origin; history.

provender /'prɒvɪndə/ *noun* 1 fodder. 2 *jocular* food.

proverb /'prɒvɜːb/ *noun* short pithy saying in general use.
■ adage, aphorism, apophthegm, maxim, saw, saying.

proverbial /prə'vɜːbɪəl/ *adjective* 1 notorious. 2 of or referred to in proverbs. □ **proverbially** *adverb*.
■ 1 customary, famous, *colloquial* legendary, time-honoured, traditional, well known. 2 aphoristic, axiomatic, clichéd.

provide /prə'vaɪd/ *verb* (**-ding**) 1 supply. 2 (usually + *for*, *against*) make due preparation. 3 (usually + *for*) take care of person etc. with money, food, etc. 4 (often + *that*) stipulate. □ **provider** *noun*.
■ 1 afford, allot, allow, contribute, donate, endow, equip, fix up with, *slang* fork out, furnish, give, grant, lay on, lend, offer, present, produce, purvey, spare, stock, supply, yield. 2 arrange, make provision, plan, prepare; (*provide for*) anticipate, cater for.

provided /prə'vaɪdɪd/ *adjective* supplied. ● *conjunction* (also **providing**) (often + *that*) on condition or understanding (that).

providence /'prɒvɪd(ə)ns/ *noun* 1 protective care of God or nature. 2 (**Providence**) God. 3 foresight, thrift.
■ 1 divine intervention.

provident /'prɒvɪd(ə)nt/ *adjective* having or showing foresight; thrifty.
■ careful, economical, far-sighted, forward-looking, frugal, judicious, prudent, thrifty.

providential /prɒvɪ'denʃ(ə)l/ *adjective* 1 of or by divine foresight or intervention. 2 opportune, lucky. □ **providentially** *adverb*.
■ 2 felicitous, fortunate, happy, lucky, opportune, timely.

province /'prɒvɪns/ *noun* 1 principal administrative division of country etc. 2 (**the provinces**) whole of country outside capital. 3 sphere of action. 4 branch of learning.

provincial /prə'vɪnʃ(ə)l/ *adjective* 1 of province(s). 2 unsophisticated, uncultured. ● *noun* 1 inhabitant of province(s). 2 unsophisticated or uncultured person. □ **provincialism** *noun*.
■ *adjective* 1 local, parochial, regional. 2 backward, boorish, insular, narrow-minded, parochial, rural, rustic, small-minded, uncultivated, uncultured, unsophisticated.

provision /prə'vɪʒ(ə)n/ *noun* 1 providing. 2 (in *plural*) food and drink, esp. for expedition. 3

legal or formal stipulation. ● *verb* supply with provisions.
■ 2 (*provisions*) food, foodstuff, groceries, *jocular* provender, rations, requirements, stocks, stores, subsistence, supplies, victuals.

provisional *adjective* 1 providing for immediate needs only; temporary. 2 (**Provisional**) of the unofficial wing of the IRA. ● *noun* (**Provisional**) member of unofficial wing of IRA. □ **provisionally** *adverb*.
■ *adjective* 1 conditional, interim, stopgap, temporary, tentative, transitional.

proviso /prə'vaɪzəʊ/ *noun* (*plural* **-s**) 1 stipulation. 2 limiting clause. □ **provisory** *adjective*.
■ condition, exception, limitation, provision, qualification, requirement, restriction, rider, stipulation.

provocation /prɒvə'keɪʃ(ə)n/ *noun* 1 provoking, being provoked. 2 cause of annoyance.
■ 1 *disputed* aggravation, incitement, taunting, teasing. 2 cause, grievance, grounds, incentive, incitement, inducement, justification, motivation, motive, reason, stimulus, taunts, teasing.

provocative /prə'vɒkətɪv/ *adjective* (usually + *of*) tending or intended to provoke anger, lust, interest, etc. □ **provocatively** *adverb*.
■ [*of anger*] *disputed* aggravating, annoying, infuriating, irksome, irritating, maddening, provoking, teasing, vexing; [*of lust*] alluring, arousing, erotic, pornographic, *colloquial* raunchy, seductive, sensual, sensuous, sexy, tantalizing, tempting.

provoke /prə'vəʊk/ *verb* (**-king**) 1 (often + *to*, *to do*) rouse, incite. 2 call forth; cause. 3 (usually + *into*) irritate; stimulate. 4 tempt. □ **provoker** *noun*.
■ 1 encourage, incite, induce, inspire, motivate, move, prompt, rouse, spur, stimulate, stir, urge on. 2 activate, arouse, awaken, bring about, call forth, cause, elicit, encourage, excite, foment, generate, give rise to, induce, initiate, inspire, instigate, kindle, motivate, promote, prompt, spark off, start. 3 *disputed* aggravate, anger, annoy, enrage, exasperate, gall, goad, incense, incite, inflame, infuriate, insult, irk, irritate, madden, offend, outrage, pique, *colloquial* rile, rouse, stimulate, stir up, tease, torment, upset, vex, *colloquial* wind up, work up, worry.

provost /'prɒvəst/ *noun* 1 head of some colleges. 2 head of cathedral chapter. 3 /prə'vəʊ/ (in full **provost marshal**) head of military police in camp or on active service.

prow /praʊ/ *noun* 1 bow of ship. 2 pointed or projecting front part.

prowess /'praʊɪs/ *noun* 1 skill, expertise. 2 valour, gallantry.
■ 1 ability, adeptness, adroitness, aptitude, cleverness, competence, dexterity, excellence, expertise, genius, mastery, proficiency, skill, talent. 2 boldness, bravery, courage, daring,

archaic doughtiness, gallantry, heroism, mettle, spirit, valour.

prowl /praʊl/ *verb* (often + *about, around*) roam, esp. stealthily in search of prey, plunder, etc. ● *noun* prowling. □ **prowler** *noun*.
■ *verb* creep, lurk, roam, rove, skulk, slink, sneak, steal.

prox. *abbreviation* proximo.

proximate /ˈprɒksɪmət/ *adjective* nearest, next before or after.

proximity /prɒkˈsɪmɪtɪ/ *noun* nearness.
■ closeness, nearness, propinquity.

proximo /ˈprɒksɪməʊ/ *adjective* of next month.

proxy /ˈprɒksɪ/ *noun* (*plural* **-ies**) **1** authorization given to deputy. **2** person authorized to deputize. **3** document authorizing person to vote on another's behalf. **4** vote so given.

prude *noun* excessively squeamish or sexually modest person. □ **prudery** *noun*. **prudish** *adjective*. **prudishly** *adverb*. **prudishness** *noun*.
■ □ **prudish** decorous, illiberal, intolerant, narrow-minded, old-fashioned, old-maidish, priggish, prim, prissy, proper, puritanical, rigid, shockable, strait-laced, strict.

prudent /ˈpruːd(ə)nt/ *adjective* **1** cautious. **2** politic. □ **prudence** *noun*. **prudently** *adverb*.
■ advisable, careful, cautious, circumspect, discreet, economical, far-sighted, frugal, judicious, politic, proper, provident, reasonable, sagacious, sage, sensible, shrewd, thoughtful, thrifty, vigilant, watchful, wise.

prudential /pruːˈdenʃ(ə)l/ *adjective* of or showing prudence.

prune[1] *noun* dried plum.

prune[2] *verb* (**-ning**) **1** (often + *down*) trim (tree etc.) by cutting away dead or overgrown parts. **2** (usually + *off, away*) remove (branches etc.) thus. **3** reduce (costs etc.). **4** (often + *of*) clear superfluities from. **5** remove (superfluities).
■ **1, 2** clip, cut back, lop, pare down, trim. **4, 5** see CUT *verb* 2–3.

prurient /ˈprʊərɪənt/ *adjective* having or encouraging unhealthy sexual curiosity. □ **prurience** *noun*.

Prussian /ˈprʌʃ(ə)n/ *adjective* of Prussia. ● *noun* native of Prussia. □ **Prussian blue** deep blue (pigment).

prussic acid /ˈprʌsɪk/ *noun* highly poisonous liquid.

pry /praɪ/ *verb* (**pries, pried**) (usually + *into* etc.) **1** inquire impertinently. **2** look inquisitively. □ **prying** *adjective*.
■ be curious, be inquisitive, *colloquial* be nosy, delve, ferret, inquire, interfere, intrude, investigate, meddle, nose about, peer, poke about, *colloquial* poke one's nose in, search, *colloquial* snoop. □ **prying** see INQUISITIVE 1.

PS *abbreviation* postscript.

psalm /sɑːm/ *noun* **1** (also **Psalm**) sacred song. **2** (**the (Book of) Psalms**) book of these in Old Testament.

psalmist /ˈsɑːmɪst/ *noun* author or composer of psalm(s).

psalmody /ˈsɑːmədɪ/ *noun* practice or art of singing psalms.

Psalter /ˈsɔːltə/ *noun* **1** Book of Psalms. **2** (**psalter**) version or copy of this.

psaltery /ˈsɔːltərɪ/ *noun* (*plural* **-ies**) ancient and medieval musical stringed instrument played by plucking.

psephology /sɪˈfɒlədʒɪ/ *noun* statistical study of voting etc. □ **psephologist** *noun*.

pseudo /ˈsjuːdəʊ/ *adjective* **1** sham. **2** insincere. ● *noun* (*plural* **-os**) pretentious or insincere person.

pseudo- *combining form* (also **pseud-** before vowel) **1** false, not genuine. **2** resembling, imitating.

pseudonym /ˈsjuːdənɪm/ *noun* fictitious name, esp. of author.
■ alias, assumed name, false name, incognito, nickname, *nom de plume*, pen-name, sobriquet, stage name.

psoriasis /səˈraɪəsɪs/ *noun* skin disease with red scaly patches.

PSV *abbreviation* public service vehicle.

psych /saɪk/ *verb colloquial* **1** (usually + *up*) prepare mentally. **2** (often + *out*) intimidate. **3** (usually + *out*) analyse (person's motivation etc.).

psyche /ˈsaɪkɪ/ *noun* **1** soul; spirit. **2** mind.

psychedelic /saɪkəˈdelɪk/ *adjective* **1** expanding the mind's awareness. **2** hallucinatory. **3** vivid in colour, design, etc.

psychiatry /saɪˈkaɪətrɪ/ *noun* study and treatment of mental disease. □ **psychiatric** /-kɪˈætrɪk/ *adjective*. **psychiatrist** *noun*.

psychic /ˈsaɪkɪk/ *adjective* **1** (of person) regarded as having paranormal powers; clairvoyant. **2** (of process, phenomenon, etc.) paranormal, supernatural. **3** of the soul or mind. ● *noun* psychic person; medium.
■ *adjective* **1** clairvoyant, telepathic. **2** extrasensory, magical, metaphysical, mystic, occult, paranormal, preternatural, psychical, supernatural. **3** mental, psychical, psychological, spiritual. ● *noun* astrologer, clairvoyant, crystal-gazer, fortune-teller, medium, spiritualist.

psychical *adjective* **1** concerning psychic phenomena or faculties. **2** of the soul or mind.

psycho- *combining form* of mind or psychology.

psychoanalysis /saɪkəʊəˈnælɪsɪs/ *noun* treatment of mental disorders by bringing repressed fears etc. into conscious mind. □ **psychoanalyse** /-ˈænəl-/ *verb* (**-sing**). **psychoanalyst** /-ˈænəl-/ *noun*. **psychoanalytical** /-ænəˈlɪt-/ *adjective*.

psychokinesis /saɪkəʊkɪˈniːsɪs/ *noun* movement of objects by telepathy.

psychological /saɪkəˈlɒdʒɪk(ə)l/ *adjective* **1** of

the mind. **2** of psychology. **3** *colloquial* imaginary. □ **psychological block** inhibition caused by emotion. **psychological moment** best time to achieve purpose. **psychological warfare** campaign to reduce enemy's morale. □ **psychologically** *adverb*.

■ **1** cerebral, emotional, mental, subconscious, *esp. Philosophy* subjective, subliminal, unconscious.

psychology /saɪˈkɒlədʒɪ/ *noun* (*plural* **-ies**) **1** study of human mind. **2** treatise on or theory of this. **3** mental characteristics. □ **psychologist** *noun*.

psychopath /ˈsaɪkəpæθ/ *noun* **1** mentally deranged person, esp. with abnormal social behaviour. **2** mentally or emotionally unstable person. □ **psychopathic** /-ˈpæθ-/ *adjective*.

psychosis /saɪˈkəʊsɪs/ *noun* (*plural* **-choses** /-siːz/) severe mental derangement involving loss of contact with reality.

psychosomatic /saɪkəʊsəˈmætɪk/ *adjective* **1** (of disease) mental, not physical, in origin. **2** of both mind and body.

psychotherapy /saɪkəʊˈθerəpɪ/ *noun* treatment of mental disorder by psychological means. □ **psychotherapist** *noun*.

psychotic /saɪˈkɒtɪk/ *adjective* of or suffering from psychosis. ● *noun* psychotic person.

PT *abbreviation* physical training.

pt *abbreviation* **1** part. **2** pint. **3** point. **4** port.

PTA *abbreviation* parent–teacher association.

ptarmigan /ˈtɑːmɪgən/ *noun* bird of grouse family.

Pte. *abbreviation* Private (soldier).

pteridophyte /ˈterɪdəfaɪt/ *noun* flowerless plant.

pterodactyl /terəˈdæktɪl/ *noun* large extinct flying reptile.

PTO *abbreviation* please turn over.

ptomaine /ˈtəʊmeɪn/ *noun* any of a group of compounds (some toxic) in putrefying matter.

pub *noun colloquial* public house.

■ *archaic* alehouse, bar, *colloquial* boozer, *archaic* hostelry, inn, *colloquial* local, public house, *US* saloon, *archaic* or *literary* tavern, wine bar.

puberty /ˈpjuːbətɪ/ *noun* period of sexual maturing.

■ adolescence, pubescence, sexual maturity, teens.

pubes[1] /ˈpjuːbiːz/ *noun* (*plural* same) lower part of abdomen.

pubes[2] *plural* of PUBIS.

pubescence /pjuːˈbes(ə)ns/ *noun* **1** beginning of puberty. **2** soft down on plant or animal. □ **pubescent** *adjective*.

pubic /ˈpjuːbɪk/ *adjective* of pubes or pubis.

pubis /ˈpjuːbɪs/ *noun* (*plural* **pubes** /-biːz/) front portion of hip bone.

public /ˈpʌblɪk/ *adjective* **1** of the people as a whole. **2** open to or shared by all. **3** done or existing openly. **4** of or from government. **5** involved in community affairs. **6** well known. ● *noun* **1** (treated as *singular* or *plural*) (members of) community as a whole. **2** section of community. □ **go public 1** (of company) start selling shares on open market. **2** reveal one's plans. **in public** publicly, openly. **public address system** equipment of loudspeakers etc. **public convenience** public lavatory. **public figure** famous person. **public house** place selling alcoholic drink for consumption on premises. **public lending right** right of authors to payment when their books are lent by public libraries. **public relations** professional promotion of company, product, etc. **public school 1** independent fee-paying school. **2** *US, Australian, Scottish, etc.* non-fee-paying school. **public-spirited** ready to do things for the community. **public transport** buses, trains, etc. available for public use on fixed routes. **public utility** organization supplying water, gas, etc. to community. □ **publicly** *adverb*.

■ *adjective* **1** civic, civil, collective, communal, community, democratic, general, majority, national, popular, social, universal. **2** accessible, available, common, familiar, free, known, open, shared, unconcealed, unrestricted, visible, well known. **4** government, national, state. **6** see PROMINENT **3**. ● *noun* **1** (*the public*) citizens, the community, the country, the nation, people, the populace, society, voters.

publican /ˈpʌblɪkən/ *noun* keeper of public house.

publication /pʌblɪˈkeɪʃ(ə)n/ *noun* **1** publishing. **2** published book, periodical, etc.

■ **1** advertising, announcement, appearance, broadcasting, declaration, disclosure, dissemination, issuing, printing, proclamation, production, promulgation, publicizing, reporting. **2** see BOOK *noun* **1,2**, MAGAZINE **1**.

publicist /ˈpʌblɪsɪst/ *noun* publicity agent; public relations officer.

publicity /pʌbˈlɪsɪtɪ/ *noun* **1** (means of attracting) public attention. **2** (material used for) advertising.

■ **1** attention, ballyhoo, fame, *slang* hype, limelight, notoriety. **2** advertisement, advertising, marketing, promotion.

publicize /ˈpʌblɪsaɪz/ *verb* (also **-ise**) (**-zing** or **-sing**) advertise; make publicly known.

■ advertise, *slang* hype, *colloquial* plug, promote, publish, puff.

publish /ˈpʌblɪʃ/ *verb* **1** prepare and issue (book, magazine, etc.) for public sale. **2** make generally known. **3** formally announce.

■ **1** bring out, circulate, issue, make available, print, produce, put on sale, release. **2** advertise, announce, broadcast, communicate, declare, disclose, disseminate, divulge, leak, make known, make public, proclaim, promulgate, publicize, put about, report, reveal, spread.

publisher *noun* person or firm that publishes books etc.

puce /pjuːs/ *adjective & noun* purple-brown.

puck[1] *noun* rubber disc used in ice hockey.

puck[2] *noun* mischievous sprite. □ **puckish** *adjective*. **puckishly** *adverb*. **puckishness** *noun*.

pucker /'pʌkə/ *verb* (often + *up*) gather into wrinkles, folds, or bulges. ● *noun* such wrinkle etc.

■ *verb* compress, contract, crease, crinkle, draw together, purse, screw up, squeeze, tighten, wrinkle.

pudding /'pʊdɪŋ/ *noun* 1 sweet cooked dish. 2 savoury dish containing flour, suet, etc. 3 sweet course of meal. 4 kind of sausage.

puddle /'pʌd(ə)l/ *noun* 1 small (dirty) pool. 2 clay made into watertight coating.

pudenda /pjuː'dendə/ *plural noun* genitals, esp. of woman.

pudgy /'pʌdʒɪ/ *adjective* (**-ier**, **-iest**) *colloquial* plump, podgy.

puerile /'pjʊəraɪl/ *adjective* childish, immature. □ **puerility** /-'rɪl-/ *noun* (*plural* **-ies**).

■ babyish, boyish, childish, immature, infantile, *often derogatory* juvenile, silly.

puerperal /pjuː'ɜːpər(ə)l/ *adjective* of or due to childbirth.

puff *noun* 1 short quick blast of breath or wind. 2 sound (as) of this. 3 vapour or smoke sent out in one blast. 4 light pastry cake. 5 gathered material in dress etc. 6 unduly favourable review, advertisement, etc. ● *verb* 1 emit puff(s). 2 smoke or move with puffs. 3 (usually in *passive*; often + *out*) put out of breath. 4 pant. 5 (usually + *up*, *out*) inflate. 6 (usually as **puffed up** *adjective*) elate; make boastful. 7 advertise in exaggerated terms. □ **puff-adder** large venomous African viper. **puffball** ball-shaped fungus. **puff pastry** pastry consisting of thin layers.

■ *noun* 1–3 blast, blow, breath, cloud, draught, flurry, gust, whiff, wisp. ● *verb* 1 blow, breathe, exhale. 2 *slang* drag, draw, inhale, pull, smoke, suck. 4 blow, gasp, huff, pant, wheeze. 5 balloon, billow, distend, enlarge, inflate, rise, swell.

puffin /'pʌfɪn/ *noun* N. Atlantic and N. Pacific auk with short striped bill.

puffy *adjective* (**-ier**, **-iest**) 1 swollen; puffed out. 2 *colloquial* short-winded.

pug *noun* (in full **pug-dog**) dog of small breed with flat nose. □ **pug-nose** short flat or snub nose.

pugilist /'pjuːdʒɪlɪst/ *noun* boxer. □ **pugilism** *noun*. **pugilistic** /-'lɪs-/ *adjective*.

pugnacious /pʌg'neɪʃəs/ *adjective* disposed to fight. □ **pugnaciously** *adverb*. **pugnacity** /-'næs-/ *noun*.

■ aggressive, antagonistic, argumentative, bellicose, belligerent, combative, contentious, disputatious, excitable, fractious, hostile, hot-tempered, litigious, militant, quarrelsome, unfriendly, warlike.

puissance /'pwiːsɑ̃s/ *noun* jumping of large obstacles in showjumping.

puissant /'pwiːsɒnt/ *adjective literary* powerful; mighty.

puke /pjuːk/ *verb & noun* (**-king**) *slang* vomit. □ **pukey** *adjective*.

pukka /'pʌkə/ *adjective colloquial* 1 genuine. 2 reliable.

pulchritude /'pʌlkrɪtjuːd/ *noun literary* beauty. □ **pulchritudinous** /-'tjuːdɪnəs/ *adjective*.

pull /pʊl/ *verb* 1 exert force on (thing etc.) to move it to oneself or origin of force. 2 exert pulling force. 3 extract by pulling. 4 damage (muscle etc.) by abnormal strain. 5 proceed with effort. 6 (+ *on*) draw (weapon) against (person). 7 attract. 8 draw (liquor) from barrel etc. 9 (+ *at*) pluck at. 10 (often + *on*, *at*) inhale or drink deeply; suck. ● *noun* 1 act of pulling. 2 force thus exerted. 3 influence; advantage. 4 attraction. 5 deep draught of liquor. 6 prolonged effort. 7 handle etc. for applying pull. 8 printer's rough proof. 9 suck at cigarette. □ **pull back** retreat. **pull down** demolish. **pull in** 1 arrive to take passengers. 2 move to side of or off road. 3 *colloquial* earn. 4 *colloquial* arrest. **pull-in** *noun* roadside café etc. **pull off** 1 remove. 2 win; manage successfully. **pull oneself together** recover control of oneself. **pull out** 1 take out. 2 depart. 3 withdraw. 4 leave station or stop. 5 move towards off side. **pull-out** *noun* removable section of magazine. **pull person's leg** deceive person playfully. **pull round, through** (cause to) recover from illness. **pull strings** exert (esp. clandestine) influence. **pull through** get through illness, danger, or difficulty. **pull together** work in harmony. **pull up** 1 (cause to) stop moving. 2 pull out of ground. 3 reprimand. 4 check oneself.

■ *verb* 1 drag, draw, haul, jerk, lug, pluck, tow, trail, tug, wrench, *colloquial* yank. 3 draw, extract, pull out, remove, take out. 9 (*pull at*) jerk, pluck at, tug at, wrench, *colloquial* yank. □ **pull off** 1 see DETACH 1. **pull out** 3 see WITHDRAW 5. **pull round, through** see RECOVER 2. **pull together** see COOPERATE. **pull up** 1 see HALT[1] *verb*. 3 see REPRIMAND *verb*.

pullet /'pʊlɪt/ *noun* young hen, esp. less than one year old.

pulley /'pʊlɪ/ *noun* (*plural* **-s**) 1 grooved wheel(s) for cord etc. to run over, mounted in block and used to lift weight etc. 2 wheel or drum mounted on shaft and turned by belt, used to increase speed or power.

Pullman /'pʊlmən/ *noun* (*plural* **-s**) 1 luxurious railway carriage or motor coach. 2 sleeping car.

pullover *noun* knitted garment put on over the head.

pullulate /'pʌljʊleɪt/ *verb* (**-ting**) 1 sprout. 2 swarm. 3 develop. 4 (+ *with*) abound with. □ **pullulation** *noun*.

pulmonary /'pʌlmənərɪ/ *adjective* 1 of lungs. 2 having (organs like) lungs. 3 affected with or subject to lung disease.

pulp *noun* 1 fleshy part of fruit etc. 2 soft shapeless mass, esp. of materials for papermaking. 3

cheap fiction. ● *verb* reduce to or become pulp. □ **pulpy** *adjective*. **pulpiness** *noun*.

■ *noun* **2** mash, mush, paste, pap, purée. ● *verb* crush, liquidize, mash, pound, pulverize, purée, smash, squash.

pulpit /'pʊlpɪt/ *noun* **1** raised enclosed platform for preaching from. **2** (**the pulpit**) preachers collectively; preaching.

pulsar /'pʌlsɑː/ *noun* cosmic source of regular rapid pulses of radiation.

pulsate /pʌl'seɪt/ *verb* (**-ting**) **1** expand and contract rhythmically. **2** throb, vibrate, quiver. □ **pulsation** *noun*.

■ beat, drum, oscillate, palpitate, pound, pulse, quiver, reverberate, throb, tick, vibrate.

pulse[1] *noun* **1** rhythmical throbbing of arteries. **2** each beat of arteries or heart. **3** throb or thrill of life or emotion. **4** general feeling. **5** single vibration of sound, electromagnetic radiation, etc. **6** rhythmical (esp. musical) beat. ● *verb* (**-sing**) pulsate.

■ *noun* **6** beat, drumming, oscillation, pounding, pulsation, rhythm, throb, ticking, vibration.

pulse[2] *noun* (treated as *singular* or *plural*) (plant producing) edible seeds of peas, beans, lentils, etc.

pulverize /'pʌlvəraɪz/ *verb* (also **-ise**) (**-zing** or **-sing**) **1** reduce or crumble to powder or dust. **2** *colloquial* demolish. **3** *colloquial* crush. □ **pulverization** *noun*.

puma /'pjuːmə/ *noun* large tawny American feline.

pumice /'pʌmɪs/ *noun* (in full **pumice stone**) **1** light porous lava used as abrasive. **2** piece of this.

pummel /'pʌm(ə)l/ *verb* (**-ll-**; *US* **-l-**) strike repeatedly, esp. with fists.

pump[1] *noun* **1** machine or device for raising or moving liquids or gases. **2** act of pumping. ● *verb* **1** (often + *in*, *out*, *up*, etc.) raise, remove, inflate, empty, etc. (as) with pump. **2** work pump. **3** persistently question (person) to elicit information. **4** move vigorously up and down. □ **pump iron** *colloquial* exercise with weights.

■ *verb* **1** (*pump out*) drain, draw off, empty, force out, siphon (off); (*pump up*) blow up, fill, inflate.

pump[2] *noun* **1** plimsoll. **2** light shoe for dancing etc.

pumpernickel /'pʌmpənɪk(ə)l/ *noun* wholemeal rye bread.

pumpkin /'pʌmpkɪn/ *noun* **1** large yellow or orange fruit used as vegetable. **2** plant bearing it.

pun *noun* humorous use of word(s) with two or more meanings; play on words. ● *verb* (**-nn-**) (usually + *on*) make pun(s).

Punch *noun* grotesque humpbacked puppet in *Punch and Judy* shows.

punch[1] *verb* **1** strike with fist. **2** make hole in (as) with punch. **3** pierce (hole) thus. ● *noun* **1** blow with fist. **2** *colloquial* vigour; effective force. **3** instrument or machine for piercing holes or

impressing design in leather, metal, etc. □ **pull one's punches** avoid using full force. **punchball** stuffed or inflated ball used for practice in punching. **punch-drunk** stupefied (as) with repeated punches. **punchline** words giving point of joke etc. **punch-up** *colloquial* fist-fight; brawl. □ **puncher** *noun*.

■ *verb* **1** beat, *slang* biff, box, clout, cuff, hit, prod, pummel, slog, *US* slug, *colloquial* sock, strike, thump. **2, 3** see PIERCE 1–3.

punch[2] *noun* hot or cold mixture of wine or spirit with water, fruit, spices, etc. □ **punch-bowl 1** bowl for punch. **2** deep round hollow in hill.

punchy *adjective* (**-ier**, **-iest**) vigorous, forceful.

punctilio /pʌŋk'tɪlɪəʊ/ *noun* (*plural* **-s**) **1** delicate point of ceremony or honour. **2** petty formality.

punctilious /pʌŋk'tɪlɪəs/ *adjective* **1** attentive to formality or etiquette. **2** precise in behaviour. □ **punctiliously** *adverb*. **punctiliousness** *noun*.

punctual /'pʌŋktʃʊəl/ *adjective* observing appointed time; prompt. □ **punctuality** /-'æl-/ *noun*. **punctually** *adverb*.

■ in good time, on the dot, on time, prompt.

punctuate /'pʌŋktʃʊeɪt/ *verb* (**-ting**) **1** insert punctuation marks in. **2** interrupt at intervals.

■ **2** break, interrupt, intersperse.

punctuation *noun* (system of) punctuating. □ **punctuation mark** any of the marks used in writing to separate sentences, phrases, etc.

puncture /'pʌŋktʃə/ *noun* **1** prick, pricking. **2** hole made by this, esp. in pneumatic tyre. ● *verb* (**-ring**) **1** make or suffer puncture (in). **2** deflate.

■ *noun* **1** perforation, pinprick, prick, pricking, rupture. **2** *colloquial* blow-out, burst tyre, flat, flat tyre, hole, leak, opening, perforation, pinprick, rupture. ● *verb* **1** go through, penetrate, perforate, pierce, prick, rupture. **2** deflate, let down.

pundit /'pʌndɪt/ *noun* **1** (also **pandit**) learned Hindu. **2** expert.

pungent /'pʌndʒ(ə)nt/ *adjective* **1** having sharp or strong taste or smell. **2** biting, caustic. □ **pungency** *noun*.

■ **1** acid, acrid, aromatic, astringent, caustic, harsh, hot, peppery, piquant, seasoned, sharp, sour, spicy, stinging, strong, tangy. **2** biting, bitter, caustic, incisive, mordant, sarcastic, scathing, trenchant.

punish /'pʌnɪʃ/ *verb* **1** inflict penalty on (offender) or for (offence). **2** tax, abuse, or treat severely. □ **punishable** *adjective*. **punishment** *noun*.

■ **1** castigate, chasten, chastise, correct, discipline, exact retribution from, make an example of, pay back, penalize, scold, teach a lesson. □ **punishment** chastisement, correction, discipline, forfeit, imposition, just deserts, penalty, punitive measure, retribution, revenge, sentence.

punitive /'pjuːnɪtɪv/ *adjective* **1** inflicting or intended to inflict punishment. **2** extremely severe.

■ **1** disciplinary, penal, retaliatory, retributive, revengeful, vindictive.

punk *noun* **1** (in full **punk rock**) deliberately outrageous style of rock music. **2** (in full **punk rocker**) fan of this. **3** *esp. US* hooligan, lout.

punkah /'pʌŋkə/ *noun* large swinging fan on frame worked by cord or electrically.

punnet /'pʌnɪt/ *noun* small basket for fruit etc.

punster /'pʌnstə/ *noun* maker of puns.

punt¹ *noun* square-ended flat-bottomed boat propelled by long pole. ● *verb* travel or carry in punt.

punt² *verb* kick (football) dropped from hands before it reaches ground. ● *noun* such kick.

punt³ *verb* **1** *colloquial* bet. **2** *colloquial* speculate in shares etc. **3** (in some card games) lay stake against bank. ● *noun* bet.

punt⁴ /pʊnt/ *noun* chief monetary unit of Republic of Ireland.

punter *noun colloquial* **1** person who gambles or bets. **2** customer, client.

puny /'pju:nɪ/ *adjective* (**-ier, -iest**) **1** undersized. **2** feeble.

■ **1** diminutive, dwarf, small, stunted, underdeveloped, undernourished, undersized. **2** feeble, frail, sickly, weak.

pup *noun* young dog, wolf, rat, seal, etc. ● *verb* (**-pp-**) give birth to (pups).

pupa /'pju:pə/ *noun* (*plural* **pupae** /-pi:/) insect in stage between larva and imago.

pupil¹ /'pju:pɪl/ *noun* person being taught.

■ apprentice, beginner, disciple, follower, learner, novice, scholar, schoolboy, schoolchild, schoolgirl, student, tiro.

pupil² /'pju:pɪl/ *noun* opening in centre of iris of eye.

puppet /'pʌpɪt/ *noun* **1** small figure moved esp. by strings as entertainment. **2** person controlled by another. □ **puppet state** country apparently independent but actually under control of another power. □ **puppetry** *noun*.

■ **1** doll, dummy, marionette.

puppy /'pʌpɪ/ *noun* (*plural* **-ies**) **1** young dog. **2** conceited young man. □ **puppy fat** temporary fatness of child or adolescent. **puppy love** calf love.

purblind /'pɜ:blaɪnd/ *adjective* **1** partly blind, dim-sighted. **2** obtuse, dull. □ **purblindness** *noun*.

purchase /'pɜ:tʃəs/ *verb* (**-sing**) buy. ● *noun* **1** buying. **2** thing bought. **3** firm hold on thing; leverage. **4** equipment for moving heavy objects. □ **purchaser** *noun*.

■ *verb* acquire, buy, get, invest in, obtain, pay for, procure, secure. ● *noun* **2** acquisition, *colloquial* buy, investment. **3** grasp, grip, hold, leverage, support.

purdah /'pɜ:də/ *noun* screening of Muslim or Hindu women from strangers.

pure /pjʊə/ *adjective* **1** unmixed, unadulterated.

2 absolute; sheer. **3** chaste. **4** not morally corrupt; guiltless. **5** sincere. **6** not discordant. **7** (of science) abstract; not applied. □ **pureness** *noun*.

purity *noun*.

■ **1** authentic, genuine, natural, neat, real, solid, sterling, straight, unadulterated, unalloyed, uncontaminated, undiluted, unmixed, unpolluted, untainted. **2** absolute, complete, downright, out and out, perfect, sheer, thorough, total, true, unmitigated, unqualified, utter. **3, 4** blameless, chaste, decent, good, impeccable, innocent, irreproachable, maidenly, modest, moral, proper, sinless, stainless, virginal, virtuous. **7** abstract, academic, conjectural, conceptual, hypothetical, speculative, theoretical.

pure-bred *adjective* (of animal) bred from parents of same breed. ● *noun* such an animal.

purée /'pjʊəreɪ/ *noun* smooth pulp of vegetables or fruit etc. ● *verb* (**-ées, -éed**) make purée of.

purely *adverb* **1** in a pure way. **2** merely, solely. **3** exclusively.

purgative /'pɜ:gətɪv/ *adjective* **1** serving to purify. **2** strongly laxative. ● *noun* purgative thing.

■ *noun* aperient, cathartic, enema, laxative, purge.

purgatory /'pɜ:gətərɪ/ *noun* (*plural* **-ies**) **1** place or state of spiritual cleansing, esp. after death and before entering heaven. **2** place or state of temporary suffering or expiation. ● *adjective* purifying. □ **purgatorial** /-'tɔ:rɪəl/ *adjective*.

purge /pɜ:dʒ/ *verb* (**-ging**) **1** (often + *of, from*) make physically or spiritually clean. **2** remove by cleansing. **3** rid of unacceptable members. **4** empty (bowels). **5** *Law* atone for (offence). ● *noun* **1** purging. **2** purgative.

■ *verb* **1** clean out, cleanse, clear, empty, purify, wash out. **3** eject, eliminate, eradicate, expel, get rid of, liquidate, oust, remove, root out.

purify /'pjʊərɪfaɪ/ *verb* (**-ies, -ied**) **1** clear of extraneous elements; make pure. **2** (often + *of, from*) cleanse. □ **purification** *noun*. **purificatory** /-fɪkeɪtərɪ/ *adjective*.

■ clarify, clean, cleanse, clear, decontaminate, disinfect, distil, filter, fumigate, purge, refine, sanitize, sterilize.

purist /'pjʊərɪst/ *noun* stickler for correctness, esp. in language. □ **purism** *noun*.

puritan /'pjʊərɪt(ə)n/ *noun* **1** (**Puritan**) *historical* member of English Protestant group regarding Reformation as incomplete. **2** purist member of any party. **3** strict observer of religion or morals. ● *adjective* **1** (**Puritan**) *historical* of Puritans. **2** scrupulous in religion or morals. □ **puritanical** /-'tæn-/ *adjective*. **puritanically** /-'tæn-/ *adverb*. **puritanism** *noun*.

■ *noun* **3** ascetic, fanatic, killjoy, moralist, prude, zealot. □ **puritanical** ascetic, austere, moralistic, narrow-minded, pietistic, prim, proper, prudish, rigid, self-denying, self-disciplined, severe, stern, stiff-necked, strait-laced, strict, temperate, unbending, uncompromising.

purl¹ *noun* **1** knitting stitch with needle moved in

opposite to normal direction. **2** chain of minute loops. ● *verb* knit with purl stitch.

purl² *verb* flow with babbling sound.

purler /'pɜːlə/ *noun colloquial* heavy fall.

purlieu /'pɜːljuː/ *noun* (*plural* **-s**) **1** person's limits or usual haunts. **2** *historical* tract on border of forest. **3** (in *plural*) outskirts; outlying region.

purlin /'pɜːlɪn/ *noun* horizontal beam along length of roof.

purloin /pə'lɔɪn/ *verb formal* or *jocular* steal, pilfer. □ **purloiner** *noun*.

purple /'pɜːp(ə)l/ *noun* **1** colour between red and blue. **2** purple robe, esp. of emperor etc. **3** cardinal's scarlet official dress. ● *adjective* of purple. ● *verb* (**-ling**) make or become purple. □ **purplish** *adjective*.

purport *verb* /pə'pɔːt/ **1** profess; be intended to seem. **2** (often + *that*) have as its meaning. ● *noun* /'pɜːpɔːt/ **1** ostensible meaning. **2** tenor of document or statement. □ **purportedly** *adverb*.

purpose /'pɜːpəs/ *noun* **1** object to be attained; thing intended. **2** intention to act; resolution, determination. **3** reason for existing; use. ● *verb* (**-sing**) have as one's purpose, intend. □ **on purpose** intentionally. **to good, little, no, etc. purpose** with good, little, no, etc. effect or result. **to the purpose 1** relevant. **2** useful.

■ *noun* **1** aim, ambition, aspiration, design, end, goal, hope, intent, intention, motivation, motive, object, objective, plan, point, target, wish. **2** determination, devotion, drive, firmness, persistence, resolution, resolve, steadfastness, tenacity, will, zeal. **3** advantage, application, benefit, good (*what's the good of it?*), point, practicality, rationale, use, usefulness, utility, value. ● *verb* see INTEND.

purposeful *adjective* **1** having or indicating purpose. **2** intentional. □ **purposefully** *adverb*. **purposefulness** *noun*.

■ calculated, decided, decisive, deliberate, determined, devoted, firm, intentional, persistent, positive, resolute, steadfast, stubborn, tenacious, unwavering, wilful, zealous.

purposeless *adjective* having no aim or plan.

■ aimless, *archaic* bootless, empty, gratuitous, meaningless, pointless, senseless, unnecessary, useless, vacuous, wanton.

purposely *adverb* on purpose.

■ consciously, deliberately, intentionally, knowingly, on purpose, wilfully.

purposive /'pɜːpəsɪv/ *adjective* **1** having, serving, or done with a purpose. **2** purposeful.

purr /pɜː/ *verb* **1** make low vibratory sound of cat expressing pleasure. **2** (of machinery etc.) run smoothly and quietly. ● *noun* purring sound.

purse /pɜːs/ *noun* **1** small pouch for carrying money in. **2** *US* handbag. **3** funds. **4** sum given as present or prize. ● *verb* (**-sing**) **1** (often + *up*) contract (esp. lips). **2** become wrinkled. □ **hold the purse strings** have control of expenditure.

■ *noun* **1** pocketbook, pouch, wallet. **2** bag, handbag.

purser /'pɜːsə/ *noun* ship's officer who keeps accounts, esp. head steward in passenger vessel.

pursuance /pə'sjuːəns/ *noun* (+ *of*) carrying out or observance (of plan, rules, etc.).

pursuant /pə'sjuːənt/ *adverb* (+ *to*) in accordance with.

pursue /pə'sjuː/ *verb* (**-sues**, **-sued**, **-suing**) **1** follow with intent to overtake, capture, or harm. **2** proceed along. **3** engage in (study etc.). **4** carry out (plan etc.). **5** seek after. **6** continue to investigate etc. **7** persistently importune or assail. □ **pursuer** *noun*.

■ **1** chase, follow, go after, hound, hunt, run after, shadow, stalk, *colloquial* tail, trace, track down, trail. **2** continue, follow, keep on, persevere in, persist in, proceed along, stick with. **3, 4** be committed to, carry on, conduct, continue, dedicate oneself to, engage in, proceed with, *formal* prosecute. **5** aim for, aspire to, *colloquial* go for, seek (after), strive for, try for. **6** inquire into, investigate.

pursuit /pə'sjuːt/ *noun* **1** pursuing. **2** occupation or activity pursued. □ **in pursuit of** pursuing.

■ **1** chase, chasing, following, hue and cry, hunt, hunting, shadowing, stalking, tracking down, trail. **2** activity, employment, enthusiasm, hobby, interest, obsession, occupation, pastime, pleasure.

purulent /'pjʊərʊlənt/ *adjective* of, containing, or discharging pus. □ **purulence** *noun*.

purvey /pə'veɪ/ *verb* provide or supply food etc. as one's business. □ **purveyor** *noun*.

purview /'pɜːvjuː/ *noun* **1** scope of document etc. **2** range of physical or mental vision.

pus /pʌs/ *noun* thick yellowish liquid produced from infected tissue.

push /pʊʃ/ *verb* **1** exert force on (thing) to move it away. **2** cause to move thus. **3** exert such force. **4** thrust forward or upward. **5** (cause to) project. **6** press, depress. **7** (often + *on*) move forward. **8** make (one's way) forcibly or persistently. **9** exert oneself. **10** (often + *to, into, to do*) urge, impel. **11** (often + *for*) pursue (claim etc.) persistently. **12** promote, advertise. **13** *colloquial* sell (drug) illegally. ● *noun* **1** act of pushing. **2** force thus exerted. **3** vigorous effort. **4** determination. **5** use of influence to advance person. □ **give or get the push** *colloquial* dismiss, be dismissed. **push around** *colloquial* bully. **push-bike** *colloquial* bicycle. **pushchair** child's folding chair on wheels. **push off** *colloquial* go away. **pushover** *colloquial* opponent or difficulty easily overcome.

■ *verb* **1** advance, drive, force, hustle, impel, move, nudge, propel, set in motion, shove, thrust. **7** (*push on*) see ADVANCE *verb* 1. **8** elbow, force, jostle, nudge, press, ram, shove, thrust. **10** browbeat, bully, coerce, compel, constrain, dragoon, encourage, force, hurry, hustle, impel, importune, incite, induce, influence, *colloquial* lean on, motivate, nag, persuade, pressurize, prompt, put pressure on, spur, stimulate, urge. **12** advertise, boost, make known, market, *colloquial* plug, promote, publicize. □ **push around** see BULLY[1] *verb*. **push off** see DEPART 1,2.

pusher *noun colloquial* seller of illegal drugs.

pushing *adjective* **1** pushy. **2** *colloquial* having nearly reached (specified age).

pushy *adjective* (**-ier**, **-iest**) *colloquial* excessively self-assertive. □ **pushily** *adverb*. **pushiness** *noun*.

pusillanimous /pjuːsɪˈlænɪməs/ *adjective formal* cowardly; timid. □ **pusillanimity** /-ləˈnɪm-/ *noun*.

puss /pʊs/ *noun colloquial* **1** cat. **2** sly or coquettish girl.

pussy /ˈpʊsɪ/ *noun* (*plural* **-ies**) (also **pussy-cat**) *colloquial* cat. □ **pussyfoot** *colloquial* move stealthily, equivocate. **pussy willow** willow with furry catkins.

pustulate /ˈpʌstjʊleɪt/ *verb* (**-ting**) form into pustules.

pustule /ˈpʌstjuːl/ *noun* pimple containing pus. □ **pustular** *adjective*.

put /pʊt/ *verb* (**-tt-**; *past & past participle* **put**) **1** move to or cause to be in specified place, position, or state. **2** (often + *on*, *to*) impose. **3** (+ *for*) substitute (thing) for (another). **4** express in specified way. **5** (+ *into*) express or translate in (words etc.). **6** (+ *at*) estimate at. **7** (+ *into*) invest (money) in. **8** (+ *on*) stake (money) on. **9** (+ *to*) submit for attention to. **10** hurl (shot etc.) as sport. ● *noun* throw of shot. □ **put about** spread (rumour etc.). **put across 1** make understood. **2** achieve by deceit. **put away 1** restore to usual place. **2** lay aside for future. **3** imprison. **4** consume (food or drink). **put back 1** restore to usual place. **2** change (meeting etc.) to later time. **3** move back hands of (clock or watch). **put by** lay aside for future. **put down 1** suppress. **2** *colloquial* snub. **3** record in writing. **4** enter on list. **5** kill (old etc. animal). **6** pay as deposit. **7** (+ *as*, *for*) account or reckon. **8** (+ *to*) attribute to. **put-down** *colloquial* snub or humiliating criticism. **put in 1** spend (time). **2** insert. **3** submit (claim). **4** (+ *for*) be candidate for (election etc.). **put off 1** postpone. **2** evade (person) with excuse. **3** dissuade. **4** disconcert. **put on 1** clothe oneself with. **2** cause (light etc.) to operate. **3** make (transport) available. **4** stage (play etc.). **5** advance hands of (clock or watch). **4** feign. **5** increase one's weight by (specified amount). **put out 1** disconcert; annoy. **2** inconvenience. **3** extinguish. **4** throw out. **put over** put across. **put through 1** complete. **2** connect by telephone. **put together 1** make from parts. **2** combine (parts) into whole. **put up 1** build. **2** raise. **3** lodge (person). **4** engage in (fight etc.). **5** propose. **6** provide (money) as backer. **7** display (notice). **8** offer for sale etc. **put-up** *adjective* (usually in phrase **put-up job**) fraudulently presented or devised. **put upon** (usually in *passive*) *colloquial* unfairly burden or deceive. **put (person) up to** instigate him or her to. **put up with** endure, tolerate.

■ *verb* **1** arrange, deploy, deposit, dispose, fix, hang, lay, leave, locate, park, place, plonk, position, rest, set down, settle, situate, stand, station. **2** attach, attribute, cast, fix, impose, inflict, lay, pin. **4, 5** express, formulate, frame, phrase, say, state, utter, voice, word, write. **9** advance, bring forward, offer, outline, present, propose, submit, suggest, tender. □ **put across 1** see COMMUNICATE 1. **put back 1** see RETURN *verb* 2. **put by** SAVE[1] *verb* 2,3. **put down 1** see SUPPRESS 1. **5** see KILL *verb* 1. **put in 2** see INSERT *verb*, INSTALL 1. **put off 1** see POSTPONE. **put out 3** see EXTINGUISH 1. **4** see EJECT 1. **put over** see COMMUNICATE 1. **put up 2** see RAISE *verb* 1;3. **3** see ACCOMMODATE 1.

putative /ˈpjuːtətɪv/ *adjective formal* reputed, supposed.

■ alleged, assumed, conjectural, presumed, reputed, rumoured, supposed.

putrefy /ˈpjuːtrɪfaɪ/ *verb* (**-ies**, **-ied**) **1** become or make putrid; go bad. **2** fester. **3** become morally corrupt. □ **putrefaction** /-ˈfæk-/ *noun*. **putrefactive** /-ˈfæk-/ *adjective*.

■ **1** decay, decompose, go bad, go off, moulder, rot, spoil.

putrescent /pjuːˈtres(ə)nt/ *adjective* rotting. □ **putrescence** *noun*.

putrid /ˈpjuːtrɪd/ *adjective* **1** decomposed, rotten. **2** noxious. **3** corrupt. **4** *slang* contemptible; very unpleasant. □ **putridity** /-ˈtrɪd-/ *noun*.

■ **1** bad, decaying, decomposing, mouldy, putrefying, rotten, rotting, spoilt. **2** fetid, foul, noxious, rank, stinking.

putsch /pʊtʃ/ *noun* attempt at revolution.

putt /pʌt/ *verb* (**-tt-**) strike (golf ball) on putting green. ● *noun* putting stroke. □ **putting green** smooth turf round hole on golf course.

puttee /ˈpʌtɪ/ *noun historical* long strip of cloth wound round leg for protection and support.

putter[1] *noun* golf club used in putting.

putter[2] *US* = POTTER[1].

putty /ˈpʌtɪ/ *noun* paste of chalk, linseed oil, etc. for fixing panes of glass etc. ● *verb* (**-ies**, **-ied**) fix, fill, etc. with putty.

puzzle /ˈpʌz(ə)l/ *noun* **1** difficult or confusing problem. **2** problem or toy designed to test ingenuity etc. ● *verb* (**-ling**) **1** perplex. **2** (usually + *over* etc.) be perplexed. **3** (usually as **puzzling** *adjective*) require much mental effort. **4** (+ *out*) solve using ingenuity etc. □ **puzzlement** *noun*.

■ *noun* **1** difficulty, *disputed* dilemma, enigma, mystery, paradox, poser, problem, quandary, question. **2** *colloquial* brain-teaser, conundrum, poser, problem, question, riddle. ● *verb* **1** baffle, bewilder, confound, confuse, floor, *colloquial* flummox, mystify, nonplus, perplex, set thinking, stump, stymie, worry. **2** (*puzzle over*) see CONSIDER 1. **3** (**puzzling**) ambiguous, baffling, bewildering, confusing, cryptic, enigmatic, impenetrable, inexplicable, insoluble, *colloquial* mind-boggling, mysterious, mystifying, perplexing, strange, unaccountable, unanswerable, unfathomable, worrying. **4** (*puzzle out*) see SOLVE.

PVC *abbreviation* polyvinyl chloride, a plastic used for pipes, electrical insulation, etc.

pyaemia /paɪˈiːmɪə/ *noun* (*US* **pyemia**) severe bacterial infection of blood.

pygmy /ˈpɪgmɪ/ (also **pigmy**) *noun* (*plural* **-ies**) **1** member of dwarf people of esp. equatorial Africa. **2** very small person, animal, or thing. ● *adjective* very small.

■ *adjective* dwarf, lilliputian, midget, small, tiny, undersized

pyjamas /pəˈdʒɑːməz/ *plural noun* (*US* **pajamas**) **1** suit of trousers and top for sleeping in etc. **2** loose trousers worn in some Asian countries.

pylon /ˈpaɪlən/ *noun* tall structure esp. as support for electric cables.

pyorrhoea /paɪəˈrɪə/ *noun* (*US* **pyorrhea**) **1** gum disease. **2** discharge of pus.

pyramid /ˈpɪrəmɪd/ *noun* **1** monumental (esp. ancient Egyptian) stone structure with square base and sloping sides meeting at apex. **2** solid of this shape with base of 3 or more sides. **3** pyramid-shaped thing. □ **pyramidal** /-ˈræm-/ *adjective*.

pyre /ˈpaɪə/ *noun* pile of combustible material, esp. for burning corpse.

pyrethrum /paɪˈriːθrəm/ *noun* **1** aromatic chrysanthemum. **2** insecticide from its dried flowers.

Pyrex /ˈpaɪəreks/ *noun proprietary term* a hard heat-resistant glass.

pyrites /paɪˈraɪtiːz/ *noun* (in full **iron pyrites**) yellow sulphide of iron.

pyromania /paɪərəʊˈmeɪnɪə/ *noun* obsessive desire to start fires. □ **pyromaniac** *noun & adjective*.

pyrotechnics /paɪərəʊˈtekniks/ *plural noun* **1** art of making fireworks. **2** display of fireworks. □ **pyrotechnic** *adjective*.

pyrrhic /ˈpɪrɪk/ *adjective* (of victory) achieved at too great cost.

python /ˈpaɪθ(ə)n/ *noun* large snake that crushes its prey.

pyx /pɪks/ *noun* vessel for consecrated bread of Eucharist.

Qq

Q *abbreviation* (also **Q.**) question.

QC *abbreviation* Queen's Counsel.

QED *abbreviation* which was to be proved (*quod erat demonstrandum*).

QM *abbreviation* Quartermaster.

qr. *abbreviation* quarter(s).

qt *abbreviation* quart(s).

qua /kwɑ:, kweɪ/ *conjunction* in the capacity of.

quack[1] *noun* harsh sound made by ducks. ● *verb* utter this sound.

quack[2] *noun* **1** unqualified practitioner, esp. of medicine. **2** *slang* any doctor. □ **quackery** *noun*.

quad /kwɒd/ *colloquial noun* **1** quadrangle. **2** quadruplet. **3** quadraphonics. ● *adjective* quadraphonic.

quadrangle /ˈkwɒdræŋg(ə)l/ *noun* **1** 4-sided plane figure, esp. square or rectangle. **2** 4-sided court, esp. in college etc. □ **quadrangular** /-ˈræŋgjʊlə/ *adjective*.
■ **2** courtyard, enclosure, *colloquial* quad, yard.

quadrant /ˈkwɒdrənt/ *noun* **1** quarter of circle or sphere or of circle's circumference. **2** optical instrument for measuring angle between distant objects.

quadraphonic /kwɒdrəˈfɒnɪk/ *adjective* (of sound reproduction) using 4 transmission channels. □ **quadraphonically** *adverb*. **quadraphonics** *plural noun*.

quadrate *adjective* /ˈkwɒdrət/ square; rectangular. ● *noun* /ˈkwɒdrət, -dreɪt/ rectangular object. ● *verb* /kwɒˈdreɪt/ **(-ting)** make square.

quadratic /kwɒˈdrætɪk/ *Mathematics adjective* involving the square (and no higher power) of unknown quantity or variable. ● *noun* quadratic equation.

quadriceps /ˈkwɒdrɪseps/ *noun* 4-headed muscle at front of thigh.

quadrilateral /kwɒdrɪˈlætər(ə)l/ *adjective* having 4 sides. ● *noun* 4-sided figure.

quadrille /kwɒˈdrɪl/ *noun* **1** square dance. **2** music for this.

quadruped /ˈkwɒdrʊped/ *noun* 4-footed animal, esp. mammal.

quadruple /ˈkwɒdrʊp(ə)l/ *adjective* **1** fourfold; having 4 parts. **2** (of time in music) having 4 beats in bar. ● *noun* fourfold number or amount. ● *verb* /kwɒˈdru:p(ə)l/ multiply by 4.

quadruplet /ˈkwɒdrʊplɪt/ *noun* each of 4 children born at one birth.

quadruplicate *adjective* /kwɒˈdru:plɪkət/ **1** fourfold. **2** of which 4 copies are made. ● *verb* /-keɪt/ **(-ting)** multiply by 4.

quaff /kwɒf/ *verb literary* **1** drink deeply. **2** drain (cup etc.) in long draughts.

quagmire /ˈkwɒgmaɪə, ˈkwæg-/ *noun* **1** muddy or boggy area. **2** hazardous situation.
■ **1** bog, fen, marsh, mire, *literary* morass, mud, slough, swamp.

quail[1] *noun* (*plural* same or **-s**) small game bird related to partridge.

quail[2] *verb* flinch; show fear.
■ back away, be apprehensive, blench, cower, cringe, falter, flinch, quake, recoil, shrink, tremble, wince.

quaint *adjective* attractively odd or old-fashioned. □ **quaintly** *adverb*. **quaintness** *noun*.
■ antiquated, antique, charming, curious, eccentric, fanciful, fantastic, odd, offbeat, old-fashioned, old-world, outlandish, peculiar, picturesque, strange, *derogatory* twee, unconventional, unexpected, unfamiliar, unusual, whimsical.

quake *verb* **(-king)** shake, tremble. ● *noun colloquial* earthquake.
■ *verb* convulse, heave, quaver, quiver, rock, shake, shiver, shudder, stagger, sway, tremble, vibrate, wobble.

Quaker *noun* member of Society of Friends. □ **Quakerism** *noun*.

qualification /kwɒlɪfɪˈkeɪʃ(ə)n/ *noun* **1** accomplishment fitting person for position or purpose. **2** thing that modifies or limits. **3** qualifying, being qualified. □ **qualificatory** /ˈkwɒl-/ *adjective*.
■ **1** ability, aptitude, capability, capacity, competence, eligibility, experience, fitness, know-how, knowledge, proficiency, quality, skill, suitability. **2** caveat, condition, exception, limitation, modification, proviso, reservation, restriction. **3** certification, training.

qualified /ˈkwɒlɪfaɪd/ *adjective* **1** competent or legally entitled to do something. **2** eligible. **3** limited, restricted.
■ **1** able, authorized, capable, certificated, certified, competent, equipped, experienced, expert, fit, licensed, practised, professional, proficient, skilled, trained, well informed. **2** eligible, suitable. **3** cautious, conditional, equivocal, guarded, half-hearted, limited, modified, provisional, reserved, restricted.

qualify /ˈkwɒlɪfaɪ/ *verb* **(-ies, -ied)** **1** make competent or fit for purpose or position. **2** make legally entitled. **3** (usually + *for*) satisfy conditions. **4** modify, limit. **5** moderate, mitigate. **6**

Grammar (of word) attribute quality to (esp. noun). **7** (+ *as*) be describable as. □ **qualifier** *noun.*

■ **1** equip, fit, prepare. **2** authorize, empower, entitle, make eligible, permit, sanction. **3** become eligible, get through, make the grade, meet requirements, pass. **4** limit, modify, restrict. **5** abate, lessen, mitigate, moderate, modulate, restrain, soften, temper, weaken.

qualitative /'kwɒlɪtətɪv/ *adjective* concerned with quality as opposed to quantity. □ **qualitatively** *adverb.*

quality /'kwɒlɪtɪ/ *noun* (*plural* **-ies**) **1** excellence. **2** degree of excellence. **3** attribute, faculty. **4** relative nature or character. **5** timbre. ● *adjective* of high quality.

■ *noun* **1** *colloquial* class, excellence, merit, value, worth. **2** calibre, class, condition, grade, rank, sort, standard, status, value, worth. **3** attribute, characteristic, distinction, feature, mark, peculiarity, property, trait.

qualm /kwɑːm/ *noun* **1** misgiving. **2** scruple of conscience. **3** momentary faint or sick feeling.

quandary /'kwɒndərɪ/ *noun* (*plural* **-ies**) **1** perplexed state. **2** practical dilemma.

■ *colloquial* catch-22, confusion, difficulty, dilemma, perplexity, plight, predicament, uncertainty.

quango /'kwæŋɡəʊ/ *noun* (*plural* **-s**) semi-public administrative body appointed by government.

quanta *plural* of QUANTUM.

quantify /'kwɒntɪfaɪ/ *verb* (**-ies**, **-ied**) **1** determine quantity of. **3** express as quantity. □ **quantifiable** *adjective.*

quantitative /'kwɒntɪtətɪv/ *adjective* **1** concerned with quantity as opposed to quality. **2** measured or measurable by quantity.

quantity /'kwɒntɪtɪ/ *noun* (*plural* **-ies**) **1** property of things that is measurable. **2** size, extent, weight, amount, or number. **3** specified or considerable amount, number, etc.; portion. **4** (in *plural*) large amounts or numbers. **5** length or shortness of vowel sound or syllable. **6** *Mathematics* value, component, etc. that may be expressed in numbers. □ **quantity surveyor** person who measures and prices building work.

■ **1, 2** amount, bulk, extent, length, magnitude, mass, measure, number, size, volume, weight. **3** aggregate, amount, consignment, dosage, dose, expanse, length, load, lot, measure, number, part, portion, proportion, quantum, sum, total, volume.

quantum /'kwɒntəm/ *noun* (*plural* **-ta**) **1** discrete amount of energy proportional to frequency of radiation it represents. **2** required or allowed amount. □ **quantum mechanics, theory** theory assuming that energy exists in discrete units.

quarantine /'kwɒrəntiːn/ *noun* **1** isolation imposed on person or animal to prevent infection or contagion. **2** period of this. ● *verb* (**-ning**) put in quarantine.

quark¹ /kwɑːk/ *noun Physics* component of elementary particles.

quark² /kwɑːk/ *noun* kind of low-fat curd cheese.

quarrel /'kwɒr(ə)l/ *noun* **1** severe or angry dispute. **2** break in friendly relations. **3** cause of complaint. ● *verb* (**-ll-**; *US* **-l-**) **1** (often + *with*) find fault. **2** dispute. **3** break off friendly relations. □ **quarrelsome** *adjective.*

■ *noun* **1** altercation, argument, bickering, *colloquial* bust-up, clash, conflict, confrontation, contention, controversy, debate, difference, disagreement, dispute, fight, *colloquial* hassle, misunderstanding, *colloquial* row, *colloquial* ructions, scene, slanging match, squabble, tiff, wrangle. **2** conflict, discord, disharmony, dissension, division, feud, rift, rupture, schism, split, strife, vendetta. ● *verb* **1** (*quarrel with*) see DISPUTE *verb* 3. **2** argue, be at loggerheads, be at odds, bicker, clash, conflict, contend, cross swords, differ, disagree, dispute, dissent, fall out, feud, fight, hassle, *colloquial* row, squabble, wrangle. □ **quarrelsome** aggressive, angry, argumentative, bad-tempered, cantankerous, choleric, contentious, contrary, cross, defiant, disagreeable, dyspeptic, explosive, fractious, impatient, irascible, irritable, peevish, petulant, pugnacious, querulous, quick-tempered, *colloquial* stroppy, testy, truculent, unfriendly, volatile.

quarry¹ /'kwɒrɪ/ *noun* (*plural* **-ies**) place from which stone etc. is extracted. ● *verb* (**-ies**, **-ied**) extract (stone etc.) from quarry. □ **quarry tile** unglazed floor-tile.

■ *noun* excavation, mine, pit, working. ● *verb* dig out, excavate, extract, mine.

quarry² /'kwɒrɪ/ *noun* (*plural* **-ies**) **1** intended victim or prey. **2** object of pursuit.

■ game, kill, object, prey, victim.

quart /kwɔːt/ *noun* liquid measure equal to quarter of gallon; two pints (1.136 litre).

quarter /'kwɔːtə/ *noun* **1** each of 4 equal parts. **2** period of 3 months. **3** point of time 15 minutes before or after any hour. **4** 25 US or Canadian cents. **5** coin worth this. **6** part of town, esp. as occupied by particular class. **7** point of compass. **8** region at this. **9** direction, district. **10** source of supply. **11** (in *plural*) lodgings. **12** (in *plural*) accommodation of troops etc. **13** one-fourth of a lunar month. **14** mercy towards enemy etc. on condition of surrender. **15** grain measure equivalent to 8 bushels. **16** *colloquial* one-fourth of a pound weight. ● *verb* **1** divide into quarters. **2** put (troops etc.) into quarters. **3** provide with lodgings. **4** *Heraldry* place (coats of arms) on 4 quarters of shield. □ **quarterback** player in American football who directs attacking play. **quarter day** day on which quarterly payments are due. **quarterdeck** part of ship's upper deck near stern. **quarter-final** match or round preceding semifinal. **quarter-hour** period of 15 minutes. **quartermaster 1** regimental officer in charge of quartering, rations, etc. **2** naval petty officer in charge of steering, signals, etc.

■ *noun* **6, 8** area, direction, district, division, locality, neighbourhood, part, region, *US* section, *Military* sector, territory, vicinity, zone. **11, 12** (*quarters*) abode, accommodation, barracks, billet, domicile, dwelling place, home, housing, lodgings, residence, rooms, shelter. ● *verb* **2** accommodate, billet, board, house, lodge, put up, shelter, station.

quarterly *adjective* produced or occurring once every quarter of year. ● *adverb* once every quarter of year. ● *noun* (*plural* **-ies**) quarterly journal.

quartet /kwɔːˈtet/ *noun* **1** musical composition for 4 performers. **2** the performers. **3** any group of 4.

quarto /ˈkwɔːtəʊ/ *noun* (*plural* **-s**) size of book or page made by folding sheet of standard size twice to form 4 leaves.

quartz /kwɔːts/ *noun* silica in various mineral forms. ● *adjective* (of clock or watch) operated by vibrations of electrically driven quartz crystal.

quasar /ˈkweɪzɑː/ *noun* starlike object with large red shift.

quash /kwɒʃ/ *verb* **1** annul; reject as not valid. **2** suppress, crush.

■ **1** abolish, annul, cancel, invalidate, overrule, overthrow, reject, rescind, reverse, revoke. **2** see QUELL 1.

quasi- /ˈkweɪzaɪ/ *combining form* **1** seemingly; not really. **2** almost.

quaternary /kwəˈtɜːnərɪ/ *adjective* having 4 parts.

quatrain /ˈkwɒtreɪn/ *noun* 4-line stanza.

quatrefoil /ˈkætrəfɔɪl/ *noun* **1** leaf consisting of 4 leaflets. **2** design or ornament in this shape.

quaver /ˈkweɪvə/ *verb* **1** (esp. of voice or sound) vibrate, shake, tremble. **2** sing or say with quavering voice. ● *noun* **1** *Music* note half as long as crotchet. **2** trill in singing. **3** tremble in speech. □ **quavery** *adjective*.

■ *verb* **1** falter, fluctuate, oscillate, pulsate, quake, quiver, shake, shiver, shudder, tremble, vibrate, waver.

quay /kiː/ *noun* artificial landing-place for loading and unloading ships. □ **quayside** land forming or near quay.

■ dock, harbour, jetty, landing stage, pier, wharf.

queasy /ˈkwiːzɪ/ *adjective* (**-ier**, **-iest**) **1** (of person) nauseous. **2** (of stomach) easily upset. **3** (of conscience etc.) overscrupulous. □ **queasily** *adverb*. **queasiness** *noun*.

■ **1** bilious, ill, nauseated, nauseous, poorly, queer, sick, squeamish, unwell.

queen *noun* **1** (as title usually **Queen**) female sovereign. **2** (in full **queen consort**) king's wife. **3** woman, country, or thing pre-eminent of its kind. **4** fertile female among bees, ants, etc. **5** most powerful piece in chess. **6** court card depicting queen. **7** (**the Queen**) national anthem when sovereign is female. **8** *offensive slang* male

homosexual. ● *verb* convert (pawn in chess) to queen when it reaches opponent's side of board. □ **queen mother** king's widow who is mother of sovereign. **Queen's Bench** division of High Court of Justice. **Queen's Counsel** counsel to the Crown, taking precedence over other barristers. **the Queen's English** English language correctly written or spoken. □ **queenly** *adjective* (**-ier**, **-iest**).

Queensberry Rules /ˈkwiːnzbərɪ/ *plural noun* standard rules, esp. of boxing.

queer *adjective* **1** strange, odd, eccentric. **2** suspect; of questionable character. **3** slightly ill; faint. **4** *offensive slang* (esp. of a man) homosexual. ● *noun offensive slang* homosexual. ● *verb slang* spoil; put out of order. □ **in Queer Street** *slang* in difficulty, esp. in debt. □ **queerness** *noun*.

■ *adjective* **1** aberrant, abnormal, anomalous, atypical, bizarre, cranky, curious, deviant, different, eccentric, eerie, exceptional, extraordinary, freakish, funny, incongruous, inexplicable, irrational, mad, odd, offbeat, outlandish, peculiar, puzzling, quaint, remarkable, *colloquial* rum, singular, strange, unaccountable, uncanny, uncommon, unconventional, unexpected, unnatural, unorthodox, unusual, *colloquial* weird. **2** *slang* fishy, mysterious, questionable, shady (*customer*), *colloquial* shifty, suspect, suspicious. **3** see ILL *adjective* 1. **4** see HOMOSEXUAL *adjective*.

quell *verb* **1** crush, suppress (rebellion etc.). **2** subdue (fears etc.).

■ **1** crush, overcome, put down, quash, repress, subdue, suppress. **2** allay, alleviate, calm, mitigate, moderate, mollify, pacify, soothe, subdue.

quench *verb* **1** satisfy (thirst) by drinking. **2** extinguish (fire or light). **3** cool, esp. with water. **4** stifle, suppress.

■ **1** allay, appease, cool, *formal* sate, satisfy, slake. **2** damp down, douse, extinguish, put out, smother, snuff out. **4** quell, repress, stifle, suppress.

quern *noun* hand mill for grinding corn.

querulous /ˈkwerʊləs/ *adjective* complaining, peevish. □ **querulously** *adverb*.

query /ˈkwɪərɪ/ *noun* (*plural* **-ies**) **1** question. **2** question mark. ● *verb* (**-ies**, **-ied**) **1** ask, inquire. **2** call in question. **3** dispute accuracy of.

quest *noun* **1** search, seeking. **2** thing sought, esp. by medieval knight. ● *verb* (often + *about*; often + *after*, *for*) go about in search of something.

■ *noun* **1** expedition, exploration, hunt, mission, pursuit, search, voyage of discovery. ● *verb* (*quest after*) see SEEK 1–2.

question /ˈkwestʃ(ə)n/ *noun* **1** sentence worded or expressed so as to seek information or answer. **2** doubt or dispute about matter. **3** raising of such doubt etc. **4** matter to be discussed or decided. **5** problem requiring solution. ● *verb* **1** ask questions of. **2** subject (person) to examination. **3** throw doubt on. □ **be just a question of time** be certain to happen sooner or later. **be a question of** be at issue; be a problem. **call in or into question** express doubts about. **in question** being discussed or referred to. **out of the question** not worth questioning; impossible. **question mark** punctuation mark (?) indicating question (see panel). **question master** person presiding over quiz game etc. **question time** period in Parliament when MPs may question ministers. □ **questioner** *noun*. **questioning** *adjective & noun*. **questioningly** *adverb*.

■ *noun* **2, 3** argument, controversy, debate, difficulty, dispute, doubt, misgiving, objection, uncertainty. **4** issue, matter, point. **5** *colloquial* brain-teaser, conundrum, demand, enquiry, inquiry, mystery, *colloquial* poser, problem, puzzle, query, request, riddle. ● *verb* **1, 2** ask, cross-examine, cross-question, debrief, enquire of, examine, grill, inquire of, interrogate, interview, probe, pump, quiz. **3** argue over, be sceptical about, call into question, cast doubt upon, challenge, dispute, doubt, enquire about, impugn, inquire about, object to, oppose, quarrel with, query.

questionable *adjective* doubtful as regards truth, quality, honesty, wisdom, etc.

■ arguable, borderline, debatable, disputable, doubtful, dubious, *colloquial* iffy, moot (*point*), problematical, shady (*customer*), suspect, suspicious, uncertain, unclear, unprovable, unreliable.

questionnaire /kwestʃə'neə/ *noun* list of questions for obtaining information esp. for statistical analysis.

■ catechism, opinion poll, quiz, survey, test.

queue /kjuː/ *noun* line or sequence of people, vehicles, etc. waiting their turn. ● *verb* (**-s, -d, queuing** or **queueing**) (often + *up*) form or join queue. □ **queue-jump** push forward out of turn in queue.

■ *noun* chain, column, *colloquial* crocodile, file, *US* line, line-up, procession, row, string, succession, tailback, train. ● *verb* line up.

quibble /'kwɪb(ə)l/ *noun* **1** petty objection; trivial point of criticism. **2** evasion. ● *verb* (**-ling**) use quibbles.

■ *noun* **1** see OBJECTION. ● *verb* carp, cavil, equivocate, object, split hairs, wrangle.

quiche /kiːʃ/ *noun* savoury flan.

quick *adjective* **1** moving fast. **2** taking only a short time. **3** arriving or happening after only a short time; prompt. **4** with only a short interval.

5 alert, intelligent. **6** lively, agile, nimble. **7** (of temper) easily roused. **8** *archaic* living. ● *adverb* quickly. ● *noun* **1** soft sensitive flesh, esp. below nails or skin. **2** seat of emotion. □ **quicklime** unslaked lime. **quicksand 1** area of loose wet sand that sucks in anything placed on it. **2** treacherous situation etc. **quickset** (of hedge etc.) formed of cuttings, esp. hawthorn. **quicksilver** mercury. **quickstep** fast foxtrot. **quick-tempered** easily angered. **quick-witted** quick to grasp situation, make repartee, etc. **quick-wittedness** *noun*. □ **quickly** *adverb*. **quickness** *noun*.

■ *adjective* **1** breakneck, brisk, expeditious, express, fast, *poetical* or *literary* fleet, headlong, high-speed, *colloquial* nippy, precipitate, rapid, smart (*pace*), spanking, speedy, swift. **2** brief, fleeting, momentary, passing, perfunctory, short, short-lived, temporary, transitory. **3** abrupt, early, hasty, hurried, immediate, instant, instantaneous, precipitate, prompt, punctual, ready, sudden, summary, unhesitating. **5** acute, alert, apt, astute, bright, clever, intelligent, nimble, perceptive, quick-witted, sharp, shrewd, smart. **6** adroit, agile, animated, brisk, deft, dexterous, energetic, lively, nimble, spirited, spry, vigorous. **8** see ALIVE 1.

quicken *verb* **1** make or become quicker; accelerate. **2** give life or vigour to; rouse. **3** (of woman) reach stage in pregnancy when movements of foetus can be felt. **4** (of foetus) begin to show signs of life.

■ **1** accelerate, expedite, go faster, hasten, hurry, speed up. **2** see ANIMATE *verb* 1, AROUSE 1.

quid[1] *noun slang* (*plural* same) one pound sterling.

quid[2] *noun* lump of tobacco for chewing.

quid pro quo /kwɪd prəʊ 'kwəʊ/ *noun* (*plural* **quid pro quos**) gift, favour, etc. exchanged for another.

quiescent /kwɪ'es(ə)nt/ *adjective* inert; dormant. □ **quiescence** *noun*.

quiet /'kwaɪət/ *adjective* **1** with little or no sound or motion. **2** of gentle or peaceful disposition; reserved. **3** unobtrusive; not showy. **4** not overt; disguised. **5** undisturbed; uninterrupted; not busy. ● *noun* **1** silence; stillness. **2** undisturbed state; tranquillity. ● *verb* (often + *down*) make or become quiet; calm. □ **be quiet** (esp. in *imperative*) cease talking etc. **keep quiet** (often + *about*) say nothing. **on the quiet** secretly. □ **quietly** *adverb*. **quietness** *noun*.

■ *adjective* **1** calm, hushed, inactive, inaudible, low, motionless, noiseless, *Music* pianissimo, silent, soft, *sotto voce*, soundless, still. **2** calm,

Question mark ?

This is used instead of a full stop at the end of a sentence to show that it is a question, e.g.

Have you seen the film yet?
You didn't lose my purse, did you?

It is **not** used at the end of a reported question, e.g.

I asked you whether you'd seen the film yet.

composed, contemplative, contented, gentle, introverted, meditative, meek, mild, modest, peaceable, placid, reserved, reticent, retiring, serene, shy, taciturn, thoughtful, uncommunicative, unforthcoming, unsociable, withdrawn. **3** restful, soft, subdued, unobtrusive. **5** cloistered, isolated, lonely, peaceful, private, restful, secluded, sequestered, sheltered, tranquil, unadventurous, undisturbed, unexciting, unfrequented, untroubled.

quieten *verb* (often + *down*) make or become quiet or calm.
■ calm, compose, deaden, dull, hush, lull, muffle, mute, pacify, sedate, silence, soften, soothe, stifle, subdue, suppress, tone down, tranquillize.

quietism *noun* passive contemplative attitude towards life. □ **quietist** *noun & adjective.*

quietude /'kwaɪɪtjuːd/ *noun* state of quiet.

quietus /kwaɪ'iːtəs/ *noun* release from life; death; final riddance.

quiff *noun* man's tuft of hair brushed upwards in front.

quill *noun* **1** (in full **quill-feather**) large feather in wing or tail. **2** hollow stem of this. **3** (in full **quill pen**) pen made of quill. **4** (usually in *plural*) porcupine's spine.

quilt *noun* bedspread, esp. of quilted material. ● *verb* line bedspread or garment with padding enclosed between layers of fabric by lines of stitching. □ **quilter** *noun.* **quilting** *noun.*

quin *noun colloquial* quintuplet.

quince *noun* (tree bearing) acid pear-shaped fruit used in jams etc.

quincentenary /kwɪmsen'tiːnərɪ/ *noun* (*plural* **-ies**) **1** 500th anniversary. **2** celebration of this. ● *adjective* of this anniversary.

quinine /'kwɪmiːn/ *noun* bitter drug used as a tonic and to reduce fever.

Quinquagesima /kwɪŋkwə'dʒesɪmə/ *noun* Sunday before Lent.

quinquennial /kwɪŋ'kwenɪəl/ *adjective* **1** lasting 5 years. **2** recurring every 5 years. □ **quinquennially** *adverb.*

quintessence /kwɪn'tes(ə)ns/ *noun* **1** (usually + *of*) purest and most perfect form, manifestation, or embodiment of quality etc. **2** highly refined extract. □ **quintessential** /-tɪ'sen-/ *adjective.* **quintessentially** /-tɪ'sen-/ *adverb.*

quintet /kwɪn'tet/ *noun* **1** musical composition for 5 performers. **2** the performers. **3** any group of 5.

quintuple /'kwɪntjʊp(ə)l/ *adjective* fivefold; having 5 parts. ● *noun* fivefold number or amount. ● *verb* (**-ling**) multiply by 5.

quintuplet /'kwɪntjʊplɪt/ *noun* each of 5 children born at one birth.

quip *noun* clever saying; epigram. ● *verb* (**-pp-**) make quips.

quire *noun* 25 sheets of paper.

quirk *noun* **1** peculiarity, foible. **2** trick of fate. □ **quirky** *adjective* (**-ier, -iest**).

■ **1** caprice, eccentricity, foible, idiosyncrasy, kink, oddity, peculiarity, whim. **2** aberration, fluke, trick, twist, vagary.

quisling /'kwɪzlɪŋ/ *noun* collaborator with invading enemy.

quit *verb* (**-tting**; *past & past participle* **quitted** or **quit**) **1** give up; let go; abandon. **2** *US* cease, stop. **3** leave or depart from. ● *adjective* (+ *of*) rid of.
■ *verb* **1** abandon, abdicate, discontinue, drop, forsake, give up, let go, *colloquial* pack it in, relinquish, renounce, resign from, retire from, withdraw from. **2** *formal* cease, desist from, discontinue, leave off, stop. **3** decamp from, depart from, desert, exit from, go away from, leave, walk out (on), withdraw.

quitch *noun* couch grass.

quite *adverb* **1** completely; altogether; absolutely. **2** rather; to some extent. **3** (often + *so*) *said to indicate agreement.* □ **quite a**, **quite some** a remarkable. **quite a few** *colloquial* a fairly large number (of). **quite something** *colloquial* a remarkable thing or person.
■ **1** absolutely, altogether, completely, entirely, perfectly, thoroughly, totally, unreservedly, utterly, wholly. **2** comparatively, fairly, moderately, *colloquial* pretty, rather, relatively, somewhat, to some extent.

quits *adjective* on even terms by retaliation or repayment. □ **call it quits 1** acknowledge that things are now even. **2** agree to stop quarrelling.
■ equal, even, level, repaid, revenged, square.

quiver[1] /'kwɪvə/ *verb* tremble or vibrate with slight rapid motion. ● *noun* quivering motion or sound.
■ *verb* flicker, fluctuate, flutter, oscillate, palpitate, pulsate, quake, quaver, shake, shiver, shudder, tremble, vibrate, wobble.

quiver[2] /'kwɪvə/ *noun* case for arrows.

qui vive /kiː viːv/ *noun* □ **on the qui vive** on the alert.

quixotic /kwɪk'sɒtɪk/ *adjective* extravagantly and romantically chivalrous. □ **quixotically** *adverb.*
■ fanciful, foolhardy, idealistic, impracticable, impractical, romantic, *colloquial* starry-eyed, unrealistic, unrealizable, unselfish, Utopian, visionary.

quiz *noun* (*plural* **quizzes**) **1** test of knowledge, esp. as entertainment. **2** interrogation, examination. ● *verb* examine by questioning.
■ *noun* **1** see COMPETITION 2. **2** exam, examination, interrogation, questioning, questionnaire, test. ● *verb* see QUESTION *verb* 1,2.

quizzical /'kwɪzɪk(ə)l/ *adjective* mocking; gently amused. □ **quizzically** *adverb.*
■ amused, curious, intrigued, perplexed, puzzled, questioning.

quod *noun slang* prison.

quoin /kɔɪn/ *noun* **1** external angle of building.

2 cornerstone. **3** wedge used in printing or gunnery.

quoit /kɔɪt/ *noun* **1** ring thrown to encircle peg. **2** (in *plural*) game using these.

quondam /ˈkwɒndæm/ *adjective* that once was; former.

quorate /ˈkwɔːreɪt/ *adjective* constituting or having quorum.

Quorn /kwɔːn/ *noun proprietary term* vegetable protein food made from fungus.

quorum /ˈkwɔːrəm/ *noun* minimum number of members that must be present to constitute valid meeting.

quota /ˈkwəʊtə/ *noun* **1** share to be contributed to or received from total. **2** number of goods, people, etc. stipulated or permitted.

■ **1** allocation, allowance, apportionment, cut, part, portion, proportion, ration, share.

quotable *adjective* worth quoting.

quotation /kwəʊˈteɪʃ(ə)n/ *noun* **1** passage or remark quoted. **2** quoting, quoted. **3** contractor's estimate. □ **quotation marks** inverted commas (' ' or " ") used at beginning and end of quotation

etc. (see panel).

■ **1** citation, cutting, excerpt, extract, passage, piece, *colloquial* quote, reference, selection. **3** estimate, price, *colloquial* quote, tender, valuation.

quote *verb* (**-ting**) **1** cite or appeal to as example, authority, etc. **2** (+ *as*) cite (author etc.) as proof, evidence, etc. **3** repeat or copy out passage from. **4** (+ *from*) cite (author, book, etc.). **5** (as *interjection*) *used in dictation etc. to indicate opening quotation marks.* **6** (often + *at*) state price of. **7** state (price) for job. ● *noun colloquial* **1** passage quoted. **2** (usually in *plural*) quotation marks. **3** price quoted.

■ *verb* **1, 2** adduce, appeal to, cite, instance, mention, refer to. **3, 4** cite, repeat, reproduce. **6, 7** estimate, tender.

quoth /kwəʊθ/ *verb* (only in 1st & 3rd persons) *archaic* said.

quotidian /kwɒˈtɪdɪən/ *adjective* **1** occurring or recurring daily. **2** commonplace, trivial.

quotient /ˈkwəʊʃ(ə)nt/ *noun* result of division sum.

q.v. *abbreviation* which see (*quod vide*).

··

Quotation marks ' ' " "

Also called inverted commas, these are used:

1 round a direct quotation (closing quotation marks come after any punctuation which is part of the quotation), e.g.

> *He said, 'That is nonsense.'*
> *'That', he said, 'is nonsense.'*
> *'That, however,' he said, 'is nonsense.'*
> *Did he say, 'That is nonsense'?*
> *He asked, 'Is that nonsense?'*

2 round a quoted word or phrase, e.g.

> *What does 'integrated circuit' mean?*

3 round a word or phrase that is not being used in its central sense, e.g.

> *the 'king' of jazz*
> *He said he had enough 'bread' to buy a car.*

4 round the title of a book, song, poem, magazine article, television programme, etc. (but not a book of the Bible), e.g.

> *'Hard Times' by Charles Dickens*

5 as double quotation marks round a quotation within a quotation, e.g.

> *He asked, 'Do you know what "integrated circuit" means?'*

In handwriting, double quotation marks are usual.

··

Rr

R *abbreviation* (also **R.**) **1** *Regina.* **2** *Rex.* **3** River. **4** (also ®) registered as trademark. □ **R & D** research and development.

r. *abbreviation* (also **r**) **1** right. **2** radius.

RA *abbreviation* **1** Royal Academy or Academician. **2** Royal Artillery.

rabbet /'ræbɪt/ *noun* step-shaped channel cut along edge or face of wood etc. to receive edge or tongue of another piece. ● *verb* (**-t-**) **1** join with rabbet. **2** make rabbet in.

rabbi /'ræbaɪ/ *noun* (*plural* **-s**) **1** Jewish religious leader. **2** Jewish scholar or teacher, esp. of the law. □ **rabbinical** /rə'bɪn-/ *adjective.*

rabbit /'ræbɪt/ *noun* **1** burrowing mammal of hare family. **2** its fur. ● *verb* (**-t-**) **1** hunt rabbits. **2** (often + *on, away*) *colloquial* talk pointlessly; chatter. □ **rabbit punch** blow with edge of hand on back of neck.

rabble /'ræb(ə)l/ *noun* **1** disorderly crowd; mob. **2** contemptible or inferior set of people. **3** (**the rabble**) lower classes of the populace. □ **rabble-rouser** person who stirs up rabble, esp. to agitate for social change. **rabble-rousing** *adjective & noun.*

> ■ **1** crowd, gang, *derogatory* herd, *usually derogatory* horde, mob, swarm, throng. **3** (**the rabble**) *hoi polloi*, the masses, the populace, (the) riff-raff.

Rabelaisian /ræbə'leɪzɪən/ *adjective* exuberantly and coarsely humorous.

rabid /'ræbɪd/ *adjective* **1** affected with rabies; mad. **2** violent. **3** fanatical. □ **rabidity** /rə'bɪd-/ *noun.*

rabies /'reɪbiːz/ *noun* contagious viral disease of esp. dogs; hydrophobia.

RAC *abbreviation* Royal Automobile Club.

raccoon /rə'kuːn/ *noun* (also **racoon**) (*plural* same or **-s**) **1** N. American mammal with bushy tail. **2** its fur.

race[1] *noun* **1** contest of speed or to be first to achieve something. **2** (in *plural*) series of races for horses etc. **3** strong current in sea or river. **4** channel. ● *verb* (**-cing**) **1** take part in race. **2** have race with. **3** (+ *with*) compete in speed with. **4** cause to race. **5** go at full speed. **6** (usually as **racing** *adjective*) follow or take part in horse racing. □ **racecourse** ground for horse racing. **racehorse** one bred or kept for racing. **race meeting** sequence of horse races at one place. **racetrack 1** racecourse. **2** track for motor racing. **racing car** one built for racing. **racing driver** driver of racing car.

> ■ *noun* **1** chase, competition, contest, heat. ● *verb* **2** compete with, contest with, try to beat. **5** career, dash, fly, gallop, hasten, hurry, move fast, run, rush, speed, sprint, *colloquial* tear, zip, zoom. □ **racetrack** *noun* circuit, racecourse.

race[2] *noun* **1** each of the major divisions of humankind, each having distinct physical characteristics. **2** group of people, animals, or plants connected by common descent. **3** any great division of living creatures. □ **race relations** relations between members of different races in same country.

> ■ **2** breed, clan, ethnic group, family, folk, genus, kind, lineage, nation, people, species, stock, tribe, variety.

raceme /rə'siːm/ *noun* flower cluster with flowers attached by short stalks at equal distances along stem.

racer /'reɪsə/ *noun* **1** horse, yacht, bicycle, etc. of kind used for racing. **2** person or thing that races.

racial /'reɪʃ(ə)l/ *adjective* **1** of or concerning race. **2** on grounds of or connected with difference in race. □ **racially** *adverb.*

> ■ **1** ethnic, folk, genetic, national, tribal.

racialism *noun* = RACISM. □ **racialist** *noun & adjective.*

racism *noun* **1** (prejudice based on) belief in superiority of particular race. **2** antagonism towards other races. □ **racist** *noun & adjective.*

> ■ bigotry, chauvinism, discrimination, intolerance, prejudice, racialism, xenophobia. □ **racist** *adjective* bigoted, chauvinist, discriminatory, intolerant, prejudiced, racialist, xenophobic.

rack[1] *noun* **1** framework, usually with rails, bars, etc., for holding things. **2** cogged or toothed rail or bar engaging with wheel, pinion, etc. **3** *historical* instrument of torture stretching victim's joints. ● *verb* **1** inflict suffering on. **2** *historical* torture on rack. □ **rack one's brains** make great mental effort. **rack-rent** extortionate rent.

> ■ *noun* **1** frame, framework, holder, scaffold, scaffolding, shelf, stand, support. ● *verb* **1** see TORTURE *verb.*

rack[2] *noun* destruction (esp. in **rack and ruin**).

rack[3] *verb* (often + *off*) draw off (wine etc.) from lees.

racket[1] /'rækɪt/ *noun* (also **racquet**) **1** bat with round or oval frame strung with catgut, nylon, etc., used in tennis etc. **2** (in *plural*) game like squash but in larger court.

racket[2] *noun* **1** uproar, din. **2** *slang* scheme for obtaining money etc. by dishonest means. **3** *slang* dodge; sly game. **4** *colloquial* line of business.

racketeer /rækɪˈtɪə/ *noun* person who operates dishonest business. □ **racketeering** *noun.*

raconteur /rækɒnˈtɜː/ *noun* teller of anecdotes.

racoon = RACCOON.

racy *adjective* (**-ier, -iest**) **1** lively and vigorous in style. **2** risqué. **3** of distinctive quality. □ **raciness** *noun.*

rad *noun* unit of absorbed dose of ionizing radiation.

RADA /ˈrɑːdə/ *abbreviation* Royal Academy of Dramatic Art.

radar /ˈreɪdɑː/ *noun* **1** radio system for detecting the direction, range, or presence of objects. **2** apparatus for this. □ **radar trap** device using radar to detect speeding vehicles.

raddled /ˈræd(ə)ld/ *adjective* worn out.

radial /ˈreɪdɪəl/ *adjective* **1** of or arranged like rays or radii. **2** having spokes or radiating lines. **3** acting or moving along such lines. **4** (in full **radial-ply**) (of tyre) having fabric layers arranged radially. ● *noun* radial-ply tyre. □ **radially** *adverb.*

radian /ˈreɪdɪən/ *noun* SI unit of plane angle (about 57°).

radiant /ˈreɪdɪənt/ *adjective* **1** emitting or issuing in rays. **2** beaming with joy etc. **3** splendid, dazzling. ● *noun* point or object from which heat or light radiates. □ **radiance** *noun.* **radiantly** *adverb.*

■ *adjective* **1** beaming, bright, brilliant, gleaming, glowing, incandescent, luminous, phosphorescent, *literary* refulgent, shining. **2** see HAPPY **1**. **3** see BRILLIANT *adjective* **1**.

radiate /ˈreɪdɪeɪt/ *verb* (**-ting**) **1** emit rays of light, heat, etc. **2** be emitted in rays. **3** emit or spread from centre. **4** transmit or demonstrate.

■ **1, 2** beam, gleam, glow, shine. **3** beam, diffuse, emanate, emit, give off, send out, shed, spread. **4** diffuse, give out, shed, spread, transmit.

radiation *noun* **1** radiating. **2** emission of energy as electromagnetic waves. **3** energy thus transmitted, esp. invisibly. **4** (in full **radiation therapy**) treatment of cancer etc. using e.g. X-rays or ultraviolet light. □ **radiation sickness** sickness caused by exposure to radiation such as gamma rays.

radiator *noun* **1** device for heating room etc. by circulation of hot water etc. **2** engine-cooling device in motor vehicle or aircraft.

radical /ˈrædɪk(ə)l/ *adjective* **1** fundamental; forming the basis; primary. **2** far-reaching; thorough. **3** advocating fundamental reform. **4** of the root of a number or plant. ● *noun* **1** person holding radical views. **2** atom or group of atoms forming base of compound and remaining unchanged during reactions. **3** quantity forming or expressed as root of another. □ **radicalism** *noun.* **radically** *adverb.*

■ *adjective* **1** basic, cardinal, deep-seated, elementary, essential, fundamental, primary, principal, profound. **2** complete, comprehensive, drastic, entire, exhaustive, far-reaching, thorough, thoroughgoing. **3** extreme, extremist, revolutionary, subversive.

radicchio /rəˈdiːkɪəʊ/ *noun* (*plural* **-s**) chicory with purplish leaves.

radicle /ˈrædɪk(ə)l/ *noun* part of seed that develops into root.

radii *plural* of RADIUS.

radio /ˈreɪdɪəʊ/ *noun* (*plural* **-s**) **1** transmission and reception of messages etc. by electromagnetic waves of radio frequency. **2** apparatus for receiving, broadcasting, or transmitting radio signals. **3** sound broadcasting (station or channel). ● *verb* (**-es, -ed**) **1** send (message) by radio. **2** send message to (person) by radio. **3** communicate or broadcast by radio. □ **radio-controlled** controlled from a distance by radio. **radio telephone** one operating by radio. **radio telescope** aerial system for analysing radiation in the radio-frequency range from stars etc.

■ *noun* **2** CB, ghetto-blaster, receiver, set, transistor, transmitter, walkie-talkie, wireless. ● *verb* **1** broadcast, send out, transmit.

radioactive *adjective* of or exhibiting radioactivity.

radioactivity *noun* spontaneous disintegration of atomic nuclei, with emission of usually penetrating radiation or particles.

radiocarbon *noun* radioactive isotope of carbon.

radiogram /ˈreɪdɪəʊgræm/ *noun* **1** combined radio and record player. **2** picture obtained by X-rays etc. **3** telegram sent by radio.

radiograph /ˈreɪdɪəʊgrɑːf/ *noun* **1** instrument recording intensity of radiation. **2** picture obtained by X-rays etc. ● *verb* obtain picture of by X-rays, gamma rays, etc. □ **radiographer** /-ˈɒgrəfə/ *noun.* **radiography** /-ˈɒgrəfɪ/ *noun.*

radiology /reɪdɪˈɒlədʒɪ/ *noun esp. Medicine* study of X-rays and other high-energy radiation. □ **radiologist** *noun.*

radiophonic *adjective* of electronically produced sound, esp. music.

radioscopy /reɪdɪˈɒskəpɪ/ *noun* examination by X-rays etc. of objects opaque to light.

radiotherapy *noun* treatment of disease by X-rays or other forms of radiation.

radish /ˈrædɪʃ/ *noun* **1** plant with crisp pungent root. **2** this root, esp. eaten raw.

radium /ˈreɪdɪəm/ *noun* radioactive metallic element.

radius /ˈreɪdɪəs/ *noun* (*plural* **radii** /-dɪaɪ/ or **-es**) **1** straight line from centre to circumference of circle or sphere. **2** distance from a centre. **3** bone of forearm on same side as thumb.

radon /ˈreɪdɒn/ *noun* gaseous radioactive inert element arising from disintegration of radium.

RAF *abbreviation* Royal Air Force.

raffia /'ræfɪə/ *noun* **1** palm tree native to Madagascar. **2** fibre from its leaves.

raffish /'ræfɪʃ/ *adjective* **1** disreputable, rakish. **2** tawdry.

raffle /'ræf(ə)l/ *noun* fund-raising lottery with prizes. ● *verb* (**-ling**) (often + *off*) sell by raffle.

raft /rɑːft/ *noun* flat floating structure of wood etc., used for transport.

rafter /'rɑːftə/ *noun* any of sloping beams forming framework of roof.

■ beam, girder, joist.

rag¹ *noun* **1** torn, frayed, or worn piece of woven material. **2** remnant. **3** (in *plural*) old or worn clothes. **4** *derogatory* newspaper. □ **ragbag** miscellaneous collection. **rag doll** stuffed cloth doll. **ragtime** form of highly syncopated early jazz. **the rag trade** *colloquial* the clothing business. **ragwort** yellow-flowered ragged-leaved plant.

■ **1** cloth, scrap; (*rags*) bits and pieces, ribbons, shreds, tatters. **2** fragment, remnant, scrap, shred.

rag² *noun* **1** fund-raising programme of stunts etc. staged by students. **2** prank. **3** rowdy celebration. **4** disorderly scene. ● *verb* (**-gg-**) **1** tease; play rough jokes on. **2** engage in rough play.

ragamuffin /'rægəmʌfɪn/ *noun* child in ragged dirty clothes.

rage *noun* **1** violent anger. **2** fit of this. **3** temporary fashion. ● *verb* (**-ging**) **1** be full of anger. **2** (often + *at*, *against*) speak furiously. **3** be violent; be at its height. **4** (as **raging** *adjective*) extreme, very painful. □ **all the rage** very popular, fashionable.

■ *noun* **1** see ANGER *noun*. ● *verb* **1** be angry, boil, fume, go berserk, lose control, *colloquial* see red, seethe. **2** fulminate, fume, rail, rant, rave, storm, thunder.

ragged /'rægɪd/ *adjective* **1** torn; frayed. **2** in ragged clothes. **3** with a broken or jagged outline or surface. **4** lacking finish, smoothness, or uniformity.

■ **1** frayed, in ribbons, old, patched, patchy, ravelled, *archaic* rent, ripped, rough, shabby, tattered, *colloquial* tatty, threadbare, torn, unravelled, untidy, worn out. **2** rough, shabby, tattered, *colloquial* tatty, unkempt, untidy. **3** jagged, rough-edged, serrated, uneven, zigzag. **4** disorganized, erratic, imperfect, irregular, rough, uneven.

raglan /'ræglən/ *adjective* (of sleeve) running up to neck of garment.

ragout /ræ'guː/ *noun* highly seasoned stew of meat and vegetables.

raid *noun* **1** rapid surprise attack by armed forces or thieves. **2** surprise visit by police etc. to arrest suspects or seize illicit goods. ● *verb* **1** make raid on. **2** plunder. □ **raider** *noun*.

■ *noun* **1** assault, attack, *colloquial* blitz, foray, incursion, inroad, invasion, onslaught, sally, sortie, strike, swoop. ● *verb* **1** assault, attack, descend on, invade, pounce on, rush, storm, swoop (down) on. **2** loot, maraud, pillage, plunder, ransack, rifle, rob, sack, steal from, strip. □ **raider** attacker, brigand, invader, looter, marauder, outlaw, pillager, pirate, plunderer, ransacker, robber, rustler, thief.

rail¹ *noun* **1** bar used to hang things on or as protection, part of fence, top of banisters, etc. **2** steel bar(s) making railway track. **3** railway. ● *verb* provide or enclose with rail(s). □ **railcard** pass entitling holder to reduced rail fares.

rail² *verb* (often + *at*, *against*) complain or protest strongly; rant.

rail³ *noun* marsh wading bird.

railing *noun* (often in *plural*) fence or barrier made of rails.

raillery /'reɪlərɪ/ *noun* good-humoured ridicule.

railroad *noun esp. US* railway. ● *verb* (often + *into*, *through*) coerce, rush.

railway /'reɪlweɪ/ *noun* **1** track or set of tracks of steel rails on which trains run. **2** organization and people required to work such a system. □ **railwayman** male railway employee.

■ **1** line, *esp. US* railroad, rails, track.

raiment /'reɪmənt/ *noun archaic* clothing.

rain *noun* **1** condensed atmospheric moisture falling in drops. **2** fall of these. **3** falling liquid or objects. **4** (**the rains**) rainy season. ● *verb* **1** (after *it*) rain falls. **2** fall or send down like rain. **3** (after *it*) send in large quantities. **4** lavishly bestow. □ **raincoat** waterproof or water-resistant coat. **rainfall** total amount of rain falling within given area in given time. **rainforest** tropical forest with heavy rainfall. **take a rain check on** reserve right to postpone taking up (offer) until convenient.

■ *noun* **1** drizzle, precipitation, raindrops, rainfall. **2** cloudburst, deluge, downpour, rainstorm, shower, squall. ● *verb* **1** *colloquial* bucket down, drizzle, pelt, pour, *colloquial* rain cats and dogs, spit, teem.

rainbow /'reɪnbəʊ/ *noun* arch of colours formed in sky by reflection, refraction, and dispersion of sun's rays in falling rain etc. ● *adjective* many-coloured. □ **rainbow trout** large trout originally of N. America.

rainstorm /'reɪnstɔːm/ *noun* storm with heavy rain.

rainy *adjective* (**-ier**, **-iest**) (of weather, day, climate, etc.) in or on which rain is falling or much rain usually falls. □ **rainy day** time of need in the future.

■ damp, drizzly, showery, wet.

raise /reɪz/ *verb* (**-sing**) **1** put or take into higher position. **2** (often + *up*) cause to rise or stand up or be vertical. **3** increase amount, value, or strength of. **4** promote. **5** (often + *up*) build up, construct. **6** levy, collect. **7** cause to be heard or considered. **8** bring up; educate. **9** breed. **10** remove (embargo). **11** rouse. ● *noun* **1** *Cards* increase in stake or bid. **2** *US* rise in salary. □ **raise a laugh** cause others to laugh. **raise Cain, hell, the roof** *colloquial* be very angry; cause an uproar. **raise from the dead** restore to life. **raise one's glass to** toast.

■ *verb* **1** elevate, heave up, hoist, hold up, jack up, lift, pick up, put up, rear. **2** augment, boost, increase, inflate, put up, up. **4** exalt, prefer, promote, upgrade. **5** build, construct, create, erect, set up. **6** amass, collect, get, make, receive, solicit. **7** advance, bring up, broach, express, introduce, mention, moot, originate, pose, present, put forward, suggest. **8** bring up, care for, educate, look after, nurture, rear. **9** breed, cultivate, farm, grow, look after, nurture, produce, propagate, rear. **11** activate, arouse, awaken, build up, buoy up, encourage, engender, enlarge, excite, foment, foster, heighten, incite, kindle, motivate, provoke, rouse, stimulate, uplift. □ **raise from the dead** see RESURRECT 1.

raisin /'reɪz(ə)n/ *noun* dried grape.

raison d'être /reɪzɔ̃ 'detr/ *noun* (*plural* **raisons d'être** same pronunciation) purpose that accounts for, justifies, or originally caused thing's existence. [French]

raj /'rɑːdʒ/ *noun* (**the raj**) *historical* British rule in India.

raja /'rɑːdʒə/ *noun* (also **rajah**) *historical* Indian king or prince.

rake[1] *noun* **1** implement with long handle and toothed crossbar for drawing hay etc. together, smoothing loose soil, etc. **2** similar implement. ● *verb* (**-king**) **1** collect or gather (as) with rake. **2** ransack; search thoroughly. **3** direct gunfire along (line) from end to end. □ **rake in** *colloquial* amass (profits etc.). **rake-off** *colloquial* commission or share. **rake up** revive (unwelcome) memory of.

rake[2] *noun* dissolute man of fashion.

rake[3] *verb* (**-king**) set or be set at sloping angle. ● *noun* **1** raking position or build. **2** amount by which thing rakes.

rakish *adjective* dashing, jaunty; dissolute. □ **rakishly** *adverb*.

rallentando /rælən'tændəʊ/ *Music adverb & adjective* with gradual decrease of speed. ● *noun* (*plural* **-s** or **-di** /-dɪ/) rallentando passage.

rally /'rælɪ/ *verb* (**-ies, -ied**) **1** (often + *round*) bring or come together as support or for action. **2** recover after illness etc.; revive. **3** (of prices etc.) increase after fall. ● *noun* (*plural* **-ies**) **1** rallying, being rallied. **2** mass meeting. **3** competition for motor vehicles over public roads. **4** extended exchange of strokes in tennis etc. □ **rallycross** motor racing across country.

■ *verb* **1** assemble, come together, convene, get together, marshal, muster, organize, reassemble, reform, regroup, round up, summon. **2** see RECOVER 2. ● *noun* **2** assembly, *colloquial* demo, demonstration, gathering, march, mass meeting, protest. **3** see COMPETITION 2.

RAM *abbreviation* **1** Royal Academy of Music. **2** random-access memory.

ram *noun* **1** uncastrated male sheep. **2** (**the Ram**) zodiacal sign or constellation Aries. **3** falling weight of pile-driving machine. **4** hydraulic water pump. ● *verb* (**-mm-**) **1** force into place. **2** (usually + *down, in*, etc.) beat down or drive in by blows. **3** (of ship, vehicle, etc.) strike, crash against. □ **ram-raid** robbery of shop in which entry is gained by ramming vehicle into window. **ram-raider** *noun*. **ram-raiding** *noun*.

■ *verb* **1** compress, cram, crowd, crush, drive, force, jam, pack, press, push, *colloquial* squash, squeeze, tamp down, wedge. **3** bump, butt, collide with, crash into, hit, slam into, smash into, strike.

Ramadan /'ræmədæn/ *noun* ninth month of Muslim year, with strict fasting from sunrise to sunset.

ramble /'ræmb(ə)l/ *verb* (**-ling**) **1** walk for pleasure. **2** talk or write incoherently. ● *noun* walk taken for pleasure.

■ *verb* **1** hike, range, roam, rove, tramp, trek, stroll, walk, wander. **2** digress, drift, maunder, *colloquial* rabbit on, rattle on, wander, *colloquial* witter on. ● *noun* hike, tramp, trek, walk.

rambler *noun* **1** person who rambles. **2** straggling or spreading rose.

rambling *adjective* **1** wandering. **2** disconnected, incoherent. **3** (of house, town, street, etc.) irregularly arranged, spread out. **4** (of plant) straggling, climbing.

■ **2** aimless, circumlocutory, confused, diffuse, digressive, disconnected, discursive, disjointed, illogical, incoherent, jumbled, muddled, periphrastic, roundabout, unstructured, verbose, wandering, wordy. **3** asymmetrical, extensive, irregular, labyrinthine, sprawling, straggling, straggly, tortuous, twisting, winding, zigzag.

RAMC *abbreviation* Royal Army Medical Corps.

ramekin /'ræmɪkɪn/ *noun* small dish for baking and serving individual portion of food.

ramification /ræmɪfɪ'keɪʃ(ə)n/ *noun* **1** (usually in *plural*) consequence. **2** subdivision.

■ **1** by-product, complication, consequence, effect, implication, offshoot, result, upshot. **2** branch, division, extension, subdivision.

ramify /'ræmɪfaɪ/ *verb* (**-ies, -ied**) (cause to) form branches or subdivisions; branch out.

ramp *noun* **1** slope joining two levels of ground, floor, etc. **2** stairs for entering or leaving aircraft. **3** transverse ridge in road making vehicles slow down.

■ **1** acclivity, gradient, incline, rise, slope.

rampage *verb* /ræm'peɪdʒ/ (**-ging**) **1** (often + *about*) rush wildly. **2** rage, storm. ● *noun* /'ræmpeɪdʒ/ wild or violent behaviour. □ **on the rampage** rampaging.

■ *verb* behave violently, go berserk, go wild, lose control, race about, rage, run amok, run riot, rush about, storm about. ● *noun* frenzy, riot, tumult, uproar, vandalism, violence. □ **on the rampage** see WILD *adjective* 2.

rampant /'ræmpənt/ *adjective* **1** unchecked; flourishing excessively. **2** rank, luxuriant. **3** *Heraldry* (of lion etc.) standing on left hind foot with forepaws in air. **4** fanatical. □ **rampancy** *noun*.

rampart /'ræmpɑːt/ *noun* **1** defensive broad-topped wall. **2** defence, protection.

ramrod *noun* **1** rod for ramming down charge of muzzle-loading firearm. **2** thing that is very straight or rigid.

ramshackle /'ræmʃæk(ə)l/ *adjective* rickety, tumbledown.

■ broken-down, crumbling, decrepit, derelict, dilapidated, flimsy, jerry-built, rickety, ruined, run-down, shaky, tottering, tumbledown, unsafe, unstable, unsteady.

ran *past* of RUN.

ranch /rɑːntʃ/ *noun* **1** cattle-breeding establishment, esp. in US & Canada. **2** farm where other animals are bred. ● *verb* farm on ranch. □ **rancher** *noun*.

rancid /'rænsɪd/ *adjective* (of fat or fatty foods) smelling or tasting rank and stale. □ **rancidity** /-'sɪd-/ *noun*.

rancour /'ræŋkə/ *noun* (*US* **rancor**) inveterate bitterness; malignant hate. □ **rancorous** *adjective*.

rand *noun* monetary unit of South Africa.

random /'rændəm/ *adjective* made, done, etc. without method or conscious choice. □ **at random** without particular aim. **random-access** (of computer memory) having all parts directly accessible. □ **randomly** *adverb*.

■ accidental, adventitious, aimless, arbitrary, casual, chance, fortuitous, haphazard, hit-and-miss, indiscriminate, irregular, serendipitous, stray, unconsidered, unplanned, unpremeditated, unspecific, unsystematic.

randy /'rændɪ/ *adjective* (**-ier**, **-iest**) eager for sexual satisfaction.

ranee /'rɑːnɪ/ *noun* (also **rani**) (*plural* **-s**) *historical* raja's wife or widow.

rang *past* of RING².

range /reɪndʒ/ *noun* **1** region between limits of variation, esp. scope of operation. **2** such limits. **3** area relevant to something. **4** distance attainable by gun or projectile. **5** distance between gun etc. and target. **6** row, series, etc., esp. of mountains. **7** area with targets for shooting. **8** fireplace for cooking. **9** area over which a thing is distributed. **10** distance that can be covered by vehicle without refuelling. **11** stretch of open land for grazing or hunting. ● *verb* (**-ging**) **1** reach; extend; vary between limits. **2** (usually in *passive*) line up; arrange. **3** rove, wander. **4** traverse in all directions. □ **rangefinder** instrument for determining distance of object.

■ *noun* **1** area, compass, distance, diversity, extent, field, gamut, limit, orbit, radius, reach, scope, selection, span, spectrum, sphere, spread, sweep, variety. **6** chain, file, line, rank, row, series, string, tier. ● *verb* **1** differ, extend, fluctuate, go, reach, spread, stretch, vary. **2** see RANK¹ *verb* 3. **3** see ROAM.

ranger *noun* **1** keeper of royal or national park, or of forest. **2** (**Ranger**) senior Guide.

rangy /'reɪndʒɪ/ *adjective* (**-ier**, **-iest**) tall and slim.

rani = RANEE.

rank¹ *noun* **1** position in hierarchy; grade of advancement; place in scale. **2** distinct social class, grade of dignity or achievement. **3** high social position. **4** row or line. **5** single line of soldiers drawn up abreast. **6** place where taxis wait for customers. ● *verb* **1** have rank or place. **2** classify; give a certain grade to. **3** arrange in rank. □ **rank and file** (usually treated as *plural*) ordinary members of organization. **the ranks** common soldiers.

■ *noun* **1**, **2** birth, blood, caste, class, condition, echelon, grade, level, position, standing, station, status, stratum, title. **4** column, file, formation, line, queue, row, series, tier. ● *verb* **1** rate, stand. **2** categorize, class, classify, grade, rate, sort. **3** align, arrange, array, dispose, line up, order, organize, range, set out in order.

rank² *adjective* **1** luxuriant; coarse; choked with weeds etc. **2** foul-smelling; loathsome. **3** flagrant; gross, complete.

■ **1** see ABUNDANT 1. **2** see SMELLY.

rankle /'ræŋk(ə)l/ *verb* (**-ling**) cause persistent annoyance or resentment.

ransack /'rænsæk/ *verb* **1** pillage, plunder. **2** thoroughly search. □ **ransacker** *noun*.

■ **1** despoil, loot, pillage, plunder, raid, ravage, rob, sack, strip, wreck. **2** *colloquial* comb, explore, rake through, rummage through, scour, search, turn upside down.

ransom /'rænsəm/ *noun* sum demanded or paid for release of prisoner. ● *verb* **1** buy freedom or restoration of. **2** hold (prisoner) to ransom. **3** release for a ransom. □ **hold to ransom 1** keep (prisoner) and demand ransom. **2** demand concessions from by threats.

■ *noun* payment, *colloquial* pay-off, price. ● *verb* **1** buy the release of, deliver, redeem.

rant *verb* speak loudly, bombastically, or violently. ● *noun* piece of ranting. □ **rant and rave** express anger noisily and forcefully.

ranunculus /rə'nʌŋkjʊləs/ *noun* (*plural* **-luses** or **-li** /-laɪ/) plant of genus including buttercup.

RAOC *abbreviation* Royal Army Ordnance Corps.

rap¹ *noun* **1** smart slight blow. **2** sound of this; tap. **3** *slang* blame, punishment. **4** rhythmic monologue recited to music. **5** (in full **rap music**) style of rock music with words recited. ● *verb* (**-pp-**) **1** strike smartly. **2** make sharp tapping sound. **3** criticize adversely. **4** *Music* perform rap. □ **take the rap** suffer the consequences. □ **rapper** *noun* *Music*.

■ *verb* **1** see HIT *verb* 1. **2** knock, tap. **3** see CRITICIZE 1.

rap² *noun* the least bit.

rapacious /rə'peɪʃəs/ *adjective* grasping, extortionate, predatory. □ **rapacity** /-'pæs-/ *noun*.

rape¹ *noun* **1** act of forcing esp. woman or girl to

have sexual intercourse unwillingly. **2** (often + *of*) violent assault or plunder. ● *verb* (**-ping**) commit rape on.

■ *noun* **1** assault, sexual attack. **2** see PILLAGE *noun*. ● *verb* assault, defile, deflower, *archaic* dishonour, force oneself on, *archaic* ravish, violate.

rape² *noun* plant grown as fodder and for oil from its seed.

rapid /'ræpɪd/ *adjective* (**-er, -est**) quick, swift. ● *noun* (usually in *plural*) steep descent in river bed, with swift current. □ **rapid eye movement** jerky movement of eyes during dreaming. □ **rapidity** /rə'pɪd-/ *noun*. **rapidly** *adverb*.

■ *adjective* breakneck, brisk, expeditious, express, fast, *poetical* or *literary* fleet, hasty, headlong, high-speed, hurried, immediate, impetuous, instant, instantaneous, *colloquial* nippy, precipitate, prompt, quick, smooth, speedy, swift, unchecked, uninterrupted. ● *noun* (*rapids*) cataract, waterfall, white water.

rapier /'reɪpɪə/ *noun* light slender sword for thrusting.

rapine /'ræpaɪn/ *noun rhetorical* plundering.

rapist *noun* person who commits rape.

rapport /ræ'pɔː/ *noun* communication or relationship, esp. when useful and harmonious.

rapprochement /ræ'prɒʃmɑ̃/ *noun* resumption of harmonious relations, esp. between states. [French]

rapscallion /ræp'skæljən/ *noun archaic* rascal.

rapt *adjective* **1** absorbed; intent. **2** carried away with feeling or thought.

rapture /'ræptʃə/ *noun* **1** ecstatic delight. **2** (in *plural*) great pleasure or enthusiasm or expression of it. □ **rapturous** *adjective*.

■ **1** bliss, delight, ecstasy, elation, euphoria, exaltation, happiness, joy, pleasure, thrill.

rare¹ *adjective* (**-r, -st**) **1** seldom done, found, or occurring; uncommon. **2** exceptionally good. **3** of less than usual density. □ **rareness** *noun*.

■ **1** abnormal, atypical, curious, exceptional, extraordinary, few and far between, infrequent, irreplaceable, limited, occasional, odd, out of the ordinary, peculiar, scarce, singular, special, strange, surprising, uncommon, unfamiliar, unusual.

rare² *adjective* (**-r, -st**) (of meat) underdone.

rarebit *noun* see WELSH RAREBIT.

rarefy /'reərɪfaɪ/ *verb* (**-ies, -ied**) (often as **rarefied** *adjective*) **1** make or become less dense or solid. **2** refine. **3** make (idea etc.) subtle. □ **rarefaction** /-'fækʃ(ə)n/ *noun*.

rarely *adverb* seldom, not often.

raring /'reərɪŋ/ *adjective* (esp. in phrase **raring to go**) *colloquial* eager.

rarity /'reərətɪ/ *noun* (*plural* **-ies**) **1** rareness. **2** uncommon thing.

rascal /'rɑːsk(ə)l/ *noun* dishonest or mischievous person. □ **rascally** *adjective*.

■ blackguard, *colloquial or jocular* bounder, devil, good-for-nothing, imp, knave, mischief-maker, miscreant, ne'er-do-well, *archaic* rapscallion, rogue, scallywag, *colloquial* scamp, scoundrel, troublemaker, *colloquial* villain, wastrel.

rase = RAZE.

rash¹ *adjective* reckless, hasty, impetuous. □ **rashly** *adverb*. **rashness** *noun*.

■ careless, foolhardy, hare-brained, hasty, headlong, headstrong, heedless, hot-headed, hurried, ill-advised, ill-considered, impetuous, imprudent, impulsive, incautious, indiscreet, injudicious, madcap, precipitate, reckless, risky, thoughtless, unthinking, wild.

rash² *noun* **1** skin eruption in spots or patches. **2** (usually + *of*) sudden widespread occurrence.

■ **1** eruption, spots. **2** see OUTBREAK.

rasher /'ræʃə/ *noun* thin slice of bacon or ham.

rasp /rɑːsp/ *noun* **1** coarse file. **2** grating noise or utterance. ● *verb* **1** scrape roughly or with rasp. **2** make grating sound. **3** say gratingly. **4** grate on.

■ *verb* **1** abrade, file, grate, rub, scrape. **2, 3** croak, grate, jar, screech; (*rasping*) see HARSH 1.

raspberry /'rɑːzbərɪ/ *noun* (*plural* **-ies**) **1** red fruit like blackberry. **2** shrub bearing this. **3** *colloquial* sound made by blowing through lips, expressing derision or disapproval.

Rastafarian /ræstə'feərɪən/ (also **Rasta** /'ræstə/) *noun* member of Jamaican sect regarding Haile Selassie of Ethiopia (d. 1975) as God. ● *adjective* of this sect.

rat *noun* **1** large mouselike rodent. **2** *colloquial* unpleasant or treacherous person. ● *verb* (**-tt-**) **1** hunt or kill rats. **2** (also + *on*) *colloquial* inform (on). **3** (also + *on*) *colloquial* desert, betray. □ **ratbag** *slang* obnoxious person. **rat race** *colloquial* fiercely competitive struggle.

ratable = RATEABLE.

ratatouille /rætə'tuːɪ/ *noun* dish of stewed onions, courgettes, tomatoes, aubergines, and peppers.

ratchet /'rætʃɪt/ *noun* **1** set of teeth on edge of bar or wheel with catch ensuring motion in one direction only. **2** (in full **ratchet-wheel**) wheel with rim so toothed.

rate¹ *noun* **1** numerical proportion between two sets of things or as basis of calculating amount or value. **2** charge, cost, or value; measure of this. **3** pace of movement or change. **4** (in *plural*) tax levied by local authorities according to value of buildings and land occupied. ● *verb* (**-ting**) **1** estimate worth or value of. **2** assign value to. **3** consider, regard as. **4** (+ *as*) rank or be considered as. **5** subject to payment of local rate. **6** deserve. □ **at any rate** in any case; whatever happens. **at this rate** if this example is typical. **rate-capping** *historical* imposition of upper limit on local authority rates. **ratepayer** person liable to pay rates.

■ *noun* **2** amount, charge, cost, fare, fee, figure, payment, price, scale, tariff, wage. **3** pace, speed, tempo, velocity. ● *verb* **1, 2** appraise, assess, compute, estimate, evaluate, gauge, grade, judge, measure, prize, put a price on, rank, reckon, value, weigh. **3** class, classify, consider, judge, rank, reckon, regard as. **6** be worthy of, deserve, merit.

rate² *verb* scold.
■ see REPRIMAND *verb*.

rateable /'reɪtəb(ə)l/ *adjective* (also **ratable** /'reɪtəb(ə)l/) liable to rates. □ **rateable value** value at which business etc. is assessed for rates.

rather /'rɑːðə/ *adverb* **1** by preference. **2** (usually + *than*) more truly; as a more likely alternative. **3** more precisely. **4** to some extent. **5** /rɑːˈðɜː/ most emphatically.
■ **1** more willingly, preferably, sooner. **4** fairly, moderately, *colloquial* pretty, quite, relatively, slightly, somewhat.

ratify /'rætɪfaɪ/ *verb* (**-ies, -ied**) confirm or accept by formal consent, signature, etc. □ **ratification** *noun*.
■ approve, authorize, confirm, endorse, sanction, sign, validate, verify.

rating /'reɪtɪŋ/ *noun* **1** placing in rank or class. **2** estimated standing of person as regards credit etc. **3** non-commissioned sailor. **4** (usually in *plural*) popularity of a broadcast as determined by estimated size of audience.
■ **1** classification, evaluation, grade, grading, mark, order, placing, ranking.

ratio /'reɪʃɪəʊ/ *noun* (*plural* **-s**) quantitative relation between similar magnitudes.
■ balance, correlation, correspondence, proportion, relationship.

ratiocinate /rætɪˈɒsɪneɪt/ *verb* (**-ting**) *literary* reason, esp. using syllogisms. □ **ratiocination** *noun*.

ration /'ræʃ(ə)n/ *noun* **1** official allowance of food, clothing, etc., in time of shortage. **2** (usually in *plural*) fixed daily allowance of food. ● *verb* **1** limit (food etc. or people) to fixed ration. **2** (usually + *out*) share (out) in fixed quantities.
■ *noun* **1** allocation, allotment, allowance, amount, helping, measure, percentage, portion, quota, share. **2** (*rations*) food, necessaries, necessities, provisions, stores, supplies. ● *verb* **1** conserve, control, limit, restrict. **2** (*ration out*) allocate, allot, apportion, distribute, dole out, give out, parcel out, share out.

rational /'ræʃ(ə)n(ə)l/ *adjective* **1** of or based on reason. **2** sensible. **3** endowed with reason. **4** rejecting what is unreasonable. **5** *Mathematics* expressible as ratio of whole numbers. □ **rationality** /-'næl-/ *noun*. **rationally** *adverb*.
■ **2** balanced, clear-headed, considered, judicious, logical, lucid, normal, reasonable, reasoned, sane, sensible, sound, thoughtful, wise. **3** enlightened, intelligent, logical, reasoning, thinking.

rationale /ræʃəˈnɑːl/ *noun* fundamental reason; logical basis.
■ argument, case, cause, excuse, explanation, grounds, justification, logical basis, principle, reason, reasoning, theory, vindication.

rationalism *noun* practice of treating reason as basis of belief and knowledge. □ **rationalist** *noun & adjective*. **rationalistic** /-'lɪs-/ *adjective*.

rationalize *verb* (also **-ise**) (**-zing** or **-sing**) **1** (often + *away*) offer rational but specious explanation of (behaviour or attitude). **2** make logical and consistent. **3** make (industry etc.) more efficient by reducing waste. □ **rationalization** *noun*.
■ **1** account for, elucidate, excuse, explain, justify, provide a rationale for, *literary* ratiocinate, think through, vindicate. **3** see REORGANIZE.

ratline /'rætlɪn/ *noun* (also **ratlin**) (usually in *plural*) any of the small lines fastened across ship's shrouds like ladder rungs.

rattan /rəˈtæn/ *noun* **1** palm with long thin many-jointed stems. **2** cane of this.

rattle /'ræt(ə)l/ *verb* (**-ling**) **1** (cause to) give out rapid succession of short sharp sounds. **2** cause such sounds by shaking something. **3** move or travel with rattling noise. **4** (usually + *off*) say or recite rapidly. **5** (usually + *on*) talk in lively thoughtless way. **6** *colloquial* disconcert, alarm. ● *noun* **1** rattling sound. **2** device or plaything made to rattle. □ **rattlesnake** poisonous American snake with rattling rings on tail. □ **rattly** *adjective*.
■ *verb* **1** agitate, clatter, jar, jiggle about, joggle, jolt, shake about, vibrate. **4** (*rattle off*) see RECITE 1. **5** (*rattle on*) see RAMBLE *verb* 2, TALK *verb* 1. **6** alarm, discomfit, discompose, disconcert, disturb, fluster, frighten, make nervous, put off, unnerve, upset, worry.

rattling *adjective* **1** that rattles. **2** brisk, vigorous. ● *adverb colloquial* remarkably (good etc.).

ratty /'rætɪ/ *adjective* (**-ier, -iest**) *colloquial* irritable, angry.

raucous /'rɔːkəs/ *adjective* harsh-sounding; hoarse. □ **raucously** *adverb*. **raucousness** *noun*.
■ ear-splitting, harsh, husky, grating, jarring, noisy, rasping, rough, screeching, shrill, squawking, strident.

raunchy /'rɔːntʃɪ/ *adjective* (**-ier, -iest**) *colloquial* sexually boisterous.

ravage /'rævɪdʒ/ *verb* (**-ging**) devastate, plunder. ● *noun* (usually in *plural*; + *of*) destructive effect of.
■ *verb* damage, despoil, destroy, devastate, lay waste, loot, pillage, plunder, raid, ransack, ruin, sack, spoil, wreak havoc on, wreck.

rave *verb* (**-ving**) **1** talk furiously, wildly, or deliriously. **2** (usually + *about, over*) speak with rapturous admiration. **3** *colloquial* enjoy oneself freely. ● *noun colloquial* **1** highly enthusiastic review. **2** (also **rave-up**) lively party.

■ *verb* **1** fulminate, fume, rage, rant, roar, storm, thunder. **2** be enthusiastic, *colloquial* enthuse, go into raptures, gush, rhapsodize.

ravel /'ræv(ə)l/ *verb* (**-ll-**; *US* **-l-**) **1** entangle, become entangled. **2** fray out.

raven /'reɪv(ə)n/ *noun* large glossy black crow with hoarse cry. ● *adjective* glossy black.

ravening /'ræv(ə)nɪŋ/ *adjective* **1** hungrily seeking prey. **2** voracious.

ravenous /'rævənəs/ *adjective* **1** very hungry. **2** voracious; rapacious. □ **ravenously** *adverb*. **ravenousness** *noun*.

■ **1** *colloquial* famished, hungry, *colloquial* starved, *colloquial* starving. **2** greedy, insatiable, piggish, rapacious, ravening, voracious.

raver *noun colloquial* uninhibited pleasure-loving person.

ravine /rə'viːn/ *noun* deep narrow gorge.

raving *noun* (usually in *plural*) wild or delirious talk. ● *adjective colloquial* utter, absolute. ● *adverb colloquial* utterly, absolutely.

ravioli /rævɪ'əʊlɪ/ *noun* small square pasta envelopes containing meat, spinach, etc.

ravish /'rævɪʃ/ *verb* **1** *archaic* rape (woman). **2** enrapture.

■ **1** see RAPE[1] *verb*. **2** bewitch, captivate, capture, charm, delight, enchant, enrapture, entrance, spellbind, transport.

ravishing *adjective* lovely, beautiful. □ **ravishingly** *adverb*.

■ see BEAUTIFUL 1.

raw *adjective* **1** uncooked. **2** in natural state; not processed or manufactured. **3** inexperienced, untrained. **4** stripped of skin. **5** unhealed; sensitive to touch. **6** (of weather) cold and damp. **7** crude; lacking finish. □ **in the raw 1** in its natural state. **2** naked. **raw-boned** gaunt. **raw deal** unfair treatment. **rawhide 1** untanned hide. **2** rope or whip of this. **raw material** material from which manufactured goods are made. □ **rawness** *noun*.

■ **2** crude, natural, unprocessed, unrefined, untreated. **3** green, ignorant, immature, inexperienced, innocent, new, unseasoned, untrained, untried. **4, 5** bloody, chafed, grazed, inflamed, painful, red, rough, scraped, scratched, sensitive, sore, tender, vulnerable. **6** see COLD *adjective* 1.

Rawlplug /'rɔːlplʌg/ *noun proprietary term* cylindrical plug for holding screw in masonry.

ray[1] *noun* **1** single line or narrow beam of light. **2** straight line in which radiation travels. **3** (in *plural*) radiation. **4** trace or beginning of enlightening influence. **5** any of set of radiating lines, parts, or things. **6** marginal part of daisy etc.

■ **1** beam, shaft, streak, stream. **4** flicker, gleam, glimmer, hint, indication, scintilla, sign, trace.

ray[2] *noun* large edible marine fish with flat body.

ray[3] *noun* (also **re**) *Music* second note of scale in tonic sol-fa.

rayon /'reɪɒn/ *noun* textile fibre or fabric made from cellulose.

raze *verb* (also **rase**) (**-zing** or **-sing**) completely destroy; tear down.

■ bulldoze, demolish, destroy, flatten, level, tear down.

razor /'reɪzə/ *noun* instrument for shaving. □ **razorbill** auk with sharp-edged bill. **razorblade** flat piece of metal with sharp edge, used in safety razor. **razor-edge, razor's edge 1** keen edge. **2** sharp mountain ridge. **3** critical situation. **4** sharp line of division.

razzle /'ræz(ə)l/ *noun colloquial* spree. □ **razzle-dazzle 1** excitement; bustle. **2** extravagant publicity.

razzmatazz /ræzmə'tæz/ *noun* (also **razzamatazz** /ræzə-/) *colloquial* **1** glamorous excitement. **2** insincere activity.

RC *abbreviation* Roman Catholic.

Rd. *abbreviation* Road.

RE *abbreviation* **1** Religious Education. **2** Royal Engineers.

re[1] /reɪ, riː/ *preposition* **1** in the matter of. **2** about, concerning.

re[2] = RAY[3].

re- *prefix attachable to almost any verb or its derivative, meaning*: once more, anew, afresh; back. For words starting with *re-* that are not found below, the root-words should be consulted.

reach *verb* **1** (often + *out*) stretch out; extend. **2** (often + *for*) stretch hand etc. **3** get as far as. **4** get to or attain. **5** make contact with. **6** pass, hand. **7** take with outstretched hand. **8** *Nautical* sail with wind abeam. ● *noun* **1** extent to which hand etc. can be reached out, influence exerted, etc. **2** act of reaching out. **3** continuous extent, esp. of river or canal. □ **reach-me-down** *colloquial* ready-made garment. □ **reachable** *adjective*.

■ *verb* **1** (*reach out*) see EXTEND 2. **2** (*reach for*) grasp for, put out one's hand for, stretch for, try to get. **3, 4** achieve, arrive at, attain, come to, get to, go as far as, *colloquial* make. **5** communicate with, contact, get hold of, get in touch with, touch. **7** grasp, take. ● *noun* **1** compass, distance, orbit, range, scope, sphere.

react /rɪ'ækt/ *verb* **1** (often + *to*) respond to stimulus; change or behave differently due to some influence. **2** (often + *with*) undergo chemical reaction (with other substance). **3** (often + *against*) respond with repulsion to; tend in reverse or contrary direction.

■ **1** act, answer, behave, conduct oneself, reciprocate, reply, respond, retaliate, retort, take revenge; (*react to*) see COUNTER[2] *verb*.

reaction /rɪ'ækʃ(ə)n/ *noun* **1** reacting; response. **2** bad physical response to drug etc. **3** occurrence of condition after its opposite. **4** tendency to oppose change or reform. **5** interaction of substances undergoing chemical change.

■ **1** answer, backlash, *slang* comeback, counter, countermove, effect, feedback, reciprocation, rejoinder, reply, reprisal, response, retaliation, retort, revenge, riposte.

reactionary *adjective* tending to oppose (esp. political) change or reform. ● *noun* (*plural* **-ies**) reactionary person.
■ *adjective* conservative, old-fashioned, traditionalist, unprogressive. ● *noun* conservative, diehard, *colloquial* stick-in-the-mud, traditionalist.

reactivate /rɪˈæktɪveɪt/ *verb* (**-ting**) restore to state of activity. □ **reactivation** *noun*.

reactive /rɪˈæktɪv/ *adjective* **1** showing reaction. **2** reacting rather than taking initiative. **3** susceptible to chemical reaction.

reactor *noun* (in full **nuclear reactor**) device in which nuclear chain reaction is used to produce energy.

read *verb* (*past & past participle* **read** /red/) **1** reproduce (written or printed words) mentally or (often + *aloud, out, off*, etc.) vocally. **2** (be able to) convert (written or printed words or other symbols) into intended words or meaning. **3** interpret. **4** (of meter) show (figure). **5** interpret state of (meter). **6** study (subject) at university. **7** (as **read** /red/ *adjective*) versed in subject (esp. literature) by reading. **8** (of computer) copy or transfer (data). **9** hear and understand (over radio). **10** substitute (word etc.) for incorrect one. ● *noun* **1** spell of reading. **2** *colloquial* book etc. as regards readability. □ **take as read** treat (thing) as if it has been agreed.
■ *verb* **1** devour, dip into, glance at, look over, peruse, pore over, review, scan, skim, study. **2** decipher, decode, interpret, make out, understand.

readable *adjective* **1** able to be read. **2** interesting to read. □ **readability** *noun*.
■ **1** clear, comprehensible, decipherable, distinct, easy, intelligible, legible, neat, plain, understandable. **2** absorbing, compulsive, engaging, enjoyable, entertaining, gripping, interesting, stimulating, well written.

reader *noun* **1** person who reads. **2** book intended for reading practice. **3** device for producing image that can be read from microfilm etc. **4** (also **Reader**) university lecturer of highest grade below professor. **5** publisher's employee who reports on submitted manuscripts. **6** printer's proof-corrector.

readership *noun* **1** readers of a newspaper etc. **2** (also **Readership**) position of Reader.

readily *adverb* **1** without reluctance; willingly. **2** easily.
■ **1** cheerfully, eagerly, freely, gladly, happily, promptly, quickly, ungrudgingly, unhesitatingly, voluntarily, willingly. **2** easily, effortlessly.

readiness *noun* **1** prepared state. **2** willingness. **3** facility. **4** promptness in argument or action.

reading *noun* **1** act of reading. **2** matter to be

read. **3** literary knowledge. **4** entertainment at which something is read. **5** figure etc. shown by recording instrument. **6** interpretation or view taken. **7** interpretation made (of music etc.). **8** presentation of bill to legislature.

ready /ˈredɪ/ *adjective* (**-ier, -iest**) **1** with preparations complete. **2** in fit state. **3** willing. **4** (of income etc.) easily secured; at hand. **5** fit for immediate use. **6** prompt, quick, enthusiastic. **7** (+ *to do*) about to. **8** provided beforehand. ● *adverb* **1** (usually in *combination*) beforehand. **2** in readiness. ● *noun slang* **1** (**the ready**) ready money. **2** (**readies**) bank notes. ● *verb* (**-ies, -ied**) prepare. □ **at the ready** ready for action. **ready-made**, **ready-to-wear** (esp. of clothes) made in standard size; not to measure. **ready money** cash, actual coin. **ready reckoner** book or table listing standard numerical calculations.
■ *adjective* **1** *colloquial* all set, arranged, complete, done, finalized, finished, organized, prepared, primed, set, set up, waiting. **2** equipped, fit, *colloquial* psyched up, ripe, trained. **3** agreeable, consenting, content, disposed, eager, game, glad, inclined, in the mood, keen, keyed up, minded, open, pleased, predisposed, *colloquial* raring to go, willing. **4** accessible, at hand, available, convenient, obtainable. **6** acute, adroit, alert, apt, immediate, prompt, quick, quick-witted, rapid, sharp, smart, speedy. **7** (*ready to*) about to, close to, *disputed* liable to, likely to, on the point of, on the verge of, poised to.

reagent /riːˈeɪdʒ(ə)nt/ *noun* substance used to produce chemical reaction.

real *adjective* **1** actually existing or occurring. **2** genuine. **3** appraised by purchasing power. ● *adverb Scottish & US colloquial* really, very. □ **real ale** beer regarded as brewed in traditional way. **real estate** property such as land and houses. **real tennis** original form of tennis played on indoor court.
■ *adjective* **1** actual, authentic, corporeal, existing, factual, genuine, material, natural, palpable, physical, tangible, visible. **2** authenticated, bona fide, earnest, genuine, heartfelt, honest, legal, legitimate, official, positive, sincere, sound, true, truthful, unaffected, undoubted, unfeigned, unquestionable, valid, verifiable.

realism *noun* **1** practice of regarding things in their true nature and dealing with them as they are. **2** fidelity to nature in representation. □ **realist** *noun*.
■ **1** clear-sightedness, common sense, objectivity, practicality, pragmatism. **2** authenticity, fidelity, naturalism, verisimilitude.

realistic /rɪəˈlɪstɪk/ *adjective* **1** regarding things as they are. **2** facing facts; based on facts rather than ideals. **3** reasonable. □ **realistically** *adverb*.
■ **1** authentic, convincing, faithful, graphic, lifelike, natural, recognizable, representational, true to life, truthful, vivid. **2** businesslike, clear-sighted, common-sense, down-to-earth, hard-headed, *colloquial* hard-nosed, level-headed, logical, matter-of-fact, no-nonsense, objective, practical, pragmatic, rational, sensible, tough, unemotional,

unsentimental; (*of plan etc.*) feasible, possible, practicable, viable, workable. **3** acceptable, adequate, fair, genuine, justifiable, moderate, reasonable.

reality /rɪˈælɪtɪ/ *noun* (*plural* **-ies**) **1** what is real or existent or underlies appearances. **2** (+ *of*) real nature of. **3** real existence; being real. **4** likeness to original. □ **in reality** in fact.
■ **1** actuality, authenticity, certainty, fact, life, *slang* nitty-gritty, real life, the real world, truth, *archaic* verity.

realize *verb* (also **-ise**) (**-zing** or **-sing**) **1** (often + *that*) be or become fully aware of. **2** understand clearly. **3** convert into actuality. **4** convert into money. **5** acquire (profit). **6** be sold for. □ **realizable** *adjective*. **realization** *noun*.
■ **1, 2** accept, appreciate, apprehend, be aware of, become conscious of, *colloquial* catch on to, comprehend, conceive of, *colloquial* cotton on to, grasp, know, perceive, recognize, see, sense, *colloquial* twig, understand, wake up to. **3** accomplish, achieve, bring about, complete, effect, effectuate, fulfil, implement, make a reality of, obtain, perform, put into effect. **5** bring in, clear, earn, fetch, make, net, obtain, produce.

really /ˈrɪəlɪ/ *adverb* **1** in fact. **2** very. **3** I assure you. **4** *expression of mild protest or surprise*.

realm /relm/ *noun* **1** *formal* kingdom. **2** domain.
■ **1** country, domain, empire, kingdom, monarchy, principality. **2** see SPHERE 3.

realty /ˈriːəltɪ/ *noun* real estate.

ream *noun* **1** 500 sheets of paper. **2** (in *plural*) large quantity of writing.

reap *verb* **1** cut (grain etc.) as harvest. **2** receive as consequences of actions. □ **reaper** *noun*.
■ **1** cut, garner, gather in, glean, harvest, mow. **2** acquire, bring in, collect, get, obtain, receive, win.

rear[1] *noun* **1** back part of anything. **2** space or position at back. **3** *colloquial* buttocks. ● *adjective* at the back. □ **bring up the rear** come last. **rear admiral** naval officer below vice admiral. □ **rearmost** *adjective*.
■ *noun* **1** back, end, stern (*of ship*), tail-end. **3** see BUTTOCK. ● *adjective* back, end, hind, hinder, hindmost, last, rearmost.

rear[2] *verb* **1** bring up and educate. **2** breed and care for. **3** cultivate. **4** (of horse etc.) raise itself on hind legs. **5** raise (one's head). **6** build.
■ **1–3** breed, bring up, care for, cultivate, educate, feed, look after, nurse, nurture, produce, raise, train. **5** elevate, hold up, lift, raise, uplift. **6** see BUILD *verb* 1.

rearguard *noun* troops detached to protect rear, esp. in retreat. □ **rearguard action 1** engagement undertaken by rearguard. **2** defensive stand or struggle, esp. when losing.

rearm /riːˈɑːm/ *verb* arm again, esp. with improved weapons. □ **rearmament** *noun*.

rearrange /riːəˈreɪndʒ/ *verb* (**-ging**) arrange in different way or order. □ **rearrangement** *noun*.

■ change, change round, regroup, reorder, reorganize, reshuffle, swap round, switch round, transpose. □ **rearrangement** change, reorganization, reshuffle, transposition.

rearward /ˈrɪəwəd/ *noun* rear. ● *adjective* to the rear. ● *adverb* (also **rearwards**) towards the rear.

reason /ˈriːz(ə)n/ *noun* **1** motive, cause, or justification. **2** fact adduced or serving as this. **3** intellectual faculty by which conclusions are drawn. **4** sanity. **5** sense; sensible conduct. **6** moderation. ● *verb* **1** form or try to reach conclusions by connected thought. **2** (+ *with*) use argument with person by way of persuasion. **3** (+ *that*) conclude or assert in argument. **4** (+ *out*) think out. □ **reasoning** *noun*.
■ *noun* **1** aim, apology, argument, case, cause, defence, excuse, explanation, goal, grounds, incentive, intention, justification, motivation, motive, object, objective, occasion, point, pretext, purpose, rationale, spur, stimulus, vindication. **3** brains, intellect, intelligence, judgement, logic, perspicacity, rationality, reasoning, thought. **4** mind, rationality, saneness, sanity. **5** common sense, *colloquial* gumption, intelligence, *colloquial* nous, reasonableness, sense, understanding, wisdom, wit. ● *verb* **1** cerebrate, intellectualize, *literary* ratiocinate, theorize, think, use one's head. **2** (*reason with*) argue with, debate with, discuss with, expostulate with, remonstrate with. **3** argue, assert, calculate, conclude, consider, deduce, estimate, figure out, hypothesize, infer, intellectualize, judge, resolve, theorize, work out. **4** (*reason out*) figure out, think out, work out. □ **reasoning** analysis, argument, cerebration, deduction, line of thought, logic, proof, rationalization, theorizing, thinking.

reasonable *adjective* **1** having sound judgement; moderate; ready to listen to reason; sensible. **2** sound; based on reason. **3** inexpensive. **4** tolerable. □ **reasonableness** *noun*. **reasonably** *adverb*.
■ **1** calm, helpful, honest, intelligent, moderate, rational, realistic, sane, sensible, sincere, sober, thinking, thoughtful, unemotional, wise. **2** arguable, believable, credible, defensible, justifiable, logical, plausible, practical, reasoned, sound, tenable, viable, well thought out. **3** cheap, competitive, inexpensive, moderate. **4** acceptable, appropriate, average, fair, ordinary, proper, right, suitable, tolerable, unexceptionable.

reassure /riːəˈʃʊə/ *verb* (**-ring**) **1** restore confidence to. **2** confirm in opinion etc. □ **reassurance** *noun*. **reassuring** *adjective*.
■ **1** assure, bolster, buoy up, calm, cheer, comfort, encourage, hearten, set (person's) mind at rest, support, uplift. □ **reassuring** see SOOTHING, SUPPORTIVE.

rebate[1] /ˈriːbeɪt/ *noun* **1** partial refund. **2** deduction from sum to be paid; discount.

rebate[2] /ˈriːbeɪt/ *noun & verb* (**-ting**) rabbet.

rebel *noun* /ˈreb(ə)l/ **1** person who fights against, resists, or refuses allegiance to, established government. **2** person etc. who resists authority or control. ● *adjective* /ˈreb(ə)l/ rebellious. ● *verb* /rɪˈbel/ (**-ll-**) (usually + *against*) **1** act as rebel. **2** feel or show repugnance.

■ *noun* anarchist, apostate, dissenter, freedom fighter, heretic, iconoclast, insurgent, malcontent, maverick, mutineer, nonconformist, recusant, resistance fighter, revolutionary, schismatic. ● *adjective* see REBELLIOUS. ● *verb* **1** disobey, dissent, fight, kick over the traces, mutiny, revolt, rise up, run riot, take a stand; (*rebel against*) see DEFY 1.

rebellion /rɪˈbeljən/ *noun* open resistance to authority, esp. organized armed resistance to established government.

■ defiance, disobedience, insubordination, insurgency, insurrection, mutiny, rebelliousness, resistance, revolt, revolution, rising, schism, sedition, uprising.

rebellious /rɪˈbeljəs/ *adjective* **1** disposed to rebel. **2** in rebellion. **3** unmanageable. □ **rebelliously** *adverb*. **rebelliousness** *noun*.

■ *slang* bolshie, defiant, difficult, disaffected, disloyal, disobedient, incorrigible, insubordinate, insurgent, intractable, malcontent, mutinous, obstinate, quarrelsome, rebel, recalcitrant, refractory, resistant, revolutionary, seditious, uncontrollable, ungovernable, unmanageable, unruly, wild.

rebirth /ˈriːbɜːθ/ *noun* **1** new birth or beginning. **2** revival.

■ reawakening, regeneration, renaissance, renewal, resurgence, resurrection, return, revival.

rebound *verb* /rɪˈbaʊnd/ **1** spring back after impact. **2** (+ *upon*) have adverse effect on (doer). ● *noun* /ˈriːbaʊnd/ **1** rebounding; recoil. **2** reaction. □ **on the rebound** while still recovering from emotional shock, esp. rejection by lover.

■ *verb* **1** bounce, recoil, ricochet, spring back. **2** (*rebound upon*) backfire on, recoil on.

rebuff /rɪˈbʌf/ *noun* rejection of person who makes advances, offers help, etc.; snub. ● *verb* give rebuff to.

■ *noun* brush-off, check, discouragement, refusal, rejection, slight, snub. ● *verb* cold-shoulder, decline, discourage, refuse, reject, repulse, slight, snub, spurn, turn down.

rebuild /riːˈbɪld/ *verb* (*past & past participle* **-built** /-bɪlt/) build again.

■ reassemble, reconstruct, recreate, redevelop, refashion, regenerate, remake, restore.

rebuke /rɪˈbjuːk/ *verb* (**-king**) express sharp disapproval to (person) for fault; censure. ● *noun* rebuking, being rebuked.

■ *verb* admonish, castigate, censure, *archaic* chide, *formal* reprehend, reprimand, reproach, *formal* reprove, scold, upbraid.

rebus /ˈriːbəs/ *noun* (*plural* **rebuses**) representation of word (esp. name) by pictures etc. suggesting its parts.

rebut /rɪˈbʌt/ *verb* (**-tt-**) **1** refute, disprove. **2** force back. □ **rebuttal** *noun*.

recalcitrant /rɪˈkælsɪtrənt/ *adjective* **1** obstinately disobedient. **2** objecting to restraint. □ **recalcitrance** *noun*.

recall /rɪˈkɔːl/ *verb* **1** summon to return. **2** recollect, remember; bring back to memory. **3** revoke, annul. **4** revive, resuscitate. ● *noun* (also /ˈriːkɔːl/) **1** summons to come back. **2** act of remembering. **3** ability to remember. **4** possibility of recalling.

■ *verb* **1** bring back, call in, summon, withdraw. **2** see REMEMBER 2.

recant /rɪˈkænt/ *verb* withdraw and renounce (belief or statement) as erroneous or heretical. □ **recantation** /riːkænˈteɪʃ(ə)n/ *noun*.

recap /ˈriːkæp/ *colloquial verb* (**-pp-**) recapitulate. ● *noun* recapitulation.

recapitulate /riːkəˈpɪtjʊleɪt/ *verb* (**-ting**) summarize; restate briefly. □ **recapitulation** *noun*.

recast /riːˈkɑːst/ *verb* (*past & past participle* **recast**) **1** cast again. **2** put into new form. **3** improve arrangement of. ● *noun* **1** recasting. **2** recast form.

recce /ˈrekɪ/ *colloquial noun* reconnaissance. ● *verb* (**recced, recceing**) reconnoitre.

recede /rɪˈsiːd/ *verb* (**-ding**) **1** go or shrink back. **2** be left at an increasing distance. **3** slope backwards. **4** decline in force or value.

■ **1** ebb, fall back, go back, regress, retire, retreat, return, shrink back, sink, subside, withdraw. **4** abate, decline, dwindle, fade, lessen, sink, slacken, subside, wane.

receipt /rɪˈsiːt/ *noun* **1** receiving, being received. **2** written or printed acknowledgement of payment received. **3** (usually in *plural*) amount of money received. ● *verb* place written or printed receipt on (bill). □ **in receipt of** having received.

■ *noun* **1** acceptance, delivery, reception. **2** acknowledgement, proof of purchase, sales slip, ticket. **3** (*receipts*) gains, gate, income, proceeds, profits, return, takings.

receive /rɪˈsiːv/ *verb* (**-ving**) **1** take or accept (thing offered, sent, or given). **2** acquire. **3** have conferred, inflicted, etc. on one. **4** react to (news etc.) in particular way. **5** stand force or weight of. **6** consent to hear or consider. **7** admit; entertain as guest. **8** greet, welcome. **9** be able to hold. **10** convert (broadcast signals) into sound or pictures. **11** (as **received** *adjective*) accepted as authoritative or true. □ **Received Pronunciation** standard pronunciation of English in Britain (see panel at ACCENT).

■ **1, 2** accept, acquire, be given, be paid, be sent, collect, come by, come into, derive, earn, gain, get, gross, inherit, make, net, obtain, take. **3** (*receive an honour*) be awarded, collect, gain, win; (*receive an injury*) bear, be subjected to, endure, experience, meet with, suffer, sustain, undergo. **7, 8** accommodate, admit, entertain, greet, let in, meet, show in, welcome.

receiver *noun* **1** part of telephone containing earpiece. **2** (in full **official receiver**) person appointed to administer property of bankrupt person etc. or property under litigation. **3** radio or television receiving apparatus. **4** person who receives stolen goods.

receivership *noun* ▢ **in receivership** being dealt with by receiver.

recent /'riːs(ə)nt/ *adjective* **1** not long past; that happened or existed lately. **2** not long established; modern. ▢ **recently** *adverb*.

> ■ **2** brand new, contemporary, current, fresh, just out, (the) latest, modern, new, novel, present-day, up to date.

receptacle /rɪ'septək(ə)l/ *noun* object or space used to contain something.

reception /rɪ'sepʃ(ə)n/ *noun* **1** receiving, being received. **2** way in which person or thing is received. **3** social occasion for receiving guests, esp. after wedding. **4** place where visitors register on arriving at hotel, office, etc. **5** (quality of) receiving of broadcast signals. ▢ **reception room** room for receiving guests, clients, etc.

> ■ **2** greeting, response, welcome. **3** see PARTY 1.

receptionist *noun* person employed to receive guests, clients, etc.

receptive /rɪ'septɪv/ *adjective* able or quick to receive ideas etc. ▢ **receptively** *adverb*. **receptiveness** *noun*. **receptivity** /riːsep'tɪv-/ *noun*.

> ■ amenable, flexible, interested, open, open-minded, responsive, susceptible, sympathetic, tractable, welcoming, well disposed.

recess /rɪ'ses/ *noun* **1** space set back in wall. **2** (often in *plural*) remote or secret place. **3** temporary cessation from work, esp. of Parliament. ● *verb* **1** make recess in. **2** place in recess. **3** *US* take recess; adjourn.

> ■ *noun* **1** alcove, apse, bay, cavity, corner, cranny, hollow, indentation, niche, nook. **3** adjournment, break, *colloquial* breather, breathing-space, interlude, intermission, interval, respite, rest, time off.

recession /rɪ'seʃ(ə)n/ *noun* **1** temporary decline in economic activity or prosperity. **2** receding, withdrawal.

> ■ **1** decline, depression, downturn, slump.

recessive /rɪ'sesɪv/ *adjective* **1** tending to recede. **2** (of inherited characteristic) appearing in offspring only when not masked by inherited dominant characteristic.

recherché /rə'ʃeəʃeɪ/ *adjective* **1** carefully sought out. **2** far-fetched.

recidivist /rɪ'sɪdɪvɪst/ *noun* person who relapses into crime. ▢ **recidivism** *noun*.

recipe /'resɪpɪ/ *noun* **1** statement of ingredients and procedure for preparing dish etc. **2** (+ *for*) certain means to.

> ■ **1** directions, formula, instructions, method, procedure. **2** formula, prescription.

recipient /rɪ'sɪpɪənt/ *noun* person who receives something.

reciprocal /rɪ'sɪprək(ə)l/ *adjective* **1** in return. **2** mutual. **3** inversely corresponding. **4** *Grammar* expressing mutual relation. ● *noun* *Mathematics* function or expression so related to another that their product is unity. ▢ **reciprocally** *adverb*.

> ■ *adjective* **2** exchanged, mutual, reciprocated, requited, returned. **3** complementary, corresponding.

reciprocate /rɪ'sɪprəkeɪt/ *verb* (**-ting**) **1** requite, return. **2** (+ *with*) give in return. **3** interchange. **4** (of machine part) move backwards and forwards. ▢ **reciprocation** *noun*.

> ■ **2** (*reciprocate with*) give in return, match with, repay with, respond with. **3** exchange, interchange, swap.

reciprocity /resɪ'prɒsɪtɪ/ *noun* **1** condition of being reciprocal. **2** mutual action. **3** give and take.

recital /rɪ'saɪt(ə)l/ *noun* **1** reciting, being recited. **2** concert of classical music by soloist or small group. **3** (+ *of*) detailed account of (facts etc.); narrative.

> ■ **1** narration, recitation, rehearsal, repetition. **2** concert, performance, programme. **3** account, description, narration, narrative, recounting, relation.

recitation /resɪ'teɪʃ(ə)n/ *noun* **1** reciting. **2** piece recited.

> ■ **1** declaiming, declamation, delivery, narration, performance, presentation, reading, recital, rendition, speaking, telling. **2** monologue, narration, piece, reading.

recitative /resɪtə'tiːv/ *noun* passage of singing in speech rhythm, esp. in narrative or dialogue section of opera or oratorio.

recite /rɪ'saɪt/ *verb* (**-ting**) **1** repeat aloud or declaim from memory. **2** enumerate.

> ■ **1** articulate, declaim, deliver, narrate, perform, present, quote, rattle off, recount, reel off, rehearse, relate, repeat, speak, tell.

reckless /'reklɪs/ *adjective* disregarding consequences or danger etc. ▢ **recklessly** *adverb*. **recklessness** *noun*.

> ■ brash, careless, crazy, daredevil, desperate, devil-may-care, foolhardy, hare-brained, *colloquial* harum-scarum, hasty, heedless, impetuous, imprudent, impulsive, inattentive, incautious, indiscreet, injudicious, irresponsible, mad, madcap, negligent, rash, thoughtless, unconsidered, unwise, wild.

reckon /'rekən/ *verb* **1** (often + *that*) think, consider. **2** count or compute by calculation. **3** (+ *on*) rely or base plans on. **4** (+ *with, without*) take (or fail to take) into account.

> ■ **1** see THINK *verb* 1. **2** add up, appraise, assess, calculate, compute, count, enumerate, estimate, evaluate, figure out, gauge, tally, total, value, work out.

reckoning *noun* **1** calculating. **2** opinion. **3** settlement of account.

reclaim /rɪˈkleɪm/ *verb* **1** seek return of (one's property etc.). **2** bring (land) under cultivation from sea etc. **3** win back from vice, error, or waste condition. □ **reclaimable** *adjective*. **reclamation** /reklə-/ *noun*.

■ **1** get back, recapture, recover, redeem, regain. **3** redeem, reform, regenerate, reinstate, rescue, restore, salvage, save.

recline /rɪˈklaɪn/ *verb* (**-ning**) assume or be in horizontal or leaning position.

■ lean back, lie, loll, lounge, repose, rest, sprawl, stretch out.

recluse /rɪˈkluːs/ *noun* person given to or living in seclusion. □ **reclusive** *adjective*.

■ anchoress, anchorite, hermit, loner, solitary.

recognition /rekəɡˈnɪʃ(ə)n/ *noun* recognizing, being recognized.

recognizance /rɪˈkɒɡnɪz(ə)ns/ *noun Law* **1** bond by which person undertakes to observe some condition. **2** sum pledged as surety for this.

recognize /ˈrekəɡnaɪz/ *verb* (also **-ise**) (**-zing** or **-sing**) **1** identify as already known. **2** realize or discover nature of. **3** (+ *that*) realize or admit. **4** acknowledge existence, validity, character, or claims of. **5** show appreciation of; reward. □ **recognizable** *adjective*.

■ **1** detect, diagnose, discern, distinguish, identify, know, name, notice, perceive, pick out, place, put a name to, recall, recollect, remember, see, *colloquial* spot. **2, 3** accept, acknowledge, admit, appreciate, be aware of, concede, confess, grant, realize, understand. **4** acknowledge, approve, back, endorse, legitimize, ratify, sanction, support, validate. **5** acknowledge, honour, pay tribute to, reward, salute. □ **recognizable** detectable, distinctive, distinguishable, identifiable, known, noticeable, perceptible, undisguised, unmistakable, visible.

recoil *verb* /rɪˈkɔɪl/ **1** jerk or spring back in horror, disgust, or fear. **2** shrink mentally in this way. **3** rebound. **4** (of gun) be driven backwards by discharge. ● *noun* /ˈriːkɔɪl/ act or sensation of recoiling.

■ *verb* **1, 2** blench, draw back, falter, flinch, jerk back, jump, quail, shrink, shy away, start, wince. **3** see REBOUND *verb* 1.

recollect /rekəˈlekt/ *verb* remember; call to mind.

■ recall, remember, reminisce about, think back to.

recollection /rekəˈlekʃ(ə)n/ *noun* **1** act or power of recollecting. **2** thing recollected. **3** person's memory. **4** time over which it extends.

recommend /rekəˈmend/ *verb* **1** suggest as fit for purpose or use; praise. **2** advise (course of action etc.). **3** (of qualities etc.) make acceptable or desirable. **4** (+ *to*) commend or entrust to. □ **recommendation** *noun*.

■ **1** applaud, approve of, back, commend, favour, *colloquial* plug, praise, push, put in a good word for, speak well of, support, vouch for. **2** advise,

advocate, counsel, exhort, prescribe, propose, put forward, suggest, urge. □ **recommendation** advice, advocacy, approbation, approval, backing, commendation, counsel, reference, seal of approval, support, testimonial.

recompense /ˈrekəmpens/ *verb* (**-sing**) **1** make amends to; compensate. **2** reward or punish. ● *noun* **1** reward. **2** compensation; retribution.

reconcile /ˈrekənsaɪl/ *verb* (**-ling**) **1** make friendly again after estrangement. **2** (usually **reconcile oneself** or in *passive*; + *to*) make resigned to. **3** settle (quarrel etc.). **4** harmonize; make compatible. **5** show compatibility of. □ **reconcilable** /-ˈsaɪl-/ *adjective*. **reconciler** *noun*. **reconciliation** /-sɪlɪˈeɪʃ(ə)n-/ *noun*.

■ **1** bring together, conciliate, placate, reunite, settle differences between. **2** (*be reconciled to*) accept, adjust to, resign oneself to, submit to.

recondite /ˈrekəndaɪt/ *adjective* abstruse; obscure.

recondition /riːkənˈdɪʃ(ə)n/ *verb* **1** overhaul, renovate. **2** make usable again.

■ make good, overhaul, rebuild, renew, renovate, repair, restore.

reconnaissance /rɪˈkɒnɪs(ə)ns/ *noun* **1** survey of region to locate enemy or ascertain strategic features. **2** preliminary survey.

■ examination, exploration, inspection, investigation, observation, *colloquial* recce, reconnoitring, scouting, spying, survey.

reconnoitre /rekəˈnɔɪtə/ *verb* (*US* **reconnoiter**) (**-ring**) make reconnaissance (of).

■ *slang* case, *colloquial* check out, examine, explore, gather intelligence (about), inspect, investigate, patrol, scout, scrutinize, spy, survey, *slang* suss out.

reconsider /riːkənˈsɪdə/ *verb* consider again, esp. for possible change of decision.

■ change one's mind, come round, reappraise, reassess, re-examine, rethink, review one's position, think better of.

reconstitute /riːˈkɒnstɪtjuːt/ *verb* (**-ting**) **1** reconstruct. **2** reorganize. **3** rehydrate (dried food etc.). □ **reconstitution** /-ˈtjuːʃ(ə)n/ *noun*.

reconstruct /riːkənˈstrʌkt/ *verb* **1** build again. **2** form impression of (past events) by assembling evidence. **3** re-enact (crime). **4** reorganize. □ **reconstruction** *noun*.

■ **1** see REBUILD. **3** act out, recreate, rerun.

record *noun* /ˈrekɔːd/ **1** evidence etc. constituting account of occurrence, statement, etc. **2** document etc. preserving this. **3** (in full **gramophone record**) disc carrying recorded sound in grooves, for reproduction by record player. **4** facts known about person's past, esp. criminal convictions. **5** best performance or most remarkable event of its kind. ● *verb* /rɪˈkɔːd/ **1** put in writing or other permanent form for later reference. **2** convert (sound etc.) into permanent form for later reproduction. □ **have a record** have criminal conviction. **off the record** unofficially; confidentially. **on record** officially recorded; publicly known. **recorded delivery** Post Office service in which dispatch and receipt are recorded. **record player** apparatus for reproducing sounds from gramophone records.

■ *noun* **1, 2** account, annals, archives, catalogue, chronicle, diary, documentation, dossier, file, journal, log, memorandum, minutes, narrative, note, register, report, transactions. ● *verb* **1** chronicle, document, enter, inscribe, list, log, minute, note, put down, register, set down, take down, transcribe, write down. **2** keep, preserve, tape, tape-record, video. □ **record player** gramophone, phonograph, turntable.

recorder /rɪˈkɔːdə/ *noun* **1** apparatus for recording. **2** woodwind musical instrument. **3** (also **Recorder**) barrister or solicitor serving as part-time judge.

recording /rɪˈkɔːdɪŋ/ *noun* **1** process of recording sound etc. for later reproduction. **2** material or programme recorded.

■ **2** performance, release.

recordist /rɪˈkɔːdɪst/ *noun* person who records sound.

recount /rɪˈkaʊnt/ *verb* narrate; tell in detail.

■ communicate, describe, detail, impart, narrate, recite, relate, report, tell, unfold.

re-count *verb* /riːˈkaʊnt/ count again. ● *noun* /ˈriːkaʊnt/ re-counting, esp. of votes.

recoup /rɪˈkuːp/ *verb* **1** recover or regain (loss). **2** compensate or reimburse for loss.

recourse /rɪˈkɔːs/ *noun* **1** resort to possible source of help. **2** person or thing resorted to.

recover /rɪˈkʌvə/ *verb* **1** regain possession, use, or control of. **2** return to health, consciousness, or normal state or position. **3** secure by legal process. **4** make up for; retrieve. □ **recoverable** *adjective*.

■ **1** find, get back, recapture, reclaim, recoup, regain, repossess, restore, retrieve, salvage, trace, track down, win back. **2** be on the mend, come round, convalesce, get better, heal, improve, mend, pull round, pull through, rally, recuperate, regain one's strength, revive, survive, take a turn for the better. **4** get compensation for, make good, make up for, redeem, retrieve.

re-cover /riːˈkʌvə/ *verb* **1** cover again. **2** provide (chairs etc.) with new cover.

recovery *noun* (*plural* **-ies**) recovering, being recovered.

■ advance, cure, deliverance, healing, improvement, progress, rally, recapture, reclamation, recuperation, repossession, restoration, retrieval, revival, salvage, salvaging, upturn.

recreant /ˈrekrɪənt/ *literary adjective* cowardly. ● *noun* coward.

re-create /riːkrɪˈeɪt/ *verb* (**-ting**) **1** create anew. **2** reproduce. □ **re-creation** *noun*.

recreation /rekrɪˈeɪʃ(ə)n/ *noun* **1** (means of)

entertaining oneself. **2** pleasurable activity. □ **recreation ground** public land for sports etc. □ **recreational** *adjective*.

■ amusement, distraction, diversion, enjoyment, entertainment, fun, games, hobby, leisure, pastime, play, pleasure, relaxation, sport.

recriminate /rɪˈkrɪmɪneɪt/ *verb* (**-ting**) make mutual or counter accusations. □ **recrimination** *noun*. **recriminatory** /-nət(ə)rɪ/ *adjective*.

■ □ **recrimination** accusation, *slang* comeback, counter-attack, reprisal, retaliation, retort.

recrudesce /riːkruːˈdes/ *verb* (**-cing**) *formal* (of disease, problem, etc.) break out again. □ **recrudescence** *noun*. **recrudescent** *adjective*.

recruit /rɪˈkruːt/ *noun* **1** newly enlisted serviceman or servicewoman. **2** new member of a society etc. ● *verb* **1** enlist (person) as recruit. **2** form (army etc.) by enlisting recruits. **3** replenish, reinvigorate. □ **recruitment** *noun*.

■ *noun* **1** conscript, trainee. **2** apprentice, beginner, greenhorn, initiate, learner, neophyte, new boy, new girl, novice, tiro, trainee. ● *verb* **1** advertise for, conscript, draft, engage, enlist, enrol, register, sign on, sign up, take on. **2** assemble, mobilize, muster, raise.

rectal /ˈrekt(ə)l/ *adjective* of or by means of rectum.

rectangle /ˈrektæŋg(ə)l/ *noun* plane figure with 4 straight sides and 4 right angles. □ **rectangular** /-ˈtæŋgjʊlə/ *adjective*.

rectify /ˈrektɪfaɪ/ *verb* (**-ies, -ied**) **1** adjust or make right. **2** purify, esp. by repeated distillation. **3** convert (alternating current) to direct current. □ **rectifiable** *adjective*. **rectification** /-fɪˈkeɪʃ(ə)n/ *noun*.

■ **1** amend, correct, cure, fix, make good, put right, repair, revise.

rectilinear /rektɪˈlɪnɪə/ *adjective* **1** bounded or characterized by straight lines. **2** in or forming straight line.

rectitude /ˈrektɪtjuːd/ *noun* moral uprightness.

recto /ˈrektəʊ/ *noun* (*plural* **-s**) **1** right-hand page of open book. **2** front of printed leaf.

rector /ˈrektə/ *noun* **1** incumbent of C. of E. parish where in former times all tithes passed to incumbent. **2** head priest of church or religious institution. **3** head of university or college. □ **rectorship** *noun*.

rectory *noun* (*plural* **-ies**) rector's house.

rectum /ˈrektəm/ *noun* (*plural* **-s**) final section of large intestine.

recumbent /rɪˈkʌmbənt/ *adjective* lying down; reclining.

■ flat, flat on one's back, horizontal, lying down, prone, reclining, stretched out, supine.

recuperate /rɪˈkuːpəreɪt/ *verb* (**-ting**) **1** recover from illness, exhaustion, loss, etc. **2** regain (health, loss, etc.). □ **recuperation** *noun*. **recuperative** /-rətɪv/ *adjective*.

■ **1** convalesce, get better, heal, improve, mend, rally, recover, regain strength, revive.

recur /rɪˈkɜː/ *verb* (**-rr-**) **1** occur again or repeatedly. **2** (+ *to*) go back to in thought or speech. **3** (as **recurring** *adjective*) (of decimal fraction) with same figure(s) repeated indefinitely.
■ **1** be repeated, come back again, happen again, persist, reappear, repeat, return.

recurrent /rɪˈkʌrənt/ *adjective* recurring. □ **recurrence** *noun*.
■ cyclical, frequent, intermittent, iterative, periodic, persistent, recurring, regular, repeated, repetitive, returning.

recusant /ˈrekjʊz(ə)nt/ *noun* **1** person refusing submission or compliance. **2** *esp. historical* one who refused to attend services of the Church of England. □ **recusancy** *noun*.

recycle /riːˈsaɪk(ə)l/ *verb* (**-ling**) convert (waste) to reusable material. □ **recyclable** *adjective*.
■ reclaim, recover, retrieve, reuse, salvage, use again.

red *adjective* (**-dd-**) **1** of colour from that of blood to deep pink or orange. **2** flushed. **3** bloodshot. **4** (of hair) reddish-brown. **5** having to do with bloodshed, burning, violence, or revolution. **6** *colloquial* communist. ● *noun* **1** red colour, paint, clothes, etc. **2** *colloquial* communist. □ **in the red** in debt or deficit. **red admiral** butterfly with red bands. **red-blooded** virile, vigorous. **redbrick** (of university) founded in the 19th or early 20th c. **red card** *Football* card shown by referee to player being sent off. **red carpet** privileged treatment of eminent visitor. **redcoat** *historical* British soldier. **Red Crescent** equivalent of Red Cross in Muslim countries. **Red Cross** international relief organization. **redcurrant 1** small red edible berry. **2** shrub bearing it. **red-faced** embarrassed, ashamed. **red flag 1** symbol of revolution. **2** danger signal. **red-handed** in act of crime. **redhead** person with red hair. **red herring** irrelevant diversion. **red-hot 1** heated until red. **2** *colloquial* highly exciting or excited. **3** *colloquial* (of news) completely new. **red lead** red oxide of lead as pigment. **red-letter day** joyfully noteworthy or memorable day. **red light 1** stop signal. **2** warning. **red meat** meat that is red when raw (e.g. beef). **red neck** conservative working-class white in southern US. **red pepper 1** cayenne pepper. **2** red fruit of capsicum. **red rag** thing that excites rage. **redshank** sandpiper with bright red legs. **red shift** displacement of spectrum to longer wavelengths in light from receding galaxies. **redstart** red-tailed songbird. **red tape** excessive bureaucracy or formality. **redwing** thrush with red underwings. **redwood** tree with red wood. □ **reddish** *adjective*. **redness** *noun*.
■ *adjective* **1** blood-red, brick-red, cardinal, carmine, cerise, cherry, crimson, damask, flame-coloured, magenta, maroon, rose, ruby, scarlet, Titian, vermilion, wine-coloured. **2** blushing, embarrassed, florid, flushed, glowing,

rosy, rubicund, ruddy. **4** auburn, carroty, chestnut, flame-coloured, foxy, orange, russet. □ **red herring** see DECOY.

redden *verb* make or become red; blush.
■ blush, colour, flush, glow.

redeem /rɪˈdiːm/ *verb* **1** buy back; recover by expenditure of effort. **2** make single payment to cancel (regular charge etc.). **3** convert (tokens or bonds) into goods or cash. **4** deliver from sin and damnation. **5** (often as **redeeming** *adjective*) make amends or compensate for. **6** (**redeem oneself**) make up for former fault. **7** buy freedom of. **8** save, rescue, reclaim. **9** fulfil (promise). □ **redeemable** *adjective*.
■ **1** buy back, reclaim, recover, repurchase, win back. **3** cash in, exchange for cash, trade in. **6** (**redeem oneself**) see ATONE. **7, 8** see LIBERATE 1.

redeemer *noun* one who redeems. □ **the Redeemer** Christ.

redemption /rɪˈdempʃ(ə)n/ *noun* redeeming, being redeemed.

redeploy /riːdɪˈplɔɪ/ *verb* send (troops, workers, etc.) to new place or task. □ **redeployment** *noun*.

rediffusion /riːdɪˈfjuːʒ(ə)n/ *noun* relaying of broadcast programmes, esp. by cable from central receiver.

redolent /ˈredələnt/ *adjective* **1** (+ *of, with*) strongly suggestive of. **2** strongly smelling. □ **redolence** *noun*.
■ **1** (*redolent of*) reminiscent of, suggestive of. **2** aromatic, fragrant, perfumed, scented, smelling.

redouble /riːˈdʌb(ə)l/ *verb* (**-ling**) **1** make or grow greater or more intense or numerous. **2** double again.

redoubt /rɪˈdaʊt/ *noun Military* outwork or fieldwork without flanking defences.

redoubtable /rɪˈdaʊtəb(ə)l/ *adjective* formidable.

redound /rɪˈdaʊnd/ *verb* **1** (+ *to*) make great contribution to (one's advantage etc.). **2** (+ *upon, on*) come back or recoil upon.

redress /rɪˈdres/ *verb* remedy; put right again. ● *noun* **1** reparation. **2** (+ *of*) redressing of.

reduce /rɪˈdjuːs/ *verb* (**-cing**) **1** make or become smaller or less. **2** (+ *to*) bring by force or necessity to. **3** convert to another (esp. simpler) form. **4** bring lower in status, rank, or price. **5** lessen one's weight or size. **6** make (sauce etc.) more concentrated by boiling. **7** weaken. **8** impoverish. **9** subdue. □ **reduced circumstances** poverty after relative prosperity. □ **reducible** *adjective*.
■ **1** abbreviate, abridge, clip, compress, contract, curtail, cut, cut back, cut down, decimate, decline, decrease, detract from, devalue, diminish, dock (*wages*), dwindle, ease up on, halve, lessen, limit, lower, minimize, moderate, narrow, prune, shorten, shrink, slash, slim down, tone down, trim, truncate, whittle. **3** break down, break up, convert, simplify. **4** degrade, demote, downgrade, humble, lower, move down, put down. **6** concentrate, condense, thicken. **7** see WEAKEN (WEAK). **8** impoverish, ruin.

reduction /rɪ'dʌkʃ(ə)n/ *noun* **1** reducing, being reduced. **2** amount by which prices etc. are reduced. **3** smaller copy of picture etc. □ **reductive** *adjective*.

■ **1** contraction, curtailment, cutback, deceleration (*of speed*), decimation, decline, decrease, diminution, drop, impairment, lessening, limitation, loss, moderation, narrowing, remission, shortening, shrinkage, weakening. **2** concession, cut, depreciation, devaluation, discount, rebate, refund.

redundant /rɪ'dʌnd(ə)nt/ *adjective* **1** superfluous. **2** that can be omitted without loss of significance. **3** no longer needed at work and therefore unemployed. □ **redundancy** *noun* (*plural* **-ies**).

■ **1, 2** excessive, inessential, non-essential, superfluous, supernumerary, surplus, unnecessary, unneeded, unwanted. **3** see UNEMPLOYED 1.

reduplicate /rɪ'djuːplɪkeɪt/ *verb* (**-ting**) **1** make double. **2** repeat. □ **reduplication** *noun*.

re-echo /riː'ekəʊ/ *verb* (**-es, -ed**) echo repeatedly; resound.

reed *noun* **1** firm-stemmed water or marsh plant. **2** tall straight stalk of this. **3** vibrating part of some wind instruments. □ **reedy** *adjective* (**-ier, -iest**).

reef[1] *noun* **1** ridge of rock or coral etc. at or near surface of sea. **2** lode of ore. **3** bedrock surrounding this.

reef[2] *noun* each of several strips across sail, for taking it in etc. ● *verb* take in reef(s) of (sail). □ **reef-knot** symmetrical double knot.

reefer *noun* **1** *slang* marijuana cigarette. **2** thick double-breasted jacket.

reek *verb* **1** (often + *of*) smell unpleasantly. **2** have suspicious associations. ● *noun* **1** foul or stale smell. **2** *esp. Scottish* smoke. **3** vapour; exhalation.

■ *noun* **1** *archaic* miasma, *colloquial* pong, smell, stench, stink.

reel *noun* **1** cylindrical device on which thread, paper, film, wire, etc. are wound. **2** device for winding and unwinding line as required, esp. in fishing. **3** lively folk or Scottish dance. **4** music for this. ● *verb* **1** wind on reel. **2** (+ *in, up*) draw in or up with reel. **3** stand, walk, etc. unsteadily. **4** be shaken physically or mentally. **5** dance reel. □ **reel off** recite rapidly and without apparent effort.

■ *noun* **1** bobbin, spool. ● *verb* **3** falter, lurch, pitch, rock, roll, stagger, stumble, sway, totter, waver, wobble. **4** spin, swim, whirl. □ **reel off** see RECITE 1.

re-entrant /riː'entrənt/ *adjective* (of angle) pointing inwards.

re-entry /riː'entrɪ/ *noun* (*plural* **-ies**) act of entering again, esp. (of spacecraft etc.) of re-entering earth's atmosphere.

reeve *noun historical* **1** chief magistrate of town or district. **2** official supervising landowner's estate.

ref[1] *noun colloquial* referee.

ref[2] *noun colloquial* reference.

refectory /rɪ'fektərɪ/ *noun* (*plural* **-ies**) dining-room, esp. in monastery or college. □ **refectory table** long narrow table.

refer /rɪ'fɜː/ *verb* (**-rr-**) (usually + *to*) **1** have recourse to (some authority or source of information). **2** send on or direct. **3** make allusion or be relevant. □ **referred pain** pain felt in part of body other than actual source. □ **referable** *adjective*.

■ (*refer to*) **1** consult, go to, look at, resort to, study, turn to. **2** direct to, guide to, hand over to, pass on to, recommend to, send to. **3** allude to, bring up, cite, comment on, draw attention to, make reference to, mention, name, point to, quote, speak of, specify, touch on.

referee /refə'riː/ *noun* **1** umpire, esp. in football or boxing. **2** person referred to for decision in dispute etc. **3** person willing to testify to character of applicant for employment etc. ● *verb* (**-rees, -reed**) act as referee (for).

■ *noun* **1, 2** adjudicator, arbiter, arbitrator, judge, mediator, umpire.

reference /'refərəns/ *noun* **1** referring to some authority. **2** scope given to such authority. **3** (+ *to*) relation, respect, or allusion to. **4** direction to page, book, etc. for information. **5** passage or book cited. **6** written testimonial. **7** person giving it. □ **reference book** book for occasional consultation. **with reference to** regarding; about. □ **referential** /-'ren-/ *adjective*.

■ **1** referral. **3** allusion, intimation, mention, remark. **4, 5** citation, example, illustration, instance, note, quotation. **6** endorsement, recommendation, testimonial. **7** referee. □ **with reference to** see REGARDING.

referendum /refə'rendəm/ *noun* (*plural* **-s** or **-da**) vote on political question open to entire electorate.

referral /rɪ'fɜːr(ə)l/ *noun* referring of person to medical specialist etc.

refill *verb* /riː'fɪl/ fill again. ● *noun* /'riːfɪl/ **1** thing that refills. **2** act of refilling. □ **refillable** *adjective*.

■ *verb* fill up, refuel, renew, replenish, top up.

refine /rɪ'faɪn/ *verb* (**-ning**) **1** free from impurities or defects. **2** (esp. as **refined** *adjective*) make or become more elegant or cultured. **3** (esp. as **refined** *adjective*) make or become more subtle.

■ **1** clarify, cleanse, clear, decontaminate, distil, process, purify, treat. **2** civilize, cultivate, improve, perfect, polish; (**refined**) aristocratic, civilized, courteous, courtly, cultivated, cultured, dignified, educated, elegant, genteel, gentlemanly, gracious, ladylike, polished, polite, *colloquial* posh, pretentious, prissy, sophisticated, stylish, tasteful, *colloquial* upper-crust, urbane, well bred, well brought up. **3** (**refined**) delicate, elegant, fastidious, nice, precise, sensitive, sophisticated, subtle.

refinement *noun* **1** refining, being refined. **2**

fineness of feeling or taste; elegance. **3** added development or improvement. **4** subtle reasoning. **5** fine distinction.

> ■ **2** breeding, *colloquial* class, courtesy, cultivation, delicacy, discernment, discrimination, elegance, finesse, gentility, graciousness, polish, pretentiousness, sensitivity, sophistication, style, taste, urbanity. **3** alteration, change, development, enhancement, improvement, modification, perfection. **5** distinction, nicety, nuance, subtlety.

refiner *noun* person or firm refining crude oil, metal, sugar, etc.

refinery *noun* (*plural* **-ies**) place where oil etc. is refined.

refit *verb* /riːˈfɪt/ (**-tt-**) make or become serviceable again by repairs etc. ● *noun* /ˈriːfɪt/ refitting.

reflate /riːˈfleɪt/ *verb* (**-ting**) cause reflation of (currency, economy, etc.).

reflation *noun* inflation of financial system to restore previous condition after deflation. □ **reflationary** *adjective*.

reflect /rɪˈflekt/ *verb* **1** throw back (light, heat, sound, etc.). **2** (of mirror etc.) show image of; reproduce to eye or mind. **3** correspond in appearance or effect to. **4** bring (credit, discredit, etc.). **5** (usually + *on*, *upon*) bring discredit. **6** (often + *on*, *upon*) meditate. **7** (+ *that*, *how*, etc.) consider.

> ■ **1** echo, mirror, return, send back, shine back, throw back. **3** bear witness to, correspond to, demonstrate, evidence, exhibit, illustrate, indicate, match, point to, reveal, show. **6, 7** brood, cerebrate, deliberate, meditate, ponder, ruminate, think; (*reflect on* or *upon*) chew over, consider, contemplate, mull over, reminisce about.

reflection /rɪˈflekʃ(ə)n/ *noun* **1** reflecting, being reflected. **2** reflected light, heat, colour, or image. **3** thinking; reconsideration. **4** (often + *on*) thing bringing discredit. **5** (often + *on*, *upon*) comment. **6** (usually + *of*) evidence.

> ■ **2** echo, image, likeness. **3** cerebration, cogitation, consideration, contemplation, deliberation, meditation, pondering, rumination, self-examination, study, thinking, thought. **4** aspersion, censure, criticism, discredit, imputation, reproach, shame, slur. **6** demonstration, evidence, indication, manifestation, result.

reflective *adjective* **1** (of surface) reflecting. **2** (of mental faculties) concerned in reflection or

thought. **3** thoughtful. □ **reflectively** *adverb*.

> ■ **1** glittering, lustrous, shiny, silvery. **3** see
> THOUGHTFUL 1.

reflector *noun* **1** piece of glass or metal for reflecting light in required direction. **2** telescope etc. using mirror to produce images.

reflex /ˈriːfleks/ *adjective* **1** (of action) independent of will. **2** (of angle) larger than 180°. ● *noun* **1** reflex action. **2** sign; secondary manifestation. **3** reflected light or image. □ **reflex camera** camera in which image is reflected by mirror to enable correct focusing.

reflexive /rɪˈfleksɪv/ *Grammar adjective* **1** (of word or form) referring back to subject (e.g. *myself* in *I hurt myself*) (see panel). **2** (of verb) having reflexive pronoun as object. ● *noun* reflexive word or form.

reflexology /riːflekˈsɒlədʒɪ/ *noun* massage to areas of soles of feet. □ **reflexologist** *noun*.

reform /rɪˈfɔːm/ *verb* **1** make or become better. **2** abolish or cure (abuse etc.). ● *noun* **1** removal of abuses, esp. political. **2** improvement. □ **reformable** *adjective*. **reformative** *adjective*.

> ■ *verb* **1** ameliorate, amend, better, change, convert, correct, improve, mend, purge, put right, reconstitute, reconstruct, rectify, regenerate, remodel, reorganize, revolutionize, save.

reformation /refəˈmeɪʃ(ə)n/ *noun* **1** reforming or being reformed, esp. radical improvement in political, religious, or social affairs. **2** (**the Reformation**) 16th-c. movement for reform of abuses in Roman Church ending in establishment of Reformed or Protestant Churches.

reformatory /rɪˈfɔːmətərɪ/ *noun* (*plural* **-ies**) *US* & *historical* institution for reform of young offenders. ● *adjective* producing reform.

reformer *noun* advocate of reform.

reformism *noun* policy of reform rather than abolition or revolution. □ **reformist** *noun* & *adjective*.

refract /rɪˈfrækt/ *verb* deflect (light) at certain angle when it enters obliquely from another medium. □ **refraction** *noun*. **refractive** *adjective*.

refractor *noun* **1** refracting medium or lens. **2** telescope using lens to produce image.

refractory /rɪˈfræktərɪ/ *adjective* **1** stubborn, unmanageable, rebellious. **2** resistant to treatment. **3** hard to fuse or work.

Reflexive pronoun

Reflexive pronouns (*himself*, *yourselves*, etc.) are used in two ways:

1 for a direct or indirect object that refers to the same person or thing as the subject of the clause:

> *They didn't hurt themselves.*
> *He wanted it for himself.*

2 for emphasis:

> *She said so herself.*
> *I myself do not believe her.*

refrain[1] /rɪ'freɪn/ *verb* (+ *from*) avoid doing (action).

■ (*refrain from*) abstain from, avoid, *formal* cease, desist from, do without, *formal* eschew, *formal* forbear, leave off, *US* quit, renounce, stop.

refrain[2] /rɪ'freɪn/ *noun* recurring phrase or lines, esp. at ends of stanzas.

refresh /rɪ'freʃ/ *verb* **1** give fresh spirit or vigour to. **2** revive (memory).

■ **1** cool, energize, enliven, fortify, freshen, invigorate, perk up, quench the thirst of, reanimate, rejuvenate, renew, restore, resuscitate, revitalize, revive, slake (*thirst*). **2** activate, awaken, jog, prod, prompt, revive, stimulate.

refresher *noun* **1** something that refreshes, esp. drink. **2** extra fee to counsel in prolonged lawsuit. □ **refresher course** course reviewing or updating previous studies.

refreshing *adjective* **1** restoring energy. **2** interesting because unfamiliar. □ **refreshingly** *adverb.*

■ **1** bracing, cool, enlivening, exhilarating, inspiriting, invigorating, restorative, reviving, stimulating, thirst-quenching, tingling, tonic. **2** different, fresh, interesting, new, novel, original, unexpected, unfamiliar, unforeseen, unpredictable, welcome.

refreshment *noun* **1** refreshing, being refreshed. **2** (usually in *plural*) food or drink.

■ **2** (*refreshments*) drinks, eatables, *colloquial* eats, food, nibbles, snacks.

refrigerant /rɪ'frɪdʒərənt/ *noun* substance used for refrigeration. ● *adjective* cooling.

refrigerate /rɪ'frɪdʒəreɪt/ *verb* (**-ting**) cool or freeze (esp. food). □ **refrigeration** *noun.*

■ chill, cool, freeze, ice, keep cold.

refrigerator *noun* cabinet or room in which food etc. is refrigerated.

refuge /'refjuːdʒ/ *noun* **1** shelter from pursuit, danger, or trouble. **2** person or place offering this.

■ **1** asylum, cover, protection, safety, sanctuary, security, shelter. **2** bolt-hole, cover, harbour, haven, hideaway, hideout, hiding place, retreat, sanctuary, shelter, stronghold.

refugee /refjʊ'dʒiː/ *noun* person taking refuge, esp. in foreign country, from war, persecution, etc.

■ displaced person, émigré, exile, fugitive, outcast, runaway.

refulgent /rɪ'fʌldʒ(ə)nt/ *adjective literary* shining; gloriously bright. □ **refulgence** *noun.*

refund /rɪ'fʌnd/ **1** pay back (money etc.). **2** reimburse. ● *noun* /'riːfʌnd/ **1** act of refunding. **2** sum refunded. □ **refundable** /rɪ'fʌn-/ *adjective.*

■ *verb* give back, pay back, reimburse, repay, return. ● *noun* rebate, repayment.

refurbish /riː'fɜːbɪʃ/ *verb* **1** brighten up. **2** redecorate. □ **refurbishment** *noun.*

refusal /rɪ'fjuːz(ə)l/ *noun* **1** refusing, being refused. **2** (in full **first refusal**) chance of taking thing before it is offered to others.

■ **1** brush-off, denial, rebuff, rejection, veto.

refuse[1] /rɪ'fjuːz/ *verb* (**-sing**) **1** withhold acceptance of or consent to. **2** not grant (request) made by (person). **3** (often + *to do*) indicate unwillingness. **4** (of horse) be unwilling to jump (fence etc.).

■ **1** decline, *colloquial* pass up, rebuff, reject, repudiate, say no to, spurn, turn down, veto. **2** deny, deprive of, disallow, withhold. **4** baulk at, jib at.

refuse[2] /'refjuːs/ *noun* items rejected as worthless; waste.

■ detritus, dirt, *US* garbage, junk, litter, rubbish, *esp. US* trash, waste.

refusenik /rɪ'fjuːznɪk/ *noun* **1** *historical* Soviet Jew refused permission to emigrate to Israel. **2** person who refuses to follow orders, esp. as protest.

refute /rɪ'fjuːt/ *verb* (**-ting**) **1** prove falsity or error of. **2** rebut by argument. **3** *disputed* deny or contradict (without argument). □ **refutation** /refjʊ'teɪʃ(ə)n/ *noun.*

USAGE The use of *refute* to mean 'deny, contradict' is considered incorrect by some people. *Repudiate* can be used instead.

■ **1, 2** counter, discredit, disprove, negate, prove wrong, rebut.

reg /redʒ/ *noun colloquial* registration mark.

regain /rɪ'geɪn/ *verb* obtain possession or use of after loss.

■ be reunited with, find, get back, recapture, reclaim, recoup, recover, repossess, retake, retrieve, return to, win back.

regal /'riːg(ə)l/ *adjective* **1** of or by monarch(s). **2** magnificent. □ **regality** /rɪ'gæl-/ *noun.* **regally** *adverb.*

■ **1** imperial, kingly, majestic, princely, queenly, royal, sovereign. **2** grand, lordly, magnificent, majestic, noble, palatial, splendid, stately.

regale /rɪ'geɪl/ *verb* (**-ling**) **1** entertain lavishly with feasting. **2** (+ *with*) entertain with (talk etc.).

regalia /rɪ'geɪlɪə/ *plural noun* insignia of royalty or an order, mayor, etc.

regard /rɪ'gɑːd/ *verb* **1** gaze on. **2** heed; take into account. **3** look upon or think of in specified way. ● *noun* **1** gaze; steady look. **2** attention, care. **3** esteem. **4** (in *plural*) expression of friendliness in letter etc. □ **as regards** about; in respect of. **in this regard** on this point. **in, with regard to** in respect of.

■ *verb* **1** *literary* behold, contemplate, eye, gaze at, gaze on, keep an eye on, look at, note, observe, scrutinize, stare at, view, watch. **3** account, consider, *formal* deem, *formal* esteem, judge, look upon, perceive, rate, reckon, think of, view, *colloquial* weigh up; (*regard highly*) esteem, respect, value. ● *noun* **1** gaze, look, scrutiny, stare.

2 attention, care, concern, consideration, deference, heed, notice, sympathy, thought. **3** admiration, affection, appreciation, approbation, approval, deference, esteem, favour, honour, love, respect, reverence, veneration.

regardful *adjective* (+ *of*) mindful of.

regarding *preposition* concerning; in respect of.
■ about, *colloquial* apropos, concerning, connected with, involving, on the subject of, pertaining to, re, respecting, with reference to, with regard to.

regardless *adjective* (+ *of*) without regard or consideration for. ● *adverb* without paying attention.
■ *adjective* (*regardless of*) careless about, despite, heedless of, indifferent to, neglectful of, notwithstanding, unconcerned about, unmindful of.

regatta /rɪ'gætə/ *noun* event consisting of rowing or yacht races.

regency /'ri:dʒənsɪ/ *noun* (*plural* **-ies**) **1** office of regent. **2** commission acting as regent. **3** regent's or regency commission's period of office. **4** (**Regency**) (in UK) period from 1811 to 1820.

regenerate *verb* /rɪ'dʒenəreɪt/ (**-ting**) **1** bring or come into renewed existence. **2** improve moral condition of. **3** impart new, more vigorous, or spiritually higher life or nature to. **4** regrow or cause (new tissue) to regrow. ● *adjective* /-rət/ **1** spiritually born again. **2** reformed. □ **regeneration** *noun*. **regenerative** /-rətɪv/ *adjective*.

regent /'ri:dʒ(ə)nt/ *noun* person acting as head of state because monarch is absent, ill, or a child. ● *adjective* (after noun) acting as regent.

reggae /'regeɪ/ *noun* W. Indian style of music with strongly accented subsidiary beat.

regicide /'redʒɪsaɪd/ *noun* **1** person who kills or helps to kill a king. **2** killing of a king.

regime /reɪ'ʒi:m/ *noun* (also **régime**) **1** method of government. **2** prevailing system. **3** regimen.
■ **1** administration, control, discipline, government, leadership, management, order, reign, rule, system.

regimen /'redʒɪmən/ *noun* prescribed course of exercise, way of life, and diet.

regiment *noun* /'redʒɪmənt/ **1** permanent unit of army consisting of several companies, troops, or batteries. **2** (usually + *of*) large or formidable array or number. ● *verb* /-ment/ **1** organize in groups or according to system. **2** form into regiment(s). □ **regimentation** /-men-/ *noun*.
■ *verb* **1** arrange, control, discipline, organize, regulate, systematize.

regimental /redʒɪ'ment(ə)l/ *adjective* of a regiment. ● *noun* (in *plural*) military uniform, esp. of particular regiment.

Regina /rɪ'dʒaɪnə/ *noun* **1** (after name) reigning queen. **2** *Law* the Crown. [Latin]

region /'ri:dʒ(ə)n/ *noun* **1** geographical area or division, having definable boundaries or characteristics. **2** administrative area, esp. in Scotland. **3** part of body. **4** sphere, realm. □ **in the region of** approximately. □ **regional** *adjective*. **regionally** *adverb*.
■ **1, 2** area, country, department, district, division, expanse, land, locality, neighbourhood, part, place, province, quarter, *Military* sector, territory, tract, vicinity, zone.

register /'redʒɪstə/ *noun* **1** official list. **2** book in which items are recorded for reference. **3** device recording speed, force, etc. **4** compass of voice or instrument. **5** form of language used in particular circumstances. **6** adjustable plate for regulating draught etc. ● *verb* **1** set down formally; record in writing. **2** enter or cause to be entered in register. **3** send (letter) by registered post. **4** record automatically; indicate. **5** make mental note of. **6** show (emotion etc.) in face etc. **7** make impression. □ **registered post** postal procedure with special precautions and compensation in case of loss. **register office** state office where civil marriages are conducted and births, marriages, and deaths are recorded.
■ *noun* **1, 2** archive(s), catalogue, chronicle, diary, directory, file, index, inventory, journal, ledger, list, record, roll. ● *verb* **1** make official, minute, present, record, set down, submit, write down. **2** catalogue, check in (*as hotel guest*), enlist, enrol, enter, enter one's name, join, list, log, sign in, sign on. **5** keep in mind, make a note of, mark, notice, take account of. **6** betray, display, divulge, express, indicate, manifest, reflect, reveal, show.

registrar /redʒɪ'strɑː/ *noun* **1** official keeping register. **2** chief administrator in university etc. **3** hospital doctor training as specialist.

registration /redʒɪ'streɪʃ(ə)n/ *noun* registering, being registered. □ **registration mark, number** combination of letters and numbers identifying vehicle.

registry /'redʒɪstrɪ/ *noun* (*plural* **-ies**) place where registers or records are kept. □ **registry office** register office (the official name).

Regius professor /'ri:dʒɪəs/ *noun* holder of university chair founded by sovereign or filled by Crown appointment.

regress *verb* /rɪ'gres/ **1** move backwards. **2** return to former stage or state. ● *noun* /'ri:gres/ act of regressing. □ **regression** /rɪ'greʃ(ə)n/ *noun*. **regressive** /rɪ'gresɪv/ *adjective*.
■ *verb* **1** fall back, go back, move backwards, retreat, slip back. **2** backslide, degenerate, deteriorate, retrogress, revert, slip back.

regret /rɪ'gret/ *verb* (**-tt-**) **1** feel or express sorrow, repentance, or distress over (action or loss). **2** say with sorrow or remorse. ● *noun* sorrow, repentance, or distress over action or loss. □ **regretful** *adjective*. **regretfully** *adverb*.
■ *verb* bemoan, be sad (about), bewail, deplore, feel remorse (about), grieve (about), lament, mourn, repent (of), reproach oneself (about), rue, weep (for). ● *noun* bad conscience, compunction, contrition, disappointment, grief, guilt, penitence,

pricking of conscience, remorse, repentance, sadness, self-accusation, self-condemnation, self-reproach, shame, sorrow. □ **regretful** apologetic, ashamed, bad, conscience-stricken, contrite, disappointed, guilty, penitent, remorseful, repentant, rueful, sad, sorry.

regrettable *adjective* undesirable, unwelcome; deserving censure. □ **regrettably** *adverb*.
■ deplorable, disappointing, distressing, lamentable, reprehensible, sad, shameful, undesirable, unfortunate, unhappy, unlucky, unwanted, upsetting, woeful, wrong.

regular /'regjʊlə/ *adjective* **1** acting, done, or recurring uniformly; orderly. **2** habitual, usual. **3** conforming to rule or principle. **4** conforming to correct procedure etc. **5** symmetrical. **6** *Grammar* (of verb etc.) following normal type of inflection. **7** *colloquial* absolute, thorough. **8** (of soldier etc.) permanent, professional. ● *noun* **1** regular soldier. **2** *colloquial* regular customer, visitor, etc. **3** one of regular clergy. □ **regularity** /-'lærɪtɪ/ *noun*. **regularize** *verb* (also **-ise**) (**-zing** or **-sing**). **regularly** *adverb*.
■ *adjective* **1** consistent, constant, dependable, equal, even, fixed, measured, ordered, orderly, periodic, predictable, recurring, reliable, repeated, rhythmic, steady, systematic, uniform, unvarying. **2** accustomed, common, commonplace, customary, everyday, familiar, frequent, habitual, normal, ordinary, routine, scheduled, typical, usual. **3, 4** conventional, established, known, normal, official, orthodox, prevailing, proper, standard, traditional. **5** even, symmetric, symmetrical. ● *noun* **2** frequenter, *habitué*, patron.

regulate /'regjʊleɪt/ *verb* (**-ting**) **1** control by rule. **2** subject to restrictions. **3** adapt to requirements. **4** adjust (clock, watch, etc.) to work accurately. □ **regulator** *noun*.
■ **1** administer, conduct, control, direct, govern, manage, monitor, order, organize, oversee, restrict, supervise. **3, 4** adjust, alter, balance, change, get right, moderate, modify, set, vary.

regulation *noun* **1** regulating, being regulated. **2** prescribed rule. ● *adjective* in accordance with regulations, of correct pattern etc.
■ *noun* **2** by-law, commandment, decree, dictate, directive, edict, law, order, ordinance, requirement, restriction, rule, ruling, statute.

regulo /'regjʊləʊ/ *noun* (usually + numeral) number on scale denoting temperature in gas oven.

regurgitate /rɪ'gɜːdʒɪteɪt/ *verb* (**-ting**) **1** bring (swallowed food) up again to mouth. **2** reproduce (information etc.). □ **regurgitation** *noun*.

rehabilitate /riːhə'bɪlɪteɪt/ *verb* (**-ting**) **1** restore to normal life by training etc., esp. after imprisonment or illness. **2** restore to former privileges or reputation or to proper condition. □ **rehabilitation** *noun*.

rehash *verb* /riː'hæʃ/ put into new form without significant change or improvement. ● *noun* /'riːhæʃ/ **1** material rehashed. **2** rehashing.

rehearsal /rɪ'hɜːs(ə)l/ *noun* **1** trial performance or practice. **2** rehearsing.
■ **1** *colloquial* dry run, dummy run, exercise, practice, preparation, run-through, try-out.

rehearse /rɪ'hɜːs/ *verb* (**-sing**) **1** practise before performing in public. **2** recite or say over. **3** give list of; enumerate. □ **rehearsed** *adjective*.
■ **1** drill, go over, practise, prepare, run over, run through, try out. □ **rehearsed** calculated, practised, pre-arranged, premeditated, prepared, scripted, studied, thought out.

Reich /raɪx/ *noun* former German state, esp. Third Reich (1933–45).

reign /reɪn/ *verb* **1** be king or queen. **2** prevail. **3** (as **reigning** *adjective*) currently holding title. ● *noun* **1** sovereignty, rule. **2** sovereign's period of rule.
■ *verb* **1** be on the throne, command, govern, have power, hold sway, rule, wear the crown. ● *noun* **1** administration, ascendancy, command, government, jurisdiction, power, rule, sovereignty.

reimburse /riːɪm'bɜːs/ *verb* (**-sing**) repay (person); refund. □ **reimbursement** *noun*.

rein /reɪn/ *noun* (in *singular* or *plural*) **1** long narrow strap used to guide horse. **2** means of control. ● *verb* **1** (+ *back*, *up*, *in*) pull back or up or hold in (as) with reins. **2** govern, control.

reincarnate *verb* /riːɪn'kɑːneɪt/ (**-ting**) give esp. human form to again. ● *adjective* /-nət/ reincarnated.

reincarnation /riːɪnkɑː'neɪʃ(ə)n/ *noun* rebirth of soul in new body.
■ rebirth, transmigration.

reindeer /'reɪndɪə/ *noun* (*plural* same or **-s**) sub-arctic deer with large antlers.

reinforce /riːɪn'fɔːs/ *verb* (**-cing**) support or strengthen, esp. with additional personnel or material. □ **reinforced concrete** concrete with metal bars etc. embedded in it.
■ add to, assist, augment, back up, bolster, buttress, fortify, help, hold up, prop up, stiffen, strengthen, supplement, support, toughen.

reinforcement *noun* **1** reinforcing, being reinforced. **2** (in *plural*) additional personnel, equipment, etc.
■ **2** (*reinforcements*) auxiliaries, backup, help, reserves, support.

reinstate /riːɪn'steɪt/ *verb* (**-ting**) **1** replace in former position. **2** restore to former privileges. □ **reinstatement** *noun*.
■ **1** recall, rehabilitate, restore, take back, welcome back.

reinsure /riːɪn'ʃʊə/ *verb* (**-ring**) insure again (esp. of insurer transferring risk to another insurer). □ **reinsurance** *noun*.

reiterate /riː'ɪtəreɪt/ *verb* (**-ting**) say or do again or repeatedly. □ **reiteration** /-'reɪʃ(ə)n/ *noun*. **reiterative** /-rətɪv/ *adjective*.

reject *verb* /rɪ'dʒekt/ **1** put aside or send back as not to be used, done, or complied with. **2** refuse to accept or believe in. **3** rebuff. ● *noun* /'riːdʒekt/ rejected thing or person. □ **rejection** /rɪ'dʒek-/ *noun*.

■ *verb* **1** brush aside, cast off, discard, discount, dismiss, eliminate, exclude, jettison, junk, put aside, scrap, send back, throw away, throw out. **2** decline, refuse, renounce, say no to, turn down, veto. **3** disown, *colloquial* drop, give the cold shoulder to, jilt, rebuff, renounce, repel, repudiate, repulse, *colloquial* send packing, shun, spurn, turn one's back on.

rejoice /rɪ'dʒɔɪs/ *verb* (**-cing**) **1** feel joy; be glad. **2** (+ *in, at*) take delight in.

■ be happy, celebrate, delight, exult, glory, revel, triumph.

rejoin[1] /riː'dʒɔɪn/ *verb* join again; reunite.

rejoin[2] /rɪ'dʒɔɪn/ *verb* say in answer; retort.

rejoinder /rɪ'dʒɔɪndə/ *noun* reply, retort.

rejuvenate /rɪ'dʒuːvəneɪt/ *verb* (**-ting**) make (as if) young again. □ **rejuvenation** *noun*.

relapse /rɪ'læps/ *verb* (**-sing**) (usually + *into*) fall back (into worse state after improvement). ● *noun* relapsing, esp. deterioration in patient's condition after partial recovery.

■ *verb* backslide, degenerate, deteriorate, fall back, lapse, regress, revert, sink back, slip back, weaken. ● *noun* degeneration, deterioration, recurrence (*of illness*), regression, reversion, setback, worsening.

relate /rɪ'leɪt/ *verb* (**-ting**) **1** narrate, recount. **2** (usually + *to, with*) connect in thought or meaning. **3** (+ *to*) have reference to. **4** (+ *to*) feel connected or sympathetic to.

■ **1** communicate, describe, detail, divulge, impart, make known, narrate, present, recite, recount, rehearse, report, reveal, tell. **2** associate, compare, connect, consider together, coordinate, correlate, couple, join, link. **3** (*relate to*) appertain to, apply to, have a bearing on, be relevant to, concern, go with, pertain to, refer to. **4** (*relate to*) be friends with, empathize with, fraternize with,

handle, have a relationship with, identify with, socialize with, understand.

related *adjective* connected, esp. by blood or marriage.

■ affiliated, akin, allied, associated, cognate, comparable, connected, consanguineous, interconnected, interdependent, interrelated, joined, joint, linked, parallel, reciprocal, relative, similar, twin.

relation /rɪ'leɪʃ(ə)n/ *noun* **1** connection between people or things. **2** relative. **3** (in *plural*) dealings (with others). **4** narration.

■ **2** kinsman, kinswoman, member of the family, relative; (*relations*) kin, kith and kin. **4** see NARRATION (NARRATE).

relationship *noun* **1** state of being related. **2** connection, association. **3** *colloquial* emotional association between two people.

■ **1** consanguinity, kinship. **2** affiliation, affinity, association, attachment, bond, closeness, connection, correlation, correspondence, interconnection, interdependence, link, parallel, pertinence, rapport, ratio, similarity, tie, understanding. **3** affair, alliance, friendship, intrigue, liaison, love affair, romance, sexual relations.

relative /'relətɪv/ *adjective* **1** in relation or proportion to something else; implying comparison or relation. **2** (+ *to*) having application or reference to. **3** *Grammar* (of word, esp. pronoun) referring to expressed or implied antecedent and attaching subordinate clause to it (e.g. *which, who*); (of clause) attached to antecedent by relative word (see panel). ● *noun* **1** person connected by blood or marriage. **2** species related to another by common origin. **3** relative word, esp. pronoun. □ **relative density** ratio between density of substance and that of a standard (usually water or air). □ **relatively** *adverb*.

■ *adjective* **1** comparative, proportional, proportionate, related; (*relative to*) commensurate with, corresponding to. **2** see RELEVANT. ● *noun* **1** see RELATION 2.

Relative clause

A relative clause is a subordinate clause used to add to the meaning of a noun. A relative clause is usually introduced by a relative pronoun (*who, which, that*).

Restrictive relative clauses are distinguished from non-restrictive relative clauses by punctuation. A non-restrictive relative clause has commas round it, e.g.

Please approach any member of our staff, who will be pleased to help, and discuss your needs.

The shopkeeper who left the commas out turned this into a restrictive relative clause, implying that there were other members of staff who would not be pleased to help!

The relative pronoun *whom* (the objective case of *who*) is now used only in formal writing.

The person whom he hit was a policeman. (formal)
The person who he hit was a policeman. (less formal)

The relative pronoun may be omitted if it is the object of the relative clause:

The person he hit was a policeman.

relativity /relə'tɪvɪtɪ/ *noun* **1** relativeness. **2** *Physics* theory based on principle that all motion is relative and that light has constant velocity in a vacuum.

relax /rɪ'læks/ *verb* **1** make or become less stiff, rigid, or tense. **2** make or become less formal or strict. **3** reduce (attention, efforts). **4** cease work or effort. **5** (as **relaxed** *adjective*) at ease, unperturbed.

> ■ **1** calm down, cool down, ease (up), let go, loosen, release, relieve, soften, unbend, unclench, unfasten, unwind. **2** curb, mitigate, moderate, temper, tone down. **3** abate, decrease, diminish, ease, lessen, moderate, reduce, slacken, weaken. **4** ease up, rest, slow down, take it easy, *colloquial* unwind. **5** (**relaxed**) at ease, blasé, calm, carefree, casual, comfortable, contented, cool, cosy, easy, easygoing, free and easy, friendly, good-humoured, happy, happy-go-lucky, informal, insouciant, *colloquial* laid-back, lax, leisurely, light-hearted, nonchalant, peaceful, restful, serene, slack, tranquil, unconcerned, unhurried, untroubled.

relaxation /riːlæk'seɪʃ(ə)n/ *noun* **1** relaxing. **2** rest or recreation.

> ■ **1** abatement, alleviation, diminution, lessening, *colloquial* let-up, loosening up, mitigation, moderation, slackening, weakening. **2** diversion, ease, leisure, pleasure, recreation, repose, rest.

relay /'riːleɪ/ *noun* **1** fresh set of people etc. to replace tired ones. **2** supply of material similarly used. **3** relay race. **4** device activating electric circuit. **5** device transmitting broadcast. **6** relayed transmission. ● *verb* /also rɪ'leɪ/ receive (esp. broadcast message) and transmit to others. □ **relay race** one between teams of which each member in turn covers part of distance.

> ■ *noun* **6** broadcast, programme, transmission.
> ● *verb* broadcast, communicate, pass on, send out, spread, televise, transmit.

release /rɪ'liːs/ *verb* (**-sing**) **1** (often + *from*) set free, liberate, unfasten. **2** allow to move from fixed position. **3** make (information) public. **4** issue (film etc.) generally. ● *noun* **1** liberation from restriction, duty, or difficulty. **2** handle, catch, etc. that releases part of mechanism. **3** item made available for publication. **4** film, record, etc. that is released. **5** releasing of film etc.

> ■ *verb* **1** acquit, allow out, deliver, discharge, emancipate, excuse, exonerate, free, let go, let loose, let off, liberate, loose, pardon, rescue, save, set free, set loose, unchain, unfasten, unfetter, unleash, unshackle, untie. **2** fire off, launch, let fly, let off, send off. **3** circulate, disseminate, distribute, issue, make available, present, publish, put out, send out, unveil.

relegate /'relɪgeɪt/ *verb* (**-ting**) **1** consign or dismiss to inferior position. **2** transfer (team) to lower division of league. **3** banish. □ **relegation** *noun*.

> ■ **1** demote, downgrade, put down. **3** banish, exile.

relent /rɪ'lent/ *verb* **1** relax severity. **2** yield to compassion.

> ■ acquiesce, be merciful, capitulate, give in, give way, relax, show pity, soften, weaken, yield.

relentless *adjective* **1** unrelenting. **2** unceasing. □ **relentlessly** *adverb*.

> ■ **1** cruel, dogged, fierce, hard-hearted, implacable, inexorable, intransigent, merciless, obdurate, obstinate, pitiless, remorseless, ruthless, uncompromising, unfeeling, unforgiving, unmerciful, unyielding. **2** continuous, incessant, non-stop, persistent, unceasing, unrelieved, unstoppable.

relevant /'relɪv(ə)nt/ *adjective* (often + *to*) bearing on or pertinent to matter in hand. □ **relevance** *noun*.

> ■ appertaining, applicable, apposite, appropriate, apropos, apt, connected, essential, fitting, germane, linked, material, pertinent, proper, related, relative, significant, suitable, suited, to the point.

reliable /rɪ'laɪəb(ə)l/ *adjective* that may be relied on. □ **reliability** *noun*. **reliably** *adverb*.

> ■ certain, conscientious, consistent, constant, dependable, devoted, efficient, faithful, honest, infallible, loyal, predictable, proven, punctilious, regular, reputable, responsible, safe, solid, sound, stable, staunch, steady, sure, trusted, trustworthy, *archaic* or *jocular* trusty, unchanging, unfailing.

reliance /rɪ'laɪəns/ *noun* (+ *in*, *on*) trust or confidence in. □ **reliant** *adjective*.

relic /'relɪk/ *noun* **1** object interesting because of its age or associations. **2** part of holy person's body or belongings kept as object of reverence. **3** surviving custom, belief, etc. from past age. **4** (in *plural*) what is left. **5** (in *plural*) dead body or remains of person.

> ■ **1** heirloom, keepsake, memento, reminder, souvenir, token. **4** (*relics*) see REMAINS 1. **5** (*relics*) see REMAINS 3.

relict /'relɪkt/ *noun* object surviving in primitive form.

relief /rɪ'liːf/ *noun* **1** (feeling accompanying) alleviation of or deliverance from pain, distress, etc. **2** feature etc. that diversifies monotony or relaxes tension. **3** assistance given to people in special need. **4** replacing of person(s) on duty by another or others. **5** person(s) thus bringing relief. **6** thing supplementing another in some service. **7** method of carving, moulding, etc., in which design projects from surface. **8** piece of sculpture etc. in relief. **9** effect of being done in relief given by colour or shading etc. **10** vividness, distinctness. □ **relief map** one showing hills and valleys by shading or colouring etc.

> ■ **1** abatement, alleviation, assuagement, comfort, deliverance, diversion, ease, easing, *colloquial* let-up, mitigation, palliation, relaxation, release, respite, rest. **3** aid, assistance, help, support. **5** see SUBSTITUTE *noun* **1**.

relieve /rɪ'liːv/ *verb* (**-ving**) **1** bring or give relief to. **2** reduce (pain, distress, etc.). **3** mitigate tedium of. **4** release (person) from duty by acting as or providing substitute. **5** (+ *of*) take (burden or duty) away from. □ **relieve oneself** urinate, defecate. □ **relieved** *adjective*.

■ **2** abate, alleviate, assuage, calm, comfort, console, cure, diminish, dull, ease, help, lessen, lift, lighten, mitigate, moderate, palliate, reduce, relax, soften, soothe. **5** (*relieve of*) disburden of, disencumber of, release from, rescue from, rid of, unburden of.

religion /rɪ'lɪdʒ(ə)n/ *noun* **1** belief in super-human controlling power, esp. in personal God or gods entitled to obedience. **2** study of religious belief. **3** particular system of faith and worship.

■ **1** belief, faith, theism. **2** divinity, theology. **3** creed, cult, denomination, faith, persuasion, sect.

religiosity /rɪlɪdʒɪ'ɒsɪtɪ/ *noun* state of being reli-gious or too religious.

religious /rɪ'lɪdʒəs/ *adjective* **1** devoted to reli-gion; devout. **2** of or concerned with religion. **3** of or belonging to monastic order. **4** scrupulous. ● *noun* (*plural* same) person bound by monastic vows. □ **religiously** *adverb*.

■ *adjective* **1** churchgoing, devout, God-fearing, godly, pious, reverent, righteous, saintly, spiritual. **2** devotional, divine, holy, sacramental, sacred, scriptural, theological.

relinquish /rɪ'lɪŋkwɪʃ/ *verb* **1** give up; let go. **2** resign; surrender. □ **relinquishment** *noun*.

■ concede, give in, hand over, part with, submit, surrender, yield.

reliquary /'relɪkwərɪ/ *noun* (*plural* **-ies**) recep-tacle for relic(s).

relish /'relɪʃ/ *noun* **1** (often + *for*) liking or enjoy-ment. **2** appetizing flavour. **3** attractive quality. **4** thing eaten with plainer food to add flavour. **5** (+ *of*) distinctive flavour or taste of. ● *verb* **1** get pleasure out of; enjoy greatly. **2** anticipate with pleasure.

■ *noun* **1** appetite, delight, enjoyment, enthusiasm, gusto, pleasure, zest. **2, 4** flavour, piquancy, savour, tang, taste. ● *verb* **1** appreciate, delight in, enjoy, like, love, revel in, savour, take pleasure in.

reluctant /rɪ'lʌkt(ə)nt/ *adjective* (often + *to do*) unwilling, disinclined. □ **reluctance** *noun*. **reluctantly** *adverb*.

■ averse, disinclined, grudging, hesitant, loath, unenthusiastic, unwilling.

rely /rɪ'laɪ/ *verb* (**-ies**, **-ied**) (+ *on*, *upon*) **1** depend with confidence on. **2** be dependent on.

■ (*rely on*) *colloquial* bank on, count on, depend on, have confidence in, lean on, put one's faith in, *colloquial* swear by, trust.

REM *abbreviation* rapid eye movement.

remade *past* and *past participle* of REMAKE.

remain /rɪ'meɪn/ *verb* **1** be left over. **2** stay in same place or condition; be left behind. **3** con-tinue to be. □ **remaining** *adjective*.

■ **2** *archaic* abide, be left, carry on, continue, endure, keep on, linger, live on, persevere, persist, stay, *colloquial* stay put, survive, *archaic* tarry, wait. **3** continue (to be), stay. □ **remaining** see RESIDUAL.

remainder /rɪ'meɪndə/ *noun* **1** residue. **2** re-maining people or things. **3** number left after subtraction or division. **4** (any of) copies of book left unsold. ● *verb* dispose of remainder of (book) at reduced prices.

■ *noun* **1, 2** balance, excess, remains, remnants, residue, residuum, the rest, surplus.

remains /rɪ'meɪnz/ *plural noun* **1** what remains after other parts have been removed or used. **2** relics of antiquity etc. **3** dead body.

■ **1** crumbs, debris, detritus, dregs, fragments, leftovers, oddments, odds and ends, offcuts, relics, remainder, remnants, residue, rubble, ruins, scraps, traces, vestiges, wreckage. **2** antiquities, archaeological remains, relics, ruins, traces. **3** ashes, body, bones, carcass, corpse, relics.

remake *verb* /riː'meɪk/ (**-king**; *past* and *past par-ticiple* **remade**) make again or differently. ● *noun* /'riːmeɪk/ remade thing, esp. cinema film.

■ *verb* piece together, rebuild, reconstitute, reconstruct, redo, renew.

remand /rɪ'mɑːnd/ *verb* return (prisoner) to custody, esp. to allow further inquiry. ● *noun* recommittal to custody. □ **on remand** in custody pending trial. **remand centre** institution for remand of accused people.

remark /rɪ'mɑːk/ *verb* **1** (often + *that*) say by way of comment. **2** (usually + *on*, *upon*) make comment. **3** *archaic* take notice of. ● *noun* **1** comment, thing said. **2** noticing.

■ *verb* **1, 2** assert, comment, declare, mention, note, observe, pass comment, reflect, say, state. **3** heed, mark, notice, observe, perceive, see, take note of. ● *noun* **1** comment, mention, observation, opinion, reflection, statement, thought, utterance, word.

remarkable *adjective* worth notice; excep-tional, striking. □ **remarkably** *adverb*.

■ amazing, astonishing, astounding, conspicuous, curious, different, distinguished, exceptional, extraordinary, important, impressive, marvellous, memorable, notable, noteworthy, odd, out of the ordinary, outstanding, peculiar, phenomenal, prominent, signal, significant, singular, special, strange, striking, surprising, *colloquial* terrific, *colloquial* tremendous, uncommon, unforgettable, unusual, wonderful.

REME /'riːmɪ/ *abbreviation* Royal Electrical and Mechanical Engineers.

remedial /rɪ'miːdɪəl/ *adjective* **1** affording or intended as a remedy. **2** (of teaching) for slow or disadvantaged pupils.

remedy /'remɪdɪ/ *noun* (*plural* **-ies**) (often + *for*, *against*) **1** medicine or treatment. **2** means of removing anything undesirable or setting things right. **3** redress. ● *verb* (**-ies, -ied**) rectify, make good. □ **remediable** /rɪ'miːdɪəb(ə)l/ *adjective*.

■ *noun* **1** antidote, cure, drug, elixir, medicament, medication, medicine, nostrum, palliative, panacea, prescription, restorative, therapy, treatment. **2** answer, antidote, corrective, countermeasure, cure, help, nostrum, panacea, solution. **3** redress, reparation. ● *verb* alleviate, ameliorate, answer, control, correct, counteract, cure, fix, heal, help, mend, mitigate, palliate, put right, rectify, redress, relieve, repair, solve, treat.

remember /rɪ'membə/ *verb* **1** (often + *to do, that*) keep in the memory; not forget. **2** bring back into one's thoughts. **3** acknowledge in making gift etc. **4** convey greetings from.

■ **1** be mindful of, celebrate, commemorate, have a memory of, have in mind, keep in mind, learn, memorize, observe, recognize, retain. **2** be nostalgic about, recall, recollect, reminisce about, review, think back to.

remembrance /rɪ'membrəns/ *noun* **1** remembering, being remembered. **2** recollection. **3** keepsake, souvenir. **4** (in *plural*) greetings conveyed through third person.

remind /rɪ'maɪnd/ *verb* (usually + *of, to do, that*) cause (person) to remember or think of.

■ jog the memory of, prompt.

reminder *noun* **1** thing that reminds. **2** (often + *of*) memento.

■ **1** aide-mémoire, cue, hint, *colloquial* memo, memorandum, mnemonic, note, prompt. **2** heirloom, keepsake, memento, relic, souvenir.

reminisce /remɪ'nɪs/ *verb* (**-cing**) indulge in reminiscence.

■ be nostalgic, look back, recall, remember, review, think back.

reminiscence /remɪ'nɪs(ə)ns/ *noun* **1** remembering things past. **2** (in *plural*) *literary* account of things remembered.

■ **1** memory, recollection, remembrance. **2** (*reminiscences*) account, anecdotes, memoirs, memories.

reminiscent *adjective* **1** (+ *of*) reminding or suggestive of. **2** concerned with reminiscence.

■ **1** (*reminiscent of*) evocative of, recalling, redolent of, similar to, suggestive of.

remiss /rɪ'mɪs/ *adjective* careless of duty; negligent.

■ careless, dilatory, forgetful, irresponsible, lax, negligent, slack, thoughtless.

remission /rɪ'mɪʃ(ə)n/ *noun* **1** reduction of prison sentence for good behaviour. **2** remittance of debt etc. **3** diminution of force etc. **4** (often + *of*) forgiveness (of sins etc.).

remit *verb* /rɪ'mɪt/ (**-tt-**) **1** refrain from exacting or inflicting (debt, punishment, etc.). **2** abate, slacken. **3** send (esp. money). **4** (+ *to*) refer to some authority. **5** (+ *to*) send back to lower court. **6** postpone, defer. **7** pardon (sins etc.). ● *noun*

/'riːmɪt/ **1** terms of reference of committee etc. **2** item remitted.

■ *verb* **1** cancel, let off, settle. **2** abate, decrease, ease off, lessen, relax, slacken. **3** dispatch, forward, pay, send, transmit.

remittance *noun* **1** money sent. **2** sending of money.

■ **1** allowance, fee, payment.

remittent *adjective* (of disease etc.) abating at intervals.

remix *verb* /riː'mɪks/ mix again. ● *noun* /'riːmɪks/ remixed recording.

remnant /'remnənt/ *noun* **1** small remaining quantity. **2** piece of cloth etc. left when greater part has been used or sold.

■ **1** bit, butt, fragment, leftover, oddment, offcut, remainder, residue, scrap, trace, vestige; (*remnants*) remains. **2** bit, end, offcut.

remodel /riː'mɒd(ə)l/ *verb* (**-ll-**; *US* **-l-**) **1** model again. **2** reconstruct.

■ see RENEW 1.

remold *US* = REMOULD.

remonstrate /'remənstreɪt/ *verb* (**-ting**) (+ *with*) make protest; argue forcibly with. □ **remonstrance** /rɪ'mɒnstrəns/ *noun*. **remonstration** *noun*.

remorse /rɪ'mɔːs/ *noun* **1** bitter repentance. **2** compunction. **3** mercy.

■ **1, 2** bad conscience, compunction, contrition, grief, guilt, mortification, pangs of conscience, penitence, pricking of conscience, regret, repentance, sadness, self-accusation, self-reproach, shame, sorrow.

remorseful *adjective* filled with repentance. □ **remorsefully** *adverb*.

■ ashamed, conscience-stricken, contrite, grief-stricken, guilt-ridden, guilty, penitent, regretful, repentant, rueful, sorry.

remorseless *adjective* **1** without compassion. **2** relentless. □ **remorselessly** *adverb*.

■ cruel, heartless, implacable, inexorable, intransigent, merciless, obdurate, pitiless, relentless, ruthless, uncompromising, unforgiving, unkind, unmerciful, unrelenting, unremitting.

remote /rɪ'məʊt/ *adjective* (**-r, -st**) **1** distant in place or time. **2** secluded. **3** distantly related. **4** slight, faint. **5** aloof, not friendly. □ **remote control** (device for) control of apparatus etc. from a distance. □ **remotely** *adverb*. **remoteness** *noun*.

■ **1** distant, far-away, far-flung, far-off, outlying, out of reach, unreachable. **2** cut off, desolate, godforsaken, hard to find, inaccessible, isolated, lonely, out of the way, secluded, solitary, unfrequented, *colloquial* unget-at-able. **4** doubtful, implausible, improbable, negligible, outside, poor, slender, slight, small, unlikely. **5** abstracted, aloof, cold, cool, detached, haughty, preoccupied, reserved, stand-offish, uninvolved, withdrawn.

remould verb /ri:'məʊld/ (US **remold**) **1** mould again; refashion. **2** reconstruct tread of (tyre). ● noun /'ri:məʊld/ remoulded tyre.

removal /rɪ'mu:v(ə)l/ noun **1** removing, being removed. **2** transfer of furniture etc. on moving house. **3** dismissal (from job etc.). **4** killing.

■ **1** elimination, eradication, eviction, extraction, taking away, taking out, withdrawal. **2** move, relocation, transfer, transportation. **3** deposition, dethronement, dislodgement, dismissal, displacement, ejection, expulsion, firing, ousting, colloquial sacking, unseating. **4** elimination, eradication, extermination, killing, liquidation, murder, purge, purging.

remove /rɪ'mu:v/ verb (**-ving**) **1** take off or away from place occupied; get rid of. **2** convey to another place. **3** dismiss. **4** cause to be no longer available. **5** kill. **6** (in passive; + from) be distant in condition from. **7** (as **removed** adjective) (esp. of cousins) separated by a specified number of generations. ● noun **1** distance; degree of remoteness. **2** stage in gradation. **3** form or division in some schools. □ **removable** adjective.

■ verb **1** abstract, amputate (limb), banish, clear away, cut off, cut out, delete, detach, disconnect, dispense with, dispose of, colloquial do away with, esp. literary doff (a hat), eject, eliminate, eradicate, erase, evict, excise, exile, expel, expunge, extract, get rid of, peel off, pull out, purge, root out, rub out, separate, strike out, strip off, sweep away, take away, take off, take out, throw out, undo, unfasten, uproot, wash off, wipe (tape recording), wipe out. **2** carry away, convey, move, take away, transfer, transport. **3** depose, discharge, dismiss, displace, expel, fire, get rid of, kick out, oust, colloquial sack, send away, throw out, turn out. **4** abolish, colloquial do away with, eliminate, get rid of, take away, withdraw.

remunerate /rɪ'mju:nəreɪt/ verb (**-ting**) pay for service rendered. □ **remuneration** noun. **remunerative** /-rətɪv/ adjective.

Renaissance /rɪ'neɪs(ə)ns/ noun **1** revival of classical art and literature in 14th–16th c. **2** period of this. **3** style of art and architecture developed by it. **4** (**renaissance**) any similar revival. □ **Renaissance man** person with many talents.

renal /'ri:n(ə)l/ adjective of kidneys.

renascent /rɪ'næs(ə)nt/ adjective springing up anew; being reborn. □ **renascence** noun.

rend verb (past & past participle **rent**) archaic tear or wrench forcibly.

■ literary cleave, lacerate, pull apart, rip, rupture, shred, split, tear.

render /'rendə/ verb **1** cause to be or become. **2** give in return; pay as due. **3** (often + to) give (assistance). **4** (often + to) show (obedience etc.). **5** present; submit. **6** archaic hand over. **7** represent; portray; perform. **8** translate. **9** (often + down) melt (fat) down. **10** cover (stone or brick) with plaster. □ **rendering** noun.

■ **1** cause to be, make. **2** give, pay, repay, return. **5, 6** formal cede, deliver, furnish, give, hand over, offer, present, proffer, provide, submit, surrender, tender, yield. **7** execute, interpret, perform, play, produce, sing.

rendezvous /'rɒndɪvu:/ noun (plural same /-vu:z/) **1** agreed or regular meeting-place. **2** meeting by arrangement. ● verb (**rendezvouses** /-vu:z/; **rendezvoused** /-vu:d/; **rendezvousing** /-vu:ɪŋ/) meet at rendezvous.

■ noun **2** appointment, assignation, colloquial date, engagement, meeting, archaic tryst.

rendition /ren'dɪʃ(ə)n/ noun interpretation or rendering of dramatic or musical piece.

renegade /'renɪgeɪd/ noun deserter of party or principles.

■ apostate, backslider, defector, deserter, fugitive, heretic, mutineer, outlaw, rebel, runaway, traitor, turncoat.

renege /rɪ'ni:g, rɪ'neɪg/ verb (**-ging**) (often + on) go back on (promise etc.).

■ (renege on) abjure, back out of, break, default on, fail to keep, go back on, rat on, repudiate, welsh on.

renew /rɪ'nju:/ verb **1** make new again; restore to original state. **2** replace. **3** repeat. **4** resume after interruption. **5** grant or be granted continuation of (licence etc.). □ **renewable** adjective. **renewal** noun.

■ **1** bring up to date, colloquial do up, give a facelift to, improve, mend, modernize, overhaul, recondition, reconstitute, recreate, redecorate, redesign, redevelop, redo, refit, refresh, refurbish, regenerate, reintroduce, rejuvenate, remake, remodel, renovate, repaint, repair, restore, resume, colloquial resurrect, revamp, revitalize, revive, touch up, transform, update. **2** refill, replace, replenish. **3** confirm, reaffirm, reiterate, repeat, restate. **4** come back to, pick up again, recommence, restart, resume, return to.

rennet /'renɪt/ noun curdled milk from calf's stomach, or artificial preparation, used in making cheese etc.

renounce /rɪ'naʊns/ verb (**-cing**) **1** consent formally to abandon. **2** repudiate; decline further association with.

■ abandon, abdicate from, abjure, abstain from, desert, discard, disown, formal eschew, forgo, forsake, forswear, give up, quit, reject, relinquish, repudiate, resign from, spurn, surrender.

renovate /'renəveɪt/ verb (**-ting**) restore to good condition; repair. □ **renovation** noun. **renovator** noun.

■ see RENEW 1. □ **renovation** improvement, modernization, overhaul, reconditioning, redevelopment, refit, refurbishment, renewal, repair, restoration, transformation, updating.

renown /rɪ'naʊn/ noun fame; high distinction. □ **renowned** adjective.

■ □ **renowned** celebrated, distinguished, eminent, famous, illustrious, noted, prominent, well known.

rent[1] *noun* **1** periodical payment for use of land or premises. **2** payment for hire of machinery etc. ● *verb* **1** (often + *from*) take, occupy, or use for rent. **2** (often + *out*) let or hire for rent. **3** (often + *at*) be let at specified rate.

■ *noun* **2** fee, hire, instalment, payment, rental. ● *verb* **1** charter, hire, lease. **2** (*rent out*) charter, hire (out), lease, let (out).

rent[2] *noun* **1** tear in garment etc. **2** gap, cleft, fissure.

■ **1** see SPLIT *noun* 2.

rent[3] *past & past participle* of REND.

rental /'rent(ə)l/ *noun* **1** amount paid or received as rent. **2** act of renting.

rentier /'rãtɪeɪ/ *noun* person living on income from property or investments. [French]

renunciation /rɪmʌnsɪ'eɪʃ(ə)n/ *noun* renouncing; self-denial; giving up of things.

reorganize /ri:'ɔ:gənaɪz/ *verb* (also **-ise**) (**-zing** or **-sing**) organize differently. □ **reorganization** *noun*. **reorganizer** *noun*.

■ rationalize, rearrange, redeploy, reshuffle, restructure.

rep[1] *noun colloquial* representative, esp. salesperson.

rep[2] *noun colloquial* **1** repertory. **2** repertory theatre or company.

repair[1] /rɪ'peə/ *verb* **1** restore to good condition after damage or wear. **2** set right or make amends for. ● *noun* **1** (result of) restoring to sound condition. **2** good or relative condition for working or using. □ **repairable** *adjective*. **repairer** *noun*.

■ *verb* **1** darn, fix, mend, overhaul, patch (up), put right, refit, renew, restore, service. **2** make amends for, make good, put right, rectify, set right.

repair[2] /rɪ'peə/ *verb* (usually + *to*) resort; go.

reparable /'repərəb(ə)l/ *adjective* that can be made good.

reparation /repə'reɪʃ(ə)n/ *noun* **1** making amends. **2** (esp. in *plural*) compensation.

repartee /repɑ:'ti:/ *noun* (making of) witty retorts.

repast /rɪ'pɑ:st/ *noun formal* meal.

repatriate /ri:'pætrɪeɪt/ *verb* (**-ting**) return (person) to native land. □ **repatriation** *noun*.

repay /ri:'peɪ/ *verb* (*past & past participle* **repaid**) **1** pay back (money). **2** make repayment to (person). **3** make return for (action etc.); requite. □ **repayable** *adjective*. **repayment** *noun*.

■ **1** give back, pay back, refund, reimburse, settle (*a debt*). **2** compensate, pay back, recompense, refund, reimburse, remunerate. **3** avenge, pay back, reciprocate, requite, retaliate, return, reward, take revenge for.

repeal /rɪ'pi:l/ *verb* annul, revoke. ● *noun* repealing.

■ *verb* abolish, abrogate, annul, cancel, invalidate, nullify, rescind, reverse, revoke.

repeat /rɪ'pi:t/ *verb* **1** say or do over again. **2** recite; report. **3** recur. ● *noun* **1** repeating. **2** thing repeated, esp. broadcast. **3** *Music* passage intended to be repeated. □ **repeatable** *adjective*. **repeatedly** *adverb*.

■ *verb* **1** do again, duplicate, redo, rehearse, replay, replicate, reproduce, rerun, show again. **2** echo, quote, recapitulate, recite, re-echo, regurgitate, reiterate, report, restate, retell, say again.

repeater *noun* **1** person or thing that repeats. **2** firearm that fires several shots without reloading. **3** watch that strikes last quarter etc. again when required. **4** device for retransmitting electrical message.

repel /rɪ'pel/ *verb* **1** drive back; ward off. **2** be repulsive or distasteful to. **3** resist mixing with. **4** push away from itself.

■ **1** drive away, drive back, fend off, fight off, hold off, keep at bay, keep away, parry, push away, rebuff, reject, repulse, resist, ward off, withstand. **2** alienate, disgust, nauseate, offend, put off, revolt, sicken, *colloquial* turn off.

repellent /rɪ'pel(ə)nt/ *adjective* **1** that repels. **2** repulsive. ● *noun* substance that repels.

■ *adjective* **2** see REPULSIVE.

repent /rɪ'pent/ *verb* **1** (often + *of*) feel sorrow about one's actions etc. **2** wish one had not done; resolve not to continue (wrongdoing etc.). □ **repentance** *noun*. **repentant** *adjective*.

■ bemoan, bewail, lament, regret, reproach oneself for, rue. □ **repentance** contrition, guilt, penitence, regret, remorse, self-accusation, self-reproach, shame, sorrow. **repentant** apologetic, ashamed, conscience-stricken, contrite, grief-stricken, guilt-ridden, guilty, penitent, regretful, remorseful, rueful, sorry.

repercussion /ri:pə'kʌʃ(ə)n/ *noun* **1** indirect effect or reaction following event etc. **2** recoil after impact.

repertoire /'repətwɑ:/ *noun* stock of works that performer etc. knows or is prepared to perform.

repertory /'repətərɪ/ *noun* (*plural* **-ies**) **1** performance of various plays for short periods by one company. **2** repertory theatres collectively. **3** store of information etc. **4** repertoire. □ **repertory company** one performing plays from repertoire. **repertory theatre** one with repertoire of plays.

■ **3** collection, repertoire, repository, reserve, stock, store, supply.

repetition /repə'tɪʃ(ə)n/ *noun* **1** repeating, being repeated. **2** thing repeated. **3** copy. □ **repetitious** *adjective*. **repetitiousness** *noun*. **repetitive** /rɪ'petətɪv/ *adjective*.

■ □ **repetitive** boring, continual, incessant, iterative, monotonous, recurrent, repeated, repetitious, tautologous, tedious, unchanging, unvaried.

repine /rɪˈpaɪn/ *verb* (**-ning**) (often + *at*, *against*) fret; be discontented.

replace /rɪˈpleɪs/ *verb* (**-cing**) **1** put back in place. **2** take place of; be or provide substitute for. **3** (often + *with*, *by*) fill up place of. **4** renew. □ **replaceable** *adjective*.

■ **1** put back, reinstate, restore, return. **2** come after, deputize for, follow, oust, stand in for, substitute for, succeed, supersede, supplant, take over from, take the place of. **4** change, renew, substitute.

replacement *noun* **1** replacing, being replaced. **2** person or thing that replaces another.

■ **2** deputy, locum, proxy, stand-in, substitute, successor, understudy.

replay *verb* /riːˈpleɪ/ play (match, recording, etc.) again. ● *noun* /ˈriːpleɪ/ replaying of match, recorded incident in game, etc.

replenish /rɪˈplenɪʃ/ *verb* (often + *with*) fill up again. □ **replenishment** *noun*.

■ fill up, refill, renew, restock, top up.

replete /rɪˈpliːt/ *adjective* (often + *with*) **1** well fed. **2** filled or well supplied. □ **repletion** *noun*.

■ **1** full, gorged, *formal* sated, satiated, stuffed, well fed. **2** crammed, full, *colloquial* jam-packed, overloaded, stuffed.

replica /ˈreplɪkə/ *noun* **1** exact copy, esp. duplicate made by original artist. **2** model, esp. small-scale.

■ **1** carbon copy, *colloquial* clone, copy, duplicate, facsimile, imitation, likeness, reproduction. **2** see MODEL *noun* 1,3.

replicate /ˈreplɪkeɪt/ *verb* make replica of. □ **replication** *noun*.

reply /rɪˈplaɪ/ *verb* (**-ies**, **-ied**) **1** (often + *to*) make an answer; respond. **2** say in answer. ● *noun* (*plural* **-ies**) **1** replying. **2** what is replied.

■ *verb* **1** (*reply to*) see ACKNOWLEDGE 2, COUNTER[2] *verb*. **2** answer, rejoin, respond, retort. ● *noun* **2** acknowledgement, answer, *slang* comeback, reaction, rejoinder, response, retort, riposte.

report /rɪˈpɔːt/ *verb* **1** bring back or give account of; tell as news; describe, esp. as eyewitness. **2** make official or formal statement. **3** (often + *to*) bring to attention of authorities. **4** (often + *to*) present oneself as arrived. **5** take down, write description of, etc. for publication. **6** (+ *to*) be responsible to. ● *noun* **1** account given or opinion formally expressed after investigation. **2** description, reproduction, or summary of speech, law case, scene, etc., esp. for newspaper publication or broadcast. **3** common talk; rumour. **4** repute. **5** periodical statement on (esp. pupil's) work etc. **6** sound of gunshot. □ **reportedly** *adverb*.

■ *verb* **1, 2** announce, broadcast, circulate, communicate, declare, describe, disclose, divulge, document, give an account of, proclaim, publish, put out, record, recount, reveal, state, tell. **3** complain about, denounce, inform against. **4** announce oneself, check in, clock in, introduce oneself, make oneself known, present oneself, sign in. ● *noun* **1, 2** account, announcement, article, communication, communiqué, description, dispatch, narrative, record, statement, story, write-up. **6** bang, blast, boom, crack, detonation, discharge, explosion, noise.

reporter *noun* person employed to report news etc. for media.

■ columnist, commentator, correspondent, journalist, newscaster, newspaperman, newspaperwoman, news presenter, photojournalist.

repose[1] /rɪˈpəʊz/ *noun* **1** rest; inactivity. **2** sleep. **3** tranquillity. ● *verb* (**-sing**) **1** rest. **2** lie, esp. when dead.

■ *noun* **1, 2** inactivity, quiescence, relaxation, respite, rest, sleep, *poetical* slumber. **3** calm, calmness, comfort, ease, peace, peacefulness, poise, quiet, quietness, serenity, stillness, tranquillity.

repose[2] /rɪˈpəʊz/ *verb* (**-sing**) (+ *in*) place (trust etc.) in.

repository /rɪˈpɒzɪtərɪ/ *noun* (*plural* **-ies**) **1** place where things are stored or may be found. **2** receptacle. **3** (often + *of*) book, person, etc. regarded as store of information, recipient of secrets etc.

reprehend /reprɪˈhend/ *verb formal* rebuke, blame.

reprehensible /reprɪˈhensɪb(ə)l/ *adjective* blameworthy.

■ blameworthy, culpable, deplorable, disgraceful, immoral, objectionable, regrettable, remiss, shameful, unworthy, wicked.

represent /reprɪˈzent/ *verb* **1** stand for; correspond to. **2** symbolize. **3** be specimen of. **4** present likeness of to mind or senses. **5** (often + *as*, *to be*) describe or depict; declare. **6** (**represent oneself as**) pose as. **7** (+ *that*) allege that. **8** show or play part of. **9** be substitute, deputy, or spokesperson for. **10** be elected by as member of legislature etc.

■ **1, 2** correspond to, embody, epitomize, express, indicate, mean, personify, signify, stand for, symbolize, typify. **3** be an example of, exemplify, illustrate, typify. **5** characterize, declare, define, delineate, depict, describe, draw, paint, picture, portray, reflect, show, sketch. **6** (**represent oneself as**) assume the guise of, impersonate, masquerade as, pose as, present oneself as, pretend to be. **8** act as, act out, enact, perform, play, portray, present. **9** act for, act on behalf of, deputize for, speak for, stand in for, substitute for.

representation /reprɪzenˈteɪʃ(ə)n/ *noun* **1** representing, being represented. **2** thing that represents another.

■ **2** depiction, figure, icon, image, imitation, likeness, model, picture, portrait, portrayal, resemblance, semblance, statue.

representational *adjective* (of art) seeking to portray objects etc. realistically.

representative /reprɪˈzentətɪv/ *adjective* **1** typical of class. **2** containing typical specimens of all or many classes. **3** (of government etc.) of elected deputies or based on representation. ● *noun* **1** (+ *of*) sample, specimen, or typical embodiment of. **2** agent; salesperson. **3** delegate; substitute. **4** deputy, esp. in representative assembly.

■ *adjective* **1** archetypal, average, characteristic, illustrative, normal, typical. **3** chosen, democratic, elected, elective, popular. ● *noun* **2** agent, *colloquial* rep, salesman, salesperson, saleswoman, traveller. **3** ambassador, consul, delegate, deputy, diplomat, emissary, envoy, legate, proxy, spokesman, spokesperson, spokeswoman, stand-in, substitute. **4** congressman, councillor, deputy, Member of Parliament, MP.

repress /rɪˈpres/ *verb* **1** keep under; put down. **2** suppress (esp. unwelcome thought). □ **repressed** *adjective*. **repression** *noun*. **repressive** *adjective*.

■ **1** control, crush, curb, frustrate, inhibit, keep down, limit, oppress, overcome, put down, quell, restrain, subdue, subjugate, suppress. **2** bottle up, restrain, stifle, suppress. □ **repressed** *of person* cold, frigid, frustrated, inhibited, neurotic, prim, tense, undemonstrative, *colloquial* uptight; *of emotions* bottled up, hidden, latent, subconscious, suppressed, unconscious, unfulfilled. **repression** authoritarianism, censorship, coercion, control, despotism, dictatorship, oppression, restraint, subjugation, totalitarianism, tyranny. **repressive** authoritarian, autocratic, brutal, coercive, cruel, despotic, dictatorial, fascist, harsh, illiberal, oppressive, restricting, severe, totalitarian, tyrannical, undemocratic, unenlightened.

reprieve /rɪˈpriːv/ *verb* (**-ving**) **1** remit or postpone execution of. **2** give respite to. ● *noun* reprieving, being reprieved.

■ *verb* commute a sentence, forgive, let off, pardon, postpone execution, set free, spare. ● *noun* amnesty, pardon, postponement, respite, stay of execution.

reprimand /ˈreprɪmɑːnd/ *noun* official rebuke. ● *verb* rebuke officially.

■ *noun* admonition, castigation, censure, condemnation, criticism, *colloquial* dressing down, lecture, lesson, rebuke, remonstration, reproach, *formal* reproof, scolding, *colloquial* slating, *colloquial* talking-to, *colloquial* telling-off, *colloquial* ticking-off, upbraiding. ● *verb* admonish, berate, blame, *colloquial* carpet, castigate, censure, *archaic* chide, condemn, correct, criticize, disapprove of, find fault with, lecture, pull up, *slang* rap, rate, rebuke, *formal* reprehend, reproach, *formal* reprove, scold,

colloquial slate, take to task, teach a lesson, *colloquial* tell off, *colloquial* tick off, upbraid.

reprint *verb* /riːˈprɪnt/ print again. ● *noun* /ˈriːprɪnt/ **1** reprinting of book etc. **2** quantity reprinted.

reprisal /rɪˈpraɪz(ə)l/ *noun* act of retaliation.

■ counter-attack, getting even, repayment, retaliation, retribution, revenge, vengeance.

reprise /rɪˈpriːz/ *noun Music* repeated passage or song etc.

repro /ˈriːprəʊ/ *noun* (*plural* **-s**) *colloquial* reproduction, copy.

reproach /rɪˈprəʊtʃ/ *verb* express disapproval to (person) for fault etc. ● *noun* **1** rebuke, censure. **2** (often + *to*) thing that brings discredit.

■ *verb* censure, criticize, rebuke, reprimand, scold, upbraid. ● *noun* **1** blame, censure, condemnation, criticism, disapproval, opprobrium, rebuke, scorn. **2** discredit, disgrace.

reproachful *adjective* full of or expressing reproach. □ **reproachfully** *adverb*.

■ admonitory, censorious, condemnatory, critical, disapproving, disparaging, reproving, scornful, withering.

reprobate /ˈreprəbeɪt/ *noun* unprincipled or immoral person.

reproduce /riːprəˈdjuːs/ *verb* (**-cing**) **1** produce copy or representation of. **2** produce further members of same species by natural means. **3** (**reproduce itself**) produce offspring. □ **reproducible** *adjective*.

■ **1** copy, counterfeit, duplicate, forge, imitate, mimic, photocopy, print, redo, reissue, repeat, reprint, simulate. **2, 3** *literary* beget young, breed, increase, multiply, procreate, produce offspring, propagate, spawn.

reproduction /riːprəˈdʌkʃ(ə)n/ *noun* **1** reproducing, esp. of further members of same species. **2** copy of work of art. ● *adjective* (of furniture etc.) imitating earlier style. □ **reproductive** *adjective*.

■ *noun* **1** breeding, cloning, increase, multiplying, procreation, proliferation, propagation, spawning. **2** copy, duplicate, facsimile, fake, forgery, imitation, likeness, print, replica.

reproof /rɪˈpruːf/ *noun formal* **1** blame. **2** rebuke.

reprove /rɪˈpruːv/ *verb* (**-ving**) *formal* rebuke.

reptile /ˈreptaɪl/ *noun* **1** cold-blooded scaly animal of class including snakes, lizards, etc. **2** grovelling or repulsive person. □ **reptilian** /-ˈtɪl-/ *adjective*.

republic /rɪˈpʌblɪk/ *noun* state in which supreme power is held by the people or their elected representatives.

republican *adjective* **1** of or characterizing republic(s). **2** advocating or supporting republican government. ● *noun* **1** supporter or advocate of republican government. **2** (**Republican**) member of political party styled 'Republican'. □ **republicanism** noun.

repudiate /rɪ'pjuːdɪeɪt/ verb (-ting) 1 disown; disavow; deny. 2 refuse to recognize or obey (authority) or discharge (obligation or debt).
□ **repudiation** noun

> ■ 1 deny, disagree with, discard, disown, dispute, rebuff, reject, renounce, scorn, turn down. 2 go back on, recant, renounce, rescind, retract, reverse, revoke.

repugnance /rɪ'pʌgnəns/ noun 1 aversion, antipathy. 2 inconsistency or incompatibility of ideas etc.

repugnant /rɪ'pʌgn(ə)nt/ adjective 1 distasteful. 2 contradictory.

> ■ 1 see REPULSIVE.

repulse /rɪ'pʌls/ verb (-sing) 1 drive back. 2 rebuff, reject. ● noun 1 defeat. 2 rebuff.

repulsion /rɪ'pʌlʃ(ə)n/ noun 1 aversion, disgust. 2 Physics tendency of bodies to repel each other.

repulsive /rɪ'pʌlsɪv/ adjective causing aversion or loathing. □ **repulsively** adverb.

> ■ abhorrent, abominable, colloquial beastly, disagreeable, disgusting, distasteful, distressing, foul, gross, hateful, hideous, loathsome, nasty, nauseating, nauseous, objectionable, obnoxious, odious, offensive, off-putting, repellent, repugnant, revolting, colloquial sick, sickening, ugly, unattractive, unpalatable, unpleasant, unsavoury, unsightly, vile.

reputable /'repjʊtəb(ə)l/ adjective of good reputation; respectable.

> ■ dependable, esteemed, famous, good, highly regarded, honourable, honoured, prestigious, reliable, respectable, respected, trustworthy, unimpeachable, well thought of, worthy.

reputation /repjʊ'teɪʃ(ə)n/ noun 1 what is generally said or believed about character of person or thing. 2 credit; respectability.

> ■ character, archaic fame, name, prestige, renown, repute, standing, stature, status.

repute /rɪ'pjuːt/ noun reputation. ● verb (as **reputed** adjective) be generally considered. □ **reputedly** adverb.

> ■ verb (reputed) alleged, assumed, believed, considered, formal deemed, famed, judged, purported, reckoned, regarded, rumoured, said, supposed, thought.

request /rɪ'kwest/ noun 1 asking for something. 2 thing asked for. ● verb 1 ask to be given, allowed, etc. 2 (+ to do) ask (person) to do something. 3 (+ that) ask that.

> ■ noun appeal, application, call, demand, entreaty, petition, plea, prayer, requisition, solicitation, literary supplication. ● verb 1 appeal for, apply for, ask for, beg, beseech, call for, claim, demand, desire, entreat, implore, petition for, pray for, requisition, seek, solicit, literary supplicate for. 2 adjure, appeal to, apply to, ask, beg, beseech, entreat, implore, importune, invite, petition, require, literary supplicate.

Requiem /'rekwɪəm/ noun (also **requiem**) esp. RC Church mass for the dead.

require /rɪ'kwaɪə/ verb (-ring) 1 need; depend on for success etc. 2 lay down as imperative. 3 command; instruct. 4 demand; insist on. □ **required** adjective. **requirement** noun.

> ■ 1 be missing, be short of, call for, demand, depend on, lack, necessitate, need, want. 3 coerce, command, compel, direct, force, instruct, make, oblige, order, put pressure on, request. 4 call for, demand, insist on. □ **required** see REQUISITE. **requirement** condition, demand, essential, necessity, need, precondition, prerequisite, provision, proviso, qualification, sine qua non, stipulation.

requisite /'rekwɪzɪt/ adjective required, necessary. ● noun (often + for) thing needed.

> ■ adjective compulsory, essential, imperative, indispensable, mandatory, necessary, needed, obligatory, prescribed, required, set, stipulated.

requisition /rekwɪ'zɪʃ(ə)n/ noun 1 official order laying claim to use of property or materials. 2 formal written demand. ● verb demand use or supply of.

> ■ noun 2 application, authorization, demand, mandate, order, request, voucher. ● verb appropriate, commandeer, confiscate, demand, expropriate, occupy, order, request, seize, take over, take possession of.

requite /rɪ'kwaɪt/ verb (-ting) 1 make return for. 2 reward; avenge. 3 (often + for) give in return. □ **requital** noun.

reredos /'rɪədɒs/ noun ornamental screen covering wall above back of altar.

rescind /rɪ'sɪnd/ verb abrogate, revoke, cancel. □ **rescission** /-'sɪʒ-/ noun.

rescue /'reskjuː/ verb (-ues, -ued, -uing) 1 (often + from) save or set free from danger or harm. 2 recover. ● noun rescuing, being rescued. □ **rescuer** noun.

> ■ verb 1 deliver, emancipate, extricate, free, let go, liberate, loose, ransom, release, save, set free. 2 get back, recover, retrieve, salvage. ● noun deliverance, emancipation, freeing, liberation, recovery, release, relief, salvage.

research /rɪ'sɜːtʃ, 'riːsɜːtʃ/ noun systematic investigation of materials, sources, etc. to establish facts. ● verb do research into (subject) or for (book etc.). □ **researcher** noun.

> ■ noun analysis, enquiry, examination, experimentation, exploration, fact-finding, inquiry, investigation, scrutiny, searching, study. ● verb colloquial check out, delve into, investigate, probe, search, study.

resemble /rɪ'zemb(ə)l/ verb (-ling) be like; have similarity to. □ **resemblance** noun.

> ■ approximate to, bear resemblance to, be similar to, compare with, look like, mirror, sound like, take after. □ **resemblance** affinity, closeness, coincidence, comparability, comparison, conformity, congruity, correspondence, equivalence, likeness, similarity, similitude.

resent /rɪ'zent/ *verb* feel indignation at; be aggrieved by. □ **resentful** *adjective*. **resentfully** *adverb*. **resentment** *noun*.

■ begrudge, dislike, envy, feel bitter about, grudge, grumble at, object to, take exception to, take umbrage at. □ **resentful** aggrieved, angry, annoyed, begrudging, bitter, disgruntled, displeased, embittered, envious, grudging, hurt, indignant, irked, jaundiced, jealous, malicious, offended, *colloquial* peeved, put out, rancorous, spiteful, unfriendly, ungenerous, upset, vexed, vindictive. **resentment** anger, animosity, bitterness, discontent, envy, grudge, hatred, hurt, ill will, indignation, irritation, jealousy, malevolence, malice, pique, rancour, spite, unfriendliness, vexation, vindictiveness.

reservation /rezə'veɪʃ(ə)n/ *noun* 1 reserving, being reserved. 2 thing reserved (e.g. room in hotel). 3 spoken or unspoken limitation or exception. 4 (in full **central reservation**) strip of land between carriageways of road. 5 area reserved for occupation of aboriginal peoples. 6 area reserved as habitat for wildlife.

■ 2 appointment, booking. 3 condition, doubt, hesitation, misgiving, proviso, qualification, qualm, reluctance, reticence, scepticism, scruple. 6 see RESERVE *noun* 9.

reserve /rɪ'zɜːv/ *verb* (**-ving**) 1 put aside or keep back for later occasion or special use. 2 order to be retained or allocated for person at particular time. 3 retain; secure. ● *noun* 1 thing reserved for future use. 2 limitation or exception attached to something. 3 self-restraint; reticence. 4 company's profit added to capital. 5 (in *singular* or *plural*) assets kept readily available. 6 (in *singular* or *plural*) troops withheld from action to reinforce or protect others. 7 (in *singular* or *plural*) forces outside regular ones but available in emergency. 8 extra player chosen as possible substitute in team. 9 land reserved for special use, esp. as habitat.

■ *verb* 1 earmark, hoard, hold back, keep, keep back, preserve, put aside, retain, save, set aside, stockpile, store up. 2 *colloquial* bag, book, order, pay for. 3 keep, retain, secure. ● *noun* 1 cache, fund, hoard, nest egg, reservoir, savings, stock, stockpile, store, supply. 3 aloofness, caution, modesty, quietness, reluctance, reticence, self-consciousness, self-effacement, shyness, stand-offishness, taciturnity, timidity. 6, 7 backup; (*reserves*) auxiliaries, reinforcements. 8 deputy, replacement, standby, stand-in, substitute, understudy. 9 game park, preserve, protected area, reservation, safari park, sanctuary.

reserved *adjective* 1 reticent, uncommunicative. 2 set apart for particular use.

■ 1 see RETICENT (RETICENCE).

reservist *noun* member of reserve forces.

reservoir /'rezəvwɑː/ *noun* 1 large natural or artificial lake as source of water supply. 2 receptacle for fluid. 3 supply of facts etc.

reshuffle /riː'ʃʌf(ə)l/ *verb* (**-ling**) 1 shuffle again. 2 change posts of (government ministers etc.). ● *noun* reshuffling.

reside /rɪ'zaɪd/ *verb* (**-ding**) 1 have one's home. 2 (+ *in*) (of right etc.) be vested in. 3 (+ *in*) (of quality) be present in.

■ 1 (*reside in*) dwell in, inhabit, live in, lodge in, occupy, settle in.

residence /'rezɪd(ə)ns/ *noun* 1 residing. 2 place where one resides. 3 house, esp. large one. □ **in residence** living or working at specified place.

■ 2 abode, address, domicile, dwelling, dwelling place, habitation, home, house, quarters, seat.

resident /'rezɪd(ə)nt/ *noun* 1 (often + *of*) permanent inhabitant. 2 guest staying at hotel. ● *adjective* 1 residing, in residence. 2 living at one's workplace etc. 3 (+ *in*) located in.

■ *noun* 1 citizen, denizen, dweller, householder, inhabitant, local, native. ● *adjective* 1 in residence, permanent, remaining, staying.

residential /rezɪ'denʃ(ə)l/ *adjective* 1 suitable for or occupied by dwellings. 2 used as residence. 3 connected with residence.

residual /rɪ'zɪdjʊəl/ *adjective* left as residue or residuum.

■ abiding, continuing, leftover, outstanding, persisting, remaining, surviving, unconsumed, unused.

residuary /rɪ'zɪdjʊərɪ/ *adjective* 1 of the residue of an estate. 2 residual.

residue /'rezɪdjuː/ *noun* 1 remainder; what is left over. 2 what remains of estate when liabilities have been discharged.

residuum /rɪ'zɪdjʊəm/ *noun* (*plural* **-dua**) 1 substance left after combustion or evaporation. 2 residue.

resign /rɪ'zaɪn/ *verb* 1 (often + *from*) give up job, position, etc. 2 relinquish, surrender. 3 (**resign oneself to**) accept (situation etc.) reluctantly.

■ 1, 2 abandon, abdicate, *colloquial* chuck in, forsake, give up, leave, quit, relinquish, renounce, retire, stand down, step down, surrender, vacate. 3 (**resign oneself to**) see ACCEPT 5.

resignation /rezɪg'neɪʃ(ə)n/ *noun* 1 resigning, esp. from job or office. 2 reluctant acceptance of the inevitable.

resigned *adjective* 1 (often + *to*) having resigned oneself; resolved to endure. 2 indicative of this. □ **resignedly** /-nɪdlɪ/ *adverb*.

■ see PATIENT *adjective*.

resilient /rɪ'zɪlɪənt/ *adjective* 1 resuming original form after compression etc. 2 readily recovering from setback. □ **resilience** *noun*.

■ 1 bouncy, elastic, plastic, pliable, rubbery, springy, supple. 2 adaptable, buoyant, irrepressible, strong, tough, unstoppable.

resin /'rezɪn/ *noun* 1 sticky secretion of trees and plants. 2 (in full **synthetic resin**) organic compound made by polymerization etc. and used in plastics. ● *verb* (**-n-**) rub or treat with resin. □ **resinous** *adjective*.

resist /rɪ'zɪst/ *verb* 1 withstand action or effect of. 2 abstain from (pleasure etc.). 3 strive against;

oppose. **4** offer opposition. □ **resistible** *adjective*.
■ **1** check, confront, face up to, hold one's ground against, hold out against, keep at bay, stand up to, withstand. **2** see ABSTAIN 1. **3, 4** counteract, defy, fight, hinder, impede, inhibit, oppose, struggle against.

resistance /rɪ'zɪst(ə)ns/ *noun* **1** resisting. **2** power to resist. **3** ability to withstand disease. **4** impeding effect exerted by one thing on another. **5** *Physics* property of hindering passage of electric current, heat, etc. **6** resistor. **7** secret organization resisting regime, esp. in occupied country. □ **resistant** *adjective*.
■ □ **resistant** defiant, hostile, intransigent, invulnerable, obstinate, opposed, refractory, stubborn, uncooperative, unresponsive, unyielding; (*resistant to, against*) impervious to, invulnerable to, opposed to, proof against, unaffected by, unsusceptible to, unyielding to.

resistor *noun* device having resistance to passage of electric current.

resit *verb* /ri:'sɪt/ (**-tt-**; *past & past participle* **resat**) sit (exam) again after failing. ● *noun* /'ri:sɪt/ **1** resitting of exam. **2** exam for this.

resoluble /rɪ'zɒljʊb(ə)l/ *adjective* **1** resolvable. **2** (+ *into*) analysable into.

resolute /'rezəlu:t/ *adjective* determined, decided; purposeful. □ **resolutely** *adverb*. **resoluteness** *noun*.
■ adamant, bold, committed, constant, courageous, decided, decisive, determined, dogged, firm, immovable, immutable, indefatigable, inflexible, obstinate, persevering, persistent, pertinacious, relentless, resolved, single-minded, staunch, steadfast, strong-minded, strong-willed, stubborn, tireless, unbending, undaunted, unflinching, unshakeable, unswerving, untiring, unwavering.

resolution /rezə'lu:ʃ(ə)n/ *noun* **1** resolute temper or character. **2** thing resolved on. **3** formal expression of opinion of meeting. **4** (+ *of*) solving of question etc. **5** resolving, being resolved.
■ **1** boldness, commitment, constancy, determination, devotion, doggedness, firmness, obstinacy, perseverance, persistence, pertinacity, purposefulness, resolve, single-mindedness, staunchness, steadfastness, stubbornness, tenacity, will-power. **2** commitment, oath, pledge, promise, resolve, undertaking, vow. **3** decision, motion, proposal, proposition, statement. **4** answer, disentanglement, settlement, solution, sorting out.

resolve /rɪ'zɒlv/ *verb* (**-ving**) **1** make up one's mind; decide firmly. **2** cause to do this. **3** solve, settle. **4** (+ *that*) pass resolution by vote. **5** (often + *into*) (cause to) separate into constituent parts; analyse. **6** *Music* convert or be converted into concord. ● *noun* **1** firm mental decision. **2** determination. □ **resolved** *adjective*.
■ *verb* **1** agree, conclude, decide, determine, fix, make a decision, make up one's mind, opt, settle,

undertake. **3** answer, clear up, disentangle, figure out, settle, solve, sort out, work out. **4** decide, elect, pass a resolution, vote. ● *noun* see RESOLUTION 1.

resonant /'rezənənt/ *adjective* **1** echoing, resounding; continuing to sound. **2** causing reinforcement or prolongation of sound, esp. by vibration. □ **resonance** *noun*.
■ **1** booming, echoing, full, pulsating, resounding, reverberant, reverberating, rich, ringing, sonorous, thunderous, vibrant, vibrating.

resonate /'rezəneɪt/ *verb* (**-ting**) produce or show resonance; resound. □ **resonator** *noun*.

resort /rɪ'zɔːt/ *noun* **1** place frequented, esp. for holidays etc. **2** thing to which recourse is had; expedient. **3** (+ *to*) recourse to; use of. ● *verb* (+ *to*) **1** turn to as expedient. **2** go often or in numbers to. □ **in the or as a last resort** when all else has failed.
■ *noun* **1** holiday town, retreat, spa, watering place. **2** alternative, course of action, expedient, option, recourse, refuge, remedy, reserve. ● *verb* (*resort to*) **1** fall back on, have recourse to, make use of, turn to, use. **2** frequent, go to, *slang* hang out in, haunt, invade, patronize, visit.

resound /rɪ'zaʊnd/ *verb* **1** (often + *with*) ring, echo. **2** produce echoes; go on sounding; fill place with sound. **3** be much talked of. **4** produce sensation.
■ **1, 2** boom, echo, pulsate, resonate, reverberate, ring, rumble, thunder, vibrate.

resounding *adjective* **1** ringing, echoing. **2** unmistakable; emphatic.
■ **1** see RESONANT 1.

resource /rɪ'zɔːs/ *noun* **1** expedient, device. **2** (often in *plural*) means available. **3** (often in *plural*) stock that can be drawn on. **4** (in *plural*) country's collective wealth. **5** (in *plural*) person's inner strength. **6** skill in devising expedients. ● *verb* (**-cing**) provide with resources.
■ **2–4** (*resources*) assets, capital, funds, materials, means, money, possessions, property, raw materials, reserves, riches, wealth.

resourceful *adjective* good at devising expedients. □ **resourcefully** *adverb*. **resourcefulness** *noun*.
■ clever, creative, enterprising, imaginative, ingenious, innovative, inspired, inventive, original, skilful, smart, talented.

respect /rɪ'spekt/ *noun* **1** deferential esteem. **2** (+ *of, for*) heed, regard. **3** detail, aspect. **4** reference, relation. **5** (in *plural*) polite greetings. ● *verb* **1** regard with deference or esteem. **2** treat with consideration. **3** spare. □ **respectful** *adjective*. **respectfully** *adverb*.
■ *noun* **1** admiration, appreciation, awe, consideration, courtesy, deference, esteem, homage, honour, liking, love, politeness, regard, reverence, tribute, veneration. **3** aspect, attribute, characteristic, detail, element, facet, feature, particular, point, property, quality, trait, way.

● *verb* **1** admire, appreciate, be polite to, defer to, esteem, have high regard for, honour, look up to, pay homage to, revere, reverence, think well of, value, venerate. □ **respectful** admiring, civil, considerate, cordial, courteous, deferential, dutiful, gentlemanly, gracious, humble, ladylike, obliging, polite, proper, reverent, reverential, servile, subservient, thoughtful, well mannered.

respectable *adjective* **1** of acceptable social standing; decent in appearance or behaviour. **2** reasonably good in condition, appearance, size, etc. □ **respectability** *noun*. **respectably** *adverb*.

■ **1** chaste, decent, decorous, dignified, genteel, honest, honourable, law-abiding, modest, presentable, proper, refined, respected, seemly, unimpeachable, upright, worthy. **2** see CONSIDERABLE 1.

respecting *preposition* with regard to.

respective /rɪ'spektɪv/ *adjective* of or relating to each of several individually.

■ individual, own, particular, personal, relevant, separate, several, special, specific.

respectively *adverb* for each separately or in turn, and in the order mentioned.

respiration /respə'reɪʃ(ə)n/ *noun* **1** breathing. **2** single breath in or out. **3** plant's absorption of oxygen and emission of carbon dioxide.

respirator /'respəreɪtə/ *noun* **1** apparatus worn over mouth and nose to filter inhaled air. **2** apparatus for maintaining artificial respiration.

respire /rɪ'spaɪə/ *verb* (**-ring**) **1** breathe. **2** inhale and exhale. **3** (of plant) carry out respiration. □ **respiratory** /-'spɪr-/ *adjective*.

respite /'respaɪt/ *noun* **1** interval of rest or relief. **2** delay permitted before discharge of obligation or suffering of penalty.

■ **1** break, *colloquial* breather, holiday, intermission, interruption, interval, *colloquial* let-up, lull, pause, recess, relaxation, relief, rest, time off, time out, vacation. **2** delay, hiatus, pause, reprieve, stay.

resplendent /rɪ'splend(ə)nt/ *adjective* brilliant; dazzlingly or gloriously bright. □ **resplendence** *noun*.

■ bright, brilliant, dazzling, glittering, shining, splendid.

respond /rɪ'spɒnd/ *verb* **1** answer, reply. **2** (often + *to*) act etc. in response.

■ **1** answer, counter, reply, retort; (*respond to*) acknowledge, return. **2** see REACT 1.

respondent *noun* defendant, esp. in appeal or divorce case. ● *adjective* in position of defendant.

response /rɪ'spɒns/ *noun* **1** answer, reply. **2** action, feeling, etc. caused by stimulus etc. **3** (often in *plural*) part of liturgy said or sung in answer to priest.

■ **1** acknowledgement, answer, *slang* comeback, counter, feedback, reaction, rejoinder, reply, retort, riposte. **2** reaction, reflex.

responsibility /rɪspɒnsə'bɪlɪtɪ/ *noun* (*plural*

-ies) **1** (often + *for*, *of*) being responsible. **2** authority. **3** person or thing for which one is responsible.

responsible /rɪ'spɒnsəb(ə)l/ *adjective* **1** (often + *to*, *for*) liable to be called to account. **2** morally accountable for actions. **3** of good credit and repute; trustworthy. **4** (often + *for*) being the cause. **5** involving responsibility. □ **responsibly** *adverb*.

■ **1, 2** accountable, answerable, liable. **3** concerned, conscientious, creditable, dependable, diligent, dutiful, ethical, honest, law-abiding, loyal, mature, moral, reliable, sensible, sober, steady, thinking, thoughtful, trustworthy. **4** at fault, culpable, guilty, to blame. **5** burdensome, decision-making, executive, important, managerial, top.

responsive /rɪ'spɒnsɪv/ *adjective* **1** (often + *to*) responding readily (to some influence); sympathetic. **2** answering; by way of answer. □ **responsiveness** *noun*.

■ **1** alert, alive, aware, impressionable, interested, open, perceptive, receptive, sensitive, sharp, sympathetic, warm-hearted, wide awake, willing.

rest[1] *verb* **1** cease from exertion or action. **2** be still or asleep, esp. to recover strength. **3** lie in death. **4** give relief or repose to. **5** be left without further investigation or discussion. **6** (+ *on*, *upon*, *against*) place, lie, or lean on. **7** (+ *on*, *upon*) depend on. **8** (as **rested** *adjective*) refreshed by resting. ● *noun* **1** repose or sleep; resting; inactivity. **2** break. **3** prop or support for steadying something. **4** *Music* (sign denoting) interval of silence. □ **at rest** not moving; not agitated or troubled. **come to rest** stop moving. **rest-cure** prolonged rest as medical treatment. **rest home** place where elderly or convalescent people are cared for. **restroom** *esp. US* public lavatory. **set at rest** settle; reassure.

■ *verb* **1, 2** be still, doze, idle, laze, lie back, lie down, lounge, *colloquial* nod off, recline, relax, sleep, *colloquial* snooze, take a nap, take it easy, unwind. **6** lean, place, position, prop, set, stand, support. **7** (*rest on*) depend on, hang on, hinge on, rely on, turn on. ● *noun* **1** ease, idleness, inactivity, indolence, leisure, loafing, nap, quiet, relaxation, relief, repose, respite, siesta, sleep. **2** break, *colloquial* breather, breathing-space, hiatus, holiday, interlude, intermission, interval, *colloquial* let-up, lull, pause, recess, respite, time off, vacation. **3** base, brace, bracket, holder, prop, stand, support, trestle, tripod. □ **come to rest** see HALT[1] *verb*.

rest[2] *noun* (**the rest**) remainder or remaining parts or individuals. ● *verb* **1** remain in specified state. **2** (+ *with*) be left in the charge of. □ **for the rest** as regards anything else.

■ *noun* (**the rest**) see REMAINDER *noun* 1, 2.

restaurant /'restərɒnt/ *noun* public premises where meals may be bought and eaten.

■ bistro, brasserie, buffet, café, cafeteria, canteen, carvery, *US* diner, dining room, eating place, grill, refectory, snack bar, steakhouse.

restaurateur /restərə'tɜ:/ *noun* keeper of restaurant.

restful *adjective* quiet, soothing.

■ calm, calming, comfortable, leisurely, peaceful, quiet, relaxed, relaxing, soothing, still, tranquil, undisturbed, unhurried, untroubled.

restitution /restɪ'tju:ʃ(ə)n/ *noun* 1 restoring of property etc. to its owner. 2 reparation.

restive /'restɪv/ *adjective* 1 fidgety. 2 intractable; resisting control.

restless *adjective* 1 without rest. 2 uneasy, agitated. 3 fidgeting; unable to stay still. □ **restlessly** *adverb*. **restlessness** *noun*.

■ 1 disturbed, interrupted, sleepless, unsettled, wakeful. 2, 3 agitated, anxious, edgy, excitable, fidgety, highly-strung, hyperactive, impatient, *colloquial* jittery, jumpy, nervous, on tenterhooks, restive, skittish, troubled, uneasy, worked up, worried.

restoration /restə'reɪʃ(ə)n/ *noun* 1 restoring, being restored. 2 model or drawing representing supposed original form of thing. 3 (**Restoration**) re-establishment of British monarchy in 1660.

restorative /rɪ'stɒrətɪv/ *adjective* tending to restore health or strength. ● *noun* restorative food, medicine, etc.

restore /rɪ'stɔ:/ *verb* (**-ring**) 1 bring back to original state by rebuilding, repairing, etc. 2 give back. 3 reinstate; bring back to former place, condition, or use. 4 bring back to good health. 5 make restoration of (extinct animal, ruined building, etc.). □ **restorer** *noun*.

■ 1 clean, *colloquial* do up, fix, make good, mend, rebuild, recondition, reconstruct, refurbish, renew, renovate, replace, touch up. 2 bring back, give back, make restitution for, put back, replace, return. 3 bring back, re-establish, rehabilitate, reinstate, reintroduce, rekindle, revive. 4 cure, nurse, rejuvenate, resuscitate, revitalize.

restrain /rɪ'streɪn/ *verb* 1 (usually + *from*) check or hold in; keep under control. 2 repress. 3 confine. □ **restrainable** *adjective*. **restrained** *adjective*.

■ 1, 2 check, control, curb, govern, hold back, inhibit, keep back, keep under control, limit, regulate, rein in, repress, restrict, stifle, stop, subdue, suppress. 3 arrest, bridle, confine, detain, fetter, handcuff, harness, imprison, incarcerate, jail, keep under lock and key, lock up, manacle, muzzle, pinion, tie up. □ **restrained** see CALM *adjective* 2, DISCREET 3.

restraint /rɪ'streɪnt/ *noun* 1 restraining, being restrained. 2 restraining agency or influence. 3 self-control; moderation. 4 reserve of manner.

restrict /rɪ'strɪkt/ *verb* 1 confine, limit. 2 withhold from general disclosure. □ **restriction** *noun*.

■ 1 circumscribe, confine, control, cramp, delimit, enclose, impede, imprison, inhibit, keep within bounds, limit, regulate, restrain. □ **restriction** ban, check, constraint, control, curb, curfew, inhibition, limit, limitation, proviso, qualification, regulation, restraint, rule, stipulation.

restrictive /rɪ'strɪktɪv/ *adjective* restricting. □ **restrictive practice** agreement or practice that limits competition or output in industry.

result /rɪ'zʌlt/ *noun* 1 consequence, issue. 2 satisfactory outcome. 3 answer etc. got by calculation. 4 (in *plural*) list of scores, winners, etc. in sporting events or exams. ● *verb* 1 (often + *from*) arise as consequence. 2 (+ *in*) end in.

■ *noun* 1 conclusion, consequence, effect, end product, fruit, issue, outcome, repercussion, upshot. 3 answer, product, score, total. ● *verb* 1 arise, be produced, come about, develop, emanate, emerge, ensue, follow, happen, issue, occur, proceed, spring, stem, turn out. 2 (*result in*) see CAUSE *verb* 1.

resultant *adjective* resulting. ● *noun* force etc. equivalent to two or more acting in different directions at same point.

resume /rɪ'zju:m/ *verb* (**-ming**) 1 begin again; recommence. 2 take again or back. □ **resumption** /-'zʌmp-/ *noun*. **resumptive** /-'zʌmp-/ *adjective*.

■ 1 begin again, carry on, continue, proceed, recommence, reconvene, reopen, restart. □ **resumption** continuation, recommencement, reopening, restart.

résumé /'rezjʊmeɪ/ *noun* summary.

resurgent /rɪ'sɜ:dʒ(ə)nt/ *adjective* rising or arising again. □ **resurgence** *noun*.

resurrect /rezə'rekt/ *verb* 1 raise or rise from dead. 2 *colloquial* revive practice or memory of.

■ 1 breathe new life into, bring back, raise (from the dead), restore to life, resuscitate, revive, rise (from the dead). 2 see RENEW 1.

resurrection /rezə'rekʃ(ə)n/ *noun* 1 rising from the dead. 2 revival from disuse or decay etc.

resuscitate /rɪ'sʌsɪteɪt/ *verb* (**-ting**) 1 revive from unconsciousness or apparent death. 2 revive, restore. □ **resuscitation** *noun*.

retail /'ri:teɪl/ *noun* sale of goods to the public in small quantities. ● *adjective* & *adverb* by retail; at retail price. ● *verb* 1 sell by retail. 2 (often + *at, of*) (of goods) be sold by retail. 3 (also /rɪ'teɪl/) recount. □ **retailer** *noun*.

retain /rɪ'teɪn/ *verb* 1 keep possession of; continue to have, use, etc. 2 keep in mind. 3 hold (moisture). 4 keep in place; hold fixed. 5 secure services of (esp. barrister) by preliminary fee.

■ 1 hang on to, hold, hold back, keep, keep control of, maintain, preserve, reserve, save. 2 keep in mind, learn, memorize, remember. 3 absorb, soak up.

retainer *noun* 1 fee for securing person's services. 2 faithful servant. 3 reduced rent paid to retain unoccupied accommodation. 4 person or thing that retains.

retake *verb* /ri:'teɪk/ (**-king**; *past* **retook**; *past participle* **retaken**) 1 take (photograph, exam, etc.) again. 2 recapture. ● *noun* /'ri:teɪk/ 1 filming, recording, etc. again. 2 taking of exam etc. again.

retaliate /rɪˈtælɪeɪt/ *verb* (**-ting**) repay in kind; attack in return. □ **retaliation** *noun.* **retaliatory** /-ˈtæljət-/ *adjective.*

■ avenge oneself, be revenged, counter-attack, exact retribution, get even, *colloquial* get one's own back, give tit for tat, hit back, pay back, repay, retort, revenge oneself, seek retribution, settle a score, strike back, take revenge, wreak vengeance. □ **retaliation** counter-attack, reprisal, retribution, revenge, vengeance.

retard /rɪˈtɑːd/ *verb* **1** make slow or late. **2** delay progress or accomplishment of. □ **retardant** *adjective* & *noun.* **retardation** /riː-/ *noun.*

■ check, delay, handicap, hinder, hold back, hold up, impede, obstruct, postpone, put back, set back, slow down.

retarded *adjective* backward in mental or physical development.
■ see BACKWARD 3.

retch *verb* make motion of vomiting.

retention /rɪˈtenʃ(ə)n/ *noun* retaining, being retained.

retentive /rɪˈtentɪv/ *adjective* **1** tending to retain. **2** (of memory) not forgetful.

rethink *verb* /riːˈθɪŋk/ (*past* & *past participle* **rethought** /-ˈθɔːt/) consider again, esp. with view to making changes. ● *noun* /ˈriːθɪŋk/ rethinking, reassessment.

reticence /ˈretɪs(ə)ns/ *noun* **1** avoidance of saying all one knows or feels. **2** taciturnity. □ **reticent** *adjective.*

■ □ **reticent** aloof, antisocial, bashful, cautious, cold, cool, demure, diffident, discreet, distant, modest, quiet, remote, reserved, restrained, retiring, secretive, self-conscious, self-effacing, shy, silent, stand-offish, taciturn, timid, uncommunicative, undemonstrative, unemotional, unforthcoming, unresponsive, unsociable, withdrawn.

reticulate *verb* /rɪˈtɪkjʊleɪt/ (**-ting**) divide or be divided in fact or appearance into network. ● *adjective* /rɪˈtɪkjʊlət/ reticulated. □ **reticulation** *noun.*

retina /ˈretɪnə/ *noun* (*plural* **-s** or **-nae** /-niː/) light-sensitive layer at back of eyeball. □ **retinal** *adjective.*

retinue /ˈretɪnjuː/ *noun* group of people attending important person.
■ attendants, company, entourage, followers, hangers-on, servants, train.

retire /rɪˈtaɪə/ *verb* (**-ring**) **1** leave office or employment, esp. because of age. **2** cause (employee) to retire. **3** withdraw, retreat. **4** seek seclusion or shelter. **5** go to bed. **6** *Cricket* (of batsman) suspend one's innings. □ **retired** *adjective.*

■ **1** give up, leave, quit, resign. **3, 4** become reclusive, cloister oneself, go away, go into retreat, retreat from the world, sequester oneself, withdraw.

retirement *noun* **1** retiring. **2** period spent as retired person. **3** seclusion. □ **retirement pension** pension paid by state to retired people above certain age.

retiring *adjective* shy; fond of seclusion.

retort[1] /rɪˈtɔːt/ *noun* incisive, witty, or angry reply. ● *verb* **1** say by way of retort. **2** repay in kind.

■ *noun* answer, *slang* comeback, rebuttal, rejoinder, reply, response, retaliation, riposte.
● *verb* **1** answer, counter, react, rejoin, reply, respond, return. **2** see RETALIATE.

retort[2] /rɪˈtɔːt/ *noun* **1** vessel with long downward-bent neck for distilling liquids. **2** vessel for heating coal to generate gas.

retouch /riːˈtʌtʃ/ *verb* improve (esp. photograph) by minor alterations.

retrace /rɪˈtreɪs/ *verb* (**-cing**) **1** go back over (one's steps etc.). **2** trace back to source or beginning.

retract /rɪˈtrækt/ *verb* **1** withdraw (statement etc.). **2** draw or be drawn back or in. □ **retractable** *adjective.* **retraction** *noun.*

■ **1** cancel, disclaim, disown, forswear, have second thoughts about, recant, renounce, repeal, repudiate, rescind, reverse, revoke, withdraw. **2** draw in, pull back, pull in.

retractile /rɪˈtræktaɪl/ *adjective* retractable.

retread *verb* /riːˈtred/ **1** (*past* **retrod**; *past participle* **retrodden**) tread (path etc.) again. **2** (*past* and *past participle* **retreaded**) put new tread on (tyre). ● *noun* /ˈriːtred/ retreaded tyre.

retreat /rɪˈtriːt/ *verb* **1** go back, retire. **2** recede. ● *noun* **1** (signal for) act of retreating. **2** withdrawing into privacy. **3** place of seclusion or shelter. **4** period of seclusion for prayer and meditation.

■ *verb* **1** back away, back down, climb down, decamp, depart, evacuate, fall back, flee, go away, leave, move back, pull back, retire, run away, take flight, take to one's heels, turn tail, withdraw. **2** ebb, flow back, recede, shrink back. ● *noun* **1** departure, escape, evacuation, exit, flight, retirement, withdrawal. **3** asylum, den, haven, hideaway, hideout, hiding place, refuge, resort, sanctuary, shelter.

retrench /rɪˈtrentʃ/ *verb* cut down expenses; reduce amount of (costs); economize. □ **retrenchment** *noun.*

retrial /riːˈtraɪəl/ *noun* retrying of case.

retribution /retrɪˈbjuːʃ(ə)n/ *noun* recompense, usually for evil; vengeance. □ **retributive** /rɪˈtrɪb-/ *adjective.*

■ compensation, quid pro quo, recompense, redress, reprisal, retaliation, revenge, satisfaction, vengeance.

retrieve /rɪˈtriːv/ *verb* (**-ving**) **1** regain possession of; find again. **2** obtain (information in computer). **3** (of dog) find and bring in (game). **4** (+ *from*) rescue from (bad state etc.). **5** restore to good state. **6** repair, set right. □ **retrievable** *adjective*. **retrieval** *noun*.

■ **1** bring back, come back with, fetch back, find, get back, recapture, reclaim, recoup, recover, regain, repossess, trace, track down. **5, 6** make up for, redeem, repair, rescue, restore, salvage, save.

retriever *noun* dog of breed used for retrieving game.

retro /ˈretrəʊ/ *slang adjective* reviving or harking back to past. ● *noun* (*plural* **retros**) retro fashion or style.

retro- *combining form* backwards, back.

retroactive /retrəʊˈæktɪv/ *adjective* having retrospective effect.

retrod *past of* RETREAD.

retrodden *past participle of* RETREAD.

retrograde /ˈretrəgreɪd/ *adjective* **1** directed backwards. **2** reverting, esp. to inferior state. ● *verb* **1** move backwards. **2** decline, revert.

■ *adjective* **1** backward, retreating, retrogressive, reverse. **2** backward, negative, regressive, retrogressive.

retrogress /retrəˈgres/ *verb* **1** move backwards. **2** deteriorate. □ **retrogression** *noun*. **retrogressive** *adjective*.

retrorocket /ˈretrəʊrɒkɪt/ *noun* auxiliary rocket for slowing down spacecraft etc.

retrospect /ˈretrəspekt/ *noun* □ **in retrospect** when looking back.

retrospection /retrəˈspekʃ(ə)n/ *noun* looking back into the past.

retrospective /retrəˈspektɪv/ *adjective* **1** looking back on or dealing with the past. **2** (of statute etc.) applying to the past as well as the future. ● *noun* exhibition etc. showing artist's lifetime development. □ **retrospectively** *adverb*.

■ *adjective* **1** backward-looking, nostalgic.

retroussé /rəˈtruːseɪ/ *adjective* (of nose) turned up at tip.

retroverted /ˈretrəʊvɜːtɪd/ *adjective* (of womb) inclining backwards.

retry /riːˈtraɪ/ *verb* (**-ies, -ied**) try (defendant, law case) again.

retsina /retˈsiːnə/ *noun* resin-flavoured Greek white wine.

return /rɪˈtɜːn/ *verb* **1** come or go back. **2** bring, put, or send back. **3** pay back; give in response. **4** yield (profit). **5** say in reply. **6** send (ball) back in tennis etc. **7** state in answer to formal demand. **8** elect as MP etc. ● *noun* **1** coming or going back. **2** putting, giving, sending, or paying back. **3** what is returned. **4** (in full **return ticket**) ticket for journey to place and back again. **5** (in *singular* or *plural*) proceeds, profit. **6** (in *singular* or *plural*) coming in of these. **7** formal statement or report. **8** (in full **return match, game**) second game between same opponents. **9** (announcement of) person's election as MP etc. □ **by return (of post)** by the next available post in the return direction. **returning officer** official conducting election in constituency etc. and announcing result.

■ *verb* **1** backtrack, come back, crop up again, do a U-turn, double back, go back, happen again, reappear, reassemble, reconvene, recur, re-enter, regress, resurface, retrace one's steps, revert, turn back. **2** bring back, put back, repatriate, replace, restore, send back. **3** give back, pay back, refund, reimburse, repay. **7** deliver, give, proffer, report. ● *noun* **1** advent, arrival, comeback, reappearance, *formal* recrudescence, recurrence, re-emergence, re-entry, re-establishment, repetition, reversion. **2** reimbursement, reinstatement, repayment, replacement, restitution, restoration, retrieval. **5** benefit, earnings, gain, income, interest, proceeds, profit, yield.

returnee /rɪtɜːˈniː/ *noun* person who returns home, esp. after war service.

reunify /riːˈjuːnɪfaɪ/ *verb* (**-ies, -ied**) restore to political unity. □ **reunification** *noun*.

reunion /riːˈjuːnjən/ *noun* **1** reuniting, being reunited. **2** social gathering, esp. of former associates.

reunite /riːjuːˈnaɪt/ *verb* (**-ting**) (cause to) come together again.

reuse *verb* /riːˈjuːz/ (**-sing**) use again. ● *noun* /riːˈjuːs/ second or further use. □ **reusable** *adjective*.

Rev. *abbreviation* Reverend.

rev *colloquial noun* (in *plural*) revolutions of engine per minute. ● *verb* (**-vv-**) **1** (of engine) revolve. **2** (often + *up*) cause (engine) to run quickly.

revalue /riːˈvæljuː/ *verb* (**-ues, -ued, -uing**) give different, esp. higher, value to (currency etc.). □ **revaluation** *noun*.

revamp /riːˈvæmp/ *verb* **1** renovate, revise. **2** patch up.

Revd *abbreviation* Reverend.

reveal /rɪˈviːl/ *verb* **1** display, show; allow to appear. **2** (often as **revealing** *adjective*) disclose, divulge.

■ **1** bare, display, exhibit, expose, lay bare, show, take the wraps off, uncover, undress, unearth, unfold, unmask, unveil. **2** announce, betray, bring to light, communicate, confess, declare, dig up, disclose, divulge, expose, leak, *colloquial* let on, let out, let slip, make known, proclaim, publish, show up, *colloquial* spill the beans about, tell.

reveille /rɪˈvælɪ/ *noun* military waking-signal.

revel /ˈrev(ə)l/ *verb* (**-ll-**; *US* **-l-**) **1** make merry; be riotously festive. **2** (+ *in*) take keen delight in. ● *noun* (in *singular* or *plural*) revelling. □ **reveller** *noun*. **revelry** *noun* (*plural* **-ies**).

■ *verb* **1** carouse, celebrate, *colloquial* have a spree, have fun, *colloquial* live it up, make merry, *colloquial* paint the town red. **2** (*revel in*) see ENJOY 1. ● *noun* carnival, festival, fête, jamboree, party, *colloquial* rave-up, *colloquial* shindig, *colloquial* spree; (*revels*) see REVELRY. □ **revelry** carousing, celebration, conviviality, debauchery, festivity, fun, gaiety, high jinks, jollification, jollity, junketing, *colloquial* living it up, merrymaking, revelling, revels, roistering, *colloquial* spree.

revelation /revə'leɪʃ(ə)n/ *noun* **1** revealing. **2** knowledge supposedly disclosed by divine or supernatural agency. **3** striking disclosure or realization. **4** (**Revelation** or *colloquial* **Revelations**) last book of New Testament.

■ **3** admission, announcement, communiqué, confession, declaration, disclosure, discovery, exposé, exposure, *colloquial* eye-opener, leak, news, proclamation, publication, unmasking, unveiling.

revelatory /revə'leɪt(ə)rɪ, 'rev(ə)lət(ə)rɪ/ *adjective* yielding a revelation.

revenge /rɪ'vendʒ/ *noun* **1** (act of) retaliation. **2** desire for this. ● *verb* (**-ging**) **1** avenge. **2** (**revenge oneself** or in *passive*; often + *on*, *upon*) inflict retaliation.

■ *noun* **1** reprisal, retaliation, retribution, vengeance. **2** spitefulness, vindictiveness. ● *verb* **1** avenge, repay. **2** (*be revenged*) see RETALIATE.

revengeful *adjective* eager for revenge.

revenue /'revənju:/ *noun* **1** income, esp. annual income of state. **2** department collecting state revenue.

■ **1** gain, income, interest, money, proceeds, profits, receipts, returns, takings, yield.

reverberate /rɪ'vɜːbəreɪt/ *verb* (**-ting**) **1** (of sound, light, or heat) be returned or reflected repeatedly. **2** return (sound etc.) thus. **3** (of event) produce continuing effect. □ **reverberant** *adjective*. **reverberation** *noun*. **reverberative** /-rətɪv/ *adjective*.

■ **1** boom, echo, pulsate, resonate, resound, ring, rumble, throb, thunder, vibrate.

revere /rɪ'vɪə/ *verb* (**-ring**) regard with deep and affectionate or religious respect.

■ admire, adore, adulate, *RC Church* beatify, esteem, glorify, honour, idolize, pay homage to, praise, respect, reverence, value, venerate, worship.

reverence /'revərəns/ *noun* **1** revering, being revered. **2** deep respect. ● *verb* (**-cing**) treat with reverence.

■ *noun* admiration, adoration, adulation, awe, deference, devotion, esteem, glorification, homage, honour, idolization, praise, respect, veneration, worship.

reverend /'revərənd/ *adjective* (esp. as title of member of clergy) deserving reverence. □ **Reverend Mother** Mother Superior of convent.

reverent /'revərənt/ *adjective* feeling or showing reverence. □ **reverently** *adverb*.

■ adoring, awed, deferential, devoted, devout, pious, prayerful, religious, respectful, reverential, solemn.

reverential /revə'renʃ(ə)l/ *adjective* of the nature of, due to, or characterized by reverence. □ **reverentially** *adverb*.

reverie /'revərɪ/ *noun* fit of musing; daydream.

■ daydream, dream, fantasy, meditation.

revers /rɪ'vɪə/ *noun* (*plural* same /-'vɪəz/) (material of) turned-back front edge of garment.

reverse /rɪ'vɜːs/ *verb* (**-sing**) **1** turn the other way round or up; turn inside out. **2** convert to opposite character or effect. **3** (cause to) travel backwards. **4** make (engine) work in contrary direction. **5** revoke, annul. ● *adjective* **1** backward; upside down. **2** opposite or contrary in character or order; inverted. ● *noun* **1** opposite or contrary. **2** contrary of usual manner. **3** piece of misfortune; disaster. **4** reverse gear or motion. **5** reverse side. **6** side of coin etc. bearing secondary design. **7** verso of printed leaf. □ **reverse the charges** have recipient of telephone call pay for it. **reverse gear** gear used to make vehicle etc. go backwards. **reversing light** light at rear of vehicle showing it is in reverse gear. □ **reversal** *noun*. **reversible** *adjective*.

■ *verb* **1** change, invert, overturn, transpose, turn inside out, turn round, turn upside down. **3** back, drive backwards. **5** abandon, annul, cancel, countermand, invalidate, negate, nullify, overturn, quash, repeal, rescind, retract, revoke, undo. ● *adjective* backward, contrary, converse, inverse, inverted, opposite. ● *noun* **1** antithesis, contrary, converse, opposite. **3** defeat, difficulty, disaster, failure, misfortune, mishap, problem, reversal, setback, upset, *literary* vicissitude. **5** back, rear, underside, verso, wrong side.

reversion /rɪ'vɜːʃ(ə)n/ *noun* **1** return to previous state or earlier type. **2** legal right (esp. of original owner) to possess or succeed to property on death of present possessor.

revert /rɪ'vɜːt/ *verb* **1** (+ *to*) return to (former condition, practice, subject, opinion, etc.). **2** return by reversion. □ **revertible** *adjective*.

review /rɪ'vju:/ *noun* **1** general survey or assessment. **2** survey of past. **3** revision, reconsideration. **4** published criticism of book, play, etc. **5** periodical in which events, books, etc. are reviewed. **6** inspection of troops etc. ● *verb* **1** survey, look back on. **2** reconsider, revise. **3** hold review of (troops etc.). **4** write review of (book etc.). □ **reviewer** *noun*.

■ *noun* **1** assessment, examination, report, study, survey. **2** *colloquial* post-mortem. **3** reappraisal, reassessment, recapitulation, reconsideration, re-examination, revision. **4** appreciation, assessment, commentary, criticism, critique, evaluation, judgement, notice, write-up. ● *verb* **1** assess, consider, examine, go over, inspect, scrutinize, study, survey, take stock of, *colloquial* weigh up. **2** reassess, recapitulate, reconsider, re-examine, revise. **4** appraise, assess, criticize, evaluate, judge.

revile /rɪ'vaɪl/ *verb* (**-ling**) abuse verbally.

revise /rɪ'vaɪz/ *verb* (**-sing**) **1** examine and improve or amend. **2** reconsider and alter (opinion etc.). **3** go over (work etc.) again, esp. for examination. □ **revisory** *adjective*.

■ **1** adapt, alter, amend, change, correct, edit, emend, improve, modify, overhaul, polish up, rectify, redo, rehash, rephrase, revamp, reword, rework, rewrite, update. **2** alter, change, modify, reconsider. **3** brush up, cram, go over, learn, study, *colloquial* swot.

revision /rɪ'vɪʒ(ə)n/ *noun* **1** revising, being revised. **2** revised edition or form.

revisionism *noun often derogatory* revision or modification of orthodoxy, esp. of Marxism. □ **revisionist** *noun & adjective.*

revitalize /ri:'vaɪtəlaɪz/ *verb* (also **-ise**) (**-zing** or **-sing**) imbue with new vitality. □ **revitalization** /-'zeɪʃ(ə)n/ *noun.*

revival /rɪ'vaɪv(ə)l/ *noun* **1** reviving, being revived. **2** (campaign to promote) reawakening of religious fervour. **3** new production of old play etc.
■ **1, 2** reawakening, rebirth, recovery, renaissance, renewal, restoration, resurgence, resurrection, resuscitation, return, revitalization, upsurge.

revivalism *noun* promotion of esp. religious revival. □ **revivalist** *noun & adjective.*

revive /rɪ'vaɪv/ *verb* (**-ving**) come or bring back to consciousness, life, vigour, use, or notice.
■ awaken, bring back to life, cheer up, come back to life, come round, come to, freshen, invigorate, quicken, rally, reawaken, recover, refresh, renew, restore, *colloquial* resurrect, resuscitate, revitalize, rouse, strengthen, waken.

revivify /rɪ'vɪvɪfaɪ/ *verb* (**-ies**, **-ied**) restore to life, strength, or activity. □ **revivification** *noun.*

revoke /rɪ'vəuk/ *verb* (**-king**) **1** rescind, withdraw, cancel. **2** *Cards* fail to follow suit though able to. ● *noun Cards* revoking. □ **revocable** /'revəkəb(ə)l/ *adjective.* **revocation** /revə-'keɪʃ(ə)n/ *noun.*

revolt /rɪ'vəult/ *verb* **1** rise in rebellion. **2** affect with disgust. **3** (often + *at, against*) feel revulsion. ● *noun* **1** insurrection. **2** sense of disgust. **3** rebellious mood.
■ *verb* **1** disobey, dissent, mutiny, rebel, riot, rise up. **2** appal, disgust, nauseate, offend, outrage, repel, sicken, upset. ● *noun* **1** coup, *coup d'état,* insurrection, mutiny, putsch, rebellion, revolution, rising, takeover, uprising.

revolting *adjective* disgusting, horrible. □ **revoltingly** *adverb.*
■ see OFFENSIVE *adjective* 2.

revolution /revə'lu:ʃ(ə)n/ *noun* **1** forcible overthrow of government or social order. **2** fundamental change. **3** revolving. **4** single completion of orbit or rotation.
■ **1** see REVOLT *noun* 1. **2** change, reorganization, reorientation, shift, transformation, turn-about, upheaval, upset, U-turn. **3, 4** circuit, cycle, gyration, orbit, rotation, spin, turn.

revolutionary *adjective* **1** involving great change. **2** of political revolution. ● *noun* (*plural* **-ies**) instigator or supporter of political revolution.

■ *adjective* **1** avant-garde, challenging, creative, different, experimental, extremist, innovative, new, novel, progressive, radical. **2** insurgent, mutinous, rebel, rebellious, seditious, subversive. ● *noun* anarchist, extremist, freedom fighter, insurgent, mutineer, rebel, terrorist.

revolutionize *verb* (also **-ise**) (**-zing** or **-sing**) change fundamentally.

revolve /rɪ'vɒlv/ *verb* (**-ving**) **1** turn round; rotate. **2** move in orbit. **3** ponder in the mind. **4** (+ *around*) be centred on.
■ **1, 2** circle, go round, gyrate, orbit, pirouette, pivot, reel, rotate, spin, swivel, turn, twirl, wheel, whirl.

revolver *noun* pistol with revolving chambers enabling user to fire several shots without reloading.

revue /rɪ'vju:/ *noun* theatrical entertainment of usually comic sketches and songs.

revulsion /rɪ'vʌlʃ(ə)n/ *noun* **1** abhorrence. **2** sudden violent change of feeling.
■ **1** abhorrence, aversion, disgust, hatred, loathing, outrage, repugnance.

reward /rɪ'wɔ:d/ *noun* **1** return or recompense for service or merit. **2** requital for good or evil. **3** sum offered for detection of criminal, recovery of lost property, etc. ● *verb* give or serve as reward to. □ **rewarding** *adjective.*
■ *noun* award, bonus, bounty, compensation, decoration, favour, honour, medal, payment, prize, recompense, remuneration, requital, return, tribute. ● *verb* compensate, decorate, honour, recompense, remunerate, repay. □ **rewarding** see PROFITABLE 2, WORTHWHILE (WORTH).

rewind /ri:'waɪnd/ *verb* (*past & past participle* **rewound** /-'waʊnd/) wind (film, tape, etc.) back.

rewire /ri:'waɪə/ *verb* (**-ring**) provide with new electrical wiring.

rework /ri:'wɜ:k/ *verb* revise; refashion; remake. □ **reworking** *noun.*

Rex *noun* **1** (after name) reigning king. **2** *Law* the Crown. [Latin]

rhapsodize /'ræpsədaɪz/ *verb* (also **-ise**) (**-zing** or **-sing**) speak or write rhapsodies.
■ be expansive, effuse, *colloquial* enthuse, go into raptures.

rhapsody /'ræpsədɪ/ *noun* (*plural* **-ies**) **1** enthusiastic or extravagant speech or composition. **2** melodic musical piece often based on folk culture. □ **rhapsodic** /-'sɒd-/ *adjective.*

rhea /'ri:ə/ *noun* large flightless S. American bird.

rheostat /'ri:əstæt/ *noun* instrument used to control electric current by varying resistance.

rhesus /'ri:səs/ *noun* (in full **rhesus monkey**) small Indian monkey. □ **rhesus factor** antigen occurring on red blood cells of most humans and some other primates. **rhesus-positive, -negative** having or not having rhesus factor.

rhetoric /'retərɪk/ *noun* **1** art of persuasive

speaking or writing. **2** language intended to impress, esp. seen as inflated, exaggerated, or meaningless.
■ **1** eloquence, expressiveness, gift of the gab, oratory. **2** bombast, grandiloquence.

rhetorical /rɪ'tɒrɪk(ə)l/ *adjective* **1** expressed artificially or extravagantly. **2** of the nature of rhetoric. □ **rhetorical question** question asked not for information but to produce effect. □ **rhetorically** *adverb*.
■ **1** artificial, bombastic, florid, flowery, fustian, grandiloquent, grandiose, high-flown, insincere, ornate, pretentious, verbose, wordy. **2** oratorical.

rheumatic /ruː'mætɪk/ *adjective* of, caused by, or suffering from rheumatism. ● *noun* **1** person suffering from rheumatism. **2** (in *plural*, often treated as *singular*) *colloquial* rheumatism. □ **rheumatic fever** fever with pain in the joints. □ **rheumatically** *adverb*. **rheumaticky** *adjective colloquial*.

rheumatism /'ruːmətɪz(ə)m/ *noun* disease marked by inflammation and pain in joints etc.

rheumatoid /'ruːmətɔɪd/ *adjective* having the character of rheumatism. □ **rheumatoid arthritis** chronic progressive disease causing inflammation and stiffening of joints.

rhinestone /'raɪnstəʊn/ *noun* imitation diamond.

rhino /'raɪnəʊ/ *noun* (*plural* same or **-s**) *colloquial* rhinoceros.

rhinoceros /raɪ'nɒsərəs/ *noun* (*plural* same or **-roses**) large thick-skinned animal with usually one horn on nose.

rhizome /'raɪzəʊm/ *noun* underground rootlike stem bearing both roots and shoots.

rhododendron /rəʊdə'dendrən/ *noun* (*plural* **-s** or **-dra**) evergreen shrub with large flowers.

rhomboid /'rɒmbɔɪd/ *adjective* (also **rhomboidal** /-'bɔɪd-/) like a rhombus. ● *noun* quadrilateral of which only opposite sides and angles are equal.

rhombus /'rɒmbəs/ *noun* (*plural* **-buses** or **-bi** /-baɪ/) oblique equilateral parallelogram, e.g. diamond on playing card.

rhubarb /'ruːbɑːb/ *noun* **1** (stalks of) plant with fleshy leaf-stalks cooked and eaten as dessert. **2** *colloquial* indistinct conversation or noise, from repeated use of word 'rhubarb' by stage crowd.

rhyme /raɪm/ *noun* **1** identity of sound at ends of words or verse-lines. **2** (in *singular* or *plural*) rhymed verse. **3** use of rhyme. **4** word providing rhyme. ● *verb* (**-ming**) **1** (of words or lines) produce rhyme. **2** (+ *with*) be or use as rhyme with. **3** write rhymes; put into rhyme. □ **rhymer** *noun*.
■ *noun* **2** doggerel, jingle, poem, verse.

rhythm /'rɪð(ə)m/ *noun* **1** periodical accent and duration of notes in music. **2** type of structure formed by this. **3** measured flow of words in verse or prose. **4** *Physiology* pattern of successive strong and weak movements. **5** regularly occurring sequence of events. □ **rhythm method** con-

traception by avoiding sexual intercourse near times of ovulation. □ **rhythmic** *adjective*. **rhythmical** *adjective*. **rhythmically** *adverb*.
■ **1** accent, beat, measure, metre, pattern, pulse, stress, tempo, throb, time. □ **rhythmic** beating, measured, metrical, pulsing, regular, repeated, steady, throbbing.

rib *noun* **1** each of the curved bones joined to spine and protecting organs of chest. **2** joint of meat from this part of animal. **3** supporting ridge, timber, rod, etc. across surface or through structure. **4** combination of plain and purl stitches producing ribbed design. ● *verb* (**-bb-**) **1** provide or mark (as) with ribs. **2** *colloquial* tease. □ **ribcage** wall of bones formed by ribs round chest. **rib-tickler** something amusing. □ **ribbed** *adjective*. **ribbing** *noun*.

ribald /'rɪb(ə)ld/ *adjective* irreverent; coarsely humorous. □ **ribaldry** *noun*.
■ bawdy, coarse, disrespectful, earthy, *colloquial* jocular naughty, obscene, racy, *colloquial* rude, scurrilous, smutty, vulgar.

riband /'rɪbənd/ *noun* ribbon.

ribbon /'rɪbən/ *noun* **1** narrow strip or band of fabric. **2** material in this form. **3** ribbon worn to indicate some honour, membership of sports team, etc. **4** long narrow strip. **5** (in *plural*) ragged strips. □ **ribbon development** building of houses along main road outwards from town.
■ **1, 2, 4** band, braid, line, strip, stripe, tape, trimming. **5** (*in ribbons*) see RAGGED 1.

riboflavin /raɪbəʊ'fleɪvɪn/ *noun* (also **riboflavine** /-viːn/) vitamin of B complex, found in liver, milk, and eggs.

ribonucleic acid /raɪbəʊnjuː'kliːɪk/ *noun* substance controlling protein synthesis in cells.

rice *noun* (grains from) swamp grass grown esp. in Asia. □ **rice-paper** edible paper made from pith of an oriental tree and used for painting and in cookery.

rich *adjective* **1** having much wealth. **2** splendid, costly; valuable. **3** abundant, ample. **4** (often + *in*, *with*) abounding; fertile. **5** (of food) containing much fat, spice, etc. **6** (of colour, sound, or smell) mellow, strong and full. **7** highly amusing or ludicrous. □ **richness** *noun*.
■ **1** affluent, *colloquial* flush, *slang* loaded, moneyed, opulent, prosperous, wealthy, *colloquial* well-heeled, well off, well-to-do. **2** costly, elaborate, expensive, lavish, luxurious, precious, priceless, splendid, sumptuous, valuable. **3** abundant, ample, bountiful, copious, *literary* plenteous, plentiful, profuse, prolific, teeming. **4** fecund, fertile, fruitful, productive. **5** cloying, creamy, fat, fattening, fatty, full-flavoured, heavy, highly-flavoured, luscious, sumptuous, sweet. **6** deep, full, intense, strong, vibrant, vivid, warm.

riches *plural noun* abundant means; valuable possessions.
■ affluence, fortune, means, money, opulence, plenty, possessions, prosperity, resources, wealth.

richly *adverb* **1** in a rich way. **2** fully, thoroughly.

Richter scale /ˈrɪktə/ *noun* scale of 0–10 for representing strength of earthquake.

rick[1] *noun* stack of hay etc.

rick[2] (also **wrick**) *noun* slight sprain or strain. ● *verb* slightly strain or sprain.

rickets /ˈrɪkɪts/ *noun* (treated as *singular* or *plural*) children's deficiency disease with softening of the bones.

rickety /ˈrɪkɪtɪ/ *adjective* **1** shaky, insecure. **2** suffering from rickets.

■ **1** dilapidated, flimsy, frail, insecure, ramshackle, shaky, tottering, tumbledown, unsteady, weak, wobbly.

rickshaw /ˈrɪkʃɔː/ *noun* (also **ricksha** /-ʃə/) light two-wheeled hooded vehicle drawn by one or more people.

ricochet /ˈrɪkəʃeɪ/ *noun* **1** rebounding of esp. shell or bullet off surface. **2** hit made after this. ● *verb* (**-cheted** /-ʃeɪd/ or **-chetted** /-ʃetɪd/; **-cheting** /-ʃeɪɪŋ/ or **-chetting** /-ʃetɪŋ/) (of projectile) make ricochet.

ricotta /rɪˈkɒtə/ *noun* soft Italian cheese.

rid *verb* (**-dd-**; *past & past participle* **rid**) (+ *of*) make (person, place) free of. □ **get rid of** be freed of.

■ (*rid of*) clear of, deliver from, free of, purge of, rescue from, save from. □ **get rid of** see DESTROY 2, REMOVE *verb* 1; 3–4.

riddance /ˈrɪd(ə)ns/ *noun* □ **good riddance** expression of relief at getting rid of something or someone.

ridden *past participle* of RIDE.

riddle[1] /ˈrɪd(ə)l/ *noun* **1** verbal puzzle or test, often with trick answer. **2** puzzling fact, thing, or person. ● *verb* (**-ling**) speak in riddles.

■ *noun* **1** *colloquial* brain-teaser, conundrum, *colloquial* poser, problem, puzzle, question. **2** enigma, mystery, puzzle.

riddle[2] /ˈrɪd(ə)l/ *verb* (**-ling**) **1** (usually + *with*) make many holes in, esp. with gunshot. **2** (in *passive*) fill, permeate. **3** pass through riddle. ● *noun* coarse sieve.

■ *verb* **1** honeycomb, pepper, perforate, pierce, puncture. **3** filter, screen, sieve, sift, strain. ● *noun* filter, screen, sieve.

ride *verb* (**-ding**; *past* **rode**; *past participle* **ridden** /ˈrɪd(ə)n/) **1** travel or be carried on (bicycle, horse, etc.) or in (vehicle). **2** (often + *on, in*) travel or be carried (on horseback or bicycle, or in vehicle). **3** cross, be conveyed over. **4** be carried or supported by. **5** float buoyantly. **6** (as **ridden** *adjective*) (+ *by, with*) dominated by or infested with. ● *noun* **1** journey or spell of riding in vehicle, on horse, etc. **2** path (esp. through woods) for riding on. **3** amusement for riding on at fairground. □ **ride up** (of garment) work upwards when worn. **take for a ride** *colloquial* hoax, deceive.

■ *verb* **1** control, handle, manage, sit on, steer. **2** be carried, cycle, journey, pedal, travel. ● *noun* **1** see JOURNEY *noun*.

rider *noun* **1** person riding. **2** additional remark following statement, verdict, etc.

ridge *noun* **1** line of junction of two surfaces sloping upwards towards each other. **2** long narrow hilltop; mountain range. **3** any narrow elevation across surface. □ **ridge pole** horizontal pole of long tent. **ridgeway** road along ridge.

■ **1** crest, top, top edge. **2** arête, crest, edge, saddle.

ridicule /ˈrɪdɪkjuːl/ *noun* derision, mockery. ● *verb* (**-ling**) make fun of; mock; laugh at.

■ *noun* badinage, banter, burlesque, caricature, derision, gibing, invective, jeering, jibing, lampoon, laughter, mockery, parody, raillery, *colloquial* ribbing, sarcasm, satire, scorn, sneers, taunts, teasing. ● *verb* be sarcastic, be satirical about, burlesque, caricature, chaff, deride, gibe at, jeer at, jibe at, joke about, lampoon, laugh at, make fun of, make jokes about, mimic, mock, parody, pillory, poke fun at, *colloquial* rib, satirize, scoff at, *colloquial* send up, sneer at, *slang* take the mickey out of, taunt, tease, travesty.

ridiculous /rɪˈdɪkjuləs/ *adjective* **1** deserving to be laughed at. **2** unreasonable. □ **ridiculously** *adverb*. **ridiculousness** *noun*.

■ absurd, amusing, comic, comical, crazy, daft, eccentric, farcical, foolish, funny, grotesque, hilarious, illogical, irrational, laughable, ludicrous, mad, nonsensical, preposterous, senseless, silly, stupid, unbelievable, unreasonable, *colloquial* weird, zany.

riding[1] /ˈraɪdɪŋ/ *noun* sport or pastime of travelling on horseback.

riding[2] /ˈraɪdɪŋ/ *noun historical* former division of Yorkshire.

Riesling /ˈriːzlɪŋ/ *noun* (white wine made from) type of grape.

rife *adjective* **1** widespread. **2** (+ *with*) abounding in.

■ **1** abundant, common, prevalent, widespread.

riff *noun* short repeated phrase in jazz etc.

riffle /ˈrɪf(ə)l/ *verb* (**-ling**) **1** (often + *through*) leaf quickly through (pages). **2** shuffle (cards). ● *noun* **1** riffling. **2** *US* patch of ripples in stream etc.

riff-raff /ˈrɪfræf/ *noun* rabble, disreputable people.

rifle[1] /ˈraɪf(ə)l/ *noun* **1** gun with long rifled barrel. **2** (in *plural*) troops armed with these. ● *verb* (**-ling**) make spiral grooves in (gun etc.) to make projectile spin. □ **rifle range** place for rifle practice.

rifle[2] /ˈraɪf(ə)l/ *verb* (**-ling**) **1** (often + *through*) search and rob. **2** carry off as booty.

rift *noun* **1** crack, split; cleft. **2** disagreement, dispute. □ **rift valley** one formed by subsidence of section of earth's crust.

■ **1** breach, break, chink, cleft, crack, fracture, gap, gulf, opening, split. **2** alienation, conflict, difference, disagreement, division, schism, separation.

rig¹ *verb* (**-gg-**) **1** provide (ship) with rigging. **2** (often + *out*, *up*) fit with clothes or equipment. **3** (+ *up*) set up hastily or as makeshift. ● *noun* **1** arrangement of ship's masts, sails, etc. **2** equipment for special purpose. **3** oil rig. **4** *colloquial* style of dress, uniform. □ **rig-out** *colloquial* outfit of clothes. □ **rigger** *noun*.
■ *verb* **2** (*rig out*) equip, fit out, kit out, provision, set up, supply. ● *noun* **1** rigging, tackle. **2** apparatus, clothes, equipment, gear, kit, outfit, stuff, tackle.

rig² *verb* (**-gg-**) manage or fix fraudulently. ● *noun* trick, swindle.

rigging *noun* ship's spars, ropes, etc.
■ rig, tackle.

right /raɪt/ *adjective* **1** just; morally or socially correct. **2** correct, true. **3** preferable, suitable. **4** in good or normal condition. **5** on or towards east side of person or thing facing north. **6** (also **Right**) *Politics* of the Right. **7** (of side of fabric etc.) meant to show. **8** *colloquial* real, complete. ● *noun* **1** what is just; fair treatment. **2** fair claim; legal or moral entitlement. **3** right-hand part, region, or direction. **4** *Boxing* right hand. **5** *Boxing* blow with this. **6** (often **Right**) *Politics* conservatives collectively. ● *verb* **1** (often **right itself**) restore to proper, straight, or vertical position. **2** correct; set in order. **3** avenge; make reparation for. ● *adverb* **1** straight. **2** *colloquial* immediately. **3** (+ *to*, *round*, *through*, etc.) all the way. **4** (+ *off*, *out*, etc.) completely. **5** quite, very. **6** justly, properly, correctly, truly. **7** on or to right side. ● *interjection colloquial: expressing agreement or consent*. □ **by right(s)** if right were done. **in the right** having justice or truth on one's side. **put right 1** set in order; repair, cure. **2** correct. **right angle** angle of 90°. **right-angled** *adjective*. **right away (or off)** immediately. **right-hand** on right side. **right-handed 1** naturally using right hand for writing etc. **2** made by or for right hand. **3** turning to right. **4** (of screw) turning clockwise to tighten. **right-hander** right-handed person or blow. **right-hand man, woman** indispensable or chief assistant. **Right Honourable** *title of certain high officials, e.g. Privy Counsellors*. **right-minded, -thinking** having sound views and principles. **right of way 1** right to pass over another's ground. **2** path subject to such right. **3** precedence granted to one vehicle over another. **Right Reverend** *title of bishop*. **right wing 1** more conservative section of political party etc. **2** right side of football etc. team. **right-wing** conservative, reactionary. **right-winger** member of right wing. □ **rightness** *noun*. **rightward** *adjective & adverb*. **rightwards** *adverb*.
■ *adjective* **1** decent, ethical, fair, good, honest, honourable, just, law-abiding, lawful, moral, principled, responsible, righteous, right-minded, upright, virtuous. **2** accurate, apposite, appropriate, apt, correct, exact, factual, faultless,

fitting, genuine, perfect, precise, proper, sound, suitable, true, truthful, valid, *formal* veracious. **3** advantageous, beneficial, best, convenient, good, normal, preferable, preferred, recommended, sensible, usual. **5** right-hand, starboard = *right facing bow of ship*. **6** conservative, reactionary, right-wing, *colloquial* Tory. ● *noun* **1** decency, equity, ethics, fairness, goodness, honesty, integrity, justice, morality, propriety, reason, truth, virtue. **2** authority, commission, entitlement, facility, franchise, freedom, liberty, licence, position, power, prerogative, privilege, title. ● *verb* **1** pick up, set upright, stand upright, straighten up. **2** amend, correct, make amends for, put right, rectify, redress, remedy, repair, set right. □ **put right 1** see REPAIR¹ *verb* 1–2.

righteous /ˈraɪtʃəs/ *adjective* morally right; virtuous, law-abiding. □ **righteously** *adverb*. **righteousness** *noun*.
■ blameless, ethical, God-fearing, good, guiltless, honest, just, law-abiding, moral, pure, upright, upstanding, virtuous.

rightful *adjective* **1** legitimately entitled to (position etc.). **2** that one is entitled to. □ **rightfully** *adverb*.
■ authorized, bona fide, correct, just, lawful, legal, legitimate, licensed, *formal* licit, proper, real, true, valid.

rightly *adverb* justly, correctly, properly, justifiably.

rigid /ˈrɪdʒɪd/ *adjective* **1** not flexible, unbendable. **2** inflexible; harsh. □ **rigidity** /-ˈdʒɪd-/ *noun*. **rigidly** *adverb*.
■ **1** adamantine, firm, hard, inelastic, inflexible, set, solid, steely, stiff, strong, unbending, wooden. **2** harsh, immovable, inflexible, intransigent, obdurate, obstinate, punctilious, rigorous, stern, strict, stubborn, unbending, uncompromising, unkind, unrelenting, unyielding.

rigmarole /ˈrɪgmərəʊl/ *noun* **1** complicated procedure. **2** rambling tale etc.

rigor *US* = RIGOUR.

rigor mortis /rɪgə ˈmɔːtɪs/ *noun* stiffening of body after death.

rigorous /ˈrɪgərəs/ *adjective* **1** strict, severe. **2** exact, accurate; thorough. **3** (of weather) severe, cold. □ **rigorously** *adverb*. **rigorousness** *noun*.
■ **1** demanding, exacting, harsh, rigid, severe, strict, stringent, tough, uncompromising, undeviating, unsparing, unswerving. **2** accurate, conscientious, exact, meticulous, painstaking, precise, punctilious, scrupulous, thorough. **3** cold, extreme, hard, harsh, inclement, inhospitable, severe, unfriendly, unpleasant.

rigour /ˈrɪgə/ *noun* (*US* **rigor**) **1** severity, strictness, harshness. **2** (in *plural*) harsh conditions. **3** strict application or observance etc.

rile *verb* (**-ling**) *colloquial* anger, irritate.

rill *noun* small stream.

rim *noun* **1** edge or border, esp. of something circular. **2** outer ring of wheel, holding tyre. **3** part of spectacle frames around lens. □ **rimless** *adjective.* **rimmed** *adjective.*

■ **1** border, brim, brink, circumference, edge, lip, perimeter, periphery.

rime *noun* **1** frost. **2** hoar-frost. ● *verb* (**-ming**) cover with rime.

rind /raɪnd/ *noun* tough outer layer or covering of fruit and vegetables, cheese, bacon, etc.

■ crust, husk, peel, skin.

ring[1] *noun* **1** circular band, usually of metal, worn on finger. **2** circular band of any material. **3** line or band round cylindrical or circular object. **4** mark or part etc. resembling ring. **5** ring in cross-section of tree representing one year's growth. **6** enclosure for circus, boxing, betting at races, etc. **7** people or things arranged in circle. **8** such arrangement. **9** combination of traders, politicians, spies, etc. acting together. **10** gas ring. **11** disc or halo round planet, moon, etc. ● *verb* **1** (often + *round, about, in*) encircle. **2** put ring on (bird etc.). □ **ring-binder** loose-leaf binder with ring-shaped clasps. **ring-dove** wood-pigeon. **ring finger** finger next to little finger, esp. on left hand. **ringleader** instigator in crime or mischief etc. **ringmaster** director of circus performance. **ring-pull** (of tin) having ring for pulling to break seal. **ring road** bypass encircling town. **ringside** area immediately beside boxing or circus ring etc. **ringworm** skin infection forming circular inflamed patches.

■ *noun* **2–4** band, bracelet, circle, circlet, collar, eyelet, girdle, halo, hoop, loop, ringlet. **6** arena, enclosure, rink. **9** association, band, gang, group, *colloquial* mob, organization, syndicate. **11** aureole, corona, halo. ● *verb* **1** bind, circle, encircle, enclose, encompass, gird, surround.

ring[2] *verb* (*past* **rang**; *past participle* **rung**) **1** (often + *out* etc.) give clear resonant sound. **2** make (bell) ring. **3** call by telephone. **4** (usually + *with, to*) (of place) resound, re-echo. **5** (of ears) be filled with sensation of ringing. **6** (+ *in, out*) usher in or out with bell-ringing. **7** give specified impression. ● *noun* **1** ringing sound or tone. **2** act of ringing bell. **3** sound caused by this. **4** *colloquial* telephone call. **5** set of esp. church bells. **6** specified feeling conveyed by words etc. □ **ring back** make return telephone call to. **ring off** end telephone call. **ring up 1** make telephone call (to). **2** record (amount) on cash register.

■ *verb* **1** chime, clang, jangle, jingle, knell, peal, resonate, resound, reverberate, sound, tinkle, toll. **3** call, *slang* give a buzz, *colloquial* phone, ring up, telephone. **4** re-echo, resonate, resound, reverberate. ● *noun* **1** chime, clang, jangle, jingle, knell, peal, resonance, reverberation, tinkle, tintinnabulation, tolling. **4** *slang* buzz, call.

ringlet /ˈrɪŋlɪt/ *noun* curly lock of esp. long hair.

rink *noun* **1** area of ice for skating, curling, etc. **2** enclosed area for roller-skating. **3** building containing either of these. **4** strip of bowling green. **5** team in bowls or curling.

rinse *verb* (**-sing**) **1** (often + *through, out*) wash or treat with clean water etc. **2** wash lightly. **3** put through clean water after washing. **4** (+ *out, away*) remove by rinsing. ● *noun* **1** rinsing. **2** temporary hair tint.

■ *verb* **1** clean, cleanse, flush, sluice, swill, wash.

riot /ˈraɪət/ *noun* **1** disturbance of peace by crowd. **2** loud revelry. **3** (+ *of*) lavish display of. **4** *colloquial* very amusing thing or person. ● *verb* make or engage in riot. □ **run riot 1** throw off all restraint. **2** spread uncontrolled. □ **rioter** *noun.* **riotous** *adjective.*

■ *noun* **1** affray, brawl, commotion, disturbance, fracas, fray, hubbub, imbroglio, insurrection, mass protest, mêlée, mutiny, *colloquial* punch-up, revolt, rising, *colloquial* row, *colloquial* rumpus, *colloquial* shindig, tumult, uproar. ● *verb* brawl, fight, go on the rampage, go wild, mutiny, rampage, rebel, revolt, rise up, run riot. □ **riotous** anarchic, boisterous, chaotic, disorderly, lawless, mutinous, noisy, obstreperous, rebellious, rowdy, tumultuous, uncivilized, uncontrollable, undisciplined, ungovernable, unrestrained, unruly, uproarious, violent, wild.

RIP *abbreviation* may he, she, or they rest in peace (*requiesca(n)t in pace*).

rip *verb* (**-pp-**) **1** tear or cut quickly or forcibly away or apart. **2** make (hole etc.) thus. **3** make long tear or cut in. **4** come violently apart; split. ● *noun* **1** long tear or cut. **2** act of ripping. □ **let rip** *colloquial* (allow to) proceed or act without restraint or interference. **ripcord** cord for releasing parachute from its pack. **rip off** *colloquial* swindle, exploit; steal. **rip-off** *noun colloquial* **1** swindle. **2** financial exploitation. □ **ripper** *noun.*

■ *verb* **1** pull apart, tear apart. **2, 3** cut, gash, lacerate, *archaic* rend, rupture, shred, slit, tear. **4** *archaic* rend, rupture, split, tear.

riparian /raɪˈpeərɪən/ *adjective* of or on river-bank.

ripe *adjective* **1** ready to be reaped, picked, or eaten. **2** mature. **3** (often + *for*) fit, ready. □ **ripen** *verb.* **ripeness** *noun.*

■ **1** mature, mellow, ready. □ **ripen** age, develop, mature, mellow.

riposte /rɪˈpɒst/ *noun* **1** quick retort. **2** quick return thrust in fencing. ● *verb* (**-ting**) deliver riposte.

ripple /ˈrɪp(ə)l/ *noun* **1** ruffling of water's surface; small wave(s). **2** gentle lively sound, e.g. of laughter or applause. **3** slight variation in strength of current etc. **4** ice cream with veins of syrup. ● *verb* (**-ling**) **1** (cause to) form or flow in ripples. **2** show or sound like ripples.

■ *noun* **1** see WAVE *noun* 1,2. ● *verb* **1** agitate, disturb, make waves, purl, ruffle, stir.

rise /raɪz/ *verb* (**-sing**; *past* **rose** /rəʊz/; *past participle* **risen** /ˈrɪz(ə)n/) **1** come or go up; ascend; soar. **2** project or swell upwards. **3** appear above horizon. **4** get up from lying, sitting, or kneeling. **5** get out of bed. **6** (of meeting etc.) adjourn. **7** reach higher level. **8** make social progress. **9** (often + *up*) rebel. **10** come to surface. **11** react to provocation. **12** have origin; begin to flow.

● *noun* **1** rising. **2** upward slope. **3** increase in amount, extent, pitch, etc. **4** increase in salary. **5** increase in status or power. **6** height of step, incline, etc. **7** origin. □ **give rise to** cause, induce. **get, take a rise out of** *colloquial* provoke reaction from. **on the rise** on the increase.

■ *verb* **1** arise, ascend, climb, come up, fly up, go up, levitate, lift, mount, soar, take off. **2** loom, stand out, stick up, tower. **4** get to one's feet, get up, stand up. **7** escalate, go up, grow, increase, soar, spiral (upwards). **9** (*rise up*) see REBEL *verb* **1**. ● *noun* **1** ascension, ascent, climb. **2** acclivity, ascent, bank, climb, elevation, hill, incline, ramp, ridge, slope. **3** escalation, gain, increase, increment, jump, leap, upsurge, upswing, upturn.

riser *noun* **1** person who rises from bed. **2** vertical piece between treads of staircase.

risible /ˈrɪzɪb(ə)l/ *adjective* laughable, ludicrous.

rising *adjective* **1** advancing. **2** approaching specified age. **3** going up. ● *noun* insurrection. □ **rising damp** moisture absorbed from ground into wall.

risk *noun* **1** chance of danger, injury, loss, etc. **2** exposure to this. **3** person or thing causing risk or regarded as source of risk. ● *verb* **1** expose to risk. **2** venture on. **3** take chances of. □ **at risk** exposed to danger. **at one's (own) risk** accepting responsibility for oneself. **at the risk of** with the possibility of (adverse consequences).

■ *noun* **1, 2** chance, danger, hazard, likelihood, peril, possibility. **3** gamble, liability, speculation, uncertainty, venture. ● *verb* **1** endanger, gamble, hazard, imperil, jeopardize, venture. **2** *colloquial* chance, dare, gamble on, venture on.

risky *adjective* (**-ier, -iest**) **1** involving risk. **2** risqué. □ **riskily** *adverb*. **riskiness** *noun*.

■ **1** chancy, dangerous, *slang* dicey, hazardous, *colloquial* iffy, perilous, precarious, unsafe.

risotto /rɪˈzɒteʊ/ *noun* (*plural* **-s**) Italian savoury rice dish cooked in stock.

risqué /ˈrɪskeɪ/ *adjective* (of story etc.) slightly indecent.

rissole /ˈrɪsəʊl/ *noun* fried cake of minced meat coated in breadcrumbs.

ritardando /rɪtɑːˈdændəʊ/ *adverb, adjective, & noun* (*plural* **-s** or **-di** /-dɪ/) *Music* = RALLENTANDO.

rite *noun* religious or solemn ceremony or observance. □ **rite of passage** (often in *plural*) event marking change or stage in life.

ritual /ˈrɪtʃʊəl/ *noun* **1** prescribed order esp. of religious ceremony. **2** solemn or colourful pageantry etc. **3** procedure regularly followed. ● *adjective* of or done as ritual or rite. □ **ritually** *adverb*.

■ *noun* **1** ceremonial, ceremony, liturgy, observance, rite, sacrament, service, tradition. **3** custom, practice, procedure, routine.

ritualism *noun* regular or excessive practice of ritual. □ **ritualist** *noun*. **ritualistic** /-ˈlɪs-/ *adjective*. **ritualistically** /-ˈlɪs-/ *adverb*.

rival /ˈraɪv(ə)l/ *noun* person or thing that competes with another or equals another in quality. ● *verb* (**-ll-**; *US* **-l-**) **1** be rival of. **2** be comparable to; seem or be as good as.

■ *noun* adversary, antagonist, challenger, competitor, contender, contestant, enemy, opponent, opposition. ● *verb* **1** challenge, compete with, contend with, contest, emulate, oppose, struggle with, undercut, vie with. **2** be as good as, compare with, equal, match, measure up to.

rivalry *noun* (*plural* **-ies**) being rivals; competition.

■ antagonism, competition, competitiveness, conflict, contention, feuding, opposition, strife.

riven /ˈrɪv(ə)n/ *adjective literary* split, torn.

river /ˈrɪvə/ *noun* **1** large natural stream of water flowing to sea, lake, etc. **2** copious flow. □ **riverside** ground along river bank.

■ **1** brook, *Scottish* burn, rivulet, stream, tributary, watercourse, waterway.

rivet /ˈrɪvɪt/ *noun* nail or bolt for joining metal plates etc. ● *verb* (**-t-**) **1** join or fasten with rivets. **2** fix; make immovable. **3** (+ *on, upon*) direct intently. **4** (esp. as **riveting** *adjective*) engross.

riviera /rɪvɪˈeərə/ *noun* coastal subtropical region, esp. that of SE France and NW Italy.

rivulet /ˈrɪvjʊlɪt/ *noun* small stream.

RLC *abbreviation* Royal Logistics Corps.

RM *abbreviation* Royal Marines.

rm. *abbreviation* room.

RN *abbreviation* Royal Navy.

RNA *abbreviation* ribonucleic acid.

RNLI *abbreviation* Royal National Lifeboat Institution.

roach *noun* (*plural* same or **-es**) small freshwater fish.

road *noun* **1** way with prepared surface for vehicles, etc. **2** route. **3** (usually in *plural*) piece of water near shore in which ships can ride at anchor. □ **any road** *dialect* anyway. **in the** or **one's road** *dialect* forming obstruction. **on the road** travelling. **roadbed 1** foundation of road or railway. **2** *US* part of road for vehicles. **roadblock** barrier on road to detain traffic. **road fund licence** = TAX DISC. **road hog** *colloquial* reckless or inconsiderate motorist etc. **roadhouse** inn etc. on main road. **road metal** broken stone for road-making. **roadshow** touring entertainment etc., esp. radio or television series broadcast from changing venue. **roadstead** sea road for ships. **road tax** tax payable on vehicles. **road test** test of vehicle's roadworthiness. **roadway** part of road used by vehicles. **roadworks** construction or repair of roads. **roadworthy** (of vehicle) fit to be used on road. □ **roadworthiness** *noun*.

■ **1** alley, avenue, boulevard, bypass, byroad, byway, carriageway, causeway, clearway, crescent, cul-de-sac, drive, driveway, *US* freeway, highway, lane, motorway, roadway, route, street, thoroughfare, *US* and *historical* turnpike, way. **2** route, way.

roadie *noun colloquial* assistant of touring band etc., responsible for equipment.

roadside *noun* strip of land beside road.

roadster *noun* open car without rear seats.

roam *verb* **1** ramble, wander. **2** travel unsystematically over, through, or about.

■ amble, drift, meander, prowl, ramble, range, rove, saunter, stray, stroll, *colloquial* traipse, travel, walk, wander.

roan *adjective* (esp. of horse) with coat thickly interspersed with hairs of another colour. ● *noun* roan animal.

roar /rɔː/ *noun* **1** loud deep hoarse sound as of lion. **2** loud laugh. ● *verb* **1** (often + *out*) utter loudly, or make roar, roaring laugh, etc. **2** travel in vehicle at high speed. □ **roaring drunk** very drunk and noisy. **roaring forties** stormy ocean tracts between latitudes 40° and 50°S. **roaring success** great success. **roaring twenties** decade of 1920s.

■ *verb* **1** bellow, cry out, growl, howl, shout, snarl, thunder, yell, yowl.

roast *verb* **1** cook or be cooked by exposure to open heat or in oven. **2** criticize severely. ● *adjective* roasted. ● *noun* **1** (dish of) roast meat. **2** meat for roasting. **3** process of roasting.

rob *verb* (**-bb-**) (often + *of*) **1** take unlawfully from, esp. by force. **2** deprive of. □ **robber** *noun*. **robbery** *noun* (*plural* **-ies**).

■ **1** burgle, hold up, loot, mug, pilfer from, pillage, plunder, ransack, rifle, steal from. □ **robber** bandit, brigand, burglar, cat burglar, embezzler, *historical* highwayman, housebreaker, looter, mugger, pickpocket, pirate, shoplifter, swindler, thief. **robbery** burglary, embezzlement, hold-up, larceny, looting, mugging, pilfering, pillage, plunder, sacking, shoplifting, stealing, theft, thieving.

robe *noun* **1** long loose garment, esp. (often in *plural*) as indication of rank, office, etc. **2** *esp. US* dressing gown. ● *verb* (**-bing**) **1** clothe in robe. **2** dress.

■ *noun* **1** cloak, dress, frock, gown, habit, vestment. ● *verb* see DRESS *verb* 1.

robin /ˈrɒbɪn/ *noun* (also **robin redbreast**) small brown red-breasted bird.

Robin Hood *noun* person who steals from rich to give to poor.

robot /ˈrəʊbɒt/ *noun* **1** automaton resembling or functioning like human. **2** automatic mechanical device. **3** machine-like person. □ **robotic** /-ˈbɒt-/ *adjective*. **robotize** *verb* (also **-ise**) (**-zing** or **-sing**).

■ **1** android, automaton, bionic man, bionic woman, mechanical man, mechanical woman. **2** automaton.

robotics /rəʊˈbɒtɪks/ *plural noun* (usually treated as *singular*) science or study of robot design and operation.

robust /rəʊˈbʌst/ *adjective* (**-er**, **-est**) **1** strong, esp. in health and physique. **2** (of exercise etc.) vigorous. **3** straightforward. **4** (of statement etc.) bold. □ **robustly** *adverb*. **robustness** *noun*.

■ **1** athletic, brawny, fit, hale and hearty, hardy, healthy, hearty, muscular, powerful, rugged, sound, strong, sturdy, tough, vigorous.

roc *noun* gigantic bird of Eastern legend.

rock[1] *noun* **1** solid part of earth's crust. **2** material or projecting mass of this. **3** (**the Rock**) Gibraltar. **4** large detached stone. **5** *US* stone of any size. **6** firm support or protection. **7** hard sweet usually as peppermint-flavoured stick. **8** *slang* precious stone, esp. diamond. □ **on the rocks** *colloquial* **1** short of money. **2** (of marriage) broken down. **3** (of drink) served with ice cubes. **rock-bottom** very lowest (level). **rock cake** bun with rough surface. **rock crystal** crystallized quartz. **rock face** vertical surface of natural rock. **rock garden** rockery. **rock plant** plant that grows on or among rocks. **rock salmon** catfish, dogfish, etc. **rock salt** common salt as solid mineral.

■ **2** crag, outcrop, tor. **4, 5** boulder, stone.

rock[2] *verb* **1** move gently to and fro; set, keep, or be in such motion; (cause to) sway. **2** shake, reel, oscillate. **3** shock. ● *noun* **1** rocking motion. **2** rock and roll. **3** popular music influenced by this. □ **rock and roll, rock 'n' roll** popular dance music with heavy beat and blues influence. **rocking chair** chair on rockers or springs. **rocking horse** toy horse on rockers or springs.

■ *verb* **1** move to and fro, oscillate, sway, swing. **2** lurch, oscillate, pitch, reel, roll, shake, toss, totter, wobble. **3** see SHOCK[1] *verb* 2.

rocker *noun* **1** device for rocking, esp. curved bar etc. on which something rocks. **2** rocking-chair. **3** rock music devotee, esp. leather-clad motorcyclist.

rockery *noun* (*plural* **-ies**) pile of rough stones with soil between them for growing rock plants on.

rocket /ˈrɒkɪt/ *noun* **1** firework or signal propelled to great height after ignition. **2** engine operating on same principle. **3** rocket-propelled missile, spacecraft, etc. ● *verb* (**-t-**) **1** move rapidly upwards or away. **2** bombard with rockets.

rocketry *noun* science or practice of rocket propulsion.

rocky[1] *adjective* (**-ier**, **-iest**) of, like, or full of rocks.

■ pebbly, rough, rugged, stony.

rocky[2] *adjective* (**-ier**, **-iest**) *colloquial* unsteady, tottering.

■ see UNSTEADY 1.

rococo /rəˈkəʊkəʊ/ *adjective* of ornate style of art, music, and literature in 18th-c. Europe. ● *noun* this style.

rod *noun* **1** slender straight round stick or bar. **2** cane for flogging. **3** fishing rod. **4** *historical* measure of length (5½ yds).

■ **1** bar, baton, cane, dowel, pole, rail, shaft, spoke, staff, stick, strut, wand.

rode *past of* RIDE.

rodent /ˈrəʊd(ə)nt/ *noun* mammal with strong incisors and no canine teeth (e.g. rat, squirrel, beaver).

rodeo /ˈrəʊdɪəʊ/ *noun* (*plural* **-s**) **1** exhibition of cowboys' skills. **2** round-up of cattle for branding etc.

roe[1] *noun* **1** (also **hard roe**) mass of eggs in female fish. **2** (also **soft roe**) male fish's milt.

roe[2] *noun* (*plural* same or **-s**) (also **roe-deer**) small kind of deer. □ **roebuck** male roe.

roentgen /ˈrʌntjən/ *noun* (also **röntgen**) unit of exposure to ionizing radiation.

rogation /rəʊˈɡeɪʃ(ə)n/ *noun* (usually in *plural*) litany of the saints chanted on the 3 days (**Rogation Days**) before Ascension Day.

roger /ˈrɒdʒə/ *interjection* **1** your message has been received and understood. **2** *slang* I agree.

rogue /rəʊɡ/ *noun* **1** dishonest or unprincipled person. **2** *jocular* mischievous person. **3** wild fierce animal driven or living apart from herd. **4** inferior or defective specimen. □ **roguery** *noun* (*plural* **-ies**). **roguish** *adjective*. **roguishness** *noun*.

■ **1** blackguard, charlatan, cheat, con man, criminal, fraud, knave, quack, *archaic* rapscallion, rascal, ruffian, scoundrel, swindler, trickster, villain, wastrel, wretch. **2** devil, imp, mischief-maker, *archaic* rapscallion, rascal, scallywag, *colloquial* scamp, wretch.

roister /ˈrɔɪstə/ *verb* (esp. as **roistering** *adjective*) revel noisily; be uproarious. □ **roisterer** *noun*.

role *noun* (also **rôle**) **1** actor's part. **2** person's or thing's function. □ **role model** person on whom others model themselves. **role-playing, -play** acting of characters or situations as aid in psychotherapy, teaching, etc. **role-play** *verb*.

■ **1** character, part. **2** contribution, duty, function, job, position, post, task.

roll /rəʊl/ *verb* **1** (cause to) move or go in some direction by turning over and over on axis. **2** rotate. **3** make cylindrical or spherical by revolving between two surfaces or over on itself. **4** gather into mass. **5** (often + *along, by,* etc.) move or be carried on or as if on wheels. **6** flatten with roller. **7** sway or rock. **8** proceed unsteadily. **9** undulate; show undulating motion or surface. **10** sound with vibration. ● *noun* **1** rolling motion or gait. **2** undulation. **3** act of rolling. **4** rhythmic rumbling sound. **5** anything forming cylinder by being turned over on itself without folding. **6** small loaf of bread for one person. **7** official list or register. □ **roll-call** calling of list of names to establish presence. **rolled gold** thin coating of gold applied by roller to base metal. **rolled oats** husked and crushed oats. **roll in 1** arrive (in quantity). **2** wallow in. **rolling mill** machine or factory for rolling metal into shape. **rolling pin** roller for pastry. **rolling stock** company's

railway or (*US*) road vehicles. **rollmop** rolled pickled herring fillet. **roll-neck** having high loosely turned-over collar. **roll-on** applied by means of rotating ball. **roll-on roll-off** (of ship etc.) in which vehicles are driven directly on and off. **roll-top desk** desk with flexible cover sliding in curved grooves. **roll up 1** *colloquial* arrive. **2** make into roll. **roll-up** *noun* hand-rolled cigarette. **strike off the rolls** debar from practising as solicitor.

■ *verb* **1, 2** go round, move round, revolve, rotate, run, somersault, spin, tumble, turn. **3** coil, curl, furl, twist, wind. **6** flatten, level off, level out, smooth. **7, 8** lumber, lurch, pitch, reel, rock, stagger, sway, toss, totter, wallow, welter. ● *noun* **5** cylinder, reel, scroll, spool, tube. **7** catalogue, directory, index, inventory, list, listing, record, register. □ **roll in 1** see ARRIVE 1. **roll up 1** see ARRIVE 1.

roller *noun* **1** revolving cylinder for smoothing, flattening, crushing, spreading, etc. **2** small cylinder on which hair is rolled for setting. **3** long swelling wave. □ **roller bearing** bearing with cylinders instead of balls. **roller coaster** switchback at fair etc. **roller-skate** *noun* **1** frame with small wheels, strapped to shoes. **2** boot with small wheels underneath. ● *verb* move on roller-skates. **roller towel** towel with ends joined held on roller.

rollicking /ˈrɒlɪkɪŋ/ *adjective* jovial, exuberant.

roly-poly /ˈrəʊlɪˈpəʊlɪ/ *noun* (*plural* **-ies**) (also **roly-poly pudding**) pudding of rolled-up suet pastry covered with jam and boiled or baked. ● *adjective* podgy, plump.

ROM *noun* *Computing* read-only memory.

Roman /ˈrəʊmən/ *adjective* **1** of ancient Rome or its territory or people. **2** of medieval or modern Rome. **3** Roman Catholic. **4** (**roman**) (of type) plain and upright, used in ordinary print. **5** (of the alphabet etc.) based on the ancient Roman system with letters A–Z. ● *noun* (*plural* **-s**) **1** citizen of ancient Roman Republic or Empire, or of modern Rome. **2** Roman Catholic. **3** (**roman**) roman type. □ **Roman candle** firework discharging coloured sparks. **Roman Catholic** ● *adjective* of part of Christian Church acknowledging Pope as its head. ● *noun* member of this. **Roman Catholicism** *noun*. **Roman Empire** *historical* that established in 27 BC and divided in AD 395. **Roman law** law code of ancient Rome, forming basis of many modern codes. **Roman nose** one with high bridge. **roman numerals** numerals expressed in letters of Roman alphabet. □ **romanize** *verb* (also **-ise**) (**-zing** or **-sing**). **romanization** *noun*.

romance /rəʊˈmæns/ *noun* (also /ˈrəʊ-/) **1** idealized, poetic, or unworldly atmosphere or tendency. **2** love affair. **3** (work of) literature concerning romantic love, stirring action, etc. **4** medieval tale of chivalry. **5** exaggeration; picturesque falsehood. ● *adjective* (**Romance**) (of a language) descended from Latin. ● *verb* (**-cing**) **1** exaggerate, fantasize. **2** woo.

■ *noun* **1** adventure, colour, excitement, fascination, glamour, mystery. **2** affair, amour, attachment, intrigue, liaison, love affair, *colloquial* relationship. **3** idyll, love story, novel.

Romanesque /rəʊməˈnesk/ *noun* style of European architecture *c.* 900–1200, with massive vaulting and round arches. ● *adjective* of this style.

Romanian /rəʊˈmeɪnɪən/ (also **Rumanian** /ruː-/) *noun* native, national, or language of Romania. ● *adjective* of Romania or its people, or language.

romantic /rəʊˈmæntɪk/ *adjective* **1** of, characterized by, or suggestive of romance. **2** inclined towards or involving romance in love. **3** imaginative, visionary. **4** (of literature or music etc.) concerned more with emotion than with form. **5** (also **Romantic**) of the 18th–19th-c. romantic movement or style in European arts. ● *noun* **1** romantic person. **2** romanticist. □ **romantically** *adverb*.

■ *adjective* **1** colourful, dreamlike, exotic, fabulous, fairy-tale, glamorous, idyllic, nostalgic, picturesque. **2** affectionate, amorous, emotional, erotic, loving, passionate, sexy, *colloquial* soppy, tender. **3** chimerical, idealistic, illusory, impractical, improbable, quixotic, *colloquial* starry-eyed, unrealistic, unworkable, Utopian, visionary. **4** emotional, heart-warming, nostalgic, sentimental, sloppy, tender.

romanticism /rəʊˈmæntɪsɪz(ə)m/ *noun* (also **Romanticism**) adherence to romantic style in literature, art, etc. □ **romanticist, Romanticist** *noun*.

romanticize /rəʊˈmæntɪsaɪz/ *verb* (also **-ise**) (**-zing** or **-sing**) **1** make romantic. **2** exaggerate. **3** indulge in romance.

Romany /ˈrɒmənɪ/ *noun* (*plural* **-ies**) **1** Gypsy. **2** language of Gypsies. ● *adjective* of Gypsies or Romany language.

Romeo /ˈrəʊmɪəʊ/ *noun* (*plural* **-s**) passionate male lover or seducer.

romp *verb* **1** play roughly and energetically. **2** (+ *along, past,* etc.) *colloquial* proceed without effort. ● *noun* spell of romping. □ **romp in, home** *colloquial* win easily.

rompers *plural noun* (also **romper suit**) young child's one-piece garment.

rondeau /ˈrɒndəʊ/ *noun* (*plural* **-x** same pronunciation or /-z/) short poem with two rhymes only, and opening words used as refrains.

rondel /ˈrɒnd(ə)l/ *noun* rondeau.

rondo /ˈrɒndəʊ/ *noun* (*plural* **-s**) musical form with recurring leading theme.

röntgen = ROENTGEN.

rood /ruːd/ *noun* **1** crucifix, esp. on rood-screen. **2** quarter-acre. □ **rood-screen** carved screen separating nave and chancel.

roof /ruːf/ *noun* (*plural* **roofs** /ruːvz/) **1** upper covering of building. **2** top of covered vehicle etc. **3** top interior surface of oven, cave, mine, etc. ● *verb* **1** (often + *in, over*) cover with roof. **2** be roof of. □ **roof of the mouth** palate. **roof-rack** framework for luggage on top of vehicle. **rooftop**

1 outer surface of roof. **2** (in *plural*) tops of houses etc.

rook[1] /rʊk/ *noun* black bird of crow family nesting in colonies. ● *verb colloquial* **1** charge (customer) extortionately. **2** win money at cards etc., esp. by swindling.

rook[2] /rʊk/ *noun* chess piece with battlement-shaped top.

rookery *noun* (*plural* **-ies**) colony of rooks, penguins, or seals.

rookie /ˈrʊkɪ/ *noun slang* recruit.

room /ruːm/ *noun* **1** space for, or occupied by, something. **2** capacity; scope. **3** part of building enclosed by walls. **4** (in *plural*) apartments or lodgings. ● *verb US* have room(s); lodge. □ **room service** provision of food etc. in hotel bedroom.

■ *noun* **1, 2** area, capacity, *colloquial* elbow room, freedom, latitude, leeway, margin, play, scope, space, territory. **3** cell, *archaic* chamber. **4** (*rooms*) see LODGING 2.

roomy *adjective* (**-ier, -iest**) having much room; spacious. □ **roominess** *noun*.

■ big, capacious, commodious, large, sizeable, spacious, voluminous.

roost /ruːst/ *noun* bird's perch. ● *verb* (of bird) settle for rest or sleep.

rooster *noun* domestic cock.

root[1] /ruːt/ *noun* **1** part of plant below ground conveying nourishment from soil. **2** (in *plural*) fibres or branches of this. **3** plant with edible root. **4** such root. **5** (in *plural*) emotional attachment or family ties in a place. **6** embedded part of hair or tooth etc. **7** basic cause, source. **8** *Mathematics* number which multiplied by itself a given number of times yields a given number, esp. square root. **9** core of a word. ● *verb* **1** (cause to) take root. **2** (esp. as **rooted** *adjective*) fix or establish firmly. **3** pull up by roots. □ **root out** find and get rid of. **rootstock 1** rhizome. **2** plant into which graft is inserted. **3** source from which offshoots have arisen. **take root 1** begin to draw nourishment from the soil. **2** become established. □ **rootless** *adjective*.

■ *noun* **1** radicle, rhizome, tap root, tuber. **7** base, basis, bottom, cause, foundation, *poetical* fount, origin, seat, source, starting point. □ **root out** see REMOVE *verb* 1.

root[2] /ruːt/ *verb* **1** (often + *up*) turn up (ground) with snout etc. in search of food. **2** (+ *around, in,* etc.) rummage. **3** (+ *out, up*) extract by rummaging. **4** (+ *for*) *US slang* encourage by applause or support.

rope *noun* **1** stout cord made by twisting together strands of hemp or wire etc. **2** (+ *of*) string of onions, pearls etc. **3** (**the rope**) (halter for) execution by hanging. ● *verb* (**-ping**) **1** fasten or catch with rope. **2** (+ *off, in*) enclose with rope. □ **know, learn, or show the ropes** know, learn, show how to do a thing properly. **rope into** persuade to take part (in).

■ *noun* **1** cable, cord, halyard, hawser, lanyard, lariat, lasso, line, tether. **2** strand, string. ● *verb* **1** bind, fasten, hitch, lash, moor, tether, tie.

ropy *adjective* (also **ropey**) (**-ier, -iest**) *colloquial* poor in quality. □ **ropiness** *noun*.

Roquefort /'rɒkfɔ:/ *noun proprietary term* soft blue ewe's-milk cheese.

rorqual /'rɔ:kw(ə)l/ *noun* whale with dorsal fin.

rosaceous /rəʊ'zeɪʃəs/ *adjective* of plant family including the rose.

rosary /'rəʊzərɪ/ *noun* (*plural* **-ies**) *RC Church* **1** repeated sequence of prayers. **2** string of beads for keeping count in this.

rose¹ /rəʊz/ *noun* **1** prickly shrub bearing fragrant red, pink, yellow, or white flowers. **2** this flower. **3** pinkish-red colour or (usually in *plural*) complexion. **4** rose-shaped design. **5** fitting on ceiling from which electric light hangs by cable. **6** spray nozzle of watering-can etc. **7** (in *plural*) *used to express ease, luck, etc.* ● *adjective* rose-coloured. □ **rosebowl** bowl for cut roses, esp. given as prize. **rosebud** **1** bud of rose. **2** pretty girl. **rose-coloured 1** pinkish-red. **2** cheerful, optimistic. **rose-hip** fruit of rose. **rose-water** perfume made from roses. **rose-window** circular window with roselike tracery. **rosewood** close-grained wood used in making furniture.

rose² *past* of RISE.

rosé /'rəʊzeɪ/ *noun* light pink wine. [French]

rosemary /'rəʊzmərɪ/ *noun* evergreen fragrant shrub used as herb.

rosette /rəʊ'zet/ *noun* rose-shaped ornament made of ribbons etc. or carved in stone etc.

rosin /'rɒzɪn/ *noun* resin, esp. in solid form. ● *verb* (**-n-**) rub with rosin.

RoSPA /'rɒspə/ *abbreviation* Royal Society for the Prevention of Accidents.

roster /'rɒstə/ *noun* list or plan of turns of duty etc. ● *verb* place on roster.

rostrum /'rɒstrəm/ *noun* (*plural* **rostra** or **-s**) platform for public speaking etc.

rosy /'rəʊzɪ/ *adjective* (**-ier, -iest**) **1** pink, red. **2** optimistic, hopeful. □ **rosiness** *noun*.

rot *verb* (**-tt-**) **1** undergo decay by putrefaction. **2** perish; waste away. **3** cause to rot; make rotten. ● *noun* **1** decay, rottenness. **2** *slang* nonsense. **3** decline in standards etc. ● *interjection: expressing incredulity or ridicule.* □ **rot-gut** *slang* cheap harmful alcohol.

■ *verb* **1, 2** corrode, crumble, decay, decompose, degenerate, deteriorate, disintegrate, fester, go bad, go off, moulder, perish, putrefy, spoil. ● *noun* **1** corrosion, corruption, decay, decomposition, deterioration, disintegration, mould, mouldiness, putrefaction. **2** see NONSENSE 1.

rota /'rəʊtə/ *noun* list of duties to be done or people to do them in turn.

■ list, roster, schedule.

rotary /'rəʊtərɪ/ *adjective* acting by rotation. ● *noun* (*plural* **-ies**) **1** rotary machine. **2** (**Rotary**; in full **Rotary International**) worldwide charitable society of businessmen.

■ *adjective* gyrating, revolving, rotating, rotatory, spinning, turning, twirling, twisting, whirling.

rotate /rəʊ'teɪt/ *verb* (**-ting**) **1** move round axis or centre; revolve. **2** arrange or take in rotation. □ **rotatory** /'rəʊtətərɪ/ *adjective*.

■ **1** go round, gyrate, move round, pirouette, pivot, reel, revolve, roll, spin, swivel, turn, twiddle, twirl, twist, wheel, whirl. **2** alternate, pass round, share out, take in turn, take turns.

rotation *noun* **1** rotating, being rotated. **2** recurrent series or period; regular succession. **3** growing of different crops in regular order. □ **rotational** *adjective*.

rote *noun* (usually in **by rote**) mechanical repetition (in order to memorize).

rotisserie /rəʊ'tɪsərɪ/ *noun* **1** restaurant etc. where meat is roasted. **2** revolving spit for roasting food.

rotor /'rəʊtə/ *noun* **1** rotary part of machine. **2** rotating aerofoil on helicopter.

rotten /'rɒt(ə)n/ *adjective* (**-er, -est**) **1** rotting or rotted; fragile from age etc. **2** morally or politically corrupt. **3** *slang* disagreeable, unwell. □ **rotten borough** *historical* (before 1832) English borough electing MP though having very few voters. □ **rottenness** *noun*.

■ **1** bad, corroded, crumbling, decayed, decaying, decomposed, disintegrating, foul, mouldering, mouldy, *colloquial* off, overripe, perished, putrid, rusty, smelly, tainted, unsound. **2** see IMMORAL.

rotter *noun slang* objectionable person.

Rottweiler /'rɒtvaɪlə/ *noun* black-and-tan dog noted for ferocity.

rotund /rəʊ'tʌnd/ *adjective* plump, podgy. □ **rotundity** *noun*.

rotunda /rəʊ'tʌndə/ *noun* circular building, esp. domed.

rouble /'ru:b(ə)l/ *noun* (also **ruble**) monetary unit of Russia etc.

roué /'ru:eɪ/ *noun* (esp. elderly) debauchee.

rouge /ru:ʒ/ *noun* red cosmetic used to colour cheeks. ● *verb* (**-ging**) **1** colour with or apply rouge. **2** blush.

rough /rʌf/ *adjective* **1** having uneven surface; not smooth or level. **2** shaggy; coarse. **3** (of weather, sea, etc.) violent. **4** not mild, quiet, or gentle. **5** (of wine) harsh. **6** insensitive. **7** unpleasant, severe. **8** lacking finish etc. **9** rudimentary. **10** approximate. ● *adverb* in a rough way. ● *noun* **1** (usually **the rough**) hardship. **2** rough ground. **3** hooligan. **4** unfinished or natural state. ● *verb* **1** make rough. **2** (+ *out, in*) sketch or plan roughly. □ **rough-and-ready** rough or crude but effective; not over-particular. **rough-and-tumble** ● *adjective* irregular, disorderly. ● *noun* scuffle. **roughcast** ● *noun* plaster of lime and gravel. ● *verb* coat with this. **rough diamond 1** uncut diamond. **2** rough but honest person. **rough house** *slang* disturbance; rough fight. **rough it** *colloquial* do without basic comforts. **rough justice 1** treatment that is approximately fair. **2** unfair treatment. **roughneck** *colloquial* **1** worker on oil rig. **2** rough person. **rough up** *slang* attack violently. □ **roughen** *verb*. **roughly** *adverb*. **roughness** *noun*.

■ *adjective* **1** broken, bumpy, coarse, craggy, irregular, jagged, knobbly, lumpy, pitted, rocky, rugged, rutted, stony, uneven. **2** bristly, calloused, chapped, coarse, hairy, harsh, leathery, ragged, scratchy, shaggy, unshaven, wrinkled. **3** agitated, choppy, stormy, tempestuous, turbulent, violent, wild. **4** (*rough voice*) cacophonous, discordant, grating, gruff, harsh, hoarse, husky, rasping, raucous, strident, unmusical, unpleasant; (*rough manners, a rough fellow*) badly behaved, bluff, blunt, brusque, churlish, ill-bred, impolite, loutish, rowdy, rude, surly, ugly, uncivil, uncivilized, undisciplined, unfriendly; (*rough treatment*) brutal, cruel, insensitive, painful, severe, thuggish, tough, violent. **6** see UNKIND. **7** demanding, difficult, exacting, hard, severe, taxing, tough, unpleasant. **8, 9** amateurish, careless, clumsy, crude, hasty, imperfect, incomplete, inept, rough-and-ready, rudimentary, unfinished, unpolished, unskilful. **10** approximate, general, hasty, imprecise, inexact, *colloquial* sketchy, vague. □ **roughly** about, approximately, around, close to, nearly.

roughage *noun* fibrous material in food, stimulating intestinal action.

roughshod /ˈrʌfʃɒd/ □ **ride roughshod over** treat arrogantly.

roulade /ruˈlɑːd/ *noun* **1** filled rolled piece of meat, sponge, etc. **2** quick succession of notes.

roulette /ruːˈlet/ *noun* gambling game with ball dropped on revolving numbered wheel.

round /raʊnd/ *adjective* **1** shaped like circle, sphere, or cylinder. **2** (of person, figure) rotund, plump. **3** done with circular motion. **4** (of number etc.) without odd units. **5** entire, continuous, complete. **6** candid. **7** (of voice etc.) sonorous. ● *noun* **1** round object. **2** revolving motion; circular or recurring course. **3** series. **4** route for deliveries, inspection, etc. **5** drink etc. for each member of group. **6** one bullet, shell, etc. **7** slice of bread. **8** sandwich made from two slices. **9** joint of beef from haunch. **10** one period of play etc. **11** one stage in competition. **12** playing of all holes in golf course once. **13** song for unaccompanied voices overlapping at intervals. **14** rung of ladder. **15** (+ *of*) circumference or extent of. ● *adverb* **1** with circular motion. **2** with return to starting point or change to opposite position. **3** to, at, or affecting circumference, area, group, etc. **4** in every direction from a centre. **5** measuring (specified distance) in girth. ● *preposition* **1** so as to encircle or enclose. **2** at or to points on circumference of. **3** with successive visits to. **4** within a radius of; having as central point. **5** so as to pass in curved course. **6** having thus passed. ● *verb* **1** give or take round shape. **2** pass round (corner etc.). **3** (usually + *up, down*) express (number) approximately. □ **in the round 1** with all angles or features shown or considered. **2** with audience all round theatre stage. **Round-head** *historical* member of Parliamentary party in English Civil War. **round off** make complete or less angular. **round on** attack unexpectedly. **round out** provide with more details; finish. **round robin 1** petition with signatures in circle to conceal order of writing. **2** tournament in which each competitor plays every other. **round-shouldered** having shoulders bent forward and back rounded. **Round Table** international charitable association. **round table** assembly for discussion, esp. at conference. **round the clock** all day and night. **round trip** trip to one or more places and back. **round up** gather or bring together. **round-up** *noun* **1** rounding-up. **2** summary.

■ *adjective* **1** annular, ball-shaped, bulbous, circular, curved, cylindrical, disc-shaped, globular, hoop-shaped, *formal* orbicular, orb-shaped, ring-shaped, spherical, spheroid. **2** ample, fat, full, plump, rotund, rounded. ● *noun* **10, 11** bout, contest, game, heat, stage. ● *verb* **2** skirt, travel round, turn. □ **round off** see COMPLETE *verb* 1–2. **round on** see ATTACK *verb* 1. **round-shouldered** humpbacked, hunchbacked, stooping. **round up** see ASSEMBLE 2.

roundabout *noun* **1** road junction with traffic passing in one direction round central island. **2** revolving device in children's playground; merry-go-round. ● *adjective* **1** circuitous, indirect; circumlocutory.

■ *noun* **1** traffic island. **2** carousel, merry-go-round, whirligig. ● *adjective* circuitous, circular, circumlocutory, devious, indirect, long, meandering, oblique, rambling, tortuous, twisting, winding.

roundel /ˈraʊnd(ə)l/ *noun* **1** circular mark. **2** small disc, medallion.

roundelay /ˈraʊndɪleɪ/ *noun* short simple song with refrain.

rounders /ˈraʊndəz/ *noun* team game in which players hit ball and run through round of bases.

roundly *adverb* bluntly, severely.

rouse /raʊz/ *verb* (**-sing**) **1** (cause to) wake. **2** (often + *up*) make or become active or excited. **3** anger. **4** evoke (feelings). □ **rousing** *adjective*.

■ **1** arise, arouse, awaken, call, get up, wake up. **2** agitate, animate, electrify, excite, galvanize, goad, incite, inflame, provoke, spur on, stimulate, stir up, *colloquial* wind up, work up.

roustabout /ˈraʊstəbaʊt/ *noun* **1** labourer on oil rig. **2** unskilled or casual labourer.

rout /raʊt/ *noun* **1** disorderly retreat of defeated troops. **2** overthrow, defeat. ● *verb* **1** put to flight. **2** defeat.

■ *verb* conquer, crush, defeat, overpower, overthrow, overwhelm, put to flight, *colloquial* send packing.

route /ruːt/ *noun* way taken (esp. regularly) from one place to another. ● *verb* (**-teing**) send etc. by particular route. □ **route march** training march for troops.

■ *noun* course, direction, itinerary, journey, path, road, way.

routine /ruːˈtiːn/ *noun* **1** regular course or procedure; unvarying performance of certain acts. **2** set sequence in dance, comedy act, etc. **3** sequence of instructions to computer. ● *adjective*

1 performed as routine. **2** of customary or standard kind. □ **routinely** *adverb*.

■ *noun* **1** custom, *colloquial* drill, habit, method, pattern, plan, practice, procedure, schedule, system, way. **2** act, number, performance, programme, set piece. ● *adjective* accustomed, commonplace, customary, everyday, familiar, habitual, humdrum, normal, ordinary, perfunctory, planned, regular, run-of-the-mill, scheduled, standard, uneventful, usual, well rehearsed.

roux /ruː/ *noun* (*plural* same) mixture of fat and flour used in sauces etc.

rove /rəʊv/ *verb* (**-ving**) **1** wander without settling; roam. **2** (of eyes) look about.

rover *noun* wanderer.

row[1] /rəʊ/ *noun* **1** line of people or things. **2** line of seats in theatre etc. □ **in a row 1** forming a row. **2** *colloquial* in succession.

■ **1** chain, column, cordon, file, line, queue, rank, sequence, series, string, tier.

row[2] /rəʊ/ *verb* **1** propel (boat) with oars. **2** convey thus. ● *noun* **1** spell of rowing. **2** trip in rowing boat. □ **rowing boat** small boat propelled by oars. □ **rower** *noun*.

row[3] /raʊ/ *colloquial noun* **1** loud noise, commotion. **2** quarrel, dispute. **3** severe reprimand. ● *verb* **1** make or engage in row. **2** reprimand.

■ *noun* **1** commotion, fuss, hubbub, hullabaloo, noise, racket, *colloquial* rumpus, tumult, uproar. **2** altercation, argument, controversy, disagreement, dispute, fight, fracas, quarrel, *colloquial* ructions, slanging match, squabble. ● *verb* **1** see QUARREL *verb* 2.

rowan /'rəʊən/ *noun* **1** (in full **rowan tree**) mountain ash. **2** (in full **rowan-berry**) its scarlet berry.

rowdy /'raʊdɪ/ *adjective* (**-ier, -iest**) noisy and disorderly. ● *noun* (*plural* **-ies**) rowdy person. □ **rowdily** *adverb*. **rowdiness** *noun*. **rowdyism** *noun*.

■ *adjective* badly behaved, boisterous, disorderly, ill-disciplined, irrepressible, lawless, noisy, obstreperous, riotous, rough, turbulent, undisciplined, unruly, violent, wild.

rowel /'raʊəl/ *noun* spiked revolving disc at end of spur.

rowlock /'rɒlək/ *noun* device for holding oar in place.

royal /'rɔɪəl/ *adjective* **1** of, suited to, or worthy of king or queen. **2** in service or under patronage of king or queen. **3** of family of king or queen. **4** splendid. **5** on great scale. ● *noun colloquial* member of royal family. □ **royal blue** deep vivid blue. **Royal Commission** commission of inquiry appointed by Crown at request of government. **royal flush** straight poker flush headed by ace. **royal jelly** substance secreted by worker bees and fed to future queen bees. **Royal Navy** British navy. **royal 'we'** use of 'we' instead of 'I' by single person. □ **royally** *adverb*.

■ *adjective* **1** imperial, kingly, majestic, princely, queenly, regal, sovereign, stately. **4** see SPLENDID 1.

royalist *noun* supporter of monarchy, *esp. historical* of King's side in English Civil War.

royalty *noun* (*plural* **-ies**) **1** being royal. **2** royal people. **3** member of royal family. **4** percentage of profit from book, public performance, patent, etc. paid to author etc. **5** royal right (now esp. over minerals) granted by sovereign. **6** payment made by producer of minerals etc. to owner of site etc.

RP *abbreviation* Received Pronunciation.

RPI *abbreviation* retail price index.

rpm *abbreviation* revolutions per minute.

RSA *abbreviation* **1** Royal Society of Arts. **2** Royal Scottish Academy. **3** Royal Scottish Academician.

RSC *abbreviation* Royal Shakespeare Company.

RSM *abbreviation* Regimental Sergeant-Major.

RSPB *abbreviation* Royal Society for the Protection of Birds.

RSPCA *abbreviation* Royal Society for the Prevention of Cruelty to Animals.

RSV *abbreviation* Revised Standard Version (of Bible).

RSVP *abbreviation* please answer (*répondez s'il vous plaît*).

Rt. Hon. *abbreviation* Right Honourable.

Rt Revd *abbreviation* (also **Rt. Rev.**) Right Reverend.

rub *verb* (**-bb-**) **1** move hand etc. firmly over surface of. **2** (usually + *against, in, on, over*) apply (hand etc.) thus. **3** polish, clean, or make dry by rubbing. **4** abrade, chafe, or make sore or bare by rubbing. **5** (+ *in, into, through, over*) apply by rubbing. **6** (often + *together, against, on*) move with friction or slide (objects) against each other. **7** get frayed or worn by friction. ● *noun* **1** action or spell of rubbing. **2** impediment or difficulty. □ **rub down** dry or smooth or clean by rubbing. **rub it in** emphasize fact etc. **rub off** (usually + *on*) be transferred by contact; be transmitted. **rub out** erase with rubber. **rub up the wrong way** irritate.

■ *verb* **1** caress, knead, massage, smooth, stroke. **3** buff, burnish, polish, scour, scrub, shine, wipe. **4** abrade, chafe, graze, scrape, wear away. □ **rub it in** see EMPHASIZE. **rub out** see ERASE 1. **rub up the wrong way** see ANNOY 1.

rubato /ruːˈbɑːtəʊ/ *noun Music* (*plural* **-s** or **-ti** /-tɪ/) temporary disregarding of strict tempo.

rubber[1] /'rʌbə/ *noun* **1** elastic substance made from latex of plants or synthetically. **2** piece of this or other substance for erasing pencil marks. **3** (in *plural*) *US* galoshes. □ **rubber band** loop of rubber to hold papers etc. **rubberneck** *colloquial* (be) inquisitive sightseer. **rubber plant 1** tropical plant often grown as house-plant. **2** (also **rubber tree**) tree yielding latex. **rubber stamp 1** device for inking and imprinting on surface. **2** (person giving) mechanical endorsement of actions etc. **rubber-stamp** approve automatically. □ **rubberize** *verb* (also **-ise**) (**-zing** or **-sing**). **rubbery** *adjective*.

rubber[2] /'rʌbə/ *noun* series of games between same sides or people at whist, bridge, cricket, etc.

rubbish /'rʌbɪʃ/ *noun* **1** waste or worthless matter; litter; trash. **2** (often as *interjection*) nonsense. ● *verb colloquial* criticize contemptuously. □ **rubbishy** *adjective*.

■ **1** debris, detritus, dregs, dross, filth, flotsam and jetsam, *US* garbage, junk, leavings, leftovers, litter, lumber, *colloquial* muck, odds and ends, offal, offcuts, refuse, rejects, rubble, scrap, slops, sweepings, *esp. US* trash, waste. **2** see NONSENSE 1.

rubble /'rʌb(ə)l/ *noun* rough fragments of stone, brick, etc.

rubella /ru:'belə/ *noun formal* German measles.

Rubicon /'ru:bɪkɒn/ *noun* point from which there is no going back.

rubicund /'ru:bɪkʌnd/ *adjective* ruddy, red-faced.

ruble = ROUBLE.

rubric /'ru:brɪk/ *noun* **1** heading or passage in red or special lettering. **2** explanatory words. **3** established custom or rule. **4** direction for conduct of divine service in liturgical book.

ruby /'ru:bɪ/ *noun* (*plural* **-ies**) **1** crimson or rose-coloured precious stone. **2** deep red colour. ● *adjective* ruby-coloured. □ **ruby wedding** 40th wedding anniversary.

RUC *abbreviation* Royal Ulster Constabulary.

ruche /ru:ʃ/ *noun* frill or gathering of lace etc. □ **ruched** *adjective*.

ruck[1] *noun* **1** (**the ruck**) main group of competitors not likely to overtake leaders. **2** undistinguished crowd of people or things. **3** *Rugby* loose scrum.

ruck[2] *verb* (often + *up*) crease, wrinkle. ● *noun* crease, wrinkle.

rucksack /'rʌksæk/ *noun* bag carried on back, esp. by hikers.

ruckus /'rʌkəs/ *noun esp. US* row, commotion.

ruction /'rʌkʃ(ə)n/ *noun colloquial* **1** disturbance, tumult. **2** (in *plural*) row.

rudder /'rʌdə/ *noun* flat piece hinged to vessel's stern or rear of aeroplane for steering. □ **rudderless** *adjective*.

ruddy /'rʌdɪ/ *adjective* (**-ier, -iest**) **1** freshly or healthily red. **2** reddish. **3** *colloquial* bloody, damnable. □ **ruddiness** *noun*.

■ **1** flushed, fresh, glowing, healthy, red, sunburnt.

rude *adjective* **1** impolite, offensive. **2** roughly made or done. **3** primitive, uneducated. **4** abrupt, sudden. **5** *colloquial* indecent, lewd. **6** vigorous, hearty. □ **rudely** *adverb*. **rudeness** *noun*.

■ **1** abrupt, abusive, bad-mannered, bad-tempered, blasphemous, blunt, boorish, brusque, cheeky, churlish, coarse, *derogatory* common, condescending, contemptuous, discourteous, disparaging, disrespectful, foul, graceless, gross, *colloquial* ignorant, ill-bred, ill-mannered, impertinent, impolite, improper,

impudent, in bad taste, inconsiderate, insolent, insulting, loutish, mocking, naughty, oafish, offensive, offhand, patronizing, peremptory, personal (*remarks*), saucy, scurrilous, shameless, tactless, unchivalrous, uncivil, uncomplimentary, uncouth, ungracious, unmannerly, unprintable, vulgar. **2** awkward, basic, bumbling, clumsy, crude, inartistic, primitive, rough, rough-hewn, simple, unpolished, unskilful, unsubtle. **3** primitive, uneducated, unrefined, unsophisticated. **4** abrupt, startling, sudden, unexpected. **5** see NAUGHTY 2, OBSCENE 1. □ **rudeness** abuse, *colloquial* backchat, bad manners, boorishness, cheek, churlishness, condescension, contempt, discourtesy, disrespect, impertinence, impudence, incivility, insolence, insults, oafishness, tactlessness, vulgarity.

rudiment /'ru:dɪmənt/ *noun* **1** (in *plural*) elements or first principles of subject. **2** (in *plural*) imperfect beginning of something undeveloped. **3** vestigial or undeveloped part or organ. □ **rudimentary** /-'mentərɪ/ *adjective*.

■ **1** (**rudiments**) basic principles, basics, elements, essentials, first principles, foundations, fundamentals. □ **rudimentary** basic, crude, elementary, embryonic, immature, initial, introductory, preliminary, primitive, provisional, undeveloped.

rue[1] *verb* (**rues, rued, rueing** or **ruing**) repent of; wish undone or non-existent.

rue[2] *noun* evergreen shrub with bitter strong-scented leaves.

rueful *adjective* genuinely or humorously sorrowful. □ **ruefully** *adverb*. **ruefulness** *noun*.

ruff[1] *noun* **1** projecting starched frill worn round neck. **2** projecting or coloured ring of feathers or hair round bird's or animal's neck. **3** domestic pigeon.

ruff[2] *verb* trump at cards. ● *noun* trumping.

ruffian /'rʌfɪən/ *noun* violent lawless person.

■ *colloquial* brute, bully, desperado, gangster, hoodlum, hooligan, lout, mugger, rogue, scoundrel, thug, tough, villain, *slang* yob.

ruffle /'rʌf(ə)l/ *verb* (**-ling**) **1** disturb smoothness or tranquillity of. **2** upset calmness of (person). **3** gather into ruffle. **4** make (esp. hair) untidy. **5** (often + *up*) (of bird) erect (feathers) in anger, display, etc. ● *noun* frill of lace etc.

■ *verb* **1** agitate, disturb, ripple, stir. **2** annoy, confuse, disconcert, disquiet, fluster, irritate, nettle, *colloquial* rattle, *colloquial* throw, unnerve, unsettle, upset, vex, worry. **4** derange, disarrange, disorder, mess up, rumple, tangle, tousle.

rufous /'ru:fəs/ *adjective* reddish-brown.

rug *noun* **1** floor-mat. **2** thick woollen wrap or coverlet.

■ **2** blanket, coverlet.

Rugby /'rʌgbɪ/ *noun* (in full **Rugby football**) team game played with oval ball that may be kicked or carried. □ **Rugby League** Rugby with teams of 13. **Rugby Union** Rugby with teams of 15.

rugged /'rʌgɪd/ *adjective* **1** (esp. of ground) rough, uneven. **2** (of features) furrowed, irregular. **3** harsh. **4** robust. **5** unpolished, rough. □ **ruggedly** *adverb.* **ruggedness** *noun.*

■ **1** bumpy, craggy, irregular, jagged, pitted, rocky, rough, stony, uneven. **2** craggy, furrowed, lined, weather-beaten. **3** arduous, difficult, hard, harsh, onerous, rough, severe, tough. **4** burly, hardy, husky, muscular, robust, strong, sturdy. **5** rough, uncultured, ungraceful, unpolished, unrefined.

rugger /'rʌgə/ *noun colloquial* Rugby.

ruin /'ruːɪn/ *noun* **1** wrecked or spoiled state. **2** downfall. **3** loss of property or position. **4** (in *singular* or *plural*) remains of building etc. that has suffered ruin. **5** cause of ruin. ● *verb* **1** bring to ruin. **2** spoil, damage. **3** (esp. as **ruined** *adjective*) reduce to ruins. □ **ruination** *noun.*

■ *noun* **2** breakdown, collapse, destruction, downfall, end, failure, fall, ruination, wreck. **3** bankruptcy, collapse, crash, downfall, failure, insolvency, undoing. **4** (*ruins*) debris, remains, rubble, wreckage. ● *verb* **1** see DESTROY 1. **2** see SPOIL *verb* 1,2. **3** demolish, destroy, devastate, flatten, shatter, wreck; (**ruined**) crumbling, derelict, dilapidated, fallen down, in ruins, ramshackle, ruinous, tumbledown, uninhabitable, unsafe.

ruinous *adjective* **1** bringing ruin; disastrous. **2** dilapidated.

■ **1** apocalyptic, calamitous, cataclysmic, catastrophic, crushing, destructive, devastating, dire, disastrous, fatal, harmful, injurious, pernicious, shattering. **2** see RUIN *verb* 3.

rule *noun* **1** compulsory principle governing action. **2** prevailing custom, standard; normal state of things. **3** government, dominion. **4** straight measuring device; ruler. **5** code of discipline of religious order. **6** *Printing* thin line or dash. ● *verb* (**-ling**) **1** dominate; keep under control. **2** (often + *over*) have sovereign control of. **3** (often + *that*) pronounce authoritatively. **4** make parallel lines across (paper). **5** make (straight line) with ruler etc. □ **as a rule** usually. **rule of thumb** rule based on experience or practice, not theory. **rule out** exclude.

■ *noun* **1** axiom, decree, guideline, law, ordinance, precept, principle, regulation, ruling, statute. **2** convention, custom, norm, routine, standard. **3** administration, ascendancy, authority, command, control, domination, dominion, empire, government, influence, jurisdiction, management, mastery, oversight, power, regime, reign, sovereignty, supervision, supremacy, sway. ● *verb* **1** administer, command, control, direct, dominate, govern, guide, hold sway, lead, manage, run, superintend. **2** see REIGN *verb* 1. **3** decide, decree, *formal* deem, determine, find, judge, pronounce, resolve. □ **rule out** see EXCLUDE 2.

ruler *noun* **1** person exercising government or dominion. **2** straight strip of plastic etc. used to draw or measure.

■ **1** administrator, chief, emir, emperor, empress, governor, *historical* kaiser, king, lawmaker, leader, lord, manager, monarch, potentate, president,

prince, princess, queen, *historical* raja, regent, sovereign, sultan, *historical* suzerain, *historical* tsar, *historical* tsarina, viceroy.

ruling *noun* authoritative pronouncement.

rum¹ *noun* spirit distilled from sugar cane or molasses. □ **rum baba** sponge cake soaked in rum syrup.

rum² *adjective* (**-mm-**) *colloquial* queer, strange.

Rumanian = ROMANIAN.

rumba /'rʌmbə/ *noun* **1** ballroom dance of Cuban origin. **2** music for this.

rumble /'rʌmb(ə)l/ *verb* (**-ling**) **1** make continuous deep sound as of thunder. **2** (+ *along, by, past,* etc.) (esp. of vehicle) move with such sound. **3** *slang* see through, detect. ● *noun* rumbling sound.

rumbustious /rʌm'bʌstʃəs/ *adjective colloquial* boisterous, uproarious.

ruminant /'ruːmɪnənt/ *noun* animal that chews the cud. ● *adjective* **1** of ruminants. **2** meditative.

ruminate /'ruːmɪneɪt/ *verb* (**-ting**) **1** meditate, ponder. **2** chew the cud. □ **rumination** *noun.* **ruminative** /-nətɪv/ *adjective.*

rummage /'rʌmɪdʒ/ *verb* (**-ging**) **1** search, esp. unsystematically. **2** (+ *up, out*) find among other things. ● *noun* rummaging. □ **rummage sale** *esp. US* jumble sale.

rummy /'rʌmɪ/ *noun* card game played usually with two packs.

rumour /'ruːmə/ (*US* **rumor**) *noun* (often + *of, that*) general talk, assertion, or hearsay of doubtful accuracy. ● *verb* (usually in *passive*) report by way of rumour.

■ *noun* chat, *colloquial* chit-chat, gossip, hearsay, news, prattle, report, scandal, tittle-tattle, whisper.

rump *noun* **1** hind part of mammal or bird, esp. buttocks. **2** remnant of parliament etc. □ **rump steak** cut of beef from rump.

rumple /'rʌmp(ə)l/ *verb* (**-ling**) crease, ruffle.

rumpus /'rʌmpəs/ *noun colloquial* row, uproar.

run *verb* (**-nn-**; *past* **ran**; *past participle* **run**) **1** go at pace faster than walk. **2** go or travel hurriedly, briefly, etc. **3** flee. **4** advance smoothly or (as) by rolling or on wheels. **5** (cause to) be in action or operation. **6** be current or operative. **7** (of bus, train, etc.) travel on its route. **8** (of play etc.) be presented. **9** extend; have course or tendency. **10** compete or enter (horse etc.) in race etc. **11** (often + *for*) seek election. **12** (cause to) flow or emit liquid. **13** spread rapidly. **14** perform (errand). **15** publish (article etc.). **16** direct (business etc.). **17** own and use (vehicle). **18** smuggle. **19** (of thought, the eye, etc.) pass quickly. **20** (of tights etc.) ladder. ● *noun* **1** running. **2** short excursion. **3** distance travelled. **4** general tendency. **5** regular route. **6** continuous stretch, spell, or course. **7** (often + *on*) high general demand. **8** quantity produced at one time. **9** general or average type or class. **10** point scored in cricket or baseball. **11** (+ *of*) free use of. **12** animal's regular track. **13** enclosure for fowls etc. **14** range of pasture. **15** ladder in tights etc. **16** *Music* rapid scale passage. □ **give (person) the run-around** deceive, evade. **on the run** fleeing. **runabout** light car or aircraft. **run across** happen to meet. **run after** pursue. **run away** (often + *from*) flee, abscond. **runaway** *noun* person, animal, vehicle, etc. running away or out of control. **run down 1** knock down. **2** reduce numbers of. **3** (of clock etc.) stop. **4** discover after search. **5** *colloquial* disparage. **rundown** *noun* **1** reduction in numbers. **2** detailed analysis. **run-down** *adjective* **1** dilapidated, decayed. **2** exhausted. **run dry** cease to flow. **run in 1** run (vehicle, engine) carefully when new. **2** *colloquial* arrest. **run-in** *noun colloquial* quarrel. **run into 1** collide with. **2** encounter. **3** reach as many as. **run low, short** become depleted; have too little. **run off 1** flee. **2** produce (copies) on machine. **3** decide (race) after tie or heats. **4** write or recite fluently. **run-of-the-mill** ordinary, not special. **run on 1** continue in operation. **2** speak volubly. **3** continue on same line as preceding matter. **run out 1** come to an end. **2** (+ *of*) exhaust one's stock of. **3** put down wicket of (running batsman). **run out on** *colloquial* desert. **run over 1** (of vehicle) knock down or crush. **2** overflow. **3** review quickly. **run through 1** examine or rehearse briefly. **2** deal successively with. **3** spend money rapidly. **4** pervade. **5** pierce with blade. **run-through** *noun* rehearsal. **run to 1** have money or ability for. **2** reach (amount etc.). **3** show tendency to. **run up 1** accumulate (debt etc.). **2** build or make hurriedly. **3** raise (flag). **run-up** *noun* (often + *to*) preparatory period. **run up against** meet with (difficulty etc.). **runway** specially prepared airfield surface for taking off and landing.

■ *verb* **1, 2** bolt, canter, career, dash, gallop, hare, hurry, jog, race, rush, scamper, *colloquial* scoot, scurry, scuttle, speed, sprint, *colloquial* tear, trot. **3** see ESCAPE *verb* 1, FLEE. **5** behave, function, go, perform, work. **7** go, operate, ply, travel. **12** cascade, dribble, flow, gush, leak, pour, spill, stream, trickle. **16** administer, conduct, control, direct, govern, look after, maintain, manage, rule, supervise. ● *noun* **1** canter, dash, gallop, jog, race, sprint, trot. **2** drive, excursion, jaunt, journey, *colloquial* joyride, ride, *colloquial* spin, trip. **6** chain, course, period, sequence, series, spell, stretch. **13** compound, coop, enclosure, field, paddock, pen. □ **run across** see MEET[1] *verb* 1. **run after** see PURSUE 1. **run away** see ESCAPE *verb* 1, FLEE. **run into 2** see MEET[1] *verb* 1.

rune *noun* **1** letter of earliest Germanic alphabet. **2** similar character of mysterious or magic significance. □ **runic** *adjective*.

rung[1] *noun* **1** step of ladder. **2** strengthening crosspiece of chair etc.

rung[2] *past participle* of RING[2].

runnel /'rʌn(ə)l/ *noun* **1** brook. **2** gutter.

runner *noun* **1** racer. **2** creeping rooting plant-stem. **3** groove, rod, etc. for thing to slide along or on. **4** sliding ring on rod etc. **5** messenger. **6** long narrow ornamental cloth or rug. **7** (in full **runner bean**) kind of climbing bean. □ **runner-up** (*plural* **runners-up** or **runner-ups**) competitor taking second place.

■ **1** athlete, jogger, racer, sprinter. **2** offshoot, shoot, sucker, tendril. **5** courier, dispatch rider, errand-boy, errand-girl, messenger.

running *noun* act or manner of running race etc. ● *adjective* **1** continuous. **2** consecutive. **3** done with a run. □ **in or out of the running** with good or poor chance of success. **running commentary** verbal description of events in progress. **running knot** one that slips along rope etc. to allow tightening. **running mate** *US* **1** vice-presidential candidate. **2** horse setting pace for another. **running repairs** minor or temporary repairs. **running water** flowing water, esp. on tap.

runny *adjective* (**-ier, -iest**) **1** tending to run or flow. **2** excessively fluid.

■ fluid, free-flowing, liquid, running, thin, watery.

runt *noun* **1** smallest pig etc. of litter. **2** undersized person.

rupee /ruːˈpiː/ *noun* monetary unit of India, Pakistan, etc.

rupiah /ruːˈpiːə/ *noun* monetary unit of Indonesia.

rupture /'rʌptʃə/ *noun* **1** breaking, breach. **2** breach in relationship. **3** abdominal hernia. ● *verb* (**-ring**) **1** burst (cell, membrane, etc.). **2** sever (connection). **3** affect with or suffer hernia.

■ *noun* **1** breach, break, burst, cleavage, fracture, puncture, rift, split. **2** break-up, rift, schism, separation, split. ● *verb* **1** break, burst, fracture, part, separate, split. **2** break, sever.

rural /'rʊər(ə)l/ *adjective* in, of, or suggesting country.

■ agrarian, agricultural, Arcadian, bucolic, countrified, pastoral, rustic, sylvan.

ruse /ruːz/ *noun* stratagem, trick.

rush[1] *verb* **1** go, move, flow, or act precipitately or with great speed. **2** move or transport with great haste. **3** perform or deal with hurriedly. **4** force (person) to act hastily. **5** attack or capture by sudden assault. ● *noun* **1** rushing. **2** violent advance or attack. **3** sudden flow. **4** period of great activity. **5** sudden migration of large numbers. **6** (+ *on, for*) strong demand for a commodity. **7** (in *plural*) *colloquial* first uncut prints of film. ● *adjective* done hastily. □ **rush hour** time each day when traffic is heaviest.

■ *verb* **1** bolt, burst, bustle, canter, career, charge, dash, fly, gallop, *colloquial* get a move on, hare, hasten, hurry, jog, make haste, race, run, scamper, *colloquial* scoot, scramble, scurry, scuttle, shoot, speed, sprint, stampede, *colloquial* step on it, *colloquial* tear, trot, zoom. ● *noun* **1** bustle, dash, haste, hurry, panic, pressure, race, scramble, speed, urgency. **2** charge, onslaught, stampede. **3** flood, gush, spate, surge.

rush[2] *noun* **1** marsh plant with slender pith-filled stem. **2** its stem esp. used for making basketware etc.

rusk *noun* slice of bread rebaked as light biscuit, esp. for infants.

russet /'rʌsɪt/ *adjective* reddish-brown. ● *noun*

1 russet colour. **2** rough-skinned russet-coloured apple.

Russian /'rʌʃ(ə)n/ *noun* **1** native or national of Russia or (loosely) former USSR. **2** person of Russian descent. **3** language of Russia. ● *adjective* **1** of Russia or (loosely) former USSR or its people. **2** of or in Russian. □ **Russian roulette** firing of revolver held to one's head after spinning cylinder with one chamber loaded. **Russian salad** mixed diced cooked vegetables with mayonnaise.

rust *noun* **1** reddish corrosive coating formed on iron etc. by oxidation. **2** plant disease with rust-coloured spots. **3** reddish-brown. ● *verb* **1** affect or be affected with rust. **2** become impaired through disuse. □ **rustproof** not susceptible to corrosion by rust.

■ *verb* **1** corrode, crumble away, oxidize, rot.

rustic /'rʌstɪk/ *adjective* **1** of or like country people or country life. **2** unsophisticated. **3** of rough workmanship. **4** made of untrimmed branches or rough timber. **5** *Architecture* with roughened surface. ● *noun* country person; peasant. □ **rusticity** /-'tɪs-/ *noun*.

■ *adjective* **1** see RURAL. **2** artless, clumsy, crude, naive, oafish, plain, rough, simple, uncomplicated, uncultured, unpolished, unsophisticated.

rusticate /'rʌstɪkeɪt/ *verb* (-ting) **1** expel temporarily from university. **2** retire to or live in the country. **3** make rustic. □ **rustication** *noun*.

rustle /'rʌs(ə)l/ *verb* (-ling) **1** (cause to) make sound as of dry blown leaves. **2** steal (cattle or horses). ● *noun* rustling sound. □ **rustle up** *colloquial* produce at short notice. □ **rustler** *noun*.

rusty *adjective* (-ier, -iest) **1** rusted, affected by rust. **2** stiff with age or disuse. **3** (of knowledge etc.) impaired by neglect. **4** rust-coloured. **5** discoloured by age.

■ **1** corroded, oxidized, rotten. **3** forgotten, out of practice, unused. **5** discoloured, stained, tarnished.

rut[1] *noun* **1** deep track made by passage of wheels. **2** fixed (esp. tedious) practice or routine. ● *verb* (-tt-) (esp. as **rutted** *adjective*) mark with ruts.

■ *noun* **1** channel, furrow, groove, indentation, track, trough, wheel-mark. **2** habit, pattern, routine, treadmill.

rut[2] *noun* periodic sexual excitement of male deer etc. ● *verb* (-tt-) be affected with rut.

ruthless /'ruːθlɪs/ *adjective* having no pity or compassion. □ **ruthlessly** *adverb*. **ruthlessness** *noun*.

■ bloodthirsty, brutal, callous, cruel, dangerous, ferocious, fierce, hard, heartless, inexorable, inhuman, merciless, pitiless, relentless, *colloquial* sadistic, unfeeling, unrelenting, unsympathetic, vicious, violent.

RV *abbreviation* Revised Version (of Bible).

rye /raɪ/ *noun* **1** cereal plant. **2** grain of this, used for bread, fodder, etc. **3** (in full **rye whisky**) whisky distilled from rye.

Ss

S. *abbreviation* (also **S**) **1** Saint. **2** south(ern).

s. *abbreviation* **1** second(s). **2** *historical* shilling(s). **3** son.

SA *abbreviation* **1** Salvation Army. **2** South Africa. **3** South Australia.

sabbath /ˈsæbəθ/ *noun* religious rest-day kept by Christians on Sunday and Jews on Saturday.

sabbatical /səˈbætɪk(ə)l/ *adjective* (of leave) granted at intervals to university teacher for study or travel. ● *noun* period of sabbatical leave.

saber *US* = SABRE.

sable /ˈseɪb(ə)l/ *noun* (*plural* same or **-s**) **1** small dark-furred mammal. **2** its skin or fur. **3** *esp. poetical* black colour. ● *adjective* **1** *Heraldry* black. **2** *esp. poetical* dark, gloomy.

sabot /ˈsæbəʊ/ *noun* wooden or wooden-soled shoe.

sabotage /ˈsæbətɑːʒ/ *noun* deliberate destruction or damage, esp. for political purpose. ● *verb* (**-ging**) **1** commit sabotage on. **2** destroy, spoil.
■ *noun* damage, destruction, disruption, vandalism, wrecking. ● *verb* cripple, damage, destroy, disable, disrupt, incapacitate, ruin, *colloquial* throw a spanner in the works (of), undermine, vandalize, wreck.

saboteur /sæbəˈtɜː/ *noun* person who commits sabotage.

sabre /ˈseɪbə/ *noun* (*US* **saber**) **1** curved cavalry sword. **2** light fencing-sword. □ **sabre-rattling** display or threat of military force.

sac *noun* membranous bag in animal or plant.

saccharin /ˈsækərɪn/ *noun* a sugar substitute.

saccharine /ˈsækəriːn/ *adjective* excessively sentimental or sweet.

sacerdotal /sækəˈdəʊt(ə)l/ *adjective* of priests or priestly office.

sachet /ˈsæʃeɪ/ *noun* small bag or packet containing shampoo, perfumed substances, etc.

sack[1] *noun* **1** large strong bag for coal, food, mail, etc. **2** amount held by sack. **3** (**the sack**) *colloquial* dismissal. **4** (**the sack**) *US slang* bed. ● *verb* **1** put in sack(s). **2** *colloquial* dismiss from employment. □ **sackcloth** coarse fabric of flax or hemp.
■ *noun* **1** bag, pouch. **3** (**the sack**) *colloquial* the boot, *slang* the chop, dismissal, redundancy. ● *verb* **2** axe, discharge, dismiss, fire, give notice to, *colloquial* give the boot to, *slang* give the chop to, lay off, make redundant.

sack[2] *verb* plunder and destroy (town etc.). ● *noun* such sacking.

■ *verb* see DESTROY 1, PLUNDER *verb* 1.

sack[3] *noun historical* white wine from Spain etc.

sackbut /ˈsækbʌt/ *noun* early form of trombone.

sacking *noun* sackcloth.

sacral /ˈseɪkr(ə)l/ *adjective* of sacrum.

sacrament /ˈsækrəmənt/ *noun* **1** symbolic Christian ceremony, esp. Eucharist. **2** sacred thing. □ **sacramental** /-ˈmen-/ *adjective*.

sacred /ˈseɪkrɪd/ *adjective* **1** (often + *to*) dedicated to a god; connected with religion. **2** safeguarded or required, esp. by tradition or religion; inviolable. □ **sacred cow** *colloquial* idea or institution unreasonably held to be above criticism. □ **sacredness** *noun*.
■ **1** blessed, blest, consecrated, dedicated, divine, godly, hallowed, holy, religious, revered, sanctified, venerable, venerated. **2** see SACROSANCT.

sacrifice /ˈsækrɪfaɪs/ *noun* **1** voluntary relinquishing of something valued. **2** thing thus relinquished. **3** loss entailed. **4** slaughter of animal or person, or surrender of possession, as offering to deity. **5** animal, person, or thing thus offered. ● *verb* (**-cing**) **1** give up. **2** (+ *to*) devote to. **3** offer or kill (as) sacrifice. □ **sacrificial** /-ˈfɪʃ-/ *adjective*.
■ *noun* **4** immolation, oblation, offering. ● *verb* **1** abandon, forfeit, forgo, give up, let go, lose, relinquish, renounce, surrender. **3** immolate, kill, offer up, slaughter, yield up.

sacrilege /ˈsækrɪlɪdʒ/ *noun* violation of what is sacred. □ **sacrilegious** /-ˈlɪdʒəs/ *adjective*.
■ blasphemy, desecration, disrespect, heresy, impiety, irreverence, profanation. □ **sacrilegious** atheistic, blasphemous, disrespectful, heretical, impious, irreligious, irreverent, profane, ungodly.

sacristan /ˈsækrɪst(ə)n/ *noun* person in charge of sacristy and church contents.

sacristy /ˈsækrɪstɪ/ *noun* (*plural* **-ies**) room in church for vestments, vessels, etc.

sacrosanct /ˈsækrəʊsæŋkt/ *adjective* most sacred; inviolable. □ **sacrosanctity** /-ˈsæŋkt-/ *noun*.
■ inviolable, inviolate, protected, respected, sacred, secure, untouchable.

sacrum /ˈseɪkrəm/ *noun* (*plural* **sacra** or **-s**) triangular bone between hip-bones.

sad *adjective* (**-dd-**) **1** sorrowful. **2** causing sorrow; regrettable. **3** deplorable. □ **sadden** *verb*. **sadly** *adverb*. **sadness** *noun*.

■ **1** abject, blue, broken-hearted, careworn, cheerless, crestfallen, dejected, depressed, desolate, despairing, desperate, despondent, disappointed, disconsolate, discontented, discouraged, disgruntled, disheartened, disillusioned, dismal, dispirited, dissatisfied, distressed, doleful, *literary* dolorous, *colloquial* down, downcast, downhearted, dreary, forlorn, friendless, funereal, gloomy, glum, grave, grief-stricken, grieving, heartbroken, heavy, heavy-hearted, homesick, hopeless, in low spirits, in the doldrums, joyless, *formal* lachrymose, lonely, long-faced, low, lugubrious, melancholy, miserable, moody, moping, morose, mournful, pathetic, penitent, pessimistic, piteous, pitiable, pitiful, plaintive, poignant, regretful, rueful, saddened, serious, sober, sombre, sorrowful, sorry, tearful, troubled, unhappy, unsatisfied, upset, wistful, woebegone, woeful, wretched. **2** calamitous, depressing, disastrous, discouraging, dismal, dispiriting, distressing, grievous, heartbreaking, heart-rending, lamentable, *colloquial* morbid, moving, painful, regrettable, touching, tragic, unfortunate, unwelcome, upsetting. **3** see DEPLORABLE, UNSATISFACTORY. □ **sadden** break (person's) heart, depress, disappoint, discourage, dishearten, dismay, dispirit, distress, grieve, upset. **sadness** bleakness, care, dejection, depression, desolation, despair, despondency, disappointment, disillusionment, dissatisfaction, distress, dolour, gloom, glumness, grief, heartbreak, heaviness, homesickness, hopelessness, loneliness, melancholy, misery, moping, moroseness, mournfulness, pessimism, poignancy, regret, ruefulness, seriousness, sombreness, sorrow, tearfulness, trouble, unhappiness, wistfulness, woe.

saddle /ˈsæd(ə)l/ *noun* **1** seat of leather etc. fastened on horse etc. **2** bicycle etc. seat. **3** joint of meat consisting of the two loins. **4** ridge rising to a summit at each end. ● *verb* (**-ling**) **1** put saddle on (horse etc.). **2** (+ *with*) burden with task etc. □ **saddle-bag 1** each of pair of bags laid across back of horse etc. **2** bag attached behind bicycle etc. saddle.

saddler *noun* maker of or dealer in saddles etc. □ **saddlery** *noun* (*plural* **-ies**).

sadism /ˈseɪdɪz(ə)m/ *noun* **1** *colloquial* enjoyment of cruelty to others. **2** sexual perversion characterized by this. □ **sadist** *noun*. **sadistic** /səˈdɪs-/ *adjective*. **sadistically** /səˈdɪs-/ *adverb*.

■ □ **sadistic** barbarous, beastly, brutal, cruel, inhuman, monstrous, perverted, pitiless, ruthless, vicious.

sadomasochism /seɪdəʊˈmæsəkɪz(ə)m/ *noun* sadism and masochism in one person. □ **sadomasochist** *noun*. **sadomasochistic** /-ˈkɪs-/ *adjective*.

s.a.e. *abbreviation* stamped addressed envelope.

safari /səˈfɑːrɪ/ *noun* (*plural* **-s**) expedition, esp. in Africa, to observe or hunt animals. □ **safari park** area where wild animals are kept in open for viewing.

safe *adjective* **1** uninjured. **2** affording security; free of danger; not risky. **3** reliable, sure. **4** prevented from escaping or doing harm. **5** cautious; moderate. ● *noun* **1** strong lockable cupboard for valuables. **2** ventilated cupboard for provisions. □ **safe conduct** immunity from arrest or harm. **safe deposit** building containing strongrooms and safes for hire. **safe keeping** protection. □ **safely** *adverb*.

■ *adjective* **1** alive and well, all right, in one piece, intact, sound, undamaged, unharmed, unhurt, uninjured, unscathed, well, whole. **2** defended, foolproof, guarded, harmless, immune, impregnable, innocuous, protected, secure, secured, shielded, tame. **3** certain, dependable, reliable, sound, sure, tried and tested, trustworthy; *of vehicle* airworthy, roadworthy, seaworthy. **5** careful, cautious, circumspect, moderate, tame. □ **safe keeping** care, charge, custody, guardianship, keeping, protection.

safeguard *noun* protecting proviso, circumstance, etc. ● *verb* guard or protect (rights etc.).

■ *verb* care for, defend, keep safe, look after, protect, shelter, shield.

safety /ˈseɪftɪ/ *noun* being safe; freedom from danger. □ **safety belt** belt or strap preventing injury, esp. seat belt. **safety catch** device preventing accidental operation of gun trigger or machinery. **safety curtain** fireproof curtain to divide theatre auditorium from stage. **safety match** match that ignites only on specially prepared surface. **safety net** net placed to catch acrobat etc. in case of fall. **safety pin** pin with guarded point. **safety razor** razor with guard to prevent user cutting skin. **safety valve 1** valve relieving excessive pressure of steam. **2** means of harmlessly venting excitement etc.

■ cover, dependability, harmlessness, immunity, invulnerability, protection, refuge, reliability, sanctuary, security, shelter.

saffron /ˈsæfrən/ *noun* **1** deep yellow colouring and flavouring from dried crocus stigmas. **2** colour of this. ● *adjective* deep yellow.

sag *verb* (**-gg-**) **1** sink or subside. **2** have downward bulge or curve in middle. ● *noun* state or amount of sagging. □ **saggy** *adjective*.

■ *verb* bend, dip, droop, drop, fall, flop, hang down, sink, slump.

saga /ˈsɑːgə/ *noun* **1** long heroic story, esp. medieval Icelandic or Norwegian. **2** long family chronicle. **3** long involved story.

sagacious /səˈgeɪʃəs/ *adjective* showing insight or good judgement. □ **sagacity** /-ˈgæs-/ *noun*.

sage[1] *noun* aromatic herb with dull greyish-green leaves.

sage[2] *noun* wise man. ● *adjective* wise, judicious, experienced. □ **sagely** *adverb*.

Sagittarius /sædʒɪˈteərɪəs/ *noun* ninth sign of zodiac.

sago /ˈseɪgəʊ/ *noun* (*plural* **-s**) **1** starch used in puddings etc. **2** (in full **sago palm**) any of several tropical trees yielding this.

sahib /sɑːb/ *noun historical: form of address to European men in India.*

said *past & past participle* of SAY.

sail *noun* **1** piece of material extended on rigging to catch wind and propel vessel. **2** ship's sails collectively. **3** voyage or excursion in sailing vessel. **4** wind-catching apparatus of windmill. ● *verb* **1** travel on water by use of sails or engine-power. **2** begin voyage. **3** navigate (ship etc.). **4** travel on (sea). **5** glide or move smoothly or with dignity. **6** (often + *through*) *colloquial* succeed easily. □ **sailboard** board with mast and sail, used in windsurfing. **sailcloth 1** material for sails. **2** kind of coarse linen. **sailing boat, ship, etc.** vessel moved by sails. **sailplane** kind of glider. **under sail** with sails set.
■ *noun* **3** cruise, journey, passage, voyage. ● *verb* **1** cruise, steam, travel. **2** put to sea, set sail. **3** captain, navigate, pilot, skipper, steer.

sailor *noun* seaman or mariner, esp. below officer's rank. □ **bad, good sailor** person very liable or not liable to seasickness.
■ mariner, old salt, sea dog, seafarer, seaman, yachtsman, yachtswoman.

sainfoin /'sænfɔɪn/ *noun* pink-flowered plant used as fodder.

saint /seɪnt, before a name usually sənt/ *noun* **1** holy or canonized person, regarded as deserving special veneration. **2** very virtuous person. ● *verb* (as **sainted** *adjective*) holy, virtuous. □ **sainthood** *noun.* **saintlike** *adjective.* **saintly** (**-ier, -iest**) *adjective.* **saintliness** *noun.*
■ □ **saintly** angelic, blessed, blest, chaste, godly, good, holy, innocent, moral, pious, pure, religious, righteous, seraphic, sinless, virginal, virtuous.

sake[1] *noun* □ **for the sake of 1** out of consideration for; in the interest of. **2** in order to please, get, etc.
■ □ **for the sake of 1** on account of, to the advantage of, on behalf of, for the benefit of, for the good of, in the interest of, for the welfare of.

sake[2] /'sɑːkɪ/ *noun* Japanese rice wine.

salaam /sə'lɑːm/ *noun* **1** (*chiefly as Muslim greeting*) Peace! **2** low bow. ● *verb* make salaam.

salacious /sə'leɪʃəs/ *adjective* **1** erotic. **2** lecherous. □ **salaciousness** *noun.* **salacity** /-'læs-/ *noun.*

salad /'sæləd/ *noun* cold mixture of usually raw vegetables etc. often with dressing. □ **salad cream** creamy salad dressing. **salad days** period of youthful inexperience. **salad dressing** sauce of oil, vinegar, etc. for salads.

salamander /'sæləmændə/ *noun* **1** newt-like amphibian formerly supposed to live in fire. **2** similar mythical creature.

salami /sə'lɑːmɪ/ *noun* (*plural* **-s**) highly-seasoned sausage, originally Italian.

sal ammoniac /sæl ə'məʊnɪæk/ *noun* ammonium chloride.

salary /'sælərɪ/ *noun* (*plural* **-ies**) fixed regular payment by employer to employee. ● *verb* (**-ies, -ied**) (usually as **salaried** *adjective*) pay salary to.
■ *noun* compensation, earnings, emolument, income, pay, payment, remuneration, stipend, wages.

sale *noun* **1** exchange of commodity for money etc.; act or instance of selling. **2** amount sold. **3** temporary offering of goods at reduced prices. **4** event at which goods are sold. □ **on, for sale** offered for purchase. **saleroom** room where auctions are held. **salesman, salesperson, saleswoman** person employed to sell goods etc.
■ **1** marketing, selling, trade, traffic, transaction, vending. □ **salesman, salesperson, saleswoman** assistant, auctioneer, representative, sales assistant, shop assistant.

saleable *adjective* fit or likely to be sold. □ **saleability** *noun.*

salesmanship *noun* skill in selling.

salient /'seɪlɪənt/ *adjective* **1** prominent, conspicuous. **2** (of angle) pointing outwards. ● *noun* **1** salient angle. **2** outward bulge in military line.

saline /'seɪlaɪn/ *adjective* **1** containing or tasting of salt(s). **2** of salt(s). ● *noun* **1** salt lake, spring, etc. **2** saline solution. □ **salinity** /sə'lɪn-/ *noun.*

saliva /sə'laɪvə/ *noun* colourless liquid produced by glands in mouth. □ **salivary** *adjective.*
■ dribble, spit, spittle, sputum.

salivate /'sælɪveɪt/ *verb* (**-ting**) secrete saliva, esp. in excess.

sallow[1] /'sæləʊ/ *adjective* (**-er, -est**) (esp. of complexion) yellowish.
■ anaemic, bloodless, colourless, etiolated, pale, pallid, pasty, unhealthy, wan, yellowish.

sallow[2] /'sæləʊ/ *noun* **1** low-growing willow. **2** shoot or wood of this.

sally /'sælɪ/ *noun* (*plural* **-ies**) **1** witticism. **2** military rush. **3** excursion. ● *verb* (**-ies, -ied**) **1** (usually + *out, forth*) set out for walk etc. **2** make sally.

salmon /'sæmən/ *noun* (*plural* same) large silver-scaled fish with orange-pink flesh. ● *adjective* orange-pink. □ **salmon-pink** orange-pink. **salmon trout** large silver-coloured trout.

salmonella /sælmə'nelə/ *noun* (*plural* **-llae** /-liː/) **1** bacterium causing food poisoning. **2** such food poisoning.

salon /'sælɒn/ *noun* **1** room or establishment of hairdresser, fashion designer, etc. **2** *historical* meeting of eminent people at fashionable home. **3** reception room of large house.

saloon /sə'luːn/ *noun* **1** large room or hall on ship, in hotel, etc., or for specified purpose. **2** saloon car. **3** *US* drinking bar. **4** saloon bar. □ **saloon bar** more comfortable bar in public house. **saloon car** car with body closed off from luggage area.

salsa /'sælsə/ *noun* **1** dance music of Cuban origin. **2** kind of spicy tomato sauce.

salsify /'sælsɪfɪ/ *noun* (*plural* **-ies**) plant with long fleshy edible root.

salt /sɔːlt/ *noun* **1** (also **common salt**) sodium chloride, esp. mined or evaporated from sea water, and used esp. for seasoning or preserving food. **2** *Chemistry* substance formed in reaction of an acid with a base. **3** piquancy, wit. **4** (in *singular* or *plural*) substance resembling salt in taste, form, etc. **5** (esp. in *plural*) substance used as laxative. **6** (also **old salt**) experienced sailor. ● *adjective* containing, tasting of, or preserved with salt. ● *verb* **1** cure, preserve, or season with salt. **2** sprinkle salt on (road etc.). □ **salt away, down** *slang* put (money etc.) by. **salt cellar** container for salt at table. **salt marsh** marsh flooded by tide. **salt mine** mine yielding rock salt. **salt of the earth** finest or most honest people. **salt pan** vessel, or hollow near sea, used for getting salt by evaporation. **salt-water** of or living in sea. **take with a pinch or grain of salt** be sceptical about. **worth one's salt** efficient, capable.

■ *adjective* brackish, briny, saline, salted, salty, savoury.

salting *noun* (esp. in *plural*) marsh overflowed by sea.

saltire /'sɔːltaɪə/ *noun* X-shaped cross.

saltpetre /sɔːlt'piːtə/ *noun* (*US* **saltpeter**) white crystalline salty substance used in preserving meat and in gunpowder.

salty *adjective* (**-ier**, **-iest**) **1** tasting of or containing salt. **2** witty, piquant. □ **saltiness** *noun*.

salubrious /sə'luːbrɪəs/ *adjective* health-giving. □ **salubrity** *noun*.

■ health-giving, healthy, hygienic, invigorating, nice, pleasant, refreshing, sanitary, wholesome.

saluki /sə'luːkɪ/ *noun* (*plural* **-s**) dog of tall slender silky-coated breed.

salutary /'sæljʊtərɪ/ *adjective* producing good effect.

salutation /sælju:'teɪʃ(ə)n/ *noun formal* sign or expression of greeting.

salute /sə'luːt/ *noun* **1** gesture of respect, homage, greeting, etc. **2** *Military etc.* prescribed gesture or use of weapons or flags as sign of respect etc. ● *verb* (**-ting**) **1** make salute (to). **2** greet. **3** commend.

■ *noun* **1** acknowledgement, gesture, greeting, *formal* salutation, wave. ● *verb* **2** acknowledge, address, greet, hail. **3** see HONOUR *verb* 2.

salvage /'sælvɪdʒ/ *noun* **1** rescue of property from sea, fire, etc. **2** saving and utilization of waste materials. **3** property or materials salvaged. ● *verb* (**-ging**) save from wreck etc. □ **salvageable** *adjective*.

■ *noun* **1** reclamation, recovery, rescue, retrieval, salvation, saving. **2** recycling. ● *verb* conserve, preserve, reclaim, recover, recycle, redeem, rescue, retrieve, reuse, save.

salvation /sæl'veɪʃ(ə)n/ *noun* **1** saving, being saved. **2** deliverance from sin and damnation. **3** religious conversion. **4** person or thing that saves. □ **Salvation Army** worldwide

quasi-military Christian charitable organization.

■ **1** deliverance, escape, help, preservation, rescue, saving. **2** deliverance, redemption.

Salvationist *noun* member of Salvation Army.

salve[1] *noun* **1** healing ointment. **2** (often + *for*) thing that soothes. ● *verb* (**-ving**) soothe.

■ *noun* **1** balm, cream, embrocation, emollient, liniment, lotion, ointment, unguent. ● *verb* alleviate, appease, assuage, comfort, ease, mitigate, mollify, soothe.

salve[2] *verb* (**-ving**) save from wreck, fire, etc. □ **salvable** *adjective*.

salver /'sælvə/ *noun* tray for drinks, letters, etc.

salvo /'sælvəʊ/ *noun* (*plural* **-es** or **-s**) **1** simultaneous firing of guns etc. **2** round of applause.

sal volatile /sæl və'lætɪlɪ/ *noun* solution of ammonium carbonate, used as smelling salts.

SAM *abbreviation* surface-to-air missile.

Samaritan /sə'mærɪt(ə)n/ *noun* **1** (in full **good Samaritan**) charitable or helpful person. **2** member of counselling organization.

samba /'sæmbə/ *noun* **1** ballroom dance of Brazilian origin. **2** music for this. ● *verb* (**-bas**, **-baed** or **-ba'd** /-bəd/, **-baing** /-bəɪŋ/) dance samba.

same *adjective* **1** identical. **2** unvarying. **3** exactly like, equivalent. **4** just mentioned. ● *pronoun* (**the same**) the same person or thing. ● *adverb* (**the same**) in the same manner. □ **all or just the same** nevertheless. **at the same time 1** simultaneously. **2** notwithstanding. □ **sameness** *noun*.

■ *adjective* **1** actual, identical, selfsame. **2** consistent, constant, unaltered, unchanged, uniform, unvaried, unvarying. **3** analogous, comparable, corresponding, duplicate, equal, equivalent, indistinguishable, interchangeable, matching, parallel, similar, synonymous, twin.

samosa /sə'məʊsə/ *noun* Indian fried triangular pastry containing spiced vegetables or meat.

samovar /'sæməvɑː/ *noun* Russian tea-urn.

Samoyed /'sæməjed/ *noun* **1** member of a northern Siberian people. **2** (also **samoyed**) dog of white Arctic breed.

sampan /'sæmpæn/ *noun* small boat used in Far East.

samphire /'sæmfaɪə/ *noun* cliff plant used in pickles.

sample /'sɑːmp(ə)l/ *noun* **1** small representative part or quantity. **2** specimen. **3** typical example. ● *verb* (**-ling**) **1** take samples of. **2** try qualities of. **3** experience briefly.

■ *noun* bit, cross-section, demonstration, example, foretaste, illustration, indication, instance, model, pattern, selection, snippet, specimen, taste, trailer (*of film*), trial offer. ● *verb* experience, inspect, taste, test, try.

sampler /'sɑːmplə/ *noun* piece of embroidery worked to show proficiency.

samurai /'sæmʊraɪ/ *noun* (*plural* same) **1** Japanese army officer. **2** *historical* member of Japanese military caste.

sanatorium /sænə'tɔːrɪəm/ *noun* (*plural* **-riums** or **-ria**) **1** residential clinic, esp. for convalescents and the chronically sick. **2** accommodation for sick people in school etc.
■ **1** clinic, convalescent home, hospital, nursing home, rest home.

sanctify /'sæŋktɪfaɪ/ *verb* (**-ies, -ied**) **1** consecrate; treat as holy. **2** purify or free from sin. **3** sanction. □ **sanctification** *noun*.
■ **1** *RC Church* beatify, bless, canonize, consecrate, hallow. **2** cleanse, purge, purify.

sanctimonious /sæŋktɪ'məʊnɪəs/ *adjective* ostentatiously pious. □ **sanctimoniously** *adverb*. **sanctimoniousness** *noun*. **sanctimony** /'sæŋktɪmənɪ/ *noun*.
■ canting, *colloquial* holier-than-thou, hypocritical, insincere, moralizing, pietistic, pious, self-righteous, sententious, *colloquial* smarmy, smug, superior, unctuous.

sanction /'sæŋkʃ(ə)n/ *noun* **1** approval by custom or tradition. **2** express permission. **3** confirmation of law etc. **4** penalty or reward attached to law. **5** moral impetus for obedience to rule. **6** (esp. in *plural*) (esp. economic) action to coerce state to conform to agreement etc. ● *verb* **1** authorize, countenance. **2** make (law etc.) binding.
■ *noun* **1, 2** agreement, approval, authorization, blessing, consent, encouragement, endorsement, permission, support. **3** authorization, confirmation, endorsement, legalization, licence, ratification, validation. ● *verb* **1** agree to, allow, approve, authorize, confirm, consent to, endorse, give one's blessing to, give permission for, permit, support. **2** authorize, legalize, legitimize, license, ratify, validate.

sanctity /'sæŋktɪtɪ/ *noun* **1** holiness, sacredness. **2** inviolability.
■ **1** divinity, godliness, grace, holiness, piety, sacredness, saintliness.

sanctuary /'sæŋktʃʊərɪ/ *noun* (*plural* **-ies**) **1** holy place. **2** place where birds, wild animals, etc. are protected. **3** (place of) refuge.
■ **1** chapel, church, holy of holies, holy place, sanctum, shrine, temple. **2** conservation area, park, preserve, reservation, reserve. **3** asylum, haven, protection, refuge, retreat, safety, shelter.

sanctum /'sæŋktəm/ *noun* (*plural* **-s**) **1** holy place, esp. in temple or church. **2** *colloquial* person's den.

sand *noun* **1** fine grains resulting from erosion of esp. siliceous rocks. **2** (in *plural*) grains of sand. **3** (in *plural*) expanse of sand. **4** (in *plural*) sandbank. ● *verb* smooth or treat with sandpaper or sand. □ **sandbag** ● *noun* bag filled with sand, esp. for making temporary defences. ● *verb* defend or hit with sandbag(s). **sandbank** sand forming shallow place in sea or river. **sandblast** ● *verb* treat with jet of sand driven by com-

pressed air or steam. ● *noun* this jet. **sandcastle** model castle of sand on beach. **sand dune**, **sand-hill** dune. **sand martin** bird nesting in sandy banks. **sandpaper** ● *noun* paper with abrasive coating for smoothing or polishing wood etc. ● *verb* treat with this. **sandpiper** bird inhabiting wet sandy places. **sandpit** hollow or box containing sand for children to play in. **sandstone** sedimentary rock of compressed sand. **sandstorm** storm with clouds of sand raised by wind.
■ *noun* **3** (*sands*) beach, seaside, shore, *esp. poetical* strand.

sandal /'sænd(ə)l/ *noun* shoe with openwork upper or no upper, fastened with straps.

sandal-tree /'sændəltriː/ *noun* tree yielding sandalwood.

sandalwood /'sændəlwʊd/ *noun* scented wood of sandal-tree.

sandwich /'sænwɪdʒ/ *noun* **1** two or more slices of bread with filling. **2** layered cake with jam, cream, etc. ● *verb* **1** put (thing, statement, etc.) between two of different kind. **2** squeeze in between others. □ **sandwich-board** each of two advertising boards worn front and back. **sandwich course** course with alternate periods of study and work experience.

sandy *adjective* (**-ier, -iest**) **1** containing or covered with sand. **2** (of hair) reddish. **3** sand-coloured.

sane *adjective* **1** of sound mind; not mad. **2** (of opinion etc.) moderate, sensible. □ **saneness** *noun*.
■ **1** *colloquial* all there, balanced, compos mentis, in one's right mind, level-headed, lucid, normal, of sound mind, rational, sensible, stable, well balanced. **2** see SOUND[2] *adjective* 2.

sang *past* of SING.

sang-froid /sɑ̃'frwɑː/ *noun* calmness in danger or difficulty.

sangria /sæŋ'griːə/ *noun* Spanish drink of red wine with fruit etc.

sanguinary /'sæŋgwɪnərɪ/ *adjective* bloody; bloodthirsty.

sanguine /'sæŋgwɪn/ *adjective* **1** optimistic. **2** (of complexion) florid, ruddy.
■ **1** buoyant, cheerful, confident, expectant, hopeful, optimistic, positive.

Sanhedrin /'sænɪdrɪn/ *noun* court of justice and supreme council in ancient Jerusalem.

sanitarium /sænɪ'teərɪəm/ *noun* (*plural* **-s** or **-ria**) *US* sanatorium.

sanitary /'sænɪtərɪ/ *adjective* **1** (of conditions etc.) affecting health. **2** hygienic. □ **sanitary towel** (*US* **sanitary napkin**) absorbent pad used during menstruation. □ **sanitariness** *noun*.
■ **2** aseptic, bacteria-free, clean, disinfected, germ-free, healthy, hygienic, pure, salubrious, sterile, sterilized, uncontaminated, unpolluted, wholesome.

sanitation /sænɪ'teɪʃ(ə)n/ *noun* **1** sanitary conditions. **2** maintenance etc. of these. **3** disposal of sewage, refuse, etc.

sanitize /'sænɪtaɪz/ *verb* (also **-ise**) (**-zing** or **-sing**) **1** make sanitary; disinfect. **2** *colloquial* censor.

sanity /'sænɪtɪ/ *noun* **1** being sane. **2** moderation.

sank *past* of SINK.

Sanskrit /'sænskrɪt/ *noun* ancient and sacred language of Hindus in India. ● *adjective* of or in Sanskrit.

Santa Claus /'sæntə klɔːz/ *noun* person said to bring children presents at Christmas.

sap[1] *noun* **1** vital juice of plants. **2** vitality. **3** *slang* foolish person. ● *verb* (**-pp-**) **1** drain of sap. **2** weaken. □ **sappy** *adjective* (**-ier, -iest**).
■ *noun* **1** fluid, moisture, vital juices. **2** lifeblood, vigour, vitality. ● *verb* **2** see EXHAUST *verb* 1.

sap[2] *noun* tunnel or trench for concealed approach to enemy. ● *verb* (**-pp-**) **1** dig saps. **2** undermine.

sapient /'seɪpɪənt/ *adjective literary* **1** wise. **2** aping wisdom. □ **sapience** *noun*.

sapling /'sæplɪŋ/ *noun* young tree.

sapper *noun* **1** digger of saps. **2** private of Royal Engineers.

sapphire /'sæfaɪə/ *noun* **1** transparent blue precious stone. **2** its colour. ● *adjective* (also **sapphire blue**) bright blue.

saprophyte /'sæprəfaɪt/ *noun* plant or micro-organism living on dead organic matter.

saraband /'særəbænd/ *noun* **1** slow Spanish dance. **2** music for this.

Saracen /'særəs(ə)n/ *noun* Arab or Muslim of time of Crusades.

sarcasm /'sɑːkæz(ə)m/ *noun* ironically scornful remark(s). □ **sarcastic** /sɑːˈkæstɪk/ *adjective*. **sarcastically** /sɑːˈkæstɪkəlɪ/ *adverb*.
■ acerbity, asperity, contumely, derision, irony, malice, mockery, ridicule, satire, scorn.
□ **sarcastic** acerbic, acidulous, biting, caustic, contemptuous, cutting, demeaning, derisive, disparaging, hurtful, ironic, ironical, mocking, satirical, scathing, sharp, sneering, spiteful, taunting, trenchant, venomous, vitriolic, withering, wounding.

sarcophagus /sɑːˈkɒfəgəs/ *noun* (*plural* **-gi** /-gaɪ/) stone coffin.

sardine /sɑːˈdiːn/ *noun* (*plural* same or **-s**) young pilchard etc. tinned tightly packed.

sardonic /sɑːˈdɒnɪk/ *adjective* bitterly mocking; cynical. □ **sardonically** *adverb*.
■ bitter, black, cruel, cynical, grim, heartless, malicious, mocking, mordant, scornful, wry.

sardonyx /'sɑːdənɪks/ *noun* onyx in which white layers alternate with yellow or orange ones.

sargasso /sɑːˈgæsəʊ/ *noun* (*plural* **-s** or **-es**) seaweed with berry-like air-vessels.

sarge *noun slang* sergeant.

sari /'sɑːrɪ/ *noun* (*plural* **-s**) length of material draped round body, worn traditionally by Hindu etc. women.

sarky /'sɑːkɪ/ *adjective* (**-ier, -iest**) *slang* sarcastic.

sarong /səˈrɒŋ/ *noun* garment of long strip of cloth tucked round waist or under armpits.

sarsaparilla /sɑːsəpəˈrɪlə/ *noun* **1** dried roots of esp. smilax used to flavour drinks and medicines and formerly as tonic. **2** plant yielding these.

sarsen /'sɑːs(ə)n/ *noun* sandstone boulder carried by ice in glacial period.

sarsenet /'sɑːsnɪt/ *noun* soft silk fabric used esp. for linings.

sartorial /sɑːˈtɔːrɪəl/ *adjective* of clothes or tailoring. □ **sartorially** *adverb*.

SAS *abbreviation* Special Air Service.

sash[1] *noun* strip or loop of cloth worn over one shoulder or round waist.
■ band, belt, cummerbund, girdle, waistband.

sash[2] *noun* frame holding glass in window sliding up and down in grooves.

sass *US colloquial noun* impudence. ● *verb* be impudent to. □ **sassy** *adjective* (**-ier, -iest**).

sassafras /'sæsəfræs/ *noun* **1** small N. American tree. **2** medicinal preparation from its leaves or bark.

Sassenach /'sæsənæk/ *noun Scottish usually derogatory* English person.

Sat. *abbreviation* Saturday.

sat *past & past participle* of SIT.

Satan /'seɪt(ə)n/ *noun* the Devil.

satanic /səˈtænɪk/ *adjective* **1** of or like Satan. **2** hellish, evil.
■ demonic, devilish, diabolical, evil, fiendish, hellish, infernal, wicked.

Satanism *noun* worship of Satan. □ **Satanist** *noun*.

satchel /'sætʃ(ə)l/ *noun* small bag, esp. for carrying school books.
■ bag, school bag, shoulder bag.

sate *verb* (**-ting**) *formal* **1** gratify fully. **2** surfeit.

sateen /sæˈtiːn/ *noun* glossy cotton fabric like satin.

satellite /'sætəlaɪt/ *noun* **1** heavenly or artificial body orbiting earth or other planet. **2** (in full **satellite state**) small country controlled by another. ● *adjective* **1** transmitted by satellite. **2** receiving signal from satellite.
■ *noun* **1** moon, planet; [*artificial*] spacecraft, sputnik.

satiate /'seɪʃɪeɪt/ *verb* (**-ting**) sate. □ **satiation** *noun*.

satiety /səˈtaɪɪtɪ/ *noun formal* being sated.

satin /'sætɪn/ *noun* silk etc. fabric glossy on one side. ● *adjective* smooth as satin. □ **satinwood** kind of yellow glossy timber. □ **satiny** *adjective*.

satire /'sætaɪə/ *noun* **1** ridicule, irony, etc. used to expose folly, vice, etc. **2** literary work using satire. □ **satirical** /sə'tɪrɪk(ə)l/ *adjective*. **satirically** /sə'tɪrɪkəlɪ/ *adverb*.

■ **1** caricature, derision, invective, irony, mockery, parody, ridicule, scorn. **2** burlesque, caricature, lampoon, parody, *colloquial* send-up, *colloquial* spoof, *colloquial* take-off, travesty. □ **satirical** critical, derisive, disparaging, disrespectful, ironic, irreverent, mocking, sarcastic, scornful.

satirist /'sætərɪst/ *noun* **1** writer of satires. **2** satirical person.

satirize /'sætəraɪz/ *verb* (also **-ise**) (**-zing** or **-sing**) attack or describe with satire.

■ burlesque, caricature, criticize, deride, hold up to ridicule, lampoon, laugh at, make fun of, mimic, mock, parody, pillory, ridicule, *colloquial* send up, *colloquial* take off, travesty.

satisfaction /sætɪs'fækʃ(ə)n/ *noun* **1** satisfying, being satisfied. **2** thing that satisfies. **3** atonement; compensation.

■ **1** comfort, content, contentment, delight, enjoyment, fulfilment, gratification, happiness, joy, pleasure, pride, self-satisfaction. **2** comfort, delight, joy, pleasure.

satisfactory /sætɪs'fæktərɪ/ *adjective* adequate; causing satisfaction. □ **satisfactorily** *adverb*.

■ acceptable, adequate, all right, competent, fair, good enough, not bad, passable, pleasing, satisfying, sufficient, suitable, tolerable, up to scratch.

satisfy /'sætɪsfaɪ/ *verb* (**-ies**, **-ied**) **1** meet expectations or wishes of. **2** be adequate for. **3** meet (an appetite or want). **4** rid (person) of an appetite or want. **5** pay. **6** fulfil, comply with. **7** convince. □ **satisfied** *adjective*. **satisfying** *adjective*.

■ **1, 4** appease, assuage, comfort, content, fulfil, gratify, make happy, pacify, placate, please. **3** appease, assuage, fill, fulfil, gratify, meet, quench, *formal* sate, satiate, serve (*a need*), slake (*thirst*), supply. **5** discharge, pay, settle. **6** comply with, fulfil, meet. □ **satisfied** see CONTENTED.

satsuma /sæt'suːmə/ *noun* kind of tangerine.

saturate /'sætʃəreɪt/ *verb* (**-ting**) **1** fill with moisture. **2** fill to capacity. **3** cause (substance) to absorb, hold, etc. as much as possible of another substance. **4** supply (market) beyond demand. **5** (as **saturated** *adjective*) (of fat) containing the most possible hydrogen atoms.

■ **1** drench, fill, impregnate, permeate, soak, souse, steep, suffuse, wet.

saturation *noun* saturating, being saturated. □ **saturation point** stage beyond which no more can be absorbed or accepted.

Saturday /'sætədeɪ/ *noun* day of week following Friday.

Saturnalia /sætə'neɪlɪə/ *noun* (*plural* same or **-s**) **1** ancient Roman festival of Saturn. **2** (**saturnalia**) (treated as *singular* or *plural*) scene of wild revelry.

saturnine /'sætənaɪn/ *adjective* of gloomy temperament or appearance.

satyr /'sætə/ *noun* **1** *Greek & Roman Mythology* part-human part-animal woodland deity. **2** lecherous man.

sauce /sɔːs/ *noun* **1** liquid or viscous accompaniment to food. **2** something that adds piquancy. **3** *colloquial* impudence. ● *verb* (**-cing**) *colloquial* be impudent to. □ **sauce-boat** jug or dish for serving sauce. **saucepan** cooking vessel usually with handle, used on hob.

■ *noun* **1** condiment, gravy, ketchup, relish. **3** see INSOLENCE (INSOLENT). □ **saucepan** cauldron, pan, pot, skillet, stockpot.

saucer /'sɔːsə/ *noun* shallow circular dish, esp. for standing cup on.

saucy *adjective* (**-ier**, **-iest**) impudent, cheeky. □ **saucily** *adverb*. **sauciness** *noun*.

sauerkraut /'saʊəkraʊt/ *noun* German dish of pickled cabbage.

sauna /'sɔːnə/ *noun* **1** period spent in room with steam bath. **2** this room.

saunter /'sɔːntə/ *verb* stroll. ● *noun* leisurely walk.

saurian /'sɔːrɪən/ *adjective* of or like a lizard.

sausage /'sɒsɪdʒ/ *noun* **1** seasoned minced meat etc. in edible cylindrical case. **2** sausage-shaped object. □ **sausage meat** minced meat for sausages etc. **sausage roll** sausage meat in pastry cylinder.

sauté /'səʊteɪ/ *adjective* fried quickly in a little fat. ● *noun* food cooked thus. ● *verb* (*past & past participle* **sautéd** or **sautéed**) cook thus.

savage /'sævɪdʒ/ *adjective* **1** fierce, cruel. **2** wild, primitive. ● *noun* **1** *derogatory* member of primitive tribe. **2** brutal or barbarous person. ● *verb* (**-ging**) **1** attack and maul. **2** attack verbally. □ **savagely** *adverb*. **savagery** *noun* (*plural* **-ies**).

■ *adjective* **1** barbaric, barbarous, beastly, bestial, blistering, bloodthirsty, bloody, brutal, callous, cold-blooded, cruel, demonic, diabolical, ferocious, fierce, heartless, inhuman, merciless, murderous, pitiless, ruthless, *colloquial* sadistic, unfeeling, vicious, violent. **2** barbarian, barbaric, feral, primitive, uncivilized, uncultivated, undomesticated, uneducated, untamed, wild. ● *noun* **1** barbarian. **2** barbarian, beast, brute, fiend. ● *verb* **1** attack, bite, claw, lacerate, maul, mutilate.

savannah /sə'vænə/ *noun* (also **savanna**) grassy plain in tropical or subtropical region.

savant /'sæv(ə)nt/ *noun* (*feminine* **savante** same pronunciation) learned person.

save[1] *verb* (**-ving**) **1** (often + *from*) rescue or preserve from danger or harm. **2** (often + *up*) keep for future use. **3** (often + *up*) put aside money for future use. **4** relieve (person) from spending (money, time, etc.); prevent exposure to (annoyance etc.). **5** prevent need for. **6** rescue spiritually. **7** *Football etc.* avoid losing (match). **8** *Football etc.* prevent (goal) from being scored.

● *noun Football etc.* act of saving goal. □ **savable**, **saveable** *adjective*. **saver** *noun*.

■ *verb* **1** bail out, defend, deliver, free, guard, keep safe, liberate, preserve, protect, ransom, recover, redeem, release, rescue, retrieve, safeguard, salvage, set free, shelter, shield. **2, 3** be frugal, be sparing with, be thrifty, collect, conserve, economize, hoard, hold back, hold on to, invest, keep, lay aside, put by, put in a safe place, reserve, retain, scrape together, set aside, *colloquial* stash away, store up. **4** obviate, preclude, prevent, spare, stop.

save² *preposition & conjunction archaic or poetical* except; but.

saveloy /'sævəlɔɪ/ *noun* highly seasoned sausage.

saving *noun* **1** anything saved. **2** an economy. **3** (usually in *plural*) money saved. **4** act of preserving or rescuing. ● *preposition* **1** except. **2** without offence to. □ **-saving** making economical use of specified thing. **saving grace** redeeming feature.

■ *noun* **2** cut, discount, economy, reduction. **3** (*savings*) capital, funds, investments, nest egg, reserves, resources, riches, wealth.

saviour /'seɪvjə/ *noun* (*US* **savior**) **1** person who saves from danger etc. **2** (**the, our Saviour**) Christ.

■ **1** champion, defender, deliverer, guardian, liberator, rescuer.

savoir faire /sævwɑː 'feə/ *noun* ability to behave appropriately; tact. [French]

savory¹ /'seɪvərɪ/ *noun* aromatic herb used in cookery.

savory² *US* = SAVOURY.

savour /'seɪvə/ (*US* **savor**) *noun* **1** characteristic taste, flavour, etc. **2** tinge or hint. ● *verb* **1** appreciate, enjoy. **2** (+ *of*) imply, suggest.

■ *noun* **1** flavour, piquancy, relish, smell, tang, taste, zest. ● *verb* **1** appreciate, delight in, enjoy, relish, smell, taste.

savoury /'seɪvərɪ/ (*US* **savory**) *adjective* **1** with appetizing taste or smell. **2** (of food) salty or piquant; not sweet. **3** pleasant. ● *noun* (*plural* **-ies**) savoury dish.

■ *adjective* **1** appetizing, delicious, flavoursome, piquant, tasty.

savoy /sə'vɔɪ/ *noun* rough-leaved winter cabbage.

savvy /'sævɪ/ *slang verb* (**-ies, -ied**) know. ● *noun* knowingness, understanding. ● *adjective* (**-ier, -iest**) *US* knowing, wise.

saw¹ *noun* implement with toothed blade etc. for cutting wood etc. ● *verb* (*past participle* **sawn** or **sawed**) **1** cut or make with saw. **2** use saw. **3** make to-and-fro sawing motion. □ **sawdust** fine wood fragments produced in sawing. **sawfish** (*plural* same or **-es**) large sea fish with toothed flat snout. **sawmill** factory for sawing wood into planks. **sawtooth(ed)** serrated.

■ *verb* **1, 2** see CUT *verb* 1.

saw² *past* of SEE¹.

saw³ *noun* proverb, maxim.

■ see SAYING.

sawyer /'sɔːjə/ *noun* person who saws timber.

sax *noun colloquial* saxophone.

saxe /sæks/ *noun & adjective* (in full **saxe blue**; as *adjective* often hyphenated) light greyish-blue.

saxifrage /'sæksɪfreɪdʒ/ *noun* small-flowered rock-plant.

Saxon /'sæks(ə)n/ *noun* **1** *historical* member or language of Germanic people that occupied parts of England in 5th–6th c. **2** Anglo-Saxon. ● *adjective* **1** *historical* of the Saxons. **2** Anglo-Saxon.

saxophone /'sæksəfəʊn/ *noun* keyed brass reed instrument used esp. in jazz. □ **saxophonist** /sæk'spfən-/ *noun*.

say *verb* (*3rd singular present* **says** /sez/; *past & past participle* **said** /sed/) **1** utter, remark; express. **2** state; indicate. **3** (in *passive*; usually + *to do*) be asserted. **4** (+ *to do*) *colloquial* direct, order to. **5** convey (information). **6** adduce, plead. **7** decide. **8** take as example or as near enough. **9** (**the said**) *Law* or *jocular* the previously mentioned. ● *noun* **1** opportunity to express view. **2** share in decision. □ **say-so** *colloquial* **1** power of decision. **2** mere assertion.

■ *verb* **1, 2** affirm, allege, announce, answer, articulate, assert, asseverate, *formal* aver, bruit abroad, come out with, comment, communicate, convey, declare, disclose, divulge, ejaculate, enunciate, exclaim, express, indicate, intimate, maintain, mention, mouth, phrase, pronounce, read out, recite, rejoin, remark, repeat, reply, report, respond, retort, reveal, signify, state, suggest, tell, utter. **5** communicate, convey, disclose, divulge, impart, indicate, reveal.

saying *noun* maxim, proverb, etc.

■ adage, aphorism, apophthegm, axiom, catchphrase, catchword, cliché, dictum, epigram, expression, formula, maxim, motto, phrase, precept, proverb, quotation, remark, saw, slogan, statement, tag, truism, watchword.

sc. *abbreviation* scilicet.

scab *noun* **1** crust over healing cut, sore, etc. **2** skin disease. **3** plant disease. **4** *colloquial derogatory* blackleg. ● *verb* (**-bb-**) **1** form scab. **2** *colloquial derogatory* act as blackleg. □ **scabby** *adjective* (**-ier, -iest**)

■ *noun* **4** *derogatory* blackleg, strikebreaker.

scabbard /'skæbəd/ *noun historical* sheath of sword etc.

scabies /'skeɪbiːz/ *noun* contagious skin disease causing itching.

scabious /'skeɪbɪəs/ *noun* plant with pin-cushion-shaped flowers.

scabrous /'skeɪbrəs/ *adjective* **1** rough, scaly. **2** indecent.

scaffold /'skæfəʊld/ *noun* **1** scaffolding. **2** *historical* platform for execution of criminal.

scaffolding *noun* **1** temporary structure of poles, planks, etc. for building work. **2** materials for this.

scald /skɔːld/ *verb* **1** burn (skin etc.) with hot liquid or vapour. **2** heat (esp. milk) to near boiling point. **3** (usually + *out*) clean with boiling water. ● *noun* burn etc. caused by scalding.

scale¹ *noun* **1** each of thin horny plates protecting skin of fish and reptiles. **2** thing resembling this. **3** incrustation inside kettle etc. **4** tartar on teeth. ● *verb* (**-ling**) **1** remove scale(s) from. **2** form or come off in scales. □ **scaly** *adjective* (**-ier, -iest**).

■ *noun* **1** flake, lamina, plate. **3** caking, coating, crust, deposit, encrustation, fur, incrustation. **4** plaque, tartar.

scale² *noun* **1** (often in *plural*) weighing machine. **2** (also **scale-pan**) pan of weighing-balance. □ **tip, turn the scales 1** be decisive factor. **2** (+ *at*) weigh (specified amount).

■ **1** (*scales*) balance, weighing machine.

scale³ *noun* **1** graded classification system. **2** ratio of reduction or enlargement in map, picture, etc. **3** relative dimensions. **4** *Music* set of notes at fixed intervals, arranged in order of pitch. **5** set of marks on line used in measuring etc. **6** rule determining distances between these. **7** rod on which these are marked. ● *verb* (**-ling**) **1** climb. **2** represent in proportion. **3** reduce to common scale. □ **scale down, up** make or become smaller or larger in proportion. **to scale** uniformly in proportion.

■ *noun* **1** classification, gradation, graduation, hierarchy, ladder, order, progression, ranking, sequence, series. **2** proportion, ratio. **3** see SIZE¹ *noun* **1**. **5** calibration. ● *verb* **1** ascend, clamber up, climb, go up, mount.

scalene /ˈskeɪliːn/ *adjective* (of triangle) having unequal sides.

scallion /ˈskæljən/ *noun esp. US* shallot, spring onion.

scallop /ˈskæləp/ *noun* **1** edible bivalve with fan-shaped ridged shells. **2** (in full **scallop shell**) one shell of this, esp. used for cooking or serving food on. **3** (in *plural*) ornamental edging of semicircular curves. ● *verb* (**-p-**) ornament with scallops.

scallywag /ˈskælɪwæg/ *noun* scamp, rascal.

scalp *noun* **1** skin and hair on head. **2** *historical* this cut off as trophy by N. American Indian. ● *verb historical* take scalp of.

scalpel /ˈskælp(ə)l/ *noun* small surgical knife.

scam *noun US slang* trick, fraud.

scamp *noun colloquial* rascal, rogue.

scamper /ˈskæmpə/ *verb* run and skip. ● *noun* act of scampering.

■ *verb* dash, frisk, frolic, gambol, hasten, hurry, play, romp, run, rush, scuttle.

scampi /ˈskæmpɪ/ *plural noun* large prawns.

scan *verb* (**-nn-**) **1** look at intently. **2** glance at quickly. **3** (of verse etc.) be metrically correct. **4** examine (surface etc.) for radioactivity etc. **5** traverse (region) with radar etc. beam. **6** resolve (picture) into elements of light and shade for esp. television transmission. **7** analyse metre of (line etc.). **8** obtain image of (part of body) using scanner. ● *noun* **1** scanning. **2** image obtained by scanning.

■ *verb* **1** check, examine, explore, eye, gaze at, investigate, look at, pore over, scrutinize, search, stare at, study, survey, view, watch. **2** flip through, glance at, read quickly, skim, thumb through.

scandal /ˈskænd(ə)l/ *noun* **1** disgraceful event; public outrage. **2** malicious gossip. □ **scandalmonger** /-mʌŋɡə/ person who spreads scandal.

■ **1** discredit, disgrace, dishonour, disrepute, embarrassment, ignominy, infamy, notoriety, obloquy, outrage, sensation, shame. **2** calumny, defamation, gossip, innuendo, libel, rumour, slander, slur, smear, tittle-tattle.

scandalize *verb* (also **-ise**) (**-zing** or **-sing**) offend morally; shock.

■ affront, appal, disgust, horrify, offend, outrage, shock, upset.

scandalous *adjective* **1** causing disgrace or outrage. **2** containing scandal. □ **scandalously** *adverb*.

■ **1** disgraceful, disgusting, dishonourable, disreputable, ignominious, immodest, immoral, improper, indecent, indecorous, infamous, licentious, notorious, outrageous, shameful, shocking, sinful, sordid, unmentionable, unspeakable, wicked. **2** calumnious, defamatory, libellous, scurrilous, slanderous, untrue.

Scandinavian /skændɪˈneɪvɪən/ *noun* native or inhabitant, or family of languages, of Scandinavia. ● *adjective* of Scandinavia.

scanner *noun* **1** device for scanning. **2** diagnostic apparatus measuring radiation, ultrasound reflections, etc. from body.

scansion /ˈskænʃ(ə)n/ *noun* metrical scanning of verse.

■ metre, prosody, rhythm.

scant *adjective* barely sufficient; deficient.

scanty *adjective* (**-ier, -iest**) **1** of small extent or amount. **2** barely sufficient. □ **scantily** *adverb*. **scantiness** *noun*.

■ inadequate, insufficient, meagre, mean, *colloquial* measly, *colloquial* mingy, minimal, scant, scarce, skimpy, small, sparing, sparse, stingy.

scapegoat /ˈskeɪpɡəʊt/ *noun* person blamed for others' faults.

■ dupe, *slang* fall guy, victim.

scapula /ˈskæpjʊlə/ *noun* (*plural* **-lae** /-liː/ or **-s**) shoulder blade.

scapular /ˈskæpjʊlə/ *adjective* of scapula. ● *noun* monastic short cloak.

scar¹ *noun* **1** mark left on skin etc. by wound etc. **2** emotional damage. ● *verb* (**-rr-**) (esp. as **scarred**

adjective) mark with or form scar(s).
■ *noun* **1** blemish, cicatrice, cut, disfigurement, mark. ● *verb* blemish, damage, deface, disfigure, injure, mark, scratch, spoil.

scar[2] *noun* (also **scaur**) steep craggy part of mountainside.

scarab /'skærəb/ *noun* **1** kind of beetle. **2** gem cut in form of beetle.

scarce /skeəs/ *adjective* in short supply; rare. ● *adverb archaic* or *literary* scarcely. □ **make oneself scarce** *colloquial* keep out of the way; disappear.
■ *adjective* few and far between, hard to come by, hard to find, inadequate, infrequent, in short supply, insufficient, lacking, meagre, rare, scant, scanty, sparse, thin on the ground, tight, uncommon, unusual.

scarcely /'skeəslɪ/ *adverb* hardly; only just.
■ barely, hardly, only just.

scarcity *noun* (*plural* **-ies**) lack or shortage.
■ dearth, famine, inadequacy, insufficiency, lack, need, paucity, poverty, rarity, shortage, want.

scare /skeə/ *verb* (**-ring**) **1** frighten. **2** (as **scared** *adjective*) (usually + *of*) frightened. **3** (usually + *away, off*, etc.) drive away by frightening. ● *noun* sudden fright or alarm, esp. caused by rumours. □ **scarecrow 1** human figure used for frightening birds away from crops. **2** *colloquial* badly dressed or grotesque person. **scaremonger** /-mʌŋgə/ person who spreads scare(s).
■ *verb* **1** alarm, dismay, frighten, intimidate, make afraid, make (person) jump, menace, panic, shake, shock, startle, terrorize, threaten, unnerve. ● *noun* fright, jolt, shock, start.

scarf[1] *noun* (*plural* **scarves** /skɑːvz/ or **-s**) piece of material worn round neck or over head for warmth or ornament.
■ muffler, shawl, stole.

scarf[2] *verb* join ends of (timber etc.) by thinning or notching them and bolting them together. ● *noun* (*plural* **-s**) joint made thus.

scarify /'skærɪfaɪ/ *verb* (**-ies, -ied**) **1** make slight incisions in. **2** scratch. **3** criticize etc. mercilessly. **4** loosen (soil). □ **scarification** *noun*.

scarlatina /skɑːlə'tiːnə/ *noun* scarlet fever.

scarlet /'skɑːlət/ *adjective* of brilliant red tinged with orange. ● *noun* scarlet colour, pigment, clothes, etc. □ **scarlet fever** infectious fever with scarlet rash. **scarlet pimpernel** wild plant with small esp. scarlet flowers.

scarp *noun* steep slope, esp. inner side of ditch in fortification. ● *verb* make perpendicular or steep.

scarper /'skɑːpə/ *verb slang* run away; escape.

scarves *plural* of SCARF[1].

scary *adjective* (**-ier, -iest**) *colloquial* frightening.
■ *colloquial* creepy, eerie, frightening, hair-raising, *colloquial* horrible, *colloquial* spooky, unnerving.

scat *noun* wordless jazz singing. ● *verb* (**-tt-**) sing scat.

scathing /'skeɪðɪŋ/ *adjective* witheringly scornful. □ **scathingly** *adverb*.
■ biting, caustic, critical, humiliating, mordant, satirical, savage, scornful, tart, withering.

scatology /skæ'tɒlədʒɪ/ *noun* preoccupation with excrement or obscenity. □ **scatological** /-tə'lɒdʒ-/ *adjective*.

scatter /'skætə/ *verb* **1** throw about, strew. **2** cover by scattering. **3** (cause to) flee. **4** (cause to) disperse. **5** (as **scattered** *adjective*) wide apart; sporadic. **6** *Physics* deflect or diffuse (light, particles, etc.). ● *noun* **1** act of scattering. **2** small amount scattered. **3** extent of distribution. □ **scatterbrain** person lacking concentration. **scatterbrained** *adjective*.
■ *verb* **1** broadcast, disseminate, intersperse, shed, shower, sow, spread, sprinkle, strew, throw about. **3, 4** break up, disband, disintegrate, dispel, disperse, divide, separate. □ **scatterbrained** absent-minded, careless, crazy, disorganized, forgetful, frivolous, hare-brained, inattentive, muddled, *colloquial* not with it, *colloquial* scatty, silly, thoughtless, unreliable, unsystematic, vague.

scatty /'skætɪ/ *adjective* (**-ier, -iest**) *colloquial* lacking concentration. □ **scattily** *adverb*. **scattiness** *noun*.

scavenge /'skævɪndʒ/ *verb* (**-ging**) (usually + *for*) search for and collect (discarded items).
■ forage, rummage, scrounge, search.

scavenger /'skævɪndʒə/ *noun* **1** person who scavenges. **2** animal etc. feeding on carrion.

SCE *abbreviation* Scottish Certificate of Education.

scenario /sɪ'nɑːrɪəʊ/ *noun* (*plural* **-s**) **1** synopsis of film, play, etc. **2** imagined sequence of future events.

USAGE *Scenario* should not be used in standard English to mean 'situation', as in *It was an unpleasant scenario.*
■ **1** framework, outline, plan, scheme, storyline, structure, summary.

scene /siːn/ *noun* **1** place of actual or fictitious occurrence. **2** incident. **3** public display of emotion, temper, etc. **4** piece of continuous action in a play, film, book, etc. **5** piece(s) of scenery for a play. **6** landscape, view. **7** *colloquial* area of interest or activity. □ **behind the scenes 1** out of view of audience. **2** secret, secretly. **scene-shifter** person who moves scenery in theatre.
■ **1** area, locale, locality, location, place, position, setting, site, situation, spot, whereabouts. **3** altercation, argument, *colloquial* carry-on, commotion, disturbance, furore, fuss, incident, quarrel, row, tantrum, to-do, upset. **4** act, chapter, episode, part, passage, section, sequence. **6** landscape, panorama, picture, scenery, sight, spectacle, view, vista.

scenery /'si:nərɪ/ *noun* **1** features (esp. picturesque) of landscape. **2** backcloths, properties, etc. representing scene in a play etc.
■ **1** landscape, panorama, prospect, scene, view, vista. **2** backdrop, flats, set, setting.

scenic /'si:nɪk/ *adjective* **1** picturesque. **2** of scenery. □ **scenically** *adverb*.
■ attractive, beautiful, breathtaking, grand, impressive, lovely, panoramic, picturesque, pretty, spectacular.

scent /sent/ *noun* **1** characteristic, esp. pleasant, smell. **2** liquid perfume. **3** smell left by animal. **4** clues etc. leading to discovery. **5** power of scenting. ● *verb* **1** discern by smell. **2** sense. **3** (esp. as **scented** *adjective*) make fragrant.
■ *noun* **1** aroma, bouquet, fragrance, nose, odour, perfume, redolence, smell. **2** aftershave, perfume. **3** spoor, track, trail. ● *verb* **1** see SMELL *verb* **1**. **3** (**scented**) aromatic, fragrant, musky, odoriferous, odorous, perfumed, redolent, sweet-smelling.

scepter *US* = SCEPTRE.

sceptic /'skeptɪk/ *noun* (*US* **skeptic**) sceptical person, esp. one who questions truth of religions, or the possibility of knowledge. □ **scepticism** /-sɪz(ə)m/ *noun*.
■ agnostic, cynic, disbeliever, doubter, scoffer, unbeliever. □ **scepticism** agnosticism, cynicism, disbelief, distrust, doubt, *literary* dubiety, incredulity, mistrust, suspicion.

sceptical /'skeptɪk(ə)l/ *adjective* (*US* **skeptical**) inclined to doubt accepted opinions; critical; incredulous. □ **sceptically** *adverb*.
■ agnostic, cynical, disbelieving, distrustful, doubting, dubious, incredulous, mistrustful, questioning, scoffing, suspicious, uncertain, unconvinced, unsure.

sceptre /'septə/ *noun* (*US* **scepter**) staff borne as symbol of sovereignty.

schedule /'ʃedju:l/ *noun* **1** timetable. **2** list, esp. of rates or prices. ● *verb* (**-ling**) **1** include in schedule. **2** make schedule of. **3** list (building) for preservation. □ **on schedule** at time appointed. **scheduled flight, service, etc.** regular public one.
■ *noun* **1** agenda, calendar, diary, itinerary, list, plan, programme, scheme, timetable. **2** inventory, list, register. ● *verb* **1, 2** appoint, arrange, assign, book, earmark, organize, plan, programme, time, timetable.

schema /'ski:mə/ *noun* (*plural* **schemata** or **-s**) synopsis, outline, diagram.

schematic /skɪ'mætɪk/ *adjective* of or as scheme or diagram. ● *noun* diagram, esp. of electronic circuit.

schematize /'ski:mətaɪz/ *verb* (also **-ise**) (**-zing** or **-sing**) put in schematic form.

scheme /ski:m/ *noun* **1** systematic arrangement. **2** artful plot. **3** plan of action or work; outline, syllabus, etc. ● *verb* (**-ming**) plan, esp. secretly or deceitfully. □ **schemer** *noun*. **scheming** *adjective*.

■ *noun* **1** arrangement, design, system. **2** conspiracy, dodge, intrigue, machinations, manoeuvre, plot, ploy, *slang* racket, ruse, stratagem, subterfuge, tactic. **3** approach, blueprint, design, draft, idea, method, outline, plan, procedure, programme, project, proposal, scenario, strategy, system. ● *verb* collude, connive, conspire, *colloquial* cook something up, hatch a plot, intrigue, machinate, manoeuvre, plan, plot.

scherzo /'skeətsəʊ/ *noun* (*plural* **-s**) *Music* vigorous and lively movement or composition.

schism /'skɪz(ə)m/ *noun* division of esp. religious group into sects etc. □ **schismatic** /-'mæt-/ *adjective & noun*.

schist /ʃɪst/ *noun* layered crystalline rock.

schizo /'skɪtsəʊ/ *offensive colloquial adjective* schizophrenic. ● *noun* (*plural* **-s**) schizophrenic person.

schizoid /'skɪtsɔɪd/ *adjective* tending to schizophrenia. ● *noun* schizoid person.

schizophrenia /skɪtsə'fri:nɪə/ *noun* mental disorder marked by disconnection between thoughts, feelings, and actions. □ **schizophrenic** /-'fren-/ *adjective & noun*.

schmaltz /ʃmɔ:lts/ *noun colloquial* sickly sentimentality. □ **schmaltzy** *adjective* (**-ier, -iest**).

schnapps /ʃnæps/ *noun* any of various spirits drunk in N. Europe.

schnitzel /'ʃnɪts(ə)l/ *noun* veal escalope.

scholar /'skɒlə/ *noun* **1** learned person. **2** holder of scholarship. **3** person of specified academic ability. □ **scholarly** *adjective*.
■ **1** academic, *colloquial* egghead, expert, *colloquial* highbrow, intellectual, professor, pundit, savant. **3** see PUPIL[1]. □ **scholarly** academic, bookish, brainy, deep, erudite, *colloquial* highbrow, intellectual, knowledgeable, learned, lettered, widely-read.

scholarship *noun* **1** learning, erudition. **2** award of money etc. towards education.
■ **1** education, erudition, knowledge, learning, research, schooling, wisdom. **2** award, bursary, endowment, exhibition, fellowship, grant.

scholastic /skə'læstɪk/ *adjective* of schools, education, etc.; academic.

school[1] /sku:l/ *noun* **1** educational institution for pupils up to 19 years old or (*US*) at any level. **2** school buildings, pupils, staff, etc. **3** (time given to) teaching. **4** university department or faculty. **5** group of artists, disciples, etc. following or holding similar principles, opinions, etc. **6** instructive circumstances. ● *verb* **1** send to school. **2** discipline, train, control. **3** (as **schooled** *adjective*) (+ *in*) educated, trained in. □ **schoolboy, schoolchild, schoolgirl** one who attends school. **school leaver** person who has just left school. **schoolmaster, schoolmistress, schoolteacher** teacher in school. **schoolmasterly** having qualities of schoolmaster. **schoolroom** room used for lessons, esp. in private house.

■ *noun* **1** academy, college, educational institution, institute, seminary. ● *verb* **1, 2** see EDUCATE.

school[2] /skuːl/ *noun* shoal of fish, whales, etc.

schooling *noun* education.

schooner /'skuːnə/ *noun* **1** two-masted fore-and-aft rigged ship. **2** large glass, esp. for sherry. **3** *US & Australian* tall beer glass.

schottische /ʃɒ'tiːʃ/ *noun* kind of slow polka.

sciatic /saɪ'ætɪk/ *adjective* **1** of hip or sciatic nerve. **2** of or having sciatica. □ **sciatic nerve** large nerve from pelvis to thigh.

sciatica /saɪ'ætɪkə/ *noun* neuralgia of hip and leg.

science /'saɪəns/ *noun* **1** branch of knowledge involving systematized observation, experiment, and induction. **2** knowledge so gained. **3** pursuit or principles of this. **4** skilful technique. □ **science fiction** fiction with scientific theme. **science park** area containing science-based businesses.

■ **4** skill, technique.

scientific /saɪən'tɪfɪk/ *adjective* **1** following systematic methods of science. **2** systematic, accurate. **3** of or concerned with science.

■ **2** analytical, methodical, meticulous, orderly, organized, precise, rational, regulated, rigorous, systematic.

scientist /'saɪəntɪst/ *noun* student or expert in science.

■ *colloquial* boffin, researcher, technologist.

sci-fi /'saɪfaɪ/ *noun colloquial* science fiction.

scilicet /'saɪlɪset/ *adverb* that is to say.

scimitar /'sɪmɪtə/ *noun* curved oriental sword.

scintilla /sɪn'tɪlə/ *noun* **1** trace. **2** spark.

scintillate /'sɪntɪleɪt/ (**-ting**) **1** (esp. as **scintillating** *adjective*) talk or act cleverly. **2** sparkle, twinkle. □ **scintillation** *noun*.

■ **1** (**scintillating**) brilliant, clever, dazzling, effervescent, lively, sparkling, vivacious, witty. **2** coruscate, dazzle, flash, glitter, sparkle, twinkle.

scion /'saɪən/ *noun* **1** shoot cut for grafting. **2** young member of family.

scissors /'sɪzəz/ *plural noun* (also **pair of scissors** *singular*) cutting instrument with pair of pivoted blades.

sclerosis /sklə'rəʊsɪs/ *noun* **1** abnormal hardening of tissue. **2** (in full **multiple sclerosis**) serious progressive disease of nervous system. □ **sclerotic** /-'rɒt-/ *adjective*.

scoff[1] *verb* (usually + *at*) speak derisively; mock. ● *noun* mocking words, taunt. □ **scoffer** *noun*.

■ *verb* be sarcastic, be scornful, gibe, jeer, laugh, mock, poke fun, sneer, tease; (*scoff at*) belittle, deride, disparage, ridicule, taunt.

scoff[2] *colloquial verb* eat (food) greedily. ● *noun* food.

scold /skəʊld/ *verb* **1** rebuke. **2** find fault noisily. ● *noun archaic* nagging woman.

■ *verb* **1** admonish, berate, blame, *colloquial* carpet, castigate, censure, *archaic* chide, criticize, find fault with, nag, rate, rebuke, *formal* reprehend, reprimand, reproach, *formal* reprove, *colloquial* slate, *colloquial* tell off, *colloquial* tick off, upbraid. **2** carp, complain, find fault, nag, rail.

sconce *noun* wall-bracket holding candlestick or light-fitting.

scone /skɒn, skəʊn/ *noun* small cake of flour etc. baked quickly.

scoop /skuːp/ *noun* **1** short-handled deep shovel. **2** long-handled ladle. **3** excavating part of digging machine etc. **4** device for serving ice cream etc. **5** quantity taken up by scoop. **6** scooping movement. **7** exclusive news item. **8** large profit made quickly. ● *verb* **1** (usually + *out*) hollow out or (usually + *up*) lift (as) with scoop. **2** forestall (rival newspaper etc.) with scoop. **3** secure (large profit etc.), esp. suddenly.

■ *noun* **2** ladle, spoon. **7** exclusive, inside story, the latest, revelation. ● *verb* **1** dig, excavate, gouge, hollow, scrape, shovel, spoon.

scoot /skuːt/ *verb* (esp. in *imperative*) *colloquial* **1** shoot along. **2** depart, flee.

scooter *noun* **1** child's toy with footboard on two wheels and long steering-handle. **2** low-powered motorcycle.

scope *noun* **1** range; extent of ability, outlook, etc. **2** opportunity.

■ **1** ambit, area, breadth, compass, competence, extent, field, limit, range, reach, span, sphere, terms of reference. **2** capacity, chance, *colloquial* elbow room, freedom, latitude, leeway, liberty, opportunity, outlet, room, space.

scorch *verb* **1** burn or discolour surface of with dry heat. **2** become so discoloured etc. **3** (as **scorching** *adjective*) *colloquial* (of weather) very hot. **4** (as **scorching** *adjective*) *colloquial* (of criticism etc.) stringent. ● *noun* mark of scorching. □ **scorched earth policy** policy of destroying everything that might be of use to invading enemy.

■ *verb* **1** blacken, brand, burn, char, heat, roast, sear, singe.

scorcher *noun colloquial* extremely hot day.

score *noun* **1** number of points, goals, etc. made by player or side in game etc. **2** respective scores at end of game. **3** act of gaining esp. goal. **4** (*plural* same or **-s**) (set of) 20. **5** (in *plural*) a great many. **6** reason, motive. **7** *Music* copy of composition with parts arranged one below another. **8** music for film or play. **9** notch, line, etc. made on surface. **10** record of money owing. ● *verb* (**-ring**) **1** win, gain. **2** make (points etc.) in game. **3** keep score. **4** mark with notches etc. **5** have an advantage. **6** *Music* (often + *for*) orchestrate or arrange (piece of music). **7** *slang* obtain drugs illegally. **8** *slang* make sexual conquest. □ **keep (the) score** register points etc. as they are made. **score (points) off** *colloquial* humiliate, esp. verbally.

scoreboard large board for displaying score in match etc. **settle a (or the) score 1** requite obligation. **2** avenge injury or offence.

■ *noun* **1** amount, count, marks, points, reckoning, result, sum, tally, total. **9** cut, groove, incision, line, mark, nick, scrape, scratch, slash. ● *verb* **1** achieve, chalk up, earn, gain, make, win. **3** add up, count, keep an account, keep the tally. **4** cut, engrave, gouge, incise, mark, scrape, scratch, slash. **6** orchestrate, write out.

scoria /'skɔːrɪə/ *noun* (*plural* **scoriae** /-riː/) **1** (fragments of) cellular lava. **2** slag.

scorn *noun* disdain, contempt, derision. ● *verb* **1** hold in contempt. **2** reject or refuse to do as unworthy.

■ *noun* contempt, contumely, derision, detestation, disdain, disgust, dislike, dismissal, disparagement, disrespect, jeering, mockery, rejection, ridicule, scoffing, sneering, taunting. ● *verb* deride, despise, disapprove of, disdain, dislike, dismiss, disparage, hate, insult, jeer at, laugh at, look down on, make fun of, mock, reject, ridicule, scoff at, sneer at, sniff at, spurn, taunt, *colloquial* turn up one's nose at.

scornful *adjective* (often + *of*) contemptuous. □ **scornfully** *adverb*.

■ condescending, contemptuous, derisive, disdainful, dismissive, disparaging, disrespectful, haughty, insulting, jeering, mocking, patronizing, sarcastic, satirical, scathing, scoffing, sneering, snide, *colloquial* snooty, supercilious, superior, taunting, withering.

Scorpio /'skɔːpɪəʊ/ *noun* eighth sign of zodiac.

scorpion /'skɔːpɪən/ *noun* lobster-like arachnid with jointed stinging tail.

Scot *noun* native of Scotland.

Scotch *adjective* Scottish, Scots. ● *noun* **1** Scottish, Scots. **2** Scotch whisky. □ **Scotch broth** meat soup with pearl barley etc. **Scotch egg** hard-boiled egg in sausage meat. **Scotch fir** Scots pine. **Scotch mist** thick mist and drizzle. **Scotch terrier** small rough-coated terrier. **Scotch whisky** whisky distilled in Scotland.

USAGE *Scots* or *Scottish* is preferred to *Scotch* in Scotland, except in the compound nouns given above.

scotch *verb* **1** decisively put an end to. **2** *archaic* wound without killing.

scot-free *adverb* unharmed; unpunished.

Scots *adjective* Scottish. ● *noun* **1** Scottish. **2** form of English spoken in (esp. Lowlands of) Scotland. □ **Scotsman**, **Scotswoman** Scot. **Scots pine** kind of pine tree.

Scottish *adjective* of Scotland or its inhabitants. ● *noun* (**the Scottish**) (treated as *plural*) people of Scotland.

scoundrel /'skaʊndr(ə)l/ *noun* unscrupulous villain; rogue.

■ blackguard, *colloquial* blighter, *colloquial or jocular* bounder, cad, good-for-nothing, *colloquial* heel, knave, miscreant, rascal, rogue, ruffian, scallywag, *colloquial* scamp, *colloquial* villain, wretch.

scour[1] /skaʊə/ *verb* **1** rub clean. **2** (usually + *away*, *off*, etc.) clear by rubbing. **3** clear out (pipe etc.) by flushing through. ● *noun* scouring, being scoured. □ **scourer** *noun*.

■ *verb* **1** abrade, buff, burnish, clean, cleanse, polish, rub, scrape, scrub, shine, wash.

scour[2] /skaʊə/ *verb* search thoroughly.

■ *colloquial* comb, forage through, hunt through, rake through, ransack, rummage through, search, turn upside down.

scourge /skɜːdʒ/ *noun* **1** person or thing regarded as causing suffering. **2** whip. ● *verb* (**-ging**) **1** whip. **2** punish, oppress.

■ *noun* **1** affliction, bane, curse, evil, misery, misfortune, plague, torment, woe. **2** see WHIP *noun* 1. ● *verb* **1** beat, *slang* belt, flagellate, flog, horsewhip, lash, whip.

Scouse /skaʊs/ *colloquial* *noun* **1** Liverpool dialect. **2** (also **Scouser**) native of Liverpool. ● *adjective* of Liverpool.

scout /skaʊt/ *noun* **1** person sent out to get information or reconnoitre. **2** search for this. **3** talent-scout. **4** (also **Scout**) member of (originally boys') association intended to develop character. ● *verb* **1** (often + *for*) seek information etc. **2** (often + *about*, *around*) make search. **3** (often + *out*) *colloquial* explore. □ **Scoutmaster** person in charge of group of Scouts. □ **scouting** *noun*.

■ *noun* **1** lookout, spy. ● *verb* explore, hunt around, investigate, look about, reconnoitre, search, *colloquial* snoop, spy.

Scouter *noun* adult leader of Scouts.

scowl /skaʊl/ *noun* sullen or bad-tempered look. ● *verb* wear scowl.

■ *verb* frown, glower, grimace, look daggers, lour.

scrabble /'skræb(ə)l/ *verb* (**-ling**) scratch or grope busily about. ● *noun* **1** scrabbling. **2** (**Scrabble**) *proprietary term* game in which players build up words from letter-blocks on board.

scrag *noun* **1** (also **scrag-end**) inferior end of neck of mutton. **2** skinny person or animal. ● *verb* (**-gg-**) *slang* **1** strangle, hang. **2** handle roughly; beat up.

scraggy *adjective* (**-ier**, **iest**) thin and bony. □ **scragginess** *noun*.

■ bony, emaciated, gaunt, lanky, lean, scrawny, skinny, thin, underfed.

scram *verb* (**-mm-**) (esp. in *imperative*) *colloquial* go away.

scramble /'skræmb(ə)l/ *verb* (**-ling**) **1** clamber, crawl, climb, etc. **2** (+ *for*, *at*) struggle with competitors (for thing or share). **3** move hastily. **4** mix indiscriminately. **5** cook (eggs) by stirring in heated pan. **6** alter sound frequencies of (broadcast or telephone conversation) so as to make it unintelligible without special receiver. **7** (of fighter aircraft or pilot) take off rapidly. ● *noun* **1** scrambling. **2** difficult climb or walk. **3** (+ *for*) eager or confused struggle or competition for. **4** motorcycle race over rough ground. **5** emergency take-off by fighter aircraft.

■ *verb* **1** clamber, climb, crawl, grope, scrabble. **2** compete, contend, fight, jostle, push, scuffle, strive, struggle, tussle, vie. **3** dash, hasten, hurry, run, rush, scurry. **4** confuse, jumble, mix up. ● *noun* **3** commotion, confusion, free-for-all, mêlée, race, rush, scrimmage, struggle.

scrambler *noun* **1** device for scrambling telephone conversations. **2** motorcycle used for scrambles.

scrap[1] *noun* **1** small detached piece; fragment. **2** waste material. **3** discarded metal for reprocessing. **4** (with negative) smallest piece or amount. **5** (in *plural*) odds and ends. **6** (in *plural*) bits of uneaten food. ● *verb* (**-pp-**) discard as useless. □ **scrapbook** book in which cuttings etc. are kept. **scrap heap 1** collection of waste material. **2** state of being discarded as useless. **scrapyard** place where (esp. metal) scrap is collected.

■ *noun* **1** bit, fragment, piece, rag, remnant, shard, shred, sliver, snippet. **2** junk, litter, refuse, rejects, rubbish, waste. **4** atom, bit, crumb, fraction, fragment, grain, hint, iota, jot, mite, molecule, morsel, particle, piece, scintilla, shred, sliver, speck, trace. **5** (*scraps*) leavings, odds and ends, offcuts, remains, remnants, residue. ● *verb* abandon, cancel, discard, *slang* ditch, drop, give up, jettison, throw away, write off.

scrap[2] *colloquial noun* fight or rough quarrel. ● *verb* (**-pp-**) have scrap.

■ *noun* argument, fight, quarrel, scuffle, *colloquial* set-to, squabble, tiff, tussle, wrangle. ● *verb* argue, bicker, fight, quarrel, spar, squabble, tussle, wrangle.

scrape *verb* (**-ping**) **1** move hard edge across (surface), esp. to smooth or clean. **2** (+ *away, off*, etc.) remove by scraping. **3** rub (surface) harshly against another. **4** scratch or damage by scraping. **5** excavate by scraping. **6** draw or move with sound (as) of scraping. **7** produce such sound from. **8** (often + *along, by, through*, etc.) move while (almost) touching. **9** narrowly achieve. **10** (often + *by, through*) barely manage. **11** (often + *by, through*) pass exam etc. with difficulty. **12** (+ *together, up*) provide or amass with difficulty. **13** be economical. **14** make clumsy bow. **15** (+ *back*) draw (hair) tightly back. ● *noun* **1** act or sound of scraping. **2** scraped place; graze. **3** *colloquial* predicament caused by rashness. □ **scraper** *noun*.

■ *verb* **4** abrade, bark, damage, graze, injure, lacerate, scratch, scuff, skin, wound. **12** (*scrape together*) see COLLECT[1] *verb* 1. ● *noun* **2** abrasion, graze, injury, laceration, scratch, scuff, wound. **3** difficulty, escapade, plight, prank, predicament, trouble.

scrapie /'skreɪpɪ/ *noun* viral disease of sheep.

scrappy *adjective* (**-ier, -iest**) **1** consisting of scraps. **2** incomplete.

■ **2** bitty, careless, disjointed, fragmentary, imperfect, incomplete, inconclusive, *colloquial* sketchy, slipshod, unfinished, unpolished, unsatisfactory.

scratch *verb* **1** score or wound superficially, esp. with sharp object. **2** scrape with the nails to relieve itching. **3** make or form by scratching. **4** (+ *out, off, through*) erase. **5** withdraw from race or competition. **6** (often + *about, around*, etc.) scratch ground etc. in search. **7** (often + *about, around*, etc.) search haphazardly. ● *noun* **1** mark, wound, or sound made by scratching. **2** act of scratching oneself. **3** *colloquial* trifling wound. **4** starting line for race etc. **5** position of those receiving no handicap. ● *adjective* **1** collected by chance. **2** collected or made from whatever is available. **3** with no handicap given. □ **from scratch 1** from the beginning. **2** without help. **up to scratch** up to required standard.

■ *verb* **1** abrade, claw at, cut, damage, dent, gash, gouge, graze, groove, incise, injure, lacerate, mark, scarify, score, scrape, scuff, wound. ● *noun* **1** abrasion, dent, gash, graze, groove, indentation, injury, laceration, line, mark, score, scrape, scuff, wound. □ **up to scratch** see SATISFACTORY.

scratchy *adjective* (**-ier, -iest**) **1** tending to make scratches or scratching noise. **2** causing itchiness. **3** (of drawing etc.) careless. □ **scratchily** *adverb*. **scratchiness** *noun*.

scrawl *verb* write in hurried untidy way. ● *noun* **1** hurried writing. **2** scrawled note. □ **scrawly** *adjective* (**-ier, -iest**). ■ *verb* doodle, scribble.

scrawny /'skrɔːnɪ/ *adjective* (**-ier, -iest**) lean, scraggy.

scream *noun* **1** piercing cry (as) of terror or pain. **2** *colloquial* hilarious occurrence or person. ● *verb* **1** emit scream. **2** utter in or with scream. **3** move with scream. **4** laugh uncontrollably. **5** be blatantly obvious.

■ *noun* **1** bawl, caterwaul, cry, howl, roar, screech, shout, shriek, squeal, wail, yell, yowl. ● *verb* **1, 2** bawl, caterwaul, cry, howl, roar, screech, shout, shriek, squeal, wail, yell, yowl.

scree *noun* (in *singular* or *plural*) **1** small loose stones. **2** mountain slope covered with these.

screech *noun* harsh scream or squeal. ● *verb* utter with or make screech. □ **screech-owl** barn owl.

screed *noun* **1** long usually tiresome letter or harangue. **2** layer of cement etc. applied to level a surface.

screen *noun* **1** fixed or movable upright partition for separating, concealing, or protecting from heat etc. **2** thing used to conceal or shelter. **3** concealing stratagem. **4** protection thus given. **5** blank surface on which images are projected. **6** (**the screen**) cinema industry; films collectively. **7** windscreen. **8** large sieve. **9** system for detecting disease, ability, attribute, etc. ● *verb* **1** shelter, hide. **2** protect from detection, censure, etc. **3** (+ *off*) shut off or conceal behind screen. **4** show (film etc.). **5** prevent from causing, or protect from, electrical interference. **6** test (person or group) for disease, reliability, loyalty, etc. **7** sieve. □ **screenplay** film script. **screen printing** printing process with ink forced through areas of sheet of fine mesh. **screen test** audition for film part. **screenwriter** person who writes for cinema.

■ *noun* **1** blind, curtain, divider, partition. **2** camouflage, cover, disguise, shelter, shield, smokescreen. **3, 4** blind, concealment, cover, front, protection, smokescreen. **8** filter, mesh, riddle, sieve, strainer. ● *verb* **1, 2** camouflage, cloak, conceal, cover, disguise, guard, hide, mask, protect, safeguard, shade, shelter, shield, shroud, veil. **3** divide, partition off, subdivide, wall off. **6** *colloquial* check out, examine, investigate, vet.

screw /skruː/ *noun* **1** cylinder or cone with spiral ridge running round it outside (**male screw**) or inside (**female screw**). **2** (in full **woodscrew**) metal male screw with slotted head and sharp point. **3** (in full **screw-bolt**) blunt metal male screw on which nut is threaded. **4** straight screw used to exert pressure. **5** (in *singular* or *plural*) instrument of torture acting thus. **6** (in full **screw propeller**) propeller with twisted blades. **7** one turn of screw. **8** (+ *of*) small twisted-up paper (of tobacco etc.). **9** oblique curling motion (of ball). **10** *slang* prison warder. ● *verb* **1** fasten or tighten (as) with screw(s). **2** turn (screw). **3** (of ball etc.) swerve. **4** (+ *out*, *of*) extort from; swindle. □ **screwball** *US slang* crazy or eccentric person. **screwdriver** tool for turning screws by putting tool's tip into screw's slot. **screw up 1** contract, crumple, or contort. **2** summon up (courage etc.). **3** *slang* bungle or spoil. **4** *slang* upset; disturb mentally. **screw-up** *noun slang* bungle.

■ *noun* **7** rotation, turn, twist. ● *verb* **1** see FASTEN 1. **2** rotate, turn, twist. ● **screw up 1** see TWIST *verb* 1–3. **3** see BUNGLE *verb* 1.

screwy *adjective* (**-ier**, **-iest**) *slang* **1** mad, eccentric. **2** absurd. □ **screwiness** *noun*.

scribble /ˈskrɪb(ə)l/ *verb* (**-ling**) **1** write or draw carelessly or hurriedly. **2** *jocular* be author or writer. ● *noun* **1** scrawl. **2** hasty note etc.

■ *verb* **1** doodle, scrawl.

scribe *noun* **1** ancient or medieval copyist of manuscripts. **2** pointed instrument for marking wood etc. **3** *colloquial* writer. ● *verb* (**-bing**) mark with scribe. □ **scribal** *adjective*.

■ *noun* **1** amanuensis, clerk, copyist, secretary, transcriber. **3** see WRITER.

scrim *noun* open-weave fabric for lining, upholstery, etc.

scrimmage /ˈskrɪmɪdʒ/ *noun* tussle, brawl. ● *verb* (**-ging**) engage in scrimmage.

scrimp *verb* skimp.

scrip *noun* **1** provisional certificate of money

subscribed to company etc. **2** extra share(s) instead of dividend.

script *noun* **1** text of play, film, or broadcast (see panel at DIRECT SPEECH). **2** handwriting. **3** typeface imitating handwriting. **4** alphabet or other system of writing. **5** examinee's written answer(s). ● *verb* write script for (film etc.). □ **scriptwriter** person who writes scripts for films etc.

■ *noun* **1** libretto, screenplay, text, words. **2** calligraphy, handwriting, penmanship.

scripture /ˈskrɪptʃə/ *noun* **1** sacred writings. **2** (**Scripture**, **the Scriptures**) the Bible. □ **scriptural** *adjective*.

■ **2** (**Scripture**, **the Scriptures**) Holy Writ, the Bible, the Good Book, the Gospel, the Holy Bible, the Word of God.

scrivener /ˈskrɪvənə/ *noun historical* **1** copyist; drafter of documents. **2** notary.

scrofula /ˈskrɒfjʊlə/ *noun* disease with glandular swellings. □ **scrofulous** *adjective*.

scroll /skrəʊl/ *noun* **1** roll of parchment or paper. **2** book in ancient roll form. **3** ornamental design imitating roll of parchment. ● *verb* (often + *down*, *up*) move (display on VDU screen) to view later or earlier material.

scrotum /ˈskrəʊtəm/ *noun* (*plural* **scrota** or **-s**) pouch of skin enclosing testicles. □ **scrotal** *adjective*.

scrounge /skraʊndʒ/ *verb* (**-ging**) obtain (things) by cadging. □ **on the scrounge** scrounging. □ **scrounger** *noun*.

■ beg, *colloquial* cadge, importune.

scrub[1] *verb* (**-bb-**) **1** clean by hard rubbing, esp. with hard brush. **2** (often + *up*) (of surgeon etc.) clean and disinfect hands etc. before operating. **3** *colloquial* cancel. **4** pass (gas etc.) through scrubber. ● *noun* scrubbing, being scrubbed.

■ *verb* **1** brush, clean, rub, scour, wash. **3** see CANCEL 1.

scrub[2] *noun* **1** brushwood or stunted trees etc. **2** land covered with this. □ **scrubby** *adjective* (**-ier**, **-iest**).

scrubber *noun* **1** *slang* promiscuous woman. **2** apparatus for purifying gases etc.

scruff[1] *noun* back of neck.

scruff[2] *noun colloquial* scruffy person.

scruffy /ˈskrʌfɪ/ *adjective* (**-ier**, **-iest**) *colloquial* shabby, slovenly, untidy. □ **scruffily** *adverb*. **scruffiness** *noun*.

■ bedraggled, dirty, dishevelled, disordered, dowdy, frowzy, messy, ragged, shabby, slatternly, slovenly, *colloquial* tatty, ungroomed, unkempt, untidy, worn out.

scrum *noun* **1** scrummage. **2** *colloquial* scrimmage. □ **scrum-half** *Rugby* half-back who puts ball into scrum.

scrummage /ˈskrʌmɪdʒ/ *noun Rugby* massed forwards on each side pushing to gain possession of ball thrown on ground between them.

scrump /skrʌmp/ *verb colloquial* steal (fruit) from orchard or garden.

scrumptious /'skrʌmpʃəs/ *adjective colloquial* delicious.

scrumpy /'skrʌmpɪ/ *noun colloquial* rough cider.

scrunch *verb* **1** (usually + *up*) crumple. **2** crunch. ● *noun* crunch.

scruple /'skru:p(ə)l/ *noun* (often in *plural*) **1** moral concern. **2** doubt caused by this. ● *verb* (**-ling**) (+ *to do*; usually in negative) hesitate owing to scruples.

■ *noun* compunction, conscience, doubt, hesitation, misgiving, qualm. ● *verb* (*scruple to*) be reluctant to, have a conscience about, hesitate to, hold back from, think twice about.

scrupulous /'skru:pjʊləs/ *adjective* **1** conscientious, thorough. **2** careful to avoid doing wrong. **3** over-attentive to details. □ **scrupulously** *adverb*. **scrupulousness** *noun*.

■ **1, 3** careful, cautious, conscientious, diligent, exacting, fastidious, finicky, meticulous, minute, neat, painstaking, precise, punctilious, rigid, rigorous, strict, systematic, thorough. **2** ethical, fair-minded, honest, honourable, just, moral, principled, proper, upright, upstanding.

scrutineer /skru:tɪ'nɪə/ *noun* person who scrutinizes ballot papers.

scrutinize /'skru:tɪnaɪz/ *verb* (also **-ise**) (**-zing** or **-sing**) subject to scrutiny.

■ analyse, check, examine, inspect, investigate, probe, sift, study.

scrutiny /'skru:tɪnɪ/ *noun* (*plural* **-ies**) **1** critical gaze. **2** close examination. **3** official examination of ballot papers.

■ **2** analysis, examination, inspection, investigation, probing, search, study.

scuba /'sku:bə/ *noun* (*plural* **-s**) aqualung. □ **scuba-diving** swimming underwater using scuba.

scud *verb* (**-dd-**) **1** move straight and fast; skim along. **2** *Nautical* run before wind. ● *noun* **1** scudding. **2** vapoury driving clouds or shower.

scuff *verb* **1** graze or brush against. **2** mark or wear out (shoes etc.) thus. **3** shuffle or drag feet. ● *noun* mark of scuffing.

scuffle /'skʌf(ə)l/ *noun* confused struggle or fight at close quarters. ● *verb* (**-ling**) engage in scuffle.

scull *noun* **1** each of pair of small oars. **2** oar used to propel boat from stern. **3** (in *plural*) sculling race. ● *verb* propel with scull(s).

scullery /'skʌlərɪ/ *noun* (*plural* **-ies**) back kitchen; room where dishes are washed etc.

sculpt *verb* sculpture.

sculptor /'skʌlptə/ *noun* (*feminine* **sculptress**) person who sculptures.

sculpture /'skʌlptʃə/ *noun* **1** art of making 3-dimensional forms by chiselling, carving, modelling, casting, etc. **2** work of sculpture. ● *verb*

(**-ring**) **1** represent in or adorn with sculpture. **2** practise sculpture. □ **sculptural** *adjective*.

■ *noun* **2** bas-relief, bust, carving, cast, relief, statue, statuette; (*sculptures*) marbles. ● *verb* **1** carve, cast, chisel, fashion, form, hew, model, sculpt, shape.

scum *noun* **1** layer of dirt etc. at surface of liquid. **2** *derogatory* worst part, person, or group. ● *verb* (**-mm-**) **1** remove scum from. **2** form scum (on). □ **scumbag** *slang* contemptible person. □ **scummy** *adjective* (**-ier**, **-iest**).

■ *noun* **1** dirt, film, foam, froth, impurities, suds.

scupper[1] /'skʌpə/ *noun* hole in ship's side draining water from deck.

scupper[2] /'skʌpə/ *verb slang* **1** sink (ship, crew). **2** defeat or ruin (plan etc.). **3** kill.

scurf *noun* dandruff. □ **scurfy** *adjective* (**-ier**, **-iest**).

scurrilous /'skʌrɪləs/ *adjective* grossly or obscenely abusive. □ **scurrility** /skə'rɪl-/ *noun* (*plural* **-ies**). **scurrilously** *adverb*. **scurrilousness** *noun*.

■ abusive, calumnious, coarse, defamatory, derogatory, disparaging, foul, indecent, insulting, libellous, low, obscene, offensive, opprobrious, scabrous, shameful, slanderous, vile, vulgar.

scurry /'skʌrɪ/ *verb* (**-ies**, **-ied**) run hurriedly, scamper. ● *noun* (*plural* **-ies**) **1** scurrying sound or movement. **2** flurry of rain or snow.

scurvy /'skɜ:vɪ/ *noun* disease resulting from deficiency of vitamin C. ● *adjective* (**-ier**, **-iest**) paltry, contemptible. □ **scurvily** *adverb*.

scut *noun* short tail, esp. of hare, rabbit, or deer.

scutter /'skʌtə/ *verb* & *noun colloquial* scurry.

scuttle[1] /'skʌt(ə)l/ *noun* **1** coal scuttle. **2** part of car body between windscreen and bonnet.

scuttle[2] /'skʌt(ə)l/ *verb* (**-ling**) **1** scurry. **2** flee in undignified way. ● *noun* **1** hurried gait. **2** precipitate flight.

scuttle[3] /'skʌt(ə)l/ *noun* hole with lid in ship's deck or side. ● *verb* (**-ling**) let water into (ship) to sink it.

scythe /saɪð/ *noun* mowing and reaping implement with long handle and curved blade. ● *verb* (**-thing**) cut with scythe.

SDLP *abbreviation* (in N. Ireland) Social Democratic and Labour Party.

SDP *abbreviation historical* (in UK) Social Democratic Party.

SE *abbreviation* south-east(ern).

sea *noun* **1** expanse of salt water covering most of earth. **2** area of this. **3** large inland lake. **4** (motion or state of) waves of sea. **5** (+ *of*) vast quantity or expanse of. ● *adjective* **1** found in or near sea; of sea. **2** used at sea. **3** of shipping. □ **at sea 1** in ship on the sea. **2** confused. **sea anchor** bag to reduce drifting of ship. **sea anemone** polyp with petal-like tentacles. **seabed** ocean floor. **seaboard** coastline; coastal region. **sea dog** old sailor. **seafarer** traveller by sea. **seafood** edible marine fish or shellfish. **seafront** part of seaside town facing sea. **seagoing** designed for open sea. **seagull** = GULL[1]. **sea horse** small fish with head like horse's. **seakale** plant with young shoots used as vegetable. **sea legs** ability to keep one's balance at sea. **sea level** mean level of sea's surface, used in reckoning heights of hills etc. and as barometric standard. **sea lion** large, eared seal. **seaman 1** person whose work is at sea; sailor. **2** sailor below rank of officer. **seaplane** aircraft designed to take off from and land on water. **seaport** town with harbour. **sea salt** salt got by evaporating sea water. **seascape** picture or view of sea. **seashell** shell of salt-water mollusc. **seashore** land next to sea. **seasick** nauseous from motion of ship at sea. **seasickness** noun. **seaside** sea coast, esp. as holiday resort. **sea urchin** small marine animal with spiny shell. **seaweed** plant growing in sea. **seaworthy** fit to put to sea.

■ noun **1, 2** slang briny, poetical deep, archaic main, ocean. ● adjective **1** aquatic, marine, maritime, oceanic, salt-water. **2, 3** marine, maritime, nautical, naval, seafaring, seagoing.
□ **seaside** beach, coast, sands, seashore, shore.

seafaring /'siːfɛːrɪŋ/ adjective & noun travelling by sea, esp. regularly.

seal[1] noun **1** piece of stamped wax etc. attached to document or to receptacle, envelope, etc. to guarantee authenticity or security. **2** metal stamp etc. used in making seal. **3** substance or device used to close gap etc. **4** anything regarded as confirmation or guarantee. **5** decorative adhesive stamp. ● verb **1** close securely or hermetically. **2** stamp, fasten, or fix with seal. **3** certify as correct with seal etc. **4** (often + up) confine securely. **5** settle, decide. **6** (+ off) prevent access to or from. □ **sealing wax** mixture softened by heating and used for seals.

■ verb **1** close, fasten, lock, make airtight, make watertight, plug, secure, shut, stick down, stop up. **3** affirm, authenticate, confirm, corroborate, endorse, guarantee, ratify, sign, validate, verify. **5** clinch, conclude, decide, finalize, settle.

seal[2] noun fish-eating amphibious marine mammal with flippers. ● verb hunt seals.

sealant noun material for sealing, esp. to make watertight.

seam noun **1** line where two edges join, esp. of cloth or boards. **2** fissure between parallel edges. **3** wrinkle. **4** stratum of coal etc. ● verb **1** join with seam. **2** (esp. as **seamed** adjective) mark or score with seam. □ **seamless** adjective.

■ noun **1** join, stitching. **4** bed, layer, lode, stratum, vein.

seamstress /'siːmstrɪs/ noun woman who sews.

seamy adjective (**-ier, -iest**) **1** disreputable, sordid. **2** showing seams. □ **seaminess** noun.

■ **1** disreputable, distasteful, nasty, repulsive, shameful, sordid, squalid, unattractive, unpleasant, unsavoury, unwholesome.

seance /'seɪɑ̃s/ noun meeting at which spiritualist attempts to contact the dead.

sear /sɪə/ verb **1** scorch, cauterize. **2** cause anguish to. **3** brown (meat) quickly.

search /sɜːtʃ/ verb **1** examine thoroughly to find something. **2** (often + for) make investigation. **3** (+ out) look for; seek out. **4** (as **searching** adjective) keenly questioning; thorough. ● noun **1** act of searching. **2** investigation. □ **searchlight 1** outdoor lamp designed to throw strong beam of light in any direction. **2** light or beam from this. **search party** group of people conducting organized search. **search warrant** official authorization to enter and search building. □ **searcher** noun. **searchingly** adverb.

■ verb **1** check, colloquial comb, examine, slang frisk, inspect, ransack, rifle through, rummage through, scour, scrutinize. **2** cast about, explore, ferret about, hunt, investigate, look, nose about, poke about, prospect, seek. **3** (search out) hunt for, look for, seek (out), track down. **4 (searching)** see INQUISITIVE 2, THOROUGH 1. ● noun **1** hunt, look, pursuit, quest. **2** check, enquiry, examination, inspection, investigation, probe, scrutiny.

season /'siːz(ə)n/ noun **1** each of climatic divisions of year. **2** proper or suitable time. **3** time when something is plentiful, active, etc. **4 (the season)** (also **high season**) busiest period at resort etc. **5** colloquial season ticket. ● verb **1** flavour with salt, herbs, etc. **2** enhance with wit etc. **3** moderate. **4** (esp. as **seasoned** adjective) make or become suitable by exposure to weather or experience. □ **in season 1** (of food) available plentifully. **2** (of animal) on heat. **season ticket** ticket entitling holder to unlimited travel, access, etc. in given period.

■ noun **1–3** period, phase, time. ● verb **1** flavour, colloquial pep up, salt, spice. **4** age, harden, mature, ripen.

seasonable adjective **1** suitable to season. **2** opportune.

USAGE Seasonable is sometimes confused with seasonal.

■ **2** appropriate, apt, convenient, favourable, fitting, opportune, propitious, suitable, timely, well timed.

seasonal adjective of, depending on, or varying with seasons.

USAGE Seasonal is sometimes confused with seasonable.

seasoning noun salt, herbs, etc. as flavouring for food.

■ condiments, dressing, flavouring, herbs, relish, salt, sauce, spice, zest.

seat noun **1** thing made or used for sitting on. **2** buttocks. **3** part of garment covering them. **4** part of chair etc. on which buttocks rest. **5** place for one person in theatre etc. **6** position as MP, committee member, etc., or right to occupy it. **7** machine's supporting or guiding part. **8** location. **9** country mansion. **10** posture on horse. ● verb **1** cause to sit. **2** provide sitting accommodation for. **3** (as **seated** adjective) sitting. **4** establish in position. □ **seat belt** belt securing seated person in vehicle or aircraft.

■ *noun* **1** bench, chair, couch, form, pew, pillion, place, saddle, settee, settle, sofa, stall, stool, throne. **2** see BUTTOCK. **9** see RESIDENCE 2. ● *verb* **1** (*seat oneself*) see SIT 1.

seating *noun* **1** seats collectively. **2** sitting accommodation.

sebaceous /sɪ'beɪʃəs/ *adjective* fatty; secreting oily matter.

Sec. *abbreviation* (also **sec.**) secretary.

sec[1] *noun colloquial* (in phrases) second, moment.

sec[2] *adjective* (of wine) dry.

sec. *abbreviation* second(s).

secateurs /sekə'tɜ:z/ *plural noun* pruning clippers.
■ clippers, cutters.

secede /sɪ'si:d/ *verb* (**-ding**) withdraw formally from political or religious body.

secession /sɪ'seʃ(ə)n/ *noun* seceding. □ **secessionist** *noun & adjective*.

seclude /sɪ'klu:d/ *verb* (**-ding**) **1** keep (person, place) apart from others. **2** (esp. as **secluded** *adjective*) screen from view.
■ **2** (**secluded**) cloistered, concealed, cut off, hidden, inaccessible, isolated, lonely, monastic, private, remote, screened, sequestered, sheltered, shut away, solitary, unfrequented, unvisited.

seclusion /sɪ'klu:ʒ(ə)n/ *noun* secluded state or place.
■ concealment, hiding, isolation, loneliness, privacy, remoteness, retirement, separation, shelter, solitariness.

second[1] /'sekənd/ *adjective* **1** next after first. **2** additional. **3** subordinate; inferior. **4** comparable to. ● *noun* **1** runner-up; person or thing coming second. **2** second gear. **3** (in *plural*) inferior goods. **4** (in *plural*) *colloquial* second helping or course. **5** assistant to boxer, duellist, etc. ● *verb* formally support (nomination, proposal, etc.). □ **second-best** next after best. **second class** second-best group, category, postal service, or accommodation. **second-class** ● *adjective* **1** of or belonging to second class. **2** inferior in quality, status, etc. ● *adverb* by second class. **second cousin** child of parent's first cousin. **second fiddle** subordinate position. **second-guess** *colloquial* **1** anticipate by guesswork. **2** criticize with hindsight. **second-hand 1** (of goods) having had previous owner. **2** (of information etc.) obtained indirectly. **second in command** officer next in rank to commanding or chief officer. **second nature** acquired tendency that has become instinctive. **second-rate** inferior. **second sight** clairvoyance. **second string** alternative course of action etc. **second thoughts** revised opinion. **second to none** surpassed by no other. **second wind** renewed capacity for effort after breathlessness or tiredness. □ **seconder** *noun*.
■ *adjective* **2** added, additional, alternative, duplicate, extra, following, further, later, matching, next, other, repeated, subsequent. ● *noun* **5** assistant, deputy, helper, right-hand man,

right-hand woman, second in command, stand-in, subordinate, supporter, understudy, vice-. ● *verb* back, give approval to, side with, support. □ **second-hand 1** hand-me-down, old, used, worn. **2** indirect, secondary, vicarious. **second-rate** commonplace, indifferent, inferior, low-grade, mediocre, middling, ordinary, poor, second-best, second-class, undistinguished, unexciting, uninspiring.

second[2] /'sekənd/ *noun* **1** SI unit of time (1/60 of minute). **2** 1/60 of minute of angle. **3** *colloquial* very short time.
■ **3** flash, instant, *colloquial* jiffy, moment, *colloquial* tick, twinkling.

second[3] /sɪ'kɒnd/ *verb* transfer (person) temporarily to another department etc. □ **secondment** *noun*.
■ move, reassign, relocate, shift, transfer.

secondary /'sekəndərɪ/ *adjective* **1** coming after or next below what is primary. **2** derived from what is primary. **3** supplementing what is primary. **4** (of education etc.) following primary. ● *noun* (*plural* **-ies**) secondary thing. □ **secondary colour** result of mixing two primary colours.
■ *adjective* **1** inessential, inferior, lesser, lower, minor, non-essential, second, second-rate, subordinate, unimportant. **2** derivative, second-hand, unoriginal. **3** ancillary, auxiliary, backup, extra, reinforcing, reserve, spare, subsidiary, supplementary, supporting, supportive.

secondly *adverb* **1** furthermore. **2** as a second item.

secrecy /'si:krəsɪ/ *noun* **1** being secret. **2** keeping of secrets.

secret /'si:krɪt/ *adjective* **1** not (to be) made known or seen. **2** working etc. secretly. **3** liking secrecy. ● *noun* **1** thing (to be) kept secret. **2** mystery. **3** effective but not widely known method. □ **in secret** secretly. **secret agent** spy. **secret police** police operating secretly for political ends. **secret service** government department concerned with espionage. □ **secretly** *adverb*.
■ *adjective* **1** arcane, clandestine, classified, concealed, confidential, covert, cryptic, disguised, encoded, esoteric, hidden, hushed up, *colloquial* hush-hush, inaccessible, incomprehensible, intimate, mysterious, occult, personal, private, recondite, secluded, sensitive, shrouded, top-secret, undisclosed, unknown, unpublished. **2** clandestine, covert, stealthy, surreptitious, undercover, underground. **3** see SECRETIVE.

secretariat /sekrɪ'teərɪət/ *noun* **1** administrative office or department. **2** its members or premises.

secretary /'sekrɪtərɪ/ *noun* (*plural* **-ies**) **1** employee who deals with correspondence, records, making appointments, etc. **2** official of society etc. who writes letters, organizes business, etc. **3** principal assistant of government minister, ambassador, etc. □ **secretary bird** long-legged crested African bird. **Secretary-General** principal administrative officer of organization. **Secretary of State** head of major government department, (in US) foreign minister. □ **secretarial** /-'teərɪəl/ *adjective*.

■ **1** amanuensis, clerk, personal assistant, scribe, shorthand typist, *esp. US* stenographer, typist.

secrete /sɪ'kri:t/ *verb* (**-ting**) **1** (of cell, organ, etc.) produce and discharge (substance). **2** conceal. □ **secretory** *adjective*.

■ **1** discharge, emit, excrete, exude, give off, leak, ooze, produce, release. **2** cloak, conceal, cover up, disguise, enshroud, hide, mask, put away, put into hiding.

secretion /sɪ'kri:ʃ(ə)n/ *noun* **1** process or act of secreting. **2** secreted substance.

■ **1** discharge, emission, escape, excretion, leakage, release. **2** discharge, emission.

secretive /'si:krətɪv/ *adjective* inclined to make or keep secrets; uncommunicative. □ **secretively** *adverb*. **secretiveness** *noun*.

■ enigmatic, furtive, mysterious, quiet, reserved, reticent, secret, *colloquial* shifty, silent, taciturn, tight-lipped, uncommunicative, unforthcoming, withdrawn.

sect *noun* **1** group sharing (usually unorthodox) religious etc. doctrines. **2** religious denomination.

■ cult, denomination, faction, group, order, party, persuasion.

sectarian /sek'teərɪən/ *adjective* **1** of sect(s). **2** bigoted in following one's sect. ● *noun* member of a sect. □ **sectarianism** *noun*.

■ *adjective* **1** clannish, cliquish, denominational, factional, partisan. **2** bigoted, dogmatic, exclusive, fanatical, inflexible, narrow, narrow-minded, partial, partisan, prejudiced, rigid.

section /'sekʃ(ə)n/ *noun* **1** each of parts into which something is divisible or divided. **2** part cut off. **3** subdivision. **4** *US* area of land. **5** *US* district of town. **6** surgical separation or cutting. **7** cutting of solid by plane. **8** resulting figure or area of this. **9** thin slice cut off for microscopic examination. ● *verb* **1** arrange in or divide into sections. **2** compulsorily commit to psychiatric hospital.

■ *noun* **1**, **3** bit, branch, chapter, compartment, component, department, division, element, fraction, group, instalment, leg (*of journey*), part, passage, piece, portion, sector, segment, slice, stage, subdivision, subsection. **2** fragment, part, piece, portion, sample, slice. **5** district, quarter, zone.

sectional *adjective* **1** of a social group. **2** partisan. **3** made in sections. **4** local rather than general. □ **sectionally** *adverb*.

sector /'sektə/ *noun* **1** branch of an enterprise, the economy, etc. **2** *Military* portion of battle area. **3** plane figure enclosed between two radii of circle etc.

■ **1** see SECTION *noun* 1,3. **2** area, district, division, part, quarter, region, zone.

secular /'sekjʊlə/ *adjective* **1** not concerned with religion; not sacred. **2** (of clerics) not monastic. □ **secularism** *noun*. **secularization** *noun*. **secularize** *verb* (also **-ise**) (**-zing** or **-sing**).

■ **1** civil, earthly, lay, material, mundane, non-religious, temporal, terrestrial, worldly.

secure /sɪ'kjʊə/ *adjective* **1** untroubled by danger or fear. **2** safe. **3** fastened or fixed so as not to give way. **4** reliable, stable. ● *verb* (**-ring**) **1** make secure or safe. **2** fasten or close securely. **3** obtain. □ **securely** *adverb*.

■ *adjective* **1** certain, confident, cosy, immune, protected, safe, snug, sure, unquestioning, untroubled. **2** defended, guarded, impregnable, invulnerable, protected, safe, sheltered, shielded. **3** bolted, burglar-proof, closed, fast, fastened, firm, fixed, foolproof, immovable, locked, shut, solid, tight, unyielding. **4** certain, firm, reliable, solid, sound, stable, steady, strong, sure. ● *verb* **1** defend, guard, make safe, preserve, protect, shelter, shield. **2** anchor, attach, bolt, close, fasten, fix, lock, make fast, screw down, tie down. **3** acquire, come by, gain, get, obtain, procure, win.

security *noun* (*plural* **-ies**) **1** secure condition or feeling. **2** thing that guards or guarantees. **3** safety against espionage, theft, etc. **4** organization for ensuring this. **5** thing deposited as guarantee for undertaking or loan. **6** (often in *plural*) document as evidence of loan, certificate of stock, bonds, etc. □ **security guard** person employed to protect security of buildings etc. **security risk** person or thing threatening security.

sedan /sɪ'dæn/ *noun* **1** (in full **sedan chair**) *historical* enclosed chair for one person, usually carried on poles by two. **2** *US* saloon car.

sedate /sɪ'deɪt/ *adjective* tranquil; serious. ● *verb* (**-ting**) put under sedation. □ **sedately** *adverb*. **sedateness** *noun*.

■ *adjective* calm, collected, composed, controlled, conventional, cool, decorous, deliberate, dignified, equable, even-tempered, formal, grave, imperturbable, level-headed, peaceful, prim, proper, quiet, sensible, serene, serious, slow, sober, solemn, staid, strait-laced, tranquil, unruffled. ● *verb* calm, tranquillize.

sedation *noun* treatment with sedatives.

sedative /'sedətɪv/ *noun* calming drug or influence. ● *adjective* calming, soothing.

■ *noun* anodyne, barbiturate, depressant, narcotic, opiate, sleeping pill, soporific, tranquillizer. ● *adjective* anodyne, calming, narcotic, relaxing, soothing, soporific, tranquillizing.

sedentary /'sedəntərɪ/ *adjective* **1** sitting. **2** (of work etc.) done while sitting. **3** (of person) disinclined to exercise.

■ **1** seated, sitting. **3** immobile, inactive.

sedge *noun* grasslike waterside or marsh plant. □ **sedgy** *adjective*.

sediment /'sedɪmənt/ *noun* **1** dregs. **2** matter deposited on land by water or wind. □ **sediment-ary** /-'men-/ *adjective*. **sedimentation** *noun*.

■ **1** deposit, dregs, grounds, lees, precipitate, remains, residue, sludge.

sedition /sɪ'dɪʃ(ə)n/ *noun* conduct or speech inciting to rebellion. □ **seditious** *adjective*.

■ agitation, incitement, insurrection, mutiny, rabble-rousing, treachery, treason.

seduce /sɪ'djuːs/ *verb* **(-cing) 1** entice into sexual activity or wrongdoing. **2** coax or lead astray. □ **seducer** *noun*.

■ **1** corrupt, debauch, deflower, deprave, *archaic* dishonour, rape, *archaic* ravish, violate. **2** allure, beguile, charm, deceive, decoy, ensnare, entice, inveigle, lead astray, lure, mislead, tempt.

seduction /sɪ'dʌkʃ(ə)n/ *noun* **1** seducing, being seduced. **2** tempting or attractive thing.

■ **1** allurement, beguilement, enticement, temptation.

seductive /sɪ'dʌktɪv/ *adjective* alluring, en-ticing. □ **seductively** *adverb*. **seductiveness** *noun*.

■ alluring, appealing, attractive, bewitching, captivating, charming, coquettish, enchanting, enticing, flirtatious, inviting, irresistible, persuasive, provocative, sexy, tantalizing, tempting.

sedulous /'sedjʊləs/ *adjective* persevering, dili-gent, painstaking. □ **sedulity** /sɪ'djuː-/ *noun*. **sed-ulously** *adverb*. **sedulousness** *noun*.

see[1] *verb* **(sees**; *past* **saw**; *past participle* **seen) 1** perceive with the eyes. **2** have or use this power. **3** discern mentally; understand. **4** watch; witness (event etc.). **5** ascertain. **6** imagine, foresee. **7** look at. **8** meet. **9** meet regularly. **10** visit; be visited by. **11** reflect; get clarification. **12** (+ *in*) find attractive in. **13** escort, conduct. **14** experience. **15** ensure. □ **see about 1** attend to. **2** consider. **see off 1** be present at departure of. **2** *colloquial* get the better of. **see over** inspect; tour. **see red** *colloquial* become enraged. **see through 1** not be deceived by. **2** support (person) during difficult time. **3** complete (project). **see-through** *adjective* translucent. **see to 1** attend to. **2** repair. **see to it** (+ *that*) ensure that. **see you** (also **see you later**) *colloquial* goodbye.

■ **1** *literary* behold, catch sight of, descry, discern, discover, distinguish, espy, glimpse, identify, look at, make out, mark, note, notice, observe, perceive, recognize, regard, sight, *colloquial* spot, spy, view, watch, witness. **3** appreciate, apprehend, comprehend, discern, fathom, follow, *colloquial* get the hang of, grasp, know, perceive, realize, take in, understand. **4** attend, be a spectator at, view, watch, witness. **6** *disputed* anticipate, conceive, envisage, foresee, foretell, imagine, picture, visualize. **8** encounter, meet, run into, talk to, visit. **9** court, go out with, *colloquial* have a date with, meet, socialize with, visit, woo. **11** consider, decide, mull over, reflect on, think about, *colloquial*

weigh up. **13** accompany, conduct, escort. **14** endure, experience, go through, suffer, survive, undergo. □ **see to 1** see ORGANIZE 3.

see[2] *noun* **1** area under (arch)bishop's authority. **2** (arch)bishop's office or jurisdiction.

seed *noun* **1** part of plant capable of developing into another such plant. **2** seeds collectively, esp. for sowing. **3** semen. **4** prime cause, beginning. **5** offspring. **6** *Tennis etc.* seeded player. ● *verb* **1** place seed(s) in. **2** sprinkle (as) with seed. **3** sow seeds. **4** produce or drop seed. **5** remove seeds from (fruit etc.). **6** place crystal etc. in (cloud) to produce rain. **7** *Tennis etc.* designate (competitor in knockout tournament) so that strong compet-itors do not meet each other until later rounds. **8** *Tennis etc.* arrange (order of play) thus. □ **go, run to seed 1** cease flowering as seed develops. **2** become degenerate, unkempt, etc. **seedbed 1** bed prepared for sowing. **2** place of development. **seedpearl** very small pearl. **seed potato** potato kept for planting. **seedsman** dealer in seeds.

■ *noun* **1** ovule, pip, spore, stone. **3** semen, sperm. ● *verb* **1, 3** see SOW[1] 1.

seedling *noun* young plant raised from seed.

seedy *adjective* **(-ier, -iest) 1** shabby. **2** *colloquial* unwell. **3** full of seed.

seeing *conjunction* (usually + *that*) considering that, inasmuch as, because.

seek *verb* (*past & past participle* **sought** /sɔːt/) **1** (often + *for*, *after*) search, inquire. **2** try or want to obtain or reach. **3** request. **4** endeavour. □ **seek out** search for and find. □ **seeker** *noun*.

■ **1** (*seek for* or *after*) go after, hunt for, inquire after, look for, pursue, quest after, search for. **2** aim at, apply for, aspire to, desire, go after, hope for, pursue, quest after, strive after, try for, want, wish for. **3** ask for, beg for, demand, request, solicit. **4** aim, aspire, attempt, endeavour, strive, try.

seem *verb* (often + *to do*) appear; give the impres-sion.

■ appear, feel, give an impression of being, have an appearance of being, look, pretend to be, sound.

seeming *adjective* apparent but doubtful. □ **seemingly** *adverb*.

seemly /'siːmlɪ/ *adjective* **(-ier, -iest)** in good taste; decorous. □ **seemliness** *noun*.

seen *past participle* of SEE[1].

seep *verb* ooze, percolate.

■ dribble, drip, exude, flow, leak, ooze, percolate, run, soak, trickle.

seepage *noun* **1** act of seeping. **2** quantity that seeps.

seer /sɪə/ *noun* **1** person who sees. **2** prophet, visionary.

■ **2** clairvoyant, fortune-teller, oracle, prophet, prophetess, psychic, sibyl, soothsayer.

seersucker /'sɪəsʌkə/ *noun* thin cotton etc. fabric with puckered surface.

see-saw /'siːsɔː/ *noun* **1** long board supported

in middle so that children etc. sitting on ends move alternately up and down. **2** this game. **3** up-and-down or to-and-fro motion, contest, etc. ● *verb* **1** play or move (as) on see-saw. **2** vacillate. ● *adjective & adverb* with up-and-down or to-and-fro motion.

seethe /siːð/ *verb* (**-thing**) **1** boil, bubble. **2** be very angry, resentful, etc.
■ **1** boil, bubble, foam, froth, simmer, stew. **2** be angry, rage, simmer.

see you *interjection colloquial* (also as **see you later**) goodbye.

segment *noun* /ˈsegmənt/ **1** part cut off or separable from other parts. **2** part of circle or sphere cut off by intersecting line or plane. ● *verb* /segˈment/ divide into segments. □ **segmental** /-ˈment-/ *adjective*. **segmentation** *noun*.
■ *noun* **1** bit, division, element, fraction, fragment, part, piece, portion, section, slice, subdivision, subsection, wedge.

segregate /ˈsegrɪgeɪt/ *verb* (**-ting**) **1** put apart; isolate. **2** separate (esp. ethnic group) from the rest of the community. □ **segregation** *noun*. **segregationist** *noun & adjective*.
■ compartmentalize, cut off, exclude, isolate, keep apart, put apart, separate, sequester, set apart, shut out. □ **segregation** apartheid, discrimination, isolation, quarantine, seclusion, separation.

seigneur /semˈjɜː/ *noun* feudal lord. □ **seigneurial** *adjective*.

seine /sem/ *noun* large vertical fishing net. ● *verb* (**-ning**) fish with seine.

seismic /ˈsaɪzmɪk/ *adjective* of earthquake(s).

seismograph /ˈsaɪzməgrɑːf/ *noun* instrument for recording earthquake details. □ **seismographic** /-ˈgræf-/ *adjective*.

seismology /saɪzˈmɒlədʒɪ/ *noun* the study of earthquakes. □ **seismological** /-məˈlɒdʒ-/ *adjective*. **seismologist** *noun*.

seize /siːz/ *verb* (**-zing**) **1** take hold of, esp. forcibly or suddenly. **2** arrest (person); take prisoner. **3** (often + *on, upon*) take possession of, esp. forcibly or by legal power. **4** take advantage of. **5** comprehend quickly or clearly. **6** affect suddenly. **7** (also **seise**) (usually + *of*) *Law* put in possession of. □ **seize up 1** (of mechanism) become jammed. **2** (of part of body etc.) become stiff.
■ **1** catch, clutch, grab, grasp, grip, *slang* nab, pluck, snatch, take. **2** abduct, apprehend, arrest, capture, catch, *colloquial* collar, detain, *slang* nab, take into custody, take prisoner. **3** (*seize property*) appropriate, commandeer, confiscate, hijack, impound, repossess, steal, take away; (*seize a country*) annex, capture, invade, occupy, take over. □ **seize up 1** see STICK² 5.

seizure /ˈsiːʒə/ *noun* **1** seizing, being seized. **2** sudden attack of epilepsy, apoplexy, etc.

■ **1** abduction, annexation, appropriation, arrest, capture, confiscation, hijacking, invasion, sequestration, theft, usurpation. **2** attack, convulsion, epileptic fit, fit, paroxysm, spasm, stroke.

seldom /ˈseldəm/ *adverb* rarely, not often.
■ infrequently, occasionally, rarely.

select /sɪˈlekt/ *verb* choose, esp. with care. ● *adjective* **1** chosen for excellence or suitability. **2** exclusive. □ **select committee** parliamentary committee conducting special inquiry. □ **selector** *noun*.
■ *verb* appoint, cast (*actor for role*), choose, decide on, elect, nominate, opt for, pick, settle on, single out, vote for. ● *adjective* **1** best, choice, chosen, excellent, exceptional, favoured, finest, first-class, first-rate, hand-picked, preferred, prime, selected, special, top-quality. **2** closed, elite, exclusive, privileged, restricted.

selection /sɪˈlekʃ(ə)n/ *noun* **1** selecting, being selected. **2** person or thing selected. **3** things from which choice may be made. **4** = NATURAL SELECTION.
■ **1** choice, election. **2** choice, option, pick, preference. **3** assortment, range, variety.

selective *adjective* **1** of or using selection. **2** able to select. **3** selecting what is convenient. □ **selectively** *adverb*. **selectivity** /-ˈtɪv-/ *noun*.
■ **3** careful, *colloquial* choosy, discerning, discriminating, particular.

selenium /sɪˈliːnɪəm/ *noun* non-metallic element in some sulphide ores.

self *noun* (*plural* **selves**/selvz/) **1** individuality, essence. **2** object of introspection or reflexive action. **3** one's own interests or pleasure. **4** concentration on these.

self- *combining form: expressing reflexive action, automatic or independent action, or sameness.* □ **self-addressed** addressed to oneself. **self-adhesive** (of envelope etc.) adhesive, esp. without wetting. **self-aggrandizement** enriching oneself; making oneself powerful. **self-assertive** confident or assertive in promoting oneself, one's claims, etc. **self-assertion** *noun*. **self-assured** self-confident. **self-catering** providing cooking facilities but no food. **self-centred** preoccupied with oneself. **self-centredness** *noun*. **self-confessed** openly admitting oneself to be. **self-confident** having confidence in oneself. **self-confidence** *noun*. **self-conscious** nervous, shy, embarrassed. **self-consciously** *adverb*. **self-contained 1** uncommunicative. **2** complete in itself. **self-control** control of oneself, one's behaviour, etc. **self-critical** critical of oneself, one's abilities, etc. **self-defence** defence of oneself, one's reputation, etc. **self-denial** abstinence, esp. as discipline. **self-deprecating** belittling oneself. **self-destruct** (of device etc.) explode or disintegrate automatically, esp. when pre-set to do so. **self-determination 1** nation's right to determine own government etc. **2** free will. **self-effacing**

retiring; modest. **self-employed** working as freelance or for one's own business etc. **self-employment** *noun*. **self-esteem** good opinion of oneself. **self-evident** needing no proof or explanation. **self-explanatory** not needing explanation. **self-financing** not needing subsidy. **self-fulfilling** (of prophecy etc.) assured fulfilment by its utterance. **self-governing** governing itself or oneself. **self-government** *noun*. **self-help** use of one's own abilities etc. to achieve success etc. **self-image** one's conception of oneself. **self-important** conceited, pompous. **self-importance** *noun*. **self-indulgent 1** indulging one's own pleasures, feelings, etc. **2** (of work of art etc.) lacking control. **self-indulgence** *noun*. **self-interest** one's personal interest or advantage. **self-interested** *adjective*. **self-made** successful or rich by one's own efforts. **self-opinionated** obstinate in one's opinion. **self-pity** pity for oneself. **self-portrait** portrait of oneself by oneself. **self-possessed** unperturbed; cool. **self-possession** *noun*. **self-preservation 1** keeping oneself safe. **2** instinct for this. **self-raising** (of flour) containing a raising agent. **self-reliance** reliance on one's own abilities etc. **self-reliant** *adjective*. **self-respect** respect for oneself. **self-restraint** self-control. **self-righteous** smugly sure of one's righteousness. **self-righteously** *adverb*. **self-righteousness** *noun*. **self-rule** self-government. **self-sacrifice** selflessness, self-denial. **self-satisfied** complacent. **self-satisfaction** *noun*. **self-seeking** selfish. **self-service** with customers helping themselves and paying cashier afterwards. **self-starter 1** electric device for starting engine. **2** ambitious person with initiative. **self-styled** called so by oneself. **self-sufficient** capable of supplying one's own needs. **self-sufficiency** *noun*. **self-willed** obstinately pursuing one's own wishes. **self-worth** self-esteem.

■ □ **self-confident** assertive, assured, bold, collected, cool, fearless, independent, outgoing, poised, positive, self-assured, self-possessed, self-reliant, sure of oneself. **self-conscious** awkward, bashful, blushing, coy, diffident, embarrassed, ill at ease, insecure, nervous, reserved, self-effacing, sheepish, shy, timid, uncomfortable. **self-contained 1** aloof, cold, reserved, self-reliant, uncommunicative, undemonstrative, unemotional. **2** complete, independent, separate. **self-control** calmness, composure, coolness, patience, resolve, restraint, self-command, self-denial, self-discipline, self-possession, self-restraint, will-power. **self-denial** abstemiousness, abstinence, moderation, self-abnegation, self-sacrifice, temperance, unselfishness. **self-employed** freelance, independent. **self-esteem** assurance, confidence, pride, self-confidence, self-respect. **self-explanatory** apparent, axiomatic, blatant, clear, manifest, obvious, patent, plain, recognizable, self-evident, understandable, unmistakable, visible. **self-governing** autonomous, free, independent, sovereign. **self-important** arrogant, bombastic, conceited, grandiloquent, haughty, magisterial, ostentatious, pompous, pontifical, pretentious, self-centred,

sententious, smug, *colloquial* snooty, *colloquial* stuck-up, supercilious, vainglorious. **self-indulgence** extravagance, gluttony, greed, hedonism, pleasure, profligacy, self-gratification, selfishness. **self-indulgent 1** dissipated, epicurean, extravagant, gluttonous, gormandizing, greedy, hedonistic, immoderate, intemperate, pleasure-loving, profligate, selfish, sybaritic. **self-reliant** autonomous, independent, self-contained, self-sufficient, self-supporting. **self-respect** dignity, honour, integrity, morale, pride, self-confidence, self-esteem. **self-righteous** complacent, *colloquial* goody-goody, *colloquial* holier-than-thou, mealy-mouthed, pietistic, pious, pompous, priggish, proud, sanctimonious, self-important, self-satisfied, smug, superior, vain. **self-sufficient** autonomous, independent, self-reliant, self-supporting. **self-willed** determined, dogged, forceful, headstrong, inflexible, intractable, intransigent, mulish, obstinate, pig-headed, single-minded, stiff-necked, stubborn, uncontrollable, uncooperative, wilful.

selfhood /'selfhʊd/ *noun* personal individuality.

selfish *adjective* **1** concerned chiefly with one's own interests or pleasure. **2** actuated by or appealing to self-interest. □ **selfishness** *noun*.

■ acquisitive, avaricious, covetous, demanding, egocentric, egotistic(al), grasping, greedy, inconsiderate, mean, mercenary, miserly, self-absorbed, self-centred, self-indulgent, self-interested, self-seeking, self-serving, stingy, thoughtless, uncaring, ungenerous, unhelpful, unsympathetic, worldly. □ **selfishness** acquisitiveness, avarice, covetousness, egotism, greed, meanness, miserliness, niggardliness, possessiveness, self-indulgence, self-interest, self-love, self-regard, stinginess, thoughtlessness.

selfless *adjective* unselfish.

selfsame /'selfseɪm/ *adjective* (**the selfsame**) the very same; the identical.

sell *verb* (*past & past participle* **sold** /səʊld/) **1** exchange or be exchanged for money. **2** stock for sale; be dealer in. **3** (*at, for*) have specified price. **4** betray or prostitute for money etc. **5** advertise; publicize. **6** cause to be sold. **7** *colloquial* make (person) enthusiastic about (idea etc.). ● *noun colloquial* **1** manner of selling. **2** deception, disappointment. □ **sell-by date** latest recommended date of sale. **sell off** sell at reduced prices. **sell out 1** sell (all one's stock or shares etc.). **2** betray; be treacherous. **sell-out** *noun* **1** commercial success. **2** betrayal. **sell short** disparage, underestimate. **sell up** sell one's business, house, etc.

■ *verb* **1** auction, barter, exchange, sell off, trade, trade in (*traded in my car*), vend. **2** carry, deal in, handle, hawk, offer for sale, peddle, retail, stock, trade in, traffic in, vend. **5** advertise, market, merchandise, package, promote, publicize, push, tout.

seller *noun* **1** person who sells. **2** thing that sells well or badly as specified. □ **seller's market** time when goods are scarce and expensive.

■ **1** agent, broker, dealer, hawker, *esp. US & Scottish* merchant, pedlar, *colloquial* rep, representative, retailer, salesman, salesperson, saleswoman, shop assistant, shopkeeper, stockist, storekeeper, supplier, trader, tradesman, traveller, vendor, wholesaler.

Sellotape /'seləteɪp/ *noun proprietary term* adhesive usually transparent cellulose tape. ● *verb* (**sellotape**) (**-ping**) fix with Sellotape.

selvage /'selvɪdʒ/ *noun* (also **selvedge**) edge of cloth woven to prevent fraying.

selves *plural* of SELF.

semantic /sɪ'mæntɪk/ *adjective* of meaning in language.

semantics *plural noun* (usually treated as *singular*) branch of linguistics concerned with meaning.

semaphore /'seməfɔ:/ *noun* **1** system of signalling with arms or two flags. **2** railway signalling apparatus with arm(s). ● *verb* (**-ring**) signal or send by semaphore.

semblance /'sembləns/ *noun* (+ *of*) appearance, show of.

semen /'si:mən/ *noun* reproductive fluid of males.

semester /sɪ'mestə/ *noun* half-year term in universities.

semi /'semɪ/ *noun colloquial* (*plural* **-s**) semi-detached house.

semi- *prefix* **1** half. **2** partly.

semibreve /'semɪbri:v/ *noun Music* note equal to 4 crotchets.

semicircle /'semɪsɜ:k(ə)l/ *noun* half of circle or its circumference. □ **semicircular** /-'sɜ:kjʊlə/ *adjective*.

semicolon /semɪ'kəʊlən/ *noun* punctuation mark (;) of intermediate value between comma and full stop (see panel).

semiconductor /semɪkən'dʌktə/ *noun* substance that is a poor electrical conductor when either pure or cold and a good conductor when either impure or hot.

semi-detached /semɪdɪ'tætʃt/ *adjective* (of

house) joined to another on one side only. ● *noun* such house.

semifinal /semɪ'faɪn(ə)l/ *noun* match or round preceding final. □ **semifinalist** *noun*.

seminal /'semɪn(ə)l/ *adjective* **1** of seed, semen, or reproduction. **2** germinal. **3** (of idea etc.) providing basis for future development.

■ **2** basic, formative, germinal, primary. **3** basic, constructive, creative, fertile, formative, imaginative, important, influential, innovative, new, original, productive.

seminar /'semɪnɑ:/ *noun* **1** small class for discussion etc. **2** short intensive course of study. **3** specialists' conference.

seminary /'semɪnərɪ/ *noun* (*plural* **-ies**) training college for priests etc. □ **seminarist** *noun*.

semipermeable /semɪ'pɜ:mɪəb(ə)l/ *adjective* (of membrane etc.) allowing small molecules to pass through.

semiprecious /semɪ'preʃəs/ *adjective* (of gem) less valuable than a precious stone.

semi-professional /semɪprə'feʃən(ə)l/ *adjective* **1** (of footballer, musician, etc.) paid for activity but not relying on it for living. **2** of semi-professionals. ● *noun* semi-professional person.

semiquaver /'semɪkweɪvə/ *noun Music* note equal to half a quaver.

semi-skimmed /semɪ'skɪmd/ *adjective* (of milk) with some of cream skimmed off.

Semite /'si:maɪt/ *noun* member of peoples supposedly descended from Shem, including Jews and Arabs.

Semitic /sɪ'mɪtɪk/ *adjective* **1** of Semites, esp. Jews. **2** of languages of family including Hebrew and Arabic.

semitone /'semɪtəʊn/ *noun* half a tone in musical scale.

semivowel /'semɪvaʊəl/ *noun* **1** sound intermediate between vowel and consonant. **2** letter representing this.

semolina /semə'li:nə/ *noun* **1** hard round grains of wheat used for puddings etc. **2** pudding of this.

Semtex /'semteks/ *noun proprietary term* odourless plastic explosive.

Semicolon ;

This is used:

1 between clauses that are too short or too closely related to be made into separate sentences; such clauses are not usually connected by a conjunction, e.g.

To err is human; to forgive, divine.
You could wait for him here; on the other hand I could wait in your place; this would save you valuable time.

2 between items in a list which themselves contain commas, if it is necessary to avoid confusion, e.g.

The party consisted of three teachers, who had already climbed with the leader; seven pupils; and two parents.

SEN *abbreviation* State Enrolled Nurse.

Sen. *abbreviation* **1** Senior. **2** Senator.

senate /'senɪt/ *noun* **1** upper house of legislature in some countries. **2** governing body of some universities or (*US*) colleges. **3** ancient Roman state council.

senator /'senətə/ *noun* member of senate. □ **senatorial** /-'tɔː-/ *adjective*.

send *verb* (*past & past participle* **sent**) **1** order or cause to go or be conveyed. **2** cause to become. **3** send message etc. **4** grant, bestow, inflict; cause to be. **5** (+ *forth*, *off*, *out*, etc.) emit; give off; give out. □ **send away** dismiss. **send away for** order (goods) by post. **send down 1** rusticate or expel from university. **2** send to prison. **send for 1** summon. **2** order by post. **send off 1** dispatch. **2** attend departure of. **send-off** *noun* party etc. at departure of person. **send off for** send away for. **send on** transmit further or in advance of oneself. **send up** *colloquial* ridicule (by mimicking). **send-up** *noun colloquial* parody, satire. □ **sender** *noun*.

■ **1** address, consign, convey, deliver, direct, dispatch, fax, forward, mail, post, remit, ship, transmit; (*send a missile*) fire, launch, project, propel, release, shoot. **5** (*send out*) see EMIT.
□ **send away** see DISMISS 1. **send down 2** see IMPRISON 1. **send for 1** see SUMMON 1,2. **send-off** see GOODBYE. **send up** see PARODY *verb*.

senescent /sɪ'nes(ə)nt/ *adjective* growing old. □ **senescence** *noun*.

seneschal /'senɪʃ(ə)l/ *noun* steward of medieval great house.

senile /'siːnaɪl/ *adjective* **1** of old age. **2** mentally or physically infirm because of old age. □ **senile dementia** illness of old people with loss of memory etc. □ **senility** /sɪ'nɪl-/ *noun*.

■ **2** declining, doddery, in one's dotage, *colloquial* past it.

senior /'siːnɪə/ *adjective* **1** higher in age or standing. **2** (placed after person's name) senior to relative of same name. ● *noun* **1** senior person. **2** one's elder or superior. □ **senior citizen** old-age pensioner. □ **seniority** /-'ɒr-/ *noun*.

■ *adjective* **1** chief, elder, higher, high-ranking, major, older, principal, superior, well established.

senna /'senə/ *noun* **1** cassia. **2** laxative from leaves and pods of this.

señor /sen'jɔː/ *noun* (*plural* **señores** /-rez/) title used of or to Spanish-speaking man.

señora /sen'jɔːrə/ *noun: title used of or to Spanish-speaking esp. married woman.*

señorita /senjə'riːtə/ *noun: title used of or to young Spanish-speaking esp. unmarried woman.*

sensation /sen'seɪʃ(ə)n/ *noun* **1** feeling in one's body. **2** awareness, impression. **3** intense feeling, esp. in community. **4** cause of this. **5** sense of touch.

■ **1, 2** awareness, feeling, perception, sense. **3** commotion, excitement, furore, outrage, scandal, stir, thrill.

sensational *adjective* **1** causing or intended to cause public excitement etc. **2** *colloquial* wonderful. □ **sensationalism** *noun*. **sensationalist** *noun & adjective*. **sensationalize** *verb* (also **-ise**) (**-zing** or **-sing**).

■ **1** amazing, astonishing, astounding, breathtaking, electrifying, exciting, hair-raising, lurid, melodramatic, shocking, spine-tingling, startling, stimulating, stirring, surprising, thrilling, unbelievable, unexpected. **2** extraordinary, *colloquial* fabulous, *colloquial* fantastic, *colloquial* great, marvellous, remarkable, spectacular, superb, wonderful.

sense *noun* **1** any of bodily faculties transmitting sensation. **2** sensitiveness of any of these. **3** ability to perceive. **4** (+ *of*) consciousness of. **5** (+ *of*) appreciation, instinct. **6** practical wisdom. **7** meaning of word etc. **8** intelligibility, coherence. **9** prevailing opinion. **10** (in *plural*) sanity; ability to think. ● *verb* (**-sing**) **1** perceive by sense(s). **2** be vaguely aware of. **3** (of machine etc.) detect. □ **make sense** be intelligible or practicable. **make sense of** show or find meaning of. **sense of humour** see HUMOUR 3.

■ *noun* **1, 2** faculty, feeling, sensation. **4, 5** appreciation, awareness, consciousness, instinct, intuition, perception, understanding. **6** brains, cleverness, *colloquial* gumption, intellect, intelligence, judgement, logic, *colloquial* nous, reason, reasoning, understanding, wisdom, wit. **7, 8** coherence, connotation, denotation, drift, gist, import, intelligibility, interpretation, meaning, message, point, purport, significance, signification, substance. ● *verb* **1, 2** be aware of, detect, discern, divine, feel, guess, have a hunch, intuit, notice, perceive, *colloquial* pick up vibes, realize, suspect, understand. **3** see DETECT 2.
□ **make sense of** see UNDERSTAND 1.

senseless *adjective* **1** pointless, foolish. **2** unconscious. □ **senselessly** *adverb*. **senselessness** *noun*.

■ **1** absurd, crazy, fatuous, meaningless, pointless, purposeless, silly, stupid. **2** anaesthetized, comatose, insensate, insensible, knocked out, stunned, unconscious.

sensibility *noun* (*plural* **-ies**) **1** capacity to feel. **2** (exceptional) sensitiveness. **3** (in *plural*) tendency to feel offended etc.

USAGE *Sensibility* should not be used in standard English to mean 'possession of good sense'.

sensible /'sensɪb(ə)l/ *adjective* **1** having or showing good sense. **2** perceptible by senses. **3** (of clothing etc.) practical. **4** (+ *of*) aware of. □ **sensibly** *adverb*.

■ **1** calm, cool, discreet, discriminating, intelligent, judicious, level-headed, logical, prudent, rational, realistic, reasonable, reasoned, sage, sane, sound, thoughtful, wise. **2** corporeal, existent, material, palpable, perceptible, physical, real, tangible, visible. **3** comfortable, functional, no-nonsense, practical, useful. **4** (*sensible of*) acquainted with, alert to, alive to, appreciative of, aware of, *formal* cognizant of, in touch with, mindful of, responsive to, *colloquial* wise to.

sensitive /'sensɪtɪv/ *adjective* **1** (often + *to*) acutely affected by external impressions; having sensibility. **2** easily offended or hurt. **3** considerate of others' feelings. **4** (often + *to*) responsive to or recording slight changes of condition. **5** *Photography* responding (esp. rapidly) to light. **6** (of topic etc.) requiring tact or secrecy. □ **sensitively** *noun*. **sensitiveness** *noun*. **sensitivity** /-'tɪv-/ *noun* (*plural* **-ies**).

■ **1** impressionable, perceptive, receptive, responsive, susceptible; (*sensitive to*) affected by, attuned to, aware of. **2** delicate, emotional, fragile, hypersensitive, susceptible, temperamental, tender, thin-skinned, touchy, volatile, vulnerable. **3** considerate, perceptive, receptive, responsive, sympathetic, tactful, thoughtful, understanding. **4** (*sensitive to*) affected by, attuned to, responsive to, susceptible to. **6** controversial, delicate, touchy, tricky.

sensitize /'sensɪtaɪz/ *verb* (also **-ise**) (**-zing** or **-sing**) make sensitive. □ **sensitization** *noun*.

sensor /'sensə/ *noun* device to detect or measure a physical property.

sensory /'sensərɪ/ *adjective* of sensation or senses.

sensual /'sensjʊəl/ *adjective* **1** of physical, esp. sexual, pleasure. **2** enjoying, giving, or showing this. □ **sensuality** /-'æl-/ *noun*. **sensually** *adverb*.

USAGE *Sensual* is sometimes confused with *sensuous*.

■ animal, bodily, carnal, fleshly, physical, pleasure-loving, self-indulgent, sexual, sexy, voluptuous, worldly.

sensuous /'sensjʊəs/ *adjective* of or affecting senses, esp. aesthetically. □ **sensuously** *adverb*. **sensuousness** *noun*.

USAGE *Sensuous* is sometimes confused with *sensual*.

■ beautiful, emotional, gratifying, luxurious, rich.

sent *past* & *past participle* of SEND.

sentence /'sent(ə)ns/ *noun* **1** grammatically complete series of words with (implied) subject and predicate (see panel). **2** punishment allotted to person convicted in criminal trial. **3** declaration of this. ● *verb* (**-cing**) **1** declare sentence of. **2** condemn.

■ *noun* **2, 3** decision, judgement, pronouncement, punishment, ruling. ● *verb* condemn, pass judgement on.

sententious /sen'tenʃəs/ *adjective* **1** pompously moralizing. **2** affectedly formal. **3** using maxims. □ **sententiousness** *noun*.

sentient /'senʃ(ə)nt/ *adjective* capable of perception and feeling. □ **sentience** *noun*. **sentiently** *adverb*.

sentiment /'sentɪmənt/ *noun* **1** mental feeling. **2** (often in *plural*) opinion. **3** emotional or irrational view(s). **4** tendency to be swayed by feeling. **5** mawkish tenderness.

■ **1** emotion, feeling, sensibility. **2** attitude, belief, idea, judgement, opinion, outlook, thought, view.

sentimental /sentɪ'ment(ə)l/ *adjective* **1** of or showing sentiment. **2** showing or affected by emotion rather than reason. □ **sentimentalism** *noun*. **sentimentalist** *noun*. **sentimentality** /-'tæl-/ *noun*. **sentimentalize** *verb* (also **-ise**) (**-zing** or **-sing**). **sentimentally** *adverb*.

■ compassionate, emotional, gushing, indulgent, maudlin, mawkish, mushy, nostalgic, overdone, over-emotional, romantic, sloppy, soft-hearted, *colloquial* soppy, sugary, sympathetic, tearful, tender, unrealistic, warm-hearted, *colloquial* weepy, *slang* yucky. □ **sentimentality** emotionalism, mawkishness, nostalgia, romanticism, slush.

sentinel /'sentɪn(ə)l/ *noun* sentry.

sentry /'sentrɪ/ *noun* (*plural* **-ies**) soldier etc. stationed to keep guard. □ **sentry box** cabin to shelter standing sentry.

■ guard, lookout, patrol, picket, sentinel, watch, watchman.

sepal /'sep(ə)l/ *noun* division or leaf of calyx.

separable /'sepərəb(ə)l/ *adjective* able to be separated. □ **separability** *noun*.

■ detachable, distinguishable, fissile, removable.

separate *adjective* /'sepərət/ forming unit by itself; existing apart; disconnected, distinct, individual. ● *noun* /'sepərət/ (in *plural*) articles of

---

Sentence

A sentence is the basic unit of language in use and expresses a complete thought. There are three types of sentence, each starting with a capital letter, and each normally ending with a full stop, a question mark, or an exclamation mark:

Statement: *You're happy.*
Question: *Is it raining?*
Exclamation: *I wouldn't have believed it!*

A sentence, especially a statement, often has no punctuation at the end in a public notice, a newspaper headline, or a legal document, e.g.

Government cuts public spending

A sentence normally contains a subject and a verb, but may not, e.g.

What a mess! *Where?* *In the sink.*

dress not parts of suits. ● *verb* /'sepəreɪt/ (**-ting**) **1** make separate, sever. **2** prevent union or contact of. **3** go different ways. **4** (esp. as **separated** *adjective*) cease to live with spouse. **5** secede. **6** divide or sort into parts or sizes. **7** (often + *out*) extract or remove (ingredient etc.). □ **separately** *adverb*. **separateness** *noun*. **separator** *noun*.

USAGE *Separate, separation,* etc. are not spelt with an *e* in the middle.

■ *adjective* apart, autonomous, cloistered, cut off, detached, different, discrete, distinct, divided, divorced, fenced off, free-standing, independent, individual, isolated, particular, peculiar, secluded, segregated, separated, shut off, solitary, unattached, unconnected, unique, unrelated, unshared, withdrawn. ● *verb* **1** break up, cut off, detach, disconnect, disengage, disentangle, dismember, dissociate, divide, fence off, fragment, hive off, isolate, keep apart, part, pull apart, segregate, sever, split, *literary* sunder, take apart, uncouple, unfasten, unhook, unravel, unyoke. **3** bifurcate, branch, diverge, fork. **4** become estranged, break up, divorce, part, part company, split up. **7** abstract, extract, filter out, remove, set apart, sift out, winnow.

separation /sepə'reɪʃ(ə)n/ *noun* **1** separating, being separated. **2** arrangement by which couple remain married but live apart.

■ **1** amputation, detachment, disconnection, dismemberment, dissociation, division, fission, fragmentation, parting, partition, rift, severance, split. **2** break, break-up, estrangement, rift, split.

separatist /'sepərətɪst/ *noun* person who favours separation, esp. political independence. □ **separatism** *noun*.

sepia /'si:pɪə/ *noun* **1** dark reddish-brown colour or paint. **2** brown tint used in photography.

sepoy /'si:pɔɪ/ *noun historical* Indian soldier under European, esp. British, discipline.

sepsis /'sepsɪs/ *noun* septic condition.

Sept. *abbreviation* September.

sept *noun* clan, esp. in Ireland.

September /sep'tembə/ *noun* ninth month of year.

septet /sep'tet/ *noun* **1** musical composition for 7 performers. **2** the performers. **3** any group of 7.

septic /'septɪk/ *adjective* contaminated with bacteria; putrefying. □ **septic tank** tank in which sewage is disintegrated through bacterial activity.

■ diseased, festering, infected, inflamed, poisoned, purulent, putrefying, putrid, suppurating.

septicaemia /septɪ'si:mɪə/ *noun* (*US* **septicemia**) blood poisoning.

septuagenarian /septjʊədʒɪ'neərɪən/ *noun* person between 70 and 79 years old.

Septuagesima /septjʊə'dʒesɪmə/ *noun* third Sunday before Lent.

Septuagint /'septjʊədʒɪnt/ *noun* ancient Greek version of Old Testament.

septum /'septəm/ *noun* (*plural* **septa**) partition such as that between nostrils.

sepulchral /sɪ'pʌlkr(ə)l/ *adjective* **1** of tomb or burial. **2** funereal, gloomy.

sepulchre /'sepəlkə/ (*US* **sepulcher**) *noun* tomb, burial cave or vault. ● *verb* (**-ring**) lay in sepulchre.

sequel /'si:kw(ə)l/ *noun* **1** what follows. **2** novel, film, etc. that continues story of earlier one.

■ **1** consequence, continuation, development, follow-up, issue, outcome, result, upshot. **2** continuation, follow-up.

sequence /'si:kwəns/ *noun* **1** succession. **2** order of succession. **3** set of things belonging next to one another; unbroken series. **4** episode or incident in film etc.

■ **1–3** arrangement, chain, concatenation, course, cycle, line, order, procession, programme, progression, range, row, run, series, set, string, succession, train. **4** clip, episode, excerpt, extract, scene, section.

sequential /sɪ'kwenʃ(ə)l/ *adjective* forming sequence or consequence. □ **sequentially** *adverb*.

sequester /sɪ'kwestə/ *verb* **1** (esp. as **sequestered** *adjective*) seclude, isolate. **2** sequestrate.

sequestrate /'si:kwɪstreɪt/ *verb* (**-ting**) **1** confiscate. **2** take temporary possession of (debtor's estate etc.). □ **sequestration** *noun*.

sequin /'si:kwɪn/ *noun* circular spangle on dress etc. □ **sequined**, **sequinned** *adjective*.

sequoia /sɪ'kwɔɪə/ *noun* extremely tall Californian conifer.

sera *plural* of SERUM.

seraglio /sə'rɑːlɪəʊ/ *noun* (*plural* **-s**) **1** harem. **2** *historical* Turkish palace.

seraph /'serəf/ *noun* (*plural* **-im** or **-s**) member of highest of 9 orders of angels. □ **seraphic** /sə'ræfɪk/ *adjective*.

Serb *noun* **1** native of Serbia. **2** person of Serbian descent. ● *adjective* Serbian.

Serbian /'sɜːbɪən/ *noun* **1** Slavonic dialect of Serbs. **2** Serb. ● *adjective* of Serbs or their dialect.

Serbo-Croat /sɜːbəʊ'krəʊæt/ (also **Serbo-Croatian** /-krəʊ'eɪʃ(ə)n/) *noun* main official language of former Yugoslavia, combining Serbian and Croatian dialects. ● *adjective* of this language.

serenade /serə'neɪd/ *noun* **1** piece of music performed at night, esp. under lover's window. **2** orchestral suite for small ensemble. ● *verb* (**-ding**) perform serenade to.

serendipity /serən'dɪpɪtɪ/ *noun* faculty of making happy discoveries by accident. □ **serendipitous** *adjective*.

serene /sɪ'riːn/ *adjective* (**-r**, **-st**) **1** clear and calm. **2** placid, unperturbed. □ **serenely** *adverb*. **serenity** /-'ren-/ *noun*.

■ **1** calm, idyllic, peaceful, placid, pleasing, quiet, restful, still, tranquil, unclouded, unruffled. **2** collected, composed, contented, cool, easygoing, equable, even-tempered, imperturbable, pacific, peaceable, peaceful, placid, poised, self-possessed, undisturbed, *colloquial* unflappable, unperturbed, unruffled, untroubled.

serf *noun* **1** *historical* labourer not allowed to leave the land on which he worked. **2** oppressed person; drudge. □ **serfdom** *noun*.

serge *noun* durable woollen fabric.

sergeant /'sɑːdʒ(ə)nt/ *noun* **1** non-commissioned army or RAF officer next below warrant officer. **2** police officer next below inspector. □ **sergeant major** warrant officer assisting adjutant of regiment or battalion.

serial /'sɪərɪəl/ *noun* story published, broadcast, or shown in instalments. ● *adjective* of, in, or forming series. □ **serial killer** person who murders repeatedly. □ **serially** *adverb*.

serialize *verb* (also **-ise**) (**-zing** or **-sing**) publish or produce in instalments. □ **serialization** *noun*.

series /'sɪəriːz/ *noun* (*plural* same) **1** number of similar or related things, events, etc.; succession, row, set. **2** *Broadcasting* set of related but individually complete programmes. □ **in series 1** in ordered succession. **2** (of set of electrical circuits) arranged so that same current passes through each circuit.

■ **1** arrangement, chain, concatenation, course, cycle, line, order, procession, programme, progression, range, row, run, sequence, set, string, succession, train.

serif /'serɪf/ *noun* fine cross-line at extremities of printed letter.

serious /'sɪərɪəs/ *adjective* **1** thoughtful, earnest. **2** important; requiring thought. **3** not negligible; dangerous. **4** sincere, in earnest. **5** (of music, literature, etc.) intellectual, not popular. □ **seriously** *adverb*. **seriousness** *noun*.

■ **1** careful, committed, conscientious, determined, diligent, earnest, grave, grim, hard-working, humourless, long-faced, pensive, poker-faced, sedate, sober, solemn, sombre, staid, stern, straight-faced, thoughtful, unsmiling. **2** deep, heavy, important, intellectual, momentous, profound, significant, weighty. **3** acute, calamitous, critical, crucial, dangerous, grave, grievous, life-threatening, nasty, severe, urgent, vital. **4** genuine, honest, in earnest, sincere.

serjeant /'sɑːdʒ(ə)nt/ *noun* (in full **serjeant-at-law**, *plural* **serjeants-at-law**) *historical* barrister of highest rank. □ **serjeant-at-arms** official of court, city, or parliament, with ceremonial duties.

sermon /'sɜːmən/ *noun* **1** discourse on religion or morals, esp. delivered in church. **2** admonition, reproof.

■ **1** address, discourse, homily, lecture, lesson, talk.

sermonize *verb* (also **-ise**) (**-zing** or **-sing**) (often + *to*) moralize.

serous /'sɪərəs/ *adjective* **1** of or like serum; watery. **2** (of gland etc.) having serous secretion.

serpent /'sɜːpənt/ *noun* **1** snake, esp. large. **2** cunning or treacherous person.

serpentine /'sɜːpəntaɪn/ *adjective* **1** of or like serpent. **2** coiling, sinuous. **3** cunning, treacherous. ● *noun* soft usually dark green rock, sometimes mottled.

■ *adjective* **2** coiling, labyrinthine, meandering, roundabout, sinuous, snaking, tortuous, twisting, winding.

SERPS *abbreviation* State Earnings-Related Pension Scheme.

serrated /sə'reɪtɪd/ *adjective* with sawlike edge. □ **serration** *noun*.

■ cogged, crenellated, indented, jagged, notched, sawlike, toothed, zigzag.

serried /'serɪd/ *adjective* (of ranks of soldiers etc.) close together.

serum /'sɪərəm/ *noun* (*plural* **sera** or **-s**) **1** liquid separating from clot when blood coagulates, esp. used for inoculation. **2** watery fluid in animal bodies.

servant /'sɜːv(ə)nt/ *noun* **1** person employed for domestic work. **2** devoted follower or helper.

■ **1** assistant, attendant, *colloquial* dogsbody, domestic, drudge, factotum, *usually derogatory* flunkey, *colloquial* help, helper, *usually derogatory* hireling, lackey, maid, maidservant, manservant, menial, *derogatory* minion, retainer, *colloquial derogatory* skivvy, slave, valet, *historical* vassal; (*servants*) retinue.

serve *verb* (**-ving**) **1** do service for. **2** be servant to. **3** carry out duty. **4** (+ *in*) be employed in (esp. armed forces). **5** be useful to or serviceable for. **6** meet needs; perform function. **7** go through due period of (apprenticeship, prison sentence, etc.). **8** go through (specified period) of imprisonment etc. **9** (often + *up*) present (food) to eat. **10** act as waiter. **11** attend to (customer etc.). **12** (+ *with*) supply with (goods). **13** treat (person) in specified way. **14** *Law* (often + *on*) deliver (writ etc.). **15** *Law* (+ *with*) deliver writ etc. to. **16** set (ball) in play at tennis etc. **17** (of male animal) copulate with (female). ● *noun Tennis etc.* service. □ **serve (person) right** be his or her deserved misfortune. □ **server** *noun*.

■ *verb* **1, 2** aid, assist, attend, be at (person's) beck and call, help, look after, minister to, wait upon, work for. **3** officiate. **4** (*serve in*) be employed in, fight in, work in. **5, 6** answer, do, satisfy, suffice. **7, 8** complete, endure, go through, pass, spend, survive. **9** deal out, dish up, distribute, dole out, give out, present. **10** wait. **11** assist, attend to, help, look after, wait on. **12** (*serve with*) make available, provide, sell, supply.

service /'sɜːvɪs/ *noun* **1** (often in *plural*) work done or doing of work for employer or for community etc. **2** work done by machine etc. **3** assistance or benefit given. **4** provision of some public need, e.g. transport or (often in *plural*) water, gas, etc. **5** employment as servant. **6** state or period of employment. **7** Crown or public department or organization. **8** (in *plural*) the armed forces. **9** ceremony of worship. **10** liturgical form for this. **11** (routine) maintenance and repair of machine etc. after sale. **12** assistance given to customers. **13** serving of food etc. **14** quality of this. **15** nominal charge for this. **16** (in *plural*) motorway service area. **17** set of dishes etc. for serving meal. **18** act of serving in tennis etc. **19** person's turn to serve. **20** game in which one serves. ● *verb* (**-cing**) **1** maintain or repair (car, machine, etc.). **2** provide service for. □ **at (person's) service** ready to serve him or her. **of service** useful. **service area** area near road supplying petrol, refreshments, etc. **service charge** additional charge for service in restaurant etc. **service flat** one in which domestic service etc. is provided. **service industry** one providing services, not goods. **serviceman, servicewoman** person in armed services. **service road** one giving access to houses etc. lying back from main road. **service station** establishment selling petrol etc. to motorists.

■ *noun* **1** employment, labour, ministering, ministry, work. **3** aid, assistance, benefit, care, favour, help, kindness, support. **4** supply, system, utility. **5, 6** employ, employment, labour, work. **7** department, organization. **9, 10** ceremony, liturgy, meeting, rite, ritual, worship. **11** checking, maintenance, overhaul, repair, servicing. **12** advice, assistance, attention, care, help. ● *verb* **1** check, maintain, mend, overhaul, repair, tune.

serviceable *adjective* **1** useful, usable. **2** durable but plain. □ **serviceability** *noun*.

■ **1** functional, practical, usable, useful. **2** dependable, durable, hard-wearing, lasting, strong, tough.

serviette /sɜ:vɪˈet/ *noun* table napkin.

servile /ˈsɜ:vaɪl/ *adjective* **1** of or like slave(s). **2** fawning, subservient. □ **servility** /-ˈvɪl-/ *noun*.

■ **2** abject, acquiescent, craven, cringing, deferential, fawning, flattering, grovelling, humble, ingratiating, low, menial, obsequious, slavish, submissive, subservient, sycophantic, toadying, unctuous.

serving *noun* helping of food.

■ helping, plateful, portion, ration.

servitude /ˈsɜ:vɪtju:d/ *noun* slavery, subjection.

servo- /ˈsɜ:vəʊ/ *combining form* power-assisted.

sesame /ˈsesəmɪ/ *noun* **1** E. Indian plant with oil-yielding seeds. **2** its seeds.

sesqui- /ˈseskwɪ/ *combining form* one and a half.

sessile /ˈsesaɪl/ *adjective* **1** *Biology* attached directly by base without stalk or peduncle. **2** fixed, immobile.

session /ˈseʃ(ə)n/ *noun* **1** period devoted to an activity. **2** assembly of parliament, court, etc. **3** single meeting for this. **4** period during which such meetings are regularly held. **5** academic year. □ **in session** assembled for business, not on vacation. □ **sessional** *adjective*.

■ **1** period, term, time. **2, 3** assembly, conference, discussion, hearing, meeting, sitting.

set *verb* (**-tt-**; *past & past participle* **set**) **1** put, lay, or stand in certain position etc. **2** apply. **3** fix or place ready; dispose suitably for use, action, or display. **4** adjust hands or mechanism of (clock, trap, etc.). **5** insert (jewel) in ring etc. **6** lay (table) for meal. **7** style (hair) while damp. **8** (+ *with*) ornament or provide (surface) with. **9** bring into specified state; cause to be. **10** harden, solidify. **11** (of sun, moon, etc.) move towards or below earth's horizon. **12** show (story etc.) as happening in a certain time or place. **13** (+ *to do*) cause (person) to do specified thing. **14** (+ *present participle*) start (person, thing) doing something. **15** present or impose as work to be done, problem to be solved, etc. **16** exhibit as model etc. **17** initiate (fashion etc.). **18** establish (record etc.). **19** determine, decide. **20** appoint, establish. **21** put parts of (broken or dislocated bone, limb, etc.) together for healing. **22** provide (song, words) with music. **23** arrange (type) or type for (book etc.). **24** (of tide, current, etc.) have a certain motion or direction. **25** (of face) assume hard expression. **26** (of eyes etc.) become motionless. **27** have a certain tendency. **28** (of blossom) form into fruit. **29** (of dancer) take position facing partner. **30** (of hunting dog) take rigid attitude indicating presence of game. ● *noun* **1** group of linked or similar things or persons. **2** section of society. **3** collection of objects for specified purpose. **4** radio or television receiver. **5** *Tennis etc.* group of games counting as unit towards winning match. **6** *Mathematics* collection of things sharing a property. **7** direction or position in which something sets or is set. **8** slip, shoot, bulb, etc. for planting. **9** setting, stage furniture, etc. for play, film, etc. **10** setting of sun, hair, etc. **11** = SETT. ● *adjective* **1** prescribed or determined in advance. **2** unchanging, fixed. **3** prepared for action. **4** (+ *on, upon*) determined to get, achieve, etc. □ **set about 1** begin; take steps towards. **2** *colloquial* attack. **set aside 1** put to one side. **2** keep for future. **3** disregard or reject. **set back 1** place further back in space or time. **2** impede or reverse progress of. **3** *colloquial* cost (person) specified amount. **setback** reversal or arrest of progress. **set down 1** record in writing. **2** allow to alight. **set forth 1** begin journey. **2** expound. **set free** release. **set in 1** begin; become established. **2** insert. **set off 1** begin journey. **2** detonate (bomb etc.). **3** initiate, stimulate. **4** cause (person) to start laughing etc. **5** adorn, enhance. **6** (+ *against*) use as compensating item against. **set on** (cause or urge to) attack. **set one's heart on** want eagerly. **set one's sights on** aim at. **set out 1** begin journey. **2** exhibit, arrange. **3** (+ *to do*) intend to. **set piece** formal or elaborate arrangement, esp. in art or literature. **set sail 1** hoist sails. **2** begin voyage. **set square** right-angled triangular plate for drawing lines at certain angles. **set theory** study or use of sets in mathematics. **set to** begin doing something vigorously. **set-to** *noun* (*plural* **-tos**) *colloquial* fight, argument. **set up 1** place in position or view. **2** start; establish. **3** equip, prepare. **4** *collo-*

quial cause (person) to look guilty or foolish.
set-up *noun* **1** arrangement or organization. **2** manner or structure of this. **3** instance of setting person up. **set upon** set on.

■ *verb* **1, 3** arrange, assign, deploy, deposit, dispose, lay, leave, locate, lodge, park, place, plant, plonk, put, position, rest, set down, set out, settle, situate, stand, station. **4** adjust, correct, put right, rectify, regulate. **5** embed, fasten, fix. **10** congeal, firm, gel, harden, *colloquial* jell, stiffen, take shape. **15** ask, express, formulate, frame, phrase, pose, present, put, put forward, suggest, write. **19, 20** allocate, allot, appoint, decide, designate, determine, establish, identify, name, ordain, prescribe, settle. ● *noun* **1, 3** batch, bunch, category, class, clique, collection, combination, group, kind, series, sort. **4** apparatus, receiver. **9** scene, scenery, setting. ● *adjective* **1** advertised, agreed, arranged, defined, definite, fixed, pre-arranged, predetermined, prepared, scheduled, standard. **2** established, fixed, invariable, predictable, regular, stable, unchanging, unvarying. **3** fit, prepared, ready.
□ **set about 1** see BEGIN 1. **2** see ATTACK *verb* 1.
setback blow, check, complication, defeat, delay, difficulty, disappointment, hindrance, hitch, hold-up, impediment, misfortune, obstacle, problem, relapse, reverse, snag, upset. **set free** see LIBERATE 1. **set off 1** see DEPART 1,2. **2** see EXPLODE 1,2. **set on** see ATTACK *verb* 1. **set out 1** see DEPART 1,2. **set up 2** see ESTABLISH 1.

sett *noun* (also **set**) **1** badger's burrow. **2** paving-block.

settee /se'ti:/ *noun* sofa.
■ chaise longue, couch, sofa.

setter *noun* dog of long-haired breed trained to stand rigid on scenting game.

setting *noun* **1** position or manner in which thing is set. **2** surroundings. **3** period, place, etc. of story, film, etc. **4** frame etc. for jewel. **5** music to which words are set. **6** cutlery etc. for one person at table. **7** operating level of machine.
■ **1, 2** background, context, environment, environs, frame, habitat, locale, location, place, position, site, surroundings. **3** background, context, set.

settle¹ /'set(ə)l/ *verb* (**-ling**) **1** (often + *down*, *in*) establish or become established in abode or lifestyle. **2** (often + *down*) regain calm after disturbance. **3** (often + *down*) adopt regular or secure way of life. **4** (often + *down to*) apply oneself to. **5** (cause to) sit down or come to rest. **6** place (thing) in position. **7** make or become composed, etc. **8** arrange, deal with; make orderly. **9** determine, decide, agree on. **10** resolve (dispute etc.). **11** agree to terminate (lawsuit). **12** (+ *for*) accept or agree to. **13** pay (bill); discharge (debt). **14** (as **settled** *adjective*) established. **15** colonize. **16** subside, sink; (cause to) compact. □ **settle up** pay money owed etc.
■ **1** become established, make one's home, set up home, stay. **5** alight, come to rest, land, make oneself comfortable, *colloquial* park oneself,

pause, rest, roost, sit down. **6** deploy, deposit, dispose, lay, locate, lodge, park, place, plant, position, put, rest, set, set down, situate, stand, station. **7** see CALM *verb*. **8** arrange, conclude, deal with, decide, organize, put in order, straighten out. **9** agree, choose, decide, determine, establish, fix. **10** end, put an end to, reconcile, resolve, sort out. **13** clear, discharge, pay, pay off, square. **15** colonize, occupy, people, populate. **16** compact, fall, go down, sink, subside.

settle² /'set(ə)l/ *noun* high-backed bench, often with box under seat.

settlement *noun* **1** settling, being settled. **2** place occupied by settlers. **3** small village. **4** political etc. agreement. **5** arrangement ending dispute. **6** terms on which property is given to person. **7** deed stating these. **8** amount or property given. **9** payment of account.
■ **2, 3** camp, colony, community, encampment, kibbutz, outpost, post, town, village. **4, 5** agreement, arbitration, arrangement, contract.

settler *noun* person who settles in newly developed region.
■ colonist, frontiersman, immigrant, newcomer, pioneer.

seven /'sev(ə)n/ *adjective & noun* one more than six. □ **seventh** *adjective & noun*.

seventeen /sevən'ti:n/ *adjective & noun* one more than sixteen. □ **seventeenth** *adjective & noun*.

seventy /'sevəntɪ/ *adjective & noun* (*plural* **-ies**) seven times ten. □ **seventieth** *adjective & noun*.

sever /'sevə/ *verb* **1** divide, break, or make separate, esp. by cutting. **2** end (contract, relationship, etc.).
■ **1** amputate, break, cut, cut off, detach, disconnect, part, remove, separate, split. **2** abandon, break off, discontinue, end, put an end to, suspend, terminate.

several /'sevr(ə)l/ *adjective* **1** a few; quite a large number. **2** *formal* separate, respective. ● *pronoun* a few; quite a large number. □ **severally** *adverb*.
■ *adjective* **1** assorted, certain, different, *archaic* divers, a few, a handful of, many, miscellaneous, a number of, some, sundry, a variety of, various.

severance /'sevr(ə)ns/ *noun* **1** severing. **2** severed state. □ **severance pay** payment to employee on termination of contract.

severe /sɪ'vɪə/ *adjective* **1** rigorous and harsh. **2** not negligible; worrying. **3** forceful. **4** extreme. **5** exacting. **6** unadorned. □ **severely** *adverb*. **severity** /-'ver-/ *noun*.
■ **1** aloof, brutal, cold, cold-hearted, cruel, disapproving, dour, Draconian, forbidding, glowering, grave, grim, hard, harsh, inexorable, merciless, obdurate, oppressive, pitiless, punitive, relentless, rigorous, stern, stony, strict, stringent, unbending, uncompromising, unkind, unsmiling, unsympathetic, unyielding. **2** acute, critical, dangerous, drastic, fatal, great, intense, keen, life-threatening, mortal, nasty, serious, sharp,

terminal, troublesome. **3, 4** adverse, bad, cold, extreme, fierce, inclement, stormy, violent, *colloquial* wicked. **5** arduous, demanding, difficult, exacting, onerous, punishing, taxing, tough. **6** austere, bare, chaste, plain, simple, Spartan, stark, unadorned.

sew /səʊ/ *verb* (*past participle* **sewn** or **sewed**) fasten, join, etc. with needle and thread or sewing machine. □ **sewing machine** machine for sewing or stitching.
  ■ baste, darn, hem, mend, repair, stitch, tack.

sewage /'suːɪdʒ/ *noun* waste matter carried in sewers. □ **sewage farm, works** place where sewage is treated.
  ■ effluent, waste.

sewer /'suːə/ *noun* (usually underground) conduit for carrying off drainage water and waste matter.
  ■ see DRAIN *noun* 1.

sewerage /'suːərɪdʒ/ *noun* system of or drainage by sewers.

sewing /'səʊɪŋ/ *noun* material or work to be sewn.
  ■ dressmaking, embroidery, mending, needlework, stitching.

sewn *past participle* of SEW.

sex *noun* **1** group of males or females collectively. **2** fact of belonging to either group. **3** sexual instincts, desires, activity, etc. **4** *colloquial* sexual intercourse. ● *adjective* of or relating to sex or sexual differences. ● *verb* **1** determine sex of. **2** (as **sexed** *adjective*) having specified sexual appetite. □ **sex appeal** sexual attractiveness. **sex life** person's sexual activity. **sex symbol** person famed for sex appeal.
  ■ *noun* **1, 2** gender, sexuality. **4** carnal knowledge, coition, coitus, consummation of marriage, copulation, coupling, *usually jocular* fornication, intercourse, intimacy, lovemaking, mating, sexual intercourse, sexual relations, union.

sexagenarian /seksədʒɪ'neərɪən/ *noun* person between 60 and 69 years old.

Sexagesima /seksə'dʒesɪmə/ *noun* second Sunday before Lent.

sexism *noun* prejudice or discrimination against people (esp. women) because of their sex. □ **sexist** *adjective & noun*.
  ■ chauvinism, male chauvinism, sexual discrimination.

sexless *adjective* **1** neither male nor female. **2** lacking sexual desire or attractiveness.

sextant /'sekst(ə)nt/ *noun* optical instrument for measuring angle between distant objects, esp. sun and horizon in navigation.

sextet /seks'tet/ *noun* **1** musical composition for 6 performers. **2** the performers. **3** any group of 6.

sexton /'sekst(ə)n/ *noun* person who looks after church and churchyard, often acting as bell-ringer and gravedigger.

sextuple /'sekstjuːp(ə)l/ *adjective* sixfold.

sextuplet /'sekstjʊplɪt/ *noun* each of 6 children born at one birth.

sexual /'sekʃʊəl/ *adjective* of sex, the sexes, or relations between them. □ **sexual intercourse** insertion of man's penis into woman's vagina. □ **sexually** *adverb*.
  ■ carnal, erotic, genital, procreative, reproductive, sexy, venereal.

sexuality /sekʃʊ'ælɪtɪ/ *noun* **1** fact of belonging to one of sexes. **2** sexual characteristics, impulses, etc.
  ■ **1** gender, sex.

sexy *adjective* (**-ier, -iest**) **1** sexually attractive or provocative. **2** sexually aroused. **3** concerned with sex. **4** *colloquial* (of project etc.) exciting. □ **sexily** *adverb*. **sexiness** *noun*.
  ■ **1** aphrodisiac, arousing, attractive, desirable, *colloquial* dishy, erotic, flirtatious, pornographic, provocative, *colloquial* raunchy, salacious, seductive, sensual, sexual, *colloquial* steamy, suggestive, sultry, titillating, torrid, voluptuous. **2** amorous, *formal* concupiscent, lascivious, lecherous, lewd, libidinous, lubricious, lustful, passionate, prurient, randy, salacious.

SF *abbreviation* science fiction.

Sgt. *abbreviation* Sergeant.

sh *interjection* hush.

shabby /'ʃæbɪ/ *adjective* (**-ier, -iest**) **1** faded and worn, dingy, dilapidated. **2** poorly dressed. **3** contemptible. □ **shabbily** *adverb*. **shabbiness** *noun*.
  ■ **1, 2** bedraggled, dilapidated, dingy, dirty, disreputable, dowdy, drab, faded, frayed, grubby, mangy, moth-eaten, ragged, run-down, *colloquial* scruffy, seedy, tattered, *colloquial* tatty, threadbare, unattractive, worn, worn out. **3** base, contemptible, despicable, disagreeable, discreditable, dishonest, dishonourable, disreputable, ignoble, low-down, mean, nasty, shameful, shoddy, unfair, unfriendly, ungenerous, unkind, unworthy.

shack *noun* roughly built hut or cabin. ● *verb* (+ *up*) *slang* cohabit.
  ■ *noun* cabin, hovel, hut, lean-to, shanty, shed.

shackle /'ʃæk(ə)l/ *noun* **1** metal loop or link closed by bolt; coupling link. **2** fetter. **3** (usually in *plural*) restraint. ● *verb* (**-ling**) fetter, impede, restrain.

shad *noun* (*plural* same or **-s**) large edible marine fish.

shade *noun* **1** comparative darkness caused by shelter from direct light and heat. **2** area so sheltered. **3** darker part of picture etc. **4** a colour, esp. as darker or lighter than one similar. **5** comparative obscurity. **6** slight amount. **7** lampshade. **8** screen moderating light. **9** (in *plural*) *esp. US colloquial* sunglasses. **10** *literary* ghost. **11** slightly different variety. **12** (in *plural*; + *of*) reminder of. ● *verb* (**-ding**) **1** screen from light. **2** cover or moderate light of. **3** darken, esp. with parallel lines to represent shadow etc. **4** (often +

away, off, into) pass or change gradually. ▫ **put in the shade** appear or be very superior to. ▫ **shading** *noun*.

■ *noun* **1, 2, 5** see SHADOW *noun* 1. **4** colour, hue, intensity, tinge, tint, tone. **8** awning, blind, canopy, covering, curtain, parasol, screen, shelter, shield, umbrella. **11** degree, difference, nuance, variation. ● *verb* **1, 2** camouflage, conceal, cover, hide, mask, obscure, protect, screen, shield, shroud, veil. **3** cross-hatch, darken, fill in, hatch.

shadow /ˈʃædəʊ/ *noun* **1** shade; patch of shade. **2** dark shape projected by body blocking out light. **3** inseparable attendant or companion. **4** person secretly following another. **5** (with negative) slightest trace. **6** insubstantial remnant. **7** shaded part of picture. **8** gloom, sadness. ● *verb* **1** cast shadow over. **2** secretly follow and watch. ▫ **shadow-boxing** boxing against imaginary opponent. **Shadow Cabinet, Minister, etc.** members of opposition party holding posts parallel to those of government.

■ *noun* **1** darkness, dimness, dusk, gloom, obscurity, penumbra, semi-darkness, shade, umbra. **2** outline, shape, silhouette. **5** see HINT *noun* 3. ● *verb* **2** dog, follow, hunt, *colloquial* keep tabs on, keep watch on, pursue, stalk, *colloquial* tail, track, trail, watch.

shadowy *adjective* **1** vague, obscure. **2** giving shade; full of shadows. **3** ghostly.

■ **1** dark, dim, faint, hazy, ill-defined, indefinite, indistinct, nebulous, obscure, unclear, unrecognizable, vague. **2** see SHADY 1. **3** see GHOSTLY (GHOST).

shady /ˈʃeɪdɪ/ *adjective* (**-ier, -iest**) **1** giving or situated in shade. **2** disreputable; of doubtful honesty.

■ **1** cool, dark, dim, gloomy, leafy, shaded, shadowy, sheltered, sunless. **2** devious, dishonest, disreputable, dubious, *slang* fishy, questionable, *colloquial* shifty, suspicious, unreliable, untrustworthy.

shaft /ʃɑːft/ *noun* **1** narrow usually vertical space for access to mine or (in building) for lift, ventilation, etc. **2** (+ *of*) ray of (light). **3** (+ *of*) stroke of (lightning). **4** handle of tool etc. **5** long narrow part supporting, connecting, or driving thicker part(s) etc. **6** *archaic* arrow, spear. **7** *archaic* its long slender stem. **8** hurtful or provocative remark. **9** each of pair of poles between which horse is harnessed to vehicle. **10** central stem of feather. **11** column, esp. between base and capital.

■ **1** duct, pit, tunnel, well. **2** beam, gleam, ray, streak. **4, 5** column, handle, pillar, pole, post, rod, shank, stanchion, stem, stick, upright.

shag *noun* **1** coarse tobacco. **2** rough mass of hair. **3** (crested) cormorant. ● *adjective* (of carpet) with long rough pile.

shaggy *adjective* (**-ier, -iest**) **1** hairy, rough-haired. **2** tangled. ▫ **shaggy-dog story** lengthy 'joke' without funny ending. ▫ **shagginess** *noun*.

■ bushy, dishevelled, fleecy, hairy, hirsute, matted, rough, tangled, tousled, unkempt, unshorn, untidy, woolly.

shagreen /ʃæˈɡriːn/ *noun* **1** kind of untanned granulated leather. **2** sharkskin.

shah /ʃɑː/ *noun historical* ruler of Iran.

shake *verb* (**-king**; *past* **shook** /ʃʊk/; *past participle* **shaken**) **1** move violently or quickly up and down or to and fro. **2** (cause to) tremble or vibrate. **3** agitate, shock, disturb. **4** weaken, impair. **5** *colloquial* shake hands. ● *noun* **1** shaking, being shaken. **2** jerk, shock. **3** (**the shakes**) *colloquial* fit of trembling. ▫ **shake down 1** settle or cause to fall by shaking. **2** become comfortably settled or established. **shake hands** (often + *with*) clasp hands, esp. at meeting or parting or as sign of bargain. **shake off 1** get rid of. **2** evade. **shake up 1** mix (ingredients) or restore to shape by shaking. **2** disturb or make uncomfortable. **3** rouse from lethargy etc. **shake-up** *noun* upheaval; reorganization.

■ *verb* **1** brandish, flourish, gyrate, jar, jerk, jiggle, joggle, jolt, oscillate, sway, swing, twirl, twitch, vibrate, wag, *colloquial* waggle, wave, *colloquial* wiggle. **2** convulse, heave, quake, quiver, rattle, rock, shiver, shudder, sway, throb, totter, tremble, vibrate, waver, wobble. **3** agitate, alarm, distress, disturb, frighten, perturb, *colloquial* rattle, shock, startle, surprise, *colloquial* throw, unnerve, unsettle, upset.

shaker *noun* **1** person or thing that shakes. **2** container for shaking together ingredients of cocktails etc.

Shakespearian /ʃeɪkˈspɪərɪən/ *adjective* (also **Shakespearean**) of Shakespeare.

shako /ˈʃækəʊ/ *noun* (*plural* **-s**) cylindrical plumed military peaked cap.

shaky *adjective* (**-ier, -iest**) **1** unsteady, trembling. **2** infirm, weak. **3** unreliable. ▫ **shakily** *adverb*. **shakiness** *noun*.

■ **1** faltering, quavering, quivering, rickety, *colloquial* rocky, shaking, trembling, tremulous, unsteady, wobbly. **2** decrepit, dilapidated, feeble, flimsy, frail, infirm, insecure, precarious, ramshackle, unsound, weak. **3** nervous, tentative, uncertain, underconfident, unpromising, unreliable, unsound.

shale *noun* soft rock that splits easily. ▫ **shaly** *adjective*.

shall *auxiliary verb* (*3rd singular present* **shall**) used to form future tenses.

shallot /ʃəˈlɒt/ *noun* onion-like plant with cluster of small bulbs.

shallow /ˈʃæləʊ/ *adjective* **1** of little depth. **2** superficial, trivial. ● *noun* (often in *plural*) shallow place. ▫ **shallowness** *noun*.

■ **2** empty, facile, foolish, frivolous, glib, insincere, puerile, silly, simple, skin-deep, slight, superficial, trivial, unconvincing, unscholarly, unthinking.

sham *verb* (**-mm-**) feign; pretend (to be). ● *noun* **1** imposture, pretence. **2** bogus or false person or thing. ● *adjective* pretended, counterfeit.

■ *verb* counterfeit, fake, feign, imitate, make believe, pretend, simulate. ● *noun* counterfeit, fake, fiction, fraud, hoax, imitation, make-believe, pretence, put-up job, simulation. ● *adjective* artificial, bogus, counterfeit, ersatz, fake, false, fictitious, fraudulent, imitation, make-believe, mock, *colloquial* pretend, pretended, simulated, synthetic.

shamble /ˈʃæmb(ə)l/ *verb* (**-ling**) walk or run awkwardly, dragging feet. ● *noun* shambling gait.

shambles *plural noun* (usually treated as *singular*) **1** *colloquial* mess, muddle. **2** butcher's slaughterhouse. **3** scene of carnage.

■ **1** chaos, confusion, devastation, disorder, mess, muddle, *colloquial* tip.

shambolic /ʃæmˈbɒlɪk/ *adjective colloquial* chaotic, disorganized.

shame *noun* **1** humiliation caused by consciousness of guilt or folly. **2** capacity for feeling this. **3** state of disgrace or discredit. **4** person or thing that brings disgrace etc. **5** wrong or regrettable thing. ● *verb* (**-ming**) **1** bring disgrace on; make ashamed. **2** (+ *into*, *out of*) force by shame into or out of.

■ *noun* **1** chagrin, distress, embarrassment, guilt, humiliation, loss of face, mortification, remorse. **3** degradation, discredit, disgrace, dishonour, ignominy, infamy, obloquy, opprobrium, vilification. **5** outrage, pity, scandal, wickedness. ● *verb* **1** abash, chagrin, chasten, discomfit, disconcert, discountenance, disgrace, embarrass, humble, humiliate, mortify, show (person) up.

shamefaced *adjective* **1** showing shame. **2** bashful.

■ **1** abashed, ashamed, chagrined, hangdog, humiliated, mortified, penitent, red-faced, remorseful, repentant, sorry. **2** bashful, coy, embarrassed, modest, self-conscious, sheepish, shy, timid.

shameful *adjective* disgraceful, scandalous. □ **shamefully** *adverb*. **shamefulness** *noun*.

■ base, compromising, contemptible, degrading, demeaning, deplorable, discreditable, disgraceful, dishonourable, embarrassing, humiliating, ignoble, ignominious, infamous, *colloquial* infra dig, inglorious, low, lowering, mean, mortifying, outrageous, reprehensible, scandalous, undignified, unworthy, wicked.

shameless *adjective* **1** having or showing no shame. **2** impudent. □ **shamelessly** *adverb*. **shamelessness** *noun*.

■ barefaced, bold, brazen, cheeky, cool, defiant, flagrant, hardened, immodest, impenitent, improper, impudent, incorrigible, indecorous, insolent, rude, shocking, unabashed, unashamed, unblushing, unconcealed, undisguised, unrepentant, unselfconscious.

shammy /ˈʃæmɪ/ *noun* (*plural* **-ies**) *colloquial* chamois leather.

shampoo /ʃæmˈpuː/ *noun* **1** liquid for washing hair. **2** similar substance for washing cars, carpets, etc. ● *verb* (**-poos**, **-pooed**) wash with shampoo.

shamrock /ˈʃæmrɒk/ *noun* trefoil, as national emblem of Ireland.

shandy /ˈʃændɪ/ *noun* (*plural* **-ies**) beer with lemonade or ginger beer.

shanghai /ʃæŋˈhaɪ/ *verb* (**-hais**, **-haied**, **-haiing**) *colloquial* trick or force (person) to do something, esp. be sailor.

shank *noun* **1** leg. **2** lower part of leg. **3** shaft or stem, esp. joining tool's handle to its working end.

shan't /ʃɑːnt/ shall not.

shantung /ʃænˈtʌŋ/ *noun* soft undressed Chinese silk.

shanty[1] /ˈʃæntɪ/ *noun* (*plural* **-ies**) hut, cabin. □ **shanty town** area with makeshift housing.

shanty[2] /ˈʃæntɪ/ *noun* (*plural* **-ies**) (in full **sea shanty**) sailors' work song.

shape *noun* **1** outline. **2** form. **3** specific form or guise. **4** good or specified condition. **5** person or thing seen indistinctly. **6** mould, pattern. ● *verb* (**-ping**) **1** give a certain form to; fashion, create. **2** influence. **3** (usually + *up*) show promise. **4** adapt. **5** (+ *to*) make conform to. □ **take shape** assume distinct form; develop. □ **shapable** *adjective* (also **shapeable**).

■ *noun* **1**, **2** body, build, configuration, contour, figure, form, outline, physique, profile, silhouette. **6** form, model, mould, pattern. ● *verb* **1** carve, cast, cut, fashion, form, model, mould, sculpt, sculpture, whittle. **4** adapt, adjust, fit, modify, tailor.

shapeless *adjective* lacking definite or attractive shape. □ **shapelessness** *noun*.

■ amorphous, deformed, distorted, formless, indeterminate, irregular, misshapen, nebulous, twisted, undefined, unformed, unshapely, unstructured, vague.

shapely *adjective* (**-ier**, **-iest**) **1** of pleasing shape. **2** well proportioned. □ **shapeliness** *noun*.

■ attractive, *literary* comely, *colloquial* curvaceous, elegant, good-looking, graceful, neat, trim, voluptuous, well proportioned.

shard *noun* broken fragment of pottery, glass, etc.

share /ʃeə/ *noun* **1** portion of whole given to or taken from person. **2** each of equal parts into which company's capital is divided, entitling owner to proportion of profits. ● *verb* (**-ring**) **1** get, have, or give share of. **2** (often + *out*) divide and distribute. **3** (+ *in*) participate in. **4** (often as **shared** *adjective*) have or use with another or others. □ **shareholder** owner of shares in a company. **share-out** division and distribution.

■ *noun* **1** allocation, allotment, allowance, bit, cut, division, due, fraction, helping, part, percentage, piece, portion, proportion, quota, ration, serving, *slang* whack. ● *verb* **1**, **2** allocate, allot, apportion, deal out, distribute, divide, dole out, partake of, portion out, ration out, split. **3** (*share in*) be involved in, cooperate in, join in, participate in, take part in. **4 (shared)** see JOINT *adjective*.

shark *noun* **1** large voracious sea fish. **2** *colloquial* swindler, extortioner. □ **sharkskin 1** skin of shark. **2** smooth slightly shiny fabric.

sharp *adjective* **1** having edge or point able to cut or pierce. **2** tapering to a point or edge. **3** abrupt, steep, angular. **4** well defined. **5** (of cold, pain, etc.) severe, intense. **6** pungent, acid. **7** shrill, piercing. **8** (of words etc.) harsh, cutting. **9** acute, sensitive, clever. **10** unscrupulous. **11** vigorous, brisk. **12** *Music* above true pitch. **13** *Music* a semitone higher than note named. ● *noun* **1** *Music* sharp note. **2** *Music* sign (#) indicating this. **3** *colloquial* swindler, cheat. ● *adverb* **1** punctually. **2** suddenly. **3** at a sharp angle. **4** *Music* above true pitch. □ **sharp-eyed** having good sight; observant. **sharp practice** barely honest dealings. **sharpshooter** skilled marksman. **sharp-witted** keenly perceptive or intelligent. □ **sharpen** *verb*. **sharpener** *noun*. **sharply** *adverb*. **sharpness** *noun*

■ *adjective* **1, 2** acute, arrow-shaped, cutting, fine, jagged, keen, needle-sharp, pointed, razor-sharp, sharpened, spiky, tapering. **3** abrupt, acute, angular, hairpin, marked, precipitous, sheer, steep, sudden, vertical. **4** clear, defined, distinct, focused, well defined. **5** acute, biting, bitter, excruciating, extreme, intense, keen, painful, piercing, severe, stabbing, stinging, sudden, violent. **6** acid, acrid, bitter, caustic, hot, piquant, pungent, sour, spicy, tangy, tart. **7** clear, ear-splitting, high, high-pitched, penetrating, piercing, shrieking, shrill, strident. **8** acerbic, acid, acidulous, barbed, biting, caustic, critical, cutting, harsh, hurtful, incisive, malicious, mocking, mordant, pointed, sarcastic, sardonic, scathing, spiteful, tart, trenchant, unkind, venomous, vitriolic. **9** acute, alert, artful, astute, attentive, bright, clever, crafty, *colloquial* cute, discerning, eagle-eyed, incisive, intelligent, keen, observant, penetrating, perceptive, probing, quick, quick-witted, searching, shrewd, watchful. □ **sharpen** file, grind, hone, strop, whet. **sharpener** file, grindstone, hone, strop, whetstone.

sharper *noun* swindler, esp. at cards.

shatter /'ʃætə/ *verb* **1** break suddenly in pieces. **2** severely damage; destroy. **3** (esp. in *passive*) severely upset. **4** (usually as **shattered** *adjective*) *colloquial* exhaust.

■ **1** break, break up, burst, crack, crush, dash to pieces, demolish, disintegrate, explode, *colloquial* pulverize, shiver, smash, smash to smithereens, splinter. **2** see DESTROY 1. **4 (shattered)** see WEARY *adjective* 1.

shave *verb* (**-ving**; *past participle* **shaved** or (as *adjective*) **shaven**) **1** remove (bristles, hair) with razor. **2** remove hair with razor from (leg, head, etc.) or from face of (person). **3** reduce by small amount. **4** pare (wood etc.) to shape it. **5** miss or pass narrowly. ● *noun* **1** shaving, being shaved. **2** narrow miss or escape.

shaver *noun* **1** thing that shaves. **2** electric razor. **3** *colloquial* young lad.

shaving *noun* (esp. in *plural*) thin paring of wood.

shawl *noun* large usually rectangular piece of fabric worn over shoulders etc. or wrapped round baby.

she *pronoun* (as subject of verb) the female person or animal in question.

s/he *pronoun: written representation of* 'he or she'.

sheaf *noun* (*plural* **sheaves**) bundle of things laid lengthways together and usually tied, esp. reaped corn or collection of papers. ● *verb* make into sheaves.

■ *noun* bunch, bundle, file, ream.

shear *verb* (*past* **sheared**; *past participle* **shorn** or **sheared**) **1** clip wool off (sheep etc.). **2** remove by cutting. **3** cut with scissors, shears, etc. **4** strip bare. **5** deprive. **6** (often + *off*) distort, be distorted, or break. ● *noun* **1** strain produced by pressure in structure of substance. **2** (in *plural*) (also **pair of shears** *singular*) scissor-shaped clipping or cutting instrument. □ **shearer** *noun*. ■ *verb* **1, 2** clip, cut, trim.

sheath /ʃiːθ/ *noun* (*plural* **-s** /ʃiːðz/) **1** close-fitting cover, esp. for blade. **2** condom. □ **sheath knife** dagger-like knife carried in sheath.

■ **1** casing, covering, *historical* scabbard.

sheathe /ʃiːð/ *verb* (**-thing**) **1** put into sheath. **2** encase or protect with sheath.

■ cocoon, cover, encase, enclose, put away, wrap.

sheaves *plural* of SHEAF.

shebeen /ʃɪˈbiːn/ *noun esp. Irish* unlicensed drinking place.

shed[1] *noun* one-storeyed building for storage or shelter or as workshop etc.

■ hut, hutch, lean-to, outhouse, shack, shelter, storehouse.

shed[2] *verb* (**-dd-**; *past & past participle* **shed**) **1** let, or cause to, fall off. **2** take off (clothes). **3** reduce (electrical power load). **4** cause to fall or flow. **5** disperse, diffuse, radiate. **6** get rid of. □ **shed light** give or cast light. **shed light on** help to explain.

■ **1** cast off, discard, drop, let fall, moult, spill, throw off. **2** cast off, *esp. literary* doff, remove, strip, take off. **4** discharge, drop, pour out, shower, spill. **5** diffuse, disperse, emit, radiate, scatter, spread. **6** abandon, cast off, discard, drop, get rid of. □ **shed light** see SHINE *verb* 1. **shed light on** see EXPLAIN 1,2.

she'd /ʃiːd/ **1** she had. **2** she would.

sheen *noun* lustre, brightness.

■ brightness, burnish, glaze, gleam, glint, gloss, lustre, patina, polish, radiance, reflection, shimmer, shine.

sheep *noun* (*plural* same) **1** mammal with thick

woolly coat, esp. kept for its wool or meat. **2** timid, silly, or easily-led person. **3** (usually in *plural*) member of minister's congregation. □ **sheep-dip** preparation or place for cleansing sheep of vermin etc. **sheepdog 1** dog trained to guard and herd sheep. **2** dog of breed suitable for this. **sheepfold** enclosure for sheep. **sheepshank** knot for shortening rope temporarily. **sheepskin** sheep's skin with wool on.

■ **1** ewe, lamb, ram, wether.

sheepish *adjective* embarrassed or shy; ashamed. □ **sheepishly** *adverb.*

■ abashed, ashamed, bashful, coy, docile, embarrassed, guilty, meek, mortified, reticent, self-conscious, self-effacing, shamefaced, shy, timid.

sheer[1] *adjective* **1** mere, complete. **2** (of cliff etc.) perpendicular. **3** (of textile) diaphanous. ● *adverb* **1** directly. **2** perpendicularly.

■ *adjective* **1** absolute, *literary* arrant, complete, downright, out and out, plain, pure, simple, thoroughgoing, total, unadulterated, unalloyed, unmitigated, unmixed, unqualified, utter. **2** abrupt, perpendicular, precipitous, steep, vertical. **3** diaphanous, filmy, fine, flimsy, gauzy, gossamer, see-through, thin, translucent, transparent.

sheer[2] *verb* **1** swerve or change course. **2** (often + *away, off*) turn away, esp. from person that one dislikes or fears.

sheet[1] *noun* **1** rectangular piece of cotton etc. as part of bedclothes. **2** broad thin flat piece of paper, metal, etc. **3** wide expanse of glass, ice, water, flame, etc. ● *verb* **1** cover (as) with sheet. **2** (of rain etc.) fall in sheets. □ **sheet metal** metal rolled or hammered etc. into thin sheets. **sheet music** music published in separate sheets.

■ *noun* **2** folio, leaf, page. **3** (*sheet of glass*) pane, panel, plate; (*sheet of ice, water, etc.*) area, blanket, coating, covering, expanse, film, lamina, layer, membrane, skin, surface, veneer.

sheet[2] *noun* rope at lower corner of sail to control it. □ **sheet anchor 1** emergency anchor. **2** person or thing depended on as last hope.

sheikh /ʃeɪk/ *noun* **1** chief or head of Arab tribe, family, or village. **2** Muslim leader.

sheila /ˈʃiːlə/ *noun Australian & NZ slang* girl, young woman.

shekel /ˈʃek(ə)l/ *noun* **1** chief monetary unit of Israel. **2** *historical* weight and coin in ancient Israel etc. **3** (in *plural*) *colloquial* money.

shelduck /ˈʃeldʌk/ *noun* (*plural* same or **-s**; *masculine* **sheldrake**, *plural* same or **-s**) brightly coloured wild duck.

shelf *noun* (*plural* **shelves**) **1** wooden etc. board projecting from wall or forming part of bookcase or cupboard. **2** ledge on cliff face etc. **3** reef, sandbank. □ **on the shelf 1** (of woman) considered past marriageable age. **2** put aside. **shelf-life** time for which stored thing remains usable. **shelf mark** code on book to show its place in library.

■ **1** ledge, mantelpiece; (*shelves*) shelving.

shell *noun* **1** hard outer case of many molluscs, tortoise, egg, nut-kernel, seed, etc. **2** explosive artillery projectile. **3** hollow container for fireworks, cartridges, etc. **4** light racing boat. **5** framework of vehicle etc. **6** walls of unfinished or gutted building etc. ● *verb* **1** remove shell or pod from. **2** fire shells at. □ **come out of one's shell** become less shy. **shellfish 1** aquatic mollusc with shell. **2** crustacean. **shell out** *colloquial* pay (money). **shell-shock** nervous breakdown caused by warfare. **shell-shocked** *adjective.* □ **shell-like** *adjective.*

■ *noun* **1** carapace (*of tortoise*), case, casing, covering, crust, exterior, hull, husk, outside, pod. **2** cartridge, projectile. ● *verb* **2** barrage, bomb, bombard, fire at, shoot at, strafe. □ **shellfish** bivalve, crustacean, mollusc.

she'll /ʃiːl/ she will; she shall.

shellac /ʃəˈlæk/ *noun* resin used for making varnish. ● *verb* (**-ck-**) varnish with shellac.

shelter /ˈʃeltə/ *noun* **1** protection from danger, bad weather, etc. **2** place providing this. **3** thing providing protection or serving as shield. ● *verb* **1** act or serve as shelter to; shield. **2** take shelter. □ **sheltered** *adjective.*

■ *noun* **1** cover, protection, refuge, safety, sanctuary, security. **2** accommodation, asylum, haven, home, house, housing, hut, lee, lodging, refuge, resting place, sanctuary. **3** barrier, cover, fence, roof, screen, shield, umbrella. ● *verb* **1** defend, enclose, guard, harbour, hide, keep safe, protect, safeguard, screen, secure, shade, shield. □ **sheltered** see QUIET *adjective* 5.

shelve *verb* (**-ving**) **1** put aside, esp. temporarily. **2** put on shelf. **3** provide with shelves. **4** (of ground) slope.

■ **1** defer, hold in abeyance, lay aside, postpone, put off. **4** see SLOPE *verb* 1.

shelving *noun* **1** shelves. **2** material for shelves.

shepherd /ˈʃepəd/ *noun* (*feminine* **shepherdess**) **1** person who tends sheep. **2** pastor. ● *verb* **1** tend (sheep). **2** marshal or guide like sheep. □ **shepherd's pie** minced meat baked with covering of (esp. mashed) potato.

sherbet /ˈʃɜːbət/ *noun* flavoured effervescent powder or drink.

sherd *noun* potsherd.

sheriff /ˈʃerɪf/ *noun* **1** (also **High Sheriff**) chief executive officer of Crown in county, administering justice etc. **2** *US* chief law-enforcing officer of county. **3** (also **sheriff-depute**) *Scottish* chief judge of county or district.

sherry /ˈʃerɪ/ *noun* (*plural* **-ies**) fortified wine originally from Spain.

she's /ʃiːz/ **1** she is. **2** she has.

Shetland pony /ˈʃetlənd/ *noun* pony of small hardy breed.

shew *archaic* = SHOW.

shiatsu /ʃɪˈætsuː/ *noun* Japanese therapy involving pressure on specific points of body.

shibboleth /ˈʃɪbəleθ/ *noun* long-standing

formula, doctrine, phrase, etc. espoused by party or sect.

shied *past & past participle* of SHY².

shield /ʃiːld/ *noun* **1** piece of defensive armour held in front of body when fighting. **2** person or thing giving protection. **3** shield-shaped trophy. **4** protective plate or screen in machinery etc. **5** representation of shield for displaying person's coat of arms. ● *verb* protect, screen.

■ *noun* **2** barrier, bulwark, defence, guard, protection, safeguard, screen, shelter. **5** escutcheon. ● *verb* cover, defend, guard, keep safe, protect, safeguard, screen, shade, shelter.

shier *comparative* of SHY¹.

shiest *superlative* of SHY¹.

shift *verb* **1** (cause to) change or move from one position to another. **2** remove, esp. with effort. **3** *slang* hurry. **4** *US* change (gear). ● *noun* **1** shifting. **2** relay of workers. **3** period for which they work. **4** device, expedient, trick. **5** woman's loose straight dress. **6** displacement of spectral line. **7** key on keyboard for switching between lower and upper case etc. **8** *US* gear lever in motor vehicle. □ **make shift** manage; get along. **shift for oneself** rely on one's own efforts. **shift one's ground** alter stance in argument etc.

■ *verb* **1** adjust, alter, budge, change, displace, move, reposition, switch, transfer, transpose. **2** budge, dislodge, get rid of, remove. ● *noun* **1** adjustment, alteration, change, move, switch, transfer, transposition. **2** crew, gang, group, team, workforce. **3** period, stint. □ **shift for oneself** see MANAGE 3.

shiftless *adjective* lacking resourcefulness; lazy. □ **shiftlessness** *noun*.

■ idle, indolent, ineffective, inefficient, inept, irresponsible, lazy, unambitious, unenterprising.

shifty *adjective* (**-ier, -iest**) *colloquial* evasive, deceitful.

■ artful, canny, crafty, cunning, deceitful, designing, devious, dishonest, evasive, foxy, furtive, scheming, secretive, shady, slippery, sly, treacherous, tricky, untrustworthy, wily.

Shiite /ˈʃiːaɪt/ *noun* member of esp. Iranian branch of Islam opposed to Sunnis. ● *adjective* of this branch.

shillelagh /ʃrˈleɪlɪ/ *noun* Irish cudgel.

shilling /ˈʃɪlɪŋ/ *noun* **1** *historical* former British coin and monetary unit, worth 1/20 of pound. **2** monetary unit in some other countries.

shilly-shally /ˈʃɪlɪʃælɪ/ *verb* (**-ies, -ied**) be undecided, vacillate.

shimmer /ˈʃɪmə/ *verb* shine tremulously or faintly. ● *noun* tremulous or faint light.

■ *verb* flicker, glimmer, glisten, ripple, shine.

shin *noun* **1** front of leg below knee. **2** cut of beef from this part. ● *verb* (**-nn-**) (usually + *up, down*) climb quickly using arms and legs. □ **shin-bone** tibia.

shindig /ˈʃɪndɪg/ *noun* (also **shindy**) *colloquial* **1** lively noisy party. **2** brawl, disturbance.

shine *verb* (**-ning**; *past & past participle* **shone** /ʃɒn/ or **shined**) **1** emit or reflect light; be bright; glow. **2** (of sun, star, etc.) be visible. **3** cause to shine. **4** be brilliant; excel. **5** (*past* and *past participle* **shined**) polish. ● *noun* **1** light, brightness. **2** polish, lustre. □ **take a shine to** *colloquial* take a liking to.

■ *verb* **1** beam, be luminous, blaze, coruscate, dazzle, flare, flash, glare, gleam, glint, glisten, glitter, glow, phosphoresce, radiate, reflect, scintillate, shed light, shimmer, sparkle, twinkle. **4** be brilliant, be clever, do well, excel, make one's mark, stand out. **5** brush, buff, burnish, clean, polish. ● *noun* brightness, burnish, coruscation, glaze, gleam, glint, gloss, glow, luminosity, lustre, patina, phosphorescence, polish, radiance, sheen, shimmer, sparkle.

shiner *noun colloquial* black eye.

shingle¹ /ˈʃɪŋg(ə)l/ *noun* small rounded pebbles on seashore. □ **shingly** *adjective*.

■ gravel, pebbles, stones.

shingle² /ˈʃɪŋg(ə)l/ *noun* **1** rectangular wooden tile used on roofs etc. **2** *archaic* shingled hair. ● *verb* (**-ling**) **1** roof with shingles. **2** *archaic* cut (woman's hair) short and tapering.

shingles /ˈʃɪŋg(ə)lz/ *plural noun* (usually treated as *singular*) painful viral infection of nerves with rash, esp. round waist.

Shinto /ˈʃɪntəʊ/ *noun* (also **Shintoism**) Japanese religion with worship of ancestors and nature-spirits.

shinty /ˈʃɪntɪ/ *noun* (*plural* **-ies**) **1** game resembling hockey. **2** stick or ball for this.

shiny *adjective* (**-ier, -iest**) **1** having shine. **2** (of clothing) with nap worn off.

■ **1** bright, brilliant, burnished, gleaming, glistening, glossy, glowing, luminous, lustrous, phosphorescent, polished, reflective, shimmering, shining, sleek, smooth.

ship *noun* **1** large seagoing vessel. **2** *US* aircraft. **3** spaceship. **4** *colloquial* boat. ● *verb* (**-pp-**) **1** transport, esp. in ship. **2** take in (water) over ship's side etc. **3** lay (oars) at bottom of boat. **4** fix (rudder etc.) in place. **5** embark. **6** be hired to work on ship. □ **shipmate** fellow member of ship's crew. **ship off** send away. **shipshape** trim, neat, tidy. **shipwreck** ● *noun* **1** destruction of ship by storm or collision etc. **2** ship so destroyed. ● *verb* (usually in *passive*) cause to suffer this. **shipwright** **1** shipbuilder. **2** ship's carpenter. **shipyard** place where ships are built.

■ *noun* **4** boat, craft. ● *verb* **1** carry, convey, deliver, ferry, move, send, transport.

shipment *noun* **1** goods shipped. **2** act of shipping goods etc.

shipper *noun* person or company that ships goods.

shipping *noun* **1** transport of goods etc. **2** ships collectively.

shire /ʃaɪə/ *noun* county. □ **shire horse** heavy powerful horse.

shirk *verb* avoid (duty, work, etc.). □ **shirker** *noun*.

■ avoid, dodge, evade, get out of, neglect, shun; (*shirk work*) malinger, *slang* skive, *colloquial* slack.

shirr *noun* elasticated gathered threads forming smocking. ● *verb* gather (material) with parallel threads. □ **shirring** *noun*.

shirt *noun* upper-body garment of cotton etc., usually with sleeves and collar. □ **in shirt-sleeves** not wearing jacket. **shirt dress, shirt-waister** dress with bodice like shirt.

shirty *adjective* (**-ier, -iest**) *colloquial* annoyed. □ **shirtily** *adverb*. **shirtiness** *noun*.

shish kebab /ʃɪʃ/ *noun* pieces of meat and vegetables grilled on skewer.

shiver[1] /ʃɪvə/ *verb* tremble with cold, fear, etc. ● *noun* **1** momentary shivering movement. **2** (**the shivers**) attack of shivering. □ **shivery** *adjective*.

■ *verb* quake, quaver, quiver, shake, shudder, tremble, twitch, vibrate. ● *noun* **1** flutter, *frisson*, quiver, shake, shudder, tremor, vibration.

shiver[2] /ʃɪvə/ *noun* (esp. in *plural*) small fragment, splinter. ● *verb* break into shivers.

shoal[1] *noun* multitude, esp. of fish swimming together. ● *verb* form shoal(s).

shoal[2] *noun* **1** area of shallow water. **2** submerged sandbank. ● *verb* (of water) become shallow.

shock[1] *noun* **1** violent collision, impact, etc. **2** (thing causing) sudden and disturbing emotional effect. **3** acute prostration following wound, pain, etc. **4** electric shock. **5** disturbance in stability of organization etc. ● *verb* **1** horrify, outrage. **2** cause shock. **3** affect with electric or pathological shock. □ **shock absorber** device on vehicle etc. for absorbing shock and vibration. **shockproof** resistant to effects of shock. **shock therapy** electroconvulsive therapy. **shock wave** moving region of high air pressure caused by explosion etc. □ **shockable** *adjective*.

■ *noun* **1** blow, collision, impact, jolt, thud. **2** bombshell, dismay, distress, fright, surprise, thunderbolt, upset. **3** trauma. ● *verb* **1** appal, disgust, horrify, nauseate, offend, outrage, repel, revolt, scandalize, sicken. **2** alarm, amaze, astonish, astound, confound, daze, dismay, distress, dumbfound, frighten, *colloquial* give (person) a turn, jar, jolt, numb, paralyse, petrify, rock, scare, shake, stagger, startle, stun, stupefy, surprise, *colloquial* throw, traumatize, unnerve.

shock[2] *noun* unkempt or shaggy mass of hair.

shocker *noun colloquial* **1** shocking person or thing. **2** sensational novel etc.

shocking *adjective* **1** causing shock; scandalous. **2** *colloquial* very bad. □ **shocking pink** vibrant shade of pink. □ **shockingly** *adverb*.

shod *past & past participle* of SHOE.

shoddy /ʃɒdɪ/ *adjective* (**-ier, -iest**) **1** poorly made or done. **2** counterfeit. □ **shoddily** *adverb*. **shoddiness** *noun*.

■ **1** careless, cheap, flimsy, gimcrack, inferior, jerry-built, meretricious, messy, nasty, negligent, poor, rubbishy, second-rate, shabby, slipshod, sloppy, slovenly, *colloquial* tacky, *colloquial* tatty, tawdry, *esp. US* trashy, untidy.

shoe /ʃuː/ *noun* **1** foot-covering of leather etc., esp. one not reaching above ankle. **2** protective metal rim for horse's hoof. **3** thing like shoe in shape or use, e.g. brake shoe. ● *verb* (**shoes, shoeing**; *past & past participle* **shod**) fit with shoe(s). □ **-shod** having shoes of specified kind. **shoehorn** curved implement for easing heel into shoe. **shoelace** cord for lacing shoe. **shoemaker** person who makes shoes. **shoestring 1** shoelace. **2** *colloquial* small esp. inadequate amount of money. **shoe-tree** shaped block for keeping shoe in shape.

shone *past & past participle* of SHINE.

shoo *interjection: used to frighten animals etc. away.* ● *verb* (**shoos, shooed**) **1** utter such sound. **2** (usually + *away*) drive away thus.

shook *past* of SHAKE.

shoot /ʃuːt/ *verb* (*past & past participle* **shot**) **1** cause (weapon) to discharge missile. **2** (often + *at*) discharge (arrow, bullet, etc.). **3** kill or wound with bullet, arrow, etc. **4** send out or discharge rapidly. **5** come or go swiftly or suddenly. **6** (of plant) put forth buds etc. **7** (of bud etc.) appear. **8** hunt game etc. with gun. **9** film, photograph. **10** *esp. Football* score or take shot at (goal). **11** (often + *up*) *slang* inject (drug). ● *noun* **1** young branch or sucker. **2** hunting party or expedition. **3** land on which game is shot. □ **shooting gallery** place for shooting at targets with rifles etc. **shooting star** small rapidly moving meteor. **shooting stick** walking stick with foldable seat.

■ *verb* **1, 2** discharge, fire, let fly. **2** (*shoot at*) *colloquial* blast, bombard, fire on, open fire on, shell, snipe at, strafe, take pot-shots at. **3** gun down, hit, kill. **5** bolt, dart, dash, fly, hurtle, leap, race, run, rush, speed, spring, streak. **6, 7** bud, burgeon, develop, flourish, grow, put out shoots, spring up, sprout. ● *noun* **1** branch, bud, offshoot, sprout, sucker.

shop *noun* **1** place for retail sale of goods or services. **2** act of shopping. **3** place for making or repairing something. **4** *colloquial* place of business etc. ● *verb* (**-pp-**) **1** go to shop(s) to make purchases. **2** *slang* inform against. □ **shop around** look for best bargain. **shop assistant** person serving in shop. **shop floor 1** production area in factory etc. **2** workers as distinct from management. **shopkeeper** owner or manager of shop. **shoplift** steal goods while appearing to shop. **shoplifter** *noun*. **shoplifting** *noun*. **shop-soiled** soiled or faded by display in shop. **shop steward** elected representative of workers in factory etc. **shopwalker** supervisor in large shop. **talk shop** talk about one's occupation. □ **shopper** *noun*.

■ *noun* **1** boutique, cash and carry, emporium, establishment, outlet, retailer, *esp. US* store, supermarket. □ **shopkeeper** dealer, *esp. US & Scottish* merchant, retailer, stockist, *US* storekeeper, supplier, trader, tradesman. □ **shopper** buyer, customer, patron.

shopping *noun* **1** purchase of goods. **2** goods bought. □ **shopping centre** area containing many shops.

■ **2** goods, purchases. □ **shopping centre** arcade, complex, hypermarket, mall, precinct.

shore¹ *noun* **1** land adjoining sea, lake, etc. **2** (usually in *plural*) country. □ **on shore** ashore. **shoreline** line where shore meets water.

■ **1** bank, beach, coast, edge, foreshore, sands, seashore, seaside, strand.

shore² *verb* (**-ring**) (often + *up*) support (as if) with prop(s) or beam(s).

■ (*shore up*) see SUPPORT *verb* 1,2.

shorn *past participle* of SHEAR.

short *adjective* **1** measuring little from end to end or from head to foot. **2** not lasting long. **3** (usually + *of*, *on*) deficient; scanty. **4** concise, brief. **5** curt, uncivil. **6** (of memory) unable to remember distant events. **7** (of vowel or syllable) having the lesser of two recognized durations. **8** (of pastry) easily crumbled. **9** (of a drink of spirits) undiluted. ● *adverb* **1** before the natural or expected time or place; abruptly. **2** rudely. ● *noun* **1** short circuit. **2** *colloquial* short drink. **3** short film. ● *verb* short-circuit. □ **short back and sides** short simple haircut. **shortbread**, **shortcake** rich crumbly biscuit or cake made of flour, butter, and sugar. **short-change** cheat, esp. by giving insufficient change. **short circuit** electric circuit through small resistance, esp. instead of through normal circuit. **short-circuit** *verb* **1** cause short circuit in. **2** have short circuit. **3** shorten or avoid by taking short cut. **shortcoming** deficiency, defect. **short cut** path or course shorter than usual or normal. **shortfall** deficit. **short-handed**, **-staffed** understaffed. **shorthorn** animal of breed of cattle with short horns. **short list** list of candidates from whom final selection will be made. **short-list** *verb* put on short list. **short-lived** ephemeral. **short-range 1** having short range. **2** relating to immediate future. **short shrift** curt or dismissive treatment. **short sight** inability to focus except at close range. **short-tempered** easily angered. **short-term** of or for a short period of time. **short-winded** easily becoming breathless. □ **shorten** *verb*. **shortness** *noun*.

■ *adjective* **1** diminutive, dumpy, dwarfish, little, midget, petite, *colloquial* pint-sized, slight, small, squat, stubby, stumpy, stunted, tiny, *esp. Scottish* wee. **2** brief, cursory, curtailed, ephemeral, fleeting, momentary, passing, quick, short-lived, temporary, transient, transitory. **3** deficient, inadequate, insufficient, lacking, limited, low, meagre, scanty, scarce, sparse, wanting. **4** abbreviated, abridged, compact, concise, cut, pocket, pocket-sized, shortened, succinct. **5** abrupt, bad-tempered, blunt, brusque, cross, curt, gruff, grumpy, impolite, irritable, laconic, sharp, *colloquial* snappy, taciturn, terse, testy, uncivil, unfriendly, unkind, unsympathetic.

□ **shortcoming** bad habit, defect, deficiency, drawback, failing, failure, fault, flaw, foible, imperfection, limitation, vice, weakness, weak point. **short-tempered** abrupt, acerbic, brusque, crabby, cross, crusty, curt, gruff, irascible, irritable, peevish, peremptory, shrewish, *colloquial* snappy, testy, touchy, waspish. □ **shorten** abbreviate, abridge, compress, condense, curtail, cut, cut down, cut short, diminish, dock, lop, précis, prune, reduce, shrink, summarize, take up (*clothes*), telescope, trim, truncate.

shortage *noun* (often + *of*) deficiency; lack.

■ absence, dearth, deficiency, deficit, insufficiency, lack, paucity, poverty, scarcity, shortfall, want.

shortening *noun* fat for pastry.

shorthand /ˈʃɔːthænd/ *noun* **1** method of rapid writing using special symbols. **2** abbreviated or symbolic mode of expression. □ **shorthand typist** typist qualified to take and transcribe shorthand.

shortly *adverb* **1** (often + *before*, *after*) soon. **2** curtly.

■ **1** *archaic* anon, before long, by and by, directly, presently, soon.

shorts *plural noun* **1** trousers reaching to knees or higher. **2** *US* underpants.

short-sighted *adjective* **1** having short sight. **2** lacking imagination or foresight. □ **short-sightedly** *adverb*. **short-sightedness** *noun*.

■ **1** myopic, near-sighted. **2** improvident, unadventurous, unimaginative.

shot¹ *noun* **1** firing of gun etc. **2** attempt to hit by shooting or throwing etc. **3** single missile for gun etc. **4** (*plural* same or **-s**) small lead pellet of which several are used for single charge. **5** (treated as *plural*) these collectively. **6** photograph. **7** film sequence. **8** stroke or kick in ball game. **9** *colloquial* attempt, guess. **10** person of specified skill in shooting. **11** heavy metal ball thrown in shot-put. **12** *colloquial* drink of spirits. **13** *colloquial* injection of drug etc. □ **shotgun** gun for firing small shot at short range. **shotgun wedding** *colloquial* wedding enforced because of bride's pregnancy. **shot in the arm** *colloquial* **1** stimulus, encouragement. **2** alcoholic drink. **shot in the dark** mere guess. **shot-put** athletic contest in which shot is thrown. **shot-putter** *noun*.

■ **1** bang, blast, crack, discharge, explosion, report. **3** ball, bullet, missile, pellet, projectile, round, slug. **6** angle, photograph, picture, snap, snapshot. **9** attempt, chance, *colloquial* crack, endeavour, go, *colloquial* stab, try. **10** marksman, markswoman, sharpshooter.

shot² *past & past participle* of SHOOT. ● *adjective* woven so as to show different colours at different angles.

should /ʃʊd/ *auxiliary verb* (*3rd singular present* **should**) **1** *used in reported speech.* **2** *expressing obligation, likelihood, or tentative suggestion.* **3** *used to form conditional clause or* (*in 1st person*) *conditional mood.*

shoulder /'ʃəʊldə/ *noun* **1** part of body to which arm, foreleg, or wing is attached. **2** either of two projections below neck. **3** animal's upper foreleg as joint of meat. **4** (also in *plural*) shoulder regarded as supportive, comforting, etc. **5** strip of land next to road. **6** part of garment covering shoulder. ● *verb* **1** push with shoulder. **2** make one's way thus. **3** take on (burden, responsibility, etc.) □ **shoulder bag** bag that can be hung from shoulder. **shoulder blade** either flat bone of upper back. **shoulder-length** (of hair etc.) reaching to shoulders. **shoulder pad** pad in garment to bulk out shoulder. **shoulder to shoulder 1** side by side. **2** with united effort. **shoulder strap 1** strap going over shoulder from front to back of garment. **2** strap suspending bag etc. from shoulder.

shouldn't /'ʃʊd(ə)nt/ should not.

shout /ʃaʊt/ *verb* **1** speak or cry loudly. **2** say or express loudly. ● *noun* loud cry calling attention or expressing joy, defiance, approval, etc. □ **shout down** reduce to silence by shouting.

■ *verb* bawl, bellow, *slang* belt out, call, cheer, clamour, cry out, exclaim, howl, rant, roar, scream, screech, shriek, vociferate, whoop, yell, yelp, yowl.

shove /ʃʌv/ *verb* (**-ving**) **1** push, esp. vigorously or roughly. **2** *colloquial* put casually. ● *noun* act of shoving. □ **shove-halfpenny** form of shovelboard played with coins etc. on table. **shove off 1** start from shore, mooring, etc. in boat. **2** *slang* depart.

■ *verb* **1** barge into, crowd, drive, elbow, hustle, impel, jostle, nudge, press, prod, push, shoulder, thrust.

shovel /'ʃʌv(ə)l/ *noun* spadelike scoop used to shift earth or coal etc. ● *verb* (**-ll-**; *US* **-l-**) move (as) with shovel. □ **shovelboard** game played esp. on ship's deck by pushing discs over marked surface.

■ *verb* clear, dig, scoop, shift.

shoveller /'ʃʌvələ/ *noun* (also **shoveler**) duck with shovel-like beak.

show /ʃəʊ/ *verb* (*past participle* **shown** or **showed**) **1** be seen. **2** allow or cause to be seen; manifest. **3** exhibit; offer for inspection. **4** express or indicate (one's feelings). **5** accord, grant (favour, mercy, etc.). **6** (of feelings etc.) be manifest. **7** instruct by example; make understood. **8** demonstrate, prove. **9** present image of. **10** (often + *in*, *round*, etc.) conduct, lead. **11** *colloquial* appear, arrive. ● *noun* **1** showing. **2** spectacle, exhibition, display. **3** public entertainment or performance. **4** outward appearance; impression produced. **5** ostentation; mere display. **6** *colloquial* undertaking, business. □ **good** (**or bad or poor**) **show!** *colloquial* that was well (or badly) done. **showbiz** *colloquial* show business. **show business** *colloquial* the entertainment profession. **showcase** glass case

or event for displaying goods or exhibits. **showdown** final test or confrontation. **show house, flat** furnished and decorated new house or flat on show to prospective buyers. **showjumping** competitive jumping on horseback. **show off 1** display to advantage. **2** *colloquial* act pretentiously. **show-off** *noun colloquial* person who shows off. **show of hands** raised hands indicating vote for or against. **show-piece** excellent specimen suitable for display. **showroom** room where goods are displayed for sale. **show trial** judicial trial designed to frighten or impress the public. **show up 1** make or be visible or conspicuous. **2** expose. **3** humiliate. **4** *colloquial* appear or arrive. **show willing** show willingness to help etc.

■ *verb* **1** appear, be seen, be visible, catch the eye, come out, emerge, make an appearance, *colloquial* materialize, peep (through), stand out, stick out. **2, 3** bare, display, exhibit, expose, make public, manifest, open up, present, produce, reveal, uncover. **4** betray, demonstrate, disclose, divulge, express, indicate, lay bare, make public, manifest, reveal. **5** accord, bestow, confer, grant, treat with. **6** be apparent, be manifest, be seen. **7** clarify, describe, elucidate, explain, instruct, teach, tell. **8** attest, bear out, confirm, corroborate, demonstrate, evince, exemplify, manifest, point out, prove, substantiate, verify, witness. **9** depict, give a picture of, illustrate, picture, portray, represent, symbolize. **10** conduct, direct, escort, guide, indicate, lead, steer, usher. ● *noun* **2** demonstration, display, exhibition, exposition, fair, pageant, presentation, spectacle. **3** drama, entertainment, performance, play, presentation, production. **4** appearance, demonstration, façade, illusion, impression, pose, pretence, threat. **5** affectation, exhibitionism, flamboyance, ostentation, pretentiousness, showing off. □ **showdown** confrontation, crisis. **show off 2** see BOAST *verb* 1. **show-off** *colloquial* big-head, boaster, braggart, egotist, exhibitionist, poser, poseur, swaggerer. **show up 3** see HUMILIATE. **4** see ARRIVE 1.

shower /'ʃaʊə/ *noun* **1** brief fall of rain, snow, etc. **2** brisk flurry of bullets, dust, etc. **3** sudden copious arrival of gifts, honours, etc. **4** (also **shower-bath**) bath or cubicle in which water is sprayed from above. ● *verb* **1** descend, send, or give in shower. **2** take shower-bath. **3** (+ *upon*, *with*) bestow lavishly. □ **showery** *adjective*.

■ *noun* **4** douche. ● *verb* **1** deluge, drop, rain, spatter, splash, spray, sprinkle. **3** (*shower with*) bestow, heap, inundate with, lavish, load with, overwhelm with.

showing *noun* **1** display. **2** quality of performance, achievement, etc. **3** evidence; putting of case etc.

shown *past participle* of SHOW.

showy *adjective* (**-ier**, **-iest**) **1** gaudy. **2** striking. □ **showily** *adverb*. **showiness** *noun*.

■ bright, conspicuous, elaborate, fancy, flamboyant, flashy, florid, fussy, garish, gaudy, lavish, loud, lurid, ornate, ostentatious, over the top, pretentious, striking, trumpery, vulgar.

shrank *past* of SHRINK.

shrapnel /'ʃræpn(ə)l/ *noun* fragments of exploded bomb etc.

shred *noun* **1** scrap, fragment. **2** least amount. ● *verb* (**-dd-**) tear, cut, etc. to shreds. □ **shredder** *noun.*

■ *noun* **1** bit, fragment, piece, remnant, scrap, sliver, snippet, strip; (*shreds*) rags, ribbons, tatters. **2** atom, bit, fragment, grain, hint, iota, jot, scintilla, speck, trace. ● *verb* destroy, grate, rip up, tear.

shrew *noun* **1** small long-snouted mouselike animal. **2** bad-tempered or scolding woman. □ **shrewish** *adjective.*

shrewd *adjective* astute; clever. □ **shrewdly** *adverb.* **shrewdness** *noun.*

■ acute, artful, astute, calculating, canny, clever, crafty, cunning, discerning, discriminating, foxy, ingenious, intelligent, knowing, observant, perceptive, percipient, perspicacious, quick-witted, sage, sharp, sly, smart, wily, wise.

shriek *noun* shrill cry or sound. ● *verb* **1** make a shriek. **2** say in shrill tones.

■ *noun* & *verb* cry, scream, screech, squawk, squeal.

shrike *noun* bird with strong hooked beak.

shrill *adjective* piercing and high-pitched. ● *verb* sound or utter shrilly. □ **shrillness** *noun.* **shrilly** *adverb.*

■ *adjective* ear-splitting, high, high-pitched, jarring, penetrating, piercing, piping, screaming, screeching, sharp, shrieking, strident, treble, whistling.

shrimp *noun* (*plural* same or **-s**) **1** small edible crustacean. **2** *colloquial* very small person.

shrine *noun* **1** sacred or revered place. **2** casket or tomb holding relics.

■ **1** altar, chapel, church, holy of holies, holy place, place of worship, sanctum. **2** casket, reliquary, tomb.

shrink *verb* (*past* **shrank**; *past participle* **shrunk** or (esp. as *adjective*) **shrunken**) **1** become or make smaller, esp. by action of moisture, heat, or cold. **2** (usually + *from*) recoil, flinch. ● *noun slang* psychiatrist. □ **shrink-wrap** enclose (article) in material that shrinks tightly round it.

■ *verb* **1** contract, decrease, diminish, dwindle, lessen, narrow, reduce, shorten, shrivel. **2** back off, cower, cringe, flinch, hang back, quail, recoil, retire, shy away, wince, withdraw.

shrinkage *noun* **1** process or degree of shrinking. **2** allowance for loss by theft or wastage.

shrivel /'ʃrɪv(ə)l/ *verb* (**-ll-**; *US* **-l-**) contract into wrinkled or dried-up state.

■ become parched, become wizened, curl (up), dehydrate, desiccate, droop, dry out, dry up, shrink, wilt, wither, wrinkle.

shroud /ʃraʊd/ *noun* **1** wrapping for corpse. **2** something which conceals. **3** rope supporting mast. ● *verb* **1** clothe (corpse) for burial. **2** cover, disguise.

■ *noun* **1** winding-sheet. **2** blanket, cloak, cloud, cover, mantle, mask, pall, veil. ● *verb* camouflage, cloak, conceal, cover, disguise, enshroud, envelop, hide, mask, screen, swathe, veil, wrap up.

Shrove Tuesday /ʃrəʊv/ *noun* day before Ash Wednesday.

shrub *noun* woody plant smaller than tree and usually branching from near ground. □ **shrubby** *adjective.*

■ bush.

shrubbery *noun* (*plural* **-ies**) area planted with shrubs.

shrug *verb* (**-gg-**) draw up (shoulders) momentarily as gesture of indifference, ignorance, etc. ● *noun* shrugging movement. □ **shrug off** dismiss as unimportant by or as if by shrugging.

shrunk (also **shrunken**) *past participle* of SHRINK.

shudder /'ʃʌdə/ *verb* **1** shiver from fear, cold, etc. **2** feel strong repugnance, fear, etc. **3** vibrate. ● *noun* act of shuddering.

■ *verb* **1** convulse, jerk, quake, quiver, shake, shiver, squirm, tremble. **3** judder, rattle, shake, vibrate.

shuffle /'ʃʌf(ə)l/ *verb* (**-ling**) **1** drag or slide (feet) in walking. **2** mix up or rearrange (esp. cards). **3** be evasive. **4** keep shifting one's position. ● *noun* **1** shuffling action or movement. **2** change of relative positions. **3** shuffling dance. □ **shuffle off** remove; get rid of.

■ *verb* **1** drag one's feet, scrape, shamble, slide. **2** confuse, disorganize, intermix, intersperse, jumble, mix, mix up, rearrange, reorganize.

shufti /'ʃʊftɪ/ *noun* (*plural* **-s**) *colloquial* look, glimpse.

shun *verb* (**-nn-**) avoid; keep clear of.

■ avoid, disdain, *formal* eschew, flee, give the cold shoulder to, keep clear of, rebuff, reject, shy away from, spurn, steer clear of, turn away from.

shunt *verb* **1** move (train etc.) to another track. **2** (of train) be shunted. **3** redirect. ● *noun* **1** shunting, being shunted. **2** conductor joining two points in electric circuit for diversion of current. **3** *slang* collision of vehicles.

shush /ʃʊʃ/ *interjection* & *verb* hush.

shut *verb* (**-tt-**; *past* & *past participle* **shut**) **1** move (door, window, lid, etc.) into position to block opening. **2** shut door etc. of. **3** become or be capable of being shut. **4** become or make closed for trade. **5** fold or contract (book, hand, telescope). **6** bar access to (place). □ **shut down 1** close. **2** cease working. **shut-eye** *colloquial* sleep. **shut in** confine; encircle. **shut off 1** stop flow of (water, gas, etc.). **2** separate. **shut one's eyes (or ears or heart or mind) to** refuse to or pretend not to see (or hear or feel sympathy for or think about). **shut out 1** exclude. **2** screen from view. **3** prevent. **shut up 1** close all doors and windows of. **2** imprison. **3** put away in box etc. **4** (esp. in *imperative*) *colloquial* stop talking.

■ **1–3** bolt, close, fasten, latch, lock, seal, secure, slam. □ **shut in** see CONFINE 1, IMPRISON 2. **shut off 2** see ISOLATE 1,2. **shut out 1** see EXCLUDE 1. **shut up 2** see CONFINE 1, IMPRISON 1–2. **4** see SILENCE *verb*.

shutter *noun* **1** movable hinged cover for window. **2** device for exposing film in camera. ● *verb* provide or close with shutter(s).

■ *noun* **1** blind, louvre, screen.

shuttle /'ʃʌt(ə)l/ *noun* **1** part of loom which carries weft-thread between threads of warp. **2** thread-carrier for lower thread in sewing machine. **3** train, bus, aircraft, etc. used in shuttle service. **4** space shuttle. ● *verb* (**-ling**) (cause to) move to and fro like shuttle. □ **shuttlecock** cork with ring of feathers, or similar plastic device, struck to and fro in badminton. **shuttle diplomacy** negotiations conducted by mediator travelling between disputing parties. **shuttle service** transport system operating to and fro over short distance.

shy¹ *adjective* (**-er, -est**) **1** timid and nervous in company; self-conscious. **2** easily startled. ● *verb* (**shies, shied**) (usually + *at*) (esp. of horse) start back or aside in fright. ● *noun* sudden startled movement. □ **-shy** showing fear or dislike of. □ **shyly** *adverb*. **shyness** *noun*.

■ *adjective* apprehensive, backward, bashful, cautious, chary, coy, diffident, hesitant, inhibited, introverted, modest, mousy, nervous, reserved, reticent, retiring, self-conscious, self-effacing, sheepish, timid, timorous, underconfident, wary, withdrawn.

shy² *verb* (**shies, shied**) throw, fling. ● *noun* (*plural* **shies**) throw, fling.

■ *verb* see THROW *verb* 1,2.

shyster /'ʃaɪstə/ *noun colloquial* person who acts unscrupulously or unprofessionally.

SI *abbreviation* international system of units of measurement (*Système International*).

si /si:/ *noun Music* te.

Siamese /saɪə'miːz/ *noun* (*plural* same) **1** native or language of Siam (now Thailand). **2** (in full **Siamese cat**) cat of cream-coloured dark-faced short-haired breed with blue eyes. ● *adjective* of Siam. □ **Siamese twins** twins joined together at birth.

sibilant /'sɪbɪlənt/ *adjective* **1** hissing. **2** sounded with hiss. ● *noun* sibilant speech sound or letter. □ **sibilance** *noun*.

sibling /'sɪblɪŋ/ *noun* each of two or more children having one or both parents in common.

■ brother, sister.

sibyl /'sɪbɪl/ *noun* pagan prophetess.

sic *adverb* used or spelt thus (confirming form of quoted words). [Latin]

sick *adjective* **1** vomiting, disposed to vomit. **2** ill, unwell. **3** (often + *of*) *colloquial* disgusted; surfeited. **4** *colloquial* cruel, morbid, perverted,

offensive. ● *noun colloquial* vomit. ● *verb* (esp. + *up*) *colloquial* vomit. □ **sickbay** place for sick people. **sickbed** invalid's bed. **sick leave** leave granted because of illness. **sick pay** pay given during sick leave. **take sick** *colloquial* be taken ill.

■ *adjective* **1** airsick, bilious, carsick, nauseated, nauseous, queasy, seasick, squeamish, vomiting. **2** afflicted, ailing, bedridden, diseased, ill, indisposed, infirm, laid up, poorly, queer, sickly, *colloquial* under the weather, unhealthy, unwell. **3** (*sick of*) annoyed by, bored with, disgusted by, fed up with, glutted with, nauseated by, *formal* sated with, sickened by, tired of, weary of. **4** see MORBID 1. ● *verb* (*sick up*) see VOMIT *verb* 1.

sicken *verb* **1** make or become sick, disgusted, etc. **2** (often + *for*) show symptoms of illness. **3** (as **sickening** *adjective*) disgusting. **4** (as **sickening** *adjective*) *colloquial* very annoying. □ **sickeningly** *adverb*.

■ **1** appal, be sickening to, disgust, nauseate, offend, repel, revolt, turn (person's) stomach. **2** *slang* catch a bug, fail, fall ill, *colloquial* take sick, weaken; (*sicken for*) catch, come down with, contract. **3** (*sickening*) see REPULSIVE.

sickle /'sɪk(ə)l/ *noun* short-handled implement with semicircular blade for reaping, lopping, etc.

sickly *adjective* (**-ier, -iest**) **1** apt to be ill; weak. **2** faint, pale. **3** causing sickness; nauseating. **4** mawkish, weakly sentimental.

■ **1** ailing, anaemic, delicate, drawn, feeble, frail, ill, pale, pallid, peaky, unhealthy, unwholesome, wan, weak. **3** nasty, nauseating, obnoxious, off-putting, unpleasant. **4** cloying, maudlin, mawkish, mushy, syrupy.

sickness *noun* **1** being ill; disease. **2** vomiting, nausea.

■ **1** see ILLNESS 1–2. **2** biliousness, nausea, queasiness, vomiting.

side *noun* **1** each of inner or outer surfaces of object, esp. as distinct from top and bottom or front and back or ends. **2** right or left part of person's or animal's body. **3** part of object, place, etc. that faces specified direction or that is on observer's right or left. **4** either surface of thing regarded as having two. **5** aspect of question, character, etc. **6** each of sets of opponents in war, game, etc. **7** cause or position represented by this. **8** part or region near edge. **9** *colloquial* television channel. **10** each of lines bounding triangle, rectangle, etc. **11** position nearer or farther than, or to right or left of, dividing line. **12** line of descent through father or mother. **13** spinning motion given to ball by striking it on side. **14** *slang* swagger; assumption of superiority. ● *adjective* **1** of, on, from, or to side. **2** oblique, indirect. **3** subordinate, subsidiary, not main. ● *verb* (**-ding**) **1** take side in dispute etc. **2** (+ *with*) be on or join same side as. □ **on the side 1** as sideline. **2** illicitly. **3** *US* as side dish. **sideboard** table or flat-topped chest with drawers and cupboards for crockery etc. **sideboards, sideburns** short side-whiskers. **side by side** standing close together, esp. for mutual encouragement.

sidecar passenger car attached to side of motorcycle. **side drum** small double-headed drum. **side effect** secondary (usually undesirable) effect. **sidekick** *colloquial* close associate. **sidelight 1** light from side. **2** small light at side of front of vehicle etc. **sideline 1** work etc. done in addition to one's main activity. **2** (usually in *plural*) line bounding side of sports pitch etc. **3** (usually in *plural*) space just outside these for spectators to sit. **side-saddle** ● *noun* saddle for woman riding with both legs on same side of horse. ● *adverb* sitting thus on horse. **sideshow** minor show or stall in exhibition, fair, etc. **sidesman** assistant churchwarden. **side-splitting** causing violent laughter. **sidestep** ● *noun* step taken sideways. ● *verb* avoid, evade. **sidetrack** divert from course, purpose, etc. **sidewalk** *US* pavement. **side-whiskers** hair left unshaven on cheeks. **take sides** support either of (usually) two opposing sides in argument etc.

■ *noun* **1** elevation, face, facet, flank, surface. **5** angle, aspect, facet, perspective, slant, view. **6** army, camp, faction, interest, party, sect, team. **7** attitude, point of view, position, school of thought, standpoint, view, viewpoint. **8** border, boundary, brim, brink, edge, fringe, limit, margin, perimeter, rim, verge. ● *verb* **2** (*side with*) ally with, back, favour, form an alliance with, go along with, join up with, partner, support, team up with. □ **sidestep** *verb* avoid, circumvent, dodge, evade, skirt round. **sidetrack** deflect, distract, divert.

sidelong *adjective* directed to the side. ● *adverb* to the side.

sidereal /saɪˈdɪərɪəl/ *adjective* of or measured or determined by stars.

sideways *adverb* & *adjective* **1** to or from a side. **2** with one side facing forward.

■ *adjective* crabwise, indirect, lateral, oblique, sidelong.

siding *noun* short track by side of railway line for shunting etc.

sidle /ˈsaɪd(ə)l/ *verb* (**-ling**) walk timidly or furtively.

siege /siːdʒ/ *noun* surrounding and blockading of town, castle, etc. □ **lay siege to** conduct siege of. **raise siege** end it.

■ blockade. □ **lay siege to** see BESIEGE 1,2.

siemens /ˈsiːmənz/ *noun* (*plural* same) SI unit of electrical conductance.

sienna /sɪˈenə/ *noun* **1** kind of reddish- or yellowish-brown earth used as pigment. **2** its colour.

sierra /sɪˈerə/ *noun* long jagged mountain chain, esp. in Spain or Spanish America.

siesta /sɪˈestə/ *noun* afternoon nap or rest in hot countries.

sieve /sɪv/ *noun* utensil with network or perforated bottom through which liquids or fine particles can pass. ● *verb* (**-ving**) sift.

■ *noun* colander, riddle, screen, strainer. ● *verb* see SIFT 1–2.

sift *verb* **1** separate with or cause to pass through sieve. **2** sprinkle through perforated container. **3** closely examine details of; analyse. **4** (of snow, light, etc.) fall as if from sieve.

■ **1** filter, riddle, screen, separate, sieve, strain. **2** sieve, sprinkle. **3** analyse, examine, investigate, review, scrutinize, sort out, winnow.

sigh /saɪ/ *verb* **1** emit long deep audible breath in sadness, weariness, relief, etc. **2** yearn. **3** express with sighs. ● *noun* **1** act of sighing. **2** sound (like that) made in sighing.

■ *noun* **1** exhalation. **2** moan, sough.

sight /saɪt/ *noun* **1** faculty of seeing. **2** seeing, being seen. **3** thing seen. **4** range of vision. **5** (usually in *plural*) noteworthy features of a place. **6** device for assisting aim with gun or observation with telescope etc. **7** aim or observation so gained. **8** *colloquial* unsightly person or thing. **9** *colloquial* great deal. ● *verb* **1** get sight of. **2** observe presence of. **3** aim (gun etc.) with sight. □ **at first sight** on first glimpse or impression. **catch sight of** begin to see. **lose sight of** cease to see or be aware of. **on, at sight** as soon as person or thing is seen. **set one's sights on** aim at. **sight-read** read (music) at sight. **sight-screen** *Cricket* large white screen placed near boundary in line with wicket to help batsman see ball. **sightseer** person visiting sights of place. **sightseeing** *noun*.

■ *noun* **1** eyesight, seeing, vision, visual perception. **2** glance, glimpse, look, peep. **3** display, exhibition, scene, show, spectacle. **4** field of vision, gaze, range of vision, view, visibility. ● *verb* **1, 2** *literary* behold, descry, discern, distinguish, espy, glimpse, make out, notice, observe, perceive, recognize, see, *colloquial* spot. □ **catch sight of** see SEE¹ 1. **sightseer** globe-trotter, holidaymaker, tourist, tripper, visitor.

sighted *adjective* not blind. □ **-sighted** having specified vision.

sightless *adjective* blind.

sign /saɪn/ *noun* **1** indication of quality, state, future event, etc. **2** mark, symbol, etc. **3** motion or gesture used to convey information, order, etc. **4** signboard. **5** each of the 12 divisions of the zodiac. ● *verb* **1** write one's name on (document etc.) as authorization. **2** write (one's name) thus. **3** communicate by gesture. □ **sign away or over** convey (property, rights, etc.) by signing document. **signboard** board bearing name, symbol, etc. displayed outside shop, inn, etc. **sign in 1** sign register on arrival. **2** get (person) admitted by signing register. **sign language** series of signs used esp. by deaf or dumb people for communication. **sign off** end contract, work, etc. **sign on** register to obtain unemployment benefit. **sign out** sign register on departing. **signpost** ● *noun* post etc. showing directions of roads. ● *verb* provide with signpost(s). **sign up 1** engage (person). **2** enlist in armed forces. **3** commit (person or oneself) by signing; enrol. **signwriter** person who paints signboards etc.

■ *noun* **1** augury, clue, forewarning, *colloquial* give-away, hint, indication, indicator, intimation, manifestation, marker, omen, pointer, portent, presage, proof, reminder, signal, spoor (*of animal*), suggestion, symptom, token, trace, vestige, warning. **2** badge, brand, cipher, device, emblem, flag, hieroglyph, ideogram, ideograph, insignia, logo, mark, monogram, rebus, symbol, trade mark. **4** advertisement, notice, placard, poster, signboard. ● *verb* **1, 2** autograph, countersign, endorse, inscribe, write. **3** see SIGNAL¹ *verb*.

□ **sign away or over** see TRANSFER *verb* 1,2. **sign off** see FINISH *verb* 1. **sign up 2** see ENLIST 1. **signpost** *noun* pointer, road sign, sign.

signal¹ /'sɪgn(ə)l/ *noun* **1** sign, esp. pre-arranged one, conveying information or direction. **2** message of such signs. **3** event which causes immediate activity. **4** *Electricity* transmitted impulses or radio waves. **5** *Electricity* sequence of these. **6** device on railway giving instructions or warnings to train drivers etc. ● *verb* (**-ll-**; US **-l-**) **1** make signal(s) (to). **2** (often + *to do*) transmit, announce, or direct by signal(s). □ **signal box** building from which railway signals are controlled. **signalman** railway signal operator.

■ *noun* **1** communication, cue, gesticulation, gesture, go-ahead, indication, indicator, motion, nod, password, sign, tip-off, token, warning, wave, wink. **4** emission, output, transmission, waves.
● *verb* beckon, communicate, flag, gesticulate, gesture, indicate, motion, nod, notify, semaphore, sign, wave, wink.

signal² /'sɪgn(ə)l/ *adjective* remarkable, noteworthy. □ **signally** *adverb*.

signalize *verb* (also **-ise**) (**-zing** or **-sing**) **1** make conspicuous or remarkable. **2** indicate.

signatory /'sɪgnətərɪ/ *noun* (*plural* **-ies**) party that has signed an agreement, esp. a treaty. ● *adjective* having signed such an agreement.

signature /'sɪgnətʃə/ *noun* **1** person's name or initials used in signing. **2** act of signing. **3** *Music* key signature. **4** *Music* time signature. **5** section of book made from one sheet folded and cut. □ **signature tune** tune used esp. in broadcasting to announce a particular programme, performer, etc.

■ **1** autograph, endorsement, mark, name.

signet /'sɪgnɪt/ *noun* small seal. □ **signet ring** ring with seal set in it.

■ seal, stamp.

significance /sɪg'nɪfɪkəns/ *noun* **1** importance; being significant. **2** meaning. **3** extent to which result deviates from hypothesis such that difference is due to more than errors in sampling.

■ **1** force, import, importance, relevance, usefulness, value, weight. **2** denotation, idea, implication, import, meaning, message, point, purport, sense, signification.

significant /sɪg'nɪfɪkənt/ *adjective* **1** having or conveying meaning. **2** important. □ **significant figure** *Mathematics* digit conveying information about a number containing it. □ **significantly** *adverb*.

■ **1** eloquent, expressive, indicative, informative, knowing, meaningful, pregnant, revealing, suggestive, symbolic, tell-tale. **2** big, consequential, considerable, historic, important, influential, memorable, newsworthy, noteworthy, relevant, salient, serious, sizeable, valuable, vital, worthwhile.

signify /'sɪgnɪfaɪ/ *verb* (**-ies**, **-ied**) **1** be sign or symbol of. **2** represent, mean, denote. **3** make known. **4** be of importance; matter. □ **signification** *noun*.

■ **1–3** announce, be a sign of, betoken, communicate, connote, convey, denote, express, foretell, impart, imply, indicate, intimate, make known, mean, reflect, represent, reveal, signal, suggest, symbolize, tell, transmit. **4** be important, be significant, count, matter, merit consideration.

signor /'siːnjɔː/ *noun* (*plural* **-i** /-'njɔːriː/) title used of or to Italian man.

signora /siː'njɔːrə/ *noun: title used of or to Italian esp. married woman.*

signorina /siːnjə'riːnə/ *noun: title used of or to Italian unmarried woman.*

Sikh /siːk/ *noun* member of Indian monotheistic sect.

silage /'saɪlɪdʒ/ *noun* **1** green fodder stored in silo. **2** storage in silo.

silence /'saɪləns/ *noun* **1** absence of sound. **2** abstinence from speech or noise. **3** neglect or omission to mention, write, etc. ● *verb* (**-cing**) make silent, esp. by force or superior argument.

■ *noun* **1** calm, calmness, hush, noiselessness, peace, quiet, quietness, quietude, soundlessness, stillness, tranquillity. **2** dumbness, muteness, reticence, speechlessness, taciturnity.
● *verb* deaden, gag, hush, keep quiet, muffle, mute, muzzle, quieten, repress, *colloquial* shut up, smother, stifle, suppress.

silencer *noun* device for reducing noise made by gun, vehicle's exhaust, etc.

silent /'saɪlənt/ *adjective* **1** not speaking. **2** making or accompanied by little or no sound. **3** unspoken. **4** saying little. □ **silently** *adverb*.

■ **1** dumb, *colloquial* mum, mute, speechless, voiceless. **2** hushed, inaudible, muffled, muted, noiseless, quiet, soundless, still. **3** implicit, implied, mute, tacit, understood, unexpressed, unspoken, unuttered. **4** dumb, laconic, *colloquial* mum, quiet, reserved, reticent, taciturn, tight-lipped, tongue-tied, uncommunicative, unforthcoming.

silhouette /sɪluː'et/ *noun* **1** dark outline or shadow in profile against lighter background. **2** contour, outline, profile. **3** portrait in profile showing outline only, usually cut from paper or in black on white. ● *verb* (**-tting**) represent or show in silhouette.

■ *noun* contour, form, outline, profile, shadow, shape.

silica /'sɪlɪkə/ *noun* silicon dioxide, occurring as quartz and as main constituent of sand etc. □ **siliceous** /sɪ'lɪʃəs/ *adjective*.

silicate /ˈsɪlɪkeɪt/ *noun* compound of metal(s), silicon, and oxygen.

silicon /ˈsɪlɪkən/ *noun* non-metallic element occurring in silica and silicates. □ **silicon chip** silicon microchip.

silicone /ˈsɪlɪkəʊn/ *noun* any organic compound of silicon with high resistance to cold, heat, water, etc.

silicosis /ˌsɪlɪˈkəʊsɪs/ *noun* lung disease caused by inhaling dust containing silica.

silk *noun* **1** fine strong soft lustrous fibre produced by silkworms. **2** thread or cloth made from this. **3** (in *plural*) cloth or garments of silk. **4** *colloquial* Queen's Counsel. □ **silk-screen printing** screen printing. **silkworm** caterpillar which spins cocoon of silk. **take silk** become Queen's Counsel.

silken *adjective* **1** of or resembling silk. **2** soft, smooth, lustrous.

silky *adjective* (**-ier**, **-iest**) **1** like silk in smoothness, softness, etc. **2** suave. □ **silkily** *adverb*.

■ **1** delicate, fine, glossy, lustrous, satiny, sleek, smooth, soft, velvety.

sill *noun* slab of wood, stone, etc. at base of window or doorway.

silly /ˈsɪlɪ/ *adjective* (**-ier**, **-iest**) **1** foolish, imprudent. **2** weak-minded. **3** *Cricket* (of fielder or position) very close to batsman. ● *noun* (*plural* **-ies**) *colloquial* silly person. □ **silliness** *noun*.

■ *adjective* **1** absurd, asinine, brainless, childish, crazy, daft, *colloquial* dopey, *colloquial* dotty, fatuous, flighty, fond, foolish, frivolous, grotesque, half-baked, hare-brained, idiotic, ill-advised, illogical, immature, impractical, imprudent, inadvisable, inane, infantile, irrational, jokey, laughable, light-hearted, ludicrous, mad, meaningless, mindless, misguided, naive, nonsensical, playful, pointless, preposterous, ridiculous, scatterbrained, *colloquial* scatty, senseless, shallow, simplistic, *colloquial* soppy, stupid, thoughtless, unintelligent, unreasonable, unsound, unwise, wild, witless. **2** *colloquial* dim-witted, empty-headed, feather-brained, feeble-minded, half-witted, simple, simple-minded, stupid, weak-minded.

silo /ˈsaɪləʊ/ *noun* (*plural* **-s**) **1** pit or airtight structure in which green crops are stored for fodder. **2** tower or pit for storage of grain, cement, etc. **3** underground storage chamber for guided missile.

silt *noun* sediment in channel, harbour, etc. ● *verb* (often + *up*) block or be blocked with silt. ■ *noun* alluvium, deposit, mud, ooze, sediment, slime, sludge.

silvan = SYLVAN.

silver /ˈsɪlvə/ *noun* **1** greyish-white lustrous precious metal. **2** coins or articles made of or looking like this. **3** colour of silver. ● *adjective* of or coloured like silver. ● *verb* **1** coat or plate with silver. **2** provide (mirror-glass) with backing of tin amalgam etc. **3** make silvery. **4** turn grey or white. □ **silver birch** common birch with silvery white bark. **silverfish** (*plural* same or **-es**) **1** small silvery wingless insect. **2** silver-coloured fish. **silver jubilee** 25th anniversary of reign. **silver medal** medal awarded as second prize. **silver paper** aluminium foil. **silver plate** articles plated with silver. **silver-plated** plated with silver. **silver sand** fine pure kind used in gardening. **silver screen** (usually **the silver screen**) cinema films collectively. **silverside** upper side of round of beef. **silversmith** worker in silver. **silver wedding** 25th anniversary of wedding.

silvery *adjective* **1** like silver in colour or appearance. **2** having clear soft ringing sound.

simian /ˈsɪmɪən/ *adjective* **1** of anthropoid apes. **2** resembling ape, monkey. ● *noun* ape or monkey.

similar /ˈsɪmɪlə/ *adjective* **1** like, alike. **2** (often + *to*) having resemblance. □ **similarity** /-ˈlær-/ *noun* (*plural* **-ies**). **similarly** *adverb*.

■ akin, alike, analogous, comparable, compatible, congruous, coordinating, corresponding, equal, equivalent, harmonious, homogeneous, identical, indistinguishable, like, matching, parallel, related, the same, toning, twin, uniform, well matched; (*similar to*) redolent of, reminiscent of, resembling. □ **similarity** affinity, closeness, congruity, correspondence, equivalence, homogeneity, kinship, likeness, match, parallelism, relationship, resemblance, sameness, similitude, uniformity.

simile /ˈsɪmɪlɪ/ *noun* esp. poetical comparison of two things using *like* or *as* (see panel).

similitude /sɪˈmɪlɪtjuːd/ *noun* **1** guise, appearance. **2** comparison or its expression.

Simile

A simile is a figure of speech involving the comparison of one thing with another of a different kind, using *as* or *like*, e.g.

The water was as clear as glass.
Cherry blossom lay like driven snow upon the lawn.

Everyday language is rich in similes:

with *as*:	as like as two peas	as poor as a church mouse
	as strong as an ox	as rich as Croesus
with *like*:	spread like wildfire	run like the wind
	sell like hot cakes	like a bull in a china shop

simmer /'sɪmə/ verb 1 be or keep just below boiling point. 2 be in state of suppressed anger or laughter. ● noun simmering state. □ **simmer down** become less agitated.

■ verb 1 boil, bubble, cook, seethe, stew. 2 fume, seethe, smoulder.

simnel cake /'sɪmn(ə)l/ noun rich fruit cake, usually with almond paste.

simony /'saɪmənɪ/ noun buying or selling of ecclesiastical privileges.

simoom /sɪ'muːm/ noun hot dry dust-laden desert wind.

simper /'sɪmpə/ verb 1 smile in silly affected way. 2 utter with simper. ● noun such smile.

simple /'sɪmp(ə)l/ adjective (-r, -st) 1 easily understood or done; presenting no difficulty. 2 not complicated or elaborate; plain. 3 not compound or complex. 4 absolute, unqualified, straightforward. 5 foolish, feeble-minded. 6 artless, unsophisticated. 7 humble, lowly. □ **simple-minded** foolish, feeble-minded. **simple-mindedness** noun. □ **simpleness** noun.

■ 1 clear, comprehensible, easy, foolproof, intelligible, lucid, straightforward, uncomplicated, understandable, user-friendly. 2 austere, basic, classical, elementary, fundamental, plain, severe, stark, unadorned, unembellished. 5 see FOOLISH. 6 artless, candid, childlike, frank, guileless, honest, ingenuous, innocent, naive, natural, sincere, unaffected, unassuming, unpretentious, unsophisticated. 7 humble, lowly, modest, ordinary, unpretentious.

simpleton /'sɪmpəlt(ə)n/ noun stupid or gullible person.

simplicity /sɪm'plɪsɪtɪ/ noun fact or condition of being simple.

simplify /'sɪmplɪfaɪ/ verb (-ies, -ied) make simple or simpler. □ **simplification** /-fɪ'keɪʃ(ə)n/ noun.

■ clarify, explain, paraphrase, prune, streamline, unravel, untangle.

simplistic /sɪm'plɪstɪk/ adjective excessively or affectedly simple. □ **simplistically** adverb.

■ facile, inadequate, naive, oversimple, oversimplified, shallow, silly, superficial.

simply adverb 1 in a simple way. 2 absolutely. 3 merely.

simulate /'sɪmjʊleɪt/ verb (-ting) 1 pretend to be, have, or feel. 2 counterfeit. 3 reproduce conditions of (situation etc.), e.g. for training. □ **simulation** noun. **simulator** noun.

■ 1, 2 act, counterfeit, dissimulate, fake, feign, imitate, play-act, pretend, sham.

simultaneous /sɪməl'teɪnɪəs/ adjective (often + with) occurring or operating at same time. □ **simultaneity** /-tə'neɪɪtɪ/ noun. **simultaneously** adverb.

■ coinciding, concurrent, contemporaneous, parallel, synchronized, synchronous.

sin noun 1 breaking of divine or moral law. 2 offence against good taste etc. ● verb (-nn-) 1 commit sin. 2 (+ against) offend against. □ **sinless** adjective. **sinlessness** noun. **sinner** noun.

■ noun 1 corruption, depravity, desecration, devilry, error, evil, fault, guilt, immorality, impiety, iniquity, irreverence, misdeed, offence, peccadillo, profanation, sacrilege, sinfulness, transgression, archaic trespass, ungodliness, unrighteousness, vice, wickedness, wrong, wrongdoing. ● verb 1 do wrong, err, fall from grace, go astray, lapse, misbehave, offend, stray, transgress. 2 (sin against) offend against, archaic trespass against, violate. □ **sinner** evildoer, malefactor, miscreant, offender, reprobate, transgressor, wrongdoer.

since preposition throughout or within period after. ● conjunction 1 during or in time after. 2 because. ● adverb from that time or event until now.

sincere /sɪn'sɪə/ adjective (-r, -st) 1 free from pretence. 2 genuine, honest, frank. □ **sincerity** /-'ser-/ noun.

■ candid, direct, earnest, frank, genuine, guileless, heartfelt, honest, open, real, serious, simple, straight, straightforward, true, truthful, unaffected, unfeigned, upright, wholehearted. □ **sincerity** candour, directness, earnestness, frankness, genuineness, honesty, honour, integrity, openness, straightforwardness, trustworthiness, truthfulness, uprightness.

sincerely adverb in a sincere way. □ **Yours sincerely** written before signature at end of informal letter.

sine noun ratio of side opposite angle (in right-angled triangle) to hypotenuse.

sinecure /'saɪnɪkjʊə/ noun position that requires little or no work but usually yields profit or honour.

sine die /saɪneɪ 'diːeɪ/ adverb formal indefinitely. [Latin]

sine qua non /saɪneɪ kwɑː 'nəʊn/ noun indispensable condition or qualification. [Latin]

sinew /'sɪnjuː/ noun 1 tough fibrous tissue joining muscle to bone; tendon. 2 (in plural) muscles, strength. 3 framework of thing. □ **sinewy** adjective.

■ □ **sinewy** brawny, muscular, strapping, strong, tough, wiry.

sinful adjective committing or involving sin. □ **sinfully** adverb. **sinfulness** noun.

■ bad, corrupt, damnable, depraved, erring, evil, fallen, guilty, immoral, impious, iniquitous, irreligious, irreverent, profane, sacrilegious, ungodly, unholy, unrighteous, vile, wicked, wrong, wrongful.

sing verb (past **sang**; past participle **sung**) 1 utter musical sounds, esp. words in set tune. 2 utter (song, tune). 3 (of wind, kettle, etc.) hum, buzz, or whistle. 4 slang become informer. 5 (+ of) literary celebrate in verse. □ **sing out** shout. **sing the praises of** commend (person) highly.

singsong *noun* session of informal singing. ● *adjective* (of voice) monotonously rising and falling. □ **singable** *adjective*. **singer** *noun*.
■ **1, 2** carol, chant, chirp, chorus, croon, hum, intone, serenade, trill, vocalize, warble, whistle, yodel. □ **singer** chorister, crooner, diva, minstrel, precentor, prima donna, songster, troubadour, vocalist; (*singers*) choir, chorus.

singe /smdʒ/ *verb* (**-geing**) **1** burn superficially. **2** burn off tips or edges of (esp. hair). ● *noun* superficial burn.
■ *verb* blacken, burn, char, scorch, sear.

single /'sɪŋg(ə)l/ *adjective* **1** one only; not double or multiple. **2** united, undivided. **3** of or for one person or thing. **4** solitary. **5** taken separately. **6** unmarried. **7** (with negative or in questions) even one. ● *noun* **1** single thing, esp. room in hotel. **2** (in full **single ticket**) ticket for one-way journey. **3** pop record with one piece of music on each side. **4** *Cricket* hit for one run. **5** (usually in *plural*) game with one player on each side. ● *verb* (**-ling**) (+ *out*) choose for special attention. □ **single-breasted** (of coat etc.) with only one vertical row of buttons, and overlapping little at front. **single-decker** bus with only one deck. **single file** ● *noun* line of people arranged one behind another. ● *adverb* going one behind another. **single-handed** without help. **single-handedly** *adverb*. **single-minded** intent on only one aim. **single-mindedness** *noun*. **single parent** parent bringing up child or children alone. □ **singly** /'sɪŋglɪ/ *adverb*.
■ *adjective* **1, 4** exclusive, individual, isolated, lone, odd, one, only, singular, sole, solitary, unique, unparalleled. **3** individual, personal. **5** distinct, individual, separate. **6** celibate, free, unattached, unmarried. ● *verb* (*single out*) see CHOOSE 1. □ **single-handed** alone, independent, solitary, unaided, unassisted, without help. **single-minded** dedicated, determined, devoted, dogged, fanatical, obsessive, persevering, resolute, steadfast, tireless, unswerving, unwavering.

singlet /'sɪŋglɪt/ *noun* sleeveless vest.

singleton /'sɪŋgəlt(ə)n/ *noun* player's only card of particular suit.

singular /'sɪŋgjʊlə/ *adjective* **1** unique. **2** outstanding. **3** extraordinary, strange. **4** *Grammar* denoting one person or thing. ● *noun Grammar* singular word or form. □ **singularity** /-'lær-/ *noun* (*plural* **-ies**). **singularly** *adverb*.
■ *adjective* **1** see DISTINCTIVE, SINGLE *adjective* 1,4. **2** see OUTSTANDING 1. **3** abnormal, curious, different, eccentric, exceptional, extraordinary, odd, peculiar, rare, remarkable, strange, unusual.

Sinhalese /smhə'liːz/ *noun* (*plural* same) **1** member of a people from N. India now forming majority of population of Sri Lanka. **2** their language. ● *adjective* of this people or language.

sinister /'sɪnɪstə/ *adjective* **1** suggestive of evil; ominous. **2** suggestive of dishonesty. **3** wicked, criminal. **4** *Heraldry* on left side of shield etc. (i.e. to observer's right).

■ **1** dark, disquieting, disturbing, forbidding, frightening, gloomy, inauspicious, menacing, *formal* minatory, ominous, threatening, upsetting. **2** furtive, questionable, shady, suspect. **3** bad, corrupt, criminal, dishonest, evil, illegal, malevolent, malignant, nefarious, treacherous, unworthy, villainous, wicked.

sink *verb* (*past* **sank** or **sunk**; *past participle* **sunk** or (as *adjective*) **sunken**) **1** fall or come slowly downwards. **2** disappear below horizon. **3** go or penetrate below surface of liquid. **4** go to bottom of sea etc. **5** settle down. **6** decline in strength and vitality. **7** descend in pitch or volume. **8** send (ship) to bottom of sea. **9** cause or allow to sink or penetrate. **10** cause failure of. **11** dig (well); bore (shaft). **12** engrave (die). **13** invest (money). **14** cause (ball) to enter pocket at billiards or hole at golf etc. ● *noun* **1** plumbed-in basin, esp. in kitchen. **2** place where foul liquid collects. **3** place of vice. □ **sinking fund** money set aside for eventual repayment of debt.
■ *verb* **1** decline, descend, droop, drop, fall, go down, go lower, plunge, sag, slip down, slump, subside. **2** disappear, go down, set (*sun sets*), vanish. **4** be engulfed, be submerged, founder, go down, go under. **6** collapse, decline, diminish, droop, dwindle, ebb, fade, fail, fall, subside, weaken. **7** decline, descend, diminish, drop, fade, fall, subside. **8** *slang* scupper, scuttle. **11** bore, dig, drill, excavate. ● *noun* **1** basin, stoup.

sinker *noun* weight used to sink fishing or sounding line.

Sino- /'saɪnəʊ/ *combining form* Chinese.

sinology /saɪ'nɒlədʒɪ/ *noun* study of China and its language, history, etc. □ **sinologist** *noun*.

sinuous /'sɪnjʊəs/ *adjective* with many curves; undulating. □ **sinuosity** /-'ɒs-/ *noun*.

sinus /'saɪnəs/ *noun* either of cavities in skull communicating with nostrils.

sinusitis /saɪnə'saɪtɪs/ *noun* inflammation of sinus.

sip *verb* (**-pp-**) drink in small mouthfuls. ● *noun* **1** small mouthful of liquid. **2** act of taking this.
■ *verb* drink, lap, sample, taste.

siphon /'saɪf(ə)n/ *noun* **1** tube shaped like inverted V or U with unequal legs, used for transferring liquid from one container to another by atmospheric pressure. **2** bottle from which fizzy water is forced by pressure of gas. ● *verb* (often + *off*) **1** conduct or flow through siphon. **2** divert or set aside (funds etc.).

sir /sɜː/ *noun* **1** *polite form of address or reference to a man*. **2** (**Sir**) *title used before forename of knight or baronet*.

sire *noun* **1** male parent of animal, esp. stallion. **2** *archaic: form of address to king*. **3** *archaic* father or other male ancestor. ● *verb* (**-ring**) beget.

siren /'saɪərən/ *noun* **1** device for making loud prolonged signal or warning sound. **2** *Greek Mythology* woman or winged creature whose singing lured unwary sailors on to rocks. **3** dangerously fascinating woman.

sirloin /'sɜ:lɔɪn/ *noun* best part of loin of beef.

sirocco /sɪ'rɒkəʊ/ *noun* (*plural* **-s**) **1** Saharan simoom. **2** hot moist wind in S. Europe.

sisal /'saɪs(ə)l/ *noun* fibre from leaves of agave.

siskin /'sɪskɪn/ *noun* small songbird.

sissy /'sɪsɪ/ (also **cissy**) *colloquial noun* (*plural* **-ies**) effeminate or cowardly person. ● *adjective* (**-ier, -iest**) effeminate; cowardly.

sister /'sɪstə/ *noun* **1** woman or girl in relation to her siblings. **2** female fellow member of trade union, sect, human race, etc. **3** member of female religious order. **4** senior female nurse. □ **sister-in-law** (*plural* **sisters-in-law**) **1** husband's or wife's sister. **2** brother's wife. □ **sisterly** *adjective*.

sisterhood *noun* **1** relationship (as) of sisters. **2** society of women bound by monastic vows or devoting themselves to religious or charitable work. **3** community of feeling among women.

sit *verb* (**-tt-**; *past & past participle* **sat**) **1** support body by resting buttocks on ground, seat, etc. **2** cause to sit; place in sitting position. **3** (of bird) perch or remain on nest to hatch eggs. **4** (of animal) rest with hind legs bent and buttocks on ground. **5** (of parliament, court, etc.) be in session. **6** (usually + *for*) pose (for portrait). **7** (+ *for*) be MP for (constituency). **8** (often + *for*) take (exam). □ **be sitting pretty** be comfortably placed. **sit back** relax one's efforts. **sit down 1** sit after standing. **2** cause to sit. **3** (+ *under*) suffer tamely (humiliation etc.). **sit in** occupy place as protest. **sit-in** *noun*. **sit in on** be present as guest etc. at (meeting). **sit on 1** be member of (committee etc.). **2** *colloquial* delay action about. **3** *slang* repress or snub. **sit out 1** take no part in (dance etc.). **2** stay till end of. **3** sit outdoors. **sit tight** *colloquial* **1** remain firmly in one's place. **2** not yield. **sit up 1** rise from lying to sitting. **2** sit firmly upright. **3** defer going to bed. **4** *colloquial* become interested, aroused, etc. **sit-up** *noun* physical exercise of sitting up from supine position without using arms or hands.

■ **1** be seated, *colloquial* park oneself, rest, seat oneself, settle, *colloquial* squat, take a seat, take the weight off one's feet. **5** assemble, be in session, convene, gather, get together, meet. **6** model, pose. **8** be a candidate in, go in for, take, write.

sitar /'sɪtɑ:/ *noun* long-necked Indian lute.

sitcom /'sɪtkɒm/ *noun colloquial* situation comedy.

site *noun* **1** ground chosen or used for town or building. **2** ground set apart for some purpose. ● *verb* (**-ting**) locate, place.

■ *noun* area, campus, ground, location, place, plot, position, setting, situation, spot. ● *verb* see SITUATE.

sitter *noun* **1** person who sits for portrait etc. **2** babysitter.

sitting *noun* **1** continuous period spent engaged in an activity. **2** time during which assembly is engaged in business. **3** session in which meal is served. ● *adjective* **1** having sat down. **2** (of animal or bird) still. **3** (of MP etc.) current.

□ **sitting room** room in which to sit and relax.

■ □ **sitting room** drawing-room, living room, lounge, *archaic* parlour.

***situ** see IN SITU.

situate /'sɪtjʊeɪt/ *verb* (**-ting**) (usually in *passive*) place or put in position, situation, etc.

■ establish, install, locate, place, position, put, set up, site, station.

situation *noun* **1** place and its surroundings. **2** circumstances; position; state of affairs. **3** *formal* paid job. □ **situation comedy** broadcast comedy series involving characters dealing with awkward esp. domestic or everyday situations. □ **situational** *adjective*.

■ **1** area, locale, locality, location, place, position, setting, site, spot. **2** case, circumstances, condition, plight, position, predicament, state of affairs. **3** employment, job, place, position, post.

six *adjective & noun* **1** one more than five. **2** *Cricket* hit scoring six runs. □ **hit, knock for six** *colloquial* utterly surprise or defeat.

sixpence /'sɪkspəns/ *noun* **1** sum of 6 (esp. old) pence. **2** *historical* coin worth this.

sixpenny /'sɪkspənɪ/ *adjective* costing or worth 6 (esp. old) pence.

sixteen /sɪks'ti:n/ *adjective & noun* one more than fifteen. □ **sixteenth** *adjective & noun*.

sixth *adjective & noun* **1** next after fifth. **2** any of 6 equal parts of thing. □ **sixth form** form in secondary school for pupils over 16. **sixth-form college** separate college for pupils over 16. **sixth sense** supposed intuitive or extrasensory faculty.

sixty /'sɪkstɪ/ *adjective & noun* (*plural* **-ies**) six times ten. □ **sixtieth** *adjective & noun*.

sizable = SIZEABLE.

size¹ *noun* **1** relative bigness or extent of a thing; dimensions, magnitude. **2** each of classes into which things are divided by size. ● *verb* (**-zing**) sort in sizes or by size. □ **size up** *colloquial* form judgement of.

■ *noun* **1** amount, area, bigness, breadth, bulk, capacity, depth, dimensions, extent, gauge, height, immensity, largeness, length, magnitude, mass, measure, measurement, proportions, scale, scope, volume, weight, width. □ **size up** see ASSESS 1.

size² *noun* sticky solution used for glazing paper and stiffening textiles etc. ● *verb* (**-zing**) treat with size.

sizeable *adjective* (also **sizable**) fairly large.

■ big, considerable, decent, generous, large, largish, significant, worthwhile.

sizzle /'sɪz(ə)l/ *verb* (**-ling**) **1** sputter or hiss, esp. in frying. **2** *colloquial* be very hot. ● *noun* sizzling sound. □ **sizzling** *adjective & adverb*.

SJ *abbreviation* Society of Jesus.

skate¹ *noun* **1** ice-skate. **2** roller skate. ● *verb* (**-ting**) **1** move, glide, or perform (as) on skates. **2** (+ *over*) refer fleetingly to; disregard. □ **skate-**

board ● *noun* short narrow board on roller-skate wheels for riding on standing up. ● *verb* ride on skateboard. □ **skater** *noun*.

| ■ *verb* **1** glide, skim, slide.

skate[2] *noun* (*plural* same or **-s**) large edible marine flatfish.

skedaddle /skɪ'dæd(ə)l/ *verb* (**-ling**) *colloquial* run away; retreat hastily.

skein /skem/ *noun* **1** quantity of yarn etc. coiled and usually loosely twisted. **2** flock of wild geese etc. in flight.

skeleton /'skelɪt(ə)n/ *noun* **1** hard framework of bones etc. of animal. **2** supporting framework or structure of thing. **3** very thin person or animal. **4** useless or dead remnant. **5** outline sketch. ● *adjective* having only essential or minimum number of people, parts, etc. □ **skeleton key** key fitting many locks. □ **skeletal** *adjective*.

| ■ *noun* **1** bones, frame. **2** frame, framework, structure.

skerry /'skerɪ/ *noun* (*plural* **-ies**) *Scottish* reef; rocky islet.

sketch *noun* **1** rough or unfinished drawing or painting. **2** rough draft; general outline. **3** short usually humorous play. **4** short descriptive piece of writing. ● *verb* **1** make or give sketch of. **2** make sketches. □ **sketchbook** (also **sketchblock, sketch pad**) pad of paper used for drawing and sketching. **sketch map** roughly drawn map.

| ■ *noun* **1** drawing, picture. **2** design, diagram, draft, outline, plan, skeleton. **3** performance, scene, skit, turn. **4** description, profile, vignette. ● *verb* **1** depict, draft, draw, indicate, outline, plan, portray, represent. **2** see DRAW *verb* 7–9.

sketchy *adjective* (**-ier**, **-iest**) **1** giving only a rough outline. **2** *colloquial* insubstantial or imperfect, esp. through haste. □ **sketchily** *adverb*.

| ■ bitty, crude, cursory, hasty, hurried, imperfect, incomplete, inexact, perfunctory, rough, scrappy, undeveloped, unfinished, unpolished.

skew *adjective* oblique, slanting, set askew. ● *noun* slant. ● *verb* **1** make skew. **2** distort. **3** move obliquely.

skewbald /'skju:bɔ:ld/ *adjective* (of animal) with irregular patches of white and another colour. ● *noun* skewbald animal, esp. horse.

skewer /'skju:ə/ *noun* long pin for holding meat compactly together while cooking. ● *verb* fasten together or pierce (as) with skewer.

ski /ski:/ *noun* (*plural* **-s**) **1** each of pair of long narrow pieces of wood etc. fastened under feet for travelling over snow. **2** similar device under vehicle. ● *verb* (**skis**; **ski'd** or **skied** /ski:d/; **skiing**) travel on skis. □ **skier** *noun*.

skid *verb* (**-dd-**) **1** (of vehicle etc.) slide esp. sideways or obliquely on slippery road etc. **2** cause (vehicle) to skid. ● *noun* **1** act of skidding. **2** runner used as part of landing-gear of aircraft. □ **skid-pan** slippery surface for drivers to prac-

tise control of skidding. **skid row** *US slang* district frequented by vagrants.

| ■ *verb* **1** aquaplane, glide, slide, slip.

skiff *noun* light boat, esp. for rowing or sculling.

skilful /'skɪlfʊl/ *adjective* (*US* **skillful**) having or showing skill. □ **skilfully** *adverb*. **skilfulness** *noun*.

| ■ able, accomplished, adept, adroit, apt, artful, capable, clever, competent, consummate, crafty, cunning, deft, dexterous, experienced, expert, gifted, handy, ingenious, masterful, masterly, practised, professional, proficient, qualified, shrewd, skilled, smart, talented, trained, versatile, versed, workmanlike.

skill *noun* **1** practised ability, expertness, technique. **2** craft, art, etc. requiring skill.

| ■ **1** ability, accomplishment, adroitness, aptitude, art, artistry, capability, cleverness, competence, craft, cunning, deftness, dexterity, experience, expertise, facility, flair, gift, ingenuity, knack, mastery, professionalism, proficiency, prowess, shrewdness, talent, technique, workmanship. **2** art, craft, handicraft, science, technique.

skilled *adjective* **1** skilful. **2** (of work or worker) requiring or having skill or special training.

| ■ **1** see SKILFUL. **2** experienced, expert, practised, qualified, skilful, trained, versed.

skillet /'skɪlɪt/ *noun* **1** long-handled metal cooking pot. **2** *US* frying-pan.

skim *verb* (**-mm-**) **1** take scum or cream etc. from surface of (liquid). **2** barely touch (surface) in passing over. **3** (often + *over*) deal with or treat (matter) superficially. **4** (often + *over*, *along*) glide lightly. **5** read or look over superficially. □ **skim, skimmed milk** milk with cream removed.

| ■ **4** aquaplane, coast, fly, glide, sail, skate, skid, slide, slip. **5** dip into, leaf through, look through, scan, skip through, thumb through.

skimp *verb* (often + *on*) **1** economize. **2** supply meagrely; use too little of.

skimpy *adjective* (**-ier**, **-iest**) meagre, insufficient.

skin *noun* **1** flexible covering of body. **2** skin removed from animal. **3** material made from this. **4** complexion. **5** outer layer or covering. **6** film like skin on liquid etc. **7** container for liquid, made of animal's skin. ● *verb* (**-nn-**) **1** strip skin from. **2** graze (part of body). **3** *slang* swindle. □ **skin-deep** superficial. **skin-diver** person who swims under water without diving suit. **skin-diving** *noun*. **skinflint** miser. **skin graft 1** surgical transplanting of skin. **2** skin thus transferred. **skintight** very close-fitting.

| ■ *noun* **2**, **3** coat, fur, hide, pelt. **5** casing, coat, coating, covering, exterior, husk, integument, membrane, outside, peel, rind, shell, surface. ● *verb* **1** excoriate, flay, pare, peel, shell, strip. □ **skin-deep** insubstantial, shallow, superficial, trivial, unimportant.

skinful *noun colloquial* enough alcohol to make one drunk.

skinny *adjective* (**-ier, -iest**) thin, emaciated.
■ bony, emaciated, gaunt, lanky, scraggy, thin, wasted.

skint *adjective slang* having no money.

skip[1] *verb* (**-pp-**) **1** move along lightly, esp. by taking two hops with each foot in turn. **2** frisk, gambol. **3** jump lightly esp. over skipping rope. **4** move quickly from one subject etc. to another. **5** omit or make omissions in reading. **6** *colloquial* not attend etc. **7** *colloquial* leave hurriedly. ● *noun* skipping movement or action. □ **skipping rope** length of rope turned over head and under feet while jumping.
■ *verb* **1–3** bound, caper, cavort, dance, frisk, gambol, hop, jump, leap, prance, romp, spring. **5** avoid, forget, ignore, leave out, miss out, neglect, omit, overlook, pass over, skim through. **6** be absent from, *US* cut, miss, play truant from.

skip[2] *noun* **1** large container for refuse etc. **2** container in which men or materials are lowered or raised in mines etc.

skipjack *noun* (in full **skipjack tuna**) (*plural* same or **-s**) small Pacific tuna.

skipper /ˈskɪpə/ *noun* captain of ship, aircraft, team, etc. ● *verb* be captain of.

skirl *noun* shrill sound of bagpipes. ● *verb* make skirl.

skirmish /ˈskɜːmɪʃ/ *noun* **1** minor battle. **2** short argument etc. ● *verb* engage in skirmish.
■ *noun* **1** brush, fight, fray, scrimmage, *colloquial* set-to, tussle. ● *verb* see FIGHT *verb* 1.

skirt *noun* **1** woman's garment hanging from waist, or this part of complete dress. **2** part of coat etc. that hangs below waist. **3** hanging part at base of hovercraft. **4** (in *singular* or *plural*) border, outlying part. **5** flank of beef etc. ● *verb* **1** go or be along or round edge of. **2** avoid dealing with (question etc.). □ **skirting board** narrow board etc. round bottom of room-wall.
■ *verb* **1** border, bypass, circle, encircle, go round, pass round, surround. **2** avoid, bypass, dodge, evade, sidestep, steer clear of.

skit *noun* light piece of satire; burlesque.
■ burlesque, parody, satire, sketch, *colloquial* spoof, *colloquial* take-off.

skittish /ˈskɪtɪʃ/ *adjective* **1** lively, playful. **2** (of horse etc.) nervous; inclined to shy.

skittle /ˈskɪt(ə)l/ *noun* pin used in game of skittles, in which number of wooden pins are set up to be bowled or knocked down.

skive *verb* (**-ving**) (often + *off*) *slang* evade work; play truant. □ **skiver** *noun*.

skivvy /ˈskɪvɪ/ *noun* (*plural* **-ies**) *colloquial* derogatory female domestic servant.

skua /ˈskjuːə/ *noun* large predatory seabird.

skulduggery /skʌlˈdʌgərɪ/ *noun* trickery; unscrupulous behaviour.

skulk *verb* lurk or conceal oneself or move stealthily.

skull *noun* **1** bony case of brain. **2** bony frame-work of head. **3** head as site of intelligence. □ **skull and crossbones** representation of skull over two crossed thigh-bones, esp. on pirate flag or as emblem of death. **skullcap** close-fitting peakless cap.

skunk *noun* (*plural* same or **-s**) **1** black white-striped bushy-tailed mammal, emitting powerful stench when attacked. **2** *colloquial* contemptible person.

sky /skaɪ/ *noun* (*plural* **skies**) (in *singular* or *plural*) atmosphere and outer space seen from the earth. □ **sky blue** bright clear blue. **skydiving** sport of performing acrobatic manoeuvres under free fall before opening parachute. **sky-high** as if reaching the sky, very high. **skylark** *noun* lark that sings while soaring. ● *verb* play tricks and practical jokes. **skylight** window in roof. **skyline** outline of hills, buildings, etc. against sky. **sky-rocket** ● *noun* firework shooting into air and exploding. ● *verb* rise steeply. **skyscraper** very tall building.
■ air, atmosphere, *literary* firmament, heavens, space, stratosphere, *poetical* welkin.

slab *noun* **1** flat thickish esp. rectangular piece of solid material. **2** mortuary table.
■ **1** block, chunk, hunk, lump, piece, slice, wedge.

slack[1] *adjective* **1** (of rope etc.) not taut; loose. **2** (of trade) sluggish. **3** inactive; negligent, remiss. **4** (of tide etc.) neither ebbing nor flowing. ● *noun* **1** slack part of rope etc. **2** slack period. **3** (in *plural*) casual trousers. ● *verb* **1** slacken. **2** *colloquial* take a rest; be lazy. □ **slack off** loosen. **slack up** reduce level of activity or speed. □ **slackness** *noun*.
■ *adjective* **1** drooping, flaccid, floppy, limp, loose, sagging. **2** inactive, quiet, slow, slow-moving, sluggish. **3** careless, dilatory, disorganized, easygoing, idle, inattentive, indolent, lax, lazy, listless, neglectful, negligent, permissive, relaxed, remiss, slothful, unbusinesslike, uncaring, undisciplined. ● *verb* **2** be lazy, idle, malinger, neglect one's duty, shirk, *slang* skive.

slack[2] *noun* coal dust; coal fragments.

slacken *verb* make or become slack. □ **slacken off** slack off.
■ abate, decrease, ease, ease off, lessen, loosen, lower, moderate, reduce, relax, release, slow down.

slacker *noun* shirker.
■ good-for-nothing, idler, *colloquial* lazybones, malingerer, shirker, *slang* skiver, sluggard.

slag *noun* refuse left after ore has been smelted etc. ● *verb* (**-gg-**) **1** form slag. **2** (often + *off*) *slang* insult, slander. □ **slag-heap** hill of refuse from mine etc.

slain *past participle* of SLAY.

slake *verb* (**-king**) **1** assuage or satisfy (thirst etc.). **2** cause (lime) to heat and crumble by action of water.
■ **1** allay, assuage, cool, ease, quench, relieve, satisfy.

slalom /'slɑːləm/ *noun* downhill ski-race on zigzag course between artificial obstacles.

slam[1] *verb* (-mm-) **1** shut, throw, or put down violently or with bang. **2** *slang* criticize severely. ● *noun* sound or action of slamming.
| ■ *verb* **1** bang, shut. **2** see CRITICIZE **1**.

slam[2] *noun* winning of all tricks at cards.

slander /'slɑːndə/ *noun* false and damaging utterance about person. ● *verb* utter slander about. □ **slanderer** *noun*. **slanderous** *adjective*.
| ■ *noun* backbiting, calumny, defamation, denigration, insult, libel, lie, misrepresentation, obloquy, scandal, slur, smear, vilification. ● *verb* blacken the name of, calumniate, defame, denigrate, disparage, libel, malign, misrepresent, *archaic* or *US* slur, smear, traduce, vilify.
□ **slanderous** abusive, calumnious, cruel, damaging, defamatory, disparaging, false, hurtful, insulting, libellous, lying, malicious, mendacious, scurrilous, untrue, vicious.

slang *noun* very informal words, phrases, or meanings, not regarded as standard and often peculiar to profession, class, etc. ● *verb* use abusive language (to). □ **slanging match** prolonged exchange of insults. □ **slangy** *adjective*.
| ■ *verb* see INSULT *verb* **1**. □ **slanging match** see QUARREL *noun* **1**.

slant /slɑːnt/ *verb* **1** slope; (cause to) lie or go obliquely. **2** (often as **slanted** *adjective*) present (news etc.) in biased or particular way. ● *noun* **1** slope; oblique position. **2** point of view, esp. biased one. ● *adjective* sloping, oblique. □ **slanting** *adjective*.
| ■ *verb* **1** be at an angle, be skewed, incline, lean, shelve, slope, tilt. **2** bias, colour, distort, prejudice, twist, weight. ● *noun* **1** angle, bevel, camber, cant, diagonal, gradient, incline, list, pitch, rake, ramp, slope, tilt. **2** approach, attitude, bias, distortion, emphasis, imbalance, one-sidedness, perspective, point of view, prejudice, standpoint, view, viewpoint. □ **slanting** see OBLIQUE *adjective* **1**.

slantwise *adverb* aslant.

slap *verb* (-pp-) **1** strike (as) with palm of hand. **2** lay forcefully. **3** put hastily or carelessly. ● *noun* slapping stroke or sound. ● *adverb* suddenly, fully, directly. □ **slapdash** hasty, careless. **slap-happy** *colloquial* cheerfully casual. **slapstick** boisterous comedy. **slap-up** *colloquial* lavish.
| ■ *verb* **1** hit, smack, spank.

slash *verb* **1** cut or gash with knife etc. **2** (often + *at*) deliver or aim cutting blows. **3** reduce (prices etc.) drastically. **4** criticize harshly. ● *noun* **1** slashing cut. **2** *Printing* oblique stroke. **3** *slang* act of urinating.
| ■ *verb* **1** cut, gash, hack, slice, slit.

slat *noun* long narrow strip of wood, plastic, or metal, used in fences, venetian blinds, etc.

slate *noun* **1** fine-grained bluish-grey rock easily split into thin smooth plates. **2** piece of this used

esp. in roofing or *historical* for writing on. **3** colour of slate. **4** list of nominees for office etc. ● *verb* (-ting) **1** roof with slates. **2** *colloquial* criticize severely. **3** *US* make arrangements for (event etc.). **4** *US* nominate for office. ● *adjective* of (colour of) slate. □ **slating** *noun*. **slaty** *adjective*.

slattern /'slæt(ə)n/ *noun* slovenly woman. □ **slatternly** *adjective*.

slaughter /'slɔːtə/ *verb* **1** kill (animals) for food etc. **2** kill (people) ruthlessly or in large numbers. **3** *colloquial* defeat utterly. ● *noun* act of slaughtering. □ **slaughterhouse** place for slaughter of animals for food. □ **slaughterer** *noun*.
| ■ *verb* **1** butcher, kill. **2** annihilate, butcher, kill, massacre, murder, slay. ● *noun* bloodshed, butchery, carnage, killing, massacre, murder. □ **slaughterhouse** abattoir, shambles.

Slav /slɑːv/ *noun* member of group of peoples of central and eastern Europe speaking Slavonic languages. ● *adjective* of the Slavs.

slave *noun* **1** person who is owned by and has to serve another. **2** drudge; hard worker. **3** (+ *of, to*) obsessive devotee. ● *verb* (-ving) work very hard. □ **slave-driver 1** overseer of slaves. **2** hard taskmaster. **slave trade** dealing in slaves, esp. African blacks.
| ■ *noun* **1** *historical* serf, servant, *literary* thrall, *historical* vassal. **2** *colloquial* dogsbody, drudge, toiler. ● *verb* drudge, exert oneself, grind away, labour, sweat, toil. □ **slave-driver 2** despot, hard taskmaster, tyrant.

slaver[1] *noun* *historical* ship or person engaged in slave trade.

slaver[2] /'slævə/ *verb* dribble; drool. ● *noun* **1** dribbling saliva. **2** flattery. **3** drivel.
| ■ *verb* dribble, drool, foam at the mouth, salivate, slobber, spit.

slavery /'sleɪvərɪ/ *noun* **1** condition of slave. **2** drudgery. **3** practice of having slaves.
| ■ **1** bondage, captivity, enslavement, *historical* serfdom, servitude, subjugation, *historical* vassalage.

Slavic /'slɑːvɪk/ *adjective* & *noun* Slavonic.

slavish /'sleɪvɪʃ/ *adjective* **1** like slaves. **2** without originality. □ **slavishly** *adverb*.
| ■ **1** abject, cringing, fawning, grovelling, humiliating, menial, obsequious, servile, submissive, sycophantic. **2** imitative, unimaginative, unoriginal.

Slavonic /slə'vɒnɪk/ *adjective* of group of languages including Russian, Polish, and Czech. ● *noun* Slavonic group of languages.

slay *verb* (*past* **slew** /sluː/; *past participle* **slain**) kill. □ **slayer** *noun*.
| ■ assassinate, *slang* bump off, butcher, destroy, dispatch, execute, exterminate, *colloquial* finish off, kill, martyr, massacre, murder, put down, put to death, slaughter.

sleaze *noun* *colloquial* sleaziness.

sleazy /'sliːzɪ/ *adjective* (**-ier**, **-iest**) squalid, tawdry. □ **sleazily** *adverb*. **sleaziness** *noun*.

> ■ cheap, contemptible, dirty, disreputable, low-class, mean, mucky, run-down, seedy, slovenly, sordid, squalid, unprepossessing.

sled *noun* & *verb* (**-dd-**) *US* sledge.

sledge *noun* vehicle on runners for use on snow. ● *verb* (**-ging**) travel or carry on sledge.

> ■ *noun* bobsleigh, *US* sled, sleigh, toboggan.

sledgehammer /'sledʒhæmə/ *noun* large heavy hammer.

sleek *adjective* **1** (of hair, skin, etc.) smooth and glossy. **2** (of vehicle) smooth, streamlined. **3** looking well fed and comfortable. ● *verb* make sleek. □ **sleekly** *adverb*. **sleekness** *noun*.

> ■ *adjective* **1** brushed, glossy, lustrous, shining, shiny, silken, silky, smooth, soft, velvety, well groomed. **2** graceful, smooth, streamlined, trim. **3** comfortable, contented, thriving, well fed.

sleep *noun* **1** condition in which eyes are closed, muscles and nerves relaxed, and consciousness suspended. **2** period of this. **3** state like sleep, e.g. rest, quiet, death. ● *verb* (*past & past participle* **slept**) **1** be or fall asleep. **2** spend the night. **3** provide sleeping accommodation for. **4** (+ *with, together*) have sexual intercourse. **5** (+ *on*) defer (decision) until next day. **6** (+ *through*) fail to be woken by. **7** be inactive or dead. **8** (+ *off*) cure by sleeping. □ **sleeping bag** padded bag to sleep in when camping etc. **sleeping car, carriage** railway coach with berths. **sleeping partner** partner not sharing in actual work of firm. **sleeping pill** pill to induce sleep. **sleeping policeman** ramp etc. in road to slow traffic. **sleepwalk** walk about while asleep. **sleepwalker** *noun*. □ **sleeping** *adjective*. **sleepless** *adjective*. **sleeplessness** *noun*.

> ■ *noun* **1, 2** catnap, doze, *colloquial* forty winks, *slang* kip, nap, repose, rest, *colloquial* shut-eye, siesta, *poetical* slumber, *colloquial* snooze. **3** coma, dormancy, hibernation, repose, rest, torpor, unconsciousness. ● *verb* **1** catnap, *slang* doss down, doze, drop off, drowse, fall asleep, go to bed, *colloquial* have forty winks, *slang* kip, *colloquial* nod off, rest, *poetical* slumber, *colloquial* snooze, take a nap. **7** be dormant, hibernate. □ **sleepwalker** noctambulist, somnambulist. □ **sleeping** see ASLEEP *adjective* 1. **sleepless** awake, conscious, disturbed, insomniac, restless, wakeful, watchful, wide awake.

sleeper *noun* **1** sleeping person or animal. **2** beam supporting railway track. **3** sleeping car. **4** ring worn in pierced ear to keep hole open.

sleepy *adjective* (**-ier**, **-iest**) **1** feeling need of sleep. **2** quiet, inactive. □ **sleepily** *adverb*. **sleepiness** *noun*.

> ■ **1** comatose, *colloquial* dopey, drowsy, lethargic, sluggish, somnolent, tired, torpid, weary. **2** boring, dull, inactive, quiet, restful, slow-moving, soporific, unexciting. □ **sleepiness** drowsiness, lassitude, lethargy, somnolence, tiredness, torpor.

sleet *noun* **1** snow and rain together. **2** hail or snow melting as it falls. ● *verb* (after *it*) sleet falls. □ **sleety** *adjective*.

sleeve *noun* **1** part of garment covering arm. **2** cover for gramophone record. **3** tube enclosing rod etc. □ **up one's sleeve** in reserve. □ **sleeved** *adjective*. **sleeveless** *adjective*.

sleigh /sleɪ/ *noun* sledge, esp. for riding on. ● *verb* travel on sleigh.

sleight of hand /slaɪt/ *noun* dexterity, esp. in conjuring.

slender /'slendə/ *adjective* (**-er**, **-est**) **1** of small girth or breadth; slim. **2** slight, scanty, meagre.

> ■ **1** fine, graceful, lean, narrow, slight, slim, svelte, sylphlike, tenuous, thin, trim. **2** feeble, inadequate, meagre, scanty, slight, slim, small, tenuous.

slept *past & past participle* of SLEEP.

sleuth /sluːθ/ *colloquial noun* detective. ● *verb* investigate crime etc.

slew[1] /sluː/ *verb* (often + *round*) turn or swing to new position. ● *noun* such turn.

slew[2] *past* of SLAY.

slice *noun* **1** thin flat piece or wedge cut from something. **2** share. **3** kitchen utensil with thin broad blade. **4** stroke sending ball obliquely. ● *verb* (**-cing**) **1** (often + *up*) cut into slices. **2** (+ *off*) cut off. **3** (+ *into, through*) cut (as) with knife. **4** strike (ball) with slice.

> ■ *noun* **1** layer, piece, rasher, shaving, sliver, wedge. **2** cut, helping, part, portion, share. ● *verb* **1** carve, cut, divide. **2** (*slice off*) cut off, pare, shave off, trim, whittle.

slick *adjective* **1** skilful, efficient. **2** superficially dexterous; glib. **3** sleek, smooth. ● *noun* patch of oil etc., esp. on sea. ● *verb colloquial* make smooth or sleek. □ **slickly** *adverb*. **slickness** *noun*.

> ■ *adjective* **1** adroit, artful, clever, cunning, deft, dexterous, efficient, quick, skilful, smart. **2** glib, meretricious, plausible, *colloquial* smarmy, smooth, smug, specious, suave, superficial, tricky, unctuous, untrustworthy, urbane, wily. **3** glossy, oiled, shiny, sleek, smooth.

slide *verb* (*past & past participle* **slid**) **1** (cause to) move along smooth surface touching it always with same part. **2** move quietly or smoothly. **3** glide over ice without skates. **4** (often + *into*) pass unobtrusively. ● *noun* **1** act of sliding. **2** rapid decline. **3** smooth slope down which people or things slide. **4** track for sliding, esp. on ice. **5** part of machine or instrument that slides. **6** mounted transparency viewed with projector. **7** piece of glass holding object for microscope. **8** hairslide. **9** landslide. □ **let things slide** be negligent; allow deterioration. **slide rule** ruler with sliding central strip, graduated logarithmically for rapid calculations. **sliding scale** scale of fees, taxes, wages, etc. that varies according to some other factor.

> ■ *verb* **1** aquaplane, coast, glide, glissade, plane, skate, skid, skim, slip, slither, toboggan. **2** creep, slink, slip, slither, steal. **3** glide, glissade. ● *noun* **9** avalanche, landslide, landslip.

slight /slaɪt/ *adjective* **1** small, insignificant. **2** inadequate. **3** slender, frail-looking. ● *verb* treat disrespectfully; ignore. ● *noun* act of slighting. □ **slightly** *adverb*. **slightness** *noun*.

■ *adjective* **1, 2** imperceptible, inadequate, inconsequential, inconsiderable, insignificant, insufficient, little, minor, negligible, scanty, slim (*chance*), small, superficial, trifling, trivial, unimportant. **3** delicate, diminutive, flimsy, fragile, frail, petite, sickly, slender, slim, svelte, sylphlike, thin, tiny, weak. ● *verb* see INSULT *verb* 1. ● *noun* see INSULT *noun*. □ **slightly** hardly, moderately, only just, scarcely.

slim *adjective* (**-mm-**) **1** not fat, slender. **2** small, insufficient. ● *verb* (**-mm-**) **1** (often + *down*) become slim, esp. by dieting etc. **2** make slim. □ **slimline 1** of slender design. **2** not fattening. □ **slimmer** *noun*.

■ *adjective* **1** fine, graceful, lean, narrow, slender, svelte, sylphlike, thin, trim. **2** little, negligible, remote, slender, slight, small, unlikely. ● *verb* **1** diet, lose weight.

slime *noun* oozy or sticky substance.

■ *colloquial* muck, mucus, mud, ooze, sludge.

slimy *adjective* (**-ier, -iest**) **1** like, covered with, or filled with slime. **2** *colloquial* disgustingly obsequious. □ **sliminess** *noun*.

■ **1** clammy, greasy, mucous, muddy, oily, oozy, slippery, *colloquial* slippy, slithery, *colloquial* squidgy, *colloquial* squishy, wet.

sling[1] *noun* **1** strap etc. used to support or raise thing. **2** bandage supporting injured arm. **3** strap etc. used to throw small missile. ● *verb* (*past & past participle* **slung**) **1** suspend with sling. **2** *colloquial* throw. □ **sling-back** shoe held in place by strap above heel. **sling one's hook** *slang* go away.

■ *verb* **2** cast, *colloquial* chuck, fling, *colloquial* heave, hurl, launch, let fly, lob, pelt, pitch, propel, shoot, shy, throw, toss.

sling[2] *noun* sweetened drink of spirits (esp. gin) with water.

slink *verb* (*past & past participle* **slunk**) (often + *off, away, by*) move stealthily or guiltily.

■ creep, edge, prowl, skulk, slither, sneak, steal.

slinky *adjective* (**-ier, -iest**) (of garment) close-fitting and sinuous.

■ clinging, close-fitting, graceful, sexy, sinuous, sleek.

slip[1] *verb* (**-pp-**) **1** slide unintentionally or momentarily; lose footing or balance. **2** go with sliding motion. **3** escape or fall because hard to grasp. **4** go unobserved or quietly. **5** make careless or slight mistake. **6** fall below standard. **7** place stealthily or casually. **8** release from restraint or connection. **9** (+ *on, off*) pull (garment) easily or hastily on or off. **10** escape from; evade. ● *noun* **1** act of slipping. **2** careless or slight error. **3** pillowcase. **4** petticoat. **5** (in *singular* or *plural*) slipway. **6** *Cricket* fielder behind wicket on off side. **7** *Cricket* (in *singular*

or *plural*) this position. □ **give (person) the slip** escape from; evade. **let slip 1** release. **2** utter inadvertently. **3** miss (opportunity). **slip away** escape. **slip-knot 1** knot that can be undone by pull. **2** running knot. **slip of the pen (or tongue)** small unintentional written (or spoken) mistake. **slip-on** (of shoes or clothes) easily slipped on or off. **slipped disc** displaced disc between vertebrae. **slip road** road for entering or leaving motorway etc. **slipstream** current of air or water driven backwards by propeller etc. **slip up** *colloquial* make mistake. **slip-up** *noun colloquial* mistake, blunder. **slipway** ramp for shipbuilding or landing boats.

■ *verb* **1** aquaplane, coast, glide, glissade, skate, ski, skid, skim, slide, slither, stumble, trip. **4** creep, edge, slink, sneak, steal. ● *noun* **2** accident, *slang* bloomer, blunder, error, fault, *faux pas*, impropriety, inaccuracy, indiscretion, lapse, miscalculation, mistake, oversight, slip of the pen, slip of the tongue, *colloquial* slip-up. □ **give (person) the slip** see ELUDE 1. **let slip 2** see REVEAL 2. **slip away** see ESCAPE *verb* 1. **slip up** see BLUNDER *verb* 1.

slip[2] *noun* **1** small piece of paper, esp. for making notes. **2** cutting from plant for grafting or planting.

■ **1** note, piece, sheet, strip.

slippage *noun* act or instance of slipping.

slipper *noun* light loose indoor shoe.

slippery /'slɪpərɪ/ *adjective* **1** difficult to grasp, stand on, etc., because smooth or wet. **2** unreliable, unscrupulous. □ **slipperiness** *noun*.

■ **1** glassy, greasy, icy, lubricated, oily, slimy, *colloquial* slippy, slithery, smooth, wet. **2** crafty, cunning, devious, evasive, hard to pin down, *colloquial* shifty, sly, *colloquial* smarmy, smooth, sneaky, specious, tricky, unreliable, untrustworthy, wily.

slippy *adjective* (**-ier, -iest**) *colloquial* slippery.

slipshod *adjective* careless, slovenly.

■ careless, disorganized, lax, messy, slapdash, sloppy, slovenly, untidy.

slit *noun* straight narrow incision or opening. ● *verb* (**-tt-**; *past & past participle* **slit**) **1** make slit in. **2** cut in strips.

■ *noun* aperture, breach, break, chink, cleft, crack, cut, fissure, gap, gash, hole, incision, opening, rift, slot, split, tear, vent. ● *verb* **1** cut, gash, slice, split, tear.

slither /'slɪðə/ *verb* slide unsteadily. ● *noun* act of slithering. □ **slithery** *adjective*.

■ *verb* creep, glide, slide, slink, slip, snake, worm.

sliver /'slɪvə/ *noun* long thin slice or piece. ● *verb* cut or split into slivers.

■ *noun* chip, flake, piece, shard, shaving, snippet, splinter, strip.

slob *noun colloquial derogatory* lazy, untidy, or fat person.

slobber /'slɒbə/ *verb & noun* slaver. □ **slobbery** *adjective*.

■ *verb* dribble, drool, salivate, slaver. ● *noun* dribble, saliva, slaver.

sloe *noun* **1** blackthorn. **2** its small bluish-black fruit.

slog *verb* (**-gg-**) **1** hit hard and usually unskilfully. **2** work or walk doggedly. ● *noun* **1** heavy random hit. **2** hard steady work or walk. **3** spell of this.

slogan /'sləʊgən/ *noun* **1** catchy phrase used in advertising etc. **2** party cry, watchword.

■ battle-cry, catchphrase, catchword, jingle, motto, saying, war cry, watchword.

sloop /sluːp/ *noun* small one-masted fore-and-aft rigged vessel.

slop *verb* (**-pp-**) **1** (often + *over*) spill over edge of vessel. **2** spill or splash liquid on. ● *noun* **1** liquid spilled or splashed. **2** (in *plural*) dirty waste water, wine, etc. **3** (in *singular* or *plural*) unappetizing liquid food.

slope *noun* **1** inclined position, direction, or state. **2** piece of rising or falling ground. **3** difference in level between two ends or sides of a thing. **4** place for skiing. ● *verb* (**-ping**) **1** have or take slope; slant. **2** cause to slope. □ **slope off** *slang* go away, esp. to evade work etc. □ **sloping** *adjective*.

■ *noun* **1–3** acclivity, angle, ascent, bank, bevel, camber, cant, decline, declivity, descent, dip, drop, fall, gradient, hill, incline, pitch, rake, ramp, rise, scarp, slant, tilt. ● *verb* **1** ascend, bank, decline, descend, dip, fall, incline, lean, pitch, rise, shelve, slant, tilt, tip. **2** angle, incline, lean, slant, tilt, tip. □ **sloping** see OBLIQUE *adjective* 1.

sloppy *adjective* (**-ier, -iest**) **1** wet, watery, too liquid. **2** careless, untidy. **3** foolishly sentimental. □ **sloppily** *adverb*. **sloppiness** *noun*.

■ **1** liquid, runny, sloshy, slushy, squelchy, watery, wet. **2** careless, dirty, disorganized, lax, messy, slapdash, slipshod, slovenly, unsystematic, untidy. **3** see SENTIMENTAL.

slosh *verb* **1** (often + *about*) splash or flounder. **2** *slang* hit, esp. heavily. **3** *colloquial* pour (liquid) clumsily. ● *noun* **1** slush. **2** act or sound of splashing. **3** *slang* heavy blow.

sloshed *adjective slang* drunk.

sloshy /'slɒʃɪ/ *adjective* (**-ier, -iest**) **1** watery, slushy. **2** sentimental.

slot *noun* **1** slit in machine etc. for something (esp. coin) to be inserted. **2** slit, groove, etc. for thing. **3** allotted place in schedule. ● *verb* (**-tt-**) **1** (often + *in, into*) place or be placed (as if) into slot. **2** provide with slot(s). □ **slot machine** machine worked by insertion of coin, esp. delivering small items or providing amusement.

■ *noun* **1, 2** aperture, breach, break, channel, chink, cleft, crack, cut, fissure, gap, gash, groove, hole, incision, opening, rift, slit, split, vent. **3** place, position, space, spot, time.

sloth /sləʊθ/ *noun* **1** laziness, indolence. **2** slow-moving arboreal S. American mammal.

■ **1** apathy, idleness, indolence, inertia, laziness, lethargy, sluggishness, torpor.

slothful *adjective* lazy. □ **slothfully** *adverb*. **slothfulness** *noun*.

slouch /slaʊtʃ/ *verb* stand, move, or sit in drooping fashion. ● *noun* **1** slouching posture or movement. **2** *slang* incompetent or slovenly worker etc. □ **slouch hat** hat with wide flexible brim.

■ *verb* droop, hunch, loll, lounge, sag, shamble, slump, stoop.

slough[1] /slaʊ/ *noun* swamp, miry place. □ **Slough of Despond** state of hopeless depression.

slough[2] /slʌf/ *noun* part that animal (esp. snake) casts or moults. ● *verb* (often + *off*) cast or drop as slough.

Slovak /'sləʊvæk/ *noun* **1** member of Slavonic people inhabiting Slovakia. **2** their language. ● *adjective* of this people or language.

sloven /'slʌv(ə)n/ *noun* untidy or careless person.

Slovene /'sləʊviːn/ (also **Slovenian** /-'viːnɪən/) *noun* **1** member of Slavonic people in Slovenia. **2** their language. ● *adjective* of Slovenia or its people or language.

slovenly *adjective* careless and untidy; unmethodical. ● *adverb* in a slovenly way. □ **slovenliness** *noun*.

■ *adjective* careless, disorganized, disreputable, lax, messy, shoddy, slapdash, slatternly, sloppy, thoughtless, unmethodical, untidy.

slow /sləʊ/ *adjective* **1** taking relatively long time to do thing(s); acting, moving, or done without speed. **2** not conducive to speed. **3** (of clock etc.) showing earlier than correct time. **4** dull-witted, stupid. **5** tedious. **6** slack, sluggish. **7** (of fire or oven) not very hot. **8** (of photographic film) needing long exposure. **9** reluctant. ● *adverb* slowly. ● *verb* (usually + *down, up*) (cause to) move, act, or work with reduced speed or vigour. □ **slowcoach** *colloquial* slow person. **slow motion 1** speed of film or videotape in which actions etc. appear much slower than usual. **2** simulation of this in real action. **slow-worm** small European legless lizard. □ **slowly** *adverb*. **slowness** *noun*.

■ *adjective* **1** careful, cautious, crawling, dawdling, delayed, deliberate, dilatory, gradual, lagging, late, lazy, leisurely, lingering, loitering, measured, moderate, painstaking, phlegmatic, plodding, protracted, slow-moving, sluggardly, sluggish, steady, tardy, torpid, unhurried, unpunctual. **4** backward, dense, dim, dull, obtuse, stupid, *colloquial* thick. **6** inactive, quiet, slack, sluggish. **9** hesitant, reluctant, unenthusiastic, unwilling. ● *verb* (*slow down, up*) brake, decelerate, ease up, hold back, reduce speed.

sludge *noun* **1** thick greasy mud or sediment. **2** sewage. □ **sludgy** *adjective*.

■ **1** mire, *colloquial* muck, mud, ooze, precipitate, sediment, silt, slime, slurry, slush.

slug[1] *noun* **1** slimy shell-less mollusc. **2** bullet, esp. irregularly shaped. **3** missile for airgun. **4** *Printing* metal bar for spacing. **5** mouthful of liquor.

slug² *US verb* (**-gg-**) hit hard. ● *noun* hard blow.

sluggard /'slʌɡəd/ *noun* lazy person. □ **sluggardly** *adjective*.

sluggish *adjective* inert; slow-moving. □ **sluggishly** *adverb*. **sluggishness** *noun*.

■ apathetic, dull, idle, inactive, indolent, inert, lazy, lethargic, lifeless, listless, phlegmatic, slothful, slow, stagnant, torpid, unresponsive.

sluice /sluːs/ *noun* **1** (also **sluice-gate, -valve**) sliding gate or other contrivance for regulating volume or flow of water. **2** water so regulated. **3** (also **sluice-way**) artificial water-channel. **4** place for or act of rinsing. ● *verb* (**-cing**) **1** provide or wash with sluice(s). **2** rinse. **3** (of water) rush out (as if) from sluice.

■ *verb* **1, 2** flush, rinse, swill, wash.

slum *noun* **1** house unfit for human habitation. **2** (often in *plural*) overcrowded and squalid district in city. ● *verb* (**-mm-**) visit slums, esp. out of curiosity. □ **slum it** *colloquial* put up with conditions less comfortable than usual. □ **slummy** *adjective*.

slumber /'slʌmbə/ *verb & noun poetical* sleep.

■ **see** SLEEP *noun* 1,2, *verb* 1.

slump *noun* sudden severe or prolonged fall in prices and trade. ● *verb* **1** undergo slump. **2** sit or fall heavily or limply.

■ *noun* collapse, crash, decline, depression, dip, downturn, drop, fall, falling-off, plunge, recession, trough. ● *verb* **1** collapse, crash, decline, dive, drop, fall off, plummet, plunge, recede, sink, slip, take a nosedive, worsen. **2** *colloquial* collapse, droop, flop, hunch, loll, lounge, sag, slouch, subside.

slung *past & past participle* of SLING¹.

slunk *past & past participle* of SLINK.

slur *verb* (**-rr-**) **1** sound (words, musical notes, etc.) so that they run into one another. **2** *archaic* or *US* put slur on (person, character). **3** (usually + *over*) pass over lightly. ● *noun* **1** imputation of wrongdoing. **2** act of slurring. **3** *Music* curved line joining notes to be slurred.

■ *verb* **1** garble, lisp, mumble. ● *noun* **1** affront, aspersion, calumny, imputation, innuendo, insinuation, insult, libel, slander, smear, stigma.

slurp *colloquial verb* eat or drink noisily. ● *noun* sound of slurping.

slurry /'slʌrɪ/ *noun* thin semi-liquid cement, mud, manure, etc.

■ mud, ooze, slime.

slush *noun* **1** thawing snow. **2** silly sentimentality. □ **slush fund** reserve fund, esp. for bribery. □ **slushy** *adjective* (**-ier, -iest**).

slut *noun derogatory* slovenly or promiscuous woman. □ **sluttish** *adjective*.

sly *adjective* (**-er, -est**) **1** crafty, wily. **2** secretive. **3** knowing, insinuating. □ **on the sly** secretly. □ **slyly** *adverb*. **slyness** *noun*.

■ **1, 2** artful, canny, conniving, crafty, cunning, deceitful, designing, devious, disingenuous, foxy, furtive, guileful, insidious, scheming, secretive, *colloquial* shifty, shrewd, sneaky, stealthy, surreptitious, treacherous, tricky, underhand, wily. **3** arch, insinuating, knowing, mischievous, roguish, snide.

smack¹ *noun* **1** sharp slap or blow. **2** hard hit. **3** loud kiss. **4** loud sharp sound. ● *verb* **1** slap. **2** part (lips) noisily in anticipation of food. **3** move, hit, etc. with smack. ● *adverb colloquial* **1** with a smack. **2** suddenly; violently. **3** exactly.

■ *verb* **1** hit, pat, slap, spank. **3** see HIT *verb* 1.

smack² (+ *of*) *verb* **1** taste of. **2** suggest. ● *noun* flavour or suggestion of.

smack³ *noun* single-masted sailing boat.

smack⁴ *noun slang* heroin; other hard drug.

smacker *noun slang* **1** loud kiss. **2** £1. **3** *US* $1.

small /smɔːl/ *adjective* **1** not large or big. **2** not great in importance, amount, number, etc. **3** not much. **4** insignificant. **5** of small particles. **6** on small scale. **7** poor, humble. **8** mean. **9** young. ● *noun* **1** slenderest part, esp. of back. **2** (in *plural*) *colloquial* underwear, esp. as laundry. ● *adverb* into small pieces. □ **small arms** portable firearms. **small change** coins, not notes. **small fry 1** unimportant people. **2** children. **smallholding** agricultural holding smaller than farm. **small hours** night-time after midnight. **small-minded** petty; narrow in outlook. **smallpox** *historical* acute contagious disease with fever and pustules usually leaving scars. **small print** matter printed small, esp. limitations in contract. **small-scale** made or occurring in small amounts or to a lesser degree. **small talk** trivial social conversation. **small-time** *colloquial* unimportant, petty. □ **smallness** *noun*.

■ *adjective* **1** baby, bantam, compact, concise, cramped, diminutive, *colloquial* dinky, dwarf, exiguous, fine, fractional, infinitesimal, lean, lilliputian, little, microscopic, midget, *colloquial* mini, miniature, *colloquial* minuscule, minute, narrow, petite, *colloquial* pint-sized, pocket-sized, poky, portable, pygmy, short, slender, slight, *colloquial* teeny, thin, tiny, toy, undersized, *esp.* Scottish wee, *colloquial* weeny. **2, 3** inadequate, insufficient, meagre, modest, *colloquial* piddling, scant, scanty, skimpy, unsatisfactory. **4** inconsequential, insignificant, minor, negligible, nugatory, slim (*chance*), slight, trifling, trivial, unimportant. **8** mean, *colloquial* measly, miserly, niggardly, parsimonious, stingy, ungenerous. □ **small arms** see WEAPON 1. **small-minded** bigoted, grudging, hidebound, illiberal, intolerant, mean, narrow, narrow-minded, old-fashioned, parochial, petty, prejudiced, rigid, selfish, trivial, unimaginative.

smarmy /'smɑːmɪ/ *adjective* (**-ier, -iest**) *colloquial* ingratiating. □ **smarmily** *adverb*. **smarminess** *noun*.

smart *adjective* **1** well groomed, neat. **2** bright and fresh in appearance. **3** stylish, fashionable. **4** clever, ingenious, quick-witted. **5** quick, brisk.

6 painfully severe; sharp, vigorous. ● *verb* **1** feel or give pain. **2** rankle. **3** (+ *for*) suffer consequences of. ● *noun* sharp pain; stinging sensation. ● *adverb* smartly. □ **smartish** *adjective* & *adverb*. **smartly** *adverb*. **smartness** *noun*.

■ *adjective* **1, 3** chic, dapper, dashing, elegant, fashionable, modish, *colloquial* natty, neat, *colloquial* posh, *slang* snazzy, *soigné(e)*, spruce, stylish, tidy, trim, well dressed, well groomed. **2** bright, clean, fresh, gleaming. **4** acute, adept, artful, astute, bright, clever, crafty, *colloquial* cute, discerning, ingenious, intelligent, perceptive, perspicacious, quick, quick-witted, shrewd, streetwise. **5** brisk, *slang* cracking, fast, forceful, quick, rapid, rattling, speedy, swift. **6** painful, sharp, stinging, vigorous. ● *verb* **1** see HURT *verb* 2.

smarten *verb* (usually + *up*) make or become smart.

smash *verb* **1** (often + *up*) break to pieces. **2** bring or come to destruction, defeat, or disaster. **3** (+ *into*, *through*) move forcefully. **4** (+ *in*) break with crushing blow. **5** strike or throw forcefully. **6** hit (ball) hard, esp. downwards. ● *noun* **1** act or sound of smashing. **2** (in full **smash hit**) very successful play, song, etc. ● *adverb* with smash. □ **smash-and-grab** robbery with goods snatched from broken shop window etc.

■ *verb* **1** break, crumple, crush, demolish, destroy, shatter, squash, wreck. **2** see DEFEAT *verb* 1, DESTROY 1. **3** (*smash into*) bang into, bash into, bump into, collide with, crash into, hit, knock into, ram into, run into, slam into, strike. **5** bang, bash, batter, bump, crash, hammer, hit, knock, pound, ram, slam, strike, thump, *colloquial* wallop.

smashing *adjective colloquial* excellent, wonderful.

smattering /ˈsmætərɪŋ/ *noun* slight knowledge.

smear /smɪə/ *verb* **1** daub or mark with grease etc. **2** smudge. **3** defame. ● *noun* **1** action or instance of smearing. **2** defamation. **3** material smeared on microscope slide etc. for examination. **4** specimen of this. □ **smear test** cervical smear. □ **smeary** *adjective*.

■ *verb* **1** dab, daub, plaster, rub, spread, wipe. **2** blot, smudge. **3** attack, besmirch, blacken, calumniate, defame, discredit, libel, malign, slander, stigmatize, tarnish, vilify. ● *noun* **1** blot, daub, mark, smudge, stain, streak. **2** aspersion, calumny, defamation, imputation, innuendo, insinuation, libel, slander, slur, stigma, vilification.

smell *noun* **1** sense of odour perception. **2** property perceived by this. **3** unpleasant odour. **4** act of inhaling to ascertain smell. ● *verb* (*past* & *past participle* **smelt** or **smelled**) **1** perceive or examine by smell. **2** stink. **3** seem by smell to be. **4** (+ *of*) emit smell of. **5** (+ *of*) suggest. **6** detect. **7** have or use sense of smell. □ **smelling salts** sharp-smelling substances sniffed to relieve faintness.

■ *noun* **2** aroma, bouquet, fragrance, nose, odour, perfume, redolence, scent, whiff. **3** mephitis, *archaic* miasma, *colloquial* pong, reek, stench,

stink, whiff. ● *verb* **1** scent, sniff. **2** *colloquial* hum, *colloquial* pong, reek, stink, whiff.

smelly *adjective* (**-ier**, **-iest**) strong- or evil-smelling.

■ fetid, foul, foul-smelling, gamy, high, malodorous, mephitic, miasmic, musty, *literary* noisome, odorous, *colloquial* off, *colloquial* pongy, pungent, putrid, rank, reeking, rotten, stinking.

smelt¹ *verb* **1** melt (ore) to extract metal. **2** obtain (metal) thus. □ **smelter** *noun*.

smelt² *past* & *past participle* of SMELL.

smelt³ *noun* (*plural* same or **-s**) small edible green and silver fish.

smidgen /ˈsmɪdʒɪn/ *noun* (also **smidgeon**, **smidgin**) *colloquial* small bit or amount.

smilax /ˈsmaɪlæks/ *noun* any of several climbing plants.

smile *verb* (**-ling**) **1** have or assume facial expression of amusement or pleasure, with ends of lips turned upward. **2** express by smiling. **3** give (smile). **4** (+ *on*, *upon*) favour. ● *noun* **1** act of smiling. **2** smiling expression or aspect.

■ *verb* **1** beam, grin, leer, simper, smirk, sneer. ● *noun* beam, grin, leer, simper, smirk, sneer.

smirch *verb* & *noun* stain, smear.

smirk *noun* conceited or silly smile. ● *verb* give smirk.

smite *verb* (**-ting**; *past* **smote**; *past participle* **smitten** /ˈsmɪt(ə)n/) *esp. archaic* or *literary* **1** hit. **2** chastise; defeat. **3** (in *passive*) affect strongly; fascinate.

smith *noun* **1** blacksmith. **2** worker in metal. **3** craftsman.

smithereens /smɪðəˈriːnz/ *plural noun* small fragments.

smithy /ˈsmɪðɪ/ *noun* (*plural* **-ies**) blacksmith's workshop; forge.

smitten *past participle* of SMITE.

smock *noun* loose shirtlike garment, often adorned with smocking. ● *verb* adorn with smocking.

smocking *noun* ornamentation on cloth made by gathering it tightly with stitches.

smog *noun* dense smoky fog. □ **smoggy** *adjective* (**-ier**, **-iest**).

smoke *noun* **1** visible vapour from burning substance. **2** act of smoking tobacco etc. **3** *colloquial* cigarette, cigar. ● *verb* (**-king**) **1** inhale and exhale smoke of (cigarette etc.). **2** do this habitually. **3** emit smoke or visible vapour. **4** darken or preserve with smoke. □ **smoke bomb** bomb emitting dense smoke on bursting. **smoke-free 1** free from smoke. **2** where smoking is not permitted. **smoke out 1** drive out by means of smoke. **2** drive out of hiding etc. **smokescreen 1** cloud of smoke concealing esp. military operations. **2** ruse for disguising activities. **smokestack 1** funnel of locomotive or steamship. **2** tall chimney.

■ *noun* **1** exhaust, fog, fumes, gas, smog, steam, vapour. **3** cigar, cigarette, cheroot, *slang* fag. ● *verb* **1** inhale, puff at. **3** fume, smoulder.

smoker *noun* **1** person who habitually smokes tobacco. **2** compartment on train where smoking is permitted.

smokestack /'sməʊkstæk/ *noun* **1** funnel of steamer. **2** chimney, esp. of locomotive or factory.

smoky *adjective* (**-ier, -iest**) **1** emitting, filled with, or obscured by, smoke. **2** coloured by or like smoke. **3** having flavour of smoked food.

■ **1, 2** clouded, dirty, foggy, grimy, hazy, sooty.

smolder *US* = SMOULDER.

smooch /smuːtʃ/ *verb* kiss and caress. ● *noun* smooching.

smooth /smuːð/ *adjective* **1** having even surface; free from projections and roughness. **2** that can be traversed uninterrupted. **3** (of sea etc.) calm, flat. **4** (of journey etc.) easy. **5** not harsh in sound or taste. **6** conciliatory, slick. **7** not lumpy. **8** not jerky. ● *verb* **1** (often + *out, down*) make or become smooth. **2** (often + *out, down, over, away*) get rid of (differences, faults, etc.). ● *noun* smoothing touch or stroke. □ **smooth-tongued** insincerely flattering. □ **smoothly** *adverb*. **smoothness** *noun*.

■ *adjective* **1** burnished, even, flat, glassy, glossy, horizontal, level, plane, polished, regular, satiny, shiny, silken, silky, sleek, soft, unbroken, velvety. **3** calm, flat, peaceful, placid, quiet, restful, still, unruffled. **4** comfortable, easy, effortless, fluent, steady, uneventful, uninterrupted, unobstructed. **5** agreeable, bland, mellow, mild, pleasant, soft, soothing. **6** convincing, facile, glib, insincere, plausible, polite, self-assured, self-satisfied, slick, smug, sophisticated, suave, untrustworthy, urbane. **7** creamy, flowing, runny. ● *verb* **1** buff, burnish, even out, file, flatten, iron, level, level off, plane, polish, press, roll out, sand, sandpaper.

smorgasbord /'smɔːgəsbɔːd/ *noun* **1** Swedish hors d'oeuvres. **2** buffet meal with various esp. savoury dishes.

smote *past of* SMITE.

smother /'smʌðə/ *verb* **1** suffocate, stifle. **2** (+ *in, with*) overwhelm or cover with (kisses, gifts, etc.). **3** extinguish (fire) by heaping with ashes etc. **4** have difficulty breathing. **5** (often + *up*) suppress, conceal.

■ **1** asphyxiate, choke, stifle, suffocate. **3** see EXTINGUISH 1. **5** see SUPPRESS 2.

smoulder /'sməʊldə/ (*US* **smolder**) *verb* **1** burn without flame or internally. **2** (often as **smouldering** *adjective*) (of person) show silent emotion. ● *noun* smouldering.

■ *verb* **1** burn, smoke. **2** (**smouldering**) see ANGRY 1.

smudge *noun* blurred or smeared line, mark, etc. ● *verb* (**-ging**) **1** make smudge on or with. **2** become smeared or blurred. □ **smudgy** *adjective*.

■ *verb* blot, blur, dirty, mark, smear, stain, streak.

smug *adjective* (**-gg-**) self-satisfied. □ **smugly** *adverb*. **smugness** *noun*.

■ complacent, conceited, *colloquial* holier-than-thou, priggish, self-important, self-righteous, self-satisfied.

smuggle /'smʌg(ə)l/ *verb* (**-ling**) **1** import or export illegally, esp. without paying duties. **2** convey secretly. □ **smuggler** *noun*. **smuggling** *noun*.

smut *noun* **1** small piece of soot. **2** spot or smudge made by this. **3** obscene talk, pictures, or stories. **4** fungous disease of cereals. ● *verb* (**-tt-**) mark with smut(s). □ **smutty** *adjective* (**-ier, -iest**).

snack *noun* light, casual, or hasty meal. □ **snack bar** place where snacks are sold.

■ bite, *colloquial* elevenses, nibble, refreshments. □ **snack bar** buffet, café, cafeteria, fast-food restaurant.

snaffle /'snæf(ə)l/ *noun* (in full **snaffle-bit**) simple bridle-bit without curb. ● *verb* (**-ling**) *colloquial* steal, seize.

snag *noun* **1** unexpected obstacle or drawback. **2** jagged projection. **3** tear in material etc. ● *verb* (**-gg-**) catch or tear on snag.

■ *noun* **1** catch, complication, difficulty, drawback, hindrance, hitch, impediment, obstacle, obstruction, problem, setback, stumbling block. ● *verb* catch, jag, rip, tear.

snail *noun* slow-moving mollusc with spiral shell.

snake *noun* **1** long limbless reptile. **2** (also **snake in the grass**) traitor, secret enemy. ● *verb* (**-king**) move or twist like a snake. □ **snakes and ladders** board game with counters moved up 'ladders' and down 'snakes' **snakeskin** ● *noun* skin of snake. ● *adjective* made of snakeskin.

■ *noun* ophidian, serpent. ● *verb* crawl, creep, meander, twist and turn, wander, worm, zigzag.

snaky *adjective* **1** of or like a snake. **2** sinuous. **3** treacherous.

snap *verb* (**-pp-**) **1** break sharply. **2** (cause to) emit sudden sharp sound. **3** open or close with snapping sound. **4** speak irritably. **5** (often + *at*) make sudden audible bite. **6** move quickly. **7** photograph. ● *noun* **1** act or sound of snapping. **2** crisp biscuit. **3** snapshot. **4** (in full **cold snap**) sudden brief period of cold weather. **5** card game in which players call 'snap' when two similar cards are exposed. **6** vigour. ● *adverb* with snapping sound. ● *adjective* done without forethought. □ **snapdragon** plant with two-lipped flowers. **snap-fastener** press-stud. **snap out of** *slang* get out of (mood etc.) by sudden effort. **snapshot** informal or casual photograph. **snap up** accept (offer etc.) hastily or eagerly.

■ *verb* **1** break, crack, fracture, give way, part, split. **2** click, crack, pop. **4** bark, growl, snarl. **5** bite, gnash, nip, snatch. ● *adjective* see SUDDEN.

snapper *noun* any of several edible marine fish.

snappish *adjective* curt, ill-tempered.

snappy *adjective* (**-ier, -iest**) *colloquial* **1** brisk, lively. **2** neat and elegant. **3** snappish. □ **snappily** *adverb*.

snare /sneə/ *noun* **1** trap, esp. with noose, for birds or animals. **2** trap, trick; temptation. **3** (in *singular* or *plural*) twisted strings of gut, hide, or wire stretched across lower head of side drum to produce rattle. **4** (in full **snare drum**) side drum with snares. ● *verb* (-**ring**) catch in snare; trap.
■ *noun* **1** ambush, booby trap, gin, noose, trap. ● *verb* capture, catch, ensnare, entrap, net, trap.

snarl[1] *verb* **1** growl with bared teeth. **2** speak angrily. ● *noun* act or sound of snarling.

snarl[2] *verb* **1** (often + *up*) twist, entangle, hamper movement of (traffic etc.). **2** (often + *up*) become entangled. ● *noun* tangle. □ **snarl-up** *colloquial* **1** muddle, entanglement. **2** traffic jam.
■ *verb* confuse, entangle, jam, knot, tangle, twist.

snatch *verb* **1** (often + *away, from*) seize quickly, eagerly, or unexpectedly. **2** steal by grabbing. **3** *slang* kidnap. **4** (+ *at*) try to seize; take eagerly. ● *noun* **1** act of snatching. **2** fragment of song, talk, etc. **3** short spell of activity etc.
■ *verb* **1** catch, clutch, grab, grasp, lay hold of, pluck, seize, take, wrench away, wrest away. **2** see STEAL *verb* **1**. **3** abduct, kidnap.

snazzy /'snæzɪ/ *adjective* (-**ier**, -**iest**) *slang* smart, stylish, showy.

sneak *verb* **1** go or convey furtively. **2** *slang* steal unobserved. **3** *slang* tell tales. **4** (as **sneaking** *adjective*) furtive, persistent and puzzling. ● *noun* **1** mean-spirited, underhand person. **2** *slang* tell-tale. ● *adjective* acting or done without warning; secret. □ **sneak thief** person who steals without breaking in. □ **sneaky** *adjective* (-**ier**, -**iest**).
■ *verb* **1** creep, prowl, skulk, slink, stalk, steal. **3** *slang* grass, inform, report, *slang* snitch, tell tales. **4** (**sneaking**) furtive, half-formed, intuitive, lurking, nagging, niggling, persistent, private, secret, uncomfortable, unconfessed, undisclosed, unproved, worrying. □ **sneaky** cheating, contemptible, crafty, deceitful, despicable, devious, dishonest, furtive, low-down, mean, nasty, shady, *colloquial* shifty, sly, stealthy, treacherous, underhand, unscrupulous, untrustworthy.

sneaker *noun slang* soft-soled shoe.

sneer *noun* derisive smile or remark. ● *verb* **1** (often + *at*) make sneer. **2** utter with sneer. □ **sneering** *adjective*. **sneeringly** *adverb*.
■ *verb* **1** be contemptuous, be scornful, boo, curl one's lip, hiss, hoot, jeer, laugh, mock, scoff; (*sneer at*) see DENIGRATE, RIDICULE *verb*.

sneeze *noun* sudden involuntary explosive expulsion of air from irritated nostrils. ● *verb* (-**zing**) make sneeze. □ **not to be sneezed at** *colloquial* worth having or considering.

snick *verb* **1** make small notch or cut in. **2** *Cricket* deflect (ball) slightly with bat. ● *noun* such notch or deflection.

snicker /'snɪkə/ *noun & verb* snigger.

snide *adjective* sneering, slyly derogatory.

sniff *verb* **1** inhale air audibly through nose. **2** (often + *up*) draw in through nose. **3** smell scent of by sniffing. ● *noun* act or sound of sniffing. □ **sniff at** show contempt for. **sniffer dog** *colloquial* dog trained to find drugs or explosives by scent.
■ *verb* **1** see SNIVEL *verb* **1**. **3** scent, smell. □ **sniff at** see SCORN *verb*.

sniffle /'snɪf(ə)l/ *verb* (-**ling**) sniff repeatedly or slightly. ● *noun* **1** act of sniffling. **2** (in *singular* or *plural*) cold in the head causing sniffling.

snifter /'snɪftə/ *noun slang* small alcoholic drink.

snigger /'snɪgə/ *noun* half-suppressed laugh. ● *verb* utter snigger.
■ *verb* chuckle, giggle, laugh, snicker, titter.

snip *verb* (-**pp**-) cut with scissors etc., esp. in small quick strokes. ● *noun* **1** act of snipping. **2** piece snipped off. **3** *slang* something easily done. **4** *slang* bargain.
■ *verb* clip, cut, dock, nick, nip, trim.

snipe *noun* (*plural* same or -**s**) wading bird with long straight bill. ● *verb* (-**ping**) **1** fire shots from hiding usually at long range. **2** (often + *at*) make sly critical attack. □ **sniper** *noun*.
■ *verb* **1** fire, shoot, take pot-shots. **2** (*snipe at*) see CRITICIZE **1**.

snippet /'snɪpɪt/ *noun* **1** small piece cut off. **2** (usually in *plural*) scrap of information etc. **3** (usually in *plural*) short extract from book etc.
■ **1** fragment, morsel, particle, piece, scrap, shred, snatch. **3** bit, cutting, extract, fragment, part, passage, portion, quotation, section.

snitch *slang verb* **1** steal. **2** (often + *on*) inform on person. ● *noun* informer.

snivel /'snɪv(ə)l/ *verb* (-**ll**-; *US* -**l**-) **1** sniffle. **2** weep with sniffling. **3** show maudlin emotion. ● *noun* act of snivelling.
■ *verb* **1** sniff, sniffle, snuffle. **2** blubber, cry, *colloquial* grizzle, mewl, sob, weep, whimper, whine, *colloquial* whinge.

snob *noun* person who despises people with inferior social position, wealth, intellect, tastes, etc. □ **snobbery** *noun*. **snobbish** *adjective*. **snobbishness** *noun*. **snobby** *adjective* (-**ier**, -**iest**).
■ □ **snobbish** affected, conceited, condescending, disdainful, elitist, haughty, *colloquial* highfalutin, hoity-toity, lofty, lordly, patronizing, pompous, *colloquial* posh, pretentious, self-important, smug, *colloquial* snooty, *colloquial* stuck-up, supercilious, superior, *colloquial* toffee-nosed.

snood /snu:d/ *noun* woman's loose hairnet.

snook /snu:k/ *noun slang* contemptuous gesture with thumb to nose and fingers spread. □ **cock a snook (at) 1** make this gesture (at). **2** show contempt (for).

snooker /'snuːkə/ *noun* **1** game played on oblong cloth-covered table with 1 white, 15 red, and 6 other coloured balls. **2** position in this game where direct shot would give points to opponent. ● *verb* **1** subject (player) to snooker. **2** (esp. as **snookered** *adjective*) *slang* thwart; defeat.

snoop /snuːp/ *colloquial verb* **1** pry into another's affairs. **2** (often + *about, around*) investigate (often stealthily) transgressions of rules etc. ● *noun* act of snooping. □ **snooper** *noun*.

■ *verb* be inquisitive, butt in, interfere, intrude, investigate, meddle, nose about, *colloquial* poke one's nose in, pry, sneak, spy. □ **snooper** busybody, detective, investigator, meddler, sneak, spy.

snooty /'snuːtɪ/ *adjective* (**-ier, -iest**) *colloquial* supercilious, snobbish. □ **snootily** *adverb*.

snooze /snuːz/ *colloquial noun* short sleep, nap. ● *verb* (**-zing**) take snooze.

snore *noun* snorting or grunting sound of breathing during sleep. ● *verb* (**-ring**) make this sound.

snorkel /'snɔːk(ə)l/ *noun* device for supplying air to underwater swimmer or submerged submarine. ● *verb* (**-ll-**; *US* **-l-**) use snorkel.

snort *noun* **1** explosive sound made by driving breath violently through nose, esp. by horses, or by humans to show contempt, incredulity, etc. **2** *colloquial* small drink of liquor. **3** *slang* inhaled dose of powdered cocaine. ● *verb* **1** make snort. **2** *slang* inhale (esp. cocaine). **3** express or utter with snort.

snot *noun slang* nasal mucus.

snotty *adjective* (**-ier, -iest**) *slang* **1** running or covered with nasal mucus. **2** snooty. **3** contemptible. □ **snottily** *adverb*. **snottiness** *noun*.

snout /snaʊt/ *noun* **1** projecting nose (and mouth) of animal. **2** *derogatory* person's nose. **3** pointed front of thing.

■ **1** muzzle, nose, proboscis, trunk.

snow /snəʊ/ *noun* **1** frozen vapour falling to earth in light white flakes. **2** fall or layer of this. **3** thing resembling snow in whiteness or texture etc. **4** *slang* cocaine. ● *verb* **1** (after *it*) snow falls. **2** (+ *in, over, up*, etc.) confine or block with snow. □ **snowball** ● *noun* snow pressed into ball for throwing in play. ● *verb* **1** throw or pelt with snowballs. **2** increase rapidly. **snow-blind** temporarily blinded by glare from snow. **snowbound** prevented by snow from going out. **snowcap** snow-covered mountain peak. **snowdrift** bank of snow piled up by wind. **snowdrop** spring-flowering plant with white drooping flowers. **snowed under** overwhelmed, esp. with work. **snowflake** each of the flakes in which snow falls. **snow goose** white Arctic goose. **snowline** level above which snow never melts entirely. **snowman** figure made of snow. **snowplough** device for clearing road of snow. **snowshoe** racket-shaped attachment to boot for walking on surface of snow. **snowstorm** heavy fall of snow, esp. with wind. **snow white** pure white. □ **snowy** *adjective* (**-ier, iest**).

SNP *abbreviation* Scottish National Party.

Snr. *abbreviation* Senior.

snub *verb* (**-bb-**) rebuff or humiliate in a sharp or cutting way. ● *noun* snubbing, rebuff. ● *adjective* (of nose) short and turned up.

■ *verb* be rude to, brush off, cold-shoulder, disdain, humiliate, insult, offend, *colloquial* put (person) down, rebuff, reject, scorn, squash.

snuff[1] *noun* charred part of candlewick. ● *verb* trim snuff from (candle). □ **snuff it** *slang* die. **snuff out 1** extinguish (candle). **2** put an end to (hopes etc.).

■ *verb* extinguish, put out. □ **snuff it** see DIE[1] 1. **snuff out 1** see EXTINGUISH 1.

snuff[2] *noun* powdered tobacco or medicine taken by sniffing. ● *verb* take snuff.

snuffle /'snʌf(ə)l/ *verb* (**-ling**) **1** make sniffing sounds. **2** speak nasally. **3** breathe noisily, esp. with blocked nose. ● *noun* snuffling sound or speech.

snug *adjective* (**-gg-**) **1** cosy, comfortable, sheltered. **2** close-fitting. ● *noun* small room in pub. □ **snugly** *adverb*.

■ *adjective* **1** comfortable, *colloquial* comfy, cosy, enclosed, friendly, intimate, protected, reassuring, relaxed, relaxing, restful, safe, secure, sheltered, soft, warm. **2** close-fitting, neat, well tailored.

snuggle /'snʌg(ə)l/ *verb* (**-ling**) settle or move into warm comfortable position.

so[1] /səʊ/ *adverb* **1** to such an extent. **2** in this or that manner or state. **3** also. **4** indeed, actually. **5** very. **6** thus. ● *conjunction* (often + *that*) **1** consequently. **2** in order that. **3** and then. **4** (introducing question) after that. □ **so-and-so 1** particular but unspecified person or thing. **2** *colloquial* objectionable person. **so as to** in order to. **so-called** commonly called but often incorrectly. **so long** *colloquial* goodbye. **so so** *colloquial* only moderately good or well.

so[2] = SOH.

soak *verb* **1** make or become thoroughly wet through saturation. **2** (of rain etc.) drench. **3** (+ *in, up*) absorb (liquid, knowledge, etc.). **4** (+ *in, into, through*) penetrate by saturation. **5** *colloquial* extort money from. **6** *colloquial* drink heavily. ● *noun* **1** soaking. **2** *colloquial* hard drinker. □ **soakaway** arrangement for disposal of waste water by percolation through soil. □ **soaked** *adjective*.

■ *verb* **1** bathe, drench, immerse, marinate, pickle, saturate, souse, steep, submerge, wet. **2** drench, saturate, wet. **3** (*soak up*) see ABSORB 1,2. □ **soaked** see WET *adjective* 1.

soaking *adjective* (in full **soaking wet**) wet through.

■ see WET *adjective* 1.

soap *noun* **1** cleansing substance yielding lather when rubbed in water. **2** *colloquial* soap opera. ● *verb* apply soap to. □ **soapbox** makeshift stand for street orator. **soap opera** domestic broadcast serial. **soap powder** powdered soap usually with additives, for washing clothes etc. **soapstone** steatite. **soapsuds** suds.

soapy *adjective* (**-ier, -iest**) **1** of or like soap. **2** containing or smeared with soap. **3** unctuous, flattering.

soar /sɔː/ *verb* **1** fly or rise high. **2** reach high level or standard. **3** fly without flapping wings or using motor power.

■ **1** ascend, climb, fly, rise, tower. **2** escalate, increase, rise, rocket, shoot up, spiral. **3** float, fly, glide, hang, hover.

sob *verb* (**-bb-**) **1** inhale convulsively, usually with weeping. **2** utter with sobs. ● *noun* act or sound of sobbing. □ **sob story** *colloquial* story or explanation appealing for sympathy.

■ *verb* blubber, cry, gasp, snivel, weep, whimper.

sober /ˈsəʊbə/ *adjective* (**-er, -est**) **1** not drunk. **2** not given to drink. **3** moderate, tranquil, serious. **4** (of colour) dull. ● *verb* (often + *down*, *up*) make or become sober. □ **soberly** *adverb*.

■ *adjective* **1** clear-headed, in control, lucid, rational. **2** abstemious, *slang* on the wagon, teetotal, temperate. **3** calm, composed, dignified, grave, level-headed, moderate, peaceful, quiet, restrained, sedate, self-controlled, sensible, serene, serious, solemn, staid, steady, subdued, temperate, tranquil, unexciting. **4** colourless, drab, dull, plain, sombre.

sobriety /səˈbraɪɪtɪ/ *noun* being sober.

sobriquet /ˈsəʊbrɪkeɪ/ *noun* (also **soubriquet** /ˈsuː-/) nickname.

Soc. *abbreviation* **1** Socialist. **2** Society.

soccer /ˈsɒkə/ *noun* Association football.

sociable /ˈsəʊʃəb(ə)l/ *adjective* liking company; gregarious, friendly. □ **sociability** *noun*. **sociably** *adverb*.

■ affable, approachable, clubbable, companionable, convivial, extroverted, friendly, gregarious, hospitable, neighbourly, outgoing, social, warm, welcoming.

social /ˈsəʊʃ(ə)l/ *adjective* **1** of society or its organization, esp. of relations of (classes of) people. **2** living in communities. **3** gregarious; interdependent. ● *noun* social gathering. □ **social climber** *derogatory* person anxious to gain higher social status. **social science** study of society and social relationships. **social security** state assistance to the poor and unemployed. **social services** welfare services provided by the State, esp. education, health care, and housing. **social work** professional or voluntary work with people in need of help or welfare. **social worker** *noun*. □ **socially** *adverb*.

■ *adjective* **1** collective, communal, community, general, group, organized, popular, public. **3** gregarious, interdependent, sociable. ● *noun* dance, *colloquial* disco, *colloquial* do, gathering, *colloquial* get-together, party, reception, reunion, soirée.

socialism *noun* **1** political and economic theory advocating state ownership and control of means of production, distribution, and exchange. **2** social system based on this. □ **socialist** *noun* & *adjective*. **socialistic** /-ˈlɪs-/ *adjective*.

socialite /ˈsəʊʃəlaɪt/ *noun* person moving in fashionable society.

socialize /ˈsəʊʃəlaɪz/ *verb* (also **-ise**) (**-zing** or **-sing**) **1** mix socially. **2** make social. **3** organize in a socialistic way.

■ **1** associate, be sociable, entertain, fraternize, get together, go out together, join in, keep company, mix.

society /səˈsaɪətɪ/ *noun* (*plural* **-ies**) **1** organized and interdependent community. **2** system and organization of this. **3** (members of) aristocratic part of this. **4** mixing with other people, companionship, company. **5** association, club. □ **societal** *adjective*.

■ **1, 2** civilization, community, culture, nation, people, the public. **4** camaraderie, companionship, company, fellowship, friendship. **5** academy, alliance, association, brotherhood, circle, club, *US* fraternity, group, guild, league, organization, sisterhood, *US* sorority, union.

sociology /səʊsɪˈɒlədʒɪ/ *noun* study of society and social problems. □ **sociological** /-əˈlɒdʒ-/ *adjective*. **sociologist** *noun*.

sock[1] *noun* **1** knitted covering for foot and lower leg. **2** insole.

sock[2] *colloquial verb* hit hard. ● *noun* hard blow. □ **sock it to** attack or address vigorously.

socket /ˈsɒkɪt/ *noun* hollow for thing to fit into etc., esp. device receiving electric plug, light bulb, etc.

Socratic /səˈkrætɪk/ *adjective* of Socrates or his philosophy.

sod *noun* **1** turf; piece of turf. **2** surface of ground.

soda /ˈsəʊdə/ *noun* **1** any of various compounds of sodium in common use. **2** (in full **soda water**) effervescent water used esp. with spirits etc. as drink. □ **soda fountain 1** device supplying soda water. **2** shop or counter with this.

sodden /ˈsɒd(ə)n/ *adjective* **1** saturated, soaked through. **2** stupid, dull, etc. with drunkenness.

sodium /ˈsəʊdɪəm/ *noun* soft silver-white metallic element. □ **sodium bicarbonate** white compound used in baking-powder. **sodium chloride** common salt. **sodium lamp** lamp using sodium vapour and giving yellow light. **sodium nitrate** white powdery compound in fertilizers etc.

sofa /ˈsəʊfə/ *noun* long upholstered seat with raised back and ends. □ **sofa bed** sofa that can be converted into bed.

■ chaise longue, couch, settee.

soffit /ˈsɒfɪt/ *noun* undersurface of arch, lintel, etc.

soft *adjective* **1** not hard; easily cut or dented, malleable. **2** (of cloth etc.) smooth, fine, not rough. **3** mild. **4** (of water) low in mineral salts which prevent lathering. **5** not brilliant or glaring. **6** not strident or loud. **7** sibilant. **8** not sharply defined. **9** gentle, conciliatory. **10** compassionate, sympathetic. **11** feeble, half-witted, silly, sentimental. **12** *colloquial* easy. **13** (of drug) not highly addictive. ● *adverb* softly. □ **have a soft spot for** be fond of. **softball** form of baseball with softer larger ball. **soft-boiled** (of egg) boiled leaving yolk soft. **soft-centred 1** having soft centre. **2** soft-hearted. **soft drink** non-alcoholic drink. **soft fruit** small stoneless fruit. **soft furnishings** curtains, rugs, etc. **soft-hearted** tender, compassionate. **soft option** easier alternative. **soft palate** back part of palate. **soft pedal** pedal on piano softening tone. **soft-pedal** *verb* refrain from emphasizing. **soft sell** restrained salesmanship. **soft soap** *colloquial* persuasive flattery. **soft-spoken** having gentle voice. **soft target** vulnerable person or thing. **soft touch** *colloquial* gullible person, esp. over money. **software** computer programs. **softwood** wood of coniferous tree. □ **softly** *adverb*. **softness** *noun*.

■ *adjective* **1** compressible, crumbly, elastic, flabby, flexible, floppy, limp, malleable, mushy, plastic, pliable, pliant, pulpy, spongy, springy, squashy, squeezable, supple, tender, yielding. **2** downy, feathery, fleecy, fluffy, furry, satiny, silky, sleek, smooth, velvety. **3** balmy, delicate, gentle, light, mild, pleasant, warm. **5** dim, faint, muted, pale, pastel, subdued. **6** faint, low, mellifluous, muted, peaceful, quiet, relaxing, restful, soothing, subdued. **10** see SOFT-HEARTED. **12** *colloquial* cushy, easy, undemanding. □ **soft-hearted** benign, compassionate, conciliatory, easygoing, generous, indulgent, kind, kind-hearted, lax, lenient, merciful, permissive, sentimental, soft, sympathetic, tender, tender-hearted, tolerant, understanding.

soften /'sɒf(ə)n/ *verb* **1** make or become soft(er). **2** (often + *up*) reduce strength, resistance, etc. of. □ **softener** *noun*.

■ **1** abate, alleviate, cushion, deaden, decrease, deflect, diminish, ease, ease up, give in, give way, *colloquial* let up, lighten, lower, mellow, melt, mitigate, moderate, mollify, muffle, pacify, palliate, quell, quieten, relax, subdue, succumb, temper, tone down, turn down, yield. **2** see WEAKEN (WEAK).

softie *noun* (also **softy**) (*plural* **-ies**) *colloquial* weak, silly, or soft-hearted person.

soggy /'sɒgɪ/ *adjective* (**-ier**, **-iest**) sodden, water-logged.

■ boggy, drenched, dripping, heavy (*soil*), marshy, muddy, saturated, soaked, sodden, sopping, waterlogged, wet.

soh *noun* (also **so**) *Music* fifth note of scale in tonic sol-fa.

soigné /swɑːnjeɪ/ *adjective* (*feminine* **soignée** same pronunciation) carefully arranged; well groomed. [French]

soil[1] *noun* **1** upper layer of earth, in which plants grow. **2** ground, territory.

■ **1** clay, dirt, earth, ground, humus, land, loam, marl, topsoil. **2** ground, land, territory.

soil[2] *verb* **1** make dirty; smear, stain. **2** discredit;

defile. ● *noun* **1** dirty mark. **2** filth, refuse. □ **soil pipe** discharge-pipe of lavatory.

■ *verb* **1** *poetical* befoul, besmirch, blacken, contaminate, defile, dirty, muddy, pollute, smear, stain, sully, tarnish. **2** besmirch, blacken, defile, discredit, sully, tarnish.

soirée /'swɑːreɪ/ *noun* evening party.

sojourn /'sɒdʒ(ə)n/ *noun* temporary stay. ● *verb* stay temporarily.

sola /'səʊlə/ *noun* pithy-stemmed E. Indian swamp plant. □ **sola topi** sun-helmet made from pith of this.

solace /'sɒləs/ *noun* comfort in distress or disappointment. ● *verb* (**-cing**) give solace to.

■ *noun* comfort, consolation, reassurance, relief. ● *verb* see CONSOLE[1].

solan /'səʊlən/ *noun* (in full **solan goose**) large gooselike gannet.

solar /'səʊlə/ *adjective* of or reckoned by sun. □ **solar battery, cell** device converting solar radiation into electricity. **solar panel** panel absorbing sun's rays as energy source. **solar plexus** complex of nerves at pit of stomach. **solar system** sun and the planets etc. whose motion is governed by it.

solarium /sə'leərɪəm/ *noun* (*plural* **-ria**) room with sunlamps, glass roof, etc.

sold *past & past participle* of SELL.

solder /'sɒldə/ *noun* fusible alloy used for joining metals, wires, etc. ● *verb* join with solder. □ **soldering iron** tool for melting and applying solder.

soldier /'səʊldʒə/ *noun* **1** member of army, esp. (in full **common soldier**) private or NCO. **2** *colloquial* bread finger, esp. for dipping in egg. ● *verb* serve as soldier. □ **soldier on** *colloquial* persevere doggedly. □ **soldierly** *adjective*.

■ *noun* **1** conscript, fighter, fighting man, fighting woman, infantryman, mercenary, NCO, private, recruit, serviceman, servicewoman, trooper, warrior; (*soldiers*) troops. □ **soldier on** see PERSIST.

soldiery *noun* soldiers collectively.

sole[1] *noun* **1** undersurface of foot. **2** part of shoe, sock, etc. below foot, esp. part other than heel. **3** lower surface or base of plough, golf-club head, etc. ● *verb* (**-ling**) provide with sole.

sole[2] *noun* (*plural* same or **-s**) type of flatfish.

sole[3] *adjective* one and only; single; exclusive. □ **solely** *adverb*.

■ exclusive, individual, lone, one, only, single, singular, solitary, unique.

solecism /'sɒlɪsɪz(ə)m/ *noun* **1** mistake of grammar or idiom. **2** offence against etiquette.

solemn /'sɒləm/ *adjective* **1** serious and dignified. **2** formal. **3** awe-inspiring. **4** of cheerless manner. **5** grave. □ **solemness** *noun*. **solemnity** /sə'lem-/ *noun* (*plural* **-ies**). **solemnly** *adverb*.

■ **1, 2** ceremonial, ceremonious, dignified, ecclesiastical, formal, grand, holy, important, liturgical, momentous, pompous, religious, ritualistic, stately. **3** august, awe-inspiring, awesome, grand, imposing, impressive. **4** earnest, gloomy, glum, grave, grim, long-faced, reserved, sedate, serious, sober, sombre, staid, straight-faced, thoughtful, unsmiling.

solemnize /'sɒləmnaɪz/ *verb* (also **-ise**) (**-zing** or **-sing**) **1** duly perform (esp. marriage ceremony). **2** make solemn. □ **solemnization** *noun*.

solenoid /'səʊlənɔɪd/ *noun* cylindrical coil of wire acting as magnet when carrying electric current.

sol-fa /'sɒlfɑː/ *noun* system of syllables representing musical notes.

solicit /sə'lɪsɪt/ *verb* (**-t-**) **1** seek repeatedly or earnestly. **2** (of prostitute) accost (person) concerning sexual activity. □ **solicitation** *noun*.

■ **1** ask, beg, entreat, importune, invite, petition, seek, *literary* supplicate.

solicitor /sə'lɪsɪtə/ *noun* lawyer qualified to advise clients and instruct barristers.

solicitous /sə'lɪsɪtəs/ *adjective* **1** showing concern. **2** (+ *to do*) eager, anxious to. □ **solicitously** *adverb*. **solicitousness** *noun*.

■ **1** attentive, caring, concerned, considerate, sympathetic. **2** see ANXIOUS 3.

solicitude /sə'lɪsɪtjuːd/ *noun* being solicitous.

solid /'sɒlɪd/ *adjective* (**-er**, **-est**) **1** of firm and stable shape; not liquid or fluid. **2** of such material throughout; not hollow. **3** alike all through. **4** sturdily built; not flimsy. **5** 3-dimensional; of solids. **6** sound, reliable. **7** uninterrupted. **8** unanimous. ● *noun* **1** solid substance or body. **2** (in *plural*) solid food. ● *adverb* solidly. □ **solid-state** using electronic properties of solids to replace those of valves. □ **solidity** /sə'lɪd-/ *noun*. **solidly** *adverb*. **solidness** *noun*.

■ *adjective* **1** concrete, firm, hard, rigid, unmoving. **2** compact, dense, impenetrable, impermeable. **3** pure, unadulterated, unalloyed, unmixed. **4** firm, fixed, immovable, robust, sound, stable, steady, stout, strong, sturdy, substantial, unbending, unyielding, well made. **5** cubic, rounded, spherical, three-dimensional. **6** authentic, authoritative, cogent, coherent, convincing, dependable, effective, genuine, incontrovertible, indisputable, irrefutable, provable, proven, real, reliable, sound, stalwart, strong, tangible, trustworthy, unwavering, vigorous, weighty. **7** complete, continuous, entire, unbroken, uninterrupted, unrelieved, whole. **8** unanimous, undivided, united.

solidarity /sɒlɪ'dærɪtɪ/ *noun* **1** unity, esp. political or in industrial dispute. **2** mutual dependence.

■ **1** accord, agreement, coherence, cohesion, concord, harmony, like-mindedness, unanimity, unity.

solidify /sə'lɪdɪfaɪ/ *verb* (**-ies**, **-ied**) make or become solid.

■ cake, clot, coagulate, congeal, crystallize, freeze, harden, *colloquial* jell, set, thicken.

soliloquy /sə'lɪləkwɪ/ *noun* (*plural* **-quies**) **1** talking without or regardless of hearers. **2** this part of a play. □ **soliloquize** *verb* (also **-ise**) (**-zing** or **-sing**).

■ monologue, speech.

solipsism /'sɒlɪpsɪz(ə)m/ *noun* theory that self is all that exists or can be known.

solitaire /'sɒlɪteə/ *noun* **1** jewel set by itself. **2** ring etc. with this. **3** game for one player who removes pegs etc. from board on jumping others over them. **4** *US* card game for one person.

solitary /'sɒlɪtərɪ/ *adjective* **1** living or being alone; not gregarious; lonely. **2** secluded. **3** single. ● *noun* (*plural* **-ies**) **1** recluse. **2** *colloquial* solitary confinement. □ **solitary confinement** isolation in separate prison cell. □ **solitariness** *noun*.

■ *adjective* **1** alone, antisocial, cloistered, companionless, friendless, isolated, lonely, *esp. US* lonesome, reclusive, unsociable, withdrawn. **2** desolate, distant, hidden, inaccessible, isolated, out of the way, private, remote, secluded, sequestered, unfrequented, unknown. **3** individual, one, only, single, sole. ● *noun* **1** anchoress, anchorite, hermit, loner, recluse.

solitude /'sɒlɪtjuːd/ *noun* **1** being solitary. **2** solitary place.

■ **1** friendlessness, isolation, loneliness, privacy, remoteness, retirement, seclusion.

solo /'səʊləʊ/ *noun* (*plural* **-s**) **1** piece of music or dance performed by one person. **2** thing done by one person, esp. unaccompanied flight. **3** (in full **solo whist**) type of whist in which one player may oppose the others. ● *verb* (**-es**, **-ed**) perform a solo. ● *adjective* & *adverb* unaccompanied, alone.

■ *adverb* alone, individually, on one's own, unaccompanied.

soloist /'səʊləʊɪst/ *noun* performer of solo.

solstice /'sɒlstɪs/ *noun* either of two times (**summer, winter solstice**) when sun is farthest from equator.

soluble /'sɒljʊb(ə)l/ *adjective* **1** that can be dissolved. **2** that can be solved. □ **solubility** *noun*.

■ **1** dissolving, melting. **2** explicable, manageable, solvable, understandable.

solution /sə'luːʃ(ə)n/ *noun* **1** (means of) solving a problem. **2** conversion of solid or gas into liquid by mixture with liquid. **3** state or substance resulting from this. **4** dissolving, being dissolved.

■ **1** answer, clarification, conclusion, elucidation, explanation, explication, key, outcome, resolution, solving, unravelling, working out. **3** blend, compound, emulsion, infusion, mixture, suspension.

solve *verb* (**-ving**) answer, remove, or deal with (problem). □ **solvable** *adjective*.

■ answer, clear up, crack, decipher, elucidate, explain, explicate, figure out, interpret, puzzle out, resolve, unravel, work out.

solvency /ˈsɒlvənsɪ/ *noun* being financially solvent.

solvent /ˈsɒlv(ə)nt/ *adjective* **1** able to pay one's debts. **2** able to dissolve or form solution. ● *noun* solvent liquid etc.

somatic /səˈmætɪk/ *adjective* of the body; not of the mind.

sombre /ˈsɒmbə/ *adjective* (also US **somber**) dark, gloomy, dismal. □ **sombrely** *adverb*. **sombreness** *noun*.

■ black, bleak, cheerless, dark, dim, dismal, doleful, drab, dreary, dull, funereal, gloomy, grave, grey, joyless, lowering, lugubrious, melancholy, morose, mournful, sad, serious, sober.

sombrero /sɒmˈbreərəʊ/ *noun* (*plural* **-s**) broad-brimmed hat worn esp. in Latin America.

some /sʌm/ *adjective* **1** unspecified amount or number of. **2** unknown, unspecified. **3** approximately. **4** considerable. **5** at least a small amount of. **6** such to a certain extent. **7** *colloquial* a remarkable. ● *pronoun* some people or things; some number or amount. ● *adverb colloquial* to some extent. □ **somebody** ● *pronoun* some person. ● *noun* important person. **some day** at some time in the future. **somehow 1** for some reason. **2** in some way; by some means. **someone** somebody. **something 1** unspecified or unknown thing. **2** unexpressed or intangible quantity or quality. **3** *colloquial* notable person or thing. **sometime 1** at some time. **2** former(ly). **sometimes** occasionally. **somewhat** to some extent. **somewhere** (in or to) some place.

■ □ **somewhat** fairly, moderately, *colloquial* pretty, quite, rather, *colloquial* sort of.

somersault /ˈsʌməsɒlt/ *noun* leap or roll in which one turns head over heels. ● *verb* perform somersault.

somnambulism /sɒmˈnæmbjʊlɪz(ə)m/ *noun* sleepwalking. □ **somnambulant** *adjective*. **somnambulist** *noun*.

somnolent /ˈsɒmnələnt/ *adjective* **1** sleepy, drowsy. **2** inducing drowsiness. □ **somnolence** *noun*.

son /sʌn/ *noun* **1** male in relation to his parent(s). **2** male descendant. **3** (+ *of*) male member of (family etc.). **4** male inheritor of a quality etc. **5** *form of address, esp. to boy*. □ **son-in-law** (*plural* **sons-in-law**) daughter's husband.

sonar /ˈsəʊnɑː/ *noun* **1** system for detecting objects under water by reflected sound. **2** apparatus for this.

sonata /səˈnɑːtə/ *noun* musical composition for one or two instruments in several related movements.

song *noun* **1** words set to music or for singing. **2** vocal music. **3** composition suggestive of song. **4** cry of some birds. □ **for a song** *colloquial* very cheaply. **songbird** bird with musical call. **song thrush** common thrush. **songwriter** writer of (music for) songs.

■ **1** air, anthem, ballad, carol, chant, ditty, *colloquial* hit, hymn, lullaby, melody, number, nursery rhyme, tune.

songster /ˈsɒŋstə/ *noun* (*feminine* **songstress**) **1** singer. **2** songbird.

sonic /ˈsɒnɪk/ *adjective* of or using sound or sound waves. □ **sonic bang, boom** noise made by aircraft flying faster than sound.

sonnet /ˈsɒnɪt/ *noun* poem of 14 lines with fixed rhyme scheme.

sonny /ˈsʌnɪ/ *noun colloquial*: familiar form of address to young boy.

sonorous /ˈsɒnərəs/ *adjective* **1** having a loud, full, or deep sound. **2** (of speech etc.) imposing. □ **sonority** /səˈnɒr-/ *noun* (*plural* **-ies**).

■ **1** deep, full, loud, powerful, resonant, resounding, reverberant, rich, ringing.

soon /suːn/ *adverb* **1** in a short time. **2** relatively early. **3** readily, willingly. □ **sooner or later** at some future time. □ **soonish** *adverb*.

■ **1** *archaic* anon, before long, in a minute, presently, quickly, shortly, straight away. **2** early, quickly, speedily; (*sooner*) before, earlier. **3** readily, willingly; (*sooner*) preferably, rather.

soot /sʊt/ *noun* black powdery deposit from smoke.

■ dirt, grime.

soothe /suːð/ *verb* (**-thing**) **1** calm. **2** soften, mitigate. □ **soothing** *adjective*.

■ allay, appease, assuage, calm, comfort, compose, ease, mitigate, mollify, pacify, quiet, relieve, salve, settle, still, tranquillize. □ **soothing** balmy, calming, comforting, emollient, gentle, healing, mild, palliative, peaceful, pleasant, reassuring, relaxing, restful.

soothsayer /ˈsuːθseɪə/ *noun* seer, prophet.

sooty *adjective* (**-ier**, **-iest**) **1** covered with soot. **2** black; brownish black.

sop *noun* **1** thing given or done to pacify or bribe. **2** piece of bread etc. dipped in gravy etc. ● *verb* (**-pp-**) (+ *up*) soak up.

sophism /ˈsɒfɪz(ə)m/ *noun* false argument, esp. one meant to deceive.

sophist /ˈsɒfɪst/ *noun* captious or clever but fallacious reasoner. □ **sophistic** /səˈfɪs-/ *adjective*. **sophistical** /səˈfɪstɪk(ə)l/ *adjective*.

sophisticate /səˈfɪstɪkət/ *noun* sophisticated person.

sophisticated /səˈfɪstɪkeɪtɪd/ *adjective* **1** worldly-wise, cultured, elegant. **2** highly developed and complex. □ **sophistication** *noun*.

■ **1** *slang* cool, cosmopolitan, cultivated, cultured, elegant, fashionable, polished, *colloquial* posh, pretentious, refined, stylish, urbane, worldly, worldly-wise. **2** advanced, clever, complex, complicated, elaborate, ingenious, intricate, involved, subtle.

sophistry /'sɒfɪstrɪ/ *noun* (*plural* **-ies**) **1** use of sophisms. **2** a sophism.

sophomore /'sɒfəmɔː/ *noun US* second-year university or high-school student.

soporific /sɒpə'rɪfɪk/ *adjective* inducing sleep. ● *noun* soporific drug or influence. □ **soporifically** *adverb*.

■ *adjective* boring, deadening, drowsy, hypnotic, sedative, sleepy, somnolent.

sopping *adjective* drenched.

soppy *adjective* (**-ier**, **-iest**) *colloquial* **1** mawkishly sentimental. **2** silly, foolish.

soprano /sə'prɑːnəʊ/ *noun* (*plural* **-s**) **1** highest singing voice. **2** singer with this. ● *adjective* having range of soprano.

sorbet /'sɔːbeɪ/ *noun* **1** water-ice. **2** sherbet.

sorcerer /'sɔːsərə/ *noun* (*feminine* **sorceress**) magician, wizard. □ **sorcery** *noun* (*plural* **-ies**).

■ conjuror, enchanter, enchantress, magician, magus, medicine man, necromancer, *archaic* warlock, witch, witch-doctor, wizard. □ **sorcery** black magic, charms, conjuring, diabolism, incantations, magic, necromancy, the occult, spells, voodoo, witchcraft, wizardry.

sordid /'sɔːdɪd/ *adjective* **1** dirty, squalid. **2** ignoble, mercenary. □ **sordidly** *adverb*. **sordidness** *noun*.

■ **1** dingy, dirty, disreputable, filthy, foul, miserable, *colloquial* mucky, nasty, offensive, polluted, putrid, ramshackle, seamy, seedy, sleazy, slummy, squalid, ugly, unclean, undignified, unpleasant, unsanitary, wretched. **2** avaricious, base, corrupt, covetous, degenerate, despicable, dishonourable, ignoble, ignominious, immoral, mean, mercenary, rapacious, selfish, shabby, shameful, unethical, unscrupulous.

sore *adjective* **1** painful. **2** suffering pain. **3** aggrieved, vexed. **4** *archaic* grievous, severe. ● *noun* sore place, subject, etc. ● *adverb archaic* grievously, severely. □ **soreness** *noun*.

■ *adjective* **1** aching, bruised, burning, chafed, chapped, delicate, grazed, hurting, inflamed, lacerated, painful, raw, red, rubbed, sensitive, smarting, stinging, tender. **3** aggrieved, annoyed, hurt, irked, *colloquial* peeved, put out, resentful, upset, vexed. *noun* abrasion, abscess, boil, bruise, burn, carbuncle, gall, gathering, graze, infection, inflammation, injury, laceration, pimple, rawness, redness, scrape, spot, swelling, ulcer, wound.

sorely *adverb* extremely.

sorghum /'sɔːgəm/ *noun* tropical cereal grass.

sorority /sə'rɒrɪtɪ/ *noun* (*plural* **-ies**) *US* female students' society in university or college.

sorrel[1] /'sɒr(ə)l/ *noun* sour-leaved herb.

sorrel[2] /'sɒr(ə)l/ *adjective* of light reddish-brown colour. ● *noun* **1** this colour. **2** sorrel animal, esp. horse.

sorrow /'sɒrəʊ/ *noun* **1** mental distress caused by loss, disappointment, etc. **2** cause of sorrow.

● *verb* **1** feel sorrow. **2** mourn. □ **sorrowful** *adjective*.

■ *noun* **1** affliction, anguish, dejection, depression, desolation, despair, desperation, despondency, disappointment, discontent, disgruntlement, dissatisfaction, distress, *literary* dolour, gloom, glumness, grief, guilt, heartache, heartbreak, heaviness, homesickness, hopelessness, loneliness, melancholy, misery, mourning, penitence, regret, remorse, repentance, sadness, suffering, tearfulness, tribulation, trouble, unhappiness, wistfulness, woe, wretchedness. **2** affliction, disappointment, misery, misfortune, suffering, tribulation, trouble, woe. ● *verb* agonize, grieve, lament, mourn, weep; (*sorrow for, over*) bemoan, bewail, regret. □ **sorrowful** broken-hearted, dejected, disconsolate, distressed, doleful, grief-stricken, heartbroken, long-faced, lugubrious, melancholy, miserable, mournful, regretful, rueful, sad, saddened, sombre, sorry, tearful, unhappy, upset, woebegone, woeful, wretched.

sorry /'sɒrɪ/ *adjective* (**-ier**, **-iest**) **1** pained, regretful, penitent. **2** feeling pity. **3** wretched; in poor state. □ **sorry for oneself** dejected.

■ **1** apologetic, ashamed, conscience-stricken, contrite, guilt-ridden, penitent, regretful, remorseful, repentant, shamefaced. **2** compassionate, concerned, pitying, sympathetic, understanding.

sort *noun* **1** class, kind. **2** *colloquial* person of specified kind. ● *verb* (often + *out*, *over*) arrange systematically. □ **of a sort**, **of sorts** *colloquial* barely deserving the name. **out of sorts 1** slightly unwell. **2** in low spirits. **sort of** *colloquial* as it were; to some extent. **sort out 1** separate into sorts. **2** select from miscellaneous group. **3** disentangle; put into order. **4** solve. **5** *colloquial* deal with or punish.

■ *noun* **1** brand, breed, category, class, classification, description, family, form, genre, genus, group, kind, make, mark, nature, quality, race, set, species, strain, stock, type, variety. ● *verb* arrange, assort, catalogue, categorize, classify, divide, file, grade, group, order, organize, put in order, rank, systematize, tidy. □ **sort out 2** choose, segregate, select, separate, set aside. **4** attend to, clear up, cope with, deal with, find an answer to, grapple with, handle, manage, organize, put right, resolve, solve, straighten out.

sortie /'sɔːtɪ/ *noun* **1** sally, esp. from besieged garrison. **2** operational military flight. ● *verb* (**sortieing**) make sortie.

SOS *noun* (*plural* **SOSs**) **1** international code-signal of extreme distress. **2** urgent appeal for help.

sot *noun* habitual drunkard. □ **sottish** *adjective*.

sotto voce /sɒtəʊ 'vəʊtʃɪ/ *adverb* in an undertone. [Italian]

sou /suː/ *noun* (*plural* **-s**) **1** *colloquial* very small amount of money. **2** *historical* former French coin of low value.

soubrette /suː'bret/ *noun* **1** pert maidservant etc. in comedy. **2** actress taking this part.

soubriquet = SOBRIQUET.

soufflé /'su:fleɪ/ *noun* light spongy dish made with stiffly beaten egg white.

sough /saʊ, sʌf/ *noun* moaning or rustling sound, e.g. of wind in trees. ● *verb* make this sound.

sought /sɔːt/ *past & past participle* of SEEK. □ **sought after** much in demand.

souk /suːk/ *noun* market-place in Muslim countries.

soul /səʊl/ *noun* 1 spiritual or immaterial part of person. 2 moral, emotional, or intellectual nature of person. 3 personification, pattern. 4 an individual. 5 animating or essential part. 6 energy, intensity. 7 soul music. □ **soul-destroying** tedious, monotonous. **soul mate** person ideally suited to another. **soul music** type of black American music. **soul-searching** introspection.

■ *noun* 1 psyche, spirit. 4 see PERSON 1.

soulful *adjective* having, expressing, or evoking deep feeling. □ **soulfully** *adverb*.

■ eloquent, emotional, expressive, fervent, heartfelt, inspiring, moving, passionate, profound, sincere, spiritual, stirring, uplifting, warm.

soulless *adjective* 1 lacking sensitivity or noble qualities. 2 undistinguished, uninteresting.

■ cold, inhuman, insincere, mechanical, perfunctory, routine, spiritless, superficial, trite, unemotional, unfeeling, uninspiring, unsympathetic.

sound¹ /saʊnd/ *noun* 1 sensation produced in ear when surrounding air etc. vibrates. 2 vibrations causing this. 3 what is or may be heard. 4 idea or impression given by words. ● *verb* 1 (cause to) emit sound. 2 utter, pronounce. 3 convey specified impression. 4 give audible signal for. 5 test condition of by sound produced. □ **sound barrier** high resistance of air to objects moving at speeds near that of sound. **sound effect** sound other than speech or music produced artificially for film, broadcast, etc. **sounding board** 1 person etc. used to test or disseminate opinion(s). 2 canopy projecting sound towards audience. **sound off** 1 talk loudly. 2 express one's opinions forcefully. **soundproof** ● *adjective* impervious to sound. ● *verb* make soundproof. **sound system** equipment for reproducing sound. **soundtrack** 1 sound element of film or videotape. 2 recording of this available separately. **sound wave** wave of compression and rarefaction by which sound is transmitted in air etc. □ **soundless** *adjective*. **soundlessly** *adverb*. **soundlessness** *noun*.

■ *noun* 1 din, noise, resonance, timbre, tone. ● *verb* 1 be heard, echo, resonate, resound, reverberate, ring. 2 articulate, produce, pronounce, utter, voice. 4 announce, declare, signal.

sound² /saʊnd/ *adjective* 1 healthy; not diseased or rotten; uninjured. 2 correct, well founded. 3 financially secure. 4 undisturbed. 5 thorough. ● *adverb* soundly. □ **soundly** *adverb*. **soundness** *noun*.

■ *adjective* 1 durable, edible (*of food*), fit, healthy, hearty, in good shape, robust, secure, solid, strong, sturdy, tough, undamaged, uninjured, unscathed, vigorous, well, whole, wholesome. 2 balanced, coherent, common-sense, convincing, correct, judicious, logical, orthodox, prudent, rational, reasonable, reasoned, sane, sensible, well founded, wise. 3 dependable, established, profitable, recognized, reliable, reputable, safe, secure, viable.

sound³ /saʊnd/ *verb* 1 test depth or quality of bottom of (sea, river, etc.). 2 (often + *out*) inquire (esp. discreetly) into views etc. of (person); investigate (matter, views, etc.).

■ 1 fathom, plumb, probe. 2 (*sound out*) check, examine, inquire of, investigate, probe, research, survey, test, try.

sound⁴ /saʊnd/ *noun* strait (of water).

sounding *noun* 1 measurement of depth of water. 2 (in *plural*) region near enough to shore for sounding. 3 (in *plural*) cautious investigation.

soup /suːp/ *noun* liquid food made by boiling meat, fish, or vegetables. ● *verb* (usually + *up*) *colloquial* 1 increase power of (engine). 2 enliven. □ **in the soup** *colloquial* in difficulties. **soup kitchen** place supplying free soup etc. to the poor. **soup spoon** large round-bowled spoon. □ **soupy** *adjective* (**-ier**, **-iest**).

■ *noun* broth, consommé.

soupçon /'suːpsɔ̃/ *noun* small quantity, trace.

sour /saʊə/ *adjective* 1 having acid taste or smell (as) from unripeness or fermentation. 2 (of food, esp. milk) bad because of fermentation. 3 morose, bitter. 4 unpleasant, distasteful. 5 (of soil) dank. ● *verb* make or become sour. □ **sour grapes** resentful disparagement of something coveted. **sourpuss** *colloquial* bad-tempered person. □ **sourly** *adverb*. **sourness** *noun*.

■ *adjective* 1 acid, acidic, acidulous, bitter, citrus, lemony, pungent, sharp, tangy, tart, unripe, vinegary. 2 bad, curdled, *colloquial* off, rancid, turned. 3 acerbic, bad-tempered, bitter, caustic, cross, crusty, curmudgeonly, cynical, disaffected, disagreeable, grudging, grumpy, ill-natured, irritable, jaundiced, peevish, petulant, *colloquial* snappy, testy, unpleasant.

source /sɔːs/ *noun* 1 place from which river or stream issues. 2 place, person, or thing from which something originates. 3 person, book, etc. providing information. □ **at source** at point of origin or issue.

■ 1 head, origin, spring, start, well-head, well-spring. 2 author, *literary* begetter, beginning, cause, creator, derivation, initiator, originator, root, starting point. 3 informant.

souse /saʊs/ *verb* (**-sing**) 1 immerse in pickle or other liquid. 2 (as **soused** *adjective*) *colloquial* drunk. 3 (usually + *in*) soak (thing). ● *noun* 1 pickle made with salt. **2** *US* food in pickle. **3** a plunge or drenching in water.

soutane /suːˈtɑːn/ *noun* cassock of RC priest.

south /saʊθ/ *noun* **1** point of horizon opposite north. **2** corresponding compass point. **3** (usually **the South**) southern part of world, country, town, etc. ● *adjective* **1** towards, at, near, or facing south. **2** (of wind) from south. ● *adverb* **1** towards, at, or near south. **2** (+ *of*) further south than. □ **southbound** travelling or leading south. **south-east, -west** point midway between south and east or west. **southpaw** *colloquial* left-handed person, esp. boxer. **south-south-east, south-south-west** point midway between south and south-east or south-west. □ **southward** *adjective, adverb, & noun.* **southwards** *adverb.*

southerly /ˈsʌðəlɪ/ *adjective & adverb* **1** in southern position or direction. **2** (of wind) from south.

southern /ˈsʌð(ə)n/ *adjective* of or in south. □ **Southern Cross** constellation with stars forming cross. **southern lights** aurora australis. □ **southernmost** *adjective.*

southerner *noun* native or inhabitant of south.

souvenir /suːvəˈnɪə/ *noun* memento of place, occasion, etc.
 ■ heirloom, keepsake, memento, relic, reminder.

sou'wester /saʊˈwestə/ *noun* **1** waterproof hat with broad flap at back. **2** SW wind.

sovereign /ˈsɒvrɪn/ *noun* **1** supreme ruler, esp. monarch. **2** *historical* British gold coin nominally worth £1. ● *adjective* **1** supreme. **2** self-governing. **3** royal. **4** (of remedy etc.) effective. □ **sovereignty** *noun* (*plural* **-ies**).
 ■ *noun* **1** emperor, empress, king, monarch, prince, princess, queen, ruler. ● *adjective* **1** absolute, all-powerful, dominant, highest, supreme, unlimited. **2** autonomous, independent, self-governing. **3** see ROYAL *adjective* 1.

soviet /ˈsəʊvɪət/ *noun* **1** elected council in former USSR. **2** (**Soviet**) citizen of former USSR. ● *adjective* of former USSR.

sow[1] /səʊ/ *verb* (*past* **sowed**; *past participle* **sown** or **sowed**) **1** scatter (seed) on or in earth. **2** (often + *with*) plant with seed. **3** initiate.
 ■ **1** broadcast, disseminate, plant, scatter, seed, spread.

sow[2] /saʊ/ *noun* adult female pig.

soy *noun* (in full **soy sauce**) sauce made from pickled soya beans.

soya /ˈsɔɪə/ *noun* (in full **soya bean**) (seed of) leguminous plant yielding edible oil and flour.

sozzled /ˈsɒz(ə)ld/ *adjective colloquial* very drunk.

spa /spɑː/ *noun* **1** curative mineral spring. **2** resort with this.

space *noun* **1** continuous expanse in which things exist and move. **2** amount of this taken by thing or available. **3** interval between points or objects; empty area. **4** outdoor urban recreation area. **5** outer space. **6** interval of time. **7** expanse of paper used in writing, available for advertising, etc. **8** blank between printed, typed, or written words etc. **9** *Printing* piece of metal separating words etc. ● *verb* (**-cing**) **1** set or arrange at intervals. **2** put spaces between. □ **space age** era of space travel. **space-age** *adjective* very modern. **spacecraft** vehicle for travelling in outer space. **spaceman, spacewoman** astronaut. **space out** spread out (more) widely. **spaceship** spacecraft. **space shuttle** spacecraft for repeated use. **space station** artificial satellite as base for operations in outer space. **spacesuit** sealed pressurized suit for astronaut in space. **space-time** fusion of concepts of space and time as 4-dimensional continuum.
 ■ *noun* **2** area, capacity, *colloquial* elbow room, expanse, extent, latitude, leeway, margin, room, scope, spaciousness, volume. **3** area, blank, break, chasm, distance, gap, hiatus, hole, interval, lacuna, opening, place, vacuum. **5** the cosmos, emptiness, endlessness, infinity, the universe; (*space travel*) cosmic, extraterrestrial, interplanetary, interstellar. **6** break, duration, gap, hiatus, intermission, interval, lacuna, lapse, pause, slot, span, spell, stretch, time, wait. ● *verb* **1** see ARRANGE 1.

spacious /ˈspeɪʃəs/ *adjective* having ample space; roomy. □ **spaciously** *adverb.* **spaciousness** *noun.*
 ■ ample, big, broad, capacious, commodious, extensive, large, open, roomy, sizeable, vast, wide.

spade[1] *noun* long-handled digging tool with rectangular metal blade. □ **spadework** hard preparatory work. **spadeful** *noun* (*plural* **-s**).

spade[2] *noun* playing card of suit denoted by black inverted heart-shaped figures with short stems.

spaghetti /spəˈgetɪ/ *noun* pasta in long thin strands. □ **spaghetti western** cowboy film made cheaply in Italy.

span[1] *noun* **1** full extent from end to end. **2** each part of bridge between supports. **3** maximum lateral extent of aeroplane or its wing or of bird's wing etc. **4** distance between outstretched tips of thumb and little finger; 9 inches. ● *verb* (**-nn-**) **1** extend from side to side or end to end of. **2** bridge (river etc.).
 ■ *noun* **1** breadth, compass, distance, duration, extent, interval, length, period, reach, scope, stretch, term, width. ● *verb* arch over, bridge, cross, extend across, go over, pass over, reach over, straddle, stretch over, traverse.

span[2] *past* of SPIN.

spandrel /ˈspændrɪl/ *noun* space between curve of arch and surrounding rectangular moulding, or between curves of adjoining arches and moulding above.

spangle /ˈspæŋg(ə)l/ *noun* small piece of glittering material, esp. one of many used to ornament dress etc. ● *verb* (**-ling**) (esp. as **spangled** *adjective*) cover (as) with spangles.

Spaniard /ˈspænjəd/ *noun* native or national of Spain.

spaniel /'spænj(ə)l/ *noun* dog of breed with long silky coat and drooping ears.

Spanish /'spænɪʃ/ *adjective* of Spain. ● *noun* language of Spain.

spank *verb & noun* slap, esp. on buttocks.
■ hit, slap, smack.

spanker *noun Nautical* fore-and-aft sail on mizen-mast.

spanking *adjective* **1** brisk. **2** *colloquial* striking, excellent. ● *adverb colloquial* very. ● *noun* slapping on buttocks.

spanner /'spænə/ *noun* tool for turning nut on bolt etc. □ **spanner in the works** *colloquial* impediment.

spar¹ *noun* stout pole, esp. as ship's mast etc.

spar² *verb* (**-rr-**) **1** make motions of boxing. **2** argue. ● *noun* **1** sparring. **2** boxing match. □ **sparring partner 1** boxer employed to spar with another as training. **2** person with whom one enjoys arguing.
■ *verb* **1** box, exchange blows, fight, *colloquial* scrap. **2** see ARGUE 1.

spar³ *noun* easily split crystalline mineral.

spare /speə/ *adjective* **1** not required for ordinary or present use; extra. **2** for emergency or occasional use. **3** lean, thin. **4** frugal. ● *noun* spare part. ● *verb* (**-ring**) **1** afford to give; dispense with. **2** refrain from killing, hurting, etc. **3** not inflict. **4** be frugal or grudging of. □ **go spare** *colloquial* become very angry. **spare (person's) life** not kill. **spare part** duplicate, esp. as replacement. **spare rib** closely trimmed rib of esp. pork. **spare time** leisure. **spare tyre** *colloquial* roll of fat round waist. **to spare** left over. □ **sparely** *adverb*. **spareness** *noun*.
■ *adjective* **1, 2** additional, auxiliary, extra, free, inessential, in reserve, leftover, odd, remaining, superfluous, supernumerary, supplementary, surplus, unnecessary, unneeded, unused, unwanted. **3** see THIN *adjective* 4. ● *verb* **1** afford, allow, donate, give, give up, manage without, part with, provide, sacrifice. **2** be merciful to, deliver, forgive, free, have mercy on, let go, let off, liberate, pardon, redeem, release, reprieve, save.

sparing *adjective* **1** frugal, economical. **2** restrained. □ **sparingly** *adverb*.
■ see ECONOMICAL, MISERLY (MISER).

spark *noun* **1** fiery particle of burning substance. **2** (often + *of*) small amount. **3** flash of light between electric conductors etc. **4** this for firing explosive mixture in internal-combustion engine. **5** flash of wit etc. **6** (also **bright spark**) lively or clever person. ● *verb* **1** emit spark(s). **2** (often + *off*) stir into activity; initiate. □ **spark plug, sparking plug** device for making spark in internal-combustion engine. □ **sparky** *adjective*.
■ *noun* **2** see PARTICLE 2. **3** flash, flicker, gleam, glint, scintilla, sparkle. ● *verb* **2** (*spark off*) ignite, kindle, provoke, trigger.

sparkle /'spɑːk(ə)l/ *verb* (**-ling**) **1** (seem to) emit sparks; glitter. **2** scintillate. **3** (esp. as **sparkling**

adjective) (of wine etc.) effervesce. ● *noun* **1** glitter. **2** lively quality. □ **sparkly** *adjective*.
■ *verb* **1** coruscate, flash, flicker, gleam, glint, glitter, scintillate, shine, spark, twinkle, wink. **3** (**sparkling**) aerated, bubbly, carbonated, effervescent, fizzy.

sparkler *noun* **1** sparkling firework. **2** *colloquial* gem, esp. diamond.

sparrow /'spærəʊ/ *noun* small brownish-grey bird. □ **sparrowhawk** small hawk.

sparse /spɑːs/ *adjective* thinly scattered. □ **sparsely** *adverb*. **sparseness** *noun*. **sparsity** *noun*.
■ few and far between, inadequate, light, little, meagre, scanty, scarce, scattered, sparing, spread out, thin, thin on the ground.

Spartan /'spɑːt(ə)n/ *adjective* **1** of ancient Sparta. **2** austere, rigorous. ● *noun* native or citizen of Sparta.
■ *adjective* **2** abstemious, ascetic, austere, bare, bleak, disciplined, frugal, hard, harsh, plain, rigid, rigorous, severe, simple, stern, strict.

spasm /'spæz(ə)m/ *noun* **1** sudden involuntary muscular contraction. **2** convulsive movement or emotion etc. **3** (usually + *of*) *colloquial* brief spell.
■ **1** contraction, convulsion, fit, jerk, paroxysm, seizure, throe, twitch. **2** attack, eruption, fit, outburst, paroxysm. **3** bout, burst, fit, spell.

spasmodic /spæz'mɒdɪk/ *adjective* of or in spasms; intermittent. □ **spasmodically** *adverb*.
■ by fits and starts, erratic, fitful, intermittent, interrupted, irregular, jerky, occasional, on and off, periodic, sporadic.

spastic /'spæstɪk/ *adjective* of or having cerebral palsy. ● *noun* spastic person.

spat¹ *past & past participle* of SPIT¹.

spat² (usually in *plural*) *historical* short gaiter covering shoe.

spate *noun* **1** river-flood. **2** large amount or number (of similar events etc.).
■ **1** deluge, flood, inundation, torrent. **2** deluge, flood, flow, inundation, onrush, run, rush, torrent.

spathe /speɪð/ *noun* large bract(s) enveloping flower-cluster.

spatial /'speɪʃ(ə)l/ *adjective* of space. □ **spatially** *adverb*.

spatter /'spætə/ *verb* splash or scatter in drips. ● *noun* **1** splash. **2** pattering.
■ *verb* bespatter, daub, pepper, scatter, shower, slop, speckle, splash, splatter, spray, sprinkle.

spatula /'spætjʊlə/ *noun* broad-bladed implement used esp. by artists and in cookery.

spawn *verb* **1** (of fish, frog, etc.) produce (eggs). **2** be produced as eggs or young. **3** produce or generate in large numbers. ● *noun* **1** eggs of fish, frogs, etc. **2** white fibrous matter from which fungi grow.

spay *verb* sterilize (female animal) by removing ovaries.

speak *verb* (*past* **spoke**; *past participle* **spoken** /'spəʊk(ə)n/) **1** utter words in ordinary way. **2** utter (words, the truth, etc.). **3** converse. **4** (+ *of*, *about*) mention. **5** (+ *for*) act as spokesman for. **6** (+ *to*) speak with reference to or in support of. **7** deliver speech. **8** (be able to) use (specified language) in speaking. **9** convey idea. **10** (usually + *to*) affect. □ **speak for itself** be sufficient evidence. **speaking clock** telephone service announcing correct time. **speak one's mind** give one's frank opinion. **speak out** give one's opinion courageously. **speak up** speak (more) loudly. **speak up for** speak in support of.

■ **1, 2** answer, articulate, ask, declare, ejaculate, enunciate, exclaim, express oneself, pipe up, pronounce, recite, say something, state, talk, tell, use one's voice, utter, verbalize, vocalize, voice. **3** chat, communicate, confer, converse, discourse, talk. **4** (*speak about*) see MENTION *verb* 1, DISCUSS. **7** declaim, harangue, hold forth, lecture, preach, soliloquize, *jocular* speechify; (*speak to*) see ADDRESS *verb* 3. **8** communicate in, converse in, express oneself in, talk. □ **speak one's mind** say what one thinks, speak out, state one's opinion, voice one's thoughts.

speaker *noun* **1** person who speaks, esp. in public. **2** person who speaks specified language. **3** (**Speaker**) presiding officer of legislative assembly. **4** loudspeaker.

■ **1** lecturer, mouthpiece, orator, spokesperson.

spear *noun* **1** thrusting or hurling weapon with long shaft and sharp point. **2** tip and stem of asparagus, broccoli, etc. ● *verb* pierce or strike (as) with spear. □ **spearhead** ● *noun* **1** point of spear. **2** person(s) leading attack or challenge. ● *verb* act as spearhead of (attack etc.). **spearmint** common garden mint.

■ *noun* **1** assegai, harpoon, javelin, lance, pike.

spec¹ *noun colloquial* speculation. □ **on spec** as a gamble.

spec² *noun colloquial* specification.

special /'speʃ(ə)l/ *adjective* **1** exceptional. **2** peculiar, specific. **3** for particular purpose. **4** for children with special needs. ● *noun* special constable, train, edition of newspaper, dish on menu, etc. □ **Special Branch** police department dealing with political security. **special constable** person assisting police in routine duties or in emergencies. **special effects** illusions created by props, camera-work, etc. **special licence** licence allowing immediate marriage without banns. **special pleading** biased reasoning. □ **specially** *adverb*.

■ *adjective* **1** different, distinguished, exceptional, extraordinary, important, memorable, momentous, notable, noteworthy, odd, out of the ordinary, rare, remarkable, significant, strange, uncommon, unconventional, unorthodox, unusual. **2, 3** characteristic, distinctive, especial, idiosyncratic, individual, particular, peculiar, personal, singular, specialized, specific, unique, unmistakable.

specialist *noun* **1** person trained in particular branch of profession, esp. medicine. **2** person specially studying subject or area. □ **specialism** /-lɪz(ə)m/*noun*.

■ **1** consultant, expert. **2** authority, connoisseur, expert, fancier (*pigeon fancier*), master, professional, pundit, researcher.

speciality /speʃɪ'ælɪtɪ/ *noun* (*plural* **-ies**) **1** special subject, product, activity, etc. **2** special feature or skill.

■ **1** claim to fame, field, line, specialization, esp. US specialty. **2** expertise, forte, genius, esp. US specialty, strength, strong point, talent.

specialize *verb* (also **-ise**) (**-zing** or **-sing**) **1** (often + *in*) become or be specialist. **2** (often + *in*) devote oneself to an interest, skill, etc. **3** (esp. in *passive*) adapt for particular purpose. **4** (as **specialized** *adjective*) of a specialist. □ **specialization** *noun*.

■ **1, 2** (*specialize in*) be best at, concentrate on, devote oneself to, have a reputation for. **4** (**specialized**) esoteric, expert, specialist, unfamiliar.

specialty /'speʃəltɪ/ *noun* (*plural* **-ies**) *esp. US* speciality.

specie /'spiːʃiː/ *noun* coin as opposed to paper money.

species /'spiːʃɪz/ *noun* (*plural* same) **1** group of animals or plants within genus. **2** class of things having common characteristics. **3** kind, sort.

■ **2, 3** breed, class, genus, kind, race, sort, type, variety.

specific /spə'sɪfɪk/ *adjective* **1** clearly defined. **2** relating to particular subject; peculiar. **3** exact; giving full details. **4** *archaic* (of medicine etc.) for particular disease. ● *noun* **1** *archaic* specific medicine. **2** specific aspect. □ **specific gravity** relative density. □ **specifically** *adverb*. **specificity** /-'fɪs-/ *noun*.

■ *adjective* **1, 3** clear-cut, defined, definite, detailed, exact, explicit, express, fixed, identified, itemized, known, named, particular, precise, predetermined, specified, unequivocal. **2** individual, particular, peculiar, special.

specification /spesɪfɪ'keɪʃ(ə)n/ *noun* **1** specifying. **2** (esp. in *plural*) detailed description of work (to be) done or of invention, patent, etc.

specify /'spesɪfaɪ/ *verb* (**-ies**, **-ied**) **1** name or mention expressly or as condition. **2** include in specifications.

■ define, denominate, detail, enumerate, establish, identify, itemize, list, name, particularize, set out, spell out, state, stipulate.

specimen /'spesɪmɪn/ *noun* **1** individual or sample taken as example of class or whole, esp. in experiments etc. **2** *colloquial usually derogatory* person of specified sort.

■ **1** example, exemplar, illustration, instance, model, pattern, representative, sample.

specious /'spiːʃəs/ *adjective* plausible but wrong.

■ casuistic, deceptive, misleading, plausible, seductive.

speck *noun* **1** small spot or stain. **2** particle. ● *verb* (esp. as **specked** *adjective*) mark with specks.

■ *noun* **1** dot, fleck, mark, speckle, spot, trace. **2** bit, crumb, fleck, grain, mite, mote, particle.

speckle /'spek(ə)l/ *noun* speck, esp. one of many markings. ● *verb* (**-ling**) (esp. as **speckled** *adjective*) mark with speckles.

■ *verb* (**speckled**) blotchy, brindled, dappled, dotted, flecked, freckled, mottled, patchy, spattered, spotted, spotty, sprinkled, stippled.

specs *plural noun colloquial* spectacles.

spectacle /'spektək(ə)l/ *noun* **1** striking, impressive, or ridiculous sight; object of public attention. **2** public show. **3** (in *plural*) pair of lenses in frame supported on nose and ears, to correct defective eyesight.

■ **1** display, exhibition, scene, sight, wonder. **2** ceremony, display, exhibition, extravaganza, pageant, parade, show. **3** (*spectacles*) see GLASS *noun* 11.

spectacled *adjective* wearing spectacles.

spectacular /spek'tækjʊlə/ *adjective* striking, impressive, lavish. ● *noun* spectacular performance. □ **spectacularly** *adverb*.

■ *adjective* beautiful, breathtaking, colourful, dramatic, elaborate, *colloquial* eye-catching, impressive, magnificent, ostentatious, sensational, showy, splendid, *colloquial* stunning.

spectator /spek'teItə/ *noun* person who watches a show, game, incident, etc. □ **spectator sport** sport attracting many spectators. □ **spectate** *verb* (**-ting**).

■ beholder, bystander, eyewitness, looker-on, observer, onlooker, passer-by, viewer, watcher, witness; (*spectators*) audience, crowd.

specter *US* = SPECTRE.

spectra *plural* of SPECTRUM.

spectral /'spektr(ə)l/ *adjective* **1** of or like spectres or spectra. **2** ghostly.

spectre /'spektə/ *noun* (*US* **specter**) **1** ghost. **2** haunting presentiment.

■ **1** apparition, ghost, phantom, spirit, vision, wraith.

spectroscope /'spektrəskəʊp/ *noun* instrument for recording and examining spectra. □ **spectroscopic** /-'skɒp-/ *adjective*. **spectroscopy** /-'trɒskəpɪ/ *noun*.

spectrum /'spektrəm/ *noun* (*plural* **-tra**) **1** band of colours as seen in rainbow etc. **2** entire or wide range of subject, emotion, etc. **3** arrangement of electromagnetic radiation by wavelength.

■ **2** compass, extent, gamut, orbit, range, scope, series, span, spread, sweep, variety.

speculate /'spekjʊleɪt/ *verb* (**-ting**) **1** (usually + *on*, *upon*, *about*) theorize, conjecture. **2** deal in commodities etc. in expectation of profiting from fluctuating prices. □ **speculation** *noun*. **speculator** *noun*.

■ **1** conjecture, consider, hypothesize, meditate, ponder, reflect, ruminate, surmise, theorize, think, *colloquial* weigh up, wonder. **2** gamble, play the market, take a chance, wager.

speculative /'spekjʊlətɪv/ *adjective* **1** of or based on speculation. **2** (of investment) risky.

■ **1** abstract, conjectural, doubtful, hypothetical, notional, suppositional, supposititious, theoretical, unfounded, unproven, untested. **2** chancy, *slang* dicey, *colloquial* dodgy, hazardous, *colloquial* iffy, risky, uncertain, unpredictable, unreliable, unsafe.

sped *past & past participle* of SPEED.

speech *noun* **1** faculty, act, or manner of speaking. **2** formal public address. **3** language, dialect. □ **speech day** annual prize-giving day in school. **speech therapy** treatment for defective speech.

■ **1** articulation, communication, declamation, delivery, diction, elocution, enunciation, expression, language, pronunciation, speaking, talking, utterance. **2** address, discourse, disquisition, harangue, homily, lecture, monologue, oration, presentation, sermon, soliloquy, *slang* spiel, talk, tirade. **3** dialect, idiom, jargon, language, parlance, register, talk, tongue.

speechify /'spiːtʃɪfaɪ/ *verb* (**-ies**, **-ied**) *jocular* make speeches.

speechless *adjective* temporarily silenced by emotion etc. □ **speechlessness** *noun*.

■ dumb, dumbfounded, dumbstruck, inarticulate, *colloquial* mum, mute, nonplussed, silent, thunderstruck, tongue-tied, voiceless.

speed *noun* **1** rapidity. **2** rate of progress or motion. **3** gear on bicycle. **4** relative sensitivity of photographic film to light. **5** *slang* amphetamine. ● *verb* (*past & past participle* **sped**) **1** go or send quickly. **2** (*past & past participle* **speeded**) travel at illegal or dangerous speed. **3** *archaic* be or make prosperous or successful. □ **speedboat** fast motor boat. **speed limit** maximum permitted speed on road etc. **speed up** increase speed. **speedway 1** (dirt track for) motorcycle racing. **2** *US* road or track for fast vehicles. □ **speeder** *noun*.

■ *noun* **1** alacrity, briskness, *archaic* celerity, dispatch, expeditiousness, fleetness, haste, hurry, quickness, rapidity, speediness, swiftness. **2** pace, rate, tempo, velocity. ● *verb* **1** *slang* belt, bolt, bowl along, canter, career, dart, dash, flash, flit, fly, gallop, go like the wind, hasten, hurry, hurtle, make haste, *colloquial* nip, *colloquial* put one's foot down, race, run, rush, shoot, sprint, - stampede, streak, *colloquial* tear, zoom. **2** break the speed limit, exceed the speed limit. □ **speed up** see ACCELERATE 1.

speedometer /spiː'dɒmɪtə/ *noun* instrument on vehicle indicating its speed.

speedwell /'spiːdwel/ *noun* small blue-flowered herbaceous plant.

speedy *adjective* (**-ier**, **-iest**) **1** rapid. **2** prompt.

□ **speedily** *adverb.* **speediness** *noun.*
■ **1** expeditious, fast, *poetical* or *literary* fleet, nimble, quick, rapid, swift. **2** hasty, hurried, immediate, precipitate, prompt, unhesitating.

speleology /spi:lɪˈɒlədʒɪ/ *noun* the study of caves etc.

spell[1] *verb* (*past & past participle* **spelt** or **spelled**) **1** write or name correctly the letters of (word etc.). **2** (of letters) form (word etc.). **3** result in; signal. □ **spell out 1** make out letter by letter. **2** explain in detail. □ **speller** *noun.*
■ **3** augur, bode, foretell, indicate, mean, portend, presage, signal, signify, suggest. □ **spell out 2** see CLARIFY 1.

spell[2] *noun* **1** words used as charm. **2** effect of these. **3** fascination.
■ **1** charm, incantation, magic formula. **2** bewitchment, charm, conjuring, enchantment, sorcery, witchcraft, witchery. **3** allure, captivation, charm, enthralment, fascination, glamour, magic.

spell[3] *noun* **1** (fairly) short period. **2** period of some activity or work.
■ **1** interval, period, phase, season. **2** session, stint, stretch, term, time, turn, *Nautical* watch.

spellbind /ˈspelbaɪnd/ *verb* (*past & past participle* **spellbound**) **1** bind with spell; entrance. **2** (as **spellbound** *adjective*) entranced, fascinated.
■ **1** bewitch, charm, enchant, entrance, hypnotize. **2** (**spellbound**) bewitched, captivated, charmed, enchanted, enthralled, entranced, fascinated, transported.

spelling *noun* **1** way word is spelt. **2** ability to spell.

spelt[1] *past & past participle* of SPELL[1].

spelt[2] *noun* kind of wheat giving very fine flour.

spend *verb* (*past & past participle* **spent**) **1** pay out (money). **2** use or consume (time or energy). **3** use up. **4** (as **spent** *adjective*) having lost force or strength. □ **spendthrift** extravagant person. □ **spendable** *adjective.* **spender** *noun.*
■ **1** *slang* blue, consume, *slang* cough up, disburse, expend, *slang* fork out, fritter, get through, invest, *colloquial* lash out, pay out, *colloquial* shell out, *colloquial* splash out, *colloquial* splurge, squander. **2** consume, devote, expend, fill, occupy, pass, use, waste. **3** see EXHAUST *verb* 1. □ **spendthrift** prodigal, profligate, waster, wastrel.

sperm *noun* (*plural* same or **-s**) **1** spermatozoon. **2** semen. □ **sperm bank** store of semen for artificial insemination. **sperm whale** large whale hunted for spermaceti.

spermaceti /spɜ:məˈsetɪ/ *noun* white waxy substance used for ointments etc.

spermatozoon /spɜ:mətəʊˈzəʊən/ *noun* (*plural* **-zoa**) fertilizing cell of male organism.

spermicide /ˈspɜ:mɪsaɪd/ *noun* substance that kills spermatozoa. □ **spermicidal** /-ˈsaɪd-/ *adjective.*

spew *verb* **1** (often + *up*) vomit. **2** (often + *out*) (cause to) gush.

sphagnum /ˈsfægnəm/ *noun* (*plural* **-na**) (in full **sphagnum moss**) moss growing in bogs, used as packing etc.

sphere /sfɪə/ *noun* **1** solid figure with every point on its surface equidistant from centre. **2** ball, globe. **3** field of action, influence, etc. **4** place in society. **5** *historical* each of revolving shells in which heavenly bodies were thought to be set.
■ **1, 2** ball, globe, globule, orb, spheroid. **3** area, department, discipline, domain, field, preserve, province, range, realm, scope, speciality, subject, territory. **4** caste, class, domain, milieu, position, rank, society, station, stratum, walk of life.

spherical /ˈsferɪk(ə)l/ *adjective* **1** shaped like sphere. **2** of spheres. □ **spherically** *adverb.*
■ **1** ball-shaped, globe-shaped, globular, rotund, round, spheroidal.

spheroid /ˈsfɪərɔɪd/ *noun* spherelike but not perfectly spherical body. □ **spheroidal** /-ˈrɔɪd-/ *adjective.*

sphincter /ˈsfɪŋktə/ *noun* ring of muscle closing and opening orifice.

Sphinx /sfɪŋks/ *noun* **1** ancient Egyptian stone figure with lion's body and human or animal head. **2** (**sphinx**) inscrutable person.

spice *noun* **1** aromatic or pungent vegetable substance used as flavouring. **2** spices collectively. **3** piquant quality. **4** slight flavour. ● *verb* (**-cing**) **1** flavour with spice. **2** enhance.
■ *noun* **1** flavouring, relish, seasoning. **3** colour, excitement, gusto, interest, *colloquial* pep, piquancy, sharpness, stimulation, vigour, zest.

spick and span *adjective* **1** trim and clean. **2** smart, new-looking.

spicy *adjective* (**-ier, -iest**) **1** of or flavoured with spice. **2** piquant; improper. □ **spiciness** *noun.*
■ **1** aromatic, fragrant, gingery, hot, peppery, piquant, pungent, seasoned, spiced, tangy, zestful.

spider /ˈspaɪdə/ *noun* 8-legged arthropod, many species of which spin webs esp. to capture insects as food. □ **spider plant** house plant with long narrow leaves.

spidery *adjective* elongated and thin.

spiel /ʃpiːl/ *noun slang* glib speech or story; sales pitch.

spigot /ˈspɪgət/ *noun* **1** small peg or plug. **2** device for controlling flow of liquid in tap.

spike[1] *noun* **1** sharp point. **2** pointed piece of metal, esp. forming top of iron railing. **3** metal point on sole of running shoe to prevent slipping. **4** (in *plural*) spiked running shoes. **5** large nail. ● *verb* (**-king**) **1** put spikes on or into. **2** fix on or pierce with spike. **3** *colloquial* add alcohol to (drink). **4** *colloquial* contaminate. □ **spike (person's) guns** defeat his or her plans.
■ *noun* **1, 2** barb, nail, pin, point, projection, prong, skewer, spine, stake, tine. ● *verb* **2** impale, perforate, pierce, skewer, spear, spit, stab, stick.

spike[2] *noun* cluster of flower heads on long stem.

spikenard /ˈspaɪknɑːd/ *noun* **1** tall sweet-smelling plant. **2** *historical* aromatic ointment formerly made from this.

spiky *adjective* (**-ier, -iest**) **1** like a spike; having spikes. **2** *colloquial* irritable.

spill[1] *verb* (*past & past participle* **spilt** or **spilled**) **1** allow (liquid etc.) to fall or run out of container, esp. accidentally. **2** (of liquid etc.) fall or run out thus. **3** throw from vehicle, saddle, etc. **4** (+ *into, out*, etc.) leave quickly. **5** *slang* divulge (information etc.). **6** shed (blood). ● *noun* **1** spilling, being spilt. **2** tumble, esp. from horse or vehicle. □ **spill the beans** *colloquial* divulge secret etc. □ **spillage** *noun*.

■ *verb* **1, 2** brim over, flow, overflow, pour, run, slop, splash, upset. **3** discharge, drop, scatter, shed, throw, tip.

spill[2] *noun* thin strip of wood, paper, etc. for lighting candle etc.

spillikin /ˈspɪlɪkɪn/ *noun* **1** splinter of wood etc. **2** (in *plural*) game in which thin rods are removed one at a time from heap without disturbing others.

spilt *past & past participle* of SPILL[1].

spin *verb* (**-nn-**; *past* **spun** or **span**; *past participle* **spun**) **1** (cause to) turn or whirl round rapidly. **2** make (yarn) by drawing out and twisting together fibres of wool etc. **3** make (web etc.) by extruding fine viscous thread. **4** (of person's head) be in a whirl. **5** tell or compose (story etc.). **6** toss (coin). **7** (as **spun** *adjective*) made into threads. ● *noun* **1** revolving motion; whirl. **2** rotating dive of aircraft. **3** secondary twisting motion e.g. of ball in flight. **4** *colloquial* brief drive, esp. in car. □ **spin bowler** *Cricket* one who imparts spin to ball. **spin-drier, -dryer** machine for drying clothes by spinning them in rotating drum. **spin-dry** *verb*. **spinning wheel** household implement for spinning yarn, with spindle driven by wheel with crank or treadle. **spin-off** incidental result, esp. from technology. **spin out** prolong. **spin a yarn** tell story.

■ *verb* **1** gyrate, pirouette, revolve, rotate, swirl, turn, twirl, twist, wheel, whirl. **4** be giddy, reel, suffer vertigo, swim, whirl. □ **spin out** see PROLONG 1.

spina bifida /ˌspaɪnə ˈbɪfɪdə/ *noun* congenital spinal defect, with protruding membranes.

spinach /ˈspɪnɪdʒ/ *noun* green vegetable with edible leaves.

spinal /ˈspaɪn(ə)l/ *adjective* of spine. □ **spinal column** spine. **spinal cord** cylindrical nervous structure within spine.

spindle /ˈspɪnd(ə)l/ *noun* **1** slender rod for twisting and winding thread in spinning. **2** pin or axis on which something revolves. **3** turned piece of wood used as banister etc.

■ **2** axis, axle, pin, rod, shaft.

spindly *adjective* (**-ier, -iest**) long or tall and thin.

spindrift /ˈspɪndrɪft/ *noun* spray on surface of sea.

spine *noun* **1** series of vertebrae extending from skull; backbone. **2** needle-like outgrowth of animal or plant. **3** part of book enclosing page-fastening. **4** ridge, sharp projection. □ **spine-chiller** suspense or horror film, story, etc. **spine-chilling** *adjective*. **spine-tingling** thrilling, pleasurably frightening.

■ **1** backbone, spinal column, vertebrae. **2** barb, needle, point, prickle, prong, quill, spike, spur, thorn.

spineless *adjective* lacking resoluteness. □ **spinelessness** *noun*.

■ cowardly, craven, faint-hearted, feeble, helpless, irresolute, lily-livered, *formal* pusillanimous, soft, timid, unheroic, weak, *colloquial* wimpish.

spinet /spɪˈnet/ *noun historical* small harpsichord with oblique strings.

spinnaker /ˈspɪnəkə/ *noun* large triangular sail used at bow of yacht.

spinner *noun* **1** spin bowler. **2** person or thing that spins, esp. manufacturer engaged in spinning. **3** spin-drier. **4** revolving bait or lure in fishing.

spinneret /ˈspɪnəret/ *noun* spinning-organ in spider etc.

spinney /ˈspɪnɪ/ *noun* (*plural* **-s**) small wood; thicket.

spinster /ˈspɪnstə/ *noun* unmarried woman. □ **spinsterhood** *noun*.

spiny *adjective* (**-ier, -iest**) having (many) spines.

spiraea /spaɪˈriːə/ *noun* (*US* **spirea**) garden plant related to meadowsweet.

spiral /ˈspaɪər(ə)l/ *adjective* **1** coiled in a plane or as round a cylinder or cone. **2** having this shape. ● *noun* **1** spiral curve. **2** progressive rise or fall. ● *verb* (**-ll-**; *US* **-l-**) **1** move in spiral course. **2** (of prices etc.) rise or fall continuously. □ **spiral staircase** circular staircase round central axis.

■ *adjective* coiled, corkscrew, turning, whorled. ● *noun* **1** coil, curl, helix, screw, whorl. ● *verb* **1** turn, twist. **2** see FALL *verb* 1, RISE *verb* 7.

spirant /ˈspaɪərənt/ *adjective* uttered with continuous expulsion of breath. ● *noun* spirant consonant.

spire *noun* **1** tapering structure, esp. on church tower. **2** any tapering thing.

■ **1** pinnacle, steeple.

spirea *US* = SPIRAEA.

spirit /ˈspɪrɪt/ *noun* **1** person's essence or intelligence; soul. **2** rational being without material body. **3** ghost. **4** attitude; prevailing tendency. **5** person's character. **6** type of person. **7** distilled volatile liquid. **8** (usually in *plural*) distilled alcoholic liquor. **9** courage, vivacity. **10** essential as opposed to formal meaning. **11** (in *plural*) mood. ● *verb* (**-t-**) (usually + *away, off*, etc.) convey mysteriously. □ **spirit gum** quick-drying gum for attaching false hair. **spirit lamp** lamp burning methylated or other volatile spirit. **spirit level** device used to test horizontality.

■ *noun* **1** breath, mind, psyche, soul. **3** apparition, bogey, demon, devil, genie, ghost, ghoul, *colloquial* gremlin, incubus, nymph, phantasm, phantom, poltergeist, *literary* shade, shadow, spectre, *colloquial* spook, sprite, sylph, vision, visitant, wraith, zombie. **4** atmosphere, attitude, feeling, mood, tendency. **8** (*spirits*) see ALCOHOL 2. **9** animation, bravery, cheerfulness, confidence, courage, daring, determination, dynamism, energy, enthusiasm, fire, fortitude, *colloquial* get-up-and-go, go, *colloquial* guts, heroism, liveliness, mettle, morale, motivation, optimism, pluck, resolve, valour, verve, vivacity, will-power, zest. **10** aim, essence, heart, intention, meaning, purpose, sense.

spirited *adjective* lively, courageous. □ **-spirited** in specified mood. □ **spiritedly** *adverb*.

■ active, animated, assertive, brave, brisk, buoyant, courageous, daring, determined, dynamic, energetic, enterprising, enthusiastic, frisky, gallant, *colloquial* gutsy, intrepid, lively, mettlesome, plucky, positive, resolute, sparkling, sprightly, vigorous, vivacious.

spiritless *adjective* lacking vivacity or courage.

■ apathetic, cowardly, defeatist, despondent, dispirited, dull, irresolute, lacklustre, languid, lethargic, lifeless, listless, melancholy, negative, passive, slow, unenterprising, unenthusiastic.

spiritual /ˈspɪrɪtʃʊəl/ *adjective* **1** of spirit. **2** religious; divine; inspired. **3** refined, sensitive. ● *noun* (also **Negro spiritual**) religious song originally of American blacks. □ **spirituality** /-ˈæl-/ *noun*. **spiritually** *adverb*.

■ *adjective* **1** incorporeal, inner, psychic, psychical. **2** devotional, devout, divine, heavenly, holy, religious, sacred, unworldly.

spiritualism *noun* belief in, and practice of, communication with the dead, esp. through mediums. □ **spiritualist** *noun*. **spiritualistic** /-ˈlɪs-/ *adjective*.

spirituous /ˈspɪrɪtʃʊəs/ *adjective* **1** very alcoholic. **2** distilled as well as fermented.

spit[1] *verb* (**-tt-**; *past & past participle* **spat** or **spit**) **1** eject saliva from mouth. **2** do this as gesture of contempt. **3** (usually + *out*) eject (food, saliva, etc.) from mouth. **4** utter vehemently. **5** (of fire etc.) throw out with explosion. **6** make spitting noise. **7** (of rain etc.) fall lightly. ● *noun* **1** spittle. **2** spitting. □ **spitfire** fiery-tempered person. **spitting distance** *colloquial* very short distance. **spitting image** *colloquial* exact counterpart or likeness.

■ *verb* **1** dribble, expectorate, salivate, splutter. **3** (*spit out*) see DISCHARGE *verb* 4. **4–6** splutter, sputter. ● *noun* **1** dribble, saliva, spittle, sputum. □ **spitting image** see TWIN *noun* 2.

spit[2] *noun* **1** rod for skewering meat for roasting over fire etc. **2** point of land projecting into sea.

3 spade-depth of earth. ● *verb* (**-tt-**) pierce (as) with spit. □ **spit-roast** roast on spit.

spite *noun* ill will, malice. ● *verb* (**-ting**) hurt, thwart. □ **in spite of** notwithstanding.

■ *noun* animosity, animus, antagonism, *slang* bitchiness, bitterness, cattiness, gall, hate, hatred, hostility, ill feeling, ill will, malevolence, malice, maliciousness, malignity, rancour, resentment, spleen, venom, vindictiveness. ● *verb* see ANNOY 1.

spiteful *adjective* malicious. □ **spitefully** *adverb*. **spitefulness** *noun*.

■ acid, acrimonious, *slang* bitchy, bitter, catty, cruel, cutting, hateful, hostile, hurtful, ill-natured, malevolent, malicious, nasty, poisonous, punitive, rancorous, resentful, revengeful, sharp, snide, sour, unforgiving, venomous, vicious, vindictive.

spittle /ˈspɪt(ə)l/ *noun* saliva.

spittoon /spɪˈtuːn/ *noun* vessel to spit into.

spiv *noun colloquial* man, esp. flashily-dressed one, living from shady dealings. □ **spivvish** *adjective*. **spivvy** *adjective*.

splash *verb* **1** (cause to) scatter in drops. **2** wet or stain by splashing. **3** (usually + *across, along, about*, etc.) move with splashing. **4** jump or fall into water etc. with splash. **5** display (news) conspicuously. **6** decorate with scattered colour. **7** spend (money) ostentatiously. ● *noun* **1** act or noise of splashing. **2** quantity splashed. **3** mark of splashing. **4** prominent news feature, display, etc. **5** patch of colour. **6** *colloquial* small quantity of soda water etc. (in drink). □ **splashback** panel behind sink etc. to protect wall from splashes. **splashdown** alighting of spacecraft on sea. **splash down** *verb*. **splash out** *colloquial* spend money freely.

■ *verb* **1, 2** bespatter, shower, slop, *colloquial* slosh, spatter, spill, splatter, spray, sprinkle, squirt. **3** dabble, paddle, wade. **5** blazon, display, exhibit, flaunt, publicize, show, spread. □ **splash out** see SPEND 1.

splat *colloquial noun* sharp splattering sound. ● *adverb* with splat. ● *verb* (**-tt-**) fall or hit with splat.

splatter /ˈsplætə/ *verb & noun* splash, esp. with continuous noisy action; spatter.

splay *verb* **1** spread apart. **2** (of opening) have sides diverging. **3** make (opening) with divergent sides. ● *noun* surface at oblique angle to another. ● *adjective* splayed.

■ *verb* slant, spread.

spleen *noun* **1** abdominal organ regulating quality of blood. **2** moroseness, irritability.

splendid /ˈsplendɪd/ *adjective* **1** magnificent; glorious, dignified. **2** excellent. □ **splendidly** *adverb*.

■ **1** admirable, awe-inspiring, beautiful, brilliant, costly, dazzling, dignified, elegant, glittering, *colloquial* glorious, *colloquial* gorgeous, grand, handsome, imposing, impressive, lavish, luxurious, magnificent, majestic, noble, ornate, ostentatious, palatial, *colloquial* posh, *literary* refulgent, regal, resplendent, rich, royal, showy, spectacular, *colloquial* splendiferous, stately, sublime, sumptuous. **2** excellent, *colloquial* fabulous, *colloquial* fantastic, fine, first-class, great, marvellous, outstanding, *colloquial* super, *colloquial* superb, supreme, wonderful.

splendiferous /splenˈdɪfərəs/ *adjective colloquial* splendid.

splendour /ˈsplendə/ *noun* (*US* **splendor**) **1** dazzling brightness. **2** magnificence.

■ **1** brightness, brilliance, dazzle, glitter, *literary* refulgence. **2** beauty, ceremony, costliness, display, elegance, glitter, glory, grandeur, luxury, magnificence, majesty, nobility, ostentation, pomp, pomp and circumstance, richness, show, spectacle, stateliness, sumptuousness.

splenetic /splɪˈnetɪk/ *adjective* bad-tempered, peevish.

splenic /ˈsplenɪk/ *adjective* of or in spleen.

splice *verb* (**-cing**) **1** join (ropes) by interweaving strands. **2** join (pieces of wood, tape, etc.) by overlapping. **3** (esp. as **spliced** *adjective*) *colloquial* join in marriage. ● *noun* join made by splicing.

■ *verb* **1** entwine, intertwine, join, knit, tie together. **3** bind, *formal* conjoin, join, marry, unite.

splint *noun* strip of wood etc. bound to broken limb while it heals. ● *verb* secure with splint.

splinter /ˈsplɪntə/ *noun* small sharp fragment of wood, stone, glass, etc. ● *verb* split into splinters; shatter. □ **splinter group** small group that has broken away from larger group. □ **splintery** *adjective*.

■ *noun* chip, flake, fragment, shard, shaving, shiver, sliver. ● *verb* break, chip, crack, fracture, shatter, shiver, smash, split.

split *verb* (**-tt-**; *past & past participle* **split**) **1** break, esp. lengthwise or with grain; break forcibly. **2** (often + *up*) divide into parts, esp. equal shares. **3** divide into branches. **4** (often + *off*, *away*) remove or be removed by breaking or dividing. **5** (usually + *on*, *over*, etc.) divide into disagreeing or hostile parties. **6** cause fission of (atom). **7** *slang* leave, esp. suddenly. **8** (usually + *on*) *colloquial* inform. **9** (of head) suffer severe headache. **10** (as **splitting** *adjective*) (of headache) severe. ● *noun* **1** splitting. **2** place where thing is split. **3** disagreement, schism. **4** (in *plural*) feat of leaping or sitting with legs straight and pointing in opposite directions. □ **split hairs** make oversubtle distinctions. **split infinitive** one with adverb etc. inserted between *to* and verb (see note below). **split-level** with more than one level. **split one's sides** be convulsed with laughter. **split personality** condition of alternating personalities. **split pin** metal cotter with its two ends splayed out after passing through hole. **split second** very short time. **split-second** *adjective* **1** very rapid. **2** (of timing) very accurate. **split up 1** separate. **2** end relationship.

USAGE Split infinitives, as in *I want to quickly sum up* and *One's job is to really get to know everybody*, are common in informal English, but many people consider them incorrect and prefer *I want to sum up* or *I want to sum up quickly*. They should therefore be avoided in formal English, but note that just changing the order of words can alter the meaning, e.g. *One's job is really to get to know everybody*.

■ *verb* **1** break, chop, *literary* cleave, crack, cut, *archaic* rend, rip apart, rip open, slash, slice, slit, tear. **2** allocate, allot, apportion, distribute, divide, halve, separate, share. **3** bifurcate, branch, diverge, divide, fork. **5** break up, divide, divorce, go separate ways, move apart, part, separate. **8** see INFORM 2. ● *noun* **2** break, chink, cleavage, cleft, crack, cranny, crevice, fissure, furrow, gash, groove, leak, opening, rent, rift, rip, rupture, slash, slit, tear. **3** breach, dichotomy, difference, dissension, divergence of opinion, division, divorce, estrangement, quarrel, schism, separation.

splodge *colloquial noun* daub, blot, smear. ● *verb* (**-ging**) make splodge on. □ **splodgy** *adjective*.

splosh *colloquial verb* move with splashing sound. ● *noun* **1** splashing sound. **2** splash of water etc.

splotch *noun & verb* splodge. □ **splotchy** *adjective*.

splurge *colloquial noun* **1** sudden extravagance. **2** ostentatious display or effort. ● *verb* (**-ging**) (usually + *on*) make splurge.

splutter /ˈsplʌtə/ *verb* **1** speak or express in choking manner. **2** emit spitting sounds. **3** speak rapidly or incoherently. ● *noun* spluttering speech or sound.

spoil *verb* (*past & past participle* **spoilt** or **spoiled**) **1** make or become useless or unsatisfactory. **2** reduce enjoyment etc. of. **3** ruin character of by over-indulgence. **4** decay, go bad. ● *noun* (usually in *plural*) **1** plunder; stolen goods. **2** profit or advantages accruing from success or position. □ **spoilsport** person who spoils others' enjoyment. **spoilt for choice** having excessive number of choices.

■ *verb* **1, 2** blight, blot, blotch, bungle, damage, deface, destroy, disfigure, harm, injure, make a mess of, mar, mess up, ruin, stain, undermine, undo, upset, vitiate, worsen, wreck. **3** coddle, cosset, dote on, indulge, make a fuss of, mollycoddle, over-indulge, pamper. **4** curdle, decay, decompose, go bad, go off, moulder, perish, putrefy, rot, turn.

spoiler *noun* **1** device on aircraft to increase drag. **2** device on vehicle to improve road-holding at speed.

spoilt *past & past participle* of SPOIL.

spoke[1] *noun* each of rods running from hub to rim of wheel. □ **put a spoke in (person's) wheel** thwart, hinder.

spoke[2] *past* of SPEAK.

spoken *past participle* of SPEAK. ● *adjective* uttered in speech. □ **spoken for** claimed.

■ *adjective* oral, unwritten, verbal, viva voce.

spokesman /'spəʊksmən/ *noun* (*feminine* **spokeswoman**) person who speaks for others; representative.

spokesperson /'spəʊkspɜ:s(ə)n/ *noun* (*plural* **-s** or **spokespeople**) spokesman or spokeswoman.

■ mouthpiece, representative, spokesman, spokeswoman.

spoliation /spəʊli'eɪʃ(ə)n/ *noun* plundering, pillage.

spondee /'spɒndi:/ *noun* metrical foot of two long syllables. □ **spondaic** /-'deɪɪk/ *adjective*.

sponge /spʌndʒ/ *noun* **1** sea animal with porous body wall and tough elastic skeleton. **2** this skeleton or piece of porous rubber etc. used in bathing, cleaning, etc. **3** thing like sponge in consistency, esp. sponge cake. **4** act of sponging. ● *verb* (**-ging**) **1** wipe or clean with sponge. **2** (often + *out*, *away*, etc.) wipe off or rub out (as) with sponge. **3** (often + *up*) absorb (as) with sponge. **4** (often + *on*, *off*) live as parasite. □ **sponge bag** waterproof bag for toilet articles. **sponge cake**, **pudding** one of light spongelike consistency. **sponge rubber** porous rubber.

■ *verb* **1** clean, cleanse, mop, rinse, wash, wipe. **4** (*sponge on*, *off*) be dependent on, *colloquial* cadge from, scrounge from.

sponger *noun* parasitic person.

spongy *adjective* (**-ier**, **-iest**) like a sponge; porous, elastic, absorbent.

■ absorbent, compressible, elastic, porous, soft, springy, yielding.

sponsor /'spɒnsə/ *noun* **1** person who pledges money to charity in return for specified activity by someone. **2** patron of artistic or sporting activity etc. **3** company etc. financing broadcast in return for advertising. **4** person introducing legislation. **5** godparent at baptism. ● *verb* be sponsor for. □ **sponsorship** *noun*.

■ *noun* **1**, **2** backer, benefactor, donor, patron, promoter, supporter. ● *verb* back, finance, fund, help, patronize, promote, subsidize, support, underwrite. □ **sponsorship** aegis, auspices, backing, benefaction, funding, patronage, promotion, support.

spontaneous /spɒn'teɪnɪəs/ *adjective* **1** acting, done, or occurring without external cause; unplanned. **2** instinctive, automatic, natural. □ **spontaneity** /-tə'neɪətɪ/ *noun*. **spontaneously** *adverb*.

■ **1** ad lib, extempore, impromptu, impulsive, off the cuff, unplanned, unpremeditated, unprepared, unrehearsed, voluntary. **2** automatic, instinctive, instinctual, involuntary, mechanical, natural, reflex, unconscious, unconstrained, unforced, unthinking.

spoof /spu:f/ *noun* & *verb colloquial* **1** parody. **2** hoax, swindle.

spook /spu:k/ *colloquial noun* ghost. ● *verb* esp.

US frighten, unnerve; become alarmed. □ **spooky** *adjective* (**-ier**, **-iest**).

■ □ **spooky** creepy, eerie, frightening, ghostly, haunted, mysterious, *colloquial* scary, uncanny, unearthly, weird.

spool /spu:l/ *noun* **1** reel on which something is wound. **2** revolving cylinder of angler's reel. ● *verb* wind on spool.

■ *noun* **1** bobbin, reel.

spoon /spu:n/ *noun* **1** utensil with bowl and handle for putting food in mouth or for stirring etc. **2** spoonful. **3** spoon-shaped thing, esp. (in full **spoon-bait**) revolving metal fish-lure. ● *verb* **1** (often + *up*, *out*) take (liquid etc.) with spoon. **2** hit (ball) feebly upwards. □ **spoonbill** wading bird with broad flat-tipped bill. **spoon-feed 1** feed with spoon. **2** give help etc. to (person) without demanding any effort from recipient. □ **spoonful** *noun* (*plural* **-s**).

■ □ **spoon-feed** cosset, help, indulge, mollycoddle, pamper, spoil.

spoonerism /'spu:nərɪz(ə)m/ *noun* (usually accidental) transposition of initial sounds of two or more words.

spoor /spʊə/ *noun* animal's track or scent.

■ footprints, scent, traces, track.

sporadic /spə'rædɪk/ *adjective* occurring only sparsely or occasionally. □ **sporadically** *adverb*.

■ erratic, fitful, intermittent, irregular, occasional, periodic, scattered, separate, unpredictable.

spore *noun* reproductive cell of ferns, fungi, protozoa, etc.

sporran /'spɒrən/ *noun* pouch worn in front of kilt.

sport *noun* **1** game or competitive activity usually involving physical exertion. **2** these collectively. **3** (in *plural*) meeting for competition in athletics. **4** amusement, fun. **5** *colloquial* sportsman; good fellow. **6** *colloquial* person with specified attitude to games, rules, etc. ● *verb* **1** amuse oneself; play about. **2** wear or exhibit, esp. ostentatiously. □ **sports car** low-built fast car. **sports coat**, **jacket** man's informal jacket. **sports ground** piece of land used for sport. **sportswear 1** clothes for sports. **2** informal clothes.

■ *noun* **1**, **2** activity, athletics, exercise, game(s), pastime, physical education, physical training, recreation. **4** amusement, fun. **5** *colloquial* badinage, banter, diversion, enjoyment, entertainment, fun, humour, jesting, joking, merriment, play, pleasure, raillery, teasing. ● *verb* **1** caper, cavort, divert oneself, frisk about, frolic, gambol, *colloquial* lark about, play about, romp, skip about. **2** display, exhibit, flaunt, show off, wear. □ **sports ground** arena, court, field, ground, pitch, playground, playing area, playing field, recreation ground, stadium.

sporting *adjective* **1** of or interested in sport. **2** generous, fair. □ **sporting chance** some possibility of success. □ **sportingly** *adverb*.

■ **2** considerate, fair, generous, good-humoured, honourable, sportsmanlike.

sportive *adjective* playful.
■ coltish, frisky, kittenish, light-hearted, playful, sprightly, waggish.

sportsman /'spɔːtsmən/ *noun* (*feminine* **sportswoman**) 1 person engaging in sport. 2 fair and generous person. □ **sportsmanlike** *adjective*. **sportsmanship** *noun*.

sportsperson /'spɔːtspɜːs(ə)n/ *noun* (*plural* **-s** or **sportspeople**) sportsman or sportswoman.
■ contestant, participant, player, sportsman, sportswoman.

sporty *adjective* (**-ier, -iest**) *colloquial* 1 fond of sport. 2 rakish, showy.
■ 1 active, athletic, energetic, fit. 2 casual, informal, loud, rakish, showy, *slang* snazzy.

spot *noun* 1 small mark differing in colour etc. from surface it is on. 2 pimple, blemish. 3 particular place; locality. 4 particular part of one's body or character. 5 *colloquial* one's (regular) position in organization, programme, etc. 6 *colloquial* small quantity. 7 drop (of rain etc.). 8 spotlight. 9 *colloquial* difficult situation. ● *verb* (**-tt-**) 1 *colloquial* pick out. 2 *colloquial* recognize. 3 *colloquial* catch sight of. 4 watch for and take note of (trains, talent, etc.). 5 (esp. as **spotted** *adjective*) mark with spots. 6 make spots; rain slightly. □ **on the spot** 1 at scene of event. 2 *colloquial* in position demanding response or action. 3 without delay. 4 without moving backwards or forwards. **spot cash** money paid immediately after sale. **spot check** sudden or random check. **spotlight** ● *noun* 1 beam of light directed on small area. 2 lamp projecting this. 3 full publicity. ● *verb* direct spotlight on. **spot on** *colloquial* precise(ly). **spotted dick** suet pudding containing currants. **spot-weld** join (metal surfaces) by welding at points. □ **spotter** *noun*.
■ *noun* 1 blot, blotch, dot, fleck, mark, patch, smudge, speck, speckle, stain, stigma. 2 birthmark, blemish, blotch, boil, discoloration, freckle, mole, pimple, pock, pock-mark, *esp. US slang* zit; (*spots*) acne, impetigo, rash. 3 locale, locality, location, neighbourhood, place, point, position, scene, setting, site, situation. 6 bit, *colloquial* smidgen. 7 bead, blob, drop. 9 difficulties, *disputed* dilemma, fix, *colloquial* jam, mess, predicament, quandary. ● *verb* 1 see SEE¹ 1. 5 blot, discolour, fleck, mark, mottle, smudge, spatter, speckle, splash, spray, stain.

spotless *adjective* absolutely clean or pure; unblemished. □ **spotlessly** *adverb*.
■ blameless, clean, faultless, flawless, fresh, immaculate, innocent, irreproachable, laundered, pure, unblemished, unmarked, unspotted, unsullied, untarnished, white.

spotty *adjective* (**-ier, -iest**) 1 marked with spots. 2 patchy, irregular.
■ 1 blotchy, dappled, flecked, freckled, mottled, pimply, pock-marked, spattered, speckled, *colloquial* splodgy, spotted.

spouse /spaʊz/ *noun* husband or wife.

■ *colloquial* better half, helpmate, husband, partner, wife.

spout /spaʊt/ *noun* 1 projecting tube or lip for pouring from teapot, kettle, jug, fountain, roof-gutter, etc. 2 jet of liquid. ● *verb* 1 discharge or issue forcibly in jet. 2 utter at length or pompously. □ **up the spout** *slang* 1 useless, ruined. 2 pregnant.
■ *noun* 1 duct, gargoyle, jet, lip, nozzle, outlet, rose (*of watering can*). 2 see JET¹ *noun* 1. ● *verb* 1 discharge, emit, erupt, flow, gush, jet, pour, shoot, spew, spit, spurt, squirt, stream. 2 see TALK *verb* 1.

sprain *verb* wrench (ankle, wrist, etc.) causing pain or swelling. ● *noun* such injury.

sprang *past* of SPRING.

sprat *noun* small sea fish.

sprawl *verb* 1 sit, lie, or fall with limbs spread out untidily. 2 spread untidily; straggle. ● *noun* 1 sprawling movement, position, or mass. 2 straggling urban expansion.
■ *verb* 1 flop, lean back, lie, loll, lounge, recline, relax, slouch, slump, spread out, stretch out. 2 be scattered, branch out, spread (out), straggle.

spray¹ *noun* 1 water etc. flying in small drops. 2 liquid intended for spraying. 3 device for spraying. ● *verb* 1 throw (liquid) as spray. 2 sprinkle (as) with spray. 3 (of tom-cat) mark environment with urine to attract females. □ **spray-gun** device for spraying paint etc. □ **sprayer** *noun*.
■ *noun* 1 drizzle, droplets, fountain, mist, shower, splash, sprinkling. 3 aerosol, atomizer, spray-gun, sprinkler, vaporizer. ● *verb* 1, 2 diffuse, disperse, scatter, shower, spatter, splash, sprinkle.

spray² *noun* 1 sprig with flowers or leaves, small branch. 2 ornament in similar form.
■ 1 arrangement, bouquet, branch, bunch, corsage, posy, sprig.

spread /spred/ *verb* (*past & past participle* **spread**) 1 (often + *out*) open, extend, unfold. 2 (often + *out*) cause to cover larger area. 3 (often + *out*) have wide or increasing extent. 4 (cause to) become widely known. 5 (cause to) cover; apply. 6 lay (table). ● *noun* 1 act, capability, or extent of spreading. 2 diffusion. 3 breadth. 4 increased girth. 5 difference between two rates, prices. etc. 6 *colloquial* elaborate meal. 7 paste for spreading on bread etc. 8 bedspread. 9 printed matter spread across more than one column. □ **spread eagle** figure of eagle with legs and wings extended as emblem. **spreadeagled** 1 placed with arms and legs spread out. 2 utterly defeated. **spreadsheet** computer program for handling tabulated figures etc., esp. in accounting.
■ *verb* 1 display, extend, fan out, lay out, open out, unfold, unfurl, unroll. 3 broaden, enlarge, expand, extend, lengthen, mushroom, proliferate, sprawl, widen. 4 advertise, broadcast, circulate, diffuse, disperse, disseminate, distribute, divulge, give out, make known, pass on, proclaim, promote, promulgate, publicize, publish, transmit. 5 apply,

cover, plaster, scatter, smear, strew. **6** arrange, lay, set. ● *noun* **1** broadening, development, expansion, extension, growth, increase, proliferation. **2** broadcasting, circulation, diffusion, dispersal, dissemination, distribution, passing on, promotion, promulgation. **3** breadth, compass, extent, size, span, stretch, sweep. **6** see MEAL¹.

spree *noun colloquial* **1** extravagant outing. **2** bout of drinking etc.
■ **1** fling, outing, *colloquial* splurge. **2** *slang* binge, debauch, fling, frolic, orgy, revel.

sprig *noun* **1** small branch or shoot. **2** ornament resembling this, esp. on fabric. ● *verb* (**-gg-**) ornament with sprigs.

sprightly /'spraɪtlɪ/ *adjective* (**-ier, -iest**) vivacious, lively. □ **sprightliness** *noun*.
■ active, agile, animated, brisk, energetic, jaunty, lively, nimble, perky, playful, spirited, sportive, spry, vivacious.

spring *verb* (*past* **sprang**; *past participle* **sprung**) **1** rise rapidly or suddenly; leap. **2** move rapidly (as) by action of a spring. **3** (usually + *from*) originate. **4** (usually + *up*) (cause to) act or appear unexpectedly. **5** *slang* contrive escape of (person from prison etc.). **6** (usually as **sprung** *adjective*) provide with springs. ● *noun* **1** jump, leap. **2** recoil. **3** elasticity. **4** elastic device usually of coiled metal used esp. to drive clockwork or for cushioning in furniture or vehicles. **5** season of year between winter and summer. **6** (often + *of*) early stage of life etc. **7** place where water, oil, etc. wells up from earth. **8** basin or flow so formed. **9** motive for or origin of action, custom, etc. □ **spring a leak** develop leak. **spring balance** device measuring weight by tension of spring. **springboard 1** flexible board for leaping or diving from. **2** source of impetus. **spring-clean** ● *noun* thorough cleaning of house, esp. in spring. ● *verb* clean thus. **spring greens** young cabbage leaves. **spring onion** young onion eaten raw. **spring roll** Chinese fried pancake filled with vegetables etc. **spring tide** tide with greatest rise and fall. **springtime** season or period of spring.
■ *verb* **1** bounce, bound, hop, jump, leap, pounce, vault. **3** (*spring from*) come from, derive from, proceed from, stem from. **4** (*spring up*) appear, arise, burst forth, come up, develop, emerge, germinate, grow, shoot up, sprout. ● *noun* **1** bounce, bound, hop, jump, leap, pounce, vault. **3** buoyancy, elasticity, give, resilience. **4** coil, mainspring. **7** *poetical* fount, fountain, geyser, source (*of river*), spa, well, well-spring.

springbok /'sprɪŋbɒk/ *noun* (*plural* same or **-s**) S. African gazelle.

springer *noun* small spaniel.

springy *adjective* (**-ier, -iest**) elastic.
■ *colloquial* bendy, elastic, flexible, pliable, resilient, spongy, stretchy, supple.

sprinkle /'sprɪŋk(ə)l/ *verb* (**-ling**) **1** scatter or fall in small drops or particles. **2** (often + *with*) subject to sprinkling. ● *noun* (usually + *of*) light shower, sprinkling.

■ *verb* drip, dust, pepper, scatter, shower, spatter, splash, spray, strew.

sprinkler *noun* device for sprinkling lawn or extinguishing fires.

sprinkling *noun* small sparse number or amount.

sprint *verb* run short distance at top speed. ● *noun* **1** such run. **2** similar short effort in cycling, swimming, etc. □ **sprinter** *noun*.
■ *verb* dash, hare, race, run, speed, *colloquial* tear.

sprit *noun* small diagonal spar from mast to upper outer corner of sail. □ **spritsail** /'sprɪts(ə)l/ sail extended by sprit.

sprite *noun* elf, fairy.

spritzer /'sprɪtsə/ *noun* drink of white wine with soda water.

sprocket /'sprɒkɪt/ *noun* projection on rim of wheel engaging with links of chain.

sprout /spraʊt/ *verb* **1** put forth (shoots etc.). **2** begin to grow. ● *noun* **1** plant shoot. **2** Brussels sprout.
■ *verb* **1** develop, grow, put forth. **2** bud, come up, develop, emerge, germinate, grow, shoot up, spring up. ● *noun* **1** bud, shoot.

spruce¹ *adjective* of trim appearance; smart. ● *verb* (**-cing**) (usually + *up*) make or become smart. □ **sprucely** *adverb*. **spruceness** *noun*.
■ *adjective* clean, dapper, elegant, groomed, *colloquial* natty, neat, *colloquial* posh, smart, tidy, trim, well dressed, well groomed, well turned out. ● *verb* (**spruce up**) see TIDY *verb*.

spruce² *noun* **1** conifer with dense conical foliage. **2** its wood.

sprung *past participle* of SPRING.

spry /spraɪ/ *adjective* (**-er, -est**) lively, nimble. □ **spryly** *adverb*.

spud *noun* **1** *colloquial* potato. **2** small narrow spade for weeding. ● *verb* (**-dd-**) (+ *up, out*) remove with spud.

spumante /spuːˈmæntɪ/ *noun* Italian sparkling white wine.

spume /spjuːm/ *noun & verb* (**-ming**) froth, foam. □ **spumy** *adjective* (**-ier, -iest**).

spun *past & past participle* of SPIN. □ **spun silk** cheap material containing waste silk.

spunk *noun colloquial* mettle, spirit. □ **spunky** *adjective* (**-ier, -iest**).

spur *noun* **1** small spike or spiked wheel attached to rider's heel for urging horse forward. **2** stimulus, incentive. **3** spur-shaped thing, esp. projection from mountain (range), branch road or railway, or hard projection on cock's leg. ● *verb* (**-rr-**) **1** prick (horse) with spur. **2** (often + *on*) incite, encourage. **3** stimulate (interest etc.). □ **on the spur of the moment** on impulse.
■ *noun* **2** encouragement, goad, impetus, incentive, incitement, inducement, motivation, motive, prod, prompting, stimulus, urging. **3** branch, projection. ● *verb* **2** animate, egg on, encourage, impel, incite, motivate, pressure, pressurize, prick, prod, prompt, stimulate, urge.

spurge *noun* plant with acrid milky juice.

spurious /'spjʊərɪəs/ *adjective* not genuine, fake.

spurn *verb* reject with disdain or contempt.

■ disown, give the cold shoulder to, jilt, rebuff, reject, renounce, repel, repudiate, repulse, shun, snub, turn one's back on.

spurt *verb* **1** (cause to) gush out in jet or stream. **2** make sudden effort. ● *noun* **1** sudden gushing out; jet. **2** short burst of speed, growth, etc.

sputnik /'spʊtnɪk/ *noun* Russian artificial earth satellite.

sputter /'spʌtə/ *verb* & *noun* splutter.

sputum /'spjuːtəm/ *noun* thick coughed-up mucus.

spy *noun* (*plural* **spies**) **1** person secretly collecting and reporting information for a government, company, etc. **2** person watching others secretly. ● *verb* (**spies**, **spied**) **1** discern, see. **2** (often + *on*) act as spy. □ **spyglass** small telescope. **spyhole** peephole. **spy out** explore or discover, esp. secretly. □ **spying** *noun*.

■ *noun* contact, double agent, fifth columnist, *slang* grass, infiltrator, informant, informer, *slang* mole, private detective, secret agent, *colloquial* snooper, stool-pigeon, undercover agent. ● *verb* **1** see SEE[1] 1. **2** eavesdrop, gather intelligence, *colloquial* snoop; (*spy on*) keep under surveillance, *colloquial* tail, trail, watch. □ **spying** detective work, eavesdropping, espionage, intelligence, *colloquial* snooping, surveillance.

sq. *abbreviation* square.

Sqn. Ldr. *abbreviation* Squadron Leader.

squab /skwɒb/ *noun* **1** young esp. unfledged pigeon etc. **2** short fat person. **3** stuffed cushion, esp. as part of car-seat. **4** sofa. ● *adjective* short and fat.

squabble /'skwɒb(ə)l/ *noun* petty or noisy quarrel. ● *verb* (**-ling**) engage in squabble.

■ *verb* argue, bicker, clash, quarrel, *colloquial* row, wrangle.

squad /skwɒd/ *noun* **1** small group sharing task etc., esp. of soldiers or police officers. **2** team. □ **squad car** police car.

squaddie *noun* (also **squaddy**) (*plural* **-ies**) *slang* **1** recruit. **2** private.

squadron /'skwɒdrən/ *noun* **1** unit of RAF with 10–18 aircraft. **2** detachment of warships employed on particular service. **3** organized group etc., esp. cavalry division of two troops. □ **squadron leader** RAF officer commanding squadron, next below wing commander.

squalid /'skwɒlɪd/ *adjective* **1** filthy, dirty; mean in appearance. **2** sordid, morally degrading.

■ **1** dingy, dirty, disgusting, filthy, foul, insalubrious, mean, mucky, nasty, poverty-stricken, repulsive, run-down, sleazy, slummy, sordid, ugly, uncared-for, unpleasant, wretched. **2** corrupt, degrading, dishonest, dishonourable, disreputable, immoral, scandalous, shabby, shameful, sordid, unethical, unworthy.

squall /skwɔːl/ *noun* **1** sudden or violent gust or storm. **2** discordant cry; scream. ● *verb* utter (with) squall; scream. □ **squally** *adjective*.

squalor /'skwɒlə/ *noun* filthy or squalid state.

squander /'skwɒndə/ *verb* spend wastefully.

■ *slang* blow, *slang* blue, dissipate, fritter, misuse, *colloquial* splurge, use up, waste.

square /skweə/ *noun* **1** rectangle with 4 equal sides. **2** object of (roughly) this shape. **3** open area enclosed by buildings. **4** product of number multiplied by itself. **5** L- or T-shaped instrument for obtaining or testing right angles. **6** *slang* conventional or old-fashioned person. ● *adjective* **1** square-shaped. **2** having or in form of a right angle. **3** angular; not round. **4** designating unit of measure equal to area of square whose side is one of the unit specified. **5** (usually + *with*) level, parallel. **6** (usually + *to*) perpendicular. **7** sturdy, squat. **8** arranged. **9** (also **all square**) with no money owed. **10** (also **all square**) (of scores) equal. **11** fair, honest. **12** direct. **13** *slang* conventional, old-fashioned. ● *adverb* squarely. ● *verb* (**-ring**) **1** make square. **2** multiply (number) by itself. **3** (usually + *to*, *with*) make or be consistent; reconcile. **4** (often as **squared** *adjective*) mark out in squares. **5** settle (bill etc.). **6** place (shoulders etc.) squarely facing forwards. **7** *colloquial* pay, bribe. **8** make scores of (match etc.) equal. □ **square brackets** brackets of the form [ ] (see panel at BRACKET). **square dance** dance with 4 couples facing inwards from 4 sides. **square deal** fair bargain or treatment. **square leg** *Cricket* fielding position on batsman's leg side nearly opposite stumps. **square meal** substantial meal. **square-rigged** having 4-sided sails set across length of ship. **square root** number that multiplied by itself gives specified number. □ **squarely** *adverb*.

■ *noun* **3** piazza. **6** *often derogatory* bourgeois, conformist, conservative, diehard, *colloquial* fuddy-duddy, old fogey, *colloquial* stick-in-the-mud, traditionalist. ● *adjective* **11** above board, decent, equitable, ethical, fair, honest, honourable, proper, *colloquial* straight. ● *verb* **4** (squared) checked, chequered, criss-crossed. **5** see SETTLE[1] 13.

squash[1] /skwɒʃ/ *verb* **1** crush or squeeze flat or into pulp. **2** (often + *into*) *colloquial* force into small space; crowd. **3** belittle; bully. **4** suppress. ● *noun* **1** crowd; crowded state. **2** drink made of crushed fruit. **3** (in full **squash rackets**) game played with rackets and small ball in closed court. □ **squashy** *adjective* (**-ier**, **-iest**).

■ *verb* **1** compress, crumple, crush, flatten, mangle, mash, pound, press, pulp, smash, stamp on, tamp down, tread on. **2** cram, crowd, pack, push, ram, shove, squeeze, stuff, thrust, wedge. **3** crush, humiliate, *colloquial* put down, silence, snub. **4** control, put down, quash, quell, repress, suppress. □ **squashy** mushy, pulpy, shapeless, soft, spongy, squelchy, yielding.

squash[2] /skwɒʃ/ *noun* (*plural* same or **-es**) **1** trailing annual plant. **2** gourd of this.

squat /skwɒt/ *verb* (**-tt-**) **1** sit on one's heels, or

on ground with knees drawn up. **2** *colloquial* sit down. **3** act as squatter. ● *adjective* (**-tt-**) short and thick; dumpy. ● *noun* **1** squatting posture. **2** place occupied by squatter(s).
■ *verb* **1** crouch, sit. ● *adjective* dumpy, plump, podgy, short, stocky, thick, thickset.

squatter *noun* person who inhabits unoccupied premises without permission.

squaw *noun* N. American Indian woman or wife.

squawk *noun* **1** harsh cry. **2** complaint. ● *verb* utter squawk.

squeak *noun* **1** short high-pitched cry or sound. **2** (also **narrow squeak**) narrow escape. ● *verb* **1** emit squeak. **2** utter shrilly. **3** (+ *by*, *through*) *colloquial* pass narrowly. **4** *slang* turn informer.

squeaky *adjective* (**-ier**, **-iest**) making squeaking sound. □ **squeaky clean** *colloquial* **1** completely clean. **2** above criticism. □ **squeakily** *adverb.* **squeakiness** *noun.*

squeal *noun* prolonged shrill sound or cry. ● *verb* **1** make, or utter with, squeal. **2** *slang* turn informer. **3** *colloquial* protest vociferously.

squeamish /'skwi:mɪʃ/ *adjective* **1** easily nauseated. **2** fastidious. □ **squeamishly** *adverb.* **squeamishness** *noun.*
■ **2** *colloquial* choosy, dainty, fastidious, finicky, overscrupulous, particular, *colloquial* pernickety, prim, prissy, prudish, scrupulous.

squeegee /'skwi:dʒi:/ *noun* rubber-edged implement on handle, for cleaning windows etc.

squeeze *verb* (**-zing**) **1** (often + *out*) exert pressure on, esp. to extract moisture. **2** reduce in size or alter in shape by squeezing. **3** force or push into or through small or narrow space. **4** harass; pressure. **5** (usually + *out of*) get by extortion or entreaty. **6** press (person's hand) in sympathy etc. **7** hold (person) closely. ● *noun* **1** squeezing, being squeezed. **2** close embrace. **3** crowd; crowded state. **4** small quantity produced by squeezing. **5** restriction on borrowing and investment. □ **squeeze-box** *colloquial* accordion, concertina. □ **squeezable** *adjective.*
■ *verb* **1, 2** compress, crush, flatten, mangle, pinch, press, squash, stamp on, tread on, wring; (*squeeze out*) expel, extrude, force out. **3** cram, crowd, pack, push, ram, shove, *colloquial* squash, stuff, tamp, thrust, wedge. **6, 7** clasp, embrace, enfold, grip, hug, press.

squelch *verb* **1** make sucking sound as of treading in thick mud. **2** move with squelching sound. **3** disconcert, silence. ● *noun* act or sound of squelching. □ **squelchy** *adjective.*

squib *noun* **1** small hissing firework. **2** satirical essay.

squid *noun* (*plural* same or **-s**) 10-armed marine cephalopod.

squidgy /'skwɪdʒɪ/ *adjective* (**-ier**, **-iest**) *colloquial* squashy, soggy.

squiffy /'skwɪfɪ/ *adjective* (**-ier**, **-iest**) *slang* slightly drunk.

squiggle /'skwɪg(ə)l/ *noun* short curling line, esp. in handwriting. □ **squiggly** *adjective.*

squint *verb* **1** have eyes turned in different directions. **2** (often + *at*) look sidelong. ● *noun* **1** squinting condition. **2** stealthy or sidelong glance. **3** *colloquial* glance, look. **4** oblique opening in church wall.

squire *noun* **1** country gentleman, esp. chief landowner of district. **2** *historical* knight's attendant. ● *verb* (**-ring**) (of man) escort (woman).

squirearchy /'skwaɪərɑːkɪ/ *noun* (*plural* **-ies**) landowners collectively.

squirm *verb* **1** wriggle, writhe. **2** show or feel embarrassment. ● *noun* squirming movement.
■ *verb* **1** twist, wriggle, writhe.

squirrel /'skwɪr(ə)l/ *noun* **1** bushy-tailed usually tree-living rodent. **2** its fur. **3** hoarder. ● *verb* (**-ll-**; *US* **-l-**) (often + *away*) hoard.

squirt *verb* **1** eject (liquid etc.) in jet. **2** be ejected thus. **3** splash with squirted substance. ● *noun* **1** jet of water etc. **2** small quantity squirted. **3** syringe. **4** *colloquial* insignificant person.
■ *verb* **1, 2** ejaculate, eject, gush, jet, send out, shoot, spit, splash, spout, spray, spurt.

squish *colloquial noun* slight squelching sound. ● *verb* **1** move with squish. **2** squash. □ **squishy** *adjective* (**-ier**, **-iest**).

Sr. *abbreviation* Senior.

SRN *abbreviation* State Registered Nurse.

SS *abbreviation* **1** steamship. **2** Saints. **3** *historical* Nazi special police force (*Schutzstaffel*).

SSE *abbreviation* south-south-east.

SSW *abbreviation* south-south-west.

St *abbreviation* Saint.

St. *abbreviation* Street.

st. *abbreviation* stone (weight).

stab *verb* (**-bb-**) **1** pierce or wound with knife etc. **2** (often + *at*) aim blow with such weapon. **3** cause sharp pain to. ● *noun* **1** act or result of stabbing. **2** sharp pain. **3** *colloquial* attempt. □ **stab in the back** ● *noun* treacherous attack. ● *verb* betray.
■ *verb* **1** bayonet, cut, injure, jab, lance, perforate, pierce, puncture, skewer, spike, stick, thrust, transfix, wound. ● *noun* **1** cut, jab, prick, puncture, thrust, wound, wounding. **2** see PAIN *noun* 1. **3** see TRY *noun* 1.

stability /stə'bɪlɪtɪ/ *noun* being stable.
■ balance, constancy, durability, equilibrium, firmness, immutability, permanence, reliability, solidity, soundness, steadiness, strength.

stabilize /'steɪbɪlaɪz/ *verb* (also **-ise**) (**-zing** or **-sing**) make or become stable. □ **stabilization** *noun.*
■ balance, keep upright, settle, steady.

stabilizer *noun* (also **-iser**) **1** device to keep aircraft or (in *plural*) child's bicycle steady. **2** food additive for preserving texture.

stable /'steɪb(ə)l/ *adjective* (**-r**, **-st**) **1** firmly fixed or established; not fluctuating or changing. **2** not easily upset or disturbed. ● *noun* **1** building for keeping horses. **2** establishment for training racehorses. **3** racehorses of particular stable. **4** people, products, etc. having common origin or affiliation. **5** such origin or affiliation. ● *verb* (**-ling**) put or keep in stable. □ **stable lad** person employed in stable. □ **stably** *adverb*.

■ *adjective* **1** balanced, constant, continuing, durable, established, firm, fixed, immutable, lasting, long-lasting, permanent, predictable, solid, sound, steadfast, steady, strong, sturdy, unchanging, unwavering. **2** balanced, even-tempered, reasonable, sane, sensible.

stableman /ˈsteɪb(ə)lmən/ *noun* person employed in stable.

stabling *noun* accommodation for horses.

staccato /stəˈkɑːtəʊ/ *esp. Music adverb & adjective* with each sound sharply distinct. ● *noun* (*plural* **-s**) staccato passage or delivery.

stack *noun* **1** (esp. orderly) pile or heap. **2** haystack. **3** *colloquial* large quantity. **4** number of chimneys standing together. **5** smokestack; tall factory chimney. **6** stacked group of aircraft. **7** part of library where books are compactly stored. ● *verb* **1** pile in stack(s). **2** arrange (cards, circumstances, etc.) secretly for cheating. **3** cause (aircraft) to fly in circles while waiting to land.

■ *noun* **1, 3** accumulation, heap, hill, hoard, mound, mountain, pile, quantity, stock, stockpile, store. **2** cock, haycock, haystack, rick. ● *verb* **1** accumulate, amass, assemble, build up, collect, gather, heap, load, mass, pile, stockpile.

stadium /ˈsteɪdɪəm/ *noun* (*plural* **-s**) athletic or sports ground with tiered seats for spectators.

■ amphitheatre, arena, ground, sports ground.

staff /stɑːf/ *noun* **1** stick or pole for walking, as weapon, or as symbol of office. **2** supporting person or thing. **3** people employed in a business etc. **4** those in authority in a school etc. **5** group of army officers assisting officer in high command. **6** (*plural* **-s** or **staves**) *Music* set of usually 5 parallel lines to indicate pitch of notes by position. ● *verb* provide (institution etc.) with staff. □ **staff nurse** one ranking just below a sister.

■ *noun* **1** baton, cane, crook, crosier, flagstaff, pike, pole, rod, sceptre, shaft, stake, standard, stick, wand. **3** assistants, crew, employees, establishment, hands, personnel, officers, team, workers, workforce. **6** stave. ● *verb* man, run.

stag *noun* **1** male deer. **2** person who applies for new shares to sell at once for profit. □ **stag beetle** beetle with antler-like mandibles. **stag-party** *colloquial* party for men only.

stage *noun* **1** point or period in process or development. **2** raised platform, esp. for performing plays etc. on. **3** (**the stage**) theatrical profession. **4** scene of action. **5** regular stopping place on route. **6** distance between stopping places. **7** section of space rocket with separate engine. ● *verb* (**-ging**) **1** put (play etc.) on stage. **2** organ-

ize and carry out. □ **stagecoach** *historical* coach running on regular route. **stage direction** instruction in a play about actors' movements, sound effects, etc. **stage door** entrance from street to backstage part of theatre. **stage fright** performer's fear of audience. **stage-manage** arrange and control as or like stage manager. **stage manager** person responsible for lighting and mechanical arrangements on stage. **stage-struck** obsessed with becoming actor. **stage whisper** loud whisper meant to be overheard.

■ *noun* **1** juncture, period, phase, point, time. **2** apron, dais, performing area, platform, podium, proscenium, rostrum. **6** leg, section. ● *verb* **1** mount, perform, present, produce, put on. **2** arrange, get up, mount, organize, put on, set up, stage-manage.

stagecraft /ˈsteɪdʒkrɑːft/ *noun* skill or experience in writing or staging plays.

stagger /ˈstægə/ *verb* **1** (cause to) walk unsteadily. **2** shock, confuse. **3** arrange (events etc.) so that they do not coincide. **4** arrange (objects) so that they are not in line. ● *noun* **1** staggering movement. **2** (in *plural*) disease, esp. of horses and cattle, causing staggering.

■ *verb* **1** falter, lurch, reel, rock, stumble, sway, teeter, totter, waver, wobble. **2** amaze, astonish, astound, confuse, dismay, dumbfound, flabbergast, shake, shock, startle, stun, stupefy, surprise, worry.

staggering *adjective* astonishing, bewildering. □ **staggeringly** *adverb*.

staging /ˈsteɪdʒɪŋ/ *noun* **1** presentation of play etc. **2** (temporary) platform. **3** shelves for plants in greenhouse. □ **staging post** regular stopping place, esp. on air route.

stagnant /ˈstægnənt/ *adjective* **1** (of liquid) motionless, without current. **2** dull, sluggish. □ **stagnancy** *noun*.

■ **1** motionless, sluggish, stale, standing, static, still. **2** see SLUGGISH.

stagnate /stægˈneɪt/ *verb* (**-ting**) be or become stagnant. □ **stagnation** *noun*.

■ degenerate, deteriorate, idle, languish, stand still, stay still, vegetate.

stagy /ˈsteɪdʒɪ/ *adjective* (also **stagey**) (**-ier**, **-iest**) theatrical, artificial, exaggerated.

staid *adjective* sober, steady, sedate.

stain *verb* **1** discolour or be discoloured by action of liquid sinking in. **2** spoil, damage. **3** colour (wood, etc.) with penetrating substance. **4** treat with colouring agent. ● *noun* **1** discoloration, spot, mark. **2** blot, blemish. **3** dye etc. for staining. □ **stained glass** coloured glass in leaded window etc.

■ *verb* **1** blacken, blemish, blot, contaminate, dirty, discolour, mark, smudge, soil, tarnish. **2** besmirch, damage, defile, disgrace, shame, spoil, sully, taint. **3, 4** colour, dye, tinge, tint. ● *noun* **1** blemish, blot, blotch, discoloration, mark, smear, smudge, speck, spot. **2** blemish, blot, stigma. **3** colouring, dye, pigment, tinge, tint.

stainless *adjective* **1** without stains. **2** not liable to stain. □ **stainless steel** chrome steel resisting rust and tarnish.

stair *noun* **1** each of a set of fixed indoor steps. **2** (usually in *plural*) such a set. □ **staircase** flight of stairs and supporting structure. **stair-rod** rod securing carpet between two steps. **stairway** staircase. **stairwell** shaft for staircase.

■ **1** riser, step, tread. **2** (*stairs*) escalator (= *moving stairs*), flight of stairs, staircase, stairway, steps.

stake *noun* **1** stout sharpened stick driven into ground as support, boundary mark, etc. **2** *historical* post to which person was tied to be burnt alive. **3** sum of money etc. wagered on event. **4** (often + *in*) interest or concern, esp. financial. **5** (in *plural*) prize money, esp. in horse race, such race. ● *verb* (**-king**) **1** secure or support with stake(s). **2** (+ *off*, *out*) mark off (area) with stakes. **3** wager. **4** establish (claim). **5** *US colloquial* support, esp. financially. □ **at stake** risked; to be won or lost. **stake out** *colloquial* place under surveillance. **stake-out** *noun esp. US colloquial* period of surveillance.

■ *noun* **1** pale, paling, picket, pile, pillar, pole, post, rod, shaft, standard, stick, upright. **3** bet, pledge, wager. ● *verb* **1** fasten, hitch, secure, tether, tie up. **2** (*stake out*) define, delimit, demarcate, enclose, fence in, mark off, outline. **3** bet, *colloquial* chance, gamble, hazard, risk, venture, wager. **4** establish, put on record, state.

stalactite /'stæləktaɪt/ *noun* icicle-like deposit of calcium carbonate hanging from roof of cave etc.

stalagmite /'stæləgmaɪt/ *noun* icicle-like deposit of calcium carbonate rising from floor of cave etc.

stale *adjective* **1** not fresh; musty, insipid, or otherwise the worse for age or use. **2** trite, unoriginal. **3** (of athlete or performer) impaired by excessive training. ● *verb* (**-ling**) make or become stale. □ **staleness** *noun*.

■ *adjective* **1** dry, hard, limp, mouldy, musty, *colloquial* off, old, past its best, tasteless. **2** banal, clichéd, familiar, hackneyed, mouldy, old-fashioned, out of date, overused, stock, threadbare, tired, trite, uninteresting, unoriginal, worn out.

stalemate *noun* **1** *Chess* position counting as draw in which player cannot move except into check. **2** deadlock. ● *verb* (**-ting**) **1** *Chess* bring (player) to stalemate. **2** bring to deadlock.

■ *noun* **2** deadlock, impasse, standstill.

Stalinism /'stɑːlɪnɪz(ə)m/ *noun* centralized authoritarian form of socialism associated with Stalin. □ **Stalinist** *noun & adjective*.

stalk¹ /stɔːk/ *noun* **1** main stem of herbaceous plant. **2** slender attachment or support of leaf, flower, fruit, etc. **3** similar support for organ etc. in animal.

■ **1** branch, shaft, stem, trunk. **2** shoot, stem, twig.

stalk² /stɔːk/ *verb* **1** pursue (game, enemy) stealthily. **2** stride; walk in a haughty way. **3** *formal* or *rhetorical* move silently or threateningly through (place). ● *noun* **1** stalking of game. **2** haughty gait. □ **stalking-horse 1** horse concealing hunter. **2** pretext concealing real intentions or actions. □ **stalker** *noun*.

■ *verb* **1** chase, dog, follow, hound, hunt, pursue, shadow, *colloquial* tail, track, trail. **2** prowl, rove, stride, strut.

stall¹ /stɔːl/ *noun* **1** trader's booth or table in market etc. **2** compartment for one animal in stable or cowhouse. **3** fixed, usually partly enclosed, seat in choir or chancel of church. **4** (usually in *plural*) each of seats on ground floor of theatre. **5** stalling of engine or aircraft. **6** condition resulting from this. ● *verb* **1** (of vehicle or its engine) stop because of overload on engine or inadequate supply of fuel to it. **2** (of aircraft or its pilot) lose control because speed is too low. **3** cause to stall. □ **stallholder** person in charge of stall in market etc.

■ *noun* **1** booth, counter, kiosk, stand, table.

stall² /stɔːl/ *verb* **1** play for time when being questioned etc. **2** delay, obstruct.

■ be obstructive, delay, hang back, haver, hesitate, obstruct, pause, play for time, postpone, prevaricate, procrastinate, put off, stonewall, stop, temporize, waste time.

stallion /'stæljən/ *noun* uncastrated adult male horse.

stalwart /'stɔːlwət/ *adjective* **1** strong, sturdy. **2** courageous, resolute, reliable. ● *noun* stalwart person, esp. loyal comrade.

■ *adjective* **1** see STRONG *adjective* 1. **2** brave, courageous, dependable, determined, faithful, indomitable, intrepid, redoubtable, reliable, resolute, staunch, steadfast, trustworthy, valiant.

stamen /'steɪmən/ *noun* organ producing pollen in flower.

stamina /'stæmɪnə/ *noun* physical or mental endurance.

■ endurance, energy, *colloquial* grit, indomitability, resilience, staunchness, staying power.

stammer /'stæmə/ *verb* **1** speak haltingly, esp. with pauses or rapid repetitions of same syllable. **2** (often + *out*) utter (words) in this way. ● *noun* **1** tendency to stammer. **2** instance of stammering.

■ *verb* **1** falter, hesitate, hum and haw, splutter, stumble, stutter.

stamp *verb* **1** bring down (one's foot) heavily, esp. on ground. **2** (often + *on*) crush or flatten in this way. **3** walk heavily. **4** impress (design, mark, etc.) on surface. **5** impress (surface) with pattern etc. **6** affix postage or other stamp to. **7** assign specific character to; mark out. ● *noun* **1** instrument for stamping. **2** mark or design made by this. **3** impression of official mark required to be made on deeds, bills of exchange, etc., as evidence of payment of tax. **4** small adhesive piece of paper as evidence of payment, esp. postage stamp. **5** mark, label, etc. on commodity as evidence of quality etc. **6** act or sound of stamping foot. **7** characteristic mark. **8** quality. ◻ **stamp duty** duty imposed on certain kinds of legal document. **stamping ground** *colloquial* favourite haunt. **stamp on 1** impress (idea etc.) on (memory etc.). **2** suppress. **stamp out 1** produce by cutting out with die etc. **2** put end to.

■ *verb* **1, 3** stomp, thump. **2** (*stamp on*) crush, flatten, trample. **4, 5** brand, emboss, engrave, impress, imprint, label, mark, print, punch. ● *noun* **1** die, punch. **2, 3** brand, hallmark, impression, imprint, print, seal. **7** characteristic, mark, sign. ◻ **stamp on 2** see SUPPRESS **2**. **stamp out 2** see ELIMINATE **1**, SUPPRESS **1**.

stampede /stæm'piːd/ *noun* **1** sudden flight or hurried movement of animals or people. **2** response of many people at once to a common impulse. ● *verb* (**-ding**) (cause to) take part in stampede.

■ *noun* charge, dash, flight, panic, rout, rush. ● *verb* bolt, career, charge, dash, frighten, gallop, panic, rout, run, rush, scatter, sprint, take to one's heels, *colloquial* tear.

stance /stɑːns/ *noun* **1** standpoint, attitude. **2** position of body, esp. when hitting ball etc.

stanch /stɑːntʃ, stɔːntʃ/ *verb* (also **staunch** /stɔːntʃ/) **1** restrain flow of (esp. blood). **2** restrain flow from (esp. wound).

stanchion /'stɑːnʃ(ə)n/ *noun* upright post or support.

stand *verb* (*past & past participle* **stood** /stʊd/) **1** have, take, or maintain upright or stationary position, esp. on feet or base. **2** be situated. **3** be of specified height. **4** be in specified state. **5** set in upright or specified position. **6** move to and remain in specified position; take specified attitude. **7** remain valid or unaltered. **8** *Nautical* hold specified course. **9** endure, tolerate. **10** provide at one's own expense. **11** (often + *for*) be candidate (for office etc.). **12** act in specified capacity. **13** undergo (trial). ● *noun* **1** cessation from progress; stoppage. **2** *Military* (esp. in **make a stand**) halt made to repel attack. **3** (esp. in **make a stand**) resistance to attack or compulsion. **4** position taken up; attitude adopted. **5** rack, set of shelves, etc. for storage or support. **6** open-fronted stall or structure for trader, exhibitor, etc. **7** standing-place for vehicles. **8** raised structure to sit or stand on. **9** *US* witness-box. **10** each halt made for performance on tour. **11** group of growing plants. ◻ **as it stands 1** in its present condition. **2** in the present circumstances. **stand by 1** stand nearby. **2** look on without interfering. **3** uphold, support (person). **4** adhere to (promise etc.). **5** be ready for action. **stand down** withdraw from position or candid-

acy. **stand for 1** represent, signify, imply. **2** *colloquial* endure, tolerate. **stand in** (usually + *for*) deputize for. **stand-in** *noun* deputy, substitute. **stand off 1** move or keep away. **2** temporarily dismiss (employee). **stand-off half** *Rugby* half-back forming link between scrum-half and three-quarters. **stand on** insist on; observe scrupulously. **stand out 1** be prominent or outstanding. **2** (usually + *against, for*) persist in opposition or support. **standpipe** vertical pipe extending from water supply, esp. one connecting temporary tap to mains. **standpoint** point of view. **standstill** stoppage; inability to proceed. **stand to** *Military* **1** stand ready for attack. **2** abide by. **3** be likely or certain to. **stand to reason** be obvious. **stand up 1** rise to one's feet. **2** come to, remain in, or place in standing position. **3** (of argument etc.) be valid. **4** *colloquial* fail to keep appointment with. **stand-up** *adjective* **1** (of meal) eaten standing. **2** (of fight) violent, thorough. **3** (of collar) not turned down. **4** (of comedian) telling jokes to audience. **stand up for** support, side with. **stand up to 1** face (opponent) courageously. **2** be resistant to (wear, use, etc.).

■ *verb* **1** arise, get to one's feet, get up, rise. **2** be, be situated, exist. **5** arrange, deposit, erect, locate, place, position, put up, set up, situate, station, up-end. **7** be unchanged, continue, remain valid, stay. **9** abide, bear, endure, put up with, suffer, tolerate, *colloquial* wear. ● *noun* **5** base, pedestal, rack, support, tripod, trivet. **6** booth, kiosk, stall. **8** grandstand, terraces. ◻ **stand by 3** see SUPPORT *verb* **4**. **stand for 1** see SYMBOLIZE **1**. **stand in** see DEPUTIZE. **stand out 1** see SHOW *verb* **1**. **standpoint** angle, attitude, belief, opinion, perspective, point of view, position, stance, vantage point, view, viewpoint. **standstill** dead end, deadlock, halt, hold-up, impasse, jam, stalemate, stop, stoppage. **stand up for** see SUPPORT *verb* **4**, PROTECT. **stand up to** see RESIST **1**.

standard /'stændəd/ *noun* **1** object, quality, or measure serving as basis, example, or principle to which others conform or should conform or by which others are judged. **2** level of excellence etc. required or specified. **3** ordinary procedure, quality, etc. **4** distinctive flag. **5** upright support or pipe. **6** shrub standing without support, or grafted on upright stem and trained in tree form. ● *adjective* **1** serving or used as standard. **2** of normal or prescribed quality, type, or size. ◻ **standard-bearer 1** person who carries distinctive flag. **2** prominent leader in cause. **standard English** most widely accepted dialect of English (see panel). **standard lamp** lamp on tall upright with base. **standard of living** degree of material comfort of person or group. **standard**

Standard English

Standard English is the dialect of English used by most educated English speakers and is spoken with a variety of accents (see language panel at ACCENT). While not *in itself* any better than any other dialect, standard English is the form of English normally used for business dealings, legal work, diplomacy, teaching, examinations, and in all formal written contexts.

time uniform time established by law or custom in country or region.

■ *noun* **1** archetype, benchmark, criterion, example, exemplar, gauge, guide, guideline, ideal, measure, model, paradigm, pattern, requirement, rule, sample, specification, touchstone, yardstick. **2** level, quality. **3** average, level, mean, norm. **4** banner, colours, ensign, flag, pennant. **5** column, pillar, pole, post, support, upright. ● *adjective* accepted, accustomed, approved, average, basic, classic, common, conventional, customary, definitive, established, everyday, familiar, habitual, normal, official, ordinary, orthodox, popular, prevailing, prevalent, recognized, regular, routine, set, staple (*diet*), stock, traditional, typical, universal, usual.

standardize *verb* (also **-ise**) (**-zing** or **-sing**) cause to conform to standard. □ **standardization** *noun*.

■ average out, equalize, homogenize, normalize, regiment, stereotype, systematize.

standby /'stæn(d)baɪ/ *noun* (*plural* **-s**) **1** person or thing ready if needed in emergency. **2** readiness for duty. ● *adjective* **1** ready for immediate use. **2** (of tickets) not booked in advance.

standing *noun* **1** esteem, repute, esp. high. **2** duration. ● *adjective* **1** that stands, upright. **2** established, permanent. **3** (of jump, start, etc.) performed with no run-up. □ **standing order** instruction to banker to make regular payments. **standing orders** rules governing procedure in a parliament, council, etc. **standing ovation** prolonged applause from audience that has risen to its feet. **standing room** space to stand in.

stand-offish /stænd'ɒfɪʃ/ *adjective* cold or distant in manner. □ **stand-offishly** *adverb*. **stand-offishness** *noun*.

■ aloof, antisocial, cold, cool, distant, frosty, haughty, remote, reserved, reticent, retiring, secretive, self-conscious, *colloquial* snooty, taciturn, unapproachable, uncommunicative, unforthcoming, unfriendly, unsociable, withdrawn.

stank *past* of STINK.

stanza /'stænzə/ *noun* group of lines forming division of poem, etc.

staphylococcus /stæfɪlə'kɒkəs/ *noun* (*plural* **-cocci** /-kaɪ/) bacterium sometimes forming pus. □ **staphylococcal** *adjective*.

staple[1] /'steɪp(ə)l/ *noun* shaped piece of wire with two points for fastening papers together, fixing netting to post, etc. ● *verb* (**-ling**) fasten with staple(s). □ **stapler** *noun*.

staple[2] /'steɪp(ə)l/ *noun* **1** principal or important article of commerce. **2** chief element; main component. **3** fibre of cotton, wool, etc. with regard to its quality. ● *adjective* **1** main, principal. **2** important as product or export.

■ *adjective* **1** basic, chief, important, main, principal, standard.

star *noun* **1** celestial body appearing as luminous point in night sky. **2** large luminous gaseous body such as the sun. **3** celestial body regarded as influencing fortunes etc. **4** conventional image of star with radiating lines or points. **5** famous or brilliant person; leading performer. ● *adjective* outstanding. ● *verb* (**-rr-**) **1** appear or present as leading performer(s). **2** (esp. as **starred** *adjective*) mark, set, or adorn with star(s). □ **starfish** (*plural* same or **-es**) sea creature with 5 or more radiating arms. **stargazer** *colloquial usually derogatory* or *jocular* astronomer or astrologer. **starlight** light of stars. **starlit 1** lit by stars. **2** with stars visible. **Stars and Stripes** US national flag. **star turn** main item in entertainment etc. □ **stardom** *noun*. **starless** *adjective*.

■ *noun* **1** asteroid, celestial body, comet, evening star, falling star, heavenly body, lodestar, morning star, nova, shooting star, supernova. **4** asterisk, pentagram. **5** attraction, big name, celebrity, diva, draw, idol, leading lady, leading man, personage, prima donna, starlet, superstar.

starboard /'stɑːbəd/ *noun* right-hand side of ship or aircraft looking forward. ● *verb* turn (helm) to starboard.

starch *noun* **1** white carbohydrate obtained chiefly from cereals and potatoes. **2** preparation of this for stiffening fabric. **3** stiffness of manner; formality. ● *verb* stiffen (clothing) with starch. □ **starchy** *adjective* (**-ier**, **-iest**).

■ ■ **starchy** aloof, conventional, formal, prim, stiff, unfriendly.

stare /steə/ *verb* (**-ring**) (usually + *at*) look fixedly, esp. in curiosity, surprise, horror, etc. ● *noun* staring gaze. □ **stare (person) in the face** be evident or imminent. **stare out** stare at (person) until he or she looks away.

■ *verb* gape, *colloquial* gawp, gaze, glare, goggle, peer; (*stare at*) contemplate, examine, eye, scrutinize, study, watch.

stark *adjective* **1** sharply evident. **2** desolate, bare. **3** absolute. ● *adverb* completely, wholly. □ **starkly** *adverb*.

■ *adjective* **1** clear, evident, obvious, plain, sharp. **2** austere, bare, bleak, depressing, desolate, dreary, gloomy, grim. **3** absolute, complete, perfect, sheer, thoroughgoing, total, unqualified, utter.

starkers /'stɑːkəz/ *adjective slang* stark naked.

starlet /'stɑːlɪt/ *noun* promising young performer, esp. film actress.

starling /'stɑːlɪŋ/ *noun* gregarious bird with blackish speckled lustrous plumage.

starry *adjective* (**-ier**, **-iest**) **1** full of stars. **2** starlike. □ **starry-eyed** *colloquial* **1** romantic but impractical. **2** euphoric.

start *verb* **1** begin. **2** set in motion or action. **3** set oneself in motion or action. **4** (often + *out*) begin journey etc. **5** (often + *up*) (cause to) begin operating. **6** (often + *up*) establish. **7** give signal to (competitors) to start in race. **8** (often + *up*, *from*, etc.) jump in surprise, pain, etc. **9** rouse (game etc.). ● *noun* **1** beginning. **2** starting place of race etc. **3** advantage given at beginning of race etc. **4** advantageous initial position in life, business, etc. **5** sudden movement of surprise, pain, etc. □ **starting block** shaped block against which runner braces feet at start of race. **starting price** odds ruling at start of horse race.

■ *verb* **1, 2** activate, begin, *formal* commence, embark on, *colloquial* get cracking on, *colloquial* get off the ground, launch, set in motion. **3, 4** depart, embark, get going, get under way, *slang* hit the road, *colloquial* kick off, leave, move off, proceed, set off, set out. **6** *literary* beget, create, engender, establish, found, give birth to, inaugurate, initiate, instigate, institute, introduce, launch, open, originate, pioneer, set up. **8** blench, draw back, flinch, jerk, jump, quail, recoil, shy, spring up, twitch, wince. ● *noun* **1** beginning, birth, *formal* commencement, creation, dawn, establishment, founding, *poetical* fount, inauguration, inception, initiation, institution, introduction, launch, onset, opening, origin, outset, point of departure, spring, springboard. **3** advantage, edge, head start. **5** jump, shock, surprise.

starter *noun* **1** device for starting vehicle engine etc. **2** first course of meal. **3** person giving signal to start race. **4** horse or competitor starting in race. □ **for starters** *colloquial* to start with.

startle /'stɑːt(ə)l/ *verb* (**-ling**) shock, surprise. □ **startling** *adjective*.

■ agitate, alarm, catch unawares, disturb, frighten, give (person) a start, jolt, make (person) jump, make (person) start, scare, shake, shock, surprise, take aback, take by surprise, upset. □ **startling** see SURPRISING (SURPRISE).

starve *verb* (**-ving**) **1** (cause to) die of hunger or suffer from malnourishment. **2** (esp. as **starved** or **starving** *adjectives*) *colloquial* feel very hungry. **3** suffer from mental or spiritual want. **4** (+ *of*) deprive of. **5** compel by starvation. □ **starvation** *noun*.

■ **2** (**starved, starving**) see HUNGRY 1. □ **starvation** deprivation, *archaic* famine, hunger, malnutrition, undernourishment, want.

stash *colloquial verb* (often + *away*) **1** conceal; put in safe place. **2** hoard. ● *noun* **1** hiding place. **2** thing hidden.

state *noun* **1** existing condition or position of person or thing. **2** *colloquial* excited or agitated mental condition. **3** *colloquial* untidy condition. **4** political community under one government. **5** this as part of federal republic. **6** civil government. **7** pomp. **8** (**the States**) USA. ● *adjective* **1** of, for, or concerned with state. **2** reserved for or done on ceremonial occasions. ● *verb* (**-ting**) **1** express in speech or writing. **2** fix, specify. □ **lie in state** be laid in public place of honour before burial. **state of the art** current stage of esp. technological development. **state-of-the-art** absolutely up to date. **stateroom 1** state apartment. **2** large private cabin in passenger ship.

■ *noun* **1** circumstances, condition, fitness, health, mood, shape, situation. **2** *colloquial* flap, panic, plight, predicament, *colloquial* tizzy. **4**

country, land, nation. ● *verb* **1** affirm, announce, assert, asseverate, *formal* aver, communicate, declare, express, formulate, proclaim, put into words, report, say, speak, submit, talk, testify, voice. **2** see SPECIFY.

stateless *adjective* having no nationality or citizenship.

stately *adjective* (**-ier, -iest**) dignified, imposing. □ **stately home** large historic house, esp. one open to public. □ **stateliness** *noun*.

■ august, dignified, distinguished, elegant, formal, grand, imperial, imposing, impressive, lofty, majestic, noble, pompous, regal, royal, solemn, splendid, striking. □ **stately home** see MANSION 1.

statement *noun* **1** stating, being stated. **2** thing stated. **3** formal account of facts. **4** record of transactions in bank account etc. **5** notification of amount due to tradesman etc.

■ **1–3** account, affirmation, announcement, annunciation, assertion, bulletin, comment, communication, communiqué, declaration, disclosure, explanation, message, notice, proclamation, proposition, report, testament, testimony, utterance. **5** account, bill, invoice.

statesman /'steɪtsmən/ *noun* (*feminine* **stateswoman**) distinguished and capable politician or diplomat. □ **statesmanlike** *adjective*. **statesmanship** *noun*.

■ diplomat, politician.

static /'stætɪk/ *adjective* **1** stationary; not acting or changing. **2** *Physics* concerned with bodies at rest or forces in equilibrium. ● *noun* **1** static electricity. **2** atmospherics. □ **static electricity** electricity not flowing as current.

■ *adjective* **1** constant, fixed, immobile, immovable, inert, invariable, motionless, passive, stable, stagnant, stationary, steady, still, unchanging, unmoving.

statics *plural noun* (usually treated as *singular*) science of bodies at rest or forces in equilibrium.

station /'steɪʃ(ə)n/ *noun* **1** regular stopping place on railway line. **2** person or thing's allotted place, building, etc. **3** centre for particular service or activity. **4** establishment involved in broadcasting. **5** military or naval base. **6** inhabitants of this. **7** position in life; rank, status. **8** *Australian & NZ* large sheep or cattle farm. ● *verb* **1** assign station to. **2** put in position. □ **stationmaster** official in charge of railway station. **stations of the cross** *RC Church* series of images representing events in Christ's Passion. **station wagon** esp. *US* estate car.

■ *noun* **1** halt, railway station, stopping place, terminus, train station. **2** location, place, position, post, situation. **3, 5** base, centre, depot, headquarters, office. **4** channel, company, transmitter, wavelength. **7** caste, class, level, place, position, rank, *formal* situation, standing, status. ● *verb* **1** assign, garrison, post. **2** locate, place, position, put, site, situate, spot, stand.

stationary *adjective* **1** not moving. **2** not meant to be moved. **3** unchanging.

■ **1** at a standstill, at rest, halted, inert, motionless, parked, pausing, standing, static, still, stock-still, unmoving. **2** fixed, immobile, immovable. **3** see CONSTANT *adjective* 3.

stationer *noun* dealer in stationery.

stationery *noun* writing materials, office supplies, etc.

statistic /stə'tɪstɪk/ *noun* statistical fact or item.

statistical *adjective* of statistics. □ **statistically** *adverb*.

statistics *plural noun* **1** (usually treated as *singular*) science of collecting and analysing significant numerical data. **2** such data. □ **statistician** /stætɪs'tɪʃ(ə)n/ *noun*.

■ **2** data, figures, information, numbers.

statuary /'stætʃʊərɪ/ *adjective* of or for statues. ● *noun* **1** statues collectively. **2** making statues.

statue /'stætʃuː/ *noun* sculptured figure of person or animal, esp. life-size or larger.

■ carving, figure, sculpture, statuette.

statuesque /stætʃʊ'esk/ *adjective* like statue, esp. in beauty or dignity.

■ dignified, elegant, imposing, impressive, poised, stately, upright.

statuette /stætʃʊ'et/ *noun* small statue.

stature /'stætʃə/ *noun* **1** height of (esp. human) body. **2** calibre (esp. moral); eminence.

■ **1** build, height, size, tallness. **2** eminence, esteem, greatness, recognition, status.

status /'steɪtəs/ *noun* **1** rank, social position, relative importance. **2** superior social etc. position. □ **status quo** /'kwəʊ/ existing conditions. **status symbol** possession etc. intended to indicate owner's superiority.

■ **1** class, grade, importance, level, position, prominence, rank, reputation, significance, standing, station, stature, title. **2** see PRESTIGE.

statute /'stætʃuːt/ *noun* **1** written law passed by legislative body. **2** rule of corporation, founder, etc., intended to be permanent.

statutory /'stætʃʊtərɪ/ *adjective* required or enacted by statute.

staunch[1] /stɔːntʃ/ *adjective* trustworthy, loyal. □ **staunchly** *adverb*. **staunchness** *noun*.

■ see STEADFAST.

staunch[2] = STANCH.

stave *noun* **1** each of curved slats forming sides of cask. **2** *Music* staff. **3** stanza, verse. ● *verb* (**-ving**; *past & past participle* **stove** /stəʊv/ or **staved**) (usually + *in*) **1** break hole in; damage. **2** crush by forcing inwards. □ **stave off** (*past & past participle* **staved**) avert or defer (danger etc.).

stay[1] *verb* **1** continue in same place or condition; not depart or change. **2** (often + *at, in, with*) reside

temporarily. **3** *archaic* or *literary* stop, check. **4** (esp. in *imperative*) pause. **5** postpone (judgement etc.). **6** assuage (hunger etc.), esp. for short time. ● *noun* **1** act or period of staying. **2** suspension or postponement of sentence, judgement, etc. **3** prop, support. **4** (in *plural*) *historical* (esp. boned) corset. □ **stay-at-home** (person) rarely going out. **staying power** endurance. **stay the night** remain overnight. **stay put** *colloquial* remain where it is put or where one is. **stay up** not go to bed (until late).

■ *verb* **1** *archaic* or *dialect* bide, carry on, continue, endure, hang about, hold out, keep on, last, linger, live on, loiter, persist, remain, survive, *archaic* tarry, wait. **2** *archaic* abide, be accommodated, be a guest, be housed, board, dwell, live, lodge, reside, settle, sojourn, *colloquial* stop, visit. **3** see DELAY *verb* 2. **5** see DELAY *verb* 1. ● *noun* **1** holiday, sojourn, stop, stopover, visit. **2** see DELAY *noun*.

stay[2] *noun* **1** rope supporting mast, flagstaff, etc. **2** supporting cable on aircraft. □ **staysail** sail extended on stay.

■ see SUPPORT *noun* 2.

stayer *noun* person or animal with great endurance.

STD *abbreviation* subscriber trunk dialling.

stead /sted/ *noun* □ **in (person's, thing's) stead** as substitute. **stand (person) in good stead** be advantageous or useful to him or her.

steadfast /'stedfɑːst/ *adjective* constant, firm, unwavering. □ **steadfastly** *adverb*. **steadfastness** *noun*.

■ committed, constant, dedicated, dependable, determined, devoted, faithful, firm, loyal, patient, persevering, reliable, resolute, resolved, single-minded, sound, stalwart, staunch, steady, strong, true, trustworthy, *archaic* or *jocular* trusty, unchanging, unfaltering, unflinching, unswerving, unwavering.

steady /'stedɪ/ *adjective* (**-ier, -iest**) **1** firmly fixed or supported; unwavering. **2** uniform, regular. **3** constant, persistent. **4** (of person) serious and dependable. **5** regular, established. ● *verb* (**-ies, -ied**) make or become steady. ● *adverb* steadily. ● *noun* (*plural* **-ies**) *colloquial* regular boyfriend or girlfriend. □ **steady state** unvarying condition, esp. in physical process. □ **steadily** *adverb*. **steadiness** *noun*.

■ *adjective* **1** balanced, fast, firm, immovable, poised, safe, secure, settled, solid, stable. **2, 3** ceaseless, changeless, consistent, constant, continuous, dependable, endless, even, incessant, invariable, never-ending, non-stop, perpetual, persistent, regular, reliable, repeated, rhythmic, round the clock, unbroken, unchanging, undeviating, unfaltering, unhurried, uniform, uninterrupted, unrelieved, unremitting, unvarying. **4** see STEADFAST. ● *verb* balance, brace, calm, control, keep still, secure, soothe, stabilize, support, tranquillize.

steak /steɪk/ *noun* thick slice of meat (esp. beef) or fish, usually grilled or fried. □ **steakhouse** restaurant specializing in beefsteaks.

steal *verb* (*past* **stole**; *past participle* **stolen** /'stəʊl(ə)n/) **1** take (another's property) illegally or without right or permission, esp. in secret. **2** obtain surreptitiously, insidiously, or artfully. **3** (+ *in*, *out*, *away*, *up*, etc.) move, esp. silently or stealthily. ● *noun* **1** *US colloquial* act of stealing; theft. **2** *colloquial* easy task; bargain. □ **steal a march on** gain advantage over by surreptitious means. **steal the show** outshine other performers, esp. unexpectedly. □ **stealer** *noun*. **stealing** *noun*.

■ *verb* **1** annex, appropriate, arrogate, commandeer, confiscate, embezzle, expropriate, filch, hijack, *slang* knock off, *colloquial* lift, loot, make off with, misappropriate, *slang* nick, peculate, pilfer, pillage, *slang* pinch, pirate, plagiarize, plunder, poach, *formal* or *jocular* purloin, *colloquial* rip off, seize, shoplift, snatch, *slang* sneak, *slang* snitch, *colloquial* swipe, take, thieve, usurp, *colloquial* walk off with. **3** creep, slink, slip, sneak, tiptoe. □ **stealing** burglary, embezzlement, fraud, hijacking, larceny, looting, misappropriation, mugging, peculation, pilfering, pillage, piracy, plagiarism, plundering, poaching, *formal* or *jocular* purloining, robbery, *colloquial* scrumping, shoplifting, theft, thieving.

stealth /stelθ/ *noun* secrecy; secret behaviour.

stealthy *adjective* (**-ier**, **-iest**) done or moving with stealth. □ **stealthily** *adverb*.

■ clandestine, concealed, covert, disguised, furtive, imperceptible, inconspicuous, quiet, secret, secretive, sly, sneaky, surreptitious, underhand, unobtrusive.

steam *noun* **1** gas into which water is changed by boiling. **2** condensed vapour formed from this. **3** power obtained from steam. **4** *colloquial* power, energy. ● *verb* **1** cook (food) in steam. **2** give off steam. **3** move under steam power. **4** (+ *ahead*, *away*, etc.) *colloquial* proceed or travel fast or with vigour. □ **let off steam** relieve pent-up energy or feelings. **steamboat** steam-driven boat. **steam engine** one worked or propelled by steam. **steam iron** electric iron that emits steam. **steamroller** ● *noun* **1** heavy slow-moving vehicle with roller, used to flatten newly made roads. **2** crushing power or force. ● *verb* crush or move forcibly or indiscriminately. **steamship** steam-driven ship. **steam train** train pulled by steam engine. **steam up 1** cover or become covered with condensed steam. **2** (as **steamed up** *adjective*) *colloquial* angry, excited.

■ *noun* **1** condensation, haze, mist, vapour.

steamer *noun* **1** steamboat. **2** vessel for steaming food in.

steamy *adjective* (**-ier**, **-iest**) **1** like or full of steam. **2** *colloquial* erotic.

■ **1** blurred, close, clouded, cloudy, damp, fogged over, foggy, hazy, humid, misted over, misty, moist, muggy, sticky, sultry, sweaty, sweltering. **2** see SEXY 1.

steatite /'stɪətaɪt/ *noun* impure form of talc, esp. soapstone.

steed *noun archaic* or *poetical* horse.

steel *noun* **1** strong malleable low-carbon iron alloy, used esp. for making tools, weapons, etc. **2** strength, firmness. **3** steel rod for sharpening knives. ● *adjective* of or like steel. ● *verb* harden, make resolute. □ **steel band** band playing chiefly calypso-style music on instruments made from oil drums. **steel wool** fine steel shavings used as abrasive. **steelworks** factory producing steel. **steelyard** balance with graduated arm along which weight is moved.

steely *adjective* (**-ier**, **-iest**) **1** of or like steel. **2** severe, resolute.

steep[1] *adjective* **1** sloping sharply. **2** (of rise or fall) rapid. **3** *colloquial* exorbitant, unreasonable. **4** *colloquial* exaggerated, incredible. ● *noun* steep slope, precipice. □ **steepen** *verb*. **steeply** *adverb*. **steepness** *noun*.

■ *adjective* **1** abrupt, bluff, headlong, perpendicular, precipitous, sharp, sheer, sudden, vertical. **3** see EXPENSIVE.

steep[2] *verb* soak or bathe in liquid. ● *noun* **1** act of steeping. **2** liquid for steeping. □ **steep in 1** imbue with. **2** make deeply acquainted with (subject etc.).

■ *verb* see SOAK *verb* 1.

steeple /'stiːp(ə)l/ *noun* tall tower, esp. with spire, above roof of church. □ **steeplechase 1** horse race with ditches, hedges, etc. to jump. **2** cross-country foot race. **steeplejack** repairer of tall chimneys, steeples, etc.

■ pinnacle, point, spire.

steer[1] *verb* **1** guide (vehicle, ship, etc.) with wheel, rudder, etc. **2** direct or guide (one's course, other people, conversation, etc.) in specified direction. □ **steer clear of** avoid. **steering column** column on which steering wheel is mounted. **steering committee** one deciding order of business, course of operations etc. **steering wheel** wheel by which vehicle etc. is steered. **steersman** person who steers ship.

■ **1** be at the wheel, control, direct, drive, guide, navigate, pilot. **2** direct, guide, lead. □ **steer clear of** see AVOID.

steer[2] *noun* bullock.

steerage *noun* **1** act of steering. **2** *archaic* cheapest part of ship's accommodation.

steering *noun* apparatus for steering vehicle etc.

stegosaurus /stegə'sɔːrəs/ *noun* (*plural* **-ruses**) large dinosaur with two rows of vertical plates along back.

stela /'stiːlə/ *noun* (*plural* **stelae** /-liː/) (also **stele** /'stiːl/) ancient upright slab or pillar, usually inscribed and sculptured, esp. as gravestone.

stellar /'stelə/ *adjective* of star or stars.

stem[1] *noun* **1** main body or stalk of plant. **2** stalk of fruit, flower, or leaf. **3** stem-shaped part, e.g. slender part of wineglass. **4** *Grammar* root or main part of noun, verb, etc. to which inflections are added. **5** main upright timber at bow of ship. ● *verb* (**-mm-**) (+ *from*) spring or originate from.

■ *noun* **1, 2** peduncle, shoot, stalk, stock, trunk.
● *verb* arise, come, derive, develop, emanate, flow, issue, originate, proceed, result, spring, sprout.

stem² *verb* (**-mm-**) check, stop.
■ see CHECK *verb* 2.

stench *noun* foul smell.
■ mephitis, *colloquial* pong, reek, stink.

stencil /'stensɪl/ *noun* **1** thin sheet in which pattern is cut, placed on surface and printed, inked over, etc. **2** pattern so produced. ● *verb* (**-ll-**; *US* **-l-**) **1** (often + *on*) produce (pattern) with stencil. **2** mark (surface) in this way.

Sten gun *noun* lightweight sub-machine-gun.

stenographer /stɛ'nɒgrəfə/ *noun esp. US* shorthand typist.

stentorian /stɛn'tɔːrɪən/ *adjective* loud and powerful.

step *noun* **1** complete movement of leg in walking or running. **2** distance so covered. **3** unit of movement in dancing. **4** measure taken, esp. one of several in course of action. **5** progress. **6** surface of stair, stepladder, etc. tread. **7** short distance. **8** sound or mark made by foot in walking etc. **9** degree in scale of promotion, precedence, etc. **10** stepping in unison or to music. **11** state of conforming. **12** (in *plural*) stepladder. ● *verb* (**-pp-**) **1** lift and set down foot or alternate feet in walking. **2** come or go in specified direction by stepping. **3** make progress in specified way. **4** (+ *off*, *out*) measure (distance) by stepping. **5** perform (dance). □ **mind, watch one's step** be careful. **step by step** gradually; cautiously. **step down** resign. **step in 1** enter. **2** intervene. **stepladder** short ladder with flat steps and folding prop. **step on it** *colloquial* hurry. **step out 1** be active socially. **2** take large steps. **step out of line** behave inappropriately or disobediently. **step up** increase, intensify.

■ *noun* **1** footstep, pace, stride, tread. **4** action, initiative, manoeuvre, measure, move, phase, procedure, stage; (*take steps*) see BEGIN 3. **5** advance, move, movement, progress, progression. **6** doorstep, rung, stair, tread; (*steps*) stairs, staircase, stairway. **8** footfall, footprint, footstep, tread. **9** degree, grade, level, notch, rung, stage, tier. **12** (*steps*) ladder, stepladder. ● *verb* **1** stamp, stride, tread, walk; (*step on*) see TRAMPLE 1. **2** see WALK *verb* 1–5. □ **step down** see RESIGN 1,2. **step in 1** see ENTER 1. **2** see INTERVENE 2,4;5. **step on it** see HURRY *verb* 1. **step up** see INCREASE *verb*.

step- *combining form* related by remarriage of parent. □ **stepchild, stepdaughter, stepson** one's husband's or wife's child by previous partner. **stepfather, stepmother, step-parent** mother's or father's spouse who is not one's own parent. **stepbrother, stepsister** child of one's step-parent by previous partner.

stephanotis /stɛfə'nəʊtɪs/ *noun* fragrant tropical climbing plant.

steppe /stɛp/ *noun* level grassy treeless plain.

stepping stone *noun* **1** raised stone in stream,

muddy place, etc. used to help in crossing. **2** means to end; stage of progress.

stereo /'sterɪəʊ/ *noun* (*plural* **-s**) **1** stereophonic sound reproduction or equipment. **2** stereoscope. ● *adjective* **1** stereophonic. **2** stereoscopic.

stereo- *combining form* solid; 3-dimensional.

stereophonic /sterɪəʊ'fɒnɪk/ *adjective* using two or more channels, to give effect of naturally distributed sound.

stereoscope /'sterɪəskəʊp/ *noun* device for producing 3-dimensional effect by viewing two slightly different photographs together. □ **stereoscopic** /-'skɒp-/ *adjective*.
■ □ **stereoscopic** solid-looking, three-dimensional.

stereotype /'sterɪəʊtaɪp/ *noun* **1** person or thing seeming to conform to widely accepted type. **2** such type, idea, or attitude. **3** printing plate cast from mould of composed type. ● *verb* (**-ping**) **1** (esp. as **stereotyped** *adjective*) cause to conform to type; standardize. **2** print from stereotype. **3** make stereotype of.
■ *noun* **2** formula, model, pattern, type. ● *verb* **1** (**stereotyped**) cliché'd, conventional, formalized, hackneyed, predictable, standard, standardized, stock, typecast, unoriginal.

sterile /'steraɪl/ *adjective* **1** not able to produce crop, fruit, or young; barren. **2** lacking ideas or originality; unproductive. **3** free from microorganisms etc. □ **sterility** /stə'rɪl-/ *noun*.
■ **1** arid, barren, childless, fruitless, infertile, lifeless, unfruitful, unproductive. **2** abortive, barren, dry, fruitless, hopeless, pointless, unfruitful, unproductive, unprofitable, useless. **3** antiseptic, aseptic, clean, disinfected, germ-free, hygienic, pure, sanitary, sterilized, uncontaminated, uninfected, unpolluted.

sterilize /'sterɪlaɪz/ *verb* (also **-ise**) (**-zing** or **-sing**) **1** make sterile. **2** deprive of reproductive power. □ **sterilization** *noun*.
■ **1** clean, cleanse, decontaminate, disinfect, fumigate, pasteurize, purify. **2** castrate, emasculate, geld, neuter, perform a vasectomy on, spay.

sterling /'stɜːlɪŋ/ *adjective* **1** of or in British money. **2** (of coin or precious metal) genuine; of standard value or purity. **3** (of person etc.) genuine, reliable. ● *noun* British money. □ **sterling silver** silver of 92½% purity.

stern¹ *adjective* severe, grim; authoritarian. □ **sternly** *adverb*. **sternness** *noun*.
■ adamant, austere, authoritarian, critical, dour, forbidding, frowning, grim, hard, harsh, inflexible, obdurate, resolute, rigid, rigorous, serious, severe, strict, stringent, *colloquial* tough, unbending, uncompromising, unrelenting, unremitting.

stern² *noun* rear part, esp. of ship or boat.
■ aft, back, rear end.

sternum /'stɜːnəm/ *noun* (*plural* **-na** or **-nums**) breastbone.

steroid /ˈstɪərɔɪd/ *noun* any of group of organic compounds including many hormones, alkaloids, and vitamins.

sterol /ˈsterɒl/ *noun* naturally occurring steroid alcohol.

stertorous /ˈstɜːtərəs/ *adjective* (of breathing etc.) laboured and noisy.

stet *verb* (**-tt-**) (usually written on proof-sheet etc.) ignore or cancel (alteration); let original stand.

stethoscope /ˈsteθəskəʊp/ *noun* instrument used in listening to heart, lungs, etc.

stetson /ˈstets(ə)n/ *noun* slouch hat with wide brim and high crown.

stevedore /ˈstiːvədɔː/ *noun* person employed in loading and unloading ships.

stew *verb* **1** cook by long simmering in closed vessel. **2** *colloquial* swelter. **3** (of tea etc.) become bitter or strong from infusing too long. ● *noun* **1** dish of stewed meat etc. **2** *colloquial* agitated or angry state.

■ *verb* **1** boil, braise, casserole, simmer. ● *noun* **1** casserole, goulash, hash, hotpot, ragout.

steward /ˈstjuːəd/ *noun* **1** passengers' attendant on ship, aircraft, or train. **2** official managing meeting, show, etc. **3** person responsible for supplies of food etc. for college, club, etc. **4** property manager. □ **stewardship** *noun*.

■ **1** attendant, waiter. **2** marshal, officer, official.

stewardess /stjuːəˈdes/ *noun* female steward, esp. on ship or aircraft.

■ attendant, steward, waitress.

stick[1] *noun* **1** short slender length of wood, esp. for use as support or weapon. **2** thin rod of wood etc. for particular purpose. **3** gear lever. **4** joystick. **5** sticklike piece of celery, dynamite, etc. **6** (often **the stick**) punishment, esp. by beating. **7** *colloquial* adverse criticism. **8** *colloquial* person, esp. when dull or unsociable. □ **stick insect** insect with twiglike body.

■ **1** branch, stalk, twig. **2** bar, baton, cane, club, cue, pole, rod, staff, stake, wand.

stick[2] *verb* (*past & past participle* **stuck**) **1** (+ *in, into, through*) thrust, insert (thing or its point). **2** stab. **3** (+ *in, into, on*, etc.) fix or be fixed (as) by pointed end. **4** fix or be fixed (as) by adhesive etc. **5** lose or be deprived of movement or action through adhesion, jamming, etc. **6** *colloquial* put in specified position or place. **7** remain. **8** *colloquial* endure, tolerate. **9** (+ *at*) *colloquial* persevere with. □ **stick around** *colloquial* linger. **stick at it** *colloquial* persevere. **sticking plaster** adhesive plaster for wounds etc. **stick-in-the-mud** *colloquial* unprogressive or old-fashioned person. **stick it out** *colloquial* endure to the end. **stick out** (cause to) protrude. **stick out for** persist in demanding. **stick together** become or remain united. **stick to one's guns** see GUN. **stick up 1** be or make erect or protruding upwards. **2** fasten to upright surface. **3** *colloquial* rob or threaten with gun. **stick up for** support, defend. **stick with** support; persevere with.

■ **1, 2** bore, dig, impale, jab, penetrate, pierce, pin, poke, prick, prod, punch, puncture, run through, spear, spike, spit, stab, thrust, transfix. **3** attach, fasten, fix, nail, pin, tack. **4** adhere, affix, agglutinate, bind, bond, cement, cling, fasten, fuse together, glue, gum, paste, solder, weld. **5** become trapped, get bogged down, seize up, jam, wedge. **7** be fixed, continue, endure, keep on, last, linger, persist, remain, stay. **8** see TOLERATE 2,3. **9** (*stick at*) see CONTINUE 1. □ **stick at it** see PERSIST. **stick out** see PROTRUDE 2. **stick together** see UNITE 1. **stick up 1** see PROTRUDE 2. **stick up for** see DEFEND 1. **stick with** see SUPPORT *verb* 4.

sticker *noun* adhesive label.

stickleback /ˈstɪk(ə)lbæk/ *noun* small spiny-backed fish.

stickler /ˈstɪklə/ *noun* (+ *for*) person who insists on something.

sticky *adjective* (**-ier, -iest**) **1** tending or intended to stick or adhere. **2** glutinous, viscous. **3** (of weather) humid. **4** *colloquial* difficult, awkward. **5** *colloquial* unpleasant, painful. □ **sticky wicket** *colloquial* difficult situation. □ **stickiness** *noun*.

■ **1** adhesive, glued, gummed, self-adhesive. **2** gluey, glutinous, *colloquial* gooey, gummy, tacky, viscous. **3** clammy, close, damp, dank, humid, moist, muggy, steamy, sultry.

stiff *adjective* **1** rigid, inflexible. **2** hard to bend, move, turn, etc. **3** hard to cope with; needing strength or effort. **4** severe, strong. **5** formal, constrained. **6** (of muscle, person, etc.) aching from exertion, injury, etc. **7** (of esp. alcoholic drink) strong. ● *noun slang* corpse. □ **bore, scare person stiff** *colloquial* bore or scare person to extreme degree. **stiff-necked** obstinate, haughty. **stiff upper lip** appearance of firmness or fortitude. □ **stiffen** *verb*. **stiffly** *adverb*. **stiffness** *noun*.

■ *adjective* **1, 2** compact, dense, firm, hard, heavy, inelastic, inflexible, rigid, semi-solid, solid, solidified, thick, tough, unbending, unyielding, viscous. **3** arduous, challenging, difficult, exacting, exhausting, hard, laborious, tiring, tough, uphill. **4** (*stiff opposition*) determined, dogged, obstinate, powerful, resolute, strong, stubborn, unyielding, vigorous; (*stiff penalties*) cruel, drastic, excessive, harsh, hurtful, merciless, pitiless, punishing, punitive, relentless, rigorous, severe, strict; (*stiff wind*) brisk, fresh, strong. **5** artificial, awkward, cold, constrained, forced, formal, graceless, haughty, inelegant, laboured, mannered, pedantic, self-conscious, stand-offish, starchy, stilted, stuffy, tense, ungainly, unnatural, wooden. **6** arthritic, immovable, painful, rheumatic, taut, tight. **7** alcoholic, potent, strong. □ **stiffen** clot, coagulate, congeal, harden, *colloquial* jell, set, solidify, thicken, tighten, toughen.

stifle /ˈstaɪf(ə)l/ *verb* (**-ling**) **1** suppress. **2** feel or make unable to breathe easily; suffocate. □ **stifling** *adjective*.

■ **1** check, control, crush, curb, deaden, destroy, extinguish, keep back, kill off, muffle, quash, repress, restrain, silence, stamp out, stop, suppress, withhold. **2** asphyxiate, choke, smother, strangle, suffocate, throttle.

stigma /'stɪgmə/ *noun* (*plural* **-s** or **stigmata** /-mətə or -'mɑːtə/) **1** shame, disgrace. **2** part of pistil that receives pollen in pollination. **3** (**stigmata**) marks like those on Christ's body after the Crucifixion, appearing on bodies of certain saints etc.
■ **1** blot, brand, disgrace, dishonour, mark, reproach, shame, slur, stain, taint.

stigmatize /'stɪgmətaɪz/ *verb* (also **-ise**) (**-zing** or **-sing**) (often + *as*) brand as unworthy or disgraceful.
■ brand, condemn, defame, denounce, disparage, label, mark, pillory, slander, vilify.

stile *noun* set of steps etc. allowing people to climb over fence, wall, etc.

stiletto /stɪ'letəʊ/ *noun* (*plural* **-s**) **1** short dagger. **2** (in full **stiletto heel**) long tapering heel of shoe. **3** pointed implement for making eyelets etc.

still[1] *adjective* **1** with little or no movement or sound. **2** calm, tranquil. **3** (of drink) not effervescing. ● *noun* **1** deep silence. **2** static photograph, esp. single shot from cinema film. ● *adverb* **1** without moving. **2** even now; at particular time. **3** nevertheless. **4** (+ *comparative*) even, yet, increasingly. ● *verb* make or become still; quieten. □ **stillbirth** birth of dead child. **stillborn 1** born dead. **2** abortive. **still life** painting or drawing of inanimate objects. □ **stillness** *noun*.
■ *adjective* **1, 2** at rest, calm, even, flat, hushed, immobile, inert, lifeless, motionless, noiseless, pacific, peaceful, placid, quiet, restful, serene, silent, smooth, soundless, stagnant, static, stationary, tranquil, unmoving, unruffled, untroubled, windless. ● *verb* allay, appease, assuage, calm, lull, pacify, quieten, settle, silence, soothe, subdue, suppress, tranquillize.

still[2] *noun* apparatus for distilling spirits etc.

stilt *noun* **1** either of pair of poles with foot supports for walking at a distance above ground. **2** each of set of piles or posts supporting building etc.

stilted *adjective* (of literary style etc.) stiff and unnatural.

Stilton /'stɪlt(ə)n/ *noun proprietary term* strong rich esp. blue-veined cheese.

stimulant /'stɪmjʊlənt/ *adjective* stimulating esp. bodily or mental activity. ● *noun* **1** stimulant substance. **2** stimulating influence.
■ *noun* **1** antidepressant, pick-me-up, restorative, *colloquial* shot in the arm, tonic. **2** see STIMULUS.

stimulate /'stɪmjʊleɪt/ *verb* (**-ting**) **1** act as stimulus to. **2** animate, excite, rouse. □ **stimulating** *adjective*. **stimulation** *noun*. **stimulative** /-lətɪv/ *adjective*. **stimulator** *noun*.
■ activate, arouse, awaken, cause, encourage, excite, fan, fire, foment, galvanize, goad, incite, inflame, inspire, instigate, invigorate, kindle, motivate, prick, prompt, provoke, quicken, rouse, set off, spur, stir up, titillate, urge, whet.

□ **stimulating** arousing, challenging, exciting, exhilarating, inspirational, inspiring, interesting, intoxicating, invigorating, provocative, rousing, stirring, thought-provoking, titillating.

stimulus /'stɪmjʊləs/ *noun* (*plural* **-li** /-laɪ/) thing that rouses to activity.
■ encouragement, fillip, goad, incentive, inducement, inspiration, prompting, provocation, spur, stimulant.

sting *noun* **1** sharp wounding organ of insect, nettle, etc. **2** inflicting of wound with this. **3** wound itself. **4** pain caused by it. **5** painful quality or effect. **6** pungency, vigour. ● *verb* (*past & past participle* **stung**) **1** wound with sting. **2** be able to sting. **3** feel or cause tingling physical pain or sharp mental pain. **4** (+ *into*) incite, esp. painfully. **5** *slang* swindle; charge heavily. □ **stinging nettle** nettle with stinging hairs. **stingray** broad flatfish with stinging tail.
■ *noun* **2–4** bite, pain, prick, stab, tingle. ● *verb* **1** bite, nip, prick, wound. **3** hurt, pain, prick, smart, tingle, wound.

stingy /'stɪndʒɪ/ *adjective* (**-ier**, **-iest**) niggardly, mean. □ **stingily** *adverb*. **stinginess** *noun*.
■ *of person* cheese-paring, close, close-fisted, covetous, mean, *colloquial* mingy, miserly, niggardly, parsimonious, penny-pinching, tight-fisted, ungenerous; *of amount, etc.* inadequate, insufficient, meagre, *colloquial* measly, scanty, small.

stink *verb* (*past* **stank** or **stunk**; *past participle* **stunk**) **1** emit strong offensive smell. **2** (often + *out*) fill (place) with stink. **3** (+ *out* etc.) drive (person) out etc. by stink. **4** *colloquial* be or seem very unpleasant. ● *noun* **1** strong offensive smell. **2** *colloquial* loud complaint; fuss. □ **stink bomb** device emitting stink when opened.
■ *verb* **1** see SMELL *verb* 2. ● *noun* **1** see SMELL *noun* 3.

stinker *noun slang* **1** particularly annoying or unpleasant person. **2** very difficult problem etc.

stinking *adjective* **1** that stinks. **2** *slang* very objectionable. ● *adverb slang* extremely and usually objectionably.

stint *verb* **1** (often + *on*) supply (food, aid, etc.) meanly or grudgingly. **2** (often **stint oneself**) supply (person etc.) in this way. ● *noun* allotted amount or period of work.

stipend /'staɪpend/ *noun* salary, esp. of clergyman.

stipendiary /staɪ'pendjərɪ/ *adjective* receiving stipend. ● *noun* (*plural* **-ies**) person receiving stipend. □ **stipendiary magistrate** paid professional magistrate.

stipple /'stɪp(ə)l/ *verb* (**-ling**) **1** draw, paint, engrave, etc. with dots instead of lines. **2** roughen surface of (paint, cement, etc.). ● *noun* **1** stippling. **2** effect of stippling.

stipulate /'stɪpjʊleɪt/ *verb* (**-ting**) demand or specify as part of bargain etc. □ **stipulation** *noun*.

■ demand, insist on, require, specify.
□ **stipulation** condition, demand, prerequisite, proviso, requirement, specification.

stir *verb* (**-rr-**) **1** move spoon etc. round and round in (liquid etc.), esp. to mix ingredients. **2** cause to move, esp. slightly. **3** be or begin to be in motion. **4** rise from sleep. **5** arouse, inspire, excite. **6** *colloquial* cause trouble by gossiping etc. ● *noun* **1** act of stirring. **2** commotion, excitement. □ **stir-fry** ● *verb* fry rapidly while stirring. ● *noun* stir-fried dish. **stir up 1** mix thoroughly by stirring. **2** stimulate, incite. □ **stirring** *adjective*.

■ *verb* **1** agitate, beat, blend, churn, mingle, mix, scramble, whisk. **2, 3** see MOVE *verb* 2. **4** arise, bestir oneself, *colloquial* get a move on, get going, get up, move, rise, show signs of life. **5** activate, affect, arouse, awaken, challenge, disturb, electrify, excite, exhilarate, fire, impress, inspire, kindle, move, resuscitate, revive, rouse, stimulate, touch, upset. ● *noun* **2** see COMMOTION. □ **stirring** affecting, arousing, challenging, dramatic, electrifying, emotional, emotion-charged, emotive, exciting, exhilarating, heady, impassioned, inspirational, inspiring, interesting, intoxicating, invigorating, moving, provocative, provoking, rousing, spirited, stimulating, thought-provoking, thrilling, titillating, touching.

stirrer /'stə:rə/ *noun* **1** thing or person that stirs. **2** troublemaker, agitator.

stirrup /'stɪrəp/ *noun* support for horse-rider's foot, suspended by strap from saddle. □ **stirrup-cup** cup of wine etc. offered to departing traveller, originally rider.

stitch *noun* **1** single pass of needle, or result of this, in sewing, knitting, or crochet. **2** particular method of sewing etc. **3** least bit of clothing. **4** sharp pain in side induced by running etc. ● *verb* sew, make stitches (in). □ **in stitches** *colloquial* laughing uncontrollably. **stitch up** join or mend by sewing.

■ *verb* darn, mend, repair, sew, tack.

stoat *noun* mammal of weasel family with brown fur turning mainly white in winter.

stock *noun* **1** store of goods etc. ready for sale or distribution. **2** supply or quantity of things for use. **3** equipment or raw material for manufacture, trade, etc. **4** farm animals or equipment. **5** capital of business. **6** shares in this. **7** reputation, popularity. **8** money lent to government at fixed interest. **9** line of ancestry. **10** liquid made by stewing bones, vegetables, etc. **11** fragrant garden plant. **12** plant into which graft is inserted. **13** main trunk of tree etc. **14** (in *plural*) *historical* timber frame with holes for feet in which offenders were locked as public punishment. **15** base, support, or handle for implement or machine. **16** butt of rifle etc. **17** (in *plural*) supports for ship during building or repair. **18** band of cloth worn round neck. ● *adjective* **1** kept regularly in stock for sale or use. **2** commonly use; hackneyed. ● *verb* **1** have (goods) in stock. **2** provide (shop, farm, etc.) with goods, livestock, etc. □ **in stock** available immediately for sale.

out of stock not available immediately for sale. **stockbroker** member of Stock Exchange dealing in stocks and shares. **stock car** specially strengthened car used in racing where deliberate bumping is allowed. **Stock Exchange 1** place for dealing in stocks and shares. **2** dealers working there. **stock-in-trade** requisite(s) of trade or profession. **stock market 1** Stock Exchange. **2** transactions on this. **stockpile** ● *noun* reserve supply of accumulated stock. ● *verb* accumulate stockpile (of). **stockpot** pot for making soup stock. **stockroom** room for storing goods in stock. **stock-still** motionless. **stocktaking** making inventory of stock. **stock up** (often + *with*) provide with or get stocks or supplies (of). **stockyard** enclosure for sorting or temporary keeping of cattle. **take stock 1** make inventory of one's stock. **2** (often + *of*) review (situation etc.).

■ *noun* **1** commodities, goods, merchandise, range, wares. **2** cache, hoard, reserve, reservoir, stockpile, store, supply. **4** animals, beasts, cattle, herds, livestock. **9** ancestry, blood, descent, dynasty, extraction, family, forebears, genealogy, line, lineage, parentage, pedigree. **10** broth, soup. ● *adjective* **2** accustomed, banal, clichéd, common, commonplace, conventional, customary, expected, hackneyed, ordinary, predictable, regular, routine, run-of-the-mill, set, standard, staple, stereotyped, tired, traditional, trite, unoriginal, usual. ● *verb* **1** carry, deal in, handle, have available, keep, keep in stock, market, offer, provide, sell, supply, trade in. □ **out of stock** sold out, unavailable. **take stock 2** (*take stock of*) see REVIEW *verb* 1.

stockade /stɒˈkeɪd/ *noun* line or enclosure of upright stakes. ● *verb* (**-ding**) fortify with this.
■ *noun* fence, paling, palisade, wall.

stockinet /stɒkɪˈnet/ *noun* (also **stockinette**) elastic knitted fabric.

stocking /'stɒkɪŋ/ *noun* knitted covering for leg and foot, of nylon, wool, silk, etc. □ **stocking stitch** alternate rows of plain and purl.

stockist *noun* dealer in specified types of goods.
■ dealer, *esp. US & Scottish* merchant, retailer, seller, shopkeeper, supplier.

stocky *adjective* (**-ier, -iest**) short and strongly built. □ **stockily** *adverb*.
■ burly, compact, dumpy, heavy-set, short, solid, squat, stubby, sturdy, thickset.

stodge *noun colloquial* heavy fattening food.

stodgy *adjective* (**-ier, -iest**) **1** (of food) heavy, filling. **2** dull, uninteresting. □ **stodginess** *noun*.
■ **1** filling, heavy, indigestible, solid, starchy. **2** boring, dull, ponderous, stuffy, tedious, tiresome, turgid, unexciting, unimaginative, uninteresting.

stoic /'stəʊɪk/ *noun* person having great self-control in adversity. □ **stoical** *adjective*. **stoicism** /-ɪsɪz(ə)m/ *noun*.
■ □ **stoical** calm, cool, disciplined, impassive, imperturbable, long-suffering, patient, philosophical, phlegmatic, resigned, stolid,

uncomplaining, unemotional, unexcitable, *colloquial* unflappable.

stoke *verb* (**-king**) **1** (often + *up*) feed and tend (fire, furnace, etc.). **2** *colloquial* fill oneself with food. □ **stokehold** compartment in steamship containing its boilers and furnace. **stokehole** space for stokers in front of furnace.
  ■ *verb* **1** feed, fuel, tend.

stoker *noun* person who tends furnace, esp. on steamship.

stole[1] *noun* **1** woman's garment like long wide scarf worn over shoulders. **2** strip of silk etc. worn similarly by priest.
  ■ **1** cape, shawl, wrap.

stole[2] *past* of STEAL.

stolen *past participle* of STEAL.

stolid /'stɒlɪd/ *adjective* not easily excited or moved; impassive, unemotional. □ **stolidity** /-'lɪdɪtɪ/ *noun*. **stolidly** *adverb*.
  ■ bovine, dull, heavy, immovable, impassive, lumpish, phlegmatic, stoical, unemotional, unimaginative, wooden.

stomach /'stʌmək/ *noun* **1** internal organ in which food is digested. **2** lower front of body. **3** (usually + *for*) appetite, inclination, etc. ● *verb* (usually in negative) endure. □ **stomach-ache** pain in stomach. **stomach pump** syringe for forcing liquid etc. into or out of stomach.
  ■ *noun* **2** abdomen, belly, *slang* gut, *colloquial* insides, paunch, pot belly, *colloquial* tummy.
  ● *verb* see TOLERATE 2,3. □ **stomach-ache** colic, *colloquial* collywobbles, gripes, *colloquial* tummy-ache.

stomp *verb* tread or stamp heavily. ● *noun* lively jazz dance with heavy stamping.

stone *noun* **1** solid non-metallic mineral matter; rock. **2** small piece of this. **3** stone as material for building etc. **4** piece of shaped stone, esp. as monument. **5** hard case of kernel in some fruits. **6** hard morbid concretion in body. **7** (*plural* same) unit of weight (14 lb, 6.35 kg). **8** precious stone. ● *verb* (**-ning**) **1** pelt with stones. **2** remove stones from (fruit). □ **Stone Age** prehistoric period when weapons and tools were made of stone. **stone-cold** completely cold. **stone-cold sober** completely sober. **stonecrop** succulent rock plant. **stone-dead** completely dead. **stone-deaf** completely deaf. **stone fruit** fruit with flesh enclosing stone. **stoneground** (of flour) ground with millstones. **stone's throw** short distance. **stonewall 1** obstruct with evasive answers etc. **2** *Cricket* bat with excessive caution. **stoneware** impermeable and partly vitrified but opaque ceramic ware. **stonewashed** (esp. of denim) washed with abrasives to give worn or faded look. **stonework** masonry.
  ■ *noun* **2** cobble, pebble, *US* rock; (*stones*) gravel, scree, shingle. **3** block, flagstone, sett, slab. **4** gravestone, headstone, memorial, monolith, obelisk, tablet, tombstone. **5** pip, seed. **8** see JEWEL *noun* 1.

stoned *adjective slang* drunk; drugged.

stony *adjective* (**-ier**, **-iest**) **1** full of stones. **2** hard, rigid. **3** unfeeling, unresponsive. □ **stony-broke** *slang* entirely without money. □ **stonily** *adverb*.
  ■ **1** pebbly, rocky, rough, shingly. **3** adamant, chilly, cold, cold-hearted, expressionless, frigid, hard, hard-boiled, heartless, hostile, icy, indifferent, insensitive, merciless, pitiless, steely, stony-hearted, uncaring, unemotional, unfeeling, unforgiving, unfriendly, unresponsive, unsympathetic.

stood *past & past participle* of STAND.

stooge *colloquial noun* **1** person acting as butt or foil, esp. for comedian. **2** assistant or subordinate, esp. for unpleasant work. **3** person controlled by another. ● *verb* (**-ging**) **1** (+ *for*) act as stooge for. **2** (+ *about*, *around*, etc.) move about aimlessly.
  ■ *noun* **1** butt, dupe, *slang* fall guy, foil, straight man. **3** cat's-paw, lackey, puppet.

stool /stuːl/ *noun* **1** single seat without back or arms. **2** footstool. **3** (usually in *plural*) faeces. □ **stool-pigeon 1** person acting as decoy. **2** police informer.

stoop *verb* **1** bend down. **2** stand or walk with shoulders habitually bent forward. **3** (+ *to do*) condescend to. **4** (+ *to*) descend to (shameful act). ● *noun* stooping posture.
  ■ *verb* **1** bend, bow, crouch, duck, kneel, lean, squat. **2** hunch one's shoulders. **3, 4** condescend, degrade oneself, deign, descend, humble oneself, lower oneself, sink.

stop *verb* (**-pp-**) **1** put an end to progress, motion, or operation of; discontinue. **2** effectively hinder or prevent. **3** come to an end. **4** cease from motion, speaking, or action. **5** defeat. **6** *colloquial* remain; stay for short time. **7** (often + *up*) block or close up (hole, leak, etc.). **8** not permit or supply as usual. **9** instruct bank to withhold payment on (cheque). **10** fill (tooth). **11** press (violin etc. string) to obtain required pitch. ● *noun* **1** stopping, being stopped. **2** place where bus, train, etc. regularly stops. **3** full stop. **4** device for stopping motion at particular point. **5** change of pitch effected by stopping string. **6** (in organ) row of pipes of one character. **7** knob etc. operating these. **8** (in camera etc.) diaphragm. **9** effective diameter of lens. **10** device for reducing this. **11** plosive sound. □ **pull out all the stops** make extreme effort. **stopcock** externally operated valve regulating flow through pipe etc. **stopgap** temporary substitute. **stop off, over** break one's journey; **stopover** break in journey. **stop press** late news inserted in newspaper after printing has begun. **stopwatch** watch that can be instantly started and stopped, used in timing of races etc. □ **stoppable** *adjective*.
  ■ *verb* **1** break off, call a halt to, *formal* cease, conclude, cut off, desist from, end, finish, halt, *colloquial* knock off, leave off, *colloquial* pack in, pause, put an end to, put a stop to, *US* quit, refrain from, rest from, suspend, terminate. **2** arrest, bar, block, check, curb, cut off, delay, detain, frustrate, hamper, hinder, hold up,

immobilize, impede, intercept, interrupt, nip in the bud, obstruct, put a stop to, stanch, stem, suppress, thwart. **3** be over, *formal* cease, come to an end, finish, peter out. **4** come to rest, draw up, halt, pull up. **6** have a holiday, remain, rest, sojourn, spend time, stay, visit. **7** block, bung up, close, fill in, plug, seal. ● *noun* **1** ban, break, cessation, close, conclusion, end, finish, halt, pause, rest, standstill, stopover, stoppage, termination. **2** destination, stage, station, stopping place, terminus. □ **stopover** break, sojourn, stay, stop, visit.

stoppage *noun* **1** interruption of work due to strike etc. **2** (in *plural*) sum deducted from pay, for tax, etc. **3** condition of being blocked or stopped.

stopper *noun* plug for closing bottle etc.
■ bung, cork, plug.

storage /'stɔːrɪdʒ/ *noun* **1** storing of goods etc. **2** method of, space for, or cost of storing. □ **storage battery, cell** one for storing electricity. **storage heater** electric heater releasing heat stored outside peak hours.

store *noun* **1** quantity of something kept ready for use. **2** (in *plural*) articles gathered for particular purpose. **3** (in *plural*) supply of, or place for keeping, these. **4** department store. **5** *esp. US* shop. **6** (often in *plural*) shop selling basic necessities. **7** warehouse for keeping furniture etc. temporarily. **8** device in computer for keeping retrievable data. ● *verb* (**-ring**) **1** (often + *up, away*) accumulate for future use. **2** put (furniture etc.) in a store. **3** stock or provide with something useful. **4** keep (data) for retrieval. □ **in store 1** in reserve. **2** to come. **3** (+ *for*) awaiting. **storehouse** storage place. **storekeeper 1** person in charge of stores. **2** *US* shopkeeper. **storeroom** storage room.

■ *noun* **1** accumulation, cache, fund, hoard, quantity, reserve, reservoir, stock, stockpile, supply. **2** (*stores*) see PROVISION 2. **3** see STOREHOUSE. **4–6** outlet, retailer, shop, supermarket. ● *verb* **1** accumulate, aggregate, deposit, hoard, keep, lay by, lay in, lay up, preserve, put away, reserve, save, set aside, *colloquial* stash away, stockpile, stock up, stow away. □ **storehouse** depository, depot, repository, stockroom, storage, store, storeroom, stores, warehouse.

storey /'stɔːrɪ/ *noun* (*plural* **-s**) rooms etc. on one level of building.
■ deck, floor, level, stage, tier.

stork *noun* long-legged usually white wading bird.

storm *noun* **1** violent disturbance of atmosphere with high winds and usually thunder, rain, or snow. **2** violent disturbance in human affairs. **3** (+ *of*) shower of missiles or blows. **4** (+ *of*) outbreak of applause, hisses, etc. **5** assault on fortified place. ● *verb* **1** attack or capture by storm. **2** rush violently. **3** rage; be violent. **4** bluster. □ **storm centre 1** comparatively calm centre of cyclonic storm. **2** centre round which

controversy etc. rages. **storm cloud** heavy rain cloud. **storm troops 1** shock troops. **2** *historical* Nazi political militia. **take by storm 1** capture by direct assault. **2** quickly captivate.

■ *noun* **1** blizzard, cloudburst, cyclone, deluge, dust storm, electrical storm, gale, hailstorm, hurricane, mistral, monsoon, rainstorm, sandstorm, simoom, sirocco, snowstorm, squall, tempest, thunderstorm, tornado, typhoon, whirlwind. **2** see TUMULT. **3** barrage, outbreak, outburst, shower. **5** see ATTACK *noun* 1. ● *verb* **1** see ATTACK *verb* 1.

stormy *adjective* (**-ier**, **-iest**) **1** of or affected by storms. **2** (of wind etc.) violent. **3** full of angry feeling or outbursts. □ **stormily** *adverb*.
■ **2** blustery, choppy, gusty, raging, rough, squally, tempestuous, thundery, turbulent, violent, wild, windy. **3** fierce, furious, tempestuous, tumultuous, turbulent, vehement, violent, wild.

story /'stɔːrɪ/ *noun* (*plural* **-ies**) **1** account of real or imaginary events; tale, anecdote. **2** history of person, institution, etc. **3** plot of novel, play, etc. **4** article in newspaper. **5** material for this. **6** *colloquial* fib. □ **storyline** narrative or plot of novel, play, etc. **storyteller 1** person who tells or writes stories. **2** *colloquial* liar. **storytelling** *noun* & *adjective*.

■ **1** account, allegory, anecdote, chronicle, epic, fable, fiction, history, legend, myth, narration, narrative, novel, parable, recital, record, romance, saga, tale, *colloquial* yarn. **3** plot, scenario. **4** article, dispatch, exclusive, feature, news item, piece, report, scoop. **6** falsehood, fib, lie, *colloquial* tall story, untruth. □ **storyteller** author, biographer, narrator, raconteur, teller.

stoup /stuːp/ *noun* **1** basin for holy water. **2** *archaic* flagon, beaker.

stout /staʊt/ *adjective* **1** rather fat, corpulent. **2** thick, strong. **3** brave, resolute. ● *noun* strong dark beer. □ **stout-hearted** courageous. □ **stoutly** *adverb*. **stoutness** *noun*.

■ *adjective* **1** beefy, big, bulky, burly, chubby, corpulent, fat, fleshy, heavy, *colloquial* hulking, overweight, plump, portly, solid, stocky, strapping, thickset, tubby, well built. **2** durable, robust, sound, strong, sturdy, substantial, thick, tough. **3** bold, brave, courageous, fearless, gallant, heroic, intrepid, plucky, resolute, spirited, valiant.

stove[1] /stəʊv/ *noun* closed apparatus burning fuel or using electricity etc. for heating or cooking. □ **stove-pipe** pipe carrying smoke and gases from stove to chimney.
■ boiler, cooker, fire, furnace, heater, oven, range.

stove[2] *past & past participle* of STAVE.

stow /stəʊ/ *verb* pack (goods, cargo, etc.) tidily and compactly. □ **stow away 1** place (thing) out of the way. **2** hide oneself on ship etc. to travel free. **stowaway** person who stows away.
■ load, pack, put away, *colloquial* stash away, store.

stowage *noun* **1** stowing. **2** place for this.

straddle /'stræd(ə)l/ *verb* (**-ling**) **1** sit or stand across (thing) with legs wide apart. **2** be situated on both sides of. **3** spread legs wide apart.

strafe /strɑːf/ *verb* (**-fing**) bombard; attack with gunfire.

straggle /'stræg(ə)l/ *verb* (**-ling**) **1** lack compactness or tidiness. **2** be dispersed or sporadic. **3** trail behind in race etc. ● *noun* straggling group. □ **straggler** *noun*. **straggling** *adjective*. **straggly** *adjective*.

■ *verb* **1** dangle, sprawl, spread out. **2** be dispersed, be scattered, scatter, spread out, stray, string out. **3** dawdle, drift, fall behind, lag, loiter, trail. □ **straggling** see DISORGANIZE 2, LOOSE *adjective* 1,2.

straight /streɪt/ *adjective* **1** not curved; bent, crooked, or curly. **2** successive, uninterrupted. **3** ordered; level; tidy. **4** honest, candid. **5** (of thinking etc.) logical. **6** (of theatre, music, etc.) not popular or comic. **7** unmodified. **8** (of a drink) undiluted. **9** *colloquial* (of person etc.) conventional, respectable. **10** *colloquial* heterosexual. ● *noun* **1** straight part, esp. concluding stretch of racetrack. **2** straight condition. **3** *colloquial* conventional person. **4** *colloquial* heterosexual. ● *adverb* **1** in straight line; direct. **2** in right direction. **3** correctly. □ **go straight** (of criminal) become honest. **straight away** immediately. **straight face** intentionally expressionless face. **straight fight** *Politics* contest between two candidates only. **straightforward 1** honest, frank. **2** (of task etc.) simple. **straightforwardness** *noun*. **straight man** comedian's stooge. **straight off** *colloquial* without hesitation. □ **straightness** *noun*.

■ *adjective* **1** direct, linear, unbending, undeviating, unswerving. **2** consecutive, continuous, non-stop, sustained, unbroken, uninterrupted, unrelieved. **3** aligned, even, flat, level, neat, orderly, organized, regular, right, shipshape, smooth, sorted out, spruce, square, tidy, true. **4** see STRAIGHTFORWARD 1. □ **straight away** at once, directly, immediately, instantly, now, without delay. **straightforward 1** blunt, candid, direct, forthright, frank, genuine, honest, lucid, open, plain, sincere, straight, truthful. **2** easy, simple, uncomplicated.

straighten *verb* **1** (often + *out*) make or become straight. **2** (+ *up*) stand erect after bending.

■ **1** disentangle, rearrange, sort out, tidy, unbend, uncurl, unravel, untangle, untwist.

strain[1] *verb* **1** stretch tightly; make or become taut or tense. **2** injure or weaken by overuse or excessive demands. **3** exercise (oneself, one's senses, thing, etc.) intensely; press to extremes. **4** strive intensely. **5** distort from true intention or meaning. **6** clear (liquid) of solid matter by passing it through sieve etc. ● *noun* **1** act of straining. **2** force exerted in this. **3** injury caused by straining muscle etc. **4** severe mental or physical demand or exertion. **5** snatch of music or poetry. **6** tone or tendency in speech or writing.

■ *verb* **1** pull, stretch, tauten, tighten, tug. **2** damage, exhaust, hurt, injure, overtax, overwork,

pull, rick, sprain, tear, tire out, twist, weaken, wear out, weary, wrench. **3** exercise, push to the limit, stretch, tax. **4** attempt, endeavour, exert oneself, labour, make an effort, strive, struggle, toil, try. **6** drain, draw off, filter, percolate, purify, riddle, screen, separate, sieve, sift. ● *noun* **4** anxiety, difficulty, effort, exertion, hardship, pressure, stress, tension, worry.

strain[2] *noun* **1** breed or stock of animals, plants, etc. **2** characteristic tendency.

■ **1** see ANCESTRY.

strained *adjective* **1** constrained, artificial. **2** (of relationship) distrustful, tense. **3** (of interpretation) far-fetched. **4** weary, tense.

■ **1** artificial, constrained, false, forced, insincere, self-conscious, stiff, unnatural. **2** distrustful, embarrassed, tense, uncomfortable, uneasy. **3** far-fetched, incredible, laboured, unlikely, unreasonable. **4** drawn, tense, tired, weary.

strainer *noun* device for straining liquids.

■ colander, filter, riddle, sieve.

strait *noun* **1** (in *singular* or *plural*) narrow channel connecting two large bodies of water. **2** (usually in *plural*) difficulty, distress. □ **strait-jacket 1** strong garment with long sleeves for confining violent prisoner etc. **2** restrictive measures. **strait-laced** puritanical.

straitened /'streɪt(ə)nd/ *adjective* of or marked by poverty.

strand[1] *verb* **1** run aground. **2** (as **stranded** *adjective*) in difficulties, esp. without money or transport. ● *noun esp. poetical* foreshore, beach.

■ *verb* **1** beach, ground, run aground, wreck; (**stranded**) shipwrecked, stuck. **2** (**stranded**) abandoned, deserted, forsaken, helpless, high and dry, marooned.

strand[2] *noun* **1** each of twisted threads or wires making rope, cable, etc. **2** single thread or strip of fibre. **3** lock of hair. **4** element, component.

■ **1, 2** fibre, filament, string, thread, wire.

strange /streɪndʒ/ *adjective* **1** unusual, peculiar, surprising, eccentric. **2** (often + *to*) unfamiliar, foreign. **3** (+ *to*) unaccustomed to. **4** not at ease. □ **strangely** *adverb*. **strangeness** *noun*.

■ **1** abnormal, astonishing, atypical, baffling, bewildering, bizarre, cranky, curious, eccentric, eerie, exceptional, extraordinary, fantastic, funny, grotesque, inexplicable, insoluble, irregular, mysterious, mystifying, odd, out of the ordinary, outré, peculiar, perplexing, puzzling, quaint, queer, rare, remarkable, singular, sinister, surprising, surreal, unaccountable, unaccustomed, uncommon, unconventional, unexpected, unheard-of, *disputed* unique, unnatural, untypical, unusual, *colloquial* weird, zany. **2** alien, different, exotic, foreign, little known, new, novel, outlandish, out of the way, remote, unexplored, unfamiliar, unmapped. **3** (*strange to*) fresh to, new to, unaccustomed to, unfamiliar with, unused to. □ **strangeness** abnormality, bizarreness, eccentricity, eeriness, extraordinariness, irregularity, mysteriousness, novelty, oddity, oddness, outlandishness, peculiarity, quaintness, queerness, rarity, singularity, unconventionality, unfamiliarity.

stranger *noun* **1** person new to particular place or company. **2** (often + *to*) person one does not know.

■ **1** alien, foreigner, guest, newcomer, outsider, visitor.

strangle /'stræŋg(ə)l/ *verb* (**-ling**) **1** squeeze windpipe or neck of, esp. so as to kill. **2** hamper or suppress (movement, cry, etc.). □ **stranglehold 1** deadly grip. **2** complete control. □ **strangler** *noun*.

■ **1** asphyxiate, choke, garrotte, smother, stifle, suffocate, throttle. **2** see SUPPRESS 2.

strangulate /'stræŋgjʊleɪt/ *verb* (**-ting**) compress (vein, intestine, etc.), preventing circulation.

■ bind, compress, constrict, squeeze.

strangulation *noun* **1** strangling, being strangled. **2** strangulating.

■ **1** asphyxiation, garrotting, suffocation.

strap *noun* **1** strip of leather etc., often with buckle, for holding things together etc. **2** narrow strip of fabric forming part of garment. **3** loop for grasping to steady oneself in moving vehicle. ● *verb* (**-pp-**) **1** (often + *down, up*, etc.) secure or bind with strap. **2** beat with strap. □ **straphanger** *colloquial* standing passenger in bus or train. **strap-hang** *verb*. □ **strapless** *adjective*.

■ *noun* **1** band, belt, strop, thong, webbing. ● *verb* **1** see FASTEN 1.

strapping *adjective* large and sturdy.

strata *plural* of STRATUM.

USAGE It is a mistake to use the plural form *strata* when only one stratum is meant.

stratagem /'strætədʒəm/ *noun* **1** cunning plan or scheme. **2** trickery.

■ **1** artifice, device, dodge, manoeuvre, plan, ploy, ruse, scheme, subterfuge, tactic, trick.

strategic /strə'ti:dʒɪk/ *adjective* **1** of or promoting strategy. **2** (of materials) essential in war. **3** (of bombing or weapons) done or for use as longer-term military policy. □ **strategically** *adverb*.

■ **1** calculated, deliberate, politic, tactical.

strategy /'strætɪdʒɪ/ *noun* (*plural* **-ies**) **1** long-term plan or policy. **2** art of war. **3** art of moving troops, ships, aircraft, etc. into favourable positions. □ **strategist** *noun*.

■ **1** approach, design, manoeuvre, method, plan, plot, policy, procedure, programme, scenario, scheme, tactics.

stratify /'strætɪfaɪ/ *verb* (**-ies, -ied**) (esp. as **stratified** *adjective*) arrange in strata, grades, etc. □ **stratification** *noun*.

stratosphere /'strætəsfɪə/ *noun* layer of atmo-

sphere above troposphere, extending to about 50 km from earth's surface.

stratum /'strɑːtəm/ *noun* (*plural* **strata**) **1** layer or set of layers of any deposited substance, esp. of rock. **2** atmospheric layer. **3** social class.

■ **1** layer, seam, thickness, vein.

straw *noun* **1** dry cut stalks of grain. **2** single stalk of straw. **3** thin tube for sucking drink through. **4** insignificant thing. **5** pale yellow colour. □ **clutch at straws** try any remedy in desperation. **straw vote, poll** unofficial ballot as test of opinion.

■ **1** stalks, stubble.

strawberry /'strɔːbərɪ/ *noun* (*plural* **-ies**) **1** pulpy red fruit having surface studded with yellow seeds. **2** plant bearing this. □ **strawberry mark** reddish birthmark.

stray *verb* **1** wander from the right place, from one's companions, etc.; go astray. **2** deviate. ● *noun* strayed animal or person. ● *adjective* **1** strayed, lost. **2** isolated, occasional.

■ *verb* **1** get lost, get separated, go astray, meander, ramble, range, roam, rove, straggle, wander. **2** deviate, digress, diverge, drift, get off the subject, go off at a tangent, veer. ● *adjective* **1** abandoned, homeless, lost, roaming, roving, wandering. **2** accidental, casual, chance, haphazard, isolated, lone, occasional, odd, random, single.

streak *noun* **1** long thin usually irregular line or band, esp. of colour. **2** strain or trait in person's character. **3** spell, period. ● *verb* **1** mark with streaks. **2** move very rapidly. **3** *colloquial* run naked in public.

■ *noun* **1** band, bar, dash, line, mark, score, smear, stain, striation, strip, stripe, stroke, vein. **2** component, element, strain, touch, trace. **3** period, run, series, spate, spell, stretch, time. ● *verb* **1** smear, smudge, stain. **2** dart, dash, flash, fly, gallop, hurtle, rush, *colloquial* scoot, speed, sprint, *colloquial* tear, whip, zoom.

streaky *adjective* (**-ier, -iest**) **1** marked with streaks. **2** (of bacon) with streaks of fat.

■ **1** barred, lined, smeary, smudged, streaked, striated, stripy, veined.

stream *noun* **1** body of running water, esp. small river. **2** current, flow. **3** group of schoolchildren of similar ability taught together. ● *verb* **1** move as stream. **2** run with liquid. **3** be blown in wind. **4** emit stream of (blood etc.). **5** arrange (schoolchildren) in streams. □ **on stream** in operation or production.

■ *noun* **1** beck, brook, *Scottish* burn, channel, freshet, rill, river, rivulet, watercourse. **2** cascade, cataract, current, deluge, effluence, flood, flow, fountain, gush, jet, outpouring, rush, spate, spurt, surge, tide, torrent. ● *verb* **1** cascade, course, deluge, flood, flow, gush, issue, pour, run, spill, spout, spurt, squirt, surge, well.

streamer *noun* **1** long narrow strip of ribbon or paper. **2** long narrow flag.

■ **2** banner, flag, pennant, pennon.

streamline *verb* (**-ning**) (often as **streamlined** *adjective*) **1** give (vehicle etc.) form which presents least resistance to motion. **2** make simple or more efficient.
■ (**streamlined**) **1** aerodynamic, elegant, graceful, sleek, smooth. **2 see** EFFICIENT 1.

street *noun* **1** road in city, town, or village. **2** this with buildings on each side. □ **on the streets** living by prostitution. **streetcar** *US* tram. **street credibility, cred** *slang* acceptability within fashionable urban subculture. **street light** (also **street lamp**) light or lamp for illuminating road etc. **streetwalker** prostitute seeking customers in street. **streetwise** knowing how to survive modern urban life.
■ avenue, road, roadway, terrace.

strength *noun* **1** being strong; degree or manner of this. **2** person or thing giving strength. **3** number of people present or available. □ **from strength to strength** with ever-increasing success. **on the strength of** on basis of.
■ **1** backbone, brawn, capacity, commitment, condition, courage, determination, energy, firmness, fitness, force, *colloquial* grit, health, might, muscle, perseverance, persistence, power, resilience, resolution, resolve, robustness, sinew, spirit, stamina, stoutness, sturdiness, tenacity, toughness, vigour.

strengthen *verb* make or become stronger.
■ back up, bolster, boost, brace, build up, buttress, consolidate, corroborate, encourage, enhance, fortify, harden, hearten, increase, justify, prop up, reinforce, stiffen, substantiate, support, tone up, toughen.

strenuous /'strenjʊəs/ *adjective* **1** using or requiring great effort. **2** energetic. □ **strenuously** *adverb*.
■ **1** arduous, back-breaking, burdensome, demanding, difficult, exhausting, gruelling, hard, Herculean, laborious, punishing, stiff, taxing, tough, uphill. **2** active, committed, determined, dogged, dynamic, eager, energetic, indefatigable, pertinacious, resolute, spirited, strong, tenacious, tireless, unremitting, vigorous, zealous.

streptococcus /streptə'kɒkəs/ *noun* (*plural* **-cocci** /-kaɪ/) bacterium causing serious infections. □ **streptococcal** *adjective*.

streptomycin /streptəʊ'maɪsɪn/ *noun* antibiotic effective against many disease-producing bacteria.

stress *noun* **1** pressure, tension. **2** quantity measuring this. **3** physical or mental strain. **4** emphasis. ● *verb* **1** emphasize. **2** subject to stress.
■ *noun* **1** pressure, strain, tension. **3** anxiety, difficulty, distress, hardship, pressure, strain, tenseness, tension, trauma, worry. **4** accent, accentuation, beat, emphasis, importance, significance, underlining, urgency, weight. ● *verb* **1** accent, accentuate, assert, draw attention to, emphasize, feature, highlight, insist on, mark,

repeat, spotlight, underline, underscore. **2** burden, distress, overstretch, pressure, pressurize, push to the limit, tax, weigh down.

stressful *adjective* causing stress.
■ anxious, difficult, taxing, tense, tiring, traumatic, worrying.

stretch *verb* **1** draw, be drawn, or be able to be drawn out in length or size. **2** make or become taut. **3** place or lie at full length or spread out. **4** extend limbs and tighten muscles after being relaxed. **5** have specified length or extension, extend. **6** strain or exert extremely. **7** exaggerate. ● *noun* **1** continuous extent, expanse, or period. **2** stretching, being stretched. **3** *colloquial* period of imprisonment, service, etc. □ **at a stretch** in one period. **stretch a point** agree to something not normally allowed. **stretch one's legs** exercise oneself by walking. **stretch out 1** extend (limb etc.). **2** last; prolong. □ **stretchable** *adjective*. **stretchy** *adjective* (**-ier, -iest**).
■ *verb* **1** broaden, crane (*one's neck*), dilate, distend, draw out, elongate, enlarge, expand, extend, flatten out, inflate, lengthen, open out, pull out, spread out, swell, widen. **2** tauten, tighten. **5** be unbroken, continue, disappear, extend, go, reach out, spread. **6** overextend, overtax, push to the limit, strain, tax. ● *noun* **1** of *country* area, distance, expanse, length, span, spread, sweep, tract; *of time* period, spell, stint, term, time. **3** spell, stint, term, time.

stretcher *noun* **1** two poles with canvas etc. between for carrying person in lying position. **2** brick etc. laid along face of wall.

strew /struː/ *verb* (*past participle* **strewn** or **strewed**) **1** scatter over surface. **2** (usually + *with*) spread (surface) with scattered things.
■ disperse, distribute, litter, scatter, spread, sprinkle.

'strewth = 'STRUTH.

striated /straɪ'eɪtɪd/ *adjective* marked with slight ridges or furrows. □ **striation** *noun*.

stricken /'strɪkən/ *archaic past participle* of STRIKE. ● *adjective* affected or overcome (with illness, misfortune, etc.).

strict *adjective* **1** precisely limited or defined; without deviation. **2** requiring complete obedience or exact performance. □ **strictly** *adverb*. **strictness** *noun*.
■ **1** absolute, accurate, binding, complete, correct, defined, exact, hard and fast, inflexible, invariable, meticulous, perfect, precise, right, rigid, scrupulous, stringent, tight, unchangeable. **2** austere, authoritarian, autocratic, firm, harsh, merciless, no-nonsense, rigorous, severe, stern, stringent, tyrannical, uncompromising.

stricture /'strɪktʃə/ *noun* (usually in *plural*; often + *on, upon*) critical or censorious remark.

stride *verb* (**-ding**; *past* **strode**; *past participle* **stridden** /'strɪd(ə)n/) **1** walk with long firm steps. **2** cross with one step. **3** bestride. ● *noun* **1** single long step. **2** length of this. **3** gait as determined by length of stride. **4** (usually in *plural*) progress.

□ **take in one's stride** manage easily.

■ *verb* **1** see WALK *verb* 1–5. ● *noun* **1, 2** pace, step.

strident /ˈstraɪd(ə)nt/ *adjective* loud and harsh. □ **stridency** *noun*. **stridently** *adverb*.

■ clamorous, discordant, grating, harsh, jarring, loud, noisy, raucous, screeching, shrill, unmusical.

strife *noun* conflict, struggle.

■ animosity, arguing, bickering, competition, conflict, discord, disharmony, dissension, enmity, fighting, friction, hostility, quarrelling, rivalry, unfriendliness.

strike *verb* (**-king**; *past* **struck**; *past participle* **struck** or *archaic* **stricken**) **1** deliver (blow). **2** inflict blow on. **3** come or bring sharply into contact with. **4** propel or divert with blow. **5** (cause to) penetrate. **6** ignite (match) or produce (sparks etc.) by rubbing. **7** make (coin) by stamping. **8** produce (musical note) by striking. **9** (of clock) indicate (time) with chime etc. **10** (of time) be so indicated. **11** attack suddenly. **12** (of disease) afflict. **13** cause to become suddenly. **14** reach, achieve. **15** agree on (bargain). **16** assume (attitude). **17** find (oil etc.) by drilling. **18** come to attention of or appear to. **19** (of employees) engage in strike. **20** lower or take down (flag, tent, etc.). **21** take specified direction. ● *noun* **1** act of striking. **2** employees' organized refusal to work until grievance is remedied. **3** similar refusal to participate. **4** sudden find or success. **5** attack, esp. from air. □ **on strike** taking part in industrial etc. strike. **strikebreaker** person working or employed in place of strikers. **strike home** deal effective blow. **strike off 1** remove with stroke. **2** delete. **strike out 1** hit out. **2** act vigorously. **3** delete. **strike up 1** start (acquaintance, conversation, etc.), esp. casually. **2** begin playing (tune etc.).

■ *verb* **1, 2** beat, hammer, hit, knock, rap, smack, thump, *colloquial* whack. **3** bang against, bang into, collide with, hit, knock into, run into, smash into. **4** drive, hit, impel, propel, *colloquial* swipe. **6** ignite, light. **9** chime, ring, sound. **11** affect, afflict, assail, attack, beset, hit. **18** dawn on, hit, impress, occur to. **19** come out, *colloquial* down tools, stop work, take industrial action, walk out, withdraw labour, work to rule. **20** dismantle, lower, pull down, remove, take down. ● *noun* **2** industrial action, stoppage, walk-out. **5** assault, attack, bombardment.

striker *noun* **1** employee on strike. **2** *Football* attacking player positioned forward.

striking *adjective* impressive; noticeable. □ **strikingly** *adverb*.

■ affecting, amazing, arresting, conspicuous, distinctive, extraordinary, glaring, imposing, impressive, memorable, noticeable, obvious, out of the ordinary, outstanding, prominent, showy, *colloquial* stunning, telling, unmistakable, unusual.

string *noun* **1** twine, narrow cord. **2** length of this or similar material used for tying, holding together, pulling, forming head of racket, etc. **3** piece of catgut, wire, etc. on musical instrument, producing note by vibration. **4** (in *plural*) stringed instruments in orchestra etc. **5** (in *plural*) condition or complication attached to offer etc. **6** set of things strung together. **7** tough side of bean-pod etc. ● *verb* (*past & past participle* **strung**) **1** fit with string(s). **2** thread on string. **3** arrange in or as string. **4** remove strings from (bean-pod etc.). □ **string along** *colloquial* **1** deceive. **2** (often + *with*) keep company (with). **string-course** raised horizontal band of bricks etc. on building. **string up 1** hang up on strings etc. **2** kill by hanging. **3** (usually as **strung up** *adjective*) make tense.

■ *noun* **1** cable, cord, fibre, line, rope, twine. **6** chain, file, line, procession, progression, queue, row, sequence, series, stream, succession, train. ● *verb* **3** connect, join, line up, link.

stringed *adjective* (of musical instrument) having strings.

stringent /ˈstrɪndʒ(ə)nt/ *adjective* (of rules etc.) strict, precise. □ **stringency** *noun*. **stringently** *adverb*.

stringer *noun* **1** longitudinal structural member in framework, esp. of ship or aircraft. **2** *colloquial* freelance newspaper correspondent.

stringy *adjective* (**-ier, -iest**) like string; fibrous.

■ chewy, fibrous, gristly, sinewy, tough.

strip[1] *verb* (**-pp-**) **1** (often + *of*) remove clothes or covering from; undress. **2** (often + *off*) undress oneself. **3** (often + *of*) deprive (person) of property or titles. **4** leave bare. **5** (often + *down*) remove accessory fittings of or take apart (machine etc.). **6** remove old paint etc. from (surface) with solvent. **7** damage thread of (screw) or teeth of (gearwheel). ● *noun* **1** act of stripping, esp. in striptease. **2** *colloquial* distinctive outfit worn by sports team. □ **strip club** club where striptease is performed. **striptease** entertainment in which performer slowly and erotically undresses.

■ *verb* **1, 4** bare, clear, defoliate, denude, *literary* disrobe, divest, *esp. literary* doff, excoriate, expose, flay, lay bare, peel, skin, uncover, undress. **2** bare oneself, *literary* disrobe, divest oneself, expose oneself, get undressed, *colloquial* peel off, uncover oneself, undress. **5** (*strip down*) see DISMANTLE 1.

strip[2] *noun* long narrow piece. □ **strip cartoon** comic strip. **strip light** tubular fluorescent lamp. **tear (person) off a strip** *colloquial* rebuke.

■ band, belt, fillet, lath, line, ribbon, shred, slat, sliver, stripe, swath.

stripe *noun* **1** long narrow band or strip differing in colour or texture from surface on either side of it. **2** *Military* chevron etc. denoting military rank. □ **stripy** *adjective* (**-ier, -iest**).

■ **1** band, bar, chevron, line, ribbon, streak, striation, strip, stroke, swath.

striped *adjective* having stripes.

■ banded, barred, lined, streaky, striated, stripy.

stripling /ˈstrɪplɪŋ/ *noun* youth not yet fully grown.

stripper *noun* **1** device or solvent for removing paint etc. **2** performer of striptease.

strive *verb* (**-ving**; *past* **strove** /strəʊv/; *past participle* **striven** /ˈstrɪv(ə)n/) **1** try hard. **2** (often + *with*, *against*) struggle.

> ■ **1** attempt, do one's best, endeavour, make an effort, strain, struggle, try. **2** see FIGHT *verb* 1;3.

strobe *noun colloquial* stroboscope.

stroboscope /ˈstrəʊbəskəʊp/ *noun* lamp producing regular intermittent flashes. □ **stroboscopic** /-ˈskɒp-/ *adjective*.

strode *past* of STRIDE.

stroke *noun* **1** act of striking. **2** sudden disabling attack caused esp. by thrombosis. **3** action or movement, esp. as one of series or in game etc. **4** slightest action. **5** single complete action of moving wing, oar, etc. **6** whole motion of piston either way. **7** mode of moving limbs in swimming. **8** single mark made by pen, paint brush, etc. **9** detail contributing to general effect. **10** sound of striking clock. **11** oarsman nearest stern, who sets time of stroke. **12** act or spell of stroking. ● *verb* (**-king**) **1** pass hand gently along surface of (hair, fur, etc.). **2** act as stroke of (boat, crew). □ **at a stroke** by a single action. **on the stroke of** punctually at. **stroke of (good) luck** unexpected fortunate event.

> ■ *noun* **1** blow, hit, knock, *colloquial* swipe, *colloquial* whack. **2** apoplexy, attack, embolism, fit, seizure, spasm, thrombosis. **3** action, move, movement. **8** flourish, gesture, line, mark, movement, sweep. ● *verb* **1** caress, fondle, massage, pass one's hand over, pat, pet, rub, soothe, touch.

stroll /strəʊl/ *verb* walk in leisurely fashion. ● *noun* leisurely walk. □ **strolling players** *historical* actors etc. going from place to place performing.

> ■ *verb & noun* amble, meander, saunter, walk, wander.

strong *adjective* (**stronger** /ˈstrɒŋgə/, **strongest** /-gɪst/) **1** physically powerful; vigorous, robust; performed with muscular strength. **2** difficult to damage, capture, overcome, escape from, etc. **3** assertive; determined; steadfast. **4** (of suspicion, belief, etc.) firmly held; intensely felt. **5** powerfully affecting senses or mind etc. **6** (of argument, evidence, etc.) convincing. **7** (of drink, solution, etc.) with large proportion of alcohol etc. **8** powerful in numbers or equipment etc. **9** (of measure) drastic. **10** (of verb) forming inflections by vowel change in root syllable. ● *adverb* strongly. □ **come on strong** act forcefully. **going strong** *colloquial* thriving. **strongarm** using force. **strongbox** strongly made box for valuables. **stronghold 1** fortress. **2** centre of support for a cause etc. **strong language** swearing. **strong-minded** determined. **strongroom** strongly built room for valuables. **strong suit** thing in which one excels. □ **strongish** *adjective*. **strongly** *adverb*.

> ■ *adjective* **1** athletic, beefy, brawny, burly, fit, hale and hearty, hardy, hefty, husky, mighty, muscular, powerful, robust, sinewy, stalwart, strapping, sturdy, tough, vigorous, well built, wiry. **2** durable, hard, hard-wearing, heavy-duty, impregnable, indestructible, permanent, reinforced, resilient, robust, solid, sound, stout, substantial, thick, unbreakable, well made. **3** assertive, assiduous, committed, decisive, dependable, determined, dictatorial, doctrinaire, dogmatic, domineering, dynamic, energetic, fearless, forceful, formidable, independent, obstinate, positive, reliable, resolute, stalwart, steadfast, stout, strong-minded, strong-willed, stubborn, tenacious, tyrannical, unswerving, unwavering, vigorous. **4** deep-rooted, deep-seated, earnest, enthusiastic, fervent, fierce, firm, genuine, intense, keen, loyal, passionate, rabid, sedulous, staunch, true, vehement, zealous. **5** (*strong colour*, *light*) bright, brilliant, clear, dazzling, garish, glaring, vivid; (*strong taste*, *smell*) concentrated, highly-flavoured, hot, intense, noticeable, obvious, overpowering, prominent, pronounced, pungent, sharp, spicy, unmistakable. **6** clear-cut, cogent, compelling, convincing, evident, forceful, influential, persuasive, plain, solid, telling, undisputed. **7** alcoholic, concentrated, intoxicating, potent, undiluted. **8** formidable, invincible, large, numerous, powerful, unconquerable, well armed, well equipped, well trained. **9** aggressive, Draconian, drastic, extreme, harsh, high-handed, ruthless, severe, tough, unflinching, violent. □ **stronghold 1** bastion, bulwark, castle, citadel, fastness, fort, fortification, fortress, garrison.

strontium /ˈstrɒntɪəm/ *noun* soft silver-white metallic element. □ **strontium-90** radioactive isotope of this.

strop *noun* **1** device, esp. strip of leather, for sharpening razors. **2** *colloquial* bad temper. ● *verb* (**-pp-**) sharpen on or with strop.

stroppy /ˈstrɒpɪ/ *adjective* (**-ier**, **-iest**) *colloquial* bad-tempered; awkward to deal with.

strove *past* of STRIVE.

struck *past & past participle* of STRIKE.

structuralism *noun* doctrine that structure rather than function is important. □ **structuralist** *noun & adjective*.

structure /ˈstrʌktʃə/ *noun* **1** constructed unit, esp. building. **2** way in which thing is constructed. **3** framework. ● *verb* (**-ring**) give structure to; organize. □ **structural** *adjective*. **structurally** *adverb*.

> ■ *noun* **1** building, complex, construction, edifice, erection, pile, superstructure. **2** arrangement, composition, configuration, constitution, design, fabric, form, formation, make-up, order, organization, plan, shape, system. **3** see FRAMEWORK 1–2. ● *verb* arrange, build, construct, design, form, frame, organize, shape, systematize.

strudel /ˈstruːd(ə)l/ *noun* thin leaved pastry filled esp. with apple and baked.

struggle /ˈstrʌg(ə)l/ *verb* (**-ling**) **1** violently try to get free. **2** (often + *for*, *to do*) make great efforts under difficulties. **3** (+ *with*, *against*) fight against. **4** (+ *along*, *up*, etc.) make one's way with difficulty. **5** (esp. as **struggling** *adjective*) have difficulty in getting recognition or a living. ● *noun* **1** act or period of struggling; vigorous effort. **2** hard or confused contest.

■ *verb* **1** squirm, strain, wriggle, writhe. **2** endeavour, exert oneself, labour, make an effort, strain, strive, toil, try, work hard, wrestle. **3** see FIGHT *verb* 1;3. **4** flounder, scramble, stumble. ● *noun* **1** challenge, effort, endeavour, exertion, labour.

strum *verb* (**-mm-**) (often + *on*) play on (stringed or keyboard instrument), esp. carelessly or unskilfully. ● *noun* strumming sound.

strumpet /'strʌmpɪt/ *noun archaic* prostitute.

strung *past & past participle* of STRING.

strut *noun* **1** bar in framework to resist pressure. **2** strutting gait. ● *verb* (**-tt-**) **1** walk in stiff pompous way. **2** brace with strut(s).

'struth /struːθ/ *interjection* (also **'strewth**) *colloquial: exclamation of surprise.*

strychnine /'strɪkniːn/ *noun* highly poisonous alkaloid.

stub *noun* **1** remnant of pencil, cigarette, etc. **2** stump. **3** counterfoil of cheque, receipt, etc. ● *verb* (**-bb-**) **1** strike (one's toe) against something. **2** (usually + *out*) extinguish (cigarette etc.) by pressing lighted end against something.

■ *noun* **1**, **2** butt, end, remains, remnant, stump. ● *verb* **1** see HIT *verb* 1.

stubble /'stʌb(ə)l/ *noun* **1** cut stalks of corn etc. left in ground after harvest. **2** short stiff hair or bristles, esp. on unshaven face. □ **stubbly** *adjective.*

■ **1** stalks, straw. **2** beard, bristles, five o'clock shadow, hair, roughness. □ **stubbly** bristly, prickly, rough, unshaven.

stubborn /'stʌbən/ *adjective* obstinate; inflexible. □ **stubbornly** *adverb.* **stubbornness** *noun.*

■ defiant, determined, difficult, disobedient, dogged, dogmatic, headstrong, inflexible, intractable, intransigent, mulish, obdurate, obstinate, opinionated, persistent, pertinacious, pig-headed, recalcitrant, refractory, rigid, self-willed, tenacious, uncompromising, uncontrollable, uncooperative, unmanageable, unreasonable, unyielding, wayward, wilful.

stubby *adjective* (**-ier**, **-iest**) short and thick.

stucco /'stʌkəʊ/ *noun* (*plural* **-es**) plaster or cement for coating walls or moulding into architectural decorations. ● *verb* (**-es**, **-ed**) coat with stucco.

stuck *past & past participle* of STICK². ● *adjective* **1** not able to move. **2** baffled. □ **get stuck into** *slang* start in earnest. **stuck for** at a loss for; needing. **stuck-up** *colloquial* conceited, snobbish. **stuck with** *colloquial* unable to get rid of.

■ *adjective* **1** bogged down, cemented, fast, fastened, firm, fixed, glued, immovable. **2** baffled, beaten, held up, stumped, stymied. □ **stuck-up** arrogant, *colloquial* big-headed, bumptious, *colloquial* cocky, conceited, condescending, *colloquial* high and mighty, patronizing, proud, self-important, snobbish, *colloquial* snooty, supercilious, *colloquial* toffee-nosed.

stud¹ *noun* **1** large projecting nail, knob, etc. as surface ornament. **2** double button, esp. for use in shirt-front. ● *verb* (**-dd-**) **1** set with studs. **2** (as **studded** *adjective*) (+ *with*) thickly set or strewn with.

stud² *noun* **1** number of horses kept for breeding etc. **2** place where these are kept. **3** stallion. □ **at stud** (of stallion) hired out for breeding. **stud-book** book giving pedigrees of horses. **stud-farm** place where horses are bred. **stud poker** poker with betting after dealing of cards face up.

student /'stjuːd(ə)nt/ *noun* person who is studying, esp. at place of higher or further education. □ **studentship** *noun.*

■ apprentice, disciple, learner, postgraduate, pupil, scholar, schoolchild, trainee, undergraduate.

studio /'stjuːdɪəʊ/ *noun* (*plural* **-s**) **1** workroom of sculptor, painter, photographer, etc. **2** place for making films, recordings, or broadcasts. □ **studio couch** couch that can be converted into a bed; **studio flat** one-roomed flat.

studious /'stjuːdɪəs/ *adjective* **1** diligent in study or reading. **2** painstaking. □ **studiously** *adverb.*

■ **1** academic, assiduous, attentive, bookish, brainy, diligent, earnest, hard-working, intellectual, scholarly, thoughtful.

study /'stʌdɪ/ *noun* (*plural* **-ies**) **1** acquiring knowledge, esp. from books. **2** (in *plural*) pursuit of academic knowledge. **3** private room for reading, writing, etc. **4** piece of work, esp. in painting, done as exercise or preliminary experiment. **5** portrayal, esp. in literature, of character, behaviour, etc. **6** *Music* composition designed to develop player's skill. **7** thing worth observing. **8** thing that is or deserves to be investigated. ● *verb* (**-ies**, **-ied**) **1** make study of. **2** scrutinize. **3** devote time and thought to understanding subject etc. or achieving desired result. **4** (as **studied** *adjective*) deliberate; affected.

■ *verb* **1**, **2** analyse, consider, contemplate, enquire into, examine, give attention to, investigate, learn about, look at, peruse, ponder, pore over, read, research, scrutinize, survey, think about, weigh. **3** cram, learn, *slang* mug up, read, *colloquial* swot, work. **4** (**studied**) calculated, conscious, contrived, deliberate, intentional, planned, premeditated.

stuff *noun* **1** material; fabric. **2** substance or things not needing to be specified. **3** particular knowledge or activity. **4** woollen fabric. **5** nonsense. **6** (**the stuff**) *colloquial* supply, esp. of drink or drugs. ● *verb* **1** pack (receptacle) tightly. **2** (+ *in*, *into*) force or cram (thing). **3** fill out skin to restore original shape of (bird, animal, etc.). **4** fill (bird, piece of meat, etc.) with mixture, esp. before cooking. **5** (also **stuff oneself**) eat greedily. **6** push, esp. hastily or clumsily. **7** (usually in *passive*; + *up*) block up (nose etc.). **8** *slang derogatory* dispose of. □ **get stuffed** *slang* go away; get lost. **stuff and nonsense** something ridiculous or incredible.

■ *noun* **1** components, constituents, fabric, ingredients, material, matter, substance. **2** accoutrements, articles, belongings, bits and pieces, *slang* clobber, effects, gear, impedimenta, junk, objects, paraphernalia, possessions, tackle, things. **4** cloth, fabric, material, textile. ● *verb* **1, 3, 4** cram, fill, pack, pad. **2** compress, cram, crowd, force, jam, pack, press, ram, shove, squeeze, stow, thrust, tuck. **6** push, shove, stick, thrust.

stuffing *noun* **1** padding for cushions etc. **2** mixture used to stuff food, esp. before cooking.
■ **1** filling, lining, padding, quilting, wadding. **2** forcemeat.

stuffy *adjective* (**-ier, -iest**) **1** (of room etc.) lacking fresh air. **2** dull, uninteresting. **3** conventional, narrow-minded. **4** (of nose etc.) stuffed up. □ **stuffily** *adverb*. **stuffiness** *noun*.
■ **1** airless, close, fetid, *colloquial* fuggy, fusty, heavy, muggy, musty, oppressive, stale, steamy, stifling, suffocating, sultry, unventilated, warm. **2, 3** boring, conventional, dreary, dull, formal, humourless, narrow-minded, old-fashioned, pompous, prim, staid, stodgy, strait-laced, uninteresting.

stultify /ˈstʌltɪfaɪ/ *verb* (**-ies, -ied**) make ineffective or useless, esp. by routine or from frustration. □ **stultification** *noun*.

stumble /ˈstʌmb(ə)l/ *verb* (**-ling**) **1** accidentally lurch forward or have partial fall. **2** (often + *along*) walk with repeated stumbles. **3** speak clumsily. **4** (+ *on, upon, across*) find by chance. ● *noun* act of stumbling. □ **stumbling block** circumstance causing difficulty or hesitation.
■ *verb* **1, 2** blunder, falter, flounder, lurch, miss one's footing, reel, slip, stagger, totter, trip, tumble. **3** become tongue-tied, falter, hesitate, pause, stammer, stutter. □ **stumbling block** bar, difficulty, hindrance, hurdle, impediment, obstacle, snag.

stump *noun* **1** part of cut or fallen tree still in ground. **2** similar part (of branch, limb, tooth, etc.) cut off or worn down. **3** *Cricket* each of 3 uprights of wicket. ● *verb* **1** (of question etc.) be too difficult for; baffle. **2** (as **stumped** *adjective*) at a loss. **3** *Cricket* put batsman out by touching stumps with ball while batsman is out of the crease. **4** walk stiffly or clumsily and noisily. **5** *US* traverse (district) making political speeches. □ **stump up** *colloquial* produce or pay (money required).
■ *verb* **1** baffle, bewilder, confound, confuse, defeat, *colloquial* flummox, mystify, outwit, perplex, puzzle, stymie. □ **stump up** see PAY *verb* 2.

stumpy *adjective* (**-ier, -iest**) short and thick. □ **stumpiness** *noun*.

stun *verb* (**-nn-**) **1** knock senseless; stupefy. **2** bewilder, shock.
■ **1** daze, knock out, numb, stupefy. **2** amaze, astonish, astound, bewilder, confound, confuse, dumbfound, flabbergast, shock, stagger, stupefy.

stung *past & past participle* of STING.

stunk *past & past participle* of STINK.

stunner *noun colloquial* stunning person or thing.

stunning *adjective colloquial* extremely attractive or impressive. □ **stunningly** *adverb*.
■ see BEAUTIFUL 1, STUPENDOUS.

stunt[1] *verb* retard growth or development of.
■ see CHECK *verb* 2.

stunt[2] *noun* **1** something unusual done to attract attention. **2** trick; daring manoeuvre. □ **stunt man** man employed to take actor's place in performing dangerous stunts.
■ exploit, feat, trick.

stupefy /ˈstjuːpɪfaɪ/ *verb* (**-ies, -ied**) **1** make stupid or insensible. **2** astonish. □ **stupefaction** *noun*.

stupendous /stjuːˈpendəs/ *adjective* **1** amazing. **2** of vast size or importance. □ **stupendously** *adverb*.
■ amazing, colossal, enormous, exceptional, extraordinary, huge, *colloquial* incredible, marvellous, miraculous, notable, phenomenal, prodigious, remarkable, *colloquial* sensational, singular, special, staggering, *colloquial* stunning, *colloquial* tremendous, unbelievable, wonderful.

stupid /ˈstjuːpɪd/ *adjective* (**-er, -est**) **1** unintelligent, slow-witted. **2** typical of stupid person. **3** uninteresting. **4** in state of stupor. □ **stupidity** /-ˈpɪd-/ *noun* (*plural* **-ies**). **stupidly** *adverb*.
■ **1** addled, asinine, *slang* barmy, *slang* boneheaded, bovine, brainless, *colloquial* clueless, crazy, *colloquial* cretinous, dense, *colloquial* dim, doltish, *colloquial* dopey, dull, *colloquial* dumb, empty-headed, feather-brained, feeble-minded, foolish, *colloquial* gormless, half-witted, idiotic, ignorant, imbecilic, ineducable, lacking, lumpish, *colloquial* moronic, naive, obtuse, scatterbrained, silly, simple, simple-minded, slow, *colloquial* slow on the uptake, slow-witted, subnormal, *colloquial* thick, *colloquial* thickheaded, unintelligent, unperceptive, witless. **2** absurd, *slang* barmy, crack-brained, crass, crazy, *colloquial* dumb, fatuous, feeble, foolish, futile, half-baked, hare-brained, idiotic, ill-advised, imbecilic, inane, irrational, irresponsible, laughable, ludicrous, lunatic, mad, mindless, nonsensical, pointless, puerile, rash, reckless, ridiculous, risible, senseless, silly, thoughtless, unjustifiable, unthinking, unwise, vacuous. **4** dazed, semi-conscious, stunned, stupefied. □ **stupidity** absurdity, crassness, denseness, dullness, *colloquial* dumbness, fatuity, fatuousness, folly, foolishness, futility, idiocy, ignorance, imbecility,

inanity, lunacy, madness, mindlessness, naivety, pointlessness, recklessness, silliness, slowness, thoughtlessness.

stupor /'stju:pə/ *noun* 1 dazed or torpid state. 2 utter amazement.
■ 1 coma, daze, inertia, insensibility, lassitude, lethargy, numbness, shock, torpor, trance, unconsciousness.

sturdy /'stɜ:dɪ/ *adjective* (**-ier, -iest**) 1 robust; strongly built. 2 vigorous. □ **sturdily** *adverb*. **sturdiness** *noun*.
■ 1 athletic, brawny, burly, durable, hardy, healthy, hefty, husky, muscular, powerful, robust, solid, sound, stalwart, stocky, strapping, strong, substantial, tough, vigorous, well built, well made. 2 determined, firm, indomitable, resolute, staunch, steadfast, strong, uncompromising, vigorous.

sturgeon /'stɜ:dʒ(ə)n/ *noun* (*plural* same or **-s**) large edible fish yielding caviar.

stutter /'stʌtə/ *verb* & *noun* stammer.
■ *verb* stammer, stumble.

sty[1] /staɪ/ *noun* (*plural* **sties**) 1 enclosure for pigs. 2 filthy room or dwelling.

sty[2] /staɪ/ *noun* (also **stye**) (*plural* **sties** or **styes**) inflamed swelling on edge of eyelid.

Stygian /'stɪdʒɪən/ *adjective literary* murky, gloomy.

style /staɪl/ *noun* 1 kind or sort, esp. in regard to appearance and form (of person, house, etc.). 2 manner of writing, speaking, etc. 3 distinctive manner of person, artistic school, or period. 4 correct way of designating person or thing. 5 superior quality or manner; elegance. 6 fashion in dress etc. 7 implement for scratching or engraving. 8 part of flower supporting stigma. ● *verb* (**-ling**) 1 design or make etc. in particular style. 2 designate in specified way.
■ *noun* 1 see FORM *noun* 3, KIND *noun* 2. 2 language, mode, phraseology, phrasing, register, sentence structure, tenor, tone, wording. 3 approach, character, custom, habit, idiosyncrasy, manner, method, way. 5 chic, dash, elegance, flair, flamboyance, panache, polish, refinement, smartness, sophistication, stylishness, taste. 6 cut, design, fashion, look, mode, pattern, shape, tailoring, type, vogue.

stylish *adjective* fashionable, elegant. □ **stylishly** *adverb*. **stylishness** *noun*.
■ à la mode, chic, *colloquial* classy, contemporary, dapper, elegant, fashionable, modern, modish, *colloquial* natty, *colloquial* posh, smart, *slang* snazzy, sophisticated, *colloquial often derogatory* trendy, up to date.

stylist /'staɪlɪst/ *noun* 1 designer of fashionable styles. 2 hairdresser. 3 stylish writer or performer.

stylistic /staɪ'lɪstɪk/ *adjective* of literary or artistic style. □ **stylistically** *adverb*.

stylized /'staɪlaɪzd/ *adjective* (also **-ised**) painted, drawn, etc. in conventional non-realistic style.

stylus /'staɪləs/ *noun* (*plural* **-luses**) 1 needle-like point for producing or following groove in gramophone record. 2 ancient pointed writing implement.

stymie /'staɪmɪ/ (also **stimy**) *noun* (*plural* **-ies**) 1 *Golf* situation where opponent's ball lies between one's ball and the hole. 2 difficult situation. ● *verb* (**stymying** or **stymieing**) obstruct, thwart.

styptic /'stɪptɪk/ *adjective* serving to check bleeding. ● *noun* styptic substance.

styrene /'staɪri:n/ *noun* liquid hydrocarbon used in making plastics etc.

suave /swɑ:v/ *adjective* smooth; polite; sophisticated. □ **suavely** *adverb*. **suavity** *noun*.

sub *colloquial noun* 1 submarine. 2 subscription. 3 substitute. 4 sub-editor. ● *verb* (**-bb-**) 1 (usually + *for*) act as substitute. 2 lend or advance (sum) to (person) against expected income. 3 sub-edit.

sub- *prefix* 1 at, to, or from lower position. 2 secondary or inferior position. 3 nearly; more or less.

subaltern /'sʌbəlt(ə)n/ *noun Military* officer below rank of captain, esp. second lieutenant.

sub-aqua /sʌb'ækwə/ *adjective* (of sport etc.) taking place under water.

subaquatic /sʌbə'kwætɪk/ *adjective* 1 of aquatic habits or kind. 2 underwater.

subatomic /sʌbə'tɒmɪk/ *adjective* occurring in, or smaller than, an atom.

subcommittee *noun* committee formed from main committee for special purpose.

subconscious /sʌb'kɒnʃəs/ *adjective* of part of mind that is not fully conscious but influences actions etc. ● *noun* this part of the mind. □ **subconsciously** *adverb*.
■ *adjective* deep-rooted, hidden, inner, intuitive, latent, repressed, subliminal, suppressed, unacknowledged, unconscious.

subcontinent /'sʌbkɒntɪnənt/ *noun* large land mass, smaller than continent.

subcontract *verb* /sʌbkən'trækt/ 1 employ another contractor to do (work) as part of larger project. 2 make or carry out subcontract. ● *noun* /sʌb'kɒntrækt/ secondary contract. □ **subcontractor** /-'træktə/ *noun*.

subculture /'sʌbkʌltʃə/ *noun* social group or its culture within a larger culture.

subcutaneous /sʌbkju:'teɪnɪəs/ *adjective* under the skin.

subdivide /sʌbdɪ'vaɪd/ *verb* (**-ding**) divide again after first division. □ **subdivision** /'sʌbdɪvɪʒ(ə)n/ *noun*.

subdue /səb'dju:/ *verb* (**-dues, -dued, -duing**) 1 conquer, suppress; tame. 2 (as **subdued** *adjective*) softened, lacking in intensity. 3 (as **subdued** *adjective*) (of person) quiet, restrained.

■ **1** check, curb, hold back, keep under, moderate, quieten, repress, restrain, subjugate, suppress, tame, temper. **2 (subdued)** calm, hushed, low, mellow, muted, peaceful, placid, quiet, soft, soothing, toned down, tranquil, unobtrusive. **3 (subdued)** chastened, crestfallen, depressed, downcast, grave, quiet, reflective, repressed, restrained, sad, serious, silent, sober, solemn, thoughtful.

sub-editor /sʌb'edɪtə/ *noun* **1** assistant editor. **2** person who prepares material for printing. □ **sub-edit** *verb* (**-t-**).

subheading /'sʌbhedɪŋ/ *noun* subordinate heading or title.

subhuman /sʌb'hjuːmən/ *adjective* (of behaviour, intelligence, etc.) less than human.

subject *noun* /'sʌbdʒɪkt/ **1** theme of discussion, description, or representation. **2** (+ *for*) person, circumstance, etc. giving rise to specified feeling, action, etc. **3** branch of study. **4** word or phrase representing person or thing carrying out action of verb (see panel). **5** person other than monarch living under government. **6** *Philosophy* thinking or feeling entity; conscious self. **7** *Music* theme; leading motif. ● *adjective* /'sʌbdʒɪkt/ **1** (+ *to*) liable or exposed to. **2** (+ *to*) conditional on. **3** owing obedience to government etc. ● *adverb* /'sʌbdʒɪkt/ (+ *to*) conditionally on. ● *verb* /səb'dʒekt/ **1** (+ *to*) make liable or expose to. **2** (usually + *to*) subdue (person, nation, etc.) to superior will. □ **subject matter** subject or theme of book, speech, etc; matter treated in lawsuit etc. □ **subjection** *noun*.

■ *noun* **1** affair, business, issue, matter, point, proposition, question, theme, thesis, topic. **3** area, branch of knowledge, course, discipline, field. **5** citizen, national, passport-holder, taxpayer, voter. ● *adjective* **1** (*subject to*) exposed to, liable to, prone to, susceptible to, vulnerable to. **2** (*subject to*) conditional on, contingent on, dependent on. **3** captive, dependent, enslaved, oppressed, ruled, subjugated. ● *verb* **1** (*subject to*) expose to, lay open to, submit to. **2** see SUBJUGATE.

subjective /səb'dʒektɪv/ *adjective* **1** (of art, written history, opinion, etc.) not impartial or literal. **2** *esp. Philosophy* of individual consciousness or perception; imaginary, partial, distorted. **3** *Grammar* of the subject. □ **subjectively** *adverb*. **subjectivity** /sʌbdʒek'tɪv-/ *noun*.

■ **1, 2** biased, emotional, gut, idiosyncratic, individual, intuitive, partial, personal, prejudiced, self-centred.

subjoin /sʌb'dʒɔɪn/ *verb* add (illustration, anecdote, etc.) at the end.

sub judice /sʌb 'dʒuːdɪsɪ/ *adjective Law* under judicial consideration and therefore prohibited from public discussion. [Latin]

subjugate /'sʌbdʒʊgeɪt/ *verb* (**-ting**) conquer; bring into subjection. □ **subjugation** *noun*. **subjugator** *noun*.

■ beat, conquer, control, crush, defeat, dominate, enslave, enthral, get the better of, master, oppress, overcome, overpower, overrun, put down, quash, quell, subdue, subject, tame, triumph over, *literary* vanquish.

subjunctive /səb'dʒʌŋktɪv/ *Grammar adjective* (of mood) expressing wish, supposition, or possibility. ● *noun* subjunctive mood or form.

sublease *noun* /'sʌbliːs/ lease granted by tenant to subtenant. ● *verb* /sʌb'liːs/ (**-sing**) lease to subtenant.

sublet /sʌb'let/ *verb* (**-tt-**; *past & past participle* **-let**) lease to subtenant.

sub-lieutenant /sʌblef'tenənt/ *noun* officer ranking next below lieutenant.

sublimate *verb* /'sʌblɪmeɪt/ (**-ting**) **1** divert energy of (primitive impulse etc.) into socially more acceptable activity. **2** sublime (substance). **3** refine, purify. ● *noun* /'sʌblɪmət/ sublimated substance. □ **sublimation** *noun*.

■ *verb* **1** channel, convert, divert, redirect. **3** idealize, purify, refine.

sublime /sə'blaɪm/ *adjective* (**-r, -st**) **1** of most exalted kind. **2** awe-inspiring. **3** arrogantly undisturbed. ● *verb* (**-ming**) **1** convert (substance) from solid into vapour by heat (and usually allow to solidify again). **2** make sublime. **3** become pure (as if) by sublimation. □ **sublimely** *adverb*. **sublimity** /-'lɪm-/ *noun*.

■ *adjective* **1** ecstatic, elated, elevated, exalted, great, heavenly, high, high-minded, lofty, noble, spiritual, transcendent.

subliminal /səb'lɪmɪn(ə)l/ *adjective* **1** *Psychology* below threshold of sensation or consciousness. **2** too faint or rapid to be consciously perceived. □ **subliminally** *adverb*.

Subject

The subject of a sentence is the person or thing that carries out the action of the verb and can be identified by asking the question 'who or what' before the verb, e.g.

The goalkeeper *made a stunning save*.
Hundreds of books *are now available on CD-ROM*.

In a passive construction, the subject of the sentence is in fact the person or thing to which the action of the verb is done, e.g.

I *was hit by a ball*.
Has the programme *been broadcast yet*?

sub-machine-gun /sʌbmə'ʃiːngʌn/ *noun* hand-held lightweight machine-gun.

submarine /sʌbmə'riːn/ *noun* vessel, esp. armed warship, which can be submerged and navigated under water. ● *adjective* existing, occurring, done, or used below surface of sea. □ **submariner** /-'mærmə/ *noun*.

submerge /səb'mɜːdʒ/ *verb* (**-ging**) **1** place, go, or dive beneath water. **2** overwhelm with work, problems, etc. □ **submergence** *noun.* **submersion** *noun.*

■ **1** cover, dip, dive, drench, drown, dunk, engulf, flood, go down, go under, immerse, inundate, plummet, sink, soak, subside, swamp. **2** drown, flood, inundate, overwhelm, swamp.

submersible /səb'mɜːsɪb(ə)l/ *noun* submarine operating under water for short periods. ● *adjective* capable of submerging.

submicroscopic /sʌbmaɪkrə'skɒpɪk/ *adjective* too small to be seen by ordinary microscope.

submission /səb'mɪʃ(ə)n/ *noun* **1** submitting, being submitted. **2** thing submitted. **3** submissive attitude etc.

■ **1** acquiescence, capitulation, compliance, giving in, surrender, yielding. **2** argument, claim, contention, contribution, entry, idea, offering, presentation, proposal, suggestion, tender, theory. **3** see SUBMISSIVENESS (SUBMISSIVE).

submissive /səb'mɪsɪv/ *adjective* humble, obedient. □ **submissively** *adverb.* **submissiveness** *noun.*

■ accommodating, acquiescent, amenable, biddable, compliant, deferential, docile, humble, meek, obedient, passive, pliant, resigned, servile, slavish, supine, tame, tractable, unassertive, uncomplaining, unresisting, weak, yielding. □ **submissiveness** acquiescence, compliance, deference, docility, humility, meekness, obedience, passivity, resignation, servility, submission, subservience, tameness.

submit /səb'mɪt/ *verb* (**-tt-**) **1** (often + *to*) cease resistance; yield. **2** present for consideration. **3** (+ *to*) subject or be subjected to (process, treatment, etc.). **4** *Law* argue, suggest.

■ **1** accede, bow, capitulate, concede, give in, knuckle under, succumb, surrender, yield; (*submit to*) see ACCEPT 5, OBEY 1. **2** advance, enter, give in, hand in, offer, present, proffer, propose, propound, put forward, state, suggest. **3** (*submit to*) see UNDERGO.

subnormal /sʌb'nɔːm(ə)l/ *adjective* below or less than normal, esp. in intelligence.

subordinate *adjective* /sə'bɔːdɪnət/ (usually + *to*) of inferior importance or rank; secondary, subservient. ● *noun* /sə'bɔːdɪnət/ person working under authority of another. ● *verb* /sə'bɔːdɪneɪt/ (**-ting**) (usually + *to*) make or treat as subordinate. □ **subordinate clause** clause serving as noun, adjective, or adverb within sentence (see panel at CLAUSE). □ **subordination** *noun.*

■ *adjective* inferior, junior, lesser, lower, menial, minor, secondary, subservient, subsidiary. ● *noun* aide, assistant, employee, inferior, junior, menial, servant, *usually derogatory* underling.

suborn /sə'bɔːn/ *verb* induce esp. by bribery to commit perjury or other crime.

subpoena /sə'piːnə/ *noun* writ ordering person's attendance in law court. ● *verb* (*past & past participle* **-naed** or **-na'd**) serve subpoena on.

sub rosa /sʌb 'rəʊzə/ *adjective & adverb* in confidence or in secret. [Latin]

subscribe /səb'skraɪb/ *verb* (**-bing**) **1** (usually + *to, for*) pay (specified sum) esp. regularly for membership of organization or receipt of publication etc. **2** (usually + *to, for*) contribute to fund, for cause, etc. **3** (usually + *to*) agree with (opinion etc.). □ **subscribe to** arrange to receive (periodical etc.) regularly.

■ **1, 2** (*subscribe to*) contribute to, donate to, give to, patronize, sponsor, support. **3** (*subscribe to*) advocate, agree with, approve of, back, believe in, condone, consent to, endorse, give one's blessing to.

subscriber *noun* person who subscribes, esp. person paying regular sum for hire of telephone line. □ **subscriber trunk dialling** making of trunk calls by subscriber without assistance of operator.

■ patron, sponsor, supporter.

subscript /'sʌbskrɪpt/ *adjective* written or printed below the line. ● *noun* subscript number etc.

subscription /səb'skrɪpʃ(ə)n/ *noun* **1** act of subscribing. **2** money subscribed. **3** membership fee, esp. paid regularly.

■ **2** fee, payment, remittance. **3** contribution, dues, fee.

subsequent /'sʌbsɪkwənt/ *adjective* (usually + *to*) following specified or implied event. □ **subsequently** *adverb.*

■ consequent, ensuing, following, future, later, next, resultant, resulting, succeeding, successive.

subservient /səb'sɜːvɪənt/ *adjective* **1** servile. **2** (usually + *to*) instrumental. **3** (usually + *to*) subordinate. □ **subservience** *noun.*

subside /səb'saɪd/ *verb* (**-ding**) **1** become tranquil; diminish. **2** (of water etc.) sink. **3** (of ground) cave in. **4** (of person) sink into chair etc. □ **subsidence** /-'saɪd-, 'sʌbsɪd-/ *noun.*

....

Subordinate clause

See panel at CLAUSE.

....

■ **1** abate, calm down, decline, decrease, die down, diminish, dwindle, ebb, lessen, melt away, moderate, quieten, recede, shrink, slacken, wear off. **2** drop, ebb, fall, go down, recede, sink. **3** cave in, collapse, drop, sink. **4** *colloquial* collapse, descend, lower oneself, settle, sink.

subsidiary /səb'sɪdɪərɪ/ *adjective* **1** supplementary; additional. **2** (of company) controlled by another. ● *noun* (*plural* **-ies**) subsidiary company, person, or thing.

■ *adjective* **1** additional, ancillary, auxiliary, complementary, contributory, inferior, lesser, minor, secondary, subordinate, supplementary, supporting.

subsidize /'sʌbsɪdaɪz/ *verb* (also **-ise**) (**-zing** or **-sing**) **1** pay subsidy to. **2** support by subsidies.

■ aid, back, finance, fund, maintain, promote, sponsor, support, underwrite.

subsidy /'sʌbsɪdɪ/ *noun* (*plural* **-ies**) **1** money contributed esp. by state to keep prices at desired level. **2** any monetary grant.

■ aid, backing, financial help, funding, grant, maintenance, sponsorship, subvention, support.

subsist /səb'sɪst/ *verb* **1** (often + *on*) keep oneself alive; be kept alive. **2** remain in being; exist.

subsistence *noun* **1** subsisting. **2** means of supporting life. **3** minimal level of existence, income, etc. □ **subsistence farming** farming in which almost all produce is consumed by farmer's household.

subsoil /'sʌbsɔɪl/ *noun* soil just below surface soil.

subsonic /sʌb'sɒnɪk/ *adjective* of speeds less than that of sound.

substance /'sʌbst(ə)ns/ *noun* **1** particular kind of material. **2** reality; solidity. **3** essence of what is spoken or written. **4** wealth and possessions. □ **in substance** generally; essentially.

■ **1** fabric, material, matter, stuff. **2** actuality, body, concreteness, corporeality, reality, solidity. **3** core, essence, gist, import, meaning, significance, subject matter, theme. **4** see WEALTH 1,2.

substandard /sʌb'stændəd/ *adjective* of lower than desired standard.

■ disappointing, inadequate, inferior, poor, shoddy, unworthy.

substantial /səb'stænʃ(ə)l/ *adjective* **1** of real importance or value. **2** large in size or amount. **3** of solid structure. **4** commercially successful; wealthy. **5** largely true. **6** real; existing. □ **substantially** *adverb*.

■ **1, 2** big, consequential, considerable, generous, great, important, large, significant, sizeable, worthwhile. **3** durable, hefty, massive, solid, sound, stout, strong, sturdy, well built, well made.

substantiate /səb'stænʃɪeɪt/ *verb* (**-ting**) support or prove truth of (charge, claim, etc.). □ **substantiation** *noun*.

substantive /'sʌbstəntɪv/ *adjective* **1** actual, real, permanent. **2** substantial. ● *noun* noun. □ **substantively** *adverb*.

substitute /'sʌbstɪtjuːt/ *noun* **1** person or thing acting or serving in place of another. **2** artificial alternative to a food etc. ● *verb* (**-ting**) (often + *for*) **1** put in place of another. **2** act as substitute. ● *adjective* acting as substitute. □ **substitution** *noun*.

■ *noun* **1** alternative, deputy, locum, proxy, relief, replacement, reserve, stand-in, stopgap, substitution, supply, surrogate, understudy. **2** alternative, ersatz, imitation, replacement. ● *verb* **1** change, exchange, interchange, replace, swap, switch. **2** (*substitute for*) cover for, deputize for, double for, relieve, stand in for, supplant, take the place of, understudy. ● *adjective* acting, alternative, deputy, ersatz, imitation, relief, reserve, standby, supply, surrogate, temporary.

substratum /'sʌbstrɑːtəm/ *noun* (*plural* **-ta**) underlying layer.

subsume /səb'sjuːm/ *verb* (**-ming**) (usually + *under*) include under particular rule, class, etc.

subtenant /'sʌbtenənt/ *noun* person renting room or house etc. from its tenant. □ **subtenancy** *noun* (*plural* **-ies**).

subtend /sʌb'tend/ *verb* (of line) be opposite (angle, arc).

subterfuge /'sʌbtəfjuːdʒ/ *noun* attempt to avoid blame etc., esp. by lying or deceit.

subterranean /sʌbtə'reɪnɪən/ *adjective* underground.

subtext *noun* underlying theme.

subtitle /'sʌbtaɪt(ə)l/ *noun* **1** subordinate or additional title of book etc. **2** caption of cinema film, esp. translating dialogue. ● *verb* (**-ling**) provide with subtitle(s).

subtle /'sʌt(ə)l/ *adjective* (**-r, -st**) **1** hard to detect or describe. **2** (of scent, colour, etc.) faint, delicate. **3** perceptive; able to make fine distinctions. **4** ingenious. □ **subtlety** *noun* (*plural* **-ies**). **subtly** *adverb*.

■ **1** arcane, elusive, indirect, mysterious, recondite. **2** delicate, elusive, faint, fine, gentle, mild, slight, understated, unobtrusive. **3** acute, nice, perceptive, refined, sophisticated. **4** discriminating, clever, cunning, ingenious, shrewd.

subtract /səb'trækt/ *verb* (often + *from*) deduct (number etc.) from another. □ **subtraction** *noun*.

■ debit, deduct, remove, take away, take off.

subtropical /sʌb'trɒpɪk(ə)l/ *adjective* **1** bordering on the tropics. **2** characteristic of such regions.

suburb /'sʌbɜːb/ *noun* outlying district of city.

■ (*suburbs*) fringes, outer areas, outskirts, *usually derogatory* suburbia.

suburban /sə'bɜːbən/ *adjective* **1** of or characteristic of suburbs. **2** *derogatory* provincial in outlook. □ **suburbanite** *noun*.

■ **1** outer, outlying, residential.

suburbia /sə'bɜːbɪə/ *noun usually derogatory* suburbs and their inhabitants etc.

subvention /səb'venʃ(ə)n/ *noun* subsidy.

subversive /səb'vɜːsɪv/ *adjective* seeking to overthrow (esp. government). ● *noun* subversive person. □ **subversion** *noun.* **subversively** *adverb.* **subversiveness** *noun.*

■ *adjective* challenging, disruptive, insurrectionary, questioning, radical, revolutionary, seditious, traitorous, treacherous, treasonous, undermining, unsettling.

subvert /səb'vɜːt/ *verb* overthrow or weaken (government etc.).

■ challenge, corrupt, destroy, disrupt, overthrow, overturn, pervert, ruin, undermine, upset, wreck.

subway /'sʌbweɪ/ *noun* 1 underground passage, esp. for pedestrians. 2 *US* underground railway.

■ 1 tunnel, underpass.

subzero /sʌb'zɪərəʊ/ *adjective* (esp. of temperature) lower than zero.

succeed /sək'siːd/ *verb* 1 (often + *in*) have success; prosper. 2 (of plan etc.) be successful. 3 follow in order. 4 (often + *to*) come into inheritance, office, title, or property. ● **succeeding** *adjective.*

■ 1 *colloquial* arrive, be a success, do well, flourish, get on, *colloquial* make it, prosper, thrive. 2 be effective, *colloquial* catch on, produce results, work. 3, 4 be successor to, come after, follow, inherit from, replace, take over from. □ **succeeding** see SUBSEQUENT.

success /sək'ses/ *noun* 1 accomplishment of aim; favourable outcome. 2 attainment of wealth, fame, etc. 3 successful person or thing. □ **successful** *adjective.* **successfully** *adverb.*

■ 1 accomplishment, achievement, attainment, completion, effectiveness. 2 fame, good fortune, prosperity, wealth. 3 *colloquial* hit, sensation, triumph, victory, winner. □ **successful** best-selling, booming, celebrated, effective, effectual, famed, famous, flourishing, fruitful, leading, lucrative, moneymaking, popular, productive, profitable, prosperous, rewarding, thriving, top, unbeaten, *colloquial* useful, victorious, well known, well off, winning.

succession /sək'seʃ(ə)n/ *noun* 1 following in order. 2 series of things or people following one another. 3 succeeding to inheritance, office, or esp. throne. 4 right to succeed to one of these. 5 set of people with such right. □ **in succession** one after another. **in succession to** as successor of.

■ 1, 2 chain, flow, line, procession, progression, run, sequence, series, string.

successive /sək'sesɪv/ *adjective* following in succession; consecutive. □ **successively** *adverb.*

■ consecutive, continuous, succeeding, unbroken, uninterrupted.

successor /sək'sesə/ *noun* (often + *to*) person or thing that succeeds another.

■ heir, inheritor, replacement.

succinct /sək'sɪŋkt/ *adjective* brief, concise. □ **succinctly** *adverb.* **succinctness** *noun.*

■ brief, compact, concise, condensed, epigrammatic, neat, pithy, short, terse, to the point.

succour /'sʌkə/ (*US* **succor**) *archaic* or *formal noun* help, esp. in time of need. ● *verb* give succour to.

succulent /'sʌkjʊlənt/ *adjective* 1 juicy. 2 (of plant) thick and fleshy. ● *noun* succulent plant. □ **succulence** *noun.*

■ *adjective* juicy, luscious, moist, mouth-watering, palatable, rich. 2 fleshy, lush, thick.

succumb /sə'kʌm/ *verb* (usually + *to*) 1 give way; be overcome. 2 die.

■ 1 accede, be overcome, capitulate, give in, give up, give way, submit, surrender, yield.

such *adjective* 1 (often + *as*) of kind or degree specified or suggested. 2 so great or extreme. 3 unusually, abnormally. ● *pronoun* such person(s) or thing(s). □ **as such** as being what has been specified. **such-and-such** particular but unspecified. **suchlike** *colloquial* of such kind.

suck *verb* 1 draw (liquid) into mouth by suction. 2 draw liquid from in this way. 3 roll tongue round (sweet etc.) in mouth. 4 make sucking action or noise. 5 (usually + *down*) engulf or drown in sucking movement. ● *noun* act or period of sucking. □ **suck in** 1 absorb. 2 involve (person). **suck up** 1 absorb. 2 (often + *to*) *colloquial* behave in a servile way.

■ □ **suck up** 1 absorb, draw up, pull up, soak up. 2 (*suck up to*) see FLATTER 1.

sucker *noun* 1 person easily duped or cheated. 2 (+ *for*) person susceptible to. 3 rubber etc. cap adhering by suction. 4 similar part of plant or animal. 5 shoot springing from plant's root below ground.

suckle /'sʌk(ə)l/ *verb* (**-ling**) feed (young) from breast or udder.

suckling /'sʌklɪŋ/ *noun* unweaned child or animal.

sucrose /'suːkrəʊz/ *noun* kind of sugar obtained from cane, beet, etc.

suction /'sʌkʃ(ə)n/ *noun* 1 sucking. 2 production of partial vacuum so that external atmospheric pressure forces fluid into vacant space or causes adhesion of surfaces.

Sudanese /suːdə'niːz/ *adjective* of Sudan. ● *noun* (*plural* same) native or national of Sudan.

sudden /'sʌd(ə)n/ *adjective* done or occurring unexpectedly or abruptly. □ **all of a sudden** suddenly. □ **suddenly** *adverb.* **suddenness** *noun.*

■ abrupt, brisk, hasty, hurried, impetuous, impulsive, precipitate, quick, rash, sharp, snap, startling, surprising, swift, unannounced, unconsidered, unexpected, unforeseeable, unforeseen, unlooked-for, unplanned, unpremeditated.

sudorific /suːdəˈrɪfɪk/ *adjective* causing sweating. ● *noun* sudorific drug.

suds *plural noun* froth of soap and water. □ **sudsy** *adjective*.

■ bubbles, foam, froth, lather, soapsuds.

sue *verb* (**sues, sued, suing**) **1** begin lawsuit against. **2** (often + *for*) make application to law court for compensation etc. **3** (often + *to, for*) make plea to person for favour.

■ **1** indict, institute legal proceedings against, proceed against, prosecute, *esp. Law* summons, take legal action against. **3** see ENTREAT.

suede /sweɪd/ *noun* leather with flesh side rubbed into nap.

suet /ˈsuːɪt/ *noun* hard fat surrounding kidneys of cattle and sheep, used in cooking etc. □ **suety** *adjective*.

suffer /ˈsʌfə/ *verb* **1** undergo pain, grief, etc. **2** undergo or be subjected to (pain, loss, punishment, grief, etc.). **3** tolerate. □ **sufferable** *adjective*. **sufferer** *noun*. **suffering** *noun*.

■ **1** ache, agonize, be punished, hurt, smart. **2, 3** bear, cope with, endure, experience, feel, go through, live through, put up with, stand, tolerate, undergo, withstand.

sufferance *noun* tacit permission or toleration. □ **on sufferance** tolerated but not supported.

suffice /səˈfaɪs/ *verb* (**-cing**) be enough; meet needs of. □ **suffice it to say** I shall say only this.

■ answer, be sufficient, do, satisfy, serve.

sufficiency /səˈfɪʃənsɪ/ *noun* (*plural* **-ies**) (often + *of*) sufficient amount.

sufficient /səˈfɪʃ(ə)nt/ *adjective* sufficing, adequate. □ **sufficiently** *adverb*.

■ adequate, enough, satisfactory.

suffix /ˈsʌfɪks/ *noun* letter(s) added to end of word to form derivative. ● *verb* add as suffix.

suffocate /ˈsʌfəkeɪt/ *verb* (**-ting**) **1** kill, stifle, or choke by stopping breathing, esp. by fumes etc. **2** be or feel suffocated. □ **suffocating** *adjective*. **suffocation** *noun*.

■ **1** asphyxiate, choke, smother, stifle, strangle, throttle.

suffragan /ˈsʌfrəgən/ *noun* bishop assisting diocesan bishop.

suffrage /ˈsʌfrɪdʒ/ *noun* right of voting in political elections.

suffragette /ˌsʌfrəˈdʒet/ *noun historical* woman who agitated for women's suffrage.

suffuse /səˈfjuːz/ *verb* (**-sing**) (of colour, moisture, etc.) spread throughout or over from within. □ **suffusion** /-ʒ(ə)n/ *noun*.

sugar /ˈʃʊgə/ *noun* **1** sweet crystalline substance obtained from sugar cane and sugar beet, used in cookery, confectionery, etc. **2** *Chemistry* soluble usually sweet crystalline carbohydrate, e.g. glucose. **3** *esp. US colloquial* darling (as term of address). ● *verb* sweeten or coat with sugar. □ **sugar beet** white beet yielding sugar. **sugar cane** tall stout perennial tropical grass yielding sugar. **sugar daddy** *slang* elderly man who lavishes gifts on young woman. **sugar loaf** conical moulded mass of hard refined sugar.

■ *verb* sweeten.

sugary *adjective* **1** containing or resembling sugar. **2** cloying, sentimental. □ **sugariness** *noun*.

■ **1** glazed, iced, sugared, sweet, sweetened. **2** cloying, honeyed, sentimental, sickly.

suggest /səˈdʒest/ *verb* **1** (often + *that*) propose (theory, plan, etc.). **2** hint at. **3** evoke (idea etc.). **4** (**suggest itself**) (of idea etc.) come into person's mind.

■ **1** advise, advocate, counsel, moot, move, propose, propound, put forward, raise, recommend, urge. **2, 3** call to mind, communicate, evoke, hint (at), imply, indicate, insinuate, intimate, make one think of, mean, signal.

suggestible *adjective* capable of being influenced by suggestion. □ **suggestibility** *noun*.

suggestion /səˈdʒestʃ(ə)n/ *noun* **1** suggesting. **2** thing suggested. **3** slight trace; hint. **4** insinuation of belief or impulse into the mind.

■ **1** counselling, prompting, urging. **2** advice, counsel, offer, plan, proposal, recommendation. **3** breath, hint, idea, indication, intimation, notion, suspicion, touch, trace.

suggestive /səˈdʒestɪv/ *adjective* **1** (usually + *of*) conveying a suggestion. **2** (of remark, joke, etc.) suggesting something indecent. □ **suggestively** *adverb*.

■ **1** evocative, expressive, indicative, reminiscent, thought-provoking. **2** see INDECENT 1.

suicidal /suːɪˈsaɪd(ə)l/ *adjective* **1** (of person) liable to commit suicide. **2** of or tending to suicide. **3** destructive to one's own interests. □ **suicidally** *adverb*.

■ **1** see DESOLATE *adjective* 3. **3** kamikaze, self-destructive.

suicide /ˈsuːɪsaɪd/ *noun* **1** intentional self-killing. **2** person who commits suicide. **3** action destructive to one's own interests etc.

sui generis /sjuːˈɑːdʒenerɪs/ *adjective* of its own kind; unique. [Latin]

suit /suːt, sjuːt/ *noun* **1** set of usually matching clothes consisting usually of jacket and trousers or skirt. **2** clothing for particular purpose. **3** any of the 4 sets into which pack of cards is divided. **4** lawsuit. ● *verb* **1** go well with (person's appearance). **2** meet requirements of. **3** be convenient. **4** (**suit oneself**) do as one chooses. **5** be in harmony with. **6** make fitting; adapt. **7** (as **suited** *adjective*) appropriate; well fitted. □ **suitcase** flat case for carrying clothes, usually with hinged lid.

■ *noun* **1** costume, ensemble, outfit. **2** see CLOTHES 1. ● *verb* **1** become, fit, look good on. **2** conform to, fill one's needs, fit in with, gratify, please, satisfy, tally with. **3** be convenient, be suitable. **5** go with, harmonize with, match. **6** accommodate, adapt, fit, tailor.

suitable *adjective* (usually + *to, for*) well fitted for purpose; appropriate to occasion. □ **suitability** *noun*. **suitably** *adverb*.

■ acceptable, applicable, apposite, appropriate, apt, becoming, befitting, congenial, convenient, correct, decent, decorous, fit, fitting, handy, *archaic* meet, opportune, pertinent, proper, relevant, right, satisfactory, seemly, tasteful, timely, well chosen, well judged, well timed.

suite /swiːt/ *noun* **1** set of rooms, furniture, etc. **2** *Music* set of instrumental pieces.

suitor /'suːtə/ *noun* **1** man who woos woman. **2** plaintiff or petitioner in lawsuit.

sulfur etc. *US* = SULPHUR etc.

sulk *verb* be sulky. ● *noun* (also **the sulks**) fit of sullen silence.

■ *verb* be sullen, brood, mope, pout.

sulky /'sʌlkɪ/ *adjective* (**-ier, -iest**) sullen and unsociable from resentment or ill temper. □ **sulkily** *adverb*.

sullen /'sʌlən/ *adjective* **1** sulky, morose. **2** (of sky) dull, gloomy. □ **sullenly** *adverb*. **sullenness** *noun*.

■ **1** antisocial, bad-tempered, brooding, churlish, crabby, cross, disgruntled, dour, glum, grim, grudging, ill-humoured, lugubrious, moody, morose, out of sorts, petulant, pouting, resentful, silent, sour, stubborn, sulking, sulky, surly, uncommunicative, unforgiving, unfriendly, unhappy, unsociable. **2** cheerless, dark, dismal, dull, gloomy, grey, leaden, sombre.

sully /'sʌlɪ/ *verb* (**-ies, -ied**) spoil purity or splendour of (reputation etc.).

sulphate /'sʌlfeɪt/ *noun* (*US* **sulfate**) salt or ester of sulphuric acid.

sulphide /'sʌlfaɪd/ *noun* (*US* **sulfide**) binary compound of sulphur.

sulphite /'sʌlfaɪt/ *noun* (*US* **sulfite**) salt or ester of sulphurous acid.

sulphonamide /sʌl'fɒnəmaɪd/ *noun* (*US* **sulfonamide**) kind of antibiotic drug containing sulphur.

sulphur /'sʌlfə/ *noun* (*US* **sulfur**) pale yellow non-metallic element burning with blue flame and stifling smell. □ **sulphur dioxide** colourless pungent gas formed by burning sulphur in air and dissolving it in water.

sulphuric /sʌl'fjʊərɪk/ *adjective* (*US* **sulfuric**) of or containing sulphur with valency of 6. □ **sulphuric acid** dense highly corrosive oily acid.

sulphurous /'sʌlfərəs/ *adjective* (*US* **sulfurous**) **1** of or like sulphur. **2** containing sulphur with

valency of 4. □ **sulphurous acid** unstable weak acid used e.g. as bleaching agent.

sultan /'sʌlt(ə)n/ *noun* Muslim sovereign.

sultana /sʌl'tɑːnə/ *noun* **1** seedless raisin. **2** sultan's wife, mother, concubine, or daughter.

sultanate /'sʌltəneɪt/ *noun* position of or territory ruled by sultan.

sultry /'sʌltrɪ/ *adjective* (**-ier, -iest**) **1** (of weather) oppressively hot. **2** (of person) passionate, sensual. □ **sultriness** *noun*.

■ **1** close, hot, humid, muggy, oppressive, steamy, stifling, stuffy, warm. **2** erotic, passionate, provocative, seductive, sensual, sexy, voluptuous.

sum *noun* **1** total resulting from addition. **2** amount of money. **3** arithmetical problem. **4** (esp. in *plural*) *colloquial* arithmetic work, esp. elementary. ● *verb* (**-mm-**) find sum of. □ **in sum** briefly; to sum up. **summing-up 1** judge's review of evidence given to jury. **2** recapitulation of main points of argument etc. **sum up 1** (esp. of judge) give summing-up. **2** form or express opinion of (person, situation, etc.). **3** summarize.

■ *noun* **1** aggregate, amount, number, quantity, reckoning, result, score, tally, total, whole. □ **sum up 1, 3** see SUMMARIZE.

sumac /'suːmæk/ *noun* (also **sumach**) **1** shrub with reddish fruits used as spice. **2** dried and ground leaves of this for use in tanning and dyeing.

summarize /'sʌməraɪz/ *verb* (also **-ise**) (**-zing** or **-sing**) make or be summary of.

■ abridge, condense, encapsulate, give the gist of, outline, précis, *colloquial* recap, recapitulate, review, simplify, sum up.

summary /'sʌmərɪ/ *noun* (*plural* **-ies**) brief account giving chief points. ● *adjective* brief; without details or formalities. □ **summarily** *adverb*.

■ *noun* abridgement, abstract, condensation, digest, epitome, gist, outline, précis, recapitulation, résumé, review, summation, summing-up, synopsis.

summation /sə'meɪʃ(ə)n/ *noun* **1** finding of total or sum. **2** summarizing.

summer /'sʌmə/ *noun* **1** warmest season of year. **2** (often + *of*) mature stage of life etc. □ **summer house** light building in garden etc. for use in summer. **summer pudding** dessert of soft fruit pressed in bread casing. **summer school** course of lectures etc. held in summer, esp. at university. **summer time** period from March to October when clocks etc. are advanced one hour. **summertime** season or period of summer. □ **summery** *adjective*.

■ □ **summery** bright, hot, sunny, tropical, warm.

summit /'sʌmɪt/ *noun* **1** highest point, top. **2** highest level of achievement or status. **3** (in full **summit conference, meeting, etc.**) discussion between heads of governments.

■ **1** apex, crown, head, height, peak, pinnacle, top.
2 acme, apogee, climax, culmination, high point,
pinnacle, zenith.

summon /'sʌmən/ *verb* **1** order to come or
appear, esp. in law court. **2** (usually + *to do*) call
on. **3** call together. **4** (often + *up*) gather (courage,
resources, etc.).
■ **1, 2** command, demand, invite, order, send for,
subpoena. **3** assemble, call, convene, convoke,
gather together, muster, rally. **4** (*summon up*) call
on, draw on, gather, invoke, muster.

summons /'sʌmənz/ *noun* (*plural* **sum-
monses**) authoritative call to attend or do something, esp. to appear in court. ● *verb esp. Law*
serve with summons.

sumo /'suːməʊ/ *noun* Japanese wrestling in
which only soles of feet may touch ground.

sump *noun* **1** casing holding oil in internal-
combustion engine. **2** pit, well, etc. for collecting
superfluous liquid.

sumptuary /'sʌmptʃʊərɪ/ *adjective Law* regulating (esp. private) expenditure.

sumptuous /'sʌmptʃʊəs/ *adjective* costly;
splendid, magnificent. □ **sumptuously** *adverb*.
sumptuousness *noun*.

Sun. *abbreviation* Sunday.

sun *noun* **1** the star round which the earth travels
and from which it receives light and warmth. **2**
this light or warmth. **3** any star. ● *verb* (**-nn-**)
(often **sun oneself**) expose to sun. □ **sunbathe**
bask in sun, esp. to tan one's body. **sunbeam** ray
of sunlight. **sunblock** lotion protecting skin from
sun. **sunburn** inflammation of skin from exposure to sun. **sunburnt** affected by sunburn.
sundial instrument showing time by shadow of
pointer in sunlight. **sundown** sunset. **sunflower**
tall plant with large golden-rayed flowers. **sunglasses** tinted spectacles to protect eyes from
glare. **sunlamp** lamp giving ultraviolet rays for
therapy or artificial suntan. **sunlight** light from
sun. **sunlit** illuminated by sun. **sun lounge** room
with large windows etc. to receive much sunlight. **sunrise** (time of) sun's rising. **sunroof**
opening panel in car's roof. **sunset** (time of) sun's
setting. **sunshade 1** parasol. **2** awning. **sunshine**
1 sunlight. **2** area illuminated by it. **3** fine
weather. **4** cheerfulness. **sunspot** dark patch on
sun's surface. **sunstroke** acute prostration from
excessive heat of sun. **suntan** brownish skin
colour caused by exposure to sun. **suntrap** sunny
place, esp. sheltered from wind. **sunup** *esp. US*
sunrise. □ **sunless** *adjective*.
■ □ **sunbathe** bask, sun oneself, tan oneself.
sunlight daylight, sun, sunbeams, sunshine.
sunrise dawn, daybreak. **sunset** dusk, evening,
poetical gloaming, nightfall, sundown, twilight.
sunshade awning, canopy, parasol. □ **sunless**
cheerless, cloudy, dark, dismal, dreary, dull,
gloomy, grey, overcast, sombre.

sundae /'sʌndeɪ/ *noun* ice cream with fruit,
nuts, syrup, etc.

Sunday /'sʌndeɪ/ *noun* **1** day of week following
Saturday. **2** Christian day of worship. **3** collo-

quial newspaper published on Sundays.
□ **month of Sundays** *colloquial* very long period.
Sunday school religious class held on Sundays
for children.

sunder /'sʌndə/ *verb literary* sever; keep apart.

sundry /'sʌndrɪ/ *adjective* various, several.
● *noun* (*plural* **-ies**) (in *plural*) oddments,
accessories, etc. not mentioned individually.
□ **all and sundry** everyone.
■ *adjective* assorted, different, *archaic* divers,
miscellaneous, mixed, various.

sung *past participle* of SING.

sunk *past* and *past participle* of SINK.

sunken *adjective* **1** that has sunk. **2** lying below
general surface. **3** (of eyes, cheeks, etc.) shrunken, hollow.
■ **2** submerged, underwater. **3** concave,
depressed, hollow, hollowed.

Sunni /'sʌnɪ/ *noun* (*plural* same or **-s**) **1** one of
two main branches of Islam. **2** adherent of this.

sunny *adjective* (**-ier, -iest**) **1** bright with or
warmed by sunlight. **2** cheerful. □ **sunnily**
adverb. **sunniness** *noun*.
■ **1** bright, clear, cloudless, fair, fine, summery,
sunlit, unclouded. **2** see CHEERFUL 1.

sup[1] *verb* (**-pp-**) **1** drink by sips or spoonfuls. **2**
esp. Northern English colloquial drink (alcohol).
● *noun* sip of liquid.

sup[2] *verb* (**-pp-**) *archaic* take supper.

super /'suːpə/ *adjective colloquial* excellent,
unusually good. ● *noun colloquial* **1** superintendent. **2** supernumerary.

super- *combining form* **1** on top, over, beyond. **2**
to extreme degree. **3** extra good or large of its
kind. **4** of higher kind.

superabundant /suːp(ə)rə'bʌnd(ə)nt, sjuː-/
adjective abounding beyond what is normal.
□ **superabundance** *noun*.

superannuate /suːpər'ænjʊeɪt/ *verb* (**-ting**) **1**
pension (person) off. **2** dismiss or discard as too
old. **3** (as **superannuated** *adjective*) too old for
work or use.
■ **1** pension off, retire. **3** (**superannuated**)
discarded, disused, obsolete, old, thrown out, worn
out.

superannuation *noun* **1** pension. **2** payment
made to obtain pension.
■ **1** annuity, pension.

superb /suː'pɜːb/ *adjective* **1** *colloquial* excellent.
2 magnificent. □ **superbly** *adverb*.
■ admirable, excellent, fine, first-class, first-rate,
grand, impressive, marvellous, splendid,
superior.

supercargo /'suːpəkɑːgəʊ/ *noun* (*plural* **-es**)
person in merchant ship managing sales etc. of
cargo.

supercharge /'suːpətʃɑːdʒ/ *verb* (**-ging**) **1**
(usually + *with*) charge (atmosphere etc.) with
energy, emotion, etc. **2** use supercharger on.

supercharger *noun* device forcing extra air or fuel into internal-combustion engine.

supercilious /su:pə'sılıəs/ *adjective* haughtily contemptuous. □ **superciliously** *adverb*. **superciliousness** *noun*.

supererogation /su:pərerə'geɪʃ(ə)n/ *noun* doing of more than duty requires. □ **supererogatory** /-ɪ'rɒɡət(ə)rɪ/ *adjective*.

superficial /su:pə'fıʃ(ə)l/ *adjective* 1 of or on the surface; lacking depth. 2 swift, cursory; not thorough. 3 apparent, not real. 4 (esp. of person) of shallow feelings etc. □ **superficiality** /-ʃɪ'æl-/ *noun*. **superficially** *adverb*.

■ 1 cosmetic, external, exterior, outward, shallow, skin-deep, slight, surface. 2 careless, casual, cursory, desultory, facile, hasty, hurried, inattentive, lightweight, oversimplified, passing, perfunctory, simplistic, sweeping (*generalization*), swift, unconvincing, uncritical, undiscriminating, unquestioning, unscholarly. 4 frivolous, shallow, simple-minded, simplistic, trivial.

superfluity /su:pə'flu:ɪtɪ/ *noun* (*plural* -ies) 1 being superfluous. 2 superfluous amount or thing.

superfluous /su:'pɜ:flʊəs/ *adjective* more than is needed or wanted; needless.

■ excess, excessive, extra, needless, redundant, spare, superabundant, surplus, unnecessary, unneeded, unwanted.

supergrass /'su:pəɡrɑ:s/ *noun colloquial* police informer implicating many people.

superhuman /su:pə'hju:mən/ *adjective* exceeding normal human capacity or power.

■ divine, godlike, Herculean, heroic, metaphysical, phenomenal, prodigious, supernatural.

superimpose /su:pərɪm'pəʊz/ *verb* (-sing) (usually + *on*) place (thing) on or above something else. □ **superimposition** /-pə'zɪʃ(ə)n/ *noun*.

■ overlay, place on top of.

superintend /su:pərɪn'tend/ *verb* manage; supervise (work etc.). □ **superintendence** *noun*.

■ administer, be in charge of, be the supervisor of, conduct, control, direct, look after, manage, organize, oversee, preside over, run, supervise, watch over.

superintendent /su:pərɪn'tend(ə)nt/ *noun* 1 police officer above rank of chief inspector. 2 person who superintends. 3 director of institution etc.

superior /su:'pɪərɪə/ *adjective* 1 higher in rank, position, quality, etc. 2 high-quality. 3 supercilious. 4 (often + *to*) better or greater in some respect. 5 written or printed above the line. ● *noun* 1 person superior to another, esp. in rank. 2 head of monastery etc. □ **superiority** /-'ɒr-/ *noun*.

■ *adjective* 1 better, *colloquial* classier, greater, higher, higher-born, loftier, more important, more impressive, nobler, senior, upmarket, upper. 2 choice, exclusive, fine, first-class, first-rate, select, top, unrivalled. 3 arrogant, condescending, contemptuous, disdainful, elitist, haughty, *colloquial* high and mighty, lofty, paternalistic, patronizing, self-important, smug, snobbish, *colloquial* snooty, *colloquial* stuck-up, supercilious.

superlative /su:'pɜ:lətɪv/ *adjective* 1 of highest degree; excellent. 2 *Grammar* (of adjective or adverb) expressing highest or very high degree of quality etc. denoted by simple word (see panel). ● *noun* 1 *Grammar* superlative expression or word. 2 (in *plural*) high praise. 3 (in *plural*) exaggerated language.

■ *adjective* 1 best, choicest, consummate, excellent, finest, first-rate, incomparable, matchless, peerless, supreme, *colloquial* tiptop, *colloquial* top-notch, unrivalled, unsurpassed.

superman *noun colloquial* man of exceptional powers or achievement.

supermarket /'su:pəmɑ:kɪt/ *noun* large self-service store selling food, household goods, etc.

supernatural /su:pə'nætʃər(ə)l/ *adjective* not attributable to, or explicable by, natural or physical laws; magical; mystical. ● *noun* (**the supernatural**) supernatural forces etc. □ **supernaturally** *adverb*.

■ *adjective* abnormal, ghostly, inexplicable, magical, metaphysical, miraculous, mysterious, mystic, occult, other-worldly, paranormal, preternatural, psychic, spiritual, uncanny, unearthly, unnatural, weird.

Superlative

The superlative form of an adjective is used to say that something is the supreme example of its kind. Superlative adjectives are formed in two ways: generally, short words add *-est* to the base form, e.g.

smallest, fastest, greatest

Often, the base form alters, e.g.

biggest, finest, easiest

Long words take *most* in front of them, e.g.

most beautiful, most informative

Superlatives are normally used with *the*:

the smallest, the most beautiful

supernova /suːpəˈnəʊvə/ *noun* (*plural* **-vae** /-viː/ or **-vas**) star that suddenly increases very greatly in brightness.

supernumerary /suːpəˈnjuːmərəri/ *adjective* **1** in excess of normal number. **2** engaged for extra work. **3** (of actor) with non-speaking part. ● *noun* (*plural* **-ies**) supernumerary person or thing.

superphosphate /suːpəˈfɒsfeɪt/ *noun* fertilizer made from phosphate rock.

superpower /ˈsuːpəpaʊə/ *noun* extremely powerful nation.

superscript /ˈsuːpəskrɪpt/ *adjective* written or printed above. ● *noun* superscript number or symbol.

supersede /suːpəˈsiːd/ *verb* (**-ding**) **1** take place of. **2** put or use another in place of. □ **supersession** /-ˈseʃ-/ *noun*.

supersonic /suːpəˈsɒnɪk/ *adjective* of or having speed greater than that of sound. □ **supersonically** *adverb*.

superstar /ˈsuːpəstɑː/ *noun* extremely famous or renowned actor, musician, etc.

superstition /suːpəˈstɪʃ(ə)n/ *noun* **1** belief in the supernatural. **2** irrational fear of the unknown or mysterious. **3** practice, belief, or religion based on this. □ **superstitious** *adjective*.
■ **3** delusion, illusion, myth, old wives' tale.
□ **superstitious** credulous, groundless, illusory, irrational, mythical, unfounded, unprovable.

superstore /ˈsuːpəstɔː/ *noun* very large supermarket.

superstructure /ˈsuːpəstrʌktʃə/ *noun* **1** structure built on top of another. **2** upper part of building, ship, etc.

supertanker /ˈsuːpətæŋkə/ *noun* very large tanker.

supertax /ˈsuːpətæks/ *noun* surtax.

supervene /suːpəˈviːn/ *verb* (**-ning**) *formal* occur as interruption in or change from some state. □ **supervention** *noun*.

supervise /ˈsuːpəvaɪz/ *verb* (**-sing**) oversee, superintend. □ **supervision** /-ˈvɪʒ(ə)n/ *noun*. **supervisor** *noun*. **supervisory** *adjective*.
■ administer, be in charge of, conduct, control, direct, govern, invigilate (*an exam*), keep an eye on, lead, look after, manage, organize, oversee, preside over, run, superintend, watch over.
□ **supervision** administration, conduct, control, direction, government, invigilation, management, organization, oversight, running, surveillance. **supervisor** administrator, chief, controller, director, executive, foreman, forewoman, *colloquial* gaffer, head, inspector, invigilator, leader, manager, organizer, overseer, superintendent, timekeeper.

superwoman *noun colloquial* woman of exceptional ability or power.

supine /ˈsuːpaɪn/ *adjective* **1** lying face upwards. **2** inactive, indolent. ● *noun* type of Latin verbal noun.

■ *adjective* **1** face upwards, flat on one's back, recumbent. **2** see PASSIVE 3.

supper /ˈsʌpə/ *noun* meal taken late in day, esp. evening meal less formal and substantial than dinner.

supplant /səˈplɑːnt/ *verb* take the place of, esp. by underhand means.
■ displace, dispossess, eject, expel, oust, replace, supersede, topple, unseat.

supple /ˈsʌp(ə)l/ *adjective* (**-r**, **-st**) easily bent; pliant, flexible. □ **suppleness** *noun*.
■ bending, *colloquial* bendy, elastic, flexible, graceful, limber, lithe, plastic, pliable, pliant, resilient, soft.

supplement *noun* /ˈsʌplɪmənt/ **1** thing or part added to improve or provide further information. **2** additional charge. **3** separate section of newspaper etc. ● *verb* /ˈsʌplɪment/ provide supplement for. □ **supplemental** /-ˈment(ə)l/ *adjective*. **supplementary** /-ˈmentəri/ *adjective*. **supplementation** *noun*.
■ *noun* **1** addendum, addition, appendix, codicil, continuation, extra, postscript, sequel. **2** extra, surcharge. **3** extra, insert, magazine. ● *verb* add to, augment, boost, complement, extend, reinforce, top up. □ **supplementary** accompanying, added, additional, ancillary, auxiliary, complementary, excess, extra, new, supportive.

suppliant /ˈsʌplɪənt/ *adjective* supplicating. ● *noun* humble petitioner.

supplicate /ˈsʌplɪkeɪt/ *verb* (**-ting**) *literary* make humble petition to or for. □ **supplicant** *noun*. **supplication** *noun*. **supplicatory** /-kətəri/ *adjective*.
■ □ **supplication** appeal, entreaty, petition, plea, prayer, request, solicitation.

supply /səˈplaɪ/ *verb* (**-ies**, **-ied**) **1** provide (thing needed). **2** (often + *with*) provide (person etc. with something). **3** make up for (deficiency etc.). ● *noun* (*plural* **-ies**) **1** provision of what is needed. **2** stock, store. **3** (in *plural*) provisions, equipment, etc. for army, expedition, etc. **4** person, esp. teacher, acting as temporary substitute. □ **supply and demand** quantities available and required, as factors regulating price. □ **supplier** *noun*.
■ *verb* **1, 2** cater to, contribute, deliver, distribute, donate, endow, equip, feed, furnish, give, hand over, pass on, produce, provide, purvey, sell, stock. ● *noun* **1** delivery, distribution, provision, provisioning. **2** cache, hoard, quantity, reserve, reservoir, stock, stockpile, store. **3** (*supplies*) equipment, food, necessities, provisions, rations. □ **supplier** dealer, provider, purveyor, retailer, seller, shopkeeper, vendor, wholesaler.

support /səˈpɔːt/ *verb* **1** carry all or part of weight of. **2** keep from falling, sinking, or failing. **3** provide for. **4** strengthen; encourage; give help to. **5** corroborate; bear out. **6** speak in favour of. **7** take secondary part to (actor etc.). **8** perform secondary act to (main act) at pop concert.

● *noun* **1** supporting, being supported. **2** person or thing that supports. □ **in support of** so as to support. □ **supportable** *adjective*. **supportive** *adjective*. **supportively** *adverb*. **supportiveness** *noun*.

■ *verb* **1, 2** bear, bolster, buttress, carry, hold up, keep up, prop up, reinforce, shore up, strengthen, sustain, underpin. **3** bring up, feed, finance, fund, keep, look after, maintain, nourish, provide for, sustain. **4** aid, allow, approve, assist, back, be faithful to, be interested in, bolster, buoy up, comfort, contribute to, encourage, espouse (*a cause*), fight for, follow, give to, help, patronize, pay money to, promote, rally round, reassure, side with, sponsor, stand by, stand up for, stay with, stick up for, stick with, subsidize, sustain, work for. **5** bear out, confirm, corroborate, defend, endorse, explain, justify, ratify, substantiate, uphold, validate, verify. **6** advocate, agree with, argue for, back, champion, defend, favour, speak up for. ● *noun* **1** aid, approval, assistance, backing, backup, bolstering, contribution, cooperation, encouragement, fortifying, friendship, help, interest, loyalty, patronage, protection, reassurance, reinforcement, *archaic* or *formal* succour. **2** brace, bracket, buttress, crutch, foundation, frame, pillar, post, prop, sling, stanchion, stay, strut, substructure, trestle, truss, underpinning; (*financial support*) aid, backing, donation, expenses, funding, keep, maintenance, sponsorship, subsidy, subsistence, upkeep. □ **supportive** caring, concerned, encouraging, favourable, heartening, helpful, interested, kind, loyal, positive, reassuring, sustaining, sympathetic, understanding.

supporter *noun* person or thing that supports particular cause, team, sport, etc.
■ adherent, admirer, advocate, aficionado, ally, apologist, assistant, champion, collaborator, defender, devotee, enthusiast, fan, fanatic, follower, helper, *usually derogatory* henchman, second, seconder, upholder, voter.

suppose /sə'pəʊz/ *verb* (**-sing**) (often + *that*) **1** assume; be inclined to think. **2** take as possibility or hypothesis. **3** require as condition. **4** (as **supposed** *adjective*) presumed. □ **be supposed to 1** be expected or required to. **2** (in negative) ought not; not be allowed to. **I suppose so** *expression of hesitant agreement*.
■ **1** accept, assume, believe, conclude, conjecture, *colloquial* expect, guess, infer, judge, postulate, presume, presuppose, speculate, surmise, suspect, take for granted, think. **2** daydream, fancy, fantasize, hypothesize, imagine, postulate, pretend, theorize. **4** (**supposed**) see HYPOTHETICAL, PUTATIVE. □ **be supposed to 1** be due to, be expected to, have a duty to, be meant to, be required to.

supposedly /sə'pəʊzɪdlɪ/ *adverb* as is generally believed.

supposition /sʌpə'zɪʃ(ə)n/ *noun* what is supposed or assumed. □ **suppositional** *adjective*.
■ assumption, belief, conjecture, fancy, guess, guesstimate, hypothesis, inference, notion, opinion, presumption, speculation, surmise, theory, thought.

suppositious /sʌpə'zɪʃəs/ *adjective* hypothetical.

suppository /sə'pɒzɪtərɪ/ *noun* (*plural* **-ies**) solid medical preparation put into rectum or vagina to melt.

suppress /sə'pres/ *verb* **1** put an end to. **2** prevent (information, feelings, etc.) from being seen, heard, or known. **3** *Electricity* partially or wholly eliminate (interference etc.). **4** *Electricity* equip (device) to reduce interference due to it. □ **suppressible** *adjective*. **suppression** *noun*. **suppressor** *noun*.
■ **1** conquer, *colloquial* crack down on, crush, end, finish off, halt, overcome, overthrow, put an end to, put down, quash, quell, stamp out, stop, subdue. **2** bottle up, censor, choke back, conceal, cover up, hide, hush up, keep quiet about, keep secret, muffle, mute, obstruct, prohibit, repress, restrain, silence, smother, stamp on, stifle, strangle.

suppurate /'sʌpjʊreɪt/ *verb* (**-ting**) **1** form or secrete pus. **2** fester. □ **suppuration** *noun*.

supra- *prefix* above.

supranational /su:prə'næʃən(ə)l/ *adjective* transcending national limits.

supremacy /su:'preməsɪ/ *noun* (*plural* **-ies**) **1** being supreme. **2** highest authority.
■ ascendancy, dominance, domination, dominion, lead, mastery, predominance, pre-eminence, sovereignty, superiority.

supreme /su:'pri:m/ *adjective* **1** highest in authority or rank. **2** greatest; most important. **3** (of penalty, sacrifice, etc.) involving death. □ **supremely** *adverb*.
■ **1** chief, head, highest, sovereign, top. **2** best, choicest, consummate, crowning, culminating, excellent, finest, first-rate, greatest, highest, incomparable, matchless, outstanding, paramount, peerless, predominant, pre-eminent, prime, principal, superlative, surpassing, *colloquial* tiptop, top, *colloquial* top-notch, ultimate, unbeatable, unbeaten, unparalleled, unrivalled, unsurpassable, unsurpassed.

supremo /su:'pri:məʊ/ *noun* (*plural* **-s**) supreme leader.

surcharge /'sɜ:tʃɑ:dʒ/ *noun* additional charge or payment. ● *verb* (**-ging**) exact surcharge from.

surd *adjective* (of number) irrational. ● *noun* surd number.

sure /ʃʊə/ *adjective* **1** (often + *of, that*) convinced. **2** having or seeming to have adequate reason for belief. **3** (+ *of*) confident in anticipation or knowledge of. **4** reliable, unfailing. **5** (+ *to do*) certain to. **6** undoubtedly true or truthful. ● *adverb colloquial* certainly. □ **make sure** make or become certain; ensure. **sure-fire** *colloquial* certain to succeed. **sure-footed** never stumbling. **to be sure** admittedly, indeed, certainly. □ **sureness** *noun*.

■ *adjective* **1, 2** assured, certain, confident, convinced, decided, definite, persuaded, positive. **4** dependable, effective, established, faithful, firm, infallible, loyal, reliable, resolute, safe, secure, solid, steadfast, steady, trustworthy, *archaic* or *jocular* trusty, undeviating, unerring, unfailing, unfaltering, unflinching, unswerving, unwavering. **5** (*sure to*) bound to, certain to. **6** accurate, clear, convincing, guaranteed, indisputable, inescapable, inevitable, infallible, proven, reliable, true, unchallenged, undeniable, undisputed, undoubted, verifiable.

surely *adverb* **1** with certainty or safety. **2** *added to statement to express strong belief in its correctness.*

surety /ˈʃuːrətɪ/ *noun* (*plural* **-ies**) **1** money given as guarantee of performance etc. **2** person taking responsibility for another's debt, obligation, etc.

surf *noun* foam of sea breaking on rock or (esp. shallow) shore. ● *verb* engage in surfing. □ **surfboard** long narrow board used in surfing. □ **surfer** *noun*.

surface /ˈsɜːfɪs/ *noun* **1** the outside of a thing. **2** any of the limits of a solid. **3** top of liquid, soil, etc. **4** outward or superficial aspect. **5** *Geometry* thing with length and breadth but no thickness. ● *verb* (**-cing**) **1** give (special) surface to (road, paper, etc.). **2** rise or bring to surface. **3** become visible or known. **4** *colloquial* wake up; get up. □ **surface mail** mail not carried by air. **surface tension** tension of surface of liquid, tending to minimize its surface area.

■ *noun* **1** coat, coating, covering, crust, exterior, façade, integument, interface, outside, shell, skin, top, veneer. **2** face, facet, plane, side. **4** exterior, façade, face, outside, top. ● *verb* **1** coat, cover, laminate, veneer. **2, 3** appear, arise, come to light, come up, crop up, emerge, *colloquial* materialize, pop up, rise.

surfeit /ˈsɜːfɪt/ *noun* **1** excess, esp. in eating or drinking. **2** resulting fullness. ● *verb* (**-t-**) **1** overfeed. **2** (+ *with*) (cause to) be wearied through excess.

■ *noun* **1** excess, flood, glut, over-abundance, over-indulgence, oversupply, plethora, superfluity, surplus.

surfing *noun* sport of riding surf on board.

surge *noun* **1** sudden rush. **2** heavy forward or upward motion. **3** sudden increase (in price etc.). **4** sudden but brief increase in pressure, voltage, etc. **5** surging motion of sea, waves, etc. ● *verb* (**-ging**) **1** move suddenly and powerfully forwards. **2** (of sea etc.) swell.

■ *noun* **1, 2** burst, gush, onrush, onset, outpouring, rush, upsurge, wave. **3, 4** increase, rise, upsurge. **5** heave, surf, swell, waves. ● *verb* **1** flow, gush, pour, push, rush, stampede, stream, sweep. **2** billow, heave, rise, roll, swell, well up.

surgeon /ˈsɜːdʒ(ə)n/ *noun* **1** medical practitioner qualified to practise surgery. **2** naval or military medical officer.

surgery /ˈsɜːdʒərɪ/ *noun* (*plural* **-ies**) **1** manual or instrumental treatment of injuries or disorders of body. **2** place where or time when doctor, dentist, etc. gives advice and treatment to patients, or MP, lawyer, etc. gives advice.

■ **1** operation. **2** clinic, consulting room, health centre, infirmary, medical centre, sickbay.

surgical /ˈsɜːdʒɪk(ə)l/ *adjective* **1** of or by surgery or surgeons. **2** used for surgery. **3** (of appliance) worn to correct deformity etc. **4** (esp. of military action) swift and precise. □ **surgical spirit** methylated spirits used for cleansing etc. □ **surgically** *adverb*.

surly /ˈsɜːlɪ/ *adjective* (**-ier**, **-iest**) bad-tempered, unfriendly. □ **surliness** *noun*.

■ bad-tempered, boorish, cantankerous, churlish, crabby, cross, crotchety, crusty, curmudgeonly, dyspeptic, gruff, grumpy, ill-natured, ill-tempered, irascible, miserable, morose, peevish, rough, rude, sulky, sullen, testy, touchy, uncivil, unfriendly, ungracious, unpleasant.

surmise /səˈmaɪz/ *noun* conjecture. ● *verb* (**-sing**) (often + *that*) infer doubtfully; suppose; guess.

■ *verb* assume, believe, conjecture, *colloquial* expect, fancy, gather, guess, hypothesize, imagine, infer, judge, postulate, presume, presuppose, sense, speculate, suppose, suspect, think.

surmount /səˈmaʊnt/ *verb* **1** overcome (difficulty, obstacle). **2** (usually in *passive*) cap, crown. □ **surmountable** *adjective*.

surname /ˈsɜːneɪm/ *noun* name common to all members of family.

surpass /səˈpɑːs/ *verb* **1** outdo; be better than. **2** (as **surpassing** *adjective*) greatly exceeding; excelling others.

■ **1** beat, better, eclipse, exceed, excel, go beyond, leave behind, outclass, outdistance, outdo, outshine, outstrip, overshadow, top, transcend, worst.

surplice /ˈsɜːplɪs/ *noun* loose full-sleeved white vestment worn by clergy etc.

surplus /ˈsɜːpləs/ *noun* **1** amount left over when requirements have been met. **2** excess of income over spending. ● *adjective* exceeding what is needed or used.

■ *noun* **1** balance, excess, extra, glut, oversupply, remainder, residue, superfluity, surfeit.

surprise /səˈpraɪz/ *noun* **1** unexpected or astonishing thing. **2** emotion caused by this. **3** catching or being caught unawares. ● *adjective* made, done, etc. without warning. ● *verb* (**-sing**) **1** affect with surprise. **2** (usually in *passive*; + *at*) shock, scandalize. **3** capture by surprise. **4** come upon (person) unawares. **5** (+ *into*) startle, betray, etc. (person) into doing something. □ **surprising** *adjective*. **surprisingly** *adverb*.

■ *noun* **1** blow, bolt from the blue, bombshell, *colloquial* eye-opener, jolt, shock. **2** alarm, amazement, astonishment, consternation, dismay, incredulity, stupefaction, wonder. ● *verb*

1, 2 amaze, astonish, astound, disconcert, dismay, dumbfound, flabbergast, *colloquial* knock for six, nonplus, rock, shatter, shock, stagger, startle, stun, stupefy, take aback, *colloquial* throw; (*surprised*) incredulous, speechless, struck dumb, thunderstruck. **3, 4** capture, catch out, catch red-handed, come upon, detect, discover, take unawares. □ **surprising** amazing, astonishing, astounding, disconcerting, extraordinary, *colloquial* incredible, shocking, staggering, startling, *colloquial* stunning, sudden, unexpected, unforeseen, unlooked-for, unplanned, unpredictable, upsetting.

surreal /sə'rɪəl/ *adjective* unreal; dreamlike; bizarre.

surrealism /sə'rɪəlɪz(ə)m/ *noun* 20th-c. movement in art and literature aiming to express subconscious mind by dream imagery etc. □ **surrealist** *noun* & *adjective*. **surrealistic** /-'lɪs-/ *adjective*. **surrealistically** /-'lɪs-/ *adverb*.

surrender /sə'rendə/ *verb* **1** hand over, relinquish. **2** submit, esp. to enemy. **3** (often **surrender oneself**; + *to*) yield to habit, emotion, influence, etc. **4** give up rights under (life-insurance policy) in return for smaller sum received immediately. ● *noun* surrendering.

■ *verb* **1** abandon, *formal* cede, deliver up, forgo, give up, hand over, part with, relinquish, renounce, waive. **2** acquiesce, capitulate, cave in, collapse, concede, fall, give in, give oneself up, give up, give way, resign, submit, succumb, throw in the towel, yield. ● *noun* capitulation, giving in, resignation, submission.

surreptitious /sʌrəp'tɪʃəs/ *adjective* done by stealth; underhand. □ **surreptitiously** *adverb*.

■ clandestine, concealed, covert, crafty, disguised, furtive, hidden, private, secret, secretive, *colloquial* shifty, sly, sneaky, stealthy, underhand.

surrogate /'sʌrəgət/ *noun* **1** substitute. **2** deputy, esp. of bishop. □ **surrogate mother** woman who conceives and gives birth to child on behalf of woman unable to do so. □ **surrogacy** *noun*.

surround /sə'raʊnd/ *verb* come or be all round; encircle, enclose. ● *noun* border or edging, esp. area between walls and carpet. □ **surrounding** *adjective*.

■ *verb* beset, besiege, cocoon, cordon off, encircle, enclose, encompass, engulf, envelop, girdle, hedge in, hem in, ring, skirt, trap, wrap. □ **surrounding** adjacent, adjoining, bordering, local, nearby, neighbouring.

surroundings *plural noun* things in neighbourhood of, or conditions affecting, person or thing; environment.

■ ambience, area, background, context, environment, environs, location, milieu, neighbourhood, setting, vicinity.

surtax /'sɜːtæks/ *noun* additional tax, esp. on high incomes.

surtitle /'sɜːtaɪt(ə)l/ *noun* caption translating words of opera, projected on to screen above stage.

surveillance /sə'veɪləns/ *noun* close watch undertaken by police etc., esp. on suspected person.

■ observation, reconnaissance, scrutiny, supervision, watch.

survey *verb* /sə'veɪ/ **1** take or present general view of. **2** examine condition of (building etc.). **3** determine boundaries, extent, ownership, etc. of (district etc.). ● *noun* /'sɜːveɪ/ **1** general view or consideration. **2** investigation of public opinion etc. **3** surveying of property. **4** result of this. **5** map or plan made by surveying.

■ *verb* **1, 2** appraise, assess, estimate, evaluate, examine, inspect, investigate, look over, review, scrutinize, study, view, *colloquial* weigh up. **3** map out, measure, plan out, plot, reconnoitre, triangulate. ● *noun* **1, 2** appraisal, assessment, census, count, evaluation, examination, inquiry, inspection, investigation, poll, review, scrutiny, study. **5** map, plan.

surveyor /sə'veɪə/ *noun* person who surveys land and buildings, esp. professionally.

survival /sə'vaɪv(ə)l/ *noun* **1** surviving. **2** relic.

■ **1** continuance, continued existence, persistence, subsistence.

survive /sə'vaɪv/ *verb* (**-ving**) **1** continue to live or exist. **2** live or exist longer than. **3** come alive through or continue to exist in spite of (danger, accident, etc.). □ **survivable** *adjective*. **survivor** *noun*.

■ **1** bear up, carry on, continue, endure, keep going, last, live, persist, remain. **3** come through, live through, outlast, outlive, pull through, weather, withstand.

sus = SUSS.

susceptibility *noun* (*plural* **-ies**) **1** being susceptible. **2** (in *plural*) person's feelings.

susceptible /sə'septəb(ə)l/ *adjective* **1** impressionable, sensitive; easily moved by emotion. **2** (+ *to*) accessible or sensitive to. **3** (+ *of*) allowing, admitting of (proof etc.).

■ **1** impressionable, responsive, sensitive, suggestible, vulnerable. **2** (*susceptible to*) affected by, disposed to, given to, inclined to, liable to, open to, predisposed to, prone to, responsive to, sensitive to, vulnerable to.

suspect *verb* /səs'pekt/ **1** be inclined to think. **2** have impression of the existence or presence of. **3** (often + *of*) mentally accuse; doubt innocence, genuineness, or truth of. ● *noun* /'sʌspekt/ suspected person. ● *adjective* /'sʌspekt/ subject to suspicion or distrust.

■ *verb* **1** believe, conjecture, consider, guess, imagine, infer, presume, speculate, suppose, surmise, think. **3** call into question, disbelieve, distrust, doubt, have suspicions about, mistrust. ● *adjective* doubtful, dubious, inadequate, questionable, shady, suspected, suspicious, unconvincing, unreliable, unsatisfactory, untrustworthy.

suspend /səs'pend/ *verb* **1** hang up. **2** keep inoperative or undecided temporarily. **3** debar temporarily from function, office, etc. **4** (as **suspended** *adjective*) (of particles or body in fluid) floating between top and bottom. □ **suspended animation** temporary deathlike condition. **suspended sentence** judicial sentence remaining unenforced on condition of good behaviour.

> ■ **1** dangle, hang, swing. **2** adjourn, break off, defer, delay, discontinue, freeze, hold in abeyance, hold up, interrupt, postpone, put off, shelve. **3** debar, dismiss, exclude, expel, lay off, lock out, send down.

suspender *noun* **1** attachment to hold up stocking or sock by its top. **2** (in *plural*) *US* pair of braces. □ **suspender belt** woman's undergarment with suspenders.

suspense /səs'pens/ *noun* state of anxious uncertainty or expectation. □ **suspenseful** *adjective*.

> ■ anticipation, anxiety, apprehension, doubt, drama, excitement, expectancy, expectation, insecurity, irresolution, nervousness, not knowing, tension, uncertainty, waiting.

suspension /səs'penʃ(ə)n/ *noun* **1** suspending, being suspended. **2** means by which vehicle is supported on its axles. **3** substance consisting of particles suspended in fluid. □ **suspension bridge** bridge with roadway suspended from cables supported by towers.

suspicion /səs'pɪʃ(ə)n/ *noun* **1** unconfirmed belief; distrust. **2** suspecting, being suspected. **3** (+ *of*) slight trace of.

> ■ **1** apprehension, apprehensiveness, caution, distrust, doubt, *literary* dubiety, dubiousness, guess, hunch, impression, misgiving, mistrust, presentiment, qualm, scepticism, uncertainty, wariness. **3** glimmer, hint, inkling, shadow, suggestion, tinge, touch, trace.

suspicious /səs'pɪʃəs/ *adjective* **1** prone to or feeling suspicion. **2** indicating or justifying suspicion. □ **suspiciously** *adverb*.

> ■ **1** apprehensive, chary, disbelieving, distrustful, doubtful, dubious, incredulous, in doubt, mistrustful, sceptical, uncertain, unconvinced, uneasy, wary. **2** disreputable, dubious, *slang* fishy, peculiar, questionable, shady, suspect, suspected, unreliable, untrustworthy.

suss /sʌs/ *verb* (also **sus**) (**-ss-**) *slang* (usually + *out*) **1** investigate; inspect. **2** understand; work out.

sustain /səs'tem/ *verb* **1** bear weight of; support, esp. for long period. **2** encourage, support. **3** endure, stand. **4** (of food) nourish. **5** undergo (defeat, injury, loss, etc.). **6** (of court etc.) decide in favour of; uphold. **7** substantiate, corroborate. **8** keep up (effort etc.). □ **sustainable** *adjective*.

> ■ **1** see SUPPORT *verb* 1,2. **2** see SUPPORT *verb* 4. **8** continue, extend, keep alive, keep going, keep up, maintain, prolong.

sustenance /'sʌstməns/ *noun* **1** nourishment, food. **2** means of support.

> ■ **1** eatables, edibles, food, foodstuffs, nourishment, nutriment, *jocular* provender, provisions, rations, victuals.

suture /'su:tʃə/ *noun* **1** joining edges of wound or incision by stitching. **2** stitch or thread etc. used for this. ● *verb* (**-ring**) stitch (wound, incision).

suzerain /'su:zərən/ *noun* **1** *historical* feudal overlord. **2** *archaic* sovereign or state having some control over another state that is internally self-governing. □ **suzerainty** *noun*.

svelte /svelt/ *adjective* slim, slender, graceful.

SW *abbreviation* south-west(ern).

swab /swɒb/ *noun* **1** absorbent pad used in surgery. **2** specimen of secretion etc. taken for examination. **3** mop etc. for cleaning or mopping up. ● *verb* (**-bb-**) **1** clean with swab. **2** (+ *up*) absorb (moisture) with swab. **3** mop clean (ship's deck).

swaddle /'swɒd(ə)l/ *verb* (**-ling**) wrap tightly in bandages, wrappings, etc. □ **swaddling-clothes** narrow bandages formerly wrapped round newborn child to restrain its movements.

swag *noun* **1** *slang* thief's booty. **2** *Australian & NZ* traveller's bundle. **3** festoon of flowers, foliage, drapery, etc.

> ■ **1** booty, loot, plunder, takings.

swagger /'swægə/ *verb* walk or behave arrogantly or self-importantly. ● *noun* swaggering gait or manner. □ **swaggerer** *noun*.

> ■ *verb* parade, prance, *colloquial* show off, strut, *colloquial* swank.

swain *noun* **1** *archaic* country youth. **2** *poetical* young lover or suitor.

swallow[1] /'swɒləʊ/ *verb* **1** make or let (food etc.) pass down one's throat. **2** accept meekly or gullibly. **3** repress (emotion). **4** (often + *up*) engulf; absorb; make disappear. **5** say (words etc.) indistinctly. ● *noun* **1** act of swallowing. **2** amount swallowed.

> ■ *verb* **1** consume, drink, eat, gulp down, guzzle, ingest, take down. **4** (*swallow up*) absorb, assimilate, consume, enclose, enfold, engulf, swamp.

swallow[2] /'swɒləʊ/ *noun* migratory swift-flying bird with forked tail. □ **swallow-dive** dive with arms spread sideways. **swallow-tail 1** deeply forked tail. **2** butterfly etc. with this.

swam *past* of SWIM.

swamp /swɒmp/ *noun* piece of wet spongy ground. ● *verb* **1** submerge, inundate. **2** cause to fill with water and sink. **3** overwhelm with numbers or quantity. □ **swampy** *adjective* (**-ier**, **-iest**).

> ■ *noun* bog, fen, marsh, marshland, *literary* morass, mud, mudflats, quagmire, salt marsh, slough, wetlands. ● *verb* deluge, drench, engulf, envelop, flood, immerse, inundate, overcome, overwhelm, sink, submerge, swallow up. □ **swampy** boggy, marshy, muddy, soft, soggy, unstable, waterlogged, wet.

swan /swɒn/ *noun* large web-footed usually white waterfowl with long flexible neck. ● *verb* (**-nn-**) (usually + *about, off,* etc.) *colloquial* move about casually or with superior manner. □ **swansong** person's last work or performance before death, retirement, etc.

swank *colloquial noun* ostentation, swagger. ● *verb* show off. □ **swanky** *adjective* (**-ier, -iest**).

swap /swɒp/ (also **swop**) *verb* (**-pp-**) exchange, barter. ● *noun* **1** act of swapping. **2** thing suitable for swapping.

sward /swɔːd/ *noun literary* expanse of short grass.

swarf /swɔːf/ *noun* fine chips or filings of stone, metal, etc.

swarm[1] /swɔːm/ *noun* **1** cluster of bees leaving hive etc. with queen bee to establish new colony. **2** large group of insects, birds, or people. **3** (in *plural*; + *of*) great numbers. ● *verb* **1** move in or form swarm. **2** (+ *with*) be overrun or crowded with.

■ *noun* **1, 2** army, cloud, crowd, *usually derogatory* horde, host, multitude, throng. ● *verb* **1** cluster, congregate, crowd, flock, gather, mass, throng. **2** (*swarm with*) see TEEM[1] 2.

swarm[2] /swɔːm/ *verb* (+ *up*) climb (rope, tree, etc.) clasping or clinging with arms and legs.

■ (*swarm up*) see CLIMB *verb* 1.

swarthy /ˈswɔːðɪ/ *adjective* (**-ier, -iest**) dark-complexioned; dark in colour.

■ brown, dark, dark-complexioned, dark-skinned, dusky, tanned.

swashbuckler /ˈswɒʃbʌklə/ *noun* swaggering adventurer. □ **swashbuckling** *adjective & noun.*

■ □ **swashbuckling** *adjective* adventurous, bold, daredevil, daring, dashing, macho, manly, swaggering.

swastika /ˈswɒstɪkə/ *noun* **1** ancient symbol formed by equal-armed cross with each arm continued at a right angle. **2** this with clockwise continuations as symbol of Nazi Germany.

swat /swɒt/ *verb* (**-tt-**) **1** crush (fly etc.) with blow. **2** hit hard and abruptly. ● *noun* act of swatting.

swatch /swɒtʃ/ *noun* **1** sample, esp. of cloth. **2** collection of samples.

swath /swɔːθ/ *noun* (also **swathe** /sweɪð/) **1** ridge of cut grass, corn, etc. **2** space left clear by mower, scythe, etc.

swathe /sweɪð/ *verb* (**-thing**) bind or wrap in bandages, garments, etc.

sway *verb* **1** (cause to) move unsteadily from side to side. **2** oscillate irregularly; waver. **3** have influence over. ● *noun* **1** influence; rule, government. **2** swaying motion.

■ *verb* **1, 2** bend, fluctuate, lean from side to side, oscillate, rock, roll, swing, undulate, wave, waver. **3** affect, bias, bring round, convert, convince, influence, persuade, win over.

swear /sweə/ *verb* (*past* **swore**; *past participle* **sworn**) **1** state or promise on oath. **2** cause to take oath. **3** *colloquial* insist. **4** (often + *at*) use profane or obscene language. **5** (+ *by*) appeal to as witness or guarantee of oath. **6** (+ *by*) *colloquial* have great confidence in. □ **swear in** admit to office etc. by administering oath. **swear off** *colloquial* promise to keep off (drink etc.). **swear word** profane or obscene word.

■ **1, 3** affirm, asseverate, attest, *formal* aver, *formal* avow, declare, give one's word, insist, pledge, promise, state on oath, take an oath, testify, *formal* vouchsafe, vow. **4** blaspheme, curse, execrate, utter profanities. □ **swear word** blasphemy, curse, execration, expletive, four-letter word, *formal* imprecation, oath, obscenity, profanity.

sweat /swet/ *noun* **1** moisture exuded through pores, esp. when one is hot or nervous. **2** state or period of sweating. **3** *colloquial* state of anxiety. **4** *colloquial* drudgery, effort. **5** *colloquial* laborious task or undertaking. **6** condensed moisture on surface. ● *verb* (*past* and *past participle* **sweated** or *US* **sweat**) **1** exude sweat. **2** be terrified, suffer, etc. **3** (of wall etc.) show surface moisture. **4** (cause to) toil or drudge. **5** emit like sweat. **6** make (horse, athlete, etc.) sweat by exercise. **7** (as **sweated** *adjective*) (of goods, labour, etc.) produced by or subjected to exploitation. □ **no sweat** *colloquial* no bother; no trouble. **sweatband** band of absorbent material inside hat or round head, wrist, etc. to soak up sweat. **sweatshirt** sleeved cotton sweater. **sweatshop** workshop where sweated labour is employed. □ **sweaty** *adjective* (**-ier, -iest**).

■ *verb* **1** perspire. **4** see WORK *verb* 1. □ **sweaty** clammy, damp, moist, perspiring, sticky, sweating.

sweater *noun* woollen etc. pullover.

Swede *noun* **1** native or national of Sweden. **2** (**swede**) large yellow variety of turnip.

Swedish /ˈswiːdɪʃ/ *adjective* of Sweden. ● *noun* language of Sweden.

sweep *verb* (*past & past participle* **swept**) **1** clean or clear (room, area, etc.) (as) with a broom. **2** (often + *up*) collect or remove (dirt etc.) by sweeping. **3** (+ *aside, away,* etc.) dismiss abruptly. **4** (+ *along, down,* etc.) drive or carry along with force. **5** (+ *off, away,* etc.) remove or clear forcefully. **6** traverse swiftly or lightly. **7** impart sweeping motion to. **8** glide swiftly; go majestically. **9** (of landscape etc.) be rolling or spacious. ● *noun* **1** act or motion of sweeping. **2** curve in road etc. **3** range, scope. **4** chimney sweep. **5** sortie by aircraft. **6** *colloquial* sweepstake. □ **sweep the board** **1** win all the money in gambling game. **2** win all possible prizes etc. **sweepstake** form of gambling on horse races etc. in which money staked is divided among those who have drawn numbered tickets for winners.

■ *verb* **1** brush, clean, clear, dust, tidy up. **5** (*sweep away*) see REMOVE *verb* 1. **8** see MOVE *verb* 4.

sweeping *adjective* **1** wide in range or effect. **2** generalized, arbitrary. ● *noun* (in *plural*) dirt etc. collected by sweeping.

■ *adjective* **1** see GENERAL *adjective* 1. **2** see SUPERFICIAL 2.

sweet *adjective* **1** tasting like sugar, honey, etc. **2** smelling pleasant like roses, perfume, etc.; fragrant. **3** melodious. **4** fresh. **5** not sour or bitter. **6** gratifying, attractive. **7** amiable, gentle. **8** *colloquial* pretty. **9** (+ *on*) *colloquial* fond of; in love with. ● *noun* **1** small shaped piece of sugar or chocolate confectionery. **2** sweet dish forming course of meal. □ **sweet and sour** cooked in sauce with sugar, vinegar, etc. **sweetbread** pancreas or thymus of animal, as food. **sweet-brier** single-flowered fragrant-leaved wild rose. **sweetcorn** sweet-flavoured maize kernels. **sweetheart** either of pair of lovers. **sweetmeat** *archaic* **1** a sweet. **2** a small fancy cake. **sweet pea** climbing garden annual with scented flowers in many colours. **sweet pepper** fruit of capsicum. **sweet potato** tropical plant with edible tuberous roots. **sweet-talk** flatter in order to persuade. **sweet tooth** liking for sweet-tasting things. **sweet william** garden plant with close clusters of sweet-smelling flowers. □ **sweetish** *adjective*. **sweetly** *adverb*.

■ *adjective* **1** cloying, honeyed, luscious, mellow, saccharine, sickly, sugary, sweetened, syrupy, treacly. **2** aromatic, fragrant, perfumed, scented, sweet-scented, sweet-smelling. **3** dulcet, euphonious, harmonious, mellifluous, melodious, musical, pleasant, silvery, soothing, tuneful. **7** affectionate, amiable, charming, dear, endearing, engaging, friendly, genial, gentle, gracious, lovable, *colloquial* lovely, nice, pretty, unselfish, winning. ● *noun* **1** bon-bon, *US* candy, drop, fondant, pastille, *colloquial* sweetie, *archaic* sweetmeat, toffee; (*sweets*) confectionery. **2** *colloquial* afters, dessert, pudding.

sweeten *verb* **1** make or become sweet(er). **2** make agreeable or less painful. □ **sweetening** *noun*.

■ **1** sugar. **2** appease, assuage, calm, mellow, mollify, pacify, soothe.

sweetener *noun* **1** thing that sweetens. **2** *colloquial* bribe.

sweetie *noun colloquial* **1** a sweet. **2** sweetheart.

sweetness *noun* being sweet; fragrance. □ **sweetness and light** (esp. uncharacteristic) mildness and reason.

swell *verb* (*past participle* **swollen** /'swəʊlən/ or **-ed**) **1** (cause to) grow bigger, louder, or more intense. **2** rise or raise up. **3** (+ *out*) bulge out. **4** (of heart etc.) feel full of joy, pride, etc. **5** (+ *with*) be hardly able to restrain (pride etc.). ● *noun* **1** act or state of swelling. **2** heaving of sea etc. with unbreaking rolling waves. **3** crescendo. **4** mechanism in organ etc. for gradually varying volume. **5** *colloquial* fashionable or stylish person. ● *adjective esp. US colloquial* fine, excellent. □ **swelled head** (also **swollen head**) *colloquial* conceit. **swollen-headed** *colloquial* conceited.

■ *verb* **1** augment, blow up, boost, build up, dilate, enlarge, expand, extend, grow, heighten, increase, intensify, mushroom, raise, rise, step up. **3** (*swell out*) balloon, belly (out), billow, bloat, blow up, bulge out, distend, expand, fatten, fill out, inflate, puff up.

swelling *noun* abnormally swollen place, esp. on body.

■ blister, boil, bulge, bump, distension, enlargement, excrescence, hump, inflammation, knob, lump, node, nodule, prominence, protrusion, protuberance, tumescence, tumour.

swelter /'sweltə/ *verb* be uncomfortably hot. ● *noun* sweltering condition. □ **sweltering** *adjective*.

■ □ **sweltering** hot, humid, muggy, oppressive, steamy, sticky, stifling, sultry, torrid, tropical.

swept *past & past participle* of SWEEP.

swerve *verb* (**-ving**) (cause to) change direction, esp. suddenly. ● *noun* swerving motion.

■ *verb* career, deviate, diverge, dodge about, sheer off, swing, turn aside, veer, wheel.

swift *adjective* **1** rapid, quick. **2** prompt. ● *noun* swift-flying long-winged migratory bird. □ **swiftly** *adverb*. **swiftness** *noun*.

■ *adjective* agile, brisk, expeditious, fast, *poetical* or *literary* fleet, fleet-footed, hasty, hurried, nimble, *colloquial* nippy, prompt, quick, rapid, speedy, sudden.

swig *colloquial verb* (**-gg-**) drink in large draughts. ● *noun* swallow of liquid, esp. of large amount.

swill *verb* **1** (often + *out*) rinse; pour water over or through. **2** drink greedily. ● *noun* **1** swilling. **2** mainly liquid refuse as pig-food.

■ *verb* **1** bathe, clean, rinse, wash. **2** see DRINK *verb* 1.

swim *verb* (**-mm-**; *past* **swam**; *past participle* **swum**) **1** propel body through water with limbs, fins, etc. **2** perform (stroke) or cross (river etc.) by swimming. **3** float on liquid. **4** appear to undulate, reel, or whirl. **5** (of head) feel dizzy. **6** (+ *in*, *with*) be flooded. ● *noun* act or spell of swimming. □ **in the swim** *colloquial* involved in or aware of what is going on. **swimming bath, pool** pool constructed for swimming. **swimming costume** bathing costume. **swimsuit** swimming costume, esp. one-piece for women and girls. **swimwear** clothing for swimming in. □ **swimmer** *noun*.

■ *verb* **1** bathe, take a dip. □ **swimming bath, pool** baths, lido. **swimsuit** bathing costume, bikini, swimwear, trunks.

swimmingly *adverb colloquial* smoothly; without obstruction.

swindle /'swɪnd(ə)l/ *verb* (**-ling**) (often + *out of*) cheat of money etc.; defraud. ● *noun* **1** act of swindling. **2** fraudulent person or thing. □ **swindler** *noun*.

■ *verb colloquial* bamboozle, cheat, *slang* con, *literary* cozen, deceive, defraud, *colloquial* diddle, *slang* do, double-cross, dupe, exploit, *slang* fiddle, fleece, fool, gull, hoax, hoodwink, *colloquial* pull a fast one on, *colloquial* rook, *colloquial* take for a ride, trick, welsh (*on a bet*). ● *noun* **1** cheating, chicanery, deception, double-dealing, fraud, knavery, sharp practice, trickery. **2** cheat, *slang* con, confidence trick, fraud, hoax, *slang* racket, *colloquial* rip-off, *colloquial* swizz, trick.

□ **swindler** charlatan, cheat, cheater, con man, counterfeiter, double-crosser, extortioner, forger, fraud, hoaxer, impostor, knave, mountebank, quack, racketeer, scoundrel, *colloquial* shark, *colloquial* shyster, trickster, *colloquial* twister.

swine *noun* (*plural* same) **1** *formal* or *US* pig. **2** (*plural* same or **-s**) *colloquial* disgusting person; unpleasant or difficult thing. □ **swinish** *adjective*.

swing *verb* (*past & past participle* **swung**) **1** (cause to) move with to-and-fro or curving motion. **2** sway or hang like pendulum or door etc. **3** oscillate. **4** move by gripping something and leaping etc. **5** walk with swinging gait. **6** (cause to) change direction. **7** (+ *round*) move to face opposite direction. **8** (+ *at*) attempt to hit. **9** *colloquial* (of party etc.) be lively. **10** have decisive influence on (voting etc.). **11** change from one opinion, mood, etc. to another. **12** *colloquial* be executed by hanging. ● *noun* **1** act, motion, or extent of swinging. **2** swinging or smooth gait, rhythm, or action. **3** seat slung by ropes, chains, etc. for swinging on or in. **4** spell of swinging thus. **5** smooth rhythmic jazz or jazzy dance music. **6** amount by which votes etc. change from one side to another. □ **swingboat** boat-shaped swing at fairs etc. **swing-bridge** bridge that can be swung aside to let ships etc. pass. **swing-door** door that swings in either direction and closes by itself when released. **swings and roundabouts** situation allowing equal gain and loss. **swing-wing** (aircraft) with wings that can pivot to point sideways or backwards. □ **swinger** *noun*.

■ *verb* **1–3** be suspended, dangle, flap, fluctuate, hang loosely, move from side to side, move to and fro, oscillate, revolve, rock, roll, sway, swivel, turn, twirl, wave about, zigzag. **6** deviate, divert, go off course, swerve, turn, veer. **7** (*swing round*) pivot, swivel, wheel. **10** affect, bias, bring round, convert, convince, govern, influence, persuade, sway, win over. **11** change, fluctuate, oscillate, shift, transfer, vacillate, vary, waver. ● *noun* **1** oscillation, sway, sweep. **6** change, fluctuation, movement, shift, variation.

swingeing /ˈswɪndʒɪŋ/ *adjective* **1** (of blow etc.) forcible. **2** huge, far-reaching.

swipe *colloquial verb* (**-ping**) **1** (often + *at*) hit hard and recklessly. **2** steal. ● *noun* reckless hard hit or attempt to hit.

■ *verb* **1** hit, lash out at, strike, swing at. **2** see STEAL *verb* 1.

swirl *verb* move, flow, or carry along with whirling motion. ● *noun* **1** swirling motion. **2** twist, curl. □ **swirly** *adjective*.

■ *verb* boil, churn, circulate, curl, eddy, seethe, spin, surge, twirl, twist, whirl.

swish *verb* **1** swing (cane, scythe, etc.) audibly through air, grass, etc. **2** move with or make swishing sound. ● *noun* swishing action or sound. ● *adjective colloquial* smart, fashionable.

Swiss *adjective* of Switzerland. ● *noun* (*plural* same) native or national of Switzerland. □ **Swiss roll** cylindrical cake, made by rolling up thin flat sponge cake spread with jam etc.

switch *noun* **1** device for making and breaking connection in electric circuit. **2** transfer, changeover, deviation. **3** flexible shoot cut from tree. **4** light tapering rod. **5** *US* railway points. ● *verb* **1** (+ *on*, *off*) turn (electrical device) on or off. **2** change or transfer (position, subject, etc.). **3** exchange. **4** whip or flick with switch. □ **switchback 1** ride at fair etc. with extremely steep ascents and descents. **2** similar railway or road. **switchboard** apparatus for varying connections between electric circuits, esp. in telephony. **switched-on** *colloquial* up to date; aware of what is going on. **switch off** *colloquial* cease to pay attention.

■ *verb* **2** change, divert, redirect, shift, transfer, turn. **3** change, exchange, replace, reverse, substitute, swap.

swivel /ˈswɪv(ə)l/ *noun* coupling between two parts etc. so that one can turn freely without the other. ● *verb* (**-ll-**; *US* **-l-**) turn (as) on swivel; swing round. □ **swivel chair** chair with revolving seat.

■ *verb* gyrate, pirouette, pivot, revolve, rotate, spin, swing, turn, twirl, wheel.

swizz *noun* (also **swiz**) *colloquial* **1** something disappointing. **2** swindle.

swizzle /ˈswɪz(ə)l/ *noun* **1** *colloquial* frothy mixed alcoholic drink, esp. of rum or gin and bitters. **2** *colloquial* swizz. □ **swizzle-stick** stick used for frothing or flattening drinks.

swollen *past participle* of SWELL.

swoon /swuːn/ *verb & noun literary* faint.

swoop /swuːp/ *verb* **1** (often + *down*) come down with rush like bird of prey. **2** (often + *on*) make sudden attack. ● *noun* act of swooping; sudden pounce.

■ *verb* **1** descend, dive, drop, fall, fly down, lunge, plunge, pounce. **2** (*swoop on*) see RAID *verb* 1.

swop = SWAP.

sword /sɔːd/ *noun* weapon with long blade for cutting or thrusting. □ **put to the sword** kill. **sword dance** dance with brandishing of swords, or steps about swords laid on ground. **swordfish** (*plural* same or **-es**) large sea fish with swordlike upper jaw. **swordplay 1** fencing. **2** repartee; lively arguing. **swordsman** person of (usually specified) skill with sword. **swordstick** hollow walking stick containing sword blade.

■ *poetical* blade, *historical* cutlass, dagger, foil, rapier, sabre, scimitar.

swore *past* of SWEAR.

sworn *past participle* of SWEAR. ● *adjective* bound (as) by oath.

swot *colloquial verb* (**-tt-**) **1** study hard. **2** (usually + *up*, *up on*) study (subject) hard or hurriedly. ● *noun usually derogatory* person who swots.

swum *past participle* of SWIM.

swung *past & past participle* of SWING.

sybarite /'sɪbəraɪt/ *noun* self-indulgent or luxury-loving person. □ **sybaritic** /-'rɪt-/ *adjective*.

sycamore /'sɪkəmɔː/ *noun* 1 large maple tree. 2 its wood. 3 *US* plane tree. 4 *US* its wood.

sycophant /'sɪkəfænt/ *noun* flatterer, toady. □ **sycophancy** *noun*. **sycophantic** /-'fæn-/ *adjective*.

■ □ **sycophantic** *colloquial* crawling, flattering, obsequious, servile, *colloquial* smarmy, toadying, unctuous.

syllabic /sɪ'læbɪk/ *adjective* of or in syllables. □ **syllabically** *adverb*.

syllable /'sɪləb(ə)l/ *noun* unit of pronunciation forming whole or part of word, usually consisting of vowel sound with consonant(s) before or after (see panel). □ **in words of one syllable** plainly, bluntly.

syllabub /'sɪləbʌb/ *noun* dessert of cream or milk sweetened and whipped with wine etc.

syllabus /'sɪləbəs/ *noun* (*plural* **-buses** or **-bi** /-baɪ/) programme or outline of course of study, teaching, etc.

■ course, curriculum, outline, programme.

syllogism /'sɪlədʒɪz(ə)m/ *noun* form of reasoning in which from two propositions a third is deduced. □ **syllogistic** /-'dʒɪs-/ *adjective*.

sylph /sɪlf/ *noun* 1 elemental spirit of air. 2 slender graceful woman. □ **sylphlike** *adjective*.

sylvan /'sɪlv(ə)n/ *adjective* (also **silvan**) 1 of the woods. 2 having woods. 3 rural.

■ 1 arboreal, leafy, tree-covered, wooded.

symbiosis /sɪmbaɪ'əʊsɪs/ *noun* (*plural* **-bioses** /-siːz/) 1 (usually mutually advantageous) association of two different organisms living attached to one another etc. 2 mutually advantageous connection between people. □ **symbiotic** /-'ɒt-/ *adjective*.

symbol /'sɪmb(ə)l/ *noun* 1 thing generally regarded as typifying, representing, or recalling something. 2 mark, sign, etc. representing object, idea, process, etc. □ **symbolic** /-'bɒl-/ *adjective*. **symbolically** /-'bɒl-/ *adverb*.

■ badge, brand, character, cipher, coat of arms, crest, emblem, figure, hieroglyph, icon, ideogram, ideograph, image, insignia, logo, mark, monogram, motif, pictogram, pictograph, sign, token, trade mark. □ **symbolic** allegorical,

emblematic, figurative, meaningful, metaphorical, representative, significant, suggestive, symptomatic, token (*gesture*).

symbolism *noun* 1 use of symbols. 2 symbols. 3 artistic movement or style using symbols to express ideas, emotions, etc. □ **symbolist** *noun*.

symbolize *verb* (also **-ise**) (**-zing** or **-sing**) 1 be symbol of. 2 represent by symbol(s).

■ 1 be a sign of, betoken, communicate, connote, denote, epitomize, imply, indicate, mean, represent, signify, stand for, suggest. 2 denote, indicate, represent, signify.

symmetry /'sɪmɪtrɪ/ *noun* (*plural* **-ies**) 1 correct proportion of parts. 2 beauty resulting from this. 3 structure allowing object to be divided into parts of equal shape and size. 4 possession of such structure. 5 repetition of exactly similar parts facing each other or a centre. □ **symmetric** *adjective*. **symmetrical** /-'met-/ *adjective*. **symmetrically** /-'met-/ *adverb*.

■ □ **symmetrical** balanced, even, proportional, regular.

sympathetic /sɪmpə'θetɪk/ *adjective* 1 of or expressing sympathy. 2 likeable, pleasant. 3 (+ *to*) favouring (proposal etc.). □ **sympathetically** *adverb*.

■ 1 benevolent, caring, charitable, comforting, commiserating, compassionate, concerned, consoling, empathetic, friendly, humane, interested, kind-hearted, kindly, merciful, pitying, soft-hearted, solicitous, sorry, supportive, tender, tolerant, understanding, warm.

sympathize /'sɪmpəθaɪz/ *verb* (also **-ise**) (**-zing** or **-sing**) (often + *with*) 1 feel or express sympathy. 2 agree. □ **sympathizer** *noun*.

■ 1 (*sympathize with*) be sorry for, comfort, commiserate with, condole with, console, empathize with, feel for, identify with, pity, understand. 2 (*sympathize with*) agree with, favour, go along with, support.

sympathy /'sɪmpəθɪ/ *noun* (*plural* **-ies**) 1 sharing of another's feelings. 2 (often + *with*) sharing or tendency to share emotion, sensation, condition, etc. of another person. 3 (in *singular* or *plural*) compassion; commiseration; condolences. 4 (often + *with*) agreement (with person etc.) in opinion or desire. □ **in sympathy** (often + *with*) having, showing, or resulting from sympathy.

Syllable

A syllable is the smallest unit of speech that can be pronounced in isolation, such as *a*, *at*, *ta*, or *tat*. A word can be made up of one or two or more syllables:

> *cat*, *fought*, and *twinge* each have one syllable;
> *rating*, *deny*, and *collapse* each have two syllables;
> *excitement*, *superman*, and *telephone* each have three syllables;
> *America* and *complicated* each have four syllables;
> *examination* and *uncontrollable* each have five syllables.

■ **1–3** commiseration, compassion, concern, condolence, consideration, empathy, feeling, fellow feeling, kindness, mercy, pity, solicitousness, tenderness, understanding. **4** affinity, agreement, concord, rapport, unanimity.

symphony /'sɪmfənɪ/ *noun* (*plural* **-ies**) musical composition in several movements for full orchestra. ▫ **symphony orchestra** large orchestra playing symphonies etc. ▫ **symphonic** /-'fɒn-/ *adjective*.

symposium /sɪm'pəʊzɪəm/ *noun* (*plural* **-sia**) conference, or collection of essays, on particular subject.

symptom /'sɪmptəm/ *noun* **1** physical or mental sign of disease or injury. **2** sign of existence of something. ▫ **symptomatic** /-'mæt-/ *adjective*.

■ characteristic, evidence, feature, indication, manifestation, mark, marker, sign, warning, warning sign. ▫ **symptomatic** characteristic, indicative, representative, suggestive, typical.

synagogue /'sɪnəgɒg/ *noun* building for Jewish religious instruction and worship.

sync /sɪŋk/ (also **synch**) *colloquial noun* synchronization. ● *verb* synchronize. ▫ **in or out of sync** (often + *with*) according or agreeing well or badly.

synchromesh /'sɪŋkrəʊmeʃ/ *noun* system of gear-changing, esp. in vehicles, in which gear-wheels revolve at same speed during engagement. ● *adjective* of this system.

synchronize /'sɪŋkrənaɪz/ *verb* (also **-ise**) (**-zing** or **-sing**) **1** (often + *with*) make or be synchronous (with). **2** make sound and picture of (film etc.) coincide. **3** cause (clocks etc.) to show same time. ▫ **synchronization** *noun*.

synchronous /'sɪŋkrənəs/ *adjective* (often + *with*) existing or occurring at same time.

syncopate /'sɪŋkəpeɪt/ *verb* (**-ting**) **1** displace beats or accents in (music). **2** shorten (word) by omitting syllable or letter(s) in middle. ▫ **syncopation** *noun*.

syncope /'sɪŋkəpɪ/ *noun* **1** *Grammar* syncopation. **2** *Medicine* fainting through fall in blood pressure.

syncretize /'sɪŋkrətaɪz/ *verb* (also **-ise**) (**-zing** or **-sing**) attempt to unify or reconcile differing schools of thought. ▫ **syncretic** /-'kret-/ *adjective*. **syncretism** *noun*.

syndicalism /'sɪndɪkəlɪz(ə)m/ *noun historical* movement for transferring industrial control and ownership to workers' unions. ▫ **syndicalist** *noun*.

syndicate *noun* /'sɪndɪkət/ **1** combination of people, commercial firms, etc. to promote some common interest. **2** agency supplying material simultaneously to a number of periodicals etc. **3** group of people who gamble, organize crime, etc. ● *verb* /'sɪndɪkeɪt/ (**-ting**) **1** form into syndicate. **2** publish (material) through syndicate. ▫ **syndication** *noun*.

syndrome /'sɪndrəʊm/ *noun* **1** group of concur-rent symptoms of disease. **2** characteristic combination of opinions, emotions, etc.

synod /'sɪnəd/ *noun* Church council of clergy and lay people.

synonym /'sɪnənɪm/ *noun* word or phrase that has same meaning as or similar meaning to another word or phrase.

synonymous /sɪ'nɒnɪməs/ *adjective* **1** (often + *with*) having same meaning. **2** suggestive of; associated with.

synopsis /sɪ'nɒpsɪs/ *noun* (*plural* **synopses** /-siːz/) summary; outline.

synoptic /sɪ'nɒptɪk/ *adjective* of or giving synopsis. ▫ **Synoptic Gospels** those of Matthew, Mark, and Luke.

syntax /'sɪntæks/ *noun* **1** grammatical arrangement of words. **2** rules or analysis of this. ▫ **syntactic** /-'tæk-/ *adjective*.

synthesis /'sɪnθəsɪs/ *noun* (*plural* **-theses** /-siːz/) **1** putting together of parts or elements to make up complex whole. **2** *Chemistry* artificial production of (esp. organic) substances from simpler ones.

■ amalgamation, blend, coalescence, combination, composite, compound, fusion, integration, union.

synthesize /'sɪnθəsaɪz/ *verb* (also **-ise**) (**-zing** or **-sing**) make synthesis of.

synthesizer *noun* (also **-iser**) electronic, usually keyboard, instrument producing great variety of sounds.

synthetic /sɪn'θetɪk/ *adjective* **1** produced by synthesis, esp. to imitate natural product. **2** affected, insincere. ● *noun* synthetic substance. ▫ **synthetically** *adverb*.

■ *adjective* **1** artificial, bogus, concocted, counterfeit, ersatz, fabricated, fake, made up, man-made, manufactured, mock, *colloquial* phoney, simulated, spurious, unnatural.

syphilis /'sɪfəlɪs/ *noun* a contagious venereal disease. ▫ **syphilitic** /-'lɪt-/ *adjective*.

Syrian /'sɪrɪən/ *noun* native or national of Syria. ● *adjective* of Syria.

syringa /sɪ'rɪŋgə/ *noun* shrub with white scented flowers.

syringe /sɪ'rɪndʒ/ *noun* device for drawing in quantity of liquid and ejecting it in fine stream. ● *verb* (**-ging**) sluice or spray with syringe.

■ *noun* hypodermic, needle.

syrup /'sɪrəp/ *noun* (*US* **sirup**) **1** sweet sauce of sugar dissolved in boiling water, often flavoured or medicated. **2** condensed sugar-cane juice; molasses, treacle. **3** excessive sweetness of manner. ▫ **syrupy** *adjective*.

system /'sɪstəm/ *noun* **1** complex whole; set of connected things or parts; organized group of things. **2** set of organs in body with common structure or function. **3** human or animal body as organized whole. **4** method, scheme of action, procedure, or classification. **5** orderliness. **6** set of principles forming philosophy, form of government, etc. **7 (the system)** prevailing political or social order, esp. seen as oppressive. □ **get (thing) out of one's system** get rid of (anxiety etc.). **systems analysis** analysis of complex process etc. so as to improve its efficiency, esp. by using computer.

■ **1** network, organization, set-up, structure. **4** approach, arrangement, categorization, classification, logic, method, methodology, *modus operandi*, order, plan, practice, principles, procedure, process, routine, rules, scheme, science, technique, theory. **5** see ORDER *noun* 1,2, TIDINESS (TIDY). **6** code, constitution, discipline, philosophy, regime, set of principles.

systematic /sɪstə'mætɪk/ *adjective* **1** methodical; according to system. **2** deliberate. □ **systematically** *adverb*.

■ **1** businesslike, categorized, classified, codified, constitutional, coordinated, logical, methodical, neat, ordered, orderly, organized, planned, rational, regimented, routine, scientific, structured, tidy, well arranged, well organized, well rehearsed, well run.

systematize /'sɪstəmətaɪz/ *verb* (also **-ise**) (**-zing** or **-sing**) make systematic. □ **systematization** *noun*.

■ arrange, catalogue, categorize, classify, codify, organize, rationalize, regiment, standardize, tabulate.

systemic /sɪ'stemɪk/ *adjective* **1** *Physiology* of the whole body. **2** (of insecticide etc.) entering plant tissues via roots and shoots. □ **systemically** *adverb*.

Tt

T *noun* □ **to a T** exactly; to a nicety. **T-bone** T-shaped bone, esp. in steak from thin end of loin. **T-junction** junction, esp. of two roads, in shape of T. **T-shirt** short-sleeved casual top. **T-square** T-shaped instrument for drawing right angles.

t. *abbreviation* (also **t**) **1** ton(s). **2** tonne(s).

TA *abbreviation* Territorial Army.

ta /tɑː/ *interjection colloquial* thank you.

tab[1] *noun* **1** small piece of material attached to thing for grasping, fastening, identifying, etc. **2** *US colloquial* bill. **3** distinguishing mark on officer's collar. □ **keep tabs on** *colloquial* have under observation or in check.

tab[2] *noun* tabulator.

tabard /'tæbəd/ *noun* **1** herald's official coat emblazoned with arms of sovereign. **2** woman's or girl's sleeveless jerkin. **3** *historical* knight's short emblazoned garment worn over armour.

tabasco /tə'bæskəʊ/ *noun* **1** pungent pepper. **2** (**Tabasco**) *proprietary term* sauce made from this.

tabby /'tæbɪ/ *noun* (*plural* **-ies**) grey or brownish cat with dark stripes.

tabernacle /'tæbənæk(ə)l/ *noun* **1** *historical* tent used as sanctuary by Israelites during Exodus. **2** niche or receptacle, esp. for bread and wine of Eucharist. **3** Nonconformist meeting-house.

tabla /'tæblə/ *noun* pair of small Indian drums played with hands.

table /'teɪb(ə)l/ *noun* **1** flat surface on legs used for eating, working at, etc. **2** food provided at table. **3** group seated for dinner etc. **4** set of facts or figures arranged esp. in columns. **5** multiplication table. ● *verb* (**-ling**) **1** bring forward for discussion at meeting etc. **2** *esp. US* postpone consideration of. □ **at table** taking a meal. **tablecloth** cloth spread over table. **tableland** plateau. **tablespoon 1** large spoon for serving etc. **2** (also **tablespoonful**) amount held by this. **table tennis** game played with small bats on table divided by net. **tableware** dishes etc. for meals. **table wine** wine of ordinary quality. **turn the tables** (often + *on*) reverse circumstances to one's advantage.

■ *noun* **4** catalogue, chart, diagram, graph, index, inventory, list, register, schedule, tabulation, timetable. ● *verb* **1** bring forward, offer, proffer, propose, submit.

tableau /'tæbləʊ/ *noun* (*plural* **-x** /-z/) **1** picturesque presentation. **2** group of silent motionless people representing stage scene.

table d'hôte /tɑːb(ə)l 'dəʊt/ *noun* meal from set menu at fixed price.

tablet /'tæblɪt/ *noun* **1** small solid dose of medicine etc. **2** bar of soap etc. **3** flat slab of stone etc., esp. inscribed.

■ **1** capsule, drop, lozenge, pastille, pellet, pill. **2** bar, block, chunk, piece, slab. **3** gravestone, headstone, memorial, plaque, plate, tombstone.

tabloid /'tæblɔɪd/ *noun* small-sized, often popular or sensational, newspaper.

taboo /tə'buː/ *noun* (*plural* **-s**) **1** ritual isolation of person or thing as sacred or accursed. **2** prohibition. ● *adjective* avoided or prohibited, esp. by social custom. ● *verb* (**-oos**, **-ooed**) **1** put under taboo. **2** exclude or prohibit, esp. socially.

■ *noun* **1** anathema, curse. **2** ban, interdiction, prohibition, proscription. ● *adjective* banned, censored, disapproved of, forbidden, interdicted, prohibited, proscribed, rude, unacceptable, unlawful, unmentionable, unnameable.

tabor /'teɪbə/ *noun historical* small drum.

tabular /'tæbjʊlə/ *adjective* of or arranged in tables.

tabulate /'tæbjʊleɪt/ *verb* (**-ting**) arrange (figures, facts) in tabular form. □ **tabulation** *noun*.

■ catalogue, index, list, pigeon-hole, systematize.

tabulator *noun* device on typewriter etc. for advancing to sequence of set positions in tabular work.

tachograph /'tækəɡrɑːf/ *noun* device in vehicle to record speed and travel time.

tachometer /tə'kɒmɪtə/ *noun* instrument measuring velocity or rate of shaft's rotation (esp. in vehicle).

tacit /'tæsɪt/ *adjective* implied or understood without being stated. □ **tacitly** *adverb*.

■ implicit, implied, silent, undeclared, understood, unexpressed, unsaid, unspoken, unvoiced.

taciturn /'tæsɪtɜːn/ *adjective* saying little; uncommunicative. □ **taciturnity** /-'tɜːn-/ *noun*.

■ mute, quiet, reserved, reticent, silent, tight-lipped, uncommunicative, unforthcoming.

tack[1] *noun* **1** small sharp broad-headed nail. **2** *US* drawing-pin. **3** long stitch for fastening materials lightly or temporarily together. **4** (in sailing) direction. **5** temporary change of direction. **6** course of action or policy. ● *verb* **1** (often + *down* etc.) fasten with tacks. **2** stitch lightly together. **3** (+ *to, on, on to*) add, append. **4** change ship's course by turning head to wind. **5** make series of such tacks.

■ *noun* **2** drawing-pin, pin, tin-tack. **4** bearing, course, direction. **6** approach, course, direction, line, policy, procedure, technique. ● *verb* **1** fasten, nail, pin. **2** sew, stitch. **3** (*tack on*) see ADD 1. **4** beat against the wind, change course, go about, zigzag.

tack² *noun* horse's saddle, bridle, etc.

tack³ *noun colloquial* cheap or shoddy material; tat, kitsch.

tackle /'tæk(ə)l/ *noun* **1** equipment for task or sport. **2** rope(s), pulley(s), etc. used in working sails, hoisting weights, etc. **3** tackling in football etc. ● *verb* (**-ling**) **1** try to deal with (problem etc.). **2** grapple with (opponent). **3** confront (person) in discussion. **4** intercept or stop (player running with ball etc.). □ **tackle-block** pulley over which rope runs. □ **tackler** *noun*.

■ *noun* **1** accoutrements, apparatus, *slang* clobber, equipment, fittings, gear, implements, kit, outfit, paraphernalia, rig, tools. **2** rig, rigging. **3** attack, block, challenge, interception, intervention. ● *verb* **1** address (oneself to), apply oneself to, attempt, attend to, combat, come to grips with, concentrate on, confront, cope with, deal with, face up to, focus on, get involved in, grapple with, handle, have a go at, manage, set about, settle down to, sort out, take on, undertake. **2** attack, grapple with, take on. **3** challenge, confront. **4** attack, challenge, intercept, stop, take on.

tacky¹ /'tæki/ *adjective* (**-ier**, **-iest**) slightly sticky.

■ adhesive, gluey, *colloquial* gooey, gummy, sticky, viscous, wet.

tacky² /'tæki/ *adjective* (**-ier**, **-iest**) *colloquial* **1** in poor taste. **2** cheap, shoddy.

taco /'tækəʊ/ *noun* (*plural* **-s**) Mexican dish of meat etc. in crisp folded tortilla.

tact *noun* **1** adroitness in dealing with people or circumstances. **2** intuitive perception of right thing to do or say. □ **tactful** *adjective*. **tactfully** *adverb*. **tactfulness** *noun*. **tactless** *adjective*. **tactlessly** *adverb*. **tactlessness** *noun*.

■ adroitness, consideration, delicacy, diplomacy, discernment, discretion, finesse, judgement, perceptiveness, politeness, *savoir faire*, sensitivity, tactfulness, thoughtfulness, understanding. □ **tactful** adroit, appropriate, considerate, courteous, delicate, diplomatic, discreet, judicious, perceptive, polite, politic, sensitive, thoughtful, understanding. **tactless** blundering, blunt, boorish, bungling, clumsy, discourteous, gauche, heavy-handed, hurtful, impolite, impolitic, inappropriate, inconsiderate, indelicate, indiscreet, inept, insensitive, maladroit, misjudged, rude, thoughtless, uncivil, uncouth, undiplomatic, unkind.

tactic /'tæktɪk/ *noun* piece of tactics.

tactical *adjective* **1** of tactics. **2** (of bombing etc.) done in immediate support of military or naval operation. **3** adroitly planning or planned. □ **tactically** *adverb*.

■ **3** artful, calculated, clever, deliberate, planned, politic, prudent, shrewd, skilful, strategic.

tactics /'tæktɪks/ *plural noun* (also treated as *singular*) **1** disposition of armed forces, esp. in warfare. **2** procedure calculated to gain some end. **3** skilful device(s). □ **tactician** /-'tɪʃ-/ *noun*.

■ **2, 3** approach, campaign, course of action, design, device, manoeuvre, manoeuvring, plan, ploy, policy, procedure, ruse, scheme, stratagem, strategy.

tactile /'tæktaɪl/ *adjective* **1** of sense of touch. **2** perceived by touch. □ **tactility** /-'tɪl-/ *noun*.

tadpole /'tædpəʊl/ *noun* larva of frog, toad, etc. at stage of living in water and having gills and tail.

taffeta /'tæfɪtə/ *noun* fine lustrous silk or silk-like fabric.

taffrail /'tæfreɪl/ *noun* rail round ship's stern.

tag *noun* **1** label, esp. to show address or price. **2** metal point of shoelace etc. **3** loop or flap for handling or hanging thing. **4** loose or ragged end. **5** trite quotation; stock phrase. ● *verb* (**-gg-**) **1** furnish with tag(s). **2** (often + *on*, *on to*) join, attach. □ **tag along** (often + *with*) go along; accompany passively.

■ *noun* **1** docket, label, marker, slip, sticker, tab, ticket. **5** see SAYING. ● *verb* **1** identify, label, mark, ticket.

tagliatelle /tæljə'teli/ *noun* ribbon-shaped pasta.

tail¹ *noun* **1** hindmost part of animal, esp. extending beyond body. **2** thing like tail in form or position, esp. rear part of aeroplane, vehicle, etc., hanging part of back of shirt or coat, end of procession, luminous trail following comet, etc. **3** inferior, weak, or last part of anything. **4** (in *plural*) *colloquial* tailcoat. **5** (in *plural*) *colloquial* evening dress with this. **6** (in *plural*) reverse of coin turning up in toss. **7** *colloquial* person following another. ● *verb* **1** remove stalks of (fruit etc.). **2** *colloquial* follow closely. □ **tailback** long queue of traffic caused by obstruction. **tailboard** hinged or removable back of lorry etc. **tailcoat** man's coat divided at back into tails and cut away in front. **tail-end** hindmost or lowest or last part. **tailgate 1** tailboard. **2** rear door of estate car. **tail-light, -lamp** *US* rear light on vehicle etc. **tail off, away** gradually diminish and cease. **tailpiece 1** final part of thing. **2** decoration at end of chapter etc. **tailplane** horizontal aerofoil at tail of aircraft. **tailspin 1** aircraft's spinning dive. **2** state of panic. **tail wind** one blowing in direction of travel. □ **tailless** *adjective*.

■ *verb* **2** dog, follow, hunt, pursue, shadow, stalk, track, trail. □ **tail off** see DECLINE *verb* 1.

tail² *Law noun* limitation of ownership, esp. of estate limited to person and his heirs. ● *adjective* so limited.

tailor /'teɪlə/ *noun* maker of (esp. men's) outer garments to measure. ● *verb* **1** make (clothes) as tailor. **2** make or adapt for special purpose. **3** work as tailor. □ **tailor-made 1** made by tailor. **2**

made or suited for particular purpose. □ **tailored** *adjective*.

taint *noun* **1** spot or trace of decay, corruption, etc. **2** corrupt condition; infection. ● *verb* **1** affect with taint; become tainted. **2** (+ *with*) affect slightly with.

> ■ *verb* **1** adulterate, besmirch, blacken, blemish, contaminate, damage, defile, dirty, dishonour, harm, infect, poison, pollute, ruin, slander, smear, soil, spoil, stain, sully, tarnish.

take *verb* (**-king**; *past* **took** /tʊk/; *past participle* **taken**) **1** lay hold of. **2** acquire, capture, earn, win. **3** regularly buy (newspaper etc.). **4** occupy. **5** make use of. **6** be effective. **7** consume; use up. **8** accommodate. **9** carry; accompany. **10** remove; steal. **11** catch; be infected with. **12** be affected by (pleasure etc.). **13** ascertain and record. **14** grasp mentally; understand. **15** accept; submit to. **16** deal with or regard in specified way. **17** (+ *for*) regard as being. **18** teach; be taught or examined in. **19** submit to (exam). **20** make (photograph). **21** have as necessary accompaniment, requirement, or part. **22** assume, choose. **23** subtract. ● *noun* **1** amount taken or caught. **2** scene or film sequence photographed continuously. □ **take after** resemble (parent etc.). **take against** begin to dislike. **take apart 1** dismantle. **2** *colloquial* defeat. **3** *colloquial* criticize severely. **take away 1** remove or carry elsewhere. **2** subtract. **take-away 1** (cooked meal) bought at restaurant for eating elsewhere. **2** restaurant selling this. **take back 1** retract (statement). **2** convey to original position. **3** carry in thought to past time. **4** return or accept back (goods). **take down 1** write down (spoken words). **2** dismantle (structure). **3** lower (garment). **take heart** be encouraged. **take-home pay** employee's pay after deduction of tax etc. **take in 1** receive as lodger etc. **2** undertake (work) at home. **3** make (garment etc.) smaller. **4** understand. **5** cheat. **6** include. **take it 1** (often + *that*) assume. **2** *colloquial* endure difficulty (in specified way). **take it out of** exhaust strength of. **take (person's) life** kill. **take off 1** remove (clothing). **2** deduct. **3** *colloquial* mimic. **4** begin a jump. **5** become airborne. **6** (of scheme etc.) become successful. **take-off** *noun* **1** becoming airborne. **2** *colloquial* act of mimicking. **take on 1** undertake. **2** acquire. **3** engage. **4** agree to oppose at game. **5** *colloquial* show strong emotion. **take one's time** not hurry. **take out 1** remove. **2** escort on outing. **3** get (licence etc.). **take over 1** succeed to management or ownership of. **2** assume control. **takeover** *noun*. **take part 1** have share. **2** be involved. **take to 1** begin. **2** have recourse to. **3** form liking for. **take up 1** adopt as pursuit. **2** accept (offer etc.). **3** occupy (time or space). **4** absorb. **5** shorten (garment). **6** pursue (matter). **7** (often + *on*) interrupt or correct (speaker). □ **taker** *noun*.

> ■ *verb* **1** clasp, clutch, grab, grasp, grip, hold, lay hold of, pick up, pluck, seize, snatch. **2** abduct, acquire, arrest, capture, carry away, cart off, catch, corner, detain, ensnare, entrap, gain, get, secure, win. **5** engage, hire, make use of, travel by, use. **7** consume, drink, eat, exhaust, have, swallow, use

up. **8** accommodate, carry, contain, have room for, hold. **9** accompany, bring, carry, conduct, convey, escort, ferry, fetch, guide, lead, transfer, transport. **10** appropriate, *colloquial* lift, *slang* nick, *slang* pinch, pocket, remove, steal, *colloquial* walk off with. **15** abide, accept, bear, brook, endure, receive, stand, stomach, submit to, suffer, tolerate, undergo, withstand. **18** give lessons in, have lessons in, learn about, read, study, teach. **21** demand, necessitate, need, require. **22** adopt, assume, choose, select. **23** deduct, subtract, take away. □ **take after** see RESEMBLE. **take against** see DISLIKE *verb*. **take back 1** see WITHDRAW 2. **take in 1** see ACCOMMODATE 1. **4** see UNDERSTAND 1. **5** see DECEIVE 1. **take (person's) life** see KILL *verb* 1. **take off 1** see REMOVE *verb* 1. **3** see IMITATE 2. **take on 1** see UNDERTAKE 1. **take out 1** see REMOVE *verb* 1. **takeover** amalgamation, incorporation, merger. **take part 2** see PARTICIPATE. **take up 1** see BEGIN 1. **2** see UNDERTAKE 1. **3** see OCCUPY 2.

taking *adjective* attractive, captivating. ● *noun* (in *plural*) money taken in business etc.

> ■ *noun* (**takings**) earnings, gains, gate, income, proceeds, profits, receipts, revenue.

talc *noun* **1** talcum powder. **2** translucent mineral formed in thin plates.

talcum /'tælkəm/ *noun* **1** talc. **2** (in full **talcum powder**) usually perfumed powdered talc for toilet use.

tale *noun* **1** narrative or story, esp. fictitious. **2** allegation or gossip, often malicious.

> ■ **1** account, anecdote, chronicle, narration, narrative, report, *slang* spiel, story, *colloquial* yarn.

talent /'tælənt/ *noun* **1** special aptitude or gift. **2** high mental ability. **3** people of talent. **4** *colloquial* attractive members of opposite sex. **5** ancient weight and money unit. □ **talent-scout, -spotter** person seeking new talent, esp. in sport or entertainment. □ **talented** *adjective*.

> ■ **1, 2** ability, accomplishment, aptitude, brains, brilliance, capacity, cleverness, expertise, facility, faculty, flair, genius, gift, ingenuity, knack, know-how, prowess, skill, strength, versatility. □ **talented** able, accomplished, artistic, brilliant, clever, distinguished, expert, gifted, inspired, proficient, skilful, skilled, versatile.

talisman /'tælɪzmən/ *noun* (*plural* **-s**) thing believed to bring good luck or protect from harm.

> ■ amulet, charm, fetish, mascot.

talk /tɔːk/ *verb* **1** (often + *to*, *with*) converse or communicate verbally. **2** have power of speech. **3** (often + *about*) express; utter; discuss. **4** use (language). **5** gossip. **6** betray secret. ● *noun* **1** conversation. **2** particular mode of speech. **3** short address or lecture. **4** rumour or gossip. **5** its theme. **6** *colloquial* empty words or boasting. **7** (often in *plural*) discussions, negotiations. □ **talk big** *colloquial* talk boastfully. **talk down 1** silence by loud or persistent talking. **2** guide (pilot, aircraft) to landing by radio. **3** (+ *to*) speak patronizingly to. **talk into** persuade by talking. **talk of 1** discuss. **2** express intention of. **talk over** discuss. **talk round** persuade to change opinion etc. **talk to** rebuke, scold. □ **talker** noun.

■ verb **1** chat, chatter, commune, communicate, confer, converse, deliver a speech, discourse, discuss, enunciate, exchange views, have a conversation, hold forth, lecture, negotiate, pipe up, pontificate, preach, rattle on, say something, sermonize, speak, spout, verbalize, vocalize; (talk to) see ADDRESS verb 3. **2** communicate, speak, use language, use one's voice, vocalize. **3** express, utter; (talk about) see DISCUSS. **4** communicate in, express oneself in, speak. **5** see GOSSIP verb. **6** blab, confess, give information, slang grass, inform, colloquial let on, colloquial spill the beans, slang squeal, tell, tell tales. ● noun **1** chat, slang chinwag, colloquial chit-chat, confabulation, conference, conversation, dialogue, discourse, discussion, intercourse, powwow, words. **2** see SPEECH 3. **3** address, diatribe, exhortation, harangue, lecture, oration, pep talk, presentation, sermon, speech, tirade. **4** gossip, hearsay, rumour, tattle, tittle-tattle. **5** blarney, slang hot air, derogatory verbiage, words.

talkative /'tɔːkətɪv/ adjective fond of talking.
■ chatty, communicative, effusive, eloquent, expansive, garrulous, gossipy, long-winded, loquacious, open, prolix, unstoppable, verbose, vocal, voluble, wordy.

talkie noun colloquial early film with soundtrack.

talking adjective **1** that talks or can talk. **2** expressive. ● noun action or process of talking. □ **talking of** while we are discussing. **talking point** topic for discussion. **talking-to** colloquial scolding.

tall /tɔːl/ adjective **1** of more than average height. **2** of specified height. **3** higher than surroundings. ● adverb as if tall; proudly. □ **tallboy** tall chest of drawers. **tall order** unreasonable demand. **tall ship** high-masted sailing ship. **tall story** colloquial extravagant tale. □ **tallness** noun.
■ adjective **1** see BIG adjective 1. **3** colossal, giant, gigantic, high, lofty, soaring, towering.

tallow /'tæləʊ/ noun hard (esp. animal) fat melted down to make candles, soap, etc.

tally /'tælɪ/ noun (plural -ies) **1** reckoning of debt or score. **2** mark registering number of objects delivered or received. **3** historical piece of notched wood for keeping account. **4** identification ticket or label. **5** counterpart, duplicate. ● verb (-ies, -ied) **1** (often + with) agree, correspond. **2** (often + up) reckon by tally.
■ noun **1** addition, count, reckoning, record, sum, total. ● verb **1** accord, agree, coincide, concur, correspond, match up, square. **2** (tally up) add (up), calculate, compute, count (up), reckon, total, work out.

tally-ho /tælɪ'həʊ/ interjection: huntsman's cry as signal on seeing fox.

Talmud /'tælmʊd/ noun body of Jewish civil and ceremonial law. □ **Talmudic** /-'mʊd-/ adjective. **Talmudist** noun.

talon /'tælən/ noun claw, esp. of bird of prey.

talus /'teɪləs/ noun (plural **tali** /-laɪ/) ankle-bone supporting tibia.

tamarind /'tæmərɪnd/ noun **1** tropical evergreen tree. **2** its fruit pulp used as food and in drinks.

tamarisk /'tæmərɪsk/ noun seaside shrub usually with small pink or white flowers.

tambour /'tæmbʊə/ noun **1** drum. **2** circular frame for stretching embroidery-work on.

tambourine /tæmbə'riːn/ noun small shallow drum with jingling discs in rim, shaken or banged as accompaniment.

tame adjective **1** (of animal) domesticated; not wild or shy. **2** uninteresting, insipid. ● verb (-ming) **1** make tame, domesticate. **2** subdue. □ **tamely** adverb. **tameness** noun. **tamer** noun.
■ adjective **1** amenable, approachable, biddable, broken in, compliant, disciplined, docile, domesticated, fearless, friendly, gentle, house-trained, manageable, meek, mild, obedient, safe, sociable, subdued, submissive, tamed, tractable, trained, unafraid. **2** bland, boring, dull, feeble, flat, insipid, lifeless, tedious, unadventurous, unexciting, uninspiring, uninteresting, vapid, colloquial wishy-washy. ● verb **1** break in, domesticate, train. **2** conquer, curb, discipline, humble, keep under, master, mollify, mute, quell, repress, subdue, subjugate, suppress, temper, tone down.

Tamil /'tæmɪl/ noun **1** member of a people inhabiting South India and Sri Lanka. **2** their language. ● adjective of this people or language.

tam-o'-shanter /tæmə'ʃæntə/ noun floppy woollen beret of Scottish origin.

tamp verb ram down tightly.

tamper /'tæmpə/ verb (+ with) meddle or interfere with.
■ (tamper with) alter, fiddle about with, interfere with, make adjustments to, meddle with, tinker with.

tampon /'tæmpɒn/ noun plug of cotton wool etc. used esp. to absorb menstrual blood.

tan[1] noun **1** suntan. **2** yellowish-brown colour. **3** bark of oak etc. used for tanning. ● adjective yellowish-brown. ● verb (-nn-) **1** make or become brown by exposure to sun. **2** convert (raw hide) into leather. **3** slang thrash. □ **tanned** adjective.
■ verb **1** bronze, brown, burn, colour, darken. □ **tanned** brown, sunburnt, weather-beaten.

tan[2] abbreviation tangent.

tandem /'tændəm/ noun **1** bicycle with two or more seats one behind another. **2** vehicle driven tandem. ● adverb with two or more horses harnessed one behind another. □ **in tandem 1** one behind the other. **2** alongside each other. **3** together.

tandoor /'tændʊə/ noun clay oven.

tandoori /tænˈdʊərɪ/ *noun* spiced food cooked in tandoor.

tang *noun* **1** strong taste or smell. **2** characteristic quality. **3** part of tool by which blade is held firm in handle. □ **tangy** *adjective* (**-ier, -iest**).

■ **1** acidity, bite, edge, piquancy, pungency, savour, sharpness, spiciness, zest. □ **tangy** acid, appetizing, bitter, fresh, piquant, pungent, refreshing, sharp, spicy, strong, tart.

tangent /ˈtændʒ(ə)nt/ *noun* **1** straight line, curve, or surface touching but not intersecting curve. **2** ratio of sides opposite and adjacent to acute angle in right-angled triangle. □ **at a tangent** diverging from previous course or from what is relevant. □ **tangential** /-ˈdʒenʃ(ə)l/ *adjective*.

tangerine /tændʒəˈriːn/ *noun* **1** small sweet-scented fruit like orange; mandarin. **2** deep orange-yellow colour.

tangible /ˈtændʒɪb(ə)l/ *adjective* **1** perceptible by touch. **2** definite; clearly intelligible; not elusive. □ **tangibility** *noun.* **tangibly** *adverb.*

■ **1** concrete, corporeal, material, palpable, physical, real, solid, tactile, touchable. **2** actual, concrete, definite, palpable, perceptible, positive, provable, real, substantial.

tangle /ˈtæŋg(ə)l/ *verb* (**-ling**) **1** intertwine or become twisted or involved in confused mass; entangle. **2** complicate. **3** (+ *with*) become involved with. ● *noun* tangled mass or state. □ **tangled** *adjective.* **tangly** *adjective.*

■ *verb* **1** catch, enmesh, ensnare, entangle, entrap, entwine, foul up, intertwine, interweave, ravel, scramble, snarl up, trap, twist. **2** complicate, confuse, mix up, muddle. **3** (*tangle with*) become involved with, confront, cross. ● *noun* coil, complication, confusion, jumble, jungle, knot, labyrinth, maze, mesh, mess, muddle, scramble, twist, web. □ **tangled** see DISHEVELLED, INTRICATE.

tango /ˈtæŋgəʊ/ *noun* (*plural* **-s**) (music for) slow South American ballroom dance. ● *verb* (**-goes, -goed**) dance tango.

tank *noun* **1** large receptacle for liquid, gas, etc. **2** heavy armoured fighting vehicle moving on continuous tracks. □ **tank engine** steam engine with integral fuel and water containers. □ **tankful** *noun* (*plural* **-s**).

■ **1** aquarium, basin, cistern, reservoir.

tankard /ˈtæŋkəd/ *noun* (contents of) tall beer mug with handle.

tanker *noun* ship, aircraft, or road vehicle for carrying liquids, esp. oil, in bulk.

tanner *noun* person who tans hides.

tannery *noun* (*plural* **-ies**) place where hides are tanned.

tannic /ˈtænɪk/ *adjective* of tan. □ **tannic acid** yellowish organic compound used in cleaning, dyeing, etc.

tannin /ˈtænɪn/ *noun* any of several substances extracted from tree-barks etc. and used in tanning etc.

Tannoy /ˈtænɔɪ/ *noun proprietary term* type of public address system.

tansy /ˈtænzɪ/ *noun* (*plural* **-ies**) aromatic herb with yellow flowers.

tantalize /ˈtæntəlaɪz/ *verb* (also **-ise**) (**-zing** or **-sing**) **1** torment with sight of the unobtainable. **2** raise and then dash the hopes of. □ **tantalization** *noun.*

■ bait, entice, frustrate, keep on tenterhooks, lead on, *colloquial* plague, provoke, taunt, tease, tempt, titillate, torment.

tantamount /ˈtæntəmaʊnt/ *adjective* (+ *to*) equivalent to.

tantra /ˈtæntrə/ *noun* any of a class of Hindu or Buddhist mystical or magical writings.

tantrum /ˈtæntrəm/ *noun* (esp. child's) outburst of bad temper or petulance.

Taoiseach /ˈtiːʃəx/ *noun* prime minister of Irish Republic.

tap[1] *noun* **1** device by which flow of liquid or gas from pipe or vessel can be controlled. **2** act of tapping telephone. **3** taproom. ● *verb* (**-pp-**) **1** provide (cask) with tap. **2** let out (liquid) thus. **3** draw sap from (tree) by cutting into it. **4** draw supplies or information from; discover and exploit. **5** connect listening device to (telephone etc.). □ **on tap 1** ready to be drawn off. **2** *colloquial* freely available. **taproom** room in pub serving drinks on tap. **tap root** tapering root growing vertically downwards.

■ *noun* **1** *esp. US* faucet, spigot, stopcock, valve.

tap[2] *verb* (**-pp-**) **1** (+ *at, on, against*, etc.) strike or cause to strike lightly. **2** (often + *out*) make by taps. **3** tap-dance. ● *noun* **1** light blow or rap. **2** tap-dancing. **3** metal attachment on dancer's shoe. □ **tap-dance** ● *noun* rhythmic dance performed in shoes with metal taps. ● *verb* perform this. **tap-dancer** *noun.* **tap-dancing** *noun.*

■ *verb* **1, 2** hit, knock, rap, strike. ● *noun* **1** knock, rap.

tapas /ˈtæpæs/ *plural noun* small savoury esp. Spanish dishes.

tape *noun* **1** narrow woven strip of cotton etc. for fastening etc. **2** this across finishing line of race. **3** (in full **adhesive tape**) strip of adhesive plastic etc. for fastening, masking, insulating, etc. **4** magnetic tape. **5** tape recording. **6** tape-measure. ● *verb* (**-ping**) **1** tie up or join with tape. **2** apply tape to. **3** (+ *off*) seal off with tape. **4** record on magnetic tape. **5** measure with tape. □ **have (person, thing) taped** *colloquial* understand fully. **tape deck** machine for using audiotape (separate from speakers etc.). **tape machine 1** device for recording telegraph messages. **2** tape recorder. **tape-measure** strip of tape or thin flexible metal marked for measuring. **tape recorder** apparatus for recording and replaying sounds on magnetic tape. **tape-record** *verb.* **tape recording** *noun.* **tapeworm** tapelike worm parasitic in alimentary canal.

■ *noun* **1** band, belt, binding, braid, fillet, ribbon, strip, stripe. **4, 5** audiotape, cassette, magnetic tape, tape recording, videotape.

taper /'teɪpə/ *noun* **1** wick coated with wax etc. for conveying flame. **2** slender candle. ● *verb* (often + *off*) **1** (cause to) diminish in thickness towards one end. **2** make or become gradually less.

■ *noun* **1** lighter, spill. ● *verb* **1** attenuate, become narrower, narrow, thin. **2** (*taper off*) see DECLINE *verb* 1.

tapestry /'tæpɪstrɪ/ *noun* (*plural* **-ies**) **1** thick fabric in which coloured weft threads are woven to form pictures or designs. **2** (usually wool) embroidery imitating this. **3** piece of this.

tapioca /tæpɪ'əʊkə/ *noun* starchy granular foodstuff prepared from cassava.

tapir /'teɪpə/ *noun* small piglike mammal with short flexible snout.

tappet /'tæpɪt/ *noun* lever etc. in machinery giving intermittent motion.

tar[1] *noun* **1** dark thick inflammable liquid distilled from wood, coal, etc. **2** similar substance formed in combustion of tobacco. ● *verb* (**-rr-**) cover with tar.

tar[2] *noun colloquial* sailor.

taramasalata /tærəməsə'lɑːtə/ *noun* (also **taramosalata**) dip made from roe, olive oil, etc.

tarantella /tærən'telə/ *noun* (music for) whirling Southern Italian dance.

tarantula /tə'ræntjʊlə/ *noun* **1** large hairy tropical spider. **2** large black spider of Southern Europe.

tarboosh /tɑː'buːʃ/ *noun* cap like fez.

tardy /'tɑːdɪ/ *adjective* (**-ier**, **-iest**) **1** slow to act, come, or happen. **2** delaying; delayed. □ **tardily** *adverb*. **tardiness** *noun*.

tare[1] /teə/ *noun* **1** vetch, esp. as cornfield weed or fodder. **2** (in *plural*) *Biblical* injurious cornfield weed.

tare[2] /teə/ *noun* **1** allowance made for weight of packing around goods. **2** weight of vehicle without fuel or load.

target /'tɑːgɪt/ *noun* **1** mark fired at, esp. round object marked with concentric circles. **2** person, objective, or result aimed at. **3** butt of criticism etc. ● *verb* (**-t-**) **1** single out as target. **2** aim, direct.

■ *noun* **2** aim, ambition, end, goal, hope, intention, objective, purpose. **3** butt, object, quarry, victim.

tariff /'tærɪf/ *noun* **1** table of fixed charges. **2** duty on particular class of goods. **3** list of duties or customs due.

■ **1** charges, price list, schedule. **2** customs, duty, excise, impost, levy, tax, toll.

tarlatan /'tɑːlət(ə)n/ *noun* thin stiff muslin.

Tarmac /'tɑːmæk/ *noun proprietary term* **1** tarmacadam. **2** area surfaced with this. ● *verb* (**tarmac**) (**-ck-**) lay tarmacadam on.

tarmacadam /tɑːmə'kædəm/ *noun* bitumenbound stones etc. used as paving.

tarn *noun* small mountain lake.

tarnish /'tɑːnɪʃ/ *verb* **1** (cause to) lose lustre. **2**

impair (reputation etc.). ● *noun* **1** tarnished state. **2** stain, blemish.

■ *verb* **1** blacken, corrode, dirty, discolour, soil, spoil, stain, taint. **2** blemish, blot, calumniate, defame, denigrate, disgrace, dishonour, mar, ruin, spoil, stain, sully.

taro /'tɑːrəʊ/ *noun* (*plural* **-s**) tropical plant with edible tuberous roots.

tarot /'tærəʊ/ *noun* (in *singular* or *plural*) pack of 78 cards used in fortune-telling.

tarpaulin /tɑː'pɔːlɪn/ *noun* **1** waterproof cloth, esp. of tarred canvas. **2** sheet or covering of this.

tarragon /'tærəgən/ *noun* aromatic herb.

tarry[1] /'tɑːrɪ/ *adjective* (**-ier**, **-iest**) of or smeared with tar.

tarry[2] /'tærɪ/ *verb* (**-ies**, **-ied**) *archaic* linger, stay, wait.

■ dawdle, delay, hang about, hang back, linger, loiter, pause, procrastinate, temporize, wait.

tarsal /'tɑːs(ə)l/ *adjective* of the ankle-bones. ● *noun* tarsal bone.

tarsus /'tɑːsəs/ *noun* (*plural* **tarsi** /-saɪ/) bones of ankle and upper foot.

tart[1] *noun* pastry case containing fruit, jam, etc. □ **tartlet** *noun*.

■ flan, pastry, pasty, patty, pie, quiche, tartlet, turnover.

tart[2] *noun slang* prostitute; promiscuous woman. ● *verb* (+ *up*) *colloquial* smarten or dress up, esp. gaudily. □ **tarty** *adjective* (**-ier**, **-iest**).

■ *noun* see PROSTITUTE.

tart[3] *adjective* **1** sharp-tasting, acid. **2** (of remark etc.) cutting, biting. □ **tartly** *adverb*. **tartness** *noun*.

■ **1** acid, acidic, acidulous, astringent, biting, citrus, harsh, lemony, piquant, pungent, sharp, sour, tangy. **2** see SHARP *adjective* 8.

tartan /'tɑːt(ə)n/ *noun* (woollen cloth woven in) pattern of coloured stripes crossing at right angles, esp. denoting a Scottish Highland clan.

Tartar /'tɑːtə/ *noun* **1** member of group of Central Asian people including Mongols and Turks. **2** their Turkic language. **3** (**tartar**) harsh or formidable person. □ **tartar sauce** mayonnaise with chopped gherkins etc.

tartar /'tɑːtə/ *noun* **1** hard deposit that forms on teeth. **2** deposit forming hard crust in wine casks.

tartaric /tɑː'tærɪk/ *adjective* of tartar. □ **tartaric acid** organic acid found esp. in unripe grapes.

tartrazine /'tɑːtrəziːn/ *noun* brilliant yellow dye from tartaric acid, used to colour food etc.

task /tɑːsk/ *noun* piece of work to be done. ● *verb* make great demands on. □ **take to task** rebuke, scold. **task force** specially organized unit for task. **taskmaster**, **taskmistress** person who makes others work hard.

■ *noun* activity, assignment, burden, business, charge, chore, duty, employment, enterprise, errand, imposition, job, mission, requirement, test, undertaking, work. □ **take to task** see REPRIMAND *verb*.

Tass *noun* official news agency of the former Soviet Union.

tassel /'tæs(ə)l/ *noun* 1 tuft of hanging threads etc. as ornament. 2 tassel-like flowerhead of plant. □ **tasselled** *adjective* (*US* **tasseled**).

taste /teɪst/ *noun* 1 (faculty of perceiving) sensation caused in mouth by contact with substance. 2 flavour. 3 small sample of food etc. 4 slight experience. 5 (often + *for*) liking, predilection. 6 aesthetic discernment in art, clothes, conduct, etc. ● *verb* (**-ting**) 1 perceive or sample flavour of. 2 eat small portion of. 3 experience. 4 (often + *of*) have specified flavour. □ **taste bud** organ of taste on surface of tongue.

■ *noun* 2 character, flavour, relish, savour. 3 bit, bite, morsel, mouthful, nibble, piece, sample, titbit. 5 appetite, appreciation, fancy, fondness, inclination, leaning, liking, partiality, predilection, preference. 6 breeding, cultivation, culture, discernment, discretion, discrimination, education, elegance, fashion sense, finesse, judgement, perception, perceptiveness, polish, refinement, sensitivity, style, tastefulness. ● *verb* 1 sample, savour, test, try. 2 nibble, partake of, sip.

tasteful *adjective* done in or having good taste. □ **tastefully** *adverb*. **tastefulness** *noun*.

■ aesthetic, artistic, attractive, charming, correct, cultivated, decorous, dignified, discerning, discreet, discriminating, elegant, fashionable, in good taste, judicious, nice, polite, proper, refined, restrained, sensitive, smart, stylish, tactful, well judged.

tasteless *adjective* 1 flavourless. 2 having or done in bad taste. □ **tastelessly** *adverb*. **tastelessness** *noun*.

■ 1 bland, characterless, flavourless, insipid, mild, uninteresting, watered-down, watery, weak, *colloquial* wishy-washy. 2 cheap, coarse, crude, flashy, garish, gaudy, graceless, improper, inartistic, in bad taste, indecorous, indelicate, inelegant, injudicious, in poor taste, loud, meretricious, ugly, unattractive, uncouth, uncultivated, undiscriminating, unfashionable, unimaginative, unpleasant, unrefined, unseemly, unstylish, vulgar.

taster *noun* 1 person employed to test food or drink by tasting. 2 small sample.

tasting *noun* gathering at which food or drink is tasted and evaluated.

tasty *adjective* (**-ier**, **-iest**) 1 of pleasing flavour; appetizing. 2 *colloquial* attractive. □ **tastiness** *noun*.

■ 1 appetizing, delectable, delicious, flavoursome, luscious, mouth-watering, nice, palatable, piquant, savoury, *colloquial* scrumptious, tangy, toothsome, *colloquial* yummy.

tat[1] *noun colloquial* tatty things; junk.

tat[2] *verb* (**-tt-**) do, or make by, tatting.

ta-ta /tæ'tɑː/ *interjection colloquial* goodbye.

tatter /'tætə/ *noun* (usually in *plural*) rag; irregularly torn cloth, paper, etc. □ **in tatters** *colloquial* 1 torn in many places. 2 ruined.

■ (*tatters*) bits, pieces, rags, ribbons, shreds.

tattered *adjective* in tatters.

■ frayed, ragged, rent, ripped, shredded, *colloquial* tatty, threadbare, torn, worn out.

tatting /'tætɪŋ/ *noun* (process of making) kind of handmade knotted lace.

tattle /'tæt(ə)l/ *verb* (**-ling**) prattle, chatter; gossip. ● *noun* gossip; idle talk.

tattoo[1] /tə'tuː/ *verb* (**-oos**, **-ooed**) 1 mark (skin) by puncturing and inserting pigment. 2 make (design) thus. ● *noun* such design. □ **tattooer** *noun*. **tattooist** *noun*.

tattoo[2] /tə'tuː/ *noun* 1 evening signal recalling soldiers to quarters. 2 elaboration of this with music and marching etc. as entertainment. 3 drumming, rapping; drumbeat.

tatty /'tætɪ/ *adjective* (**-ier**, **-iest**) *colloquial* 1 tattered. 2 shabby; inferior; tawdry. □ **tattily** *adverb*. **tattiness** *noun*.

■ 1 frayed, old, patched, ragged, ripped, *colloquial* scruffy, shabby, tattered, torn, threadbare, untidy, worn out. 2 see TAWDRY.

taught *past & past participle* of TEACH.

taunt *noun* insult; provocation. ● *verb* insult; provoke contemptuously.

■ *verb* annoy, goad, insult, jeer at, ridicule, tease, torment.

taupe /təʊp/ *noun* grey tinged with esp. brown.

Taurus /'tɔːrəs/ *noun* second sign of zodiac.

taut *adjective* 1 (of rope etc.) tight. 2 (of nerves etc.) tense. 3 (of ship etc.) in good condition. □ **tauten** *verb*. **tautly** *adverb*. **tautness** *noun*.

■ 1, 2 firm, rigid, stiff, strained, stretched, tense, tight.

tautology /tɔː'tɒlədʒɪ/ *noun* (*plural* **-ies**) repetition of same thing in different words. □ **tautological** /-tə'lɒdʒ-/ *adjective*. **tautologous** /-ləgəs/ *adjective*.

■ duplication, long-windedness, pleonasm, prolixity, repetition, *derogatory* verbiage, verbosity, wordiness. □ **tautological**, **tautologous** long-winded, otiose, pleonastic, prolix, redundant, repetitious, repetitive, superfluous, verbose, wordy.

tavern /'tæv(ə)n/ *noun archaic* or *literary* inn, pub.

■ *archaic* alehouse, *archaic* hostelry, inn, *colloquial* local, *colloquial* pub, public house.

taverna /tə'vɜːnə/ *noun* Greek restaurant.

tawdry /'tɔːdrɪ/ *adjective* (**-ier**, **-iest**) showy but worthless; gaudy.

■ cheap, common, flashy, garish, gaudy, inferior, meretricious, showy, tasteless, *colloquial* tatty, tinny, vulgar, worthless.

tawny /'tɔːnɪ/ *adjective* (**-ier**, **-iest**) of orange-brown colour. □ **tawny owl** reddish-brown European owl.

tax *noun* **1** money compulsorily levied by state on person, property, business, etc. **2** (+ *on*, *upon*) strain, heavy demand. ● *verb* **1** impose tax on. **2** deduct tax from. **3** make demands on. **4** (often + *with*) charge. **5** call to account. □ **tax avoidance** minimizing tax payment by financial manoeuvring. **tax-deductible** (of expenses) legally deductible from income before tax assessment. **tax disc** licence on vehicle certifying payment of road tax. **tax evasion** illegal non-payment of taxes. **tax-free** exempt from tax. **taxman** *colloquial* inspector or collector of taxes. **taxpayer** person who pays taxes. **tax return** declaration of income etc. for taxation purposes.

> ■ *noun* **1** charge, customs, due, duty, excise, imposition, impost, levy, rates, tariff, *historical* tithe, toll, *historical* tribute. ● *verb* **1** assess, exact, impose a tax on, levy a tax on. **3** burden, exhaust, overwork, pressure, pressurize, strain, tire, try. **4** (*tax with*) accuse of, blame for, censure for, charge with, reproach for, *formal* reprove for.

taxation /tæk'seɪʃ(ə)n/ *noun* imposition or payment of tax.

taxi /'tæksɪ/ *noun* (*plural* **-s**) (in full **taxi-cab**) car plying for hire and usually fitted with taximeter. ● *verb* (**taxis**, **taxied**, **taxiing** or **taxying**) **1** (of aircraft) go along ground before or after flying. **2** go or carry in taxi. □ **taxi rank** (*US* **taxi stand**) place where taxis wait to be hired.

> ■ *noun* cab, hackney carriage, minicab.

taxidermy /'tæksɪdɜːmɪ/ *noun* art of preparing, stuffing, and mounting skins of animals. □ **taxidermist** *noun*.

taximeter /'tæksɪmiːtə/ *noun* automatic fare-indicator in taxi.

taxon /'tæks(ə)n/ *noun* (*plural* **taxa**) any taxonomic group.

taxonomy /tæk'sɒnəmɪ/ *noun* classification of living and extinct organisms. □ **taxonomic** /-sə'nɒm-/ *adjective*. **taxonomical** /-sə'nɒm-/ *adjective*. **taxonomist** *noun*.

tayberry /'teɪbərɪ/ *noun* (*plural* **-ies**) hybrid fruit between blackberry and raspberry.

TB *abbreviation* **1** tubercle bacillus. **2** tuberculosis.

tbsp. *abbreviation* tablespoonful.

te /tiː/ *noun* (also **ti**) seventh note of scale in tonic sol-fa.

tea *noun* **1** (in full **tea plant**) Asian evergreen shrub or small tree. **2** its dried leaves. **3** infusion of these leaves as drink. **4** infusion made from other leaves etc. **5** light meal in afternoon or evening. □ **tea bag** small permeable bag of tea for infusion. **tea break** pause in work for drinking tea. **tea caddy** container for tea. **teacake** light usually toasted sweet bun. **tea chest** light metal-lined wooden box for transporting tea. **tea cloth** tea towel. **tea cosy** cover to keep teapot warm. **teacup 1** cup from which tea is drunk. **2** amount it holds. **tea leaf** leaf of tea, esp. (in *plural*) after infusion. **teapot** pot with handle and spout, in which tea is made. **tearoom** small unlicensed café. **tea rose** rose with scent like tea. **teaset** set of crockery for serving tea. **teashop** tearoom. **teaspoon 1** small spoon for stirring tea etc. **2** (also **teaspoonful**) amount held by this. **tea towel** cloth for drying washed crockery etc. **tea trolley** (*US* **tea wagon**) small trolley from which tea is served.

teach *verb* (*past & past participle* **taught** /tɔːt/) **1** give systematic information, instruction, or training to (person) or about (subject, skill). **2** practise this as a profession. **3** advocate as moral etc. principle. **4** (+ *to do*) instruct to. **5** (+ *to do*) *colloquial* discourage from. □ **teach person a lesson** punish person. □ **teachable** *adjective*.

> ■ **1** advise, brainwash, coach, counsel, demonstrate to, discipline, drill, edify, educate, enlighten, familiarize with, give lessons in, ground in, impart knowledge to, implant knowledge in, inculcate habits in, indoctrinate, inform, instruct, lecture, school, train, tutor.

teacher *noun* person who teaches, esp. in school.

> ■ adviser, coach, counsellor, demonstrator, don, educator, governess, guide, guru, instructor, lecturer, maharishi, master, mentor, mistress, *archaic* pedagogue, preacher, preceptor, professor, rabbi, reader, schoolmaster, schoolmistress, schoolteacher, trainer, tutor.

teaching *noun* **1** teacher's profession. **2** (often in *plural*) what is taught; doctrine.

> ■ **1** education, guidance, instruction, training. **2** doctrine, dogma, gospel, precept, principle, tenet.

teak *noun* a hard durable wood.

teal *noun* (*plural* same) small freshwater duck.

team *noun* **1** set of players etc. in game or sport. **2** set of people working together. **3** set of draught animals. ● *verb* **1** (usually + *up*) join in team or in common action. **2** (+ *with*) coordinate with; match. □ **team-mate** fellow member of team. **team spirit** willingness to act for communal good. **teamwork** combined effort; cooperation.

> ■ *noun* **1** club, line-up, side, squad. **2** band, corps, crew, force, gang, group, partnership, squad, unit.

teamster /'tiːmstə/ *noun* **1** *US* lorry driver. **2** driver of team.

tear[1] /teə/ *verb* (*past* **tore**; *past participle* **torn**) **1** (often + *up*) pull (apart) with some force. **2** make (hole, rent) thus. **3** undergo this. **4** (+ *away*, *off*, *at*, etc.) pull violently. **5** violently disrupt. **6** *colloquial* go hurriedly. ● *noun* **1** hole etc. caused by tearing. **2** torn part of cloth etc. □ **tear apart 1** search exhaustively. **2** criticize forcefully. **3** divide utterly. **4** distress greatly. **tearaway** *colloquial* unruly young person. **tearing hurry** *colloquial* great hurry. **tear into** *colloquial* **1** severely reprimand. **2** start (activity) vigorously. **tear to shreds** *colloquial* criticize thoroughly.

> ■ *verb* **1**, **2** claw, gash, lacerate, mangle, pull apart, *archaic* rend, rip, rupture, scratch, sever, shred, slit, snag, split. ● *noun* **1** cut, fissure, gap, gash, hole, laceration, opening, rent, rip, slit, split.

tear[2] /tɪə/ *noun* drop of clear salty liquid secreted from eye and shed esp. in grief. □ **in tears** weeping. **tear-drop** single tear. **tear-duct** drain carrying tears to or from eye. **tear gas** gas causing severe irritation to the eyes.

■ □ **in tears** blubbering, *slang* blubbing, crying, sobbing, weeping.

tearful *adjective* in, given to, or accompanied with tears. □ **tearfully** *adverb*. **tearfulness** *noun*.

■ blubbering, crying, emotional, in tears, *formal* lachrymose, sad, snivelling, sobbing, weeping, *colloquial* weepy, wet-cheeked, whimpering.

tease /tiːz/ *verb* (**-sing**) **1** make fun of; irritate. **2** entice sexually while refusing to satisfy desire. **3** pick (wool etc.) into separate fibres. **4** raise nap on (cloth) with teasels etc. **5** (+ *out*) extract or obtain by careful effort. ● *noun* **1** *colloquial* person fond of teasing. **2** act of teasing. □ **teasing** *noun*.

■ *verb* **1**, **2** *disputed* aggravate, annoy, badger, bait, chaff, goad, harass, irritate, laugh at, make fun of, mock, *colloquial* needle, nettle, pester, *colloquial* plague, provoke, pull (person's) leg, *colloquial* rib, ridicule, tantalize, taunt, torment, vex, worry. □ **teasing** badinage, banter, chaffing, joking, mockery, provocation, raillery, *colloquial* ribbing, ridicule, taunts.

teasel /ˈtiːz(ə)l/ *noun* (also **teazel**, **teazle**) **1** plant with prickly flower heads, used dried for raising nap on cloth. **2** other device used for this.

teaser *noun colloquial* hard question or problem.

teat *noun* **1** nipple on breast or udder. **2** rubber etc. nipple for sucking milk from bottle.

teazel (also **teazle**) = TEASEL.

TEC /tek/ *abbreviation* Training and Enterprise Council.

tec *noun colloquial* detective.

tech /tek/ *noun* (also **tec**) *colloquial* technical college.

technic /ˈteknɪk/ *noun* **1** (usually in *plural*) technology. **2** (usually in *plural*) technical terms, methods, etc. **3** technique.

technical *adjective* **1** of the mechanical arts and applied sciences. **2** of a particular subject, craft, etc. **3** using technical language; specialized. **4** due to mechanical failure. **5** in strict legal sense. □ **technical knockout** referee's ruling that boxer has lost because he is unfit to continue. □ **technically** *adverb*.

■ **1** industrial, mechanical, technological, scientific. **3** complicated, detailed, esoteric, expert, professional, specialized.

technicality /teknɪˈkælɪtɪ/ *noun* (*plural* **-ies**) **1** being technical. **2** technical expression. **3** technical point or detail.

technician /tekˈnɪʃ(ə)n/ *noun* **1** person doing practical or maintenance work in laboratory etc. **2** person skilled in artistic etc. technique. **3** expert in practical science.

■ **1** engineer, mechanic.

Technicolor /ˈteknɪkʌlə/ *noun* **1** *proprietary term* process of colour cinematography. **2** (usually **technicolour**) *colloquial* vivid or artificial colour.

technique /tekˈniːk/ *noun* **1** mechanical skill in art. **2** method of achieving purpose, esp. by manipulation. **3** manner of execution in music, painting, etc.

■ **1** art, artistry, cleverness, craft, craftsmanship, expertise, facility, know-how, proficiency, skill, talent, workmanship. **2** approach, dodge, knack, manner, means, method, mode, procedure, routine, system, trick, way.

technocracy /tekˈnɒkrəsɪ/ *noun* (*plural* **-ies**) (instance of) rule or control by technical experts.

technocrat /ˈteknəkræt/ *noun* exponent or advocate of technocracy. □ **technocratic** /-ˈkræt-/ *adjective*.

technology /tekˈnɒlədʒɪ/ *noun* (*plural* **-ies**) **1** knowledge or use of mechanical arts and applied sciences. **2** these subjects collectively. □ **technological** /-nəˈlɒdʒ-/ *adjective*. **technologically** /-nəˈlɒdʒ-/ *adverb*. **technologist** *noun*.

■ □ **technological** automated, computerized, electronic, scientific.

tectonic /tekˈtɒnɪk/ *adjective* **1** of building or construction. **2** of changes in the earth's crust.

tectonics *plural noun* (usually treated as *singular*) study of earth's large-scale structural features.

teddy /ˈtedɪ/ *noun* (also **Teddy**) (*plural* **-ies**) (in full **teddy bear**) soft toy bear.

Teddy boy /ˈtedɪ/ *noun colloquial* 1950s youth with Edwardian-style clothing, hair, etc.

tedious /ˈtiːdɪəs/ *adjective* tiresomely long, wearisome. □ **tediously** *adverb*. **tediousness** *noun*.

■ banal, boring, dreary, dry, dull, endless, humdrum, irksome, laborious, long-drawn(-out), long-winded, monotonous, prolonged, repetitious, slow, soporific, tiresome, tiring, unexciting, uninteresting, vapid, wearing, wearisome, wearying.

tedium /ˈtiːdɪəm/ *noun* tediousness.

■ boredom, dreariness, dullness, ennui, long-windedness, monotony, repetitiousness, slowness, tediousness.

tee[1] *noun* letter T.

tee[2] *noun* **1** cleared space from which golf ball is struck at start of play for each hole. **2** small wood or plastic support for golf ball used then. **3** mark aimed at in bowls, quoits, curling, etc. ● *verb* (**tees**, **teed**) (often + *up*) place (ball) on tee. □ **tee off 1** make first stroke in golf. **2** *colloquial* start, begin.

teem[1] *verb* **1** be abundant. **2** (+ *with*) be full of; swarm with.

■ **1** abound, be abundant, proliferate. **2** (*teem with*) be alive with, be full of, be infested with, be overrun by, bristle with, crawl with, seethe with, swarm with.

teem[2] *verb* (often + *down*) pour (esp. of rain).
■ see RAIN *verb* 1.

teen *adjective* teenage.

teenage /'ti:neɪdʒ/ *adjective* of or characteristic of teenagers. □ **teenaged** *adjective*.

teenager /'ti:neɪdʒə/ *noun* person in teens.
■ adolescent, boy, girl, juvenile, youngster, youth.

teens /ti:nz/ *plural noun* years of one's age from 13 to 19.

teensy /'ti:nzɪ/ *adjective* (**-ier, -iest**) *colloquial* teeny.

teeny /'ti:nɪ/ *adjective* (**-ier, -iest**) *colloquial* tiny.

teepee = TEPEE.

teeter /'ti:tə/ *verb* totter; stand or move unsteadily.

teeth *plural* of TOOTH.

teethe /ti:ð/ *verb* (**-thing**) grow or cut teeth, esp. milk teeth. □ **teething ring** ring for infant to bite on while teething. **teething troubles** initial troubles in an enterprise etc.

teetotal /ti:'təʊt(ə)l/ *adjective* advocating or practising total abstinence from alcohol. □ **teetotalism** *noun*. **teetotaller** *noun*.
■ abstemious, abstinent, *slang* on the wagon, self-denying. □ **teetotaller** abstainer, non-drinker.

TEFL /'tef(ə)l/ *abbreviation* teaching of English as a foreign language.

Teflon /'teflɒn/ *noun proprietary term* non-stick coating for kitchen utensils.

Tel. *abbreviation* (also **tel.**) telephone.

tele- *combining form* 1 at or to a distance. 2 television. 3 by telephone.

telecast /'telɪkɑ:st/ *noun* television broadcast.
● *verb* transmit by television. □ **telecaster** *noun*.

telecommunication /telɪkəmju:nɪ'keɪʃ(ə)n/ *noun* 1 communication over distances by cable, fibre optics, satellites, radio, etc. 2 (in *plural*) technology of this.

telefax /'telɪfæks/ *noun* fax.

telegram /'telɪgræm/ *noun* message sent by telegraph.
■ cable, cablegram, radiogram, telex, *colloquial* wire.

telegraph /'telɪgrɑ:f/ *noun* (device or system for) transmitting messages to a distance by making and breaking electrical connection.
● *verb* (often + *to*) send message or communicate by telegraph. □ **telegraphist** /tɪ'legrə-/ *noun*.

telegraphic /telɪ'græfɪk/ *adjective* 1 of or by telegraphs or telegrams. 2 economically worded.
□ **telegraphically** *adverb*.

telegraphy /tɪ'legrəfɪ/ *noun* communication by telegraph.

telekinesis /telɪkaɪ'ni:sɪs/ *noun* supposed paranormal force moving objects at a distance.
□ **telekinetic** /-'net-/ *adjective*.

telemessage /'telɪmesɪdʒ/ *noun* message sent by telephone or telex and delivered in printed form.

telemetry /tɪ'lemətrɪ/ *noun* process of recording readings of instrument and transmitting them by radio. □ **telemeter** /tɪ'lemɪtə/ *noun*.

teleology /ti:lɪ'ɒlədʒɪ/ *noun* (*plural* **-ies**) *Philosophy* explanation of phenomena by purpose they serve. □ **teleological** /-ə'lɒdʒ-/ *adjective*.

telepathy /tɪ'lepəθɪ/ *noun* supposed paranormal communication of thoughts. □ **telepathic** /telɪ'pæθɪk/ *adjective*. **telepathically** /telɪ'pæθ-/ *adverb*.
■ □ **telepathic** clairvoyant, psychic.

telephone /'telɪfəʊn/ *noun* 1 apparatus for transmitting sound (esp. speech) to a distance. 2 instrument used in this. 3 system of communication by network of telephones. ● *verb* (**-ning**) 1 send (message) or speak to by telephone. 2 make telephone call. □ **on the telephone** having or using a telephone. **telephone book, directory** book listing telephone subscribers and numbers. **telephone booth, box, kiosk** booth etc. with telephone for public use. **telephone number** number used to call a particular telephone. □ **telephonic** /-'fɒn-/ *adjective*. **telephonically** /-'fɒn-/ *adverb*.
■ *noun* 2 *colloquial* blower, handset, *colloquial* phone. ● *verb* call, dial, *colloquial* give (person) a bell, *slang* give (person) a buzz, give (person) a call, *colloquial* phone, ring, ring up.

telephonist /tɪ'lefənɪst/ *noun* operator in telephone exchange or at switchboard.

telephony /tɪ'lefənɪ/ *noun* transmission of sound by telephone.

telephoto /telɪ'fəʊtəʊ/ *noun* (*plural* **-s**) (in full **telephoto lens**) lens used in telephotography.

telephotography /telɪfə'tɒgrəfɪ/ *noun* photographing of distant object with combined lenses giving large image. □ **telephotographic** /-fəʊtə'græf-/ *adjective*.

teleprinter /'telɪprɪntə/ *noun* device for sending, receiving, and printing telegraph messages.

teleprompter /'telɪprɒmptə/ *noun* device beside etc. television camera that slowly unrolls script out of sight of audience.

telesales /'telɪseɪlz/ *plural noun* selling by telephone.

telescope /'telɪskəʊp/ *noun* 1 optical instrument using lenses or mirrors to magnify distant objects. 2 radio telescope. ● *verb* (**-ping**) 1 press or drive (sections of tube etc.) one into another. 2 close or be capable of closing thus. 3 compress.
■ *verb* 3 abbreviate, collapse, compress, elide, shorten.

telescopic /telɪ'skɒpɪk/ *adjective* 1 of or made with telescope. 2 (esp. of lens) able to magnify distant objects. 3 consisting of sections that telescope. □ **telescopic sight** telescope on rifle etc. used for sighting. □ **telescopically** *adverb*.
■ 3 collapsible, expanding, extending, retractable.

teletext /'telɪtekst/ *noun* computerized information service transmitted to subscribers' televisions.

telethon /'telɪθɒn/ *noun* long television programme to raise money for charity.

televise /'telɪvaɪz/ *verb* (**-sing**) transmit by television.
- ■ broadcast, relay, send out, transmit.

television /'telɪvɪʒ(ə)n/ *noun* **1** system for reproducing on a screen visual images transmitted (with sound) by radio signals or cable. **2** (in full **television set**) device with screen for receiving these signals. **3** television broadcasting. □ **televisual** /-'vɪʒʊəl/ *adjective*.
- ■ **2** *colloquial* the box, monitor, receiver, *colloquial* telly, TV.

telex /'teleks/ (also **Telex**) *noun* international system of telegraphy using teleprinters and public telecommunication network. ● *verb* send, or communicate with, by telex.

tell *verb* (*past & past participle* **told** /təʊld/) **1** relate in speech or writing. **2** make known; express in words. **3** (often + *of, about*) divulge information; reveal secret etc. **4** utter. **5** (+ *to do*) direct, order to. **6** decide about, distinguish. **7** (often + *on*) produce marked effect or influence. □ **tell apart** distinguish between. **tell off** *colloquial* scold. **telling-off** *noun*. **tell-tale** *noun* **1** person who tells tales. **2** automatic registering device. ● *adjective* serving to reveal or betray something. **tell tales** report discreditable fact about another.
- ■ **1, 2** acquaint with, advise, announce, assure, communicate, describe, disclose, divulge, explain, express, impart, inform, make known, narrate, notify, portray, promise, recite, recount, rehearse, relate, report, reveal. **3** see TALK *verb* 6. **4** see SPEAK 1,2. **5** command, direct, instruct, order. **6** calculate, comprehend, decide, discover, discriminate, distinguish, identify, notice, recognize, see. □ **tell off** see REPRIMAND *verb*.

teller *noun* **1** person employed to receive and pay out money in bank etc. **2** person who counts votes. **3** person who tells esp. stories.
- ■ **1** bank clerk, cashier. **3** author, narrator, raconteur, storyteller.

telling *adjective* having marked effect; striking. □ **tellingly** *adverb*.
- ■ considerable, effective, influential, potent, powerful, significant, striking, weighty.

telly /'telɪ/ *noun* (*plural* **-ies**) *colloquial* television.

temerity /tɪ'merɪtɪ/ *noun* rashness, audacity.

temp *colloquial noun* temporary employee, esp. secretary. ● *verb* work as temp.

temper /'tempə/ *noun* **1** mental disposition; mood. **2** fit of anger; irritation, anger. **3** tendency to become angry. **4** composure, calmness. **5** metal's hardness or elasticity. ● *verb* **1** bring (clay, metal) to proper consistency or hardness. **2** (often + *with*) moderate, mitigate.

- ■ *noun* **1** attitude, character, disposition, frame of mind, humour, make-up, mood, personality, state of mind, temperament. **2** anger, fit of anger, fury, irritation, *colloquial* paddy, passion, rage, tantrum, *literary* wrath. **3** churlishness, hot-headedness, ill humour, irascibility, irritability, peevishness, petulance, surliness, unpredictability, volatility. **4** calmness, composure, *slang* cool, coolness, equanimity, sang-froid, self-control, self-possession. ● *verb* **1** harden, strengthen, toughen. **2** assuage, lessen, mitigate, moderate, modify, modulate, reduce, soften, soothe, tone down.

tempera /'tempərə/ *noun* method of painting using emulsion e.g. of pigment with egg.

temperament /'temprəmənt/ *noun* person's or animal's nature and character.
- ■ attitude, character, disposition, frame of mind, humour, make-up, mood, nature, personality, spirit, state of mind, temper.

temperamental /temprə'ment(ə)l/ *adjective* **1** regarding temperament. **2** unreliable, moody. **3** *colloquial* (of thing) unpredictable. □ **temperamentally** *adverb*
- ■ **1** characteristic, congenital, constitutional, inherent, innate, natural. **2, 3** capricious, changeable, emotional, erratic, excitable, explosive, fickle, highly-strung, impatient, inconsistent, inconstant, irascible, irritable, mercurial, moody, neurotic, passionate, sensitive, touchy, undependable, unpredictable, unreliable, *colloquial* up and down, variable, volatile.

temperance /'tempərəns/ *noun* **1** moderation, esp. in eating and drinking. **2** abstinence, esp. total, from alcohol.
- ■ **1** abstemiousness, continence, moderation, self-discipline, self-restraint. **2** abstinence, sobriety, teetotalism.

temperate /'tempərət/ *adjective* **1** avoiding excess, moderate. **2** (of region or climate) mild.
- ■ **1** calm, controlled, disciplined, moderate, reasonable, restrained, self-possessed, sensible, sober, stable, steady.

temperature /'temprɪtʃə/ *noun* **1** measured or perceived degree of heat or cold of thing, region, etc. **2** *colloquial* body temperature above normal.

tempest /'tempɪst/ *noun* violent storm.
- ■ cyclone, gale, hurricane, storm, tornado, tumult, typhoon, whirlwind.

tempestuous /tem'pestʃʊəs/ *adjective* stormy, turbulent. □ **tempestuously** *adverb*. **tempestuousness** *noun*.
- ■ fierce, furious, stormy, tumultuous, turbulent, vehement, violent, wild.

tempi *plural* of TEMPO.

template /'templɪt/ *noun* thin board or plate used as guide in drawing, cutting, drilling, etc.

temple[1] /'temp(ə)l/ *noun* building for worship, or treated as dwelling place, of god(s).

■ church, mosque, pagoda, place of worship, sanctuary, shrine, synagogue.

temple[2] /'temp(ə)l/ *noun* flat part of side of head between forehead and ear.

tempo /'tempəʊ/ *noun* (*plural* **-pos** or **-pi** /-piː/) **1** speed at which music is (to be) played. **2** speed, pace.

■ beat, pace, pulse, rate, rhythm, speed, time.

temporal /'tempər(ə)l/ *adjective* **1** worldly as opposed to spiritual; secular. **2** of time. **3** of the temples of the head.

■ **1** earthly, fleshly, material, materialistic, mortal, mundane, non-religious, secular, terrestrial, worldly.

temporary /'tempərərɪ/ *adjective* lasting or meant to last only for limited time. ● *noun* (*plural* **-ies**) person employed temporarily. □ **temporarily** *adverb*.

■ *adjective* acting, brief, ephemeral, *literary* evanescent, fleeting, fugitive, impermanent, interim, makeshift, momentary, passing, provisional, short, short-lived, short-term, stopgap, transient, transitory.

temporize /'tempəraɪz/ *verb* (also **-ise**) (**-zing** or **-sing**) **1** avoid committing oneself, so as to gain time; procrastinate. **2** comply temporarily.

tempt *verb* **1** entice, incite to what is forbidden. **2** allure, attract. **3** risk provoking. □ **tempter** *noun*. **tempting** *adjective*. **temptingly** *adverb*. **temptress** *noun*.

■ **1** bait, bribe, cajole, coax, decoy, entice, incite, inveigle, offer incentives, persuade. **2** allure, attract, captivate, fascinate, lure, seduce, tantalize. □ **tempting** see APPETIZING, ATTRACTIVE.

temptation /temp'teɪʃ(ə)n/ *noun* **1** tempting, being tempted; incitement, esp. to wrongdoing. **2** attractive thing or course of action.

■ **1** allurement, cajolery, coaxing, enticement, incitement, inducement, persuasion, seduction, wooing. **2** allurement, attraction, bait, draw, enticement, inducement, lure, pull, snare.

ten *adjective* & *noun* one more than nine. □ **the Ten Commandments** rules of conduct given by God to Moses. □ **tenth** *adjective* & *noun*.

tenable /'tenəb(ə)l/ *adjective* **1** maintainable against attack or objection. **2** (+ *for*, *by*) (of office etc.) that can be held for period or by (person etc.). □ **tenability** *noun*.

■ **1** arguable, believable, conceivable, credible, creditable, defendable, defensible, justifiable, legitimate, logical, plausible, rational, reasonable, sensible, sound, supportable, understandable, viable.

tenacious /tɪ'neɪʃəs/ *adjective* **1** (often + *of*) keeping firm hold. **2** persistent, resolute. **3** (of memory) retentive. □ **tenaciously** *adverb*. **tenacity** /-'næs-/ *noun*.

■ **1** firm, strong, tight. **2** determined, dogged, firm, intransigent, obdurate, obstinate, persistent, pertinacious, resolute, single-minded, steadfast,

stubborn, uncompromising, unfaltering, unshakeable, unswerving, unwavering, unyielding.

tenancy /'tenənsɪ/ *noun* (*plural* **-ies**) (duration of) tenant's status or possession.

tenant /'tenənt/ *noun* **1** person who rents land or property from landlord. **2** (often + *of*) occupant of place. □ **tenantless** *adjective*.

■ **1** leaseholder, lessee, lodger. **2** inhabitant, occupant, occupier, resident.

tenantry *noun* tenants of estate etc.

tench *noun* (*plural* same) freshwater fish of carp family.

tend[1] *verb* **1** (often + *to*) be apt or inclined. **2** be moving; hold a course.

■ **1** be apt, be disposed, be inclined, *disputed* be liable, be prone, have a tendency, incline.

tend[2] *verb* take care of; look after.

■ attend to, care for, cultivate, guard, keep, keep an eye on, look after, manage, mind, minister to, mother, nurse, protect, supervise, take care of, treat, watch.

tendency /'tendənsɪ/ *noun* (*plural* **-ies**) (often + *to*, *towards*) leaning, inclination.

■ bias, disposition, drift, inclination, instinct, leaning, liability, partiality, penchant, predilection, predisposition, proclivity, proneness, propensity, readiness, susceptibility, trend.

tendentious /ten'denʃəs/ *adjective* *derogatory* designed to advance a particular cause; biased; controversial. □ **tendentiously** *adverb*. **tendentiousness** *noun*.

tender[1] /'tendə/ *adjective* (**tenderer**, **tenderest**) **1** not tough or hard. **2** delicate, fragile. **3** susceptible to pain or grief; painful. **4** touching. **5** loving, affectionate; compassionate. **6** requiring tact. **7** immature. □ **tenderfoot** (*plural* **-s** or **-feet**) novice, newcomer. **tender-hearted** easily moved. **tender-heartedness** *noun*. **tenderloin** middle part of loin of pork. **tender mercies** *ironic* harsh treatment. □ **tenderly** *adverb*. **tenderness** *noun*.

■ **1** eatable, edible, soft, succulent. **2** dainty, delicate, fragile, frail, vulnerable, weak. **3** aching, inflamed, painful, sensitive, smarting, sore. **4** emotional, heartfelt, moving, poignant, romantic, sentimental, stirring, touching. **5** affectionate, amorous, caring, compassionate, concerned, considerate, fond, gentle, humane, kind, loving, merciful, pitying, soft-hearted, sympathetic, tender-hearted, warm-hearted. **7** green, immature, impressionable, inexperienced, vulnerable, young, youthful.

tender[2] /'tendə/ *verb* **1** offer, present (services, resignation, payment, etc.). **2** (often + *for*) make tender. ● *noun* offer to execute work or supply goods at fixed price.

tender[3] /'tendə/ *noun* **1** person who looks after people or things. **2** supply vessel attending larger one. **3** truck attached to steam locomotive and carrying fuel etc.

tenderize *verb* (also **-ise**) (**-zing** or **-sing**) render (meat) tender by beating etc.

tendon /'tend(ə)n/ *noun* tough fibrous tissue connecting muscle to bone etc.

tendril /'tendrɪl/ *noun* slender leafless shoot by which some climbing plants cling.

tenebrous /'tenɪbrəs/ *adjective literary* dark, gloomy.

tenement /'tenmənt/ *noun* **1** room or flat within house or block of flats. **2** (also **tenement house, block**) house or block so divided.

tenet /'tenɪt/ *noun* doctrine, principle.

tenfold *adjective & adverb* ten times as much or many.

tenner /'tenə/ *noun colloquial* £10 or $10 note.

tennis /'tenɪs/ *noun* ball game played with rackets on court divided by net. □ **tennis elbow** sprain caused by overuse of forearm muscles.

tenon /'tenən/ *noun* wooden projection shaped to fit into mortise of another piece.

tenor /'tenə/ *noun* **1** male singing voice between alto and baritone. **2** singer with this. **3** (usually + *of*) general purport; prevailing course of one's life or habits. ● *adjective* having range of tenor.

tenosynovitis /ˌtenəʊsaɪməˈvaɪtɪs/ *noun* repetitive strain injury, esp. of wrist.

tenpin bowling *noun* game in which ten pins or skittles are bowled at in alley.

tense[1] *adjective* **1** stretched tight. **2** strained. **3** causing tenseness. ● *verb* (**-sing**) make or become tense. □ **tense up** become tense. □ **tensely** *adverb*. **tenseness** *noun*.

■ *adjective* **1** rigid, strained, stretched, taut, tight. **2** anxious, apprehensive, edgy, excited, fidgety, highly-strung, intense, *colloquial* jittery, jumpy, nervous, on edge, on tenterhooks, overwrought, restless, strained, stressed, strung up, touchy, uneasy, *colloquial* uptight, worried. **3** exciting, fraught, nerve-racking, stressful, worrying.

tense[2] *noun* **1** form of verb indicating time of action etc. **2** set of such forms for various persons and numbers.

tensile /'tensaɪl/ *adjective* **1** of tension. **2** capable of being stretched. □ **tensile strength** resistance to breaking under tension.

tension /'tenʃ(ə)n/ *noun* **1** stretching, being stretched. **2** mental strain or excitement. **3** strained state. **4** stress produced by forces pulling apart. **5** degree of tightness of stitches in knitting and machine sewing. **6** voltage.

■ **1** pull, strain, stretching, tautness, tightness. **2** anxiety, apprehension, edginess, excitement, nervousness, stress, suspense, unease, worry.

tent *noun* portable shelter or dwelling of canvas etc.

tentacle /'tentək(ə)l/ *noun* slender flexible appendage of animal, used for feeling, grasping, or moving.

tentative /'tentətɪv/ *adjective* **1** experimental. **2** hesitant, not definite. □ **tentatively** *adverb*.

■ **1** experimental, exploratory, preliminary, provisional, speculative. **2** cautious, diffident, doubtful, half-hearted, hesitant, inconclusive, indecisive, indefinite, nervous, shy, timid, uncertain, uncommitted, unsure, *colloquial* wishy-washy.

tenterhooks /'tentəhʊks/ *plural noun* □ **on tenterhooks** in suspense; distracted by uncertainty.

tenuous /'tenjʊəs/ *adjective* **1** slight, insubstantial. **2** oversubtle. **3** thin, slender. □ **tenuity** /-'juːɪtɪ/ *noun*. **tenuously** *adverb*.

■ **1** flimsy, fragile, insubstantial, slender, slight, weak. **3** attenuated, fine, slender, slight, thin.

tenure /'tenjə/ *noun* **1** (often + *of*) holding of property or office. **2** conditions or period of this. **3** guaranteed permanent employment, esp. as lecturer. □ **tenured** *adjective*.

tepee /'tiːpiː/ *noun* (also **teepee**) N. American Indian's conical tent.

tepid /'tepɪd/ *adjective* **1** lukewarm. **2** unenthusiastic.

■ **1** lukewarm, warm. **2** see APATHETIC (APATHY).

tequila /tɪˈkiːlə/ *noun* Mexican liquor made from agave.

tercel /'tɜːs(ə)l/ *noun* (also **tiercel** /'tɪəs(ə)l/) male hawk.

tercentenary /ˌtɜːsenˈtiːnərɪ/ *noun* (*plural* **-ies**) **1** 300th anniversary. **2** celebration of this.

tergiversate /'tɜːdʒɪvəseɪt/ *verb* (**-ting**) **1** change one's party or principles. **2** make conflicting or evasive statements. □ **tergiversation** *noun*. **tergiversator** *noun*.

term *noun* **1** word for definite concept, esp. specialized. **2** (in *plural*) language used; mode of expression. **3** (in *plural*) relation, footing. **4** (in *plural*) stipulations. **5** (in *plural*) charge, price. **6** limited period. **7** period of weeks during which instruction is given or during which law court holds sessions. **8** *Logic* word(s) which may be subject or predicate of proposition. **9** *Mathematics* each quantity in ratio or series. **10** *Mathematics* part of algebraic expression. **11** completion of normal length of pregnancy. ● *verb* call, name. □ **come to terms with** reconcile oneself to. **in terms of** with reference to. **terms of reference 1** scope of inquiry etc. **2** definition of this. □ **termly** *adjective*.

■ *noun* **1** *formal* appellation, designation, epithet, expression, name, phrase, title, word. **4** (*terms*) conditions, provisions, provisos, specifications, stipulations. **5** (*terms*) charges, fees, prices, rates, schedule, tariff. **6** duration, period, season, span, spell, stretch, time. **7** semester, session.

termagant /'tɜːməgənt/ *noun* overbearing woman; virago.

terminable /'tɜːmɪnəb(ə)l/ *adjective* able to be terminated.

terminal /'tɜːmɪn(ə)l/ *adjective* **1** (of condition or disease) fatal. **2** (of patient) dying. **3** of or forming limit or terminus. ● *noun* **1** terminating thing;

extremity. **2** bus or train terminus; air terminal. **3** point of connection for closing electric circuit. **4** apparatus for transmission of messages to and from computer, communications system, etc. □ **terminally** *adverb*.

■ *adjective* **1** deadly, fatal, incurable, killing, lethal, mortal. ● *noun* **2** airport, terminus. **3** connection, connector, coupling. **4** keyboard, VDU, workstation.

terminate /'tɜːmɪneɪt/ *verb* (**-ting**) **1** bring or come to an end. **2** (+ *in*) end in.

■ **1** bring to an end, *formal* cease, come to an end, discontinue, end, finish, *colloquial* pack in, phase out, stop, wind up.

termination *noun* **1** terminating, being terminated. **2** ending, result. **3** induced abortion.

terminology /tɜːmɪ'nɒlədʒɪ/ *noun* (*plural* **-ies**) system of specialized terms. □ **terminological** /-nə'lɒdʒɪ-/ *adjective*.

■ argot, cant, jargon, language, nomenclature, phraseology, terms, vocabulary.

terminus /'tɜːmɪnəs/ *noun* (*plural* **-ni** /-naɪ/ or **-nuses**) point at end of railway or bus route or of pipeline etc.

■ destination, last stop, station, terminal.

termite /'tɜːmaɪt/ *noun* antlike insect destructive to timber.

tern *noun* seabird with long pointed wings and forked tail.

ternary /'tɜːnərɪ/ *adjective* composed of 3 parts.

terrace /'terəs/ *noun* **1** flat area on slope for cultivation. **2** level paved area next to house. **3** row of houses built in one block of uniform style. **4** terrace house. **5** tiered standing accommodation for spectators at sports ground. ● *verb* (**-cing**) form into or provide with terrace(s). □ **terrace(d) house** house in terrace.

terracotta /terə'kɒtə/ *noun* **1** unglazed usually brownish-red earthenware. **2** its colour.

terra firma /terə 'fɜːmə/ *noun* dry land; firm ground.

terrain /tə'reɪn/ *noun* tract of land, esp. in military or geographical contexts.

■ country, ground, land, landscape, territory, topography.

terra incognita /terə ɪŋ'kɒgnɪtə/ *noun* unexplored region. [Latin]

terrapin /'terəpɪn/ *noun* N. American edible freshwater turtle.

terrarium /tə'reərɪəm/ *noun* (*plural* **-s** or **-ria**) **1** place for keeping small land animals. **2** transparent globe containing growing plants.

terrestrial /tə'restrɪəl/ *adjective* **1** of or on the earth; earthly. **2** of or on dry land.

■ **1** earthly, mundane.

terrible /'terɪb(ə)l/ *adjective* **1** *colloquial* very great, bad, or incompetent. **2** causing or likely to cause terror; dreadful.

■ **1** acute, *colloquial* appalling, *colloquial* awful, bad, *colloquial* beastly, distressing, grave, insupportable, intolerable, loathsome, nasty, nauseating, outrageous, revolting, *colloquial* shocking, terrific, unbearable, vile. **2** appalling, *poetical* awful, dreadful, fearful, fearsome, formidable, frightening, frightful, ghastly, gruesome, harrowing, hideous, horrendous, horrible, horrific, horrifying, shocking, terrific, terrifying.

terribly *adverb* **1** *colloquial* very, extremely. **2** in terrible manner.

terrier /'terɪə/ *noun* small active hardy dog.

terrific /tə'rɪfɪk/ *adjective* **1** *colloquial* huge; intense; excellent. **2** causing terror. □ **terrifically** *adverb*.

■ **1** see BIG *adjective* 1, EXCELLENT, EXTREME *adjective* 1, VIOLENT 2.

terrify /'terɪfaɪ/ *verb* (**-ies**, **-ied**) fill with terror. □ **terrifying** *adjective*. **terrifyingly** *adverb*.

■ appal, dismay, frighten, horrify, petrify, shock, terrorize. □ **terrifying** see FRIGHTENING (FRIGHTEN).

terrine /tə'riːn/ *noun* (earthenware vessel for) pâté or similar food.

territorial /terɪ'tɔːrɪəl/ *adjective* of territory or district. ● *noun* (**Territorial**) member of Territorial Army. □ **Territorial Army** local volunteer reserve force. **territorial waters** waters under state's jurisdiction, esp. part of sea within stated distance of shore. □ **territorially** *adverb*.

territory /'terɪtərɪ/ *noun* (*plural* **-ies**) **1** extent of land under jurisdiction of ruler, state, etc. **2** (**Territory**) organized division of a country, esp. if not yet admitted to full rights of a state. **3** sphere of action etc.; province. **4** representative's sales area. **5** area defended by animal or human, or by team etc. in game.

■ **1** area, colony, country, demesne, district, domain, dominion, enclave, land, neighbourhood, precinct, province, purlieu, region, *Military* sector, state, terrain, tract, zone. **3** see SPHERE 3.

terror /'terə/ *noun* **1** extreme fear. **2** terrifying person or thing. **3** *colloquial* troublesome or tiresome person, esp. child. **4** terrorism.

■ **1** alarm, awe, consternation, dismay, dread, fear, fright, *slang* funk, horror, panic, shock, trepidation.

terrorist *noun* person using esp. organized violence to secure political ends. □ **terrorism** *noun*.

■ assassin, bomber, desperado, gunman, hijacker.

terrorize *verb* (also **-ise**) (**-zing** or **-sing**) **1** fill with terror. **2** use terrorism against.

■ browbeat, bully, coerce, cow, frighten, intimidate, menace, persecute, terrify, threaten, torment, tyrannize.

terry /'terɪ/ *noun* looped pile fabric used for nappies, towels, etc.

terse /tɜːs/ *adjective* (**-r**, **-st**) **1** concise, brief. **2**

curt. □ **tersely** *adverb.* **terseness** *noun.*

■ **1** brief, compact, concentrated, concise, crisp, epigrammatic, incisive, laconic, pithy, short, succinct, to the point. **2** abrupt, brusque, curt, short, *colloquial* snappy.

tertiary /'tɜːʃərɪ/ *adjective* of third order, rank, etc.

Terylene /'terɪliːn/ *noun proprietary term* synthetic polyester textile fibre.

TESL /'tes(ə)l/ *abbreviation* teaching of English as a second language.

tesla /'tezlə/ *noun* SI unit of magnetic flux density.

tessellated /'tesəleɪtɪd/ *adjective* **1** of or resembling mosaic. **2** finely chequered.

tessellation /tesə'leɪʃ(ə)n/ *noun* close arrangement of polygons, esp. in repeated pattern.

test *noun* **1** critical examination or trial of person's or thing's qualities. **2** means, procedure, or standard for so doing. **3** minor exam. **4** *colloquial* test match. ● *verb* **1** put to test. **2** try severely; tax. □ **test card** still television picture outside normal programme hours. **test case** *Law* case setting precedent for other similar cases. **test drive** drive taken to judge vehicle's performance. **test-drive** *verb* take test drive in. **test match** international cricket or Rugby match, usually in series. **test out** put (theory, machine, etc.) to practical test. **test-tube** thin glass tube closed at one end, used for chemical tests etc. **test-tube baby** *colloquial* baby conceived elsewhere than in a mother's body. □ **tester** *noun.*

■ *noun* **1, 2** analysis, appraisal, assay, assessment, audition, check, check-up, evaluation, examination, inspection, interrogation, investigation, trial, try-out. **3** exam, examination, quiz. ● *verb* **1** analyse, appraise, assay, assess, audition, check, evaluate, examine, experiment with, inspect, interrogate, investigate, probe, question, quiz, screen, try out.

testaceous /tes'teɪʃəs/ *adjective* having hard continuous shell.

testament /'testəmənt/ *noun* **1** a will. **2** (usually + *to*) evidence, proof. **3** *Biblical* covenant. **4** (**Testament**) division of Bible. □ **testamentary** /-'ment-/ *adjective.*

testate /'testeɪt/ *adjective* having left valid will at death. ● *noun* testate person. □ **testacy** /-təsɪ/ *noun* (*plural* **-ies**).

testator /tes'teɪtə/ *noun* (*feminine* **testatrix** /-trɪks/) (esp. deceased) person who has made a will.

testes *plural* of TESTIS.

testicle /'testɪk(ə)l/ *noun* male organ that secretes spermatozoa, esp. one of pair in scrotum of man and most mammals.

testify /'testɪfaɪ/ *verb* (**-ies**, **-ied**) **1** (often + *to*) bear witness. **2** give evidence. **3** affirm, declare.

■ affirm, attest, *formal* aver, bear witness, declare, give evidence, proclaim, state on oath, swear, vouch, witness.

testimonial /testɪ'məʊnɪəl/ *noun* **1** certificate of character, conduct, or qualifications. **2** gift presented as mark of esteem.

■ **1** character reference, commendation, recommendation, reference.

testimony /'testɪmənɪ/ *noun* (*plural* **-ies**) **1** witness's statement under oath etc. **2** declaration, statement of fact. **3** evidence.

■ **1, 2** affidavit, assertion, declaration, deposition, evidence, statement, submission. **3** see EVIDENCE *noun* 3.

testis /'testɪs/ *noun* (*plural* **testes** /-tiːz/) testicle.

testosterone /te'stɒstərəʊn/ *noun* male sex hormone.

testy /'testɪ/ *adjective* (**-ier**, **-iest**) irascible, short-tempered. □ **testily** *adverb.* **testiness** *noun.*

tetanus /'tetənəs/ *noun* bacterial disease causing painful spasm of voluntary muscles.

tetchy /'tetʃɪ/ *adjective* (**-ier**, **-iest**) peevish, irritable. □ **tetchily** *adverb.* **tetchiness** *noun.*

tête-à-tête /teɪtɑː'teɪt/ *noun* private conversation between two people. ● *adverb* privately without third person.

tether /'teðə/ *noun* rope etc. confining grazing animal. ● *verb* fasten with tether. □ **at the end of one's tether** at the limit of one's patience, resources, etc.

■ *noun* chain, cord, fetter, halter, lead, leash, restraint, rope. ● *verb* chain up, fasten, fetter, leash, restrain, rope, secure, tie up.

tetra- *combining form* four.

tetragon /'tetrəgɒn/ *noun* plane figure with 4 sides and angles. □ **tetragonal** /tɪ'trægən-/ *adjective.*

tetrahedron /tetrə'hiːdrən/ *noun* (*plural* **-dra** or **-s**) 4-sided triangular pyramid. □ **tetrahedral** *adjective.*

Teutonic /tjuː'tɒnɪk/ *adjective* **1** of Germanic peoples or languages. **2** German.

text *noun* **1** main part of book. **2** original document, esp. as distinct from paraphrase etc. **3** passage of Scripture, esp. as subject of sermon. **4** subject, theme. **5** (in *plural*) books prescribed for study. **6** data in textual form, esp. in word processor. □ **textbook** book used in studying, esp. standard book in any subject. **text editor** computing program allowing user to edit text.

■ **1** content, contents, matter, subject matter, words. **3** line, passage, quotation, sentence, verse. **4** argument, motif, subject, theme, topic. **5** (*texts*) books, textbooks, works, writings.

textile /'tekstaɪl/ *noun* (often in *plural*) fabric, esp. woven. ● *adjective* **1** of weaving or cloth. **2** woven.

■ *noun* cloth, fabric, material, stuff.

textual /'tekstʃʊəl/ *adjective* of, in, or concerning a text.

texture /'tekstʃə/ *noun* **1** feel or appearance of

surface or substance. **2** arrangement of threads in textile fabric. ● *verb* (**-ring**) (usually as **textured** *adjective*) **1** provide with texture. **2** provide (vegetable protein) with texture like meat. □ **textural** *adjective*.

■ *noun* **1** appearance, consistency, feel, grain, quality, surface, touch. **2** weave.

Thai /taɪ/ *noun* (*plural* same or **-s**) native, national, or language of Thailand. ● *adjective* of Thailand.

thalidomide /θəˈlɪdəmaɪd/ *noun* sedative drug found in 1961 to cause foetal malformation when taken early in pregnancy.

than /ðən/ *conjunction: introducing comparison.*

thane /θeɪn/ *noun historical* **1** holder of land from English king by military service, or from Scottish king and ranking below earl. **2** clan-chief.

thank /θæŋk/ *verb* **1** express gratitude to. **2** hold responsible. ● *noun* (in *plural*) **1** gratitude. **2** *colloquial* (as *interjection*) *expression of gratitude.* □ **thanksgiving** expression of gratitude, esp. to God. **Thanksgiving (Day)** US national holiday on fourth Thurs. in Nov. **thanks to** as result of. **thank you** *polite formula expressing gratitude.*

■ *verb* **1** express thanks, say thank you, show gratitude. ● *noun* **1** (*thanks*) acknowledgement, appreciation, gratefulness, gratitude, recognition, thanksgiving. □ **thanks to** as a result of, because of, owing to, through.

thankful *adjective* grateful, pleased; expressive of thanks. □ **thankfulness** *noun*.

■ appreciative, contented, glad, grateful, happy, indebted, pleased, relieved.

thankfully *adverb* **1** in a thankful way. **2** let us be thankful that.

USAGE The use of *thankfully* to mean 'let us be thankful that' is common, but it is considered incorrect by some people.

thankless *adjective* **1** not feeling or expressing gratitude. **2** (of task etc.) unprofitable, unappreciated.

■ **1** unappreciative, ungrateful. **2** *archaic* bootless, futile, profitless, unappreciated, unrecognized, unrewarded, unrewarding.

that /ðæt/ *adjective* (*plural* **those** /ðəʊz/) **1** *used to describe the person or thing nearby, indicated, just mentioned, or understood.* **2** *used to specify the further or less immediate of two.* ● *pronoun* (*plural* **those** /ðəʊz/) **1** that one. **2** the one, the person, etc. /ðət/ **3** (*plural* **that**) who, whom, which (*used to introduce a defining relative clause*). ● *adverb* **1** (+ adjective or adverb) to that degree; so. **2** (with negative) *colloquial* very. ● *conjunction* /ðət/ *used to introduce a subordinate clause expressing esp. a statement, purpose, or result.* □ **at that** moreover; then. **that is (to say)** in other words; more correctly or intelligibly.

thatch /θætʃ/ *noun* roofing of straw, reeds, etc. ● *verb* cover with thatch. □ **thatcher** *noun*.

thaw /θɔː/ *verb* **1** (often + *out*) pass from frozen into liquid or unfrozen state. **2** (of weather) become warm enough to melt ice etc. **3** warm into life, animation, cordiality, etc. ● *noun* **1** thawing. **2** warmth of weather that thaws.

■ *verb* **1** defrost, de-ice, melt, unfreeze. **2** heat up, warm up. **3** melt, relax, soften, warm.

the /ðɪ, ðə, ðiː/ *adjective* (called the definite article) **1** *denoting person(s) or thing(s) already mentioned or known about.* **2** *describing as unique.* **3** (+ adjective) which is, who are, etc. **4** (with *the* stressed) best known. **5** *used with noun which represents or symbolizes a group, activity, etc.* ● *adverb* (preceding comparatives in expressions of proportional variation) in or by that degree; on that account.

theatre /ˈθɪətə/ *noun* (*US* **theater**) **1** building or outdoor area for dramatic performances. **2** writing, production, acting, etc. of plays. **3** room or hall for lectures etc. with seats in tiers. **4** operating theatre. **5** scene or field of action.

■ **1** auditorium, hall, opera house, playhouse. **2** acting, drama, plays, *colloquial* show business, the stage, Thespian arts.

theatrical /θɪˈætrɪk(ə)l/ *adjective* **1** of or for theatre or acting. **2** calculated for effect; showy. ● *noun* (in *plural*) dramatic performances. □ **theatricality** /-ˈkæl-/ *noun*. **theatrically** *adverb*.

■ *adjective* **1** dramatic, histrionic, Thespian. **2** affected, artificial, calculated, exaggerated, forced, melodramatic, ostentatious, overacted, overdone, over the top, showy, stagy, stilted, unconvincing, unnatural.

thee /ðiː/ *pronoun archaic* (as object of verb) you (singular).

theft /θeft/ *noun* act of stealing.

■ burglary, larceny, pilfering, robbery, stealing, thievery.

their /ðeə/ *adjective* of or belonging to them.

theirs /ðeəz/ *pronoun* the one(s) belonging to them.

theism /ˈθiːɪz(ə)m/ *noun* belief in gods or a god. □ **theist** *noun*. **theistic** /-ˈɪstɪk/ *adjective*.

them /ðem, ð(ə)m/ *pronoun* **1** (as object of verb) the people or things in question. **2** (as object of verb) people in general. **3** (as object of verb) people in authority. **4** *colloquial* they. ● *adjective slang* or *dialect* those.

theme /θiːm/ *noun* **1** subject or topic of talk etc. **2** *Music* leading melody in a composition. **3** *US* school exercise on given subject. □ **theme park** amusement park based on unifying idea. **theme song, tune** signature tune. □ **thematic** /θɪˈmætɪk/ *adjective*. **thematically** /θɪˈmæt-/ *adverb*.

■ **1** argument, core, essence, gist, idea, issue, keynote, point, subject, text, thesis, thread, topic. **2** air, melody, motif, subject, tune.

themselves /ðəmˈselvz/ *pronoun* **1** *emphatic form of* THEY *or* THEM. **2** *reflexive form of* THEM.

then /ðen/ *adverb* **1** at that time. **2** after that, next. **3** in that case; accordingly. ● *adjective* such at that time. ● *noun* that time. □ **then and there** immediately and on the spot.

thence /ðens/ *adverb* (also **from thence**) *archaic* or *literary* **1** from that place. **2** for that reason. □ **thenceforth, thenceforward** from that time on.

theo- *combining form* God or god(s).

theocracy /θɪ'ɒkrəsɪ/ *noun* (*plural* **-ies**) form of government by God or a god directly or through a priestly order etc. □ **theocratic** /θɪə'krætɪk/ *adjective*.

theodolite /θɪ'ɒdəlaɪt/ *noun* surveying instrument for measuring angles.

theology /θɪ'ɒlədʒɪ/ *noun* (*plural* **-ies**) study or system of (esp. Christian) religion. □ **theologian** /θɪə'ləʊdʒ-/ *noun.* **theological** /θɪə'lɒdʒ-/ *adjective.*

| ■ divinity, religion, religious studies.

theorem /'θɪərəm/ *noun esp. Mathematics* **1** general proposition not self-evident but demonstrable by argument. **2** algebraic rule.

theoretical /θɪə'retɪk(ə)l/ *adjective* **1** concerned with knowledge but not with its practical application. **2** based on theory rather than experience. □ **theoretically** *adverb.*

| ■ **1** abstract, academic, ideal, impractical, pure (*science*). **2** conjectural, hypothetical, notional, *formal* putative, speculative, suppositious, unproven, untested.

theoretician /θɪərə'tɪʃ(ə)n/ *noun* person concerned with theoretical part of a subject.

theorist /'θɪərɪst/ *noun* holder or inventor of a theory.

theorize /'θɪəraɪz/ *verb* (also **-ise**) (**-zing** or **-sing**) evolve or indulge in theories.

| ■ conjecture, guess, hypothesize, speculate.

theory /'θɪərɪ/ *noun* (*plural* **-ies**) **1** supposition or system of ideas explaining something, esp. one based on general principles. **2** speculative view. **3** abstract knowledge or speculative thought. **4** exposition of principles of a science etc. **5** collection of propositions to illustrate principles of a mathematical subject.

| ■ **1** argument, assumption, belief, conjecture, explanation, guess, hypothesis, idea, notion, speculation, supposition, surmise, thesis, view. **4** laws, principles, rules, science.

theosophy /θɪ'ɒsəfɪ/ *noun* (*plural* **-ies**) philosophy professing to achieve knowledge of God by direct intuition, spiritual ecstasy, etc. □ **theosophical** /θɪə'sɒf-/ *adjective.* **theosophist** *noun.*

therapeutic /θerə'pjuːtɪk/ *adjective* **1** of, for, or contributing to the cure of diseases. **2** soothing; conducive to well-being. □ **therapeutically** *adverb.*

| ■ **1** corrective, curative, healing, medicinal, remedial, restorative. **2** beneficial, healthy, helpful, salubrious.

therapeutics *plural noun* (usually treated as

singular) branch of medicine concerned with cures and remedies.

therapy /'θerəpɪ/ *noun* (*plural* **-ies**) nonsurgical treatment of disease etc. □ **therapist** *noun.*

| ■ cure, healing, remedy, treatment. □ **therapist** counsellor, healer, psychoanalyst, psychotherapist.

there /ðeə/ *adverb* **1** in, at, or to that place or position. **2** at that point. **3** in that respect. **4** *used for emphasis in calling attention.* **5** *used to indicate the fact or existence of something.* ● *noun* that place. ● *interjection* **1** *expressing confirmation, triumph, etc..* **2** *used to soothe a child etc.* □ **thereabout(s)** near that place, amount, or time. **thereafter** *formal* after that. **thereby** by that means or agency. **therefore** for that reason; accordingly, consequently. **therein** *formal* in that place or respect. **thereof** *formal* of that or it. **thereto** *formal* **1** to that or it. **2** in addition. **thereupon** **1** in consequence of that. **2** directly after that.

| ■ □ **therefore** accordingly, consequently, hence, so, *formal* thus.

therm /θɜːm/ *noun* unit of heat; former UK unit of gas supplied.

thermal /'θɜːm(ə)l/ *adjective* of, for, producing, or retaining heat. ● *noun* rising current of warm air. □ **thermal unit** unit for measuring heat. □ **thermally** *adverb.*

thermionic valve /θɜːmɪ'ɒnɪk/ *noun* device giving flow of electrons in one direction from heated substance, used esp. in rectification of current and in radio reception.

thermo- *combining form* heat.

thermodynamics /θɜːməʊdaɪ'næmɪks/ *plural noun* (usually treated as *singular*) science of relationship between heat and other forms of energy. □ **thermodynamic** *adjective.*

thermoelectric /θɜːməʊɪ'lektrɪk/ *adjective* producing electricity by difference of temperatures.

thermometer /θə'mɒmɪtə/ *noun* instrument for measuring temperature, esp. graduated glass tube containing mercury or alcohol.

thermonuclear /θɜːməʊ'njuːklɪə/ *adjective* **1** relating to nuclear reactions that occur only at very high temperatures. **2** (of bomb etc.) using such reactions.

thermoplastic /θɜːməʊ'plæstɪk/ *adjective* becoming plastic on heating and hardening on cooling. ● *noun* thermoplastic substance.

Thermos /'θɜːməs/ *noun* (in full **Thermos flask**) *proprietary term* vacuum flask.

thermosetting /'θɜːməʊsetɪŋ/ *adjective* (of plastics) setting permanently when heated.

thermosphere /'θɜːməsfɪə/ *noun* region of atmosphere beyond mesosphere.

thermostat /'θɜːməstæt/ *noun* device for automatic regulation of temperature. □ **thermostatic** /-'stæt-/ *adjective.* **thermostatically** /-'stæt-/ *adverb.*

thesaurus /θɪˈsɔːrəs/ *noun* (*plural* **-ri** /-raɪ/ or **-ruses**) dictionary of synonyms etc.

these *plural* of THIS.

thesis /ˈθiːsɪs/ *noun* (*plural* **theses** /-siːz/) 1 proposition to be maintained or proved. 2 dissertation, esp. by candidate for higher degree.
■ 1 argument, assertion, contention, hypothesis, idea, opinion, postulate, premise, premiss, proposition, theory, view. 2 disquisition, dissertation, essay, monograph, paper, tract, treatise.

Thespian /ˈθespɪən/ *adjective* of drama. ● *noun* actor or actress.

they /ðeɪ/ *pronoun* (as subject of verb) 1 the people or things in question. 2 people in general. 3 people in authority.

they'd /ðeɪd/ 1 they had. 2 they would.

they'll /ðeɪəl/ they will; they shall.

they're /ðeə/ they are.

they've /ðeɪv/ they have.

thiamine /ˈθaɪəmɪn/ *noun* (also **thiamin**) B vitamin found in unrefined cereals, beans, and liver.

thick /θɪk/ *adjective* 1 of great or specified extent between opposite surfaces. 2 (of line etc.) broad, not fine. 3 closely set; dense; crowded. 4 (usually + *with*) densely filled or covered. 5 firm in consistency. 6 made of thick material. 7 muddy; impenetrable. 8 *colloquial* stupid. 9 (of voice) indistinct. 10 (of accent) marked. 11 *colloquial* intimate. ● *noun* thick part of anything. ● *adverb* thickly. □ **a bit thick** *colloquial* unreasonable, intolerable. **in the thick of** in the busiest part of. **thickhead** *colloquial* stupid person. **thickheaded** *adjective*. **thickset** *adjective* 1 heavily or solidly built. 2 set or growing close together. **thick-skinned** not sensitive to criticism. **through thick and thin** under all conditions; in spite of all difficulties. □ **thickly** *adverb*.
■ *adjective* 1 broad, bulky, chunky, fat, stout, sturdy, wide. 2 broad, fat, wide. 3 abundant, bushy, compact, dense, impassable, impenetrable, luxuriant, numerous, packed, plentiful, solid. 4 alive, bristling, chock-full, choked, covered, crammed, crawling, crowded, filled, full, jammed, packed, swarming, teeming. 5 clotted, coagulated, concentrated, condensed, firm, glutinous, heavy, jellied, stiff, viscid, viscous. 6 bulky, deep, heavy, substantial, woolly.

thicken *verb* 1 make or become thick(er). 2 become more complicated.
■ 1 coagulate, clot, congeal, firm up, gel, *colloquial* jell, reduce, solidify, stiffen.

thickener *noun* substance used to thicken liquid.

thickening *noun* 1 thickened part. 2 = THICKENER.

thicket /ˈθɪkɪt/ *noun* tangle of shrubs or trees.

thickness *noun* 1 being thick. 2 measure of this. 3 layer.

■ 1, 2 breadth, density, depth, fatness, viscosity, width. 3 coating, layer, seam, stratum.

thief /θiːf/ *noun* (*plural* **thieves** /θiːvz/) person who steals, esp. secretly.
■ bandit, brigand, burglar, cat burglar, embezzler, *historical* highwayman, housebreaker, kleptomaniac, looter, mugger, peculator, pickpocket, pilferer, pirate, *formal* or *jocular* purloiner, robber, safe-cracker, shoplifter, stealer, swindler.

thieve /θiːv/ *verb* (**-ving**) be a thief; steal. □ **thievery** *noun*. **thieving** *adjective* & *noun*.
■ □ **thieving** (*adjective*) dishonest, light-fingered, rapacious; (*noun*) see STEALING (STEAL).

thievish *adjective* given to stealing.

thigh /θaɪ/ *noun* part of leg between hip and knee. □ **thigh-bone** femur.

thimble /ˈθɪmb(ə)l/ *noun* metal or plastic cap worn to protect finger and push needle in sewing.

thimbleful *noun* (*plural* **-s**) small quantity, esp. of drink.

thin /θɪn/ *adjective* (**-nn-**) 1 having opposite surfaces close together; of small thickness or diameter. 2 (of line etc.) narrow, fine. 3 made of thin material. 4 lean, not plump. 5 not dense or copious. 6 of slight consistency. 7 weak; lacking an important ingredient. 8 (of excuse etc.) transparent, flimsy. ● *adverb* thinly. ● *verb* (**-nn-**) 1 make or become thin(ner). 2 (often + *out*) make or become less dense, crowded, or numerous. □ **thin on the ground** few. **thin on top** balding. **thin-skinned** sensitive to criticism. □ **thinly** *adverb*. **thinness** *noun*.
■ *adjective* 1, 2 attenuated, fine, narrow, skinny, slender, slim, spindly. 3 delicate, diaphanous, filmy, fine, flimsy, gauzy, insubstantial, light, see-through, sheer (*silk*), translucent, transparent. 4 anorexic, bony, cadaverous, emaciated, gangling, gaunt, lanky, lean, rangy, scraggy, scrawny, skeletal, skinny, slender, slight, slim, small, spare, spindly, underfed, undernourished, underweight, wiry. 5 meagre, rarefied (*atmosphere*), scanty, scarce, scattered, sparse, wispy. 6 dilute, fluid, runny, sloppy, watery, weak. 8 feeble, flimsy, implausible, tenuous, transparent, unconvincing. ● *verb* 1 attenuate, reduce, trim. 2 decrease, dilute, diminish, disperse, prune, reduce, trim, water down, weaken, weed out.

thine /ðaɪn/ *archaic pronoun* yours (singular). ● *adjective* your (singular).

thing /θɪŋ/ *noun* 1 any possible object of thought or perception including people, material objects, events, qualities, details, ideas, utterances, and acts. 2 *colloquial* one's special interest. 3 (**the thing**) *colloquial* what is proper, fashionable, needed, important, etc. 4 (in *plural*) personal belongings, clothing, or equipment. 5 (in *plural*) affairs, circumstances. □ **have a thing about** *colloquial* be obsessed by or prejudiced about.

■ **1** (*material object*) apparatus, artefact, article, contrivance, device, entity, gadget, implement, invention, item, object, utensil; (*event*) *colloquial* affair, circumstance, deed, event, eventuality, happening, incident, occurrence, phenomenon; (*idea, detail, utterance, etc.*) concept, concern, detail, fact, factor, feeling, idea, matter, point, statement, thought; (*act*) act, action, chore, deed, job, responsibility, task. **4** (*things*) baggage, belongings, clothing, equipment, gear, luggage, possessions, stuff. **5** (*things*) affairs, circumstances, conditions, life. □ **have a thing about** be neurotic about, be obsessed with, be passionate about, be preoccupied with, have an aversion to, have a fixation about, *slang* have a hang-up about, have a phobia about.

thingummy /ˈθɪŋəmɪ/ *noun* (*plural* -**ies**) (also **thingumabob** /-məbɒb/, **thingumajig** /-mədʒɪg/) *colloquial* person or thing whose name one forgets or does not know.

think /θɪŋk/ *verb* (*past & past participle* **thought** /θɔːt/) **1** be of opinion. **2** (+ *of*, *about*) consider. **3** exercise mind. **4** form ideas; imagine. **5** have half-formed intention. ● *noun colloquial* act of thinking. □ **think better of** change one's mind about (intention) after reconsideration. **think out 1** consider carefully. **2** devise. **think over** reflect on. **think-tank** *colloquial* group of experts providing advice and ideas on national or commercial problems. **think twice** avoid hasty action etc. **think up** *colloquial* devise. □ **thinkable** *adjective*.

■ *verb* **1** accept, admit, assume, be convinced, believe, be under the impression, conclude, consider, *formal* deem, estimate, feel, guess, judge, presume, reckon, suppose, surmise. **2** (*think about*) attend to, chew over, consider, contemplate, dwell on, give thought to, mull over, ponder, remember, remind oneself of. **3** brood, cogitate, concentrate, contemplate, deliberate, meditate, muse, ponder, rack one's brains, reason, reflect, reminisce, ruminate, use one's intelligence, work things out, worry. **4** daydream, dream, fancy, fantasize, imagine. □ **think better of** see RECONSIDER. **think up** see DEVISE 1.

thinker *noun* **1** person who thinks in specified way. **2** person with skilled or powerful mind.

■ **2** *colloquial* brain, innovator, inventor, mastermind, philosopher, sage, savant, scholar.

thinking *adjective* intelligent, rational. ● *noun* opinion, judgement.

■ *adjective* see INTELLIGENT, THOUGHTFUL 1.

thinner *noun* solvent for diluting paint etc.

third /θɜːd/ *adjective & noun* **1** next after second. **2** any of 3 equal parts of thing. □ **third degree** severe and protracted interrogation by police etc. **third man** *Cricket* fielder near boundary behind slips. **third party** another party besides the two principals. **third-party insurance** insurance against damage or injury suffered by person other than the insured. **third-rate** inferior; very poor. **Third World** developing countries of Africa, Asia, and Latin America. □ **thirdly** *adverb*.

thirst /θɜːst/ *noun* **1** (discomfort caused by) need to drink. **2** desire, craving. ● *verb* (often + *for*, *after*) feel thirst.

■ *noun* **1** dryness, thirstiness. **2** appetite, craving, desire, eagerness, hunger, itch, longing, lust, passion, urge, wish, yearning, *colloquial* yen.
● *verb* (*thirst for*, *after*) crave, desire, hunger for, long for, strive after, want, wish for, yearn for.

thirsty /ˈθɜːstɪ/ *adjective* (-**ier**, -**iest**) **1** feeling thirst. **2** (of land, season, etc.) dry, parched. **3** (often + *for*, *after*) eager. **4** *colloquial* causing thirst. □ **thirstily** *adverb*. **thirstiness** *noun*.

■ **1** dehydrated, *colloquial* dry, *colloquial* parched. **3** avid, craving, desirous, eager, greedy, hankering, itching, longing, voracious, yearning.

thirteen /θɜːˈtiːn/ *adjective & noun* one more than twelve. □ **thirteenth** *adjective & noun*.

thirty /ˈθɜːtɪ/ *adjective & noun* (*plural* -**ies**) three times ten. □ **thirtieth** *adjective & noun*.

this /ðɪs/ *adjective* (*plural* **these** /ðiːz/) **1** used to describe the person or thing nearby, indicated, just mentioned, or understood. **2** used to specify the nearer or more immediate of two. **3** the present (morning, week, etc.). ● *pronoun* (*plural* **these** /ðiːz/) this one. ● *adverb* (+ adjective or adverb) to this degree or extent.

thistle /ˈθɪs(ə)l/ *noun* **1** prickly plant, usually with globular heads of purple flowers. **2** this as Scottish national emblem. □ **thistledown** down containing thistle-seeds. □ **thistly** *adjective*.

thither /ˈðɪðə/ *adverb archaic* or *formal* to that place.

tho' = THOUGH.

thole /θəʊl/ *noun* (in full **thole-pin**) **1** pin in gunwale of boat as fulcrum for oar. **2** each of two such pins forming rowlock.

thong /θɒŋ/ *noun* narrow strip of hide or leather.

thorax /ˈθɔːræks/ *noun* (*plural* -**races** /-rəsiːz/ or -**raxes**) part of the body between neck and abdomen. □ **thoracic** /-ˈræs-/ *adjective*.

thorn /θɔːn/ *noun* **1** sharp-pointed projection on plant. **2** thorn-bearing shrub or tree. □ **thornless** *adjective*.

■ **1** barb, needle, prickle, spike, spine.

thorny *adjective* (-**ier**, -**iest**) **1** having many thorns. **2** (of subject) problematic; causing disagreement.

■ **1** barbed, bristly, prickly, scratchy, sharp, spiky, spiny. **2** see DIFFICULT 1.

thorough /ˈθʌrə/ *adjective* **1** complete, unqualified; not superficial. **2** acting or done with great care etc. **3** absolute. □ **thoroughbred** *adjective* **1** of pure breed. **2** high-spirited. ● *noun* such animal, esp. horse. **thoroughfare** public way open at both ends, esp. main road. **thoroughgoing** thorough, complete. □ **thoroughly** *adverb*. **thoroughness** *noun*.

■ **1** complete, comprehensive, deep, detailed, exhaustive, extensive, full, in-depth, penetrating, probing, searching, systematic, thoroughgoing, total, unqualified. **2** assiduous, attentive, careful, conscientious, diligent, efficient, methodical, meticulous, observant, orderly, organized, painstaking, particular, scrupulous, thoughtful, watchful. **3** absolute, *literary* arrant, complete, downright, out and out, perfect, *colloquial* proper, sheer, thoroughgoing, total, unmitigated, unmixed, unqualified, utter.

those *plural* of THAT.

thou[1] /ðaʊ/ *pronoun archaic* (as subject of verb) you (singular).

thou[2] /θaʊ/ *noun* (*plural* same or **-s**) *colloquial* **1** thousand. **2** one thousandth.

though /ðəʊ/ (also **tho'**) *conjunction* **1** in spite of the fact that. **2** even if. **3** and yet. ● *adverb colloquial* however; all the same.

thought[1] /θɔːt/ *noun* **1** process, power, faculty, etc. of thinking. **2** particular way of thinking. **3** sober reflection, consideration. **4** care or concern. **5** idea, notion. **6** intention, purpose. **7** (usually in *plural*) one's opinion.
■ **1, 3** brooding, cerebration, cogitation, concentration, consideration, contemplation, daydreaming, deliberation, intelligence, introspection, meditation, mental activity, musing, pensiveness, *literary* ratiocination, rationality, reason, reasoning, reflection, reverie, rumination, study, thinking, worrying. **4** attention, care, concern, consideration, kindness, regard, solicitude, thoughtfulness. **5** belief, concept, conception, conclusion, conjecture, conviction, idea, notion, observation, opinion. **6** aim, design, dream, expectation, hope, intention, objective, plan, prospect, vision.

thought[2] *past & past participle* of THINK.

thoughtful *adjective* **1** engaged in or given to meditation. **2** giving signs of serious thought. **3** considerate. □ **thoughtfully** *adverb*. **thoughtfulness** *noun*.
■ **1** absorbed, abstracted, anxious, attentive, brooding, contemplative, dreamy, grave, introspective, meditative, pensive, philosophical, rapt, reflective, serious, solemn, studious, thinking, wary, watchful, worried. **2** careful, conscientious, diligent, exhaustive, intelligent, methodical, meticulous, observant, orderly, organized, painstaking, rational, scrupulous, sensible, systematic, thorough. **3** attentive, caring, compassionate, concerned, considerate, friendly, good-natured, helpful, kind, obliging, public-spirited, solicitous, unselfish.

thoughtless *adjective* **1** careless of others' feelings. **2** careless of consequences. **3** caused by lack of thought. □ **thoughtlessly** *adverb*. **thoughtlessness** *noun*.
■ **1** cruel, heartless, impolite, inconsiderate, insensitive, rude, selfish, tactless, uncaring, undiplomatic, unfeeling, unkind. **2, 3** absent-minded, careless, forgetful, hasty, heedless, ill-considered, impetuous, inadvertent, inattentive, injudicious, irresponsible, mindless, negligent, rash, reckless, scatterbrained, stupid, unobservant, unthinking.

thousand /ˈθaʊz(ə)nd/ *adjective & noun* **1** (*plural* same) ten hundred. **2** (**thousands**) *colloquial* large number. □ **thousandth** *adjective & noun*.

thrall /θrɔːl/ *noun literary* **1** (often + *of, to*) slave. **2** slavery. □ **thraldom** *noun*.

thrash /θræʃ/ *verb* **1** beat or whip severely. **2** defeat thoroughly. **3** move or fling (esp. limbs) violently. □ **thrash out** discuss to conclusion.
■ **1** beat, birch, cane, chastise, flay, flog, hit, lash, scourge, whip. **2** see DEFEAT *verb* 1.

thread /θred/ *noun* **1** spun-out cotton, silk, glass, etc. **2** length of this. **3** thin cord of twisted yarns used esp. in sewing and weaving. **4** continuous aspect of thing. **5** spiral ridge of screw. ● *verb* **1** pass thread through (needle). **2** put (beads) on thread. **3** arrange (material in strip form, e.g. film) in proper position on equipment. **4** pick (one's way) through maze, crowded place, etc. □ **threadbare 1** (of cloth) so worn that nap is lost and threads showing. **2** (of person) shabby. **3** (of idea etc.) hackneyed. **threadworm** parasitic threadlike worm.
■ *noun* **1** fibre, filament, strand, yarn. **2, 3** cord, line, string, twine, yarn. **4** continuity, course, direction, drift, line of thought, plot, storyline, tenor, theme. ● *verb* **4** (*thread one's way*) file, pass, pick one's way, weave, wind. □ **threadbare 1** frayed, old, ragged, tattered, *colloquial* tatty, worn, worn out. **2** *colloquial* scruffy, shabby.

threat /θret/ *noun* **1** declaration of intention to punish or hurt. **2** indication of something undesirable coming. **3** person or thing regarded as dangerous.
■ **1** intimidation, menace, warning. **2** forewarning, intimation, omen, portent, presage, warning. **3** danger, hazard, menace, risk.

threaten /ˈθret(ə)n/ *verb* **1** use threats towards. **2** be sign or indication of (something undesirable). **3** (+ *to do*) announce one's intention to do (undesirable thing). **4** give warning of infliction of (harm etc.). **5** put in danger. **6** (as **threatened** *adjective*) (of species etc.) likely to become extinct. □ **threatening** *adjective*.
■ **1** browbeat, bully, cow, frighten, intimidate, menace, pressurize, terrorize. **2** forebode, foreshadow, forewarn of, portend, presage, warn of. **5** endanger, imperil, jeopardize, put at risk. □ **threatening** forbidding, grim, impending, looming, menacing, *formal* minatory, ominous, portentous, sinister, stern, ugly, unfriendly, worrying.

three /θriː/ *adjective & noun* one more than two. □ **three-cornered 1** triangular. **2** (of contest etc.) between 3 people etc. **three-dimensional** having or appearing to have length, breadth, and depth. **three-legged race** race for pairs with right leg of one tied to other's left leg. **threepence** /ˈθrepəns/ sum of 3 pence. **threepenny** /ˈθrepənɪ/ costing 3 pence. **three-piece** (suit or suite) consisting of 3 items. **three-ply 1** (wool etc.) having 3 strands. **2** (plywood) having 3 layers. **three-point turn** method of turning vehicle in narrow space by moving forwards, backwards, and forwards again. **three-quarter** *Rugby* any of 3 or 4 players just behind half-backs. **the three Rs** reading, writing, and arithmetic.

■ *noun* triad, trio, triplet, triumvirate.
□ **three-dimensional** solid, stereoscopic.

threefold *adjective & adverb* three times as much or many.

threesome *noun* group of 3 people.

threnody /'θrenədɪ/ *noun* (*plural* **-ies**) song of lamentation.

thresh *verb* beat out or separate grain from (corn etc.). □ **thresher** *noun*.

threshold /'θreʃəʊld/ *noun* **1** plank or stone forming bottom of doorway. **2** point of entry. **3** limit below which stimulus causes no reaction.

■ **1** doorstep, doorway, entrance, sill. **2** see BEGINNING 1,2.

threw *past of* THROW.

thrice *adverb archaic* or *literary* 3 times.

thrift *noun* frugality; economical management. □ **thriftless** *adjective*. **thrifty** *adjective* (**-ier**, **-iest**).

■ □ **thrifty** careful, economical, frugal, parsimonious, provident, prudent, skimping, sparing.

thrill *noun* **1** wave or nervous tremor of emotion or sensation. **2** throb, pulsation. ● *verb* **1** (cause to) feel thrill. **2** quiver or throb (as) with emotion. □ **thrilling** *adjective*.

■ *noun* **1** *slang* buzz, excitement, *frisson*, *colloquial* kick, shiver, tingle, titillation, tremor. ● *verb* **1** arouse, delight, electrify, excite, galvanize, rouse, stimulate, stir, titillate. □ **thrilling** see EXCITING (EXCITE).

thriller *noun* sensational or exciting play, story, etc.

■ crime story, detective story, mystery, *colloquial* whodunit.

thrips *noun* (*plural* same) insect harmful to plants.

thrive *verb* (**-ving**; *past* **throve** or **thrived**; *past participle* **thriven** /'θrɪv(ə)n/ or **thrived**) **1** prosper. **2** grow vigorously. □ **thriving** *adjective*.

■ **1** boom, do well, flourish, prosper, succeed. **2** bloom, burgeon, come on, develop, expand, flourish, grow, increase, make strides. □ **thriving** see PROSPEROUS 2, VIGOROUS (VIGOUR).

thro' = THROUGH.

throat *noun* **1** gullet, windpipe. **2** front of neck. **3** *literary* narrow passage or entrance.

throaty *adjective* (**-ier**, **-iest**) (of voice) hoarsely resonant.

■ deep, gravelly, gruff, guttural, hoarse, husky, rasping, rough, thick.

throb *verb* (**-bb-**) **1** pulsate. **2** vibrate with persistent rhythm or with emotion. ● *noun* throbbing; violent beat or pulsation.

■ *verb* beat, palpitate, pound, pulsate, pulse, vibrate.

throe *noun* (usually in *plural*) violent pang. □ **in the throes of** struggling with the task of.

■ convulsion, pain, pang, paroxysm, spasm; (*throes*) labour, labour pains.

thrombosis /θrɒm'bəʊsɪs/ *noun* (*plural* **-boses** /-siːz/) coagulation of blood in blood vessel or organ.

■ blood clot, embolism.

throne *noun* **1** ceremonial chair for sovereign, bishop, etc. **2** sovereign power. ● *verb* (**-ning**) enthrone.

throng *noun* (often + *of*) crowd, esp. of people. ● *verb* **1** come in multitudes. **2** fill (as) with crowd.

■ *noun* assembly, crowd, crush, gathering, *usually derogatory* horde, jam, mass, mob, multitude, swarm.

throstle /'θrɒs(ə)l/ *noun* song thrush.

throttle /'θrɒt(ə)l/ *noun* **1** lever etc. operating valve controlling flow of steam or fuel in engine. **2** throat. ● *verb* (**-ling**) **1** choke, strangle. **2** control (engine etc.) with throttle. □ **throttle back, down** reduce speed of (engine etc.) by throttling.

■ *verb* **1** asphyxiate, choke, strangle, suffocate.

through /θruː/ (also **thro'**, *US* **thru**) *preposition* **1** from end to end or side to side of. **2** between, among. **3** from beginning to end of. **4** by agency, means, or fault of; by reason of. **5** *US* up to and including. ● *adverb* **1** through something; from end to end. **2** to the end. ● *adjective* **1** (of journey etc.) done without change of line, vehicle, etc. **2** (of traffic) going through a place to its destination. **3** (of road) open at both ends. □ **be through** *colloquial* (often + *with*) **1** have finished. **2** cease to have dealings. **through and through** thoroughly, completely. **throughput** amount of material put through a manufacturing etc. process or a computer.

throughout /θruː'aʊt/ *preposition* right through; from end to end of. ● *adverb* in every part or respect.

throve *past of* THRIVE.

throw /θrəʊ/ *verb* (*past* **threw** /θruː/; *past participle* **thrown**) **1** propel through space. **2** force violently into specified position or state. **3** turn or move (part of body) quickly or suddenly. **4** project (rays, light, etc.); cast (shadow). **5** bring to the ground. **6** *colloquial* disconcert. **7** (+ *on*, *off*, etc.) put (clothes etc.) carelessly or hastily on, off, etc. **8** cause (dice) to fall on table etc. **9** obtain (specified number) thus. **10** cause to pass or extend suddenly to another state or position. **11** move (switch, lever). **12** shape (pottery) on wheel. **13** have (fit, tantrum, etc.). **14** give (a party). ● *noun* **1** throwing, being thrown. **2** distance a thing is or may be thrown. **3** (**a throw**) *slang* each, per item. □ **throw away 1** discard as unwanted. **2** waste; fail to make use of. **throw-away** *adjective* **1** to be thrown away after (one) use. **2** deliberately underemphasized. **throw back** (usually in *passive*; + *on*) compel to rely on. **throwback** (instance of) reversion to ancestral character. **throw in 1** interpose (word, remark). **2** include at no extra cost. **3** throw (football) from edge of pitch where it has gone out of play. **throw-in** *noun* throwing in of football from edge of pitch. **throw in the towel** admit defeat. **throw off 1** discard; contrive to get rid of. **2** write or utter in offhand way. **throw open** (often + *to*) **1** cause to be suddenly or widely open. **2** make accessible. **throw out 1** put out forcibly or suddenly. **2** discard as unwanted. **3** reject. **throw over** desert, abandon. **throw together 1** assemble hastily. **2** bring into casual contact. **throw up 1** abandon. **2** resign from. **3** vomit. **4** erect hastily. **5** bring to notice.

■ *verb* **1, 2** bowl, *slang* bung, cast, *colloquial* chuck, fling, *colloquial* heave, hurl, launch, lob, pelt, pitch, propel, put (*the shot*), send, shy, *colloquial* sling, toss. **4** cast, project, shed. **5** dislodge, floor, shake off, throw down, throw off, unseat, upset. **6** see DISCONCERT. □ **throw away 1** see DISCARD 1. **throw-away 1** disposable. **2** casual, offhand, passing, unimportant. **throw out 1** see EXPEL 1. **throw up 3** see VOMIT *verb* 1. **5** see PRODUCE *verb* 2.

thrum *verb* (**-mm-**) **1** play (stringed instrument) monotonously or unskilfully. **2** (often + *on*) drum idly. ● *noun* **1** such playing. **2** resultant sound.

thrush[1] *noun* kind of songbird.

thrush[2] *noun* fungus infection of throat, esp. in children, or of vagina.

thrust *verb* (*past & past participle* **thrust**) **1** push with sudden impulse or with force. **2** (+ *on*) impose (thing) forcibly on. **3** (+ *at, through*) pierce, stab; lunge suddenly. **4** make (one's way) forcibly. **5** (as **thrusting** *adjective*) aggressive, ambitious. ● *noun* **1** sudden or forcible push or lunge. **2** forward force exerted by propeller or jet etc. **3** strong attempt to penetrate enemy's line or territory. **4** remark aimed at person. **5** stress between parts of arch etc. **6** (often + *of*) theme, gist.

■ *verb* **1** drive, force, impel, poke, press, prod, propel, push, ram, send, shove, stick. **2** (*thrust on*) force on, impose on, press on, urge on. **3** jab, lunge, pierce, plunge, poke, stab, stick. **4** butt, elbow, force, push, ram, shoulder, shove.

thud /θʌd/ *noun* low dull sound as of blow on non-resonant thing. ● *verb* (**-dd-**) make thud; fall with thud.

thug /θʌg/ *noun* vicious or brutal ruffian. □ **thuggery** *noun*. **thuggish** *adjective*.

■ bully, criminal, delinquent, desperado, gangster, hoodlum, hooligan, mugger, rough, ruffian, tough, troublemaker, vandal, *slang* yob.

thumb /θʌm/ *noun* **1** short thick finger on hand, set apart from other 4. **2** part of glove for thumb. ● *verb* **1** soil or wear with thumb. **2** turn over pages with thumb. **3** request or get (lift) by sticking out thumb. □ **thumb index** set of lettered grooves cut down side of book etc. for easy reference. **thumbnail** ● *noun* nail of thumb. ● *adjec-*

tive concise. **thumbscrew** instrument of torture for squeezing thumbs. **thumbs up, down** indication of approval or rejection. **under (person's) thumb** dominated by him or her.

thump /θʌmp/ *verb* **1** beat heavily, esp. with fist. **2** throb strongly. **3** (+ *at, on*, etc.) knock loudly. ● *noun* (sound of) heavy blow.

thumping *adjective colloquial* huge.

thunder /'θʌndə/ *noun* **1** loud noise accompanying lightning. **2** resounding loud deep noise. **3** strong censure. ● *verb* **1** sound with or like thunder. **2** move with loud noise. **3** utter loudly. **4** (+ *against* etc.) make violent threats. □ **thunderbolt 1** flash of lightning with crash of thunder. **2** unexpected occurrence or announcement. **3** supposed bolt or shaft as destructive agent. **thunderclap** crash of thunder. **thundercloud** electrically charged cumulus cloud. **thunderstorm** storm with thunder and lightning. **thunderstruck** amazed. □ **thunderous** *adjective*. **thundery** *adjective*.

■ *noun* **1, 2** clap, crack, peal, roll, rumble. □ **thunderous** booming, deafening, loud, reverberant, reverberating, roaring, rumbling.

thundering *adjective colloquial* huge.

Thur. *abbreviation* (also **Thurs.**) Thursday.

thurible /'θjʊərɪb(ə)l/ *noun* censer.

Thursday /'θɜːzdeɪ/ *noun* day of week following Wednesday.

thus /ðʌs/ *adverb formal* **1** in this way; like this. **2** accordingly; as a result or inference. **3** to this extent; so.

■ **2** accordingly, consequently, for this reason, hence, so, therefore.

thwack *verb* hit with heavy blow. ● *noun* heavy blow.

thwart /θwɔːt/ *verb* frustrate, foil. ● *noun* rower's seat.

■ *verb* baffle, baulk, block, check, foil, frustrate, hinder, impede, obstruct, prevent, stand in the way of, stop, stump.

thy /ðaɪ/ *adjective* (also **thine**, esp. before vowel) *archaic* your (singular).

thyme /taɪm/ *noun* herb with aromatic leaves.

thymol /'θaɪmɒl/ *noun* antiseptic made from oil of thyme.

thymus /'θaɪməs/ *noun* (*plural* **thymi** /-maɪ/) ductless gland near base of neck.

thyroid /'θaɪrɔɪd/ *noun* thyroid gland. □ **thyroid cartilage** large cartilage of larynx forming Adam's apple. **thyroid gland 1** large ductless gland near larynx secreting hormone which regulates growth and development. **2** extract of this.

thyself /ðaɪ'self/ *pronoun archaic* **1** emphatic *form of* THOU[1] *or* THEE. **2** *reflexive form of* THEE.

ti = TE.

tiara /tɪ'ɑːrə/ *noun* **1** jewelled ornamental band worn on front of woman's hair. **2** 3-crowned diadem formerly worn by pope.

tibia /'tɪbɪə/ *noun* (*plural* **tibiae** /-bɪiː/) inner of two bones extending from knee to ankle.

tic *noun* (in full **nervous tic**) spasmodic contraction of muscles, esp. of face.

tick[1] *noun* **1** slight recurring click, esp. of watch or clock. **2** *colloquial* moment. **3** small mark (✓) to denote correctness etc. ● *verb* **1** make sound of tick. **2** (often + *off*) mark with tick. □ **tick off** *colloquial* reprimand. **ticking-off** *noun*. **tick over 1** (of engine) idle. **2** function at basic level. **tick-tack** kind of manual semaphore used by racecourse bookmakers. **tick-tock** ticking of large clock etc.

tick[2] *noun* parasitic arachnid or insect on animals.

tick[3] *noun colloquial* financial credit.

tick[4] *noun* **1** case of mattress or pillow. **2** ticking.

ticker *noun colloquial* **1** heart. **2** watch. **3** *US* tape machine. □ **ticker-tape** paper strip from tape machine, esp. as thrown from windows to greet celebrity.

ticket /'tɪkɪt/ *noun* **1** piece of paper or card entitling holder to enter place, participate in event, travel by public transport, etc. **2** notification of traffic offence etc. **3** certificate of discharge from army or of qualification as ship's master, pilot, etc. **4** price etc. label. **5** *esp. US* list of candidates put forward by group, esp. political party. **6** *esp. US* principles of party. **7** (**the ticket**) *colloquial* what is needed. ● *verb* (**-t-**) attach ticket to.

■ *noun* **1** coupon, pass, permit, token, voucher. **4** docket, label, marker, tab, tag.

ticking *noun* strong usually striped material to cover mattresses etc.

tickle /'tɪk(ə)l/ *verb* (**-ling**) **1** touch or stroke lightly so as to produce laughter and spasmodic movement. **2** excite agreeably; amuse. **3** catch (trout etc.) by rubbing it so that it moves backwards into hand. ● *noun* act or sensation of tickling.

ticklish /'tɪklɪʃ/ *adjective* **1** sensitive to tickling. **2** difficult to handle.

■ **2** awkward, delicate, difficult, risky, thorny, touchy, tricky.

tidal /'taɪd(ə)l/ *adjective* related to, like, or affected by tides. □ **tidal wave 1** exceptionally large ocean wave, esp. one caused by underwater earthquake. **2** widespread manifestation of feeling etc.

tidbit *US* = TITBIT.

tiddler /'tɪdlə/ *noun colloquial* **1** small fish, esp. stickleback or minnow. **2** unusually small thing.

tiddly[1] /'tɪdlɪ/ *adjective* (**-ier**, **-iest**) *colloquial* slightly drunk.

tiddly[2] /'tɪdlɪ/ *adjective* (**-ier**, **-iest**) *colloquial* little.

tiddly-wink /'tɪdlɪwɪŋk/ *noun* **1** counter flicked with another into cup. **2** (in *plural*) this game.

tide *noun* **1** regular rise and fall of sea due to attraction of moon and sun. **2** water as moved by this. **3** time, season. **4** trend of opinion, fortune,

or events. ● *verb* (**-ding**) (**tide over**) temporarily provide with what is needed. □ **tidemark 1** mark made by tide at high water. **2** *colloquial* line of dirt round bath, or on person's face between washed and unwashed parts. **tideway** tidal part of river.

tidings /'taɪdɪŋz/ *noun archaic* or *jocular* (treated as *singular* or *plural*) news.

tidy /'taɪdɪ/ *adjective* (**-ier**, **-iest**) **1** neat, orderly. **2** (of person) methodical. **3** *colloquial* considerable. ● *noun* (*plural* **-ies**) receptacle for odds and ends. ● *verb* (**-ies**, **-ied**) (often + *up*) make (oneself, room, etc.) tidy; put in order. □ **tidily** *adverb*. **tidiness** *noun*.

■ *adjective* **1** neat, orderly, presentable, shipshape, smart, spick and span, spruce, straight, trim, uncluttered, well groomed, well kept. **2** businesslike, careful, methodical, meticulous, organized, systematic, well organized. ● *verb* arrange, clean up, groom, neaten, put in order, rearrange, reorganize, set straight, smarten, spruce up, straighten, *colloquial* titivate.
□ **tidiness** meticulousness, neatness, order, orderliness, organization, smartness, system.

tie *verb* (**tying**) **1** attach or fasten with cord etc. **2** form into knot or bow. **3** (often + *down*) restrict, bind. **4** (often + *with*) make same score as another competitor. **5** bind (rafters etc.) by crosspiece etc. **6** *Music* unite (notes) by tie. ● *noun* **1** cord etc. used for fastening. **2** strip of material worn round collar and tied in knot at front. **3** thing that unites or restricts people. **4** equality of score, draw, or dead heat among competitors. **5** match between any pair of players or teams. **6** rod or beam holding parts of structure together. **7** *Music* curved line above or below two notes of same pitch that are to be joined as one. □ **tie-break, -breaker** means of deciding winner when competitors have tied. **tie-dye** method of producing dyed patterns by tying string etc. to keep dye from parts of fabric. **tie in** (often + *with*) have close association. **tiepin** ornamental pin to hold necktie in place. **tie up 1** fasten with cord etc. **2** invest (money etc.) so that it is not immediately available for use. **3** fully occupy (person). **4** bring to satisfactory conclusion. **tie-up** *noun* connection, association.

■ *verb* **1** attach, bind, chain, do up, fasten, hitch, join, knot, lash, moor, rope, secure, splice, tether, truss up. **4** be equal, be level, be neck and neck, draw.

tied *adjective* **1** (of dwelling house) occupied subject to tenant's working for house's owner. **2** (of public house etc.) bound to supply only particular brewer's liquor.

tier /tɪə/ *noun* row, rank, or unit of structure, as one of several placed one above another. □ **tiered** *adjective*.

■ course (*of bricks*), layer, level, line, order, range, rank, row, stage, storey, stratum, terrace.

tiercel = TERCEL.

tiff *noun* slight or petty quarrel.

tiger /'taɪgə/ *noun* **1** large Asian animal of cat

family, with yellow-brown coat with black stripes. **2** fierce, formidable, or energetic person. □ **tiger-cat** any moderate-sized feline resembling tiger. **tiger lily** tall garden lily with dark-spotted orange flowers.

tight /taɪt/ *adjective* **1** closely held, drawn, fastened, fitting, packed, etc. **2** impermeable, impervious. **3** tense, stretched. **4** *colloquial* drunk. **5** *colloquial* stingy. **6** (of money or materials) not easily obtainable. **7** stringent, demanding. **8** presenting difficulties. **9** produced by or requiring great exertion or pressure. ● *adverb* tightly. □ **tight corner** difficult situation. **tight-fisted** stingy. **tight-lipped** restraining emotion; determinedly reticent. **tightrope** high tightly stretched rope or wire on which acrobats etc. perform. □ **tighten** *verb*. **tightly** *adverb*. **tightness** *noun*.

■ *adjective* **1** close, close-fitting, compact, constricted, crammed, cramped, crowded, dense, fast, firm, fixed, immovable, packed, secure, snug. **2** airtight, impermeable, impervious, leak-proof, sealed, waterproof, watertight. **3** rigid, stiff, stretched, taut, tense. **4** see DRUNK *adjective* 1. **5** see MISERLY (MISER). **6** see SCARCE *adjective*. **7** harsh, inflexible, precise, rigorous, severe, strict, stringent. □ **tighten** clamp down, close, close up, constrict, fasten, screw up, squeeze, stiffen, stretch, tauten, tense.

tights *plural noun* thin close-fitting stretch garment covering legs, feet, and lower torso.

tigress /ˈtaɪgrɪs/ *noun* female tiger.

tilde /ˈtɪldə/ *noun* mark (˜) placed over letter, e.g. Spanish *n* in *señor*.

tile *noun* thin slab of concrete, baked clay, etc. for roofing, paving, etc. ● *verb* (**-ling**) cover with tiles. □ **tiler** *noun*.

tiling *noun* **1** process of fixing tiles. **2** area of tiles.

till[1] *preposition* up to; as late as. ● *conjunction* **1** up to time when. **2** so long that.

USAGE In all senses, *till* can be replaced by *until*, which is more formal in style.

till[2] *noun* money-drawer in bank, shop, etc., esp. with device recording amount and details of each purchase.

till[3] *verb* cultivate (land).

■ cultivate, dig, farm, plough, work.

tillage *noun* **1** preparation of land for growing crops. **2** tilled land.

tiller /ˈtɪlə/ *noun* bar by which boat's rudder is turned.

tilt *verb* **1** (cause to) assume sloping position or heel over. **2** (+ *at*) thrust or run at with weapon. **3** (+ *with*) engage in contest with. ● *noun* **1** tilting. **2** sloping position. **3** (of medieval knights etc.) charging with lance against opponent or mark. □ **(at) full tilt 1** at full speed. **2** with full force.

■ *verb* **1** angle, bank, cant, careen, heel over, incline, lean, list, slant, slope, tip. **2, 3** fight, *historical* joust, thrust.

tilth *noun* **1** tillage, cultivation. **2** cultivated soil.

timber /ˈtɪmbə/ *noun* **1** wood for building, carpentry, etc. **2** piece of wood, beam, esp. as rib of vessel. **3** large standing trees. **4** (as *interjection*) warning that tree is about to fall.

■ **1** beams, boarding, boards, laths, logs, lumber, planks, posts, tree trunks, wood. **2** see BEAM *noun* 1. **3** forest, trees, woodland, woods.

timbered *adjective* **1** made (partly) of timber. **2** (of land) wooded.

timbre /ˈtæmbə/ *noun* distinctive character of musical sound or voice apart from its pitch and volume.

timbrel /ˈtɪmbr(ə)l/ *noun archaic* tambourine.

time *noun* **1** indefinite continuous progress of past, present, and future events etc. regarded as a whole. **2** more or less definite portion of this; historical or other period. **3** allotted or available portion of time. **4** definite or fixed point or portion of time. **5** (**a time**) indefinite period. **6** occasion. **7** moment etc. suitable for purpose. **8** (in *plural*) (preceded by numeral etc.) *expressing multiplication*. **9** lifetime. **10** (in *singular* or *plural*) conditions of life or of period. **11** *slang* prison sentence. **12** apprenticeship. **13** date or expected date of childbirth or death. **14** measured amount of time worked. **15** rhythm or measure of musical composition. ● *verb* (**-ming**) **1** choose time for. **2** do at chosen or appropriate time. **3** ascertain time taken by. □ **at the same time 1** simultaneously. **2** nevertheless. **at times** now and then. **from time to time** occasionally. **in no time 1** rapidly. **2** in a moment. **in time 1** not late; early enough. **2** eventually. **3** following time of music etc. **on time** punctually. **time and (or time and time) again** on many occasions. **time-and-motion** measuring efficiency of industrial etc. operations. **time bomb** one designed to explode at pre-set time. **time capsule** box etc. containing objects typical of present time, buried for future discovery. **time-consuming** using much or too much time. **time-honoured** esteemed by tradition or through custom. **timekeeper 1** person who records time. **2** watch or clock as regards accuracy. **timekeeping 1** keeping of time. **2** punctuality. **time-lag** interval between cause and effect. **time off** (also **time out**) time used for rest or different activity. **timepiece** clock, watch. **time-server** person who adapts his or her opinions to suit prevailing circumstances. **time-share** share in property under time-sharing scheme. **time-sharing 1** use of holiday home by several joint owners at different times of year. **2** use of computer by several people for different operations at the same time. **time sheet** sheet of paper for recording hours worked. **time-shift** move from one time to another. **time signal** audible indication of exact time of day. **time signature** *Music* indication of rhythm. **time switch** one operating automatically at pre-set time. **timetable** ● *noun* **1** table showing times of public transport services. **2** scheme of lessons, etc. ● *verb* include or arrange in such schedule. **time-worn** impaired by age. **time zone** range of longitudes where a common standard time is used.

■ *noun* **2** age, days, epoch, era, period. **3, 5** duration, interval, period, phase, season, session, spell, stretch, term, while. **4, 6, 7** date, hour, instant, juncture, moment, occasion, opportunity, point. **15** beat, measure, rhythm, tempo. ● *verb* **1** fix, judge, organize, plan, programme, schedule, timetable. **3** clock. □ **timetable** ● *noun* **2** agenda, calendar, curriculum, diary, list, programme, roster, rota, schedule.

timeless *adjective* not affected by passage of time. □ **timelessness** *noun*.

■ ageless, deathless, eternal, everlasting, immortal, immutable, indestructible, permanent, unchanging, undying, unending.

timely *adjective* (**-ier**, **-iest**) opportune; coming at right time. □ **timeliness** *noun*.

■ appropriate, apt, fitting, suitable.

timer *noun* person or device that measures time taken.

timid /ˈtɪmɪd/ *adjective* (**-er**, **-est**) easily alarmed; shy. □ **timidity** /-ˈmɪd-/ *noun*. **timidly** *adverb*.

■ afraid, apprehensive, bashful, chicken-hearted, cowardly, coy, diffident, faint-hearted, fearful, frightened, modest, mousy, nervous, *formal* pusillanimous, reserved, retiring, scared, sheepish, shrinking, shy, spineless, tentative, timorous, unadventurous, unheroic, *colloquial* wimpish.

timing *noun* **1** way thing is timed. **2** regulation of opening and closing of valves in internal-combustion engine.

timorous /ˈtɪmərəs/ *adjective* timid, frightened. □ **timorously** *adverb*.

timpani /ˈtɪmpənɪ/ *plural noun* (also **tympani**) kettledrums. □ **timpanist** *noun*.

tin *noun* **1** silvery-white metal used esp. in alloys and in making tin plate. **2** container of tin or tin plate, esp. for preserving food. **3** tin plate. ● *verb* (**-nn-**) **1** preserve (food) in tin. **2** cover or coat with tin. □ **tin foil** foil of tin, aluminium, or tin alloy, used to wrap food. **tin hat** *colloquial* military steel helmet. **tin-opener** tool for opening tins. **tin-pan alley** world of composers and publishers of popular music. **tin plate** sheet steel coated with tin. **tinpot** cheap, inferior. **tinsnips** clippers for cutting sheet metal. **tin-tack** TACK[1] coated with tin.

tincture /ˈtɪŋktʃə/ *noun* **1** (often + *of*) slight flavour or tinge. **2** medicinal solution of drug in alcohol. ● *verb* (**-ring**) **1** colour slightly; tinge, flavour. **2** (often + *with*) affect slightly.

tinder /ˈtɪndə/ *noun* dry substance readily taking fire from spark. □ **tinder-box** *historical* box with tinder, flint, and steel for kindling fires.

tine *noun* prong, tooth, or point of fork, comb, antler, etc.

ting *noun* tinkling sound as of bell. ● *verb* (cause to) emit this.

tinge /tɪndʒ/ *verb* (**-ging**) (often + *with*; often in *passive*) colour slightly. ● *noun* **1** tendency to or trace of some colour. **2** slight admixture of feeling or quality.

tingle /ˈtɪŋg(ə)l/ *verb* (**-ling**) feel or cause slight pricking or stinging sensation. ● *noun* tingling sensation.

■ *verb* itch, prickle, sting, tickle. ● *noun* itch, itching, pins and needles, prickling, stinging, thrill, tickle, tickling.

tinker /ˈtɪŋkə/ *noun* **1** itinerant mender of kettles, pans, etc. **2** *Scottish & Irish* Gypsy. **3** *colloquial* mischievous person or animal. ● *verb* **1** (+ *at, with*) work in amateurish or desultory way. **2** work as tinker.

■ *verb* **1** dabble, fiddle, fool about, mess about, play about.

tinkle /ˈtɪŋk(ə)l/ *verb* (**-ling**) (cause to) make short light ringing sounds. ● *noun* tinkling sound.

tinnitus /ˈtɪnɪtəs/ *noun Medicine* condition with ringing in ears.

tinny *adjective* (**-ier**, **-iest**) **1** like tin. **2** flimsy. **3** (of sound) thin and metallic.

■ **2** cheap, flimsy, inferior, insubstantial, poor quality, shoddy, tawdry.

tinsel /ˈtɪns(ə)l/ *noun* **1** glittering decorative metallic strips, threads, etc. **2** superficial brilliance or splendour. □ **tinselled** *adjective*.

■ **2** glitter, gloss, show, sparkle.

tint *noun* **1** variety of colour. **2** tendency towards or admixture of different colour. **3** faint colour spread over surface. ● *verb* apply tint to; colour.

■ *noun* **1** colour, hue, shade, tone. **2** tincture, tinge, touch. **3** colouring, dye, stain, wash.

tintinnabulation /tɪntɪmæbjʊˈleɪʃ(ə)n/ *noun* ringing of bells.

tiny /ˈtaɪnɪ/ *adjective* (**-ier**, **-iest**) very small.

■ diminutive, dwarf, imperceptible, infinitesimal, insignificant, lilliputian, microscopic, midget, *colloquial* mini, miniature, *colloquial* minuscule, minute, negligible, pygmy, small, *colloquial* teeny, unimportant, *esp. Scottish* wee, *colloquial* weeny.

tip[1] *noun* **1** extremity, esp. of small or tapering thing. **2** small piece or part attached to end of thing. **3** light touch. ● *verb* (**-pp-**) **1** provide with tip. **2** strike or touch lightly. □ **tiptop** *colloquial* first-rate; of highest excellence.

■ **1** apex, crown, end, extremity, head, peak, pinnacle, point, summit, top, vertex. **2** cap, crown, ferrule.

tip[2] *verb* (**-pp-**) **1** (often + *over*, *up*) (cause to) lean or slant. **2** (+ *into* etc.) overturn; cause to overbalance. **3** (+ *into* etc.) discharge contents of (container etc.) thus. ● *noun* **1** tilt. **2** place where refuse is tipped. **3** *colloquial* untidy place.

■ *verb* **1** careen, incline, lean, list, slant, slope, tilt; (*tip over*) see OVERTURN 1. **2, 3** drop off, dump, empty, pour out, spill, unload, upset. ● *noun* **2** dump, rubbish heap.

tip[3] *verb* (**-pp-**) **1** give small present of money to, esp. for service. **2** name as likely winner of race or contest. ● *noun* **1** small present of money given esp. for service. **2** piece of private or special information, esp. regarding betting or investment. **3** piece of advice. □ **tip off** give warning, hint, or inside information to. **tip-off** *noun* hint, warning, etc.

■ *verb* **1** remunerate, reward. ● *noun* **1** baksheesh, gift, gratuity, present, reward. **2, 3** advice, clue, forecast, hint, *colloquial* pointer, prediction, suggestion, tip-off, warning.

tippet /'tɪpɪt/ *noun* cape or collar of fur etc.

tipple /'tɪp(ə)l/ *verb* (**-ling**) drink intoxicating liquor habitually or repeatedly in small quantities. ● *noun colloquial* alcoholic drink. □ **tippler** *noun*.

tipster /'tɪpstə/ *noun* person who gives tips about horse racing etc.

tipsy /'tɪpsɪ/ *adjective* (**-ier, -iest**) **1** slightly drunk. **2** caused by or showing intoxication.

tiptoe /'tɪptəʊ/ *noun* the tips of the toes. ● *verb* (**-toes, -toed, -toeing**) walk on tiptoe or stealthily. ● *adverb* (also **on tiptoe**) with heels off the ground.

TIR *abbreviation* international road transport (*transport international routier*).

tirade /tar'reɪd/ *noun* long vehement denunciation or declamation.

tire[1] /taɪə/ *verb* (**-ring**) **1** make or grow weary. **2** exhaust patience or interest of. **3** (in *passive*; + *of*) have had enough of. □ **tiring** *adjective*.

■ **1** debilitate, drain, enervate, exhaust, fatigue, flag, *slang* knacker, overtire, sap, *colloquial* shatter, take it out of, tax, weaken, wear out, weary. **2** bore, weary. **3** (*be tired of*) be bored with, be fed up with, be impatient with, be sick of. □ **tiring** debilitating, demanding, difficult, exhausting, fatiguing, hard, laborious, strenuous, taxing, wearying.

tire[2] *US* = TYRE.

tired *adjective* **1** weary; ready for sleep. **2** (of idea) hackneyed. □ **tiredly** *adverb*. **tiredness** *noun*.

■ **1** see WEARY *adjective* 1. □ **tiredness** drowsiness, exhaustion, fatigue, inertia, lassitude, lethargy, listlessness, sleepiness, weariness.

tireless *adjective* not tiring easily; energetic. □ **tirelessly** *adverb*. **tirelessness** *noun*.

■ determined, diligent, dogged, dynamic, energetic, hard-working, indefatigable, persistent, pertinacious, resolute, sedulous, unceasing, unfaltering, unflagging, untiring, unwavering, vigorous.

tiresome *adjective* **1** tedious. **2** *colloquial* annoying. □ **tiresomely** *adverb*.

■ **1** boring, dull, monotonous, tedious, tiring, unexciting, uninteresting, wearisome, wearying. **2** annoying, bothersome, distracting, exasperating, inconvenient, infuriating, irksome, irritating, maddening, petty, troublesome, trying, unwelcome, upsetting, vexatious, vexing.

tiro /'taɪərəʊ/ *noun* (also **tyro**) (*plural* **-s**) beginner, novice.

tissue /'tɪʃuː/ *noun* **1** any of the coherent collections of cells of which animals or plants are made. **2** tissue-paper. **3** disposable piece of thin absorbent paper for wiping, drying, etc. **4** fine woven esp. gauzy fabric. **5** (often + *of*) connected series (of lies etc.). □ **tissue-paper** thin soft paper for wrapping etc.

tit[1] *noun* any of various small birds.

tit[2] *noun* □ **tit for tat** blow for blow; retaliation.

Titan /'taɪt(ə)n/ *noun* (often **titan**) person of superhuman strength, intellect, or importance.

titanic /tar'tænɪk/ *adjective* gigantic, colossal.

titanium /tar'teɪnɪəm/ *noun* dark grey metallic element.

titbit /'tɪtbɪt/ *noun* (*US* **tidbit**) **1** dainty morsel. **2** piquant item of news etc.

titchy /'tɪtʃɪ/ *adjective* (**-ier, -iest**) *colloquial* very small.

tithe /taɪð/ *historical noun* one-tenth of annual produce of land or labour taken as tax for Church. ● *verb* (**-thing**) **1** subject to tithes. **2** pay tithes.

Titian /'tɪʃ(ə)n/ *adjective* (of hair) bright auburn.

titillate /'tɪtɪleɪt/ *verb* (**-ting**) **1** excite, esp. sexually. **2** tickle. □ **titillation** *noun*.

titivate /'tɪtɪveɪt/ *verb* (**-ting**) *colloquial* **1** smarten. **2** put finishing touches to. □ **titivation** *noun*.

title /'taɪt(ə)l/ *noun* **1** name of book, work of art, etc. **2** heading of chapter etc. **3** title-page. **4** caption or credit in film etc. **5** name denoting person's status. **6** championship in sport. **7** legal right to ownership of property. **8** (+ *to*) just or recognized claim to. ● *verb* give title to. □ **title deed** legal document constituting evidence of a right. **title-holder** person holding (esp. sporting) title. **title-page** page at beginning of book giving title, author, etc. **title role** part in play etc. from which its title is taken.

■ *noun* **2** caption, heading, headline, inscription, rubric. **5** *formal* appellation, designation, form of address, office, position, rank, status. **7, 8** claim, entitlement, interest, ownership, possession, right. ● *verb* call, designate, entitle, label, name, tag.

titled *adjective* having title of nobility or rank.

■ aristocratic, noble, upper-class.

titmouse /'tɪtmaʊs/ *noun* (*plural* **titmice**) small active tit.

titrate /tar'treɪt/ *verb* (**-ting**) ascertain quantity of constituent in (solution) by adding measured amounts of reagent. □ **titration** *noun*.

titter /'tɪtə/ *verb* laugh covertly; giggle. ● *noun* covert laugh.

■ *verb* chortle, chuckle, giggle, laugh, snicker, snigger.

tittle /'tɪt(ə)l/ *noun* particle; whit.

tittle-tattle /'tɪt(ə)ltæt(ə)l/ *noun & verb* (**-ling**) gossip, chatter.

tittup /'tɪtəp/ *verb* (**-p-** or **-pp-**) go friskily or jerkily; bob up and down; canter. ● *noun* such gait or movement.

titular /ˈtɪtjʊlə/ *adjective* **1** of or relating to title. **2** existing or being in name only.
■ **2** nominal, *formal* putative, so-called, theoretical, token.

tizzy /ˈtɪzɪ/ *noun* (*plural* **-ies**) *colloquial* state of nervous agitation.

TNT *abbreviation* trinitrotoluene.

to /tə, before vowel tʊ, when stressed tuː/ *preposition* **1** in direction of. **2** as far as; not short of. **3** according to. **4** compared with. **5** involved in; comprising. **6** *used to introduce indirect object of verb etc., to introduce or as substitute for infinitive, or to express purpose, consequence, or cause.* ● *adverb* **1** in normal or required position or condition. **2** (of door) nearly closed. □ **to and fro 1** backwards and forwards. **2** (repeatedly) from place to place. **to-do** fuss, commotion. **toing and froing 1** constant movement to and fro. **2** great or dispersed activity.

toad *noun* **1** froglike amphibian breeding in water but living chiefly on land. **2** repulsive person. □ **toadflax** plant with yellow or purple flowers. **toad-in-the-hole** sausages baked in batter. **toadstool** fungus (usually poisonous) with round top and slender stalk.

toady /ˈtəʊdɪ/ *noun* (*plural* **-ies**) sycophant. ● *verb* (**-ies, -ied**) (+ *to*) behave servilely to; fawn on. □ **toadyism** *noun*.

toast *noun* **1** sliced bread browned on both sides by radiant heat. **2** person or thing in whose honour company is requested to drink. **3** call to drink or instance of drinking thus. ● *verb* **1** brown by heat, warm at fire etc. **2** drink to the health or in honour of. □ **toasting-fork** long-handled fork for toasting bread etc. **toastmaster, toastmistress** person announcing toasts at public occasion. **toast rack** rack for holding slices of toast at table.
■ *verb* **1** brown, grill. **2** drink to, pay tribute to, raise one's glass to.

toaster *noun* electrical device for making toast.

tobacco /təˈbækəʊ/ *noun* (*plural* **-s**) **1** plant of American origin with leaves used for smoking, chewing, or snuff. **2** its leaves, esp. as prepared for smoking.

tobacconist /təˈbækənɪst/ *noun* dealer in tobacco.

toboggan /təˈbɒgən/ *noun* long light narrow sledge for sliding downhill, esp. over snow. ● *verb* ride on toboggan.

toby jug /ˈtəʊbɪ/ *noun* jug or mug in shape of stout man in 3-cornered hat.

toccata /təˈkɑːtə/ *noun Music* composition for keyboard instrument, designed to exhibit performer's touch and technique.

tocsin /ˈtɒksɪn/ *noun* alarm bell or signal.

today /təˈdeɪ/ *adverb* **1** on this present day. **2** nowadays. ● *noun* **1** this present day. **2** modern times.

toddle /ˈtɒd(ə)l/ *verb* (**-ling**) **1** walk with young child's short unsteady steps. **2** *colloquial* walk, stroll. **3** *colloquial* (usually + *off*, *along*) depart. ● *noun* toddling walk.

toddler *noun* child just learning to walk.

toddy /ˈtɒdɪ/ *noun* (*plural* **-ies**) sweetened drink of spirits and hot water.

toe *noun* **1** any of terminal projections of foot or paw. **2** part of footwear that covers toes. **3** lower end or tip of implement etc. ● *verb* (**toes, toed, toeing**) touch with toe(s). □ **on one's toes** alert. **toecap** (reinforced) part of boot or shoe covering toes. **toe-hold 1** slight foothold. **2** small beginning or advantage. **toe the line** conform, esp. under pressure. **toenail** nail of each toe.

toff *noun slang* upper-class person.

toffee /ˈtɒfɪ/ *noun* **1** firm or hard sweet made of boiled butter, sugar, etc. **2** this substance. □ **toffee-apple** toffee-coated apple. **toffee-nosed** *colloquial* snobbish, pretentious.

tofu /ˈtəʊfuː/ *noun* curd of mashed soya beans.

tog[1] *colloquial noun* (in *plural*) clothes. ● *verb* (**-gg-**) (+ *out*, *up*) dress.

tog[2] *noun* unit of thermal resistance of quilts etc.

toga /ˈtəʊgə/ *noun historical* ancient Roman citizen's loose flowing outer garment.

together /təˈgeðə/ *adverb* **1** in(to) company or conjunction. **2** simultaneously. **3** one with another. **4** uninterruptedly. ● *adjective colloquial* well organized; self-assured; emotionally stable. □ **togetherness** *noun*.
■ *adverb* **1, 3** collectively, cooperatively, hand in hand, in chorus, in unison, jointly, shoulder to shoulder, side by side. **2** all at once, at the same time, concurrently, simultaneously. **4** consecutively, continuously, uninterruptedly.

toggle /ˈtɒg(ə)l/ *noun* **1** short bar used like button for fastening clothes. **2** *Computing* key or command which alternately switches function on and off.

toil *verb* **1** work laboriously or incessantly. **2** make slow painful progress. ● *noun* labour; drudgery. □ **toiler** *noun*. **toilsome** *adjective*.
■ *verb* drudge, exert oneself, grind away, labour, *colloquial* plug away, slave away, slog, struggle, sweat, work. ● *noun* donkey-work, drudgery, effort, exertion, industry, labour, work.

toilet /ˈtɔɪlɪt/ *noun* **1** lavatory. **2** process of washing oneself, dressing, etc. □ **toilet paper** paper for cleaning oneself after using lavatory. **toilet roll** roll of toilet paper. **toilet water** dilute perfume used after washing.
■ **1** convenience, latrine, lavatory, *colloquial* loo, privy, urinal, water-closet, WC. **2** dressing, grooming, making up, washing.

toiletries /ˈtɔɪlɪtriːz/ *plural noun* articles or cosmetics used in washing, dressing, etc.

toilette /twɑːˈlet/ *noun* process of washing oneself, dressing, etc.

toils /tɔɪlz/ *plural noun* net, snare.

token /ˈtəʊkən/ *noun* **1** symbol, reminder, mark. **2** voucher. **3** thing equivalent to something else, esp. money. ● *adjective* **1** perfunctory. **2** chosen by tokenism to represent a group. □ **token strike** brief strike to demonstrate strength of feeling.

■ *noun* **1** badge, emblem, evidence, expression, indication, keepsake, mark, marker, memento, proof, reminder, sign, souvenir, symbol, testimony. **2** coupon, voucher. **3** coin, counter, disc.
● *adjective* cosmetic, dutiful, emblematic, insincere, nominal, perfunctory, representative, superficial, symbolic.

tokenism *noun* granting of minimum concessions.

told *past & past participle* of TELL.

tolerable /'tɒlərəb(ə)l/ *adjective* **1** endurable. **2** fairly good. □ **tolerably** *adverb*.

■ **1** acceptable, allowable, bearable, endurable, sufferable, supportable. **2** adequate, all right, average, fair, mediocre, middling, *colloquial* OK, ordinary, passable, satisfactory.

tolerance /'tɒlərəns/ *noun* **1** willingness or ability to tolerate. **2** permitted variation in dimension, weight, etc.

■ **1** acceptance, broad-mindedness, charity, fairness, forbearance, forgiveness, lenience, open-mindedness, openness, patience, permissiveness, sufferance, sympathy, toleration, understanding. **2** allowance, clearance, fluctuation, play, variation.

tolerant /'tɒlərənt/ *adjective* **1** disposed to tolerate others. **2** (+ *of*) enduring or patient of.

■ **1** big-hearted, broad-minded, charitable, easygoing, fair, forbearing, forgiving, generous, indulgent, lax, lenient, liberal, magnanimous, open-minded, patient, permissive, soft, sympathetic, understanding, unprejudiced.

tolerate /'tɒləreɪt/ *verb* (**-ting**) **1** allow the existence or occurrence of without authoritative interference. **2** endure. **3** find or treat as endurable. **4** be able to take or undergo without harm. □ **toleration** *noun*.

■ **1** accept, admit, allow, brook, condone, countenance, permit, put up with, sanction, *colloquial* stand for, *colloquial* wear. **2, 3** abide, bear, endure, make allowances for, put up with, stand, *colloquial* stick, stomach, suffer, take, undergo, *colloquial* wear, weather. **4** stand, stand up to, survive, take, weather, withstand.

toll¹ /təʊl/ *noun* **1** charge to use bridge, road, etc. **2** cost or damage caused by disaster etc. □ **toll gate** barrier preventing passage until toll is paid.

■ **1** charge, dues, duty, fee, levy, payment, tariff, tax.

toll² /təʊl/ *verb* **1** (of bell) ring with slow uniform strokes. **2** ring (bell) thus. **3** announce or mark (death etc.) thus. **4** (of bell) strike (the hour). ● *noun* tolling or stroke of bell.

■ *verb* chime, peal, ring, sound, strike.

toluene /'tɒljʊiːn/ *noun* colourless liquid hydrocarbon used in manufacture of explosives etc.

tom *noun* (in full **tom-cat**) male cat.

tomahawk /'tɒməhɔːk/ *noun* N. American Indian war-axe.

tomato /tə'mɑːtəʊ/ *noun* (*plural* **-es**) **1** glossy red or yellow fleshy edible fruit. **2** plant bearing this.

tomb /tuːm/ *noun* **1** burial vault. **2** grave. **3** sepulchral monument. □ **tombstone** memorial stone over grave.

■ **1, 2** burial chamber, burial place, catacomb, crypt, grave, last resting place, sepulchre, vault. **3** mausoleum, memorial, monument. □ **tombstone** gravestone, headstone.

tombola /tɒm'bəʊlə/ *noun* kind of lottery.

tomboy /'tɒmbɔɪ/ *noun* girl who enjoys rough noisy recreations. □ **tomboyish** *adjective*.

tome *noun* large book or volume.

tomfool /tɒm'fuːl/ *noun* fool. ● *adjective* foolish. □ **tomfoolery** *noun*.

Tommy /'tɒmɪ/ *noun* (*plural* **-ies**) *colloquial* British private soldier.

tommy-gun /'tɒmɪɡʌn/ *noun* sub-machine-gun.

tomorrow /tə'mɒrəʊ/ *adverb* **1** on day after today. **2** in future. ● *noun* **1** the day after today. **2** the near future.

tomtit *noun* tit, esp. blue tit.

tom-tom /'tɒmtɒm/ *noun* kind of drum usually beaten with hands.

ton /tʌn/ *noun* **1** measure of weight equalling 2,240 lb (**long ton**) or 2,000 lb (**short ton**). **2** metric ton. **3** unit of measurement of ship's tonnage. **4** (usually in *plural*) *colloquial* large number or amount. **5** *slang* speed of 100 m.p.h. **6** *slang* score of 100.

tonal /'təʊn(ə)l/ *adjective* of or relating to tone or tonality.

tonality /tə'nælɪtɪ/ *noun* (*plural* **-ies**) **1** relationship between tones of a musical scale. **2** observance of single tonic key as basis of musical composition. **3** colour scheme of picture.

tone *noun* **1** sound, esp. with reference to pitch, quality, and strength. **2** (often in *plural*) modulation of voice to express emotion etc. **3** manner of expression in writing or speaking. **4** musical sound, esp. of definite pitch and character. **5** general effect of colour or of light and shade in picture. **6** tint or shade of colour. **7** prevailing character of morals, sentiments, etc. **8** proper firmness of body. **9** state of (good) health. ● *verb* (**-ning**) **1** give desired tone to. **2** alter tone of. **3** (often + *in*) harmonize. □ **tone-deaf** unable to perceive differences in musical pitch. **tone down** make or become softer in tone. **tone up** make or become stronger in tone. □ **toneless** *adjective*. **tonelessly** *adverb*. **toner** *noun*.

■ *noun* **1, 4** note, sound. **2** accent, colouring, expression, feel, inflection, intonation, modulation, note, phrasing, pitch, quality, sonority, sound, timbre. **3** manner, note, style, vein. **6** colour, hue, shade, tinge, tint. **7** air, atmosphere, character, effect, feeling, mood, spirit, style, temper, tenor, vein. ● *verb* **3** (*tone in*) see HARMONIZE 2. □ **tone down** see SOFTEN 1. **tone up** see STRENGTHEN.

tongs *plural noun* implement with two arms for grasping coal, sugar, etc.

tongue /tʌŋ/ *noun* 1 muscular organ in mouth used in tasting, swallowing, speaking, etc. 2 tongue of ox etc. as food. 3 faculty or manner of speaking. 4 particular language. 5 thing like tongue in shape. ● *verb* (**-guing**) use tongue to articulate (notes) in playing wind instrument. □ **tongue-in-cheek** ironic(ally). **tongue-tied** too shy to speak. **tongue-twister** sequence of words difficult to pronounce quickly and correctly.

■ *noun* 4 dialect, idiom, language, parlance, patois, speech. □ **tongue-tied** dumb, dumbfounded, inarticulate, lost for words, mute, silent, speechless.

tonic /ˈtɒnɪk/ *noun* 1 invigorating medicine. 2 anything serving to invigorate. 3 tonic water. 4 *Music* keynote. ● *adjective* invigorating. □ **tonic sol-fa** musical notation used esp. in teaching singing. **tonic water** carbonated drink with quinine.

■ *noun* 1, 2 boost, fillip, pick-me-up, refresher, restorative, stimulant.

tonight /təˈnaɪt/ *adverb* on present or approaching evening or night. ● *noun* the evening or night of today.

tonnage /ˈtʌnɪdʒ/ *noun* 1 ship's internal cubic capacity or freight-carrying capacity. 2 charge per ton on freight or cargo.

tonne /tʌn/ *noun* 1,000 kg.

tonsil /ˈtɒns(ə)l/ *noun* either of two small organs on each side of root of tongue.

tonsillectomy /tɒnsəˈlektəmɪ/ *noun* (*plural* **-ies**) surgical removal of tonsils.

tonsillitis /tɒnsəˈlaɪtɪs/ *noun* inflammation of tonsils.

tonsorial /tɒnˈsɔːrɪəl/ *adjective usually jocular* of hairdresser or hairdressing.

tonsure /ˈtɒnʃə/ *noun* 1 shaving of crown or of whole head as clerical or monastic symbol. 2 bare patch so made. ● *verb* (**-ring**) give tonsure to.

too *adverb* 1 to a greater extent than is desirable or permissible. 2 *colloquial* very. 3 in addition. 4 moreover.

took *past* of TAKE.

tool /tuːl/ *noun* 1 implement for working on something by hand or by machine. 2 thing used in activity. 3 person merely used by another. ● *verb* 1 dress (stone) with chisel. 2 impress design on (leather). 3 (+ *along, around,* etc.) *slang* drive or ride esp. in a casual or leisurely way.

■ *noun* 1 aid, apparatus, appliance, contraption, contrivance, device, gadget, implement, instrument, invention, machine, mechanism, utensil, weapon; (*tools*) gear, hardware.

toot /tuːt/ *noun* sound (as) of horn etc. ● *verb* 1 sound (horn etc.). 2 give out such sound.

tooth /tuːθ/ *noun* (*plural* **teeth**) 1 each of a set of hard structures in jaws of most vertebrates, used for biting and chewing. 2 toothlike part or projec-

tion, e.g. cog of gearwheel, point of saw or comb, etc. 3 (often + *for*) taste, appetite. 4 (in *plural*) force, effectiveness. □ **fight tooth and nail** fight fiercely. **get one's teeth into** devote oneself seriously to. **in the teeth of 1** in spite of. 2 contrary to. 3 directly against (wind etc.). **toothache** pain in teeth. **toothbrush** brush for cleaning teeth. **toothpaste** paste for cleaning teeth. **toothpick** small sharp stick for removing food lodged between teeth. □ **toothed** *adjective.* **toothless** *adjective.*

■ □ **toothed** cogged, crenellated, indented, jagged, serrated.

toothsome *adjective* (of food) delicious.

toothy *adjective* (**-ier, -iest**) having large, numerous, or prominent teeth.

tootle /ˈtuːt(ə)l/ *verb* (**-ling**) 1 toot gently or repeatedly. 2 (usually + *around, along,* etc.) *colloquial* move casually.

top¹ *noun* 1 highest point or part. 2 highest rank or place. 3 person occupying this. 4 upper end; head. 5 upper surface; upper part. 6 cover or cap of container etc. 7 garment for upper part of body. 8 utmost degree; height. 9 (in *plural*) *colloquial* person or thing of best quality. 10 (esp. in *plural*) leaves etc. of plant grown chiefly for its root. 11 *Nautical* platform round head of lower mast. ● *adjective* highest in position, degree, or importance. ● *verb* (**-pp-**) 1 furnish with top, cap, etc. 2 be higher or better than; surpass; be at or reach top of. 3 *slang* kill. 4 hit golf ball above centre. □ **on top of 1** fully in command of. 2 very close to. 3 in addition to. **on top of the world** *colloquial* exuberant. **over the top** to excess; outrageous. **top brass** *colloquial* high-ranking officers. **topcoat 1** overcoat. 2 final coat of paint etc. **top dog** *colloquial* victor; master. **top drawer** *colloquial* high social position or origin. **top dress** apply fertilizer on top of (earth) without ploughing it in. **top-flight** of highest rank of achievement. **top hat** tall silk hat. **top-heavy** overweighted at top. **topknot** knot, tuft, crest, or bow worn or growing on top of head. **top-level** of highest level of importance or prestige. **topmast** mast on top of lower mast. **top-notch** *colloquial* first-rate. **top off** put end or finishing touch to. **top secret** of utmost secrecy. **topside 1** outer side of round of beef. 2 side of ship above waterline. **topsoil** top layer of soil. **top up 1** complete (amount). 2 fill up (partly empty container). **top-up** *noun* addition; amount that completes or quantity that fills something. □ **topmost** *adjective.*

■ *noun* 1 acme, apex, apogee, crest, crown, culmination, head, height, high point, peak, pinnacle, summit, tip, vertex, zenith. 4 cap, cover, covering, lid, stopper. ● *adjective slang* ace, best, choicest, finest, first, foremost, greatest, highest, incomparable, leading, maximum, peerless, pre-eminent, prime, principal, supreme, topmost, unequalled, winning. ● *verb* 1 cap, complete, cover, crown, decorate, finish off, garnish, surmount. 2 beat, be higher than, better, cap, exceed, excel, outdo, outstrip, surpass, transcend.

top[2] *noun* toy spinning on point when set in motion.

topaz /ˈtəʊpæz/ *noun* semiprecious transparent stone, usually yellow.

tope *verb* (**-ping**) *archaic* or *literary* drink alcohol to excess, esp. habitually. □ **toper** *noun*.

topi /ˈtəʊpɪ/ *noun* (also **topee**) (*plural* **-s**) hat, esp sun-helmet.

topiary /ˈtəʊpɪərɪ/ *adjective* of or formed by clipping shrubs, trees, etc. into ornamental shapes. ● *noun* topiary art.

topic /ˈtɒpɪk/ *noun* subject of discourse, conversation, or argument.
■ issue, matter, point, question, subject, talking point, text, theme, thesis.

topical *adjective* dealing with current affairs, etc. □ **topicality** /-ˈkæl-/ *noun*.
■ contemporary, current, recent, timely, up to date.

topless *adjective* **1** without a top. **2** (of garment) leaving breasts bare. **3** (of woman) bare-breasted. **4** (of place) where women go or work bare-breasted.

topography /təˈpɒɡrəfɪ/ *noun* **1** detailed description, representation, etc. of features of a district. **2** such features. □ **topographer** *noun*. **topographical** /tɒpəˈɡræf-/ *adjective*.
■ **2** features, geography, lie of the land.

topology /təˈpɒlədʒɪ/ *noun* study of geometrical properties unaffected by changes of shape or size. □ **topological** /tɒpəˈlɒdʒ-/ *adjective*.

topper *noun colloquial* top hat.

topping *noun* thing that tops, esp. sauce on dessert etc.

topple /ˈtɒp(ə)l/ *verb* (**-ling**) **1** (often + *over*, *down*) (cause to) fall as if top-heavy. **2** overthrow.
■ **1** bring down, collapse, fall, fell, knock down, overbalance, overturn, throw down, tip over, tumble, upset. **2** defeat, oust, overthrow, unseat.

topsy-turvy /tɒpsɪˈtɜːvɪ/ *adverb & adjective* **1** upside down. **2** in utter confusion.

toque /təʊk/ *noun* woman's close-fitting brimless hat.

tor *noun* hill, rocky peak.

torch *noun* **1** battery-powered portable lamp. **2** thing lit for illumination. **3** source of heat, light, or enlightenment. □ **carry a torch for** have (esp. unreturned) love for.
■ **1** flashlight. **2** *poetical* brand, lamp.

tore *past* of TEAR[1].

toreador /ˈtɒrɪədɔː/ *noun* bullfighter, esp. on horseback.

torment *noun* /ˈtɔːment/ (cause of) severe bodily or mental suffering. ● *verb* /tɔːˈment/ **1** subject to torment. **2** tease or worry excessively. □ **tormentor** /-ˈmen-/ *noun*.

■ *noun* affliction, agony, anguish, distress, harassment, misery, ordeal, pain, persecution, plague, scourge, suffering, torture, vexation, woe, worry, wretchedness. ● *verb* afflict, annoy, bait, bedevil, bother, bully, distress, harass, hurt, inflict pain on, intimidate, nag, persecute, pester, *colloquial* plague, tease, torture, vex, victimize, worry.

torn *past participle* of TEAR[1].

tornado /tɔːˈneɪdəʊ/ *noun* (*plural* **-es**) violent storm over small area, with whirling winds.

torpedo /tɔːˈpiːdəʊ/ *noun* (*plural* **-es**) cigar-shaped self-propelled underwater or aerial missile that explodes on hitting ship. ● *verb* (**-es**, **-ed**) **1** destroy or attack with torpedo(es). **2** make ineffective. □ **torpedo boat** small fast warship armed with torpedoes.

torpid /ˈtɔːpɪd/ *adjective* **1** sluggish, apathetic. **2** numb. **3** dormant. □ **torpidity** /-ˈpɪd-/ *noun*.
■ **1** apathetic, dull, inactive, indolent, inert, lackadaisical, languid, lethargic, lifeless, listless, passive, phlegmatic, slothful, slow, slow-moving, sluggish, somnolent, spiritless. **3** see DORMANT 1.

torpor /ˈtɔːpə/ *noun* torpid condition.

torque /tɔːk/ *noun* **1** twisting or rotary force, esp. in machine. **2** *historical* twisted metal neck-lace worn by ancient Gauls and Britons.

torrent /ˈtɒrənt/ *noun* **1** rushing stream of liquid. **2** downpour of rain. **3** (in *plural*; usually + *of*) violent flow. □ **torrential** /təˈrenʃ(ə)l/ *adjective*.
■ **1, 3** cascade, deluge, effusion, flood, flow, gush, inundation, outpouring, overflow, rush, spate, stream, tide. **2** deluge, downpour, flood. □ **torrential** copious, heavy, relentless, teeming, violent.

torrid /ˈtɒrɪd/ *adjective* **1** intensely hot. **2** scorched, parched. **3** passionate, intense. □ **torridity** /-ˈrɪdɪtɪ/ *noun*.

torsion /ˈtɔːʃ(ə)n/ *noun* twisting. □ **torsional** *adjective*.

torso /ˈtɔːsəʊ/ *noun* (*plural* **-s**) **1** trunk of human body. **2** statue of this.

tort *noun* breach of legal duty (other than under contract) with liability for damages. □ **tortious** /ˈtɔːʃəs/ *adjective*.

tortilla /tɔːˈtiːjə/ *noun* thin flat originally Mexican maize cake eaten hot.

tortoise /ˈtɔːtəs/ *noun* slow-moving reptile with horny domed shell. □ **tortoiseshell 1** mottled yellowish-brown turtle-shell. **2** cat or butterfly with markings resembling tortoiseshell.

tortuous /ˈtɔːtʃʊəs/ *adjective* **1** winding. **2** devious, circuitous. □ **tortuously** *adverb*.
■ **1** bent, circuitous, contorted, convoluted, corkscrew, crooked, curling, curvy, labyrinthine, meandering, serpentine, sinuous, turning, twisted, twisting, twisty, wandering, winding, zigzag. **2** circuitous, complicated, convoluted, devious, indirect, involved, roundabout.

torture /ˈtɔːtʃə/ *noun* **1** infliction of severe

bodily pain, esp. as punishment or means of persuasion. **2** severe physical or mental pain. ● *verb* (**-ring**) subject to torture. □ **torturer** *noun*. **torturous** *adjective*.

■ *noun* **1** cruelty, degradation, humiliation, persecution, punishment, torment. **2** affliction, agony, anguish, distress, misery, pain, plague, scourge, suffering. ● *verb* afflict, agonize, be cruel to, bully, cause pain to, distress, hurt, inflict pain on, persecute, *colloquial* plague, rack, torment.

Tory /'tɔːrɪ/ *colloquial noun* (*plural* **-ies**) member of Conservative party. ● *adjective* Conservative. □ **Toryism** *noun*.

tosa /'təʊsə/ *noun* dog of a mastiff breed.

tosh *noun colloquial* rubbish, nonsense.

toss *verb* **1** throw up, esp. with hand. **2** roll about, throw, or be thrown, restlessly or from side to side. **3** throw lightly or carelessly. **4** throw (coin) into air to decide choice etc. by way it falls. **5** (often + *for*) settle question or dispute with (person) thus. **6** (of bull etc.) fling up with horns. **7** coat (food) with dressing etc. by shaking it. ● *noun* **1** tossing. **2** fall, esp. from horseback. □ **toss one's head** throw it back, esp. in anger, impatience, etc. **toss off 1** drink off at a draught. **2** dispatch (work) rapidly or easily. **toss up** toss coin. **toss-up** *noun* **1** doubtful matter. **2** tossing of coin.

■ *verb* **1**, **3** bowl, cast, *colloquial* chuck, fling, flip, *colloquial* heave, hurl, lob, pitch, shy, *colloquial* sling, throw. **2** bob, dip, flounder, lurch, pitch, plunge, reel, rock, roll, shake, twist and turn, writhe, yaw.

tot[1] *noun* **1** small child. **2** dram of liquor.

tot[2] *verb* (**-tt-**) (usually + *up*) add; mount. □ **tot up to** amount to.

total /'təʊt(ə)l/ *adjective* **1** complete; comprising the whole. **2** absolute, unqualified. ● *noun* whole sum or amount. ● *verb* (**-ll-**; *US* **-l-**) **1** (often + *to*, *up to*) amount to. **2** calculate total of. □ **totality** /-'tæl-/ *noun* (*plural* **-ies**). **totally** *adverb*.

■ *adjective* **1** complete, comprehensive, entire, full, gross, overall, whole. **2** absolute, downright, out and out, outright, perfect, sheer, thorough, thoroughgoing, unalloyed, unmitigated, unqualified, utter. ● *noun* aggregate, amount, *colloquial* lot, sum, totality, whole. ● *verb* **1** add up to, amount to, come to, make. **2** add up, calculate, compute, count, find the sum of, reckon up, totalize, tot up, work out.

totalitarian /təʊtælɪ'teərɪən/ *adjective* of one-party government requiring complete subservience to state. □ **totalitarianism** *noun*.

■ absolute, arbitrary, authoritarian, autocratic, despotic, dictatorial, fascist, illiberal, oppressive, tyrannous, undemocratic, unrepresentative.

totalizator /'təʊtəlaɪzeɪtə/ *noun* (also **totalisator**) **1** device showing number and amount of bets staked on race when total will be divided among those betting on winner. **2** this betting system.

totalize /'təʊtəlaɪz/ *verb* (also **-ise**) (**-zing** or **-sing**) combine into a total.

tote[1] *noun slang* totalizator.

tote[2] *verb* (**-ting**) *esp. US colloquial* carry, convey. □ **tote bag** large and capacious bag.

totem /'təʊtəm/ *noun* **1** natural object (esp. animal) adopted esp. among N. American Indians as emblem of clan or individual. **2** image of this. □ **totem-pole** post with carved and painted or hung totem(s).

toto see IN TOTO.

totter /'tɒtə/ *verb* **1** stand or walk unsteadily or feebly. **2** shake; be about to fall. ● *noun* unsteady or shaky movement or gait. □ **tottery** *adjective*.

■ *verb* **1** dodder, falter, reel, rock, stagger, stumble, teeter, tremble, waver, wobble. **2** see SHAKE *verb* 2.

toucan /'tuːkən/ *noun* tropical American bird with large bill.

touch /tʌtʃ/ *verb* **1** come into or be in physical contact with. **2** (often + *with*) bring hand etc. into contact with. **3** bring (two things) into contact. **4** rouse tender or painful feelings in. **5** strike lightly. **6** (usually in negative) disturb, harm; affect; have dealings with; consume, use. **7** concern. **8** reach as far as. **9** (usually in negative) approach in excellence. **10** modify. **11** (as **touched** *adjective*) *colloquial* slightly mad. **12** (usually + *for*) *slang* request and get money etc. from (person). ● *noun* **1** act of touching. **2** sense of feeling. **3** quality perceived by touch. **4** small amount; trace. **5** (**a touch**) slightly. **6** *Music* manner of playing keys or strings. **7** *Music* instrument's response to this. **8** artistic, literary, etc. style or skill. **9** *slang* act of requesting and getting money etc. from person. **10** *Football* part of field outside touchlines. □ **in touch** (often + *with*) **1** in communication. **2** up to date. **3** aware, conscious. **touch-and-go** critical; risky. **touch at** *Nautical* call at (port etc.). **touch down** (of aircraft) alight. **touchdown** *noun*. **touchline** side limit of football etc. pitch. **touch off 1** explode by touching with match etc. **2** initiate (process) suddenly. **touch on, upon 1** refer to or mention briefly or casually. **2** verge on. **touch-paper** paper impregnated with nitre for igniting fireworks etc. **touchstone 1** dark schist or jasper for testing alloys by marking it with them. **2** criterion. **touch-type** type without looking at keys. **touch-typist** *noun*. **touch up 1** give finishing touches to; retouch. **2** *slang* molest sexually. **touch wood** touch something wooden to avert ill luck. **touchwood** readily inflammable rotten wood. □ **touchable** *adjective*.

■ *verb* **1** abut (on), adjoin, be in contact with, come together, lean against, meet. **2** brush, caress, contact, dab, feel, finger, fondle, graze, handle, kiss, manipulate, massage, nuzzle, pat, *colloquial* paw, pet, push, rub, stroke, tap, tickle. **4** affect, arouse, awaken, concern, disturb, impress, influence, inspire, move, stimulate, stir, upset; (*touched*) see EMOTIONAL 1. **8** attain, reach, rise to. **9** be in the same league as, compare with, equal, match, parallel, rival. **11** (**touched**) see MAD 1. ● *noun* **1** brush, caress, dab, pat, stroke, tap. **2**, **3** feel, feeling, texture. **4** bit, dash, drop, hint, intimation, suggestion, suspicion, taste, tinge,

trace. **8** ability, capability, experience, expertise, facility, feel, flair, gift, knack, manner, sensitivity, skill, style, technique, understanding, way.
□ **touch off 1** see IGNITE 1. **2** see BEGIN 1. **touch on 1** see MENTION *verb* 1. **touch up 1** see IMPROVE 1.

touché /tu:ˈʃeɪ/ *interjection: acknowledging justified accusation or retort, or hit in fencing.* [French]

touching *adjective* moving; pathetic. ● *preposition literary* concerning. □ **touchingly** *adverb*.
■ *adjective* see EMOTIONAL 3.

touchy *adjective* (**-ier, -iest**) apt to take offence; over-sensitive. □ **touchily** *adverb*. **touchiness** *noun*.
■ edgy, highly-strung, hypersensitive, irascible, irritable, *colloquial* jittery, jumpy, nervous, over-sensitive, peevish, querulous, quick-tempered, sensitive, short-tempered, *colloquial* snappy, temperamental, tense, testy, tetchy, thin-skinned, unpredictable, waspish.

tough /tʌf/ *adjective* **1** hard to break, cut, tear, or chew. **2** able to endure hardship; hardy. **3** stubborn, difficult. **4** *colloquial* acting sternly. **5** *colloquial* (of luck etc.) hard. **6** *colloquial* criminal, violent. ● *noun* tough person, esp. ruffian. □ **toughen** *verb*. **toughness** *noun*.
■ *adjective* **1** durable, hard-wearing, indestructible, lasting, rugged, sound, stout, strong, substantial, unbreakable, well built, well made; *of meat* chewy, hard, gristly, leathery, rubbery, uneatable. **2** beefy, brawny, burly, hardy, muscular, robust, stalwart, strong, sturdy. **3** arduous, baffling, demanding, difficult, exacting, exhausting, gruelling, hard, intractable, knotty, laborious, mystifying, obdurate, obstinate, perplexing, puzzling, resilient, resistant, resolute, stiff, strenuous, stubborn, taxing, tenacious, thorny, troublesome, unyielding. **4** cold, cool, hard-boiled, hardened, *colloquial* hard-nosed, inhuman, merciless, ruthless, severe, stern, stony, uncaring, unsentimental, unsympathetic.
□ **toughen** harden, reinforce, strengthen.

toupee /ˈtu:peɪ/ *noun* hairpiece to cover bald spot.

tour /tʊə/ *noun* **1** holiday journey or excursion including stops at various places. **2** walk round; inspection. **3** spell of military or diplomatic duty. **4** series of performances, matches, etc. at different places. ● *verb* **1** (often + *through*) go on a tour. **2** make a tour of (country etc.). □ **on tour** (esp. of sports team, theatre company, etc.) touring. **tour operator** travel agent specializing in package holidays.
■ *noun* **1** drive, excursion, expedition, jaunt, journey, outing, ride, trip. **2** circuit, inspection, walk, walkabout. ● *verb* do the rounds of, explore, go round, travel round, visit.

tour de force /tʊə də ˈfɔːs/ *noun* (*plural* **tours de force** same pronunciation) outstanding feat or performance. [French]

tourer *noun* car or caravan for touring in.

tourism *noun* commercial organization and operation of holidays.

tourist *noun* **1** holiday traveller. **2** member of touring sports team. □ **tourist class** lowest class of passenger accommodation in ship, aeroplane, etc.
■ **1** day tripper, holidaymaker, sightseer, traveller, tripper, visitor.

tourmaline /ˈtʊəməliːn/ *noun* mineral with unusual electric properties and used as gem.

tournament /ˈtʊənəmənt/ *noun* **1** large contest of many rounds. **2** display of military exercises. **3** *historical* pageant with jousting.
■ **1** championship, competition, contest, event, match, meeting, series.

tournedos /ˈtʊənədəʊ/ *noun* (*plural* same /-dəʊz/) small thick piece of fillet of beef.

tourney /ˈtʊənɪ/ *noun* (*plural* **-ies**) tournament. ● *verb* (**-eys, -eyed**) take part in tournament.

tourniquet /ˈtʊənɪkeɪ/ *noun* device for stopping flow of blood through artery by compression.

tousle /ˈtaʊz(ə)l/ *verb* (**-ling**) **1** make (esp. hair) untidy. **2** handle roughly.

tout /taʊt/ *verb* **1** (usually + *for*) solicit custom persistently; pester customers. **2** solicit custom of or for. **3** spy on racehorses in training. ● *noun* person who touts.

tow[1] /təʊ/ *verb* pull along by rope etc. ● *noun* towing, being towed. □ **in tow 1** being towed. **2** accompanying or in the charge of a person. **on tow** being towed. **towpath** path beside river or canal originally for horse towing boat.
■ *verb* drag, draw, haul, lug, pull, trail, tug.

tow[2] /təʊ/ *noun* fibres of flax etc. ready for spinning. □ **tow-headed** having very light-coloured or tousled hair.

towards /təˈwɔːdz/ *preposition* (also **toward**) **1** in direction of. **2** as regards; in relation to. **3** as a contribution to; for. **4** near.

towel /ˈtaʊəl/ *noun* absorbent cloth, paper, etc. for drying after washing etc. ● *verb* (**-ll-**; *US* **-l-**) rub or dry with towel.

towelling *noun* thick soft absorbent cloth used esp. for towels.

tower /ˈtaʊə/ *noun* **1** tall structure, often part of castle, church, etc. **2** fortress etc. with tower. **3** tall structure housing machinery etc. ● *verb* **1** (usually + *above, up*) reach high; be superior. **2** (as **towering** *adjective*) high, lofty. **3** (as **towering** *adjective*) violent. □ **tower block** tall building of offices or flats. **tower of strength** person who gives strong emotional support.
■ *noun* **1** belfry, campanile, minaret, pagoda, spire, steeple, turret. **2** castle, fort, fortress, *historical* keep. ● *verb* **1** ascend, dominate, loom, rear, rise, soar, stand out, stick up. **2** (**towering**) colossal, gigantic, high, huge, imposing, lofty, mighty, soaring, tall. **3** (**towering**) extreme, fiery, immoderate, intemperate, intense, mighty, overpowering, passionate, unrestrained, vehement, violent.

town /taʊn/ *noun* **1** densely populated area, between city and village in size. **2** London or the chief city or town in area. **3** central business area in neighbourhood. □ **go to town** *colloquial* act or work with energy or enthusiasm. **on the town** *colloquial* enjoying urban nightlife. **town clerk** *US & historical* official in charge of records etc. of town. **town gas** manufactured gas for domestic etc. use. **town hall** headquarters of local government, with public meeting rooms etc. **town house** town residence, esp. one of terrace. **town planning** planning of construction and growth of towns. **township 1** *South African* urban area for occupation by black people. **2** *US & Canadian* administrative division of county, or district 6 miles square. **3** *Australian & NZ* small town. **townsman, townswoman** inhabitant of town. **townspeople** inhabitants of town.

■ **1** borough, city, community, conurbation, municipality, township, urban district.

townie /'taʊnɪ/ *noun* (also **townee** /-'niː/) *derogatory* inhabitant of town.

toxaemia /tɒk'siːmɪə/ *noun* (*US* **toxemia**) **1** blood poisoning. **2** increased blood pressure in pregnancy.

toxic /'tɒksɪk/ *adjective* **1** poisonous. **2** of poison. □ **toxicity** /-'sɪs-/ *noun*.

■ **1** dangerous, deadly, harmful, lethal, noxious, poisonous.

toxicology /tɒksɪ'kɒlədʒɪ/ *noun* study of poisons. □ **toxicological** /-kə'lɒdʒ-/ *adjective*. **toxicologist** *noun*.

toxin /'tɒksɪn/ *noun* poison produced by living organism.

toy *noun* **1** plaything. **2** thing providing amusement. **3** diminutive breed of dog etc. ● *verb* (usually + *with*) **1** amuse oneself; flirt. **2** move thing idly. □ **toy boy** *colloquial* woman's much younger boyfriend. **toyshop** shop selling toys.

trace[1] *verb* (**-cing**) **1** find signs of by investigation. **2** (often + *along, through, to,* etc.) follow or mark track, position, or path of. **3** (often + *back*) follow to origins. **4** copy (drawing etc.) by marking its lines on superimposed translucent paper. **5** mark out, delineate, or write, esp. laboriously. ● *noun* **1** indication of existence of something; vestige. **2** very small quantity. **3** track, footprint. **4** mark left by instrument's moving pen etc. □ **trace element** chemical element occurring or required, esp. in soil, only in minute amounts. □ **traceable** *adjective*.

■ *verb* **1–3** detect, discover, find, follow, get back, recover, retrieve, seek out, track down. **4** copy, draw, go over. **5** see OUTLINE *verb* 1. ● *noun* **1** clue, evidence, *colloquial* give-away, hint, indication, intimation, mark, remains, sign, token, vestige. **2** see BIT[1] 1. **3** footmark, footprint, spoor, track, trail.

trace[2] *noun* each of two side-straps, chains, or ropes by which horse draws vehicle. □ **kick over the traces** become insubordinate or reckless.

■ □ **kick over the traces** see REBEL *verb* 1.

tracer *noun* **1** bullet etc. made visible in flight

by flame etc. emitted. **2** artificial radioisotope which can be followed through body by radiation it produces.

tracery /'treɪsərɪ/ *noun* (*plural* **-ies**) **1** decorative stone openwork, esp. in head of Gothic window. **2** lacelike pattern.

trachea /trə'kiːə/ *noun* (*plural* **-cheae** /-'kiːiː/) windpipe.

tracing *noun* **1** traced copy of drawing etc. **2** act of tracing. □ **tracing-paper** translucent paper for making tracings.

track *noun* **1** mark(s) left by person, animal, vehicle, etc. **2** (in *plural*) such marks, esp. footprints. **3** rough path. **4** line of travel. **5** continuous railway line. **6** racecourse; circuit; prepared course for runners. **7** groove on gramophone record. **8** single song etc. on gramophone record, CD, or magnetic tape. **9** band round wheels of tank, tractor, etc. ● *verb* **1** follow track of. **2** trace (course, development, etc.) from vestiges. □ **in one's tracks** *colloquial* where one stands; instantly. **make tracks** *colloquial* depart. **make tracks for** *colloquial* go in pursuit of or towards. **track down** reach or capture by tracking. **tracker dog** police dog tracking by scent. **track events** running-races. **track record** person's past achievements. **track shoe** runner's spiked shoe. **track suit** warm outfit worn for exercising etc. □ **tracker** *noun*.

■ *noun* **1** footmark, footprint, mark, scent, spoor, trace, trail, wake (*of ship*). **4** bridle path, bridleway, cart track, footpath, path, road, route, trail, way. **5** line, *esp. US* railroad, rails, railway. **6** circuit, course, dirt track, racecourse, racetrack. ● *verb* **1** chase, dog, follow, hound, hunt, pursue, shadow, stalk, *colloquial* tail, trace, trail. □ **make tracks** see DEPART 1,2. **track down** see TRACE[1] *verb* 1–3.

tract[1] *noun* **1** (esp. large) stretch of territory. **2** bodily organ or system.

tract[2] *noun* pamphlet, esp. containing propaganda.

tractable /'træktəb(ə)l/ *adjective* easily managed; docile. □ **tractability** *noun*.

traction /'trækʃ(ə)n/ *noun* **1** hauling, pulling. **2** therapeutic sustained pull on limb etc. □ **traction-engine** steam or diesel engine for drawing heavy load.

tractor /'træktə/ *noun* **1** vehicle for hauling farm machinery etc. **2** traction-engine.

trad *colloquial noun* traditional jazz. ● *adjective* traditional.

trade *noun* **1** buying and selling. **2** this between nations etc. **3** business merely for profit (as distinct from profession). **4** business of specified nature or time. **5** skilled handicraft. **6** (**the trade**) people engaged in specific trade. **7** *US* transaction, esp. swap. **8** (usually in *plural*) trade wind. ● *verb* (**-ding**) **1** (often + *in, with*) engage in trade; buy and sell. **2** exchange. **3** (+ *for*) *US* swap. **4** (usually + *with, for*) have transaction. □ **trade in** exchange (esp. used article) in part payment for another. **trade mark 1** device or name legally registered to represent a company or product. **2** distinctive characteristic. **trade name** name by which a thing is known in a trade, or given by a manufacturer to a product, or under which a business trades. **trade off** exchange as compromise. **trade-off** *noun* balance, compromise. **trade on** take advantage of. **tradesman, tradeswoman** person engaged in trade, esp. shopkeeper. **trade(s) union** organized association of workers in trade, profession, etc. formed to further their common interests. **trade-unionist** member of trade union. **trade wind** constant wind blowing towards equator from NE or SE. □ **trader** *noun*.

■ *noun* **1, 2** barter, business, buying and selling, commerce, dealing, exchange, industry, marketing, merchandising, trading, traffic, transactions. **5** calling, career, craft, employment, job, line, occupation, profession, pursuit, work. **7** deal, exchange, swap, transaction. ● *verb* **1** buy and sell, deal, do business, have dealings, market, merchandise, retail, sell, traffic. □ **trade in** see EXCHANGE *verb*. **trade on** see EXPLOIT *verb* 1. □ **trader** broker, buyer, dealer, *esp. US & Scottish* merchant, retailer, salesman, saleswoman, seller, shopkeeper, stockist, supplier, tradesman, tradeswoman, trafficker, vendor.

tradescantia /ˌtrædɪsˈkæntɪə/ *noun* (usually trailing) plant with large blue, white, or pink flowers.

trading *noun* engaging in trade. □ **trading estate** area designed for industrial and commercial firms. **trading post** store etc. in remote region. **trading-stamp** token given to customer and exchangeable in quantity usually for goods.

tradition /trəˈdɪʃ(ə)n/ *noun* **1** custom, opinion, or belief handed down to posterity, esp. orally or by practice. **2** handing down of these.

■ belief, convention, custom, folklore, habit, institution, practice, rite, ritual, routine, usage.

traditional *adjective* **1** of, based on, or obtained by tradition. **2** (of jazz) in style of early 20th c. □ **traditionally** *adverb*.

■ **1** accustomed, conventional, customary, established, familiar, folk, habitual, handed down, historic, normal, old, orthodox, popular, regular, time-honoured, typical, unwritten, usual.

traditionalism *noun* respect or support for tradition. □ **traditionalist** *noun & adjective*.

traduce /trəˈdjuːs/ *verb* (-**cing**) slander. □ **traducement** *noun*. **traducer** *noun*.

traffic /ˈtræfɪk/ *noun* **1** vehicles moving on public highway, in air, or at sea. **2** (usually + *in*) trade, esp. illegal. **3** coming and going of people or goods by road, rail, air, sea, etc. **4** dealings between people etc. **5** (volume of) messages transmitted through communications system. ● *verb* (-**ck-**) **1** (often + *in*) deal, esp. illegally. **2** barter. □ **traffic island** raised area in road to divide traffic and provide refuge for pedestrians. **traffic jam** traffic at standstill. **traffic light(s)** signal controlling road traffic by coloured lights. **traffic warden** person employed to control movement and parking of road vehicles. □ **trafficker** *noun*.

■ *noun* **3** conveyance, movements, shipping, transport, transportation. ● *verb* see TRADE *verb* 1.

tragedian /trəˈdʒiːdɪən/ *noun* author of or actor in tragedies.

tragedienne /trədʒiːdɪˈen/ *noun* actress in tragedies.

tragedy /ˈtrædʒɪdɪ/ *noun* (*plural* **-ies**) **1** serious accident. **2** sad event. **3** play with tragic unhappy ending.

■ **1, 2** adversity, affliction, blow, calamity, catastrophe, disaster, misfortune.

tragic /ˈtrædʒɪk/ *adjective* **1** disastrous, distressing, very sad. **2** of tragedy. □ **tragically** *adverb*.

■ **1** appalling, *colloquial* awful, calamitous, catastrophic, depressing, dire, disastrous, distressing, dreadful, fatal, fearful, funereal, hapless, ill-fated, ill-omened, ill-starred, inauspicious, lamentable, pathetic, piteous, pitiful, sad, sorrowful, *colloquial* terrible, unfortunate, unlucky, woeful, wretched.

tragicomedy /trædʒɪˈkɒmədɪ/ *noun* (*plural* **-ies**) drama or event combining comedy and tragedy.

trail *noun* **1** track or scent left by moving person, thing, etc. **2** beaten path, esp. through wild region. **3** long line of people or things following behind something. **4** part dragging behind thing or person. ● *verb* **1** draw or be drawn along behind. **2** (often + *behind*) walk wearily. **3** follow trail of; pursue. **4** be losing in contest. **5** (usually + *away, off*) peter out. **6** (of plant etc.) grow or hang over wall, along ground, etc. **7** hang loosely. □ **trailing edge** rear edge of aircraft's wing.

■ *noun* **1** evidence, footmarks, footprints, marks, scent, signs, spoor, traces, wake (*of ship*). **2** path, pathway, route, track, way. ● *verb* **1** dangle, drag, draw, haul, pull, tow. **2** (*trail behind*) see DAWDLE. **3** chase, follow, hunt, pursue, shadow, stalk, *colloquial* tail, trace, track down.

trailblazer /ˈtreɪlbleɪzə/ *noun* **1** person who marks new track. **2** pioneer; innovator. □ **trailblazing** *noun & adjective*.

trailer *noun* **1** set of extracts from film etc. shown in advance to advertise it. **2** vehicle pulled by another. **3** *US* caravan.

train *verb* **1** (often + *to do*) teach (person etc.) specified skill, esp. by practice. **2** undergo this process. **3** bring or come to physical efficiency by exercise, diet, etc. **4** (often + *up, along*) guide growth of (plant). **5** (usually as **trained** *adjective*) make (mind etc.) discerning through practice etc. **6** (often + *on*) point, aim. ● *noun* **1** series of railway carriages or trucks drawn by engine. **2** thing dragged along behind or forming back part of dress etc. **3** succession or series of people, things, events, etc. **4** group of followers, retinue. □ **in train** arranged; in preparation. **train-bearer** person holding up train of another's robe etc. **train-spotter** person who collects numbers of railway locomotives. □ **trainee** /-ˈniː/ *noun*.

■ *verb* **1** coach, discipline, drill, educate, instruct, practise, prepare, rehearse, school, teach, tutor. **3** do exercises, exercise, get fit, practise, prepare oneself, work out. **6** see AIM *verb* 2. ● *noun* **3** see

SEQUENCE 1–3. **4** cortège, entourage, escort, followers, guard, retainers, retinue, staff.
□ **trainee** apprentice, beginner, cadet, learner, novice, pupil, starter, student, tiro.

trainer *noun* **1** person who trains horses, athletes, etc. **2** aircraft or simulator used to train pilots. **3** soft running shoe.
■ **1** coach, instructor, teacher, tutor.

training /'treɪnɪŋ/ *noun* process of teaching or learning a skill etc.

traipse *colloquial verb* (**-sing**) tramp or trudge wearily. ● *noun* tedious journey on foot.

trait /treɪ/ *noun* characteristic.
■ attribute, characteristic, feature, idiosyncrasy, peculiarity, property, quality, quirk.

traitor /'treɪtə/ *noun* (*feminine* **traitress**) person guilty of betrayal or disloyalty. □ **traitorous** *adjective*.
■ betrayer, collaborator, defector, *Military* deserter, double-crosser, fifth columnist, informer, Judas, quisling, renegade, turncoat.

trajectory /trə'dʒektərɪ/ *noun* (*plural* **-ies**) path of object moving under given forces.

tram *noun* (also **tramcar**) electrically powered passenger road vehicle running on rails. □ **tramlines 1** rails for tram. **2** *colloquial* either pair of parallel lines at edge of tennis etc. court.

trammel /'træm(ə)l/ *noun* **1** (usually in *plural*) impediment, restraint. **2** kind of fishing net. ● *verb* (**-ll-**; *US* **-l-**) hamper.

tramp *verb* **1** walk heavily and firmly. **2** go on walking expedition. **3** walk laboriously across or along. **4** (often + *down*) tread on, stamp on. **5** live as tramp. ● *noun* **1** itinerant vagrant or beggar. **2** sound of person or people walking or marching. **3** long walk. **4** *slang derogatory* promiscuous woman.
■ *verb* **1** plod, stamp, stomp, stride, stump, toil, *colloquial* traipse, trudge. **2** footslog, hike, march, ramble, trek, walk. **4** (*tramp down*) see TRAMPLE 1. ● *noun* **1** beggar, *slang* dosser, down-and-out, drifter, homeless person, rover, traveller, vagabond, vagrant, wanderer. **3** hike, march, trek, trudge, walk.

trample /'træmp(ə)l/ *verb* (**-ling**) **1** tread under foot. **2** crush thus. □ **trample on 1** tread heavily on. **2** treat roughly or with contempt.
■ **1** stamp on, step on, tramp down, tread on, walk on, walk over. **2** crush, flatten, squash, *colloquial* squish.

trampoline /'træmpəliːn/ *noun* canvas sheet connected by springs to horizontal frame, used for acrobatic exercises. ● *verb* (**-ning**) use trampoline.

trance /trɑːns/ *noun* **1** sleeplike state. **2** hypnotic or cataleptic state. **3** such state as supposedly entered into by medium. **4** rapture, ecstasy.
■ **1–3** daydream, daze, dream, hypnotic state, reverie, semi-consciousness, spell, stupor.

tranny /'trænɪ/ *noun* (*plural* **-ies**) *colloquial* transistor radio.

tranquil /'træŋkwɪl/ *adjective* serene, calm, undisturbed. □ **tranquillity** /-'kwɪl-/ *noun*. **tranquilly** *adverb*.
■ calm, collected, composed, dispassionate, halcyon (*days*), *colloquial* laid-back, peaceful, placid, quiet, restful, sedate, serene, sober, still, undisturbed, unemotional, unexcited, unruffled, untroubled.

tranquillize *verb* (also **-ise**; *US* also **tranquilize**) (**-zing** or **-sing**) make tranquil, esp. by drug etc.

tranquillizer *noun* (also **-iser**; *US* also **tranquilizer**) drug used to diminish anxiety.
■ barbiturate, bromide, narcotic, opiate, sedative.

trans- *prefix* **1** across, beyond. **2** on or to other side of. **3** through.

transact /træn'zækt/ *verb* perform or carry through (business etc.).

transaction /træn'zæk∫(ə)n/ *noun* **1** piece of commercial or other dealing. **2** transacting of business. **3** (in *plural*) published reports of discussions and lectures at meetings of learned society.
■ **1** agreement, bargain, business, contract, deal, negotiation, proceeding. **3** (*transactions*) see PROCEEDING 3.

transatlantic /trænzət'læntɪk/ *adjective* **1** beyond or crossing the Atlantic. **2** American. **3** *US* European.

transceiver /træn'siːvə/ *noun* combined radio transmitter and receiver.

transcend /træn'send/ *verb* **1** go beyond or exceed limits of. **2** excel, surpass.
■ **1** see EXCEED 2. **2** beat, excel, outdo, outstrip, rise above, surpass, top.

transcendent *adjective* **1** excelling, surpassing. **2** transcending human experience. **3** (esp. of God) existing apart from, or not subject to limitations of, material universe. □ **transcendence** *noun*. **transcendency** *noun*.

transcendental /trænsen'dent(ə)l/ *adjective* **1** a priori; not based on experience; intuitively accepted. **2** abstract; vague. □ **Transcendental Meditation** meditation seeking to induce detachment from problems, anxiety, etc.

transcontinental /trænzkɒntɪ'nent(ə)l/ *adjective* extending across a continent.

transcribe /træn'skraɪb/ *verb* (**-bing**) **1** copy out. **2** write out (notes etc.) in full. **3** record for subsequent broadcasting. **4** *Music* adapt for different instrument etc. □ **transcriber** *noun*. **transcription** /-'skrɪp-/ *noun*.
■ **1, 2** copy out, render, reproduce, translate, transliterate, write out. **3** see RECORD *verb* 1.

transcript /'trænskrɪpt/ *noun* written copy.

transducer /trænz'djuːsə/ *noun* device for changing a non-electrical signal (e.g. pressure) into an electrical one (e.g. voltage).

transept /'trænsept/ *noun* **1** part of cross-shaped church at right angles to nave. **2** either arm of this.

transfer *verb* /træns'fɜː/ (**-rr-**) **1** convey, remove, or hand over (thing etc.). **2** make over possession of (thing, right, etc.) to person. **3** move, change, or be moved to another group, club, etc. **4** change from one station, route, etc. to another to continue journey. **5** convey (design etc.) from one surface to another. ● *noun* /'trænsfɜː/ **1** transferring, being transferred. **2** design etc. (to be) conveyed from one surface to another. **3** football player etc. who is transferred. **4** document effecting conveyance of property, a right, etc. □ **transferable** /-'fɜːrəb(ə)l/ *adjective*. **transference** /'trænsfərəns/ *noun*.

■ *verb* **1, 2** bring, carry, convey, deliver, displace, ferry, hand over, make over, move, pass on, pass over, remove, shift, sign away, sign over, take, transport, transpose. **3** change, move, relocate, second, shift, switch, transplant.

transfigure /træns'fɪgə/ *verb* (**-ring**) change appearance of; make more elevated or idealized. □ **transfiguration** *noun*.

transfix /træns'fɪks/ *verb* **1** paralyse with horror or astonishment. **2** pierce with sharp implement or weapon.

transform /træns'fɔːm/ *verb* **1** change form, appearance, character, etc. of, esp. considerably. **2** change voltage etc. of (alternating current). □ **transformation** /-fə'meɪ-/ *noun*.

■ **1** adapt, alter, change, convert, improve, metamorphose, modify, mutate, rebuild, reconstruct, remodel, revolutionize, transfigure, translate, *jocular* transmogrify, transmute, turn. □ **transformation** adaptation, alteration, change, conversion, improvement, metamorphosis, modification, mutation, permutation, reconstruction, revolution, transfiguration, transition, translation, *jocular* transmogrification, transmutation, turn-about.

transformer *noun* apparatus for reducing or increasing voltage of alternating current.

transfuse /træns'fjuːz/ *verb* (**-sing**) **1** transfer (blood or other liquid) into blood vessel to replace that lost. **2** permeate. □ **transfusion** *noun*.

transgress /trænz'gres/ *verb* **1** infringe (law etc.). **2** overstep (limit laid down). **3** sin. □ **transgression** *noun*. **transgressor** *noun*.

■ □ **transgression** crime, error, fault, lapse, misdeed, misdemeanour, offence, sin, wickedness, wrongdoing.

transient /'trænzɪənt/ *adjective* of short duration; passing. □ **transience** *noun*.

■ brief, ephemeral, *literary* evanescent, fleeting, fugitive, impermanent, momentary, passing, quick, short, short-lived, temporary, transitory.

transistor /træn'zɪstə/ *noun* **1** semiconductor device capable of amplification and rectification. **2** (in full **transistor radio**) portable radio using transistors.

transistorize *verb* (also **-ise**) (**-zing** or **-sing**) equip with transistors rather than valves.

transit /'trænzɪt/ *noun* **1** going; conveying, being conveyed. **2** passage, route. **3** apparent passage of heavenly body across meridian of place or across sun or planet. □ **in transit** (while) going or being conveyed.

■ **1** conveyance, journey, movement, moving, passage, shipment, transfer, transportation, travel.

transition /træn'zɪʃ(ə)n/ *noun* passage or change from one place, state, condition, style, etc. to another. □ **transitional** *adjective*. **transitionally** *adverb*.

■ alteration, change, changeover, conversion, development, evolution, modification, movement, passing, progress, progression, shift, transformation, transit.

transitive /'trænsɪtɪv/ *adjective* (of verb) requiring direct object expressed or understood (see panel).

transitory /'trænzɪtərɪ/ *adjective* not lasting; brief, fleeting.

translate /træn'sleɪt/ *verb* (**-ting**) **1** (often + *into*) express sense of in another language or in another form. **2** be translatable. **3** interpret. **4** move or change, esp. from one person, place, or condition to another. □ **translatable** *adjective*. **translation** *noun*. **translator** *noun*.

■ **1** change, convert, decode, elucidate, explain, express, gloss, interpret, paraphrase, render, reword, spell out, transcribe. **3** construe, interpret, read, understand. **4** see TRANSFORM 1. □ **translation** decoding, gloss, interpretation,

---

Transitive verb

A transitive verb is one that has a direct object, e.g.

John was reading a book

(where *a book* is the direct object).

An intransitive verb is one that does not have a direct object, e.g.

John was reading.

Some verbs are always transitive, e.g. *bury, foresee, rediscover*; others are always intransitive, e.g. *dwell, grovel, meddle*. Many, as *read* in the examples above, are used both transitively and intransitively.

paraphrase, rendering, transcription, transliteration, version. **translator** interpreter, linguist.

transliterate /trænz'lɪtəreɪt/ verb (-**ting**) represent (word etc.) in closest corresponding characters of another script. □ **transliteration** noun.

translucent /trænz'luːs(ə)nt/ adjective allowing light to pass through diffusely; semitransparent. □ **translucence** noun.

transmigrate /trænzmaɪ'greɪt/ verb (-**ting**) (of soul) pass into different body. □ **transmigration** noun.

transmission /trænz'mɪʃ(ə)n/ noun **1** transmitting, being transmitted. **2** broadcast programme. **3** device transmitting power from engine to axle in vehicle.

■ **1** broadcasting, carriage, communication, conveyance, diffusion, dispatch, dissemination, relaying, sending, shipment, shipping, transfer, transference, transport, transportation. **2** broadcast, programme, relay, show, telecast.

transmit /trænz'mɪt/ verb (-**tt**-) **1** pass or hand on; transfer. **2** communicate or be medium for (ideas, emotions, etc.). **3** allow (heat, light, sound, etc.) to pass through. **4** broadcast (programme). **5** send (signal) by telegraph wire. □ **transmissible** adjective. **transmittable** adjective.

■ **1** convey, dispatch, disseminate, forward, pass on, post, send, transfer, transport. **2** see COMMUNICATE 1. **3** see CONDUCT verb 4. **4, 5** broadcast, cable, fax, colloquial phone, radio, relay, telegraph, telephone, telex, colloquial wire.

transmitter noun **1** person or thing that transmits. **2** equipment used to transmit radio etc. signals.

transmogrify /trænz'mɒɡrɪfaɪ/ verb (-**ies**, -**ied**) jocular transform, esp. in magical or surprising way. □ **transmogrification** noun.

transmute /trænz'mjuːt/ verb (-**ting**) **1** change form, nature, or substance of. **2** historical change (base metals) into gold. □ **transmutation** noun.

transom /'trænsəm/ noun **1** horizontal bar in window or above door. **2** (in full **transom window**) window above this.

transparency /træns'pærənsɪ/ noun (plural -**ies**) **1** being transparent. **2** picture (esp. photograph) to be viewed by light passing through it.

transparent /træns'pærənt/ adjective **1** able to be seen through. **2** (of disguise, pretext, etc.) easily discerned. **3** (of quality etc.) obvious. **4** easily understood; frank. □ **transparently** adverb.

■ **1** clear, crystalline, diaphanous, filmy, gauzy, limpid, pellucid, see-through, sheer. **2, 3** see OBVIOUS. **4** see CANDID 1.

transpire /træns'paɪə/ verb (-**ring**) **1** (of secret, fact, etc.) come to be known. **2** disputed happen. **3** emit (vapour, moisture) or be emitted through pores of skin etc. □ **transpiration** /-spɪ-/ noun.

USAGE The use of transpire to mean 'happen' is considered incorrect by some people.

transplant verb /træns'plɑːnt/ **1** plant elsewhere. **2** transfer (living tissue or organ) to another part of body or to another body. ● noun /'trænsplɑːnt/ **1** transplanting of organ or tissue. **2** thing transplanted. □ **transplantation** noun.

■ verb **1** displace, move, relocate, reposition, resettle, shift, transfer, uproot.

transport verb /træns'pɔːt/ **1** take to another place. **2** historical deport (criminal) to penal colony. **3** (as **transported** adjective) (usually + with) affected with strong emotion. ● noun /'trænspɔːt/ **1** system of transporting. **2** means of conveyance. **3** ship, aircraft, etc. used to carry troops, military stores, etc. **4** (esp. in plural) vehement emotion. □ **transportable** /-'pɔːt-/ adjective.

■ verb **1** bear, carry, convey, fetch, haul, move, remove, send, shift, ship, take, transfer. **2** see DEPORT 1. ● noun **1** conveyance, haulage, removal, shipment, shipping, transportation. **2** carrier, conveyance, US transportation, vehicle, slang wheels.

transportation /trænspɔː'teɪʃ(ə)n/ noun **1** (system of) conveying, being conveyed. **2** US means of transport. **3** historical deporting of criminals.

transporter noun vehicle used to transport other vehicles, heavy machinery, etc. □ **transporter bridge** bridge carrying vehicles etc. across water on suspended moving platform.

transpose /træns'pəʊz/ verb (-**sing**) **1** cause (two or more things) to change places. **2** change position of (thing) in series or (word(s)) in sentence. **3** Music write or play in different key. □ **transposition** /-pə'zɪʃ(ə)n/ noun.

■ **1, 2** change, exchange, interchange, move round, rearrange, reverse, substitute, swap, switch, transfer.

transsexual /træns'sekʃʊəl/ (also **transexual**) adjective having physical characteristics of one sex and psychological identification with the other. ● noun **1** transsexual person. **2** person who has had sex change.

transship /træns'ʃɪp/ verb (-**pp**-) transfer from one ship or conveyance to another. □ **transshipment** noun.

transubstantiation /trænsəbstænʃɪ'eɪʃ(ə)n/ noun conversion of Eucharistic elements wholly into body and blood of Christ.

transuranic /trænzjʊ'rænɪk/ adjective Chemistry (of element) having higher atomic number than uranium.

transverse /'trænzvɜːs/ adjective situated, arranged, or acting in crosswise direction. □ **transversely** adverb.

■ crosswise, diagonal, oblique.

transvestism /trænz'vestɪz(ə)m/ noun habitual wearing of clothes of the opposite sex.

transvestite /trænz'vestaɪt/ noun person, esp. man, given to transvestism.

trap *noun* **1** device, often baited, for catching animals. **2** arrangement or trick to catch (out) unsuspecting person. **3** device for releasing clay pigeon to be shot at or greyhound at start of race etc. **4** curve in drainpipe etc. that fills with liquid and forms seal against return of gas. **5** two-wheeled carriage. **6** trapdoor. **7** *slang* mouth. ● *verb* (**-pp-**) **1** catch (as) in trap. **2** catch (out) using trick etc. **3** furnish with traps. □ **trapdoor** door in floor, ceiling, or roof.

■ *noun* **1** gin, net, noose, pitfall, snare. **2** ambush, booby trap, deception, mantrap, pitfall, ploy, snare, trick. ● *verb* **1** ambush, capture, catch, corner, ensnare, entrap, net, snare. **2** catch out, deceive, dupe, inveigle, trick.

trapeze /trə'piːz/ *noun* crossbar suspended by ropes as swing for acrobatics etc.

trapezium /trə'piːzɪəm/ *noun* (*plural* **-s** or **-zia**) **1** quadrilateral with only one pair of sides parallel. **2** *US* trapezoid.

trapezoid /'træpɪzɔɪd/ *noun* **1** quadrilateral with no sides parallel. **2** *US* trapezium.

trapper *noun* person who traps wild animals, esp. for their fur.

trappings /'træpɪŋz/ *plural noun* **1** ornamental accessories. **2** (esp. ornamental) harness for horse.

■ **1** accessories, accompaniments, accoutrements, adornments, appointments, decorations, equipment, finery, fittings, furnishings, gear, ornaments, paraphernalia, things, *colloquial* trimmings.

Trappist /'træpɪst/ *noun* monk of order vowed to silence. ● *adjective* of this order.

trash *noun* **1** *esp. US* worthless or waste stuff; rubbish. **2** *esp. US* nonsense. **3** worthless person(s). ● *verb slang* wreck, vandalize. □ **trash can** *US* dustbin. □ **trashy** *adjective* (**-ier**, **-iest**).

■ *noun* **1** debris, *US* garbage, junk, litter, refuse, rubbish, sweepings, waste. **2** see NONSENSE 1.

trauma /'trɔːmə/ *noun* (*plural* **traumata** /-mətə/ or **-s**) **1** emotional shock. **2** physical injury; resulting shock. □ **traumatic** /-'mæt-/ *adjective*. **traumatize** *verb* (also **-ise**) (**-zing** or **-sing**).

travail /'træveɪl/ *literary noun* **1** laborious effort. **2** pangs of childbirth. ● *verb* make laborious effort, esp. in childbirth.

travel /'træv(ə)l/ *verb* (**-ll-**; *US* **-l-**) **1** go from one place to another; make journey(s), esp. long or abroad. **2** journey along or through. **3** cover (distance). **4** *colloquial* withstand long journey. **5** go from place to place as salesperson. **6** move or proceed as specified. **7** *colloquial* move quickly. **8** pass from point to point. **9** (of machine or part) move or operate in specified way. ● *noun* **1** travelling, esp. abroad. **2** (often in *plural*) spell of this. **3** range, rate, or mode of motion of part in machinery. □ **travel agency** agency making arrangements for travellers. **travel-sick** nauseous owing to motion in travelling. □ **travelling** *adjective*.

■ *verb* **1** commute, gad about, *colloquial* gallivant, go, journey, make a trip, migrate, move, proceed, progress, ramble, roam, rove, tour, trek, trip, voyage, wander. ● *noun* **1** globe-trotting, moving around, touring, tourism, travelling, wandering. **2** (*travels*) excursion, expedition, exploration, journey, pilgrimage, safari, tour, trek, trip, voyage. □ **travelling** homeless, itinerant, migrant, migratory, mobile, nomadic, peripatetic, restless, roaming, roving, touring, vagrant, wandering.

travelled *adjective* (*US* **traveled**) experienced in travelling.

traveller *noun* (*US* **traveler**) **1** person who travels or is travelling. **2** Gypsy. **3** travelling salesperson. □ **traveller's cheque** cheque for fixed amount, cashed on signature for equivalent in other currencies. **traveller's joy** wild clematis.

■ **1** commuter, explorer, globe-trotter, hiker, hitchhiker, holidaymaker, migrant, passenger, pilgrim, rambler, stowaway, tourist, tripper, voyager, wanderer, wayfarer. **3** *colloquial* rep, representative, salesman, saleswoman.

travelogue /'trævəlɒg/ *noun* film or illustrated lecture about travel.

traverse *verb* /trə'vɜːs/ (**-sing**) **1** travel or lie across. **2** consider or discuss whole extent of. ● *noun* /'trævəs/ **1** sideways movement. **2** traversing. **3** thing that crosses another. □ **traversable** *adjective*. **traversal** *noun*.

travesty /'trævɪstɪ/ *noun* (*plural* **-ies**) grotesque parody; ridiculous imitation. ● *verb* (**-ies**, **-ied**) make or be travesty of.

trawl *verb* **1** fish with trawl or seine or in trawler. **2** catch by trawling. **3** (often + *for*, *through*) search thoroughly. ● *noun* **1** trawling. **2** (in full **trawl-net**) large wide-mouthed fishing net dragged by boat along sea bottom.

trawler *noun* boat used for trawling.

tray *noun* **1** flat board with raised rim for carrying dishes etc. **2** shallow lidless box for papers or small articles, sometimes forming drawer in cabinet etc.

treacherous /'tretʃərəs/ *adjective* **1** guilty of or involving violation of faith or betrayal of trust. **2** not to be relied on; deceptive. □ **treacherously** *adverb*. **treachery** *noun*.

■ **1** deceitful, disloyal, double-crossing, double-dealing, duplicitous, faithless, false, perfidious, sneaky, unfaithful, untrustworthy. **2** dangerous, deceptive, hazardous, misleading, perilous, risky, shifting, unpredictable, unreliable, unsafe, unstable. □ **treachery** betrayal, dishonesty, disloyalty, double-dealing, duplicity, faithlessness, infidelity, perfidy, treason, untrustworthiness.

treacle /'triːk(ə)l/ *noun* **1** syrup produced in refining sugar. **2** molasses. □ **treacly** *adjective*.

tread /tred/ *verb* (*past* **trod**; *past participle* **trodden** or **trod**) **1** (often + *on*) set one's foot down. **2** walk on. **3** (often + *down*, *in*, *into*) press (down) or crush with feet. **4** perform (steps etc.) by walking. ● *noun* **1** manner or sound of walking. **2** top surface of step or stair. **3** thick moulded part of vehicle tyre for gripping road. **4** part of wheel or sole of shoe etc. that touches ground. □ **treadmill 1** device for producing motion by treading on steps on revolving cylinder. **2** similar device used for exercise. **3** monotonous routine work. **tread water** maintain upright position in water by moving feet and hands.

■ *verb* **1** see WALK *verb* 1–5; (*tread on*) crush, squash underfoot, stamp on, step on, trample, walk on.

treadle /'tred(ə)l/ *noun* lever moved by foot and imparting motion to machine.

treason /'tri:z(ə)n/ *noun* (in full **high treason**) violation of allegiance to sovereign (e.g. plotting assassination) or state (e.g. helping enemy). □ **treasonous** *adjective*.

■ betrayal, mutiny, rebellion, sedition, treachery.

treasonable *adjective* involving or guilty of treason.

treasure /'treʒə/ *noun* **1** precious metals or gems. **2** hoard of them. **3** accumulated wealth. **4** thing valued for rarity, workmanship, associations, etc. **5** *colloquial* beloved or highly valued person. ● *verb* (**-ring**) **1** value highly. **2** (often + *up*) store up as valuable. □ **treasure hunt 1** search for treasure. **2** game in which players seek hidden object. **treasure trove** treasure of unknown ownership found hidden.

■ *noun* **1–3** cache, cash, fortune, gold, hoard, jewels, riches, treasure trove, valuables, wealth. ● *verb* **1** adore, appreciate, cherish, esteem, love, prize, rate highly, value, venerate, worship. **2** guard, keep safe, preserve.

treasurer *noun* person in charge of funds of society etc.

treasury /'treʒərɪ/ *noun* (*plural* **-ies**) **1** place where treasure is kept. **2** funds or revenue of state, institution, or society. **3** (**Treasury**) (offices and officers of) department managing public revenue of a country. □ **Treasury bench** government front bench in parliament. **treasury bill** bill of exchange issued by government to raise money for temporary needs.

■ **1** bank, coffers, exchequer, hoard, repository, storeroom, vault. **3** exchequer.

treat *verb* **1** act, behave towards, or deal with in specified way. **2** apply process to. **3** apply medical care or attention to. **4** present or handle (subject) in literature or art. **5** (often + *to*) provide with food, drink, or entertainment at one's own expense. **6** (often + *with*) negotiate terms. **7** (often + *of*) give exposition. ● *noun* **1** event or circumstance that gives great pleasure. **2** meal, entertainment, etc. designed to do this. **3** (**a treat**) *colloquial* extremely good or well. □ **treatable** *adjective*.

■ *verb* **1** behave towards, consider, deal with, handle, manage, regard, tackle, use. **2** process. **3** attend to, care for, cure, dress, heal, look after, medicate, nurse, prescribe for, tend. **5** entertain,

pay for, provide for, regale. ● *noun* **2** entertainment, gift, outing, surprise.

treatise /'tri:tɪz/ *noun* literary composition dealing esp. formally with subject.

■ disquisition, dissertation, essay, monograph, pamphlet, paper, thesis, tract.

treatment *noun* **1** process or manner of behaving towards or dealing with person or thing. **2** medical care or attention.

■ **1** care, conduct, dealings, handling, management, manipulation, organization, reception, usage, use. **2** cure, healing, medication, nursing, remedy, therapy.

treaty /'tri:tɪ/ *noun* (*plural* **-ies**) **1** formal agreement between states. **2** agreement between people, esp. for purchase of property.

■ agreement, alliance, armistice, compact, concordat, contract, covenant, convention, deal, entente, pact, peace, protocol, settlement, truce, understanding.

treble /'treb(ə)l/ *adjective* **1** threefold, triple; 3 times as much or many. **2** high-pitched. ● *noun* **1** treble quantity or thing. **2** (voice of) boy soprano. **3** high-pitched instrument. **4** high-frequency sound of radio, record player, etc. ● *verb* (**-ling**) multiply or be multiplied by 3. □ **trebly** *adverb*.

tree *noun* **1** perennial plant with woody self-supporting main stem and usually unbranched for some distance from ground. **2** shaped piece of wood for various purposes. **3** family tree. ● *verb* (**trees, treed**) cause to take refuge in tree. □ **treecreeper** small creeping bird feeding on insects in tree-bark. **tree-fern** large fern with upright woody stem. **tree surgeon** person who treats decayed trees in order to preserve them. □ **treeless** *adjective*.

trefoil /'trefɔɪl/ *noun* **1** plant with leaves of 3 leaflets. **2** 3-lobed ornamentation, esp. in tracery windows.

trek *verb* (**-kk-**) make arduous journey, esp. (*historical*) travel or migrate by ox-wagon. ● *noun* **1** such journey. **2** each stage of it. □ **trekker** *noun*.

trellis /'trelɪs/ *noun* (in full **trellis-work**) lattice of light wooden or metal bars, esp. support for climbing plants.

tremble /'tremb(ə)l/ *verb* (**-ling**) **1** shake involuntarily with emotion, cold, etc. **2** be affected with extreme apprehension. ● *noun* trembling, quiver. □ **trembly** *adjective* (**-ier**, **-iest**).

■ *verb* quake, quaver, quiver, rock, shake, shiver, shudder, vibrate.

tremendous /trɪ'mendəs/ *adjective colloquial* **1** remarkable, considerable, excellent. **2** awe-inspiring, overpowering. □ **tremendously** *adverb*.

■ **1** see REMARKABLE, BIG *adjective* 1, EXCELLENT. **2** alarming, appalling, *poetical* awful, fearful, fearsome, frightening, frightful, horrifying,

823 tremolo | tribute

shocking, startling, *colloquial* terrible, *colloquial* terrific.

tremolo /'tremələʊ/ *noun* (*plural* **-s**) tremulous effect in music.

tremor /'tremə/ *noun* **1** shaking, quivering. **2** thrill (of fear, exultation, etc.). **3** (in full **earth tremor**) slight earthquake.
■ **1** agitation, quavering, quiver, shaking, trembling, vibration. **3** earthquake, seismic disturbance.

tremulous /'tremjʊləs/ *adjective* trembling. □ **tremulously** *adverb*.
■ agitated, *colloquial* jittery, jumpy, quivering, shaking, shivering, trembling, trembly, vibrating.

trench *noun* deep ditch, esp. one dug by troops as shelter from enemy's fire. ● *verb* **1** dig trench(es) in. **2** make series of trenches (in) so as to bring lower soil to surface. □ **trench coat 1** lined or padded waterproof coat. **2** loose belted raincoat.

trenchant /'trentʃ(ə)nt/ *adjective* incisive, terse, vigorous. □ **trenchancy** *noun*. **trenchantly** *adverb*.

trencher /'trentʃə/ *noun historical* wooden etc. platter for serving food.

trencherman /'trentʃəmən/ *noun* eater.

trend *noun* **1** general direction and tendency. **2** fashion. ● *verb* **1** turn away in specified direction. **2** have general tendency. □ **trend-setter** person who leads the way in fashion etc. **trend-setting** *adjective*.
■ *noun* **1** bent, bias, direction, drift, inclination, leaning, movement, shift, tendency. **2** craze, fad, fashion, mode, rage, style, *colloquial* thing, vogue.

trendy *colloquial often derogatory adjective* (**-ier**, **-iest**) fashionable. ● *noun* (*plural* **-ies**) fashionable person. □ **trendily** *adverb*. **trendiness** *noun*.
■ *adjective* all the rage, contemporary, *slang* cool, fashionable, in, (the) latest, modern, stylish, up to date, voguish.

trepan /trɪ'pæn/ *historical noun* surgeon's cylindrical saw for making opening in skull. ● *verb* (**-nn-**) perforate (skull) with trepan.

trepidation /trepɪ'deɪʃ(ə)n/ *noun* fear, anxiety.

trespass /'trespəs/ *verb* (usually + *on*, *upon*) **1** enter unlawfully (on another's land, property, etc.). **2** encroach. **3** (+ *against*) *archaic* offend. ● *noun* **1** act of trespassing. **2** *archaic* sin, offence. □ **trespasser** *noun*.
■ *verb* (**trespass on**) encroach on, infringe on, intrude on, invade.

tress *noun* **1** lock of hair. **2** (in *plural*) hair.

trestle /'tres(ə)l/ *noun* **1** supporting structure for table etc. consisting of two frames fixed at an angle or hinged or of bar with two divergent pairs of legs. **2** (in full **trestle-table**) table of board(s) laid on trestles. **3** (in full **trestle-work**) open braced framework to support bridge etc.

trews *plural noun* close-fitting usually tartan trousers.

tri- *combining form* three (times).

triad /'traɪæd/ *noun* group of 3 (esp. notes in chord). □ **triadic** /-'æd-/ *adjective*.

trial /'traɪəl/ *noun* **1** judicial examination and determination of issues between parties by judge with or without jury. **2** test. **3** trying thing or person. **4** match held to select players for team. **5** contest for horses, dogs, motorcycles, etc. □ **on trial 1** being tried in court of law. **2** being tested. **trial run** preliminary operational test.
■ **1** case, court martial, enquiry, examination, hearing, inquisition, judicial proceeding, lawsuit, tribunal. **2** attempt, check, *colloquial* dry run, experiment, rehearsal, test, testing, trial run, try-out. **3** affliction, burden, difficulty, hardship, nuisance, ordeal, *colloquial* pain in the neck, pest, problem, tribulation, trouble, worry.

triangle /'traɪæŋg(ə)l/ *noun* **1** plane figure with 3 sides and angles. **2** any 3 things not in straight line, with imaginary lines joining them. **3** implement etc. of this shape. **4** musical instrument of steel rod bent into triangle, struck with small steel rod. **5** situation involving 3 people. □ **triangular** /-'æŋgjʊlə/ *adjective*.
■ □ **triangular** three-cornered, three-sided.

triangulate /traɪ'æŋgjʊleɪt/ *verb* (**-ting**) divide (area) into triangles for surveying purposes. □ **triangulation** *noun*.

triathlon /traɪ'æθlən/ *noun* athletic contest of 3 events. □ **triathlete** *noun*.

tribe *noun* **1** (in some societies) group of families under recognized leader with blood etc. ties and usually having common culture and dialect. **2** any similar natural or political division. **3** *usually derogatory* set or number of people, esp. of one profession etc. or family. □ **tribesman**, **tribeswoman** member of tribe. □ **tribal** *adjective*.
■ **1, 2** clan, dynasty, family, group, *usually derogatory* horde, house, nation, pedigree, people, race, stock, strain.

tribulation /trɪbjʊ'leɪʃ(ə)n/ *noun* great affliction.

tribunal /traɪ'bju:n(ə)l/ *noun* **1** board appointed to adjudicate on particular question. **2** court of justice.

tribune /'trɪbju:n/ *noun* **1** popular leader, demagogue. **2** (in full **tribune of the people**) *Roman History* officer chosen by the people to protect their liberties.

tributary /'trɪbjʊtərɪ/ *noun* (*plural* **-ies**) **1** stream etc. that flows into larger stream or lake. **2** *historical* person or state paying or subject to tribute. ● *adjective* that is a tributary.

tribute /'trɪbju:t/ *noun* **1** thing said or done or given as mark of respect or affection etc. **2** (+ *to*) indication of (some praiseworthy quality). **3** *historical* periodic payment by one state or ruler to another. **4** *historical* obligation to pay this.
■ **1** accolade, appreciation, commendation, compliment, eulogy, glorification, homage, honour, panegyric, praise, recognition, respect, testimony; (**pay tribute to**) see HONOUR *verb* 2.

trice *noun* □ **in a trice** in an instant.

triceps /'traɪseps/ *noun* muscle (esp. in upper arm) with 3 points of attachment.

triceratops /traɪ'serətɒps/ *noun* large dinosaur with 3 horns.

trichinosis /trɪkɪ'nəʊsɪs/ *noun* disease caused by hairlike worms.

trichology /trɪ'kɒlədʒɪ/ *noun* study of hair. □ **trichologist** *noun*.

trichromatic /traɪkrə'mætɪk/ *adjective* 3-coloured.

trick *noun* 1 thing done to deceive or outwit; hoax. 2 illusion. 3 knack. 4 feat of skill or dexterity. 5 unusual action learned by animal. 6 foolish or discreditable act; joke. 7 idiosyncrasy. 8 cards played in one round. 9 point gained in this. ● *verb* 1 deceive by trick. 2 (+ *into*) cause to do something by trickery. 3 swindle. 4 take by surprise.

■ *noun* 1 cheat, *slang* con, deceit, deception, device, dodge, fraud, hoax, imposture, manoeuvre, ploy, pretence, ruse, scheme, stratagem, stunt, subterfuge, swindle, trap, wile. 2 deception, illusion, sleight of hand. 3 art, knack, secret, skill, technique. 4, 5 antic, feat, stunt. 6 gag, hoax, joke, *colloquial* leg-pull, practical joke, prank, stunt. 7 characteristic, habit, idiosyncrasy, mannerism, peculiarity, way. ● *verb* 1–3 *colloquial* bamboozle, bluff, cheat, *slang* con, *literary* cozen, deceive, defraud, *colloquial* diddle, dupe, fool, hoax, hoodwink, *colloquial* kid, mislead, outwit, pull (person's) leg, swindle, take in.

trickery *noun* deception; use of tricks.

■ bluffing, cheating, chicanery, deceit, deception, dishonesty, double-dealing, duplicity, fraud, *slang* funny business, guile, hocus-pocus, *colloquial* jiggery-pokery, knavery, legerdemain, magic, skulduggery, sleight of hand, slyness, swindling, trick.

trickle /'trɪk(ə)l/ *verb* (**-ling**) 1 (cause to) flow in drops or small stream. 2 come or go slowly or gradually. ● *noun* trickling flow. □ **trickle charger** *Electricity* device for slow continuous charging of battery.

■ *verb* 1 dribble, drip, drizzle, drop, exude, flow, leak, ooze, percolate, run, seep.

trickster /'trɪkstə/ *noun* deceiver, rogue.

tricky *adjective* (**-ier, -iest**) 1 requiring care and adroitness. 2 crafty, deceitful. □ **trickily** *adverb*. **trickiness** *noun*.

tricolour /'trɪkələ/ *noun* (*US* **tricolor**) flag of 3 colours, esp. French national flag.

tricot /'trɪkəʊ/ *noun* knitted fabric.

tricycle /'traɪsɪk(ə)l/ *noun* 3-wheeled pedal-driven vehicle.

trident /'traɪd(ə)nt/ *noun* 3-pronged spear.

Tridentine /traɪ'dentaɪn/ *adjective* of traditional RC orthodoxy.

triennial /traɪ'enɪəl/ *adjective* 1 lasting 3 years. 2 recurring every 3 years.

trifle /'traɪf(ə)l/ *noun* 1 thing of slight value or importance. 2 small amount. 3 (**a trifle**) somewhat. 4 dessert of sponge cake with custard, cream, fruit, etc. ● *verb* (**-ling**) 1 talk or act frivolously. 2 (+ *with*) treat frivolously; flirt heartlessly with.

■ *verb* 1 dabble, fiddle, fool about, play about.

trifling *adjective* 1 unimportant. 2 frivolous.

■ see TRIVIAL 1.

trigger /'trɪgə/ *noun* 1 movable device for releasing spring or catch and so setting off mechanism, esp. of gun. 2 event etc. that sets off chain reaction. ● *verb* (often + *off*) set (action, process) in motion; precipitate. □ **trigger-happy** apt to shoot on slight provocation.

trigonometry /trɪgə'nɒmətrɪ/ *noun* branch of mathematics dealing with relations of sides and angles of triangles, and with certain functions of angles. □ **trigonometric** /-nə'met-/ *adjective*. **trigonometrical** /-nə'met-/ *adjective*.

trike *noun colloquial* tricycle.

trilateral /traɪ'lætər(ə)l/ *adjective* 1 of, on, or with 3 sides. 2 involving 3 parties.

trilby /'trɪlbɪ/ *noun* (*plural* **-ies**) soft felt hat with narrow brim and indented crown.

trilingual /traɪ'lɪŋgw(ə)l/ *adjective* speaking or in 3 languages.

trill *noun* 1 quavering sound, esp. quick alternation of notes. 2 bird's warbling. 3 pronunciation of letter *r* with vibrating tongue. ● *verb* 1 produce trill. 2 warble (song). 3 pronounce (*r* etc.) with trill.

■ *verb* 2 sing, twitter, warble, whistle.

trillion /'trɪljən/ *noun* (*plural* same) 1 million million. 2 million million million. 3 (**trillions**) *colloquial* large number. □ **trillionth** *adjective* & *noun*.

trilobite /'traɪləbaɪt/ *noun* kind of fossil crustacean.

trilogy /'trɪlədʒɪ/ *noun* (*plural* **-ies**) set of 3 related novels, plays, operas, etc.

trim *verb* (**-mm-**) 1 make neat or tidy or of required size or shape, esp. by cutting away irregular or unwanted parts. 2 (+ *off*, *away*) cut off. 3 ornament. 4 adjust balance of (ship, aircraft) by arranging cargo etc. 5 arrange (sails) to suit wind. ● *noun* 1 state of readiness or fitness. 2 ornament, decorative material. 3 trimming of hair etc. ● *adjective* (**-mm-**) 1 neat. 2 in good order; well arranged or equipped.

■ *verb* 1 clip, crop, cut, dock, pare down, prune, shape, shear, shorten, snip, tidy. 3 see DECORATE 1. ● *adjective* compact, neat, orderly, shipshape, smart, spruce, tidy, well groomed, well kept, well ordered.

trimaran /'traɪməræn/ *noun* vessel like catamaran, with 3 hulls side by side.

trimming *noun* 1 ornamental addition to dress, hat, etc. 2 (in *plural*) *colloquial* usual accompaniments.

trinitrotoluene /tramaɪtrə'tɒljʊiːn/ *noun* (also **trinitrotoluol** /-'tɒljʊɒl/) a high explosive.

trinity /'trɪnɪtɪ/ *noun* (*plural* **-ies**) **1** being 3. **2** group of 3. **3** (**the Trinity**) the 3 persons of the Christian Godhead. □ **Trinity Sunday** Sunday after Whit Sunday.

trinket /'trɪŋkɪt/ *noun* trifling ornament, esp. piece of jewellery.

trio /'triːəʊ/ *noun* (*plural* **-s**) **1** group of 3. **2** musical composition for 3 performers. **3** the performers.

trip *verb* (**-pp-**) **1** (often + *up*) (cause to) stumble, esp. by catching foot. **2** (+ *up*) (**cause** to) commit fault or blunder. **3** run lightly. **4** make excursion to place. **5** operate (mechanism) suddenly by knocking aside catch etc. **6** *slang* have drug-induced hallucinatory experience. ● *noun* **1** journey or excursion, esp. for pleasure. **2** stumble, blunder. **3** tripping, being tripped up. **4** nimble step. **5** *slang* drug-induced hallucinatory experience. **6** device for tripping mechanism etc. □ **trip-wire** wire stretched close to ground to operate alarm etc. if disturbed.

> ■ *verb* **1** catch one's foot, fall, stumble, totter, tumble. **3** caper, dance, frisk, gambol, run, skip. **4** see TRAVEL *verb* 1. ● *noun* **1** day out, drive, excursion, expedition, holiday, jaunt, journey, outing, ride, tour, visit, voyage.

tripartite /traɪ'pɑːtaɪt/ *adjective* **1** consisting of 3 parts. **2** shared by or involving 3 parties.

tripe *noun* **1** first or second stomach of ruminant, esp. ox, as food. **2** *colloquial* nonsense, rubbish.

triple /'trɪp(ə)l/ *adjective* **1** threefold; having 3 parts. **2** involving 3 parties. **3** 3 times as much or as many. ● *noun* **1** threefold number or amount. **2** set of 3. ● *verb* (**-ling**) multiply by 3. □ **triple crown** winning of 3 important sporting events. **triple jump** athletic contest comprising hop, step, and jump. □ **triply** *adverb*.

triplet /'trɪplɪt/ *noun* **1** each of 3 children or animals born at one birth. **2** set of 3 things, esp. of notes played in time of two.

triplex /'trɪpleks/ *adjective* triple, threefold.

triplicate *adjective* /'trɪplɪkət/ **1** existing in 3 examples or copies. **2** having 3 corresponding parts. **3** tripled. ● *noun* /'trɪplɪkət/ each of 3 copies or corresponding parts. ● *verb* (**-ting**) /'trɪplɪkeɪt/ **1** make in 3 copies. **2** multiply by 3. □ **triplication** *noun*.

tripod /'traɪpɒd/ *noun* 3-legged or 3-footed stand, stool, table, or utensil.

tripos /'traɪpɒs/ *noun* honours exam for primary degree at Cambridge University.

tripper *noun* person who goes on pleasure trip.

triptych /'trɪptɪk/ *noun* picture etc. with 3 panels usually hinged vertically together.

trireme /'traɪriːm/ *noun* ancient Greek warship, with 3 files of oarsmen on each side.

trisect /traɪ'sekt/ *verb* divide into 3 (usually equal) parts. □ **trisection** *noun*.

trite *adjective* hackneyed. □ **tritely** *adverb*. **triteness** *noun*.

> ■ banal, commonplace, hackneyed, ordinary, pedestrian, predictable, uninspired, uninteresting.

tritium /'trɪtɪəm/ *noun* radioactive isotope of hydrogen with mass about 3 times that of ordinary hydrogen.

triumph /'traɪʌmf/ *noun* **1** state of victory or success. **2** great success or achievement. **3** supreme example. **4** joy at success. ● *verb* **1** (often + *over*) gain victory; be successful. **2** *Roman History* ride in triumph. **3** (often + *over*) exult.

> ■ *noun* **1, 2** accomplishment, achievement, conquest, coup, *colloquial* hit, smash hit, success, victory, walkover, win. **4** celebration, elation, exultation, joy, jubilation, rapture. ● *verb* **1** be victorious, prevail, succeed, take the honours, win; (*triumph over*) see DEFEAT *verb* 1.

triumphal /traɪ'ʌmf(ə)l/ *adjective* of, used in, or celebrating a triumph.

> USAGE *Triumphal*, as in *triumphal arch*, should not be confused with *triumphant*.

triumphant /traɪ'ʌmf(ə)nt/ *adjective* **1** victorious, successful. **2** exultant. □ **triumphantly** *adverb*.

> USAGE See note at TRIUMPHAL.

> ■ **1** conquering, dominant, successful, victorious, winning. **2** boastful, *colloquial* cocky, elated, exultant, gleeful, gloating, immodest, joyful, jubilant, proud.

triumvirate /traɪ'ʌmvərət/ *noun* ruling group of 3 men.

trivalent /traɪ'veɪlənt/ *adjective Chemistry* having a valency of 3. □ **trivalency** *noun*.

trivet /'trɪvɪt/ *noun* iron tripod or bracket for pot or kettle to stand on.

trivia /'trɪvɪə/ *plural noun* trifles, trivialities.

trivial /'trɪvɪəl/ *adjective* **1** of small value or importance. **2** concerned only with trivial things. □ **triviality** /-'æl-/ *noun* (*plural* **-ies**). **trivially** *adverb*.

> ■ **1** fiddling, *colloquial* footling, frivolous, inconsequential, inconsiderable, inessential, insignificant, little, meaningless, minor, negligible, paltry, pettifogging, petty, *colloquial* piddling, *colloquial* piffling, silly, slight, small, superficial, trifling, unimportant, worthless.

trivialize *verb* (also **-ise**) (**-zing** or **-sing**) make or treat as trivial; minimize. □ **trivialization** *noun*.

trochee /'trəʊkiː/ *noun* metrical foot of one long followed by one short syllable. □ **trochaic** /trə'keɪɪk/ *adjective*.

trod *past* and *past participle* of TREAD.

trodden *past participle* of TREAD.

troglodyte /'trɒglədaɪt/ *noun* cave dweller.

troika /'trɔɪkə/ *noun* Russian vehicle drawn by 3 horses abreast.

Trojan /'trəʊdʒ(ə)n/ *adjective* of ancient Troy. ● *noun* **1** native or inhabitant of ancient Troy. **2** person who works, fights, etc. courageously. □ **Trojan Horse** person or device planted to bring about enemy's downfall.

troll[1] /trəʊl/ *noun* supernatural cave-dwelling giant or dwarf in Scandinavian mythology.

troll[2] /trəʊl/ *verb* fish by drawing bait along in water.

trolley /'trɒlɪ/ *noun* (*plural* **-s**) **1** table, stand, or basket on wheels or castors for serving food, carrying luggage etc., gathering purchases in supermarket, etc. **2** low truck running along rails. **3** (in full **trolley-wheel**) wheel attached to pole etc. for collecting current from overhead electric wire to drive vehicle. □ **trolley bus** electric bus using trolley-wheel.

trollop /'trɒləp/ *noun* disreputable girl or woman.

trombone /trɒm'bəʊn/ *noun* musical wind instrument made of brass, with sliding tube. □ **trombonist** *noun*.

troop /tru:p/ *noun* **1** assembled company; assemblage of people or animals. **2** (in *plural*) soldiers, armed forces. **3** cavalry unit commanded by captain. **4** artillery unit. **5** group of 3 or more Scout patrols. ● *verb* (+ *in*, *out*, *off*, etc.) come together or move in a troop. □ **troop the colour** transfer flag ceremonially at public mounting of garrison guards. **troop-ship** ship for transporting troops.

trooper *noun* **1** private soldier in cavalry or armoured unit. **2** *Australian & US* mounted or State police officer. **3** cavalry horse. **4** troop-ship.

trope *noun* figurative use of word.

trophy /'trəʊfɪ/ *noun* (*plural* **-ies**) **1** cup etc. as prize in contest. **2** memento of any success.
- **1** award, cup, laurels, medal, palm, prize. **2** memento, reminder, souvenir.

tropic /'trɒpɪk/ *noun* **1** parallel of latitude 23° 27′ N. (**tropic of Cancer**) or S. (**tropic of Capricorn**) of Equator. **2** (**the Tropics**) region lying between these.

tropical *adjective* of or typical of the Tropics.

troposphere /'trɒpəsfɪə/ *noun* layer of atmosphere extending about 8 km upwards from earth's surface.

trot *verb* (**-tt-**) **1** (of person) run at moderate pace. **2** (of horse) proceed at steady pace faster than walk. **3** traverse (distance) thus. ● *noun* **1** action or exercise of trotting. **2** (**the trots**) *slang* diarrhoea. □ **on the trot** *colloquial* **1** in succession. **2** continually busy. **trot out** *colloquial* introduce (opinion etc.) repeatedly or tediously.

troth /trəʊθ/ *noun archaic* **1** faith, fidelity. **2** truth.

trotter *noun* **1** (usually in *plural*) animal's foot, esp. as food. **2** horse bred or trained for trotting.

troubadour /'tru:bədʊə/ *noun* **1** singer; poet. **2** French medieval poet singing of love.

trouble /'trʌb(ə)l/ *noun* **1** difficulty, distress; vexation, affliction. **2** inconvenience; unpleasant exertion. **3** cause of this. **4** perceived failing. **5** malfunction. **6** disturbance. **7** (in *plural*) public disturbances. ● *verb* (**-ling**) **1** cause distress to; disturb. **2** (as **troubled** *adjective*) anxious, uneasy. **3** be disturbed. **4** afflict; cause pain etc.

to. **5** subject or be subjected to inconvenience or unpleasant exertion. □ **in trouble 1** likely to incur censure or punishment. **2** *colloquial* pregnant and unmarried. **take (the) trouble** exert oneself to do something. **troublemaker** person who habitually causes trouble. **troubleshooter 1** mediator in dispute. **2** person who traces and corrects faults in machinery etc.
- *noun* **1** adversity, affliction, anxiety, burden, difficulty, distress, grief, hardship, illness, misery, misfortune, pain, problem, sadness, sorrow, suffering, trial, tribulation, unhappiness, vexation, worry. **2, 3** bother, care, concern, effort, exertion, inconvenience, labour, pains, struggle, thought. **5** breakdown, defect, failure, fault, malfunction. **6** bother, commotion, conflict, discontent, discord, disorder, dissatisfaction, disturbance, fighting, fuss, misbehaviour, misconduct, naughtiness, *colloquial* row, strife, turmoil, unpleasantness, unrest, violence. ● *verb* **1, 4** afflict, agitate, alarm, annoy, bother, concern, distress, disturb, exasperate, grieve, harass, *colloquial* hassle, hurt, irk, irritate, molest, nag, pain, perturb, pester, *colloquial* plague, put out, ruffle, torment, upset, vex, worry. **2** (**troubled**) see WORRY *verb* 4. **5** bother, exert oneself, impose on, *formal* incommode, inconvenience, put out, take pains.
- □ **troublemaker** *agent provocateur*, agitator, criminal, culprit, delinquent, hooligan, malcontent, mischief-maker, offender, rabble-rouser, rascal, ringleader, ruffian, scandalmonger, stirrer, vandal, wrongdoer.

troublesome *adjective* causing trouble, annoying.
- annoying, badly behaved, bothersome, disobedient, disorderly, distressing, inconvenient, irksome, irritating, naughty, pestilential, rowdy, *colloquial* tiresome, trying, uncooperative, unruly, upsetting, vexatious, vexing, wearisome, worrying.

trough /trɒf/ *noun* **1** long narrow open receptacle for water, animal feed, etc. **2** channel or hollow like this. **3** elongated region of low barometric pressure.

trounce /traʊns/ *verb* (**-cing**) inflict severe defeat, beating, or punishment on.

troupe /tru:p/ *noun* company of actors, acrobats, etc.

trouper *noun* **1** member of theatrical troupe. **2** staunch colleague.

trousers /'traʊzəz/ *plural noun* two-legged outer garment from waist usually to ankles. □ **trouser suit** woman's suit of trousers and jacket.
- breeches, culottes, dungarees, jeans, jodhpurs, knickerbockers, *proprietary term* Levis, overalls, *US* pants, shorts, slacks, trews, trunks.

trousseau /'tru:səʊ/ *noun* (*plural* **-s** or **-x** /-z/) bride's collection of clothes etc.

trout /traʊt/ *noun* (*plural* same or **-s**) fish related to salmon.

trove /trəʊv/ *noun* treasure trove.

trowel /'traʊəl/ *noun* **1** flat-bladed tool for

spreading mortar etc. **2** scoop for lifting small plants or earth.

troy *noun* (in full **troy weight**) system of weights used for precious metals etc.

truant /ˈtruːənt/ *noun* **1** child who does not attend school. **2** person who avoids work etc. ● *adjective* idle, wandering. ● *verb* (also **play truant**) be truant. □ **truancy** *noun* (*plural* **-ies**).

■ *noun* absentee, malingerer, runaway, shirker, *slang* skiver, *slang* wag. ● *verb* (**play truant**) be absent, desert, malinger, *slang* skive, stay away. □ **truancy** absenteeism, malingering, shirking, *slang* skiving.

truce *noun* temporary agreement to cease hostilities.

■ armistice, ceasefire, moratorium, pact, peace, suspension of hostilities, treaty.

truck[1] *noun* **1** lorry. **2** open railway wagon for freight.

truck[2] *noun* □ **have no truck with** avoid dealing with.

trucker *noun esp. US* long-distance lorry driver.

truckle /ˈtrʌk(ə)l/ *noun* (in full **truckle-bed**) low bed on wheels, stored under another. ● *verb* (**-ling**) (+ *to*) submit obsequiously to.

truculent /ˈtrʌkjʊlənt/ *adjective* aggressively defiant. □ **truculence** *noun*. **truculently** *adverb*.

trudge *verb* (**-ging**) **1** walk laboriously. **2** traverse (distance) thus. ● *noun* trudging walk.

true *adjective* (**-r, -st**) **1** in accordance with fact or reality. **2** genuine. **3** loyal, faithful. **4** (+ *to*) accurately conforming to (type, standard). **5** correctly positioned or balanced; level. **6** exact, accurate. ● *adverb* **1** *archaic* truly. **2** accurately. **3** without variation. □ **out of true** out of alignment.

■ *adjective* **1** accurate, actual, confirmed, correct, exact, factual, faithful, faultless, flawless, literal, real, realistic, *formal* veracious, verified, veritable. **2** authentic, authorized, genuine, legal, legitimate, proper, real, rightful, valid, veritable. **3** confirmed, constant, dedicated, dependable, devoted, faithful, firm, honest, honourable, loyal, reliable, responsible, sincere, staunch, steadfast, steady, trustworthy, *archaic* or *jocular* trusty, unswerving, upright. **6** accurate, correct, exact, perfect, precise, right, *colloquial* spot on, unerring.

truffle /ˈtrʌf(ə)l/ *noun* **1** rich-flavoured underground fungus. **2** sweet made of soft chocolate mixture.

trug *noun* shallow oblong garden-basket.

truism /ˈtruːɪz(ə)m/ *noun* self-evident or hackneyed truth.

truly /ˈtruːlɪ/ *adverb* **1** sincerely. **2** really. **3** loyally. **4** accurately. □ **Yours truly 1** *written before signature at end of informal letter*. **2** *jocular* I, me.

trump[1] *noun* **1** playing card(s) of suit temporarily ranking above others. **2** (in *plural*) this suit. **3** *colloquial* helpful or excellent person. ● *verb* **1** defeat with trump. **2** *colloquial* outdo. □ **come or**

turn up trumps *colloquial* **1** turn out well or successfully. **2** be extremely successful or helpful. **trump card 1** card belonging to, or turned up to determine, trump suit. **2** *colloquial* valuable resource. **trump up** fabricate, invent (accusation, excuse, etc.).

trump[2] *noun archaic* trumpet-blast.

trumpery /ˈtrʌmpərɪ/ *noun* **1** worthless finery. **2** rubbish. ● *adjective* **1** showy but worthless; trashy. **2** shallow.

trumpet /ˈtrʌmpɪt/ *noun* **1** brass musical instrument with flared mouth and bright penetrating tone. **2** trumpet-shaped thing. **3** sound (as) of trumpet. ● *verb* (**-t-**) **1** blow trumpet. **2** (of elephant) make trumpet. **3** proclaim loudly. □ **trumpeter** *noun*.

truncate /trʌŋˈkeɪt/ *verb* (**-ting**) cut off top or end of; shorten. □ **truncation** *noun*.

truncheon /ˈtrʌntʃ(ə)n/ *noun* short club carried by police officer.

■ baton, club, cudgel, staff, stick.

trundle /ˈtrʌnd(ə)l/ *verb* (**-ling**) roll or move, esp. heavily or noisily.

trunk *noun* **1** main stem of tree. **2** body without limbs or head. **3** large luggage-box with hinged lid. **4** *US* boot of car. **5** elephant's elongated prehensile nose. **6** (in *plural*) men's close-fitting shorts worn for swimming etc. □ **trunk call** long-distance telephone call. **trunk line** main line of railway, telephone system, etc. **trunk road** important main road.

■ **1** bole, shaft, stalk, stem, stock. **2** body, torso. **3** box, case, chest, coffer, crate. **5** nose, proboscis.

truss *noun* **1** framework supporting roof, bridge, etc. **2** supporting surgical appliance for hernia etc. sufferers. **3** bundle of hay or straw. **4** cluster of flowers or fruit. ● *verb* **1** tie up (fowl) for cooking. **2** (often + *up*) tie (person) with arms to sides. **3** support with truss(es).

trust *noun* **1** firm belief that a person or thing may be relied on. **2** confident expectation. **3** responsibility. **4** *Law* arrangement involving trustees. **5** *Law* property so held. **6** group of trustees. **7** association of companies for reducing competition. ● *verb* **1** place trust in; believe in; rely on. **2** (+ *with*) give (person) charge of. **3** (often + *that*) hope earnestly that a thing will take place. **4** (+ *to*) consign (thing) to (person). **5** (+ *in*) place reliance in. **6** (+ *to*) place (esp. undue) reliance on. □ **in trust** (of property) managed by person(s) on behalf of another. **trustworthy** deserving of trust; reliable. **trustworthiness** *noun*. □ **trustful** *adjective*.

■ *noun* **1** assurance, belief, certainty, certitude, confidence, conviction, credence, faith, reliance. **4** trusteeship. ● *verb* **1, 5, 6** *colloquial* bank on, believe in, be sure of, confide in, count on, depend on, have confidence in, have faith in, rely on. **3** assume, expect, hope, imagine, presume, suppose, surmise. □ **trustworthy** constant, dependable, ethical, faithful, honest, honourable, loyal, moral, *colloquial* on the level, principled, reliable, responsible, safe, sensible, sincere, steadfast, steady, straightforward, true, *archaic* or *jocular* trusty, truthful, upright. □ **trustful** confiding, credulous, gullible, innocent, trusting, unquestioning, unsuspecting, unsuspicious, unwary.

trustee /trʌsˈtiː/ *noun* person or member of board managing property in trust with legal obligation to administer it solely for purposes specified. □ **trusteeship** *noun*.

trusting *adjective* having trust or confidence. □ **trustingly** *adverb*.

trusty *adjective* (**-ier**, **-iest**) *archaic* or *jocular* trustworthy. ● *noun* (*plural* **-ies**) prisoner given special privileges for good behaviour.

truth /truːθ/ *noun* (*plural* **truths** /truːðz/) **1** quality or state of being true. **2** what is true or accepted as true.

■ **1** accuracy, authenticity, correctness, exactness, factuality, genuineness, integrity, reliability, truthfulness, validity, veracity, *archaic* verity. **2** axiom, fact, maxim, truism, *archaic* verity.

truthful *adjective* **1** habitually speaking the truth. **2** (of story etc.) true. □ **truthfully** *adverb*. **truthfulness** *noun*.

■ accurate, candid, correct, credible, earnest, factual, faithful, forthright, frank, honest, proper, realistic, reliable, right, sincere, straight, straightforward, true, trustworthy, valid, *formal* veracious, unvarnished.

try *verb* (**-ies**, **-ied**) **1** attempt, endeavour. **2** test (quality); test by use or experiment; test qualities of. **3** make severe demands on. **4** examine effectiveness of for purpose. **5** ascertain state of fastening of (door etc.). **6** investigate and decide (case, issue) judicially. **7** (often + *for*) subject (person) to trial. **8** (+ *for*) apply or compete for. **9** (+ *for*) seek to attain. ● *noun* (*plural* **-ies**) **1** attempt. **2** *Rugby* touching-down of ball by player behind opposing goal line, scoring points and entitling player's side to a kick at goal. □ **try one's hand** (often + *at*) have attempt. **try it on** *colloquial* test how much unreasonable behaviour etc. will be tolerated. **try on** put (clothes etc.) on to test fit etc. **try-on** *noun colloquial* **1** act of trying it on or trying on clothes etc. **2** attempt to deceive. **try out 1** put to the test. **2** test thoroughly. **try-out** *noun* experimental test.

■ *verb* **1** aim, attempt, endeavour, *formal* essay, exert oneself, have a go at, *colloquial* have a stab at, make an effort, strain, strive, struggle, undertake, venture. **2** appraise, *colloquial* check out, evaluate, examine, experiment with, investigate, sample, test, try out. ● *noun* **1** attempt, *slang* bash, *colloquial* crack, effort, endeavour, go, *colloquial* shot, *colloquial* stab.

trying *adjective* annoying, exasperating; hard to bear.

■ see ANNOYING (ANNOY), TIRESOME 2.

tryst /trɪst/ *noun archaic* meeting, esp. of lovers.

tsar /zɑː/ *noun* (also **czar**) (*feminine* **tsarina** /-ˈriːnə/) *historical* emperor of Russia. □ **tsarist** *noun & adjective*.

tsetse /ˈtsetsɪ/ *noun* African fly feeding on blood and transmitting disease.

tsp. *abbreviation* (*plural* **tsps.**) teaspoonful.

TT *abbreviation* **1** Tourist Trophy. **2** tuberculin-tested. **3** teetotal(ler).

tub *noun* **1** open flat-bottomed usually round vessel. **2** tub-shaped (usually plastic) carton. **3** *colloquial* bath. **4** *colloquial* clumsy slow boat. ● *verb* (**-bb-**) plant, bathe, or wash in tub. □ **tub-thumper** *colloquial* ranting preacher or orator.

■ *noun* **1** barrel, butt, cask, drum, keg, pot, vat.

tuba /ˈtjuːbə/ *noun* (*plural* **-s**) low-pitched musical wind instrument made of brass.

tubby /ˈtʌbɪ/ *adjective* (**-ier**, **-iest**) short and fat. □ **tubbiness** *noun*.

tube *noun* **1** long hollow cylinder. **2** soft metal or plastic cylinder sealed at one end and having screw cap at other. **3** hollow cylindrical bodily organ. **4** *colloquial* London underground. **5** cathode ray tube, esp. in television. **6** (**the tube**) *esp. US colloquial* television. **7** *US* thermionic valve. **8** inner tube. ● *verb* (**-bing**) **1** equip with tubes. **2** enclose in tube.

■ *noun* **1** capillary, conduit, cylinder, duct, hose, main, pipe.

tuber /ˈtjuːbə/ *noun* short thick rounded root or underground stem of plant.

tubercle /ˈtjuːbək(ə)l/ *noun* small rounded swelling on part or in organ of body, esp. as characteristic of tuberculosis. □ **tubercle bacillus** bacterium causing tuberculosis. □ **tuberculous** /-ˈbɜːkjʊləs/ *adjective*.

tubercular /tjʊˈbɜːkjʊlə/ *adjective* of or affected with tuberculosis.

tuberculin /tjʊˈbɜːkjʊlɪn/ *noun* preparation from cultures of tubercle bacillus used in diagnosis and treatment of tuberculosis. □ **tuberculin-tested** (of milk) from cows shown to be free of tuberculosis.

tuberculosis /tjʊbɜːkjʊˈləʊsɪs/ *noun* infectious bacterial disease marked by tubercles, esp. in lungs.

tuberose /ˈtjuːbərəʊz/ *noun* plant with creamy-white fragrant flowers.

tuberous /ˈtjuːbərəs/ *adjective* **1** having tubers. **2** of or like a tuber.

tubing *noun* **1** length of tube. **2** quantity of or material for tubes.

tubular /ˈtjuːbjʊlə/ *adjective* **1** tube-shaped. **2** having or consisting of tubes.

TUC *abbreviation* Trades Union Congress.

tuck *verb* **1** (often + *in*, *up*) draw, fold, or turn outer or end parts of (cloth, clothes, etc.) close together. **2** (often + *in*, *up*) push in edges of bedclothes around (person). **3** draw together into small space. **4** stow (thing) away in specified place or way. **5** make stitched fold in (cloth etc.). ● *noun* **1** flattened fold sewn in garment etc. **2** *colloquial* food, esp. cakes and sweets. □ **tuck in**

colloquial eat heartily. **tuck shop** shop selling sweets etc. to schoolchildren.

■ *verb* **4** place, put away, shove, store, stow, stuff.

tucker /'tʌkə/ *noun Australian & NZ slang* food. ● *verb* (esp. in *passive*; often + *out*) *US & Australian colloquial* tire.

Tudor /'tjuːdə/ *adjective* **1** of royal family of England from Henry VII to Elizabeth I. **2** of this period (1485–1603). **3** of the architectural style of this period.

Tues. *abbreviation* (also **Tue.**) Tuesday.

Tuesday /'tjuːzdeɪ/ *noun* day of week following Monday.

tufa /'tjuːfə/ *noun* **1** porous rock formed round mineral springs. **2** tuff.

tuff *noun* rock formed from volcanic ash.

tuft *noun* bunch of threads, grass, feathers, hair, etc. held or growing together at base. □ **tufted** *adjective*. **tufty** *adjective*.

■ bunch, clump, cluster, tussock.

tug *verb* (**-gg-**) **1** (often + *at*) pull hard or violently. **2** tow (vessel) by tugboat. ● *noun* **1** hard, violent, or jerky pull. **2** sudden emotion. **3** (also **tugboat**) small powerful boat for towing ships. □ **tug of war** trial of strength between two sides pulling opposite ways on a rope.

■ *verb* drag, draw, haul, heave, jerk, lug, pluck, pull, twitch, wrench, *colloquial* yank.

tuition /tjuː'ɪʃ(ə)n/ *noun* **1** teaching. **2** fee for this.

tulip /'tjuːlɪp/ *noun* **1** bulbous spring-flowering plant with showy cup-shaped flowers. **2** its flower. □ **tulip-tree** tree with tulip-like flowers.

tulle /tjuːl/ *noun* soft fine silk etc. net for veils and dresses.

tumble /'tʌmb(ə)l/ *verb* (**-ling**) **1** (cause to) fall suddenly or headlong. **2** fall rapidly in amount etc. **3** roll, toss. **4** move or rush in headlong or blundering fashion. **5** (often + *to*) *colloquial* grasp meaning of. **6** fling or push roughly or carelessly. **7** perform acrobatic feats, esp. somersaults. **8** rumple, disarrange. ● *noun* **1** fall. **2** somersault or other acrobatic feat. □ **tumbledown** falling or fallen into ruin; dilapidated. **tumble-drier, -dryer** machine for drying washing in heated rotating drum. **tumble-dry** *verb*.

■ *verb* **1** collapse, drop, fall, flop, pitch, roll, stumble, topple, trip up. **2** collapse, drop, fall, nosedive, plummet. **6** dump, fling, shove, spill, throw, toss. **8** disarrange, jumble, mix up, rumple. □ **tumbledown** broken down, crumbling, decrepit, derelict, dilapidated, ramshackle, rickety, ruined, shaky, tottering.

tumbler *noun* **1** drinking glass without handle or foot. **2** acrobat. **3** part of mechanism of lock.

tumbrel /'tʌmbr(ə)l/ *noun* (also **tumbril**) *historical* open cart in which condemned people were carried to guillotine during French Revolution.

tumescent /tjʊ'mes(ə)nt/ *adjective* swelling. □ **tumescence** *noun*.

tumid /'tjuːmɪd/ *adjective* **1** swollen, inflated. **2** pompous. □ **tumidity** /-'mɪd-/ *noun*.

tummy /'tʌmɪ/ *noun* (*plural* **-ies**) *colloquial* stomach. □ **tummy-ache** pain in stomach.

tumour /'tjuːmə/ *noun* (*US* **tumor**) abnormal or morbid swelling in the body.

tumult /'tjuːmʌlt/ *noun* **1** uproar, din. **2** angry demonstration by mob; riot. **3** conflict of emotions etc. □ **tumultuous** /tjʊ'mʌltʃʊəs/ *adjective*.

■ ado, agitation, chaos, commotion, confusion, din, disturbance, excitement, ferment, fracas, frenzy, hubbub, hullabaloo, riot, *colloquial* rumpus, storm, strife, tempest, unrest, upheaval, uproar, welter. □ **tumultuous** agitated, boisterous, confused, excited, frenzied, hectic, passionate, stormy, tempestuous, turbulent, unrestrained, unruly, violent, wild.

tumulus /'tjuːmjʊləs/ *noun* (*plural* **-li** /-laɪ/) ancient burial mound.

tun *noun* **1** large cask. **2** brewer's fermenting-vat.

tuna /'tjuːnə/ *noun* (*plural* same or **-s**) **1** large edible marine fish. **2** (in full **tuna-fish**) its flesh as food.

tundra /'tʌndrə/ *noun* vast level treeless Arctic region with permafrost.

tune *noun* **1** melody. **2** correct pitch or intonation. ● *verb* (**-ning**) **1** put (musical instrument) in tune. **2** (often + *in*) adjust (radio etc.) to desired frequency etc. **3** adjust (engine etc.) to run smoothly. □ **change one's tune 1** voice different opinion. **2** become more respectful. **tune up** bring instrument(s) to proper pitch. **tuning fork** two-pronged steel fork giving particular note when struck.

■ *noun* **1** air, melody, motif, song, strain, theme. ● *verb* **1** adjust, attune. **2, 3** adjust, calibrate, regulate, set.

tuneful *adjective* melodious, musical. □ **tunefully** *adverb*. **tunefulness** *noun*.

■ catchy, euphonious, mellifluous, melodic, melodious, musical, pleasant, singable, sweet-sounding.

tuneless *adjective* unmelodious, unmusical. □ **tunelessly** *adverb*.

tuner *noun* **1** person who tunes pianos etc. **2** part of radio or television receiver for tuning.

tungsten /'tʌŋst(ə)n/ *noun* heavy steel-grey metallic element.

tunic /'tjuːnɪk/ *noun* **1** close-fitting short coat of police or military uniform. **2** loose often sleeveless garment.

tunnel /'tʌn(ə)l/ *noun* **1** underground passage dug through hill, or under river, road, etc. **2** underground passage dug by animal. ● *verb* (**-ll-**; *US* **-l-**) **1** (+ *through, into*) make tunnel through (hill etc.). **2** make (one's way) so. □ **tunnel vision 1** restricted vision. **2** *colloquial* inability to grasp wider implications of situation etc.

■ *noun* **1** mine, passage, passageway, shaft, subway, underpass. **2** burrow, hole. ● *verb* **1** burrow, dig, excavate, mine, penetrate.

tunny /'tʌnɪ/ *noun* (*plural* same or **-ies**) tuna.

tuppence = TWOPENCE.

tuppenny = TWOPENNY.

Tupperware /'tʌpəweə/ *noun proprietary term* range of plastic containers for food.

turban /'tɜ:bən/ *noun* **1** man's headdress of fabric wound round cap or head, worn esp. by Muslims and Sikhs. **2** woman's hat resembling this.

turbid /'tɜ:bɪd/ *adjective* **1** muddy, thick; not clear. **2** confused, disordered. □ **turbidity** /-'bɪd-/ *noun*.

USAGE *Turbid* is sometimes confused with *turgid*.

turbine /'tɜ:baɪn/ *noun* rotary motor driven by flow of water, gas, etc.

turbo- *combining form* turbine.

turbocharger /'tɜ:bəʊtʃɑ:dʒə/ *noun* (also **turbo**) supercharger driven by turbine powered by engine's exhaust gases.

turbojet /'tɜ:bəʊdʒet/ *noun* **1** jet engine in which jet also operates turbine-driven air-compressor. **2** aircraft with this.

turboprop /'tɜ:bəʊprɒp/ *noun* **1** jet engine in which turbine is used as in turbojet and also to drive propeller. **2** aircraft with this.

turbot /'tɜ:bət/ *noun* (*plural* same or **-s**) large flatfish valued as food.

turbulent /'tɜ:bjʊlənt/ *adjective* **1** disturbed, in commotion. **2** (of flow of air, water, etc.) varying irregularly. **3** riotous, restless. □ **turbulence** *noun*. **turbulently** *adverb*.

■ **1** agitated, boisterous, confused, disordered, excited, hectic, passionate, restless, seething, turbid, unrestrained, violent, volatile, wild. **2** blustery, bumpy, choppy (*sea*), rough, stormy, tempestuous, violent, wild, windy. **3** badly behaved, disorderly, lawless, obstreperous, riotous, rowdy, undisciplined, unruly.

tureen /tjʊə'ri:n/ *noun* deep covered dish for soup.

turf *noun* (*plural* **-s** or **turves**) **1** short grass with surface earth bound together by its roots. **2** piece of this cut from ground. **3** slab of peat for fuel. **4** (**the turf**) horse racing. **5** (**the turf**) racecourse. ● *verb* **1** cover (ground) with turf. **2** (+ *out*) *colloquial* expel, eject. □ **turf accountant** bookmaker. □ **turfy** *adjective*.

■ *noun* **1** grass, grassland, green, lawn, *literary* sward.

turgid /'tɜ:dʒɪd/ *adjective* **1** swollen, inflated. **2** (of language) pompous, bombastic. □ **turgidity** /-'dʒɪd-/ *noun*.

USAGE *Turgid* is sometimes confused with *turbid*.

■ **2** affected, bombastic, flowery, fulsome, grandiose, high-flown, overblown, pompous, pretentious, stilted, wordy.

Turk *noun* native or national of Turkey.

turkey /'tɜ:kɪ/ *noun* (*plural* **-s**) **1** large originally American bird bred for food. **2** its flesh. □ **turkeycock** male turkey.

Turkish *adjective* of Turkey. ● *noun* language of Turkey. □ **Turkish bath 1** hot-air or steam bath followed by massage etc. **2** (in *singular* or *plural*) building for this. **Turkish carpet** thick-piled woollen carpet with bold design. **Turkish delight** kind of gelatinous sweet. **Turkish towel** one made of cotton terry.

turmeric /'tɜ:mərɪk/ *noun* **1** E. Indian plant of ginger family. **2** its rhizome powdered as flavouring or dye.

turmoil /'tɜ:mɔɪl/ *noun* **1** violent confusion. **2** din and bustle.

■ bedlam, bustle, chaos, commotion, confusion, disorder, disturbance, ferment, hubbub, hullabaloo, pandemonium, riot, *colloquial* row, *colloquial* rumpus, tumult, turbulence, unrest, upheaval, uproar, welter.

turn *verb* **1** move around point or axis; give or receive rotary motion. **2** change from one side to another; invert, reverse. **3** give new direction to. **4** take new direction. **5** aim in certain way. **6** (+ *into*) change in nature, form, or condition to. **7** (+ *to*) set about. **8** (+ *to*) have recourse to. **9** (+ *to*) consider next. **10** become. **11** (+ *against*) make or become hostile to. **12** (+ *on, upon*) face hostilely. **13** change colour. **14** (of milk) become sour. **15** cause (milk) to become sour. **16** (of stomach) be nauseated. **17** cause (stomach) to be nauseated. **18** (of head) become giddy. **19** translate. **20** move to other side of; go round. **21** pass age or time of. **22** (+ *on*) depend on. **23** send, put; cause to go. **24** remake (sheet, shirt collar, etc.). **25** make (profit). **26** divert (bullet). **27** shape (object) in lathe. **28** give (esp. elegant) form to. ● *noun* **1** turning; rotary motion. **2** changed or change of direction or tendency. **3** point of turning or change. **4** turning of road. **5** change of direction of tide. **6** change in course of events. **7** tendency; formation. **8** opportunity, obligation, etc. that comes successively to each of several people etc. **9** short walk or ride. **10** short performance on stage, in circus, etc. **11** service of specified kind. **12** purpose. **13** *colloquial* momentary nervous shock. **14** *Music* ornament of principal note with those above and below it. □ **in turn** in succession. **take (it in) turns** act alternately. **turn-about 1** turning about. **2** radical or abrupt change. **turncoat** person who changes sides. **turn down 1** reject. **2** reduce volume or strength of (sound, heat, etc.) by turning knob. **3** fold down. **turn in 1** hand in. **2** achieve. **3** incline inwards. **4** *colloquial* go to bed. **turnkey** *archaic* jailer. **turn off 1** stop flow or working of by means of tap, switch, etc. **2** enter side road. **3** *colloquial* cause to lose interest. **turn-off 1** turning off a road. **2** *colloquial* something that repels or causes loss of interest. **turn of phrase** linguistic expression. **turn on 1** start flow or working of by means of tap, switch, etc. **2** *colloquial* arouse, esp. sexually. **turn one's back on** see BACK. **turn out 1** expel. **2** extinguish (light etc.). **3** dress; equip. **4** produce (goods etc.). **5** empty; clean out. **6** (cause to) assemble. **7** prove to be the case; result. **8** (usually + *to be*) be found. **turnout 1** number of people who attend meeting etc. **2** equipage. **turn over 1** reverse position of. **2** cause (engine etc.) to run. **3** (of engine) start running. **4** consider thoroughly. **5** (+ *to*) transfer care or conduct of (person, thing) to (person). **turnover 1** turning over. **2** gross amount of money taken in business. **3** rate of sale and replacement of goods. **4** rate at which people enter and leave employment etc. **5** small pie with pastry folded over filling. **turnpike** *US & historical* road on which toll is charged. **turnstile** revolving gate with arms. **turntable** circular revolving plate or platform. **turn tail** turn one's back; run away. **turn the corner 1** pass round corner. **2** pass critical point in illness, difficulty, etc. **turn to** begin work. **turn turtle** capsize. **turn up 1** increase (volume or strength of) by turning knob etc. **2** discover; reveal. **3** be found. **4** happen; arrive. **5** shorten (garment etc.). **6** fold over or upwards. **turn-up** *noun* **1** turned-up end of trouser leg. **2** *colloquial* unexpected happening. **turn up one's nose** see NOSE.

■ *verb* **1** circle, coil, curl, gyrate, loop, orbit, pivot, revolve, roll, rotate, spin, spiral, swivel, twirl, twist, whirl, wind. **2** flip over, invert, reverse, turn over, turn upside down. **3, 4** bend, change direction, corner, deviate, divert, go round a corner, negotiate a corner, shift, swerve, veer, wheel, yaw. **6** (*turn into*) become, be transformed into, change into, convert into, develop into, grow into, make into, metamorphose into, remake as, transform into. **22** (*turn on*) depend on, hinge on, pivot on, revolve around. ● *noun* **1** circle, coil, curve, cycle, loop, pirouette, revolution, roll, rotation, spin, twirl, twist, whirl. **2** deviation, reversal, shift, U-turn. **3** crossroads, junction, turning, turning point. **4** angle, bend, corner, curve, hairpin bend, loop, meander, zigzag. **8** chance, go, innings, opportunity, *colloquial* shot, stint. **10** see PERFORMANCE 3. **13** fright, scare, shock, start. □ **turn down 1** see REJECT *verb* 2. **turn off 1** disconnect, switch off. **2** see DEVIATE. **3** see REPEL 2. **turn on 2** see ATTRACT 3. **turn out 1** see EXPEL 1. **4** see PRODUCE *verb* 1. **7** see HAPPEN 1. **turn over 1** see OVERTURN 1. **4** see CONSIDER 1. **turnover 2** business, revenue. **turn tail** see ESCAPE *verb* 1. **turn up 2** see DISCOVER 1, 2. **4** see ARRIVE 1.

turner *noun* lathe-worker.

turnery *noun* **1** objects made on lathe. **2** work with lathe.

turning *noun* **1** road branching off another. **2** place where this occurs. **3** use of lathe. **4** (in *plural*) chips or shavings from this. □ **turning circle** smallest circle in which vehicle can turn. **turning point** point at which decisive change occurs.

■ □ **turning point** watershed.

turnip /ˈtɜːnɪp/ *noun* **1** plant with globular root. **2** its root as vegetable.

turpentine /ˈtɜːpəntaɪn/ *noun* **1** resin from any of various trees. **2** (in full **oil of turpentine**) volatile inflammable oil distilled from turpentine and used in mixing paints etc.

turpitude /ˈtɜːpɪtjuːd/ *noun formal* depravity, wickedness.

turps *noun colloquial* oil of turpentine.

turquoise /ˈtɜːkwɔɪz/ *noun* **1** opaque semi-precious stone, usually greenish-blue. **2** this colour. ● *adjective* of this colour.

turret /ˈtʌrɪt/ *noun* **1** small tower, esp. decorating building. **2** usually revolving armoured structure for gun and gunners on ship, fort, etc. **3** rotating holder for tools in lathe etc. □ **turreted** *adjective*.

turtle /ˈtɜːt(ə)l/ *noun* aquatic reptile with flippers and horny shell. □ **turtle-neck** high close-fitting neck on knitted garment.

turtle-dove /ˈtɜːt(ə)ldʌv/ *noun* wild dove noted for soft cooing and affection for its mate.

tusk *noun* long pointed tooth, esp. projecting beyond mouth as in elephant, walrus, or boar. □ **tusked** *adjective*.

tussle /ˈtʌs(ə)l/ *noun & verb* (**-ling**) struggle, scuffle.

tussock /ˈtʌsək/ *noun* clump of grass etc.

tut = TUT-TUT.

tutelage /ˈtjuːtɪlɪdʒ/ *noun* **1** guardianship. **2** being under this. **3** tuition.

tutelary /ˈtjuːtɪlərɪ/ *adjective* **1** serving as guardian or protector. **2** of guardian.

tutor /ˈtjuːtə/ *noun* **1** private teacher. **2** university teacher supervising studies or welfare of assigned undergraduates. ● *verb* act as tutor (to). □ **tutorship** *noun*.

tutorial /tjuːˈtɔːrɪəl/ *adjective* of tutor or tuition. ● *noun* period of tuition for single student or small group.

tutti /ˈtʊtɪ/ *Music adjective & adverb* with all instruments or voices together. ● *noun* (*plural* **-s**) tutti passage.

tut-tut /tʌtˈtʌt/ (also **tut**) *interjection: expressing rebuke or impatience.* ● *noun* such exclamation. ● *verb* (**-tt-**) exclaim thus.

tutu /ˈtuːtuː/ *noun* (*plural* **-s**) dancer's short skirt of stiffened frills.

tuxedo /tʌkˈsiːdəʊ/ *noun* (*plural* **-s** or **-es**) *US* (suit including) dinner jacket.

TV *abbreviation* television.

twaddle /ˈtwɒd(ə)l/ *noun* silly writing or talk.

twain *adjective & noun archaic* two.

twang *noun* **1** sound made by plucked string of musical instrument, bow, etc. **2** nasal quality of voice. ● *verb* (cause to) emit twang. □ **twangy** *adjective*.

tweak *verb* **1** pinch and twist; jerk. **2** adjust finely. ● *noun* such action.

twee *adjective* (**tweer** /ˈtwiːə/, **tweest** /ˈtwiːɪst/) *derogatory* affectedly dainty or quaint.

tweed *noun* **1** rough-surfaced woollen cloth usually of mixed colours. **2** (in *plural*) clothes of tweed.

tweedy *adjective* (**-ier**, **-iest**) **1** of or dressed in tweed. **2** heartily informal.

tweet *noun* chirp of small bird. ● *verb* make this noise.

tweeter *noun* loudspeaker for high frequencies.

tweezers /'twi:zəz/ *plural noun* small pair of pincers for picking up small objects, plucking out hairs, etc.

twelfth *adjective & noun* **1** next after eleventh. **2** any of twelve equal parts of thing. □ **Twelfth Night** evening of 5 Jan.

twelve /twelv/ *adjective & noun* one more than eleven.

twenty /'twentɪ/ *adjective & noun* (*plural* **-ies**) twice ten. □ **twentieth** *adjective & noun*.

twerp *noun slang* stupid or objectionable person.

twice *adverb* **1** two times; on two occasions. **2** doubly.

twiddle /'twɪd(ə)l/ *verb* (**-ling**) twist or play idly about. ● *noun* act of twiddling. □ **twiddle one's thumbs 1** make them rotate round each other. **2** have nothing to do.
 ■ *verb* fiddle with, fidget with, fool with, mess with, twirl, twist.

twig[1] *noun* very small branch of tree or shrub.
 ■ branch, offshoot, shoot, stalk, stem, stick.

twig[2] *verb* (**-gg-**) *colloquial* understand, realize.

twilight /'twaɪlaɪt/ *noun* **1** light from sky when sun is below horizon, esp. in evening. **2** period of this. **3** faint light. **4** period of decline. □ **twilight zone 1** decrepit urban area. **2** undefined or intermediate area.
 ■ **1** dusk, evening, *archaic* or *poetical* eventide, *poetical* gloaming, gloom, half-light, nightfall, sundown, sunset.

twilit /'twaɪlɪt/ *adjective* dimly illuminated (as) by twilight.

twill *noun* fabric woven with surface of parallel diagonal ridges. □ **twilled** *adjective*.

twin *noun* **1** each of closely related pair, esp. of children or animals born at a birth. **2** counterpart. ● *adjective* forming, or born as one of, twins. ● *verb* (**-nn-**) **1** join closely. **2** (+ *with*) pair with. **3** bear twins. **4** link (town) with one abroad for social and cultural exchange. □ **twin bed** each of pair of single beds. **twin set** woman's matching cardigan and jumper. **twin town** town twinned with another.
 ■ *noun* **2** *colloquial* clone, counterpart, double, duplicate, lookalike, match, pair, *colloquial* spitting image. ● *adjective* balancing, corresponding, double, duplicate, identical, indistinguishable, matching, paired, similar, symmetrical.

twine *noun* **1** strong coarse string of twisted strands of fibre. **2** coil, twist. ● *verb* (**-ning**) **1** coil, twist. **2** form (string etc.) by twisting strands.

twinge /twɪndʒ/ *noun* sharp momentary local pain.

twinkle /'twɪŋk(ə)l/ *verb* (**-ling**) **1** shine with rapidly intermittent light. **2** sparkle. **3** move rapidly. ● *noun* **1** sparkle or gleam of eyes. **2** twinkling light. **3** light rapid movement. □ **in a twinkle (or a twinkling or the twinkle of an eye)** in an instant. □ **twinkly** *adjective*.

twirl *verb* spin, swing, or twist quickly and lightly round. ● *noun* **1** twirling. **2** flourish made with pen.
 ■ *verb* gyrate, pirouette, revolve, rotate, spin, turn, twiddle, twist, wheel, whirl, wind.

twist *verb* **1** change the form of by rotating one end and not the other or the two ends opposite ways. **2** undergo such change. **3** wrench or distort by twisting. **4** wind (strands etc.) about each other. **5** form (rope etc.) thus. **6** (cause to) take spiral form. **7** take winding course. **8** move in winding manner. **9** (+ *off*) break off by twisting. **10** misrepresent meaning of (words). **11** *colloquial* cheat. **12** (as **twisted** *adjective*) perverted. **13** dance the twist. ● *noun* **1** twisting, being twisted. **2** thing made by twisting. **3** point at which thing twists. **4** *usually derogatory* peculiar tendency of mind, character, etc. **5** unexpected development. **6** (**the twist**) 1960s dance with twisting hips. □ **twisty** *adjective* (**-ier, -iest**).
 ■ *verb* **1–3** buckle, contort, crinkle, crumple, distort, screw up, sprain, turn, warp, wrench, wrinkle. **4, 5** braid, entangle, entwine, intertwine, interweave, plait, tangle, weave, wind. **6–8** bend, coil, corkscrew, curl, curve, loop, revolve, rotate, screw, spin, spiral, squirm, turn, twirl, wind, wreathe, wriggle, writhe, zigzag. **9** see WRENCH *verb* 1,2. **10** alter, change, falsify, misquote, misrepresent. **12** (**twisted**) see PERVERT *verb* 3. ● *noun* **1** rotation, spin, turn, twirl, wind. **3** bend, coil, curl, kink, knot, loop, tangle, turn, zigzag. **5** revelation, surprise ending. □ **twisty** circuitous, coiled, contorted, crooked, curving, curvy, indirect, looped, meandering, misshapen, roundabout, serpentine, sinuous, snaking, tortuous, twisted, twisting, twisting and turning, winding, zigzag.

twister *noun colloquial* swindler.

twit[1] *noun slang* foolish person.

twit[2] *verb* (**-tt-**) reproach, taunt, usually good-humouredly.

twitch *verb* **1** quiver or jerk spasmodically. **2** pull sharply at. ● *noun* **1** twitching movement. **2** pang, twinge. □ **twitchy** *adjective* (**-ier, -iest**).
 ■ *verb* **1** fidget, flutter, jerk, jump, start, tremble. **2** see JERK[1] *verb*. ● *noun* **1** blink, convulsion, flutter, jerk, jump, spasm, tic, tremor.

twitter /'twɪtə/ *verb* **1** (esp. of bird) utter succession of light tremulous sounds. **2** utter or express thus. ● *noun* **1** twittering. **2** *colloquial* tremulously excited state.

two /tu:/ *adjective & noun* one more than one. □ **two-dimensional 1** having or appearing to have length and breadth but no depth. **2** superficial. **two-edged** having both good and bad effect; ambiguous. **two-faced** insincere. **two-handed 1** having 2 hands. **2** used with both hands or by 2 people. **twopence** /'tʌpəns/ **1** sum of 2 pence. **2** (esp. with negative) *colloquial* thing of little value. **twopenny** /'tʌpənɪ/ **1** costing twopence. **2** *colloquial* cheap, worthless. **two-piece** (suit etc.) comprising 2 matching parts. **two-ply 1** (wool etc.) having 2 strands. **2** (plywood) having 2 layers. **two-step** dance in march or polka time. **two-stroke** (of internal-combustion engine) having power cycle completed in one up-and-down movement of piston. **two-time** *colloquial* **1** be unfaithful to. **2** swindle. **two-tone** having two colours or sounds. **two-way 1** involving or operating in two directions. **2** (of radio) capable of transmitting and receiving signals.

■ *noun* couple, duet, duo, pair, twosome.

twofold *adjective & adverb* twice as much or many.

twosome *noun* two people together.

tycoon /taɪˈkuːn/ *noun* business magnate.

tying *present participle* of TIE.

tyke /taɪk/ *noun* (also **tike**) **1** objectionable or coarse man. **2** small child.

tympani = TIMPANI.

tympanum /'tɪmpənəm/ *noun* (*plural* **-s** or **-na**) **1** middle ear; eardrum. **2** vertical space forming centre of pediment. **3** space between lintel and arch above door etc.

type /taɪp/ *noun* **1** sort, class, kind. **2** person, thing, or event exemplifying class or group. **3** *colloquial* person, esp. of specified character. **4** object, idea, or work of art serving as model. **5** small block with raised character on upper surface for printing. **6** printing types collectively. **7** typeset or printed text. ● *verb* (**-ping**) **1** write with typewriter. **2** typecast. **3** assign to type; classify. □ **-type** made of; resembling; functioning as. **typecast** cast (performer) repeatedly in similar roles. **typeface 1** inked surface of type. **2** set of characters in one design. **typescript** typewritten document. **typesetter 1** compositor. **2** composing machine. **typewriter** machine with keys for producing printline characters. **typewritten** produced thus.

■ *noun* **1** category, class, classification, form, genre, group, kind, mark, sort, species, variety. **2, 4** archetype, embodiment, epitome, example, model, pattern, personification, prototype, standard. **5–7** characters, font, fount, lettering, letters, print, printing, typeface.

typhoid /'taɪfɔɪd/ *noun* (in full **typhoid fever**) infectious bacterial fever attacking intestines.

typhoon /taɪˈfuːn/ *noun* violent hurricane in E. Asian seas.

typhus /'taɪfəs/ *noun* an acute infectious fever.

typical /'tɪpɪk(ə)l/ *adjective* **1** serving as characteristic example. **2** (often + *of*) characteristic of particular person or thing. □ **typicality** /-ˈkæl-/ *noun*. **typically** *adverb*.

■ average, characteristic, conventional, normal, ordinary, orthodox, predictable, representative, standard, stock, unsurprising, usual.

typify /'tɪpɪfaɪ/ *verb* (**-ies, -ied**) **1** be typical of. **2** represent by or as type. □ **typification** *noun*.

typist /'taɪpɪst/ *noun* (esp. professional) user of typewriter.

typo /'taɪpəʊ/ *noun* (*plural* **-s**) *colloquial* typographical error.

typography /taɪˈpɒɡrəfɪ/ *noun* **1** printing as an art. **2** style and appearance of printed matter. □ **typographer** *noun*. **typographical** /-pəˈɡræf-/ *adjective*. **typographically** /-pəˈɡræf-/ *adverb*.

tyrannical /tɪˈrænɪk(ə)l/ *adjective* acting like or characteristic of tyrant.

■ absolute, authoritarian, autocratic, *colloquial* bossy, cruel, despotic, dictatorial, domineering, harsh, high-handed, illiberal, imperious, oppressive, overbearing, ruthless, severe, totalitarian, tyrannous, undemocratic, unjust.

tyrannize /'tɪrənaɪz/ *verb* (also **-ise**) (**-zing** or **-sing**) (often + *over*) treat despotically.

tyrannosaurus /tɪrænəˈsɔːrəs/ *noun* (*plural* **-ruses**) very large carnivorous dinosaur with short front legs and powerful tail.

tyranny /'tɪrənɪ/ *noun* (*plural* **-ies**) **1** cruel and arbitrary use of authority. **2** rule by tyrant. **3** period of this. **4** state thus ruled. □ **tyrannous** *adjective*.

tyrant /'taɪərənt/ *noun* **1** oppressive or cruel ruler. **2** person exercising power arbitrarily or cruelly.

■ autocrat, despot, dictator, hard taskmaster, oppressor, slave-driver.

tyre /'taɪə/ *noun* (*US* **tire**) rubber covering, usually inflated, placed round vehicle's wheel for cushioning and grip.

tyro = TIRO.

tzatziki /tsætˈsiːkɪ/ *noun* Greek dish of yoghurt with cucumber and garlic.

Uu

U¹ □ **U-boat** *historical* German submarine. **U-turn 1** U-shaped turn of vehicle to face in opposite direction. **2** reversal of policy.

U² *abbreviation* (of film classified as suitable for all) universal.

UB40 *abbreviation* **1** card for claiming unemployment benefit. **2** *colloquial* unemployed person.

ubiquitous /juː'bɪkwɪtəs/ *adjective* **1** (seemingly) present everywhere simultaneously. **2** often encountered. □ **ubiquity** *noun*.

UCAS /'juːkas/ *abbreviation* Universities and Colleges Admissions Service.

UCCA /'ʌkə/ *abbreviation historical* Universities Central Council on Admissions.

UDA *abbreviation* Ulster Defence Association.

udder /'ʌdə/ *noun* baglike milk-producing organ of cow etc.

UDI *abbreviation* unilateral declaration of independence.

UDR *abbreviation* Ulster Defence Regiment.

UEFA /juː'eɪfə/ *abbreviation* Union of European Football Associations.

UFO /'juːfəʊ/ *noun* (also **ufo**) (*plural* **-s**) unidentified flying object.

ugh /əx, ʌg/ *interjection: expressing disgust etc.*

Ugli /'ʌglɪ/ *noun* (*plural* **-lis** or **-lies**) *proprietary term* mottled green and yellow citrus fruit.

ugly /'ʌglɪ/ *adjective* (**-ier, -iest**) **1** unpleasant to eye, ear, mind, etc. **2** discreditable. **3** threatening, dangerous. **4** morally repulsive. □ **ugly duckling** person lacking early promise but blossoming later. □ **uglify** *verb* (**-ies, -ied**). **ugliness** *noun*.

■ **1** deformed, disfigured, disgusting, displeasing, dreadful, frightful, ghastly, grim, grisly, grotesque, gruesome, hideous, *colloquial* horrible, *colloquial* horrid, ill-favoured, inartistic, inelegant, loathsome, misshapen, monstrous, nasty, objectionable, odious, offensive, plain, repellent, repulsive, revolting, shocking, sickening, tasteless, *colloquial* terrible, unattractive, unpleasant, unprepossessing, unsightly, *colloquial* vile. **3** angry, cross, dangerous, forbidding, hostile, menacing, ominous, sinister, surly, threatening, unfriendly. **4** see VILE 2.

UHF *abbreviation* ultra-high frequency.

uh-huh /'ʌhʌ/ *interjection colloquial* yes.

UHT *abbreviation* ultra heat treated (esp. of milk, for long keeping).

UK *abbreviation* United Kingdom.

Ukrainian /juː'kreɪnɪən/ *noun* native, national, or language of Ukraine. ● *adjective* of Ukraine.

ukulele /juːkə'leɪlɪ/ *noun* small 4-stringed guitar.

ulcer /'ʌlsə/ *noun* **1** (often pus-forming) open sore on or in body. **2** corrupting influence. □ **ulcerous** *adjective*.

ulcerate /'ʌlsəreɪt/ *verb* (**-ting**) form into or affect with ulcer. □ **ulceration** *noun*.

ullage /'ʌlɪdʒ/ *noun* **1** amount by which cask etc. falls short of being full. **2** loss by evaporation or leakage.

ulna /'ʌlnə/ *noun* (*plural* **ulnae** /-niː/) **1** longer bone of forearm, opposite thumb. **2** corresponding bone in animal's foreleg or bird's wing. □ **ulnar** *adjective*.

ulster /'ʌlstə/ *noun* long loose overcoat of rough cloth.

Ulsterman /'ʌlstəmən/ *noun* (*feminine* **Ulsterwoman**) native of Ulster.

ult. *abbreviation* ultimo.

ulterior /ʌl'tɪərɪə/ *adjective* not admitted; hidden, secret.

■ concealed, covert, hidden, personal, private, secondary, secret, undeclared, underlying, undisclosed, unexpressed.

ultimate /'ʌltɪmət/ *adjective* **1** last, final. **2** fundamental, basic. ● *noun* **1** (**the ultimate**) best achievable or imaginable. **2** final or fundamental fact or principle. □ **ultimately** *adverb*.

■ *adjective* **1** closing, concluding, eventual, extreme, final, furthest, last, terminal, terminating. **2** basic, fundamental, primary, root, underlying.

ultimatum /ʌltɪ'meɪtəm/ *noun* (*plural* **-s**) final statement of terms, rejection of which could cause hostility etc.

ultimo /'ʌltɪməʊ/ *adjective* of last month.

ultra /'ʌltrə/ *adjective* extreme, esp. in religion or politics. ● *noun* extremist.

ultra- *combining form* **1** extreme(ly), excessive(ly). **2** beyond.

ultra-high /ʌltrə'haɪ/ *adjective* (of frequency) between 300 and 3000 megahertz.

ultramarine /ʌltrəmə'riːn/ *noun* (colour of) brilliant deep blue pigment. ● *adjective* of this colour.

ultrasonic /ʌltrə'sɒnɪk/ *adjective* of or using sound waves pitched above range of human hearing. □ **ultrasonically** *adverb*.

ultrasound /'ʌltrəsaʊnd/ *noun* ultrasonic waves.

ultraviolet /ʌltrə'vaɪələt/ *adjective* of or using radiation just beyond violet end of spectrum.

ultra vires /ʌltrə 'vaɪəriːz/ *adverb & adjective* beyond one's legal power or authority. [Latin]

ululate /'juːljʊleɪt/ *verb* (**-ting**) howl, wail. □ **ululation** *noun*.

um *interjection: representing hesitation or pause in speech*.

umbel /'ʌmb(ə)l/ *noun* flower-cluster with stalks springing from common centre. □ **umbellate** *adjective*.

umbelliferous /ʌmbə'lɪfərəs/ *adjective* (of plant, e.g. parsley or carrot) bearing umbels.

umber /'ʌmbə/ *noun* (colour of) dark brown earth used as pigment. ● *adjective* umbercoloured.

umbilical /ʌm'bɪlɪk(ə)l/ *adjective* of navel. □ **umbilical cord** cordlike structure attaching foetus to placenta.

umbilicus /ʌm'bɪlɪkəs/ *noun* (*plural* **-ci** /-saɪ/ or **-cuses**) navel.

umbra /'ʌmbrə/ *noun* (*plural* **-s** or **-brae** /-briː/) shadow cast by moon or earth in eclipse.

umbrage /'ʌmbrɪdʒ/ *noun* offence taken.

umbrella /ʌm'brelə/ *noun* **1** collapsible cloth canopy on central stick for protection against rain, sun, etc. **2** protection, patronage. **3** coordinating agency.

umlaut /'ʊmlaʊt/ *noun* **1** mark (¨) over vowel, esp. in German, indicating change in pronunciation. **2** such a change.

umpire /'ʌmpaɪə/ *noun* person enforcing rules and settling disputes in game, contest, etc. ● *verb* (**-ring**) (often + *for*, *in*, etc.) act as umpire (in).
■ *noun* adjudicator, arbiter, arbitrator, judge, moderator, official, *colloquial* ref, referee.

umpteen /'ʌmptiːn/ *adjective & noun colloquial* very many. □ **umpteenth** *adjective & noun*.

UN *abbreviation* United Nations.

un- *prefix* **1** *added to adjectives, nouns, and adverbs, meaning:* not; non-; reverse of; lack of. **2** *added to verbs, verbal derivatives, etc. to express contrary or reverse action, deprivation of, or removal from*. For words starting with *un-* that are not found below, the root-words should be consulted.

unable /ʌn'eɪb(ə)l/ *adjective* not able.
■ impotent, incompetent, powerless, unfit, unprepared, unqualified.

unacceptable /ʌnək'septəb(ə)l/ *adjective* not acceptable. □ **unacceptably** *adverb*.
■ bad, forbidden, illegal, improper, inadequate, inadmissible, inappropriate, inexcusable, insupportable, intolerable, invalid, taboo, unsatisfactory, unsuitable, wrong.

unaccompanied /ʌnə'kʌmpənɪd/ *adjective* alone.
■ alone, lone, single-handed, sole, solo, unaided, unescorted.

unaccountable /ʌnə'kaʊntəb(ə)l/ *adjective* **1** without explanation; strange. **2** not answerable for one's actions. □ **unaccountably** *adverb*.
■ **1** see INEXPLICABLE.

unaccustomed /ʌnə'kʌstəmd/ *adjective* **1** (usually + *to*) not accustomed. **2** unusual.
■ **2** see STRANGE 1.

unadopted /ʌnə'dɒptɪd/ *adjective* (of road) not maintained by local authority.

unadulterated /ʌnə'dʌltəreɪtɪd/ *adjective* **1** pure. **2** complete, utter.

unadventurous /ʌnəd'ventʃərəs/ *adjective* **1** (of person) not adventurous. **2** not involving adventure; not risky.
■ **1** cautious, cowardly, spiritless, timid, unimaginative. **2** cloistered, limited, protected, sheltered, unexciting.

unaffected /ʌnə'fektɪd/ *adjective* **1** (usually + *by*) not affected. **2** free from affectation. □ **unaffectedly** *adverb*.

unalloyed /ʌnə'lɔɪd/ *adjective* complete, pure.

unalterable /ʌn'ɔːltərəb(ə)l/ *adjective* not able to be changed. □ **unalterably** *adverb*.
■ see IMMUTABLE.

unambiguous *adjective* /ʌnæm'bɪgjʊəs/ not ambiguous; clear. □ **unambiguously** *adverb*.
■ see DEFINITE 2.

un-American /ʌnə'merɪkən/ *adjective* **1** uncharacteristic of Americans. **2** contrary to US interests; treasonable.

unanimous /juː'nænɪməs/ *adjective* **1** all in agreement. **2** (of vote etc.) by all without exception. □ **unanimity** /-nə'nɪm-/ *noun*. **unanimously** *adverb*.
■ **1** see UNITED (UNITE).

unannounced /ʌnə'naʊnst/ *adjective* not announced; without warning.

unanswerable /ʌn'ɑːnsərəb(ə)l/ *adjective* that cannot be answered or refuted.

unapproachable /ʌnə'prəʊtʃəb(ə)l/ *adjective* **1** inaccessible. **2** (of person) unfriendly, aloof.

unasked /ʌn'ɑːskt/ *adjective* not asked.
■ see UNINVITED.

unassailable /ʌnə'seɪləb(ə)l/ *adjective* that cannot be attacked or questioned.

unassuming /ʌnə'sjuːmɪŋ/ *adjective* not pretentious; modest.
■ see MODEST 1;5.

unattached /ʌnə'tætʃt/ *adjective* **1** not engaged, married, etc. **2** (often + *to*) not attached to particular organization etc.
■ **1** available, single, uncommitted, unmarried, unspoken for. **2** autonomous, free, independent, separate.

unattractive /ʌnə'træktɪv/ *adjective* ugly; not attractive. □ **unattractively** *adverb*. **unattractiveness** *noun*.
■ characterless, colourless, displeasing, dull, inartistic, inelegant, nasty, objectionable, off-putting, plain, repellent, repulsive, tasteless, ugly, uninviting, unpleasant, unprepossessing, unsightly.

unauthorized /ʌnˈɔːθəraɪzd/ *adjective* (also **-ised**) not authorized.
■ illegal, illegitimate, illicit, irregular, unapproved, unlawful, unofficial.

unavoidable /ʌnəˈvɔɪdəb(ə)l/ *adjective* not avoidable. □ **unavoidability** /-ˈbɪlɪtɪ/*noun*. **unavoidably** *adverb*.
■ certain, compulsory, destined, fated, fixed, ineluctable, inescapable, inevitable, inexorable, mandatory, necessary, obligatory, predetermined, required, sure, unalterable.

unaware /ʌnəˈweə/ *adjective* 1 (usually + *of*, *that*) not aware. 2 unperceptive. ● *adverb* unawares.
■ *adjective* 1 (*unaware of*) see IGNORANT 2.

unawares /ʌnəˈweəz/ *adverb* 1 unexpectedly. 2 inadvertently.

unbalanced /ʌnˈbælənst/ *adjective* 1 not balanced. 2 biased. 3 emotionally unstable.
■ 1 asymmetrical, irregular, lopsided, off-centre, shaky, uneven, unstable, wobbly. 2 biased, bigoted, one-sided, partial, partisan, prejudiced, unfair, unjust. 3 see MAD 1.

unbearable /ʌnˈbeərəb(ə)l/ *adjective* not bearable. □ **unbearably** *adverb*.
■ insufferable, insupportable, intolerable, overpowering, overwhelming, unacceptable, unendurable.

unbeatable /ʌnˈbiːtəb(ə)l/ *adjective* not beatable.
■ see INVINCIBLE.

unbecoming /ʌnbɪˈkʌmɪŋ/ *adjective* 1 not suiting or flattering. 2 (usually + *to, for*) not suitable; indecorous. □ **unbecomingly** *adverb*.
■ 1 unattractive, unflattering. 2 dishonourable, improper, inappropriate, indecorous, indelicate, offensive, tasteless, unbefitting, undignified, ungentlemanly, unladylike, unseemly, unsuitable.

unbeknown /ʌnbɪˈnəʊn/ *adjective* (also **unbeknownst** /-ˈnəʊnst/) (+ *to*) without the knowledge of.

unbelief /ʌnbɪˈliːf/ *noun* lack of (esp. religious) belief. □ **unbeliever** *noun*. **unbelieving** *adjective*.
■ □ **unbeliever** see NON-BELIEVER. **unbelieving** see INCREDULOUS.

unbelievable /ʌnbɪˈliːvəb(ə)l/ *adjective* not believable. □ **unbelievably** *adverb*.
■ see INCREDIBLE 1 .

unbend /ʌnˈbend/ *verb* (*past & past participle* **unbent**) 1 straighten. 2 relax; become affable.
■ 1 straighten, uncurl, untwist. 2 loosen up, relax, rest, *colloquial* unwind.

unbending /ʌnˈbendɪŋ/ *adjective* 1 inflexible. 2 firm, austere.
■ see INFLEXIBLE 2.

unbiased /ʌnˈbaɪəst/ *adjective* (also **unbiassed**) not biased; impartial.
■ balanced, disinterested, enlightened, even-handed, fair, impartial, independent, just, neutral, non-partisan, objective, open-minded, reasonable, unbigoted, undogmatic, unprejudiced.

unblushing /ʌnˈblʌʃɪŋ/ *adjective* shameless; frank.

unbosom /ʌnˈbʊz(ə)m/ *verb* 1 disclose (thoughts etc.). 2 (**unbosom oneself**) disclose one's thoughts etc.

unbounded /ʌnˈbaʊndɪd/ *adjective* infinite.

unbreakable /ʌnˈbreɪkəb(ə)l/ *adjective* not breakable.
■ see INDESTRUCTIBLE.

unbridled /ʌnˈbraɪd(ə)ld/ *adjective* unrestrained, uncontrolled.

unbroken /ʌnˈbrəʊk(ə)n/ *adjective* 1 not broken or interrupted. 2 not tamed. 3 not surpassed.
■ 1 see CONTINUOUS, WHOLE *adjective* 1.

uncalled-for /ʌnˈkɔːldfɔː/ *adjective* (of remark etc.) rude and unnecessary.
■ see UNNECESSARY 1.

uncanny /ʌnˈkænɪ/ *adjective* (**-ier**, **-iest**) seemingly supernatural; mysterious. □ **uncannily** *adverb*. **uncanniness** *noun*.

uncapped /ʌnˈkæpt/ *adjective Sport* (of player) not yet awarded his or her cap or never having been selected to represent his or her country.

uncared-for /ʌnˈkeədfɔː/ *adjective* neglected.
■ see DERELICT *adjective* 1.

uncaring /ʌnˈkeərɪŋ/ *adjective* lacking compassion.
■ see CALLOUS 1.

unceasing /ʌnˈsiːsɪŋ/ *adjective* not ceasing; continuous. □ **unceasingly** *adverb*.
■ see CONTINUOUS.

unceremonious /ʌnserɪˈməʊnɪəs/ *adjective* 1 abrupt; discourteous. 2 informal. □ **unceremoniously** *adverb*.

uncertain /ʌnˈsɜːt(ə)n/ *adjective* 1 not knowing certainly. 2 not known certainly. 3 unreliable. 4 changeable. □ **in no uncertain terms** clearly and forcefully. □ **uncertainly** *adverb*. **uncertainty** *noun* (*plural* **-ies**).
■ 1 ambivalent, doubtful, dubious, hazy, insecure, in two minds, self-questioning, unclear, unconvinced, undecided, unsure, vague, wavering. 2 ambiguous, arguable, chancy, confusing, conjectural, enigmatic, equivocal, hazardous, hazy, *colloquial* iffy, imprecise, incalculable, inconclusive, indefinite, indeterminate, problematical, puzzling, questionable, risky, speculative, touch-and-go, unclear, unconvincing, undecided, undetermined, unforeseeable, unknown, unresolved, woolly. 3 hit-and-miss, unpredictable, unreliable, unsure. 4 changeable, erratic, fitful, inconstant, irregular, precarious, unpredictable, unreliable, unsettled, variable.

unchanging /ʌn'tʃeɪndʒɪŋ/ *adjective* not changing.
■ see CONSTANT *adjective* 3.

uncharitable /ʌn'tʃærɪtəb(ə)l/ *adjective* severe in judging others. □ **uncharitably** *adverb*.
■ see UNKIND.

uncharted /ʌn'tʃɑːtɪd/ *adjective* not mapped or surveyed.

uncivilized /ʌn'sɪvɪlaɪzd/ *adjective* (also **-ised**) **1** not civilized. **2** rough; not cultured.
■ **1** anarchic, backward, barbarian, barbaric, barbarous, disorganized, primitive, savage, wild. **2** antisocial, brutish, philistine, rough, uncouth, uncultured, uneducated, unenlightened, unsophisticated.

uncle /'ʌŋk(ə)l/ *noun* parent's brother or brother-in-law. □ **Uncle Sam** *colloquial* US government.

unclean /ʌn'kliːn/ *adjective* **1** not clean. **2** unchaste. **3** religiously impure.
■ **1** see DIRTY *adjective* 1.

unclear /ʌn'klɪə/ *adjective* **1** not clear; obscure. **2** not certain.
■ **1** see OBSCURE *adjective* 1,2. **2** see UNCERTAIN 1–2.

unclothe /ʌn'kləʊð/ *verb* **1** remove clothes of. **2** expose. □ **unclothed** *adjective*.
■ **1** see UNDRESS *verb* 2. □ **unclothed** see NAKED 1.

uncomfortable /ʌn'kʌmftəb(ə)l/ *adjective* **1** not comfortable. **2** uneasy. □ **uncomfortably** *adverb*.
■ **1** bleak, cold, comfortless, cramped, hard, inconvenient, lumpy, painful, restrictive, stiff, tight, tight-fitting. **2** awkward, distressing, embarrassing, nervous, restless, troubled, uneasy, worried.

uncommon /ʌn'kɒmən/ *adjective* unusual, remarkable. □ **uncommonly** *adverb*.
■ see UNUSUAL.

uncommunicative /ʌnkə'mjuːnɪkətɪv/ *adjective* not wanting to communicate.
■ see TACITURN.

uncomplimentary /ʌnkɒmplɪ'mentərɪ/ *adjective* not complimentary; insulting.
■ censorious, critical, deprecatory, depreciatory, derogatory, disapproving, disparaging, insulting, pejorative, rude, scathing, slighting, unfavourable, unflattering.

uncompromising /ʌn'kɒmprəmaɪzɪŋ/ *adjective* stubborn, unyielding. □ **uncompromisingly** *adverb*.
■ see INFLEXIBLE 2.

unconcealed /ʌnkən'siːld/ *adjective* not concealed; obvious.
■ see OBVIOUS.

unconcern /ʌnkən'sɜːn/ *noun* calmness; indifference; apathy. □ **unconcerned** *adjective*.

unconditional /ʌnkən'dɪʃən(ə)l/ *adjective* not subject to conditions; complete. □ **unconditionally** *adverb*.
■ absolute, categorical, complete, full, outright, total, unequivocal, unlimited, unqualified, unreserved, unrestricted, wholehearted.

uncongenial /ʌnkən'dʒiːnɪəl/ *adjective* not congenial.
■ alien, antipathetic, disagreeable, unattractive, unfriendly, unpleasant, unsympathetic.

unconquerable /ʌn'kɒŋkərəb(ə)l/ *adjective* not conquerable.
■ see INVINCIBLE.

unconscionable /ʌn'kɒnʃənəb(ə)l/ *adjective* **1** without conscience. **2** excessive.

unconscious /ʌn'kɒnʃəs/ *adjective* **1** not conscious; not awake. **2** (usually + *of*) not aware. **3** not intentional; involuntary. **4** subconscious. ● *noun* normally inaccessible part of mind affecting emotions etc. □ **unconsciously** *adverb*. **unconsciousness** *noun*.
■ *adjective* **1** anaesthetized, blacked out, comatose, concussed, *colloquial* dead to the world, insensible, knocked out, senseless, sleeping. **2** (*unconscious of*) blind to, deaf to, ignorant of, insensible of, oblivious of, unaware of. **3** accidental, automatic, gut, impulsive, inadvertent, instinctive, involuntary, reflex, spontaneous, unintended, unintentional, unthinking, unwitting. **4** repressed, subconscious, subliminal, suppressed. □ **unconsciousness** blackout, coma, faint, sleep.

unconsidered /ʌnkən'sɪdəd/ *adjective* **1** not considered; disregarded. **2** not premeditated.

unconstitutional /ʌnkɒnstɪ'tjuːʃən(ə)l/ *adjective* in breach of political constitution or procedural rules.

uncontrollable /ʌnkən'trəʊləb(ə)l/ *adjective* not controllable; wild. □ **uncontrollably** *adverb*.
■ see UNDISCIPLINED.

unconventional /ʌnkən'venʃ(ə)l/ *adjective* not bound by convention; not orthodox. □ **unconventionality** /-'nælɪtɪ/ *noun*. **unconventionally** *adverb*.
■ abnormal, atypical, cranky, eccentric, exotic, futuristic, idiosyncratic, independent, inventive, non-conforming, non-standard, odd, offbeat, original, peculiar, progressive, revolutionary, strange, surprising, unaccustomed, unorthodox, *colloquial* way-out, wayward, *colloquial* weird, zany.

unconvincing /ʌnkən'vɪnsɪŋ/ *adjective* not convincing. □ **unconvincingly** *adverb*.
■ implausible, improbable, incredible, invalid, spurious, unbelievable, unlikely.

uncooperative /ʌnkəʊ'ɒpərətɪv/ *adjective* not cooperative.

■ obstructive, recalcitrant, selfish, unhelpful, unwilling.

uncork /ʌnˈkɔːk/ *verb* **1** draw cork from (bottle). **2** vent (feelings).

uncouple /ʌnˈkʌp(ə)l/ *verb* (**-ling**) release from couples or coupling.

uncouth /ʌnˈkuːθ/ *adjective* uncultured, rough.

uncover /ʌnˈkʌvə/ *verb* **1** remove cover or covering from. **2** disclose.

■ **1** bare, dig up, *literary* disrobe, exhume, strip, take the wraps off, undress, unearth, unmask, unveil, unwrap. **2** come across, detect, disclose, discover, expose, locate, reveal, show, unearth.

uncrowned /ʌnˈkraʊnd/ *adjective* having status but not name of.

unction /ˈʌŋkʃ(ə)n/ *noun* **1** anointing with oil etc. as religious rite or medical treatment. **2** oil etc. so used. **3** soothing words or thought. **4** excessive or insincere flattery. **5** (pretence of) deep emotion.

unctuous /ˈʌŋktʃʊəs/ *adjective* **1** unpleasantly flattering. **2** greasy. □ **unctuously** *adverb*. **unctuousness** *noun*.

uncut /ʌnˈkʌt/ *adjective* **1** not cut. **2** (of book) with pages sealed or untrimmed. **3** (of film) not censored. **4** (of diamond) not shaped. **5** (of fabric) with looped pile.

undamaged /ʌnˈdæmɪdʒd/ *adjective* not damaged; intact.

■ see PERFECT *adjective* 2.

undefended /ʌndɪˈfendɪd/ *adjective* not defended.

■ defenceless, exposed, helpless, insecure, unarmed, unfortified, unguarded, unprotected, vulnerable, weaponless.

undemanding /ʌndɪˈmɑːndɪŋ/ *adjective* not demanding; easily satisfied.

■ see EASY *adjective* 1.

undemonstrative /ʌndɪˈmɒnstrətɪv/ *adjective* not expressing feelings outwardly. □ **undemonstratively** *adverb*.

■ see ALOOF *adjective*.

undeniable /ʌndɪˈnaɪəb(ə)l/ *adjective* indisputable; certain. □ **undeniably** *adverb*.

under /ˈʌndə/ *preposition* **1** in or to position lower than; below; beneath. **2** inferior to; less than. **3** undergoing; liable to. **4** controlled or bound by. **5** classified or subsumed in. ● *adverb* in or to lower condition or position. ● *adjective* lower.

under- *prefix* added to verbs, nouns, adjectives, and adverbs, indicating: **1** below, beneath. **2** lower in status than; subordinate to. **3** insufficiently, incompletely.

underachieve /ʌndərəˈtʃiːv/ *verb* (**-ving**) do less well than might be expected, esp. academically. □ **underachiever** *noun*.

underarm *adjective* & *adverb* Cricket etc. with arm below shoulder level.

underbelly *noun* (*plural* **-ies**) under surface of animal etc., esp. as vulnerable to attack.

underbid /ʌndəˈbɪd/ *verb* (**-dd-**; *past* and *past participle* **-bid**) **1** make lower bid than. **2** *Bridge etc.* bid too little (on).

undercarriage *noun* **1** wheeled retractable landing structure beneath aircraft. **2** supporting framework of vehicle etc.

undercharge /ʌndəˈtʃɑːdʒ/ *verb* (**-ging**) charge too little to.

underclothes *plural noun* (also **underclothing**) clothes worn under others, esp. next to skin.

■ lingerie, *colloquial* smalls, undergarments, *colloquial* underthings, underwear, *colloquial* undies.

undercoat *noun* **1** layer of paint under another. **2** (in animals) under layer of hair etc.

undercook /ʌndəˈkʊk/ *verb* cook insufficiently.

undercover /ʌndəˈkʌvə/ *adjective* **1** surreptitious. **2** spying incognito.

undercroft *noun* crypt.

undercurrent *noun* **1** current below surface. **2** underlying often contrary feeling, force, etc.

■ **2** atmosphere, feeling, hint, sense, suggestion, trace, undertone.

undercut *verb* /ʌndəˈkʌt/ (**-tt-**; *past & past participle* **-cut**) **1** sell or work at lower price than. **2** strike (ball) to make it rise high. **3** undermine. ● *noun* /ˈʌndəkʌt/ underside of sirloin.

underdeveloped /ʌndədɪˈveləpt/ *adjective* **1** immature. **2** (of country etc.) with unexploited potential.

underdog *noun* **1** oppressed person. **2** loser in fight etc.

underdone /ʌndəˈdʌn/ *adjective* undercooked.

underemployed /ʌndərɪmˈplɔɪd/ *adjective* not fully occupied.

underestimate *verb* /ʌndərˈestɪmeɪt/ (**-ting**) form too low an estimate of. ● *noun* /ʌndərˈestɪmət/ estimate that is too low. □ **underestimation** /ˈmeɪʃ(ə)n/ *noun*.

■ *verb* belittle, depreciate, dismiss, disparage, minimize, miscalculate, misjudge, underrate, undervalue.

underexpose /ʌndərɪkˈspəʊz/ *verb* (**-sing**) expose (film) for too short a time. □ **underexposure** *noun*.

underfed /ʌndəˈfed/ *adjective* malnourished.

underfelt *noun* felt laid under carpet.

underfloor /ʌndəˈflɔː/ *adjective* (esp. of heating) beneath floor.

underfoot /ʌndəˈfʊt/ *adverb* (also **under foot**) **1** under one's feet. **2** on the ground.

underfunded /ʌndəˈfʌndɪd/ *adjective* provided with insufficient money.

undergarment *noun* piece of underclothing.

undergo /ʌndəˈɡəʊ/ *verb* (*3rd singular present*

-goes; *past* **-went**; *past participle* **-gone** /-'gɒn/) be subjected to; endure.

■ bear, be subjected to, endure, experience, go through, live through, put up with, stand, submit (oneself) to, suffer, withstand.

undergraduate /ʌndə'grædjʊət/ *noun* person studying for first degree.

underground *adverb* /ʌndə'graʊnd/ **1** beneath the ground. **2** in(to) secrecy or hiding. ● *adjective* /'ʌndəgraʊnd/ **1** situated underground. **2** secret, subversive. **3** unconventional. ● *noun* /'ʌndəgraʊnd/ **1** underground railway. **2** secret subversive group or activity.

■ *adjective* **1** buried, hidden, subterranean, sunken. **2** clandestine, secret, subversive, unofficial.

undergrowth *noun* dense shrubs etc., esp. in wood.

■ brush, bushes, ground cover, plants, vegetation.

underhand *adjective* **1** secret, deceptive. **2** *Cricket etc.* underarm. ● *adverb* in underhand manner.

underhanded /ʌndə'hændɪd/ *adjective* & *adverb* = UNDERHAND. □ **underhandedly** *adverb*. **underhandedness** *noun*.

underlay[1] *verb* /ʌndə'leɪ/ (*past & past participle* **-laid**) lay thing under (another) to support or raise. ● *noun* /'ʌndəleɪ/ thing so laid (esp. under carpet).

underlay[2] *past* of UNDERLIE.

underlie /ʌndə'laɪ/ *verb* (**-lying**; *past* **-lay**; *past participle* **-lain**) **1** lie under (stratum etc.). **2** (esp. as **underlying** *adjective*) be basis of. **3** exist beneath superficial aspect of.

underline /ʌndə'laɪn/ *verb* (**-ning**) **1** draw line under (words etc.). **2** emphasize.

underling /'ʌndəlɪŋ/ *noun usually derogatory* subordinate.

undermanned /ʌndə'mænd/ *adjective* having insufficient crew or staff.

undermine /ʌndə'maɪn/ *verb* (**-ning**) **1** injure or wear out insidiously or secretly. **2** wear away base of. **3** make excavation under.

■ **1** destroy, erode, ruin, sabotage, sap, subvert, weaken. **2** erode, wear away. **3** burrow under, dig under, excavate, mine under, tunnel under, undercut.

underneath /ʌndə'ni:θ/ *preposition* **1** at or to lower place than; below. **2** on inside of. ● *adverb* **1** at or to lower place. **2** inside. ● *noun* lower surface or part. ● *adjective* lower.

undernourished /ʌndə'nʌrɪʃt/ *adjective* insufficiently nourished. □ **undernourishment** *noun*.

underpants *plural noun* undergarment for lower part of torso.

underpass *noun* road etc. passing under another; subway.

underpay /ʌndə'peɪ/ *verb* (*past* and *past parti-*

ciple **-paid**) pay too little to (person) or for (thing). □ **underpayment** *noun*.

underpin /ʌndə'pɪn/ *verb* (**-nn-**) **1** support from below with masonry etc. **2** support, strengthen.

underprivileged /ʌndə'prɪvɪlɪdʒd/ *adjective* **1** less privileged than others. **2** having below average income, rights, etc.

■ deprived, destitute, disadvantaged, downtrodden, impoverished, needy, oppressed, poor.

underrate /ʌndə'reɪt/ *verb* (**-ting**) have too low an opinion of.

underscore /ʌndə'skɔ:/ *verb* (**-ring**) underline.

undersea *adjective* below sea or its surface.

■ subaquatic, submarine, underwater.

underseal *verb* seal underpart of (esp. vehicle against rust etc.).

under-secretary /ʌndə'sekrətərɪ/ *noun* (*plural* **-ies**) subordinate official, esp. junior minister or senior civil servant.

undersell /ʌndə'sel/ *verb* (*past & past participle* **-sold**) sell at lower price than (another seller).

undershirt *noun esp. US* vest.

undershoot /ʌndə'ʃu:t/ *verb* (*past & past participle* **-shot**) land short of (runway etc.).

undershot *adjective* **1** (of wheel) turned by water flowing under it. **2** (of lower jaw) projecting beyond upper jaw.

underside *noun* lower side or surface.

undersigned /ʌndə'saɪnd/ *adjective* whose signature is appended.

undersized /'ʌndə'saɪzd/ *adjective* smaller than average.

underspend /ʌndə'spend/ *verb* (*past* and *past participle* **-spent**) spend less than (expected amount) or too little.

understaffed /ʌndə'stɑ:ft/ *adjective* having too few staff.

understand /ʌndə'stænd/ *verb* (*past & past participle* **-stood**) **1** comprehend; perceive meaning, significance, or cause of. **2** know how to deal with. **3** (often + *that*) infer; take as implied. □ **understandable** *adjective*. **understandably** *adverb*.

■ **1** appreciate, apprehend, be conversant with, *colloquial* catch on, comprehend, *colloquial* cotton on to, decipher, decode, fathom, figure out, follow, gather, *colloquial* get, grasp, interpret, know, learn, make out, make sense of, master, perceive, realize, recognize, see, take in, *colloquial* twig. **2** be in sympathy with, empathize with, sympathize with.

understanding *noun* **1** intelligence; ability to understand. **2** individual's perception of situation. **3** sympathy. **4** agreement, esp. informal. ● *adjective* **1** having understanding or insight. **2** sympathetic. □ **understandingly** *adverb*.

■ *noun* **1** ability, acumen, brains, cleverness, discernment, insight, intellect, intelligence, judgement, penetration, perceptiveness, percipience, sense, wisdom. **2** appreciation, apprehension, awareness, cognition, comprehension, grasp, knowledge. **3** compassion, consideration, empathy, fellow feeling, harmony, kindness, sympathy, tolerance. **4** accord, agreement, arrangement, bargain, compact, contract, deal, entente, pact, settlement, treaty.

understate /ʌndə'steɪt/ *verb* (**-ting**) **1** express in restrained terms. **2** represent as being less than it really is. □ **understatement** *noun*.
■ belittle, make light of, minimize, play down, soft-pedal.

understudy /'ʌndəstʌdɪ/ *noun* (*plural* **-ies**) person ready to take another's role when required, esp. in theatre. ● *verb* (**-ies, -ied**) **1** study (role etc.) for this purpose. **2** act as understudy to.

undersubscribed /ʌndəsəb'skraɪbd/ *adjective* without sufficient subscribers, participants, etc.

undertake /ʌndə'teɪk/ *verb* (**-king**; *past* **-took**; *past participle* **-taken**) **1** agree to perform or be responsible for; engage in. **2** (usually + *to do*) promise. **3** guarantee, affirm.
■ **1** accept responsibility for, attempt, attend to, begin, *formal* commence, commit oneself to, cope with, deal with, embark on, grapple with, handle, manage, tackle, take on, take up, try. **2** agree, consent, covenant, guarantee, pledge, promise.

undertaker /'ʌndəteɪkə/ *noun* professional funeral organizer.

undertaking /ʌndə'teɪkɪŋ/ *noun* **1** work etc. undertaken; enterprise. **2** promise. **3** /'ʌn-/ professional funeral management.
■ **1** affair, business, enterprise, project, task, venture. **2** agreement, assurance, contract, guarantee, pledge, promise, vow.

underthings *plural noun colloquial* underclothes.

undertone *noun* **1** subdued tone. **2** underlying quality or feeling.

undertow *noun* current below sea surface contrary to surface current.

underused /ʌndə'juːzd/ *adjective* not used to capacity.

undervalue /ʌndə'væljuː/ *verb* (**-ues, -ued, -uing**) **1** value insufficiently. **2** underestimate.
■ belittle, depreciate, dismiss, disparage, minimize, miscalculate, misjudge, underestimate, underrate.

underwater /ʌndə'wɔːtə/ *adjective* situated or done under water. ● *adverb* under water.
■ *adjective* subaquatic, submarine, undersea.

underwear *noun* underclothes.

underweight /ʌndə'weɪt/ *adjective* below normal weight.

underwent *past* of UNDERGO.

underwhelm /ʌndə'welm/ *verb jocular* fail to impress.

underworld *noun* **1** those who live by organized crime. **2** mythical home of the dead.

underwrite /ʌndə'raɪt/ *verb* (**-ting**; *past* **-wrote**; *past participle* **-written**) **1** sign and accept liability under (insurance policy). **2** accept (liability) thus. **3** undertake to finance or support. **4** engage to buy all unsold stock in (company etc.). □ **underwriter** /'ʌn-/ *noun.*

undeserved /ʌndɪ'zɜːvd/ *adjective* not deserved. □ **undeservedly** /-vɪdlɪ/ *adverb*.
■ unearned, unfair, unjustified, unmerited, unwarranted.

undesirable /ʌndɪ'zaɪərəb(ə)l/ *adjective* unpleasant, objectionable. ● *noun* undesirable person. □ **undesirability** /'bɪlɪtɪ/ *noun*.
■ *adjective* see OBJECTIONABLE 1.

undies /'ʌndɪz/ *plural noun colloquial* (esp. women's) underclothes.

undisciplined /ʌn'dɪsɪplɪnd/ *adjective* not disciplined.
■ anarchic, chaotic, disobedient, disorderly, disorganized, intractable, rebellious, uncontrollable, uncontrolled, ungovernable, unmanageable, unruly, unsystematic, untrained, wild, wilful.

undiscriminating /ʌndɪ'skrɪmɪneɪtɪŋ/ *adjective* lacking good judgement.
■ see INDISCRIMINATE 1, SUPERFICIAL 2.

undisguised /ʌndɪs'gaɪzd/ *adjective* not disguised; overt.
■ see OBVIOUS.

undistinguished /ʌndɪ'stɪŋgwɪʃt/ *adjective* not distinguished; ordinary.
■ see ORDINARY.

undo /ʌn'duː/ *verb* (*3rd singular present* **-does**; *past* **-did**; *past participle* **-done**; *present participle* **-doing**) **1** unfasten. **2** annul. **3** ruin prospects, reputation, or morals of.
■ **1** detach, disconnect, disengage, loose, loosen, open, part, separate, unbind, unbuckle, unbutton, unchain, unclasp, unclip, uncouple, unfasten, unfetter, unhook, unleash, unlock, unpick, unpin, unscrew, unseal, unshackle, unstick, untether, untie, unwrap, unzip. **2** annul, cancel out, invalidate, nullify, quash, reverse, wipe out. **3** destroy, mar, ruin, spoil, undermine, vitiate, wreck.

undoing *noun* **1** (cause of) ruin. **2** reversing of action etc. **3** unfastening.

undone /ʌn'dʌn/ *adjective* **1** not done. **2** not fastened. **3** *archaic* ruined.

undoubted /ʌn'daʊtɪd/ *adjective* certain; not questioned. □ **undoubtedly** *adverb*.
■ see INDISPUTABLE. □ **undoubtedly** certainly, definitely, doubtless, indubitably, of course, surely, undeniably, unquestionably.

undreamed /ʌnˈdriːmd, ʌnˈdremt/ *adjective* (also **undreamt** /ʌnˈdremt/) (often + *of*) not thought of; never imagined.

undress /ʌnˈdres/ *verb* **1** take off one's clothes. **2** take clothes off (person). ● *noun* **1** ordinary dress, esp. as opposed to (full-dress) uniform. **2** naked or scantily clad state.

■ *verb* **1** *literary* disrobe, divest oneself, *colloquial* peel off, shed one's clothes, strip off, take off one's clothes, uncover oneself. **2** *literary* disrobe, divest, strip, unclothe.

undressed /ʌnˈdrest/ *adjective* **1** no longer dressed. **2** (of food) without dressing. **3** (of leather) untreated.

■ **1** see NAKED 1.

undue /ʌnˈdjuː/ *adjective* excessive, disproportionate. □ **unduly** *adverb*

■ see EXCESSIVE.

undulate /ˈʌndjʊleɪt/ *verb* (**-ting**) (cause to) have wavy motion or look. □ **undulation** *noun*.

undying /ʌnˈdaɪɪŋ/ *adjective* **1** immortal. **2** never-ending.

■ see ETERNAL 1.

unearth /ʌnˈɜːθ/ *verb* discover by searching, digging, or rummaging.

unearthly /ʌnˈɜːθlɪ/ *adjective* **1** supernatural; mysterious. **2** *colloquial* absurdly early.

unease /ʌnˈiːz/ *noun* nervousness, anxiety.

uneasy /ʌnˈiːzɪ/ *adjective* (**-ier**, **-iest**) disturbed or uncomfortable in body or mind. □ **uneasily** *adverb*. **uneasiness** *noun*.

■ anxious, apprehensive, awkward, concerned, distressed, disturbed, edgy, fearful, insecure, *colloquial* jittery, nervous, restive, restless, tense, troubled, uncomfortable, unsettled, worried.

uneducated /ʌnˈedjʊkeɪtɪd/ *adjective* not educated.

■ see IGNORANT 1.

unemotional /ʌnɪˈməʊʃən(ə)l/ *adjective* lacking emotion. □ **unemotionally** *adverb*.

■ apathetic, clinical, cold, cool, dispassionate, frigid, hard-hearted, heartless, impassive, indifferent, objective, unfeeling, unmoved, unresponsive.

unemployable /ʌnɪmˈplɔɪəb(ə)l/ *adjective* unfit for paid employment.

unemployed /ʌnɪmˈplɔɪd/ *adjective* **1** out of work. **2** not used.

■ **1** jobless, laid off, *colloquial* on the dole, out of work, redundant, unwaged. **2** see IDLE *adjective* 2.

unemployment /ʌnɪmˈplɔɪmənt/ *noun* lack of employment. □ **unemployment benefit** state payment made to unemployed worker.

unencumbered /ʌnɪmˈkʌmbəd/ *adjective* **1** (of estate) having no liabilities. **2** free; not burdened.

unendurable /ʌnɪmˈdjʊərəb(ə)l/ *adjective* unable to be endured.

■ see UNBEARABLE.

unenthusiastic /ʌnɪmθjuːzɪˈæstɪk/ *adjective* not enthusiastic. □ **unenthusiastically** *adverb*.

■ see APATHETIC (APATHY), UNINTERESTED.

unequal /ʌnˈiːkw(ə)l/ *adjective* **1** not equal. **2** of variable quality. **3** (of contest) unfair. □ **unequally** *adverb*.

■ **1** different, differing, disparate, dissimilar. **2** uneven, variable, varying. **3** biased, ill-matched, one-sided, unbalanced, uneven, unfair, unjust.

unequalled /ʌnˈiːkwəld/ *adjective* without equal; superior to others.

■ incomparable, inimitable, matchless, peerless, supreme, surpassing, unmatched, unparalleled, unrivalled, unsurpassed.

unequivocal /ʌnɪˈkwɪvək(ə)l/ *adjective* not ambiguous; plain, unmistakable. □ **unequivocally** *adverb*.

UNESCO /juːˈneskəʊ/ *abbreviation* (also **Unesco**) United Nations Educational, Scientific, and Cultural Organization.

unethical /ʌnˈeθɪk(ə)l/ *adjective* not ethical; unscrupulous. □ **unethically** *adverb*.

■ see IMMORAL.

uneven /ʌnˈiːv(ə)n/ *adjective* **1** not level. **2** of variable quality. **3** (of contest) unequal. □ **unevenly** *adverb*. **unevenness** *noun*.

■ **1** asymmetrical, bent, broken, bumpy, crooked, irregular, jagged, lopsided, pitted, rough, rutted, undulating, wavy. **2** erratic, fitful, fluctuating, inconsistent, spasmodic, unpredictable, unsteady, variable, varying. **3** ill-matched, one-sided, unbalanced, unequal, unfair.

uneventful /ʌnɪˈventfʊl/ *adjective* not eventful. □ **uneventfully** *adverb*.

■ see UNEXCITING.

unexceptionable /ʌnɪkˈsepʃənəb(ə)l/ *adjective* entirely satisfactory.

USAGE *Unexceptionable* is sometimes confused with *unexceptional*.

unexceptional /ʌnɪkˈsepʃən(ə)l/ *adjective* normal, ordinary.

USAGE *Unexceptional* is sometimes confused with *unexceptionable*.

unexciting /ʌnɪkˈsaɪtɪŋ/ *adjective* lacking excitement; dull.

■ boring, dreary, dry, dull, humdrum, monotonous, ordinary, predictable, quiet, repetitive, routine, soporific, straightforward, tedious, uneventful, uninspiring, uninteresting, vapid, wearisome.

unexpected /ʌnɪkˈspektɪd/ *adjective* not expected. □ **unexpectedly** *adverb*.

■ accidental, chance, fortuitous, sudden, surprising, unforeseen, unhoped-for, unlooked-for, unplanned, unpredictable, unusual.

unfailing /ʌnˈfeɪlɪŋ/ *adjective* **1** not failing. **2** constant; reliable. □ **unfailingly** *adverb*.

unfair /ʌnˈfeə/ *adjective* unjust; not fair or impar-

tial. □ **unfairly** *adverb.* **unfairness** *noun.*
▪ see UNJUST.

unfaithful /ʌn'feɪθfʊl/ *adjective* not faithful, esp. adulterous. □ **unfaithfully** *adverb.* **unfaithfulness** *noun.*
■ adulterous, deceitful, disloyal, double-dealing, duplicitous, faithless, false, fickle, inconstant, perfidious, traitorous, treacherous, treasonable, unreliable, untrue, untrustworthy.
□ **unfaithfulness** adultery, duplicity, infidelity, perfidy, treachery, treason.

unfamiliar /ʌnfə'mɪlɪə/ *adjective* not familiar. □ **unfamiliarity** /-lɪ'ærɪtɪ/ *noun.*
▪ see STRANGE 2.

unfashionable /ʌn'fæʃənəb(ə)l/ *adjective* not fashionable. □ **unfashionably** *adverb.*
■ dated, obsolete, old-fashioned, *colloquial* out, outmoded, passé, superseded, unstylish.

unfasten /ʌn'fɑːs(ə)n/ *verb* 1 open; loosen. 2 detach.
▪ see UNDO 1.

unfavourable /ʌn'feɪvərəb(ə)l/ (*US* **favorable**) *adjective* not favourable; adverse. □ **unfavourably** *adverb.*
■ adverse, attacking, bad, contrary, critical, disapproving, discouraging, hostile, ill-disposed, inauspicious, negative, opposing, uncomplimentary, undesirable, unenviable, unfriendly, unhelpful, unkind, unpromising, unpropitious, unsatisfactory, unsympathetic.

unfeeling /ʌn'fiːlɪŋ/ *adjective* unsympathetic, harsh.
▪ see CALLOUS.

unfinished /ʌn'fɪnɪʃt/ *adjective* not finished; incomplete.
■ imperfect, incomplete, rough, *colloquial* sketchy, uncompleted, unpolished.

unfit /ʌn'fɪt/ *adjective* 1 (often + *for, to do*) not fit; unsuitable. 2 in poor health. □ **unfitness** *noun.*
■ 1 ill-equipped, inadequate, inappropriate, incapable, incompetent, unsatisfactory, unsuitable, unsuited, useless. 2 feeble, flabby, ill, unhealthy.

unfitting /ʌn'fɪtɪŋ/ *adjective* not fitting or suitable.

unflagging /ʌn'flægɪŋ/ *adjective* tireless, persistent.
▪ see TIRELESS.

unflappable /ʌn'flæpəb(ə)l/ *adjective colloquial* imperturbable. □ **unflappability** /-'bɪlɪtɪ/ *noun.*

unfledged /ʌn'fledʒd/ *adjective* 1 inexperienced. 2 not fledged.

unflinching /ʌn'flɪntʃɪŋ/ *adjective* not flinching; steadfast. □ **unflinchingly** *adverb.*
▪ see RESOLUTE.

unfold /ʌn'fəʊld/ *verb* 1 open out. 2 reveal. 3 become opened out. 4 develop.

unforeseen /ʌnfɔː'siːn/ *adjective* not foreseen.
▪ see UNEXPECTED.

unforgettable /ʌnfə'getəb(ə)l/ *adjective* memorable, wonderful.
▪ see MEMORABLE 1–2.

unforgivable /ʌnfə'gɪvəb(ə)l/ *adjective* not forgivable.
■ inexcusable, mortal (*sin*), reprehensible, shameful, unjustifiable, unpardonable, unwarrantable.

unfortunate /ʌn'fɔːtʃənət/ *adjective* 1 unlucky. 2 unhappy. 3 regrettable. 4 disastrous. ● *noun* unfortunate person. □ **unfortunately** *adverb.*
▪ *adjective* 1 see UNLUCKY 1. 3 see REGRETTABLE.

unfounded /ʌn'faʊndɪd/ *adjective* (of rumour etc.) without foundation.

unfreeze /ʌn'friːz/ *verb* (-zing; *past* **unfroze**; *past participle* **unfrozen**) 1 (cause to) thaw. 2 derestrict (assets etc.).

unfriendly /ʌn'frendlɪ/ *adjective* (-ier, -iest) not friendly. □ **unfriendliness** *noun.*
■ aggressive, aloof, antagonistic, antisocial, cold, cool, detached, disagreeable, distant, forbidding, frigid, haughty, hostile, ill-disposed, ill-natured, impersonal, indifferent, inhospitable, menacing, nasty, obnoxious, offensive, remote, reserved, rude, sour, stand-offish, starchy, stern, supercilious, threatening, unapproachable, uncivil, uncongenial, unenthusiastic, unforthcoming, unkind, unneighbourly, unresponsive, unsociable, unsympathetic, unwelcoming.

unfrock /ʌn'frɒk/ *verb* defrock.

unfurl /ʌn'fɜːl/ *verb* unroll; spread out.

ungainly /ʌn'geɪnlɪ/ *adjective* awkward, clumsy.
▪ see AWKWARD 2.

unget-at-able /ʌnget'ætəb(ə)l/ *adjective colloquial* inaccessible.

ungodly /ʌn'gɒdlɪ/ *adjective* 1 impious, wicked. 2 *colloquial* outrageous. □ **ungodliness** *noun.*
▪ 1 see IRRELIGIOUS 2.

ungovernable /ʌn'gʌvənəb(ə)l/ *adjective* uncontrollable, violent.
▪ see UNDISCIPLINED.

ungracious /ʌn'greɪʃəs/ *adjective* discourteous, grudging.

ungrateful /ʌn'greɪtfʊl/ *adjective* not feeling or showing gratitude. □ **ungratefully** *adverb.*
■ displeased, ill-mannered, rude, selfish, unappreciative, unthankful.

ungreen /ʌn'griːn/ *adjective* 1 harmful to environment. 2 not concerned with protection of environment.

unguarded /ʌnˈgɑːdɪd/ *adjective* **1** incautious, thoughtless. **2** not guarded.

unguent /ˈʌŋgwənt/ *noun* ointment, lubricant.

ungulate /ˈʌŋgjʊlət/ *adjective* hoofed. ● *noun* hoofed mammal.

unhallowed /ʌnˈhæləʊd/ *adjective* **1** unconsecrated. **2** not sacred; wicked.

unhand /ʌnˈhænd/ *verb rhetorical* or *jocular* take one's hands off; release (person).

unhappy /ʌnˈhæpɪ/ *adjective* (**-ier, -iest**) **1** miserable. **2** unfortunate. **3** unsuitable. **4** disastrous. ◻ **unhappily** *adverb*. **unhappiness** *noun*.

■ **1** dejected, depressed, disaffected, discontented, disgruntled, disillusioned, dispirited, displeased, dissatisfied, *colloquial* down, downcast, fed up, gloomy, grumpy, miserable, morose, mournful, sad, sorrowful, sulky, sullen, unsatisfied. **2** see UNLUCKY 1. **3** see UNSUITABLE.

unhealthy /ʌnˈhelθɪ/ *adjective* (**-ier, -iest**) **1** in poor health. **2** harmful to health; unwholesome. **3** *slang* dangerous. ◻ **unhealthily** *adverb*.

■ **1** ailing, debilitated, delicate, diseased, feeble, frail, ill, infected, infirm, poorly, sick, sickly, suffering, unsound, unwell, valetudinarian, weak. **2** deleterious, detrimental, dirty, harmful, insalubrious, insanitary, noxious, polluted, unhygienic, unwholesome.

unheard-of /ʌnˈhɜːdɒv/ *adjective* unprecedented.

■ see UNUSUAL.

unhelpful /ʌnˈhelpfʊl/ *adjective* not helpful.

■ disobliging, inconsiderate, negative, slow, uncivil, uncooperative, unwilling.

unhinge /ʌnˈhɪndʒ/ *verb* (**-ging**) **1** take (door etc.) off hinges. **2** (esp. as **unhinged** *adjective*) derange; disorder (mind).

unholy /ʌnˈhəʊlɪ/ *adjective* (**-ier, -iest**) **1** profane, wicked. **2** *colloquial* dreadful, outrageous.

unhorse /ʌnˈhɔːs/ *verb* (**-sing**) throw (rider) from horse.

unhygienic /ʌnhaɪˈdʒiːnɪk/ *adjective* not hygienic. ◻ **unhygienically** *adverb*.

■ see UNHEALTHY 2.

uni /ˈjuːnɪ/ *noun* (*plural* **-s**) *esp. Australian & NZ colloquial* university.

uni- *combining form* having or composed of one.

Uniate /ˈjuːnɪət/ *adjective* of Church in E. Europe or Near East acknowledging papal supremacy but retaining its own liturgy etc. ● *noun* member of such Church.

unicameral /juːnɪˈkæmər(ə)l/ *adjective* having one legislative chamber.

UNICEF /ˈjuːnɪsef/ *abbreviation* United Nations Children's Fund.

unicellular /juːnɪˈseljʊlə/ *adjective* consisting of a single cell.

unicorn /ˈjuːnɪkɔːn/ *noun* mythical horse with single straight horn.

unicycle /ˈjuːnɪsaɪk(ə)l/ *noun* one-wheeled cycle used by acrobats etc.

unidentifiable /ʌnaɪˈdentɪfaɪəb(ə)l/ *adjective* unable to be identified.

■ anonymous, camouflaged, disguised, hidden, undetectable, unidentified, unknown, unrecognizable.

unidentified /ʌnaɪˈdentɪfaɪd/ *adjective* not identified.

■ anonymous, incognito, mysterious, nameless, unfamiliar, unknown, unmarked, unnamed, unrecognized, unspecified.

unification /juːnɪfɪˈkeɪʃ(ə)n/ *noun* unifying, being unified. ◻ **Unification Church** religious organization funded by Sun Myung Moon. ◻ **unificatory** *adjective*.

uniform /ˈjuːnɪfɔːm/ *adjective* **1** unvarying. **2** constant over a period. **3** conforming to same standard or rule. ● *noun* distinctive clothing worn by members of same organization etc. ◻ **uniformed** *adjective*. **uniformity** /-ˈfɔːm-/ *noun*. **uniformly** *adverb*.

■ *adjective* **1, 2** consistent, constant, even, homogeneous, predictable, regular, same, unbroken, unchanging, unvaried, unvarying. **3** homogeneous, identical, indistinguishable, regular, same, similar, standard. ● *noun* costume, livery, outfit.

unify /ˈjuːnɪfaɪ/ *verb* (**-ies, -ied**) make or become united or uniform.

■ amalgamate, bring together, coalesce, combine, consolidate, fuse, harmonize, integrate, join, merge, unite, weld together.

unilateral /juːnɪˈlætər(ə)l/ *adjective* done by or affecting one side only. ◻ **unilaterally** *adverb*.

unilateralism *noun* unilateral disarmament. ◻ **unilateralist** *noun* & *adjective*.

unimaginative /ʌnɪˈmædʒɪnətɪv/ *adjective* lacking imagination; dull. ◻ **unimaginatively** *adverb*.

■ banal, boring, clichéd, derivative, dull, hackneyed, inartistic, obvious, ordinary, prosaic, stale, trite, uninspired, uninteresting, unoriginal.

unimpeachable /ʌnɪmˈpiːtʃəb(ə)l/ *adjective* beyond reproach.

unimportant /ʌnɪmˈpɔːt(ə)nt/ *adjective* not important.

■ ephemeral, forgettable, immaterial, inconsequential, inconsiderable, inessential, insignificant, irrelevant, lightweight, minor, negligible, peripheral, petty, secondary, slight, small, trifling, trivial, valueless, worthless.

uninhabitable /ʌnɪnˈhæbɪtəb(ə)l/ *adjective* not able to be inhabited.

■ condemned, in bad repair, unusable.

uninhabited /ʌnɪnˈhæbɪtɪd/ *adjective* not inhabited.

■ abandoned, deserted, desolate, empty, tenantless, uncolonized, unoccupied, unpeopled, unpopulated, vacant.

uninhibited /ʌnɪnˈhɪbɪtɪd/ *adjective* not inhibited.

■ abandoned, candid, casual, easygoing, frank, informal, natural, open, outgoing, outspoken, relaxed, spontaneous, unbridled, unconstrained, unrepressed, unreserved, unrestrained, unselfconscious, wild.

unintelligent /ʌnɪnˈtelɪdʒ(ə)nt/ *adjective* not intelligent. □ **unintelligently** *adverb*.

■ see STUPID 1.

unintelligible /ʌnɪnˈtelɪdʒɪb(ə)l/ *adjective* not intelligible; impossible to understand. □ **unintelligibility** *noun*. **unintelligibly** *adverb*.

■ see INCOMPREHENSIBLE.

unintentional /ʌnɪnˈtenʃən(ə)l/ *adjective* not intentional. □ **unintentionally** *adverb*.

■ accidental, fortuitous, inadvertent, involuntary, unconscious, unintended, unplanned, unthinking, unwitting.

uninterested /ʌnˈɪntrəstɪd/ *adjective* not interested; unconcerned.

■ apathetic, bored, incurious, indifferent, lethargic, passive, phlegmatic, unconcerned, unenthusiastic, uninvolved, unresponsive.

uninteresting /ʌnˈɪntrəstɪŋ/ *adjective* not interesting.

■ boring, dreary, dry, dull, flat, monotonous, obvious, ordinary, predictable, tedious, unexciting, uninspiring, vapid, wearisome.

uninterrupted /ʌnɪntəˈrʌptɪd/ *adjective* not interrupted; continuous. □ **uninterruptedly** *adverb*.

■ see CONTINUOUS.

uninvited /ʌnɪnˈvaɪtɪd/ *adjective* not invited; not asked.

■ gratuitous, unasked, unbidden, unsolicited, unwelcome.

uninviting /ʌnɪnˈvaɪtɪŋ/ *adjective* unattractive, repellent.

■ see UNATTRACTIVE.

union /ˈjuːnjən/ *noun* 1 uniting, being united. 2 whole formed from parts or members. 3 trade union. 4 marriage. 5 concord. 6 university social club or debating society. □ **Union flag, Jack** national flag of UK.

■ 1 alliance, amalgamation, association, coalition, combination, confederation, conjunction, federation, fusion, grafting, integration, joining together, marriage, marrying, merger, mixture, synthesis, unification, unity, welding. 2 alliance, amalgam, association, blend, coalition, compound, confederation, federation, fusion, mixture, synthesis. 4 marriage, matrimony, partnership, wedlock.

unionist *noun* 1 member of trade union. 2 advocate of trade unions. 3 (usually **Unionist**) supporter of continued union between Britain and Northern Ireland. □ **unionism** *noun*.

unionize *verb* (also **-ise**) (**-zing** or **-sing**) organize in or into trade union. □ **unionization** *noun*.

unique /juːˈniːk/ *adjective* 1 being the only one of its kind; having no like, equal, or parallel. 2 *disputed* remarkable. □ **uniquely** *adverb*. **uniqueness** *noun*.

USAGE The use of *unique* to mean 'remarkable' is considered incorrect by some people.

■ 1 distinctive, incomparable, lone, one-off, peerless, second to none, single, singular, unequalled, unparalleled, unrepeatable, unrivalled.

unisex /ˈjuːnɪseks/ *adjective* (of clothing etc.) designed for both sexes.

unison /ˈjuːnɪs(ə)n/ *noun* 1 concord. 2 coincidence in pitch of sounds or notes.

unit /ˈjuːnɪt/ *noun* 1 individual thing, person, or group, esp. for calculation. 2 smallest component of complex whole. 3 quantity chosen as standard of measurement. 4 smallest share in unit trust. 5 part with specified function in complex mechanism. 6 fitted item of furniture, esp. as part of set. 7 subgroup with special function. 8 group of buildings, wards, etc. in hospital. 9 single-digit number, esp. 'one'. □ **unit cost** cost of producing one item. **unit trust** company investing contributions from many people in various securities.

■ 1, 2, 5 component, constituent, element, entity, item, module, part, piece, portion, section, segment.

Unitarian /juːnɪˈteərɪən/ *noun* member of religious body maintaining that God is one person not Trinity. □ **Unitarianism** *noun*.

unitary /ˈjuːnɪtərɪ/ *adjective* 1 of unit(s). 2 marked by unity or uniformity.

unite /jʊˈnaɪt/ *verb* (**-ting**) 1 join together, esp. for common purpose. 2 join in marriage. 3 (cause to) form physical or chemical whole. □ **United Kingdom** Great Britain and Northern Ireland. **United Nations** (treated as *singular* or *plural*) international peace-seeking organization. **United States (of America)** federal republic of 50 states, mostly in N. America and including Alaska and Hawaii. □ **united** *adjective*.

■ 1 ally, amalgamate, associate, bring together, collaborate, combine, *literary* commingle, confederate, connect, consolidate, conspire, cooperate, couple, federate, go into partnership, harmonize, incorporate, integrate, interlock, join, join forces, link, link up, marry, merge, mingle, mix, stick together, tie up, unify, weld (together). 2 see MARRY 1. 3 amalgamate, blend, coalesce, combine, fuse, incorporate, integrate, merge, mix. □ **united** agreed, allied, coherent, collective, common, concerted, coordinated, corporate, harmonious, integrated, joint, like-minded, *colloquial disputed* mutual, shared, solid, unanimous, undivided.

unity /ˈjuːnɪtɪ/ *noun* (*plural* **-ies**) 1 oneness; being one. 2 interconnecting parts making a whole. 3 the whole made. 4 solidarity; harmony between people etc. 5 the number 'one'.

■ **1** coherence, integrity, oneness, wholeness. **4** accord, agreement, concord, consensus, harmony, like-mindedness, rapport, solidarity, unanimity.

universal /juːnɪˈvɜːs(ə)l/ *adjective* of, belonging to, or done etc. by all; applicable to all cases. ● *noun* term, characteristic, or concept of general application. □ **universal coupling, joint** one transmitting rotary power by a shaft at any angle. **universal time** Greenwich Mean Time. □ **universality** /-ˈsæl-/ *noun*. **universally** *adverb*.

■ *adjective* all-embracing, all-round, boundless, common, comprehensive, cosmic, general, global, international, omnipresent, pandemic, prevailing, prevalent, total, ubiquitous, unbounded, unlimited, widespread, worldwide.

universe /ˈjuːnɪvɜːs/ *noun* **1** all existing things; Creation. **2** all humankind.

■ **1** cosmos, Creation, the heavens, macrocosm.

university /juːnɪˈvɜːsɪtɪ/ *noun* (*plural* **-ies**) **1** educational institution of advanced learning and research, conferring degrees. **2** members of this.

unjust /ʌnˈdʒʌst/ *adjective* not just. □ **unjustly** *adverb*. **unjustness** *noun*.

■ biased, bigoted, indefensible, inequitable, one-sided, partial, partisan, prejudiced, undeserved, unfair, unjustified, unlawful, unmerited, unreasonable, unwarranted, wrong, wrongful.

unjustifiable /ʌnˈdʒʌstɪfaɪəb(ə)l/ *adjective* not justifiable. □ **unjustifiably** *adverb*.

■ excessive, immoderate, indefensible, inexcusable, unacceptable, unconscionable, unforgivable, unjust, unreasonable, unwarranted.

unkempt /ʌnˈkempt/ *adjective* dishevelled, untidy.

unkind /ʌnˈkaɪnd/ *adjective* not kind; cruel, harsh. □ **unkindly** *adverb*. **unkindness** *noun*.

■ abrasive, *colloquial* beastly, brutal, callous, caustic, cold-blooded, critical, cruel, discourteous, disobliging, hard, hard-hearted, harsh, heartless, hurtful, ill-natured, impolite, inconsiderate, inhuman, inhumane, insensitive, malevolent, malicious, mean, merciless, nasty, pitiless, rigid, rough, ruthless, *colloquial* sadistic, savage, selfish, severe, sharp, spiteful, stern, tactless, thoughtless, uncaring, uncharitable, unchristian, unfeeling, unfriendly, unpleasant, unsympathetic, unthoughtful, vicious.

unknown /ʌnˈnəʊn/ *adjective* (often + *to*) not known; unfamiliar. ● *noun* unknown thing, person, or quantity. □ **unknown quantity** mysterious or obscure person or thing. **Unknown Soldier, Warrior** unidentified soldier symbolizing nation's dead in war.

■ *adjective* anonymous, disguised, incognito, little known, mysterious, nameless, obscure, strange, uncharted, undiscovered, undistinguished, unexplored, unfamiliar, unheard-of, unidentified, unmapped, unnamed, unrecognized, unspecified.

unlawful /ʌnˈlɔːfʊl/ *adjective* illegal; not permissible. □ **unlawfully** *adverb*. **unlawfulness** *noun*.

■ see ILLEGAL.

unleaded /ʌnˈledɪd/ *adjective* (of petrol etc.) without added lead.

unleash /ʌnˈliːʃ/ *verb* **1** free from leash or restraint. **2** set free to pursue or attack.

unleavened /ʌnˈlev(ə)nd/ *adjective* made without yeast etc.

unless /ʌnˈles/ *conjunction* if not; except when.

unlettered /ʌnˈletəd/ *adjective* illiterate.

unlike /ʌnˈlaɪk/ *adjective* not like; different. ● *preposition* differently from. □ **unlikeness** *noun*.

unlikely /ʌnˈlaɪklɪ/ *adjective* (**-ier**, **-iest**) **1** improbable. **2** (+ *to do*) not expected to. **3** unpromising.

■ **1** doubtful, dubious, far-fetched, implausible, improbable, incredible, suspect, suspicious, *colloquial* tall (*story*), unbelievable, unconvincing, *colloquial* unthinkable; [*of possibility etc.*] distant, faint, outside, remote, slight.

unlimited /ʌnˈlɪmɪtɪd(ə)n/ *adjective* having no limit.

■ see BOUNDLESS.

unlisted /ʌnˈlɪstɪd/ *adjective* not included in list, esp. of Stock Exchange prices or telephone numbers.

unload /ʌnˈləʊd/ *verb* **1** remove load from (vehicle etc.). **2** remove (load) from vehicle etc. **3** remove ammunition from (gun). **4** *colloquial* get rid of.

■ **1, 2, 4** disburden, discharge, drop off, dump, empty, offload, take off, unpack.

unlock /ʌnˈlɒk/ *verb* **1** release lock of. **2** release or disclose by unlocking. **3** release feelings etc. from.

unlooked-for /ʌnˈlʊktfɔː/ *adjective* unexpected.

unloved /ʌnˈlʌvd/ *adjective* not loved.

■ friendless, unpopular, unvalued.

unlucky /ʌnˈlʌkɪ/ *adjective* (**-ier**, **-iest**) **1** not fortunate or successful; wretched. **2** disastrous. **3** bringing bad luck. **4** ill-judged. □ **unluckily** *adverb*.

■ **1** accident-prone, cursed, hapless, *colloquial* jinxed, luckless, unfortunate, unhappy, unsuccessful, wretched. **2** calamitous, disastrous, dreadful, tragic, unfortunate, untimely, unwelcome. **3** cursed, fateful, ill-fated, ill-omened, ill-starred, inauspicious, *colloquial* jinxed, ominous, unfavourable.

unman /ʌnˈmæn/ *verb* (**-nn-**) deprive of courage, self-control, etc.

unmanageable /ʌnˈmænɪdʒəb(ə)l/ *adjective* not (easily) managed or controlled.

■ see UNDISCIPLINED.

unmannerly /ʌnˈmænəlɪ/ *adjective* ill-mannered.

unmarried /ʌnˈmærɪd/ *adjective* not married; single.
■ available, celibate, free, single, unattached, unwed.

unmask /ʌnˈmɑːsk/ *verb* **1** remove mask from. **2** expose true character of. **3** remove one's mask.

unmentionable /ʌnˈmenʃənəb(ə)l/ *adjective* unsuitable for polite conversation. ● *noun* (in *plural*) *jocular* undergarments.
■ *adjective* see TABOO *adjective*.

unmistakable /ʌnmɪˈsteɪkəb(ə)l/ *adjective* clear, obvious, plain. □ **unmistakably** *adverb*.
■ see DEFINITE 2, OBVIOUS.

unmitigated /ʌnˈmɪtɪɡeɪtɪd/ *adjective* **1** not modified. **2** absolute.

unmoved /ʌnˈmuːvd/ *adjective* **1** not moved. **2** constant in purpose. **3** unemotional.

unnameable /ʌnˈneɪməb(ə)l/ *adjective* that cannot be named, esp. too bad to be named.

unnamed /ʌnˈneɪmd/ *adjective* not named.
■ see UNIDENTIFIED.

unnatural /ʌnˈnætʃər(ə)l/ *adjective* **1** contrary to nature; not normal. **2** lacking natural feelings. **3** artificial. **4** forced. □ **unnaturally** *adverb*. **unnaturalness** *noun*.
■ **1** abnormal, bizarre, eccentric, eerie, extraordinary, fantastic, freak, freakish, inexplicable, magic, magical, odd, outlandish, preternatural, queer, strange, supernatural, unaccountable, uncanny, unusual, weird. **2** callous, cold-blooded, cruel, hard-hearted, heartless, inhuman, inhumane, monstrous, perverse, perverted, *colloquial* sadistic, savage, stony-hearted, unfeeling, unkind. **3** artificial, fabricated, imitation, man-made, manufactured, simulated, synthetic. **4** affected, artificial, bogus, contrived, fake, false, feigned, forced, insincere, laboured, overdone, *colloquial* phoney, pretended, pseudo, put on, self-conscious, stagy, stiff, stilted, theatrical, uncharacteristic, unspontaneous.

unnecessary /ʌnˈnesəsərɪ/ *adjective* **1** not necessary. **2** superfluous. □ **unnecessarily** *adverb*.
■ **1** dispensable, expendable, inessential, needless, non-essential, uncalled-for, unjustified, unneeded, unwanted, useless. **2** excessive, extra, redundant, supererogatory, superfluous, surplus.

unnerve /ʌnˈnɜːv/ *verb* (**-ving**) deprive of confidence etc.

unobjectionable /ʌnəbˈdʒekʃənəb(ə)l/ *adjective* acceptable.

unobtrusive /ʌnəbˈtruːsɪv/ *adjective* not making oneself or itself noticed. □ **unobtrusively** *adverb*.
■ see INCONSPICUOUS.

unofficial /ʌnəˈfɪʃ(ə)l/ *adjective* not officially authorized or confirmed. □ **unofficial strike**

strike not ratified by trade union. □ **unofficially** *adverb*.
■ informal, off the record, private, secret, unauthorized, unconfirmed, undocumented, unlicensed.

unorthodox /ʌnˈɔːθədɒks/ *adjective* not orthodox. □ **unorthodoxly** *adverb*. **unorthodoxy** *noun*.
■ see UNCONVENTIONAL.

unpack /ʌnˈpæk/ *verb* **1** open and empty. **2** take (thing) from package etc.

unpaid /ʌnˈpeɪd/ *adjective* **1** (of debt) not paid. **2** not receiving payment for work etc.
■ **1** due, outstanding, owing, payable, unsettled. **2** honorary, unremunerative, unsalaried, voluntary.

unpalatable /ʌnˈpælətəb(ə)l/ *adjective* (of food, suggestion, etc.) disagreeable, distasteful.
■ disgusting, distasteful, inedible, nasty, nauseating, *colloquial* off, rancid, sickening, sour, tasteless, unacceptable, unappetizing, uneatable, unpleasant.

unparalleled /ʌnˈpærəleld/ *adjective* unequalled.
■ see UNEQUALLED.

unpardonable /ʌnˈpɑːdənəb(ə)l/ *adjective* not able to be pardoned.
■ see UNFORGIVABLE.

unparliamentary /ʌnpɑːləˈmentərɪ/ *adjective* contrary to proper parliamentary usage. □ **unparliamentary language** oaths, abuse.

unperceptive /ʌnpəˈseptɪv/ *adjective* not perceptive; unobservant. □ **unperceptively** *adverb*. **unperceptiveness** *noun*.
■ inattentive, slow, stupid, uncritical, undiscriminating, unobservant, unresponsive.

unpick /ʌnˈpɪk/ *verb* undo sewing of.

unplaced /ʌnˈpleɪst/ *adjective* not placed as one of the first 3 in race etc.

unplanned /ʌnˈplænd/ *adjective* not planned.
■ see SPONTANEOUS 1.

unpleasant /ʌnˈplez(ə)nt/ *adjective* disagreeable. □ **unpleasantly** *adverb*. **unpleasantness** *noun*.
■ abhorrent, *colloquial* abominable, antisocial, *colloquial* appalling, atrocious, *colloquial* awful, bad, bad-tempered, *colloquial* beastly, bitter, coarse, crude, despicable, detestable, diabolical, dirty, disagreeable, disgusting, displeasing, distasteful, *colloquial* dreadful, evil, execrable, fearful, fearsome, filthy, foul, frightful, *colloquial* ghastly, grim, grisly, gruesome, harsh, hateful, hellish, hideous, *colloquial* horrible, *colloquial* horrid, horrifying, improper, indecent, inhuman, irksome, loathsome, *colloquial* lousy, malevolent, malicious, mucky, nasty, nauseating, objectionable, obnoxious, odious, offensive, off-putting, repellent, repugnant, repulsive, revolting, rude, *colloquial* shocking, sickening, sickly, sordid, sour, spiteful, squalid, *colloquial*

terrible, ugly, unattractive, uncouth, undesirable, unfriendly, unkind, unpalatable, unsavoury, unwelcome, upsetting, vexing, vicious, vile, vulgar.

unplug /ʌn'plʌg/ *verb* (**-gg-**) **1** disconnect (electrical device) by removing plug from socket. **2** unstop.

unplumbed /ʌn'plʌmd/ *adjective* **1** not plumbed. **2** not fully explored or understood.

unpopular /ʌn'pɒpjʊlə/ *adjective* not popular; disliked. □ **unpopularity** /-'lær-/ *noun.*

■ despised, disliked, friendless, hated, ignored, minority (*interests*), out of favour, rejected, shunned, unfashionable, unloved, unwanted.

unpractised /ʌn'præktɪst/ *adjective* (*US* **unpracticed**) **1** not experienced or skilled. **2** not put into practice.

unprecedented /ʌn'presɪdentɪd/ *adjective* having no precedent; unparalleled.

unpredictable /ʌnprɪ'dɪktəb(ə)l/ *adjective* not predictable. □ **unpredictability** /-'bɪlɪtɪ/ *noun.* **unpredictably** *adverb.*

■ changeable, surprising, uncertain, unexpected, unforeseeable, variable.

unprejudiced /ʌn'predʒʊdɪst/ *adjective* not prejudiced.

■ see UNBIASED.

unpremeditated /ʌnpri:'medɪteɪtɪd/ *adjective* not planned beforehand.

■ see SPONTANEOUS 1.

unprepared /ʌnprɪ'peəd/ *adjective* not prepared beforehand; not ready. □ **unpreparedness** *noun.*

■ caught out, ill-equipped, surprised, taken off guard, unready.

unprepossessing /ʌnpri:pə'zesɪŋ/ *adjective* unattractive.

unpretentious /ʌnprɪ'tenʃəs/ *adjective* modest, simple; not putting on excessive display. □ **unpretentiously** *adverb.* **unpretentiousness** *noun.*

■ humble, modest, plain, simple, straightforward, unaffected, unassuming, unostentatious, unsophisticated.

unprincipled /ʌn'prɪnsɪp(ə)ld/ *adjective* lacking or not based on moral principles.

unprintable /ʌn'prɪntəb(ə)l/ *adjective* too offensive or indecent to be printed.

unproductive /ʌnprə'dʌktɪv/ *adjective* not productive. □ **unproductively** *adverb.* **unproductiveness** *noun.*

■ arid, barren, fruitless, futile, ineffective, infertile, pointless, sterile, unfruitful, unprofitable, unrewarding, useless, valueless, worthless.

unprofessional /ʌnprə'feʃən(ə)l/ *adjective* **1** contrary to professional standards. **2** unskilled, amateurish. □ **unprofessionally** *adverb.*

■ **1** casual, lax, negligent, unethical, unfitting, unprincipled, unseemly, unworthy. **2** amateurish, incompetent, inefficient, inexpert, shoddy, sloppy, unskilful, unskilled.

unprofitable /ʌn'prɒfɪtəb(ə)l/ *adjective* not profitable. □ **unprofitably** *adverb.*

■ futile, loss-making, pointless, uncommercial, uneconomic, ungainful, unproductive, unremunerative, unrewarding, worthless.

unprompted /ʌn'prɒmptɪd/ *adjective* spontaneous.

unprovable /ʌn'pru:vəb(ə)l/ *adjective* not able to be proved.

■ doubtful, inconclusive, questionable, undemonstrable, unsubstantiated, unverifiable.

unpunctual /ʌn'pʌŋktʃʊəl/ *adjective* not punctual. □ **unpunctuality** /-tjʊ'ælɪtɪ/ *noun.*

■ behindhand, belated, delayed, detained, last-minute, late, overdue, tardy, unreliable.

unputdownable /ʌnpʊt'daʊnəb(ə)l/ *adjective colloquial* compulsively readable.

unqualified /ʌn'kwɒlɪfaɪd/ *adjective* **1** not qualified or competent. **2** complete.

unquestionable /ʌn'kwestʃənəb(ə)l/ *adjective* that cannot be disputed or doubted. □ **unquestionably** *adverb.*

unquote /ʌn'kwəʊt/ *interjection: used in dictation etc. to indicate closing quotation marks.*

unravel /ʌn'ræv(ə)l/ *verb* (**-ll-**; *US* **-l-**) **1** make or become unknitted, unknotted, etc. **2** solve (mystery etc.). **3** undo (knitted fabric).

■ **1** disentangle, free, sort out, straighten out, undo, untangle. **2** clear up, solve, sort out, work out.

unreal /ʌn'rɪəl/ *adjective* **1** not real; imaginary. **2** *slang* incredible.

■ **1** chimerical, false, fanciful, hypothetical, illusory, imaginary, imagined, make-believe, non-existent, phantasmal, *colloquial* pretend, pseudo, sham.

unrealistic /ʌnrɪə'lɪstɪk/ *adjective* **1** not true to life. **2** idealistic; not practical. □ **unrealistically** *adverb.*

■ **1** inaccurate, non-representational, unconvincing, unlifelike, unnatural, unrecognizable. **2** delusory, fanciful, idealistic, impossible, impracticable, impractical, overambitious, quixotic, romantic, silly, visionary, unreasonable, unworkable.

unreasonable /ʌn'ri:zənəb(ə)l/ *adjective* **1** excessive. **2** not heeding reason. □ **unreasonably** *adverb.*

■ **1** see EXCESSIVE. **2** see IRRATIONAL 1,2.

unrecognizable /ʌn'rekəgnaɪzəb(ə)l/ *adjective* (also **-isable**) not able to be recognized.

■ see UNIDENTIFIABLE.

unregenerate /ʌnrɪ'dʒenərət/ *adjective* obstinately wrong or bad.

unrelated /ʌnrɪ'leɪtɪd/ *adjective* not related.
■ beside the point, different, extraneous, independent, irrelevant, unconnected.

unrelenting /ʌnrɪ'lentɪŋ/ *adjective* 1 not abating. 2 merciless.

unreliable /ʌnrɪ'laɪəb(ə)l/ *adjective* not reliable; erratic. □ **unreliability** /-'bɪlɪtɪ/ *noun*.
■ changeable, deceptive, erratic, fallible, false, fickle, flimsy, inaccurate, inconsistent, irresponsible, misleading, suspect, treacherous, unconvincing, undependable, unpredictable, unsound, unstable, untrustworthy.

unrelieved /ʌnrɪ'liːvd/ *adjective* monotonously uniform.

unremarked /ʌnrɪ'mɑːkt/ *adjective* not mentioned or remarked on.

unremitting /ʌnrɪ'mɪtɪŋ/ *adjective* incessant. □ **unremittingly** *adverb*.

unremunerative /ʌnrɪ'mjuːnərətɪv/ *adjective* unprofitable.

unrepentant /ʌnrɪ'pent(ə)nt/ *adjective* not repentant; impenitent. □ **unrepentantly** *adverb*.
■ brazen, confirmed, conscienceless, hardened, impenitent, incorrigible, incurable, inveterate, irredeemable, shameless, unapologetic, unashamed, unblushing, unreformable, unregenerate.

unrequited /ʌnrɪ'kwaɪtɪd/ *adjective* (of love etc.) not returned.

unreserved /ʌnrɪ'zɜːvd/ *adjective* without reservation. □ **unreservedly** /-vɪdlɪ/ *adverb*.

unrest /ʌn'rest/ *noun* disturbance, turmoil, trouble.

unripe /ʌn'raɪp/ *adjective* not ripe.
■ green, immature, sour, unready.

unrivalled /ʌn'raɪv(ə)ld/ *adjective* (*US* **unrivaled**) having no equal.
■ see UNEQUALLED.

unroll /ʌn'rəʊl/ *verb* 1 open out from rolled-up state. 2 display; be displayed.

unruffled /ʌn'rʌf(ə)ld/ *adjective* calm.

unruly /ʌn'ruːlɪ/ *adjective* (**-ier, -iest**) undisciplined, disorderly. □ **unruliness** *noun*.
■ see UNDISCIPLINED.

unsafe /ʌn'seɪf/ *adjective* not safe; dangerous.
■ see DANGEROUS.

unsatisfactory /ʌnsætɪs'fæktərɪ/ *adjective* poor, unacceptable. □ **unsatisfactorily** *adverb*.
■ defective, deficient, disappointing, displeasing, dissatisfying, faulty, frustrating, imperfect, inadequate, incompetent, inefficient, inferior, insufficient, lacking, not good enough, poor, sad, unacceptable, unhappy, unsatisfying, wretched.

unsaturated /ʌn'sætʃəreɪtɪd/ *adjective* Chemistry (of fat) containing double or triple molecular bonds and therefore capable of combining with hydrogen.

unsavoury /ʌn'seɪvərɪ/ *adjective* (*US* **unsavory**) 1 disgusting. 2 (esp. morally) offensive.

unscathed /ʌn'skeɪðd/ *adjective* uninjured, unharmed.

unschooled /ʌn'skuːld/ *adjective* uneducated, untrained.

unscientific /ʌnsaɪən'tɪfɪk/ *adjective* not scientific in method etc. □ **unscientifically** *adverb*.

unscramble /ʌn'skræmb(ə)l/ *verb* (**-ling**) decode; interpret (scrambled transmission etc.).

unscreened /ʌn'skriːnd/ *adjective* 1 (esp. of coal) not passed through screen. 2 not checked, esp. for security or medical problems. 3 not having screen. 4 not shown on screen.

unscrew /ʌn'skruː/ *verb* 1 unfasten by removing screw(s). 2 loosen (screw).

unscripted /ʌn'skrɪptɪd/ *adjective* (of speech etc.) delivered impromptu.

unscrupulous /ʌn'skruːpjʊləs/ *adjective* without scruples; unprincipled. □ **unscrupulously** *adverb*. **unscrupulousness** *noun*.
■ amoral, conscienceless, corrupt, *colloquial* crooked, cunning, dishonest, dishonourable, immoral, improper, self-interested, shameless, slippery, sly, unconscionable, unethical, untrustworthy.

unseasonal /ʌn'siːzən(ə)l/ *adjective* not typical of the time or season.

unseat /ʌn'siːt/ *verb* 1 remove from (esp. parliamentary) seat. 2 dislodge from horseback etc.

unseeing /ʌn'siːɪŋ/ *adjective* 1 unobservant. 2 blind. □ **unseeingly** *adverb*.

unseemly /ʌn'siːmlɪ/ *adjective* (**-ier, -iest**) 1 indecent. 2 unbecoming. □ **unseemliness** *noun*.
■ 2 see UNBECOMING 2.

unseen /ʌn'siːn/ *adjective* 1 not seen; invisible. 2 (of translation) to be done without preparation.
● *noun* unseen translation.
■ *adjective* 1 see INVISIBLE.

unselfconscious /ʌnself'kɒnʃəs/ *adjective* not self-conscious; natural. □ **unselfconsciously** *adverb*.

unselfish /ʌn'selfɪʃ/ *adjective* concerned about others; sharing. □ **unselfishly** *adverb*. **unselfishness** *noun*.
■ altruistic, caring, charitable, considerate, disinterested, generous, humanitarian, kind, liberal, magnanimous, open-handed, philanthropic, public-spirited, self-effacing, selfless, self-sacrificing, thoughtful, ungrudging, unstinting.

unsettled /ʌn'set(ə)ld/ *adjective* 1 restless, disturbed. 2 open to further discussion; liable to change. 3 not paid.

unsex /ʌn'seks/ *verb* deprive of qualities of one's (esp. female) sex.

unshakeable /ʌn'ʃeɪkəb(ə)l/ *adjective* firm; obstinate.

unsightly /ʌn'saɪtlɪ/ *adjective* ugly. □ **unsightliness** *noun*.
■ see UGLY 1.

unskilful /ʌn'skɪlfʊl/ *adjective* not having or showing skill. □ **unskilfully** *adverb*.
■ amateurish, bungled, clumsy, crude, incompetent, inept, inexpert, maladroit, rough-and-ready, shoddy, unprofessional.

unskilled /ʌn'skɪld/ *adjective* lacking or (of work) not needing special skills.
■ inexperienced, unqualified, untrained.

unsociable /ʌn'səʊʃəb(ə)l/ *adjective* disliking company.

USAGE *Unsociable* is sometimes confused with *unsocial*.
■ see UNFRIENDLY.

unsocial /ʌn'səʊʃ(ə)l/ *adjective* **1** not social; not suitable for or seeking society. **2** outside normal working day. **3** antisocial.

USAGE *Unsocial* is sometimes confused with *unsociable*.

unsolicited /ʌnsə'lɪsɪtɪd/ *adjective* voluntary.

unsophisticated /ʌnsə'fɪstɪkeɪtɪd/ *adjective* artless, simple, natural.
■ artless, childlike, guileless, ingenuous, innocent, *colloquial* lowbrow, naive, plain, provincial, simple, simple-minded, straightforward, unaffected, uncomplicated, unostentatious, unpretentious, unrefined, unworldly.

unsound /ʌn'saʊnd/ *adjective* **1** not sound; unhealthy, rotten. **2** weak. **3** unreliable; ill-founded.
■ **1** see ROTTEN 1, UNHEALTHY 1. **2** see WEAK 1. **3** see UNRELIABLE.

unsparing /ʌn'speərɪŋ/ *adjective* **1** lavish. **2** merciless.

unspeakable /ʌn'spiːkəb(ə)l/ *adjective* **1** that words cannot express. **2** indescribably bad. □ **unspeakably** *adverb*.
■ **1** indescribable, ineffable, inexpressible, nameless, unutterable. **2** abominable, appalling, dreadful, horrible, indescribable, nameless, *colloquial* shocking, *colloquial* terrible, unutterable.

unspecified /ʌn'spesɪfaɪd/ *adjective* not specified.
■ see UNIDENTIFIED.

unstable /ʌn'steɪb(ə)l/ *adjective* (**-r, -st**) **1** likely to fall. **2** not stable emotionally. **3** changeable.
■ **1** see UNSTEADY 1. **2, 3** capricious, changeable, fickle, inconsistent, inconstant, mercurial, shifting, unpredictable, unsteady, variable, volatile.

unsteady /ʌn'stedɪ/ *adjective* (**-ier, -iest**) **1** not firm. **2** changeable. **3** not regular. □ **unsteadily** *adverb*. **unsteadiness** *noun*.

■ **1** flimsy, frail, insecure, precarious, rickety, *colloquial* rocky, shaky, tottering, unbalanced, unsafe, unstable, wobbly. **2, 3** changeable, erratic, flickering, fluctuating, inconstant, intermittent, irregular, quavering, quivering, trembling, tremulous, variable, wavering.

unstick /ʌn'stɪk/ *verb* (*past & past participle* **unstuck**) separate (thing stuck to another). □ **come unstuck** *colloquial* fail.

unstinting /ʌn'stɪntɪŋ/ *adjective* lavish; limitless. □ **unstintingly** *adverb*.

unstressed /ʌn'strest/ *adjective* not pronounced with stress.

unstring /ʌn'strɪŋ/ *verb* (*past & past participle* **unstrung**) **1** remove string(s) of (bow, harp, etc.). **2** take (beads etc.) off string. **3** (esp. as **unstrung** *adjective*) unnerve.

unstructured /ʌn'strʌktʃəd/ *adjective* **1** without structure. **2** informal.

unstudied /ʌn'stʌdɪd/ *adjective* easy, natural, spontaneous.

unsuccessful /ʌnsək'sesfʊl/ *adjective* not successful. □ **unsuccessfully** *adverb*.
■ [*of actions, ventures, etc.*] abortive, failed, fruitless, futile, ill-fated, ineffective, ineffectual, loss-making, sterile, unavailing, unproductive, unprofitable, unsatisfactory, useless, vain, worthless; [*of people*] beaten, defeated, foiled, hapless, losing, luckless, unlucky, *literary* vanquished.

unsuitable /ʌn'suːtəb(ə)l, ʌn'sjuːtəb(ə)l/ *adjective* not suitable. □ **unsuitability** /-'bɪlɪtɪ/ *noun*. **unsuitably** *adverb*.
■ ill-chosen, ill-judged, ill-timed, inapposite, inappropriate, incongruous, inept, irrelevant, unbefitting, unfitting, unhappy, unsatisfactory, unseasonable, unseemly, untimely.

unsung /ʌn'sʌŋ/ *adjective* not celebrated; unrecognized.

unsure /ʌn'ʃʊə/ *adjective* not sure. □ **unsureness** *noun*.
■ see UNCERTAIN 1.

unsurpassable /ʌnsə'pɑːsəb(ə)l/ *adjective* that cannot be surpassed. □ **unsurpassably** *adverb*.

unsurpassed /ʌnsə'pɑːst/ *adjective* not surpassed.
■ see UNEQUALLED.

unsuspecting /ʌnsəs'pektɪŋ/ *adjective* not suspecting.
■ see CREDULOUS.

unswerving /ʌn'swɜːvɪŋ/ *adjective* steady, constant. □ **unswervingly** *adverb*.

unsympathetic /ʌnsɪmpə'θetɪk/ *adjective* not sympathetic. □ **unsympathetically** *adverb*.

■ apathetic, cool, cold, dispassionate, hard-hearted, heartless, impassive, indifferent, insensitive, neutral, pitiless, reserved, ruthless, stony, stony-hearted, unaffected, uncaring, uncharitable, unconcerned, unfeeling, uninterested, unkind, unmoved, unpitying, unresponsive.

unsystematic /ʌnsɪstə'mætɪk/ *adjective* not systematic. □ **unsystematically** *adverb*.
■ anarchic, chaotic, confused, disorderly, disorganized, haphazard, illogical, jumbled, muddled, *colloquial* shambolic, sloppy, unmethodical, unplanned, unstructured, untidy.

unthinkable /ʌn'θɪŋkəb(ə)l/ *adjective* **1** unimaginable, inconceivable. **2** *colloquial* highly unlikely or undesirable.
■ **1** see INCONCEIVABLE.

unthinking /ʌn'θɪŋkɪŋ/ *adjective* **1** thoughtless. **2** unintentional, inadvertent. □ **unthinkingly** *adverb*.
■ **1** see THOUGHTLESS 2,3. **2** see UNINTENTIONAL.

untidy /ʌn'taɪdɪ/ *adjective* (**-ier, -iest**) not neat or orderly. □ **untidily** *adverb*. **untidiness** *noun*
■ bedraggled, blowzy, careless, chaotic, cluttered, confused, dishevelled, disordered, disorderly, disorganized, haphazard, higgledy-piggledy, in disarray, jumbled, littered, messy, muddled, rumpled, *colloquial* scruffy, shabby, *colloquial* shambolic, slapdash, sloppy, slovenly, straggly, tangled, topsy-turvy, tousled, uncared-for, uncombed, ungroomed, unkempt, unsystematic, upside down.

untie /ʌn'taɪ/ *verb* **1** undo; unfasten. **2** release from bonds etc.
■ cast off (*boat*), disentangle, free, loosen, release, unbind, undo, unfasten, unknot, untether.

until /ən'tɪl/ *preposition & conjunction* = TILL[1].

USAGE *Until*, as opposed to *till*, is used especially at the beginning of a sentence and in formal style, as in *Until you told me, I had no idea* or *He resided there until his decease.*

untimely /ʌn'taɪmlɪ/ *adjective* **1** inopportune. **2** premature.

untiring /ʌn'taɪərɪŋ/ *adjective* tireless.

unto /'ʌntʊ/ *preposition archaic* to.

untold /ʌn'təʊld/ *adjective* **1** not told. **2** immeasurable.

untouchable /ʌn'tʌtʃəb(ə)l/ *adjective* that may not be touched. ● *noun* Hindu of group believed to defile higher castes on contact.

untoward /ʌntə'wɔːd/ *adjective* **1** inconvenient, unlucky. **2** awkward. **3** refractory. **4** unseemly.

untrammelled /ʌn'træm(ə)ld/ *adjective* not hampered.

untried /ʌn'traɪd/ *adjective* not tried or tested.
■ experimental, innovatory, new, novel, unproved, untested.

untroubled /ʌn'trʌb(ə)ld/ *adjective* not troubled; calm.
■ carefree, peaceful, straightforward, undisturbed, uninterrupted, unruffled.

untrue /ʌn'truː/ *adjective* **1** not true; contrary to facts. **2** (often + *to*) not faithful.
■ **1** see FALSE 1. **2** see UNFAITHFUL.

untrustworthy /ʌn'trʌstwɜːðɪ/ *adjective* not trustworthy. □ **untrustworthiness** *noun*.
■ see DISHONEST.

untruth /ʌn'truːθ/ *noun* **1** being untrue. **2** lie. □ **untruthful** *adjective*. **untruthfulness** *noun*.
■ **2** see LIE[2] *noun* 1. □ **untruthful** see LYING *adjective*.

unused *adjective* **1** /ʌn'juːzd/ never used. **2** /ʌn'juːzd/ not in use. **3** /ʌn'juːst/ (+ *to*) not accustomed to.
■ **1** blank, clean, fresh, in mint condition, intact, new, pristine, unopened, untouched, unworn.

unusual /ʌn'juːʒʊəl/ *adjective* **1** not usual. **2** remarkable. □ **unusually** *adverb*.
■ abnormal, atypical, curious, different, exceptional, extraordinary, *colloquial* freakish, funny, irregular, odd, out of the ordinary, peculiar, queer, rare, remarkable, singular, strange, surprising, uncommon, unconventional, unexpected, unfamiliar, unheard-of, *disputed* unique, unnatural, unorthodox, untypical, unwonted.

unutterable /ʌn'ʌtərəb(ə)l/ *adjective* inexpressible; beyond description. □ **unutterably** *adverb*.
■ see INDESCRIBABLE 1.

unvarnished /ʌn'vɑːnɪʃt/ *adjective* **1** not varnished. **2** plain, direct, simple.

unveil /ʌn'veɪl/ *verb* **1** uncover (statue etc.) ceremonially. **2** reveal (secrets etc.).

unversed /ʌn'vɜːst/ *adjective* (usually + *in*) not experienced or skilled.

unwanted /ʌn'wɒntɪd/ *adjective* not wanted.
■ see UNNECESSARY 1.

unwarrantable /ʌn'wɒrəntəb(ə)l/ *adjective* (also **unwarranted**) unjustified.
■ see UNJUSTIFIABLE.

unwary /ʌn'weərɪ/ *adjective* not cautious. □ **unwarily** *adverb*. **unwariness** *noun*
■ see CARELESS 2.

unwashed /ʌn'wɒʃt/ *adjective* not washed or clean. □ **the great unwashed** *colloquial* the rabble.

unwavering /ʌn'weɪvərɪŋ/ *adjective* not wavering; resolute.
■ see RESOLUTE.

unwelcome /ʌn'welkəm/ *adjective* not welcome or acceptable.
■ disagreeable, unacceptable, undesirable, uninvited, unpopular, unwanted.

unwell /ʌn'wel/ *adjective* ill.
■ see ILL *adjective* 1.

unwholesome /ʌn'həʊlsəm/ *adjective* **1** detrimental to moral or physical health. **2** unhealthy-looking.
■ **1** see UNHEALTHY 2. **2** see SICKLY 1.

unwieldy /ʌn'wiːldɪ/ *adjective* (**-ier, -iest**) cumbersome or hard to manage owing to size, shape, etc.
■ awkward, bulky, clumsy, cumbersome, inconvenient, ungainly, unmanageable.

unwilling /ʌn'wɪlɪŋ/ *adjective* reluctant. □ **unwillingly** *adverb*. **unwillingness** *noun*.
■ averse, disinclined, grudging, half-hearted, hesitant, ill-disposed, indisposed, lazy, loath, opposed, reluctant, resistant, slow, uncooperative, unenthusiastic, unhelpful.

unwind /ʌn'waɪnd/ *verb* (*past* and *past participle* **unwound**) **1** draw out or become drawn out after having been wound. **2** *colloquial* relax.

unwise /ʌn'waɪz/ *adjective* not wise; foolish. □ **unwisely** *adverb*.
■ daft, foolhardy, foolish, ill-advised, ill-judged, illogical, impolitic, imprudent, inadvisable, indiscreet, inexperienced, injudicious, irrational, irresponsible, mistaken, obtuse, perverse, rash, reckless, senseless, short-sighted, silly, stupid, thoughtless, unintelligent, unperceptive, unreasonable.

unwitting /ʌn'wɪtɪŋ/ *adjective* **1** not knowing; unaware. **2** unintentional. □ **unwittingly** *adverb*.

unwonted /ʌn'wəʊntɪd/ *adjective* not customary or usual.

unworldly /ʌn'wɜːldlɪ/ *adjective* **1** spiritual. **2** naive. □ **unworldliness** *noun*.
■ **1** see SPIRITUAL *adjective* 2.

unworthy /ʌn'wɜːðɪ/ *adjective* (**-ier, -iest**) **1** (often + *of*) not worthy or befitting. **2** discreditable, unseemly. □ **unworthiness** *noun*.
■ **1** unbecoming, unbefitting, unsuitable; (*unworthy of*) beneath. **2** contemptible, despicable, discreditable, dishonourable, disreputable, ignoble, mediocre, second-rate, shameful, substandard, undeserving.

unwritten /ʌn'rɪt(ə)n/ *adjective* **1** not written. **2** (of law etc.) based on tradition or judicial decision, not on statute.
■ **1** oral, spoken, verbal.

unyielding /ʌn'jiːldɪŋ/ *adjective* not yielding; firm.
■ see INFLEXIBLE 2.

up *adverb* **1** towards or in higher place or place regarded as higher, e.g. the north, a capital. **2** to or in erect or required position. **3** in or into active condition. **4** in stronger position. **5** (+ *to, till*, etc.) to specified place, person, or time. **6** higher in price. **7** completely. **8** completed. **9** into compact, accumulated, or secure state. **10** having risen. **11** happening, esp. unusually. ● *preposition* **1** upwards and along, through, or into. **2** at higher part of. ● *adjective* directed upwards. ● *noun* spell of good fortune. ● *verb* (**-pp-**) **1** *colloquial* start (abruptly or unexpectedly) to speak or act. **2** raise. □ **on the up (and up)** *colloquial* steadily improving. **up against 1** close to. **2** in(to) contact with. **3** *colloquial* confronted with. **up and about (or doing)** having risen from bed; active. **up-and-coming** *colloquial* (of person) promising, progressing. **up and down 1** to and fro (along). **2** in every direction. **3** *colloquial* in varying health or spirits. **up for** available for or standing for (sale, office, etc.). **upstate** *US* (in, to, or of) provincial, esp. northern, part of a state. **upstream** ● *adverb* against flow of stream etc. ● *adjective* moving upstream. **up to 1** until. **2** below or equal to. **3** incumbent on. **4** capable of. **5** occupied or busy with. **up to date** see DATE¹. **uptown** *US* (in, into, or of) residential part of town or city. **upwind** in the direction from which the wind is blowing.

upbeat *noun Music* unaccented beat. ● *adjective colloquial* optimistic, cheerful.

upbraid /ʌp'breɪd/ *verb* (often + *with, for*) chide, reproach.

upbringing *noun* child's rearing.
■ breeding, bringing up, care, education, instruction, nurture, raising, rearing, teaching, training.

up-country /ʌp'kʌntrɪ/ *adjective* & *adverb* inland.

update *verb* /ʌp'deɪt/ (**-ting**) bring up to date. ● *noun* /'ʌpdeɪt/ **1** updating. **2** updated information etc.
■ *verb* amend, correct, modernize, review, revise.

up-end /ʌp'end/ *verb* set or rise up on end.

upfront /ʌp'frʌnt/ *colloquial adverb* (usually **up front**) **1** at the front; in front. **2** (of payments) in advance. ● *adjective* **1** honest, frank, direct. **2** (of payments) made in advance.

upgrade /ʌp'greɪd/ *verb* (**-ding**) **1** raise in rank etc. **2** improve (equipment etc.).
■ **2** enhance, expand, improve.

upheaval /ʌp'hiːv(ə)l/ *noun* sudden esp. violent change or disturbance.
■ chaos, commotion, confusion, disorder, disruption, disturbance, revolution, to-do, turmoil.

uphill *adverb* /ʌp'hɪl/ up a slope. ● *adjective* /'ʌphɪl/ **1** sloping up; ascending. **2** arduous.
■ *adjective* **2** arduous, difficult, exhausting, gruelling, hard, laborious, stiff, strenuous, taxing, tough.

uphold /ʌp'həʊld/ *verb* (*past* & *past participle* **upheld**) **1** support. **2** maintain, confirm. □ **upholder** *noun*.
■ back, champion, confirm, defend, endorse, maintain, preserve, protect, stand by, support, sustain.

upholster /ʌp'həʊlstə/ *verb* provide (furniture) with upholstery. □ **upholsterer** *noun*.

upholstery *noun* 1 covering, padding, springs, etc. for furniture. 2 upholsterer's work.

upkeep *noun* 1 maintenance in good condition. 2 cost or means of this.

■ 1 care, conservation, keep, maintenance, operation, preservation, running.

upland /'ʌplənd/ *noun* (usually in *plural*) higher parts of country. ● *adjective* of these parts.

uplift *verb* /ʌp'lɪft/ 1 raise. 2 (esp as **uplifting** *adjective*) elevate morally or emotionally. ● *noun* /'ʌplɪft/ 1 elevating influence. 2 support for breasts etc.

■ *verb* 2 (**uplifting**) civilizing, edifying, educational, enlightening, ennobling, enriching, humanizing, improving, spiritual.

upmarket /ʌp'mɑːkɪt/ *adjective* & *adverb* of or to more expensive sector of market.

upon /ə'pɒn/ *preposition* on.

USAGE *Upon* is usually more formal than *on*, but it is standard in *once upon a time* and *upon my word*.

upper /'ʌpə/ *adjective* 1 higher in place; situated above. 2 superior in rank etc. ● *noun* part of shoe or boot above sole. □ **on one's uppers** *colloquial* extremely short of money. **upper case** capital letters. **upper class** highest class of society, esp. the aristocracy. **upper crust** *colloquial* the aristocracy. **upper-crust** *colloquial* of or relating to the aristocracy. **upper-cut** hit upwards with arm bent. **the upper hand** dominance, control.

■ *adjective* 1 elevated, higher, raised, superior, upstairs. 2 see SUPERIOR *adjective* 1.

uppermost *adjective* 1 highest. 2 predominant. ● *adverb* on or to the top.

■ *adjective* 1 highest, loftiest, supreme, top, topmost.

uppity /'ʌpɪtɪ/ *adjective* (also **uppish**) *colloquial* self-assertive, arrogant.

upright /'ʌpraɪt/ *adjective* 1 erect, vertical. 2 (of piano) with vertical strings. 3 honourable, honest. ● *noun* 1 upright post or rod, esp. as structural support. 2 upright piano. □ **uprightness** *noun*.

■ *adjective* 1 erect, on end, perpendicular, vertical. 3 conscientious, fair, good, high-minded, honest, honourable, incorruptible, just, moral, principled, righteous, *colloquial* straight, true, trustworthy, upstanding, virtuous. ● *noun* 1 column, pole, post, vertical.

uprising *noun* insurrection.

uproar *noun* tumult, violent disturbance.

■ bedlam, brawling, chaos, clamour, commotion, confusion, din, disorder, disturbance, furore, hubbub, hullabaloo, noise, outburst, outcry, pandemonium, racket, riot, *colloquial* row, *colloquial* ructions, *colloquial* rumpus, tumult, turbulence, turmoil.

uproarious /ʌp'rɔːrɪəs/ *adjective* 1 very noisy.

2 provoking loud laughter; very funny. □ **uproariously** *adverb*.

uproot /ʌp'ruːt/ *verb* 1 pull (plant etc.) up from ground. 2 eradicate. 3 displace (person).

■ 1, 2 *literary* deracinate, destroy, eliminate, eradicate, extirpate, get rid of, grub up, pull up, remove, root out, tear up, weed out.

upset *verb* /ʌp'set/ (**-tt-**; *past & past participle* **upset**) 1 overturn. 2 disturb temper, digestion, or composure of. 3 disrupt. 4 defeat. ● *noun* /'ʌpset/ 1 disturbance. 2 surprising result. ● *adjective* /ʌp'set, 'ʌp-/ disturbed.

■ *verb* 1 capsize, destabilize, overturn, spill, tip over, topple. 2 agitate, alarm, annoy, disconcert, dismay, distress, disturb, excite, fluster, frighten, grieve, irritate, offend, perturb, rub up the wrong way, ruffle, scare, unnerve, worry. 3 affect, alter, change, confuse, disorganize, disrupt, hinder, interfere with, interrupt, spoil. 4 defeat, overthrow, topple, *literary* vanquish.

upshot *noun* outcome, conclusion.

upside down /ʌpsaɪd 'daʊn/ *adverb* & *adjective* 1 with upper and lower parts reversed; inverted. 2 in(to) total disorder.

■ 1 inverted, topsy-turvy, upturned, wrong way up.

upstage /ʌp'steɪdʒ/ *adjective* & *adverb* nearer back of theatre stage. ● *verb* (**-ging**) 1 move upstage to make (another actor) face away from audience. 2 divert attention from (person) to oneself.

upstairs *adverb* /ʌp'steəz/ to or on an upper floor. ● *adjective* /'ʌpsteəz/ situated upstairs. ● *noun* /ʌp'steəz/ upper floor.

upstanding /ʌp'stændɪŋ/ *adjective* 1 standing up. 2 strong and healthy. 3 honest.

upstart *noun* newly successful, esp. arrogant, person. ● *adjective* 1 that is an upstart. 2 of upstarts.

■ *noun* social climber, *colloquial usually derogatory* yuppie.

upsurge *noun* upward surge.

upswept *adjective* (of hair) combed to top of head.

upswing *noun* upward movement or trend.

uptake *noun* 1 (esp. in phrases **quick or slow on the uptake**) *colloquial* understanding. 2 taking up (of offer etc.).

uptight /ʌp'taɪt/ *adjective colloquial* 1 nervously tense; angry. 2 *US* rigidly conventional.

upturn *noun* /'ʌptɜːn/ upward trend, improvement. ● *verb* /ʌp'tɜːn/ turn up or upside down.

upward /'ʌpwəd/ *adverb* (also **upwards**) towards what is higher, more important, etc. ● *adjective* moving or extending upwards. □ **upwardly** *adverb*.

■ *adjective* ascending, going up, rising, uphill.

uranium /jʊ'reɪnɪəm/ *noun* radioactive heavy grey metallic element, capable of nuclear fission and used as source of nuclear energy.

urban /'ɜːbən/ *adjective* of, living in, or situated

in city or town. □ **urban guerrilla** terrorist operating in urban area.

■ built-up, metropolitan, suburban.

urbane /ɜːˈbeɪn/ *adjective* suave; elegant. □ **urbanity** /-ˈbæn-/ *noun*.

urbanize /ˈɜːbənaɪz/ *verb* (also **-ise**) (**-zing** or **-sing**) make urban, esp. by destroying rural quality of (district). □ **urbanization** *noun*.

urchin /ˈɜːtʃɪn/ *noun* **1** mischievous, esp. ragged, child. **2** sea urchin.

Urdu /ˈʊədu:/ *noun* Persian-influenced language related to Hindi, used esp. in Pakistan.

urea /jʊəˈriːə/ *noun* soluble nitrogenous compound contained esp. in urine.

ureter /jʊəˈriːtə/ *noun* duct carrying urine from kidney to bladder.

urethra /jʊəˈriːθrə/ *noun* (*plural* **-s**) duct carrying urine from bladder.

urge /ɜːdʒ/ *verb* (**-ging**) **1** (often + *on*) drive forcibly; hasten. **2** entreat or exhort earnestly or persistently. **3** (often + *on*, *upon*) advocate (action, argument, etc.) emphatically. ● *noun* **1** urging impulse or tendency. **2** strong desire.

■ *verb* **1** accelerate, compel, drive, egg on, force, goad, hasten, impel, incite, induce, move on, prod, prompt, propel, push, spur, stimulate. **2** appeal to, beg, beseech, chivvy, encourage, entreat, exhort, implore, importune, invite, nag, persuade, plead with, press, solicit. **3** advise, advocate, counsel, recommend. ● *noun* **1** compulsion, drive, impetus, impulse, inclination, instinct, pressure. **2** craving, desire, eagerness, hunger, itch, longing, thirst, wish, yearning, *colloquial* yen.

urgent /ˈɜːdʒ(ə)nt/ *adjective* **1** requiring immediate action or attention. **2** importunate. □ **urgency** *noun*. **urgently** *adverb*.

■ **1** acute, compelling, dire, essential, exigent, high-priority, immediate, imperative, important, inescapable, instant, necessary, pressing, top-priority, unavoidable. **2** eager, earnest, forceful, importunate, insistent, persistent, persuasive, solicitous.

uric acid /ˈjʊərɪk/ *noun* constituent of urine.

urinal /jʊəˈraɪn(ə)l/ *noun* place or receptacle for urinating by men.

urinary /ˈjʊərɪnərɪ/ *adjective* of or relating to urine.

urinate /ˈjʊərɪneɪt/ *verb* (**-ting**) discharge urine. □ **urination** *noun*.

urine /ˈjʊərɪn/ *noun* waste fluid secreted by kidneys and discharged from bladder.

urn *noun* **1** vase with foot, used esp. for ashes of the dead. **2** large vessel with tap, in which tea etc. is made or kept hot.

urology /jʊəˈrɒlədʒɪ/ *noun* study of the urinary system. □ **urological** /-rəˈlɒdʒ-/ *adjective*.

ursine /ˈɜːsaɪn/ *adjective* of or like a bear.

US *abbreviation* United States.

us /ʌs, əs/ *pronoun* **1** used by speaker or writer to refer to himself or herself and one or more others

as object of verb. **2** used for ME[1] by sovereign in formal contexts or by editorial writer in newspaper. **3** *colloquial* we.

USA *abbreviation* United States of America.

usable /ˈjuːzəb(ə)l/ *adjective* that can be used.

■ acceptable, current, functional, functioning, operating, operational, serviceable, valid, working.

USAF *abbreviation* United States Air Force.

usage /ˈjuːsɪdʒ/ *noun* **1** use; treatment. **2** customary practice; established use (esp. of language).

use *verb* /juːz/ (**using**) **1** cause to act or serve for purpose; bring into service. **2** treat in specified way. **3** exploit for one's own ends. **4** (as **used** *adjective*) second-hand. ● *noun* /juːs/ **1** using, being used. **2** right or power of using. **3** benefit, advantage. **4** purpose. **5** custom, usage. □ **in use** being used. **make use of 1** use. **2** benefit from. **used to** /juːst/ ● *adjective* accustomed to. ● *verb* used before other verb to describe habitual action (e.g. I *used to live here*). **use up 1** consume. **2** find use for (leftovers etc.).

USAGE The usual negative and question forms of *used to* are, for example, *You didn't use to go there* and *Did you use to go there?* Both are, however, rather informal, so it is better in formal language to use *You used not to go there* and a different expression such as *Were you in the habit of going there?* or *Did you go there when you lived in London?*

■ *verb* **1** administer, apply, employ, exercise, handle, make use of, operate, put to use, utilize, wield, work. **3** see EXPLOIT *verb* 2. **4** (**used**) cast-off, hand-me-down, second-hand. ● *noun* **1** application, employment, usage. **3** advantage, benefit, service, utility. **4** advantage, benefit, necessity, need, point, profit, purpose, usefulness, value, worth. □ **use up 1** consume, drink, eat, exhaust, expend, spend, waste.

useful *adjective* **1** that can be used to advantage; helpful, beneficial. **2** *colloquial* creditable, efficient. □ **usefully** *adverb*. **usefulness** *noun*.

■ **1** advantageous, beneficial, constructive, convenient, effective, good, handy, helpful, invaluable, positive, practical, productive, profitable, salutary, serviceable, utilitarian, valuable, worthwhile. **2** capable, competent, effectual, efficient, proficient, skilful, successful, talented.

useless *adjective* **1** serving no purpose; unavailing. **2** *colloquial* feeble, ineffectual. □ **uselessly** *adverb*. **uselessness** *noun*.

■ **1** fruitless, futile, hopeless, ineffective, pointless, unavailing, unprofitable, unsuccessful, vain, worthless. **2** broken down, *slang* clapped out, dead, *slang* dud, feeble, impractical, incapable, incompetent, ineffective, ineffectual, inefficient, lazy, unhelpful, unskilful, unsuccessful, untalented, unusable.

user *noun* **1** person who uses a thing. **2** *colloquial* drug addict. □ **user-friendly** (of computer, program, etc.) easy to use.

usher /ˈʌʃə/ *noun* **1** person who shows people to

their seats in cinema, church, etc. **2** doorkeeper of court etc. ● *verb* **1** act as usher to. **2** (usually + *in*) announce; show in.

usherette /ʌʃə'ret/ *noun* female usher, esp. in cinema.

USSR *abbreviation historical* Union of Soviet Socialist Republics.

usual /'juːʒəl/ *adjective* customary; habitual. □ **as usual** as is (or was) usual. □ **usually** *adverb*.

■ accepted, accustomed, average, common, conventional, customary, everyday, expected, familiar, general, habitual, natural, normal, official, ordinary, orthodox, predictable, prevalent, recognized, regular, routine, standard, stock, traditional, typical, unexceptional, unsurprising, well known, widespread, wonted.

usurer /'juːʒərə/ *noun* person who practises usury.

usurp /jʊ'zɜːp/ *verb* seize (throne, power, etc.) wrongfully. □ **usurpation** /juːzə'p-/ *noun*. **usurper** *noun*.

■ appropriate, assume, commandeer, seize, steal, take, take over.

usury /'juːʒərɪ/ *noun* **1** lending of money at interest, esp. at exorbitant or illegal rate. **2** interest at this rate. □ **usurious** /'ʒʊərɪəs/ *adjective*.

utensil /juː'tens(ə)l/ *noun* implement or vessel, esp. for kitchen use.

■ appliance, device, gadget, implement, instrument, machine, tool.

uterus /'juːtərəs/ *noun* (*plural* **uteri** /-raɪ/) womb. □ **uterine** /-raɪn/ *adjective*.

utilitarian /juːtɪlɪ'teərɪən/ *adjective* **1** designed to be useful rather than attractive. **2** of utilitarianism. ● *noun* adherent of utilitarianism.

utilitarianism *noun* doctrine that actions are justified if they are useful or benefit majority.

utility /juː'tɪlɪtɪ/ *noun* (*plural* **-ies**) **1** usefulness. **2** useful thing. **3** public utility. ● *adjective* basic and standardized. □ **utility room** room for domestic appliances, e.g. washing machine, boiler, etc. **utility vehicle** vehicle serving various functions.

utilize /'juːtɪlaɪz/ *verb* (also **-ise**) (**-zing** or **-sing**) turn to account; use. □ **utilization** *noun*.

utmost /'ʌtməʊst/ *adjective* farthest, extreme, greatest. ● *noun* the utmost point, degree, etc. □ **do one's utmost** do all that one can.

Utopia /juː'təʊpɪə/ *noun* imagined perfect place or state. □ **Utopian, utopian** *adjective*.

utter[1] /'ʌtə/ *adjective* complete, absolute. □ **utterly** *adverb*. **uttermost** *adjective*.

utter[2] /'ʌtə/ *verb* **1** emit audibly. **2** express in words. **3** *Law* put (esp. forged money) into circulation.

■ **1, 2** articulate, come out with, express, pronounce, say, speak, talk, verbalize, vocalize, voice.

utterance *noun* **1** uttering. **2** thing spoken. **3** power or manner of speaking.

UV *abbreviation* ultraviolet.

uvula /'juːvjʊlə/ *noun* (*plural* **uvulae** /-liː/) fleshy part of soft palate hanging above throat. □ **uvular** *adjective*.

uxorious /ʌk'sɔːrɪəs/ *adjective* excessively fond of one's wife.

Vv

V[1] *noun* (also **v**) (Roman numeral) 5.

V[2] *abbreviation* volt(s).

v. *abbreviation* **1** verse. **2** versus. **3** very. **4** verb. **5** *vide*.

vac *noun colloquial* vacation.

vacancy /'veɪkənsɪ/ *noun* (*plural* **-ies**) **1** being vacant. **2** unoccupied post, place, etc.
■ **2** job, opening, place, position, post, *formal* situation.

vacant *adjective* **1** not filled or occupied. **2** not mentally active; showing no interest. □ **vacant possession** ownership of unoccupied house etc. □ **vacantly** *adverb*.
■ **1** abandoned, available, bare, blank, clear, deserted, empty, free, hollow, open, unfilled, uninhabited, unoccupied, unused, usable, void. **2** absent-minded, abstracted, blank, deadpan, dreamy, expressionless, far-away, fatuous, inattentive, vacuous.

vacate /və'keɪt/ *verb* (**-ting**) leave vacant; cease to occupy.
■ abandon, depart from, desert, evacuate, get out of, give up, leave, quit, withdraw from.

vacation /və'keɪʃ(ə)n/ *noun* **1** fixed holiday period, esp. in law courts and universities. **2** *US* holiday. **3** vacating, being vacated.

vaccinate /'væksɪmeɪt/ *verb* (**-ting**) inoculate with vaccine to immunize against disease. □ **vaccination** *noun*.

vaccine /'væksiːn/ *noun* preparation used for inoculation, originally cowpox virus giving immunity to smallpox.

vacillate /'væsɪleɪt/ *verb* (**-ting**) fluctuate in opinion or resolution. □ **vacillation** *noun*. **vacillator** *noun*.

vacuous /'vækjʊəs/ *adjective* **1** expressionless. **2** unintelligent. □ **vacuity** /və'kjuːɪtɪ/ *noun*. **vacuously** *adverb*.
■ apathetic, blank, empty-headed, expressionless, inane, mindless, stupid, uncomprehending, unintelligent, vacant.

vacuum /'vækjʊəm/ *noun* (*plural* **-s** or **vacua**) **1** space entirely devoid of matter. **2** space or vessel from which air has been completely or partly removed by pump etc. **3** absence of normal or previous content. **4** (*plural* **-s**) *colloquial* vacuum cleaner. ● *verb colloquial* clean with vacuum cleaner. □ **vacuum brake** brake worked by exhaustion of air. **vacuum cleaner** machine for removing dust etc. by suction. **vacuum flask** vessel with double wall enclosing vacuum so that contents remain hot or cold. **vacuum-packed** sealed after partial removal of air. **vacuum tube** tube containing near-vacuum for free passage of electric current.
■ *noun* **1, 3** emptiness, space, void.

vagabond /'vægəbɒnd/ *noun* wanderer, esp. idle one. ● *adjective* wandering; having no settled habitation or home.

vagary /'veɪgərɪ/ *noun* (*plural* **-ies**) caprice; eccentric act or idea.
■ caprice, fancy, fluctuation, quirk, uncertainty, whim; (*vagaries*) unpredictability.

vagina /və'dʒaɪnə/ *noun* (*plural* **-s** or **-nae** /-niː/) canal joining womb and vulva of female mammal. □ **vaginal** *adjective*.

vagrant /'veɪgrənt/ *noun* person without settled home or regular work. ● *adjective* wandering, roving. □ **vagrancy** *noun*.
■ *noun* beggar, down-and-out, homeless person, itinerant, tramp, traveller, vagabond, wanderer, wayfarer.

vague /veɪg/ *adjective* **1** uncertain, ill-defined. **2** not clear-thinking; inexact. □ **vaguely** *adverb*. **vagueness** *noun*.
■ **1** ambiguous, amorphous, blurred, broad, confused, diffuse, dim, equivocal, general, generalized, hazy, ill-defined, imprecise, indefinable, indefinite, indescribable, indistinct, inexact, loose, misty, nebulous, shadowy, uncertain, unclear, undefined, unrecognizable, unspecific, woolly. **2** absent-minded, careless, confused, disorganized, evasive, forgetful, inattentive, inexact, scatterbrained, thoughtless, uncertain, unsure.

vain *adjective* **1** conceited. **2** empty, trivial. **3** unavailing, useless. □ **in vain** without result or success, lightly or profanely. □ **vainly** *adverb*.
■ **1** arrogant, *colloquial* big-headed, boastful, *colloquial* cocky, conceited, egotistic(al), haughty, narcissistic, proud, self-important, self-satisfied, *colloquial* stuck-up, vainglorious. **3** abortive, fruitless, futile, ineffective, pointless, senseless, unavailing, unproductive, unrewarding, unsuccessful, useless, worthless.

vainglory /veɪn'glɔːrɪ/ *noun* extreme vanity, boastfulness. □ **vainglorious** *adjective*.

valance /'væləns/ *noun* short curtain round bedstead, above window, etc.

vale *noun* (*archaic* except in place names) valley.

valediction /vælɪ'dɪkʃ(ə)n/ *noun formal* **1** bidding farewell. **2** words used in this. □ **valedictory** *adjective* & *noun* (*plural* **-ies**).

valence /'veɪləns/ *noun* valency.

valency /'veɪlənsɪ/ *noun* (*plural* **-ies**) combining-power of an atom measured by number of hydrogen atoms it can displace or combine with.

valentine /'væləntaɪn/ *noun* **1** (usually anonymous) letter or card sent as mark of love on St Valentine's Day (14 Feb.). **2** sweetheart chosen on that day.

valerian /və'lɪərɪən/ *noun* any of various kinds of flowering herb.

valet /'vælɪt/ *noun* gentleman's personal servant. ● *verb* (**-t-**) act as valet (to).

valetudinarian /ˌvælɪtjuːdɪ'neərɪən/ *noun* person of poor health or unduly anxious about health. ● *adjective* of a valetudinarian.

valiant /'væljənt/ *adjective* brave. □ **valiantly** *adverb*.

■ bold, brave, courageous, *archaic* doughty, gallant, heroic, plucky, stalwart, stout-hearted, valorous.

valid /'vælɪd/ *adjective* **1** (of reason, objection, etc.) sound, defensible. **2** legally acceptable; not yet expired. □ **validity** /və'lɪd-/ *noun*.

■ **1** convincing, defensible, legitimate, logical, sound, well founded, well grounded. **2** acceptable, allowed, approved, authentic, authorized, bona fide, current, genuine, lawful, legal, legitimate, official, permissible, permitted, proper, ratified, rightful, suitable, usable.

validate /'vælɪdeɪt/ *verb* (**-ting**) make valid, ratify. □ **validation** *noun*.

■ authenticate, authorize, certify, endorse, legalize, legitimize, ratify.

valise /və'liːz/ *noun US* small portmanteau.

Valium /'vælɪəm/ *noun proprietary term* the tranquillizing drug diazepam.

valley /'vælɪ/ *noun* (*plural* **-s**) low area between hills, usually with stream or river.

■ canyon, chasm, coomb, dale, defile, dell, dingle, glen, gorge, *US* gulch, gully, hollow, ravine, *archaic* vale.

valour /'vælə/ *noun* (*US* **valor**) courage, esp. in battle. □ **valorous** *adjective*.

■ bravery, courage, pluck.

valuable /'væljʊəb(ə)l/ *adjective* of great value, price, or worth. ● *noun* (usually in *plural*) valuable thing.

■ *adjective* advantageous, beneficial, constructive, costly, dear, esteemed, expensive, helpful, invaluable, irreplaceable, positive, precious, priceless, prized, profitable, treasured, useful, valued, worthwhile.

valuation /ˌvæljʊ'eɪʃ(ə)n/ *noun* **1** estimation (esp. by professional valuer) of thing's worth. **2** estimated value.

value /'væljuː/ *noun* **1** worth, desirability, or qualities on which these depend. **2** worth as estimated. **3** amount for which thing can be exchanged in open market. **4** equivalent of thing. **5** (in full **value for money**) something well worth money spent. **6** ability of thing to serve a purpose or cause an effect. **7** (in *plural*) one's principles,

priorities, or standards. **8** *Music* duration of note. **9** *Mathematics* amount denoted by algebraic term. ● *verb* (**-ues, -ued, -uing**) **1** estimate value of. **2** have high or specified opinion of. □ **value added tax** tax levied on rise in value of services and goods at each stage of production. **value judgement** subjective estimate of worth etc. □ **valueless** *adjective*.

■ *noun* **1, 6** advantage, benefit, importance, merit, significance, use, usefulness, utility, worth. **3** cost, price, worth. ● *verb* **1** assess, evaluate, price. **2** appreciate, care for, cherish, esteem, have a high regard for, hold dear, love, prize, respect, treasure.

valuer *noun* person who estimates or assesses values.

valve *noun* **1** device controlling flow through pipe etc., usually allowing movement in one direction only. **2** structure in organ etc. allowing flow of blood etc. in one direction only. **3** thermionic valve. **4** device to vary length of tube in trumpet etc. **5** half-shell of oyster, mussel, etc.

valvular /'vælvjʊlə/ *adjective* **1** having valve(s). **2** having form or function of valve.

vamoose /və'muːs/ *verb US slang* depart hurriedly.

vamp[1] *noun* upper front part of boot or shoe. ● *verb* **1** (often + *up*) repair, furbish, or make by patching or piecing together. **2** improvise musical accompaniment.

vamp[2] *colloquial noun* woman who uses sexual attraction to exploit men. ● *verb* allure or exploit (man).

vampire /'væmpaɪə/ *noun* **1** supposed ghost or reanimated corpse sucking blood of sleeping people. **2** person who preys on others. **3** (in full **vampire bat**) bloodsucking bat.

van[1] *noun* covered vehicle or closed railway truck for transporting goods etc.

van[2] *noun* **1** vanguard. **2** forefront.

vanadium /və'neɪdɪəm/ *noun* hard grey metallic element used to strengthen steel.

vandal /'vænd(ə)l/ *noun* person who wilfully or maliciously damages property. □ **vandalism** *noun*.

■ delinquent, hooligan, ruffian, troublemaker.

vandalize /'vændəlaɪz/ *verb* (also **-ise**) (**-zing** or **-sing**) destroy or damage wilfully or maliciously (esp. public property).

vane *noun* **1** weather vane. **2** blade of windmill, ship's propeller, etc.

vanguard /'vænɡɑːd/ *noun* **1** foremost part of advancing army etc. **2** leaders of movement etc.

vanilla /və'nɪlə/ *noun* **1** tropical fragrant climbing orchid. **2** extract of its fruit (**vanilla-pod**), or synthetic substitute, used as flavouring.

vanish /'vænɪʃ/ *verb* **1** disappear. **2** cease to exist. □ **vanishing point** point at which receding parallel lines appear to meet.

■ die out, disappear, disperse, dissolve, evaporate, fade, go away, melt away.

vanity /'vænɪtɪ/ noun (plural **-ies**) **1** conceit about one's attainments or appearance. **2** futility; unreal thing. □ **vanity bag, case** woman's make-up bag or case.

■ **1** arrogance, colloquial big-headedness, conceit, egotism, narcissism, pride, self-esteem.

vanquish /'væŋkwɪʃ/ verb literary conquer, overcome.

vantage /'vɑːntɪdʒ/ noun **1** (also **vantage-point**) place giving good view. **2** advantage, esp. in tennis.

vapid /'væpɪd/ adjective insipid, dull, flat. □ **vapidity** /və'pɪd-/ noun.

vapor US = VAPOUR.

vaporize /'veɪpəraɪz/ verb (also **-ise**) (**-zing** or **-sing**) change into vapour. □ **vaporization** noun.

■ dry up, evaporate.

vaporizer /'veɪpəraɪzə/ noun device that vaporizes substances.

vaporous /'veɪpərəs/ adjective in the form of or consisting of vapour.

vapour /'veɪpə/ noun (US **vapor**) **1** moisture or other substance diffused or suspended in air, e.g. mist, smoke. **2** gaseous form of substance. □ **vapour trail** trail of condensed water from aircraft etc.

■ **1** exhalation, fog, fumes, haze, archaic miasma, mist, smoke, steam. **2** gas.

variable /'veərɪəb(ə)l/ adjective **1** changeable, adaptable. **2** apt to vary; not constant. **3** Mathematics (of quantity) indeterminate; able to assume different numerical values. ● noun variable thing or quantity. □ **variability** noun.

■ adjective **1** adaptable, changeable. **2** capricious, changeable, erratic, fickle, fitful, fluctuating, fluid, inconsistent, inconstant, mercurial, literary mutable, protean, shifting, temperamental, uncertain, unpredictable, unreliable, unstable, unsteady, colloquial up and down, vacillating, varying, volatile, wavering.

variance /'veərɪəns/ noun **1** (usually after at) difference of opinion; dispute. **2** discrepancy.

variant adjective **1** differing in form or details from standard. **2** having different forms. ● noun variant form, spelling, type, etc.

variation /veərɪ'eɪʃ(ə)n/ noun **1** varying; departure from normal kind, standard, type, etc. **2** extent of this. **3** thing that varies from type. **4** Music theme in changed or elaborated form.

■ **1, 2** alteration, change, conversion, deviation, difference, discrepancy, diversification, diversity, elaboration, modification, permutation, variety. **3** variant, variety, version.

varicose /'værɪkəʊs/ adjective (esp. of vein etc.) permanently and abnormally dilated.

variegated /'veərɪgeɪtɪd/ adjective **1** with irregular patches of different colours. **2** having leaves of two or more colours. □ **variegation** noun.

variety /və'raɪətɪ/ noun (plural **-ies**) **1** diversity; absence of uniformity. **2** collection of different things. **3** class of things differing from rest in same general class. **4** member of such class. **5** (+ of) different form of thing, quality, etc. **6** Biology subdivision of species. **7** series of dances, songs, comedy acts, etc.

■ **1** change, difference, diversity, unpredictability, variation. **2** array, assortment, blend, collection, combination, jumble, medley, miscellany, mixture, multiplicity. **3, 4** brand, breed, category, class, form, kind, make, sort, species, strain, type.

various /'veərɪəs/ adjective **1** different, diverse. **2** several. □ **variously** adverb.

USAGE Various (unlike several) is not a pronoun and therefore cannot be used with of, as in Various of the guests arrived late.

■ **1** assorted, contrasting, different, differing, dissimilar, diverse, heterogeneous, miscellaneous, mixed, motley, varied, varying. **2** multifarious, several, sundry.

varnish /'vɑːnɪʃ/ noun resinous solution used to give hard shiny transparent coating. ● verb **1** coat with varnish. **2** conceal with deceptively attractive appearance.

varsity /'vɑːsɪtɪ/ noun (plural **-ies**) colloquial university.

vary /'veərɪ/ verb (**-ies**, **-ied**) **1** be or become different; be of different kinds. **2** modify, diversify. □ **varied** adjective. **varying** adjective.

■ **1** change, deviate, differ, fluctuate, go up and down, vacillate. **2** adapt, adjust, alter, convert, modify, reset, switch, transform, upset. □ **varied, varying** see VARIOUS 1.

vascular /'væskjʊlə/ adjective of or containing vessels for conveying blood, sap, etc.

vas deferens /væs 'defərenz/ noun (plural **vasa deferentia** /veɪsə defə'renʃɪə/) sperm duct of testicle.

vase /vɑːz/ noun vessel used as ornament or container for flowers.

vasectomy /və'sektəmɪ/ noun (plural **-ies**) removal of part of each vas deferens, esp. for sterilization.

Vaseline /'væsɪliːn/ noun proprietary term type of petroleum jelly used as ointment etc.

vassal /'væs(ə)l/ noun **1** humble dependant. **2** historical holder of land by feudal tenure. □ **vassalage** noun.

vast /vɑːst/ adjective immense, huge. □ **vastly** adverb. **vastness** noun.

■ big, boundless, broad, colossal, enormous, extensive, gigantic, great, huge, immeasurable, immense, infinite, interminable, large, limitless, mammoth, massive, measureless, monumental, never-ending, titanic, colloquial tremendous, unbounded, unlimited, voluminous, wide.

VAT abbreviation value added tax.

vat noun tank, esp. for holding liquids in brewing, dyeing, and tanning.

Vatican /'vætɪkən/ noun palace or government of Pope in Rome.

vaudeville /ˈvɔːdəvɪl/ *noun esp. US* variety entertainment.

vault /vɔːlt/ *noun* **1** arched roof. **2** vaultlike covering. **3** underground room as place of storage. **4** underground burial chamber. **5** act of vaulting. ● *verb* **1** leap or spring, esp. using hands or pole. **2** spring over in this way. **3** (esp. as **vaulted** *adjective*) make in form of vault. **4** (esp. as **vaulted** *adjective*) provide with vault(s).
∎ *noun* **3, 4** basement, cavern, cellar, crypt, undercroft. ● *verb* **1** bound, clear, hurdle, jump, leap, leapfrog, spring.

vaunt /vɔːnt/ *verb & noun literary* boast.

VC *abbreviation* Victoria Cross.

VCR *abbreviation* video cassette recorder.

VD *abbreviation* venereal disease.

VDU *abbreviation* visual display unit.

veal *noun* calf's flesh as food.

vector /ˈvektə/ *noun* **1** *Mathematics & Physics* quantity having both magnitude and direction. **2** carrier of disease.

veer /vɪə/ *verb* **1** change direction, esp. (of wind) clockwise. **2** change in opinion, course, etc.
∎ change direction, dodge, shift, swerve, tack, turn, wheel.

vegan /ˈviːgən/ *noun* person who does not eat animals or animal products. ● *adjective* using or containing no animal products.

vegetable /ˈvedʒtəb(ə)l/ *noun* plant, esp. edible herbaceous plant. ● *adjective* of, derived from, or relating to plant life or vegetables as food.

vegetarian /vedʒɪˈteərɪən/ *noun* person who does not eat meat or fish. ● *adjective* excluding animal food, esp. meat. ▫ **vegetarianism** *noun*.

vegetate /ˈvedʒɪteɪt/ *verb* (**-ting**) **1** lead dull monotonous life. **2** grow as plants do.
∎ **1** be inactive, do nothing, go to seed, idle, lose interest, stagnate.

vegetation /vedʒɪˈteɪʃ(ə)n/ *noun* plants collectively; plant life.
∎ flora, greenery, plants.

vegetative /ˈvedʒɪtətɪv/ *adjective* **1** concerned with growth and development rather than sexual reproduction. **2** of vegetation.

vehement /ˈviːəmənt/ *adjective* showing or caused by strong feeling; ardent. ▫ **vehemence** *noun*. **vehemently** *adverb*.
∎ animated, ardent, eager, enthusiastic, excited, fervent, fierce, forceful, heated, impassioned, intense, passionate, powerful, strong, vigorous, violent.

vehicle /ˈviːɪk(ə)l/ *noun* **1** conveyance used on land or in space. **2** thing or person as medium for thought, feeling, or action. **3** liquid etc. as medium for suspending pigments, drugs, etc. ▫ **vehicular** /vɪˈhɪkjʊlə/ *adjective*.

veil /veɪl/ *noun* **1** piece of usually transparent material attached to woman's hat or otherwise forming part of headdress, esp. to conceal or protect face. **2** piece of linen etc. as part of nun's headdress. **3** thing that hides or disguises. ● *verb* **1** cover with veil. **2** (esp. as **veiled** *adjective*) partly conceal. ▫ **beyond the veil** in the unknown state of life after death. **draw a veil over** avoid discussing. **take the veil** become nun.
∎ *verb* camouflage, cloak, conceal, cover, disguise, hide, mask, shroud.

vein /veɪn/ *noun* **1** any of tubes carrying blood to heart. **2** (in general use) any blood vessel. **3** rib of leaf or insect's wing. **4** streak of different colour in wood, marble, cheese, etc. **5** fissure in rock filled with ore. **6** specified character or tendency; mood. ▫ **veined** *adjective*.
∎ **5** bed, course, deposit, line, lode, seam, stratum. **6** see MOOD¹ 1.

Velcro /ˈvelkrəʊ/ *noun proprietary term* fastener consisting of two strips of fabric which cling when pressed together.

veld /velt/ *noun* (also **veldt**) *South African* open country.

veleta /vəˈliːtə/ *noun* ballroom dance in triple time.

vellum /ˈveləm/ *noun* **1** fine parchment, originally calfskin. **2** manuscript on this. **3** smooth writing paper imitating vellum.

velociraptor /vɪˈlɒsɪræptə/ *noun* small carnivorous dinosaur with short front legs.

velocity /vɪˈlɒsɪtɪ/ *noun* (*plural* **-ies**) speed, esp. of inanimate things.

velour /vəˈlʊə/ *noun* (also **velours** same pronunciation) plushlike fabric.

velvet /ˈvelvɪt/ *noun* **1** soft fabric with thick short pile on one side. **2** furry skin on growing antler. ● *adjective* of, like, or soft as velvet. ▫ **on velvet** in advantageous or prosperous position. **velvet glove** outward gentleness cloaking firmness or inflexibility. ▫ **velvety** *adjective*.

velveteen /velvɪˈtiːn/ *noun* cotton fabric with pile like velvet.

Ven. *abbreviation* Venerable.

venal /ˈviːn(ə)l/ *adjective* **1** able to be bribed. **2** involving bribery; corrupt. ▫ **venality** /-ˈnæl-/ *noun*.

USAGE *Venal* is sometimes confused with *venial*.

vend *verb* offer (esp. small wares) for sale. ▫ **vending machine** slot machine selling small items. ▫ **vendor** *noun*.

vendetta /venˈdetə/ *noun* **1** blood feud. **2** prolonged bitter quarrel.

veneer /vɪˈnɪə/ *noun* **1** thin covering of fine wood. **2** (often + *of*) deceptively pleasing appearance. ● *verb* apply veneer to (wood etc.).
∎ *noun* **1** coating, covering, finish, layer, surface. ● *verb* see COVER *verb* 1.

venerable /ˈvenərəb(ə)l/ *adjective* **1** entitled to deep respect on account of age, character, etc. **2** *title of* archdeacon. ▫ **venerability** /-ˈbɪlɪtɪ/ *noun*.

■ **1** aged, ancient, august, dignified, esteemed, estimable, honourable, honoured, old, respectable, respected, revered, reverenced, venerated, worshipped, worthy.

venerate /'venəreɪt/ *verb* (**-ting**) regard with deep respect. □ **veneration** *noun*.

■ adore, esteem, hero-worship, honour, idolize, look up to, pay homage to, respect, revere, reverence, worship.

venereal /vɪ'nɪərɪəl/ *adjective* **1** of sexual desire or intercourse. **2** of venereal disease. □ **venereal disease** disease contracted by sexual intercourse with infected person.

Venetian /vɪ'niːʃ(ə)n/ *noun* native, citizen, or dialect of Venice. ● *adjective* of Venice. □ **venetian blind** window-blind of adjustable horizontal slats.

vengeance /'vendʒ(ə)ns/ *noun* punishment inflicted for wrong to oneself or to one's cause. □ **with a vengeance** to extreme degree; thoroughly, violently.

■ reprisal, retaliation, retribution, revenge, tit for tat.

vengeful /'vendʒfʊl/ *adjective* seeking vengeance; vindictive. □ **vengefulness** *noun*.

■ avenging, bitter, rancorous, revengeful, spiteful, unforgiving, vindictive.

venial /'viːnɪəl/ *adjective* (of sin or fault) pardonable, not mortal. □ **veniality** /-'æl-/ *noun*.

USAGE *Venial* is sometimes confused with *venal*.

venison /'venɪs(ə)n/ *noun* deer's flesh as food.

Venn diagram *noun* diagram using overlapping and intersecting circles etc. to show relationships between mathematical sets.

venom /'venəm/ *noun* **1** poisonous fluid of esp. snakes. **2** malignity; virulence of feeling, language, or conduct. □ **venomous** *adjective*. **venomously** *adverb*.

■ **1** poison, toxin. □ **venomous** deadly, lethal, poisonous, toxic.

venous /'viːnəs/ *adjective* of, full of, or contained in veins.

vent[1] *noun* **1** opening for passage of air etc. **2** outlet; free expression. **3** anus, esp. of lower animal. ● *verb* give vent or free expression to.

■ *noun* **1** aperture, cut, duct, gap, hole, opening, orifice, outlet, passage, slit, slot, split. ● *verb* articulate, express, give vent to, make known, release, utter, ventilate, voice.

vent[2] *noun* slit in garment, esp. in back of jacket.

ventilate /'ventɪleɪt/ *verb* (**-ting**) **1** cause air to circulate freely in (room etc.). **2** air (question, grievance, etc.). □ **ventilation** *noun*.

■ **1** aerate, air, freshen, oxygenate.

ventilator *noun* **1** appliance or aperture for ventilating room etc. **2** apparatus for maintaining artifical respiration.

ventral /'ventr(ə)l/ *adjective* of or on abdomen.

ventricle /'ventrɪk(ə)l/ *noun* **1** cavity in body. **2** hollow part of organ, esp. brain or heart.

ventricular /ven'trɪkjʊlə/ *adjective* of or shaped like ventricle.

ventriloquism /ven'trɪləkwɪz(ə)m/ *noun* skill of speaking without moving the lips. □ **ventriloquist** *noun*.

venture /'ventʃə/ *noun* **1** risky undertaking. **2** commercial speculation. ● *verb* (**-ring**) **1** dare; not be afraid. **2** dare to go. **3** dare to make or put forward. **4** expose to risk; stake. **5** take risks. □ **Venture Scout** senior Scout.

■ *noun* enterprise, experiment, gamble, risk, speculation, undertaking. ● *verb* **1** see ATTEMPT *verb* **1**, PRESUME **2**. **3** advance, dare, proffer, put forward. **4, 5** bet, *colloquial* chance, dare, gamble, risk, speculate, stake, wager.

venturesome *adjective* disposed to take risks.

■ adventurous, bold, courageous, daring, *archaic* doughty, fearless, intrepid.

venue /'venjuː/ *noun* appointed place for match, meeting, concert, etc.

■ location, meeting place, rendezvous.

Venus fly-trap /'viːnəs/ *noun* insectivorous plant.

veracious /və'reɪʃəs/ *adjective formal* truthful, true. □ **veracity** /-'ræs-/ *noun*.

veranda /və'rændə/ *noun* (sometimes partly covered) platform along side of house.

verb *noun* word used to indicate action, event, state, or change (see panel).

verbal *adjective* **1** of words. **2** oral; not written. **3** of a verb. **4** (of translation) literal. □ **verbally** *adverb*.

■ **1** lexical, linguistic. **2** oral, said, spoken, unwritten, vocal, word of mouth.

verbalize *verb* (also **-ise**) (**-zing** or **-sing**) put into words.

verbatim /vɜ:'beɪtɪm/ *adverb & adjective* in exactly the same words.

■ *adjective* exact, faithful, literal, precise, word for word.

verbena /vɜ:'biːnə/ *noun* (*plural* same) plant of genus of herbs and small shrubs with fragrant flowers.

verbiage /'vɜ:bɪɪdʒ/ *noun derogatory* unnecessary number of words.

verbose /vɜ:'bəʊs/ *adjective* using more words than are needed. □ **verbosity** /-'bɒs-/ *noun*.

■ diffuse, garrulous, long-winded, loquacious, prolix, rambling, repetitious, talkative, voluble, wordy. □ **verbosity** beating about the bush, circumlocution, diffuseness, garrulity, long-windedness, loquacity, periphrasis, prolixity, repetition, *derogatory* verbiage, wordiness.

verdant /'vɜ:d(ə)nt/ *adjective* (of grass, field, etc.) green, lush. □ **verdancy** *noun*.

verdict /'vɜːdɪkt/ *noun* **1** decision of jury. **2** decision, judgement.

> ■ adjudication, assessment, conclusion, decision, finding, judgement, opinion.

verdigris /'vɜːdɪgriː/ *noun* greenish-blue substance that forms on copper or brass.

verdure /'vɜːdjə/ *noun literary* green vegetation or its colour.

verge[1] *noun* **1** edge, border; brink. **2** strip of land at side of road etc., usually covered in grass.

> ■ **1** bank, border, boundary, brim, brink, edge, lip, margin, side, threshold.

verge[2] *verb* (**-ging**) **1** (+ *on*) border on. **2** incline downwards or in specified direction.

verger /'vɜːdʒə/ *noun* **1** caretaker and attendant in church. **2** officer carrying staff before dignitaries of cathedral etc.

verify /'verɪfaɪ/ *verb* (**-ies, -ied**) **1** establish truth or correctness of by examination etc. **2** fulfil, bear out. □ **verifiable** *adjective.* **verification** /-fɪ'keɪʃ(ə)n/ *noun.*

> ■ affirm, ascertain, attest to, authenticate, bear out, bear witness to, check out, confirm, corroborate, demonstrate the truth of, establish, prove, show the truth of, substantiate, support, uphold, validate, vouch for. □ **verifiable** demonstrable, provable.

verily /'verɪlɪ/ *adverb archaic* truly, really.

verisimilitude /verɪsɪ'mɪlɪtjuːd/ *noun* appearance of being true or real.

> ■ authenticity, realism.

veritable /'verɪtəb(ə)l/ *adjective* real; rightly so called.

verity /'verɪtɪ/ *noun* (*plural* **-ies**) **1** true statement. **2** *archaic* truth.

vermicelli /vɜːmɪ'tʃelɪ/ *noun* pasta in long slender threads.

vermicide /'vɜːmɪsaɪd/ *noun* drug used to kill intestinal worms.

vermiform /'vɜːmɪfɔːm/ *adjective* worm-shaped. □ **vermiform appendix** small blind tube extending from caecum in man and some other mammals.

vermilion /və'mɪljən/ *noun* **1** brilliant scarlet pigment made esp. from cinnabar. **2** colour of this. ● *adjective* of this colour.

vermin /'vɜːmɪn/ *noun* (usually treated as *plural*) **1** mammals and birds harmful to game, crops, etc. **2** parasitic worms or insects. **3** vile people.

> ■ **1, 2** parasites, pests.

verminous *adjective* of the nature of or infested with vermin.

vermouth /'vɜːməθ/ *noun* wine flavoured with aromatic herbs.

vernacular /və'nækjʊlə/ *noun* **1** language or dialect of country. **2** language of particular class or group. **3** homely speech. ● *adjective* (of language) of one's own country; not foreign or formal.

> ■ *adjective* common, everyday, indigenous, local, native, ordinary, popular, vulgar.

vernal /'vɜːn(ə)l/ *adjective* of or in spring.

•••

Verb

A verb says what a person or thing does, and can describe:

> an action, e.g. *run, hit*
> an event, e.g. *rain, happen*
> a state, e.g. *be, have, seem, appear*
> a change, e.g. *become, grow*

Verbs occur in different forms, usually in one or other of their tenses. The most common tenses are:

the simple present tense:	*The boy walks down the road.*
the continuous present tense:	*The boy is walking down the road.*
the simple past tense:	*The boy walked down the road.*
the continuous past tense:	*The boy was walking down the road.*
the perfect tense:	*The boy has walked down the road.*
the future tense:	*The boy will walk down the road.*

Each of these forms is a finite verb, which means that it is in a particular tense and that it changes according to the number and person of the subject, as in

> *I am*   *you walk*
> *we are*   *he walks*

An infinitive is the form of a verb that usually appears with *to*, e.g.

> *to wander, to look, to sleep.*

(See also panels at PARTICIPLE, PASSIVE, TRANSITIVE VERB.)

•••

vernier /ˈvɜːnɪə/ *noun* small movable scale for reading fractional parts of subdivisions on fixed scale of measuring instrument.

veronica /vəˈrɒnɪkə/ *noun* speedwell.

verruca /vəˈruːkə/ *noun* (*plural* **verrucae** /-siː/ or **-s**) wart or similar growth, esp. on foot.

versatile /ˈvɜːsətaɪl/ *adjective* **1** turning easily or readily from one subject or occupation to another; skilled in many subjects or occupations. **2** having many uses. □ **versatility** /-ˈtɪl-/ *noun*.

▪ **1** adaptable, all-round, flexible, gifted, resourceful, skilful, talented. **2** all-purpose, handy, multi-purpose, useful.

verse *noun* **1** poetry. **2** stanza of poem or song. **3** each of short numbered divisions of Bible.

▪ **1** poetry, rhyme.

versed /vɜːst/ *adjective* (+ *in*) experienced or skilled in.

▪ (*versed in*) accomplished in, competent in, experienced in, expert in, knowledgeable about, practised in, proficient in, skilled in, trained in.

versicle /ˈvɜːsɪk(ə)l/ *noun* short sentence, esp. each of series in liturgy said or sung by minister or priest, answered by congregation.

versify /ˈvɜːsɪfaɪ/ *verb* (**-ies, -ied**) **1** turn into or express in verse. **2** compose verses. □ **versification** /-frˈkeɪʃ(ə)n/ *noun*. **versifier** *noun*.

version /ˈvɜːʃ(ə)n/ *noun* **1** account of matter from particular point of view. **2** particular edition or translation of book etc. **3** form or variant of thing.

▪ **1** account, description, portrayal, reading, rendition, report, story. **2** adaptation, edition, interpretation, rendering, translation. **3** design, form, kind, mark, model, style, type, variant.

verso /ˈvɜːsəʊ/ *noun* (*plural* **-s**) **1** left-hand page of open book. **2** back of printed leaf.

versus /ˈvɜːsəs/ *preposition* against.

vertebra /ˈvɜːtɪbrə/ *noun* (*plural* **-brae** /-briː/) each segment of backbone. □ **vertebral** *adjective*.

vertebrate /ˈvɜːtɪbrət/ *adjective* having backbone. ● *noun* vertebrate animal.

vertex /ˈvɜːteks/ *noun* (*plural* **-tices** /-tɪsiːz/ or **-texes**) **1** highest point; top, apex. **2** meeting-point of lines that form angle.

vertical /ˈvɜːtɪk(ə)l/ *adjective* **1** at right angles to horizontal plane. **2** in direction from top to bottom of picture etc. **3** of or at vertex. ● *noun* vertical line or plane. □ **vertical take-off** take-off of aircraft directly upwards. □ **vertically** *adverb*.

▪ *adjective* **1** erect, perpendicular, precipitous, sheer, upright.

vertiginous /vɜːˈtɪdʒɪnəs/ *adjective* of or causing vertigo.

vertigo /ˈvɜːtɪɡəʊ/ *noun* dizziness.

▪ dizziness, giddiness, light-headedness.

vervain /ˈvɜːveɪn/ *noun* any of several verbenas, esp. one with small blue, white, or purple flowers.

verve *noun* enthusiasm, energy, vigour.

very /ˈverɪ/ *adverb* **1** in high degree. **2** (+ *own* or superlative adjective) in fullest sense. ● *adjective* real; properly so called etc. □ **very good, well** *formula of consent or approval*. **very high frequency** 30–300 megahertz (in radio). **Very Reverend** *title of dean*.

▪ *adverb* **1** acutely, enormously, especially, exceedingly, extremely, greatly, highly, *colloquial* jolly, most, noticeably, outstandingly, particularly, really, remarkably, *colloquial* terribly, truly, uncommonly, unusually.

vesicle /ˈvesɪk(ə)l/ *noun* small bladder, blister, or bubble.

vespers /ˈvespəz/ *plural noun* evening church service.

vessel /ˈves(ə)l/ *noun* **1** hollow receptacle, esp. for liquid. **2** ship or boat, esp. large one. **3** duct or canal holding or conveying blood, sap, etc.

▪ **1** see CONTAINER 1. **2** barque, boat, craft, ship.

vest *noun* **1** undergarment worn on upper part of body. **2** *US & Australian* waistcoat. ● *verb* **1** (+ *with*) bestow (powers, authority, etc.) on. **2** (+ *in*) confer (property or power) on (person) with immediate fixed right of future possession. □ **vested interest 1** personal interest in state of affairs, usually with expectation of gain. **2** *Law* interest (usually in land or money held in trust) recognized as belonging to person.

vestal virgin /ˈvest(ə)l/ *noun* virgin consecrated to Vesta, Roman goddess of hearth and home, and vowed to chastity.

vestibule /ˈvestɪbjuːl/ *noun* lobby, entrance hall.

vestige /ˈvestɪdʒ/ *noun* **1** trace, evidence. **2** slight amount, particle. **3** *Biology* part or organ now atrophied that was well developed in ancestors. □ **vestigial** /-ˈtɪdʒɪəl/ *adjective*.

vestment /ˈvestmənt/ *noun* ceremonial garment worn by priest etc.

vestry /ˈvestrɪ/ *noun* (*plural* **-ies**) room or part of church for keeping vestments etc. in.

vet *noun colloquial* veterinary surgeon. ● *verb* (**-tt-**) make careful and critical examination of (scheme, work, candidate, etc.).

▪ *verb colloquial* check out, examine, investigate, review, scrutinize.

vetch *noun* plant of pea family largely used for fodder.

veteran /ˈvetərən/ *noun* **1** old soldier or long-serving member of any group. **2** *US* ex-serviceman or -woman. ● *adjective* of or for veterans. □ **veteran car** one made before 1905.

▪ *noun* **1** old hand, old soldier, survivor. **2** ex-serviceman, ex-servicewoman, old soldier. ● *adjective* experienced, mature, old, practised.

veterinarian /vetərɪˈneərɪən/ *noun formal* veterinary surgeon.

veterinary /ˈvetərɪnərɪ/ *adjective* of or for diseases and injuries of animals. □ **veterinary surgeon** person qualified to treat animals.

veto /'vi:təʊ/ *noun* (*plural* **-es**) **1** right to reject measure etc. unilaterally. **2** rejection, prohibition. ● *verb* (**-oes**, **-oed**) **1** reject (measure etc.). **2** forbid.

■ *noun* **2** ban, embargo, prohibition, proscription, refusal, rejection, thumbs down. ● *verb* ban, bar, blackball, block, disallow, dismiss, forbid, prohibit, proscribe, quash, refuse, reject, rule out, say no to, turn down, vote against.

vex *verb* **1** annoy, irritate. **2** *archaic* grieve, afflict.

■ **1** *disputed* aggravate, anger, annoy, bother, displease, exasperate, harass, irritate, provoke, put out, trouble, upset, worry.

vexation /vek'seɪʃ(ə)n/ *noun* **1** vexing, being vexed. **2** annoying or distressing thing.

vexatious /vek'seɪʃ(ə)s/ *adjective* **1** causing vexation. **2** *Law* lacking sufficient grounds for action and seeking only to annoy defendant.

vexed *adjective* (of question) much discussed.

VHF *abbreviation* very high frequency.

via /'vaɪə/ *preposition* by way of; through.

viable /'vaɪəb(ə)l/ *adjective* **1** (of plan etc.) feasible, esp. economically. **2** (esp. of foetus) capable of living and surviving independently. □ **viability** *noun*.

■ **1** achievable, feasible, operable, possible, practicable, practical, realistic, reasonable, supportable, sustainable, workable.

viaduct /'vaɪədʌkt/ *noun* long bridge carrying railway or road over valley.

vial /'vaɪəl/ *noun* small glass vessel.

viands /'vaɪəndz/ *plural noun formal* articles of food.

viaticum /vaɪ'ætɪkəm/ *noun* (*plural* **-ca**) Eucharist given to dying person.

vibes /vaɪbz/ *plural noun colloquial* **1** vibrations, esp. feelings communicated. **2** vibraphone.

vibrant /'vaɪbrənt/ *adjective* **1** vibrating. **2** resonant. **3** (often + *with*) thrilling. **4** (of colour) bright and striking. □ **vibrancy** *noun*.

■ **1** pulsating, quivering, throbbing, trembling, vibrating. **2** see RESONANT 1. **3** alert, alive, dynamic, electric, energetic, lively, living, thrilling, vivacious.

vibraphone /'vaɪbrəfəʊn/ *noun* percussion instrument with motor-driven resonators under metal bars giving vibrato effect.

vibrate /vaɪ'breɪt/ *verb* (**-ting**) **1** move rapidly to and fro. **2** (of sound) throb, resonate. **3** (+ *with*) quiver with. **4** swing to and fro; oscillate. □ **vibratory** *adjective*.

■ **1, 3** fluctuate, judder, quake, quiver, shake, shiver, shudder, throb, tremble. **2** pulsate, resonate, reverberate, throb. **4** oscillate, swing.

vibration *noun* **1** vibrating. **2** (in *plural*) mental (esp. occult) influence. **3** (in *plural*) atmosphere or feeling communicated.

■ **1** juddering, oscillation, pulsation, quivering, resonance, reverberation, shaking, shivering, shuddering, throbbing, trembling, tremor.

vibrato /vɪ'brɑːtəʊ/ *noun* tremulous effect in musical pitch.

vibrator *noun* device that vibrates, esp. instrument used in massage or sexual stimulation.

viburnum /vaɪ'bɜːnəm/ *noun* shrub with pink or white flowers.

vicar /'vɪkə/ *noun* **1** incumbent of C. of E. parish where in former times incumbent received stipend rather than tithes. **2** any member of the clergy.

vicarage *noun* vicar's house.

vicarious /vɪ'keərɪəs/ *adjective* **1** experienced indirectly. **2** acting or done etc. for another. **3** deputed, delegated. □ **vicariously** *adverb*.

■ **1** indirect, second-hand. **2** surrogate.

vice[1] *noun* **1** immoral conduct. **2** particular form of this. **3** bad habit. □ **vice ring** group of criminals organizing prostitution. **vice squad** police department concerned with prostitution.

■ **1, 2** badness, corruption, degeneracy, degradation, depravity, evil, evildoing, immorality, iniquity, lechery, profligacy, promiscuity, sin, venality, villainy, wickedness, wrongdoing. **3** bad habit, blemish, defect, failing, fault, flaw, foible, imperfection, shortcoming, weakness.

vice[2] *noun* (*US* **vise**) clamp with two jaws for holding an object being worked on.

vice- *combining form* **1** person acting in place of. **2** person next in rank to.

vice-chancellor /vaɪs'tʃɑːnsələ/ *noun* deputy chancellor (esp. administrator of university).

viceregal /vaɪs'riːg(ə)l/ *adjective* of viceroy.

vicereine /'vaɪsreɪn/ *noun* **1** viceroy's wife. **2** woman viceroy.

viceroy /'vaɪsrɔɪ/ *noun* ruler on behalf of sovereign in colony, province, etc.

vice versa /vaɪs 'vɜːsə/ *adjective* with order of terms changed; other way round.

Vichy water /'viːʃi/ *noun* effervescent mineral water from Vichy in France.

vicinity /vɪ'sɪnɪtɪ/ *noun* (*plural* **-ies**) **1** surrounding district. **2** (+ *to*) nearness to. □ **in the vicinity (of)** near (to).

■ **1** area, district, environs, locale, locality, neighbourhood, precincts, purlieus, region, *Military* sector, territory, zone. **2** closeness, nearness, propinquity, proximity.

vicious /'vɪʃəs/ *adjective* **1** (of animals) bad-tempered, savage. **2** cruel, evil, spiteful. **3** violent, severe. **4** corrupt. □ **vicious circle** self-perpetuating, harmful sequence of cause and effect. □ **viciously** *adverb*. **viciousness** *noun*.

■ **1** aggressive, bad-tempered, dangerous, ferocious, fierce, savage, *colloquial* snappy, untamed, wild. **2** atrocious, bad, barbaric, barbarous, beastly, *slang* bitchy, bloodthirsty, brutal, callous, cruel, cutting, depraved, diabolical, evil, fiendish, fierce, heartless, heinous, hurtful, immoral, inhuman, malicious, *US* mean, merciless, monstrous, murderous, nasty, perverted, pitiless, rancorous, ruthless, *colloquial* sadistic, savage, sinful, spiteful, unfeeling, venomous, vile, villainous, vindictive, violent, vitriolic, wicked. **3** fierce, savage, severe, violent.

vicissitude /vɪˈsɪsɪtjuːd/ *noun literary* change, esp. of fortune.

■ alteration, change, flux, instability, mutability, mutation, shift, uncertainty, unpredictability, variability.

victim /ˈvɪktɪm/ *noun* **1** person or thing destroyed or injured. **2** prey; dupe. **3** creature sacrificed to a god etc.

■ **1** casualty, fatality, martyr, sufferer. **2** butt, dupe, prey, target. **3** offering, sacrifice.

victimize *verb* (also **-ise**) (**-zing** or **-sing**) **1** single out for punishment or unfair treatment. **2** make (person etc.) a victim. □ **victimization** *noun*.

■ bully, cheat, discriminate against, exploit, intimidate, oppress, persecute, pick on, prey on, take advantage of, terrorize, torment, use.

victor /ˈvɪktə/ *noun* conqueror; winner of contest.

■ champion, conqueror, prizewinner, winner.

Victoria Cross /vɪkˈtɔːrɪə/ *noun* highest decoration for conspicuous bravery in armed services.

Victorian /vɪkˈtɔːrɪən/ *adjective* **1** of time of Queen Victoria. **2** prudish, strict. ● *noun* person of this time.

Victoriana /vɪktɔːrɪˈɑːnə/ *plural noun* articles, esp. collectors' items, of Victorian period.

victorious /vɪkˈtɔːrɪəs/ *adjective* **1** conquering, triumphant. **2** marked by victory. □ **victoriously** *adverb*.

■ **1** champion, conquering, first, leading, prevailing, successful, top, top-scoring, triumphant, unbeaten, undefeated, winning.

victory /ˈvɪktərɪ/ *noun* (*plural* **-ies**) success in battle, war, or contest.

■ conquest, mastery, success, superiority, supremacy, triumph, walkover, win.

victual /ˈvɪt(ə)l/ *noun* (usually in *plural*) food, provisions. ● *verb* (**-ll-**; *US* **-l-**) **1** supply with victuals. **2** lay in supply of victuals. **3** eat victuals.

victualler /ˈvɪtlə/ *noun* (*US* **victualer**) **1** person who supplies victuals. **2** (in full **licensed victualler**) publican licensed to sell alcohol.

vicuña /vɪˈkjuːnə/ *noun* **1** S. American mammal with fine silky wool. **2** cloth made from its wool. **3** imitation of this.

vide /ˈviːdeɪ/ *verb* (in *imperative*) see; consult. [Latin]

videlicet /vɪˈdeliset/ *adverb* that is to say; namely.

video /ˈvɪdɪəʊ/ *adjective* **1** relating to recording or reproduction of moving pictures on magnetic tape. **2** of broadcasting of these. ● *noun* (*plural* **-s**) **1** such recording or broadcasting. **2** *colloquial* video recorder. **3** film etc. recorded on videotape.

● *verb* (**-oes**, **-oed**) record on videotape. □ **video cassette** cassette of videotape. **video game** computer game played on television screen. **video nasty** *colloquial* horrific or pornographic video film. **video (cassette) recorder** apparatus for recording and playing videotapes.

videotape *noun* magnetic tape for recording television pictures and sound. ● *verb* (**-ping**) record on this.

vie /vaɪ/ *verb* (**vying**) (often + *with*) contend, compete; strive for superiority.

■ compete, contend, strive, struggle.

Vietnamese /vɪetnəˈmiːz/ *adjective* of Vietnam. ● *noun* (*plural* same) native, national, or language of Vietnam.

view /vjuː/ *noun* **1** range of vision. **2** what is seen. **3** scene, prospect, picture etc. of this. **4** opinion. **5** inspection by eye or mind. ● *verb* **1** look at; survey visually or mentally. **2** form mental impression or opinion of. **3** watch television. □ **in view of** considering. **on view** being shown or exhibited. **viewdata** news and information service from computer source, connected to TV screen by telephone link. **viewfinder** part of camera showing field of photograph. **viewpoint** point of view. **with a view to** with hope or intention of.

■ *noun* **1** sight, vision. **2, 3** aspect, landscape, outlook, panorama, perspective, picture, prospect, scene, scenery, seascape, sight, spectacle, vista. **4** attitude, belief, conviction, idea, judgement, notion, opinion, perception, position, thought. **5** examination, inspection, look, scrutiny, survey. ● *verb* **1** *literary* behold, consider, contemplate, examine, eye, gaze at, inspect, observe, perceive, regard, scan, stare at, survey, witness. **2** see REGARD *verb* 3. **3** look at, see, watch. □ **viewpoint** angle, perspective, point of view, position, slant, standpoint.

viewer *noun* **1** television-watcher. **2** device for looking at film transparencies etc.

vigil /ˈvɪdʒɪl/ *noun* **1** keeping awake during night etc., esp. to keep watch or pray. **2** eve of festival or holy day.

vigilance *noun* watchfulness, caution. □ **vigilant** *adjective*.

■ □ vigilant alert, attentive, awake, careful, circumspect, eagle-eyed, observant, on one's guard, on one's toes, on the watch, sharp, wakeful, wary, watchful, wide awake.

vigilante /vɪdʒɪˈlæntɪ/ *noun* member of self-appointed group for keeping order etc.

vignette /viːˈnjet/ *noun* **1** short description; character sketch. **2** illustration not in definite border. **3** photograph etc. with background shaded off.

vigour /ˈvɪgə/ *noun* (*US* **vigor**) **1** activity and strength of body or mind. **2** healthy growth. **3** animation. □ **vigorous** *adjective*. **vigorously** *adverb*.

■ animation, dynamism, energy, fitness, force, forcefulness, gusto, health, life, liveliness, might, potency, power, robustness, spirit, stamina, strength, verve, *colloquial* vim, virility, vitality, vivacity, zeal, zest. □ **vigorous** active, alive, animated, brisk, dynamic, energetic, fit, flourishing, forceful, full-blooded, *colloquial* full of beans, growing, hale and hearty, healthy, lively, lusty, potent, prosperous, red-blooded, robust, spirited, strenuous, strong, thriving, virile, vital, vivacious, zestful.

Viking /'vaɪkɪŋ/ *noun* Scandinavian raider and pirate of 8th–11th c.

vile *adjective* **1** disgusting. **2** depraved. **3** *colloquial* abominably bad. □ **vilely** *adverb*. **vileness** *noun*.

■ **1** abominable, disgusting, execrable, filthy, foul, hateful, horrible, loathsome, nasty, nauseating, obnoxious, odious, offensive, repellent, repugnant, repulsive, revolting, sickening, ugly. **2** base, contemptible, degenerate, depraved, despicable, evil, immoral, low, perverted, sinful, ugly, vicious, wicked. **3** see WICKED 4.

vilify /'vɪlɪfaɪ/ *verb* (**-ies, -ied**) speak ill of; defame. □ **vilification** *noun*.

■ abuse, calumniate, defame, denigrate, deprecate, disparage, revile, *colloquial* run down, slander, smear, speak evil of, traduce, vituperate.

villa /'vɪlə/ *noun* **1** country house; mansion. **2** rented holiday home, esp. abroad. **3** detached or semi-detached house in residential district.

village /'vɪlɪdʒ/ *noun* group of houses etc. in country district, larger than hamlet and smaller than town.

villager *noun* inhabitant of village.

villain /'vɪlən/ *noun* **1** wicked person. **2** chief wicked character in play, story, etc. **3** *colloquial* professional criminal. **4** *colloquial* rascal.

■ **1** blackguard, criminal, evildoer, malefactor, miscreant, reprobate, rogue, scoundrel, sinner, wretch. **3** see CRIMINAL *noun*. **4** see RASCAL.

villainous *adjective* wicked.

■ bad, corrupt, criminal, dishonest, evil, sinful, treacherous, vile, wicked.

villainy *noun* (*plural* **-ies**) wicked behaviour or act.

villein /'vɪlɪn/ *noun historical* feudal tenant entirely subject to lord or attached to manor. □ **villeinage** *noun*.

vim *noun colloquial* vigour, energy.

vinaigrette /vɪnɪ'gret/ *noun* salad dressing of oil and wine vinegar.

vindicate /'vɪndɪkeɪt/ *verb* (**-ting**) **1** clear of suspicion. **2** establish existence, merits, or justice of. □ **vindication** *noun*. **vindicator** *noun*. **vindicatory** *adjective*.

vindictive /vɪn'dɪktɪv/ *adjective* tending to seek revenge. □ **vindictively** *adverb*. **vindictiveness** *noun*.

■ avenging, malicious, nasty, punitive, rancorous, revengeful, spiteful, unforgiving, vengeful, vicious.

vine *noun* trailing or climbing woody-stemmed plant, esp. bearing grapes.

vinegar /'vɪnɪgə/ *noun* sour liquid produced by fermentation of wine, malt, cider, etc. □ **vinegary** *adjective*.

vineyard /'vɪnjɑːd/ *noun* plantation of grape-vines, esp. for wine-making.

vingt-et-un /væ̃teɪ'œ̃/ *noun* = PONTOON[1]. [French]

vino /vi:nəʊ/ *noun slang* wine, esp. of inferior kind.

vinous /'vaɪnəs/ *adjective* of, like, or due to wine.

vintage /'vɪntɪdʒ/ *noun* **1** season's produce of grapes. **2** wine from this. **3** grape-harvest. **4** season of this. **5** wine of high quality from particular year and district. **6** year etc. when thing was made. **7** thing made etc. in particular year etc. ● *adjective* **1** of high or peak quality, esp. from past period. **2** of a past season. □ **vintage car** car made 1917–1930.

■ *adjective* **1** choice, classic, fine, good, high-quality, mature, mellowed, seasoned, venerable. **2** see OLD 4.

vintner /'vɪntnə/ *noun* wine merchant.

vinyl /'vaɪnɪl/ *noun* any of group of plastics made by polymerization.

viol /'vaɪəl/ *noun* medieval stringed instrument similar in shape to violin.

viola[1] /vɪ'əʊlə/ *noun* musical instrument like violin but larger and of lower pitch.

viola[2] /'vaɪələ/ *noun* any plant of genus including violet and pansy, esp. cultivated hybrid.

viola da gamba /vɪəʊlə də 'gæmbə/ *noun* viol held between player's legs.

violate /'vaɪəleɪt/ *verb* (**-ting**) **1** disregard; break (oath, law, etc.). **2** treat profanely. **3** break in on; disturb. **4** rape. □ **violation** *noun*. **violator** *noun*.

■ **1** breach, break, contravene, defy, disobey, disregard, flout, ignore, infringe, overstep, sin against, transgress. **2** defile, desecrate, profane. **3** disturb, invade. **4** abuse, assault, attack, debauch, *archaic* dishonour, force oneself on, rape, *archaic* ravish. □ **violation** breach, contravention, defiance, flouting, infringement, invasion, offence, transgression.

violence /'vaɪələns/ *noun* **1** being violent. **2** violent conduct or treatment. **3** unlawful use of force. □ **do violence to** act contrary to; outrage.

violent /'vaɪələnt/ *adjective* **1** involving or using great physical force. **2** intense, vehement. **3** (of death) resulting from violence or poison. □ **violently** *adverb*.

■ **1** barbaric, berserk, bloodthirsty, brutal, cruel, damaging, dangerous, desperate, destructive, devastating, explosive, ferocious, fierce, frenzied, furious, hard, harmful, headstrong, homicidal, murderous, powerful, riotous, rough, rowdy, ruinous, ruthless, savage, strong, swingeing, tempestuous, turbulent, uncontrollable, uncontrolled, unruly, vicious, wild. **2** acute, forceful, furious, impassioned, intense, powerful, severe, strong, *colloquial* terrific, vehement, wild.

violet /'vaɪələt/ *noun* **1** plant with usually purple, blue, or white flowers. **2** bluish-purple colour at opposite end of spectrum from red. **3** paint, clothes, or material of this colour. ● *adjective* of this colour.

violin /vaɪə'lɪn/ *noun* high-pitched musical instrument with 4 strings played with bow. □ **violinist** *noun*.

violoncello /vaɪələn'tʃeləʊ/ *noun* (*plural* **-s**) *formal* cello.

VIP *abbreviation* very important person.
| ■ celebrity, dignitary.

viper /'vaɪpə/ *noun* **1** small venomous snake. **2** malignant or treacherous person.

virago /vɪ'rɑːgəʊ/ *noun* (*plural* **-s**) fierce or abusive woman.

viral /'vaɪər(ə)l/ *adjective* of or caused by virus.

virgin /'vɜːdʒɪn/ *noun* **1** person who has never had sexual intercourse. **2** (**the Virgin**) Christ's mother Mary. ● *adjective* **1** not yet used etc. **2** virginal. □ **the Virgin birth** doctrine of Christ's birth from virgin mother. □ **virginity** /və'dʒɪn-/ *noun*.

virginal *adjective* of or befitting a virgin. ● *noun* (usually in *plural*) legless spinet in box.

Virginia creeper /və'dʒɪnɪə/ *noun* vine cultivated for ornament.

Virgo /'vɜːgəʊ/ *noun* sixth sign of zodiac.

virile /'vɪraɪl/ *adjective* **1** having masculine vigour or strength. **2** sexually potent. **3** of man as distinct from woman or child. □ **virility** /-'rɪl-/ *noun*.
| ■ **1** macho, manly, masculine, potent, vigorous.

virology /vaɪ'rɒlədʒɪ/ *noun* study of viruses.

virtual /'vɜːtʃʊəl/ *adjective* being so for practical purposes though not strictly or in name. □ **virtual reality** computer-generated images, sounds, etc. that appear real to the senses. □ **virtually** *adverb*.

virtue /'vɜːtʃuː/ *noun* **1** moral goodness. **2** particular form of this. **3** chastity, esp. of woman. **4** good quality. **5** efficacy. □ **by or in virtue of** on account of; because of.
| ■ **1** decency, fairness, goodness, high-mindedness, honesty, honour, integrity, justice, morality, nobility, rectitude, respectability, righteousness, uprightness, worthiness. **3** abstinence, chastity, honour, innocence, purity, virginity. **4** advantage, asset, good point, merit, quality, redeeming feature, strength.

virtuoso /vɜːtʃʊ'əʊsəʊ/ *noun* (*plural* **-si** /-siː/ or **-sos**) highly skilled artist, esp. musician. □ **virtuosity** /-'ɒs-/ *noun*.
| ■ expert, genius, maestro, prodigy, wizard.

virtuous /'vɜːtʃʊəs/ *adjective* **1** morally good. **2** *archaic* chaste. □ **virtuously** *adverb*.
| ■ **1** blameless, decent, ethical, exemplary, fair, God-fearing, good, *colloquial* goody-goody,

high-minded, high-principled, honest, honourable, irreproachable, just, law-abiding, moral, noble, praiseworthy, principled, respectable, right, righteous, right-minded, sincere, spotless, trustworthy, uncorrupted, unimpeachable, upright, worthy. **2** chaste, decent, innocent, pure, unsullied, virginal.

virulent /'vɪrʊlənt/ *adjective* **1** poisonous. **2** (of disease) violent. **3** bitterly hostile. □ **virulence** *noun*. **virulently** *adverb*.
| ■ **1, 2** dangerous, deadly, lethal, life-threatening, noxious, pernicious, poisonous, toxic, venomous. **3** acrimonious, bitter, hostile, malicious, malign, malignant, mordant, nasty, spiteful, splenetic, vicious, vitriolic.

virus /'vaɪərəs/ *noun* **1** microscopic organism able to cause diseases. **2** computer virus.

visa /'viːzə/ *noun* endorsement on passport etc., esp. allowing holder to enter or leave country.

visage /'vɪzɪdʒ/ *noun literary* face.

vis-à-vis /viːzə'viː/ *preposition* in relation to; in comparison with. ● *adverb* opposite. [French]

viscera /'vɪsərə/ *plural noun* internal organs of body. □ **visceral** *adjective*.

viscid /'vɪsɪd/ *adjective* glutinous, sticky.

viscose /'vɪskəʊz/ *noun* **1** viscous form of cellulose used in making rayon etc. **2** fabric made from this.

viscount /'vaɪkaʊnt/ *noun* British nobleman ranking between earl and baron.

viscountess /'vaɪkaʊntɪs/ *noun* **1** viscount's wife or widow. **2** woman holding rank of viscount.

viscous /'vɪskəs/ *adjective* **1** glutinous, sticky. **2** semifluid; not flowing freely. □ **viscosity** /-kɒs-/ *noun* (*plural* **-ies**).
| ■ gluey, glutinous, sticky, syrupy, thick, viscid.

visibility /vɪzɪ'bɪlɪtɪ/ *noun* **1** being visible. **2** range or possibility of vision as determined by light and weather.

visible /'vɪzɪb(ə)l/ *adjective* **1** able to be seen, perceived, or discovered. **2** in sight; apparent, open, obvious. □ **visibly** *adverb*.
| ■ apparent, clear, conspicuous, detectable, discernible, distinct, evident, manifest, noticeable, observable, obvious, open, perceivable, perceptible, plain, recognizable, unconcealed, undisguised, unmistakable.

vision /'vɪʒ(ə)n/ *noun* **1** act or faculty of seeing; sight. **2** thing or person seen in dream or trance. **3** thing seen in imagination. **4** imaginative insight. **5** foresight; good judgement in planning. **6** beautiful person etc. **7** TV or cinema picture, esp. of specified quality.
| ■ **1** eyesight, perception, sight. **2** apparition, chimera, ghost, hallucination, illusion, mirage, phantasm, phantom, spectre, spirit, wraith. **3** conception, daydream, dream, fantasy, idea, image, mental picture. **4, 5** far-sightedness, foresight, imagination, insight, understanding.

visionary *adjective* **1** given to seeing visions or to fanciful theories. **2** having vision or foresight. **3** unpractical. **4** not real; imaginary. ● *noun* (*plural* **-ies**) visionary person.

■ *adjective* **1, 2** dreamy, fanciful, far-sighted, futuristic, idealistic, imaginative, mystical, prophetic, quixotic, romantic, speculative, transcendental, Utopian. **3** idealistic, impractical, unpractical, unrealistic, unworkable, Utopian. **4** see IMAGINARY. ● *noun* dreamer, idealist, mystic, poet, prophet, romantic, seer.

visit /'vɪzɪt/ *verb* (**-t-**) **1** go or come to see (person, place, etc.). **2** stay temporarily with or at. **3** (of disease, calamity, etc.) attack. **4** (often + *upon*) inflict punishment for (sin). ● *noun* **1** act of visiting. **2** temporary stay with person or at place. **3** (+ *to*) occasion of going to doctor etc. **4** formal or official call.

■ *verb* **1** call on, come to see, descend on, *colloquial* drop in on, go to see, *colloquial* look up, pay a call on, pop in on. **2** sojourn with, stay with. ● *noun* **1, 2** call, sojourn, stay, stop.

visitant /'vɪzɪt(ə)nt/ *noun* visitor, esp. ghost etc.

visitation /vɪzɪ'teɪʃ(ə)n/ *noun* **1** official visit of inspection. **2** trouble etc. seen as divine punishment.

visitor *noun* **1** person who visits. **2** migrant bird.

■ **1** caller, foreigner, guest, holidaymaker, migrant, sightseer, tourist, traveller, tripper; (*visitors*) company.

visor /'vaɪzə/ *noun* **1** movable part of helmet covering face. **2** shield for eyes, esp. one at top of vehicle windscreen.

vista /'vɪstə/ *noun* **1** view, esp. through avenue of trees or other long narrow opening. **2** mental view of long succession of events.

■ **1** landscape, outlook, panorama, prospect, scene, scenery, seascape, view. **2** outlook, prospect, view.

visual /'vɪʒʊəl/ *adjective* of or used in seeing. □ **visual display unit** device displaying data of computer on screen. □ **visually** *adverb*.

visualize *verb* (also **-ise**) (**-zing** or **-sing**) imagine visually. □ **visualization** *noun*.

■ conceive, dream up, envisage, imagine, picture.

vital /'vaɪt(ə)l/ *adjective* **1** of or essential to organic life. **2** essential to existence, functioning, matter in hand, etc; indispensable. **3** paramount; very great. **4** full of life or activity. **5** *archaic* fatal. ● *noun* (in *plural*) vital organs, e.g. lungs and heart. □ **vital statistics 1** those relating to number of births, marriages, deaths, etc. **2** *jocular* measurements of woman's bust, waist, and hips. □ **vitally** *adverb*.

■ *adjective* **1** enlivening, invigorating, life-giving, quickening, vitalizing. **2** compulsory, crucial, essential, fundamental, imperative, important, indispensable, mandatory, necessary, needed, pressing, primary, relevant, requisite. **3** alive, animate, animated, dynamic, energetic,

exuberant, lively, sparkling, spirited, sprightly, vigorous, vivacious, zestful.

vitality /vaɪ'tælɪtɪ/ *noun* **1** animation, liveliness. **2** ability to survive or endure.

■ **1** animation, dynamism, energy, exuberance, go, life, liveliness, sparkle, spirit, sprightliness, vigour, *colloquial* vim, vivacity, zest. **2** endurance, life, stamina, strength, vigour.

vitalize *verb* (also **-ise**) (**-zing** or **-sing**) **1** endow with life. **2** make lively or vigorous. □ **vitalization** *noun*.

vitamin /'vɪtəmɪn/ *noun* any of various substances present in many foods and essential to health and growth.

vitaminize *verb* (also **-ise**) (**-zing** or **-sing**) introduce vitamins into (food).

vitiate /'vɪʃɪeɪt/ *verb* (**-ting**) **1** impair, debase. **2** make invalid or ineffectual.

viticulture /'vɪtɪkʌltʃə/ *noun* cultivation of grapes.

vitreous /'vɪtrɪəs/ *adjective* of or like glass.

vitrify /'vɪtrɪfaɪ/ *verb* (**-ies**, **-ied**) change into glass or glassy substance, esp. by heat. □ **vitrification** *noun*.

vitriol /'vɪtrɪəl/ *noun* **1** sulphuric acid or sulphate. **2** caustic speech or criticism. □ **vitriolic** /-'ɒl-/ *adjective*.

■ □ **vitriolic** abusive, acid, biting, bitter, caustic, cruel, destructive, hostile, hurtful, malicious, savage, scathing, vicious, vindictive, virulent.

vitro see IN VITRO.

vituperate /vɪ'tjuːpəreɪt, vaɪ'tjuːpəreɪt/ *verb* (**-ting**) criticize abusively. □ **vituperation** *noun*. **vituperative** /-rətɪv/ *adjective*.

■ abuse, berate, calumniate, censure, defame, denigrate, deprecate, disparage, reproach, revile, *colloquial* run down, slander, upbraid, vilify.

viva[1] /'vaɪvə/ *colloquial noun* (*plural* **-s**) viva voce. ● *verb* (**vivas, vivaed, vivaing**) viva-voce.

viva[2] /'viːvə/ *interjection* long live. ● *noun* cry of this as salute etc. [Italian]

vivacious /vɪ'veɪʃəs/ *adjective* lively, animated. □ **vivacity** /vɪ'væsɪtɪ/ *noun*.

■ animated, bubbly, cheerful, ebullient, energetic, high-spirited, light-hearted, lively, merry, positive, spirited, sprightly.

vivarium /vaɪ'veərɪəm/ *noun* (*plural* **-ria** or **-s**) **1** glass bowl etc. for keeping animals for scientific study. **2** place for keeping animals in (nearly) their natural conditions.

viva-voce *verb* (**-voces, -voceed, -voceing**) examine orally.

viva voce /vaɪvə 'vəʊtʃɪ/ *adjective* oral. ● *adverb* orally. ● *noun* oral exam.

vivid /'vɪvɪd/ *adjective* **1** (of light or colour) bright, strong, intense. **2** (of memory, description, etc.) lively, incisive, graphic. □ **vividly** *adverb*. **vividness** *noun*.

■ **1** bright, brilliant, colourful, dazzling, fresh, gaudy, gay, gleaming, glowing, intense, rich, shining, showy, strong, vibrant. **2** clear, detailed, graphic, imaginative, lifelike, lively, memorable, powerful, realistic, striking.

vivify /'vɪvɪfaɪ/ *verb* (**-ies**, **-ied**) give life to; animate.

viviparous /vɪ'vɪpərəs/ *adjective* bringing forth young alive.

vivisect /'vɪvɪsekt/ *verb* perform vivisection on.

vivisection /vɪvɪ'sekʃ(ə)n/ *noun* surgical experimentation on living animals for scientific research. □ **vivisectionist** *noun.*

vixen /'vɪks(ə)n/ *noun* **1** female fox. **2** spiteful woman.

viz. *abbreviation* videlicet.

vizier /vɪ'zɪə/ *noun historical* high official in some Muslim countries.

V-neck *noun* V-shaped neckline on pullover etc.

vocabulary /və'kæbjʊlərɪ/ *noun* (*plural* **-ies**) **1** words used by language, book, branch of science, or author. **2** list of these. **3** person's range of language.
■ **2** dictionary, glossary, lexicon, phrase book.

vocal /'vəʊk(ə)l/ *adjective* **1** of or uttered by voice. **2** speaking one's feelings freely. □ **vocal cords** voice-producing part of larynx. □ **vocally** *adverb.*
■ **1** oral, said, spoken, sung, voiced. **2** communicative, forthcoming, loquacious, outspoken, talkative, vociferous.

vocalist *noun* singer.

vocalize *verb* (also **-ise**) (**-zing** or **-sing**) **1** form (sound) or utter (word) with voice. **2** articulate, express. □ **vocalization** *noun.*

vocation /vəʊ'keɪʃ(ə)n/ *noun* **1** divine call to, or sense of suitability for, career or occupation. **2** employment, trade, profession. □ **vocational** *adjective.*
■ **1** call, calling. **2** calling, career, employment, job, life's work, occupation, profession, trade.

vocative /'vɒkətɪv/ *noun* case of noun used in addressing person or thing. ● *adjective* of or in this case.

vociferate /və'sɪfəreɪt/ *verb* (**-ting**) **1** utter noisily. **2** shout, bawl. □ **vociferation** *noun.*

vociferous /və'sɪfərəs/ *adjective* **1** noisy, clamorous. **2** loud and insistent in speech. □ **vociferously** *adverb.*

vodka /'vɒdkə/ *noun* alcoholic spirit distilled esp. in Russia from rye etc.

vogue /vəʊg/ *noun* **1** (**the vogue**) prevailing fashion. **2** popular use. □ **in vogue** in fashion. □ **voguish** *adjective.*
■ **1** craze, fad, fashion, latest thing, mode, rage, style, taste, trend. □ **in vogue** see FASHIONABLE.

voice *noun* **1** sound formed in larynx and uttered by mouth, esp. in speaking, singing, etc. **2** ability to produce this. **3** use of voice; spoken or written expression. **4** opinion so expressed. **5** right to express opinion. **6** *Grammar* set of verbal forms showing whether verb is active or passive. ● *verb* (**-cing**) **1** express. **2** (esp. as **voiced** *adjective*) utter with vibration of vocal cords. □ **voice-over** commentary in film by unseen speaker.
■ *noun* **1–3** accent, articulation, expression, inflection, intonation, sound, speaking, speech, tone, utterance. **4, 5** say, vote. ● *verb* **1** see SPEAK 1,2.

voiceless *adjective* **1** dumb, speechless. **2** *Phonetics* uttered without vibration of the vocal cords.

void *adjective* **1** empty, vacant. **2** not valid or binding. ● *noun* empty space; sense of loss. ● *verb* **1** invalidate. **2** excrete.
■ *adjective* **1** blank, empty, unoccupied, vacant. **2** annulled, cancelled, inoperative, invalid, unenforceable, useless. ● *noun* blank, emptiness, nothingness, space, vacancy, vacuum.

voile /vɔɪl/ *noun* thin semi-transparent fabric.

vol. *abbreviation* volume.

volatile /'vɒlətaɪl/ *adjective* **1** changeable in mood; flighty. **2** unstable. **3** evaporating rapidly. □ **volatility** /-'tɪl-/ *noun.*
■ **1** changeable, erratic, fickle, flighty, inconstant, lively, mercurial, temperamental, unpredictable, *colloquial* up and down, variable. **2** explosive, sensitive, unstable.

vol-au-vent /'vɒləʊvɑ̃/ *noun* small round case of puff pastry with savoury filling.

volcanic /vɒl'kænɪk/ *adjective* of, like, or produced by volcano.

volcano /vɒl'keɪnəʊ/ *noun* (*plural* **-es**) mountain or hill from which lava, steam, etc. escape through earth's crust.

vole *noun* small plant-eating rodent.

volition /və'lɪʃ(ə)n/ *noun* act or power of willing. □ **of one's own volition** voluntarily.

volley /'vɒlɪ/ *noun* (*plural* **-s**) **1** simultaneous firing of a number of weapons. **2** bullets etc. so fired. **3** (usually + *of*) torrent (of abuse etc.). **4** *Tennis, Football etc.* playing of ball before it touches ground. ● *verb* (**-eys**, **-eyed**) return or send by volley. □ **volleyball** game for two teams of 6 hitting large ball by hand over net.
■ *noun* **1** barrage, bombardment, burst, cannonade, fusillade, salvo, shower. **3** barrage, outpouring, shower, storm, torrent.

volt /vəʊlt/ *noun* SI unit of electromotive force. □ **voltmeter** instrument measuring electric potential in volts.

voltage *noun* electromotive force expressed in volts.

volte-face /vɒlt'fɑːs/ *noun* (*plural* **voltes-face** same pronunciation) complete change of position in one's attitude or opinion.

voluble /'vɒljʊb(ə)l/ *adjective* speaking or spoken fluently or with continuous flow of words. □ **volubility** *noun.* **volubly** *adverb.*

■ chatty, fluent, garrulous, glib, loquacious, talkative, wordy.

volume /'vɒljuːm/ *noun* **1** single book forming part or all of work. **2** solid content, bulk. **3** space occupied by gas or liquid. **4** (+ *of*) amount or quantity of. **5** (+ *of*) moving mass of (water, smoke, etc.). **6** quantity or power of sound.

■ **1** book, tome. **2** aggregate, amount, bulk, capacity, dimensions, mass, measure, quantity, size.

voluminous /və'luːmɪnəs/ *adjective* **1** large in volume; bulky. **2** (of drapery etc.) loose and ample. **3** written or writing at great length.

■ **1, 2** ample, big, billowing, bulky, capacious, cavernous, enormous, extensive, gigantic, great, huge, immense, large, mammoth, massive, roomy, spacious, vast.

voluntary /'vɒləntrɪ/ *adjective* **1** done, acting, or given willingly. **2** unpaid. **3** (of institution) supported or built by charity. **4** brought about by voluntary action. **5** (of muscle, limb, etc.) controlled by will. ● *noun* (*plural* **-ies**) organ solo played before or after church service. □ **voluntarily** *adverb*.

■ *adjective* **1** elective, free, optional, spontaneous, willing. **2** honorary, unpaid, unsalaried. **4** conscious, deliberate, intended, intentional, planned, premeditated, wilful.

volunteer /vɒlən'tɪə/ *noun* person who voluntarily undertakes task or enters military etc. service. ● *verb* **1** (often + *to*) undertake or offer voluntarily. **2** (often + *for*) be volunteer.

■ *verb* **1** be willing, offer, propose, put oneself forward. **2** see ENLIST 1.

voluptuary /və'lʌptʃʊərɪ/ *noun* (*plural* **-ies**) person who seeks luxury and sensual pleasure.

voluptuous /və'lʌptʃʊəs/ *adjective* **1** of, tending to, occupied with, or derived from, sensuous or sensual pleasure. **2** (of woman) curvaceous and sexually desirable. □ **voluptuously** *adverb*. **voluptuousness** *noun*.

■ **1** erotic, hedonistic, luxurious, pleasure-loving, self-indulgent, sensual, sensuous, sybaritic. **2** attractive, buxom, *colloquial* curvaceous, desirable, sexy, shapely, *colloquial* well endowed.

vomit /'vɒmɪt/ *verb* (**-t-**) **1** eject (contents of stomach) through mouth; be sick. **2** (of volcano, chimney, etc.) eject violently; belch forth. ● *noun* matter vomited from stomach.

■ *verb* **1** be sick, bring up, disgorge, heave, *slang* puke, regurgitate, retch, *colloquial* sick up, spew up, throw up.

voodoo /'vuːduː/ *noun* religious witchcraft as practised esp. in W. Indies. ● *verb* (**-doos, -dooed**) affect by voodoo; bewitch.

voracious /və'reɪʃəs/ *adjective* **1** greedy in eating; ravenous. **2** very eager. □ **voraciously** *adverb*. **voraciousness** *noun*. **voracity** /-'ræs-/ *noun*.

■ **1** gluttonous, greedy, hungry, insatiable, ravenous, thirsty. **2** avid, eager, fervid, keen.

vortex /'vɔːteks/ *noun* (*plural* **-texes** or **-tices** /-tɪsiːz/) **1** whirlpool; whirlwind. **2** whirling motion or mass. **3** thing viewed as destructive or devouring.

■ **1, 2** eddy, whirlpool, whirlwind.

votary /'vəʊtərɪ/ *noun* (*plural* **-ies**; *feminine* **votaress**) (usually + *of*) **1** person dedicated to service of god or cult. **2** devotee of a person, occupation etc.

vote *noun* **1** formal expression of choice or opinion by ballot, show of hands, etc. **2** (usually **the vote**) right to vote. **3** opinion expressed by vote. **4** votes given by or for particular group. ● *verb* (**-ting**) **1** (often + *for*, *against*) give vote. **2** enact etc. by majority of votes. **3** *colloquial* pronounce by general consent. **4** (often + *that*) suggest, urge. □ **vote down** defeat (proposal etc.) by voting. **vote in** elect by voting. **vote with one's feet** *colloquial* indicate opinion by one's presence or absence.

■ *noun* **1** ballot, election, plebiscite, poll, referendum, show of hands. ● *verb* **1** ballot, cast one's vote; (*vote for*) choose, elect, nominate, opt for, pick, return, select, settle on.

voter *noun* person voting or entitled to vote.

votive /'vəʊtɪv/ *adjective* given or consecrated in fulfilment of vow.

vouch /vaʊtʃ/ *verb* (+ *for*) answer or be surety for.

■ (*vouch for*) answer for, back, certify, endorse, guarantee, speak for, sponsor, support.

voucher *noun* **1** document exchangeable for goods or services. **2** receipt.

■ **1** coupon, ticket, token.

vouchsafe /vaʊtʃ'seɪf/ *verb* (**-fing**) *formal* **1** condescend to grant. **2** (+ *to do*) condescend to.

vow /vaʊ/ *noun* solemn, esp. religious, promise. ● *verb* **1** promise solemnly. **2** *archaic* declare solemnly.

■ *noun* assurance, guarantee, oath, pledge, promise, undertaking, word of honour. ● *verb* **1** give an assurance, give one's word, guarantee, pledge, promise, swear, take an oath.

vowel /'vaʊəl/ *noun* **1** speech sound made by vibrations of vocal cords, but without audible friction. **2** letter(s) representing this.

USAGE The (written) vowels of English are customarily said to be *a, e, i, o,* and *u,* but *y* can be either a consonant (as in *yet*) or a vowel (as in *by*), and combinations of these six, such as *ee* in *keep, ie* in *tied,* and *ye* in *rye,* are just as much vowels.

vox pop *noun colloquial* popular opinion as represented by informal comments.

vox populi /vɒks 'pɒpjʊlaɪ/ *noun* public opinion; popular belief. [Latin]

voyage /'vɔɪdʒ/ *noun* journey, esp. long one by sea or in space. ● *verb* (**-ging**) make voyage. □ **voyager** *noun*.

■ *noun* cruise, journey, passage. ● *verb* cruise, sail, travel.

voyeur /vwɑːˈjɜː/ *noun* **1** person who derives sexual pleasure from secretly observing others' sexual activity or organs. **2** (esp. covert) spectator. □ **voyeurism** *noun*. **voyeuristic** /-ˈrɪs-/ *adjective*.

vs. *abbreviation* versus.

VSO *abbreviation* Voluntary Service Overseas.

VTOL /ˈviːtɒl/ *abbreviation* vertical take-off and landing.

vulcanite /ˈvʌlkənaɪt/ *noun* hard black vulcanized rubber.

vulcanize /ˈvʌlkənaɪz/ *verb* (also **-ise**) (**-zing** or **-sing**) make (rubber etc.) stronger and more elastic by treating with sulphur at high temperature. □ **vulcanization** *noun*.

vulgar /ˈvʌlɡə/ *adjective* **1** coarse; of or characteristic of the common people. **2** in common use; prevalent. □ **vulgar fraction** fraction expressed by numerator and denominator (e.g. ½), not decimally (e.g. 0.5). **the vulgar tongue** native or vernacular language. □ **vulgarity** /-ˈɡær-/ *noun* (*plural* **-ies**). **vulgarly** *adverb*.

■ **1** churlish, coarse, *derogatory* common, crude, foul, gaudy, gross, ill-bred, impolite, improper, inartistic, in bad taste, indecent, indecorous, inelegant, insensitive, low, *colloquial* lowbrow, obscene, offensive, plebeian, rude, tasteless, tawdry, uncouth, ungentlemanly, unladylike, unrefined, unsophisticated.

vulgarian /vʌlˈɡeərɪən/ *noun* vulgar (esp. rich) person.

vulgarism *noun* vulgar word or expression.

vulgarize /ˈvʌlɡəraɪz/ *verb* (also **-ise**) (**-zing** or **-sing**) **1** make vulgar. **2** spoil by popularizing. □ **vulgarization** *noun*.

Vulgate /ˈvʌlɡeɪt/ *noun* 4th-c. Latin version of Bible.

vulnerable /ˈvʌlnərəb(ə)l/ *adjective* **1** easily wounded or harmed. **2** (+ *to*) open to attack, injury, or criticism. □ **vulnerability** *noun*.

■ **1** at risk, defenceless, helpless, sensitive, thin-skinned, touchy, unguarded, unprotected, weak. **2** (*vulnerable to*) exposed to, liable to, susceptible to, wide open to.

vulpine /ˈvʌlpaɪn/ *adjective* **1** of or like fox. **2** crafty, cunning.

vulture /ˈvʌltʃə/ *noun* **1** large carrion-eating bird of prey. **2** rapacious person.

vulva /ˈvʌlvə/ *noun* (*plural* **-s**) external female genitals.

vv. *abbreviation* verses.

vying *present participle* of VIE.

Ww

W. *abbreviation* (also **W**) **1** watt(s). **2** west(ern).

w. *abbreviation* **1** wicket(s). **2** wide(s). **3** with.

wacky /'wækɪ/ *adjective* (**-ier, -iest**) *slang* crazy.

wad /wɒd/ *noun* **1** lump of soft material to keep things apart or in place or to block hole. **2** roll of banknotes. ● *verb* (**-dd-**) **1** stop up or fix with wad. **2** line, stuff, or protect with wadding.
- ■ *noun* **1** bundle, lump, mass, pack, pad, plug, roll.

wadding *noun* soft fibrous material for stuffing quilts, packing fragile articles in, etc.
- ■ filling, lining, packing, padding, stuffing.

waddle /'wɒd(ə)l/ *verb* (**-ling**) walk with short steps and swaying motion. ● *noun* such walk.

wade *verb* (**-ding**) **1** walk through water, mud, etc., esp. with difficulty. **2** (+ *through*) go through (tedious task, book, etc.). **3** (+ *into*) *colloquial* attack (person, task). ● *noun* spell of wading. □ **wade in** *colloquial* make vigorous attack or intervention.
- ■ *verb* **1** paddle, splash.

wader *noun* **1** long-legged waterfowl. **2** (in *plural*) high waterproof boots.

wadi /'wɒdɪ/ *noun* (*plural* **-s**) rocky watercourse in N. Africa etc., dry except in rainy season.

wafer /'weɪfə/ *noun* **1** very thin light crisp biscuit. **2** disc of unleavened bread used in Eucharist. **3** disc of red paper stuck on legal document instead of seal. □ **wafer-thin** very thin.

waffle[1] /'wɒf(ə)l/ *colloquial noun* aimless verbose talk or writing. ● *verb* (**-ling**) indulge in waffle. □ **waffly** *adjective*.
- ■ *noun* evasiveness, padding, prevarication, prolixity, *derogatory* verbiage, wordiness. ● *verb* beat about the bush, blather, hedge, prattle, prevaricate.

waffle[2] /'wɒf(ə)l/ *noun* small crisp batter cake. □ **waffle-iron** utensil for cooking waffles.

waft /wɒft/ *verb* convey or be conveyed smoothly (as) through air or over water. ● *noun* whiff.
- ■ *verb* bear, be borne, carry, convey, drift, float, puff, transmit, transport, travel.

wag[1] *verb* (**-gg-**) shake or wave to and fro. ● *noun* single wagging motion. □ **wagtail** small bird with long tail.
- ■ *verb* bob, flap, move to and fro, nod, oscillate, rock, shake, sway, undulate, *colloquial* waggle, wave, *colloquial* wiggle.

wag[2] *noun* **1** facetious person. **2** *slang* truant.
- ■ **1** see COMEDIAN 1,3. **2** see TRUANT *noun*.

wage *noun* (in *singular* or *plural*) employee's regular pay, esp. paid weekly. ● *verb* (**-ging**) carry on (war etc.). □ **wage earner** person who works for wages.
- ■ *noun* compensation, earnings, emolument, honorarium, income, pay, recompense, remuneration, reward, salary, stipend. ● *verb* carry on, conduct, engage in, fight, prosecute, pursue, undertake.

waged *adjective* in regular paid employment.

wager /'weɪdʒə/ *noun & verb* bet.
- ■ *noun* see BET *noun* 1–2. *verb* see BET *verb*.

waggish *adjective* playful, facetious. □ **waggishly** *adverb*. **waggishness** *noun*.

waggle /'wæg(ə)l/ *verb* (**-ling**) *colloquial* wag.

wagon /'wægən/ *noun* (also **waggon**) **1** 4-wheeled vehicle for heavy loads. **2** open railway truck. □ **on the wagon** *slang* abstaining from alcohol. **wagon-load** as much as wagon can carry.

wagoner *noun* (also **waggoner**) driver of wagon.

waif *noun* **1** homeless and helpless person, esp. abandoned child. **2** ownerless object or animal.

wail *noun* **1** prolonged plaintive inarticulate cry of pain, grief, etc. **2** sound resembling this. ● *verb* **1** utter wail. **2** lament or complain persistently.
- ■ *verb* caterwaul, complain, cry, howl, lament, moan, shriek, weep, yowl.

wain *noun archaic* wagon.

wainscot /'weɪnskət/ *noun* (also **wainscoting**) boarding or wooden panelling on room-wall.

waist *noun* **1** part of human body between ribs and hips; narrowness marking this. **2** circumference of waist. **3** narrow middle part of anything. **4** part of garment encircling waist. **5** *US* bodice, blouse. **6** part of ship between forecastle and quarterdeck. □ **waistband** strip of cloth forming waist of garment. **waistcoat** usually sleeveless and collarless waist-length garment. **waistline** outline or size of waist.
- ■ **1** middle, waistline. □ **waistband** belt, cummerbund, girdle.

wait *verb* **1** defer action until expected event occurs. **2** await (turn etc.). **3** (of thing) remain in readiness. **4** (usually as **waiting** *noun*) park briefly. **5** act as waiter or attendant. **6** (+ *on, upon*) await convenience of. **7** (+ *on, upon*) be attendant to. ● *noun* **1** act or period of waiting. **2** (usually + *for*) watching for enemy. **3** (in *plural*) *archaic* street singers of Christmas carols. □ **waiting-list** list of people waiting for thing not immediately available. **waiting-room** room for people to wait in, esp. at surgery or railway station.

■ *verb* **1** bide one's time, delay, halt, hang about, hang on, hesitate, hold back, keep still, linger, mark time, pause, remain, rest, *colloquial* sit tight, stand by, stay, stop, *archaic* tarry. **5** serve. ● *noun* **1** delay, halt, hesitation, hiatus, hold-up, intermission, interval, pause, postponement, rest, stay, stop, stoppage.

waiter *noun* (*feminine* **waitress**) person who serves at hotel or restaurant tables.

waive *verb* (**-ving**) refrain from insisting on or using.

■ abandon, *formal* cede, disclaim, dispense with, forgo, give up, relinquish, remit, renounce, resign, sign away, surrender.

waiver *noun* Law (document recording) waiving.

wake[1] *verb* (**-king**; *past* **woke**; *past participle* **woken** /'wəʊk(ə)n/) **1** (often + *up*) (cause to) cease to sleep. **2** (often + *up*) (cause to) become alert. **3** *archaic* (except as **waking** *adjective* & *noun*) be awake. **4** disturb with noise. **5** evoke. ● *noun* **1** (chiefly in Ireland) vigil beside corpse before burial. **2** attendant lamentations and merrymaking. **3** (usually in *plural*) annual holiday in (industrial) N. England. □ **wake up to** realize.

■ *verb* **1, 2** arouse, awaken, become conscious, bestir oneself, bring to life, call, come to life, disturb, galvanize, get up, rise, rouse, stimulate, stir, waken. **3 (waking)** see CONSCIOUS 1. ● *noun* **1** funeral, vigil. □ **wake up to** see REALIZE 1,2.

wake[2] *noun* **1** track left on water's surface by moving ship etc. **2** turbulent air left by moving aircraft. □ **in the wake of** following; as result of.

■ path, track, trail, turbulence, wash.

wakeful *adjective* **1** unable to sleep; sleepless. **2** vigilant. □ **wakefully** *adverb*. **wakefulness** *noun*.

■ **1** awake, insomniac, restless, sleepless. **2** alert, on the qui vive, vigilant, watchful.

waken /'weɪkən/ *verb* make or become awake.

walk /wɔːk/ *verb* **1** move by lifting and setting down each foot in turn, never having both feet off the ground at once. **2** (of quadruped) go with slowest gait. **3** travel or go on foot. **4** take exercise thus. **5** traverse (distance) in walking; tread floor or surface of. **6** cause to walk with one. ● *noun* **1** act of walking; ordinary human gait. **2** slowest gait of animal. **3** person's manner of walking. **4** distance walkable in specified time. **5** excursion on foot. **6** place or track meant or fit for walking. □ **walkabout 1** informal stroll by royal person etc. **2** Australian Aboriginal's period of wandering. **walk away with** *colloquial* win easily. **walking frame** tubular metal frame to assist elderly or disabled people in walking. **walking stick** stick carried for support when walking. **walk off with** *colloquial* **1** steal. **2** win easily. **walk of life** one's occupation. **walk-on part** short or non-speaking dramatic role. **walk out 1** depart suddenly or angrily. **2** stop work in protest. **walk-out** *noun*. **walk out on** desert. **walkover** easy victory. **walk the streets** be prostitute.

walkway passage or path for walking along. □ **walkable** *adjective*.

■ *verb* **1–5** amble, creep, dodder, footslog, hike, hobble, limp, lope, lurch, march, mince, pace, pad, paddle, parade, perambulate, plod, promenade, prowl, ramble, saunter, scuttle, shamble, shuffle, slink, stagger, stalk, stamp, steal, step, stomp, stride, stroll, strut, stumble, swagger, tiptoe, *colloquial* toddle, totter, *colloquial* traipse, tramp, trample, tread, trek, troop, trot, trudge, waddle, wade. ● *noun* **3** bearing, carriage, gait, stride. **5** constitutional, hike, promenade, ramble, saunter, stroll, *colloquial* traipse, tramp, trek, trudge, turn. **6** alley, path, pathway, pavement. □ **walk away with** see WIN *verb* 1. **walk off with 1** see STEAL *verb* 1. **walk out 2** see STRIKE *verb* 19. **walk out on** see DESERT[1] 1,2.

walker *noun* **1** person etc. that walks. **2** framework in which baby can walk unaided. **3** walking frame.

■ **1** hiker, pedestrian, rambler.

walkie-talkie /wɔːkɪ'tɔːkɪ/ *noun* portable two-way radio.

Walkman /'wɔːkmən/ *noun* (*plural* **-s**) *proprietary term* type of personal stereo.

wall /wɔːl/ *noun* **1** continuous narrow upright structure of usually brick or stone, enclosing or dividing a space or supporting a roof. **2** thing like wall in appearance or effect. **3** outermost layer of animal or plant organ, cell, etc. ● *verb* **1** (esp. as **walled** *adjective*) surround with wall. **2** (usually + *up*, *off*) block with wall. **3** (+ *up*, *in*) enclose within sealed space. □ **go to the wall** fare badly in competition. **up the wall** *colloquial* crazy; furious. **wallflower 1** fragrant garden plant. **2** *colloquial* woman not dancing because partnerless. **wall game** Eton form of football. **wallpaper** ● *noun* paper for covering interior walls of rooms. ● *verb* decorate with wallpaper. **wall-to-wall 1** fitted to cover whole floor. **2** *colloquial* ubiquitous.

■ *noun* **1** barricade, bulwark, dyke, fortification, parapet, rampart. **2** barrier, divider, fence, hedge, obstacle, partition, screen. ● *verb* **3** (*wall in*) see ENCLOSE 1.

wallaby /'wɒləbɪ/ *noun* (*plural* **-ies**) small kangaroo-like marsupial.

wallah /'wɒlə/ *noun slang* person connected with a specified occupation or thing.

wallet /'wɒlɪt/ *noun* small flat case for holding banknotes etc.

■ notecase, pocketbook, pouch, purse.

wall-eye *noun* eye with whitish iris or outward squint. □ **wall-eyed** *adjective*.

wallop /'wɒləp/ *colloquial verb* (**-p-**) thrash, beat. ● *noun* **1** whack. **2** beer.

wallow /'wɒləʊ/ *verb* **1** roll about in mud etc. **2** (+ *in*) indulge unrestrainedly in. ● *noun* **1** act of wallowing. **2** place where animals wallow.

■ *verb* **1** roll about, welter. **2** (*wallow in*) glory in, indulge oneself in, luxuriate in, revel in, take delight in.

wally /ˈwɒlɪ/ noun (plural **-ies**) slang foolish or incompetent person.

walnut /ˈwɔːlnʌt/ noun **1** tree with aromatic leaves and drooping catkins. **2** its nut. **3** its timber.

walrus /ˈwɔːlrəs/ noun (plural same or **walruses**) long-tusked amphibious arctic mammal. □ **walrus moustache** long thick drooping moustache.

waltz /wɔːls/ noun **1** ballroom dance in triple time. **2** music for this. ● verb **1** dance waltz. **2** (often + in, out, round, etc.) colloquial move easily, casually, etc.

wampum /ˈwɒmpəm/ noun strings of shell-beads formerly used by N. American Indians for money, ornament, etc.

wan /wɒn/ adjective (**-nn-**) pale; weary-looking. □ **wanly** adverb.
■ anaemic, ashen, bloodless, colourless, exhausted, faint, feeble, livid, pale, pallid, pasty, sickly, tired, waxen, worn.

wand /wɒnd/ noun **1** fairy's or magician's magic stick. **2** staff as sign of office etc. **3** Music colloquial conductor's baton.
■ baton, rod, staff, stick.

wander /ˈwɒndə/ verb **1** (often + in, off, etc.) go from place to place aimlessly. **2** meander. **3** diverge from path etc. **4** talk or think incoherently; be inattentive or delirious. □ **wanderlust** eagerness to travel or wander; restlessness. □ **wanderer** noun. **wandering** adjective.
■ **1** drift, go aimlessly, prowl, ramble, range, roam, rove, saunter, stroll, travel about, walk. **2** curve, meander, snake, twist and turn, wind, zigzag. **3** deviate, drift, err, stray, swerve, veer. **4** be inattentive, digress, drift, go off at a tangent, ramble, stray. □ **wandering** see NOMADIC (NOMAD).

wane verb (**-ning**) **1** (of moon) decrease in apparent size. **2** decrease in power, vigour, importance, size, etc. ● noun process of waning. □ **on the wane** declining.
■ verb decline, decrease, dim, diminish, dwindle, ebb, fade, fail, fall off, lessen, peter out, shrink, subside, taper off, weaken.

wangle /ˈwæŋg(ə)l/ colloquial verb (**-ling**) contrive to obtain (favour etc.). ● noun act of wangling.

wannabe /ˈwɒnəbɪ/ noun slang avid fan who apes person admired; anyone wishing to be someone else.

want /wɒnt/ verb **1** (often + to do) desire; wish for possession of. **2** need. **3** (+ to do) colloquial should. **4** (usually + for) lack; be without or fall short by. **5** (as **wanted** adjective) (of suspected criminal etc.) sought by police. ● noun **1** lack, deficiency. **2** poverty, need. **3** desire.
■ verb **1** aspire to, covet, crave, desire, colloquial fancy, hanker after, colloquial have a yen for, hunger for, itch for, like, long for, miss, pine for, prefer, set one's heart on, thirst after, thirst for,

wish for, yearn for. **2** demand, need, require. **4** be short of, be without, lack, miss, need, require.
● noun **1** absence, dearth, deficiency, insufficiency, lack, scarcity, shortage. **2** famine, hunger, need, penury, poverty, privation. **3** demand, desire, need, requirement, wish.

wanting adjective **1** lacking (in quality or quantity); unequal to requirements. **2** absent.

wanton /ˈwɒnt(ə)n/ adjective **1** licentious. **2** capricious, arbitrary. **3** luxuriant, wild. ● noun literary licentious person. □ **wantonly** adverb.

wapiti /ˈwɒpɪtɪ/ noun (plural **-s**) large N. American deer.

war /wɔː/ noun **1** armed hostility, esp. between nations. **2** specific period of this. **3** hostility between people. **4** (often + on) efforts against crime, poverty, etc. ● verb (**-rr-**) **1** (as **warring** adjective) rival; fighting. **2** make war. □ **at war** engaged in war. **go to war** begin war. **on the warpath 1** going to war. **2** colloquial seeking confrontation. **wage war** carry on war. **war crime** crime violating international laws of war. **war cry 1** phrase or name shouted to rally troops. **2** party slogan. **war dance** dance performed by primitive peoples before battle or after victory. **warhead** explosive head of missile. **warhorse 1** historical trooper's horse. **2** colloquial veteran soldier. **war memorial** monument to those killed in (a) war. **warmonger** /-mʌŋgə/ person who promotes war. **warmongering** noun & adjective. **warpaint 1** paint put on body esp. by N. American Indians before battle. **2** colloquial make-up. **warship** ship used in war.
■ noun **1** campaign, combat, conflict, fighting, hostilities, military action, strife, warfare. **3** assault, battle, campaign, crusade, fight, offensive. □ **wage war** see FIGHT verb **1**.

warble /ˈwɔːb(ə)l/ verb (**-ling**) sing in a gentle trilling way. ● noun warbling sound.

warbler noun bird that warbles.

ward /wɔːd/ noun **1** separate division or room of hospital etc. **2** administrative division, esp. for elections. **3** minor etc. under care of guardian or court. **4** (in plural) corresponding notches and projections in key and lock. **5** archaic guardianship. □ **ward off 1** parry (blow). **2** avert (danger etc.). **wardroom** officers' mess in warship.
■ **3** charge, dependant, minor. □ **ward off** avert, beat off, block, chase away, check, deflect, fend off, forestall, parry, push away, repel, repulse, stave off, thwart, turn aside.

-ward /wəd/ suffix (also **-wards**) added to nouns of place or destination and to adverbs of direction and forming: **1** adverbs (usually **-wards**) meaning 'towards the place etc.' **2** adjectives (usually **-ward**) meaning 'turned or tending towards'. **3** nouns meaning 'the region towards or about'.

warden /ˈwɔːd(ə)n/ noun **1** supervising official. **2** president or governor of institution. **3** traffic warden.

warder /ˈwɔːdə/ noun (feminine **wardress**) prison officer.

■ guard, jailer, keeper, prison officer.

wardrobe /'wɔːdrəʊb/ *noun* **1** large cupboard for storing clothes. **2** stock of clothes. **3** theatre's costume department. ◻ **wardrobe master, mistress** person in charge of theatrical wardrobe.

wardship *noun* tutelage.

ware *noun* **1** things of specified kind made usually for sale. **2** (usually in *plural*) articles for sale.

■ **2** (*wares*) commodities, goods, merchandise, produce, stock, supplies.

warehouse *noun* **1** building in which goods are stored. **2** wholesale or large retail store. ● *verb* (**-sing**) store in warehouse.

■ *noun* **1** depository, depot, store, storehouse.

warfare /'wɔːfeə/ *noun* waging war; campaigning.

warlike *adjective* **1** hostile. **2** soldierly. **3** military.

■ **1** aggressive, bellicose, belligerent, hawkish, hostile, militant, militaristic, pugnacious, warmongering, warring. **3** martial, military.

warlock /'wɔːlɒk/ *noun archaic* sorcerer.

warm /wɔːm/ *adjective* **1** of or at fairly high temperature. **2** (of person) with skin at natural or slightly raised temperature. **3** (of clothes) affording warmth. **4** hearty, enthusiastic. **5** sympathetic, friendly, loving. **6** *colloquial* dangerous, hostile. **7** *colloquial* (in game) near object sought. **8** *colloquial* near to guessing. **9** (of colour) reddish or yellowish, suggesting warmth. **10** (of scent in hunting) fresh and strong. ● *verb* make or become warm. ● *noun* **1** act of warming. **2** warmth. ◻ **warm-blooded** (of animals) having blood temperature well above that of environment. **warm-hearted** kind, friendly. **warmheartedness** *noun*. **warming-pan** *historical* flat closed vessel holding hot coals for warming beds. **warm up 1** make or become warm. **2** prepare for performance etc. by practising. **3** reach temperature for efficient working. **4** reheat (food). **warm-up** *noun*. ◻ **warmly** *adverb*. **warmth** *noun*.

■ *adjective* **1** close, hot, lukewarm, subtropical, sultry, summery, temperate, tepid, warmish. **3** cosy, thermal, thick, winter, woolly. **4** ardent, emotional, enthusiastic, excited, fervent, impassioned, passionate. **5** affable, affectionate, cordial, friendly, genial, kind, loving, sympathetic, warm-hearted. ● *verb* heat, melt, thaw, thaw out.

warn /wɔːn/ *verb* **1** (often + *of, that*) inform of impending danger or misfortune. **2** (+ *to do*) advise (person) to take certain action. **3** (often + *against*) inform (person) about specific danger. ◻ **warn off** tell (person) to keep away (from).

■ admonish, advise, alert, caution, counsel, forewarn, give a warning, give notice, inform, notify, raise the alarm, remind, tip off.

warning *noun* what is said or done or occurs to warn person.

■ admonition, advance notice, advice, augury, caution, caveat, forewarning, hint, indication, notice, notification, omen, portent, premonition, presage, prophecy, reminder, sign, signal, threat, tip-off.

warp /wɔːp/ *verb* **1** make or become distorted, esp. through heat, damp, etc. **2** make or become perverted or strange. **3** haul (ship etc.) by rope attached to fixed point. ● *noun* **1** warped state. **2** mental perversion. **3** lengthwise threads in loom. **4** rope used in warping ship.

■ *verb* **1** become deformed, bend, buckle, contort, curl, curve, deform, distort, kink, twist.

warrant /'wɒrənt/ *noun* **1** thing that authorizes an action. **2** written authorization, money voucher, etc. **3** written authorization allowing police to carry out search or arrest. **4** certificate of service rank held by warrant officer. ● *verb* **1** serve as warrant for; justify. **2** guarantee. ◻ **warrant officer** officer ranking between commissioned and non-commissioned officers.

■ *noun* **1**–**3** authorization, certification, document, entitlement, guarantee, licence, permit, sanction, voucher, warranty. ● *verb* **1** see JUSTIFY 1,2.

warranty /'wɒrəntɪ/ *noun* (*plural* **-ies**) **1** undertaking as to ownership or quality of thing sold etc., often accepting responsibility for repairs needed over specified period. **2** authority; justification.

warren /'wɒrən/ *noun* **1** network of rabbit burrows. **2** densely populated or labyrinthine building or district.

warrior /'wɒrɪə/ *noun* person skilled in or famed for fighting.

wart /wɔːt/ *noun* **1** small round dry growth on skin. **2** protuberance on skin of animal, surface of plant, etc. ◻ **wart-hog** African wild pig. ◻ **warty** *adjective*.

wary /'weərɪ/ *adjective* (**-ier, -iest**) on one's guard; circumspect, cautious. ◻ **warily** *adverb*. **wariness** *noun*.

■ alert, apprehensive, attentive, *colloquial* cagey, careful, cautious, chary, circumspect, distrustful, heedful, observant, on one's guard, on the lookout, suspicious, vigilant, watchful.

was *1st & 3rd singular past* of BE.

wash /wɒʃ/ *verb* **1** cleanse with liquid. **2** (+ *out, off, away*, etc.) remove or be removed by washing. **3** wash oneself or one's hands (and face). **4** wash clothes, dishes, etc. **5** (of fabric or dye) bear washing without damage. **6** bear scrutiny; be believed or acceptable. **7** (of river etc.) touch. **8** (of liquid) carry along in specified direction. **9** sweep, move, splash. **10** (+ *over*) occur without affecting (person). **11** sift (ore) by action of water. **12** brush watery colour over. **13** *poetical* moisten. ● *noun* **1** washing, being washed. **2** clothes for washing or just washed. **3** motion of agitated water or air, esp. due to passage of vessel or aircraft. **4** kitchen slops given to pigs. **5** thin, weak, inferior, or animals' liquid food. **6** liquid to spread over surface to cleanse, heal, or colour. □ **washbasin** basin for washing one's hands etc. **washboard 1** ribbed board for washing clothes. **2** this as percussion instrument. **wash down 1** wash completely. **2** (usually + *with*) accompany or follow (food). **washed out 1** faded, pale. **2** *colloquial* exhausted. **washed up** *esp. US slang* defeated, having failed. **wash one's hands of** decline responsibility for. **wash out 1** clean inside of by washing. **2** *colloquial* cause to be cancelled because of rain. **wash-out** *noun colloquial* complete failure. **washroom** *esp. US* public toilet. **washstand** piece of furniture for holding washbasin, soap-dish, etc. **wash up 1** wash (dishes etc.) after use. **2** *US* wash one's face and hands. **3** (of sea) carry on to shore. □ **washable** *adjective*.

■ *verb* **1** clean, cleanse, flush, launder, mop, rinse, scrub, shampoo, sluice, sponge down, swab down, swill, wipe. **3** bath, bathe, *colloquial* perform one's ablutions, shower. **9** break, dash, flow, lap, pound, roll, splash. ● *noun* **1** *colloquial* ablutions, bath, rinse, shampoo, shower. □ **wash-out** disappointment, *colloquial* disaster, failure, *slang* flop.

washer *noun* **1** person or thing that washes. **2** flat ring placed between two surfaces or under plunger of tap, nut, etc. to tighten joint or disperse pressure.

washerwoman *noun* laundress.

washing *noun* clothes etc. for washing or just washed. □ **washing machine** machine for washing clothes. **washing powder** soap powder or detergent for washing clothes. **washing-up 1** washing of dishes etc. **2** dishes etc. for washing.

■ laundry, the wash.

washy *adjective* (**-ier, -iest**) **1** too watery or weak. **2** lacking vigour.

wasn't /'wɒz(ə)nt/ was not.

Wasp /wɒsp/ *noun* (also **WASP**) *US usually derogatory* middle-class white American [Anglo-Saxon] Protestant.

wasp /wɒsp/ *noun* stinging insect with black and yellow stripes. □ **wasp-waist** very slender waist.

waspish *adjective* irritable, snappish.

wassail /'wɒseɪl/ *archaic noun* festive drinking. ● *verb* make merry.

wastage /'weɪstɪdʒ/ *noun* **1** amount wasted. **2** loss by use, wear, or leakage. **3** (also **natural wastage**) loss of employees other than by redundancy.

waste *verb* (**-ting**) **1** use to no purpose or for inadequate result or extravagantly. **2** fail to use. **3** (often + *on*) give (advice etc.) without effect. **4** (in *passive*) fail to be appreciated or used properly. **5** (often + *away*) wear away; make or become weak. **6** devastate. ● *adjective* **1** superfluous; no longer needed. **2** uninhabited, not cultivated. ● *noun* **1** act of wasting. **2** waste material. **3** waste region. **4** diminution by wear. **5** waste pipe. □ **go, run to waste** be wasted.

wasteland 1 land not productive or developed. **2** spiritually or intellectually barren place or time. **waste paper** used or valueless paper. **waste pipe** pipe carrying off waste material. **waste product** useless by-product of manufacture or organism.

■ *verb* **1** dissipate, fritter, misspend, misuse, *colloquial* splurge, squander, use up. **5** become emaciated, become thin, become weaker, pine, weaken. ● *adjective* **1** discarded, extra, superfluous, unusable, unused, unwanted, worthless. **2** bare, barren, derelict, empty, overgrown, run-down, uncared-for, uncultivated, undeveloped, unproductive, wild. ● *noun* **1** extravagance, indulgence, prodigality, profligacy, self-indulgence. **2** debris, dregs, effluent, excess, *US* garbage, junk, leavings, leftovers, litter, offcuts, refuse, remnants, rubbish, scrap, scraps, *esp. US* trash, wastage.

wasteful *adjective* **1** extravagant. **2** causing or showing waste. □ **wastefully** *adverb*. **wastefulness** *noun*.

■ excessive, extravagant, improvident, imprudent, lavish, prodigal, profligate, reckless, spendthrift, thriftless, uneconomical, unthrifty.

waster *noun* **1** wasteful person. **2** *colloquial* wastrel.

wastrel /'weɪstr(ə)l/ *noun* good-for-nothing person.

watch /wɒtʃ/ *verb* **1** keep eyes fixed on. **2** keep under observation; follow observantly. **3** (often + *for*) be in alert state, be vigilant; take heed. **4** (+ *over*) look after; take care of. ● *noun* **1** small portable timepiece for wrist or pocket. **2** state of alert or constant attention. **3** *Nautical* usually 4-hour spell of duty. **4** *historical* (member of) body of men patrolling streets at night. □ **keep watch** be watchful; guard. **on the watch** waiting for anticipated occurrence. **watchdog 1** dog guarding property. **2** person etc. monitoring others' rights etc. **watching brief** brief of barrister who follows case for client not directly concerned. **watchman** man employed to look after empty building etc. at night. **watch one's step** be cautious. **watch out** (often + *for*) be on one's guard. **watch-tower** tower for observing prisoners, attackers, etc. **watchword** phrase summarizing guiding principle. □ **watcher** *noun* (also in *combination*).

■ *verb* **1** contemplate, eye, gaze at, keep one's eyes on, look at, mark, note, observe, regard, see, stare at, view. **2** follow, keep an eye on, keep watch on, monitor, observe, spy on. **3** attend, concentrate, heed, keep an eye open, pay attention, pay heed, take notice. **4** (*watch over*) care for, chaperon, defend, guard, keep an eye on, keep watch on, look after, mind, protect, safeguard, shield, superintend, supervise, take care of, take charge of, tend. □ **keep watch** see GUARD *verb* 2,3. **on the watch** see WATCHFUL. **watchman** custodian, guard, lookout, nightwatchman, security guard, sentinel, sentry, watch. **watch one's step** see BEWARE 1. □ **watcher** looker-on, observer, onlooker, spectator, viewer, witness; (*watchers*) audience.

watchful *adjective* **1** accustomed to watching. **2** on the watch. □ **watchfully** *adverb*. **watchfulness** *noun*.

■ alert, attentive, eagle-eyed, heedful, observant, on the lookout, on the qui vive, on the watch, quick, sharp-eyed, vigilant.

water /'wɔːtə/ *noun* **1** transparent colourless liquid found in seas and rivers etc. and in rain etc. **2** sheet or body of water. **3** (in *plural*) part of sea or river. **4** (often **the waters**) mineral water at spa etc. **5** state of tide. **6** solution of specified substance in water. **7** transparency and lustre of gem. **8** (usually in *plural*) amniotic fluid. ● *verb* **1** sprinkle or soak with water. **2** supply (plant or animal) with water. **3** secrete water. **4** (as **watered** *adjective*) (of silk etc.) having irregular wavy finish. **5** take in supply of water. □ **make water** urinate. **water-bed** mattress filled with water. **water biscuit** thin unsweetened biscuit. **water buffalo** common domestic Indian buffalo. **water-butt** barrel used to catch rainwater. **water cannon** device giving powerful water-jet to disperse crowd etc. **water chestnut** corm from a sedge, used in Chinese cookery. **water-closet** lavatory that can be flushed. **watercolour 1** paint made with pigment diluted with water (not oil). **2** picture painted or art of painting with this. **watercourse 1** stream of water. **2** bed of this. **watercress** pungent cress growing in running water. **water-diviner** dowser. **water down 1** dilute. **2** make less forceful or horrifying. **waterfall** stream or river falling over precipice or down steep hill. **waterfowl** bird(s) frequenting water. **waterfront** part of town adjoining river etc. **waterhole** shallow depression in which water collects. **water ice** flavoured and frozen water and sugar. **watering can** portable container for watering plants. **watering hole 1** pool where animals drink. **2** *slang* bar. **watering place 1** watering hole. **2** spa or seaside resort. **water jump** jump over water in steeplechase etc. **water level 1** surface of water. **2** height of this. **3** water table. **water lily** aquatic plant with floating leaves and flowers. **waterline** line along which surface of water touches ship's side. **waterlogged** saturated or filled with water. **water main** main pipe in water supply system. **waterman** boatman plying for hire. **watermark** faint design in paper identifying maker etc. **water-meadow** meadow periodically flooded by stream. **water melon** large dark green melon with red pulp and watery juice. **water-mill** mill worked by waterwheel. **water pistol** toy pistol shooting jet of water. **water polo** game played by swimmers with ball like football. **water power** mechanical force from weight or motion of water. **waterproof** ● *adjective* impervious to water. ● *noun* such garment or material. ● *verb* make waterproof. **water-rat** water vole. **water rate** charge for use of public water supply. **water-repellent** not easily penetrated by water. **water-resistant** able to resist, but not entirely prevent, penetration of water. **watershed 1** line between waters flowing to different river basins. **2** turning point in events. **waterside** edge of sea, lake, or river. **water-ski** each of pair of skis on which person is towed by motor boat across water. **waterspout** gyrating column of water and spray between sea and cloud. **water-table** plane below which ground is saturated with water. **watertight 1** so closely fastened or fitted that water cannot leak through. **2** (of argument etc.) unassailable. **water tower** tower with elevated tank to give pressure for distributing water. **water vole** aquatic vole. **waterway** navigable channel. **waterwheel** wheel driven by water to drive machinery or to raise water. **water-wings** inflated floats used to support person learning to swim. **waterworks 1** establishment for managing water supply. **2** *colloquial* shedding of tears. **3** *colloquial* urinary system. □ **waterless** *adjective*.

■ *noun* **2** lake, ocean, pond, pool, river, sea, stream. ● *verb* **1, 2** damp, dampen, douse, drench, flood, hose, inundate, irrigate, moisten, saturate, soak, souse, spray, sprinkle, wet. □ **water down 1** see DILUTE *verb*. **waterfall** cascade, cataract, falls. **waterlogged** boggy, marshy, saturated, soaked, sodden, soggy, watery. **waterproof** ● *adjective* damp-proof, impermeable, impervious, sealed, water-repellent, water-resistant, watertight, weatherproof. ● *noun* cape, *colloquial* mac, mackintosh.

watery *adjective* **1** containing too much water. **2** too thin in consistency. **3** of or consisting of water. **4** vapid, uninteresting. **5** (of colour) pale. **6** (of sun, moon, or sky) rainy-looking. **7** (of eyes) moist.

■ **1** see WET *adjective* 1. **2** dilute, diluted, liquid, runny, sloppy, tasteless, thin, watered-down, weak, *colloquial* wishy-washy. **3** aqueous, fluid, liquid. **4** bland, characterless, insipid, tasteless, vapid. **7** damp, moist, tear-filled, tearful, *colloquial* weepy, wet.

watt /wɒt/ *noun* SI unit of power.

wattage *noun* amount of electrical power expressed in watts.

wattle[1] /'wɒt(ə)l/ *noun* **1** interlaced rods and sticks used for fences etc. **2** Australian acacia with fragrant golden yellow flowers. □ **wattle and daub** network of rods and twigs plastered with clay or mud as building material.

wattle[2] /'wɒt(ə)l/ *noun* fleshy appendage hanging from head or neck of turkey etc.

wave *verb* (**-ving**) **1** move (hand etc.) to and fro in greeting or as signal. **2** direct (person) or express (greeting etc.) by waving. **3** show sinuous or sweeping motion. **4** give such motion to. **5** give undulating form to. **6** have such form. ● *noun* **1** moving ridge of water between two depressions. **2** long body of water curling into arch and breaking on shore. **3** thing compared to this. **4** gesture of waving. **5** curved shape in hair. **6** temporary occurrence or heightening of condition or influence. **7** disturbance carrying motion, heat, light, sound, etc. through esp. fluid medium. **8** single curve in this. □ **wave aside** dismiss as intrusive or irrelevant. **waveband** radio wavelengths between certain limits. **wave down** wave to (vehicle or driver) to stop. **wavelength 1** distance between successive crests of wave. **2** this as distinctive feature of radio waves from a transmitter. **3** *colloquial* person's way of thinking.

■ *verb* **1, 2** gesticulate, gesture, indicate, sign, signal. **3, 4** billow, brandish, flail about, flap, flourish, fluctuate, flutter, move to and fro, ripple, shake, sway, swing, twirl, undulate, waft, wag, *colloquial* waggle, *colloquial* wiggle, zigzag. ● *noun* **1, 2** billow, breaker, ridge, ripple, roller, swell, undulation, wavelet. **4** flourish, gesticulation, gesture, shake, sign, signal. **6** current, fashion, flood, ground swell, outbreak, surge, tendency, tide, trend, upsurge. □ **wave aside** see DISMISS 3,4. **wavelength 2** channel, station, waveband.

wavelet *noun* small wave.

waver /'weɪvə/ *verb* be or become unsteady or irresolute; begin to give way.

■ be in two minds, be unsteady, change, falter, flicker, hesitate, quake, quaver, quiver, shake, shiver, shudder, sway, teeter, tergiversate, totter, tremble, vacillate, wobble.

wavy *adjective* (**-ier, -iest**) having waves or alternate contrary curves. □ **waviness** *noun*.

■ curling, curly, curving, heaving, rippling, rolling, sinuous, undulating, up and down, winding, zigzag.

wax[1] *noun* **1** sticky pliable yellowish substance secreted by bees as material of honeycomb. **2** this bleached and purified for candles, modelling, etc. **3** any similar substance. ● *verb* **1** cover or treat with wax. **2** remove hair from (legs etc.) using wax. □ **waxwork 1** object, esp. lifelike dummy, modelled in wax. **2** (in *plural*) exhibition of wax dummies.

wax[2] *verb* **1** (of moon) increase in apparent size. **2** grow larger or stronger. **3** become.

waxen *adjective* **1** smooth or pale like wax. **2** *archaic* made of wax.

waxy /'wæksɪ/ *adjective* (**-ier, -iest**) resembling wax in consistency or in its surface.

way *noun* **1** road, track, path, street. **2** course, route; direction. **3** method, means. **4** style, manner. **5** habitual course of action. **6** personal peculiarity. **7** normal course of events. **8** distance (to be) travelled. **9** unimpeded opportunity or space to advance. **10** advance; progress. **11** specified condition or state. **12** respect, sense. ● *adverb colloquial* far. □ **by the way** incidentally. **by way of 1** by means of. **2** as a form of. **3** passing through. **give way 1** yield under pressure. **2** give precedence. **in the way, in (person's) way** forming obstruction (to). **lead the way** act as guide or leader. **make one's way 1** go. **2** prosper. **make way for 1** allow to pass. **2** be superseded by. **out of the way 1** not forming obstruction. **2** disposed of. **3** unusual. **4** remote. **pay its or one's way 1** cover costs. **2** pay one's expenses as they arise. **under way** in motion or progress. **way back** *colloquial* long ago. **wayfarer** traveller, esp. on foot. **wayfaring** *noun*. **waylay 1** lie in wait for. **2** stop to accost or rob. **way of life** principles or habits governing one's actions. **way-out** *colloquial* unusual, eccentric. **wayside** (land at) side of road.

■ *noun* **1** see ROAD 1. **2** course, direction, path, route. **3** approach, avenue, course, knack, manner, means, method, mode, *modus operandi*, path, procedure, process, system, technique. **4** fashion, manner, mode, style. **5** custom, habit, *modus vivendi*, practice, routine, tradition. **6** characteristic, eccentricity, idiosyncrasy, oddity, peculiarity. **8** distance, haul, journey. **10** advance, headway, movement, progress. **12** aspect, circumstance, detail, feature, particular, respect. □ **waylay** accost, ambush, attack, await, *colloquial* buttonhole, detain, intercept, lie in wait for, pounce on, surprise.

wayward /'weɪwəd/ *adjective* **1** childishly self-willed. **2** capricious. □ **waywardness** *noun*.

■ **1** disobedient, headstrong, naughty, obstinate, self-willed, stubborn, uncontrollable, uncooperative, wilful.

WC *abbreviation* **1** water-closet. **2** West Central.

W/Cdr. *abbreviation* Wing Commander.

we /wiː/ *pronoun* **1** *used by speaker or writer to refer to himself or herself and one or more others as subject of verb.* **2** *used for I*[2] *by sovereign in formal contexts or by editorial writer in newspaper.*

weak *adjective* **1** lacking in strength, power, or number. **2** lacking in vigour; sickly. **3** lacking in resolution. **4** unconvincing. **5** dilute, watery. **6** (of verb) forming inflections by suffix. □ **weak-kneed** *colloquial* lacking resolution. **weak-minded 1** mentally deficient. **2** lacking resolution. □ **weaken** *verb*.

■ **1** breakable, brittle, decrepit, defenceless, delicate, exposed, feeble, flawed, flimsy, fragile, frail, frangible, helpless, inadequate, insubstantial, rickety, shaky, slight, substandard, tender, thin, unguarded, unprotected, unsafe, unsound, unsteady, unsubstantial, vulnerable; *of colour, light, sound, etc.* dim, distant, fading, faint, indistinct, pale, poor, unclear, vague. **2** anaemic, debilitated, delicate, enervated, exhausted, feeble, frail, helpless, ill, infirm, listless, low, poorly, puny, sickly, slight, thin, tired out, wasted, weakly, weedy. **3** cowardly, fearful, impotent, indecisive, ineffective, ineffectual, irresolute, powerless, *formal* pusillanimous, spineless, timid, timorous, unassertive, weak-minded, *colloquial* wimpish. **4** feeble, flimsy, hollow, lame, *colloquial* pathetic, poor, shallow, unbelievable, unconvincing, unsatisfactory. **5** dilute, diluted, tasteless, thin, watery. □ **weaken** abate, debilitate, decline, decrease, dilute, diminish, dwindle, ebb, emasculate, enervate, enfeeble, erode, exhaust, fade, flag, give in, give way, impair, lessen, lower, reduce, sag, sap, soften, thin down, undermine, wane, water down, yield.

weakling *noun* feeble person or animal.

■ coward, milksop, *colloquial* pushover, runt, *colloquial* softie, *colloquial* weed, *colloquial* wimp.

weakly *adverb* in a weak way. ● *adjective* (**-ier, -iest**) sickly; not robust.

weakness *noun* **1** being weak. **2** weak point. **3** self-indulgent liking.

■ **1** debility, decrepitude, delicacy, feebleness, flimsiness, fragility, frailty, impotence, incapacity, infirmity, lassitude, softness, vulnerability. **2** Achilles heel, blemish, defect, error, failing, fault, flaw, foible, imperfection, inadequacy, mistake, shortcoming, weak spot. **3** affection, fancy, fondness, inclination, liking, partiality, penchant, predilection, soft spot, taste.

weal[1] *noun* ridge raised on flesh by stroke of rod or whip. ● *verb* raise weals on.

weal[2] *noun literary* welfare.

wealth /welθ/ *noun* **1** riches. **2** being rich. **3** abundance.

■ **1, 2** affluence, assets, capital, fortune, *derogatory* lucre, means, money, opulence, possessions, property, prosperity, riches, substance. **3** abundance, bounty, copiousness, cornucopia, mine, plenty, profusion, store, treasury.

wealthy *adjective* (**-ier**, **-iest**) having abundance, esp. of money.

■ affluent, *colloquial* flush, *slang* loaded, moneyed, opulent, privileged, prosperous, rich, *colloquial* well-heeled, well off, well-to-do.

wean *verb* **1** accustom (infant or other young mammal) to food other than mother's milk. **2** (often + *from*, *away from*) disengage (from habit etc.) by enforced discontinuance.

weapon /wepən/ *noun* **1** thing designed, used, or usable for inflicting bodily harm. **2** means for gaining advantage in a conflict. □ **weaponless** *adjective*.

■ **1** (*weapons*) armaments, armoury, arms, arsenal, magazine, munitions, ordnance, small arms, weaponry.

weaponry *noun* weapons collectively.

wear /weə/ *verb* (*past* **wore**; *past participle* **worn**) **1** have on one's person as clothing, ornament, etc. **2** exhibit (expression etc.). **3** *colloquial* (usually in negative) tolerate. **4** (often + *away*, *down*) damage or deteriorate gradually by use or attrition. **5** make (hole etc.) by attrition. **6** (often + *out*) exhaust. **7** (+ *down*) overcome by persistence. **8** (+ *well* etc.) endure continued use or life. **9** (of time) pass, esp. tediously. ● *noun* **1** wearing, being worn. **2** things worn; fashionable or suitable clothing. **3** (in full **wear and tear**) damage from continuous use. □ **wear off** lose effectiveness or intensity. **wear out 1** use or be used until useless. **2** tire or be tired out. □ **wearer** *noun*.

■ *verb* **1** be dressed in, clothe oneself in, dress in, have on, present oneself in. **2** adopt, assume, display, exhibit, show. **4** damage, fray, mark, scuff, weaken; (*wear away*) see ERODE. **6** (*wear out*) see WEARY *verb*. **8** (*wear well*) endure, last, stand the test of time, survive. □ **wear off** see SUBSIDE 1.

wearisome /'wɪərɪsəm/ *adjective* tedious, monotonous.

■ boring, dreary, exhausting, monotonous, repetitive, tedious, tiring, troublesome, wearying.

weary /'wɪərɪ/ *adjective* (**-ier**, **-iest**) **1** very tired; intensely fatigued. **2** (+ *of*) tired of. **3** tiring, tedious. ● *verb* (**-ies**, **-ied**) make or become weary. □ **wearily** *adverb*. **weariness** *noun*.

■ *adjective* **1** *colloquial* beat, *colloquial* dead beat, dog-tired, drained, drawn, drowsy, enervated, exhausted, *colloquial* fagged, fatigued, flagging, footsore, jaded, jet-lagged, *slang* knackered, limp, listless, prostrate, *colloquial* shattered, sleepy, spent, tired, tired out, wearied, *colloquial* whacked, worn, worn out. **2** (*weary of*) fed up with, impatient with, *colloquial* sick of, tired of. ● *verb* become bored, become tired, debilitate, drain, enervate, exhaust, fatigue, flag, *slang* knacker, overtire, sap, *colloquial* shatter, take it out of, tax, tire, weaken, wear out.

weasel /'wiːz(ə)l/ *noun* small ferocious reddish-brown flesh-eating mammal.

weather /'weðə/ *noun* atmospheric conditions at specified place or time as regards heat, cloudiness, humidity, sunshine, wind, and rain etc. ● *verb* **1** expose to or affect by atmospheric changes; season (wood). **2** be discoloured or worn thus. **3** come safely through (storm etc.). **4** get to windward of. □ **make heavy weather of** *colloquial* exaggerate difficulty of. **under the weather** *colloquial* indisposed. **weather-beaten** affected by exposure to weather. **weatherboard 1** sloping board attached at bottom of door to keep out rain. **2** each of series of overlapping horizontal boards on wall. **weathercock 1** weather vane in form of cock. **2** inconstant person. **weather forecast** prediction of likely weather. **weather vane** revolving pointer on church spire etc. to show direction of wind.

■ *noun* climate, the elements, meteorological conditions. ● *verb* **3** see SURVIVE 3. □ **under the weather** see ILL *adjective* 1.

weatherproof /'weðəpruːf/ *adjective* resistant to effects of bad weather, esp. rain. ● *verb* make weatherproof.

weave[1] *verb* (**-ving**; *past* **wove** /wəʊv/; *past participle* **woven**) **1** form (fabric) by interlacing threads. **2** form (threads) into fabric, esp. in loom. **3** (+ *into*) make (facts etc.) into story or connected whole. **4** make (story etc.) thus. ● *noun* style of weaving.

■ *verb* **1** braid, criss-cross, entwine, interlace, intertwine, interweave, knit, plait. **2** compose, create, make, put together.

weave[2] *verb* (**-ving**) move repeatedly from side to side; take intricate course.

■ dodge, make one's way, tack, twist and turn, wind, zigzag.

weaver *noun* **1** person who weaves fabric. **2** (in full **weaver-bird**) tropical bird building elaborately woven nest.

web *noun* **1** woven fabric. **2** amount woven in one piece. **3** complex structure or series. **4** cobweb or similar tissue. **5** membrane connecting toes of aquatic bird or other animal. **6** large roll of paper for printing. □ **web-footed** having toes connected by web. □ **webbed** *adjective*.

■ **3** criss-cross, lattice, mesh, net, network.

webbing *noun* strong narrow closely woven fabric for belts etc.

weber /'veɪbə/ *noun* SI unit of magnetic flux.

Wed. *abbreviation* (also **Weds.**) Wednesday.

wed *verb* (**-dd-**; *past* and *past participle* **wedded** or **wed**) **1** *usually formal* or *literary* marry. **2** unite. **3** (as **wedded** *adjective*) of or in marriage. **4** (as **wedded** *adjective*) (+ *to*) obstinately attached to (pursuit etc.).

we'd /wiːd/ **1** we had. **2** we should; we would.

wedding /'wedɪŋ/ *noun* marriage ceremony. □ **wedding breakfast** meal etc. between wedding and departure for honeymoon. **wedding cake** rich decorated cake served at wedding reception. **wedding ring** ring worn by married person.
■ marriage, nuptials, union.

wedge *noun* **1** piece of tapering wood, metal, etc., used for forcing things apart or fixing them immovably etc. **2** wedge-shaped thing. ● *verb* (**-ging**) **1** secure or force open or apart with wedge. **2** (+ *in*, *into*) pack or force (thing, oneself) in or into. □ **thin end of the wedge** *colloquial* small beginning that may lead to something more serious.
■ *verb* **2** cram, force, jam, pack, squeeze, stick.

wedlock /'wedlɒk/ *noun* married state. □ **born in or out of wedlock** born of married or unmarried parents.

Wednesday /'wenzdeɪ/ *noun* day of week following Tuesday.

wee *adjective* (**weer** /'wiːə/, **weest** /'wiːɪst/) **1** *esp.* *Scottish* little. **2** (esp. in phrase **a wee bit**) *colloquial* tiny.

weed *noun* **1** wild plant growing where it is not wanted. **2** *colloquial* feeble or thin and weak-looking person. **3** (**the weed**) *slang* marijuana. **4** (**the weed**) *slang* tobacco. ● *verb* **1** rid of weeds or unwanted parts. **2** (+ *out*) sort out and remove (inferior or unwanted parts etc.). **3** (+ *out*) rid of inferior or unwanted parts etc. **4** remove or destroy weeds.

weeds *plural noun* (in full **widow's weeds**) *archaic* deep mourning worn by widow.

weedy *adjective* (**-ier**, **-iest**) **1** weak, feeble. **2** full of weeds.

week *noun* **1** 7-day period reckoned usually from Saturday midnight. **2** any 7-day period. **3** the 6 days between Sundays. **4** the 5 days Monday to Friday. **5** period of work done during week. □ **weekday** day other than (Saturday or) Sunday. **weekend** Saturday and Sunday.

weekly *adjective* done, produced, or occurring once a week. ● *adverb* once a week. ● *noun* (*plural* **-ies**) weekly newspaper or periodical.

weeny /'wiːnɪ/ *adjective* (**-ier**, **-iest**) *colloquial* tiny.

weep *verb* (*past & past participle* **wept**) **1** shed tears. **2** (often + *for*) lament over. **3** be covered with or send forth drops. **4** come or send forth in drops; exude liquid. **5** (as **weeping** *adjective*) (of tree) have drooping branches. ● *noun* spell of weeping.
■ *verb* **1** bawl, *slang* blub, blubber, cry, *colloquial* grizzle, mewl, moan, shed tears, snivel, sob, wail, whimper, whine. **2** (*weep for*) bemoan, bewail, lament over.

weepie *noun* *colloquial* sentimental or emotional film, play, etc.

weepy *adjective* (**-ier**, **-iest**) *colloquial* inclined to weep; tearful.

weevil /'wiːvɪl/ *noun* destructive beetle feeding esp. on grain.

weft *noun* threads woven across warp to make fabric.

weigh /weɪ/ *verb* **1** find weight of. **2** balance in hand (as if) to guess weight of. **3** (often + *out*) take definite weight of (substance); measure out (specified weight). **4** estimate relative value or importance of. **5** (+ *with*, *against*) compare with. **6** be of specified weight or importance. **7** have influence. **8** (often + *on*) be heavy or burdensome (to). **9** raise (anchor). □ **weighbridge** weighing machine for vehicles. **weigh down 1** bring down by weight. **2** oppress. **weigh in** (of boxer before contest, or jockey after race) be weighed. **weigh-in** *noun*. **weighing machine** machine for weighing large weights. **weigh in with** *colloquial* advance (argument etc.) confidently. **weigh one's words** carefully choose words to express something. **weigh up** *colloquial* form estimate of.
■ **1, 3** measure. **4** assess, consider, contemplate, evaluate, judge, ponder, reflect on, think about, *colloquial* weigh up. **7** be important, carry weight, count, *slang* cut any ice, have weight, matter. □ **weigh down 2** see BURDEN *verb*. **weighing machine** balance, scales, spring balance, weighbridge. **weigh up** see EVALUATE 1.

weight /weɪt/ *noun* **1** force on a body due to earth's gravitation. **2** heaviness of body. **3** quantitative expression of a body's weight. **4** scale of such weights. **5** body of known weight for use in weighing or weight training. **6** heavy body, esp. used in mechanism etc. **7** load, burden. **8** influence, importance. **9** preponderance (of evidence etc.). ● *verb* **1** attach a weight to. **2** hold down with a weight. **3** impede, burden. **4** bias. □ **pull one's weight** do fair share of work. **weightlifting** sport of lifting heavy objects. **weight training** physical training using weights. □ **weightless** *adjective*.
■ *noun* **2** density, heaviness, mass, tonnage. **7** burden, load, pressure, strain. **8** authority, credibility, emphasis, force, gravity, importance, power, seriousness, significance, substance, value, worth. ● *verb* **1, 2** ballast, hold down, keep down, load, make heavy, weigh down. **4** bias, load.

weighting *noun* extra pay in special cases.

weighty *adjective* (**-ier**, **-iest**) **1** heavy. **2** momentous. **3** deserving attention. **4** influential, authoritative. □ **weightiness** *noun*.

weir /wɪə/ *noun* dam across river to retain water and regulate its flow.

weird /wɪəd/ *adjective* **1** uncanny, supernatural. **2** *colloquial* queer, incomprehensible. □ **weirdly** *adverb.* **weirdness** *noun.*

■ **1** creepy, eerie, ghostly, mysterious, preternatural, *colloquial* scary, *colloquial* spooky, supernatural, unaccountable, uncanny, unearthly, unnatural. **2** abnormal, bizarre, cranky, curious, eccentric, funny, grotesque, odd, outlandish, peculiar, queer, quirky, strange, unconventional, unusual, *colloquial* way-out, zany.

weirdo /'wɪədəʊ/ *noun* (*plural* **-os**) *colloquial* odd or eccentric person.

welch = WELSH.

welcome /'welkəm/ *noun* kind or glad greeting or reception. ● *interjection: expressing such greeting.* ● *verb* (**-ming**) receive with welcome. ● *adjective* **1** gladly received. **2** (+ *to*) cordially allowed or invited to. □ **make welcome** receive hospitably.

■ *noun* greeting, reception, *formal* salutation. ● *verb* accept, appreciate, approve of, delight in, greet, hail, like, receive, want. ● *adjective* **1** acceptable, accepted, agreeable, appreciated, desirable, gratifying, nice, pleasant, pleasing, pleasurable.

weld *verb* **1** join (pieces of metal or plastic) using heat, usually from electric arc. **2** fashion into effectual or homogeneous whole. ● *noun* welded joint. □ **welder** *noun.*

■ *verb* **1** bond, cement, fasten, fuse, join, solder. **2** see UNITE **1**.

welfare /'welfeə/ *noun* **1** well-being, happiness; health and prosperity (of person, community, etc.). **2** (**Welfare**) financial support from state. □ **welfare state 1** system of social services controlled or financed by government. **2** state operating this. **welfare work** organized effort for welfare of poor, disabled, etc.

■ **1** advantage, benefit, felicity, good, happiness, health, interest, prosperity, well-being.

welkin /'welkɪn/ *noun poetical* sky.

well¹ *adverb* (**better, best**) **1** in satisfactory way. **2** with distinction. **3** in kind way. **4** thoroughly, carefully. **5** with heartiness or approval. **6** probably, reasonably. **7** to considerable extent. **8** *slang* extremely. ● *adjective* (**better, best**) **1** in good health. **2** in satisfactory state or position. **3** advisable. ● *interjection: expressing astonishment, resignation, etc., or introducing speech.* □ **as well 1** in addition. **2** advisable, desirable. **3** reasonably. **as well as** in addition to. **well adjusted** (**well-adjusted** before noun) mentally and emotionally stable. **well advised** prudent. **well and truly** decisively, completely. **well appointed** (**well-appointed** before noun) properly equipped or fitted out. **well away 1** having made considerable progress. **2** *colloquial* fast asleep or drunk. **well balanced** (**well-balanced** before noun) sane, sensible. **well behaved** (**well-behaved** before noun) having good conduct. **well-being** happiness, health, prosperity. **well born** (**well-born** before noun) of noble family. **well bred** (**well-bred** before noun) having

or showing good breeding or manners. **well built** (**well-built** before noun) big, strong, and shapely. **well-connected** related to good families. **well developed** (**well-developed** before noun) **1** fully grown. **2** of generous size. **well disposed** (**well-disposed** before noun) (often + *towards*) friendly, sympathetic. **well earned** (**well-earned** before noun) fully deserved. **well endowed** (**well-endowed** before noun) **1** well provided with money etc. **2** *colloquial* (of man) having large genitals; (of woman) large-breasted. **well founded** (**well-founded** before noun) based on good evidence. **well groomed** (**well-groomed** before noun) with carefully tended hair, clothes, etc. **well-heeled** *colloquial* wealthy. **well informed** (**well-informed** before noun) having much knowledge or information. **well intentioned** (**well-intentioned** before noun) having or showing good intentions. **well judged** (**well-judged** before noun) opportunely, skilfully, or discreetly done. **well kept** (**well-kept** before noun) kept in good condition. **well known** (**well-known** before noun) known to many. **well meaning, meant** (**well-meaning, -meant** before noun) well intentioned. **well-nigh** almost. **well off** (**well-off** before noun) **1** rich. **2** fortunately situated. **well read** (**well-read** before noun) having read (and learnt) much. **well-spoken** articulate or refined in speech. **well-to-do** prosperous. **well tried** (**well-tried** before noun) often tested with good result. **well-wisher** person who wishes another well. **well worn** (**well-worn** before noun) much used, trite.

■ *adjective* **1** fit, hale, healthy, hearty, in fine fettle, lively, robust, sound, strong, thriving, vigorous. **2** all right, fine, *colloquial* OK, satisfactory. □ **well behaved** cooperative, disciplined, docile, dutiful, good, hard-working, law-abiding, manageable, nice, obedient, polite, quiet, well trained. **well bred** courteous, courtly, cultivated, decorous, genteel, polite, proper, refined, sophisticated, urbane, well brought up, well mannered. **well built** athletic, big, brawny, burly, hefty, muscular, powerful, stocky, strapping, strong, sturdy, upstanding. **well known** celebrated, eminent, familiar, famous, illustrious, noted, notorious, prominent, renowned. **well meaning** good-natured, kind, obliging, sincere, well intentioned, well meant. **well off 1** affluent, comfortable, moneyed, prosperous, rich, *colloquial* well-heeled, well-to-do. **well-spoken** articulate, educated, polite, refined.

well² *noun* **1** shaft sunk in ground to obtain water, oil, etc. **2** enclosed space resembling well-shaft, e.g. central space in building for staircase, lift, light, or ventilation. **3** source. **4** (in *plural*) spa. **5** inkwell. **6** railed space in law court. ● *verb* (+ *out, up*) rise or flow as water from well. □ **well-head, -spring** source.

■ *noun* **1** bore, gusher, shaft. **3** fountain, source, spring, well-spring.

we'll /wi:l/ we shall; we will.

wellington /'welɪŋt(ə)n/ *noun* (in full **wellington boot**) waterproof rubber boot usually reaching knee.

welly /'welɪ/ noun (plural **-ies**) colloquial wellington.

Welsh adjective of Wales. ● noun **1** language of Wales. **2** (**the Welsh**) (treated as plural) the Welsh people. □ **Welshman**, **Welshwoman** native of Wales. **Welsh rarebit** dish of melted cheese etc. on toast.

welsh verb (also **welch** /welt∫/) **1** (of loser of bet, esp. bookmaker) evade an obligation. **2** (+ on) fail to carry out promise to (person). **3** (+ on) fail to honour (obligation).

welt noun **1** leather rim sewn to shoe-upper for sole to be attached to. **2** weal. **3** ribbed or reinforced border of garment. **4** heavy blow. ● verb **1** provide with welt. **2** raise weals on; thrash.

welter /'weltə/ verb **1** roll, wallow. **2** (+ in) be soaked in. ● noun **1** general confusion. **2** disorderly mixture.

welterweight /'weltəweɪt/ noun amateur boxing weight (63.5–67 kg).

wen noun benign tumour on skin.

wench noun jocular girl, young woman.

wend verb □ **wend one's way** go.

went past of GO¹.

wept past & past participle of WEEP.

were 2nd singular past, plural past, and past subjunctive of BE.

we're /wɪə/ we are.

weren't /wɜ:nt/ were not.

werewolf /'weəwʊlf/ noun (plural **-wolves**) Mythology human being who changes into wolf.

Wesleyan /'wezlɪən/ adjective of Protestant denomination founded by John Wesley. ● noun member of this denomination.

west noun **1** point of horizon where sun sets at equinoxes. **2** corresponding compass point. **3** (usually **the West**) European civilization. **4** (usually **the West**) western part of world, country, town, etc. ● adjective **1** towards, at, near, or facing west. **2** (of wind) from west. ● adverb **1** towards, at, or near west. **2** (+ of) further west than. □ **go west** slang be killed or wrecked etc. **westbound** travelling or leading west. **West End** fashionable part of London. **west-north-west**, **west-south-west** point midway between west and north-west or southwest. □ **westward** adjective, adverb, & noun. **westwards** adverb.

westering /'westərɪŋ/ adjective (of sun) nearing the west.

westerly /'westəlɪ/ adjective & adverb **1** in western position or direction. **2** (of wind) from west. ● noun (plural **-ies**) wind from west.

western /'west(ə)n/ adjective of or in west. ● noun film or novel about cowboys in western N. America. □ **westernize** verb (also **-ise**) (**-zing** or **-sing**). **westernmost** adjective.

westerner noun native or inhabitant of west.

wet adjective (**-tt-**) **1** soaked or covered with water or other liquid. **2** (of weather) rainy. **3** (of paint) not yet dried. **4** used with water. **5** collo-

quial feeble. ● verb (**-tt-**; past and past participle **wet** or **wetted**) **1** make wet. **2** urinate in or on. ● noun **1** liquid that wets something. **2** rainy weather. **3** colloquial feeble or spiritless person. **4** colloquial liberal Conservative. **5** colloquial drink. □ **wet behind the ears** immature, inexperienced. **wet blanket** gloomy person discouraging cheerfulness etc. **wet-nurse** ● noun woman employed to suckle another's child. ● verb **1** act as wet-nurse to. **2** colloquial treat as if helpless. □ **wetness** noun.

■ adjective **1** awash, bedraggled, clammy, damp, dank, dewy, drenched, dripping, moist, saturated, sloppy, soaked, soaking, sodden, soggy, sopping, soused, spongy, submerged, waterlogged, watery, wringing. **2** drizzly, pouring, rainy, showery, teeming. **3** runny, sticky, tacky. ● verb **1** dampen, douse, drench, irrigate, moisten, saturate, soak, spray, sprinkle, steep, water. ● noun **1** dampness, dew, humidity, liquid, moisture. **2** damp, drizzle, rain.

wether /'weðə/ noun castrated ram.

wetland /wetlænd/ noun (usually in plural) saturated area of land; marsh.

we've /wi:v/ we have.

Wg. Cdr. abbreviation Wing Commander.

whack colloquial verb **1** hit forcefully. **2** (as **whacked** adjective) tired out. ● noun **1** sharp or resounding blow. **2** slang share.

whacking colloquial adjective large. ● adverb very.

whale noun (plural same or **-s**) large fishlike marine mammal. ● verb (**-ling**) hunt whales. □ **whalebone** elastic horny substance in upper jaw of some whales.

whaler noun whaling ship or seaman.

wham interjection colloquial: expressing forcible impact.

wharf /wɔ:f/ noun (plural **wharves** /wɔ:vz/ or **-s**) quayside structure for loading or unloading of moored vessels. ● verb **1** moor (ship) at wharf. **2** store (goods) on wharf.

what /wɒt/ interrogative adjective: used in asking someone to specify one or more things from an indefinite number. ● adjective (usually in exclamation) how great; how remarkable. ● relative adjective the or any … that. ● interrogative pronoun **1** what thing(s). **2** what did you say? ● relative pronoun **1** the things which. **2** anything that. □ **whatever 1** anything at all that. **2** no matter what. **3** (with negative or in questions) at all; of any kind. **what for?** colloquial for what reason? **what have you** colloquial anything else similar. **whatnot** unspecified thing. **what not** colloquial other similar things. **whatsoever** whatever. **know what's what** colloquial have common sense; know what is useful or important. **what with** colloquial because of.

wheat noun **1** cereal plant bearing dense 4-sided seed-spikes. **2** its grain used for flour etc. □ **wheat germ** wheat embryo extracted as source of vitamins. **wheatmeal** flour from wheat with some bran and germ removed.

wheatear /'wiːtɪə/ *noun* small migratory bird.

wheaten *adjective* made of wheat.

wheedle /'wiːd(ə)l/ *verb* (**-ling**) **1** coax by flattery or endearments. **2** (+ *out*) get (thing) from person or cheat (person) of thing by wheedling.

wheel *noun* **1** circular frame or disc revolving on axle and used to propel vehicle or other machinery. **2** wheel-like thing. **3** motion as of wheel. **4** movement of line of men etc. with one end as pivot. **5** (in *plural*) *slang* car. ● *verb* **1** turn on axis or pivot. **2** swing round in line with one end as pivot. **3** (often + *about, around*) (cause to) change direction or face another way. **4** push or pull (wheeled thing, or its load or occupant). **5** go in circles or curves. □ **wheel and deal** engage in political or commercial scheming. **wheelbarrow** small cart with one wheel at front and two handles. **wheelbase** distance between axles of vehicle. **wheelchair** disabled person's chair on wheels. **wheel-spin** rotation of vehicle's wheels without traction. **wheels within wheels 1** intricate machinery. **2** *colloquial* indirect or secret agencies. **wheelwright** maker or repairer of wheels.

■ *noun* **1** circle, disc, hoop, ring. ● *verb* **1, 2** circle, gyrate, pivot, revolve, rotate, spin, swing round, swivel, turn, whirl. **3** spin round, swerve, swing round, swivel, turn, veer. **5** circle, move in circles, orbit.

wheelie *noun slang* manoeuvre on bicycle or motorcycle with front wheel off the ground.

wheeze *verb* (**-zing**) breathe or utter with audible whistling sound. ● *noun* **1** sound of wheezing. **2** *colloquial* clever scheme. □ **wheezy** *adjective* (**-ier, -iest**).

■ *verb* breathe noisily, gasp, pant, puff.

whelk *noun* spiral-shelled marine mollusc.

whelp *noun* **1** young dog, puppy. **2** *archaic* cub. **3** ill-mannered child or youth. ● *verb* give birth to puppies.

when *interrogative adverb* at what time. ● *relative adverb* (time etc.) at or on which. ● *conjunction* **1** at the or any time that. **2** as soon as. **3** although. **4** after which; and then; but just then. ● *pronoun* what time; which time. □ **whenever, whensoever 1** at whatever time; on whatever occasion. **2** every time that.

whence *archaic* or *formal interrogative adverb* from what place. ● *relative adverb* (place etc.) from which. ● *conjunction* to the place from which.

where /weə/ *interrogative adverb* **1** in or to what place. **2** in what direction. **3** in what respect. ● *relative adverb* (place etc.) in or to which. ● *conjunction* **1** in or to the or any place, direction, or respect in which. **2** and there. ● *interrogative pronoun* what place. ● *relative pronoun* the place in or to which. □ **whereabouts** ● *interrogative adverb* approximately where. ● *noun* person's or thing's location. **whereas 1** in contrast or comparison with the fact that. **2** taking into consideration the fact that. **whereby** by what or which means. **wherefore** *archaic* for

what or which reason. **wherein** *formal* in what or which. **whereof** *formal* of what or which. **whereupon** immediately after which. **wherever 1** anywhere at all that. **2** no matter where. **wherewithal** /-wɪðɔːl/ *colloquial* money etc. needed for a purpose.

■ □ **whereabouts** *noun* location, place, position, site, situation.

wherry /'werɪ/ *noun* (*plural* **-ies**) **1** light rowing boat, usually for carrying passengers. **2** large light barge.

whet *verb* (**-tt-**) **1** sharpen. **2** stimulate (appetite etc.). □ **whetstone** stone for sharpening cutting-tools.

whether /'weðə/ *conjunction: introducing first or both of alternative possibilities.*

whew /hwjuː/ *interjection: expressing astonishment, consternation, or relief.*

whey /weɪ/ *noun* watery liquid left when milk forms curds. □ **whey-faced** pale, esp. with fear.

which *interrogative adjective: used in asking someone to specify one or more things from a definite set of alternatives.* ● *relative adjective* being the one just referred to; and this or these. ● *interrogative pronoun* which person(s) or thing(s). ● *relative pronoun* which thing(s). □ **whichever 1** any which. **2** no matter which.

whiff *noun* **1** puff of air, smoke, etc. **2** smell. **3** (+ *of*) trace of. **4** small cigar.

■ **1** breath, puff. **2** see SMELL *noun* 2–3. **3** see HINT *noun* 3.

Whig *noun historical* member of British political party succeeded by Liberals. □ **Whiggery** *noun.* **Whiggish** *adjective.* **Whiggism** *noun.*

while *noun* period of time. ● *conjunction* **1** during the time that; for as long as; at the same time as. **2** although, whereas. ● *verb* (**-ling**) (+ *away*) pass (time etc.) in leisurely or interesting way. ● *relative adverb* (time etc.) during which. □ **for a while** for some time. **in a while** soon. **once in a while** occasionally.

whilst /waɪlst/ *adverb & conjunction* while.

whim *noun* sudden fancy; caprice.

■ caprice, desire, fancy, impulse, urge.

whimper /'wɪmpə/ *verb* make feeble, querulous, or frightened sounds. ● *noun* such sound.

whimsical /'wɪmzɪk(ə)l/ *adjective* **1** capricious. **2** fantastic. □ **whimsicality** /-'kæl-/ *noun.* **whimsically** *adverb.*

whimsy /'wɪmzɪ/ *noun* (*plural* **-ies**) whim.

whin *noun* (in *singular* or *plural*) gorse. □ **whinchat** small songbird.

whine *noun* **1** long-drawn complaining cry (as) of dog or child. **2** querulous tone or complaint. ● *verb* (**-ning**) **1** emit or utter whine(s). **2** complain.

■ *verb* complain, cry, *colloquial* grizzle, groan, moan, snivel, wail, weep, whimper, *colloquial* whinge.

whinge /wɪndʒ/ *verb* (**-geing** or **-ging**) *colloquial* complain peevishly.

whinny /'wɪnɪ/ *noun* (*plural* **-ies**) gentle or joyful neigh. ● *verb* (**-ies, -ied**) emit whinny.

whip *noun* **1** lash attached to stick, for urging on or for punishing. **2** person appointed by political party to control its discipline and tactics in Parliament. **3** whip's written notice requesting member's attendance. **4** food made with whipped cream etc. **5** whipper-in. ● *verb* (**-pp-**) **1** beat or urge on with whip. **2** beat (eggs, cream, etc.) into froth. **3** take or move suddenly or quickly. **4** *slang* steal. **5** *slang* excel. **6** *slang* defeat. **7** bind with spirally wound twine. **8** sew with overcast stitches. □ **whipcord** tightly twisted cord. **(the) whip hand** advantage, control; **whiplash** sudden jerk. **whipper-in** huntsman's assistant who manages hounds. **whipping boy** scapegoat. **whip-round** *colloquial* informal collection of money among group of people. **whipstock** handle of whip. **whip up** excite (feeling etc.).

■ *noun* **1** birch, cane, cat, *historical* cat-o'-nine-tails, crop, horsewhip, lash, scourge, switch. ● *verb* **1** beat, birch, cane, flagellate, flog, hit, horsewhip, lash, scourge, *slang* tan, thrash. **2** beat, whisk.

whippersnapper /'wɪpəsnæpə/ *noun* **1** small child. **2** insignificant but presumptuous person.

whippet /'wɪpɪt/ *noun* crossbred dog of greyhound type, used for racing.

whippoorwill /'wɪpʊəwɪl/ *noun* N. American nightjar.

whirl *verb* **1** swing round and round; revolve rapidly. **2** (+ *away*) convey or go rapidly in car etc. **3** send or travel swiftly in orbit or curve. **4** (of brain etc.) seem to spin round. ● *noun* **1** whirling movement. **2** state of intense activity or confusion. □ **give it a whirl** *colloquial* attempt it. **whirlpool** circular eddy in sea, river, etc. **whirlwind** ● *noun* whirling mass or column of air. ● *adjective* very rapid.

■ *verb* **1, 3** circle, gyrate, pirouette, revolve, rotate, spin, swivel, turn, twirl, twist, wheel. **4** reel, spin. □ **whirlpool** eddy, maelstrom, swirl, vortex, whirl. **whirlwind** *noun* cyclone, hurricane, tornado, typhoon, vortex, waterspout.

whirligig /'wɜːlɪɡɪɡ/ *noun* **1** spinning or whirling toy. **2** merry-go-round. **3** revolving motion.

whirr *noun* continuous buzzing or softly clicking sound. ● *verb* (**-rr-**) make this sound.

whisk *verb* **1** (+ *away, off*) brush with sweeping movement. **2** (+ *away, off*) take suddenly. **3** whip (cream, eggs, etc.). **4** convey or go lightly or quickly. **5** wave (object). ● *noun* **1** whisking movement. **2** utensil for whipping eggs, cream, etc. **3** bunch of twigs, bristles, etc. for brushing or dusting.

■ *verb* **3** beat, mix, stir, whip. ● *noun* **2** beater, mixer.

whisker /'wɪskə/ *noun* **1** (usually in *plural*) hair on cheeks or sides of face of man. **2** each of bristles on face of cat etc. **3** *colloquial* small dis-

tance. □ **whiskered** *adjective*. **whiskery** *adjective*.

■ **1** (*whiskers*) bristles, hairs, moustache.

whisky /'wɪskɪ/ *noun* (*Irish & US* **whiskey**) (*plural* **-ies** or **-eys**) spirit distilled esp. from malted barley.

whisper /'wɪspə/ *verb* **1** speak using breath instead of vocal cords. **2** talk or say in barely audible tone or confidential way. **3** rustle, murmur. ● *noun* **1** whispering speech or sound. **2** thing whispered.

■ *verb* **1, 2** breathe, hiss, murmur, mutter. **3** murmur, rustle, sough. ● *noun* **1** murmur, undertone. **2** gossip, hearsay, rumour.

whist *noun* card game, usually for two pairs of opponents. □ **whist drive** whist-party with players moving on from table to table.

whistle /'wɪs(ə)l/ *noun* **1** clear shrill sound made by forcing breath through lips contracted to narrow opening. **2** similar sound made by bird, wind, missile, etc. **3** instrument used to produce such sound. ● *verb* (**-ling**) **1** emit whistle. **2** give signal or express surprise or derision by whistling. **3** (often + *up*) summon or give signal to thus. **4** produce (tune) by whistling. **5** (+ *for*) seek or desire in vain. □ **whistle-stop 1** *US* small unimportant town on railway. **2** politician's brief pause for electioneering speech on tour.

■ *noun* **3** hooter, pipe, siren. ● *verb* **4** blow, pipe.

Whit *noun* Whitsuntide. ● *adjective* of Whitsuntide. □ **Whit Sunday** 7th Sunday after Easter, commemorating Pentecost.

whit *noun* particle; least possible amount.

white *adjective* **1** of colour produced by reflection or transmission of all light; of colour of snow or milk. **2** pale. **3** of the human racial group having light-coloured skin. **4** albino. **5** (of hair) having lost its colour. **6** (of coffee) with milk or cream. ● *noun* **1** white colour, paint, clothes, etc. **2** (in *plural*) white garments worn in cricket, tennis, etc. **3** (player using) lighter-coloured pieces in chess etc. **4** egg white. **5** whitish part of eyeball round iris. **6** white person. □ **white ant** termite. **whitebait** small silvery-white food-fish. **white cell** leucocyte. **white-collar** (of worker or work) non-manual, clerical, professional. **white corpuscle** leucocyte. **white elephant** useless possession. **white feather** symbol of cowardice. **white flag** symbol of surrender. **white goods** large domestic electrical equipment. **white heat 1** degree of heat making metal glow white. **2** state of intense anger or passion. **white-hot** *adjective*. **white hope** person expected to achieve much. **white horses** white-crested waves. **white lead** mixture containing lead carbonate used as white pigment. **white lie** harmless or trivial untruth. **white magic** magic used for beneficent purposes. **white meat** poultry, veal, rabbit, and pork. **White Paper** government report giving information. **white pepper** pepper made by grinding husked berry. **white sauce** sauce of flour, melted butter, and milk or cream. **white slave** woman entrapped for prostitution. **white spirit** light petroleum as solvent. **white sugar** purified sugar.

white tie man's white bow tie as part of full evening dress. **white water** shallow or foamy stretch of water. **white wedding** wedding where bride wears formal white dress. **whitewood** light-coloured wood, esp. prepared for staining etc. □ **whiten** verb. **whitener** noun. **whiteness** noun. **whitish** adjective.

■ adjective **1** chalky, cream, ivory, milky, silver, snow white, snowy, whitish. **2** see PALE¹ adjective 1. □ **whiten** blanch, bleach, etiolate, fade, lighten, pale.

whitewash /'waɪtwɒʃ/ noun **1** solution of chalk or lime for whitening walls etc. **2** means of glossing over faults. ● verb **1** apply whitewash (to). **2** gloss over; clear of blame etc.

whither /'wɪðə/ archaic interrogative adverb to what place. ● relative adverb (place etc.) to which.

whiting¹ /'waɪtɪŋ/ noun (plural same) small edible sea fish.

whiting² /'waɪtɪŋ/ noun ground chalk used in whitewashing etc.

whitlow /'wɪtləʊ/ noun inflammation near fingernail or toenail.

Whitsun /'wɪts(ə)n/ noun Whitsuntide. ● adjective of Whitsuntide.

Whitsuntide noun weekend or week including Whit Sunday.

whittle /'wɪt(ə)l/ verb (**-ling**) **1** (often + at) pare (wood etc.) by cutting thin slices or shavings from surface. **2** (often + away, down) reduce by repeated subtractions.

whiz (also **whizz**) noun sound made by object moving through air at great speed. ● verb (**-zz-**) move with or make a whiz. □ **whiz-kid** colloquial brilliant or highly successful young person.

WHO abbreviation World Health Organization.

who /huː/ interrogative pronoun **1** what or which person(s). **2** what sort of person(s). ● relative pronoun (person or persons) that. □ **whoever**, **whosoever 1** the or any person(s) who. **2** no matter who.

whoa /wəʊ/ interjection: used to stop or slow horse etc.

who'd /huːd/ **1** who had. **2** who would.

whodunit /huːˈdʌnɪt/ noun (also **whodunnit**) colloquial detective story, play, or film.

whole /həʊl/ adjective **1** uninjured, unbroken, intact, undiminished. **2** not less than; all, all of. ● noun **1** complete thing. **2** all of a thing. **3** (+ of) all members etc. of. □ **on the whole** all things considered. **wholefood** food not artificially processed or refined. **wholehearted 1** completely devoted. **2** done with all possible effort or sincerity. **wholeheartedly** adverb. **wholemeal** meal or flour made from whole grains of wheat. □ **wholeness** noun.

■ adjective **1** complete, entire, healthy, in one piece, intact, integral, perfect, sound, total, unabbreviated, unabridged, unbroken, uncut, undamaged, undivided, unedited, unexpurgated, unharmed, unhurt, uninjured, unscathed. **2** complete, entire, full, total.

wholesale /'həʊlseɪl/ noun selling in large quantities, esp. for retail by others. ● adjective & adverb **1** by wholesale. **2** on a large scale. ● verb (**-ling**) sell wholesale. □ **wholesaler** noun.

■ adjective **2** comprehensive, extensive, general, global, indiscriminate, mass, total, universal, widespread.

wholesome adjective **1** promoting physical, mental, or moral health. **2** prudent. □ **wholesomeness** noun.

■ **1** beneficial, good, healthful, health-giving, healthy, hygienic, nourishing, nutritious, salubrious, sanitary.

wholly /'həʊllɪ/ adverb **1** entirely; without limitation. **2** purely.

whom /huːm/ pronoun (as object of verb) who. □ **whomever** (as object of verb) whoever. **whomsoever** (as object of verb) whosoever.

whoop /huːp, wuːp/ noun **1** cry expressing excitement etc. **2** characteristic drawing-in of breath after cough in whooping cough. ● verb utter whoop. □ **whooping cough** /'huːpɪŋ/ infectious disease, esp. of children, with violent convulsive cough.

whoopee /wʊˈpiː/ interjection: expressing wild joy. □ **make whoopee** /'wʊpɪ/ colloquial **1** make merry. **2** make love.

whoops /wʊps/ interjection colloquial: apology for obvious mistake.

whop verb (**-pp-**) slang **1** thrash. **2** defeat.

whopper noun slang **1** big specimen. **2** great lie.

whopping adjective colloquial huge.

whore /hɔː/ noun **1** prostitute. **2** derogatory promiscuous woman. □ **whorehouse** brothel.

whorl /wɜːl/ noun **1** ring of leaves etc. round stem. **2** one turn of spiral. □ **whorled** adjective.

whortleberry /'wɜːt(ə)lberɪ/ noun (plural **-ies**) bilberry.

who's /huːz/ **1** who is. **2** who has.

USAGE Because it has an apostrophe, who's is easily confused with whose. They are each correctly used in Who's there? (= Who is there?), Who's taken my pen? (= Who has taken my pen?), and Whose book is this? (= Who does this book belong to?).

whose /huːz/ interrogative pronoun & adjective of whom. ● relative adjective of whom or which.

why /waɪ/ interrogative adverb for what reason or purpose. ● relative adverb (reason etc.) for which. ● interjection: expressing surprise, impatience, reflection, or protest. □ **whys and wherefores** reasons; explanation.

WI abbreviation **1** West Indies. **2** Women's Institute.

wick noun strip or thread feeding flame with fuel.

wicked /'wɪkɪd/ adjective (**-er**, **-est**) **1** sinful, immoral. **2** spiteful. **3** playfully malicious. **4** colloquial very bad. **5** slang excellent. □ **wickedly** adverb. **wickedness** noun.

■ **1** abominable, base, corrupt, criminal, depraved, diabolical, dissolute, evil, foul, guilty, heinous, immoral, impious, incorrigible, indefensible, infamous, iniquitous, insupportable, intolerable, irreligious, irresponsible, lawless, lost (*soul*), machiavellian, murderous, nefarious, obscene, offensive, perverted, scandalous, shameful, sinful, sinister, ungodly, unprincipled, unregenerate, unrighteous, unscrupulous, vile, villainous, violent, wrong. **2** *colloquial* beastly, ill-tempered, malevolent, malicious, spiteful, vicious. **3** devilish, mischievous, naughty, rascally, roguish. **4** *colloquial* abominable, atrocious, *colloquial* awful, bad, *colloquial* foul, *colloquial* terrible, *colloquial* vile. □ **wickedness** baseness, depravity, enormity, evil, guilt, heinousness, immorality, infamy, iniquity, irresponsibility, knavery, malice, misconduct, naughtiness, sin, sinfulness, spite, *formal* turpitude, ungodliness, unrighteousness, vileness, villainy, wrong, wrongdoing.

wicker /ˈwɪkə/ *noun* osiers etc. woven together as material for chairs, baskets, etc. □ **wickerwork** 1 wicker. 2 things made of wicker.

wicket /ˈwɪkɪt/ *noun* 1 *Cricket* 3 upright stumps with bails in position defended by batsman. 2 *Cricket* ground between the two wickets. 3 *Cricket* state of this. 4 *Cricket* batsman's being got out. 5 (in full **wicket-door, -gate**) small door or gate, esp. beside or in larger one. □ **wicketkeeper** fielder stationed close behind batsman's wicket.

wide *adjective* 1 having sides far apart; broad, not narrow. 2 (following measurement) in width. 3 extending far; not restricted. 4 liberal; not specialized. 5 open to full extent. 6 (+ *of*) not within reasonable distance of; far from. ● *adverb* 1 to full extent. 2 far from target etc. ● *noun* wide ball. □ **-wide** extending over whole of. **wide awake** 1 fully awake. 2 *colloquial* wary or knowing. **wide ball** *Cricket* ball judged by umpire to be beyond batsman's reach. **wide-eyed** surprised, naive. **wide-ranging** covering an extensive range. **widespread** widely distributed. □ **widen** *verb*.

■ *adjective* 1 ample, broad, expansive, extensive, large, panoramic, roomy, spacious, vast, yawning. 3 all-embracing, broad, catholic, comprehensive, eclectic, encyclopedic, extensive, far-reaching, inclusive, sweeping, wide-ranging, widespread. 4 broad, broad-minded, general, liberal, unprejudiced. 5 extended, open, outspread, outstretched. 6 off course, off target. □ **widespread** common, endemic, extensive, far-reaching, general, global, pandemic, pervasive, prevalent, rife, universal, wholesale. □ **widen** augment, broaden, dilate, distend, enlarge, expand, extend, flare, increase, open out, spread, stretch.

widely *adverb* 1 far apart. 2 extensively. 3 by many people. 4 considerably.

widgeon /ˈwɪdʒ(ə)n/ *noun* (also **wigeon**) kind of wild duck.

widow /ˈwɪdəʊ/ *noun* woman who has lost her husband by death and not married again. ● *verb* 1 make into widow or widower. 2 (as **widowed** *adjective*) bereft by death of spouse. □ **widow's peak** V-shaped growth of hair on forehead. □ **widowhood** *noun*.

widower /ˈwɪdəʊə/ *noun* man who has lost his wife by death and not married again.

width *noun* 1 measurement from side to side. 2 large extent. 3 liberality of views etc. 4 piece of material of full width. □ **widthways** *adverb*.

■ **1** breadth, broadness, calibre (*of gun*), compass, diameter, distance across, extent, span, thickness.

wield /wiːld/ *verb* 1 hold and use. 2 control; exert (power).

■ **1** brandish, flourish, handle, hold, manage, ply, use, wave. 2 employ, exercise, exert, have, possess, use.

wife *noun* (*plural* **wives**) married woman, esp. in relation to her husband. □ **wifely** *adjective*.

wig *noun* artificial head of hair.

wigeon = WIDGEON.

wiggle /ˈwɪg(ə)l/ *colloquial verb* (**-ling**) move from side to side etc. ● *noun* 1 wiggling movement. 2 kink in line etc. □ **wiggly** *adjective* (**-ier**, **-iest**).

wight /waɪt/ *noun archaic* person.

wigwam /ˈwɪgwæm/ *noun* N. American Indian's hut or tent.

wilco /ˈwɪlkəʊ/ *interjection colloquial:* expressing compliance or agreement.

wild /waɪld/ *adjective* 1 in original natural state; not domesticated, cultivated, or civilized. 2 unrestrained, disorderly. 3 tempestuous. 4 intensely eager; frantic. 5 (+ *about*) *colloquial* enthusiastically devoted to. 6 *colloquial* infuriated. 7 random, ill-aimed, rash. ● *adverb* in a wild way. ● *noun* wild place; desert. □ **like wildfire** with extraordinary speed. **run wild** grow or stray unchecked or undisciplined. **wild card** 1 card having any rank chosen by its player. 2 person or thing usable in several different ways. **wildcat** ● *noun* hot-tempered or violent person. ● *adjective* 1 (of strike) sudden and unofficial. 2 reckless; financially unsound. **wild-goose chase** foolish or hopeless quest. **wildlife** wild animals collectively. **Wild West** western US in lawless times. □ **wildly** *adverb*. **wildness** *noun*.

■ *adjective* 1 *of animals* feral, free, undomesticated, untamed; *of country* deserted, desolate, natural, overgrown, remote, rough, rugged, uncultivated, unenclosed, unfarmed, uninhabited; *of people* barbaric, barbarous, primitive, savage, uncivilized. 2 boisterous, disorderly, lawless, noisy, obstreperous, on the rampage, out of control, riotous, rowdy, uncontrollable, uncontrolled, undisciplined, ungovernable, unmanageable, unrestrained, unruly, uproarious, violent. 3 blustery, stormy, tempestuous, turbulent, violent, windy. 4 berserk, eager, excited, frantic, hysterical, mad, uninhibited, unrestrained. 7 crazy, fantastic, impetuous, inaccurate, irrational, random, rash, reckless, silly, unreasonable, unthinking.

wildebeest /'wɪldəbiːst/ *noun* (*plural* same or -**s**) gnu.

wilderness /'wɪldənɪs/ *noun* **1** desert; uncultivated area. **2** confused assemblage.
■ **1** desert, jungle, waste, wasteland, wild(s).

wile *noun* (usually in *plural*) stratagem, trick.
● *verb* (-**ling**) lure.
■ *noun* artifice, gambit, *colloquial* game, machination, manoeuvre, plot, ploy, ruse, stratagem, subterfuge, trick.

wilful /'wɪlfʊl/ *adjective* (*US* **willful**) **1** intentional, deliberate. **2** obstinate, self-willed. □ **wilfully** *adverb*.
■ **1** calculated, conscious, deliberate, intended, intentional, premeditated, purposeful, voluntary. **2** *colloquial* bloody-minded, determined, dogged, headstrong, immovable, intransigent, obdurate, obstinate, perverse, pig-headed, refractory, self-willed, stubborn, uncompromising, unyielding, wayward.

will[1] *auxiliary verb* (*3rd singular present* **will**) **1** *used to form future tenses.* **2** *expressing request as question.* **3** be able to. **4** have tendency to. **5** be likely to.

will[2] *noun* **1** faculty by which person decides what to do. **2** fixed desire or intention. **3** will-power. **4** legal written directions for disposal of one's property etc. after death. **5** disposition towards others. ● *verb* **1** try to cause by will-power. **2** intend, desire. **3** bequeath by will. □ **at will** whenever one wishes. **will-power** control exercised by deliberate purpose over impulse. **with a will** vigorously.
■ *noun* **1** volition. **2** aim, commitment, desire, inclination, intent, intention, longing, purpose, resolution, resolve, wish. **3** determination, resolution, resolve, self-control, volition, will-power. **5** attitude, disposition, feeling. ● *verb* **1** command, encourage, force, influence, inspire, persuade. **2** desire, intend, require, want, wish. **3** bequeath, hand down, leave, pass on.

willing /'wɪlɪŋ/ *adjective* **1** ready to consent to undertake. **2** given etc. by willing person. □ **willingly** *adverb*. **willingness** *noun*.
■ **1** acquiescent, agreeable, amenable, assenting, *formal* complaisant, compliant, consenting, content, cooperative, disposed, docile, eager, game, happy, helpful, inclined, keen, pleased, prepared, obliging, ready, well disposed.

will-o'-the-wisp /wɪləðə'wɪsp/ *noun* **1** phosphorescent light seen on marshy ground. **2** elusive person.

willow /'wɪləʊ/ *noun* waterside tree with pliant branches yielding osiers. □ **willowherb** plant with leaves like willow. **willow-pattern** conventional Chinese design of blue on white china etc.

willowy *adjective* **1** lithe and slender. **2** having willows.

willy-nilly /wɪlɪ'nɪlɪ/ *adverb* whether one likes it or not.

wilt *verb* **1** wither, droop. **2** lose energy. ● *noun* plant disease causing wilting.
■ **1** become limp, droop, flop, sag, shrivel, wither. **2** droop, fade, fail, flag, flop, languish, sag, tire, weaken.

wily /'waɪlɪ/ *adjective* (-**ier**, -**iest**) crafty, cunning.
■ artful, astute, canny, clever, crafty, cunning, deceptive, designing, devious, dishonest, disingenuous, furtive, guileful, ingenious, knowing, scheming, *colloquial* shifty, shrewd, sly, tricky, underhand.

wimp *noun colloquial* feeble or ineffectual person. □ **wimpish** *adjective*.

wimple /'wɪmp(ə)l/ *noun* headdress covering neck and sides of face, worn by some nuns.

win *verb* (-**nn**-; *past & past participle* **won** /wʌn/) **1** secure as result of fight, contest, bet, etc. **2** be victor; be victorious in. ● *noun* victory in game etc. □ **win the day** be victorious in battle, argument, etc. **win over** gain support of. **win through, out** overcome obstacles.
■ *verb* **1** achieve, acquire, carry off, collect, come away with, earn, gain, get, obtain, pick up, receive, secure, *colloquial* walk away with. **2** be victorious, come first, conquer, overcome, prevail, succeed, triumph.

wince *noun* start or involuntary shrinking movement of pain etc. ● *verb* (-**cing**) give wince.

winceyette /wɪnsɪ'et/ *noun* lightweight flannelette.

winch *noun* **1** crank of wheel or axle. **2** windlass.
● *verb* lift with winch.

wind[1] /wɪnd/ *noun* **1** air in natural motion. **2** breath, esp. as needed in exertion or playing wind instrument. **3** power of breathing easily. **4** empty talk. **4** gas generated in bowels etc. **5** wind instruments of orchestra etc. **6** scent carried by the wind. ● *verb* **1** exhaust wind of by exertion or blow. **2** make (baby) bring up wind after feeding. **3** detect presence of by scent. □ **get wind of** begin to suspect. **get, have the wind up** *colloquial* become, be frightened. **in the wind** *colloquial* about to happen. **put the wind up** *colloquial* frighten. **take the wind out of (person's) sails** frustrate by anticipation. **windbag** *colloquial* person who talks a lot but says little of value. **windbreak** thing that breaks force of wind. **windcheater** windproof jacket. **windfall 1** fruit blown down by wind. **2** unexpected good fortune, esp. legacy. **wind instrument** musical instrument sounded by air current. **wind-jammer** merchant sailing ship. **windmill 1** mill worked by action of wind on sails. **2** toy with curved vanes revolving on stick. **windpipe** air-passage between throat and lungs. **windscreen** screen of glass at front of car etc. **windscreen wiper** rubber etc. blade to clear windscreen of rain etc. **windshield** *US* windscreen. **wind-sock** canvas cylinder or cone on mast to show direction of wind. **windswept** exposed to high winds. **wind-tunnel** enclosed chamber for testing (models or parts of) aircraft etc. in winds of known velocities. □ **windless** *adjective*.

■ *noun* **1** air current, blast, breath, breeze, cyclone, draught, gale, gust, hurricane, monsoon, puff, squall, tempest, tornado, whirlwind, *literary* zephyr. **4** flatulence. □ **windswept** bare, bleak, desolate, exposed, unprotected, windy.

wind² /waɪnd/ *verb* (*past & past participle* **wound** /waʊnd/) **1** go in spiral, crooked, or curved course. **2** make (one's way) thus. **3** wrap closely; surround (as) with coil. **4** coil; provide with coiled thread etc. **5** wind up (clock etc.). ● *noun* bend or turn in course. □ **wind down 1** lower by winding. **2** unwind. **3** approach end gradually. **winding-sheet** sheet in which corpse is wrapped for burial. **wind up 1** coil whole of. **2** tighten coiling or coiled spring of. **3** *colloquial* increase intensity of. **4** *colloquial* provoke to anger etc. **5** bring to conclusion; end. **6** arrange affairs of and dissolve (company). **7** cease business and go into liquidation. **8** *colloquial* arrive finally. **wind-up** *noun* **1** conclusion. **2** *colloquial* attempt to provoke. □ **winding** *adjective*.

■ *verb* **1** bend, curve, loop, meander, ramble, slew, snake, spiral, turn, twist, twist and turn, veer, zigzag. **3** see WRAP *verb* **1**. **4** coil, curl, furl, loop, reel, roll, spiral, turn, twine, twist, wreathe. □ **wind up 5** see FINISH *verb* **1**. □ **winding** see TORTUOUS **1**.

windlass /'wɪndləs/ *noun* machine with horizontal axle for hauling or hoisting.

window /'wɪndəʊ/ *noun* **1** opening, usually with glass, in wall etc. to admit light etc. **2** the glass itself. **3** space for display behind window of shop. **4** window-like opening. **5** transparent part in envelope showing address. **6** opportunity for study or action. □ **window-box** box placed outside window for cultivating plants. **window-dressing 1** art of arranging display in shop window etc. **2** adroit presentation of facts etc. to give falsely favourable impression. **window-pane** glass pane in window. **window-seat 1** seat below window. **2** seat next to window in aircraft etc. **window-shop** look at displays in shop windows without buying anything.

windsurfing *noun* sport of riding on water on sailboard. □ **windsurf** *verb*. **windsurfer** *noun*.

windward /'wɪndwəd/ *adjective & adverb* on or towards side from which wind is blowing. ● *noun* this direction.

windy *adjective* (**-ier, -iest**) **1** stormy with or exposed to wind. **2** generating or characterized by flatulence. **3** *colloquial* wordy. **4** *colloquial* apprehensive, frightened. □ **windiness** *noun*.

■ **1** blowy, blustery, boisterous, breezy, draughty, fresh, gusty, squally, stormy, tempestuous, windswept.

wine *noun* **1** fermented grape juice as alcoholic drink. **2** fermented drink resembling this made from other fruits etc. **3** colour of red wine. ● *verb* (**-ning**) **1** drink wine. **2** entertain with wine. □ **wine bar** bar or small restaurant where wine is main drink available. **wine cellar 1** cellar for storing wine. **2** its contents. **wineglass** glass for wine, usually with stem and foot. **winepress** press in which grape juice is extracted for

wine. **wine waiter** waiter responsible for serving wine.

wing *noun* **1** each of the limbs or organs by which bird etc. flies. **2** winglike part supporting aircraft. **3** projecting part of building. **4** *Football etc.* forward player at either end of line. **5** *Football etc.* side part of playing area. **6** (in *plural*) sides of theatre stage. **7** extreme section of political party. **8** flank of battle array. **9** part of vehicle over wheel. **10** air-force unit of several squadrons. ● *verb* **1** travel or traverse on wings. **2** wound in wing or arm. **3** equip with wings. **4** enable to fly; send in flight. □ **on the wing** flying. **take under one's wing** treat as protégé. **take wing** fly away. **wing-case** horny cover of insect's wing. **wing-chair** chair with side-pieces at top of high back. **wing-collar** man's high stiff collar with turned-down corners. **wing commander** RAF officer next below group captain. **wing-nut** nut with projections to turn it by. **wingspan** measurement right across wings. □ **winged** *adjective*.

winger *noun Football etc.* wing player.

wink *verb* **1** (often + *at*) close and open (one eye) quickly, esp. as signal. **2** close eye(s) momentarily. **3** (of light) twinkle. **4** (of indicator) flash on and off. ● *noun* **1** act of winking. **2** *colloquial* short sleep. □ **wink at** purposely avoid seeing; pretend not to notice.

■ *verb* **1, 2** bat (*eyelid*), blink, flutter. **3** flash, flicker, sparkle, twinkle.

winkle /'wɪŋk(ə)l/ *noun* edible sea snail. ● *verb* (**-ling**) (+ *out*) extract with difficulty.

winner *noun* **1** person who wins. **2** successful thing.

■ **1** *slang* champ, champion, conquering hero, conqueror, medallist, prizewinner, title-holder, victor. **2** see SUCCESS **3**.

winning *adjective* **1** having or bringing victory. **2** attractive. ● *noun* (in *plural*) money won. □ **winning post** post marking end of race. □ **winningly** *adverb*.

■ **1** champion, conquering, first, leading, prevailing, successful, top, top-scoring, triumphant, unbeaten, undefeated, victorious. **2** see ATTRACTIVE.

winnow /'wɪnəʊ/ *verb* **1** blow (grain) free of chaff etc. **2** (+ *out, away, from*, etc.) rid grain of (chaff etc.). **3** sift, examine.

winsome /'wɪnsəm/ *adjective* attractive, engaging. □ **winsomely** *adverb*. **winsomeness** *noun*.

winter /'wɪntə/ *noun* coldest season of year. ● *verb* (usually + *at, in*) spend the winter. □ **winter garden** garden of plants flourishing in winter. **wintergreen** kind of plant remaining green all winter. **winter sports** sports practised on snow or ice. **wintertime** season or period of winter.

wintry /'wɪntrɪ/ *adjective* (**-ier, -iest**) **1** characteristic of winter. **2** lacking warmth. □ **wintriness** *noun*.

■ arctic, chilly, cold, frigid, frosty, icy, snowy.

winy *adjective* (**-ier, -iest**) wine-flavoured.

wipe *verb* (**-ping**) **1** clean or dry surface of by rubbing. **2** rub (cloth) over surface. **3** spread (liquid etc.) over surface by rubbing. **4** (often + *away, off,* etc.) clear or remove by wiping. **5** (often + *away, off,* etc.) erase, eliminate. ● *noun* **1** act of wiping. **2** piece of specially treated cloth for wiping. □ **wipe out 1** utterly destroy or defeat. **2** clean inside of. **wipe up 1** dry (dishes etc.). **2** take up (liquid etc.) by wiping.

■ *verb* **1** clean, cleanse, dry, dust, mop, polish, rub, scour, sponge, swab, wash. **3** rub, smear, spread. □ **wipe out 1** see DESTROY 1–2.

wiper *noun* windscreen wiper.

wire *noun* **1** metal drawn out into thread or slender flexible rod. **2** piece of this. **3** length of this used for fencing or to carry electric current etc. **4** *colloquial* telegram. ● *verb* (**-ring**) **1** provide, fasten, strengthen, etc. with wire. **2** (often + *up*) install electrical circuits in. **3** *colloquial* telegraph. □ **get one's wires crossed** become confused. **wire-haired** (of dog) having stiff wiry hair. **wire netting** netting made of meshed wire. **wire-tapping** tapping of telephone wires. **wire wool** mass of fine wire for scouring. **wireworm** destructive larva of a kind of beetle.

■ *noun* **3** cable, flex, lead. **4** cable, cablegram, telegram.

wireless *noun* **1** radio. **2** radio receiving set.

wiring *noun* system or installation of electrical circuits.

wiry *adjective* (**-ier, -iest**) **1** sinewy; untiring. **2** like wire; tough and coarse.

■ **1** lean, muscular, sinewy, strong, thin, tough. **2** coarse, stiff, tough.

wisdom /ˈwɪzdəm/ *noun* **1** experience, knowledge, and the power of applying them. **2** prudence; common sense. **3** wise sayings. □ **wisdom tooth** hindmost molar usually cut at age of about 20.

■ **1, 2** astuteness, common sense, discernment, discrimination, good sense, insight, intelligence, judgement, judiciousness, penetration, perceptiveness, perspicacity, prudence, rationality, reason, sagacity, sapience, sense, understanding.

wise[1] /waɪz/ *adjective* **1** having, showing, or dictated by wisdom. **2** prudent, sensible. **3** having knowledge. **4** suggestive of wisdom. **5** *US colloquial* alert, crafty. □ **be, get wise to** *colloquial* be, become aware of. **wisecrack** *colloquial noun* smart remark. ● *verb* make wisecrack. **wise guy** *colloquial* know-all. **wise man** wizard, esp. one of the Magi. **wise up** esp. *US colloquial* inform; get wise. □ **wisely** *adverb*.

■ **1** astute, discerning, intelligent, penetrating, perceptive, perspicacious, sagacious, sage, shrewd, sound, thoughtful, understanding. **2** advisable, appropriate, diplomatic, expedient, judicious, politic, proper, prudent, rational, reasonable, right, sagacious, sage, sensible. **3** enlightened, erudite, informed, knowledgeable, well informed.

wise[2] /waɪz/ *noun archaic* way, manner, degree.

-wise /waɪz/ *combining form: added to nouns to form adjectives and adverbs:* **1** in the manner or direction of (e.g. *clockwise, lengthwise*). **2** with reference to (e.g. *weatherwise*).

wiseacre /ˈwaɪzeɪkə/ *noun* person who affects to be wise.

wish *verb* **1** (often + *for*) have or express desire or aspiration. **2** want, demand. **3** express one's hopes for. **4** *colloquial* foist. ● *noun* **1** desire, request. **2** expression of this. **3** thing desired. □ **wishbone** forked bone between neck and breast of fowl. **wish-fulfilment** tendency of unconscious wishes to be satisfied in fantasy. **wishing-well** well at which wishes are made.

■ *verb* **1** aspire, choose, crave, desire, fancy, hope, yearn; (*wish for*) see WANT *verb* 1. **2** ask, demand, request, require, want. ● *noun* **1, 2** aim, ambition, appetite, aspiration, craving, desire, *colloquial* fancy, hankering, hope, inclination, itch, keenness, longing, objective, request, urge, want, yearning, *colloquial* yen.

wishful *adjective* (often + *to do*) desiring. □ **wishful thinking** belief founded on wishes rather than facts.

wishy-washy /ˈwɪʃɪwɒʃɪ/ *adjective colloquial* **1** feeble or poor in quality or character. **2** weak, watery.

wisp *noun* **1** small bundle or twist of straw etc. **2** small separate quantity of smoke, hair, etc. **3** small thin person. □ **wispy** *adjective* (**-ier, -iest**).

■ **2** shred, strand, streak. □ **wispy** flimsy, fragile, gossamer, insubstantial, light, streaky, thin.

wisteria /wɪˈstɪərɪə/ *noun* (also **wistaria** /-tear-/) climbing plant with blue, purple, or white hanging flowers.

wistful /ˈwɪstfʊl/ *adjective* yearning; mournfully expectant or wishful. □ **wistfully** *adverb*. **wistfulness** *noun*.

■ forlorn, longing, melancholy, mournful, nostalgic, pensive, regretful, sad, thoughtful, yearning.

wit *noun* **1** (in *singular* or *plural*) intelligence, understanding. **2** (in *singular*) imaginative and inventive faculty. **3** amusing ingenuity of speech or ideas. **4** person noted for this. □ **at one's wit's** or **wits' end** utterly at a loss or in despair. **have** or **keep one's wits about one** be alert. **out of one's wits** mad. **to wit** that is to say; namely.

■ **1** see INTELLIGENCE 1. **3** banter, cleverness, comedy, facetiousness, humour, ingenuity, jokes, puns, quickness, quips, repartee, witticisms. **4** comedian, comic, humorist, *historical* jester, joker, wag.

witch *noun* **1** woman supposed to have dealings with Devil or evil spirits. **2** old hag. **3** fascinating girl or woman. □ **witchcraft 1** use of magic. **2** bewitching charm. **witch-doctor** tribal magician of primitive people. **witch, wych hazel 1** N. American shrub. **2** astringent lotion from its bark. **witch-hunt** campaign against people suspected of unpopular or unorthodox views.

■ **1** enchantress, sibyl, sorceress. **2** crone, gorgon, hag, harridan, shrew, virago. □ **witchcraft 1** black magic, charms, enchantment, incantations, magic, necromancy, the occult, occultism, sorcery, spells, voodoo, witchery, wizardry.

witchery /'wɪtʃərɪ/ *noun* witchcraft.

with /wɪð/ *preposition: expressing instrument or means used, company, parting of company, cause, possession, circumstances, manner, agreement, disagreement, antagonism, understanding, regard.* □ **with child** *literary* pregnant. **with it** *colloquial* **1** up to date. **2** alert and comprehending. **with that** thereupon.

withdraw /wɪð'drɔː/ *verb* (*past* **-drew**; *past participle* **-drawn**) **1** pull or take aside or back. **2** discontinue, cancel, retract. **3** remove, take away. **4** take (money) out of an account. **5** retire or go apart. **6** (as **withdrawn** *adjective*) unsociable. □ **withdrawal** *noun*.

■ **1** draw back, pull away, pull back, retract, take back. **2** abjure, back down on, call back, cancel, go back on, recall, rescind, retract, take back. **3** extract, pull out, remove, take away, take out. **4** remove, take out. **5** back away, back out, *colloquial* chicken out, cry off, draw back, *colloquial* drop out, fall back, leave, move back, pull back, pull out, quit, recoil, retire, retreat, run away, scratch, secede, shrink back. **6** (**withdrawn**) bashful, diffident, distant, introverted, private, quiet, reclusive, remote, reserved, retiring, shy, silent, solitary, taciturn, timid, uncommunicative.

withe = WITHY.

wither /'wɪðə/ *verb* **1** (often + *up*) make or become dry and shrivelled. **2** (often + *away*) deprive of or lose vigour or freshness. **3** (esp. as **withering** *adjective*) blight with scorn etc. □ **witheringly** *adverb*.

■ **1** become dry, become limp, dehydrate, desiccate, droop, dry out, dry up, flop, sag, shrink, shrivel, waste away, wilt. **2** decline, droop, fail, flag, flop, languish, wilt.

withers /'wɪðəz/ *plural noun* ridge between horse's shoulder-blades.

withhold /wɪð'həʊld/ *verb* (*past & past participle* **-held**) **1** refuse to give, grant, or allow. **2** hold back, restrain.

■ **1** deny, refuse. **2** check, conceal, control, hide, hold back, keep back, keep secret, repress, reserve, restrain, retain, suppress.

within /wɪ'ðɪn/ *adverb* **1** inside. **2** indoors. **3** in spirit. ● *preposition* **1** inside. **2** not beyond or out of. **3** not transgressing or exceeding. **4** not further off than.

without /wɪ'ðaʊt/ *preposition* **1** not having, feeling, or showing. **2** free from. **3** in absence of. **4** with neglect or avoidance of. **5** *archaic* outside. ● *adverb archaic* or *literary* **1** outside. **2** out of doors.

withstand /wɪð'stænd/ *verb* (*past & past participle* **-stood**) oppose; hold out against.

■ bear, brave, confront, cope with, defy, endure, fight, grapple with, hold out against, last out against, oppose, put up with, resist, stand up to, *colloquial* stick, survive, take, tolerate, weather.

withy /'wɪðɪ/ *noun* (*plural* **-ies**) tough flexible shoot, esp. of willow.

witless *adjective* foolish; crazy.

witness /'wɪtnɪs/ *noun* **1** eyewitness. **2** person giving sworn testimony. **3** person attesting another's signature to document. **4** (+ *to, of*) person or thing whose existence etc. attests or proves something. ● *verb* **1** be eyewitness of. **2** be witness to (signature etc.). **3** serve as evidence or indication of. **4** give or be evidence. □ **bear witness** (often + *to*) **1** attest truth (of). **2** state one's belief (in). **witness-box** (*US* **-stand**) enclosed space in law court from which witness gives evidence.

■ *noun* **1** bystander, eyewitness, looker-on, observer, onlooker, spectator, viewer, watcher. ● *verb* **1** attend, *literary* behold, be present at, look on, note, notice, observe, see, view, watch. □ **bear witness 1** see TESTIFY.

witter /'wɪtə/ *verb* (often + *on*) *colloquial* chatter annoyingly or on trivial matters.

witticism /'wɪtɪsɪz(ə)m/ *noun* witty remark.

wittingly /'wɪtɪŋlɪ/ *adverb* consciously, intentionally.

witty *adjective* (**-ier**, **-iest**) showing verbal wit. □ **wittily** *adverb*. **wittiness** *noun*.

■ amusing, clever, comic, droll, facetious, funny, humorous, ingenious, intelligent, jocular, quick-witted, sarcastic, sharp-witted, waggish.

wives *plural* of WIFE.

wizard /'wɪzəd/ *noun* **1** sorcerer, magician. **2** person of extraordinary powers. ● *adjective slang* wonderful. □ **wizardry** *noun*.

■ *noun* **1** enchanter, magician, magus, sorcerer, *archaic* warlock, witch-doctor.

wizened /'wɪz(ə)nd/ *adjective* shrivelled-looking.

WNW *abbreviation* west-north-west.

WO *abbreviation* Warrant Officer.

woad *noun* **1** plant yielding blue dye. **2** this dye.

wobble /'wɒb(ə)l/ *verb* (**-ling**) **1** sway from side to side. **2** stand or go unsteadily; stagger. **3** waver, vacillate. ● *noun* wobbling motion. □ **wobbly** *adjective* (**-ier**, **-iest**).

■ *verb* **1, 2** be unsteady, oscillate, quake, quiver, rock, shake, sway, teeter, totter, tremble, vibrate, waver. □ **wobbly** insecure, loose, rickety, *colloquial* rocky, shaky, teetering, tottering, unbalanced, unsafe, unstable, unsteady.

woe *noun* **1** affliction; bitter grief. **2** (in *plural*) calamities. □ **woebegone** dismal-looking.

■ **1** affliction, anguish, dejection, despair, distress, grief, heartache, melancholy, misery, misfortune, sadness, sorrow, suffering, trouble, unhappiness, wretchedness. □ **woebegone** crestfallen, dejected, dismal, downhearted, forlorn, gloomy, melancholy, miserable, sad, sorry for oneself, woeful, wretched.

woeful *adjective* **1** sorrowful. **2** causing or feeling affliction. **3** very bad. □ **woefully** *adverb*.

wok *noun* bowl-shaped frying-pan used in esp. Chinese cookery.

woke *past* of WAKE[1].

woken *past participle* of WAKE[1].

wold /wəʊld/ *noun* high open uncultivated land or moor.

wolf /wʊlf/ *noun* (*plural* **wolves** /wʊlvz/) **1** wild animal related to dog. **2** *slang* man who seduces women. ● *verb* (often + *down*) devour greedily. □ **cry wolf** raise false alarm. **keep the wolf from the door** avert starvation. **wolfhound** dog of kind used originally to hunt wolves. **wolfsbane** an aconite. **wolf-whistle** man's whistle to attractive woman. □ **wolfish** *adjective*.

wolfram /'wʊlfrəm/ *noun* **1** tungsten. **2** tungsten ore.

wolverine /'wʊlvəriːn/ *noun* N. American animal of weasel family.

wolves *plural* of WOLF.

woman /'wʊmən/ *noun* (*plural* **women** /'wɪmɪn/) **1** adult human female. **2** the female sex. **3** *colloquial* wife, girlfriend.

■ **1** *slang* bird, *slang* chick, *US slang* dame, *archaic* damsel, female, *colloquial* girl, lady, *esp. Scottish & Northern English* or *poetical* lass, *archaic* maid, *archaic* maiden, matron, *Australian & NZ slang* sheila, squaw. **3** bride, *colloquial* girl, girlfriend, *colloquial* lady, mistress, wife.

womanhood *noun* **1** female maturity. **2** womanliness. **3** womankind.

womanish *adjective derogatory* effeminate, unmanly.

womanize *verb* (also **-ise**) (**-zing** or **-sing**) (of man) be promiscuous. □ **womanizer** *noun*.

womankind *noun* (also **womenkind**) women in general.

womanly *adjective* having or showing qualities associated with women. □ **womanliness** *noun*.

womb /wuːm/ *noun* organ of conception and gestation in female mammals.

wombat /'wɒmbæt/ *noun* burrowing plant-eating Australian marsupial.

women /'wɪmɪn/ *plural* of WOMAN. □ **women's libber** *colloquial* supporter of women's liberation. **women's liberation, lib** *colloquial* movement for release of women from subservient status. **women's rights** human rights of women giving equality with men.

womenfolk *noun* **1** women in general. **2** women in family.

won *past* & *past participle* of WIN.

wonder /'wʌndə/ *noun* **1** emotion, esp. admiration, excited by what is unexpected, unfamiliar, or inexplicable. **2** strange or remarkable thing, specimen, event, etc. ● *adjective* having amazing properties etc. ● *verb* **1** (often + *at*) be filled with wonder. **2** (+ *that*) be surprised to find that. **3** be curious to know. □ **no or small wonder** it is not

surprising. **wonderland 1** fairyland. **2** place of surprises or marvels.

■ *noun* **1** admiration, amazement, astonishment, awe, bewilderment, curiosity, fascination, respect, reverence, stupefaction, surprise, wonderment. **2** marvel, miracle, phenomenon, prodigy, sensation. ● *verb* **1** (*wonder at*) see ADMIRE. **3** ask oneself, be curious, be inquisitive, conjecture, ponder, question oneself, speculate.

wonderful *adjective* very remarkable or admirable. □ **wonderfully** *adverb*.

■ amazing, astonishing, astounding, extraordinary, impressive, *colloquial* incredible, marvellous, miraculous, phenomenal, remarkable, surprising, unexpected, *poetical* wondrous.

wonderment *noun* surprise, awe.

wondrous /'wʌndrəs/ *poetical adjective* wonderful. ● *adverb* wonderfully.

wonky /'wɒŋkɪ/ *adjective* (**-ier**, **-iest**) *slang* **1** crooked. **2** unsteady. **3** unreliable.

wont /wəʊnt/ *adjective archaic* or *literary* (+ *to do*) accustomed to. ● *noun formal* or *jocular* custom, habit.

won't /wəʊnt/ will not.

wonted /'wəʊntɪd/ *adjective* habitual, usual.

woo *verb* (**woos**, **wooed**) **1** court; seek love of. **2** try to win. **3** seek support of. **4** coax, importune.

■ **1** *colloquial* chat up, court, *archaic* make love to. **2, 3** attract, cultivate, pursue, seek, try to get. **4** cajole, coax, importune, persuade.

wood /wʊd/ *noun* **1** hard fibrous substance of tree. **2** this for timber or fuel. **3** (in *singular* or *plural*) growing trees occupying piece of ground. **4** wooden cask for wine etc. **5** wooden-headed golf club. **6** ball in game of bowls. □ **out of the wood(s)** clear of danger or difficulty. **wood anemone** wild spring-flowering anemone. **woodbine** honeysuckle. **woodchuck** N. American marmot. **woodcock** game bird related to snipe. **woodcut 1** relief cut on wood. **2** print made from this. **woodcutter** person who cuts timber. **woodland** wooded country. **woodlouse** small land crustacean with many legs. **woodman** forester. **woodpecker** bird that taps tree trunks to find insects. **woodpigeon** dove with white patches round neck. **wood pulp** wood fibre prepared for papermaking. **woodwind** wind instrument(s) of orchestra made originally of wood. **woodwork 1** making of things in wood. **2** things made of wood. **woodworm 1** beetle larva that bores in wood. **2** resulting condition of wood.

■ **2** see TIMBER 1. **3** (*wood* or *woods*) coppice, copse, forest, grove, jungle, orchard, plantation, spinney, thicket, trees, woodland. □ **woodwork 1** carpentry, joinery.

wooded *adjective* having woods.

■ afforested, *literary* bosky, forested, sylvan, timbered, tree-covered, woody.

wooden /'wʊd(ə)n/ *adjective* **1** made of wood. **2** like wood. **3** stiff, clumsy. **4** expressionless.

□ **woodenly** *adverb.* **woodenness** *noun.*
■ **1** ligneous, timber, wood. **3, 4** dead, emotionless, expressionless, hard, inflexible, lifeless, rigid, stiff, stilted, unbending, unemotional, unnatural.

woody *adjective* (**-ier, -iest**) **1** wooded. **2** like or of wood.
■ **1** see WOODED. **2** fibrous, hard, ligneous, tough, wooden.

woof¹ /wʊf/ *noun* gruff bark of dog. ● *verb* give woof.

woof² /wuːf/ *noun* weft.

woofer /'wuːfə/ *noun* loudspeaker for low frequencies.

wool /wʊl/ *noun* **1** fine soft wavy hair forming fleece of sheep etc. **2** woollen yarn, cloth, or garments. **3** wool-like substance. □ **wool-gathering** absent-mindedness. **the Woolsack** Lord Chancellor's seat in House of Lords.

woollen /'wʊlən/ (*US* **woolen**) *adjective* made (partly) of wool. ● *noun* **1** woollen fabric. **2** (in *plural*) woollen garments.

woolly *adjective* (**-ier, -iest**) **1** bearing or covered with wool. **2** like wool; woollen. **3** indistinct. **4** confused. ● *noun* (*plural* **-ies**) *colloquial* woollen (esp. knitted) garment.
■ *adjective* **1** wool-bearing. **2** cuddly, downy, fleecy, furry, fuzzy, hairy, shaggy, soft, wool, woollen. **3, 4** ambiguous, blurry, confused, hazy, ill-defined, indefinite, indistinct, uncertain, unclear, unfocused, vague.

woozy /'wuːzɪ/ *adjective* (**-ier, -iest**) *colloquial* **1** dizzy. **2** slightly drunk.

word /wɜːd/ *noun* **1** meaningful element of speech, usually shown with space on either side of it when written or printed. **2** speech as distinct from action. **3** one's promise or assurance. **4** (in *singular* or *plural*) thing said, remark, conversation. **5** (in *plural*) text of song or actor's part. **6** (in *plural*) angry talk. **7** news, message. **8** command. ● *verb* put into words; select words to express. □ **word-blindness** dyslexia. **word for word** in exactly the same words; literally. **the Word (of God)** the Bible. **word of honour** assurance given on one's honour. **word of mouth** speech (only). **word-perfect** having memorized one's part etc. perfectly. **word processor** computer software or hardware for storing text entered from keyboard, incorporating corrections, and producing printout. **word-process** *verb.* **word processing** *noun.*
■ *noun* **1** expression, name, term. **3** see PROMISE *noun* **1**. **7** see NEWS **1**. ● *verb* articulate, express, phrase. □ **word for word** see VERBATIM *adjective.*

wording *noun* form of words used.
■ choice of words, expression, language, phraseology, phrasing, style, terminology.

wordsmith /'wɜːdsmɪθ/ *noun* skilled user of words.

wordy *adjective* (**-ier, -iest**) using or expressed in (too) many words. □ **wordiness** *noun.*

■ chatty, diffuse, digressive, discursive, garrulous, long-winded, loquacious, pleonastic, prolix, rambling, repetitious, talkative, unstoppable, verbose, voluble, *colloquial* windy.

wore *past* of WEAR.

work /wɜːk/ *noun* **1** application of effort to a purpose; use of energy. **2** task to be undertaken. **3** thing done or made by work; result of action. **4** employment, occupation, etc., esp. as means of earning money. **5** literary or musical composition. **6** actions or experiences of specified kind. **7** (in *plural*) operative part of clock etc. **8** (**the works**) *colloquial* all that is available or needed; full treatment. **9** (in *plural*) operations of building or repair. **10** (in *plural*; often treated as *singular*) factory. **11** (usually in *plural* or in *combination*) defensive structure. ● *verb* **1** be engaged in activity. **2** be employed in certain work. **3** make efforts. **4** be craftsman in (material). **5** operate or function, esp. effectively. **6** operate, manage, control. **7** put or keep in operation or at work; cause to toil. **8** cultivate (land). **9** produce as result. **10** *colloquial* arrange. **11** knead, hammer; bring to desired shape or consistency. **12** do, or make by, needlework etc. **13** (cause to) make way or make (way) slowly or with difficulty. **14** gradually become (loose etc.) by motion. **15** artificially excite. **16** purchase with labour instead of money. **17** obtain money for by labour. **18** (+ *on, upon*) influence. **19** be in motion or agitated; ferment. □ **worked up** angry, excited, or tense. **workaday** ordinary, everyday, practical. **work-basket** basket for sewing materials. **workbench** bench for manual work, esp. carpentry. **workbox** box for tools, needlework, etc. **workday** day on which work is usually done. **work experience** temporary experience of employment for young people. **workforce 1** workers engaged or available. **2** number of these. **workhouse** *historical* public institution for the poor. **work in** find place for. **workload** amount of work to be done. **workman 1** man employed to do manual labour. **2** person who works in specified manner. **workmanlike** showing practised skill. **workmanship** degree of skill in doing task or of finish in product. **workmate** person working alongside another. **work off** get rid of by work or activity. **work out 1** solve (sum) or find (amount) by calculation. **2** understand (problem, person, etc.). **3** be calculated. **4** have result. **5** provide for all details of. **6** engage in physical exercise. **workout** *noun* session of physical exercise. **work over 1** examine thoroughly. **2** *colloquial* treat with violence. **workplace** place at which person works; office, factory, etc. **workroom** room arranged for working in. **workshop 1** room or building in which goods are manufactured. **2** place or meeting for concerted activity. **work-shy** disinclined to work. **workstation 1** location of stage in manufacturing process. **2** computer terminal. **worktop** flat (esp. kitchen) surface for working on. **work to rule** follow official working rules exactly to reduce efficiency as protest. **work-to-rule** *noun.* **work up 1** bring gradually to efficient or advanced state. **2** advance gradually. **3** elaborate or excite by degrees. **4** mingle (ingredients). **5** learn (subject) by study.

■ *noun* **1** donkey-work, drudgery, effort, exertion, *colloquial* fag, *slang* graft, *colloquial* grind, industry, labour, slavery, slog, spadework, strain, struggle, *colloquial* sweat, toil, *literary* travail. **2** assignment, chore, commission, duty, errand, job, mission, project, responsibility, task, undertaking. **4** business, calling, career, employment, job, livelihood, living, *métier*, occupation, post, profession, *formal* situation, trade. ● *verb* **1** *colloquial* beaver (away), be busy, drudge, exert oneself, grind away, labour, peg away, *colloquial* plug away, potter about, slave, slog away, sweat, toil, *literary* travail. **3** exert oneself, make efforts, strain, strive, struggle. **5** act, be effective, function, go, operate, perform, run, succeed. **7** drive, employ, exploit, use, utilize. □ **workforce** employees, staff, workers. **workmanship** art, artistry, competence, craft, craftsmanship, expertise, handicraft, handiwork, skill, technique. **work out 1** see CALCULATE 1. **workshop 1** factory, mill, smithy, studio, workroom, works. **work up 2** see DEVELOP 1. **3** see EXCITE 1.

workable *adjective* that can be worked, will work, or is worth working. □ **workability** /-'bɪlɪtɪ/ *noun*.

worker *noun* **1** manual or industrial etc. employee. **2** neuter bee or ant. **3** person who works hard.

■ **1** artisan, breadwinner, craftsman, employee, hand, labourer, navvy, operative, operator, peasant, tradesman, wage earner, working man, working woman, workman; (*workers*) staff, workforce.

working *adjective* **1** engaged in work. **2** while so engaged. **3** functioning, able to function. ● *noun* **1** activity of work. **2** functioning. **3** mine, quarry. **4** (usually in *plural*) mechanism. □ **working capital** capital used in conducting a business. **working class** social class employed for wages, esp. in manual or industrial work. **working-class** *adjective*. **working day 1** workday. **2** part of day devoted to work. **working knowledge** knowledge adequate to work with. **working lunch** lunch at which business is conducted. **working order** condition in which machine works. **working party** committee appointed to study and advise on some question.

■ **1** see EMPLOYED (EMPLOY). **3** see OPERATIONAL (OPERATION).

world /wɜːld/ *noun* **1** the earth, or a planetary body like it. **2** the universe; all that exists. **3** time, state, or scene of human existence. **4** (**the, this world**) mortal life. **5** secular interests and affairs. **6** human affairs; active life. **7** average, respectable, or fashionable people or their customs or opinions. **8** all that concerns or all who belong to specified class or sphere of activity. **9** vast amount. ● *adjective* of or affecting all nations. □ **out of this world** *colloquial* extremely good etc. **think the world of** have very high regard for. **world-class** of standard considered high throughout world. **world-famous** known throughout the world. **world music** pop music

incorporating ethnic elements. **world war** one involving many important nations. **world-weary** bored with human affairs. **world-wide** ● *adjective* occurring or known in all parts of the world. ● *adverb* throughout the world.

■ *noun* **1** earth, globe, planet. **8** area, circle, domain, field, milieu, sphere.

worldly *adjective* (**-ier**, **-iest**) **1** temporal, earthly. **2** experienced in life; sophisticated, practical. **3** devoted to pursuit of wealth, pleasure, etc.; materialistic. □ **worldly-wise** prudent in one's dealings with world.

■ **1** earthly, fleshly, human, material, mundane, physical, profane, secular, temporal. **3** avaricious, covetous, greedy, materialistic, selfish.

worm /wɜːm/ *noun* **1** any of several types of creeping invertebrate animal with long slender body and no limbs. **2** larva of insect. **3** (in *plural*) internal parasites. **4** insignificant or contemptible person. **5** spiral of screw. ● *verb* **1** crawl, wriggle. **2** (**worm oneself**) insinuate oneself (into favour etc.). **3** (+ *out*) obtain (secret etc.) by cunning persistence. **4** rid (dog etc.) of worms. □ **worm-cast** convoluted mass of earth left on surface by burrowing earthworm. **wormeaten 1** eaten into by worms. **2** decayed, dilapidated.

■ *verb* **1** crawl, creep, slither, squirm, wriggle, writhe.

wormwood /'wɜːmwʊd/ *noun* **1** plant with bitter aromatic taste. **2** bitter humiliation. **3** source of this.

wormy *adjective* (**-ier**, **-iest**) **1** full of worms. **2** wormeaten.

worn *past participle* of WEAR. ● *adjective* **1** damaged by use or wear. **2** looking tired and exhausted.

■ *adjective* **1** frayed, moth-eaten, old, ragged, *colloquial* scruffy, shabby, tattered, *colloquial* tatty, thin, threadbare, worn out. **2** see WEARY *adjective* 1.

worry /'wʌrɪ/ *verb* (**-ies**, **-ied**) **1** be anxious. **2** harass, importune; be trouble or anxiety to. **3** shake or pull about with teeth. **4** (as **worried** *adjective*) uneasy. ● *noun* (*plural* **-ies**) **1** thing that causes anxiety or disturbs tranquillity. **2** disturbed state of mind; anxiety. □ **worry beads** string of beads manipulated with fingers to occupy or calm oneself. □ **worrier** *noun*.

■ *verb* **1** agonize, be anxious, brood, feel uneasy, fidget, fret. **2** agitate, annoy, badger, bother, disquiet, distress, disturb, exercise, harass, *colloquial* hassle, importune, irritate, molest, nag, perplex, perturb, pester, *colloquial* plague, tease, threaten, torment, trouble, upset, vex. **4** (**worried**) afraid, agitated, agonized, alarmed, anxious, apprehensive, bothered, concerned, distraught, distressed, disturbed, edgy, fearful, fraught, fretful, insecure, nervous, *colloquial* nervy, neurotic, obsessed, on edge, overwrought, perplexed, perturbed, tense, troubled, uncertain, uneasy, unhappy, upset, vexed. ● *noun* **1** affliction, annoyance, bother, burden, care, concern, misgiving, problem, trial, tribulation, trouble, vexation. **2** agitation, anxiety, apprehension, disquiet, distress, fear, neurosis, perplexity, perturbation, tension, unease, uneasiness.

worse /wɜːs/ *adjective* **1** more bad. **2** in or into worse health or worse condition. ● *adverb* **1** more badly. **2** more ill. ● *noun* **1** worse thing(s). **2 (the worse)** worse condition. □ **the worse for wear 1** damaged by use. **2** injured. **worse off** in a worse (esp. financial) position. □ **worsen** *verb*.

■ □ **worsen** aggravate, decline, degenerate, deteriorate, exacerbate, fail, heighten, increase, intensify, weaken.

worship /'wɜːʃɪp/ *noun* **1** homage or service to deity. **2** acts, rites, or ceremonies of this. **3** adoration, devotion. **4 (His, Her, Your Worship)** *title used of or to mayor, magistrate, etc.* ● *verb* **(-pp-;** *US* **-p-) 1** adore as divine; honour with religious rites. **2** idolize. **3** attend public worship. **4** be full of adoration. □ **worshipper** *noun*.

■ *noun* **1, 2** adoration, adulation, deification, devotion, glorification, homage, idolatry, love, praise, reverence, veneration. ● *verb* **1, 2** admire, adore, adulate, be devoted to, deify, dote on, exalt, extol, glorify, hero-worship, idolize, kneel before, laud, lionize, look up to, love, *archaic* magnify, pay homage to, praise, pray to, put on a pedestal, revere, reverence, venerate.

worshipful *adjective* (also **Worshipful**) *archaic* honourable, distinguished (esp. in old titles of companies or officers).

worst /wɜːst/ *adjective* most bad. ● *adverb* most badly. ● *noun* worst part or possibility. ● *verb* get the better of; defeat. □ **at (the) worst** in the worst possible case. **do your worst** *expression of defiance*. **get the worst of it** be defeated. **if the worst comes to the worst** if the worst happens.

worsted /'wʊstɪd/ *noun* **1** fine woollen yarn. **2** fabric made from this.

wort /wɜːt/ *noun* infusion of malt before it is fermented into beer.

worth /wɜːθ/ *adjective* **1** of value equivalent to. **2** such as to justify or repay. **3** possessing property equivalent to. ● *noun* **1** value. **2** equivalent of money etc. in commodity etc. □ **worth it** (*colloquial*), **worth (one's) while**, **worthwhile** worth the time or effort spent; of value or importance.

■ *noun* **1** benefit, cost, good, importance, merit, price, quality, significance, use, usefulness, utility, value. □ **worthwhile** advantageous, beneficial, enriching, fruitful, fulfilling, gainful, gratifying, helpful, important, invaluable, meaningful, productive, profitable, remunerative, rewarding, satisfying, significant, useful, valuable, worthy.

worthless *adjective* without value or merit. □ **worthlessness** *noun*.

■ *archaic* bootless, dispensable, disposable, frivolous, futile, good-for-nothing, hollow, insignificant, meaningless, meretricious, paltry, pointless, poor, rubbishy, *esp. US* trashy, trifling, trivial, trumpery, unimportant, unproductive, unprofitable, unusable, useless, vain, valueless.

worthy /'wɜːðɪ/ *adjective* **(-ier, -iest) 1** deserving respect; estimable. **2** entitled to recognition. **3** (usually + *of*) deserving. **4** (+ *of*) adequate or suitable for the dignity etc. of. ● *noun* (*plural* **-ies**) **1** worthy person. **2** person of some distinction. □ **worthiness** *noun*.

■ *adjective* **1, 2** admirable, commendable, creditable, decent, deserving, estimable, good, honourable, laudable, meritorious, praiseworthy, reputable, respectable, worthwhile.

would *auxiliary verb* (*3rd singular present* **would**) **1** *used in reported speech or to form conditional mood.* **2** *expressing habitual past action, request as question, or probability.* □ **would-be** desiring or aspiring to be.

wouldn't /'wʊd(ə)nt/ would not.

wound[1] /wuːnd/ *noun* **1** injury done by cut or blow etc. to living tissue. **2** pain inflicted on feelings; injury to reputation. ● *verb* inflict wound on.

■ *noun* **1** bite, cut, damage, gash, graze, hurt, injury, laceration, lesion, mutilation, puncture, scar, scratch, sore, stab, sting, trauma, weal, welt. **2** blow, distress, hurt, injury, mortification, pain, slight, trauma. ● *verb* bite, claw, cut, damage, gash, gore, graze, harm, hit, hurt, impale, injure, knife, lacerate, maim, mangle, maul, mutilate, pain, scratch, shoot, stab, sting, torture, traumatize.

wound[2] *past & past participle* of WIND[2]. □ **wound up** excited; tense; angry.

wove *past* of WEAVE[1].

woven *past participle* of WEAVE[1].

wow /waʊ/ *interjection: expressing astonishment or admiration.* ● *noun slang* sensational success. ● *verb slang* impress greatly.

WP *abbreviation* word processor.

WPC *abbreviation* woman police constable.

w.p.m. *abbreviation* words per minute.

WRAC *abbreviation historical* Women's Royal Army Corps.

wrack *noun* **1** seaweed cast up or growing on seashore. **2** destruction.

WRAF *abbreviation historical* Women's Royal Air Force.

wraith /reɪθ/ *noun* **1** ghost. **2** spectral appearance of living person supposed to portend that person's death.

wrangle /'ræŋg(ə)l/ *noun* noisy argument or dispute. ● *verb* **(-ling)** engage in wrangle.

wrap *verb* **(-pp-) 1** (often + *up*) envelop in folded or soft encircling material. **2** (+ *round*, *about*) arrange or draw (pliant covering) round (person). ● *noun* **1** shawl, scarf, etc.; wrapper. **2** *esp. US* wrapping material. □ **take the wraps off** disclose. **under wraps** in secrecy. **wraparound**, **wrapround 1** (esp. of clothing) designed to wrap round. **2** curving round at edges. **wrap-over** ● *adjective* (of garment) overlapping when worn. ● *noun* such garment. **wrapped up in** engrossed or absorbed in. **wrap up 1** *colloquial* finish off (matter). **2** put on warm clothes.

■ *verb* **1** bind, bundle up, cloak, cocoon, conceal, cover, do up, encase, enclose, enfold, enshroud, envelop, hide, insulate, lag, muffle, pack, package, shroud, surround, swaddle, swathe, wind. ● *noun* **1** cape, cloak, mantle, poncho, shawl, stole, wrapper.

wrapper *noun* **1** cover for sweet, book, posted newspaper, etc. **2** loose enveloping robe or gown.

wrapping *noun* (esp. in *plural*) material used to wrap; wraps, wrappers. □ **wrapping paper** strong or decorative paper for wrapping parcels.

wrasse /ræs/ *noun* (*plural* same or **-s**) brilliant-coloured edible sea fish.

wrath /rɒθ/ *noun literary* extreme anger. □ **wrathful** *adjective*.

wreak *verb* **1** (usually + *upon*) give play to (vengeance etc.). **2** cause (damage etc.).

wreath /riːθ/ *noun* (*plural* **-s** /riːðz/) **1** flowers or leaves wound together into ring, esp. as ornament for head or door or for laying on grave etc. **2** curl or ring of smoke, cloud, or soft fabric.

wreathe /riːð/ *verb* (**-thing**) **1** encircle (as) with or like wreath. **2** (+ *round*) wind (one's arms etc.) round (person etc.). **3** move in wreaths. **4** twist (flowers etc.) into wreath.

■ **1** adorn, decorate, encircle, festoon. **4** intertwine, interweave, twine, twist, weave.

wreck *noun* **1** sinking or running aground of ship. **2** ship that has suffered wreck. **3** destruction, ruin. **4** greatly damaged building, thing, or person. ● *verb* **1** seriously damage (vehicle etc.). **2** ruin (hopes etc.). **3** cause wreck of (ship).

■ *noun* **2** hulk, shipwreck, wreckage. **3** demolition, destruction, devastation, loss, obliteration, overthrow, ruin, termination, undoing. ● *verb* **1** annihilate, break up, crumple, crush, dash to pieces, demolish, destroy, devastate, ruin, shatter, smash, write off. **2** annihilate, crush, dash, demolish, destroy, ruin, shatter, smash, spoil. **3** capsize, founder, scuttle, sink, shipwreck.

wreckage *noun* **1** wrecked material. **2** remnants of wreck. **3** act of wrecking.

■ **1, 2** bits, debris, flotsam and jetsam, fragments, pieces, remains, rubble, ruins.

wrecker *noun* person or thing that wrecks or destroys, esp. (*historical*) person who tries from shore to bring about shipwreck for plunder or profit.

Wren *noun historical* member of former Women's Royal Naval Service.

wren *noun* small usually brown short-winged songbird.

wrench *noun* **1** violent twist or oblique pull or tearing off. **2** tool for gripping and turning nuts etc. **3** painful uprooting or parting etc. ● *verb* **1** twist or pull violently round or sideways. **2** (often + *off*, *away*, etc.) pull with wrench. **3** injure (limb etc.) by wrenching.

■ *verb* **1, 2** force, jerk, lever, prize, pull, rip, tear, tug, twist, wrest, wring, *colloquial* yank. **3** rick, sprain, strain, twist.

wrest *verb* **1** wrench away from person's grasp. **2** (+ *from*) obtain by effort or with difficulty.

wrestle /'res(ə)l/ *noun* **1** contest in which two opponents grapple and try to throw each other to ground. **2** hard struggle. ● *verb* (**-ling**) **1** have wrestling match. **2** (often + *with*) struggle. **3** (+ *with*) do one's utmost to deal with. □ **wrestler** *noun*.

■ *verb* battle, contend, fight, grapple, strive, struggle, tussle.

wretch *noun* **1** unfortunate or pitiable person. **2** reprehensible person.

■ **1** beggar, down-and-out, pauper, unfortunate. **2** see VILLAIN 1.

wretched /'retʃɪd/ *adjective* (**-er**, **-est**) **1** unhappy, miserable. **2** unwell. **3** of bad quality; contemptible. **4** unsatisfactory, displeasing. □ **wretchedly** *adverb*. **wretchedness** *noun*.

■ **1** dejected, depressed, dispirited, downhearted, hapless, melancholy, miserable, pathetic, pitiable, pitiful, sad, unfortunate. **3, 4** see UNSATISFACTORY.

wriggle /'rɪg(ə)l/ *verb* (**-ling**) **1** twist or turn body with short writhing movements. **2** make wriggling motions. **3** (+ *along*, *through*, etc.) go thus. **4** be evasive. ● *noun* wriggling movement. □ **wriggly** *adjective*.

■ *verb* **1, 2** squirm, twist, *colloquial* wiggle, writhe. **3** crawl, snake, worm, zigzag.

wring *verb* (*past & past participle* **wrung**) **1** squeeze tightly. **2** (often + *out*) squeeze and twist, esp. to remove liquid. **3** break by twisting. **4** distress, torture. **5** extract by squeezing. **6** (+ *out*, *from*) obtain by pressure or importunity. ● *noun* act of wringing. □ **wringing (wet)** so wet that water can be wrung out. **wring one's hands** clasp them as gesture of grief. **wring the neck of** kill (chicken etc.) by twisting neck.

■ *verb* **1** clasp, compress, crush, grip, press, squeeze. **6** coerce, exact, extort, extract, force.

wringer *noun* device for wringing water from washed clothes etc.

wrinkle /'rɪŋk(ə)l/ *noun* **1** crease in skin or other flexible surface. **2** *colloquial* useful hint; clever expedient. ● *verb* (**-ling**) **1** make wrinkles in. **2** form wrinkles. □ **wrinkled** *adjective*. **wrinkly** *adjective* (**-ier**, **-iest**).

■ *noun* **1** corrugation, crease, crinkle, crow's-foot, dimple, fold, furrow, gather, line, pleat, pucker, ridge, ripple. ● *verb* corrugate, crease, crinkle, crumple, fold, furrow, gather, pleat, pucker up, ridge, ripple, ruck up, rumple, screw up. □ **wrinkled** corrugated, creased, crinkly, crumpled, furrowed, lined, pleated, ridged, rumpled, screwed up, shrivelled, undulating, wavy, wizened, wrinkly.

wrist *noun* **1** joint connecting hand and forearm. **2** part of garment covering wrist. □ **wrist-watch** small watch worn on strap etc. round wrist.

wristlet *noun* band or ring to strengthen, guard, or adorn wrist.

writ *noun* formal written court order to do or not do specified act.

write *verb* (**-ting**; *past* **wrote**; *past participle* **written** /'rɪt(ə)n/) **1** mark paper or other surface with symbols, letters, or words. **2** form or mark (such symbols etc.). **3** form or mark symbols of (word, document, etc.). **4** fill or complete with writing. **5** put (data) into computer store. **6** (esp. in *passive*) indicate (quality or condition) by appearance. **7** compose for reproduction or publication. **8** (usually + *to*) write and send letter. **9** convey (news etc.) by letter. **10** state in book etc. **11** (+ *into, out of*) include or exclude (character, episode) in or from story. □ **write down** record in writing. **write in** send suggestion etc. in writing, esp. to broadcasting station. **write off 1** cancel (debt etc.). **2** acknowledge as lost. **3** completely destroy. **4** (+ *for*) order or request by post. **write-off** *noun* thing written off, esp. vehicle etc. so damaged as not to be worth repair. **write up** write full account of. **write-up** *noun* written or published account; review.

■ **1, 2** inscribe, pen, print, scrawl, scribble. **3** copy, draft, draw up, jot down, note, put in writing, record, set down, take down, transcribe. **7** compile, compose. **8** correspond, *formal or jocular* indite, pen, send. □ **write off 1** see CANCEL 1. **3** DESTROY 1.

writer *noun* person who writes, esp. author. □ **writer's cramp** muscular spasm due to excessive writing.

■ amanuensis, author, clerk, columnist, contributor, copyist, correspondent, dramatist, essayist, hack, journalist, librettist, novelist, *colloquial derogatory* pen-pusher, playwright, poet, reporter, *colloquial* scribe, scriptwriter, wordsmith.

writhe /raɪð/ *verb* (**-thing**) **1** twist or roll oneself about (as) in acute pain. **2** suffer mental torture.

■ **1** coil, contort, jerk, squirm, struggle, thrash about, twist, wriggle.

writing *noun* **1** written words etc. **2** handwriting. **3** literary composition. **4** (usually in *plural*) writer's works. □ **in writing** in written form. **the writing on the wall** ominously significant event etc. **writing pad** pad of paper for drawing on.

■ **1** characters, cuneiform, hieroglyphs, inscription, letters, notation, runes. **2** calligraphy, copperplate, handwriting, longhand, penmanship, printing, scrawl, scribble, script, shorthand. **3** authorship, belles-lettres, composition, journalism, letters, literature. **4** article, book, composition, document, essay, letter, manuscript, opus, publication, text, typescript, work; (*writings*) correspondence, literature, poetry, prose.

written *past participle* of WRITE. ● *adjective* recorded in symbols, letters, words, etc. on paper or other surface.

■ *adjective* documentary, in black and white, inscribed, in writing, set down, transcribed, typewritten.

WRNS *abbreviation historical* Women's Royal Naval Service.

wrong *adjective* **1** mistaken; not true; in error.

2 unsuitable; less or least desirable. **3** contrary to law or morality. **4** amiss; out of order. ● *adverb* in wrong manner or direction; with incorrect result. ● *noun* **1** what is morally wrong. **2** unjust action. ● *verb* **1** treat unjustly. **2** mistakenly attribute bad motives to. □ **do wrong** behave immorally or illegally; sin. **get wrong** misunderstand (person, statement, etc). **go wrong 1** take wrong path. **2** stop functioning properly. **3** depart from virtuous behaviour. **in the wrong** responsible for quarrel, mistake, or offence. **wrongdoer** person who behaves immorally or illegally. **wrongdoing** *noun*. **wrong-foot** *colloquial* catch off balance or unprepared. **wrong-headed** perverse and obstinate. **wrong side** worse or undesirable or unusable side. **wrong way round** in opposite of normal orientation or sequence. □ **wrongly** *adverb*. **wrongness** *noun*.

■ *adjective* **1** erroneous, fallacious, false, imprecise, improper, inaccurate, incorrect, inexact, misinformed, mistaken, specious, unfounded, untrue. **2** ill-advised, ill-considered, ill-judged, impolitic, imprudent, inappropriate, incongruous, inconvenient, injudicious, misguided, misjudged, unacceptable, undesirable, unhelpful, unsound, unsuitable, unwise. **3** bad, base, blameworthy, corrupt, criminal, *colloquial* crooked, deceitful, dishonest, dishonourable, evil, felonious, illegal, illegitimate, illicit, immoral, iniquitous, irresponsible, mendacious, reprehensible, sinful, unethical, unfair, unjust, unjustifiable, unlawful, unprincipled, unscrupulous, vicious, villainous, wicked, wrongful. **4** abnormal, amiss, bad, broken down, defective, faulty, out of order, unusable. ● *verb* **1** abuse, be unfair to, cheat, damage, harm, hurt, ill-treat, injure, maltreat, mistreat. **2** do an injustice to, malign, misrepresent, traduce. □ **do wrong** see MISBEHAVE. **wrongdoer** *esp. historical* convict, criminal, *colloquial* crook, culprit, delinquent, evildoer, lawbreaker, malefactor, mischief-maker, miscreant, offender, sinner, transgressor. **wrongdoing** crime, delinquency, disobedience, evil, immorality, indiscipline, iniquity, malpractice, misbehaviour, mischief, naughtiness, offence, sin, sinfulness, wickedness.

wrongful *adjective* unwarranted, unjustified. □ **wrongfully** *adverb*.

wrote *past* of WRITE.

wroth /rəʊθ/ *adjective archaic* angry.

wrought /rɔːt/ *archaic past & past participle* of WORK. □ **wrought iron** form of iron suitable for forging or rolling; not cast.

wrung *past & past participle* of WRING.

WRVS *abbreviation* Women's Royal Voluntary Service.

wry /raɪ/ *adjective* (**-er, -est**) **1** distorted; turned to one side. **2** contorted in disgust, disappointment, or mockery. **3** (of humour) dry and mocking. □ **wryneck** small woodpecker able to turn head over shoulder. □ **wryly** *adverb*. **wryness** *noun*.

■ **1** askew, aslant, awry, bent, contorted, crooked, deformed, distorted, lopsided, twisted, uneven. **2** contorted, crooked, twisted. **3** droll, dry, ironic, mocking, sardonic.

WSW *abbreviation* west-south-west.

wt *abbreviation* weight.

wych hazel /wɪtʃ/ witch hazel.

WYSIWYG /'wɪzɪwɪg/ *adjective: indicating that text on computer screen and printout correspond exactly (what you see is what you get).*

X[1] *noun* (also **x**) **1** (Roman numeral) 10. **2** first unknown quantity in algebra. **3** unknown or unspecified number, person, etc. **4** cross-shaped symbol, esp. used to indicate position or incorrectness, to symbolize kiss or vote, or as signature of person who cannot write. □ **X-ray** *noun* **1** electromagnetic radiation of short wavelength able to pass through opaque bodies. **2** photograph made by X-rays. ● *verb* photograph, examine, or treat with X-rays.

X[2] *adjective* (of film) classified as suitable for adults only.

xenophobe /'zenəfəʊb/ *noun* person given to xenophobia. ● *adjective* characteristic of a xenophobe; xenophobic.

xenophobia /zenə'fəʊbɪə/ *noun* hatred or fear of foreigners. □ **xenophobic** *adjective*.

Xerox /'zɪərɒks/ *noun proprietary term* **1** type of photocopier. **2** copy made by it. ● *verb* (**xerox**) make Xerox of.

Xmas /'krɪsməs, 'eksməs/ *noun colloquial* Christmas.

xylophone /'zaɪləfəʊn/ *noun* musical instrument of graduated wooden or metal bars struck with small wooden hammers.

Yy

Y *noun* (also **y**) **1** second unknown quantity in algebra. **2** Y-shaped thing.

yacht /jɒt/ *noun* **1** light sailing vessel for racing or cruising. **2** larger usually power-driven vessel for cruising. ● *verb* race or cruise in yacht. □ **yachtsman**, **yachtswoman** person who yachts.

yah /jɑː/ *interjection: expressing derision, defiance, etc.*

yahoo /jɑːˈhuː/ *noun* bestial person.

Yahweh /ˈjɑːweɪ/ *noun* Jehovah.

yak *noun* long-haired Tibetan ox.

yam *noun* **1** tropical or subtropical climbing plant. **2** edible starchy tuberous root of this. **3** *US* sweet potato.

yang *noun* (in Chinese philosophy) active male principle of universe (compare YIN).

Yank *noun colloquial often derogatory* American.

yank *verb & noun colloquial* pull with jerk.

Yankee /ˈjæŋkɪ/ *noun colloquial* **1** Yank. **2** *US* inhabitant of New England or of northern States.

yap *verb* (**-pp-**) **1** bark shrilly or fussily. **2** *colloquial* talk noisily, foolishly, or complainingly. ● *noun* sound of yapping.

yard¹ *noun* **1** unit of linear measure (3 ft, 0.9144 m.). **2** this length of material. **3** square or cubic yard. **4** spar slung across mast for sail to hang from. **5** (in *plural*; + *of*) *colloquial* a great length. □ **yard-arm** either end of ship's yard. **yardstick** **1** standard of comparison. **2** rod a yard long usually divided into inches etc.

yard² *noun* **1** piece of enclosed ground, esp. attached to building or used for particular purpose. **2** *US & Australian* garden of house.
■ **1** court, courtyard, enclosure, *colloquial* quad, quadrangle.

yardage *noun* number of yards of material etc.

yarmulke /ˈjɑːməlkə/ *noun* (also **yarmulka**) skullcap worn by Jewish men.

yarn *noun* **1** spun thread for weaving, knitting, etc. **2** *colloquial* story, traveller's tale, anecdote. ● *verb colloquial* tell yarns.
■ *noun* **1** fibre, strand, thread. **2** account, anecdote, fiction, narrative, story, tale.

yarrow /ˈjærəʊ/ *noun* perennial plant, esp. milfoil.

yashmak /ˈjæʃmæk/ *noun* veil concealing face except eyes, worn by some Muslim women.

yaw *verb* (of ship, aircraft, etc.) fail to hold straight course; go unsteadily. ● *noun* yawing of ship etc. from course.

yawl *noun* **1** kind of sailing boat. **2** small fishing boat.

yawn *verb* **1** open mouth wide and inhale, esp. when sleepy or bored. **2** (often as **yawning** *adjective*) gape; be wide open. ● *noun* act of yawning.
■ *verb* **2** (**yawning**) gaping, open, wide.

yaws /jɔːz/ *plural noun* (usually treated as *singular*) contagious tropical skin disease.

yd *abbreviation* (*plural* **yds**) yard (measure).

ye /jiː/ *pronoun archaic* (as subject of verb) you (plural).

yea /jeɪ/ *archaic adverb* yes. ● *noun* 'yes' vote.

yeah /jeə/ *adverb colloquial* yes.

year /jɪə/ *noun* **1** time occupied by one revolution of earth round sun, approx. 365¼ days. **2** period from 1 Jan. to 31 Dec. inclusive. **3** period of 12 calendar months. **4** (in *plural*) age, time of life. **5** (usually in *plural*) *colloquial* very long time. □ **yearbook** annual publication bringing information on some subject up to date.

yearling *noun* animal between one and two years old.

yearly *adjective* **1** done, produced, or occurring once every year. **2** of or lasting a year. ● *adverb* once every year.
■ *adjective* **1** annual.

yearn /jɜːn/ *verb* be filled with longing, compassion, or tenderness. □ **yearning** *noun & adjective*.
■ ache, desire, hanker, have a craving, hunger, itch, long, pine, want.

yeast *noun* greyish-yellow fungus, got esp. from fermenting malt liquors and used as fermenting agent, to raise bread, etc.

yeasty *adjective* (**-ier**, **-iest**) **1** frothy. **2** in ferment. **3** working like yeast.

yell *noun* **1** sharp loud cry. **2** shout. ● *verb* cry, shout.

yellow /ˈjeləʊ/ *adjective* **1** of the colour of lemons, buttercups, etc. **2** having yellow skin or complexion. **3** *colloquial* cowardly. ● *noun* yellow colour, paint, clothes, etc. ● *verb* turn yellow. □ **yellow-belly** *colloquial* coward. **yellow card** card shown by referee to football-player being cautioned. **yellow fever** tropical virus fever with jaundice etc. **yellowhammer** bunting of which male has yellow head, neck, and breast. **Yellow Pages** *proprietary term* telephone directory on yellow paper, listing and classifying business subscribers. **yellow streak** *colloquial* trace of cowardice. □ **yellowish** *adjective*. **yellowness** *noun*. **yellowy** *adjective*.

■ *adjective* **1** chrome, cream, gold, golden, lemon, orange.

yelp *noun* sharp shrill bark or cry as of dog in excitement or pain. ● *verb* utter yelp.

yen[1] *noun* (*plural* same) chief monetary unit of Japan.

yen[2] *colloquial noun* intense desire or longing. ● *verb* (**-nn-**) feel longing.

yeoman /ˈjəʊmən/ *noun* **1** *esp. historical* man holding and farming small estate. **2** member of yeomanry force. □ **Yeoman of the Guard** member of bodyguard of English sovereign.

yeomanry *noun* (*plural* **-ies**) **1** group of yeomen. **2** *historical* volunteer cavalry force in British army.

yes *adverb* **1** *indicating affirmative reply to question, statement, request, command, etc.* **2** (**yes?**) indeed?, is that so? **3** (**yes?**) what do you want? ● *noun* utterance of word yes. □ **yes-man** *colloquial* weakly acquiescent person.

yesterday /ˈjestədeɪ/ *adverb* on the day before today. ● *noun* the day before today.

yesteryear /ˈjestəjɪə/ *noun archaic* or *rhetorical* **1** last year. **2** the recent past.

yet *adverb* **1** up to now or then. **2** (with negative or in questions) so soon as, or by, now or then. **3** again; in addition. **4** in the remaining time available. **5** (+ *comparative*) even. **6** nevertheless. ● *conjunction* but nevertheless.

yeti /ˈjetɪ/ *noun* supposed manlike or bearlike Himalayan animal.

yew *noun* **1** dark-leaved evergreen coniferous tree. **2** its wood.

YHA *abbreviation* Youth Hostels Association.

Yiddish /ˈjɪdɪʃ/ *noun* language used by Jews in or from Europe. ● *adjective* of this language.

yield /jiːld/ *verb* **1** produce or return as fruit, profit, or result. **2** concede, give up. **3** (often + *to*) surrender, submit, defer. **4** (as **yielding** *adjective*) soft and pliable. **5** (as **yielding** *adjective*) submissive. **6** (+ *to*) give right of way to. ● *noun* amount yielded or produced.

■ *verb* **1** bear, earn, generate, pay out, produce, provide, return, supply. **2** *formal* cede, concede, give up, relinquish, surrender. **3** acquiesce, agree, assent, bow, capitulate, cave in, comply, defer, give in, give way, knuckle under, submit, succumb, surrender, throw in the towel. **4** (**yielding**) see FLEXIBLE 1, SPONGY. **5** (**yielding**) see SUBMISSIVE. ● *noun* crop, earnings, gain, harvest, income, interest, output, proceeds, produce, product, profit, return, revenue.

yin *noun* (in Chinese philosophy) passive female principle of universe (compare YANG).

yippee /jɪˈpiː/ *interjection: expressing delight or excitement.*

YMCA *abbreviation* Young Men's Christian Association.

yob /jɒb/ *noun* (also **yobbo**, *plural* **-s**) *slang* lout, hooligan. □ **yobbish** *adjective*.

yodel /ˈjəʊd(ə)l/ *verb* (**-ll-**; *US* **-l-**) sing with melodious inarticulate sounds and frequent changes between falsetto and normal voice, in manner of Swiss mountain-dwellers. ● *noun* yodelling cry.

yoga /ˈjəʊgə/ *noun* **1** Hindu system of meditation and asceticism. **2** system of physical exercises and breathing control used in yoga.

yoghurt /ˈjɒgət/ *noun* (also **yogurt**) rather sour semi-solid food made from milk fermented by added bacteria.

yogi /ˈjəʊgɪ/ *noun* (*plural* **-s**) devotee of yoga.

yoke *noun* **1** wooden crosspiece fastened over necks of two oxen etc. and attached to plough or wagon to be pulled. **2** (*plural* same or **-s**) pair (of oxen etc.). **3** object like yoke in form or function, e.g. wooden shoulder-piece for carrying pair of pails, top part of garment from which rest hangs. **4** sway, dominion; servitude. **5** bond of union, esp. of marriage. ● *verb* (**-king**) **1** put yoke on. **2** couple or unite (pair). **3** link (one thing) to (another). **4** match or work together.

yokel /ˈjəʊk(ə)l/ *noun* country bumpkin.

yolk /jəʊk/ *noun* yellow inner part of egg.

Yom Kippur /jɒm ˈkɪpə/ *noun* most solemn religious fast day of Jewish year; Day of Atonement.

yon *adjective* & *adverb literary* & *dialect* yonder.

yonder /ˈjɒndə/ *adverb* over there; at some distance in that direction; in place indicated. ● *adjective* situated yonder.

yore *noun literary* □ **of yore** formerly; of long ago.

york *verb Cricket* bowl out with yorker.

yorker *noun Cricket* ball that pitches immediately under bat.

Yorkist /ˈjɔːkɪst/ *noun historical* follower of House of York, esp. in Wars of the Roses. ● *adjective* of House of York.

Yorkshire pudding /ˈjɔːkʃə/ *noun* baked batter usually eaten with roast beef.

Yorkshire terrier /jɔːkʃə/ *noun* small longhaired blue and tan kind of terrier.

you /juː/ *pronoun* **1** the person(s) or thing(s) addressed. **2** one, a person.

you'd /juːd/ **1** you had. **2** you would.

you'll /juːl/ you will; you shall.

young /jʌŋ/ *adjective* (**younger** /ˈjʌŋgə/, **youngest** /ˈjʌŋgɪst/) **1** not far advanced in life, development, or existence; not yet old. **2** immature, inexperienced. **3** youthful; of or characteristic of youth. ● *noun* offspring, esp. of animals. □ **youngish** *adjective*.

■ *adjective* **1** adolescent, baby, early, growing, immature, juvenile, new, newborn, pubescent, teenage, under age, undeveloped, unfledged, youngish, youthful. **2** babyish, boyish, callow, childish, girlish, green, immature, inexperienced, infantile, *often derogatory* juvenile, naive, puerile, unfledged. **3** see YOUTHFUL. ● *noun* babies, brood, children, family, issue, litter, offspring, progeny.

youngster *noun* child; young person.

your /jɔː/ *adjective* of or belonging to you.

you're /jɔː/ you are.

yours /jɔːz/ *pronoun* the one(s) belonging to you.

yourself /jɔːˈself/ *pronoun* (*plural* **yourselves**): *emphatic and reflexive form of* YOU.

youth /juːθ/ *noun* (*plural* **-s** /juːðz/) **1** being young; early part of life, esp. adolescence. **2** quality or condition characteristic of the young. **3** young man. **4** (treated as *plural*) young people collectively. □ **youth club** place for young people's leisure activities. **youth hostel** any of chain of cheap lodgings where (esp. young) holidaymakers can stay for the night.

■ **1** adolescence, babyhood, boyhood, childhood, girlhood, growing up, immaturity, infancy, minority, pubescence, salad days, teens. **3** adolescent, boy, juvenile, *colloquial* kid, lad, minor, stripling, teenager, youngster.

youthful *adjective* young or still having characteristics of youth. □ **youthfulness** *noun*.

■ fresh, lively, sprightly, vigorous, well preserved, young, young-looking.

you've /juːv/ you have.

yowl /jaʊl/ *noun* loud wailing cry (as) of cat or dog in distress. ● *verb* utter yowl.

yo-yo /ˈjəʊjəʊ/ *noun* (*plural* **yo-yos**) toy consisting of pair of discs with deep groove between

them in which string is attached and wound, and which can be made to fall and rise.

yr. *abbreviation* **1** year(s). **2** younger. **3** your.

yrs. *abbreviation* **1** years. **2** yours.

YTS *abbreviation* Youth Training Scheme.

yuan /juːˈɑːn/ *noun* (*plural* same) chief monetary unit of China.

yucca /ˈjʌkə/ *noun* white-flowered plant with swordlike leaves, often grown as house plant.

yuck /jʌk/ *interjection* (also **yuk**) *slang: expression of strong distaste.*

yucky *adjective* (also **yukky**) (**-ier**, **-iest**) *slang* **1** messy, repellent. **2** sickly, sentimental.

Yugoslav /ˈjuːgəslɑːv/ *adjective* of Yugoslavia. ● *noun* native or national of former Yugoslavia. □ **Yugoslavian** /-ˈslɑːv-/ *adjective & noun.*

yuk = YUCK.

yukky = YUCKY.

yule *noun* (in full **yule-tide**) *archaic* festival of Christmas. □ **yule-log** large log burnt at Christmas.

yummy /ˈjʌmɪ/ *adjective* (**-ier**, **-iest**) *colloquial* tasty, delicious.

yuppie /ˈjʌpɪ/ *noun* (also **yuppy**) (*plural* **-ies**) *colloquial usually derogatory* young ambitious professional person working in city.

YWCA *abbreviation* Young Women's Christian Association.

Zz

zabaglione /zæbə'ljəʊnɪ/ *noun* Italian dessert of whipped and heated egg yolks, sugar, and wine.

zany /'zeɪnɪ/ *adjective* (**-ier**, **-iest**) comically idiotic; crazily ridiculous.
■ absurd, clownish, crazy, eccentric, idiotic, *slang* loony, mad, madcap, playful, ridiculous, silly, *slang* wacky.

zap *verb* (**-pp-**) *slang* **1** kill, destroy. **2** attack; hit hard.

zeal *noun* **1** fervour, eagerness. **2** hearty persistent endeavour. □ **zealous** /'zeləs/ *adjective*.
■ earnestness, enthusiasm, fervour. □ **zealous** conscientious, diligent, eager, earnest, enthusiastic, fervent, keen, passionate.

zealot /'zelət/ *noun* extreme partisan; fanatic.
■ bigot, extremist, fanatic, partisan, radical.

zebra /'zebrə, 'ziː-/ *noun* (*plural* same or **-s**) African black and white striped horselike animal. □ **zebra crossing** striped street-crossing where pedestrians have precedence.

Zeitgeist /'tsaɪtgaɪst/ *noun* spirit of times. [German]

Zen *noun* form of Buddhism emphasizing meditation and intuition.

zenith /'zenɪθ/ *noun* **1** point of heavens directly overhead. **2** highest point (of power, prosperity, etc.).
■ **2** acme, apex, apogee, climax, height, highest point, peak, pinnacle, summit, top.

zephyr /'zefə/ *noun literary* mild gentle breeze.

zero /'zɪərəʊ/ *noun* (*plural* **-s**) **1** figure 0, nought, nil. **2** point on scale of thermometer etc. from which positive or negative quantity is reckoned. **3** (in full **zero-hour**) hour at which planned, esp. military, operation is timed to begin. **4** (in full **zero-hour**) crucial moment. **5** lowest or earliest point. ● *adjective* no, not any. ● *verb* (**zeroes**, **zeroed**) adjust (instrument etc.) to zero. □ **zero in on 1** take aim at. **2** focus attention on. **zero-rated** on which no VAT is charged.
■ *noun* **1** archaic naught, nil, nothing, nought, *esp. US slang* zilch. □ **zero in on 1** see AIM *verb* 2.

zest *noun* **1** piquancy. **2** keen interest or enjoyment; relish, gusto. **3** outer layer of orange or lemon peel. □ **zestful** *adjective*.
■ **2** appetite, eagerness, energy, enjoyment, enthusiasm, exuberance, hunger, interest, liveliness, pleasure, thirst, zeal.

zigzag /'zɪgzæg/ *adjective* with abrupt alternate right and left turns. ● *noun* zigzag line; thing having sharp turns. ● *adverb* with zigzag manner or course. ● *verb* (**-gg-**) move in zigzag course.
■ *adjective* crooked, in and out, indirect, meandering, serpentine, twisting, winding. ● *verb* bend, curve, meander, snake, tack, twist, wind.

zilch *noun esp. US slang* nothing.

zillion /'zɪljən/ *noun* (*plural* same) *colloquial* **1** indefinite large number. **2** (**zillions**) very large number.

Zimmer frame /'zɪmə/ *noun proprietary term* kind of walking frame.

zinc *noun* greyish-white metallic element.

zing *colloquial noun* vigour, energy. ● *verb* move swiftly, esp. with shrill sound.

zinnia /'zɪnɪə/ *noun* garden plant with showy flowers.

zip *noun* **1** light sharp sound. **2** energy, vigour. **3** (in full **zip-fastener**) fastening device of two flexible strips with interlocking projections, closed or opened by sliding clip along them. ● *verb* (**-pp-**) **1** (often + *up*) fasten with zip-fastener. **2** move with zip or at high speed.

zipper *noun esp. US* zip-fastener.

zircon /'zɜːkən/ *noun* translucent varieties of zirconium silicate cut into gems.

zirconium /zə'kəʊnɪəm/ *noun* grey metallic element.

zit *noun esp. US slang* pimple.

zither /'zɪðə/ *noun* stringed instrument with flat soundbox, placed horizontally and played by plucking.

zloty /'zlɒtɪ/ *noun* (*plural* same or **-s**) chief monetary unit of Poland.

zodiac /'zəʊdɪæk/ *noun* belt of heavens including all apparent positions of sun, moon, and planets as known to ancient astronomers, and divided into 12 equal parts (**signs of the zodiac**).

zombie /'zɒmbɪ/ *noun* **1** corpse said to have been revived by witchcraft. **2** *colloquial* dull or apathetic person.

zone *noun* **1** area having particular features, properties, purpose, or use. **2** well-defined region of more or less beltlike form. **3** area between two concentric circles. **4** encircling band of colour etc. **5** *archaic* girdle, belt. ● *verb* (**-ning**) **1** encircle as or with zone. **2** arrange or distribute by zones. **3** assign as or to specific area. □ **zonal** *adjective*.
■ *noun* **1**, **2** area, belt, district, domain, locality, neighbourhood, province, quarter, region, *US* section, *Military* sector, sphere, territory, tract, vicinity.

zonked /zɒŋkt/ *adjective slang* (often + *out*) exhausted; intoxicated.

zoo *noun* zoological garden.

■ menagerie, safari park, zoological gardens.

zoological /zəʊə'lɒdʒɪk(ə)l, zuː-ə-/ *adjective* of zoology. ▫ **zoological garden(s)** public garden or park with collection of animals for exhibition and study.

USAGE See note at ZOOLOGY.

zoology /zəʊ'ɒlədʒɪ, zuː'ɒl-/ *noun* scientific study of animals. ▫ **zoologist** *noun*.

USAGE The second pronunciation given for *zoology*, *zoological*, and *zoologist* (with the first syllable pronounced as in *zoo*), although extremely common, is considered incorrect by some people.

zoom *verb* **1** move quickly, esp. with buzzing sound. **2** cause aeroplane to mount at high speed and steep angle. **3** (often + *in*, *in on*) (of camera) change rapidly from long shot to close-up (of). ● *noun* aeroplane's steep climb. ▫ **zoom lens** lens allowing camera to zoom by varying focal length.

■ *verb* **1** career, dart, dash, hurry, hurtle, race, rush, shoot, speed, whiz, zip.

zoophyte /'zəʊəfaɪt/ *noun* plantlike animal, esp. coral, sea anemone, or sponge.

zucchini /zuː'kiːnɪ/ *noun* (*plural* same or -s) *esp. US & Australian* courgette.

zygote /'zaɪɡəʊt/ *noun Biology* cell formed by union of two gametes.

Reverse Dictionary Supplement

Compiled by
David Edmonds

A

aardvark *alternative term*: ant bear
Aaron's beard *alternative term*: rose of Sharon
abalone *alternative term*: ear shell
abandoned child *alternative term*: foundling
abandonment *abandonment of claim etc.*: waiver
abbreviation *adjectives*: acrologic, acrological
abele *alternative term*: white poplar
abominable snowman *alternative term*: yeti
about *combining forms*: circum-, peri-
about to happen imminent, impending
about-turn volte-face
above *combining forms*: epi-, super-, supra-, sur-, trans-
absence without permission □ *French leave* □ *child absent without permission from school etc.*: truant
absolute power or dictatorship autocracy, despotism, totalitarianism
absurdity □ *absurd misrepresentation*: travesty □ *seemingly absurd but in fact true statement*: paradox □ *demonstration of a statement's absurdity by developing it to its logical conclusion*: reductio ad absurdum
academic □ *academic conference*: colloquium □ *academic thesis etc.*: dissertation
accent *Irish accent*: brogue
accepted *generally accepted, believed, etc.*: received
accessory fruit *technical term*: pseudocarp
account book ledger
across *combining forms*: dia-, trans-
acting □ *combining form*: pro- □ *person acting for absent etc. doctor*: locum □ *person acting for absent etc. monarch*: regent
actor □ *sardonic term for actor*: Thespian □ *bad actor*: ham □ *actor who has prepared another actor's role, in order to replace him if necessary*: understudy □ *actor who performs in silence*: mime
acupuncture *technical term*: stylostixis
acupressure *Japanese acupressure therapy*: shiatsu
addition □ *addition to will etc.*: codicil □ *addition to a collection etc.*: accession
additional □ *combining form*: epi- □ *additional charge*: surcharge □ *additional clause to a parliamentary bill, jury's verdict, or other document*: rider
address □ *address used as a collecting-point for mail*: accommodation address □ *address for a letter to be left at a post office until called for*: poste restante □ *African polite form of address to a man*:

bwana □ *Indian polite form of address to a man*: sahib □ *Turkish polite form of address to a man*: effendi
adjective □ *technical terms*: modifier, qualifier, determiner, attributive adjective, predicative adjective □ *abusive or disparaging adjective*: epithet
admiration *deserving admiration*: commendable, estimable, laudable, admirable, praiseworthy
admission □ *admission ritual to tribe etc.*: initiation □ *admission ceremony to university etc.*: matriculation □ *right of admission*: entrée, entry
adultery □ *man whose wife has committed adultery*: cuckold □ *person alleged in a divorce case to have committed adultery etc.*: respondent □ *person alleged in a divorce case to have committed adultery with the respondent*: co-respondent
advance *advance payment*: ante
adverb *technical term*: modifier, qualifier
advertisement □ *catchphrase used in an advertisement*: slogan □ *simple tune used in an advertisement*: jingle □ *large board to display advertisements*: hoarding □ *person who writes the text for advertisements*: copywriter □ *stick up unauthorized advertisements*: fly-post
adviser *influential but unofficial adviser(s) to a person in authority*: guru, kitchen cabinet
afraid of *combining form*: -phobe
after *combining forms*: epi-, post-
afterbrain *technical term*: myencephalon
afternoon □ *adjective*: postmeridian □ *afternoon sleep*: siesta □ *afternoon performance*: matinée
again *combining forms*: ana-, re-
against *combining forms*: anti-, contra-, counter-, ob-
agnail *alternative term*: hangnail
agreed □ *agreed by everyone*: unanimous □ *general agreement*: consensus
air □ *combining forms*: aero-, atmo-, pneum(o)- □ *adjective*: pneumatic
airship □ *technical term*: dirigible □ *German military airship used in First World War*: Zeppelin □ *cabin etc. suspended beneath an airship*: gondola
airsock *alternative term*: windsock
airtight *adjective*: hermetic
alcoholism □ *technical term*: dipsomania □ *delusions etc. caused by alcoholism*: delirium tremens
alfalfa *alternative term*: lucerne
all *combining forms*: omni-, pan-, panto-
allergy *medicine used to treat allergies*: antihistamine
alligator pear *alternative term*: avocado

all-in *alternative term*: freestyle

all-knowing *alternative term*: omniscient

all-powerful *alternative term*: omnipotent

all together *alternative terms*: en bloc, en masse

almond □ *adjective*: amygdalate □ *almond paste, used on cakes etc.*: marzipan □ *scald almonds to remove skin*: blanch □ *almond-shaped*: amygdaloid

alone *combining forms*: mon-, mono-, uni- □ *person who lives alone*: recluse

almost *combining form*: quasi-

alpine house chalet

altar □ *altar canopy*: baldacchino, ciborium □ *embroidered etc. hanging in front of altar*: frontal □ *sculpture etc. on wall behind altar*: reredos

altar boy *alternative terms*: acolyte, server

alternative energy *alternative term*: renewable energy

altitude sickness *alternative term*: mountain sickness

amenity bed *alternative term*: pay bed

American eagle *alternative term*: bald eagle

American Indian Amerindian, Native American, Red Indian

among *combining form*: inter-

among other things inter alia

amoretto *alternative term*: cherub, putto

ancient *combining forms*: archaeo-, palaeo-

angle □ *combining form*: -gon □ *instrument to measure or draw angles*: protractor, set square

aniline *technical term*: phenylamine

animal □ *combining forms*: theri-, zoo- □ *animals of a particular region*: fauna □ *animal used to pull carts, ploughs, etc.*: draught animal □ *animal used to carry loads*: beast of burden

ankh *alternative term*: crux ansata

ankle *ankle-covering, worn over shoe etc.*: gaiter, spat

ankle bones *technical terms*: astragalus, talus

annual ring *alternative term*: tree ring

anointing □ *ritual anointing for religious purposes*: unction □ *oil used for ritual anointing*: chrism

answer *witty answer that occurs to one after the opportunity to make it has gone*: esprit de l'escalier

ant □ *adjective*: formic □ *combining form*: myrmec(o)- □ *study of ants*: myrmecology

ant bear *alternative term*: aardvark

antidote *supposed antidote to all poisons*: mithridate

antique *alternative term*: object of virtu

antler □ *flat section of antler*: palm □ *prong of antler*: tine

anus □ *combining form*: proct(o)- □ *surgical construction of an artificial anus*: colostomy □ *muscle closing the anus*: sphincter

anvil *anvil in ear, technical term*: incus

apart *combining form*: dia-

ape *adjective*: simian

Aphrodite *Latin name*: Venus

appeal *litigant who appeals to a higher court*: appellant

appearance *combining form*: -phany

appendix □ *medical term*: vermiform appendix □ *surgical removal of appendix*: appendectomy

appetite *adjective*: orectic

appetizer □ *first course of a meal*: hors d'oeuvre, starter □ *small open sandwich etc. served as appetizer*: canapé □ *alcoholic drink taken before a meal as an appetizer*: aperitif

apple □ *apple brandy*: Calvados □ *apple of one's eye*: cynosure

approved school *official term*: community home

aquilegia columbine

Arab □ *Arab sailing boat*: dhow □ *Arab covered market*: souk □ *Arab quarter in town*: kasbah □ *Arab prince etc.*: emir, sheik □ *Arab cloak*: burnous, djellaba □ *Arab headdress*: keffiyeh

archer *astrological term*: sagittarius

Ares *Latin name*: Mars

argument *adjective*: eristic

arm □ *adjective*: brachial □ *arm of octopus etc.*: tentacle

armed forces *adjective*: military

armpit □ *adjective*: axillary □ *technical term*: axilla

around *combining forms*: amph-, circum-, epi-, peri-

arrogance *arrogance leading to one's downfall*: hubris

arrow □ *arrow for crossbow*: bolt, quarrel □ *case for arrows*: quiver

art *vulgar or sentimental art*: kitsch

Artemis *Latin name*: Diana

artery *hardening of the arteries, technical term*: arteriosclerosis

artist □ *artist's studio*: atelier □ *artist's complete output*: corpus, oeuvre

ash □ *adjectives*: cinerary, cinerous □ *container for cremated ashes*: urn

assumed name alias

Athena *Latin name*: Minerva

athlete's foot *technical term*: tinea pedis

atom smasher *technical term*: accelerator

attack *medical combining form*: -lepsy

autumn crocus meadow saffron

away *combining forms*: ap-, apo-, ec-, ex-

B

baby □ *set of clothes etc for a new-born baby*: layette □ *discourage a baby from breast-feeding*: wean □ *apparatus providing special environment for a premature baby*: incubator □ *abandoned baby of unknown parentage*: foundling □ *baby secretly substituted for another*: changeling

Bacchus □ *Greek name*: Dionysus □ *female follower of Bacchus*: Maenad □ *staff carried by Bacchus' followers*: thyrsus

back □ *combining forms*: dors-, not- □ *adjective*: dorsal □ *lying on one's back*: supine □ *back of a leaf of paper*: verso

back again *combining forms*: ana-, re-, retr(o)-

backbone □ *adjectives*: spinal, myeloid □ *technical term*: spinal column □ *having a backbone*: vertebrate □ *having no backbone*: invertebrate □ *joint of meat containing a backbone*: chine

back country *alternative terms*: hinterland, outback

bacon-and-eggs *alternative term*: bird's-foot trefoil

bad *combining forms*: caco-, dys-, mal-, mis-

bad breath *technical term*: halitosis

badger's burrow sett

bagpipes □ *pipe on bagpipes on which the tune is played*: chanter □ *pipe on bagpipes used to produce a continuous bass note*: drone

balance □ *adjective*: equilibrious □ *noun*: equilibrium □ *astrological term*: libra

ball *adjective*: globular, spherical

ball and socket joint *technical term*: enarthrosis

ballerina *ballerina's short skirt*: tutu

bandage *bandage etc. bound tight to stop the flow of blood*: tourniquet

barber *adjective*: tonsorial

barking deer muntjac

barrel □ *person who makes barrels*: cooper □ *plank from which barrels are made*: stave □ *metal band compressing a barrel's staves*: hoop □ *open a barrel*: broach

basket □ *basket for picnic food or laundry*: hamper □ *basket for strawberries etc.*: punnet □ *basket for garden vegetables*: trug □ *basket on a bicycle or donkey*: pannier

bastardy *heraldic indication of bastardy*: bend sinister

bath □ *adjective*: balneal □ *hot bath with underwater jets*: jacuzzi™ □ *steam bath*: Turkish bath □ *hot-air bath*: sauna

battle *the ultimate battle, or one causing huge destruction*: Armageddon

beach *adjective*: littoral

beach flea *alternative term*: sand-hopper

beads □ *large string of beads used in prayer*: rosary □ *small string of beads used in prayer*: chaplet

beam □ *beam supporting a ceiling etc.*: joist □ *beam supporting joists*: summer □ *beam above a window, door etc.*: lintel □ *horizontal beam dividing a window*: transom □ *vertical beam dividing a window*: mullion

bean *adjective*: leguminous

bean aphid *alternative term*: blackfly

bear *adjective*: ursine

bearer *combining forms*: -fer, -phore, -phorous

bearing *combining form*: -ferous

beast *adjective*: bestial, animal, feral

becoming *combining form*: -escent

bed □ *canvas bed suspended by cords at its ends*: hammock □ *Japanese quilted mattress used on the floor as a bed*: futon □ *canopy over a bed*: tester

bedsore *technical term*: decubitus ulcer

bee □ *adjective*: apian □ *female bee*: queen □ *male bee*: drone □ *group of beehives*: apiary

beekeeper *technical term*: apiarist

beetle □ *adjective*: coleopterous □ *sacred beetle of ancient Egypt*: scarab

before □ *combining forms*: ante-, fore-, pre- □ *feeling, when in a new situation, of having experienced it before*: déjà vu

beggar *adjective*: mendicant

begging the question *technical term*: petitio principii

beginning □ *combining form*: -escent □ *adjectives*: embryonic, incipient, inceptive, inchoate, nascent

behaviour *person's distinctive behaviour*: trait, quirk, mannerism, idiosyncrasy

being *combining form*: onto-

bell □ *bell rung to instruct people to return to their houses*: curfew □ *bell rung for the recitation of Roman Catholic prayers commemorating the Incarnation*: angelus □ *art of bell-ringing*: campanology □ *alarm bell*: tocsin

belladonna *alternative term*: deadly nightshade

bellflower *alternative term*: campanula

bell tower campanile

below □ *combining forms*: hypo-, infra-, sub- □ *below the threshold of consciousness*: subliminal

belt □ *belt worn by some army officers, with a strap over the shoulder*: Sam Browne □ *similar belt, carrying cartridges*: bandoleer □ *ornamental belt, worn with men's evening dress*: cummerbund □ *ornamental belt, won by champion boxer*: Lonsdale Belt

bench □ *long wooden bench with high back*: settle □ *upholstered bench against wall in restaurant etc.*: banquette

bends *technical terms*: caisson disease, decompression sickness

beneath □ *combining forms*: hypo-, infra-, sub- □ *beneath one's dignity*: infra dig

beside *combining form*: para-

best *best of all*: crème de la crème

between *combining form*: inter-

beyond □ *combining forms*: hyper-, meta-, para-, super-, supra-, sur-, trans-, ultra- □ *beyond one's authority*: ultra vires □ *beyond what is necessary*: supererogatory, de trop

bicycle □ *bicycle for two riders, one seated behind the other*: tandem □ *bicycle with one wheel*: monocycle, unicycle □ *early bicycle with one very large and one small wheel*: penny-farthing

big toe *technical term*: hallux

big wheel *alternative term*: Ferris wheel

bile *combining form*: chole-

bilharzia *technical term*: schistostomiasis

billionth *combining form*: nano-

bindweed *alternative term*: convolvulus

biological classification *technical term*: taxonomy

bird □ *combining form*: ornith- □ *adjectives*: avian, ornithic □ *study of birds*: ornithology □ *mythical bird, said to burn itself every 500 years and rise again from the ashes*: phoenix

birth □ *combining form*: -genesis □ *adjective*:

natal □ *giving birth by means of eggs*: oviparous □ *giving birth to live offspring*: viviparous □ *giving birth from eggs hatched within the body*: ovoviviparous

bishop □ *adjective*: episcopal □ *bishop's hat*: mitre □ *bishop's staff*: crosier □ *bishop's area of authority*: diocese, see □ *chief bishop*: primate

black □ *combining forms*: melan- □ *black box in an aircraft, technical term*: flight recorder

blackcurrant syrup cassis

blackhead *technical term*: comedo

black hole □ *technical term in astronomy*: collapsar □ *boundary of black hole*: event horizon

black lung *technical terms*: pneumoconiosis, anthracosis

black magic □ diabolism, the occult □ *black magic as practised on Haiti*: voodoo □ *black magic as practised in the West Indies*: obeah

blackthorn *alternative term*: sloe

bladder □ *combining form*: cyst- □ *adjective*: vesical

blame □ *free from blame*: exculpate, exonerate □ *person made to bear the blame for another's wrongdoing*: scapegoat, whipping boy

bleeder *medical technical term*: haemophiliac

blind gut *technical term*: caecum

blind worm *alternative term*: slow-worm

blink *technical term*: nictitate

blood □ *combining forms*: haem-, haemat- □ *adjectives*: haemal, haematic, sanguineous □ *blood transfer*: transfusion □ *artificial purification of the blood*: haemodialysis

blood clot *combining form*: thromb(o)-

blood feud *alternative term*: vendetta

blood poisoning *technical term*: septicaemia, toxaemia

blood pressure □ *high blood pressure*: hypertension □ *low blood pressure*: hypotension □ *instrument for measuring blood pressure*: sphygmomanometer

blunder *social blunder*: gaffe, faux pas

blush *adjective*: erubescent

body □ *combining forms*: somat-, -some □ *adjective*: corporal □ *entertainer who twists his body into abnormal positions*: contortionist

bogbean *alternative term*: buckbean

bog myrtle *alternative term*: sweet gale

bomb □ *hand-thrown bomb*: grenade □ *crude hand-thrown petrol bomb*: Molotov cocktail □ *bomb containing jellied petrol*: napalm bomb

bone □ *combining form*: osteo- □ *adjectives*: osseous, osteal □ *person who manipulates bones to ease pain etc.*: osteopath □ *brittleness of bones in the old*: osteoporosis □ *bone-house in church etc.*: charnel house

book □ *combining form*: biblio- □ *account-book*: ledger □ *list of books*: bibliography

bookplate *alternative term*: ex-libris

borderland *borderland between England and Wales or Scotland*: marches

born □ *born in wedlock*: legitimate □ *born out of wedlock*: illegitimate, natural

both *combining forms*: ambi-, amphi-, bi-

bottle □ *unmarked bottle for serving wine or water*: carafe, decanter □ *large bottle for acids etc.*: carboy

bow □ *traditional Muslim bow of greeting*: salaam □ *former Chinese bow of greeting*: kowtow

bowls □ *large black ball used in bowls*: wood □ *small white ball used in bowls*: jack □ *French bowls*: boules, pétanque

brain □ *combining forms*: encephal-, cerebr(o)- □ *adjective*: cerebral □ *technical term*: encephalon

branch *adjective*: ramose

breast □ *combining form*: mast- □ *adjectives*: mammary, pectoral □ *chemical polymer used in breast implants*: silicone □ *surgical removal of a breast*: mastectomy □ *surgical removal of a breast tumour*: lumpectomy

breastbone *technical term*: sternum

breastwork *alternative term*: parapet

breath *combining form*: spiro-

bridge □ *many-arched bridge carrying road or railway*: viaduct □ *many-arched bridge carrying river or canal*: aqueduct □ *raisable bridge in front of castle etc.*: drawbridge

bring □ *bring back to life*: resuscitate, reanimate, revivify □ *bring up (food etc.)*: regurgitate

bristle *adjective*: setaceous

broadcast *simultaneous broadcast of a programme on radio and television*: simulcast

bronze *combining form*: chalco-

brother □ *combining form*: fratr(i)- □ *adjective*: fraternal □ *murder of one's brother*: fratricide

brown coal *technical term*: lignite

brown lung *technical term*: byssinosis

brown owl *alternative term*: tawny owl

building □ *adjectives*: architectural, tectonic □ *sham building erected as a landscape decoration etc.*: folly

bulge *adjectives*: bulbous, tumescent

bull □ *adjective*: taurine □ *astrological term*: taurus

bundle *adjectives*: fascicular, fasciculate

burden *adjective*: onerous

burial *adjectives*: funerary, sepulchral

busy Lizzie *alternative term*: balsam

butter *clarified butter, used in Indian cuisine*: ghee

butterfly *butterfly expert*: lepidopterist

butterfly bush *alternative term*: buddleia

butterfly nut *alternative term*: wing nut

buttock *technical term*: natis (pl. nates)

buyer *let the buyer beware*: caveat emptor

buzzing *buzzing in the ears*: tinnitus

C

cabbage salad coleslaw

cable □ *cable for securing a ship to a pier*: hawser □ *cable for steadying a mast etc.*: guyrope

caisson disease *alternative terms*: decompression sickness, bends

cake shop *alternative term*: patisserie

calamus *alternative term*: sweet flag

calceolaria *alternative term*: slipperwort

calf love *alternative term*: puppy love

call in or **up** invoke

Cambridge University □ *Cambridge college annual feast*: Commemoration □ *Cambridge college servant*: gyp □ *Cambridge first-degree examination or course*: tripos □ *person gaining first-class honours in the Cambridge mathematical tripos*: wrangler

camel □ *camel with one hump*: dromedary □ *camel with two humps*: Bactrian camel

camellia *alternative term*: japonica

camera □ *crosswise movement of a camera*: pan □ *move a camera towards or away from object*: track □ *bring an object into close or distant camera focus*: zoom

campanula *alternative term*: bellflower

canal □ *path along side of a canal*: towpath □ *boat used on Venetian canals*: gondola □ *bridge to carry a canal over a valley, road, etc.*: aqueduct

cancer □ *combining form*: carcin- □ *technical term*: carcinoma □ *cancer treatment by drugs*: chemotherapy □ *cancer treatment by X-rays*: radiotherapy

cancerous *technical term*: carcinomatous, malignant

candlestick □ *candlestick attached to wall*: sconce □ *suspended multi-light candlestick*: chandelier □ *Jewish liturgical candlestick*: menorah

cane *cane carried by military officers*: swagger stick

cannibal *adjective*: anthropophagous

car □ *old and inefficient car*: banger, jalopy, rattletrap, tin lizzie □ *car that is modified to give high performance*: hot rod

carbohydrate *combining form*: -ose

career *summary of a person's career and education*: curriculum vitae

carnation *alternative term*: clove pink

carrying *combining forms*: -fer, -ferous, -phore, -phorous

cart *cart used in the French Revolution to convey condemned persons to the guillotine*: tumbril

Carthage *adjective*: Punic

cartilage *combining form*: chondr(o)-

case history *technical term*: anamnesis

cassava *alternative term*: manioc

cast off □ *cast off an old skin (of a snake etc.)*: slough □ *the skin so cast off*: slough □ *action of casting off a skin*: ecdysis

castrate □ *castrated man*: eunuch □ *castrated male singer in baroque opera or the papal chapel*: castrato □ *castrated cockerel*: capon □ *castrated stallion*: gelding □ *castrated ram*: wether

cat *adjective*: feline

Catherine wheel *alternative term*: pinwheel

cattle *adjective*: bovine

cauliflower ear *technical term*: aural hematoma

cause *adjective*: aetiological

causing *combining forms*: -genesis, -genous, -facient, -fic, -otic

cave *combining form*: speleo-

cell *combining forms*: -cyt-, cyto-, -cyte, -blast, -plast

cement □ *cement used between bricks*: pointing □ *cement used between tiles*: grout □ *cement used to cover a floor*: screed □ *cement used to cover a wall*: parget

centre *combining form*: mes-

ceremony □ *admission ceremony*: initiation □ *ceremony to make an award*: investiture □ *ceremony to place a person in office*: induction □ *ceremony to denote a turning-point in a person's life*: rite of passage □ *memorial ceremony*: commemoration

Ceres *Greek name*: Demeter

chalk *adjective*: calcareous

chamber *adjective*: cameral

chance *adjective*: fortuitous

change □ *combining forms*: -trop-, -tropic, tropo- □ *radical change*: quantum leap □ *change sides*: apostatize □ *change of the Eucharistic elements*: transubstantiation □ *person who changes his principles to suit the times*: trimmer, time-server

change of life *technical term*: menopause

charity *adjective*: eleemosynary

Charlemagne *adjectives*: Carolingian, Carlovingian

Charles I and II *adjective*: Caroline

cheek *adjectives*: buccal, malar

cheekbone *technical term*: zygomatic bone

cheese □ *adjective*: caseous □ *sprinkled with grated cheese and browned*: au gratin

chemical *combining forms*: chem-, chemi-, chemo-

cherry brandy *alternative term*: kirsch

cherub *technical terms in art*: amoretto, putto

chess □ *winning position in chess*: checkmate □ *draw in chess*: stalemate □ *opening tactic in chess*: gambit

chest □ *adjectives*: pectoral, thoracic □ *technical term*: thorax

chew *chew the cud, technical term*: ruminate

chicken pox *technical term*: varicella

chickpea □ *chickpea paste*: hummus □ *chickpea rissole*: felafel

child □ *combining form*: paedo-, paedi- □ *child under state guardianship*: ward of court □ *nursery for young children*: crèche

childbirth □ *technical terms*: confinement, parturition □ *adjective*: puerperal □ *medical care and study of those giving birth*: obstetrics □ *doctor providing such care, or person making such study*: obstetrician □ *nurse attending at childbirth*: midwife □ *matter discharged after childbirth*: afterbirth

Chinese □ *combining form*: Sino- □ *Chinese frying pan*: wok □ *Chinese game played with small tiles*: mah-jong □ *Chinese therapy by needles*: acupuncture □ *Chinese official*: mandarin □ *study of Chinese culture etc.*: Sinology □ *Chinese gooseberry*: kiwi fruit □ *Chinese ink*: Indian ink

choice □ *difficult choice*: dilemma □ *choice with no real alternatives*: Hobson's choice □ *choice made to allocate scarce resources*: triage

church □ *adjective*: ecclesiastical □ *church*

usher: verger □ *churchwarden's assistant*: sidesman □ *church gravedigger etc.*: sexton □ *forms of church service*: liturgy □ *church assembly*: synod, convocation □ *church court*: consistory □ *church law*: canon □ *expel from a church*: excommunicate □ *grotesque stone figure on the outside of a church*: gargoyle □ *roofed gate in a churchyard, for cover when starting the burial service*: lich gate □ *a tenth of one's income given to the Church*: tithe

cider *strong and rough cider*: scrumpy

circle □ *combining form*: cycl- □ *imagined circle joining the earth's poles*: meridian □ *imagined circle round the earth equidistant from its poles*: equator □ *prehistoric circle of stones etc.*: henge

city □ *adjectives*: civic, urban □ *chief city*: metropolis □ *large city made by the fusion of several towns or cities*: megalopolis

classification □ *classification of plants and animals*: taxonomy □ *classification of plants and animals by genus and species*: Linnaean nomenclature, binomial nomenclature □ *classification according to rank*: hierarchy □ *classification according to shared ancestry*: cladistics

clay □ *clay used for pottery*: argil □ *clay used to make reddish pottery*: terracotta □ *thin clay used to decorate pottery*: slip □ *clay used for bricks and walls*: adobe □ *clay used as a filter*: fuller's earth

clerical collar *alternative term*: dog collar

climb *climb down a sheer cliff etc. using ropes*: abseil

clock □ *clock mechanism*: escapement □ *art or study of clock-making*: horology □ *precise clock*: chronometer

cloth □ *cloth-merchant*: mercer, draper □ *roll of cloth in a shop etc.*: bolt □ *cloth to cover a corpse*: shroud, winding sheet

clothes □ *adjective*: sartorial □ *clothes for a new baby*: layette □ *liturgical clothes*: vestments □ *clothes designer*: couturier

cloud *adjective*: nebulous

clove pink *alternative term*: carnation

club □ *adjectives*: clavate, claviform □ *Irish club*: shillelagh □ *Australian aborigine's club*: waddy □ *African club*: knobkerrie □ *veto someone's proposed membership of a club etc.*: blackball

coal miner's lung *technical terms*: pneumoconiosis, anthracosis

coast □ *adjective*: littoral □ *scenic coast road*: corniche

coat □ *coat with flour, sugar, etc.*: dredge □ *coat with plaster or cement*: render □ *coat with planks etc.*: clad

codes □ *study of codes*: cryptography, cryptology □ *deciphering of codes*: cryptanalysis

coffee □ *strong black coffee made under steam pressure*: espresso □ *coffee topped with frothed milk*: cappuccino □ *stimulant in coffee*: caffeine

coffin □ *stone coffin*: sarcophagus □ *stand for a coffin*: bier, catafalque □ *coffin-carrier*: pallbearer

coin □ *adjective*: nummary □ *face of a coin*: obverse □ *back of a coin*: reverse □ *ridges on a coin's edge*: milling □ *study of coins*: numismatics

cold □ *combining forms*: cryo-, psychro- □ *sleepy etc. state brought on by extreme cold*: hypothermia

cold sore *technical term*: herpes labialis

collarbone *technical term*: clavicle

collection □ *collection of writings etc.*: anthology, miscellany, omnibus □ *collection of miscellaneous items*: farrago, job lot

collective farm □ *collective farm in Israel*: kibbutz □ *collective farm in Russia*: kolkhoz

collector □ *collector of bygones*: antiquary □ *collector of beer mats*: tegestologist □ *collector of books*: bibliophile □ *collector of butterflies and moths*: lepidopterist □ *collector of coins and medals*: numismatist □ *collector of matchboxes*: phillumenist □ *collector of stamps*: philatelist

college □ *college dining room*: hall, refectory □ *college doorkeeper*: porter □ *college doorkeeper's room*: lodge □ *college principal's apartments*: lodgings □ *annual college feast*: gaudy, commemoration

colour □ *adjective*: chromatic □ *range of colours*: spectrum

columbine *alternative term*: aquilegia

combat □ *medieval mock-combat between mounted knights*: joust □ *place for such combat*: lists □ *mock sea battle staged in a Roman arena*: naumachia

combatant *person who fought in a Roman arena to entertain*: gladiator

combination *combination of businesses*: conglomerate, consortium, syndicate, cartel

command *adjectives*: mandatory, preceptive

command economy *alternative term*: planned economy

comment *comment made in passing*: obiter dictum

common fraction *alternative term*: simple fraction

Common Market *official name*: European Community

common noun *technical term*: appellative

complaint □ *adjective*: querulous □ *government official investigating complaints*: ombudsman

complete *combining form*: hol(o)-

complex fraction *alternative term*: compound fraction

compliance *minimal compliance with a law etc.*: tokenism

compressed air *adjective*: pneumatic

conclusion □ *conclusion derived by logic*: deduction, inference □ *conclusion inferred from a limited number of instances*: generalization □ *conclusion wrongly inferred*: non sequitur

condition *combining forms*: -osis, -tude

connoisseur □ *connoisseur of food and drink*: gourmet, gastronome □ *connoisseur of antiques etc.*: virtuoso

conqueror *Spanish conqueror of South America*: conquistador

contact *spread by contact*: contagious

contain *combining form*: -fer-

container □ *container for fluids*: reservoir, cistern □ *sealed container for a measured amount of medicine etc.*: ampoule □ *container for molten metal*: crucible □ *container for wine or oil*: ampulla, cruse

□ *container for tea*: caddy □ *container for petrol or water*: jerrycan □ *container for relics*: reliquary

continental quilt *alternative term*: duvet

contradiction *apparent contradiction used for rhetorical effect*: oxymoron

contrast *contrast of light and shade in a picture etc*.: chiaroscuro

cooked *lightly cooked*: al dente

cooking *adjective*: culinary

copper □ *combining forms*: chalc-, cupr- □ *adjectives*: cupric, cuprous

copy □ *copying the work of another and claiming it as one's own*: plagiarism, piracy □ *exact genetic copy*: clone

corn on the cob *alternative term*: maize

corpse □ *combining form*: necr- □ *corpse used for medical research*: cadaver □ *dissection of a corpse*: post-mortem, autopsy □ *building etc. for storing corpses*: mortuary, morgue □ *deep-freezing of corpses*: cryonics □ *preservation of a corpse by injecting chemicals*: embalmment □ *destruction of a corpse by fire*: cremation □ *burial of a corpse*: interment □ *corpse revived by witchcraft*: zombie

correct *combining form*: ortho-

cot death *technical term*: sudden infant death syndrome

cottage pie *alternative term*: shepherd's pie

cough □ *technical term*: tussis □ *cough medicine*: expectorant

counterpoint *adjective*: contrapuntal

country *adjectives*: rural, pastoral

cowboy □ *South American cowboy*: gaucho □ *cowboy's leather overtrousers*: chaps

coyote *alternative term*: prairie wolf

crab *astrological term*: cancer

crane-fly *alternative term*: daddy-long-legs

criminal □ *criminal who betrays his fellows to the police* (Brit): grass □ *criminal intent, technical term*: mens rea

criticism *person etc. thought to be above criticism*: sacred cow

crow *adjective*: corvine

crown □ *crown worn by a nobleman*: coronet □ *crown worn by the pope*: tiara

crux ansata *alternative term*: ankh

cud-chewer *technical term*: ruminant

culture □ *person having no cultural interests*: philistine □ *study of primitive cultures*: ethnology

cup *Eucharistic cup*: chalice □ *cup used by Christ at the Last Supper*: Holy Grail

Cupid *Greek name*: Eros

curve *adjective*: sinuous

cut *combining forms*: -tom-, -tomy

D

daddy-long-legs *alternative term*: crane-fly

dancer *dancer's close-fitting garment covering the torso, and sometimes the arms and legs*: leotard

danger □ *hidden danger*: pitfall □ *danger inherent in a task etc*.: occupational hazard

dalton *alternative term*: atomic mass unit

daughter *adjective*: filial

dawn *adjective*: auroral

day □ *adjective*: diurnal □ *day in which hours of daylight and darkness are equal*: equinox □ *longest or shortest day*: solstice

day blindness *technical term*: hemeralopia

dayfly *alternative term*: mayfly

Day of Atonement *alternative term*: Yom Kippur

dead □ *service for the dead*: requiem □ *medical examination of a dead person*: post-mortem □ *medical examiner of dead person*: pathologist □ *published history of a dead person*: obituary □ *tomb-inscription*: epitaph □ *summon up the dead by magic*: necromancy

dead end □ *road with no exit at its far end*: cul-de-sac □ *deadlock in argument or discussion*: impasse, stalemate

deadly nightshade *alternative term*: belladonna

dean *adjective*: decanal

death □ *combining form*: mori-, necr-, -thanasia □ *adjectives*: fatal, lethal, mortal □ *causing death*: lethal, fatal, terminal □ *at the point of death*: moribund □ *death inflicted to relieve suffering*: euthanasia □ *death of body tissue*: necrosis, mortification, gangrene □ *stiffness of joints after death*: rigor mortis □ *magistrate investigating cause of person's death*: coroner □ *reminder of death's inevitability*: memento mori □ *after-death*: posthumous

decay □ *combining form*: sapr- □ *decay of teeth or bones*: caries □ *decayed organic matter in the soil*: humus

deceive *easily deceived*: credulous, gullible

decompose *able to be decomposed by bacteria*: biodegradable

decompression sickness *alternative terms*: caisson sickness, the bends

deep *combining form*: bath-

deer □ *adjective*: cervine □ *deer meat*: venison □ *deer's track*: slot

degree □ *degree awarded to a candidate who was ill at the time of the examination*: aegrotat □ *degree conferred when the graduate is elsewhere*: in absentia

delay □ *adjective*: dilatory □ *delay by non-cooperation*: stonewall □ *delay by lengthy speeches*: filibuster

delusion *delusions of being persecuted*: paranoia

Demeter *Latin name*: Ceres

dentist □ *dentist who corrects the position of teeth*: orthodontist □ *dentist's assistant who cleans teeth*: hygienist

descent □ *direct descent*: lineal □ *descent by a parallel line*: collateral □ *of the male line of descent*: patrilineal □ *of the female line of descent*: matrilineal

desire □ *adjective, technical term*: orectic □ *desire another's property*: covet

despair *despair at imagined lack of progress*: accidie

destruction □ *destruction from within*: sabotage □ *destruction of revered objects or ideas*: iconoclasm □ *malicious or purposeless destruction*: vandalism □ *total destruction*: holocaust

detail *subtle detail*: nicety, quibble, niggle, technicality, punctilio

devil □ *adjectives*: diabolic, diabolical □ *worship of the devil*: diabolism

dial □ *conventional watch etc. dial with moving hands*: analog □ *watch etc. dial with changing numerical display*: digital

Diana *Greek name*: Artemis

diaphragm *medical adjective*: phrenic

dictator □ *title of German dictator*: führer □ *title of Italian dictator*: duce □ *title of Spanish dictator*: caudillo □ *small group exercising dictatorial powers*: junta

dictionary □ *small dictionary at the back of a textbook etc.*: glossary, vocabulary □ *dictionary of places etc.*: gazetteer □ *dictionary of synonyms and antonyms*: thesaurus □ *dictionary in which the definition precedes the headword (as here)*: reverse dictionary □ *person who compiles dictionaries*: lexicographer

difference □ *subtle difference*: nuance □ *difference in brightness in a picture*: contrast

different □ *combining forms*: allo-, aniso-, heter-, vari- □ *of many different colours*: motley, pied, variegated □ *having a different content*: heterogeneous

difficult *combining form*: dys-

digestion *adjective*: peptic

dinner *adjective*: prandial

Dionysus □ *Latin name*: Bacchus □ *female follower of Dionysus*: Maenad □ *staff carried by Dionysus' followers*: thyrsus

disappointing *disappointing outcome*: anticlimax, bathos

discharge *combining forms*: -rrhoea, -rrhagia

discontinue *discontinue meetings of a parliament etc. without dissolution*: prorogue

discovery □ *method of discovery by trial and error*: heuristic □ *faculty of making fortunate discoveries*: serendipity

discuss □ *discuss publicly*: ventilate, air □ *avoid discussion*: fence, prevaricate

disease □ *combining forms*: nos(o)-, patho-, -pathy, -osis □ *temporary abatement of a disease*: remission □ *general outbreak of a disease*: epidemic □ *resumption of a disease*: recrudescence □ *study of disease*: pathology □ *group of symptoms indicating a particular disease*: syndrome □ *denoting a disease passed on by physical contact*: contagious □ *denoting a disease often or only found in a certain region or race*: endemic

diseased *combining forms*: dys-, -otic

dislike *person or thing particularly disliked*: bête noire

dismiss *dismiss with dishonour (from the armed forces etc.)*: cashier

disseminated sclerosis *alternative term*: multiple sclerosis

dissolution *combining forms*: lyso-, -lys-, -lysis

distance *combining form*: tel(e)-

distant *ultimately distant spot*: ultima Thule

distillation flask retort

distinction □ *subtle distinction*: nicety, nuance □ *over-subtle distinction*: hair-splitting, quibble

ditch *hidden ditch separating gardens from parkland*: ha-ha

diver □ *diver's compressed-air apparatus*: scuba, aqualung □ *diver's enclosed vessel for deep-sea observations*: bathyscaphe □ *painful condition suffered by diver after sudden reduction of pressure*: the bends, caisson disease, decompression sickness

divide *combining form*: -sect

divine *divine for water*: dowse

division □ *combining form*: schiz(o)- □ *division into opposing factions etc.*: polarization, schism

divorce □ *spouse initiating a divorce action*: applicant □ *spouse against whom a divorce action is brought*: respondent □ *person cited in a divorce action as having committed adultery with the partner being sued*: co-respondent □ *court's provisional divorce ruling*: decree nisi □ *court's final divorce ruling*: decree absolute □ *financial support to be given by a former spouse after divorce*: maintenance

doctor □ *doctor in charge of a particular branch of medicine at a hospital*: consultant □ *hospital doctor assisting a consultant*: registrar □ *junior hospital doctor*: houseman □ *family doctor*: general practitioner □ *replacement doctor*: locum

document □ *document containing a sworn statement*: affidavit □ *document recording a contract*: deed □ *document showing ownership of a property*: title deed □ *document recording the transfer of ownership of a property*: conveyance □ *document written entirely by its author*: holograph □ *document signed by its author*: autograph

doer *combining forms*: -tor, -tress, -trix

dog □ *adjective*: canine □ *female dog*: bitch □ *male dog*: dog □ *give birth to dogs*: whelp

dog collar *alternative term*: clerical collar

done *something done and unalterable*: fait accompli

doorman □ *doorman at an hotel or theatre etc.*: commissionaire □ *doorman at a block of flats*: concierge □ *doorman at a college etc.*: porter

downwards *combining form*: cata-

drawing □ *combining form*: -graphy □ *drawing of a machine etc. showing its parts as if separated by an explosion*: exploded view □ *drawing of a machine etc. with parts of its casing removed to show inner workings*: cutaway □ *drawing of a vertical aspect of a building*: elevation □ *drawing of a floor layout of a building*: plan

dream □ *combining form*: oneir(o)- □ *adjective*: oneiric

drift anchor *alternative term*: sea anchor

dripstone *alternative term*: hood mould

drug □ *combining forms*: pharmaco-, narco- □ *drug that sharpens the senses*: stimulant □ *drug that dulls the senses*: narcotic □ *drug producing hallucinations*: psychedelic, hallucinogenic □ *hormonal drug used by athletes to improve performance*: steroid □ *inject a drug directly into a vein*: mainline □ *cure of addiction by complete* *deprivation of drugs*: cold turkey □ *cure of addiction by progressive deprivation of drugs*: withdrawal

drum □ *pitched bowl-shaped drum*: timpano, kettledrum □ *drum with resonating strings along its underside*: snare drum □ *drum in Latin American band*: bongo □ *jazz drum beaten with the hands*: tom-tom □ *Indian drum*: tabla

dry *combining form*: xero-

dummy *jointed dummy used by artists*: lay figure

dung □ *combining form*: copro- □ *dung-eating, technical term*: coprophagous □ *dung of seabirds sold as a fertilizer*: guano

duty □ *adjective*: deontic □ *beyond the call of duty*: supererogatory

duvet *alternative term*: continental quilt

dwarf □ *dwarf bean*: French bean, kidney bean □ *dwarf plant or tree as cultivated in Japan*: bonsai

E

each other *adjectives*: mutual, reciprocal

eagle *adjective*: aquiline

eagle's nest *alternative term*: eyrie

ear □ *adjective*: aural □ *combining forms*: ot-, oto-

earache *technical term*: otalgia

eardrum *technical terms*: tympanic membrane, tympanum

ear, nose, and throat *technical term*: otorhinolaryngology

ear-shaped *adjective*: auriculate

ear shell *alternative term*: abalone

earth *adjectives*: terrestrial, telluric

earth *combining form*: geo-

earthquake *adjective*: seismic

earwax *technical term*: cerumen

east *adjective*: oriental

Easter *adjective*: Paschal

Easter cactus *alternative term*: Christmas cactus

East Germany *official title*: German Democratic Republic

eating □ *combining forms*: -phag-, -phagous, -vorous □ *eating all foods*: omnivorous □ *meat-eating*: carnivorous □ *plant-eating*: herbivorous □ *eating grasses and cereals*: graminivorous □ *fish-eating*: piscivorous □ *eating corpses*: necrophagous □ *eating dung*: coprophagous

ebonite *alternative term*: vulcanite

ecology *technical term*: bionomics

ecstatic speech *technical term*: glossolalia

eel-shaped *adjective*: anguilliform

efficiency *analysis of workplace efficiency*: operational research

egg *combining forms*: -oo-, -ovi-, -ovo-

egg-shaped *adjective*: oval, ovate, ovoid

eglantine *alternative term*: sweetbrier

Egyptian scripts demotic, hieratic

Egyptian tomb mastaba

eight *combining form*: octo-, octa-

eighty-year-old *alternative term*: octogenarian

election □ *election campaign*: hustings □ *study of voting at elections*: psephology

electric eye *alternative term*: photocell

electric □ *electric shock treatment*: electroconvulsive therapy □ *electric supply failure*: outage

electronic music keyboard moog synthesizer

elements *table of the chemical elements arranged by atomic number*: periodic table

elephant □ *elephant driver*: mahout □ *seat on elephant's back*: howdah

eleven *combining form*: hendeca-

elf □ *alternative term*: pixie □ *in Irish folklore*: leprechaun

emotion *adjective*: affective

emotional release *in response to a moving play, novel, etc.*: catharsis

emotional shock *technical term*: trauma

emperor □ *emperor of Germany*: Kaiser □ *emperor of Japan*: Mikado □ *emperor of Russia*: Tsar

end □ *combining forms*: □ *purpose*: tel-, tele- □ *tip*: acro-

end of the world *theological study of the end of the world*: eschatology

enemy *adjective*: inimical

English *combining form*: Anglo-

English-speaking *adjective*: anglophone

engraving *adjective*: glyptic

enlightenment *theological term in Buddhism or Hinduism*: nirvana

enteric fever *alternative term*: typhoid fever

entertain *adjective*: amusing, diverting

entire *combining forms*: pan-, panto-

environment *combining form*: eco-

enzyme *combining form*: -ase

equal *combining form*: equi-, iso-

equal in size *adjective*: coextensive, coterminous

equivalent return quid pro quo

Eros *Latin name*: Cupid

erosion *projecting wall or fence to limit sea's erosion of coast*: groyne

error in logic fallacy

escape *person who entertains audiences by demonstrating skill in escaping*: escapologist

escort □ *female escort for young woman*: chaperone, duenna □ *male escort for older woman*: gigolo

Eskimo □ *Eskimo ice-house*: igloo □ *Eskimo sledge-dog*: husky, malamute □ *Eskimo canoe*: kayak □ *Eskimo inhabitant of the islands off Alaska*: Aleut □ *Eskimo inhabitant of North America or Greenland*: Inuit

essential condition prerequisite, sine qua non

estimator *one who estimates the cost of a proposed building etc.*: quantity surveyor

estragon *alternative term*: tarragon

euphrasy *alternative term*: eyebright

evaporating rapidly *technical term*: volatile

event □ *important event*: milestone, landmark □ *possible sequence of events*: scenario

everyday speech *technical terms*: demotic, vernacular

everything *combining forms*: pan-, panto-

evidence *object shown in court as evidence*: exhibit

evil *averting evil*: apotropaic

evil spirit □ *spirit said to take female form to seduce a sleeping man*: succubus □ *spirit said to take male form to seduce a sleeping woman*: incubus □ *person posssessed by an evil spirit*: demoniac □ *drive out evil spirits*: exorcize

examination □ *combining forms*: -opsy, -scopy □ *examination of financial accounts*: audit □ *verbal examination*: oral, viva □ *supervisor of persons taking a written examination*: invigilator □ *medical examination of a corpse*: autopsy, post-mortem □ *medical examination of tissue from a living body*: biopsy □ *theological examination of heretic etc.*: inquisition □ *mental examination of one's thoughts etc.*: introspection

example □ *example to be imitated*: paradigm □ *example cited to justify similar action*: precedent □ *cite as an example*: adduce

exceeding *combining forms*: super-, ultra-

excessive *combining form*: hyper-

excrement □ *combining form*: copro-, scato- □ *eating excrement, technical term*: coprophagous □ *excrement of seabirds sold as a fertilizer*: guano

exempt from blame exonerate

existence *combining form*: onto-

existing situation status quo

expelling *combining form*: -fuge

experience □ *in handling tricky social or business situations etc.*: savoir faire □ *a short but unpleasant interview etc.*: mauvais quart d'heure

experimentation *on living animals*: vivisection

explanation □ *provisional explanation*: hypothesis □ *of a difficult word in a text etc.*: gloss

explosive □ *explosive material in a missile's warhead*: payload □ *explosive charge to propel a rocket etc.*: propellant □ *explosive situation*: powder keg, tinderbox

extermination *extermination of an entire nation or race*: genocide

external *combining form*: exo-

extra *combining form*: super-, ultra-

eye □ *adjectives*: ocular, ophthalmic □ *combining form*: ophthalmo- □ *medical specialist for vision problems*: oculist, optician, optometrist □ *an eye for an eye, legal concept*: lex talionis

eyeblack *alternative term*: mascara

eyebright *alternative term*: euphrasy

eyelash *technical term*: cilium

eyelid *adjective*: palpebral

eyeshadow *alternative term*: kohl

eye socket *technical term*: orbit

eyestrain *technical term*: asthenopia

eye tooth *technical term*: canine

F

face □ *combining form*: -hedron □ *with an unexpressive face*: deadpan, inscrutable, poker-faced

facing □ *combining forms*: -ward, -wards □ *lying facing downwards*: prone □ *lying facing upwards*: supine

fact *an unalterable fact*: fait accompli

false *combining form*: pseud(o)-

false fruit *technical term*: pseudocarp

family *narrowest family unit, consisting of a couple and their children only*: nuclear family

family tree *alternative terms*: genealogy, pedigree

fantasy □ *fantasy world*: Cockaigne, cloud-cuckoo-land, Utopia □ *person living in a fantasy world*: Walter Mitty

Far East *adjective*: oriental

far sight *technical terms*: hyperopia, hypermetropia, presbyopia

farming *adjective*: agr-

fast *combining form*: tach-

fat □ *combining forms*: lipo-, seb(o)-, steat(o)- □ *adjective*: sebaceous

fate □ *fate in Hindu and Buddhist thought*: karma □ *fate in Islamic thought*: kismet

father □ *combining form*: patr(i)- □ *adjective*: paternal □ *murder of one's father*: patricide

fault □ *fault-finding*: captious, carping, niggling □ *minor personal fault*: foible, peccadillo

faulty *combining form*: dys-

Faunus *Greek name*: Pan

favouritism *favouritism towards one's relatives*: nepotism

fear □ *combining form*: -phobia □ *fear of confined spaces*: claustrophobia □ *fear of foreigners*: xenophobia □ *fear of public places*: agoraphobia □ *fear of homosexuals*: homophobia □ *fear of heights*: acrophobia □ *fear of water*: hydrophobia

feast *adjective*: festal

Feast of Lights *alternative term*: Hannukkah

Feast of Tabernacles *alternative term*: Sukkoth

Feast of Weeks *alternative term*: Shavuoth

fee □ *initial fee paid to a barrister*: retainer □ *further fee paid to a barrister*: refresher □ *fee paid to cover expenses etc. of someone doing 'unpaid' work*: honorarium □ *percentage fee on sales made etc.*: commission □ *fee paid to an author etc. for copies sold or performances given*: royalty

feeding *combining forms*: troph-, -trophy

feelings □ *combining form*: -pathy □ *ability to share another's feelings*: empathy

female *combining forms*: gyno-, -gyn-, -ess, -tress, -trix

ferroconcrete *alternative term*: reinforced concrete

fever *technical term*: pyrexia

field *adjective*: campestral

film □ *combining form*: cine- □ *film expert or enthusiast*: cineaste

filtration *filtration process for blood of patient suffering kidney failure*: dialysis

final □ *final part of a speech*: peroration □ *final part of a play*: denouement, epilogue □ *final part of a piece of music*: coda

finger □ *combining form*: dactyl(o)- □ *adjective*: digital

fingerprint *technical term*: dactylogram

fire □ *combining form*: pyro- □ *fire for burning a corpse*: pyre □ *person starting fires for malicious purposes*: arsonist □ *mythical creature living in fire*: salamander

fireplace □ *grid at front of fireplace to keep in burning material*: fender □ *shelf along side of fireplace for kettle etc.*: hob □ *stand for kettle etc. at front of fireplace*: trivet □ *stand to support logs in a fireplace*: andiron, firedog □ *metal plate at the back of a fireplace*: reredos

first □ *combining forms*: proto-, ur- □ *first example*: prototype □ *first appearance of a performer*: debut □ *first performance*: premiere □ *first-year student at a university*: freshman

fish □ *combining forms*: ichthy(o)-, pisc- □ *adjective*: piscine □ *fish eggs*: spawn □ *fish sperm*: milt

fishes *astrological term*: pisces

fishing □ *adjective*: piscatorial □ *catch fish with one's hands*: guddle

five □ *combining forms*: pent-, quin-, quinque- □ *five-sided figure*: pentagon □ *five-pointed star*: pentagram □ *group of five*: pentad

flag *adjective*: vexillary

flat □ *top-floor flat*: penthouse □ *flat on two or more floors, with its own outside door*: maisonette □ *flat kept for occasional use*: pied-à-terre □ *large building divided into flats*: tenement

fleet □ *fleet of warships*: armada □ *fleet of merchant ships*: argosy □ *fleet of small ships*: flotilla

flesh □ *combining forms*: carn-, sarc(o)- □ *adjective*: carnal

float □ *float attached to side of a canoe etc*: outrigger □ *float supporting a bridge*: pontoon □ *float used to raise sunken ships*: caisson

flood □ *adjective*: diluvial □ *sudden flood*: flash flood □ *before the (biblical) Flood*: antediluvian

floor □ *floor of a building having principal reception rooms etc.*: piano nobile □ *floor set in a building between main floors*: mezzanine □ *floor of wood blocks*: parquet

flour *adjective*: farinaceous

flow *combining forms*: rheo-, -rrhoea, -rrhagia

flower □ *combining forms*: antho-, flor-, anthous □ *adjective*: floral □ *sweet liquid collected by bees from flowers*: nectar □ *fine dust collected by bees from flowers*: pollen □ *flower that keeps its colour when dried*: immortelle

fluid □ *body fluid in early medicine*: humour □ *body fluid surrounding embryo*: amniotic fluid □ *body fluid around joints*: sinovia

fodder □ *fodder of fermented grass etc.*: silage □ *tall fodder plant with yellow flowers*: rape

fond *combining forms*: phil(o)-, -phile

food □ *adjective*: alimentary □ *food for the gods*: ambrosia □ *food for pigs*: swill □ *food for horses*: tack □ *seasoning for food*: condiment □ *food additive used in Chinese cuisine*: monosodium glutamate □ *shop selling foreign foods*: delicatessen □ *denoting food prepared in accordance with Jewish law*: kosher □ *denoting food unacceptable to Jewish law*: tref □ *food poisoning*: botulism, salmonellosis

fool's gold *technical term*: iron pyrites

foot □ *combining forms*: pedi-, -pod, -pode □ *wart growing on feet*: verruca □ *specialist treating hands and feet*: chiropodist

forehead *adjectives*: frontal

foreign □ *combining form*: xeno- □ *foreign girl who does domestic work in return for keep and English lessons*: au pair

foreskin □ *technical term*: prepuce □ *removal of the foreskin*: circumcision

forest *adjective*: sylvan

form *combining forms*: morpho-, -morphic

formal logic *alternative term*: symbolic logic

fortification □ *fortification of wooden stakes*: palisade, stockade □ *concrete fortification, with loopholes for guns etc.*: blockhouse □ *underground fortified shelter*: bunker

fortune telling □ *fortune telling from lines on the hand*: palmistry □ *fortune telling from the stars*: astrology □ *fortune telling from playing cards*: cartomancy □ *fortune telling from dreams*: oneiromancy □ *fortune telling by drawing lots*: sortilege

found object *alternative term*: objet trouvé

four □ *combining forms*: quadr-, tetr- □ *four children born at a birth*: quadruplets □ *four-legged animal*: quadruped □ *four-line verse stanza*: quatrain □ *four-track stereophonic sound*: quadraphony

fowl □ *adjective*: gallinaceous □ *castrated fowl*: capon □ *fowl's edible offal*: giblets

fox □ *adjective*: vulpine □ *female fox*: vixen □ *male fox*: dog □ *fox's lair*: earth □ *fox's tail*: brush

fraction □ *number placed above the line in a fraction*: numerator □ *number placed below the line in a fraction*: denominator □ *fraction equal to less than one*: proper fraction □ *fraction equal to more than one*: improper fraction

France *combining forms*: Franco-, Gallo-

freeze *combining form*: cryo-

French bean *alternative terms*: dwarf bean, haricot, kidney bean

friction *combining form*: tribo-

frog *adjective*: batrachian

front □ *front of a building*: façade □ *front of an army*: vanguard □ *front of a leaf of paper*: recto

fruit *combining forms*: fruct-, -carp

fruit fly *alternative term*: drosophila

fruit sugar *technical term*: fructose

fungus □ *combining forms*: myco-, -mycete □ *edible fungus growing underground*: truffle

furnace □ *furnace for steel*: blast furnace □ *furnace for pottery*: kiln □ *furnace for rubbish*: incinerator

fusion bomb *alternative term*: thermonuclear bomb

G

gall *combining form*: chole-

gallery *exterior gallery on an upper floor*: loggia

game *game killed during a day's shoot etc.*: bag

gangrene *technical terms*: necrosis, mortification

garden □ *formal garden with paths between small beds etc.*: knot garden □ *garden pavilion with view*: gazebo □ *garden shelter*: alcove, arbour, bower □ *ornamental hedge-clipping in a garden*: topiary

garlic □ *adjective*: alliaceous □ *garlic mayonnaise*: aioli

gas □ *combining forms*: aero-, pneum(o)- □ *laboratory gas burner*: Bunsen burner □ *gas in the digestive tract*: flatulence □ *foul-smelling gas*: mephitis, effluvium □ *gas formerly thought to fill all space*: ether

gas mask *technical term*: respirator

gate □ *revolving gate*: turnstile □ *fortified gate*: barbican □ *back gate*: postern

gear □ *gear system causing the parts to revolve at the same speed before engagement*: synchromesh □ *system changing cycle gears by moving the chain*: derailleur

general assistant factotum

German shepherd dog *alternative term*: alsatian

germ warfare *alternative term*: biological warfare

gift of tongues *technical term*: glossolalia

glandular fever *technical term*: infectious mononucleosis

glass *adjective*: vitreous

goat *adjectives*: caprine, hircine

goose □ *adjective*: anserine □ *group of geese*: gaggle □ *group of geese flying in formation*: skein

geranium *alternative term*: pelargonium

germ □ *technical term*: pathogen □ *blood protein counteracting germs*: antibody □ *germ provoking the production of antibodies*: antigen

German measles *technical term*: rubella

ghost □ *ghostly double of a living person*: doppelgänger □ *ghost that throws things about*: poltergeist □ *ghostly emanation from a medium during a seance*: ectoplasm

give *person who gives*: donor

glandular fever *technical term*: infectious mononucleosis

Glasgow *adjective*: Glaswegian

glass □ *combining form*: vitr- □ *adjectives*: vitreous

glass fibre *alternative term*: optical fibre

glue-sniffing *technical term*: solvent abuse

gnu *alternative term*: wildebeest

goat □ *adjectives*: caprine, hircine □ *male goat*: billy goat □ *female goat*: nanny goat □ *fabric made from goat hair*: mohair □ *astrological term*: capricorn

god □ *combining form*: the- □ *adjective*: divine □ *belief in a single god*: monotheism □ *belief in many gods*: polytheism □ *belief that God is identical with the created universe*: pantheism □ *drink of the gods*: nectar □ *food of the gods*: ambrosia □ *blood of the gods*: ichor □ *woodland god*: satyr, faun □ *creator-god*: demiurge □ *god's appearance to men*: epiphany, theophany □ *of a god taking animal form*: zoomorphic □ *of a god taking human form*: anthropomorphic □ *belief that there can be no sure evidence of a god's existence*: agnosticism □ *belief that there is no god*: atheism

gold □ *combining forms*: auri-, chryso-, -chrys- □ *gold in bulk*: bullion □ *gold bar*: ingot □ *lump of natural gold*: nugget □ *search for natural gold*: prospect □ *stone said to turn base metals to gold*: philosopher's stone

goose *adjective*: anserine

goose-flesh *technical term*: horripilation

government □ *combining forms*: -archy, -cracy, -nomy □ *moral authority given to a government by its election majority*: mandate □ *transfer of governmental power to regional authorities*: devolution □ *organization that is independent but government-sponsored*: quango

gradual □ *gradual development*: evolution □ *gradual absorption*: osmosis

grain □ *combining form*: grani- □ *grain-eating*: granivorous □ *grain fungus*: ergot □ *funnel for dispensing grain*: hopper □ *gather leftover grain from a harvest field*: glean □ *separate chaff from grain by the wind*: winnow □ *separate chaff from grain by beating*: thresh □ *storage tower or pit for threshed grain*: silo □ *storehouse for threshed grain*: granary

grammar □ *mistake in grammar*: solecism □ *mistake in grammar made by inappropriate application of a rule*: hypercorrection

grape □ *grape harvest*: vintage □ *fermenting grape juice*: must □ *remains of grapes after pressing*: marc

grandfather clock *alternative term*: long-case clock

grass □ *adjectives*: graminaceous, gramineous □ *grass-eating*: graminivorous □ *circle of darker grass in lawn etc.*: fairy ring □ *clump of grass dislodged by horse's hoof etc.*: divot □ *synthetic grass surface used on sports fields*: AstroTurf™

grassland □ *extensive grassland in Russia*: steppe □ *extensive grassland in North America*: prairie □ *extensive grassland in South America*: pampas □ *extensive grassland in warm regions*: savannah □ *extensive grassland in South Africa*: veldt

grave □ *adjective*: sepulchral □ *prehistoric grave mound*: barrow, tumulus

Greek □ *combining form*: Graeco-, Hellen- □ *adjective*: Hellenic □ *Greek restaurant*: taverna □ *Greek resin-flavoured wine*: retsina □ *Greek mandolin*: bouzouki □ *white skirt in Greek men's traditional dress*: fustanella □ *citadel of ancient Greek city*: acropolis

green □ *combining forms*: chlor(o)- □ *adjective*: verdant □ *green pepper*: capsicum □ *green pigment in plants*: chlorophyll □ *green crystallized crust forming on exposed copper, brass, etc.*: verdigris

groin *adjective*: inguinal

groove *adjective*: sulcate

group □ *group of people of equal social status*: peer group □ *group of people living together and sharing all property*: commune □ *group of people pressing a common interest*: lobby □ *group of actors etc.*: troupe □ *group of businesses*: consortium, syndicate, cartel

guard *adjective*: custodial

guardian *adjective*: tutelary

guide □ *moral* guide: mentor, guru □ *tourists' guide*: cicerone

guillotine □ *cart carrying prisoners to the guillotine*: tumbrel □ *woman knitting by the guillotine*: tricoteuse

guilt □ *produce arguments or evidence to lessen someone's guilt*: extenuate, mitigate □ *feeling of guilt*: compunction

guitar *small disc used to pluck a guitar's strings*: plectrum

gullet *technical term*: oesophagus

gum □ *technical term*: gingiva □ *gum disease caused by plaque, with bleeding etc.*: gingivitis

gunfire □ *simultaneous fire from all the guns on one side of a ship*: broadside □ *rapid burst of gunfire*: fusillade, volley

gunman *hidden gunman*: sniper

guru *Hindu guru*: maharishi

gut *adjective*: visceral

gypsy □ *gypsy person, or their language*: Romany □ *Romany word for 'man'*: rom □ *Romany word for a non-gypsy*: gorgio □ *Italian gypsy*: Zingaro □ *Hungarian gypsy*: tzigane □ *itinerant tinker or scrap-metal dealer*: didicoi

H

habit □ *strange habit*: eccentricity, idiosyncrasy, mannerism □ *of a person possessed by compulsive habits*: inveterate, pathological

hair □ *combining forms*: pil-, -trich- □ *adjective*: capillary □ *bristling of the hair in fear etc.*: gooseflesh □ *removal of unwanted hair*: depilation □ *having tightly curled hair*: ulotrichan □ *study of hair and its diseases*: trichology

hairdressing *adjective*: tonsorial

hair oil brilliantine, pomade, Macassar oil

half □ *combining forms*: demi-, hemi-, semi- □ *half-board*: demi-pension □ *half-line of verse*: hemistich

hallucination □ *producing or produced by hallucinations*: psychedelic □ *hallucinations etc. suffered by alcoholics*: delirium tremens

hammer □ *hammer used by auctioneers etc.*: gavel □ *diagnostic hammer used by doctors*: plexor □ *flat part of a hammer head, used for striking*: face □ *rounded or wedge-shaped part of a hammer head, opposite to the face*: peen □ *V-shaped device for removing nails, set opposite to the face*: claw □ *technical term for a bone in the ear*: malleus

hand □ *combining forms*: chiro-, manu- □ *adjective*: manual, palmate □ *able to use both hands equally well*: ambidextrous

hand over *hand over a person to a foreign power for trial etc.*: extradite

handle □ *handle of a sword or knife*: haft, hilt □ *handle of an axe or hammer*: helve □ *handle of a whip or fishing rod*: stock

handwriting *psychological study of handwriting*: graphology

hangnail *alternative term*: agnail

hard *combining form*: scler(o)-

hard coal *alternative term*: anthracite

hardening of the arteries *technical term*: arteriosclerosis

hare □ *adjective*: leporine □ *female hare*: doe □ *male hare*: buck □ *young hare*: leveret □ *hare-hunting*: coursing

haricot *alternative term*: French bean

hat □ *cowboy's hat*: stetson □ *Mexican hat*: sombrero □ *academic hat*: square, mortarboard, bonnet □ *soft cloth hat with brims at front and back, and earflaps that may be tied up*: deerstalker □ *hat of stiffened straw with a low flat crown*: boater □ *sailor's oilskin hat*: sou'wester

hate *combining forms*: mis-, -phobe, -phobia, -phobic

hatred □ *hatred of men*: misandry □ *hatred of women*: misogyny □ *hatred of people*: misanthropy

head *combining forms*: cephalo-, -cephal-, -capit-

headache *severe headache with nausea and impaired vision*: migraine

headband □ *Arab's headband*: agal □ *Jew's liturgical headband*: frontlet

health *person obsessed by his own health*: hypochondriac, valetudinarian

hearing □ *combining form*: audi- □ *adjectives*: acoustic, auditory

heart □ *combining form*: cardi- □ *adjective*: cardiac □ *heart specialist*: cardiologist

heart attack *technical term*: coronary thrombosis, myocardial infarction

heartbeat □ *electrically traced record of a heartbeat*: electrocardiogram □ *irregular heartbeat*: arrhythmia □ *abnormally slow heartbeat*: bradycardia □ *abnormally fast heartbeat*: tachycardia

heat □ *combining forms*: cal(o)-, therm(o)-, -thermy □ *adjectives*: thermal, caloric □ *heat milk etc. to increase shelf-life*: pasteurize □ *heat spiced wine or ale*: mull

heating □ *underfloor heating system in Roman houses*: hypocaust □ *progressive heating of the earth's atmosphere due to breaches in ozone layer*: global warming, greenhouse effect

hedge-trimming *ornamental hedge-trimming*: topiary

hedgehog *adjective*: erinaceous

heel *combining form*: -calc- ·

heel bone *technical term*: calcaneus

height □ *combining forms*: acro-, alt-, hyps- □ *dizziness caused by heights etc.*: vertigo □ *fear of heights*: acrophobia □ *instrument measuring an aircraft's height*: altimeter

heir *adjective*: hereditary

Hermes □ *Latin name*: Mercury □ *Hermes' snake-twined staff*: caduceus

hermit □ *adjective*: eremitic □ *hermit living on the top of a pillar*: stylite

hiccup *technical term*: singultus

hidden □ *combining form*: crypt(o)- □ *hidden store*: cache, stash

higher *combining forms*: super-, supra-

Hindu □ *Hindu teacher*: guru, maharishi, pandit □ *Hindu ascetic*: fakir □ *Hindu state of blessedness*: nirvana □ *Hindu erotic classic*: Karma Sutra □ *Hindu seclusion of women*: purdah □ *Hindu widow's self-cremation*: suttee □ *Hindu meditation technique poupular in the West*: Transcendental Meditation

hip □ *hip bone*: innominate bone, coxa □ *hip joint*: coxa □ *hip socket for thigh bone*: acetabulum

hives *technical term*: urticaria

holy *combining form*: hagi(o)-, hier(o)-

holy war □ *by Christians to recover the Holy Land*: crusade □ *by Muslims against infidels*: jihad

honey □ *alcoholic drink made from honey*: mead □ *sweetmeat made of honey and sesame flour*: halva □ *liquid collected by bees from flowers to make honey*: nectar

hook □ *hooked pole used to land large fish etc.*: gaff □ *hooked device on a rope thrown to gain purchase on the top of a wall etc.*: grappling iron, grapnel

hoop *hoop attached to a skirt to support it*: farthingale

hormone □ *hormone secreted when under stress*: adrenaline □ *hormone regulating blood sugar levels*: insulin □ *hormone used by athletes to inprove performance*: steroid □ *hormone used to treat allergies and arthritis*: cortisone □ *hormone governing female secondary sexual characteristics*: oestrogen □ *hormones governing male secondary sexual characteristics*: androgen, testosterone

horn □ *combining form*: kerat(o)- □ *adjective*: corneous □ *horn of plenty*: cornucopia

horse □ *combining forms*: equi-, hippo- □ *adjective*: equine □ *small prehistoric horse*: eohippus □ *female horse*: mare □ *young female horse*: filly □ *castrated male horse*: gelding □ *uncastrated male horse*: stallion, entire horse □ *young male horse*: colt □ *thoroughbred horses*: bloodstock □ *wild American horse*: mustang, bronco □ *person who rides horses*: equestrian □ *person who shoes horses*: farrier □ *horse-slaughterer*: knacker

hospital *hospital for the terminally ill*: hospice

hot water □ *natural hot spring*: geyser □ *pan of hot water above which food may be cooked or kept warm*: bain-marie

house □ *Eskimo's house made of ice blocks*: igloo □ *Russian summer residence*: dacha □ *traditional wooden house in Switzerland*: chalet □ *traditional conical stone house of southern Italy*: trullo □ *children's play-house*: Wendy house

housemaid's knee *technical term*: prepatellar bursitis

huge *combining forms*: mega-, megalo-, macro-

human □ *combining forms*: -anthrop(o)- □ *attribution of human form or behaviour to gods, animals, or inanimate objects*: anthropomorphism □ *assumption of human form by a god, concept, etc.*: embodiment, incarnation □ *attribution of human emotions etc. to inanimate objects*: pathetic fallacy

hundred *combining forms*: cent-, hecto-

Hungarian □ *Hungarian cavalryman*: hussar □ *Hungarian gypsy*: tzigane □ *Hungarian stew*: goulash □ *Hungarian person or his language*: Magyar

hunting □ *adjective*: venatic □ *animal etc. pursued by hunters*: quarry □ *time of year when hunting etc. is permitted*: open season □ *artificial scent used in sham hunts*: drag

husband □ *monarch's husband*: consort □ *husband of unfaithful wife*: cuckold □ *servility of a husband towards his wife*: uxoriousness □ *custom or state of having only one husband at a time*: monandry □ *custom or state of having several husbands at a time*: polyandry

hymn □ *hymn sung as the clergy etc. enter the church for a service*: introit □ *hymn sung during a procession*: processional □ *hymn sung as the clergy etc. leave the church after a service*: recessional □ *Lutheran hymn or its music*: chorale

I

ice □ *adjective*: glacial □ *river of ice*: glacier □ *floating sheet of ice*: floe □ *large floating block of ice*: iceberg □ *area of water crowded with floating blocks of ice*: pack ice □ *thin transparent layer of ice on road etc.*: black ice □ *drink poured over crushed ice*: frappé □ *water ice made from fruit etc.*: sorbet □ *Italian ice cream of various flavours with glacé fruits etc.*: cassata

identical □ *identical twins, technical term*: monozygotic twins □ *genetically identical organism*: clone

illegal □ *official's illegal use of powers or funds entrusted to him*: malversation □ *alcohol distilled illegally in Ireland*: poteen □ *alcohol distilled illegally in the USA*: moonshine

illegitimacy *heraldic indication of illegitimacy*: bar sinister

illness □ *feign illness to avoid work etc.*: malinger □ *denoting a physical illness that has a psychological cause*: psychosomatic □ *denoting an illness caused by medical intervention*: iatrogenic

illusion □ *illusion seen in a desert*: mirage □ *illusion seen on mountain peaks*: Brocken spectre □ *illusionist technique of mural painting*: trompe l'oeil

illustration □ *illustration at the front of a book*: frontispiece □ *illustration used to fill the page at the end of a chapter etc.*: tailpiece □ *illustration of a machine etc. showing the parts separated for clarity*: exploded view □ *illustration of a machine etc. showing its casing cut away*: cutaway

immature *immature works of an artist etc.*: juvenilia

immigrant *immigrant worker in Germany*: Gastarbeiter

immunity □ *immunity offered to previous offenders*: amnesty □ *immunity from local laws enjoyed by foreign diplomats*: extraterritoriality

imprisonment □ *wartime imprisonment of enemy aliens*: internment □ *imprisonment with forced labour*: penal servitude □ *writ to assess the legality of someone's imprisonment*: habeas corpus

impurities *add impurities to food or drink*: adulterate

in *combining forms*: endo-, entro-, intra-, intro-

incidental *incidental remark in a legal judgement*: obiter dictum

income □ *person's income before taxes are deducted*: gross income □ *person's income after taxes have been deducted*: net income, disposable income □ *adequate income*: competence

inconsistency *statement containing two apparently inconsistent elements*: paradox, oxymoron

Indian □ *Indian ruler*: maharaja, raja, nawab, nizam □ *Indian soldier*: sepoy □ *Indian elephant-driver*: mahout □ *Indian fan*: punkah □ *Indian corn, alternative term*: maize □ *flight of steps leading down to a river in India*: ghat □ *Indian ink, alternative term*: Chinese ink

indigestion □ *technical term*: dyspepsia □ *bloated feeling resulting from indigestion*: flatulence

individual *combining form*: idio-

industrial disputes □ *use of a third party to negotiate a settlement*: conciliation □ *recourse to a third party who adjudicates a settlement*: arbitration

inferior *combining forms*: infra-, sub-

inflammation *medical combining form*: -itis

informer *criminal supplying information to the police*: stool-pigeon, nark, grass

inhabitant *original inhabitant*: aboriginal, autochthon

inscription *study of ancient inscriptions*: epigraphy

insect □ *combining form*: entomo- □ *study of insects*: entomology □ *insect in immature grub-like form*: larva □ *insect in inactive stage between larva and adult*: pupa, chrysalis □ *larva of certain insects which develops directly into the adult stage*: nymph □ *transformation of an insect between these stages*: metamorphosis □ *mature insect*: imago □ *insect's feeding tube*: proboscis □ *insect excrement*: frass □ *insect of greenfly or blackfly type, living on plant juices*: aphid

interest □ *interest paid on capital only*: simple interest □ *interest paid on capital and on accumulated interest of previous periods*: compound interest □ *lowest available rate of interest on a bank loan*: prime rate

interval □ *interval between two successive reigns etc.*: interregnum □ *music etc. performed in a theatre interval*: intermezzo, entr'acte

intestines □ *combining form*: enter(o)- □ *pig's intestines prepared as food*: chitterlings □ *pain in the intestines*: colic

into *combining form*: intro-

introductory *combining form*: fore-

invention *document granting an inventor sole right to the exploitation of his work*: patent

investment □ *list of investments made*: portfolio □ *certificate assuring ownership of investments*: securities □ *company holding a wide and changing share portfolio and inviting clients to invest in the whole*: unit trust □ *person living off dividends from investments etc.*: rentier

inward *combining form*: intro-

ion □ *ion having a negative charge*: anion □ *ion having a positive charge*: cation

Ireland □ *adjective*: Hibernian □ *Celtic language of Ireland*: Erse □ *citizen of Ireland, especially if an Erse-speaker*: Gael □ *area of Ireland where Erse is spoken*: Gaeltacht □ *citizen of Northern Ireland who wishes to retain political links with the UK*: Unionist, Loyalist □ *citizen of Ireland who seeks the political unification of the island*: Nationalist

Irish □ *Irish social gathering*: ceilidh □ *Irish accent*: brogue □ *Irish cudgel*: shillelagh □ *Irish police force*: Garda

iron □ *combining forms*: ferro-, ferri-, sider(o)- □ *adjectives*: ferrous □ *block of crude cast iron*: pig

irrigation □ *irrigation device of a bucket on a pole*: shadouf □ *irrigation device of buckets on a wheel*: Noria

island □ *adjective*: insular □ *island on a lake or river*: ait, holm, eyot □ *group of islands*: archipelago □ *low coral island*: cay, key

Israeli □ *Israeli nationalist*: Zionist □ *Israeli collective farm*: kibbutz □ *Isaeli smallholders' co-operative*: moshav

itch □ *technical term*: pruritus □ *itchy feeling as if of ants crawling over the skin*: formication

J

Jamaican *Jaimaican religion regarding Haile Selassie as God*: Rastafarianism

Japanese □ *Japanese emperor*: mikado □ *Japanese art of paper-folding*: origami □ *Japanese wrestling*: sumo □ *Japanese warrior*: samurai □ *ritual suicide required of dishonoured Japanese warrior etc.*: hara-kiri □ *Japanese art of self-defence*: judo, jujitsu, aikido □ *Japanese sport of fencing with wooden swords*: kendo □ *Japanese suicide pilot*: kamikaze □ *Japanese prostitute*: geisha □ *Japanese alcoholic drink made from rice*: sake □ *Japanese dwarf tree*: bonsai □ *Japanese puppet theatre*: bunraku □ *Japanese traditional theatre*: Noh □ *Japanese popular theatre*: kabuki □ *Japanese poem of 17 syllables*: haiku

japonica *alternative term*: camellia

jar *storage jar in classical times*: amphora

jaundice □ *technical term*: icterus □ *liver disease producing jaundice*: hepatitis

Java *Javan percussion orchestra*: gamelan

jaw □ *combining forms*: -gnath-, -gnathic □ *adjective*: gnathic □ *paralysis of the jaws*: lockjaw, trismus

jelly □ *jelly made from meat or fish stock*: aspic □ *dish served in aspic*: galantine

jester □ *jester's cap*: coxcomb □ *jester's baton*: bauble □ *jester's particoloured suit*: motley

Jew □ *combining form*: Judaeo- □ *food etc. that conforms to Jewish dietary regulations*: kosher □ *food etc. that does not conform to Jewish dietary regulations*: tref □ *Jewish unleavened bread*: matzo □ *Jewish seven-branched candlestick*: menorah □ *Orthodox Jew's skullcap*: yarmulke □ *Jewish* *girl's coming of age ceremony*: bat mitzvah □ *Jewish boy's coming of age ceremony*: bar mitzvah □ *language used by Jews of central and eastern Europe*: Yiddish □ *language used by some mediterranean Jews*: Ladino □ *Jewish quarter in a city*: ghetto □ *organized massacre of Jews in 19th-c. Russia etc.*: pogrom □ *Hitler's programme for the extermination of European Jews*: Holocaust □ *Jewish term for non-Jew*: goy

job *job in which no work is required*: sinecure

joint □ *combining forms*: arthr-, -arthr- □ *painful inflammation of the joints*: arthritis

judge □ *adjective*: judicial □ *judge's office for private hearings etc.*: chambers □ *judge's order for enforcement of a law etc.*: injunction □ *expert adviser who sits with a judge in technical cases*: assessor □ *attempt to corrupt a judge*: embracery

judo □ *judo teacher*: judoka □ *judo suit*: judogi □ *judo mat*: dojo

jump □ *sprung stick for making large jumps*: pogo stick □ *sheet stretched taut for jumping on*: trampoline

justice □ *system of justice where the judge or magistrate acts as prosecutor*: inquisitorial system □ *system of justice where the judge or magistrate adjudicates between prosecution and defence*: accusatorial system □ *out-of-court negotiations between prosecution and defence lawyers to secure a reduced charge in return for an admission of guilt*: plea bargaining

K

kidney □ *combining forms*: nephr-, ren-, -ren- □ *adjective*: renal, nephritic

kidney bean *alternative term*: dwarf bean, French bean

kidney machine *technical term*: haemodialyser

kidney stone *technical term*: renal calculus, renal concretion

kill □ *kill by beheading*: decapitate □ *kill by suffocation*: asphyxiate □ *kill selectively, to reduce a herd etc.*: cull □ *killing one's brother*: fratricide □ *killing one's father*: patricide □ *killing one's mother*: matricide □ *killing a parent or other near relative*: parricide □ *killing oneself*: suicide □ *killing a sovereign*: regicide □ *killing a whole race*: genocide □ *mercy killing*: euthanasia

killer *combining form*: -cide

king □ *adjectives*: royal, regal □ *person who governs during a king's illness etc.*: regent □ *disease formerly thought to be cured by the sovereign's touch*: king's evil

kitchen □ *adjective*: culinary □ *kitchen on a ship or aircraft*: galley

kiwi *technical term*: apteryx

kiwi fruit *alternative term*: Chinese gooseberry

kneecap *technical term*: patella

knee-jerk *technical term*: patellar reflex

kidney vetch *alternative terms*: ladies' fingers, okra

knife *knife-maker*: cutler

knotwork *ornamental knotwork made with string*: macramé

knowledge □ *combining forms*: -gnosis, -nomy, -sophy □ *scholarly knowledge*: erudition □ *rote knowledge*: pedantry □ *shallow knowledge*: sciolism □ *instinctive knowledge*: intuition □ *social knowledge*: savoir-faire □ *knowledge before the event*: precognition □ *knowledge after the event*: hindsight □ *knowledge of many subjects*: polymathy □ *knowledge of everything*: omniscience

L

lake □ *adjective*: lacustrine □ *Scottish lake*: loch □ *Irish lake*: lough □ *mountain lake*: tarn □ *lake made by blocked-up loop of river*: oxbow lake □ *study of lakes*: limnology

ladies' fingers *alternative terms*: kidney vetch, okra

Lama □ *chief Lama of Tibet*: Dalai Lama □ *second Lama of Tibet*: Panchen Lama, Tashi Lama

lament □ *Irish lament*: keen □ *Scottish lament*: pibroch

land □ *adjective*: terrestrial □ *right of way over another's land*: easement □ *ownership of land or the land owned*: domain □ *a government's right to take privately owned land into public use*: eminent domain □ *the taking of such land*: expropriation □ *land given for the support of a beneficed clergyman*: glebe □ *land in Holland etc. reclaimed from the sea*: polder □ *narrow strip of land projecting into water*: peninsula □ *narrow strip of land connecting two larger areas*: isthmus □ *narrow strip of land projecting into the holdings of others*: panhandle

language □ *combining forms*: lingu-, -glot □ *adjective*: linguistic □ *everyday language*: vernacular □ *simplified language, often drawn from several sources, used by foreign traders etc.*: pidgin, lingua franca □ *form of a native language that has been corrupted by colonists' speech*: creole □ *basic sound unit in a language*: phoneme □ *basic meaning unit in a language*: semanteme, sememe □ *basic word unit in a language*: morpheme □ *distinctive language of an individual*: idiolect □ *distinctive language of a region*: dialect □ *language as people actually use it*: parole □ *language as described in grammar books*: langue □ *study of language*: linguistics

large *combining forms*: macro-, maxi-, mega-, megalo-

laser *laser-produced three-dimensional image*: hologram

laughing jackass *alternative term*: kookaburra

law □ *adjective*: legal □ *redress of an injustice offered or gained by law*: remedy □ *required by law*: liable □ *academic study of law*: jurisprudence

lead *combining forms*: plumb-

leader □ *combining forms*: -agogue, -arch □ *nominal leader*: figurehead, front man, puppet

leaf □ *combining forms*: -foli-, -phyll- □ *adjectives*: foliaceous, foliate □ *leaves in general*: foliage □ *leaf-stalk*: petiole □ *strip of leaves*: defoliate

leap year □ *adjective*: bissextile □ *technical term*: intercalary year

learning □ *learning from a course in a book or computer*: programmed learning □ *learning through tapes played while asleep*: hypnopaedia □ *learning by controlled trial and error*: heuristic

lease □ *person granting a lease*: lessor □ *person taking a lease*: lessee

leather □ *leather formerly used for writing*: parchment □ *leather strap formerly used to punish Scottish schoolchildren*: tawse □ *impressed ornamentation on leather*: tooling

leave □ *leave to be absent from school*: exeat □ *leave taken without asking permission*: French leave

left □ *combining form*: laev(o)- □ *adjective*: sinistral □ *left-hand page in a book*: verso □ *left-handed person*: southpaw □ *left side of a ship as seen by one facing its prow*: port

leg □ *adjective*: crural □ *swollen vein on the leg*: varicose vein □ *metal support strapped to a broken etc. leg*: calliper

lemon *adjectives*: citric, citrous, citrine

lens □ *variable opening for a camera lens*: aperture □ *camera lens allowing rapid changes in magnification*: zoom lens □ *uneven focus of an eye due to a fault in the cornea or lense*: astigmatism

leprosy *technical term*: Hansen's disease

let *let the buyer beware*: caveat emptor

letter □ *adjective*: epistolary, literal □ *letter sent to all bishops by the Pope*: encyclical □ *letter which each recipient is asked to copy out and send to several others*: chain letter □ *letter sent by a woman breaking off a relationship*: Dear John □ *conventional letter of thanks for hospitality etc.*: Collins □ *opening greeting in a letter*: salutation □ *message added to a letter after the writer's signature*: postscript □ *write out in the letters of a different alphabet*: transliterate

level □ *social level*: stratum, echelon □ *set level to each other, making a single flat surface*: flush □ *device with an air-bubble in liquid to show if surfaces are level*: spirit level

lice *infestation with lice*: pediculosis

lie □ *adjective*: mendacious □ *telling lies when under oath to speak the truth*: perjury □ *lie detector*: polygraph

life □ *combining form*: bio-, vit- □ *adjectives*: animate, vital □ *bodily processes that support life*: metabolism □ *study of living organisms*: physiology □ *long life*: longevity

lifeboat *ship's crane for a lifeboat*: davit

lift □ *lift for food in restaurant etc.*: dumb waiter □ *continuously moving lift with doorless compartments*: paternoster

light *combining forms*: lumin-, photo-, -phos-, -phot-

like *combining forms*: -esque, -oid, -ose

liker *combining forms*: phil(o)-, -phile

lilac *alternative term*: syringa

lime *combining form*: calci-

line □ *line of latitude*: parallel □ *line of longitude*: meridian

lion □ *adjective*: leonine □ *astrological term*: leo

lip □ *combining form*: labi(o)- □ *adjective*: labial

live □ *living on land*: terrestrial □ *living in or near water*: aquatic □ *living in the sea*: marine □ *able to live on land and in water*: amphibious

liver □ *combining form*: hepat- □ *adjective*: hepatic □ *inflammation of the liver, causing jaundice*: hepatitis □ *degeneration of the liver due to alcoholism or hepatitis*: cirrhosis

Liverpool *adjective*: Liverpudlian

lizard □ *combining forms*: sauro-, -saur, -saurus □ *adjective*: saurian □ *lizard that can change its colour for camouflage*: chameleon □ *mythical lizard said to live in fire*: salamander

loan translation *alternative term*: calque

locomotive *frame on the top of an electric locomotive that rises to the overhead wires*: pantograph

loin *adjective*: lumbar

logic □ *false step in reasoning*: fallacy, non sequitur, paralogism □ *deliberately misleading step in reasoning*: sophism □ *disproof of a proposition by demonstrating the absurdity of its consequences*: reductio ad absurdum □ *system of logical reasoning that moves from a general rule to a particular instance*: deduction □ *system of logical reasoning that derives a general rule from particular instances*: induction □ *logical proposition that is verified by the meanings of the words that make it*: analytic proposition □ *logical proposition that is verified by experience*: synthetic proposition

lockjaw *technical term*: trismus

long sight *technical terms*: hypermetropia, hyperopia, presbyopia

lorry □ *articulated lorry's skid into a V-shape*: jackknife □ *device recording a lorry driver's speeds and spells of driving*: tachograph □ *lorry's unladen weight*: tare □ *large covered lorry for furniture etc.*: pantechnicon

loudspeaker □ *loudspeaker for low-pitched sounds*: woofer □ *loudspeaker for high-pitched sounds*: tweeter

love □ *combining forms*: philo-, -phil-, -phile □ *adjectives*: amorous, amatory

loyalty *group loyalty*: esprit de corps

lucerne *alternative term*: alfalfa

luggage *rotating luggage delivery system at an airport etc.*: carousel

lung □ *combining form*: pneumo- □ *adjective*: pulmonary

lying □ *lying face-downwards*: prone □ *lying face-upwards*: supine

M

machine □ *adjective*: mechanical □ *person who behaves like a machine*: automaton □ *person opposed to the introduction of machines*: Luddite

mad cow disease *technical term*: bovine spongiform encephalitis

mad dog *disease caused by the bite of a mad dog*: rabies

made to order *technical term*: bespoke

Mafia □ *Neapolitan Mafia*: Camorra □ *US Mafia*: Cosa Nostra □ *leader of US Mafia*: capo, godfather

magic *object thought to have magic powers*: amulet, fetish, juju, talisman

magistrate *professional magistrate*: stipendiary magistrate

magnetism □ *destroy an object's magnetism*: degauss □ *personal magnetism*: charisma

maidenhead *medical term*: hymen

maize *alternative term*: Indian corn

making *combining forms*: -facient, -fic, -poiesis

malaria □ *drug that cures malaria*: quinine □ *type of mosquito that carries malaria*: anopheles

Malayan □ *Malayan village*: kampong □ *Malayan dagger*: kris □ *Malayan garment*: sarong

male □ *combining forms*: andro-, -andr- □ *aggressive maleness*: machismo □ *development of male characteristics is women*: virilism

mammal □ *mammal with incisor teeth*: rodent □ *mammal that chews the cud*: ruminant □ *thick-skinned mammal (e.g. rhinoceros)*: pachyderm

man □ *combining forms*: andro-, anthropo-, -andr-, -anthrop- □ *adjectives*: male, virile

Manchester *adjective*: Mancunian

mania □ *mania for drink*: dipsomania □ *mania for books*: bibliomania □ *mania for starting fires*: pyromania □ *mania for power or self-aggrandizement*: megalomania □ *manic obsession with a single idea*: monomania □ *mania for stealing*: kleptomania

manioc *alternative term*: cassava

manipulation □ *therapeutic manipulation of bones*: osteopathy □ *manipulation of electoral boundaries for party advantage*: gerrymandering

manners *code of good manners*: etiquette

manuscript □ *manuscript written by the author of the text it contains*: autograph □ *manuscript wholly written by the author of the text it contains*: holograph □ *manuscript with a text written over an earlier text*: palimpsest □ *sheepskin or goatskin prepared for use as a manuscript*: parchment □ *calfskin prepared for use as a manuscript*: vellum

Manx *Manx emblem of three legs*: triskelion

many *combining forms*: multi-, poly-, pluri-

marble *adjective*: marmoreal

marriage □ *combining form*: -gam- □ *adjectives*: conjugal, connubial, marital, matrimonial, nuptial □ *unsuccessful marriage*: misalliance □ *marriage with a social inferior*: mésalliance □ *marriage formalized by a legal ceremony only*: civil marriage □ *clothing etc. collected by a bride before her marriage*: trousseau, bottom drawer □ *property etc. brought by a bride to her marriage*: dowry □ *crime of being simultaneously married to several spouses*: bigamy □ *practice of being simultaneously married to several spouses*: polygamy □ *practice of having only one spouse at a time*: monogamy □ *practice of living together without being married*: cohabitation, common-law marriage

Mars *Greek name*: Ares

marsh □ *adjective*: paludal □ *marsh gas*: methane □ *moving light seen over marshes when the methane ignites*: will-o'-the-wisp, ignis fatuus

mask □ *mask to protect the eyes*: visor □ *mask to aid breathing*: respirator □ *mask with attached cloak*: domino

massage *massage treatment using fragrant oils*: aromatherapy

master *adjective*: magisterial

matchbox *collector of matchbox labels*: phillumenist

matter *combining form*: hyl-

mattress □ *mattress stuffed with straw*: pallet, palliasse □ *strong cloth used to cover mattresses, pillows, etc.*: ticking

meadow saffron *alternative term*: autumn crocus

meal □ *meal taken as breakfast and lunch*: brunch □ *self-service meal*: buffet □ *light meal*: tiffin, collation □ *restaurant meal with a fixed global price and offering few alternatives*: table d'hôte □ *restaurant meal chosen from a range of separately priced dishes*: à la carte

meaning □ *adjective*: semantic □ *general meaning of a text etc.*: burden, gist, gravamen □ *word having the same meaning as another*: synonym □ *word having the opposite meaning to another*: antonym

measles *technical term*: morbilli, rubella

measurement □ *combining forms*: -metr-, -metry □ *adjectives*: mensural, metrical

meat □ *cold cooked meats*: charcuterie □ *meat minced for stuffing*: forcemeat □ *seasoned smoked beef*: pastrami □ *German pork sausage*: bratwurst □ *Italian peppered pork and beef sausage*: pepperoni □ *Italian garlic sausage*: salami □ *spiced Italian pork sausage*: mortadella □ *Italian ham*: prosciutto □ *meat cooked very rare*: au bleu □ *meat cooked rare*: saignant □ *medium-cooked meat*: à point □ *well-cooked meat*: bien cuit

medical examination *combining form*: -opsy

medical treatment □ *combining form*: -pathy □ *medical treatment of children*: paediatrics □ *medical treatment of old people*: geriatrics □ *medical treatment of women*: gynaecology □ *medical treatment of the skin*: dermatology □ *medical treatment of bones and muscles*: orthopaedics □ *medical treatment of the blood*: haematology □ *medical treatment of the nervous system*: neurology □ *medical teatment of mental diseases*: psychiatry □ *medical treatment by small doses of drugs that would induce the disease*: homoeopathy □ *medical treatment by drugs that resist the disease*: allopathy

medicine *combining form*: pharm(aco)-

meeting □ *meeting for academic discussion*: colloquium, seminar, symposium □ *meeting for church government*: synod, consistory □ *meeting of cardinals to elect a pope*: conclave □ *meeting of political delegates etc.*: congress, convention □ *mass meeting of supporters etc.*: rally □ *meeting of heads of state*: summit □ *minimum attendance required for a meeting to be valid*: quorum

membrane □ *membrane dividing the thorax from the abdomen*: diaphragm □ *membrane lining the abdomen*: peritoneum □ *membrane blocking a virgin's vagina*: hymen

memory □ *loss of memory*: amnesia, oblivion □ *formula etc. used to aid memorization or recall*: mnemonic

men □ *rule by men*: patriarchy □ *hatred of men*: misandry □ *party for men*: stag party

menstruation □ *first onset of menstruation at puberty*: menarche □ *menstrual blood*: menses □ *painful or difficult menstruation*: dysmenorrhoea □ *abnormal absence of menstruation*: amenorrhoea □ *cessation of menstruation in middle age*: menopause

Mercury □ *Greek name*: Hermes □ *Mercury's snake-twined staff*: caduceus

mercy killing *technical term*: euthanasia

middle □ *combining forms*: medi-, mes- □ *adjectives*: medial, median □ *middle ear*: tympanum

military □ *swift and intense military attack*: blitzkrieg □ *military officer assisting a senior officer*: adjutant, aide-de-camp □ *military officers who plan a campaign*: general staff □ *long-term military plans*: strategy □ *short-term military plans*: tactics □ *provision of military manpower and supplies*: logistics □ *military stores and materials*: ordnance □ *military court*: court martial

milk □ *combining forms*: lact-, galact- □ *adjectives*: lactic, lacteal

million *combining form*: mega-

millionth *combining form*: micro-

mind *adjective*: mental

Minerva *Greek name*: Athena

mirror *adjective*: catoptric

misfortune *delight in the misfortunes of others*: schadenfreude

mix □ *mix to make uniform throughout*: homogenize □ *mix to create something different*: synthesize □ *mix socially with*: fraternize

mock orange *alternative term*: syringa

modification *modification to parliamentary bill or judicial verdict*: rider

moisture □ *combining form*: hygro- □ *full of moisture*: saturated, desiccated □ *void of moisture*: dehydrated

mole *technical term*: naevus

Monaco *adjective*: Monegasque

money □ *adjectives*: pecuniary, monetary, numismatic □ *money paid to ensure secrecy*: hush money □ *money paid as a political bribe*: slush money □ *money paid as consolation to a redundant etc. executive*: golden handshake, golden parachute □ *extra money paid to employees working in a high cost-of-living area*: weighting □ *dispose of money so as to conceal its illegal origins*: launder

mongolism *technical term*: Down's syndrome

monkey *adjective*: simian

moon □ *combining forms*: lun-, selen- □ *adjective*: lunar

mortgage □ *person granting a mortgage*: mortgagee □ *person taking out a mortgage*: mortgager

Moscow *adjective*: Muscovite

mosque □ *mosque tower*: minaret □ *person calling the faithful to prayer from a minaret*: muezzin □ *mosque's pulpit*: mimbar □ *niche in a mosque's wall facing Mecca*: mimbar

moss □ *combining form*: bryo- □ *study of mosses*: bryology

mother □ *combining form*: matri- □ *adjective*: maternal □ *murder of one's mother*: matricide

motion *adjective*: kinetic

mountain sickness *alternative term*: altitude sickness

mouse *adjective*: murine

mouth □ *combining forms*: or-, stomato-, -stom-, -stome □ *adjectives*: oral, buccal

much *combining forms*: multi-, poly-

muscle *muscle-building drug used by athletes etc.*: anabolic steroid

musician *street musician*: busker

Muslim □ *Muslim name for God*: Allah □ *Muslim scriptures*: Koran □ *Muslim month-long fast*: Ramadan □ *Muslim pilgrimage to Mecca*: haj □ *Muslim mystic*: dervish, sufi □ *Muslim who calls the faithful to prayer*: muezzin □ *Muslim religious leader*: ayatollah, imam, mullah □ *Muslim holy war*: jihad □ *Muslim prince*: emir □ *Muslim princess*: begum □ *Muslim judge*: cadi □ *Muslim chronological era*: Hegira □ *Muslim food regulations*: halal □ *Muslim term for forbidden foods*: haram □ *Muslim seclusion of women*: purdah □ *Muslim woman's veil*: yashmak □ *Muslim woman's overgarment*: chador

N

nail □ *adjective*: ungual □ *dead skin at the base of a nail*: cuticle □ *piece of torn skin beside a nail*: agnail □ *inflammation near a nail*: whitlow

name □ *combining forms*: onom-, nomin-, -nym □ *adjective*: onomastic □ *false name*: pseudonym, alias, nom de plume

Naples *adjective*: Neapolitan

Native American *alternative terms*: American Indian, Amerindian, Red Indian

navel □ *technical term*: umbilicus □ *adjective*: umbilical

navigation *navigation based on computation of position from speed and direction of travel*: dead reckoning

Nazi □ *official title*: National Socialist □ *Nazi emblem*: swastika □ *Nazi marching step*: goose step □ *Nazi secret police*: Gestapo □ *Nazi regional governor*: Gauleiter

neck □ *adjective*: jugular □ *fold of skin hanging from a bird's neck*: wattle □ *fold of skin hanging from the necks of cattle*: dewlap

Neptune *Greek name*: Poseidon

nerve □ *combining form*: neur(o)- □ *adjective*: neural

net □ *adjective*: retiform □ *woman's hairnet*: snood □ *Roman gladiator armed with net*: retiarius

nettle-rash *technical term*: urticaria

new □ *combining forms*: ana-, neo- □ *new thing*: innovation □ *new word*: neologism

newspaper □ *newspaper with large pages*: broadsheet □ *newspaper with small pages*: tabloid

night □ *combining forms*: noct-, nyct- □ *adjective*: nocturnal

night blindness *technical term*: nyctalopia

non-interference *government policy of non-interference*: laissez-faire

non-violence □ *Hindu and Buddhist principle of non-violence towards all living things*: ahimsa □ *non-violent resistance as a form of political protest*: civil disobedience □ *non-violent resistance as advocated by Gandhi in India*: satyagraha

north *adjective*: boreal

northern lights *technical term*: aurora borealis

nose □ *combining forms*: nas(o)-, -rhin(o)- □ *adjectives*: nasal, rhinal □ *hooked nose*: Roman nose □ *straight nose*: Grecian nose

nosebleed *technical term*: epistaxis

nostril □ *technical term*: naris (*plural* nares) □ *adjective*: narial

not *combining forms*: a-, an,- dis-, un-

notebook *notebook containing a personal collection of literary quotations etc.*: commonplace book

noun *adjective*: nominal

novel □ *novel depicting real persons or events but with changed names*: roman à clef □ *novel depicting its hero's early life*: Bildungsroman □ *family novel, usually dealing with several generations*: roman-fleuve □ *novel presented as a series of letters*: epistolary novel

nuclear reactor □ *type of nuclear reactor producing more nuclear fuel than it consumes*: breeder □ *overheating and destruction of a nuclear reactor's core*: meltdown

number □ *number indicating quantity*: cardinal number □ *number indicating position in a sequence*: ordinal number □ *whole number*: integer □ *number system based on 10*: decimal system □ *number system based on 0 and 1*: binary system □ *number system based on 12*: duodecimal system

nut *combining forms*: nuci-

nutrition *combining forms*: troph-, -troph-

nymph □ *tree nymph*: hamadryad □ *wood nymph*: dryad □ *mountain nymph*: oread □ *river nymph*: naiad □ *sea nymph*: nereid □

O

oath □ *evidence given under oath*: deposition □ *written statement made under oath*: affidavit □ *solicitor entitled to administer oaths*: Commissioner for Oaths

offal □ *deer's offal*: umbles □ *fowl's offal*: giblets

official *government official investigating complaints against public bodies*: ombudsman

oil □ *combining form*: ole- □ *adjective*: oleaginous □ *sacramental oil*: chrism, unguent

okra *alternative terms*: kidney vetch, ladies' fingers

old *combining forms*: archaeo-, palaeo-

old age □ *combining form*: geront- □ *mental and physical decay characteristic of old age*: senility □ *study of old age*: geriatrics

old woman *adjective*: anile

one *combining forms*: mon(o)-, uni-

one and a half *combining form*: sesqui-

opera □ *word-book of an opera*: libretto □ *running translation of an opera displayed above the stage*: surtitles □ *famous female opera singer*: diva □ *person teaching opera singers in their music*: répétiteur

opposite □ *opposite side of the world*: antipodes □ *word having the opposite sense*: antonym

orbit □ *point in an orbit furthest from the earth, moon, sun*: apogee, apolune, aphelion □ *point in an orbit closest to the earth, moon, sun*: perigee, perilune, perihelion □ *orbit that keeps a satellite fixed over a terrestrial point*: geostationary orbit □ *star etc. round which a satellite orbits*: primary

order □ *order for supplies*: requisition □ *order for work to be undertaken*: commission □ *order sent from a higher to a lower court*: mandamus □ *order for a person to attend a court*: summons, subpoena □ *court order requiring a certain actions to be performed or avoided*: writ, injunction

organization □ *organization sponsored but not controlled by government*: quango □ *detailed practical organization required to implement a plan*: logistics

origin □ *combining forms*: -genesis, -geny □ *geographical origin of a work of art*: provenance □ *study of the origins of words*: etymology □ *study of the origins of names*: onomastics

Orkneys *adjective*: Orcadian

ostrich *adjective*: struthious

other *combining form*: heter(o)-

otter *otter's lair*: holt, lodge

out *combining forms*: e-, ec-, ex-

ovary □ *combining form*: oophor- □ *immature ovum in the ovary*: oocyte □ *ovary cavity for the ovum*: follicle

over *combining forms*: hyper-, super-, supra-, sur-, trans-

overeating *compulsive overeating*: bulimia

Oxford University □ *Oxford University annual feast*: encaenia □ *Oxford University formal dress*: subfusc □ *Oxford college annual feast*: gaudy □ *Oxford college servant*: scout

P

pain □ *combining forms*: alg-, -algia □ *pain that shoots along a nerve*: neuralgia □ *pain felt away from its real source*: referred pain

painting □ *painting on wet plaster*: fresco □ *painting on dry plaster*: secco □ *painting intended to give a deceptive three-dimensional view*: trompe l'oeil □ *painting in shades of grey to imitate sculpture, masonry, etc.*: grisaille □ *painting in shades of a single colour*: monochrome □ *small cracks on an old painting's surface*: craquelure □ *reappearance of traces of earlier painting*: pentimento

pair *combining form*: zyg-

pancake □ *French pancake*: crêpe □ *Russian pancake*: blini

paper □*front side of a sheet of paper*: recto □ *reverse side of a sheet of paper*: verso □ *maker's emblem etc. in a sheet of paper*: watermark □ *quality of paper used for top copies*: bond □ *quality of paper used for carbon copies etc.*: bank □ *art of folding paper into decorative shapes*: origami

parachute □ *cord pulled by the parachuter to open a parachute*: ripcord □ *cord fixed to the aircraft to open a jumper's parachute*: static line □ *expanding part of a parachute that arrests and directs its movement*: canopy □ *ropes that hold and control a parachute's canopy*: shrouds □ *sort of parachute used to decelerate a landing aircraft*: drogue parachute

paralysis □ *combining form*: -plegia □ *paralysis from the neck down*: quadriplegia, tetraplegia □ *paralysis from the waist down*: paraplegia □ *paralysis of one side of the body*: hemiplegia □ *paralysis of a single limb*: monoplegia

parish *adjective*: parochial

parrot □ *adjective*: psittacine □ *pneumonia-like disease caught by humans from parrots*: psittacosis

part □ *combining forms*: mero-, -merous □ *composed of similar parts*: homogeneous □ *composed of dissimilar parts*: heterogeneous

Passover □ *adjective*: paschal □ *Jews' name for Passover*: Pesach □ *Passover ceremonies and feast*: Seder □ *Passover bread*: matzo

pastry □ *place where pastries are sold*: patisserie □ *soft light pastry for éclairs etc.*: choux pastry □ *light pastry used in sausage rolls etc.*: puff pastry □ *Greek pastry rolled into thin leaves*: filo pastry

patch □ *having black and white patches*: piebald □ *having patches of white and of some other colour (not black)*: skewbald

path □ *raised path used by models in a fashion show*: catwalk □ *raised path over land liable to flooding*: causeway □ *country path for walkers and horseriders*: bridlepath □ *path alongside a canal*: towpath

pause □ *pause for food, sleep, private discussion, etc. in a court or parliamentary session*: adjournment □ *pause for holidays in a parliamentary session*: recess □ *pause for holidays in a court session*: vacation □ *pause in the middle of a line of verse*: caesura

pay bed *technical term*: amenity bed

payment □ *divorced person's payment to former spouse*: maintenance □ *advance payment made for club membership, or for a series of performances, issues of a journal, etc.*: subscription □ *payment made for services not officially charged for*: honorarium □ *payment made in kind*: truck □ *initial payment made to a barrister*: retainer □ *subsequent payment made to a barrister in a long case*: refresher

peacock *adjective*: pavonine

Peking *currently preferred transliteration*: Beijing

permission □ *permission to be absent from school*: exeat □ *ecclesiatical permission to publish a book*: imprimatur □ *absence without permission*: French leave

permit *customs permit for the temporary import of a motor vehicle*: carnet

petrol bomb □ *crude bomb made by filling a bottle with petrol*: Molotov cocktail □ *jellied petrol used in US incendiary bombs in Vietnam etc.*: napalm

picture □ *simplified picture used to represent a word in some ancient writing systems*: pictograph □ *picture puzzle in which a word is represented by pictures of objects whose names make its syllables*: rebus

pig □ *adjective*: porcine □ *pig's offal used as food*: chitterlings, haslet □ *pig's feet used as food*: trotters □ *smallest piglet in a litter*: runt

piles *technical term*: haemorrhoids

pillar □ *combining forms*: styl-, -stylar □ *prehistoric ring of pillars*: henge □ *classical pillar carved to resemble a man*: telamon □ *classical pillar carved to resemble a woman*: caryatid □ *early Christian saint living on the top of a pillar*: stylite □ *Amerindian carved pillar*: totem pole

pilot *Japanese suicide pilot*: kamikaze

pimento *alternative term*: pimiento

pinwheel *alternative term*: Catherine wheel

pipe □ *long-stemmed clay pipe*: churchwarden □ *Amerindian peace pipe*: calumet □ *oriental smoker's pipe in which the smoke is passed through water*: hookah, narghile

pitch *drop in pitch of a sound that passes the hearer and moves away*: Doppler effect

pith helmet *alternative term*: sola topi

pituitary gland *technical term*: hypophysis

pivot □ *pivot on a rudder*: pintle □ *pivot on a large gun*: trunnion

place □ *combining form*: top- □ *list of places*: gazetteer □ *'feel' of a place*: genius loci

plain □ *plain in Russia*: steppe □ *plain in South Africa*: veldt □ *grassy plain in warm countries*: savannah □ *Arctic plain*: tundra

planning □ *planning method that evaluates a complex set of alternatives*: critical path analysis □ *practical planning, especially of transport*: logistics □ *planning schedule*: PERT chart

plant □ *combining forms*: phyto-, -phyte □ *plant living for one year only*: annual □ *plant living for two years only*: biennial □ *plant living for three or more years*: perennial □ *use by green plants of sunlight energy*: photosynthesis

plant louse *technical term*: aphid

planned economy *alternative term*: command economy

plaster □ *decorative plasterwork*: pargeting □ *fine plaster for frescos etc.*: stucco □ *roughen a plaster surface to aid adhesion*: key □ *smooth a plaster surface*: float

plastic □ *sheet plastic used as glazing etc.*: Perspex™ □ *plastic-coated cloth used for tablecloths etc.*: American cloth □ *plastic lamination for kitchen work surfaces etc.*: Formica™ □ *plastic used for gramophone records etc.*: vinyl □ *plastic used in paints*: acrylic, vinyl □ *plastic used for packing*: expanded polystyrene

plastic surgery *technical term*: anaplasty

platform □ *platform for a gibbet etc.*: scaffold □ *platform for election speeches*: hustings

pleasure □ *pleasure-loving*: hedonistic □ *pleasure derived from the suffering of others*: Roman holiday □ *pleasure gained from the contemplation of others' misfortunes*: schadenfreude

plug □ *plug for the vent of a cask*: spigot, spile □ *plug for the muzzle of a large gun*: tampion □ *plug for a cannon's touch-hole*: spike

poem □ *poem celebrating a marriage*: epithalamium, prothalamium □ *poem about rural life*: bucolic, eclogue, georgic □ *poem lamenting a person's death*: elegy, threnody □ *five-line nonsense poem*: limerick □ *Japanese three-line poem of 17 syllables*: haiku □ *poem constructed so that certain letters from each line form a name etc.*: acrostic

poet □ *successful poet at an Eisteddfodd*: bard □ *French medieval poet*: troubadour, trouvère □ *Scandinavian medieval poet*: skald

Poseidon □ *Latin name*: Neptune □ *Poseidon's three-pronged spear*: trident

poison □ *combining forms*: toxi-, toxo- □ *poison produced by a fungus on peanuts*: aflatoxin □ *poison produced by a fungus on cereals*: ergot □ *poison drunk by Socrates*: hemlock □ *cure for a poison*: antitoxin, antivenin

pole *pole used to push a punt etc.*: quant

police □ *police van*: Black Maria □ *police kit for assembling a likeness of a wanted person*: identikit, photofit

policy □ *published policy statement*: manifesto □ *reversal of policy*: about-face, volte-face, U-turn

polio *technical terms*: poliomyelitis, infantile paralysis

politics □ *political agenda driven by practical needs rather than moral principles*: realpolitik □ *persistent dissemination of political propaganda via the media*: agitprop □ *discarded political system*: ancien régime □ *political opposition in a one-party state*: dissidence □ *splinter group within a political party*: faction, caucus □ *political enthusiast*: activist, militant, Young Turk

poll □ *public poll on some issue of current concern*: plebiscite, referendum □ *officer who counts the votes cast in a poll*: scrutineer □ *officer administering a poll and announcing its result*: returning officer

pope □ *adjective*: papal □ *pope's triple crown*: tiara □ *pope's letter to the Church*: bull, brief, encyclical □ *pope's ambassador*: nuncio □ *clergyman acting as a pope's representative*: legate □ *pope's administrative staff*: curia □ *meeting of cardinals to elect a new pope*: conclave

population □ *combining form*: dem(o)- □ *study of population statistics*: demography

possession □ *useless possession*: white elephant □ *possession giving social prestige*: status symbol

post-mortem □ *technical term*: autopsy □ *doctor conducting post-mortem examination*: pathologist □ *magistrate conducting post-mortem judicial inquiry*: coroner

posture *cross-legged position with the legs resting on opposite thighs*: lotus position

pouch □ *kangaroo's pouch*: marsupium □ *Scotsman's pouch*: sporran

power □ *combining form*: dynam(o)- □ *absolute power*: carte blanche □ *transfer of power from central to regional authorities*: devolution

prairie wolf *alternative term*: coyote

pregnancy □ *technical term*: cyesis □ *adjectives*: antenatal, prenatal □ *craving for strange foods during pregnancy*: pica □ *custom in some cultures of the husband's taking to his bed during the latter stages of a pregnancy*: couvade □ *spontaneous expulsion of the foetus early in pregnancy*: miscarriage □ *medically induced expulsion or destruction of an unviable foetus*: abortion □ *diagnostic sampling of amniotic fluid during pregnancy*: amniocentesis □ *toxic condition during pregnancy*: eclampsia □ *false pregnancy*: pseudocyesis

price □ *lowest price at which an auctioned item may be sold*: reserve price □ *raise a previously agreed price*: gazump

prickly heat *technical term*: miliaria

priest □ *adjective*: sacerdotal □ *priest's robes*: vestments □ *Roman Catholic priest's hat*: biretta □ *Anglican priest's house*: rectory, vicarage □ *Roman Catholic priest's house*: presbytery □ *Buddhist priest in China or Japan*: bonze □ *Orthodox priest in Greece*: pope, papas □ *Orthodox priest in Russia*: pope

principle □ *principle that if anything can go wrong it will*: Murphy's law, sod's law □ *principle that employees are always promoted beyond their abilities*: Peter principle □ *principle that work expands to fill the time available*: Parkinson's law

prison □ *Nazi prison camp*: stalag □ *Soviet labour prison*: gulag

prisoner *prisoner who has won privileges by good behaviour*: trusty

prize □ *prize given to near-winner*: consolation prize, proxime accessit □ *prize given to worst contestant*: booby prize, wooden spoon

problem □ *problem-solving by application of logic*: vertical thinking □ *problem-solving by a seemingly illogical thought process*: lateral thinking □ *problem-solving by random trial and error*: heuristic

producing *combining forms*: -facient, -fer, -fic, -gen, -genic, -genous

property □ *legal document transferring ownership of property*: conveyance □ *government's right to seize private property for state use*: eminent domain □ *seize property for the repayment of a debt*: distrain, sequester □ *repossess a mortgaged property upon failure of payments*: foreclose

prophet □ *prophet of doom*: Jeremiah □ *prophet of doom who is ignored*: Cassandra

pulp □ *pulp of pressed grapes*: marc □ *pulp of pressed apples*: pomace

punishment □ *combining form*: pen(o)- □ *adjective*: penal □ *punishment seen as a deterrent to others*: exemplary punishment □ *punishment seen as society's revenge on the criminal*: retributive punishment □ *study of punishment*: penology

puppy love *alternative term*: calf love

purification *purification of the emotions through drama etc.*: catharsis

pus □ *combining form*: pyo- □ *adjective*: purulent

putto *alternative terms*: amoretto, cherub

Q

queen *adjectives*: royal, regal
question □ *set of questions and answers used as a means of instruction*: catechism □ *question returned diplomat etc. about his misson*: debrief
quick □ *quick and efficient*: expeditious □ *quick and careless*: perfunctory

R

rabbit □ *female rabbit*: doe □ *male rabbit*: buck □ *very young rabbit*: kitten □ *disease fatal to rabbits*: myxomatosis
rabies *technical term*: hydrophobia
radioactivity □ *instrument for measuring radioactivity*: Geiger counter □ *atmospheric radioactivity after a nuclear explosion*: fallout □ *radioactive substance whose passage though the body is monitored for diagnostic purposes*: tracer
rain □ *combining form*: pluvi(o)- □ *rain cloud*: nimbus □ *rainy season in India etc.*: monsoon □ *spraying chemicals into a cloud to produce rain*: seeding
rainbow *band of colours seen in the rainbow*: spectrum
rally *rally of Scouts and/or Guides*: jamboree
random *of music allowing for some random elements in its performance*: aleatoric
rapid *combining form*: tach(o)-, tach(y)-
raven *adjective*: corvine
ray *adjective*: radial
read □ *inability to read due to ignorance*: illiteracy □ *inability to read due to brain damage*: alexia □ *difficulty with reading due to brain dysfunction*: dyslexia
reason *adjective*: rational
recent *combining form*: neo-
record □ *combining form*: -gram □ *set of records, papers, etc. on a particular topic*: dossier □ *record of a person's education and career*: curriculum vitae □ *record of a business meeting*: minutes □ *record of a learned society's meetings*: proceedings, transactions □ *collection of written etc. records*: archive
recorder *combining form*: -graph
recruitment □ *former services' recruitment unit, employing force and trickery*: pressgang □ *entice (esp. senior) employees away from other companies*: headhunt
rectum *combining form*: proct(o)-
red *combining forms*: erythr(o)-, rhod(o)-, rub(i)
Red Indian *alternative terms*: American Indian, Amerindian, Native American
refuse □ *refuse to do business with*: boycott □ *refuse to socialize with*: ostracize
registration plate *specially purchased vehicle registration plates that contain the owner's initials etc.*: vanity plates
reign □ *adjective*: regnal □ *period between two reigns*: interregnum
related □ *related by blood*: consanguineous □ *related through marriage or adoption*: affined □ *related through the paternal line*: agnate □ *related through the maternal line*: cognate □ *(of words) related by having a common source*: cognate □ *related at a distance of x generations*: x times removed
relative density *apparatus measuring a liquid's relative density*: hydrometer
religion □ *religious belief in the existence of a single god*: monotheism □ *religious belief in the existence of several gods*: polytheism □ *religious belief in counterbalanced forces of good and evil*: dualism □ *religious belief that God created the world but has had no further involvement with it*: deism □ *religious belief that God created the world and continues to be active in it*: theism □ *religious belief that God and the universe are identical*: pantheism
remote *remote area*: ultima Thule
renewable energy *alternative term*: alternative energy
rent □ *nominal rent*: peppercorn rent □ *excessive rent*: rack-rent □ *person living on rental income*: rentier
replacement □ *temporary replacement for doctor etc.*: locum □ *fertile woman replacing a would-be mother unable to bear children*: surrogate
report □ *government report with proposals for public discussion*: green paper □ *government report with proposals for legislation*: white paper
reproduction □ *combining forms*: gon-, -gen-, -genesis □ *reproducing by means of eggs*: oviparous □ *reproducing live offspring*: viviparous □ *reproducing by giving birth from eggs hatched within the body*: ovoviviparous
reptile *combining form*: herpet(o)-
retort *witty retort that comes to mind after the chance to make it has gone*: esprit de l'escalier
rhyme □ *rhyme between final stressed syllables*: masculine rhyme □ *rhyme between words with final unstressed syllables*: feminine rhyme □ *false rhyme between words that look but do not sound the same*: eye-rhyme □ *game of inventing successive lines of rhyming verse*: crambo
rib *adjective*: costal
riches *imaginary land of great riches*: eldorado
rickets *technical term*: rachitis
right □ *combining forms*: □ *hand*: dextro- □ *correct, upright*: ortho- □ *right of way etc. enjoyed over another's property*: easement □ *right of way etc. that one must allow another over one's property*: servitude □ *right side of a ship as seen by one facing its prow*: starboard
ring □ *adjective*: annular □ *ring for the leash on a dog's collar*: terret □ *leather ring for Scout's neckerchief*: woggle □ *finger ring having a seal instead of a stone*: signet ring □ *plain ring worn in a pierced ear to prevent its healing*: sleeper □ *ring inserted in the lip*: labret □ *ring of muscle*: sphincter □ *ring of light round the sun or moon*: aureole, corona
ringing *persistent ringing sound heard in one or both ears*: tinnitus
ringworm *technical term*: tinea pedis
risk *risk inherent in a particular activity*: occupational hazard

ritual □ *admission ritual*: initiation □ *ritual marking a new stage in life*: rite of passage □ *ritual pouring of liquid*: libation

river □ *adjectives*: fluvial, potamic, riverine □ *ice river*: glacier □ *small island in a river*: ait, eyot □ *horseshoe-shaped bend in a river's course*: oxbow □ *triangular area, with many streams, at a river's mouth*: delta □ *wide area of water at a river's mouth*: estuary □ *low dam in a river to regulate its flow*: weir □ *dry river bed*: wadi □ *high wave moving up a river at the spring tide*: bore, eagre

river bank *adjective*: riparian

road □ *scenic coast road*: corniche □ *road on which no stopping is permitted*: clearway □ *road with no exit*: cul-de-sac □ *rise in a road's surface towards the centre, to assist drainage*: camber □ *hump built across a road to limit speeds*: sleeping policeman

rock □ *combining forms*: litho-, petro-, -lith-, -lite □ *loose pieces of rock on a hillside*: scree

rocket □ *rocket's curving course*: trajectory □ *scaffold supporting a space rocket before take-off*: gantry

rod □ *rod said to indicate underground springs etc. by twitching*: dowsing rod □ *bundle of rods with an axe, carried before Roman magistrates*: fasces

root □ *combining forms*: rhiz-, -radic- □ *adjective*: radical

rope □ *adjective*: funicular □ *ship's heavy rope for mooring etc.*: hawser □ *secure a rope*: belay □ *interweave two ropes*: splice □ *bind a rope-end to prevent fraying*: whip □ *descend a rock face using a double rope coiled round the body*: abseil

rot *combining form*: sapr-

row *combining forms*: stich-, -stichous

rowing boat □ *support for rowing boat's oar*: rowlock □ *seat for oarsman*: thwart □ *rowing boat for a single oarsman*: scull □ *steersman in a rowing boat*: cox □ *oarsman next to the cox*: stroke

rule □ *combining forms*: -archy, -cracy □ *rules for social behaviour*: etiquette □ *procedural rules for diplomatic etc. occasions*: protocol □ *rules for the grammatical arangement of words in a language*: syntax □ *rules of boxing*: Queensberry Rules

ruler □ *combining forms*: -arch, -crat □ *former chief magistrate at Genoa and Venice*: doge □ *Nazi ruler of Germany*: führer □ *former rulers in India*: nawab, nizam □ *former ruler of Iran*: shah □ *Islamic rulers*: ayatollah, caliph, emir □ *Fascist ruler of Italy*: duce □ *former Japanese rulers*: mikado, shogun □ *Ottoman rulers*: aga, bey, khedive, pasha, sultan □ *Spanish military dictator*: caudillo □ *former ruler of Tibet*: Dalai Lama □ *former ruler of Russia*: tsar □ *ruling group (often military officers) following a coup d'état*: junta

rumour □ *false, often malicious, rumour*: canard □ *source of rumours*: bush telegraph, grapevine

runic alphabet *technical term*: futhorc

running *combining form*: -dromous

rupture *technical term*: hernia

Russian □ *Russian script*: Cyrillic □ *old Russian woman*: babushka □ *set of Russian babushka dolls*: matrioshka □ *Russian cavalryman*: cossack □ *Russian country cottage*: dacha □ *Russian citadel*: kremlin □ *Russian guitar*: balalaika □ *Russian pancake*: blini □ *Russian beetroot soup*: bortsch □ *Russian beer*: kvass □ *Russian tea urn*: samovar

S

sacred *combining form*: hier(o)-

saddle *second saddle on a horse or motorcycle*: pillion

safety *safety switch in a locomotive cab that cuts the engine unless constantly depressed by the driver*: dead man's handle

sailor □ *ordinary sailor*: rating □ *sailor's canvas bed*: hammock □ *dried bread formerly eaten by sailors*: hard tack, ship's biscuit □ *punish a sailor by dragging him beneath the ship*: keelhaul

saint □ *combining form*: hagi(o)- □ *declare a person to be a saint*: canonize □ *person arguing for a saint's canonization*: postulator □ *person arguing against a saint's canonization*: devil's advocate

Saint Vitus' dance *technical term*: Sydenham's chorea

same □ *combining form*: taut(o)- □ *of the same age or time*: coetaneous, coeval, contemporary □ *of the same size*: commensurate □ *of the same extent or meaning*: coterminous □ *of the same shape*: congruent □ *having the same meaning*: synonymous

satellite *communications etc. satellite orbiting at a fixed position relative to the earth*: geostationary satellite, geosynchronous satellite

sausage □ *seasoned smoked sausage*: saveloy □ *small thin spicy sausage*: chipolata □ *German pork sausage*: bratwurst □ *Italian peppered pork and beef sausage*: pepperoni □ *Italian garlic sausage*: salami □ *spiced Italian pork sausage*: mortadella

saying □ *wise saying*: aphorism, epigram □ *trite saying*: platitude, cliché, bromide

scale □ *scale for wind velocities*: Beaufort scale □ *scale for earthquake intensities*: Richter scale □ *scale for child intelligence*: Binet–Simon scale □ *relating to a twelve-tone musical scale*: chromatic □ *relating to an eight-tone musical scale*: diatonic

scales *astrological term*: libra

scaly *technical term*: squamose

scarlet fever *technical term*: scarlatina

scent *dried petals used for scent*: pot-pourri

scissors *tailor's serrated scissors*: pinking shears

scorpion *astrological term*: scorpio

screen □ *sliding screen in a Japanese house*: shoji □ *screen in an Indian house concealing women from view*: purdah

screw □ *screw with a cross-shaped slot*: Phillips screw □ *screw with a hexagonal slot*: Allen screw

scriptures □ *Islamic scriptures*: Koran □ *Sikh scriptures*: Granth □ *Hindu scriptures*: Veda □ *Buddhist scriptures*: Tripitaka □ *Zoroastrian scriptures*: Avesta

scurvy *adjective*: scorbutic

sea *adjectives*: marine, maritime

second *combining forms*: deut-, deutero-

secret societies □ *Sicilian secret criminal and political organization*: Mafia □ *Neapolitan branch of the Mafia*: Camorra □ *US branch of the Mafia*: Cosa Nostra □ *Chinese secret criminal gang*: Tong, Triad □ *US secret society promoting White supremacy*: Klu Klux Klan □ *international secret society with allegedly social purposes*: Freemasonry

security *security given for a loan*: collateral

seed *adjective*: seminal

seizure *seizure of a debtor's property*: distraint, sequestration

self □ *combining form*: aut(o)- □ *self-government*: autonomy, autarchy □ *self-sufficiency*: autarky

sell □ *selling by sending out unsolicited items and then demanding payment if they are not returned*: inertia selling □ *selling through a hierarchy of agents*: pyramid selling □ *sell goods by association (e.g. inscribed sweatshirts at a pop concert)*: merchandize □ *sell goods abroad at a giveaway price, to maintain their home price*: dump

seller □ *combining form*: -monger □ *person selling from door to door*: hawker, pedlar □ *person selling fruit etc. in a street market*: costermonger □ *person selling a specified type of goods*: chandler □ *former seller of quack medicines etc. at fairs*: mountebank

sentence □ *sentence containing every letter of the alphabet*: pangram □ *sentence that tails off uncompleted*: aposiopesis □ *prison sentence to be served only upon re-offending*: suspended sentence □ *reduction of a prison sentence for good behaviour*: remission

sentimentality *sentimentality in music or art*: kitsch, schmaltz

servant □ *military officer's servant*: batman □ *junior public-school boy who acts as servant to a senior boy*: fag □ *Cambridge college servant*: gyp □ *Oxford college servant*: scout □ *Indian servant operating a large ceiling fan*: punkah wallah

sesame □ *paste made from sesame seeds*: tahini □ *sweet made from sesame seeds*: halva

seven □ *combining forms*: hept(a)-, sept(i)- □ *adjective*: septenary

sexual activity *adjective*: venereal

shakes *technical term*: Parkinson's disease

shape *combining forms*: morph(o)-, -form, -morphic

share □ *list of an investor's shares*: portfolio □ *share-buying company selling to the public shares in its whole portfolio*: unit trust □ *offer shares for sale*: float □ *periodic payment made by a successful company to its shareholders*: dividend □ *shares offering a guaranteed dividend*: gilts □ *speculator who sells shares because he expects their price to fall*: bear □ *speculator who buys shares because he expects their price to rise*: bull □ *speculator who buys new share issues for a quick resale*: stag

sharp □ *combining form*: oxy- □ *sharpness of a picture*: definition □ *mental sharpness*: acuity

shed □ *shed feathers or fur*: moult □ *shed an outer skin or shell*: slough □ *shedding its leaves annually*: deciduous

sheep □ *adjective*: ovine □ *sheep's brain disease thought to cause BSE*: scrapie □ *castrated male sheep, leader of the flock*: bellwether

sheet *sheet for a corpse*: shroud

shell □ *combining forms*: concho-, -conch- □ *fragments of an exploding artillery shell*: shrapnel

shell-shock *technical term*: combat neurosis

shepherd *adjective*: bucolic

shepherd's pie *alternative term*: cottage pie

shield □ *shield bearing a coat of arms*: escutcheon □ *knob in the centre of a shield*: boss, umbo □ *Roman legionaries' roof of linked shields*: testudo

shin bone *technical term*: tibia

shingles *technical term*: herpes zoster

ship □ *adjective*: marine, maritime □ *line painted on a ship's side to show permitted submersion levels*: Plimsoll line □ *list of a ship's cargo*: bill of lading, manifest □ *dock worker employed to unload a ship*: stevedore □ *recovery of a wrecked or abandoned ship*: salvage □ *cargo thrown overboard from a ship to lighten it in a storm*: jetsam □ *cargo washed overboard from a ship*: flotsam □ *cargo thrown overboard from a ship but marked with buoys etc. for later recovery*: lagan □ *common room for a warship's senior officers*: wardroom □ *common room for a warship's junior officers*: gunroom

shock *shock that may cause lasting psychological harm*: trauma

shock treatment *technical term*: electroconvulsive therapy

shoot □ *shoot growing from a plant's roots etc.*: sucker □ *shoot prepared for planting or grafting*: scion, slip □ *climbing plant's shoot used to gain support*: tendril

shore *adjective*: littoral

short *combining form*: brach-

short-sightedness *technical term*: myopia

shoulder blade *technical term*: scapula

sickle *adjective*: falcate

sickly *sickly person*: valetudinarian

sided *combining forms*: -gon, -gonal

sight □ *combining form*: -scopy □ *adjective*: visual

signal □ *bell rung as an alarm*: tocsin □ *signalling system based on combinations of long and short flashes, marks, or sounds*: Morse □ *signalling system based on flags hand-held in various positions*: semaphore □ *signalling system used by bookmakers' assistants*: tick-tack

silence *Cistercian monk vowed to silence*: Trappist

silver *adjective*: argent-

simple fraction *alternative term*: common fraction

singer □ *range of notes a singer can sing*: compass, register □ *range within which the majority of notes in a song fall*: tessitura

single *combining forms*: mono-, uni-

sister □ *combining form*: soror(i)- □ *murder of a sister*: sororicide

situation *perplexing situation*: dilemma, predicament

six *combining forms*: hexa-, hexi-, sexa-, sexi-

sixth sense *perception by a 'sixth sense'*: extrasensory perception

skin □ *combining forms*: derm(o)-, dermat(o)- □ *technical term*: cutis, dermis □ *adjective*: cutaneous □ *beneath the skin*: hypodermic, subcutaneous □ *blemish on the skin*: naevus, macula, stigma □ *strip off the skin*: flay □ *shed a skin*: slough □ *shedding of a skin*: slough, ecdysis

skirt □ *ballet dancer's stiff short skirt*: tutu □ *short skirt as part of traditional Greek male dress*: fustanella □ *padding formerly worn under the rear of a skirt*: bustle □ *hoops formerly supporting a skirt*: farthingale

skull □ *combining forms*: cephal(o)-, -cephal- □ *technical term*: cranium □ *study of the size and shape of the skull as a supposed indicator of character and mental ability*: phrenology □ *bore a hole in the skull for surgical purposes*: trepan, trephine

skullcap □ *skullcap worn by some Roman Catholic clergymen*: zucchetto □ *skullcap worn by male Orthodox Jews*: yarmulka

slave *adjective*: servile

sleep □ *combining forms*: hypn(o)-, narc(o)-, somni-, somno- □ *learning while asleep*: hypnopaedia □ *sleep with dreaming and eye movements*: paradoxical sleep, REM sleep □ *shallow sleep induced by surgical anaesthesia*: twilight sleep □ *sleep through the winter*: hibernate □ *sleep through the summer*: aestivate

sleeping sickness □ *technical term*: encephalitis lethargica, trypanosomiasis □ *African fly causing sleeping sickness*: tsetse

sleepwalking *technical terms*: somnambulism, noctambulism

slip of the tongue □ *technical term*: lapsus linguae □ *slip of the tongue thought to reveal the speaker's true thoughts*: Freudian slip

sloe *alternative term*: blackthorn

slope □ *combining forms*: clin-, -clin- □ *steep slope at the end of a plateau*: escarpment □ *slope of a stage etc.*: rake □ *slope of a road etc.*: gradient □ *skier's diagonal route across sloping ground*: traverse

slow □ *combining form*: brady- □ *Chinese system of slow exercises*: t'ai chi ch'uan

slum clearance *alternative term*: urban renewal

small □ *combining forms*: micro-, mini-, nano-, -cle, -ule □ *smallest possible*: marginal, minimal, minuscule □ *infinitely small*: infinitesimal □ *small amount*: soupçon, smidgen, vestige

smallpox *technical term*: variola

smell □ *adjectives*: □ *sense of smell*: olfactory □ *stink*: mephitic, hircine

smelling salts *technical term*: sal volatile

snake □ *adjective*: anguine □ *snake's poison*: venom □ *antidote to this*: serum, antivenin

snapdragon *alternative term*: antirrhinum

sneezing *technical term*: sternutation

soccer *technical term*: Association Football

social □ *socially correct*: comme il faut □ *social rules or custom*: etiquette □ *social blunder*: gaffe, faux pas □ *social skills*: savoir-faire □ *social climber*: arriviste, parvenu □ *social prestige*: cachet □ *gaining social status*: upwardly mobile □ *losing social status*: déclassé

society □ *person ostracized by society*: pariah □ *group thought to have a hidden but pervasive control of society*: the Establishment

solar system *mechanical model of the solar system*: orrery

sole of the foot *adjectives*: plantar, volar

solvent □ *universal solvent sought by alchemists*: alkahest □ *strong solvent attacking most substances*: aqua regia

son *adjective*: filial

song □ *improvised West Indian song on topical theme*: calypso □ *sailors' work song*: shanty □ *gondolier's song*: barcarole □ *Renaissance secular part-song*: madrigal □ *German art-song*: lied

soot *adjective*: fuliginous

sound □ *combining forms*: audi-, phon(o)-, -phony □ *adjectives*: acoustic, sonic □ *of sound recorded and reproduced via a single channel*: monophonic □ *of sound recorded and reproduced via several channels*: streophonic □ *of sound recorded and reproduced via two separate channels*: binaural □ *of sound recorded and reproduced via four separate channels*: quadraphonic □ *slow pitch-distortion of recorded sound*: wow □ *fast pitch-distortion of recorded sound*: flutter □ *name for the indefinite sound often made by English vowels*: schwa

south *adjectives*: austral, meridional

South Africa □ *South African barbecue*: braai □ *South African native club*: knobkerrie □ *South African native spear*: assegai □ *South African whip*: sjambok □ *South African cattle pound*: kraal □ *small town in South Africa*: dorp □ *South African wagon encampment*: laager □ *open bush in South Africa*: bundu □ *veranda in South Africa*: stoep □ *former South African policy of racial segregation*: apartheid

South American □ *South American cloak having a hole for the head*: poncho □ *South American cowboy*: gaucho

Soviet □ *Soviet party official*: commissar □ *Soviet secret police*: KGB □ *Soviet forced labour camp*: gulag □ *Soviet collective farm*: kolkhoz □ *Soviet worker who achieves exceptional output*: stakhanovite □ *underground publishing in Soviet Russia*: samizdat □ *Soviet youth organization*: Komsomol

speak *that cannot be spoken*: ineffable

specific gravity □ *technical term*: relative density □ *apparatus measuring a liquid's specific gravity*: hydrometer

spectacles □ *spectacles supported by a nose clip*: pince nez □ *single eyeglass*: monocle □ *pair of eyeglasses on a long handle*: lorgnette □ *spectacles with combined lenses to give near and far vision*: bifocals

speech □ *combining forms*: logo-, phono-, -log-, -phon(o)-, -logue, -phone, -phony □ *adjective*: oral □ *inability to express or understand speech due to brain damage*: aphasia □ *inability to express speech due to loss of voice*: aphonia

speed □ *combining form*: tach- □ *speed at which an object can defy gravity*: escape velocity □ *object's maximum possible air speed*: terminal velocity □ *instrument measuring a vehicle's speed*: speedometer □ *instrument measuring an engine's speed*: rev counter, tachometer □ *automatic regulator of an engine's speed*: governor □ *automatic recorder of a vehicle's speed*: tachograph

spelling *technical term*: orthography

spirit □ *combining forms*: pneumat- □ *spirit of the age*: zeitgeist □ *spirit of a place*: genius loci, numen

spiritualist □ *spiritualist thought to be able to contact the dead*: medium □ *spiritualist meeting for contact with the dead*: seance □ *substance said to exude from a spritualist medium during a trance*: ectoplasm □ *boards used for messages in a spiritualist seance*: ouija board, planchette □ *form of spiritualism practised by some Native Americans, Aleuts, etc.*: shamanism

split *combining form*: schiz(o)-

squint *technical term*: strabismus

squirrel *squirrel's nest*: drey

staff □ *bishop's staff*: crosier □ *monarch's staff*: sceptre □ *beadle's staff*: mace □ *verger's staff*: verge □ *Dionysus' staff*: thyrsus □ *Hermes' staff*: caduceus

stain *brownish stain on the paper of a book or engraving*: foxing

stained glass *lead strip holding pieces of stained glass*: came

stamp collecting *technical term*: philately

standard *standard used for comparison*: benchmark, control, yardstick

star □ *combining forms*: astr-, sider(o)- □ *adjectives*: astral, sidereal, stellar □ *cluster of stars*: asterism □ *exploding star*: nova □ *large cool star*: red giant □ *small cool star*: red dwarf □ *group of stars thought to form a particular figure*: constellation □ *star that is the brightest in its constellation*: alpha □ *measure of a star's brightness*: magnitude □ *building with a domed ceiling for displaying images of the stars*: planetarium

start □ *start a car from another car's battery*: jump-start □ *start a car by pushing it and then engaging the gears*: bump-start

state *combining forms*: -osis, -tude

statement *legal statement made under oath*: affidavit, deposition

steal □ *steal someone's ideas*: plagiarize □ *steal from money entrusted to one*: embezzle, peculate, defalcate □ *steal small items from the workplace*: pilfer □ *person who knowingly buys or stores stolen goods*: receiver □ *person who finds a buyer for stolen goods*: fence □ *compulsive urge to steal, regardless of need*: kleptomania

stirrup bone *technical term*: stapes

stomach □ *combining form*: gastr(o)- □ *adjective*: gastric

stomach-ache *technical term*: gastralgia

stone □ *combining forms*: lapid-, lith(o)-, petr(o)- □ *adjective*: lithic □ *large standing stone in a prehistoric monument*: megalith □ *prehistoric stone chamber tomb*: dolmen □ *stone coffin*: sar-

cophagus □ *person who shapes building stone or builds with it*: mason, stonemason □ *grotesque stone figure serving as rainwater spout*: gargoyle □ *stone believed by alchemists to turn base metals into gold*: philosophers' stone

store □ *secret store*: cache, stash □ *funnel-shaped store for coal, grain, etc.*: hopper

storm *still area at the centre of a storm*: eye

strangle *execute a criminal by strangling*: garrotte

stroke *technical term*: cerebral haemorrhage

study □ *combining form*: -logy □ *study of the universe*: cosmology □ *study of the stars*: astronomy □ *study of mankind*: anthropology □ *study of primitive cultures*: ethnology □ *study of statistics of births, deaths, and disease*: demography □ *study of language*: philology □ *study of living organisms*: physiology □ *study of the skin*: dermatology □ *study of diseases*: pathology □ *study of resistance to infection*: immunology □ *study of tumours*: oncology □ *study of poisons*: toxicology □ *study of voting at elections*: psephology □ *study of crime*: criminology □ *study of punishment*: penology □ *study of family trees*: genealogy □ *study of the soil*: pedology □ *study of mosses*: bryology □ *study of fossils*: palaeontology □ *study of earthquakes*: seismology □ *study of the weather*: meteorology □ *study of unidentified flying objects*: ufology

stuffing □ *stuffing dead animals*: taxidermy □ *stuffing made of chopped meat or vegetables*: forcemeat

substitute *fraudulently substituted*: supposititious

subtraction □ *number from which subtraction is to be made*: minuend □ *number to be subtracted*: subtrahend

sugar □ *combining forms*: glyc(o)-, sacchar- □ *adjective*: saccharine □ *hormone regulating the blood sugar level*: insulin □ *disease characterized by excess sugar in the blood and urine*: diabetes mellitus

sugar pea *alternative term*: mangetout

summer □ *adjective*: aestival □ *resumption of summer weather in the autumn*: Indian summer

summer house *raised summer house with a view*: gazebo, belvedere

sun □ *combining forms*: heli-, sol- □ *adjective*: solar □ *sun's highest point in the sky*: zenith □ *orbiting planet's furthest point from the sun*: aphelion □ *orbiting planet's nearest point to the sun*: perihelion

sunburn *technical term*: erythema solare

supporting *combining form*: pro-

surgical cutting *combining forms*: -tom-, -tome, -tomy

surgical opening *combining form*: -stomy

surgical removal *combining form*: -ectomy

surveyor □ *surveyor's rotating telescope for measuring angles*: theodolite □ *surveyor's incised mark in wall etc.*: benchmark □ *surveyor's striped sight-pole*: ranging pole

survive *capable of surviving independently*: viable

suspicious *pathologically suspicious*: paranoid

sweat □ *technical term*: hidrosis □ *adjective*: hidrotic

sweating sickness *technical term*: miliary fever

sweet □ *excessively sweet*: cloying □ *sweet-voiced*: mellifluous

Swiss □ *Swiss state*: canton □ *Swiss breakfast food of cereals, dried fruit, and nuts*: muesli □ *Swiss mountaineers' style of song*: yodelling

symbol □ *identifying symbol used for a company, product, etc.*: logo, trade mark □ *symbol replacing a word*: logogram □ *system of symbols, each of which represents a syllable in a certain language*: syllabary □ *system of symbols, each of which represents a word in a certain language*: ideograms

symptom *set of symptoms whose joint presence indicates a particular disease*: syndrome

syringa *alternative terms*: lilac, mock orange

T

table □ *table of the elements arranged to group those of similar chemical structure*: periodic table □ *table giving the results of various mathematical calculations*: ready reckoner

tail □ *combining forms*: caud-, -urous □ *adjective*: caudal □ *fox's tail*: brush □ *rabbit or deer's tail*: scut

tailor *adjective*: sartorial

tar □ *tar used to preserve wood*: creosote □ *tar used on roofs and roads*: bitumen □ *tar mixed with gravel etc. for road-making*: asphalt

target □ *disk thrown up as a shooting target*: clay pigeon □ *revolving target in a medieval tilt-yard*: quintain

tawny owl *alternative term*: brown owl

taxation □ *adjective*: fiscal □ *taxation of income*: direct taxation □ *taxation of expenditure*: indirect taxation □ *avoidance of tax liability by legal means*: tax avoidance □ *avoidance of tax liability by dishonest means*: tax evasion □ *former tax of 10% payable to the Church*: tithe □ *former tax levied upon every adult*: poll tax

teacher *teacher engaged to give a few lessons at each of several schools*: peripatetic

tear *adjective*: lachrymal

tear gas *alternative term*: CS gas

telephone □ *telephone link for a computer*: modem □ *direct emergency telephone line between heads of state*: hotline

temper *temper metal or glass by heating and cooling*: anneal

temperament □ *of a gloomy temperament*: saturnine □ *of a changeable temperament*: mercurial, volatile

temperature □ *temperature-controlled switch*: thermostat □ *cooling effect of the wind upon air temperature*: chill factor, wind-chill factor

ten *combining forms*: deca-, deci-

tent □ *Native American tent*: teepee, wigwam □ *large tent for flower shows etc.*: marquee □ *tent shrine used by the ancient Israelites*: tabernacle

territory *national policy of regaining former ter-ritories*: revanchism, irredentism

test *test of actors or musicians applying for work*: audition

thermometer □ *thermometer that plots the temperature on a revolving graph*: thermograph □ *thermometer for low temperatures*: cryometer □ *thermometer for high temperatures*: pyrometer □ *pair of thermometers that measure humidity*: psychrometer

thermonuclear bomb *alternative term*: fusion bomb

thigh bone *technical term*: femur

thing □ *thing as perceived by the senses*: phenomenon □ *thing as conceived by the mind*: noumenon

thinking □ *thinking in which problems are solved by logical deduction*: vertical thinking □ *thinking in which problems are solved by apparently illogical association of ideas*: lateral thinking

this side *combining form*: cis-

thoroughbred *thoroughbred horses*: blood-stock

thousand *combining forms*: kilo-, milli-

thousand million *combining form*: giga-

thousand millionth *combining form*: nano-

thousandth *combining form*: milli-

threat □ *threat made by a hostile military build-up*: sabre-rattling □ *constant threat of disaster*: sword of Damocles

three □ *combining forms*: ter-, tri- □ *adjectives*: ternary, treble, triple □ *occurring once in, or lasting for, three years*: triennial □ *Three Wise Men*: Magi □ *three in one*: triune □ *painting etc. covering three panels*: triptych □ *ancient ship with three banks of oars*: trireme □ *three-dimensional picture produced by lasers*: hologram

threshold *adjective*: liminal

ticket *person buying up tickets to resell at inflated prices*: tout

tide □ *tide that rises highest*: spring tide □ *tide that rises least*: neap tide □ *rising tide*: flood tide □ *falling tide*: ebb tide

tile □ *wooden exterior tile for roofs and walls*: shingle □ *curved interlocking roof tile*: pantile

time □ *combining forms*: chron(o)-, temp- □ *adjective*: chronological, temporal □ *ticking device that helps musicians keep time*: metronome □ *law setting a time limit for initiating a prosecution*: statute of limitations

times over *combining form*: -fold

toast □ *thin crisp toast*: Melba toast □ *small piece of toast served on soup or a salad*: crouton

tomb □ *large and elaborate tomb*: mausoleum □ *inscription on a tomb*: epitaph

tongue □ *combining forms*: gloss(o)- □ *adjectives*: glossal, lingual

tooth □ *combining forms*: dent-, odont-, -odont □ *adjective*: dental □ *narrow tooth used to cut*: incisor □ *broad tooth used to grind*: molar □ *pointed tooth at front corner of mouth*: canine □ *tooth emerging at the back of the jaw during adulthood*: wisdom tooth □ *tooth decay*: caries □ *bacterial film on teeth*: plaque □ *hard yellowish deposit forming on teeth*: tartar □ *alloy used to fill* *teeth*: amalgam □ *teeth present in a mouth*: dentition □ *toothed wheel*: cog □ *toothed projection on a wheel or cylinder*: sprocket

toothache *technical term*: odontalgia

touch *adjective*: tactile

tournament *tournament for medieval knights*: joust

tower □ *stepped temple tower in ancient Mesopotamia*: ziggurat □ *ancient Scottish tower*: broch □ *mosque tower*: minaret

trade □ *adjective*: mercantile □ *trade restrictions imposed upon a foreign country until it changes its policies*: sanctions

training *training mock-up of an aircraft's flight deck etc.*: simulator

transplant *drug given to prevent rejection of a transplanted organ*: immunosuppressor

treaty □ *formal acceptance of a treaty*: accession □ *formal rejection of a treaty*: denunciation □ *basic draft of a treaty*: protocol

tree □ *combining forms*: arbor-, dendro-, dendri-, silv(i)- □ *adjective*: arboreal □ *type of tree that sheds its leaves annually*: deciduous □ *type of tree that retains its leaves*: evergreen □ *botanical garden devoted to trees*: arboretum

tree ring *alternative term*: annual ring

trellis □ *trellis along which the branches of fruit trees are trained*: espalier □ *trellis carrying climbing plants over a garden path or arbour*: pergola

trial and error *trial-and-error method of solving problems*: heuristic

triangle □ *triangle with three equal sides*: equilateral triangle □ *triangle with two equal sides*: isosceles triangle □ *triangle with unequal sides*: scalene □ *longest side of a right-angled triangle*: hypotenuse

tumour □ *combining forms*: onco-, -cele, -oma □ *tumour that does not seriously threaten health*: benign □ *tumour that spreads out of control and returns after treatment*: malignant

tunnel *tunnel dug under an enemy's defences*: sap

turn □ *combining forms*: trop-, -trop-, -tropic □ *turn in office etc. assigned by rote*: Buggins' turn □ *turn into stone*: petrify □ *turn into bone*: ossify

turning □ *combining forms*: trop-, -tropism, -tropy □ *turning force*: torque □ *crucial turning point*: Rubicon, watershed

twelve □ *combining form*: dodeca- □ *adjectives*: duodecimal, duodenary □ *twelve-tone musical system*: serialism, dodecaphony

twenty *adjective*: vigesimal

twice □ *combining forms*: bi-, di-, duo-, semi- □ *occurring twice a year*: biannual, semi-annual

twilight *adjective*: crepuscular

twin □ *combining form*: zyg- □ *twin-hulled boat*: catamaran

trust *adjective*: fiduciary

turpentine *adjective*: terebinthine

twins *astrological term*: gemini

two □ *combining forms*: ambi-, bi-, di-, du(o)- □ *adjectives*: binary, double, dual □ *cut in two*:

bisect □ *having two parts*: binary, dual □ *two-sided*: bilateral □ *living for, or occurring once every, two years*: biennial □ *having two chambers (of a parliament etc.)*: bicameral □ *painting etc. covering two panels*: diptych □ *two-faced*: duplicitous

U

unanimously *technical term*: nem. con.

unarmed combat *sports giving skill in unarmed combat*: martial arts

uncle *adjective*: avuncular

unconsciousness □ *long period of deep unconsciousness*: coma □ *state of unconsciousness with bodily rigidity*: catalepsy, catatonia

under *combining forms*: hypo-, infra-, sub-

underground □ *underground cemetery*: catacomb □ *underground railway in London*: tube □ *underground railway in Paris*: metro □ *underground railway in Rome*: metropolitana □ *underground railway in New York*: subway

undermine □ *undermine a fortification by tunnelling beneath it*: sap □ *undermine an organization by establishing agents within it*: infiltrate

understanding □ *sympathetic understanding*: empathy □ *informal diplomatic understanding negotiated between two nations*: entente cordiale

underwater □ *sealed underwater chamber for repair workers etc.*: caisson □ *underwater wall reaching to the surface to provide a dry area for repairs etc.*: coffer □ *divers' underwater vessel open at the bottom and filled with air*: diving bell □ *submarine-like vessel for deep underwater exploration*: bathyscaphe

unequal *combining form*: aniso-

unity *pursuit of unity between all Christian churches*: ecumenism

union □ *enforced union of Austria with Germany in 1938*: Anschluss □ *temporary union between political parties to form a government*: coalition □ *temporary union between business companies undertaking a large project*: consortium □ *secret union between firms to prevent competition*: cartel □ *secret union of purchasers at an auction etc. to force down prices*: ring

urinate *technical term*: micturate

urine □ *duct by which urine passes from the kidney to the bladder*: ureter □ *duct by which urine passes from the bladder to the kidney*: urethra □ *substance causing increased production of urine*: diuretic □ *tube inserted into the body for draining off urine*: catheter □ *horse and cattle urine*: stale

uterus □ *combining forms*: hyster(o)-, metr-, uter(o)- □ *surgical scraping of the uterus*: dilatation and curettage. □ *vacuuming the uterus as a means of abortion*: vacuum aspiration □ *diagnostic sampling of fluid from a pregnant uterus*: amniocentesis □ *surgical removal of the uterus*: hysterectomy

V

V *V-shaped pattern*: chevron

vaccine *supplementary dose of vaccine*: booster

vagina □ *combining form*: colp- □ *membrane partially blocking the entrance of a virgin's vagina*: hymen □ *surgical cutting of the vagina to ease childbirth*: episiotomy

valley □ *valley in Scotland or Ireland*: glen □ *valley in Wales*: cwm □ *wooded valley*: dene

value *loss of value due to wear and tear*: depreciation

vegetarian *strict vegetarian who avoids all animal products*: vegan

vein □ *combining forms*: phleb(o)-, vene-, veni-, veno- □ *adjective*: venous □ *swollen vein in the legs*: varicose vein □ *in or into a vein*: intravenous □ *surgical opening of a vein*: phlebotomy, venesection

Venice □ *former ruler of Venice*: Doge □ *small Venetian passenger boat*: gondola □ *song of Venetian gondoliers*: barcarole □ *Venetian water bus*: vaporetto

Venus *Greek name*: Aphrodite

verse □ *metrical analysis of verse*: scansion □ *theory and practice of versification*: prosody □ *metrical unit in versification*: foot □ *central pause in a line of verse*: caesura

viceroy *adjective*: viceregal

vine □ *cultivation of vines*: viticulture □ *insect that destroys vines*: phylloxera

vinegar *adjective*: acetic

virgin *astrological term*: virgo

virgin birth *technical term*: parthenogenesis

voice □ *combining forms*: phon(o)-, -phone, -phony □ *adjective*: vocal

vote □ *chairman's vote to decide a tied poll*: casting vote □ *vote given to exclude a candidate*: blackball □ *person empowered to cast another's vote*: proxy □ *parliamentary vote*: division

voting □ *voting strategy aimed at defeating an otherwise strong candidate or party*: tactical voting □ *study of voting patterns etc.*: psephology

W

wagon *wagon for condemned prisoners in the French Revolution*: tumbril

wake *signal for waking in an army camp etc.*: reveille

walking *combining form*: -grade

walking stick □ *walking stick with a handle that makes a seat*: shooting stick □ *walking stick's metal tip*: ferrule

wall □ *adjectives*: □ *of a building*: mural □ *in the body*: parietal □ *building's wall of two layers with a gap between*: cavity wall □ *layer of cement etc. on a wall surface*: rendering □ *row of spikes or broken glass set on a wall's top*: cheval-de-frise □ *rounded bricks etc. at a wall's top*: coping □ *watertight wall dividing the interior of a ship etc.*: bulkhead □ *wall of a body cavity*: paries

wandering □ *wandering in search of trade*: itinerant □ *wandering in search of adventure*: errant

war □ *adjective*: martial □ *of a war waged without nuclear weapons*: conventional □ *person favouring recourse to war*: hawk □ *person avoiding recourse to war*: dove

wasp *adjective*: vespine

water □ *combining forms*: aqua-, aqui-, hydr- □ *adjectives*: aqueous, aquatic □ *operated by water*: hydraulic □ *temporary vertical water pipe with a tap*: standpipe

water-carrier *astrological term*: aquarius

water on the brain *technical term*: hydrocephalus

weakness □ *minor weakness of character etc.*: foible □ *weak spot*: Achilles' heel

wealth □ *wealth or its pursuit seen as a corrupting influence*: Mammon □ *source of wealth*: bonanza □ *fabulous place of great wealth*: eldorado

wear *gradual wearing down*: attrition, erosion

weather □ *low-pressure weather system*: cyclone □ *high-pressure weather system*: anticyclone □ *line on a weather map linking places with the same atmospheric pressure*: isobar □ *line on a weather map linking places with the same temperature*: isotherm □ *balloon-borne radio transmitter sending weather information*: radiosonde

weaving □ *threads running lengthways in weaving*: weft, woof □ *threads running crossways in weaving*: warp □ *cylinder holding a weaver's thread*: bobbin □ *double-ended bobbin used on a mechanical loom*: shuttle

week *adjective*: hebdomadal

well *well in which the water rises by natural pressure through a borehole*: artesian well

Welsh □ *adjectives*: Cambrian, Cymric □ *Welsh Nationalist Party*: Plaid Cymru □ *Welsh competition for poets and musicians*: eisteddfod □ *Welsh poetry sung in counterpoint to a traditional harp melody*: penillion

west *adjective*: occidental

West Indian □ *West Indian song improvised on a topical theme*: calypso □ *West Indian popular music with a strong secondary beat*: reggae □ *West Indian sorcery*: obeah, voodoo

whiplash injury *technical term*: hyperextension-hyperflexion injury

white □ *combining forms*: leuc(o)-, leuk(o)- □ *white-skinned person*: Caucasian □ *person or animal having white skin and hair due to a pigment defect*: albino

white ant *alternative term*: termite

white whale *alternative term*: beluga

whooping cough *technical term*: pertussis

widow □ *widow holding a title from her late husband*: dowager □ *estate etc. left a widow by her late husband's will*: jointure

wife *adjective*: uxorial

will □ *adjectives*: □ *wish*: volitional, voluntary □ *legal document*: testamentary □ *person making a will*: testator □ *person appointed to carry out he terms of a will*: executor □ *gift made in a will*: bequest, legacy □ *person receiving a gift from a will*: beneficiary □ *legal authentication of a will*: probate

wildebeest *alternative term*: gnu

wind □ *combining form*: anemo- □ *instrument for measuring wind speed*: anemometer □ *scale for wind velocities*: Beaufort scale □ *build-up of gas in the digestive tract causing the breaking of wind*: flatulence □ *humid southerly wind in southern Europe*: sirocco □ *cold northerly wind blowing down the Rhone*: mistral □ *warm southerly wind blowing off the Alps*: föhn

window □ *adjective*: fenestral □ *window made of vertically sliding glazed sections*: sash window □ *side-hinged window*: casement □ *small window over a door etc.*: fanlight □ *small diamond-shaped pane of window-glass*: quarry □ *ornamental stonework subdividing a window*: tracery □ *angled wall-opening for a window*: embrasure

windpipe *technical term*: trachea

wine □ *combining form*: vin- □ *adjective*: vinous □ *spice and warm wine*: mull □ *wine expert*: oenologist □ *wine merchant*: vintner □ *wine waiter*: sommelier □ *charge made for serving the customer's own wine at a restaurant*: corkage

wing □ *combining forms*: pter(o)-, -pter- □ *adjective*: alar

winter □ *adjectives*: hibernal, hiemal □ *sleep through the winter*: hibernate

wire *wires used to start a car from the battery of another*: jump leads

wisdom tooth *technical term*: third molar

witch □ *gathering of witches*: coven □ *witch's attendant spirit*: familiar □ *male witch*: warlock

without *combining forms*: a-, an-

witness □ *witness's evidence given in court*: testimony □ *sworn statement made by a witness out of court*: deposition □ *lying by a witness under oath*: perjury

wolf □ *adjective*: lupine □ *person who changes into a wolf*: lycanthrope, werewolf

woman □ *combining forms*: gyn(o)-, gynaeco- □ *adjective*: feminine □ *woman with intellectual or literary pretensions*: bluestocking □ *arrogant and domineering woman*: prima donna □ *woman whose husband is often absent*: grass widow

□ *party for women only*: hen party □ *hatred of women*: mysogyny

wood □ *combining forms*: ligno-, ligni-, xylo-, xyli- □ *wooden plate*: trencher □ *ornamental inlay of wood, ivory, etc.*: marquetry

womb *technical term*: uterus

word □ *combining forms*: lexi-, logo-, logi-, -nym □ *adjective*: verbal □ *study of the meaning of words*: semantics □ *study of the forms of words*: morphology

word-blindness *technical term*: alexia

work □ *combining form*: erg(o)- □ *belief that work has an intrinsic moral value*: work ethic □ *person addicted to work*: workaholic

works *complete works of an artist etc.*: oeuvre, corpus

worm □ *combining form*: vermi- □ *adjectives*: vermicular, vermiform

worship *combining form*: -latry

wrist □ *technical term*: carpus □ *adjective*: carpal

wrong *combining forms*: caco-, mal-, mis-

X

X-rays □ *study or use of X-rays*: radiography □ *X-ray of a section through the body*: tomography □ *X-ray of body tissue*: computerized axial tomography □ *treatment of cancer etc. by X-rays*: radiotherapy

Y

youth *artistic creations of one's youth, often later suppressed as immature*: juvenilia

Z

zigzag *zigzag course taken by a vessel sailing into the wind*: tacking, traverse

zinc *coat a metal with zinc*: galvanize